LITERARY CULTURES OF
LATIN AMERICA

A COMPARATIVE HISTORY

LITERARY HISTORY PROJECT

UNDER THE AUSPICES OF THE SOCIAL SCIENCES
AND HUMANITIES RESEARCH COUNCIL OF CANADA
AND THE UNIVERSITY OF TORONTO

RESEARCH DIRECTOR
Mario J. Valdés, University of Toronto

CODIRECTOR
Linda Hutcheon, University of Toronto

Hutcheon, Linda, and Mario J. Valdés, eds.
Rethinking Literary History: A Dialogue on Theory.
New York: Oxford University Press, 2002.

Valdés, Mario J., and Djelal Kadir, eds.
Literary Cultures of Latin America: A Comparative History.
3 vols. New York: Oxford University Press, 2004.

Cornis-Pope, Marcel, and John Neubauer, eds.
History of Literary Cultures in East-Central Europe.
Forthcoming.

LITERARY CULTURES OF
LATIN AMERICA

A COMPARATIVE HISTORY

Mario J. Valdés
and
Djelal Kadir
Editors

Volume I
CONFIGURATIONS OF
LITERARY CULTURE

OXFORD

UNIVERSITY PRESS
2004

Page Design & Production
Publication Services

Project Manager
Susan Yates

Designer
Lori Martinsek

Editorial Manager
Rob Siedenburg

Editorial Staff
Jerome Colburn, Al Davis, Philip D. Hamer, David Mason, Jennifer Putman,
Scott Stocking, Rebecca Taylor

Production Manager
Foti Kutil

Production Staff
Kelly Applegate, Pamela J. Broderick-Rhoades, Elisa Laird, Carol McGilliuray,
Paul Mitchell, Steven Sansone, James Torbit, Eric R. Tucker

Indexing Staff
Alysia Cooley, Benjamin Moreland, Louise Toft, Joyce Wiehagen,
Debora Mori Benencase Ayers, Neil Ching

Art
Ben Coblentz, Jason Pankoke, Guoliang Wu

OXFORD
University Press

Oxford   New York
Auckland   Bangkok   Buenos Aires   Cape Town   Chennai
Dar es Salaam   Delhi   Hong Kong   Istanbul   Karachi   Kolkata
Kuala Lumpur   Madrid   Melbourne   Mexico City   Mumbai
Nairobi   São Paulo   Shanghai   Taipei   Tokyo   Toronto

Copyright © 2004 by Oxford University Press, Inc.

Published by Oxford University Press, Inc.
198 Madison Avenue, New York, New York, 10016
http://www.oup.com/us

Oxford is a registered trademark of Oxford University Press

Library of Congress Cataloging-in-Publication Data

Literary cultures of Latin America : a comparative history / edited by
Mario J. Valdés and Djelal Kadir.
      v. ; cm.
  Includes bibliographical references and index.
  Contents: v. 1 Configurations of literary culture -- v. 2
Institutional modes and cultural modalities -- v. 3 Latin American
literary culture.
  ISBN 0-19-512621-1 (set : alk. paper) -- ISBN 0-19-517540-9 (v. 1 :
alk. paper) -- ISBN 0-19-517541-7 (v. 2 : alk. paper) -- ISBN
0-19-517542-5 (v. 3 : alk. paper)
  1. Latin American literature--History and criticism. 2. Literature
and society--Latin America. I. Valdés, Mario J. II. Kadir, Djelal.
  PQ7081.A1L525 2004
  860.9'98--dc22
                              2003027353

Printing Number: 9 8 7 6 5 4 3 2 1

Printed in the United States of America
on acid-free paper

ACKNOWLEDGMENTS

The editors are pleased to acknowledge the contributions of the following individuals and institutions to the realization of this *Literary Cultures of Latin America: A Comparative History.* The project began in 1994 and was completed in 2004.

Phase One: Rethinking Literary History, 1994–1996
Mario J. Valdés organized a weeklong meeting of twenty-five scholars from various disciplines to respond to his position paper on "Rethinking Literary History," under the auspices of the Rockefeller Foundation of New York in the Bellagio Conference Center in Lake Como, Italy.

Phase Two: Meetings, 1996–1998
Three meetings at the University of Toronto of the twenty-seven Research Coordinators, the salary of the Administrative Director, the Research Centre, and staff were funded by the Social Sciences and Humanities Research Council of Canada and the University of Toronto. The salary of the Director of the Project was funded by Northern Telecom through the Northern Telecom Professorship in Ibero-American Studies. A meeting at Duke University organized by Alberto Moreiras was funded by the research office of Duke University. A meeting in Bogotá, Colombia, organized by Victoria Peralta was funded by the Colombian Research Council. A meeting in St. Louis organized by Randolph Pope was funded by the Washington University Research Fund. A meeting at the École Normale Supérieure in Paris, organized by Mario J. Valdés, was funded by that institution. A meeting in Rio de Janeiro organized by Eduardo de Faria Coutinho was funded by the Brazilian Research Council.

The ten parts of *Literary Cultures of Latin America: A Comparative History* were coordinated by the following scholars:
Volume One
Part One: Beatriz Garza Cuarón (Mexico), Luis Millones (Peru), Hervé Théry (France).
Part Two: Heloisa Buarque de Hollanda, Marlyse Meyer, Beatriz Resende (Brazil), and Cynthia Steele (United States).
Part Three: Raúl Antelo (Brazil/Argentina), Eugenia Meyer (Mexico), Zuzana M. Pick (Canada), Eneida María de Souza (Brazil), Juan Villegas (Chile/United States).
Volume Two
Part One: Lisa Block de Behar (Uruguay), Tania Franco Carvalhal (Brazil).
Part Two: Randolph Pope (Chile/United States), Flora Sussekind (Brazil).
Part Three: Eduardo de Faria Coutinho (Brazil), Victoria Peralta (Colombia).
Volume Three
Part One: Doris Sommer (United States), María Consuelo Cunha Campos (Brazil).
Part Two: Wander Melo Miranda (Brazil), Alberto Moreiras (Spain/United States), Iris Zavala (Puerto Rico/Spain).
Part Three: Elizabeth Monasterios (Bolivia/Canada), Juan Villegas (Chile/United States).
Part Four: Renato Cordeiro Gomes and Marilia Rothier Cardoso (Brazil), Djelal Kadir (United States).

Phase Three: Translation and Revision, 1998–2001
Two-thirds of the 205 texts in the *History* were written in languages other than English and were translated. Translation services were paid out of the operating budget of the Research Centre. The following are our translators: from Portuguese, Nair Maria Anaya-Ferreira, Idelber Avelar, Stephen A. Berg, Paulo Henriques Britto, Thomas LaBorie Burns, María Clara Galery, Glaucia Renate Gonçalves, Paulo Lemos Horta, and Lis Horta Moriconi; from Spanish, Charlotte Broad de Mena, Colman Hogan, Jessica Johnson, and Suzanne D. Stephens; from French, Marie Carrière and Wendy J. Eberle.

Phase Four: Copyediting, 2001–2004
Texts were edited by Linda Hutcheon and María Elena de Valdés. Documentation of texts and dates of authors was completed by María Elena de Valdés and her staff.

We wish to thank Susan Yates of Publication Services for her valuable assistance throughout this long copyediting period.

We also wish to acknowledge the kind permission given by the following photographers and artist for the reproduction of their work: Jack Delano, Lois Greenfield, Sebastião Salgado, and Jack Vartoogian (photographers), and María Luisa de Villa (artist).

Finally, the project would not have been possible without the full cooperation and support of the John P. Robarts Research Library of the University of Toronto, the Chief Librarian Carol R. Moore, and her staff.

CONTENTS

Volume I
Configurations of Literary Culture

PART ONE

PARAMETERS OF LITERARY CULTURE

PART TWO

FROM THE MARGINS OF LITERARY HISTORY

PART THREE

PLURALITY OF DISCOURSE IN LATIN AMERICAN CULTURE

CONTENTS OF OTHER VOLUMES

Volume II

Institutional Modes and Cultural Modalities

INTRODUCTION
Walter D. Mignolo

PART ONE

CULTURAL INSTITUTIONS

Volume III

Latin American Literary Culture:

Subject to History

INTRODUCTION
Wander Melo Miranda

PART ONE

FISSURED FOUNDATIONS: NOSTALGIA AND NEW BEGINNINGS

PART TWO

INTERNAL BORDERS: CULTURAL CONFLICTS AND STATE DISCOURSE

PART THREE

LIMINALITY AND CENTRALITY OF LITERARY CULTURES IN THE TWENTIETH CENTURY

PART FOUR

LITERARY CULTURE IN THE TWENTIETH CENTURY

INTRODUCTION

BEYOND LITERARY HISTORY

Mario J. Valdés

The people of Latin America have diverse and extremely rich literary cultures that bring together three traditions into one heterogeneous flux. Latin American literary culture partakes unequally, discontinuously, and without any uniformity of three very distinct cultures: first, the Amerindian, especially in Mesoamerica and the Andean region; second, the European, predominantly Spanish and Portuguese (but also having some French and Italian characteristics); third, the African cultures which are today still of major consequence in Brazil and the Caribbean region. In some regions European traditions have mixed with one of the two other traditions, but in other regions (predominantly those that were sparsely populated before the sixteenth century, Argentina, Chile, Uruguay, and the Rio Grande do Sul State in southern Brazil) European traditions are still the primary basis for cultural life. African culture is a deeply rooted tradition in former slave-holding areas but almost nonexistent in other parts of the continent. Some forty percent of the African slaves brought to the Americas during the colonial period went to Brazil, and another forty percent went to the Spanish, French, and British Caribbean; another fifteen percent went to the rest of Spanish America, and less than five percent went to what is now the United States (a fact that is not often noted in African American Studies that are restricted to African culture in the United States). Although the Caribbean and Brazil are today the principal areas of African influence, all of Latin America has been affected by multiple elements of popular culture coming from these regions. In terms of literature, the early manifestations in the sixteenth century were typical of those under colonial rule: The imported European expression stood alone in authority, along with an uneven policy aimed at the ultimate eradication of all traces of either the pre-Columbian or the African cultures. In spite of the large scale and wanton destruction of the other cultures (the burning of the Mayan library, the persecution of the educated elite among the Aztecs, Maya, and Incas), the Spanish and Portuguese colonial administration failed to destroy the past and were sometimes thwarted in their attempts to do so by the Spanish and Portuguese religious orders: especially by the Franciscans and Jesuits. It has been primarily in the twentieth century that the sometimes underground streams of Amerindian and African cultures have emerged to contest their role in Latin America's literary culture and to end centuries of rejection–and of surreptitious influence.

Not only would it be presumptuous of us to claim originality in the aims of this history of Latin American literary culture, it would be untrue. We are working in the tradition and direction outlined by Pedro Henríquez Ureña more than a

half-century ago in his landmark work *Literary Currents in Hispanic America* [1945; *Las corrientes literarias en la América Hispánica*, 1949]. The distinguished Colombian critic Rafael Gutiérrez Girardot claims, and perhaps rightly so, that Henríquez Ureña did not at first see the magnitude of his departure from traditional literary history and only in retrospect came to understand that he had written the first and, until now, only history of literary cultures of Latin America. It may be that Henríquez Ureña was obliged to take this unprecedented route because he was writing in English for an English-speaking readership who did not share in the Latin American legacy; he was a Latin American looking at the Latin American continent from the outside. This fact does not in any way diminish the accomplishment and significance of this ground-breaking work. But perhaps by looking at the cultural imaginary of Latin America from the outside, he was obliged to consider the validity of the designation "Latin American literature" rather than, say, Argentinean or Mexican literature. His first response was vehemently to resist the attempt to impose any form of homogeneity of an abstract nature. Twenty years before, in *La utopía de América* (1925), he had written that the individual differences of writers across the continent are real differences resulting from diversity in climate, language, and traditions, but that these differences, instead of leading to division and discord, had come together in a unity of cultural heterogeneity in dialogue. In the same years that Henríquez Ureña was writing his *Literary Currents*, Marc Bloch and the French historians of the Annales school had also taken on the challenge of writing a social history of heterogeneity. The parallel is not meant to indicate more than the fact that this was a time of critical rethinking in historiography and that a common cause had arisen in bringing together the empirical, ideological, and aesthetic aspects of life both by those historians in France and the great scholar from Santo Domingo.

If the proposed writing of a history of cultural heterogeneity is the first major debt we owe to this scholar, it is not the only one; there are at least three other important links between the present work and *Literary Currents*. Henríquez Ureña was the first literary historian of this region to incorporate comparative practices into the historical narrative, constantly relating writers and texts to other writers and never isolating them. Another innovation on the part of Henríquez Ureña was to make artistic, scientific, religious, and political discourse part of the same cultural process. This change in perspective cannot be underestimated, for it necessarily repositions the literary text within a cultural process of variegated discourse and thus avoids the all too common absurdities (into which uninformed literary criticism so easily falls) of attributing influences from one literary text to the other, without taking into account the plurality of discourses that interact in the cultural habitat. Finally, we would be remiss if we did not point out that our response to the central historiographic problem of periodization and the internal structure of a history of literary culture has, in part, been a response to Henríquez Ureña, but also to Fernand Braudel. Henríquez Ureña fully understood that, although Latin American literatures are, for the most part, written in European languages, they are not European. For, as he so often pointed out, Latin America did not have a medieval period; its Renaissance was parallel to but not the same as that of Spain and Portugal. What happens in Latin America in the sixteenth and seventeenth centuries, in fact, breaks down all classifications based on European models. Henríquez Ureña's solution was to bring together social, political, and economic indicators of culture in the Americas and thus develop a separate periodization for Latin America. His five large divisions are the foundation of a new society (1492–1600), the two centuries of institutionalization (1600–1780), the Enlightenment and Independence (1780–1830), the chaos of the independent republics (1830–1900), and the first period of modernity (1900–1945). These divisions are still too limiting for our purposes here, but they have served as a starting point for us to explore and develop our own temporal paradigm. The basic difference between Henríquez Ureña's divisions and our model is that the breaks differ somewhat from section to section, and this is so because the issues examined differ. But the debt to his work should not be underestimated, because both his history and ours are dialectic processes of inquiry. When, in our history, we write about the development of the printing press as part of the history of literary production, our time span is relatively short; if, however, we write about the mutations of form in the short poem, the period will be long. These temporal structures are in marked contrast with the arbitrary period formats of positivism. The most arbitrary of these in Latin American literary histories is the scheme of generations used by Enrique Anderson-Imbert some ten years after *Literary Currents*; without a doubt, this was a major retreat in historiographic development. Anderson Imbert's literary history was designed as if literature were the work of a homogeneous group that shared the same sociological characteristics and constituted an unmistakable intellectual and artistic leadership. Such a situation has never existed in Latin America, except at the most local level in the isolation of the hinterland.

Our concept of the heterogeneous unity of differences in this project is above all a dialectic concept; in Ricoeur's terms, it is the necessary conflict of interpretations that makes up a literary culture. In historical terms, the process of culture is always subject to internal as well as external forces in the society in question. To offer a brief example, one of the most discussed examples of literary escapism is the poetry written in Mexico during the most violent years of the Mexican revolution (1910–1918). It broke with the tradition of social engagement among writers, which had developed rapidly after the end of colonial censorship. But as Octavio Paz and others have recognized, escapism was a necessary response to violence and was itself a political statement; the fact that some of the best work was written in exile should not be lost on us (e.g., Amado Nervo).

The work of Pedro Henríquez Ureña was the first (although limited attempt) to write a history of literary culture. It opened the conceptual door that we have entered, a half-century later, with the advantage of collaborative research from a plethora of related disciplines coordinated into a comparative history with the help of electronic systems. An endearing primitivism of sorts still appears in much of the literary history that has been written in the last quarter-century. The force, logic, and validity of contextualization–so often invoked or rejected in the debate on the future of literary history–is never dismissed on historical or logical grounds, but rather for practical reasons. David Perkins puts it succinctly for our generation. He argues that literary interpretation has, in most cases, been based on a more or less crude construction of context by the literary historian; in other words, the historian interprets the text first and then builds up the context that will bolster the interpretation. This primitive, cause-and-effect linkage between context and text risks discrediting the entire operation. Writing about one text (*The Madwoman in the Attic*), Perkins states flatly: "The contextualizing is, in a sense, bogus" (138). But Perkins is at a loss to understand the aim and purpose of dialectic contextualization as practiced by Stephen Greenblatt: "His essay combines two intentions that are logically separate: to interpret the play and to exemplify the processes of circulation and negotiation among cultural discourses and institutions" (151). Perkins argues that if one can interpret the text without the context (as he claims Greenblatt did), then why bother to build up the context? Yet, the historical aim of that essay lies in the very relation between the interpreted text and the sociocultural context. Greenblatt is not claiming cause and effect, but rather participation, contestation, and interaction of significances in the historian's construction of literary culture. It would be unthinkable for carpenters setting out to build a cabin, for example, to make their own nails, cut and plane the boards from the tree trunk, haul the gravel needed for the foundations, and so forth. No doubt they could, if they were in such dire straits that there was no other choice. Fortunately for our would-be carpenters, there are others who can provide building materials of much better quality than those they could make themselves and with an incomparably better use of time and effort than they could ever hope to achieve working in isolation. Yet literary historians have subscribed to analogous primitive working conditions that no self-respecting carpenter would accept by choice.

The context of literature–understood as the literary culture in which texts are conceived, written, and read–is an area of research with multiple interlacing specializations: cultural geography, the demographics of culture, the history of production and reception, the linguistic registers of culture, the sociology of literary movements, and the history of ideas, to name but a few. Could not literary historians avail themselves of this research in the same way those carpenters procured the best nails, lumber, and fittings for their job? I have yet to hear a good reason why not. The primary reason is likely neither inertia nor unawareness of these collateral fields of inquiry, but rather the fear of leaving the safe haven of years of disciplinary work. This fear is as irrational as it is international. Even in the heart of interdisciplinary exchange, at the distinguished École Normale Supérieure of Paris–the former home base of Althusser and Derrida–the leading professors of literature rejected even the possibility of dialogue across disciplines because they "could only work in their area of specialization." Our position is that the most effective form of literary history today is a contextualized literary history, and either we learn to work in and with the research of corollary fields, or we will be condemned to increasing isolation and irrelevance. But there is also a cautionary note to be added. In the development of cultural context, we must still defer examination of some elements and foreground others; in other words, there is an implicit bias in constructing any model that is unavoidable. For example, in our case there was a conscious decision to take geography first, then demographic inquiry, followed by linguistics, before going on to consider social and political issues affecting literary culture.

This heuristic device becomes a category error if we transfer our perspective and, of course, the biases of our approach to the phenomenon itself (as happens in a remark like "the economic conditions of the lower classes in Paris are always in the background of the scenes that were played out in the meetings of the Estates General"). In society, as in culture, there is no background or foreground; these descriptors are simply useful devices used in the emplotment of history. In the life of communities, there are social forces that compel people to act, and there are the relations and interrelations of those who share the same time and place. With regard to the purported impasse created by either the amalgam of disciplines or the excess of information, our response is simple. We take from many disciplines and respect their sense of domain and of the imposed limitations of their methods. But our approach is not eclectic; it is a highly developed hermeneutics of culture which builds the context both historically and formally as a conscious heuristic model.

The term "*cultural imaginary,*" as used in this history, is the collective expression of communities that creates significations of identity. It affects singular human beings insofar as they all live in language-speaking communities of one size or another. Language in these volumes is considered as habitat but also as institution. As habitat, it is the center of a person's space of experience; as institution, it is the rule-governed instrument of domination in the exercise of power within the community, but also a weapon to subvert the discourse of power. The cultural imaginary is a foundational aspect of all human society, large or small, and in some cases also of conglomerates of disparate social groups (as we will contend is the case in Latin America). The imaginary consists of forms, images, emblems, flags, and so forth, but most of it is made up of modes of signification in the community. It has its origin in the commonalities of shared habitat, and when the local level of kinship is exceeded, it becomes self-generating, completely entwined with the development of a common language. The cultural imaginary can expand or contract; it can also bifurcate, as the concept of cultural identity changes.

Literature, in the broad sense as used in this history, is one of the main sources of the imaginary and as such provides its historicality. Along with the literary sources of the imaginary, we must also emphasize the role of ritual and celebrations, which are often maintained and developed through an oral tradition with no written texts. Finally, we must also take into consideration that there have always been popular sources of literary culture. The most potent contemporary source of popular culture is television and, in Latin America, specifically the "*telenovela*" [soap opera]. It is incumbent upon us to make clear that the cultural imaginary does not develop freely but, on the contrary, is constantly subject to constraints and powerful forces, both benign and destructive. We should distinguish between those constraints that are intrinsic–such as the geography of the community in question, for example, the formidable natural boundaries of Chile in contrast to the complete lack of effective territorial demarcations between Mexico and the United States (except for a shallow river or a barbed-wire fence)–and other limitations that are external to the community itself, such as war or natural disaster. There are also limitations, sometimes the most severe, that are internal to the community itself–such as ideological division, or religious or ethnic marginalization of parts of the community.

One of the difficulties of writing literary history is that, like all writing, it must unfold in a linear fashion; the historian is only too well aware that linear narrative oversimplifies and is prone to one-sidedness. The reader of literary history ought to be given the larger network of cultural relationships that are at play in the particular detail, but how can we describe multiple perspectives and yet maintain a sense of historical narrative discourse? The cross-references and we are using in this history open up the discussion to simultaneous development on several dimensions of cultural intercourse.

From its beginnings in France, comparative literary study has been related to literary history, but at the same time removed from it, and this was due primarily to the strong identification of literary history with nationalist aspirations among the European states. But it was perhaps inevitable that, as comparative studies grew in number around the world, a time would finally arrive when literary history could be envisaged beyond the nation-state. Comparative literary history could be described today as a collaborative interdisciplinary study of the production and reception of literature in specific social and cultural contexts. The nation need no longer be the model.

The decade of the 1960s was a time of challenge and change in comparative literature in general because of the rise of literary theory. It was not long before the simple paradigm of comparative literary history as a series of national entries under a common and perhaps reductive logic ("Symbolism in Hungary," for instance) was challenged as a mere anthology of national literature summaries. The first and most successful comparative literary history was the late Albert S. Gérard's two volume *European Language Writing in Sub-Saharan Africa* (1984). The lessons learned in this pioneering work were of great significance for the development of literary history. One of the most important was the strong case he made with regard to the artificial nature of linguistic boundaries. Languages are not unbreakable walls. Gérard pointed out that the comparative aim of comparative literary histories would be lost if we could not free ourselves of the arbitrary limitations of our Eurocentric biases. He argued convincingly that areas like the Mediterranean could not be engaged without careful study of relations between European languages and Arabic, Hebrew, and Turkish, that the comparative study of the medieval Iberian peninsula had to concern itself with Arabic and Hebrew besides Latin, Old Spanish, Old Portuguese, and Medieval Catalan. Gerard also challenged the purportedly autonomous nature of literature and the concomitant notion that rejected the need to contextualize the writing within society. A second interdisciplinary model to be put into practice was the one developed by James Arnold and his colleagues in their comparative literary history of the Caribbean. The first of three volumes was published in 1994, the second in 1997, and the third in 2001. Arnold and his team developed a grid of cultural and linguistic factors affecting the entire Caribbean area from the sixteenth century to the end of the twentieth century. The most innovative aspect of this history is its coordination of literatures as the narrative expression of linguistic communities across five centuries.

Without minimizing the importance of all these projects and taking advantage of the many lessons they have taught us, we feel that the most ambitious model to date is the one used in the present history. It is based on the concept of progressive development from a conceptual frame to multiple synopsis of cultural institutions and centers, and culminating with a narrative description of the cultural imaginary. The frame is constructed on the basis of the cultural geography, the demographic changes, the linguistic diversity, and the sociological and economic conditions of cultural production in Latin America. The synoptic network then follows the travel routes in use in Latin America for centuries as the channels of commercial and cultural communication. Books, writers, ideas, and systems of representation moved from one center to another and responded to one institution or another: The Venezuelan Andrés Bello left a profound mark on Chile; Pedro Henríquez Ureña from Santo Domingo becomes part of the intellectual leadership in Mexico. Ideas and ideologies regarding the Amerindian run throughout the whole of Latin America from Bartolomé de las Casas in the sixteenth century to Rosario Castellanos in the twentieth.

This model of comparative literary history is, therefore, not only a construct (as are all histories), but it is also, and above all, a construct that deconstructs itself in order to remain an open history. By contrast, if in Dilthey's philosophy the past is an unknown horizon in need of interpretation, then texts are, above all, reflections on meanings that have been lost and have to be reconstructed. In other words, history is a horizon, and the past as a whole is the object of study. Texts are the means to the end of knowing the past. Heidegger's contribution to hermeneutics was a radical change from this. To read a text from the sixteenth century, for example, is to gain a small part of that time, but history is no longer the object of study of an unknown that can be known and mastered through the historian's efforts. History becomes the way in which historians construct the past and concomitantly understand their own time, place, and experience. There still remains the implicit bias brought about by the linear mode of historical discourse, the bias that asserts that the past offers continuous development leading to the present and pointing toward the future. In literary history, this bias can be seen in those almost endless lists of precursors leading to a major canonical work, followed by those equally long lists of successors.

But Foucault completely changed our approach to history, without any recourse to a return to totalizing narrative history. What was the historian to do? Was narrative history obsolete? Foucault was determined to rethink history as discontinuity. But how do we write history as discontinuity? His own work, shifting from archeology to genealogy, does not help, for he, too, was caught in the trap of thinking as an "other" and yet retaining his own historicity. A history of discontinuities might be an open history; however, the open history we describe in this introduction and put into practice in the three volumes is open insofar as it is designed as multiple dialectic encounters whose tensional developments must be interpreted by the reader and linked up to other moments that have become defining moments in the line of inquiry pursued by the particular reader of the history. The term "literary culture" is used here and throughout the volumes to designate an interactive network of sociolinguistic factors that make possible the communication and circulation of images, stories, beliefs, and other imaginative forms by which a community identifies itself. Literary works both are located in the historical process of production and reception and, at the same time, can also occasionally be suspended from it, since they can reenter at different times and places and under very different circumstances than those that obtained at the time of original composition. By considering literary culture as a field of production of the community's imaginary, we are compelled to follow a form of reading that examines texts according to the role they play in the constitution of the social and aesthetic identity of the community, the nation or, in our case, the entire continent we call Latin America. The multiple links between cultural identity and other forms of social power have usually been present only by inference in the literary histories of the past. Our contributors meet the new challenge head-on. The blindness to the power of the legitimating role of literature is only one of the many consequences of the intellectual and social isolation into which literary history had fallen.

In order to offer a historical account of literary culture we must emphasize both the scope and the focal points of our inquiry. Our scope is the entire hermeneutic arc of operations, beginning with ourselves as participants in literary reception. It is premised on our study of the vast area of cultural pre-understanding that Ricoeur calls the pre-figurative dimension, and reaches out, through our explanations, to the refigurative dimension of the imaginary in the social interaction of criticism, commentary, and history—which is nothing more or less than the process of world making in which we all participate. Our collective critical focus moves through a vast array of cultural artifacts and closes in on events of production and reception that have had a distinctive role in the development of the cultural imaginary of Latin America.

Historical writing is a privileged "grasping together" of discrete documents from the past, thereby giving them the meaning of an "event." Literary history creates events related to the production and reception of literature. The question has always been what elements of the past are significant for literary history as distinct from economic history or the history of ideas? In contrast to most of our predecessors, we have asked disturbing questions, such as how one can discuss the publication of a book of poetry and not take cognizance of the conditions under which the book was written or the conditions that prevail in the community into which it is received? This is the challenge of a history of literary culture. It can be neither the cumulative record of everything that has been published nor the compilation of themes and topics that have been treated by the literary histories of the past. A history of literary culture is possible only if we recognize that our sense of the past is made in the present. At any given point in the writing of the historical record, our knowledge of the past is partial and reflects present concerns and perspectives. The quest for what happened in the literary culture of the past is constituted by the gradual expansion of multiple points of view and the recognition that data are meaningless until they are given historicity. The significance of the events of the literary past is important today because of the meaning we derive from those events. When, for example, we discuss the historicity of Sor Juana Inés de la Cruz, we must be prepared not only to consider the differences in our many and varied descriptions of the context surrounding specific acts of composition, but also to recognize that the historical event itself is a construct. The meaning of a historical event in traditional literary history is determined by its role in a linear development; but in a comparative history of literary culture there is a weblike construct that is proposed as the context of production and reception and that establishes the dialectic framework for a debate of the conflict of interpretations.

If the literary text, its composition and reading, forms the historical subject matter of a history of literary culture, the text must be seen as more than a book; it must be construed as the nucleus of a historical event, an event that multiplies into many subsequent events and is subject to marked discontinuities as well as continuities. Can we imagine the delineation of a historical map of literary culture that is not a map of only one particular period in history? These volumes offer a historical map that situate the changing points of convergence and dissipation of cultural production through five hundred years. The database for such a map would be massive, even for one contiguous linguistic area, but if we take on the entire Latin American continent in all its diversity and heterogeneity, such an undertaking would be beyond the competence or, indeed, beyond the control of individual historians. This is the conclusion we reached when we envisaged such a history; therefore, a great deal of our own time and effort has gone into the organization and coordination of an international team of two hundred forty-two scholars to develop this history of literary cultures.

The Model for a Comparative History of Literary Culture

The description of the organizational plan should begin with the basics. There are three parts to this model, each building on the previous one, as already mentioned: the frame, the synopsis, and the narrative. The frame of cultural production is constructed in terms of cultural geography, the demographics of divergence and convergence of peoples, and the linguistic variables over this long duration of five centuries. This is followed by the factoring-in of the individual component of unquestioned foundational figures who changed the course of development of the imaginary, as well as the social, economic, and political conditions under which literary culture developed. However, this frame would be seriously flawed if it did not also bring into consideration the ideological power of social and state authority to fashion an official version of literary culture, excluding or relegating to the extreme margins all expression that did not perpetuate the elite's self-image of its culture as the only one. In most literary histories this has meant that as much as ninety percent of Latin American cultural production has gone unnoticed. The strongest evidence available to offset this gross distortion is the unacknowledged richness of Latin American discourses, including the religious, political, and scientific discourses as well as the historical and fictive.

What manner of frame is this that begins with the empirical, goes on to the ideological, and ends up with the plurality of discourses? It is a frame for literary culture that can be used to engage the innumerable specific uses of the imaginary without naming them all: a frame, as Ortega y Gasset said in another context, that both contains and excludes. We must contain the components of cultural formation, but we must exercise extreme caution with what we exclude, for even in the sixteenth century, as the Spanish and Portuguese authorities found out, Descartes, Erasmus, and Cervantes were very much in evidence, despite the laws enacted to keep them out.

Words can never be excluded altogether, as the Cuban landholders discovered when they tried to sever all communication with Haiti in the nineteenth century, fearing that their illiterate African slaves would communicate with the Haitians and somehow, in spite of illiteracy and language differences, learn of the slave revolt. Thus the function of containment is much more in evidence than any possible exclusion. The contraband book trade has always been more powerful than the full might of state authorities.

Such is the first part of our model and consequently the first volume of this history. The synopsis sections then map the cultural concentrations of production of literary culture. Literature in all its guises is produced by people coming together in specific places and slowly building their numbers until there is a necessary critical mass to be able to attract others to join. Societies offer places to meet and exchange goods as well as stories, opinions, and ideas and, in so doing, producers and consumers of cultural products make a group into a community. These places vary from one period to another and from one region to another, but in Latin America their history begins with the convergence of European and Amerindian institutions, with the attempt of the former to eradicate the latter—only to discover with time that their imported institutions of schools, academies, and museums would change because the displaced Amerindian cultural institutions lived on, altering and accelerating the mutation of European models.

But there is also another institution that was imported and almost immediately began to mutate: literature. This is not that curious nineteenth-century concept of autonomous literary writing but rather the tradition of writing used to teach, entertain, protest, praise God, express love, and also dream of utopic worlds. But literature did not only come from Europe fully developed to be altered in America. Literature was an institution that the colonial administrators who followed the conquerors tried to impose in place of the Amerindian literatures, but it was also a process. What did happen was that literatures in Spanish on both sides of the Atlantic developed at the same time. Mateo Alemán, Cervantes, Lope de Vega, Quevedo, Calderón are all contemporaries of Alonso de Ercilla, Ruiz de Alarcón, Bernardo de Balbuena, to name but a few in the Americas whose work marked the beginning of the bifurcation. The literary construct of expression is, indeed, one of the most important and most neglected of all cultural institutions, and so it is that we examine it closely in this history. Finally, the culmination of this mapping of cultural concentration arrives at a macro- level analysis of cultural centers throughout the continent, from Havana and Mexico City in the north to Buenos Aires and Santiago in the south. These are the places of production of literary culture.

The last part of this comparative history recognizes that we are still in need of historical narrativization. Even Fernand Braudel eventually had to write a narrative of life in the Mediterranean world. The danger here, of course, was that we might succumb to the traditional linear narrative of writers and their ideas (and books and their composition) in complete isolation from the social context in which they were created. Such linear narratives are not effective history; they are political legitimation. Therefore, with caution and with fascination, we turned to writing the history of Latin America's cultural imaginary from the bifurcated agony of the conquest and colonization to the chaotic struggle for cultural identity in the eighteenth and nineteenth centuries, culminating in the breakdown in the twentieth century of the structures established during the long colonial period. Now we present a fuller description of each volume:

Volume I

In 1970 Foucault wrote in what would be later titled *The Discourse on Language*: "in any society the production of discourse is at once controlled, selected, organized, and redistributed according to a number of procedures whose role is to avert its powers" (216). Therefore, if we approach literature as a discourse of social power, we are confronted with the realities of control and exclusion. In Volume I, the first part of our Latin American history of literary culture establishes the geographic, demographic, linguistic, and social dimensions of Latin American literatures as social discourse and, in the second part, turns to the legacy of exclusions established by literary histories (subdivided into two large subtopics: gender and sexual orientations, and ethnic marginalization). But beyond the subject matter of literature, there is a far more powerful force that provokes exclusions, and that is the perceived place in society of the speakers themselves. Not every speaking subject is considered to have an equal voice in the community of letters. The insane, the very young, the unlettered, and women are among those who have not had access to the discursive exchange of literature. These exclusions are the result of the dominant social forces that compete for control of the production and dissemination of literature and respond vigorously to any purported threat. In addition, as Foucault reminds us, there are also forces internal to the historiographic enterprise that limit access; the writing of history and the response to predecessors establishes, directly or indirectly, norms for inclusion. What are the norms that have dominated Latin American literary history? For the most part, they have been Eurocentric notions about nature and humanity as a binary opposition, which makes the question of verisimilitude into a circular argument that considers true to life whatever the society in question considers the quotidian to be in the struggle against nature (usually equated with barbarity). More subtle ideas, such as truth and honesty, become logocentric notions of domination. These historical truth claims and their severe limitations can be confronted only within the larger context of social discourse that engages but is not subject to Eurocentric biases of the literary histories of the past. Thus it is that the third part of this first volume contextualizes literary discourse within social discourse. Our response to Foucault's challenge throughout this first volume is to establish the diversity of speaking voices in Latin America, all with stories to tell and songs to sing and encounters to reenact in performance. The nonrecognition of these voices (which have never been silent) has had a marked effect on the elaboration of the symbolic expression of the imaginary. There have been numerous streams of literature for more than five hundred years with multiple crossings from one to the other, but nevertheless all but one has been absent from the historical record. Therefore, in this last part of the volume we attempt to contextualize the traditions of Latin America: the European-based traditions, primarily but not exclusively those of Spain and Portugal, with the Amerindian and the African traditions.

Volume II

It is not enough to state that the multiple institutions of society exercise power over discourse and attempt to control it. The exercise of power must be deconstructed. Whether control is partial or effective, what matters is the impact and effect these social structures have had on the development of literary culture. The second volume advances the historical description of centuries of discursive diversity by looking closely at the institutions throughout the Americas and thus linking the geographic factors in the development of cultural centers with the social forces that have produced the similarities and differences across Latin America. Recognizing that literature has its own history of form, the second part of this second volume pays attention to the mutations of literary form in Latin America in these hybrid cultures that are so different from Europe and yet so often imitative of its rituals and mannerisms. The syncretic transformations of literary form must be understood as a response to these opposing forces. The third part of the second volume pulls together the preceding sections of the first two volumes by elaborating the history of the centers of literary culture of all Latin America from the northern border of Mexico to the southern limits of South America. The various regions themselves have been designated via the history of transportation and population movements. At the end of these two volumes we are finally prepared to enter into the narrative of the cultural imaginary of Latin America.

Volume III

If the exclusionary practices of society have been considered in terms of the control of discourse, let us not forget that these are all external social forces that affect the cultural imaginary. But there is also an internal drive within these societies that is quite unpredictable: It can be seen in the sudden eruption of passionate interest in specific topics or texts such as the pre-Hispanic past or the postmodern. For our purposes, let us call this the discourse of the communities of critical commentary that build up and surround primary texts from the past and the present (as brilliantly expressed by the literary historian Sara Castro-Klarén). It is only by means of the most extreme manipulation and rationalization by the historian that a smooth and coherent sense of order can be imposed on this unpredictable flow of commentary. These are what Foucault calls the societies of discourse whose only social function is self-preservation as the dominant sector, a status that is protected by restricting access to cultural exchange. Cultural criticism throughout Europe and the Americas has been just such a domain. Foucault never hesitates to point out that the history of such societies of discourse is a history of discontinuity marked by radical changes in the social appropriation of discourse. The history of the cultural imaginary must therefore not only engage the profoundly split vision of Latin American writing, forever caught between celebration and lament; it must also map out the history of the communities of critical commentary and the almost constant series of changes in direction, especially during the eighteenth and nineteenth centuries. The insight gained from the research in previous volumes comes into play here.

How, we can ask, is it possible to write a historical account of literature, if each literary text is to be treated as caught in a discontinuous flux, as a work that may or may not prompt the emergence of commentary? One response is that the history of literary culture cannot be told in the traditional mode of a descriptive narration of cause and effect. The historical examination of the texts that have provoked explosions of critical commentary is addressed in the second part of the third volume by analyzing the structures of transculturation and describing the conditions of the emergence of the literary text as an event in the literary culture. I turn to Foucault once again. In *The Discourse on Language* he writes:

History has long since abandoned its attempts to understand events in terms of cause and effect in the formless unity of some great evolutionary process . . . . But it did this not to rediscover structures that were prior, alien and even hostile to the event. It was rather to establish the diverse, intersecting, often divergent, but never autonomous series that enable us to circumscribe the "locus" of the event, the margins of its unpredictability, the conditions of its emergence. (230)

If literary history is to be considered history, it must begin by rethinking the nature of literature as both part of the social discourse and at the same time as a text, an event whose locus must be circumscribed. The text as historical event is the key to a history of literary culture. The last leg of this long journey of three volumes is an attempt to lay the foundation for the consideration of the events of literary history in the twentieth century. The text as historical event can be addressed by establishing the material conditions for its production as part of the literary culture, its radical discontinuity in terms of the unpredictable nature of commentary, and finally in terms of its power to transcend the local and to enter the diverse but related literary cultures of Latin America. The editors and writers of this collaborative literary history have built up a kind of hypertext for the reader to open up and unfold one historical narrative after another. And what is the truth claim we put forward? That the information we give is as accurate as we have been able to make it and that the history of literary cultures is a process and not a fixed representation of the past. This is our interpretation of Ricoeur's call for effective history and our response to Foucault's history of discontinuities.

How to Read This Comparative History

Any one of the three sections of the first volume is a good place to begin, since the reader will enter into either the empirical, the ideological, or the discursive areas of literary culture–from which multiple indicators will point to the follow-up sections. The second volume will allow the reader to enter into collective cultural constructs, since it concentrates on cultural modalities, discursive modes, institutional sanctions, and cultural centers that both attract and irradiate ideas, images, ideals, dreams, and passionate denunciations throughout wider and wider circles of distribution and influence. These cultural centers make up the constellation of major and lesser concentrations of literary activity, which are linked not only to each other but to expatriate centers in places such as Paris and New York. The third volume is the story of identity and focuses on modes of representation and the resultant narrative web that connects the cultural centers with each other and with European and (English-speaking) North American centers. These collective threads construct the fabric of the shared culture and identify the key role of certain individual writers whose works have become major cultural forces. The reader of the third volume will encounter the richness of the cultural imaginary. Authors such as Sor Juana, Rubén Darío, Pablo Neruda, Machado de Assis, Jorge Luis Borges, Clarice Lispector, or Gabriel García Márquez, whose writings have been translated and transmitted far beyond their place of origin, become the major indicators of the cultural reality of Latin America. But when taken out of that local context, they create yet another Latin America–one that exists elsewhere–in the fabulations created by cultural distance. Like the first two, the third volume has its own specific structure and logic. The central focus is on the specifici-

ties of the phenomenon of transculturation as it pertains to the special cases within Latin America.

The structure of this history is designed to provide the configuration of an open history, one that neither hides the assumptions of the past nor replaces them with new ones, but rather challenges such presumptions as, for example, the claims of elite class priority, or notions of racial superiority or of male dominance. All of these presumptions have been part of the cultural history of Latin America, and all have been inscribed to a greater or lesser extent in history and, especially, literary history. Our task in this history has been, first, to describe these presumptions of authority; second, to describe the effects they have had as historical norms; third, to confront them with the exclusions and marginalizations of discourse; and fourthly, to work out an effective history of the dialectic tension that persists to this day in the double vision of Latin America.

This history of literary cultures both acknowledges a prolonged period of over five hundred years of maturation and opens up a new millennium of heightened interaction in the community of critical commentators of Latin America. The dialogue (and debate) between the best scholars in this field is now a well-established tradition; what we have done is to invite new participants, our readers, into the discussion. The editors and coordinators of these volumes recognize and respond to the hermeneutic principle that historiography always involves the narrative possibilities of the past dialectically linked with the perspective of the present-day historian: The historical past is a construct we build conceptually by means of ideas made possible because of present debates. So it is that the reader of this history will not find a recitation of dates, facts, or events. Instead, the historical materials we have been able to bring together are laid out in a grid, subject to the multiple viewpoints of 242 scholars and open to the interpretation of the reader. At this particular moment, at the start of the twenty-first century, we would do well to be mindful of the admonition of Francisco Goya from the nineteenth century: "El sueño de la razón produce monstruos" ["The dream of reason produces monsters"]. Positivism was such a dream, as is the neoliberalism of the International Monetary Fund. Yet to abandon reason is to revert to the irrational tyranny of ambition and greed. The dialectics of collaborative research give us the advantage of initiating a continuous dialogue with the past, engaging our rational faculties as we explain our collective experience. Thus, we may also be able to avoid the dream of reason that, in our time, continues to produce the monsters of multinational communication conglomerates and the sleep of reason that allows the growth of rabid nationalism, which, more often than not, has served as a cover for gross political and economic exploitation of the many by the few. In seeking a model of shared culture, this history of literary culture aims to go beyond the limits of both imperial domination and divisive nationalism; it rejects master narratives that replicate such domination and blindness.

In conclusion, for whom is this history written and to what end? It is written for those inside and outside of the Americas who are interested in the exploration of a very distinct and complex shared history of literary culture. It aims to be a readable, perspectival account, and also to create a research tool that continuously opens up new lines of inquiry, one that does not close upon an official history or a master text, or reduce questions to one version and one interpretation. Nineteenth-century literary history, in its various forms, did tend to impose closure; one of its tasks was the contextualizing of literature in history according to certain specific universal models–from Hegel's unified spirit of an age to Dilthey's characteristic *Geist*, in which the "context" was cultural (philosophic, religious, legal, aesthetic, scientific) but not really material, social, or political. For over a century now, there has been a rejection of literary history as serious *historical* scholarship; its demise as a discipline within literary studies has been expected for more than forty years, certainly since North American New Criticism dismissed historicism. But history is an essential part of all inquiry.

Recent critics of literary history have been just as suspicious of its possibilities as their predecessors had been un-self-consciously confident of being able to attain objective truth.

As we write at the start of the new century, under the diverse influences of, to name a few, cultural anthropology, communications theory, cultural semiotics, hermeneutics, critical legal theory, the new geography, the new history, and the theories of Michel Foucault and Pierre Bourdieu, there is a much more supple sense of the possible intersections of the literary and its wider socio-political contexts. It is instructive for us to inquire as to why it has taken so long for literary history to transcend its canonical limitations. To a large extent, Latin American histories of literature were written within a small close-knit community of the lettered elite. We have already noted some of the great exceptions of people like Henríquez Ureña, who was able to see beyond his social and academic status into the rich manifold of the popular base of literature and lament the failure of scholarship to encompass it. He considered his own work to be a first step, and it was.

The complex mass of cultural discourse contained in this comparative history–two hundred and five texts from seven separate disciplines– raises no more of a problem for the reader than that encountered in reading the results of any research project on culture. In the first volume, it may be the disciplinary distance in the succession of texts rather than any complicated discursive structure that will prove somewhat daunting. The second volume is on much more familiar ground for literary scholars, since institutions, textual forms, and cultural centers are all part of the literary historicity traditionally considered as the author's context. The difficulty here may be the problematizing of these conditions of composition, as political, social and economic factors are brought to bear. The third volume, because of its extensive use of current thinking on miscegenation, alterity, and misogamy, is the most challenging because of the diversity of voices coming forth in the extraordinary range of cultural indicators in the flux of the cultural imaginary, but the reader who will stay with it will be richly rewarded.

The case for the "unity" of the whole of this historical project has been argued on numerous occasions over the last five years among the participants with little agreement. Since totalizing narrative has been deconstructed and the conventions of writing effective history have come down to good writing, the Gadamerian metaphor of "play" may prove useful in the effort to break the impasse. If we play a game such as soccer (football), we must subscribe to the rules of the game, the established size of the field, the ball, and so forth, as well as agreeing upon the length of the game. However, all of these pregame agreements in no way determine how the game will be played. In this history, there is a unified design, and the standard rules of documentation are strictly observed. Although each writer is his or her own player, she or he is also part of a team, sometimes working together to write a

section. We can look upon this ten-section history as a soccer tournament of ten games in which the reader plays; winners and losers will be determined by how well the reader plays with the section's team.

The sequence or order of the texts is also explicitly displayed through the descriptive titles and subtitles of the history and the multiple texts that serve as prefaces or introductions to a volume, a part, or a section. Each major component is keyed into the design of frame, synopsis, and narrative. What is the ultimate result? The history is in itself unfinished, since there are no grand conclusions or even a kind of summing up. The result we have endeavored to obtain is that of a continuing and meaningful encounter between reader and text, and implicitly between texts themselves that complement or contest each other. Collectively we seek to respond to F. W. Bateman–in agreement with his assessment of history and in disagreement with his view on literature: "History is committed by its nature to the expositions of *differences* between one temporal event or period and another. A country in which no such differences can be distinguished is a country without a history.... Literature, on the other hand, is necessarily 'esemplastic', to use Coleridge's term. The emphasis in it is on similarities rather than differences... like oil and water literature and history will not mix" (116). No scholar would seriously seek to mix or confuse history and literature, but an effective history of literature should be a constant play between the historian's explanation and the reader's understanding.

Consider the prophetic words of Roland Barthes in *On Racine* some thirty years ago: "literary history is possible only if it becomes sociological, if it is concerned with activities and institutions, not with individuals"(161). Barthes did not write such a history, but we have. For the generation of literary historians who have worked their way through Foucault, the ruptures, breaks, gaps, and unexpected recycling of human activity in the past are not impediments to historical research but rather are the material of study. Neat groupings of works and authors, the orderly succession of images, tropes, plots are nothing more than the utopic fantasy of literary historians and, as with all utopian visions, lurking behind there is an ideology–which in this case is the Comtean positivism that conquered Latin America in the second half of the nineteenth century, from Mexico to Brazil. The oxymoron "order and progress" became a metaphor for modernity.

As we complete this history at the beginning of the twenty-first century, we understand that the sense of order imposed on Latin American literary culture by our emplotment of data and circumstance must self-deconstruct and rid itself of all vestiges of totalizing history. The dialectic of historical explanation and reader understanding is a dialectic in constant motion and so keeps the inquiry open; understanding is always incomplete, and therefore explanations must be provided again and again. In this history of Latin American literary culture, the reader will encounter many equally cogent and informed emplotments of Latin America's cultural past. Readers do not have to deconstruct this history; we have done it for them by mapping out multiple trajectories of historical emplotment.

In closing this introduction, we want to thank María Elena de Valdés, who corrected and coordinated all of the documentation for the three volumes and who was the control center for the entire project. Linda Hutcheon was responsible for the final copyediting of all the essays. Special thanks are also in order for the twenty-seven section coordinators for their enthusiasm, trust, and dedication to this history, beginning with our first meeting in February 1996. Our research assistants were an invaluable asset to all our authors. We want to acknowledge the assistance of Wendy Eberle, Jonathan Rollins, Adriana Spahr, and, especially, Cristina Santos, who has been with us throughout the entire five years. Three undergraduate students of extraordinary skill and dedication worked on the second phase of the project; thanks to Alexandra Pimenidis, Nancy Grande, and Katya Rosadiuk for their part. We want to thank the Social Sciences and Humanities Research Council of Canada for awarding us the principal grant that made this project and its historical enterprises possible. At a time when political isolation has raised a potential threat to international cooperation, it is with pleasure that we acknowledge that the Canadian granting agency was solely guided by questions of scholarly value. The University of Toronto—through the Vice-President, Research, Heather Munroe-Blum; the former Dean of Arts and Science, Marsha Chandler; and the present Dean, Carl G. Amrhein—has supported the Literary History Project with extraordinary resources and encouragement. Finally, we wish to acknowledge that the Robarts Research Library has been the very heart of the research effort in putting together these volumes. We wish to thank Chief Librarian Carol R. Moore and her staff, especially Sharon Brown, Shawn Meikle, Maureen Morin, Gayle Garlock, and Terry Correia, for their time, expert assistance, and good cheer. To our fellow authors, we extend our warmest congratulations for a job well done. Our publishing partners in this history, Oxford University Press, Fondo de Cultura Económica, and Universidade de Minas Gerais, have had an important part of the planning of the volumes that we gratefully acknowledge.

We invite our readers to explore the rich diversity of Latin American literary cultures.

Works Cited

Anderson-Imbert, Enrique. 1954. *Historia de la literatura hispanoamericana*. 2 vols. Mexico City: Fondo de Cultura Económica.

Arnold, A. James, ed. 1994–2001. *A History of Literature in the Caribbean*. 3 vols. Amsterdam: John Benjamins.

Barthes, Roland. 1983. *On Racine*. Trans. Richard Howard. New York: Performing Arts Journal Publications.

Bateson, F. W. 1970–71. "Literary History: Non-Subject Par Excellence." *New Literary History* 2: 115–122.

Bloch, Marc. [1952] 1996. *Apología para la historia*. Trans. María Jiménez and Danielle Zaslavsky. Mexico City: Instituto Nacional de Antropología e Historia, Fondo de Cultura Económica.

Bourdieu, Pierre. 1993. *The Field of Cultural Production: Essays on Art and Literature*. Ed. and Intro. Randal Johnson. Trans. Richard Nice, R. Swyer, Claud DuVerlie, and Juliette Parnell. New York: Columbia University Press.

Braudel, Fernand. 1972. *The Mediterranean and the Mediterranean World in the Age of Philip II*. Trans. Siân Reynolds. 2 vols. New York: Harper and Row.

Castro-Klarén, Sara. 1999. "Mimicry Revisited: Latin America, a Post-Colonial Theory and the Location of Knowledge." In *El debate de la postcolonialidad en Latinoamérica: Una postmodernidad periférica o cambio de paradigma en el pensamiento latinoamericano*. Ed. Alfonso de Toro and Fernando de Toro. Madrid: Iberoamericana; Frankfurt am Main: Vervuert. 137–164.

Foucault, Michel. 1972. "The Discourse on Language." Trans. Rupert Sawyer. In *The Archeology of Knowledge*. New York: Random House. 215–237.

Gérard, Albert S. 1986. *European-Language Writing in Sub-Saharan Africa*. 2 vols. Budapest: Akadémiai Kiadó.

Henríquez Ureña, Pedro. 1949. *Las corrientes literarias en la América Hispánica*. Mexico: Fondo de Cultura Económica.

Perkins, David. 1992. *Is Literary History Possible?* Baltimore: Johns Hopkins University Press.

Ricoeur, Paul. 1984. *Time and Narrative*. Trans. Kathleen McLaughlin and David Pellauer. 3 vols. Chicago: University of Chicago Press.

SERIES OVERVIEW

RETHINKING LITERARY HISTORY—COMPARATIVELY

Mario J. Valdés and Linda Hutcheon,
General Series Editors

The proliferation in the last few decades of both new literary histories and essays, and books on the topic of writing literary history would suggest that this is a fitting time to explore not only the problematizing challenges that new methodological paradigms have raised, but also the new concrete possibilities opened up by precisely these challenges. In this spirit, and with the financial support of the Major Collaborative Research Initiatives program of the Social Sciences and Humanities Research Council of Canada and the University of Toronto, two large teams of scholars from North and South America and Europe have worked together to find new models of rethinking the way literary history is written in two of the more culturally complex parts of the world: Latin America and East Central Europe. Each of these new projects, in its own way, takes a very different tack on the writing of literary history than have other histories, which have traditionally been organized around nations or national languages.

In order to begin to explain the shared theoretical grounding that unites both *Literary Cultures of Latin America* and *The Comparative History of East Central European Literary Cultures: Nineteenth and Twentieth Centuries*, let us look at the four words of our title here, each of which on the surface seems benign but in fact opens up onto large areas of both contention and excitement today: "Rethinking Literary History—Comparatively." Clearly, to *rethink* is not only to think once again; it is to think anew. This does not involve revisionism or revising: It is not a question of correcting, altering, amending, or improving. To rethink is to reconsider, and here we intend all the associations of care and attentiveness and serious reflection that go with the notion of consideration. One of the things that has consistently been rethought over the centuries is the very concept of the *literary*: Its boundaries have been extended from the view of literature as only imaginative writing, to include many other categories of discourse—fictional as well as documentary, oral as well as written, popular as well as "elite." This inclusive and nonnormative notion of literature is not new to the early twenty-first century, but it has been theorized anew, with the help of, among others, post-structuralist and feminist thinking, which has allowed research to cross cultural and national language borders in productive ways. A significant result of this theorizing (as the examples of these volumes show) has been the articulation of new and more complex ways to think through the already

acknowledged importance of both literature and literary history to more general categories of social and cultural history.

Thus, this broadening of the object of study not only increases the number of types of texts to be examined by literary historians but also expands the historical contexts in which such texts will, of necessity, have to be considered. In this case, the *history* of literature then turns out to be the multiple and complex histories of its production, but also of its reception. Literary historians over the centuries have always been aware of the complexity of literary production, but the new methodological paradigms developed by various critical theories in the last few decades have made it impossible not to add to this an awareness of the equally complicated and equally significant nature of literary reception. What has come to be called the "literary institution"—the field in which literary experience occurs—is, therefore, as much a part of this history as is the development of styles or genres. Because we are now aware of these dimensions, economic, political, and broader cultural and social perspectives on issues such as race or gender must be brought to bear in the constructing of any "literary" history today in a different way than they might have in the past. As theorized by postcolonial and gender theorists, these perspectives help make conscious the ideological underpinnings of the experience of producing and responding to literature—and, of course, of writing literary histories.

It is because of this sort of rethinking that the recent critical reconsiderations of history as a discipline were bound to have inevitable repercussions on the conceptualizing of what a literary history can and should be. Indeed, what is at stake in the move from the more traditional national model of literary history to a *comparative* one can be seen best by analogy to the discipline of history and to historiography. In the introduction to the English translation of the first book of his monumental three-volume, *Civilisation matérielle, économie et capitalisme, 15e–18e siècle* [*Civilisation and Capitalism 15–18 Century*, 1981], the French historian Fernand Braudel described his project as comparative, as moving dialectically between past and present, between concrete observation and an awareness of the heterogeneity and complexity of life (25). A comparative literary history would not only try to keep in the foreground this dialectic hermeneutic movement between past and present but would try to do something analogous to what Braudel and the Annales school accomplished in their moving of history's emphasis from the events of politics and diplomacy to, on the one hand, a study of the broader circumstances (demographic, geographical, climatic, etc.) conditioning such events and, on the other, a parallel and very detailed scrutiny of the quantified, concrete material data of life of the past, thus expanding the sense of what constituted historical evidence. A "comparative" literary history would move from this life as it is *lived* to how it is *told*. Just as Braudel's *La Méditerranée et le monde méditerranéen à l'époque de Philippe II* brought together such diverse elements as the religion, history, geography, technology, agriculture, and general intellectual trends of this place at this time, so the specific comparative literary histories of Latin America and East Central Europe study literature in contexts beyond the aesthetic and formal, taking into account relevant political, anthropological, economic, geographic, historical, demographic, and sociological research in articulating the contexts of a community's literature. For this reason, these projects have, by definition, become interdisciplinary ones, and the teams of researchers have included scholars from the social sciences as well as humanities.

These comparative literary histories seek to do something very different from what national literary histories have done, both in their traditional forms and in their recent, quite differently formatted ones (such as Hollier's *A New History of French Literature*).

As Benedict Anderson argues in his influential study, *Imagined Communities: Reflections on the Origin and Spread of Nationalism*, nationhood is a matter of "imagined community" (7). In Europe, he claims, that sense of collective identity was conceived in the nineteenth century and born largely of the printed word and the literary genre we know as the novel—though others would, no doubt, want to argue for the centrality of drama or even opera (see, for example, Lindenberger 257). This general intertwining of the literary and the national, however, is not one to be abandoned in a comparative literary history, but to limit oneself to it would be to downplay the power of other "imagined communities" based on, say, language or geographic region rather than nation. Either of these categories might foreground the artificiality, not to say fragility, of national borders: After all such borders, as historical entities, have changed often and, indeed, change constantly.

In addition, any monolithic construction of a national literary history risks marginalizing or even excluding the literary creations of even those working within those borders, but in other languages or other cultural traditions. There are other complicating factors, too, that suggest the need for a more flexible and integrative concept of the scope and scale of literary history than might be implied when the focus is on a single language (often acting as a synecdoche of a nation): Besides the obvious fact that people can and often do participate in several language communities at once, texts, as well as ideas and images, pass from one language to another through the medium of translation. Films are released in many languages at the same time; novels are simultaneously published around the world in translation; plays are performed on several continents in different languages. A comparative literary history is also, therefore, the history both made possible by and even demanded of our age of international information access and electronic technology.

These two projects address these possibilities and fulfil these demands in very specific and individual ways as dictated by their particular, appropriate choice of focus and methodology (which will be explained by the editors' introductions). Despite this necessary particularity of engagement, as we have been suggesting, they are united by a certain, general shared methodological and theoretical grounding on which they have built in order to put into practice the insights that such a journal as *New Literary History* has been theorizing, in issue after issue, for over twenty years. It is *in practice*, as well as theory, that these volumes seek to rethink literary history—comparatively.

Fernand Braudel called his own historical work comparative not only because it crossed traditional disciplinary boundaries but because it involved what he called the "dialectic of past and present." (25) Similarly, literary history is inevitably the history of the past as read through the present. It cannot be simply a cumulative record of all that has been written or performed or even a compilation of themes or forms. The literary past—that is, the past of both literature's production and its reception—is unavoidably interpreted in the light of the present, and present knowledge of it will, therefore, be partial and provisional, but not insignificant for all that. A comparative literary history would have to acknowledge the epistemological limitations that its hermeneutic situation creates: Each historian is situated as a real person living in a linguistic and cultural community, and it is from that specific position that he or she engages in what phenomenologists call the horizon of the past. The texts of that past were created by people in a specific language, at a specific moment, in a specific place; but the literary historian is also a historical being, "situated" with similar particularity. The community of readers of any text, as Hans-Georg Gadamer argued, is historically constituted, but is never limited to its creator's contemporaries in the past.

This hermeneutic underpinning of a "situated" literary history is only one of the senses in which there is a "dialectic of past and present." As the work of Hayden White and others has shown, it is in the present that the historian shapes and orders the events of the past, *making* meaning even more than *recording* it. In Anglo-American literary criticism, the rise of what has been called the New Historicism is an example of a post-New Critical (formalist) return to the historical embeddedness of literature. It also marks a specifically literary engaging of the issues that historians have been debating for some time now, provoked by the work of Marxists, feminists, and theorists of race, ethnicity, and sexual choice.

The implications of this notion of the "situatedness" of the historian dovetail with those created by the new awareness of (and openness about) the interpretive and narrating act of history-writing. And these all have special resonance for the literary historian: Perspective, interpretation, and narration are among the staples of the study of literature, as much as history. Just as a work such as Emmanuel Le Roy Ladurie's *Carnival in Romans* (1979) challenged the convention of historical narrative as objective, neutral, impersonal, and transparent; so, too, does fiction such as Salman Rushdie's *Midnight's Children* or E. L. Doctorow's *Ragtime*. The inevitable self-consciousness of literary historians, when they are faced with such historiographic metafictional texts cannot but condition their sense of what the "imaginative reconstruction" (Gottschalk 48) of the past in the present might entail. History's explanatory or narrative "emplotments," to use Hayden White's term, are never innocent or without consequences. To admit any of this is, in some way, to challenge the cognitive status of historical knowledge as it had come to be known in empirical and positivist terms in the nineteenth century. Ground-breaking work, such as Paul Ricoeur's multivolumed *Temps et récit,* with its painstaking study of the reconfiguration and refiguration of time by narrative—both historical and fictive—has provided the kind of necessary bridge between those cognitive challenges faced by the discipline of history and those that need to be considered in writing about the past of literature. As a human construct, literary history, too, is a narrativizing of literary "events," and its "archive" is a textualized one in only a more immediately self-evident way than is the archive of all historiography.

Such analogies between the writing of history and the writing of literary history are also possible because of what intellectual historian Dominick LaCapra has articulated in terms of "the postulates of unity, continuity, and mastery of a documentary repertoire" that have underpinned both endeavors in the past and which, thus, have come under close scrutiny in the wake of poststructuralist, postcolonial, and other critiques that point to discontinuities, gaps, ruptures, or exclusions rather than linear development, evolution, or continuity (32). This means that the very task of the historian has to be rethought. In White's words, "a specifically *historical* inquiry is born less of the necessity to establish that certain events *occurred* than of the desire to determine what certain events might *mean* for a given group, society, or culture's conception of its present tasks and future prospects" (487). With this kind of shift from validation to signification, it is not hard to see where the push might have come for literary historians, as well, to reconceptualize historical process to include the relations between texts and the contexts of production—and reception. The kind of question asked of historiography for decades should also be (and is also being) asked of literary history writing today: "How did (a given) phenomenon enter the system entitled history and how has the system of historical writing acquired effective discursive power?" (Cohen 206). The Foucaultian linking of power and knowledge points here, as elsewhere in contemporary theorizing, to an awareness that, while events did occur in the past, we give meaning to—that is, we name and constitute—those "events" as "historical facts" by selection and narrative positioning. And those acts are carried out by people who are as "situated" in the particularities of such things as time and place, language and gender. (So too are the people who first produced the literature being studied.) It is in this sense, perhaps, that we should read Nietzsche's admonition in *The Use and Abuse of History:* "*You can explain the past only by what is most powerful in the present*" (40; his italics). The present is what always gives the past whatever meaning accrues to it. This is not a defeatist invalidation of the process of history-writing; it is merely a frank acknowledgment of a hermeneutic reality.

In literary history, as theorists as diverse as Robert Weimann, Ralph Cohen, and Claudio Guillén have shown, the "events" of the past to be ordered and given meaning are, in this case, literary texts—as they are produced and received—and, for the historian as interpreter, these texts act as both documents of the past and experiences of the present. This is another of the senses in which these two projects involve a "dialectic of past and present." In openly confronting this duality and in reflexively engaging with the fact (and consequences) of the power that accompanies the shaping and ordering process that constitutes the writing of any history, a comparative literary history would foreground

these methodological frameworks (hermeneutic, poststructuralist, postcolonial, feminist, and so on) and directly address its own theoretical assumptions regarding both texts and contexts (sociocultural, economic, political, aesthetic). Such is the theory. How successfully this has been achieved *in practice* is up to the readers of these volumes to decide. With hundreds of contributors living in many countries and doing their research under radically differing working conditions, it will be clear why this is the kind of vast venture that is possible only in an age of electronic communication among scholars and computer access to bibliographic sources previously unavailable to many.

In full awareness of the current debates in historiography, then, and necessarily drawing on the work of experts in the other adjacent fields of anthropology, sociology, geography, fine art, music, communications, economics, and political science as well as history, these comparative literary histories seek not only to address specific instances of historical exclusions and inclusions, but to rethink the very categories of selection and ordering used in the writing of literary history. Comparative literary history looks to recast literary works as historical "events" within a dynamic cultural context of reception and transmission. This undertaking has necessitated the reexamination of certain historiographic blind spots involving such matters as the institutional promotion or suppression of literature. It has also involved a questioning of the basic assumptions of historical narrative, including those of narrative time frame and narrative authority.

Our general model, adapted to literary ends from Braudel's historical one, calls for the separate and detailed elaboration of the broader social context along with the narration of literary "events" in an attempt to redress some of the omissions of the past by confronting issues such as the social institutions that have been important in the production and reception of literature or the politics of readership in a given community. This model eschews periodization based on either empirical evidence (dates of birth and death of writers, publication dates) or interpretive or generic categories ("late romantic prose" or "neoclassical drama"), and substitutes, instead, alternative time frames of reception in which, for example, specific literary works can be examined as mobile attractors of larger cultural forces: to use examples from other areas, *The Tempest* as a postcolonial historical text or *Don Quijote* as a twentieth-century mediator of Spanish literary identity (in Unamuno, Ortega y Gasset, and Azorín). This has meant expanding the scope of what constitutes the "literary" as well as what a "period" might entail. As Denis Hollier put it in his Introduction to *A New History of French Literature:* "Today it is increasingly difficult to draw one solid line of demarcation between the inside and the outside of a work of art; sometimes it is even impossible to distinguish between form and background" (xxv).

This expansion of scope, however, does not do away with, but rather only intensifies, the need to acknowledge that the act of narrativizing—of writing a literary history of any kind—imposes a sense of order and, inevitably, closure upon the literary "events" under scrutiny. The question of narrative authority is one that our related metatheoretical volume, *Rethinking Literary History* (with contributions from Stephen Greenblatt, Walter Mignolo, Marshall Brown, Homi Bhabha, and the two of us), and the individual histories all address, for this authority is linked not only to the multiple truth claims that historical narratives propose but to the historians' causal explanations themselves. The exercise of narrative authority is more blatant, perhaps, in such nineteenth-century histories as the first volumes of Michelet's *Histoire de la Révolution Française*, but it is a constant in historical writing, for this process involves selecting and sorting evidence, organizing it into a narrative sequence, and thus interpreting it and giving it meaning. Literary histories are no different: They too give form and coherence to data. The task set by a *comparative* literary history is all the more complex, because such a project must deal with multiple social and demographic factors, sometimes of long duration. That more than one such historical narrative should—and inevitably will—be offered in each of these collaborative volumes is a sign of the interpretive complexity of both the data and the narrativization process itself. Literature does not exist in isolation from the culture in which it is "experienced"—that is, the culture in which it is both produced and received. While acknowledging the undeniable specificity of language or nation, we feel it is now time to consider as well other, more comparative configurations for the historical knowledge of literature.

On a more personal note, as general editors, we are often asked (as the particular volume editors are as well): Why would we willingly give up eight years of our life to organize and edit these large collaborative projects? To answer with candor, our academic and professional explanations, given above, do not tell the whole story. There is also what is almost a moral imperative involved. In our case, our separate scholarly work on narrative identity has given us cause to distinguish the identity of the self from that of things: The latter kind of identity comes down, in the final analysis, to the recognition of stability and even immutability, as illustrated by the genetic code of a living organism. Narrative identity, in contrast, changes; one could even say that it swims in a fast-flowing narrative stream. The mutability of fictional characters in the stories we tell and read is recognized and accepted because characters are emplotted along with the story itself. But the notion of narrative identity is of the greatest importance in an inquiry into the identity of peoples and nations as well, for these, too, possess the same dramatic character of narrative identity—this time, in the stories we have told each other about who we are and who our "others" are. All too often, this narrative identity of peoples and nations has been

confused with that of a fixed thing. In our present concern with the comparative history of literary cultures of different peoples, we, along with the many authors of these volumes, have been careful to point to the contingency of the turning points in the story that contribute to the overall significance of the history as well as the place accorded to the protagonists. To recognize this is, perhaps, to begin to free ourselves of prejudice concerning the identity claimed by different peoples for themselves and for their "others," which so often has produced arrogance, fear, and even hatred. These volumes aim to enhance an understanding—among the peoples of Latin America and East Central Europe—that the similarities they share with others are a response to human needs, drawing upon a common cultural imaginary, and so, too, are their differences. This is the moral imperative of a comparative literary history.

Works Cited

Anderson, Benedict. 1983. *Imagined Communities: Reflections on the Origin and Spread of Nationalism*. London: Verso.

Braudel, Fernand. 1981. *The Structures of Everyday Life: The Limits of the Possible*. Trans. Sian Reynolds. London: Collins. Vol. 1 of *Civilisation and Capitalism 15–18 Century*. 3 vols.

Cohen, Sande. 1978. "Structuralism and the Writing of Intellectual History." *History and Theory* 17.2: 175–206.

Gottschalk, Louis. 1969. *Understanding History: A Primer of Historical Method*. 2d. ed. New York: Knopf.

Hollier, Denis, ed. 1989. *A New History of French Literature*. Cambridge: Harvard University Press.

Hutcheon, Linda. 1988. *A Poetics of Postmodernism: History, Theory, Fiction*. London and New York: Routledge.

LaCapra, Dominick. 1985. *History and Criticism*. Ithaca, NY: Cornell University Press.

Lindenberger, Herbert. 1984. *Opera: the Extravagant Art*. Ithaca, NY: Cornell University Press.

Nietzsche, Friedrich. 1957. *The Use and Abuse of History*. Trans. Adrian Collins. Ed. Julius Kraft. Indianapolis, IN, and New York: Liberal Arts Press and Bobbs-Merrill.

White, Hayden. 1986. "Historical Pluralism." *Critical Inquiry*. 12.3: 480–93.

COEDITOR'S INTRODUCTION

HISTORY AFTER HISTORY

Djelal Kadir

Latin American historiography today, whether literary or more broadly cultural, inevitably tracks a delicate course through national and separatist articulations, especially a transnationally constructed historiographic project such as the present one, an endeavor that involves 242 contributors from twenty-two different countries. The Argentine/Mexican cultural anthropologist Néstor García Canclini, in his *La globalización imaginada* [Imagined Globalization], would wish to make this delineation between the national and the separatist into a counterpoint. He would do so in juxtaposing discrepant usages of concepts such as "multiculturalism" in Latin America and the United States of America. García Canclini undertakes this contrapuntal parsing on the way to articulating what he calls a "supranational culture" that corresponds to an epoch of globalization and the production of social institutions and historical subjects, consistent, in Alberto Moreiras' phrase, "with the cultural logic of multinational capitalism." I invoke these distinguished critics of Latin American culture as much for recalling their insightful critiques as for the symptomatic echoes in their lexicon that resonates so unmistakably with such key figures in contemporary cultural discourse as the United States' Fredric Jameson and Europe's Slavoj Žižek.

These symptomatic resonances carry a certain explanatory power; principally, they point to the fact that critical and historical discourses inevitably exceed the linguistic and cognitive circumscriptions of cultural particularity and national boundaries. It has been the task of comparative studies to trace and diagnose those transnational imbrications and transdiscursive crossings, and this is precisely the animating impetus of the present literary history, a dynamic that surpasses and de-defines the traditional narratives of nation and national literary history. As such, the focus of the current project passes through the fissures of its construction, the infra-history of the history, so to speak.

If history is a cognitive map of the life it narrates, the figuration of that cartography is inevitably symptomatic of the cognitive processes of the cartographers and, in the case of our collective endeavors, of the negotiations and accommodations that articulate this construct. García Canclini's expressed desideratum of a "supranational culture," then, may well be embodied in the very pages of this collaboration, involving, as it does, the large, multinational team of contributors that the making of this project has required. What, no doubt, may also be embodied in the historiographic culture inhabiting these pages are the fault lines, the textual and textural biases that attest, paradoxically, to the simultaneously utopian *and* inevitable character of "supranational" formations. The greatest inevitability, in this regard, may well be that whatever may be deemed "supranational" is certainly not

immune to the centripetal interpellations of hegemonic discourse (except in the reverie of those who believe they actually inhabit a postnational era). Operating under such illusions are likely to be those who would see Althusser's ideological state apparatuses melt into thin air, like everything that is solid, especially since 1989, simply by rhetorically de-linking state and nation in that clenched binomial of the "nation-state." Clearly, the global climate of the New World Order at the beginning of the twenty-first century suggests otherwise, and thus requires a more complex understanding of history and of the historical present.

The discursive counterpoints, the jockeying juxtapositions, the allegiances, now insightful, now blind, that may suffuse the formative blocks of this project may aspire, in some cases, to be novel and unprecedented. These too, however, are qualitatively coterminous with the sempiternal vicissitudes of historiography, since historical time has sought to displace time immemorial. It might be instructive to note this constancy of history's history, particularly since the lay expectation from history is the documenting of discontinuities and the narration of particularist contingencies that move narrative along by ruptures and raptures rather than by recurrent leaps and lapses.

History and nation have been intricately enmeshed in mutual engendering from their very beginning. *Nation* peels back etymologically to *nature* and birth. History as narrative has emerged perennially as the certification of that birth, inasmuch as historical narration, like national literature, has been used to validate a people's collective cultural existence. The history of literature, for its part, invariably ends up articulating the narratives of such self-confirmations as meta-narrative, since historiography sutures received narrations in plotting its own discourse. There is no logical necessity for this to be so. This, nonetheless, has been the precedent and practice of history and of literary history since people first sought to hold past and future oblivion at bay. The history of its histories illustrates that Latin America, as multinational hemisphere and "supranational culture," as some would have it, has not been an exception in this regard.

Most historiographers and philosophers of history have come to appreciate the humbling predicament of the historian, whose efforts are invariably framed by contingency in the process of trying to frame the contingent into narrative circumscription. And most historians, unless they be little more than programmatic propagandists, appreciate as well that, far from purveying explanatory answers to a culture's contingencies, history's narrative tries to reconstruct the questions to which those cultural peripeties and their by-products respond. And if our history raises more questions than it answers, as I suspect to be the case, this too should be considered a felicitous outcome.

Few, if any, histories begin without a self-conscious alertness to the nature of the historical enterprise itself. Hence, the self-attestation of the primal historians, who begin by inscribing themselves into the narrative of their histories. Thucydides, and no less Herodotus before him, begin their narrations by identifying themselves by name and provenance: "Herodotus of Halicarnassus here presents his *historiê* . . ." and "Thucydides, an Athenian, wrote . . . ." Such precedents have proved defining for historiography, and they have established as well the relationship of history to culture. This relationship has oscillated over the centuries between the history of representation and the representation of history. In practice, this translates into defining history as a narrative about an existing culture, on the one hand, and history as the narration of culture into existence, on the other. While these two strands are inextricably entwined and mutually repercussive, historiographic practice has sought to maintain the dichotomy, often hierarchically, so that between the two, the latter–history as the narration of culture into existence–has, starting with Thucydides, proved preeminent. Thucydides assumed the role of scriptor for the deeds and destinies of Hellas, expressly those linked to the Peloponnesian War, which were defining of Greek culture and in which Thucydides himself was enmeshed as a general of the Athenian armies.

This culturally structuring role of historical narrative would soon metamorphose, yielding first the project of history as made by those who would make themselves into the culture represented through their narratives. Such self-making through narration is codified as the eighteenth century's "new science," and the locus classicus of its theorization is in the 1725–1730 work of Giambattista Vico, which goes by the very scientific title of *Principi di una scienza nuova* [Principles of a New Science]. This narrative self-making would find its unquestionable legitimacy (or what ethno-nationalist believers have come to consider as beyond questioning) in the blood rights of ethnic and racial identity, as articulated by Johann Gottfried Herder in his *Ideen zur Philosophie der Geschichte der Menschheit* (1784–1791; *Outlines of the Philosophy of Man*, 1800). This redoubled foundation of historical narrative, predicated on the self as differentiated identity formation, has proved most resilient, finding its late twentieth-century refigurations in the critical idiom of constructedness where cultures and their history are concerned. Simultaneously, such eighteenth-century discursive formations would eventuate in the "natural" privileging of those human subjects whose history a particular narrative is said to be as the most appropriate agents for performing those constructions.

Performativity and construction, then, become the operative modes of narrating these cultural/national identities into historical and political existence. Through such narrative self-engenderment, cultures or nations are made naturally essential, even when, in current critical discourse, "naturalization" is deemed essentializing and essentialism perniciously reductive. "Strategic essentialism" is the self-exculpating byword of those who would prefer their performative identities constructed through culturalism, even as they engage in a tactically and politically expedient form of naturalism.

"Natural Histories" have been the prototypes of historical narration in the Latin American new world, as are "true histories." One thinks, inevitably, of Fernando González de Oviedo, Emperor Charles V's royal court chronicler and primal naturalizer of America's strange new world. One thinks too of Hernán Cortés's foot soldier in the conquest of Tenochtitlan-Mexico, Bernal Díaz del Castillo. His memorial history deemed itself to be the "true history," in contradistinction to Francisco López de Gómara's "official history," a claim to authenticity that serves as precedent for the authentication of testamental narrative and the authenticity of the "native subject," for whom narrated events are said to be experiential. While González de Oviedo derives his formative discourse of natural history from Pliny, Bernal Díaz del Castillo's historical attestation rests, ultimately, on the self-privileging agency of bearing witness that, as François Hartog suggests, is founded on Herodotus and the notion of *autopsis* ("I have seen"), itself derived from Book 23 of Homer's *Iliad*. This is the scene of the chariot race organized around the funeral of Patroclus and the ensuing dispute between Ajax and Idomeneus as to who is leading the race and which of the two has the better eyesight in determining the front runner. The upshot of the argument, Hartog notes, is that the observer or spectator as "[a]n eyewitness, [is one who] knows because he has seen. The *histôr*, then would first and foremost be an oculus and the *historiê* an affair, if not a story, of the eye" (87).

The true knowledge in the matter, however, is the knowledge derived not from testimonial attestation or sight, but from adjudicating what is seen, that is, educing the *evidence* in the public sphere (*historiês apodexis,* in Herodotus's opening terms). In the dispute between Ajax and Idomeneus, the truth comes to rest not in their eyesight, but on the public adjudication by Agamemnon, who is not a witness, but who makes the truth visible, nonetheless. This, according to André Sauge, is the true *histôr*. And this, reiterates Hertog, is the historic transition from seeing to knowing, troped in the French lexicon of these historiographers as a passing from *voir* (to see) to *savoir* (to know). Ultimately, as we shall see shortly, "true history" will redound, starting with Homer, yet again, to the enunciation of the narrative persona who has neither seen nor lived the events he or she narrates, something which was overlooked by Bernal Díaz del Castillo. The distant beneficiaries of his legacy in the genre of Latin American *testimonio* at the end of the twentieth century continued to do likewise, a history of "true history" expediently ignored still among ethnocentric and nationalist self-authenticators.

Percolated through Herder's and Vico's eighteenth-century science, especially since the 1980s, Bernal Díaz del Castillo's historiographic misrecognition would find its exacerbated avatars in the shrillness of ethnic and racial authenticity among the testimonial genre's acolytes. This would particularly be so among those speaking from the context of the so-called "culture wars" in the United States, which mimetically reflected Latin American cultural discourse on and in Latin America. The "naturalism" of this late modernity at the end of the twentieth century and its privileging of the testamental informant construe, *mutatis mutandis,* with those early narrative prototypes that gave historical density and epistemic reality to the American hemisphere through the hegemonic discourse of naturalization and self-authentication. Thus, that discursive formation that came to define late modernity and that goes by the code term of "multiculturalism" is more accurately reflected in its own praxes as a form of "multinaturalism," whereby difference is performed as self-differentiation, and differentiation yields, naturally, one's "authentic" identity. Néstor García Canclini, who sought to differentiate Latin American "multiculturalism" from U.S. (I do not say Anglo American, because the United

States is more than Anglo in this regard) multiculturalism, may wish to see this difference as cohesively national in the case of Latin America and as culturally separatist in the case of the United States. Nonetheless, García Canclini's schematic counterpoint, even if it could be pragmatically sustainable, amounts to little more than a matter of degree, with one mode of partition occurring at the level of nationalism and the other on an ethnicist or racial plain. In either case, historical reality demonstrates that these would-be differences are simply symptoms of discrepant modes of diversity management on the part of the state and its cultural/governmental institutions, an entangling form of superintendence in which intellectuals like García Canclini inexorably become complicit, willingly or inadvertently.

This, in short, is the discursive climate in which the present history has evolved. It is neither inevitable nor logically necessary that these should be the operative parameters for cultural narration and historiographic discourse. An alternative precedent, either bracketed or elided altogether by the vested expediencies of self-affirmation and self-privileging formations in national(ist) and ethno-national discourses, has always existed alongside the very prototypes of historical narration that ended up being cultural dominants in engendering the narratives of historiography that have become de facto and hegemonically operative.

That alternative prototype, like the one that has proved paradigmatically hegemonic, also exists in the ancient Greek historians and, ultimately, as I have already suggested, is also derived from Homer. I am referring to that defining precedent at the end of Book VIII (lines 486–498) in the *Odyssey* that, *pace* David Hume (about whom more shortly), figures as the primal scene of history, that is, of historical narration. This is the scene at the court of Nausikaa's father, King Alkínoös, where Odysseus hears for the first time the story of his own vicissitudes, specifically the episode of the Trojan horse, sung by the blind Phaiakian bard Demódokos. Here, for the first recorded time, someone (the primal Greek Odysseus) hears his own story as history told by a stranger, the non-Greek Demódokos, who is ethnically not one of the subjects of the narrative; nor was he there, in Troy, with the Greeks to witness the story that he narrates. This, I believe, is the primal scene of history as historiography's repressed alterity. That the foundational text of cultural identity and national pedagogy of the Greeks, the *Odyssey,* should contain its periphrastic alterity embedded within it may be the hope for history other than the official history of ethnocentric or nationalist self-privileging. That occluded alterity is the perennial exclusion that is always present, and usually silenced, in the narration of nations and in the vested interest of the self-serving.

In the nearly decade-long process of the making of the present history, I have often concluded that one's, or a people's, history should best be narrated by someone else. This would have the added virtue of foreclosing on history being written, as is the case most often, by the victors. This prospect, though it has often been lost to history, was not lost on Herodotus, who introduces himself and his *historiê apodexis* (the public presentation of his researches) simultaneously with the Persian *logioi,* "the learned Persians," that is, the Barbarians, whose invoked presence on the first page gives the Greek historian's narrative a citational base, a discursive frame that originates in the non-Greek narrators.

That someone by the name of Djelal Kadir should be collaborating in the construction of the present historical enterprise, and as co-editor, at that, may not be altogether unrelated to this primal scene of history and its vicissitudes. And the various reactions to such intrusion of cultural alterity, particularly in a history that coincides chronologically with a cultural moment when all history is deemed to be the history of vertiginous identity, makes the aptness of recalling those distant origins of historiography compelling. History's propensity as self-affirmation continues to be a hegemonic enterprise. The ethno-national non-self, even if, or especially as strategy of "differential inclusion," as Deleuze and Guattari would have it, in the narrative formation of this history of Latin American literary culture, has often had to seek refuge in the smiling impicty of Oscar Wilde, who made it everyone's responsibility to be implausible. In the long process of this history's making, such implausibility has not escaped the irritation and outright aggression of some, or the bemused perplexity of others. The unforgettable displeasure of a long-forgotten would-be contributor, aroused by the fact that the role of scribe and recapitulator for the conceptualizing colloquia of this history should have been the present scriptor, a non-Latin and a non-Latin American, betrayed the insuperable role of history as perennially speaking the ethno-cultural self into narrative existence. The Roman diptych of *jus solis* and *jus sanguinis* as criteria for citizenship and pertinence, juridical or discursive, has obviously not faded in New World Latinity, as it has not in most parts of the world. That ethno-racialized legacy, instituted within historiography's enterprise by Johann Gottfried von Herder, continues unabated. Even though Ernest Renan, in his 1882 Sorbonne lecture "Qu'est-ce qu'une nation?" ["What Is a Nation?"], reminded historiography that historians ineluctably misunderstand their own history and that historical error is a crucial factor in the creation of a nation—and even though the Cuban José Martí would dilate expressly on Renan's insight two years later, in his 1884 essay "Escenas europeas," by noting that human history is not a chapter in the history of zoology—such umbrage more than a hundred years later at the incipient meetings of this project, starting in 1993 at the Bellagio Center of the Rockefeller Foundation and with intermittent regularity in more subtle and not-so-subtle variants thereafter, is no less symptomatic of the history of history. For those so vexed, history continues to be the narrative of self-definition by the ethno-national self. Meanwhile, for the well-meaning liberal, history has never ceased to be an echoic identity narrative, a tale told by the idiosyncratic catchpoles of a culture, who triumphantly proclaim idiosyncrasies that would make "their culture" identical to itself.

Nor have the insidious strains of globalization in the so-called postnational age managed to liberate those essentialist adherents to proprietary rights from the clenched embrace of ethno-biology as a defining instrument of culture. In a trenchant invocation of Herder's zoologization of the human, Giorgio Agamben, in such monitory books as *Homo Sacer,* reminds us that in the counterpoint between nature and culture at the end of the twentieth century, but most notably at that century's most bellicose and baleful midpoint, the authenticators of genealogies still militate for the naturalization of the human as "bare life," a political move for the expedient manageability of bodies—ethnic, national, and racial—as objects of biopower and biopolitcs. The discursive avatars of Latin American *mestizaje* (miscegenation) as hybridity in such magical terrain as the "third space" of some recent studies of culture find their divining rods crooked back on themselves as exacerbated particularity tangled in intersubjective and psychologistic metaphor. They find the explicatory power they seek in such asymmetrical propinquity vitiated by the reductive essentialization of the cultures they inevitably reify and hypostasize into juxtaposition. Such representations, we have since come to realize, are little more than aleatory projects of metaphor that trap, and trope, their objects of scrutiny into rhetorical simulacra. In retrospect, we can now discern that those endeavors willy-nilly collude through modes of cultural and institutional interpellation in the production of manageably articulated subjects and identities.

The submission of those late twentieth-century endeavors to any rigorous ideological critique now reveals the unalloyed hyperreality of cultural and subjective individuation as precipitated by the pervasive thrust of global capital, an exacerbation of difference in which those late twentieth-century theoretical projects have been inadvertently and inexorably complicit. In the recrudescent empire of the New World Order that ushered in the twenty-first century, differentiation of identities has intensified beyond the ethnic, the national, the racial, or the generic to the extremes of tailored subjectivity and subjection. Here, each individual subject is greeted by name and preference, offered customized goods to taste and proclivity every time one logs on to the World Wide Web as one's own "user name" and password. Those on the short end of the digital divide, as always, become relegated to the status of spectral drones in the production of what hypothetically sustains phantom capital, just as the use and utility of those who log on serve as their code of entry, or suction, into capital's digital beltway. For those who, in Jacques Derrida's terms, would wish to be identical to themselves to the exclusion of all and everyone else, such extremes of identity differentiation are nothing short of the fulfillment of the Chinese mixed blessing of wishing one what one wants, with all wants now designed to duly reflect individual and individuated subjectivity as difference in the extreme.

As we have seen in the Homeric primal scene of the history of history, cautionary tales that might mitigate such cultural and discursive self-invagination are not lacking. Historical memory, however, has been wont to lapse precipitously in the autolepses, or self-seizures, of ethno-nationalism, hence historiography's foundering on human agency as the performative self-enactment of identity. Stephen Greenblatt has diagnosed such fables of identity as "hardening instantly into alleged reality" (53), a symptom, he says, of "the pragmatic, strategic appropriation of the national model of literary history—with its teleological, developmental narrative of progress—in order to confer authority on an emergent group. This appropriation permits the group's leading figures to make political and institutional, as well as cultural claims" (54). These are, of course, self-privileging claims of biopower and naturalized authorization that reinscribe hegemonic discourse through national, ethnic, or tribal self-differentiation. That Greenblatt should be writing, in this instance, of the recent *Cambridge History of Latin American Literature* (1996) is not altogether irrelevant to the present discussion. What underlies the symptoms diagnosed by Greenblatt is the elision or repression of that perennial Homeric alterity in the history of historiography, predictably enough in the case under Greenblatt's scrutiny, since such cultural paradigm of history has its genesis in a cultural space-time other than one's own.

David Hume, in his essay "Of the Populousness of Ancient Nations," had already framed such self-mirroring in eighteenth-century historiography when he pronounced "[t]he first page of Thucydides is, in my opinion, the commencement of real history" (248). Thucydides' first page, of course, is a disoursive locus in which the historian, an Athenian general in the very conflict he narrates, inscribes himself as the narrative voice of his own culture and of the internecine strife that pitted Hellas against itself in the Peloponnesian War. An extreme nominalist who pressed rationalism and causality to the ends of skepticism, Hume, nonetheless, would write a most exhaustive *History of England* (1754–1762), despite the fact that he consigned the narrative of rational causality to the condition of ancillary to custom and belief, and relegated mind to a bundle of perceptions.

Hume's exaltation of Thucydides' narrative as the beginning of all real history (Thucydides, in fact, never uses the Greek term *historiê*, or any of its lexical cognates) would resonate in such imperial historians as Edward Gibbon and, in the next century, in Thomas Babington Macaulay, not so much for the "scientific" self-reflexivity Hume detected in the first page of Thucydides as for the Athenian's chapter devoted to Pericles' funeral oration at the end of the first year of the war. That inventory of Athens' munificent bequest to civilization clearly appealed to the civilizing mission of imperial Britain. It was, I suspect, this timely relevance of Thucydides à propos the British historical moment, and not Hume's, or Gibbon's, or Macaulay's ignorance of Homer and Herodotus, that elevated the Athenian general Thucydides to the status of ur-historian for these Britons. Their legacy in this regard, as hegemonic discourse, has clearly not diminished. It has simply permeated historical discourse as ubiquitous global replication as far as the Americas.

Though humbling in the process, there is something strongly presumptive in any effort to recompose history. I do not say to write a new history, because the presuppositions implicit in such a claim would vitiate the effort at the outset. A felt need for undertaking any rehistoricization assumes that the existing archive of histories is in need of an amendment. That is, the amending historians presume on the unsettled status of what previous historians had believed settled. Just as powerfully, any historiographic enterprise assumes some degree of discursive completion, however provisional, in the historical process, at the end of whose course the historians position themselves. History, in this sense, figures as aftereffect and as recapitulation of a narrative process. This process encompasses treatment of a history's subject matter (in our case, literature), the previous histories of/on that subject (literary histories), and, not least, the histories of the human subjects who constituted both the matter of history (literary authors, readers, promoters, censors) and the historical efforts of those human agencies (literary historians) that preceded the current historiographer(s). In his 1874 essay "Idea for a Universal History from a Cosmopolitan Point of View," Immanuel Kant hoped that "[h]owever obscure their causes, history, which is concerned with narrating" these phenomena (11), might be susceptible to certain universal laws. Finding none, Kant would delegate to "Nature—or better, [to] Providence" (25) any such purposefulness; failing that also, he would default to that philosopher's stone he refers to as "the Idea."

If this characterization of a historiographic undertaking tends to make history a supposititious and recursive endeavor, such a portrayal is not unjustified, to the degree that it characterizes the historian's actual predicament. It would be peculiarly anomalous for historians to claim that the discursive formations they take as narrative objects are not founded in the past, lest they be defined as futurologists or considered to be presentist diagnosticians of the moment deemed momentous. (Historians over the centuries have not been immune to such temptations or to State imperatives, to assume such roles, nonetheless). It would be likewise incongruous with the ends of historiography (founded, after all, on the preservation of *kleos,* or *fama,* for posterity) to eschew the purposive projections of the historian's narrative into the as yet undefined memory of the future and of future readers. This is not to say that the course of history and the processes of historiography unfold in a linear continuity on which, at certain strategic points, historians halt to glance backward and assess their itinerary. This sort of flattening out of the historical process and of the historiographic enterprise is far from capturing the complexity that makes history necessary and the historian a perennial necessity. The first, necessary history, is the force of inevitability in human life; the second, the perennial necessity of the historian, reflects the endemic insufficiency in human understanding, which seeks some explanation for what history makes inevitable.

For the technical philosopher, whose explanation of unfolding processes would be leveraged on "necessary and sufficient reason," the phenomenon of a "necessary history" would seem an oxymoron, as Kant's predicament in the 1874 essay on the subject symptomatically avers. In the philosopher's logic, when the inevitability of the necessary and the contingency of the historical converge, we can only have a contradiction, if not an outright antinomy. We know that the first, contradiction, can be negotiated, while the latter, antinomy, is resolutely irresolvable. The philosopher shuns the first and cloaks the latter in sufficient reason. It is left to the historian, then, to live with the contradictions. And while the disambiguation of contradictions through reason's logical "Idea" might make for a good philosopher, it certainly would make for a poor historian, who, alas, is condemned, at least since Aristotle, to pursue some articulation of what he or she deems the world to be, no matter how ambiguous, rather than devolve upon what reasonably, or ideally, might or ought to be.

This, in sum, constitutes the adventure of the present writer and his collaborators in this history. To undertake such an enterprise at a time deemed by some to be the "end of history" is more urgent than ever. Historical junctures in which cultural dominants and hegemonic discourses judge the moment to be beyond or outside history are precisely when the enterprise of historiography becomes most imperative. The sentencing of history to exception is little more than the affirmation of one's own historical apotheosis at the cost of banishing the history of everyone else. The reduction of history to the chronicle of one's own identity (cultural, national, racial, or ethnic) and the reification of human subjectivity to the measure of one's difference are no less an elision of the complexity of historical life. Such "strategic essentialism," some would say, should be considered a counter-hegemonic intervention. But, as history illustrates, this form of intervention can be little more than a mimetic replication that ineluctably colludes with those who would pronounce the last judgement on history. Julia Kristeva had already warned us, not without some prophetic accuracy, as it turns out, of the consequences of what she had foreseen in the last decade of the twentieth century as precisely such unintended collusion between hegemony and would-be counter-hegemony in cultural discourse: "In years to come it is likely that we could witness a loss of concern for personal freedom, which was one of the essential assets in the *Declaration of the Rights of Man and Citizen,* to the advantage of subjective, sexual, nationalist, and religious protectionism that will freeze evolutionary potentialities

of men and women, reducing them to the identification needs of their originary groups" (2).

By the beginning of the twenty-first century, Kristeva's admonition already seems rather quaint, a sobering lesson in how precipitously the realization of prophecy morphs into nostalgia, because, by now, authenticity and self-affirmation of one's difference, whether as part of a group or as individual, is a niche category of speculative exchange, marketing, and consumption in the global machinery of empire and its insidiously pervasive capital that works to assure everyone's complicity through the very self-differentiations of identity with which one would counter such collusion. The pragmatics of social, political, economic, and cultural life illustrate how little, if any, emancipatory yield there has been in the vertiginous intensification of individuated identities. On the contrary, sharply honed and laser-accurate instruments of speculative capital operate with a suppleness that make Althusser's ideological state apparatuses seem rather clunky. Such panopticism and global reach manage to target and transform everything and everyone into deterritorialized abstraction, where what's paramount are symbolic operations that lighten and dematerialize not only production and capital, but also human agency and historical subjectivity.

Not so long ago, one could tether such buoyancy to the technologies of the state and their coaxing or coercive instrumentalities. Or, one could anchor even nomadic identities to differentiated performativity, as Judith Butler averred, or to the affectivity and affectation of one's continental drifts, as Emily Apter proclaimed. By now, at this side of the new century's threshold, even in that ventriloquy of consensual hallucination that served as virtual definition of culture, however, it has become all but impossible to ascertain whether consent is indeed consensual or spectrally and inexorably mediated. As Jorge Luis Borges prophesied some six decades ago, the world may have indeed become "Tlön," and the histories of its cultural artifacts, verbal or otherwise, may be, at once, yet so many more symptoms and instruments of an encyclopedic omniverse.

How does one dare, then, to construct a history such as the present one under such circumstances? Clearly one does not, most certainly not as one, and not as a single, univocal history. Hence, the assemblage of comparatist scholarly collaboration and the resulting network of this cooperative ars combinatoria for the production of the present history. History as solo performance, or as echoic tribal discourse of the like-minded, would be little short of solipsism in a context as culturally diverse and multinational as Latin America, and it would certainly be so in a current discursive environment of scholarly polyglossia and contending ideological agendas. To the degree that these pluralities coexist in conversation here, I can only hope that coexistence might yield a richer and more multifaceted historical narrative than a soliloquy of the differentiated voice, individual or tribal, that has tended to convert itself into its own simulacrum and hyperreality.

Some eighteen years before Stephen Greenblatt's comments, cited above, on the *Cambridge History of Latin American Literature,* in a now classic 1983 essay Fredric Jameson had already diagnosed modernity's cultural dominant in similar terms. Jameson noted "a dialectical intensification of the autoreferentiality of all modern culture, which tends to turn upon itself and designate its own cultural production as its content" ("Postmodernism and Consumer Society" 14). Jameson's insight applies no less to historiography than it does to other cultural narratives. The polyphony of contrapuntal and crosshatched collaborative history we have earnestly pursued in this project hopefully has succeeded in moving history beyond that soliloquy and cultural solipsism. As the pervasiveness of imperial capital and the technologies of the state collude to individuate human agency and cultural subjectivity to extreme states of exception and hyperreality, collaborative efforts such as this, with few illusions, may well be our only recourse for safeguarding a modicum of civil society in the face of ubiquitous control and global capitalization of culture. This kind of solidarity and this sort of historiography, like the literature it historicizes, may be among the few modes of resistance that remain against the unmitigated etiolation of human agency.

Such endeavors, like all human initiative, might still not be immune to illusion, a predicament Borges mapped with irony, Althusser through ideology, and Foucault as governmentality. Nevertheless, the alternative to cultural engagement, even as consensual hallucination, would be quiescence and immobility. Between praxis and thanatopraxis, historical life and history tend toward the contingencies of the former, rather than the totalization of the latter. History still tacks its paradoxical course between the necessity of the first and the inevitability of the second. In this regard, and in this instance, the historian too is subject to history. The illusion of immunity from its ambiguities may well continue to be the metaphysician's domain. And only those who are irreparably convinced that they have triumphed over history can exempt themselves from it by declaring its end.

Works Cited

Agamben, Giorgio. 1998. *Homo Sacer: Sovereign Power and Bare Life.* Trans. Daniel Heller-Roazen. Stanford: Stanford University Press.

Althusser, Louis. 1972. "Ideology and Ideological State Apparatuses (Notes Towards An Investigation)." *Lenin and Philosophy, and Other Essays.* Trans. Ben Brewster. New York: Monthly Review Press. 127–86.

Apter, Emily. 1999. *Continental Drift: From National Characters to Virtual Subjects.* Chicago: University of Chicago Press.

Bhabha, Homi K. 1994. *The Location of Culture.* London and New York: Routledge.

Borges, Jorge Luis. 1996. "Tlön Uqbar Orbis Tertius." *Obras completas I.* Buenos. Aires: Emecé. 431–443.

Butler, Judith. 1997. *Excitable Speech: A Politics of Performance.* London and New York: Routledge.

Deleuze, Gilles and Felix Guattari. 1987. *A Thousand Plateaus: Capitalism and Schizophrenia.* Trans. Brian Massumi. Minneapolis: University of Minnesota Press.

Derrida, Jacques. 1991. *L'autre cap.* Paris: Les Editions de Minuit.

Díaz del Castillo, Bernal. 1968. *Historia verdadera de la conquista de la Nueva España [por] Bernal Díaz del Castillo.* 2nd ed. Madrid : Espasa-Calpe.

Fernández de Oviedo y Valdés, Gonzalo. 1944-45. *Historia general y natural de las Indias: islas y tierra-firme del mar Océano/por el capitán Gonzalo Fernández de Oviedo y Valdés.* Asunción del Paraguay: Editorial Guarania.

Foucault, Michel. 1991. "Governmentality." *The Foucault Effect: Studies in Governmentality.* Ed. Graham Burchell, et al. London: Harvester Wheatsheaf. 87–104.

García Canclini, Néstor. 1999. *La globalización imaginada.* Mexico and Buenos Aires: Editorial Paidos.

González Echevarría, Roberto, and Enrique Pupo Walker, eds. 1996. *The Cambridge History of Latin American Literature.* Cambridge: Cambridge University Press.

Greenblatt, Stephen. 2001. "Racial Memory and Literary History." PMLA 116.1: 48–63.

Hartog, François. 1992. "Herodotus and the Historiographical Operation." *Diacritics* 22.2: 83–93.

Herder, Johann Gottfried von. 1997. *On World History: An Anthology/ Johann Gottfried Herder.* Ed. Hans Adler and Ernest A. Menze. Armonk, NY.: M. E. Sharpe.

Herodotus. 1996. *The Histories.* Trans. Aubrey de Sélincourt. Harmondsworth: Penguin Classics.

Homer. *The Iliad.* 1974. Trans. Robert Fitzgerald. Garden City, NY: Anchor Press/Doubleday.

——. *The Odyssey.* 1963. Trans. Robert Fitzgerald. Garden City, NY: Anchor Press/Doubleday.

Hume, David. 1877. "Essay XXXIII: Of the Populousness of Ancient Nations." *Essays, Moral, Political, and Literary.* London: Ward, Lock, & Co. 222–69.

Jameson, Fredric. 1984. "Postmodernism: the Cultural Logic of Late Capitalism." *New Left Review* 146: 59–92.

——. 1998. "'End of Art' or 'End of History'?" *The Cultural Turn: Selected Writings on the Postmodern, 1983–1998.* New York: Verso. 73–92.

——. 1998 ."Postmodernism and Consumer Society." *The Cultural Turn: Selected Writings on the Postmodern, 1983–1998.* New York: Verso. 1–20.

Kant, Immanuel. 1963. "Idea for a Universal History from a Cosmopolitan Point of View (1874)." *On History. Immanuel Kant.* Ed. Lewis White Beck. Indianapolis and New York: The Bobbs-Merrill Co., Inc. 11–26.

Kristeva, Julia. 1993. *Nations Without Nationalism.* Trans. Leon S. Roudiez. New York: Columbia University Press.

López de Gómara, Francisco. 1988. *Historia de la conquista de México/ Francisco López de Gómara.* Ed. Juan Miralles Ostos. Mexico: Editorial Porrúa.

Martí, José. 1964. "Escenas europeas." *Obras completas.* Havana: Editorial Nacional de Cuba. Vol.14, 449–50.

Moreiras, Alberto. 2001. *The Exhaustion of Difference : The Politics of Latin American Cultural Studies.* Durham : Duke University Press.

Renan, Ernest. 1947–1961. "Qu'est-ce qu'une nation?" *Oeuvres completes.* Paris: Calmann-Lévy. I: 887–907.

Sauge, André. 1992. *De l'épopée à l'histoire: Fondement de la notion d'histoire.* Frankfurt: Peter Lang.

Thucydides. 1960. *The Peloponnesian War.* Trans. Benjamin Jowett. New York: Bantam Books.

Vico, Giambattista. 1948. *The New Science of Giambattista Vico.* Trans. 3d ed., 1744, Thomas Goddard Bergin and Max Harold Fisch. Ithaca: Cornell University Press.

Yudice, George. 2001. Translator's "Introduction" to *Consumers: Globalization and Multicultural Conflicts* by Néstor García Canclini. Minneapolis: University of Minnesota Press. ix–xxxviii.

Zizek, Slavoj. 1997. "Multiculturalism, or, the Cultural Logic of Multinational Capitalism." *New Left Review* 225: 28–51.

INTRODUCTION TO VOLUME I

FOR A MORE INCLUSIVE LITERARY HISTORY OF LATIN AMERICA

Luisa Campuzano

During the last quarter of the twentieth century, Latin American literary studies focused on finding new critical strategies with which to confront transformations in this field as well as the challenges they have themselves engendered. These new critical strategies have been frequently expressed by incisive theories (Fernández Retamar; Rincón; Cornejo Polar) as well as through a number of collective (Losada Guido; Pizarro; González Echevarría and Pupo–Walker) and individual projects that have involved the complete or partial rewriting of the literary history of the continent (Lienhard; Harrison; González Echevarría; Rama [1982, 1986]; Ramos; Ludmer; Sommer; Franco; Molloy; Mignolo). All this has inevitably meant both a restating of the field of study and a more or less exacting examination of the principles and trajectory of literary studies. These approaches have not been unaware of the critical and epistemological context of this period, but they have not been submissively dependent on or subordinate to it.

Intelligent and well-documented studies on the historiography of Spanish American literature have been published (Rincón [1986]; Losada Guido; Gutiérrez Girardot; Miliani; Pizarro; González Stephan; González Echevarría and Pupo–Walker) that are permeated with the same climate of debate, questioning the principles of traditional disciplinary practice, whether or not derived from the passion engendered by the new projects. These review the structure of the field of study and raise questions that are basically aimed in two directions: where to establish the boundaries of what pertains to Latin America and where those boundaries are in relation to the concept of literature.

This collaborative history, *Literary Cultures of Latin America*, as a project located on the diachronic axis of the historiography of Latin American literary production, has benefited from the shared experiences that have preceded its publication and reveal the common concerns of those responsible. But it also has felt free to reject recent procedures that have been revealed as unprofitable or that cannot be reconciled with the principles derived from its other configurative dimension: the synchronic axis to which it belongs as part of a larger project, notably *Rethinking Literary History—Comparatively,* with its guiding proposition: "'Comparative' literary history is also, perhaps, the history both made possible by and even demanded by our age of international information access and electronic technology. . . . It is in practice, as well as theory, that we seek to 'rethink' 'literary' 'history' 'comparatively'" (Valdés and Hutcheon 4).

Thus this history coincides with the different proposals of inclusion formulated in other histories of Latin American literature compiled at the end of the twentieth century and to a great extent supersedes them. In fact, it incorporates the literature of Brazil, the different expressions of Amerindian and Afro-Latin American cultures, the literature of Hispanic communities within the United States, and that of other minorities and alternative cultures, such as the work of Jewish, women, gay, and lesbian writers. Discourses and registers that are either partially or totally overlooked and ignored by the traditional canon are also included, such as religious, scientific, and political discourse; different forms of oral literature; and theater and theatricalities as well as many diverse literary manifestations of mass and popular culture. However, the most important aspects of this history are the principles and methods that determine the incorporation of these discourses. This is not just a question of expanding the geographical area under consideration and consequently the linguistic area involved. Nor is it simply a matter of accepting a greater or lesser quantity of what hitherto has been excluded, but rather of recognizing that a truly fresh and significant literary history is not delineated by content determined by the field of study but rather by the methodological and ideological postulates that are realized here.

Thus, for example, the fact of including Brazilian literature, even though this without doubt demonstrates an important shift toward a substantially broader scope than that of traditional literary historiography, has little meaning if this body of work is treated as a separate and exclusive contribution. It is necessary to establish the boundaries and sequential nature of the subject so that differences stand out, so that what links this corpus to or differentiates it from Spanish American literature is made clear in terms of specific moments and particular aspects as much in the process itself. This is, in fact, the purpose behind this history, which is organized in such a way that it not only permits but also stimulates the transition from one literature to another, thus bypassing the old concern for achieving effects of false contiguity or impossible continuity through regionalization and division into periods that were finally always forced, incomplete, and fallible. On the other hand, to continue with this example, the inclusion of Brazilian literature, when unaccompanied by other inclusions and the resultant tactical accommodations, far from resolving the question of setting boundaries, could lead to an exacerbation of the situation, given that the linguistic diversity of Latin America and its broad range of textual production go beyond the conventional frontiers of what is "Latin American" in both chronological and geographical terms. Invasions and imperial occupation, both during the long pre-Hispanic period and during the centuries that followed the Conquest; the United States' expansion westward and into the Caribbean; and many varied forms of internal migration, population shifts, and mass immigration–whether under duress or purportedly voluntary–that have been provoked by different social causes, have promoted the constant renewal of texts as linguistic and culturally hybrid products whose context could not have been ignored in a literary history project like this, whose focus is both comparative and social.

Even so, in contrast to other constructions of what constitutes Latin America established in important historiographic works of the preceding decade (Osorio; Pizarro), this history does not explicitly include the English-, French-, and Dutch-speaking cultures of the Caribbean. These have already been handled substantially, both on an individual basis and with regard to their mutual interrelationship in terms of dialogue with the literary cultures of the Spanish West Indies. This latter theme has received particular attention in the three volumes of *A History of Literature in the Caribbean* edited by A. James Arnold, which form a part of the collection entitled *A Comparative History of Literatures in European Languages*, from which initially arose this project, *Literary Cultures of Latin America*. The highly productive interpretation of literature in Cuba, Puerto Rico, and the Dominican Republic derived from the Caribbean cultural context (as relevant, on its own terms, as this one) is an excellent example of the character of "intermediate zones" (Oviedo I 25) that many of the countries' and even regions of the continent exhibit. These allow for, rather than demand, very distinct frameworks as well as different approaches to tactical abridgement, a requisite for a comparative strategy such as that adopted by this history.

It seems evident, therefore, that such an enterprise cannot be the work of one individual or even of a team of literary academics, since a profoundly multidisciplinary approach is required to achieve the aims proposed. But it is also evident that this history cannot achieve the eminence for which it strives if there does not exist at the same time a minimal consensus among the authors in the face of this density of dialogue as it emerges from very varied disciplines, specialties, perspectives, experiences, and nationalities–in other words, from the diversity that the collaborators have brought to the project. Thus the design, organization, and creation of *Literary Cultures of Latin America*, apart from the participation of many researchers involved in the direct study of these literary cultures, has required the collaboration of specialists in many varied disciplines. This has been very clear in the writing of the first volume, the responsibility of seventy authors from fourteen countries, notably Latin America (forty-seven), Europe (ten), the United States (ten), and Canada (three). On the other hand, this history, like any other that endeavors to do likewise, cannot claim to be exhaustive without running the risk of losing the threads of thematic meaning out of which it is woven. It is therefore a selective history with the proviso that the criteria employed for such selection do not legitimize an exclusive aesthetic valuation but are rather analytic bases derived from the assumption that literature is a social praxis. These foundations confer a privileged status on *everything*, since they reveal the different specificities of the literary production of the continent.

The first volume of this comparative and social history, *Configurations of Literary Culture*, is a construction that establishes the material and textual bases of the literary cultures of the continent and thus serves as a general framework for the three volumes. The initial part, "Parameters of Literary Culture," containing twenty-one chapters, provides the relevant empirical information and perspectives needed in order to understand the conditions within which these literary cultures developed. Thus it begins with an elucidation of the geographic, demographic, and linguistic framework, which spans the three first sections. This is the only continent that carries the most accepted and at the same time controversial of denominations: "Latin America" (Rojas-Mix, passim). This naming is the sign of a culture, which, rather than constituting it (Chapter 1), is the result of the need for legitimization of a European political ideology, notably Bonapartist imperialism (see Canfora). This widespread acceptance of a single name for the region came at a time when the notable geographical, demographic, and linguistic diversity was recognized, thereby creating a historical and cultural community that today is defined more through the extraordinary variety of cultural elements that provide internal cohesion, markedly distinguishing it from the United States–the "other" America–than through those links that once connected it with its ancient metropoli. For this reason José Martí most emphatically baptized this historical and cultural community "Our America," an identification that bears a strong ideological mark but that was formulated from within on behalf of the region and thus fundamentally intended to confront the America that was not "ours."

In addition to the effects of a comparative history that underlines those very differences that allow the discovery of community, the perspective provided here on Latin America over a long period through looking at its cultural geography is enormously productive. On the one hand, the documentation of the variety of landscapes and climates, of the vast proportions of its spaces, of the devastating cataclysms that entrap it, and of the exploitation of natural resources of every kind, is here deployed by literary researchers as some of the keys to understanding the hundreds of symbolic constructions that have modeled the culture of the continent. But beginning this comparative history with an entry into the material from the perspective of cultural geography is also enormously important in its unveiling of the paradoxes inherent in Latin America's population (which would have tremendous influence both on its constitution as a historical and cultural community and on its future). These paradoxes shed important light on the principles that dominated the organization of colonial space in particular. The basic fact is without precedent: Almost a thousand cities were founded by the Spanish and Portuguese between the sixteenth and eighteenth centuries. These cities were established to export whatever was extracted from the continent, while simultaneously exercising political control over the immediate environment. Many of these cities were subjected to varied kinds of political, religious, and judicial control and coordination over centuries or were linked together as enclaves located on lines of communication or as academic centers, thus consolidating a historical and cultural community that transcended the balkanization produced by independence. The Spanish colonies became important cultural loci that constructed the diversity and continuity of the literary culture of the continent precisely through their interrelationships.

Moving on from demography, the impressive evolution of the urban network of many of these settlements (as years passed, what were once just villages and factories have become some of the most populated cities in the world) offers new and fertile possibilities for the interpretation of Latin American literary cultures. The unfolding of this dynamic of urban growth allows for the comprehension of the distinct tensions between colony and metropolis, nation and continent, local and universal, both in the long term and at successive moments of change when these cultures were constituting and developing their differences. The comparative and particular study of the principal cultural centers in which Latin American literature was produced, viewed as microcosmic projections of the continent and, simultaneously, as spaces of multiple cultural heterogeneity, is taken up in the second volume of this history, titled *Institutional Modes and Cultural Modalities,* in its third part. This is preceded by reviews of the cultural institutions and of the textual models that sustained and modeled the discourses expressed in these centers.

Undoubtedly a linguistic mapping of the continent constitutes the most productive means of making evident Latin America's ethnic plurality at the start of the third millennium and, at the same time, its history of different migrations, both internal and external, prior to and after the Conquest, that have left their mark on these cultures. Some of these languages, with their ancient, extensive, and varied forms of artistic expression, resisted and survived centuries of repression and marginalization. They reveal an extraordinary vitality, not only as a means of communication but also as a vehicle of creation for millions of Latin Americans. Despite this, others are severely threatened by newer mass communication, and it appears that many are now on an irreversible road to extinction or have already disappeared. Meanwhile, the Spanish and Portuguese languages, which have a little more than half of their documented history in Latin America, count approximately 500 million speakers. While the peculiar process of Brazil's constitution as an independent nation preserved the territorial unity of the colony, and with it that of the language, the dismemberment of the Spanish Empire into various nations as a result of the Wars of Independence led to a fear (until well into the twentieth century) of linguistic fragmentation, similar to what befell Latin in the late Roman world. But in fact Spanish, though subjected to every kind of influence, juxtaposition, and linguistic borrowing, has conserved its unity, while enriching itself with multiple regional nuances, fundamentally in terms of vocabulary and phonetics as well as, to a lesser extent, including morphosyntactic changes (where the unity is extraordinary). There is no doubt that the expansion of primary education, though still insufficient, and the influx of the mass media have contributed to this linguistic unity and the knowledge shared by speakers in different Latin American nations regarding the most recognizable and distinctive features of American variants of the Spanish language. On the other hand, it must be remembered that, at the same time in the sixteenth century, but on the opposite shore of the Atlantic, Spain was reading elegant poetry written in the Italian mode by Boscán and Garcilaso, the ironic realism of *El Lazarillo de Tormes* on the sorrows of poverty, the conquistadors' bewildered descriptions of a new world and the narratives of their exploits, and the moral indignation of Fray Bartolomé de Las Casas as he denounced the genocide of American indigenous peoples.

To return to the structure of this volume: After an analysis of the most important figures of the respective literary cultures of Latin America, representatives in turn of very distinct geographical (section 1), demographic (section 2), and linguistic (section 3) considerations, the fourth section of the first part concentrates on the history of the literary production in colonial Latin America. This region is regarded a "contact zone" (Pratt), where, on the one hand, syncretism and heterogeneity make hybridization a characteristic feature and, on the other, the ideological constructions that will legitimate the identity of these future nations were formulated. "Access and Participation in the Literary Cultures of Latin America" is the final section of this part; it is this section that addresses the dynamic production-consumption-valuation of literary culture in conjunction with the affirmation of national identity as a consequence of the founding of the new republics. Examples of different moments and continental regions and their relationship with other model cultures are used to study "the sociological and political conditions that have determined who participated as 'writers,' how they related to their readership, and the fundamental change in the symbolic works as creators of identity" (Introduction to Part I).

The second part of this volume, "From the Margins of Literary History," introduces a wide range of voices hitherto excluded from the literary history of a continent that despite its own history of colonialism, imperialism, and internal colonialism, such as that of anti-imperialist struggles, is not exempt from racism, anti-Semitism, sexism, and homophobia. Special emphasis is placed on underlining the parameters of marginality in Latin America, in order to indicate that the most common exclusion is economic and thus that poverty is the great source of marginalization in the literary system (Introduction to Part II). Lacking both habits and living conditions that stimulate or permit reading, but also lacking a minimum of economic resources to buy books or magazines and, in fact, belonging in the majority to the large number of the illiterate that exist in the continent, the poor that populate its cities and countryside are not only located on the periphery of traditional literary production (which they have barely come to grips with through the survival of orality, or through exceptional means like the *testimonio*), but they have also been kept marginalized from the formative debates on identity. There is equal emphasis given here to the fact that Latin America has had no lack (but rather an abundance) of political methods of marginalization whose most obvious manifestations are censorship and the persecution of writers imposed by dictatorships and totalitarian governments. One of the immediate consequences, and a powerful one in the context of the literary process, is exile. Even when the regime responsible for it has disappeared, forced exile leaves permanent scars in the literary fabric, manifesting breaks in the weave, interruptions, or definitive shifts to another environment or context of production and reception. Continuing along the same lines of analysis, the authors of this ground-breaking section point out that what is considered as peripheral in Europe and the United States and what is experienced as marginal in Latin America are fundamentally different: Latin America is entirely periphery, when viewed from the perspective of the hegemonical centers of New York, London, or Paris (Introduction to Part II).

There are two sections to this part, consisting of nineteen chapters; the texts are grouped under the headings "Configurations of Socioeconomic, Racial, and Ethnic Alterity in Literary History" and "Gender and Sexual Orientation in the Historical Formation of the Cultural Imaginary." These essays recover, study, and evaluate those voices previously excluded from Latin American literary history that emerge from the different geographical, linguistic, and chronological regions mapped out in the first section of the volume. In so doing they confirm two of the main observations made by the authors whose texts introduce this theme: the avoidance of the issue of poverty in literary histories of Hispanic-America and the tremendous role of racism throughout Latin America. In the latter case, this section explores the heretofore unacknowledged fact of noncanonical writers' productivity and, at the same time, the almost limitless capacity for avoiding recognition of ideologies and cultural constructions that are at the origins of racism, in particular the ideology of *mestizaje* (Chapter 23). It is important, however, to emphasize that the proposal to include the periphery, far from annulling differences, should have the opposite effect of unscoring them and their particularities in a way that does not inhibit their contestatory and subversive character (Introduction to Part II). Thus the majority of the essays gathered in the first part of this section cover indigenous and Afro-Latin American textualities excluded by a literary historiography that, though not accustomed to make amends in recognizing itself as imitatively Eurocentric, also very rarely accepts that the *encomienda*, slavery, and the discriminatory practices that emerged there lie at the roots of the social exclusions that they enact. This part also explores a recently constituted critical space: that of the Judeo-Latin American literary culture, one of considerable magnitude and importance in various zones of the continent.

The histories of the Latin-American literature thus far have been literary histories of a markedly masculine focus, revealing an almost total lack of works authored by women (which, if included, are almost always there as exceptions, as followers or minor voices). Their study is reduced to forms codified by the canon as representative of the "feminine," for example, various lyrical expressions. Even though feminist studies of Latin American literature during the colonial period and the nineteenth century have demonstrated the prolonged existence of an abundant textual production by women throughout the continent, most of these texts are not included in literary histories because they do not fit into the canonical stylistic and formal structures valued by male historians. This exclusion has been maintained because, arguably, women's writing could provide evidence, in one way or another, of a dangerous transgression of the social control imposed on women that keeps them on the periphery of all activity considered to be in the public domain. This disqualifying absence of the feminine from literary history has been refuted in recent years, not only by exemplary rescue work performed on texts and authors previously excluded from the literary institution, but also through the subversion of the discriminatory ideology that has been at its root. This has meant a recovery of the locus of the enunciation of difference, with a consequent reclaiming of texts from the periphery and of alternative textual practices now recognized and legitimized by a century-long exercise in discourse once fraudulently silenced by power. A similar strategy directs the work here destined to unveil the importance of "homotextuality" in the complex of Latin American literature from a new critical perspective that, in less than a decade, has achieved particular relevance in academic circles.

The third and final part of this volume, "Plurality of Discourse in Latin American Culture," is subdivided into five sections and contains a total of twenty-four chapters. Coverage of the religious, political, and scientific discourses appears in the first section. These are viewed from a plurality of theoretical perspectives, but the focus of analysis is on a specific space and time, cutting through broad zones of the continent from Colonial times through to the present day. In Latin America, public discourse has always been held captive, from the early years of the Conquest on, by the hegemonic sectors of societies whose religious, political, and military legitimacy was sanctioned by the written word; therefore there existed an urgent need to demonstrate, investigate, understand, discuss, and organize through writing the different dimensions of life in this so-called "new" world–a world whose fate was dependent upon and determined by the European world whose prestige, in turn, relied on the antiquity of its institutions and instruments of power. In Latin America, the prose essay appears very early on in comparison with other forms of expression or is used in combination with these others to produce a discursive hybridization that was as efficient as it was characteristic. During the nineteenth century and for a good part of the twentieth, independent ideas on the formation of new nations, social and cultural progress, and the search for identity are among the many themes that would nurture the Latin American essay as one of the most outstanding, productive, and polemical creations of the continent's literature. Thus, the first part of the last section of this volume proposes new readings of religious, scientific, and political reflexive-discursive prose from Hispanic America and Brazil from the sixteenth century to the present.

The second section of this part focuses on contemporary literature, through one of the fundamental axes that articulate Latin American discursive heterogeneity: the oral literary tradition. There exist many distinct and fully legitimate forms corresponding to cultures that have developed diverse media through which to express, transmit, and preserve their textual production. Eurocentric prejudices with regard to writing, combined with the political and social subservience of both indigenous and Africans as a result of the conquest and slavery, have demeaned the image of their oral production (Lienhard 1994, 371–2). Both textual manifestations among Mesoamerican, Andean, Amazonian, and West Indian cultures and the hybrid forms developed from European models in the Southern Cone or Brazil are covered in six essays.

The study of the plurality and diversity in theater and theatrical discourse, whose presence in the continent dates back to the pre-Hispanic period, provides other diachronic revisions of the Latin American literary cultures that, in terms of Spanish America, began in the period prior to the Conquest, and, in Portuguese, during the nineteenth century. These new perspectives, while focusing on their specific literary domain, also introduce the conflict between text and scenario, illuminating, complementing, and revealing issues raised by other approaches to literary cultures on the continent. This methodology is applied to Afro-Latin American theater and contemporary Mayan theater, for example, using perspectives that emphasize the intercultural nature of productions of oral character that are destined to create local identifications, yet that operate in society in our times when traditional popular culture must intersect with the media, mass culture, and the manipulations of the marketplace. The fourth section of this part is dedicated to investigating these transformations that have been generated by traditional popular culture as a result of both the exhaustion of the expressive or communicative effectiveness of some manifestations and the intervention of the market and mass culture with its resultant resemantization of existing forms or promotion of new ones. The relationship between traditional popular culture and mass culture within contemporary literature is central to this section.

An excellent means of probing into the complexities of popular culture can be seen in the analysis of the historical process of popular urban culture in Mexico City, the largest city in Latin America and indeed the world, in almost all its manifestations during the period from the Porfiriato to the 1950s, a period during which the commercial mechanisms that exploited mass culture began to be activated. Equally revealing are the continental impact of the carnival, the embodiment of some of the most significant of Afro-Brazilian religious manifestations and the mixed fortunes of the history of the Brazilian serial novel. Both testify to the forms of intercultural syncretism present in traditional popular culture and its capacity for transmutation and, at the same time, for permanence. The Mexican *corrido*–a musical epic ballad and the most long-lasting and widespread musical form in which the peninsular romance was reinvented in Spanish America–is a prime example of how the exchange between popular culture and mass culture takes place. It has renewed and maintained its capacity to represent symbolically the conflicts of the society from which it emerged and the communities of emigrants that broke away from that society; it has reinforced popular identifications in a vast continental framework in which both contemporary and traditional productions interact. Seen from another perspective, the *corrido* also, like other forms of popular music on the continent, has been adopted and catalogued most productively by researchers into the contexts of regional or national literatures. This is a sign of the massive impact of popular music, offering not only an intertextual basis in various authors and genres but also a decided literary value. This is the case, for example, with the tango and, in particular, the myths that have been constructed from it, as one can read in another very recent history of Latin American literature (Puccini and Yurkievich, II, 404–13) or in the texts of the lyricists of the 1960s–1970s included in anthologies of contemporary Cuban poetry.

On the other hand, an aspect that this section cannot avoid covering is the presence of popular culture and mass literature in canonic Latin American letters, in both Spanish and Portuguese, during the last decades. This impact of mass culture, far from being visible only in quotes or apposite parodies, manifests itself in creative forms of appropriation or resemantization of themes, personalities, spaces, and languages. In some cases (for example, the detective story or kitsch novel) this process has provoked real changes in narrative and marked significant literary tendencies in different countries. For these reasons, and given the important role that it plays in the daily life of the great urban masses that make up the majority of the population of the continent (combined with its circulation on a global scale as the representative image of Latin America), the soap opera is also a cause for reflection and analysis in this section.

Finally, a broad and well-documented study of the historical course of cinema in Latin America and the culturally rich dialogues it has promoted in the modernizing process of the continent concludes the third part of the first volume.

The initial, largely factual framework, made up of empirical data, makes it possible to establish and, above all, evaluate, from both comparative and social perspectives, the factors that have intervened in the complex and particular process of development experienced by the literary cultures of the continent. This volume acts as the basis from which the texts in the volumes that follow cover the historical development of Latin American literary culture through the study of institutions, textual models, and the cultural centers participating in its production, concluding in the third volume with the history of the bifurcated cultural imaginary of Latin America from the sixteenth century to the end of the twentieth century.

Translation by Jessica Johnson

Works Cited

Arnold, A. James, ed. 1994–2001. *A History of Literature in the Caribbean.* 3 vols. Amsterdam: John Benjamins Publishing Company.

Canfora, Luciano. 1980. *Ideologie del classicismo.* Torino: Einaudi.

Cornejo Polar, Antonio. 1989. *La formación de la tradición literaria en el Perú.* Lima: Centro de Estudios y Publicaciones.

Fernández Retamar, Roberto. 1977. *Para una teoría de la literatura hispanoamericana.* Mexico City: Nuestro Tiempo.

Franco, Jean. 1984. *Plotting Women: Gender and Representation in Mexico.* New York: Columbia University Press.

González Echevarría, Roberto. 1990. *Myth and Archive: A Theory of Latin American Narrative.* Cambridge: Cambridge University Press.

— and Enrique Pupo-Walker, eds. 1996. *The Cambridge History of Latin American Literature.* 3 vols. New York: Cambridge University Press.

González Stephan, Beatriz. 1987. *La historiografía literaria del liberalismo hispano-americano del siglo XIX.* Havana: Casa de las Américas.

Gutierrez Girardot, Rafael. 1989. *Temas y problemas de una historia social de la literatura hispanoamericana.* Bogota: Ediciones Cave Canem.

Harrison, Regina. 1989. *Signs, Songs, and Memory in the Andes: Translating Quechua Language and Culture.* Austin: University of Texas Press.

Lienhard, Martin. 1992. *La voz y su huella: Escritura y conflicto étnico-cultural en América Latina, 1492–1988.* Lima: Editorial Horizonte.

——. 1994. "Oralidad." *Revista de Crítica Literaria Latinoamericana* 20.40: 371–74.

Losada Guido, Alejandro. 1983. *La literatura en la sociedad de América Latina: Perú y el Río de la Plata, 1837-1880.* Frankfurt [am Main]: Vervuert.

Ludmer, Josefina. 1988. *El género gauchesco: Un tratado sobre la patria.* Buenos Aires: Editorial Sudamericana.

Mignolo, Walter. 1995. *The Darker Side of the Renaissance: Literacy, Territoriality, and Colonization.* Ann Arbor: University of Michigan Press.

Miliani, Domingo. 1985. *Tríptico venezolano: Narrativa, pensamiento, crítica.* Caracas: Fundación Cultural de Venezuela.

Molloy, Sylvia. 1991. *At Face Value: Autobiographical Writing in Spanish America.* Cambridge and New York: Cambridge University Press.

Osorio Tejeda, Nelson, coordinator. 1995. *Diccionario enciclopédico de las letras de América Latina.* 3 vol. Caracas: Ayacucho/Monte Avila.

Oviedo, José Miguel. 1995–2001. *Historia de la literatura hispanoamericana.* 3 vols. Madrid: Alianza Editorial.

Pizarro, Ana, ed. 1987. *Hacia una historia de la literatura latinoamericana.* Mexico City: Colegio de México, Centro de Estudios Lingüísticos y Literarios.

Pratt, Mary Louise. 1992. *Imperial Eyes: Travel Writing and Transculturation.* London and New York: Routledge.

Puccini, Dario, and Saul Yurkievich, eds. 2000. *Storia della civiltà letteraria ispanoamericana.* Vol. I. *Dell'età precolombina all'ottocento.* Vol. II. *L'ultimo ottocento e il novecento.* Torino: Tipografico-Editrice Torinense.

Rama, Angel. 1982. *Transculturación narrativa en América Latina.* Mexico City: Siglo Veintiuno Editores.

———. 1986. *La novela en América Latina: Panoramas 1920–1980.* Xalapa, Mexico: Universidad Veracruzana.

Ramos, Julio. 1989. *Desencuentros de la modernidad en América Latina: Literatura y política en el siglo XIX.* Mexico City: Fondo de Cultura Económica.

Rincón, Carlos. 1995. *La no simultaneidad de lo simultáneo: Postmodernidad, globalización y culturas en América Latina.* Bogota: Editorial Universidad Nacional.

Rojas-Mix, Miguel. 1991. *Los cien nombres de América: eso que descubrió Colón.* Barcelona: Lumen.

Sommer, Doris. 1991. *Foundational Fictions: The National Romances of Latin America.* Berkeley: University of California Press.

Valdés, Mario and Linda Hutcheon. 1994. "Rethinking Literary History–Comparatively." New York. American Council of Learned Societies, 1994.

PART ONE

PARAMETERS OF LITERARY CULTURE
INTRODUCTION

Mario J. Valdés

If we contextualize literary texts within the socioeconomic and political parameters of Latin American history, it becomes evident that neither the texts nor the authors remain the fixed center of inquiry. But what then is the center? The fixed center has been replaced, whether we are aware of it or not, by numerous movable points of convergence in the cities and communities that make up the Latin American continent. These dynamic, and therefore changing, points of intersection mark the coming together of two powerful modes of expression. One is the use of the imagination in written discourse; the other is the use of the imagination, either in oral discourse or in various forms of plastic representation. The former is definitely European in origin and formal definition; the latter is autochthonous. Of course, these two modes go on independently of each other and do not have to converge, but when they do, there is an encounter full of hybrid possibilities, certainly unique to the American continent. The languages, the use of space and proportion, the sense of the cosmos, the sense of identity and alterity from two different worlds converge and explode. How do we map these strange, unexpected but continuous convergences?

This opening part of the history of Latin American literary cultures functions as a macro-frame for the entire three volumes. A brief statement of purpose is called for before turning to the workings of this part. The historizing of literature should not be construed as conferring a specific referential meaning on the hundreds of authors and works we treat in this comparative history, for we are not advocating a return to Dilthey's historicist concept of meaning. Neither do we accept the essentialist argument that construes a purported, timeless meaning to certain canonical works. Our aim as literary historians is to reinsert the cultural products of the past into the field of production from which they emerged and in which they continue to function, and in so doing bring out their historical value as significant contributions to the present habitat of Latin America and its cultural imaginary. The parameters of this historical context have been built up by successive inquiries into the geographic indicators, the demographic processes, the linguistic diversity and its political dimension, the history of ideas, and the nodal thinkers who have moved this historical process, and, finally, the social indicators of accessibility and participation in the literary culture.

The complex nature of the literary text demands a more elaborate concept of historical events than is usual in literary histories–a concept that recognizes both the text's relationship to the sociocultural context and its own unique capacity

to create and yet to refer to lived reality. In this part there is no attempt to deal with this kind of polar referentiality. The task at hand is to establish the contextual variables across time. The contributors to this history are from many disciplines, but the inquiry for all of us is focused on a set of operating principles that make our collaborative history a unique instrument for future scholarship.

First, although literature in Latin America has been a sociocultural phenomenon for the better part of five centuries, the historical description of Latin American literatures has been constructed in almost complete isolation from the social context. There are multiple historical factors inside and outside Latin America that suggest reasons why this has been so. It is our task in this history to open up a new era of historical study of cultural contextualization as the foundation for the study of Latin American literatures. Our approach is comparative and is informed by contemporary hermeneutics in both the humanities (Gadamer, Ricoeur, Vattimo) and the social sciences (Foucault, Bourdieu, García Canclini).

Second, literature is considered in this history as texts–both written and oral and of many different origins–but as texts that participate in the community as a source of the cultural imaginary. No single individual, institution, or state confers the status of "literature" on specific works; it is society itself that finds in texts a symbolic representational value. Communities have social needs and concerns whether dealing with the individual, the individual's interaction with the group, or collectively within the group itself, and literature is the response to the societal imperative of remaking the world in all of its vicissitudes, individually and collectively.

Third, the term "cultural imaginary" that we use in this history refers to the relational matrix of ideas, images, concepts of representation, and, above all, beliefs that interact within a community, thus giving identity to a multiplicity of discrete works as a symbolic whole. Further, throughout this history, we stress that the cultural imaginary is grounded in an empirical reality of language, land, people, and a way of life that together make up the cultural habitat.

The key to the writing and the reading of this history is that it is comparative and emphasizes the differences between central highlands and coastal regions, between the metropolises and rural life, between the European and the Amerindian languages, between the strong African presence in former slave-holding regions and its absence in other areas where economic development did not involve the use of slaves. All of these differences and sharp contrasts are part of a common history of the ex-colonies of Spain and Portugal in the Americas. This is a history of dialectical continuities as well as significant differences. Although this history is indebted to the philosophers and scholars we have duly recognized, our greatest debt is to our predecessors in the revision of Latin American literary history, especially Pedro Henríquez Ureña, Angel Rama, Antonio Candido, and Antonio Cornejo-Polar. We have learned from them that we must probe the demands society makes on writers if we are to understand the dialectical continuities of Latin American history. In our approach, the lived experience of the writer is neither cultivated nor denied; it is situated within the web of empirical, ideological, and symbolic relations that are constantly being spun out and broken.

In this part, we map out the land and its people, as participating in the historical process of making communities and thereby making literature. The part opens with cultural geography, because of our conviction that the spatial aspects of the habitat are of primary importance to a history of the production of symbolic works. Bourdieu reminds us: "Symbolic goods are a two-faced reality: a commodity and a symbolic object. Their specifically cultural value and their commercial value remain relatively independent, although the economic sanction may come to reinforce their cultural consecration"(113). The makers of symbolic works as members of their communities are studied in terms of the demographic changes in those communities; therefore, the second basic component of the habitat is the movement and change in its population. This demographic dimension obviously works at a macrosocial level and, together with the cultural geography that precedes it and the linguistic diversity that follows it, establishes the contextual base of the habitat.

The third component of the context is the linguistic diversity of Latin America. In this case, as in the two other empirical subsections, there is no attempt to be (or intent to be) either complete in our description or exhaustive in our coverage. Our aim is to bring out the functional realities of linguistic diversity amongst the peoples of the continent we now call Latin America. Few non-specialists are aware of the hundreds of Amerindian languages that still function in the early twenty-first century as vigorous centers of their communities;

nor are many aware of the complex interactions they effect on a daily basis with the mainstream European languages. There is no greater example of full bilingualism than that of Paraguay's Spanish- and Guaraní-speaking population. Even within Latin America, this is a unique literary culture. Another fascinating aspect of the linguistic diversity of Latin America is the development of two immense heteroglossic regions: Mesoamerica in the North and Amazonía in the South. The literary culture of these two regions remains virtually unmapped territory for the historical study of literary culture. We propose to begin to remedy the situation.

The fourth section of this part puts together cultural geography, demographics, and social linguistics to highlight those catalytic figures in Latin America who altered the direction of intellectual and ideological production of symbolic works. The fifth and final section examines the sociological and political conditions that have determined who participated as "writers," how they related to their readership, and the fundamental change in the symbolic works as creators of identity.

In the same way as we now recognize that the binary opposition between traditional and modern cultural practices has no historical validity, we should also dismiss the categorical distinctions between elite, popular, and mass culture as arbitrary and not supported by the historical record. The fact that our past histories of culture have been constructed on the basis of these distinctions makes it imperative to revise cultural historiography of literature by deconstructing these "common-sense categories" of a self-serving elite. The primary task for the historian of literary culture is to examine the relations of the various social sectors and not get entrapped in pre-established categories of literary history. A history of literary culture would account for the market of symbolic production; the multiple symbolic products entering the market constantly meet, clash, sometimes merge together, but, more often than not, mutate.

To use the expression of García Canclini, what we need today are nomadic social sciences and humanities that cross and criss-cross the territory of the other without losing their identity. This is the aim of this comparative history of Latin American literary cultures.

SECTION I
GEOGRAPHIC FACTORS AND THE FORMATION OF CULTURAL TERRAIN FOR LITERARY PRODUCTION

CHAPTER 1

THE FORMATION OF A CULTURAL TERRITORY

Hervé Théry

This chapter builds on elements of the first part, "Des Amériques au Sud," of the volume *Amérique latine,* volume III of *Géographie Universelle,* Belin/Reculs, Paris 1992, edited by Claude Bataillon, Jean-Paul Deler, and Hervé Théry. It is based chiefly on the chapters "Ce que latine veut dire" and "Modèles de l'organisation de l'espace" by Claude Bataillon, Jean-Paul Deler, and Hervé Théry and partially on the chapters "Un continent et des territoires" and "Perspectives cavalières et terres de parcours" by Claude Laugénie (with the collaboration of Jean-Pierre Tihay) and "Des populations et de leur mouvement" by Janine Brisseau-Loiaza.

As its name indicates, Latin America is a cultural construction: It is the only continent in the world whose name bears a qualifying adjective signifying the culture that shaped it. The repercussions of this fact can be traced not only in the region's cultural productions (in the usual sense of the term, and notably in its literatures), but also in its material civilization and geography. Since the arrival of the European conquerors, the territory has borne the mark of its appropriation by the Iberian peoples who imposed a durable model of cultural values that organized its space. From the beginning, the territory was organized to facilitate the extraction of natural resources, giving rise to an archipelago of small, autonomous, outward-looking centers at both local and regional levels. These local production units—and the towns founded by the conquerors to organize and coordinate their activities—formed the base from which to take over a new and radically different world.

However, American nature has taken its revenge. Its boundless distances, its dangers, and the diversity of its landscapes have imposed their own constraints, linked or separated the emergent centers, and had an effect on the people's spirit. While working from the same model, the inhabitants of each center evolved in a unique fashion as they put down roots in this new world and, in turn, accommodated it to their own image. They then progressively conquered new spaces as they migrated and extended the scope of their activities and their horizons. The creation of such broad-ranging centers, which functioned in part as cultural centers, tended to precede the construction of nations. Quite often, these nations developed when one of the expanding centers took over and unified a space and then grew to national scale—due partly to its economic range, but even more so to the political and cultural control it exercised, leading to other centers declining or remaining isolated. The genesis of cultural centers in Latin America is thus entwined with that of nations—their centers of gravity, backyards, and peripheries.

A Model and Its Variants

After the arrival of the European conquerors, the America that today is called "Latin" was built initially by the Europeans and for the Europeans, for the purpose of exporting its agricultural and mineral wealth. From the sixteenth century onward, the exploitation of resources responded, above all, to external demand. Beginning with the various Latin American nations' independence, the liberalization of trade and the development and diversification of the needs of, first, Europe, and then, the United States only augmented this outward orientation. Nuances aside, this remains a dominant trait of national economies. "Gold fevers" abounded: for the golden fleece (wool), the golden bean (cacao), white gold (nitrate), green gold (banana), and black gold (petroleum). The economic histories of most of these states are characterized by a series of cycles of mineral extraction or agricultural speculation, which were important as phases of prosperity for the elites and as stages in the evolution of spatial organization. Today many countries continue to be economically dependent on the international market for the demand for a limited range of their primary or barely transformed resources. The qualifiers "sugar" island, "petroleum" nation, and "banana" republic retain in part their caricatured relevance, despite some progress in the diversification of economies and exports.

The majority of the capitals are port cities: cities located close to the seaboard or cities linked to a neighboring port. Where they are located in the interior—in Colombia, Ecuador, or Mexico—the axis linking the capital to the principal port has determined how space is organized. The only two landlocked countries, Bolivia and Paraguay, have never stopped seeking an ocean or fluvial port access. On another scale, the vigorous economic outward orientation has diffused the general model of organizing space for exploiting and exporting resources.

This model's basic structure links the area of production with the most direct transportation route to the outlet. The historical evolution of productive Latin American space offers a large inventory of reproductions of and variations on this general model. In privileging what could be called asymmetrical flux with a perpendicular orientation toward the seaboard, this model of spatial organization has caused new equipment and infrastructures to be located according to the caprice of circumstances (often to the detriment of establishing large-scale national or continental networks) and has contributed to the atomization and discontinuous arrangement of the territory and to the multiplication of poorly connected centers.

Thus the future Latin American nations were structured from the very beginning primarily as an archipelago of local urban centers—economic, political, and cultural units—because such was the model of spatial organization imported by the conquerors.

The City-Territory

For the several thousand Spanish and Portuguese adventurers who in the sixteenth century were able to appropriate a continent in less than a generation, the city was the cornerstone of colonial order. Fernand Braudel clearly understood the significance of the seizure of the American expanses, where every city established, however modest, was an advantage gained, and every city that grew was a modest victory, but a victory nonetheless, in what remains even now the greatest urbanization enterprise in history. In three centuries, close to a thousand cities were founded: The Spanish cities, the most numerous, were established primarily during the sixteenth century; other cities, in particular the Portuguese ones, were established in the eighteenth century. Initially, these were modest military posts, often isolated in the heart of vast, hostile expanses. Not all survived; however, the network of those that did constitutes nothing less than the heritage of the greatest intentional and coherent urbanization project in the world. It is not at all surprising that, by the end of the eighteenth century, Latin America was the most urbanized region on the planet, with a growth rate of 15 percent, a third greater than that of Europe. This precipitous, colonial urban domination profoundly affected the spatial organization of the continent.

During the different phases of this epic period of discovery and conquest, each founding of a city was above all a political act, an intervention by a colonial state establishing its jurisdiction over the surrounding area in order to control its people and resources, all the while ensuring that both the conquest and the indispensable link with the distant metropolis were protected. In the great centers of autochthonous populations, colonial urbanization was often most dense where pre-Columbian urbanization had been so. The exemplary and symbolic cases of Cuzco and Mexico City are exceptional; however, some of the most important colonial establishments—such as Guatemala City, Bogotá, Quito, Lima, and La Paz—issued from this type of reproduction in rupture. In the eighteenth century, most of the twenty to twenty-five cities having more than 20,000 inhabitants had no indigenous roots. These included large mining centers, such as Potosí, Quito, and Huancavelica in the Andean highlands and Zacatecas in the northern Mexican desert; ports and centers of colonial commercial monopoly, such as Havana, Cartagena, Panamá, and Callao; and rectorial centers of the empire's subdivisions, such as Santiago de Chile, Caracas, and Buenos Aires. Apart from these masterpieces of the colonial apparatus—cities of functionaries, ship-owners,

merchants, and miners—the urban network consisted primarily of large boroughs. These boroughs were the local arenas of power, sites of the residences of Spanish-born and *criollo* (Spanish-descended but American-born) landowners who lived off rural revenues and who were sometimes endowed with an office in the manufacturing industry. In a parallel movement, from the sixteenth century onward the native peasantry, which until then had been dispersed among hamlets, was subjected to a large-scale regrouping into villages. These were the famous indigenous "reductions." In the view of the colonial authorities, the enterprise would facilitate their control over the local population and its evangelization and promote the payment of tributes and the mobilization and exploitation of labor. The cities were reserved for the Spanish while the suburbs, established around a parish church, were home to the Indians, grouped according to ethnicity. The ethno-cultural dualism of colonial society, evidenced by the unequal coexistence of two republics—Spanish and Indian—each having its own rules, was expressed spatially in the dual will of the conquerors to gather and to separate.

If a colonial urban model exists, it is certainly that of the Spanish empire, which made up the world's largest ensemble of cities laid out in checkerboard pattern. This model includes large cities as well as modest market towns. The city also represented a model of and window onto the "civilization" that policed and confronted the "barbarianism" of the conquered.

In the beginning, and in the heart of the city, was the generative kernel, most often a square; the direction of its contours determined the grid pattern of the streets. This was the ostentatious center of religious and civil power. The main church and city hall were situated here, along with the seat of supreme political authority: the viceroy, president of the assembly, governor, or his representative. It has remained so to this day. To own a house there, or a parcel of land in the immediate area, was a sign of power and privilege. As ceremonial and festive open space, as rupture in the established order, it gained by the symbolic value that the collective imagination of the pre-Columbian indigenous populations attached to the exterior (as opposed to the interior). As theatre of the city, this seat of power was in fact the center of all demonstrations: of power, with the ceremonial parades and proclamations; of faith, with the religious processions and liturgies; and of gaiety and barter, with the festivals and markets. It represented the meeting place of the two republics.

From this central place, a series of concentric circles organized the urban space and the vast territory under municipal jurisdiction. Apart from the privately owned buildings of the powerful, those belonging to the principal religious orders—churches, convents, colleges, and hospitals—were concentrated in the first circle. Craftsmen's workshops were located by specialization in certain streets and quarters of the second circle, which was reserved for these less fortunate Spaniards and *criollos*. The third circle might be composed of native suburbs grouped around a church. Beyond, similar structures defined the model of the city-territory, at once symbolic of the symbiosis of the city and its rural environment and indicative of the ethno-cultural dualism that organized space.

A Civilization of the Great Estate

Along with the proliferation of cities, another important imprint of Iberian colonization is the omnipresence of the great rural estate, which remains the dominant model of agricultural production. The introduction of stock farming, a colonial innovation, contributed to the diffusion of the great estate model while permitting human beings to exercise control and appropriate vast spaces. If the network of cities was set up mainly in the sixteenth century, the widespread establishment and expansion of great estates took place chiefly in the seventeenth. This development peaked during the Republican Period, when the class of great landowners held hegemony in postcolonial society—a status they retained up until the 1930s and sometimes even well after.

At the origin of the great estate lie juridical and social practices dating from the first colonization. As compensation for their participation in colonialization, the conquerors were granted lands by the Crown, *mercedes de tierra* or *sesmarias,* theoretically irrevocable, with their size determined by the beneficiary's rank. In principle, all land adjudged as such property should have been granted without prejudice to the autochthonous populations. However, no land was of interest that did not have a certain economic value, and since the conquerors were loath to work it themselves, it was the control of indigenous manpower that constituted the main stakes in calculating land value (see **Map 1**). The most powerful conquerors, therefore, managed to be delegated administrative supervision of a territory and its population, the *encomienda,* which gave them the right to distribute the workers among economic activities (mining, agriculture, construction, portage); in exchange, the beneficiary was expected to supervise the Indians' conversion to Christianity and to ensure the security of the territory. In addition, early on the financial needs of the Crown induced the authorities to legitimize many situations involving the illegal appropriation of land—illegal, it must be stressed, under Spanish and Portuguese law—by accepting sums having no relation to the value of the illegally acquired property. The introduction of the rule of the transmission of inheritances, privileging the eldest family member, helped ensure the continuity of possession of the great estate, once constituted as such. Ultimately, the economic situation even of the first colonial century favored the takeover of enormous expanses of land. This period was marked by the concentration and restriction of native lands in and peripheral to new villages—a result of the politics of reduction—and by the various traumas of conquest that led to a brutal depopulation.

The shift toward this institution and the variations in the economic situation thus provided the base from which these innumerable estates—*haciendas, fazendas,* and *estancias*—could be expanded and progressively consolidated. The estates were dedicated to agriculture or livestock breeding and, along with the cities and mines, constituted the web of colonial presence, symbolizing colonial control over space and the population. But what diversity is contained within this category of the great estate! On the one hand, there is the traditional, ideal type of *hacienda,* which produces for a narrow market or exists self-sufficiently, requiring no investments and commanding a subjugated labor force; on the other, there is the plantation, which produces on a large scale for the market, has heavy investments, and employs a salaried workforce. Between these two extreme structures of agricultural production—the one seigniorial, the other frankly capitalist—a wide range of subtle variations can be observed over time and space. In culturally dualistic societies, where races and classes are intertwined, the great estate system of production, which combined feudal and capitalist traits, imposed itself not only as a form of appropriation and exploitation of land,

but perhaps even more as an institutional structure, the keystone of traditional rural society.

By monopolizing the production factors of earth and water, the great estate imposed dependence on its rural environment. Only one part, located at the heart of the estate and made up of the best lands–namely, the reserve–was exploited directly by the proprietor, who had access to either a salaried workforce or free labor provided in exchange for the use of a scanty parcel of land. These dependent peasants lived within a first circle of small farms inside the estate's borders; sometimes they were given additional parcels of land for tenant farming under conditions that obliged them to supplement their income by renting their own labor to the landowner. Around the estate, the domestic units of the independent peasants from neighboring villages or the indigenous communities constituted a second circle of small farms, whose expansion in periods of demographic growth was blocked. The great estate was, finally, also a way of life tied to the prestige and social status conferred by the possession of land and its riches and, thus, to the importance ensured by strict control over a population enchained by a pitiless patriarchal authority or by the variegated network of parentage and patronage. The ensemble of these social relationships contributed in large part to establishing the local power of these landowners and, for nearly two centuries, to making them representatives of a landed *criollo* oligarchy characterized by this symbiosis among landed wealth, economic power, forms of regional or local dictatorship, and political influence.

Today the space, the mentalities, and the social relations retain the traces of a system whose abuses were suppressed by agrarian reforms. Rural space remains unequally distributed in Latin America between a majority of small farms, whose size does not permit them to meet the needs of a peasant family, and a minority of large, specialized agricultural operations producing for national or international markets.

Map 1.

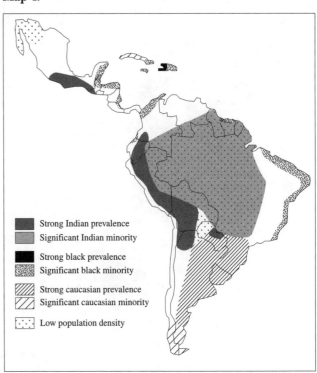

Strong Indian prevalence

Significant Indian minority

Strong black prevalence

Significant black minority

Strong caucasian prevalence

Significant caucasian minority

Low population density

Sowers and Pavers

The America called "Latin" cannot be reduced to an Iberian stamp on an Indian ground. One reason is that the Iberian conquerors came from two countries, Spain and Portugal, whose different traditions, applied to distinct areas, produced different results and divergent styles of development, notably with regards to the relationship to space. These are but nuances, however, for other issues complicated the situation. The *conquistadores* were soon faced with a serious labor problem. They had recourse first to African slaves, then to free workers from Europe and Asia. This importation of labor has not only a history but a geography as well, and after four centuries the end results are diverse local combinations, an ethno-cultural mosaic with specific local dominants.

Nothing so illustrates the difference between the two ancient colonial empires as what remains of their cities. The Portuguese cities had neither the same plan nor the same function as the Spanish (see **Map 2**). Contrasting the manner in which the two types were laid out, the Brazilian historian Sérgio Buarque de Holanda (1902–1982), in *Raizes do Brasil* [1936; Roots of Brazil], distinguishes between the Portuguese "sower" and the Spanish "paver" and opposes the rigorous checkerboard of the Spanish city to the amiable whimsy of Portuguese cities. The first visitors described the Portuguese cities as built without order, with poorly laid-out streets; the first Governor General of Brazil complained of not being able to enclose Santos and São Vicente with walls because of their anarchic construction. The disorder of Bahia, the first capital, was noted by a voyager of the eighteenth century, who remarked that the main square, where the viceroy's palace stood, seemed to be placed there as though by sheer accident. Even the sites for these cities were rarely chosen rationally, as in the Spanish empire, but more often according to the ever-changing needs of the moment.

Map 2.

Occupied or canvassed spaces

Spain Portugal
　　　　1600–1650
　　　　18th century

☆ Viceroyalty capital
◉ Capital of "audiencia" later state capital
• Capital of "audiencia" without a state

□ English holding
◇ Dutch holding
△ French holding
○ Spanish holding

🔷 Jesuits
🔷 Franciscans

This fact becomes all the more startling considering the way in which the same voyagers underscore the splendor of the homes of the sugar mill masters, who had only a small pied-à-terre in town where they hardly ever stayed. This is easier to understand if we bear in mind that these towns were often, and above all, centers of commerce: The Portuguese practiced a Phoenician style of colonization, as opposed to the Roman style of the Spanish. Whereas Spanish policy in the New World aimed at pursuing the secular struggle against infidels and at making the colonies into an "organic extension" of the metropolis, Brazil was for the Portuguese never more than a site of passage and rapid acquisition of wealth.

This attitude of the Portuguese is evident in their fear of venturing too deeply into the interior and reducing their presence on the coast, over which their mastery was uncertain. Tomé de Sousa, the first Governor General, expressly forbade such movement, and in 1554 at São Vicente the order revoking the command to occupy the Piratininga *campos* (the site of the future São Paulo) caused such confusion that the local authorities insisted on seeing the original text. The Portuguese authorities preferred that the colonies be able to send their products to Portugal at low cost; they therefore concentrated their colonization close to the coastline or at least along navigable routes, such as the São Francisco. This planning resulted in a prudent colonization–realistic, commercial, and nonoppressive–which for a long time distinguished the development of that half of the continent. Frei Vicente do Salvador, in the seventeenth century, commented ironically on the Portuguese in Brazil, who stayed along the shore "scrabbling at the coastline like crabs." It was all the more surprising then that these timid colonies had their share of reckless explorers, whose progress toward the west allowed the Portuguese, in less than two centuries, to conquer more than half the continent–well beyond the limit set by the Treaty of Tordesillas–a territory that extended south along the mouth of the Amazon.

In this enterprise one group in particular played a crucial role–the *bandeirantes,* the slave hunters based in São Paulo. It was from this little Jesuit establishment that the great exploration expeditions fanned out to hunt slaves, natural resources, and minerals. São Paulo was a village where more Tupí was spoken than Portuguese; it was a pioneer village, perhaps because exploration was the only resource open to this poorly set up group in a distant outpost. São Paulo became the testing ground for Brazilian unity: Its *bandeirantes* were the first to have concrete knowledge of the space that would become Brazil and to link their destiny to the exploration and exploitation of resources.

Other Immigrations

On the two shores of Iberian America, the demand to develop new resources resulted in important changes because it entailed importing new populations, neither Indian nor Iberian. Outside the densely populated zones, which were able to overcome the demographic shock associated with the Conquest, the Indian population could not provide the labor necessary for the colonial enterprises of mines and plantations. In the Caribbean, on the Atlantic coast of Brazil, African slaves had been used from the sixteenth century onward. The result was a massive displacement of Africans, which markedly affected the composition of the population: Already in 1650 the black population in South America–at 380,000–equaled the white, and in 1829 Alexander von Humboldt estimated the number of blacks in

Latin America at 4.4 million, of which almost 2 million lived in Brazil (excluding mulattos). In total, close to 6.5 million Africans landed, of whom 3.5 million were destined for Brazil alone. Taking into account the mortality rate on the slave ships, Brazil represented 9 to 10 million men and women torn from Africa. They were distributed to the plantations, notably sugar, and their arrival was essential for the development of certain regions, such as the Brazilian Northeast, where sugar constituted the first stable economic activity. The role that this forced immigration played in the genesis of the country was, at the time, acknowledged with the saying, "No blacks, no sugar, no Brazil."

Undoubtedly, this dependency on the forced immigration of African slaves restrained Brazilian plantation owners from abolishing slavery until 1888, making Brazil the last country in the world to give in to pressure from Great Britain, then champion of abolitionism. This policy of resistance was shortsighted, however, for soon after abolition the slave trade was replaced by the free immigration of contract workers. In part, this immigration took the form of an unscrupulous importing of Asian workers. These immigrants would migrate to the cities at the end of their contracts on the plantations, become tradespeople or market-gardeners, and form settlements. Their presence is still noticeable today in these key and lucrative businesses. These policies, then, were responsible for establishing groups of Chinese in areas previously inhabited by slaves or in newly opened zones, notably on the Pacific coast of Peru (between 1860 and 1874, 75,000 Chinese laborers arrived in this area); East Indians in Guyana and the British West Indies; and Japanese in southern Brazil (200,000 arrived between 1884 and 1939).

In Brazil, European immigrants outnumbered Asians. The political and economic crises in Europe during the first half of the nineteenth century, particularly in Italy and Germany, presented the plantation owners (and the United States) with the opportunity to recruit candidates for the great transatlantic voyage. Argentina thus received, between 1857 and 1930, more than six million immigrants, nearly four million of whom settled when the country had only 1.7 million inhabitants (at its first census in 1869). Brazil received more than four million European immigrants between 1824 and 1939, of whom 34 percent were Italians, 29 percent Portuguese, and 14 percent Spanish, while the 170,000 Germans gave a unique physical coloring to the southern states.

There were other immigrants who arrived in smaller numbers but who had a disproportionate importance due either to their isolation in closed colonies (such as the Mennonites of Russian origin in the Paraguayan Chaco, the Welsh colony in Patagonia, or the Dutch colony in the Brazilian Paraná) or to their place in a small economic sector where knowledge and solidarity played significant roles. The latter is the case with the Basques in Argentina or, on a more limited scale, the people from Barcelonette (in the French Alps) in Mexico, who from the base of their alpine valley built a commercial and industrial empire. This category also includes the Levantine tradespeople of Brazil, where a common classification distinguished among *Turcos,* small peddlers recently arrived from the Ottoman Empire who became, with increasing economic success, *Arabes* or *Sirios* and, in the best cases, *Libaneses.*

An Amerindian foundation, Iberian conquerors, African slaves, European and Asian immigrants–many peoples contributed to the genesis of the Latin American population.

From this history emerged a geography, for the proportion of these groups was not by any means the same in all places, and from the differences emerges a distinct contrast between the countries where one element or another dominates–namely, in the regions with an Amerindian, African, or European majority (or strong minority). Indian America corresponds to the physical centers of the ancient empires–the Andean and Mesoamerican Cordillera–and to the sparsely populated zones in the heart of the continent, where the outsider population was more limited. Black Latin America is that of the old slave plantations: the West Indies, the Caribbean coastline of Colombia, and the Brazilian Northeast. White Latin America occupies the temperate zones of the south, where nineteenth-century European immigrants were concentrated: Argentina, Uruguay, and southern Brazil.

Still, this is not to say that there is segregation or any clear line of demarcation. Latin America is certainly the region of the world where creolization has been most intense. This creolization–more of a forced submission than is sometimes admitted, as it was imposed upon slaves of color by white masters–has muddied all the classifications attempted by "specialists." Count Gobineau, author of *Essai sur l'inégalité des races humaines* [1884; Essay on the Inequality of Human Races], was very unhappy in Brazil as a diplomat in Rio in 1869: He viewed miscegenation as the greatest of evils and considered the complete absence of pure blood in Brazil to be catastrophic. The mixing of Blacks, Indians, and Europeans had extended, in his opinion, so as to encompass the whole of Brazilian society, which he considered degeneration.

This situation made any thought of segregation impossible, for no one could be certain of his or her racial purity. Jorge Amado (1912–2000) ridicules his militantly racist fictional character when, at the end of his novel *Tenda dos milagres* [1969; The Tent of Miracles], he is discovered to have a cumbersome black ancestry. However, this does not mean that Latin America is free of all racial tension: First, certain regions are split between two ethnicities having unequal demographic and economic weight; second, a troubling inverse correlation between the pigmentation of the skin and the level of income can be observed almost everywhere.

The societies that took possession of the continent had to contend constantly with a new environment that, in turn, transformed their vision of the world.

The Continent and Its Territories

For Latin Americans, the environment is such a powerful presence that it is constantly represented in literature, beginning with the first chroniclers in the sixteenth century through to the poets of today and including the nativist novelists: Alonso de Ercilla y Zúñiga (1533–1594) evoked the dangerous exhalations of the volcanoes, *respiradores de la tierra;* in Gabriel García Márquez's (b. 1927) *Cien años de soledad* [1967; *One Hundred Years of Solitude*], the character Rebecca eats earth in order not to forget the "ancestral taste of elemental minerals"; Pablo Neruda identified with the "great astral plain" and the giant trees of the Chilean "frontier."

From earthquakes to volcanic eruptions and including tidal waves, cyclones, and landslides, the list of cataclysms that have marked Latin American history is long. Distances, volumes, and contrasts all take on dimensions unknown in Europe. One need only glance at a map of the Amazon and its network of tributaries to be struck by the gigantic scale:

7,200 kilometers in length, this river drains into a basin of more than six million square kilometers, and it has an outflow at the mouth estimated at 200,000 cubic meters per second—more than twice that of the Congo! At 4,000 kilometers in length, the Paraná is not far behind, rivaling the Mekong. And the distances! At the time of the discovery of California, Cape Horn sailors took fifteen months to go around South America. Today it takes seven days and seven nights for coaches to travel the Pan-American Highway from Santiago de Chile to Caracas, ten hours by plane to get from Buenos Aires to Mexico City, and many days by bus, railway, and jeep, with sharp detours and river fordings, to traverse the continent!

Tellurism (the impact of the Earth on its inhabitants), excess, enormity, immensity—these commonplaces, evoked already by the discoverers of America, have not changed over time. For the geographer, they are somewhat simplistic subjective perceptions; however, their merit lies in the fact that they reflect for us the image of nature as imperious and omnipresent. It is from this perspective that we address American nature and space—not in order to set the scene, to present a frontispiece, or to elaborate the decor of social theatre but simply to understand how these physical settings function and, above all, how the Latin American peoples made use of them, understood them, and managed or ignored them.

This colonized space coincides with a primarily tropical region. Although South America extends to a latitude of 55 degrees south in the Antarctic waters, close to 84 percent of its surface lies between the tropics. A tropical region of Hispano-Portuguese colonization and European immigration—these traits make Latin America unique. It is this unique combination that led Pierre Gourou to speak of the "European tropics" in *Les pays tropicaux* [1947; *The Tropical World*, 1953]. This audacious abbreviation, which barely acknowledges Latin Americans, nevertheless summarizes perfectly what distinguishes this America from the Asia and Africa of the same latitudes.

The Stable Americas of Plates and Basins

The second differentiating factor is of a structural order. There are, in fact, two Americas: the America of plates, plateaus, and basins and the America of mountain ranges. The former is that of vast spaces; it is geodynamically stable. The latter is that of the highlands, a domain of ecological mosaics regulated by altitude and escalation; it is a turbulent and unstable America.

In Central America, plates, plateaus, and basins are continuous with the North American Great Plains. They make up the eastern framework of South America. To the north, the mountains of the Guyanas rise up and are crowned by an extraordinary horizontal plateau that is bordered on all sides by giant escarpments, dotted by the highest waterfalls in the world. The enormous Brazilian plateau, rising on its Atlantic edge and covered in many places in primary sandstone, widens to the west and inclines to the south under the Cretaceous basalt that encroaches on the Precambrian kernel of Uruguay. At the southernmost point, the Patagonian triangle, itself elevated, is so often masked by the spread of the Andes that one would hesitate to include it in the same category if it had not retained its plateau aspect.

This world of plates is characterized by horizontality. The eroded surfaces—the pediplanes—seem to slice into the crystalline rock and fight with the sandstone platforms covering them. *Chapadas, tabuleiros*—these large horizontal causeways, which are sometimes set high, do not present an insurmountable topographical obstacle. Pioneers, soldiers, and *bandeirantes* have all crossed them without difficulty. And today the Brazilians easily travel the feverish tangle of roads laid into the red earth.

The America of plates harbors a variety of minerals whose inventory, incidentally, is far from complete. These include the largest known deposits of hematite—mountains of iron, like that of Itabira—as well as an incalculable number of rare ores discovered as a result of the demands of modern metallurgy. The undulations that create rifts in the rock formations seem to date from a distant past, at least from the Tertiary epoch (a division of the Cenozoic era marked by major geographic changes). Even the faults that direct the loosening of the famous sugarloaves of Rio de Janeiro and of the Serra do Mar were reactivated during the Quaternary (the later Cenozoic). The soils of the sandstone plateaus have also suffered such long-term disintegration that they have been demineralized and impoverished by incessant leaching. As one traverses these immense spaces, the feeling of stability asserts itself, and one can understand how these environments function only by decoding their distant heritage. This does not mean that they are any less fragile, however.

None of this holds true for the plains, where recent or current deposits and alluviation dominate. The Amazon basin provides an extraordinary illustration of this phenomenon. A veritable trap for sediments, the plate is to be found at a depth of from 2,500 to 4,000 meters. Reliefs are formed by low and finely chiseled hills, between which the great rivers wind lazily. This is the perfect plain, immense and contourless. Subsidence is so strong here that the bed of the Amazon lies only at an altitude of 65 meters, even at a distance of 3,000 kilometers from the mouth. Apart from the rapids, the indolent waters wind slowly into lakes, whose forms change according to the changing water levels. Here the slope is so gentle that the tides can be felt a thousand kilometers upstream from the mouth of the river.

Upstream, at the foot of the Andes, the basin opens onto the piedmont plains of the *llanos*. These plains would extend into impressive peri-Andean boulevards up to the Chaco were it not for the rivers and the forests that make the terrain impassable. Clearings are sporadic, and only recently have pioneer agricultural land clearings created new openings. Finally, to the south the groove of Paraguay opens out with the Paraná plain, in the Pampa. There, too, subsidence regulates the development of near-perfect surfaces. The drainage is unpredictable; it is curiously aerated in the Pampa, which is covered in volcanic loess, and marshy in the Pantanal, where the smallest obstacle to flow plus a rise in water level transform the plain into an immense expanse of blackish waters (of nearly 150,000 square kilometers). Only grassy islands, which are used for pasture during the rainy season, emerge.

The Turbulent America of the Cordilleras

The same gigantic dimensions are found in the Latin America of the Cordillera, but here the range of environments is far more varied and full of contrasts. Despite the altitude, the vigor of the contours, the tectonic mobility, and hindrances to circulation, men were more willing (and were willing at an earlier stage) to exploit the area. Whereas the Latin America of the plains and plateaus was and remains unpopulated or nearly so, the Cordilleras were home to the great Amerindian civilizations. These were more centralized, and they understood how to create the political tools necessary to manage the vast spaces to ensure an environment suitable to their survival.

Nowhere else on earth does there exist a mountainous meridian purview as imposing as that of the Andean Cordillera. This enormous voussoir (upthrust wedge), which forms the western edge of the continent and which, in the median zone, frequently exceeds 5,000 meters in altitude (6,959 meters with the Aconcagua), develops over tens of thousands of kilometers. Clearly meridian at the latitude of Chile, the range divides into branches near the northwest, molding itself along the old Hercynian lines as it widens to some 500 or 600 kilometers. It narrows to 150 kilometers near the equator and again in the south near Argentina, due to the progressive encroachment of the eastern epicontinental secondary mountain ranges. Finally, at its two extremities, it links with island chains: the Shetlands and Orkneys to the south and the Caribbean to the north via the Venezuelan Andes, with one branch verging toward the Panamá isthmus and Central America to join, past the Mexican volcanic axis, with the mountains of North America.

The Andes, whose geological history is extremely complex, harbor a rich store of metals; the stanniferous axis of Bolivia and the copper of Chile and Peru are often mined by small, fly-by-night establishments (as in the Land of a Thousand Mines in the Chilean Norte Chico) or exploited by large conglomerates. The particulars of the range's orogenesis (the process of its formation) can be deduced from this history: the wedge's great and brittle movement; the ongoing volcanic action associated with this swelling; and a postorogenetic seismic mobility all the more damaging today as it strikes urban centers that have more complicated infrastructure than before.

The vast, protracted lifting that created the current chain collapsed a number of vaulted axes. These intermediary gaps compartmentalize the Cordillera, subdividing it into parallel chains bordered by large, brittle undulations. Three or four chains in succession extend from the Pacific to the eastern sub-Andean plains, separated by intermountain corridors that are at times continuous and at other times arranged in garlands. These are the many *valles centrales* and *valles longitudinales*. The bulk of the population is concentrated in these valleys, which stretch from Managua, Costa Rica, the valley of Magdalena, the Quito basin, and the Bolivian *altiplano* and its great lakes to the endless Chilean *valle central*, which, in fact, is more of a piedmont plain than an intra-Andean basin. From Quito to Maule, and skirting Cuzco, the Incas knew how to take advantage of these strings of basins to control the Andes. The same holds true for the Aztecs, whose settlement is supported by a series of basins backing onto the Mexican volcanic axis.

No Andean state today escapes the medianizing force that the Cordillera impose on spaces, making them conform to the same model: the median axes that concentrate the population and cities alternate with the less-populated Cordillera bordering. The flow of exchange–the movement of people and products–runs perpendicularly across the Cordillera, primarily toward the Pacific, imitating the traditional tropism of the colonial economy. Apart from these privileged lines, this habitual movement often reduces the coastal Cordillera to human deserts. Colombia and southern Chile offer remarkable examples of this phenomenon.

Andean and Mesoamerican orogenesis is inseparable from volcanic and seismic activity. In response to upheaval come fissural eruptions, which have created high *mesas,* and the Quaternary manifests itself with regular volcanic activity, as in the Mexican volcanic axis, the Caribo-Guatemalan alignment, the volcanoes of the central Colombian Cordillera, and the numerous systems that regularly punctuate the Andean summit down to Tierra del Fuego. *Mochos* or *puntiagudos* volcanoes with "pointed" craters raise their rocky silhouette in the central deserts and their ice-capped peaks in the humid tropical or temperate regions of Colombia or Chile. "Protective guardians of towns and villages," they often dominate the intermountain depressions that serve as catchment basins for their deposits. The soil may be rich, but catastrophic eruptions are frequent and dramatic. The zones of "volcanic silence" correspond to portions of the Cordillera having no longitudinal depressions, while seismic activity confers a cataclysmic tone on the Andean dynamism that is comparable to that of the Pacific "firebelt." This activity is part of life in the American mountains. It feeds beliefs and myths. It is, however, quickly forgotten as soon as speculation leads to systematic development. The recent example of the Mexican catastrophe of 1985 is, in this regard, sadly revelatory.

The continent is equally rich in bioclimatic environments: From the Amazonian rainforests to the deserts of Chile, these are among the most diverse in the world. They will not be explored here, but they are described superbly in literature. Of note here is that the laws of nature differentiate among spaces and offer Latin-American societies several Americas. There is nothing surprising in this; after all, the domain extends across two hemispheres and into temperate lands. What attracts the geographer's attention is the arrangement of these spaces. They are not distributed as straightforwardly as is usual, given the layout of zones. Certainly one does find homogenous spaces in the Amazonian equator, and the enormous meridian roll of the Cordillera, from the Tierra del Fuego to Mexico, does impose a singular bioclimatic distribution to the general schema. More commonly, though, one finds large transitional areas, arid or humid diagonals, and immense interior mosaics with floating isohyets (lines connecting areas of equal rainfall) characterized by climatic irregularity. They strike the continent broadside from the Chaco to northeast Brazil. These patterns reflect the reciprocal influences of mechanisms operating at the low and mid-latitudes, marking America with a "meridian permeability" that is, without a doubt, the most remarkable trait of its geography. With the upthrust of the Cordillera and since the end of the Tertiary epoch, the important reserve of Amazonia diversifies as it adapts to the multitude of ecological conditions. The same polymorphism can be observed in the forests of southern Chile, where there is ample evidence of a tropical legacy. The laurifoliates, myrtifoliates, creepers, epiphytes, semi-arboreal mosses, and the same bamboo undergrowth as in the Serra do Mar suggest comparisons with tropical rain forests.

Continuity, inherited flora, and hardiness–the American stocks offer an extraordinary diversification of species, making this one of the world's genetic laboratories. It is hardly surprising that corn, the most ubiquitous plant, comes from the Americas. By exploiting its properties, first pre-Columbian farmers and then modern agronomy have made corn a universal plant through hybridization, the accidental modification of its genetic information, and even genetic drift. It is not the only plant to spread from the Americas: the Chilean strawberry, squash, beans, tomatoes, tobacco, and potatoes have been spread over vast ecological domains the world over.

This diversity, however, does not explain everything, for human space cannot be superimposed upon natural space. If the laws of nature and the limits they impose determined the scope of activity of societies, American geography would be a strange bouquet of paradoxes: the great empty spaces of the immense tropical or temperate plains and accumulations on the divided territories of the Cordillera or the Caribbean.

Cavalier Prospects and Lands of Many Pathways

The land here is marked by great empty spaces, whereas similar areas on other continents are hives of human activity. One need only compare the population density maps of the Amazon and Orinoco deltas with those of their Asian counterparts. As regards the use of space, with the exception perhaps of the Paraná, the great basin saddles are generally underused. The same holds true for the Andean thresholds. Numerous routes descend the Andes toward Amazonia, crossing passes more than 4,000 meters in height, while the pass of Porcullo near Marañon, at an elevation of only 2,150 meters, is poorly developed. It has only an oil pipeline and a poorly marked road. The sites of Asunción and Santa Cruz, which were quite accessible and allowed the possibility of the Brazilian platform linking complementary spaces, were used only briefly in the early days of colonization. And this is not to mention the late colonization of the temperate lands of Chile and Argentina, the Pampa, and the Pacific coast of Mexico.

It is astonishing also that the unifying tendencies observable in certain environments have hardly come into play in America. The Caribbean Sea, for example, a region of archipelagoes, is a world far too fragmentary for it to pretend to the ranks of the inland Mediterranean Sea. Similarly, despite the formidable main highway that is the Amazon, the river has not constituted a sufficient link to counteract tribal and linguistic divisions in the equatorial rain forest. Conversely, despite the difficult orographical conditions the Andes and the central Mexican plateau have made way for homogenous civilizations with strong infrastructures and wide territorial scopes of influence. Highly organized civilizations have even developed in northeast Guatemala, an ordinary region where nothing seemed to encourage such wonders.

This list of paradoxes could be multiplied infinitely if one did not sense that they assume a kind of ideal rationality with respect to land use—that is, the environment's supposed "assets," "potential," and "vocations." In reality, the space and the relationships that people have with nature cannot be understood without turning attention to history and to the societies involved. The maps say so. The occupational gradient of America is organized along obscure littorals, be they dry, tropical, or temperate. Conversely, the interior of the continent is often empty, or nearly so. From all available evidence, this distribution does not correspond to natural determining factors but is inscribed in the logic of the history of conquest and prolonged by the colonial system.

When the Spanish and Portuguese *conquistadores* arrived in America, they found sparsely populated spaces, along with large centers in the Andean highlands and the Mexican Meseta. After the dazzling cavalcades of the first decades, the occupation quickly crystallized in those places that offered gold, silver, and Indian labor. Apart from mining operations, colonization rapidly turned to the appropriation of land, chiefly through animal breeding. Thus for a long time two systems of relating to space coexisted: that of the pre-Columbian farmers and that of the European animal breeders. The former managed their lands in a manner closer to nature; the latter preferred occupation and appropriation, consuming immense spaces. This often conflicting duality in land use remains even today one of the main features of Latin America. Because pre-Columbian farmers contributed little to the genesis of cultural centers, apart from a few old indigenous centers, we will not dwell on them here. The breeders, however, contributed largely to structuring new spaces and developing new cities.

The Epic of Animal Breeding

If the Amerindians were not breeders, neither did the *conquistadores* bring with them the tradition of the Iberian *huerta*. Heirs of the Reconquest, the Spanish who arrived on the continent were cavalrymen, conquerors of space who pursued their struggle against the infidel in the New World. While the same did not exactly hold for the little Portuguese colony, nonetheless in a few decades colonization had transformed this America of open spaces into immense *saltus* more or less converted into savanna, which encroached upon the pre-Columbian islands of *ager*.

Colonial animal breeding was one of the essential means of appropriating space. It took off like a powder trail in the American savanna, beginning with the *solturas*, the pack animals the Spanish and the Portuguese judiciously deposited among the islands, notably in the Caribbean. Beginning in 1525, horses and cattle were released first in the Orinoco plains, then in Pernambuco and Bahia. They spread all along the Pacific coast. In the 1520s the horse arrived in the continent's north. In 1534, Mendoza introduced it from Santiago de Chile to Buenos Aires. After a few decades, the population and reproduction of livestock underwent such a dazzling expansion that wild herds sometimes preceded the conquerors themselves. Even today, the plains of Beni give a sense of what these "livestock mines" were like, these *vaquerías* where the herds were less domestic livestock than wild game, more tracked than raised in the easily flooded, difficult-to-access savannas.

Pierre Deffontaines has described the development of this system. Cattle were used not only for their meat, dried or salted, but also for their by-products of leather and fats. They provided the driving force behind the plantations in the northeast. The oxcart became the main mode of transport in Portuguese America and later in the Argentinean pampas. With the breeding of animals came a flow of traffic, networks, roads, *pasos,* and official and clandestine routes—a life of large-scale relationships and exchanges. *Tambos,* or roadhouses, and trade fairs stretched along the large livestock traffic routes, created *ex nihilo.*

Breeding supported the development of the *latifundio* property system that progressively structured America. From the seventeenth century onward, the system became so ubiquitous that farmers had to protect themselves from livestock. The peasants erected hedges of bamboo or *aveloes* in the *brejos* of northeastern Brazil; they created a farmland crisscrossed by willows, poplars, and eucalyptus in Colombia and built drystone walls in Mexico, Ecuador, and Chile; sometimes they even dug deep trenches, the *zanjas* of Minas. Pasture fences, and the noticeable transformations wrought by them, did not play a part until much later, notably in the ovine zones of the Pampa, which were stripped of trees; wire fences were supported by posts made of *quebracho,* the tree of a Chaco deforested, if not devastated, by the demands of the breeders.

Such essential moments must be revisited in order to account for the apparent paradoxes in the occupation of space in Latin America: mountains populated by farmers; plains free of agriculture and devoted to extensive animal breeding supported by the latifundiary system; and forests stripped almost bare by a tradition of clearing, gathering, and harvesting. In short, the distribution of roles owes more to history than to the natural "vocations" of the environments. Even if the plantation economy developed quite early, notably in the islands and on the Brazilian coast (sugar, then cacao), modern large-scale agriculture appeared only belatedly in America. The result is a loose command of space, vast expanses left nearly empty—an ensemble of factors that clarifies the nature of the relationship Latin-Americans maintain with nature.

Vastness

The sheer vastness of America results more from an absence of control than from its physical size, for which equivalents can be found in Asia or Africa. In other words, it is a result of underpopulation, underoccupation, the predominance of the large estate, and the extensiveness of the systems of production. Where it reigns, the *latifundio* has not permitted peasant societies to develop. The relations the agricultural worker, or *péon,* has are not with the land, the soil, or the district but with the supervisor. The poverty of the vocabulary of nature and space bears witness to this fact. Place names are devoted to saints rather than places. Areas merit no designation more precise than *campos* (fields, the countryside) or *sertão* (the bush)—and, from a certain point of view, all savannas are *sertão.* One distinguishes among *el cerro, el monte, la mata, el alto, el bajo,* but not much more. All environments are the same for the worker who, driven to the margins of the *hacienda,* finds work in another *campo.* If he transfers to another supervisor, the distances are measured in hours of transportation by horseback, truck, or bus.

Once a peasant society does take root, however, it develops a full vocabulary for nature that reveals its hold over places. The peasants of the Brazilian Agreste distinguish among the *topos de gerais, brejos, pé da serras,* and *açudes* (equivalent, more or less, to high plateaus, high oasis, piedmonts, and hilltop lakes), which are environments rather than topographies. This is nothing compared to the wealth of the Indian languages, which designate the spaces, soils, vegetation, and fauna with remarkable precision. The Ashuar of eastern Ecuador have elaborated typologies of streams and rivers, and the Kayapo Indians of Brazil distinguish among dozens of types of ashes resulting from slash-and-burn techniques, and for every type of crop they elaborate particular blends of humus.

Apart from strictly utilitarian vocabularies, such as classifications of "friendly" medicinal plants according to their benefits or properties, the vernacular languages often reveal a true "socialization of nature," a rich symbolics of interactions. Behind the crude appearance of converted clearings, which in reality reproduce the structure of the forests, hide unsuspected riches of a disorder that is actually a social order projected onto "domesticated nature." This has nothing in common with the anonymous nature of the well-traveled lands, with their exasperating monotony of *fazendas* or *haciendas,* so vast that—from Patagonia in the south to Llanos by way of Goiás, and from central Cuba to the Mexican northwest—they reproduce the same social structures, the same hierarchies, and the same landscapes.

The Horseman, Space, and the Road

American vastness was not born simply of the latifundiary system. It also forms an integral part of the colonial epic of the horse. While the Jivaro Indian opened up and demarcated his territory on foot, and the Quechua Indian traversed the Sierra,

the Spaniard measured distances in horseback rides—a perceptible difference that explains his particular perception of space. The horse gave him absolute supremacy and great mobility—no roads, no routes, but the ability to get around vast expanses, to dominate immense areas whose populations were under Spanish control. Overall, it provided a means of mastering distance, no matter how the space was occupied. The Indians of the Pampa adopted this form of mobility for their livestock hunts and raids, as did the Indians of North America, whose forays extended into central Mexico.

Today, when applied to the extensive, dominant systems of production, to activities that, in the *haciendas,* are more a matter of guarding than breeding livestock, horse-powered movement implies a whole category of relations to the land, the soil, fertility, water, and erosion. While the peasant or Amazonian Indian manages his ecological capital, the latifundian remains unaware of it. He covers a domain whose value is defined solely by its expanse. In America, it is less the quality of the soil than its surface and speculative prospects that attract pioneers.

On another scale, by linking distant regions, the horse allowed for the development of complex organizations of space. Large road systems, punctuated with roadhouses, united disparate areas: from Asuncion toward the Atlantic, from Quito to Cauca, from Magdalena to Panamá, and from Mexico City to San Francisco. In the Cordillera during the seventeenth century, mule trains born of gold smuggling created new links between the piedmonts and the plains. The horse allowed the Spaniard to find pathways other than those of the Indians. The Incas created their traffic network by taking advantage of the ridges; the conqueror preferred to follow valleys or slopes, thus exposing his roads and settlements to the effects of runoff, floods, and landslides in the rainy season. The roads that plunge down the eastern Bolivian Cordillera toward the Yungas, and those that cut across the coffee terrace in Colombia, are studded with *animitas* indicating countless accidental deaths. The road also compresses space and the use that is made of it. The Indian, the *seringueiro* (hevea tapper), and even the *bandeirantes* scattered into the mountains or the rainforest, no matter how difficult these were to penetrate. Today's roads have relegated to oblivion numerous pathways, those which, in Peru or Bolivia, led to the lost cities of the rain forest—Machu Picchu is only the most famous among them—as well as those used by collectors of quinquina bark and by rubber tappers. Even the Jesuit foundations of the Amazonian or Patagonian slopes of the Andes were excavated only belatedly. For example, it took many years of expeditions into the forests of southern Chile to rediscover, at the end of the nineteenth century, access to San Carlos de Bariloche from the Gulf of Reloncavi (see **Map 3**).

Today America is the domain of the road: The Pan-American Highway is traversed by trucks bearing improbable cargoes; mountain roads take peasants in their Sunday best, hanging from small trucks or jeeps, to market towns; dusty trails through the *campos* are swallowed by flashy buses, their roofs laden with frightened poultry and bundles of grain; the rocky trails of the fluvial terraces are built by communities of peasants; and the cinder trails of the volcanic piedmont are traveled by the winch trucks of logging expeditions. There is always a road in America to access the least-populated territory, even at the price of the consumption of vehicles, an incredible accident rate, and erosion by runoff or landslide.

Map 3.

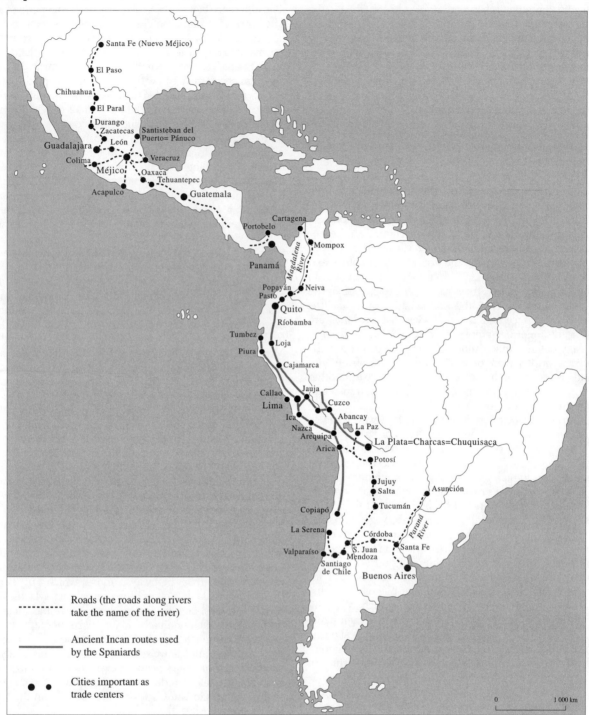

Roads (the roads along rivers
take the name of the river)

Ancient Incan routes used
by the Spaniards

Cities important as
trade centers

At the same time, there remain vacant spaces and roadways to be built. There are still journeys to be made and adventures to be had. There are inaccessible regions dying of entropy, unexplored areas accessible only through the images of aerial photography, radar, and satellites.

The Recourse to Vacant Spaces

Whether natural or the result of history, vastness can be a handicap. Latin Americans have made it a resource and, at times, a recourse. Underpopulation, neglect, and the reign of the *latifundio* are accompanied by an extraordinary mobility

in land occupation. The notion of the "frontier" in Frederick Jackson Turner's sense still hovers over the temperate lands of Chile and Argentina, the plateaus of the *cerrados*, Amazonia, the Venezuelan *llanos*, and even the Caribbean coast of Mexico. Today the nations themselves institute or take part in this mobility. Planning organizations, *agropecuarios* institutes, centers for agrarian reform, regional banks, and innumerable experts all make use of technical means for analyzing space that have been developed by Latin America's big neighbor to the north and constantly plan large-scale development projects. One imagines reconstructions of space on an immense scale. Similarly, an appetite for lands and concessions has been awakened. For the past twenty years, the map has lured planners, at times to the detriment of real knowledge of the environments concerned, their function, and the societies that use them. Ecological conservation has rarely been a concern of pioneer epics, past or recent. Alongside unarguable successes, many setbacks must be recorded in the accounts of hasty or speculative exploitations.

For more than a century, thus, reserves of vacant land have constituted a permanent resource in Latin America. But the recourse to space–a windfall during periods of speculation, a relentless pursuit or diversion from the problems of regions or nations in crisis–is quite often accompanied by an exploitation of minimal value at maximal ecological expense. In this sense, American space reflects its history well and, from the point of view that concerns us here, that of newer, developing countries. According to Claude Lévi-Strauss, nature in Latin America is sufficiently sought after by man to allow enough time for the creation of imbalances but not enough that a slow and steady cohabitation could elevate it to the level of landscape.

Space, reputed to be free, is seen as a resource, even if it is poorly understood. But the societies that view it thus sometimes forget that space is not simply there to buttress their own activities, and they pay the price when nature painfully reminds them of this fact.

The Uneasy Land
The three main natural limitations of the continent–the altitude and steepness of the Cordillera, catastrophic events, and climatic fluctuations and hazards–have been experienced in diverse ways. There are limitations that transform themselves into assets; there are adaptations that have become constraints. From the Cordillera to the treacherous lands of Amazonia, there are numerous examples of societies that have at times learned to accommodate the most drastic limitations and, if need be, to develop and take advantage of them. There are others, however, that have aggravated these limitations, as demonstrated by certain recently colonized spaces. There are those, finally, that submit with a surprising passivity, with the accumulated acts of negligence in the face of the natural elements amounting to a fatalism bordering on abnegation.

More spectacular, and more constraining, perhaps, than the slopes, altitude, and terracing, the natural catastrophes that strike the subcontinent are another constant in its history. Their incidence, nevertheless, has changed. Volcanic and seismic activity and tropical hurricanes affect the societies and economies of today more harshly. Among these, earthquakes are the most spectacular and the most serious.

Plate tectonics theory helps to explain the genesis of these phenomena. The thrusting or "subduction" of the Pacific oceanic plate (the Nazca plate) under the continental plate induces these two plates to draw closer together at an overall rate of five or six centimeters per year in Peru and Chile. Tremendous energy accumulates at certain points along this fault and is released brutally and unpredictably. The depth of these centers increases, then, as the subduction's surface plunges. In this way, the earthquakes may be superficial or intermediate in severity to the west (from 50 to 250 kilometers) and deep to the east, in Brazil (from 500 to 700 kilometers).

The indirect effects of these earthquakes are often even more catastrophic than their direct impact: Rivers are rerouted; lakes are brutally emptied or sealed; glaciers are ruptured; and there are lake floods and mudslides. Many manifestations can affect even valleys quite distant from the zones around the epicenters and can result in real tragedies. One example: the 60,000 victims at Yungay in Peru in 1970.

One notes that history rarely records earthquakes striking only rural areas, where the effects are diluted. The destruction of a single adobe house entails little damage. Collective memory is more sensitized to urban destruction. Santiago de Cuba, Port Royal, Antigua, Guatemala la Nueva, San Salvador, Cuzco, Managua, and Mexico City–many cities have been devastated and rebuilt. There have been many catastrophes whose amplitude has grown with the urbanization of Latin America, the increasing complexity of networks and civil engineering, and the enormous extent of construction projects. Ultimately, it is not unusual for earthquakes to punctuate Latin American economic life. They reveal ruptures and form landmarks. Thus the 1972 earthquake represented a turning point for Nicaragua. It was during this time that the Somoza clan confiscated international aid, became a financial group, and founded banks and insurance companies. These ventures, in a country of seismic activity, constitute lucrative enterprises. It was also at this time that the clan began to split. Seismic destruction brought into play considerable sums of money. By depriving the bourgeoisie of the profits from reconstruction, Somoza succeeded in precipitating his own downfall. It was a pivotal date, in fact, just as 1985 was for Mexico City, where the earthquake unleashed the discontent of the urban middle classes: The party in power at the time would find itself a minority in the 1988 presidential elections.

Latin American societies in part adapted their strong cultural model to these new territories and in turn reshaped these territories after their own image. They preferred to occupy certain areas and to leave enormous empty spaces in between, thereby establishing a highly unequal territorial occupation that persists today.

The Archipelago of Population: Centers and Borders
With an overall population density of twenty inhabitants per square kilometer, South American space is not very populous. This statistic, however, disguises the higher population densities of the Caribbean (more than 200 individuals per square kilometer for eleven states, and 643 people per square kilometer for Barbados) and certain regions of the high Andean and Mexican plateaus. Population distribution in the archipelago, while ancient, was accentuated by colonization and, more recently, by the politics of development, which concentrated people along the coasts and in the cities.

In the dense population centers of the Mesoamerican highlands and the Andes, the pre-Columbian heritage was reinforced by European colonization, which was installed there for fiscal, sanitary, and strategic reasons and for mining development. The capital cities of Mexico and Guatemala still lie at an altitude of about 2,500 meters, and their rural population density is more than 100 inhabitants per square kilometer. Higher in the Andes, the level described as "temperate" (around 2,500 to 3,500 meters) has been favored, notably in the basins and the high valleys of the center and the north; here population densities are often higher than 50 inhabitants per square kilometer, reaching 100 near Lake Titicaca, which is at 4,000 meters. The Caribbean islands, especially the small ones, often appear to be populated beyond their capacities, with average densities at more than seventy inhabitants per square kilometer, except in the Bahamas. Many of the interior mountains, however, are uninhabited, a fact that accentuates the density of the coastal regions, and parks have been created in those areas where, in the eighteenth century, fugitive slaves would hide.

The existence of large spaces with low population densities (often less than one inhabitant per square kilometer) accentuates the impression of immensity and underpopulation. These are regions with far more challenging environmental conditions (the North Mexican desert, cold Southern Patagonia, the high slopes of the Andes, the humid windward coasts of the isthmus, and especially Amazonia, the vast hinterland of several of the South American countries). There are, however, mining agglomerations at an altitude of more than 5,000 meters, and railways come close to that. Some Indian groups adapted to the desert, the cold, and above all the Amazonian rain forest; they were driven back, marginalized, and often wiped out by the new masters of the land. These spaces appear empty only in the context of European colonization, which privileged the coasts, the easily accessible temperate or tropical regions, and places where the forms of development remain either very selective—ports, mines, cities—or very extensive. So, apart from the Caribbean, each country has its own interior "frontier," open to the population and often associated with a political border, which the country tries to manage for reasons of geostrategy or to solve its economic problems.

The opening of new lands was made possible by the opening of new roads, whose main reason for being does not seem to have been the widely promoted colonization. These roads, most often the work of military governments, were above all strategic: They were designed to mark out the territory, to open up ill-consolidated regions that were poorly linked to the more populated areas of each country. The proof lies in the trans-Amazonian highways of Brazil, as attested to by the writings of General Golbery do Couto e Silva, a geopolitician and professor of the Brazilian Military Academy. These new roads, however, have altered the conditions of accessibility to entire regions: Manaus has been linked by road to southern Brazil, and not only by more than 6,000 kilometers of fluvial and marine coastal navigation; Santa Cruz de Sierra can claim its status as the capital of Western Bolivia and as rival to La Paz all the more now that it is better linked to the high Andean plateaus.

Geopolitical axes first and foremost, these new roads should have proved the medium for colonization on a large scale. Though they may involve enormous areas, however, these pioneer fronts have not had a decisive impact at a demographic level: In Brazil, where the phenomenon was most widespread, the state of São Paulo received more migrants between 1970 and 1980 than all the pioneer regions (which were then fully active) combined; in the other countries the rural exodus to the large cities everywhere surpassed by far the migration to new lands. Centripetal tendencies remained stronger—and more far-reaching—than centrifugal tendencies.

Mobilities and Migrations

As a land of Indians often practicing itinerant agriculture, immigrants from three continents, pioneers, and displaced country folk on the move to the cities, Latin America has always been marked by the strong spatial mobility of its population. The rural exodus, which was exacerbated by highly inegalitarian agrarian structures, was, for a long time, quite impressive. It is difficult to say whether it has slowed down today; it may just be less definitive in that those who find only temporary work (urban or rural) outside their native base periodically return home. Life for many Latin Americans currently

consists of a series of individual or family displacements, either within their home country or abroad, with urban stays of varying durations for work or study, supported or not by family. As in North America, everyone has thus retained the risk-taking spirit and adaptability of the immigrant; but in Latin America, poverty and political problems are also powerful factors influencing migration.

Much of the migratory flow extends beyond the borders; the motivations are often the same as for internal migration, although the determination and decision-making influences are somewhat different, notably in the cases of political exile. Three destinations are privileged: the former European metropolises, the United States, and richer neighboring countries. At the time of the various independences in the Caribbean, there were exoduses to Great Britain and the Netherlands, which today restrict and closely monitor such immigration. Spain continues to attract businessmen, students, and well-to-do retirees. In the United States, there were more than 4 million legally established, often naturalized, Spanish speakers in 1950 and close to 15 million in 1980 (9 million from Mexico, 2 million from Puerto Rico, and 800,000 from Cuba), to which can be added some 6 million illegal immigrants.

Levels of development—the demand for cheap labor—determined migration among neighboring countries, with the flow moving from the poorer or more densely populated countries to the wealthier ones: from Haiti to the Dominican Republic, from Guatemala to Belize or Mexico, from overpopulated El Salvador to its neighbors, from Barbados or Jamaica to Trinidad. Certain countries were highly attractive during periods of economic prosperity. Argentina in the 1950s attracted Paraguayans, Bolivians, and Chileans; in 1978, it received 2.5 million Latin American immigrants, the vast majority of whom were hired farm hands or workers from the *villas miserias,* the shantytowns of Buenos Aires. Between 1973 and 1979, nearly 3 million South Americans headed toward petroleum-rich Venezuela (a number equal to one-fifth of the country's 1979 population); the great majority were Colombians, notably women, but also Dominicans, Chileans, and Argentineans who came for political or economic reasons and often poorer Ecuadorians and Peruvians. Even when illegal, these immigrants provide both the cheap labor and the technicians the country lacks. The language community, the ease of communication, the tradition of welcoming, and the solidarity of democracies with those exiled by dictatorships facilitate these migrations among countries, which remain open to Europeans, particularly Latins, who rush in during periods of prosperity. The main movement, however, is toward the cities; the large urban centers today are the major areas of population concentration.

Metropolization and Giant Cities

Due to the age of the urban network, the dependence on the exterior, and the level of development, the rates of urbanization in Latin America are the highest in the Third World: 70 percent in 1985 (almost three Latin Americans in four, versus one in two in 1960). In each country, more than 40 percent of the overall urban population tends to reside in the largest city, generally the capital. There is, then, an unequal distribution within the urban network, with a significant gap between the largest and second-largest cities and too few well-equipped and attractive smaller cities. In the Latin America of the 1950s, only six towns exceeded the million-inhabitants mark;

twenty years later, fifteen were recorded, and in this period their total population tripled, reaching 40 million. At the end of the 1980s, the number of metropolises with a population of one or more million was estimated at roughly thirty, and their cumulative population was estimated at 100 million inhabitants; in India, which is 1.7 times more populated, these metropolises total 50 million inhabitants, or half that in Latin America. Taking into account cities having a current population of half a million, one Latin American in four has the large-city lifestyle; this proportion remains at the level of one in eight for the African continent and is slightly higher for the ensemble of Third World countries.

By the early twenty-first century, more than 200 million people–probably half the citizens of the subcontinent–will reside in these sprawling metropolises, which include four of the ten giant cities of the planet: Mexico City, São Paulo, Rio de Janeiro, and Buenos Aires–all urban nebulae that have already passed the symbolic 10 million mark. Heading the world's list of urban gigantism, Mexico City and São Paulo have an annual population growth rate equivalent to the entire population of European cities such as Bordeaux, Seville, and Stuttgart, while Bogotá and Lima will soon be almost as populous as Paris, probably reaching populations of 12 million. The extraordinary growth rate and expansion of these metropolises proceed according to an evolutionary logic in which certain traits of the dynamics of large industrial cities are combined with the specific characteristics of underdevelopment, as if, in the final analysis, Mexico City were at once Paris plus Cairo, and São Paulo were New York and Calcutta or Manila.

The phenomenon of metropolization is linked directly to the powerful historical tendency that favors the growth of the main city (generally, the state capital) to the detriment of other centers subordinate to it in the hierarchy of national urban networks. In light of the situation prevalent in most industrialized countries, and with respect to the possibility of a more balanced national economic growth rate, the concentration of people, equipment, and service and production industries in a dominant center appears more of a handicap. Upsetting the urban network, the logical consequence of creating a balance, however, would be, for many specialists, an obstacle to implementing more egalitarian development.

If this state of affairs has deep roots in the historical tradition–first colonial, then republican–of strong administrative centralization in the capitals, which was and remains the privileged channel of relations with the outside, the relentless movement of people can be attributed to the effects of full-blown phases of industrialization in the twentieth century and the general crisis in the countryside. This phenomenon of blatant urban "macrocephaly" depends to a large extent on the advantages of localization offered by the main city. At first, during the phase of industrialization, through importation, the development of enterprises was stimulated by the availability of national capital, the presence of the most important market in the country, and poorly distributed facilities in the rest of the region. More recently, with the phase of internationalization of capital and of industrial production, companies seek as a priority a suitably technological and economical environment, conditions of employment, and ready access to the world market that only a large metropolis can assure them. Induced by the expansion of economic activity and the demands of the population, the tertiary sector finds in the big city an environment that privileges rapid expansion and that, moreover, allows the state apparatus to develop significantly.

Finally, the great disparities in revenue and standards of living that, in all the countries, favor the metropolises, sustain a steady flow of floating populations seeking social advancement, a better standard of living, or even, quite often, simply survival, including those for whom the city appears as the last refuge from societies torn apart by rising insecurity and violence or for victims of natural catastrophes.

It is not surprising, then, that the national capitals tend to coincide with the main centers of nonagricultural economic activity and are the most populated cities in each country. The notable exceptions of Ecuador and Brazil correspond to a marked urban "bicephaly," in which the major metropolis is not the capital, while the capital, in turn, retains considerable economic and demographic weight (see **Map 4**). Thus Guayaquil outstrips Quito and São Paulo has the upper hand over Rio de Janeiro; moreover, the creation of a new capital at Brasília in the 1950s has further distorted the case of Brazil. Between 10 percent and 20 percent, and frequently between one-quarter and one-third, of the national population is concentrated often within an almost insignificant surface area of a few hundred square kilometers–that is, a few hundredths of the surface area of the largest countries. It is not unusual to find in this small area one half or two thirds of the companies and industrial employment, more than half of the public service jobs, and often 75 percent to 80 percent of all banking and financial institutions. With 40 percent of the isthmus population, the city of Panamá has 58 percent of the industrial jobs, 64 percent of the commercial jobs, and 83 percent of the banking and national service jobs. The city participates at a rate of 71 percent, 82 percent, and 91 percent, respectively, in the production of the gross national product in each of these economic sectors. The metropolitan area of Lima assembles nearly one-third of all Peruvians within 0.3 percent of the national territory, has 70 percent of the industrial operations, records 80 percent of all banking deposits, registers 40 percent of the secondary school student and 55 percent of the university student populations, and has half of all hospital beds and two-thirds of the country's doctors. The most important and extensive of these metropolitan nebulae often incorporate several of the most populated municipalities in the country, which in some cases emerged only a generation ago. Villa el Salvador, on the periphery of Lima, was only desert in 1970 and today numbers nearly 300,000 inhabitants; in the metropolitan region of Mexico City, Netzahualcoyotl, built upon a site experts in 1950 declared uninhabitable and sometimes described as the world's largest shantytown, is, with its 2 million citizens, the fourth-largest city in Mexico.

Heartland, Key Region

There are even more ancient roots to this movement to consolidate the heartland, combined with the movement toward metropolization. Many of these core regions played a catalytic role in the creation of a national identity when the Spanish colonial empire was disintegrating and rupturing. In these central regions, whether based in the main centers of the Andean or Mexican indigenous population or born from the expansion of the great agricultural frontiers in the nineteenth and twentieth centuries–for example, the Paulist plateau, Argentinean pampa, and Colombian Andes–the high rural densities, relative or absolute, and the presence of one or more important cities, including the capital, have favored a cumulative economic growth, stimulated by the growth of the main urban market, the extension of transportation networks, and the distribution

Map 4.

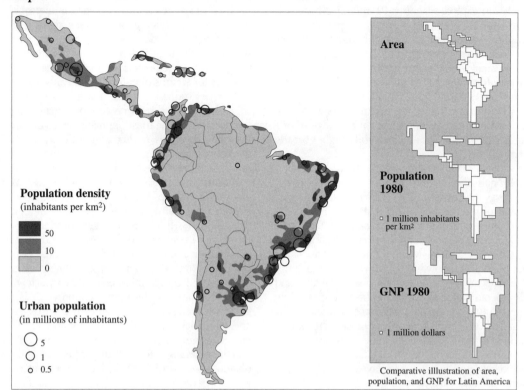

Population density
(inhabitants per km²)

50
10
0

Urban population
(in millions of inhabitants)

5
1
0.5

Area

Population
1980

□ 1 million inhabitants
per km²

GNP 1980

□ 1 million dollars

Comparative illlustration of area,
population, and GNP for Latin America

of technological innovations and production investments. Today these regions enjoy a quality and density of infrastructures and production sites far superior to those of the rest of the country, which is consequently identified as an outlying "desert" as compared to the "preferred" central region.

The reality of the matter is not quite so neat, because the exploitation of valuable natural resources (hydrocarbons, mines) gives rise to considerable investments, including infrastructures, that sometimes benefit outlying regions, and because the national policies that manage the territory redirect the concentration of capital. Certain decentralization policies at times systematically link space and strategic interests at the borders, notably in zones of conflict: The national armies are often widely deployed there for many years; massive programs of road creation or agricultural settlement have come into being; and poles of decentralized industrial development have been created. Moreover, national aerial networks have played a role in structuring centers of activity peripheral to each country's political and economic center. Then there is the transfer of the Brazilian capital from Rio de Janeiro to Brasília, a stunning symbol of the movement toward the western interior. This success has inspired other projects: Argentina has envisaged the creation of a new capital at Viedma in order to move its center of gravity toward the south and Patagonia; in Peru, the possibility of an eastern settlement in Amazonia or the central Andes is being explored.

It is unlikely that this kind of deliberate alteration will profoundly affect the hierarchy of urban centers in Latin America, for this network is one of the oldest and strongest structures in place on the continent. Other factors have emerged in the past decade, however, that could alter the predominance of the capitals in some places: the growing resistance to centralism and the decentralization movement linked to democratization, but also the relentless effect of the drug traffic

Map 5.

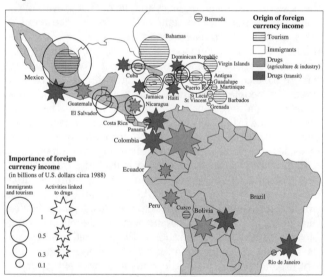

Origin of foreign
currency income

Tourism
Immigrants
Drugs
(agriculture & industry)
Drugs (transit)

Importance of foreign
currency income
(in billions of U.S. dollars circa 1988)

Immigrants
and tourism

Activities linked
to drugs

1
0.5
0.3
0.1

from south to north (see **Map 5**). The network of secondary centers, some of which are also important cultural centers, could provide the basis for future cross-border and transnational reconstructions, which would make feasible the recent attempts at regional integration in Mercosur and Alena.

The territorial organization implied by the cultural model by which Latin America has lived for five centuries could change if this cultural model were also to change. However, it is likely that the harbingers of such change would be detected at the local and regional levels. Therefore, we need to examine closely the past and present configurations of the cultural centers in each of the large regional bodies.

Translation by Wendy J. Eberle

Works Cited

Amado, Jorge. 1969. *Tenda dos milagres*. São Paulo: Martins.

Buarque de Holanda, Sérgio. 1936. *Raizes do Brasil*. Rio de Janeiro: Olympio.

Deffontaines, Pierre. 1938. "Rapports fonctionnels entre les agglomérations urbaines et rurales: un exemple en pays de colonisation, le Brésil." *Comptes rendus du Congrès international de géographie d'Amsterdam*. Leiden: E. J. Brills.

García Márquez, Gabriel. 1967. *Cien años de soledad*. Buenos Aires: Editorial Sudamericana.

Gobineau, Arthur, comte de. 1884. *Essai sur l'inégalité des races humaines*. Paris: Firmin-Didot.

Gourou, Pierre. 1976. *L'Amérique tropicale et australe*. Paris: Hachette.

Levi-Strauss, Claude. 1955. *Tristes tropiques*. Paris: Plon.

CHAPTER 2

FROM THE NEW SPAIN OF CORTÉS TO THE MEXICAN, CENTRAL AMERICAN, AND CARIBBEAN MOSAIC

Alain Musset

The Spanish built the first strongholds for their overseas empire around the American Mediterranean. From the short-lived city of Isabela, founded by Christopher Columbus on the north coast of Santo Domingo, to the powerful Mexico City, raised by Cortés on the ruins of ancient Tenochtitlan, a whole series of cities has structured a space long situated at the heart of the economic, political, and cultural systems established by the conquerors of the New World (see **Map 1**). Paradoxically, this vast grouping (baptized at the beginning of the sixteenth century under the highly symbolic name of New Spain) is today a frontier, and at times a periphery, of the Latin American world. In the West Indies–a multitude of islands, which no fleet, no matter how powerful, could master–a number of foreign influences competed with the monopoly that the Spanish Crown pretended to exercise. In Central America, divided into as many states as there were provinces during the Colonial period, the small numbers of Spaniards encouraged communities of settlers to pull back and be diverted to other areas because of the lack of natural resources. Mexico, one of the pillars of Latin America, did not start to lean toward North America until 1992, when it signed the North American Free Trade Agreement (NAFTA) with the United States and Canada; already in the seventeenth century, the entire western subcontinent bore the name *America mexicana*. Between 1836 and 1853, the loss of territories located beyond the Rio Grande (Rio Bravo for the Mexicans) did not erase the Spanish influence in regions under U.S. domination. At the dawn of the third millennium, northern Mexico and the southwestern United States still constitute a vast frontier zone where two civilizations rub shoulders, confront each other, and sometimes blend together.

To understand the complexity of this large assemblage, it is necessary first to focus on the causes and consequences of such geographic and political parceling and then to examine how the cities founded by the Spanish in the Caribbean basin favored the emergence of a genuine *criollo* consciousness, a blend of Hispanism and Americanism. Between the epochs of Discovery and Independence, networks of cities took shape. They permitted the development of urban hierarchies that were not replaced during the spectacular demographic boom of the second half of the twentieth century. The permanence of these structures, often inherited from the Colonial period, helps explain why, unlike other Latin American regions, the nations of the former New Spain have coalesced around sometimes medium-sized urban centers that form the crucible of local elites seeking a territory and an identity.

A Sea and Two Archipelagoes

Initially founded by Hernán Cortés on the ruins of the Aztec empire, New Spain did not confine itself to the borders of today's Mexico, but in the sixteenth century took over the

Map 1.

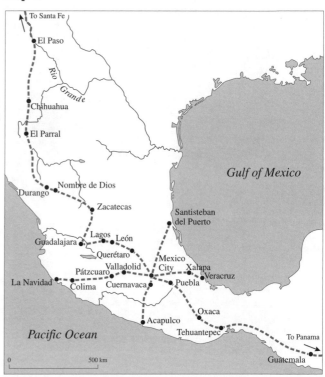

entire Caribbean basin, including the Antilles and part of what is now Venezuela but excluding the District of Panama (see **Map 2**). In his second report to Charles V, Cortés justified the choice of this prestigious name on the basis of what were, in his view, similarities between the newly conquered kingdom and the Iberian peninsula: the expanse and fertility of the spaces yet to be discovered, the wide variety of climates, and the wealth of the civilizations subjugated to the Hapsburg crown (Cortés 96). The land of conquest and creolization, New Spain also became a laboratory for colonial town planning and the heart of Hispanic-American culture.

In many respects, though, the processes of identification and imitation that had facilitated the transmission to America of a Spanish model based on the city have functioned more in the domain of municipal powers and urban culture than in the concrete shape of the cities. This explains the considerable number of homonymous cities located on either side of the Atlantic. For the Spanish conquerors, Seville–where, every year, fleets would depart and arrive–remained for a long time the ultimate cultural and civilizing reference point. For that reason, in 1509 Juan de Esquivel, Christopher Columbus's former traveling companion, decided to found a

Map 2.

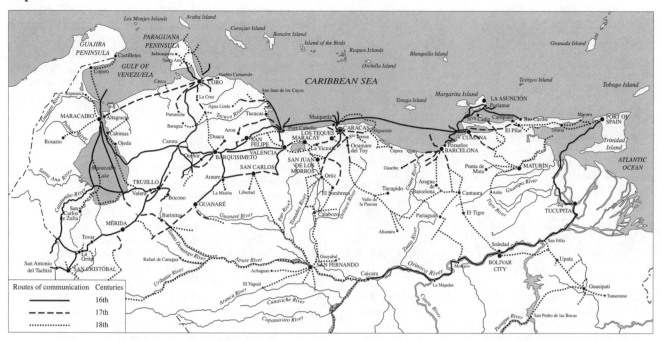

new city in Jamaica called Sevilla la Nueva. Ten years later, dazzled by the first large indigenous city he had discovered on the east coast of Mexico, Cortés rebaptized the ancient Cempoala as Seville; today little remains of this city but a few ruins surrounded by sugarcane fields.

During the first century of Conquest, the Spanish founded dozens of cities in the vast space of the American Mediterranean. However, despite appearances, the processes of urbanization and the formation of urban spheres of influence have neither complied with the same criteria in all cases nor followed the same evolutionary path; this explains in large part the heterogeneity of the area's cultural regions. Geographic factors have played an important role in the compartmentalization of these different areas. In the islands, as on the continent, the tortured contours and the scarcity of territory serve to exacerbate regional contrasts. A few dozen kilometers suffice to pass from the temperate climate of the Guatemalan *altiplano*, where coffee and corn got the better of the pine forests, to the hot and humid lands of Petén, whose tropical vegetation has buried the ruins of Tikal. In many respects, the Caribbean islands and the Central American isthmus resemble two archipelagoes facing each other. In fact, Central America extends over more than 2000 kilometers and stretches from the eighth to the eighteenth parallel, covering an area of 540,000 square kilometers. This corridor narrows progressively toward the south to a width of 80 kilometers at the Panama Canal. Despite the cultural standardization wrought by Spanish colonization, seven independent nations have formed in this area. At a regional level, Guatemala, Honduras, and Nicaragua–each having an area of more than 100,000 square kilometers–are regarded as giants. Next to them, Belize and El Salvador, at around 20,000 square kilometers, are considerably smaller.

These political divisions can be explained in part by the extreme parceling of physical and demographic units. For El Salvador alone, at 21,000 square kilometers, some sixty morphologic units (alternating between basins and elevations) can

be demarcated. Though distances may be short, a very tortured natural setting contributes to the compartmentalization and fragmentation of space. The marked unevenness of the terrain accentuates the climatic contrasts in this complexly structured zone. The creased Paleozoic ranges of the Mexican Chiapas, which end in northern Nicaragua, resurface in Guatemala; fractures and gaps from cave-ins scar their contours and are emphasized by the multitude of volcanic cones. In Nicaragua, the central depression is occupied by two lakes (Managua, or Xolotlán, and Nicaragua, or Cocibolca) whose total surface area exceeds 9000 square kilometers. This is the largest Latin American lake formation after Lake Titicaca, which is shared by Peru and Bolivia.

This general arrangement has limited the length and average flow of the medium-sized rivers. Their undulating contours and highly variable rate of flow (between the dry and rainy seasons) rarely allow them to be used as communication routes. For a long time, the Dulce River (Guatemala), the San Juan River (Nicaragua), and the Chagres (Panama) allowed small boats to penetrate into the interior; today, however, the traffic has been reduced and is purely local. Rather than increasing accessibility in Central America, the rivers are obstacles to be crossed or circumvented. At right angles to the main axis of the isthmus, they heighten a general compartmentalization that encourages the insularity of the different regions. For this reason, Central America has functioned more as a border than as a bridge between the two continents and as a primary zone of smuggling in the eighteenth century (see **Map 3**). The mountain chain of Tabarasa, which reaches a height of nearly 3500 meters, constitutes a barrier between Panama and Costa Rica that is difficult to cross. To the southwest, near Colombia, the dense forest of Darién forms a small Amazonia still little explored, where the Pan-American Highway loses itself in the famous Darién Gap.

The emergent lands of the Caribbean archipelago make up a somewhat smaller surface area of around 233,000 square kilometers. However, from the western point of Cuba

Map 3.

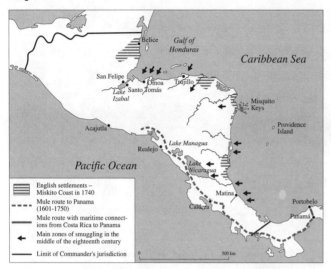

to the island of Aruba, which faces Venezuela's Lake Maracaibo, the Caribbean arc extends over 4700 kilometers between the tenth and twenty-third parallels and between the sixtieth and eighty-fifth meridians. More so than for Central America, this archipelago is characterized by its dispersal. Here, distances play a fundamental role in problems of communication, and the lack of land is of central concern. With its 105,000 square kilometers, Cuba alone represents nearly half of the total surface area of the Caribbean islands. As the second largest island at 76,500 square kilometers, Hispaniola seems like a giant next to Grenada, whose 330 square kilometers comprise an independent state. Despite this relatively modest total surface area, Hispaniola is divided into two countries of different languages and cultures, Haiti and the Dominican Republic. The insularity has reinforced the specific local characteristics of these minuscule territories. Continued political liaisons are rare and fragile, even for territories formerly linked by a colonial power. Thus, Antigua and Barbuda represent a surface area of 442 square kilometers for 90,000 inhabitants, but the representatives of Barbuda (3000 inhabitants) accuse their neighbors of political domination and, for several years, have been threatening to form an independent state.

Within this vast geographic assemblage, characterized as much by the fragmentation and dispersal of political structures as by the narrowness of the cultural regions, Mexico, with its 1,971,000 square kilometers and 92 million inhabitants (1995 census), is a giant. But there, too, the appearance of political unity founded on the predominant role of Mexico City–which brings together 20 million citizens–poorly masks the great regional disparities. The concentration of power, means of communication, and cultural activities in the federal capital only serves to accentuate its contrast with a large number of isolated secondary centers, whose sphere of influence is often reduced to the borders of their administrative districts. The main performances, plays, concerts, and exhibitions are staged in Mexico City. Only the famous international festival, Cervantino, based in Guanajuato, can compete with this cultural abundance– but only for a period of fifteen days. The central role played by Mexico City in the life of the nation has an ancient ancestry, for before the Spanish Conquest the city

of Tenochtitlan had already played this very role in the most densely populated zone of Mesoamerica. Without a doubt, this is one of the unique characteristics of Mexico in a Latin America that has undergone profound social and spatial mutations from the pre-Hispanic period through the Colonial era to modern times: Since the emergence of Aztec civilization, the basin of Mexico City has remained the center of gravity in a country whose many regions aspire to emancipate themselves from the excessively weighty influence of the capital.

Spanish City, *Criollo* Consciousness

In Mexico and Central America, the current nations formed around the principal urban centers founded by the conquerors, these new cities (often of reduced size) have truly shaped the crucible of a *criollo* culture, at once European in its origins and American in its biological and cultural relationships. After the Conquest, there was a decline, more or less rapid, of the major Indian towns in favor of the Spanish cities. Considered the centers of demonic cults, these towns fell victim to systematic destruction: Their populations were decimated by epidemic illnesses imported from Europe, and the traditional marketplaces were forced to compete with new consumer centers. In fact, the Spanish rarely settled in existing native cities. They preferred cities that followed European criteria for urban planning.

Thus, in Mexico, the city of Puebla was founded in 1531 between two Indian villages, Tlaxcala and Cholula. The Tlaxcaltecans, who helped Cortés take over Mexico, enjoyed their friendship with the conquerors . . . for a time. In 1543, the seat of the bishopric was transferred from Tlaxcala to Puebla–a symbolic gesture that consolidated the new city's control over the territories subject to the Crown in this part of New Spain, governed until then (at least in theory) from the old indigenous capital. The old ceremonial and political center of the Purépechas, Tzin-Tzun-Tzan (Michoacán, Mexico), also suffered as a result of decisions made by the Spanish before the middle of the sixteenth century. Whereas the first conquerors chose to establish themselves there, Friar Pedro de Gante y Vasco de Quíroga, a prelate famous for his tendency to take positions favorable to the Indians, decided to transfer the seat of his bishopric to Pátzcuaro. This move led to the rapid decline of the little town, which found itself obligated, at the end of the sixteenth century, to request the king's assistance in obtaining minimal autonomy over its territory. In recognition of its loyal service and prestigious past, a royal decree of 22 November 1593, detached it from the jurisdiction of Pátzcuaro and accorded it the title of county town (*cabecera*). This decree released it from the obligation to furnish provisions and free manual labor to a town whose inhabitants, before the Conquest, were under its authority (Manuscript 3000, fol. 139).

On several occasions the Crown indicated to the conquerors how a site was to be chosen, and how the future town and its territory were to be organized. Beginning in 1513, such instructions were given to Pedrarias Dávila, the founder of Panama. He had to verify the number of points along the coast where inhabitants could settle in order to protect and ensure the reprovisioning of ships. It should be recalled that the American Spanish city was based on a geometric ideal. In New Spain, only those cities located in mountainous regions (often mining towns) deviated from the imposed schema, which was characterized by the same checkerboard plan, a grid work of wide streets, and a central square (the parade ground) where the church or cathedral, viceroy's palace, and town hall were located.

In the Caribbean, the first space the Spanish dominated, however, the plans of the earliest settlements often lacked clarity and consistency, though Santo Domingo (founded in 1498 and moved four years later to the right bank of the Río Ozoma) and Santiago de Cuba (erected on its current site in 1514) were organized around a central square, with orthogonal streets, in the style of the Roman military camps. Gonzalo Fernández de Oviedo, moreover, could declare, not without some satisfaction, that the streets of his city, Santo Domingo, were traced with string and compass, which guaranteed their rectilinear and highly civilized geometric character (*Historia general y natural de las Indias* [General and Natural History of the Indies] 77). With the founding of Panama and Veracruz in 1519, the idea of a regular latticework was imposed on the soldiers who followed Pedrarias Dávila and Hernán Cortés. In Mexico, Alonso García Bravo sketched an orthogonal city plan with a central parade ground on the ruins of Tenochtitlan. This ideal schema, interrupted by the numerous canals that crisscrossed the old indigenous capital, materialized several years later with the founding of Puebla, which was made up of rectangular blocks of 180 meters by 90 meters, separated by streets 13 meters wide.

Despite the recommendations of the great architects of the Renaissance, who could only conceive of a city encircled by walls, fortified cities did not appear around the Caribbean basin until quite late—primarily in the seventeenth century—on the coastlines menaced by pirates and privateers. The combat techniques used against the Indians help explain this absence of fortifications. Wide rectilinear streets worked to the advantage of cavalry charges and firearms against an enemy armed with bows, clubs, swords, and spears. Conversely, traditional enclosures offered more effective protection against European enemies armed with cannons and firearms. In New Spain, Veracruz and Campeche (founded in 1540) soon took shelter behind their walls, which often proved useless, while the formidable ramparts of San Juan (constructed in 1521 after Villa de Caparra was abandoned), bristling with redoubts and bastions, are even today a source of admiration and pride for Puerto Ricans.

Progressively, the Spanish managed to put in place a vast network of more or less insular cities that enabled them to supervise territories greater than the human resources available to the Iberian peninsula would normally have allowed. The first of these were established on the coast, in order to maintain permanent contact with the metropolis and to facilitate maritime trade: This is the case for nearly all the urban centers founded in the Caribbean during the first phase of the Conquest and organization of American space. These cities of merchants and the military never exerted broad cultural influence. In order to ensure the morality and security of its inhabitants, the New Ordinances of Discovery and Population, promulgated in 1573, even underscored that it was necessary to avoid overpopulating the ports, whose inhabitants were subjected not only to the menace of pirate ships but also to the temptations of easy money. In a world composed of small, autonomous cells, these cities nevertheless played an important role in that they opened regional life to the exterior, maintained contact with the metropolis, and organized the intercontinental flow that was the backbone of the Spanish empire.

The principal cities founded by the Spanish in this part of America, then, were erected in the interior, on the high plateaus or in mountain basins and valleys. This was the case for Mexico (1521), Puebla (1531), Guadalajara (1532), and, in Central America, Santiago de Guatemala (1527, moved in 1545 and then again in 1775) and Cartago (1564), former capital of the province of Costa Rica (see **Map 4**). In this, the Spanish followed the recommendations of Hippocrates and Galen, the great doctors of antiquity, according to whom the hot and humid climate of the tropical zones was harmful not only to the health of the body but also to that of the spirit (and consequently, the soul) (Hippocrates 115). By invoking the temperate climate enjoyed by their little city–neither too hot nor to cold, and similar to Spain's–the inhabitants of Santa María de Comayagua (Honduras) claimed the title of *ciudad* and the role of capital for the Central American isthmus, to the detriment of unfortunate Panama, which, according to them, was crushed by the torrid tropical heat (1539) (Archivo General de Indias, 43 N. 76). However, by adhering to these hygienic precepts, the conquerors also settled near the main indigenous groups, whom they could put to work in their vast agricultural operations. A secondary logic behind the location of urban centers was thus superimposed on the primary, strictly tied to the control of maritime routes.

In the middle of the sixteenth century, the discovery of rich veins of silver in the center and to the north of New Spain, and also in Central America (Harbor Master's Office of Guatemala), led to the development of a third type of Spanish city. These new urban centers, founded in the mountainous regions, did not conform to the norms of geometry and regularity theoretically in force on the whole continent. In Mexico, Taxco (1528), Zacatecas (1548), and Guanajuato (c. 1553) owed their architectural splendor to the wealth accumulated by a few mining families. In Honduras, Tegucigalpa,

Map 4.

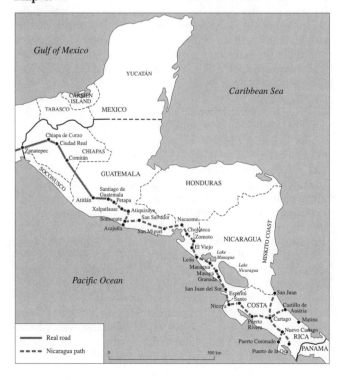

never having been formally founded, developed anarchically around a few mineral deposits discovered between 1540 and 1546. Despite the efforts of the royally appointed governors, the local authorities never succeeded in imposing urban design plans that were poorly adaptable to both the terrain and the mentality of the inhabitants, city dwellers in name only. In 1635, just a few years after the informal founding of San José del Parral (today the state of Chihuahua, Mexico), the *alcalde mayor* attempted to conform the city center to a checkerboard pattern; his efforts, however, were limited to regularizing a tiny part of the town where the majority of the houses were built into a hillside in outlying neighborhoods centered around mine shafts and the *haciendas* of the *beneficio de plata* (Cramaussel).

In the Hispanic-American world in general, and in New Spain in particular, the city rapidly became the heart and soul, not only of *criollo* culture, but also of an embryonic patriotism. Thus in 1637, after suffering through several catastrophic floods, the inhabitants of Mexico City received the order from the King to abandon the site of ancient Tenochtitlan, which had been founded by the Aztecs in a marshy zone, in order to establish a new city safe from the vagaries of the lake. After having acknowledged receipt of the document and having approved its contents, according to custom, the aldermen crossed swords with Crown representatives. At first, they were content to invoke the human and financial cost that such a move would entail. Next, they cited the tales, more or less historic, of floods prior to the Conquest, under the pretext that they were no less shrewd than the Indians who, after having encountered similar problems, were able to resist the temptation to move. The opponents of the move found an unexpected ally in the viceroy, Marquis de Cerralvo, who refused to take on the enormous responsibility of this task, and who supported the claims of the inhabitants of Mexico City. Without formally disobeying its king and after a brave struggle, the *criollo* city thus won the right not to be moved to the lake's west bank, preferring to drain the waters that threatened their security. Today Mexico City has nearly 20 million inhabitants who daily suffer the effects of a particularly aggressive, centuries-old hydraulic policy for managing the natural environment (see **Map 5**). This undeniable victory by the *criollos* led to the disappearance of the lakeside settlements that had flourished in the Mexico basin before the arrival of the conquerors. In a sense, this victory marks the success of the urbanization process desired by the Crown at the beginning of the sixteenth century to anchor the Spanish city in the heart of the territories in order better to dominate them.

But the failure of this move is also the first visible sign of the appearance of a *criollo* and "Mexican" consciousness that successfully opposed the will of the peninsular authorities. In fact, according to one of the adversaries of the transfer project, the Mexicans of the old city would never have agreed to abandon their site, despite the ravages of the floods. Why? Because, as Father Cavo reminds us in the *Relación Universal legitima y verdadera del sitio en que está fundada la muy noble, insigne y muy leal Ciudad de México* [1637; Universal, Legitimate, and True Report of the Site on Which the Most Noble, Renowned, and Most Loyal City of Mexico Was Founded], they "loved their country as one must love it." Barely a century after its founding, the city of Mexico, capital of New Spain, had thus become the "homeland" of the Mexican *criollos*, whose political and blood ties to the metropolis were becoming blurred over time. In fact, the material conditions of

urban reality (the land, the ground, the buildings–public and private) did not mask the essential core of the problem that a move to another site posed: The Spanish city has a spiritual existence that neither man nor natural environment can touch, and on which its true identity is based. In 1775, when the Crown ordered Santiago de Guatemala to be transferred to its new site after the violent earthquakes of 1773 destroyed a large part of the city, an initial rupture was introduced among the king, the Church, and the municipality–the three elements that ensure the existence and the continuity of the Spanish city in America. In a way, this move served as a basis for the independence claims of the Guatemalan *criollos* who, in the letters and reports with which they inundated the Council of the Indies during this period, used and abused the term Patria to designate their ruined city.

Continuity and Change in the Urban Hierarchies

This awareness of a *criollo* consciousness on the part of the city-dwellers of New Spain was heightened by the increasing cultural importance of cities in lands subject to the Spanish monarchy. The populations of the mining towns or port cities rarely felt the need to affirm an independent cultural identity by developing "parasitic" activities that would have influenced the rhythms of commercial transactions or slowed the extraction of mineral ores. Even in Panama, seat of the Audience of Tierra Firme, there were very few men of letters and individuals dedicated to the life of the spirit. In 1607, of a total of 5702 inhabitants, the white population (which constituted the urban elite) totaled only 1267 persons, compared to 4009 blacks (most of whom were registered slaves). The city's four convents together included fewer than thirty members of religious orders, and these were known for their weak ecclesiastical training and distaste for study (Mena García).

In contrast, in the administrative centers founded in the hearts of areas favored by the great pre-Columbian civilizations, a whole society of legal professionals, landowners, and cultured monks encouraged the emergence of an original urban culture, even if highly dependent on the traditions and fashions imported from Spain. In Mexico, cultural creolization was encouraged by certain religious orders such as the Franciscans, who, in founding the college of Santa Cruz de Tlatelolco (1536), attempted to shape the young Indian nobility according to the methods and objectives of European education. Despite the failure of this effort (by 1565, the establishment had fallen into complete decadence), the creation of colleges in the main urban centers during the Colonial period favored the emergence of a *criollo* intellectual elite and accentuated the split between the cities endowed with a real educational system and those whose children were forced to go abroad to pursue their studies.

The city of Mexico quickly rose to the top of this hierarchy, thanks to the establishment in 1553 of its university, which allowed it to extend its influence over the whole of New Spain. The first subjects taught in this prestigious institution were theology, law (canon and civil), arts, rhetoric, and grammar. Subsequently, the field of instruction was extended to include medicine and languages (indigenous or eastern). The Jesuits knew to draw on a papal bull of 1621 that gave them the right to grant university diplomas to students who had completed five years of study in one of their colleges, on the condition that the college be situated more than 70 leagues from the university. Thus, the colleges of Santo Tomas de Guadalajara and San Javier de Mérida came to the fore as

Map 5.

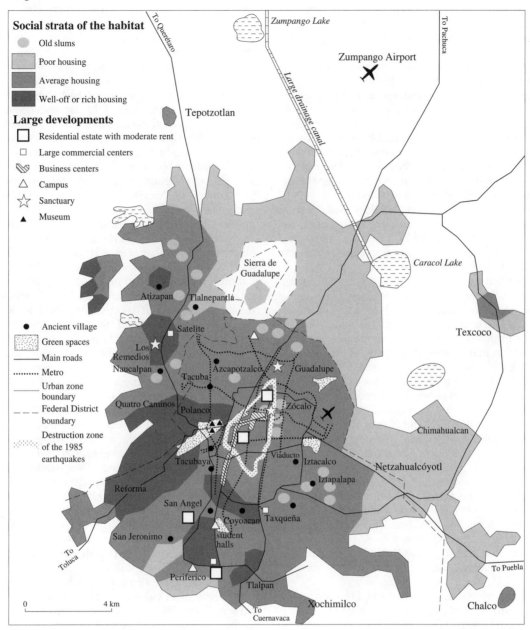

Social strata of the habitat
- Old slums
- Poor housing
- Average housing
- Well-off or rich housing

Large developments
- Residential estate with moderate rent
- Large commercial centers
- Business centers
- Campus
- Sanctuary
- Museum

- Ancient village
- Green spaces
- Main roads
- Metro
- Urban zone boundary
- Federal District boundary
- Destruction zone of the 1985 earthquakes

To Querétaro
Zumpango Lake
To Pachuca
Zumpango Airport
Large drainage canal
Tepotzotlan
Sierra de Guadalupe
Caracol Lake
Atizapan
Tlalnepantla
Texcoco
Satelite
Los Remedios
Naucalpan
Tacuba
Azcapotzalco
Guadalupe
Quatro Caminos
Polanco
Zócalo
Chimahualcan
Viaducto
Iztacalco
Netzahualcóyotl
Tacubaya
Iztapalapa
Reforma
San Angel
Coyoacan
Taxqueña
San Jeronimo
student halls
To Toluca
Periferico
Tlalpan
To Puebla
Xochimilco
To Cuernavaca
Chalco

0   4 km

important centers of study and training on the regional level, augmenting their host city's sphere of influence. By the end of the Colonial period (1792), a new university was founded at Guadalajara, a sign of the importance of the ancient capital of New Galicia in the economic and cultural geography of New Spain.

In Central America, conversely, the capital of the Harbor Master General's Office of Guatemala had to wait until 1676 to witness the birth of the Real y Ponficia Universidad de San Carlos, whose statutes were not confirmed by Pope Innocent IX until 1687. But the intellectual prestige of the Colonial cities can also be measured by the printing houses, which enabled the distribution of works–primarily of a religious nature–written by the *criollo* elite. In 1539 Mexico, the first American city to benefit from this essential means of spreading Hispanic culture, celebrated the opening of a branch office of the Seville printer, Johan Cromberger. A century later, in 1642, the first book

came off the presses of Pedro Quiñones, who was based in Puebla, and in 1660 Santiago de Guatemala celebrated the arrival of its first press. However, before the end of the Colonial period, only three other cities in this part of America had such a workshop: Oaxaca (1720), Guadalajara (1793), and Veracruz (1794).

The cultural hierarchy established little by little among the urban centers was also based on criteria that were more subjective, but whose importance to the collective mentality cannot be overlooked. While the Spanish city, unlike other European cities, wished itself to be and had pretensions of being noble, this claim was not made in the same way on both sides of the Atlantic. Like all good aristocrats, the city liked to display its titles, its heraldry, and its coats of arms. According to its means, its economic resources, and the importance of its population, it could claim the status of either *villa* or *ciudad*. Having obtained that, it desired even more to increase its prestige and to establish its authority. During the Colonial period, the passage from one category to another was even more important in that it symbolized the economic and social success of its inhabitants (Demélas-Bohy et al). Mexico, capital of the viceroyalty of New Spain, quickly attained the title of "*ciudad muy noble, insigne y muy leal*" ("very noble, illustrious, and very loyal city"). But loyalty to the king or the courage of the inhabitants–values long recognized in Spain–were combined in America with new qualities. The memory of an heroic struggle against the Indians, the selection of a particularly favorable site, or simply the existence of a temperate climate that agreeably recalled Spain's, sufficed to support a request to the king by a "city" having a population of barely a few hundred inhabitants, and whose main buildings were the only ones constructed of durable materials.

The Crown's granting of titles and heraldry established a hierarchy among the urban centers in New Spain (and more generally throughout the New World) and a system that, despite numerous upheavals, was not dismantled when the countries attained independence. Even today, the scale of urban values is often measured according to the rank occupied by the city in the hierarchy of ancient noble titles. Thus, Mexico has retained three major political categories inherited directly from the Colonial period–*pueblo, villa*, and *ciudad*–to which are added references to particular economic activities (mineral, for certain mining sites) or other types of groupings (*congregación*). This hierarchy was not always fixed, however, and a city could still move from one category to another in accord with a loss or gain in political or demographic significance. Between the 1980 and 1990 censuses, eight little towns in the state of Oaxaca (one of the most rural in the country) slid from the honorific status of *villa* to the less prestigious *pueblo*–the only Mexican villages to be submitted to such an affront. Conversely, the *congregación* of Santiago Jocotepec, formerly Monte Negro, rose to the title of *pueblo*, the *pueblo* of Santiago Tejupan became a *villa*, and the *villa* of Pinotepa Nacional attained the enviable status of *ciudad*. During the same period, from a total of 2393 municipalities, thirty-two *villas* climbed one level, and twenty-three others passed directly from *pueblo* to *ciudad*, such as the little village of Tixpéhual (Yucatán), which numbered less than 3000 inhabitants in 1990.

These examples show that the demographic criterion is not the only argument used to justify the change in political category of Mexican towns. The municipal functions, cultural status, and image of the city still play an important role in the perception of the urban condition. The case of Guatemala is particularly revelatory of the notion of the city based more on the town's spirit than on physical urban appearances. The 1950 census, in an attempt to be modern and innovative, decided to include within the category of "urban zones" all centers with populations of more than 2000, as well as towns with at least 1500 inhabitants and with an assured supply of drinking water. This definition, which took quantitative and qualitative aspects into account, was not retained, however. Later censuses (1964 and 1973) used more traditional criteria, because the Guatemalan authorities had by then considered as urban all those towns that, according to the law, belonged to the higher echelons of the political hierarchy: *ciudad, villa,* and *pueblo*. These legal and administrative subtleties were all the more important in locating the border between the urban and rural worlds, because, first, the countries of the isthmus, like the islands of the Caribbean, based their economy on export agriculture, and, second, without exception, the towns long remained marginal to the country that produced the essential wealth.

In fact, as administrative and legal centers where the important landowners could reside, these cities did not really play a driving role and, up to the twentieth century, were often of mediocre size. Trujillo, the main Honduran port during much of the Colonial period, had barely twenty Spanish families in 1594. At the end of the sixteenth century, the town of Cartago, capital of the province of Costa Rica, was home to at most eighty Spanish families (around 400 people). On the eve of Independence, its population was just over 8000 inhabitants, of whom 600 were Spaniards and *criollos*. During the same period, Granada and Léon, the two cities that quarreled over control of Nicaragua, had a comparable size. With nearly 12,000 inhabitants, San Salvador was at the time one of the most populous cities in the region, yet still far behind Guatemala, seat of the Harbor Master's Office, at 25,000. In this context, the Cuban port of Havana, with its 50,000 inhabitants by the mid-seventeenth century, seemed to be disproportionately large, though on the demographic scale it could not rival the major Mexican cities. In 1820, while the city of Mexico approached 180,000 inhabitants, Puebla, the second city, barely exceeded 60,000, and Guadalajara, which today has more than 3 million inhabitants, had hardly more than 45,000.

The nineteenth century did not do away with the urban hierarchy established since the Colonial period, even if, in the old Harbor Master General's Office of Guatemala, certain political capitals were moved from one city to another. Founded in 1737 under the name of Villa Nueva de la Boca del Monte, San José thus became the capital of Costa Rica in 1823 at the expense of the ancient Cartago, too often hit by earthquakes. In 1858, Managua, a little town of secondary importance, was chosen as seat of Nicaraguan power in order to cut short old rivalries between the liberals of Léon and the conservatives of Granada. In Honduras, more personal reasons, it seemed, compelled President Soto to abandon the aristocratic Comayagua for Tegucigalpa (1880). Even in countries where the rural world had preserved much of its demographic importance, the twentieth century was marked by a strong growth in major urban centers and by a hypertrophy of the capitals, to the detriment of a homogeneous urban network. These giant cities concentrated the essential industrial and service activities and augmented the regional disparities. As the main centers of attraction, they underwent and still sustain an unprecedented demographic growth. Managua has thus grown from 110,000 inhabitants to more than a million today and is now home to more than a quarter of the Nicaraguan population. Guatemala City, which numbers around 2.3 million inhabitants or 25 percent of the total population, has two-thirds of the country's urban population. In Salvador, the situation is even more critical. The civil war during the 1980s prompted the flight of at least 500,000 people, who for the most part found refuge on the outskirts of the capital. At the end of the decade, San Salvador numbered around 2.6 million inhabitants, or nearly half of all Salvadorans, before the return of civil peace led to a gradual decline in growth.

City and Nation in Mexico and the Caribbean Basin

Even in the less urbanized countries, the city–the crucible of *criollo* consciousness and main refuge of the middle classes (even when reduced to a minimum)–became the true focal point for national identity. Until the end of the Colonial period, and even afterward, the countryside was kept dependent on the urban centers, which monopolized the activities of commerce and exchange, and also of administration and law. However, these cities, often reduced in size and forced to compete, had only limited influence on regional organization, while they sped up the development of a particularly acute parochialism among the urban elites. These particularities formed the basis for the dissent that followed the wars of independence and, on the isthmus, ruptured the short-lived Central American federation (1823-1838). The problems in communication encountered by the Spanish in this part of America allowed neither for a true network of cities to emerge nor for relations of exchange and complementarity to be maintained. The Caribbean islands—divided by the European powers, separated by the sea, and focused on the plantations located in the interior—had limited interrelationships. On the continent, roads were few and often badly maintained, though the most important ones, called royal highways (*caminos reales*), did allow for cart travel and did link the main urban centers. These large highways made it possible for specific activities to develop, such as Costa Rica's breeding of mules for the lucrative trade on the Panama isthmus. In these underpopulated and poorly controlled regions, however, the dangers were many. Thus, travelers taking the *camino real* from Panama to Porto Belo were perpetually exposed to hostile flora and fauna, pernicious fevers, or attacks by runaway slaves and pirates.

To the weak influence of the cities must be added the imprecise nature of the administrative structures. Until the end of the Colonial period, the lands washed by the Caribbean Sea were officially dependent upon the viceroyalty of New Spain—except, of course, for the territories not belonging to the Spanish Crown. Panama, whose economic life was tied to the silver mines of Potosi, was attached to the South American continent—that is, to the viceroyalty of Peru and then, after its formation in 1717, to New Granada's. This administrative adherence did not favor the unity of the territories concerned because it was in large part fictitious. In reality, Central America was not governed from Mexico but from Guatemala City, seat of the Harbor Master General of Guatemala. The West Indies were responsible to the Harbor Master General of Cuba, whose capital was Havana. Viceroyalties and Harbor Masters' offices were divided into several *audiencias* (courts of appeal with a large administrative domain), which allowed for the population to be more closely managed but further fragmented the regional political fabric: There were *audiencias* for Mexico, Guadalajara, Santo Domingo, Guatemala, and Panama. This was the administrative framework of Spanish America up until the Bourbon reforms of the eighteenth century, which would introduce the system of intendancy. To this should be added the religious divisions (provinces of religious orders or bishoprics) and the system of the co-regiments and the *Alcaldias mayores*, centered in the main cities.

On 15 September 1821, Central America declared its independence from Spain after ten years of armed conflict. The following year, it formed an alliance with the Mexican empire of Iturbide to create a vast political body that extended from California all the way down to, but not including, Panama, and covering an area of more than 4 million square kilometers. However, a decade of war against a common enemy had not succeeded in forging a Central American nation or in

shaping a cohesive space within the isthmus. This failure is explained in part by the fact that the American patriotism claimed by the *criollos* applied chiefly at the local, if not the municipal, level. Contrary to traditional belief, this coming to consciousness is ancient: After the first stage of the Conquest the urban elites of each province attempted to impose administrative boundaries in order to protect themselves against incursions by neighboring cities. Thus, in 1531, the aldermen of the city of Léon (Nicaragua) petitioned the king to establish an official border between their province and Honduras, whose inhabitants were accused of wishing to invade them (Argüello 63).

After Independence, centrifugal forces quickly thwarted the efforts toward union demanded by the first revolutionaries. Ruptures often followed the more or less theoretical boundaries imposed by the Crown, with each province becoming introverted and focused around its main city. The first rupture occurred in 1823, when Central America detached itself from the Mexican Empire during the fall of Agustín de Iturbide. The old Harbor Master's Office of Guatemala regained its autonomy, while losing Chiapas, which was reclaimed by Mexico. A Central American federation was then formed that assembled five states: Guatemala, El Salvador, Honduras, Nicaragua, and Costa Rica. Panama did not yet belong to this group, for until 1903, the definitive date of its independence, it was only a province of Colombia. Fifteen years later, a second rupture led to the definitive separation of these states. The division of the isthmus countries, however, was not completed. The English in Belize had succeeded in forming a true colony, which turned its back on Spanish Central America. In 1862, Mexico officially recognized the British presence, but it would take until 1893 to set the borders between the two regions—and another century for Guatemala to officially relinquish all claims to that territory!

In the West Indies, the independence movements had a less homogeneous history than on the continent, due to the multiplicity of the colonial controls that weighed upon them. If Haiti was the first independent republic on the American continent (with the exception of the United States in North America), Cuba separated from Spain only at the end of the nineteenth century. Furthermore, numerous islands remain politically dependent upon a European home country, such as Martinique and Guadeloupe, French *départements* since 1946. In fact, after the Second World War, the only independent islands in the West Indies were Haiti, the Dominican Republic, and Cuba. Puerto Rico, torn from Spain's grasp by the United States in 1898 after the war that led to Cuban independence, had become a U.S. territory. It was only progressively, and blow by blow, that the former European possessions became free countries by profiting from the wave of decolonization after the war. This movement was accompanied by an extreme division of political units, furthering the division of cultural regions. In fact, even within large linguistic groups, the Caribbean territories quickly became a puzzle for the colonial administrations, which struggled in vain to enforce arbitrary groupings as a method of managing a space spread over several hundred kilometers, riddled with hostile enclaves, and poorly linked to the major center.

The former French sugar islands did not escape these insular rivalries, which are still deeply felt. Seat of the General Government of the Antilles under the former administration, Martinique exercised a political domination over Guadeloupe that was enhanced by commercial privileges bestowed by the

Crown on the inhabitants of Saint Pierre, nicknamed the "Paris of the Antilles," until its destruction in 1902 by a burning cloud spewed from Mount Pelée. Since this catastrophe, the city of Fort-de-France has become the intellectual capital of the francophone islands of the Caribbean. Before, their English rivals had attempted to impose a certain unity on the islands they had colonized. Beginning in 1674, the Leeward Islands (Anguilla, St. Kitts, Nevis, Monserrat, Antigua, and Barbuda) were grouped under the same authority, but quite quickly the internal rivalries and local particularities undermined this federation, which was officially dissolved in 1798. The same fate befell the "Federal Colony of Leeward Islands," created in 1871 and abolished in 1956. That same year, the ambitious "British West Indies Federation" was created, joining together Jamaica and the collection of little anglophone Caribbean islands, excluding the Virgin Islands. The constitution provided for the creation of a parliament, a federal supreme court, and a common government. The central administration was set up at Port of Spain on the island of Trinidad, but the federal authorities had very little power, and the largest islands refused to provide financial support to their partners and to replace the English Crown in this area. In 1961, Jamaica withdrew from the federation; Trinidad followed a year later.

The large islands of the West Indies with a Spanish language and culture followed an identical course, and in many respects the former island of Hispaniola is an extreme case of territorial division. Shared between two states, Haiti and the Dominican Republic, it is the result of a turbulent colonial history followed by wars of independence fought in a disorganized manner. The Treaty of Ryswick, signed in 1697, gave France official possession of the western part of the island, at the expense of the Spanish. Until the end of the eighteenth century, the colony of Saint-Dominigue, administered from 1789 onward by the city of Port-au-Prince, was to remain the jewel in the crown of its colonial domain in the West Indies. Subjected to the repercussions of the French Revolution several months later, the colony experienced its first blood-washed insurrection in 1791. In an effort to subdue the black population, the French colonists allied themselves in turn with the English or the Spanish. But neither they nor the troops sent by Bonaparte could put a stop to a movement that made famous a champion of the black cause: Toussaint-Louverture. After having participated in the uprising, he agreed to lead the island in the name of France. Taken prisoner by General Leclerc's soldiers, he died in prison, but in 1804 Haitian independence was declared. Nevertheless, there were numerous sources of discord among groups having divergent interests. The Spanish profited from the conflicts between the blacks and the mulattos and regained provisional control of the eastern part of the island. A new bid to unite the island, initiated in 1821, failed when the minority whites of Santo Domingo rose up against the black control of Haiti in 1844. The split was confirmed definitively in 1863 with the proclamation of the independence of the Dominican Republic. Since then, relations between the two states sharing the same island have remained strained.

The remarkable political and cultural unity of Mexico, founded on the hegemony of a city (Mexico City), contrasts sharply with the extraordinary dispersal of cultural regions in Central America and in the Caribbean. However, if the vertical and horizontal divisions of Mexican society are taken into account, several socioeconomic, ethnic, and cultural groups can be identified as confirming (but also redividing) the traditional schemas: northern and southern, urban and rural, rich and poor, Indian and *mestizo*. In 1990, Louis B. Casagrande thus spoke of the five nations of Mexico, insisting on the profound disparities that justified this division of the Mexican people. In this, he revisited an older geopolitical representation proposed by the North American journalist Joel Garreau, who in 1981 published a book titled *The Nine Nations of North America*, in which he presented the very controversial notion of Mexamerica. This transborder nation would gather together the populations located on either side of the Rio Grande (Río Bravo for the Mexicans), united by linguistic bonds (Spanish), economic links (migratory flux, the flow of capital, *maquiladora* industry), and cultural ties (religion, music, culinary practices). All of the northern Mexican states would belong to this vast space, which would extend far into the United States, into the old provinces lost by Mexico between 1836 and 1853 (Texas, California, New Mexico, Arizona).

The fact is that the cities located on the Mexican side of the border have few relationships among themselves, while they function symbiotically with their twin cities in the United States: Such is the case for Tijuana and San Diego, or Ciudad Juárez and El Paso. The flow of merchandise, capital, and people always follows a north-south axis rather than an east-west one, as the organization of the main axes of traffic shows. Thus there exist true transborder corridors that unite the zones of production in the south and the areas of consumption in the north. More than 40 million people are collected under this "nation," whose principal urban centers would be Los Angeles, San Diego, Houston, and Albuquerque in the north, and Monterrey, Ciudad Juárez, and Tijuana in the south. In fact, Mexamerica, real or imagined, would be nothing without the Spanish populations located "on the other side" of the Río Bravo, for the 22 million Spanish-speakers (of whom at least 15 million are from Mexico) living in the United States play an economic and political role of increasing importance in both their country of origin and their adopted land. The money sent by workers who have settled in California or New Mexico supports entire families who have remained behind in the villages of Guerrero and Michoacán.

In the United States, Mexicans have long suffered from systematic discrimination, at once numeric, economic, and cultural. Imported en masse to provide seasonal labor (as *braceros*) in the large agricultural operations of the Southwest, working under difficult conditions and for starvation wages, they have nevertheless come to an awareness of their strength and their identity. As early as 1949, a film directed by Anthony Mann with Ricardo Montalban in the main role (*Border Incident*) dealt with the issue of the traffic of illegal immigrants between Mexico and the United States. In 1995, U.S. authorities turned back without consideration nearly 1.4 million applicants for temporary or permanent immigration. Even if this statistic has to be contextualized—the same individuals make several attempts before they succeed in getting across—it does translate into a reality: There is a potent economic boundary, a split between two worlds, that gives full meaning to the concept of Mexamerica. The role of the Chicanos who have settled, legally or illegally, in the United States thus remains very ambiguous. Poor in contrast to the wealthy mainstream U.S. population, they are rich in the eyes of underprivileged, lower-class Mexicans. Despite their rapid demographic growth, they had to wait until the 1960s before they could openly claim their cultural identity and rebel against an Anglo-Saxon–dominated society, which they felt exploited them, while treating them with contempt. On 16 September 1965 a strike, initiated in Delano, California, by the union leader César Chávez, mobilized grape pickers for nearly five years and affected production in the entire region; this movement earned him the hostility of a large number of his compatriots, who could no longer earn their living by crossing the border. In 1967 the evangelist Reyes López Tijerina became famous for attempting forcibly to seize the courthouse of Tierra Amarilla, the Río Arriba county seat in New Mexico. Jailed repeatedly by state authorities, he became a symbol of the Spanish-speaking workers' resistance movement against U.S. imperialism.

The first significant political victory of the Chicano movement dates from 1969, when the party led by Rudolfo González ("The Crusade for Justice") won the municipal elections in Crystal City, Colorado. In order better to assert the identity of his supporters, Rudolfo González campaigned under the sign of *la Raza* (the Race) and the mythical city of Aztlan, where the Aztecs originated. This return to imaginary and utopian pre-Hispanic roots offered the Chicano people a new way to negotiate their identity between the predominantly Anglo-Saxon world and their Mexican heritage. Since those heroic times, the Spanish-speaking community of the United States has acquired a new status. It is on its way to becoming the principal ethnic minority in the country (10.2 percent of the population in 1995, and nearly 18 percent predicted by the year 2000), leaving the black population in second place. It has created its own culture, a blend of the "American way of life" and Mexican traditions, a culture that marks a departure from its "natural" boundaries–the U.S. southwestern states–and extends not only to northern and central Mexico but also to the urban centers on the Atlantic coast. The *tejano* music of Spanish-speaking Texans has thus established itself both north and south of the Río Bravo, and its most famous representative, the singer Selena (who was killed in 1995), remains the symbol of a community whose members are now able to breach the barriers of language, economics, and race that segment U.S. society.

Thanks to the economic ties established with the United States and concretized by NAFTA, the cultural region of Mexico today largely exceeds the political borders imposed by history. However, the internal tensions are growing ever stronger, and ancient regional capitals like Guadalajara (Jalisco), Monterrey (Nuevo Léon), or Mérida (Yucatán) are reclaiming more and more autonomy within the framework of a federation that wishes to be less dominated by Mexico City. They base their claims on the existence of a cultural identity too long overshadowed by the revolutionary ideals of the party in power, the Institutional Revolutionary Party (PRI), which claimed to be its sole heir. But the emergence of a genuine local power (marked since the mid-1980s by several electoral victories by opposition parties), the recent flourishing of intermediary cities, and the insurrection of Chiapas (launched on 1 January 1994, the day NAFTA came into effect) have demonstrated that the Mexican cultural region, far from being the manifestation of a single voice, rests on different types of creolization and on many centers of the expression and diffusion of national identity.

Translation by Wendy J. Eberle

Works Cited

Argüello Argüello, Alfonso. 1994. *Historia de Léon Viejo*. Léon: Editorial Hospicio.

Archivo General de Indias. *Guatemala*. 43, n. 76. Seville.

Border Incident. 1949. Screenplay by John C. Higgins. Dir. Anthony Mann. MGM.

Cepeda, Fernando de. 1975. *Relación Universal legítima y verdadera del sitio en que está fundada la muy noble, insigne y muy leal Ciudad de México*. Comp. Fernando de Cepeda et al. 1637. 1st facsimile edition. Mexico City: Secretaria de Obras Públicas.

Cortés, Hernán. 1983. *Cartas de Relación*. Mexico City: Porrúa.

Cramaussel, Chantal. 1997. "L'urbanisme espagnol et les cités minières d'Amérique, la ville de Parral au XVIIième siècle." *De Séville à Lima*. Ed. Alain Musset and Pablo Emilio Pérez Mallaína. Paris: VEP-LGU. 33-58.

Demélas-Bohy, Marie-Danielle, and Julián Montemayor. 1997. "Noblesses citadines, de l'Espagne à l'Amérique." *De Séville à Lima*. Ed. Alain Musset and Pablo Emilio Pérez Mallaína. Paris: VEP-LGU. 79-100.

Fernández de Oviedo, Gonzalo. 1959. *Historia general y natural de las Indias*. Vol. 1. Madrid: BAE.

Garreau, Joel. 1981. *The Nine Nations of North America*. Boston: Houghton Mifflin.

Hippocrates. 1800. *Traité des airs, des eaux et des lieux* [On Airs, Waters, and Places]. Paris: Imprimerie de Baudelot et Eberhart.

Mena García, Carmen. 1984. *La sociedad de Panamá en el siglo XVI*. Seville: Diputación Provincial de Sevilla.

Ms. 3000, fol. 139. 1593. Biblioteca Nacional, Madrid.

CHAPTER 3

THE ANDEAN COUNTRIES

Jean-Paul Deler

It was in the Orinoco delta in August 1498, during his third voyage, that Christopher Columbus identified the American *Terra Firma* for the first time. The following year, Alonzo de Ojeda and Americo Vespucci recognized the south coast of Margarita Island and gave it the name of "Little Venice"; in 1511, the Spanish founded Acha there–the first, and provisional, urban creation on the continent. It was only in 1520, however, that the city of Cumana was founded, a year after Vera Cruz was established at the lower end of the Gulf of Mexico. In 1545, a quarter of a century later and several thousand kilometers to the south, after the extensive pillaging of the treasures of the Incan Empire, the discovery of Cerro Rico, a veritable mountain of silver in the heart of the high Andean plateaus, and the founding of Potosí put the seal of success on the conquest of the Andean world and its Amazonian margins. The epic widely identified–here perhaps more than elsewhere in the New World–with the quest for the fabulous wealth of a mythic Eldorado gave way to the economic reality of developing mineral resources. The first Viceroyalty of Peru (1543) brought together the Andean territories, excluding Venezuela (which belonged to the Viceroyalty of New Spain) but including the isthmus of Panama, which by then was serving as passage to the South Sea.

Terra Firma, Eldorado, and Mountain of Silver

Today, from the mangrove-fringed gutters of the mouth of the Venezuelan Orinoco on the Caribbean coast to the immense desert horizons of the Bolivian Lipez highlands bordering the Tropic of Capricorn, five nation states share 4.7 million square kilometers spread over thirty-five degrees of latitude. Between the southeast Pacific and the Amazon basin, filled by the largest tropical rainforest on the planet, this space is home to the world's largest mountain system. American nature has arrayed an unequalled kaleidoscope of landscapes and environments. It might be objected that the immense Andean Cordillera extends over 10,000 kilometers–all the way to the Tierra del Fuego and thus across a territory of seven countries; however, for the southernmost countries, the mountain crest is situated rather on the margins of their national territory, where it is seen more as a "backdrop." Thus Argentina identifies above all with the Atlantic and the *pampas,* while Chile is less Andean than situated "at the foot of the Andes"; and the mountain range along the southern frontier, which falls into the subtropical or temperate climatic zones, is nearly empty of inhabitants.

If the five Andean countries of the intertropical zone– Venezuela, Colombia, Ecuador, Peru, and Bolivia–constitute a specific cultural region in the heart of Latin America, they do not owe this status exclusively to the ecological effect of the Andean mountain range, nor even to the traits assumed during the Iberian conquest. In the interplay of complex variables considered over the long course of history, above and beyond the indisputable differences among countries or vast regional transborder groups, the relationships between space and societies have created a specific community in the very heart of the Andean domain.

To begin with, this space was the stage for the almost "insular" blossoming of one of the great centers of Amerindian culture in the New World. In this part of the Andes, brilliant pre-Hispanic rural civilizations developed that populated the tropical mountains to a height of nearly 5000 meters. In the sixteenth century, structures of the densest Spanish colonization were grafted onto the pre-Columbian state structures, which ranged from the nascent to the vigorous. In the beginning of the nineteenth century, the territory from the plains of the Apure to the valleys of the Chuquisaca was liberated from Spanish control by the epic efforts of Simón Bolívar and his lieutenants; their victories in the name of independence led to the establishment of one of the world's first national republican states. Nearly five centuries of complex interbreeding between the Hispanic Latin world and the Andean Indian world shaped a lasting and original cultural zone, which later kept clear of the great European immigration movement that preceded World War I. Today this zone groups together 100 million inhabitants and the strongest concentration of communities descended from the pre-Columbian autochthonous (indigenous) population. The formation of the regional group of the Andean Community at the end of the 1960s aimed to develop new forms of solidarity and cooperation among the "sister republics" which might be able to shake off the border controversies of another age. This Andean Community, however, also returns indisputably to shared historic roots. It must face the hard realities of economic and social integration without leaving behind a certain symbolic lyricism, which nourishes its histories.

However, and this should come as no great surprise, the different countries involved are not equally Andean. The variations in the mountain range at the heart of each region, the densities and varying levels of development among the populations, the degree of urbanization and infrastructures, and the relative economic weight of the so-called mountain regions serve in part to explain the observable differences (Dollfus 165). The place which the Andes–or what is interpreted as "Andean"–hold in the discourse of intellectuals (including writers) and politicians, and also in the symbolic order or the imagination of the societies, reveals something more pronounced than mere nuances among the five countries.

The Cordillera: The Backbone

One cannot minimize the important impact of the Andean environment, which the eponymous qualifier of "cultural region" underscores. The Andes serve at once as common denominator and link for the cultural region and as a specific constraint on the subspaces in its heart. In the tropical zone, in fact, the "cold" or "temperate" mountain altitudes, which do not experience winter weather, have attracted settlements and facilitated migrations. Through the impressive continuity of its contours and an upthrust wedge whose altitudes frequently exceed 4000 meters along its longitude, the mountain system serves as a backbone for the whole, while simultaneously and vigorously parceling out the land beneath it. The terrain's configuration introduces certain specific models for structuring space, notably the tripartition of each national territory into the following: coastal regions of varying expanses (*costa*); the powerful mountain ranges (*sierra*); and the vast interior plains, all of which incorporate part of the Amazon basin (*selva, llanos, oriente*). The very architecture of the Cordillera introduces many nuances. In Bolivia and southern Peru, it spreads out to a width of 500 to 600 kilometers, fitting neatly into the vast *altiplano,* which coincides, in part, with the endoreic basin of Lake Titicaca. Near the equator, it narrows into two volcanic chains that frame a longitudinal fissure whose width barely exceeds 100 kilometers. In Colombia and Venezuela, the range terminates in large fingers enframing the great gaps of the Cauca, the Magdalena, and Lake Maracaibo, which open onto the Caribbean coast.

It is also to the Andes that this intertropical segment of South America owes its wide range of bioclimatic environments: from the glaciers hanging from the Cordillera or the large volcanoes covered in dense forest to the savannas of the Amazonian piedmonts; from the misty deserts of southern Peru (which receive a few millimeters of precipitation annually) to the extremely wet regions of the Choco (with six to ten meters of rain), such as the valley of Atrato. As a true synthesis of the world's mountain landscapes, the extreme diversity of the ecosystems reflects the range of locations corresponding to specific combinations of gradations in temperature and humidity, to the play of systems of slopes, and to the effects of weather fronts and coverage with respect to the dominant atmospheric changes. Thus, important contrasts exist between the equatorial, moist, green Andes and the tropical or subtropical, brown, dry Andes. To the former correspond the high surfaces covered in *páramos* (high grasslands) and the symmetrical, forested slopes. To the latter correspond the *punas,* the high steppes, whose faces are extremely dissymmetrical, and which are overrun with herds of ruminants (llamas and alpacas) and sheep. To the east the slopes and piedmonts, exposed to the dominant atmospheric flux, have good precipitation and are well forested, while to the west the slopes are arid and overlook a coastal desert dotted with oases, cooled by the air rising from cold waters whose coastal drift to the north forms the Humboldt Current. The southern Cordillera system introduces deformations into the zonal distribution of the large bioclimactic environments, further accentuating the dissymmetry in the huge slopes and their piedmonts.

The Vigor of Amerindian Roots

For several thousand years now, human communities have been numerous in the intertropical section of the Andean range. Population density has been concentrated particularly in the high valleys and basins located at between 2000 and 3500 meters, but agriculture is sustainable up to an altitude of over 4000 meters, and in certain mining sites permanent settlements can be found at elevations of higher than 5000 meters. Before the Spanish Conquest, the Andean region included the main centers of dense population in South America: the Tairona country of the Sierra Nevada in Santa Marta, in Colombia; the Chibcha and Kara country of the Northern Andes; the Aymara world of the *altiplano* of Lake Titicaca; and the vast valleys and basins of the Incan world. Extending over a million square kilometers between the equator and the southern tropic, the Incan Empire probably numbered 12 million inhabitants and, over the entire region, some 15 million. The pre-Columbian civilizations were undergirded by many peasant populations, well adapted to the diversity and specificity of their environments. In village communities, which were organized in collectives according to lineage with endogamous tendencies, land was not under private ownership; rather, it was shared among families that engaged in collective labor for agricultural methods and projects of communal interest. The land was subject to periodic redistribution. Belonging to a village community created a network of solidarity and reciprocity through a whole system of rights and obligations, which guaranteed strong group cohesion. Agriculture activities produced a surplus sufficient for the needs of a significant nonpeasant population. Thanks to ecological diversity, the range of production was considerable: from tubers–among them numerous varieties of potato–to corn and beans; from peanuts and cassava to cotton and cacao, the latter for ritual use; llamas and alpacas bred in the Andean *punas*. The variability of the environments either motivated the communities of the Andes to organize themselves into a "vertical archipelago" of lands, sometimes separated by a distance of several days on foot, and assigned production of complementary crops, or stimulated active commercial activity among communities occupying different ecological levels (Murra 430).

Today, the population of Amerindian origin is calculated at close to 20 million–higher than it was in 1492, and representing nearly 20 percent of the current total population of the five republics. From Ecuador to northeast Argentina, 12 million people still speak Quechua, for the Incan language was disseminated widely by the colonial clergy; 1.5 million people speak Aymara. The proportion of Indians in the national population varies considerably from one country to the next, and the southern Andes contrast with the northern. Indians make up more than 60 percent of the population of Bolivia and between one third and one half in Ecuador and Peru; in Colombia and Venezuela especially, the natives registered by census are far fewer; the Selvatic ethnic groups, present everywhere, are fragmented into small groups, with the exception of the Jivaro in Ecuador and Peru, or the Tupí-Guaraní in Bolivia. The unequal geographic distribution of Indian populations weighs heavily on the question of social justice, for, from southern Colombia to Bolivia, in many of the poorest rural regions, Indians often represent half and often as much as 80 percent of the local peasant population. However, several million Indians have also migrated to the cities and the large metropolises, such as La Paz, Quito, Lima, Guayaquil, and Bogotá. Since the 1970s, an Indian reawakening has taken place, marked by a return to the valorization of cultural traditions and to certain technologies (particularly agricultural), and also by the demand for a state more attentive to issues raised by the multiethnic and multicultural character of the national societies. New struggles to reclaim ancestral lands have emerged; radio programs and primary school programs in the native languages have been developed, which are indicators of a more widely assumed bilingualism, even in the cities. In the course of the first half of the twentieth century, literature–notably through the powerful nativist current particularly widespread throughout the Andean world (Ecuador, Peru, and Bolivia)–have contributed greatly to helping certain elites take stock of the importance of the ethnic divisions that constitute national societies when it comes to the question of the Indian, deprived of ancestral land and culture. A relatively new phenomenon in terms of its amplitude, the demands of the Indian population could well increase.

Urbanizing Colonization

From the second third of the sixteenth century onward, the Spanish laid the foundations in the Andes for exceptional colonization, in terms of both spatial deployment and long-term commitment. Their mastery over populations, resulting in control and exploitation of the indigenous people, and mastery of space was achieved through a network of cities and the villages subordinate to them and the assimilation of lands into the framework of large rural estates.

In the former empire of the Incas—and in a few rare cases, beyond its borders—colonial urbanization grafted itself partially onto a dense network of pre-Columbian centers but with a perceptible modification in the hierarchy (see **Map 1**). More often there is a certain continuity of situation more than an actual permanence of site. The exemplary and symbolic case of Cuzco, from this point of view, has remained the exception. The famous illustrated manuscript of *Nueva corónica y buen gobierno* [New Chronicle and Good Government], written in his twilight years by Felipe Guamán Poma de Ayala (1524?–1613), who was the son of an Indian noblewoman and adopted by a Spaniard, was witness to the first decades of the Conquest and the last guardians of the pre-Columbian oral tradition; it demonstrates well the rich relation between the Spanish and pre-Columbian urban systems, while simultaneously emphasizing the new importance of the city in the colonial system. Poma de Ayala thus offers a kind of a guide to the principal Spanish cities from Cartagena to Potosí at the turning point between the sixteenth and seventeenth centuries (982–1093). Only a few of the most important colonial Andean cities remain, all emerging from a kind of reproduction through fission, as manifested by their place names and by their location in proximity to the prestigious pre-Columbian sites of power: Bogotá, Quito and Cuenca (Tomebamba), Tumbes, Cajamarca and Trujillo (Chan-Chan), Lima (Pachacamac) and Huamanga, La Paz (Choqueyapu) and Sucre (Chuquisaca). Cuzco remains the exception: here, urbanism and architecture offer a unique cultural synthesis; here, Incan foundations and *criollo* constructions, superposition and syncretism, serve as signatures of a *mestizaje*. Garcilaso de la Vega el Inca (1539-1616), son of the imperial city and one of the leaders among those of mixed blood in the New World, made himself the bard of this *mestizaje* as he sought to reconcile the victors and the vanquished in his *Comentarios Reales de los Incas* [Royal Commentaries on the Incas], published in 1609.

In the Andean world, as in the New World as a whole, the appropriation of colonial territory was linked to the establishment of central sites, which were at once the seat or way station of the new powers, the residence of new masters, and the symbol and model of the dominant civilization. Their location was determined by a set of imperatives, including the particular distribution of densely populated regions and proximity to coveted natural resources—the mines, in particular—and to strategic control points for the essential link with the metropolis. Thus, Buritica, Castrovirreyna, Huancavelica, Potosí, Oruro, and other ephemeral cities tied to the exploitation of gold deposits in the Amazonian slopes of the Andes are products of the mining enterprise. The ports and corridors of the commercial monopoly, such as Coro, Cumana, Cartagena, or Santa Marta on the Caribbean coast and Guayaquil,

Paita, Callao, or Arica on the Pacific are the result of colonial metropolis structuring (see **Map 2**). Tocuyo and Caracas, Popayan and Tunja, Riobamba and Guaranda, Ica and Arequipa, Mizque and Tarija, all major centers of the empire's subdivisions, are products of territorial administration and control; whereas Guanare and Jaén de la Frontera, Chachapoyas and Santa Cruz de la Sierra are the result of border vigilance. In the course of the seventeenth century, on the eastern borders of the Andean region, religious congregations (Dominican, Franciscan, Jesuit) also gathered the local populations together in missions, such as those of Orinoco, of Mocoa and Sucumbios, of Maynas, and of Mojos and Chiquitos.

The colonial Andean territory was organized around the city of the Spanish (the *vecinos*) and the criollos, whether it be a *ciudad* (city), *villa* (village) or simply an *asiento* (settling), according to its importance and position in the urban hierarchy. In the immediate periphery, a periurban ring juxtaposed communal lands (*ejidos*) and lands granted to the principal religious communities (in return for their social role), with indigenous suburbs often associated with manufacturing industries (the *obrajes*) or the production of building materials, and the few hectares of cultivated land (the *chacras*) assigned to each city dweller. In the second circle, where the native population was most dense, space was unequally distributed between territories recognized as belonging to the Indian communities and lands that the Spanish had appropriated for their own use in the form of large agricultural estates (*haciendas* and *estancias*). From the sixteenth century onward, a large part of the native population was resettled to indigenous reservations. These were villages planned around a hundred homesteads and true replicas in miniature of Spanish cities; located at the heart of a defined region and having a ringed structure, with family parcels close to the village and peripheral lands cultivated collectively, they designated a more or less complete and regular sphere of influence around the main center. Certain manufacturing activities (*obrajes*) were sometimes associated with these indigenous villages or large estates. On the margins of the colonial administrative district, whose borders were long uncertain and fluid, was often a third ring of lands. These lands were difficult to traverse or of limited accessibility and mediocre agricultural value, and sometimes developed into zones of refuge for populations fleeing the labor force, or were held by particularly rebellious ethnic groups. Only the exploitation of mineral wealth or the trajectory of an important journey drove the Spanish to assert their discontinuous presence or selective control in those areas. Such was the model of organization and space dominated by the colonial city (Deler 1992, 352).

Almost all of these urban centers were located at the top of the hierarchy of the colonial administrative network (*corregimientos, audiencias,* vice-kingdoms, intendancies later). The possibilities of local economic autonomy, if not quasi-autarchy, in many cases reinforced the system's modular character. The symbiosis of the little town and its territorial jurisdiction was all the more marked for those city-dwellers living on income generated from the exploitation of the large land holdings in the outlying area. The most widespread urban standard was the large market town: It was the local power relay and site of the residences of Spanish or *criollo* landowners who lived off local rural rents and who sometimes were endowed with a manufacturing office, particularly in textile workshops (*obrajes, obrajillos*). However, this network of towns should be viewed in the devastating demographic

Map 1.

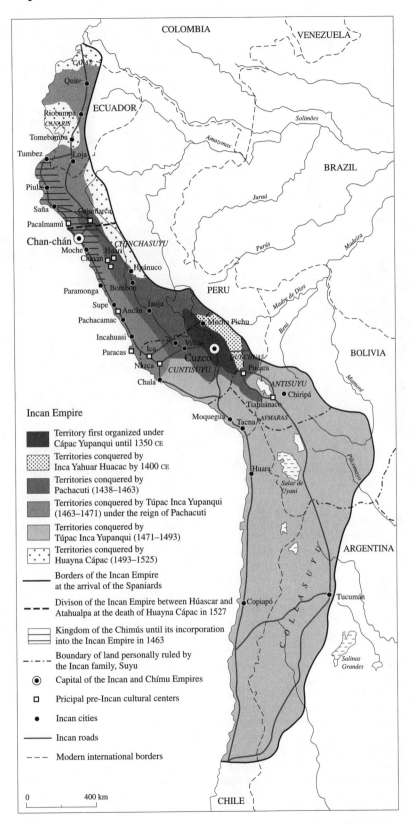

COLOMBIA

VENEZUELA

CAÑAS

Quite

ECUADOR

Solimões

Riobampa
CAÑARIS

Tomebamba

Amazonas

BRAZIL

Tumbez

Loja

Juruá

Piula

Saña

Cajamarca

Pacalmamú

Purús

Madeira

Chan-chán

Moche

CHINCHASUYU

Huari

Chavin

Huánuco

Paramonga

Bombón

PERU

Madre de Dios

Supe

Jauja

Ancán

Pachacamac

Machu Pichu

Beni

BOLIVIA

Incahuasi

Paracas

Vilcas

Ica

Cuzco

QUICHUAS

Nazca

CUNTISUYU

Pucara

Chala

ANTISUYU

Mamoré

Chiripá

Tiahuánaco

Moquegua

Tacna

AYMARAS

Incan Empire

Territory first organized under
Cápac Yupanqui until 1350 CE

Territories conquered by
Inca Yahuar Huacac by 1400 CE

Territories conquered by
Pachacuti (1438–1463)

Territories conquered by Túpac Inca Yupanqui
(1463–1471) under the reign of Pachacuti

Territories conquered by
Túpac Inca Yupanqui (1471–1493)

Territories conquered by
Huayna Cápac (1493–1525)

Borders of the Incan Empire
at the arrival of the Spaniards

Divison of the Incan Empire between Húascar and
Atahualpa at the death of Huayna Cápac in 1527

Kingdom of the Chimús until its incorporation
into the Incan Empire in 1463

Boundary of land personally ruled by
the Incan family, Suyu

Capital of the Incan and Chímu Empires

Pricipal pre-Incan cultural centers

Incan cities

Incan roads

Modern international borders

Huara

Salar de
Uyuni

Pilcomayo

ARGENTINA

COLLASUYU

Copiapó

Tucumán

Salinas
Grandes

0   400 km

CHILE

Map 2.

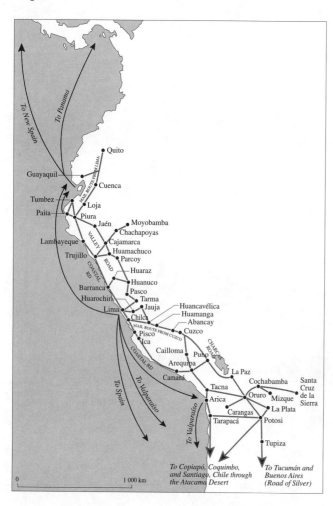

Map 3.

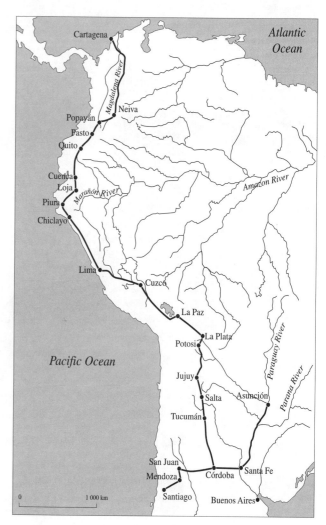

context of the Conquest, which considerably reduced the indigenous population, whose numbers did not stop shrinking globally until the end of the eighteenth century. Around 1800, in fact, the Andean region had fewer than 4 million inhabitants spread over 4 million square kilometers: this averaged to one inhabitant per square kilometer, or rather, three inhabitants per square kilometer of the "useful" part of the territories—namely, the coastal plains and the Andes, for the eastern forested plains, virtually devoid of inhabitants, covered two thirds of the space under consideration. In reality, more than 80 percent of this population lived far from the coasts, in the Cordillera, at more than 2000 meters above sea level.

Dominating the network of small cities and towns lying within the fragmented Andean archipelago, the most prestigious colonial centers gathered together a truly diversified urban society, composed of a large number of religious figures and clerics, groups of crown officials, and merchants (see **Map 3**). Also included were ship and mine owners because of their economic role and their place in the colonial commercial circuit. This aristocracy (or *criollo* and peninsular elite) rubbed shoulders with a majority population of servants and native artisans. Naturally it was these principal cities that emerged as the authentic centers of literary and artistic culture during the Colonial period. They contributed to the expression of a real cultural creolization, often by means of the clerical culture: "al mestizo, no le quedaba más

remedio que buscar su 'salvación' individual abrazando el sacerdocio: y el cultivo de las letras formaba parte de la actividad sacerdotal" ("for the *mestizo,* no other avenue remained but to seek out his individual 'salvation' while embracing the priesthood: and the cultivation of letters made up part of the priestly activity") (Cueva 21). The different religious orders, moreover, maintained schools and colleges close to the convents, and, in the eighteenth century, the Jesuits played a role of primary intellectual and cultural importance thanks to their network of educational establishments. There were also the seminaries and universities, where, as in Spain, arts, medicine, law, and theology were taught: from the sixteenth century in Lima and Bogotá; from the seventeenth century in Quito, Chuquisaca (Sucre), and Cusco; and from the eighteenth century in Caracas. Convents, colleges, and universities had important libraries at their disposal, to which were added those set up, notably during the second half of the eighteenth century, by certain wealthy clerics or officials with an interest in the arts and sciences. The book was a precious cultural commodity imported from Spain—through contraband when it was necessary to get around regulations or the censors; but there were also local presses in Lima and, in the eighteenth century, in Bogotá, Quito, Cartagena, and later Guayaquil.

Academies and literary salons proliferated in the second half of the eighteenth century along with groups concerned with the local economy, such as the famous *Sociedades de amigos del pais*. Finally, the press emerged as a force at the end of the colonial period, and a few news magazines and literary journals circulated in Lima, Bogotá, and Quito. Between 1750 and 1820, this cultural situation, with its subtleties and hierarchies, involved some twenty cities in the Andean world. The twelve cities, which numbered around 20,000 inhabitants, found themselves unequally divided between the regions located to the north of the equator (three centers) and those found to the south (nine centers, including Lima, which had reached 50,000 inhabitants).

The City—Stake and Force in a Precocious Liberation

The very nature of the colonial urban model of the city-territory and the ethnic fragmentation of Andean society placed the cities at the heart of developments and contradictions in the process of Independence. Emancipation was a matter of concern for the greater part of the urban population, and especially the dominant *criollo* faction, which included the large landowners and the mixed-race castes who were the majority urban population. However, the Indian peasantry—which made up three quarters of the total population and was subject to the triple imposition of tribute, forced labor, and bills of trade—tended to intervene in the emancipation process when mobilized as a native group, as often under the banner of the *Libertador* as under the banner of the Crown, and subject to the whims of its local *criollo* or autochthonous elite masters and the mood of the moment.

Between 1809 and 1824, many Andean cities took their turn at the heart of the turbulence: some as centers of insurrection, such as Chuquisaca (Sucre), Cochabamba, Santa Cruz, La Paz, Cuzco, Quito, and Santa Fé de Bogotá; others as centers of resistance and loyalism, such as Caracas, Popayan, Lima, Callao, and Cartagena. They were important stakes for the liberation armies, who sought to rally their elite members or to rouse the plebeians in order to subjugate them. Some cities were besieged or made victims of loyalist suppression. Decisive battles, on one side or the other, were fought at their gates, as at Guaqui (La Paz, 1811), Boyaca (Bogotá, 1819), Carabobo (Caracas, 1821), Pichincha (Quito, 1822), Ayacucho (1824), and Callao (1826); the two *Libertadores*, Bolívar and San Martín, had their famous meeting at Guayaquil in 1822. No one voice, however, emerged from these fragmented and fractious local urban societies, where the often partisan patricians also hedged their bets in their own best interest for the long or short term.

The interplay among the cities emerged from the hazards of the geopolitics of Independence, and around the difficult and somewhat paradoxical crystallization of republican nation-states, which arose from the disaggregation of this part of the Spanish empire. One of the paradoxes of emancipation is this impossible formation of a unified political structure, designed according to a Bolivarian dream, and the exploding of a culturally homogeneous *criollo* society: that is, the exploding of a region of civilization where no religious opposition existed, where the dominant elites spoke the same language, shared the same long history, and had recourse to the same statutory and juridical reference points; in short, the exploding of a space exempt from painful ethnic divisions. In this sense, what was at stake was the political rupture between American *criollos* and metropolitan Spaniards and not, properly speaking, the specifically colonial split between *criollos* and Indians (Deler 1993,144).

Chronicle of a Disintegration Foretold

The birth of the Andean nation-states as five *criollo* republics, ultimately less "sisters" than rivals, would seem all the more paradoxical given that the national level—that intermediary stage between the imperial (or worldwide) and the regional (or local) appeared a priori the most "foreign" to the political culture of the *criollo* elites. The latter, in fact, often had pancontinental commercial interests linked to international movements of exchange. These interests existed on a supranational level in the same way that their new cosmopolitan aspirations pertain to the new ideas of the Europe of "Light" and of "Progress." Their power rested, moreover, on essentially regional and urban bases, on municipal traditions that had generated a patriotism rooted at an infra-national level. This is despite the fact that intermediary levels of solidarity also existed, not exempt from rivalries and based on geographical proximities: that is, the old complementarities between neighboring cities (notably the interior and coastal) which enlarged the horizon of these "little countries."

The constraints proper to society's mastery of a space characterized by meridian elongation are well known. An examination of the long pre-Columbian period reveals that pan-Andean cultural horizons tied to imperial political constructs, in which the Incan empire was the ultimate link, and periods of withdrawal alternated with the fading of civilizations known as "regional development"—that is, the most limited territorial scope. In the Andean America of the beginning of the nineteenth century, the low median densities, the distribution of population and activities in an archipelago, and the widespread territorial compartmentalization, where "usable" spaces were separated by vast, unpopulated expanses, all contributed to making it difficult, if not discouraging, to create any kind of unifying pan-Andean political formation. The weakly hierarchized administrative chain, to which the recurrent colonial model of the city-territory contributed, was not foreign to this area either; it also allows us to understand this "chronicle of a disintegration foretold"—the gradual, conflicted stabilization of this part of the Andean world into five republican states. For several decades, the post-Colonial state structures, poorly secured, oscillated between two ephemeral "supranational" endeavors: large federations and lively regionalism. Great Colombia thus only managed to unite present-day Colombia, Ecuador, Venezuela, and Panama between 1822 and 1830, while between 1836 and 1839 a Peruvian-Bolivian confederation struggled to take shape on the basis of the association of three states: Bolivian (around La Paz), south Peruvian (around Arequipa), and north Peruvian (around Lima). Conversely, periods of inter-regional conflict, led by the *caudillos* (leaders) and supported by the elites of the main cities, weakened the still insecure new states. On four separate occasions between 1830 and 1880, Ecuador was close to erupting, with antagonistic powers established in Quito and Guayaquil, sometimes even in Cuenca or Loja. The nineteenth century in Colombia was a long oscillation between centralist and federalist constitutional options, in the context of the vigorous claims for regional autonomies which set in opposition the valley of Cauca around Popayan, the eastern highlands around Bogotá, and the Atlantic coastline around Cartagena. In Peru, the Andean south distrusted Lima's centralism, and Arequipa was a center for regionalist expression and contestation. These centrifugal tensions coincided at times with overt or latent conflicts on the borders of the still insecure republics.

These conditions for the emergence of the nation-state finally leave the impression that the explosion of the Spanish imperial Andean system could have been produced along lines of division different from those which were prevalent among the five states. Two, three, four, or even six republics could just as easily have come into being; or the five that did emerge could have been drawn with borders quite different from today's. For the establishment of the latter, particularly in the Cordillera, *criollo* ambitions, dissension, and compromises led to the partition of territories culturally quite homogeneous (such as in the Aymara country around Lake Titicaca and the region of Pasto) or of economically distinct zones (such as the area around the commercial axis of Cuenca-Loja-Piura).

Until well into the nineteenth century, the Andean domain would have a hard time absorbing the disruptive effects of the death of colonialism: on the one hand, there were economic disruptions, with the crises in mining and internal trade circuits, and the Panama maritime route declined, dethroned by the Antarctic route, which, nevertheless, isolated the central Andes; on the other hand, there were the ravages and disorder wrought by twenty years of American civil wars, prolonged by excessive turmoil and instability in the new republics created by internal rivalries among *caudillos,* who were supported by diverse regional interests. A kind of autarkic withdrawal of Andean society into the rural world followed, in an effort to preserve poorly competitive economies from ruin. The nineteenth century was, moreover, a period of expansion for the large estates, often to the detriment of lands held by indigenous communities. Additionally, with their small population distributed over vast areas, the young states constituted fragile aggregates of provinces where traditional structures and manipulations by the *caciques* (local bosses) persisted and reinforced each other.

Opening, Europeanization, and Modernization

With the liberalization of economic exchange as a result of the development and diversification of European, then North American, demands, Andean economic activity was progressively redeployed over the course of the nineteenth century. Republican history is thus marked by various cycles: mining operations (gold and tin in Bolivia; guano and nonferrous metals in Peru; petroleum in Venezuela), the harvest of natural resources (latex, exotic nuts, and the precious woods from the tropical forests), agricultural speculation (wool, cotton, and sugarcane in Peru; cacao and bananas in Ecuador; leather, coffee, and bananas in Colombia; coffee and livestock in Venezuela). These cycles proved to be phases of prosperity for the elites, and were brought about through the transformation and organization of space, notably with the development of ports and railways; however, they rarely constituted periods of accumulation. This economy, fundamentally focused on external markets, favored the development of tropical plantations, most often in the coastal regions (the oases of Peru, the plains of Guayas, Ecuador) or in certain sectors, like the "coffee belt" on the humid slopes of the Cordillera between altitudes of 800 and 1800 meters (in Colombia and Venezuela especially, and more sporadically elsewhere). Mining operations led either to the establishment of large centers of production, as for petroleum in Venezuela and copper in Peru, or to the formation of strip mining, as in Bolivia (tin, silver) or the central Andes of

Peru (silver, lead, zinc). Given the ever-changing nature of the large cities, the traditional Andean rural areas were progressively marginalized, while a large pioneer movement to colonize the eastern piedmont of the Andes gathered momentum. These economic transformations and contrasting regional dynamics corresponded to an upheaval of the old colonial urban hierarchies at the heart of each national territory. Beginning in the final quarter of the nineteenth century, the reincorporation of the Andean region into the international market in primary resources was especially profitable for the coastal and port cities, the mining towns, and the capital cities, which were the chief beneficiaries, especially the most densely populated ones. The transformation of society and urban modernization was accelerated during the decade from 1910 to 1920, under the double impetus of the opening of the Panama Canal (which shortened distances between the Pacific coast and Europe or the northwest United States) and the demands of those fighting in World War I.

The transformation of the Andean world also had an effect on the morals and mentality of a society in the process of emancipating itself from an old colonial structure of orders and castes that was marked by vertical barriers drawn on the basis of individual status and varying degrees of creolization. Demographic growth, new occupations, the expansion of education, urban anonymity, and new class solidarities (with the notable appearance of the first industrial working class) modified the face of the cities as much as the modernization of ways of life or surroundings. Small local business developed for these urban populations, who henceforth would shop for their daily needs using fractional currency. The physical appearance of the cities was altered and, at the turn of the nineteenth and twentieth centuries, most of the major towns saw the arrival of what Lima had acquired access to between 1840 and 1870: drinking water and public lighting, sewage systems, urban transport, and an industrial infrastructure. These transformations generally affected the coastal towns and ports before the towns located in the interior, and among the latter, often the capitals or the towns along the railroad lines before the rest. The towns grew. City centers were graced with public buildings and modern facilities modeled on the French, Italian, or English residences of the new local and cosmopolitan middle classes; in the neighborhoods around the railroad station or port, a manufacturing base (particularly food and textile industries) or energy facilities (petroleum refineries, electricity-generating stations) took hold.

The National Urban Networks in the 1920s

By the end of the 1920s, the network of Andean cities (thirty-two of which had over 20,000 inhabitants) had nearly tripled in size in one century. Only Lima and Bogotá exceeded 100,000 inhabitants. Eight others had more than 50,000: the other capitals, Caracas, Quito, and La Paz, the ports of Barranquilla, Cartagena, Guayaquil, and Callao, and Medellín, which had become the first Colombian industrial center, the Manchester of the Andes. On these foundations, however, the rate of urbanization had not yet reached ten percent, with around 1.5 million city-dwellers per 17 million people; this rate is higher in the north (Colombia, Ecuador, but excluding Venezuela) than in the south (Peru, Bolivia), and in the least populous country in each group (Ecuador, Bolivia). During this period, for the most part, the main themes of the national urban networks, and even the rough outline of their hierarchical organization, were already in place.

In the Bolivian Andes, the recommencement of mining operations (silver, nonferrous metals, tin) reactivated the cities of the *altiplano* (Oruro, Potosí, La Paz) just when, on the neighboring Chilean coast, the export of nitrates stimulated the development of the Iquique and Antofagasta ports. Moreover, Arequipa made a fortune from the export of wool from the sheep, goats, llamas, and alpacas of the *altiplano*. Urban growth went hand in hand with the development of export crops: sugar cane and long-fiber cotton in the oases of the Peruvian coast, around Lima, Trujillo, Chiclayo, and Piura; cacao in the plains of Guayas, around Guayaquil; coffee on the slopes of the Colombian Cordillera, where Antioquian colonization had grown into a powerful movement, emerging from the plateaus of Medellín. Its southward progression was accompanied by the founding of cities such as Manizales and Armenia. Finally, with the supply of goods to the city, the development of national markets stimulated the transformation of agriculture in certain favorably situated regions to the benefit of market towns: Huancayo, which is linked to Lima by the mining railway of the central Andes; Cochabamba, which is close to the Bolivian mining *altiplano;* or even Ambato on the Guayaquil-Quito railroad line.

Nearly everywhere, urban growth and modernization progressed in tandem with the development of primary resource exports and the correlative progress made possible by the steam engine, which opened up the continent by rail in the southern Andes, by river navigation on the network of the Guayas and the Magdalena, or a combination of the two. From the 1930s onward, a few strong structures were in place. The rather dense urbanization of the equatorial Cordillera between Cuenca and Cucutá contrasted with the looser urbanization of the tropical Cordillera and the *altiplano;* the string of coastal cities between Guayaquil and Lima engaged in export agriculture contrasted to the weak urbanization of the adjacent Andes. Furthermore, differences in the hierarchical structure of the national networks emerge: the clear preeminence of the Lima-Callao allegiance (more than 300,000 inhabitants) over the remainder of a little-differentiated Peruvian network; the Ecuadorian diarchy, established as a result of the competition between two complementary cities, the estuary port and the Andean capital; the polycentrism of the Colombian network; the decentering of the new Bolivian capital, La Paz, which replaced Sucre, settled sleepily into a valley not far from Potosí, which has been eclipsed by Oruro; the vitality of the Venezuelan sub-coastal urban axis of Caracas-Maracaibo (see **Map 4**).

This development of new economic regions while others remained quite traditional (notably in the most landlocked parts of the Andean massif), as well as this urban push, stimulated the modernization of society. The improvement in education and in living and market conditions had an influence on the burgeoning middle class. These economic and social changes found an echo in the birth of literary movements that bore witness to the diversity of, and contradictions in, the territories and national societies. In its regionalist and nativist currents–the latter concerning Ecuador, Peru, and Bolivia almost exclusively–the Andean novel always presents the American landscape, social and economic upheavals, and the native question from the perspective of the nation-state. "It was possible to nationalize our literature, at least in part thanks to the 'provincialism' of the social class to which the

Map 4.

new writers belonged, as opposed to the 'cosmopolitanism' of the aristocracy, which was also imposed as an indisputable value upon those under the protection of the upper class" (66), wrote Agustin Cueva concerning Ecuadorian literature. And for Antonio Cornejo Polar, "the nativist novel had to understand itself as a cultural exercise located in the conflicted intersection of two sociocultural systems, entering into a dialogue which is often polemical, and expressing, at the level to which it corresponds, one of the substantive problems of nationality: its divided and conflicted constitution" (88). He adds that "the nativist novel is the most exact literary representation of Peru's mode of existence" (88).

The Strong Metropolitan Pressure from the 1950s

Urbanization accelerated after the rupture linked to the unexpected economic and social crises from around 1920 to 1930. As a result of an unprecedented rural exodus, city dwellers became the majority in all countries, albeit at an unequal rate. The level of urban population everywhere surpassed the 50 percent limit: in Venezuela from the 1950s onward; in Colombia and Peru in the 1960s; later in Ecuador and Bolivia. The time of arrival in the metropolises also proved a determining factor. In the 1990s, when the rate of urbanization exceeded 80 percent in Venezuela and 70 percent in Colombia and Peru, not to mention Ecuador and Bolivia, half of all city dwellers lived in centers of 500,000 or more. In terms of migration, the most attractive cities of the different national networks–namely, the leading capitals–

underwent the most spectacular growth through a vast move-ment of metropolization with which industrialization, substi-tuted by imports, proved incapable of keeping pace.

At the end of the 1950s, the region had only five cities of more than 500,000 inhabitants, of which three had more than 1 million (Caracas, Bogotá, Lima). In the mid-1990s, it had twenty-one, of which ten were metropolises of over a million, and these included one third of the population of the five countries, versus 10 percent around 1960. The marked dispar-ities in income and standard of living, both of which are higher in the metropolises, cause a population flow, as people seek social advancement, a better standard of living, or even simple survival–especially when the city appears as the ulti-mate refuge for societies torn apart by violence and uncer-tainty and that are prey to natural catastrophes. Nevertheless, it is the natural increase in urban crowding that mainly deter-mines the direction of movement; the number of inhabitants in the densely populated neighborhoods grows two or three times as fast as that of the cities themselves, whose growth rates remain more elevated than those of the national popula-tion. This pressure of the young urban population, as it con-fronts a job and housing market still affected by the 1970–1980 economic crisis, has spurred the growth and develop-ment of the so-called "informal" or "underground" economy, which, with the tendency toward disengagement from the state, has become increasingly prominent.

This growth of Andean metropolises paves the way for the challenge of mass urban poverty. There are millions of low-income city dwellers, segregated in either the slums (having a historic center and the surrounding rundown zones), or to an ever more peripheral location, especially in the popular new neighborhoods. The precarious state of lots and buildings, the lack or insufficiency of infrastructure and even the most basic urban services, and the informal nature of economic activities whose usefulness to society is not always recognized are the usual lot of the majority in the big cities. Strategies of survival are developed that demand imag-ination, creativity, and a low capital investment. The "inevi-tability" of these unending suburbs of shantytowns is not accepted. Ancient bonds are maintained or reappear; new ones are forged. Through neighborhood struggles, the inhab-itants express their will to improve their precarious condi-tions of existence; they also reveal a consciousness of their own capacity for intervention as producers of political and social alternatives in the face of an urban process that at once absorbs and excludes them.

The Fractures in the Andean Community

At the start of the twentieth-first century, even as cultural relations are maintained among the five Andean countries, differences tend to assert themselves, particularly among the large metropolises. Bogotá, Caracas, and Lima belong to a network of world metropolitan centers, though neither Quito nor La Paz does. Between Caracas, the most North American of the Andean metropolises, and La Paz, the most Amerin-dian, the distance is not simply one of demographics. Social situations, context, and economic dynamics create great gaps between the republican sisters of the Bolivarian family. In the 1990s, Venezuela and Colombia had a gross domestic prod-uct nearly equivalent to that of the three other countries com-bined, and 10 times higher than Bolivia's alone; these differences bear no direct relationship to the respective demographic weight of the groups.

The Andean Community, created in 1969 and inspired by the Bolivarian dream of unity, tended to favor a process of regional integration among the five countries through the pro-gressive lowering of customs barriers between member coun-tries, the establishment of common external tariffs, and the harmonization of social and economic policies, particularly in the industrial domain. Although the group of five countries is looked upon as the third potential giant in Latin America, alongside Brazil and Mexico, in reality its stature is small. The lack of realism of the programs envisaged, the rigidity of implementation mechanisms, the broken commitments, and the mutual reprisals help explain the faint progress and rela-tive failures. In the mid-1980s, years of serious economic recession still felt to varying degrees in each country, the invi-olable egoism of the states too often prevailed over the part-nership, given the constraints of the liberalism of the times, the weight of the debt, and the insistent "recommendations" of the International Monetary Fund.

More than a quarter century after its creation, the Andean Community, which seems to have been gradually drained of its meaning and substance by the rise of nationalist and com-peting economic policies, has difficulty in catching its second wind; this is all at a time when the Latin American and world markets are reconstructing themselves, when Mexico has joined NAFTA, and when Brazil and Argentina are rushing to build the Mercosur. This regionalist organization separates the three member states in the north from the two to the south. The former are the most populated (with two thirds of the region's population) and the most urbanized; they pro-vide nearly three quarters of the GNP, and Colombia and Ven-ezuela in particular have increasingly directed their trade toward Mexico and the Caribbean. Bolivia reinforces its tra-ditional economic ties with the Mercosur countries, while Peru attempts to develop its strengths alone, along the lines of the Chilean model. Would the promoters of Andean eco-nomic integration then be condemned to "plow the seas" fol-lowing the example of Simón Bolívar?

Translation by Wendy J. Eberle

Works Cited

Bataillon, Claude, Jean-Paul Deler, and Hervé Thery. 1991. *Amérique latine*. Serie Géographie Universelle 3. Paris: Belin-RECLUS.

Cornejo Polar, Antonio. 1980. *Literatura y sociedad en el Perú: La novela indigenista*. Lima: Lasontay.

Cueva, Agustín. 1976. Entre la ira y la esperanza. Quito: Ediciones Solitierra.

Deler, Jean-Paul. 1992. "Ciudades andinas: viejos y nuevos modelos." *Ciudades de los Andes. Visión histórica y contemporánea*. Comp. Eduardo King-man Garcés. Quito: Institut Français d'Etudes Andines-Centro de Investigaciones CUIDAD. 351–374.

———. 1993. "Une urbanisation andine." *L'Amérique du Sud au XIXe et XXe siècles*. Ed. Hélène Rivière d'Arc. Paris: Armand Colin.

Dollfus, Olivier. 1991. *Territorios andinos: reto y memoria*. Lima: Instituto Francés de Estudios Andinos-Instituto de Estudios Peruanos.

Garcilaso de la Vega, Inca. 1976. *Comentarios reales de Los Incas*. [1609.] Caracas: Biblioteca Ayacucho.

Murra, John V. 1972. "El 'control vertical' de un máximo de pisos ecológicos en la economía de las sociedades andinas." *Visita de la Provincia de León de Huánuco*. [1562.] Iñigo Ortiz de Zuñiga, visitador. Huánuco: Universidad Hermilio Valdizan. 429–476.

Poma de Ayala, Felipe Guamán. 1936. *Nueva corónica y buen gobierno*. [1615?.] Facsimile ed. Paris: Institut d'Ethnologie.

CHAPTER 4

BRAZIL:
A CONTINENT, AN ARCHIPELAGO

Hervé Théry

Brazil bears the stamp of a cultural model imported from Iberian Europe to an even greater degree than the rest of Latin America, because the native presence was much smaller and more dispersed in Brazil than in the great empires of Mexico and Peru. Because of its language, culture, and unique traits–including its geography and the manner in which first the Portuguese and then the Brazilians organized its space–it constitutes a variation. One of Brazil's unique traits has to do with the very existence of the country, its unity and size. Today it occupies nearly half of South America, but its initial borders encompassed only a narrow band of coastline. How and why has Brazil become what it is–a giant country, the sole inheritor of the Portuguese empire of America–while the Spanish empire exploded into some twenty pieces? The question is a pointed one, given that for a long time the territory of Brazil was composed of a series of poorly connected islands, each specializing in a particular area of export production. What centripetal forces preserved the country's cohesion against such powerful centrifugal forces? Within this composite whole are found a series of unique centers, each of unequal weight and dynamism, some on a path of expansion, others clearly in decline, still others (notably in Amazonia) emerging. How has this point been reached? What was the play of powers and influences, the territorial division among these economic, political, and cultural centers?

The Construction of a Continent

Paradoxically, Brazil in great measure owes its existence, or at least its current expanse, to the pressure of foreign rivalries that forced Portugal to take seriously a conquest begun reluctantly, and then to extend and consolidate it. Without this pressure, it is uncertain that the country would have had the same destiny. This pressure, however, does not explain everything: The expansion of the Brazilian territory is due, in fact, to the coincidence of deliberate and sustained political action and striking pioneer dynamism. Little by little, this domain was conquered, constructed, and consolidated.

Why Does Brazil Exist?

When Pedro Alvares Cabral discovered Brazil on April 22, 1500, his goal was not to conquer new lands: The major objective of the Portuguese Crown was a monopoly on Oriental spices, and the newly conquered land represented little more than a stopover point for off-course ships. It was a poor conquest indeed in comparison with the treasures the Spanish were extracting from their new domains. For the Portuguese settlement to be consolidated, it would take new rivalries, notably those with French adventurers: Many navigators, primarily the Normans, established trading posts and entered into alliances with the natives. This competition forced the Portuguese Crown to undertake a policy of

systematic colonization; it was also one of the reasons for the creation of *capitanias hereditarias* ("hereditary captaincies") in 1532. By assigning vast portions of the new colony to worthy Portuguese, the king hoped to protect his sovereignty, which was limited until 1559 to a few coastal sites between Itamaracá (to the north of the present-day city of Recife) and São Vicente (now São Paulo). It was largely to protect their threatened flank that the Portuguese then advanced northward to Belém in 1616, a move that allowed them to control the mouth of the Amazon.

The attempts at colonization by France and Holland can be situated in this context: "Antarctic France," founded by Nicolas Durand de Villegaignon in 1555 in the Bay of Rio, disappeared under the blows of the Portuguese as early as 1560. In 1612, Daniel de la Touche, Lord of La Ravardière, founded the colony called "equinoctial France" in Maranhão; the colony's central city was Saint-Louis (named in homage to Louis XIII), whose name the Portuguese retained as São Luis after the reconquest of 1613. The attempts to establish Dutch colonies were more widespread and successful. The first, at Bahia in 1624, was easily repulsed, but the Dutch reclaimed control in 1630 at Pernambuco; they then conquered a vast territory that extended from Alagoas to Paraíba and, later, all the way to Rio Grande do Norte, Ceará, and Maranhão. They were not expelled until 1654.

This was the end of the last serious attempt by Northern Europeans to gain a foothold in Brazil. They turned next to the Caribbean, which they transformed into "sugar islands." The continent became less attractive, and the new colonial powers of France, Holland, and England contented themselves with three bridgeheads in Guyana. It was thus due as much to the disinterest of its rivals as to its own energies that Portugal was able to create a vast continental empire.

The battle, however, was not truly won, for this immense country was fragile and could explode at any moment, should royal authority weaken. One need only look to the fate of the colonial Spanish empire, which shattered into pieces when its metropolis, weakened by the wars in Europe, surrendered control. Napoleon was one of the unwitting creators of Brazilian unity: The advance of his troops into the Iberian Peninsula caused one of the great "bifurcations" in Brazil and Latin America when the Portuguese court, fleeing, decided to take refuge in Brazil, whereas the king of Spain chose to remain in place. Had the Portuguese king decided otherwise, and given the natural diversity of the Brazilian territory and the large variety of economic units created between 1500 and 1808, it is possible that this space could have given birth to a series of Portuguese-speaking countries of a size and originality comparable to the old fragments of the Spanish empire: In Salvador and Recife, in the cities of Minas Gerais, in Rio de Janeiro

This text is based in part on elements of the sixth part, "le Brésil," of *Amérique latine*, the third volume of the *Géographie Universelle*, Belin/Reclus, Paris 1992, edited by Claude Bataillon, Jean-Paul Deler, and Hervé Théry. For the most part I have drawn on my own contributions, with the exception of certain passages on the Northeast, which were written by Bernard Bret.

and São Paulo there were groups ready to do as their counterparts in Lima, Mexico, Quito, and Bogotá had done. The Brazil of the beginning of the nineteenth century, at the moment of independence (1822), was economically and racially diverse, even as it retained a profound administrative and cultural unity. In many respects, as massive as it is, Brazil has long functioned, and still functions in part, as an archipelago.

For more than four centuries, Brazil's economy was structured on a series of cycles. A few major products constituted the mainstay of its exports (sugar from the sixteenth century until the turn of the eighteenth century; gold in the eighteenth century; coffee in the nineteenth and twentieth centuries; and rubber at the beginning of the twentieth century). The formation of the Brazilian archipelago is due to this succession of speculations, each of which concerned a different region: Sugar in the Northeast, gold in Minas Gerais, coffee in the Southeast, and rubber in Amazonia all left their mark while fostering settlement in regions until then uninhabited and imposing a certain style on social relations and spatial organization.

But the consequences of such formation reach farther and affect the functioning of the entire national territory. Throughout the nineteenth century and during the first half of the twentieth century, Brazil was a collection of agricultural export units, a mosaic of quasi-autonomous regions formed in the course of one cycle. Each was centered on the production of an export commodity that fed into a network of transport routes leading to a seaport, and each, in turn, was constituted of smaller production units (large estates or plantations). One can speak all the more legitimately of a Brazilian archipelago since these units were linked only by the navigation route extending along the Atlantic coast: During World War II, when Brazil was fighting on the side of the Allies, only a few German submarines sufficed to cut off all communication along the length of coast between Rio and Salvador, and thus between the North and the South, for there was no interior connection apart from the highly precarious navigation route of São Francisco.

Under these conditions, how can one explain the fact that Brazil has enough cohesion to keep it from breaking up and to allow it to grow and become the immense country it is today? If Brazilian unity is due largely to the political control of the territory, its expansion was the work of pioneers. This was a stunning conquest, a true territorial explosion that was only much later followed by consolidation and the full exploitation of Brazil's capabilities.

The Bandeiras

The most striking episode in this expansion was that of the *bandeiras* (pioneering expeditions), whose main center of activity was a town born of a Jesuit college, São Paulo. This small town was more than half Indian, with Tupí spoken more than Portuguese, and was the base for expeditions composed of a handful of *bandeira*-carrying whites and a few hundred Indians who rallied to the cause and were knowledgeable about the area's resources. The tributaries of the Paraná could take them into the interior. These expeditions would last for years, in the course of which the *bandeirantes* (expedition members) fanned out over hundreds of kilometers, sometimes stopping to plant corn or cassava and to await the harvest. From the tributaries of the left bank of the Paraná, they headed south down the La Plata River, west along the tributaries of the right bank, or north, rejoining the Amazonian network. What lured these adventurers was profit, for their

intent was to capture Indians to work in the coastal sugar plantations. The *bandeirantes* quickly found themselves in conflict with the Portuguese and the Spanish Jesuits, who were trying to gather together and convert the Indians, for the mission villages proved a tempting hunting ground. Later, the *bandeirantes* turned to prospecting for precious metals and stones. They discovered the gold veins of Minas Gerais at the end of the seventeenth century (and defended them against the colonists fresh from Portugal), of Goiás in 1718, and of Mato Grosso in 1725.

There were other reasons for their adventuring. The taste for war and violence cannot be disregarded, and the men of São Paulo–called *Paulistas*–were present, as volunteers or conscripts, in the Indian wars of the northeastern interior and in the war against the Dutch. Finally, the taste for adventure and exploration played a role. How else are we to understand these interminable and dangerous journeys through unknown territory? The people of modern São Paulo can trace their entrepreneurial spirit and pioneer character back to the *bandeirantes*. They even christened the first commercial airplane produced at São José dos Campos *Bandeirante* and exported it to a number of countries, notably France and the United States. But if the pioneers cleared routes, inventoried resources, and discovered and founded new "islands," the relationships among them were still precarious, indeed dangerous: The gold convoys between Minas Gerais and Rio de Janeiro–to say nothing of the expeditions to Goiás or Mato Grosso–were often attacked. The responsibility for truly extending and occupying the territory, for laying out a grid of reliable and durable connections, fell to the animal breeders.

The Progress of the Animal Breeders and the Conquest of Amazonia

From the age of sugar onward the animal breeders occupied the semi-arid brush of the *sertão*, breeding beef cattle in order to supply the coastal plantations with dried meat, leather, and the draft animals needed for running the sugar mills. The gold mines, too, required these animals, and the breeding regions were extended toward the interior, both north and south. The breeders, who had reached the São Francisco River before the discovery of gold in its high valley, penetrated even farther, for the mines provided new prospects for them. Toward the north, starting from the bend in the river, they occupied the future states of Piauí and Ceará and pushed as far as Maranhão to Amazonia. To the south, the need to transport gold led to mule breeding in the *campos*, the then sparsely populated grassy savannas. This breeding, supported by well-established routes and markets, gave a decisive impetus to extending the Portuguese domain southward toward the Spanish domains.

Breeding, then, more than gold, contributed to expanding Brazilian space by creating stable routes and way stations. The *fazendas* were permanent support stations scattered across the immense expanses. From the *fazendas* the livestock traveled to the coastline via established paths from watering place to watering place, the *estradas boiadeiras*, which were comparable to the trails of the United States West. Along these trails, many of which became modern-day roads, small towns offered stopover points, pastures for rest, and, occasionally, marketplaces. A number of these towns, including Feira de Santana and Campina Grande, became large cities. The breeding world–a predominantly white world without slaves, a violent world but one more egalitarian than that of plantations and mines—surrounded and extended the sugar and gold zones in a vast, moving, but organized belt, where the pioneer spirit of the *bandeirantes* was sustained as the conquered space was consolidated and homogenized.

Before the country could achieve its current dimensions, however, the immense Amazonian Basin had to be conquered. This was accomplished starting at the end of the eighteenth century and occurred without any economic justification. It has been noted that the Portuguese crown was compelled to secure the mouth of the Amazon to stave off foreign privateers. From there, the military and the Jesuits established their forts and missions farther and farther upstream. They were anxious to advance as quickly as possible because other militias and missionaries—emissaries of the king of Spain—were progressing through the Amazon Basin. With such competition, even during the time when the crowns of Spain and of Portugal were worn by the same king (1580–1640), the advance was rapid, despite the poverty of means. The fort of Manaus was founded in 1669, and missions were spaced along the river beginning in the middle of the seventeenth century. By the time the Jesuits were expelled in 1759, the conquest was nearly complete. Throughout the eighteenth century, the movement expanded, progressing along the Amazon's tributaries. At key points—straits, waterfalls, and established boundaries on the large tributaries—forts were constructed, often with stone imported from Portugal. They still stand in the jungle—immense buildings facing regions still practically deserted, pointing their rusty cannons toward an empty frontier. They could easily recall the fort of *Il deserto dei Tartari* by Dino Buzzatti if it were not clear from maps of the region that these forts mark the present-day border: Everywhere they have effectively functioned as locked gates. The only changes to this border have been as a result of Brazilian conquests.

Immense territorial gains were made in Amazonia with limited means: a few hundred soldiers and a few dozen clergy. Economic exploitation was limited to hunting and the harvest of a few plants, roots, gums, and resins in the jungle; the dreams of wealth fed by myths (the lake of gold, Eldorado) never materialized. Driving this activity was the desire of the Portuguese, whether servants of the Crown or of the Church, to extend their domain. Two factors favored this ambition. First, it was easy for the Portuguese to advance upstream on the rivers, while for the Spanish the Andean Cordillera constituted a formidable obstacle. Second, Spanish resistance was weak and inconsistent, for Amazonia did not pull much weight in an empire based on the Indian masses and the Peruvian and Mexican mines and whose lines of communication passed more along the Caribbean islands and the Rio de la Plata than by this distant and inconvenient river.

Discoveries of new resources, pastoral pressure, and political will conspired to promote the impressive expansion of the Portuguese territory. In 1750 when the Treaty of Madrid outlined the Spanish and Portuguese empires, Brazil had reached its current boundaries in nearly all directions. Important rectifications involving a total of several hundred thousands of square kilometers were made until the beginning of the twentieth century. Nearly all of these adjustments were favorable to Brazil; Brazilian diplomats, notably the famous Baron of Rio Branco, effectively supported pioneer pressure by putting into law what had been established in fact by the Brazilian adventurers. Each border adjustment, minor on the Brazilian scale, represented the acquisition of tens of thousands of square kilometers: When, in 1901, the president of the Swiss Federal Council ruled in favor of Brazil against France in their dispute over the borders of French Guiana, he increased the Brazilian territory by more than 70,000 square kilometers.

Pioneer dynamism and the efforts of crown agents thus did a great deal to expand Brazil, to "push back the meridian" established by the Pope's arbitration at Tordesillas in 1494, and to give Brazil its continental dimensions. Internally, however, the formation of the country's present-day centers resulted from a series of economic cycles that framed the country's history from the sixteenth century to the beginning of the twentieth century.

Economic Cycles and Cultural Centers

The economic cycle is an essential notion in Brazilian history, and cycles have their own geography, their own inscription in space (see **Maps** 1 and 2). At the local level, these cycles have given birth to coherent rural and urban landscapes structured socially according to the period. The cycle of sugar production is characterized by slave plantations, the contrast between the houses of the master and of the slave, the monoculture of cane, and the concentration of land ownership. In the same fashion, the baroque cities of Minas Gerais owe their existence to the cycle of gold and diamond production; the cities' very names recall the product extracted (gold at Ouro Preto, diamonds at Diamantina). On a regional scale, the geography of cycles is manifest, on the one hand, in the framework of circulation created to link each region of production with external markets (thus concretizing in the terrain the export logic of the system) and, on the other hand, in the economic gradient that is a function of the distance to the means of exportation. In the sugar cycle, the Northeast is an export port, a coastline inhabited by sugarcane plantations, while the interior supplies plantations with the animals necessary for agricultural work. Similarly, the needs of the gold cycle led to breeding being undertaken at sites quite distant from the gold-producing regions and to the opening of a traffic route toward Rio de Janeiro for shipping the metal. The state of São Paulo, situated on land deforested for plantations, was built in the course of the coffee cycle by the pioneer vanguard, which traversed it from east to west. Its space was framed by the railways that transported coffee to the port of Santos; the road network followed later, confirming this trend, and today the region is heir to the by-products of the coffee period. The same principle of organizing space for product export was applied in a different way in Amazonia, where the traffic system was the same as the hydrographic network. The banks of the waterways were favored, and confluents became crossroads and privileged sites in the birth and growth of cities.

In all cases, whatever the exports and means of transport, the system of development was translated regionally through a hierarchization of space and urban centers according to an exogenous logic. This is why, on the national scale, the geography of the production cycles does not reveal a logically endogenous—that is, Brazilian—constitution of economic space. Brazilian space opposes the coast and the interior, both for population distribution and for the degree of integration into the world economy: It consists of zones of space derived from the export function of the cycles. The juxtaposition of regional organizations made Brazilian space into an incoherent archipelago, and it is surprising that political unity was attained without a corresponding economic necessity. This archipelago-like structure would last until a territorial integration was created under the direction of São Paulo–

Map 1.

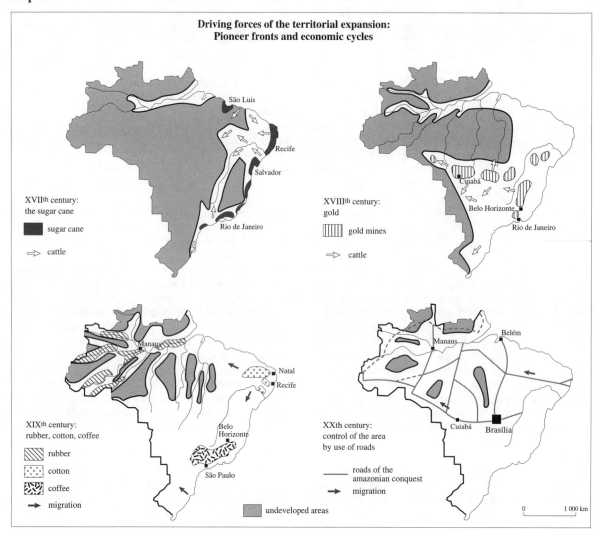

Map 2.

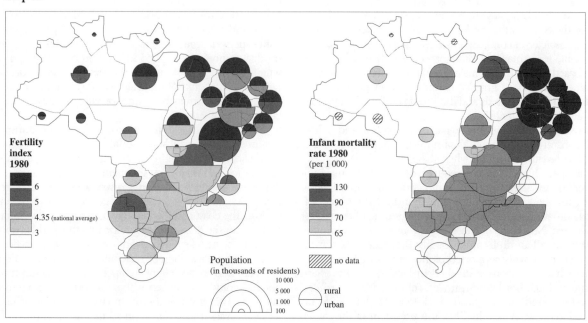

in other words, when Brazil freed itself in 1930 from the logic of its production cycles.

From this history emerged a geography that can be read starting from the former center in the Northeast, passing through the current center of gravity supported by the three capitals of Rio de Janeiro, São Paulo, and Brasília, and to the pioneer regions of Amazonia, a periphery on the way to integration.

The Ancient Center

Stretching from Maranhão to Bahia, the Northeast is an immense region whose demographic weight is considerable, even though its population has dropped relative to the other members of the Federation. The Northeast has often been described as the problem region of Brazil: Here social issues spring up with greater urgency and the economy is more vulnerable to natural hazards. However, the Northeast was the first center of colonial Brazil, and this anteriority is one of the factors contributing to the current regional crisis. The migration of the Brazilian economic center and social structures following those economic cycles is key to understanding the present situation. It is important, however, not to reduce the Northeast to this image of poverty: It is one of the most original and complex regions of Brazil and differs the most from the neighboring Spanish-speaking countries. One could say of the Northeasterners that they were the "vertical founders" of Brazil, those who planted the deep roots of the nation, just as the people of São Paulo were the "horizontal founders," those who gave the country its breadth. In both popular and highbrow literature, music, and cinema, the Northeasterners often rank number one, even if this ranking is bestowed from Rio, São Paulo, or abroad. In Brazil, with its brief history, the Northeast is the only place where, for better or worse, a certain historical depth is felt.

The First Brazil

Space in the Northeast was organized according to the imprint left by the colonial period. It was the first Brazil, not only because Cabral disembarked in 1500 on the coast of what is today the south of the Bahia state, but above all because it was there that the economy first blossomed: The choice of Salvador da Bahia as capital in 1548 bears witness to the importance of this region to the economy of the period. The sugar cycle, a fundamental stage in the genesis of the nation and the territory, created an economic structure (the establishment of the agricultural export system), a social structure (the establishment of the system of slavery), and a spatial structure from which the Northeast has inherited much in its present-day geography.

The basic unit was the sugarcane plantation. From the beginning, technical constraints (the necessity of treating the cane immediately upon cutting it) made the *engenho,* the sugar mill, into an agro-industrial unit that furnished the external market with a refined, not raw, product–sugar. Incorporating a nonagricultural value into the exported product would have provided further opportunities for the region if internal social conditions and relations with the metropolis had permitted profits to be reinvested on site to diversify the economy. They did not: The sugar cycle was not a period of capital accumulation, and, far from ensuring regional economic development, it left the Northeast as a backwater of underdevelopment and dependency.

This process can be explained by the period's social structures, which, between the slave-owning planters and the slaves themselves, did not comprise sufficient intermediate layers to create a viable market. Under these conditions, there was no place in the region for the planters' profits to be applied for diversifying the production apparatus. The profits from the cane financed the progress of the cane–that is, the despoilment of the Indians, the enslavement of the Africans, and, finally, the consolidation of an inegalitarian society and an outward dependency.

Slavery, the social system of the exploitation of labor, was consistent with the spatial system of the export of the fruits of this labor. Also, the Northeast was already peripheral with regard to the European center. It was the center of a colony, a globally dominated space. The sugarcane fields, as is the case today, occupied the coastline, while the interior was the domain of extensive animal breeding for plantation use. The fact that the geographic distribution of the activities was adapted to the bioclimatic framework changes nothing of the significance of the system: Activities were zoned according to the distance from the export ports, which concretized the relationship with the colonial power. The current administrative map of the region–with states, such as Pernambuco, that thrust inward from a narrow maritime strip–recalls this colonial logic, which incorporated conquered lands into world trade.

The legacy of this sugar cycle is multifaceted. It is demographic in that it provided the occasion for importing black peoples from Africa. It is economic in that the cane is still in place. It is social, for the large property structure has endured. It is cultural, for the Africans brought with them their customs and religions. It can be seen in the landscape, for the period has left an abundant architectural inheritance that speaks volumes about the society of its time: The old plantations with their master house, chapel, slave houses, and the remains of the pillories remind one that, in this moment of prosperity, the majority of the population lived in poverty, in servitude, and subject to violence. Gilberto Freyre has interpreted this opposition of the master's *casa grande* and the slaves' *senzala* as the matrix of Northeasternness, the combat region where the relations between the classes and the races were forged in old Brazil. To understand the present-day geography of the Northeast thus demands an understanding of why the socio-economic system was not capable of adapting to the changes that emerged after the sugar cycle, which had given the region its initial structure.

The Present-Day Transformations

After more than a century of attempts at development, the Northeast is still the region of Brazil having the most serious difficulties. Still, substantial changes have marked the region, giving it an appreciable potential for production. In agriculture, the production of new crops is attempted with greater or lesser success. Sugarcane, as noted, occupied the coastal zone. Rather than diversifying the use of the region's soil, the production of fuel alcohol provided a new opportunity for speculation and spread cane plantations everywhere on the well-watered slopes of the Agreste. This onslaught of cane did not progress without negative social consequences, for it posed a serious threat to the food-producing crops in these densely populated regions and threatened the agrarian structure of moderate land development. The establishment of vast irrigated areas on the São Francisco and its main tributaries has allowed cane to persist.

Other crops–fruits and vegetables in particular–were planted in the irrigated areas opened in the interior. Since the 1970s, coffee has become a large-scale operation on the Chapada Diamantina of Bahia and on the plateau of Conquista. The severe frosts that ravaged the plantations of São Paulo and Paraná accelerated the trend toward growing agricultural products better suited to the climate, if not to the quality of the soil. While coffee made way for cane and soybeans in the south, in the Northeast coffee growers made good use of lands that traditionally had been used for extensive breeding. All the same, breeding was not cut back on a regional scale; on the contrary, its progress has increased pressures on the soil and threatened agriculture.

In industry, the progress in mechanical and chemical industries is particularly noteworthy and is more clear-cut than the development in traditional industries, such as textiles and leather. But the most pertinent perspective for regional analysis is the location of these new industrial establishments. Three cities have benefited the most, though unevenly so, from industrial development: Salvador has profited the most, Recife somewhat, and Fortaleza to a small extent. These localizations can be understood in light of particular options. As soon as these factories were inscribed in an increasingly national logic of distribution and required financial and material ties with São Paulo and the surrounding areas, it was increasingly tempting to choose the most accessible points in the Northeast, those with the best infrastructures and that were the most suited to industry–in short, only those in a position to guarantee the kind of physical, economic, and human environment that would promote successful investments.

In Salvador, favored by its oil wells and by its relative proximity to the Southeast, the industrial center of Aratu and the nationally important petrochemical pole of Camaçaria were created. It is there, more so than in Recife and Fortaleza and far from the centers of national decision-making, that the industrial Northeast demonstrates the most spectacular development. Generally, industry is barely established in the smallest towns. It is well developed in cities such as Feira de Santana and João Pessoa because these two areas function in symbiosis with the nearby metropolises of Salvador and Recife, respectively. However, São Luis, today the modest capital of Maranhão, has undergone considerable industrial transformation, for it has become the railway outlet of the *serra* of Carajás; its modern port ships out copper ore, while a factory transforms into aluminum the bauxite extracted along the Rio Trombetas; an iron and steel industry is planned. The birth of this industrial pole in the western part of the Northeast perceptibly alters the regional economic geography, dominated until now by the dilution of activities of progress toward the west.

Economic growth, as it has evolved, has a selective impact on the Northeast, privileging those points reputed to be the most able to turn a profit on the original investments of the Southeast. This leads to the reinforcement of the large coastal developments and the inability of mid-sized cities and small towns to attract investment, despite the recent concern of developers to channel growth into the interior. Migratory flux serves only to accentuate this urban gigantism and to aggravate the unemployment among city dwellers. In the context of a rapid demographic growth, the agricultural transformations expel inhabitants from the countryside, while industries rely more on machines than on manual labor. How then to make a living if not in service activities often emerging from the so-called "informal" sector? There

has been considerable deviation from the initially sketched prospects for development.

These economic and social distortions, which can be observed at the regional level, are perhaps due ultimately to the fact that the increasing integration of the Northeast into the national economy poses the question of the very maintenance of a regional economy. For a long time, the region has been tied to the Brazilian center: Its physical integration, earlier realized quite precariously through São Francisco, was reinforced by the roads and by the relative proximity between the Bahian west and the capital, Brasília. Human integration has existed since the Northeasterners began to migrate toward the vital centers of Brazil in search of construction work. Financial integration was achieved when the São Paulo capital saw in the Northeast a space made attractive by the fiscal arrangements in place there. What remains in the economic system that is specific to the Northeast if not the localization of certain crops dictated by the natural conditions and the capacity of this space to play the role of submissive periphery to the São Paulo center?

The Center and Its Three Capitals

All available indications show that the Southeast (the states of São Paulo, Rio de Janeiro, Minas Gerais, and Espírito Santo) is the core region of Brazil from all perspectives: industrial, agricultural, financial, intellectual, and cultural. What remains to be understood is how this situation came into being and why, as a case unique in Latin America, this region has not one or two capitals, but three (see **Map 3**).

Why Is This the Center?

The environment and natural resources are not the determining factors in making this region the center of Brazil. The Bay of Guanabara, site of Rio de Janeiro, is certainly one of the most beautiful places in the world, but the coastal plain is narrow, and the steep slopes of the Serra do Mar close by are one of the few topographical obstacles that opposed European penetration in a country where plains and plateaus dominate. This same obstacle can be found in the state of São

Map 3.

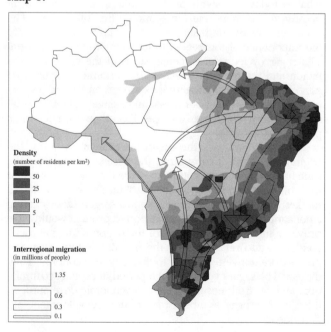

Paulo, and for a long time these steep slopes blocked the Portuguese colonists of the old colony of São Vicente (today surrounded by the city of Santos) from the modest establishment erected by the Jesuits on the other side of the plateau, the seed of São Paulo. Once established, São Paulo became a convenient point of departure for the *bandeirantes*, who followed the tributaries of the Paraná into the interior; this ease, however, was relative, since the expeditions were for the most part made on foot.

The region also offers few or no climatic or soil advantages: Cultivation of sugarcane was possible but was less productive than in the rich soils of the Northeast, which was closer to the European markets. It was not until the nineteenth century and the development of coffee production that a natural asset emerged: the *terra rôxa* (violet earth), which is particularly suitable for cultivating coffee trees. Even this asset could not be fully exploited, however, for when the pioneer vanguard arrived in the north of Paraná, an important natural boundary was reached—frost. Therefore, reasons for the region's centrality must be sought elsewhere, in the populations and their enterprises. It has been said that the principal asset of São Paulo was its pioneer spirit. In the first few decades of its existence, the colony had scarcely any resources apart from the hunt for slaves and *drogas do sertão*, the fruits of the harvest collected in the uncharted interior. It was during these explorations that the men of São Paulo found gold and emeralds, explored the interior, "pushed back the meridian," extended the domain of the king of Portugal, and forged an undeniable dynamism.

Practically the same is true for the development of coffee production; a vast pioneer vanguard swept through the state of São Paulo. Introduced in the Northeast from French Guiana, the coffee tree was cultivated without much success. With the increase in world demand, coffee was cultivated in the state of Rio de Janeiro, in the old framework of the slave plantations inherited from the sugar era. After the pioneer vanguard crossed the valley of Paraíba and arrived in the state of São Paulo, the latter changed in size and in nature. Pressure from Great Britain had, by the middle of the nineteenth century, made the importation of slaves difficult, and, even within Brazil, abolitionist movements were growing stronger. The planters of São Paulo were thus compelled to find other sources of labor: They organized and financed European immigration, alone and with the support of the state government of São Paulo, which they controlled directly.

The planters' organizational energy allowed for the development of the railroad network, which allowed the wave of coffee cultivation to move into the interior. At regular intervals, the coffee companies created way stations, many of which became towns. The largest towns knew to play up their admittedly provisory role in order to develop a collection and distribution network linked to the railroad and thus to create a zone of influence for themselves. The role of these networks was such that the regions ended up taking the names of the railroad companies servicing them: Mogiana, Alta Sorocabana, Noroeste. In all these cases, then, initiative counted for more than resources. Neither negligible nor determining, resources were well employed. The same was true when the real boom occurred, the one that saw São Paulo become the industrial core of the country.

The point of departure is easily identified as the crisis of 1929, as is its impetus—the substitution of imports. But why was there a boom in this region? This is a fundamental question for understanding present-day Brazil, a question to which it is not easy to give a persuasive response, for if the "ingredients" of development can be inventoried without too much difficulty, it is not so simple to say why, when they are assembled, a reaction is produced that leads to the formation of a new complex that cannot be reduced to the sum of its parts. In any case, it is clear that São Paulo was the only place in the country where all the necessary conditions for an industrial initiative were found, though they were not necessarily present in sufficient numbers.

First and foremost was the accumulation of capital. The expansion of coffee cultivation had made São Francisco the top-producing region in the world and had made its planters into prosperous entrepreneurs. The slump produced by the 1929 crisis would have been dramatic had the Brazilian government not decided to support its currency through large-scale spending. As the depression continued, it was necessary to destroy stocks, sometimes by spectacularly burning millions of bags of coffee, sometimes in locomotive engines. One might contest the use made of public monies by and for the coffee barons, but the fact is that these measures freed capital for other activities. This capital was concentrated in the hands of men who had proven themselves on the plantations and had gained experience in the development, commercialization, recruitment, and management of a large and unequally qualified labor force—in short, as heads of enterprises. The presence of these groups of entrepreneurs was not the least of Brazil's assets in the 1930s, and it is without doubt that presence that was most lacking in the other countries of Latin America, notably Argentina, where the landowning mentality remained dominant.

These planters from São Paulo did not have to look far to reinvest their capital, for their region offered both a market and a reservoir of labor. The immigrants who left Europe in the mid-nineteenth century and were recruited for the coffee plantations were already consumers of industrial products and were often, if not qualified workers, at least good recruits for an emerging industry. These immigrants also formed a solvent market that otherwise would not have existed in Brazil. Less marked by slavery than other regions, the state of São Paulo, despite the glaring inequalities between the rich planters and their employees, was the least inegalitarian and most populous society, for the influx of immigrants had, since 1890, made the Southeast the most densely populated region in the country. Add customs protection, indispensable for the birth of these industries, and all the necessary elements for an initial industrial boom are found. It was the good fortune of the Southeast to have protection at just the right moment, when international competition was weakened, and to be able then to preserve these embryonic industries, which presupposed a continual and active will: In the conjunction of various resources, all favorable to profit, lies the strength of this region, the real cause of both its initial boom and its current position of power.

Three Capitals

The center of modern agriculture and industry, the Southeast is also the nerve center of Brazil, its tertiary center of production. This sector holds more than 45 percent of the active population. Yet it is important to distinguish where the real commercial and financial power, the best services, the influential media, the political and administrative power, lie. It is no longer a question of the Southeast region but of the three cities where everything happens: Rio de Janeiro, São Paulo, and Brasília. Macrocephaly is a constant in Latin America, and Brazil is an exception only in that it shares the functions of the capital among three poles. Except, on a more modest scale, for Colombia (with Bogotá, Medellín, and Calí), this situation is unique on the continent. The reasons for such distribution are simple, but the balance is unstable because Rio's share is progressively declining as the city is being stripped of its main assets.

The first shock was the loss of Rio's original status of capital. A modest little town, but the most convenient port for exporting the Minas Gerais gold, when it became the colony's capital in 1763, Rio was still quite small when the king of Portugal arrived with his court in 1808. In his efforts to turn Rio into a capital worthy of his court, the king spared no expense, and Rio owes to this period a few monuments and institutions, some of which have survived better than others. We know this old Rio today thanks to a series of works by Jean-Baptiste Debret, who participated in the 1816 French artistic mission on the king's invitation. This effort was continued under the Empire and the Old Republic (1822–1889). The federal district benefited from the efforts of the political class to make Rio both its center for work and pleasure and its showcase. A series of projects were undertaken to dazzle foreigners: *para Inglês ver*, to show the English, the dominant power of the period. On the eve of the 1929 crash, Rio was at the height of its power. No city could contest its status, neither in the already decadent Northeast nor in the still wild South, where the progress of coffee had not yet reached its apogee.

After 1919, things took a downturn. São Paulo took off and, little by little, became the economic capital. Once the division was established, however, with industry on one side and finance, culture, fashion, and leisure on the other, Rio's position was called into question more and more. One of the handsome remnants in Rio was its Stock Exchange, which until recently challenged São Paulo's. For a long time, the São Paulo press has been on equal footing with Rio's. Intellectual and cultural life has increasingly shifted to São Paulo: Art galleries, fashion boutiques, and the places where "one must be seen" have multiplied there. Lacking Rio's tourism assets, São Paulo owes more and more to its economic role and its ability to attract worthwhile activities given its financial and human resources. The specter of Salvador, divided between the poor and the tourists, haunts Rio (see **Map 4**).

The rapid development of Brasília as a national capital (1960) accounts for a great deal. The *cariocas* (the inhabitants of Rio) have long poked fun at this poor capital, which the politicians and functionaries fled every Saturday for the beaches, but they soon had to eat their words. The ministries and major administrations had to transfer to Brasília or risk having their credit cut off, and the embassies had to follow or risk a break in diplomatic relations. Once the whole state apparatus had been transferred, all the lobbies and activities

Map 4.

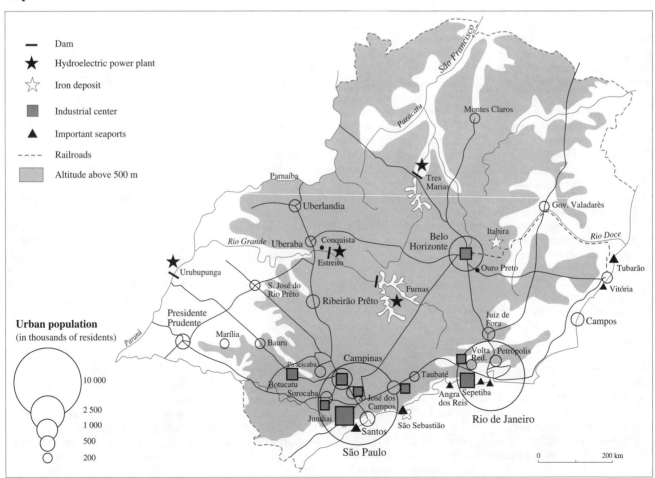

that depend on proximity to political power started to move as well, thus turning Brasília into the site where decisions are prepared, made, and contested.

Brazil is thus graced with a triple capital, a power triangle made up of unequal sides. Among them relations are many and close. One of the busiest commuter airline shuttles in the world runs between Rio and São Paulo. This service is indispensable to businessmen and runs in tandem to the hundreds of buses and trucks that congest the 400 kilometers of the Via Dutra, one of the busiest and most dangerous highways in the country. Traffic is less heavy between Rio and Brasília: Flights are numerous and frequent, but road traffic is limited to restocking Brasília. The São Paulo-Brasília axis is finally completed and, for the most part, traverses rather deserted stretches. It is not just metaphorically that the triangle Rio de Janeiro-São Paulo-Brasília can be viewed as the center of Brazil. This peripherally located center takes the form of unequal axes linking unequal points. The topographic layout is certainly a factor, but so are the distribution of power and the play of attraction among these unstable and uneasily defined poles.

It is worth looking in detail at the social geography of these capitals, for it reflects the Brazilian model by juxtaposing islands of luxury with oceans of poverty on levels of agglomeration, the city, and even neighborhoods: The poor are present at the heart of wealthy neighborhoods, where they hold low-paying jobs to supplement their income; the middle classes often settle in new neighborhoods to feel more at ease, eventually pushing out the poor. The cities that make up the center of the center as microcosm of Brazil are themselves crisscrossed with the rifts that mark the country. Even though the country has arrived at a turning point, its center appears threatened with saturation. The division of the functions of the capital among three metropolises is not sufficient to ease the congestion.

The level of concentration has begun to pose formidable problems, and the timid move toward deconcentration along the axes radiating from São Paulo has not been enough to reduce it. Already the three metropolitan regions of São Paulo, Rio de Janeiro, and Belo Horizonte total nearly 30 million inhabitants. The empty space separating them does not attenuate this problem, for the central region is experiencing a true implosion: Depressed margins have emerged around the core. Add long-depressed regions such as Espírito Santo and the north of the state of Rio de Janeiro and the central region does not seem to be doing well; it appears well off only in comparison to the truly underdeveloped regions of the distant Amazonian and Northeastern periphery.

Margins, Frontier Borderlands, Peripheries

Around this center are aureoles of decreasing degrees of development, the closer being the margins, those farther away, but still under the center's direct control, being the frontier borderlands. Finally, the distant peripheries of Amazonia are constantly being integrated into national space, at the price of sacrificing their ancient structures and their traditional autonomy (see **Map 5**).

The Margins and the Frontier Borderlands

Around the center proper is a zone of margins composed of two blocks: One includes the north of the state of Rio de Janeiro, Espírito Santo, and east Minas Gerais; the other covers the entire region of the South, apart from northern Paraná, which is almost a functional extension of the state of São

Map 5.

Formation of the Brazilian States

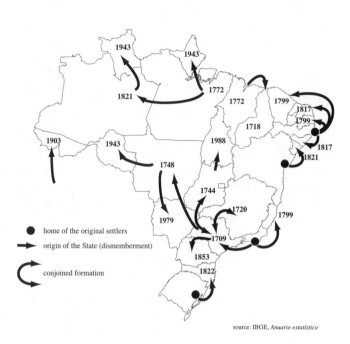

- ● home of the original settlers
- → origin of the State (dismemberment)
- ↻ conjoined formation

source: IBGE, *Anuario estatístico*

Paulo. Beyond these margins, following the secular movement of the Conquest, the pioneers integrated all of the "useful" Center-West (the forested savanna of the *cerrados*, the agricultural and pastoral glacis of the Southeast) into national space. The pioneer phase swept through nearly every part of this region, and a new wave of exploitation, focused on the three capitals, followed.

The situation of the center's borderlands is entirely different: These spaces of colonization and exploitation of natural resources are under the direct control of the center, just as at one time the frontier borderlands of medieval kingdoms, under the authority of the marquis, had their autonomy curtailed by direct allegiance to the suzerain. In these regions, which the pioneer vanguard has transformed, the importance of the center makes itself felt through the exchange of merchandise and the arrival of orders, capital, and men who furnish it. Still sparsely populated and not entirely opened, the borderlands have the advantage of being the center's point of advance in the periphery.

However, a trace of the center is found still farther afield, as far as the core of the dominated spaces. The initiatives of the center have created an archipelago of advanced posts there; these are industrial installations and agricultural investments, a network of collection and distribution that allows for the appropriation and exploitation of the interior's resources. Taking advantage of their know-how and capital, as well as favorable legislation, the entrepreneurs from the center have woven a network that makes the entire country their backyard. This unification of the national territory under the impetus, and to the benefit, of agents based in the center is one of the new aspects of Brazilian geography that has been under way for some thirty years and is close to completion: Rather than the old face of the Brazilian archipelago, we find a network whose center is well situated and whose links blanket the territory. This then is the central logic that will guide one across the vast peripheral expanses, from margins to marches, from pioneer regions to those not yet conquered.

The northern part of these margins has the lowest population density: while the populated coast is frequently contrasted with the empty interior, a clear division also is apparent between the south of the Bahia state and the north of the state of Rio de Janeiro. The latter region has not experienced a single major cycle of occupation and exploitation, since there are no resources to exploit, and it has remained in the margin of the large zones of the development of sugar, gold, and coffee industries, participating in each cycle in only a minor way. The cause of its mediocre development is probably its distance from the centers of initiative, Salvador and São Paulo. In the nineteenth century, attempts to colonize this void with German settlers failed. While this colonization proved successful in the south, in Espírito Santo the colonists, isolated and reduced to living almost at a subsistence level, saw their cultural and technical level regress. The blond-haired, blue-eyed descendants of the first colonists have resorted to the most basic slash-and-burn agriculture and are no longer able to read the piously preserved family Bibles. This decline has been christened *caboclização*, a reversion to savagery, to the level of the *caboclos*, the criollo Indian peasants. In Minas Gerais, the valley of Jequitinhonha is one of the poorest and most deprived in the state. Another sign of sparse habitation is poor definition of the frontiers of the states: The borders of Minas Gerais and Espírito Santo were still being contested at the end of the 1960s. This region is today a poorly consolidated margin, crossed by a corridor. The railroad that runs through the valley of the Rio Doce carries iron ore from Minas Gerais. This asset has been used to develop the port of embarkation, Tubarão, which is close to Vitória, as well as to develop the plants for processing ore and an iron and steel industry.

The situation in northern Paraná is quite different. Its past is glorious, for it experienced the apogee of the coffee cycle and was the most interior of the densely populated regions. Here the pioneer coffee vanguard came to rest and reached its most highly developed cultural and social forms. Here, however, coffee cultivation has reached its ecological limits: Frost is more frequent the farther south one goes, the lines of communication grow longer, the costs of transportation increase. Soil erosion is a concern and can no longer be avoided by pressing farther with migration, for the pioneer vanguard has reached its limits. The heavy frosts of 1975 destroyed millions of coffee plants, and the response was to look for new zones of production farther north in Minas Gerais, Mato Grosso, and the Bahia state. Locally, other crops, less labor-intensive than coffee, were cultivated on converted lands: wheat and soy in particular. A vast move to concentrate land was then instigated and led to the expulsion of a large number of agricultural workers and small landowners. The greater part of the expelled people headed to the large cities, while others fed the migratory currents to the Northwest, toward the two Mato Grossos and Rondônia. The Paraná North, which was well integrated into the center when it was an extension of São Paulo, thus grows closer to the South and the Center-West and forms the missing link between the zones of emigration and the pioneer receiving zones, between the center, its margins, and the exterior frontier borderlands.

The South—the three states of Paraná, Santa Catarina, and Rio Grande do Sul—constitutes an original ensemble in Brazil: Its subtropical climate allows for the cultivation of crops unknown in the rest of the country (barley, rye, olives, linen, peaches) and rules out others (coffee, cacao, sugarcane); the European colonization of the nineteenth century created a society that is more diverse and egalitarian and that enjoys both a higher standard of living than in the North and Northeast and a quality of life often superior to that in the Southeast. It is also the only region of Brazil that is truly a borderland, not only because the borders with Uruguay, Paraguay, and Argentina are the only ones in the nation that facilitate daily contact with the outside, but also because the Luso-Brazilian and pampa civilizations meet here, with the pampa carrying on into the extreme South. The prospects of regional integration with Argentina, Uruguay, and Paraguay opened by the creation of *Mercosul* (known as *Mercosur* in Spanish) give new value to this situation.

Amazonia

The pioneers who came from the South fed the pioneer vanguards of the frontier borderlands (the functional extension of the Southeast). For this reason they did not really form a new center, even if cities such as Goiânia and Campo Grande have undergone a remarkable growth that has turned them into true regional poles. But the integration of these formerly nearly empty regions was smooth, unlike what happened in Amazonia. Amazonia has a history full of sound and fury. Men struggled to take possession of it, to plant their flag in its soil, and if the Portuguese were the great winners in this race, Brazil had to struggle for a long time to keep control of its conquest. Even though large tracts of land remain virtually empty, Amazonia is no longer a new land and has not been one for a long time, but it is a disputed, poorly consolidated region that is increasingly attached to the rest of Brazil as the old Amazonia of the rivers gives way to the one organized around the roads built since the 1970s.

The pre-road Amazonia is an exemplary instance of a region structured as a network: The population distribution, the essential aspect of all economic activity, and its entire spectrum of relationships were governed by the distance from the hydrographic network, the control of resources, and river traffic. The river and its tributaries supplied water, fish and aquatic animals, and the silt that fertilizes the crops along the banks. All the human settlements were thus distributed along the banks of the Amazon's main tributaries, with the exception of a few Indian villages forced into the jungle by the onslaught of the European colonists. If the hydrographic network serves as the nervous system for the entire region, however, it has also introduced a hierarchy: All the nodes in the network were not equal, and the most strategic were occupied by cities better positioned to organize trade. The situation of the major city is logical: Belém controls the ocean outlet for the entire network, not just directly at the mouth, which is marshy and subject to a dangerous tidal bore, but on one of the many intercommunicating arms to the south of the island of Marajó, which conveniently connects river and sea navigation toward the south. The second city in the hierarchy, Manaus, occupies the confluence of the Amazon's two main tributaries: the Rio Negro, with its black waters from Colombia, and the Solimões, which carries Peru's silt in its brown waters. For the Brazilians, the spectacular confluence (where waters of different colors run side by side for several kilometers) is the starting point of the Amazon, and the city is thus well positioned to control the junction between the upstream tributaries and the main valley. Below these two capitals a hierarchy of secondary centers has been established: first cities spaced along the river (such as Santarém at the confluence of Tapajós) or along its main tributaries (such as Porto Velho at the point where the rapids interrupt navigation on the Madeira), then small towns and villages whose importance is a function of both the urban hierarchy and the waterways.

The Amazonian river system was perfectly constituted, well connected, and efficient. It satisfied the needs for both political order and economic exploitation at the lowest cost–at least from the state's point of view, for these costs were absorbed largely by "volunteers" under the strict surveillance of a few government officials and tradesmen. However, while this system was able to resist the jolts in the rush for rubber, it proved less and less satisfactory as new desires were stirred by the development of means of transportation and communication that offered the possibility of moving from the stage of harvesting to that of the real exploitation of Amazonia.

The reconquest of Amazonia under the military regime clearly had geopolitical motives. It rested chiefly on the construction of roads (of which the Transamazonian is only the most well known), colonization, and animal breeding. It was accomplished through the propagation of a highly inegalitarian model that divided the more populated, but also more ravaged, eastern Amazonia from a western Amazonia still quite empty outside of Manaus. There were inequalities also between the timber and animal breeding entrepreneurs and the mass of colonists, who tried, with an equal measure of success and failure, to develop family-run operations in a difficult environment. At the local level, territory was divided between agents of unequal power, a situation that could not proceed without shocks and violence.

Old Amazonia, however, has not disappeared, and today the two networks–the old river network upon which is superimposed the new road network–co-exist. This double stitching constitutes the principal structure of present-day Amazonia, and the coincidence–or lack of it–between the two systems decides the importance of some places and the decline of others. The large cities are supported by highway service, which brings them at last into direct communication with the South–at the price of a new dependence. If they have the good fortune to be at a contact point of the two networks, certain mid-sized towns have seen their importance reinforced, such as Porto Velho, where the road cuts across the Madeira. Others, such as Santarém and other cities along the banks of the Amazon, have fallen into decline because of their inability to integrate into the new traffic patterns. Still other cities have appeared along the new highways, born in a matter of years from modest villages (such as Imperatriz) or from nothing at all (such as Ji-Paraná): The general inversion of the traffic flow, which now runs south instead of east, destabilizes the assets of location and provokes a significant reclassification.

Between these points, in the mesh traced by the two networks, the interpolated space is itself structured by two forces: One part is planned, programmed, and governed by the state and its specialized agencies; the rest is occupied by a pioneering pressure that is uncontained and multiple. The pioneer thrust of the cattle breeders along the roads (particularly of Belém-Brasília) extends the conquest of the interior. The expansionary pressure of the landless peasants on the frontier also has a long tradition; it is stronger in the Northeast, where there is less available land, than in western Amazonia, where colonization is primarily organized by specialty firms that prefer to settle better-equipped and wealthier farmers from the South. Since the state's actions also affect eastern Amazonia more than western Amazonia, notably due to the weight of the Grand Carajás operation, a marked contrast emerges between these two spaces, which have been unequally transformed and unequally integrated into the new trade circuits. The East, more densely populated and closer to the Northeast, is covered by a denser network of meridian routes, rivers, and roads, while the West has at its disposal only interminable and poorly oriented rivers and a single road, which goes from Cuiabá to Manaus via Porto Velho: The extensions toward Acre and Roraima are still little traveled, and the western part of the Transamazonian, past Itaituba, has practically been abandoned.

To the north of the Amazon and to the west of Purus extends yet a third Amazonia, which is still virtually deserted: A few settlements along the rivers, a couple of clearings inhabited by breeders in the far north, the odd isolated mine, and a handful of military garrisons are all that exists in the immense emptiness of the jungle. The vastest empty space on the map is here, though others can be detected elsewhere: These 5 million square kilometers constitute one of the least densely populated spaces on the planet. However, this loose control is efficient: Amazonia is integrated into Brazil; its natural resources are subject to periodic harvesting; immigrants feed into the region; and state administration is present in the form of capital and representatives of the country's largest national and foreign firms. Amazonia is thus returned to the fold and progressively deprived of its aura of mystery and passion.

For more than sixty years, a grassroots economic, political, and cultural movement has helped make the Brazilian archipelago into a true continent. With the fall of the military regime in 1985, a powerful movement of decentralization emerged. Can we expect a return to regionalism, a new autonomy of the regional cultural centers? Or, parallel to the pursuit of a unified market to the benefit of São Paulo, will we witness a cultural homogenization that will cause regional cultures and identities to disappear? The future will tell. According to the evidence of a 500-year history, Brazil carries within itself both the means for unity and the seeds of diversity.

Translation by Wendy J. Eberle

CHAPTER 5

THE SOUTHERN CONE

Sébastien Velut

Nadie ignora que el sur empieza del otro lado de Rivadavia.
Nobody ignores the fact that the South begins on the other side of the Rivadavia.

—Borges 525

The three countries of the Southern Cone (Argentina, Chile, and Uruguay) occupy a privileged position in the literary canon authorized by official literary histories, often heading the list of the places most cited. At the same time, they constitute a "literary desert": the Patagonian end of the earth, emptied of men and hence of men of letters, arouses nevertheless "tempests of the imaginary" (Schneier-Madanes 227).

The Southern Cone's uniqueness can be attributed to certain traits that differentiate it from the rest of Latin America. First of all, the majority of the population is European; here, more so than elsewhere, the indigenous elements have been obliterated, with the goal of creating a virgin space for agricultural colonization. This inverse Europe enjoys a temperate, at times almost Mediterranean, climate, favorable to specific cultures; but the region also offers unique landscapes, such as the seemingly infinite stretch of the Pampas, the cold and windy Cape Horn, the mists and rains of the Valdivian forest, and the arid stretches of Moon Valley and the Atacama Desert. Thus, the familiar environment of Europeans contrasts to the American landscapes. This gap is only one of the ambiguous elements in these national identities.

These national identities were difficult to construct and to accept; as a result, these exiled peoples suffered. References to Europe and, even more, to the United States are counterbalanced by the discovery and affirmation of an American destiny at the heart of regional alliances, such as Mercosur, as well as a growing interest in the Pacific basin. In this dynamic, the position of different cultural centers in the region's bosom is challenged. Relatively young cities, such as Buenos Aires, Montevideo, and Santiago de Chile, have already seen their role modified significantly over the past few centuries. From simple villages in the outer reaches of the Spanish Empire, they became national capitals and enjoyed an enviable position among world metropolises at the beginning of the last century. This was their greatest moment of cultural influence, which today has become significantly weakened: in the current context, these capitals have to redefine their place at the continental and planetary levels and take advantage of certain trump cards, while secondary cities are struggling to find their place.

A Belated Urban Conquest

Despite maritime explorations from the beginning of the sixteenth century, the Southern Cone excited little interest on the part of the Spanish and Portuguese conquerors, who searched for the passage between the Atlantic and the Pacific that Magellan first traversed in 1521 and, especially, for gold and silver. The maritime route would be little utilized, since conditions for navigation were difficult: The Spaniards preferred to reach Lima by crossing the Panama isthmus by land rather than risk circumnavigating the continent. As for gold, the explorers found hardly any. In contrast to the Aztec and Inca empires with their prodigious and opulent cities, in this part of America they encountered only Indians who were few in number, poorly organized, and leading an extremely crude existence.

The Spaniards founded several cities during their first voyages, but without much success. The soldiers who remained behind when Buenos Aires was first founded in 1536 died of hunger and were harassed by hostile populations; in the end, they had to retreat to Asunción. Livestock, however, had been released: cattle and horses left behind at the northern and southern rivers of the Rio de la Plata multiplied amazingly due to the abundance of food and the absence of predators. These animals would subsequently be an important factor for permanent European settlements.

One of the primary concerns of the Spaniards was to equip the territories explored south of Potosí with an urban framework that would facilitate their control over the region. In contrast to the United States, where farmers homesteading on the western plains were a factor in determining the occupation of space, the way that space was structured in the Southern Cone depended, from the beginning, on the cities, which brought together a garrison, authorities representing the viceroy, clergy, and tradespeople. Each of these groups was answerable first to Lima, with relays to Tucuman and Buenos Aires in the eastern part and to Santiago in the west. This is the period when the principal cities were established.

Ever since the initial period of conquest, the Spaniards had to confront the Indians, in particular in the south and in today's Chile, where the Indians (baptized Araucans) resisted them vigorously. These battles inspired Alonso de Ercilla y Zúñiga (1533–1594), a Spanish gentleman who participated in them, to write a great epic poem, *La Araucana*, which provided certain myths that were then integrated into the makeup of the Chilean national identity. Among these myths, the territory and its "crazy geography" (Subercaseaux 325), hold a prominent place.

Chile, fértil provincia y señalada
En la region Antartica famosa,
De remotas naciones repetada
Por fuerte, principal y poderosa:
La gente que produce es tan granada,
Tan soberbia, gallarda y belicosa,
Que no ha sido por rey jamás regida,
Ni a estrangero dominio sometida.
Es Chile norte sur de gran longura
Costa del nuevo mar del sur llamado,
Tendrá del este a oeste de angostura
Cien milla por lo más ancho tomado;
Bajo del polo Antártico en altura
De veinte y siete grados prolongado
Hasta do el Oceano y Chileno

Mezclan sus aguas por angosto seno.
Y estos dos mares que pretenden
Pasando de sus términos juntarse
Baten las rocas, y sus olas tienden;
Mas es les impedido el allegarse:
Por esta parte al fin la tierra hienden,
Y pueden por aquí comunicarse.
Magallanes, señor, fué el primer hombre
Que abriendo este camino le dió nombre.
[. . .]
Digo que norte sur corre la tierra
Y bañala del oeste la marina;
A la banda del este va una sierra
Que el mismo rumbo mil leguas camina.
En medio es donde el punto de la guerra
Por uso y ejercicio mas se afina
Venús y Aman aquí no alcanzan parte,
Solo domina el iracundo Marte.
(ll. 41–56, 65–72)

Chile, my scene; a fertile land remote,
Hard by the border of Antarctic seas,
Home of a stiff-necked people, bred to arms,
Renowned in war, by neighbor nations feared;
Whose hot distempered blood alike rebels
At rule domestic and at stranger yoke.
No king among themselves they own, nor e'er,
Have bowed the knee to foreign conqueror.
Far to the North and South its shores extend
Along the borders of the uncharted main
We call the Southern Sea; from East to West
Scarcely a hundred miles this narrow land
Measures at broadest; and from where the Pole
Stands in the altitude of twenty-seven,
Runs southward to a strait, where Ocean Sea
And Chilean waters blend their meeting tides.
Those mighty seas that on opposing sides,
Beat on the escarpments of the Southern land,
Shaking the Terra Firma with the roll
Of their tempestuous surges, rage in vain,
Eager to meet and mingle, till at length
They fend the land asunder there and rush
Together through the cleft Magellan first
Of Ocean-pilots found and gave his name.
[. . .]
Due North and South the Chilean coastline runs,
Fronting along the West the Southern Main;
Upon the East a range of cloud-capped peaks
Shuts in the plain lands for a thousand leagues;
Midway between the North and South is where
Our scene of war is set; here that fierce tribe
I speak of dwells; mild Venus here no part
Has in men's lives; but Mars alone is lord.

In the cities en route from Buenos Aires to Peru, people made a living from transit and the breeding of mules sold to work in the northern mines. Cities isolated from these commercial routes languished and sometimes disappeared: this was the fate of fifteen of twenty-nine cities founded in the sixteenth century, in today's Argentina. Thus, Argentina and Chile were precociously urban, for even if the Spanish cities long remained dusty villages, they made a living from trade, and from the time of their inception had been given political, military, and religious functions. Though sparsely populated, these centers were essentially urban, and they preserved their initial political functions, eventually becoming Argentine provincial capitals. The occupation of space and regionalization here, therefore, stand in contrast to North America,

where urban foundations were laid following the development of agricultural space.

Furthermore, the urban designs of the conquerors determined the choice of sites: coming for the most part from Peru, they situated their cities inland, like Buenos Aires, which was founded for the second time in 1580 by an expedition coming this time by land, not by sea. In general, they sought to situate cities close to waterways, and this privileged basins and valleys. Today, these sites–such as Santiago de Chile–have serious atmospheric pollution problems. Also, since the Colonial age, some cities have had to be relocated or abandoned altogether because the modest rivers along whose banks they were built were subject to devastating floods. This was the case, for example, with San Juan in Argentina and Osorno in Chile. Finally, the entire Andean sector is seismic, and numerous cities have been destroyed by earthquakes, reconstructed, and sometimes relocated, as was Mendoza after the quake in 1862.

Despite its urban foundations, the Southern Cone remained of marginal significance in the Spanish imperial strategy, which was focused on Lima and Peru. The southern territories of the Andean Piedmont were only extensions of the heart of the Empire and had to serve the mining centers and, above all, Potosí. The lowlands of the South complement the tropical Andean mountains. There, the conquerors found a Mediterranean-like environment similar to that of the Iberian peninsula. The central Chilean valley and the oasis-cities of the Andean Piedmont became subject to a Mediterranean-type agricultural program, which included hydraulic development. The Pampas, however, were neglected since they were located too far from the center of the Empire. For a long time, Buenos Aires remained a big village because there was no question of utilizing the outlet of the Río de la Plata or the Paraná river system for exports: the port monopoly was firmly defended, but this did not prevent the increase in contraband from Buenos Aires (see **Map 1**).

The livestock abandoned in the Pampas multiplied rapidly. During the *vaquerías*, one could hunt, for their leather and fat, cows that had turned wild again. The carcasses, for lack of use, were left to rot. Buenos Aires became the center of this kind of activity and, despite bans, increased its exports to the Portuguese colonies of Brazil. In the seventeenth century, the city became more prominent: The viceregal government, which had established a customs house in Córdoba in 1662, moved it back to the north at the end of the century, recognizing the control over the hinterland by the port of Buenos Aires. The territory–divided among Buenos Aires, the North under the administrative control of Tucuman, and the eastern Piedmont of the Andes up to Chile–was placed under the control of Buenos Aires, which had become the capital of the viceroyalty of La Plata in 1776.

Faced with this consolidation of the Spanish settlements, the Portuguese sought control over the left bank of the Río de la Plata, which they wanted to make into the border between the empires, well beyond the Tordesillas line. The fortress of Colonia do Sacramento, founded in 1680 on a rocky point on the river's northern bank, was conceived with this aim in mind. The counterattack was late in coming: Montevideo was not created until 1736. The inhabitants of Buenos Aires, feebly supported by the Spanish Crown, whose diplomacy often undid what the colonists had obtained by force, sought to resist the Portuguese onslaught. The fortress of Colonia was taken and retaken many times. Montevideo, conceived as a counterweight to the Portuguese

Map 1.

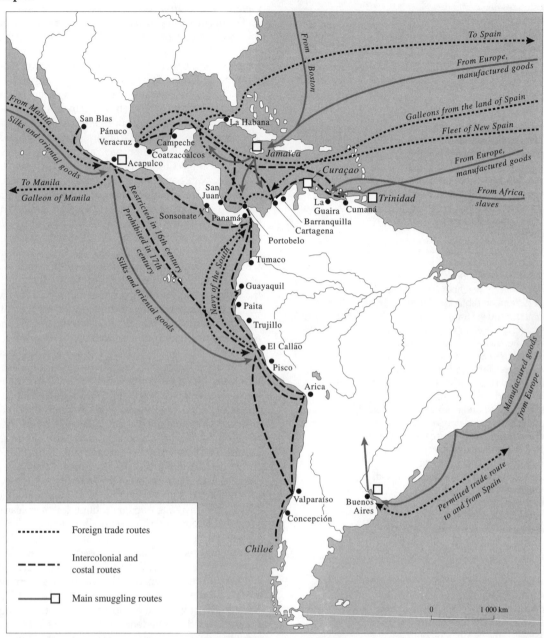

influence, quickly became a strong rival for Buenos Aires, thanks to more favorable port conditions.

Constructing Nations, Dominating Territories

By the end of the colonial period, the pattern of urban settlements north of the Montevideo–Buenos Aires–Santiago line had been set. However, the status of the cities in the future nations had not yet been determined. At the same time, these nations, newly emancipated from Spanish tutelage, had yet to be constituted. If the supremacy of Buenos Aires on the Pampas and that of Santiago in central Chile are accepted as givens, the issue of the autonomy of the interior cities, of their joining together with one capital or another, had to be resolved: Nations had to be invented. Moreover, to invent nations in the nineteenth century also meant to define territories and their boundaries.

The question was posed first for today's Uruguay, whose independence was achieved at the same time as Argentina's. General Artigas was amenable to uniting the Argentinean provinces, but only on the condition that he be given a great deal of autonomy, which the leaders of Buenos Aires were hardly inclined to grant. In 1816, the Portuguese took advantage of this dissension by occupying Uruguay, which was reclaimed in 1825 with the support of Argentina. To put an end to these conflicts, Portugal and Argentina agreed to make the Banda Oriental an independent state, a buffer between the two powers.

In Argentina, the construction of the state was a prolonged and difficult process lasting almost the entire nineteenth century. In these conflicts, the unitarians were opposed to the federalists, and the interior to Buenos Aires. The principal port of the state in gestation, Buenos Aires, was considered by the interior cities to be a threat to their independence and prosperity. In effect, the inhabitants of the port, the *porteños*, advocated free trade, which would step up the export of pampa products but jeopardize the interior's craft industry. They also wished to turn Buenos Aires into the only port for the confederated provinces of the Rio de la Plata. This move would give them a monopoly over customs, the only fiscal resource of any importance.

The fractures that cut across Argentinean society were interpreted at this time by politician and writer Domingo Faustino Sarmiento (1811–1888) as a confrontation between civilization and barbarianism. He saw in Rosas's dictatorship the revenge of the country on the city, of barbarianism on civilization. For him, as for Rosas, it was the country that vested the city; it was the gauchos who seized power and who applied to human individuals, methods used only on livestock. In this context, local caudillos like Facundo Quiroga, who provided the pretext for *Civilización y barbarie*, broke apart in order to attain power, laying waste to the country and preventing all progress of civilization. Thus the revolution of 1810, desired and realized by the cities (which were the depositories of advanced political ideas inspired by Europe), got sidetracked by the eruption of the countryside rebelling against all authority.

In fact, the extremely rough life in the distant lands favored the emergence of a unique character having a particular relation to space: the *gaucho*. The *gaucho* may have been a poor agricultural worker, but he was an excellent horseman who felt demeaned if he had to set foot on the ground, much less cultivate it. He consented only to working with livestock–rounding them up, branding and herding them–in exchange for food, shelter, and a small salary. He was employed only during the working season; then he would scatter. This man of the Pampas knew how to find food, unearth sources of water, or distinguish on the horizon dust raised by a herd from that raised by horsemen. Despising the city, he possessed a remarkable knowledge of the Pampas. For example, it was said that he needed only to taste a few blades of grass to know where he was. Weakly rooted in society, he was recruited by the *caudillos* for their expeditions, and came armed with his knife, his *boleadoras*, and a long spear with a cross blade, which usually served to cut the hocks of livestock. These troops of *montoneras*, though undisciplined, were formidable because of the mobility and endurance of their members–who had nothing to lose.

The involvement of the *gaucho* in political life after independence was brutal but short-lived, for the young republics quickly brought undisciplined citizens into line by sending them to fight against the Indians while the social structures rigidified. The *gaucho* remained, however, an agricultural worker, and literature exalted this rebel character, freely traveling the vast expanses of the new world. He was made into a paragon of pastoral virtues and provided an inexhaustible source of inspiration. This social type became a national myth in José Hernandez's (1834–1886) *Martín Fierro*, a poem about Argentinean identity.

Ah tiempos! . . . (Si era un orgullo
Ver jinetear un paisano!
Cuando era gaucho baquiano,
Anunque el potro se boliase,
No había uno que no parase
con el cabresto en la mano.
Y mientras domaban unos,
Otros al campo salían,
Y la hacienda recogían

Las manadas reuntaban
Y así sin sentir pasaban
entretenidos el día.
(ll. 181-92)

Ah times agone! To see them ride
Was a goodly sight and grand;
There was wilder horse-flesh then than now,
And the men were hardier too, I trow,
For never a breaker but got him down,
With the halter in his hand.
And while some bridled the 'pampa' colts,
And drilled them to the knee and rein,
The rangers went off in twos and threes,
Their ponchos aflap in the morning breeze,
To part the cattle and round the herds
Afar on the grassy plain.

Between Chile and Argentina, the Andes provided less a boundary than an object of contention about the borderline, as were the vast spaces of Patagonia, again occupied only by Indians. The new nations collided with the hostile and combative people of the South: In Argentina, the southern Pampas long remained unsubjugated. In Chile, the Bio-Bio River separated the European colonies from the Mapuche Indians, who resisted European pressure for a long time, just as they had formerly resisted the designs of the imperial Incas.

For the young nations, the conquest of the South in the 1870s was also a race to the frontier. The Andes, which today separate the two countries, were a natural barrier, and the Mapuches occupied both slopes. Only in 1881 did a treaty fix in principle the border between the two states along the dividing line of the waters. This precise line is now the subject of discussion. In Chile, the southern provinces could be reached only by sea or by going through Argentina because the Chilean territories are blocked by glaciers.

The Argentineans, as well, sought to control the south of the Pampas and Patagonia. These empty spaces have remained outside their dominion and can still tempt adventurers like Antoine Tounens, a solicitor from Périgueux who once proclaimed himself king of Araucania. They also served as a refuge for the Indian tribes which menaced the colonial settlements and were pushed to the south. Having become excellent horsemen, the Indians indulged in sudden attacks, pillaging and destroying the European settlements. In an effort to protect the settlements, a trench was dug over several hundred kilometers, which limited these Indian expeditions and also prevented the flight of the livestock. But, starting in 1879, Argentina carried out a veritable war against the Indian populations, who, faced with an army equipped with firearms, were quickly exterminated or pushed back to beyond the Rio Neuquén. This strategy opened up new spaces for agricultural colonization. It is an episode known as the war of the desert, a desert that barely was . . . .

The progressive domination of national space thus corresponded to the expansion of control by the capital and its elites over these new lands. In effect, besides political power, the conquest was the occasion to measure, subdivide, and allocate lands for development. The great families benefited from this division, and they obtained immense properties in the new territories, which they administered from Buenos Aires or neglected altogether while they waited for the value to increase (Gaignard 253–66). From the last third of the nineteenth century on, Argentina received an increasing influx of immigrants, attracted by the nascent prosperity. Their arrival en masse drastically changed the country.

A European Destiny?

The social classes that achieved power in Argentina came up against the same problem that the social classes in Uruguay had: These vast, agriculture-based countries were empty. The sparse population had been noted by many publicists at the time of the political battles in the middle of the century as a serious weakness for a country that had yet to be created. On this point, Sarmiento and his adversary, the lawyer Alberdi, were in agreement: only an influx of people, specifically of European people, as had benefited the United States, would permit the economy to take off. This is a program that Alberdi summed up in a famous formula: "to govern is to people."

Thus it became advisable to attract immigrants who could bring labor and technical knowledge to South America. This project also sought to modify the racial composition of the population. The *mestizos* were reputed to be lazy and incapable of working and did not seem likely to incarnate the modernization project of the leading elites. This project, inscribed in Argentina's constitution (1853–1861), began to be realized in the second half of the century. As in Uruguay, the possibility of owning land was offered to families who wanted to settle in Argentina. The two countries engaged in propaganda in those European regions from which they wished to attract inhabitants, sending their representatives to recruit candidates for immigration. They put laws in place to facilitate the arrival and work placement of newcomers. They would lodge newly arrived workers for a few days in a hotel for immigrants and help them find jobs that, in most cases, did not correspond to the promises that had attracted them in the first place. Sometimes, the welcoming country even advanced the cost of the trip, which immigrants then had to pay back within two years of their arrival. This costly system did not last, but the price of the voyage did remain low, thus permitting the seasonal immigration of unemployed agricultural workers from the Northern Hemisphere who would come to work in the Southern Cone at harvest time.

This active policy attracted an increasing flow of immigrants to the Rio de la Plata region between 1860 and 1890. It was then reduced by the economic crisis, but picked up again starting in the middle of the 1890s. It culminated with the *belle époque* at the end of the nineteenth century but was interrupted by the First World War, which saw a number of expatriates returning to their countries of origin. Immigration picked up again in the 1920s, but never reached the same levels as before the war (Bourdé 158–64).

In Argentina, the Italians made the voyage in the greatest numbers: Between 1860 and 1940, more than 2 million of the 6 million immigrants debarking in Buenos Aires were Italian–first, farmers from the northern provinces and, after 1890, the poor people of the Mezzogiorno. A similar phenomenon occurred with the Spanish, the second largest national group. First, the Basques and Galicians arrived and were followed by an increasing proportion of landless countrymen. The number of Spanish arrivals peaked around 1900, almost equaling the Italians. People of other nationalities were less numerous: The English, French, Belgians, and Germans immigrated in limited numbers, but in contrast to the Mediterranean immigrants, often either they were qualified workers having some capital or they were sent to Argentina by a company in their country of origin. Finally, in the twentieth century, a third group of immigrants appeared whom the Argentineans called Russian but who were for the most part Poles and Ukrainians, often Jews searching for an asylum from the growing anti-Semitism and pogroms in their countries of origin.

Uruguayan immigration differed from Argentinean in several respects. Except for the war years in Argentina, Uruguayan immigration was always lower, the migration balance reaching 24,000 in 1912. The national composition of immigrants was also different. There were many Italians, but the Basques, as much French as they were Spanish, also formed an important group, just as did the Brazilians from the large neighbor to the north (Kleinpenning 213–60).

In this region, and especially in Argentina, immigration did not fulfill the goals of its initiators: Not all the migrants were farmers, and even if they had been, they could not have found land to own in their adopted country. The stretches conquered after the war of the desert had been distributed to representatives of the oligarchy. Without being truly developed, the country was nonetheless divided up and possessed. The only possibility left to an immigrant was to become an agricultural worker, a farmer or sharecropper on other people's land–a lot hardly more enviable than the one they left behind, even if they were paid relatively elevated salaries for the first time. More often, they stayed in the city and little by little swelled the common urban classes. Arriving in ports, they often stayed there and found employment in the service of the leading classes or in the export of agricultural products.

In the same period, Chile did not experience an equally significant immigration. Certain Chilean politicians favored immigration, but their projects did not succeed because they feared the formation of autonomous population cores that would dilute the national identity. Colonies did exist in the south, where the Germans, in particular, settled; the national population, however, remained primarily *mestizo*. In total, Chile accepted far fewer immigrants than did Uruguay, where the national population was much smaller. At the beginning of the century, they accounted for approximately 130,000 people, among whom Peruvian and Bolivian neighbors were the most numerous. The Europeans came later, with Italians and Spaniards in equal number, followed by the Germans. This low inflow was both because Chile was not as attractive for the Europeans as Argentina and because the country did not want to attract too many immigrants. Economic development remained inferior to that in Argentina, and the availability of agricultural land was limited because such land was the property of large landowners. Free spaces lay primarily toward the south, but developing them proved difficult. Also, at that moment, Chile was rather a country of emigration, and remained so until quite recently. Its nationals found employment on the other side of the Andes: in Argentinean Patagonia.

Argentina experienced its strongest economic and demographic growth with the development of frozen meat export at the beginning of the twentieth century. The perfecting of this technique permitted pampa products to reach European markets and marked the beginning of a period of great prosperity. This export activity tended to consolidate the big cities where the livestock were gathered, slaughtered, and packaged for export in vast refrigeration units generally situated near ports. More so than agriculture, it was these industries that attracted workers, and this export activity structured national society and the territory itself.

The construction of national railroad networks strengthened the preeminence of the national capitals because the railroads organized a fan structure outward from these cities. They permitted the development of agricultural production, in particular of cereal grains and wool, but marked the ruin of small craft activities in the interior, which could not compete with the industrial products imported from Europe. The progressive expansion of the rail network also led to considerable land speculation because the property traversed increased in value. Knowing the plans for the rail line permitted one to make profits by buying and then reselling the lands concerned, sometimes sight unseen; as a result, rural land became a plaything of speculation for the most wealthy members of the bourgeoisie, who spent their profits more freely on sumptuous urban homes, luxury import items, and trips to Europe than on productive activities. While the bourgeoisie was primarily interested in cattle breeding, industrial activities in general relied on foreign capital.

Thus the great economic expansion that the countries of the La Plata region experienced at the beginning of the twentieth century, thanks to the export of their agricultural products, brought about a differentiated urban development. This development was urban because the possibility of actually owning land was limited for immigrants, who instead found employment in the city. This growth favored the cities located at the interface between the producers in the Pampas and the gateways to the global market: Montevideo, Rosario, and especially Buenos Aires, which became one of the great metropolises in the world.

Capital of a republic in full expansion, Buenos Aires aspired to being the Paris of the Southern Hemisphere. It was far from being the modest colony established by Juan de Garay or even that big village of the colonial age. Buenos Aires of the *belle époque* gave itself Parisian airs, courting Baron Haussmann's collaborators to design monuments, avenues, and parks: The Garden of Palermo is presented as a sort of Bois de Boulogne, the hippodrome as a rival for Longchamp, and the buildings in the center affected a Haussmannian elegance with additional embellishments. Considerably enriched, the port oligarchy liked to follow the latest Parisian fashions, to speak French, and, if possible, to spend part of the year in Paris. France thus set the tone for the fashion and culture, while England served as the model for agrarian and industrial improvements. Artists such as Marguerite Moreno, politicians such as Georges Clemenceau and Jean Jaurès, and writers such as Anatole France were received and fêted. Even the director of the national library, Paul Groussac, was French. However, certain people wondered to what extent this fascination with Europe was not a simple veneer, an element of the country's double-faced identity: "The external structure, amplitude, and appearances of its fast-paced and heroic life make of Buenos Aires a cosmopolitan, wealthy, world-class city with a great future. But from its inside, in its blood and style, it looks more like any other forgotten town like La Rioja, San Juan or San Luis, Catamarca or Jujuy, than a European or North American city of similar stature: Buenos Aires is the federal capital of the Republic of Argentina" (Martinez Estrada 195).

Along with these Francophile and Anglophile elites, the cities of this region attracted relatively recent immigrants who made their own mark on the national culture. The different nationalities settled in their own neighborhoods (like the Italians in La Boca, in the south of Buenos Aires) and gathered in their own clubs. Their national traits were preserved, even cultivated, and made rich contributions to the culture of the welcoming countries: In Argentina, for instance, the Spanish language was blended with Italian expressions. These cities cultivated a European culture (of variable influences), so that for the longest time, in Buenos Aires, one could publish in Spanish but also in Italian, French, and English. The provincial capitals reproduced this port model with their Spanish society and Italian clubs presided over by successful immigrants. In addition to helping newcomers, these associations were the impetus for the diversification of urban societies that formed the uniqueness of Argentinean national identity.

The Capital Question

Making Argentina a federal state led to the question of which city would be the capital. In the majority of federal states, the capital is not the major city, but in Argentina, Buenos Aires is concurrently the capital, the economic metropolis, and the largest urban center. The concentration of so much power has been of some concern ever since the nineteenth century. National unity was achieved without Buenos Aires; there was a fear that making it the capital would renew its hegemony over the federated provinces. More recently, at the end of the 1980s, president Raúl Alfonsín launched an ambitious project to relocate the capital to the south with the aim of strengthening decentralization.

The various projects (all unsuccessful) to relocate the capital all originated in an acknowledgment of failure: Buenos Aires, for one reason or another, was judged incapable of playing the role that the country expected of it. It was accused, for example, of smothering economic development by concentrating it in a metropolitan space; of favoring a policy of closed circles of initiates and functionaries cut off from the realities of the country, to the detriment of federalism and democracy; or, again, of turning toward Europe or the United States rather than formulating and serving national values. All these critiques show that the social malaise was diagnosed as a spatial problem to be treated with a spatial therapy: Relocating the capital was the means to heal the country of its current ills.

This is the case with Sarmiento, who in 1850 publicized "Argirópolis" at the very moment when the country had fallen victim to interior conflicts regarding the constitution. Sarmiento had a political project: the creation of a United States of South America by regrouping the Hispanic countries of the La Plata basin served by the great rivers, which could bring progress and prosperity. This political program rested on a spatial archway: the establishment of the capital of the federation, baptized Argirópolis (the city of silver), on the island of Martín García, the rocky point at the mouth of the Paraná. This new city, through which much river commerce could pass, would become a prosperous and industrial metropolis over which grand administrative buildings would tower, perpetuating in granite the glory of the new nation.

Sarmiento's project did not succeed, and after a brief period on the Paraná, Buenos Aires has been the capital since the province was rallied to federation. Buenos Aires at first became a provisional capital: another site would be chosen. The same Sarmiento, who had become president, used his veto against many legislative projects that foresaw the capital's relocation to different cities in the interior, arguing that it was not necessary to "distance the administration of public affairs from the most eminent men" and that the state could not finance the construction of a new capital (presidential message of 27 September 1871). Finally, in 1880, the city of Buenos Aires was ceded by the province to become the federal capital, and fifty kilometers away, a new city of La Plata, which would become the provincial capital, was founded.

One century later, the weight Buenos Aires carried led President Raúl Alfonsín to propose relocating the capital to the south. He wished to make a showpiece of political decentralization and to strengthen democracy. In contrast to Sarmiento, however, who proposed to anchor his capital on the river, Alfonsín wanted to project his capital toward Patagonia by establishing it at the southern border of the province of Buenos Aires. Thus, this project responded to a geostrategic design: the will to occupy the sparsely populated lands in the south. For precisely these reasons, Brazil had constructed Brasília on the Amazonian route. Although the Argentineans quickly abandoned this ambitious project, it did demonstrate that the weight of Buenos Aires and its role in the nation still created an eminently political problem. One can see as well that preserving the capital in its site excited little enthusiasm, and to detractors of transfer projects it appeared only as the least evil. However, as it stands, one may well wonder whether the existence of Buenos Aires is not, for the country, a stroke of good luck rather than a handicap.

The Time of Doubts

The prosperity of the *belle époque* was a fragile one: It relied on the export of agricultural products from the countries of La Plata and of nitrates and, later, leather from Chile. The fluctuations in global demand and prices were a constant threat. In Argentina, this fragility was offset in part by the emergence and consolidation of national industry which, without becoming exports, nevertheless allowed imports to be curtailed. At the same time, petroleum discovered in Patagonia triggered the populating of the area. The twentieth century, however, was also a time of doubts and difficulties, which translated spatially into the concentration of the population in cities, especially in national and provincial capitals.

The model of agro-export development weakened little by little, starting with the First World War, because the expansion of cultivated lands had reached its ecological limit. To increase production, it would be necessary to intensify cultivation, which presupposed investments and changes in methods, which the owners were not prepared to undertake. The growth in population, however, also meant an increase in internal demand, which limited export possibilities even more. In this context, the decision was made to give priority to supplying urban markets at low prices, which allowed city dwellers to feed themselves at the least cost: Agriculture subsidized the city one more time. This decision permitted the progressive development of national industry, which made Argentina (along with Brazil and Mexico) one of the three industrialized countries of Latin America. Offering jobs, industry attracted people: Buenos Aires, Rosario, Córdoba, and, to a lesser degree, Mendoza benefited from this new dynamic. At the same time, poorly competitive regions of production, notably in the northwest, experienced a marked decline.

In Chile, the dependence of the economy on leather exports, of which the country held considerable reserves, hindered industrial development. Despite a voluntary policy of industrialization, the results were limited, and annual payments from mining were divided between foreign countries exploiting the deposits (until nationalization in 1972) and the state. These funds financed the public sector, starting with the

army, rather than promoting a policy of development. Thus, they contributed to the concentration of the population in cities and not to the development of peripheral regions.

In Uruguay, there were few attempts to free the country from dependency on agricultural exports. It is true that, faced with neighbors as economically and politically powerful as Argentina and Brazil, it was difficult to see into which slot any national industry could fit. However, the great stretch of lands on which cultivation and breeding were practiced allowed the country to slow the decline that appeared inevitable. Elsewhere, many Uruguayans chose to emigrate to Argentina, where their settlement was facilitated by the proximity of the cultures and where possibilities of employment were many.

Despite the regional inequalities, the countries of the Southern Cone could boast of a well-structured welfare state, financed by exports and particularly well developed in Argentina. They had rates of elimination of illiteracy and increase in life expectancy equal to those in developed countries. In addition, the universities were subsidized and enjoyed an excellent international reputation. This high-quality social structure facilitated the regrouping of people in urban centers and helped attract a growing population who sought to benefit from these advantages. This schema was reproduced in other countries and succeeded in organizing space in a specific manner. However, the rapid growth of cities and especially of the capitals entailed new problems for urban populations: Housing was insufficient, the distances traveled every day increased, and shantytowns spread. National capitals were turned into gigantic urban organisms concentrating more than a third of the national population. The secondary cities, which benefited from this influx of people, remained far behind (see **Table 1** and **Map 2**).

The urban misery symbolized by the shantytowns is but one element in a more general crisis into which the countries of the Southern Cone were plunged starting in the 1970s. The reduction in export receipts and the difficulties of protected and hence poorly competitive national industries reduced the revenues to be distributed to the people. The attempt to make a change in policy toward the left threatened national oligarchies and foreign interests and crystallized the opposition between social groups. Allende's presidency in Chile and the terrorist actions in Argentina and Uruguay led to extremely violent military dictatorships. During these terrible years, all cultural life (which had become suspect) was suffocated and many intellectuals were forced into exile: The cultural capitals of the Southern Cone moved to New York, Paris, Madrid, and Mexico City. Shunned by nations concerned with human rights, these countries today have rediscovered democracy and liberalism.

The principal element in the current dynamic is the progressive constitution of Mercosur, which initially economically reunited Brazil, Uruguay, Paraguay, and Argentina, and with which Chile is associated. Although at first the issue was to establish a large market, this union has drastically changed the ensemble's viewpoints on the territories of the Southern Cone. In effect, it led the member countries to consider one another as partners rather than as adversaries. Moreover, by uniting Brazil with the countries of the south, Mercosur led these nations to contemplate directly a Latin American destiny, whereas since the nineteenth century, they have lived with their eyes turned toward Europe. The businessmen of the member countries have already rediscovered their common Latin origins by speaking a new lingua franca formed from Spanish and Portuguese. With a view to integration, the metropolises are seeking to play a new role, while

Table 1. *The Urban Megalapolises*

	Argentina	Chile	Uruguay
Population as of last census (thousands)	32,615	13,348	3,163
Rate of urbanization	83 percent	87 percent	87 percent
Population in the capital	11,255	5,074	1,300
Percentage of total population in the capital	34 percent	38 percent	57 percent
Secondary city	Córdoba	Valparaiso	Salto
Population of the secondary city (thousands)	1,200	793	93

Sources: National censuses of Argentina (1991), Chile (1992), Uruguay (1994)

Map 2.

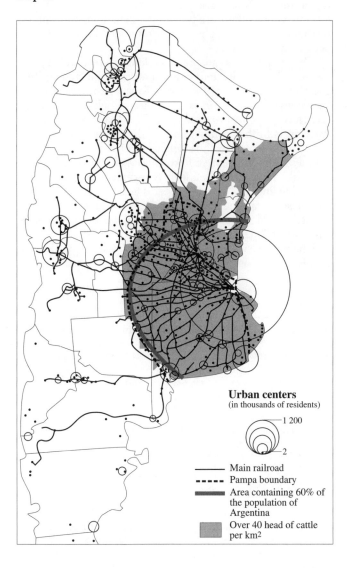

Urban centers
(in thousands of residents)

1 200

2

— Main railroad
- - - - Pampa boundary
Area containing 60% of the population of Argentina
Over 40 head of cattle per km2

becoming points of passage indebted to the interior of the new ensemble. The secondary cities, however, are looking to open up new possibilities by organizing themselves with their principal partners; this has allowed them to reduce political and administrative centralization and thus, dominance by a few very large cities. The question then is which of these two tendencies will carry the day: the increased concentration of activities and people in urban centers of more than 10 million inhabitants (São Paulo, Rio de Janeiro, Buenos Aires-Montevideo and, on a smaller scale, Santiago-Valparaiso) or the affirmation of secondary urban concentrations capable of finding a second wind and contributing to the re-establishment of equilibrium in the national territories.

Translation by Wendy J. Eberle

Works Cited

Borges, Jorge Luis. 1974. "El Sur." *Obras completas.* Vol. I. Buenos Aires: Emecé. 524–29.

Bourdé, Guy. 1974. *Urbanisation et immigration en Amérique latine.* Buenos Aires, Paris: Aubier.

Ercilla y Zúñiga, Alonso de. 1910–1918. *La Araucana.* Ed. José Toribio Medina. Vol 1. Santiago de Chile: Imprenta Elzeviriana.

Ercilla y Zúñiga, Alonso de. 1945. *La Araucana.* Trans. Walter Owen. Buenos Aires: S.A. Lamb.

Gaignard, Romain. 1989. *La Pampa argentina.* Trans. Ricardo Figueira. Buenos Aires: Solar.

Hernández, José. 1924. *Martín Fierro.* Buenos Aires: J. Roldán.

Hernández, José. 1936. *The Gaucho Martín Fierro.* Trans. Walter Owen. New York: Farrar & Rinhart.

Kleinpenning, Jan M. G. 1995. *Peopling the Purple Land: A Historical Geography of Rural Uruguay, 1500–1915.* Amsterdam: Cedla.

Martinez Estrada, Ezequiel. 1991. *Radiografía de la Pampa.* Buenos Aires: Editions Losada.

Sarmiento, Domingo Faustino. 1977. *Facundo: O, civilización y barbarie.* Ed. Nora Dottori and Silvia Zanetti. Introd. Noé Jitrik. Caracas: Biblioteca Ayacucho.

Schneier-Madanes, Graciela. 1996. *Patagonie: Une tempête d'imaginaire.* Paris: Editions Autrement.

Subercaseaux, Benjamin. 1942. *Chile o una loca geografía.* Santiago: Ercilla.

CHAPTER 6

THE AMAZON:
THE FORGOTTEN HEART

Emmanuel Lézy

Between the tenth degree north and south latitudes on the maps of South American literary production lies a vast zone of emptiness. "Amazon, that is to say, nowhere"–Alfred Jarry's phrase is applicable to this space, if only to lament the region's absence of writers. The term "the Amazon" exceeds not only the Brazilian definition of "the legal Amazon" but also, strictly speaking, the Amazon river basin (4.5 million square kilometers): It covers the entire rainforest massif (almost 7.6 million square kilometers) and integrates the Guyanese plateau. The region is both natural, being defined by the river and forest, and cultural, for its name refers also to its legendary inhabitants.

Although the Amazon's most notable characteristic is emptiness–of both inhabitants and authors–it is also considered to be a reservoir of the most tenacious Latin American myths and the most common literary clichés. The Amazons, the man-dog, and various acephalous creatures, grouped around the central myth of El Dorado, present mythic densities far surpassing human population densities and give the region a reputation as either an Eden or a "green hell." But is myth a substitute for writing? Is the scarcity of writers in this region–certainly the most vast and the most central on the continent–due to danger, to necessity? The issue is twofold: on the one hand, how to explain the literary muteness; on the other, how to justify the abundance of legends. Did the expanse (the objective, quantifiable characteristics of this region, such as surface area, vegetation or population density) or the space (the product of its organization founded on internal parceling and outward development) produce this wealth of myths while preventing literary production?

The Characteristics of the Amazonian Expanse: At the Origin of the Literary Vacuity

The Amazon opposes all attempts at penetration by writing, be it scientific or literary. This happens not only by default, for the poor population figures do, of course, handicap literary production, but also by excess: Certain of the physical and cultural traits constitute a favorable compost for growing myths.

A Human Emptiness

Population figures are important only in so far as they provide a way to order according to size. The Amazon constitutes a hole in the South American population that is obvious when one looks at both the absolute figure–almost 20 million inhabitants (Brazil has 6 million in the North and 8 million in the West Central region; Guyana has 1.3 million; the other countries have approximately 4 million)–and the population density (4 inhabitants per square kilometer in the West Central region; 1.6 per square kilometer in the North; less than 3 per square kilometer in Guyana). These figures mask a huge disequilibrium between the few populated littoral and fluvial zones (littoral Guyana, which contains 90 percent of the population, has a density of 193 inhabitants per square kilometer)

and the absolutely empty interior (with a density of 0.01 inhabitant per square kilometer). The population schema thus would have set an empty center against a more populated periphery, had the Amazon not disturbed it by creating a region that is more densely populated in the center. In general terms, then, there are two zones of emptiness surrounded by slightly more populated areas (from one to ten inhabitants per square kilometer).

The peripheral population is no longer a real unifying factor, since it is divided into nine countries (ten including Paraguay) and no fewer than five languages: Spanish and Portuguese for the main part, but also English, Dutch, and French on the Guyanese seaboard. The "Babelization" of the Amazon is further complicated by the presence of three or four Creole languages, the languages of the Asian diaspora (Chinese, Hindi, Javanese from Indonesia, Laotian, Hmong, etc.), and approximately fifteen Amerindian languages. This incredible linguistic profusion seems to be organized in a circular fashion around each zone: European languages on the coasts; Creole and diasporic languages on the peripheries; Amerindian languages in the interior.

Finally, the levels of development and wealth (see **Table 1**) are also indications of the diversity and the division.

Table 1.

France	22,464	Peru	4,680
French Guiana	600	Ecuador	4,940
Brazil	6,480	Bolivia	2,880
Venezuela	8,860	Suriname	7,922
Colombia	6,810	Guyana	3,210

GNP per capita in U.S. dollars.

Source: (United Nations, cited in *L'état du monde 2000.*) Censuses consulted are for 1990, except France (1997); Bolivia (1992); French Guiana, Peru, and Colombia (1993); and Suriname (1998).

The low Amerindian population, at less than a million people, does not provide a cultural substrate for literary culture. Apart from the political fracturing and the numerical weakness, there is hardly any linguistic or ethnic unity among aboriginal peoples. The most ancient traces of human settlement in the Amazon come from pottery dating from the tenth century BCE on the island of Marajo, at the mouth of the Amazon. Today, the linguistic panorama is dominated by three large groups: the Tupí, the Carib, and the Arawak. To these are added several, locally important groups (such as the Yanomami) and an entire ensemble of languages considered as "isolated" or "unclassified." These cultures are all oral and did not employ writing before the arrival of the Europeans.

56

One Forest, Two Rivers

The population may not lend itself very well to a literary investigation of any consequence, but the power and originality of the natural environment are primarily responsible for the production and rooting of myths.

The Amazon Rainforest: Heart or Lung?

The Amazon rainforest forms part of the great tropical rainforest that covers 4 percent of the planet (935 million hectares). It constitutes, if not the life-giving "lung," then at least the "memory" of the earth, since an estimated 50 percent of the planet's species of plants and animals is found here. Although certain species lose their foliage during the dry season, the humid, tropical rainforest is always green and has no seasonal deciduous changes. Despite the apparent chromatic uniformity, however, the shades of green are infinite and are made more subtle by the extreme variation in the distribution of light. There is a simplicity of foliage forms, but the environment has an incredible richness of flora and fauna: more than 60,000 varieties of plants, 2.5 million species of arthropods, 2000 kinds of fish, 1000 species of birds, and 300 of mammals. There are between 3000 and 5000 species of trees (from 50 to 100 per hectare). This floral diversity, to the despair of foresters (some of whom dreamt in 1975 of planting French Guiana with single resinous monophyletic crops for paper pulp), is a survival mechanism for avoiding the propagation of diseases.

From the moment one sets off in a canoe, the forest is disconcerting. On firm land, it is even worse. The images, the sounds, and the odors are no longer identifiable; the horizon is blocked by the verticality of tree trunks and invisible in the poor light. With its monochromatic impact, the triumph of the vertical line over the horizontal, and the scarcity of homogenous spatial unities, the Amazon rainforest suggests to some observers no landscape at all, no essential reference point for the occidental voyager or the geographer. It is extremely difficult, on entering such a universe, to identify its structure. Lost, the neophyte oscillates between impressions of extreme simplicity, massiveness, uniformity, and permanence and the discouraging sensation of an irreducible complexity. Certain legends concerning the tropical rainforest, despite their erroneous character, form an integral part of a cultural forest patrimony and have often played as large a role in its preservation or its exploitation as rational knowledge itself, for they directly address human fears and fantasies and not reason.

One legend about the forest has to do with its power. The luxuriance of the vegetation and the vigor of regeneration have, for a long time, given the impression that the forest soils are incredibly fertile and inexhaustible where, in fact, they are often depleted in minerals and poor in organic matter. The forest as a whole is supported by organic matter created by the rotting of its own leaves; this mechanism of autocatalysis makes it a totally closed system. Also, there is a weak layer of soil held in place by the trees' surface roots. Once those trees are uprooted and the soil has been swept away, the area is turned into a transitional zone, even into an infertile alterity.

Another important fantasy image is that of the virgin forest. As "virgin" or "primary," the forest is charged with incarnating the idea of the origin, of a prelapsarian purity: The forest would be even pre-Adamic. This notion is increasingly controversial. Not only have ecological studies shown that the notion of "primary forest" rests more on fantasy than on observation, but recent studies in ethnology insist on the importance of bio-cultural interactions between humans and their environment, even where it is thought that the Amerindians, few and far between, have barely tamed the forest's virginity. In fact, a good part of this forest today appears as little "natural" as a garden or a field of corn, and one speaks more and more of the "domestic," if not the truly cultivated, forest.

A Land Emerging from Waters

The Amazon is a gift of the rivers, primarily of the Amazon River. Its extraordinary power makes it a geographical character of legend, both the giant river and "the sea of gentle water." A fluvial basin of 7 million square kilometers, 6700 kilometers in length, draining into the largest mass of water on the planet, with an output at the mouth averaging 200,000 cubic meters per second—as such, it constitutes one-sixth of the mass of water that all the world's rivers expel into the sea. Less formidable than the Amazon, the Orinoco merits no less its Jules Vernian epithet of "splendid." With more than 2000 tributaries flowing into it, the river drains a territory of 830,000 square kilometers, of which 640,000 square kilometers lie in Venezuelan territory. In the same way that the Amazon is an important crucible of Brazilian geographical identity, the Orinoco is the essential fluvial framework of Venezuela. It extends a distance of approximately 2000 kilometers; in the delta, it reaches an average output of 35,000 cubic meters per second, and up to 100,000 cubic meters per second in spate. Each year, 200 million tons of South American sediment disappear into the sea through its reptilian mouths.

The Amazon brings together three types of currents whose tints vary according to the terrain drained. The clear, blue-green, relatively acidic waters, with low mineral salt content, from right bank tributaries like the Tapajos, the Xingu, and the Araguaia originate in the Cretaceous deposits of the central granite shield. The white waters, laden with limestone, come from the Tertiary sedimentary regions, such as the Peruvian (Putumayo, Napo, Tigre, and Marañon) and Bolivian rivers that form the Rio Madeira. Finally, the black waters of the Rio Negro and its tributaries, saturated with humic acids and poor in mineral salts, are characteristic of Guyana. These waters flow along the gently sloping banks of a forest that is flooded for most of the year. The vegetal debris that falls into the riverbed rots there, consuming oxygen and expelling carbon dioxide gas and humic acids. These rivers poorly fertilize the terrains through which they pass and have few fish. They are known as the "rivers of hunger."

The Amazon's most striking characteristic derives from the *encontras das aguas* (encounters of the waters), which mix into the brown silts of the Solimões what we might call Manichean—absolutely black and white—waters rushing from the foothills of Guyana or the central plateau. It is striking to witness the purity of the waters of the Rio Negro, which, for twenty kilometers from Manaus, refuse to merge with the eroding fertility of the Amazonian *misturação* (mixture). This magnificent and moving spectacle is repeated at the confluences of the Tocantins and the Tapajoz. (See **Figure 1**.)

The Organization of Amazonian Space: The Compost of Legends

The forms of human settlement, their very fragility, present no challenge to the magical charge of this formidable environment. On the contrary, by creating a buffer zone, the Amazonian states have somehow sacralized its inviolability.

Figure 1.

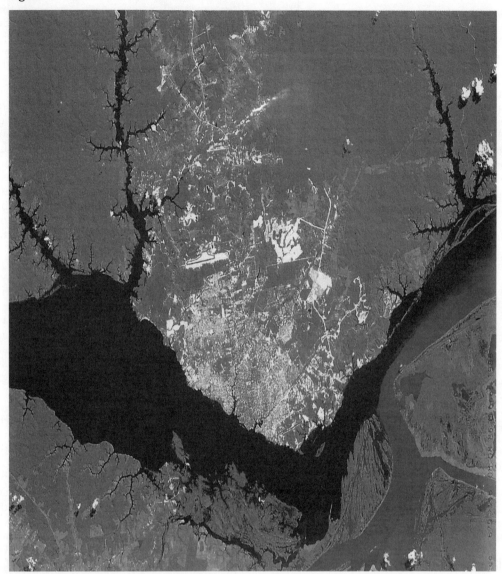

Aerial photograph of the "encounter of the waters" where the Rio Negro merges with the Solimões.

Cultural and Political Division

A Former Political No-man's Land

Since the colonization of South America, the Amazon has occupied a geopolitical dead center between the Spanish encroachment from the north (from Mexico to Chile, passing through Lima, Cuzco, and Bogotá), and the encroachment by the Portuguese, whose aim was to push the Tordesillas meridian westward by taking advantage of the privileged means of penetration that is the Amazon. This is what has permitted the entry of colonies of Northern Europeans, "long breaths and late in coming," to borrow Pierre Chaunu's expression.

The Amazon is a region of great religious diversity. The classic confrontation between Christianity and pre-Columbian spirituality is fragmented here by the schism between Catholics and Protestants: Whereas the former are concerned primarily with populating the region, the latter contributed to maintaining an empty interior. The theological dispute between the Protestant thesis of consubstantiation and the Catholic belief in transubstantiation has a geopolitical dimension. While the Catholics sought to conquer "souls" and to sketch a *fronteira* between the converted peoples and the "savages," the Protestants had their eye on the space itself and sought to draw a *frontier* (borderland) between the colonized and the indigenous lands. Beyond that, perhaps they had a greater respect for Amerindian cultures, as seen in the re-establishment of indigenous toponymy on exploration maps by the English, the Dutch, and the French. And above all, they were deeply infatuated with the legend of El Dorado and "the rich royalty of Guyana" that, after the voyage of Walter Raleigh (1595–1596), invaded the European maps. For non-Iberian countries, the birth of Guyana constitutes a "new good," a veritable colonial gospel: Not only is there gold to be found again on the land but riches to take, and these riches can be captured without pillaging by simply according protection to the invaded peoples. In this way, the soul of the European colonist, soiled by the pillaging of Mexico and Cuzco, will be saved, thanks to the promise of innocence regained that El Dorado represents.

The Common Borders of Latin America

At the beginning of the nineteenth century, the independence of the Iberian colonies consolidated Brazil's power as sole heir to the Portuguese colonies in face of the division of Spanish America, then distant from the Guyanese metropolises. At the beginning of the twentieth century, a coherent and intelligent diplomatic policy, headed by the Baron of Rio Branco, permitted Brazil to extend its Amazonian domain from Acre to Amapá at the expense of the majority of the Andean countries and of French and British Guyana.

The Amazon's political situation is thus paradoxical. On the one hand, Brazilian unity is imposed on the heart of the ensemble, solidly structured around the Amazonian groove. On the other hand, the Amazon, on its periphery, has always played the role of buffer between the different states; and all the South American countries, the Southern Cone excepted, have borders there. In 1976, the region grouped together eight countries around an "Amazonian pact" which, centered in Brazil, encompasses Bolivia, Peru, Ecuador, Colombia, Venezuela, Guyana, and Suriname. These borders are also among the most recent, the most varied in their principles, and the most volatile in terms of how they function (see **Figure 2**). The new land routes follow the same pattern as the older river routes, but the river routes move from West to East while the land routes move from North to South. The increase in size of the land route hubs of Cuíabá and Brasília contrast with the reduction of the river hubs of Manaus and Belém.

The Dependent Hinterlands

The particular position of the Amazon in the totality of the countries concerned, including Brazil, results from this border situation: It is an interior colony, distant, underpopulated, and underdeveloped–a "brow," not a brain, even less a heart. The decisions, the capital, and the culture come from the peripheral centers and make of the Amazon an object of contention, never a subject. The regular attempts to make the Amazon into an international space demonstrate perfectly the region's position of absolute dependency. The only metropolis that is properly Amazonian, Manaus, is perhaps the most foreign: Its status as a free city is the strongest symbol of this difference. From its economy to its culture (e.g., *Téatro Amazonica* is a replica in miniature of Milan's *La Scala*), Manaus's references are foreign. Today, the Brasília-driven exploitation of the Brazilian Amazon tends to surpass the former objective of national integration in favor of a continental dimension encompassing Venezuela and the French Guiana.

The Coherence and Convergence of Myths

A Circle at the Heart of the World

Without a doubt, the Amazon's situation owes more to a religious reading (in the ethnological sense of the term) than to strict geographical analysis. The meeting of the equator with the Tordesillas meridian gives the island of Marajo, at the confluence of the world's most powerful currents of fresh and salty water, a particularly pregnant symbolic position. Horizontally, the line of the equator, which only belatedly was crossed by the Europeans, is not content with inverting the direction of the flow of water in the basins. It disrupts both classical geography and Christian cosmogony. According to Ptolemy, the climate becomes drier in the south, but the existence of this zone of absolute humidity challenged his interpretation of climate. Also, the discovery of the naked and innocent "Indians" posed the problem of their position in

Figure 2. Amazon Basin Transportation Systems

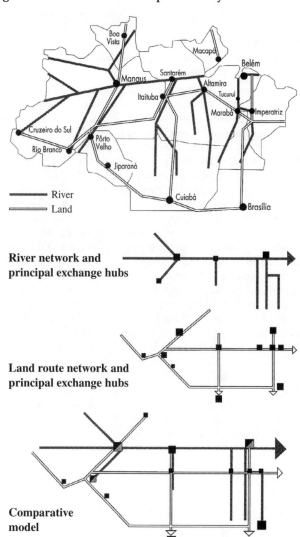

The new land routes follow the same pattern as the older river routes, but the river routes move from west to east while the land routes move from north to south. The increase in size of the land route hubs of Cuiabá and Brasília contrast with the reduction of the river hubs of Manaus and Belém.

relation to original sin: Are they angels, demons, a pre-Adamite humanity, or is it the case that "sin does not exist south of the equator"? Vertically, the Treaty of Tordesillas, since 1494, accounts for what could be the most disruptive appearance in this epoch, which opened "Modern Times" as well as access to "new lands": There is a continent between Europe and Asia. The discovery of the New World demanded the invention of a new world.

Where the vertical and the horizontal cross, at the Cardo and Decumanus of a world in gestation, the water traces a particularly tight circle around the region of the Guianas. These are the Amazon's waters, repulsed by the current of the equatorial east, which lap against the Guianese shores, are incorporated into the "current of the Guianas," and join up again with the Orinoco. The natural canal of Casiquiare also, miraculously, unites the Orinoco with the Amazon. The exceptional situation of an island in the middle of land has fascinated explorers and, up until Humboldt verified its existence in 1800, has made of the Casiquiare a mythical place. A space so strongly defined could only be a magical place, a heart of the world.

The Guyanese Amazonia: At the Convergence of Amerindian Myths and Amerindians

Eden, El Dorado, the Amazons, Canicephales, and Acephales—the Baroque people of the mythical Amazon are situated at the confluence of three major currents. The three great founding myths are Paradise, as described in the Bible and embellished by medieval tradition; the story of El Dorado, in Walter Raleigh's version; and the Indies, described by Marco Polo and the desired destination of Christopher Columbus. Each of these legends has a comparable structure: A unique and circumscribed core is opposed to a plural periphery. The latter is composed of positive elements (which spur progress toward the center) and negative elements (which prevent access).

The encounter of these three myths takes place at the center: The Manoa of El Dorado assumes the attractions of Jerusalem, with the promise of Redemption that it offers. But it is above all through the periphery's legends that there is passage from one myth to another: The presence of headless men can signal the approach of the gates of both Paradise and El Dorado. The most ubiquitous legends are those of the Amazons, signaled in the environs of Marco Polo's Indies, of El Dorado, and integrated finally by the Church in the Middle Ages into the ranks of people cast out from Eden—like the Cannibals, whose very etymology constitutes a point of trijunction of the real Caribs, the Canicephales (the dog-headed men of mythology), and the great Khan's slaves as described by Marco Polo.

As well, the natural formation of Guyana lends itself easily to the center-periphery typology and constitutes an ideal crucible for the fusing of the three myths. Thus, we find the following final schema. The center is occupied by the ideal and inaccessible city, Manoa, strongly impregnated by Christian influences. The immediate periphery is occupied by the forest over which floats a perfume of Eden. Here, there is the wealth, the fertility, the innocence, and the beauty of Eve before the fall, but also the feminine ambiguity and the tempting serpents that justify a certain frightening reading of the myths of the Amazons. Subsequent knowledge of Asia practically made a tabula rasa of the dream of the Indies, without ever ceasing to call the descendants of the cannibals "Indians."

Since its discovery, Guyana has served as a reservoir for American myths originating in other spaces and yielding, bit by bit, to rational exploitation. If this function devolved by default, with all that could not be something else becoming Guyanese, a potential weakness rapidly became an essential characteristic, and Guyana grants to the legends that it has been given a unity, a coherence that would not exist elsewhere. It went so far as to produce its own images, which were quite different from those of the ancient sources of inspiration or of its indigenous neighbors. The process is of importance, for, from that moment, the mythic burden of the Amazon ceases to be a substitute for a population or a "real" exploitation, a kind of bad grass invading the fallow field, and acquires a positive value. The attempts at colonization could never eradicate these myths completely and had to be content with varying the form. It is these enterprises of colonization that will be adapted to the fundamental character of the region.

Translation by Wendy J. Eberle

Works Cited

L'etat du monde 2000. 1999. Paris: La Découverte.

SECTION II
DEMOGRAPHICS AND THE FORMATION
OF CULTURAL CENTERS

CHAPTER 7

DEMOGRAPHY, LANGUAGE,
AND CULTURAL CENTERS

Nicolás Sánchez Albornoz

Literature does not require human agglomerations to flourish. The *Iliad* and parts of the Old Testament in the Bible are masterpieces produced in simple, scattered societies. The preceding chapters, however, have placed particular emphasis on the emergence of cities in the formation of cultural forums, and with good reason. All cultural activity involves senders and receivers, creators and consumers, and the more numerous and closer to each other they are, as happens in an urban environment, the more lively their transactions will be and the more homogeneous what they share will be. So, although in principle demography does not determine literary production, a greater demographic density favors exchanges. The characteristics of language in which it is expressed are also significant. Thus, having accepted the existence of a link between population and cultural activity, including literature and language, this chapter will review the demographic transformations of the past five hundred years, particularly those of the twentieth century, that have affected the languages and urbanization of Latin America.

Demography and Language
Words serve as the primary instrument of communication in literature. These, in turn, are grouped into languages, and have recourse to various forms of support. Languages are dependent on their speakers, whose numbers rise or fall as a result of demographic trends, and on the acceptance or rejection of their use. The past five hundred years have seen the drastic reduction of the multitude of languages native to Latin America to the benefit of two languages from outside the continent that, over the years, have far outstripped the others as regards both cultured and popular speech and writing. Spanish and Portuguese have now been firmly established as the dominant languages of today, whereas autochthonous languages have been steadily declining, in some cases becoming extinct. After several centuries, the decline of autochthonous languages has largely ended, and in some cases these communities have fully recovered. Although this is due to several factors, the demographic element constitutes the major focus of this particular study.

When Columbus set foot in America, tens of millions of Indians spoke hundreds of languages that were not always interrelated. Linguistic maps show the areas where each of these prevailed at the time. At this stage, languages, cultures, and societies corresponded exactly. Conversely, we know nothing of the linguistic component of the previous changes of horizon revealed by archaeology. What we do know of the past of these languages lacks depth. On the eve of the Europeans' arrival, some of these languages were beginning to eclipse neighboring languages, and there is evidence that these societies possessed a lively oral culture, which was rarely recorded in written form. Their dynamism was cut short in the sixteenth century by the invasion of men speaking other tongues. In comparison with the tens of millions of Indians, the handful of invaders was for many years no more than a small minority, which, nonetheless, was capable of causing social and cultural upheaval throughout the continent. These profound alterations included demographic changes.

Within a few decades, the tens of millions of Indians were reduced to a few million. Historians have discussed the scope and the reasons behind this catastrophe for years. However large the estimated size of the pre-Columbian population, at its nadir, which has been reasonably well documented, it was extremely small. Its smallness would seem to reflect a fairly sharp and undoubtedly violent fall from its starting point. Thus, for example, the hundreds of thousands or millions of natives believed to have lived on Hispaniola before European contact had been reduced to a mere handful by the time of the first census in 1775, becoming extinct before the end of the eighteenth century. The 25 million generously attributed to Central Mexico fell to less than a million in the early seventeenth-century surveys, and the nine million Andeans were reduced to just over half a million. Similar reductions were recorded in the rest of Latin America. The testimony of contemporary inhabitants confirms this impression of the decimation of the population.

Such a decline, on a scale unparalleled throughout history, cannot be the result only of the violence attributed to the conquerors. Deaths and insanity undoubtedly abounded, particularly at the outset, although the dissemination of pathogens that crept in from Europe and Africa is increasingly accepted as the main cause of depopulation. Just as certain herbaceous species and animals, whether domestic or otherwise, found America an ideal place to reproduce, in many cases displacing the indigenous flora and fauna, so the germs from the Old World discovered defenseless hosts here and clung to the ill-fated organisms until they destroyed them. Diseases that were no longer fatal in Europe recovered their virulence among the Indians, who lacked immunity. Whenever an outbreak of smallpox, chickenpox, influenza, or the plague crossed the ocean, it became free of the constraints that had contained it overseas and claimed tens of thousands of lives. These outbreaks were repeated in the New World with varying degrees of intensity and dissemination according to the climatic zone. Some became pandemic and were propagated not only throughout the occupied territories but also through unexplored land. Documents record the occurrence of epidemics at virtually ten-year intervals. As a result, the population was decimated. In addition, tropical America received a supply of germs specific to its climate, together with their transmitting agents: slave ships introduced diseases endemic to Africa but hitherto unknown, at least in their virulent forms, in Latin America. The lowlands provided an ideal environment for them to settle.

European and African diseases attacked not only healthy, resistant bodies but also organisms that were already debilitated. During the Conquest the Indians were submitted to all types of excesses. Deprived of part of their lands and harvests, subjected to grueling work circumstances, they were left with few defenses. The germs began the epidemics, but the inhabitants' physical exhaustion provided ideal conditions for their propagation. Clinical etiology requires knowledge of the social context if it is to provide a satisfactory explanation. This constant loss of life gradually reduced the size of the population and hindered its recovery. After each successive onslaught, the number of couples of childbearing age was reduced, and it declined from each generation to the next. Moreover, depression was widespread. Deprived of their gods, their government, and their heritage, the Indians were driven to extremes of suicide or abortion. Epidemics, abuse, and decisions not to reproduce combined to reduce the Indian population and, with it, its languages.

As this population declined, the number of Spaniards and Portuguese rose. Year after year, hundreds or thousands, depending on luck, disembarked and put down roots on American soil. Although often exposed to violent death, they fared better than the natives in dealing with the epidemics that followed in their wake. Few women accompanied them to help the immigrants to reproduce within their own class. Instead, Indian women bore mestizo children to the Spaniards and Portuguese; mestizos generally swelled the ranks of Europeans and spoke their languages. Out of personal preference and at the request of the authorities, the Spaniards and Portuguese settled in the cities that began to emerge in their respective domains. Although the entire territory, including the land that the Europeans had not occupied, remained under colonial jurisdiction, both they and their descendants were drawn to the administrative centers. These nuclei contained large contingents of Indians. Indigenous languages continued to be heard in the streets, although for the majority the culture was predominantly European, with a few local loan words. In Latin America, Spanish and Portuguese have been more urban than rural languages. The countryside continued to be virtually entirely Indian for many years. This duality—European city versus Indian countryside—lasted a long time and continues to this day in certain areas.

But positing such a duality involves some oversimplification. Hispaniola lost its entire Indian population in less than a century, as was mentioned earlier. A somewhat similar phenomenon occurred in the remaining Caribbean islands and along many of the tropical coasts. Soon there were territories in America with no Indians and, consequently, without this contrasting culture. The Spaniards and Portuguese found the countryside there empty, but they chose to bring in other peoples to work their lands and labor in their cities. These forced immigrants brought with them a great variety of languages that they were unable to keep up, much less spread, on American soil. The large number of languages, plus the fact that their speakers were slaves, prevented their acceptance. Their traces in today's languages are limited to a few words. It was not long before the slaves began to communicate with each other in Spanish and Portuguese. Despite being imported in great numbers, outnumbering even the whites, the slaves had relatively low survival and reproduction rates, meaning that the workforce had to be continuously replenished from Africa.

Some slaves obtained their manumission and formed small groups of free blacks, particularly in the cities. The urban castes, consisting of the latter together with mulattos and *mestizos,* blended with the European lineages and the Indian masses (or what was left of them). These castes were destined to grow. In addition to their prodigious reproductive capacity, they served as a receptacle for the constant crossing of social and ethnic barriers. Initially imbued with African or Indian culture, they gradually abandoned this in favor of European cultural expressions in their quest for social mobility. As the driving force behind the cities' progress and attached to the European group, this intermediate stratum helped reduce the Indians' initial advantage as regards population and language. On their own, the whites would have taken much longer to achieve this hegemony.

Having reached their nadir, the Indians began to rebuild their numbers despite their exhaustion and the restraints imposed by the continuous trend toward miscegenation. The ranks of this group were swollen not only by the mixture of different races but also by those who hoped to be taken for *mestizos.* Their numbers initially grew slowly, until they eventually became well established in the mid-eighteenth century. By the time Spanish America achieved its independence, the Indians had replenished their numbers and were by far the largest minority, constituting an average of 43 percent of the population. They were more numerous in some places than in others, since the natives had disappeared from certain areas many years beforehand, as mentioned earlier. Viewed from another angle, in three centuries, over half the population had stopped regarding itself as indigenous and communicating in the ancient languages. Spanish and Portuguese were now indisputably the languages of general communication. Bilingualism had spread among the Indians and, as colonization advanced, the few texts they wrote were nearly always in Spanish. Although certain ethnic groups avoided extinction and even recouped some of their demographic losses, the same could not be said of their cultural and linguistic position. By the end of the Colonial period, not only had the everyday use of ancient languages declined, but several languages had become extinct along the way, either because of the dissipation of entire linguistic groups or because they had been replaced by other Indian languages. Following the collapse of Aztec and Incan political power, the dominant Amerindian languages of these defeated empires continued to occupy ever larger expanses of land—this time led by the parish priests, who found it useful to have their parishioners exchange their language for another similar one that the clergy understood better. Thus, Nahua and Quechua were more widely spoken than they had been during the pre-Columbian period. Evangelization reinforced some native languages but simplified the linguistic panorama.

During the twentieth century the rise of the Indians reflected that of other ethnic and cultural groups in Latin America. In areas where their identity and speech have been preserved, it is not unusual for their population to equal or even surpass what it was at their peak. What they have failed to recover, however, is their original proportion. After five centuries, Indians do not even account for 5 percent of the total population, and that proportion seems likely to decrease. Over the past two centuries, the Indian population has actually grown, although at a slower rate than the rest of the population, and with a lower life expectancy than that of other groups. The demographic transition, which will be discussed subsequently, arrived too late for the Indians, who, moreover, have not had the opportunity of having their stocks replenished from overseas, as the Europeans have. During the nineteenth and twentieth centuries, migrants from Europe flocked en masse to several Latin American countries. In less than a generation, these new Latin Americans renounced their language and used those of their adopted lands. To make matters worse, in recent decades the Indians have left the countryside in droves, and in the cities they have tended to give up both their identity and their language.

The replacement of autochthonous languages by two European languages can be explained by cultural, social, and political factors, although no explanation would be complete without the demographic element. The latter changes according to the particular period involved, as we have seen. The Indians' initial numerical superiority was eroded by their inexorable decline and the trend toward mixed groups. Conversely, the intruders continued to receive reinforcements from abroad, inhabited only certain zones, and settled in the administrative and cultural capitals from which their language and culture radiated. Later, during the last two centuries, reduced to the rural sphere and enclosed in their own world, the Indians were unable to exploit the opportunities of growth that became available, so they advanced more slowly than the more open urban groups. During both these stages the differences in growth and urbanization were extremely marked.

Demography and Cultural Centers

The urbanization of Latin America dates from the beginning of the Common Era. Shortly before that time, ceremonial centers had been built, such as Chavín de Huantar or La Venta, which attracted multitudes of peasants but lacked a stable population. At the same time, the Indian chieftains created administrative capitals whose size depended on the amount of territory they dominated. By the seventh century CE, several cities performed political and religious functions, housed tens of thousands of inhabitants, and protected subordinate centers. This was the case of Teotihuacan, the capital of the urban network of the Central Valley in Mexico. Other cities soon crowned the Andean states of Huari and Tiahuanaco and the Mayan states such as Tikal and Chichén Itzá. On the eve of the Conquest, a string of cities cut through the western slope of the hemisphere from Tula to Tiahuanaco. Foremost among these were Tenochtitlan and Cuzco, capitals with large, powerful empires. All these cities were also powerful economic and cultural emporiums.

Following the European invasion of the continent, the cities fell into the hands of people who, as did the natives, preferred the urban to the rural areas. The Spaniards occupied the ancient cities, painstakingly imposing their city plans and constructing their mansions in the Renaissance style. As successors to these cities, they inherited their symbolic location of power. In the centers the conquerors placed the public buildings characteristic of their new religious functions (churches) or administrative functions (town halls). Conversely, the Indians were evicted from the urban center and relegated to districts or villages on the periphery. The cities stopped being Indian in appearance and environs, but above all, in function. In general terms, Indian society became deurbanized. Colonial cities met different criteria of development. They became links in a network, created on the basis of imperial designs, whose capital city was located in a distant metropolis. Within the cities' populations, although Indian language and cultural expression inevitably continued to exist for a long time, the dominant and therefore prestigious cultural expression was clearly Spanish. Spanish was the language of administration and education, as well as the means of communication between the various castes. Rites and beliefs were now Catholic rather than indigenous. It was not long before the colonial network, although superimposed on the previous Indian network, changed in response to political or economic causes. Certain ancient localities disappeared. Conversely, the coasts of the Caribbean became dotted with ports through which colonial trade flowed, such as Santo Domingo, Havana, Cartagena, and Veracruz. Peru was given a new capital, Lima, and built a powerful mining center, Potosí. New nuclei emerged in regions without any previous urbanization, such as Chile or Río de la Plata. On the other hand, in Brazil the Portuguese arrivals came across very few Indians, and those they did meet had no urban past. The colonizers here were therefore obliged to improvise small cities, whose plan and size could not compare with those of the Spaniards.

Two reports drafted by the highest metropolitan authorities, the *Geografía y descripción universal de las Indias* by the cosmographer López de Velasco and the *Compendio y descripción general de las Indias Occidentales* by Fr. Antonio Vázquez de Espinosa, give an account of the Spanish cities and the number of their inhabitants in 1574 and 1628. **Map 1** places at least a hundred of these at the later date. Gathering data from both these works entails a certain amount of risk, although one worth attempting. Not even a rough estimate is provided of the size of all the cities; estimates, where available, are usually given in round figures. At the same time, we do not know the number of inhabitants corresponding to each site, or whether, once a multiple has been found, it could be considered valid for all sites. Indians and *mestizos* were not included in the count, yet their activity meant that they formed an integral part of Spanish cities. Without them, the cities would not have functioned. Fortunately, the number of residents in the principal cities can sometimes be reckoned using complementary data. Separated by half a century, the two reports reflect the growth and reorganization of the urban network (see **Map 2**).

On average, Spaniards and *criollos* totaled a mere 121 per site in 1574. In other words, the majority of places mentioned were little more than towns. Inhabitants, Indians, and *mestizos* together made up a small population. Consequently, they could hardly be expected to produce an intense cultural life. Nevertheless, their administrative and economic functions belied their size and proved unmistakably urban. By 1628, the total number of these places had risen to 331, with an average of 470 residents each; in other words, nearly four times more. Thus the cities had grown in size and number in half a century. And if Vázquez de Espinosa had been interested in the language issue, he would have noted that Spanish had generally taken hold in the cities.

Map 1. Spanish Cities in 1628

Map 2.

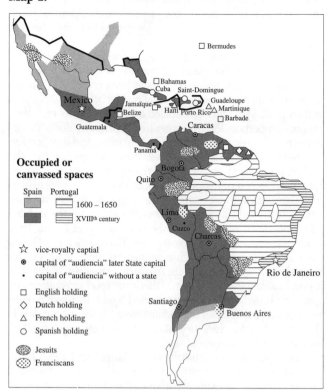

New towns were established on the border zones: Charcas and Río de la Plata. Surprisingly, Quito registered the greatest increase. The few leading cities included viceregal capitals, mining settlements, and ports. In 1628, Mexico City boasted approximately 15,000 *vecinos* (heads of households), possibly as many as 90,000 Spanish inhabitants, not counting Indians or *mestizos,* who would have considerably increased this figure. Mexico City's size made it comparable to the great European cities of the time. Lima, the capital of another viceroyalty, comprised 10,000 residents. Further south, Potosí had expanded phenomenally. The silver boom had raised the number of its residents from 400 to 4000, not counting the tens of thousands of Indians or the thousands of blacks who worked the mines. As a winter harbor for galleons, Havana also flourished during this period, with the number of its inhabitants rising from sixty to 1200. Cartagena de Indias increased from 250 to 1500 inhabitants. Regardless of numbers, many cities at that time housed educational institutions, such as colleges and universities, which, together with the printing presses, reinforced their cultural apparatus. For a long century and a half, until the eve of emancipation, the Spanish cities continued to flourish, with new ones being built in territories that had begun to prosper. Their population grew more rapidly than did that of the surrounding countryside as a result of rural and overseas emigration. In the countryside : city ratio, the latter outstripped the former. Cities increased in number of inhabitants but also in complexity and variety of functions. Their ethnic and cultural composition changed, not so much through the addition of Spaniards as through the considerable reinforcement of the intermediate layers of *mestizos* and mulattos. Greater activity fostered an increase of both production of handicrafts and commerce among these groups. The same expansion was true of the administrative and cultural services required by a larger population. Many of the convents adorning

the old cities date from this period, and theaters were also inaugurated during this time. The cities' cultural endowment also increased, although not at the same rate in all regions. In general, this expansion appears to have been achieved more quickly and to a greater extent in Mexico than in the Andes. The foundation of certain commercial or strategic centers, such as Montevideo, also dates from this period.

Independence gave cities a significant boost, enabling them to change their appearance. Several second-rate cities drew the necessary strength from this occasion to raise their surrounding territories to the rank of nation and crown themselves capital. This was true of the Central American countries and Montevideo, to cite just one example. Becoming the capital of either a nation or simply a province meant that a city's appearance, faded by economic losses, was rejuvenated by the presence of military men and government officials. The latter were briefly joined by those who had been evicted from the countryside as a result of the war. Ports, rather than cities in the interior, benefited from the increased openness to other countries produced by independence. Goods and immigrants flowed in through the ports. In the late nineteenth century, Europeans disembarked in America *en masse*. Several waves of immigrants served to populate and exploit the virgin lands, as happened in the São Paulo high tableland or the pampas of the Río de la Plata, although the majority ended up in the cities, such as Buenos Aires or Havana. Urban culture was enriched by the variety of the immigrants' cities of origin. Latin America once again looked at itself in the mirror of Europe. The state broadened its sphere of action, assuming responsibility for public education and expanding the cultural supply. Libraries open to the public, for example, date from this period.

The Western axis along which the Indian cities had been aligned was slightly modified during the Colonial period but was soon relegated to the background after independence. The cities that grew most during the nineteenth century were not the highland cities of the Pacific slope but rather the maritime cities of the Atlantic. Buenos Aires, Río de Janeiro, Montevideo, and Havana wrested from Mexico City and Lima the title of largest cities with the greatest economic and cultural activity. **Table 1** summarizes several facets of Latin American urbanization around 1900. It includes all the countries of the period with their total populations, together with three groups of cities (those with 10,000 to 19,999 inhabitants, those with 20,000 to 99,999, and those with over 100,000). Towns with fewer than 10,000 inhabitants were excluded, since they were regarded as being rural rather than urban. Each group includes the total number of cities, total number of their inhabitants, and the percentage of the latter in relation to the total population of the country. One column adds up the totals and notes the percentage of people who lived in localities with over 10,000 inhabitants. The last section in the table lists the names of the capitals of the countries and records their status, population, and the percentage of the total living in the capital.

The proliferation of republics after independence meant that many of their capitals had fewer than 100,000 inhabitants in about 1900. Moreover, in the majority of these republics, less than a tenth of the population lived in towns with over 10,000 inhabitants. The degree of urbanization of these small countries was therefore extremely low, although not very different from the rest of Latin America. Even in nations as large as Mexico and Brazil, nearly 90 percent of the population was classified as "rural," although surprisingly, Brazil boasted the second most highly populated city in the region, and no fewer than four cities with over 100,000 inhabitants. The most homogeneous and dynamic nations of the time–Argentina, Uruguay, Cuba, and Costa Rica–were exceptional in that over 25 percent of their populations lived in towns with more than 10,000 inhabitants, and over 12 percent lived in the capital itself. These countries also had the highest schooling and literacy rates. One can easily infer which parts of America were the principal centers of Spanish and Portuguese cultures at the time.

The trend toward urbanization, somewhat timid and narrowly focused at the beginning of the twentieth century, soon expanded and spread as a result of a transformation of demographic behavior, particularly during the second half of the century, which is discussed later in the chapter. This explosively growing population could not be retained in the countryside and eventually ended up in the cities. As a result, Portuguese and Spanish America became one of the most highly urbanized regions in the world, virtually equaling the United States, Oceania, and Europe in this respect and vastly surpassing Asia and Africa. In 1990, 72 percent of the population of Latin America lived in urban centers according to the census definitions, and nearly half inhabited what were unquestionably cities, with over 100,000 residents. The shift from the situation described in the **Table 1** to the current situation in less

Table 1. *Population Residing in Cities with More Than 10,000 Inhabitants c. 1900**

Country	Date	Total Population	Cities 100,000+			20,000–99,999			10,000–19,999			Percent 10,000	Capital	Rank	Population	%
			#	Pop.	%	#	Pop.	%	#	Pop.	%					
Argentina†	1895	3,955	1	664	16.8	7	294	7.4	9	117	2.9	27.1	Buenos Aires	1	664	16.8%
Bolivia†	1900	1,816	–	–	–	5	132	7.3	1	14	0.7	8.0	La Paz	11	53	2.9%
Brazil	1890	14,334	4	825	5.8	11	394	2.8	19	339	2.4	10.9	Rio de Janeiro	2	430‡	3.0%
Colombia	1905	4,144	1	117	2.9	6	199	4.8	5	72	1.7	9.4	Bogotá	8	117	2.9%
Costa Rica	1892	243	–	–	–	1	30	12.3	3	39	16.0	28.4	San José	15	30	12.3%
Cuba†	1899	1,573	1	236	15.0	5	157	9.9	7	90	5.7	30.7	La Havana	6	236	15.0%
Chile†	1895	2,696	2	379	14.1	4	135	5.0	6	74	2.8	21.8	Santiago	4	256	9.5%
Ecuador	1889	1,272	–	–	–	3	115	9.0	4	42	3.3	12.3	Quito	12	47	3.7%
Guatemala†	1893	1,501	–	–	–	4	140	9.3	9	103	6.8	16.9	Guatemala	10	72	4.8%
Honduras	1901	544	–	–	–	1	24	4.3	2	22	4.0	8.4	Tegucigalpa	17	23	4.3%
Mexico†	1900	13,607	2	446	3.3	21	816	6.0	35	467	3.4	12.7	Mexico City	3	345	2.5%
Paraguay†	1886	330	–	–	–	1	25	7.5	2	30	9.1	16.5	Asuncion	16	25	7.5%
Peru†	1876	2,622	1	101	3.9	2	63	2.4	2	31	1.2	7.4	Lima	7	101	3.9%
Puerto Rico†	1899	953	–	–	–	2	60	6.3	1	15	1.6	7.9	San Juan	14	32	3.4%
El Salvador	1892	703	–	–	–	2	56	8.0	5	52	7.4	15.4	San Salvador	13	33	4.7%
Uruguay	1900	936	1	268	28.7	–	–	–	1	13	1.4	30.0	Montevideo	5	268	28.7%
Venezuela†	1891	2,222	–	–	–	4	189	8.5	23	316	14.2	22.8	Caracas	9	72	3.3%

*Size and rank of the capitals in thousands.
†Census data.
‡Rural sectors of the Federal District excluded.

than a century signified an enormous leap, as swift as it was anomalous. Rural Latin America is now a thing of the past. The yardstick by which urbanization is measured has been extended, but Latin America has always been able to meet the most stringent requirements.

The degree of urbanization achieved by each nation varied widely. **Map 3** illustrates the existing differences in 1980. The most highly urbanized countries included Argentina and Uruguay, where over eight out of ten inhabitants lived in localities defined as urban by the census. Chile and Venezuela had joined this group, while Cuba and Costa Rica, in the lead at the beginning of the century, had lagged behind. Mexico, Colombia, Peru, and Brazil occupied an intermediate position. The least urbanized countries, as one would expect, were those in Central America.

The more cities grew, the more important the largest ones became. **Table 2** shows the distribution of larger cities by size, according to four categories: fewer than one hundred thousand inhabitants, one hundred thousand to a million inhabitants, one to four million inhabitants, and over four million. The chart spans the period from 1950 to 1980. **Map 3** shows that there has recently been a decrease in cities with fewer than a million and an increase in cities with over a million inhabitants. Among the larger cities, there are also more with over 4 million than under this figure. Cities of 4 million inhabitants, with the everyday advantages and drawbacks that this entails for its inhabitants, but with an undoubtedly greater capacity for cultural activity, are no longer unusual in Latin America. Moreover, this region currently contains four of the eight most populated cities in the world: Mexico City, São Paulo, Buenos Aires, and Río de Janeiro. Having the largest populations, however, does not mean that they occupy the same level in the cultural sphere. None of these is a world capital in this respect, although neither are they insignificant.

By the mid-twentieth century, Latin America had eight cities with over a million inhabitants (see **Table 2**), one per country except in the case of Brazil. They included Buenos Aires, Río de Janeiro, and Mexico City, followed in order of size by São Paulo, Santiago, Havana, Montevideo, and Lima. Two decades later, in 1970, cities of this size had more than doubled in number. They now totaled seventeen and had undergone significant changes as regards the order of size. Mexico City had recovered the leading position it had lost for over a century to Buenos Aires, whereas São Paulo had overtaken Río de Janeiro. Moreover, a single country, Brazil, now contained six cities with over a million inhabitants, while Mexico had three. Another twenty years later, in 1990, this trend had been exacerbated. There were now twenty-seven cities with over a million inhabitants. Mexico and São Paulo, with twenty and nineteen million inhabitants respectively, were far ahead of the rest, particularly their closest rivals, Buenos Aires and Río de Janeiro. Formerly important cities, such as Havana and Montevideo, had fallen behind. Brazil and Colombia now boasted several cities in the highest category. The great human nuclei have grown and multiplied in Latin America, and as a result of their inhabitants' demands, so have their cultural centers.

The Demographic Explosion and the Cultural Public

Consumption of cultural goods, particularly literary goods, depends on a society's level of education and its sensibility and fashions, although it is also influenced by some of the conditions in which it develops. The first of these is population size (the more inhabitants, the greater the demand for goods), modified by the degree of literacy, spatial fragmentation, and, in the case of Latin America, the number of monolingual speakers of languages other than Spanish and Portuguese. Low levels

Map 3.

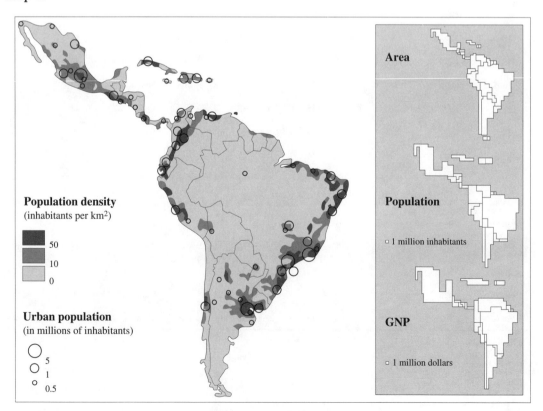

Table 2. *Cities with More Than One Million Inhabitants in 1980*

	Population (in millions)			Rank
	1950	1970	1990	
North and Central America:				
Continental				
Mexico	3.05	9.12	20.25	1
Guadalajara	0.43	1.58	3.20	12
Monterrey	0.38	1.28	3.01	15
Guatemala	0.40	0.73	1.46	27
Caribbean				
Havana	1.22	1.75	2.04	16
Santo Domingo	0.25	0.89	2.17	20
San Juan	0.47	0.70	1.49	24
South America				
Tropical				
São Paulo	2.76	8.22	18.77	2
Rio de Janeiro	3.48	7.17	11.37	4
Belo Horizonte	0.48	1.62	3.89	9
Curitiba	0.14	0.91	3.77	14
Fortaleza	0.26	0.90	2.42	19
Recife	0.83	1.82	3.04	11
Porto Alegre	0.67	1.55	3.18	13
Salvador [Bahia]	0.45	1.16	2.65	17
Brasília	0.04	0.54	2.40	22
Lima-Callao	1.05	2.92	6.78	5
Bogotá	0.70	2.37	5.27	7
Barranquilla	0.30	0.76	1.77	21
Cali	0.28	0.95	2.40	18
Medellín	0.46	1.47	3.60	10
Caracas	0.68	2.12	4.18	8
Guayaquil	0.25	0.73	1.63	24
Temperate				
Buenos Aires	5.25	8.55	11.71	3
Cordoba	0.41	0.80	1.28	26
Santiago	1.43	2.56	4.55	6
Montevideo	1.07	1.21	1.22	22

Source: United Nations. *Modalities of Urban and Rural Population Growth.* New York: 1981. *The Prospects of World Urbanization.* New York: 1987.

of literacy and linguistic exchanges effectively reduce public potential. Nowadays, in fact, Indian monolingualism tends to go hand in hand with illiteracy. In these cases, the public able to afford these goods is much smaller. Population as an indicator, therefore, requires certain adjustments. Nevertheless, it can still serve to illustrate certain points. With these restrictions in mind, let us explore the issue of the demographic explosion that lasted for much of the twentieth century and seems likely to carry on into part of our own. During this period, Latin America has grown in population and will continue to do so; its progress has exceeded all historical records. No other region in the world has grown as much or

as fast as Latin America to date. In its historical scope, the demographic explosion is comparable only to the reverse phenomenon—the collapse of the Indian population in the sixteenth and seventeenth centuries. Both occurrences, leading in opposite directions yet with an analogous caliber and degree, marked the modern history of Latin American population.

Since the last century, the world has been undergoing a change known as demographic transition. It has shifted from a regime characterized by high birth and death rates to another with noticeably fewer births and deaths. In either case, the population grows slowly, although less cruelly in the latter. This trend, although widespread, has not taken place in all areas or social levels at the same time. Deaths and births are now out of harmony. Deaths are usually the first to decline, for health reasons, whereas conceptions, which depend more on custom, remain high for a time until family expectations are modified. The disparity between the behaviors of these two variables paves the way for a huge increase in growth. In comparison with Europe and North America, Latin America joined this demographic transition fairly late, although it has gone through the various stages in far less time. The decline first in death rates and the much later fall in fertility rates have been swift, which in turn has led to unrestrained growth. From 1940, the conventional date of the beginning of the Latin American transition, to the present, the Spanish-Portuguese population of the Western hemisphere has quadrupled.

The stages of this transformation will not be recapitulated here—merely its results. **Table 3** shows the size of the population of Brazil and of the Spanish-speaking nations every twenty years, together with the projections for the next fifty years from 1940 onward. The nation continues to be the main source of statistical information and, to a great extent, the major cultural space. In Latin America, the debate on national culture is not yet over. Figures for the year 2000 are only estimates. A careful reader will be able to calculate the growth rates by country or by broader units, but we shall merely contrast the extremes. In 1940 the total number of speakers or readers in Brazil was 41.2 million. This gross mass, without the adjustments suggested at the outset, was smaller than the population of France, a country of greater cultural breadth at that time. According to these data, Brazilians numbered 2.9 and 2.1 times more than their Argentinean or Mexican neighbors. By the year 2000, Brazil would more than quadruple its population and, for this reason, would have an opulent producer and consumer market for cultural goods. Numerically speaking, it would far surpass France and would contain 4.6 and 1.7 times more inhabitants than Argentina and Mexico, respectively. These relative indices differ from the previous ones; one is much larger, the other smaller.

The demographic explosion has not only led to a considerable increase in the population size of nations but it has also produced a change in their ranking within the urban network and, one might add, as regards cultural spaces. Mexico, which in 1940 had 4.3 more inhabitants than Cuba, now has 8.8 times more. On a smaller scale, Chile, once 2.7 times larger than Uruguay, now has a population 4.6 times the size. In short, the population of Spanish-speaking nations has risen from 82 to 328 million in sixty years, while the number of Portuguese speakers has increased from 41 to 170 million. In both cases the population has virtually quadrupled, as mentioned earlier. During this period, the Portuguese-speaking population increased a tenth more than the number of Spanish speakers. These changes are not over at this point and will continue in the future.

Table 3. *Population of Latin America, 1940–2050 (in millions)*

	1940	1960	1980	2000	2050
Argentina	14.2	20.6	28.2	37.0	54.5
Bolivia	2.5	3.4	5.6	8.3	17.0
Chile	5.1	7.6	11.1	15.2	22.2
Colombia	9.1	15.5	25.8	38.9	62.4
Costa Rica	0.6	1.2	2.3	3.8	6.9
Cuba	4.6	7.0	9.7	11.2	11.3
Dominican Republic	1.8	3.2	5.6	8.5	13.1
Ecuador	2.6	4.4	8.1	12.6	21.2
Guatemala	2.2	4.0	6.9	11.4	27.2
Honduras	1.1	1.9	3.7	6.5	13.9
Mexico	19.8	37.1	69.4	98.9	146.6
Nicaragua	0.9	1.5	2.8	3.8	9.9
Panama	0.6	1.1	2.0	2.9	4.4
Paraguay	1.1	1.8	3.2	5.5	12.6
Peru	6.7	9.9	17.3	25.7	42.3
Puerto Rico	1.9	2.4	3.2	3.8	5.0
El Salvador	1.6	2.6	4.8	6.3	11.4
Uruguay	1.9	2.5	2.9	3.3	4.0
Venezuela	3.7	7.5	15.0	24.2	42.2
Total	82	135.2	227.6	327.8	528.1
Brazil	41.2	72.6	121.3	169.6	246.6
General Total	**123.2**	**207.8**	**348.9**	**497.4**	**774.7**

Source: Boletín demográfico 59 (América Latina: Proyecciones de población, 1950–2050), Santiago de Chile: 1997.

The most cautious projections for the next fifty years are given in the last column in Table 3 and assume that, by the year 2050, Brazil will have expanded again and will have reached 247 million inhabitants, while the number of Spanish speakers will have risen to 527 million. Despite being numerically large, however, this addition will be slower than that we have just described. The demographic explosion will begin to wane. In fact, there are already nations in the Southern Cone with a virtually stagnant population, prefiguring the future awaiting others. By that stage, one generation would normally merely replace another. In any case, Mexico will have become the undisputed leader of the Spanish-speaking world. By the year 2050, its population will be thirteen times larger than Cuba's and it will have increased its lead over Colombia and Argentina. Finally, there will be a greater increase in the total number of Spanish speakers in relative terms than in that of Portuguese speakers, contrary to what happened during the previous period. In a future that many of those born at the end of the twentieth century may experience, Latin American Portuguese and Spanish speakers will form two cultural blocs that will be imposing in size, with a similar sensibility. To parody the title of one of García Márquez's stories, there will be someone who will "write to the colonel," and if appropriate, perhaps even read him.

Demography is a discipline that moves confidently only among figures and one that has inherited the old humanitarian assumption that more lives equals good. Another assumption implicit in this chapter is that, all things being equal, the larger the population, the higher the degree of culture. This is not the place to discuss whether or not this is true, but having often quoted this assumption, one small proviso is appropriate: In culture, quantity is not everything.

Translation by Suzanne D. Stephens

CHAPTER 8

LINGUISTIC DIVERSITY IN MEXICO

Beatriz Garza Cuarón

Mexico is the country with the greatest linguistic diversity in the Americas (see **Map 1**). The reason for this, if one accepts the hypothesis that America was populated by groups from various parts of Asia who crossed the Bering Strait, is geography. These migrants, who spoke very different languages, had to pass through Mesoamerica. The northern part of the American continent is characterized by two great mountain ranges (the Eastern Sierra Madre and the Western Sierra Madre in Mexico) that fuse in the "Mixtec Knot" located in what is now Oaxaca, a state that presents highly complex orographic features. These ranges acted as a funnel that channeled different linguistic groups belonging to branches and families of languages that were radically unlike each other. Naturally, these groups did not necessarily stay in the region (even though today this area boasts the greatest linguistic diversity); several settled in different areas of what is now Mexico. The most telling proof of this hypothesis is the plurilingual character of Oaxaca and her neighboring states (Puebla, Veracruz, and Chiapas).

These migrations took place over very different periods. The Olmec culture, which flourished mainly in what is now the state of Veracruz, was considerably earlier than the Zapotec, Mixtec, or indeed the Mayan culture, whose languages, spoken in the mountainous area of Chiapas, are highly fragmented. In contrast, the so-called Yucatec Mayan spoken in the lowlands of the Yucatán Peninsula (today composed of the states of Yucatán, Quintana Roo, and Campeche) reveals virtually no variants of importance and is spoken over a wide area.

The Olmec Culture (approximately 3500 BCE to 1200 BCE)

The earliest Olmec settlements can be dated to around 5000 BCE, reaching their high point as sedentary communities between 2400 and 1200 BCE. During this period the population of these first farming settlements increased, ceramics were introduced, and improvements were made in both the construction of huts and the use of stone for the building of larger edifices. The society also developed some complex magical rites based on the belief that natural phenomena were possessed by spirits that had to be placated in order to obtain good harvests (Barba de Piña Chán 182–83). Subsequently between

1200 BCE and 200 CE they began to construct ceremonial centers and achieved a high level of cultural development. Indeed the Olmecs are the oldest civilization known to have achieved such an advanced cultural level.

Even though they established themselves in a fertile valley in the south of the modern state of Veracruz, the Olmecs lived more from fishing than cultivating land. Evidence points to them as the first to specialize in apiculture, and they created large stone sculptures and monolithic altars that have survived to this day (Bernal 5–6). They also began to develop a symbolic system that would become the basis for a form of ideographic writing; these symbols consisted largely of spots, claws, eyebrows, and gums, all of them linked with animals that held a particular significance for them. Thus, the claws related to the jaguar and symbolized the power of the animal, a quality the Olmecs believed that man could assume (Barba de Piña Chán 156). This basis for writing could have been passed on to the Maya, who were contemporaries of the Olmecs during their late period, given that the two cultures were not distant geographically (Bernal 23–25).

Yucatec Mayan (2500 BCE to 600 CE) and Other Mayan Languages in Chiapas

From early Preclassic times the Maya expanded southward from the north of the state of Veracruz to the Yucatán Peninsula. During this period they were probably in contact with the Olmecs and assimilated elements of their culture. In the subsequent developmental stage, known as the Classic, the Maya concentrated more in the Yucatán Peninsula. This was the period of the construction of great ceremonial centers that made use of hieroglyphic inscriptions, indicative of the development of writing, one of the most important achievements of the Mayan civilization (Manrique 1988, 84).

Even though the major ceremonial centers of the Classic Maya were located in the Yucatán Peninsula, other languages from the Mayan family were and continue to be spoken in the states of Tabasco and Chiapas (and the neighboring country of Guatemala). As previously noted, Mayan languages spoken in the Peninsula are in fact scarcely fragmented, whereas those of Chiapas show considerable fragmentation. According to Otto Schumann (34), the Mayan languages currently spoken in Chiapas are Chol, Chontal, Tojolabal, Lacandón,

Map 1.

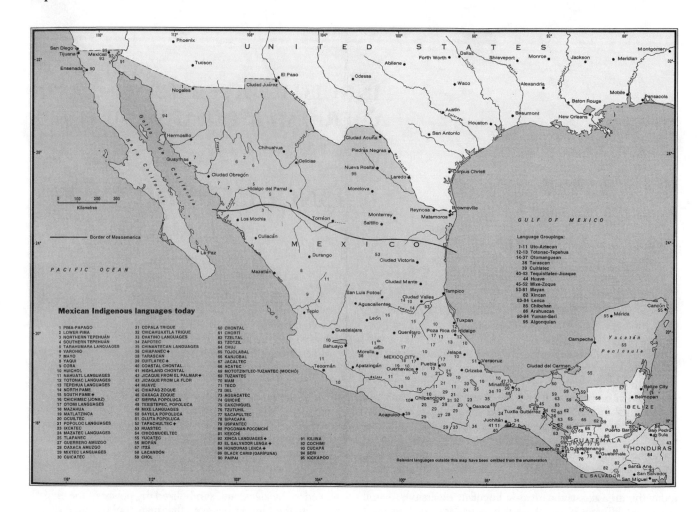

Man, Motozintleco, Tuzanteco, Chuc, Kanjobal, Jacalteco, Tzotzil, and Tzetzal. Lyle Campbell (1988) confirms that in Chiapas the Tzetzales were the carriers of the Mayan culture as evidenced by the great number of archaeological remains in the region. Chol is another important Mayan language, the presumed linguistic source for the inscriptions at Palenque.

Mixe and Zoque (approximately 1100 to 800 BCE)

The Mixe and Zoque languages of Oaxaca, Chiapas, and Veracruz have been linked to the Olmec civilization. The linguists Campbell and Kauffman cite numerous examples of borrowed vocabularies from nonrelated but similar languages as evidence for their argument. Campbell (1988) attributes the Mesoamerican calendrical system to hieroglyphic writing from the Mixe-Zoque civilization. At one stage the modern town of Juquila was one of the most important urban sites (Winter). The center of influence has since shifted to Zacatepec, the principal town of the Mixe district of Oaxaca state and the residence of a leader with a great deal of political influence among the Mixes. There is evidence that Proto-Mixe-Zoque had a syntactic structure of subject + object + verb that has changed in the modern version.

Zapotec (approximately 300 CE)

In the state of Oaxaca in southern Mexico two linguistic groups, the Zapotecs and the Mixtecs, occupy adjacent and substantial territories. Their languages, both derived from the Otopame family (**Map 1**), are very different, in the same way that German differs from the Romance languages, or as any Romance language differs from Slavic languages. Ceramics have been found in the Valley of Oaxaca that date back to between 3000 and 1400 BCE (Kowaleski et al.). Linguistic research has traced the Mixtec groups (Mixtec, Cuicatec, and Triqui) back 4000 years and the Zapotec (Zapotec and Chatino) back 2500 years. Some reconstructed lexical details have been correlated with agricultural phases in Teotihuacan (Harvey; Winter).

Around 300 CE the Zapotecs, who had mixed with the inhabitants of the highlands of Chiapas and Guatemala, developed economically and culturally to construct various ceremonial centers, including Monte Albán. Around 800 CE the Zapotec culture was in decline, and the area was subsequently invaded and the lands occupied by the Mixtecs. Codices exist that give the names of Mixtec kings dating back to around 700 CE despite the fact that the Mixtecs did not construct any great ceremonial centers. They worshipped the deity of the caves and certain sacred stones.

Today both groups have developed differences in dialect with little or no level of intelligibility between the principal dialects. A study of intelligibility between the variants of Zapotec enumerates thirty-eight Zapotec languages (less than 80 percent intelligibility) and twenty-nine Mixtec languages (less than 70 percent intelligibility; Egland). On the periphery of dialect groupings are some that have little or no intelligibility with their neighbors. These tremendous differences may be the result of contact with nonrelated languages via linguistic substrata of conquered groups or migrations from other parts of the area of the main language. As one can see, these groups are the most fragmented of the Mesoamerican languages (Garza Cuarón and Bartholomew 1263).

During the urban period in Oaxacan history (500 BCE to 800 CE), Monte Albán was the principal metropolitan center and soon became the largest. The city must have had considerable prestige and exercised great influence over the Valley of Oaxaca. The variants in the languages in this area show a greater level of intelligibility than that found in the mountain ranges of the north or south. Nevertheless, the Zapotec of Tlacolula differs greatly from that of Mitla, despite being separated by only a few kilometers within the Valley of Oaxaca. The low intelligibility could be due to the fact that Mitla was also an important urban center and larger than a city-state. It was important, and still is, as the City of the Dead (Winter).

Two groups in the west of the Zapotec region that reveal linguistic variants clearly divergent from the rest of the Zapotec languages have been given names: Papabuco and Solteco. In the past, lists of words were collected in villages where these languages are no longer spoken. However, they remain strong in nearby villages and are classified as Zapotec dialects. The northern area has two main groups that are separated by a north-south geographical divide. Low intelligibility exists for Zapotec dialects from the north of the isthmus (spoken by groups that were probably established a long time ago) and those from the Pacific side of the Isthmus of Tehuantepec (considered to have originated as a result of emigration from Zaachila after defeat by the Mixtecs). The mountainous area of the south has a substantial grouping in the center running north-south, flanked on either side by a dialectal group. This could be the result of successive migrations from the central area.

Today it would be a complex task to disentangle the sociolinguistic and historical factors for the long period that marked Zapotec predominance in Oaxaca. Suárez (1990) worked with information from seventy-six Zapotec villages in an attempt to find shared innovations that might help to define linguistic subgroups. He contrasted retentions (cognate with Chatino) with divergent words, tracing isoglosses to identify innovation. Phonological innovations can be found in the reconstruction by Fernández de Miranda. She found that various groups that emerged overlapped in such a way that they were not sufficiently well defined to establish a genetic grouping. Even so, the work is useful in its suggestion of changing centers of diffusion and migrations to different places.

Mixtec (800 CE)

This language is spoken in the western part of the state of Oaxaca and along the border with the neighboring states of Guerrero and Puebla. The large dialectal groupings have a geographic correlation. There is at least one large Mixtec group in the highlands, another in the lowlands, and one more on the Pacific coast. The large groupings of the center might suggest spheres of influence pertaining to the city-states of early Mixtec history. There is little information on the first ceremonial centers because the Mixtecs worshiped in caves or in front of nearby sacred stones. This could manifest itself linguistically in a certain amount of dialectical fragmentation.

The essential unity of the Mixtec languages, in contrast to Trique and Cuicatec, suggests that there was a period when Mixtec was spoken over a broad area. The largest subgroups reflect the geographic barriers of the Sierra Mixteca and Sierra Madre del Sur. Certain groups of isoglosses correspond generally with the geographical divisions of the highlands, lowlands, and the coastal areas and, moreover, subdivide within these major areas. Some linguistic groups have a correlation with the erstwhile city-states, while other nonadjacent subgroups are linked to the main migration routes that cross the territory from north to south (Garza Cuarón and Bartholomew 1264). Josserand (469) points out that during the high point of Mixtec civilization, the people spoke a minimum of three variants of the language. There was a court language used by the nobles, a standard commercial tongue understood throughout the Mixteca (probably the Tepescolula variant that the Dominicans used later because of its widely circulated intelligibility), and the local dialect.

Tarascan

Tarascan, also known as Purépecha, belongs to an independent linguistic family. It bears little relation to other Mesoamerican languages. Even so, as Manrique (1988, 73) points out, Morris Swadesh (1969) considers it to belong to the Mixe and Mayan families as well as the Quechua-Aymará from South America, but most linguists dispute this opinion. Prior to Cortés's arrival and the start of the Spanish Conquest, Tarascan was one of the *linguae francae* in the Nahua empire to constitute an important form of communication in Mesoamerica in what are now the states of Guanajuato, Queretaro, Guerrero, Colima, and Jalisco. Tarascan does not present many dialectical variants, even though it is now spoken only in the state of Michoacan, a region notable for its large quantity of toponyms to denominate cities, villages, lakes, mountains, valleys, and so on (for example, *Pátzcuaro, Tacámbaro, Zinapécuaro, Zitácuaro, Yuriria*, etc.).

Nahua (1100 to 1500)

Nahua, or Aztec, belongs to the Uto-Aztec linguistic family, from which various languages have emerged that were spoken from a very early period over a region extending from the United States to Central America. Classical Nahua is the most well known member of this family because it was the language spoken in the vast empire located in the Valley of Mexico that dominated almost all of the territory that makes up modern Mexico until the arrival of the Spaniards. Nahua has a system of sounds very similar to that of Spanish, and this helped both conquistadors and the religious orders to master the new language.

The Structure of the Mexica Empire

Around 1428, approximately a century prior to the arrival of Hernán Cortés, a war of expansion was undertaken by the Aztecs, Nahuas, or Mexicas (each of the three names is applicable) from the Valley of Mexico. This resulted in a series of conquests that had a profound effect on the linguistic history of the region. The Aztecs were the lords of Tenochtitlan, a city that was founded in 1325 at what is present-day Mexico City. After forming the Triple Alliance with the neighboring kingdoms of Tetzcoco and Tlacopan, they considered that they had built up their strength sufficiently to launch a war of conquest. Thanks to the Alliance they managed to gain control of almost the entire central plateau of Mexico and initiate a rapid expansion toward the valleys on the periphery, such as Toluca, Puebla, Cuernavaca, and Pachuca. The Mexica empire began to expand in all directions. At the beginning of the sixteenth century it had subjugated almost the entire area inhabited by the advanced cultures to the north except for that of the Tarascans. By 1520 they had seized territory from Tuxpán on the Gulf Coast to Jalisco on the Pacific seaboard and dominated what is now Guerrero, Oaxaca, and the isthmus of Tehuantepec in the south down to the Soconusco region in Chiapas and part of the coast of Guatemala and even farther to the south in present-day Central America. In many cases the culture of the indigenous tribes conquered by the Mexica was more advanced and refined than their own. In fact, the Mexica exercised a cultural rulership over the American continent by adopting elements of conquered civilizations as their own (especially the Mixtec and the Zapotec) while honoring by imitation past cultures (Toltec and that of Teotihuacan). The Romans, and indeed other empires throughout history, have done the same. Thus the Nahua culture was a combination of very different elements, some inherited from its ancestors and others acquired from contemporary peoples under its domination, thereby creating an original and varied synthesis.

When the Spaniards arrived, Nahua was spoken throughout almost the entire territory as a commercial language with subject and nonsubject peoples, as in the case of the Tarascans and the Maya. In time Nahua was used as a cultural language, but its predominance did not lead to a decline in the large numbers of spoken languages. Later, with the arrival of the Spanish, the number of languages actually increased as a result of tremendous linguistic fragmentation, rather similar to that of Latin in Romania. This was the consequence of isolation, marginalization, and migration. During the period of Aztec rule, communities remained in their place of origin. However, the Spaniards divided up some communities, leaving some groups isolated while others were taken far from their original location and put in contact with different groups. The conquistadors took advantage of the wide usage of Nahua to introduce their culture into territory that had once been under Mexica dominion. They also made use of two additional *linguae francae* spoken in regions independent of the Aztec empire: Yucatec Mayan and Tarascan. The evangelization, civil administration, and commercial development of New Spain were all facilitated by the employment of these three languages, known by the majority of the new subjects of the Spanish Crown. As Manrique Castañeda and Guzmán Betancourt (4652) point out, the Spanish made their own contribution to the spread of Nahua and Otomí in the northern regions, where these languages were previously not spoken.

The Substitution of Dominant Indigenous Languages by Spanish

From the beginning the Spanish monarchs were against the continuing use of indigenous languages. Their objective was to "Christianize" and "Hispanicize" all their subjects. In other words, they aimed for complete unification through the same religion and language. The missionaries considered it more important to "Christianize." The quickest way of doing so was to focus on indigenous languages and leave the task of "Hispanicization" for later. The friars began by learning Nahua and other native languages. They were instructed by the Indian nobles, who also provided information concerning their own culture and past. Various codices were made during this period narrating the history, customs, and ideas of the conquered people. In turn, the friars taught the Indians to

write using the Latin alphabet, which was then used by native scribes in combination with their previous methods of writing, notably pictographs and hieroglyphics. This form of evangelization, though undertaken using indigenous languages, imposed a new worldview and had an irrevocable impact on their cultural traditions (Pellicer 21, 31).

Missionary interest in native languages went beyond that of evangelization; a tremendous cultural legacy was also acquired. For instance by 1570, half a century after their arrival, the Franciscans, in addition to the codices written by their disciples, had written more than eighty books on indigenous languages, including grammars, vocabularies, catechisms, and translations of the Scriptures (Garza Cuarón 1990, 1991; Heath, the chapter on the Colonial period). The Spanish Crown put increasing pressure on the missionaries to impose Spanish as the sole language. This demand was the principal cause behind the dissensions and confrontations that took place between the viceregal government and the Church. Conflicts also arose within the Church, the result of some missionaries and ecclesiastical authorities supporting Hispanicization, while others continued to evangelize in native languages.

These frictions endured throughout the three centuries that marked the Colonial period. Even though Spanish was gradually imposed as the dominant language, the native tongues maintained their vigor, continuing to evolve and fragment. In fact, in 1810, the start of the War of Independence, more speakers of indigenous languages (around 60 percent of the total population) existed than Spanish speakers.

Characteristics of the Principal Indigenous Languages in Mexico Today

The linguistic situation in Mexico is highly complex. On the one hand, an enormous number of native languages continues to be used for communication within population groups that are becoming increasingly active in the future of the country. On the other hand, Spanish is still imposed as the dominant language. Currently, linguists' opinions vary as to the number of languages spoken in Mexico and the classificatory criteria under which they should be grouped. The classification presented by Suárez in *Mesoamerican Indian Languages* (1983) has been selected for this present work. One of the most widely accepted, it categorizes these indigenous languages into sixteen families or linguistic branches (see the appendix to this chapter).

Even though Mexico is fortunate to have such a great diversity of languages, as previously pointed out, it has not known how to protect them or even allow them to coexist. The provision of bilingual education and/or bicultural education has only been considered obligatory in the last few years. In the 1930s President Lázaro Cárdenas made the first move by inviting the Summer Institute of Linguistics to support a pioneer project in bilingual teaching. Subsequently, the Primer Congreso Indigenista Interamericano (First Inter-American Indigenist Congress) was celebrated in Pátzcuaro, Michoacán, in 1940. There it was agreed to subscribe to further projects in bilingual education. The declaration of the UNESCO accord, which stated that each individual had the right to be educated in his or her mother tongue, gave legitimacy to this policy (Garza Cuarón and Lastra 107–8). These bicultural projects are largely the responsibility of the Instituto Nacional Indígenista (National Indigenist Institute) and the Dirección General de Educación Indígena (Department of Indigenous

Education). However, both of these governmental agencies lack sufficient economic resources and trained personnel to perform the tasks demanded to improve bicultural education in over ninety languages.

On the other hand, some changes in the law have occurred as a result of greater participation by representative members of various indigenous communities. An outstanding example is the revision of Article 4 of the Constitution. Promulgated in 1992, the new law, as Salomón Nahmad notes (127–28), has had an impact on indigenous linguistics, culture, literature, economy, policy, and religion. In a bid to win respect for their ethnicity, indigenous communities have succeeded in developing alphabets to write their languages, as well as grammars and dictionaries. They have also succeeded in creating the Asociación de Escritores Indígenas de México (Association of Mexican Indigenous Writers), which now has a small office building and bookshop in Mexico City from which they promote their literary and linguistic work.

During most of the contact period between indigenous languages and Spanish, the former have been marginalized for various reasons. The nineteenth century was notable for a double stance; on the one hand, the use of these languages was discouraged while, on the other hand, these very languages were the subject of the first philological studies by Europeans (and some Mexicans). The situation must have been an uncomfortable one for the indigenous peoples because they were either denied all possibility of creativity unless they renounced their culture or else they were regarded as an object of study. Fortunately, in recent years, especially since 1994, they have been accorded more recognition, and there is an interest in preserving their cultures. Of course, this implies an enormous effort on their part. They have also received international support as well as help from some national government departments. Above all, this help came because reports of governmental ill-treatment of indigenous people have had worldwide coverage.

Nevertheless a lack of understanding, particularly on the part of the *mestizos,* still exists. Many Spanish speakers continue to marginalize indigenous people. Others, like anthropologists, take an interest, but regard them as an object for study or even as laboratory objects. The indigenous people respond by complaining that even though academics come to their communities, codify their language, and also probably collaborate in educational projects, sometimes advances in research go no further than the linguistic field. As research fixed in space and time, it allows no action to be taken that might allow the languages and their speakers to continue evolving and to integrate contemporary social, scientific, and technological changes.

As a result, two contrasting attitudes have emerged with regard to the education of these groups. As María de Ibarrola points out (310), the first supports an educational framework *for* the indigenous people, an "exclusive education" *by* and *for* them. Meanwhile, the second searches instead for an "articulation" of indigenous groups with the rest of the population as part of the national educational system. In general terms, the balance tends more toward the first stance, mostly because that is the wish of the indigenous communities. This does not, however, imply the rejection of teaching and instruction in Spanish. As the Mazatec poet Juan Gregorio Regina pointed out during the series of conferences entitled *Traducción de y a lenguas indígenas* [Translation of and to Indigenous Languages], Spanish is no longer a language imposed by the dominant group; it is just "another" language in Mexico that has eventually become popular and is now considered a vital part of the national scene.

The majority of the "cultural" languages consider that literature ought to be written down, but it must not be forgotten that every literature had an oral beginning. Homer and the first rhapsodists and troubadours were all oral storytellers; indeed, even today minstrels travel from village to village in China recounting stories. If these traditional forms are recognized as literature in other parts of the world, we might then ask why indigenous literature, the product of a long oral tradition, has not also received complete recognition. On arrival, the Spanish conquistadors encountered highly developed cultures that conserved many of their traditions in a kind of book known as a *codex.* Many of these were destroyed subsequently; only a few survived. They had one particular characteristic: They were not read in the same way as alphabetic texts are. This was not on account of the hieroglyphic or ideographic form of writing but because each reading implied an interpretative re-creation of the text. The reader also had to be a good orator, literate in oral tradition. Dora Pellicer (23) explains that this is due to the fact that indigenous writing conserved ideas and events but did not register exactly the words to be spoken.

The first missionaries were interested in both indigenous languages and traditions, providing the opportunity for their aristocratic informants to write new codices in which traditional forms were combined with alphabetic writing. However, the teaching of the alphabet was very limited, with the result that during the Colonial period the indigenous communities maintained their literary tradition, re-creating much material through oral means. Apart from the rewriting of many codices under the tutelage of the Catholic priesthood, indigenous people cultivated other literary forms; drama was a particular favorite. The missionaries took advantage of this taste for the stage and guided their new flock toward producing a new kind of religious theater in medieval European style, including *autos-da-fé,* mystery plays, and so on. Only some of these dramatic works were written down, however, given that most were produced orally. Even today much indigenous literature is oral and is regarded as a "social discourse"; it is a manifestation of collective memory that, through poetry, songs, myths, legends, and tales, reaffirms the identity of the community. Even so, some ethnic groups have adapted the Latin alphabet for writing down their mother tongue. Yet little written literature exists in indigenous languages, and almost all is designed to be read aloud.

Apart from the oral nature of indigenous literature, it is also characterized by genres that are shared among ethnic groups but differ from those found in literature written in Spanish. Victor de la Cruz, a Zapotec poet and researcher (334–38), explains the situation from a viewpoint based in Zapotec literary tradition and modern literature, describing the characteristics of these literary genres and providing, where possible, an equivalent or similar example from the western tradition. De la Cruz divides the genres into three groups: sacred, didactic, and entertaining. According to him the sacred genres are of three types: (1) myths, similar to the biblical writings of Catholic tradition; (2) poems, notably religious poems and songs, accompanied by musical instruments, that are sung as the accompaniment to dances during some religious ceremonies; and (3) songs or verses to accompany a melody.

Didactic genres, according to de la Cruz, exist in three varieties: (1) sermons, known among the Zapotecs as *libana* and the Nahuas as *huehuetlatolli* ("discourse of the elders"), which are beautiful didactic expositions with complicated rhetorical ornamentation, created by only the most skilled of the men; (2) proverbs, which generally sum up the teaching of the *libana* in one or two phrases; and (3) narratives, which are either stories or historical chronicles. Finally, de la Cruz explains four kinds of entertainment genres (it is worth noting that prose is almost nonexistent in an oral tradition; narratives have a rhythmic and a rhyme cadence that helps with memorization): (1) stories, which are defined as not using metaphor or any other kind of poetic embellishment; (2) lies, which bear a close relationship to tales, such that de la Cruz considers them to form a common genre divided into two at some point in history (it could be said that the difference lies in the fact that, whereas the story might be based on reality, the lie would be more of a fantastic tale); (3) jokes, that is, brief, witty, elegant, well-timed, and ironic improvisations; and (4) narratives, *tichacanitíchaci* or *tichacoquite*, characterized by wordplay; this is a literary form that has become increasingly popular.

Librado Silva, a researcher specializing in Nahua literature, draws attention to two additional classifications (345), one produced by Horcasitas and the other published in the journal *Estudios de Cultura Nahuatl*. From our point of view these classifications complement de la Cruz's classification or rather allow it to be subdivided even further so that, for example, various kinds of narrative cultivated in these literatures can be appreciated in greater detail. While working on various Nahua texts in Milpa Alta, Horcasitas uncovered the following genres: (1) myth, (2) legend, (3) the fairy story, (4) the tale of sorcery, (5) the moral example, (6) the animal story, and (7) the comic anecdote. The previously mentioned journal, on the other hand, presents only types of narratives in the Nahua language: (1) cosmogonic and etiological narratives, (2) tales of the supernatural, (3) moralizing tales, (4) local events, (5) fairy stories, and (6) comic tales. By way of conclusion it must be pointed out that none of the three classifications quoted mentions another literary form practiced since pre-Columbian times, that of drama.

Translation by Jessica Johnson

Works Cited

Barba de Piña Chán, Beatriz, 1984. "Ambiente social y mentalidad mágica: Las bases del pensamiento mágico en el México prehispánico." Ph.D. diss. Mexico City: Facultad de Filosofía y Letras, UNAM.

Bernal, Ignacio. 1969. *The Olmec World*. Trans. Doris Heyden and Fernando Horcasitas. Berkeley: University of California Press.

Campbell, Lyle. 1988. *The Linguistics of Southern Chiapas, Mexico*. (With contributions by Walter Randolph Adams and Brant Gardner). Papers of the New World Archeological Foundation, 50. Provo, UT: New World Archaeological Foundation, Brigham Young University.

Campbell, Lyle, and Terrence Kauffman. 1976. "A Linguistic Look at the Olmecs." *American Anthropologist* 41: 80–89.

Census 1980. Instituto Nacional de Estadística, Geografía e Informática (INEGI) (1990, 1995). [A census is conducted every five years to study sources of employment and geographical distribution of the population. In addition, there is a General Census of Population and Housing every decade.]

Cruz, Victor de la. 1997. "Los géneros literarios en diidxazá o la posibilidad de una retórica zapoteca." *Políticas lingüísticas en México*. Ed. Beatriz Garza Cuarón. Mexico City: Centro de Investigaciones Interdisciplinarias en Ciencias y Humanidades, UNAM. 329–40.

Egland, Steven. 1978. *La inteligibilidad interdialectal en México: Resultados de algunos sondeos*. Mexico City: Instituto Lingüístico de Verano.

Felger, Richard S. and Mary B. Moser. 1984. *People of the Desert and the Sea. Ethnobotany of the Seri Indians*. Tucson: University of Arizona Press.

Fernández de Miranda, María Teresa. 1995. *El protozapoteco*. Ed. M. J. Piper and Doris A. Bartholomew. Mexico City: El Colegio de México.

Garza Cuarón, Beatriz. 1990. "Los estudios lingüísticos en México." *Estudios de lingüística de España y México*. Ed. Violeta Demont and Beatriz Garza Cuarón. Mexico City: UNAM, El Colegio de México, and Madrid: Instituto de Cooperación Iberoamericana. 35–80.

——. 1991. "Políticas lingüísticas hacia la Nueva España durante el siglo XVIII." *Nueva Revista de Filología Hispánica* 39.2: 689–706.

Garza Cuarón, Beatriz, and Doris Bartholomew. 1996. "Languages of Intercommunication in Mexico." *Atlas of Languages of Intercultural Communication in the Pacific, Asia and the Americas*. Ed. Stephen A. Wurm, Peter Mühlhäusler, Darrell T. Tryon. Berlin and New York: Mouton de Gruyter. 1253–90.

Garza Cuarón, Beatriz, and Yolanda Lastra. 1991. "Endangered Languages in Mexico." *Endangered Languages*. Ed. Robert H. Robins and Eugenius M. Uhlenbeck. New York: Oxford University Press. 93–133.

Harvey, Herbert R. 1964. "Cultural Continuity in Central Mexico: A Case for Otomangue." *Congreso Internacional de Americanistas* 35.2: 525–32.

Heath, Shirley Brice. 1972. *Telling Tongues: Languages Policy in Mexico. Colony to Nation*. New York and London: Teachers College Press at Columbia University.

Horcasitas de Barros, María Luisa, and Ana María Crespo. 1979. *Hablantes de lenguas indígenas en México*. Mexico City: Instituto Nacional de Antropología e Historia, Colección Científica.

Ibarrola, María de. 1997. "Los grandes cambios recientes en la educación básica y sus repercusiones." *Políticas lingüísticas en México*. Ed. Beatriz Garza Cuarón. Mexico City: Centro de Investigaciones Interdisciplinarias en Ciencias y Humanidades, UNAM. 303–13.

Josserand, Judy Kathryn. 1983. "Mixtec dialect history." Ph.D. diss. Tulane University, New Orleans, LA. Ann Arbor, MI: University Microfilms.

Kowaleski, Stephen A., et al. 1983. "Tres mil años en el valle de Oaxaca: Un estudio regional de asentamientos prehispánicos." *Anales de Antropología* 22.1: 27–74.

Lastra, Yolanda. 1970. "El conejo y el coyote en chichimeco." *Tlalocan* 6:115–18.

Latorre, Felipe A., and Dolores Latorre. 1979. *The Mexican Kickapoo Indians*. Austin: University of Texas Press.

Manrique Castañeda, Leonardo. 1988. *Atlas Cultural de México: Lingüística*. Mexico City: Secretaría de Educación Pública, Instituto Nacional de Antropología e Historia y Grupo Editorial Planeta.

Manrique Castañeda, Leonardo, and Ignacio Guzmán Betancourt. 1988. "Lenguas indígenas." *Enciclopedia de México*. Vol. 8. Mexico City: Secretaría de Educación Pública.

Nahmad, Salomón. 1997. "Impactos de la reforma al Artículo Constitucional sobre la política lingüística en México." *Políticas lingüísticas en México*. Ed. Beatriz Garza Cuarón. Mexico City: Instituto de Investigaciones Interdisciplinarias en Ciencias y Humanidades, UNAM. 109–31.

Ochoa Zarzueta, Jesús Angel. 1982. *Baja California; diferenciación lingüística* (Los Mochis, Sinaloa). Sinaloa, Mexico: Universidad de Occidenta.

Pellicer, Dora. 1993. "Oralidad y escritura de la literatura indígena: Una aproximación histórica." *Situación y perspectivas de la literatura en lenguas indígenas*. Ed. Carlos Montemayor Mexico City: Consejo Nacional para la cultura y las artes. 15–51.

Regina, Juan Gregorio. 1997. *Traducción de y a lenguas indígenas*. Mexico City: Colegio de México.

Schumann, Otto. 1994. "Perfil lingüístico." *Reforma* [Mexico City] 5 February, sec. "La crónica": 34–35.

Silva, Librado. 1997. "Literatura actual en lengua náhuatl de Milpa Alta." *Políticas lingüísticas en México*. Ed. Beatriz Garza Cuarón. Mexico City: Instituto de Investigaciones Interdisciplinarias en Ciencias y Humanidades, UNAM. 341–51.

Suárez, Jorge A. 1983. *The Mesoamerican Indian Languages*. Cambridge: Cambridge University Press.

———. 1990. "La clasificación de las lenguas zapotecas." *Homenaje a Jorge A. Suárez: Lingüística indoamericana e hispánica*. Ed. Beatriz Garza Cuarón and P. Levy. Estudios de literatura y lingüística, 18. Mexico City: Centro de Estudios Lingüísticos y Literarios, El Colegio de México. 41–68.

Swadesh, Morris. 1969. *Elementos del tarasco antiguo*. Mexico City: UNAM.

Winter, Marcus. 1992. *Oaxaca: The Archaeological Record*. 2d ed. Indian People of Mexico Series, 4. Mexico City: Minutiae Mexicana.

THE PRESENT-DAY INDIGENOUS LANGUAGES OF MEXICO

(Garza Cuarón and Lastra 110–20)

Branch, Group, Families, and Languages*	Location*	Number of Speakers	Source
I. UTO-AZTEC			
(A. Numic)	(United States)		
(B. Tübatulabal)	(United States)		
(C. Hopi)	(United States)		
(D. Takic)	(United States)		
E. Pimic			
1. Pima-Pápago[†]	North of Sonora	236	Census 1980
2. Lower Pima	Yécora and other populations in the east, Sonora	553	Census 1980
3. Northern Tepehuán	Guadalupe and Calvo, Chihuahua and Vicente Guerrero, Durango	14,900	Census 1980
4. Southern Tepehuán	Mezquital and Pueblo Nuevo, Durango Huajicori, Nayarit	2,903	Census 1980
F. Taracahitic			
a. TARAHUMARA-GUARIJIO			
5. Tarahumaran languages	State of Chihuahua, mainly Guachochi, Juárez and Urique.	62,419	Census 1980
	Also Sinaloa	c. 2,000	Census 1980
6. Guarijío[†]	Chihuahua	c. 300	Suárez (1983)
b. CAHITIC			
7. Mayo	North of Sinaloa, mainly: El Fuerte; south of Sonora: Etchojoa, Navojoa, Huatabampo	56,387	Census 1980
8. Yaqui	Sonora: Guaymas and some 500 in Sinalo	9,282	Census 1980
G. Corachol			
9. Cora	Nayarit; Nayar	12,240	Census 1980
10. Huichol	Jalisco mainly, Mesquitic, Zapopan and Guadalajara; c. 9000 in Nayarit, Nayar	51,850	Census 1980
H. Aztecan			
a. NAHUA			
11. Nahua languages	Center of the Republic and the states of Durango, San Luis Potosí, Hidalgo, Veracruz, Puebla, Tlaxcala, Colima, Nayarit, Michoacán, México, Federal District, and south of Oaxaca	1,376,989	Census 1980
b. PACHUTEC[‡]	South of Oaxaca	(Extinct)	
II. TOTANAC-TEPEHUA			
A. Totonacan			

Branch, Group, Families, and Languages*	Location*	Number of Speakers	Source
12. Totonac languages	Northern region of Veracruz, mainly: Papantla, Coyutla, Zozocalco Coxquihui, Espinal, Mecatlán, Filomeno Mata, Cazones, Coacoatzintla, Tihuatlan, Chumatlán and Poza Rica; Puebla (less than 70,000): Huehuetla, Olintla, Jopala, Pantepec, Hermenegildo Galeana, Tlacuilotepec, Ixtepec, Calpan, Zapotitlán de Méndez, San Felipe Tepatla, Tepango de Rodríguez, Amixtlán, and Zongozotla	196,003	Census 1980
B. Tepehua			
13. Tepehua languages	Veracruz, mainly: Ixhuatlán de Madero, Tlachichilco, Zontecomatlán; Hidalgo, some 1500 in Huehuetla	8,487	Census 1980

III. OTOMANGUEAN

A. Otopamean

a. PAMEAN

14. North Pame	San Luis Potosí: Santa Catarina, Tamasopo, Rayón, Alaquines	5,649	Census (1980)
15. Southern Pame‡	Extinct		
16. Chichimec (Jonaz)	San Luis de la Paz, Guanajuato	c. 877	Lastra

b. OTOMIAN

OTOMI-MAZAHUA

17. Otomi languages	States of Hidalgo, Mexico, Guanajuato, Querétaro, Tlaxcala	306,190	Census 1980
18. Mazahua	Western part of the state of México, few in eastern Michoacán (in Zitácuaro)	194,125	Census 1980

MATLATZINCA- OCUILTECO

19. Matlatzinca†	San Francisco Oztotilpan, Municipality of Temazcaltepec, state of México	1,792	Suárez (1983)
20. Ocuilteco†	San Juan Atzingo, Ocuilan, Mexico	393	Suárez (1983)

B. Popolocano

a. POPOLOC-IXCATEC

21. Popoloca languages	Northern Puebla (the census of 1980 apparently includes Popoloca in the denomination of "Chocho"), northwest Oaxaca	c. 12,310	Census 1980
22. Chocho	Northeast of Oaxaca	1,912	Census 1980
23. Ixcateco†	Santa María Ixcatlán, Oaxaca	119	Suárez (1983)

b. MAZATECO

24. Mazatecan languages	Mainly in northern Oaxaca	124,176	Census 1980

C. Subtiaba-Tlapanec

25. Tlapaneco	Guerrero, mainly municipalities of Malinaltepec, Zapotitlán, Tablas, Atlixtac and Tlacoapa	55,068	Census 1980
26. (Subtiaba‡)	(Nicaragua)	Extinct	

D. Amuzgo

27. Amuzgo from Guerrero	Southeastern Guerrero	16,205	Census 1980
28. Amuzgo from Oaxaca	Southwestern Oaxaca	2,168	Census 1980

Branch, Group, Families, and Languages*	Location*	Number of Speakers	Source
E. Mixtec			
a. MIXTEC			
29. Mixtecan languages	Western Oaxaca, Eastern Guerrero, Southern Puebla	323,137	Census 1980
b. CUICATECO			
30. Cuicateco	Ex-district of Cuicatlán, Oaxaca, mainly in the municipalities of S. Tepecuixtla, S. Andrés Teotilalpan, Santos Reyes Pápalo, Concepción Pápalo and Santa María Pápalo	14,155	Census 1980
c. TRIQUE			
31. Trique from Copala	State of Oaxaca: San Juan de Copala, Municipality of Santiago Juxtlahuacan, ex-district of Juxtlahuaca	4,342	Census 1980
32. Trique from Chicahuaxtla	Western Oaxaca: San Andrés Chicahuaxtla, Santo Domingo Chicahuaxtla, Municipality of Putla, ex-district of Putla; San José Chicahuaxtla, Municipality of Sta. María Asunción Tlaxiaco, ex-district of Tlaxiaco; S. Martín Ituynoso (chief town), ex-district of Tlaxiaco	3,428	Census 1980
F. Chatino-Zapoteco			
a. CHATINO			
33. Chatino languages	Southern Oaxaca: ex-district of Juquila mainly municipalities of Santos Reyes Nopala, S. Miguel Panixtlahuaca and S. Juan Quiahije	20,543	Census 1980
b. ZAPOTECAN			
34. Zapotec	Central and eastern Oaxaca	422,937	Census 1980
G. Chinanteco			
35. Chinantecan languages	Oaxaca: mainly in the ex-districts of Tuxtepec and Choapan	77,083	Census 1980
H. Chiapanec-Mangue			
36. Chiapanec‡		Extinct	
37. (Mangue‡)	(Nicaragua)	Extinct	
IV. TARASCAN			
38. Tarasco	North central Michoacán	111,614	Census 1980
V. CUITLATECO			
39. Cuitlateco‡		Extinct	
VI. TEQUISTLATECO-JICAQUE			
A. Tequistlatecan			
40. Coastal Chontal (or Huamelula)	Huamelula and Astata in southeastern Oaxaca	1,985	Census 1980
41. Highland Chontal	Southeastern Oaxaca	6,101	Census 1980
B. Jicaque			
42. (Jicaque from El Palmar‡)	(Honduras)	Extinct	Census 1980
43. (Jicaque from La Flor)	Honduras	Extinct	

Branch, Group, Families, and Languages*	Location*	Number of Speakers	Source
VII. HUAVE			
44. Huave	Five towns on the southeastern coast of Oaxaca; (San Mateo, San Dionisio, San Francisco, Santa María and Huazontlán) in the ex-districts of Tehuantepec and Juchitán	9,972	Census 1980
VIII. MIXE-ZOQUE			
A. Zoquean			
45. Zoque from Chiapas	Municipality of Copainalá, Chapultenango, Francisco León, Ocotepec, Pantepec Tapulapan, Tapilula, and Tecpalan	25,744	Census 1980
46. Zoque from Oaxaca	Santa María Chimalapa and San Miguel Chimalapa	5,231	Census 1980
47. Popoluca from the Mountain Range (of Veracruz)	State of Veracruz, mainly Hueyapan de Ocampo, Soteapan, Acayucan and Minatitlán	19,819	Census 1980
48. Popoluca from Texistepec	Texistepec, Veracruz	797	Census 1980
B. Mixe			
a. MIXE			
49. Mixe languages	Northeastern Oaxaca	74,083	Census 1980
50. Sayula Popoluca	Sayula, Veracruz	3,025	Census 1980
51. Mixe from Oluta = Popoluca from Oluta[†]	Oluta, Veracruz	121	Census 1980
b. TAPACHULTECO			
52. Tapachulteco[‡]	(Chiapas)	Extinct	
IX. MAYAN			
A. Huastecan			
53. Huastec	San Luis Potosí: Municipalities of Aquismón, Tanjalas, Ciudad Valles, Huehuetlán, San Antonio Tampomolón, Tancuayalab. Veracruz: Municipality of Tantoyucan, Chontla, Chinamapa, Tantima and Tantoco	103,788	Census 1980
54. Chicomucelteco	(Chiapas)	Extinct	Schumann
B. Yucatecan			
55. Yucatec	Yucatán, Campeche, Quintana Roo (also spoken in Guatemala and Belize)	655,377	Census 1980
56. (Mopán)	(Belize, Guatemala)		
57. Itzá	(Guatemala)		
58. Lacandón[†]	Eastern part of Chiapas	200	Suárez (1983)
(WESTERN GROUP)			
C. Greater Tzeltalan			
a. CHOLAN			
59. Chol	Northern Chiapas: Tila, Tumbalá, Salto de Agua, Sabanilla	96,776	Census 1980
60. Chontal	Tabasco: mainly: Municipalities of Nacajuca, Centro, Centla, Macuspana, and Jonuta	60,000	Shumann
61. (Chortí)	(Guatemala)		

Branch, Group, Families, and Languages*	Location*	Number of Speakers	Source
b. TZELTALAN			
62. Tzeltal	Central Chiapas east of the Tzotziles; mainly in the municipalities of Chilón, Oxchuc, Tenejapa, Yajalón, Ocosingo and Stitala	215,145	Census 1980
63. Tzotzil	Central Chiapas, mainly the municipalities of Chamula, Chenalhó, Zinacantan, Larrainza (= San Andrés Chamula), Simojovel, El Bosque, and Chalchihuitán	133,389	Census 1980
D. Greater Kanjobalan			
a. CHUJEAN			
64. Chuj	Trinitaria, Chiapas	c. 1,500 Mexicans and c. 8,000 Guatemalan refugees	Schumann
65. Tojolabal	Mainly in the municipality of Margaritas and Altamirano, Chiapas	22,331	Census 1980
b. KANJOBALAN KANJOBAL GROUP			
66. Kanjobal	Trinitaria and Comalapa, Chiapas and Quintana Roo.	Some Mexicans and c. 10,000 refugees	Schumann
67. Jacalteco	Amatenango de la Frontera, Chiapas	c. 500 Mexicans c. 10,000 Guatemalan refugees	Schumann
68. Acateco‡	Amatenango de la Frontera, Comalapa de la Frontera, Mazapa de Madero, Chiapas	c. 100 Mexicans and a larger number of refugees	Schumann
COTOQUE			
69. Motozintleco-Tuzantec (Mochó)‡	Motozintla, Chiapas	c. 500	Schumann
70. Tuzantec‡	Tuzantán, Chiapas	c. 300	Schumann
(EASTERN GROUP)			
E. Greater Mamean			
a. MAMEAN			
71. Mam	Eastern Chiapas: Motozintla, Mazapa de Madero, Amatenango de la Frontera, Comalapa, El Porvenir, La Grandeza, Bejucal de Ocampo, Chicomucelo, Siltepec, Tuzantán, Huehuetán, Tapachula, Cacahuatán, Unión Juárez	28,000	Census 1980, Schumann
72. (Teco)	(Guatemala)		
b. IXILIAN			
73. (Ixil)	(Guatemala)		
74. (Aguacatec)	(Guatemala)		
F. Greater Quiché			
a. QUICHEAN			
75. (Quiché)	(Guatemala)		
76. (Cakchiquel)	(Guatemala)		
77. (Tzutuhil)	(Guatemala)		
78. (Sacapultec)	(Guatemala)		
79. (Sipacapa)	(Guatemala)		
b. USPANTEC			
80. (Uspanteco)	(Guatemala)		
c. POCOMAN-POCOMCHI			
81. (Pocoman-Pocomchí)	(Guatemala)		

Branch, Group, Families, and Languages*	Location*	Number of Speakers	Source
d. KEKCHI			
82. (Kekchí)	(Guatemala)		
X. XINCA			
83. (Xinca languages‡?)	(Guatemala)		
XI. LENCA			
84. (El Salvador Lenca‡)	(El Salvador)		
85. (Honduras Lenca‡)	(Honduras)		
XII. CHIBCHA§			
86. (Paya)	(Honduras)		
XIII. ARAWAKAN‖			
87. Black Carib (Garífuna)	(Honduras)		
XIV. MISUMALPA			
88. (Miskito)	(Honduras and Nicaragua)		
89. (Sumu)	(Nicaragua)		
90. (Matagalpa)	(Nicaragua)		
XV. YUMAN-SERI#			
A. Yuma#			
91. Paipai[†, #]	Ensenada, Baja California North	240	Ochoa (1982)
92. Kiliwa[†, #]	Ensenada, Baja California North	90	Ochoa (1982)
93. Cochimí[†, #]	Ensenada, Baja California North	93	Ochoa (1982)
94. Cucapá[†, #]	Ensenada, Baja California North	178	Ochoa (1982)
95. Seri[†, #]	Pitiquito, Sonora	500	Felger and Moser (1984)
XVI. ALGONQUIAN#			
96 Kickapoo[†, #]	Ranchería Nacimiento, Municipality of Melchor Múzquiz, Coahuila.	400	Latorre and Latorre (1976)

*The languages or subgroups within parentheses are found outside of Mexico.

†Languages in imminent danger of disappearing.

‡Extinct languages.

§A large family; those remaining are located in Central America and South America.

‖A large family; those remaining are located in South America.

#A family, group, or language that is not Mesoamerican.

CHAPTER 9

DOCUMENT: TZOTZIL TEXT

Juan González Hernández

Yoroal xojobal sat jtotik

Jun mal k'ak'al ta xa xch'ay sat jtotik, naka tzajal toktik xa, ko'ol xa selan chak'ucha'al oro. Ati k'alal laj kil ti va's-elanile linopaj ech'el ta yolon a ti toke yu'un slajeb xa jlikel sak ti banamile. K'alal teun xa ya'yel une, ja'to laj kil xbajlajan xa likel uni vo'etik puru k'onik chak'uni oroetik; ba ox jtzak ek u, pero ja'to chkil toj sak ch'ayel ta jk'ob, jbej chabej xa no'ox ikom pere puru uni oroetik. A ti sat jtotike tze'ej xa xa'i ech'el, ko'ol xa chak'ucha'al ch-ok', solel xmalajan ya'lel sat jun sk'anakil chak'puro oro, pere jlikel xa no'ox sak ti osile, ja'xa no'ox slajeb ora mal k'ak'al, k'alal jun stzajal, jun sk'anal sat ti jtotik ibate. Ibat yo'xu'xkuxik ti yalab snich'nabe xchi'uk xikta jutuk yabte-lik, yo'junuk yutzil, slekil, xvayik. Laj to yalbun komel jbel sk'op: ikuni nich'om, ok'om to me! Pere jech, ikom, ta jk'ob ti ya'lel yuni sate, ti jun yutzil chak'ucha'al uni oroetike.

Ta jlikel, ital ik'al tok, yu'un ik'ub o ti banomile. Sta yorail ti kuxom o'ntonale, la jkux lek te kunul ta jxokon ti sbejtikil oroe. Ja'xa no'ox laj yak sakilal xchi'uk xojobal ti bu ta jkuxe, ti bu chkux ti jbektal jta-kopale, yu'un mi ja'uk buch'utztaik yan chak'ucha'al la jta jun mal k'ak'al, ta jun tzajal mal k'ak'al, ja' no'ox jtuk jech. Lek ti mi jech la taik yan eke.

La tarde dorada

En una tarde cuando, casi metiéndose, el sol iluminaba las nubes en colores, me acerqué a esas nubes que alumbran por última vez la tarde. Al estar en aquel lugar comenzaron a caer gotas de oro sobre mí, se desvanecían entre mis manos y sólo se quedaron unas que fueron reales gotas de oro. Era el triste sol. Se despedía sonriendo con lágrimas de oro que caían de su propio ojo.

El cielo permaneció todavía unos minutos claro; era el último minuto de aquella tarde dorada, cuando el sol se fue, se fue para que sus ama-dos descansen, dejen de trabajar y pasen sueños felices. Me dejó su última palabra: "inos vemos hijito!" y quedaron en mis manos las gotas doradas de puro oro.

Al instante, nubes negras cubrieron la noche, noche de alivio que me hizo descansar juntito a las gotas de oro; sólo esas gotitas doradas ilu-minaron mi lugar de descanso, donde posan mi cuerpo y mi alma.

Creo que a nadie le ha sucedido como a mí me sucedió en esa dorada tarde del pasado, sólo a mí y espero que a ti también.

Juan González Hernández
Tzotzil, Chamula

The Golden Afternoon

One afternoon when the sun was setting, it illuminated the clouds with bright colors. I came up to those bright clouds that for the last time that afternoon filled the sky with such brilliance. While I was there drops of gold began to fall on me, they ran through my fingers and only a few drops remained. The sun was sad. He said goodbye smiling with tears of gold that fell from his eye.

The sky remained clear for a few minutes more; it was the last minute of a golden afternoon before the sun went down so that those it loves can rest, so that they can stop working and have pleasant dreams. He took his leave with these words: "See you soon!" and the drops of pure gold remained in my hand.

In a moment black clouds brought on the night, the night that soothes, that allows me to rest, next to the drops of gold. It was only those few drops of gold that illuminated my place of rest where my body and soul reposed.

I don't think that what happened to me has happened to anyone else, just me and I hope to you too.

Translation into English by Mario J. Valdés

Lucila Mondragón, Jacqueline Tello and Argelia Valdez. 1995. *Relatos Tzotziles A'yej lo'il ta sot'ilk'op*. Mexico City: Consejo Nacional para la cultura y las artes. Dirección popular de culturas populares. 8–9.

CHAPTER 10

DOCUMENT: ZAPOTEC TEXT

Santiago Fabián

¡O si da cheltelloze yel güe'o da'o risen!
¡Cha' yeto ye yaca' bi güe'onx!

Che' nac yel güe'on ca no pies
—can no pandancon—
guacja' guayonan dan repetir yeto

que nac no piesen
da guayac repite yeto
—que nac pandancon.

Pero yel güe'on
bibi de guayonan repetir yetox,
compañero qui.

Ne que ga llo'tlizen yel güe'o da'o risen.
Ga ga denx;
a ga decsen yechlasen je.

Len mejoren, mercería del Gallo,
na' de yel güe'on,
on que ne aczen.
Ba janaban, bibi de'n je.

Bibi de go'ten,
bibi llaque go'ten,
Mercería el Gallo ne aquex,
compañero qui.

Bllina' llepa' bi dependienten:
—¿Bi de yel güe'on go'to'?
—Bib yel güe'o de go'ta'.
¿O cha'lo de go'tan,
ni quia' bib de?
—Ne bi dependienten je—.

Bxi' laz co', bxi' no relojco'n,
bxi' laz con da llajlo' ganix,
biteze lle'nlo' si'ox;
pero merze yel güe'on bibi de,
bibi de go'ta'
—ne bi dependienten, llebe' nada'.

Jachela', llepabe':
¿Bi de yelnban go'to'?
llepa' bi dependiente.
Bib yel nban de go'ta', bibi de.
¡O cha' de go'ta'! . . .
¡Ni quia' yel nban bibi de!
—ne bi dependiente je.

Jachielanda' ca da tras ay,
ga bayollten llepabe':
¿Bixa yel got?
¿Bi de yel goten go'to' cha'?
llepabe'x.
Bibi yel goten llo'tanda' —nebe'y —.

Den naquen puñalen, chat uzi'o puñalen;
de yel goten naquen puñal —nebe'y;
de yel goten naquen pistole —llebe' nada'x.

—¿Bi gonla' daca'y?—llepabe'x
¡Yel güe'onan lle'nla'!

¡Yel güe'onan lle'nla'x,
compañero qui!

Santiago Fabián L. (Oral poet)
Zapotec, Yalálag, Oaxaca, Mexico

Juventud pasajera

¡Oh, qué pasajera esta juventud!
¡Si otra vez volviera a ser joven!

Si la juventud fuera como una pieza de música
—como el fandango—
que pudiera repetirla otra vez

lo mismo que una pieza
puede repetirse otra vez
como el fandango.
Pero la juventud sí
no puede repetirse otra vez,
compañeros.

En ningún lugar venden juventud.
En ningún lugar la hay;
desde siempre en ningún lugar la ha habido.

Siendo la Mercería El Gallo la mejor,
debería tener juventud,
nomás dicen.
Ya fui a pedirla y no la hay.

Que no hay para vender,
que no la pueden vender,
dicen en la Mercería El Gallo,
compañeros.

Llegando dije al dependiente:
¿No tienen juventud que vender?
-No tengo juventud que vender.
¿Cómo voy a tener para vender
si yo mismo no la tengo?
—dice el dependiente—.

Compra un repuesto, compra un reloj,
compra aquí cosas que necesitas,
todo lo que quieras comprar;
pero la mera juventud no la hay,
no la tengo para vender
—me dijo el dependiente.

Me cansé y le dije:
¿No tienes vida que vender?
le dije al dependiente.
No hay vida que vender, no la hay.
¡Si la tuviera para vender! . . .
¡Ni la mía tengo!
—dijo el dependiente.

Enfadado al fin, acabé diciendo:
¿Y muerte?
¿No tienes muerte que vender?
le dije.

Yo no tengo muerte que vender
–dijo.

Hay muerte pero es puñal;
hay muerte, es puñal;
tengo muerte pero es pistola
–me dijo.

¿Para qué quiero esas cosas?–le dije.
¡Juventud es lo que quiero!
¡Quiero juventud,
compañeros!

*Transcription and translation to Spanish by Sergio Aquino D.,
Noé Ventura P.*

Fleeting Youth

Oh, how fleeting is youth!
If only one could become young again!

If youth were like a piece of music
–like the fandango–
that could be repeated

just like a piece of music
that can be repeated
like the fandango.
But youth cannot be repeated,
my friends.

Nowhere is youth sold,
Nowhere is it found;
from the beginning it has never been found anywhere.

Since the El Gallo store is the best,
it should have youth for sale,
they say.
I went to ask for some, and there isn't any.

There isn't any to sell,
they can't sell it,
they say at the El Gallo store,
my friends.

When I got there I said to the clerk,
"Don't you have youth to sell?"
"I don't have youth to sell.
How would I have it to sell
if I myself don't have it?"
said the clerk.

"Buy a little something, buy a watch,
buy here the things that you need,
all that you want to buy,
but youth itself you won't find here.
I don't have it to sell,"
said the clerk to me.

Annoyed, I said to him,
"Don't you have life to sell?"
I said to the clerk.
"No, life is not for sale, there isn't any.
If I only had it to sell!
I don't have even my own!"
said the clerk.

Annoyed, I finished by saying,
"And death?
Don't you have death to sell?"
I said to him.
"I don't have death to sell,"
he said.

"There is death, but it is a dagger;
there is death, it is a dagger;
I have death but it is a pistol,"
he told me.

"Why do I want those things?" I said to him.
Youth is what I want!
I want youth,
my friends!

Translation into English by Stephen A. Marlett

Work Cited

Juventud pasajera: cantos de la vida y la muerte. Folleto 2. Mexico City: Summer Institute of Linguistics, 1986.

CHAPTER 11

LINGUISTIC DIVERSITY IN VENEZUELA

Marie-Claude Mattéi Muller

The indigenous population of Venezuela today numbers around 320,000, scarcely 1.5 percent of the total population of the country (22 million). Except for the Andean countries and Mesoamerica, this situation is common in a number of Latin American states. Even so, the peculiarity of Venezuela is based on the fact that these tiny ethnic minorities are precisely those that populate the frontiers (80 percent and more in some areas). This somewhat incongruous reality is well known by both national and regional authorities, who consider such populations to be "marginalized" in

many senses of the word—not only from a cultural-linguistic point of view, but also from geographic, socioeconomic, and political perspectives.

Twenty-eight indigenous languages are still spoken in Venezuela, ten of which are also spoken in the neighboring countries (Brazil, Colombia, and Surinam, as well as French Guiana and Guyana). Even so, it is necessary to point out that eight ethnic groups make up over 88 percent of the indigenous population. This means that the rest belong to very small groups, some of which are almost on the verge of extinction (see **Map 1**).

Map 1.

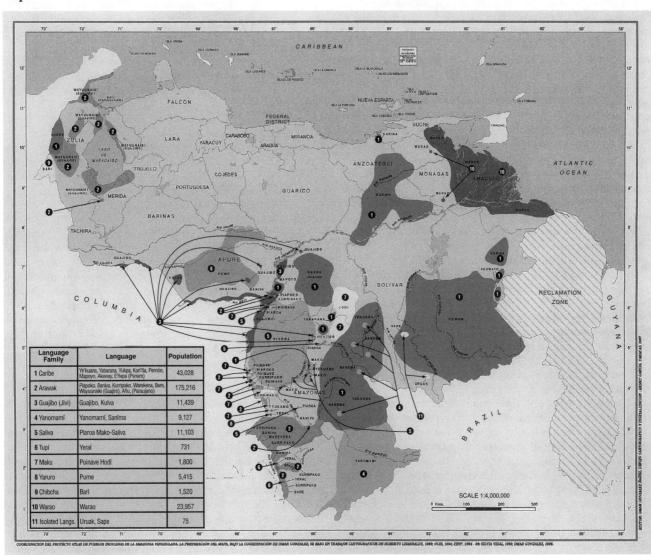

Language Family	Language	Population
1 Caribe	Ye'kuana, Yabarana, Yukpa, Kari'ña, Pemón, Mapoyo, Akaway, E'ñepa (Panare)	43,028
2 Arawak	Piapoko, Baniva, Kurripako, Warekena, Bare, Wayuunaiki (Guajiro), Añu, (Paraujano)	175,216
3 Guajibo (Jivi)	Guajibo, Kuiva	11,439
4 Yanomamï	Yanomamï, Sanïma	9,127
5 Saliva	Piaroa Mako-Saliva	11,103
6 Tupi	Yeral	731
7 Maku	Puinave Hodï	1,800
8 Yaruro	Pume	5,415
9 Chibcha	Bari	1,520
10 Warao	Warao	23,957
11 Isolated Langs.	Uruak, Sape	75

EDITOR: OMAR GONZALEZ. MAPAS: GRUPO CARTOGRAFICO I DIGITALIZACION: HENRY GARCIA, CARACAS 2007

COORDINACION DEL PROYECTO ATLAS DE PUEBLOS INDIGENAS DE LA AMAZONIA VENEZOLANA. LA PREPARACION DEL MAPA, BAJO LA COORDINACION DE OMAR GONZALEZ, SE BASO EN TRABAJOS CARTOGRAFICOS DE ROBERTO LIZARRALDE, 1983; OCEI, 1994; ZENT, 1994 - 98; SILVIA VIDAL, 1994; OMAR GONZALEZ, 1995.

These results are based on facts gained by the last indigenous census held by the OCEI (Oficina Central de Estadistica e Informática [Central Office of Statistics and Information]) in coordination with the DAI (Dirección de Asuntos Indigenistas [Department of Indigenist Affairs]) of the Education Ministry. During the taking of this census, over 80 percent of the indigenous people interviewed declared themselves as knowing a native language; more than 76 percent were already bilingual (indigenous-Spanish). Yet 20 percent of the population listed under the census as being indigenous do not communicate in their native tongue and in some cases do not understand it. Indeed, Spanish is gradually spreading as the common language, above all in communities near those with a *mestizo* population. An enormous variety of linguistic families exists in Venezuela, but two, Carib and Arawak, are the most widely spoken.

The Carib Family

This family is made up of eight ethnic groups (Akawaio, Kari'ña, Mapoyo, Panare-E'ñepa, Pemón, Yawarana, Ye'kuana, and Yukpa). An approximate calculation of Carib populations throughout the American continent in 1996 totaled 82,000 (source for Brazil: Banco de Datos do Programa Indígenas no Brasil-Instituto Socioambiental, December 1995). Venezuela, with its 43,000 Carib speakers, is the most "Carib," in the historical-linguistic sense of the word, nation in the American continent given that more than half the total population is concentrated within its territory. In fact, there still exist some 30 languages classified within the Carib family that are shared among six countries (Brazil, Colombia, French Guiana and Guyana, Surinam, and Venezuela). Many of the Carib languages spoken outside Venezuela belong to small groups of between 1000 and 2000 people, as well as even smaller ones, with populations that range from under 100 to 1000. The most important Carib group within Venezuela is the Pemón, 20,000 strong, with its different subgroups, the Arekuna, Taurepep, Kamarakoto, and Makushi. It is located in the southern part of Bolivar state on the border with Brazil. Despite an important element of bilingualism (50 percent), this group is linguistically vigorous, given that more than 5000 of the Pemón are still monolingual.

Two other groups, even though demographically smaller, remain linguistically strong. The Ye'kuana (4500 people) or De'kwana, also known as Makiritares in ethnographic literature, occupy a vast territory between the states of Bolivar and Amazonas. They are one of the most dynamic of the groups because of their knowledge and use of local flora and fauna (particularly in the field of ethnomedicine) as well as their new economic orientation (the creation of the first indigenous cooperatives, cacao production, the sale of honey, and construction of river craft) and the high quality of their craftwork. Bilingualism, which involved only 1500 individuals in 1992, is now accelerating in tandem with an increasing absorption of Western ways.

The *Panares,* who call themselves E'ñepa, are located in the northeast, on the Guiana massif in Bolivar state. Totalling over 3200 people, this is the Carib group with the highest percentage of monolingual speakers (80 percent), despite their location in *criollo* zones and areas of high mineral exploitation (bauxite, diamonds, and gold). The Kari'ña are located in the states of Anzoátegui and Monagas in the east of the country. They are also represented in Surinam (Carib) and French Guiana (Galibi). According to the 1992 indigenous census, their population totals over 11,000, but this should not be taken too literally. In fact, over 50 percent speak only Span-

ish. Almost 3000 Kari'ña are said to be bilingual, and some 300 are practically monolingual, but 92.8 percent use Spanish as the main language for communication. Moreover, today the majority of the children speak only Spanish.

The Yukpa (known as Yuko in Colombia), along with the subgroup Japrería, are to be found in the west of Venezuela on the border with Colombia. They constitute a relatively demographically important Carib group (4174 people), but the presence of the Wayuu, an extremely powerful Arawak group, and the difficulties inherent in this border region (the cultivation of marijuana and more recently of opium poppies as well as the exploitation of the forest) are having a serious effect on the linguistic and cultural vitality of this group. The majority are bilingual (Yukpa-Spanish), even though some 500 were described as monolingual in the census.

The Akawaio group, also known as the Kapon, are found on the border between Venezuela and Guyana. One of the smallest groups, it consists of only 811 individuals, all of whom are familiar with the indigenous language. Some 120 are monolingual; 454 are bilingual in Akawaio-Spanish and 70 in Akawaio-English.

Over 300 people who inhabit San Juan Manapiare and the surrounding areas in the state of Amazonas speak Yawarana. However, among the members of the population who are over five years old, 134 speak Spanish while 11 are said to be bilingual. The last monolingual speaker died in 1997, and today no child is being taught to communicate in Yawarana.

According to data published by Francia Medina (1997), Mapoyo is spoken by 124 individuals found in the Cedeño District of Bolivar state, near the Los Pijiguanos bauxite mine. Their self-appointed nomenclature is in doubt, given that the Mapoyos describe themselves as Wanai (Henley 1945 and Mattéi Muller 1975) while more recently Mattéi Muller found the name Pémono given by an informant living in the Alto Parcuito who spoke Mapoyo (work in progress). Now, only three individuals of speaking age, two very old (over 80 years), still know the Mapoyo language, but they do not practice it with their children.

One situation still needs to be clarified: the survival of some Chaimas on the east coast of the country between Puerto Piritu, Cumana, and Caripíto. Texts on this subject, written by Father Tauste and Father Ruiz Blanco, still exist that date back to the seventeenth century. However, more recently, Andrés Romero, a researcher from the University of Cumaná, is said to have found some Chaima speakers. In July 1995, a small delegation of people who identified themselves as Chaimas appeared at the Dirección de Asuntos Indígenas (Department of Indigenous Affairs) in Caracas. But to date, there is no further information as to their linguistic competence in their native language.

The Arawak Family (Arahuaca)

This is the most important group in Venezuela in terms of linguistic population, also consisting of eight ethnic groups. The Wayuu, who number around 170,000, represent not only half the indigenous population of Venezuela but also 80 percent of the Arawak family. The other ethnic groups are the Añu, Baniwa, Baré, Kurripako, Lokono, Piapoko, and Warekena.

The Wayuu, better known in ethnographic literature as the Guajiros (Wayuu being their name for themselves), are the most vigorous ethnic group in Venezuela from many points of view. Located in the northwest of the country on the border with Colombia (where an important group of the same ethnic family also lives), the Wayuu occupy mainly the Guajira Peninsula and the area around Maracaibo, capital of Zulia state and the second most important city in Venezuela. The census of 1992 reported 75 percent bilingualism, with monolingual Spanish (almost 20 percent) and Wayuu (15 percent) speakers. The importance of the Wayuu is grounded not only in their demographic strength but also particularly in their cultural-linguistic vitality and the economic and political power held by some of their members in the Zulia region. Their strong position facilitated the application of the bilingual intercultural program, discussed below, to a greater extent than in other parts of Venezuela.

The Añu, also known as Paraujanos, are found in the west of Venezuela, especially around Lake Sinamaica, the Guajira Peninsula, and the outskirts of Maracaibo. Although the population totals 17,440, the case of the Añu is even more dramatic than that of the Kari'ña, given that 99 percent speak only Spanish. The domination of their Wayuu neighbors is one of the reasons suggested to explain the brutal disappearance of this language. Among speakers over five years old, 222 acknowledged themselves as bilingual in Añu and Spanish, while the number of monolingual speakers was reduced to two now very old individuals. Some Añu have already shown their concern about the situation by asking the Dirección de Asuntos Indigenistas for help in setting up emergency rescue projects for the recovery of their cultural and linguistic heritage.

The Kurripako (also written Curripacos) are divided into small groups along the frontier between Venezuela and Colombia, south of San Fernando de Atabapo. Although very numerous on the Colombian side (some 6000 individuals), their population does not exceed 3000 on the Venezuelan side of the border. A small group called the Baniwa-Kurripako are also found in Brazilian territory. In Venezuela, 60 percent of the Kurripako are bilingual. With the exception of a few monolingual speakers, the rest now do not know how to communicate in their native language.

The Piapoko are also less numerous in Venezuela (amounting to a little over 1800) than in Colombia (approximately 5000). Located today around Puerto Ayacucho, they are almost all bilingual. The Baniwa, dispersed in small groups in Amazonas state, number little more than 1000; however, 505 are ignorant of their own language and the rest are bilingual.

The Lokono, who are sometimes classified as Arawak, are located to the south of the Orinoco delta in the eastern part of Venezuela bordering with Guyana. They have a small population (around 250 individuals) who are almost all bilingual (Lokono-Spanish or Lokono-English) with the exception of two adults who are monolingual in Lokono.

The Warekena in the south of Amazonas state constitute a small group of 428 people. Forty percent of the population now do not know the Warekena idiom; they communicate only in Spanish. The rest are largely bilingual (Warekena-Spanish), except for seven people who are monolingual.

Today the Baré, who are mainly found in Puerto Ayachucho, the capital of Amazonas state, represent in linguistic terms the most threatened group of the Arawak family. Their population totals 1226, but over 80 percent do not know the Baré language and communicate only in Spanish. The remainder know their native language but use Spanish in everyday life.

Besides these two large families (the Carib and Arawak), representatives of the Chibcha, Maku, and Tupi linguistic groups are also found in Venezuela.

The Chibcha Family

The only representative of this group are the Barí, who also have appeared in ethnographic literature as the Motilón. Without taking into consideration ethnic differences, this name was extended to all the indigenous groups inhabiting the Sierra de Perijá in the northwest section of the Venezuelan-Colombian frontier (the Motilones included the Barí and the Yukpa, the Carib group discussed above). The Barí consist of a group of 1520 people, the majority of whom are familiar with their native language; only 21 people were reported in the census as being ignorant of their mother tongue. However, the situation of the Barí is deteriorating in an alarming fashion, though to a lesser degree than that of their Yukpa neighbors, resulting from their location in this extremely conflict-ridden border zone between Venezuela and Colombia (problems of land occupation and land ownership as well as illicit drug trafficking).

The Maku Family

Two languages have been classified as belonging to this family, but this attribution is still in doubt. The Puinave, more numerous in Colombian territory, are composed of 773 individuals, the majority of whom are bilingual in Puinave and Spanish. Loukotka, taking up Rivet's argument, locates the Puinave in the Maku family, but such an association requires a more detailed comparison with the Maku groups of Colombia (Nukak and Kakwa); very limited information is currently available. Some work is now in progress on the Nukak and the Kakwa that should lead to an explanation in the near future.

The Hodi (also called the Hoti or Ho, and sometimes written Jodi) are recent arrivals in ethnographic literature, given that practically nothing was known about them prior to 1973. Located in the Sierra de Maigualida in the Alto Cuchivero between Bolivar and Amazonas states, they constitute a group of around 1000, most of whom are monolingual. Since they live isolated from *criollo* villages, only those few Hodi who live in evangelical and Catholic missions have some knowledge of Spanish. However, a part of the group has settled in Kayama, which is inhabited by a Panare group. Collaborating with Henley and Reid, the author has presented data that suggest the possibility of a Maku affiliation for the Hodi group. However, further linguistic information is lacking on the different Maku groups scattered between Venezuela, Brazil, and Colombia to consolidate this hypothesis. Work in progress in these regions may well bring a more substantial answer soon.

The Sáliba Family

The majority of the Piaroa (who call themselves Wotïhhü or Wóthïhë, also written Wótjüjä) are found in Amazonas state to the south of Puerto Ayachucho, with some enclaves near San Juan Manapiare, as well as in Bolivar state near Los Pijiguaos. Totaling 11,194, half of the population of speaking age communicate exclusively in Piaroa, an indication of great linguistic vitality. Fewer than 100 individuals do not know their mother tongue. The Piaroa group is generally associated with two subgroups that have very reduced populations.

The first of these two is the Mako, comprising 345 people, who are mostly to be found in Toki, a community in Ventuari (Amazonas state) in Ye'kuana and Yawarana territory. Almost all still speak their native language. However, their contact with the highly dominant Ye'kuana group has threatened their survival in the short term.

The second group, the Sáliba, who total just seventy-nine individuals on the Venezuelan side of the border (many more than on the Colombian), now communicate exclusively in Spanish. Seventeen people stated that they still knew their own language as well as Spanish.

The Tupí Family

The Yeral or Ñengatu language is still spoken by around 600 people in Venezuela (out of 740 people classified as Yeral in the 1992 census). The speakers of this group all know Spanish, which is the most common language used for communication. Located in Amazonas state, especially in the southern region from San Fernando de Atabapo to San Carlos de Rio Negro and San Gabriel do Cachoeira, the Yeral have progressively mixed with the Arawak groups of the area (Baniwa, Kurripako, Baré, and Warekena), which has generated an "Arawakization" of their mother tongue both in Venezuela and Brazil, the latter being inhabited by a larger number of Yeral speakers.

Independent Families

Among the independent families are four demographically important groups whose linguistic survival is not threatened in the short term (Hiwi, Piaroa, Waroa, and Yanomamï). But the danger of extinction does exist to an alarming degree for the very small groups (Mako, Sáliba, Sapé, and Uruak) and even for those that are demographically a little larger, such as the Pumé.

The Hiwi or Guajibo Group

The Guajibos call themselves the Hiwi, sometimes written Jivi, in Venezuela (Sikuani in Colombia). They total more than 11,000 individuals, the majority of whom inhabit Amazonas state around Puerto Ayachucho, except for the Kuiva subgroup, located in Apure state, which number 348 people. Eighty percent of the population over 5 years old is now bilingual in Guajibo-Spanish, but an additional 1200 are completely monolingual. Only 631 stated that they knew just the Spanish language.

The Warao Group

Situated in the Orinoco delta in Delta Amacuro state, the Warao, known as Guaraunos in some old texts, are a group now totaling 24,000 individuals. More than 50 percent still speak their native language; the rest are bilingual in Warao and Spanish. Fewer than 500 are unable to communicate in their mother tongue.

The Yanomamï Group

The Yanomamï consist of more than 20,000 people distributed between Venezuela and Brazil. More than 60 percent live in the former country (some 12,000, including the Sanïma subgroup), of which 90 percent are monolingual in their native Yanomamï. Salesian schools, organized in three missions along the Orinoco River, teach Spanish to a tiny minority. Even so, Yanomamï is still indubitably the only language of communication in this group on the Venezuelan side of the border. There are many linguistic variations—phonetic, grammatical, and lexicographical—between the Yanomamï of Brazil (also called the Yanam and the Nïnam) and those of Venezuela. Sanïma, spoken in Venezuela by 2056 people, almost all of whom are monolingual, as well as in Brazil, has been considered to date as a Yanomamï dialect. However, this language subgroup presents a complex of differences substantial enough to make it almost incomprehensible to the rest of the Yanomamï of the area. A dialectological analysis of the entire Yanomamï linguistic complex that would determine the grades of differential between subgroups and thus clarify the situation of the Sanïma is lacking at this time.

The Pumé Group

Also known by the name Yaruro, the Pumé are one of the few groups still found in Apure state (the Kuiva being the other). The Pumé total 5419 individuals, 40 percent of whom could still be exclusively Pumé speakers. The rest are now bilingual in Pumé-Spanish, with the exception of 250 who probably communicate in Spanish only. Even though a relatively important number of Pumé speakers still exist, this group is currently experiencing an accelerated state of cultural deterioration that threatens the survival of its linguistic heritage.

The Sapé Group

The Sapé, who reside in the south of Venezuela between the Pemón and the Yanomamï, are the least numerous of all the indigenous groups in Venezuela. They total twenty-eight persons, fifteen of whom are over five years old, and speak only Sapé, while ten are bilingual in Sapé and Spanish.

The Uruak Group

The Uruak, located in an area bordering that of the Sapé, share a very similar situation. Their population, forty-five strong, are almost exclusively Uruak speakers.

To sum up, almost half of the twenty-eight languages mentioned in the Venezuelan census are in danger of or on the brink of disappearing. These include three languages of the Carib family (Mapoyo, now moribund, Yawarana, and Akawaio), four from the Arawak family (Añu, Baré, Baniwa, and Warekena), one from the Piaroa group (Mako), Yeral, Sapé, and Uruak. The situation seems even more fragile when one takes into consideration the scarcity of linguistic data on these languages and the lack of a linguistic policy on the part of the national government

Research, Ethnoeducation, and Linguistic Policy

Initial information on Venezuelan indigenous languages dates back to the sixteenth and seventeenth centuries with the work undertaken by various missionaries (Ruiz Blanco, Tauste, Yangüez) in the eastern and middle parts of the Orinoco River region. The most interesting text in this regard is the *Saggio de Storia Americana* by Félipe Salvatore Gilij, a Jesuit, who was the first to outline the basis of the Carib linguistic family. A considerable lacuna in ethnolinguistic research appeared with the departure of the Jesuits in the second half of the eighteenth century and lasted until the beginning of the twentieth century. During the last 30 years, knowledge of the indigenous languages of Venezuela has increased enormously with the publication of many research projects (grammars, bilingual dictionaries, monolingual and bilingual textbooks, descriptions of phonological systems; see Bibliography). Even so, there remains much to do, and the need to do so is urgent since the languages on the point of extinction are precisely those that have been less studied to date. There are a variety projects in progress at the moment on the large groups, Carib family languages in particular, but challenges of accessibility and a lack of interest on the part of local authorities hamper linguistic work in some areas.

On 20 September 1979, the Venezuelan government passed Decree no. 283, concerning the Régimen de Educación Intercultural Bilingüe (Regulation on Intercultural Bilingual Education); The Dirección de Asuntos Indígenas

(DAI) was entrusted with the responsibility for its coordination and execution. The program began slowly, with the more numerically important groups (Wayuu, Warao, Pemón, Kari'ña, Piaroa, Hiwi, Yanomamï, Ye'kuana), aided by various specialists, anthropologists, and linguists, and occasionally with the participation of some missionaries, such as the Salesians, who were already involved in the preparation of educational material. This regulation should have been progressively implemented among all the ethnic groups that still use their native tongue, but 4 years after its official approval, the Programa de Educación Intercultural Bilingüe (Program of Intercultural Bilingual Education) began to stagnate due to a lack of funding from the DAI and a lack of interest on the part of the new political authorities. From this time onward, a number of different private initiatives–for example, one by the Salesians–and public ones proposed to extend the Régimen de Educación Intercultural Bilingüe to create what now bears the name of nichos lingüísticos ("linguistic niches") (Mosonyi 1993). With the exception of two cases that for very different reasons achieved some results (the Yanomamï in the Upper Orinoco, thanks to the support of the Salesians, and the Wayuu, the result of the cultural vigor of the group and the application of a binational program with the Wayuu of Colombia), the Programa Intercultural Bilingüe instead became a medium for the diffusion of Spanish and the "transculturization" of the ethnic minorities. The reasons for this fiasco are varied, including the lack of good indigenous or bilingual didactic material, bad training of indigenous teachers, the deteriorated state of the schools, and the total absence of supervision and continuity on the part of both regional and national authorities. The increase in research studies dedicated to minority languages in Venezuela has been mentioned previously, but few of these are oriented toward the preparation of support material for school use. The specific task of the linguists should be to dedicate themselves to a greater commitment to work together with indigenous teachers. Today the Dirección de Asuntos Indígenas (Department of Indigenous Affairs) is evaluating the program to define criteria that are more in tune with the reality of modern indigenous people and their needs. In 30 years, the situation of the native Venezuelan has changed drastically as a result of industrial and mining development (petroleum, iron, carbon, bauxite, diamonds, and gold being among the most important) in states (Anzoátegui, Amacuro, Bolivar, and Zulia in particular) that provide the natural habitat for various ethnic groups. Paradoxically, in light of such pressures, which seem to be inexorably forcing the indigenous population into extinction, new and hopeful initiatives are appearing.

The New Indigenous Voices

Along with international and intergovernmental organizations, and occasionally thanks to them and through them, a number of indigenous voices have been raised in defense of their language, culture, and land. During the last 15 years in Venezuela, many indigenous people have organized themselves into various local, regional, and national associations; CONIVE: Consejo Nacional Indio de Venezuela (Indian National Council of Venezuela), ORPIA: Organización Regional de los Pueblos Indígenas de Amazonas (Regional Organization of Indigenous Peoples of the Amazon) and the Parlamento Indígena (Indigenous

Parliament) are the most well known. These associations demand indigenous rights to education in their own language, respect for their beliefs, as well as their participation in development programs that affect their areas of residence. These indigenous initiatives, which began in a localized and sporadic fashion, now strongly dominate the regional and national picture. Various events have marked the entry of the ethnic minorities into the political scene. After the Primer Encuentro de Escritores en Lenguas Indígenas in Mexico (First Encounter of Writers in Indigenous Languages) (1994), the Encuentro Continental de Escritores en Lenguas Indígenas de América (Continental Encounter of Writers in Indigenous Languages) was organized in Venezuela (1997) with the support of UNESCO and CONICIT (Consejo Nacional de Investigación Científica y Técnica: National Council for Scientific and Technical Research). The main objective of the event was to lay the groundwork for a permanent initiative supporting the development of indigenous literature as a means of rescuing and strengthening remaining Amerindian indigenous cultures. As a result, the Asociación Venezolana de Escritores en Lenguas Indígenas (Venezuelan Association of Writers in Indigenous Languages) was set up in the country. It is still too early to predict the effectiveness of such new channels in the diffusion and promotion of languages whose practice extends far beyond that of a mere instrument of communication. It is an open secret that the indigenous languages of America are the vehicle not only of knowledge that is extremely useful to modern science, but also of collected wisdom and unsuspected poetic richness.

Translation by Jessica Johnson

Works Cited

Henley, Paul. 1975. "Wánai: aspectos del pasado y del presente del grupo indígena Mapoyo." *Antropológica* 42: 29–55.

Henley, Paul, Marie-Claude Mattéi Muller, and Howard Reid. 1994–1996. "Cultural and Linguistic Affinities of the Foraging People of Northern Amazonia: A New Perspective." *Antropologica* 83: 3–38.

Mattéi Muller, Marie-Claude. 1975. "Diferenciación lingüística Panare-Mapoyo." *Antropologica* 42: 78–95.

——. 1975. "Vocabulario básico de la lengua Mapoyo." *Antropologica* 42: 57–77.

——. (in press). "Mapoyo-Yawarana: Two Variants of the Same Language? New Outlook on the Classification of Carib Languages." *Carib Studies*. Ed. Janette Forte and Fabiola Jara Gómez. Utrecht: University of Utrecht and University of Guiana.

Medina, Francia. 1997. *Sistema fonológico de los Mapoyo*. BA thesis. Caracas: Universidad Central de Venezuela, Escuela de Antropología,.

Mosonyi, Jorge. 1993. "Resolution 954 dated 6 August 1993." *La Gaceta*, Government Publication, Ministry of Education.

Rivet, Paul, and C. Tastevin. 1920. "Affinités du Maku et du Puinave." *Journal des Américanistes de Paris* 12: 69–82.

Romero, Andrés. 1996. *A Reference Grammar of Warao: Native Languages of America*. Vol. 6. Munich: Lincom Europa.

Ruiz Blanco, Matías. 1888 [1683]. *Diccionario de la lengua de los Indios Cumanagotos Palenques*. Leipzig: Julio Platzmann.

Tauste, Francisco. 1888 [1698]. *Arte e vocabulario de la lengua de los Indios Chaymas, Cumanagotos*. Leipzig: Julio Platzmann.

Yanguez, Manuel. 1888 [1676]. *Principios y reglas de la lengua Cumanagota*. Leipzig: Julio Platzman.

CHAPTER 12

LINGUISTIC DIVERSITY
IN COLOMBIA

Jon Landaburu

Before describing Colombia's linguistic complexity, it would be beneficial to frame the discussion within the context of the entire continent. The varying circumstances of European colonization continue to be the key to understanding the linguistic situation in South America. The considerable and varied time lapses involved (some dating back to the Spanish and Portuguese Conquests, others to the immigration or colonization that has taken place in recent decades), the particular issues of pre-Columbian history relevant to individual regions, and the extreme diversity of American geography are all responsible for a range of extremely varied processes. These can be categorized according to four types of politico-linguistic contexts, in terms of the demographically dominant group within these modern states.

In South America there are regions that are predominantly "white," such as Argentina, Uruguay, southern Brazil, and, to a lesser extent, Chile. These countries enjoy a temperate climate, and in the past they were sparsely populated by indigenous Americans. During the nineteenth and twentieth centuries, they were colonized by waves of immigrants. Even though the indigenous minorities of these states have recently (particularly in Argentina and Chile) been demanding their rights, creating an "Indian problem" in countries where this phrase is almost taboo, it is patently obvious that the majority value their European descent. The diverse origins of the immigrants (generally European, sometimes Asian) and the maintenance, in some cases, of their own linguistic traditions have not prevented Spanish and Portuguese from acting as languages of integration on a mass scale in a linguistic climate that tends toward monolingualism.

In contrast, there are regions with a considerable number of Indian inhabitants who, in some areas, form the majority. This is the case for Andean countries such as Ecuador, Peru, and Bolivia, where the *campesino* population, demographically important in ancient times and later integrated politically within the Incan Empire, constitutes an extensive but marginalized mass of people who largely continue to speak variants of Quechua and Aymara. In recent years, especially in Peru, large-scale migrations have resulted in the presence of considerable numbers of Quechua speakers in the cities. Confronted by this sector, the population of Hispanic origin, although it might consider itself *criolla,* nevertheless maintains a strong linguistic loyalty to Spanish and the values of European culture. Spanish continues to make headway, but the sizes of the different language groups prevent a clear projection of the future linguistic configuration of these countries.

Paraguay is a unique case on the continent, in that Guarani, an indigenous language, is spoken by almost the entire population. The population is both culturally and genetically *mestizo.* The language has also suffered a considerable process of hybridization with Spanish, which has remained the dominant language, used for both religion and general reference. There are currently important moves toward linguistic standardization and modernization. It is important to remember that Paraguay has tribal groups in the same manner in which

all modern American states (with the exception of Uruguay) have indigenous minorities.

Brazil, Venezuela, and Colombia, in the east and north of the continent, represent social forms intermediate between the two just discussed. On the one hand, they had important indigenous settlements prior to the Iberian Conquest, even though these were never as numerous as those in the Central Andean region. On the other, this population mixed substantially with the European immigrants. Today, a large number of indigenous groups remain in these countries, but they have little demographic importance. The remainder of the population, being more of mixed race and having a strong black element of African origin, neither assert the same kind of Europeanness vaunted by the countries further south nor have the Indian reference point of the strictly Andean countries. Spanish and Portuguese are the exclusive linguistic vehicles of this sector.

The Anthropological Diversity and Linguistic Composition of the Colombian Indians

In the case of Colombia, which also participates in the Andean and Caribbean worlds, as well as those of the lowlands of the Amazon and Orinoco basins, linguistic fragmentation and the diversity of sociolinguistic elements are particularly notable. Let us look now at the little-known and chaotic reality of indigenous languages in this country.

In a country of 35 million inhabitants, a native population of fewer than 600,000, belonging to eighty-one Amerindian ethnic identities, can be found in twenty-nine of the thirty-two divisions. Some 130,000 of these individuals do not speak any Amerindian language, even though they are identified as being indigenous and have social and cultural habits that reveal them to be such. The rest speak sixty-six different languages (some important dialectal variants) that can be categorized under twenty-two linguistic families (twelve are linguistic unities while the remaining ten are isolated languages). The geographical and cultural diversity of these populations is also very great (based on evidence from the Instituto Colombiano de Antropología). Communities are found in the savannas or prairies (eastern plains of the Orinoco), the tropical rainforests (Amazon jungle, Pacific coast), the semi-arid deserts (Guajira Peninsula), the high mountain ranges (the Andes, Sierra Nevada de Santa Marta) and the deforested shoreline (Caribbean coast). They may consist of fishermen, semi-itinerant horticulturists, settled farmers, nomadic hunter-gatherers, or shepherds. A native village typical of the northeast Colombia mountains is shown in **Figure 1.**

Until very recently, the surviving remnants of the pre-Columbian indigenous population have been found in zones of refuge, difficult access, and/or insalubrious conditions (the tropical lowlands). The lowlands of the eastern area (the Orinoco and Amazon basins) have an estimated 100,000 indigenous inhabitants, while in the western lowlands (Pacific coast and the west of the Atlantic coast) there are another 100,000. The southern Andean area accounts for some

Figure 1.

Native Village in Northeast Colombia, the Sierra Nevada de Santa Marta. (Courtesy of the Instituto Colombiano de Cultura Hispánica, Santa Fe de Bogotá)

200,000 while the northern area (Guajira, the Sierra Nevada de Santa Marta, the Sierra de Perijá, and the Sierra de Motilones) accounts for a total of around 150,000.

The very limited rise of these numbers in relation to the mass of the dominant population seems more significant if one takes into account the size of these ethno-linguistic groupings. Of a total sixty-six language groups, only three have more than 50,000 members: Wayú (Guajiros), Nasa (Paeces), and Embera (Chocoes). Another twenty-nine account for populations of between 1,000 and 50,000, and thirty-four have fewer than 1,000 speakers each. It is important to evaluate these statistics while taking into account two considerations. On one hand, in global terms, the indigenous population is increasing. On the other, many of these groups are divided by the happenstance of international borders. When dealing with the problem of linguistic or ethnic survival, one must take into account the members of the same ethnolinguistic communities that live in Brazil, Venezuela, Ecuador, Panama, and Peru.

The sociolinguistic situation of these people is highly variable and largely correlates with historical antecedents and their economic, cultural, and political distance from the Spanish-speaking mainstream. To give a very general idea of this highly complex reality, the following describes a brief view of the indigenous geography of Colombia with an attempt to outline the situation of these languages in the context of their linguistic, social, and cultural environment.

Until the twentieth century, the people dwelling on the flat plains of the Amazon and Orinoco had relatively little continuous contact with European civilization. The great diversity of languages and peoples within the Amerindian world survived for much longer in these regions and continues today, though with a vigor directly proportional to their isolation from the frontier established by campesino colonization. Of the sixty-six Indian languages in Colombia, fifty are spoken in these areas. During the twentieth century, and especially in the last thirty years, this isolation has been decreasing. The colonization of the Andean-Amazonian piedmont by *mestizo campesinos* has been accelerating, displacing the indigenous population or enclosing them in fragile enclaves. The Indians of the vast Amazonian regions and the easternmost part of the plains of the Orinoco, who usually inhabit the banks of the Amazon, Putomayo, Caquetá, Apaporis, Guainía, Inírida, Guaviare, and Vichada rivers, still constitute the majority of the population. The penetration of institutions from the Colombian mainstream has increased rapidly: The Catholic Church and some traders, once practically the only white presence in these vast hinterlands, have been joined by colonizers, state functionaries from a multitude of official departments, Protestant evangelists, scientific researchers, and nongovernmental officials. The development of institutional indigenism during recent years (supposedly intended to favor the indigenous peoples) has simultaneously stepped up their transculturation, even though it might permit some to survive as autonomous entities.

Thanks to the conditions of the twentieth century, one might say that these groups are now suffering the same brutal assault inflicted on the indigenous peoples of the Andes or the coast by the Spanish colonization of the sixteenth and seventeenth centuries. The cultural and linguistic mortality, as in the past, will be considerable. The people who lived through those times developed cultural and linguistic adaptive processes that allowed their descendants to survive to the present day, protected above all by subsequent periods of isolation. In the twentieth century, the Amazon peoples experienced the first offensive of massive contact, thanks to the capacities of modern technology. Even so, the linguistic and cultural practices of these people, although threatened, are still active, and it is not an easy task to predict which ones will or will not survive. Currently there exists a real movement geared to reaffirm, rescue, and realize what is relevant to their cultures.

The settlements of the Andean range (western, central, and eastern) all disappeared during the colonial period, most notably in the nineteenth century, when the need for land, along with liberal legislation, virtually put an end to the indigenous communities. Even so, the most marginal zones, especially those where a kind of hacienda-style feudalism with a strong clerical influence was initiated, managed to maintain a strong indigenous presence. This mainly occurred in the divisions of Cauca and Nariño in the south of the country. It is interesting to see that spokesmen for supposedly vanished communities have lately appeared in the central region of the country and are now demanding their rights under indigenous law, now in their favor. These communities are very much aware of their linguistic legacy and, when possible, they implement programs of linguistic (Totoró, Pirsa) or cultural (Pasto, Tolima) recuperation. The same social conditions and system of production did not lead to linguistic fragmentation in the eastern areas, as the surviving groups are more homogeneous and numerous. Indeed, contemporary indigenous reclamation of rights began in these zones (particularly Cauca). Before spreading throughout the country with diverse demands, it originated as an agrarian movement that sought to abolish land rental obligations and other feudal throwbacks and sought to ensure land ownership. From its beginning in 1972, the indigenous approach has been different from that of other *campesino* movements, since it aims to recuperate collective ownership of the land, revitalize the culture and language, and promote traditional forms of authority.

These groups have two great advantages over the Amazon peoples. On the one hand, their secular communication with the white man–sometimes bellicose, sometimes less dramatic (although always a source of suffering)–has allowed them to have a better understanding of the dominant society and therefore arrange the most coherent adaptive strategies. On the other hand, in demographic terms, their numbers are substantial: There are 15,000 Guambianos and 100,000 Paeces. Even though they are trapped in a situation that is increasingly alien and dominating, during the last 20 years these two factors have contributed to more solid organizational structures and substantial advances in the design and execution of an educational and linguistic policy.

The Pacific coast, where the tropical forest is extremely humid and difficult to penetrate, is inhabited by the Embera and the Waunana, communities of about 60,000 who speak similar languages. These peoples lived in scattered groups at the sources of rivers and streams until two or three decades ago, when they began to create very small settlements. These have permitted the emergence of ethnic organizations and the creation of educational programs that try to promote use of the vernacular. The use of transportation has also increased communication between native peoples. Even though Embera is a very dialectized language, it is possible that the conditions are right for a "Koiné" Embera to emerge. There is an increased use of Spanish, but more in their relationship with the urban populations and the black population, which is very numerous in the region. If indigenous intercommunity and interdialectal communication continues to intensify, there is a possibility of strengthening an aboriginal vehicular language. Meanwhile the dialects are very much alive, and the promoters of a bilingual education (Embera-Spanish) face a series of obstacles in terms of standardization. Finally, the Embera are an expanding population who not only have colonized zones of the West Atlantic coast, but also have made inroads into the Amazonian piedmont. In all these new settlements, the native language continues to flourish.

The initial encounter between the Iberian conquerors and the Indians took place on the Atlantic coast. The clash was brutal, and almost all the indigenous inhabitants of the region disappeared. Some communities survived but gradually lost their language (Zenúes). Today they are reclaiming their "Indianness." In the semi-desert of the Guajira Peninsula, an inhospitable zone where indigenous peoples of diverse origins took refuge and intermixed, there emerged a culture and a people, the Wayú, who spoke an Arawakan language from Guiana. The Wayú were the only indigenous population from tropical zones who dedicated themselves to animal husbandry (cattle, goats, and horses). They knew how to maintain a brave independence in the face of the Spanish Crown and the young Colombian Republic. Today the Wayú, while constituting the most numerous ethnic group in Colombia (120,000 people), when combined with their kin in Venezuela, total 320,000 people. A high level of monolingualism exists among this group, while their economy (pasturing sheep, contraband) and habitat (isolated ranches) has kept them relatively immune to Western cultural and linguistic influences. As on the Pacific coast, the linguistic and ethnic fragmentation is minimal, physical access to their areas is difficult, and the demographic situation is more favorable to survival. Conditions supportive of a progressive expansion and modernization of the language might well exist. Also, as in the case of the Pacific coast, the fragmenting of internal political power could nevertheless create difficulties in the harmonization of this linguistic policy.

On the Atlantic coast, south of the province of Guajira, the Andean range rises with the massif of the Sierra Nevada de Santa Marta, covering an area of about some 20,000 square kilometers to a height of almost 5,000 meters above sea level. Three Indian groups live in this area, sharing the same technological and economic relationships with the natural environment, the same religious system, and very similar languages. The three groups (the Kogi, Ika, and Wiwa) together total fewer than 30,000 people. As the last of the Tairona, an important pre-Columbian civilization, they have jealously maintained their cultural and linguistic autonomy, taking advantage of the difficulties faced by strangers who try to scale such steep mountains. Multilingualism is not unusual, and a few of the people speak Spanish; at the same time, many strongly reject the world of the white man (the world of the *bunachi* or "savage"). Their various attempts at contact have, according to them, not been satisfactory, and they continue to cultivate a religious ideal based on isolation from the outside world and an exclusive dialogue with their deities. Their priests constitute a true intellectual elite who maintain, in the absence of writing, rhetorical and mnemonic practices of enormous sophistication.

Classification of Indigenous Languages

The languages of all of these peoples are highly varied, and this linguistic diversity is graphically illustrated in **Map 1.** The structural and genetic diversity of these languages directly reflects the geographic and anthropological diversity of the territory in this northwestern corner of South America, a diversity paradoxically the result of a "civilizing" or imperial unification similar to that of the central Andes region

Map 1.

Linguistic Diversity in Colombia. (Map by Jon Landaburu)

(Ecuador, Peru, Bolivia, northern Chile, and Argentina) through pre-Incan and Incan expansion. In this case too, artistic processes and the use of graphic systems did not emerge; none of the cultures in the zone managed to create writing in the sense of a codified representation of language. Nevertheless, some methods of graphic representation did exist, as seen in the numerous petroglyphs, rock paintings, ceramic codifications, body painting, and other mechanisms of mythological or ritual organization found in the area.

Direct knowledge of indigenous languages, using the precision and methodology that marks the advance of contemporary linguistics, has expanded in Colombia during recent decades, thanks to the work of the Summer Institute of Linguistics (Instituto Lingüístico de Verano), a North American missionary organization whose presence in the country dates back to 1962, and the Centro Colombiano de Estudios de Lenguas Aborígenes (CCLA) of the University of the Andes in Bogotá, which started work in 1984. We have permission to report here an important advance in the classification of genetic and geographical relationships of this complex subject (Landaburu 2000). The point of departure is Chestmir Loukotka's 1968 classification, taking into account the advances in knowledge since then.

There are twenty-two groups of languages with a probable common origin in Colombia and the surrounding regions (the frontier zones of Panama, Ecuador, Peru, Brazil, and Venezuela). These are called *estirpes* or families. These can be of continental scope (having representations in different parts of the Latin American continent), of regional scope (present in discontinuous areas in the interior of the "region"), or of localized extensive scope (languages found to be continuous within the same geographical area in the interior of the

region); in addition, there are families of single or monolingual local scope (now represented by an isolated language).

For each family, the focus is on the languages spoken today in Colombia and on an estimate of the population of the ethnic group that corresponds to the language (Ruiz Salguero and Bodnar Contreras 1995). The term *interdialectal continuum* refers to situations where various mutually intelligible dialects belonging to the same language are continuous throughout an area.

Families of Continental Scope (Present Beyond the Frontiers of the "Region")

1. *Chibcha* (seven languages). This linguistic family is probably of Central American provenance. The indigenous languages of Panama, Costa Rica, and part of Nicaragua stem from the same family (Constenla 1993). The name is a derivation of the name of the people the Spanish found in the region of Bogotá. In Colombia, there are contemporary Chibcha languages in Darien (Cuna is spoken by 1,000 Colombians and 30,000 Panamanians), in the Sierra Nevada de Santa Marta (Kogi is spoken by 7,000, Arhuaco or Ika by 13,000, Wiwa or Asrario by 1,800, and Chimila by 400), Catatumbo (Barí language, with 1,900 speakers), and western Arauca (Uwa or Tunebo language, spoken by 4,300). There has been speculation regarding the affiliation of Chibcha with languages in the south of Colombia (Paéz, Guambiano, Awa, etc.), but so far there seems to be no proof of this.

2. *Arawak* (nine languages). This linguistic family extends over most of South America, including the languages spoken in the Antilles when Columbus arrived. Probably originating from central Amazonia, it was spread through the tributaries of the Amazon and Orinoco rivers and along the coasts of the Caribbean during the last two millennia (Payne 1993). In Colombia, Arawakan languages are found in the Guajira Peninsula (Wayú has 127,000 speakers in Colombia and 180,000 in Venezuela; see Wayús in **Figure 2**), on

Figure 2.

Leaders of the Wayú People in the Guajira Peninsula, Colombia. (Courtesy of the Instituto Colombiano de Cultura Hispánica, Santa Fe de Bogotá)

the eastern plains and the Negro River region (where there are 300 speakers of Achagua, 4,500 speakers of Piapoco, a total of 7,000 Curripaco and Baniwa speakers, and 250 people who speak Baniva of Guainía and Tariano), and in the region of the Caquetá River (380 Yucuna and 280 Kabiyarí speakers).

3. *Carib* (two languages). This family, also very powerful, spread from the Guianas to the north of the entire subcontinent and the southern part of Amazonia. In Colombia, Carib is spoken in the Atlantic region, along the Magdalena and Amazon river basins, and probably in other regions as well. Today, a group exists in the Sierra de Perijá that lies partially in Colombia and partly in Venezuela (the department of Zulia). Known as the Yuko in Colombia, they number around 2,700 people, with about the same number in Venezuela. Another surviving Carib group, known as the Carijona, inhabits the Amazon area. Their population, substantially diminished in the first decades of the twentieth century, has been adapting so much to their changed environment that today only about 30 Carijona speakers are left.

4. *Quechua* (three languages). The presence of Quechua languages in Colombia is a recent phenomenon. Today Inga or Ingano is spoken (by 11,000 persons) in the department of Nariño (Aponte), in the Sibundoy valley (Putumayo), and in the department of Caquetá (the upper reaches of the Caquetá River and along the Fragua, Yuruyacu, and Orteguaza rivers). Another variation of Quechua is spoken near Puerto Asís and on the San Miguel River. Both seem to have a similarity to the Quechua dialects spoken in Ecuador and specifically those spoken in the jungle. There is a strong possibility that their appearance in Colombia and its spread is due to its diffusion as a "general language" by Catholic missionaries around the seventeenth century. There are also variants of Quechua from the Peruvian Amazon south of the Putumayo River.

5. *Tupí* (two languages). The Cocama, a tiny community, is the only representative of this great linguistic family also found in Brazil, Bolivia, Paraguay, and Argentina. It is to be found on the borders between Colombia and Brazil (280 individuals, very few of whom speak the indigenous language). There have also been reports of speakers of a *lengua geral* (Nheengatú) on the shores of the Guaviare River.

Families of Regional Scope (Various Discontinuous Areas)

1. *Tucano* (eighteen languages). This family, also of probable Central Amazonian origin, is split into two areas, western (the upper reaches of the Caquetá and Putumayo rivers) and eastern (the upper Negro and Vaupés rivers). Languages derived from this family are to be found in Brazil, Ecuador, and Peru. In Colombia, the eastern section (approximately 2,200 people speaking Coreguaje and Siona) is severely threatened by the impetus of recent colonization. This eastern area is characterized by a high percentage of multilingualism (Soerensen 1967, Gómez-Imbert 1993). Sixteen languages–Cubeo, Tanimuca, Tucano, Desano, Macuna, Tatuyo, Barasana, Carapana, Tuyuca, Yurutí, Siriano, Piratapuyo, Bará, Taiwano, Guanano, and Pisamira–are spoken by fewer than 25,000 people.

2. *Sáliba-Piaroa* (two languages). Groups from the eastern plains were catechized by Jesuits during the seventeenth century. The Sáliba live in the west (1,300 people), while the Piaroa (760 inhabitants in Colombia) are to be found near the Orinoco River in the west, the east, and also in Venezuela (5,000 speakers).

3. *Macú-Puinave* (five languages). The Macú-Puinave family, a precarious grouping of nomadic jungle-dwelling groups (the Makú are composed of the Yuhup, Hupda, Nukak, and Cacua), inhabit the Inírida River area and the jungles of the Vaupés River. Puinave, a more settled member of this family group made up of 5,200 speakers, is also to be found in Brazil and possibly Venezuela, along the Inirida River.

Families of Extensive Local Scope (Various Languages in the Same Area)

1. The eastern plains of Colombia, and possibly those of Venezuela, are inhabited by the *Guahibo* family (three languages) composed of once nomadic populations that are largely sedentary today. In Colombia, two very different languages exist at the extreme north and south: Hitnu or Macaguane (400 speakers) and Guayabero (1,200 speakers), respectively (Queixalós 1993). Between the two exist the Guahibo or Sikuaní (20,000 speakers in Colombia), a more homogeneous group, though with its own dialectal differences.

2. The *Uitoto* family (three languages) include the Caquetá-Putumayo, an interdialectal continuum of Uitoto linguistic variants (7,000 speakers), plus the Ocaina (also present in Peru) and Nonuya languages, the latter with only three speakers.

3. The *Bora* family on the Cahuinarí River has three languages: Muinane (300 speakers), Bora (400 speakers), and Miraña (450 speakers), the latter two sharing notable similarities.

4. The *Chocó* family (two languages), found on the Pacific coast from Panama to Ecuador, is spoken by more than 50,000 people. This family is divided into an interdialectal continuum of Embera variants plus Waunana (6,500 speakers), a very different language found on the San Juan River (Pardo and Aguirre 1993).

5. At the foot of the mountains on the Pacific side at Nariño and also in northwest Ecuador is the precarious *Barbacoa* linguistic family, which might include Awa (or Cuaiquer, spoken by 6,000 people) in Colombia, Chachi (or Cayapa, with 8,000 speakers), and Tsachila (or Colorado, spoken by 2,000 people) in Ecuador.

Families of Single Languages

1. In east Caucano, the Paéz family constitutes an interdialectal continuum of approximately 100,000 speakers.

2. The Guambiano family, also found in east Caucano, is an interdialectal continuum of 16,000 speakers.

3. The Ticuna, located in the Amazon, is a language belonging to an interdialectal continuum extending beyond the border with Brazil and Peru, with a total of more than 30,000 speakers.

4. In the upper Putumayo, the Cofán family is a language whose use extends to a few communities beyond the border with Ecuador (some 1,000 speakers in Colombia).

5. The Andoque family, spoken by 3,500 individuals, is located in Araracuara in the Amazon.

6. The language of the Kamsá family is spoken by 3,500 people in the valley of Sibundoy (Putumayo).

7. Tinigua, present in the Sierra de la Macarena, is dying out. There are only two speakers remaining.

8. The Yaruro family is occasionally found in Colombia on the Arauca River border with Venezuela (total of 3,000 speakers).

9. The Yagua family, with 300 speakers in Colombia and another 3,000 in Peru, is located on the border with Peru along the Putumayo and Amazon rivers.

Translation by Jessica Johnson

Works Cited

Constenla, Adolfo. 1993. "La familia Chibcha." *Estado actual de la clasificación de las lenguas indígenas de Colombia.* Ed. Jon Landaburu. Santafé de Bogotá: Instituto Caro y Cuero. 75–125.

Gómez-Imbert, Elsa. 1993. "Problemas en torno a la comparación de las lenguas tucano-orientales." *Estado actual de la clasificación de las lenguas indígenas de Colombia.* Ed. María Luisa Rodriguez de Montes. Santafé de Bogotá: Instituto Caro y Cuervo. 235–68.

Instituto Colombiano de Antropología. 1987. *Introducción a la Colombia amerindia.* Bogotá: ICA.

Instituto Lingüístico de Verano. 1997. *Bibliografía 1997: 35 años de servicio y esperanza*. Santafé de Bogotá: Instituto Lingüístico de Verano.

Landaburu, Jon. 1993. "Conclusiones del seminario sobre clasificación de lenguas indígenas de Colombia." *Estado actual de la clasificación de las lenguas indígenas de Colombia*. Ed. María Luisa Rodríguez de Montes. Santafé de Bogotá: Instituto Caro y Cuero. 313–30.

——, ed. 1994. "Estructuras sintácticas de la predicación: Lenguas amerindias de Colombia." *Buletin de l'Institut Français d'Etudes Andines* (Lima): 366-663.

——. 2000. "Clasificación de las lenguas indígenas de Colombia." *Lenguas indígenas de Colombia*. Ed. María Luisa Rodríguez de Montes and María Estela González. Santafé de Bogotá: Insituto Caro y Cuervo. 25–48.

Loukotka, Chestmir. 1968. *Classification of South American Indian Languages*. Los Angeles: University of California Press.

Pardo, Mauricio, and Daniel Aguirre. 1993. "Dialectología chocó." *Estado actual de la clasificación de las lenguas indígenas de Colombia*. Ed. María Luisa Rodríguez de Montes. Santafé de Bogotá: Instituto de Caro y Cuervo. 269–312.

Payne, L. David. 1993. "Una visión panorámica de la familia Arawak." *Estado actual de la clasificación de las lenguas indígenas de Colombia*. Ed. María Luisa Rodríguez de Montes. Santafé de Bogotá: Instituto Caro y Cuervo. 127–64.

Queixalós, Francisco. 1993. "Lenguas y dialectos de la familia Guahibo" *Estado actual de la clasificación de las lenguas indígenas de Colombia*. Ed. María Luisa Rodríguez de Montes. Santafé de Bogotá: Instituto Caro y Cuervo. 189–217.

Ruiz Salguero, Magda, and Yolanda Bodnar Contreras. 1995. *El caracter multiétnico de Colombia y sus implicaciones censales*. Santafé de Bogotá: Departamento Administrativo Nacional de Estadística (DANE).

Soerensen, Arthur P. 1967. "Multilingualism in the Northwest Amazon." *American Anthropologist* 69: 670–84.

CHAPTER 13

LINGUISTIC DIVERSITY IN THE ANDEAN COUNTRIES (ARGENTINA, BOLIVIA, CHILE, ECUADOR, AND PERU) AND PARAGUAY

Willem F. H. Adelaar

Linguistic Classification

From a linguistic point of view, the Andean area (including the Pacific Coast and the inter-Andean valleys and plateaus) was originally a region of great genetic diversity. Most of the languages in this area either were what we call "genetic isolates" or belonged to families without deep internal differentiation. From a historical-comparative point of view, the Andes continue to be problematic; it has turned out to be very difficult to establish the nature of the relationships between the languages indigenous to that area. On the eastern slopes of the Andes and in the adjacent lowland there is a mix of language isolates and small families, as well as representatives of larger families that cover substantial parts of tropical South America. Even when only the endemic groups (the isolates and small families) are taken into consideration, this is linguistically one of the most complex areas in the world.

In the Andean region, the dominant Quechuan and Aymaran languages constitute a sort of "shallow" family, which consists of a number of closely related languages and dialects. The internal differentiation of these two language groups is comparable to that of the Romance or Slavic languages. Externally, they have no relatives whose relationship would not be highly debatable. There is a large body of literature addressing the question of whether Quechuan and Aymaran are related to each other; supporting the argument that they are related are the facts that the two language groups are phonologically and typologically very similar and that they have more than 20 percent of their vocabulary in common. The fact that the discussion concerning this matter goes back to the early seventeenth century and that no consensus has been reached yet makes clear that if there is a possible genetic relationship between Quechuan and Aymaran, it is at best a remote one. Most of the similarities can be explained by intensive language contact over a considerable period of time.

From a more general typological point of view, both Quechuan and Aymaran are typically Amerindian languages with more "Pacific" than "Amazonian" characteristics. This qualification applies to Aymaran even more than to Quechuan. Characteristic of Aymaran is the presence of a four-term personal reference system based on the inclusion or noninclusion of speaker and hearer. Such a system can be reconstructed for many other Amerindian languages but has its purest and least altered manifestation in Aymaran. The Quechuan personal reference system, which is essentially like that of Aymaran, must have been constructed following an Aymaran model. The Aymaran family, also known as Jaqi or Aru, consists of the languages Aymara, Jaqaru, and Cauqui. The different

varieties of Quechuan are usually referred to as "dialects." The differences between these varieties, however, are not necessarily less important than those existing between the Aymaran languages.

Araucanian, alternatively called Mapuche or Mapudungun, is a single language with very little internal differentiation, except for its rather divergent southernmost variety, Huilliche (originally spoken near Valdivia and on Chiloé), which is now moribund. Several possible genetic links have been proposed for Araucanian. So far, none of these proposals has turned out to be more than speculative, and the language continues to stand as a genetic isolate. Of the other languages found in the Andes, many are isolates. Their state of documentation is usually so poor, however, that little can be said about possible genetic relations. From north to south, we find the following languages that can be grouped into families. Cayapa (or Chachi), Colorado (or Tsafiqui), and Cuaiquer (or Awa), situated in the northern Pacific sector of Ecuador, belong to the Barbacoan family. This family may have included some of the extinct languages of the Andean sector in Ecuador.

Among the probable isolates, we also find the extinct Atacames or Esmeraldeño language of the Ecuadorian Pacific coast. Its proposed relationships with Yaruro in Venezuela and with the Chibchan family are doubtful. Mochica, or Yunga, once spoken near Chiclayo on the Peruvian north coast, died out during the twentieth century and has no known relatives. Typologically, Mochica is very different from all the languages surrounding it; Mesoamerican connections have been suggested to explain this difference. Other languages (Cañar, Culli, Palta, Puruhá, Quingnam, Sec, and Tallan) formerly spoken in the Andes of Ecuador and in northern Peru, as well as along the coast of that area, are so poorly documented that any classification is likely to remain risky.

The Puquina language of southern Peru and Bolivia has survived in the root inventory of Callahuaya, a professional language of herb doctors living near Charazani (Bolivia). The morphology of Puquina (personal reference markers) and some lexical material suggest a relationship with the Arawakan language family. Uru-Chipaya is a small family of closely related languages. Its extant members are Chipaya and Uru (or Uchumataco). The Huarpe family in the Cuyo area of Argentina disappeared around 1700. The languages of Patagonia and the Tierra del Fuego main island also formed a family (Chon), which included Gününaküne (probably), Tehuelche, Ona, and several others. In northern Chile, the extinct Atacameño (or Kunza) language was clearly a linguistic isolate. In northwestern Argentina and neighboring Chile, Diaguita (or Kakan) has been so poorly documented that any classification of it can be only speculative. Farther south, near the extremities of the continent, we find Alacaluf (or Kaweskar), Yahgan (or Yamana), and the extinct Chono, all languages without known relatives.

Representatives of large families are frequently found east of the Andes. Of considerable importance are the Arawakan and Tupí-Guaraní families. Arawakan languages are found in Peru (Ashaninka, Asheninka, Amuesha, Campa del Pajonal, Chamicuro, Iñapari, Machiguenga, Piro, and Resígaro) and in Bolivia (Apolista, Baure, Chané, Moxo [Ignaciano and Trinitario], and Paunaca). There are many other Arawakan languages in Brazil, Colombia, and Venezuela. Tupí-Guaraní languages are found in Bolivia (Chiriguano [Avá and Izozeño], Guarayo, Pauserna, Sirionó, and Yuki), Argentina (Avá-Chiriguano, Mbyá, and Paraguayan Guaraní), and Paraguay (Aché-Guayakí, Chiripá, Paraguayan Guaraní, Mbyá, Paí, and Tapieté). The Cocama language in Peru has a Tupí-Guaraní lexical basis and represents an interesting case of language mixture as it also involves an Arawakan element. Paraguayan Guaraní is the second-largest Amerindian language of the region (after Quechua). In Bolivia, the Avá-Chiriguano language is also known as Bolivian Guaraní.

Several other language families are found in the area east of the Andes: Arawan (Culina), Boran, Bororoan (Otuque), Cahuapanan (Chayahuita and Jebero), Candoshi (Shapra), Chapacuran (Itene), Charruan, Guaicuruan (Abipon, Mocoví, Pilagá, and Toba), Hibito-Cholón, Huitotoan, Jivaroan (Achuar, Aguaruna, Huambisa, and Shuar), Lengua-Mascoi (Angaité, Guaná, Lengua, Sanapaná, and Toba Mascoi), Lule-Vilela, Matacoan (Chorotí, Mak'á, Nivaklé, and Wichi), Panoan (Amahuaca, Capanahua, Cashibo, Cashinahua, Chácobo, Mayoruna, Pacaguara, Sharanahua, Shipibo-Conibo, Yaminahua, and Yora), Tacanan (Araona, Cavineña, Ese'ejja, Reyesano, Tacana, and Toromona), Tucanoan (Orejón, Secoya, and Siona), Yaguan, Zamucoan (Ayoreo and Chamacoco), and Zaparoan (Andoa, Arabela, Cahuarano, Iquito, and Záparo). Possible language isolates or unclassified languages in the transandine area of the countries are Cofán and Huaorani in Ecuador; Aguano, Harakmbut, Muniche, Omurana, Taushiro, Tequiraca, Ticuna, and Urarina in Peru; Canichana, Cayuvava, Chiquitano, Itonama, Leco, Mosetén, Movima, and Yuracaré in Bolivia; and the extinct languages Comechingón, Sanavirón, and Querandí in Argentina.

Demographic Characteristics

Already before the Spanish Conquest, some languages were gaining territory at the expense of others. Quechuan and Aymaran probably began their expansion in the first millennium, occupying most of central and southern Peru and eventually the Bolivian highland (see **Map 1**). This expansion of Aymara into the Bolivian highland probably occurred in the late Middle Ages and must have preceded the expansion of Quechua into that area (mainly a colonial phenomenon). At the same time, Quechua expanded northward into Ecuador as a trade language and, around 1500, as a language of conquest (see **Map 2**). The extinction of most of the local languages in the Andes and along the coast of Ecuador and Northern Peru was completed during the colonial occupation and in the nineteenth century. Quechua, in particular, was very successful during the colonial administration because the Spaniards used it as an official language. Now Quechuan is subdivided into many dialects with an estimated total number of speakers oscillating between 7

Map 1.

Expansion of Aymaran languages
(±1000-1400 A.D.)

million and 10 million people in six countries: Argentina, Bolivia, Chile, Colombia, Ecuador, and Peru (see **Map 3**). Most Quechua speakers live in Bolivia, Ecuador, and Peru, with Argentina occupying the fourth place. Important Quechua dialects are Ancash Quechua, Ayacucho Quechua, Cajamarca Quechua, Cuzco Quechua, Huanca (Peru), Huánuco Quechua, Lamista (Peru), Northern Junín Quechua, Northern and Southern Bolivian Quechua, Highland and Oriente Ecuadorian Quichua, Ingano (Colombia), and Santiago del Estero Quichua. Aymara has about 2 million speakers who live mainly in Bolivia, Chile, and Peru (see **Map 4**).

Araucanian was also a language of expansion, but in its case the dynamics were entirely indigenous. During colonial times, a portion of the Araucanian people preserved their independence and some groups invaded the Argentinean pampa, where local Indian communities adopted the Araucanian language (see **Map 5**). Araucanian power was crushed at the end of the nineteenth century–in Chile, during the war of pacification, and in Argentina, during the Campaña del Desierto of the 1870s. Most observers agree that there are over a million Mapuches, but estimates of the number of speakers of the language vary enormously–from 40,000 to 500,000 (see **Map 6**).

Paraguayan Guaraní has several million speakers in Argentina, Brazil, and Paraguay. In Paraguay, it is the majoritarian language and a token of national identity. However, most speakers of Paraguayan Guaraní do not identify themselves as Amerindians. Paraguayan Guaraní is typically a

Map 2.

Limits of the Inca Empire (1532)

Map 3.

Modern distribution of Quechua

product of the colonization efforts of the Jesuits during the seventeenth and eighteenth centuries. It has a simplified structure in relation to Old Guaraní and to its more conservative relatives, such as Mbyá and Chiripá (in Brazil Nhandeva); much of the old morphophonemics has been regularized and some verbal paradigms have been lost. Part of the old, religious vocabulary has survived in Paraguayan Guaraní, but it is devoid of its original pregnant meaning. All the other Amerindian languages of the Andean region have only local importance. Many of them are already extinct or moribund, with only a handful of speakers left. On the other hand, some languages spoken by relatively small groups, such as the Asheninka and Shuar, are quite vital.

Grammatical Typology

The languages of the Andes have considerable typological variety. However, Quechuan and Aymaran are very similar. They are exclusively suffixing languages that combine extreme regularity and a rich derivational morphology. Irregular verbs and nouns are virtually absent. Some portmanteau suffixes occur in the area of person, tense, aspect, and mood, with complex verbal endings encoding both the actor and the "acted upon" of an event. Otherwise, the identification of the morphological segments is straightforward. Both Quechuan and Aymaran exhibit a relatively free constituent order, although a basic subject-object-verb order is predominant.

Nouns in Quechuan and in Aymaran are inflected for person of possessor, for case, and for number (in Ecuadorian

Quichua the possessor endings were lost). Nominalized verb forms and verbs in subordinative paradigms account for most of the complex sentences in both languages. Quechuan dialects in particular have elaborate switch-reference systems. These systems are designed to discriminate between subjects in subordinate clauses on the basis of their being or not being referentially identical with the subject in the main clause.

An interesting feature of both language groups is the existence of affixes that indicate data source and information structure. As in many Amerindian languages, there is no contrast between direct and indirect speech. Direct speech is used not only for rendering the content of utterances but also for rendering the content of thoughts. Switch-reference, direct speech, and data source are to a high degree determinative for the structure of a discourse. For instance, in a native Andean text the identity of the subject is indicated less frequently than in a European text. The identification occurs through the switch-reference system.

Araucanian is very similar to Quechuan in its structure, especially insofar as the verbal morphology is concerned. Araucanian morphology is highly complex and extremely regular. Portmanteau suffixes occur in the area of personal reference, where both subject and object are encoded in the verb. On the other hand, the Araucanian noun has very little morphology. Araucanian has one postposition denoting oblique case (*mew*) and a few postpositions with very specific meanings. Most nouns, however, remain unmarked for case, the exact relation between noun and verb being specified in

Map 4.

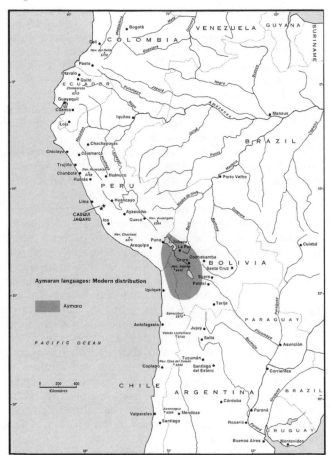

Map 5.

the verbal morphology. Personal possession is indicated by a class of possessive adjectives. They are free elements located before the head noun, rather than prefixes. Nominalized verbs and subordinate verbs characterized by special morphosyntax are used in complex sentences. Syntactically, Araucanian has a predominant subject-verb-object order.

Like several other native languages of the Southern Cone, Araucanian morphologically distinguishes singular, dual, and plural number. Characteristically, these number distinctions are also used to indicate the comitative case relation (Araucanian has no specific term or case ending for "with"). Third-person objects are encoded in the verb, with a necessity to distinguish between newly introduced objects and objects that were already in focus. Semantically, there is the curiosity that Araucanian lacks a present tense. Unmarked events are past events. Events in the present can be referred to only by derived constructions, for instance with adverbial endings or adverbs (for example, *i-n* "I ate," but *petu i-n* "I eat" or *i-meke-n* "I am busy eating"). In contrast to Quechuan and Aymaran, noun-incorporation and verb-root compounding are frequent phenomena in Araucanian.

The structure of Paraguayan Guaraní is very different from that of the great Andean languages. As a member of the Tupí stock, Guaraní has an Amazonian background and belongs to a typological area encompassing the eastern part of the subcontinent. As in many Amerindian languages, personal reference in Guaraní is indicated by means of prefixes both in verbal and in nominal constructions. Most other derivational

categories are indicated by means of postposed elements, of which the phonological status as suffixes or clitics is not always clear. The personal reference markers are divided in two sets: an "active" set indicating the actor of transitive and of most intransitive verbs, and a "stative" set indicating the subject of some intransitive verbs and of nominal predicates, the patient of transitive verbs, and a possessor with nouns.

Tense in Guaraní is indicated on nouns, by suffixes, or, adverbially, in a sentence. Some verbal tense markers are suffixes or clitics rather than adverbs. The language has several relativizing elements, which can be marked for tense as if they were nouns. In relative clauses, the relativizer, not the verb, is tense-marked. Case is marked on nouns by means of case suffixes or postpositions. Some Guaraní verbs and adjectives exhibit idiomatic (semantically unpredicted) case government. Personal pronouns can take special forms when marked for case. Noun incorporation and compounding occur in Guaraní. However, noun incorporation tends to be frozen and is not as frequent as in some of the more archaic Tupí-Guaraní languages (for example, Tupinambá). Phonologically, Paraguayan Guaraní is widely known for its suprasegmental nasality, which seems to be more systematically developed in it than in other Tupí-Guaraní languages. Suprasegmental nasality in Guaraní is based on, among other things, the existence of nasal and half-nasal allophones ([m, mb], [n, nd]) for the phonemes /m̥/, /n̥/, and so on, and on an opposition between nasal and oral vowels. Guaraní has six nasal and six oral vowels.

Map 6.

Of the other Amerindian languages found in the Andean region, some, like Quechuan, Aymaran, and Araucanian, are suffixing (for example, Cayapa, Jivaroan, Mochica, and Uru-Chipaya). Most of the other languages, however, are of the mixed type so frequently found in the Americas. They combine prefixes and suffixes as in Guaraní.

Language Policies and Intercultural Programs

Most countries of the Andean region have given some recognition to the Amerindian languages spoken in their territories. Bilingual educational programs, which at first were set up by Protestant Bible translators such as the Summer Institute of Linguistics, have a long-standing tradition in Bolivia, Ecuador, and Peru. Peru made a start toward the recognition of its indigenous linguistic heritage in 1975 when the government declared Quechua an official second language. An official spelling and standardization of six important Quechua dialects followed. But later political developments left these measures without much effect. The first experiments with bilingual education in Quechua and Spanish (in Ayacucho) date from the late 1960s. During the 1980s a sizable experimental program for bilingual education (PEEB) was set up in Puno, Peru, with the support of German development agencies. Its influence in academic, educational, and social terms has been considerable. Many bilingual textbooks were produced as a result of this program.

In Quito, Ecuador, a similar program was developed. Due to a more favorable political context, it is reported to have had more lasting results than the Peruvian project. Ecuador

has very powerful Indian movements, which benefit not only the highland population but also indigenous groups in the tropical Oriente region. Ecuador's makeup as a multicultural and a multiethnic nation is widely acknowledged on a political level. As far as Highland Quichua is concerned, a certain standardization of the language has taken place as a result of a highly successful radio-broadcasting program.

In Bolivia, the status of native cultural minorities has improved greatly due to political developments in the 1990s. Several groups now claim cultural and linguistic autonomy. The organization CIPCA (Centro de Investigación y Promoción del Campesinado) has inventoried speakers of Amerindian languages throughout the country. A large program of bilingual and intercultural education (PROEIB Andes) has been initiated recently in Cochabamba with international funding.

In Argentina, Amerindian groups receive some support locally, for instance, in the province of Santiago del Estero, where a large part of the population is Quichuaphone. Some groups in the Gran Chaco area have developed a strong ethnic conscience, sometimes leading to a rejection of the use of the Spanish language. On the whole, the position of Indian languages is weak in Argentina, despite some attempts to use Quechua for official declarations during the early days of independence. In Chile, the native population suffered from repression and the abolition of its original land rights in the 1970s and 1980s. The absence of concrete information concerning the number of Mapuche Indians and speakers of Araucanian illustrates the general lack of concern and organization. The situation appears to have improved in recent years, however, and there has been a cultural revival, which manifests itself, among other things, through theater performances in Mapudungun.

Guaraní is spoken by almost the entire population of Paraguay. Some Paraguayans are monolingual in Guaraní. Its status had long been unofficial, but the Constitution of 1992 recognized both Guaraní and Spanish as official languages, as well as the right of the people to receive education in either language. Paraguay has many private and religious institutions looking after the correct use of Guaraní (for example, El Centro de Estudios Paraguayos Antonio Guasch). The future of the other Amerindian languages in Paraguay does not seem to receive the same amount of attention.

Literature

There are a growing number of published texts in several of the indigenous Andean languages. The content of these texts mainly consists of myths, legends, and other oral traditions, such as animal fables. For most of the smaller languages, these are the only types of texts available. In the case of the languages with greater numbers of speakers (Quechua, Aymara, and Guaraní), there is a more varied assortment of texts. Several important works in Quechua date from the colonial period. Best known is the anonymous *Huarochirí manuscript*, which was written about 1600 for the idolatry fighter Francisco de Ávila (English edition by Frank Salomon and George Urioste). It contains a mythical indigenous vision of the prehistory of Central Peru, a description of secret religious practices reflecting native beliefs before the introduction of Catholicism, and a report on the subsequent ideological conflict between Indians and Spaniards. The Huarochirí manuscript has become increasingly important for the definition of national and cultural identity in the Andean countries. Some work by modern authors, such as José María Arguedas, was influenced by it.

Quechua theater attained its apogee in the late seventeenth and the eighteenth centuries. Unlike the dramatic representations of the "Death of Atahualpa," which are still performed in a traditional way in several Andean villages, colonial Quechua theater was a product of the local elite, modeled after classic Spanish theater. The topics treated were often religious. An exception is the famous play *Ollantay*, which deals with the impossible love affair of an Incan princess and an army chief of humble social extraction. Although it is written in Quechua, the versification of *Ollantay* belongs to a European tradition. Whether or not the theme itself was indigenous is a matter of debate.

Most published texts in Quechua, however, date from the twentieth century. They usually belong to an anonymous folk culture, dealing with myths, local traditions, and similar material. The pre-Columbian element is still very strong in these texts, both in the selection of topics and in the timeless way historical events are represented. An important genre among modern Quechua texts is autobiography. The anthropologists C. Escalante and R. Valderrama have collected much autobiographical material; among this material we find the autobiography of *Gregorio Condori Mamani*, an illiterate day laborer from Cuzco, and the experiences of traditional cattle thieves from Apurimac (*Nosotros los humanos–Ñuqanchik runakuna*). Almost inexhaustible is the inventory of Quechua song texts, in particular the popular *huayno*. New huayno texts are written on the occasion of any important event that takes place in Andean society, and they form an excellent mirror of the daily preoccupations of Andean people. One of the largest collections is *La sangre de los cerros–Urqukunapa yawarnin* (Rodrigo Montoya, Edwin Montoya, and Luis Montoya). Literature of an individual inspiration written in Quechua is not common, though one could mention the work of the Catholic priest Jorge Lira and the Cuzco landowner and poet Andrés Alencastre.

Aymara folklore and traditions are just as rich as those of Quechua, but there are fewer published texts. A recent anthology was published by Xavier Albó and Félix Layme (*Literatura aymara*). An example of an autibiographical text is Laura T. Briggs and Sabine Dedenbach's *Manuela Ari: An Aymara Woman's Testimony of Her Life*. The Araucanian traditional literature is of particular interest because of the importance attributed to rhetoric in that society. Mapuche leaders were selected for, among other things, their perseverance in oratorial contests, known as *wewpin*, that could last for days. Araucanian texts of the late nineteenth and early twentieth centuries are remarkably authentic and show little contact influence. They contain long and complex sentences, which are demanding even in written form. The autobiography (recorded by Moesbach in 1930) of Pascual Coña, one of the traditional leaders who remembered the last great raids against the *huinca* (white men), the pacification campaigns, and the subsequent confinement of the Mapuche in *reducciones*, is an impressive example of this genre. Storytelling (stories are called *epew*) is popular among the Araucanians, both today and in the past. An interesting example is the traditional myth of Mañkian, who turns into a rock in the ocean and continues to lure people from that spot. The daily activities of a Mapuche man called Federico are described by Segundo Llamín Canulaf in *Federico ñi nütram*.

Literature in the Guaraní language is rich and diverse in genre. However, the most important work may not have been written in Paraguayan Guaraní but in Mbyá, the dialect of one of the traditional, unmixed Guaraní tribes. The mythical texts of the Mbyá were published and translated under the name *Ayvu rapyta* [Foundations of the Word] by Léon Cadogan. These texts, which contain the core of the religious beliefs and worldview of traditional Guaraní Indians, have inspired a sizable anthropological literature. Modern Paraguayan literature is influenced by important historical events, such as the Triple Alliance war against Argentina and Brazil and the Chaco war against Bolivia, and by popular beliefs. Traditional accounts about supernatural beings, such as *Pombero* and *Jasy Jatere*, are often presented in a literary fashion. Much of this genre, represented by the work of D. Gómez Serrato among others, can be found in Antonio Guasch, *El idioma guaraní: Gramática y antología de prosa y verso*. The Guaraní counterpart of the Andean *huayno* is the *purahéi*. Any theme, regardless of whether it is of a social, religious, or romantic nature, can be expressed by these popular Paraguayan songs. Meliá Baromeu's *La lengua guaraní del Paraguay* contains a representative sample of *purahéi* texts.

The Tupí-Guaraní Languages

When the the first Portuguese explorers arrived in 1500, the coast of what is now Brazil was inhabited predominantly by speakers of Tupí-Guaraní languages (see **Map 7**). The southernmost sector of the coast, extending inland as far to the west as the Paraguay River, was occupied by the Guaraní (Carijó in Portuguese sources). Their language, Old Guaraní, was the predecessor of modern Paraguayan Guaraní. Tupí (de São Vicente) was spoken in the modern state of São Paulo. The remaining part of the Brazilian coast, from Rio de Janeiro to the mouth of the Amazon River, was inhabited by speakers of the Tupinambá (or Classical Tupí) language. The three languages were closely related, Tupinambá being the most conservative. Other languages of the Tupí-Guaraní family, itself a member of the more comprehensive Tupí stock, are found distributed in different parts of the interior of lowland South America.

The close affinity of the coastal Tupí-Guaraní languages points to a relatively recent expansion, which took place in the late Middle Ages, probably at the expense of other local populations. Its motive, apart from overpopulation, can be found in the religious beliefs of the Tupí-Guaraní people and, more particularly, in their permanent quest for a promised "land without evil" (*yvy marãe'y*) in the east. Modern Guaraní groups, such as the Mbyá, which have their homeland in the northeastern Argentinian department of Misiones and adjacent areas, still follow this practice. Some of them have reached northern Brazil in their migrations.

During the initial decades of Portuguese colonial presence in Brazil, the Tupí or Tupinambá language was known as "Língua Brasílica." In a grammar of the language, Joseph de Anchieta refers to it as "the language most employed on the coast of Brazil" (Anchieta n.p.). The Tupinambá Indians themselves were largely wiped out by the Portuguese during the sixteenth century. Some groups, however, survived, and the language continued to be used in the Brazilian colony for some time. It also developed into a so-called *língua geral* ("general language") spoken by non-Indians.

Línguas Gerais

Under the Portuguese colonial administration in Brazil, settlers of European descent often married Tupí-speaking women. Their offspring took their identity from their Portuguese fathers but spoke the language of their mothers. The varieties of Tupí that were in use among the members of this mixed population were

Map 7.

Map 8.

Map 9.

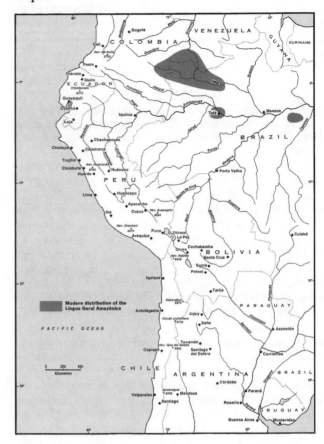

called *língua geral* ("general language," plural *línguas gerais*). Two varieties developed, one of them in the area of São Paulo (the *língua geral Paulista*) and the other in the present-day states of Pará and Maranhão (the *língua geral Amazônica*). (See **Map 8.**) The morphology of these general languages is a simplified version of that of the classical Tupí languages (Tupí de São Vicente and Tupinambá, respectively). Case endings were replaced by postpositions, the complex morphophonemics of the classical language was regularized, and some distinctions in the personal reference system were lost. These processes are reminiscent of the development of modern Paraguayan Guaraní from Old Guaraní.

The *língua geral Paulista* was generally used in southern Brazil up until the eighteenth century, among those who took part in the slaving expeditions of the *bandeirantes*. The *língua geral Paulista* was used by only a few people and disappeared sooner than the *língua geral Amazônica*, which was widely used until the end of the nineteenth century. The língua geral Amazônica survives in the Río Negro basin in northwestern Brazil, where it is locally known as Nheengatú ("good language") or *geral* (see **Map 9**). It has also spread into neighboring areas of Colombia and Venezuela, where it is called *yeral* (reflecting the Spanish spelling and pronunciation of the Portuguese *geral*).

Works Cited

Albó, Xavier. 1995. *Bolivia plurilingüe.* 3 vols. La Paz: UNICEF-Centro de Investigación y Promoción del Campesinado (CIPCA).

Albó, Xavier, and Félix Layme. 1992. *Literatura aymara: Antología.* La Paz: CIPCA/HISBOL/JAYMA.

Anchieta, Joseph de. 1990 [1595]. *Arte de grammatica da língua mais usada na costa do Brasil.* Facsimile edition. Ed. Carlos Drumond and Armando Carodoso. São Paulo: Edições Loyola.

Briggs, Laura T., and Sabine Dedenbach-Salazar Sáenz. 1995. *Manuela Ari: An Aymara Woman's Testimony of Her Life.* Bonn: Holos.

Cadogan, León. 1992. *Ayvu rapyta, Textos míticos de los Mbyá-Guaraní del Guairá.* Asunción: Fundación "León Cadogan," Centro de Estudios Antropológicos Universidad Católica "Nuestra Señora de la Asunción," "Centro de Estudios Paraguayos Antonio Guasch" (1st ed: *Boletim* no. 227, *Antropologia,* no. 5, Universidade de São Paulo, Faculdade de Filosofía, Ciências e Letras, São Paulo).

Coña, Pascual. 1984. *Testimonio de un cacique mapuche.* Re-edition of Moesbach 1930. Santiago de Chile: Pehuén.

Escalante, Carmen, and Ricardo Valderrama. 1977. *Gregorio Condori Mamani: Autobiografía.* Cuzco: Centro "Bartolomé de Las Casas."

———. 1992. *Nosotros los humanos-Ñuqanchik runakuna.* Cuzco: Centro "Bartolomé de las Casas."

Guasch, Antonio. 1956. *El idioma guaraní: Gramática y antología de prosa y verso.* 3rd ed. Asunción: Casa América-Moreno Hermanos.

Llamín Canulaf, Segundo. 1987. *Frederico ñi nütram.* 4 vols. Temuco: Imprenta y Editorial Küme Dungo.

Meliá, Baromeu. 1992. *La lengua guaraní del Paraguay.* Madrid: MAPFRE.

Moesbach, Ernesto Wilhelm de. 1930. *Vida y costumbres de los indígenas araucanos en la segunda mitad del siglo XIX.* Santiago de Chile: Imprenta Cervantes.

Montoya, Rodrigo, Luis Montoya, and Edwin Montoya. 1987. *La sangre de los cerros-Urgukunapa yawarnin.* Lima: Centro Peruano de Estudios Sociales, Mosca Azul Editores, Universidad Nacional Mayor de San Marcos.

Rodrigues, A. D. 1986. *Línguas brasileiras* [Languages of Brazil]. São Paulo: University of Brasilia.

Salomon, Frank, and George Urioste. 1991. *The Huarochirí Manuscript.* Austin: University of Texas Press.

CHAPTER 14

THE PORTUGUESE LANGUAGE IN BRAZIL

Marianne Akerberg

The fact that Brazil occupies a considerable part of South America means that Portuguese is of equal importance to Spanish on the continent. From the end of the fifteenth century, a period when both the Spanish and the Portuguese were intent on world exploration, both countries decided to come to an agreement over respective dominions. Thus the treaty of Tordesillas, signed in 1494, fixed a demarcation line between the future colonies of Spain and Portugal. When Pedro Álvares Cabral arrived in Brazil in 1500, Portugal was able to claim the land in accordance with the treaty. The name of the country was taken from the *palo de Brazil* (Brazilwood), from which a red colorant was extracted and used for dying textiles. For a long period this was the most coveted commodity exported from the Brazilian coast.

The territory was colonized by the Portuguese between the sixteenth and eighteenth centuries. Even so there were attempts on the part of the Dutch and the French to wrest control from the Portuguese. The Dutch installed themselves in the northeast, where traces of their influence can still be found in the local architecture. However, no hint of Dutch remains in the language, which is perhaps understandable because their stay in the country was relatively short. The French managed to impose the name São Luis on a city during their extremely brief colonization of the northern part of Brazil, now known as the state of Maranhão. They also tried to take over an area in the region where the city of Rio de Janeiro stands today, but without success. In fact, the greatest threat to Portuguese dominion over the country arose when the Portuguese crown, because of the lack of an heir, passed to the Spanish royal family in 1580. Had this situation continued it would have resulted in linguistic unification. However, when the Portuguese regained their independence in 1640 and João IV assumed the throne, the two languages were able to maintain their previous status.

When the Portuguese arrived in Brazil they encountered indigenous groups of which the majority, at least along the coast, spoke languages belonging to the Tupí-Guaraní linguistic family. In the beginning the small number of colonizers was not sufficient for them to impose their own language on these indigenous people. Thus initially there was a period when the Portuguese adopted the indigenous language in order to communicate and undertake transactions. Tupí, unlike other languages from the interior, has a relatively simple morphology and can be learned without difficulty, at least according to the statements of the first colonizers. This contributed to the longtime use of the simplified variant of the Tupí-Guaraní family as the most common means of communication or *língua geral*. Portuguese families also spoke it, at least in the intimacy of the home, as Father Antônio Vieira was to comment in a letter of 1694 (Monteiro 1959, 81). The Portuguese language had its own domain, being used, for example, in official events. A diglossal situation with bilingualism emerged in this first period. Tupí was used for catechizing by the Jesuits; one missionary, Father José Anchieta

(1534–1597), published a Tupí grammar entitled *Arte de gramática da língua mais usada na Costa do Brasil.* The author of sermons, chronicles, and poetry, Anchieta is considered a worthy representative of early Brazilian literature. He also wrote some poems in Tupí that exemplify this bilingual situation.

According to Serafim da Silva Neto, the first phase of colonization ended in 1654, the year in which the Portuguese succeeded in expelling the Dutch from their colonies in northeast Brazil (1963, 73). As a result of this event and, later, because of rumors of the discoveries of gold mines and veins of other metals, larger contingents of Portuguese colonizers were inspired to cross the Atlantic to try their luck in the new lands, thus reinforcing the use of the Portuguese language. At the same time, larger numbers of African slaves arrived to substitute for the depleted Indian labor force working in the sugarcane plantations of the Northeast. Because the policy with black slaves was to divide and conquer, the Portuguese proprietors tried to avoid bringing together many individuals belonging to the same linguistic group. As a consequence, the African languages were weakened. These included Bantu languages such as Kimbundu from Angola, languages such as Nagó from the Congo and Gége from Nigeria and Dahomey, as well as the Hausa languages from the Sudan-Guinea region (Diegues 1963, 92). The social distance between the slaves and their white masters was very large, and for this reason many of the former learned only the rudiments of Portuguese.

During the second phase of colonization (1654–1808), Portugal consolidated its position in Brazil. As a result, the use of the *língua franca* of Tupí origin began to diminish in densely colonized areas such as the coastal fringe northeast of the captaincies of Bahía and Pernambuco, where the economy was flourishing thanks to the cultivation of sugarcane, and which continued to attract many Portuguese settlers. Even so, Tupí persisted in Pará, Maranhão, and Amazonas in the north and in São Paulo and Rio Grande do Sul in the south, as well as in the interior of the country. For this reason the Portuguese government in 1727, alarmed at the abandonment of the Portuguese language in some parts of Brazil by their own countrymen, promulgated a decree that prohibited the use of Tupí throughout the colony (Azevedo 1964, 540). Even so, the expeditions known as *bandeiras* that penetrated into the interior continued to use the Tupí language. The social mixing of Indians, Africans, and Portuguese also meant that semi-Creole variants arose that were taken into the interior, where they endured thanks to limited contact with the Portuguese on the coast. The expulsion of the Jesuits in 1767 was another factor that contributed to the decline in the use of this *língua geral,* given that the Jesuits had a long-standing tradition of protecting indigenous languages.

The Jesuits' departure also had a negative impact on education in the colony; since their arrival in 1549, they had been responsible for all teaching in the colony, founding schools where Portuguese was taught to the sons of the Indians. They were also in charge of teaching the children of the colonizers in their colleges. Some of these, such as São Sebastião in Rio de Janeiro and Todos Santos in Bahía, were universities in embryo. The Jesuits tried to ensure that the Portuguese government officially recognized the academic studies undertaken in the college in Bahía as being equivalent to those of Évora or Coimbra. However, their sole achievement was to ensure that university courses in Brazil corresponded to a year of "Arts" in Portugal (Azevedo 1964, 529), giving them a status practically on a par with preparatory studies. Basically the Portuguese crown feared that the creation of universities in Brazil might foment independent or abolitionist ideas. For this reason young Brazilians who wished to study at the real university level were obliged to travel to Portugal.

The educational decline provoked by the expulsion of the Jesuits continued until the arrival of the royal family in 1808. Even though the Jesuits had not created sufficient infrastructure to teach a large percentage of the population (because their educational approach was somewhat elitist), without them the possibilities of study in the colony were reduced. Other religious orders such as the Franciscans tried to maintain schools and colleges but on a less ambitious scale. The lack of universities and the formation of cultural centers that could support the Portuguese spoken in Brazil meant that the speech of the elites became increasingly distanced from that of the uneducated masses who had no access to reading materials. For this reason instruction in the Portuguese language of Indian and black slaves as well as some sons of Portuguese in rural areas was achieved largely on an oral basis. Considerable documentary evidence criticizes the Portuguese spoken by the Indians, the Mamelucos (a term used to describe the offspring of an Indian and a white), and the blacks as being *deturpado* or *degenerado*. The fact that the language was not spoken well by these people is due to the social and psychological distance between those who studied it and those who spoke it as a first language (Schumann 1978, 69–100).

The third phase that saw the consolidation of the Portuguese language began, according to Serafím da Silva Neto, when the Portuguese royal family, threatened by Napoleon's invasion, fled to Brazil in 1808 (1963, 87). The Brazilians suddenly found themselves at the center of the drama. Rio de Janeiro became the capital of the entire Portuguese empire, because the court settled there along with thousands more Portuguese who had accompanied the royal family. As a consequence the land-owning elite, the hacienda owners, moved to the city. Rio became a flourishing center of social, literary, and academic life. Some faculties for higher education were established, the National Library was founded, and the printing press was introduced. The first book to be produced in the country was published in May 1808 by Regio Tipografía in Rio de Janeiro (Neto 1963, 68; Cunha 1981, 100). A press had been established in Rio some years earlier, but it was destroyed by royal decree on 6 July 1747 (Azevedo 1964, 528). In comparison with Mexico and Peru, where printing presses were established in 1534 and 1584, respectively, Brazil's cultural situation seems hardly favorable. Even so, the linguistic model was not that of Brazilian Portuguese, but the language spoken by the royal family and their entourage, which did not coincide with the norms of the majority of the inhabitants of their overseas colony. Despite this fact, the newly arrived elites did not have any decisive influence on the Brazilian way of speaking.

Other factors during this last phase complicated the linguistic unity of the country. After his arrival in Brazil with the royal family, the prince regent passed a law that allowed foreigners to hold land (Diegues 1963, 108). From that moment non-Portuguese began to migrate to Brazil. The first immigrants were mainly Germans and Italians who settled in the south of the country. This migration continued throughout the nineteenth and into the twentieth century. While the largest groups involved were German, Italian, and Japanese, Portuguese immigrants also continued to arrive during this period. Some of the European immigrants, especially the Germans, were very isolated in the southern states of Brazil, and their slight contact with the Brazilians was not sufficient for them to learn Portuguese. They created communities with their own schools that constituted small isolated pockets of foreigners in the country.

Brazilian independence, declared in 1822 by Prince Pedro when his father João VI returned to Portugal, did not imply that such freedom was linguistic or cultural. Portugal continued to be the model, and the Brazilians still had to travel to Coimbra to take university courses on many subjects, just as in previous centuries. In 1823 a statute was included in the Brazilian constitution that decreed primary school instruction would be free for all citizens. In 1827, another law ordered the foundation of primary schools in all the "cidades, vilas e lugarejos" (cities, towns, and villages). Even so, results did not live up to expectations. The government was incapable of providing education for all (Azevedo 1964, 564). For this reason the immigrants, among others, had to create schools for their own children, as mentioned previously. Meanwhile, the country continued to function without universities. Some schools of further education or faculties were established for law, medicine, engineering, and metallurgy. The founding of the first universities, those of Rio de Janeiro and São Paulo, only took place in 1931 and 1934, respectively.

As regards language, neither the Brazilian nor Portuguese literary elite accepted the validity of the changes emerging in America. Writing implied following the classical Portuguese models and applying the grammatical rules formulated in that country. Influenced by the Romantic movement, José de Alencar (1829–1877) wrote the novel *Iracema* (1865), which idealized the life of an Indian woman who fell in love with a Portuguese man. The theme itself did not create any problems, but the fact that it used some grammatical constructions of Brazilian provenance and some regional vocabulary infuriated the guardians of tradition. How dare the author abandon the norms of the Portuguese classics? They considered that "the lack of correct usage in the Portuguese language . . ., the obsession to convert Brazilian into a different language from the old Portuguese by means of bold and unjustifiable neologisms and grammatical subversions" was intolerable (Pinheiro Chagas qtd. in Cunha 1981, 15). This created a feeling of frustration that made some Brazilians propose a national language with its own characteristics. The issue of the Brazilian language, which arose at the close of the nineteenth century, continued to be a subject of debate several years into the twentieth century (see Elia 1961).

Yet the written language closely followed the Portuguese model. For this reason, written Portuguese in Brazil was rather different from the spoken version. Various writers took pains to incorporate into their texts some linguistic uses common in the country, but their efforts were not sufficient. Only with the arrival of the Modernist movement did both forms of the language achieve some kind of equality. "La Semana de Arte

Moderna" (The Week of Modern Art), responsible for initiating this movement in March 1922, finally succeeded in offering a variant of the written word that was closer to spoken Brazilian Portuguese as having the status of a literary language. As Plinio Salgado remarked, during the *Semana* there emerged "the cry of freedom against all the literary preconceptions of that past: against the artificial academicism, against the mechanization of the processes of style, against the tired Western philosophies . . . . As opposed to a classical and official concept of the language, we propose a clear dynamic conception of the Brazilian language in its historical function of existence and transformation" (qtd. in Lessa 1966, 19).

But this was by no means easy. It required the combined efforts of all the writers of the period who, inspired by the Modernist movement, declared war on the static written language that blindly followed grammatical rules in a country that had another linguistic reality. For this reason, Teyssier considered that Brazil achieved its political independence in 1822 but delayed a hundred years before obtaining its linguistic independence (1994, 89). Celebrated individuals such as Mario de Andrade (1893–1945), Oswald de Andrade (1890–1954), and Manuel Bandeira (1886–1968) were active in the movement and criticized these outdated models. Other writers, who did not take such a polemical stance, nevertheless wrote according to the Brazilian variant of Portuguese that was closer to everyday language. One of the objectives of the Congreso Brasileño de Regionalismo, the brainchild of Gilberto Freyre (1900–1987), held in Recife in 1926, was a "reaction against the conventions of classicism, academicism and Lusitanian purism" (Lessa 1966, 18).

Several characteristics of Brazilian Portuguese were not accepted by the purists. However, before describing these, some statements regarding regional or geographical differences should be made, particularly in the context of social differences observed in the American continent. According to Antenor Nacentes, to fully comprehend the linguistic geography of the area, one can divide the country into two overall groups of dialect: north and south. The main feature that sustains this division is the more open pronunciation of the pretonic vowels in the north. There also exist subdivisions of dialects in the two regions. The north can be subdivided into two variants, the Amazónica and the Nordestin, while the south has four, the Bahiana, the Fluminense (Rio de Janeiro), the Minera, and the Sulina (Nascentes 1953, 25). The Portuguese language in Brazil is generally thought to have an overall geographical unity, but only if social differences are not taken into account. This has been a consequence of the leveling of the various dialects brought from Portugal, a typical scenario when individuals of different provenance are brought together. This can also result from ignorance of all the details of these variations, because to date only a few regions have been studied in depth (Bahía, Sergipe, Paraíba, Minas Gerais), while others are still areas of research (Ceará, São Paulo, and Região Sul; cf. Brandão 1991). There is an enormous lexical variation in Brazil given that the language has to respond to extremely varied geographical, historical, climactic, and gastronomic realities.

Traditionally the variant spoken in Rio de Janeiro has been regarded as the national model. As the capital of the Portuguese court, the city acquired a status that has endured. Even so, today other cities have acquired prestige; these include São Paulo, which has enormous economic importance. As a result, other ways of speaking have been accepted, including those diffused through the mass media.

An enormous difference exists between what is considered to be the standard speech (or *lingua padrão*) spoken by the educated minority and the nonstandard (*não padrão*), spoken by the popular classes. Within the former, differences are also marked according to a series of registers. The opposite poles within the *lingua padrão* are those of spoken colloquial language and formal writing. In the latter, the rules inculcated at school are strictly adhered to, being still influenced by grammatical norms derived from the peninsular tradition. Nonstandard Portuguese cannot be precisely defined, given that its differences from standard speech are gradual (Bortoni 1981, 82). On the other hand, there is a continual social adaptation of popular usage whereby some features that were previously characterized as nonstandard have filtered into the standard version.

The differences between Brazilian and European Portuguese have been explained in terms of the influences left in the Brazilian variant by indigenous and African languages. However, this argument is difficult to prove. At most, the influence of these languages is accepted with regard to vocabulary and pronunciation. Even so, the linguistic contact did provoke the emergence of a variant with all the characteristics of a pidgin language; this is the basis of the nonstandard mode spoken by a large number of people in the rural context and in the periphery of urban areas that had limited access to education. This "language of emergence" (Neto 1963, 82) is the result of a rudimentary mastering of Portuguese for the purpose of communication between groups of different languages which also included social differences. The language of emergence is characterized by a simplification and a reduction of phonetic, morphological, and syntactic forms. This tendency toward simplification is always latent in language. Nonlinguistic factors determine whether they are socially acceptable.

The pronunciation of nonstandard Brazilian Portuguese includes examples of the elimination of the final *r* of the word (*falar > falá, doutor > doutô, senhor > sinhô*), suppression of the lateralization of the palatal (*mulher > muiê, filho > fiu*), and the frequent omission of *l* and the nasal at the end of the word (*coronel > coroné, homem > homê*).

A reduction in the verbal system has occurred in the morphology of the nonstandard language: *eu vou, ele vai, nos vai, eles vai*. Accents are only retained to differentiate the first person from the rest—hence the necessity for using pronouns. This usage has often had repercussions on the standard language. Today there are linguists who consider Brazilian Portuguese a language that lacks an indefinite subject. The plural endings of the names are eliminated by other means, for example, the morpheme of the plural of the article as in *os home*. Education has not been sufficient to eradicate many characteristics of the *não padrão*, given that the teachers themselves, particularly in the interior of the country, share this variant with the children (see Bortoni 1995, 123).

Those who have undertaken research into Brazilian Portuguese point out the archaizing nature of the language, especially in the pronunciation. This is nothing new, as this very fact has been remarked on regarding the English spoken in the United States, the French in Canada, and the Spanish of Spanish America. Joaquim Ribeiro, for example, states that "many of the so-called *Brazilianisms of expression*, even of prosody, are found to be in perfect concordance with certain particularities [of the Portuguese language] of the fourteenth and fifteenth centuries" (1959, 47). Of course, innovations do appear because a transplanted language can only with difficulty maintain the norms of the metropolis, given that the speakers, finding themselves in a new reality, need to create their own usages.

In any case the two statements manifest an ideological position that supposes the superiority and category of a language model in its place of origin. If the language of the metropolis changes, no one talks of innovations; nor are archaisms mentioned if the language maintains the norms of previous periods. The only indication for such terminology lies in the comparison of two entities that are not considered to be equal. The quantity of archaism or innovation in the colony can only provide an idea of geographic or sociocultural closeness or distance between the two regions. Even so, having expressed the previous warnings, we will continue to use these terms because they are normally used to describe such variations.

The Portuguese language had to change in a tropical environment in order to adapt to new realities. The colonizers were obliged to use words of indigenous origin to describe all the novelties they encountered. In the chronicles of the first Portuguese in Brazil, fruits and trees are given strange names such as *jabutica, jacaranda,* or *abacaxi.* Later on, with the arrival of the blacks, words of African languages were incorporated to refer to meals or to phenomena particular to their culture, such as *vatapá, candomblé,* and *acarajé* from Kimbundu or *caçula, cafuné,* and *moleque* of Yoruba derivation. Differences in the lexicon (supposedly shared by both countries) also normally exist when two territories are so far apart. For example, the word *rapariga* is preferred in Portugal while the Brazilians use *moça* (young women); in Portugal they use *comboio* and in Brazil *trem* (train); in Portugal one takes a *pequeno almoço* in the morning and in Brazil *o café da manhã* (breakfast); while the *ônibus* (bus) circulates in Brazil, the *autocarro* performs the same task in Portugal.

Today there is no apparent reason to think that Brazilian Portuguese deviates sufficiently from that of Portugal that they can be considered different languages. Currently new factors contribute to a linguistic convergence, such as the expansion of the academic system and the mass media with its international scope; the development of communications, air and land transportation, and the use of the telephone, fax, and Internet are also playing a role. The exchange between people, merchandise, and messages requires a shared and intelligible language between Brazil and Portugal that is unitary in essential matters. On the other hand, for some time now the influence has no longer been one-sided because Brazil now influences Portuguese norms through its literature, its culture, and its popular soap operas. Linguistic prestige is no longer the attribute of a single city, but rather of several. Without a doubt there is a will, either conscious or unconscious, to maintain the Portuguese linguistic community.

In contrast, a challenge still to be met is that of the sociolinguistic differences between the marginal groups, who use the nonstandard language, and the privileged elite. Certainly education is the way forward, but instruction should at the same time be given by teachers who use the standard variant. This is not always the case in rural areas or some city neighborhoods. If the Portuguese linguistic community wishes to maintain itself as such, it should take into consideration not only the few variations of cultural norms but also the language differences between the social strata, because these are important factors in terms of divergence, especially in Brazilian Portuguese.

Translation by Jessica Johnson

Works Cited

Anchieta, José de. 1990. *Arte de gramática da língua mais usada na Costa do Brasil.* São Paulo: Edições Loyola em convênio com a Vice-Postulação da Causa de Canonização do Beato José de Anchieta.

Azevedo, Fernando de. 1964. *A cultura brasileira.* 4th ed. São Paulo: Ed. Melhoramentos.

Bortoni, Stella Maris. 1981. "A concordância verbal em português: Em estudo de sua significação social." *Ensaios de lingüística aplicada ao português.* Ed. Hildo Honório Couto. Brasilia: Thesaurus. 79–101.

——. 1995. "Variação lingüística e atividades de letramento em sala de aula." *Os significados do letramento: Uma nova perspectiva sobre a prática social da escrita.* Org. Angela Kleiman. Campinas: Mercado de Letras. 119–44.

Brandão, Sílvia Figueiredo. 1991. *A geografia lingüística no Brasil.* São Paulo: Ática.

Cunha, Celso. 1981. *Língua portuguesa e realidade brasileira.* 8th ed. Rio de Janeiro: Tempo Brasileiro.

Diegues, Manuel, Jr. 1963. *Etnias e culturas do Brasil.* 3rd ed. Rio de Janeiro: Letras e Artes.

Elia, Silvio. 1961. *O problema da língua brasileira.* Rio de Janeiro: Instituto Nacional do Livro.

Lessa, Luiz Carlos. 1966. *O modernismo brasileiro e a língua portuguesa.* Rio de Janeiro: Fundação Getúlio Vargas.

Monteiro, Clovis. 1959. *Português da Europa e Português da América: Aspectos da evolução do nosso idioma.* 3rd ed. Rio de Janeiro: Livraria Acadêmica.

Nascentes, Antenor. 1953. *O linguajar carioca.* 2nd ed. Rio de Janeiro: Simões.

Neto, Serafim da Silva. 1963. *Introdução ao estudo da língua portuguesa no Brasil.* 2nd ed. Rio de Janeiro: Instituto Nacional do Livro.

Ribeiro, Joaquim. 1959. *História da romanização da América.* Rio de Janeiro: MEC.

Schumann, John H. 1978. *The Pidginization Process: A Model for Second Language Acquisition.* Rowley, MA: Newbury House.

Teyssier, Paul. 1994. *História da língua portuguesa.* 6th ed. Lisbon: Sá da Costa.

CHAPTER 15

THE PRODUCTION OF LITERARY CULTURE IN NEW SPAIN

José Joaquín Blanco

Mexico-Tenochtitlán, the capital of New Spain, produced a significant literature, including five or six world-class works, yet the inhabitants of New Spain were unaware of it. It was a multilingual, largely illiterate, nonbookish society, whose living social culture was expressed in ways other than written texts: in oral literature, multiple religious practices, music and the plastic arts, folklore and handicrafts. The new colonial society was built on the defeated but not eliminated Aztec world. The splendor of the Aztec capital could not be denied by even the most fanatic Spaniard (see **Figure** 1). Writing, particularly printed matter, constituted a dangerous minority culture, capable of disturbing order. Only the most orthodox and elementary religious propaganda and the most restricted and laudatory court poetry were able to develop freely, and

even they did not escape the occasional setback. Books were fire; most of the important works of New Spain were written as some sort of a protest against power or as an expression of nonconformity. What made them impossible in their own times is precisely what gives them their surprisingly contemporary interest and emotional force. Virtually all of them were forbidden, some were hidden, and far more were destroyed. Writing and reading were not the natural means of cultural expression and communication, but rather the most suspicious and unreliable. Among the writers of New Spain there were always some rebellious, reforming, or at least nonconformist spirits who sought more to write for themselves than merely to serve the Church or the court.

Figure 1. The Lake City of Tenochtitlan at the Time of the Conquest 1521.

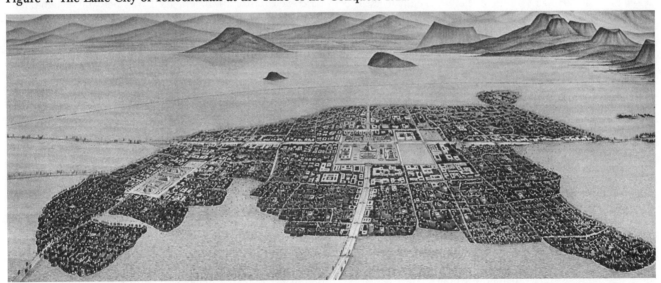

The lake city of Tenochtitlan. Photograph by Hans Ritter of mural by Luis Covarrubias in the National Museum of Anthropology in Mexico City. (Courtesy of the National Museum of Anthropology)

Since this literary culture was unknown in the late eighteenth century, when several *criollo* historians and bibliographers, following certain Spanish thinkers such as Feijoo, revised the already considerable literature of New Spain, they came to a scandalous conclusion: The authors of New Spain, particularly poets, wrote about everything but New Spain; their works were thus apparently lacking in any historical value. This opinion was reinforced during the nineteenth century, despite the fact that by then, manuscripts by leading chroniclers had begun to be edited. These, however, were scorned because of the obvious fact that they were full of either religion or conquering zeal. What could have possessed these poets, particularly those of the first century of settlement, when, despite all of the events of recent years–the encounter with a New World, the Conquest, warriors' feats, the presence of numerous indigenous cultures, the formation of new societies–all they could produce was Baroque arabesques, mannerist divertimenti, witticisms, and commentaries on classical authorities?

Everything in the literature of New Spain was worthless, the literary historians decided. This view intensified throughout the nineteenth century, and both Mexican liberals and Spanish scholars of the stature of Marcelino Menéndez y Pelayo were scandalized: How could this seemingly impoverished, useless, wasteful literature have been produced precisely in a country where so many momentous and rich historical events had taken place? Why were there no epic poems? Where was our *Araucana?* There were no novels, no critical writing, except that of Bartolomé de las Casas, who it was said, when he was not railing against the *encomenderos* (land barons), fantasized about Indian savagery as though he were discussing Athens in the tropics. The authors did not write about themselves; they were not Romantic, nor did they have a modern spirit. Similar criticism abounds in contemporary opinions of the literature of New Spain. It is obviously not a view I share. The lack of historical or historiographic value in Colonial literature is more a product of the shortsightedness of modern historians, who have wished to see certain things such as ethnology, wars, data, or political denunciations and were blind to all the rest. There was actually no sense of the "new" or of the "individual" before the Romantic and Modern eras, nor was there much intellectual criticism before the Enlightenment. There were other things, however.

There were a number of poets, throughout the colonial period but particularly during the first century, who praised the conquest, its deeds and episodes (Terrazas, Villagrá, Saavedra Guzmán, and Arias de Villalobos) or who attempted to introduce local themes, vocabulary, and atmosphere into their poems (Juan de la Cueva, Eugenio de Salazar, and González de Eslava). However, anyone hoping to find New Spain's equivalent of the old collections of ballads or Spanish *chansons de geste* would be very disappointed. We will find instead thematic extravagances and stylistic exercises, even aberrations. We have to understand that, when the poets of New Spain praise the Aztecs and the conquistadors, they are actually thinking about Renaissance or Baroque allegories of Greco-Roman or Italian cultures, or they are searching for preciosity and imaginary bravado. We might even say that these poets had turned away from their history.

The authors of the sixteenth century had not, in fact, turned from their history. It was simply that their history, culture, and interests were different from ours. They had their own ambitions, which they enthusiastically pursued, and their own small history, to which they did respond. They were far

less interested in Indians and Conquistadors of the past than in their own world as recent inhabitants of a new kingdom in which they wished to establish the Spanish language, culture, and fashions with all due haste, as well as with pomp and ceremony. And that is what we find, quite clearly, in these poems: This was their own historical discourse.

Just a few decades after the Conquest, in the mid-sixteenth century, several Spanish and *criollo* poets following the work Gutierre de Cetina (1514?–1557) and Juan de la Cueva (1543–1612) busied themselves compiling an extensive poetic compendium *Flores de baria poesía* [Flowers of Various Poetry], which included both the forms of the Spanish Renaissance and novelties imported from Italy. It was said that readers in Mexico were as familiar as those in Valladolid or Sevilla with the work of Fernando de Herrera (1534–1597). This was no mean feat in the sixteenth century for a few thousand Spaniards, *criollos,* and Spanish-speaking *mestizos* practicing a language and culture that were, first, strange and, in any case, restricted to a minority in the broad, unapproachable, multicultural, and multilingual map of the Mexico of that time. When Eslava announced that there were "more poets than manure," or when Eugenio de Salazar, Cervantes de Salazar, or Bernardo de Balbuena (1563?–1627) praised Mexico's overpopulation of scholars and doctors, we can correctly identify these sentiments as mere commonplaces of the traditional Western satires and tributes, widespread since Juvenal's time. But there is also implied here a goal that was never reached, even at the end of Spanish rule: the Castilianization and full Spanish acculturation of New Spain. Not only was there a wish to achieve this, but people struggled and eventually succeeded in their attempt to turn Mexico City into a center of Spanish language and culture that was as important as some of the main Spanish cities, a fact acknowledged by Spanish writers of the time.

The crowning achievement of the scholars of New Spain during the first century was the transfer, sowing, grafting, and cultivation of Castilian literature in this part of the world. That was their historical desire for themselves: the creation of a strictly Spanish literature in New Spain. This situation persisted until *criollo* belligerence fired writers with greater ambition, and the writings of Sor Juana Inés de la Cruz (1648–1695) and Francisco de Castro (d. 1740) emerged, together with certain poems that could not possibly have been the work of any Spaniard anywhere in the empire but were specifically and obviously produced by Mexicans, such as the *Loa del Divino Narciso* [1692; The Divine Narcissus] by Sor Juana and de Castro's *Octava maravilla* [1710; The Eighth Marvel].

Yet, in his epistle, Eugenio de Salazar (1530–1602) noted enthusiastically that a Parnassus had been created in Mexico; arts and modern sciences were cultivated; classical languages and even Italian were spoken; Spanish was spoken correctly and written well, with enough skill and mastery to be able to satisfy the most demanding of muses. These poets were less concerned about reflecting the political and multicultural reality of the new country than about impregnating it with Spanish culture and lifestyle. The time of wars and epics had passed; they were now in the era of the creation of a "new" Spain on another continent.

Among the inhabitants of New Spain, religion was not only much more important than it has been for modern Mexicans, but it was a different religion in density, profundity, and practice and, it could be said, in beliefs and dogmas. An inhabitant of New Spain would regard the most traditional bishops of today as extremely worldly Lutheran heretics. Modern Christianity has become secularized and has stripped religion of many forms of devotion, beliefs, and practices that were essential in New Spain. Particular saints, rites, brotherhoods, and churches had a social and historical importance that have been lost in our times, even for devout, believing, and practicing Christians. As one would expect in a society that is not only completely religious but also so monopolistically religious; much of its literature is devoted to ceremonies, celebrations, prayers, competitions, and church affairs. These were the texts that were most frequently written, read, and listened to, and those we least understand, since modern religion is unable to interpret them. We see dogmas and anecdotes, ideas or cultural beliefs in what was a real living culture. The existence of beings from the next world and the vital importance of these creatures had a very precise everyday reality, of which this poetry offers us as a full historical discourse. For the majority of the residents of New Spain, the most historical things that happened to them were matters from the next world. Although these poems may mean little to us today as either poetry or religion, they tell us a great deal about the internal history of this society. In other words, they contain a formidable historical discourse that neither we nor the holiest scholars are able to read. We are inevitably poor readers of this poetry: We examine it under a critical, Voltairean light, smiling at its naïveté, ignorance, hysteria, and superstitions; then we fail to give it internal credibility. This is how literature dies its inevitable death.

One may think of the missionaries' *letrillas* and couplets; of Pedro de Trejo (sixteenth century); of Hernán González de Eslava (1534–1601), of Juan Pérez Ramírez's (b. 1544?) *Desposorio espiritual entre el Pastor Pedro y la Iglesia mexicana* [1574; Spiritual Marriage Between the Shepherd Peter and the Mexican Church]; of Hortigosa (d. 1796); of Córdoba and of Matías de Bocanegra; of a talk on the conversion of the kings in Tlaxcala; of Francisco Bramón's (seventeenth century) *Sirgueros de la Virgen* [1620; Songs to the Virgin]; of the extravagant and famous *Soneto a Cristo Crucificado* [Sonnet to the Crucified Christ]; of the *Anónimo de la Pasión* [Anonymous Poem to the Passion of Christ]; and of so many others that survive as enigmatically as old oil paintings in which we can see the subject and a little color, although the vital density that blazed in them has disappeared. Even the erudite and extremely devout Father Alfonso Méndez Plancarte (1909–1955) was unable to strip them of their dusty, yellowed air of antiques from the sacristy; even he was Voltairean and condemned excessively religious effusiveness or innocence. Such extravagant devotion makes these works almost heretical from a modern point of view.

The following main groups, rather than stages, can be distinguished in the poetry of New Spain:

1. Missionary poetry, with medieval traces, was brought over for preaching and for worship and used by both the Spaniards and the Indians. This created an oral form of poetry, consisting of couplets, sonnets, décimas, allegorical plays, and carols, which was widely used for several centuries.

2. Spanish-speakers continuously added to the oral forms of poetry through the tradition of collecting ballads; this produced the *corrido* (ballad) in Mexico but was already a success by the time of Sor Juana (although the earliest recorded *corridos* were produced later). The popular Spanish ballad collections were also introduced by oral means.

3. A short-lived form of courtly-chivalrous poetry, of which Francisco de Terrazas (ca. 1524–1600) was a major exponent, was fully Renaissance in style and typically used by noble men and women. There was amatory poetry, in which the son of Hernán Cortés participated, which disappeared at the end of the sixteenth century when the chivalrous and Renaissance ideal of Spanish nobility declined in both the peninsula and its dominions (its last exponent being Luís de Sandoval y Zapata). During the Renaissance, a noble gentleman was expected to handle words as skillfully as weapons, and being a poet was virtually compulsory for both soldiers and gentlemen.

4. A powerful Baroque poetry was written by clerics, produced in monasteries but not intended for either worship or preaching but rather for the consumption of scholars in the monasteries. Balbuena and Sor Juana excelled at this form of poetry, but it was also cultivated by Carlos de Sigüenza y Góngora (1645–1700) and Francisco de Castro (d. 1740). Hundreds of poets adopted this style, with over a dozen leaving something that is still readable today.

5. Eighteenth-century didactic poetry still had baroque traces, yet it was no longer content with an audience of its own men of letters and artists; instead it pursued specific aims of education or the dissemination of knowledge and ideas or public morality (already anticipated during the previous century by Matías de Bocanegra). Eventually a neo-Classical, Rococo aesthetics developed through Fray Manuel de Navarrete (1768–1809).

These various types of poetry reveal much of the internal history of these groups; what we cannot find may simply be because we are looking for anachronisms, such as social or racial contradictions, personal effusions, or scientific, political, or philosophical curiosities typical of other eras (obviously barring exceptional cases such as certain texts by Sor Juana and Francisco de Castro). Balbuena's *Grandeza mexicana* [1604; Mexican Greatness], for example, offers extremely rich and unquestionable testimony of the degree of literary and linguistic perfection achieved by the finest men of letters in New Spain, but we are unlikely to find there *criollo* or nationalistic invocations or Casas-style "anti-colonial" diatribes, or even scientific prefigurations of a Humboldt. We find instead that, among the finest early poets, local poetry and the local use of Spanish were not that far removed from the metropolitan norms.

Throughout the viceroyalty, but particularly during the first century of settlement, the attitude of the Church and the Crown regarding indigenous histories was confusing and contradictory. On the one hand, the old codices were pursued and burnt as objects and results of idolatry; on the other, they were sought out and taken care of–copied, translated and studied, and preserved in the libraries and archives of the monasteries of New Spain and the Council of the Indies. Orders and decrees prohibiting or encouraging their preservation and study came and went; works were either treasured or burned, either preserved by ethnographers or destroyed by incendiary inquisitors.

The initial zeal of the friars, particularly Franciscans and Dominicans, produced many original, anonymous, and collective manuscripts on which the great historical works of the religious orders were based. The Indians had no alphabet (although they did have elementary phonic signs). Their writing was hieroglyphic and ideographic. Some involved pictures that required an oral explanation that only the enlightened caste of the *calmecac* could provide; these disappeared entirely during the wars and killings at Cholula and the Great Temple. After the Conquest, all that remained were a few native chiefs or *caciques*, who were second sons and thus, elders, though unaware of most secrets. These societies had been contaminated by the new culture and the new vision of the world, imposed so tragically and drastically by weapons and evangelization. Despite this, there was still much these leaders could tell; the friars encouraged them to speak and transcribed and translated their words, quickly and effectively adapting indigenous languages to the Latin alphabet (especially Nahuatl), and modifying and even distorting the culture of the Indians to adapt it to European and Christian forms. Despite tremendous odds against success, this work was done; and it is the foundation of our knowledge of ancient Mexico. Without these hybrid texts Mexican history would lack basic information that dispels the misty and fabulous legends that cover this remote period that preceded the arrival of the Spaniards. Pre-Hispanic Mexico would have been lost in silence, with no other voices than those of the visual enigmas of the paintings and sculptures that survived the wars, the evangelists' zeal, and the construction of churches and towns in New Spain.

From the time of their arrival, the Franciscans, particularly Fr. Pedro de Gante (1486–1572), set about finding a Latin alphabetical form for Nahuatl and other languages and compiling an oral history of the ancient Indians (*huehuetlatolli*), a task begun by Fr. Andrés del Olmos. They taught the Indians to write historical accounts, songs, and dialogues in an alphabetical form that would be comprehensible to the European mentality; these were immediately successful. The oldest Indian history of the Conquest, the so-called *Anales de Tlatelolco*, was written in 1528, with references to previous episodes and traditions, from the point of view of a *tlatelolca*. There are several actual "speeches by the elders" and others integrated into the friars' works (particularly in those of Bernardino de Sahagún, who also introduced the method of encouraging the Indians to talk by using questionnaires). The friar's discourses and the native responses already denoted an evangelized, colonized state; a terror of uttering idolatrous or heretical views; and a clear desire to please the priests. The native respondents told the Franciscans what they imagined the Spanish priests wanted to hear: The religion of the Mexicas was the work of the devil, and the Franciscans were devoted, austere men of God.

In the mid-sixteenth century, certain Indians raised by the Friars recorded various chronologies, songs, episodes, tales, and mythologies. From this variety of manuscripts, foremost among which are the *Anales de Cuauhtitlán* [Annals of Cuauhtitlán], the *Colección de cantares mexicanos* [Collection of Mexican Poems], the Ramírez Codex, the *Manuscrito de los romances de los señores de la Nueva España* [Manuscript of the Ballads of the Lords of New Spain], the *Libro de los coloquios* [Book of the Colloquies], and the Sahagún codices preserved in Florence and Madrid, the *Códice Aubin* [Aubin Codex], and the *Historia tolteca-chichimeca* [Toltec-Chichimec History], Angel María Garibay K. and Miguel León Portilla have selected and translated texts for various anthologies and have produced the finest studies on Nahuatl literature available to date. An excellent example of this writing is found in *Visión de los vencidos* [*The Broken Spears: The Aztec Account of the Conquest of Mexico*, 1992] by León Portilla:

En los caminos yacen dardos rotos,
los cabellos están esparcidos;
destechadas están las casas,
enrojecidos tienes sus muros.
Gusanos pululan por calles y plazas

y en las paredes están los sesos.
Rojas están las aguas,
están como teñidas,
y cuando las bebimos,
es como si bebiéramos
agua de salitre.
Golpeábamos, en tanto,
los muros de adobe,
y era nuestra herencia
una red de agujeros.

(137–138)

Broken spears lie in the roads;
we have torn our hair in our grief.
The houses are roofless now,
and their walls are red with blood.
Worms are swarming in the streets and plazas
and the walls are splattered with gore.
The water has turned red,
as if it were dyed,
and when we drink it,
it is as if we drank
saltpeter water.
We have pounded our hands in despair
against the adobe walls,
for our inheritance, our city,
is lost and dead.

The destruction of the pre-Hispanic codices was the result of something more than mere fanaticism, however. Both the Church and the Crown wished to eliminate the past and to start their rule from scratch. But the search for, and the elaboration, preservation, and study of, Indian testimonies happened for more powerful reasons than the undoubtedly noble motives of Christian charity and Renaissance enlightenment: It was essential to find out about the subjected peoples, to know them fully, or else they would be impossible to subjugate. But while theological and political polemics proliferated, and histories were just as easily fabricated as destroyed, a new materialistic, opportunistic, almost vulgar element emerged, which only served to confuse historical and literary work even further: the craving for money, power, and honors on the part of the descendants of the Indian "nobility." These passed themselves off as Indians, although they were probably almost invariably *mestizos*; in some cases, there was so much blending with the Spanish and their culture that the Indian nobility who were pressing their case for recognition seemed more like Spaniards who had recently disembarked from Spain.

During the viceroyalty, particularly during the sixteenth century, there was a great deal of disagreement concerning the treatment warranted by the Indian "nobles," the chieftains, governors of Indians, and the descendants of the conquistadors' allies. The viceregal administration needed powerful Indians to govern the people, and so, in keeping with European patterns of property and inheritance (although responding to pragmatic situations), it often granted privileges, property and honors to the Indian leaders and to the families of *caciques* who were loyal and indispensable to them. In the turmoil and extreme mortality rate of the sixteenth century, which affected males disproportionately, the men of the nobility invariably died at an early age, leaving the privileges of property and honor in the hands of women, who then married Spaniards in order to defend their inheritance. These families produced a peculiar type of increasingly *criollo mestizo* whose economic interests were based on ancient Indian history; it was the past that gave them the possibility of riches, property, positions, honors, and privileges. A vast literature of litigation was created, a bureaucratic historiography, which in turn was multiplied in size when the viceregal authorities ordered it all to be verified; these briefs sometimes produced astonishingly thick volumes.

Fernando Alvarado Tezozómoc (1530?–1600?), Chimalpahin (1579–1660), and Alva Ixtlilxóchitl (1578–1650) have generally been classified as "Indian historians," but they were not really. The true Indian version of the Conquest is only an underground thread in the works of friars and anonymous codices. These historians, instead, represented the privileged *mestizos* and generally displayed both less sympathy toward their forebears than had Bernal or the friars and a greater and somewhat tedious insistence on Christian and Spanish orthodoxy.

Fernando Alvarado Tezozómoc is the most ancient, shadowy, and interesting of the *mestizo* historians. He was said to have been the son of Cuitláhuac, although, in fact, he was only one of the many grandchildren, on the distaff side, of Moctezuma Xocoyotzin. He was born shortly after the Conquest (c. 1530) and died in the early seventeenth century. He wrote at least three works, two of which have survived: the *Crónica mexicáyotl*, in Nahuatl, and the *Crónica mexicana* (c.1598), in the clumsy Spanish of someone who has not yet been fully acculturated. His literary importance lies precisely in this aspect: Of all of the *mestizo* chroniclers, he is the closest to the culture of his elders, even though he never stopped cursing the "devil" Huitzilopochtli or fearing that he might be regarded as non-Christian. Together with Durán, he represents the strongest defense of the Mexica (Aztec) culture, at a time when it was most maligned. After the fall of Tenochtitlan, all of the peoples formerly subject to the ruling Mexicas were only too pleased to blame them for all their ills and to repeat the claims of wickedness that the Spaniards had themselves attributed to the ruling class in order to justify the frequent massacres.

Tezozómoc had access to original reports and codices, primarily the *Codex Ramírez* (or *Relación del origen de los Indios que habitan esta Nueva España, según sus historias* [Report on the Origin of the Native Peoples Who Inhabit This New Spain According to Their History], also used by Durán and Torquemada, and already translated into Spanish by the Jesuits Juan de Tovar and José de Acosta. *Crónica mexicana* tells the story of the Mexica from their fabulous origins to the Spaniards' arrival; a second part on the Conquest and the early decades of colonization may have been lost. *Crónica* was owned by Carlos de Sigüenza y Góngora, who bequeathed it to the Colegio de San Pedro y San Pablo, where the document, or at least copies of it, were consulted by Boturini, Veytia, and Clavijero. It was not published in Mexico until 1878, although it had already been brought out in London in 1848 and in a French version in Paris in 1853. *Crónica mexicáyotl* was not translated into Spanish until 1949, when Adrián León undertook the task.

Crónica mexicana is so mysterious that it almost appears to be fantastic literature; translating Mexica history into a different language and culture made everything–chronology, customs, language usage, culture, politics, religion, and wars–appear like a confusing collection of fables. It is palpable evidence of the existential confusion, the absolute destruction of awareness that the Conquest caused among the Indians, and sad evidence of the fact that, even in defeat, the Indians continued to fight among themselves, and, far from regarding themselves as ethnically and culturally united against the invaders, they insisted on their local identities, their traditional enmities (such as

Mexica against Texcocans, for example), and their caste differences in relation to the *macehuatlin* (Indian commoners). The author's faithfulness to the testimonies gathered makes the *Crónica mexicana* an abundant source of historiographic materials: his tragic cultural anguish, his confusion between the two worlds, and his astonishment at his own past (which Tezozómoc found it difficult to explain even to himself) all give us a glimpse of the mental conflict–of logic, values, and customs–of the Indian elites during the first century of the Conquest.

Domingo Francisco de San Antón Muñón Chimalpahin Cuauhtlehuanitzin, known as Chimalpahin, was born in Amecameca in the province of Chalco, in 1579, and died in Mexico City in 1660. Chalco was far from being the small village that we know today as virtually a suburb of the Federal District. It had been established as a nation long before the arrival of the Aztecs, and its rule extended over several present-day Mexican states, such as Mexico State, Guerrero, Oaxaca, Michoacán, Puebla, and Hidalgo. Chimalpahin was born into one of the leading families of Chalco that had managed to preserve some of its power even after the Conquest. He received a privileged education, which was sometimes granted to the descendants of the Indian nobility: He was educated by the Dominicans (and later, perhaps, at the Colegio de Santa Cruz Tlatelolco, which, in any case, would already have been in decline). He may have married, but in 1593, at a very early age, he joined the Church of New Spain, as a lay brother at the hermitage of San Antonio Abad. He was thereby able to obtain access both to the materials preserved by the Indians and to those preserved in the monasteries. It is unclear whether he did so out of stubborn respect for his forebears or as a means of proving either his *cacique*'s or more communal rights to the viceroy, since the Crown often acknowledged and legalized pre-Hispanic rights.

His long name accurately reflects his status: his Indian origins (Chimalpahin Cuauhtlehuanitzin), the Spanish names required at baptism (Domingo Francisco–precisely those of the founders of the prevailing monastic orders), the name of the church he served (San Antón), and the surname of the protectors of this hermitage (the Spaniards Diego de Muñón and Sancho Sánchez de Muñón). Several works in Nahuatl and Spanish are attributed to him, though some of them are lost. The surviving works are considered authentic, although they are not without gaps; nor have they been fully translated or published. They include three texts, written primarily in Nahuatl, eight historical accounts, perhaps not structured by Chimalpahin himself, entitled *Diferentes historias originales* [Various Original Histories], his *Diario* [1598–1615; Diary] and *Memorial breve acerca de la fundación de Culhuacán* [Brief Memorial on the Foundation of Culhuacán]; all written mainly during the early decades of the seventeenth century.

Paralleling the fate of several Indian and *mestizo* manuscripts, *Diferentes historias* somehow found its way into the hands of Carlos de Sigüenza y Góngora, who owned and studied it, bequeathing it to the Jesuits on his death. It was preserved in the Colegio de San Gregorio in the San Pedro y San Pablo branch in Mexico, where it was consulted and acquired by Lorenzo Boturini, from whom it was confiscated. In 1784, it was recovered by Antonio de León y Gama, whose descendants sold it during the following century to Joseph María Alexis Aubin. He, in turn, resold it in France to Eugène Goupil, an antiquarian of Mexican descent on his mother's side who eventually donated it to the Bibliothèque Nationale in Paris, where it is held to this day. Goupil decided to donate it to France instead of returning it to Mexico, not only because of the better care it would receive there—many ancient Mexican works have been preserved precisely because they were taken abroad—but because he considered Paris to be the intellectual center of the world and, therefore, a city where all men of science would have access to the text. Francisco del Paso y Troncoso photographed this text in the early twentieth century; it was not until this century, however, that part of the work of Chimalpahin was edited and translated (into Spanish and German). The *Diario* has yet to be translated, and there is no complete critical edition of the historical accounts, although in 1965 Silvia Rendón studied and translated five of them under the title *Relaciones originales de Chalco Amecamecan* [Original Reports of Chalco Amecamecan]. José Rubén Romero Galván made a further contribution in 1983 with *Octava Relación* [Eighth Report], together with a preliminary study.

Chimalpahin wrote partly to defend his family—their property rights, position, and power over *macehuatlin* Indians, as well as the right to the specific privileges granted Indian nobility (being entitled to wear Spanish clothes, bear arms, ride a horse, hold positions, and be granted honors and property). To this end, he sought to demonstrate the greatness of Chalco and the aristocratic genealogy of his family. Yet he also attempted to explain his country by incorporating it into universal history, just as the Spaniards of the Counter-Reformation had conceived it. As a historian, he was extremely loyal to his sources: paintings, codices, oral accounts, documents in Nahuatl with Latin script, Spanish texts, and a great deal of original information. His interpretation, however, is that of a convert to Christianity. Far more converted to Western culture than Tezozómoc, yet less so than Fernando de Alva Ixtlilxóchitl, he attempts to incorporate pre-Hispanic history into the biblical, theological, and political orthodoxy of the rulers, in which he too believes: the creation, original sin, the flood, the confused dispersion of peoples after the Tower of Babel, and the redemptory and providential mission of Christianity and Spain.

Chimalpahin gets lost in this cultural labyrinth: He tries to match the Mexica and Gregorian calendars, to have the Chichimecas originate in Europe, and to find local signs of the flood, Babel, and even the prophets. He compares the "prehistory" of the Indians—in other words, their lives before Christianity and the Conquest—with those of Jerusalem, Rome, and Greece. Sometimes in the form of annals and sometimes as legends, he traces the history of Chalco from the creation of the world to the viceroys, evangelization, and the tributes imposed on Indians by Colonial administration. Although Chimalpahin emphasizes the role of Chalco in Indian history (particularly regarding his grandfather, Domingo Hernández Aypochtzin, whom he makes a descendant of the founders of Chalco), he refers to a broader geographical framework; that is, he refers to the entire central region of present-day Mexico, and he records episodes involving other states, "kingdoms," or important cities such as Azcapotzalco, Texcoco, and Mexico.

The work of the most famous of these historians, Fernando de Alva Ixtlilxóchitl, arose as a result of a dispute over land, honor, and privileges; this involved an attempt to prove the chieftaincy of San Juan Teotihuacan and the author's Indian nobility through his descent from Nezahualcóyotl and Captain Ixtlilxóchitl (imposed by Cortés in Texcoco), the most important of the Indian captains to form an alliance with the

conquistadors. According to Edmundo O'Gorman, de Alva Ixtlilxóchitl's *Obras Históricas* [Historical Works] are not intended to be purely historiographical, but to serve as a reminder of merits and services that should earn recognition and rewards. It is no exaggeration to describe Ixtlilxóchitl's history as a lengthy, complicated dissertation on the merits of the author's surname, which was not even his own. Like Tezozómoc and Chimalpahin, he had access to original sources and extensive contact with the Indians, yet he is the most fully Hispanic of the three chroniclers, the one most immersed in the dominant culture. His work is distinguished from that of a Spanish friar only by his personal and familial aims and interests. Fernando de Alva Ixtlilxóchitl had, in fact, very little Indian blood in him. He was neither a de Alva nor an Ixtlilxóchitl but was the son of a Spaniard (Juan Pérez de la Peraleda) and a supposed *mestiza*, Ana Cortés Ixtlilxóchitl (who, in turn, was the daughter of the Spaniard Juan Grande), accused by the Indians of San Juan Teotihuacan of being Spanish and therefore of lacking any rights as an Indian chieftain. Strictly speaking, the historian would have lost the surname Ixtlilxóchitl from his grandparents' time and should have adopted the Spanish surnames of his immediate forebears, Fernando Pérez Grande.

Yet in the sixteenth century, calling oneself after one's saint's day was not compulsory, and Spaniards chose or invented the surnames they wished, or accepted those imposed on them by the friars or their godparents. The Texcocan captain himself, Ixtlilxóchitl, chose Cortés as a surname and had himself called Fernando in 1524: Fernando Cortés Ixtlilxóchitl. Thus the historian preserved the name Ixtlilxóchitl purely for its historical renown. It is not known why he assumed the surname of de Alva; O'Gorman surmises that this may have been due to a desire to combine the surnames of two famous Texcocan and Spanish captains in his person. Be that as it may, his children ignored the Ixtlilxóchitl surname, using Cortés instead, as well as the glamorous de Alva, calling themselves Juan, Ana, and Diego de Alva Cortés, despite the fact that their mother was called Ana Gutiérrez. All this muddle over names demonstrates the confusion and the craving for identity of the ruling or noble Indian caste, which had allied itself with the conquistadors and then the bureaucrats, and which swiftly became incorporated into the white race; all that they retained of their Indian roots was the increasingly weak and much disputed rights and privileges that the Crown recognized in certain Indian families. Furthermore, it should be noted that, in every case of distinguished *mestizos* or Indians, Indian ancestry came from the mother's side: Poor Spaniards married Indians or *mestizas* with rights in order to appropriate the wealth and privileges granted to the descendants of powerful Indians. This meant that by the third generation, all the grandchildren of the Tlatoanis were completely *criollo* and Spanish, with nothing more Indian about them than their legal status. Think, for example, of the counts and dukes of Moctezuma, some of whom even became Spanish grandees.

In any case, the historical work of Ixtlilxóchitl, who was the great-grandson of Nezahuilpilli and a distant nephew of the Mexica Cuitláhuac, was driven by the material interest in preserving the chieftaincy of San Juan Teotihuacan (highly sought after by various rivals, including the Indian community) and the honor of being descended from the kings of Texcoco, who, in his opinion, were the true pre-Hispanic emperors.

If, on the one hand, Ixtlilxóchitl spared no effort to exaggerate and even invent "Texcocan greatness" and the importance of Captain Ixtlilxóchitl in the Conquest and evangelization; on the other hand, he always identified with the Spaniards as "our men," distancing himself from the Indians as "the enemy" in his own texts, when he was discussing warriors. In any case, he justifies his work not by being an Indian himself, but by having been brought up among Indians and therefore having been introduced to the codices, poetry, and oral reports.

In Fernando de Alva Ixtlilxóchitl, we see less Indian memory than the beginnings of a *criollo* identity of New Spain–and the not-so-unusual case of a white man pretending to be Indian. (He eventually managed to preserve the chieftaincy, which his grandchildren inherited; he was also an official interpreter and governor in Texcoco, Tlalmanalco, and Chalco.) This Indian character of indomitable will prefigured the *indigenismo* that would prevail in the nationalism of an independent Mexico: a fanciful, sentimental, and somewhat opportunistic identification with Indian aristocracy and splendor, which were increasingly less well understood.

Ixtlilxóchitl was a perfect example of acculturation; thus, when he translated his ancestor Nezahualcóyotl (1402–1472), the poetic language and the ideas of any real weight are actually those of Fray Luis de León or Jorge Manrique.

Los gustos de esta vida,
Sus riquezas y mando,
son prestados;
Son substancia findiga,
En aparienica sólo matizados
Y es tan grande verdad ésta
Que a una pregunta me has de
dar respuesta;
¿Qué es de Cihuapatzin
Y de Cuauhtezontecomatzin
el valiente
Y de Acolnahuacatzin?
¿Sus voces oigo acaso?
¿Qué es de toda esa gente?
Ya están en la otra vida;
éste es el caso.

(Vol. II, 269)

The pleasures of this life,
Its wealth and command,
Are merely lent;
They are a fictitious substance,
Only apparently nuanced,
And this is so true
That you must answer one
question;
What has become of Cihuapatzin
And Cuauhtezontecomatzin
the brave
and Acolnahuacatzin?
Do I perchance hear their voices?
What has become of all these people?
They are in the next life,
that is what has happened.

Similarly, others attempt to make Nezahualcóyotl's work sound like bibilical verses, or like Horace, or Victor Hugo, or even St. John Perse. Critics have constantly sought to base the lord of Texcoco's greatness on the fact that he resembles the great Western poets, yet his poetry remains enigmatic.

The originals of Ixtlilxóchitl's work were lost, and the copies or transfers were so muddled up that, although his works began to be published in 1829, with more extensive editions in 1848 and in 1891 to 1892, it was not until 1975 that they could be read accurately, thanks to a critical edition by Edmundo O'Gorman, who separated, under five different titles, the various texts that had been randomly compiled into a single edition and whose chaos exasperated historians. The five texts are mature works, written in the early seventeenth century, that contradict each other, since they depend on different sources in regard to specific historical data, although not in regard to the general aim of making Texcoco appear as a metropolis and center of an empire, usurped by the Mexicas just before the Spaniards' arrival. The copies or transfers of these texts survived, as in the case of Alvarado Tezozómoc and Chimalpahin, because they fell into the hands of Carlos de Sigüenza y Góngora, who left them to the Colegio de San Pedro y San Pablo, where they were consulted and copied by Boturini, before experiencing the same fate as the other texts. O'Gorman separates the work of Ixtlilxóchitl as follows: *Sumaria relación de todas las cosas que han sucedido en la Nueva España, Relación sucinta en forma de memorial, Compendio histórico de los reyes de Texcoco* [1608; Summary Report of all Things that have Occurred in New Spain, Succinct Report in the Form of a Memorial Account, Historical Compendium of the Kings of Texcoco], *Sumaria relación de la historia general de esta Nueva España* [1627; Summary Report of the History of This New Spain] and *Historia de la nación chichimeca* [History of the Chichimeca Nation], which is unfinished, either because of the loss or destruction of the last sections.

More emphatically than other historians, Ixtlilxóchitl sought to incorporate his own version of Indian history (everything good was due to Texcoco) into the Christian universe. Indian and biblical dimensions were made to concur; since the infallibility of the Bible and of the Spanish Counter-Reformist interpretation of it were beyond discussion, Ixtlilxóchitl had to twist Indian information to a degree that bordered on the fantastic. This must have involved a great effort, as did the adaptation of the codices, other accounts, and poetry to his acculturated interpretation. Likewise, he tried to make Nahua chronology match the Gregorian calendar: The ancient history of the Indians had to have its creation, its flood, and its Babel, or else it was not history. The dispersion after the Tower of Babel became the origin of the various Indian migrations and the split into Toltecs and Chichimecas; thus, the central region of Mexico was turned into an upside-down Europe, with is own Holy Roman Empire, and Xólotoal as its Caesar or Constantine and the historian's ancestors, Nezahualcóyotl and Nezahualpilli, as their local Charlemagne, from whom the dubiously-named family of Ixtlilxóchitl derived their claim in the litigation for land, positions, and honors in the viceregal antechambers. For the historian, it was this family, rather than Moctezuma's, that deserved countships and dukedoms; and he even complained at length that the sons and daughters, grandchildren and relatives of Nezahualcóyotl and Nezahualpilli went around digging and scratching for something to eat and even paid taxes, as *macehuatlin* did.

The most outstanding part of Ixtlilxóchitl's work is obviously the Texcocan part, where the figure of Nezahualcóyotl is presented as a meticulous King David. He does not expressly establish this relationship, but he does draw a parallel down to the last detail; each has dynastic roots, and each one is a poet, God's favorite, and a prophet of the true God who is yet to come, but they are both sinners (Nezahualcóyotl fathering an Indian Absolom and Solomon–Tetzauhpintzintli and Nezahualpilli, respectively–from his Texcocan woman).

His sources do not support his exaggerations and interpretations; if one were to believe him about Nezahualcóyotl's penal code, then mankind would never have had a more brutal concentration camp than Texcoco, where people were executed, tortured, and mutilated for minor crimes. One might suspect, however, that Ixtlilxóchitl exaggerated the Indians' severity in order to exalt his nation and his forebears morally, depicting them as more zealous of virtue than the most enthusiastic inquisitor and thereby forgiving himself for the sins of idolatry generally attributed to the Mexicas, who would have been seen as the barbarians, the sinners, and the servants of the devil. He was not able to twist history sufficiently, however, to be able to justify the betrayal by his ancestor Ixtlilxóchitl of his own Texcocan people and his lord Cacama; nor could he paint it as a divine plan, foretold by Nezahualpilli, to facilitate both the conversion of the Indians to Christianity and the Spanish rule of the Indies.

Ixtlilxóchitl's Texcocan bias, although not entirely baseless (Texcoco was a strong, illustrious nation, prior to the Mexica and a key element of the Triple Alliance, which the Spaniards merely regarded as Moctezuma's empire), clearly underlines the degree of division among the Indians of the time of the Spaniards' arrival, particularly among the Indian aristocracy. All the kingdoms and communities were eager to separate from each other; there was no empire, but rather numerous different communities that were reluctant to unite, for union was an action that was regarded in warlike terms, as submission by the weaker to the stronger party. They all conspired against each other, even before fatal omens were noticed. They fought against their neighbors and even within the same family; at the time of Cortes' arrival, Ixtlilxóchitl was conspiring against his sister Cacama.

Fernando de Alva Ixtlilxóchitl was profoundly distressed that it was precisely because of the defeat of the Mexicas by the Spanish conquerors that the land he called the Kingdom of the Chichimeca came to be known as Mexico and acquired the prestige of Mexico-Tenochtitlan, and the Mexicas thus became the heirs to the great Toltec culture, while no one regarded Texcoco as anything more than a second-rate, dependent town. The historian himself, a century after the Conquest, continued conspiring against Tenochtitlan and seeking friendship with the Spaniards to erase the memory of the Mexicas, who, he thought, seemed to continue winning victories even after their destruction and to spread their name and prestige all over the ancient map and even ancient history. (A few decades before Ixtlilxóchitl's work, his forerunner and relative, Juan Bautista Pomar [fl. 1582], wrote *Relación de Texcoco* [Report on Texcoco], which was not, however, published until 1891.) Rancor, anger, displeasure, greed, vanity, and simply a greater incorporation into the Spanish world distinguishes Ixtlilxóchitl's work from that of Indians and other *mestizos*, and even that of *criollos* and Spaniards. It depicts not only antiquity but also the entire era of its author, what privileged, acculturated Indians (and *mestizos* and *criollos* with an interest in Indian affairs) could know, think, or imagine in the early seventeenth century. The desperate justification of the Indians' cultural and religious differences became an issue in New Spain and then Mexico that has lasted until the present.

Indian Literatures and National Literature

The work of the *mestizo* chroniclers, the descendants of the ancient powerful Indian families, overlaps with and imitates the friars' work, merely adding an emphasis on region or lineage, together with a more worldly aim. Among the friars there were already cases in which solidarity with, or sympathy toward, the conquered nations blended seamlessly with the ecclesiastic intention, such as those of Fr. Diego Durán (d. 1588?) regarding the Aztecs, the anonymous Franciscan who wrote the *Relación de Michoacán* [1541; Report on Michoacan], and Fray Diego Muñoz Camargo (ca. 1529–1599) with respect to the Tlaxcaltecs.

The tradition of compiling the oral literature of the Indians in the Latin alphabet lasted throughout the viceroyalty and afterward up to the present, producing literary miracles such as the numerous Náhoa poems, the great Mayan books (*Crónica de Nakuk Pech* [Nakuk Pech Chronicle], *Popul Vuh*, the various *Chilam Balam*, and *Rabinal Achí*), as well as several texts in the Indian languages that were and still are spoken in Mexico. Neither the Conquest nor evangelization, neither Castilianization nor electronic communications media, have been able to eliminate the country's ethnic-cultural-linguistic mosaic. This mosaic has produced many legitimate national literatures, which function as part of the reality and life of Mexico yet at the same time differ from the unifying norms of the national project, the Spanish language, and compulsory adaptation to Western culture. One has to accept the fact that the efforts of translation into Spanish and of interpretation, in order to understand these texts from the dominant Western perspective, have failed to dispel either the enigma or the radical difference of Indian literatures. Strictly speaking, every ethnic culture constitutes a national culture; many nations were comprised in New Spain, and as clandestine, hidden, or marginalized trends their identities have continued to be expressed in their own languages, with their own cultural characteristics and singularities, showing varying degrees of influence of New Spain or Mexico. Literature cannot erase what reality has established, and, although the *mestizo* population and the Mexican Spanish have been unified in one national Mexican identity since the beginning of Spanish colonization, the cultural contradictions and multiplicity that exceeded the unifying or dominant norm of national culture were not to be denied; the Nahua, Maya, Zapotec, Otomí, and Tarascan chapters constituted unusual, parallel histories that, like the communities that created and continue to create them, were rich and expressive precisely because of their differences and their opposition.

During the first century of New Spain, *mestizo* historians represented a powerful attempt to assimilate this conquered multiplicity to the dominating norm, a tradition that has continued until the present. Diego Durán of the Dominicans is an exceptional case. Like Sahagún, he may have been a converted Jew, and therefore more open to other nationalities and cultures. He became Indianized in a different way from Sahagún, however, not so much by recovering cultures as by the generosity of his interpretation. In his view, the Indians of America might have been lost Jewish tribes rather than the people of the devil, perhaps evangelized in remote times (as shown by objects, signs, and customs that were similar to Christian ones). His writings are clearly apologetic, and he already speaks of Quetzalcóatl as a saint who resembles the apostle St. Thomas, with his gospels, his crosses, his sacraments, and his penitence. Rather than rescuing an abandoned culture, he sought to establish a syncretic, *mestizo* culture.

The historical works of Tezozómoc, Chimalpahin, and Ixtlilxóchitl make curious literary reading; despite being based on codices and testimonies, they are primarily composed of legends, fables, and imagination. Their interpretation makes history unreal. In a sense, these works recall the original epic of other peoples: *Gilgamesh*, the Bible, the *Iliad*, and numerous oriental books. These texts were unable to regard what had already disappeared and been abolished as "historical." In the Spanish chronicles, the Indians of the Conquest appear far more human than in the *mestizo* chronicles, in which they are depicted as allegorical, spectral, or even mad protagonists of a nightmare. By way of an example, here is an account of Moctezuma's fears, according to Alvarado Tezozómoc's *Crónica mexicana*:

> Llamó Moctezuma á todos sus mayordomos, y dijoles: padres y abuelos mios, ¿nunca me habeis soñado alguna vez? ó si me soñaderes, decídmelo, que me holgaré en extremo de ello: así mismo se lo encargó á todos los sacerdotes y á los principales, que lo digan á sus conocidos y vecinos, para que si alguna persona me soñase, ó soñare alguna cosa, ahora sea en bien, ahora sea en mal, que me lo digan: y que se lo dijesen á muchas personas, en especial á las mujeres viejas, porque son grandes adivinadoras: sobre todo le dijesen, si viesen algunas cosas, como pronósticos, ahora sea vision ó fantasma ó lloro ó gemido, de que no parece quien sea, ó abusion, y que tengan gran cuenta de oir de noche, si anda la mujer que llama el vulgo Cihuacoatl, y qué es lo que llora, si se lo pueden preguntar, pues es como aire esta mujer, que de improviso la verán aquí: luego la verán en Xochimilco, ó en Tula, ó Chalco, con su voz y lloro. Pasados algunos dias vinieron viejos y viejas, y dijeron á los mayordomos que habian soñado, y que era tocante al rey. Lleváronlos ante Moctezuma, á los cuales dijo: [sic] uno de los viejos dijo, que habia soñado que veía que todo el templo de Huitzilopochtli, poco á poco se iba quemando, y lo iban desbaratando, y esto es, señor lo que soñé. Luego otra mujer vieja dijo: señor, soñé que tu casa la llevaba un gran rio, que piedras y vigas se las llevaba el agua. Recibió tan grande enojo de oir esto, que llamó luego á Petlacalcatl su mayordomo, y dijole: llevad luego á la cárcel a estos bellacos viejos, y mueran allí de hambre, cual vienen estos bellacos; y muchos otros viejos y principales y sahumadores, le soñaban, más no osaban á decirselo, porque no los echase en las cárceles y les cortasen las vidas. Con todo, otra vez mandó á los sacerdotes de los templos, á los ayunadores y veladores de noche, tuviesen especial cuenta de ver lo que de noche se hacia en el cielo, y las estrellas, y sueños, o visiones, o fantasmas, que ¿cómo no se lo decian?
>
> Respondiéronle: señor nuestro, hasta ahora no habemos oido ni visto ninguna cosa, ni sueño de alguna cosa grave. Con este enojo llamó a Petlacalcatl mayordomo y dijole: llevadme á todos estos bellacos á la cárcel. (682–683)

Moctezuma called all his stewards and said to them, "Fathers and grandfathers, have you never dreamt of me? Or if you do dream of me, tell me, for I would be most delighted to know." Likewise, he charged all the priests and chiefs to tell their acquaintances and neighbors, that if anyone should dream about him, whether good or bad, that they should tell him, and that they should tell many people, especially old women, because they are marvelous diviners; and particularly that they should tell him, if they say anything, like a prediction, such as a vision or a ghost or weeping or wailing, or someone who does not appear to be what he is, or an omen. And they should take care to listen at night, to see if the woman the multitudes call Cihuacóatl is there and, if they can, ask her what she is crying about, because that woman is like the air: Suddenly you see her here and then you see her in Xochimilco or Tula or Chalco, with her voice and wailing. After a few days, old men and women turned up and told the stewards that they had dreamt about the king. They took them to Moctezuma, and one of the old men said that he had dreamt he had seen the temple of Huitzilopochtli burning and being taken apart, and this, lord, was what he dreamt. Then another old woman said: I dreamt that your house was being swept away by a great river, that stones and beams were being carried along by the water. Moctezuma was so enraged when he heard this that he called Petlacálcatl his steward and said to him, "Take these old rogues to prison and let them starve to death there, the scoundrels." And many other old men and chieftains and incense burners dreamt this, yet they did not dare tell him so, for fear that he would throw them into jail and end their lives. Despite this, once again he ordered the temple priests, the fasters and the night watchmen to watch what happened in the heavens at night, and to record the stars, dreams, visions or ghosts, for why had they not told him anything? And they replied, "Lord, we have not seen or heard anything, or dreamt of anything serious." Enraged, he called Petlacálcatl, the steward, and said. "Take all these rogues to jail."

While there are obvious literary conventions operating here, the historical aim of the text is also clearly in evidence. There has been much speculation with regard to the origins of lyric poetry in ancient Mexico, ranging from onomatopoeia to modes of dramatizing religious ritual, but all attempts to organize it according to historical criteria are purely conjectural, since the oldest Indian songs were compiled after the Conquest and after the Indian converts had been evangelized and taught to read, which justifies the doubts of Menéndez y Pelayo about the works' purity, particularly since poetry loses so much in translation–especially if the informants or translators are the survivors of a catastrophe such as the conquest and colonization of Mexico, and the disciples of the evangelizers as strict as the friars. In any case, Indian poetry, and not only ancient poetry but the poetry that continues to be written to this day, warrants a separate chapter as part of the national literature, rather than a mere reference to their Spanish translations (which always end up sounding more like the Hispanic than the Indian tradition).

Moreover, the great monuments of pre-Cortesian literatures–all transferred to the Spanish alphabet and consciousness–either emerged very late, such as the *Popol Vuh,* or were stored in vast archives where they were gradually lost. In short, Indian literature has been of little or no consequence to the Spaniards, *criollos,* and *mestizos* who have successively dominated Mexican culture. Literary authors who mastered Indian languages, a feat less rare in New Spain than today, have always been the exception. Certain friars spoke these languages, first for missionary purposes, and then as part of convent culture; Nahuatl was studied in sumptuous monasteries so that writers would be able to write erudite verses in the style of Horace and Virgil in this language. Even in the twentieth century, the impact of Indian literature and myths on certain poets, such as Carlos Pellicer (1899–1977), appears more as a form of nationalistic love and interest than as a real direct influence. No Mexican poet uses Indian literatures as an immediate, essential source. Even Sor Juana's *tocotines* are charming miniatures of Hispanic work. However, several of the poets in New Spain were friars and knew and spoke Indian languages; they must have heard songs and poems, something of which might well have seeped into the forms of Spanish literature, which was famous throughout the world at that time.

It is rumored that when the early Franciscans were teaching Indian children to read, they taught the words of short Spanish poems (of which no traces remain) and may even have improvised them in Nahuatl, showing them images of the one God, Christ, the Virgin, Adam, and Eve. All that remains of the work of Fray Pedro de Gante (1490–1572) and Fray Andrés de Olmos (1486–1571), however, are the legends. Conversely, Toribio de Motolinía (1490?–1565) records that in 1538, in Tlaxcala, to celebrate the feasts of the Incarnation, the *Auto de la caída de Adán y Eva* [Mystery Play of the Fall of Adam and Eve] was performed in Nahuatl, ending with a Spanish song:

Pare qué comió
la primera casada,
para que comió
la fruta vedada
La primera casada,
ella y su marido,
a Dios han traído,
en pobre posada,
por haber comido
la fruta vedada.

(1941,109)

Oh, why did she eat,
"that first married woman,"
Oh, why did she eat
The forbidden fruit?
That first married woman,
She and her husband,
Have brought Our Lord down
To a humble abode
Because they both ate
The forbidden fruit.

(1941,96)

This also sounds rather too intentionally Christian: Starting with Genesis and original sin, it offers in short, an entire project of Messianic redemption.

The fact is that it fell to the second wave of Spanish immigration and the first generation of *criollos,* in the middle of the sixteenth century (once most of Spanish colonization had been achieved), to concern themselves with literature as art. The first *criollo* poet was Francisco de Terrazas, a poor flatterer of Cortés but a splendid singer of love affairs and women's beauty.

It was also Terrazas who gave the best literary form to the resentment of the conquistadors, *encomenderos,* and *criollos* relegated to the background by the upstart fortune-hunters and Spanish public officials favored by the Crown. It was an issue that obsessed all *criollos* until the end of the Colonial era; it is already present, in the form of the unhappy soldier, in the work of Bernal Díaz del Castillo (1492–1584) and in Gaspar Pérez de Villagrá (1555–1620), and as the descendant of the humiliated conquistador, in Juan Suárez de Peralta (1536–1589?) and Baltasar Dorantes de Carranza (fl. 1550–1604). Terrazas writes (87):

Madrastra nos has sido rigurosa
y dulce madre pía a los extraños;
con ellos de tus bienes generosa,
con nosotros repartes de tus daños.
Ingrata patria, adiós,
vive dichosa,
con hijos adoptivos largos años,
que con tu disfavor, fiero, importuno
consumiendo nos vamos uno a otro.

You have been a harsh stepmother to us
and a sweet pious mother to strangers.
You have been generous to them,
yet harmed us.
Farewell, ungrateful motherland,

may you live happily
for many years with your adoptive children,
for your fierce, importunate disfavor
is making us destroy each other.

The main forms of sixteenth-century poetry are the Italian Petrarchan style of verse, which was also used in religious matters, and immensely long, failed attempts at versified epics, in the style of *La Araucana,* the *Iliad,* or the *Aeneid,* on the deeds of the Conquest. This literature gradually became more fantastic, allegorical, or hagiographic. It also claimed anachronistically that the Aztec Empire extended towards the north, far into what is now the southwestern part of the United States. The building of the sumptuous Spanish capital of New Spain on the Aztec ruins was celebrated in excess— both out of pride and for propaganda purposes–in various eulogistic epistles and allegorico-laudatory literary descriptions. Literature's role as a ritual complement to Catholicism was already evident, with the predominance of clerics and friars as writers, although the proportion of lay authors and themes was higher in the sixteenth than in the following centuries. The emotional, administrative, social, and economic struggles between *criollos* and Spaniards were recorded, particularly through satire. There were also the beginnings of a lay theater that would travel outside Mexico City and presented a variety of productions, including the work of Juan Ruiz de Alarcón (1582–1639), who became a classic author of Spanish theater.

It has been correctly pointed out that the concept of "colonial" is an eighteenth-century, Bourbon, non-Spanish one, and characteristic of the French and English empires. Throughout most of Spanish rule, although Mexico received what could effectively be described as colonial treatment with greater exploitation, more repression, and harsher restrictions and obligations than those suffered by Spanish subjects–the concept of colony did not exist. Rather, what did was the idea of a new kingdom, similar and equivalent in theory to its European peers (such as the Spanish kingdoms of Naples, Galicia, Asturias, and Cataluña); that was what the inhabitants of New Spain at the time thought. Whether Spaniards, *criollos,* or *mestizos,* they had a view of local history that began with them as founders, thus making a clean sweep of all that had gone before and beginning a process of Castilianization of a land that was essentially regarded as virgin–once the Indians and the devil had been conquered. This is why they wished to innovate little and imitate a great deal; they sought to create very little original work and transfer instead all of Spanish literature to the Indies, in the same way one would transport methods of agriculture, cattle raising, and architecture from the metropolis to the new lands. Mediocre artisans of verse and second-rate imitators abounded, but not inventors of literature. Nowadays we can notice the local differences that this transfer produced, particularly in words borrowed from native languages, or passages of local color. What mattered to them, however, were the similarities between their transfers, grafts, and implants and the original Spanish. Let it not be said that a Spaniard in America could not write a sonnet or an octave as well as a Spaniard in Spain. It was far more meritorious to imitate a Garcilaso or a Góngora than to invent new expressions. Among this group, originality was regarded as somewhat vulgar and rather simplistic: Since the aim was to attract droves of Spaniards to these lands, erudition and skill, abundance and accuracy of imitation were favored. These writers produced, extremely successfully, a vast literary corpus that was faithfully Spanish though born in the new dominions. Only three or four poets in an entire century, including Góngora, Quevedo, Lope, surpassed Fernando de Balbuena's *Grandeza mexicana* or Sor Juana's *Primero sueño* in literary scope and perfection. It was not until Mexico's independence that the ambition to create a different form of literature from that of Spain emerged explicitly and intentionally. By then, it seemed that the inhabitants of New Spain had a great deal of Spain and very little of Mexico in them and that they were identical, except in small details, to the Spanish, a notion that disillusioned the new Mexicans. The important Jesuit historian Francisco Javier Clavijero (1731–1787) had already attacked certain poets of New Spain in his *Historia antigua de México* [1780–1781; *The History of Mexico*, 1787], with arguments that would be taken up by Altamirano in the nineteenth century.

It is unfair to reproach the poets of New Spain for keeping their eyes closed to European history. They had their eyes wide open to the making of *their* own history—their small, infinitely detailed, internal history of a graft that mutated—which can be deciphered, if not reconstructed, on the basis of these texts. The history of the establishment of European groups in Mexico, particularly members of religious orders, can be read together with recounted episodes involving the transfer and implantation of European culture into Mexico throughout the emotional and spiritual times and works of this group.

Modern readers may tend to look for other things: data from the chronicles; evidence of confrontation between two worlds, wars, the lives of the Indians, and social and racial conflicts. We wish we could find the satires of Mateo Rosas de Oquendo (b. 1559?) in every poet. We also find these things, but less in verse than in another form of literature, the prose of the chroniclers. Yet the epic richness and emotion of a Bernal del Castillo ought not to make us forget that in New Spain, just as in any other society, an extremely important part of the lives and thought of its inhabitants was devoted to the cultivation of beliefs and devotion, love and scorn, myths, and ceremonies, and above all, the living practice of a transplanted language. This is precisely what we do find in the poetry of New Spain. Denying them their internal history would be tantamount to denying it to the altar pieces, convents, and cathedrals we continue to regard as somewhat extravagant, monumental, and enigmatic. New Spain was not a Hispanicized, lettered society, but multilingual and largely illiterate. Much of the culture that we now believe to be inextricably linked to the alphabet and books actually took place orally, in conversations and pulpits, in images (emblems or altar pieces), or in ceremonies and fiestas. Few people spoke Spanish, even fewer could write it, and fewer still could read it. Indeed, authors and readers were concentrated in convents that often preferred Latin as the language of culture. The function of literature was often therefore extremely limited: sacred entertainment, plays for nuns, flattery of the powerful, and demonstrations of skill in competitions. Yet despite its restricted function, it could not fail to express much of its world.

It was certainly a literature for a minority—one that was neither the richest nor the most powerful. It was often a poor, powerless minority, struggling against the tide, the few whites or *mestizos* who tried to write something to fill the gap between the solid Indian and Spanish literary cultures to create a culture of New Spain. Their predicament largely continues to this day. Much of the criticism of the literature of New Spain here could equally fairly be applied to modern literature. Have we really, for example, been more generous and inspired about modern Indians or the Mexican Revolution than earlier writers were about ancient Indians and ancient wars? There are six or seven great authors—Cortés, Bernal del Castillo, Toribio de Motolinía, Sahagún, Sor Juana, Clavijero, Fray Servando Teresa de Mier (1763–1827)—whose work can by no means be regarded as inferior to the greatest world literature of their time. There is also a motley assortment of voices from the past that often speak to us with surprising relevance or familiarity, or sometimes with a mystery that finds current echoes in us.

Translation by Suzanne D. Stephens

Parts of this text have appeared in different formats in various publications: *Los imprescindibles; El lector novohispano. Una antología de literatura colonial Mexicana.* (Mexico City: Cal y Arena, 1996); *La literatura en la Nueva España* (Mexico City: Cal y Arena, 1989).

Works Cited

Alvarado Tezozómoc, Hernando. 1949. *Crónica mexicayotl.* Trans. Adrián León. Mexico City: Universidad Nacional Autónoma de México.

——. 1975 [1878] *Crónica mexicana.* Annotated by Manuel Orozco y Berra. Ed. José M. Vigil. Mexico City: Imprenta y Litografía de Ireneo Paz.

Balbuena, Bernardo de. 1941. *Grandeza mexicana.* Ed. Francisco Monterde. Mexico City: Universidad Nacional Autónoma de México.

Chimalpahin Cuauhtlehuanitzin, Domingo Francisco de San Antón Muñón. 1869. *Annales: 6e et 7e Rélations.* Ed. R. Siméon. Paris: Maisonneuve.

——. 1958. *Das Memorial Breve.* Ed. W. Lehmann and G. Kutscher. QGA 7. Stuttgart and Berlin: Mann.

——. 1963–1965. *Die relationen C.'s zur Geschichte Mexikos.* Ed. G. Zimmermann. 2 vols. Hamburg: Musuem für Völkerkunde.

——. 1965. *Relaciones originales de Chalco Amaquemecan.* Ed. S. Rendón. Mexico City: Fondo de Cultura Económica.

Ixtlilxóchitl, Fernando de Alva. 1975–1977. *Obras históricas.* Ed. Edmundo O'Gorman. 2 vols. Mexico City: Universidad Nacional Autónoma de México.

León Portilla, Miguel. 1959. *Visión de los vencidos: Relaciones indígenas de la Conquista.* Mexico City: Universidad Nacional Autónoma de México.

Motolinía, Fr. Toribio de Benavente o. 1941. *Historia de los Indios de la Nueva España.* Mexico City: Editorial Chavez Hayhoe.

——. 1950. *Motolinía's History of the Indians of New Spain.* Trans. and ed. Elizabeth Andros Foster. Berkeley: The Cortés Society.

Terrazas, Francisco de. 1941. *Poesías.* Ed. Antonio Castro Leal. Mexico City: Librería de Porrúa.

CHAPTER 16

THE CONTEXT OF LITERARY CULTURE IN THE CARIBBEAN

Jorge Luis Camacho

This section will identify some of the principal ideological and creative sources that inspired different tendencies in cultural production during the Colonial period in the Caribbean. The discussion is centered on the figures of Fray Bartolomé de Las Casas (1474–1566), José María Heredia (1803–1839), and José Martí (1853–1895). Each of these writers represents far more than just the sum of his works, because of the chain of effects they produced that spread through Latin America. It must be understood that this discussion is limited to the dominant historical protagonists and does not include numerous incidents and details. Moreover, only three countries within the Caribbean will be discussed: Cuba, Puerto Rico, and Santo Domingo. More detailed attention will be paid to Cuba's historical development because it has the largest population and is the center of Caribbean culture among the Spanish-speaking islands.

In October 1492 Christopher Columbus (1451–1506) and a group of sailors arrived in the West Indies. In the years that followed the task of what the Europeans thought of as discovery and conquest, other countries apart from Spain, notably England, France, and Holland, would occupy islands in Caribbean waters. Despite pirate attacks, the harsh control over commerce imposed by the Spanish crown, and contraband in all kinds of goods, a community was created in the Caribbean with strong cultural and commercial links that were reinforced by virtually constant emigration from one island to another. From the moment of the Conquest, the Spanish-speaking islands formed a historic community of tremendous importance for the development of the Spanish colonial empire. From the start, the Caribbean was the point of arrival and departure for the Spanish ships that crossed the Atlantic. Thus for a long period Cuba, Puerto Rico, and Santo Domingo developed a maritime-oriented economy, providing water, food, and other products for the Spanish vessels. Also, from the beginning, the Spanish created an *encomienda* (royal grant of land and its inhabitants) system with the dual aim of teaching Amerindians the Christian faith while enriching themselves. Once the indigenous culture was almost entirely exterminated and its resources at an end, the Spaniards sent raiding parties from the Caribbean to sack neighboring territories. One of the objectives of Cortés's expedition to the mainland was to bring new Amerindians to work in the *encomiendas* in the islands, because the original inhabitants had either died as a result of the inhuman treatment they had received or committed suicide in a desperate attempt to escape their terrible situation.

Fray Bartolomé de Las Casas, initially an adherent of the imperial policy, reacted to the methods of extermination used against the Amerindians and initiated a long campaign in defense and recognition of these unfortunates that would only end with his death (see **Figure 1**). The *Brevísima relación de la destrucción de Las Indias* [1552; *Short Account of the Destruction of the Indies*, 1992], like other texts written by the friar, was affected by his desire for justice and the reform of the imperial policy.

Figure 1.

While the *Diarios de Colón* [Diaries of Columbus], transcribed by Las Casas, represented an encounter with a fantastic world, the friar's own book bore witness to the other side of this confrontation with images of a fallen world, destroyed by cupidity and pride. Las Casas's text is presented to the reader as documentary proof of Spanish atrocities in the Indies. One of the key words in the title, from an ethical and stylistic point of view, is *brevísima* ("short"). This is a metaphorical allusion both to the book and the reality it describes. From the generic point of view, the speaker is a friar of the Dominican order with a vision of the universe that fits perfectly within the scholastic doctrine of the Catholic Church. In the prologue written to the prince, Don Felipe, the future King Philip II, Las Casas explicitly states his wish to compose a different kind of history that would feature the *estragos* ("devastation") and *perdiciones* ("ruination") that the Spaniards carried out in the Indies. In this sense, his history is only a very brief sample of the whole: "tuve por conveniente servir a Vuestra Alteza con este sumario brevísimo de muy difusa historia que de los estragos y perdiciones se podría y debería componer" ("I considered it convenient to serve Your Highness with this brief summary of the extremely widespread history of devastation and ruination that could and ought to be remedied," 69). This affirmation of epistemological certainty is based on a knowledge derived from his stature as an eyewitness reporter of the events that he describes: "hablo con la verdad por lo que sé y he visto todo el dicho tiempo" ("I speak the truth from what I know and what I have seen all this time," 74).

Thus the adjective *brevísima* of the title (the superlative of *breve* and placed at the beginning of the phrase, thereby reinforcing its value) seems to refer equally to both the document and the reality that is described. Its predicate, which he modifies, attempts to make explicit that the *Brevísima relación* could be more extensive; to write a history in all its *particularidades* ("details"), for example, could take up thousands of sheets. However, the writer, in this case the friar, has preferred to reduce it to a few chapters "para que con más facilidad Vuestra Alteza las pueda leer" ("so that Your Highness would be able to read it with greater facility," 68). This interpretation of the title that explains and describes the history is also applicable to the reality of the situation. The adjective also implies that the reality on which the document is based abounds in horrendous events such as those narrated by the author, and that it would be simply impossible to describe all the monstrous deeds that occurred during the period. In reality, this is perhaps the first rhetorical resource that the friar's discourse uses to persuade the reader. Several times in the book Las Casas laments that "son tantas las particularidades que en estas matanzas y perdiciones de aquellas gentes ha habido, que en mucha escriptura no podrían caber" ("so many are the details relevant to the killing and ruination of these people that even writing at length they could not all be included," 83). Las Casas's text is revealed to the reader as a discourse on what has been lost, not only in terms of human lives but also in terms of discourse, a discourse that has been irremediably lost to history for lack of a witness narrator. His discourse is one of lament for the loss of the empty spaces of a history that cannot explain "de mil partes una" ("even one detail in a thousand," 83).

In fact, writing and the form chosen seem to be inefficient vehicles for and in Las Casas's discourse, a place where history loses its "details." Here the friar is renouncing a global discourse. He seems to be telling us that only fragments, the residue of memory, have survived. This is the *topos* of memory as an agent of truth, a *topos* of classical rhetoric and the source of the authenticity of his writing. Fundamentally what is not said is just as important as or more so than what is said. The title, then, functions as a double key that opens simultaneously a metahistoric document and reality itself. It is the other history of the Conquest, the history, suppressed by official discourse, of repressed places. Thus text, narrator, and reality are mutually implicated, one links to the other, overflows, and is erected as its own point of reference. With Las Casas, history becomes a deconstruction, a patient dismantling of the motives and causes of the Conquest.

Las Casas did not undertake this task only in the *Brevísima relación*. In the prologue to his *Historia de las Indias,* the Dominican friar analyzes the four causes or motives that, since the time of Aristotle, have inspired historians to write of the past, notably "manifestar su elocuencia para ganar fama y gloria; complacer a los príncipes, alabando sus obras ilustres; restablecer en su integridad la verdad alterada por otros; dar

a conocer los hechos notables caídos en el olvido" (3; "to manifest their eloquence to win fame and glory; to please princes by praising their illustrious deeds; to restore to its original integrity the truth that was altered by others; to bring to light notable deeds that have been forgotten"). This criticism of previous historiography emphasizes not only the rhetorical form in which history was expressed, but also the truth that some have either altered or forgotten. If the less erudite (or ethical) had written to display their eloquence and to please princes, Las Casas would write to reestablish truth and bring forgotten deeds to light. In other words, Las Casas was conscious of his motivation and was fully aware of his task as historian. For this reason he criticized previous historiography written by the Greeks, Chaldeans, Romans, Jews, and Christians. Las Casas was also criticizing contemporary historians and chroniclers, even when he did not mention them by name (Oviedo and Cortés in particular). Thus he draws the line between himself and the others, between his writing and that of the rest. Even so, despite the fact that the majority of historians of the Indies favored "testimony" as the indispensable condition for the writing of history (Pastor 97), Las Casas alone was concerned with legitimizing his position with the rhetorical (and very Renaissance) resource of citing authorities. Las Casas mentions the *Etymologíae* of Saint Isidore of Seville, which requires the historian to include eyewitness accounts (*Historia* 6), though he does not follow this precept to the letter. Included in his discourse are the anonymous voices of other friars and of the Amerindians who play a determining role in the way one reads the text, for these are the voices that have been once again marginalized by the official discourse of the Empire.

It is appropriate to state that, even though the narrative of the friar is made up of fragments of memory, Bartolomé de Las Casas finds it both ethically and morally necessary to refer to this other history of the Conquest in order to expose what the Spaniards have left in "silence" and have worked hard to "forget." In the same way the friar swears in the *Brevísima relación* that "en Dios y en mi conciencia . . . tengo por cierto que para hacer todas las injusticias y maldades dichas . . . no dieron más causa los indios" ("by God and my conscience . . . I am convinced that, for committing all the injustices and evil mentioned . . . the Indians gave no cause," 83). Again, one must recall the role of the friar who found it ethically necessary, to be at peace with God and his conscience, to pronounce himself in favor of the Amerindians.

In fact, the *topos* of the conscience put to one side or abandoned in Spain is one of the most important in the literature of the period, as Fernando Ortiz (1881–1969) would point out. In *El diablo cojuelo* [1641; Crippled Devil], Luis Vélez de Guevara (1611–1675) makes the devil state: "No quiero que dejemos a Sevilla . . . me hallo en este lugar muy bien, porque alcanzan a él las conciencias de Indias" ("I do not wish for us to abandon Seville. . . . I find this place very good because the conscience of the Indies reaches here," 193). For Luis Vélez's devil, the Indies held the strongest right to hell's ownership, thanks to the evil that the Spaniards knew how to commit with clear conscience once there. In the same way, in his *Guzmán de Alfarache* (1599), Mateo Alemán (1547–1614?) wrote that "the surplus consciences" wandered in Seville, the headquarters of the Casa de Contrataciones, because those who embarked for the Indies did not take them with them: "que lo más de ellos, como si fuera de tanto peso y balume que se hubiera de hundir el navío con ellas, así las dejan en sus casas o a sus huéspedes, que las guarden hasta la vuelta" ("most of them, as if they were so heavy and bulky that they might sink the ship, were left behind in their houses or with their guests, so that they would guard them until their return," 349).

These quotations show that sociopolitical nonconformity was generated from the very start of the Conquest and that Las Casas was not the only one to criticize crown practices. While his strategy of confrontation is radical, the critiques of Vélez de Guevara and Mateo Alemán are no less so, though filtered through a game of masks and the carnival discourse of the devil, the vagabond, and the thief—discourse tempered by fear of official censure and prosecution by the Inquisition. For criticism to work, the attitude of the character must coincide with that of the public in such a way that corrective enthusiasm finds fertile ground for its display in the public's pathos. It is therefore not at all strange to find in the mid nineteenth century Martí and other participants in the Cuban Independence movement using *El diablo cojuelo* and the *Brevísima relación* symbolically to criticize the despotic government of the island. At the end of the nineteenth century, with the same intention, Manuel de Jesús Galván (1834–1911) in Santo Domingo would write the novel *Enriquillo,* in which he brought together the events of the uprising of the cacique mentioned by Las Casas. The appearance of the novel was praised, among others, by Martí, who speedily addressed an enthusiastic letter to the author, which, in future editions, would appear as the prologue to the novel. National history was being built on a past of rebellion and resistance.

To call on the conscience of the readers and to persuade them are the two basic aims of Las Casas's text. One way to do both was to employ a simple language and style specifically designed to "capture the good will of the reader," a trope known as *captatio benevolentiae* in sixteenth-century rhetoric (Pagden xxxvi), used along with a strategy based on persuasion in a time of violence. In all his books, though primarily in the *Brevísima relación,* Las Casas narrates straightforwardly the meeting between the Spaniards and the Caribbean Amerindians and the rest of the countries of the continent. On every page appear the cruel methods of extermination and slavery that the Spanish soldiers inflicted on the original inhabitants of these lands. At the same time Las Casas criticizes the official historians of the Empire and those discourses that assure the Europeans of their ontological superiority over the Amerindians.

To follow the development of the discovery and the Conquest from Columbus's *Diarios* and Hernán Cortés's (1485–1547) *Las cartas de relación* [Letters from Mexico], and then to arrive at the *Brevísima relación de la Destrucción de las Indias,* is to witness the emergence of Las Casas from the straitjacket imposed by the powerful discourse of the conquistadors that perpetuated the logic established by the Empire and the rule of force, discourses that were already well established and legitimized through power. At the same time, one should bear in mind the impossibility of writing outside the conceptual boundaries that transcribed universal history with its origin in the Bible and more generally the histories of Spain during the fifteenth and sixteenth centuries. Even so, it is possible to see the episteme, as Michel Foucault suggests, in terms of discontinuity and discursive resistance. We might say that the archaeology of knowledge in Bartolomé de Las Casas's work includes the physical and human pain inflicted unjustly and without reason on the native inhabitants of the Indies, a suffering with which the Dominican friar tries to make us identify. Thus Las Casas creates an ethical alternative and a different format for reading the official Spanish discourse and history, criticizing the practices and the legitimizing stratagems of power. In fact one of the great treasures of his archive is his insistent dismantling of the motives behind the Conquest: the power of gold and the slavery of the Indians as a means of enriching Spain and the violence unleashed against the Indians. This would be the explosive and challenging function of Las Casas's writing that would nourish Spanish-American *criollo* dreams of independence. While no editions of Las Casas's book could be found in Spain, they were to proliferate in America and Europe in books and journals, and served to foster the history of the vanquished, those anonymous voices silenced by the Conquest.

In the centuries that followed the Conquest, the Caribbean became the locus for the maximum expression of violence among the European powers. The resulting unequal struggle was almost constant among the different cultures, races, and economic systems. The virtually total destruction of pre-Columbian culture was followed by the emergence of different African cultures, imposed by a brutal and intensive system of exploitation through slave labor. In the nineteenth century, José María Heredia and José Martí would take up Las Casas's greatest legacy and not only change the literary history of Latin America, but also strive to lay the foundations of Cuban national consciousness.

The Colonial Legacy

While Las Casas chronicled the beginning of the conquest and the violent form whereby these new lands were annexed to the Empire, the nineteenth century witnessed the end of the colonial period and the creation of new nation-states. Once again, the West Indies provided the scenario for the violent overthrow of the old order. The independence of Haiti opened the way for the later independence of Mexico, Venezuela, Bolivia, Colombia, Argentina, Chile, Peru, and the rest of the Latin American countries. Even so, Cuba and Puerto Rico remained tied to the Spanish crown and would remain so until the 1898 intervention by the United States of America; their goal of independence would only be achieved after a long struggle full of sacrifices.

During the War of Independence the Spanish Caribbean was a strategic center and site of conflict. From Cuba, vessels filled with Spaniards and volunteers embarked to fight the troops battling for independence in South America and in Mexico. The island thus became crowded with a floating population of soldiers who left for the battlefield filled with hope and returned defeated. The constant movement of soldiers and the plantation system that had been imposed from early on were what differentiated the later development of the Spanish colonies from other European settlements in the Caribbean. The former was responsible for a high percentage of *mestizo* population and the second for the creation of an oligarchy based on the cultivation of sugar cane, tobacco, and coffee.

From the end of the eighteenth and the beginning of the nineteenth century, Cuba was experiencing an unaccustomed economic growth that converted the island, from then onward, into the world's prime supplier of sugar. Various factors contributed to this growth during the nineteenth century: the early liberalization of trade, a process that accelerated with the occupation of Havana by the English; the introduction of new and improved farming techniques; the mechanization of the economy that made it possible to introduce the new steam engines based on the invention of James Watt; and the construction in 1837 of the first railway in Latin America, the fourth oldest in the world. Other fundamental factors were the destruction of the infrastructure established for sugar and coffee production in Haiti as a result of the slave revolt; the arrival of French merchants in Cuba; and the importation of black slaves from other Caribbean islands. This economic development had, in turn, repercussions on the cultural, scientific, intellectual, and political life of most of the West Indies (Moreno Fraginals 145–169).

At the same time, the *criollo* oligarchy responsible for the principal sugar and coffee centers of the island grew stronger, while there was a corresponding increase in the quantity of slaves brought by traders in the holds of slave ships from the rest of the Caribbean and Africa. The modernization of the sugar refineries demanded more labor for harvesting the sugar cane. The importation of slaves increased to such an extent that the black population ended up presenting an authentic psychological threat to the whites after the Haitian revolt. This was the origin of their fear of the blacks. In her antislavery novel *Sab*, Cuban writer Gertrudis Gómez de Avellaneda (1814–1873) wrote: "siempre alarmados los cubanos, después del espantoso y reciente ejemplo de una isla vecina, no oían sin terror en boca de un hombre del desgraciado color cualquiera palabra que manifestase el sentimiento de sus desagrados derechos y la posibilidad de reconquistarlos" ("the Cubans were always in a state of alarm, after the terrifying and recent example of a neighboring island, and could never hear without fear words uttered by a man of unfortunate color that were expressive of their abused rights and the possibility of recovering them," 93). Gómez de Avellaneda grew up in the city of Puerto Príncipe, one of the first places on the island where the process of developing a national consciousness took root. Even so it is evident that, when she writes of "Cubans," she is referring only to the white population. The black slaves and free mulattoes did not constitute part of the idea of a nation in the nineteenth century.

The national drama of slavery–the oligarchy's desire for economic prosperity and the longing of the marginalized and poorer classes for national independence–was to develop slowly on the "loyal" island of Cuba. The poet José María Heredia, born 31 December 1803 in Santiago de Cuba, would incarnate better than anyone the dilemma that lay behind Cuban freedom in this first generation. The family history that led to Heredia's birth in Cuba is dramatic and illustrates perfectly the chaotic situation of the Caribbean countries in the opening years of the nineteenth century. In January 1801, a schooner carrying 150 passengers, the majority of them women and children, foundered off the Venezuelan coast. The passengers were Dominicans fleeing from the devastation provoked by the Haitian revolt and the imminent invasion by Toussaint L'Ouverture's troops of the island's Spanish zone. The difficult situation on ship led to a romance and later a marriage between José Francisco de Heredia and his cousin María de la Merced de Heredia y Campuzano. A year later, the danger over, the Heredias returned to Santo Domingo, but in 1803 they once again had to abandon the country. The Haitian revolutionary troops won battle after battle, making the situation at the other end of the island insupportable. This time, the new Dominican diaspora found a safe port in Cuba. At the end of the same year, the poet was born in the easternmost city of the island (Augier ix–xv).

Santo Domingo had been the first country to be colonized by the Spaniards in the New World. From its territory many conquistadors had set sail for the mainland, among them men of letters and the law (such as the Heredia family) and of the cloth (such as Morell de Santa Cruz [1684–1768]). Despite the incursions and depredations of the Haitian troops on the other side of the island, the Dominicans remained faithful to their Spanish and Catholic roots. In Cuba, Heredia had not yet reached the age of twenty when he had to emigrate from the island as a result of his involvement in conspiracy against the Spanish Crown. With the exception of a brief period spent in Cuba prior to his death, Heredia lived most of his adult life in exile. The Romantic period in Spanish America began with him. His poems celebrate the freedom of humanity and the cosmos and the fury of nature, all throbbing to the same rhythm as the poet's heart. There is no doubt that the poem that made him famous was his poem to Niagara, "terrific and sublime" (141).

> Sereno corres, majestuoso; y luego
> En ásperos peñascos quebrantado,
> Te abalanzas violento, arrebatado,
> Como el destino irresistible y ciego
> ¿Qué voz humana describir podría
> De la sirte rugiente
> La aterradora faz?

(Heredia 141)

> You flow, serene, majestic, and then
> Crashing onto sharp rugged rocks,
> Violently you dash forward, relentless,
> Like destiny, irresistible and blind
> What human voice could describe
> The terrifying spectacle
> Of this roaring chasm?

(quoted in Ellis 21)

In 1820 Heredia wrote "En el teocalli de Cholula" ["In the Pyramid of Cholula"], in which he describes visions of the Aztec rituals that he contemplates "en la profunda noche de los tiempos" ("in the deep night of time," 108). In 1832 he wrote a long poem dedicated to the "progress of science" in which he reveals familiarity with the experiments of Pascal and Torricelli. It concludes with an encomium to technology and the Montgolfier brothers' hot-air balloon that is written in a bizarre poetic form similar to that employed years afterward by Martí and the modernists: "De blanda seda refulgente globo/Hinche ligero gas: en él suspenso/Deja la tierra el físico atrevido" ("Of soft silk the balloon glows/light gas expands: suspended within/the daring physicist abandons earth," 129). Heredia died in Mexico in 1839 at the age of thirty-six after a long illness.

In 1821 the Dominicans declared their independence from Spain in Santo Domingo and, after reannexation in 1861, proclaimed it once again definitively in 1865, when the Spanish troops were expelled from the island. Indigenist literature arose as a result of this conflict with Spain, inspired by the misfortunes of the Amerindians in their clash with the European conquistadors. Thus the names Guacanagarí, Ancaona, and Enriquillo reappear in historical fiction, a considerable time after the aboriginal race had been eliminated, as expressions of the love the Dominicans had for land, liberty, and nation. Meanwhile in Puerto Rico, Alejandro Tapia y Rivera (1826–1882) was composing a series of works, especially his novel *Póstume el transmigrado* (1882), published the year of the author's demise, that would define him as a great figure of Caribbean literature in the nineteenth century.

Almost thirty years after the death of Heredia, the *grito de Lares* in Puerto Rico and the *La Demajagua* in Cuba, events that marked the beginning of the independence revolt, a long struggle was initiated; there were intervals of relative calm followed by numerous conspiracies and banishments that would not end until Cuban troops achieved total independence for the island. José Martí grew up in the shadow of this dramatic and destructive panorama and was to play a key role within it. Martí was born in 1853 to Spanish parents and died in 1895 fighting the Spanish army in a war that he organized and directed and to which he dedicated all his talent. As a young man he endured prison, forced labor, and exile for his separatist ideas. After living in various Central American countries, he made his permanent residence in New York, where he was to live for most of his adult life, conspiring against the despotic government ruling the island. Martí combined the rare abilities of politician, strategist, and writer, but his intellectual activity was not limited to Cuba alone. From the beginning Martí contributed to the most influential periodicals in both Spanish America and the United States, including *The Hour* (New York), *La opinión nacional* (Caracas), *La Nación* (Buenos Aires), and the *Partido Liberal* (Mexico). His chronicles of the literature, politics, and social life of the United States earned him the respect and admiration of writers such as Domingo Faustino Sarmiento and Rubén Darío, who was to address him as *maestro*.

Apart from his articles, Martí published two books of poetry, *Ismaelillo* (1882) and *Versos sencillos* [1891; Candid Verses] while *Versos libres* [Free Verses], composed between 1880 and 1895, appeared after his death. His literary work initiated the *Modernista* movement in Spanish America, together with that of another Cuban, Julián del Casal (1863–1893), and the Mexican Gutiérrez Najera (1859–1895). His prose and verse were enriched through the study of the Spanish classics and the literary experiments of the new French and North American literatures. His writing revealed a plasticity and chromatism previously unknown in Spanish-American prose and verse. Martí thus created what would become the characteristic stamp of the writing of the generations that followed. The writer's arsenal included elements of symbolism, expressionism, impressionism, and the great myths of the nineteenth century. But above all, what Martí sought was a reworking of what was the essence of literature–prose and verse that provoked thought, free of dogma and profoundly Spanish American.

Martí's prologue to the *Poema de Niágara* by the Venezuelan Antonio Pérez Bonalde (1846–1892) is the first reflection on the process of modernity written by a Spanish American. The end of the century witnessed a universal crisis of values in the social, political, and existential spheres. In social terms, Cuba participated in an expansion in the monetary-mercantile system combined with the development of science and technology. The unequal relationship between the United States and Latin America appeared on the political front in the expansionist policy of those who declared Manifest Destiny. This confrontation reached its climax during 1898 with the North American intervention in Cuba, which made way for the elevation of the United States to new hegemonic status in the region. At the same time, in the existential sphere, the process of demystification of the world and the loss of faith in a transcendental being accelerated. Faced with this devastating panorama, the poet emerged as a marginalized entity who took on the task of directing the brotherhood of man from the vantage point of his poetic musings.

The literature of the period abounds with criticism of religious institutions and specifically the work of the priests. In the above-mentioned prologue to *Poema del Niágara*, Martí laments that "los sacerdotes no merecen ya la alabanza ni la veneración de los poetas, ni los poetas han comenzado todavía a ser sacerdotes!" ("now the priests merit neither the hymns nor the veneration of the poets, nor have the poets yet begun tc become priests!" 1975, VII: 223). In his article on the North American poet Walt Whitman (1887), Martí criticizes the poets who weep on "empty altars," referring to this loss of faith, and asks the poet to worship a new religion that encompasses poetry, individual liberty, and the creative capacities of modern man. Martí declares:

> Ved sobre los montes, poetas que regáis con lágrimas pueriles los altares desiertos. Creíais la religión perdida, porque estaba mudando de forma sobre vuestras cabezas. Levantaos, porque vosotros sois los sacerdotes. La libertad es la religión definitiva. Y la poesía de la libertad el culto nuevo. Ella aquieta y hermosea lo presente, deduce e ilumina lo futuro, y explica el propósito inefable y seductora bondad del Universo. (1975, XIII: 136)

> Gaze on the mountains, you poets who water empty altars with childish tears. You thought religion lost because its form was changing all about you. Arise, since you are the priests. Liberty is the definitive religion and the poetry of liberty, the new liturgy. She pacifies and beautifies the present, infers and illuminates the future and explains the ineffable plan and seductive goodness of the Universe.

This fragment is fundamental for understanding the secularization process of the modern ethic at the end of the century and the replacement of faith by the creative capacities of man. Here Martí raises poetry from a plane of aesthetic and personal pleasure to a reverential, sacred level. Poetry "deduce e ilumina lo futuro, y explica el propósito inefable y seductora bondad del Universo" ("infers and illuminates the future, and explains the ineffable plan and seductive goodness of the Universe"). In other words, Martí converts poetry into an epistemological category, convinced that the poet uses a truly metaphysical method to explain "the ineffable plan" of the universe. The same discourse appears in his article entitled "Las Fiestas de la estatua de la libertad" ["The Festivities of the Statue of Liberty"], published in New York in the same year as his piece on Whitman. Martí takes this opportunity to superimpose sacred images onto the Statue of Liberty so that it becomes a religious symbol, a cult object, within the discourse of Martí's poetic imagination. "Si vaciasen la estatua en palabras, eso mismo diría" ("If they molded the statue out of words, it would say the same," 1975, XI: 113), he affirms. Initially the statue appears to be surrounded by "souls." Those who come to see her, gaze at her with devotion and weep. The statue is an "altar," another god that bears some similarity to pagan deities such as Apollo or Jupiter. Martí claims that:

> Vuelven en su presencia los ojos secos a saber lo que son lágrimas. Parecía que las almas se abrían, y volaban a cobijarse en los pliegues de su túnica, a murmurar en sus oídos, a posarse en sus hombros, a morir, como las mariposas en su luz. Parecía viva:

iera en verdad como un altar, con los vapores arrodillados a sus pies! ¡Ni el Apolo de Rodas, con la urna de fuego sobre su cabeza y la saeta de la luz en la mano fue más alto! Ni el Júpiter de Fidias, todo de oro y marfil, hijo del tiempo en que aún eran mujeres los hombres. (1975, XI: 109)

In her presence dry eyes once again know what it is to feel tears. It seemed that the souls opened up and flew to take shelter in the folds of her tunic, to murmur in her ears, to lay their heads on her shoulders, to die, like butterflies in her light. She seemed alive; she was truly like an altar with the steamships kneeling at her feet. Not even the Apollo of Rhodes with a brazier of fire on his head and the arrow of light in his hand was taller! Nor even the Jupiter of Pheidias, sculpted entirely from gold and marble, son of an epoch when men were still women.

Martí's description, "the steamships knelt at her feet," is a novel and bizarre image of the manner in which these ships worshipped liberty. The same process that empties the object of its lexical meaning and then endows it with a new significance–that of a "deity"–is repeated in the words of the orator Lesseps that Martí transcribes in the text. At the end of the article, he describes the departure of these same steam vessels from the island "converted now into an altar" (1975, XI: 115). What is important here is to understand the meaning behind this image that translates into the hope placed in human creative ability and the promise of the "emancipation" of modern man.

The poetic structure that Martí uses to describe this process forms part of the same act of worship. Poetry will praise the liberty that has been erected on a new altar. The characterization of *Modernismo* as a freedom movement, as would be claimed by Darío and Henríquez Ureña, owes more to this modern cult than is usually recognized and is strongly linked to the rejection of dogmas and the replacement of faith with poetry and liberty. The same *topos* of individual and artistic liberty, associated in Martí and Whitman with nature and the poet, reappears in the work of Lugones. In her analysis of the poetry of the Argentine poet, Gwen Kirkpatrick states that "the notion of liberty and its manifestation in the individual, in society and in art is a motif in all his early works" (79). This rebellion of forms and essences would become the anteroom of the artistic avant-garde in the twentieth century and the sign of Spanish America's cultural independence.

Translation by Jessica Johnson

Works Cited

Alemán, Mateo. 1988. *Guzmán de Alfarache.* Ed. Enrique Millares García. Barcelona: Promociones y Publicaciones Universitarias.

Augier, Angel. 1993. "Prólogo." *José Maria Heredia. Niágara y otros textos: Poesía y prosa selectas.* Ed. Angel Augier. Caracas: Biblioteca Ayacucho. ix–xxix.

Casas, Bartolomé de las. 1982. *Brevísima relación de la destrucción de las Indias.* Ed. André Saint-Lu. Madrid: Cátedra.

——. 1986. *Historia de las Indias.* Ed. André-Saint-Lu. Caracas: Biblioteca Ayacucho.

——. 1992. *A Short Account of the Destruction of the Indies.* Ed. and Trans. Nigel Griffin. Introd. Anthony Pagden. London: Penguin Books.

Colón, Cristobal. 1985. *Diario de a bordo.* Ed. Luis Arranz. Madrid: Historia 16.

Cortés, Hernán. 1993. *Cartas de Relación.* Ed. Angel Delgado Gómez. Madrid: Editorial Castalia.

Ellis, Keith, ed. and trans. 1998. *Torrente prodigioso: A Cuban Poet at Niágara Falls.* With an essay by Eliseo Diego. Toronto: Lugus Libros and Editorial José Martí.

Foucault, Michel. 1984. "Nietzsche, Genealogy, History." *The Foucault Reader.* Ed. Paul Rabinow. New York: Pantheon. 76–100.

Galván, Manuel de Jesús. 1964. *Enriquillo: Leyenda histórica dominicana.* New York: Las Americas.

Gómez de Avellaneda, Gertrudis. 1963. *Sab.* Havana: Consejo Nacional de Cultura.

Heredia, José María. 1993. *Niágara y otros textos: Poesía y prosa selectas.* Ed. Angel Augier, Caracas: Biblioteca Ayacucho.

Kirkpatrick, Gwen. 1989. *The Dissonant Legacy of Modernismo: Lugones, Herrera y Reissing, and the Voices of Modern Spanish American Poetry.* Berkeley: University of California Press.

Martí, José. 1975. *Obras completas.* 28 vols. Havana: Editorial Nacional de Cuba.

——. 1985. *Poesía completa.* Ed. Cintio Vitier, Fina García Marruz, and Emilio de Armas. Havana: Letras Cubanas.

Moreno Fraginals, Manuel. 1995. *Cuba/España España/Cuba: Historia común.* Barcelona: Grijalbo Mondadori.

Ortiz, Fernando. 1975. *Historia de una pelea cubana contra los demonios.* Havana: Editorial de Ciencias Sociales.

Pagden, Anthony. 1992. "Introduction." *Bartolomé de las Casas: Short Account of the Destruction of the Indies.* Ed. and trans. Nigel Griffin. London: Penguin Books. xiii–xlii.

Pastor, Beatriz. 1983. *Discursos narrativos de la Conquista: mitificación y emergencia.* Hanover: Ediciones del Norte.

Tapia y Rivera, Alejandro. 1968–1970. *Obras completas.* San Juan: Instituto de Cultura Puertorriqueña.

Vélez de Guevara, Luis. 1968. *El Diablo Cojuelo.* Ed. Enrique R. Cepeda and Enrique Rull. Madrid: Ediciones Alcalá.

CHAPTER 17

THE FOUNDATIONS OF
BRAZILIAN LITERARY CULTURE

Tania Franco Carvalhal

One of the characters in *Quarup*, the 1967 novel by Antônio Callado (1917–1997), poses the question, "Será que existe algum outro país com uma tão longa história de autodescobrimento?" ("Could there be another country with such a long history of self-discovery?" 285) and immediately provides the answer: "Eu duvido. Nós somos a mais sustida introspecção da História" ("I doubt it. We are History's most sustained introspection," 285). This issue of the constant affirmation of identity lies at the core of Brazilian literature. In Callado's novel, a group organizes an expedition in search of the geographic center of Brazil, with the objective of locating the heart of the country in order to establish a nationalist nucleus, free from foreign influence. The movement toward geographic interiorization taken by the party is a kind of process of self-knowledge that tells us of the search for the essence that would still be preserved in a pure state, free from exterior contamination and thus capable of defining a national identity. This is an attempt to trace a beginning, through the foundational center, where values originate and move toward the periphery; this paradigm indicates a centrifugal movement of cultural affirmation. In an allegorical form, this narration "thinks" Brazil, reflecting the national entity in its political and cultural actuality.

The preoccupation with the definition of a Brazilian identity that is expressed in Callado's text can also be applied to other Latin American countries. For this reason, the relations between one's own and the foreign, between what is here and what is there, as well as between "what is near and what is far," that surround these literatures reveal the persistent intention of finding the means of cultural identification in the literatures of the New World–as part of a totality marked by heterogeneity, thus making them distinct from the European literatures that were their sources. From this initial process of self-affirmation to the permanent search for the expression of a Brazilian specificity through its literary representation, one can see the formation of a critical consciousness. This effective procedure converts and reconfigures an originally transplanted literature, the transferred European models, into a more defined and unique form.

The reading of *Quarup* and its articulation with other important texts in Brazilian literature, such as the well-known dispute between José de Alencar (1829–1877) and Joaquim Nabuco (1849–1910) (Afrânio Coutinho), which I have discussed elsewhere (Carvalhal 1997b), allow us to transport to other thresholds the initial question of the oppositions between one's own and the foreign, the particular and the general, the legitimate and the imported. These would include the recognition of difference and the form through which identity defines and institutionalizes itself as one's own. This process of recognition takes place through the gaze of the other, the mirror on which the image is projected, deformed, and often multiplied. The old notion of the opposition between the original and the copy acquires a new dimension,

allowing for the understanding of how the chosen models gain a distinct configuration in new territories as they become adequate to new contexts.

Viewed through the intrinsic perspective of literary production, the opposition between one's own and the foreign becomes diminished, for the construction of a particularity requires the foreign element to be absorbed. Roberto Schwartz observes, in "Nacional por subtração" ["Nationalism by Elimination"], that the idea of copy opposes the national to the foreign and the original to the copy, but these oppositions are not real, since they hide what is foreign in ourselves, what is imitated in the original, and the originality in what has been imitated. The operational and methodological distinction at work in the creation of these dichotomies does not allow one to recognize an interpenetration of the foreign with one's own or of the imitated with its source of inspiration. In a certain manner, this articulation reproduces a logic that does not rest upon the principle of identity and its guaranteed prolongation of the same; instead, it rests upon a relation of alterity in which the same and the other are not exclusive but rather mutually inclusive (Collot).

In the prologue to his latest book, *Múltiples moradas: Ensayo de literatura comparada* [Multiple Dwellings: Essay on Comparative Literature], Claudio Guillén expresses a similar notion when he says that today, if he could choose a title such as the one he gave to his previous book, *Entre lo uno y lo diverso* [1985; *The Challenge of Comparative Literature*, 1993], he would prefer "The One and the Diverse," since this would suggest not comings and goings but superpositions, not dialectics but complexities (23). The recognition of a relationship of complementarity between terms previously situated in a radically antagonistic position opens new perspectives for the analysis of the processes of identity construction, as well as the procedures for literary absorption and appropriation. Guillén's example allows for the formulation of one's own identity as part of another, foreign identity. The complexity that this juxtaposition (or articulation) conveys is emphasized here, rather than the game of dialectics. Such a process of self-identification constructs a national tradition through its relationship with other traditions. Procedures such as paraphrases and parody are rendered pertinent in this process: the former in terms of acceptance and prolongation of the origin, the latter in terms of rejection and rupture.

These considerations take us back to the sources of Brazilian literature, in which the opposition between one's own and the foreign was clearly outlined. Because of its derivation from Portuguese literature, there was an early attempt to define the specificity of Brazilian literature through a contextual difference that would establish its autonomy. This is confirmed by José Aderaldo Castello (b. 1915) in the initial chapter "The Concept of Brazilian Literature" in volume 1 of *Brazilian Literature: Origins and Unity* (18) when he writes:

It is evident that in the study of the development of Brazilian literature, one cannot avoid the recognition of European and American heritages. The former had already been defined when it was transmitted to us during our formation, dating from the discovery of Brazil, whereupon ideas, attitudes, literary styles and models were transmitted. But it is clear that these occurred under the conditioning or circumstances of a new context, unchaining a process of interaction with the native landscape and culture. In this manner, the American roots are transformed and reactivated: Mutual interferences are unleashed in this entirely new physical and human landscape that constitutes Brazil.

In light of this, Castello considers this mutuality indispensable "to investigate, in order to establish to what extent the continental heterogeneity in which we are situated is a diversified product of the Eurolatin heritage transplanted to a new geographic space." He adds that "it is certainly necessary to take into account the diversification of the conditionings and what might have persisted in each country and among all countries in the Hispanic-American unity" (19).

In another study, Antonio Cândido (b. 1918) insists on the link between the foreign and the local when he says, "Brazilian colonial society was not, therefore (as the nationalist Romantic imagination might have preferred), a prolongation of the local cultures, more or less destroyed. It was the transposition of laws, customs, and the spiritual equipment of the metropolis [Portugal]. From this difference in the paces of life and cultural modalities, a Brazilian society was formed, faced from the beginning with the difficult situation deriving from the contact between primitive and advanced forms, rude and refined lives. Thus, literature was not 'born' here: It arrived ready to be transformed to the extent that a new society was formed" (1998, 10). The process of configuring a distinct form of literary expression gradually developed, followed by a twofold movement of formation. According to Cândido, there was still, "on the one hand, the vision of a new reality that had to be transformed into different 'themes' from those that nourished the literature of the metropolis. On the other hand, there was a need to adapt the literary 'forms' and genres to the expression of emotions and local reality" (1998, 12).

It is natural that, in this process of formation, "the idea that Brazilian literature *must* be interested" predominates, as Cândido reasserts in *Formation of Brazilian Literature*. According to the Brazilian critic, "the notion of *Brazilianness (brasilidade)* has been expressed in all our traditional critical writing, from Jean-Ferdinand Denis to Almeida Garret, as the description of local characteristics, acting as differential traces as well as a criterion of value" (1964, 30). One finds a preponderance of the local over the universal at the moment of the construction and self-definition of Brazilian literature, as well as an endorsement of the particular. These were strategies for the neutralization of the ties with the outside, as Jean-Ferdinand Denis (1798–1890) argues and as we will see shortly. This attitude takes place at a historical moment when Brazil, subordinated to the metropolis, was receptive to the influence of Portuguese literature and, later, to that of Italian and French literatures.

The historiographic texts are unanimous in their acknowledgment of these influences, never neglecting the contribution of European literature in the formation of the national literature. Brazilian literature included works that resulted from servile and direct appropriation of models and also the work of authors born elsewhere. This is the case, for example, with José Anchieta (1534–1597), born in the Canary Islands,

who is known as the "synthesis-figure of our sixteenth century" (Castello, 63) and also as the patriarch of Brazilian literature (Cândido 1998). These titles are not attributed to him merely because his work establishes an early site for Brazilian literary production but also because he was the author of the first book produced in Brazil and edited in Lisbon (in 1563). In reality, the literary quality of his oeuvre reflects his humanistic background and provides a variety of genres, themes, and forms. His work was not limited to catechesis (oral religious instruction) and is characterized by the use of linguistic syncretism. In relation to that, Castello praises Anchieta's critical consciousness and the appropriateness of his work to his surroundings, considering his dramaturgy as characteristic of "the interaction of an outside culture and of civilization with the autochthonous culture, under the auspices of colonization and Christianity" (65). An example of such aptness is Anchieta's use of the indigenous *língua geral* (Tupí-Guaraní), mixing it with Portuguese, Spanish, and Latin. As Cândido observes, "the extensive use of the *língua geral* in the work of Anchieta is an indication of the possibility for the development of a parallel culture in Brazil, and of a bilingual state equivalent to that which continues to exist in Paraguay (which is also a product of Jesuit catechesis). This concurrence alarmed the metropolitan authorities, who had an interest in the use of their own language as an instrument of domination and cultural homogenization, to the point that the use of the *língua geral* was prohibited in the eighteenth century in the areas where it was predominant" (1998, 17).

The imposition of Portuguese language thus works simultaneously as both a means of national unification and as a neutralizing agent of other autochthonous cultural manifestations that might have evolved eventually. A whole series of restrictions associated with difficulties in communication limit the cultural and intellectual life of the Brazilian colony. For example, all publications had to be printed in Portugal, since printing presses and typesetting facilities were prohibited in Brazil; this necessarily limited the number and nature of editions. As a result of linguistic domination, which was the expression of political control, a cultured literature developed, reproducing the polished literature of Europe in the New World. Although literary manifestations in Brazil generally mean a direct transposition of this metropolitan orientation, it is possible to recognize defining personal characteristics in the work of two authors: the *Sermons* of the Portuguese Jesuit Antonio Vieira (1608–1697) (see **Figure 1**), which constitute a classic of Brazilian and Portuguese literatures, and the work of Gregório de Matos (1633?–1696?), who was educated in the metropolis but lived for several years in Bahia, where he was born. Vieira was a notable orator and represents the decisive presence of the Jesuits in the seventeenth century, as well as being a figure of the intellectual caught between two worlds, divided between Portugal and colonial Brazil. His work is an example of religious oration at its greatest enlightening potential; this can also be found in the work of Frei Vicente do Salvador in Bahia, in that of Padre Simão de Vasconcelos about the Society of Jesus and the life of José de Anchieta, and in that of Padre Antônio de Sá in Rio de Janeiro.

The poems of Gregório de Matos also express the reality of being between two cultural realities; although he uses the consecrated forms of Portuguese poetry, the treatment of the themes is of a baroque nature. Situated between the lyric and the satiric, he can be considered a "synthesis figure of the seventeenth century" (Castello, 82). His poems portray

Figure 1.

Photograph of an engraving of Antonio Vieira (1608–1697).

the situation of an intimate relation with the metropolis, a relationship that would continue for some time, since there were no universities or schools in the colony. Young Brazilians of the elite had to study in Portugal and sometimes in France, England, or Italy, where they came under the influence of those cultures. This situation was much more common in the middle of the eighteenth century, however. The absence of institutions of higher education in Brazil until the middle of the nineteenth century, and of universities until the early twentieth century, contrasts with the situation in Hispanic-American countries, where universities were built much earlier and education was secularized (the foundation of the first universities in Hispanic America, such as those of San Marcos and Mexico, date back to the sixteenth century). Intellectuals in Brazil maintained close relations with Portugal, particularly Coimbra. The Society of Jesus and other religious orders played an essential role as educators, since they were permitted to act in the instruction and religious preparation of the population during the colonial period. The Jesuits in particular had a significant function in the development of catechesis and in the defense of the Indians from 1549 until 1759, when the Marquis de Pombal expelled them from territories under Portuguese rule. As José Aderaldo Castello points out, "in a manner that was fundamental for the general development of the process of colonization, the schools of the Society of Jesus, along with the convents of other religious orders, were the principal sites for intellectual and cultural activity of Colonial Brazil. These were situated in Salvador,

Bahia (from the sixteenth century); in Recife/Olinda, Pernambuco (from the sixteenth century); in Rio de Janeiro (from the seventeenth century); São Paulo (from the eighteenth century); Ouro Preto or Minas Gerais in the eighteenth century" (1999, 31).

The action of the Jesuits and the work that resulted from it expanded the vision of the country provided in the first foreign chronicles, starting with *Carta* by Pero Vaz de Caminha (1450?–1500): "The sixteenth century is indispensable and fundamental for the study and understanding of the origins of the formation of Brazilian literature. In its limits and insertion within the Colonial period, that century must be seen through the perspective of Christian ideals and material interests, and the confrontation with a rustic and aggressive landscape. But these did not prevent the blossoming of a sensibility, of a peculiar and imaginative consciousness that later would express the Brazilian reality and character" (Castello, 68). This search for the representation of a *Brazilianness* will be the basis for the foundation of a literary historiography of Brazil to whose beginnings we now turn. The reading of the first historiographic texts about Brazilian literature can be productive for the investigation of the question of literary self-identification. This is clear in Guilhermino Cesar's studies about the works of Bouterwek (1968a), Simonde de Sismondi (1968c), and Jean-Ferdinand Denis (1968b). The pages Cândido dedicated to the latter (1959) and the commentary of Castello (1999) further attest to the importance of these writers: They are fundamental for the understanding of the issue. In previous studies (Carvalhal 1991, 1995, 1996, 1997a, b), I have attempted to study the interrelations between these inaugural texts and the work of Machado de Assis and Mário de Andrade in Brazilian literature and also the work of Jorge Luis Borges in Argentinean literature. The possibility of interrelating these various texts, from distinct times and origins, attests to the need for a reading that moves within the scope of the juxtapositions and complexities mentioned by Guillén.

With his 1826 work, *Résumé de l'histoire littéraire du Portugal suivi du résumé de l'histoire littéraire du Brésil* [Summary of the Literary History of Portugal, Followed by Summary of the Literary History of Brazil], Jean-Ferdinand Denis was the first person to describe Brazilian literature as independent from Portugal and to situate it in relation to other literary traditions, particularly the French. This confrontation establishes the founding characteristics of Brazilian literature as well as the methodological and didactic orientation of the literary histories written by Brazilians over the course of the nineteenth century. It also explains why my investigation here encompasses both the beginnings of Brazilian literary history and the story of the origins of national identity.

The primary sources of Brazil's literary history are European works from the beginning of the century. A German, Friedrich Bouterwek (1765–1828), was the first person to undertake such a study at the end of the eighteenth century in a collective and pivotal work on Renaissance arts and sciences, *Geschichte der Poesie und Beredsamkeit seit dem Ende des 13 Jahrhunderts* [History of Poetry and Rhetoric from the End of the Thirteenth Century], published in 1805. The fourth volume of this encyclopedic work deals with Portuguese literature as well as with two Brazilian authors, Antonio José da Silva o Judeu and Claudio Manuel da Costa. It is not so much the integration of Brazilian authors that assures Bouterwek a place among the primary sources of Brazilian literary historiography; rather, it is the fact that Bouterwek was the first person to apply the historical method to the study of Portuguese literature, as Guilhermino Cesar explains in his introduction to the translation of Bouterwek's works that focus on Brazil (1968a).

Subsequently, Simonde de Sismondi (1773–1842), a Swiss who was born and died in Geneva after having lived a number of years in Lyon, France, deals with the works of three Brazilians in his 1813 work, *Histoire de la littérature du Midi* [History of the Literature of the Southern Europe]. The study considers the two authors Bouterwek includes in his volume, as well as Manuel Inácio da Silva Alvarenga (1749–1814). Although Sismondi's work appeared before Brazil's independence, he still recognizes particular features in the work of these three authors who are writing from the Portuguese colony (Cesar 1968c). However, neither Bouterwek nor Sismondi proved to be as well versed in Brazilian letters as Jean-Ferdinand Denis, who lived in Brazil from 1819 to 1821 (Cesar 1968b). Although both Bouterwek and Sismondi signal the emergence of Brazilian literature, it is Denis who, in 1826, is the first to consider it separately from Portuguese literature, as noted earlier. Only later will Romantic criticism question the new literature's claim to autonomy in relation to the metropolis.

The scope of Denis's work is comparative. "Discours Préliminaire" ["Preliminary Discourse"], a kind of introduction to his study, reveals that Denis is already alert to the problems of the relation between different literatures. Dealing with the influence of French literature on other European literatures in the eighteenth century, Denis mentions the drawback of a cultural situation based on domination and dependence, which entails the impoverishment not only of the dependent literatures, but also of the dominant literature. In order to emphasize the risk of nationalist isolation, he states: "Full of singular admiration for its great writers, proud of the influence which she exerted on Europe, France has scorned foreign literatures for a long time: In the eighteenth century, we even seemed to forget the debt which our first geniuses owed to our neighbors. Such was our way of seeing that we subjected the authors whose work we were transmitting in our language to the forms of French literature; and we must admit that other nations were instrumental in the development of our scorning prejudice: As they adopted our ideas and systems and responded to the impetus we gave. They were no longer original and we were always superior, for we were the ones they were imitating" (v).

Even today, Denis's reflection is particularly important, for it expresses the misunderstandings of cultural dependence, illustrating how the mere reproduction of foreign models leaves no room for creation as well as transformation and deformation. Seen as copy and simple reproduction of formulas, imitation is considered to be a negative force. To assess whether Denis's observations have proven accurate or whether French influences have provoked creative responses would require an examination of his assertion in the European context. In any case, Denis used his assertion as an argument in relation to his suggestions about the course to be followed by new literatures. Denis believed that every nation must draw its own literature from its precursors; it must imitate its own authors without paying tributes of admiration to foreign nations. Denis's fundamental purpose was to stimulate the emergence of a national consciousness in every nation of the New World. He states: "When peoples have said 'We wish to be ourselves,' when they have sensed their own strength, we have understood that they could become powerful rivals, and we have wanted to know them" (vi). It is interesting to note the degree of Denis's intuition about the powerful attraction of one literature for another, once that literature's difference is recognized. To be the other is already to attract that other. According to Denis, it is therefore necessary for each nation to find its own distinct character. To become the other is to become a rival, a stranger, to become different. Unfamiliarity is what identifies and characterizes the stranger, what finally defines the stranger's existence for the other who no longer sees the stranger's reproduction of one's own literature, but something that is both kindred and remote.

It is not difficult to detect in Denis's thinking the ideas of his era, notably the southern and northern European notion of the difference between man and nature that was diffused by Madame de Staël and the emerging determinism that H. Taine would later define. The unfolding universalist model presumed the idea of the established nation open to dissent; in this context, literature was becoming a useful tool both in constructing nationhood and in bringing nations closer together. The modern reader will recognize how these ideas lend themselves to the issue underlying the notion of emerging literatures—namely the tension between literary nationalism and universalism, between the need for local expression and the temptation to express the universal. Denis's conviction was that every literature must insist on its local color and enhance its own particularities. This viewpoint directs both the measures by which he judges texts and his selection of the elements he values in the authors of his study. In his reading of Santa Rita Durão's epic poem "Caramuru," Denis writes: "I believed I had to provide a reading of de Durão's work because, despite its imperfections, it is a *national* expression and amply demonstrates the goal to which American poetry must aspire" (516, my emphasis).

To be national is, therefore, to express a specific characteristic of the country in question: its first inhabitants, its legends, and its natural environment. Expressing the most typical notion of the local is indeed Denis's project. The marks of difference and the intensification of particular details are essential aspects of the expression of "local color." For Denis, European themes are in accord "with neither the climate, nature, or tradition of Brazil" (516). A new literature must correspond to the New World: Everything is yet to be done, everything has to be built. Literary independence must again correspond to political independence: "America must be as free in its poetry as in its government" (516).

Like the first European travelers, Denis was unaccustomed to the sight of an exuberant nature, and it charmed him. He was, therefore, sensitive to its particular features. Here we must contextualize Denis's work and situate it in the spirit of the era; this alone can explain his creation of the "noble savage" in his isolated forest. These are the elements that make up the essential focus of Denis's explorations into the emerging literature: the image of the New World as a kind of earthly paradise where the figure of the Indian harbors the memory of "lost virtues." We could say that Denis's characteristically Romantic thinking retains this utopian image diffused throughout Europe in the works of Montaigne and Chateaubriand. This contextualization of Denis's work points to the ways in which history and literary history reflect one another. In other words, we must return to the beginning of literary history *and* to a world that is seen as wonderful, fantastic, and utopian in the story of national beginnings.

Denis wished not only to write the history of Brazilian literature but also to be a guide to it. He clearly expresses this aspiration at the end of his introduction: "Finally, a new nation claimed the history of its literature; I have attempted to trace its principal features by indicating the path which poetry in the New World must follow" (xix). Denis again distinctly expresses his goal in the title of the first chapter in the second part of his work: "General Considerations on the Character to Be Adopted by New World Poetry." In this work he justifies his view by stating: "Having sensed the necessity of adopting institutions distinct from those imposed by Europe, Brazil already feels the need to draw its inspiration from sources which are truly its own; and in its nascent glory, Brazil will soon give us the masterpieces of this initial enthusiasm which attests to the youth of a people" (516). It is interesting to note Denis's awareness of the difference in contexts and to what extent this contextual distinction is responsible for the birth of a literature that is itself different. It is also interesting to identify in Denis's work a preoccupation with the composition of a canon made up of works expressing nationhood; he seeks to construct a tradition formed by those particular sources discovered through a search for origins. The constitution of a particular tradition would establish it as distinct from Europe's and incite authors to find models within their own literature. Such was the way a literature could constitute its classics.

Denis's contribution was essential to the formation of Brazilian nationalism. This literary nationalism, the fruit of historical conditions and Romantic inspiration, served well the first moments of Brazilian literature. In certain cases, however, the celebration of local color, on which Denis insists, has hindered the creative imagination of new poets, as Antonio Cândido argues in a chapter entitled "Franco-Brazilian Preromanticism" in his book *Formação da literatura brasileira: Momentos decisivos* [Formation of Brazilian Literature: Decisive Moments]. Denis condemns the Italian influence on the work of Claudio Manuel da Costa, finding him "too European in his images" (573). According to Denis, da Costa "disdains the natural beauty that surrounds him" (573) and lacks originality, since "his eclogues seem subjected to the poetic forms imposed by preceding centuries, as if the native of the New World were to encounter the same images as those already offered [in European literatures]" (573). The exclusivity of Denis's critical orientation had prevented him from giving a balanced evaluation of this author's work. On the contrary, Sergio Buarque de Hollanda in *Capítulos de literatura colonial* [1991, Chapters of Colonial Literature], recognizes, in a different context, the originality of da Costa's work in relation to the work of the Italian writer Metastasio. Nevertheless, Denis's questionable judgment has not stopped his work from establishing authenticity as the criteria for the historical evaluation of the new literature. These requirements will resurface with some momentum in the Romantic period and again in the Brazilian Modernist movement of 1922, which, through its general features, recuperates the Romantic and even the colonial agenda of emphasizing local color.

Before examining that resurfacing, however, the relationship between Denis's text and Joaquim María Machado de Assis's (1839–1908) well-known essay "Brazilian Literature. The Instinct of Nationality" ought to be established: The two writings are separated by a period long enough to distance one from the other, so that each becomes an account of Brazilian literature for foreign readers, providing distinctly opposite visions of this literature in two diverse periods. A contrasting simultaneous reading of these two texts is based on the premise that it is possible to read Assis's essay as a reply to the ideas conveyed by Denis. Although he does not mention the name of Denis, Assis recuperates and reverses the essence of his ideas, thus pointing toward the existence of a critical tradition in Brazilian literature wherein Denis would occupy the role of founder. Finally, Assis's text becomes a part of this same tradition, as it devours its precursor, the foreign text that examines Brazilian literature from the outside; it replaces its precursor, as it exerts a deciphering function, inverting the process by looking at literary production from the inside and eschewing "local color." In this sense, Assis's perspective recovers that of Denis, making it present through a series of allusions. Basically, both texts deal with the issue of nationality; both attempt to identify, explain, and define identity in Brazilian literature.

In his delineation of the concept of "nationality instinct," by which he means the "intimate feeling" that makes a writer a man of his time and country even when dealing with matters remote in time and space, Assis takes as his example Shakespeare, who was English even though he wrote about themes of diverse origins. This same position was adopted later, in 1951, by the Argentine writer Jorge Luis Borges (1899–1986) in his well-known text entitled "The Argentine Writer and Tradition." Borges also makes reference to the English poet as he clarifies, to his fellow Argentines, that there is no need to explore exclusively local themes, but that it is possible to borrow without fear from various cultural traditions what one desires to bring to one's own. According to Borges, "La idea de que la poesía argentina debe abundar en rasgos diferenciales argentinos y en color local argentino me parece una equivocación" ("The idea that Argentine poetry has to abound in distinctive Argentine characteristics and Argentine local color is mistaken," 269). He proclaims, "[P]odemos creer en la posibilidad de ser argentinos sin abundar en color local" ("We can believe in the possibility of being Argentines without being immersed in local color," 270) in the same manner as Assis had done in opposition to Denis. The idea that writers can write in a universal fashion will further be developed, as we shall see, by Mário de Andrade (1893–1945). Denis demands the adoption of national themes, insisting upon "local color" in opposition to those themes whose origin comes from beyond the nation's borders.

The relationship with Denis's text becomes more complex when we consider that Assis insists on undoing any correspondence between politics and literature. Assis opposes and emphasizes the discrepancy inherent in the ideas of Denis, who created a homology between political independence and literary autonomy. According to the Brazilian author, "this other independence [that of the letters] has no seventh of September nor Ipiranga countryside [date and place of the proclamation of the independence of Brazil]; it will not be made in a single day, but gradually, so that it will be enduring; it will not be the work of a single generation, or two; many will work for it until it is complete" (129). For Denis, the fundamental question regarding originality is theme. For Assis, originality lies in the treatment the author gives to a theme; it is not necessary to choose a national theme.

We have seen that Denis reads the poetry of Claudio Manuel da Costa badly, condemning him for Italian influence. Assis defends the poets of Minas Gerais, praising Gonzaga and identifying a national perspective in his work, which remains tied to the *Arcadia* tradition and the precepts of his time. Assis's opinion can be summarized in one sentence: It is a grave mistake to admire these writers' talent but not forgive them for their pastoral images. In this manner, the author of *Brás Cubas* inclines toward a school of criticism that corrects or animates invention, a criticism capable of forming individual and collective appreciation in a broad manner. In this way, Assis was as tendentious as Denis in his desire to alter the dominant nationalist orientation, while suggesting other forms, such as that of an urban and reflexive fiction, as well as promoting the adoption of literary and aesthetic criteria in opposition to the dominant criteria of the historical moment. Assis's essay can be seen as a parallel song to Denis's text, foreshadowing a nationalism of a universalistic tendency, such as Mário de Andrade would later define. The intention of building nationhood and affirming its characteristics dominates the work of de Andrade. However, he does not limit his ideas to these didactic concerns. In the innumerable letters he circulated throughout the country during the 1920s and 1930s, de Andrade advises intellectuals to write on national subjects, to deal with particular problems, and, especially, to express themselves in Brazil's Portuguese tongue.

Yet it is also necessary to distinguish in these two authors a voluntary intention from an involuntary one. If, for Denis, the involvement of national themes was indeed to be a conscious and intentional effort, for Mário de Andrade it is to be the expression (or the consequence) of a natural occurrence: that of being Brazilian. For Mário de Andrade, nationalism means "to be national," which simply means to be. This idea moves the perspective of Mário de Andrade to that of Borges, to the extent that, for both authors, Brazilian and Argentinean traditions are part of the whole of western culture. Borges writes: "Podemos manejar todos los temas europeos, manejarlos sin supersticiones, con una irreverencia que puede tener, y ya tiene, consecuencias afortunadas" ("We can treat all the European themes and treat them without superstition, with an irreverence that can have and already has fortunate consequences") (273). Taking the universe as a collective patrimony, as Assis and Mário de Andrade had done before, Borges expresses the notion that one cannot help but be national, "porque o ser argentino es una fatalidad y en ese caso lo seremos de cualquier modo, o ser argentino es una mera afectación, una máscara" ("because either being Argentinean is fate, and in that case we will be so, irrespective of all else, or being Argentinean is a mere affectation, a mask") (274).

In his day, it was difficult for Denis to see certain aspects of the question of nationhood, unlike Assis, Mário de Andrade, and Borges, who were able to develop their universalist nationalism. Yet, like Denis, Mário de Andrade would consider Brazil a manifestation of the new, a country where it was necessary to broaden possibilities, to offer guidance and suggestions. There is a coincidence of the notion of imitation, which these two authors define in relation to originality and in contrast to that which is authentic. Mário de Andrade's and Denis's perspectives were equally combative. Both wanted to raise the awareness of their contemporaries about the need for independent literary expression, that was to be inspired by primary and popular sources and the perception of social reality, which they would articulate in their own subjective ways. It is therefore de Andrade who assumes, from the inside of Brazilian literary history, the role of Denis, putting forth the notion of literary nationalism, which had developed from Denis's concept of Romantic nationalism. In de Andrade's work, Brazilian literature once again sees itself in the mirror, which reveals not only the corpus of that literature, as Roger Bastide wished (30–46), but also the gaze of the other, which recognizes it and validates it.

Mário de Andrade understood what had been an intuition for José de Alencar: A national entity would not exist in its totality without insertion of all its parts into the whole. It is for this reason that Mário de Andrade searches for a break with geography (*desgeografização*); he wanted to neutralize the emphasis placed on local particularities in order to be able to discover an underlying unity of identity, extending beyond regional differences. As Telê Porto Ancona Lopez observes in *Macunaíma: A margem e o texto* [Macunaíma: The Margin and the Text], Mário de Andrade is able to pursue his intention of "breaking up regionalism through a break with the geography of Brazil, which he does through a mixture and inversion of elements from the north and the south, and the character's panoramic journey. He makes use of regional traits but breaks away from them, because he dislocates and criticizes them" (16). Mário de Andrade thus advocates the construction of a national way of being, leaving aside nationalist amateurism. In a manner similar to Alencar's attempt at the mapping of Brazil in his fiction, de Andrade is concerned with intellectual decentralization, understood as a rupture with regional fragmentation, replacing it with the systematic creation of a national culture that would consolidate literary production, integrating it to the larger context of an international consensus. The notion of being in concert is basic for the understanding of de Andrade's ideas, for it translates into a concept of the union of distinct elements, without suggesting the dilution of regional parts into a national unity. It is not a question of assimilation, but of insertion. The former corresponds to a loss, while the latter preserves the differences.

In his letters during the 1920s to Carlos Drummond de Andrade (1902–1987), which were compiled into a volume entitled *A lição do amigo* [Lesson from a Friend], Mário de Andrade develops these concepts further, insisting on the fact that to be "national" precedes any program for nationalism. "Being national" is part of an intimate connection with the place where the writer belongs; it is the result, in other words, of the awareness of belonging to a certain place, as Assis understood it. Mário de Andrade identifies the cause for alienation among writers as a loss of one's sense of country (*despaisamento*) provoked by education through foreign books, by the contamination of foreign habits that results from the naïve mimicry that exists in all primitive beings, and also through the detailed reading, not of the great universal masterpieces of a given culture, but of its lesser and, particularly, nationalist works. This "loss of one's sense of country" is more or less fatal, undoubtedly so in a primitive country of such a small tradition as ours" (15). His criticism here is explicit: The minor works are the ones in which there is a preoccupation with being national. The greater works, in opposition, are universal– while naturally national. The imitation of the particularities of another group signifies the transplantation, the pure and simple reproduction of the foreign, while the universal masterpieces illustrate a true and creative appropriation. Mário de

Andrade adds that "it is necessary to make the country less primitive (*desprimitivar*), to accentuate tradition, to prolong it and thus to increase it" (15).

The conflict between one's own culture and the foreign runs through the concepts expressed by Mário de Andrade in his letters to Drummond on the topic of establishing a nationalist agenda. This question is taken up in *Quarup* through the prism of a political argument. It is important to observe that, in de Andrade's perspective, this opposition seems to be resolved. As an expression of extremist positions, it is operative only in radical moments. For this reason, de Andrade places the two poles (the national and the universal) in a relationship of complementarity, thus imploding any monolithic concept. The foreign is treated as a synonym for what is alien in relation to the problematic insertion of it into one's own culture; it can also be understood as one of the faces of what makes up one's identity. In de Andrade's proposal, one finds an intention to create a national tradition built upon its relation with other traditions. National literature is viewed through its dialectic or complementary relations with the Other.

The question of tradition takes us back to the contemporary novel *Quarup*, our point of departure for these reflections on the foundations of Brazilian literary culture; in that text there is an allegorical allusion to colonial Brazil. In the first chapter, which is titled "O ossuário" ("The House of Bones"), there is an underground space where the religious community stored its dead during the early centuries of the colonization of Brazil. The tradition of the colonial period is thus a kind of *ossuário*. Among the numerous historical and literary references that fill this chapter, the work of Alencar plays a prominent role. We can also ask to what extent the expedition organized in Antônio Callado's novel refers to the Scientific Commission of 1826, in which the Romantic nationalist and novelist Gonçalves Dias (1823–1864) took part in his quest to discover the real Brazil. The relations between one's own and the foreign, in their various equations, identify a Brazilian literature characteristically receptive, internally and externally, to the Other. It also serves as a guide for the reading of the cultural foundations that identify this literature.

Translation by Maria Clara Galery

Works Cited

Andrade, Mário de. 1982. *A lição do amigo: Cartas de Mário de Andrade a Carlos Drummond de Andrade anotadas pelo destinatário*. Rio de Janeiro: José Olympio.

Assis, Joaquim María Machado de. [1873] 1957. "Literatura brasileira. Instinto de nacionalidade." *Crítica literária*. Org. Mario de Alencar. Rio de Janeiro: W. M. Jackson. 129–49.

Bastide, Roger. 1958. "Sous 'La Croix du Sud.' L'Amérique Latine dans le miroir de sa littérature." *Annales* 13.1: 30–46.

Borges, Jorge Luís. 1974. "El escritor argentino y la tradición." *Discusión*. [1951]. *J. L. Borges. Obras completas*. 4 vols. Buenos Aires: Emecé. 1: 267–74.

Buarque de Hollanda, Sergio. 1991. *Capítulos de literatura colonial*. Ed. Antonio Cândido. São Paulo: Ed. Brasiliense.

Callado, Antônio. 1967. *Quarup*. Rio de Janeiro: Nova Fronteira.

Cândido, Antonio. [1959] 1964. *Formação da literatura brasileira: Momentos decisivos*. 2 vols. São Paulo: Martins Ed.

———. 1998. *Iniciação à literatura brasileira (resumo para principiantes)*. São Paulo: FFCL-USP.

Carvalhal, Tania F. 1991. "A questão do nacional (a reflexão interliterária e o início da historiografia literária brasileira)." *Dedalus* 1:49–61.

———. 1995. "The Gaze of the Other: The Mirror Image of Brazilian Literature." *Latin America as Its Literature*. Ed. Maria Elena de Valdés, Mario J. Valdés, and Richard A. Young. New York: Council on National Literatures. 105–14.

———. 1996. "A crítica da crítica: Os primórdios." *O discurso crítico na América Latina*. Org. T. F. Carvalhal. Porto Alegre: Instituto estadual do livro/Ed. da UNISINOS. 283–89.

———. 1997a. "A nação em questão: Uma leitura comparatista." *Nações/narrações: Nossas histórias e estórias*. Org. Rita T. Schmidt. Porto Alegre: Ed. UFRGS. 293–301.

———. 1997b. "O próprio e o alheio no percurso literário brasileiro." *Nacionalismo e regionalismo nas literaturas lusófonas*. Coord. Fernando Cristóvão, Maria de Lourdes Ferraz, and Alberto Carvalho. Lisboa: Ed. Cosmos. 35–46.

Castello, José Aderaldo. 1999. *A literatura brasileira: Origens e unidade* [Brazilian literature: Origins and unity]. São Paulo, EDUSP.

Cesar, Guilhermino. 1968a. *Bouterwek*. Trans. Walter Koch. Porto Alegre: Lima.

———. 1968b. *Resumo da história literária do Brasil: Ferdinand Denis*. Porto Alegre: Lima.

———. 1968c. *Simonde de Sismondi e a literatura brasileira*. Porto Alegre: Lima.

Collot, Michel. 1990. "L'Autre dans le Même." *Poétique et altérité*. Org. Michel Collot and Jean-Claude Mathieu. Paris: PENS. 25–32.

Coutinho, Afrânio. 1978. *A polêmica Alencar-Nabuco*. Rio de Janeiro: Tempo Brasileiro and UnB.

Denis, Jean-Ferdinand. 1826. *Résumé de l'histoire littéraire du Portugal suivi du résumé de l'histoire littéraire du Brésil*. Paris: Lecointe et Durey.

Guillén, Claudio. 1998. *Multiples moradas: Ensayo de literatura comparada*. Barcelona: Tusquets.

Lopez, Telê Porto Ancona. 1974. *Macunaíma: A margem e o texto*. São Paulo: HUICITEC-SCET-CEC.

Schwartz, Roberto. 1987. "Nacional por subtração." *Que horas são? Ensaios*. São Paulo: Companhia de Letras. 29–48.

CHAPTER 18

LITERARY CULTURE DURING THE PERUVIAN VICEROYALTY

Luis Millones

Vida intelectual del virreinato del Perú ("Intellectual Life in the Peruvian Viceroyalty"), by Felipe Barreda Laos, was published in 1909. In it, the elderly professor from San Marcos remarked that "Every day brought with it something else to correct, a new document to be examined" (1). This phrase could apply equally well today, when the construction of a history of vicere-gal culture is not only enhanced through the discovery of new materials but also by writers' and historians' new interpreta-tions of well-known texts. The difficulties of this historical con-struction are compounded when one wishes to provide a representative summary of a period that, in addition to span-ning three centuries, encompasses an area as large as the Andes. One solution would be to list all the important authors and works. Another possibility would be to focus on theoretical aspects, analyzing interpretative trends without mentioning concrete examples. A third option, and the one chosen here, is to select five authors whose work is representative of the Andean countries and to present their most important writings in light of the cultural development of the colonial period.

The choice has been made in order to enable literary pro-duction to be examined as though it were a polyhedron whose flat surfaces are the various forms through which writ-ers perceived reality. This is why I have decided to begin with El Inca Garcilaso de la Vega (1539–1616), whose personal stake in miscegenation made him believe he was heir to two worlds in conflict, a conflict that he believed his writing could resolve. His counterpart is Alonso de Ercilla (1533–1594), whose poem on the Araucanians, with its metrics and mean-ing, could just as easily be describing Trojan heroes or their enemies. On the opposite side of the polyhedron lies the work of the Indian Juan Santa Cruz Pachacuti (b. end 16th century), who wrote laboriously in Spanish and was far removed from the Renaissance culture of the two previous authors yet had the distinction of having transmitted the tradi-tions of the Quechua-speaking nations into Spanish.

During the sixteenth century, viceregal culture expressed its bilingual nature in many parts of Latin America, including Cuzco. The old capital of Tahuantinsuyo had created a closed, highly uniform society in which the Incan nobility and the Spaniards who had settled in the city shared both space and ideals. Thus it is hardly surprising that several nobles of Spanish descent (such as Diego de Esquivel y Navia) should have been proud to be addressed as Incan by their Indians, or that a cacique such as José Gabriel Condorcanqui (Tupac Amaru II) should have been regarded as a white man in the area. Cuzco's writers, like those from Lima, the City of Kings, were keenly aware of the fact that they were from Cuzco. This made it possible for seventeenth-century literary production to be undertaken in both Spanish and Quechua in addition to Latin, thanks to the level of education of several of Cuzco's intellectuals. This was true of Juan de Espinosa Medrano (1620?–1688) (known as "El Lunarejo" because of the con-spicuous mole on his face). His vast oeuvre, still only partially known, does not compare unfavorably with that of two other notable Baroque writers, Pedro Peralta y Barnuevo (1663–1743) and Antonio de León Pinelo (1590?–1660) (the son of converted Jews).

The last writer in this selection is Juan Pablo Viscardo Guzmán (1748–1798), one of the Jesuits expelled from the Spanish colonies, who spent his adult life in eighteenth-century Italy and England. His ideas, influenced by the Age of Enlightenment, reveal an extraordinary perception of the destiny of the *criollos* during Latin American emancipation. Far removed from El Inca Garcilaso's preoccupation with personal identity (though he nonetheless always quoted him with great care), Viscardo regarded himself and other *criollos* as victims of an anachronistic and oppressive system that had robbed them of the legitimate inheritance of their forefathers, the conquistadors. A skilled conspirator, Viscardo wrote for the British crown, providing descriptions of the Latin Ameri-can situation and possible scenarios for a liberating expedi-tion, which, in his view, would have the immediate support of the *criollos*, future governors of proven legitimacy. Viscardo's prose is brilliant. Phrases such as "The New World is our homeland, its history our own" marked the end of the colo-nial era and the beginning of the consolidation of modern republics. (Many authors and their works have necessarily been omitted from this overview. We hope that this omission will serve as an incentive to undertake another study that will continue and expand this one.)

Rewriting the Past: History and Passion in the *Comentarios Reales* of El Inca Garcilaso

"Porque el Cuzco en su imperio, fue otra Roma en el suyo" ("Because Cuzco was to its empire what Rome was to the Roman empire")–no phrase better epitomizes the work of El Inca Garcilaso de la Vega. The memory of a privileged child-hood and adolescence would haunt the old man as he hur-riedly penned three texts virtually at the same time. In 1603, he had already spent several years on the first few chapters of *Comentarios Reales* and the preface to *Florida del Inca* and was beginning *Historia General del Perú*. He lived until 1616, by which time he had managed to complete all these books, despite the illnesses that afflicted him in his later years. Signif-icantly, *Historia* (the second part of *Comentarios Reales*) was dedicated to "la gloriosísima Virgen María, nuestra señora, hija, madre y esposa virginal de su Criador" (1962, I: 53) ("the most glorious Virgin Mary, Our Lady, daughter, mother, and virgin wife of Her Creator"), as though pleading for her inter-cession during his dying moments (see **Figure 1**). The book also aims to reach "a los indios, *mestizos* y *criollos* de los reinos y provincias del grande y riquísimo imperio del Perú" (1962, I) ("the Indians, *mestizos*, and *criollos* of the kingdoms and provinces of the great, rich empire of Peru")–in other words, the public that had inspired his works. These works were writ-ten to correct those that had been produced earlier by Span-iards, who, as such, were unable to grasp the physical, social, or spiritual nature of the new continent.

Figure 1.

HISTORIA
GENERAL DEL
PERV

TRATA EL DESCVBRIMIENTO DEL,
y como lo ganaron los Españoles. Las guerras ciuiles
que huuo entre Piçarros, y Almagros, sobre la partija
de la tierra. Castigo y leuantamiēto de tiranos: y
otros sucessos particulares que en la Historia se contienen.

ESCRITA POR EL YNCA GARCILASSO DE LA
Vega, Capitan de su magestad, &c.

DIRIGIDA A LA LIMPISSIMA VIRGEN
Maria Madre de Dios, y Señora nuestra.

MARIAM NON TETIGIT

RIMVM PECCATVM.

CON PRIVILEGIO REAL.

¶ En Cordoua, Por la Vigda de Andres Barrera, y à su costa. Año, M. DC. XVII.

Cover of Historia General del Perú *by El Inca Garcilaso de la Vega.*
(Courtesy John P. Robarts Research Library, University of Toronto)

El Inca was born in Cuzco in 1539 and christened Gómez Suárez de Figueroa. He was the son of Captain Sebastián Garcilaso de la Vega Vargas and Isabel Suárez, the Spanish name of the Indian noblewoman Chimpu Ocllo, the granddaughter of the Inca Tupac Yupanqui. The future author of *Comentarios* grew up in the midst of civil wars fought between the Spanish *encomenderos* and their king, who sought to reduce the virtually feudal privileges that the first two waves of conquistadors had granted themselves. El Inca Garcilaso was raised in a home with the double advantage of having a father who was a prestigious Spanish military man and a friend of the Pizarros and a mother who was a *palla*, or member of the Inca nobility, whose lands and servants supplied the needs of the future chronicler's home. Sebastián and Isabel were not married. In 1552, the couple separated and the captain married a Spanish woman, Luisa Martel de los Ríos, while the *palla* married another Spaniard, Juan de Pedroche. The presence of El Inca Garcilaso's mother is overlooked in his biography, since the emphasis is placed instead on his need to travel to Spain to claim the privileges due to Don Sebastián and to meet his relatives. In 1559, Garcilaso journeyed to Spain with the support

of his father, who had sent him there for this purpose and in the hope that he would join a religious order. Garcilaso's time in Europe was spent mainly in Montilla, and, except for a brief sojourn in Italy as a soldier, he lived in Andalusia; although he participated in the campaign against the Moors in Alpujarras, his only significant change of residence was in 1591 to Córdoba, where he would remain until his death.

Attempts to claim his family privileges proved fruitless. El Inca was reminded that Captain Sebastián Garcilaso had fought at the battle of Huarina against troops loyal to the king of Spain. Thus, his retirement in Montilla, then a village, took an unusual turn. He lived modestly but without any financial pressures and was constantly visited by "*indianos*"–Spaniards who had made their fortune in the Americas. In Montilla, El Inca built a formidable library; in reading books on his distant homeland, he began to find the mistakes that would eventually lead him to write his own interpretation of the past. In his works, he would correct the versions that he felt had distorted the truth by blending his people's past with his personal history, a personal history in which his father was no longer a traitor, his mother was a member of a nobility equivalent to that of European courts, and he no longer bore the stigmas of being both illegitimate and *mestizo*.

Garcilaso de la Vega was well equipped for the task. In Cuzco, he had received an outstanding education, equivalent to that of any upper-class Spanish boy, thanks to his parents' relatives and friends and to his tutor. In Montilla, the inheritance left to him by his uncle Alonso de Vargas enabled him to complete his Renaissance training. From this time onward, El Inca's work can be divided into three distinct stages. First, he worked as a translator. In 1590, he published "La traduzión del Indio de los tres Diálogos de Amor de León Hebreo, hecha del Italiano en Español por Garcilaso Inga de la Vega, natural de la gran ciudad del Cuzco, cabeza de los reynos y provincias del Pirú" ("The Indian's translation of León Hebreo's three Dialogues of Love, from Italian to Spanish by Garcilaso Inga de la Vega, native of the great city of Cuzco, center of the Kingdoms and Provinces of Peru"). He subsequently became an amanuensis (Jákfalvi-Leiva 52), using as his informant the old soldier Gonzalo Silvestre, whose testimony he records in *La Florida del Inca* (1605). The book also includes two unpublished accounts by Alonso de Carmona and Juan Coles, another two witnesses of the exploits of Hernando de Soto (ca. 1500–1542), the main protagonist in this undertaking. One of the texts was given to El Inca by its author, while Juan Coles's account, badly moth-eaten, was discovered in a printer's shop (Miró Quesada 174).

For these two works, Garcilaso shared the credit. In León Hebreo's (b.ca. 1460) *Diálogos*, Garcilaso gives Hebreo full credit, even though he regards his task of translation as a second work. *La Florida* is based on Silvestre's narration and the documents Garcilaso used to write a new work. At this point, it is worth mentioning a device commonly used in the narrations of the period, that of making another, fictitious writer appear as the joint author of a literary composition. This device was used by Cervantes (1547–1616) in the second part of *Don Quixote* when he introduced the notion of the manuscripts of Cide Hamete Benengeli, the alleged author of the *Don Quijote de la Mancha*, which Cervantes had supposedly bought in Alcántara de Toledo (Cervantes 1062). In the case of *La Florida*, there is no doubt of Silvestre's existence, although the same formula is used: Garcilaso uses another person's account as a vehicle for his writing. It was only later, in *Comentarios Reales*, that he fully assumed responsibility for his writing, although the apparent false modesty of the title minimizes the work's objectives.

Garcilaso's gradual assumption of his responsibility as an author seems to coincide with his acceptance of his identity as an Indian noble. The consolidation of this process has been traced through Garcilaso's signature, which ranges from the name with which he was christened to one that reflects his self-perception as an Incan (Hernández 96–97). This acknowledgment of himself "como un indio natural de aquella tierra" (Garcilaso 1991, 94) ("as an Indian inhabitant of that land") assured the reader of his knowledge of Quechua, an essential instrument in understanding the Andean past and in repeatedly disqualifying Spanish historians. Examples of this disqualification can be found in El Inca's story of Hernando de Soto and Atahualpa (Garcilaso 1962, I: 114) and in the comments written in the margin of López de Gómara's chronicle. Of the many notes Garcilaso wrote, the following serves to illustrate this point:

> Escribe por relaciones [es decir información de segunda mano] porque los que se las daban por hacerse muy práticos con él, debían de decirle cuanto se les venía a la boca y así escribió mentiras en perjuicio de caballeros y personas muy principales que merecía que quemaran el libro. (1993, 88)

> He writes on the basis of reports [in other words, secondhand information], because those who gave it to him, thinking it would prove useful, must have told him the first thing that came to mind, and so he wrote lies which were detrimental to gentlemen and other leading figures, as a result of which the book deserved to be burnt.

Nor did he spare Alonso de Ercilla, whom he denounced for undeservedly using the title of *palla*, although Garcilaso half forgave him since this was a common mistake (1991, 64). El Inca did not regard all Spanish writings as inaccurate, however. He had only praise for Pedro Cieza de León and José de Acosta, whom he quotes frequently, and for Father Blas Valera, a *mestizo* from Chachapoyas whose command of Quechua Garcilaso praised on several occasions.

In Garcilaso's view, poor translations caused as much harm as did ignorance of the Quechua. This is reflected in the role he gives to Felipillo, the "polyglot" used by Pizarro during the meeting at Cajamarca: Felipillo's ignorance is synonymous with treason, since he takes unfair advantage of his role as a mediator between the Inca Atahualpa and his captors. Garcilaso calls him "indio trujamán y faraute . . . porque no entendía lo que interpretaba y que lo decía como un papagayo; y por decir Dios trino y uno, dijo Dios tres y uno son cuatro . . ." (1962, I: 128) ("an Indian dragoman and busybody . . . because he did not understand what he was interpreting and talked like a parrot, and instead of saying 'God, threefold and one,' he said 'God, three and one are four'"). Indian interpreters fare no better in other sixteenth- and seventeenth-century literary pieces. In *La Araucana*, Andresillo is responsible for the deception that leads to the defeat of Caupolicán (Ercilla 1993, Canto XXI).

In contrast, Garcilaso presents his work as the fruit of superior knowledge, not only because of his professed command of Quechua but also because of his status as a well-educated nobleman:

> En este tiempo tuve noticia de todo lo que vamos escribiendo, porque en mis niñeces me contaban sus historias como se cuentan las fábulas a los niños. Después, en edad más crecida me dieron larga noticia de sus leyes y gobierno, cotejando el nuevo gobierno de los españoles con el de los Incas, dividiendo en particular los delitos y las penas y el rigor de ellas. (1991, 49)

> At that time, I learned about what we are writing now, because during my childhood, I was taught history in the same way children are told fairy tales. Then, when I was older, I learned a great deal about their laws and government, by comparing the new government of the Spaniards with that of the Incas, and the way they classified crimes and punishment and the severity of the latter.

Note the author's attempts to compare the glorified past, which he heard about from his relatives, with the harsh colonial system, which he witnessed personally. At about the same time, the Indian chronicler Felipe Guamán Poma de Ayala (1524?–1613) embarked on a similar task from the provincial viewpoint of a corner of the Peruvian viceroyalty. His work has the unmistakable flavor of Spanish written by a Quechua speaker who ventured to write in another language, but this disadvantage adds merit to his work (which was not published during his lifetime). Like Garcilaso, this writer from Ayacucho sought to describe the contrast between the Inca and European governments, while at the same time expressing his disagreement with the Cuzco state, which regarded his people as a conquered nation. The title of what appears to be an immense letter to the king of Spain is particularly significant: *El primer nueva corónica y buen gobierno* [1613, 1980; The First New Chronicle and Good Government]. (See **Figure 2**.)

Figure 2.

Drawing by Guamán Poma de Ayala in El primer nueva corónica y buen gobierno *(1615) depicting the execution of Atahualpa by the Spaniards. (Courtesy of John P. Robarts Research Library, University of Toronto)*

There is yet another reason why Garcilaso was driven to record the version of history of which he was the repository. When discussing the *quipucamayos*–the experts in handling the strings, knots, and colors of the *quipus* used as an accounting system–he explains the limitations of the system: "It tells you the number but not the word." In other words, there was no verbalization, only the sense of quantity and kind. He goes on to mention the Amautas, "who were philosophers and sages" and who recorded people's memories in prose to preserve them, and the *harauicos*, "who were poets" and who wrote stories or royal messages in verse. Yet none of these arts could compare with writing: "As experience has shown, these were all transitory remedies. Because literature is what immortalizes facts . . ." (1991, 347; Jákfalvi-Leiva 58). This stake in the written word and the desire to provide an Inca version of his history do not lessen the force of the passions that emerge in the wording of *Comentarios Reales*. It is not only a question of Indian versus Spanish society, however. Within the Indian nation, Garcilaso has accounts to settle, and his book serves as an excellent instrument for this.

One of his memories of Cuzco shows the conflicting loyalties that existed during the early decades of the viceroyalty and the narrow space fought over by the Indian leaders in order to ensure access to the new rulers. This particular event took place during the feast of Corpus Christi, when the echoes of the last *encomendero* rebellion, led by Francisco Hernández Girón, had barely died away. The Cañaris were a warlike ethnic group recruited by the Europeans in their struggle to conquer Peru. Having consolidated their power, the Cañaris, like other allied groups (such as the Huancas), were rewarded by the emerging colonial government. Some of the Cañaris settled in the capital of Tahuantinsuyo and collaborated with their masters when the Manco Inca revolted in an attempt to restore the power of the Incas. One of the leaders of the indigenous group loyal to Spain was Francisco Chillchi Cañari, who performed outstandingly in this battle. When an Incan warrior challenged the Spaniards, Francisco Chillchi Cañari stole up behind him and overpowered him, cutting off his head, which he kept as a trophy. Years later, in his recollection of the feast of Corpus Christi, Garcilaso was unable to refrain from indignantly mentioning the presence of Francisco Chillchi Cañari, who, removing the blanket he wore around his shoulders like a cape, "quedó en cuerpo, con otra manta ceñida (como hemos dicho que se la ciñen cuando quieren pelear o hacer otra cosa de importancia). Llevaba en la mano derecha una cabeza de indio contrahecha, asida por los cabellos. Apenas la hubieron visto los Incas, cuando cuatro o cinco dellos arremetieron contra el Cañari y lo levantaron alto del suelo, para dar con él de cabeza en tierra" ("remained standing, with another blanket wrapped tightly around him [as we have said they do when they wish to fight or do something else important]. In his right hand, he held an Indian's deformed head by the hair. No sooner had the Incas seen him than four or five of them attacked the Cañari, lifted him up and then threw him back down, headfirst"). The commotion spread and the Spanish authorities were forced to restore calm. When asked about the incident, the oldest of the Inca nobles explained, "Este perro auca, en lugar de solemnizar la fiesta, viene con esta cabeza a recordar cosas pasadas, que estaban bien olvidadas" (Garcilaso 1962, IV: 1087) ("Instead of celebrating the feast, that *auca* dog turned up with that head to remind people of past events that are best forgotten").

Auca means warrior and, by extension, enemy or hostile person. This was the name given by the Incas to the groups that resisted the conquest or rose up after they had been subjugated. This is why Pedro de Valdivia, in the verses of *La Araucana*, called the Picunches on the south coast of the continent Promaucaes (Ercilla 1993, 98). The Cañaris, in northern Peru and Ecuador, also caused trouble for the Inca troops. They had been only partially conquered, and their relationship with Tahuantinsuyo explains their readiness to form an alliance with the Spaniards who were among the first to reach the area under Francisco Pizarro. The Cuzco nobles were understandably annoyed that the Cañaris had been given the Valley of Yucay, one of the most fertile in Cuzco. Added to this was the suspicion that Sairi Tupac, the Inca recognized by the Spaniards as the heir to Tahuantinsuyo, had died of poisoning, presumably ordered by the Cañari chiefs. Despite his retirement in Córdoba, Francisco Chillchi's swaggering continued to irk Garcilaso, who devotes several pages to the incident and has one of his protagonists express his own point of view on the last rebellion of the Incas and what he describes as Manco Inca's voluntary retirement in the mountains of Vilcamba.

Garcilaso's emotions are not aroused only by the enemies of Tahuantinsuyo. He is even more passionate about the struggles within the Indian nobility. In fact, the narrative sequence of *Comentarios Reales* differs from the well-known version of other chronicles when it reconstructs the so-called official history of the Incas. Contrary to the majority of chroniclers, who agree that the War of the Chancas, the founding era of the Incan state, was led by Pachacuti, Garcilaso de la Vega ascribes this to Viracocha, the latter's father, who, according to other chroniclers, had abandoned Cuzco (Rostworowski 210–229). In order to understand this incongruity, one should reflect on the royal families (or *panacas*) that constituted the nobility (as the Europeans called them) of Tahuantinsuyo. On becoming a ruler, each Inca created his own *panaca*, leaving that of his parents. On his death, his wives and children paid him homage by constituting a power group to preserve the material assets and servants he had acquired during his lifetime. In accordance with this, each governor was elected after a complex struggle for power among the panacas, each trying to ensure that one of the young men in its group became the future monarch. The last Incas reduced the intensity of this conflict by choosing a noble (usually a son) as a joint ruler who would succeed them. This did not prevent the struggle for power, but it did place the favorite pretender to the throne at an advantage.

Shortly before the arrival of the Europeans, the military chiefs of Atahualpa seized Cuzco and destroyed the *panaca* of Tupac Yupanqui, the grandfather of El Inca Garcilaso's mother. It was obvious that Tupac Yupanqui's panaca had supported Huascar, Atahualpa's rival, favored by certain other royal families (perhaps including Pachacuti). Consequently, Garcilaso de la Vega punished this Inca in his book, stripping him of the honor of having defeated the Chancas; Garcilaso also censured Atahualpa by establishing Huascar as the legitimate heir and Atahualpa as the son of an imaginary princess from Quito, a version that was not confirmed by other chroniclers. This interplay of passions, however, never clouds El Inca's overall judgment of the phenomenon of the Conquest; the psychological nature of the situation is perfectly depicted. In his version, the Incas defeated in war emerge as the moral victors. The parley between Hernando de Soto and Atahualpa and that with Vicente Valverde are imbued with a moving dramatic intensity that perfectly expresses the cultural distance between two conflicting worlds (Garcilaso 1962, I: 125–135).

The author's impassioned defense of the aboriginal populations had to deal with the thorny problem of their classification as infidels, for idolatry was immediately attributed to them by the Spaniards. Faithful to the culture of his times, Garcilaso wielded the argument that, for want of evangelization, as a result of their natural reasoning "rastrearon los Incas al verdadero Dios, nuestro Señor" ("the Incas tracked down the real God, our Lord," 1991, 70) and that "tenían los Incas una cruz en lugar sagrado" ("the Incas had a cross in a sacred place") (73). These signs, however, were only the beginning of a stubborn disquisition on the god Pachacámac, which the author cites as clear evidence of a cult of the Christians' supreme maker. First, he rejects Pedro Cieza de León's translation of "el que da ánima al mundo universo" ("the one who animates the universe"), which Garcilaso instead renders as "su propia y entera significación [que] quiere decir el que hace con el universo lo que el ánima con el cuerpo" ("its true and proper significance [which] means 'He who does with the universe what the spirit does with the body'") (Garcilaso 1991, 70).

This is not the place for a discussion of Garcilaso's command of his mother tongue. Time and distance had obviously worn away what had once been his native language, but the argument in favor of Pachacámac tells us far more than this. Regardless of the multitude of non-Christian religious manifestations and representations that the Andes offered the missionaries, Garcilaso seizes on the idea of "este dios no conocido" "this unknown god," 1991, 71) to conclude "que el Dios que los españoles predicaban y él [Pachacámac] era todo uno" (that the God whom the Spaniards preached and he [Pachacámac] were one and the same") (1991, 71). Depicting himself as his own informant, Garcilaso remarks, "si a mí que soy indio cristiano católico se me preguntase ahora ¿cómo se llama Dios en tu lengua? Diría Pachacámac" ("If someone should now ask me, a Catholic Christian Indian, 'What is the word for God in your language?' I would say 'Pachacámac'") (1991, 72).

This magnificent argument attempts to diminish the importance of the older gods of the Incan state, such as Illapa, the Sun, and Huiracocha, to whom Garcilaso gives a lower rank; in the case of Huiracocha, Garcilaso actually goes so far as to remark contemptuously that he does not know what the word means (1991, 72). It was obviously the devil, known as Zupay, who deceived the Indians, confusing them with his presence: "Hablaba en sus oráculos y templos y en los rincones de sus casas y en otras partes, diciéndoles que era Pachacámac y que era todas las demás cosas a que los indios atribuían deidad" ("He spoke in his oracles and temples and in the corners of their houses and elsewhere, telling them that he was Pachacámac and that he was all the other things to which the Indians attributed divinity") (1991, 71).

Modern criticism has debunked many of El Inca Garcilaso's historical affirmations, although it has acknowledged his works' literary value and the formidable influence he still wields in education, where he remains the most powerful voice in the creation of an awareness of the past among the Peruvian people. This is where the importance of *Comentarios Reales* lies; in its polished, convincing writing and in the construction of an idealized model of Incan society it has indelibly marked the country's literature and history. One should realize that, over and above his passions, Garcilaso employed the tools of modern historians in his critical use of sources and the precise, explicit development of his argument. His methodology,

however, was not aimed at complying with the assumptions of historical understanding. El Inca sought to create a personal universe whose moral coherence would serve as a counterpart to the chaos wrought by the European presence. The wars between the two and the murders, intrigues, and revenge that he observed in Peru fed the Incan utopia that he constructed during his retirement in Córdoba. From this perspective, the work of Garcilaso has achieved a timeless validity.

The Conquest as a Chanson de Geste: La Araucana

A mere two years in Chile (of the eight he spent in South America between 1555 and 1563) sufficed to inspire Alonso de Ercilla y Zúñiga (see **Figure 3**) to write the epic poem that would make him one of the most prestigious authors in Latin American literature. Born in Madrid in 1533, Ercilla followed in the footsteps of his mother (who was in the service of the Infanta María, the sister of Philip II) by joining the Spanish court as page to the future monarch. He was therefore carefully educated and had access to the cultural centers of Europe, to which he accompanied the young prince. Around 1554 news reached the court of a rebellion in Peru led by Francisco Hernández Girón, leader of the *encomenderos*, and of the death of Pedro de Valdivia in Chile, which, in the south, meant that the city of Concepción was

Figure 3.

Engraving of Alonso de Ercilla y Zúñiga (1533–1594) in Vol. 3 of La Araucana, edición del centenario *(1910). (Courtesy Thomas Fisher Library, University of Toronto)*

abandoned and the borderline was pushed back during the War of Arauco. This bad news reached Philip II in London, where he was accompanied by Ercilla. It was decided that Andrés Hurtado de Mendoza should assume the post of viceroy in Peru and that Chile should be pacified by a new governor, Jerónimo de Alderete, who would succeed the unfortunate Valdivia. Ercilla was chosen to accompany Alderete. In Panama, Governor Alderete died of fever, but Ercilla continued his voyage, accompanying Peru's new viceroy, who made his entry into Lima in June 1556. The following year an expedition set out, led by the recently appointed governor of Chile, García Hurtado de Mendoza, who was sent to recover the lands in the south of Mapocho for the Europeans. Ercilla accompanied Hurtado de Mendoza, the son of the Peruvian viceroy. This voyage and its vicissitudes inspired Ercilla's long epic poem, *La Araucana*. Ercilla went back to Spain in 1563, never to return to Latin America, and died in Madrid in 1594.

La Araucana was first published in three parts (1569, 1578, and 1589) and finally as a single volume during the same year the third part appeared; it was republished the following year (see **Figure 4**). The poem was an immediate success. The author probably died while he was preparing a fourth part of this epic poem, which was his only major work. A glance at *La Araucana* shows that it was a refined product of the Spanish Renaissance, in which historical events and the landscape served as the framework for recreating in Latin America the heroic life, intrigues, and wealth of Greek gods that was invoked by European writers from the fifteenth to seventeenth centuries. Ercilla reveals his sources of inspiration in Canto XV:

> Amor de un juicio rústico y grosero
> rompe la dura y áspera corteza,
> produce ingenio y gusto verdadero
> y pone cualquier cosa en más fineza.
> Dante, Ariosto, Petrarca y el Ibero,
> [es decir el poeta Garcilaso de la Vega]
> amor los trujo a tanta delgadeza
> que la lengua más rica y más copiosa,
> si no trata de amor, es desgustosa.

> (Ercilla 1993, 429–430)

> Love breaks through the bark-like covering
> Of a coarse and rustic judgment,
> And produces tact and wisdom,
> adding subtlety's refinement.
> Dante, Petrarch, Ariosto, and the Iberian
> [that is to say the poet Garcilaso de la Vega]
> wrought such beauty
> That the richest tongue abundant,
> Treating not of love, is irksome.

> (Ercilla 1945, 146)

This literary exercise is not devoid of historical information, particularly concerning the years the poet spent in the company of Hurtado de Mendoza. When Ercilla reached Chile, the Araucanians had already recovered much of their territory. In general terms, the people we now know as Mapuches were divided in the sixteenth century into three large groups that corresponded to their areas of concentration: The Picunches (people from the North), found from the Valley of Mapocho to the Maule River; the Araucanians, who covered the territory from the Maule River to Toltén, approximately; and the

Figure 4.

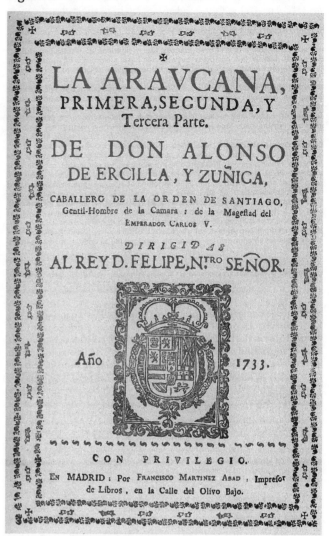

Cover of 1733 edition of La Araucana. *(Courtesy of Thomas Fisher Library, University of Toronto)*

Huilliches (people of the South) who occupied the area between this point and the Island of Chiloé (Hidalgo I: 106). The Incan expansion southward, which preceded the arrival of the Spaniards by just two decades, probably stopped at Río Maule (Betanzos 160), where the natives put up a great deal of resistance and the distance made it difficult for the Incas to receive reinforcements. This, at least, was the explanation the Incan nobles gave the Spanish chronicler. Be that as it may, the Spanish advance, originally under Diego de Almagro and then under Valdivia, found the Diaguita village (north of the Pichunches) colonized by Tahuantinsuyo, and the Pichunches themselves highly influenced by Incan culture. When Ercilla reached Chile, virtually no trace remained of Valdivia's efforts at conquering and colonizing. The conquistador had obtained permission from Francisco Pizarro in 1540 and set off to the south from Cuzco with a dozen Europeans and Indian helpers. On 12 February 1541, he founded the city of Santiago del Nuevo Extremo, which later became the base for consolidating the territory in the hands of the Spanish Crown.

This was no easy task. Rebellions abounded and, in 1550, the conquistador wrote to his representatives in the court: "It is my duty to inform you that, after having served us for five months, and sworn allegiance to His Majesty, the natives rebelled and burnt a brig that I had carefully built to send a messenger to His Majesty to tell him of myself and the land and the conquest and population of the city, and to ask Marquis Pizarro to send help in the form of soldiers, horses, and arms to force the natives to populate other cities in the future" (Valdivia 88). In his poem, Ercilla recalls with a certain amount of dismay this first stage, when the Araucanian caudillos proved outstandingly brave. Valdivia is portrayed somewhat scornfully; while many of his companions died fighting, he was captured in full flight:

Sólo quedó Valdivia acompañado
de un clérigo que acaso allí venía,
y viendo así su campo destrozado,
el mal remedio y poco compañía,
dijo: "Pues pelear es escusado,
procuremos vivir por otra vía."
Pica en esto al caballo a toda priesa
tras él corriendo el clérigo de misa.

   (Ercilla 1993, 155)

Yet Valdivia still surviving
With a friar who chanced to come there,
Prescient of defeat, and mindful
Of his flimsy force fast dwindling,
Groaned: "Excused are we from
Fighting. Other lanes of life are left us."
Leapt his spur-stung steed, eluding
E'en God's vicar, mage of Masses.

   (Ercilla 1945, 57)

In Ercilla's view, the death of the conquistador, carried out in the presence of Caupolicán, the leader of the Araucanians, was even more shameful:

Valdivia como mísero cautivo
responde, y pide humilde y obediente
que no le dé la muerte y que le jura
dejar libre la tierra en paz segura.

   (Ercilla 1993, 156)

Then Valdivia, wretched captive,
Answered, lowly and obedient,
Begging that he be not murdered,
Swearing future peace and freedom.

   (Ercilla 1945, 57)

Valdivia's plea is interrupted by an old man who breaks the conquistador's neck with a large stick made of sturdy juniper wood.

   In Ercilla's depiction of their triumph, the Araucanians are described as a tribal confederation; the poem's language recalls the various kingdoms of Greece that assembled to conquer Troy at the request of Agamemnon and Menelaus. Although the image is contrived, the geographical spheres are real, and several of the names of the tribal chieftains can be confirmed in the few records of sixteenth-century Chile. Ercilla gives the Araucanians a senate based on the Roman model, with speeches that could easily have been delivered by their European counterparts. Ercilla is, however, cautious as regards religion:

Gente es sin Dios ni ley, aunque respeta
aquel que fue del cielo derribado,
que como, a poderoso y gran profeta
es siempre en sus cantares celebrado.

Invocan su furor con falsa reta
y a todos su negocios es llamado,
teniendo cuanto dice por seguro
del próspero suceso o mal futuro.

   (Ercilla 1993, 91)

Godless, lawless, naught respecting
Save the One flung down from heaven,
Who in songs oft celebrated
Is their great and thunderous prophet,
They invoke His false-famed fury,
Chant to Him in every action,
Holding all He says as certain,
Words of dire portent and promise.

   (Ercilla 1945, 37)

   This being is explained in the Declaration that appears at the end of the poem: "Eponamón is the name given to the devil, by whom they swear when they wish to bind themselves to fulfilling what they promise" (1993, 976). It is clear that Ercilla confirms what European writers of the time believed—that Indian religions were the work of the devil.

   Eponamón's intervention is offset by the miraculous appearance of the Virgin Mary, who quenches the fury of a storm unleashed by the devil:

La tempestad cesó y el raso cielo
vistió el húmedo campo de alegría,
cuando con claro y presuroso vuelo
en una nube una mujer venía
cubierta de un hermoso y límpido velo
con tanto resplandor, que al mediodía
la claridad del sol delante della
es la que cerca dél tiene una estrella

   (Ercilla 1993, 279)

Ceased the tempest; skies of velvet
Clad the humid fields with gladness,
When in graceful flight, a goddess,
Wrapped in gauzy veils of beauty,
On a fleecy cloud swooped earthward,
Dazzling with her radiant splendor,
As the noontide sun in brilliance
Far outshines the glow of starlight.

   (Ercilla 1945, 98)

The vision then turns to the Araucanians, who, goaded by Eponamón, were preparing to attack La Imperial, a town that had run out of arms, munitions, and provisions:

Con voz blanda y delicada
les dice "¿A dónde vais, gente perdida?"
Volved, volved el paso a vuestra tierra,
no vais a la Imperial a mover guerra.
Que Dios quiere ayudar a sus cristianos
y darles sobre vos mando y potencia
pues ingratos, rebeldes, inhumanos
asi le habeis negado la obediencia.

   (Ercilla 1993, 280–281)

As she spoke with gentle chiding:
"Whither turn ye, hopeless people?"
Back, turn back! Your lands now call You!
Let the Imperial hosts go warless.
"God above would aid His Christians,
Give them power and strength to crush You.

Rebels, ingrates, beasts inhuman,
You've denied to Him obedience."

(Ercilla 1945, 98)

At this, the Araucanians fled: "Van sin orden ligeros como el viento" ("They ran pell-mell, as swiftly as the wind"). This is a recurrent motif in other accounts of the Conquest. Take, for example, the drawing of Guaman Poma de Ayala (374–75) and the accompanying text: "Santa María de la Peña of France, a beautiful woman, dressed in white raiment, whiter than the snow, her face shining more brightly than the sun. On seeing her, the Indians took fright, and it is said that she threw soil into the eyes of the Indian infidel." Just as in the War of Arauco, the Manco Inca's troops were about to seize Cuzco when the apparition foiled their plans.

From Canto XIII onward, the tone of the story changes, coinciding with the narration of the dispatch of the expedition under García Hurtado de Mendoza, for whom Ercilla spares no praise:

A tu hijo ¡Oh Marqués!, te demandamos,
en quien tanta virtud y gracia cabe
porque con su persona confiamos
que muestra desventura y mal se acabe;
de sus partes, señor, nos contentamos,
pues que por natural cosa se sabe,
y aun acá en el común es habla vieja,
que nunca del león nació la oveja.

(Ercilla 1993, 395)

We require your son, oh Marquess,
In whom dwell such grace and virtue,
For we trust that with his person.
Misery soon shall have adjournment;
With his parts we may content us,
As we presuppose his nature.
Even yet the saw is common:
   "Sheep are never sired by lions."

(Ercilla 1945, 135)

Henceforth, the *chanson de geste* becomes a series of events favorable to the Spanish troops, although emphasis is placed on the bravery of the Indians, expressed in terms of their indomitable nature. There is a progressive abandonment of a certain grandeur attributed to the Araucanians in the early cantos. Remember, for example, the heated election of the leader Caupolicán and the words of the elder Colo Colo, which are comparable to those of Nestor in the *Iliad* as he calms the fury of the heroes and demigods:

¿Qué furor es el vuestro ¡oh araucanos!,
que a perdición os lleva sin sentillo?
¿Contra vuestras entrañas tenéis manos,
y no contra el tirano en resistillo?
Teniendo tan a golpe a los cristianos
¿volvéis contra vosotros el cuchillo?
Si gana de morir os ha movido
No sea en tan bajo estado y abatido.
Volved las armas y ánimo furioso
a los pechos de aquellos que os han puesto
en dura sujeción, con afrentoso
partido, a todo el mundo manifiesto;
lanzad de voz el yugo vergonzoso
mostrad vuestro valor y fuerza en esto,
no derraméis la sangre del Estado
que para redimirnos ha quedado.

(Ercilla 1993, 114–5)

What blind rage, oh Araucanians,
Drags you, senseless, to perdition?
Will your hands pluck Indian hearts out
And not dare resist the tyrant?
In your reach are Christian devils.
Why turn knives against your brothers?
If desire for death has moved you,
Let it not be so ignoble!
Turn your spirit's heat and weapons
On the breasts of those who put you
In subjection's thrall with combat
Manifest to all, and shameful.
Fling from you the yoke outrageous.
Show your stern, heroic mettle.
Spill no blood of friends and neighbors,
Left to flow for your redemption.

(Ercilla 1945, 44)

Toward the end of the poem, the heroic tone of the Araucanians is restored, with Caopolicán being depicted as a heroic paradigm in a defeated society; only the treason of Andresillo, a *yanacona*, or servant, of the Spaniards, led to Caopolicán's defeat and subsequent captivity. His execution bears some of the signs of the death of a Spanish noble: He refuses to be executed by a black executioner, and, despite suffering the punishment of being impaled and shot with arrows at the same time, he does not die without first being baptized, thereby marking the end of the cycle of heroic deeds by the Araucanians (see **Figure 5**).

The epic does not end here, however. Ercilla inserts Philip II's claim to the kingdom of Portugal into the conclusion. This

Figure 5.

Photograph of an engraving by E. Rico depicting the judgment and sentence of Caopolicán in La Araucana, edición del centenario *(1910). (Courtesy John P. Robarts Research Library, University of Toronto)*

is not the first time that *La Araucana* has accommodated European history. Canto XVII tells of the capture of Sanquintín (a village in Picardy in the northeast of France), which was defended by Governor Coligny against the king of Spain's troops. The poet uses these episodes to heap praise on the monarch, who, according to the verses, undertakes an impeccable assault and avoids the pillaging and death of the inhabitants of the city (Ercilla 1993, 524–25).

Throughout the poem, there are wonderful digressions, such as the meeting between the poet and the sage Fitón. This meeting enables Ercilla to insert a third European episode into *La Araucana*: the Battle of Lepanto. The poet watches the scene through a crystal ball, which the necromancer shows him, saying:

> Y esta bola que ves y compostura
> es del mundo el gran término abreviado,
> que su dificilísima hechura
> cuarenta años de estudios me ha costado.
> Mas no hará en larga edad cosa futura
> ni oculto disponer de inmóvil hado
> que muy claro y patente no me sea
> y tenga aquí su muestra y viva idea
>
> *(Ercilla 1993, 649)*

> And this ball thou see'st, this crystal
> Is the world's great global symbol,
> Whose most difficult construction
> Cost me forty years of study;
> But not hap through lengthy ages,
> No caprice of Fate immobile
> Is not clearly manifested.
> Here I hold life's thoughts and patterns.
>
> *(Ercilla 1945, 216)*

Ercilla goes on to devote the entire Canto XXIII to the Battle of Lepanto, in which Juan of Austria, having successfully punished the Moors in Granada, set off to fight the Ottoman fleet on 7 October 1571. Although the event had enormous repercussions within Spain and marked a period in literature (recall that Miguel de Cervantes lost an arm in this battle, a fact of which he was extremely proud), in political terms it signified much less for the Spanish state. The following year the kingdom of Tunis, captured by Juan of Austria during this combat, was recovered by the Muslims (Elliot 238–239).

A glance at the poem shows that no praise should be spared for Ercilla and for his abilities to remember and arrange his memories and the sources he consulted and to write a captivating, convincing account in verse. Like that of El Inca Garcilaso, his work is primarily an ideological construction, and one that is beautifully written; its subsequent impact proved the success of his words. As El Inca did in Peru, Ercilla organized materials in his poem that were impossible to ignore for the identity of the Chilean people.

Writing in Anger: The Image of the Past in the Indigenous Chronicle of Santa Cruz Pachacuti

The five centuries that have elapsed since the discovery of the Americas have failed to erase the traces of aboriginal languages from Spanish. Even today, during what would appear to be the decline of some of these languages (such as Quechua), they remain stubbornly present in speech and writing. Their grammatical and phonetic features have imbued Spanish

with different sounds and altered and shifted the written language in ways that can easily be identified. Despite the intermittence of campaigns to promote bilingualism and, in some cases, the implementation of anti-indigenous policies, pre-European languages have refused to disappear. This has resulted in serious difficulties in the use of Spanish by those who spoke other languages in their childhood. If this is true of the twenty-first century, then it is easy to imagine the formidable task faced by the Indian chroniclers in the late sixteenth and early seventeenth centuries. Command of Spanish fluctuated between loan words (mainly nouns) and a primary bilingualism in which gender and verb tenses were used hesitantly. Added to this were the fluctuations in the Spanish of that time.

For the Nahuatl language of the Mexicans, a three-stage scale has been devised for the process through which speakers of aboriginal languages had to advance before becoming functionally bilingual (Lockhart 21). The chroniclers Felipe Guamán Poma de Ayala and Joan Santa Cruz Pachacuti Yamquí Salcamaygua were somewhere between the second and third stages at the time they ventured to write their texts. These writers have not been mentioned here arbitrarily. References to the Andean chronicles usually include five documents: *La Relación de antigüedades*, by Santa Cruz Pachacuti; *La Nueva Crónica* by Guaman Poma; the compilation of myths by Huarochiri, commissioned by Francisco de Avila; *La Relación*, by Titu Cussi Yupanqui; and the work of El Inca Garcilaso de la Vega. Only two of these, however, contain evidence of their authors' struggle between an original tongue and the language in which they attempted to write: Of the other three, the myths compiled by Huarochiri use the Roman alphabet, yet are written in Quechua; the text dictated by Titu Cussi was translated and written by a Spaniard (or an educated *mestizo*); and *Comentarios* and *Historia General* reveal an exceptional command of Spanish, so much so, in fact, that their author holds a privileged position in Spanish literature.

The works of Guamán Poma and Santa Cruz Pachacuti provide the clearest testimony of the tortured writing that accurately reflects the process of cultural change that took place in the Andean area. The documents were not produced for the same purpose: The lengthy letter to the king of Spain is a personal denouncement in which the author's biography and experiences are interwoven with the history of his people as well as warnings and advice aimed at the Spanish authorities in Latin American territory. *Relación de antigüedades* by Santa Cruz Pachacuti is a short moral fable in which the evangelizing background is evident in every paragraph. In writing their accounts, both authors followed the postulate established in 1550 by Carlos V, declaring that not even the most perfect Indian language could properly explain the mysteries of the holy Catholic Faith and that it was not possible to do so without creating great dissonance and imperfections (Julián de Paredes: Book VI, Title I, Law XVIII). It was therefore decided that Spanish should be introduced, and thus teachers were assigned to the Indians. This alleged superiority of Spanish was based on the conviction that its perfection was similar to that of Latin and the fact that language was the interpreter of reason, one of the benefits that man received from God (Aldrete, prologue). Moreover, Aldrete (d. 1645) himself was convinced that the conquered should receive the language of the conquerors (139), and, as happened in Spain with Latin, the same had been true in the Andes with Quechua, for the Incas' domain had been so small at the beginning that it included only Cuzco and its district for six leagues round about. Subsequently, Quechua became widely understood as the conquering Incas advanced, and they sought to introduce their courtly language from Cuzco, and they succeeded. Peru had and still has a great variety of languages; for this very reason, Quechua was known as the general language, and it was and is spoken throughout the Incan empire in an area of more than a thousand leagues (Aldrete 143–144). Aldrete had an optimistic view of the penetration of Spanish in Latin America, where "algunos indios lo pronuncian tan bien como los nuestros, lo mismo hacen todos los que tienen raza de españoles, por cualquier vía que sea, que hablan como Castilla. Los indios, aunque como he dicho, comúnmente lo saben, y entienden, pero lo usan poco por la afición que tienen a su lengua, no habiendo quien los obligue [a] usar la ajena" ("some of the Indians spoke it as well as ourselves, as did all those of Spanish descent, on either side, who speak like Castilians. The Indians, as I have already said, are usually familiar with and understand Spanish, although they rarely use it, because of their attachment to their own language, and because there is no one to force them [to] use the foreign language") (146).

There was, then, a political will that inspired the need to hispanicize the aborigines; at the same time, people believed that it was the will of God to extend the Holy Scripture as far as possible in the Spanish language, a vehicle capable of conveying the subtleties of Catholic theology.

Guamán Poma and Santa Cruz Pachacuti learned the language of the conquistadors in the shadow of the parish church, so the primary function of their writings was to contribute to the process of Christianization. Don Felipe says that his "crónica es muy útil y provechosa y es buena para enmienda de vida para los cristianos e infieles" (my "chronicle is extremely useful and beneficial and that it is helpful in correcting the lives of both Christians and infidels") (Guamán Poma 2). Joan Santa Cruz admits to being a Christian by the grace of God and, after providing a list of his parents, grandparents, and great-grandparents, describes them all as the main chieftains of this province (Canchi de Orcusuyu) and professed Christians in matters of the holy Catholic faith (Santa Cruz Pachacuti 183). There is conclusive evidence that the scholar from Ayacucho participated directly in the task of evangelization. We know little of this village headman from the highlands of Cuzco, yet the voice of Catholicism resonates throughout his work, meaning that the author was also closely involved with the work of the mission.

The greatest difficulty both writers faced was having to compare the Church's teachings with what they had assimilated in their family and community environment. This daily comparison placed the systems of values and beliefs on a battlefield where the sacred landscape of the Andes fought the environment of the Catholic Church. No one, however, could be a Catholic from the church's door inward and "pagan" or "idolatrous" from the church's door outward. The compulsory alternation between the two spheres created an ideology that caused symbols, images, and contents to be selected in such a way that the beliefs that are valid today eventually crystallized. This alternation was not religious in today's more restricted sense. For the Europeans, religion encompassed spheres that are now reserved for philosophy, education, and ethics. Every sermon expressed the knowledge and power of all these disciplines. For the Indian congregation, the voice of the preacher meant something else too: It was the voice of colonial authority, offering guidelines that covered every aspect of life and that openly contradicted the habits and customs learned in the home.

It is a well-known fact that the Spanish authorities ensured that their priests learned the indigenous languages and that, in the Peruvian viceroyalty, overt preference was given to Quechua, to such an extent, in fact, that Quechua was called the general language by the Spanish authority, not only because it was what was spoken and had been imposed by the Incas but also because it was valuable as a means of evangelization. There were many legal provisions that enforced this preference. In other parts of Latin America there was a similar preference given to the languages that had been most widely spoken prior to the Europeans' arrival. For example, the *Recopilación de leyes de los reynos de las Indias* clearly states that "que los clérigos y religiosos no sean admitidos a doctrinas sin saber la lengua general de los indios que han de administrar" ("priests, nuns, and monks would not be admitted to doctrines without knowing the general language of the Indians whom they were to administer") (Paredes, Book I, Title VI, Law XXX). Later on, it adds, "mandamos a los virreyes, presidentes, audiencias y gobernadores que estén advertidos y con particular cuidado en hacer que los curas doctrineros sepan la lengua de los indios, que han de doctrinar y administrar, pues tanto importa para el cumplimiento de su obligación y salvación de las almas de sus feligreses" ("We ordered the viceroys, magistrates, high courts, and governors to notice and ensure that the doctrinal priests should know the language of the Indians to whom they are to teach the doctrine and whom they will administer, since it is extremely important for the fulfillment of their obligations and the salvation of the souls of their parishioners") (Paredes: Book 1, Title XVIII, Law IV). Regardless of whether they were fully carried out or not, these provisions entailed a series of problems of conceptual translation. One only has to imagine the difficulties of transmitting the basic truths for Christians, such as the creation of the world or the birth of Christ, to have some idea of the extent to which the evangelizers' Quechua had to be stretched to indoctrinate the new believers.

It was this colonial Quechua, which standardized the translation of Christian concepts, that the chroniclers used in their writing. By the time Guamán Poma and Santa Cruz Pachacuti wrote, seventy years had elapsed since the episode at Cajamarca, three councils had been held in Lima, and several Quechua dictionaries and grammars, approved by Church authorities, had been compiled. There was, therefore, an established consensus on the way the mysteries of the faith and the Lord's commandments should be translated into Quechua. And although this version of written Quechua was disseminated among only a few members of the bilingual population, it undoubtedly reached these two Indian chroniclers.

However, the decision of Don Felipe and Don Joan was even more daring: They wanted to write in Spanish. Despite Guamán Poma's stated aim of addressing the king of Spain, it is doubtful that this was his main purpose (Adorno 183) or, at least, that this was his only objective. His motives probably varied during the course of preparing what was his final manuscript. The texts written in Quechua and the way he addressed his audience in the form of a sermon would suggest that he wished to reach an influential Indian public that reflected his self-image. Conversely, the chronicle by Santa Cruz Pachacuti is a linear account of the history of the Incas, with slight yet symptomatic references to the origin of man. His interest in perpetuating his thoughts is apparent in the early pages of the manuscript we know:

> ... yo como nieto y descendiente legítimo de los susodichos [se refiere a su genealogía familiar], siempre, desde que soy hombre, he procurado ser firme y estable en el misterio de mi santa fe católica, *exortándoles a los próximos que fueran a más adelante* [el subrayado es nuestro, obviamente se refiere a las generaciones futuras y en especial a su descendencia] en ser buenos cristianos con intención y celo de guardar los diez preceptos de la ley de Dios, creyendo en Jesucristo Nuestro Señor a imitación de nuestra santa madre iglesia de Roma. (Santa Cruz Pachacuti 185)

> ... as the grandson and legitimate descendant of the aforementioned [by which he means his family tree], I have always, ever since I became an adult, sought to be firm and stable in the mystery of my holy Catholic Faith, *by exhorting my fellow men to strive* [my emphasis; he is obviously referring to future generations, particularly his own descendants] to become good Christians, with the aim and fervor of respecting God's Ten Commandments, by believing in Jesus Christ our Lord, in imitation of our holy mother Church of Rome.

This document was classified as a *Relación* by Francisco de Avila (ca. 1573–1647), among whose papers the manuscript was found. In addition to having two amanuenses, probably a copyist, and the author, this manuscript also was annotated by this expurgator of idolatry (Santa Cruz Pachacuti 131).

If the aim of writing this chronicle was the one mentioned earlier, Don Joan hastens to explain the source of his knowledge: "digo que hemos oído, siendo niño noticias antiquísimas y las historias, barbarismos y fábulas del tiempo de las gentilidades, que es como sigue, que entre los naturales a las cosas de los tiempos pasados siempre las suelen parlar" ("I say that, when I was a child, I heard ancient news and stories, barbarities and fables of the times of heathendom, which is as follows, for the natives usually talk of things gone by," Santa Cruz Pachacuti 187). Like Garcilaso de la Vega, the Canchis chronicler resorts to the wisdom of the elders, on whose oral tradition he was raised. He begins Inca history with the book of Genesis, emphasizing the first couple, "Adán Eva ... cuya descendencia somos los naturales de Tahuantinsuyo, como las demás naciones que están pobladas en todo el universo ... así blancos como negros" ("Adam and Eve ... of whom, we, the Indians of Tahuantinsuyo, are the descendants, like the other nations throughout the universe, both white and black") (186). The text reflects the controversy over the humanity of the Indians and their rights as vassals of the king of Spain. By establishing a direct line of succession with the instant of creation, the chronicler ensures that the people of the Andes share the same divine origin as the rest of mankind. His reference to this origin coincides with that of Guamán Poma, albeit rather more explicitly. This was also the time of what Santa Cruz Pachacuti called *purun pacha* (wild time) or *tutayac pacha* (nighttime), when the Earth was populated by people who came from the South.

Despite the brevity of this work, one can surmise that the author makes his own point of origin (northeast of Cuzco on the outskirts of what is now the city of Sicuani) the center of his account. His version has a few incongruities when it refers to the Incas, showing that he did not belong to the ruling ethnic groups. As in the official legend, however, Santa Cruz Pachacuti assumes that the first settlers arrived from the South–in other words, from the societies established around Lake Titicaca. Hereafter he is obliged to incorporate the advent of Christ into the history of the Andes. To this end, he resorts to the Hapiñuño "devils," which used to afflict mankind but disappeared after the crucifixion at Calvary. One could interpret this as the end of the period of pagan obscurantism and, as he goes on to relate, the dawn of Christianization, beginning with the sermon by a certain Tonapa. This marks the beginning of one of several topics present in various chronicles and ethnographic versions: the sage "old gossip" clad in rags who walks from village to village, showering thanks and blessings on those who show him affection and severely punishing those who reject him. Santa Cruz Pachacuti identifies him with St. Thomas, and his pre-Pizarro evangelization is not all that different from the one Guaman Poma attributes to San Bartolomé, whom he twice depicts converting people on the edges of Lake Titicaca. The Tonapa mentioned by the chronicler is also shown to be dedicated to the same task and is shown punishing the *gaucas*, a word used in the chronicles to designate all the sacred expressions of the Indians. When Tonapa withdraws, he hands over his staff to Apo Tampo, who was to become the father of the Ayar brothers; through this shift, Santa Cruz Pachacuti adjusts his story to fit one of the best-known versions of the origin of the Incas. None of the motifs in the story attributed to Tahuantinsuyo, which follows the legend of the Ayars, is unfamiliar: One of the Ayars and his sister are turned into stone by the *guaca* Sañuc, who then receives his punishment; Ayar Manco assumes the leadership, becoming Manco Capac, whose descendants constitute the dynasty of the kings of Tahuantinsuyo.

The chronicle of Santa Cruz Pachacuti quickly became famous because of the drawing with which the author attempted to illustrate the replacement of the gold slab in the Temple of the Sun, originally placed there by Manco Capac. In the words of the chronicler, "este dicen que los hizo renovar a aquella plancha que había puesto su bisabuelo, fijándola de nuevo a la casa de Coricancha, y en toda la redonda o rededor de la plancha dicen que puso que allá detrás lo pondré para que lo vea lo que aquellos gentiles" ("they say that he made them replace the slab that had been placed there by his great-grandfather, putting it back into Coricancha's house, they say that he said he would put it back there so that it could be seen by the heathens") (Santa Cruz Pachacuti, 207–08). The drawing has sparked a number of controversies, most recently between Pierre Duviols and Tom Zuidema. The perception of the chronicler as an example of an Indian who has fully assimilated evangelization is set against the presence of thought patterns of pre-Columbian origin, which can clearly be distinguished in the chronicler's work. The truth probably lies somewhere in the middle. However convincing the education provided in the rural parishes may have been, a seventeenth-century Indian cannot have been unaffected by the place where he was born, his familial socialization, or the continuous cultural expressions that emerged from the environment of the relatives and neighbors with whom he came into contact every day. It is just as likely that Christian images should have been stripped of their content in order to be replaced by Indian values as it is that the language could have accommodated Christian concepts despite their being expressed in Quechua. The process must have been highly complex, and there are reasons to believe that both phenomena combined to create the present system of beliefs, which is not in the least pre-Columbian and is Andean to the extent that all colonial production is. If we want to believe that the ancient structures of Indian thought can be abstracted from documentary information, then we will probably have to set our sights somewhat lower and realize that, in the Peruvian sierra, particularly in the Cuzco region, even the best hypothesis has the disadvantage of the fact that there are very few documentary studies and that archaeological research is extremely limited. There is simply not enough documentary data for an undertaking of this scope (Duviols; Zuidema 101–154).

The debate mentioned earlier barely touches on this issue, although it does provide a starting point. All the chroniclers (both Spanish and Indian) who deal with Tahuantinsuyo explore the issue of its origins and are compelled to resolve the relationship between European history and the history of the Indian peoples of Latin America. One of the most erudite chroniclers, Cabello Valboa, constructed a vast history of mankind (published in 1586) in order to insert information on the Incas into it. He also took pains to establish parallel facts in order to lend force—on the basis of comparisons—to the events that had occurred in the Andes.

The Indian chroniclers faced enormous problems. They had to learn to write in another language and assimilate a perception of time that was completely alien to them, and they had to do this all under the yoke of a dominant, foreign society. One of the most serious problems was the source of their information and knowledge. Unless they had read the works of the Spanish chroniclers, their knowledge of the past was acquired through their relatives or community elders. The oral accounts they relied on had to be processed in such a way that they could be located in specific times and places; together with what they had learned in Catholic doctrine, these accounts could then be transformed into historical facts. Thus, for example, the sage Tonapa (the "old gossip" as Joan Santa Cruz Pachacuti calls him) appears in many guises in the manuscript by Huarochiri, as well as in Guaman Poma's text, and is still popular in the contemporary oral tradition. The chronicler takes this figure of the bearded man, dressed in rags, who rewards or punishes villages according to the behavior of their inhabitants, and converts him into St. Thomas, adding that it was he who converted the Indians to Christianity prior to the arrival of Pizarro (Bouysse-Cassagne 157–212; Millones 1997, 51–59; Millones 1998). Likewise, the chronicler becomes aware of the *hapiñuños* through his contemporaries, and he sets them in the pre-Christian past of the recently fabricated Andean history. This type of being is not exclusive to Joan; she also features in González Holguín's dictionary: "Fantasma o duende que solía aparecerse con dos tetas que podían asir de ellas" ("ghost or goblin usually shown with two breasts, which could be seized") (150). Guamán Poma also calls them "duende" (41) ("goblins"). And in the contemporary popular tradition, they are goblins in the shape of women with long, provocative breasts "volaban por los aires en las noches diáfanas y horas silenciosas, cogiendo a su paso y oprimiéndolas con sus pechos a gentes desprevenidas que las encontraban y se las llevaban" ("who flew through the air on clear nights when all was silent, clutching the unwary to their breasts and sweeping off with them") (M. Rigoberto Paredes 68).

What Santa Cruz Pachacuti does is historicize, lending a historical value to these traditions, which in themselves did not attempt to occupy a specific place within the trajectory from the past to the present. These events and personages were certainly not intended to be inserted in an unfamiliar chronology, such as the European one. But the chronicler would gather his information and insert it into the official European history, lending chronological meaning to the versions, or fragments of them, that came to his ears. This does not mean that the Inca state did not have its own organic version of history. Moreover, it is possible that, even before the Lords of Cuzco and even since the Wari state (CE 700), there may have been a clear conception of the past that, just as in Babylon or Egypt, served as stages of grandeur to explain to the people, the nobility, and neighboring villages the need for the rulers to have had a long and glorious past.

The chronicles of the sixteenth and seventeenth centuries are full of references to the Incas who preceded Huascar and Atahualpa. Moreover, the elders who were consulted told the Europeans that they had met Huaina Capac and that even Tupac Yupanqui could have been a historical personage in the European sense. If this was so, it means that the official version of the history of the Incan state was recorded in this way. We can speculate, with some grounds, that if Atahualpa had managed to rule, Tupac Yupanqui would have been erased from the Capac Cuna. On entering Cuzco, his "generals" pursued the members of this *panaca*, whom they then obliterated in a gruesome massacre. In other words, if Pizarro had arrived two or three years later, the list of Incas would have been different, since Tupac Yupanqui would not have been included among the ancestors of the victorious Atahualpa.

The Incas were not the only people to have written their history in accordance with the political moment. The same happens in contemporary states, of course. Yet the issue that interests us is more complex: We do not know how the *amautas* from Cuzco organized their information in order to transform it into the ideological basis justifying the fact that power lay in the hands of their rulers. The problem for us is not simply a question of the lack of writing but that the documentation by chroniclers is scarce. In Mexico, despite the unfortunate destruction of the pre-Cortesian codices, the volume of colonial texts containing indigenous ideograms is significant and permits a cross-referencing of sources, graphic characters, and illustrations that is extremely enlightening. In the Andes, however, there is very little documentation on the Incas; except for Guamán Poma's chronicle and his few drawings, there are no other illustrations of Indian society. Ideally, an iconographic corpus of the period immediately prior to Pizarro should be assembled, using mainly textiles and ceramics, to establish sequences of motifs and hierarchies of images that could then be correlated with the descriptions in the documents.

Anthropology is not all that helpful, however. Santa Cruz Pachacuti mentions specific places where proper ethnographic research could gather contemporary materials, which, by analogy, would shed light on the privileged position they hold in this chronicle. Such is the case of Vilcashuamán. According to Don Joan, the Inca Pachacuti arrived in the area with 50,000 men of war, "donde topa con siete guacas y demonios con figura de curacas muy grandes, negros y muy feos y eran llamados Ayssa Uillca, Pariacaca, Chincha Cocha, Uallallo, Chuqui Uacra y otros dos de los Cañares" ("where he came across seven *guacas* and devils in the shape of huge, black, ugly headmen, and their names were Ayssa Uillca, Pariacaca, Chincha Cocha, Uallallo, Chuqui Uacra, and another two Cañaris") (Santa Cruz Pachacuti 221). On Pachacuti's return to Vilcashuamán, "un hijo varón legítimo y mayor llamado Amaro Yupanqui, en donde estuvo algunos días" ("his first legitimate son, called Amarao Yupanqui, was born, and he stayed there for a few days") (223). According to the chronology of our chronicler, years later Huaina Capac, the grandson of Pachacuti, organized the great "fiesta de Capac Raymi en Vilcas [Vilcashumán], en donde estaba otra plancha de oro y declarado arriba [se refiere al dibujo en páginas anteriores], más medianillo" ("fiesta of Capac Raymi in Vilcas [Vilcashuamán], where there was another, medium-sized gold slab, mentioned previously, by which he means the drawing a few pages earlier") (248). Thus the region occupies a privileged place in the cultural history of the Andes. The archaeological complex at Vilcashuamán is impressive (see González Carré, Cosmópolis, and Lévano). It is located in Cangallo, a province southeast of the city of Ayacucho, about 100 kilometers away as the crow flies (although the journey today takes at least three hours). Particularly imposing are the Temple of the Sun and the square pyramid facing it; the latter is still reasonably well preserved, while the other building has now been converted into the local Catholic church, in which the bases of the Incan stone are still visible. This is not the first time that a chronicler has lent ceremonial validity to Vilcashuamán, reinforced by this Incan construction, which adds another level of validity to written testimonies. However, we lack the anthropological records to be able to suggest continuities or changes in the religious thought of what would appear to have been an important sphere in the thinking of the Incas.

Another significant issue is Santa Cruz Pachacuti's repeated interest in recording monumental festivities, to which he attributes a ceremonial and political importance. Toward the end of the chronicle, the document becomes a description of a fiesta. As we know, there were texts composed specifically for this purpose, such as *Elisio Peruano* by Gerónimo Fernández de Castro y Bocángel (1725) and *Fiestas de Lima* by Carvajal y Robles (1632). Nearer to the date of the writing of *Relación de antigüedades* there were also reports on fiestas such as the one celebrated in Pausa (Ayacucho) for the "provisioning of the viceroy in the person of the Marquis of Montesclaros" in 1607 (Rodríguez Marín 84–118). As in other examples of this literary subgenre, Santa Cruz Pachacuti inserts five festive activities that are narrated in greater detail than is any other type of event. For example, he devotes three folios (Santa Cruz Pachacuti 232–34) to describing the mock battles in which Pachacuti, Tupac Yupanqui, and "the new infante" Huaina Capac participated. Earlier in the text, another Inca summons "the frauds known as *añaysoaca, hayachuco, llama llama* and *hañamssi,* etc." to celebrate the birth of his son. These "frauds" had more than a celebratory function. They also came to denigrate, presumably through their gestures and clothes, by order of the Inca. This is what happened when Tupac Yupanqui placed the *guacas* of the conquered Collas in the midst of their troops and ordered the *hayachucos, saynatas, llama llamas,* and *chuñines* "to gallop" over them, "menos preciándolas hasta mandallos arrojar a la laguna de Orcos y a los Collas trae en triunfo al Cuzco" ("scorning them until he had them thrown into the lagoon of Orcos and had the Collas borne triumphantly into Cuzco") (Santa Cruz Pachacuti 236). Something very similar happened under the government of Huascar when he offended the Cuzco nobility by taking the *acllas* into the square and "estando todas en medio de tanto número de apo curacas y todo el reino de gente hacen salir cien indios llama llamas y hayachucos, y en el entretanto que ellos hacían sus comedias, visita a todas las doncellas, mirando a cada una manda a los llama llamas que las arremetieran a las doncellas cada uno, para usarla bestialidad en acto público, como los mismos carneros de la tierra" (Santa Cruz Pachacuti 255) ("in the midst of all these headmen, and the kingdom of the people, they ordered one hundred *llama llama* and *hayacucho* Indians to come forward, and while they were performing their plays, he visited all the maidens, and, glancing at each of them, ordered the *llama llamas* to hurl themselves against the maidens, so as to use bestiality in a public act, like the llamas themselves").

Like Guamán Poma, Don Joan also accuses Huascar of being responsible for the downfall of Tahuantinsuyo, in this case, by having resumed worship of the *guacas,* thereby paving the way for the Spaniards to restore Christianity in the Andes. This is the climax of the basic outline of the chronicle, which in the final analysis is, as mentioned earlier, a parable of Christian morality (Millones 1979, 123–161). Yet Santa Cruz Pachacuti is unable to finish his text without including a description of another festival. This time it is with the participation of the Spaniards, who, having rid themselves of Huascar and Atahualpa, entered Cuzco after the *apo curacas* had performed rituals to celebrate the vassalage that Manco Inca offered the emperor Charles V. The three protagonists of the approaching history–Pizarro, Valverde, and the new Inca–"entered with the great royal apparatus and pomp of great majesty." To an audience of natives expressing their delight, along with hundreds of Spaniards, the Marquis, with his white hair and beard, played Carlos V; Father Vicente, with his miter and cape, played St. Peter, the Roman pope (not like the impoverished St. Thomas); and Santa Cruz Pachacuti played the Inca, richly attired like a king, with a sumptuous bier and royal insignias of *capac unancha* (Santa Cruz Pachacuti 268).

How many interpretations could one make of this complex text, for which there is now a reliable edition? It should not surprise us that the chronicler from Canchis used fragments of Spanish culture, contextualized by the doctrine that made him a Christian. It is logical, then, that the mock battles, so popular at the Spanish court, should have been recreated for the Inca court by someone who had probably seen only improvised games or displays, such as those of Pausa, and imagined them in the hands of the *apo curacas* who would have done the same in pre-European times. In this case, however, the transposition from one culture did not annul the other. Even today, when dancers in Andean festivals play the role of animals, once disguised they behave like animals, imitating the noises they make and mimicking their behavior. The continuity of this type of dress and choreography has been extensively documented (as in Martínez Compañon's account). In his account, Santa Cruz Pachacuti depicts the cultural context of which he formed a part, despite the fact that the script of the events did not belong to him. By the time he was writing, the script may already have been written down, based on the versions disseminated among the Spaniards and educated Indians.

The task of writing about their people's past stretched the Indian chroniclers' capabilities to the limit. Apart from the language issue, Guamán Poma and Santa Cruz Pachacuti had to transfer the unwieldy information passed on to them by their relatives and acquaintances into the schema of European history, which was alien to them. This information combined fragments of official Incan history, stereotypes of Indian society disseminated by the Spaniards, European oral traditions, local versions of the catechisms approved by the Church, and the system of beliefs current in their regions. Despite the impression that the texts of both chroniclers give us today, their command of Spanish must have been adequate. Observe the way Guaman Poma plays with the word *procuradores* ("those who apply the law"), which he turns into *proculadrones* (a combination of *procuradores* and *ladrones* [thieves]), and with the word *peticiones* (pleas before judicial authority), which he classifies as *perdiciones* (actions that lead to ruin), an allusion to the fate of the Indians when they had recourse to the judicial power (Adorno 62–63). Consider Don Joan's reference to Tunapa, whom he calls "old loudmouth" (Santa Cruz Pachacuti 195), and by Huaina Capac's description of his sister's betrothed as "an old chieftain, a great coca eater, and very ugly" (Santa Cruz Pachacuti 246), which show the extent of his command of this foreign language.

Yet constructing a history of the Incas was an even more difficult task. Santa Cruz Pachacuti had to place all the Andean mythological references–that is, the past prior to the evangelization of St. Thomas–within a conceptual space that corresponded to the Christian devil and hell and thus constituted a permanent threat with regard to the nature of man. This is particularly clear in the history of the rulers of Cuzco, since the Incas were faithful to the teachings of Christ's disciple (as Matia Capac), received his blessings, while those who returned to the worship of the *guacas* (in other words, the devil) were unable, like Huascar, to avoid the corresponding punishment. This process of construction cannot have been easy. The chronicler had access to hundreds of stories, names of sanctuaries, rites, and festivals, which included Christian worship or were disguised for the benefit of European eyes. In his view, however, some of the figures in them were better qualified to appear in his story as Christian devils, while the activities they performed were better suited to dragging the souls of the condemned. One is struck by the prominent role given to the *hapiñuños*, who are barely referred to in other chronicles, and by the fact that the *guacas* from Vilcashuamán had notable names in the Incan religious pantheon yet were prominent chiefly in places that were far away from the Cuzco regions (such as Uallallo and Pariacaca, which are hills in the Lima sierra, and Chinchacocha, a mountain lagoon in the province of Junín). At the same time, our chronicler took care not to diverge too far from the canonical story found in other texts of the period: Manco Capac is the Ayar Manco who founds Cuzco; Matia Capac is an exemplary Inca; Pachacuti is the hero of the battles against the Chancas; and Tupac Yupanqui is the Incan warrior, while the conflict between Huascar and Atahualpa is the prelude to the end of Tahuantinsuyo.

How can one combine novel aspects of a text with the approval of established canons, the profusion of *guacas* with acquiescence to Catholic dogma, the disconcerting drawings and so few pages with so much information? No one could have written this in perfect tranquility or in the solitude of a retreat–situations that were difficult to achieve for an educated Indian such as the tormented Guamán Poma. This chronicle could have been conceived only in the everyday alternation between two worlds, which gave off sparks when they clashed. And as the title suggests, every word was eked out of a pen that wrote in anger.

The Baroque on the Frontiers of the Spanish Empire: Cuzco and the Work of Juan Espinosa Medrano

The importance of ceremonial life in the viceroyalty is borne out by the fact that more than 100 days were regarded as feast days. Although this meant little to the population scattered throughout its vast territory, in major cities such as Lima and Cuzco, fiestas filled urban spaces with music, parades and processions, bullfights, Masses, and plays. Public performances in Latin America were one of the most characteristic features of the Baroque period, whose lengthy duration left indelible traces on virtually all forms of artistic expression: from the masks worn by members of the parades to the ephemeral architecture erected along the route between the *andas*, or stages, of the processions, and from the paintings and sculptures that adorned the churches to the canvases painted to accompany the processions of images or as backdrops to the theatrical performances.

Present-day differences between Lima (with approximately 7 million inhabitants) and Cuzco (with 300,000) may obscure the parallel importance of both cities at the beginning of the colonial period. In the early seventeenth century, Cuzco had:

> una población de tres mil vecinos españoles y diez mil vecinos indios, repartidos los indios en cuatro parroquias con sus curas que los doctrinan y enseñan, y tienen un hospital muy rico, y todos tienen muchas riquezas. A esta ciudad envía el rey por corregidor un caballero de grande casa y nombre, porque la ciudad es grande, y mucho lo que tiene que gobernar y más de lo que se puede aprovechar. Tiene otras justicias y obispos con su iglesia mayor y sus canónigos y dignidades. . . . Tiene monasterios de las cuatro órdenes, poderosos y ricos, y monasterios de monjas, y rica casa de teatinos, y muchas parroquias y hospital de españoles. (León de Portocarrero 93–94)

> a population of 3,000 Spanish residents and 10,000 Indians, the Indians being divided into four parishes with their priests who taught them Catholic doctrine and educated them, and they have a very well-endowed hospital, and they are all extremely wealthy. The king sent a gentleman of an excellent family and name as chief magistrate to this city, because the city is vast and there is much to rule and more than he can utilize. It has other courts and a bishop with his church and canons and dignitaries . . . . It has monasteries of the four orders, both powerful and rich, convents, and a wealthy house of Theatines, many parishes, and a hospital for Spaniards.

In an atmosphere of this kind, cultural life had room to flourish. The second half of the sixteenth century marked the peak of the period known in Peruvian history as "civil wars," which corresponds to the time when the *encomenderos* confronted the state bureaucracy in order to preserve their rights (to possess land and Indian servants), which the crown wished to abolish. In Lima, the celebrations had gained strength through the arrival of Don Diego López de Zúñiga, count of Nieva (1561–1564), "under whose administration we recorded the first documented news of theatrical performances in our city, in praise of the Sacrament of the Eucharist, which obviously does not mean that they could not have taken place earlier . . . . A model of frivolity and detachment (a revival of a Trastamara), this disorderly, covetous ruler imposed a rule of etiquette and manners on the court at Lima in order to distribute the numerous retinue which had accompanied him from Spain, comprising over forty noblemen and chamberlains, in an orderly fashion" (Lohmann 13–14). He was also accompanied by a group of musicians and singers whose performance encouraged the authorities of the town council of Lima to enhance the splendor of the feast of Corpus Christi. Thus in 1563 the town hall organized a competition for them to "perform a mystery play and dances, in addition to what they are accustomed to," the prize for best performance being "five yards of crimson velvet" (Lohmann 15).

Entrants included the city trade guilds and other institutions (such as the university), which combined to participate in the principal fiestas. Not to be overlooked, at its own town council meeting a few years before (13 May 1560), Cuzco had agreed that, on the occasion of Corpus Christi:

> todos en aquel día se muestran alegres y regocijen y salga la procesión con toda autoridad y policía, por tanto, que además de las otras cosas que para ello se proveerán y han proveído, que se pregone públicamente que todos los oficiales de oficios mecánicos, así de sastres como de calceteros y herreros y zapateros y plateros y los demás oficios que hay en esta ciudad, saquen el dicho día sus pendones y la muestra de sus oficios y las danzas y otras cosas que nos han acostumbrado . . . y con todo ello salgan a la procesión, so pena que cada uno de los dichos oficios no saliere y sacare su oficio como se usa y acostumbra en España y en estas partes, le llevarán de pena treinta pesos al que no saliere, sin le reservar de ellos, y que estará en la cárcel quince días. (González Pujama 119)

on that day, everyone should be happy and rejoice, and join the procession with pomp and courtesy. Therefore, in addition to all the other things that would be provided, and have already been provided for this purpose, it should be publicly proclaimed that, on that day, all craftsmen in mechanical trades, including both tailors and hosiers and shoemakers and silversmiths and all the other craftsmen in this city, should display their standards and the signs of their trade and the dances and other things to which they have accustomed us . . . and join the procession. Failure on the part of any of these trades to join the procession and display their trade, as is the custom in Spain and in these parts, will be punished by a fine of thirty pesos and a fortnight in prison.

This festive urge can be observed year-round not only in the festivities recognized by the municipalities but also in every corner of the viceroyalty. Power as public performance was one of the principles of the Spanish dynasty that was exercised so widely that it blurred certain concepts: Each celebration served as an opportunity to remind vassals of their condition and of the power of their rulers, whose symbols, portraits, and flags were displayed to reaffirm the social structure in force. In this context, theatrical performances and parades played a significant role, since they depicted important personages in their proper positions. Even in places as remote from the Spanish and Indian capitals (Lima and Cuzco) as Pausa (Ayacucho), fiestas were held in 1607 to celebrate the appointment of Juan Mendoza y Luna, marquis of Montesclaros, as viceroy of Peru. There were games involving sugarcane and rings, as well as a fancy-dress parade, which included representations of Don Quixote and Sancho Panza. However, as in virtually all these types of parades, the presence of Indians proclaiming their loyalty to the king of Spain was required (Millones 1993, 122–123).

This situation was far more evident in the centers of colonial power, where the parades and dramatizations revealed the need to pay homage to His Majesty, thereby legitimizing his government. The other explicit message of these public performances was the evangelization of the Indians and respect for Christian ethics, a message aimed particularly at *criollos* and Spaniards. The following account was handed down to us by a curious observer of seventeenth-century Lima, Don José de Mugaburu, who in December 1659 witnessed the celebrations held in honor of the birth of the crown prince, the son of Philip IV and Mariana of Austria. As part of these celebrations:

> hicieron fiesta los indios, donde hubo un castillo en la plaza, y salió el rey Inga y peleó con otros dos reyes hasta que los venció y cogió el castillo; y puestos todos tres reyes ofrecieron las llaves al Príncipe que iba en un carro retratado; y salieron a la plaza todos los indios que hay en este reino, cada uno con sus trajes, que fueron más de dos mil los que salieron, que parecía toda la plaza toda plateada (*sic*) [plantada] de diferentes flores, según salieron los indios bien vestidos y con muchas galas. Hubo toros aquella tarde y salieron dos indios a garrochear a los toros. Fiesta de mucho regocijo para todos, y dicen llevaron la gala de todos, con que cesaron las fiestas. (Mugaburu 34–35)

the Indians organized a fiesta, in which there was a castle in the square, and King Inga came out and fought with the other two kings until he conquered them and seized the castle; and the three kings together handed the keys to the Prince, who rode by on a painted float, and then all the Indians in this kingdom flooded into the square, each with his costume, and over 2,000 of them went into the square, all bedecked with various flowers, and the Indians were all well-dressed and wearing their finery. There was bullfighting that afternoon, and two Indians went out to spear the bulls. It was a feast of much rejoicing for all, and they say that they all went out in their finery, after which the fiesta ended.

These celebrations lasted several months. A city such as Lima had numerous guilds that participated in the official ceremonies. The tradesmen and craftsmen, as noted earlier, used to take part in the fancy-dress parades in which either they or their hired artists acted. However, there was usually a special day when the Indian nation formally paid its respects. Its presence rounded out the political vision offered to the audience and constituted the counterpart to the mounted processions and *despejos* of the Spaniards and their progeny, sponsored by the viceroy and the town council. This festive plan obliged the colonial authorities to resort to the traditional chieftains of the Indian nation when the latter had to be mobilized. This must have been the case in the fiestas, according to the scant information provided by Mugaburu. As in other parts of the viceroyalty (Cuzco, Potosí, etc.), the Indian authorities were ordered to play the Incas. The war between these three kings was probably just another version of the "dance of Moors and Christians" brought to America by Hernán Cortés, which took the form of the death of Moctezuma and Atahualpa in New Spain and Peru. A local chieftain (or perhaps one from the North, since several chieftains of Mochica origin owned properties on the outskirts of Peru) played the role of the Inca, while others played the kings defeated in the mock castle erected on the parade ground. On handing over the keys to the portrait of the distant, ailing prince, the Indian leaders of the local community were merely renewing the pact of submission to which they were subjected.

From the little this document tells us, the European narrative would seem to have been repeated: a fight between a Moslem and a Christian king, ending with the submission and death or conversion of the infidel. However, portraying the Inca as a Christian sovereign symptomatically alters and reinforces, in both nations, the conviction that the Indian nobility, more than a century after Pizarro's arrival, was already fully Catholic.

Whether or not there is a firm basis for this belief is the subject of yet another analysis, but in any case, the actors and the script were adapted to the wishes of the viceregal authorities.

Mystery plays are allegorical, lyrico-dramatic one-act compositions that refer directly or indirectly to the Eucharist. The basic themes of mystery plays are the creation, sin, and surrender, their overt aim being to provide instruction on theological issues. Rather than having any individual personality, the characters can best be described as abstract, universal allegories. For the seventeenth-century Spanish rulers, mystery plays illustrated the moral restraint that must be taught to their vassals, while for the church they were—with their references to the Eucharist and an indispensable penance for washing away sins—a safe, sober means of celebrating the feast of Corpus Christi.

An unusual instance of this celebration took place in Peru by order of the viceroy Don Pedro Antonio Fernández de Castro, Count of Lemos (1667–1672). The program of festivities for Corpus Christi was modified to make room for the compulsory inclusion of two mystery plays by Pedro Calderón de la Barca (1600–1681), *La humildad coronada* and *El gran teatro del mundo*. This imposition was due to the desire to lend a note of sobriety to the feast, which, in the extremely devout mentality of the count of Lemos, had lost its Christian nature. He was probably referring to other celebrations, specifically the plays performed at Lurin (south of Lima), where the dances and the feast were regarded as licentious (Lohmann 208). The Lima town council program featured two plays, a parade, and two *entremeses*, or short farces. The mystery plays replaced the lay representations and were offered "with four short farces, two in each act, with a prologue in each act; the last farce to be sung and danced" (Lohmann 209). This explains both the speed with which European literary novelties sometimes reached Peru and the fact that the City of Kings sought to adapt to the canons of the mother country. By so doing, the city fulfilled one of the aims for which it was founded: It was to be the Spanish city, in contrast to the old capital of Tahuantinsuyo. In Cuzco, the intellectuals shared the same feeling of marginalization and emulation in relation to Spain as did their counterparts in Lima; yet, since it was a bilingual society, at least among the higher strata (most of the Indian population being monolingual Quechua speakers), the feasts, celebrations, and works to be recited, read, or sung could be written in Quechua.

At this point, a brief discussion of the population of the seventeenth-century Peruvian viceroyalty is in order. Once the colonial regime had been established, Spanish government activities focused on channeling what was extracted from the mines in Potosí to the mother country. This was not an easy time for the crown. The Spanish infantry regiments were fighting on many fronts, and, as a result of their defeats, they had lost ground to Dutch maritime supremacy. At the same time, the papacy and France continued to be uneasy allies, while England kept the colonies in check with raids that would eventually establish temporary strongholds for an unstoppable wave of smuggling. This situation widened the gap between Cuzco and Lima. Since the Atlantic was the port of entry for uncontrolled merchandise (particularly from Buenos Aires), merchants in Buenos Aires found a way of establishing links with Potosí through which they redirected their goods along illegal routes that avoided the land customs offices. Within the viceroyalty, this rerouting (instead of the old monopoly of the Lima merchants, who had fallen on hard times) meant that the southern region, including Cuzco, directed its production and transport system (caravans of llamas and mules) toward the new circuit, which led them away from the capital.

Consequently, the old Incan capital eventually forged its own lifestyle, with a type of miscegenation different from that of the Pacific Coast. The resident Spanish population and their *criollo* descendants came into daily contact with the Indians and *mestizos*, which led to the consolidation of a regional culture in which Quechua (like Guaraní in Paraguay) was spoken by everyone. At the same time, one should recall that Cuzco was in a situation similar to that of Mexico with a growing *mestizo* population. The Incan ethnic elite continued to occupy the same position it had held during the pre-Columbian era. The ethnic groups that had once flocked to the festivals now attended those organized by the Church and the Spanish rulers. These colorful parades, processions, and public acts in general included features that would have incurred the disapproval of the count of Lemos but which were regarded as quite natural by the Chief Magistrate of Cuzco and the aldermen.

On 14 August 1654,

la colocación del nuevo templo e iglesia catedral de esta gran ciudad del Cuzco con una procesión muy solemne que salió de la iglesia antigua (desde hoy es el Sagrario, llamado el Triunfo) con el Santísimo Sacramento y sagradas imágenes, asistiendo en ella ambos cabildos, el clero y las comunidades: dieron vuelta por las dos plazas, bien adornadas de altares, arcos triunfales, y mucha tapicería, con todo género de bailes, en la forma que se acostumbra el día de Corpus Christi. El Santísimo Sacramento fue colocado en el altar mayor en su Tabernáculo y las imágenes en sus capillas. Celebráronse luego con toda solemnidad las vísperas de la Asunción de Nuestra Señora, titular de esta santa iglesia. Y el día siguiente, sábado 15 de dicho mes, se estrenó con la misa y sermón de dicha festividad, continuándose por toda la octava la frecuencia y devoción de la ciudad y por cada noche de la octava, varios y costosos fuegos y máquinas pirotécnicas y hasta principios de setiembre [duraron] los festejos de máscaras muy lucidas, comedias, corridas de toros y otras invenciones con que los ciudadanos oficiales y gremios demostraron el común regocijo. (Esquivel y Navia 110)

the building of the new cathedral church and temple of this great city of Cuzco was celebrated with a solemn procession, which left the old church (it is now the Sacrarium, known as El Triunfo), with the Holy Sacrament and the sacred images, with the participation of both town councils, the clergy, and the communities. They walked round the two squares, adorned with altars, triumphal arches, many tapestries, and all manner of dances, in the style of the feast of Corpus Christi. The Holy Sacrament was set on the main altar in its Tabernacle, and the images placed in their chapels. They then solemnly celebrated the vespers of the Assumption of Our Lady, the saint of this holy church. And the next day, Saturday, 15th of that month, it was inaugurated with the Mass and sermon of this festivity, and the piety and frequency of devotions of the city continued the entire week, and every night, there were several costly fireworks exhibitions, and the mask festivities, plays, bullfights, and other inventions with which the official citizens and guilds demonstrated their mutual rejoicing continued until early September.

It was in this atmosphere of color, piety, and commotion that Juan Espinosa Medrano, nicknamed Lunarejo, was born, was educated, developed his talent, and thus achieved fame. He was born in a village in the south of Cuzco, in the province of Aymaraes. We do not know the exact date, but it must have been around 1620, when the literary circles of Madrid were still discussing the first manuscripts of *Las Soledades* by Luis de Góngora. Forty-two years later, El Lunarejo was to publish *Apologético en favor* on the Spanish bard he would call "The Prince of Poets and Lyricists." The book clearly explained its purpose: It was written "against Manuel de Faria y Sousa, a Portuguese nobleman."

Apologético, the best-known work of Espinosa Medrano, appears to have been the result of one of those "exercises in rhetoric given to the students of the San Antonio Abad del Cuzco Seminar" (Cisneros 54–55). Espinosa Medrano is regarded as the "finest prose writer on Gongoran *culteranismo* and Gracianian *conceptismo* in Latin America (Tamayo 261) and as such occupies a special place in Spanish literary history. As he acknowledges, by the time his book was published, its protagonists were already dead, but Espinosa Medrano declared that he was willing to continue defending Góngora. During this attempt, he reveals his social condition: "Tarde parece que salgo a esta empresa: pero vivimos muy lejos los *criollos*..." ("It seems that I have embarked on this endeavor rather late: But we *criollos* live very far away") (17). The phrase is symptomatic in that the author identifies himself as part of European culture in Latin America. It is not clear that calling oneself a *criollo* under these circumstances necessarily means being of Spanish descent. What it evidently does reveal, however, is the marginalized condition of intellectuals born in this obscure part of the Spanish empire. Quite apart from this, one should recognize the author's tremendous efforts to participate in an important polemic, despite the physical (and chronological) distances involved.

It is precisely this will to be part of the center, this desire to participate in decisions, that would characterize the culture of the viceroyalty and would do so from the perspective of the *criollos,* a view that Espinosa Medrano endorsed. One should ignore the anecdote (recorded by Esquivel and divulged by Ricardo Palma) in which, during one of his sermons, El Lunarejo is said to have asked the congregation to make room for an Indian woman he called "mother." If this indeed happened, and the woman was in fact his mother, then the phrase has a formidable rhetorical effect. However, this does not necessarily make the author an Indian, nor does it condemn him to the ambiguity of colonial miscegenation. Like Pedro Peralta y Barnuevo, another illustrious writer on a variety of subjects, El Lunarejo fought to ensure that his immense knowledge, accrued through the texts that reached the Americas, should be displayed in Europe. This is borne out by his interest in having his books sent to Spain, "in other words, to the other world, to be published and (because I am as far as one can be from a printing press) so that they can be free from horrible printer errors, because I have seen works that have been virtually ruined: with mutilated full stops, disconnected sentences, suspended syllogisms, and words that have been omitted. And since we, erroneously known as 'Spanish Americans,' are regarded as barbarians, it is hardly surprising that I should wish to prevent such vices and solecisms from being attributed to the author of the book" (Guibovich 140).

Espinosa Medrano achieved the recognition of his fellow citizens during his lifetime. In August 1681, he was admitted to the canonship while he was the parish priest of San Cristóbal,

and, as a result of the competition (on lessons and sermons), he was appointed the first canon in October of the same year (Esquivel and Navia 11, 142). Two years later, he attained the same position in the Cathedral of Cuzco (Esquivel and Navia 144). The following year, he was also made treasurer, and in 1687 he was promoted to archdeacon, a post he held until his death on 13 November 1688 (Esquivel and Navia 148–149). El Lunarejo was a prolific writer who was fluent in Quechua, Latin, and Spanish, publishing works in all three languages. He was also an outstanding preacher; a selection of his sermons was published by his students and friends as *La novena maravilla* (in Madrid in 1695). He wrote lyrical poems and plays, some of the most famous of which were composed for the festivities in honor of the count of Lemos on his entry into Cuzco in 1668. One of these may have been *El hijo pródigo*, written in Quechua, which is particularly interesting in view of the fact that the biblical parable on which it is based was rewritten using Indian personages (Kuyaj Yaya, Hanan Saya, Hurin Saya, and Kuichi) whose behavior only vaguely follows the Christian text (Basadre 267). Finally, it is interesting to reflect on Bishop Manuel de Mollinedo y Angulo's predilection for Espinosa Medrano, whom he describes as "the most meritorious figure in the bishopric because of his many significant writings and great virtue" (Guibovich 138). Who better than the patron of the Baroque in Peru to understand the writings and prose of Lunarejo?

On 8 September 1767, the viceroy Manuel Amat y Juniet, carefully following the instructions of Charles III, proceeded to enforce a royal decree of expulsion: "estrañen de España e Indias, Islas Filipinas y demás adyacentes, a los religiosos de la Compañía, así sacerdotes como coadjutores o legos que hayan hecho la primera profesión y a los novicios que quisieran seguirles y que se ocupen todas las temporalidades de la Compañia" ("to expel from Spain and the Indies, the Philippines, and adjacent countries, members of the Society of Jesus, both priests and assistants and lay brothers who have taken their vows and the novices who wished to follow them and are responsible for collecting all the tithes of the Society of Jesus") (Vargas Ugarte 1965, IV: 163–165). There is a legend, amplified by Ricardo Palma (1833–1919), that the priests were about to leave when the viceroy's men burst into their lodgings. If this were true, the Jesuits would have received advance warning of this drastic decision by the count of Aranda, a former student of theirs who had become the all-powerful minister of the king of Spain. In a courtly city such as Lima, most secrets would probably have been discovered before they reached Callao, although this does not appear to have been the case here. Moreover, Amata had taken precautions several weeks earlier (the royal dispatch reached him on August 20), pretending that he had been ordered to prepare a military expedition. To this end he gave instructions for the *San José*, moored in Callao and also known as *El Peruano*, to be prepared. He thereby distracted the attention of his fellow citizens as he prepared a swift, safe action while attempting to avoid the protests or entreaties of important members of the community who frequented Jesuit circles.

The expulsion was not entirely unheralded. Before it had been decreed in Spain and her colonies, the minister Sebastián José Carvalho e Mello, the marquis of Pombal, had managed to have the Jesuits expelled in Portugal in 1759, issuing a death sentence for those who remained in the country. They met the same fate in France, where their property was confiscated; the Society of Jesus was declared to be contrary to natural law, and its members were finally expelled in 1764. The most negative views on the Society of Jesus originated in Paris. What happened later in Spain was by no means an unusual order in this European context. To a certain extent, the arrival of the Bourbons and the need to reinforce royal authority, which was based on the French model, meant a clash with the authority of a group whose constitution had incorporated a vow of obedience to the Pope. This direct link with Rome created a conflict of interests, which was less visible but no less acute. The king of Spain enjoyed the patronage of the Holy See, which enabled him, among other privileges, to participate in the nomination of ecclesiastical authorities. This situation produced a great deal of friction between the king and his representatives in the religious orders, who felt less beholden than the regular clergy. These conflicts were exacerbated when they involved the Jesuits, who had made their autonomy a question of principle. In light of the eighteenth century, the Vatican could be regarded as a state that fully exercised its political power and was therefore in direct competition with other European kingdoms. From this point of view then the Jesuits' loyalty was permanently in doubt (Millones 1995, 225–226).

Among those expelled were the Viscardo brothers, José Anselmo and Juan Pablo, both novices who were sent to Italy. They had joined the Society of Jesus in Cuzco in 1761, when Juan Pablo, the future forerunner of Latin American emancipation, was barely thirteen. The king's decree cut short his studies. Juan Pablo obviously completed the novitiate and the juniorate, but we do not know whether he managed to complete his philosophy studies. Of the fifty years he lived, he spent eight in the Society of Jesus.

At the age of nineteen, Juan Pablo left Peru, having been one of the 500 Jesuits who carried out their pastoral duties, or were being prepared for them, in the viceroyship (which at the time had a population of more than a million and a half inhabitants). He put out to sea at Moquegua and never returned to Peru, despite his wish to do so, because of the strict prohibitions established. His father was the grand field master Don Gaspar Viscardo y Guzmán; his mother was Manuela de Zea y Andia; this couple, together with their children, constituted an important family in Pampacolca (Arequipa), where Juan Pablo was born. Once the Jesuits had been expelled and before they reached Italy, there was a brief possibility of their becoming a secularized order. The Viscardo brothers tried to take advantage of this opportunity, but the requisite proceedings do not appear to have been conducted. In any case, by 1771 José Anselmo and Juan Pablo were already living in Massacarrara, where they received a meager pension (372 copper *reales*) from the king of Spain (Vargas Ugarte n.d., 128). In 1791 when Juan Pablo Viscardo had managed to establish links with England, he managed to obtain 400 pounds sterling a year, which was equivalent to the income of a successful English professional.

His contact with London began in 1782, when the Viscardo brothers left Florence for England. In anticipation of their first meeting with the Foreign Office, they carried letters of presentation that "they had been given by Sir Horace Mann, the British ambassador at the court of Tuscany. The aim of the brothers [was] to obtain British military and political support for a project to liberate their native Peru–and indeed, all the Spanish colonies in America–from the Spanish

yoke" (Simmons 3). Not long afterward, Juan Pablo Viscardo obtained an annual allowance of 200 pounds from the British government, which he managed to double in 1791 when tension between England and Spain forced British government officials to seek his services once again. During that period, Juan Pablo had a well-paid job in the Naples consular service, and he was in a position to negotiate his new fees. The relationship between the two parties was not entirely free from periods of silence and disagreement. The fact that Spain and England were allies between 1793 and 1795 placed Viscardo in a compromising situation (Simmons 79).

Juan Pablo's forced residence in Europe prevented him from recovering his family property and claiming his due inheritance. However, by way of compensation, he witnessed the period known as the Enlightenment, which directly involved the nations with which Viscardo had close links: France, Italy, and England. It was a period of debates, publications and conspiracies, newspapers, magazines and pamphlets, café discussions, rumors, and the quest for knowledge. Juan Pablo Viscardo's status as an exile not only deprived him of his family fortune but also prevented him from joining the priesthood and returning to his homeland, facts that seem to have inspired his writings. One can assume that all these deprivations drove him to formulate his reflections in the direction identified today as the ideology of Latin American emancipation but which can also be regarded as masterpieces of Latin American prose. Other Jesuits in exile, such as Francisco Clavijero (1731–1787) and Juan de Velasco (1727–1792), used their expatriation as an opportunity to reflect on the history and origins of their native countries (Mexico and Ecuador). Viscardo preferred to adopt a more political and sociological attitude. His writings sought to achieve a continentwide validity, and his aim was to free Latin America from the colonial government.

The impact of the work of Juan Pablo Viscardo found its true scope thanks to Francisco de Miranda, who, having been born in Caracas (1756), moved to the United States to serve alongside George Washington in his fight for independence. Miranda traveled extensively through Europe (including Russia and Turkey), championing the cause of emancipation. He managed to interest the British and the Americans in his cause to such an extent that they organized two invasions to liberate Venezuela, both of which proved unsuccessful. In the first of them, in 1806, Miranda nearly lost his life; the unenthusiastic response to his improvised army reminded him that the Venezuelan revolution should begin within the country itself. Nevertheless, Miranda tried again in 1808, but the Napoleonic invasions persuaded the British to abandon their endeavor.

Miranda never met Viscardo, who died in London in February 1798, although Miranda did have access to the documents that the ex-Jesuit had left Rufus King, an envoy minister from the United States. The first edition of the most famous of his writings, *Carta a los españoles americanos*, was sent from a false address (Philadelphia) in 1799 so as not to compromise England. This brilliant document was published in several editions, not only in London but also in Buenos Aires and Bogotá (in 1816 and 1810, respectively). It was not published in Lima until 1822, although fragments of the *Carta* had already appeared in subversive proclamations during the government of the Viceroy José Fernando de Abascal (1806–1816). Nothing illustrates the value of this document better than the words of Viscardo himself. The document begins:

¡Hermanos y compatriotas!

La proximidad en que nos encontramos del cuarto siglo después de que nuestros ancestros comenzaron a establecerse en el Nuevo Mundo, es un acontecimiento demasiado notable para no atraer más seriamente nuestra atención. El descubrimiento de una tan grande parte de la tierra es y será siempre para el género humano, el acontecimiento más memorable en sus anales; pero para nosotros que somos sus habitantes, y para nuestros descendientes, es un tema de suma importancia.

El nuevo mundo es nuestra Patria, su historia es la nuestra, y es en ella que todos nuestros deberes esenciales, nuestros más caros intereses nos obligan a examinar y a considerar atentamente el estado de nuestra presente situación y las causas que en ella más han influido, para resolvernos luego, con pleno conocimiento, a tomar valientemente el partido que nos dictarán nuestros indispensables deberes hacia nosotros mismos y nuestros sucesores. (Viscardo 1998, I: 205)

Brothers and fellow countrymen!

Our proximity to the events, four centuries after our ancestors began to settle in the New World, is too important to be ignored. The discovery of such a large part of the earth is and always will be the most memorable event in the annals of mankind; but for those of us who are its inhabitants and for our descendants, it is an extremely important issue.

The New World is our homeland, its history our own, and it is because of this that our fundamental duties and our dearest interests oblige us to examine and consider the state of our present situation, and the causes that have had the greatest influence on it, to help us to decide to adopt the position dictated by our duty to both ourselves and our successors.

The text is vibrant, its arguments valid. America belongs to the descendants of its discoverers, in other words the *criollos*, who recognize it as their homeland, independent from Spain. Later on, Viscardo specifically emphasizes legal reasons ("Al haberse frustrado las legítimas esperanzas y derechos de los conquistadores . . ." 'Once the legitimate hopes and rights of the conquerors had been frustrated . . .' [Viscardo 1998, 206]), yet he also adds financial reasons:

Los impuestos del gobierno [colonial], los derechos del ministerio, y la codicia de los mercaderes autorizados a ejercer el más desenfrenado monopolio, poniéndose de acuerdo para saciarse mediante los sobreprecios al valor legítimo de las mercancías, era, pues, inevitable que la escasez no dejara opción al comprador, y como esta tiranía mercantil podía obligarnos a recurrir a nuestro trabajo para proveer a nuestras necesidades, el gobierno tomó la precaución de encadenarlo. (Viscardo 1998, 207)

[With] the [colonial] government's taxes, the rights of the ministry and the greed of the merchants authorized to organize an unbridled monopoly, making agreements to satiate themselves through surcharges on the legitimate value of the merchandise, it was obviously inevitable that these shortages would leave buyers no other option, and through this commercial tyranny, they would be able to force us to resort to our work to supply our needs, and therefore the government took the precaution of putting an end to it.

For Viscardo, looking at Spain from England or Italy, its dependence on overseas production was obvious and created a problem of high prices in Latin America, where prices rose in accordance with state controls (which favored the Spanish trade guilds). This attack on the failing monopoly of the eighteenth century served as a preamble to an analysis of the economy within the Peruvian viceroyalty: "Por respeto a la humanidad y a nuestra nación, vale más silenciar los horrores y vivencias del otro comercio exclusivo, (conocido en el Perú con el nombre de repartimiento) que se atribuyen los corregidores y Alcaldes Mayores, para la desolación de los desdichados Indios y Mestizos en particular" ("Out of respect for mankind and our nation, it is better to silence the horrors and experiences of that other exclusive trade (known in Peru as *repartimiento*) claimed by the chief magistrates and mayors to the desolation of the unfortunate Indians and *mestizos* in particular") (Viscardo 1998, 199). Here the author is referring to the compulsory sale of mainly unnecessary articles to the indigenous population in order to force them into debt and then collect these debts in the form of labor or the illicit appropriation of common land.

Added to these abuses was the fact that the Latin Americans were overlooked when it came to the exercise of authority over their own homeland, since the most important posts were reserved for the Spaniards. Viscardo reminds the rulers of the humiliation suffered two centuries earlier, when the father of Philip II arrived in Spain with a foreign court that he imposed on the environment of the Catholic monarchs: "¿Acaso no sufrieron los españoles un amargo descontento cuando algunos flamencos, súbditos como ellos de Carlos V y además compatriotas de él, ocuparon algunos puestos públicos en España?" ("Did not the Spaniards experience bitter discontent when certain Flemish, subjects, like themselves, of Charles V and moreover his fellow countrymen, occupied certain public posts in Spain?") (Viscardo 1998, 207). To the legal arguments, such as the legitimate inheritance line from conquistadors to *criollos*, and commercial arguments, such as the monopoly and *repartimiento*, Viscardo adds a third group of reasons, which to a certain extent explains the oppression of the Indians and *mestizos*. Quoting El Inca Garcilaso, he uses a short tale of the laments:

de una india [que fue] a visitar [a] su hijo, que estaba en la cárcel; supo que era de los condenados a tormento. Entró como pudo donde estaba el hijo, e en voz alta dijo: . . . Todo lo cual [tormentos y ejecuciones de Tupac Amaru I y sus seguidores, acusados de sublevarse contra el rey] permitía el Pachacámac por los pecados de las madres, que fueron traidoras a su Inca y a sus caciques y señores, por amor de los españoles. (Garcilaso 1962, IV:1161)

of an Indian woman [who went] to visit her son in prison; she knew that he had been sentenced to torture. She somehow made her way in to see her son and in a loud voice said: . . .
"Pachacámac allowed everything [the torments and executions of Tupac Amaru I and his followers, accused of rebelling against the king] because of the sins of the mothers, who had betrayed their Inca and his lords and chieftains out of love for the Spaniards."

The text is skillfully used by Viscardo to place the rights of the *criollos* over those of the *mestizos* and Indians. If one closely examines this statement, a mother's desperate plea to the god Pachacámac (whom Garcilaso classifies as the creator of the universe) lends a note of resignation to the suffering of the Indians and *mestizos*. Here the women's sin has foundational associations or, as the psychoanalysts would say, suggests a primal image. In an earlier paragraph, the sixteenth-century writer has the same person say: "pues los querían matar con tanta razón y justicia como decían que tenían para matarlos; [a los seguidores de Tupac Amaru I] que matasen también a sus madres, que la misma pena merecían por haberlos parido y criado y ayudado a sus padres, los españoles (negando a los suyos propios) a que ganasen aquel Imperio"

("Well, if they had as much right to kill them as they said they had [the followers of Tupac Amaru I] they should also kill their mothers for having borne and raised them and helped their fathers, the Spaniards–denying their own fathers–to win that Empire") (Garcilaso 1962, IV:1161).

This argument is completed in another of Viscardo's texts, *Esbozo político sobre la situación actual de América española*. In it he devotes a few paragraphs to the "lazos que unen las diferentes clases" ("links that bind the different classes"), referring to the "Estado de la sociedad entre las diferentes clases de los habitantes de las colonias" ("state of the society between the various classes of the inhabitants of the colonies"). He claims that there are significant reasons that bind the whites born in Latin America to the Indians:

> La primera de ellas es la necesidad que se tiene de estos últimos, que cumplen todas las ocupaciones subalternas de la Sociedad, desde el cuidado de los rebaños y el ejercicio de todos los oficios necesarios, hasta el trabajo doméstico. La segunda es la cordialidad natural, para con hombres con los cuales se ha crecido desde la infancia, cuya lengua hablan, cuyas costumbres conocen hasta adoptan algunas de ellas. Exceptuando aquellos criollos que han tenido nodrizas negras en los países donde había pocos indios, el resto ha sido amamantado por indias; ya se sabe cuánto afecto se conserva por aquellas mujeres de quien se reciben los tiernos y esforzados cuidados de los que las madres se excusan; afecto superado por el de las indias hacia sus niños de pecho, que llegan a preferir a sus propios hijos. (Viscardo 1988, 85)

> The first of these is the need they have of the latter, who hold all the minor positions in society, from the care of flocks and the exercise of all the necessary trades to domestic work. The second is the natural cordiality toward men with whom they have been raised since infancy, whose language they speak and whose customs they are so familiar with that they eventually adopt some of them. With the exception of a few *criollos* who have had black wet nurses in countries where there were few Indians, the rest have been suckled by Indian women; and their affection toward these women, from whom they received the tender care their mothers declined to give them, is well-known, as is the affection of the Indian women toward the children they have suckled, whom they prefer over their own offspring.

This is a fascinating text. First of all, in the ideal government of the Indies, Spaniards (or newly arrived Spanish immigrants) were overlooked because of their lack of relations with the Indians, relations that would have ensured their absolute loyalty. One should recall that many of Viscardo's writings were based on the revolt of Tupac Amaru II, the Indian chieftain José Gabriel Condorcanqui, whose warlike actions in 1780 kept the colonial government in check. From a distance, Viscardo regarded the uprising as the perfect opportunity for an intervention by the British Crown. The defeat and death of Condorcanqui meant that this incident was no longer used as a main plot device, although the idea of poor relations between Europeans and Indians continued in his narrative. Any future emancipation strategy would have to include the vast Indian population, although it also would have to be situated at a level where it did not compete with the legitimacy of the *criollos*. From this point of view, the future social conformation of the former colonies would have to emphasize a different type of link between the *criollos* destined to rule and the Indians, whose role as servants had already been predetermined. It is at this point that the conjunction of the link with the wet nurses and the aforementioned curse of their god Pachacámac

emerges. Who better than the *criollos* to understand the Indians? They shared the same mothers and were given first share of the same milk. They had no exploitative past, like the Spaniards, nor was there any doubt as to their humanity, as in the case of the Africans and their descendants. In other words, the *criollos* were their natural lords. The *mestizos* did not make up a clearly defined social state: If they were raised in Indian villages, they were indistinguishable from Indians. If they belonged to and were regarded as part of white families, then they would be part of the *criollo* group. Exceptions made the rule: There was no set of ideas proclaiming the self-identification of *mestizos* as an autonomous entity. In Viscardo's view, they could not govern Latin America as a group. Reading between the lines, one might also say that they bore the guilt attributed to their Indian mothers, and, in the last analysis, Indians and *mestizos* seem to have been interchangeable in the author's mind.

No ideological proposal would be complete without an immediate plan of action. Viscardo expresses this openly:

> Mi opinión resuelta es que el primer éxito de una expedición en el gran Mar del Sur, decidiría la suerte de toda América Española y he dicho también en mi precedente escrito, lo que siento sobre la fuerza de las circunstancias que convendrían para asegurar indefectiblemente el éxito: y esperando para la dicha de mi Patria que esta combinación pueda tener lugar, yo desearía que la aparición de la escuadra inglesa sobre las costas de Chile, siguiera muy de cerca las primeras noticias que se pudiera recibir de la declaración de la Independencia, para prevenir y obstaculizar las medidas del gobierno Español, e inclinar a los más indecisos hacia la libertad. Porque de un lado verían que Inglaterra actúa bien, y por otro lado, que es menester no rechazar las ofertas ventajosas del más fuerte. (Viscardo 1988, 97)

> It is my firm belief that the first success of an expedition in the great Sea of the South will decide the fate of all Spanish America and I have also said in my previous writing what I feel about the force of circumstances that should be in place to guarantee success; and, in the hope that this combination may occur, for the benefit of my homeland, I would wish that, on the arrival of the English squad on the coast of Chile, they should closely follow the first news of the declaration of Independence, in order to prevent and hinder any measures by the Spanish government, and nudge the undecided toward freedom. Because, on the one hand they would see that England behaves well and, on the other, they would see that it is essential not to reject the offers of those with the upper hand.

The visionary's dreams were sometimes extraordinarily specific: "la escuadra inglesa, ostentando regocijo y triunfo, pabellón blanco enarbolado, y al son de la música militar, entraría en la bella bahía de Concepción [Chile]; y apenas fuera posible, el Jefe de la Escuadra, enviaría una Diputación solemne al Gobernador y a la Magistratura de la ciudad, para anunciar a ambos la Independencia" (Viscardo 1988, 97) ("The English squad, rejoicing in their triumph, hoisting their white flag, and to the sound of military music, would enter the beautiful Bay of Concepción [Chile], and as soon as possible, the Squad Leader would send a solemn Delegation to the Governor and the Magistracy of the City, to announce Independence to both of them"). It is hardly surprising that Miranda should have been dazzled by Viscardo's writing. In 1806, the same year that the Venezuelan worthy was foundering in his country, Sir Home Popham and Lord Beresford disembarked in Buenos Aires to wrench the city from Spanish rule. To the invaders' surprise, the *criollo* and Spanish residents, organized under the French soldier Santiago Liniers (who had fought for Spain since 1775), defeated the British, taking Beresford prisoner. The following year another British expedition, six times larger than the previous one, seized Montevideo but was rebuffed with heavy losses when it attempted to recapture Buenos Aires. This reconfirmed the *criollos'* decision to be the source of their own emancipation. In Argentina, the defeat of the British proved that they could do the same. Spain was unable to resist the attacks of the colonies that had single-handedly driven back the most powerful seafaring force in the West.

It is not surprising that the lack of contact with his homeland, together with his European version of world events, should have driven Viscardo to think in the same way as Miranda and the British military leaders did later. Yet his opinion of the *criollo* group was essentially accurate, since he eventually achieved a form of emancipation that suited his immediate interests. The almost pamphleteering nature of his writings also reflects the stereotyped view of Indians, *mestizos*, and those of African descent who belonged to a society that would be different–that is, liberated–only for the *criollos*. His style is so convincing that it is easy to overlook the content of his proposal, which embodied nineteenth-century American ideals, the beginnings of which marked the end of the Spanish empire.

Translation by Suzanne D. Stephens

Works Cited

Adorno, Rolena. 1989. *Cronista y príncipe: La obra de don Felipe Guamán Poma de Ayala.* Lima: PUC.

Aldrete, Bernardo. 1606. *Del origen y principio de la lengua castellana o romance.* Roma: Carlo Vulliet.

Barreda Laos, Felipe. 1934. *Vida intelectual del virreinato peruano.* Lima: Universidad Nacional Mayor de San Marcos.

Basadre, Jorge, ed. 1938. *Literatura inca.* Biblioteca de Cultura Peruana. Paris: Desclée de Brouwer.

Betanzos, Juan de. 1987 [1551]. *Suma y narración de los Incas.* Ed., trans. María del Carmen Martín Rubio. Madrid: Ediciones Atlas.

Bouysse-Cassagne, Thérèse. 1997. "De Empédocles a Tunupa: evangelización, hagiografía y mitos." *Saberes y memorias de los Andes.* Ed. Thérèse Bouysse-Cassagne. Lima: Credal-IFEA. 157–212.

Cabello Valboa, Miguel. 1951 [1586]. *Miscelánea Antártica.* Lima: Instituto de Etnología. Universidad Mayor de San Marcos.

Carvajal y Robles, Rodrigo. 1950 [1632]. *Fiestas de Lima por el nacimiento del príncipe Baltasar Carlos.* Sevilla: Consejo Superior de Investigaciones Científicas. Escuela de Estudios Hispanoamericanos.

Cervantes, Miguel de. 1960. *Obras completas.* Madrid: Aguilar.

Cisneros, Luis J. 1987. "La polémica Faría-Espinosa Medrano: Planteamiento crítico." *Lexis* 11.1:1–62.

Duviols, Pierre. 1997. "La interpretación del dibujo de Pachacuti-Yamqui." *Saberes y memorias en los Andes.* Ed. Thérèse Bouysse-Cassagne. Lima: Credal-IFEA. 101–15.

Elliott, John H. 1977. *Imperial Spain 1469–1716.* New York: New American Library.

Ercilla y Zúñiga, Alonso de. 1993 [1569]. *La Araucana.* Ed. Isaías Lerner. Madrid: Ediciones Cátedra.

——. 1945. *The Araucaniad: A Version in English Poetry of Alonso de Ercilla y Zúñiga's "La Araucana."* Trans. Charles Maxwell Lancaster and Paul Thomas Manchester. Nashville: Vanderbilt University Press.

Espinosa Medrano, Juan de. 1982. *Apologético.* Ed. Augusto Tamayo Vargas. Caracas: Biblioteca Ayacucho.

Esquivel y Navia, Diego de. 1980 [c. 1740]. *Noticias cronológicas de la gran ciudad del Cuzco.* Lima: Fundación Ltdo. Augusto N. Wiese.

Fernández de Castro y Bocangel, Gerónimo. 1725. *Elisio peruano: Solemnidades heróicas, y festivas demostraciones de júbilos.* Lima: Francisco Sobrino Impresor del Santo Oficio.

Garcilaso de la Vega, El Inca. 1991 [1609]. *Comentarios Reales de los Incas.* Lima: Fondo de Cultura Económica.

——. 1962 [1616]. *Historia General del Perú: Segunda Parte de los Comentarios Reales.* 4 vols. Lima: Universidad Nacional Mayor de San Marcos.

González Carré, Enrique, Jorge Cosmópolis, Jorge Lévano. 1996. *La ciudad inka de Vilcashuamán.* Lima: Universidad Nacional de San Cristóbal de Huamanga.

González Holguín, Diego. 1989 [1608]. *Vocabulario de la lengua general de todo el Perú llamada lengua quichua o del Inca.* Lima: Universidad Nacional Mayor de San Marcos.

González Pujama, Laura, ed. 1982. *El libro del Cabildo de la Ciudad del Cuzco.* Lima: Instituto Riva Agüero.

Guamán Poma de Ayala, Felipe. 1980 [1615]. *El primer nueva corónica y buen gobierno.* Ed. John Murra and Rolena Adorno. Mexico City: Siglo XXI.

Guibovich, Pedro. 1982-83. "Documentos inéditos para la biografía de Espinosa Medrano." *Boletín del Instituto Riva Agüero* 12:137–45.

Hernández, Max. 1991. *Memoria del bien perdido: Identidad, conflicto y nostalgia en El Inca Garcilaso de la Vega.* Madrid: Quinto Centenario.

Hidalgo, Jorge. 1984. "The Indians of Southern South America in the Middle of the Sixteenth Century." *The Cambridge History of Latin America.* Ed. Leslie Bethell. Cambridge: Cambridge UP. 1:91–117.

Jákfalvi-Leiva, Susana. 1983. *Traducción, escritura y violencia colonizadora: Un estudio de la obra del Inca Garcilaso.* Syracuse: Maxwell School of Citizenship and Public Affairs, Syracuse University.

León de Portocarrero, Pedro. 1958. *Descripción del virreinato del Perú, crónica inédita de comienzos del siglo diecisiete.* Ed. Boleslao Lewin. Rosario: Universidad Nacional del Litoral.

Lockhart, James. 1992. "Three Experiences of Culture Contact: Nahua, Maya and Quechua." *Mester Literary Journal of the Graduate Students of the Dept. of Spanish. University of California, Los Angeles* 21.2:5–21.

Lohmann Villena, Guillermo. 1941. *Historia del arte dramático en Lima durante el Virreinato.* Lima: Universidad Católica del Perú.

López de Gómara, Francisco. 1993 [1555]. *Historia general de las Indias.* Lima: Comisión Peruana del V Centenario del Descubrimiento de América.

Martínez Compañón and Baltazar Jaime Bujanda. 1978 [1778–1788]. *La obra sobre Trujillo del Perú en el siglo XVIII.* Madrid: Ediciones Cultura Hispánica.

Millones, Luis. 1998. *De la evangelización colonial a la religiosidad popular peruana: El culto a las imágenes.* Sevilla: Fundación El Monte.

——. 1997. *El rostro de la fe: Doce ensayos sobre religiosidad andina.* Sevilla: Universidad Pablo de Olavide y Fundación El Monte.

——. 1995. *Perú colonial.* Lima: Fondo Editorial de COFIDE.

——. 1993. "El disfraz del Inca: La dramatización del pasado en los desfiles indígenas coloniales." *De la escucha a la interpretación en el Perú de hoy.* Ed. Moisés Lemlij. Lima: Biblioteca Peruana de Psicoanálisis. 118–44.

——. 1979. "Los dioses de Santa Cruz (comentarios a la crónica de Juan de Santa Cruz Pachacuti Yamqui Salcamaygua)." *Revista de Indias* 155–158:123–61.

Miró Quesada, Aurelio. 1994. *El Inca Garcilaso.* Lima: Pontificia Universidad Católica.

Mugaburu, Josephe and Francisco Mugaburu. 1935. *Diario de Lima (1640–1694). Crónica de la época colonial.* Lima: Consejo Provincial de Lima.

Paredes, Julián de. 1973 [1681]. *Recopilación de leyes de los reynos de las Indias mandadas imprimir y publicar por Carlos II.* Ed. Julián de Paredes. Madrid: Ediciones Cultura Hispánica.

Paredes, M. Rigoberto. 1976. *Mitos, supersticiones y supervivencias populares de Bolivia.* La Paz: Biblioteca de Sesquicentenario de la República.

Rodríguez Marín, Francisco. 1911. *El "Quijote" y Don Quijote en América.* Madrid: Librería de los Sucesores de Hernando.

Rostworowski, María. 1998. *Historia de Tahuantinsuyo.* Lima: Instituto de Estudios Peruanos.

Santa Cruz Pachacuti Yamqui Salcamaygua, Joan de. 1993 [1613]. *Relación de antigüedades deste reyno del Pirú.* Cuzco: IFEA y C.E.R.A. "Bartolomé de las Casas."

Simmons, Merle E. 1998. "Más en torno a las estadías de Viscardo y Guzmán en Londres." Lecture, Coloquio "El hombre y su tiempo: Juan Pablo Viscardo y Guzmán." Lima: 14–15 December.

Tamayo Vargas, Augusto. 1993. *Literatura peruana.* Lima: Peisa.

Valdivia, Pedro de. 1986 [1545–1552]. *Cartas de la relación de la conquista de Chile.* Santiago de Chile: Editorial Universitaria.

Vargas Ugarte, Rubén. n.d. *Jesuitas peruanos desterrados a Italia.* n.p. n.p. 1967? 2nd ed. Lima, n.p.

———. 1965. *Historia de la Compañía de Jesús en el Perú.* 4 vols. Burgos: Imprenta de Aldecoa.

Viscardo y Guzmán, Juan Pablo. 1998. *Obra completa.* Lima: Edición del Congreso del Perú.

———. 1988. *Obra completa.* Ed. Percy Cayo Córdova. Lima: Banco de Crédito del Perú.

Zuidema, Tom. 1997. "Pachacuti, Yamqui andino." *Saberes y memorias de los andes.* Ed. Thérèse Bouysee-Cassagne. Lima: Credal-IFEA. 115–25.

CHAPTER 19

SOCIAL HISTORY OF THE LATIN AMERICAN WRITER

Mario J. Valdés

The starting point of a social history of writers is to situate these cultural participants within the specific socioeconomic conditions in which they have worked and lived. To do so in no way diminishes the consideration of their function in producing the cultural imaginary; it simply situates this production. Why should it matter how and from what a writer lives as long as the texts he or she produces are significant? Some writers have not had to concern themselves with questions of livelihood because of their economic status in society; others have earned their living as clerks, salesmen, government employees, or more often than not in recent times, in journalism. Only a few highly successful writers actually live from their writing, and this has been so only in the last half of the twentieth century in Latin America. A writer's socioeconomic status defines his or her place in everyday life, but it does not determine a writer's place in literary culture. This dual participation in society is almost endemic to being a writer: a person who can be both marginal and culturally central to society. These general observations will serve as an introduction to the task at hand. The writers' social situation is far more complex than any literary history has heretofore considered. This omission is partially explained by the multiple factors that have to be considered, but also because of a long-standing bias against such considerations.

From an anthropological perspective the role of the writer in society is that of a cultural mediator. Individually or collectively, writers address the lettered sector of the community; they may do so in their own name or anonymously. Writers deal in values, images, ideas that have been appropriated for the specific topic of their discourse. Literary mediation is especially powerful because it carries both the possibility of the transmission of information and the skills to engage the reader's imagination and thus increase the likelihood of influencing the reader's course of action. The social and political configuration of the writer's discourse is itself a social construct made up of numerous mediations criss-crossing the population and including such varied sources as sermons, teachers' lessons, politicians' speeches, and, increasingly in the last two hundred years, the discourse of writers of fiction as well as the orality of everyday life. In the present political climate, writers are especially vulnerable since the ideological position of the writer is particularly exposed and thus subject to institutional

disapproval, exile, and even death. Although institutional attacks on writers have increased in the second half of the twentieth century, violence against writers has a long record, especially in Argentina, Brazil, Chile, and Uruguay.

Some examples taken from the beginning of journalism in Argentina can best illustrate the mediating function of writing and its dangers. One of the first of numerous short-lived newspapers printed in Buenos Aires was *Mártir o libre* (1812). It was written and published by Bernardo Monteagudo on an irregular basis, not only because of a lack of funds, but primarily because of censorship by the authorities. He printed the French Revolution's Declaration of the Rights of Man and advocated independence and a republican form of government. *Amigos de la patria* was published from 1815 to 1825 by Felipe Serrillosa. This publication was political in nature but also offered information and opinion on the cultural issues of the day. Although Serrillosa's paper was more restrained than *Mártir o libre,* it was soon the target of angry opposition from an extreme conservative Catholic paper, *Amigo de Dios y de los hombres* (which only lasted one year, 1824). The author of the editorials was anonymous. *El censor* (1812–1817) was published by Vicente Pazos Silva and José Pedro Agelo. This paper made no attempt to be anything other than a place for political debate. It ended after five years when both editors had to flee Argentina. A more moderate political paper was *El desengaño* (1816), a pro-independence Catholic newspaper. The other countries of Latin America also experienced a pronounced expansion of journalism in the early nineteenth century as part of the independence movement. The extraordinary growth in numbers and the increasing size of newspapers in the decades following independence demonstrate the communication vacuum in Colonial Latin America. Following the wars of independence, poetry and fictional narrative gradually took over a larger part of the daily or weekly newspaper. By midcentury, most of the major writers first reached their public through newspapers and only later through book publication. One of the reasons why the social history of Latin American writers is so badly served has been the almost complete social decontextualization of literary histories, which, with very few exceptions, have ignored the explosive consequences of the semiprofessional writer of occasional pieces moving toward professional status by the end of the century. The entire makeup of society changes when a class of mediators enters into the social discourse on a continuing basis of engagement.

The diverse schema that literary history uses to organize and classify writers are often quite oblivious to historical reality. For example, every literary history conventionally classifies Amado Nervo (1870–1919) as a *Modernista* poet, a follower of Manuel Gutiérrez Nájera (1859–1895), friend of Rubén Darío (1867–1916), Leopoldo Lugones (1874–1938), and Guillermo Valencia (1873–1943), whose poetry–"Perlas negras" [1898; "Black Pearls"]; "Misticas" [1898; "Mystics"]; and "Poemas" [1901; "Poems"])–is replete with French symbolist influences and generally move into the intimist mode of poetry so valued by the *Modernistas*. It is also usually noted that Nervos's significant books were written in the last ten years of his life, that is, from 1909 to 1919: *En voz baja* [1909; *In a Low Voice*], *Serenidad* [1914; Serenity], *Elevación* [1917; Elevation], *Plenitud* [1918; Plenitude], and *El estanque de los lotos* [1919; The Pool of the Lotus]. His *Amada inmóvil* [Immobile Beloved] was published posthumously in 1922. But consider how different this writer's cultural participation becomes when it is situated socially, economically, and politically. These ten extraordinary years from 1909 to 1919, when he wrote such intimate, gentle poetry, were also the years of the most violent and widespread destruction Mexico had ever experienced. The Mexican revolution of 1910 was raging at its bloodiest level in 1914, when Amado Nervo wrote *Serenidad*. The explanation lies not in any hermetic way of life but rather in the fact that, from 1905 to his death, he was in the diplomatic service, first of the Porfirio Díaz government and subsequently of all the transitional governments that followed in Mexico. He served in Madrid from 1905 to 1918. His life in Madrid was a haven of normality, far from the turmoil and bloodshed of his country. Yet he was not unaware of what was going on in Mexico. His poetry was certainly made possible because of his situation in Madrid, but in a much deeper sense the poetry was a response to the turmoil that was to ravage Mexico for almost nineteen years and about which he read from a distance. He died in Montevideo before the fighting ended. Pancho Villa was assassinated that same year, 1919, in order to pave the way for the next strongman with national power, Plutarco Elías Calles. This contextualization does not make the poetry better in any formal sense, but it does put it in another light in terms of the historical development of Mexico's literary culture (Sasso 73–76).

In this section I have two limited goals: to trace the professionalization of the writer in Latin America and to describe the diversity of the mediating function of the writer in society. Both aspects are central to the transition of Latin American cultural discourse from the long Colonial period to modernity. There are, of course, some philosophical assumptions behind this exposition, foremost of which is the idea of literary culture. My approach to literary culture is derived from key concepts developed by Paul Ricoeur and Pierre Bourdieu. In *Time and Narrative* (1984), Ricoeur introduces the idea of the prefigurative as a matrix of cultural discoursivity and, in *Distinction* (1979), Bourdieu develops the concept of habitus, in which the agent operates as a producer of cultural goods. He avoids both the trap of dehumanizing structuralism and the subjective morass of the decontextualized artist as creator. The agent, in our case, the writer, is thus considered in his or her creative capacity to mediate. In agreement with Michel Foucault, I do not consider the writer's individual or collective power as one of direct action and consequence but rather as a diffused, often concealed and unquestioned way of seeing and describing the world. This diffused sense of the world is often translated by others into political power and sometimes into economic power, but in all cases the writer's mediation in the habitus has the ultimate goal of legitimation of specific ideological directions over competing ones.

The field of literary culture encompasses all the varied discoursive modes that institutions and individuals have created in order to communicate, influence, entertain, or meet the aspirations of the social group, which, of course, usually means specific target groups within the community. Bourdieu reminds us that, in terms of cultural production, there are two fields: one of restricted production for a very specific group. as, for example, the first edition of *Piedra de sol* by Octavio Paz in 1957 [*Sunstone*, 1991], which had a printing of three hundred copies, and then there is also the field of large-scale production, as, for example, Elena Poniatowska's *Octavio Paz. Las palabras del árbol* [Octavio Paz: Words of the Tree], which was published in March 1998 with a printing of 25,000 and by December of that year had been reprinted ten times. Although both of these publications serve the same target group, they do so in two different modes of mediation: One creates a view of the world; the other communicates about the person who created it. The same division between restricted and general production is also present in mass culture. The printing run of comics in Mexico varies from a modest 80,000 to 250,000 copies a week depending on the intended audience. Given such diversity of modes of production and diffusion, we must of necessity severely limit our inquiry to the two aims already presented: a history of professionalization and the description of the mediating function of the writer in historical terms. The first deals with a sense of purpose in the writers themselves as well as the relative economic value of the writing. The second target we have set for ourselves involves an analysis of the position-taking the writer engages in as he or she responds to the demands of society. We can, as we have done, analyze these objectives separately, but we must bear in mind that in reality they are one continuous struggle to make a difference within the habitus.

The preceding subsection in this history deals with the intellectual production of literary culture in the Colonial period. In this subsection we turn to the contextualization of the primary agent of literary culture–the writer. In other words, we inquire into the history of the writer as a social subject (Chanquia Franch 42–43) and, above all, the role of mediator. Cultural mediation in the polis is as necessary as the provision of food and its distribution. A city has a stomach, but it also has a head. At the end of the twentieth century, the writer has emerged as the principal cultural mediator, and not only through the printed word but more and more via television. As Latin American cultures have gradually moved from a rural and oral culture to an urban written and oral/visual one in the twentieth and twenty-first centuries, so has the role of the writer changed. Books, newspapers, and television constitute the dominant forms of cultural mediation of the early twenty-first century, with the Internet looming as a major force. Differences and similarities between writers in Latin America, the United States, France, and India are determined by the writer's situation in what Pierre Bourdieu aptly calls the market of symbolic goods.

There are, of course, local, national, and international markets for the writers' works to be considered; our principal concern here, however, is Latin America as a market.

In Latin America, until the second half of the twentieth century, there was an extremely reduced local market, an international market that was completely dominated by the literary cultures of western Europe, especially France, and almost no national market. This state of affairs was virtually the same from the Rio de la Plata region in South America to Mexico City. The typical situation is described by the narrator in Julio Cortázar's (1914–1984) "Casa tomada" [1982; "House Taken Over"] when, on Saturday afternoons, he would stroll down to the bookstores to see whether there was anything new from France; Argentine writers were considered inconsequential. Following independence from Spain and Portugal the literate society of the new republics was entirely made up of an oligarchy educated in Europe (Coimbra for Brazilians, Paris and Madrid for Spanish Americans, in general, with the Argentine elite showing a preference for London or Paris). The new Latin American nations were prime examples of underdeveloped economies plundered of their natural resources by an avaricious international capitalism without any consideration for the development of the nations it exploited. In most respects, colonialism was merely converted into a new economic neocolonialism, in which there were only profits to be had and not even a nominal concern for the economies plundered in the name of progress. The vast majority of the population of Latin America (from 80 to 85 percent, depending on the size of the African and Amerindian populations) subsisted in the most abject poverty, illiterate, and for the most part, indentured to the oligarchy.

In terms of literary culture, this was a polarized society of extreme wealth and privilege on one side and, on the other, a hopelessly deprived population. The only economic model with which it could bear comparison was that of the medieval manor with its serfs and aristocracy. But this feudal comparison soon breaks down if we take into consideration the fact that, in nineteenth-century Latin America, the bifurcation was not only economic but also racial and linguistic. As has been pointed out in other parts of this history, only in the most exceptional cases was there a syncretic flowering of literary culture produced by the cohabitation of these two cultural extremes. El Inca Garcilaso de la Vega (1539–1616), Guamán Poma de Ayala (1524?–1613), and Sor Juana Inés de la Cruz (1648–1695) are such examples.

By the mid-nineteenth century, there was a nascent middle class that was beginning to form from the chaos of the wars of Independence. Their move towards political power occurred under the ideological banner of fervid nationalism and the need for national emblems and a national cultural imaginary. The Mexican Revolution of 1910 was only the most dramatic event of what was a relentless push for power. Francisco Madero can be taken as representative of the Mexican bourgeois class's demand for political power, and Porfirio Díaz, himself of partial Amerindian linage, is representative of the strongman who stays in power as long as the oligarchy retains control of society.

In terms of a national market of symbolic goods–the writer's larger public–the development came gradually but irrevocably from the mid-nineteenth century to the first decades of the twentieth century, during which time there were writers working as active producers of a national literary culture throughout Latin America. The three requirements to turn the avocation of writing into a recognized sector of society are (1) a professional concern by both the writer and his reading public that writing be significant (which, of course, implies the presence of critics or writers writing about writing); (2) a reading public with a broader base than the displaced oligarchy or a circle of writers reading each other (which implies both the production and the distribution of books through bookstores, libraries, etc); and (3) the introduction of improved methods of printing in order to have a marketable symbolic product. Alejo Carpentier (1904–1980) narrates, in El siglo de las luces [1962; Explosion in a Cathedral, 1963] how the French Revolution sent two modern revolutionary instruments to the Caribbean: the new printing press and the guillotine, of which the printing press would prove to be the instrument that displaced the oligarchy.

These three conditions were not present until the mid-nineteenth century throughout Latin America, but by then there was no turning back. By the end of the century the Latin American continent would display a unique hybrid literary culture with an ever increasing number of participants. The social and economic value placed on writing is difficult to gauge in statistical terms, but we can discern the combination of several factors that contributed to a steady rise in value of symbolic goods. First, there was the powerful force of nationalist ideology and the need for emblematic symbolic representations of the nation; second, there was the association of writing with civilization in the European tradition; and third, in Mesoamerica and the Andean region, there remained a profound respect for the traditions of pre-Hispanic America that had survived through the oral literary culture of the survivors. In Mesoamerica there was a profound need to overcome the tragedy endured by the people when the Spanish burned their entire libraries out of ignorance and superstition. In relative terms, it was a greater loss to historical knowledge than the burning of the library of Alexandria. The very men who destroyed the codexes lived to become aware of their crime and partially, very partially, made amends by recovering some of the lost books through the transcription of what had been saved in human memory.

The Latin America of the nineteenth century had inherited a dual tradition of writing from the Colonial period, as the preceding subsection of this volume shows by demonstrating the extent and diversity of this heritage. The Brazilian scholar José Guilherme Merquior addresses the absence of a professional class of writer during the Colonial period. He sums up the situation succinctly:

> During the colonial period, the absence of socioeconomic differentiation at a notable level and the restriction of literacy to the upper classes or to those small groups that served them in a major way impeded the possibility that writers could come from any other sector of society except that of the colonial aristocracy, and consequently made it difficult for the writing of literature to achieve a professional status. Writers of literature during the colonial period formed a small conglomerate group without definition. The sporadic and nonprofessional work of these writers corresponded to the occasional nature of their public. The presentation of a literary text was not distinguishable from a religious ceremony, a public commemoration that was its pretext, and for this very reason the writer was undistinguished as such and taken for his other role in society, priest, lawyer, or government official. The sociological presence of an intelligentsia was only in evidence in the second half of the eighteenth century

under the influence of the Enlightenment; these educated persons eventually developed into intellectual circles of enlightened administrators inspired by Bourbon Spain's reformist administrations, and in time were the vanguard of nativist rebellions and finally independence. The passing of the Latin American writer from the occasional amateur tied to the oligarchy to the literary professional from a middle-class background was not to be seen until the Romantic movement and would not be established until the last years of the nineteenth century. The status of the writer in Latin America has gone hand in hand with the increase in reading public, its diversification, the development of newspapers and book publication, and the practice of financial remuneration for literary writing. (374)

The excellent summary Merquior gives of the status of the writer in the Colonial period and the rise of the professional in the late nineteenth century is certainly an important contribution to our inquiry, but there are other facets of equal importance. His corpus of writers, both from Brazil and Spanish America, is almost entirely taken from the national canons of literature, without recognizing that the canon itself is a social construct reflecting the dominant class. This blind spot in his study leads him to the following thesis: that because writers in the Romantic spirit were distanced from the collective values of society, there developed an underlying barrier between the writer in his autonomous world and society as a whole and that this barrier would inhibit the development of Latin American literary culture well into the twentieth century. I disagree with this assessment, and would point out the circularity of the argument. If one begins with a self-selected group of noninvolved writers and exclude from consideration all writers whose writing is clearly and powerfully involved with social values, one can assert that the values of the self-selected group are evidence of the generalization. Merquior's exclusions invalidate his thesis. Who are the writers who have been excluded? First and foremost among the excluded are indigenous writers, whether writing in a European language (as most of them did) or in an Amerindian one; second in significance among the excluded are the political reformers, whose didacticism earned them the disdain of the literary historian writing under the influence of the Romantic ideal of literary autonomy (Latin American literary history in both Brazil and Spanish America begins in the Romantic period), which would never acknowledge that the aestheticist concept–that art was timeless and above material reality–was a bias of the times. Writing in antiquity and throughout the Middle Ages and into the eighteenth century in Europe would certainly not exclude the idea of instructing the reader. Finally, Merquior's premise downplays narrative prose and theatre in favor of lyric poetry, thus making it possible to overlook the theatre of the Amerindians, the *Comentarios reales* [1609–1616; *The Royal Commentaries of Peru*, 1688]; the *Nueva corónica de buen gobierno* [1615; *Letter to a King*, 1978]; and so many more of the writings from the Colonial period.

Merquior's assessment of the lack of professional writers during the Colonial period is correct, but his generalization about the reasons for this situation glosses over the continuous and intense struggle to control the ideological direction of the habitus. The polar tension that we find in Latin American literary culture from the beginning of the seventeenth century is between the lettered elite, trained in Salamanca or Coimbra, and the growing *criollo* and mestizo population, whose culture was no longer European but rather increasingly a hybrid expression of a unique worldview. This was a world

that was built on the ruins of the pre-Hispanic world and that continuously modified its unquestionably European heritage. A good example of a writer who puts Merquior's thesis in doubt is Carlos de Sigüenza y Góngora (1645–1700); as we have seen in other sections of this history, he was a Jesuit, trained in his native Mexico City, and became a leading intellectual of his time. His prose writing represents the best of American Baroque; notable works in this respect are *Primavera indiana* [1668; Spring of the Indies] and the novel *Infortunios que Alonso Ramírez padeció en poder de piratas ingleses* [1690; Misfortunes that Alonso Ramírez Suffered at the Hands of English Pirates]. Another, perhaps more striking, example to support my rebuttal of Merquior was Felipe Guamán Poma de Ayala (1524?–1613) who wrote *Nueva corónica y buen gobierno* in 1612 [New Chronicle and Good Government]. This work personifies the struggle for legitimation of the American mestizo perspective as opposed to the Spanish historiographic dismissal of everything from the New World as inferior to the European civilizing influence of the Spanish administration.

In the post-independence literary cultures, both traditions would continue to grow largely in isolation of each other but heading toward eventual confrontation, a progression marked by numerous specific instances of interaction. The social reform writing of the mid-nineteenth century began with the positivist ideas of Auguste Comte, but in short order took up John Stuart Mill's liberalism, the social philosophy of Herbert Spencer, and a plethora of ideas that were related to Darwinian social evolution. Far from being a period of Romantic idealization, it was a time of social ideals, the return of social utopianism in writing and in practice. The novels of Ignacio Manuel Altamirano (1834–1893) are a good example of social utopianism in Mexican literature. The reformation of the social order and the final defeat of barbarism is the principal thesis of Domingo Faustino Sarmiento's (1811–1888) *Facundo* (1845). Somewhat later the powerful voice of reform and anti-slavery advocacy is raised in Brazil with Joaquim Nabuco's (1849–1910) writing and oratory and the leadership of Rui Barbosa (1849–1923). Both Brazilians were a significant part of the literary culture of their country and of Latin America. Their involvement with issues of social justice was central to their writing and influence.

After mid-nineteenth century, the continent-wide debates between liberal and conservative elements of society were a dominant aspect of literary culture. In South America, Domingo Faustino Sarmiento argued for the establishment of European social values in order to civilize America, while his opponent Andrés Bello (1781–1865) championed a new American spirit that had nothing to learn from Europe. In Mexico, Ignacio Altamirano went so far as to predict the demise of peninsular Spanish as a common language between Spain and its former colonies, just as Latin had lost its vitality and given way to the Romance languages. On the other side, Mexican Francisco Pimentel (1889–1942) argued for the civilizing nature of the European heritage.

Although Chateaubriand's *Atala* (1801) became the emblematic representation of Romanticism's noble savage, its irrelevance to American reality was also argued with strong conviction. In Brazil, José de Alencar (1829–1877) gave Latin America its finest response to *Atala* in his novel *O Guaraní* (1857). Alencar was a conservative writer who opposed the abolition of slavery and, in general, was a major voice in Brazil's literary culture. *O Guaraní* was an immediate success, to the point that one of the first American operas was based on this novel. Alencar's sympathetic treatment of the Amerindian earned him the reputation of being an *indianista*, but above all, he was a writer who participated in the social issues of the day. José Fernández de Lizardi's (1776–1827) *Periquillo Sarniento* (1815; *The Itching Parrot*, 1942) (see **Figure 1**) and Manuel Antonio de Almeida's (1831–1861) *Memorias de um Sargento de Milicias* (1854; *Memoirs of a Sargent of the Militia*, 1999) are usually characterized as picaresque novels, although they owe much more to the political debates in their respective countries than to *El lazarillo de Tormes* [1554; *The Excellent History of Lazarillo de Tormes*] or *Guzmán de Alfarache* [1599, 1604; *The Rogue or the Life of Guzman de Alfarache*, 1622]. In Latin America the burning issue is and has been the exploitation of the vast majority of the population by a dominant elite. This has been so since Bartolomé de las Casas (1474–1566) wrote in the sixteenth century, persisted through the nineteenth century, and is the case even today, because the problem is still in existence. In the nineteenth century, which we recognize as the time of the beginning of the professional writer, the issue was absent only in the work of the most self-absorbed poets of the Romantic period.

Figure 1.

Lithograph in Periquillo Sarniento by José Joaquín Fernández de Lizardi (1776–1827), Edition of 1842. (Courtesy John P. Robarts Library, University of Toronto)

A professional writer not only needs a large reading public but also needs other writers. This observation is so basic that we sometimes forget why it is that, when writers begin to write for publication, they gravitate to the large cultural centers. The conditions of life in the cultural centers of Latin America at the end of the nineteenth century bear comparison to those of the cultural capitals of Europe. City plans, with the exception of Rio de Janeiro, followed the familiar grid pattern introduced at the beginning of the Colonial period; but demographically the cities were quite different from their European counterparts for a number of reasons. First, the demographic makeup of the city was stratified along ethnic and linguistic lines, and there was virtually no movement between the lower and the upper strata. Second, the cost of rapid modernization in the nation was a displaced rural population living in the most abject conditions in the city. In Buenos Aires they were immigrants from Southern Europe, in Rio de Janeiro they were former African slaves, and in Mexico City they were Mexican Amerindians (Sánchez Albornoz 180–212.) Third, the reform movement, born after independence and the establishment of republican forms of government, was highly critical of the oligarchic governments, and through the expanding daily newspapers, expressed the middle-class demand for political power. This ideological conflict intensified throughout the second half of the nineteenth century. The city was the domain of the middle class and its liberal reform policies, and it was in the city that the writer became a force for political change. The Mexican revolution of 1910 began as political agitation in the press for an end to arbitrary rule that was in favor of the oligarchy. What these writers did not realize was that, once they awakened the sleeping giant of the disenfranchised, they would not be able to control the revolution until it ran its course. Writers of all political persuasions had now entered the literary culture determined to make a difference. A notable literary example that brings together all these factors is Federico Gamboa's (1864–1939) novel *Santa* (1902), with its detailed descriptions of urban poverty and exploitation in a social system built on ethnic privilege. It was written and published at the high point of the thrust for the modernization of Mexico by Porfirio Diaz's government.

There were some striking parallels between Mexico and Brazil at the end of the nineteenth century. Both countries had vast social problems because of a displaced population; both had embraced the credo of positivism as the way to solve their problems; and both nations had a vastly increased reading public in the cities, certainly in Rio de Janeiro and Mexico City. In Brazil the reading public for literature was made up of upper middle-class students and women; the older generation of men was engrossed in political debates. The notable difference that the emergence of this larger reading public introduced was that writers no longer had to attend to the tastes and values of the Coimbra-educated upper class.

The essay and the novel very rapidly became the genre of preference for younger writers who felt the need to attend to the social, economic, and political demands that Brazil as a society had to face. An offshoot of this passion for the social health of the nation was the proliferation of debate on domestic and foreign literatures, especially by French authors. Romantic fiction had run its course and had lost its younger reading public. Works of fiction with graphic descriptions of violence and exploitation in the realist-naturalist mode made an impact, if not on the general public, then certainly on the growing student population.

Throughout Latin America the issue of the brutal exploitation of the Indian and African population became paramount. Not since the *Brevísima relación de la destrucción de las Indias* [1552; *A Short Account of the Destruction of the Indies,* 1992] of Bartolomé de las Casas (1474–1566) had there been such an outcry for social justice. In Lima, Clorinda Matto de Turner (1852–1909) published *Aves sin nido* [1889; *Birds without a Nest,* 1904] and began a line of literary development that would continue through the first half of the twentieth century with writers like Alcides Arguedas (1879–1946) in *Raza de bronce* [1919; Race of Bronze]; Jorge Icaza (1906–1978) in his powerful *Huasipungo* [1934; *The Villagers,* 1951]; Gregorio López y Fuentes (1897–1966) with *El indio* [1935; *Indio,* 1937]; Ciro Alegría's (1909–1967) *El mundo es ancho y ajeno* [1941; *Broad and Alien Is the World,* 1941]; Miguel Angel Asturias (1899–1974) with *Hombres de maiz* [1949; *Men of Maize,* 1975]; José María Arguedas' (1911–1969) *Diamantes y pedernales* [1954; Diamonds and Stones] and *Los rios profundos* [1958; *Deep Rivers,* 1978]; and Rosario Castellanos's (1925–1974) *Balún Canán* [1957; *The Nine Guardians,* 1992] and *Oficio de tinieblas* [1962; *The Book of Lamentations,* 1996].

Any historical survey of the social development and political involvement of writers in Latin America cannot fail to address the special place the *Modernista* poets held at the turn of the last century—as writers, but also notably as leaders in the literary culture of the continent. They transcended national boundaries and were the catalysts for the emergence of the concept of Hispano-American literature and Hispanic–American literary culture (Jrade 137–141). It is still an interesting topic of historical research to probe into why Brazil was not involved, for linguistic barriers were easily crossed with French writings. Most of the *Modernista* generation began writing in the wake of European Romanticism; these writers were for the most part from the lower middle class, but were drawn together by a shared sense of adventure, through what they saw as the brilliant renovation of poetry created by Parnassian and Symbolist poets, especially Stéphan Mallarmé, Paul Verlaine, and Arthur Rimbaud. This was the expression of sensation in contrast to the pictorial images of Leconte de Lisle. Throughout Hispanic America the immediate effect was a sense of rebirth of the Spanish language as a cultural force, a cultivation of creative metaphors, and above all, a departure from the commonplace. Two issues interest us here. First and foremost, a common culture was created among *Modernista* writers, a concept greatly enhanced by travel throughout the continent and the leadership of poets like Rubén Darío (1867–1916); second, in social terms, poetry was taken out of the drawing room and into the streets. In a sense poetry returned to its roots in the marketplace and in the city streets, as part of the oral tradition. It became popular for the unlettered to memorize and recite poems by Rubén Darío, José Martí (1853–1895), Manuel Gutiérrez Nájera (1859–1895), and Amado Nervo (1870–1919) to a highly receptive audience. The sonorous cadence of Darío's "Marcha triunfal" ["Triumphal March"] could be heard in any village marketplace, as can be seen in García Márquez' *Otoño del patriarca* [1975; The Autumn of the Patriarch]). The images could be recondite, the verse forms unfamiliar, but the pleasure of the language of experiences removed from the quotidian fascinated an entire continent.

In one generation, the poet went from being an occasional writer of verse for the self-legitimation of the oligarchy as part of Western civilization to becoming a public figure of national pride. The *Modernista* poetry of Spanish America for the first time reversed the stream of influence coming out of Europe. Spanish American poetry had a profound effect on the direction of Spanish peninsular literature in the early twentieth century, as is clearly evidenced by the *Sonatas* of Valle Inclán (1866–1936), and the early poetry of Juan Ramón Jiménez (1881–1958). In the capitals of Latin America, poets and writers in general became cultural leaders.

The French anthropologist Roger Bastide reminds us of the obvious social web of culture that is so often ignored in literary history:

> Since everything in a culture is bound together, it suffices to modify one of its elements for that first modification to bring about others, often unforeseen, and for the whole equilibrium of society finally to be affected by it. All the sectors articulated to each other must rearrange themselves so that society will find a new equilibrium but this new equilibrium will be different from the old one. Further, at the beginning one need only influence one cultural element, which might seem relatively neutral or peripheral vis-à-vis the culture base of a people. (45)

In Hispanic America *Modernismo* brought about one of these modifications: The break-up of the Spanish empire in America was offset by the idea of a shared culture throughout the Spanish-speaking continent that was different from Europe and also different from the English-speaking north. (Comparative history is often beset with the problem of terms that change markedly from one area to another. *Modernismo* in Spanish America refers to what is usually called avant-garde literature elsewhere, whereas in Brazil the term *modernismo* is close to U.S. and British usage, although with a very heavy injection of nationalism.) The continental scope of *Modernismo* also heightened the paradox of Latin America. On the one hand, this was a continent characterized by economic underdevelopment, easy prey for North American and European powers to dominate politically and to exploit economically. Its great cultural centers, often built on the ruins of pre-Hispanic glory, were rapidly sinking into an extreme bifurcation of wealth and poverty; the rule of law existed only on paper, for the raw power of the strongman was the only authority. On the other hand, the literary culture of Latin America had a degree of depth and sophistication surpassed only in the most developed literary cultures of Europe. This paradox has been described by many, but no one expressed it more clearly and with more vigor than Justo Sierra (1848–1912) on the eve of the Mexican Revolution: Latin America is poor, he argued, its people impoverished, and its effective political structures are primitive. It is a continent plagued by racism and constantly threatened by the military and economic intervention of the United States; yet this is a continent of cultural refinement and artistic brilliance (171ff). If we add the remarks Alfonso Reyes (1889–1959) wrote in the prologue to the 1940 edition of Sierra's *The Political Evolution of the Mexican People* (1969), we can gather that Sierra's assessment was by no means isolated: "The most difficult task confronting the Latin American intellectual is to bring about a sweeping change in the conditions of work and thought" (15).

In general, the nineteenth century was a time of independence from Europe in artistic as well as political matters. There were two ways to respond: One was the postcolonial drive to outdo the mother country in linguistic creativity; the other was to break with the European conventions altogether and to turn to new, even if hybrid, creations. Brazil witnessed both responses. Two of Brazil's major works were published within three years at the turn of the century: *Don Casmurro* [1899; *Don Casmurro*, 1966] and *Os Sertões* [1902; *Rebellion in the Backlands*, 1944]. Machado de Assis's (1839–1908) *Don Casmurro* looked back to the European origins of Brazilian literature and was the culmination of a process of maturity. It was equal to or better than any novel written in Portugal in the nineteenth century. Euclides da Cunha's (1866–1909) *Os sertões* broke with Portuguese norms and became the foundational novel for Brazil's twentieth-century literary production. Only one generation separates the two writers and only three years separate the two novels, but they manifest the difference between nineteenth- and twentieth-century concepts of art and nationhood. Both writers were at the highest expression of their professional and artistic integrity. The twentieth century honored Machado de Assis, but followed Euclides da Cunha.

In Spanish America the *Modernistas*, and especially Rubén Darío, provided the same transition. In the one sense they took the European literary models and mastered and perfected them, returning them to Spain as a culminating achievement; but in another sense Rubén Darío himself, in his later years, recognized the urgent need to turn to American reality. Of course, the anti-*Modernistas* of the early twentieth century set the course for a massive turn to the uniquely bifurcated culture of Spanish America and wrote works that responded to it. The first decades of the twentieth century were years of significant growth in the intellectual sphere, especially in Buenos Aires and Montevideo. Writers had gained an independent status of importance. Writers such as the Uruguayan José Enrique Rodó (1871–1917) set the tone of a new professionalism, moderating the strong sentiments of cultural independence from both Europe and the "materialistic Yankees." It was through his efforts and like-minded thinkers that Walt Whitman, Ralph Waldo Emerson, and Herman Melville were introduced as legitimate voices of their own culture. There was a widespread aspiration on the part of a new generation of intellectuals for a new Latin America. Foremost among these writers were Alejandro Korn (1860–1936), Pedro Henríquez Ureña (1884–1946), Alfonso Reyes (1889–1959), and Leopoldo Zea (b. 1912), to mention only a few of the most notable.

In some quarters there still remained sentiments that equated poetry with beauty and the poet as one devoted to the embellishment of life. The Brazilians had a phrase that expressed this notion admirably–"poets give us the smile of society"–but by the 1920s this way of thinking was rapidly being identified with the Colonial past. The poet as social conscience had never disappeared, although this concept was notably absent from the Colonial lettered canon. In the twentieth century, the road that would lead to César Vallejo (1892–1938) was emerging throughout the continent. A good example of this hidden but unbroken tradition can be found in José Emilio Pacheco's (b. 1939) poem on the massacre of students in Tlatelolco, using the same lines with which the sixteenth-century *Cantares Mexicanos* [*Songs of the Aztecs*, 1985] responded to the destruction of Tenochtitlan.

With the reemergence of social conscience and a professional sense of place in society came the poet's political involvement. If we look closely at the full breadth and depth of Latin American writing from Bartolomé de las Casas, El Inca Garcilaso, Guamán Poma, Lizardi, Sarmiento, Altamirano, the anonymous authors of the Amerindian tradition, Machado de Assis, José Donoso (1925–1996), Gabriel García Márquez (b. 1927), Ernesto Cardenal (b. 1925), and the prolific Carlos Fuentes (b. 1928), we discover that the social concerns of Latin America not only have been constantly raised by writers, but in terms of expressive power, those concerns have been dominant. Closely allied to this social participation is the important line of utopian thinkers among Latin American writers, from the Jesuits of the Enlightenment such as Francisco Javier Clavijero (1731–1787) to writers who are virtually unknown, like Juan Nepomuceno Adorno (d. 1814) and Ignacio Manuel Altamirano (1834–1893), to others who came to be the leading writers of their day such as José Enrique Rodó or Rui Barbosa and Pedro Henríquez Ureña or Alfonso Reyes. What they had in common, from Clavijero to Reyes, was the confrontation of cultural achievement with impoverishment of life in Latin America and the imaginative configuration of a better world.

When discussing the status of the writer in Latin America, it is important to remember that literary historians from Menéndez y Pelayo to Anderson Imbert had considered Latin American writers as an extension of a European tradition. Of course, this idea rests primarily on the linguistic dominance of Spanish and Portuguese in Latin America, but it ignores the radical differences in the economic, political and especially social configuration of the American continent that speaks these languages. Angel Rama (1926–1983) understood one of the subtle but powerful results of the basic fact that the languages of Latin America resulted from a demographic shift and not by state decree: "The (Latin American writer's) work is not the mirror reflection of the writer or his demons, but rather a mediation between a writer tied to his or her public and the brutal reality of life which finds its only coherence in their writings" (21). This interpretation does not imply a political homogeneity among Latin American writers or even an ideological consensus, but rather the fact that they express a critical perspective; they are usually on the margins of power, nearly always opposed to the aggressive foreign policy of the United States, and they are above all voices of conscience rather than revolutionaries. For a geographic summary of U.S. interventions in the region, see **Figure 2**. The decades between 1920 and 1940 were years of rapid growth and industrialization in Latin America. New technology promised to change the international status of Latin America's leading nations. The exploitation of natural resources by foreign companies was now challenged by the demand to develop these raw materials at home. This was the dream from Chile to Mexico, one which led to the expropriation of foreign-owned petroleum in Mexico in 1938.

One of the fundamental theses of this literary history is that the relationship between writers and the society in which they work is a constant symbiotic process of interaction between the creative text and the critical text. Writers respond to their material and intellectual context through their work. It is in this light that we must consider Latin American surrealism. It was much more than a creative credo; it was above all, in Latin America, a powerful response to the excesses of Positivist rationalism in the early years of the century. Literary critics throughout the 180 years of post-Colonial literary criticism have been forever trying to do the

Figure 2. U.S. Interventions in Mexico, Central America, and the Caribbean.

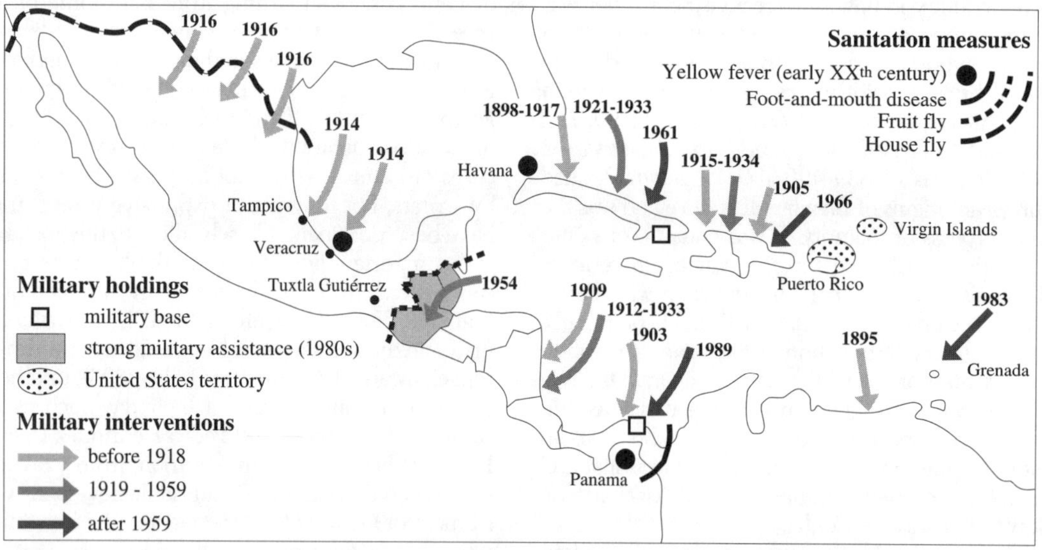

impossible: to impose critical closure on texts that nevertheless are always open to the creative reading of new and unforeseen readers. But the labor of criticism is not in vain, for although critics cannot close off the text, they often do open the minds of writers to new interpretations of their creative work, interpretations of which they have never dreamed. There can be no doubt that the literary text belongs to the reader, just as the act of writing is the property of the writer, but the making of the writer is situated in the social context, and it is this collective participation of writers in society that creates the cultural imaginary and gives meaning to the term "Latin American literature."

In cities such as Montevideo, Buenos Aires, Santiago, Rio de Janeiro, Bogotá, Lima, and Mexico City, the leading writers have turned towards the basic issues of cultural identity so aptly expressed in Oswald de Andrade's (1890–1954) *Manifesto Antropofago* [1928; Anthropophagic Manifesto]. For a short time it appeared as if poetry would lose its cutting edge and become an autonomous expression of individual genius; this period was known as Modernism in Brazil and the Avant-garde in Spanish America. But it is now evident that a literature of introversion in a continent like Latin America can only be short-lived. The problems of daily life and the ambitions of world powers are far too great to allow such movements to prosper and continue beyond a single generation. After World War II in Europe and Asia, Latin America once again was beset by a prolonged period of U.S. intervention. Guatemala, the Dominican Republic, Chile, El Salvador, and Panamá are only the most obvious examples. The result was a series of civil wars, uprisings, or military takeovers throughout the continent; as the northern neighbors exercised their domination in what was now recognized as the United States' "legitimate" sphere of influence. Writers were now at the very center of global politics.

The crisis in Latin America can be compared to the struggle for Irish independence; but in Latin America it is more complicated, for independence from the economic influence of the United States, even if American politicians ever adopted a noninterventionist policy, is possible only through the slow death of economic strangulation, as the Cuban

embargo demonstrates. Yet, in 1959, it did not look that way. Writers from all parts of Latin America joined in the celebration of the triumph of the Cuban overthrow of the Batista government. The failure of Castro's Cuba to realize its goals has led to the backlash against the left and the brutal reprisals of the right. Guerrilla movements in Argentina, Brazil, Uruguay, Colombia, Central America, and Mexico have created the most extensive ideological split amongst writers in Latin American history. There is no room for any middle ground. The military dictatorships in South America, the prolonged civil wars in Central America and Colombia, and the Tlatelolco massacre in Mexico have changed the face of Latin America. The euphoria of the 1960s ended in a bloodbath. Out of the political turmoil, new literary genres were born; others were forgotten. The testimonial took on literary sophistication in Elena Poniatowska's (b. 1933) *Noche de Tlatelolco* [1971; *Massacre in Mexico*, 1975]; poetry of social protest became poetry of cultural refiguration in the hands of José Emilio Pacheco; the novel of urban youth was taken over by television's dramatic series; and, all in all, wherever it was possible, Latin American journalism rose to a level of involvement never seen before.

The professionalization and the sharp increase in earnings experienced by writers in Latin America during the second half of the twentieth century resulted from two socioeconomic factors: the accelerated pace of technological modernization and the expansion of public education, which brought entire social sectors into the continent's literary culture. The popular base of the culture came into its own and opened a new market for symbolic goods on a massive scale through serialized melodramas on television and through mass printing of literature in the daily newspapers and in paperbacks. The works of such established writers like Carlos Fuentes and Juan Rulfo were suddenly available at the price of a newspaper. The rise in literacy among women, who, by then, made up a significant part of the work force, was one of the most significant changes in the literary culture. In one generation, a large new audience emerged, eager to participate and to have literature that engaged their own situation in society. Pierre Bourdieu has made an incisive comment on this kind of change in the symbolic market:

The development of the system of cultural production is accompanied by a process of differentiation generated by the diversity of the public at which the different categories of producers aim their products. Symbolic goods are a two-faced reality, a commodity and a symbolic object. Their specifically cultural value and their commercial value remain relatively independent although the economic sanction may come to reinforce their cultural consecration. (113)

What is the status of the writer in Latin America at the beginning of the twenty-first century? There are multiple answers to the question depending on which of the cultural centers is considered. However, a few generalizations are possible. Writers live and succeed anywhere if they know the public and are able to address their requirements. In my attempt to cope with diversity without imposing an ideological framework, I have combined the pragmatic concerns of the market with that of the status of specific writers who have figured significantly in that market. I do not accept the distinction between high and low culture or the notion that a writer who writes for a mass audience is inferior to one who writes for a specific group with shared discursive codes. A writer of a soap-opera script today is in no way inferior to the dramatist; nor is the writer of popular song lyrics inferior to the poet since, in many cases, they are one and the same person, as is the case of Washington Benavides (b. 1930) and his *Las milongas* [1975; The Milongas]. In his native Uruguay he is as well known for his popular ballads as for his books of poetry and criticism. I also reject as merely an example of reverse ethnocentrism the contemporary advocates of the ethnic popular over the upper-class elite. In what follows, I shall identify what I consider to be distinguishable sectors of reception in Latin America. In doing so, I recognize the danger about which Walter Benjamin warns:

> They [works of literature] teach him [the dialectical historian] how their function can outlast their creator, can leave his intentions behind; how their reception by the artists' contemporaries forms part of the effect that the work of art has on us ourselves today, and how this effect derives from our encounter not just with the work, but with the history that brought the work down to us. (351)

The implicit reductionism of categories must be weighed against the need to summarize. My categories are, therefore, market generalizations and not classifications of works and authors. The selection of writers has not been as arbitrary as one might think at first glance. I have selected some of the most widely read writers of Latin America of the three generations that have thus far left their mark on Latin American literary culture.

Latin America has at least five categories of public in its literary culture, or in Pierre Bourdieu's terms, the market of symbolic goods. Therefore, let us say that Latin America has a market with five distinct sectors and that there is fluid movement through at least some of these sectors. The first sector in the market is the oldest one: the academic intellectual one accustomed to issues of international interest treated within the history of ideas. In the past, as today, it has been served by specialized journals, books, and cultural supplements in the daily newspapers. For example, if we compare *Letras de Mexico* (see **Figure 3**) from 1939 to *Vuelta* from 1998 we find a continuous tradition of intellectual debate. This sector does not command mass readership, but it does offer maximum prestige.

Figure 3.

First page of Letras de Mexico, *15 January 1939. (Archive of the author)*

The second sector of the market consists of the educated middle class who reads what critics from the first sector consider significant or what has been positively valued in the United States and, to a lesser extent, Europe. This sector does not buy specialized journals but depends on newspaper reviews and television reports. Books in translation fill an important part of this sector of the market. A good number of persons who have standing in this sector read English, but they also buy translations.

The third sector of the market for Latin American writers is not in Latin America at all but is composed of the mostly English–but also French–language readership around the world that has access to Latin American writing only in translation. One medium for dissemination in this market is high-profile journals such as the *New York Review of Books* or *Lire*. It is noteworthy today that the novels of the leading Latin American writers appear simultaneously in Spanish, French, and English.

The fourth sector is the Latin American public that is illiterate or barely literate; as a group, they do not read much more than comics, but they do have access to the symbolic goods through television and, to a lesser extent, cinema. This very large sector is obviously influenced by developments in the first three sectors. The symbolic goods consumed by the nonreading public are never full texts but rather fragments of texts, summaries of texts in film, or television adaptations.

The fifth and final sector of the market is made up of multiple special-interest groups, such as feminist organizations, political organizations of the left and the right, and church-oriented groups that range from liberation theology to the traditional Vatican-bound church hierarchy and the evangelical Protestant groups financially supported by groups in the United States. This sector is so fragmented that it cannot control or influence the direction of literary culture, but any one of these groups can have a negative effect on specific writers. In this case, organization and single-mindedness make up for numbers. Of course, more often than not, an attack by one of these special-interest groups can have a positive reaction in other sectors of the market.

The most important point to be made is that these five sectors together make up the market of symbolic goods in Latin America, and writers, knowingly or not, must move through the conflicting thicket of special interests, partial knowledge, and specific agendas of opinion makers in the media. The most successful writers in Latin America have tried to control at least some sectors of the market, though with markedly different results. As evidence, I will give a brief summary of nine writers from three different generations and outline their participation in the various sectors of the market. First, there is the generation of Mario de Andrade (1893–1945), Jorge Luis Borges (1899–1986), and Miguel Angel Asturias (1899–1974); the next generation is that of João Guimarães Rosa (1908–1967), Octavio Paz (1914–1998), and Julio Cortázar (1914–1984); and the third generation is that of Clarice Lispector (1925–1977), Gabriel García Márquez (b. 1927), and Carlos Fuentes (b. 1928).

Mario de Andrade is the contemporary of Borges and Asturias, and he shares many of their concerns with art and culture. The avant-garde climate that they have in common has very different results in each writer, however. Mario de Andrade was a critic, poet, and, above all, a major force for change. His "Desvairista" movement in São Paulo was at the forefront of the Modernist revolution, which culminated in the Modern Art Week of 13–17 February 1922 in São Paulo. It would be an understatement to say that the week was an explosion of creativity; but, most of all, it was a death blow to the old literary order. Mario de Andrade's book of poems, *Paulicéia Desvairada* [1922; *Hallucinated City*, 1968] marks his lasting contribution to the change in direction in Brazilian literature. The most important legacy of the Modernist movement was a change in status for the writer. Afranio Coutinho puts it succinctly:

(After Modernism,) Brazilian generations tended more and more to renounce the amateur and dilettante spirit in the exercise of literature, taking on professional methods and attitudes in the conception and production of literary works. There was an end to self-teaching, improvisation, lack of method, lack of discipline, scattering, imprecision, disdain for the rules of composition or structure, including material; to a falsely romantic attitude of believing only in a telluric, instinctive inspiration, improvisation, paying no attention to the duties of apprenticeship in the trade, an attitude that in most cases tried to cover up weaknesses, theorizing by means of the error itself, as an attempt was made to change it into a general norm. This theory was typical of a milieu that had no organized intellectual life, no existence of its own, no normal agents of cultural production and distribution. Responsible for this effect was the absence of a university tradition in Brazil, with the result that the exercise of literature was marginal, a parasite on other activities, with the intellectual living in dependence to professions that were foreign to his calling: law, medicine, bureaucracy politics, and unspecialized teaching. (237–238)

The disparity that has existed between Brazil and its Spanish-speaking neighbors in terms of the status of its writers diminished rapidly after the decade of the 1920s, and the sense of a Latin American culture was thus enhanced.

Turning to the next figure to be considered, Miguel Angel Asturias is a primary representative of the *engagé* writer. He lived most of his adult life in exile. Deeply committed to the course of social justice in Guatemala, especially with respect to the Mayan population, after his student years of political activism, he traveled to Paris to continue his education. He remained in Paris for nine years, where he matured both intellectually and politically and developed what would be a lifelong dedication to the struggle for political and social rights for the Mayan majority. By the time he returned to Guatemala in 1933, he had written his first novel, *El señor presidente* (though it was not published until 1942; *The President*, 1963), as well as an early draft of *El alhajadito* [1961; *The Bejewelled Boy*, 1971] and *Hombres de maíz* [1949; *Men of Maize*, 1975] and had translated the *Popol-vuh* [*Popol-vuh: The Great Mythological Book of the Ancient Maya*, 1976] and the *Anales de los Xahil* [Annals of the Xahil]. While still in Paris he had published *Leyendas de Guatemala* [1930; Legends of Guatemala]. He managed to sustain himself during his nine years in Paris writing 440 newspaper articles for *El Imparcial*, an act that made him a lifelong enemy of the Guatemalan oligarchy. His return to Guatemala lasted twenty-one years (1933–1954) until a U.S.-supported military takeover ousted the elected president, Juan José Arévalo. Asturias remained a steadfast ideological activist for a democratic socialist government. He was awarded the Nobel Prize for literature in 1967 while in what was to be permanent exile. (He died in 1974.) In his final years, he served as ambassador of Guatemala to Spain, earning the violent opposition from the political left for his collaboration with the government. Four facts stand out in his life: his unrelenting struggle for social reform, especially as it concerned the Mayan majority of Guatemala; his long periods of exile, which were significant factors in his reflection on his literary culture; his work as a journalist, which turned out to be the means of earning a living but also the means of perfecting his skill as a writer; and, most significant of all, the fact that he was one of the leading writers of the twentieth century who were instrumental in writing the bifurcated literary culture of Latin America. His novel *Hombres de maíz* is a major contribution in this regard.

Asturias's work was written for and read by the first of the five groups I have described, the academic and intellectual group. After receiving the Nobel Prize in 1967, he gained readership in the second group of middle-class professionals and in the third group, the English language readership. The massive fourth group who made up the subject matter of his writing had scant access to his work. Some of the *Leyendas de Guatemala* have appeared in popular editions, but because of the long periods during which he was ostracized from Guatemala, his work is largely unknown on the popular level. Some specialized groups, those most concerned with the Mayan people, have valued his writings, however.

Jorge Luis Borges, born in the same year as Miguel Angel Asturias, is a study in contrast to the Guatemalan. There are, however, some important parallels. Both writers spent time in Europe as young men: Borges from 1914, when he was fifteen, until 1922, when he returned to Buenos Aires. Both writers had strong political views and paid the consequences of their commitment. Borges was dismissed from his job as a librarian for his opposition to fascism. (He was reinstated as Director of the National Library in 1955 and retired from this position in 1973.) Both writers wrote extensively for the press. But in most other respects the contrast between Asturias and Borges is great. Borges was not actively concerned with issues of social justice and was quite indifferent to the rest of Latin America, especially Amerindian America. He was a European in sentiment and culture, which is not to say that he did not have a major role in the intellectual life of Latin America. On the contrary, he was a major presence.

Although he was a poet and an essayist all of his life, his greatest impact was through the hybrid essay-short story form he created and made known around the world. In 1980 he was awarded the Cervantes Prize in Madrid. He never won the Nobel Prize and is perhaps the best- known unrewarded candidate in literary history. The books he published during the 1940s were to conquer an international readership; this is especially the case with *Ficciones* [1944; *Fictions*, 1985] and *El Aleph* [1949; *The Aleph*, 1970]. Politically, he underwent a subtle transition from an elitist social democrat to a moderate nationalist and a liberal democrat. His opposition to Juan Domingo Perón was as much social as it was political. His statements regarding the strongman were often excessive and marked the beginning of many unreflective political declarations. By the time of his death he had seen democracy restored to Argentina and he had become a dominant figure in world literature. Borges always wrote for an elite readership and gave no quarter to anything less than the intellectual reader who enjoyed the challenge of a master writer. To the middle class he was a name to be highly respected but rarely read; to the English reading public around the world he was a member of the international canon. Borges became what booksellers like to call a modern classic. He benefited from excellent translations into English and French. In 1999 the French published a Pléiade edition of his complete works to mark the hundredth anniversary of his birth. Although his work was unknown to the popular sector and he did not attract any of the special-interest groups, in a sense he did not need them. By the time of his death in 1986, his work was available in all the written literary languages of the world, and his name was on every list of major writers of the twentieth century.

The next generation was born during or just before the years of World War I in Europe and the Mexican Revolution in America. João Guimarães Rosa, Octavio Paz, and Julio Cortázar share some of the same social and political concerns but have played quite different roles in the literary culture of Latin America. João Guimarães Rosa, in contrast to Paz and Cortázar, could write only in his free time. He studied medicine and practiced for a while but eventually joined Brazil's diplomatic corps and moved up the ladder of this profession, obtaining the rank of ambassador in 1963 at the age of fifty-five; he died shortly after, in 1967. His works of literature are sparse because of his lack of time and relatively short life. His great achievement, *Grande Sertão: Veredas* [1956; *The Devil to Pay in the Backlands*, 1963] was, along with da Cunha's *Os Sertões* [*Rebellion in the Backlands*], one of the most important novels of the twentieth century in Brazil and certainly a classic of world literature. Guimarães Rosa's novel is part of Brazilian regionalism, but is much more in terms of Brazilian identity: It is a novel that narrates a specific sensitivity to life.

What separates Guimarães from Paz and Cortázar is the role of intellectual leader, which they fulfilled and which he did not achieve. Paz and Cortázar were, by all standards, writers above all else. Moreover, Guimarães Rosa's great novel is still largely confined to an intellectual and academic readership, even though it taps deeply into Brazil's popular culture and has had excellent translators.

Although Julio Cortázar was born in Brussels and died in Paris, he was nonetheless a Latin American writer. His political views were strong and constant. He supported liberation movements in Algeria, Cuba, Vietnam, Angola, Nicaragua–wherever U.S. hegemony manifested itself–but his powerful personal commitment was transcended in his creative work. In the 1950s, he went to Paris, where he would remain the rest of his life earning a living through his job as an interpreter at the United Nations Educational, Scientific, and Cultural Organization (UNESCO) headquarters. Cortázar was a writer's writer; his ideas on art, society, and literature were influenced by philosophy, especially Heidegger and to some extent Derrida. His short stories have become his major contribution to Latin American literary culture although his novel, *Rayuela* [1963; *Hopscotch*, 1967] is one of the most influential works of the 1960s. In many respects, his critical essays are an extension of his fiction. Cortázar wrote for an intellectual elite and disdained the commonplace that did not induce the reader to enter into a creative partnership. The middle-class reader was puzzled by the markedly indeterminate nature of his fiction. Cortázar has been one of the most influential writers in the development of postmodernism in Latin America. His work is not as well known in English as that of his compatriot Borges, but his ideas are of exceptional significance for literary thinking at the end of the twentieth century. His work is unknown by the nonreading public and is of scant interest to special-interest groups.

Octavio Paz, in contrast to Julio Cortázar, has been a dominant cultural figure of the last half-century in his own country and a significant voice worldwide. He was first and foremost a poet, but also an essayist of extraordinary skill and, in his later years, a television personality in Mexico. From the time he was seventeen years old in 1931 to his death in 1998, he was involved with literary journals. Some of these are *Barandal* (1931–1932), *Cuadernos del Valle de México* (1933–1934), *Taller* (1938–1941), *El hijo pródigo* (1943–1946), *Plural* (1971–1976), and *Vuelta* (1976–1998). From 1949 with the publication of *Libertad bajo palabra* [1960; Liberty under Oath], Paz's poetry has been a creative force of vast influence throughout Latin America, and from the publication of *El laberinto de la soledad* [1950; *Labyrinth of Solitude*, 1962], his essays have given him a major voice in Mexico, in Latin America by the 1970s, and in Europe and the United States from the 1980s. He was awarded the Cervantes Prize in 1982 and the Nobel Prize in 1990.

In the 1980s Paz entered into a partnership with Televisa, a dominant Mexican television network, to produce a series of popular programs on Mexico's cultural past, especially the pre-Hispanic civilizations and the long Colonial period. By the time of his death in 1998, he was a national icon of Mexico's cultural self-esteem. He penetrated all levels of society in spite of the fact that he was never a popularizer. The intellectual elite of Latin America has been his primary readership; the middle class has had access to his essays, if not his poetry, and to television documentaries that were aimed at them as the intended audience. The English and French reading public has had a plethora of editions, and his poetry has had, by and large, good translations. Even special-interest groups have been affected by his essays. Feminist groups have seen a national and international awakening of interest for women's writing during the Colonial period to a large extent because of his book on Sor Juana Inés de la Cruz. His steady stream of articles and books on pre-Hispanic art have stimulated major exhibits outside Mexico, the most notable being *Thirty Centuries of Mexican Art* at the Metropolitan Museum of Art in New York in 1988. Even the nonreading public in Mexico identifies him with the pre-Hispanic past because of the television programs he has presented.

The last generation of writers I will consider was born between 1924 and 1928. War in Europe had ended, although for what would be but an interlude, and this was a time when ideologies were launched that would eventually engulf the twentieth century: Communism after 1917 and Fascism after 1933. Both Carlos Fuentes and Gabriel García Márquez would be caught up in the international struggle; Clarice Lispector would stand outside.

Clarice Lispector (1925–1977) is unique in every respect. She was born in the Ukraine and immigrated to Brazil with her parents while still an infant. She wrote only in Portuguese and considered herself Brazilian. She studied law, married a diplomat, and lived the life of a diplomat's wife until 1959, a date that marks her return to Rio de Janeiro and the beginning of the most productive part of her literary career: *A maça no escuro* [1961; *The Apple in the Dark*, 1967], *A Paixão Segundo G. H.* [1964; *The Passion According to G. H.*, 1988], and *Agua Viva* [1973; *Stream of Life*, 1989]. Her writing is highly personal, mystical, and concerned with questions of being and consciousness quite unlike anything else in Latin America. Her style is characterized by a rather simple vocabulary and elliptical sentences of indeterminate meaning. One has to look to other periods of history and other genres to find ties as, for example, in the writing of St. Teresa of Ávila. She has often been compared to Virginia Woolf for the rich lyrical and introspective prose they both wrote in the same years, but Virginia Woolf's intellectual reserve and highly logical way of thinking are significantly different from Lispector's intuitive and passionate search for the phenomenology of consciousness.

Clarice Lispector is today undoubtedly the most discussed Brazilian writer of the twentieth century, both inside Brazil and in Europe and North America. This unusual and extraordinary woman rejected the notion that she was an intellectual or belonged to a specific group of writers. Her status today is, in part, due to her powerful imagery; but also because her work has come to be known by an international readership within the postmodern rethinking of literature itself. Her notebooks and journals, as well as her newspaper articles, have provided us with a full profile of this writer. By 1967 Clarice Lispector ceased to consider herself an amateur and took up writing as her only profession. The brilliance of her work in the 1960s coincided with the Spanish American boom of Fuentes, García Márquez, Cortázar, and others. *A maça no escuro* and *A paixão segundo G. H.* reached a world-wide audience through excellent translations in English, French and Spanish, but her career was truncated when, not yet fifty-two, she died of cancer on 9 December 1977, three weeks after entering the hospital. There is no question that Clarice Lispector's readership is an international, intellectual elite. Academic meetings of literary scholarship are replete with papers on her work, for the most part by readers who have read her work in translation.

Carlos Fuentes is one of the most prolific and successful writers in Latin America. Beginning with *La región más transparente* [1958; *Where the Air Is Clear*, 1960], followed by *La muerte de Artemio* Cruz [1962; *The Death of Artemio Cruz*, 1964], *Cambio de piel* [1967; *A Change of Skin*, 1967], *Terra Nostra* [1975; *Terra Nostra*, 1976], *Gringo viejo* [1985; *The Old Gringo*, 1985], *Cristóbal Nonato* [1987; *Christopher Unborn*, 1989], and his most recent novel *Los años con Laura Diaz* [1999; *The Years with Laura Diaz*, 2000], to name only some of his best known works, are all aimed at intellectual readership. But Fuentes has also become a spokesman for an independent Latin America through his newspaper articles, his essays in major journals, and his television programs. In this respect, his ideas are well-known by the middle class even if his fiction is not. His novels have all been translated into English, and, together with Paz, he enjoys a privileged position among English-language readers. Carlos Fuentes is second only to Paz in the area of iconic significance in Mexico and in Latin America. His extensive engagements in leading U.S. universities have further cemented his place as a leading intellectual. Fuentes has held strong political views and has expressed them without reservation. His staunch support of the Cuban Revolution led to his being denied a visa to visit the United States from 1963 to 1969. His criticism of U.S. policy in Latin America has been immediate and without reservation. It is this aspect of his public status that is best known by the nonreading public. Carlos Fuentes, with very few exceptions, has been a writer for the intellectual and an identity figure for the general public. Many of his political concerns are reflected in his fiction, especially in the novels dealing with the Mexican Revolution and its aftermath like *La muerte de Artemio Cruz*. In his youth he was the recipient of the guidance and friendship of two of the most distinguished figures in Mexican cultural life, first from Alfonso Reyes and later from Octavio Paz.

Gabriel García Márquez shares many of Carlos Fuentes' political views and commitments, but in contrast to him, for many years he worked as a journalist, writing chronicles and reviews of cinema and literature in Bogotá, Barranquilla, and Cartagena. He began to publish short novels in the 1950s, but it was the publication of *Cien años de soledad* [1967; *One Hundred Years of Solitude*, 1970] that changed his life and work. Although the earlier novels and short stories clearly anticipate *Cien años de soledad*, the balance of the everyday and the fantastic, the delicate structures of anticipated time, and the historical subtext do not come together until his masterpiece of 1967. From that point on, his novels have all been major works of literature: *El otoño del patriarca* [1975; *The Autumn of the Patriarch*, 1975], *Crónica de una muerte anunciada* [1981; *Chronicle of a Death Foretold*, 1982], *El amor en los tiempos del cólera* [1985; *Love in the Time of Cholera*, 1988], and *El general en su laberinto* [1989; *General in His Labyrinth*, 1990]. He was awarded the Nobel Prize in 1982. In addition to his apprenticeship as a working journalist and his major works of fiction, García Márquez has also an impressive list of film scripts to his credit, including *La increíble y triste historia de la Cándida Erendira y de su abuela desalmada* [1972; *Innocent Erendira and Other Stories*, 1978], *La fábula de la bella palomera* [1983; The Fable of the Beautiful Dove-keeper], *Un señor muy viejo con unas alas enormes* [1986; A Very Old Man with Enormous Wings]. García Márquez's *Cien años de soledad* has reached all sectors of the market of symbolic goods, if not directly as a text, through its symbolic fragments. Macondo has become emblematic of Latin America and yellow butterflies of illicit love.

By the end of the twentieth century the status of the writer in Latin America has changed so radically from a century before that it is almost unrecognizable. After the 1950s, rapid economic and political changes that brought almost all of Latin America to the brink of self-destruction—military interventions in Argentina, Chile, Brazil, Uruguay, a civil war in Colombia, a guerrilla war in Peru, a massacre in Mexico, domination by the Soviets in Cuba, followed by economic strangulation by the United States, as well as the ominous presence of the United States everywhere—had finally run their course by the 1990s. But a subtle and eventually determining change in attitude emerged among Latin American writers: the defensive cultural nationalism that had characterized the attitude of writers in the first half of the century had given way to a continentwide cultural self-confidence that Latin America was neither a European nor a U.S. cultural dependency and that, above all, Latin American writing was making a significant contribution to the world's cultural imaginary. Writers like those we have reviewed have been recognized by the major awards and prizes. Five have received Nobel Prizes: Gabriela Mistral (1945), Miguel Angel Asturias (1967), Pablo Neruda (1971), Gabriel García Márquez (1982), and Octavio Paz (1990). Thirteen were awarded Cervantes Prizes from 1977 to 2003: Alejo Carpentier (1977), Jorge Luis Borges (1979), Octavio Paz (1981), Ernesto Sábato (1984), Carlos Fuentes (1987), Augusto Roa Bastos (1989), Adolfo Bioy Cásares (1990), Dulce María Loynaz (1995), Mario Vargas Llosa (1994), Guillermo Cabrera Infante (1997), Jorge Edwards (1999), Alvaro Mutis (2001), and Gonzalo Rojas (2003).

By the 1970s, the symbolic market for Latin American writers had acquired the somewhat comic but highly descriptive name of a "boom" market. In a few years the term "magical realism" would be coined to try to describe the works of Asturias such as *Hombres de maíz*, Carlos Fuentes' *La región más transparente* and *Aura* [1962; *Aura*, 1965], and, of course, García Márquez's *Cien años de soledad*, as well as Alejo Carpentier's *El reino de este mundo* [1949; *The Kingdom of this World*, 1967], José Donoso's *El pájaro obsceno de la noche* [1970; *The Obscene Bird of Night*, 1979], Ernesto Sábato's *Sobre héroes y tumbas* [1961; *On Heroes and Tombs*, 1981], Augusto Roa Basto's *Yo el supremo* [1974; *I, the Supreme*, 1986], and the work of a younger generation. It was in the 1980s that the flood of critical commentary on postmodernity discovered the heretofore little-known writing of Latin America. The French anthropologist Roger Bastide has given us some insight into the enigma of the sudden discovery of Latin American writing, especially by English-speaking criticism. From the time of the conquest it has been recognized that Latin American culture has appeared to be strange and exotic to European eyes, and we have known that its unique mutated forms and distinct refigurations of European models have been hidden to all but the foreign specialist, but all of this has changed and it has done so in one generation. Bastide outlines the clues:

The more foreign the form of a cultural trait, the further removed it is from the recipient culture and therefore the more difficult will its acceptance be, since such a cultural trait cannot be reinterpreted into the recipient culture's terms. This does not mean, however, that it may not sometime be accepted; but if it is, it will be as an imitation or addition, not as a substitution or a replacement. Briefly it remains floating on the periphery. It is not taken up—it lacks the capacity to engender profound transformation of mentalities or sensibilities. . . . A cultural trait, whatever its form

and function, will be all the better received and integrated if it can take on a semantic value which harmonizes with the field of meanings of the recipient culture. (43–44)

In short, it is not that Latin American writing has come out of nowhere; it is primarily that western Europe and the United States arrived at postmodernity at the end of the twentieth century to discover that Latin Americans were already there and had been for some time, having created a cultural imaginary that grew out of ruptures and discontinuities that Latin American writers had been forced to transcend, transgressing logocentric European paradigms in part because Latin American cultural reality is volatile and contradictory and has been so from the time Europeans first laid claim to the Americas, having assumed that they did not already have inhabitants.

Without a doubt, the global shock waves caused by the demise of the Soviet bloc have had a profound effect on Latin American writers, and not only in Cuba, where the aftershocks have been the most intense, but also in Central America and throughout the continent for a generation that had pinned its hopes for social justice on the success of the Cuban Revolution.

To most Latin American intellectuals, the fear of U.S. military and economic domination was also a threat to cultural identity. But, perhaps because of those very fears, whether they were based on fact or not, a response was engendered in the form of a strong and sustained demonstration of cultural identity. Octavio Paz, who in his later years spoke from the political center, wrote:

The market and capitalism are not the response needed to alleviate the ills of civilization. And it is for this reason that intellectuals more than ever before must be critical now that the threat of communism has gone. . . . It is necessary to keep up critical scrutiny of power, all social power, including the state, the church, and political parties. This is a responsibility that, we, the intellectuals of the twentieth century, have not always performed. Frequently some intellectuals in all our countries of Latin America have served regimes of dictators, political parties, or church administrations that preached intolerance. (Navarrete Orta 46)

In the last decade of the twentieth century, almost every writer in Latin America has taken part in the debate that attempts to heal the wounds of the post-dictator era in Argentina, Brazil, and Chile; and also in smaller countries like El Salvador, Guatemala, and Uruguay. It still remains to be seen whether the sense of responsibility called for by Paz will be realized.

Another voice from the center right is that of Mario Vargas Llosa (b. 1936) who spoke out for a common sense of mission for Latin American writers:

Literature contributes to the improvement of the human being, because it impedes spiritual recession, self-satisfaction, immobility, paralysis, the softening of the intellectual or moral stand. Its mission is to agitate, create disquiet, alarm, maintain human beings in a state of constant dissatisfaction with themselves, its function is to stimulate without rest the will to change and better the world even when it must use the most painful of weapons, words. (353)

Alfredo Bryce Echenique (b. 1939) argues that the Latin American writer at the end of the twentieth century has restored the dream of Simón Bolívar and brought Latin America together through the plenitude of its literature. He writes that, in denial of Heidegger's idea that language is the dwelling place of being, in Latin America language had distanced itself from the reality of the continent because of its extreme nationalisms and had thus wasted the only positive legacy of Colonial rule. The challenge of remaking Latin America began with Rubén Darío and has come into its own in the twentieth century. In the nineteenth century Latin America was plagued by the absurdity of each local strongman carving out his own little impoverished country with its own flag and wild nationalism in order to feed an insatiable appetite for personal power. Latin America in its history is a continent of dictators and writers (43–45).

Over the second half of the twentieth century the social status of Latin American writers has changed in a major way, in part because of the international prestige of writers like Borges, Fuentes, García Márquez, Neruda, and Paz; but also, and perhaps of greater significance, because the usual economic support afforded by journalism has now been greatly augmented and in some countries superseded by television. There are numerous writers in Argentina, Brazil, Colombia, Mexico, and Venezuela working on scripts for television programs, and many are also the leading authors in print. An aspect that remains the same, however, is the intensity of the debate among writers themselves. The status that someone like Octavio Paz held in Mexico until his death in 1998 was not only due to his ranking within the hierarchy of cultural legitimacy but perhaps above all because of his willingness to take on all comers like a champion gladiator. Elena Poniatowska, in *Las palabras del árbol,* has given us a clear picture of the word-to-word combat of Octavio Paz and Carlos Monsiváis two decades ago (Poniatowska 177–181).

For each writer who has been consecrated in the canon of the moment, there are a hundred who will attempt to replace him or her by performing the mediating function better. This does not mean that the work of the established writer has to be diminished in the eyes of the public (or the market of symbolic goods), but rather that there will be an attempt to show that it is no longer relevant to the new sensibilities; he or she is a voice from the past. The writer's work thus constitutes the taking of a position with regard to the issues of the day, and it is this position-taking that enters the habitus. There are two distinct strategies: On the one hand, the writer can appeal to purported universal values and thus mediate the local to the universal; on the other, the writer can speak to the public in an attack mode—against real or imagined hostile pretenders to his or her place on the imagined canonical list. Alliances are part of the defensive strategy, as is the claim of independence of mind and penetrating textual commentary. Bourdieu describes the situation in these words:

> Starting from the hypothesis (of position-taking) would doubtless find its most rewarding material in an analysis of privileged references. These are not just simple indices of information exchanges, in particular, implicit or explicit borrowings of words or ideas, but as so many sorties into the common battlefield and the engagement in the network of privileged allies and adversaries proper to each category of producer. . . . The construction of the system of relations between the producers and competing, hostile, allied or neutral powers which are to be destroyed, intimidated, cajoled, annexed or won over, presumes a decisive rupture first, with naïve citalogy, since it does not go beyond any but the most basic relationships, and second, and in particular, with that naïve notion of cultural production that takes only explicit references into account. (138–139)

Although Bourdieu was for the most part basing his remarks on French culture at the beginning of the 1980s, it has an uncanny accuracy in depicting the situation in Latin America at the end of the 1990s. One of the finest recent descriptions of the network of writers in Latin America in action is Elena Poniatowska's *Octavio Paz: las palabras del árbol.* The writer of literature in Latin America in the year 2000 is in the tradition of Martí, Machado de Assis, Neruda, Vallejo, and thousands more whose lives have been lived in full awareness of language as the habitat of being and whose texts challenge the reader to engage in the redescription of the world.

Works Cited

Bastide, Roger. 1973. *Applied Anthropology.* Trans. Alice L. Morton. London: Croom Helm.

Benjamin, Walter. 1979. *One-way Street.* Trans. Edmund Jephcott and Kingsley Shorter. London: Verso.

Bourdieu, Pierre. 1993. *The Field of Cultural Production.* Trans. Randal Johnson. New York: Columbia University Press.

Bryce Echenique, Alfredo. 1992. "El escritor latinoamericano." *Hispanoamérica: La sangre del espíritu.* Ed. Victorino Polo. Murcia: Universidad de Murcia. 3–45.

Chanquia Franch, Diana. 1994. "Para investigar procesos de constitución de sujetos sociales." *Círculos de reflexión. Latinoamérica en ciencias sociales.* Ed. Hugo Zemelman. Barcelona: Anthropos. 41–46.

Coutinho, Afrânio. 1969. *An Introduction to Literature in Brazil.* Trans. Gregory Rabassa. New York, Columbia University Press.

Gutiérrez Girandot, Rafael. 1998. *Insistencias.* Bogotá: Ariel. 239–256.

———. 1976. "Pedro Henríquez Ureña y la historiografía literaria latinoamericana." *Literatura y praxis en América Latina.* Ed. Fernando Alegría et al. Caracas: Monte Avila. 29–48.

Jrade, Cathy L. 1998. *Modernismo, Modernity.* Austin: University of Texas Press.

Merquior, José Guilherme. 1972. "Situación del escritor." *América Latina en su literatura.* Ed. César Fernández Moreno. Madrid: Siglo XXI. 372–388.

Navarrete Orta, Luis. 1995. "El escritor ante el poder político en América Latina." *Literatura y política en América Latina.* Ed. Rafael di Prisco and Antonio Scocoza. Caracas: La casa de Bello. 33–47.

Poniatowska, Elena. 1998. *Octavio Paz: las palabras del árbol.* Mexico City: Plaza Janés.

Rama, Angel. 1972. "Demonios, vade retro." *Nuevos Aires* 8 (Sept.): 1–28.

Sánchez Albornoz, Nicolás. 1994. *La población de América Latina.* Madrid: Alianza.

Sasso, Javier. 1995. "Romanticismo y política en América Latina: Una reconsideración." *Esplendores y miserias en el siglo XIX.* Ed. Beatriz González Stephan et al. Caracas: Monte Avila. 75–90.

Sierra, Justo. 1969. *The Political Evolution of the Mexican People.* Trans. Charles Ramsdell. Austin: University of Texas Press.

Vargas Llosa, Mario. 1990. "Ribeyro y las sirenas." *Contra viento y marea.* 4 vols. Barcelona: Seix Barral. III: 351–355.

THE MAIN LOCATIONS
OF LATIN AMERICAN LITERATURE

Hervé Théry (École Normale Supérieure/CNRS, Paris) with the collaboration
of Cristina Santos and Jonathan Rollins (University of Toronto)

Abstract

The following statistical and cartographic analysis was produced for the Literary History Project, directed by Mario
Valdés and Linda Hutcheon under the auspices of the Social
Sciences and Research Council of Canada and the University of Toronto. It aims at providing a quantitative and cartographic basis to the notion of "cultural center" which is at
the heart of the Comparative History of Latin American Literary Cultures. The Caribbean area of English, French,
Dutch, and Creole languages is excluded because it is the
topic of another complementary project, which covers the
entire Caribbean, *A History of Literature in the Caribbean*,
edited by A. James Arnold.

While waiting for other elements to become available—
for example, totals of literary production (number of books,
editors), cultural broadcasting (creation date of the literary
Academies, Universities), and especially data on the
described places or places of action of the works themselves
(which will come later in Volume Two)—we have used as a
first indicator the number of writers born or dead in each
Latin American city. Analysis of the allocation of these
birthplaces and places of death, in time and space, constitutes a first approach to the top areas of Latin American literature, whereas analysis of the trajectories that have led
from the birthplace to the place of death provides a first idea
of the draw of these centers. If the randomness of destiny
alone is responsible for the place where they are born, it is
often a personal choice that brought writers to the place
where they died.

The Sources and Their Limits

The place and date of birth and death of Latin American writers, information that is often given at the beginning of their
bibliographical notes, have been gathered from several reference works by research assistants of this project. In all, 4,188
notes were usable; the birthplace was given in 4,170 cases and
the place of death in 1,129 cases. These places are not always
precisely indicated. It happens that with a small number of
these cases we must satisfy ourselves with the province, the
department, the state (which is acceptable), or even the country ("Peruvian author," for example).

The same goes for dates, which are sometimes summed
up as the decade ("the 1850s") or even as the century ("the
sixteenth century"). This information is sufficient for a distinct trend to appear: an increase in the number of writers
accounted for from one century to the next (from 111 in
the sixteenth century—but only 83 for the seventeenth century—to 213 for the eighteenth century, 1,516 for the nineteenth century, and 2,264 for the twentieth century). Only
the simple fact that a good many of these writers are still
alive explains that in many cases only the place and date of
birth were available. The maximum is reached in the early
1930s; fewer writers in the sample were born after this

date; it seems that some time is needed before a writer
joins the cohort of well-known writers—a length of sufficient time to achieve a certain level of success and to be
recognized by peers and critics.

Hence we can see the limits of the analysis that can be
done on these lists. It is worth only what the lists are worth,
and they evidently have some limitations:

- If they are readily available for more recent centuries than for earlier ones, it is because there are more writers today than in earlier
  times. The number of inhabitants on the continent has increased,
  and even more so the number of those who can read and write.

- It is probable that the concept sixteenth-century authors had of
  what a writer is (very broad and encompassing fields not usually
  recognized as literary) is not that which authors have today.

It is by keeping these reservations in mind—the main issue
here is writers in the most traditional meaning of the term,
and who are for the most part contemporaries—that one can
analyze their geographical distribution.

Birthplaces and Places of Death

In total, there are more than a thousand places mentioned as
the birthplace or place of death of writers, 1,061 precisely
(because we have chosen to leave out mentions such as "born
on a vessel off the coast of Maranhão" and "died near his
native state, in a shipwreck. . . ."). Among them, 712 (more
than two-thirds of the total) appear only once, and 146 (close
to 14 percent) appear only twice. Therefore more than 80 percent of places appear only once or twice, and we have left
them out, considering that only two mentions (which could be
the same if the author was born and died there) do not provide significant statistical representation. If we were to keep
these additional 858 places, often very small villages, we
would only overload the maps unnecessarily.

The distribution could be troubling for the whole analysis if certain places appear with much greater frequency. In
decreasing order, **Table 1** takes inventory of the first fifty
places, which represent two-thirds of the total of inventoried writers (the first seven represent one-fourth of the
total, and the first twenty-three represent half). A good
number of them (17 out of 50) are places with vague locations,
as mentioned above. The others are cities, some of which obtain
non-negligible scores (209 for Buenos Aires, 207 for Rio de
Janeiro), and these were the data used to produce the
maps.

The Cultural Centers of Latin America

In spite of the limitations mentioned above, representing the
data on a map provides remarkably interesting results. The
crude mapping of the places of birth and death of Latin
American writers (see **Map 1**) creates an archipelago of cultural centers that coincides closely, of course, with the urban
network of Latin America, but one that distinguishes itself on
several points:

- It is not surprising to find the principal cities of the continent in the forefront, but it is remarkable that Buenos Aires, Rio de Janeiro, and Mexico City have such close scores (around 200) when the sources used are very different. The orders of size are the same, which provides an additional argument for a comparative approach that erases national frontiers.
- There is a nice series of second-rank centers (scores between 50 and 100), of which most are national capitals, but where cities and regions having visibly strong personalities are found, such as the Rio Grande do Sul and San Juan, Puerto Rico.
- Note that the map brings out non-Latin American cities, principally European, where writers were born, or more frequently, where they died. It can clearly be seen here that Europe is part of the cultural field of Latin America.
- Even going down the list to the places that appear only three times it does not represent the entire continent. The "small" centers are generally situated close to the larger ones and draw them into cultural regions polarized by them, whereas great gaps remain, notably in the middle and south of South America. There are some empty spaces which appear to be voids on the cultural map, because no recognized writer is originally from there, but one must ask if this is the reason why no one has written about them, or if they are in fact devoid of literary culture.

Tying these numbers to the population of these towns is of course tempting, but the result is not very conclusive (see **Map 2**). At most, the flattering scores of secondary cities that already have a cultural reputation (such as Sucre, the official capital of Bolivia, San José, Costa Rica; or Asunción) are underlined. The Atlantic and Caribbean cities have better results overall, in this regard, than those of the Pacific and, of course, Europe or the United States, where Latin American writers are lost in the crowd (which is often what they want to do). We can, however, explore other avenues of research on the population distribution of writers.

If we distinguish the places of birth from the places of death (see **Map 3**), we notice—beyond the obvious fact that the first are more numerous than the second, for reasons given above—that they are also more concentrated, which can be explained by at least two reasons:

- The first is the general movement of rural exodus and metropolization that the continent has generally known, and to which writers, just like the rest of the population, are not immune.
- The second reason is more specific. Writers who have known a certain success more often than not moved to the big cultural centers to find success, or moved there once they had found it. In some cases, bio-bibliographical notes provide more detail than the birthplaces and places of death alone, indicating, for example, the successive residences of the author and even the place of forced exile. There would be enough material there for a complementary study, even if it did not have the same statistical basis.

Areas of Attraction

Places of death are fewer but more concentrated than birthplaces; thus it was tempting to determine (or at least for the main ones) the corresponding places of birth, in order to reconstruct the area of attraction for these large centers. This creates the hypothesis that these writers must have had reasons

to establish themselves in these cities to spend the remainder of their days. This approach brings back a certain homogeneity to these areas of attraction, but it also reveals the distinct differences among them, as is shown in **Map 4**.

- These six centers have a strong regional attraction that would be even stronger if one took into account the places cited only once or twice, which are usually small places near the main centers. Each cultural center shines, mainly because its nearness attracts writers born in the same cultural environment, which the maps aid in showing. This is particularly clear for Havana (with its Caribbean influence) and Caracas (in the Northern Andes).
- Certain centers have a larger recruiting area than others, notably Mexico City (all of Central America) and Buenos Aires (all of the Southern Andes). Rio de Janeiro, to this day a seat of culture and a center of attraction, attracts writers born in northeastern and southern Brazil, but it distinguishes itself by the number of writers born in the city itself.
- Finally, note that all these centers have attracted writers born in Europe, in Spain and Portugal mainly (but not exclusively: Writers of Polish, Czech, and Ukrainian origin, among others, are found in small numbers on these lists). Because some European cities show up frequently as places of death for Latin American writers, it is interesting to measure their area of attraction. For Paris, the first among them, the map shows that it is in fact the center with the greatest influence, attracting writers native to most Latin American countries. Decidedly Paris is—or at least has been—a Latin American cultural center.

An Attempt to Define Main Zones of Influence

From this series of maps, from the more global ones to those retracing the areas of attraction, we can attempt to draw a more synthetic map outlining the cultural areas of Latin America. This is represented in **Map 5**, which has the same statistical basis as **Map 1** (number of writers who were born or died in each city).

Four patterns can be distinguished:

- Some are well known and more or less unquestionable: The cultural centers of the Caribbean, of Mexico and Central America, and of northeastern and southeastern Brazil do not call for commentary. This analysis confirms their validity once again.
- Others, such as the Southern Cone and Europe, are more encompassing, but seem to have a certain coherence from the perspective of this analysis and of this project.
- Others are frankly characterized as fontier transfer points, both because spatially coherent developments on the frontiers show up on the maps, and also because it seems that culturally coherent elements have developed in the borderlands themselves. This is the case of the development in the Andes, and of an original group at the southern frontiers between Brazil, Uruguay, and Paraguay, which is worth looking into.
- Two developments of interest are the Finisterra of the southern part of the continent and the Guyano-Amazonian depths which stand out because of their noticeable lack of cultural centers. That is not surprising, because these are the main demographic voids of the continent. Their place in Latin American literature and their imaginary geographies create a beautiful paradox. The blank areas of the map can sometimes be as interesting as the areas of major activity.

Table 1. *The First Fifty Places*

Rank	City or Country	Frequency	%	Cumulative %
1	*Brazil*	265	5	5
2	*Argentina*	253	4.78	9.78
4	Buenos Aires, Argentina	209	3.95	13.73
3	Rio de Janeiro	207	3.91	17.64
5	*Mexico*	186	3.51	21.15
6	*Colombia*	156	2.95	24.09
7	Mexico City	148	2.79	26.89
8	*Chile*	129	2.44	29.32
9	Santiago de Chile	116	2.19	31.51
10	*Cuba*	99	1.87	33.38
11	Montevideo, Uruguay	91	1.72	35.1
12	*Peru*	91	1.72	36.82
13	*Venezuela*	88	1.66	38.48
14	Havana, Cuba	87	1.64	40.12
15	Caracas, Venezuela	79	1.49	41.62
16	Lima, Perú	74	1.4	43.01
17	Porto Alegre, Brazil	70	1.32	44.34
18	*Uruguay*	61	1.15	45.49
19	*Dominican Republic*	58	1.1	46.58
20	Asunción, Paraguay	57	1.08	47.66
21	*Spain*	56	1.06	48.72
22	Puerto Rico	56	1.06	49.77
23	Nicaragua	55	1.04	50.81
24	*Ecuador*	53	1	51.81
25	Santo Domingo, D. R.	57	0.98	52.79
26	*Panama*	48	0.91	53.7
27	Bogotá, Colombia	45	0,85	54.55
28	*Bolivia*	43	0.81	55.36
29	*Guatemala*	42	0.79	56.16
30	La Paz, Bolivia	42	0.79	56.95
31	Quito, Ecuador	42	0.79	57.74
32	São Paulo, SP	40	0.76	58.5
33	*Costa Rica*	39	0.74	59.23
34	Madrid, Spain	44	0.72	59.95
35	Paris, France	33	0.62	60.57
36	Recife PE	33	0.62	61.2
37	San José, Costa Rica	33	0,62	61.82
38	*El Salvador*	29	0.55	62.37
39	Guayaquil, Ecuador	28	0.53	62.9
40	*Paraguay*	24	0.45	63.35
41	San Juan, Puerto Rico	22	0.42	63.77
42	Bahia	19	0.36	64.12
43	*Honduras*	19	0.36	64.48
44	Cochabamba, Bolivia	18	0.34	64.82
45	New York, U.S.A.	18	0.34	65.16
46	Guatemala City	17	0.32	65.48
47	Cuenca, Ecuador	16	0.3	65.79
48	Guadalajara, Jalisco, Mexico	16	0.3	66.09
49	Salvador BA	16	0.3	66.39
50	León, Nicaragua	14	0.26	66.65

Map 1. Cultural Centers of Latin America (number of authors who were born or died in each place)

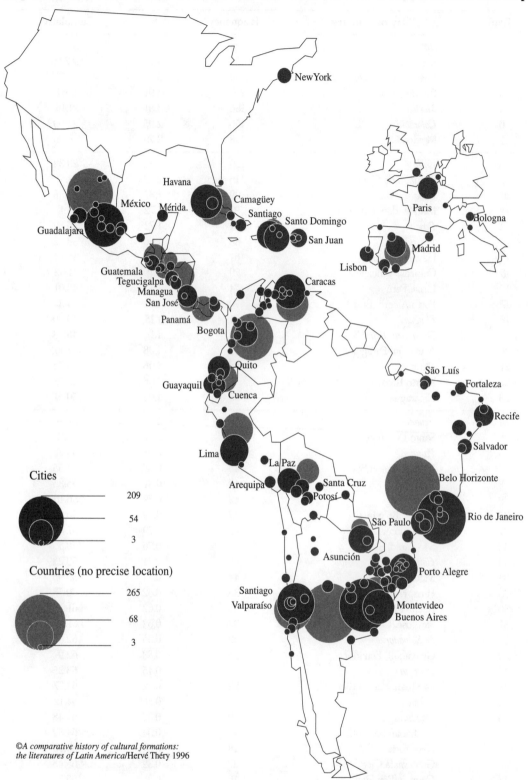

Cities

209
54
3

Countries (no precise location)

265
68
3

New York

Havana
México
Mérida.
Camagüey
Santiago
Santo Domingo
San Juan
Guadalajara

Paris
Bologna
Madrid
Lisbon

Guatemala
Tegucigalpa
Managua
San José
Panamá
Bogota
Caracas

Quito
Guayaquil
Cuenca

São Luís
Fortaleza
Recife
Salvador

Lima
La Paz
Arequipa
Santa Cruz
Potosí
Belo Horizonte
Rio de Janeiro
São Paulo
Asunción
Porto Alegre

Santiago
Valparaíso
Montevideo
Buenos Aires

©*A comparative history of cultural formations:*
the literatures of Latin America/Hervé Théry 1996

Map 2. The Literary Poles of Latin America

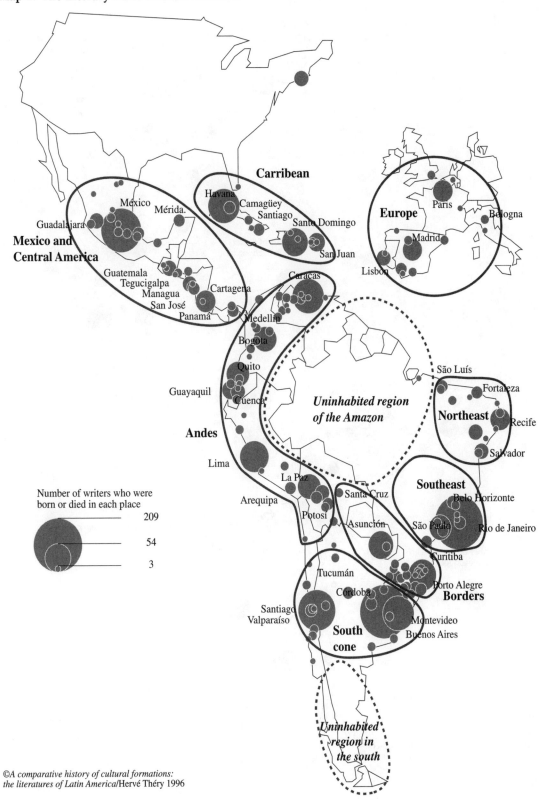

Carribean

Mexico and
Central America

Mexico
Mérida.
Guadalajara
Havana
Camagüey
Santiago
Santo Domingo
San Juan
Europe
Paris
Bologna
Madrid
Lisbon

Guatemala
Tegucigalpa
Managua
San José
Panamá
Cartagena
Caracas

Medellín
Bogotá
Quito
Guayaquil
Cuenca

Andes
Lima

La Paz
Arequipa
Potosí

Santa Cruz
Asunción
São Paulo

São Luís
Fortaleza
Recife
Salvador

Northeast

Southeast
Belo Horizonte
Rio de Janeiro
Curitiba
Porto Alegre
Borders

*Uninhabited region
of the Amazon*

Number of writers who were
born or died in each place
209
54
3

Tucumán
Cordoba
Santiago
Valparaíso
South
cone
Montevideo
Buenos Aires

*Uninhabited
region in
the south*

©*A comparative history of cultural formations:
the literatures of Latin America*/Hervé Théry 1996

Map 3. Birthplaces and Places of Death

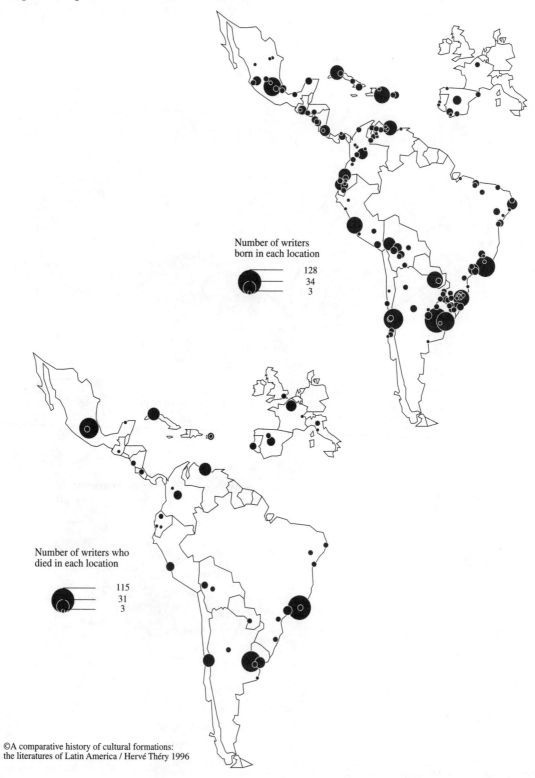

Number of writers
born in each location

128
34
3

Number of writers who
died in each location

115
31
3

©A comparative history of cultural formations:
the literatures of Latin America / Hervé Théry 1996

Map 4. Attraction of Large Literary Centers (birthplaces of writers who died in each town)

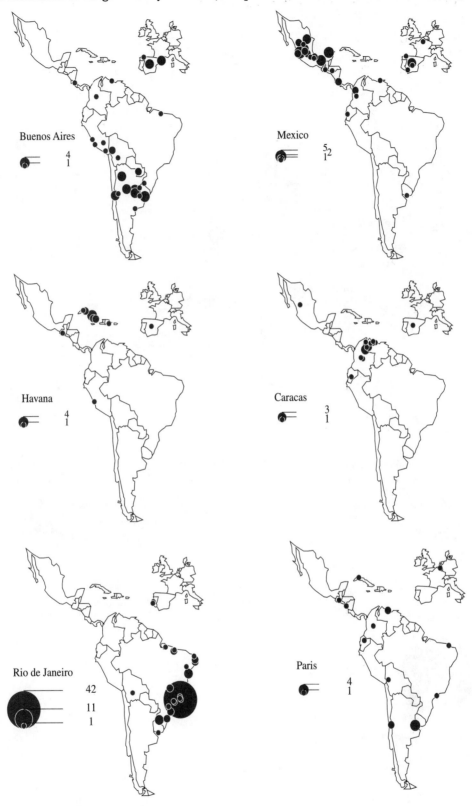

©*A comparative history of cultural formations:*
the literatures of Latin America/Hervé Théry 1996

Map 5. Writers in the City (number of writers who were born or died in each location/million residents)

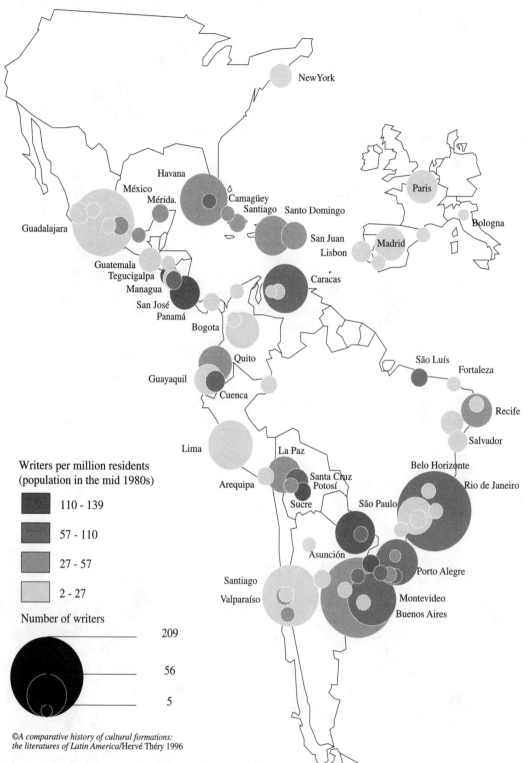

Writers per million residents
(population in the mid 1980s)

- 110 - 139
- 57 - 110
- 27 - 57
- 2 - 27

Number of writers

209

56

5

©A comparative history of cultural formations:
the literatures of Latin America/Hervé Théry 1996

New York

Havana
México
Mérida.
Guadalajara
Camagüey
Santiago
Santo Domingo
San Juan
Lisbon
Guatemala
Tegucigalpa
Managua
San José
Panamá
Bogota
Caracas
Quito
Guayaquil
Cuenca
Lima
Arequipa
La Paz
Santa Cruz
Potosí
Sucre
Santiago
Valparaíso
Asunción
São Paulo
Montevideo
Buenos Aires
Porto Alegre
Belo Horizonte
Rio de Janeiro
Salvador
Recife
Fortaleza
São Luís
Paris
Madrid
Bologna

Works Cited

Alboukrek, Aarón 1992. *Diccionario de escritores hispanoamericanos del siglo XVI al XX*. Buenos Aires: Larousse.

Coutinho, Afrânio. 1968. *A literatura no Brasil*. 7 Vols, 2nd edition. Rio de Janeiro: Ed. Sul Americana.

Faraco, Sérgio and Blasio Hugo Hickmann, eds. 1983. *Que é quem nas letras rio-grandenses: dicionário de autores contemporâneos*. Porto Alegre: Edições Porto Alegre, Prefeitura Municipal de Porto Alegre, Secretaria Municipal de Educacão e Cultura, Divisão de Cultura.

Flores, Angel. 1992. *Spanish American Authors: The Twentieth Century*. New York: Wilson.

Foster, David William, ed. 1994. *Latin American Writers on Gay and Lesbian Themes: A Bio-critical Sourcebook*. Westport, CT: Greenwood.

Gullón, Ricardo, ed. 1993. *Diccionario de literatura española e hispanoamericana*. Madrid: Alianza Editorial.

Hoeksema, Thomas, ed. 1989. *The Fertile Rhythms: Contemporary Women Poets of Mexico*. Trans. Robert Hoeksema and Romelia Enríquez. Pittsburgh: Latin American Literary Review.

Levine, Linda Gould, et al. 1993. *Spanish Women Writers: A Bio-Bibliographical Source Book*. Westport, CT: Greenwood.

Marting, Diane, ed. 1990. *Spanish American Women Writers: A Bio-bibliographical Sourcebook*. New York: Greenwood.

Paes, José Paulo, and Massaud Moisés, eds. 1980. *Pequeno dicionário de literatura brasileira*. São Paulo: Editora Cultrix.

Reichardt, Dieter, ed. 1992. *Autorenlexikon Lateinamerika*, Frankfurt: Suhrkamp.

Ryan, Bryan, ed. 1991. *Hispanic Writers: A Selection of Sketches from Contemporary Authors*. Detroit: Gale Research.

Solé, Carlos, and M. I. Abreu. 1989. *Latin American Writers*. New York: Scribner.

Stern, Irwin, ed. 1988. *Dictionary of Brazilian Literature*. New York: Greenwood.

CHAPTER 20

READING AS A HISTORICAL PRACTICE IN LATIN AMERICA
THE FIRST COLONIAL PERIOD TO THE NINETEENTH CENTURY

Juan Poblete

One of the main contributions of Latin American cultural studies has been the reappraisal of the ways in which the receivers of discourse produce signification. Jesús Martín Barbero summarizes this general theoretical change by highlighting the shift from media studies (with its attendant technological or political determinism) to the study of the mediations in the production of meaning in social communication. A more precise way of putting this is to describe the displacement that occurs in moving from the analysis of discourse and its intrinsic signification to the analysis of the social production of meaning: "Communication is not exhausted by the message. After all the time I have dedicated to semiotics, I realized that thinking about communication from the perspective of discourse analysis condemned us to thinking about signification but not about meaning, because in order to speak about the meaning of communication one has to speak about what that communication means to people" (Martín Barbero 1995, 16). These collective processes of struggling to define social semiosis have a long history on the continent and form an important part of the history of the constitution of culture itself in Latin America (Martín Barbero 1995, 31). My purpose here is to study these processes in relation to the historically variable forms of reception and reading practices conceived of as means of cultural production.

My hypothesis is twofold: first, that the relations between state and Church with respect to reading and the formation of readership and the relations between this readership and the text have undergone profound transformations throughout the history of Latin America; second, that these relations are not only merely another aspect of, but are crucial to, the forms and production of literature in the Americas. Within the confines of this essay, focusing mainly on the situation in Mexico, Argentina, and Chile, I shall make several comprehensive propositions that enable us to determine two macromoments–the Colonial and the nineteenth century–in an historical study of reading in Latin America. Central to this study are the relations among Church, state, and readership, as well as the relations between readers and texts. In both cases what are, in social terms, negotiated and disputed are the forms of authority and relative legitimacy of each of the actors involved in the determination of the meaning, function, and target audiences of cultural texts. A precondition of this semiotic debate on texts, this determination of the socially legible spaces (de Certeau) and of the actualizing practices (Bennett 1990), is the issue of access and circulation. During the period I call the colonizing moment, the Church attempted to curtail the indigenous population's access to their sources of cultural production (written and oral memories produced and transmitted through the mother-child dialogue, and between priests or intellectuals and the local population in general) in order to replace these with new

rites, texts, and communicative processes of an evangelizing nature. In the second moment under study, the proliferation and circulation of published and journalistic material opened the doors to a new agential space: that of the market. Unlike the earlier communicative processes, which, even if they did produce subordinate and loyal subjects, were clearly collective in orientation, those that were set in the marketing context of postcolonial countries during the nineteenth century were lived as (and gave the illusion of being) individual subjectivizing processes. The reader, now silent and private, experienced his or her own relation of distance from the text as an eminently personal process. Although both types of reader formations were, by definition, collective and social, the reader-text relation differed in emphasis. To these concerns should be added the market of popular writing, to which I shall return later. In all these cases, an economy of the circulation of texts presides over the forms of assigning meaning that determine their possible signification.

Reading, Production, Text

As a preliminary, reading as a cultural practice needs to be reconceptualized. Terry Eagleton's words in his essay discrediting reception studies, ironically entitled "The Revolt of the Reader," are a good reflection of the skepticism and even the disdain with which a sector of traditional criticism (Marxist and others) views these studies: "The growth of the Reader's Liberation Movement (RLM) over the past few decades has struck a decisive blow for oppressed readers everywhere, brutally proletarianized as they have been by the authorial class" (181). Having characterized the history of reception studies and humorously classified its right, central, and left wings, Eagleton concludes: "A socialist criticism is not primarily concerned with the consumer's revolution. Its task is to take over the means of production" (184). Dana Polan calls this the survival, in some contemporary Marxist trends, of a romantic vision of production that presupposes that, after this pristine and original moment, the social process of circulation and exchange of commodities and meanings is in a kind of decadence and disgrace (38).

The most recent studies on reading have endeavored precisely to counter the traditional materialist assaults, such as that of Eagleton, maintaining, on the contrary, that reception, understood as a collective activity that is culturally determined, is one of the most important aspects of the process of the social production of meaning. Far from being a reflection of the consumers' revolution, reception is the communicational moment per se in the circulation of social discourses. For example, as Michel de Certeau has indicated: "The efficiency of production implies the inertia of consumption-as-a-receptacle. . . . By challenging 'consumption' as it is conceived and (of course) confirmed by these authorial enterprises, we may be able to discover creativity where it has been denied [that] any exists" (167). Following this argument, Néstor García Canclini asks "whether by consuming we are not doing something that sustains, nurtures and, up to a certain point, constitutes a new sense of citizenship," to which he replies: "To consume is to participate in the dispute for that which society produces and for the ways of using it" (1995, 27, 44). If we recuperate the collective and productive aspects of reception, García Canclini believes, it is possible to state that "The territorial boundaries and political history of a nation, for example, are of little help in defining it at this stage. Instead it survives as an *interpretative community of consumers*, whose traditional eating and linguistic habits lead them to relate in a particular way to the objects and information circulating on the international networks" (1995, 50–51).

Martín Barbero has, in turn, emphasized just how inadequate traditional modes of analyzing contents and styles are for the comprehension of many genres of mass and popular communication. By focusing exclusively on the text or on the forms of authorial production one loses sight of the fact that what is most important in soap operas, for example, are the spaces of resignification created by the receivers in a subsequent dialogue with others: "the perception women have of a soap opera varies a lot when they tell friends and neighbours the story. . . . [W]hat the viewers see is not so significant as the dialogue. A soap opera is successful because it gives people the opportunity to talk about their lives" (1995, 56).

Finally, Tony Bennett (1990) has established what is, ultimately, the property of every text: the fact that it belongs to a public and political sphere dominated by certain discursive and reading formations that unquestionably condition the production of their meanings. The idea of a "reading formation" derives from Michel Foucault's study of discursive formations. In *The Archaeology of Knowledge*, Foucault defines a discursive formation as a certain regularity of relations among discourses that jell in one historically determined moment and space to offer an illusory (but legitimate) image of the totality of social discourses (21–70). Bennett understands a reading formation as "a set of discursive and intertextual determinations which organize and animate the practice of reading, connecting texts and readers in specific relations to one another in constituting readers as reading subjects of particular types and texts as objects-to-be-read in particular ways" (1987, 70). It is worth mentioning that this definition presupposes that both text and reading are socially and historically construed. That is to say, we are not speaking about one text that has been given different interpretations throughout its life, but of texts and readings that vary in similar ways as a result of an actualization in the here and now of their oppositional relations to other texts (discursive formation) and other reading practices (reading formation). This implies that literature is not connected, or at least not principally linked, with the forms of social power by the type of representational-ideological relation proposed by traditional Marxism. Literature is not, then, *simply and directly*, an ideology whose main function is the production of subjects receptive to its pacifying messages. It is the social and institutional mechanisms by means of which specific texts *are used and socially deployed* that constitute literature in its concrete and variable forms of social existence (see Bennett 1990).

Following this line of argument, we may contend that to read a text is to construct it, to make it signify within a social space. If every text, literary or otherwise, inevitably forms part of a semiosis that is, in principle, limitless, one of the first things that should be studied historically is the way in which texts are read, so to speak, within the limits and possibilities laid down by the practices and the spaces that institutional procedures construct in a given moment. Although I shall study two macromoments in the history of reading on the continent, I would like to put them into context by indicating the periodization of these moments in relation to those that precede, are included within, and follow the two under study. The first concerns the parallel and independent development of forms of "literacy" in pre-Columbian America and in Europe. During the second moment, the ideology of the book and the letter clash with the forms of indigenous knowledge, which from that time onward were apparently deemed inferior. This is the colonizing moment. The third moment is the emergence of a popular, Baroque, and Catholic culture during the sixteenth and seventeenth centuries (see Morandé). The fourth is the Bourbon moment in the eighteenth century, in which the modern state reared its head on the continent in order to dispute the Church's hegemony in the citizens' formation of subjectivities. The fifth is the nineteenth century, when a proto-mass and a proto-mass-media culture emerged that coincided with the political problem of national cultures, which was debated as much by state intellectuals as by those struggling outside that context. The dominant characteristics of this stage were an expansive and popular newspaper culture, the deconsecration of the book, the mechanization and economizing of its production, and a growing tendency toward mass cultural consumption. During the sixth moment, this national culture was effectively mass produced under the inspiration and force, as a rule, of cultural campaigns encouraged by the state in its attempt to construct hegemony at a time when the people and the middle classes dominated–the age, that is, of populism and popular nationalism. The last moment is that of the transnationalization of the means of mass communication and some forms of consumption and cultural production. Some of the basic territorializing and subjectivizing processes promoted by the nation-states and the Catholic Church have reached a state of crisis and face significant challenges, as do the discursive and reading formations that have characterized Latin American modernity. Globalization thus requires that the following be reconsidered: the traditional practices for the formation of citizens and worshippers, the modes of production and accumulation of cultural capital, the traditional hierarchical forms, and the symbolic profitability of the different cultural spheres.

The Colonizing Moment

Contrary to the perception held by most people, Rolena Adorno (when discussing Irving Leonard and other scholars' contributions to this topic) asserts that during the first colonial period (which I shall call the colonizing moment in order to distinguish it from the colonial period of the seventeenth and eighteenth centuries), the Church, and specifically the Inquisition that acted as its censor, seemed to take little interest in banning works of fiction, simply because these books had no dogmatic content (Adorno 1992, xvi). At least in relation to prohibition (the writs of 1531 and 1543), even if the practical results are debatable, the Spanish state, in turn, was indeed concerned with the need to ban the reading of literary fiction for reasons we might call Platonic: It fires the imagination; it persuades, seduces, and stimulates. The justification for the prohibition of works of fiction under these two royal writs was sustained by the idea that these books would corrupt not so much the soldiers as the Indians. Thus, the Queen's writ of 1531 for the officials at the Clearing House in Seville who controlled the entry of goods to America, states (in a modernized version): "I have been informed that many Romance books, vain and profane histories such as the Amadís and others of this sort have been taken to the Indies and that this is an evil exercise for the Indians and a thing which they should not spend their time on or read and hence I order you from this day forward not to grant consent to or permit any person whatsoever to take any stories or profane things through except those concerning the Christian religion" (Torre Revello iii). Despite this writ, the censorship of works of fiction did not appear to concern the ecclesiastical authorities unduly at the time; rather, they were not very efficient in actually putting it into practice (Torre Revello 40; Leal xlii). However, they were very efficient in promoting religious texts that formed part of the evangelizing (and thus legitimizing) mission in the Indian communities. As we shall see, the Church was energetically and zealously committed to the so-called persecution and eradication of every sign of idolatrous worship. In the nineteenth century, the Church discovered that the expansion of the forms of mass reproduction of works of fiction constituted a space that severely threatened their hegemony in important social sectors.

During the first colonial period, the subjectivity that the Church considered had to be conquered and reconstructed was that of the indigenous population (Gruzinski 186–228). There were two aspects to the formation of subjectivities. The negative aspect was based on the control of printed material (which included as much the persecution of ritual idolatry as that of the discourses in which the formalized part of indigenous memory was stored) and the curtailment of the maternal oral relation by imposing a third entity, the Church, which acted as a collective mother. The positive aspect of this new subjectivity was grounded in the practice of forming intellectuals and in the task of general mediation undertaken by the priests at the heart of the process of social semiosis that sought to convert the Indians into good Christians, that is, into obedient and Catholic workers.

The first (negative) aspect of this process was the making of a fetish of writing (see Lienhard), thus installing the dominance of the ideology of the Book and the Letter (see Mignolo 1995). As Martín Lienhard (41) points out: "The destruction of the ancient system, based on a balanced articulation of the stored and the live word, and the imposition of a new system in which the absolute authority of 'divine' European writing made the diabolic ancient 'writings' illegal, at the same time marginalizing oral communication, constitute the background for the emergence of 'Latin American' literature." Lienhard alludes here to the configuration of a discursive formation in pre-Hispanic societies. Both the Mesoamerican glyphs and the Quechuan *quipu* were essentially administrative forms for filing data and for fixing constituted and storable knowledge. The natural complement to these written discourses was speech. The oral form was used for discourses concerning tradition and history, such as stories and reflections that we usually place under the umbrella term of philosophy. (I shall discuss this complementariness of orality and writing in pre-Hispanic cultures later.)

In order to displace and reposition the indigenous discursive and reading formations, the missionaries undertook the twofold and paradoxical task of extirpating and preserving indigenous oral and written discourses. This resulted in the corpus of Indian-Hispanic writings that culminated in the work of Bernardino de Sahagún. This writing is an antecedent to the indigenous ethno-fiction of the nineteenth and twentieth centuries, which constructs an artificial ethnic discourse of the Other addressed to a readership outside the "exotic" culture (Lienhard 190). Unlike this discourse, the collections and chronicles of the colonizing moment were, in the end, unable to contain the subversive semiotic possibilities running through the translated and modified indigenous discourses, which would potentially be significant when reinterpreted by autochthonous readers: "What was in the end the 'explosive' character of the chronicles contaminated by indigenous discourse undoubtedly explains the censorship to which they fell victim. However excellent their official intentions (extirpation of idolatry, demonstrations of indigenous barbarity...) might have been, hardly any were printed during the period" (Lienhard 52).

When describing the discursive mechanisms that established a meeting point between the indigenous Brazilian oral tradition and the European written discourses, José Horta Nunes has studied–mainly using the methods of discourse analysis–the position constructed and prepared for the Brazilian reader, that is, the hybrid inheritor of these two discourse formations in this textual tradition: "The missionaries introduce a practice of reading oriented by the objectives of catechism and colonization. This activity develops, on the one hand, in the practice of the discourse of conversation, in the sermons, conferences, etc., and, on the other hand, in the production of new knowledge about the New World, be it in the form of reports, catechisms, grammars, or dictionaries. These activities and symbolic objects determine the construction of a position for the reader in Brazil, on the path between the discoursivity of the European and the discoursivity of the Indian" (103). This positioning of the Brazilian reader is organized within a semiotic mechanism that aspires to be total and comprehensive. A space is created so that, to each question from the indigenous oral discourse, there is one, and only one, correct Christian answer or interpretation in the written catechism discourse: "The situation of contact by missionaries manifests its form in structuring the questions and answers, determining the meanings to be read, and prohibiting the production of other interpretations" (Horta Nunes 102).

Two operations were central to the missionaries' success in this task. On the one hand, they had to plumb the depths of the indigenous oral discourse by means of written representations of dialogues and colloquies between the Indians and the missionaries, in which the former are translated and responded to in exact terms by the latter. That is to say, the missionaries wrote down the characteristic oral situations of autochthonous teaching and learning in order to reinscribe them within a Christian frame. On the other hand, the missionaries introduced the indigenous people to new knowledge and produced grammars and dictionaries, thus applying this same operation of translating one discourse into another. This became a further instrument in their mission of indoctrination.

The purpose of these textual mechanisms was to anticipate and control the Indians' interpretative semiotic responses. It is worth noting that this attempt at semiotic control occurred at the same time as the indigenous oral discourse was given expression. For this reason, this discourse is artificially constrained to a series of questions and answers, which, though extensive, limits the scope of what is utterable and pertinent in a situation that is, strictly speaking, structured in a highly hierarchical manner, even if it is formally dialogic. Perhaps the most famous example is *Los coloquios de los doce primeros misioneros de México* [The Colloquia of the First Twelve Missionaries to Mexico] by Fray Bernardino de Sahagún (1500?–1590), which Pilar Gonzalbo describes as "something like a *Summa contra Gentiles*, planned and developed for the Nahua world" (1988, 19).

The Queen's Royal Writ to the Viceroy of Mexico in 1536 placing a ban on the reading of works of fiction ratified their strategic importance. Besides being concerned with the direct moral effects of these works, what worried the Spanish Crown were what we could call their indirect ideological effects:

> Some days ago the Emperor and King gave the ruling that books of Romances of profane matters and fables should not be taken to those parts so that the Indians who knew how to read would not become addicted to them, leaving to one side the books of good and healthy doctrine, and upon reading them would not learn bad habits and so that, once it was known those books of vain histories had been composed without approval, our Holy Scriptures and books by other holy Doctors would not lose authority and credibility. For these people who have no deeply rooted Faith believe that all our books are of one authority and manner. (Torre Revello iv)

In other words, the most important reason for banning the reading and circulation of works of fiction was that they might contaminate the colonial disocursive formation. Much more detrimental to imperial plans than the direct representations of reprehensible moral acts was the idea that works of fiction, as discourses that shared the space with those of Catholic indoctrination and conversion, could subvert in the indigenous imaginary, as the Queen thought, the status and superior ideological effect of other written discourses, which the fetishizing of writing attempted to impose on Indian audiences. This subversive crack in the educational codes and practices of the Spanish priests would never disappear, because it was impossible to make a genuine and effective tabula rasa of the forms of discourse and of the production of meaning in pre-Hispanic cultures.

Cultural Semiosis

Walter Mignolo has made an extended study of what he calls "the question of the letter" and of writing (what Lienhard designates as the fetishization of writing), as well as of what he terms the processes of "colonial semiosis." The ideology of the letter and the book fundamentally consist of confusing alphabetic writing and the book, which are no more than instruments for the preservation and communication of social knowledge, with the essence and existence of this knowledge. In this way, the conquistadors ascribed the "absence" of books and letters in native cultures to an alleged lack of civilization and history. In this framework, a "lack of letters" was equivalent to a "lack of history," and orality became prehistory. This denied the pre-Hispanic cultures the right to coexist as such with the Europeans in the history of humanity: They were immediately assigned to a time and space destined to be conquered and mastered by the truth of the written history of Christianity. In contrast to this prejudice, still so ingrained today, Mignolo proposes an understanding of the indigenous discoursive and receptive formations that takes as its premise that orality is not an "antecedent" of "literacy" but an equivalent system of the practice and conceptualization of socially

relevant discourses. For our purposes here, it is worth mentioning that, in these pre-Hispanic discursive formations, certain formal discursive genres in prose (the *tlahtolli* and, particularly, the *teotlahtolli* of religious discourse and *huehuetlahtolli* of the wisdom of the elders) coexisted with other forms of poetic discourse in the sense that the communicators' bodies were an essential part of both delivery and reception. These are the *cuicatl* or canto-poetry in which music and rhythm accompanied the oral discourse (León Portilla 1989, 31–41). (I shall discuss the collective and corporal nature of these processes later.)

With the help of specialists and ethnographers, Mignolo has proposed the study of "a significant oral literary production and a conceptualization of the same based on a 'philosophy of language'" that focuses on orality rather than on writing (Mignolo 1993, 552). As in the case of the various versions of the books of *Chilam Balam* collected and preserved for centuries by different Mayan communities, this raises the issue of the presence of forms of discursive hybridity in the pre-Hispanic and European traditions. In these, "the European script that the friars were so eager to transmit in order to be more effective in the Christianization of the natives was used by the Amerindians to stabilize their past, to adapt themselves to the present, to transmit their traditions to future generations, and, in summary, to resist the colonization of language" (Mignolo 1995, 207). This gave rise to forms of adaptation and hybridity, forms of resignifying metropolitan discourses and a strategic exploitation of the available technologies–all of which have characterized the life and processes of cultural (re)production in Latin America (Adorno 1996, 35–37; García Canclini). In order to study the historical processes of these encounters of discoursive and reading formations, which are in a position of inequality in relation to political, military and, thus, epistemological power, Mignolo has coined the term "colonial semiosis." This, he proposes, helps us to overcome the ideology of the book and the letter by questioning the epistemological location of the cognitive colonial subject and the evolutionary and Eurocentric hierarchical arrangement of what are really coexistent and equivalent systems of encoding and transmitting socially and culturally relevant information. In America, these systems–the Amerindian (based on orality and alternative modes of graphic representation) and the European (based on writing and the book)–soon established a great variety of relations of interference and hybridity, which, it appears, can best be studied by using the term "colonial semiosis" (Mignolo 1995, 1–25).

Few people have given such clear and subtle insights into this process of mestizo or hybridized indigenous cultural production in the first colonizing moment as Serge Gruzinski in *La colonización de lo imaginario* [The Colonization of the Imaginary]. This study stresses the importance of understanding the historical forms of the constitution of a cultural imaginary in their frequently contradictory and complex facets. For our purposes, it is interesting to note his emphasis on the forms of cultural appropriation and resignification effected in different ways by the different sectors of a subaltern entity. This wider focus reveals, in the forms of subjectivization and in the mechanisms of reading and appropriation, that there are other forms of producing culture that are generally invisible to the learned eye focusing on the creative individuality of a specific author. In general terms, Gruzinski indicates the existence of two submoments in the history of this process of colonial acculturation. During the first, the educational and religious enterprise undertaken by the missionaries attempted to reproduce the pre-Hispanic sociocultural divisions for the benefit of their evangelizing mission. To this end, they prepared, on the one hand, two kinds of receivers: the elite, who possessed all the elements of semiotic production (reading and writing) in a bilingual, at times even multilingual (Nahuatl, Latin, Spanish), culture, and the people, who received the priests' explanations in their native tongue. In this way, they reproduced the stratification that already existed in pre-Columbian Mexican schools: *calmécac*, schools for the nobles, and *telpochcalli* for the people (López Austin 33). On the other hand, the missionaries found they needed and thus developed mixed discursive forms, which enabled them to make the most of the genres of pre-Hispanic oral culture in order to present them in a Christianized written form and content. They thus revived the ancient *cantares* (poems set to music) so that they could teach the plainsongs and Gregorian chants, and at the same time, they recycled and Christianized the stylistic conventions characteristic of indigenous discourse such as flowers, butterflies, and quetzal feathers (Gruzinski 15–76). In the same way, at least during the sixteenth century, they developed, if to a lesser degree, mixed forms of catechisms and hieroglyphic confessions in which the Christian doctrine and sins were represented graphically following pre-Hispanic conventions. They thus created both the so-called Indian Humanism of New Spain, represented by the *Colegio de Tlatelolco*, the College of Indian Grammarians, as its founder Fray Juan de Zumárraga (1468–1548) called it (Osorio Romero xxii) and Church Nahuatl, which, in Gruzinski's second proposed submoment, governed "the relations of the Indians with the clergy and with the doctrine throughout the colonial period" (Gruzinski 67; Blanco 89).

It was perhaps the success of the missionaries' educational program for the indigenous elite that condemned the project represented by the College. The first Mexican Council of 1555 "not only ordered the confiscation of all the sermons the Indians held in their possession, but also urged close attention be paid to the texts given to them in the future, 'so that they could not falsify or distort them'" (Gruzinski 63). The second Council in 1565 gave the same recommendation. Gruzinski points out how these measures alluded both to the extent to which reading was encouraged among the indigenous elite and to their ability to reproduce written materials that escaped ecclesiastical control (63). Following the spirit that inspired this control of the text and reading of the Bible, the Counter-Reformation Church decided to put an end to the missionaries' utopian project and promoted, from then on during this second submoment, uniform and limited catechization of the indigenous peoples in Church Nahuatl, which the early Indian intellectuals had helped to elaborate. This meant that the formation of relatively independent reading subjects (the subjectivization of the elite) was replaced by a more universal and homogeneous mode of viewing the indigenous population, who, realizing they had no access to the priesthood, were at once perceived as "eternal neophytes and spiritual minors," as they would be throughout their colonial existence (Gruzinski 74; Gonzalbo 1990, 98; 1988, 44). This change in policy altered the relation between subject and text. These relations were now mediated and strictly limited by the intervention that produced and regulated the semiosis that the priests sought to carry out in key spaces and discourses, such as confessionals and manuals of moral edification. Sonia Corcuera has used the phrase "from Love to Fear" to describe this shift in policy on the part of the Church before and after the Council of Trent. This phrase illustrates the transition from the full incorporation of the indigenous population to Christianity, which characterized the first period, to the pessimistic turn that catechization took when the priests felt obliged "to reduce and simplify the teaching contents in order to adapt them to the lesser ability and to the *particular intelligence* of the natives" (Corcuera 19).

The early attempts to control the literacy of the indigenous elite produced another lasting historical consequence. They marked the quasi-disappearance of the pre-Hispanic elite oral tradition connected with the "reading" of the paintings and glyphs and the beginning of an almost complete identification of orality with the indigenous culture "of the rural and urban masses" (Gruzinski 65). A natural result was the cultural configuration still familiar to us today, whereby the oral tradition is associated with the people and the countryside, and the letter with the elite living in urban centers (see Rama; Lienhard). The mass influx of the lower middle class into the large urban centers during the second half of the nineteenth century stimulated, as we shall see, a renaissance in the productive relations between orality and writing in the form of collective reading, *cordel* literature, and the art of *payadores* or gaucho singers (see **Figure 1**).

Second Moment: The Nineteenth Century, Patrician Culture-Bourgeois Culture

The colonizing configuration was followed by the real colonial moment and then the Bourbon efforts to control and direct the flow of ideas from the European Enlightenment by carefully selecting those that best suited the authoritarian and Catholic realities of America. From the time of Independence, the postcolonial states and their elitist leaders, who had often used the subversive potential of letters and the press to champion the Independence cause, attempted to reposition literature (and the production of discourse in general) within the national discursive formation. This was developed gradually and through a somewhat contradictory process. While the entry and access of the people to these discourses were limited and rationed, there was, on the one hand, an explosion of printed discourses (made possible by both liberal and conservative contributions) and, on the other, a secular attack led by the liberals on the ideological perspective inspiring the ecclesiastical censure of this thriving publishing market.

During the nineteenth century, the expansion of literature within the domestic sphere, which reached not only the female elite but also the middle classes, made the Church understand that one of the most powerful forms of secularization by which liberal ideas threatened their survival in the former colonies was now precisely the proliferation of publications addressed not only to the masculine elite in the public sphere but to an ever increasing circle of other readers (see Poblete 1999). In 1871 Ignacio Manuel Altamirano (1834–1893) indirectly mentioned the change taking effect at the time:

Ya se ve: las mujeres antes no sabían nada; el ideal del clero era la mujer ignorante, y con razón. Para dominarla a su sabor, era preciso que nada supiera. Una mujer que apenas supiera leer su devocionario, era lo más propio para hacer un instrumento ciego. Y todavía en los países atrasados, como España y México, se cree por la gente antigua que la mujer debe ser ignorante. (quoted in Ruedas de la Serna, 226)

One can already see it: before women did not know anything. The priest's ideal was, with good reason, the ignorant woman. In order to dominate her as wished, it was essential that she knew

Figure 1.

Photograph of engraving of a gaucho musical duel (payada de contrapunto). *(Courtesy of Eva Grosser Lerner and Lucio Molina y Vedia)*

nothing. A woman who could just about read her prayer book was the most suited to become a blind instrument. And in backward countries, such as Spain and Mexico, the belief is still held by old fashioned people that the woman should be ignorant.

Ambrosio Fornet states that in Cuba in the nineteenth century, "before the newspaper became a familiar object for the popular classes, religious propaganda in its various printed forms was the only 'echo' which reached all social strata" (Fornet 60).

Within this framework, the reading of literature or, more broadly speaking, of the socially circulating discourses, underwent a series of transformations determined by several new historical developments. Just as there was a growing tendency for the mass circulation of books and printed matter—obvious, at least, to the men of the time (Henríquez Ureña 59–94; Fornet; Subercaseaux 1993), so was there a separation between Church and State during the nineteenth century. These institutions no longer had the degree of identification and complementarity that had distinguished them during the colonial period (see Pike; Hamnett). The control of the production,

circulation, and interpretation of printed matter proved much more complicated and hence ineffective as soon as the secular and religious agencies began to differ in opinion. Moreover, this rise in the circulation of books and in printed matter (especially newspapers and periodicals) meant that the object of control had to be redefined. From every perspective, this was the decisive factor. Of course, the proliferation of discourses went hand in glove with the relative but important diversification of the sectors that had direct access—that is, not mediated by the priests—to this reading material. In other words, those subject to control also had to be redefined. The Indians had now been replaced by the women, first of the upper and then of the middle classes, and toward the end of the century by lower-middle-class artisans and traders. This persistent shift from the scarce and elitist book to the newspaper and relatively large amount of mass-printed matter occurred as if written discourse—which had subsumed and colonized in the book both its own medieval European origin (in documents, scrolls, folios) and the forms of non-alphabetic

writing of the *amoxtli* of the conquered indigenous peoples–
had rebelled against this compression of its origins and spread
itself out once more in the open, modern, and perishable
form of the newspaper.

Domingo Faustino Sarmiento (1811–1888) emphasized the
particular popularizing and progressive function of consistent
and mass reading of novels in the newspapers: "En el Paraguay y en Chile, todos saben leer; lo único que les falta para
no ser los dos pueblos más atrasados entre nosotros es leer.
No hay libros ni objetos [o motivaciones] para leerlos, si los
hubiera. Con las novelas y los diarios empiezan [esos lectores]
a ejercitar aquella adquisición estéril" (Sarmiento 1887–1900,
45–46; 161) ("In Paraguay and in Chile, everyone knows how
to read; the one thing they lack in order not to be the most
backward among us is actually something to read. There are
no books, no objects [or motivation] for reading, even if they
existed. With the arrival of novels and newspapers [these
readers] are beginning to exercise that heretofore sterile
acquisition"). At last, the newspaper produced this coexistence, so characteristic of the nineteenth century, of discourses
which had always belonged to clearly defined and separate
spheres and sectors: essays, politics, sentimental works of fiction and long narratives, almanacs, advice columns, police
records, business news, etc.

In this sense, one can well understand the complaint of the
Colombian Miguel A. Caro (1843–1909), an exemplary Latin
American man of letters of the nineteenth century. In "Ligera
excursión ideológica" [Light Ideological Excursion], a philosophical work on the "mental operation known as judgment
and its elements," Caro makes the following comment:

> Some will say, and not without reason, that this is a more suitable
> study for a book or a journal than a newspaper. But, just between
> us, who is going to publish a book on a point of speculative
> philosophy? Conditions in the country are such that the
> newspaper brings together the characteristics of this and that
> journal and of the book at the same time. So we have understood
> it, when editing our own . . . . We will feel rewarded if the reading
> of these brief notes shows some of those young fellow
> countrymen who unwittingly profess a belief in the sensualist
> principle the error of their ways, and if it deserves the learned
> attention of our subscribers outside the republic, who prefer the
> serious and original articles in our columns to the news items,
> stories, and frivolous and light literature in general addressed to
> another kind of readership. (1962b, 584–85)

Caro alludes here to two important points in the context of this
discussion: the place of newspapers as cultural instruments and
their public readership. In the first place, he refers to the conditions of publicity, of which the newspapers are the epitome in
countries lacking the sufficiently developed production apparatus for the book. If we consider that the function of the newspaper, the specialized journal and the book were simultaneously
incorporated into the newspaper that set out to be a de facto
textual space in which different communities of men and
women readers put into practice their distinctive sense of
belonging to the same national reading public. In the second
place, Caro distinguishes between a learned public and
"another kind of readership." This classification or class distinction among readers coincides with the reading preferences:
there is a pensive and learned sector, which reads serious articles, and another frivolous sector that spends its time reading
news items and short stories. There is a similar contrast
between learned and light literature, which suggests a repetition of, on the one hand, the traditional opposition between

two kinds of reading (the intensive and the extensive, the
learned masculine and the frivolous, light feminine reading),
and, on the other, the discursive hierarchy that makes the distinction between "the news items, stories and frivolous and
light literature in general," in other words, novelistic prose, and
poetry, the literary genre *par excellence* in Caro's opinion. In
fact, the title of his article, "Light Ideological Excursion," the
name of the newspaper (*El Tradicionista*), which Caro founded
and edited and in which the article appeared, and, finally, his
search for foreign learned readers are all signs of the climate
and the new commercial pressures with which he was forced to
come to terms in the completely new configuration proposed
by what we would today call the publishing market. He discovered that underlying that distinctive sense of belonging to the
same national reading formation was a form of cultural communion in which, at least in relation to certain discourses such
as fiction, the "classes of readers" lost their clarity of definition,
thereby merging with each other and dissolving into a more
middle class and comprehensive national bourgeois public
than the aristocracy of yesteryear.

Intensive-Extensive Reading and National Reading

During the better part of the nineteenth century, the Church
had consolidated its hold on society and had restated its
sociopolitical justification in the heart of the postcolonial
states through its control and indoctrination of women,
extolling women's virtue as submissive acceptance of their
place in society and as full compliance with sociocultural
norms in all levels of society, but especially in the popular
sector. The popularization of reading, particularly of fiction,
must have made the clergy aware of a perverse threat in the
reawakening of a sense of repression with the return of discourses other than those favored by the church, discourses
spoken from one impassioned heart to another, which the
clergy had tried so hard, over a period of three hundred
years, and at great cost, to eradicate from the American colonies. The discourses against popular fiction were the same
as those Jean-Jacques Rousseau had used to express his cen-
sorial and paradoxical fanaticism. When studying the
extraordinary case of the Frenchman Jean Ranson, an assiduous and fervent reader of Rousseau's literary work, Robert
Darnton confronted the task of historicizing reading. Darnton combines his discussion of the surviving forty-seven letters containing the readings of this good, provincial,
bourgeois man, who in many respects resembles the new
readership of what we shall later call national fiction in Latin
America, with Rousseau's work and reaches some conclusions that are very useful for this study. The paradox of the
situation of the author of *Julie, ou la Nouvelle Héloïse* was that
he had spoken out harshly against the novel and that now he
himself had written one. "Rousseau's reply in the prefaces is
deceptively simple: 'This novel is not a novel'" (Darnton 1985,
229). With this work, Rousseau had indeed proposed the creation of "another cultural form, an anti-literature literature, in
which he could defend the cause of virtue by appealing directly
to the unsophisticated" (Darnton 1985, 231).

Whereas Rousseau's proposal was a reaction against what
he considered the prevailing corruption in the French literary
salons, which even in the case of the French Encyclopedists did
little more, in his opinion, than reproduce the elitism and
moral decadence of the *ancien régime*, liberal projects in Latin
America promoting a national novel essentially attempted to
address the same problem. At issue was how to write literature

that would not only entertain readers but also educate them with the kind of knowledge and moral discipline required by the liberal champions of the new republics. The novelist Alberto Blest Gana (1830–1920), traditionally considered the father of the Chilean novel, believed he had solved the problem with his national *costumbrista* novel. He developed this theme in his famous speech of 1861 entitled "La literatura chilena. Algunas consideraciones sobre ella" [1977; "Reflections on Chilean Literature"], delivered on the incorporation of the Faculty of Humanities into the University of Chile. It essentially dealt with the need to counter the proliferation of serialized foreign novels in the newspapers of the time with a national product.

What was at stake becomes clear when one realizes that the same publishing situation that had so successfully developed literary production in Chile had meant the end of the liberal literary project of the 1830s in Cuba, where the sociopolitical and economic colonial conditions were somewhat different. Fornet points out the paradox that "Cuban narrative was left without subscribers or publishers precisely when more novels were being published and bought by readers in Cuba" (124). Their national literature had been displaced by serialized French novels and foreign romance fiction, thanks to the imperatives of the publishing market. As we shall see in the case of Chile, this denationalization of the literature that was circulating in the country was not, however, the only possible or necessary consequence of the publishing explosion and of the appearance of a new kind of reading public. This de-Cubanization, as we might call it, was a sign, even in Cuba, of the irruption into the traditional space of letters of a radically new readership (women, although mainly from the upper classes at first), which had quite a different sensitivity and literary taste from the learned elite.

Instead of trying to summarize or comment *in extenso* on that essay by Alberto Blest Gana (see, instead, Poblete 1999), I shall discuss the consequences of his proposal for this historical view of reading. In the first scene of his first novel, *Una escena social* [A Social Scene], published in serial form in 1853, Blest had written:

> Todo eso es falso, dije un día, cerrando indignado un tomo de 'La Nueva Heloísa,' 'Detesto esas virtudes lacrimosas, tan recatadas en el sensualismo que lloran sobre una falta cometida hasta encontrar de nuevo la ocasión de cometerla. Y lleno de despecho contra el pacífico ciudadano de Ginebra [Rousseau], arrojé el libro hacia la extremidad opuesta de la mesa y apoyé mi frente sobre la mano izquierda, actitud en la cual suelo quedarme largos instantes en meditación. (Blest Gana n.d., 51)

> All this is false, I said one day, indignantly closing a volume of *La Nouvelle Héloïse*. I detest those lachrymose virtues, so demurely sensual that they cry over a mistake they've made until they find another occasion to do it again. And so, disdainful of that peaceful citizen from Geneva [Rousseau], I threw the book across the table and rested my brow on my left hand, an attitude I often strike when meditating for a while.

What is worth stressing here is his dramatization of what I would call the historical conditions of the reading situation in Chile during the second half of the nineteenth century. The passage begins on a clearly metareflective level. This is a novel that *opens* with a reader indignantly closing another novel. The novel we read is a national Chilean novel and the one closed is a famous work by a French author. Blest Gana starts his literary career and his first novel, then, by proceeding to close a foreign novel; hence, the reading of the national novel begins when the reading of the foreign novel has been concluded. In this equation, one thing makes the other possible. The opening requires a closure, a beginning and an end. The question he poses is: Where does one begin and the other end? As so often happens, the border seems to unite them precisely at the moment when it separates them. Immediately afterward, the national reader-character adopts a pensive gesture typical of European sentimental literature, which Rousseau had championed and in which the Chilean protagonist would recognize the Romantic reference.

In this dramatization, the reader of A Social Scene reproduces, on another level, the paradox of the reader-character who is indignant about "those lachrymose virtues, so demurely sensual that they cry over a mistake they've made until they find another occasion to do it again." The nineteenth-century reader of a Chilean work immediately has to confront his or her moral ambiguity as a reader of novels. One could even say that the phrase perfectly describes the seductive and irrepressible mechanism that the contemporaries of Blest Gana identified, from their different ideological trenches, as the salient characteristic of novelistic fiction. The paradox here is that beginning to read is to return simultaneously to the space of the release of libidinal drives and to the site of its censure and control. Opening and closure join hands there. This highly stylized gesture of the first national reader includes, moreover, the dilemma to which the Chilean national novel, or at least that proposed by Blest Gana, attempts to respond. In this frozen moment, when the European Romantic model was utilized in order to be spurned as irrelevant, we witness the official birth of a literature whose originality and autonomy were sustained by creative dependence upon foreign models. Rather than showing a parasitic relationship, this scene truly reproduces its historical conditions of emergence.

Like Rousseau, Blest Gana proposed in this way to develop what he called a novel "of national customs" in which the Chilean reader could relate his or her own life to the text he or she was reading in such a manner that the effect would not only prove socially productive, but also be personally entertaining and transformational. That is to say, the subjective experience of reading fiction would become an act of constructing the nation. This transformation in reading practice, which attempted to combine the former ideals of moral edification through the written word with the new and modern demands of the publishing world driven fundamentally by the desire to stimulate consumption, is best understood in the context of one of the few macro-hypotheses of periodization in historical studies of reading.

In the history of European reading, Rolf Engelsing has proposed that we consider the shift from intensive to extensive reading. By intensive reading Engelsing understands discerning, thorough, and attentive rereadings of a few religious texts. Engelsing's model is the Protestant reading of the Bible; in Latin America during the first half of the nineteenth century, the equivalent would be the catechisms and prayer books that had been the first national best-sellers. This kind of reading had prevailed among Europeans from the Middle Ages to the end of the eighteenth century. According to Engelsing, a change took place at this time because the greater availability of books and writings altered reading habits and modes. Extensive reading is faster and performed on many different texts circulating in the developing publishing market (Engelsing; Chartier 1994; Darnton 1990). Domingo

Faustino Sarmiento had already understood the importance of the place of the Bible in Protestant culture, and he wondered what book could occupy a similar place in Catholic culture. His response compares the intensive and constant practice of reading the Bible in Protestant countries with the extensive reading of novels:

> Para ser católico es necesario ante todo tener fe. El catolicismo lo dice. Para ser protestante es preciso *saber leer* para leer la Biblia. . . . ¿Cuál es el libro del católico?. . . ¡Nombradlo!. . . un libro enciclopedia . . . un libro que sea cuento que interese, fantasía que exalte el espíritu, enigma que aguce la inteligencia, poesía que remonte la imaginación. . . . Mostradme ese libro. No existe. (Sarmiento 1887–1900b, 159–60)

> To be a Catholic it is necessary, first and foremost, to have faith. Catholicism dictates it. To be Protestant one must *be able to read* in order to read the Bible. . . . What is the Catholic's book? . . . Name it! . . . An encyclopedic book. . . , a book that contains an interesting story, a fantasy that exalts the spirit, an enigma that excites the intellect, poetry that gives flight to the imagination. . . . Show me this book. It does not exist.

In this text of 1856, Sarmiento alludes to the educational and progressive functions that the intensive reading of the Bible or the extensive reading of novels and serials served or might serve. He thus reveals that one of the keys to his plan for mass literacy was to exploit popular readers' potential interest in fiction. As we know, this fundamental cultural expansion was, in Sarmiento's opinion, one of the prerequisites for the extraordinary industrial and commercial development in the United States of America, the model republic: "the most effective way of raising the intellectual level of a nation, disseminating education to every social class, is to encourage the habit of reading until it becomes a distinctive feature of character and practice, as it has in Germany and the United States" (Sarmiento 1887–1900a, 396).

In 1876, the Chilean Alfredo Ovalle, responding at that time to advancements in the publishing industry in general and, in particular, to the abundance of periodicals (and within them of serialized fiction), proposed, in an article called "Los libros y los lectores" ["Books and Readers"], that readers should return to the intensive forms of reading one or two essential books and abandon superficial extensive reading: "The widespread belief that all a person has to do is read *many books in whatever way* is as mistaken as that of a certain political tendency. . . . That is why the proverb *Timeo homo unius libri* is so true. Who could be wiser than he who truly masters the Holy Bible or who could be a better linguist than he who has conversed more with Cervantes?" (Ovalle 264). In a related move, Blest Gana, armed with what I have called his "powerful transactional liberalism" (Poblete 1999, 85), proposed to his national public that, instead of accepting the cheap and facile consumerism that the mass French literary publishing industry offered them, they should decide to read a new type of national text. Based on everyday situations and realities that all could appreciate, it would not be prohibitively or discriminately dense; such an approach would permit and demand discerning reading, which would at the same time be more rewarding and entertaining. In sum, he proposed a return to semi-intensive reading, transformed by a nationalistic approach: "A menos de ser un libro cuya compresión *demande conocimientos previos y especiales*, las producciones de *amena literatura* encuentran en nuestros círculos ilustrados una acogida benévola y cordial" (Blest Gana 1859, 51) ("Unless it is a book that *demands previous and special knowledge* for its

understanding, the production of *light literature* will find a warm and benevolent welcome in our enlightened circles").

The national novel thus accomplished in practice the ideal of the new "anti-literature" reading of literature that Rousseau had offered his readers. In it, everyday life and the heart of each citizen would be directly exposed (supposedly without the mediation of traditional lettered discourses) to the impression of the word that sought to be as seductive as it was truthful and didactic. For this reason, the national novel, as Blest Gana perceived it, took great care not to demand more than what every Chilean already possessed by the mere fact of belonging to this respectable society. Poetry, in turn, exacted a particular preparation that put it beyond the bounds of many of these citizens:

> La novela, con efecto, cuenta entre la generalidad de los lectores, con un número mucho mayor de aficionados que la poesía, porque la primera está al alcance de todos, mientras que para gustar de la segunda, se ha menester de un espíritu más connaturalizado con los preceptos del arte. . . . Mientras que la poesía conserva siempre para el vulgo la apariencia de los antiguos ídolos cuyo lenguaje era comprensible únicamente a los sacerdotes del culto pagano, la novela, por el contrario, tiene un especial encanto para toda clase de inteligencias, habla el lenguaje de todos, pinta cuadros que cada cual puede a su manera comprender y aplicar y lleva la civilización hasta las clases menos cultas de la sociedad, por el atractivo de escenas de la vida ordinaria contadas con un lenguaje fácil y sencillo. (Blest Gana 1977, 119)

> The novel really has many more followers among the common run of readers than poetry, because the former is within everyone's reach, whereas one needs a spirit *au fait* with the precepts of art in order to enjoy the latter. . . . Whereas poetry always gives the appearance to the common people of the ancient idols whose language was comprehensible only to the priests of pagan worship, the novel holds a special charm for all kinds of intelligence, its language is accessible to all, it paints pictures each person can understand and apply in his own way, and it takes civilization to the least educated social classes, on account of the appeal of its scenes drawn from everyday life narrated in simple and easy language.

It is pertinent to note in passing that Blest Gana makes explicit reference to the ecclesiastical, if pagan, control of social discourses and to the contrast between this esotericism and the novel, which he favors.

In a critical article published in 1864 upon the publication of another of Blest Gana's novels, *El ideal de un calavera* [A Foolish Ideal], Benjamín Vicuña Mackenna summarized the traditional, and still influential, perception among the learned of the day:

> La novela se considera, pues, entre nosotros como una impertinencia, como un peligro, casi como un acto de mala educación, y en consecuencia los novelistas pasan por seres raros, mitad pecadores y mitad calaveras, que es preciso mirar con desconfianza, y cuyos libros no pueden leerse sino a hurtadillas, metiéndolos con astuto cuidado dentro de los sendos volúmenes del Año cristiano para que no se enfade la mamá, ni murmure el capellán o la llavera. (239)

> We consider the novel an impertinence, a danger, almost an act of bad education, and consequentially novelists are perceived as strange beings, half sinners and half scoundrels, who are best looked upon with mistrust and whose books can be read only on the sly, by placing each astutely within a volume of the *Christian Year* in order to avert mother's wrath or the complaints of housekeeper and priest.

This quotation clarifies several points in our discussion. To begin with, one understands why Blest Gana opened his first novel with that scene in which censorship, pleasure, and reading are interwoven by alluding simultaneously to the dangers and the possibilities that the culture of the period attributed to the novelistic genre. One also perceives up to what point Blest Gana's *costumbrista* novel responds to and directly represents one of the Chilean customs that most concerned the Church during this period: the insertion of the private and individual reader of fiction in the formerly quasi-exclusive space of pious texts. The hybrid Blest Gana produced in the didactic novel, then, proceeds "astutely" to legitimize another kind of reading that previously one could only do "on the sly." It thus puts the functions that the Church and State had historically assigned to written discourse and reading in touch with a new literary genre and readership.

Clearly this was not a solution that satisfied everyone. At the other end of the ideological spectrum, Miguel Antonio Caro revealed the point at which the novel as a cultural practice demanded an ideological response on the conservative band. According to Caro's cultural hierarchy, poetry, as a divinely inspired discourse, was uppermost. For this reason, he stated, when commenting on Jorge Isaacs's (1837–1895) work, that: "Mr. Isaacs is well-known in Colombia and in other Spanish American regions as a novelist and a poet, or, rather, exclusively as a poet, because *María* is not a novel (and, if considered such, it would be a bad novel), it is an idyll, a dream of love" (Caro 1962a, 1051). Regretting that Issacs had not received any financial reward for his poetic work, Caro declared: "After the publication of *María* and his *Poesías*, written when he was a spiritualist and believer, Mr. Isaacs has not written a book or anything of literary merit in twenty years. It appears that materialism has sterilized him." And he went on to say: "Sins are committed against the Holy Ghost, and, in another order of ideas, sins are committed against poetry for which there is no forgiveness. . . . This is what we deplore and this is what the muses have not pardoned, because a materialist poet is an antinomy, an impossibility" (1962a, 1050–51).

This defense of poetry and attack on the novel and the materialism of the time were, to Caro's mind, the results of a cultural proposition that endeavored to make Colombian education and literature revert to the frame of classical humanism (see Chapter 29 in Volume III). By this model, Greek and Latin poetry, as reinterpreted in a Christian and Catholic vein, was uppermost in the cultural hierarchy and openly met the functions of social distinction based on accumulated cultural capital: "literary studies simultaneously arouse, refine, and enhance intelligence. . . . The illustrious Macaulay established . . . that classical studies mark the dividing line between gentleman and savage. And could we, without seriously damaging civilization, dispense with this branch of public education, of this salutary corrective to democracies, so prone as they are to vulgarity and disorder?" (Caro 1962c, 1382). The defense of the rare and the select contained within it a desire to recuperate traditional intensive reading. This would, as we saw earlier, act as a corrective resistance, in general terms, to the egalitarian cultural and political pressures that characterized, in Caro's opinion, modern democracies; in particular, it would act as a resistance to the extensive reading typical of "frivolous and light literature addressed to another kind of readership." According to Caro, the devoted and intense reading of studies

and the careful deciphering of classical texts were the only reading practices that merited consideration.

Trying once more to create an opposition between the reading of novels and the Catholic reading of religious books, Sarmiento described the traditional learned culture of the Argentinean patriot and lawyer Dalmacio Velez Sarsfield (1800–1875) in the following way:

> Murió sin haber leído una sola novela en toda su vida; y se lamentaba a veces de no entender el libreto de las operas, por no estar en antecedentes del drama que había servido de tema [es decir, por no poder filiarlo a un texto modélico, un procedimiento típico de la cultura letrada tradicional]. Esta que parece una originalidad en quien tanto tenía el poema épico de Virgilio, que parecería abrir el ánimo a los goces de la imaginación, era sin embargo efecto de un defecto de la antigua educación monástica de nuestras Universidades. El sentimiento de lo bello no sólo no era cultivado por ningún estudio, sino que quedaba atrofiado el que nos viene de la naturaleza. Las bellas artes, las formas, la imaginación no tuvieron un altar en aquellos claustros de murallas lisas y sombrías en que se murmuraba latín, o se repetían autores de derecho o de teología. (Sarmiento 1887–1900c, 312)

> He died without having read a single novel in his entire life; and at times he regretted that he could not understand the opera libretti, because he was not familiar with the drama that might have served as the theme [that is, not to be able to affiliate it with a model text, a typical procedure in traditional learned culture]. That which appears to be an originality in a person who so possessed Virgil's epic poem that he seemed to open the spirit to the flights of fancy, was, however, the effect of a defect of ancient monastic education in our Universities. The sentiment of beauty was not only not cultivated by any study, but also atrophied that which comes to us from nature. The fine arts, the forms, the imagination had no altar in those cloisters of plain and somber walls behind which Latin was murmured, or authors of law and theology were recited.

To illustrate the effects this kind of reading would have on those who had had no training in traditional humanism, Sarmiento gave the following example:

> Dadle a una niña de quince años un libro de los que llamáis serios. No lo leerá, porque no puede concentrar su movible atención, porque su inteligencia carece de nociones, y sus ojos no están habituados a recorrer, sin fatiga y con rapidez, ese entelado de letras, de signos y de notas que contiene un libro; y sus ojos se rinden y el sueño los cierra. (1887–1990b, 160)

> Give a fifteen-year-old girl one of the books you would call serious. She will not read it, because she cannot focus her wandering attention, because her intelligence lacks the notions and she is not used to running her eyes, tirelessly and rapidly, through that puzzle of words, signs, and notes that a book contains; and her eyes would surrender and sleep would close them.

Nonetheless, the novels published in the newspapers, and thereby accessible to a new and potentially mass public, gave everyone the opportunity to exercise their dulled reading abilities. As a practice of everyday life, the reading of novels developed both intelligence and sensitivity and, in this way, made "civilization" more widely known among those who "sin su aguijón no habrían jamás tomado un libro en las manos" (Sarmiento, 1887–1900b, 160) ("would never have picked up a book without this stimulus").

The Mexican Ignacio M. Altamirano held a similar view:

> Las novelas de [Juan] Mateos, cualesquiera que sean los defectos que les eche en cara la crítica, tienen el mérito de popularizar los acontecimientos de nuestra historia nacional, que de otro modo

permanecerían desconocidos a los ojos de la multitud, supuesto que los anales puramente históricos no son fáciles de adquirir por los pobres, ni agrada su lectura por carecer del encanto que la narración novelesca sabe darles. (Altamirano 1969, 265)

Whatever defects the critics might reproach him for, [Juan] Mateos's novels have the merit of popularizing the events of our national history, which the multitude would otherwise know nothing about, since the poor would find it difficult to acquire historical annals and would not enjoy reading them as they lack the enchantment of novelistic narration.

In Mexico in 1868, Altamirano combined the positions of Sarmiento and Blest Gana in his defense of the national novel as an instrument essential to the construction of the nation. Indicating the distance between the traditional and the nationalist conception of the novel, Altamirano wrote:

No hay que decir ahora que la novela es una composición inútil y frívola, de mero pasatiempo, y de cuya lectura no se saca provecho alguno, sino por el contrario, corrupción y extravíos . . . generalmente hablando, la novela ocupa ya un lugar respetable en la literatura, y se siente su influencia en el progreso intelectual y moral de los pueblos modernos. (1991, 70)

There is no reason to say that the novel is a useless and frivolous composition, a mere pastime, from which one cannot derive any benefit; on the contrary, distortion and deviation apart, . . . generally speaking, the novel now holds a respectable position in literature and one feels its influence on the moral and intellectual progress of modern countries.

Altamirano was alluding, moreover, to a decisive epochal transformation in the transition from patrician societies to national bourgeois societies in Latin America (see Romero 1976). By this I mean the change from the pedagogy, that focused on the Greek and Latin classics and stimulated memorization of their models by repeated reading, to that which gave priority to the citizens' immediate forms of identifying with their national quotidian contexts (see Poblete 1997): "Todo lo útil que nuestros antepasados no podían hacer comprender o estudiar al pueblo bajo formas establecidas desde la Antigüedad, lo pueden hoy los modernos bajo la forma agradable y atractiva de la novela" (Altamirano 1991, 70) ("All the useful things that our forefathers could not make the people understand or study in the modes established from the time of Antiquity the moderns now can do under the pleasant and attractive mode of the novel").

This methodological change did not really take effect until the positivistic educational reforms at the end of the nineteenth century. Proof of this is that Altamirano felt obliged to add the following appeasing remarks, which reestablished the hierarchies and the traditional differences in the various ways of accumulating cultural capital:

No concluiremos este ensayo, sin advertir que nosotros hemos considerado la novela como lectura del pueblo, y hemos juzgado su importancia no por comparación con los otros géneros literarios, sino por la influencia que ha tenido y tendrá todavía en la educación de las masas. La novela es el libro de las masas. Los demás estudios, desnudos del atavío de la imaginación, y mejores por eso, sin disputa, están reservados a un círculo más inteligente y más dichoso, porque no tiene necesidad de fábulas y de poesía para sacar de ellos el provecho que desea. (1991, 76)

We should not conclude this essay before pointing out that we have regarded the novel as reading material for the people and we have judged its importance not by comparing it with other literary genres but by the influence it has exerted and will exert on the education of the masses. The novel is the book of the

masses. The other studies, bare of the fineries of the imagination, and undoubtedly better for being so, are reserved for a more intelligent and fortunate circle of people, who do not need fables and poetry to derive whatever benefit they wish.

He thus reiterated that conciliatory-conservative gesture made by Alberto Blest Gana in Chile. In discoursive and reading formations, even during the transition from the forms of literacy and cultural capital dominated by poetry and the classical writers to others in which journalistic and novelistic prose began to dominate, it appears that the new national intellectuals felt that the safest and most natural attitude was to acknowledge the legitimacy of the former and to be paternalistic toward the latter.

Other Forms of Reading

The identification of the shift from the intensive reading of a few texts, often memorized and vocalized, to the extensive and silent reading of many texts, which resulted in the deconsecration of the object and contents read, was one of the factors that permitted Blest Gana to formulate his proposal for a national semi-intensive reading readily accessible to a middle-class readership (or, to put it in other words, within the reach of the cultural capital and the interests of a very broad readership in this national society). This hypothesis of the shift from intensive to extensive reading forms one of three fundamental oppositions in current studies on the history of reading practices (Chartier 1995, 143). Another opposition is the identification of the transition, in the Middle Ages in Europe, from a reading in which comprehension presupposes the vocalization of the text to a silent and purely visual reading. The third is between the reading of intimacy, enclosure, and solitude and collective readings in communal spaces. Before concluding this essay, I would like to discuss the third of these briefly within the context of Latin America.

The entry into the world of the silent and solitary reading of the national novel should not blind us to earlier and later reading practices on the continent. I have already mentioned the presence of a form of orality practiced by the elite and of an advanced rhetoric practiced by the indigenous peoples of Mexico (León Portilla 1989). To this we should add the canto-poetry texts preserved in the codex *Cantares Mexicanos*, and my concern here is to highlight the nature of their codification and performance. Largely a product of the colonial situation during the third quarter of the sixteenth century, the *Cantares* codified the invocations of ancient history and wisdom in very formal language. John Bierhorst underlines this point by quoting the Spanish missionaries' complaints when faced with the unfathomable esotericism of these *cantares*. Given their complicated semantic and syntactic structures and the art of the singer-poets or troubadours responsible for interpreting them, the *Cantares* are an example of the interweaving of poetry, music, dance, and religion that appeared to have characterized many pre-Hispanic cultural manifestations. Bierhorst states: "There is no reliable evidence that Aztec 'poetry' was ever recited apart from music or ever committed to writing for the enjoyment of the silent reader" (42). Miguel León Portilla stresses the symbiotic relation between speech and writing in the so-called reading of the pre-Hispanic Nahuatl and Mixteca codices learned at school by those aspiring to be elders or priests. The words *amoxohtoca* (follow the book) and *tlapoa* (narrate or recite that which is contained in it) make León Portilla aware of this complex interfusion and complementarity of memorization based on formal speech and of the erudition necessary to decipher based on knowledge of pictographic language (León Portilla 1996, 19–71). The reading performances of the ancient Mexicans recall the historicity of our own acquired forms of textual deciphering and interpretation. That is to say, they indicate both the existence of other ways of reading and the productive character of our relationship with the text. They also reveal a different connection between the body of the reader and the text. For this reason, it is worth stressing the importance of the reader-interpreter in the Nahua world and in their conceptualization of sociosemiotic processes (Mignolo 1995, 109–18). As much for the elders, whose bodies were the vessels of orally transmitted wisdom, as for the young men who had to master the rhetorical art of performance, the relation between body and discourse differed from that of the Europeans whose silent and solitary reading practices began to neutralize their bodies.

Ever since this time and moving on through the excesses of the Baroque fiestas and ceremonies to the nineteenth century, these collective forms of reading and performance would always represent a potential challenge to the domination of the men of letters, the book, and writing privileges on the continent. For example, some Cuban cigar factories introduced the custom towards the end of 1865 of paying a Reader who would read out loud in order to entertain and educate the others as they worked. The Reader's pay came from the contributions of his fellow workers. Under the sociopolitical conditions of Spanish colonialism, the initiative was, however, perceived as an intolerable threat and soon suppressed. The edict prohibiting it stated: "Tolerance of public readings has turned the artisans' meetings into political groups, and this simple and hard-working social class, who do not have the necessary instruction to be able to distinguish and discern the false theories from what is useful, lawful, and just, are easily dazzled and beguiled by the exaggerated interpretation of the doctrines they are listening to" (Fornet 189). Instead of these collective readings, in which the ruling class's semiotic control subsided as the workers' abilities for semantic processing were empowered by their collectivity, the official edict proposed that they should read, in the traditional school context, texts "approved by competent authorities" in which the meaning was intentionally limited: "The reading of books that contain the Christian doctrine, the statutes of good government and the regulations laid down by the authorities, lessons that teach one how to conduct oneself with moderation and courtesy, and treatises written on trades and the arts educate and teach the least privileged classes, making them honest parents and hard-working and useful citizens of the fatherland" (Fornet 189). The subversive potential of the readings had, quite rightly, been recognized by the authorities. From 1884 to 1896, when they were once again prohibited, these collective readings in the Cuban cigar factories had sprung up once more, now dominated by the anarchic texts of José Llunás, Proudhon, and Bakunin. There were also collective readings in the cigar factories of the Cuban émigrés who were persecuted by the colonial government, in which, as Fornet puts it, they "spread the mamba ideology and created workshops which were true centres of revolutionary national culture" (Fornet 191).

Another phenomenon of the second half of the nineteenth century that Latin America shared with other regions was the development of written practices for circulating popular literatures. The work of German philologists Rudolf Lenz and Roberto Lehman-Nitsche, among others, has made it possible

for us to study these practices today (see Subercaseaux 1988; Prieto). In their quest for specific and characteristic popular practices of precapitalist cultural formations, these nineteenth-century inheritors of the zealous work of collecting data undertaken by such colonial missionaries as Fray Bernardino de Sahagún, compiled toward the end of the nineteenth century important collections of printed matter circulated among and consumed by the masses. This practice repeats, with significant modifications, the complex process of writing down, producing, and preserving the pre-Hispanic and colonial indigenous legacy. The written transcriptions enabled them to get in touch with different cultural traditions and modes of thought and circulation. Among the differences, I should highlight the popular origin of most of the producers and consumers and the mass character of the loose sheets, leaflets, collections of songs to "sing with guitar accompaniment," novels, and newspaper serials.

Like the reading in the cigar factories, different forms of appropriation and consumption of printed texts coexisted and complemented each other. On the one hand, the campaign for literacy promoted and capitalized upon by Sarmiento, Blest Gana, Altamirano, and the other nation-builders started to produce mass results. There thus emerged a growing sector of popular urban readers who demanded alternative literature and made its production possible. Although often read silently, this literature represented a fusion of many heterogeneous discursive traditions, among which the learned discourse of the elite was only one component. On the other hand, these collections are one of several sources that make us aware of the existence and scope of the collective performances and reading of popular discourses. They reflect the impact of printing and publishing on urban and rural spaces through the mass production of loose sheets and song books containing ten-line stanzas, lines celebrating God and man, *milongas*, *vidalitas*, and improvised verse duels between minstrels such as the *payadas de contrapunto*. These discursive types gave birth to what Guillermo Sunkel has called "poetic journalism" (the events of the day are narrated in verse) and "journalism without readers" (generally recited to an illiterate audience). In the twentieth century this became the industrialized world's sensationalist popular press, which exploited many of these popular themes, languages, and styles (Sunkel 80).

Finally, we should not forget the *literatura de cordel* (so named because of the cord it hung from when on sale) from the Northeast of Brazil. With historical origins similar to those of the Argentinean and Chilean songs and *payadas*, the Northeastern *folhetos* now enjoy mass distribution as a result of the strength of the publishing market. Written in verse following the metric pattern of the *sextilha* (a stanza of six heptameters), these *folhetos* represent a popular combination of the possibilities of the written word, performance, and oral transmission. The so-called reading audiences of the *literatura de cordel*, who hear it at public readings or rural fairs, delight in its characteristic oral rendering: "Although a rise in the national literacy rate means that more people can now read *folhetos*, many still prefer the oral experience. . . . [A] sizable percentage continues to read the story aloud even when they are alone. Many persons can memorize parts or even whole *folhetos* after reading them or even after hearing them. Individuals who prefer a group reading situation also tend to prefer a live poet to recordings of *cordel* tales" (Slater 34). Like the other forms of collective reading I have mentioned, *cordel* literature demonstrates the historical existence of reading and interpretative practices that relativize the apparently ahistorical naturalness of our silent, visual, solitary, and static reading practice.

Conclusion

Pedro Henríquez Ureña underlines the great concern for education on the continent after Independence and the postcolonial process of the nineteenth century by stating in his *Historia de la cultura en la América Hispánica* [*A Concise History of Latin American Culture,* 1966]: "In different places it was stipulated [at that time] that the convents should teach the people to read and write, as they had in the sixteenth century, but had subsequently neglected to do" (59). Although this is clearly a rhetorical exaggeration, it serves here as a final justification for my privileging of (only) two moments in the long history of the Americas. Besides the practical reasons mentioned at the beginning, these are two moments in which reading and writing emerge with greatest strength as important technologies in the formation of submissive subjects, worshippers, and/or citizens. During both moments, the State and the Church recognized the need to regulate the production and circulation of discourses and the forms of their deployment and interpretation. As we have seen, their attempt to do this meant they had to control social semiosis and some of the productive forms through which this was expressed; in other words, they controlled texts and reading practices. In the nineteenth century, a third element, the publishing market, complicated the earlier measures taken, because it put the relation between text and reader within the reach of a growing and increasingly diverse range of social subjects. The popular publishing market and the alternative reading practices arising from it "made it possible," in Martín Barbero's opinion, "for the popular classes to move from speech to writing [and] to change folklore into popular lore" (1987, 111).

The whole process was, of course, only possible so long as there was a continual rise in schooling and literacy rates throughout the nineteenth century. Newland has calculated that for the whole of Spanish America (the figures are higher in the large cities and for such countries as Argentina and Chile) the literacy rates, that is, reading and writing, are the following: "less than 10 per cent in 1800. . . . 15 per cent in 1850 and 27 per cent in 1900" (Newland 361). During the second half of the nineteenth century, the relative expansion of education and the eventual growth in the publishing market stimulated new forms of cultural appropriation that led to transformations in the symbolic hierarchies that had characterized discursive and reader formations until that time. Two cultural models became engaged in what would be a lengthy controversy, which in many places only ended with the positivistic educational reforms toward the end of the century, and in others continued until well into the twentieth century. I am referring here to two cultural macromechanisms in which reading and the relation between subject and text play a crucial role: on the one hand, the imitation of classical paradigms; on the other, the pseudo-individualizing and expressive subjectivization. The former consisted in internalizing and reproducing what was considered an atemporal, superior, and hierarchical model expressed in carefully chosen language (that is, the highly stratified cultural formation). An example of this mechanism is the evangelizing mission of the Church, whose forms run the gamut from the authoritarian and hierarchical relation (mediated by formal ecclesiastical language) between the faithful and the sacred text to the quasi-religious veneration of Greek and Roman humanistic culture on the

part of the Catholic conservatives of the nineteenth century. The latter seeks, by means of less exclusive modes and styles, a personal response located in nationalized time and spaces in reader and pupil (that is, the democratic and national cultural formations). Typical of this mechanism is the educational effort made on the part of the emerging nation-states to prepare citizens through a deep-rooted sense of their local cultural space. This was what Sarmiento responded to when campaigning for mass literacy, as did Alberto Blest and Ignacio Manuel Atamirano in their national novels. In both macromechanisms of cultural production, the Church, the State, and individual subjects tried to determine the ways in which texts could legitimately be deployed. These technologies of reading thus aspired, in a specific time and space, to control the semiosis of these texts, which, though potentially limitless, was historically constrained.

When discussing the possibilities and limitations of this new emphasis on readers and audiences in cultural and media studies, Jesús Martín Barbero maintains that, on the one hand, "the reinstatement of the subject as a receiver has foregrounded the existence in our society of alternative cultural forms and matrices to those of the hegemony, alternatives to the erudite and ascetic culture of the book, such as popular cultures" (Martín Barbero 1997, 9–10), thereby creating a great potential for cultural democracy in Latin America. On the other hand, it is certainly true that "the questioning of the idea of the omnipotent sender cannot be confused or compared with neo-liberal ideology which deceivingly attributes 'all power to the consumer!' and has made it impossible for society and State to make any political intervention in the regulation of production" (Martín Barbero 1997, 9). Similarly, in one of the key books on the theoretical reformulation of what Armand and Michelle Mattelart call "the return of the subject" (Mattelart and Mattelart 1988, 92), Néstor García Canclini expresses his concern about the possibility of confusing "media decentralization" (a growth in the supply of symbolic commodities that target and appeal to different audiences) with "media deregulation." Media deregulation implies that, as the state withdraws from or is withdrawn from the cultural public sphere, the transnational and monopolistic corporations split both the supply of symbolic consumer goods and access to them into unequal segments (García Canclini 1990, 347). In these circumstances, the study of mediations cannot afford to forget to analyze the properties, structure, and orientation of the media, or, as the Mattelarts put it: "A paradigm [such as that of the return of the subject] so full of potential for redesigning the social [cannot be used] to legitimize a technocratic project" (Mattelart and Mattelart 1997, 109).

In an attempt to eschew the Scylla and Charybdis of cultural studies, that is to say, the emphasis laid on structures and institutions and on subjects, I have proposed here an historical and theoretical study of the role of reading and readership in two moments in the history of Latin American literature. For this reason, it seemed important to outline the relations between the macro-agents that attempt to define the socially legible spaces (Church, State, and market) and the micro-agents or receivers who engage in historically specific reading practices in those written social spaces that we call texts.

Translation by Charlotte Broad

Works Cited

Adorno, Rolena. 1992. Introduction. *Books of the Brave.* By Irving A. Leonard. Berkeley: University of California Press. ix–xl.

———. 1996. "Cultures in Contact: Mesoamerica, the Andes and the European Written Tradition." *The Cambridge History of Latin American Literature.* Vol. I. *Discovery to Modernism.* Ed. Roberto González Echevarría and Enrique Pupo Walker. Cambridge: Cambridge University Press. 33–57.

Altamirano, Ignacio Manuel. 1969. *Crónicas de* La Semana: *De "El Renacimiento"/1869.* Mexico City: Instituto Nacional de Bellas Artes.

———. 1991. "La literatura nacional." *Los novelistas como críticos.* Ed. Norma Klahn and Wilfrido Corral. Mexico City: Fondo de Cultura Económica. 59–76.

Bennett, Tony. 1987. "Texts in History: The Determinations of Readings and Their Texts." *Post-Structuralism and the Question of History.* Ed. Derek Attridge et al. Cambridge: Cambridge University Press. 63–81.

———. 1990. *Outside Literature.* London: Routledge.

Bierhorst, John. 1985. *Cantares Mexicanos: Songs of the Aztecs.* Stanford: Stanford University Press.

Blanco, José Joaquín. 1989. *La Literatura en la Nueva España.* Conquista y *Nuevo Mundo.* Mexico City: Cal y Arena.

Blest Gana, Alberto. n.d. *La fascinación. Una escena social. La aritmética en el amor.* Santiago: Zig-Zag.

———. 1859. "De los trabajos literarios en Chile." *La Semana.* 11 June. 51–52.

———. 1977. "La literatura chilena. Algunas consideraciones sobre ella." *Testimonios y documentos de la literatura chilena* (1842–1975). Ed. José Promis. Santiago: Editorial Nascimento. 108–28. Reprint of paper read by Alberto Blest Gana at his reception into the Faculty of Humanities at the University of Chile on 3 January 1861.

Caro, Miguel Antonio. 1962a. "El Darwinismo y las misiones." *Obras.* Vol. I. Bogotá: Instituto Caro y Cuervo. 1049–107.

———. 1962b. "Ligera excursión ideológica." *Obras.* Vol. I. Bogotá: Instituto Caro y Cuervo. 583–99.

———. 1962c. "Oración de estudios pronunciada en el acto de la solemne distribución de premios del Colegio del Espíritu Santo el día 15 de noviembre de 1880." *Obras.* Vol. I. Bogotá: Instituto Caro y Cuervo. 1374–85.

Chartier, Roger. 1994. *The Order of Books.* Stanford: Stanford University Press.

———. 1995. "Labourers and Voyagers: From the Text to the Reader." *Readers and Reading.* Ed. Andrew Bennett. New York: Longman. 132–49.

Corcuera, Sonia. 1994. *Del amor al temor: Borrachez, catequesis y control en la Nueva España (1555–1771).* Mexico City: Fondo de Cultura Económica.

Darnton, Robert. 1985. "Readers Respond to Rousseau: The Fabrication of Romantic Sensitivity." *The Great Cat Massacre and Other Episodes in French Cultural History.* New York: Vintage Books. 215–56.

———. 1990. *The Kiss of Lamourette: Reflections in Cultural History.* New York: Norton.

de Certeau, Michel. 1984. *The Practice of Everyday Life.* Trans. Steven Rendall. Berkeley: University of California Press.

Eagleton, Terry. 1986. "The Revolt of the Reader." *Against the Grain. Essays 1975–1985.* London: Verso. 181–84.

Engelsing, Rolf. 1974. *Der Bürger als Leser: Lesergeschichte in Deutschland 1500–1800.* Stuttgart: Metzler.

Fornet, Ambrosio. 1994. *El Libro en Cuba: Siglos XVIII y XIX.* Havana: Editorial Letras Cubanas.

Foucault, Michel. 1972. *The Archaeology of Knowledge.* New York: Harper Colophon.

García Canclini, Néstor. 1990. *Culturas híbridas: Estrategias para entrar y salir de la modernidad.* Mexico City: Grijalbo.

———. 1995. *Consumidores y ciudadanos: Conflictos multiculturales de la globalización.* Mexico City: Grijalbo.

Gonzalbo A., Pilar. 1988. "La lectura de evangelización en la Nueva España: Seminario de la educación en México del Colegio de México." *Historia de la lectura en México.* Mexico City: Colegio de México and Ediciones del Ermitaño. 9–48.

———. 1990. *Historia de la educación en México: El mundo indígena.* Mexico City: El Colegio de México.

Gruzinski, Serge. 1991. *La colonización de lo imaginario: Sociedades indígenas y occidentalización en el México español, siglos XVI–XVIII.* Mexico City: Fondo de Cultura Económica.

Hamnett, Brian R. 1987. "La regeneración. 1875–1900." *Historia de Iberoamérica.* Tomo III. *Historia contemporánea.* Ed. Manuel Lucena Samoral. Madrid: Cátedra. 317–401.

Henríquez Ureña, Pedro. 1961. *Historia de la cultura en la América Hispánica.* Mexico City: Fondo de Cultura Económica.

Horta Nunes, José. 1994. *Formação do leitor brasileiro: Imaginario da leitura no Brasil colonial.* São Paulo: Universidade Estadual de Campinas.

Leal, Ildefonso. 1978. *Libros y bibliotecas en Venezuela colonial* (1633–1767). Vol. I. Caracas: Academia Nacional de la Historia.

León Portilla, Miguel. 1989. *Historia de la literatura mexicana: Período prehispánico.* Mexico City: Editorial Alhambra Mexicana.

———. 1996. *El destino de la palabra: De la oralidad y los códices mesoamericanos a la escritura alfabética.* Mexico City: Fondo de Cultura Económica.

Lienhard, Martín. 1992. *La voz y su huella: Escritura y conflicto étnico-cultural en América Latina 1492–1988.* Lima: Editorial Horizonte.

López Austin, Alfredo. 1996. "La enseñanza escolar entre los mexicas." *Ideas, valores y tradiciones: Ensayos sobre la historia de la educación en México.* Ed. Mílada Bazant. Zinacantepec, Mexico City: El Colegio Mexiquense. 29–40.

Martín Barbero, Jesús. 1987. *De los medios a las mediaciones: Comunicación, cultura y hegemonía.* Mexico City: Gustavo Gili.

———. 1995. *Pre-textos: Conversaciones sobre la comunicación y sus contextos.* Cali: Ediciones Universidad del Valle.

Mattelart, Armand, and Michelle Mattelart. 1988. *Pensar sobre los medios: Comunicación y crítica social.* San José, Costa Rica: Editorial DEI.

———. 1997. "Los ochenta: Retorno del sujeto y mediación tecnológica." *Proyectar la comunicación.* Ed. Jesús Martín Barbero and Armando Silva. Bogotá: Tercer Mundo Editores. 93–119.

Mignolo, Walter. 1993. "'Palabras pronunciadas con el corazón caliente': Teorías del habla, del discurso y de la escritura." *Palavra, literatura e cultura.* Vol. I. *A situação colonial.* Org. Ana Pizarro. São Paulo: Memorial-Editora da Unicamp. 527–62.

———. 1995. *The Darker Side of the Renaissance. Literacy, Territoriality and Colonization.* Ann Arbor: University of Michigan Press.

Morandé, Pedro. 1987. *Cultura y modernización en América Latina.* Madrid: Ediciones Encuentro.

Newland, Carlos. 1991. "La educación elemental en Hispanoamérica: Desde la independencia hasta la centralización de los sistemas educativos nacionales." *Hispanic American Historical Review* 71.2: 333–64.

Osorio Romero, Ignacio. 1990. *La enseñanza del Latín a los indios.* Mexico City: Universidad Nacional Autónoma de México.

Ovalle, Alfredo. 1876. "Los libros i los lectores." *La estrella de Chile.* 18 November.

Pike, Frederick B. ed. 1964. *The Conflict between Church and State in Latin America.* New York: Knopf.

Poblete, Juan. 1997. "El castellano: La nueva disciplina y el texto nacional en el fin de siglo chileno." *Revista de Crítica Cultural* 15: 22–27.

———. 1999. "La construcción social de la lectura y la novela nacional: El caso de Alberto Blest Gana en Chile." *Latin American Research Review* 34.2: 75–108.

Polan, Dana. 1993. "The Public's Fear; or, Media as Monster in Habermas, Negt and Kluge." *The Phantom Public Sphere.* Ed. Bruce Robbins. Minneapolis: University of Minnesota Press. 33–41.

Prieto, Adolfo. 1988. *El discurso criollista en la formación de la Argentina moderna.* Buenos Aires: Editorial Sudamericana.

Rama, Angel. 1984. *La ciudad letrada.* Hanover: Ediciones del Norte.

Romero, José Luis. 1976. *Latinoamérica: Las ciudades y las ideas.* Mexico City: Siglo XXI.

Ruedas de la Serna, Jorge, ed. 1996. *La misión del escritor: Ensayos mexicanos del siglo XIX.* Mexico City: Universidad Nacional Autónoma de México.

Sarmiento, Domingo Faustino. 1887–1900a. "Bibliotecas populares." *Obras completas.* Vol. 30. Buenos Aires: Moreno. 269–398.

———. 1887–1900b. "Las novelas." *Obras completas.* Vol. 45–46. Buenos Aires: Moreno. 159–163.

———. 1887–1900c. "Bosquejo de la biografía de Don Dalmacio Velez Sarfield." *Obras completas.* Vol. 27. Buenos Aires: Moreno. 299–386.

Slater, Candace. 1982. *Stories on a String: The Brazilian "Literatura do Cordel."* Berkeley: University of California Press.

Subercaseaux, Bernardo. 1988. *Fin de siglo: La epoca de Balmaceda. Modernización y cultura en Chile.* Santiago: Editorial Aconcagua.

———. 1993. *Historia del libro en Chile.* Santiago: Editorial Andrés Bello.

Sunkel, Guillermo. 1985. *Razón y pasión en la prensa popular: Un estudio sobre cultura popular, cultura de masas y cultura política.* Santiago: ILET.

Torre Revello, José. 1991. *El libro, la imprenta y el periodismo en América durante la dominación española.* Mexico City: Universidad Nacional Autónoma de México.

Vicuña Mackenna, Benjamín. 1941. "La novela en Chile. El ideal de un calavera." *Alberto Blest Gana (1830–1920), estudio biográfico y crítico.* Ed. Raúl Silva Castro. Santiago: Imprenta Universitaria. Reprint of article that originally appeared 4 January 1864 in *El Mercurio.*

CHAPTER 21

LITERARY NATIONALISM IN LATIN AMERICA

Leyla Perrone-Moises

In comparison to the great literatures of the Far East and Europe, Latin American literatures have a shorter history of variable duration: five centuries, if we consider the period of Spanish and Portuguese colonization, or two centuries, if we make literary autonomy coincide with national political independence. But if we consider the literary cultures of regions like the Andes highlands or Mesoamerica, there are two millennia to contend with. Produced and developed both in the languages of ancient indigenous cultures and as peripheral continuations of great European literatures, Latin American literatures have been forced, from the very beginning, to confront the question of identity, to cope with the contradictory oscillations between the Same and the Other. We could say that all colonial literatures face this conflict; yet we must consider their specificities if we are to avoid a generalizing postcolonial discourse that may only be partly appropriate. The specificities of Ibero-American literatures ensue from certain historical conditions that distinguish them from other colonial literatures, including those of North America. Until the nineteenth century, Spain and Portugal exploited Latin American countries by using them as reserves for the extraction of minerals and raw materials. Following the independence of the United States and the French Revolution, liberation movements erupted in all of these countries because of the aspirations of local oligarchies and with the support of England, which had the greatest interest in ridding itself of commercial rivals in that part of the globe. The working classes–Indians, blacks, and *mestizos*–had immediate and local reasons for participating in these movements, and their impact on the struggle was as heroic as it was ineffectual.

The oligarchy of Latin American countries had a European cultural formation, as the principles and values for which it fought were the ones diffused by Europe and derived from the French Revolution. Between 1810 and 1824, Latin American countries won their independence one after another. The imprisonment of the king of Spain by Napoleon's forces benefited and accelerated this liberation. Brazil's situation was unique, because King João VI of Portugal, fleeing Napoleon's armies in 1808, took refuge with his entire court in Rio de Janeiro. After the king's return to Lisbon in 1821, independence was proclaimed in 1822 by his son Pedro, who was crowned Emperor Pedro I of Brazil. These circumstances created the image, indeed the illusion, of an amicable separation without much rancor toward the motherland. Uruguay, a small territory that was disputed for a long time between the Spanish metropolis and the neighboring countries of Argentina and Brazil, did not become a republic until 1828. The independence won by all Latin American countries at the beginning of the nineteenth century was a formal independence: If these countries broke free from the Iberian yoke, they fell under the economic yoke of the great powers of Europe and would later be subjected to the powers of the United States and the World Bank.

There have been cultural and literary consequences to these events, and the aim of this chapter is to elucidate these consequences. If we are to understand how Latin American literatures distinguish themselves from other colonial and postcolonial literatures, we must consider certain facts. The cultural identity of these countries was constructed and, in certain cases, is still in the process of constructing itself, not as the recuperation of an original or autochthonous identity (in most cases obliterated by colonization), but as the affirmation of a difference at the heart of identity: a filial relation. However violent this desire for liberation, there is nonetheless an indissoluble tie to the metropolitan cultures and literatures. Therefore, the relations between Latin American literatures and European literatures do not really consist of a confrontation of diverse traditions; rather, they are a family affair (see Sommer).

The first well-read Latin Americans, often educated in Spanish and Portuguese universities, felt like European exiles in their own countries. European ideas, sentiments, and institutions, henceforth their own, seemed out of place in regions in which territorial immensity, climate, and natural environment made them appear hostile. Indeed, eighteenth-century Brazilian poets complained that nymphs could not appear at their riversides because of the heat and the mosquitoes. Even two centuries later, at his Collège de France lecture in 1983, Borges declared: "I am a European born in exile." The difference between Latin Americans and other European-colonized peoples lies in the disappearance of autochthonous cultures in most colonial parts of North America in contrast to the vast regions of Latin America. The first Latin Americans to reflect on their identity therefore faced a constitutional indeterminacy, as the liberator, Simón Bolívar, noticed in 1819:

> Nosotros ni aún conservamos los vestigios de lo que fué en otro tiempo: no somos Europeos, no somos Indios, sino una especie media entre los Aborígenes y los Españoles. Americanos por nacimiento y Europeos por derecho, nos hallamos en el conflicto de disputar a los naturales los títulos de posesión y de mantenernos en el país que nos vió nacer, contra la oposición de los invasores; así nuestro caso es el más extraordinario y complicado. (205)

> [We do not even retain the vestiges of our original being. We are not Europeans; we are not Indians; we are but a mixed species of aborigines and Spaniards. Americans by birth and European by right, we find ourselves engaged in a dual conflict: we are disputing with the natives for titles of ownership, and at the same time we are struggling to maintain ourselves in the country that gave us birth against the opposition of the invaders. Thus, our position is most extraordinary and complicated.]

Another complicating factor, which follows from this necessity of developing an identity in the image of the Other and in a place devoid of the Other's past as well as one's own, has been the double mission that the first Latin American writers proclaimed for themselves: the simultaneous creation of a country and a literature (see Candido). Literature, and particularly the novel, has had an effective role in the constitution of a national consciousness and thus in the constitution of the countries themselves. It is not purely coincidental that there happens to be a long list of Hispanic-American presidents who were also writers. Furthermore, this mission was pursued under the gaze of Europe, to which the countries of Latin America wanted to prove their worth as nations and as cultures, since they considered one synonymous with the other. Very often the same men who put pen to paper were the ones who took up arms, since literature was nothing if not political and social. This was a heavy burden on their work, prohibiting free flight of the imagination and disinterested exploration of form, as the Argentinean Ernesto Sábato and many other Latin American writers and thinkers indicated. "Un escritor nace en Francia y se encuentra, por decirlo asi con una patria hecha; aquí se debe escribir haciéndola al mismo tiempo como aquellos pioneros del lejano oeste que cultivaban la tierra con el arma al lado" (Sábato 144) [A writer born in France finds, as it were, a homeland that already exists; in Latin America, he must write it at the same time he creates it, like the pioneers of the far west who farmed the land with a gun at their side].

A number of studies on nationalism demonstrate that the nation is a collection of images and constitutes itself through its metaphors. Certain metaphors used in Latin American discourses on identity reveal the difficulties of constructing a self-image and the way this image always depends on the European other, whether seeking to imitate or reject it. The opposing metaphors of American youth and European age appeared immediately following the arrival of the Europeans. The opposing notions of new and old were already explicit labels in the designation of the New World, if considered in terms of vital strength, novelty and childhood are positive characteristics. Yet they also imply that novelty lacks a history and thus a culture, and that the child is a minor and must come to maturity in order to reach adulthood like his parents. The label *new* used extensively by Europeans in relation to "discovered" and conquered lands, indicates the intention to reduce alterity to sameness and to subject these new lands to a history that is the repetition of one's own, a history that is renewed, so to speak. Many European thinkers have regarded America as an opportunity for a new youth, and this claim, as flattering as it may appear, has weighed heavily on the shoulders of Americans. It is not unlike the obligation that some parents impose on their children to realize their own personal and unfulfilled dreams.

In the 1820s, the political economy of Latin America rapidly changed from a mercantile system inefficiently run by a bloated and corrupt colonial bureaucracy to a free-floating, precarious situation in a market economy wherein the buyers were European and United States interests and the sellers were the local Latin American producers of raw materials. Practically all manufactured goods were imported and all exports were raw materials. A good example as a kind of microcosm of the nineteenth century was the rubber boom that affected the Amazon region at the end of the century. In the chaotic conditions that followed independence, the new national literary cultures all strove for legitimacy. The nationalistic truth-claim, whether invoked by church or state, was the institutional policy of the day, subject to the political and economic demands of foreign powers. Conflicting ideologies about such issues as national history, national poets, and the making of heroes had an explosive effect on the debates over property rights of the Church, eligibility for participation in the political life of the country and the reform of the educational

system in general. These debates raged in a world where the majority of the population were still illiterate and had no idea of the political changes that had overtaken them.

As soon as Latin Americans themselves began to reflect on their identity, the metaphors employed were self-deprecating, or at least conflictual. They consisted of oppositional dichotomies that clearly reveal a sense of inferiority and dependence in relation to Europe. The most famous of these metaphors belongs to the Argentinean Domingo Faustino Sarmiento (1811–1888), who in 1845 characterized America as Barbarism in comparison to European Civilization (*Facundo*, 1845). And in 1900, in *Ariel–A la juventud de América* [1900; Ariel-To the Youth of America], the Uruguayan writer José Enrique Rodó (1871–1917) took up this theme but now invoking Greco-Roman civilization as the model for Latin America. As Richard Morse observes, Latin Americans are the only people to have ever applied the label "barbarous" to themselves rather than to others, contradicting the etymology of the word itself. The encounter (or confrontation) of civilization and barbarism has been allegorized by many novelists, such as the Argentinean José Mármol (1817–1871) (*Amalia*, 1851) or the Brazilian José de Alencar (1829–1877), who tells the unhappy love stories of his indigenous and white civilized characters (*O Guarani*, 1857; *Iracema*, 1865). Many other writers would deal with this question, such as Euclides da Cunha (1866–1909) in *Os Sertões* (1902) [*Rebellion in the Backlands*] and the Venezuelan writer Rómulo Gallegos (1884–1969) in *Doña Bárbara* (1929).

The opposition of *village* and *world* has equally pejorative connotations for America. José Marti (1853–1895) begins his famous text *Nuestra América* [Our America] with the following consideration: "Cree el aldeano vanidoso que el mundo entero es su aldea" ("The vain villager thinks his village is the world") (57). The most recent concepts of *center* and *periphery*, which certain Latin American essayists use in relation to the problems of their literatures, merely reflect Marti's thinking if, as in Marti's text, they continue to attribute all the advantages to the center. Thinking that stems from the center leads us to confuse economic and cultural dependence, and to condemn the periphery for having ideas that are always out of place, forgetting that ideas and forms fortunately circulate more freely than capital. We can see in all of these metaphors and labels the Latin Americans' sense of their underdeveloped character, in both the biological and cultural sense of the word.

As the attachment of one group to its territory and values, nationalism is not a nineteenth-century invention. However, nationalism did become a theorized concept in the nineteenth century and, due to a historical coincidence, it is at this moment that Latin American peoples embraced it. The achievements of independence by Latin American countries coincided with literary Romanticism, as was the case for many European nations. However, the latter already possessed a past that was many centuries old, as well as particular cultural features and even patriotic sentiments, which could serve as a basis for the *invention* of an identity (see Gellner; Anderson). At stake for Latin Americans was not the creation of a form for preexistent elements but indeed the very invention of this form.

Their writers received the concept of nation and nationalist sentiment from Romanticism enthusiastically. Hence, the first sets of opposition through which Latin America was trying to define itself in comparison to Europe turned into sets of paradoxes. Literature's adoption of the concept of nationalism presents the first paradox, which Borges conveys with a certain humor: "El culto argentino del color local es un reciente culto europeo que los nacionalistas deberían rechazar por foráneo" (132) ("The Argentinean cult of local color is a recent European cult, which the nationalist must refuse because it is foreign"). Nationalist demands emerge from and thrive on the rejection of an oppressive other, which imposes its own principles and values while erasing those of the particular culture. This other is an invader, a colonizer, an exploiter. In Latin America, nationalism was born of the Wars of Independence and has retained its bellicose nature, even after countries achieved political autonomy. Because it was not imposed, nationalism remained a kind of dependence that was even more insidious; it was a cultural dependence that Latin Americans experienced as a fatality insofar as the only culture left to them was the colonizer's. The other, from whom they wanted to liberate themselves, inhabited them. Their nationalism turned against ill-defined enemies, shifting according to circumstances, mixing culture, politics, and economics. They attributed all their difficulties in finding a place on the international cultural scene to the harmful intentions of others. Thus, the search for a national essence, seeking a place in an international setting, inevitably involved the paradox of reinforcing locality and provincialism, whereas the major objective was to prove the universal value of this particularity.

One of the particularities of Latin American literary nationalisms, from the Romantic movement to this day, is the exchange of claims and counter-claims that have never recognized the rational limits of their discourse, always incurring the risk of confusing political and economic reasons with aesthetic ones and of wanting to eliminate an "enemy" that, from a cultural point of view, is a historical component of the nation's own identity. Concerned with creating their own national cultures, young Latin American nations found themselves in paradoxical situations without being immediately aware of the paradoxes. This was the case throughout the nineteenth century. There are more subtle and complex reasons for cultural dependence than a nation's political and economic dependence. The first paradox of these literary nationalisms appeared in the relations to the new and old literature of France. Why was France important? Despite a few awkward attempts, it had never succeeded in colonizing Ibero-America in any real way. The reason was precisely that France was not the historical colonizer; permitting Latin Americans to idealize her; she represented, quite to the contrary, the motherland of revolution and liberty which they chose to oppose to Spain and Portugal. However, in the nineteenth century, Spanish and Portuguese metropolises themselves were highly influenced by French culture, making the turn toward France not so original in the end.

Romantic nationalism, which marked these literatures thereafter, itself came from Europe, through France. The preoccupations of Latin American writers with American nature and indigenous characters emerged from Chateaubriand's work, which had revealed a literary subject matter that came from their own homeland. Indians were at the heart of fabulous stories in which there were multiple appropriations. Indians were seen as the mythical primordial origin necessary for all nations; already practically exterminated, they could be the subject of any fantasy. Indians served as opaque screens to hide the very real daily situation of black people, which, if considered, would have raised the sensitive issue of slavery.

Throughout the nineteenth century, France was the "beacon" (a frequent metaphor employed in Latin American discourses at this time) whose light they followed. They received from France the very appellation under which they recognize themselves: *Latin* America. Napoléon III was concerned with securing France's influence in all countries threatened with the economic and cultural domination of England and the United States. He was the one to promote a Latin ideology that would ensure the annexation of Mexico and the alliance of all Latin American countries. Although the political objectives of Napoléon III were not achieved, France was assured a cultural victory. Under the influence of positivism, the ideals and symbols of the young republics were defined. Indeed, the Brazilian flag bears the logo of Auguste Comte.

At the beginning of the twentieth century, Paris was undoubtedly the cultural capital of Latin America. The real or imaginary journey to Paris was a search for identity. The return to the chosen European source (voluntarily marginal in relation to the problematic sources that Iberian cities represented) was also a necessary dissociation, so that the original Latin American country could become visible in its own identity. Exile allows this cognitive distance; yet, in the case of Latin Americans, both the return to European cultural origins and the recognition of differences increased the awareness of their own specificity. Through France, Europe revealed once again to Latin Americans the aesthetic possibilities of their cultures. The appreciation of primitive art by the avant-garde of the twentieth century was assimilated in full knowledge of the past by Latin American countries that possessed, in their own patrimony, the live manifestations of indigenous art and the active contributions of African blacks. The Latin American avant-garde claimed to have achieved the feat of being both nationalist and cosmopolitan. In a sense, this contradiction had already been set out (and remained unresolved) in the very concept of nation diffused in the Enlightenment.

As local cultures and literatures formed and asserted themselves, the idyllic relations with French culture began to sour, and a number of voices spoke out against this dependence. From the beginning of the nineteenth century, heated arguments arose between the partisans of an authentically national literature and the partisans of literature open to European influences (e.g., the Venezuelan writer Andrés Bello [1781–1865] versus the Argentinean Sarmiento; in Brazil, Alencar versus Joachim Nabuco [1849–1910]). During the twentieth century, anti-French discourses led by nationalist intellectuals intensified and were transformed into discourses calling for a national literary culture and protesting all foreign influence emanating from countries that were "developed" and, by definition, oppressive. Antonio Caso (1883–1946) stands out among intellectuals more interested in nationalism and in making a national literary culture than in reasserting universal aesthetic values. In 1923 he wrote about a Mexican national identity in these terms: "El más urgente de nuestros problemas estriba en difundir y propagar por todos los medios posibles el verdadero patriotismo, esto es, la conciencia de la colectividad mexicana" (80) ("Our most urgent problem comes down to disseminating and promoting by all possible means true patriotism, that is, an awareness of Mexican collectivity"). Therefore, the identification of a national literary culture was, he argued, as natural as the recognition of family history.

In Peru, in the same years, José Carlos Mariateguí (1894–1930) was editing and writing for *Amauta* (1926–1930), advocating the recognition of national traits as evidenced in Peruvian national literature. The Argentinean writer Velmiro Ayala Gauna (1905–1967) went further and stated that one can only call a literature a national literature if it singularizes a people and gives them a well-defined national character. This is the reason he dismisses avant-garde literature as irrelevant to the nation (9, 36). David Viñas (b. 1929), another Argentinean critic, cautions that the purported national literature is often the political requirement of the ruling oligarchy for self-legitimation and is therefore particularly susceptible to xenophobia (61).

Argentinean nationalism passed into the twentieth century with a powerful sense of Hispanism that eventually developed into a fascist ideology. Writers like Manuel Galvez (1882–1962) produced works that strongly influenced this movement: *El diario de Gabriel Quiroga* (1910) [The Diary of Gabriel Quiroga], *El solar de la raza* (1913) [The Mansion of the Race], *La pampa y su pasión* (1926) [Passion for the Pampas]. Others such as Ricardo Rojas (1882–1957) were also notable in this movement with works like *La restauración nacionalista* (1909) [Nationalist Restoration]. A more subtle nationalism is expressed in *La gloria de don Ramiro* (1908) [The Glory of Don Ramiro] by Enrique Larreta (1875–1961), often cited as the finest example of *modernista* prose; it was ideologically both part of the national declaration of Hispanic identity for Argentina and a glorification of the past. The most noteworthy of the Argentinean nationalists was Leopoldo Lugones (1874–1938). His most politically influential works were *Blasón de plata* (1909) [Silver Blazon] and *La argentinidad* (1922) [Way of Being Argentinean]. He died by his own hand just as the Second World War began and as Spain sank into its devastating civil war.

And in Brazil, always a bit different from Spanish America (but, on a deeper level, quite similar), the making of a national identity has been indelibly linked to a national literature. Afranio Coutinho considers that a national identity in literature began in 1902 with the publication of *Os Sertôes* [Rebellion in the Backlands, 1944]: "Euclides da Cunha (1866–1909) was able with one blow to pull us into Brazil, to force our eyes onto Brazilian reality, which some cosmopolites had tried to disguise in order to keep us prisoners of the European mirage. These were feelings of colonial inferiority to which as many Europeans as Brazilians were subject" (197).

Some Latin Americans developed their own generalized cultural ideal which persists to this day, and which consolidates itself on the basis of two opposite errors: the claim to a culture exclusively their own, pure of all foreign contamination, and the concept of Latin America as uniform and culturally homogeneous. If the concept of a Latin American union against hegemonic powers is perfectly comprehensible on a political and economic level, it produces confusion and misunderstanding on the level of culture and literature. First, no culture or literature, even those of hegemonic nations, has constituted itself or lives without contamination. In fact, the opposite is the case. Roman culture would not exist without Greek culture, nor Japanese culture without Chinese, and so on. The Spanish and Portuguese cultures of the colonizing countries were themselves a result of numerous assimilations. However intense our desire to recover pure sources before the arrival of the Europeans, we must recognize that these sources are forever lost. Nor were these sources ever pure; rather, they were the result of the contamination of many cultures that are themselves diverse and often opposed to one another. Latin America is therefore the result of European

culture and, far from rejecting this filiation, must claim it while also claiming what other cultures, African and indigenous, have contributed to it. Latin American identity is a *mestizo* identity. The exaltation or the rejection of any single one of these components of its identity can have ideological and political grounds, yet will never have a cultural foundation. Diversity is its richness.

The same movement that leads to the desire for an indigenous and African identity, as opposed to a white identity, leads to the exclusive valuing of folklore and poverty as specifically Latin American. Latin America is as diverse in its development as it is complex in its ethnic constitution. García Márquez's (b. 1927) village of Macondo and Guimarães Rosa's (1908–1967) *sertão* are as Latin American as Cabrera Infante's (b. 1929) Havana or Borges's Buenos Aires. The image of Latin America as unique–poor but happy, ignorant but vital–is indeed agreeable in the eyes of hegemonic cultures. Since the arrival of the Europeans, they have seen themselves through the Other's gaze. The first descriptions identified American lands with Paradise; the grandiose and marvelous natural environment was a source of awe. Yet this nature was prodigious only in comparison to European nature, long since domesticated and foreign to the natives of America who had to struggle daily against all-powerful natural forces. Latin Americans, especially in Peru and Mexico, recognized the obligation of preserving their ancient culture, an obligation that has in no small way influenced their nature as one that must be preserved because Europe's own nature has long since been sacrificed. Obviously, nature is a cultural concept, since it is through ideological mediation and the making of meaning that culture constitutes nature. In interpreting American nature, Europe conceived of it as *natural*, a view that Latin Americans came to accept. In a new opposition, they are inclined to identify with *nature*, granting Europe the privilege of *culture*. Thus, others have envisioned and often studied Latin Americans as having little history and much geography. What is highly problematic is that this common ground between European and Latin American perceptions has an element of truth to it. Despite all their troubles and sometimes because of them, Latin American countries do have a physically prodigious nature, and their inhabitants have a taste for festivities, reflecting the simple desire for survival or a happy unawareness of problems. It is not so much a question of suppressing these characteristics because they are recognized by the other, but of cherishing them with lucidity rather than as a compensation for what is missing in the other.

These difficulties with identity have often manifested themselves in the literary historiography of Latin America. These young literatures are born of old languages. As Octavio Paz observes: "En general, la vida de una literatura se confunde con la de la lengua en que está escrita; en el caso de nuestras literaturas su infancia coincide con la madurez de la lengua. Nuestros primitivos no vienen antes sino después de una tradición de siglos." (1981, 28) ("In general, the life of a literature merges with the life of the language in which it is written; in the case of our literatures, their childhood coincides with the maturity of the language. Our origins follow rather than precede a tradition of centuries"). Thus, if we write the history of Latin American literatures as a prolongation of the literatures of the mother tongues and in their image, we will tend to consider their first manifestations as childish and awkward. If we want to portray this history as autonomous, we would situate its beginnings at the moment of political autonomy, which, in practice, only prolongs this "childhood." In both cases, we forget that these literatures did not have a beginning devoid of tradition; we also forget that aesthetic value does not depend on the social situation of its producers, as discussed in the previous essay of this section. The history of Latin American literatures in relation to that of the literatures of the mother tongues is made up of constant discrepancies. Although inevitable, anachronisms did not always represent backwardness; they existed in synchrony with other, more recent developments, provoking original deviations that brought new possibilities for renewal to old forms that had been abandoned or remained undreamed of by European literatures. In Latin America, the mother tongues themselves have a double nature: as archeological reserve and revitalizing experimentation (see the texts on heteroglossia in section three by Garza Cuarón and by Akerberg).

If our political and economic history can be told in a linear fashion, simple diachrony is particularly inappropriate to our cultural and literary history. The best Latin American authors have always been both rear-guard agents of old European forms and free and audacious explorers of a possible future: Their anachronisms have often been prospective (see Rodríguez Monegal). The numerous authors who have signaled this stratified and alluvial aspect of Latin American literatures include Alejo Carpentier (1904–1980), who exploits it in his fiction, and Ángel Rama, who examines it on the level of historiography (1975; 1982). America (and I do not refer here exclusively to Latin America) is simultaneously the memory and project of Europe, the regret of a lost past and the prefiguration of a possible future. With these two words—regret and prefiguration—José Lezama Lima (1910–1976) concludes his essay "The American Expression." More recently, Brazilian poet Haroldo de Campos (1992) and Ana Pizarro (1993) have recalled the particularities of our literary history.

A large majority of Latin American literary essayists have devoted their writings to the question of identity. It would be impossible here to discuss (or even refer to) these scores of authors and thousands of pages; my intent is simply to point out a few nationalist paradoxes from this long history. If the first reflections by Latin Americans considered the question of identity in terms of a comparison with Europe, a number of thinkers have since then considered it in terms of transculturation or cultural *mestizaje*. Thus, a new paradox appears. In a general sense, nationalism has been linked to racism, to the rejection of the other. Latin American nationalism therefore often involves the praise of *mestizaje,* an ideology that we might consider as racism in disguise. At the end of the nineteenth century, certain Latin American thinkers theorized this *mestizaje* in terms of "blanching" or ameliorating racial difference.

In Mexico, the philosopher José Vasconcelos (1881–1959) published *La raza cósmica* [*The Cosmic Race*] in 1925. In it, he raises *mestizaje* to a new level of Latin American identity: ". . . llegaremos en América, antes que en parte alguna del globo, a la creación de una raza hecha con el tesoro de todas las anteriores, la raza final, la raza cósmica" (40) (" . . . we in America shall arrive, before any other part of the world, at the creation of a new race fashioned out of the treasures of all the previous ones: the final race, the cosmic race"). He argues that it is only in Latin America that there is such widespread miscegenation among Amerindians, black peoples from Africa, peoples from the Far East and Europe, a mix which, he believes, will produce the race of the future and which today has given Latin America its distinct character. However, there is a thin line between praise for the anthropological fact of miscegenation and anti-native racism.

Narrow nationalists and transnational advocates alike have used the ethnic mix of Latin America as an identity factor, but clearly it is as highly contentious today as it ever was in the past. Many intellectual approaches to ethnicity are part of the present debate. One of the participants is Martin Lienhard in his *Escritura y conflicto étnico-cultural en América Latina 1492–1988* [Writing and Ethno-cultural Conflict in Latin America 1492–1988]. Ángel Rama's use of the term *transculturation* has elicited important commentaries by Alberto Moreiras and Mabel Moraña. García Canclini's (1995) use of *hybridity* also resulted in numerous responses from intellectuals, such as Román de la Campa's "Hibridez posmoderna y transculturación: Políticas de montaje en torno a Latinoamérica" ["Postmodern Hybridity and Transculturation: Political Organization in Latin America"].   Heterogeneity was another major concept, put forward by Antonio Cornejo Polar, who proposes it as one of the distinguishing factors of Latin America. In this case, an entire volume of commentary has entered the debate on the validity or limitations of the term: *Asedios a la heterogeneidad cultural* [Contestation of Cultural Heterogeneity]. In Brazil, the alliance of a white person with an Indian could be idealized since it was so rare and so much more easily admissible than the alliances of white people with black people, who were too present and too visible as the other. With Gilberto Freyre's (1900–1987) twentieth-century work *Casa grande e senzala* [*The Master and the Slaves*], this idea was almost inverted, as intellectuals eased their conscience by declaring their black origins, which of course were remote. This premise marked them as real Brazilians, as opposed to the new European immigrants.

However, *mestizaje* is an anthropological fait accompli in Latin America and, in cultural terms, it inevitably provokes the development of original propositions. I would like to use some of these propositions as examples, to show how the synthesis that is envisaged is not the sovereign and tranquil assumption of being, as Hegel would have it, but an open dialectic charged with negativity and thus open to new adventures. In 1928, the Brazilian writer Oswald de Andrade (1890–1954) proposed a solution that would consist not in the refusal of foreign influences but in their deliberate incorporation. The metaphor he employed was the Indian practice of anthropophagy. Through the ritual of devouring their enemies, the primitive people of Brazil believed they were assimilating their qualities; this belief forced them into a preliminary evaluation of their enemies', qualities (a critical instance), qualities that would end up as a reinforcement of the devourer's capacities (an assimilative instance). Through the double process of murdering and devouring the father, the son would resolve his Oedipal complex, transforming taboo into totem. Through the voluntary and joyous appropriation in literature, this proposition was replacing what would later be called "the anxiety of influence" (see Bloom).

Oswald de Andrade's metaphor and its theoretical development sought to resolve the contradiction inherent in the double nature of the Brazilian avant-garde as both a nationalist and a cosmopolitan movement. In its own strange way, the anthropophagy of origins was, in fact, receptive to foreigners; the theory is both clever and full of humor. Later, Andrade would pursue these ideas by praising the primitive matriarchy of indigenous societies, blaming all the West's misfortunes on patriarchy and messianism. Thus, in his praise of matriarchy, he presents himself as an original nationalist. In general, the nationalist imagination is masculine: It values strength, work, and war. In contrast, the Brazilian imagination of origins, which Andrade wanted to recuperate, would embrace mildness and leisure.

In a very different tone, but with equal wit, Octavio Paz (1914–1998) always dealt with the question of European influences in terms of assimilation. In *The Labyrinth of Solitude* (1950), he envisioned the birth of Mexico as the result of the rape of an Indian woman by a European. Despite the resentment toward the rapist father, the filiation is a fact that must not only be recognized but also reclaimed by the son. According to Paz, parricide has never been a solution; renouncing European influence would mean renouncing a part of oneself because without this influence, Latin American literature and art would not be what they are (1966). Ernesto Sábato (b. 1911) also observes: "Corremos el peligro de reemplazar los males que a menudo trajo la mera imitación de la cultura europea, por el repudio de la grande y preciosa herencia que esa cultura supone, lo que sería una calamidad casi peor que la precedente" (7) ("We run the risk of replacing the pain that is often caused by the simple imitation of European culture with the rejection of a grand and precious heritage which this culture possesses; this would be a calamity almost worse than the preceding one"). In an essay in which fiction merges with criticism and imagination with reality, Lezama Lima (1910–1976) conceives Western literature as a banquet to which the American contributes the final touch of fine tobacco. Hispanic America would be a "gnostic space," open to the insemination of Spanish contributions, which in turn are the result of innumerable previous inseminations. Finally, Jorge Luis Borges contemplates this question with irony: "... podemos manejar todos los temas europeos, manejarlos sin supersticiones, con una irreverencia que puede tener, y ya tiene, consecuencias afortunadas ... debemos pensar que nuestro patrimonio es el universo" (137) ("... we can treat all European themes without superstition, with an irreverence which can have, and already has, fortunate consequences ... we must think that our patrimony is the universe").

Despite their differences, these propositions have common features that attest to their Latin American specificity. They are pacifist in that they include rather than exclude the other. Since the Wars of Independence, the implications of Latin America's nationalist discourses are no longer bellicose, acts of resistance and bombs having been purely metaphorical. Rather, Latin American metaphors of identity are erotic, turned toward the "primitive scene." Yet there remains in some of these metaphors the memory of an aggression (invasion, rape), which provokes an equally aggressive response (cannibalism) or demand (the right of the son). The question is raised in light of a solution, but is never forgotten. In Latin American reflections on identity, there is always a basic tension: the relation to the Old World that "invaded" in the sixteenth century and, today, the First World, which sets up a situation of dependence. The commemoration of origins raises problems: To commemorate the arrival of the Europeans is to commemorate a massacre, and to commemorate independence reminds us of the extent of its artificiality.

Meanwhile, a culture–or more precisely, a number of cultures–have constituted themselves in Latin American countries. Having long surpassed the stages of nationalism and liberation in the domain of formal politics, they must still acquire a true postcolonial attitude in relation to culture. They must still assume "a third nature, which is not pristine and prehistorical ... but one that derives historically and

abductively from the deprivations of the present" (Said 79). All desires depend on the Other, and for most Latin American nationalists, the most significant desire is to have their culture not only recognized but admired by the First World. This affects the production of Latin American literature itself, insofar as its international reception is often most favorable when it responds to the hegemonic cultures' own desires for evasion, exoticism, and folklore. If less standard writers are appreciated, their public is much more restricted. The general public of the First World wishes Latin Americans to be picturesque, colorful, and magical; it has difficulty seeing them as equals who are not quite identical, although their origins and histories give them the right to this recognition.

Condemned to paradox, the best Latin American writers have understood that they can and must profit from it. As evolutionist theories about man and society no longer hold, diversity and plurality can affirm themselves without complexes. Now that the legitimation and efficiency of hegemonic doxa have reached a crisis, the Latin American para-doxa can constitute a critical and liberating instance for those hegemonic cultures themselves. Construed by Europe as a world "on the side," America has always had this voluntary or involuntary tendency of being a parody of Europe. Like any past colony, America serves as a necessary mirror for Europe. That this mirror might acquire a troubling autonomy, that it might become a deformed reflection of an image that is both familiar and foreign, is the risk or the fatality of all illegitimate procreation. The son's revenge does not consist in ruminating indefinitely over his resentment against his origins, but in reclaiming his heritage and making it prosper, as he brings it the precious gift of linguistic and aesthetic difference.

Translation by Marie Carrière

Works Cited

Anderson, Benedict. 1983. *Imagined Communities: Reflections on the Origin and Spread of Nationalism*. London: Verso.

Andrade, Oswald de. 1972. "Manifesto antropófago." *Obras completas*. Vol. 4. Rio de Janeiro: Civilização Brasileira. 11–19.

Ayala Gauna, Velmiro. 1971. *¿Existe una literatura nacional?* Santa Fe, Argentina: Ediciones Colmegna.

Bloom, Harold. 1973. *The Anxiety of Influence*. New York: Oxford University Press.

Bolívar, Simón. 1939. "Discurso pronunciado por el Libertador ante el Congreso de Angostura, 15 de febrero de 1819, día de su instalación." *Proclamas y Discursos del Libertador*. Ed. Vicente Lecuna. Caracas: Lit. y Tip. del Comercio. 202–35.

Borges, Jorge Luis. 1976. *Discusión*. Madrid/Buenos Aires: Alianza-Emecé.

Campa, Román de la. 1994. "Hibridez posmoderna y transculturación: Políticas de montaje en torno a Latinoamerica." *Hispamérica* 69: 2–23.

Campos, Haroldo de. 1992. "Da razão antropofágica." *Metalinguagem & outras metas*. 4th ed. São Paulo: Perspectiva. 231–55.

Candido, Antonio. 1969. *Formação da literatura brasileira*. 3rd ed. São Paulo: Martins Fontes.

Carpentier, Alejo. 1968. *El reino de este mundo*. Montevideo: Arca.

Caso, Antonio. 1955. *El problema de México y la ideología nacional*. Mexico City: Libro-Mex. Editores.

Coutinho, Afranio. 1969. *An Introduction to Literature in Brazil*. Trans. Gregory Rabassa. New York: Columbia University Press.

García Canclini, Néstor. 1995. *Consumidores ciudadanos: Conflictos multiculturales de la globalización*. Mexico City: Grijalbo.

Gellner, Ernest. 1983. *Nations and Nationalism*. Oxford: Basil Blackwell.

Henríquez Ureña, Pedro. 1945. *Literary Currents in Hispanic America*. Cambridge: Harvard University Press.

——. 1964. *Las corrientes literarias en la América hispánica*. 3rd ed. Mexico City: Fondo de Cultura Económica.

Lezama Lima, José. 1957. *La expresión americana*. Havana: Instituto Nacional de Cultura.

Lienhard, Martin. 1992. *La voz y su huella: Escritura y conflicto étnico-cultural en América Latina 1492–1988*. Lima: Horizonte.

Martí, José. 1982. "Nuestra América." *Política de Nuestra América*. Mexico City: Siglo XXI. 37–44.

Moraña, Mabel. 1995. "De *La ciudad letrada* al imaginario nacionalista." *Esplendores y miserias del siglo XIX: Cultura y sociedad en América Latina*. Ed. Beatriz González Stephan et al. Caracas: Monte Avila. 41–51.

Moreiras, Alberto. 1997. "A Storm Blowing from Paradise: Negative Globality in Latin American Cultural Studies." *Cânones & contextos*. Ed. Eduardo Coutinho et al. Rio de Janeiro: ABRALIC. 121–36.

Morse, Richard. 1988. *O espelho de Próspero*. São Paulo: Companhia das Letras.

Paz, Octavio. 1950. *El laberinto de la soledad*. Mexico City: Fondo de Cultura Económica.

——. 1962. *The Labyrinth of Solitude*. Trans. Lysander Kemp. New York: Grove.

——. 1972. *Puertas al campo*. Barcelona: Seix Barral.

——. 1981. *In/mediaciones*. Barcelona: Seix Barral.

Pizarro, Ana, ed. 1993. *A situação colonial*. Vol. 1: *América Latina: Palavra, literatura e cultura*. Campinas: Unicamp.

Rama, Angel. 1975. "Sistema literario y sistema social en Hispanoamérica." *Literatura y praxis en América Latina*. Caracas: Monte Avila. 81–109.

——. 1982. "Autonomía literaria americana." *Sin nombre* 22.4: 7–24.

——. 1996. *The Lettered City*. Ed. and trans. John Charles Chasteen. Durham, NC: Duke University Press.

——. 1982. *Transculturación narrativa en América Latina*. Mexico City: Siglo Veintinuno Editores.

Rivas, Pierre. 1993. "París como a capital literaria da América latina." *Literatura e história na América Latina*. Ed. Ligia Chiappini and Flávio Aguiar. São Paulo: Edusp. 99–114.

Rodó, José Enrique. 1967. "Ariel-A la juventud de América." *Obras completas*. Ed. Emir Rodríquez Monegal. Madrid: Aguilar. 206–49.

Rodríguez Monegal, Emir, and Leyla Perrone-Moisés. 1983. "Isidore Ducasse et la rhétorique espagnole." *Poétique* 55: 351–77.

——. 1995. *Lautréamont austral*. Montevideo: Brecha.

Sábato, Ernesto. 1983. *La cultura en la encrucijada nacional*. 5th ed. Buenos Aires: Editorial Sudamericana.

Said, Edward W. 1990. "Yeats and Decolonization." *Nationalism, Colonialism and Literature*. Ed. Terry Eagleton, Fredric Jameson, and Edward W. Said. Minneapolis: University of Minnesota Press. 69–95.

Sarmiento, Domingo Faustino. 1976. *Facundo*. Buenos Aires: Editorial, Losada.

Sommer, Doris. 1990. "Irresistible Romance: The Foundational Fictions of Latin America." *Nation and Narration*. Ed. Homi K. Bhabha. London and New York: Routledge. 71–98.

Vasconcelos, José. 1997. *The Cosmic Race/La raza cósmica: A Bilingual Edition*. Trans. and annot. Didier T. Jaén. Baltimore: Johns Hopkins University Press.

Viñas, David. 1996. *Literatura Argentina y política*. Vol. 2. Buenos Aires: Sudamericana.

PART TWO

FROM THE MARGINS OF LITERARY HISTORY
INTRODUCTION

Cynthia Steele, Heloisa Buarque de Hollanda,
Marlyse Meyer, and Beatriz Resende

¿Qué mágicas infusiones,
de los indios herbolarios
de mi patria, entre mis letras
el hechizo derramaron?

What magical infusions
of the Indian herbalists
of my country,
have spilled their witchcraft
onto my pages?

–Sor Juana Inés de la Cruz

Sins of Omission in Spanish American History

The literary history of Spanish America is fundamentally canonical and elitist. It focuses overwhelmingly on white, male, upper- and middle-class, Catholic writers–partly because the vast majority of Latin Americans writing literature and criticism up through the 1970s fitted this profile. To adequately represent white women writers or Jewish authors from the privileged classes, let alone the abject poor, or Indian writers and those of African descent, would have required an extraordinary effort that most intellectuals did not make. At first blush we might be tempted to think that literary history in a *mestizo* or mulatto country like Mexico, Peru, or Brazil might be more inclusive of racial and ethnic differences. Certainly nationalist discourse in these countries–and particularly in postrevolutionary Mexico–pays lip service to multiculturalism and inclusiveness. However, because these national ideologies are premised on the goal of cultural assimilation, they fail to escape from an implicit hierarchy that favors the most assimilated writers. Until the past three decades there has been almost no intellectual contingent in Latin America consistently advocating for difference as a cultural and literary virtue. Difference, after all, is associated with the capacity for dissension, and in a continent whose official history is described as anarchy/chaos/civil war/despotism/barbarism/anachronism, dissension portends a failure to "progress" or "develop".

Intellectuals, like those in power, have often unselfconsciously appropriated the history of Mayan and Incan civilizations as a source of national pride, an alternative classical history to that of the Greeks and Romans. At the same time this claim to pre-Hispanic or Revolutionary Indian forefathers has usually implied no sense of brotherhood with contemporary Mexican Indians. For instance, former Mexican President Carlos Salinas de Gortari, notorious for opening the door wide to NAFTA and for the end of all pretext of agrarian reform, named his son and his official airplane Emiliano, and

he used to pose for official photographs before a portrait of Zapata. Similarly, in the realm of letters, many mainstream *ladino* (*mestizo* or *criollo*) intellectuals have seen themselves as heirs to Mexico's indigenous cultures and thus authorized to speak for these colonized peoples. As Manuel Puig (1932–1990) has shown us in *El beso de la mujer araña* [1976; *The Kiss of the Spider Woman*], having a progressive or committed ideological position does not necessarily go hand in hand with progressive positions on racial and ethnic issues, Jewish issues, or feminism and gay rights. In the nineteenth century, for instance, many committed intellectuals were impervious to the dangers of racism, sexism, and imperialism. Sarmiento's championing of "whitening" Argentina through Indian wars and European immigration is well known. Carlos Fuentes (b. 1928) cites Friedrich Engels himself as having celebrated the U.S. annexation of half of Mexico's territory. During much of the twentieth century it has not been uncommon for leftist Latin Americans to prioritize class struggle and anti-imperialism over struggles for other types of human rights, including feminism, gay rights, and Indian autonomy.

Today the lack of receptivity to difference often takes a subtler form among intellectuals. For instance, it may appear as condescension toward women's writing as "light literature" or insistence that Elena Poniatowska (b. 1933) is a journalist, not a writer. Or it may take the form of denying the existence of contemporary Indian literature. Often it takes the form of tokenism. It is increasingly common for literary historians and critics to include a brief section acknowledging difference at the end of a book or chapter, or to add a panel scheduled at the end of a conference. However, there often continues to be little sensitivity to the necessity to incorporate diverse viewpoints fully into the main body of a text or program. As Timerman notes, the flip side of total invisibility is the inability to forget difference. In literary history, this takes the form of labeling an author "a woman writer" or "an Indian writer" and discussing her or his works exclusively in relation to other members of the same minority group. There is, of course, no comparable labeling of a mainstream writer as "male" or "*criollo,*" nor is there an appreciation of the imprint of a white male writer's gender or ethnicity on his works.

As the Yucatecan novelist Dolores Bolio de Peón (b. 1880) wrote in the prologue to her 1918 novel, *Una hoja del pasado* [A Page from the Past], if the creations of a male writer are not judged primarily by the author's gender but by his skillful manipulation of language, then why should the same standards not be used in evaluating the work of women writers?

> Lector: Si tú, a ejemplo de muchos hombres, no buscas en la obra literaria de una mujer sino a la mujer (no entiendo por qué razón esto, a la inversa de lo que buscas en la del hombre, que es la literatura fuera de aquel, puesto que ellos y nosotros nos servimos de los mismos utensilios de trabajo) . . . (n.p.)

> Reader: If you, following the example of many men, look only for Woman in a woman's literary work (I don't understand why this happens, the inverse of what you look for in a man's work, which is literature outside of the person, since both they and we avail ourselves of the same tools of the trade.) . . .]

While it has not been acceptable, since the 1940s, to write literary histories of Latin America that exclude female writers altogether, it is still very common to relegate discussion of them to a separate sentence or paragraph, generally placed at the end of a lengthy discussion of male writers or of white/*mestizo* writers, as a sort of footnote or addendum. A particularly egregious recent example of this is Gerald Martin's five-page discussion of Latin American women writers of the twentieth century, which he appends to a 150-page discussion of male novelists. But such tokenism has been more generally rampant, the most obvious cases being the additions of Sor Juana (1648–1695) and Gabriela Mistral (1889–1957), Nicolás Guillén (1902–1989), Manuel Puig, and Rigoberta Menchú (b. 1959). A literary historian who has mentioned these names seems to feel satisfied that he or she has covered the minority bases. Such an approach reduces the full panoply of subjectivities present within various minority groups to those of one or two individuals. Even in testimonial fiction, no individual–not even Rigoberta Menchú–can be taken as representative of an entire ethnic group or gender. As long as access to cultural capital and means of production–to education, literacy, cultural texts, financial support, and publishers–is so violently unequal, the portrait of Latin America projected in literary histories, both at home and abroad, will continue to be hopelessly skewed.

If indigenous groups and Afro-Hispanic communities have responded to systematic exploitation and disenfranchisement with rebellion, writers from various minority groups have made innovative use of what Josefina Ludmer calls "las tretas del débil" [tricks of the weak]. For women this has often meant approaching creativity indirectly, through the domestic arts. For instance, Dolores Bolio's first forays into literature consisted of a homemade scrapbook of poems by Yucatecan writers she admired, entitled *Autographs,* and a linen tablecloth on which she embroidered the signatures of Mexican modernist poets who had graced her table (Poot Herrera 229). Like women, members of ethnic minorities have often found an outlet for creativity and self-assertion in popular culture, such as music, dance, festivals, and popular or "folk" art. Ironically, this practice of channeling creativity into acceptable spheres of behavior has, in turn, tended to reinforce the dominant class's stereotypes about black or mulatto sensuality,

Indian aesthetic taste or spirituality, female domesticity or sensibility, and so forth, and consequently to reinforce prejudices regarding these groups' intellectual and moral limitations.

The decisions regarding where to begin a history and what kind of texts to include reveal important underlying assumptions regarding the nature of colonialism, independence, and cultural sovereignty. Since the 1940s, interdisciplinary cultural histories have flourished alongside more canonical literary histories. In general the latter have responded with a much more ecumenical, inclusive conception of artistic and literary practices. One debate that persists today concerns the definition of "art," as opposed to folk art. As Carlos Montemayor (1991) has noted, Indian literatures have long been viewed as part of the oral, rather than the literary, tradition. Hence, many intellectuals in Mexico tend to see these works as appropriate objects of study for ethnographers, not literary critics. Similarly, despite Latin America's rich history of in-between genres like the chronicle and the testimonial narrative, many Latin American literary historians and critics continue to subscribe to a narrow definition of literature that excludes such genres. Because many female, indigenous, and Afro-Hispanic writers have straddled traditional genres and blurred the borders with "literature," such texts are deemed journalism or ethnography, the argument goes, not literature: Rigoberta Menchú is a political activist, not an author.

From a different perspective, during the late 1940s and 1950s liberal and leftist critics like the Venezuelan Mariano Picón-Salas (1901–1965) worked to recuperate the Colonial period and the chronicle for literary history. In Mexico, the country that has most thoroughly founded its nation-building on pride in its Indian heritage, a parallel but largely separate tradition of uncovering and publishing indigenous literary history has flourished since the 1930s, spearheaded by Angel María Garibay (1892–1967) and admirably carried on by his disciple Miguel León-Portilla (b. 1926) over the past four decades. During the 1980s, in response to indigenous autonomy movements throughout the continent, several state governments–for instance, in Oaxaca, Chiapas, Yucatán, and Michoacán–began sponsoring indigenous writing workshops. Since 1992 the Mexican novelist and classicist Carlos Montemayor (b. 1947) has played a crucial role in persuading the federal government actively to promote and publish contemporary indigenous literatures in bilingual format. Still, most Mexican literary historians and critics have continued to limit their coverage of indigenous texts to *indigenista* literature (social-protest novels and short stories written by progressive, but often paternalistic, non-Indians or *ladinos*). An interesting twist is the emergence in the 1990s of Subcomandante Insurgente Marcos, a white, middle-class urban guerrilla leader who draws heavily on Mayan mythology and the oral tradition in his lengthy, literary communiques. Over the past year several collections of his *neo-indigenista* writings have been published as books. While the issue of representation continues to be a thorny one, no one can question the sincerity of Marcos's commitment to the Ejército Zapatista de Liberación Nacional (EZLN) cause. As a semi-Indianized Che Guevara for the new century, Marcos has introduced a fascinating new wrinkle into the problem of speaking for/with/around the Other.

The work of Pedro Henríquez Ureña (1884–1946) is exemplary with regard to its representation of women and classical indigenous writers. Despite the Cuban editors' disclaimer, in the Casa de las Américas edition of his *Historia de la cultura en la América hispánica* [1947; *A Concise History of Latin American*

Culture, 1977], that some of his judgments "suffer from the ideological limitations of his era" (8), the Dominican's evaluations are generous, broad-minded, and inclusive. Writing in the 1940s, he is among the first critics to recognize the key role of transculturation in Latin America: "[In the case of] the culture implanted by the Spaniards and Portuguese in the New World . . . the very act of transplanting obliged the Europeans to modify it unconsciously. . . . Furthermore, the Indian cultures exercised quite varied influences on the European transplants" (31). He discusses the phenomenon of *tequitqui* (the introduction of indigenous motifs and elements into Colonial architecture) and defends the centrality of folk art to the world of elite art. He also notes the continuation of theater in indigenous languages, in both the Yucatán and Paraguay, up to the present day (34). In his discussion of the hundreds of sixteenth-century writers born in the Americas, Henríquez Ureña observes that many were descendants of Indians, including the "distinguished historians" Hernando Alvarado Tezozómoc (1530?–1600?) and Fernando de Alva Ixtlilxóchitl (1578–1650) (46). With regard to women writers, his coverage is also generous. Moreover, he notes both the dates on which various Latin American nations granted women the vote and the extent of female participation in federal politics. This contrasts markedly with the work from the same decade of the Chilean literary historian Arturo Torres-Ríoseco, who, for instance, remarks on indigenous historians' "imperfect command of Spanish" and argues that Sor Juana "wrote as though she were completely Spanish" (12, 33). Aside from a passing reference to Clorinda Matto de Turner (1852–1909), the only woman writer he discusses is Sor Juana.

The attitude of most Latin American literary historians toward Latin American women writers has been ambivalent, to say the least. When, in the 1960s, critics dismissed Rosario Castellanos (1925–1974) as an "indigenista writer," this led her to abandon the richest vein of her fiction in favor of more cosmopolitan, urban themes. In the process, her acute social criticism, so prescient in its treatment of the intersection of class, ethnicity, and gender, was reduced to the experiences of middle-class white and *mestiza* women. Today, even as Castellanos is canonized in the public schools and lionized by the government, she remains largely unread beyond the public school system, even in her native Chiapas. Similarly, as already noted, Mexico's foremost living woman writer, Elena Poniatowska, is still often dismissed by other Mexican authors as a journalist, rather than a novelist or fiction writer, although her readers and fans are predominantly women and university students—of both genders.

In this regard, it is instructive to compare the coverage and treatment of women authors by two preeminent critics of the past two generations. In a now classic essay on Mexican literary history orginally written in 1946 and revised in 1960 and 1995, José Luis Martínez (b. 1918) devotes considerable space and warm appreciation to numerous women writers. For instance, he praises the abundance and richness of women's poetry in the 1940s and 1950s. The publication of a new journal dedicated to women's writing, *Rueca* [Spinning Wheel], proved to be an important incentive for women poets, who contributed some of the most interesting and original writing of those years. Martínez proceeds to list Margarita Michelena (1917–1998), Castellanos, Guadalupe Amor (1920–2000), Dolores Castro (b. 1923), Margarita Paz Paredes (b. 1922), María Luisa Hidalgo (1918–2000), Concha Urquiza (1910–1945), Emma Godoy (1921–1989), Enriqueta Ochoa (b. 1928),

and Gloria Riestra (b. 1929) as names to watch; in most cases, history proved him right. He also praises the contributions of modern women novelists, short-story writers, and playwrights; although he lapses into the stereotypes of praising women dramatists' enthusiasm over their achievements, he recognizes such diverse—and in some cases sardonic—writers as Carmen Rosenzweig (b. 1925), Amparo Dávila (b. 1928), Elena Garro (1917–1998) and Guadalupe Dueñas (b. 1920). Finally, Martínez has the foresight to note the following standout on the literary scene of the 1960s, where Elena Poniatowska transformed the interview into a new genre through a mixture of malicious naivete, uncommon wit, style, and a keen awareness of how the text would be read.

On the other hand, in an essay he wrote for the same 1995 literary history in which Martínez's revised essay appears, Christopher Domínguez Michael greatly restricts his coverage of women—although he is dealing with the seventy-year period from 1920 to 1990, when they were most active. He often limits himself to listing a few of these authors' titles, omitting any commentary regarding their significance for Mexican letters. In regional literary histories and anthologies, such omissions tend to be even more pronounced. For instance, the best literary history of Oaxaca only includes one woman writer, although its Zapotec editor, the writer and critic Víctor de la Cruz, includes a number of Zapotec male authors. Only two women writers, and no Indian writers, figure in two recent literary anthologies of Chiapas (Flores and Wong). Oscar Wong nods toward the groups he has excluded in an appended "Bibliography of Authors Not Anthologized," where he lists two titles under the heading "Indian Stories," and nine women narrators among his list of the twenty-two fiction writers whom he has excluded. The only woman he has included is Castellanos. Similarly, the latest literary history of Chiapas discusses only Castellanos and Elva Macías (b. 1944), yet does mention several younger women writers (Morales Bermúdez). In one case he discounts an author's work on the basis of its "sensiblería femenina" ("feminine sensibility," echoing José Joaquín Blanco's dismissal of Rosario Castellanos' poetry, which Poniatowska in turn denounced). Similarly, in his 1999 collection of interviews with writers from Chiapas, Hernán Becerra Pino interviews ten male intellectuals but only one woman, Elva Macías.

For many readers in Mexico City and in the English-speaking world, of course, Rosario Castellanos has become synonymous with the literature of Chiapas. In response to this mythification (which is comparable to that of Gabriela Mistral in Chile), Morales Bermúdez limits his discussion of her works to a mere four pages, characterized by faint praise. He reserves his highest praise, rather, for the male poets Jaime Sabines (b. 1926) and Efraín Bartolomé (b. 1950). While Malva Flores does allude to the emergence of new Mayan literature in Chiapas, she does not include any of these authors in her anthology; Morales Bermúdez omits any mention of this work, implying with his silence that its study has no place in Spanish-language history—although, ironically, most of it is, in fact, being written in Spanish, the colonial language. These omissions seem doubly egregious in Chiapas, with its long-standing tradition of committed literature, and particularly since 1994, when the Mayan uprising brought renewed international attention to the extreme marginalization and racism endured by the state's Mayan majority.

The panorama is beginning to change, if unevenly, with the emergence of the first women, and then the first Indian, literary critics, beginning in the 1980s and 1990s. At the end of the twentieth century, there was a growing public awareness of the fundamental injustice in a *machista* society as can be seen in the SEP campaign against gender discrimination (see **Figure 1**). For instance, one of the most even-handed essays in recent Mexican literary history, with regard to gender, is an article on contemporary Mayan writers by the Yucatecan Mayan writer Jorge Miguel Cocom Pech. To some extent this response mirrors the comparatively large role that women have played in contemporary Mayan letters. Since the 1970s, black critics in the United States and Latin America have also sought to reconstruct the Afro-Hispanic literary record. Beginning in the mid-1980s, Jewish writers and critics (including a high proportion of women) have undertaken the recuperation of Sephardic and Ashkenazic Jewish cultures. (See the essay by Saúl Sosnowski in this section.) Other cultural traditions—Asian and Arabic—still remain to be written into the literary histories.

Because of Latin America's tradition of committed writing, poverty has long been a theme of its literature. Since the urban migrations of the 1960s, writers including Juan Rulfo (1918–1986) and José María Arguedas (1911–1969) have dealt directly with urban poverty. Often it seems that male artists deal with the phenomenon through the portrayal of male gangs, while women tend to focus on individual female subjectivity. Think, for instance, of Elena Poniatowska's Jesusa Palancares versus Mario Vargas Llosa's (b. 1936) male groups of "cachorros" (military cadets and soldiers); of Clarice Lispector (1925–1977) and Susana Amaral's Macabea in the novel and film versions of *The Hour of the Star* versus the boy gangs of *Tire Die* (Argentina), *Los olvidados* (Mexico), *Pixote* (Brazil), *Rodrigo D: No Future* (Colombia), or *Caluga o menta* (Chile). The past two decades have also seen a flourishing of the new urban chronicle by the likes of Poniatowska, Monsiváis, and Cristina Pacheco. However, the number of writers who, like Pacheco, are themselves products of impoverished backgrounds is minimal.

The final taboo in Latin America, as elsewhere, has been homosexuality. The 1970s and 1980s, nevertheless, saw an outpouring of gay male literature. Gay male writers like Manuel Puig, Luis Zapata (b. 1951), Pedro Lemubel, and Senel Paz (b. 1950), together with Jaime Humberto Hermosillo in cinema, have paved the way for other gay authors and directors to begin reaching mass audiences. Often this has involved collaborations between gay and straight artists, or between straight artists: for instance, Arturo Ripstein's masterful adaptation of José Donoso's (1924–1996) *El lugar sin límites* [1967; A Place Without Limits], or the film adaptations of *The Kiss of the Spider Woman* and *Strawberry and Chocolate* by Hector Babenco and Tomás Gutiérrez Alea. This has been followed during the past decade by pioneering works in gay scholarship (in journals like the Chilean *Crítica Cultural* and the Mexican *fem* and *Debate Feminista*, and in essay collections like *Masculino/femenino*). However, most of the recent scholarship about gay and lesbian writers has been published by journals and university presses based in the United States. Remarkably little literature or criticism has been published, to date, about lesbian subjectivity, however.

There are other marginalized groups, such as the elderly and the disabled, that cross class, ethnic, and gender lines and remain largely absent from Latin American letters, except as metaphors for senility or depravity. (One exception is Gaby Brimmer's and Elena Poniatowska's testimonial narrative

Figure 1.

Photograph of a poster in Mexico City. (Courtesy Eulalio Ferrer)

Gaby Brimmer.) Public debate on these issues is only just beginning. But these things change with the times, and so too do the literary histories.

The Ins and Outs of History

To speak about certain labels or established notions such as exclusion, minorities, or marginalization in a peripheral country like Brazil can be a fascinating *mistake*, a kind of insensitivity or even a misunderstanding. In order to analyze the process of exclusion and marginalization in the literary history of Brazil, we must begin by questioning the construction or invention of the country's literary canon and the processes that left certain cultural expressions out of the main body of tradition and favored others that were, in turn, privileged by literary listings that became official. Even if we understand the exclusion procedures that determine the wider framework of Western literary histories, it is necessary to identify the particular features that emerge when one examines certain national variables, such as the double dislocation of works not included in local canons and, in fact, are also marginalized by metropolitan countries. Thus, certain elements can be underlined: the situation of the cultural production of people socially marginalized by their economic condition; the conditions of cultural production in the context of the military dictatorship and of the authoritarian regimes that weakened Brazil's democratic process; the impact of an oral tradition in a society in which cultural formations are determined by time periods; the variety of the forms of transmission and hybridization of popular and high cultures; and the influence of the centrifugal force of globalization on local cultures (even when certain manifestations coming from peripheral countries manage to set an alternative route within the new configuration of forces, thus reordering the creation and transmission of culture and especially, today, multimedia transmission).

Our purpose in this introduction will be to inquire into the dynamics of the exclusion and marginalization processes in Brazilian literary culture by trying to avoid the neocanonical definitions of exclusion, especially when dealing with the notions of sexual and ethnic difference in Brazilian literature. This is why, for our evaluation of a literary text—even if it formed part of traditional historiography—we do not trust certain criteria (such as those used to explain cultural reality in the United States) or certain theoretical notions that, even if well-intentioned, are nonetheless the product of European contexts. If two negatives become a positive, what is at the margin of the periphery may risk becoming central; this is not precisely what we want, for we wish to keep an anti-hegemonic position in the context of world cultural relationships. The postmodern notion of literary history, built from a comparative perspective as we suggest here, offers a new model that allows for the inclusion of what is at the borders or in the margins. It also defends such margins, questions the authority of the canon and of history itself, decenters assumptions and inquiries, and interrogates master narratives. In creating a new history that is inclusive of the entire range of cultural relations in the Americas, this is our main challenge: To define clearly the nature of the margins in peripheral countries and to understand the dislocation strategies of what have recently been called the margins of literary history. But if we remove the condition of being at the margin of cultural production, we also risk losing the built-in resistance to the universalizing paradigm of the center. Without wanting to, we may empty it of its critical and questioning role within a history built through works created as copies, imitations, borrowings, transpositions, but also as alternatives. To transform the margins into classificatory elements in themselves risks undermining the power of such an internal disordering of culture and thus nullifying the polemical value of the margins. This may be not only a political problem but also an epistemological one. What matters is the driving force of this kind of logic, its negotiating side, its mobility to move in and out of the organized system of literary history and, thus, of the specific discursive strategies of various contexts and subsystems.

The aforementioned mistake or misunderstanding emerges originally from the notion—which was widely accepted until recently—that in Latin America, and more specifically in Brazil, "we do not have any problem" regarding not only racial issues but also gender-related questions, especially where sexual options are concerned. At least this is how Brazilians usually introduce themselves. To avoid dealing with gender or ethnic issues that may guide contemporary research does not mean a theoretical backwardness or an underdeveloped stage in the social organization where minorities are concerned. There are certain peculiarities involving situations of exclusion or marginalization that need to be taken into account. The truth is that it may be convenient to eclipse such differences and to make of this darkening process a form of cultural and even economic resistance. A different reading of the modernist notion of *anthropophagy* may be useful to understand better the subtleties of this issue. From the *Pau-Brasil Manifesto* (1924) on, avant-garde writers intended to create a modern art and literature in Brazil without becoming mere imitations of the European avant-garde movements, and thus they searched for an authentically national modern art. However, how was it possible to become modern without imitating their coveted European models, which were, in turn, valorizing primitive art forms, such as African art? At the time, then, *anthropophagy*—cannibalism—seemed to offer an image of reconciling the admiration felt toward the avant-garde movements of Europe and the desire to acquire a sense of Brazilianness, to build, by means of art, one's own cultural identity. In the context of the actual cannibalism of the native inhabitants of Brazil (that is, those who received the Portuguese colonizers) it was necessary for the enemy to show some special virtues in order to be eaten. To have the honor of being eaten and not just merely killed, the enemy must demonstrate certain virtues, such as bravery in battle and courage in defeat. Such enviable characteristics constituted the enemy's qualifications for being eaten. Cannibalism was the result of an extreme fascination with otherness and "difference"; similarly anthropophagy as a national interpretation of Brazil sought to internalize the other. Thus, the admirable qualities of the other were absorbed and, by means of this process, the uniqueness of the other was also denied. Modernist Brazil was introduced, after all, as a hospitable place, always ready to receive (and assimilate) the other, but also to devour that other.

In this new reading of the *Antropofago*, we can distinguish certain Brazilian tendencies toward eliminating differences instead of facing them. The current structure of discourse on race and gender in Brazil reflects this constant but always incomplete attempt to assimilate difference. The very possibility of this kind of representation rests on two factors. The first is the very questionable conviction that the past is irrelevant or does not exist. The second factor is directly related to the social and political organization of Brazilian elites, which is based on a master-servant relationship that ensures a vertical organization of classes in the social hierarchy—to the detriment of any possibility of establishing common interests or goals cutting through classes, races, and professional categories. Ethnic and gender questions are fundamental subjects throughout the essays offered in this section. In the context of literature written by blacks, the main exponent is Machado de Assis (1839–1908), who in fact is not only the major Brazilian author but also perhaps one of the most important prose writers in the Portuguese language. In examining the role of women and Jewish writers, the dominant figure of modern literature is Clarice Lispector (1925–1977), possibly the Brazilian author most widely studied internationally. But we must not forget Rachel de Queiróz (b. 1910), *la grande dame* of Brazilian letters, who began to earn her reputation from the moment she published her first books. Studies about "homotextuality" began in the naturalist period and reached their expressive height in contemporary literature. The main representative is Mário de Andrade (1893–1945), the favorite of the modernist canon and the most versatile of intellectuals. Does all of this mean that Brazil offers an idyllic society that has no preconceptions, and that all minorities have equal access to culture and the publication of their works? Far from it. The reality is completely different: Brazil is a country where social exclusion exacerbates extreme socioeconomic differences, a country where lordly policies and social practices have been the rule, a patriarchal, slave society. (Brazil was the last country in the Americas to abolish slavery.)

Analyzing the historiography of Brazil's cultural production–art, popular forms of expression, oral literature, and forgotten literary works that have been put aside or have not been recognized as truly literary–it is possible to identify the large gaps in the official history of Brazilian culture. However, there are certain insertion strategies that authors manage to adopt even when, historically and socially, they seemed destined to belong to these hinterlands. Therefore, it is necessary to define the notion of exclusion clearly as well as to distinguish the kinds of social and cultural exclusion to which minorities have been subjected. Given these nuances that we want to introduce here, it is evident that it would be too hasty to consider only the notions of gender and ethnic exclusion in Brazil, as one does when studying the literary production of the United States. What emerges as the pervading image is, therefore, that of the social outcast, or to be more precise, the social class of the poor, which, although worldwide in scope, in this section will be treated only as the exclusion of this sector's voice from the literary canon. As the essays will show, there are other forms of exclusion from recognized literary culture–the exclusion of blacks, women, Indians, the landless peasants, the urban homeless–and these forms usually involve multiple subjectivities. The impossibility of choosing or selecting for oneself is what defines the situation of the social outcast.

When, during the military regime of the 1970s, the movement called marginal poetry originated, its members decided to remain outside the circuit of the publishing houses and produced artisan books as a reaction to the suppression of the arts and culture of the country. This political position was also assumed in other fields: For instance, theater companies decided to organize themselves as cooperative groups. Young muscians also followed this model; however, because popular music in Brazil is so noticeable, its representatives were strongly repressed and some–like Chico Buarque de Hollanda (b. 1944), Caetano Veloso (b. 1942), and Gilberto Gil (b. 1942)–had to go into exile. In *this* kind of marginal production, there is a principle of independence, of resistance. In the world of print, an alternative cultural model was created around small newspapers, which played a fundamental role in divulging independent thought by giving voice to the group called the "AI-5 Generation," a name which alluded to the act proclaimed by the military regime in 1968, by means of which all forms of artistic and political expression were cut off. Thus, the notion of being marginal was so charged with positive connotations that certain figures such as robbers, bandits, and thieves were even mythologized. The most significant instance of the fascination exerted by the condition of marginality is that of plastic artist Hélio Oiticica (1937–1980), one of the creators of neo-Concretism in Brazil, who dedicated his innovative works to the criminals and bandits from Rio's slums. Marginal poetry greatly influenced the kind of poetry being written toward the end of the century, such as that written by Ana Cristina César (1952–1983), Torquato Neto (1944–1972), and Francisco Alvim (b. 1938).

Traditionally, the outcast is the subject of Brazilian literature. The abolitionist romantics were concerned with this figure; the republican naturalists denounced the subhuman conditions of the inhabitants of the country's capital; the regional modernists revealed the poverty of the Northeastern region in classic works such as Graciliano Ramos's (1892–1953) *Vidas secas* [1938; *Barren Lives*]. The exotic poverty of Bahia's ruffians and whores inspired Jorge Amado (1912–

2001) and made him famous. The *sertões*, the dry, backward, forgotten regions of the country, together with their history, such as the massacre of the *Canudos*, were the stage of several masterpieces such as *Os sertões* (1902) by Euclides da Cunha (1866–1909), and Guimarães Rosa's (1908–1967) *Grande Sertão: veredas* [1956; *The Devil to Pay in the Backlands,* 1967].

While the condition of being a peripheral country kept Brazil far from the cultural capitals of the world, the dictatorial regimes of Latin America increased the process of isolation. The Republic of Brazil was established in 1889, but from 1930 to 1945 the country was already undergoing its first dictatorial regime, in what became a dual process of authoritarianism and conservative modernization (which increased from 1937 on). In 1964 the democratic process was interrupted once again, and the military regime lasted until 1984. Only in 1988 was it possible to put an end to this form of government by means of a constitutional decree. The end of authoritarianism led to a democratic stage, which does not necessarily mean that there is a consolidated democratic regime or a truly democratic social organization. From the end of the dictatorship to the 1990s, Brazilian literature continued to struggle in order to achieve the level of expression that had characterized it in the 1960s. As part of the renewal process of this post-dictatorship literature–to use a term so dear to the critic Alberto Moreiras–it is now possible for the have-nots to become the real producers of culture in Brazil, and not just the producers of popular culture or other oral and traditional forms of expression. It is now quite possible for them to find the way to be included culturally by means of forms of expression that have not been the concern of academic studies and that still meet resistance in some critical works.

The notion of exclusion becomes clearer when poverty defines the role of the individual in the community in which he lives, defines his limitations as the subject of rights and duties, but, above all, defines him as subject of his own discourse, including artistic discourse. Searching for a more precise definition of poverty, we turn to Roberto Martínez Nogueira and his influential study on contemporary poverty in Argentina, *La pobreza: un programa de acción* [Poverty: An Action Program]. He argues that, although poverty is usually defined as the lack of access to certain goods and services or as the impossibility of attaining a certain income, this empirical description falls far short of the social reality, because it ignores the existential point of view of those who are deprived. Poverty is a way of life and one in which it is impossible to overlook the indirect social cost of a sector of the population that is socially recognized as such and is weakly inserted into the institutional apparatus of society. The resulting underground economy, as well as the various illegal survival tactics, have created a crisis situation everywhere in Latin America (17–23). At the start of the twenty-first century, it is fundamental to have a categorization that may explain the social exclusion of the population of a country like Brazil, where 80 percent of its inhabitants live in the cities. If, in the 1900s, the rural outcast was described as the inhabitant of the deprived regions of the country and, above all, as the victim of nature, the climate, and the immensity of the country, today the underprivileged are purely and simply the urban poor, those who remain outside society because of their socioeconomic situation and who, most of the time, are deprived of the minimum conditions of citizenship. On the contrary, the rural individual emerges as the protagonist of a new form of social organization, the Movement of the Landless (O Movimento dos Sem Terra), which is perhaps the most significant political force in a country undergoing a process of restructuring.

The severe limitations on access to education represent a decisive form of exclusion which goes from the extremes of illiteracy to those who can hardly read, much less write. Even so, in Brazil, such authors found some kind of intermediary who wrote their work for them. A singular case is that of Carolina Maria de Jesus (1914–1977), whose first book *Quarto de despejo* [1960; *Child of the Dark: The Diary of Carolina Maria de Jesus*]–a bitter diary of life in the slums–became a best-seller, with one million books sold around the world, 100,000 of which were sold in Brazil. The book was published in 1960 by journalist Audálio Dantas, who intervened in the text only in a limited way. Carolina continued to publish, and her poetic work was collected in a single volume in 1996. The poetic production of the poor tends more often to be expressed through popular music. During the 1920s, *samba* emerged in Rio de Janeiro as the artistic form of expression of the underprivileged; its lyrics dealt with poverty, life in the slums, and myths such as that of the *malandro*, the rascal, or the dunce. Today, samba has been renewed by forms derived from the main tradition, such as the *pagode* or the *sambas de enredo* of the samba schools that organize the carnival, and by other musical forms, such as funk, hip-hop, and some Brazilian variations of reggae, that come from the suburbs of the big cities like Rio or São Paulo. Thus, popular music needs to be taken into account whenever an oral tradition is discussed. For instance, funk music created in the periphery of the big urban centers is a form of social protest that incorporates a visual influence from the United States together with social criticism.

Outcasts are a central issue in the criticism of the neoliberal model that dominates the globalization process. The poor, the unemployed, the underprivileged of globalized society are the subject of sociological research (Celso Furtado and Pierre Bourdieu), of mass-culture studies (Néstor García Canclini), and of cultural criticism (George Yúdice). In the contemporary setting, the cultural manifestations of poverty acquire a new form that, while not completely leaving aside the patterns of the so-called popular culture, do not limit themselves to them. Thus, in literature the poor man represents not only a socioeconomic condition but a subjectivity, one of the last to be reconsidered. A perverse urban development resulted from the rural migration to the cities in search of better conditions of life; what followed was the building of dormitory towns around huge industrial areas and recurrent removal policies in the big cities. If it is true that this situation is not exclusive to Brazil–Celso Furtado has stated that such dislocations are caused by the social exclusion of increasingly large groups of the population in Latin American urban life–it has to do with such aggravations as new populist manifestations, official tolerance toward drug dealing, the rapid increase in criminalization in the slums, and in general the breaking up of social values.

However, something significant has changed: New subjects of artistic and literary production have increasingly emerged in those peripheral spaces that quite often are excluded from the cultural universe of big cities. In Latin America the dividing line that separated high culture from popular and mass culture is vanishing, as the next section of this history will demonstrate. Today the poverty-stricken periphery of an urban center like São Paulo produces the music that is played and consumed in the expensive clubs attended by the rich young people. Contemporary poetry circulates in the nonformal spaces of groups with certain social and behavioral habits, far from the renowned ivory tower. This kind of poetry is frequently produced in impoverished areas. Dance and theater companies of the slums, such as the *Rocinha* and *Nós no morro* [Us in the slums], have been winning awards and gaining ground in the artistic world. They are the result of a new kind of social organization created by the slums' inhabitants, who claim the condition of subjects of their own cultural reality.

One of the exclusion spaces originated in Rio de Janeiro by the removal policy during the dictatorship is the cidade de Deus (city of God), which is treated in one of the most interesting texts of Brazilian contemporary literature–the long and dense novel written by Paulo Lins (b. 1958), *Cidade de Deus* (1997). Curiously, from the moment it was published, this novel was legitimated by the critic and scholar Roberto Schwarz, who welcomed the book in these terms: "The star novel written by Paulo Lins, a 550-page bombshell about criminality in the City of God in Rio de Janeiro deserves to be welcomed like a huge event. The explosive interest of its subject, the magnitude of the task, its difficulties, its internal and different point of view, all contributed to create an unusual artistic adventure. Literature was used to explore firm possibilities which evidently do exist" (Schwarz 5). Paulo Lins's novel has no commercial appeal, because it does not offer an exotic or victimized view of the City of God. Paulo Lins's description is neither better nor worse than the one that appears in the local news; it is, however, a town seen from the inside. The narrator is an agent who places himself inside that physical space. The force of the narration lies in the difficult device of repetition–repetition of actions, pattern-like scenes that restart again and again, as if infinite fieldwork notebooks were constantly being filled. Reading this novel is not easy. The harshness, violence, and disrespect for the minimum conditions of life are presented as in a film, without mercy, without justification, without apologies, without moral or political explanations. Its logic is that of the City of God. In the novel, the City of God is a closed space; there are no exits. One can only come out dead or go to prison; perhaps one can become a born-again Christian and accept work as a bricklayer in precarious conditions. The narrative produced *within* the excluded City of God points in no direction. What becomes a path is its writing, its very existence.

Translation by Nair Anaya Ferreira

Works Cited

Blanco, José Joaquín. 1996. *Crónica literaria: Un siglo de escritores mexicanos.* Mexico City: Cal y Arena.

Bolio, Dolores. 1949 [1918]. *Una hoja del pasado. Novela.* Mérida: Editorial Club del Libro.

Bourdieu, Pierre. 1993. *The Field of Cultural Production: Essays on Art and Literature.* Ed. Randall Johnson. Cambridge: Polity Press.

Brimmer, Gaby, and Elena Poniatowska. 1979. *Gaby Brimmer.* Mexico City: Editorial Grijalbo.

Cocom Pech, Jorge Miguel. 1996. "Renacimiento de la palabra de los mayas de hoy. Ká síijil u t'an mayao'ob, bejlae." *Tierra adentro* 78 (Feb.–Mar.): 53–58.

Cruz, Víctor de la, ed. 1993. *Antología literaria de Oaxaca.* Mexico City: Universidad Autónoma "Benito Juárez" de Oaxaca.

Domínguez Michael, Christopher. 1997. *Tiros en el concierto. Literatura mexicana del siglo V.* Mexico City: Ediciones Era.

Flores, Malva, ed. 1994. *Chiapas. Voces particulares. Poesía, narrativa y teatro (Siglos XIX-XX)*. Mexico City: Consejo Nacional para la Cultura y las Artes.

Garcia Canclini, Néstor. 1995. *Consumidores y ciudadanos: Conflictos multiculturales de la globalización*. Mexico City: Grijalbo.

Henríquez Ureña, Pedro. 1979. *Historia de la cultura en la América hispánica*. Havana: Gente Nueva. (Mexico City: Fondo de Cultura Económica, 1947).

León-Portilla, Miguel. 1996. "La antigua y la nueva palabra de los pueblos indígenas." *Culturas y derechos de los pueblos indígenas de México*. Mexico City: Archivo General de la Nación and Fondo de Cultura Económica. 21–47.

Lins, Paulo. 1997. *Cidade de Deus*. São Paulo: Companhia das Letras.

Ludmer, Josefina. 1984. "Tretas del débil." *La sartén por el mango: Encuentro de escritoras latinoamericanas*. Ed. Patricia Elena González and Eliana Ortega. Río Piedras, Puerto Rico: Ediciones Huracán. 47–54.

Martin, Gerald. 1989. *Journeys through the Labyrinth. Latin American Fiction in the Twentieth Century*. London: Verso.

Martínez, José Luis, and Christopher Domínguez Michael. 1995. *La literatura mexicana del siglo XX*. Mexico City: CONACULTA.

Martínez Nogueira, Roberto. 1993. *La pobreza: Un programa de acción*. Buenos Aires: Fundación Banco de Boston.

Monsiváis, Carlos. 1996. "Versiones nacionales de lo indígena." *Culturas y derechos de los pueblos indígenas de México*. Mexico City: Archivo General de la Nación and Fondo de Cultura Económica. 55–74.

Montemayor, Carlos, ed. 1991. *Situación actual y perspectivas de la literatura en lenguas indígenas*. Mexico City: CONACULTA

———. ed . 1992. *Los escritores indígenas actuales*, 2 vols. Mexico City: Fondo Editorial Tierra Adentro/Consejo Nacional para la Cultura y las Artes. Vol. 1: Ensayo; Vol. 2: Poesía, narrativa, teatro.

Morales Bermúdez, Jesús. 1997. *Aproximaciones a la poesía y la narrativa de Chiapas*. Tuxtla Gutiérrez: Universidad de Ciencias y Artes de Chiapas.

Moreiras, Alberto. 1993. "Posdictadura y reforma del pensamiento." *Revista de crítica cultural* 7:26–35; reprtd. *Utopía(s). Seminario Internacional*. Ed. Eugenio Llona Mouat. Santiago: Ministerio de Educación. 264–76.

Picón-Salas, Mariano. 1962. *A Cultural History of Spanish America from Conquest to Independence*. Berkeley: University of California Press, 1962 (Mexico City: Fondo de Cultura Económica, 1944).

Poniatowska, Elena. 1985. "Rosario Castellanos: ¡Vida, nada te debo!" *¡Ay vida, no me mereces!* Mexico City: Joaquín Mortiz. 93–132.

Poot Herrera, Sara. 1991. "Dolores Bolio: figura literaria de vuelta de siglo." 1991. *Las voces olvidadas. Antología crítica de narradoras mexicanas nacidas en el siglo XIX*. Ed. Ana Rosa Domenella and Nora Pasternac. Mexico City: El Colegio de México. 227–46.

Schwarz, Roberto. 1997. "Uma aventura artística incomum." *Folha de São Paulo, Caderno Mais!* (September 7) 5–13.

Timerman, Jacobo. 1982. *Prisoner Without a Name, Cell Without a Number*. New York: Vintage Books.

Torres Ríoseco, Arturo. 1942. *The Epic of Latin American Literature*. Berkeley: University of California Press.

Wong, Oscar, ed. 1999. Chiapas: Dimensión de la narrativa. Antología. Mexico City: Edamex.

SECTION I
CONFIGURATIONS OF SOCIOECONOMIC, RACIAL, AND ETHNIC ALTERITY IN LITERARY HISTORY

CHAPTER 22

POVERTY IN THE HISTORY OF LITERARY CULTURES

Kathleen Newman

Though the literary representation of poverty and the literary self-representation of the poor seldom receive direct mention in the tables of contents and indexes of Spanish American literary histories of the last half-century, the category of poverty is present in numerous other guises. In the discussions of the contexts of literary production since the Conquest and Colonial period to the present, the recognition of economic hierarchies and an enduring poverty in Latin American societies is implicit in all references to social divisions of class and race, rural and urban society, oral and print cultures, elite and mass culture, and political struggles, be they on the left or right. Likewise, a review of the periodization of literature, the criteria for the delimitation of literary movements, and the categorization of authors and literary texts reveals a general denial of what perceptive historians like Jean Franco (1967; *The Modern Culture of Latin America: Society and the Artist*) have noted: that Latin American writers have more often than not taken the role of "the conscience of the nation."

The role of the intellectual as advocate for the disenfranchized, as described in the texts in this section, has changed markedly in recent decades with the debates surrounding the emergence of new forms of literary expression such as *testimonio* and with the inclusion of pre-Colombian and colonial texts previously not recognized by literary histories. This newfound source material of literary self-representation in both Spanish and the indigenous languages has presented a long-submerged face of Latin American literary cultures and has brought about a demand for a revision of the cultural past with respect to the participation of those sectors of the population victimized by economic exploitation. An important part of the historical revision that has been undertaken has been to challenge the idea of poverty as a natural phenomenon and to examine it as social violence resulting from the exercise of social power by dominant minorities. Historians of literary culture today have endeavored to give new meaning to the social context of the foundational texts of the past through identification of the traces of class domination, even in literary texts whose principal focus is not social.

A measure of the difference in the literary historian's understanding of the nature of poverty between early literary

histories and those written during the mid-twentieth century can be found in a comparison of Ricardo Rojas's (1882–1957) multivolume national literary history *La literatura argentina* [1917–1922, Argentine Literature], with Pedro Henríquez Ureña's (1884–1946) *Historia de la cultura en la América hispánica* [1947, A Concise History of Latin American Culture]. In his concluding remarks in the final volume on "Los modernos" [1922, "The Moderns"], Rojas assures the reader: "There were natural and political adversities our peoples had to overcome before forming a nation; there were multiple problems that first had to be resolved. An enormous amount of energy and thought had to go into this struggle with the desert, with barbarity, with fanaticism, with ignorance, with poverty and with the traditional obstacles left behind by colonial rule or by civil wars. All of this brought about certain anomalies in our cultural life which must be kept in mind when one examines the evolution of our literatures from an aesthetic point of view or our political evolution from a moral point of view" (990). By his association of poverty with barbarism, fanaticism, ignorance, and residual colonial impediments, Rojas locates poverty and, by extension, the poor as enemies to literature and the national culture, and asserts an equivalence between socioeconomic status and both morality and artistry. When describing contemporaneous literary production a quarter century later, in 1947, Henríquez Ureña would locate poverty as a legitimate matter for literary concern: "A part of this new literature aspires to be 'pure literature,' especially in poetry: a literature stripped of all matters that are not strictly artistic, and above all, lacking in 'anecdote,' that is, reference to events interesting in themselves rather than for the manner in which the author interprets them. But there is another part of this new literature which, in contrast, deals with human problems, be they individual or collective" (139–40). For Henríquez Ureña, this new literature of collective problems includes *indigenista* texts, *poesía negra*, the essay, and novels of the land, rural or urban work, and the Mexican Revolution. Here the writer's consciousness of the tragedy of social divisions is lauded rather than rejected.

A sample of literary histories and anthologies by Latin Americanists from the late 1940s until the late 1960s suggests that the binarism of aesthetics versus politics which Henríquez Ureña noted would underlie the periodization and categorization for at least the next two decades. Fernando Alegría's (b. 1918) *Historia de la novela hispanoamericana* [1965; History of the Hispanic American Novel], Enrique Anderson Imbert (1910–2000) and Eugenio Florit's (1903–1999) *Literatura hispanoamericana: Antología e introducción histórica* [1960; Spanish American Literature: Anthology and Introduction], Arturo Torres-Ríoseco's (1897–1971) *Historia de la literatura iberoamericana* [1965; History of Ibero-American Literature], Orlando Gómez-Gil's *Historia crítica de la literatura latinoamericana: Desde los orígenes hasta el momento actual* [1968; Critical History of Latin American Literature: From Its Origins to the Present], and Rudolf Grossman's *Historia y problemas de la literatura latinoamericana* [1969; History and Problems of Latin American Literature] do not alter significantly the chronological sequence and criteria of literary evaluation of Henríquez Ureña's *Historia de la cultura en la América hispánica*. Where considered appropriate, Anderson Imbert and Florit will note a writer's "sympathy for the Indians and for the poor" (704) or describe a "bitter novel not only because the author writes with bitterness but primarily because the reader is shaken by the description of suffering" (703). Alegría will note the vigor with which certain writers express the human condition and explicate societal contradictions. For his part, Torres-Ríoseco will find similar worth in realist novels and novels of the city and the land, assigning to the "artistic novel" the legacy of *arielismo* and to the psychological or philosophical novels the legacy of *modernismo*. Gómez-Gil will see the contemporary Latin American literature of the *generación del 50* as drawing upon "metaphysical anguish and an attitude of social protest" (717). While Grossman will employ the marked category of author to revise literary history, such as "the Indian and the mestizo as authors" in the section "La época colonial hispanoportuguesa" [The Spanish-Portuguese Colonial Period] in the table of contents (11), he leaves unmarked the literary authorship of the colonial elite. In short, poverty does not surface in these texts as a primary literary concern, but rather remains part of the given social structuration, articulated as an aspect of larger social struggles. However, one glimpses in the organization of these histories the *direct* recognition of the social role of literature that will infuse a number of Latin American literary histories written during and after the Latin American literary boom.

Perhaps the best example of a comprehensive literary history responsive to the boom is *América latina en su literatura* [Latin America in Its Literature], the anthology of literary criticism and history edited by César Fernández Moreno, underwritten by UNESCO (1972). Each of the six sections, translated as "Literature in the World," "Ruptures in the Tradition," "Literature as Experimentation," "Language and Literature," "Literature and Society," and "The Social Function of Literature," with contributions from twenty-six distinguished critics and/or writers–among them Mario Benedetti (b. 1920), Roberto Fernández Retamar (b. 1930), Juan José Saer (b. 1937), and Severo Sarduy (1937–1993)–reveals a sense that social commentary and political intervention are not merely legitimate matters for literary attention, but matters of great urgency. While the word *poverty* or *the poor* do not appear once in the table of contents, the words *revolution* and *social justice,* balanced by the word *underdevelopment,* suggest an implicit condemnation of cultural and political exclusions stemming from economic hierarchies. In the same decade, Jean Franco's general literary history *Spanish American Literature since Independence* (1973), like *Modern Culture of Latin America,* examines critically the role of the politically committed writer. So does Carlos Rincón's *Cambio actual de la noción de la literatura y otros estudios de teoría y crítica latinoamericana* [1978; Current Change in the Concept of Literature and Other Studies in Latin America. Theory and Criticism] and Ángel Rama's (1926–1983) collection of essays, written in the 1970s, *Literatura y clase social* [1983; Literature and Social Class]. Like the contributors to the UNESCO project, all three historians and critics assume literature to be integral to social change. When, in his posthumous *La ciudad letrada* [1984; *The Lettered City*], Rama explores the role of literature in social structuration from the colonial period until the first two decades of the twentieth century, he asserts an explicit role for literature in the constitution of society, in the demarcation between high and low culture, the orderly and the chaotic, print culture and oral culture, placing in question the position taken in and by a work of imaginative writing with respect to the distribution of wealth and the exclusion of power.

At the end of the 1990s, when this history was being prepared, a number of new literary histories were published that, in general periodization and categorization of literature, do not vary greatly from the paradigms present at mid-century. The best of these histories, like the histories written during and after the boom, pay close attention to the political dimension of literature and the historical events that inform the literary text. Thus, the volumes for the *Historia de la literatura hispanoamericana* [1982 and 1992; History of Hispanic American Literature], edited by Luis Iñigo Madrigal, are notable for their historical contextualization of the literary text. However, the two homonym histories from Spain, one written by José Miguel Oviedo (1997) and one written by Teodosio Fernández, Selena Millares, and Eduardo Becerra (1995), reiterate the literary trajectories set in place at mid-century. In none of these histories does the representation of poverty or the self-representation of the impoverished emerge as a primary category of analysis. Though they also do not appear as primary categories in a number of more specialized histories, these histories reveal a relevant shift in categorization that the more comprehensive histories do not. For example, in a consideration of the nature and range of current literary production and literary criticism, a number of authors assert an interstice between art and criticism where the marginalized, the hybrid, and the heterogeneous register efforts of social transformation. In *Los novelistas como críticos* [1991; Novelists as Critics], Norma Klahn and Wilfredo Corral create a counterpointed literary history in criticism where writers, such as Marta Traba in "Hipótesis sobre una escritura diferente" [1991; "Hypothesis about a Different Writing"] can suggest that women's writing occupies "a different place which has been called literary space" (212). Similar to readings based on concepts of hybridity and heterogeneity theorized by Néstor García Canclini and Antonio Cornejo Polar, respectively, the reassessment by Silvia Molloy of Alvar Núñez Cabeza de Vaca's (1490–1558) *Relación de los naufragios* [1542], ["Adventures in the Unknown Interior of America," 1983] suggests a realignment of subjectivity that positions the Spaniard to think from the perspective and place of the indigenous peoples he met during his journey. With respect to the emergent generation of poets whose work he has collected in *Antología de la poesía latinoamericana del siglo XXI: El turno y la transición* [1997; Anthology of Latin American Poetry of the Twenty-first Century: The Turn and the Transition], editor Julio Ortega suggests that "it is their turn to speak in the transition that converts their marginal and precarious place into a culture without an articulated social horizon" (15). In a culture without an as-yet-articulated social horizon, without a colonial realignment of subject position, without a space other than that of the literary text, each poet alone and all together suggest an opening toward a new dimension of literature and literary histories–wherein it would be possible to represent the determinants and consequences of poverty and present the perspectives of the poor in their own voice. They also suggest an understanding of how social systems exist simultaneously on a scale that, while inclusive of the national and the regional, extends from the local to the global–a type of knowledge in literary texts that could describe the ways in which the systemic extension of global capitalism, which has been coterminous with the centuries of Latin American literary history, makes poverty still a relevant category in literary history.

Works Cited

Alegría, Fernando. 1965. *Historia de la novela hispanoamericana.* Rev. 2nd ed. Mexico City: Ediciones de Andrea.

Anderson Imbert, Enrique, and Eugenio Florit. 1960. *Literatura hispanoamericana: Antología e introducción histórica.* New York: Holt, Rinehart and Winston.

Fernández, Teodosio, Selena Millares, and Eduardo Becerra. 1995. *Historia de la literatura hispanoamericana.* Madrid: Editorial Universitas.

Fernández Moreno, César, ed. *América latina en su literatura.* 1988. 11th ed. Paris: UNESCO; Mexico City: Siglo XXI.

Franco, Jean. 1970 [1967]. *The Modern Culture of Latin America: Society and the Artist.* Middlesex, England: Penguin Books.

——. 1973. *Spanish American Literature since Independence.* London: Ernest Benn; New York: Barnes and Noble.

García Canclini, Néstor. 1989. *Culturas híbridas: Estrategias para entrar y salir de la modernidad.* Mexico City: Grijalbo.

Gómez-Gil, Orlando. 1968. *Historia crítica de la literatura latinoamericana: Desde los orígenes hasta el momento actual.* New York: Holt, Rinehart and Winston.

Grossman, Rudolf. 1972. *Historia y problemas de la literatura latinoamericana.* Trans. Juan C. Probst. Madrid: Ediciones de la Revista de Occidente.

Henríquez Ureña, Pedro. 1970. [1947]. *Historia de la cultura en la América hispánica.* 8th ed. Mexico City: Fondo de Cultura Económica.

Iñigo Madrigal, Luis, ed. 1992–1993. *Historia de la literatura hispanoamericana.* 2 vols. Madrid: Cátedra.

Klahn, Norma, and Wilfredo Corral, eds. 1991. *Los novelistas como críticos.* 2 vols. Mexico City: Fondo de Cultura Económica and Ediciones del Norte.

Molloy, Sylvia. 1997. "Alteridad y reconocimiento en los *Naufragios de Alvar Núñez Cabeza de Vaca.*" *Writers of the Spanish Colonial Period.* Ed. David William Foster and Daniel Altamiranda. New York: Garland. 43–67.

Ortega, Julio, ed. 1997. *Antología de la poesía latinoamericana del siglo XXI: El turno y la transición.* Mexico City: Siglo XXI.

Oviedo, José Miguel. 1997. *Historia de la literatura hispanoamericana: Del Romanticismo al Modernismo.* Vol. 2. Madrid: Alianza.

Rama, Ángel. 1983. *Literatura y clase social.* Mexico City: Folios Ediciones.

——. 1984. *La ciudad letrada.* Hanover, NH: Ediciones del Norte.

Rincón, Carlos. 1978. *Cambio actual de la noción de la literatura y otros estudios de teoría y crítica latinoamericana.* Bogota: Instituto Colombiano de la Cultura.

Rojas, Ricardo. 1924–1925. *La literatura argentina.* 2nd ed., 8 vols. Buenos Aires: Librería La Facultad.

Torres-Ríoseco, Arturo. 1965. *Historia de la literatura iberoamericana.* New York: Las Américas.

Traba, Marta. 1991. "Hipótesis sobre una escritura diferente." *Los novelistas como críticos.* Ed. Norma Klahn and Wilfredo Corral. 2 vols. Mexico City: Fondo de Cultura Económica and Ediciones del Norte. 212–16.

CHAPTER 23

FIRST NATIONS, FIRST WRITERS
INDIGENOUS MEXICAN
LITERARY HISTORY

Cynthia Steele

Y bien canta, bien habla, bien conversa, bien responde, bien ruega; la palabra no es algo que se compre. No como muda, tonta, te vuelvas. Y el huso, la tablilla para tejer, hazte cargo de ellos; la labor, lo que eleva, asciende como el olor, lo que es la nobleza, el merecimiento, los libros de pintura, lo que es un modelo, el color rojo [el saber]. Así bien, al lado y junto de la gente vivirás, así merecerás parte un poquito de bebida de maíz, una tortilla doblada, una verdurita, un nopalito . . .

—Huehuehtlahtolli aztecas (palabras de consejo)
de una madre a su hija (qtd. in León-Portilla 1996, 22)

And sing well, speak well, converse well, respond well, plead well; words cannot be bought. Do not become mute, dumb. And the spindle, the loom, take charge of them; work, that which elevates, rises like scent, that which is nobility, worthiness, the painted books, that which is a model, the color red [knowledge]. And thus, alongside and together with the people shall you live, thus shall you deserve a little part, a little bit of corn gruel, a folded tortilla, a little vegetable, a little cactus . . .

—Aztec huehuehtlahtolli (words of advice)
from a mother to her daughter.

In his recent article "La antigua y la nueva palabra de los pueblos mayas" ["The Old and the New Word of the Mayan People"] Miguel León-Portilla (b. 1926) delineates five historical periods in the production of indigenous literatures in Mexico. The first corresponds to the oral tradition, codices, and stela inscriptions produced by Nahuas, Mayas, and Mixtecos before the arrival of the Spaniards. The second involves the Conquest itself, which elicited a large body of testimonial narrative and poetry regarding the indigenous sense of tragedy and loss. (See, for instance, Juan Bautista Pomar [fl. 1582] [see **Figure 1**]. Alvarado Tezozómoc [1530–1600], Chimalpahin Cuauhtlehuanitzin [1579–1660], and Fernando de Alva Ixtlilxóchitl [1578–1650].) As for the third stage, that of the three centuries of colonial rule, León-Portilla points to this as a field that has barely begun to be studied. Here we find a wealth of documents defending land titles, protesting abuses, and responding to the Spanish *requerimientos* (summons of enslavement). Also, in the eighteenth century, a new set of codices, the so-called Techialoyan Group, was produced. Independence from Spain and the rise of liberalism meant serious restrictions of indigenous judicial and property rights, with the ironic exception of the area governed by the French Empire, when Maximilian published bilingual edicts, in Spanish and Náhuatl, establishing procedures for indigenous recuperation of lands. However, these decrees were invalidated by the return of Republican rule, founded on the commitment to achieving national unity through homogeneity and monolingualism. In denying the very existence of indigenous communities, the Mexican republic denied those communities' human rights.

The fourth phase of indigenous history corresponds to the Revolution, when Emiliano Zapata, (1879a Náhuatl speaker himself, used both the Náhuatl language and allusions to the Náhuatl worldview to elicit support from *campesinos* in Tlaxcala and Puebla. (One such document spoke of "the great work we shall undertake before our dear mother the earth" [León-Portilla 1996, 37].) Article 27 of the Constitution represented a major victory for indigenous communities, because it officially acknowledged the existence of ancestral lands. Also during this fourth phase, Mexican *indigenismo* was launched under the intellectual and political leadership of Manuel Gamio. Gamio and his contemporaries

sought to integrate Indians into the Mexican nation by making Spanish their principal language and discouraging the use of indigenous languages. However, as León-Portilla points out, Gamio did defend bilingualism and was the first to officially acknowledge that Mexico is a multicultural nation. With the creation of the Instituto Indigenista Interamericano (1941) and of Cárdenas's Instituto Nacional Indigenista, other progressive intellectuals, including Alfonso Caso, Gonzalo Aguirre Beltrán, Julio de la Fuente, and Alfonso Villa Rojas, took up the assimilationist project. As León-Portilla observes, the major shortcoming of these well-meaning intellectuals was their paternalistic assumption that they, rather than the Indians, were in the best position to make decisions regarding indigenous communities (41). During this period, ethnologists from both Mexico and the United States also undertook for the first time the collection and publication, usually in English or Spanish, of the oral traditions of a number of indigenous cultures. As Carlos Montemayor notes, through this process the first contemporary indigenous authors were erroneously labeled "informants" (1992, 2:11).

This was also the golden age of *indigenista* literature, produced by progressive non-Indian intellectuals like Ermilo Abreu Gómez (1894–1971), Mauricio Magdaleno (1906–1986), Gregorio López y Fuentes (1897–1966), Francisco Rojas González (1904–1951), Eraclio Zepeda (b. 1937), B. Traven (1882–1969), and Rosario Castellanos (1925–1974). In recent years they have been followed, in Chiapas, by Jesús Morales Bermúdez (b. 1956) and Juan Pedro Viquiera Albán (b. 1934). A parallel phenomenon, which has been studied too little and was far more critical to the eventual development of indigenous written literature, was the collection, editing, and publication of indigenous folktales, creation legends, and oral history by some of these same non-Indian intellectuals, notably Abreu Gómez and Antonio Médiz Bolio (1884–1957) (for the Yucatan peninsula); Andrés Henestrosa (b. 1906) (for the Isthmus of Tehuantepec); and Carlo Antonio Castro (b. 1930), Eraclio Zepeda, and, more recently, Carlos Navarrete (b. 1945) and Jesús Morales Bermúdez (for Chiapas). These testimonies, in turn, served as an ethnographic and literary apprenticeship for indigenous youth, who, during the fifth period of indigenous literary history, assumed the task of self-ethnography, recording their own peoples' beliefs and stories. This process not only produced many important published texts, but also gave rise to the first indigenous congresses and writing workshops, which nurtured the first generation of contemporary indigenous writers in Mexico. (While León-Portilla is reluctant to date this phenomenon precisely, he cites a bilingual collection of Totonac narratives from Papantla, written by Xamanixma and published in 1974, as one of the first texts published by this new generation.) In many cases, these organic intellectuals who are publishing literature and assuming leadership positions in their communities are indigenous professionals—engineers, attorneys, linguists, anthropologists, historians, or physicists. A few examples include Jacinto Arias, a Tzotzil Ph.D. in anthropology; Natalio Hernández (b. 1947), a Nahua normal school teacher; and Víctor Toledo, a Zapotec literary critic. Many of their early works were undertaken in collaboration with Mexican and U.S. intellectuals, notably Miguel León-Portilla himself for Náhuatl cultures, Robert Laughlin for Tzotzil and Tzeltal Mayans of highland Chiapas, and Carlos Montemayor (b. 1947) for several groups, including the Zapotecs and Mixtecs of Oaxaca, and the Mayas of Chiapas and the Yucatan peninsula.

Indian literary production, in the canonical Western sense, has consisted primarily of plays, short stories, essays, and, increasingly, poetry. To date there have only been two indigenous novels, one in Zapotec and the other in Tojolabal. The transition has been made first through indigenous apprenticeship in anthropological research, followed by participation in community theatre and writing workshops. (See, for instance, Arauz, Arias, Cerero, Dzul, Dzul Chablé, Lo'il Maxiel, Méndez Guzmán, Ochoa, and Relatos tzeltales. Also, see Cocom Pech's excellent overview of contemporary Mayan literatures.) According to Montemayor (1992, II:11), the richest body of contemporary literary production is being produced in the Yucatan peninsula and on the Isthmus of Tehuantepec. The Isthmus Zapotecs, moreover, now boast three full generations of important writers, mostly centered in Juchitán: Pancho Nácar, Enrique Liekens, Gabriel López Chiñas, and Andrés Henestrosa; followed by Víctor de la Cruz (b. 1948), Manuel (b. 1949) and Macario Matus (b. 1943), and Enedino Jiménez; followed by Antonio López Pérez, Feliciano Marín, and Víctor Terán. Other well-established Indian writers include Natalio Hernández (Náhuatl), Búffalo Conde (Tzeltal), Jesús Salinas Pedraza (ñahñu), and Gerardo Can Pat and Feliciano Sánchez (Yucatec Mayan). Because few contemporary Indian writers were born before 1950, Montemayor notes, we can expect a flourishing of mature indigenous literatures over the coming years.

This literary renaissance has blossomed together with movements for indigenous autonomy and respect, both in Mexico and throughout the continent. León-Portilla notes four pivotal issues over the past two decades. These include: (1) the right to be recognized as a community (pueblo) with a distinct identity; (2) the right to participate in state and national decisions affecting their communities; (3) the right to retain and recuperate ancestral lands; and (4) the right to practice self-government or autonomy. However, the situations of Mexico's different indigenous nations vary considerably with regard to the issues of land tenure and autonomy. On the one hand, the Tzotzils and Tzeltals of Chiapas, like the Yaquis and Mayos of Sonora, have managed to retain some degree of control, through the centuries, over communal lands and self-government. On the other hand, the Otomís,

the Mayas of the Yucatan peninsula, and the Nahuas of various states, all lost their communal lands long ago, and now live dispersed among non-Indians, so recuperation of their property and achievement of political autonomy would be a daunting project for them (46).

In its struggle to win recognition, at home and abroad, for indigenous rights, the movement must avoid the pitfalls of romanticizing or idealizing native cultures. Human rights—especially those of women and of religious and political dissidents—are being abused by native governments in the name of traditionalism. Two notorious cases in Chiapas are the expulsion of thousands of Protestants from San Juan Chamula during the 1980s and 1990s, and the December 1997 massacre of alleged EZLN sympathizers—all unarmed, and predominantly women and children in Acteal, Chiapas. As Carlos Monsiváis has eloquently argued, indigenous peoples are just as prone to committing acts of intolerance, corruption, and human rights abuse as is hegemonic society. In his admiring discussion of anthropologist Guillermo Bonfil Batallas's seminal work *México profundo* (1990), Monsiváis nevertheless observes:

> en algo mitifica Bonfil al México Profundo, dejando de lado zonas muertas, limitaciones terribles, errores que son usos y costumbres petrificados. (Hoy las más graves para mí son las distorciones de la justicia comunitaria, el machismo, la oposición al control de la natalidad, y la intolerancia religiosa. El México Profundo no sólo es extraordinario; también es autoritario, intolerante, y tan capaz como sus antagonistas de asesinatos, incendios y torturas, como se probó en San Miguel Canoa, Puebla, en 1968, y los linchamientos de estos años. (69)

> to some extent Bonfil mythifies indigenous Mexico, leaving aside the dead zones, terrible limitations, errors that are petrified customs and traditions. (Today the most serious ones, to my mind, are the distortions of communal justice, the machismo, the opposition to birth control, and the religious intolerance.] Indigenous Mexico is not just extraordinary; it is also authoritarian, intolerant, and as capable as its antagonists of murder, arson and torture, as we saw in San Miguel Canoa, Puebla, in 1968, and the lynchings of these past years.)

For Monsiváis Mexican racism is one tragic symptom of the Mexican ruling class' embrace of *desarrollismo* [developmentalism], in slavish imitation of the U.S. model: "La burguesía adopta el modelo norteamericano y le copia todo, incluido el racismo" (64) ("The bourgeoisie adopts the North American model and copies them in every respect, including their racism"). As Monsiváis has argued, racism in Mexico is characterized not so much by the belief in a superior race as by the conviction that there is an inferior race—the Indians. One might add that this imitation seems part and parcel of the colonial mentality, with its internalized racism, as brilliantly described by Frantz Fanon.

Because cultural *mestizaje* has served as a keystone of the myth of national identity, the extent to which it has actually existed in Mexico has often been overstated. This is particularly true of the two class extremes in an increasingly unequal society—the bourgeoisie and the peasantry—where miscegenation has been much less widespread than in the middle and working classes. This process of uneven *mestizaje*, however, has been carefully suppressed in the demagogic rhetoric of the ruling class, which claims both Aztec princes and Indian revolutionary leaders—both Cuauhtémoc and Zapata—as their forefathers. A parallel phenomenon is the internalization of anti-Indian racism by people of Indian and mixed descent.

This accounts for the fetishization of the blue-eyed blonde as object of desire in advertising and the mass media, in a country in which a tiny minority corresponds to this phenotype. It explains the generalized disdain for the underclass, both as Indian (*campesinos* or servants, speakers of indigenous languages, erroneously called "dialects") and as *Nacos*, or de-Indianized, urban, working-class youths. The racial and cultural hybridity of this mushrooming underclass challenges the bourgeois fantasy that the face of modernization and globalization in Mexico will be predominantly middle-class, genteel, and white. At the same time, subaltern youth's predilection for international youth culture, largely emanating from the ghettoes of the United States and Europe—and in many cases arising, in turn, from diasporic cultures of Africa and the Caribbean—undermines the faith of the intellectual class that elite international culture will combine with nationalist folk culture to form the bedrock of a new American civilization. Neither tradition nor modernity holds the key to the future of Mexican culture; its twenty-first-century literatures will no doubt be as diverse, hybrid, contradictory, and dynamic as are its peoples.

Figure 1.

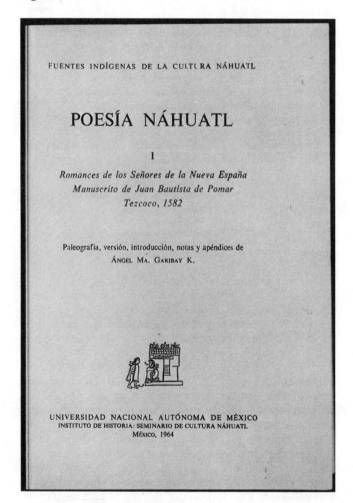

Photograph of Náhuatl *poetry volume. (Courtesy of John P. Robarts Research Library, University of Toronto)*

Works Cited

Abreu Gómez, Ermilo. 1961. *Leyendas y consejas del antiguo Yucatán.* Mexico City: Ediciones Botas.

Alcalá, Gerónimo de. 1997. *Relación de Michoacán.* Mexico City: Fondo de Cultura Económica.

Alvarado Tezozómoc, Hernando. 1949. *Chronica mexicáyotl.* Trans. Adrián León. Mexico City: UNAM, Instituto de Historia-INAH.

——.1994. *Crónica mexicana.* Ed. Mario Mariscal. Mexico City: UNAM.

Arauz, Quintín, ed. 1994. *Relatos chontales.* Mexico City: Secretaría de Educación Pública, Lenguas de México.

Arias, Jacinto. 1990. *San Pedro Chenalhó.* Tuxtla Gutiérrez: Gobierno del Estado de Chiapas. (Serie Nuestros Pueblos).

——. 1991. *El mundo numinoso de los mayas: Estructura y cambios contemporáneos.* Tuxtla Gutiérrez: Gobierno del Estado de Chiapas.

Bonfil Batalla, Guillermo. 1990. *México profundo. Una civilización negada.* Mexico City: Grijalbo/CONACULTA.

Can Pat, Gerardo. 1990. *U k'aayilo'ob in puksi'ik'al (Cantos del corazón).* Yucatán: SEP–CNCA–Culturas Populares.

——. 1993. *La Virgen de la Candelaria: Ethnohistoria de la patrona de Tibolón.* Mexico City: Instituto Nacional Indigenista.

——. 1994. *Canciones mayas tradicionales.* Mexico City: Instituto Nacional Indigenista, SEDESOL (Colección Letras Mayas Contemporáneas).

——. 1994. *La nueva canción maya.* 2 vols. Mexico City: Instituto Nacional Indigenista, SEDESOL (Colección Letras Mayas Contemporáneas).

Castellanos, Rosario. 1957. *Balún Canán.* México: Fondo de Cultura Económica.

——. 1962. *Oficio de tinieblas.* México: Joaquín Mortiz.

——. 1972. *Poesía no eres tú.* México: Fondo de Cultura Económica.

——. 1982. *Ciudad Real.* Xalapa: Universidad Veracruzana/La Letra Editores.

Castro, Carlo Antonio. 1965. *Narraciones tzeltales de Chiapas.* Xalapa: Universidad Veracruzana.

——. 1983. *Los hombres verdaderos.* Xalapa, Mexico: Universidad Veracruzana.

——. 1986. *Sk'oplal te Mejikolum/La palabra de México.* Tuxtla Gutiérrez: Gobierno del Estado de Chiapas.

Cerero, Andrés. 1988. *El vuelo de la gente nube (Narraciones zapotecas).* Mexico City: Secretaría de Educación Pública, Dirección General de Culturas Populares.

Chimalpahin Cuauhtlehuanitzin, Domingo Francisco de San Antón Muñoz. 1965. *Relaciones originales de Chalco.* Mexico City: Fondo de Cultura Económica.

Cocom Pech, Jorge Miguel. 1996. "Renacimiento de la palabra de los Mayas de hoy. Ká Siijil U T'an Mayao'ob Bejlae." *Tierra Adentro* 78 (febrero–marzo): 53–58.

Cuentos y relatos indígenas. 1989–1994. 5 vols. Ed. Juan Bañuelos. Mexico City: UNAM.

Cruz, Víctor de la, ed. 1983. *La flor de la palabra/Guie' sti' didxaza"*–edición bilingüe. *Antología de la literatura zapoteca.* 2nd ed. Mexico City: Premiá.

——. 1999. *Guie' sti' diidxazá/La flor de la palabra.* Mexico City: UNAM, Centro de Investigaciones y Estudios Superiores en Anthropología Social.

Dirección General de Culturas Populares y Dirección General de Publicaciones, Consejo Nacional para las Culturas y las Artes, ed. 1994. *Letras indígenas contemporáneas.* 10 vols. Mexico City: Editorial Diana.

Dzul, Domingo, ed. 1985. *Cuentos mayas.* Mérida: Maldonado Editores, INAH-SEP.

Dzul Chablé, Irene. 1952. *Poesía indígena de la alta planicie.* 2nd ed. Mexico City: UNAM.

——. 1953–1954. *Historia de la literatura náhuatl.* 2 vols. Mexico City: Porrúa.

——. 1963/1965/1968. *Poesía náhuatl.* 3 vols. Mexico City: UNAM, Instituto de Investigaciones Históricas.

——, ed. 1994. *Cuentos mayas tradicionales.* Mexico City: Col. Letras Mayas Contemporáneas.

Henestrosa, Andrés. 1977. *Los hombres que dispersó la danza.* Mexico City: Editorial Porrúa.

Hernández, Delfino. 1985. *Inyancui Nahua Zazanilli (Nueva narrativa náhuatl).* Mexico City: UNAM, Instituto de Investigaciones Históricas.

Huehuehtlahtolli, testimonios de la antigua palabra. 1995. Trans. Librado Silva Galeana. Mexico City: Comisión Conmemorativa del V Centenario del Encuentro de Dos Mundos, 1988; Secretaría de Educación Pública y Fondo de Cultura Económica.

Ixtlilxóchitl, Fernando de Alva. 1975–1977. *Obras completas.* 2 vols. Ed. Edmundo O'Gorman. Mexico City: UNAM, Instituto de Investigaciones Históricas.

Laughlin, Robert, and Carol Karasik, eds. 1988. *The People of the Bat: Mayan Tales and Dreams from Zinacantán.* Washington, DC: Smithsonian Institution Press.

León-Portilla, Miguel. 1989. *Yancuic Tlahtolli (Palabra Nueva): Una antología de la literatura Náhuatl contemporánea. Estudios de cultura náhuatl.* Vol. 18. Mexico City: UNAM, Instituto de Investigaciones Históricas. 361–423.

——. 1996. "La antigua y la nueva palabra de los pueblos indígenas." *Culturas y derechos de los pueblos indígenas de México.* Mexico City: Archivo General de la Nación and Fondo de Cultura Económica. 21–47.

El libro de Chilam Balam de Chumayel. 1952. Trans. Antonio Médiz Bolio. San José, Costa Rica, Mexico City: UNAM.

El libro de los cantares de Dzitbalché. 1965. Ed. Alfredo Barrera Vásquez. Mexico City: Instituto Nacional de Antropología e Historia.

El libro de los libros del Chilam Balam. 1948. Ed. Alfredo Barrera Vásquez. Mexico City: Fondo de Cultura Económica.

Médiz Bolio, Antonio. 1974. *La tierra del faisán y del venado.* Mexico City: B. Costa-Amic, Editor.

Memoria del primer encuentro de escritores en lenguas indígenas. 1990. Mexico City: CONACULTA, Dirección General de Culturas Populares.

Méndez Guzmán, Diego. 1995. *Relatos de Tenejapa.* Mexico City: Instituto Nacional Indigenista.

Monsiváis, Carlos. 1996. "Versiones nacionales de lo indígena." *Culturas y derechos de los pueblos indígenas de México.* Mexico City: Archivo General de la Nación and Fondo de Cultura Económica. 55–74.

Montemayor, Carlos, ed. 1991. *Situación actual y perspectivas de la literatura en lenguas indígenas.* Mexico City: CONACULTA.

——, ed. 1992. *Los escritores indígenas actuales.* 2 vols. Mexico City: Fondo Editorial Tierra Adentro/Consejo Nacional para la Cultura y las Artes. (Vol. 1: Ensayo; Vol. 2: Poesía, narrativa, teatro.)

——, ed. 1996. *Colección letras Mayas contemporáneas, Chiapas.* 14 vols. Mexico City: Instituto Nacional Indigenista.

——. 1996. *El cuento indígena de tradición oral. Notas sobre sus fuentes y clasificaciones.* Oaxaca: Centro de Investigaciones y Estudios Superiores en Antropología Social (CIESAS) e Instituto Oaxaqueño de las Culturas (IOC).

Morales Bermúdez, Jesús. 1984. *On O T'ian/Antigua palabra: Narrativa indígena chol.* Mexico City: Universidad Autónoma Metropolitana.

——. 1986. *Memorial del tiempo o Vía de las conversaciones.* Mexico City: Instituto Nacional de Bellas Artes.

——. 1992. *Ceremonial.* Mexico City: Consejo Nacional para la Cultura y las Artes y Gobierno del Estado de Chiapas.

——.1997. *Aproximaciones a la poesía y la narrativa de Chiapas.* Tuxtla Gutiérrez, Chiapas: Universidad de Ciencias y Artes del Estado de Chiapas.

Ochoa, Angela, ed. 1994. *Relatos huastecos.* Mexico City: Secretaría de Educación Pública, Lenguas de México.

Relatos tzeltales. 1994. Mexico City: Secretaría de Educación Pública, Lenguas de México.

Sánchez Chan, Feliciano.1994. "Juntul Kolnaal (El milpero)." *Teatro maya contemporáneo, II. Colección letras Mayas contemporáneas.* Vol. 24. Mexico City: Instituto Nacional Indigenista. 21–37.

CHAPTER 24

RECENT MAYAN INCURSIONS INTO GUATEMALAN LITERARY HISTORIOGRAPHY

Gail Ament

[M]ientras los debates intelectuales se desgastan en retóricas estériles sobre cómo entender al 'otro', los pueblos indígenas siguen viviendo las injusticias más horrendas que se han perpetuado a través de los siglos.

While intellectual debates spend themselves on sterile rhetoric about how to understand the 'other,' indigenous peoples continue living the most horrendous injustices that have been perpetuated throughout the centuries.

–Víctor Montejo

The Peruvian literary critic Antonio Cornejo Polar asserts that the vindication of plurality in Latin American culture is one of the main agenda items of recent decades: "Fue—es—el momento de la revalorización de las literaturas étnicas y otras marginales y del afinamiento de categorías críticas que intentan dar razón de ese enredado corpus. . . ." (12) ("It was and it is the time for reevaluation of ethnic and other marginal literatures and for the refinement of critical categories that try to make sense out of that tangled corpus. . . . "). He outlines a course of study that includes Ángel Rama's focus on narrative transculturation, Edmundo

Bendezú's study of "Other literature," Enrique Ballón Aguirre's discussion of diaglossic literature, and Martin Lienhard's inquiries into alternative literatures, along with his own theorization of the heterogeneous. Cornejo Polar notes that it was the work of individuals such as Miguel León-Portilla, who were able to wed the philology of indigenous languages with anthropology, that brought out the importance of colonial and modern native literatures and established the need to include them as part of the historical development of Latin American literature. For the extent of Mesoamerican culture, see **Map 1**.

Map 1.

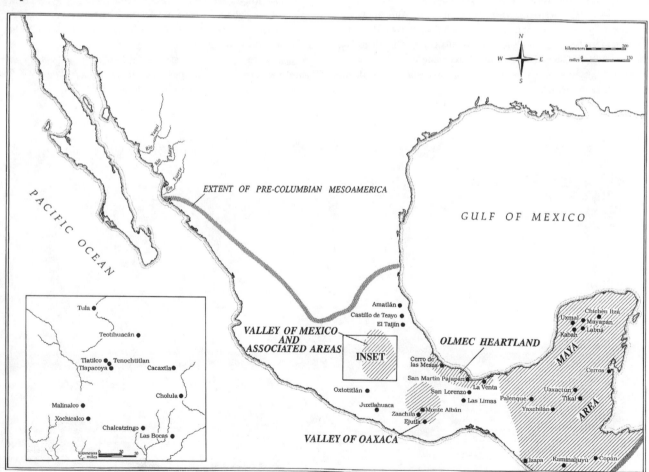

216

In a similar vein, Jean Franco comments on the abyss of cultural miscomprehension that lay between Amerindian, African, and Afro-Caribbean peoples, on the one hand, and the European elite and their descendants, on the other. The reciprocal exclusions that resulted from this miscomprehension, coupled with obstacles to writing in indigenous languages, determined that the languages and cultures of these peoples were to remain outside of representations of Latin American cultural traditions (12, 15). The abyss that Franco identifies is also apparent in literary histories of Latin America written in the past fifty years or so. Linguistic complexities, disruption of a desired sense of unity in Spanish-American letters, and lack of knowledge about Amerindian letters are the three mainstays of the exclusionary postures of literary historians. For example, Pedro Henríquez-Ureña, in his 1945 study, examines the *criollo* illusion of unity in Hispanic American culture as represented by the commonalities among European imaginings of the Indian as noble savage and of the New World as land of plenty. Decades later, Enrique Anderson-Imbert finds that, in the effort to promote a sense of the cultural unity of Spanish America, he must simply exclude Amerindian literatures from his literary history (16, 18).

In the 1960 anthology that they co-edited, Anderson-Imbert and Eugenio Florit deal somewhat more expansively with indigenous works, speculating that in Classic Mayan times there surely were individuals who spoke with refinement and employed genres of great prestige to convey artistic use of the word. They point out that what are commonly referred to as indigenous literatures are, in reality, indirect transcriptions written down by scribes after the conquest and colonization, thanks to the Latin alphabet: "It is the subject matter of ethnography, or, if you wish, of a history of literature separated linguistically from our own" (3). Despite their stated intention of including in their anthology only those selected works whose length permits their being published in their entirety, such constraints are apparently not necessary in the case of the *Popol vuh*, as the co-editors proceed to reprint two fragments from the work. In 1968, in language reminiscent of idealizing nineteenth-century Indianist writing, Orlando Gómez-Gil describes a special enchantment that he perceives in the emotion and grace of the Maya K'iché *Popol vuh*, "as if there floated over it the spirit of that conquered race, immortalized through literature" (24). Echoes of an earlier discourse, this time from Christopher Columbus's diaries of the 1490s, resound through the 1978 wording of Agustín del Saz, a Spanish historian of Ibero-American literature. Del Saz trusts that writings of the "primitives"–to which American writers so frequently allude in order to affirm their own autochthonous literary personality(7)–will eventually become better known. He predicts that university-educated Indians, or "modern primitives," will be the best collaborators in disseminating oral literature from communities of "pure Indians," some of whom speak languages of "a certain perfection," while the speech of others is "simple shrieking" (5–6). Elena de Costa's section on Mayan literature in Verity Smith's 1997 literary history of Latin America offers considerably better informed insights into genres, themes, structure, and literary conventions than do the other histories mentioned above.

However, the study of indigenous letters of Guatemala might logically begin with celestial, chronological, and dynastic records contained in hieroglyphic writing of Classical times from the first millennium CE, found etched in stone at lowland temple sites in the Petén. These records, though, are typically considered to be the scholarly domain of archaeologists and epigraphers, and thus are largely absent from Latin American literary historiography. It is, rather, two distinct periods of holocaust in Guatemalan Mayan history that frame the discussion of indigenous letters. The first is the Spanish invasion of the western highlands of the Central American isthmus in the 1520s and the decades immediately following; the second, the genocidal war of counterinsurgency that raged throughout the highlands in the 1970s and early 1980s. The few extant documents that managed to survive the flames of the first catastrophic encounter between the Spanish and the Maya, and the works transcribed shortly after the Spanish invasion, comprise what is commonly recognized in literary historiography as Mayan literature, a substratum of Guatemalan, Central American, and Mexican letters: a not easily integrated preface to the story of Latin American literature.

The second holocaust caught in its flames an entire generation of young indigenous men and women, many of whom were groomed and poised for greater interaction with, and greater relativization of, the language and culture of the dominant Ladino population. In subsequent years a few dozen eloquent Mayans have appropriated the language and literary forms of the dominant culture in order to launch a defense of their own cultural values. The result is that, in addition to acknowledging the exclusion of the colonial indigenous voice from Hispanic literary histories, we should also recognize the incursions into these histories that contemporary Mayan writers of Guatemala carry out today in an attempt to rescue Mayan culture from the ashes of both the Spanish conquest and the brutally destructive civil war.

With the arrival of the Spaniards in what came to be known as the Captaincy General of Guatemala, indigenous documents written on bark paper were destroyed because they were seen as being diabolical works, an obstacle to the proselytizing efforts of the Catholic Church. Members of the indigenous elite subsequently participated in transcribing into Roman script many cultural documents, even as scores of other writings were reduced to ashes. The few extant codices that predate the encounter of Spanish and Mayan cultures, and the Roman-character transcriptions of creation myths, land claims, genealogical records, and chronicles from the early colonial period, augment the wealth of historical and cultural information preserved through the centuries in the oral tradition, recognized as being among the richest in the world.

Of the works transcribed in early colonial times, it is the *Popol vuh* that serves as a palimpsest for linguists, ethnographers, writers, literary historians, playwrights, and even cartoonists, all of whom find fertile material for the imaginary in this sustained yet disparate record of the K'iché people. In literary histories of Latin America, the *Popol vuh* is typically catalogued with indigenous works from the Yucatan peninsula, the Valley of Mexico, and even the Andean region, in a sleight-of-hand that elides the spatial, temporal, and generic particularities of these texts and of the diverse cultures that engendered them. Few other indigenous works from the Guatemalan highlands figure in literary histories of Latin America. For example, the *Memorial de Sololá, Anales de los cakchiqueles* [Annals of the Kaqchikels]], the *Título de los señores de Otzoyá* [Title of the Lords of Otzoyá], *Título de los señores de Totonicapán* [Title of the Lords of Totonicapán], *Título de la Casa Ixcuin Nehaíb* [Title of the House of Ixcuin Nehaíb], and some dozen other indigenous texts transcribed in colonial times are invisible in the panorama of Latin American literature. However, in Guatemala in the 1950s, Adrián Recinos (1886–1962) contributed to the disinterment and wider availability of several such works, in a manner similar to that of Miguel León-Portilla in Mexico. Indigenous Mayan scholars today turn their linguistic skills to refining and revising earlier interpretations.

Within the first generations after the arrival of the Spaniards, the indigenous voice is virtually excised from written works. At present, what is most notable is the resounding silence of the past four hundred years, stretching from the late sixteenth century, through the Colonial and Independence periods, and into the latter half of the twentieth century. Literary histories of Latin America do not comment on this void. Early in the twentieth century, sixteenth-century indigenous works and elements from the oral tradition were appropriated by the dominant Ladino, or non-Mayan, culture, as foundational, but folkloric, materials contributing to the formation of a Guatemalan, Central American, or Latin American literature.

As a counterpoint to centuries of exclusion, Mayan writers and scholars since the late 1960s have been making incursions into the field of literary historiography. The terrain is not wholly congenial, even for ladino writers from within the hegemonic population. Guatemala and the other Central American countries have not historically been primary sites of cultural production and literary criticism. The region as a whole has been largely excluded from Spanish American literary historiography, an issue taken up by Ramón Luis Acevedo in his study of the Central American novel and by Magda Zavala and Seidy Araya in their discussion of Central American historiography. Writing in the early 1980s, Acevedo draws from developmentalist terminology in citing the region's status of economic underdevelopment, the lack of political influence, the limited formation of significant publishing houses in comparison to those of Mexico and Argentina, and the lack of professionally trained literary critics and historians. He points to extraliterary factors that have to do with the social, economic, and political marginalization of the region. Additionally, Acevedo notes that the low per capita income, and the high level of illiteracy, which reaches seventy percent in Guatemala, compound the problems of limited access to book distribution channels that might carry works into other Central American and Latin American countries (9–19). These factors affect the reader, the writer, publication, distribution, literary criticism, and, inevitably, the development of literary historiography as elaborated by both nationals and foreigners.

David Vela's two-volume work, *Historia de la literatura guatemalteca* [1929; History of Guatemalan Literature], and Francisco Albizúrez and Catalina Barrios y Barrios's three-volume history, published in the 1980s, are virtually the only national literary histories produced within Guatemala. Foreign academics have also contributed to discussing limited dimensions of the national literature. For example, Seymour Menton's *Historia crítica de la novela guatemalteca* [1960; Critical History of the Guatemalan Novel] and Marc Zimmerman's treatment of twentieth-century poetry and narrative in his *Literature and Resistance in Guatemala* (1995) are among those works that augment studies carried out by Guatemalans. In large part, Guatemalan literary historiography is fragmented, dispersed in cultural supplements to newspapers and magazines, literary reviews affiliated with the country's universities, prefaces and introductions to literary works, and

licentiate theses written by university students. Conference forums stimulate investigation while simultaneously ensuring that the shared fruits of this research will too often enjoy a half-life measured in days. Formal unveilings of new publications at book presentations become a vital and ceremonious means of bringing together author, publisher, supportive commentator-critic, prospective readers, and perhaps a journalist or two, in the sense of shared mission in constructing a national literary culture around works typically printed in editions of 500 or, more ambitiously, 1000 copies.

The selective inclusion or exclusion of the indigenous literary tradition within the panorama of Guatemala's national literary history reflects the ethnic and linguistic complexities in the country and the Spanish imposition of a cultural hierarchy based largely on incomprehension and rejection of autochthonous cultural values and languages. A knowledge of native languages assisted the Roman Catholic clergy in proselytizing efforts to the extent that, in the eighteenth century, a chair of Kaqchikel language was created at the national University of San Carlos (Olivera 12). Throughout the colonial period, however, Latin was the language most highly valued in the University's sphere. To a limited extent, the *criollos'* denigration of Mayan languages, and of the literary tradition carried within these languages, may reflect their struggles to institutionalize Spanish at the highest strata of the religious and cultural hierarchy supplanting Latin.

Praising the epic vitality of the *Popol vuh* (which he repeatedly refers to as "our *National Book*"), the lyrical density of the *Chilam Balam*, and the plasticity of the *Rab'inal achi*, or *Xajoj tun*, Albizúrez assigns other Mesoamerican indigenous manuscripts a documentary and historiographic value (I: 21). For his purposes, Guatemalan literature is a *mestizo* or hybrid literature written since the arrival of Pedro de Alvarado and his troops. After devoting some thirty-five pages to a discussion of select indigenous texts, this author writes that, while pre-Columbian literature serves as a substratum, it does not fit within Guatemalan literature, "*stricto sensu*, but neither is it appropriate to ignore it or to be unaware of its presence" (56). He adds that, fundamentally, an indigenous literature would consist of works created in native languages. For most intents and purposes, however, given the virtual nonexistence of literacy training in indigenous languages until recently, such expressions have circulated solely within the oral tradition. Logically, Francisco Albizúrez's definition of indigenous literature would exclude poetry and narrative written in Spanish by contemporary Mayan writers in Guatemala since the late 1960s.

The prestige enjoyed by Latin throughout the colonial period still leaves traces in Guatemalan literary historiography today. For instance, Francisco Albizúrez vacillates on the position of Mayan-language works in Guatemalan literature yet, in the same volume, his coauthor, Catalina Barrios, embraces the Latin verse of the Jesuit poet Rafael Landívar (1731–1793). Although Albizúrez defines Guatemalan literature as being written in Spanish, in Barrios's discussion of Landívar, the same logic that justified the repatriation to Guatemala of the Jesuit's remains in 1950 justifies the patriation of the exiled poet into Guatemalan letters (99–102).

What we do not have is an adequate record of indigenous creative writers who have authored works adapted from European genres. In the past thirty years there have emerged Mayan authors who utilize the language and the literary forms of the dominant culture. Their appearance on the Guatemalan literary scene is largely due to improved access to higher education, together with a growing sense of outrage over the Maya's cultural, economic, and political status in national life. In Guatemala, however, contemporary indigenous writers and scholars have produced at least three volumes that directly contribute to the broadening of this discussion. These are, namely, Luis Enrique Sam Colop's (b. 1955) doctoral dissertation on K'iché poetics; Manuel Salazar Tetzagüic's (b. 1948) study of the characteristics of Kaqchikel literature; and Gaspar Pedro González's (b. 1945) global treatment of Mayan literatures. All three of these figures have also written poetry, narrative, or both; thus, in some respects, they are their own first critics and historiographers. Additionally, there are other works penned by Mayan creative writers from which one can begin to extrapolate unique perspectives that enrich the study of marginalized literatures of Latin America.

The ladino historian Francis Polo Sifontes writes of an early colonial practice whereby, if an indigenous person wished to obtain a certain privilege for himself or for his people, he was to present a *probanza* or written evidence of his merits and lineage (x). To some extent, contemporary Mayan texts respond to this ancient obligation to put forth in writing the people's merits and lineage in a multicultural *probanza* in order to claim their rights before the Guatemalan State. While most of these works are written in Spanish, there are noteworthy instances of the new Mayan literature written in the Mayan language of the author and published in a monolingual form, typically in newspapers tied to the advancement of indigenous rights. The poetry of the Kaqchikel linguist, Martín Chacach, is one example. Mayan academics and cultural activists, and Mayan and non-Mayan linguists specializing in these languages, have the linguistic expertise to treat these works in their monolingual Mayan form; future literary criticism and historiography on these works will thus bear the imprint of this particular population of scholars, with its attendant strengths and limitations. These Mayan-language works currently entering the arena of Latin American literature will logically be inaccessible to readers and scholars who do not apply themselves to the study of indigenous languages. Furthermore, it is difficult to imagine any one individual, Maya or non-Maya, who would have the requisite erudition in all twenty Mayan languages spoken in Guatemala to be able to treat monolingual Mayan works globally, as it is difficult to imagine any one scholar who would have the linguistic agility to treat twenty-some European literatures globally.

A few dozen Guatemalan indigenous writers participate in the new Spanish-language literary discourse. While some of these have contributed modestly, with only two or three poems, others have produced numerous volumes. There is no school, movement, generation, or group of indigenous writers. As the Q'anjob'al novelist Gaspar Pedro González explains: "[The new Mayan literature] emerges not in a systematic way, not in a technical way, exactly; rather, each person autodidactically manages to express what he or she feels, manages to do a little writing without the purpose of writing literature as such, but rather to inform, to write of what is happening" (personal interview). Some Mayan authors find it more appropriate to draw from the two streams of the oral tradition—the formal poetic ceremonial tradition and storytelling—rather than from the classic works in their printed form, to which they have limited access. Manuel de Jesús Salazar Tetzagüic, a Mayan intellectual who has held major administrative posts in education, sums up this problem of accessibility: "In spite of research carried out by nationals and foreigners on literary material in indigenous languages, everything remains in archives and in publications for the erudite" (9). Salazar Tetzagüic stresses, however, that the Mayan literary tradition has always been available to the people through the oral tradition, even when it has been forced underground and marginalized: "Podemos considerar a la literatura maya como *la manifestación plena de un lenguaje que en un momento crítico de su evolución, tomó por atajos ocultos para conservarse ante el avance del idioma invasor*. En todo momento ha estado presente para la conformación de un Estado pluricultural y multilingüe, aún cuando se ha tratado de mantenerla al margen" ("We can consider Mayan literature to be *the full manifestation of a language that, in a critical moment of its evolution, took hidden byways to save itself before the advance of the invading language*. At all times it has been present for the forming of a pluricultural and multilingual State, even in those instances when it has been marginalized"; 20; emphasis in the original). Today, literary expression has an immediate political application in reforming the Guatemalan State into an entity that will be cognizant and respectful of the multicultural makeup of its population. Nevertheless, this author informs us that the poetry of the early 1970s also challenged more traditional forms of indigenous narrative and the values of the older generations of Mayans (29). In other words, this alternative written literature was marginal and oppositional, not only to hegemonic Ladino discourse, but also to hegemonic indigenous discourse.

Against the backdrop of a thirty-six-year civil war, and now in its aftermath, Mayan writers and scholars challenge the modes and the motives of literary signification as conducted by the ladino elite and by foreigners. Chronologically, the first of the contemporary Mayan writers are José Luis de León Díaz (1940-1984)—better known by his pen name, Luis de Lión—and Luis Enrique Sam Colop. Jointly, they were the founders of a new discoursivity, in that they not only were the authors of their own works, but they also have produced something more: the condition of possibility for the formation of other future texts by Mayas. In the late 1970s and early 1980s, hundreds of Guatemalan villages were razed by violence and fire in the genocidal offensive known as the counterinsurgency war. In a sense, these flames consumed the writer Luis de Lión. When he was "disappeared" in 1984, he left behind two published volumes of short fiction (*Los zopilotes* [The Vultures] and *Su segunda muerte* [His Second Death]), as well as unpublished poetry and fiction, including manuscripts of the novel *El tiempo principia en Xibalbá* [Time Begins in Xibalbá], which incorporates numerous innovative techniques of the Latin American "boom" narrative into the setting of a Guatemalan indigenous village. In this novel, the author heretically subverts the icon of the Virgin Mary, bringing her wooden form to life—and lust—under the passionate caress of the villager who has long desired to possess this most inaccessible of all ladinas. Thus, de Lión challenges the hegemony of the Catholic Church, as well as the stereotypical image of the docile and asexualized indigenous male. The poetry and narrative of de Lión attest to the loss that his disappearance represents in the earliest years of the new indigenous writing in Guatemala. He was both a product of the emerging expectations and demands of the Mayan people and a tragic victim of retaliation against individuals who could express these demands through example and through eloquence.

Along with de Lión, Luis Enrique Sam Colop is another foundational writer of the new indigenous literature of his country. As poet, literary scholar, linguist, lawyer, and newspaper columnist, Sam Colop has contributed to diverse dimensions of the Mayan cultural and political vindication movement in Guatemala. In the late 1970s, he published two volumes of short narrative and poetry: *Versos sin refugio: Quiché y español* [1978; Verses Without Refuge: K'iché and Spanish], and *La copa y la raíz* [1979; The Wine Glass and the Root]. In its phantasmagoric surrealism, "Quiché Achí guerrero" [K'iché Achi Warrior], from the latter collection, is reminiscent of scenes from *Hombres de maíz* [1949; Men of Corn] or *Leyendas de Guatemala* [1923–1928; Legends of Guatemala], by Miguel Angel Asturias (1899–1974). It also evokes the Classical Mayan ballet-drama *Xajoj tun*, or *Rab'inal achi*. In this story, the warrior endures a night of terrors populated by demon spirits condemned to the Xibalbá underworld, in the course of which he comes upon his father's tortured cadaver: ". . . vio entonces que de las manos se alzaron firmes lanzas, de los dedos de los pies, largos [sic] obsidianas . . . ; los cabellos blancos del anciano tejieron el Pop wuj, donde quiso leer su historia, pero al acercarse unas lenguas de fuego se lo impidieron . . ." (47) (". . . he saw then that from the hands there rose up strong lances, from the toes, long obsidian blades . . . ; the white hairs of the old man wove the *Popol vuh*, where he tried to read his history, but tongues of flame prevented him from approaching. . . "). Through its disintegration, his father's body offers up weapons of defense, including, significantly, a history wherein a K'iché Achi warrior might read of himself. His own hellish Xibalbá is that he is not allowed to approach his own history, for the flames drive him back.

There are intellectual prejudices, or modern-day "tongues of flame," that work against members of the Mayan intelligentsia, such as Sam Colop, who attempt to reclaim ownership of commodified Mayan literary works. For example, the researchers Anita Padia Guerchous and Manuel Vázquez-Bigi chose to base their 1991 translation of the *Xajoj tun* on the nineteenth-century French translation, rather than to utilize recent linguistic studies carried out on the K'iché-Achi language, in part by indigenous linguists. To their way of thinking, this scholarly labor falls to erudite non-Maya: "La tarea de preservar una creación y producción artística de tan formidable importancia, es demasiado grande para dejarla en manos de aquellos indígenas que pudieran emerger de la situación actual y mantener su cultura" ("The task of preserving a creation and artistic production of such formidable importance is too great to leave in the hands of those indigenous persons who might be able to emerge from the present situation and maintain their culture") (22). This assessment and various inaccuracies that he noted in the translation moved Sam Colop to write a scathing critique of the translators' colonialist assumptions and of liberties taken in the artistic recreation of the work. Their project of translating a K'iché-Achi-language work from a flawed French translation, into Spanish, often consulting a Maya Yucatec dictionary, is, for Sam Colop, "like trying to translate a work of Shakespeare from French to Spanish using a Swedish dictionary" ("Xajoj tun vs. Quiché vinak") (34). In countering the basic methodology of these two translators, Sam Colop braves the flames fanned by conventional scholarship, which would keep him from reading and analyzing his own history, in order to make an incursion into the terrain of literary historiography.

Whereas conventional literary historiography typically treats early indigenous texts as museum pieces, the Popti' writer Víctor Montejo (b. 1951) breathes new life into several of these works, finding parallels between the holocaust of the contact period and the recent genocidal violence of the counterinsurgency war. In a work coauthored with Q'anil Akab', Montejo draws from the *querella* or lament, a formal complaint to the king, composed in a legalistic epistolary form used by indigenous persons in the sixteenth and seventeenth centuries, to notify the ruling Spanish king of abuses perpetrated by *peninsulares* and *criollos* in the New World. Ostensibly, the coauthors address the work to King Juan Carlos of Spain, on the occasion of the Quincentenary in October 1992. The title, *Brevísima relación testimonial de la continua destrucción del mayab' (Guatemala)* [Brief Testimonial Chronicle of the Continuous Destruction of the Mayab (Guatemala)], borrows moral authority from the famous work of Father Bartolomé de las Casas (1474–1566), the pioneering defender of Indian rights. Montejo thus grounds the *testimonio*, and the unjust conditions that occasion it, firmly in sixteenth-century origins, bypassing Guatemalan national institutions to seek redress in a higher court.

Montejo's text is an artful and heterogeneous showcase for *testimonios* tape recorded in Guatemalan refugee camps in Chiapas, Mexico. An epigram, typically drawn from Las Casas's *Brevísima relación de la destrucción de las Indias* [1552; A Short Account of the Destruction of the Indies] or from Bishop Diego de Landa's (1524–1579) *Relación de las cosas de Yucatán* [1565; Account of the Affairs of Yucatán], introduces each lament. Lament One is preceded by the most elaborate epigrammatic arrangement: three prophecies, taken from the classic Yucatec Mayan *El libro de los libros de Chilam Balam* [Books of Chilam Balam]; the sixth and eighth predictions, communicated by indigenous informants to Bishop Sahagún; and Q'anil Akab''s recounting of premonitory visions that the villagers received in dreams, circa 1980, prior to the worst outbreaks of military violence. In their dreams, Akab' recalls, "veíamos grandes letreros dorados que aparecieron en el cielo. Otros veían filosos machetes que caían del cielo. Muchos machetes, como lluvia de machetes que se precipitaban del cielo a la tierra" ("we saw great golden signs that appeared in the sky. Others saw sharp machetes falling from the sky. Many machetes, like a rain of machetes falling from the sky to the earth") (12). This triadic overlay of omens taken from pre-Columbian, early colonial, and contemporary epochs stresses timeless and persistent qualities of the Mayan worldview, especially of the manner in which the future insinuates itself into the present by means of dreams and prognostications.

Montejo's writing serves to expose the vacuousness of the "sterile rhetoric" to which he alludes in the following: "[M]ientras los debates intelectuales se desgastan en retóricas estériles sobre cómo entender al 'otro', los pueblos indígenas siguen viviendo las injusticias más horrendas que se han perpetuado a través de los siglos" ("While intellectual debates spend themselves on sterile rhetoric about how to understand the 'other,' indigenous peoples continue living the most horrendous injustices that have been perpetuated through the centuries") (3). This statement is not wholly unrelated to the notion that, even as Mayans begin to write poetry and narrative, the *testimonio* genre calls into question the very institution of literature as an ideological apparatus of alienation and domination. One may well question how the new Mayan literature of Guatemala, and the nuances that it is beginning to introduce into literary historiography, will function as an agent of transformation.

For instance, as Mayan writers and scholars continue to critique and rewrite representations of their people and their literatures by non-Mayans, they may modify assumptions regarding such works as the *testimonio*. The recipient of the 1992 Nobel Peace Prize, Rigoberta Menchú, is definitely a formidable presence in her country, but many Maya deny that she is representative of them. For instance, a spokesperson for the Comité de Organizaciones Mayas de Guatemala (COMG) expresses the expectation that Menchú should coordinate her rhetoric more closely with that of other indigenous organizations: "[W]e have to get Rigoberta to commit herself a little, to demand a little more that she increasingly assume the discourse that we are using, an anticolonial discourse" (Bastos and Camus 183). Another COMG member expresses further reservations about Menchú's grouping of Indians and Ladinos together for the sake of national unity: "[her politics] are not an authentically Mayan politics . . . . [S]he actively manages . . . the integrationist way . . . yielding to Western culture . . ." (183). From the existing treatments of Menchú's *testimonio*, most readers of *Me llamo Rigoberta Menchú y así me nació la conciencia* [1983; *I, Rigoberta Menchú: An Indian Woman in Guatemala*] would not guess that fundamental schisms, based on ideological differences, prevent Menchú and other high-profile Mayan leaders from more closely coordinating their respective efforts.

The debate on multicultural curriculum reignited in North American academic circles by the 1999 publication of David Stoll's investigation into the veracity of Menchú's first-person narration may color the reception of creative works by other Guatemalan Mayan writers. Stoll's charge that Menchú's story is more "collective" than had been recognized previously has polarized discussion on the matter, thanks in part to journalists who neither distinguish between *testimonio* and autobiography nor see the narrative fictional qualities of both. Among Guatemalan indigenous peoples, there are other voices to heed that both nuance and enrich the conversation. It would be reductive to think that *testimonio* is the sole and inevitable textual production available to the creative subaltern; literature can be, and has been, in countless locations around the globe, instrumental in decolonizing the mind in neocolonial states. Mayan writers who care to are free to wrestle with the inadequacies and cultural restrictions that are possibly inherent in Western elitist literary forms. And they do not require the services of an educated interlocutor to do this. Thus, the writings of *la indianidad letrada* ("the indigenous lettered"), whose emergence actually predates the *testimonio* in Guatemala, continue the incursions into the institutions of literature from a different flank than does the *testimonio*. Nevertheless, their contributions are still largely imperceptible in recent literary historiography, except for several pages that Marc Zimmerman devotes to Luis de Lión, Luis Enrique Sam Colop, Calixta Domitila Canek, Víctor Montejo, and Humberto Ak'abal (b. 1952) in his 1995 study of Guatemalan oppositional literature.

Humberto Ak'abal has risen to near celebrity status in Guatemala within the past decade. Ak'abal is also a frequent guest at literary events elsewhere, in Latin America, the U.S., and Europe. Reception and evaluation of his work are intimately tied to the cultural aftermath of the armed conflict, specifically to the commemoration of the Quincentennial of 1992. When Guatemalan Ladino writers speak of "the Ak'abal phenomenon," they place him within the conjuncture of 1992 and the heightened sensitivity to indigenous demands that this commemorative year symbolically represents. Eschewing a denunciatory tone, this poet favors evocations of the daily life of his people, or of his culture's vital and cosmological interpretations of natural phenomena. Subdued and serene, the flames in Ak'abal's poetry invite reflection and communion, as the hearth warms and comforts family members, the sun's rays illuminate his beloved Momostenango landscape by day, and the playful light of the distant stars bejewels ponds and water jugs by night. Especially notable for their uniqueness are Ak'abal's onomatopoeic renderings of bird songs. The poem "Canto de pájaros" [Bird Song], for example, devotes one line each to the songs of twenty-two different birds from the western highlands of Guatemala, with each call repeated three times, followed by ellipses that prolong the melody:

Klis, klis, klis . . .
Ch'ok, ch'ok, ch'ok . . .

(318)

When the poet performs this poem in a public recital, the birds' twittering and chirping, vibrant in the natural world, seem to alight momentarily, or ephemerally, on the written page, only to soar past the suspension points and take flight, as the poet sings each bird song some six or eight times. That is, the auditory defies the written to contain it. Through the mimetic and auditory features of onomatopoeia, K'iché is made universally intelligible. The extent to which Ak'abal and his poetry modify Ladino thinking on transcultural relations has its limitations. For instance, after interviewing the poet and then dedicating some twenty pages to a discussion of his verse, including the frequent humorous elements, the Ladino author and critic Hugo Cerezo Dardón writes as though he has never actually met an indigenous person: "They say that the Indian is sad; that he has no sense of humor; that he is not a teller of jokes as the Ladinos are, nor malicious like them. In truth, I don't know. I neither affirm it nor deny it" (171).

For still another indigenous writer, the Q'anjob'al novelist Gaspar Pedro González, it is the live coals and embers, not fully extinguished after the sixteenth-century bonfires that destroyed much of the written record of his ancestors, that offer the hope of dispelling the obscurantism that cloaks his people's history. For instance, the structure of his first novel, *La otra cara* [1993; On the Other Side], adheres to Mayan cosmology, in that its thirteen chapters evoke the thirteen gods revered in this worldview. González strove to include an encyclopedic wealth of information about diverse practices and forms of knowledge that shape the daily existence of his people. In retrospect, he offers this self-critique of his novel: "In reality there was too much to write about. It was like trying to fit on one postcard . . . everything that occurs within a culture" (personal interview). This novel *is* like a postcard, mailed from the edge of Spanish-language literature. On the one side, there is a highly mimetic snapshot of life in González's community, and, *en la otra cara* ("on the other side"), a text that attempts to lead us by words deeper into that life, beyond the exotic, the picturesque, and the folkloric.

González strives to illuminate ancient Mayan writing and thought through a new literature, in order to heal the rupture between past and present cultural expressions: "We can make any kind of literature. But we can also do what is Mayan. . . . My concern is how to tie . . . the ancient period together with the present in order not to get too far off track as regards continuity . . ." (personal interview). In 1997 he published his study of pre-Columbian, early colonial, and contemporary Mayan literature, based in part on research that he has carried out in teaching courses on Mayan literature and oral tradition at Mariano Gálvez University. *Kotz'ib': Nuestra literatura maya* [*Kotz'ib': Our Mayan Literature*] stands with Enrique Sam Colop's doctoral dissertation on K'iché literature and poetics and with Manuel Salazar Tetzagüic's study of Kaqchikel oral and literary traditions as one of the major attempts to compose a new Mayan literary historiography, written by Mayans. For González, the endeavor is laden with frustration, for much of the foreign scholarship on things Mayan, which could further assist his project, is unavailable to him. Furthermore, he disparages the tendency of Western scholars to classify the various branches of his people's tradition under the rubric of folklore, "sin darles su categoría de arte, literatura o ciencia" ("without recognizing them as art, literature, or science") (99). González emphasizes that Mayan literature does not always fit within the canon of Western literature for analysis and evaluation, given that, as a cultural product, it possesses its own norms and its own canon (*Kotz'ib'* 139). Rather than overtly engage long-standing representations of Mayan literature, this author attempts to delineate for the reader the worldview that generates its own particular norms and canon in both written and oral forms of literature.

The new configurations of ethnicity being formed in Guatemala function in opposition to those established in paternalistic representations of romantic *indigenismo*, which follow Europeanizing nineteenth-century tendencies evolved from Rousseau and Chateaubriand and perpetuate colonialist discourse on the primitive Indian and the noble savage. The new configurations oppose this stereotypical view on the part of those writers who conceive of the Indian as a literary personage and symbol of national and Latin American literature. At the same time, they break with the monologic colonial model prevalent in Guatemala, as they seek to promote recognition and appreciation of diverse Mayan subjects in a variety of arenas. Today, Mayan creative writers and intellectuals participate by narrating their own views of what it means to be Mayan, at times resorting to strategic essentialism for its perceived political utility. Admittedly, they function in a frontier zone between unstable sociocultural and sociolinguistic spaces; yet, in response to the charge that their written literary production is proof of their ladinization, Mayans state that, on the contrary, their writing provides both themselves and other readers with a richer understanding of Mayan heritage, in its classical, colonial, and contemporary manifestations.

Works Cited

Acevedo, Ramón Luis. 1982. *La novela centroamericana: Desde el Popol-Vuh hasta los umbrales de la novela actual*. Río Piedras, Puerto Rico: Editorial Universitaria.

Ak'abal, Humberto. 1996. *Ajkem tzij: Tejedor de palabras*. Guatemala City: Fundación Carlos F. Novella.

Albizúrez Palma, Francisco. 1981. "Raíces indígenas." *Historia de la literatura guatemalteca*. Vol. I. By Francisco Albizúrez Palma and Catalina Barrios y Barrios. Guatemala City: Editorial Universitaria. 15–57.

——, and Catalina Barrios y Barrios. 1981. *Historia de la literatura guatemalteca*. Vol. I. Guatemala City: Editorial Universitaria.

Anderson-Imbert, Enrique. 1969. *Spanish-American Literature: A History 1492–1910*. 2 vols. 2d ed. Detroit: Wayne State University.

——, and Eugenio Florit. 1960. *Literatura hispanoamericana: Antología e introducción histórica*. New York: Holt, Rinehart and Winston. 1960.

Ballón Aguirre, Enrique and Rodolfo Cerrón Palomino, eds. 1990. *Diglosia linguo-literario y educación en el Perú: Homenaje a Alberto Escobar*. Lima: CONCYTEC.

Barrios y Barrios, Catalina. 1981. "Rafael Landívar." *Historia de la literatura guatemalteca*. Vol. I. By Francisco Albuzúrez Palma and Catalina Barrios y Barrios. Guatemala City: Editorial Universitaria. 98-115.

Bastos, Santiago, and Manuela Camus. 1993. *Quebrando el silencio: Organizaciones del Pueblo Maya y sus demandas (1986–1992)*. Guatemala City: Facultad Latinoamericana de Ciencias Sociales.

Bendezú, Edmundo. 1986. *La otra literatura peruana*. Mexico City: Fondo de Cultura Económica.

Cerezo Dardón, Hugo. 1995. *Literatura y literatos guatemaltecos*. Guatemala City: Artemis y Edinter.

Cornejo Polar, Antonio. 1994. *Escribir en el aire: Ensayo sobre la heterogeneidad sociocultural en las literaturas andinas*. Lima: Horizonte.

Costa, Elena de. 1997. "Mayan Literature." *Latin American Literature*. Ed. Verity Smith. London: Fitzroy Dearborn. 533–35.

De Lión, Luis [José Luis de León Díaz]. 1966. *Los zopilotes*. Guatemala City: Landívar.

——. 1969. *Su segunda muerte*. Guatemala City: n.p.

——. 1996. *El tiempo principia en Xibalbá*. 2d ed. Guatemala City: Artemis-Edinter.

Franco, Jean. 1993. *Historia de la literatura hispanoamericana: A partir de la Independencia*. 9th ed. rev. Barcelona: Ariel.

Gómez-Gil, Orlando. 1968. *Historia crítica de la literatura hispanoamericana*. New York: Holt, Rinehart and Winston.

González, Gaspar Pedro. 1993. *La otra cara*. 2d ed. Guatemala City: Ministerio de Cultura y Deportes.

——. 1996. Personal interview. 26 Feb.

——. 1997. *Kotz'ib': Nuestra literatura maya*. Rancho Palos Verdes, Calif.: Yax Te'.

Henríquez-Ureña, Pedro. 1945. *Literary Currents in Hispanic America*. Cambridge: Harvard University Press.

Lienhard, Martin. 1992. *La voz y su huella: Escritura y conflicto étnico-cultural en América Latina, 1492–1988*. 3rd ed. Lima: Horizonte.

Memorial de Sololá, Anales de los cakchiqueles. 1980. Transl. and intro. Adrián Recinos. *Título de los señores de Totonicapán*. Transl. Dionisio José Chonay. Guatemala City: Dirección General de Antropología e Historia: Editorial Piedra Santa.

Menchú, Rigoberta, and Elisabeth Burgos. 1983. *Me llamo Rigoberta Menchú y así me nació la conciencia*. Barcelona: Argos Vergara.

Menton, Seymour. 1960. *Historia crítica de la novela guatemalteca*. Guatemala City: Editorial Universitaria.

Montejo, Víctor, and Q'anil Akab'. 1992. *Brevísima relación testimonial de la continua destrucción del mayab' (Guatemala)*. Providence, RI: Guatemala Scholars Network.

Olivera, Otto. 1974. *La literatura en publicaciones periódicas de Guatemala (Siglo XIX)*. Tulane Studies in Romance Languages and Lit. 5. New Orleans: Tulane University.

Padia Guerchous, Anita, and Manuel Vázquez-Bigi. 1991. *Quiché Vinak: Tragedia. Nueva versión española y estudio histórico-literario del llamado 'Rabinal-Achí.'* Mexico City: Fondo de Cultura Económica.

Polo Sifontes, Francis. 1984 [1957]. "Prólogo." *Crónicas indígenas de Guatemala*. Ed. Adrián Recinos. Special publication. 29. Guatemala City: Academia de Geografía e Historia de Guatemala. vii–xviii.

Rabinal-achí: El varón de Rabinal: Ballet-drama de los indios quichés de Guatemala. 6th ed. Ed. Luis Cardoza y Aragón. N.p.: n.p., n.d.

Rama, Angel. 1982. *Transculturación narrativa en América Latina*. Mexico City: Siglo Veintiuno.

Recinos, Adrián, ed. 1984 [1957]. *Crónicas indígenas de Guatemala.* Special publication. 29. Guatemala City: Academia de Geografía e Historia de Guatemala.

Salazar Tetzagüic, Manuel de Jesús. 1995. *Rupach'uxik kina'oj qati't qamama': Características de la literatura maya kaqchikel.* 2d ed. Guatemala City: Cholsamaj.

Sam Colop, Luis Enrique. [1978]. *Versos sin refugio: Quiché y español.* [Guatemala City]: San Antonio.

——. 1979. *La copa y la raíz.* Guatemala City: RIN-78.

——. 1993. "Xajoj tun vs. Quiché vinak." *Encuentro* May-Aug.: 25–35.

——. 1994. *Maya Poetics.* Ph.D. Dissertation. Department of English, SUNY-Buffalo.

Saz, Agustín del. 1978. *Literatura iberoamericana.* Barcelona: Juventud.

Stoll, David. 1999. *Rigoberta Menchú and the Story of All Poor Guatemalans.* Boulder: Westview.

Vela, David. 1944 [1929]. *Literatura guatemalteca.* 2 vols. 2d ed. Guatemala City: Tipografía Nacional.

Zavala, Magda, and Seidy Araya. 1995. *La historiografía literaria en América Central (1957–1987).* Heredia, Costa Rica: Fundación UNA.

Zimmerman, Marc. 1995. *Literature and Resistance in Guatemala: Textual Modes and Cultural Politics from El Señor Presidente to Rigoberta Menchú.* Latin American Ser. 22. 2 vols. Athens: Ohio University Center for International Studies.

CHAPTER 25

ANDEAN INDIGENOUS EXPRESSION
RESISTING MARGINALITY

Regina Harrison

Few Andean Indians have written literary texts; however, Indians are omnipresent, not marginalized, in the literature of the central Andes. From the Colonial period up to the present day, esthetic, economic, and cultural domains are closely dependent on the persons who, poncho-clad, till patches of earth to provide food for the cities or who deftly paddle canoes and skillfully wield machetes to aid industry in the tropical forest. In the urban sprawl of cities, bilingual, apron-wearing Indian women also cook, clean, and care for non-Indian families as domestics. These images of Indians, and other depictions drawn from a vast repertoire, are abundant in South American novels, stories, poems, and popular culture.

At first, European invaders were dazzled by the accomplishment evident in the Incan culture, which spread from its Cuzco hearth to traverse the spine of the Andes from Ecuador, through Bolivia, and down to Chile (see **Map 1**). Walls covered with vast hammered gold plaques, the stone-paved road system from coast to highlands, and the abundant storage houses to ward off famine attested to skills of governance on the part of the Andean Indian leaders. Only after the spoils had been accumulated and melted down, the irrigation ditches torn apart to form the walls of Spanish villas, did the Spanish begin to look closely at these indigenous citizens who now formed part of the Spanish empire. Much of the writing in the early colonial period is attuned to the productive capacity of the Indians as seen in tribute records, land jurisdiction claims, and bills of lading. The Catholic Church similarly provided records of baptism, catechism classes, marriages, and annual certificates of confession in an effort to document the spiritual needs of the Indians. However, as late as 1611, an entry for *indio* does not appear in the ample dictionary compiled by Sebastián Covarrubias far away in Spain, despite contentious Spanish debates regarding the intellectual capacity of the Indians. Instead, another definition, that of *Peru*, best exemplifies the relationship between the Spanish and their overseas indigenous subjects: "Peru provincia famosissima . . . [d]e donde se han traido tantos millones de oro, y de plata. Y en cambio de esto se les ha comunicado la Santa Fe Catolica" ("Peru, that most famous province from which so much gold and silver has been extracted in exchange for the communication of the Holy Catholic Faith to its people") (Covarrubias 866).

Indeed, the "communication" of the Sacred Catholic Faith was under way immediately, as missionaries and soldiers began to learn the most common languages of the Andes (Quechua, Aymará, and Puquina) to best convert (and command) the aboriginal population. Therefore, it is no surprise that the first book printed in the southern Americas, in 1584, is the *Christian Doctrine and Catechism for the Instruction of the Indians* (a trilingual edition in Spanish, Quechua, and Aymará), followed closely in 1585 by companion pieces, the *Third Catechism* and the *Exposition of the Christian Doctrine*, which later was translated into Puquina (Mannheim 47). Despite these auspicious beginnings, whereby the Quechua and Aymará languages were accorded equal space in the

Map 1.

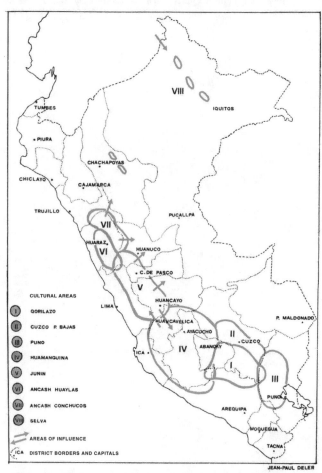

CULTURAL AREAS

- I QORILAZO
- II CUZCO P. BAJAS
- III PUNO
- IV HUAMANGUINA
- V JUNIN
- VI ANCASH HUAYLAS
- VII ANCASH CONCHUCOS
- VIII SELVA

↔ AREAS OF INFLUENCE

ICA DISTRICT BORDERS AND CAPITALS

JEAN-PAUL DELER

early literary pages of the Andean colonies, these writings (brought about mainly through the contributions of indigenous informants) were not celebratory regarding the contribution of the Andean indigenous populace. Confession manuals were used by Spanish priests, newly trained in the Quechua language, to ferret out sins, especially those of fornication and idol worship. In sermons, which make up a significant corpus of early Colonial literature, Catholic speakers continually railed against the wickedness of the Andean heathens who persisted in their beliefs and practices. However, many times the contestatory voice of the Indian can be read between the lines in Church literature. Texts published in the *Confessionario* of 1585 reveal the Indian despair. Besieged by the ravages of disease that decimated their numbers, and plagued by visiting churchmen who sought out and destroyed the sacred signs of their Andean past, it is reported that Indians questioned God's ultimate motive in creating them. Some of them went so far as to believe that God created them to live in sin, especially in the sins of promiscuity and drunkenness, and that they could not be good.

In matters of a literary tradition, the Indians of the Andes were seen as culturally disadvantaged. The writing system brought by the Spanish conquerors was a measure of the distance that separated the two cultures. Because the Spanish knew how to write, they questioned the very nature of the peoples they encountered who had no such script. The Quechua speakers, in turn, viewed the papers inscribed with Spanish letters as a magical means of communication. Felipe Guamán Poma de Ayala (1524?–1613) tells us that Atahualpa attempted to listen to the pages of the breviary at the moment of Conquest; Diego de Castro Titu Cusi Yupanqui (b. 16th C.), in his version of the conquest, states that Atahualpa was shown a book or a letter or "something he is not sure of," and goes on to say that Spaniards "day and night" speak with their papers. Yet these indigenous noblemen (and others) in time became very skilled at putting pen to paper and thus laid the foundations of a literary manuscript tradition in Quechua.

The black-and-white drawings of the indigenous chronicler Felipe Guamán Poma now are so commonly displayed on book covers, calendars, and tourist T-shirts that it is hard to believe that his manuscript languished forgotten in the Royal Library of Copenhagen until 1908. Since that date, a facsimile version has been published by the Institut d'Ethnologie (1936), and four edited versions have been published in Spanish by Posnansky (1944), Bustíos Gálvez (1956), Pease (1980), and Adorno, Murra, and Urioste (1980). Two English translations exist, one by G. R. Coulthard (1968) and the abbreviated version by Dilke (1978), but a definitive English critical edition has not yet been undertaken. An appreciation of the manuscript can easily begin with the detailed illustrations depicting harvests and rituals, male and female leaders, and the arrival of the Spanish. However, the prose text requires skillful reading for its allusions to Catholic theology, rhetorical conventions, European historiography, and Andean agricultural practices, as well as for its selections of Quechua poetry and myth. More likely to be anthologized by colonial historians rather than literary critics, Guamán Poma's text conveys the economic and social discrimination experienced by indigenous subjects in the colonies.

To consider another document, the sketch of Incan cosmology is an intriguing aspect of Juan de Santa Cruz Pachacuti Yamqui's (b. end of 15th C.) Spanish-language manuscript because the supreme god, as well as the flanking male and female sacred beings, are all linked to a patterning of constellations in the southern hemisphere. The prose text, written in a Spanish reflecting the syntax of the Quechua and Aymará languages, is difficult for nonspecialists, who are not able to sort out the intricacies of Incan dynasties, warring factions and conquests, and the descriptions of numerous celebratory rituals. However, the ritual lyrics interwoven in the text provide rich examples of a poetics based on a contrastive pair of terms in which the second element differs ever so slightly from the first. The volume of the *Relación de antigüedades deste Reyno del Pirú* edited by Pierre Duviols and César Itier [1993; Report on the Antiquities of This Kingdom of Peru] gives a facsimile version of the text, with the drawings presented as they are positioned in the manuscript, and with ample explanatory material. Formerly, only the 1879 Spanish version of the *Relación,* edited by Marcos Jiménez de la Espada, was reproduced (in 1927, 1950, 1967, and 1991 editions), and therefore errors in transcription and interpretation were transmitted over the years. An English version of the manuscript, without the Quechua verses, however, was printed by Clement Markham for the Hakluyt Society as early as 1873.

Even more information can be gathered from an indigenous Quechua manuscript that was collected from coastal villagers in the sixteenth century, probably at the behest of Father Francisco de Avila, who waged a theological battle against the Andean deities in 1608. The myths and histories written down in what is known as the Huarochiri manuscript overlap with some biblical events, such as the flood cycle, yet the text excels in representing the regional Andean conflicts between the highland and coastal ecological areas, the control of water, the invasion of the Incas, and the cults of specific deities. Hermann Trimborn's 1939 edition (barely surviving the bombing raids of World War II) presented both the German and the Quechua texts, with extensive critical commentary. Gerald Taylor is responsible for a French edition (1980) and a later Spanish-Quechua edition (1987), while Jan Szeminski edited a Polish edition (1985) and Hipólito Galante a Latin version (1942). Undoubtedly, the beauty of José María Arguedas's translation makes the 1966 Spanish-Quechua edition a literary treasure, especially aided by the editing of Pierre Duviols. A recent English edition, that of Frank Salomon and George Urioste in 1991, benefits from all the work of predecessors in understanding and accurately transcribing the Colonial text. Urioste published a Spanish translation in 1983, which is useful for this study, yet it is Salomon's meticulous anthropological introduction and notes that give this edition its merit.

Despite renewed interest at the close of the twentieth century in indigenous writers and a desire to republish the texts, appreciation of the Andean manuscripts often remains restricted to a small number of researchers in anthropology and linguistics. Because of the specialized nature of the indigenous knowledge systems presented in the texts and the conventions of stylized Colonial prose, the works are not always accessible to all readers. However, one Colonial publication, the *Comentarios reales* [The Royal Commentaries of Peru] by the *mestizo* writer El Inca Garcilaso, was widely read in the years after its publication (1609 and 1616). Seventeen editions were printed in the seventeenth and eighteenth centuries: ten in French, four in Spanish, two in English, and one in German. Notable for the vision of restitution for the heirs of the Incas as well as the histories of Incan grandeur, these two volumes were closely read by Tupac Amaru II. So inflammatory were these passages that Spanish ordinances of 1781 and 1782 demanded that all copies should be seized so as not to prejudice the Indians. With independence, revolutionary leaders (first San Martín and later Bolívar) promoted republication of the "native American" text, the *Comentarios reales.*

Although El Inca Garcilaso proudly proclaimed himself to be of mixed heritage, Indian and Spanish, and achieved significant literary recognition for his intelligent and esthetically pleasing writing, other persons of mixed race were not held in equal esteem in Colonial society. Although intermarriage between Indians, blacks, and Spanish did not occur until the second half of the seventeenth century, many children were born with ancestry in two or more of these groups as a result of nonmarital liaisons. Lists of racial taxonomies with as many as fourteen to twenty designations were common in Mexico and Peru; often "casta" paintings illustrated and identified the results of impure "Spanish" bloodlines, as in the *Quadro de historia natural, civil y geográfica del Reyno del Perú* [1799; Natural, Civil and Geographic History of the Kingdom of Peru], in which persons in their traditional clothing (Spanish and Indian) are displayed in small labeled frames organized by their "deviation" from the Spanish ideal.

Bolívar's statement in 1819 at Antofagasta, "we are not Europeans, we are not Indians," reflects the concern for identity formation that paralleled the formation of nation-states in the nineteenth century. Here, the contrast between an identity as either European or Indian is foremost, where the latter term bears the weight of prejudice in both law and social interaction. With a view to the large indigenous population, the Declaration of Independence, dated 9 July 1816, was published in Quechua and Aymará translations in Buenos Aires. So, too, were Bernardo O'Higgins's two pages addressed to the former Indians of the Incan Empire (September 1819), as well as a one-page proclamation (also in 1819) from José de San Martín regarding the liberation of Chile and Argentina.

Of course, as a symbol of independence, the Indian served literature and politics well. José Joaquín de Olmedo's (1780–1847) "La victoria de Junín: Canto a Bolívar" [1825; The Victory at Junin: Poem to Bolívar] features Huaina Capac (an Incan leader), who, from his celestial position above the battlefield in the Wars of Independence, cheers on the victorious rebel soldiers: "Oh peoples who form one people and one family, you are all my sons!" (Olmedo 115). Bolívar, a realist at least when it came to literary themes, criticized Olmedo's insistence on this point: "It is inappropriate to have Huaina Capac give preference to foreign intruders, the descendants of those who destroyed his empire" (quoted in Pérez 220). Juan Wallparrimachi Mayta (1793–1814), a Quechua-speaking Indian from Macha (Bolivia), was a soldier in the Wars of Independence, fighting alongside the 1900 members of his indigenous platoon, often using a slingshot as his weapon. He died in 1814, shot with a harquebus, yet his legacy lives on in the amorous verses he wrote, which were recovered and published in various collections in the mid-nineteenth century. Jesús Lara (1898–1980), a literary critic and novelist who searched archives for traces of Wallparrimachi, was able to recover the lyric intensity of traditional Quechua expression, as seen in the colonial writer's poetic allusions to the high-altitude Andes:

¿Ima phuyun jáqay phuyu
Yanayásqaj wasaykamun
Mamáypaj waqaninchari
Paraman tukuspa jamun.

¿Qué nube puede ser aquella nube
Que obscurecida se aproxima?
Será tal vez el llanto de mi madre
Que viene en lluvia convertido

What cloud is that cloud
which approaches darkly?
Perhaps it is my mother's lament
transformed into rain.

(Lara 1969, 148)

Variations of this sentiment are common in the popular poetry and songs of Peru, Bolivia, and Ecuador; the phrasing also resonates with the writings of José María Arguedas in the twentieth century.

Passionate amorous expression is seen in the well-known drama *Ollantay,* in which the plot concerns the plight of a non-Incan army general (Ollanta) and an Incan noblewoman (Cusi-Cuyllor), who are not allowed to "marry" because both are not of noble descent. The product of their passion, a female child by the name of Ima Sumac, begs the reigning Inca, Tupac Yapanqui, to allow the two to be recognized as a legitimate couple. Unlike his father, Pachacutec, who denied their marriage, the young Inca Tupac Yupanqui relents and pardons them. Set in the environs of Cuzco, the play reflects well the structured Incan class divisions and the regional conflicts, and is written with a controlled use of the Quechua language. The author of the manuscript is disputed, but some scholars attribute it to the priest who "discovered" the play, Father Antonio Valdez (d. 1816), who lived near Cuzco in the eighteenth century. It is said that Tupac Amaru II, the revolutionary Indian leader, saw the play represented in Tinta before his death at the hands of the Spanish in 1781. Several copies were made before the original was lost; one copy, made by Justo Apu Saharuara (1838), is of the Valdez manuscript. The other widely known version, copied by the Austrian Johann Jacob von Tschudi (published in 1853), was found in the Santo Domingo convent in Cuzco. Both manuscripts date from the eighteenth century, as determined by linguistic analysis by Mannheim, and therefore attest to a creative period in the writing of dramas, which also include *El pobre más rico* [The Richest Poor Man] and *Usca Paucar. Ollantay* has undergone several translations. The first was into Spanish by José Sebastián Barranca in 1870, Tschudi's German version appeared in 1875, Gavino Pacheco Zegarra's French translation appeared in 1878, and in 1967 an English translation by Abraham Arias Larreta was published.

Perhaps it was this literary interest in *Ollantay* that stimulated the publication of several important collections of Quechua literature. Notable is the work of José Dionisio Anchorena in his *Gramática quechua* [Lima, 1874; Quechua Grammar], in which he states his motivation for writing such a book: "White people look upon the Indians with scorn and the Indians in turn look at whites and *mestizos* with relentless hatred" (Anchorena vi). Nine grammar lessons precede a chapter on versification, in which Francisco de Quevedo (1580–1645), José de Espronceda (1808–1842), and Fray Luis de León (1527–1591) are translated to Quechua, in addition to providing samples of traditional and modern sources in Spanish and Quechua (Inca Garcilaso [1539–1616], Mariano Melgar [1790–1815], Aranda, Basagoytia). In a similar manner, in *Azucenas quechuas* [1905; Quechua Lilies], professing to correct the lack of study about "Incaic literature," Adolfo Vienrich gathered myths and poetry "from the lips [of Indians] not without some difficulty, because of their natural timidity and the fear that their ingenuous knowledge would be a thing of ridicule" (19). One year later, in 1906, he published *Fábulas quechuas* [Quechuan Fables], a bilingual edition of traditional stories.

The nineteenth century was a period of fervent collection of popular song, in both Spanish and Quechua, for publication in national anthologies. Juan León Mera (1832–1894), patterning his collection on that of Fernán Caballero (1796–1877) and Antonio Trueba (1819–1889) in Spain, published *Antología ecuatoriana: cantares del pueblo ecuatoriano* [Ecuadorian Anthology: Songs of the Ecuadorian Peoples] with backing from the Ecuadorian Academy in 1892. Of the thirty-four quatrains in Quechua, twenty-four are composed of themes of love or romantic negotiations between a "blanco señor" and an "india." Poetry written in Quechua by Luis Cordero (1833–1912), elected president of Ecuador in 1892, is also included in the anthology; his themes, however, avoid declarations of love and, instead, are fervent denunciations of the oppressive system of the church and local governments, which demanded payments from the impoverished Indians in the form of tithes and taxes.

Mera's decision to include Quechua verses is consistent with his beliefs regarding the value of the Quechua language in literary contexts. Although he was criticized fiercely in 1861 by the Chilean Amunátegui brothers, who claimed it "was not worthwhile to read a book of [Mera's] poetry, constantly turning to a dictionary or looking down at a footnote," Mera did not eliminate entirely the indigenous phrases from the second edition of his poetry. In addition, Mera is outspoken regarding the inclusion of Quechua in the formation of Hispanic-American literature: "We cannot, therefore, take up the historical study of poetry, one of our most important forms of expression, beginning with the introduction of the Spanish language and forget the language and poetry of our native people" (1868, 20–21).

Clorinda Matto de Turner (1852–1909), Mera's Peruvian colleague, shared his appreciation of Quechua and indigenous themes. She included Mera's Spanish-language poem "La madre y el hijo" ["Mother and Child"], which is critical of Andean racist attitudes toward Indians, in her manual of literature for women readers, *Elementos de literatura* [1884; Elements of Literature]. Moreover, she encouraged her compatriots to learn and use Quechua in their writing: "Why have all the writers who grace the Peruvian literary firmament chosen to ignore its language? Why can't they write in the language of their country?" (quoted in Carrillo 20). She did not criticize Mera harshly, however, even though his knowledge was often limited to the dictionaries. A fluent speaker of Quechua, Matto de Turner is responsible for Quechua publications of the books of the Apostles. However, she is better known for the *indigenista* novel *Aves sin nido* [1889; *Birds without a Nest*], which outlines the social and educational plight of the Indian, yet contains few words of Quechua.

In Bolivia, Carlos Felipe Beltrán (1816–1898) is recognized for his collections of his own creative work in Quechua, both poetry and drama, as well as the recovery of older Catholic sacred texts written in Quechua and Aymará. Paul Rivet, a Quechua and Aymará enthusiast responsible, with Georges Crequit-Montfort, for the Bibliographie des langues aymará et kic[h]ua, praised Beltrán's insightful scholarship and appreciation of indigenous culture. Heartfelt is Beltrán's description of contemporary attitudes toward the Quechua language in this poem:

Mientras que otros segando cultas flores
Te miren con desdén, mi quichua amada,
Y sin ver tu belleza virginal
. . .
A morir te condenan, desgraciada;
Yo todos te consagro mis desvelos.
Tú eres la gloria de mis pensamientos,
Tú la visión brillante de mis sueños . . .

  (quoted in Lara 1969, 165)

While others gathering cultivated flowers
look upon you with disdain, my beloved Quechua,
without seeing your Virginal beauty
. . .
They condemn you to death in disgrace.
I dedicate all my waking hours to you;
You are the glory of my thoughts,
You are the brilliant vision of my dreams . . .

Beltrán, from the region of Potosí, was ordained as a priest in 1845. He used his personal printing press to publish some thirty volumes of essays, dramas, poetry, and Quechua religious translations of the Bible. *Civilización del Indio: Antología sagrada en español, quechua, y aymará* [1889; Indian Civilization: Sacred Anthology in Spanish, Quechua, and Aymará] and *Civilización del Indio: Ramillete hispano-quechua, original con multitud de poesías originales y antiguas mejoradas* [1888; Oruro; Indian Civilization: Hispanic-Quechua Bouquet, Original Texts with Numerous Original and Ancient Poems Improved] represent his full range of interests.

With Juan León Mera's (1832–1894) publication in 1879 of *Cumandá*, a novel set in the tropical forests of Ecuador, and Matto de Turner's *Aves sin nido* in print by 1889, the *indianist* literary movement passed on to the *indigenista* phase, and an abundance of novels about Indians proliferated in the Andean countries. Written by authors who often participated in literary circles with a decidedly political agenda, these books present the face of tragedy to both Andean readers and readers in metropolitan cities worldwide. Among the most widely translated novels was Jorge Icaza's (1906–1978) *Huasipungo* (1934), a tale of unscrupulous manipulation of the Indians by landowners, the Catholic Church, foreign business interests, and Ecuadorian government officials. When the Indian protagonist's wife dies from eating rotten beef, Icaza draws upon traditional Quechua songs of lament to mark the tragic outcome in the lives of this Indian family. Although little Quechua vocabulary is included in the novel, the stark existence of the Andean Indians is graphically displayed, and the reader sympathizes with the uprising that occurs in the last pages of the novel.

Icaza readily admitted that he had no knowledge of Quechua and that his experience with indigenous communities was limited to occasional visits to the *hacienda* of his relatives. This was not the case of other novelists, such as Ciro Alegría (1909–1967), Alcides Arguedas (1879–1946), Jesús Lara (1898–1980), and José María Arguedas (1911–1969), who knew well the realities of indigenous peoples. Their solutions to the "Indian problem" shape the plots of their novels. For Alcides Arguedas, the depiction of Indians includes their magico-religious orientation, as they perform ritual ceremonies to increase the quantity of fish in the lake to ward off starvation. In view of the survival of ancient practices, Arguedas in his *Raza de bronce* [1919; Bronze Race] proposes, through the voice of a liberal *hacendado* ("*hacienda* owner"), that a politician-dictator would best shepherd the Indians into modernity. Ciro Alegría's take on the plight of the Indian supports an outcome dependent on the *mestizo* capacity to transform Andean society. Ciro Alegría's *El mundo es ancho y ajeno* [1941; *Broad and Alien is the World*] presents a symbolic contrast between a traditional leader, Maqui, and an educated and army-trained *mestizo*, Castro, who encourages Indians to participate in an armed uprising against the landlord. The Indians' military defeat in this novel does not negate the potential for a messianic rebellion in the Andes, which was seen as a means to liberate the oppressed population. *Yarwarninchij*, Jesús Lara's 1959 novel, alludes to the changes that attempted to reshape the Bolivian countryside with the decrees of the agrarian reform of the 1950s. However, in this version of Indian-ness, a priest is brought in by the wealthy landowner to persuade the Indian communities not to claim government parcels made available to them by the Bolivian revolutionary government. The armed conflict pits the Indians against the landowners, who have been forced to redistribute their lands, and against Church officials, who are the allies of the wealthy.

Surely the most recognized champion of the Indian cause is José María Arguedas, a writer who spoke Quechua as his first language and struggled with reducing the complexity of the Indian world to printed pages written in Spanish. Outspoken regarding the general attitude toward Indians and toward their language, Arguedas writes of his personal experiences: "I spent my childhood and youth reared and much loved by Indians. In 1919, on my first trip to Lima, I was chased down the streets like an animal by street gangs. They distinguished those of us who came from the mountains by our way of walking and talking. The Andes have split up Peru" (1957, 34). He goes on to confess that when he sang *waynos* he was laughed at, and the *colegio* students in Ica teased him with "No one but Indians sing that" (1938, 8). The divisions of coast and sierra are significant in Peruvian culture. José Carlos Mariátegui (1894–1930) and Luis Alberto Sánchez (1900–1994), in the pages of the periodical *Mundial* (1927), debated the centrality of the Indian problem to the political reforms they envisioned. Sánchez's sharp comments determined the debate: He claimed that neither of them (nor any other militant activists) understood well the sierra and the Indian, declaring a need for less superficiality and more study close at hand. Mariátegui's reply, that this political strategy should focus on the working class, whether Indian or *cholo*, demonstrated the degree to which his vision encompassed issues of class as well as ethnicity. Mariátegui's *Siete ensayos de interpretación de la realidad peruana* [1928; Seven Interpretative Essays of Peruvian Reality], although still oriented in part toward the recreation of another Tahuantinsuyo, includes the African Andean in its analysis of sociopolitical changes.

José María Arguedas, with his ability to speak Quechua, was encouraged by his coastal classmates at the University of San Marcos to try writing his own version of life in the highlands. This attempt brought him up against the wall of Spanish syntax that separated him from the expression of his Quechua thoughts. His attempt to create a new language form often left his expression short and choppy–"an infernal battle"; he turned to songs for inspiration as a means of conveying the deep feelings he had for the Quechua people: "I could not find any form of poetry that could express my feelings better than the poetry of Quechua songs. Those of us who speak Quechua know that this language exceeds Spanish in its capacity to express sentiments like tenderness, affection, love of nature" (1938, 16). Arguedas published his own Quechua poems, brimming with admiration for Quechua culture, in 1966; they were republished in 1972 after his tragic death. Reading Arguedas's novels and short stories presents the reader with a traditional collection of Quechua lyrics. As a singer as well as a dancer, Arguedas remembered the songs of his youth, collected in *Canto kechwa* (1938), as well as those he collected in fieldwork in the Mantaro valley and at numerous indigenous fiestas. Late in his life, he returned to these themes and began to compose his own verses in Quechua, which were published in the poetry collection *Temblor/Katatay* [Tremor/Katatay]. *Los ríos profundos* [1958; *Deep Rivers*, 1978] abounds in references to the songs that symbolize the tribulations of a young boy left in a boarding school distant from his circuit judge father and the Indians at home, who raised him as if he were their own child. The publication of this novel and others by Arguedas brought more acceptance of the theme of the Indian; Mario Vargas Llosa (b. 1936), for instance, writes eloquently of how much Arguedas's *Los ríos* served as a model for his *La ciudad y los perros* [1963; *The Time of the Hero*, 1966]. Most importantly, Arguedas influenced the direction of cultural institutions from his position as Chief in the Section of Folklore and Fine Arts in the Ministry of Culture (1948), as Head of the Institute of Ethnological Studies of the Museum of Culture (1953), and then as Director of the Casa de la Cultura in Peru (1963). His energy as an author and as an Indian activist waning, Arguedas wrote that he feared that the constant struggle would reduce him to a passive and impotent spectator in humanity's formidable struggle in Peru. He took his own life in 1969.

Arguedas worked very closely with other Andean scholars to publish translations of contemporary and pre-Columbian texts. Jorge Lira and José María Benigno Farfán both collaborated with Arguedas in translating sacred Quechua lyrics. "Apu Inca Atahuallpaman," a text collected by Farfán that is notable for its striking image of a black rainbow, was translated by Arguedas. Most notably, Arguedas worked with Pierre Duviols on the manuscript of Huarochirí, a text that is consistently praised for its literary quality. Lira, a priest who furthered the study of Quechua folklore and linguistics, is known for his *Diccionario Kkechua-Español* (1944) as well as a bilingual anthology of songs that he translated and collected, *Canto de amor* (1956). In his introduction to *Canto*, he bemoans the false image of sad, mournful Quechua poetry that was widely disseminated by Mariano Melgar, "a poet with a spirit of lamentation who found rich territory in sobs and heartrending lamentation for his most fertile sadness" (10). Melgar and other interpreters of the Quechua "spirit" wrote poems that were of poor quality and were "sickly, full of complaints, lacking in esthetics, and of a repugnant repetition," according to Lira.

J. M. B. Farfán, a professor of Quechua at the University of San Marcos, was recognized very early for his bilingual publication of dispersed Quechua lyrics from the three central Andean countries in *Poesía folklórica quechua* [1942; Quechua Folkloric Poetry]. Although he begins with reprintings of the standard selections from Guamán Poma (1524?–1613) and Inca Garcilaso, the majority of the songs were gathered by him or other collaborators throughout the Andean highlands. For Bolivia, he includes Wallparrimachi or C. F. Beltrán and other recent poetry, whereas from Ecuador he includes his own retranslations of the well-known selections found in Mera's *Antología ecuatoriana* [Ecuadorian Anthology]. His purpose, as stated in the introduction, was to gather inaccessible and out-of-print examples of Quechua literature so others could learn to appreciate it, too. Certainly, Farfán fulfills a gap in publication history. Jorge Basadre's lofty dream of putting together the first anthology of Quechua literature was abetted by his own considerable archival research skills but hampered by his omission of the original Quechua versions of the texts in *Literatura inca* [1938; Inca Literature]. Edmundo Bendezú Aybar's *Literatura quechua* [1980; Quechua Literature] is a worthy addition to the Biblioteca Ayacucho series, both for Bendezú's excellent new translation of many texts and the comprehensive chronological outline that details the importance of Quechua from the colonial period through the twentieth century. Quechua specialists, however, are not given the original Quechua texts to compare with the Spanish translations.

The Cuban anthology *Poesía quechua* [Quechua Poetry], edited by Mario Razzeto and published by Casa de las

Américas (1972), also lacks the Quechua originals and depends heavily on Basadre's selections from 1938, as well as Jesús Lara's magnificent anthology, *La literatura de los quechuas* [1960; The Quechuas' Literature]. Lara's book, an impassioned study of the origins of Quechua with lengthy analysis and more literal translations than are provided by previous scholars, was extremely influential in offering bilingual texts and sources for the originals. Of course, as Lara notes in the book's prologue, he in turn was able to benefit from the excellent bibliography of Quechua and Aymará published by Paul Rivet and Georges Crequi Montfort in the early 1950s. Lara, like J. M. Arguedas, was a Quechua speaker and sensitive to the nuances in expression that come from a daily use of the language. An advocate of the complexity of the language as well as its esthetic value, Lara fought the prejudice of those who denigrated the people, their culture, and their literature:

> ¿Es posible que el pueblo constructor de Cuzco, de Ollantaytambo y de Machu Pijchu, el pueblo que llegó a la organización social, económica y política más evolucionada de que habla la historia, el pueblo que supo cultivar las artes al extremo de que hoy día las muestras que quedan son objeto de la admiración de los propios occidentales; es posible que este pueblo no haya podido poseer el don de análisis ni llegar a la concepción de las ideas abstractas? (1969, 11)

> Is it possible that the people who built Cuzco, Ollantaytambo, and Machu Picchu, the people who achieved the advanced social, economic, and political organization described in history, the people who practiced the arts with such skill that today their works of art are the object of Western admiration–is it possible that such a people could not have mastered the discipline of close analysis or the understanding of abstract ideas?

Obviously, the answer for Lara is demonstrated in the beauty of the lyrics he published in his anthology as well as the stone monuments that also bear witness to the architectural and esthetic skill of the Incas.

A significant and carefully edited volume of Quechua songs, *La sangre en los cerros/Urqukunapa Yawarnin* [Blood on the Hills], was published by Rodrigo Montoya, Luis Montoya, and Edwin Montoya for the Centro Peruano de Estudios Sociales, Serie Cultural Peruana, in 1987. The authors scoured anthropological collections and depended on their own archives, as well as those of friends, to publish new texts that augment the more traditional collections now available in reprinted editions. Current literary interest in the voice of the subaltern has stimulated the publication of Quechua life stories and histories, which formerly had been the domain of anthropologists and sociologists. One of the most moving autobiographies was dictated by Gregorio Condori Mamani, a porter who daily earned money carrying baskets of purchases to the homes of the middle class in Cuzco. Befriended by anthropologists Ricardo Valderrama Fernández and Carmen Escalante Gutiérrez, Condori Mamani, an orphan and a modern-day Lazarillo, spun a tale of wandering from place to place in search of work and a substitute family. His loneliness is heightened when he is mistreated by society and when he buries his children, yet he expresses solace in the comfort of a known landscape, which marks incidents in his life. Furthermore, Condori Mamani revels in the myths and stories told to him; the harshness of jail was alleviated by his sharing a cell with one of the best Quechua storytellers he had ever heard. With its publication in English, this authentic, seemingly unembellished life story provides knowledge of the differences as well as the similarities that are part of the Indian perspective.

The efforts of the Centro de Estudios Regionales Andinos "Bartolomé de las Casas" (Bartolomé de las Casas Center of Andean Regional Studies) has provided a small but worthy collection of the Biblioteca de Tradición Oral Andina (Library of the Andean Oral Tradition), which is the source of publication for Condori Mamani's autobiography. Other works in the series feature similar bilingual editions of myths and short stories, with illustrative analyses of the contents. The efforts of Editorial Abya Yala in Quito have lead to the republication of many indigenous source materials, as well as contemporary collections of literary, political, and anthropological findings. In Bolivia, Silvia Rivera Cusicanqui's organization of the Taller de Historia Oral Andina (Workshop of Andean Oral History) has provided multiple texts that can serve as literary, historical, and sociological sources. A professor at the University of San Andrés, Rivera has inspired her students and shared her knowledge of the oral tradition in Aymará culture, as seen in *Pachakuti* (1991) and *La mujer andina en la historia* [1990, Women of the Andes in History].

Access to higher education and, in turn, access to the political process has enabled increased intellectual participation by the Indians in Andean society. With active organization at the local, national, and international levels, Indians are determining their fate, whether it be in decisions regarding environmental preservation, the price of admission for tourists to enter their villages, election of government officials, the extent of bilingual education, or funding for their own cultural preservation. Luis Macas, the elected leader of Ecuador's indigenous federation, has commented extensively on the activism of Indians in national politics, and Ariruma Kowii has lyrically described events of local and international scope. Now equipped with Rolodex files and fax machines as well as computers, indigenous communities publish texts for use in their schools in collaboration with the Ministry of Education and are the authors of monographs on agricultural practices as well as poetry. As authors and activists, Indians seek cultural and political representation that avoids the assimilationist models of yesteryear and instead offers a modern solution of "integration" that does not compromise their rich heritage and native identity.

Works Cited

Alegría, Ciro. 1941. *El mundo es ancho y ajeno*. Santiago: Ercilla.

Amunátegui, Miguel Luis and Gregorio Victor. 1861. *Juicio crítico sobre algunos poetas hispano-americanos*. Santiago: Ferrocarril.

Anchorena, José Dionisio. 1874. *Gramática quechua o del idioma del Imperio de los Incas*. Lima: Imprenta del Estado.

Arguedas, Alcides. 1919. *Raza de bronce. Wata-Wara*. La Paz: González y Medina.

Arguedas, José María. 1938. *Canto kechwa con un ensayo sobre la capacidad de creación artística del pueblo indio y mestizo*. Lima: Bustamante y Ballivián.

——. 1955. *Apu Inca Atahuallpaman*. Collected by J. M. B. Farfán. Trans J. M. Arguedas. Lima: Mejía Baca.

——. 1955. "Himnos quechuas católicos cuzqueños." *Folklore americano* 3.3: 121–232.

——. 1957. "Canciones quechuas." *Américas* 9.9: 30–34.

——. 1958. *Los ríos profundos*. Buenos Aires: Losada.

Basadre, Jorge. 1938. *Literatura inca. Biblioteca de cultura peruana*. Paris: De Breuwer.

Beltrán, Carlos Felipe. 1888. *Civilización del indio: Ramillete hispano-quichua original con multitud de poesías originales y antiguas mejoradas*. Oruro: Progreso.

———. 1889. *Civilización del indio: Antología sagrada en español, quichua, y aymara*. Oruro: Progreso.

Bendezú Aybar, Edmundo, ed. 1980. *Literatura quechua*. Caracas: Biblioteca Ayacucho, Arte.

Carrillo, Francisco. 1967. *Clorinda Matto de Turner y su indigenismo literario*. Lima: Biblioteca Universitaria.

Condori Mamani, Gregorio. 1977. *Gregorio Condori Mamani: autobiografía*. Biblioteca de la tradición oral andina. 2d ed. Trans. Ricardo Valderrama Fernández and Carmen Escalante Gutiérrez. Cusco: Centro de Estudios Rurales Bartolomé de las Casas.

———. 1996. *Andean Lives: Gregorio Condori Mamani and Asunta Quispe Huaman*. Eds. Ricardo Valderrama Fernández and Carmen Escalante Gutiérrez. Trans. Paul H. Gelles and Gabriela Martínez Escobar. Austin: University of Texas Press.

Confessionario para los curas de Indios. 1985 [1585]. *Corpus Hispanorum de Pace* 26-2. Madrid: Consejo Superior de Investigaciones Científicas.

Covarrubias Orozco, Sebastién. 1943 [1611]. *Tesoro de la lengua castellana, o española*. Barcelona: Horta.

Doctrina christiana y catecismo . . . 1985 [1584]. *Corpus Hispanorum de Pace* 26-2. Madrid: Consejo Superior de Investigaciones Científicas.

Farfán, José María Benigno. 1942. "Poesía folklórica quechua." *Revista del Instituto de Antropología de la Universidad Nacional de Tucumán* 2.12: 525–68.

Garcilaso de la Vega, El Inca. 1609. *Primera parte de los Comentarios reales*. Lisbon: Crasbeeck.

Guamán Poma de Ayala, Felipe. 1968 [1615]. *Nueva corónica y buen gobierno (Codex péruvien ilustré)*. Traveaux et Mémoires de L'Institut d'Ethnologie. Vol. 23. Paris: L'Institut d'Ethnologie.

———. 1980. *El primer nueva corónica y buen gobierno*. Eds. John V. Murra and Rolena Adorno. Trans. from Quechua by Jorge L. Urioste. 3 vols. Mexico City: Siglo XXI.

———. 1980. *Nueva corónica y buen gobierno*. Ed. Franklin Pease. 2 vols. Caracas: Biblioteca Ayacucho.

The Huarochirí Manuscript: A Testament of Ancient and Colonial Andean Religion. 1991 [1613]. Ed. Frank Salomon. Trans. George L. Urioste. Austin: University of Texas Press.

———. 1966 [1613]. *Dioses y hombres de Huarochirí*. Ed. Pierre Duviols. Trans. José María Arguedas. Mexico City: Siglo XXI.

Icaza, Jorge. 1934. *Huasipungo*. Quito: Talleres Nacionales.

Kowii, Ariruma. 1988. *Mutsuctsurini*. Quito: Corporación Editorial Nacional.

———. 1993. *Tsaitsik: poemas para construir el futuro*. Ibarra: Ediciones Culturales de Ibarra.

Lara, Jesús. 1959. *Yarwarninchij*. Buenos Aires: Platina.

———. 1969. *La literatura de los Quechuas: Ensayo y antología*. La Paz: Juventud.

Lira, Jorge A. 1944. *Diccionario kkechwua-español*. Tucumán: Universidad Nacional de Tucumán, Instituto de Historia, Lingüística y Folklore.

———. 1956. *Canto de amor*. Lima: Villanueva.

Macas, Luis. 1991. *El levantamiento indígena visto por sus protagonistas*. Quito: Instituto Científico de Culturas Indígenas.

Mariáteguí, José Carlos. 1943 [1928]. *Siete ensayos de interpretación de la realidad peruana*. Lima: Amauta.

Mannheim, Bruce. 1991. *The Language of the Inca since the European Invasion*. Austin: University of Texas Press.

Matto de Turner, Clorinda. 1884. *Elementos de literatura*. Arequipa: "La Bolsa".

———. 1889. *Aves sin nido*. Valencia: F. Sempere y Cía.

Mera, Juan León. 1868. *Ojeada histórico crítica de la poesía ecuatoriana*. Quito: Sanz

———. 1892. *Antología ecuatoriana: Cantares del pueblo ecuatoriano*. Quito: Universitá Central.

Montoya, Rodrigo, Luis Montoya and Edwin Montoya. 1987. *La sangre de los cerros/Urqukunapa Yawarnin: Antología de la poesía quechua que se canta en el Perú*. Lima: Centro Peruano de Estudios Sociales/Mosca Azul/Universidad Mayor San Marcos.

Ollanta. [1938] [Justiani version]. *Tragicomedia del Apu Ollantay y Cusi Coyllur: Rigores de un padre y generosidad de un Rey*. Ed. Hyppolitus Galante. Lima: Universidad Mayor San Marcos.

———. [1938] [Sahuaraura version]. *Comedia trágica que intitula los Rigores de un Padre generosidad de un Rey*. Ed. Hippolitus Galante. Lima: Universidad Mayor San Marcos.

Olmedo, José Joaquín. 1960 [1825]. "La victoria de Junín. Canto a Bolívar." *José Joaquín Olmedo: Poesía, prosa. Biblioteca Ecuatoriana Mínima*. Ed. Aureliano Espinosa Pólit. Puebla: Cajica. 101–36.

Pachacuti Yamqui Salcamagua, Joan de Santa Cruz. 1879 [1613]. *Relación de Antiguedades deste Reyno del Pirú, in Tres relaciónes de Antiguedades Peruanas*. Ed. Marcos Jiménez de Espada. Madrid: Tello.

———. 1993 [1613]. *Relación de Antiguedades deste Reyno del Pirú*. Ed. Pierre Duviols and César Itier. Cusco: Institut Français D'Etudes Andines/Centro de Estudios Regionales Andinos Bartolomé de Las Casas.

Pérez, Galo René. 1972. *Pensamiento y literatura en el Ecuador (crítica y antología)*. Quito: Casa Cultura Ecuatoriana.

Razzeto, Mario, ed. 1972. *Poesía quechua. Colección Literatura Latinoamericana Casa de las Américas*. Havana: Casa de las Américas.

Rivera Cusicanqui, Silvia. 1990. *La mujer andina en la historia*. Chukiyawu: Taller de Historia Oral Andina.

———. 1991. *Pachakuti: los aymara de Bolivia frente a medio milenio de colonialismo*. Chukiyawu: Taller de Historia Oral Andina.

Rivet, Paul, and Georges de Crequi-Monfort. 1951–1956. *Bibliographie des langues aymará et kic[h]ua*. 4 vols. Travaux et mémoires de l'Institut d'Ethnologie. Paris: Institut d'Ethnologie.

Tercero cathecismo y exposicion de la Doctrina christiana, por sermones. 1985 [1585]. *Corpus Hispanorum de Pace*, 26-2. Madrid: Consejo Superior de Investigaciones Científicas.

Titu Cusi Yupanqui, Diego de Castro. 1973 [1570]. *Relación de la conquista del Perú*. Lima: Biblioteca Universitaria.

Tschudi, Johann Jacob von. n.d. [1876]. "Ollanta: Ein alterperuanisches Drama aus der Kechuasprache." *Denkschriften der Kaiserlichen Akademie der Wissenschaften, Philosophisch-Historich Classe* 24: 167–384.

Vienrich, Adolfo. 1959 [1905]. *Azucenas quechuas*. Lima: Minerva.

———. 1961 [1906]. *Fábulas quechuas*. Lima: Lux.

CHAPTER 26

BRAZIL'S INDIGENOUS
TEXTUALITIES

Cláudia Neiva de Matos

Upon disembarking in Brazil that first tropical autumn, the first thing the velvet- and armor-clad Portuguese noticed about the dwellers of Brazil's jungles and beaches was precisely the most *evident* of all: the Indians were naked. They were *nudi e formisi* beings (as Amerigo Vespucci wrote): beautiful, healthy people, at home in the exuberant natural landscape, in the vegetation and topography that the colonial chroniclers did not tire of describing and lauding. For the European writers who then regarded the subequatorial man of the New World sympathetically, the virtue and value of being "savage" resided in the remote and yet close ties between the human and the natural: naked people, open in body and spirit, an immaculate *tabula rasa* offered to inscription in Western history. A totally visual spectacle, captured by the gaze more than the ear, the Brazilian Indian was presented from the beginning as a mute figure. In spite of the great interest aroused by their so-called gentility and the research and pedagogical efforts of the Jesuits and other pioneers in the autochthonous languages, the Europeans did not appear interested in what the Indian might have to *say.*

Most of the information we have about the Indian in the first centuries of colonization emerges from the writings of chroniclers, travelers, and missionaries. The language barrier at first justifies, but does not fully explain, the rather aphasic state that characterizes the image of the Indian in this history, which registers habits, objects, material culture, attitudes, adornments, and features in the face and the body but does not register the indigenous *text*: its speech, its authenticated word, and its proper name. In fact the text (or verbal discourse) is not the only significant expressive element in human voice. The Indians depicted by the colonial narratives do not conform to an image of total silence and immobility. They dance, make music, and sing. Most of the information produced in the period speaks of these singing and dancing manifestations, at times describing them in minute detail and foregrounding first, material elements (clothing, ornaments, and instruments), then music, and last, the vocal part (the singing).

The reception of indigenous vocalizations by the colonial chroniclers appears hesitant and contradictory. Many educated ears reacted with scandal to what seemed to them a series of "cries" and "screams." The chroniclers also related an absence of melody, and went so far as not to recognize any kind of singing there or to perceive in it a singing without words. But there were also those who saw in the New World a land of "great singers." This is the case with Michel de Montaigne (1533–1592). Disillusioned with "civilization" in a France torn apart by civil wars, the essayist in his famous "Cannibals" celebrates the "barbarian" poetry of American Indians and offers two examples: a war song (the speech of a prisoner bound for the anthropophagic ritual) and a love song. About these he comments: "Now I have conversed enough with poetry to judge this much: not only that there is nothing of the barbarous in this invention, but, moreover, that

it is perfectly anacreontic. To which may be added, that their language is soft, of a pleasing accent, with something bordering upon the Greek terminations" (Montaigne 101).

In fact the texts presented by Montaigne are far from corresponding, with any verisimilitude, to an indigenous discourse. The author does not cite his source, but it has been established that it derives from stylized versions of two texts published in *Voyage to the Land of Brazil* by Jean de Léry (1534–1611), a Calvinist who came to Brazil in the mid sixteenth century with the French Antarctic mission.

Several travelers' chronicles in the sixteenth and seventeenth centuries, such as Gabriel Soares de Sousa's (c.1540–c.1591) *Tratado Descritivo do Brazil* [1587; Descriptive Study of Brazil], refer to the Indians' musical and poetic vein, particularly that of the Tupí group, dwellers of the territories first reached by the white man. However, no document of the indigenous textualities was produced by these travelers, except for rare instances little worthy of ethnological faith, as in the case of Jean de Léry. The missionaries of the Society of Jesus, who devoted themselves to the study of the autochthonous languages, made use of them only to open the way for the evangelization of the Indians. Grammars, glossaries, and descriptions produced at the time are silent about actual indigenous textualities.

Romantic Indigenism

In the eighteenth century there seems to have occurred a decline in interest in Indians, at least outside the religious field. Information was more scarce, and references to the singing became more negative. The gaze of critical antipathy continues into the early nineteenth century. In 1803 Ribeiro de Sampaio reported a funereal oration lauding a dead man that was carried out in an "out of tune" chant, to which "attendants responded with the same lack of tone" (Sampaio, qtd. in Cameo 34). Unintelligibility, in short, continued to characterize the reception by the Europeans. The Botocudos' singing sounded "deprived of modulation" to Prince Maximilian of Wied Neuwied, who remarked: "it is known that several words that refer to war or hunting figure in this singing, but everything seemed a simple voicing without words to me" (Neuwied, qtd. in Cameo 35). About the Juri, Spix and Martius wrote: "The singing sounded now not only like snoring by the men, but the sopranos also neighed the melody and joined the abominable screaming" (Spix and Martius, qtd. in Cameo 38).

However, at that time the ongoing Independence movement drew ideological and aesthetic support from the emergent Romantic literature. Besides attributing to native characters combative, moral, and affective virtues, this writing also attributed to them the gift of the poetic word. The first Brazilian Romantic poet, Domingos José Gonçalves de Magalhães (1811–1882), picked up on suggestions from the old sixteenth-century chronicles to respond to the question posed in the thick of the discussion over national literary

231

identity: Were Brazilian Indians really poets? Magalhães answered categorically: "they were, and they still are." He complained that the missionaries did not "take the time to collect, or translate into Portuguese, the Indians' chants" (Magalhães, qtd. in Coutinho 24–25).

To the literary idea of the deeply poetic nature of the indigenous soul and language corresponds, however, an absence of documents illustrative of this nature. The field was thus open for the process of idealization to begin and, since then, a presumed, supposedly "primitive poetry" has not ceased to fascinate European poets and thinkers. In Brazil the great moment of the Indian as object of literature was Romanticism. In Romantic Indigenism, Brazilian artistic creation, particularly literature, associated the indigenous element with a poetic vision and expression of the world by assigning to the autochthonous a fundamental role in the construction of an attractive national self-image. Brazilian Romantics, critics (Joaquim Norberto de Souza e Silva, 1820–1891) as well as poets (Antonio Gonçalves Dias, 1823–1864) and novelists (José de Alencar, 1829–1877), elaborated the mythical theme of the indigenous peoples' poetic sensibility creating heroes that also shine in their singing words, capable of perceiving and expressing deep harmonies between the human soul and the virgin mother Nature. The young nation's writers thus forged a noble view that assimilated the grandiosity and beauty of the indigenous culture to the classics of antiquity and now also to the medieval bards. Despite attempts and projects by several poets, no great epic on indigenous themes was ever written. The indigenist imaginary manifested itself initially–from *Caramuru* and *Uraguai* in the eighteenth century to Gonçalves de Magalhães's *Confederação dos Tamoios* [1855, Confederation of the Tamoio]– in epic form, but it was really in the fields of the lyric, of poetry, of dramatic tension, and of novels of individual dramas that it produced its best fruit. The reason for the Indians' exclusion from the present and future history has much to do with the extreme literariness of their presentation in romanticism. The Indian is represented there as a being who is bound to disappear. With exceptions (such as *Ubirajara* and "Canção do Tamoio" ["Song of Tamoio"]), novels and poems figured or prefigured the extinction of the indigenous people; see, for instance, José de Alencar's *O Guarani* (1857) and *Iracema* (1865) and Gonçalves Dias's "Y-Juca-Pirama" (1851) and "Marabá" (1851). These are stories of exiles, pariahs, and expatriates who embody what Alfredo Bosi called the sacrificial myth of the Indian in romantic literature (176–93).

Ethnography and Literature

Since the nineteenth century and with great expansion in the twentieth, ethnographers, historians, and scholars of the backland, folklorists, anthropologists, and other social scientists have recorded indigenous narratives and analyzed them with the instruments of evolutionist genealogies, structural anthropology, linguistics, and history of religion. Among the researchers who initiated the process of shaping and systematizing this repertoire, the contributions of certain individuals deserve to be highlighted, such as those of Couto de Magalhães (*O Selvagem* [1876; The Savage]); Carlos Frederico Hartt (*Contribuições para a Etnologia do Vale do Amazonas* [1885; Contributions to the Ethnology of the Amazon Valley]); Barbosa Rodrigues (*Poranduba Amazonense* [1890; History of the Amazons]); and Capistrano de Abreu (*Rã-txa- Hu-ni-ku-i: Gramática, Textos e Vocabulário Caxinauás* [1914; Rã-txa- Hu-ni-ku-i: Cáxinauá Grammar, Texts, and Vocabulary]). More

documentation was compiled and analyzed in the twentieth century by scholars of the backland such as Field Marshal Cândido Rondon, the brothers Orlando and Cláudio Villas-Boas, and a number of contemporary ethnographers such as Claude Lévi-Strauss, Darcy Ribeiro, Berta Ribeiro, Carmem Junqueira, and Lux Vidal, among others. Notably, anthropologists have taken an interest in the vast field of mythology, utilized as a main reference point to attempt to understand the thought and language designated as "savage." A great number of documents on narratives, legends, and ancient stories has emerged as a result of that interest. These documents are generally informed by an ethnographic perspective, with few literary reflections.

If the narrative repertoire has turned out to be enriched, silence still reigns on the chants, which, of course, do lend themselves to an overtly aesthetic approach, given their more formalized textual character. However, mythological information constituted and offered to the public in this fashion led to several stylized thematizations in mainstream, erudite, written literature. Elements of indigenous legends related by ethnographers are found in numerous works of Brazilian modernism, which after romanticism is the second strongest moment of literary nationalism in the country. (The word "modernism" does not designate late nineteenth-century avant-garde poetry, as in Spanish America, but rather a Brazilian nationalist movement that emerged between the 1920s and 1950s.) Harkening back to their romantic predecessors, modernists proceeded to recreate, critically and parodically, literary emblems of the national tradition. This does not, however, imply a complete absence of that idealized image of indigenous poeticity in their works. Let us take as examples Mário de Andrade's (1893–1945) novel *Macunaíma* (1928) and the narrative poems *Martim Cererê* (1928) by Cassiano Ricardo (1895–1974) and *Cobra Norato* (1931) by Raul Bopp (1898–1984). In post-modern terms it is important to mention the novels *Quarup* (1967) by Antonio Callado (1917–1997) and *Maíra* (1977) by anthropologist Darcy Ribeiro (1922–1997).

The lens through which a reading of the Brazilian Indian has been presented to us is, as a rule, defective, giving us representations that are out of focus and full of lacunae. They promote, either by literary stylization or by their treatment of historical documentation, a double exclusion. The procedures of inscription and the modalities of ethnographic reading to which indigenous narrative prose was submitted usually ignored or blurred its aesthetic aspects and potential. The poetic or literary function of the oral tradition narratives, the indigenous ones among them, is not usually taken into account by researchers, who tend toward factual structural operations, applied first and foremost to the morphology of plot. As for the Indians' poetry, it has remained almost unknown to us; little more than hypotheses have been formulated about it. These hesitant, rough sketches have impoverished and stereotyped their object of study to the point of preventing any acute aesthetic grasp of this object. An investment in unity, simplification, and superficial exteriority has replaced research into the rich diversity of these cultures' poetry and has impeded the study of its complexity and its aesthetic and subjective dimensions. This simplifying vision, often dissimulated in processes of idealization, has been strongly denounced by Antonio Risério: "to insist on the existence of a 'primitive poetry' is to cultivate an ethnocentric superstition" (33).

Map 1.

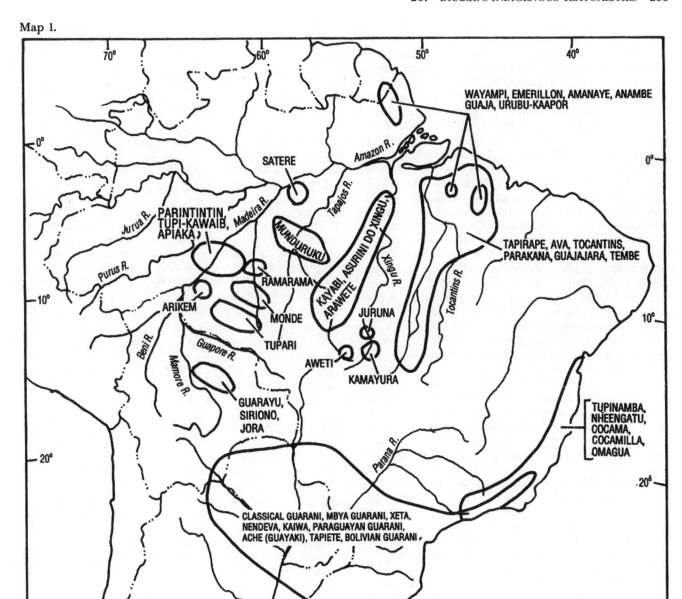

Certain circumstances and historical conditions turn what one could consider Brazilian indigenous literature (or the fraction thereof to which we have access) into something rather distinct from its counterparts in the rest of the Americas. The tropical indigenous populations, the peoples of the Brazilian jungle, were and are among the most "basic" in the American continent. That has certainly contributed to the fact that they have been more frequently imagined and represented by the West in terms of "images of paradise." A paradoxical situation was then created: On the one hand, Brazil is home to one of the literatures in which the indigenous motif is strongest, because it was most insistently cultivated in order to establish a noble image of nationality; on the other hand, this aestheticizing care was not reciprocated in the domain of research, and the verbal art of Brazilian Indians remained more unknown than those of the other autochthonous ethnicities of the New World (see **Map 1**). When the Spaniards arrived in Mesoamerica, Aztecs and Mayas already practiced highly developed forms of writing. In spite of the destruction carried out by the colonizers, numerous texts of various genres survived for posterity. Besides this legacy, the persistence of oral tradition contributed to keeping the Maya and Aztec literary cultures alive. The Andean civilizations, particularly the Inca empire, had their repertoires better registered than did their Brazilian counterparts. In North America as well, the work of compilation, including compilation of songs, was more efficacious. North American ethnopoetics also benefited from the presence of people of Indian ancestry in specialized journalism and in the university, constituting so-called "Native Studies." In Canada we have witnessed for some time now a considerable flourishing in the written and printed production of novels and poetry on the part of Indians and their descendants.

Brazil's large territorial extension incorporates a great multiplicity of indigenous groups, some of which still have virtually no contact with mainstream culture. Although a great portion of the autochthonous population has been decimated, as in other American regions, many of them remained as subjects of a living culture, and not as objects of archaeological research: Among the 1,300 languages supposedly existing in the territory at the moment of the Portuguese arrival in 1500, around 170 are still spoken. Only about half of those have been seriously researched and described by ethnologists and linguists (Ricardo 30). There is, therefore, an urgent need for research and recording still to be done so that we can have a more complete knowledge of these peoples' literature. In the universe of indigenous verbal communication as a whole, as we have seen, two great series of discursive practices can be said to constitute a literary patrimony with both social and aesthetic effects: narratives and chants, which together comprise most of their verbal art in verse and prose. Almost the totality of this patrimony came from the oral tradition. The production of written literature by individual authors is still quite exceptional. The body of published documents—such as songbooks—is small as well. We will now give a brief overview of this repertoire.

What textualities should be part of a corpus of Brazilian indigenous literature? In attempting to circumscribe it, we should keep in mind that any we choose will be a provisional configuration, subject to reconsideration according to the advances of a still incipient knowledge. The criteria with which to identify the relevant kinds of production are necessarily unstable, for in fact we still lack a firm concept of what indigenous poetic expression might be. And such a concept, were it possible to construct it, would not necessarily correspond, in any immediate fashion, to a corpus: It would rather be an ample formal and semantic system, related to a worldview that is complex and different from ours.

There is, therefore, a discursive and textual field to be explored. This field is constituted by two sets of radically uneven phenomena, constructed under different circumstances and criteria. On the one hand, there is an endless group of texts produced by nonliterate cultures without graphic notation, and these are either in narrative prose or in rhythmic verse. They are created and consumed by audio-oral means, for only small portions have been disseminated through writing (and a considerable part of those have been translated only into foreign languages, and published outside Brazil). On the other hand, there are texts authorized by first-hand writing—that is, prose and verse produced by literate indigenous individuals. We have noted above how this repertoire is still in an early stage in its constitution. Predominant here are texts produced in special situations, at times combining new circumstances of acquisition of a second language (Portuguese) with the acquisition of written expression. The basic point of reference for this group is the production carried out within the framework of programs of indigenous education connected with religious institutions, the state, and nongovernmental organizations that have substantially broadened the access by Brazilian Indians to written culture and to technical means of expression.

Indigenous Narrative

In his *Literatura oral no Brasil* [Oral Literature in Brazil], Câmara Cascudo opens the chapter dedicated to indigenous literature by evoking a scene reported by most of the rubber gatherers and cutters, travelers, and small tradesmen who have visited indigenous villages in the north and midwest of Brazil:

> Depois do jantar, noite cerrada, no pátio que uma fogueira ilumina e aquece, reúnem-se os velhos indígenas, os estrangeiros, para fumar e conversar até que o sono venha. Evocações de caçadas felizes, de pescarias abundantes, aparelhos esquecidos para prender animais de vulto, figuras de chefes mortos, lembrança de costumes passados, casos que fazem rir, mistérios da mata, assombros, explicações que ainda mais escurecem o sugestivo apelo da imaginação, todos os assuntos vão passando, examinados e lentos, no ambiente tranqüilo. (1984, 78)

> After dinner, on a dark night, in a patio warmed and lit by a bonfire, old Indians and foreigners gather to smoke and talk until sleep comes. All kind of subjects succeed each other, slowly and well-examined in that peaceful atmosphere: remembrances of fortunate hunts, apparatuses to capture bulky animals, images of dead leaders, memories of past habits, humorous stories, mysteries of the jungle, astonishing experiences, and explanations that blur even further the suggestive appeal of the imagination.

Much as in other cultures, Brazil's indigenous oral cultures are remarkably extensive and have rich and detailed narrative repertoires stored in memory and passed down from generation to generation: "O indígena conta, horas e horas. Conta, dias e dias, ou melhor, noites e noites, um milhar de estórias de guerra, caça, pesca, origem de várias coisas, o amanhecer de sua família no mundo. Todas as coisas . . . têm uma História religiosa, hierárquica, e uma literatura folclórica adjacente" ("Indians recite, for hours and hours. In fact, for days and nights, thousands of stories about war, hunting, fishing, the origin of several things, and the dawning of their families into the world. All things have a religious, hierarchical history, and an adjacent folkloric literature") (Cascudo 1984, 87). Narratives fulfill the purpose of sharing the community's wisdom and constituting the reserve and vehicle for knowledge and cultural tradition. The agents and circumstances for the transmission of this wisdom are not exactly the same in all cultures and registers, but some recurring frames of reference appear in the testimonies and research documents. For example, the task and prerogative of narrating belong first and foremost to the elderly. In different domains and conditions, mothers are important narrators as well.

The distinction among the forms of the oral tradition—myths, legends, and fables—is a question often tackled in the study of this repertoire, and it certainly consumed folklorists particularly in the first half of the twentieth century. The most complex to define is myth, a sort of "constante en movimento" 'constant in movement' (Cascudo 1984, 105) that does not exhaust itself in a textual characterization and is capable of informing imaginary representations and textualities in several formats. Legends are long, serious narratives that often treat the origin and explanation of things that populate the land, the water, and the sky, as well as of the indigenous nations and their habits; they integrate heroic elements and religious features in an atmosphere full of supernatural elements and explanations. We are told, for example, how yucca, corn, the *guaraná* fruit, and cosmic elements and phenomena appeared or were created. An animist explanation of the world is enacted here, according to which most things and human groups originated in the action of semi-divine animals in relation to human beings. This is the case, for example, in the Boa mythology, the central axis of the culture, narratives, chants, and handicraft of the Kaxinawá. Fables or stories have a shorter format and animal characters, and they thematize practical and moral aspects of everyday life. They constitute, according to Câmara Cascudo, a democratic and popular expression (1984, 88) of a frequently critical or pedagogical meaning:

> Nas fábulas pode intervir o sobrenatural, mas esse não é o elemento típico. Nas lendas é a própria atmosfera. E é preciso crer porque elas se articulam com o patrimônio da tribo que nos hospeda. Quando a fábula denuncia sua versatilidade pela etimologia, lembrando a conversa, a palavra, o entreter das horas, com humor ou tristeza nos contos evocados, a lenda, *legenda*, traz a idéia da leitura, do gráfico, a imobilidade que se reveste de um ligeiro ritual, determinando a meia certeza da credulidade. (1984, 98–99)
>
> The supernatural may intervene in fables, but it is not the typical element. In legends it is the atmosphere itself. It is necessary to believe in them because they are articulated as the patrimony of the tribe. Whereas the fable betrays its versatility through etymology, by recalling the conversation, the word, the passing of the hours with humor or sadness in the stories being evoked, the legend, *legenda*, brings to mind the idea of reading, of graphics, of the immobility that quickly becomes a ritual that determines the half certainty of incredulity.

Sometimes this effort to classify reveals commonalities between the indigenous narrative system and the ancient yet classical Western cultures, particularly the Greek. Homer's epic and Aesop's fables are constantly alluded to in this kind of comparison, and some resemblances are in fact quite clear. As for the long epic, associated with the myths of origin and the formation of social structures, the slow unfolding of the narrative, with room for digressions and details, the theme of the voyage, and the marvelous are the points of analogy. Narratives can stretch themselves out indefinitely but can also be interrupted abruptly. There are several clear resemblances to the classic epic, but one does not usually find in indigenous narratives that tone of warlike homage that echoes in the Homeric chants. Instead, the passing of time, small details, and sometimes rather crude situations are narrated. As for the fable, indigenous and ancient narratives (Aesop in particular) have in common the importance and human signification of the animal characters, as well as their critical, moral, and pedagogical purposes.

The central figures of the mythic and narrative repertoire vary from nation to nation, but some of them stand out, such as the Brazilian land turtle (*jabuti*), a protagonist in the fables of the Tupí Amazon that tells a great cycle of stories, much like the monkey, the wildcat (*onça*), and some other zoomorphic protagonists. Animals also serve the purpose of structuring and mythologically justifying the division among clans. Among the fantastic entities whose variants circulate in the cultures of different Brazilian indigenous nations, Curupira stands out. Curupira is a small Indian with his feet turned backwards, a spirit who watches over the forest and whose benevolence is sought through gifts and offerings. He is able to make hunters get lost in the jungle, but also to come to their rescue. In some regions he is conflated with Caipora, who became a rather popular dwarf in traditional northeastern narratives. But Caipora also appears as a huge, dark, taciturn man, of hairy face and body, riding an enormous wild pig. Another popular creature is Boitatá, a fire serpent who lives by the water and who was described by José de Anchieta (1534–1597) in 1560 as "coisa de fogo, [. . .]

o que é todo fogo, [. . .] um facho cintilante correndo daqui para ali" 'a thing of fire . . . made of nothing but fire . . . a scintillating flash running to-and-fro' (*Cartas, Informações, Fragmentos Históricos* [Letters, Data and Historical Fragments] qtd. in Cascudo 1972, 153).

Jurupari, presented by missionaries and colonial chroniclers as a supreme spirit of evil, played the role of demon in the discourse of the Christian catechism. However, this interpretation goes against the Manichaean Christian perspective of the Indians and was to be corrected later, by nineteenth-century ethnographers such as Stradelli, who characterized him as "a legislator-turned-divine, found at the core of all religions and primitive myths" (Ermano Stradelli, "Leggenda dell'Jurupary" ["Legend of the Jurupary"] qtd. in Cascudo 1984, 126). Sent by the sun to reform the habits of those on earth, Jurupari subverted the primitive matriarchy by transferring power to men and teaching them secrets that would be handed down to young males on the occasion of puberty initiation rites. In its incorporation of autochthonous motifs, Indigenist romantic literature notably privileged the mythic and heroic aspects of the legends of origin. The best example is José de Alencar's *Iracema* (1865), subtitled "legend of the state of Ceará." As for oral literature in Portuguese, it was more informed by genres associated with the fables, myths, and figures of the present everyday life. These modalities influenced Brazilian folklore considerably by circulating the tales in Portuguese or, until the eighteenth century, in the Tupi/Nheengatu "lingua franca" and mixing them with elements of oral narratives from Africa and Portugal.

Be that as it may, when it comes to myths of origins (ancient stories, or stories of ancestors, as the Indians call them in Portuguese) or anecdotal passages about everyday life in the forest, indigenous narrative appears as a changing text, quite hard to capture with traditional literary instruments. Usually uttered with the accompaniment of ample gesturing and dramatic resources, it demands of any analyses a poetic perspective centered on oral transmission in the presence of the body, that is to say, the narrator's performance and the reception thereof by listeners. Most of the narrative recordings made by folklorists and ethnographers are insufficient for the purposes of literary history and criticism, because they are limited to the main aspects of the plot or the configuration of myths and fail to capture the peculiarities of the indigenous narrative style. One of the first examples of more complete documentation was that carried out in the early twentieth century by historian Capistrano de Abreu, who composed his *Rã-txa- Hu-ni-ku-i* on the basis of long interviews with two young Kaxinawá.

Little by little, the methods for documenting stories have improved so that transcriptions are now closer to the original texts. Similarly to what happened in the field of oral literary manifestations as a whole, a great advance was possible with the invention and dissemination of means of registering and recording sound and image. More recently, recordings have been made in such a way that the informants' autonomy and responsibility are greater, making them more like authors and auto-ethnographers. As a result of this, some aesthetic aspects of indigenous narrative discourses have begun to become more visible to us, their distant readers. In many contemporary recordings, one witnesses the weakening–although not the disappearance–of the mediation of the ethnographer: Recordings of traditional narrators (usually the elders of the village) and their later transcription onto paper, always in their mother tongue, are generally done by other Indians; there are now texts done directly in written form, by literate Indians, in their mother tongues; there are also integral, partial, or abridged translations of texts from the original language, carried out by bilingual Indians; and we find narratives written directly in Portuguese either by bilingual Indians or even by people who have lost the use of their ancestral language but preserve part of the tradition's cultural reservoir. Examples of this repertoire are to be found in publications such as *Antes o Mundo Não Existia: A Mitologia Heróica dos Indios Desaña* [Before the World Existed: A Heroic Mythology of the Desaña Indians] by Umúsin Panlõn Kumu and Tolamãn Kenhíri, with an introduction by Berta Ribeiro. Ribeiro writes in that introduction: "In the history of Brazilian anthropology, this is the first time that indigenous people write and sign their tales of mythology.... First of all, this endows the content and form of this narrative uncontested authenticity as an expression of faith and literary construction. Second, it documents the result of the symbiosis between cultural preservationism and the use of the instrument acquired from our civilization to express it: written language" (in Kumu and Kenhíri 90). Other examples are *Torü Duü'ügü, Nosso Povo* [1985; Torü Duü'ügü, Our People], a bilingual edition of oral stories by two Ticunas; *Mantere Ma Kwé Tinhin: Histórias de Maloca Antigamente* [1988; Mantere Ma Kwé: Stories from Ancient Maloca] by Pichuvy Cinta Larga; *Histórias do Xingu: Coletâneas dos Indios Suyá, Kayaabi, Juruna, Trumai, Txucarramãe e Txicão* [1994; Stories of Xingu: Collected Items from the Suyá, Kayaabi, Juruna, Trumai, Txucarramãe and Txicão Indians], edited by Mariana K. Leal Ferreira; *Shenipabu Miyui* [1995; Stories of the Ancients], a bilingual compilation by Kaxinawá narrators, writers, and illustrators; *Vozes da Origem: Estórias sem Escrita* [1996; Voices from the Origin: Stories without Writing], a compilation of narratives by the Suruí from the state of Rondônia, edited by Betty Mindlin; and *Histórias de Ontem e de Hoje/Itxua dji aie i dji jodla* [1997; Stories from Yesterday and Today], stories by the Karipuna and Galibi-Marworno peoples, edited by Rebeca Spires. Many of the publications that make room for "authorship" (i.e., for the indigenous textual manifestation produced firsthand) are associated with programs of alternative education developed in the country through initiatives of the state, of religious institutions (such as the Missionary Indigenist Council), and above all of lay nongovernmental organizations. *Shenipabu Miyui*, for example, was done by Kaxinawá bilingual teachers within the framework of the labor carried out by the Pro-Indian Commission from the state of Acre. (This teacher training program is responsible for the production of a great number of didactic publications made by the indigenous teachers themselves and is aptly titled "an experience of authorship.")

The aforementioned instances, like many others, are narratives that originated in the oral tradition. In today's publishing world, however, one can already point out the incipient constitution of a literature written in Portuguese (and in certain cases also in the mother tongue) by Indians, often with recent access to literacy, who exercise their authorship individually or in group by creating contemporary written texts. A great part of this still small corpus is composed of the publication, in the form of didactic materials for specialized programs, of texts produced by Indians without an explicitly "literary" purpose, but in which a worldview and a poetically impressive discoursive arrangement manifest themselves. Examples are the texts

in the *Estórias de Hoje e de Antigamente dos Indios do Acre* [1984; Stories of Today and of Ancient Times of the Indians of Acre], edited by Nietta L. Monte; *Geografia Indígena* [1992; Indigenous Geography], edited by Marcia S. Rezende and Renato A. Gavazzi; and the first part of *Antologia da Floresta: Literatura Ilustrada e Selecionada pelos Professores Indígenas do Acre* [1997; Anthology of the Forest: Illustrated and Selected Literature by the Indigenous Professors of Acre], edited by Cláudia Neiva de Matos, all of them elaborated with the participation of indigenous teachers from several nations and published under the auspices of the Pro-Indian Commission of the State of Acre.

The Poetry of Indigenous Chants

The multisensorial nature of poetic manifestations in oral cultures, where words are strictly bound to voice, gesture, mise en scène—in a word, to the *body*—has been foregrounded by many specialists, among them Paul Zumthor. It is commonplace among oral literature scholars to lament and make excuses for not being able to present to the reader—and sometimes to themselves—the fullness of *meaning* of a text whose production relies so heavily on *performance*. In the written documentation, several aspects of the original event are lost, notably in the cases where expression in verbal language is indissolubly bound to singing, music, gesture, and dance. To this difficulty is added the current belief that to comprehend and interpret these texts it is indispensable to research and recognize the context in which they are produced. The premise here is that poetic expression in verbal language possesses no autonomy in a culture in which the exercise and meaning of everything is closely tied to rituals and predetermined traditions. Along these lines, ethnomusicologist Hélza Camêo has offered a fine and interesting reflection. Considering the basic "word + music + movement" formula that coalesces in artistic expression, she argues that there must still be a central line deriving from a starting point, a stimulus, an initial impulse. For the author this source that generates expression is certainly to be found in the word: "We consider singing the result of the emotional exacerbation of the word that, in the intensity of utterance, acquires musical content by becoming expressive and highly impressive" (12). How can one capture that impression? How can one open oneself up to it? How can one listen to and comprehend the Indian's poetic word? It is necessary to acknowledge the difficulties and resign oneself to giving only an incomplete and lacunary view of the subject matter. Much of the problem stems from a still fragmentary, partial, restricted observation, highly conditioned by the scarcity of information available on the topic.

At any rate, the concept of an indigenous "poetry" applies first and foremost to these chants. The notion of poetry coalesces here in the articulation of two explicitly *literary* categories: On the one hand, it points to the domain of lyric, the need for lyricism and for the cultivated intimacy of language that makes social and individual subjectivities communicate; on the other hand, it points to the text in verse, that discourse of oral culture that, by formalizing itself and favoring mnemonic fixing, becomes crystallized as *text*. In oral literatures, the textualities in verse that usually constitute the most recognizably lyric set of cultural repertoires almost always manifest themselves in chants associated with music and dance. The research into indigenous poetic expression, and the material available for it, has emerged in close association with the research into musical expression. Both were objects of a longstanding ignorance on the part of mainstream researchers, an ignorance certainly related to the lack of influence that Indians exerted on national culture. It is true that over the past decades the efforts of modern ethnomusicology and ethnolinguistics have reduced our ignorance and lack of sensibility in this matter, but much remains to be done.

Câmara Cascudo remarks that "a poética indígena foi, intrinsecamente, o elemento de menor influência na literatura oral do Brasil" ("indigenous poetics was intrinsically the least influential element in Brazil's oral literature," Cascudo 1984, 137). The narrative content of fables and legends was exported from the oral indigenous patrimony to Portuguese-language folklore and Brazilian written literature. On the contrary, chants have remained restricted to the sphere of autochthonous mother tongues, leaving as a legacy to general folklore only a few scarce verses and musical motifs, in the realm of lullabies and children's songs. In spite of that, indigenous poetry is not just an archaeological fact: Its ancient quality remains alive in the voice of indigenous singers and in the numerous autochthonous languages still spoken in Brazil. This has all recently become more accessible to us. Some of its sounds have found their way to documentary LPs or CDs, for example *A Arte Vocal dos Suyá* [1982; The Vocal Art of the Suyá], produced by A. Seeger (Museu Nacional/Tacape); *Paiter Marewá: Cantam os Suruís de Rondônia* [1984; Paiter Marewá: Sing the Suruís of Rondônia] (Memória Discos e Edições Ltda, 1984); Amazonic chants in *Música Popular do Norte* [Popular Music from the North], Vol. 4 (Marcus Pereira); *Kaapor, Cantos de Pássaros que Não Morrem* [1988; Kaapor, Songs of Birds That Do Not Die] (Unicamp/Minc-SEAC); *Bororo Vive* [1989; Bororo Lives] (Museu Rondon/UFMT); *Xingu: Cantos e Ritmos* [Xingu: Songs and Rhythms] (Philips/Phonogram); *Ñande Reko Arandu: Memória Viva Guarani* [Ñande Reko Arandu: A Live Guarani Memory] (Comunidade Solidária); and *Etenhiritipá: Cantos de Tradição Xavante* [1994; Etenhiritipá: Songs of the Xavante Tradition] (Quilombo Música/Warner Music Brasil Ltda, 1994). There are also more or less stylized versions, as in Mílton Nascimento's *Txai* (CBS, 1990) or in the compilation done by Marlui Miranda with chants from different nations, *Ihu—Todos os Sons* [1995; Ihu—All the Sounds] (Pau-Brasil), the materials which also came out in a songbook in 1996.

The access to texts is, however, more complicated, because accessibility faces obstacles that technology has not yet overcome. The words to the songs seem to have resisted the ethnographer's knowledge more than the rhythmic and melodic (instrumental and vocal) expression. The scholars who have worked most closely with indigenous verbal discourse have limited their attention to the code (linguists) and the mythological narrative structures (anthropologists, who have also usually treated these narratives as a code itself). The few translations of chants available were done in a nonsystematic fashion, with a view to anthropological research that often supplemented ethnomusicological studies. The inaugural recording was by Jean de Léry, who in his *Viagem à Terra do Brasil* [1578 (1st ed.); A Trip to the Land of Brazil] annotated lyrics and melody to a few fragments of Tupinambá chants. Very little was added to that patrimony until the twentieth century, with the exception of a few pieces presented by Couto de Magalhães in *O Selvagem* (1st edition from 1876) and the series of songs collected by Barbosa Rodrigues in *Paranduba Amazonense* (1890). More recently there are the Ariti chants collected and translated by Cândido Rondon and João Barbosa Faria in *Esboço Gramatical: Vocabulário, Lendas e*

Cânticos dos Indios Ariti (Pareci) [1948; A Grammatical Summary: Vocabulary, Legends and Chants from the Ariti (Pareci) Indians]; some ceremonial chants of the Suyá appear in ethnomusicologist Anthony Seeger's *Os Indios e Nós* [1980; The Indians and Us]; Kadiwéu shaman chants are presented by Darcy Ribeiro in *Kadiwéu: Ensaios Etnológicos sobre o Saber, o Azar e a Beleza* [1980; Kadiwéu: Ethnological Essays on Knowledge, Misfortune, and Beauty]; a shaman chant can be found in Eduardo Viveiros de Castro's *Araweté: O Povo do Ipixuna* [1992; Araweté: The People of Ipixuna]; some chants are interspersed in the Suruí narratives published by Betty Mindlin in *Vozes da Origem*; festive Kuikúro chants are analyzed by Bruna Franchetto in the essay "Tolo Kuikúro: Sing What You Can't Say" (1997); and passages of ritual chants are analyzed by Cláudia Neiva de Matos in her essay from 1999, "The Serpent's Song: Poetry by the Kaxinawá Indians" ([*cipó*] chants are ritual chants that accompany the hallucinatory experiences caused by the ingestion of a drink prepared with *cipó* and leaves from the Amazon forest). So far one cannot say that there is much individual production of written poetry by Brazilian Indians. The rare exceptions–which in fact include some texts of remarkable poetic force–again are to be found coming out of projects of special education. Some can be found, for example, in the already mentioned *Antologia da Floresta*, by the Pro-Indian Commission of the State of Acre, or in the *Livro de Poesias* [Book of Poetries] of the Institute for Anthropology and the Environment. The primary difficulty in the study of the words to the indigenous chants (that is, to a large portion of the discursive production we could call lyric) is, then, the scarcity of documentation. The fact that translating poetry is rather more difficult than translating prose has certainly contributed to these lacunae. On the other hand, the few attempts at analyzing and interpreting this material usually highlight the shamanistic and cultural functions of these chants, thus following a disciplinary line in modern anthropology that goes back to the so-called science of religion of the nineteenth century.

Colonial chroniclers often refer to the unintelligibility of what the Indians said in their chants. In fact, even if there were no language barriers, perhaps it would not have been easy for European minds and ears to understand this strongly stylized and figurative language that operates primarily with ellipsis, synthesis, and understatement. This poetic language, much like any poetic language, activates the materiality of the code and explores a metaphorical aesthetic and the zones of untranslatability. Even today great difficulties arise in the transcription of texts in verse into Portuguese. At first sight, when one attempts a translation, or even when one reads translations by others, one often has the impression that there are links missing from the text. Little by little, more consistent selections are being produced. Among these we should foreground the great potential contribution to be expected from indigenous educational programs developed over the past decades. By expanding access to writing on the part of the Indians, and by frequently investing in bilingualism and the preservation of living endogenous culture, these programs have also attempted to develop conventions of transcription for the mother tongues and to stimulate the register of texts in these languages by indigenous subjects themselves. An example is the book entitled *Nukû Mimawa* (Our Music), published in 1995 by the Pro-Indian Commission of the State of Acre. This is a compilation of lyrics to

Kaxinawá chants in the original language that emerged as a product of recordings and transcriptions done by a group of bilingual indigenous teachers.

It is interesting to note that writing, as well as the tape recorder (integral elements in the apparatus of cultural domination), have been precisely the means available to resist this domination, insofar as they have allowed for the development of work whose purpose was admittedly to revitalize the native cultural tradition by preserving from corruption and oblivion a cultural patrimony threatened by heterogeneous cultural pressures from contact with the mainstream. Joaquim Maná de Paulo, the main coordinator, writes in the introduction to *Nukû Mimawa*: "This book of Kaxinawá music was the product of work by some teachers interested in registering their culture at a moment when the Kaxinawá language began to be dominated by writing . . . . Our purpose is to make these songs part of the language disciplines in the indigenous Kaxinawá schools, where teachers can learn and teach their students–and not only their students, but everybody in the surrounding community–so that they can express themselves, learn, and strengthen our mother language *Hãtxa Kui* [true language]."

The actual language of the songs is at the same time full and circumscribed. Narratives can occasionally present some terms connected to Brazilian culture and the Portuguese language. But as mentioned before, narrative does not convey the linguistic depth of the indigenous culture. This is to be found in the chants. Chants were more rigorously conserved in their traditional form and constitute a sort of living space and textbook of the mother language in its pure form. This is what Joaquim Maná refers to when he says, "In order to know that you are speaking your language well, you have to learn several songs." This same linguistic purity is correlated to a certain degree of untranslatability: "When you sing, not a word in Portuguese comes in. In translations we see that there are a few words that cannot be translated." (This statement was made by Joaquim Maná Kaxinawá during recordings I made throughout our collaborative work of translating some *Nukû Mimawa* chants [Matos 1999].) In order to translate these chants one must count on the collaboration of bilingual Indians who are proficient in the Portuguese language and at the same time deeply connected to their original culture. There are many peculiarities to be considered in the texts' meaning and function. Frequently charged with a ritualistic function, they can play with complex symbolism by resorting to an ancient language, elliptic and stylized, that presents zones of obscurity to the Indians themselves–not only in the interpretation of meaning, but even in the understanding of some terms that are out of use or that belong to special repertoires.

As for the repertoire of chants in the indigenous languages still spoken in Brazil, it is therefore necessary to (1) record it– a fascinating task, as regarded and depicted by the researchers involved; (2) translate it–a complex and arduous task, in which to the habitual difficulties of any translation of poetic verse are added the ones created by the extreme distance and linguistic and cultural differences; and (3) read and interpret it–a multidisciplinary task, to which, however, the literary eye and ear cannot refrain from making an essential contribution. The first task is, by preference, the responsibility of indigenous researchers; it is enough that others provide them with the means to do it. The second and surely the third demand the collaboration of all interested parties. The genres are

many, and they vary in their discursive format: celebration, lyric soliloquy, exhortation, invocation, magic, cure, chants with linear lyrics, and chants with a chorus based on repetition. The themes are more varied than the first informants would have us believe, and they include everyday life, work, sensations, seduction, and feelings of love. In fact, already in 1587 Gabriel Soares de Souza noted among these "musicians of nature" the thematic and functional diversity of indigenous chants by pointing out the recurrence of mocking songs, ritual harvest songs, odes to nature, and so on.

The indigenous lyric does not work much with abstractions (which does not mean that it does not operate with metaphors). This language is bound to the concrete world by moving within strong empirical references by practicing all forms of animism. By blurring the boundaries between the literal and the figurative meanings (at least to our "foreign" comprehension), this language projects a world marked by poetic and animistic plenitude. Things of nature, such as animals, trees, the sky, stars, waters, and wind, are subjects of poetry, directly, or indirectly, by providing the metaphorical referent that allows these poems to speak of human and cultural relations. The conceptual and, let us say, existential distinction between nature and culture, which limits Western knowledge of the world, is more tenuous among the Indians; maybe it would be more accurate to say that the relation between the two terms is closer and more vital to them.

If we persist in perceiving points of contact between the chants of several indigenous cultures by attempting to capture the fundamental structures of their poetic language, what we learn at first sight does not differ much from what characterizes poetry in general: rhythm, repetitions, parallelism, and metaphorical and allegorical procedures. However, it is worth highlighting again the multiplicity of forms of motifs in these chants, easily visible after brief considerations of the available repertoire and contrasts with the traditional homogenizing perspective. The diversity observed in these groups (and among them) projects an enormous variety of genres, subject matters, stylistic procedures of a syntactical, imagistic, or semantic nature, sociocultural insertions, and modes of production and reception. One can no longer imagine indigenous poetry surrounded by a unifying veil that ignores the internal differences that help create and perceive its historicity and complexity.

Translation by Idelber Avelar

Works Cited

Abreu, Capistrano de. 1941 [1914]. *Rã-txa- Hu-ni-ku-i: Gramática, Textos e Vocabulário Caxinauás*. Rio de Janeiro: Capistrano de Abreu.

Bosi, Alfredo. 1992. "Um mito sacrificial: o indianismo de Alencar." *Dialética da Colonização*. Ed. Alfredo Bosi. São Paulo: Companhia das Letras. pp. 176–93.

Camêo, Helza. 1977. *Introdução ao estudo da música indígena brasileira*. Rio de Janeiro: Conselho Federal de Cultura e Departamento de Assuntos Culturais.

Cascudo, Luís da Câmara. 1972. *Dicionário do folclore brasileiro*. Brasília: Instituto Nacional do Livro.

———. 1984. *Literatura oral no Brasil*. Belo Horizonte; São Paulo: EDUSP.

Castro, Eduardo Viveiros de. 1992. *Araweté: o povo do Ipixuna*. São Paulo: CEDI (Centro Ecumênico de Documentação e Informação).

Cinta Larga, Pichuvy. 1988. *Mantere Ma Kwé Tinhin: histórias de maloca antigamente.* Belo Horizonte: SEGRAC-CIMI.

Ferreira, Mariana K. Leal, ed. 1994. *Histórias do Xingu: Coletâneas dos índios Suyá, Kayaabi, Juruna, Trumai, Txucarramãe e Txicão.* São Paulo: NHII/USP/FAPESP.

Franchetto, Bruna. 1997. "Tolo Kuikúro: 'Diga cantando o que não pode ser dito falando'." *Invenção do Brasil.* Revista do Museu Aberto do Descobrimento. Salvador: MINC. 57–64.

Hartt, Carlos Frederico. 1885. *Contribuições para a etnologia do vale do Amazonas.* Tomo VI. Rio de Janeiro: Arquivos do Museu Nacional.

Kumu, Umúsin Panlõn, and Tolamãn Kenhíri. 1980. *Antes o mundo não existia: a mitologia heróica dos índios Desaña.* Intro. Berta Ribeiro. São Paulo: Livraria Cultura Editora.

Léry, Jean de. 1980. *Viagem à terra do Brasil.* Belo Horizonte: Itatiaia; São Paulo: EDUSP.

Livro de poesias. N.d. São Paulo: IAMA (Instituto de Antropologia e Meio-ambiente).

Magalhães, Domingos José Gonçalves de. 1974. "Discuro sobre a história da literatura do Brasil." *Caminhos do pensamento crítico.* Ed. Afrânio Coutinho. Rio de Janeiro: Ed. Americana/Prolivro. Vol. 1: 24–25.

Magalhães, José Vieira Couto de. 1975. *O Selvagem.* Belo Horizonte: Itatiaia; São Paulo: EDUSP.

Mana de Paulo, Joaquim, ed.1995. *Nukû Mimawa.* Rio Branco: Ed. Kene Hiwa Ltda.

Matos, Cláudia Neiva de, ed. 1997. *Antología da Floresta; literatura selecionada e ilustrada pelos professores indígenas do Acre.* Rio de Janeiro: Multiletras.

——. 1999. "A Canção da serpente: poesia dos índios Kaxinawá. *Leituras do ciclo.* Ed. Ana Luiza Camargo, Maria Luci de Barros, and Raúl Antelo. Florianópolis: ABRALIC; Chapecó: Grifos. 87–97.

Mindlin, Betty, and Suruí narrators. 1996. *Vozes da origem; estórias sem escrita (narrativas dos índios Suruí de Rondônia).* São Paulo: Ed. Atica/IAMA.

Miranda, Marlui. 1996. *Ihu–todos os sons.* São Paulo: Editorial Árvore da Terra.

Montaigne, Michel de. 1986. *Essais.* Paris: Grands écrivains.

Monte, Nietta L. ed. 1984. *Estórias de hoje e de antigamente dos índios do Acre.* Rio Branco: Comissão Pró-Índio do Acre.

Rezende, Marcia S., and Renato A. Gavazzi, ed. 1992. *Geografia indígena.* Rio Branco: Comissão Pró-Índio do Acre.

Ribeiro, Darcy. 1980. *Kadiwéu; ensaios etnológicos sobre o saber, o azar e a beleza.* Petrópolis: Vozes.

Ricardo, Carlos Alberto. 1995. "Os Índios e a sociodiversidade nativa contemporânea no Brasil." *A Temática indígena na escola; novos subsídios para professores de 1º e 2º graus.* Ed. Aracy Lopes da Silva and Luís Donisete Bensi Grupioni. Brasília: MEC/MARI/UNESCO. 29–56.

Risério, Antonio. 1993. *Textos e tribos; poéticas extraocidentais nos trópicos brasileiros.* Rio de Janeiro: Imago.

Rodrigues, João Barbosa. 1890. *Poranduba amazonense.* Vol. XIV. Rio de Janeiro: Anais da Biblioteca Nacional.

Rondon, Cândido Mariano da Silva, and João Barbosa Faria. 1948. *Esboço gramatical; vocabulário; lendas e cânticos dos Índios Ariti (Pareci).* Rio de Janeiro: Imprensa Nacional.

Seeger, Anthony. 1980. *Os Índios e nós; estudos sobre sociedades tribais brasileiras.* Rio de Janeiro: Campus.

Shenipabu Miyui. 1991. Rio Branco: Comissão Pró-Índio do Acre.

Sousa, Gabriel Soares de. 1938. *Tratado descritivo do Brasil.* São Paulo: Ed. Nacional.

Spires, Rebeca, ed. 1997. *Histórias de ontem e de hoje/Itxua dji aie i dji jodla.* Oiapoque: CIMI/APIO/Governo do Amapá.

Törü Duü'ügú, nosso povo. 1985. Rio de Janeiro: Museu Nacional/SEC/MEC/SEPS/FNDE.

Zumthor, Paul. 1990. *Performance, réception, lecture.* Québec: Les Éditions du Préambule.

CHAPTER 27

AFRO-HISPANIC WRITERS IN LATIN AMERICAN LITERARY HISTORY

Rosemary Geisdorfer Feal

This essay addresses the relation of Afro-Hispanic writers to the field of Latin American literature by asking what theoretical considerations may have a bearing on the ways in which a canonical body of literary works is constructed. The numerous anthologies and histories of Latin American writing in Spanish by authors of African ancestry that have been published in Latin America, the United States, and Europe may guide us in assembling a comprehensive overview of the literature from Colonial times to the contemporary period (see representative titles in "Works Cited"). The most recent of these efforts, Vera Kutzinski's contribution to *The Cambridge History of Latin American Literature*, demonstrates how a broad and rather complete survey of Afro-Hispanic literature can also present a critical analysis of the conditions of cultural production and reception. My goal is not to summarize, synthesize, or amend the contents of these specialized anthologies and histories, but rather to inquire into the relationship between excluded or marginalized Afro-Hispanic texts–more positively denoted as emerging literatures–and the mainstream canon. I also want to discuss how different tensions or currents within Afro-Hispanic studies have had an impact on the development of the field. One tension that this article enacts is the exclusionary effect that the rubric *Afro-Hispanic* may have with respect to the literatures and cultures of Brazil, the subject of Chapter 28 in this volume. Traditionally, the language and nationality of an author have carried more weight than ethnic or cultural considerations when literary histories are assembled, unless the focus of the work is precisely a topical one (such as the pioneering studies by Janheinz Jahn: *Muntu* and *Neo-African Literature*). Afro-Hispanism generally refers to literary, cultural, and historical studies related to the African presence in countries where Spanish is spoken, whereas the diasporic experience of Africa in the Americas, a larger issue, rarely receives explicit treatment in regional literary histories.

In an earlier essay ("Feminist Interventions and the Race for Theory"), I argued that we need to recognize the importance of a canon so that we may pay tribute to the specific historical and cultural traditions of Africans in the Spanish-speaking Americas, and I noted that a canonical approach can thereby function as one method with which to contest the body of mainstream Latin American literature as it is typically presented in academic institutions. In advancing an argument of this sort, I was operating on the basis of three limited and pragmatic assumptions: (1) The canon is an imaginary construction, primarily pedagogical, that exists in the minds of scholars and teachers, who subsequently implant it in the minds of their students, as John Guilleroy proposes throughout *Cultural Capital*. (2) There is a canon of mainstream Latin American literature, from which Afro-Hispanic authors are for the most part excluded, especially outside the genre of poetry. (3) There is a discrete minority canon of

Afro-Hispanic literature, which consists of the works in Spanish by writers of African descent. Here, then, we have a set of embedded notions: the concept of canon regulates how scholars imagine our disciplines, in particular when it comes to the content of official institutions such as academic programs and literary histories; the canonical body of Latin American literature as taught in many universities and as represented in literary anthologies has excluded most writings by Afro-Hispanic authors, but scholars in Afro-Hispanism have through their critical practice constructed a growing, vital canon whose relation to the larger mainstream has yet to be solidified.

Although I am limiting my focus to Afro-Hispanism, the tension between mainstream and margin may be said to mark all struggles for canonization in Latin American literatures, as Sara Castro-Klarén argues (although she conceives of the problem differently). Her excellent discussion of canon and marginality draws on Charles Altieri's formulation: "[C]anons are essentially strategic constructs by which societies maintain their own interests, since the canon allows control over the texts a culture takes seriously and the methods of interpretation which establish the meaning of the serious" (quoted in Castro-Klarén, 7). This idea is in accord with Thomas Yingling's remark that "canonical moments are not the fruition of some natural cultural process," and his suggestion that we think of canonicity "not just as the generation of a list of validated texts but as the politically inflected codification of fantasies about collective origin or identity" (156). Castro-Klarén's literary historical account underscores the "constant challenge posed by marginalized groups and contents to the often unspoken or misspoken but well-established *norms* used for determining that elusive quality known as literary value" (8), and she shows how Latin American writers have always concentrated on "the particular, the local, the provincial, the exotic, the peripheral" (10). The challenge of marginality, then, "has impeded the formation of a stable canon in the field of Latin American letters" (17). Castro-Klarén discerns a hierarchical process that operates as follows: "The Eurocentric gaze sees its former colonies as provincial; the colonial city olympically regards the provinciality of the small town; and the small town looks down on the rural world which in turn trains its sightings on the peripheral Indian or the woman of African descent" (12). Implicit in Castro-Klarén's argument is the function of white racism as a key component of this circuit of gazes. The Latin American literary canon may be unstable, but the woman writer of African descent would come last in an order that mirrors society's larger organization in terms of class, race, nation, and gender. How else to explain her absence within the larger canon? As Debra Castillo notes in her essay in this volume, the exclusionary process of canonization means that all we can discuss are female conformists and those reformers and rebels who exist as exceptions to a writing culture defined as male (Chapter 34). Of course, it is precisely the concept of "exceptional" that reinforces the rule or norm, as Castillo's statement suggests.

At this point it would be instructive to review what the specialized Afro-Hispanic canon has looked like over time. In his article "The Emergence of Afro-Hispanic Poetry: Some Notes on Canon Formation," Edward Mullen discusses the evolution of the lexicon used to describe the corpus of literary works in question. He notes, for example, the shift from *negro* to a series of overlapping labels—*negroide, negrista, afro-cubano, mulato*. This terminology culminates "in the late seventies with the choice of the term Afro-Hispanic to refer broadly to that literature 'by, about and written to but not just for people of African descent in the Spanish speaking world'" (1988, 435; Mullen is citing Marvin Lewis's definition here). The results of Mullen's research show that, despite the proliferation in recent years of special-interest anthologies, such as *Poesía negra de América* (edited by José Luis González and Mónica Mansour), or *Sensemayá: La poesía negra en el mundo hispanohablante* (edited by Aurora de Albornoz and Julio Rodríguez-Luis), poetic works by Afro-Hispanics have not penetrated the generalist anthologies, with the exception of Cubans Plácido (Diego Gabriel de la Concepción Valdés, 1809–1844) and Nicolás Guillén (1902–1989) (1988, 449). In the ten years that have elapsed since Mullen's article appeared, we might wish to add Nancy Morejón (Cuba, b. 1944) to the list of exceptions, specifically her much-anthologized poem "Mujer negra" ["Black Woman"]. Mullen correctly attributes this predicament to the "dynamic interactions between literary, political and economic forces" (1988, 450) rather than to some kind of determinant property that literary texts might be said to have. Mullen's research inspired me to think about the related problematics of canonization with respect to Afro-Hispanic literature, particularly of the contemporary period with an emphasis on prose, and here are some excerpts from my own findings after having examined approximately fifty anthologies and literary histories.

Enrique Anderson Imbert's multiple editions of *Historia de la literatura hispanoamericana*, published in Spanish and English, have served as guideposts for generations of students and scholars. Those looking for either a panoramic or in-depth treatment of Afro-Hispanic literary history, however, will find precious little material, much of it construed in negatives. About Plácido, Anderson Imbert makes this remark: "He was an obscure figure because he was lacking the lights of a literary education and, what is worse, those of an original style" (1: 265). Were these not serious words, we might take them as a parody of the kind of canon-making judgments that smack of negative stereotypes and scorn for nonelite writers. As Anderson Imbert uses the term "oscura," which means "obscure" or "dark," it applies not to skin color but to literary quality (or rather, the lack thereof). No mention is made of Plácido's status as mulatto poet; further, the other great nineteenth-century Cuban mulatto poet and autobiographer, Juan Francisco Manzano (1797–1854), is deemed unworthy of even a line in this two-volume literary history.

The second volume of Anderson Imbert's *Historia de la literatura hispanoamericana* gives a somewhat better overview of Afro-Hispanic literary contributions to the contemporary period. Several main figures in prose fiction of African ancestry receive slight attention: Adalberto Ortiz (1914–2003), Nelson Estupiñán Bass (b. 1915) (both of Ecuador), Manuel Zapata Olivella (b. 1920), Carlos Arturo Truque (1928–1970) (both of Colombia), along with authors of non-African descent who

have contributed to the literature about blacks, such as Alejo Carpentier (1904–1980) of Cuba. Nevertheless, Anderson Imbert's critical commentary on the Afro-Hispanic authors leaves an impression similar to the one evoked in the first volume. Ortiz's *Juyungo* (1943) receives this assessment: "The novel does not have a unity of style. Imaginative sentences combined with worn clichés. Disorderly novel, not always because the author intended it" (2: 381). Vera Kutzinski, in contrast, notes that Ortiz's prose may be placed "in close proximity to the 'mainstream' of postmodern Hispanic American fiction owing to narrative fragmentation and macabre humor" (187), which suggests that Ortiz may be an important precursor to modern Spanish-American fiction rather than a novelist not in control of his discourse. Of Estupiñán Bass, author of important novels on black themes, the pronouncement "cultured novelist" (1966, 370) is all we learn from Anderson Imbert. Zapata Olivella is listed as "author of *A Saint is Born in Chimá* (misprinted "Chiná") and other intense novels" (1966, 367).

An anthology of Spanish-American literature that finds frequent use in university courses in the United States is *Texto y vida* (1991) edited by Barbara Mujica. The two short sections that refer to Afro-Hispanic literature focus on Luis Palés Matos (1898–1959) and Nancy Morejón, both Caribbean poets, only one of whom may be identified as an Afro-Hispanic; the single work of fiction mentioned in passing is Adalberto Ortiz's *Juyungo*. Despite these severe limitations, that the term *afrohispano* is even indexed in this anthology represents some progress. Giuseppe Bellini does not even mention *afrohispano* as a category in his gargantuan ode to the male mainstream, *Historia de la literatura hispanoamericana* (1985). Of the authors privileged enough to get their own section in Bellini's work, only three are women: Sor Juana Inés de la Cruz (1648–1695), of course, along with Gabriela Mistral (1889–1957) and Juana de Ibarbourou (1892–1979), grouped together. The single Afro-Hispanic author with his own section is Nicolás Guillén, and the entire literary history of Africans in the Americas must be pieced together in a series of minor notes in this encyclopedic book. The great prose writers like Manuel Zapata Olivella (Colombia) and Adalberto Ortiz (Ecuador) are squeezed into sections in microscopic type among the authors classified as "also worthy of mention." Ortiz's masterpiece, *Juyungo*, is described as a "novel of bitter protest, passionate act of love toward the race to which he himself belongs" (523). Afro-Hispanists might note with displeasure that Zapata Olivella's epic novel, *Changó, el gran putas* [1983; Shango, The Holy Motherfucker], is embedded in the fine print with much lesser known or acclaimed authors such as Ramiro Cárdenas (b. 1925), Eduardo Santa (b. 1927), and Antonio Montaña (b. 1932). Bellini does, however, devote some forty pages to pre-Columbian literatures, and refers to what he calls "the voice of the natives" or "the polemic surrounding the Indian." But blacks are not treated as natives, as subjects of polemics, or as actors in a coherent literary history, three roles that Zapata Olivella himself attributes to Africans in the New World in works such as *Claves mágicas de América* [1989; Magic Keys to America] and *Levántate mulato* [1990; Rise Up, Mulatto]. As Afro-Costa Rican author Quince Duncan (b. 1940) notes in a conversation with Afro-Uruguayan writer Cristina Rodríguez Cabral, "The 'invisibilization' of blacks is one way in which racism manifests itself" (113).

Naomi Lindstrom delivers a better outcome in her *Spanish-American Fiction: Twentieth Century* (1994), which includes in its index numerous references under the entry "African-Hispanic populations and cultures," a rubric that recognizes a fundamental aspect of Latin American history (if not literature). Unfortunately, her discussions of literary themes related to these populations and cultures point us to authors such as Rómulo Gallegos (1884–1969), Alejo Carpentier, José Lezama Lima (1910–1976), and Miguel Barnet (b. 1940), none of whom declare Afro-Hispanic ethnicity, whereas Manuel Zapata Olivella and Adalberto Ortiz both fail to receive mention in her detailed survey of this century's fiction from Latin America. We conclude from her approach, then, that Afro-Hispanic cultures are vital to our knowledge of Latin American literature, but we learn next to nothing about the writers of African descent whose works make up a large canon. In this way, blacks function as a topic but lack status as author(ities) and subjects. When excluded from critical surveys such as these, the Afro-Hispanic canon is relegated to functioning as a separate tradition and thus is not seen as collectively owned. What is worse, as Dympna Callaghan notes in another context, "the appropriation of subordinate identities by privileged whites demonstrates that endeavors to compensate for the exclusion of racial 'minorities' from the means of literary production can become the very means for continuing this exclusion" (197).

In her *La cultura moderna en América Latina* [*Modern Culture in Latin America*] Jean Franco devotes a section to "The Black," and begins with this statement: "Of the three races the black race was the last one to arrive on the Latin American continent; in slave-holding societies, of which Blacks were the base, any original culture that they were able to possess was destroyed or severely altered" (137). By designating Africans in last place in terms of arrival in the Americas, and by claiming that their original cultures were eradicated or mutilated, Franco ascribes to them a negative image as cultural outsiders, quite unlike what Cubena (Carlos Guillermo Wilson [b. 1941] of Panama) does when he uses the term "afro-exiliado" or "Afro-exile" to describe himself and his fellow diasporic people. In his work on race, ethnicity, and diasporic writing, found in "The Role of the Afro-Latin Writer and the Quincentenary" as well as in his literary prose, Cubena asserts a positive relation among all those whose labors were exploited in the Americas and who suffered discrimination (indigenous peoples, Africans, migrants within the Americas, and so forth). Franco in turn could have noted how the Africans "came with Columbus," or she could have discussed African syncretic religious practices in terms that conveyed culture building and transformation, or, following Cuban Manuel Moreno Fraginals, she might have made mention of tools of deculturation in slave-holding plantation society. But Franco's book, though slightly updated for its 1985 publication in the Mexican edition from which I cite, was originally written in the 1960s, long before the "boom" in Afro-Hispanic studies to which Mullen refers.

Could we conclude that the abundance of texts written in the second half of the twentieth century by Spanish-American writers of African descent, along with the appearance of an impressive body of criticism about Afro-Hispanic cultures, constitutes a propitious circumstance for a fuller recognition of this literature? In theory, yes, if we also make the assumption that the ideological moment is right for such a recognition to occur. The presence of certain kinds of writing has never been in itself reason enough for those texts to find their way into the mainstream canon, as feminist scholars, among

others, have documented extensively. Lillian Robinson, in her "Treason Our Text: Feminist Challenges to the Literary Canon," reiterates several points that are now commonplace in critical thinking on canon formation, and they are relevant to my discussion here. She notes that the least threatening way to incorporate an excluded point of view is to bring individuals into the established canon, one by one, in an attempt to place the authors in their rightful slot (86–87). But, as she goes on to say, this method obviously presents no challenge "to the particular notions of literary quality, timelessness, universality, and other qualities that constitute the rationale for canonicity" (87). The signal issue becomes the following, according to Robinson: "We need to understand whether the claim is being made that many of the newly recovered or validated texts by women meet existing criteria or, on the other hand, that those criteria themselves intrinsically exclude or tend to exclude women and hence should be modified or replaced" (88).

If I provisionally allow "women" to function as a term comparable to "Afro-Hispanics," it is for the purpose of showing the relationship between center and margin where canonicity is concerned. Obviously, there are major considerations elided in this equation, such as "literary blackness," to which I will return shortly. Despite the conceptual difficulties, we may nevertheless apply some of Robinson's observations to Afro-Hispanism. If we assume that the African presence in the Americas deserves sustained consideration in historical, anthropological, literary, and artistic studies, then we would actively search for the corresponding cultural products, and we would employ critical methodologies and ideologies that we deem appropriate to their interpretation. While this process seems like an obvious one, its implementation is contingent on the recognition of the value of Afro-Hispanic culture, something that seems to be lacking in many mainstream critical works and literary anthologies. This lack stands in contrast to the abundance of texts cited in the specialized work of Afro-Hispanists in North America, beginning with the pioneering books by Richard Jackson, in which we see an entire canon unfold in rich detail. There is, however, no one literary history of Afro-Hispanic literature, as Edward Mullen notes in "Afro-Hispanic and Afro-American Literary Historiography." Jackson's *The Afro-Spanish American Author*, Volumes I (1980) and II (1989), offers annotated bibliographic entries for all writers who have been the subject of critical articles and books. In Volume II, Jackson lists sixty-seven Afro-Spanish American authors, a group that forms a wide canon to be supplemented by contemporary writers not included in his survey, and by other authors who have yet to attract critical attention. Not only are there important critical overviews such as those by Jackson and Marvin Lewis (see Works Cited), but there are also numerous monographs devoted to works by single authors, such as Henry J. Richards's study of the novels of Nelson Estupiñán Bass, as well as volumes on larger questions that touch on textuality in relation to race, ethnicity, orality, literacy, sugar plantation economy, visual representations of blacks, and so on. The journals *Afro-Hispanic Review* and *Callaloo*, both published in the United States, serve as indices and guardians of the proliferation of creative and critical works by and about blacks in the Americas; the interdisciplinary *Publication of the Afro-Latin/American Research Association* entered the arena in 1997. What, then, could explain the gap between the specialized studies and journals and the generalized approaches to canon?

If we accept the observation of United States writer Toni Morrison that critical judgment is connected to pleasure in reading and recognition of oneself in the work (2), then we might be forced to conclude, pessimistically, that Latin Americanists in general have not experienced those pleasures and identities in ways that would radically alter the literary and teaching canon. A novel like Zapata Olivella's *Chambacú* (1963) is a good case in point. Highly canonical within Afro-Hispanic studies, the work is rarely listed in the mainstream Latin American canon as taught in North America, despite its having been translated into English by Jonathan Tittler. It bears little structural resemblance to the universally acclaimed magical realist works of Zapata's compatriot, the undisputed king of canon, Gabriel García Márquez (b. 1927). *Chambacú*, first published as *Corral de negros* [*Black Slum*] in 1963 by Casa de las Américas in Cuba, which awarded the novel its prize, was released in a new version in 1965 and has since gone through several editions. Richard Jackson has done a comparative study of the two versions of *Chambacú*; he documents the process through which Zapata Olivella sharpened his expression, toned down the ideological statements, giving "better art and less propaganda, an option always to be lauded in a creative artist" (1979, 148). Jackson notes that the second version "holds local officials and conditions responsible for the hunger and misery black people suffer in Colombia" (1979, 148), which therefore shifts narrative emphasis away from the United States government as the locus of all evil. Jackson concludes that the second version "continues to stand as a powerful, fast moving, and deeply committed novel of social protest, perhaps the most up-to-date black novel in Latin America insofar as literary blackness and revolutionary zeal are concerned" (1979, 151).

Zapata Olivella's novel distinctly calls for a reader trained to appreciate it in all its ideological overdeterminacy, its raw, *tremendista* style ("tremendous" in its brutal depictions), its historical underpinnings, and its sociological import. Unlike the isolated, claustrophobic interiors of *Cien años de soledad* [1967; *One Hundred Years of Solitude*], with its characters who speak in terse, abstract discourse, the action of *Chambacú* is literally out in the open, where public events such as demonstrations give way to political speeches that find their way into the novel, creating a hybrid text made up of essay, dialogue, graffiti on the walls, radio broadcasts, and so on. In fact, what makes *Chambacú* so dissonant and unfamiliar to a public accustomed to García Márquez is this particular brand of hybridity, this refusal to act like a mainstream novel performing discursive business as usual.

If we return to Lewis's definition of an Afro-Hispanic work as one "by, about and written to *but not just for* people of African descent in the Spanish speaking world" (in Mullen 1988, 435; emphasis mine), we see that *Chambacú* expressly addresses itself to a wider audience. But are audiences prepared to read this kind of novel as part of a larger Latin American canon? To do so would be to accord significance to the discourse of the margin, to read with trained eyes, to value a work in its difference, but not only *as* difference. The conversation that I cited previously between Cristina Rodríguez Cabral and Quince Duncan illustrates this problem. Rodríguez Cabral asks Duncan: "do you still think that Black authors should continue to stress the 'Afro' component? . . . [C]ould it be better to present a literature without color?"–to which Duncan replies: "While my main subject is the culture and people of the African Diaspora, I

have written about other subjects. For example, *Final de la calle* . . . is just a good novel, written by a Black author. Now from the point of view of our struggle against Eurocentrism, this is important. . . . *Final de la calle* was a demonstration that I wrote about Blacks because I chose to, not because I had to" (Duncan 114–15).

Whether the focus of Afro-Hispanic writing concerns people of the African diaspora or whether it takes up other issues altogether, it is clear that the growing interest in literatures by Afro-Hispanic writers on the part of scholars who are not devoted exclusively to that field, or even to Latin American literature, will result in increased recognition and attention for this literary and cultural area. Will Latin Americanists wait for that moment to undertake our own canon reformation? If so, why? Scholars like Castro-Klarén have already provided theoretical reasoning that should guide us as Latin Americanists in search of our own "new" literary histories. She notes how marginalized groups have continuously exerted pressure on mainstream canons: "By the telling of *their own* history, they place a claim on the land, they move the markers that delineate the sacralized space of the canon, they inject the voice of the other which destabilizes the notion that the *one* speaker is alone, forging and writing within *one* consolidated literary system. . . . As their texts, inasmuch as they are cultural artifacts with a given status, are preserved and read and even commented upon, they modify the non native terms of the ideal canon as well as the praxis of the canon by literary historians and commentators" (15–16).

Before I offer a synthesis of the prospects for canonicity with respect to Afro-Hispanic studies, let me comment briefly on some of the tensions that have already reformed that specialized canon. The question of which authors belong in the Afro-Hispanic canon has produced varying responses over the years. Richard Jackson, for example, has emphasized notions of authenticity and positive portrayals of Afro-Hispanic identity and experience in his *Black Literature and Humanism in Latin America*. This conceptual framework would tend to exclude formerly canonical texts such as Venezuelan Ramón Díaz Sánchez's (1903–1968) *Cumboto* (1950), which Stanley Cyrus has discussed in terms of "ethnic ambivalence." Jackson's formulation might also deemphasize those Afro-Hispanic works in which race and ethnicity are not primary thematic concerns. Previously, the Afro-Hispanic canon was understood to encompass works by and about blacks, yet in recent years it appears to privilege works by authors who conform to the parameters of Afro-Hispanic identity. Further, a name like Uruguayan Virginia Brindis de Salas (1908–1958) has been teetering at the edge of the canon since it was argued that her works resulted from a literary hoax, a polemic that has yet to be definitively resolved. But the Afro-Hispanic canon has been expanding in interesting directions as well. Writers like Ana Lydia Vega (b. 1946) of Puerto Rico are being read increasingly as representative of African diaspora culture, and her short stories, especially those from *Encancaranublado* (1982), have been analyzed as an integral part of the Afro-Hispanic tradition. United States Latino writers, too, are finding their way into the Afro-Latin American canon as critics take up identity and ethnicity as themes that by definition cross borders, categories, and languages.

It is important to remind ourselves that the transmission of literary knowledge–and value–within academic institutions and through literary histories has a tangible impact on collective culture, and the texts we venerate as teachers and researchers contribute to the process of canon formation. By way of conclusion I want to present three prospects for constructing canons in Afro-Hispanic studies, all of which to some extent are already functioning simultaneously. In distinction to Houston Baker's diachronic account of "generational shifts" with regard to the criticism of Afro-American literature, my categories adhere to a synchronic model applicable to canon formation. These categories may complement a historiographic approach such as the one taken by Edward Mullen, who traces the generational shifts in Afro-Hispanic studies by examining articles published in the *College Language Association Journal.* His appraisal that "in its most recent decade the journal appears to have refined and continued a strong fidelity to Afro-centric and black aesthetic schools of interpretation" (1995, 381) suggests a primary emphasis on "identity." The first construct I propose would be a canon based on the thematic content of the work in question: that is, literature about peoples of African descent in the Spanish-speaking Americas. The second draws on an affirmation of identity on the part of authors: If they foreground their African ancestry, either in their works or by extra-textual means, they belong. The third model appeals to interrelated ideological forces such as class, nation, race, gender, politics, and language as they relate to the African diaspora. This latter notion of canon, which I see as the most potent one for the current moment, still permits critics to search out previously unrecognized authors and to uphold and celebrate those writers who treat concepts of Afro-Hispanic identity in affirmative ways. Yet it also allows for a general ideological critique that could assist us not only in contesting the mainstream Latin American canon, but also in linking up with other scholars of so-called minority literatures and cultures. As Vera Kutzinski notes, "The real challenge is neither to establish a separate canon nor, for that matter, to bring select Afro-Hispanic texts into the fold of already existing canons of Latin American or Afro-American literatures. . . . What is at issue, then, is our ability (and willingness) to read Afro-Hispanic texts as evidence of the inconsistencies, irregularities, and upheavals that characterize Latin American literary, social, and political history, much more so than any unified critical narrative could even suggest" (194). The route I trace here asks us to yield some of the historical, geopolitical, or linguistic specificity of "Afro-Hispanic" as we move toward a variegated canon in which broad diasporic and postcolonial issues figure prominently. To this end, my essay should be read conjointly with the other contributions to the section of this project on exclusions in Latin American literary history, for only when we examine the mosaic of marginalities can we assemble the map for locating all the cultural products we study.

Works Cited

Albornoz, Aurora de, and Julio Rodríguez-Luis, ed. 1980. *Sensemayá: La poesía negra en el mundo hispanohablante (Antología).* Madrid: Orígenes.

Anderson Imbert, Enrique, ed. 1970. *Historia de la literatura hispanoamericana.* 2nd rev. ed. 2 Vols. Mexico City: Fondo de Cultura Económica.

Bellini, Giuseppe. 1985. *Historia de la literatura hispanoamericana.* Madrid: Castalia.

Callaghan, Dympna. 1995. "The Vicar and Virago: Feminism and the Problem of Identity." *Who Can Speak? Authority and Critical Identity.* Ed. Judith Roof and Robyn Wiegman. Urbana and Chicago: University of Illinois Press. 195–207.

Castro-Klarén, Sara. 1989. "By (T)reason of State: The Canon and Marginality in Latin American Literature." *Revista de Estudios Hispánicos* 23.2: 1–19.

Cyrus, Stanley. 1982. "Ethnic Ambivalence and Afro-Hispanic Novelists." *Afro-Hispanic Review* 1.1: 29–32.

DeCosta, Miriam. 1977. *Blacks in Hispanic Literature.* Port Washington, N.Y.: Kennikat Press.

Duncan, Quince. 1998. "A Conversation with Quince Duncan." With Cristina Rodríguez Cabral. *Publication of the Afro-Latin/American Research Association* 2: 113–18.

Feal, Rosemary Geisdorfer. 1991. "Feminist Interventions in the Race for Theory: Neither Black Nor White." *Afro-Hispanic Review* 10.3: 11–20.

Franco, Jean. 1985. *La cultura moderna en América Latina.* Mexico City: Grijalbo.

González, José Luis, and Mónica Mansour. 1976. *Poesía negra de América.* Mexico City: Era.

Guilleroy, John. 1993. *Cultural Capital: The Problem of Literary Canon Formation.* Chicago: University of Chicago Press.

Jackson, Richard. 1979. *Black Writers in Latin America.* Albuquerque: University of New Mexico Press.

——. 1980. *The Afro-Spanish American Author: An Annotated Bibliography of Criticism.* New York: Garland.

——. 1988. *Black Literature and Humanism in Latin America.* Athens: University of Georgia Press.

——. 1989. *The Afro-Spanish American Author II: The 1980s.* West Cornwall, Connecticut: Locust Hill.

Jahn, Janheinz. 1961. *Muntu: An Outline of the New African Culture.* Trans. Marjorie Grene. New York: Grove.

——. 1969. *Neo-African Literature: A History of Black Writing.* New York: Grove.

Kutzinski, Vera. 1996. "Afro-Hispanic American Literature." *The Cambridge History of Latin American Literature.* Vol. 2. Ed. Roberto González Echevarría and Enrique Pupo-Walker. Cambridge: Cambridge University Press. 164–94.

Lewis, Marvin A. 1983. *Afro-Hispanic poetry, 1940–1980: From Slavery to "Negritud" in South American Verse.* Columbia: University of Missouri Press.

——. 1987. *Treading the Ebony Path: Ideology and Violence in Contemporary Afro-Colombian Prose Fiction.* Columbia: University of Missouri Press.

——. 1992. *Ethnicity and Identity in Contemporary Afro-Venezuelan Literature: A Culturalist Approach.* Columbia: University of Missouri Press.

——. 1996. *Afro-Argentine Discourse: Another Dimension of the Black Diaspora.* Columbia: University of Missouri Press.

Lindstrom, Naomi. 1994. *Twentieth Century Spanish-American Fiction.* Austin: University of Texas Press.

Moreno Fraginals, Manuel. 1984. "Cultural Contributions and Deculturation." *Africa in Latin America: Essays on History, Culture, and Socialization.* Ed. Moreno Fraginals. Trans. Leonor Blum. New York: Holmes and Meier. 5–22.

Morrison, Toni. 1989. "Unspeakable Things Unspoken: The Afro-American Presence in American Literature." *Michigan Quarterly Review* 28.1: 1–34.

Mujica, Barbara. 1991. *Texto y vida: Introducción a la literatura hispanoamericana.* Fort Worth: Harcourt.

Mullen, Edward. 1988. "The Emergence of Afro-Hispanic Poetry: Some Notes on Canon Formation." *Hispanic Review* 56.4: 435–53.

——. 1995. "Afro-Hispanic and Afro-American Literary Historiography: Comments on Generational Shifts." *CLA Journal* 37.4: 371–89.

Ortiz, Adalberto. 1976 [1943]. *Juyungo.* Barcelona: Seix Barral.

Richards, Henry J. 1989. *La jornada novelística de Nelson Estupiñán Bass: Búsqueda de la perfección.* Quito: El Conejo.

Robinson, Lillian. 1983. "Treason Our Text: Feminist Challenges to the Literary Canon." *Tulsa Studies in Women's Literature* 2: 83–98.

Wilson, Carlos Guillermo (Cubena). 1991. "The Role of the Afro-Latin Writer and the Quincentenary (1492–1992)." *Afro-Hispanic Review* 10.3: 67–71.

Yingling, Thomas. 1995. "Fetishism, Identity, Politics." *Who Can Speak? Authority and Critical Identity.* Ed. Judith Roof and Robyn Wiegman. Urbana and Chicago: University of Illinois Press. 155–64.

Zapata Olivella, Manuel. 1990 [1963]. *Chambacú: Corral de negros.* Bogotá: Rei.

———. 1983. *Changó, el gran putas.* Bogotá: Oveja Negra.

———. 1989. *Chambacú: Black Slum.* Trans. Jonathan Tittler. Pittsburgh: Latin American Literary Review.

———. 1989. *Las claves mágicas de América.* Bogotá: Plaza y Janés.

———. 1990. *¡Levántate mulato! 'Por mi raza hablará el espíritu'.* Bogotá: Rei, Andes.

CHAPTER 28

BLACK PRESENCE IN BRAZILIAN LITERATURE
FROM THE COLONIAL PERIOD TO THE TWENTIETH CENTURY

Heloisa Toller Gomes, Gizelda Melo do Nascimento, and Leda Maria Martins

> Voltem mares, rios, instintos,
> Voltem resistindo
> nas danças dos orixás.
>
> May seas, rivers, instincts return
> Return fighting back
> in the dances of the orixás.
>
> —*Miriam Alves*

Introduction

Black authors and black characters figure less prominently than one might assume in canonical Brazilian literature during the colonial period and the eighteenth century, indebted as it remained to European models. During this period Afro-Brazilians were enslaved or impoverished and hence mostly denied access to cultural goods. Nonetheless, blacks formed a strong constitutive element in the popular and cultural imagination from the first Portuguese colonization of Brazil in mid-sixteenth century. From the start, the black population was large and, in certain regions, constituted a majority, a fact that invariably attracted foreigners' attention. In 1859 a French visitor to Salvador stated that "tudo parece negro: negros na praia, negros na cidade, negros na parte baixa, negros nos bairros altos. Tudo que corre, grita, trabalha, tudo que transporta e carrega é negro" (Avé-Lallement 20) ("Everything seems black: There are blacks on the beach, in the city, in the lower and higher neighborhoods. All that runs, shouts, works, everything that transports and bears is black").

Modern scholars of Brazilian society confirm and deepen the foreigners' empirical attestation: All spheres of Brazilian life were marked by the presence of the black slave from the beginning of colonization. In the words of Joel Rufino dos Santos, there were "escravo na roça e na cidade, na mineração, no engenho, no curral, na selva e à beira-mar; escravo do eito, de ganho" (29) ("slaves in the fields and in the city, in the mines, in the sugar plantations, in the corral, in the forest and on the coast; slaves of force, for gain"]. Black experience transcended the realm of slavery in the form of self-sufficient communities of runaway slaves known as the *quilombos*. Sociologist Darci Ribeiro (1922–1997) evokes the member of the *quilombo* as the citizen of a Brazil that was yet to be; in the *quilombos*, which produced for themselves and not for the colonial market, the black man proved the first freedom fighter, embodying the historical role of the struggle for liberty (see Ribeiro and Neto). In their statements on the black contribution to the formation of Brazil our contemporaries echo the eloquence of Joaquim Nabuco's (1849–1910) masterwork, *O Abolicionismo*:

> Em primeiro lugar, a parte da população que descende de escravos é, pelo menos, tão numerosa como a parte que descende exclusivamente de senhores: a raça negra nos deu um povo. Em segundo lugar, o que existe até hoje sobre o vasto território que se chama Brasil foi levantado ou cultivado por aquela raça; ela

construiu o nosso país. Há trezentos anos que o africano tem sido o principal instrumento da ocupação e da manutenção do nosso território pelo europeu, e que os seus descendentes se misturam com o nosso povo. Onde ele não chegou ainda, o país apresenta o aspecto com que surpreendeu aos seus primeiros descobridores. Tudo o que significa luta do homem com a natureza, conquista do solo para a habitação e cultura, estradas e edifícios, canaviais e cafezais, a casa do senhor e a senzala dos escravos, igrejas e escolas, alfândegas e correios, telégrafos e caminhos de ferro, academias e hospitais, tudo, absolutamente tudo, que existe no país, como resultado do trabalho manual, como emprego de capital, como acumulação de riqueza, não passa de uma doação gratuita da raça que trabalha à que faz trabalhar. (60)

Firstly, the black race gave us a people: The proportion of the population that descended from the slaves is as substantial as that which descends from the masters. Secondly, all that exists to this day over that vast territory called Brazil was erected or cultivated by that race–it built our country. For three hundred years the African has constituted the European's principal vehicle for the occupation and maintenance of our territory. Where the African has not arrived, the country still presents that aspect that surprised its first discoverers. Everything, absolutely everything that exists in the country as the result of labor, capital, and the accumulation of riches represents nothing more than the donation of the race that works to that which makes it work: all that signifies man's fight against nature, the conquest of the soil for the purpose of housing and cultivation, the cultivation of sugar cane and coffee, roads and buildings, churches and schools, customs and post office, telegraphs and railway tracks, academies and hospitals.

Elements of an African provenance surreptitiously were insinuated into manifestations of the erudite arts–for example, in the colonial baroque–considerably before Afro-Brazilian culture would claim the status of a cultural force in its own right. From the eighteenth century Afro-Brazilian elements were also tenaciously present in manifestations of popular culture, as in the case of the *lundu*, a popular dance of African origin. Like the popular Portuguese dances that had been condemned by Jesuits and the Inquisition, the *lundu* flowered in Brazil, above all in the time of Gregório de Matos (see Araripe 20, 170). This coy dance, sung and executed with all the rhythm and voluptuousness that choreography allows, was an ancestor of the *modinha* that proved successful in Brazil and at Lisbon's court in the eighteenth century. The *lundu* was chanted by, among others, Lerene, pseudonym for the priest of Angolan and Portuguese descent, Domingos Caldas Barbosa (1738–1800). Portuguese enthusiasm for Brazilian *modinhas* is evident in the 1786 tune, "A rabugem das velhas" ["Cantankerous Old Women"]: "And so my little rich grandma, this *modinha* just invented is a charm; it inspires passion in all" (qtd. in Araripe 200).

In this manner slaves and their descendants created a hybrid and manifold culture and made Brazil part of what convention terms Afro-America, "conjunto descontínuo de regiões marcadas pela imigração forçada de africanos e por influxos culturais poderosos provenientes da África" (Cardoso 24) ("that discontinuous collection of regions marked by the forced migration of Africans and their powerful impact on the host culture). Afro-America encompasses those regions where black slavery accounted for the predominant modes of production and therefore where African presence exerted the greatest influence. While Afro-Brazilian culture differs from other Black African cultures in some particulars–namely language and its uses–it shares certain structural elements analogous to those of other plantation cultures in the Americas. Without neglecting Afro-Brazilian culture's singularity, one must remain attentive to the numerous similarities that bind together all black cultures in America and also to their tense interactions with the cultural production of the dominant cultures. Édouard Glissant emphasizes the inter-American character of plantation culture above national and regional peculiarities:

[ç]'est dans la Plantation que, comme dans un laboratoire, nous voyons le plus évidemment à l'oeuvre les forces confrontées de l'oral et de l'écrit, une des problématiques le plus enracinées dans notre paysage contemporain. C'est là que le multilinguisme, cette dimension menacée de notre univers, pour une des premières fois constatables, se fait et se défait de manière toute organique. C'est encore dans la Plantation que la rencontre des cultures s'est manifestée avec le plus d'acuité directement observable, quoique aucun de ceux qui l'habitèrent n'eut le moindre soupçon qu'il s'agissait là véritablement d'un choc de cultures. Le métissage culturel qui nous occupe tous, nous pouvons là le surprendre quelques-unes des lois de formations. C'est dans les prolongements de la Plantation, dans ce qu'elle a enfanté au moment même où elle disparaissait comme entité fonctionelle, que s'est imposée pour nous la recherche d'historicité, cette conjonction de la passion de se définir et de l'obsession du temps, qui est aussi une des ambitions des littératures contemporaines. (75)

The plantation, like a laboratory, displays most clearly the opposed forces of the oral and the written at work–one of the most deep-rooted topics of discussion in our contemporary landscape. It is there that multilingualism, that threatened dimension of our universe, can be observed for the first time, organically forming and disintegrating. It is also within the Plantation that the meeting of cultures is most clearly and directly observable, though none of the inhabitants had the slightest hint that this was really about a clash of cultures. Here we are able to discover a few of the formational laws of the cultural *métissage* that concerns us all. It is essential that we investigate historicity–that conjunction of the passion for self-definition and an obsession with time that is also one of the ambitions of contemporary literatures.

Between four and twelve million Africans were brought by the slave trade to Brazil (the precise number remains unknown to this day). The slave trade increased dramatically during the reign of Dom Pedro I in the first half of the nineteenth century, and slave traders became important fixtures of Rio de Janeiro society. According to Clóvis Moura, by the end of the seventeenth century, Brazil's slave population numbered 1,582,000, or 47.9 percent of the total population. By 1818, another 350,000 African slaves had arrived, increasing the slave total to 52.5 percent of Brazil's total population (Moura 47).

Among the upper classes, the disguised or alleged fear of a black rebellion led to the suspicion of any social contact between slaves and freedmen. Even when the slave regime enjoyed periods of relative stability, black men faced ostracism and friction from institutions and groups that sought to exclude them socially. Evidently slaves were forbidden access to public venues and to individual and collective activities deemed threatening to the established order–among others, any action of a political nature. All forms of union and solidarity were prohibited among the slaves themselves. The ruling class believed the imposition of these anonymous conditions of existence to be essential to perpetuate the submission of slaves and the subservience of those who had been granted their freedom. These conditions were coupled with a refined and severe system of surveillance and punishment set in motion to guarantee the slaves' submission, the safety of the master and his family, and order within the slave regime (Fernandes 56–7).

Accordingly, black people's access to education was always perceived as a potential threat, as attested to by this curious passage from the conservative daily *Jornal da Província de São Paulo* (4 October 1887):

Em uma fazenda do município de Itatiba, indo á roça o seu proprietário examinar o serviço de seus escravos, em vez de encontral-os no eito, *adivinhem os leitores o que estavam elles fazendo?* Agrupados escutavam attentos a leitura do *Jornal da Província* feita por um deles cuja leitura era nada mais nada menos do que um resumo de um discurso de Conselheiro Dantas. O sr. naturalmente arrependido calou-se . . . . Em todo caso não havia perigo na leitura porque não se pregava a *insurreição.* (Schwarcz 181–2)

On a farm in the municipality of Itatiba, a landowner setting out to examine the labor of his slaves found them not at work but– can the reader guess what they were up to? In a group they sat attentive as one of them read aloud from the *Província,* more precisely, from a speech by Counselor Dantas. Regretting his discovery the landowner naturally fell silent . . . . In any event there was no danger in this reading since the speech did not preach insurrection.

Black authors would only make their presence felt in Brazilian literature during the course of the nineteenth century. Even after the abolition of slavery, reactionary mechanisms continued to act with the purpose of preserving the social and cultural status quo of old, and, in particular, of guaranteeing the subservience of former slaves and their descendants. Brazilian society remained skeptical as to the ability of a "primitive" Africa to produce true artistic manifestations, thus making difficult the black author's access to the production and marketing of cultural goods. Only in the first decades of the twentieth century would Brazil (like the West in general) recognize the value and existence of an African aesthetic; until then the intellectual milieu remained uninterested in exploring African culture. The limited number of Afro-Brazilian writers of that time was further subject to debilitating psychological pressures, not the least among them the pressure to internalize the European standards and aesthetic current within the Brazilian elite and the concomitant ideal of "whitening"–both manifest in the fiction of José do Patrocínio, as we shall see later. Yet one should remain attentive to Afro-Brazilian authors' specific social and racial predicament and engagement with the intellectual currents of the time. To become attuned to the subversive irony that often permeates Afro-Brazilian literature, one must read between the lines and be attentive to its cunning discourse of half-silences.

Blacks were doubtless excluded from the public sphere in Brazil as in all of the Americas, and this exclusion served to prolong the edifice of colonial power and its legitimating ideologies. With reference to the exclusions of the artistic world one recalls the eloquent testimony of symbolist poet Cruz e Sousa (1861–1898) in the 1898 poem "Emparedado" ["Against the Wall"]:

> ¿Artista? Loucura! Loucura! Pode lá isso ser se tu vens dessa longínqua região desolada, lá do fundo exótico dessa África sugestiva, gemente, criação dolorosa e sanguinolenta de Satãs rebelados, dessa flagelada África, grotesca e triste, melancólica, gênese assombrosa de gemidos, tetricamente fulminada pelo banzo mortal. (663)

> An Artist? Madness! Madness! You might become one if you come from that distant and desolate region, from the exotic depths of this suggestive Africa, the moaning, painful, and bloody creation of insurrecting Satans, from this flagellated Africa, grotesque, sad, and melancholic, this ghostly genesis of groans, dismally annihilated by mortal strife.

A few nineteenth-century black authors tenaciously infiltrated Brazil's realm of letters, at times even in the hope of reversing the terms of their social and cultural oppression. Despite the bitterness evident in this poem by Cruz e Sousa, the work also points to the future appearance of a new and majestic black Dante.

In turn, the literature produced by Brazil's dominant classes is marked by the almost always negated presence of the black man. In this respect, José de Alencar's (1829–1877) *O Tronco do Ipê* [1871; *The Trunk of the Ipê Tree*, published in Rio de Janeiro in 1877] allows for an exemplary reading of the betrayal of manifest authorial intentions by layers of meaning that prove destabilizing. In the folds of its textual tissue, one detects the ambivalent construction of black identity that permeates not only the plot and structure of Alencar's fiction but social interaction in Brazilian society at large. Predictably black artistic expression took root and flowered in the less oppressive soil of popular oral tradition rather than in the land of erudition. Afro-Brazilians of successive generations came to dominate popular forms of cultural expression, often marked by the fusion of the sacred and the profane that is characteristic of African cultures. In each stage of this development, the threads of the written and spoken word were interwoven in genres as diverse as dance, contests of strength and agility, idiomatic poetry, oral storytelling, and the ceremony and liturgy of African religions. Through these hybrid forms, the textual, performative, and conceptual repertoires of African civilization were translated and repatriated into Brazil's palimpsestic national narrative.

A chief constitutive element of black culture in Brazil was a performative mode of expression of broad collective appeal, a theatricality that cannot be elided within the observance of social ritual. Afro-Brazilian ritual evoked both the social and dramatic ceremonies of African traditions as well as their various forms: mimetic, expressive, and playful. Hourantier has stressed the cathartic and therapeutic nature of the performance of these rites, which "attempt to confer meaning on disorder and incorporate it into society . . . . [I]n principle it represents the celebration of a symbolic and dramatic ritual developed within the limits of the theater" (Hourantier 23).

Within the circuit of what may be termed oral textuality, the spoken word is the charge that transforms the verb into an event and a performance. Thus the spoken word breathes life into the theater of ritual and into the poetics of oral inscription. It marks the subject and performer not merely as the agent of ritual but–to the extent that the spoken word is metonymic for all language–as ritual itself. The spoken word combines past, present, and future in a spiraling discourse in which gesture and song, movement and intonation weave together the choreography of an oral and synesthetic language. In this fashion Paul Zumthor defines agency and signification: "The pronounced word does not exist (as does the written) in a purely verbal context: it necessarily takes part in a broader process, an existential predicament that the word alters in some ways and whose totality engages the bodies of the performers . . . . At the border between two semiotic realms, the corporeal attitude of gesture continuously finds its match in the inflection of voice, and vice-versa" (244).

In the vast territory of Afro-Brazilian poetic idioms, from the *Iorubá* to the *Banto*, a broad spectrum of techniques warrants investigation: the structure of rhyme, the craft of images, intertextual games: in sum everything that constitutes poetic procedure. Antônio Risério, for example, has coined the term "inter-textual phanomelopea" to define the oral traditions of the Nagô and in particular the poetry of the *Orikis* "in which verbal units revolve within a decentered textuality" (Risério 53–4). Taking a page from Karin Barber, Risério ventures that the archive of Iorubá and Afro-Brazilian oral literature represents a vast reservoir of verbal material–themes, formulae, stories, poetic idioms–that pass through the permeable borders of all genres and are incorporated into them to fulfill different functions (Barber, qtd. in Risério 52). In his recent study *Afragrafias* [Afro-graphisms] Martins ventures further that the textuality of Afro-Brazilian oral (or "non-graphic") literature necessitates the coinage of the new term *oraliture,* "a singular inscription of an oral register that–no less than the *literature* of the letter–graphs the subject onto a nation's narrative and enunciative terrain. Ora*liture,* a neologism that also points to the erasure of language, to a significant alteration in meaning constituted by difference and alterity, culture, and its symbolic representations" (Martins 1997, 21).

We may take as an example of *oraliture* the *Banto* song "O Canto de Congados," in which the singer translates the spiral memory of the crossing from Congo onto the discursive terrain of Brazil, and puns on the name of his state, Minas Gerais:

> Zum, zum, zum
> Lá no meio do mar
>
> É o canto da sereia
> Que me faz entristecer
>
> Parece que ela adivinha
> O que vai acontecer
>
> Ajudai-me rainha do mar
> Ajudai-me rainha do mar
>
> Que manda na terra
> Que manda no ar
> Ajudai-me rainha do mar
>
> Zum, zum, zum
> Lá no meio do mar
>
> É o canto da sereia
> E seus prantos muito mais

Naquele mar profundo
Adeus minas, gerais
Ajudai-me rainha do mar . . .

Zoom, zoom, zoom
There in the middle of the sea

It's the song of the siren
That comes to sadden me

It seems she can fathom
What's yet to happen

Assist me, queen of the sea
Assist me, queen of the sea

Who reigns over the earth
Who reigns in the air
Assist me, queen of the sea

Zoom, zoom, zoom
There in the middle of the sea

It's the song of the siren
Or rather of her lamentations
In the depths of that sea
So long to mines, endless mines
Assist me, queen of the sea . . .

Written and spoken word combine in the hybrid productions of today's poets, novelists, and critics, in their expression of new or renewed sentiments; the slavery of the past is fused with the complexities of the present. Afro-Brazilians have long appropriated Catholic rituals and symbols to adapt African pantheons of deities to the New World, and now they seek in the establishment's own art and discourse openings for further cultural interpenetration. Albeit with great difficulty, Afro-Brazilian *oraliture* has gained ground and an audience.

To understand this universe one must first characterize the cultural scene into which Afro-Brazilian culture has insinuated itself. One must cast a glance back toward the Colonial period and examine how the black man and his community were evoked and described as objects for the purposes of the dominant discourse. Literary references to the black experience, scant during the colonial period, increased dramatically with the calls for the abolition of slavery that greeted the beginning of the nineteenth century in Brazil. The first references were seldom admiring, as is evident by the writings of Gregório de Matos Guerra, whose experience of the Brazilian Northeast nearly spanned the seventeenth century (from his birth in Salvador in 1623 or 1633 to his death in Recife in 1696). In his "Great Baroque Rebellion," Matos dismissed the colony's people and secular and ecclesiastical dignitaries as embodiments of "Brazil's vileness" and his own native state as "Madam Lady Bahia"–stepmother to its brood and mother superior to the foreigners. Matos had only contempt for *mestizos* both of native and black blood (respectively the *caramuru* and the *mulatto*), which he regarded as arriviste and nouveau riche. In his summation Brazil constituted: "Terra tão grosseira e crassa/Que a ninguém se tem respeito,/Salvo si mostra algum jeito/De ser mulato" (qtd. in Araripe Junior 85, 89) ("A Land so vulgar and crass/That no one demands respect, /Unless he manages / To pass for mulatto").

Blacks were also present in the literature of those one may term the spiritual colonizers–the Jesuits–until the Marquis of Pombal expelled them from Portugal and its dominions in 1759. Most notably, Jesuits Antonio Vieira (1608–1697) and Giovanni Antonio Andreoni (1650–1716; under the pseudonym Antonil) wrote of the white and black protagonists of slavery in the context of the large colonial estates of seventeenth- and eighteenth-century Brazil. Antonio Vieira's concern with the slave's predicament is evident from the outset of his preaching throughout the provinces of Bahia, Pernambuco, Maranhão, and Amazônia. Eugenio Gomes notes that while Vieira formally respected the principle of "just captivity" established by the colonial Catholic church, he nonetheless represented the first voice in Brazil "to condemn in unreproachable terms, through his memorable sermons, the debasement of the human condition [under slavery]" (see the introduction to Vieira's sermons, 9). The anguished tension underlying Vieira's magnificent baroque rhetoric betrays the ambiguity of his predicament in his capacity as missionary. For while Vieira railed against the landowner's cruelty and evoked the suffering of slaves in the "sweet hell" of the sugar plantations, he sidesteps any hope for change or solace in a dimension other than the spiritual. Thus, in his preaching before the slaves on the topic of slavery (in particular, sermons XIV, XVI, XX, and XXVII of his rosary), Vieira likens their suffering to the Passion of Christ: "A paixão de Cristo parte foi de noite sem dormir, parte foi de dia sem descansar, e tais são as vossas noites e os vossos dias. Cristo despido, e vós despidos: Cristo sem comer, e vós famintos: Cristo em tudo maltratado, e vós maltratados em tudo" (Viera 315) ("Christ's Passion consisted of nights without sleep and days without rest, and such are your nights and your days. As Christ was unclad, you are unclad: as Christ went without eating, you go hungry: In everything Christ was maltreated, and you are maltreated in everything").

The tone and import of the work of Jesuit Antonil (or rather Giovanni Antonio Andreoni) are of quite a different order, as evident from his long title worth citing at length: "Brazil's Culture and Opulence through its Medicines and Mines, with Various Curious Notes as to How to Make Sugar, Plant and Reap Tobacco; and Extract Gold from Mines; and to Discover those of Silver; and of the Great Advantages this Conquest of Meridional America brings the Kingdom of PORTUGAL, through this and other Forms of Royal Contracts" (Lisbon 1711) (Araripe 184). Like his title, Antonil's infamous opening line of Chapter IX is a model of precision and perceptiveness: "Os escravos são as mãos e os pés do senhor de engenho, porque sem eles não é possível fazer, conservar e aumentar fazenda, nem ter engenho corrente" ("Slaves are the hands and the feet of the plantation owner, for without them it is not possible to accomplish anything, neither to conserve and augment, nor run the plantation"). Antonil examines Brazil's colonial order with the rationalism of a modern-day economist who always keeps in mind the property holder's interest. In contrast to Vieira, Antonil describes Brazil as "inferno dos negros, purgatório dos brancos e paraíso dos mulatos e das mulatas [as quais] depois de forras continuam a ser ruinas de muitos"–(Araripe 184) ("the black man's hell, the white man's purgatory, and paradise for mulattos and for the mulattas who continue to be the ruin of so many"). Antonil's low opinion of *mestizagem* recalls that of Gregório de Matos, in particular Matos' inference as to the value of passing for a mulatto in Brazil. In this manner, reports sent back from the distant colony confirmed racial prejudices first cultivated in, and inherited and imported from, Europe. In Brazil, these notions gradually became stereotypes and gave rise to the establishment of national myths such as that of the pleasant and amusing mulatto.

In the eighteenth century, Basílio da Gama (1740–1795) briefly digresses from his indigenist concerns to pity the African in the 1791 epic poem *O Quitubia*. At the outset of the nineteenth century, slavery was among the questions pertaining to the cultivation of land that concerned the verse of statesman and scientist José Bonifácio de Andrada e Silva, the "Patriarch of Independence" (1763–1838). Not the least of his liberal projects that were frustrated after his falling out with Brazil's first emperor, Dom Pedro I, was Bonifácio's ambitious plan to phase out slavery gradually. In his 1820 poem simply titled "O Brasil," Bonifácio advised the government to lend

> . . . socorro
> Pronto e seguro ao Índio tosco, ao Negro
> Ao pobre desvalido
>
> de forma a despedaçar:
> a imunda vestidura da pobreza
> E de brutos [fazer] homens e Heróis!
>
> *(qtd. in Candido 1981, 229)*
>
> . . . prompt and secure help
> To the coarse Indian, the Black
> To the poor and destitute
>
> in order to unravel:
> The filthy robe of poverty
> And coin from brutes men and Heroes!

In keeping with the radical secularization of Portuguese politics following Pombal's expulsion of the Jesuits, and in anticipation of the force of the successful abolitionist movement of 1870–1888, one notes here that Bonifácio's pioneering abolitionism lacks any mystical or religious import. "O Brasil" also displays the paternalistic condescension and pompous ethnocentrism that characterized nineteenth-century abolitionist sentiment among the literary and political elites in Brazil and elsewhere in the Americas, and which George Fredrickson has accurately termed a romantic racism.

To this list of the first Portuguese and Brazilian authors to represent blacks in literature one may add the name of the obscure nationalist and proto-romantic poet, José Salomé Quiroga (1810–1878). Quiroga's 1845 poem "Retrato da mulata" ["Portrait of the Mulatta"] compares his beloved's lips to coral, teeth to pearl, and breasts to lemons, and makes the expected reference to the dark hue of her *buriti* (mons veneris). It concludes with an impish invocation that sketches the stereotype of the sexually coveted and available mulatta:

> Já que pintei-te,
> Minha querida,
> Vênus nascida
> Cá no Brasil,
> Em prêmio dai-me
> *Muxoxos*, queixas,
> *Quindins, me deixas,*
> E beijos mil.
>
> Since I have painted you
> My darling,
> Venus reborn
> Here in Brazil,
> Reward me with
> Tutting, reproaches,
> Coconut sweets, and allow me
> A thousand kisses.
>
> *(qtd. in Mario de Lima 84)*

Before the romantics, the neo-Classical poets of Minas Gerais had already heralded the mulatta as the national standard of excellence for feminine beauty, a standard that would survive through the myriad aesthetic movements of the nineteenth century. While José de Alencar's 1857 romantic novel *O Guarani*

features a blonde heroine in Cecilia (lover of the native Indian Peri), the novel singles out the dark Isabel, Cecilia's cousin, as the representative of "o tipo brasileiro em toda a sua graça e formosura, com o encantador contraste de languidez e malícia, de indolência e vivacidade" (31) ("the Brazilian type in all her grace and splendor, with that charming contrast between languor and malice, indolence and vivacity").

One should note that frankness in matters sexual increased in Brazilian letters (and not merely during Romanticism) in proportion to the number of black attributes described or suggested in its female characters. Gregório de Matos's amorous lyric, for example, already distinguished between the "vulgar register" he deemed suitable for the treatment of black and mulatta women, and the "noble register" he reserved for upper-caste white women, worthy in his eyes of "a thousand [poetic] refinements" (Bosi 108–9). Trajano Galvão de Carvalho (1830–1864) figures prominently if not brilliantly within this tradition of representing the black or mulatta woman as loose. Silvio Romero has cited this native of the state of Maranhão as the first author to significantly and directly portray blacks and slaves in Brazilian poetry. Before Carvalho, Romero wrote that one or another poet had touched upon black slaves in passing, but merely in passing and always by way of a simple protest against slavery. Carvalho would have ventured one step further by placing himself in the intimate life of the slaves and by painting more realistic types (Romero 1943). Carvalho cultivated the theme of the seductive mulatta in contrast to the tragic mulatta made popular by other literatures such as that of the United States. Carvalho's poem "A crioula" ["The Creole Woman"] openly deals with sexual themes: At the outset the protagonist makes an uncanny declaration with respect to her condition, "Sou cativa . . . qu'importa? folgando/Hei de o vil cativeiro levar!" ("I am a captive . . . what does it matter? Making merry/I will take on this vile captivity!"). The protagonist embraces a *carpe diem* stance out of keeping with her slave condition, boasting of clandestine encounters with the "tender" master and with the vicar who had, during confession, seen things he would rather have touched. In Carvalho's poem sexual and racial stereotypes prove mutually reinforcing, and his political conservatism is veiled under the varnish of sexual liberation and anticlericalism.

During the Romantic period, the fiction of the young slave girl who marries out of her bondage required the absence or attenuation of the protagonist's black physical traits–as in the case of Bernardo Guimarães's (1825–1884) famous novel *A Escrava Isaura* [1875; The Slave Isaura]. Though the novel's plot and abolitionist message hinge on the fact that Isaura is indeed of mixed blood, Isaura gains the love of Álvaro precisely because she is different from her peers. In one passage she is described as:

> bela e donosa, pela correção e nobreza dos traços fisionômicos e por certa distinção nos gestos e ademanes. Ninguém diria que era uma escrava, que trabalhava entre as companheiras, e a tomaria antes por uma senhora moça que, por desenfado, fiava entre as escravas. Parecia a garça-real, alçando o colo garboso e altaneiro, entre uma chusma de pássaros vulgares. (41)
>
> beautiful and ladylike, due to the perfection and nobility of her features and a certain distinction in her gestures. No one would say that she was a slave who worked among her companions, but rather would take her for a young lady who out of amusement mingled among the slaves. She seemed like the royal heron, raising her tall and distinguished neck, among a flock of vulgar birds.

In this vein, the narrative voice of *A Escrava Isaura* exhaustively seeks to distance the heroine from her ethnic heritage, an insistence representative of the imagination of the Brazilian elite during the nineteenth century. Joaquim Manuel de Macedo's (1820–1882) 1844 romance, *A Moreninha* [The Dark-Skinned Girl], provides a further emblematic example of a heroine who is dark yet suitable for a higher station in life–that is, who does not betray the complicating ingredient of *mestizagem.* Nonetheless this ingredient would prove unavoidable in late nineteenth-century Brazilian literature.

Novelist José de Alencar betrays both a Romantic racism in his treatment of blacks and a preference for the native over the black as the mythical embodiment of Brazilian identity. Alencar would write two abolitionist plays, the 1857 *O Demônio Familiar* [The Devil You Know] and the 1860 *Mãe* [Mother], in which the hero commits suicide upon discovering that his mother is of mixed blood. In turn, Alencar's *O Demônio Familiar,* like Macedo's abolitionist 1869 novel *Vítimas-Algozes: Quadros da Escravidão* [Cruel Victims: Scenes from Slave Life], details the abyss of moral corruption destined to threaten the bourgeois family unless slavery is abolished. In all three texts the depiction of black characters is absolutely stereotypical and conventional.

In Brazilian theater history, black subjectivity and culture–though often explored as a leitmotif or object of theoretical reflections–tend to signal invisibility and what one could call "indivisibility." Blacks are invisible on the stage not merely in the literal sense of being absent from the dramatis personae, but because when they are represented, the prevalence of stereotypes reduce their alterity to the realm of ridicule. It is the reinforcement of racial stereotypes that renders blacks "indivisible" on stage, in the sense that they possess only one voice and one body, both alienating to the public. Mirian Garcia Mendes attests that blacks caught the attention of Brazilian playwrights only after 1850 and even then, as Martins Pena's (1815–1848) comedies demonstrate, only to compose a scene as extras that are not even named as characters (174). From the end of the nineteenth century, dramatic convention followed, with few exceptions, stereotypical models that endured well into the mid-twentieth century and that to some extent still shape the representation of blacks today. Among dominant images of black men, one may single out three: the loyal black man, synonymous with ignorance, passivity, and absolute submission; the criminal, an image that reflects a threat too often staged; and the caricature of the black man, prototype of ridicule and of the grotesque. In turn, the black woman's body alternatively signals the stereotypes of the docile wet nurse, the faceless and anonymous domestic servant, and the elaborate sexual fantasy of the coveted and available mulatta.

On stage, the black subject is thus not merely inverted but turned inside out, his/her textual body a site for the inscription of segregationist and racist knowledge. In Henry Louis Gates's summation of Jacques Derrida's admonition on the uses of knowledge, discourse presents itself as a system of signs that "institutes, declares, writes, inscribes and prescribes," delimiting "spaces to close frontiers. Discourse does not discern, it discriminates" (Gates 331). In the discourse of power manifest on the Brazilian stage, recognition of alterity is reduced to the negation of difference or to its grotesque fetishization. In this manner, the white man is presented as the paradigm of humanity, and a white mask mirrors beauty and the good, while on the periphery of the scene the black mask signals evil and the ridiculous. Through the syntax of these conventions of theatrical representation–opposition and exclusion, invisibility and "indivisibility"–blacks and whites enact an imaginary and deceptive dichotomy as antagonistic signs that obscure the plurality of human cultures and experience.

These distortions permeate not only the theater but, in particular, abolitionist literature in its different genres. One should note that in Brazil this literature is far from abundant: the poetry of Antonio Castro Alves (1847–1871) (see **Figure 1**), Fagundes Varela's (1841–1875) 1864 long poem, *Mauro, o Escravo* [Mauro, the Slave], and a few romances advancing the abolitionist cause, such as the aforementioned *A Escrava Isaura* and *As Vítimas Algozes.* Most of these texts focus more on slavery than on the slave, and represent the black man as the symbol of the thesis that slavery is abominable rather than as a credible human subject: His voice is rarely heard, his physical and psychological traits are grossly simplified, and the result is a quite stereotypical portrait of the slave. Castro Alves proves the exception to this rule: In his mellifluous abolitionist poetry, the male and female slave alike possess a face, voice, and gesture. Thus one can distinguish in the chorus of voices that make up "Saudação a Palmares" ["Salutation to Palmares"] not only the voice of the poet but the sounds of the rebellious *quilombo*:

Figure 1.

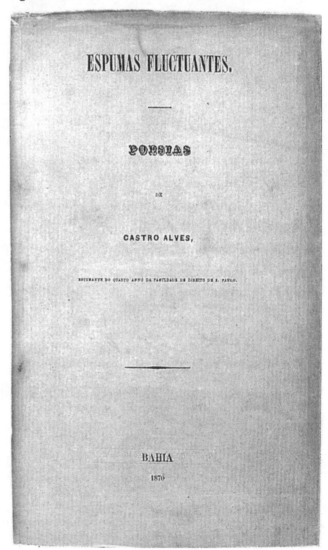

Salve! Região dos valentes
Onde os ecos estridentes
Mandam aos plainos trementes
Os gritos do caçador!
E ao longe os latidos soam,
E as trompas da caça atroam . . .
E os corvos negros revoam
Sobre o campo abrasador! . . .

　(536)

Hail! Realm of the valiant
Where echoes, strident,
Command tremendous plains
And the hunter's clamour!
Faraway the barks sound,
And the hunter's horns resound,
Over fields ablaze all around
The black ravens soar! . . .

From the mid-nineteenth century, when the intelligentsia became preoccupied with the question of what would constitute a true Brazilian people, miscegenation became a principal concern for novelists grappling with the notion of an interracial democracy. In the description of a church festivity in José de Alencar's 1862 *Lucíola*, for example, the narrator emphasizes the various hues and infinite gradations of the population of Rio de Janeiro:

> Todas as raças, desde o caucasiano sem mescla até o africano puro; todas as posições, desde as ilustrações da política, da fortuna ou do talento, até o proletário humilde e desconhecido; todas as profissões, desde o banqueiro até o mendigo [. . .] roçando a seda e a casimira pela baeta ou pelo algodão, misturando os perfumes delicados às impuras exalações, o fumo aromático do havana às acres baforadas do cigarro de palha. (12–13)

> All races were present, from the unadulterated Caucasian to the pure African; all positions, from those illustrative of the worlds of politics, fortune and talent, to the unknown and humble proletariat; all professions from banker to beggar . . . . [R]efined perfumes mixed with impure exhalations, and the aromatic smoke of the *havana* with the acrid puffs of cheap cigarettes.

Likewise, in his novel *O Ermitão de Muquém* [1869; The Hermit from Muquém], Bernardo Guimarães describes the great variety of colors and figures at a dance in the interior, detailing the presence in each pair of whites, *criollos, mestizas,* and beautiful mulattas. In both cases, the festivity is the privileged site for the democratization of the relations between social and ethnic groups, the singular space of a society free from racial discrimination.

Nonetheless, the internal contradictions of this "festive" literature become evident if one is attentive to the severe restrictions that govern interracial relationships at the described festivities. The paradox is that, while the myriad hues of miscegenation are ostentatiously flaunted in novels such as these two, in nineteenth-century Brazilian literature, the sexual union of a black man and white woman, while rare (occurring in naturalist but not romantic writing), without exception resulted in tragedy. As examples of this rule one can cite Aluísio Azevedo's (1857–1913) novel, *O Mulato* (1881), and the abolitionist play by Artur Azevedo (1855–1908) and Urbano Duarte, *O Escravocrata* [1884; The Slave-Owner]. In this unusual play of the love of a lady for her slave, the consequences prove catastrophic not only for the lovers but for the subsequent generation. The reverse equation of the sexual union of a white man and black woman proved less

threatening to Brazil's patriarchal order and was represented more frequently in its literature. Significantly, whether such an interracial coupling results in tragedy (as in Aluísio Azevedo's *O Cortiço* [1890; The Slum]) or in a happy ending (the case of *A Escrava Isaura*), nineteenth-century Brazilian literature shies away from representing and thus from confirming the fertility of such a union. In contrast, the sexual union of the white man and native woman is presented admiringly in José de Alencar's 1865 *Iracema*, where the child of suffering that Iracema gives birth to proves emblematic of a nascent Brazilian nationalism.

In the last three decades of the nineteenth century, the Brazilian intelligentsia was forced to reconsider the status of blacks following the abolition of slavery. Influenced by positivist and naturalist theories of evolution then in fashion, the intelligentsia came to accept the principle of inherent racial inequality as a scientific fact. Thus, though nineteenth-century Brazilian literature lacked an actual discourse in favor of slavery, the structure of its poetry and fiction nonetheless betrayed the workings of racist presuppositions. Miscegenation came to be seen as the basis for the Brazilian population, albeit grudgingly, by many elements of society. Intellectuals held a poor opinion of the population at large and attributed the people's shortcomings to their racial heterogeneity. While many intellectuals advocated greater miscegenation as the only possible solution to what they perceived as Brazil's racial dilemma, they did so with the belief that the hegemony and influence of the race they deemed superior would prevail. Miscegenation was to be accompanied by the greater influx of immigrants from Europe. In short, the miscegenation they supported was tantamount to a process of whitening the population.

This paradigm for miscegenation had its roots in naturalism and in the theory of evolution and rested on an ultimately racist foundation. It would only come to be called into question in Brazil in the 1930s through the work of Gilberto Freyre (1900–1987), Caio Prado Junior (1907–1990), and Sergio Buarque de Holanda (1902–1982). Before then, the adherence to racist presuppositions was manifest even in Afro-Brazilian fiction–for example, in the stereotypical characterizations of the 1877 novel *Motta Coqueiro ou a Pena de Morte* [Motta Coqueiro, or the Death Sentence] by José Patrocínio (1853–1905), himself the son of a slave. While the novel purports to denounce the infamous process whereby an innocent is sentenced to death, it indulges in the most common racial stereotypes of nineteenth-century literature: those of the asexual black man and of the sensual mulatta. The latter is, at one point, described as a Creole of sixteen going on seventeen, exuding sensuality through the sieve of her white blouse and her malicious eyes. Yet the importance of Patrocínio's novel cannot be disregarded. Silviano Santiago remarks upon the text's "extraordinary and original precision in describing African ritual (in particular, the game of conches). The images stream forth with an exuberance and precision befitting the careful collector of myths" (148). If it is true that "the text's explicit ideology recalls the manner in which whites perceived blacks," Santiago notes nonetheless that the author's insider's knowledge of black culture makes for "a complex game of intentions, for his own social and racial obsessions enter into the equation, giving free reign to an imagination that literally dominates the narrative's explicit purposes" (148). Few nineteenth-century authors were, in fact, able to transcend the racist ideology that survived the abolition of slavery and dictated the terms of the former slaves' absorption into the new order. In the literature of the late nineteenth century, physical and psychological descriptions of black and white characters perpetuated the perceived qualitative differences between them, at times almost casually. For example, while naturalist Adolfo Caminha's (1867–1897) *O Bom Crioulo* [1895; The Good Creole] deals with sexuality in a complex and sophisticated manner, his characterization of racial differences remains simplistic.

In summary, despite the intense debate surrounding slavery that preoccupied much of Europe and the young independent nations of the Americas in the nineteenth century, writers prominent in the Brazilian romantic movement of 1830–1870 proved reticent in their treatment of black characters. Native themes would only be supplanted by black subjects in Brazilian literature with the advent of naturalism and the intensification of debates surrounding the question of race in the last three decades of the century. Silvio Romero (1851–1914) pioneered the cause of black studies in Brazil by demanding the rectification of this oversight in the debates on Brazilian nationhood. Romero was among the first in the country to call for the appreciation of black culture: "If indeed the question concerns love for the races that make up our people, if we study the Indian, for what reason do we not also study the black? Why do our museums not boast an African section? Why do we not investigate black languages and religions, dances and festivities?" (qtd. in Candido 1978, 61).

Romero was not immune to the sociobiological obsession of the century's last decades, and saw in miscegenation a source of disruption and disequilibrium and the cause of "constant turbulence among the American peoples" (qtd. in Candido 1978, 62). Nonetheless, Romero proved a pioneer in his courageous statement that "Brazilian literature–like all other literatures in the world–ought to represent the positive expression of the ideas and sentiments, the intellectual and emotional state of a people. Well, our population is not Indian, black, nor Portuguese; it is above all the sum of these parts thrown into the melting pot of the New World" (qtd. in Candido 1978, 54). Thus Romero combined the prejudices then in fashion with respect to miscegenation with an appreciation of black and *mestizo* contribution to Brazilian civilization. In the latter context, Romero singled out poet Gonçalves Dias (1823–1864) as the author who is at once the most national and most Portuguese in Brazilian literature, one of the most distinct exemplars of the genuine people of Brazil. Romero concluded that Gonçalves Dias, who as the child of a Portuguese and a *Mameluca*, was a descendant of the three races that make up the national population of Brazil, and thus represented their principal tendencies.

Before the full emergence of the abolitionist movement, two books by black authors were published in the exceptional year of 1859: *Trovas Burlescas* [Burlesque Ballads] by Luíz Gama (1830–1882) and *Úrsula* by Maria Firmina dos Reis (1825–1917). Both authors preferred to publish under pseudonyms (respectively, "Getulino" and "Uma Maranhense"–meaning a native of Maranhão), a coincidence that suggests the degree to which Brazilian society was still unprepared to recognize black poetry and fiction. (We will consider Maria Firmina dos Reis' novel further under the topic of Afro-Brazilian women's literature.) The son of the legendary Nagô Luiza Mahin, a militant in the Malês Revolt, Luíz Gama was born free in Bahia but sold as a slave at the age of 10 by his white father (unidentified to this day). While a teenager he fled to São Paulo and learned to read, successively becoming a

soldier, printer, and scribe for the police. Unable to register in the Faculty of Law on account of his race, he succeeded in obtaining a license to practice law and became the first legal defender of blacks in Brazil. A distinguished journalist, orator, and poet, Gama founded São Paulo's Republican Party and Center for Abolitionism.

His poetry was produced at the crossroads of European tradition and his African heritage. To erudite European form and meter Gama brought a black social consciousness and a playfulness that was his own, inverting and confusing aesthetic and political hierarchies. Gama drew from his experience as journalist, lawyer, and political activist to characterize his contemporaries and his times. Particularly remarkable at that time was the irreverent pride he took in his African heritage, evident in the many words of African origin he incorporates into his "anti-heroic" decasyllabic verse. Gama's explorations of his rich European and African influences were never lacking in delicious self-consciousness and humor. Take for example "Lá vai verso" ["Here Comes Verse"] from the collection *Trovas Burlescas*:

> Quero que o mundo me encarando veja,
> Um retumbante *Orfeu de Carapinha*,
> Que a Lira desprezando, por mesquinha,
> Ao som decanta de Marimba augusta;
> E, qual outro Arion entre os Delfins,
> Os ávidos piratas embaindo–
> As ferrenhas palhetas vai brandindo
> Com estilo que preza a Líbia adusta.
>
> *(23)*
>
> Let the world facing me behold
> A thunderous Orpheus of Carapinha,
> Who disdains the Lyre, a meagre thing,
> Decants sounds from an august Marimba;
> And like another Arion among the dolphins
> Makes eager pirates sheathe their swords
> Brandishing against blades of iron
> With a style becoming brave Líbia.

Still in the same poem the poet invokes "The Muse from Guinea, in her jet black colour" to bid her to instruct him in the language of the Afro-Brazilian religion of *candomblé*:

> Empresta-me o cabaço d'urucungo,
> Ensina-me a brandir tua marimba,
> Inspira-me a ciência da candimba,
> Às vias me conduz d'alta grandeza.
>
> *(24)*
>
> Lend me the bark of the urucungo,
> Teach me to brandish your marimba,
> Inspire in me the science of candimba,
> From your high eminence lead me the way.

Gama did not always succeed in harmonizing the disparate and in principle mutually exclusive African and European spheres of his heritage. In contrast to his satires, his romantic lyrics often indulged the clichés and prejudices in vogue with reference to the representation of women. In his two poems of nostalgia for the impossible love of his youth, "Laura" and "Junto à Estàtua," he exalts the same woman–"A beautiful virgin with a snow-white neck, blue eyes, and golden hair." Only his satire consistently does justice to the abolitionist verve of his journalism; sadly Gama would die in 1882, six years before the abolition for which he fought.

Through his poetic versatility and political engagement with the social and racial questions of the day, Gama opened the path for two turn-of-the-century mulatto writers from Rio who would excel in fiction and journalism: Lima Barreto (1881–1922) and João Paulo Barreto (1881–1921), (best known under one of his various pseudonyms as "João do Rio"). Despite their differences in style and motivation, all three writers demonstrated audacity in making their mark within the extremely narrow and prejudiced intellectual milieu of their respective periods: the late Monarchy (the time of Luíz Gama) and the Old Republic (the time of Lima Barreto and João do Rio). Of course, the Old Republic represented our tropical belle époque, and nowhere was it more brilliantly dissected and dramatized than in the ironic fiction of the master Joaquim Maria Machado de Assis (1839–1908).

Machado's relatively infrequent concern with the black predicament during a moment of such crucial social, political, and economic upheaval in Brazil has produced a certain perplexity and much controversy among scholars. Yet we would venture to say that it is precisely in this "vacuum" that Machado accomplished a masterful sleight of hand. We must be attentive to the lacunae and silences in his work, as if contemplating the negatives of a photographic film. In turn, his critical writing is so precisely directed toward a scrutiny of the pretences and masks of the privileged classes that it is not surprising to find blacks unrepresented there, as they indeed were not in Brazilian high society. Machado de Assis did not indulge in any illusions as to the predicament of blacks in Brazilian society, as is evident not only from his fiction but from his newspaper columns. In his study of Machado, John Gledson best captures his position with respect to the abolitionist cause: For Machado, "[a]bolition did not represent a movement from darkness into light, but the simple passage from one relationship of economic and social exploitation to another" (124). Never naive, the author of *Dom Casmurro* wrote in his newspaper column, ironically entitled "Bons Dias" ("Good Days"): "in giving slaves their freedom, we accomplish no more than to give them the freedom to enter a job market where they will be hired and dismissed at will, and doubtless receive miserable salaries" (qtd. in Gledson 124).

Our own time has confirmed the perspicacity of Machado's skepticism. Giving a wide berth to the nationalist promises of abolitionists and republicans alike, Machado perceived these promises rather within the framework of an imported and misplaced European liberalism. Ever attentive to Brazilian hierarchy and its mechanisms of power, Machado foretold the destiny "of the heirs of slavery" in his newspaper writing, making explicit what remained oblique and implicit in his fiction. With startling accuracy his newspaper articles foresee that, in the passage from one economic model to another, as in a vicious game of chess, the pieces are merely rearranged on the board but the roles remain the same: "for in this society as it has been created, the pieces have to remain the same, Bishops remain Bishops, and the horse remains a horse" (Machado de Assis, "Balas de Estados," *Gazeta de Notícias*, Rio de Janeiro, 30 November 1885; qtd. in Gledson, 124).

In his criticism, Machado de Assis incisively exposes Brazil's profound inequities, and it is not too fanciful to conclude that he omits blacks as social beings in his fiction so as to more forcefully denounce the reigning social model. The latent resistance in his novels is found precisely in its blanks, in what remains unsaid and unfulfilled. Machado de Assis's work in this way attests to the increasing vitality of

the nineteenth-century Afro-Brazilian canon as also represented by Maria Firmina dos Reis, Luíz Gama, José do Patrocínio, Cruz e Sousa, João do Rio, and Lima Barreto, and it looks forward to the culturally discrete years of the beginning of the twentieth century that preceded the spectacular explosion of Brazilian Modernism in the form of the 1922 Week of Modern Art in São Paulo.

The Twentieth Century and Its Modernisms: Afro-Brazilian Literature

Nos pensamentos de esperanças
espreito de olhos baços
arregalados na insônia de aguardar
a hora de entrar em ação.

In thoughts of hope
dull eyes watch wide open
in an insomniac expectation
of the moment to enter into action.

–Miriam Alves

A general overview of the representations of blacks within Brazilian Modernist movements lies beyond the scope of this essay. Here we must be content with chronicling scientific work on Brazil's racial formation, from the pioneering efforts in the nineteenth century to the mainstream of intellectual investigation in the first decades of the twentieth century. In 1926, sociologist Gilberto Freyre helped organize, along with other writers and social scientists, the First Congress on Regionalism, partly in response to the cosmopolitan orientation of São Paulo's 1922 Week of Modern Art. Among the modernist poetry of the Northeast represented there, we can single out the experimentation with regional themes and Afro-Brazilian elements in the work of Jorge de Lima (1893–1953). During the 1920s, Modernists in São Paulo itself sought to explore the full ethnic diversity of the Brazilian popular imaginary; notable among these were the painter Tarsila do Amaral and the writer Mario de Andrade (1893–1945) who had a particular interest in Afro-Brazilian music. This music, in fact, gained fame and recognition during the 1920s largely owing to the nascent phonographic industry. Samba descended from the slums and the hills to reach the population of the main urban centers. Finally, over the objections of the purist and the prudish, samba was celebrated by the press and accepted in public venues. In the 1930s, samba schools would come to compete in tournaments during Carnival. Whether or not the mainstream relegated Afro-Brazilian music to the realm of the exotic (Rodrigues 34–5), the incontrovertible fact is that black culture gained ground at the beginning of the twentieth century after being the subject of so much persecution in the nineteenth (as evidenced by the newspapers of the day). Brazilian popular music with its African base and rhythms was already celebrated in the literature of the first years of the century: One need only think, for example, of João do Rio's newspaper articles and of the guitar player Ricardo in Lima Barreto's *Triste Fim de Policarpo Quaresma* [The Sad End of Policarpo Quaresma].

In broad terms, the influential literary Modernism of the axis Rio–São Paulo presents a confused portrait of the predicament and legacy of black culture in Brazil. This ambivalence was evident, for example, in the work of the native of São Paulo, Oswald de Andrade (1890–1954), and is illustrated in his two most famous manifestos, the *Brazil-Wood Poetry Manifesto* of 1924 and the *Anthropophagy Manifesto* of 1928. In the first manifesto, associated with his poems on colonization (part of the 1925 collection *Poesia Pau-Brasil* [Brazil-Wood Poetry]), Oswald de Andrade is attentive to the massive black presence in manifestations of contemporary popular culture: "O carnaval no Rio é o acontecimento religioso da raça." (Oswald de Andrade 1970, 5) ("In Rio, carnival is a religious event of race."). From the start the manifesto alludes to the physical and cultural presence of blacks in the urban population: "Os casebres de açafrão e de ocre nos verdes da favela, sob o azul cabralino, são fatos estéticos" (Oswald de Andrade 1970, 5) ("Saffron and ochre shacks amid the green of the hills and under the blue sky constitute aesthetic facts"). The fragmentary and open-ended structure of Andrade's masterful manifesto purposefully does not resolve the tensions between the traditional fascination with European cultural form (evident in the text's enigmatic citation of Blaise Cendars) and a formative African influence—no longer flagellated and sad as in the vision of Cruz e Souza—but confident and vibrant in its *avant la lettre* extroversion and tropical sense of humor.

In contrast, the audacious *Anthropophagy Manifesto* of 1928 curiously shies away from the complexities of Brazil's cultural inheritance and excludes blacks from its text, an attitude that would prevail in the Anthropophagy movement in general (as evident in the two phases or "teethings" of its journal in 1928–29). Instead, the Anthropophagy elected as their emblem a native "Indian," just as unrealistic and unhinged from history and society as the native of the Brazilian romanticism that they so sought to criticize. The Anthropophagy neglected Brazil's full ethnic and cultural diversity despite their repeatedly affirmed intention to ground their movement in the real soil of this nation: "O Brasil-brasileiro é que estamos construindo, dôa a quem doer, se queixe quem quizer se queixar" (Costa 10) ("We are building a Brazilian Brazil, let this hurt whom it may, over the complaints of those who choose to complain"). In the early forties, Oswald de Andrade would be cured of his case of "Anthropophagy measles" and come, in his essays, to recognize African contributions to Brazilian culture. He now took pride in the "infinite riches brought to us from Africa, and the ancestral values still guarded by the cult of the orixás" (1991, 75).

By way of contrast, family figures prominently in the writings of the native of Minas Gerais Conceição Evaristo, whose poem "Vozes Mulheres" ["Women's Voices"] traces the trajectory of her family from the slave ships to the labyrinths of the slums, retelling public events from the vantage point of those who constitute the undercurrent of official history. In this sense, the poetic subject spans time and overcomes stereotypes to give voice to a provocative counterdiscourse: Apparently subjugated voices, in fact, weave the discursive fabric of a specifically feminine genealogy invested in the figure of the mother. In this manner, the voice of the great-grandmother echoes throughout the generations until it overlaps with the poet's voice, as does hers with that of her young daughter. These murmured voices form part of a sly and cunning resistance with a rich arsenal of teachings and experiences of survival. Thus invisible genealogies recover moment-by-moment the time denied by official history. In the undercurrent of history lies the story of these mothers' resistance: silent, minute, albeit persistent revolutions. Afro-Brazilian women writers anchored their poetic and fictional universes on the figure of the family, the only site available to them for survival, in the telling of stories, and in the transmission of lived and shared experience. They sought to defend the family as a basic unit of protection against social pressures that sought to silence,

destabilize, and disaggregate familial ties among Afro-Brazilians. The woman, as head of the family, is a recurrent motif in black women's writing. Motherhood figures were portrayed less as a biological function than a social role that, in certain urgent circumstances, could pass from mother to daughter, from sister to sister, and from grandmother to granddaughter, in an infinite rosary of reciprocal care.

Central to the aforementioned works is the intention of recuperating the image of the black woman from the stereotypes prominent in literature as in the society at large. In the wake of the black movement's first wave, these crystallized images of black women were called into question by the generation of black women writers who emerged in the 1960s. No longer would black women be portrayed as either the lascivious and sexually available girl or the passive mother ready to suffer reprimand and punishment—as *Nêga Fulô* and *Mãe Preta*. Writers committed to the black movement opened alternative paths for the articulation and inscription of the word, and invited alternative readings: In their work, the black woman was presented whole, her movements more lithe, her voice unfettered.

Among contemporary Afro-Brazilian women writers, one may single out the name of Marilene Felinto (b. 1957), whose elaborate work blurs the boundaries of fiction, poetry, and journalism, and draws inspiration both from the traditions of the Northeast and from the international artistic scene. Felinto's writing plays with the borders between yesterday and today, between the subject and the world, as evident in "O Espelho da Falha" ["The Mirror of the Fault"]: "Para onde ia aquele atalho de cascalho e barro senão para o fim da tarde? Para o fim da tarde, sim, porque Sete Cidades não era um lugar, era um pedaço de tempo" (62) ("Where did that trail of red earth lead if not to the end of the afternoon? Yes, to the end of the afternoon, for Sete Cidades was not a place, it was a piece of time"). Her work contributes to what Oswald de Andrade refers to as the intersection of the past and the contemporary, of the timeless and the regional, of the Oriental and Sudanese culture, and the rhythms of the hard workers from Benin and Angola (Andrade 1991, 75).

As Oswald de Andrade's mature work suggests, awareness of the black presence in Brazil's population and culture transcends the contingencies of time and literary fashion. A critical re-evaluation of the legacy of slavery has permeated Brazilian literature in the twentieth century in all genres: poetry, drama, fiction, and the essay. No work is more important in this respect than the 1954 novel *A Menina Morta* [The Dead Girl] by Cornélio Penna (1896–1958). Penna's introspective novel represents a superb sociological and psychological portrait of the apogee of the coffee plantation culture, a rarefied and somber atmosphere. The novel's intricate and ghostly plot calls attention to the eloquence of silence and the not-spoken, achieving a symbolic density rare in modern Brazilian fiction. Its brilliant reconstruction of the world of the opulent coffee plantations of Paraíba do Sul ranges from the tapestries, crystals, and curtains of the masters' "enchanting and forbidding palaces" (37) to the realm of slaves "who did not speak and who surreptitiously ate dirt, with the hope of dying" (15). A startling filigree and plasticity characterizes Penna's language. As Luiz Costa Lima comments on this hitherto little-known work, which boasts an originality that sets it apart from the literature of its contemporaries:

One may term Cornélio Penna a novelist of the regime of slavery, as long as one does not have in mind the conciliatory vision of Gilberto Freyre. . . . A true chronicler of slavery, Penna shows us what seems to escape a sociological interpretation that focuses on phenomena: blacks not only lacked the conditions to develop class consciousness . . . they also undermined the belief-system of the master from within. If this contamination did not lead to the imposition of a dominant black culture in the real social sphere, nonetheless in the field of literature, with its much greater imaginative possibilities, where the real reveals itself to be merely one form of the possible, this dominance was achieved. (152)

Also at the margins of modernism and, ignored by the cultural elites, is the black literature of the southern states of Brazil. Thus, beyond individual figures such as Cruz e Souza, Machado de Assis, and Lima Barreto–founders of the principal literary families in black letters, in the opinion of Otàvio Ianni (209)–Brazil only slowly witnessed the gradual and collective emergence of Afro-Brazilian literature.

According to Conceição Evaristo, the principal objective of black literature is the creation of a discourse where blacks emerge as subjects of history, that develops in agreement with the black mode of being in the world, oriented toward a world vision of one's own. Evaristo clarifies that, in the writing of black literature, "we should not ground ourselves merely in references to race, but above all, focus on the manner in which the writer deals with this ethnic trait he brings within him. We speak of a literature whose creators seek the construction of a political discourse that gives the black man his voice and turns him into a subject in charge of his own representation in literature" (2). In this spirit, albeit still in a conflicted and embryonic form, we can note the presence of a black press in the city of São Paulo as early as 1915. In a first instance, the members of this press were responsible for the creation of the *Frente Negra Brasileira* (Black Brazilian Front), whose exacerbated nationalism almost brought it ideologically in line with the mainstream assimilationist right wing. Many slaves and former slaves had settled in São Paulo, and the members of the FNB now came from that city's small and incipient black bourgeoisie. Within this context the Front had as its prime objective to make the Afro-Brazilian population competitive with the European immigrants, who then dominated the job market, by teaching the masses the latest techniques employed by white immigrant labor. A brief glance at the poems published by this black press suffices to signal the ideological preoccupations that concerned this urban bourgeoisie: social injustice and the absence of solidarity among blacks and mulattos (Brookshaw 30–43).

A characteristic example of this stance is the work of Lino Guedes (1906–1991), a long-time resident of Rio and São Paulo who recuperated the figures of "Pai João" and "Mãe Preta" ["Father John" and "Black Mother"] in a poetry lacking social criticism and betraying strong assimilationist tendencies. For black culture to find regeneration, Guedes contended, it must first recognize the negative legacy of slavery in black education, morality, family life, and class and ethnic solidarity. As he writes in his collection *A Razão da Chama* [The Cause of the Fire], "Negro preto, negro preto,/sê tu um homem direito/como um cordel posto a prumo!/É só do teu proceder/que, por certo, há de nascer/a estrela do novo rumo!" (qtd. in Santos 1997,114) ("Black nigger, black nigger/be you a just man/with your pamphlet in hand!/Only from your provenance/that for certain, will emerge/the star of the new bearing!"). What makes this poem fascinating is the tension between the refusal to imitate white form and the necessity of adapting to dominant aesthetic values.

The FNB reached its peak of influence in the mid-thirties, when the newspapers *Voz da Raça* [The Voice of the Race] and *O Clarim da Alvorada* [The Bugle of Dawn] disseminated its praise of black contributions to Brazil patriotism and economic development. No contradiction was then perceived between the stated goals of taking pride in black culture and adhering to white norms of behavior, since the overall objective was assimilation to the society at large. President Getúlio Vargas dissolved the *Frente Negra Brasileira* in 1937, however. Black movements re-emerged in the mid-1940s with the creation of the *Associação dos Negros Brasileiros*, the newspapers *Alvorada* [Dawn] and *Senzala* [Slave Quarters] of 1945, and, perhaps most notably, the founding of *O Teatro Experimental do Negro* [TEN, the Black Experimental Theater]. A pioneer in the alternative scene of Brazilian theater, the Black Experimental Theater sought–through the performance of montages, parallel scenes, and texts–to deconstruct stereotypes and suggest new ways of representing black characters on stage and beyond. It made many aesthetic innovations in the realm of scenography and staging, not the least of which was the incorporation of a repertoire of non-Western props and references. Within months of its first participation in recitals and the first stagings of the work of theater troupes in 1944, the Experimental Theater was the subject of controversy. The unwelcoming attitude towards the TEN is perhaps best exemplified by Henrique Pongetti's article in the daily *O Globo* (21 October 1944), in which he wrote: "In Brazil, black theatre will not have to direct its historical message to our prejudice, but rather to our indifference." Nonetheless its first major staging of Eugene O'Neill's *Emperor Jones* at the Teatro Municipal, Rio's most prestigious theater, was acclaimed by the same columnist in the same newspaper the day after its premiere: "Each monologue in the forest earned applause for the actor in the title role. His prayer of remorse earned him two rounds of applause. Black Brazilians–as well as whites–now possess a great dramatic actor: Aguinaldo de Oliveira Camargo. An anti-academic, rustic, instinctive great actor" (*O Globo*, 5 May 1945).

In addition to its visionary cofounder Abdias do Nascimento, the Black Experimental Theater numbered among its celebrated participants: Aguinaldo de Oliveira Camargo, Ruth de Souza, Lea Garcia, Arinda Serafim, Ironildes Rodrigues, Claudiano Filho, Tibério Wilson, José Herbal, Teodorico dos Santos, Haroldo Costa, Marina Gonçalves, Mercedes Batista, Solano Trinidade, and many others. Most notable among its occasional collaborators were set designers Enrico Bianco and Santa Rosa, and director Brutus Pedreira. From its formation, the Black Experimental Theater possessed the ambition to become a broad movement of education, art, and culture; and to further this objective, it promoted various activities that expanded the range of its reach and influence. As founder Abdias Nascimento later reflected: "As the necessary and logical result of the reality and critical reflections of the Black Experimental Theater, there emerged a drama and aesthetic language for spectacle founded upon the values and from the vantage point of Afro-Brazilian culture. The Black Experimental Theater organized and sponsored courses, national contests, and conferences, increasing in this manner the opportunities for Afro-Brazilian writers to discuss and share information and experiences" (Nascimento 68).

In the fifties, the Teatro Experimental Negro edited the journal *Quilombo*, and in 1961, it published the anthology,

Drama para Negros e Prólogo para Brancos [Drama for Blacks and Prologue for Whites], still today the only anthology of its kind on the Brazilian publishing market. After its premiere at Rio's Municipal Theater, that production of *The Emperor Jones* was transferred to the Fênix Theater, ending its successful run on 8 September 1945. Following its expansion to São Paulo in 1946, the Black Experimental Theater remained a constant presence on the Brazilian stage for more than a decade. From 1945 to 1957, it staged in Rio, besides *The Emperor Jones*, O'Neill's *All God's Chillun Got Wings* (1946), and *The Dreamy Kid* (1946), Lúcio Cardoso's *O Filho Pródigo* [1947; The Prodigal Son], Joaquim Ribeiro's *Aruanda* (1948), Albert Camus's *Caligula* (1949), José Morais Pinho's *Filhos de Santo* [1949; Children of the Saint], Abdias do Nascimento's *Sortilégio* [1957; Sorcery], and the dance spectacle *Rapsódia Negra* [1952; Black Rhapsody]. Most notable among the plays staged by the Black Experimental Theater in São Paulo were Augusto Boal's *O Cavalo e o Santo* [n.d.; The Horse and the Saint] and *Filha Moça* [n.d.; The Daughter], Hermilo Borba Filho's *João Sem Terra* [c. 1955; Landless John], and Langston Hughes's *The Mulatto* [n.d.].

Júlio César Tavares has noted that the Experimental Theater's diverse range of activities and its objectives as a broad aesthetic and cultural movement requires greater critical attention, in particular with respect to the context of its emergence, its achievements, and its inherent contradictions. In his own words: "The Black Experimental Theater constituted what we may term 'a theatre of intervention,' for its ruling imperative was of a pedagogical and political nature. . . . The Black Experimental Theater appears in a national context of great upheaval, marked by the struggle against the dictatorship of the *Estado Novo* [Getúlio Vargas's New State regime] and the process of democratization through the National Constituent Assembly. In the international realm, the Experimental Theater is situated as an important link within the invisible network of cultural affirmation by members of the black diaspora and of the African continent" (81). Most relevant within this context are the discussions the Black Experimental Theater promoted on questions of culture and national identity, on racial discrimination, and on the significance of black African participation in the history and cultural life of the nation. The interventions of the Theater were seminal and its proposals radical for the time, be they in the form of conferences, debates, contests, publications, or performance: "A defining moment for the Black Experimental Theater was the Black National Convention of 1945 in São Paulo. This Convention demanded from federal legislators a law governing social relations with the intent of punishing racism. Nonetheless the Federal Congress rejected such a bill in 1946, alleging there was insufficient proof for the facts that might justify it. . . . Judge Afonso Arinos, then a federal deputy, resubmitted the bill, which was finally approved by Congress. Thus the Afonso Arinso Law was born. Despite thousands of reports of racism and discrimination, one can count on one's fingers the convictions made under this law" (Tavares 83).

Within a more strictly aesthetic realm one may note that the Black Experimental Theater was attuned to avant-garde theater groups such as *Os Comediantes* and to international movements such as that of *Negritude*. As previously mentioned, it sought collaboration with directors such as Augusto Boal and Bibi Ferreira among others. From the beginning of its operations in Rio and São Paulo to its decline in the 1960s, members and former members of the Black Experimental

Theater were responsible for the founding of other movements such as: "Solano Trindade's Brazilian Popular Theater and The Group of the New, a secession from the Black Experimental Theater, led by Haroldo Costa, later transformed into the Brazilian Folkloric Theater and finally into the Brasiliana Ballet. Both troupes privileged the staging of dances from a popular and folkloric origin: catering to the market for spectacles, in the case of the Brasiliana Ballet, and as an attempt to recuperate the authentic values of national culture, in the case of the Popular Theater" (Tavares 75).

Reviewing the Black Experimental Theater's many accomplishments, taking into account both its successes and failures, one may single out as its most influential achievement the creation of an alternative language for set design and direction in Brazilian theater—an incisive reversal of previous expressions by or about black people in Brazil. Albeit short-lived, the Black Experimental Theater contributed a singular diction and intentionality that revolutionized the spoken word and reinvented modes of expression in the theater, particularly with reference to the representation of black subjects of Afro-Brazilian culture. In many of its productions the Experimental Theater succeeded in presenting an alternative theatrical language, investing black subjectivity with dynamism, relevance, and visibility.

In its *mise-en-scène* and construction of character, the Experimental Theater sought to ascribe to the black signifier multiple meanings rather than merely one synthesis of various other signs, exploring the discourse of the other as the sign of alterity and diversity. It presented a series of images that sought to translate the broad range of black experience and memory in Brazil. The Black Experimental Theater sought to position itself as an instrument for a desired transformation in black subjectivity through various means: the deconstruction of stereotypes, the calling into question of the appearances of everyday life, the unmasking of the pretences that shape the meanings of black and white, the disruption of accepted universal and absolute truths through the deployment of irony and doublespeak, the privileging of a semiotics of mirror and shadow, the re-elaboration of formal and conceptual syntaxes, and the deployment of Afro-Brazilian rituals as structuring devices; in sum, the repositioning of black men and women as objects and subjects of expression. As founder Abdias do Nascimento would retrospectively affirm: "What is the Black Experimental Theater? In terms of its purposes it constitutes a complex organization. It was conceived fundamentally as an instrument of redemption and recuperation of Black African values, then relegated to an inferior plane in so-called Brazilian culture, where the emphasis rested on elements of a white and European provenance. Our theater would constitute a laboratory for cultural and artistic experimentation, all work, action, and production explicitly in struggle against the elitist and racist cultural supremacy of the dominant classes. The Black Experimental Theater undertook the systematic unmasking of the racial hypocrisy that pervades the nation" (Nascimento 68).

By mid-century, Brazil had witnessed the emergence of a wide-ranging black intelligentsia in Brazil, consisting of both artists and activists. Despite the residual hesitations evident in a certain insistence on African primitivism and exoticism, a black consciousness came into being that proved—as the Afro-Brazilian poet Marcio Barbosa reminds us—vital to the existence of a black literature (in Evaristo 49). One should note, however, that African influence remained most visible in the Northeast and in the states of Rio and Minas Gerais, and less so in São Paulo and the southern states where Asian and European immigration and influence prevailed in the wake of rapid industrialization. In the São Paulo of the 1950s and 1960s a young generation of black writers moved away from modernist exuberance to a more escapist and melancholic treatment of the black predicament, which amounted to an aesthetic resignation and an idealization of the interior of Brazil. In this fashion a lettered black middle class sought to find its bearings in a discriminating and forbidding white world, among them the poets Eduardo de Oliveira (b. 1926) and Oswaldo Camargo (b.1936). Oliveira wrote poems embued with a Christian symbolism, reminiscent of Cruz e Souza in their veiled manner of representing the predicament of the black subject in a white world. In contrast the aggressive poetry of Camargo is punctuated by rhetorical questions that do not wait for an answer and poignantly search for the past in the present:

> Que faço das mãos cobertas
> de um sol doído só de África?
> E do tantã nestas veias,
> turbando o ritmo ao sangue?

> *(Camargo 124)*

> What do I make of these hands
> Covered in a sun pained only in Africa?
> And what of the madness in these veins
> Which perturbs the rhythm of my blood?

In this chain of questions, melancholy infiltrates the realm of action, as if to defuse it:

> A quem oferecerás o teu suor, irmão?
> É inútil repreenderes tua história
> mesmo tresler o livro.
> Todos sabem de tua ilharga, narinas,
> crespitude,
> a cidade te encontraria, cega e bêbada,
> palpando-te os flancos, o sexo, os dentes.
> Que farás dessa cidade, irmão?

> *(Camargo 124)*

> To whom will you offer sweat, brother?
> It is useless to chastise your history
> Or even reread the book
> Everyone knows of your side, nostrils,
> Kinky hair,
> The city would meet you, blind and drunk
> Handling your flanks, sex, teeth
> What make you of this city, brother?

In the 1960s black urban poetry in Brazil became more assertive, in synch with black power movements in the United States. Solano Trinidade (1908–1973) would demand freedom for his race in a socialist style reminiscent of Jorge Amado's (1912–2001) novels in the 1940s. Roger Bastide would affectionately refer to his work as the product of the cross between Marx and *Xangô*, the Afro-Brazilian deity. Fashioning himself as poetically polygamous, Trinidade incorporated into his verses Afro-Brazilian themes and the rhythm of drums, always emphasizing the black basis for his poetry: "I am a poet of the people, *Olurum Ekê.*" In his poetry he sought to represent all the oppressed of this earth:

> Negros que escravizam
> e vendem negros na África
> não são meus irmãos.
> Negros senhores na América

> a serviço do capital
> não são meus irmãos.
> Só os negros oprimidos
> escravizados
> em luta por liberdade
> são meus irmãos.
> Para estes tenho um poema
> grande como o Nilo.

> Blacks who enslave
> and sell blacks in Africa
> are not my brothers.
> Black sirs in America
> at the service of capital
> are not my brothers.
> Only blacks who are oppressed
> enslaved
> struggling for liberty
> are my brothers.
> For them I have a poem
> as great as the Nile.

> *("Olurum Ekê," Trindade 44)*

Yet, at this fertile moment in history, the military dictatorship ushered in by the coup of 1964 silenced the expression and pruned the branches and activities of black movements in Brazil. They would regroup only with the political openness of the late 1970s and 1980s: The year 1978 saw the foundation of the newspapers *Jornegro* (São Paulo) and *Sinba* (Rio), and of *O Movimento Negro Unificado contra a Discriminação Racial* [The United Black Movement Against Racial Discrimination], later simply *O Movimento Negro Unificado*. The twentieth of November was instituted as the national day for black consciousness, and, with the aim of emphasizing black values and aggressively denouncing racism, the old symbols of "Mãe Preta" and "Pai João" were replaced by the combative Zumbi.

If, from the outset, the literary and intellectual mainstream relegated manifestations of Afro-Brazilian culture to the margins, one should be attentive to the greater degree of marginalization experienced by black women within Brazil. One is struck by the silence that envelops this figure and the absence of its representation in society–save the rare and stereotypical appearances of mulattas and black women in the media of mass communication during strategic times such as Carnival, when her absence would compromise the myth of racial democracy. In Brazil, the hegemonic cultural discourse has robbed the black woman of gesture and word, and denigrated her in representations that deny her any subjectivity. Yet concomitant with this hostile hegemonic discourse, one can also attest to black women's articulation of a counter-discourse within that narrow range allocated to them. In sum, Afro-Brazilian women have come far from the days of folkloric shows and the stages of Mardi Gras.

The difficulty of locating documents that trace black women's performance and artistic production should not prove startling. To conceive of literary production implies a certain autonomy, the ability to think and inscribe oneself in the first person. Afro-Brazilian writers have faced overwhelming difficulties in ensuring the viability of the publication of their work. Brazil's publishing market tolerates books on the topic of the black woman, with the requisite distancing demand that it be written in the third person, but it seems incapable of accepting the voice and subjectivity of an independent black woman. One should note that even on some of the rare occasions black women have succeeded in reaching a broad public–for example in the case of Carolina Maria de Jesus's (1914–1977) 1960 *Quarto de Despejo* [*Child of the Dark,* 1962]– the disbelieving literary press has not been above calling into question the identity of the author. Nonetheless, black women now constitute a significant presence in Afro-Brazilian letters. Yet even the critically acclaimed among these writers hold no illusions as to their status in society and even within alternative presses and black writers's collectives, such as the *Cadernos Negros* [Black Notebooks] organized by São Paulo's Quilombhoje, and the *Coletivo de Escritores Negros* [Black Writers' Collective] of Rio's *Negrícia*. Conceição Evaristo remarks, in a December 1992 interview, that "literature that deals with Afro-Brazilian questions is yet to make it into the mainstream. . . . Mainstream and public writing is still reserved for whites and for men" (personal interview). In an interview two years later she reflects on her own predicament: "I am a writer and a black woman: These are both difficult issues to articulate. My writing will not reach the ethnic group to which I belong because too few have access to literacy and writing and this represents a conflict for me as a writer. Our society has not trusted orality. . . . My writing is an impotent weapon, a solitary act, . . . but nonetheless it is the only one I have" (personal interview).

In the context of redressing the vacuum pertaining to the literary history of black women in Brazil, we must note Maria Lúcia de Barros Mott's fundamental and pioneering work *Escritoras Negras: Resgatando Nossa História* [Black Women Writers: Rescuing Our History]. Mott finds the first Afro-Brazilian women's literary expression in Rosa Maria Egipciaca de Vera Cruz's mid-eighteenth-century work *Sagrada Teologia do Amor Divino das Almas Peregrinas* [The Sacred Theology of the Divine Love of Pilgrim Souls]. Respecting the diversity of criteria put forward in controversies of who constitutes a black woman writer–origin, physical appearance, economic class, and choice of theme–Mott traces the work of ten writers, from the eighteenth century to the already-well-known ones of the 1960s. Rosa Vera Cruz would witness the burning of part of her manuscripts, and since her time, black women writers have suffered threats of various kinds, including doubt as to the authorship (as we have seen in the case of Carolina de Jesus) and the dust of neglect or the oblivion of the manuscript that does not find publication as in the case of Conceição Evaristo. The predicament of black women's writing reflects a society that is ill at ease and possesses many unresolved questions with respect to its racial and ethnic identity. It is within this context that one must understand the many artifices black women writers and their biographers have adopted–especially in the cases described by Mott–to see their work published, including the adoption of pseudonyms and the doctoring of their photographs to appear whiter than they were. We should not generalize or trivialize these developments, nor should we misunderstand them as attempts to deny the black African heritage. There were no other avenues open for black women to make themselves heard, to leave a mark in the public realm of letters. Maria Firmina dos Reis's novel *Úrsula* is innovative with respect to the representation of slavery; slaves are given a plot, history, and a memory. Yet, as already mentioned, she could only publish the novel under the pseudonym "Uma Maranhense" ("A Native of the State of Maranhão"). In sum, all these omissions and subterfuges with respect to identity merely mark the outsider status of Afro-Brazilian women's writing, and its subversiveness with respect to the dominant and inhibiting parameters of public and mainstream literature.

Afro-Brazilian women's literature is characterized by a persistent–but also strategic–impulse to recuperate memory through the experience of the family. For these writers, as we have seen, familial experience and memory represents an answer to the distorted representation of blacks within the dominant society. Memory was, of course, a faculty denied to slaves and their descendants. The impulse to reclaim these reminiscences, relegated to the dustbin of history and historical representation, motivates the work of prominent Afro-Brazilian writers, among them Ruth Guimarães (b. 1920), Vera Tereza de Jesus, Anajá Caetano, Aline França, Conceição Evaristo, Geni Guimarães (b. 1947), and Sônia Fátima da Conceição (b. 1951). All these writers root themselves in their own values, appropriate to the pressures of everyday life, and succeed in dramatizing and thematizing the predicament of black families outside the realm of what is institutionally encouraged and permitted. The theme of the family is further part of a strategy of maintaining group consciousness and solidarity, of demonstrating a particular form of thinking and being in the world, marked by an orientation away from individualism and towards collectivism. Notable among such treatments of the Afro-Brazilian family are Sônia Fátima da Conceição's short story; "Obsessão" ["Obsession"]; Geni Guimarães's novel, *A Cor da Ternura* [The Colour of Tenderness], Aline França's novel, *A Mulher de Aleduma* [Aleduma's Woman], and Marilene Felinto's short story, "Muslim Woman." Starting from the recognition that to be a black woman is to experience solitude, Guirmarães's novel, *A Cor da Ternura*, weaves stories of female solidarity around the plot of an Afro-Brazilian family that tries to salvage its coherence as it moves away from the ghetto. The axis for Aline França's novel is the old Aleduma, a synthesis of the universal cosmopolitan consciousness that is able to incorporate the strangeness and solitude of being, and the experience of the Afro-Brazilian woman who forces him to transcend his individual experience and engage with women's experience.

Felinto's masterful short story focuses on the fleeting encounter between women who share a sense of complicity: "Aproximei-me dela o mais espontaneamente que pude, e perguntei em inglês se ela falava minha língua (inglês, o que só me fez relembrar de súbito o quanto eu era um grandíssimo nada nos aeroportos do vasto mundo onde minha língua nativa nada era)," (18). ("I approached her as spontaneously as possible, and asked in English if she spoke my language, or English–this dissonance reminded me all of a sudden that I represented an immense nothing in the airports of this vast world where my mother tongue is worth nothing"). Author of the novels *As Mulheres de Tijucopapo* [1982; The Women of Tijucopapo] and *O Lago Encantado de Grongonzo* [1987; The Enchanted Lake of Grongonzo], Felinto commented on her literary labor in an introductory note to her first book of short stories, *Postcard*:

> Durante esses anos pensei muito em marceneiros, pedreiros, agricultores. Comparei a posição do escritor à situação absurda de um agricultor que plantasse batata e, na hora de vender o produto, não soubesse quanto cobrar–porque não tivesse clara a distinção entre o que foi trabalho seu e o que foi trabalho da terra onde a batata brotou. " E adiante: "Devo esse livro à mangueira e à romanzeira da minha casa de infância em Recife; ao ladrão que destelhou nossa cozinha de madrugada; a um carneiro todo branco, felpudo e vivo que ganhei de presente de aniversário de cinco anos; a Reinilton, ou qualquer outro nome de menino pernambucano por quem primeiro me apaixonei–devo a eles,

porque são os motivos de inspiração das primeiras histórias que escrevi na vida, longe do mercado, dos papéis e dos homens do mercado. (9–10)

During these years I thought a lot about the work of cabinet makers, stonemasons, and farmers. I compared the writer's position to the absurd situation of the farmer who, having planted a potato, is unsure of how much to ask for it, as if not wanting to make clear the distinction between his labor and that of the soil itself. . . . I owe this work to the mango tree outside my childhood home in Recife; to the thief who fell through the roof over our kitchen in the middle of the night; to the wooly and white lamb I won for my birthday when I was five; and to Renilton, or any such name for the boys of my native state of Pernambuco, such as the one for whom I first fell in love– to all these I owe this work, for they are the principal motivations for the first stories I wrote in my life, away from the market, the newspapers, and men of the market.

Representations of poor black women–the other side of the Brazilian mainstream–and of their role in familial and communal life, now transcend the realm of black women's writing and are also important features of black men's writing in Brazil. Most notable in this respect is Paulo Lins's (b. 1958)1997 novel *Cidade de Deus* [City of God], in which black women are not idealized but are nonetheless always portrayed with dignity. In the novel, children figure prominently, and are associated with the pain and burden born by black women; as in the portrait of latent brutality whereby a family self-destructs, and the women are left to mourn the deaths of their children (419). The timeless nature of the fundamental emotions that concern Lins imbues his tale of the tragedy of the poor with a terror and piety approaching that of classic tragedy. *City of God* is a novel that deals in fragments and leftovers. It represents the everyday life of the mostly black and *mestizo* inhabitants of the slum in the city of Rio known as the City of God (from which the novel takes its title, with great irony). Lins charts, on the one hand, the existential terrain of a community lacerated by poverty and violence, and the ambivalent indifference of the society that at once dominates and surrounds, despises, and fears the slum. Its most lingering image is that of the mother who desperately feels the ground for the flesh of her child, as if to put his face back together and undo the work of bullets. Similarly the novelist himself seeks to piece together bodies, dreams, and lives without foundation or future.

In its open and discontinuous structure, the work can be seen as postmodern. No central plot predominates, and the anti-narrative at work weaves together fragments of individual stories, the products of chance, dispersion, and deconstruction. No message or thesis sustains the novel, though its political interventions are sharp and there is no lack of depth in the significance of its socioeconomic, racial, political, and aesthetic concerns. Fiction ultimately bestows on its characters what life cannot: The pieces lock together; a sense of completion or, rather, recomposition is achieved. The three blocks that make up the text (the story of the Hairdresser, the story of Bené, and the story of Zé Pequeno) are discursive edifices that reproduce the solid and arid concrete blocks of the slums. Might we term this an aesthetic of abjection? Paulo Lins's novel was the result of his anthropological research and is the first ethnographic novel in Brazil not based on childhood recollections or on the author's biography. Nature is revealed as the first victim of Rio's urban sprawl: At one point the narrator notes that the guava tree, now cut down, has been replaced by a new apartment block. Other victims follow: Adults and children are killed and

women raped in an environment where honest workers are referred to, in the jargon of drug dealers, as "otários" ("suckers"). In Paulo Lins's image of the slum, cadavers appear floating in the river with an astonishing frequency, and workers, children, and gossiping women circulate within the same labyrinth of paths as the rival gangs of dealers. There are no winners or losers–all lose out in the end. Neither are there borders that might delimit clearly who makes a living under the terms of the law and who disobeys it.

Violence rules *The City of God.* This constant fighting–among rival bands of dealers or their associates, or between the police and the drug traffickers–takes place so close to the police station and yet seems to be so far from the society that enjoys the good life, the arts, and intellectual pursuits. To borrow an analogy from history, it seems that the apocalyptic movement of Canudos on behalf of the oppressed has arrived in modern Rio. And yet Paulo Lins's story is not a tale of "what if" but rather of "what is": the war of the famished right here, at the turn of the millennium, between the affluent suburbs of Barra da Tijuca and Jacarepaguá, in this splendorous Rio with its rivers and Atlantic ocean, with its lakes, mountains, and forest of eucalyptus trees. However, the analogy to the despair of nineteenth-century Canudos holds as far as the requisites of violence and destitution are concerned. Among the fighting of these dark men with their boasting mouths without teeth, with cavities for eyes, pock-marked, or simply "nervous eyes," there is no cause to fight for, or even any reasons to reach for an ideal beyond. One kills for a joint or an article of clothing, out of jealousy about a perceived or imagined betrayal, or just out of fear of being killed oneself. Here drought will not turn to rain, dry lands will not become a sea. The urban exiles, the poor, envy the ocean that seems the exclusive possession of the rich; they envy the rich their houses, automobiles, and spouses. Nonetheless, there is the occasional glimpse of harmony between nature, man, and fantasy itself: "Barbantinho (. . .) lançou-se na maré cheia, atravessou a arrebentação, descansou, olhou para o lado que estava puxando, pensou em nadar cem metros contra a correnteza. Respirou fundo para dar a primeira braçada no mais puro azul de seus desejos" (180) ("Barbantinho dove into the high tide, overcame the smashing of the waves, and, rested, looked toward the direction from which the sea was tugging him, thought of swimming a hundred meters against the current. He breathed in deeply to make the first stroke into the purest blue of his desires").

Perhaps the greatest accomplishment of Paulo Lins's work is that he bestows upon his characters a convincing humanity, with which he avoids sensationalist stereotypes and the temptations of cheap sentimentalism. In this literature of permanent struggle that will not give its readers the comfort of tears (to paraphrase the Afro-American novelist Richard Wright), there is also space for dream and for utopia. Nowhere is this more evident than in the ruminations of the bandit Bené:

O sonho de Bené era o de comprar um terreno onde tivesse água corrente, terra boa para o cultivo e pequenas casas de madeira para ele e os cocotas morarem. Era isso o que deveria fazer para viver entre pessoas de rostos límpidos por não conviverem cara a cara com a morte. Nunca pensavam em matar ninguém, embora gostassem de maconha como ele. Era esse o seu sonho: ganhar uma mina bonita, morar entre gente bonita e dançar discoteca até o fim da vida numa boa. Nada daqueles crioulos com cara nervosa e sem dentes. (352)

His dream was to buy a plot of land with running water, good land for planting and cultivation, and small wooden houses for him and the *cocotas* to live in. This is what he ought to do, to live among clean-shaven men so as not to come face to face with death. Though they might, like him, enjoy a joint, they would not consider killing a man. This was his dream: to have a pretty girl, live among beautiful people, and dance in a discotheque until the end of the world. Without a trace of those toothless *criollos* with their nervous faces.

On a different level, the novel's plot resembles a children's crusade. The children of the *City of God* are not childlike in any recognizable way; their heroes and role-models are the drug dealers for whom they serve as "remote-controlled airplanes," and who take the place of the heroes on television. Childhood does not last long in the slums: "Meu irmão, eu fumo, eu cheiro, desde nenenzinho que peço esmola, já limpei vidro de carro, já trabalhei de engraxate, já matei, já roubei... não sou criança não. Sou sujeito homem!" (410) ("My brother, I inhale, I smoke, and have begged since I was a baby, I have wiped clean the windows of automobiles and the shoes of men, I have killed, I have robbed . . . . no, I am not a child. I am a man!"). This is how an eight-year old known as "Steak with fries" greets the unfortunate and disbelieving Manoel Galinha, and explains the presence of children in a world of crime from which neither of them will be able to disentangle himself. The unraveling of these worlds at a crossroads is one of the riches of Paulo Lins's book.

Contemporary Brazilian literature is quite concerned with the expression of these "worlds at a crossroads"; male and female writers are weaving a new discourse that rewrites the history of slavery, reinterprets the import of the ethnic makeup of Brazil's population, and reveals the African heritage that has survived diaspora and near-pulverization. This is a literature that engages the negotiations between dominant and subjugated cultures and their players without false ideologies, that seeks to articulate a discursive mode conducive to "a re-territorialization, a reappropriation of the language, that seeks to lend the word a black accent" (Evaristo 57). It is a literature characterized by a dense poetic language and many specific obstacles and struggles to overcome. Cuti writes that, while "the black Brazilian writer may consider himself an orphan . . . for all the literature he knows comes from the dominant social class," the same is not true of music, where the African forefathers have bestowed a rich legacy of many forms of expression that today's artist can use as points of reference (qtd. in Evaristo 42). Despite this, Cuti perceives advances with respect to literary artistic expression: "There are black authors who are concerned with meta-language, with the structure of text, with the shape of words. . . . Defending [the freedom of inquiry] is the best way to ensure that the insidious methods of ideological domestication encounter resistance in the realm of letters. Our message does not become sterile in the camouflage of human conflict; we should reveal this conflict simply and profoundly" (qtd. in Evaristo 56–7).

Conceição Evaristo, in turn, invites us to conceive of black literature as ethno-poetics that relives the old African *griots*, guardians of memory, who sang and told a story of "the black resistance against the colonizer," who articulated "a poetics of the soil, of the African man transplanted and re-formed in the lands of diaspora." Thus, through the thread of orality, "the poet meets the word's magic power, the enchantment of speech, capable of weaving in time and space the present of yesterday's world, speech pressed and repressed in memory, and meets the word capable of inaugurating, of originating another reality" (Evaristo, respectively 52, 63). Roger Bastide likewise refers to "processes and uses of words linked to the eloquence of black storytellers" (104). Marcio Barbosa, through poetry, expresses the thought that makes reference to the *orixá* (Afro-Brazilian deities) and *exu* (the devil familiar from rituals):

E assim deixar vir
a essência orixante
o teor exuente
o fecundante, o movente
pra poder refazer
os caminhos da gente.

(qtd. in Barbosa 37)

And so allow the coming
of the essence of the orixá
the devilish meaning
fertilizing, moving
to be able to remake
the paths for the people.

In this respect, the publication of the *Cadernos Negros* [The Black Notebooks] by the Quilombhoje collective is significant. As Jamu Minka stated in 1988: "After ten consecutive years of publishing this anthology, with its ever more fertile literary life, we are reinvigorating Brazilian literature in the manner of the *Quilombos* (Societies of runaway slaves). Nonetheless, we still need a more significant presence in the mainstream media of cultural dissemination, the last taboo. Yet, we can state that, to think of Brazilian literature in its full diversity, our presence must be recognized–or else the vision of Brazilian literature would be myopic and poor" (36). Indeed, the *Notebooks* have stimulated the interest of readers and academics in Brazil and abroad.

Today the new Afro-Brazilian literature engages other countries' forms of cultural expression and the cultural production of other peoples, thus intervening, in the words of Hermógenes de Almeida at the *II Encontro de Poetas e Ficcionistas Negros Brasileiros, Rio de Janeiro* in 1986: "in history and society on its own terms, and within the cultural heritage of Humanity." This new literature reveals not so much a new history but a plurality of histories that the state and its official ideologies sought to neutralize. Antonio Risério (b. 1953) asks in his poem "Padê": "Será que a gente se entende?/Será que dá pra entender?" (qtd. in Santos 150) ("Will we be able to understand each other?/Is it possible to understand?"). Perhaps we may find an answer in the poetry of Ricardo Aleixo: "Água./Lama./Morte./Mãe do segredo/do mundo./O úmido./O que flui." (qtd. in Santos 153) ("Water./Mud./ Death./Mother of the secret/of the world/The humiditiy/that flows"), from the poem "Nanã." Or perhaps we will find it in the feminine assertiveness of Roseli Nascimento, where the play of letters in the last line spells out "sim" (yes):

olhem
olhem
olhem
nossos corpos
pairando
pairando
cintilantes
junto às estrela
assim

assim
a s
s im

   ("Olhem", qtd. in Santos 144)

look
look
look
our bodies
hovering
hovering
scintillating
next to the stars
thus
thus
t h
u s

The emergence of new and ancient voices cross and crisscross the diaspora to be reborn, outlining of new paths, and recuperating that heritage which is no longer purely African, but which enriches the imaginary of the "human man," to borrow the formulation of the storyteller Guimarães Rosa.

Translation by Paulo Horta

Works Cited

Alencar, José de. n.d. [1871]. *O Tronco do Ipê.* Rio de Janeiro: Tecnoprint.

——.1946 [1857]. *O Guarani.* Rio de Janeiro: Livraria Antunes.

——. 1960 [1857]. *O Demônio familiar. Obras completas de José de Alencar.* Rio de Janeiro: Aguilar.

——. 1975 [1975]. *Iracema.* Rio de Janeiro: Francisco Alves.

——. 1987 [1862]. *Lucíola.* São Paulo: Ática.

——. 1960 [1860]. *Mãe. Obras completas de José de Alencar.* Rio de Janeiro: Aguilar.

Andrade, Mario de. 1972. *Macunaíma: O Herói sem nenhum caráter.* 7 ed. São Paulo: Livraria Martins Editora.

Andrade, Oswald de. 1970. *Do Pau-Brasil à antropofagia e às utopias. Obras completas.* Vol 6. Rio de Janeiro: MEC/Civilização Brasileira.

——. 1991. *Ponta de Lança.* São Paulo: Editora Globo.

Araripe Junior, Tristão de Alencor. 1910. *Gregório de Matos.* 2 ed. Rio de Janeiro, Paris: Livraria Garnier.

Avé-Lallemant, Robert.1960. *Viagem pelo norte do Brasil no ano de 1859.* Trans. Eduardo Lima Castro. Rio de Janeiro: Instituto Nacional do Livro.

Azevedo, Aluísio. N.d. [1890]. *O Cortiço.* Rio de Janeiro: Tecnoprint.

——. 1958 [1881]. *O Mulato.* Rio de Janeiro: Edições de Ouro.

Azevedo, Artur and Urbano Duarte. 1985 [1884]. *O Escravocrata. Teatro de Artur Azevedo.* Rio de Janeiro: Ministério da Cultura, Instituto Nacional de Artes Cênicas.

Barbosa, Márcio. 1990. *Cadernos Negros 13—Poemas. Antologia.* São Paulo: Edição dos Autores.

Bastide, Roger. 1973. *Estudos Afro-Brasileiros.* São Paulo: Editora Perspectiva.

Bosi, Alfredo. 1974. *História concisa da literatura brasileira.* São Paulo: Editora Cultrix.

Brookshaw, David. 1978. "Quatro poetas negros brasileiros." Trans. M. Helena de Oliveira Barbosa. *Estudos Afro-asiáticos* (Rio de Janeiro) 1.2:30–43.

Caetano, Anajá. 1966. *Negra Efigênia: a paixão do Senhor Branco.* São Paulo: Edicel.

Camargo, Oswaldo. 1997. "Escolha" and "Que Farás?" *Negro Brasileiro Negro. Revista do Patrimônio Histórico e Artístico Nacional* 25:124.

Caminha, Adolfo. 1983 [1895]. *Bom Crioulo.* São Paulo: Ática.

Candido, Antonio. 1978. *Silvio Romero: Teoria, crítica e história literária.* Rio de Janeiro: L.T.C.

——. 1981. *Formação da literatura brasileira: momentos decisivos (1750–1836).* Vol. 1. Belo Horizonte: Editora Itatiaia.

Cardoso, Ciro Flamarion S. 1982. *A Afro-América: A Escravidão no novo mundo.* São Paulo: Brasiliense.

Carvalho, Trajano Galvão de, Marques Rodrigues and Gentil Homem. 1863. *Tres Lyras.* Maranhão: n.p.

Castro Alves, Antonio. 1953. *Poesias completas.* São Paulo: Edições Saraiva.

Conceição, Sônia Fátima da. 1993. "Obsessão." *Cadernos Negros: Contos. 16.* São Paulo: Editora dos Autores. 93–101.

Costa, Oswaldo. 1929. "De Antropofagia." *Revista de Antropofagia* 9:10.

Cruz e Sousa, João. 1961. *Emparedado. Obra Completa.* Rio de Janeiro: Aguilar.

Evaristo, Conceição.1990. *Cadernos Negros: Poesias 16.* São Paulo: Editora dos Autores.

Felinto, Marilene. 1991. *Postcard.* São Paulo: Iluminuras.

Fernandes, Florestan.1978. *A integração do negro na sociedade de classes.* São Paulo: Editora Ática.

França, Aline. 1985. *A mulher de Aleduma.* Salvador: Ianamá.

Fredrickson, George M. 1971. *The Black Image in the White Mind: The Debate on Afro-American Character and Destiny.* New York: Harper & Row.

Gama, Luiz. 1974 [1859]. *Trovas burlescas.* São Paulo: Três.

Gates Jr., Henry Louis, ed. 1986. *Race, Writing and Difference.* Chicago: Chicago University Press.

Gledson, John. 1986. *Machado de Assis: ficção e história.* Rio de Janeiro: Paz e Terra.

Glissant, Edouard. 1997. *Poetic of Relation.* Trans. Betsy Wing. Ann Arbor: University of Michigan Press.

Guimarães, Bernardo. N.d. [1869]. *O Ermitão de Muquém.* São Paulo: Saraiva.

——. 1983 [1875]. *A Escrava Isaura.* São Paulo: Editora Ática.

Guimarães, Geni.1991. *A Cor da ternura.* São Paulo: FTD.

Guimarães, Ruth. 1946. *Agua funda.* Porto Alegre: Globo.

Hourantier, Marie-José. 1984. *Du Ritual au théâtre-ritual: contribuitions à une esthétique théâtrale nègre-africaine.* Paris: Editions L'Harmattan.

Ianni, Otávio. 1988. "Literatura e Consciência." *Estudos Afro-Asiáticos* 15:208-17.

Jesus, Carolina Maria de. 1960. *Quarto de despejo.* São Paulo: Livraria F. Alves.

Jesus, Vera Tereza de. 1965. *Ela e a reclusão.* São Paulo: O. Livreiro.

Lima Barreto, Alfonso. 1970 [1911]. *Triste fim de Policarpo Quaresma.* São Paulo: Editora Brasiliense.

Lima, Luiz Costa. 1976. *A Perversão do trapezista: O Romance em Cornélio Penna.* Rio de Janeiro: Imago Editora.

Lima, Mario de., ed. 1922. *Coletânea de autores mineiros.* Vol. 1. Belo Horizonte: Imprensa Oficial.

Lins, Paulo. 1997. *Cidade de Deus.* São Paulo: Companhia das Letras.

Macedo, Joaquim Manuel de. 1983 [1844]. *A Moreninha.* São Paulo: Ática.

——. 1988 [1869]. *As Vítimas-algozes: Quadros da escravidão.* Rio de Janeiro: Fundação Casa de Rui Barbosa.

Martins, Leda Maria. 1995. *A Cena em sombras.* São Paulo: Perspectiva.

——. 1997. *Afrografias da memória: O Reinado do Rosário no Jatobá.* São Paulo, Belo Horizonte: Perspectiva, Mazza Edições.

Mendes, Mirian Garcia. 1982. *A Personagem negra no teatro brasileiro entre 1838 e 1888.* São Paulo: Editora Ática.

Minka, Jamu. 1988. *Caderno Negros 11—Contos*. São Paulo: Quilombhoje.

Mott, Maria Lucia de Barros. 1989. *Escritoras negras: Resgatando a nossa história*. Rio de Janeiro: CIEC.

Moura, Clóvis. 1994. *Dialética radical do Brasil negro*. São Paulo: Editora Anita Ltda.

Nabuco, Joaquim. 1977 [1883]. *O Abolicionismo*. Petrópolis: Vozes.

Nascimiento, Abdias do. 1980. *O Quilombismo: Documentos de uma militância Pan-Africana*. Petrópolis: Vozes.

Patrocínio, José do. *Motta Coqueiro ou a pena de morte*. Rio de Janeiro: Livraria F. Alves.

Penna, Cornélio. 1997 [1954]. *A Menina morta*. Rio de Janeiro: Artium Editora.

Pongetti, Henrique. 1944. "Cara ou Coroa." *O Globo*, 21 October. n.p.

Reis, Maria Firmina dos. 1988. *Úrsula: Romance original brasileiro*. Rio de Janeiro: Presença.

Ribeiro, Darci and Carlos de Araujo Moreira Neto. 1992. *A Fundação do Brasil: Testemunhos, 1500-1700*. Petrópolis: Vozes.

Risério, Antonio. 1996. *Oriki Orixá*. São Paulo: Perspectiva.

Rodrigues, Ana Maria. 1984. *Samba negro: Espoliação branca*. São Paulo: Editora Hucitec.

Romero, Silvio. 1943. *História da literatura brasileira*. Vol. 4. Rio de Janeiro: Livraria José Olimpio.

Santiago, Silviano. 1982. *Vale quanto pesa: Ensaios sobre questões político-culturais*. Rio de Janeiro: Paz e Terra.

Santos, Joel Rufino dos. 1990. *O Negro na sala de aula*. São Paulo: Editora Ática.

——, ed. 1997. *Negro brasileiro negro: Revista de patrimônio histórico e artístico nacional*. 25. IPHAN: Min. da Cultura.

Schwarcz, Lilia Moritz. 1987. *Retrato em branco e negro: Jornais, escravos e cidadãos em São Paulo no final do século XIX*. São Paulo: Companhia das Letras.

Tavares, Julio Cesar. 1988. "Teatro Experimental do Negro, Contexto, Estrutura e Acão." *Dionysus* 28: 79–85.

Trindade, Solano. 1997. "Olurum Ekê." *Negro Brasileiro Negro. Revista do Patrimônio Histórico e Artístico Nacional* 25: 122.

Varela, Fagundes. 1886. "Mauro, o escravo." *Obras completas de Fagundes Varela*. Vol. 1: *Vozes da América, Pendão auriverde, cantos religiosos. Avulsas*. Rio de Janeiro: Garnier.

Vieira, Antonio. 1972. *Sermões*. Nosso Clássicos n. 11. Rio de Janeiro: Livraria Agir Editora.

Zumthor, Paul. 1993. *A Letra e a voz: A "literatura" medieval*. Trans. Amálio Pinheiro and Jerusa P. Ferreira. São Paulo: Companhia das Letras.

CHAPTER 29

JEWISH LITERARY CULTURE IN SPANISH AMERICA

Saúl Sosnowski

The history of Latin American Jewry reflects a dazzling mosaic of sorrow and perseverance, gratification and national pride, survival and also successful integration. Even a composite picture of fleeting images is striking. For instance, Luis de Carvajal el Mozo, poet and author of a probing autobiography, nephew of Governor Luis de Carvajal, was burned at the stake in 1596 in Mexico, along with his mother and three sisters; in 1645, Jewish communities in both Amsterdam and Recife numbered 1500 souls; in eighteenth-century Paramaribo, Jews formed a literary association; Mordechay Ricardo, a Jew from Curaçao, offered refuge and assistance to Simón Bolívar; a festooned float made by the Levy family, clamoring "Viva Palestina Livre," made its way through a 1918 Brazilian carnival; Jewish gauchos sipping *maté* talked with non-Jewish gauchos in Yiddish; survivors of the Holocaust disembarked at anonymous Caribbean ports; as part of legislative and other governmental bodies, Jews fully participate in their countries' political life; the non-Jewish inhabitants of the tiny Caribbean island of St. Eustatius continue to care for the remnants of the eighteenth-century Jewish community; Portuguese language and Brazilian music echo through the paths of a *kibbutz;* Latin American Jewish literary and artistic creations dot the intellectual landscape as the products of national figures, without necessarily calling attention to Jewish motifs. There are tales of martyrdom and endurance during the Colonial period and again under repressive regimes; of ancestral rites and traditions being preserved; of active participation in nation building; of communal responsibility and support; of militancy in national affairs; and of endless queries into the very recesses of Latin American and Jewish identity that span centuries of Jewish life in Latin America.

Possibly because daily subsistence was (literally) a struggle for survival, relatively few cultural manifestations materialized before this century to chronicle Jewish life in the Americas. Over the last several decades, however, we have witnessed the emergence of an increasing body of works defined as "Latin American–Jewish literature" that respond to a composite citizenry with unique cultural imprints. It also reflects the existence of conditions enabling literature to be produced and read both inside and outside communal circles. Nevertheless, this literature continues to elicit a certain degree of curiosity on both sides of the hyphen. Such an initial reaction stems from a seemingly double definition of the exotic as seen from the cultural vantage point of the Western metropolis. Although it is a fact that Latin American literature has achieved international recognition and notable success, and that Jews have been in the region since the arrival of Columbus, it is only in recent years that a concrete segment of literary production, emanating from firmly established communities, has called forth a sustained inquiry of its character and of the very nature of its existence.

The need for a hyphen in Latin American–Jewish clearly establishes the mark of the different. It is precisely this difference, also applicable to other minority cultures, that proclaims the persistence of the distinctive amid a dominant culture. The hyphen also signals that ongoing processes of acculturation have not nullified the manifest signs of diversity. It proposes, moreover, that there is a Latin American culture that possesses a Jewish imprint or, conversely, a Latin-flavored Jewish culture. Latin American–Jewish writers who are cognizant of their hyphenated imprint recover for themselves and their readers Jewish values and traditions along with Western and more localized cultural expressions, as well as direct or inherited memories of distant beginnings, whether in Eastern European towns and villages, or in the Iberian Peninsula and Northern Africa. At the same time, they reveal through literary designs their integration into Latin America. Texts that resist a ghettoized identification and gain access to the dominant value system are promptly incorporated into their respective national literatures. To be part of a national tradition, of an ever-shifting canon, represents, in this sense, a heightened awareness on the part of the dominant culture of multiple contributions to the very definition of a plural society. On the part of the descendant of Jewish immigrants, the possibility of asserting a clear identity constitutes a rejection of designs to undermine, and ultimately to compel, the self to assimilate into a graying expression of acquiescence and uniformity.

To catalogue Latin American–Jewish writers is to bring to the fore the very definition of what constitutes "Latin American–Jewish writing"–an issue that has been addressed in varying degrees by a number of critics, among them Senkman, Sosnowski, Lindstrom, and Aizenberg, as well as others included in edited volumes that have resulted from international conferences. Jewish writers also appear in collective volumes on Latin American–Jewish writers (for instance, Finzi, Toker, and Faerman; Barylko et al.; DiAntonio and Glickman; Elkin and Merkx) and in most issues of the literary journal *Noaj* [Jerusalem]. Legal and theological prescriptions do not necessarily account for voices that speak out of a multiple heritage; nor does the fact of having been born to a Jewish mother guarantee, or warrant, a distinct literary imprint. While it may prove poetically sound to affirm that cultural-religious markings consciously or unconsciously condition writing, texts by the Argentineans Juan Gelman, Noé Jitrik, Marcos Aguinis, Santiago Kovadloff, and Arnoldo Liberman; by the Venezuelan Isaac Chocrón, and by the Peruvian Isaac Goldemberg, among others, indicate that there is ample evidence to challenge this hypothesis or, at the very least, to seriously question its general validity and the extent of its range. Ethnic politics–another complex issue that merits careful scrutiny in a separate study–has also played a role in the "coming out" of Jewish motifs in authors whose previous work did not include them, as has an age (and a fashion?) in which ethnic origins play an increasingly important role.

The dynamic interplay that defines many contemporary writers echoes the centuries-old condition of Jews who were periodically subject to coercion, expulsions, and the very real possibility of extinction. These are only echoes, for, with few exceptions, identity and free expression of the self through religious and cultural practices, as well as through social, economic, and political acceptance, are constant in the history of Latin American Jewry. In this context, it is noteworthy that, for most Latin American–Jewish writers, particularly for those born of immigrant parents, the literary allusions to religion bear a closer affinity to family tradition and lore than to a belief system. Still, because both Jewish theological and historical principles hold, among other fundamental principles, that relations among God, man, and the world are inextricably linked and that man has a commitment to the world, Judaism also finds its way into a number of literary texts. Judaism mandates preservation and life, as it commands that repression be denounced. This belief, which clearly alludes to inquisitorial chambers and to the social climate that pervaded the lives of Crypto-Jews (those who maintained their Judaism while ostensibly performing Catholic rites imposed by forced conversion), also appears in recent literary manifestations from countries that have undergone violent political upheavals and suffered from state-sponsored terrorism. It is important to note that the adoption of Judaism–through its power of survival and claims for social justice, and the view that redemption is tied to historical workings rather than solely to faith in a God-related event–is more emphatic among authors who partake of a heterodox view vis-à-vis religious conventions and who have embraced Jewish concerns after having themselves undergone the experience of repression and exile.

The profile of Jewish communities in Latin America has been defined through various migration phases. Although the majority of the approximately half million Jews who live in the region are of Ashkenazi (Central and Eastern European) ancestry, most of whom arrived beginning in the nineteenth century and through the world wars, the earliest Jewish arrivals to the Americas date back to the voyages of exploration and included *conversos* (new Christians) and a handful of Jews who managed to elude the edicts mandating the *limpieza de sangre* (purity of bloodlines).

Distance from the Crown and from the Inquisition affected the pattern of settlements in both Spanish- and Portuguese-controlled territories and, shortly thereafter, in Dutch-ruled possessions. (Suriname, Pernambuco, and Recife are important examples on the mainland, as is Curaçao in the Caribbean.) The lives of the descendants of Spanish and Portuguese *marranos,* who saw themselves as "La Nación," constitute a unique part of Jewish-Caribbean settlements that began to flourish in the seventeenth century and still await literary expression. The dominant factor in Jewish migration to Latin America and the Caribbean, whether in the sixteenth or in the twentieth century, has been the availability of a haven from persecution and access to opportunities that had been foreclosed in Europe.

In addition to various official plans aimed at attracting European immigrants, the existence of conditions that allowed for the prompt establishment of Jewish institutions and for the development of a Jewish way of life offered a significant incentive. Religious tolerance stood out, as seen in the philanthropic efforts of Baron Hirsch and the Jewish Colonization Association to save Jews from Czarist persecution. Beyond that initial drive (and as alternatives to U.S. immigration quotas), economic conditions–particularly industrial growth and a climate that fostered progress and accommodation–determined the initial immigrant inflow as

well as the sustained growth of Jewish communities. Many immigrants responded to basic industrial needs and became a defining component of the urban labor force and of nascent militant movements. In turn, socialist and anarchist convictions among the urban proletariat were a contributing factor to anti-foreign outbursts and pogroms during labor struggles, such as Argentina's "Tragic Week" of 1919. Following traditional ethnic patterns of immigration, local aid societies were established along trade lines and by city or area of origin. In wartime, the availability of visas (or of quasi-legal permits) sufficed to assist passage into one or another country. In this regard, Bolivia and the Dominican Republic (where an agricultural experiment by German-Jewish colonists took place in Sosúa) offered exemplary responses toward World War II refugees.

Today Argentina, Mexico, and Brazil have the largest Jewish communities in Latin America; Argentina's ranks first, with approximately 250,000 citizens. Its history, in terms of literary-cultural production, is both unique and paradigmatic of other countries' and therefore, will serve as a major point of reference in this section. The following facts, among many other indicators, point to a rapid cultural adaptation to the fabric of Argentinean society as well as to the preservation of varied expressions of Jewish culture: By 1898, there were three Yiddish newspapers (by 1914, there were over 40 Jewish periodicals, a prominence that has now waned with the dwindling of Yiddish speakers and the growing presence of Spanish as the communal language); the first performance of Yiddish theater was held in 1901; in 1921 the first Hebrew periodical was published in Buenos Aires; a YIVO (Yiddish Scientific Organization) branch opened in Buenos Aires in 1929; in 1911 Jewish publications in Spanish began to appear. Even this brief inventory of a few salient features underscores the prompt local development of Yiddish and Hebrew culture, along with the growth of a community in which the daily language for Jewish culture soon became Spanish. These facts also suggest that the Argentinean-Jewish community did not see its new home as a way station on the long road to Israel from a renewed diaspora. Whether in the agricultural colonies of the Jewish Colonization Association, in dismal urban conditions, or in the rising fortunes of the middle classes, the Argentinean-Jewish community established firm roots in a land that it expected to see and feel as its own. In this context it is worth noting that Zionist education as part of communal life ranged from the progressive left to the orthodox, and did prompt significant migration to Israel. Local upheaval and periodic anti-Semitic outbursts also contributed to that migration.

The process of integration, however, was not without basic conflicts rooted in the minority's mark of difference. Throughout history and in many different regions, the imposition of otherness frequently derives from the dominant culture and not necessarily from a guarded attitude of self-exclusion. Issues of adaptation, integration, acculturation, and even assimilation–the definite loss of communal identity–are mainstays of Argentinean-Jewish literature, and of similar expressions in other Latin American countries. The desire of the immigrant, particularly of the one who insisted on retaining a cultural identity and rejected assimilation into a dominant culture, was not universally embraced by the general population. At various times–most dramatically, in the 1970s and early 1980s–this rejection was also at play in deadly military and political circles. While official representatives of the Jewish minority responded loudly to any query about loyalty, others responded to suspicions by certifying with their own militancy, and all too often paid for this participation through their disappearance and death; their unfortunate integration into the mainstream of Argentina's political debacle was thus proven by their murder. Both extremes of this continuum are significant. As this dynamic interplay implies, one voice aims at obtaining total acceptance by the state of a minority's representative bodies as integral components of Argentinean society, while the other tacitly accepts integration by working through national parties or by joining alternative political movements. From an institutional standpoint, efforts to legitimize the existence of the Jewish community and the practice of a particular identity within the national mainstream emphasize the enduring vulnerability and the problematic resolution of integrationist formulas.

Several texts will further elucidate this point. For the 1910 commemoration of Argentinean independence, Alberto Gerchunoff (1883–1950) published *Los gauchos judíos* [*The Jewish Gaucho*]. In it he praised the "new Zion" ("Argentina is Palestine for the Jew," he would write in 1914) as the land of freedom, prosperity, and peace. So great was his youthful desire to integrate into Argentina that he was able to omit any reference to the xenophobic and anti-Semitic outbursts that characterized much that was written in the 1880s, as well as to pass over the restrictive laws of residence of 1902 with their particular impact on Jewish immigration. Gerchunoff, moreover, in a daring elliptical argument, adopted the legacy of Cervantes in order to inherit national legitimacy through the Spanish language and Hispanic culture. He had been in exile—he claimed—since the 1492 expulsion from Spain; having arrived in Argentina in 1889 from his native Russia, he was now home. Gerchunoff firmly believed in the power of culture to fulfill the necessary fusion to the essence of a land to which Jews would contribute their own culture as part of an advanced political project. Within new parameters, then, spiritual territoriality grounded in a sense of belonging, more than the possession of a tract of land, would guarantee the transformation of the newly arrived into a full-fledged Argentine man of letters. Gerchunoff became an insider whose integration was manifestly documented by his contributions to the literary pages of the newspaper *La Nación*. While distancing himself from unsavory political figures who also published in it, he remained rhetorically and culturally aligned with advocates of an elitist view of the national experience. Given the political and economic development of Argentina and its potential absorption of immigrants, he envisioned that the middle classes allowed a path to integration and, consequently, to safety. This very notion of safety—readily comprehensible when Jewish immigration itself was largely motivated by economic instability and officially sanctioned persecutions in several European countries—also ruled Gerchunoff's idyllic view of Argentina. Later on in life, he adjusted a number of his initial expectations, particularly as a result of World War II, local anti-Semitism, and the establishment of the State of Israel. Gerchunoff's writings—which are central to any critical reading of Argentinean-Jewish literature, of Argentinean literature in general for that period, and of Latin American–Jewish writing in general—do not reflect a naive understanding of local events. They stress, rather, the conviction that only through the unswerving affirmation of official proclamations would an immigrant who, according to local officials, did not possess the general characteristics of an ideal newcomer have the opportunity to belong, that only by adopting official culture could a hyphenated being become a "whole Argentine."

Several decades later, a generation born in Argentina and clearly more radical in its approach to local and international politics, denounced middle-class values and ideology by identifying bourgeois Jews with Judaism itself. Many rejected both of their integral components in a concerted effort to deny legitimacy to any attempt that would separate them from the national majority. By this action, they assimilated the view that a hyphenated definition nullified the possibility of being just plain Argentinean. In other words, in perceiving as viable and ideal the homogeneous whole, they adopted precisely the reactionary ideology that mandated the proscription or elimination of those who challenged the legitimacy of a purified order. In so doing, they reneged on another option: To seek acceptance as citizens poised to contribute to Argentinean society the enriched segment of their Jewish heritage. In this sense, the writings of both Germán Rozenmacher (1936–1971), most notably his often-staged play *Requiem para un viernes a la noche* [1964; *Requiem for a Friday Night*], and León Rozitchner, particularly his 1967 essay *Ser judío* [*Being Jewish*]—a text that acquired new resonance as a result of the 1994 bombing of the AMIA (Asociación Mutual Israelita Argentina) building—offer significant contributions to the debate.

Against the backdrop of the Six-Day War (1967), and bearing in mind the Jews' dual existence in the "material world" that could be anywhere and in the "imaginary field" sustained by religion and the hoped-for return to Zion, Rozitchner's major statements are anchored in the fact of being a Jew *in* Argentina. Rozitchner engages the Jewish leftists who reneged on one of their integrally defining components and addresses the assertiveness of nationality. He speaks of a segment of Argentinean Jewry that anticipated that non-Jews would act along similar lines and perceive them solely as regular Argentineans, and not primarily as an anomaly in the national body politic, that is, as interfering in Argentina's social fabric. He insists on citizenship as a birthright, on the mandatory rebuttal that every Jew must exercise against any argument that attempts to preempt him or her from the territory that by virtue of nationality is inherent to his or her being. "Ser judío" refers, then, to being Jewish in lands other than Israel, where this would have been an inconsequential dispute. The predicaments addressed in Rozitchner's essay arise out of the perception of being different and out of the demand that difference be accepted as a constituent element of being Argentinean.

By scanning texts that extend from Gerchunoff's hopes, across those of César Tiempo (pseud. Israel Zeitlin, 1906–1980), and Samuel Eichelbaum (1894–1967), to the mordant view of the vaudevillian urban characters that inhabit Mario Szichman's (b. 1945) novels, set as they are in the pivotal Peronist era, it is possible to attest to the transition from the dream that called for a Jewish renaissance through working the land, to the reality of an urban life that, at one significant level, suggested a colossal failure. Such a failure did not hinge solely on the ideological expressions of communal leadership; it rested on an entire nation and on an economic system whose inner contradictions exploded into violence and repression, and whose legacy is evident in the recovered democratic system.

Perhaps no other region of the world has generated as many pages on "'identity" as Latin America has; current interest in the construction of identities, therefore, is linked to earlier considerations. Perhaps no other Argentinean minority has so emphatically addressed the issue of its own identity as Jewish writers over the course of the twentieth century. In a region characterized by multiple ethnic groups and by a diversity of cultures that ceaselessly confront their own history while addressing the future with some justifiable (and fluctuating) trepidation, identity–in this instance based on the expressed will to be *at once* Jewish and Latin American in the various national definitions–must play a central role in these writers' intellectual map. Origins, exile, land, peoples, and hopes for historic fulfillment within national borders are important thematic threads. Interwoven with other concerns is a subtler recalling of historical markers, registering and rendering a consciousness of change that reaches toward a richly textured and varied definition of a conflictive "promised land."

The very usage of this term points to a sense of commitment to the no-longer-new land that is hardly questionable, except by unswerving extremist sectors. Without resorting to the dated fantasy that understandably enveloped Gerchunoff's eloquent pages, Jews in Argentina, as elsewhere in Latin America, have repeatedly expressed a profound commitment to their country. Oftentimes, this very sense of belonging is granted by not alluding to any minority markers at all. This would seem to be the most frequent case, as in works by authors who have not been known for using explicitly Jewish motifs, such as the Chilean Ariel Dorfman (b. 1942) and the Uruguayan Mauricio Rosencof (b. 1933)–one of the leaders of the Tupamaros. Some who once did write about the immigrant experience have also moved on to other topics, such as the Argentineans Andrés Rivera (b. 1928), Humberto Costantini (1924–1987), and, among younger authors, Marcelo Cohen (b. 1951) and Tamara Kamenszain (b. 1947). Talent and self-perception play significant roles in processes of national identification. Moreover, a correlation between openness and principles that, at the very least, nominally adhere to cultural diversity permits origins to become blurred as a mark of distinction and allows an author to be directly integrated into the nonhyphenated national culture. Argentinean examples include Bernardo Verbitsky (1907–1979), Bernardo Kordon (b. 1915), David Viñas (b. 1929), Pedro Orgambide (1929–2003), Osvaldo Dragún (1929–1999), and Liliana Heker (b. 1943), among many others; Clarice Lispector (1925–1977) would be the classic example in Brazil.

Significantly, the foundation of this position may be rooted in varying expressions of similar lines of thought. Namely, it is expected that, within Argentinean borders, it should still be possible to find a definition of peace and social justice for the wider constituency of the local and neighboring disenfranchised, not just for the persecuted of the world, and certainly not solely for Jewish communities. A high quota of murder, disappearance, and exile attests to the dedication of many to finding political solutions. But precisely that high number also allowed the juntas to identify Jews who fell during the "dirty war" and who had interests alien to the Argentinean nation–that is, who opposed the dictatorship. In this regard, Jacobo Timerman's (1923–1999) *Prisoner without a Name, Cell without a Number* (1981) can be read both as a personal testimony and as a document that presents both Jewish integration and the derivative, unreflective, agglutinating, fascist mind.

With a few notable exceptions, world history continues to demonstrate that class and ideological interests sometimes tend to dominate over other allegiances, including ethnicity and religious affiliation. Moreover, censorship and self-censorship as integral components of state-sponsored terrorism did not distinguish along ethnic or religious lines; instead, these were linked to the "occupational hazard" of the agents and were a function of their physical location (in exile or "insile"). "Teatro abierto"("Open Theater"), which included Jewish

playwrights–Aída Bortnik (b. 1942) among them–although not necessarily "Jewish themes," spoke out of the Argentine experience to probe the limits of repressed silence. It is significant that in general most Latin American–Jewish writers do not formally speak on behalf of the Jewish community; in fact, many maintain a distant and oftentimes adversarial relationship with the Jewish establishment. They do speak, however, as members of the national community. The murder and exile of intellectuals and artists who did not partake of Jewish institutional life were criminal acts directed against the entire nation, even as many were singled out in the torture chambers for being Jewish.

Doubts about Jews' loyalty can still be heard in some quarters as part of long-standing (and growing) xenophobia. Nevertheless, once barred from holding high governmental posts, Jews did acquire prominence during Alfonsín's government (although the reference to their high numbers as constitutive of "*la sinagoga radical*" has anti-Semitic undertones), and Menem appointed Jews to his cabinet. Older members of the community, learned in history and witnesses to painful memories, ponder whether Jews should acquire highly visible positions. These doubts notwithstanding, by being part of the government–which in itself reflects allegiance to drastically different ideological platforms, or at the very least to partisan ones, as even the last decade of Argentinean political life attests–Argentinean Jews have asserted that the fascist mentality will not be the sole ruler of a space it envisions as purely its own. Jewish identity, as an integral component of the hyphenated Argentinean, confronts the exclusionary vision of the world that defines the authoritarian mindset. Given Argentina's troubling history, that presence in itself, as costly as it has been, constitutes a major contribution to the broader concept that is inherent in the democratization of institutional life.

As suggested earlier, Jewish communities in Latin America did not develop uniformly or in a homogeneous fashion. They vary greatly according to the original contingent of immigrants (a birthmark that is retained in the new lands, oftentimes in separate communal clusters and organizations), class composition, and local conditions. They also range in size from a handful of isolated families in smaller cities and in rural communities to large groups in thriving centers such as Sao Paulo, Mexico City, Buenos Aires, Caracas, and Montevideo. A select number of Jewish communities, therefore, have achieved a higher intellectual and artistic profile than others. This, in itself, is not the result of values inherent to a particular country or to the originating migration sites; it responds, instead, to general community development under varying and shifting political, economic, and social conditions. National contexts clearly play an essential role in the relative acceptance of cultural products that express views other than those of the dominant culture. One pertinent example can be found in Venezuela's well-known playwright and novelist Isaac Chocrón (b. 1932). Chocrón incorporated his Sephardic-Moroccan ancestry, particularly in his novels *Rómpase en caso de incendio* [1975; *Break in Case of Fire*] and *Pájaro de mar por tierra* [1982; *Water Bird over Land*] and in the play *Clipper* (1987). While some of his works are important for retracing a pilgrimage to origins and for foregrounding the significance of Venezuelan and Jewish identity for his family of characters, these motifs are central precisely because they comment upon the mark of difference and the need to confront society with the presence of "the other." In loving (and biting) memories that recreate a Sephardic home within

Chocrón's literary system, being Jewish should also be understood as an extended metaphor for that "other" who challenges conventions adopted as norms by any dominant ruling pattern of social behavior.

A remembrance of things past–of European immigrants and of their adaptation, of Mexico's fascist youth juxtaposed with images of the Holocaust, of Mexican intellectuals and artists in a Jewish deli–is woven by the Mexican Margo Glantz (b. 1930) into her 1981 text *Las genealogías* [*The Genealogies*]. Far from engaging in the sobering deliberations that some of these topics have demanded of other authors, Jacobo Glantz, Margo's father, retained these genealogies to retrace his own immigrant past, while leaving it for his daughter to seek the meaning of the newly formed Jewish-and-Mexican being in this autobiographical novel. The elder Glantz is a portentous figure whose life threads together European origins, the family's accidental settling in Mexico, and the Yiddish culture to which he greatly contributed while also actively participating in a segment of Mexico's cultural history. A humorous synthesis of Mexico's colonial past with a more contemporary facet is found in Jacobo Glantz's response to being perceived as a threat to the Russian Revolution: He was, says Glantz, a "*judío con-verso*," a "Jew with poetry."

Mexico had long been home to a sizable Crypto-Jewish settlement. In 1528, barely nine years after the fall of Tenochtitlan, the first auto-da-fé took place in Mexico City. Descendants of Iberian Jews, nevertheless, remained in Mexico. In 1898, *El sábado secreto* [*The Secret Saturday*], dedicated to Sephardic history and language, and later to become *La luz del sábado* [*The Light of Saturday*], began publication. The subsequent arrival of Eastern European Jews generated an active Ashkenazi dimension in the cultural life of the community. The newspapers *Die Shtime* and *Der Weg*, for instance, were launched in 1939; *Prensa israelita* began in 1948, along with *Tribuna israelita* and *Mexicaner Lebn;* and a ten-volume *Enciclopedia Judaica Castellana* was published between 1948 and 1951. An increasing body of Mexican-Jewish literature, which includes the learned and skillfully crafted works of Esther Seligson (b. 1941) and Angelina Muñiz (b. 1936), the poetry of Myriam Moscona (b. 1955), and the dramas of playwright Sabina Berman (b. 1953), has been integrated into the general corpus of Mexican national literature. Other authors include Gloria Gervitz (b. 1943), whose poetry is built on Jewish motifs, Rosa Nissán (b. 1939) with her re-creation of the immigrant Sephardic experience, and Ethel Krauze (b. 1954).

The hybrid generally has negative overtones in Judaism, since Judaism is bound to protect the survival of a community held together by a set of beliefs, traditions, and rituals in the midst of challenging social constructs. As seen in these pages, the encounter of Jews with Latin America has not developed in the direction of the mixture entailed by the term *mestizaje*, which generally signals the demise of the Jewish side, but as coexistence on an equal status of the components that remain on both sides of the hyphenated being. Acculturation and estrangement tend to lead, however, to the uneasiness of the outsider/insider, to an existence on the edges of marginality in two cultures. That is precisely one of Peruvian Isaac Goldemberg's (b. 1945) defining themes in both his poetry and prose. His novel *La vida a plazos de don Jacobo Lerner* [1976; *The Fragmented Life of Don Jacob Lerner*, 2000] shows that while the Jewish father's journey is coming to a painful end, his son, deprived of protection from both Judaism and Catholicism, wavers between hope in human warmth and a

fall into irrevocable alienation. Outside, however, Peruvian-Jewish publications provide another solution: citizenship as access to "Peruvianness." As many others have across the Americas, naturalized citizens would soon learn that complete and true integration mandates that ghettoized trappings be shed, and that national concerns be internalized to construct a new composite self. That new state of being will normally have to be the new citizens' legacy to their offspring, those whose birthright included territoriality. In this context, it is worth noting that family histories constitute a topic of choice in the ample realm of the immigrants' saga: arrival and memories of the abandoned *shtetl* or European metropolis, relatively distant pogroms or the continuously echoing Holocaust, adaptation and acculturation into unfamiliar cultures, the integration of the new Latin Americans into their respective nations. Examples of such family relations are found in novels by the Argentines Mario Goloboff (b. 1939), Mario Szichman (b. 1945), and Alicia Steimberg (b. 1933), and in the work of Costa Rican Samuel Rovinski (b. 1932) and, in a humorous vein, the Colombian Azriel Bibliowicz (b. 1949).

For Latin American Jews, as for all citizens, the land of birth offers a legitimate and constitutional birthright. Along with that principle, Judaism is also seen as a condition for authenticity by writers who seek the meaning of a hyphenated existence and who strive to implement a course of action based on a plural identity. Since 1948, Israel has been the solution to the diasporic Jews' historical search for a nation. It is an available and sure option, but the territory that forever designs the individual's destiny, and to which Jews of any nationality are inextricably and fatefully accountable, is the unequivocal place of birth. A culture of daily life and of historical projections, of questions and perennial inquiries for both spiritual and material answers to the role Latin American Jews and all people play in the world, is what delineates basic cultural parameters here. The articulation of self and/in society, of being both Latin American and Jewish and not a syncretic byproduct, produces an extended sense of responsibility toward a nation and a region. It also leads to a wider concept of peoples and states.

In this context, the Holocaust and the State of Israel play major literary, historical, and ideological roles. In addition to the national, regional, and hemispheric contexts, they too are constituent elements of Jewish identity, either explicitly or as integral components whose weight is forever felt. The dominant impact of the Holocaust, of the lost hub of one of Judaism's major demographic and cultural expressions, is self-evident both in itself and in the role it has played in the patterns of immigration to Latin America. That impact is also registered through the transfer of Nazi ideologies and imagery to the region. Along a historical continuum, Israel is a land recovered, the locus where questions once extant in the diaspora have become moot. Israel appears in an intricate relational network as an object of desire, a promise fulfilled, Jewry's and Judaism's core, a challenge and a threat to overwhelming comfort under diasporic skies. Within a specific literary realm, Israel remains grounded in its symbolic form, in the historical power of memory.

Israel–as a response to exclusion, as a source and a political entity, as the state whose very existence lends strength and guarantees the survival of the Jewish people–does appear throughout Latin American–Jewish letters. Except for a few notable exceptions, it is an emblematic Israel that enters the imaginary dimension of diasporic writers, and not the milling about in an everyday nation, that intersects with Israeli letters. In other words, precisely because Israel does exist, because it is part of a historical and daily consciousness, and, above all, because it is a state and no longer just a liturgical or ideological longing, the literature produced by Latin American Jews can articulate the elements that make that hyphenated being the heir of multiple traditions and of open-ended geographical possibilities. To live in Israel—as much as abandoning it totally—constitutes one experiential option; to be a Zionist who is at the same time thoroughly committed to local national politics is another. The authors who have dealt most effectively and in greatest depth with Israel's daily issues and overarching social, political, and cultural problems are those who still live there or who were residents for an extended period of time. Among them are Ricardo Feierstein (Argentina, b. 1942), Gabriel Lerner (b. 1953; Israeli since 1972), and Samuel Pecar (b. 1922; Israeli since 1963). Jewish writers of the diaspora, even as they uphold a major emotional, rational, and tangible commitment that draws them into sharing responsibility for, and on behalf of, actions undertaken by the State of Israel, are, in the final analysis, part of a hybrid that coalesces in the category of a generic "intellectual citizen-tourist." Understandably, Israeli writers—particularly A. B. Yehoshua—have sometimes wondered why Latin American–Jewish writers who dwell on issues of identity as part of their literary self-definition would even question their place within their respective national literatures. The nation, it follows, is the site of literature and no hyphenated definition can detract from the inscription determined at birth.

If territory does in fact grant a birthright, residency in the diaspora—a life that since 1948 might be seen for the Jew as voluntary exile—problematizes a wide spectrum of relations between the land of birth and the land where, with the acquisition of nationhood, traditional Jewish allegiances have taken on a new meaning. The investment of desire to share in Israel's destiny clearly holds varying degrees of risk. On the other hand, as we have seen throughout half a century, the distance between "Jew" and "Israeli" is oftentimes blurred in persecution and death. As is often the case, to be a Jew and therefore, by popular perception, pro-Israel, is not a subject decided solely by Jews. Whether in the relatively milder forms of anti-Semitism that used to be the (tolerated) norm in many Latin American countries or under more explosive situations, the latest practitioners of theological exclusions have also taken over the task of designating who is a Jew. This is an important, albeit not new, development, and it impinges on the literary domain.

The hyphenated being, who until recently was able to measure the advances of integration, is periodically reminded of roots, origins, tacit commitments and responsibilities, and also of the cost of denial. Whether in the form of affronts or bombs, these reminders signal the locus of identity and territory. The identity that continues to be forged by Latin American–Jewish writers centers on the assertion of political rights in their respective countries of residence. In the republic of letters the emphasis is firmly placed on the Mexican, or Chilean, or Argentinean, even as the line of demarcation does bear a Jewish literary stamp—and sometimes precisely because it also carries that stamp.

Major defining elements of Latin American–Jewish literature continue to be identity, the Holocaust, remembrance of traditional and religious practices, migration and the associated aspects of integration and assimilation, and the sociohistorical and political events of the authors' countries. Humor, fantasy, and flights of historical, metaphysical, or erotic fancy are also as common in these as in any other body of works. Examples abound even within Argentinean prose fiction and poetry, as indicated by the works of Mario Satz (b. 1944), Antonio Elio Brailovsky (b. 1946), Luisa Futoransky (b. 1939), Reina Roffé (b. 1951), Ana María Shúa (b. 1951), Alejandra Pizarnik (1936–1972), Alberto Szpunberg (b. 1940), Susana Thénon (1937–1990), and, among the new generation, Sergio Chejfec (b. 1956). These are poignant indicators, all, that Latin American–Jewish writing builds on the sources that define any national literary tradition and that, from that very same position, it addresses literary exclusion as it continues to work on political recognition and inclusion.

Works Cited

Aguinis, Marcos. 1970. *La cruz invertida*. Buenos Aires: Planeta.

——. 1976. *Refugiados: Crónicas de un palestino*. Buenos Aires: Planeta.

——. 1991. *La gesta del marrano*. Buenos Aires: Planeta.

——. 1996. *Y la rama llena de frutos*. Buenos Aires: Sudamericana.

Barylko, Jaime, et al. 1986. *Pluralismo e identidad: Lo judío en la literatura latinoamericana*. Buenos Aires: Milá.

Berman, Sabina. 1985. *Teatro de Sabina Berman*. Mexico City: Editores Mexicanos Unidos.

——. 1988. *Lunas*. Mexico City: Katún.

——. 1990. *La bobe*. Mexico City: Planeta Mexicana.

——. 1994. *Un grano de arroz*. Mexico City: Seix Barral.

Bibliowicz, Azriel. 1991. *El rumor del astracán*. Bogotá: Planeta.

Bortnik, Aída. 1985. *La historia oficial. Libro cinematográfico*. Buenos Aires: Ediciones de la Urraca.

——. *Pobre mariposa* (unpublished film script).

——. 1985. *Primaveras*. Buenos Aires: Teatro Municipal Gral. San Martín.

Brailovsky, Antonio Elio. 1980. *Identidad*. Buenos Aires: Sudamericana. Reissued as *Isaac Halevy, Rey de los Judíos*. Barcelona: Tusquets, 1996.

——. 1986. *Tiempo de opresión*. Buenos Aires: Belgrano.

——. 1990. *Esta maldita lujuria*. Havana: Casa de las Américas.

——. 1995. *Me gustan sus cuernos*. Barcelona: Tusquets.

Chejfec, Sergio. 1990. *Lenta biografía*. Buenos Aires: Puntosur.

——. 1990. *Moral*. Buenos Aires: Puntosur.

——. 1992. *El aire*. Buenos Aires: Alfaguara.

——. 1997. *El llamado de la especie*. Rosario: Beatriz Viterbo.

Chocrón, Isaac. 1975. *Rómpase en caso de incendio*. Caracas: Monte Avila.

——. 1982. *Pájaro de mar por tierra*. Caracas: Monte Avila.

——. 1987. *Clipper; Simón: (teatro)*. Caracas: Alfadil.

Cohen, Marcelo. 1972. *Los pájaros también se comen*. Buenos Aires: Boedo.

——. 1981. *El instrumento más caro de la tierra*. Barcelona: Montesinos.

——. 1986. *Insomnio*. Barcelona: Muchnik.

Costantini, Humberto. 1972. *Un señor alto, rubio, de bigotes*. Buenos Aires: Centro Editor de América Latina.

——. 1966. *Cuestiones con la vida*. Buenos Aires: Canto y cuento.

——. 1967. *Una vieja historia de caminantes*. Buenos Aires: Centro Editor de América Latina.

——. 1970. *Háblenme de Funes*. Buenos Aires: Sudamericana.

——. 1974. *Más cuestiones con la vida*. Buenos Aires: Papeles de Buenos Aires.

———. 1979. *De dioses, hombrecitos y policías*. Havana: Casa de las Américas.

———. 1984. *La larga noche de Francisco Sanctis*. Buenos Aires: Bruguera.

DiAntonio, Robert, and Nora Glickman, eds. 1993. *Tradition and Innovation: Reflections on Latin American Jewish Writing*. Albany: State University of New York Press.

Dorfman, Ariel. 1981. *Viudas*. Mexico City: Siglo XXI.

———. 1982. *La última canción de Manuel Sendero*. Mexico City: Siglo XXI.

———. 1988. *Máscaras*. Buenos Aires: Sudamericana.

———. 1992. *La muerte y la doncella*. Buenos Aires: Ediciones de la Flor.

Dragún, Osvaldo. 1962. *Y nos dijeron que éramos inmortales*. Xalapa: Universidad Veracruzana.

———. 1965. *Historia de mi esquina; Los de la mesa 10; Historias para ser contadas*. Buenos Aires: G. Dávalos y G. Hernández.

———. 1981. *Teatro: Hoy se comen al flaco; Al violador*. Ottawa: GIROL.

———. 1987. (*¡Arriba, corazón!* Buenos Aires: Teatro Municipal Gral. San Martín.

Eichelbaum, Samuel. 1923. *Un hogar*. Buenos Aires: M. Gleizer.

———. 1934. *En tu vida estoy yo*. Buenos Aires: M. Gleizer.

———. 1940. *Pájaro de barro*. Buenos Aires: Sur.

———. 1942. *Un tal Servando Gómez; verguenza de querer: Divorcio nupcial*. Buenos Aires: Conducta.

———. 1952. *Un guapo del 900*. Buenos Aires: Sudamericana.

———. 1962. *Dos brasas*. Madrid: Aguilar.

———. 1966. *Rostro perdido; Subsuelo; Un cuervo sobre el imperio; Gabriel, el olvidado*. Buenos Aires: Editorial Universitaria de Buenos Aires.

———. 1967. *El judío Aarón*. Talía 32.6: 2–17.

Elkin, Judith Laikin, and Gilbert W. Merkx, eds., 1987. *The Jewish Experience in Latin America*. Boston: Allen & Unwin.

Feierstein, Ricardo. 1984. *Sinfonía inocente [El caramelo descompuesto; Entre la izquierda y la pared; Escala uno en cincuenta]*. Buenos Aires: Pardés.

———. 1988. *Mestizo*. Buenos Aires: Milá.

———. 1996. *Contraexilio y mestizaje: Ser judío en la Argentina*. Buenos Aires: Milá.

Finzi, Patricia, Eliahu Toker, and Marcos Faerman. 1992. *El imaginario judío en la literatura de América latina: Visión y realidad*. Buenos Aires: Shalom.

Futoransky, Luisa. 1968. *Babel, Babel*. Buenos Aires: La loca poesía.

———. 1983. *Son cuentos chinos*. Madrid: Hiperión.

———. 1985. *Antología (1963–1984)*. Buenos Aires: Libros de Tierra Firme.

———. 1992. *Urracas*. Buenos Aires: Planeta.

———. 1995. *La Parca, enfrente*. Buenos Aires: Libros de Tierra Firme.

Gelman, Juan. 1956. *Violín y otras cuestiones*. Buenos Aires: M. Gleizer.

———. 1962. *Gotán*. Buenos Aires: La rosa blindada.

———. 1964. *Cólera Buey*. Havana: La tertulia.

———. 1973. *Los poemas de Sidney West*. Barcelona: Llibres de Sinera.

———. 1973. *Fábulas*. Buenos Aires: La rosa blindada.

———. 1985. *La junta luz (oratorio a las Madres de la Plaza de Mayo)*. Buenos Aires: Libros de Tierra Firme.

———. 1986. *com/posiciones*. Barcelona: Llibres del Mall.

———. 1989. *Carta a mi madre*. Buenos Aires: Libros de Tierra Firme.

———. 1992. "Lo judío y la literatura en castellano." *Hispamérica* 21.62: 83–90.

———. 1993. *Antología poética (1956–1989)*. Ed. Lilián Uribe. Montevideo: Vintén.

———. 1994. *Dibaxu*. Buenos Aires: Seix Barral.

———. 1995. *Hacia el sur y otros poemas*. Buenos Aires: Espasa Calpe.

Gerchunoff, Alberto. 1910. *Los gauchos judíos*. La Plata: J. Sesé.

———. 1922. *La jofaina maravillosa: Agenda cervantina*. Buenos Aires: BABEL.

———. 1925. *La asamblea de la bohardilla*. Buenos Aires: M. Gleizer.

———. 1926. *El hombre que habló en La Sorbona*. Buenos Aires: M. Gleizer.

———. 1950. *Entre Ríos, mi país*. Buenos Aires: Futuro.

———. 1951. *Retorno a Don Quijote*. Buenos Aires: Sudamericana.

———. 1952. *Argentina, país de advenimiento*. Buenos Aires: Losada.

———. 1952. *El pino y la palmera*. Buenos Aires: Sociedad Hebraica Argentina.

Gervitz, Gloria. 1979. *Shajarit*. Mexico City: Madero.

———. 1987. *Yiskor*. Mexico City: Esnard Editores.

———. 1991. *Migraciones*. Mexico City: Fondo de Cultura Económica..

———. 1993. *Pythia*. Mexico City: Mario del Valle.

Glantz, Margo. 1978. *Las mil y una calorías; novela dietética*. Mexico City: Premiá.

———. 1979. *Doscientas ballenas azules*. Mexico City: La máquina de escribir.

———. 1980. *No pronunciarás*. Mexico City: Premiá.

———. 1981. *Las genealogías*. Mexico City: Martín Casillas.

———. 1982. *El día de tu boda*. Mexico City: Martín Casillas.

———. 1983. *La lengua en la mano*. Mexico City: Premiá.

———. 1984. *Síndrome de naufragios*. Mexico City: Joaquín Mortiz.

———. 1992. *Borrones y borradores: Reflexiones sobre el ejercicio de la escritura (ensayos de literatura colonial, de Bernal Díaz del Castillo a Sor Juana)*. Mexico City: Universidad Autónoma de México/Ediciones del equilibrista.

———. 1994. *Esguince de cintura. Ensayos sobre narrativa mexicana del siglo XX*. Mexico City: Conaculta.

Goldemberg, Isaac. 1973. *De Chepén a La Habana* (with José Kozer). New York: Bayú- Menoráh.

———. 1978. *La vida a plazos de don Jacobo Lerner*. Lima: Libre 1.

———. 1981. *Hombre de paso / Just Passing Through*. Trans. David Unger and Isaac Goldemberg. New York: Point of Contact.

———. 1984. *Tiempo al tiempo*. Hanover: Ediciones del Norte.

———. 1992. *La vida al contado*. Hanover: Ediciones del Norte.

Goloboff, Mario. 1966. *Entre la diáspora y octubre*. Buenos Aires: Stilcograf.

———. 1976. *Caballos por el fondo de los ojos*. Barcelona: Planeta.

———. 1984. *Criador de palomas*. Buenos Aires: Bruguera.

———. 1989. *La luna que cae*. Barcelona: Muchnik Editores.

———. 1990. *El soñador de Smith*. Barcelona: Muchnik Editores.

———. 1995. *Comuna verdad*. Madrid: Anaya & Mario Muchnik.

Heker, Liliana. 1966. *Los que vieron la zarza*. Buenos Aires: Jorge Alvarez.

———. 1972. *Acuario*. Buenos Aires: Centro Editor de América Latina.

———. 1977. *Un resplandor que se apagó en el mundo*. Buenos Aires: Sudamericana.

———. 1982. *Las peras del mal*. Buenos Aires: Belgrano.

———. 1987. *Zona de clivaje*. Buenos Aires: Legasa.

———. 1991. *Los bordes de lo real*. Buenos Aires: Alfaguara.

———. 1996. *El fin de la historia*. Buenos Aires: Alfaguara.

Jitrik, Noé. 1988. *Los lentos tranvías*. Mexico City: Joaquín Mortiz.

Kamenszain, Tamara. 1973. *De este lado del Mediterráneo*. Buenos Aires: Noé.

———. 1986. *La casa grande*. Buenos Aires: Sudamericana.

——. 1991. *Vida de living*. Buenos Aires: Sudamericana.

Kordon, Bernardo. 1946. *Reina del Plata*. Buenos Aires: Cronos.

——. 1972. *Los navegantes*. Buenos Aires: Losada.

——. 1981. *Alias Gardelito; Un horizonte de cemento; Kid Nandubay*. Buenos Aires: Galerna.

——. 1982. *Historias de sobrevivientes*. Buenos Aires: Bruguera.

Kovadloff, Santiago. 1982. *Una cultura de catacumbas y otros ensayos*. Buenos Aires: Botella al mar.

——. 1988. *Ben David*. Buenos Aires: Torres Aguero.

——. 1993. *El silencio primordial*. Buenos Aires: Emecé.

——. 1996. *Lo irremediable: Moisés y el espíritu trágico del judaísmo*. Buenos Aires: Emecé.

Krauze, Ethel. 1982. *Intermedio para mujeres*. México City: Océano.

——. 1985. *Fuegos y juegos*. Mexico City: Universidad Nacional Autónoma de México.

——. 1989. *He venido a buscarte*. Mexico City: Plaza & Janés.

——. 1990. *Entre la cruz y la estrella*. Mexico City: Universidad Autónoma de México.

——. 1990. *De cuerpo entero*. Mexico City: Universidad Autónoma de México.

——. 1992. *Infinita*. Mexico City: Joaquín Mortiz.

Lerner, Gabriel. 1986. *Soldados de papel*. Tel Aviv: Alfil.

Liberman, Arnoldo. 1984. *Grietas como templos: Biografía de una identidad*. Madrid: Altalena.

——. 1987. *La fascinación de la mentira*. Madrid: Altalena.

Lindstrom, Naomi. 1989. *Jewish Issues in Argentine Literature: From Gerchunoff to Szichman*. Columbia: University of Missouri Press.

Moscona, Myriam. 1983. *El último jardín*. Mexico City: El tucán de Virginia.

——. 1989. *Las visitantes*. Mexico City: Joaquín Mortiz.

——. 1992. *El árbol de los nombres*. Guadalajara: Secretaría de Cultura, Gobierno de Jalisco.

Muñiz Huberman, Angelina. 1972. *Morada interior*. Mexico City: Joaquín Mortiz.

——. 1977. *Tierra adentro*. Mexico: Joaquín Mortiz.

——. 1985. *Huerto cerrado, huerto sellado*. Mexico: Oasis.

——. 1989. *La lengua florida: Antología sefardí*. Mexico: Universidad Autónoma de México.

——. 1990. *El libro de Miriam y primicias*. Mexico City: Universidad Autónoma de México.

——. 1992. *El ojo de la creación*. Mexico City: Universidad Autónoma de México.

——. 1992. *Dulcinea encantada*. Mexico City: Joaquín Mortiz.

——. 1993. *Las raíces y las ramas: Fuentes y derivaciones de la Cábala hispanohebrea*. Mexico City: Fondo de Cultura Económica.

Nissán, Rosa. 1992. *Novia que te vea*. Mexico City: Planeta.

Orgambide, Pedro. 1964. *Memorias de un hombre de bien*. Buenos Aires: Falbo.

——. 1965. *El páramo*. Buenos Aires: G. Dávalos y G. Hernández.

——. 1967. *Los inquisidores*. Buenos Aires: Sudamericana.

——. 1976. *Historias con tangos y corridos*. Havana: Casa de las Américas.

——. 1977. *Aventuras de Edmund Ziller en tierras del Nuevo Mundo*. Mexico City: Grijalbo.

——. 1983. *El arrabal del mundo*. Buenos Aires: Bruguera.

——. 1984. *Hacer la America*. Buenos Aires: Bruguera.

——. 1985. *Pura memoria*. Buenos Aires: Bruguera.

Pecar, Samuel. 1954. *Cuentos de Kleinville*. Buenos Aires: Cimientos

——. 1960. *Los rebeldes y los perplejos*. Buenos Aires: Periplo.

——. 1984. *El hombre que hizo retroceder el tiempo*. Jerusalem: Semana.

——. 1992. *Yo soy mi alquimia*. Buenos Aires: Milá.

Pizarnik, Alejandra. 1962. *Arbol de Diana*. Buenos Aires: Sur.

——. 1968. *Extracción de la piedra de locura*. Buenos Aires: Sudamericana.

——. 1971. *La condesa sangrienta*. Buenos Aires: Acuarius.

——. 1982. *Textos de sombra y últimos poemas*. Eds. Olga Orozco and Ana Becciú. Buenos Aires: Sudamericana.

——. 1990. *Obras completas: Poesía y prosa*. Buenos Aires: Corregidor.

Rivera, Andrés. 1982. *Nada que perder*. Buenos Aires: Centro Editor de América Latina.

——. 1984. *En esta dulce tierra*. Buenos Aires: Folios.

——. 1987. *La revolución es un sueño eterno*. Buenos Aires: Grupo Editor Latinoamericano.

——. 1991. *El amigo de Baudelaire*. Buenos Aires: Alfaguara.

Roffé, Reina. 1976. *Monte de Venus*. Buenos Aires: Corregidor.

——. 1987. *La rompiente*. Buenos Aires: Puntosur.

Rosencof, Mauricio. 1988. *Teatro escogido, I: La ranas; Los caballos; El combate en el establo; El hijo que espera*. Montevideo: Túpuc Amaru.

——. 1990. *Teatro escogido, II: La valija; El saco de Antonio; ...y nuestros caballos serán blancos*. Montevideo: Túpuc Amaru.

——. 1992. *El bataraz*. Montevideo: Arca.

Rovinski, Samuel. 1985. *La víspera del sábado, in Tres obras de teatro*. San José: Editorial Costa Rica.

——. 1997. *Cuentos judíos de mi tierra*. San José: Editorial Costa Rica.

Rozenmacher, Germán. 1962. *Cabecita negra y otros cuentos*. Buenos Aires: Anuario.

——. 1967. *Los ojos del tigre*. Buenos Aires: Galerna.

——. 1970. *El avión negro* [with Roberto Cossa, Carlos Somigliana, and Ricardo Talesnik]. Buenos Aires: Talía.

——. 1971. *Cuentos completos*. Buenos Aires: Centro Editor de América Latina.

——. [1964] 1971. *Requiem para un viernes a la noche*. Buenos Aires: Talía.

——. 1987. *Simón Brumelstein, el caballero de Indias*. Buenos Aires: Argentores.

Rozitchner, León. 1967. *Ser judío*. Buenos Aires: Ediciones de la Flor.

Satz, Mario. 1976. *Los peces, los pájaros, las flores*. Buenos Aires: Sudamericana.

——. 1976. *Sol*. Barcelona: Noguer.

——. 1977. *Luna*. Barcelona: Noguer.

——. 1978. *Tierra*. Barcelona: Noguer.

——. 1980. *Marte*. Barcelona: Seix Barral.

——. 1985. *Poética de la Cábala. Senderos en el jardín del corazón*. Madrid: Altalena.

Seligson, Esther. 1978. *Luz de dos*. Mexico City City: Joaquín Mortiz.

——. 1981. *La morada en el tiempo*. Mexico City: Joaquín Mortiz.

——. 1981. *Diálogos con el cuerpo*. Mexico City: Artífice Ediciones.

——. 1988. *Indicios y quimeras: Relatos*. Mexico City: Universidad Autónoma de México.

——. 1991. *Isomorfismos*. Mexico City: Universidad Autónoma de México.

Senkman, Leonardo. 1983. *La identidad judía en la literatura argentina*. Buenos Aires: Pardés.

Shúa, Ana María. 1984. *La sueñera*. Buenos Aires: Minotauro.

——. 1990. *La fábrica del terror*. Buenos Aires: Sudamericana.

———. 1994. *Cuentos judíos con fantasmas y demonios*. Buenos Aires: Shalom.

Sosnowski, Saúl. 1984. "Latin American Jewish Writers: A Bridge towards History." *Prooftexts* 4.1: 71–92.

———. 1986. *La orilla inminente: Escritores judíos-argentinos*. Buenos Aires: Legasa.

Steimberg, Alicia. 1971. *Músicos y relojeros*. Buenos Aires: Centro Editor de América Latina.

———. 1973. *La loca 101*. Buenos Aires: Ediciones de la Flor.

———. 1981. *Su espíritu inocente*. Buenos Aires: Pomaire.

———. 1983. *Como todas las mañanas*. Buenos Aires: Celtia.

———. 1986. *El árbol del placer*. Buenos Aires: Emecé.

———. 1989. *Amatista*. Barcelona: Tusquets.

Szichman, Mario. 1969. *La crónica falsa*. Buenos Aires: Jorge Alvarez.

———. 1971. *Los judíos del Mar Dulce*. Buenos Aires: Galerna.

———. 1972. *La verdadera crónica falsa*. Buenos Aires: Centro Editor de América Latina.

———. 1981. *A las 20:25 la señora entró a la inmortalidad*. Hanover: Ediciones del Norte.

Szpunberg, Alberto. 1962. *Poemas de la mano mayor*. Buenos Aires: Gente del Sur.

———. 1987. *Apuntes (1982–1985)*. Buenos Aires: Libros de Tierra Firme.

Thénon, Susana. 1984. *Distancias*. Buenos Aires: Torres Aguero.

———. 1987. *Ova completa*. Buenos Aires: Sudamericana.

Tiempo, César [pseud. I. Zeitlin]. 1970. *Poesías completas* [*Libro para la pausa del sábado, Sabadomingo, Sábado pleno, Sabatión argentino*]. Buenos Aires: Stillman.

———. 1997. *Buenos Aires esquina sábado. Antología de César Tiempo*. Intro and ed. Eliahu Toker. Buenos Aires: Ediciones Archivo General de la Nación.

Timerman, Jacobo. 1982. *Prisoner without a Name, Cell without a Number*. Trans. Toby Talbot. New York: Vintage.

Verbitsky, Bernardo. 1941. *Es difícil empezar a vivir*. Buenos Aires: Losada.

———. 1957. *Villa miseria también es América*. Buenos Aires: Kraft.

———. 1972. *Etiquetas a los hombres*. Barcelona: Planeta.

———. 1976. *Octubre maduro*. Buenos Aires: Macondo.

———. 1977. *Hermana y sombra*. Buenos Aires: Planeta.

Viñas, David. 1958. *Los dueños de la tierra*. Buenos Aires: Losada.

———. 1966. *En la semana trágica*. Buenos Aires: Jorge Alvarez.

———. 1967. *Dar la cara*. Buenos Aires: Centro Editor de América Latina.

———. 1981. *Los hombres de a caballo*. Mexico City: Siglo XXI.

CHAPTER 30

DISPLACEMENT AND DISREGARD

BRAZILIAN-JEWISH WRITING AND THE SEARCH FOR NARRATIVE IDENTITY

Nelson H. Vieira

Approximately one-half million Jews reside in Latin America in such diverse nations as Argentina, Brazil, Mexico, Peru, and Venezuela, among others. Despite its small size in comparison to other Latin American ethnicities, the Jewish community has begun to weave a distinct cultural pattern into the social fabric of the Southern Hemisphere. However, to what extent is this pattern apparent as a contribution to the makeup of Latin American cultures and literatures? With a population of approximately 150,000, one third of the total of Latin American Jews, Brazilian Jews represent the largest Latin American Jewish community after Argentina. If one considers that Jews have been coming to Portuguese America since the early part of the sixteenth century, one can appreciate their experience as a new avenue of the Jewish Diaspora. However, since Portuguese Jews arrived as "simulated" New Christians, thereby implying an absence of their original cultural heritage and religion, one can also begin to understand their eventual cultural disappearance during the Colonial period through enforced assimilation. Is it possible that this "absented" difference continues to be manifested in diverse ways by contemporary Brazilian Jews and revealed in texts written by Brazilian-Jewish authors? Does there exist a neocolonialist proclivity toward the exclusion and subordination of Jewish writing in terms of its production and reception?

In light of the above questions, it is important to acknowledge that today's Jewish communities in Brazil are the result of immigrations occurring during the nineteenth and twentieth centuries and thus have no direct linkage to the Jewish population of colonial Brazil. Involuntary Jewish conversion was enforced in 1497 by Portugal's King Manuel I and was carried out in the colony after Brazil had been "discovered" in 1500. Except for the Dutch invasion and colonization in the Northeast during the seventeenth century (1624–1654), when Jews were "tolerated" socially and religiously, Jews did not enter Brazil as "Jews" for most of the colonial period. Not until the latter part of the eighteenth century (1773) were Jews technically free from possible persecution and able to reside in Brazil as Jews, after the obligatory New Christian label and stigma were abolished. For Portuguese-speaking Jews, the colonial atmosphere of prejudice was based on religion, politics, and the ideology of purity of blood, directed primarily at Crypto-Jews and their descendants as well as other "infidels."

Forced to simulate Christianity, New Christians were often suspected of dissimulation, as if they were all secret Judaizers. In *Cristãos Novos na Bahia* (1972), the Brazilian historian Anita Novinsky documents a picture of the history and treatment of Sephardic Jews during the Brazilian colonial era, when their status as New Christians never represented their full assimilation but rather pointed to a duality in which questions of heresy and purity of blood always dictated their living between two worlds. Obliging many Jews to practice Jewish

ritual clandestinely, the imposed conversion forced others to renounce their secret world and become "true" New Christians, a renunciation that ironically only served to underscore their never being viewed as acceptable "Old" Christians. Although the Portuguese Inquisition was never formally established in the Colony of Brazil, visitations of the Holy Office to Brazil from the end of the sixteenth century created a climate of fear that frequently resulted in denunciations and imprisonment. Such was the case of Bento Teixeira (1560–1618), author of *Prosopopea*, which is considered to be the first notable poem written in the Colony. A Portuguese New Christian as well as a diehard Crypto-Jew who was denounced in Brazil but interrogated in Lisbon for four long years, Teixeira was finally forced to renounce his Judaism in an auto-da-fé. *Prosopopea* traditionally has been read as a Christian poem, celebrating the feats and tribulations of its Christian hero, while narrating some of the Colony's growing pains. However, recent rereadings have pointed to the poem's crypto-structure and theme, suggesting the poem's dissimulating stance as well as its deftness at simulating the appearance of a Christian world. The poem's dual perspective and its focus upon persona and metamorphosis indicate that issues of alterity and difference have been experienced by Luso-Brazilian Jews since colonial times. A reassessment of the socioeconomic activities of the New Christians in the Colony also suggests their important contributions to the colonization of Brazil.

From the beginning of colonization, the New Christians and their entrepreneurial spirit played a significant role in the development of the timber industry because they were involved in the first *feitorias* or permanent trading posts in Brazil. But not all New Christians who came to the New World were secret Judaizers, traveling west solely for the purpose of practicing their Jewish faith. If this had been the case, they would have fled to other countries where they would have been free to practice their faith openly. Although their motivations were primarily economic and social, many did propagate their faith (see Cohen). The practice of dissimulation, which implied the presence of a different cultural perspective behind the simulation of the Christian mask, becomes in the history of the Jewish presence in colonial Brazil a telling manifestation of an awareness of being simultaneously an outsider and an insider, where keen insights develop an acute sensitivity to the many dimensions of difference. Perhaps one of the most noteworthy outsiders-within of the colonial period was Antonio José da Silva, known as "o Judeu"–the Jew. A twenty-one-year-old student, born in Rio de Janeiro in 1705, da Silva was to become one of Portugal's most distinguished playwrights. However, before graduating from Coimbra in 1728, he was accused of practicing Judaism and later, in 1737, denounced for the crime of heresy and apostasy. After professing his repentance to the Inquisitors, on

273

18 October 1739 Antonio José was garroted and then burned at the stake in an auto-da-fé. He was thirty-four years old. From that day, Portuguese documents regularly refer to him as "the Jew." The declared founder of Brazilian Romanticism, Domingos José de Magalhães (1811–1882) wrote a play about this historical literary figure. Entitled *António José, o Poeta e a Inquisição* [1839; Antonio José, the Poet and the Inquisition], this play's central theme is dissimulation. The suspected disguise or mask of falsehood again becomes the characteristic most associated with New Christian behavior. Also, Portugal's famous modern playwright, Bernardo Santareno (1924–1980), wrote a moving drama, *O Judeu* (1966), about da Silva's tribulations and fate within the context of Portugal's twentieth-century dictatorship and the New Christian dissimulation of its colonial past. And more recently, volume one of the mammoth bio-historical and literary treatment of the Portuguese Inquisition and the *converso* experience, *Vínculos do Fogo: Antônio José da Silva, o Judeu, e outras histórias da Inquisição em Portugal e no Brasil* [1992; Bonds of Fire: Antônio José da Silva, the Jew and Other Stories of the Inquisition in Portugal and Brazil] by the Brazilian journalist and writer Alberto Dines (b. 1932), was released by the publishing house Companhia das Letras of São Paulo. All the attention to this historical and literary figure attests to the renewed interest in the phenomenon of alterity and difference accentuated in the New Christian and Crypto-Jew/Judaizer experience. What impact did the New Christian experience actually have on Brazilian ethos and culture? Is this historical behavior representative of the way Brazilians deal with difference in the modern period?

Interestingly, despite its problematic colonial history of discrimination and, later, the fascism of the 1930s and early 1940s, Brazil became known as a veritable haven for several waves of Jewish immigrants, especially during the modern period. In terms of modern Jewish immigration, Jews began to immigrate to Brazil more openly as Jews primarily after Brazilian independence in 1822, but by this time, most of the New Christians of the earlier period had lost their Jewish identity via assimilation. The early nineteenth century witnessed the settlement of Sephardic Jews from Islamic countries, but for most of the nineteenth century, non-Iberian Jews, the Ashkenazim, represented the majority of Jewish immigration in Brazil. During the 1800s these Ashkenazim first came from Holland, Alsace-Lorraine, and Germany, but during the last decade of the century, Jews from Russia and Eastern Europe became the primary immigrants. Moroccan Jews immigrated to several parts of South America during the nineteenth century, and in Brazil they went to such regions as the Amazon. Other Sephardic Jews entered Brazil in relatively small numbers throughout the twentieth century and settled in many cities, but particularly Rio de Janeiro and São Paulo. However, the Ashkenazim first began to arrive in Brazil in larger numbers with the initial wave of European immigration in the 1880s, and specifically from Russia during the first decade of the twentieth century, via the Jewish Colonization Agency's efforts to establish Jewish agricultural settlements in the interior of Brazil's most southern state, Rio Grande do Sul. Later waves came from Eastern Europe, Poland, and Germany from the 1920s to the 1940s, but most of these twentieth-century groups of Ashkenazic immigrants came as refugees escaping the more modern forms of persecution—the pogroms and the Holocaust. However, by the turn of the earlier century, Ashkenazic and Sephardic synagogues already existed in cities such as Rio de

Janeiro. Given the history of larger waves of twentieth-century Eastern European Jewish immigration to Brazil, the majority of the present Jewish population is therefore Ashkenazic.

In a vibrant 1904 *crônica* of Jewish life in Rio, the famous Brazilian essayist João do Rio [João Paulo Barreto] (1881–1921) spoke of the "density" of the Jewish community's almost ghetto-like existence in Rio and of its colorful inhabitants, among whom were men of intellect and culture, such as the city's first *hazan* David Hornstein, a polyglot, professor, rabbi, and foreign correspondent. Many of the Jews in Rio lived in the famous Praça Onze section, which, during the 1920s, became one of the first predominantly Jewish neighborhoods in the city, also known for its varied social activities and flourishing commerce. During the early part of the twentieth century, in cities such as Rio and São Paulo, there emerged the famous *clientelchiks*, the street vendors who sold on credit, the *gringos de prestação* or *prestamistas* (as they were known in Rio), and the *russos à prestação* (as they were first called in São Paulo). Thanks to these Jewish immigrants, this type of commerce introduced a new form of business that made goods more available to the lower middle classes in Brazil. The early modern history of the Jewish community in Brazil is very much linked to the travels of these men, who shouted their wares through the various neighborhoods of the city and introduced products not accessible to the population at large. And amidst the many contributions of the Jewish culture's rich history throughout the Brazilian experience, it is their legacy of duality from the perspectives of alterity and identity that surfaces repeatedly in the literary expression of Brazilian-Jewish voices.

A climate of intermittent discrimination, more politically based, did surface much later and for a brief period during the height of Brazilian fascism in the 1930s and 1940s. Although potentially more violent than it was in actuality, the anti-Semitic atmosphere of the Vargas regime did show evidence of persecution, as exemplified in the famous case of Olga Benário Prestes, the German-Jewish political activist who participated in the 1935 Communist plot, led by her husband and leader of the Communist Party in Brazil, Luís Carlos Prestes. Seven months pregnant, Olga was deported to Hitler's Germany, where she died in a concentration camp gas chamber. It appears that the anti-Semitism allowed by the Vargas regime was a means of appeasing right-wing militants such as Plínio Salgado (1895–1975) and his green-shirted political movement, the Ação Integralista Brasileira (1932–1938), and the fascist Gustavo Barroso (1888–1959) with his anti-Semitic titles such as *Judaísmo, Maçonaria e Comunismo* [1937; Judaism, Masonry, and Communism]. The xenophobia reigning during this period had serious implications for Jews, severely limiting their opportunities. Moreover, Jewish immigration was officially restricted from 1937 to 1939, given Vargas's authoritarian Estado Novo and its refugee policy reflecting strong anti-Semitism. Nevertheless, many Jews managed to immigrate to Brazil (see Lesser).

In light of this historical experience, the folklorist Luís da Câmara Cascudo's biting remark on the contemporary Brazilian populace's attitudes toward Jews is not irrelevant: "O povo ainda vê o judeu pelos olhos quinhentistas" (93) ("The populace still sees the Jew through sixteenth-century eyes"). If this statement is true, what implications does this have for contemporary Jewish writing?

In Brazil the literary expression of this presence warrants more attention, given the emergence of writers such as Clarice Lispector (1925–1977) and Moacyr Scliar (b. 1937) who have garnered national and international renown; the former is a writer of intermittent, covert Jewish expression and the latter, a writer of overt Jewish culture. Moacyr Scliar is considered Brazil's foremost living Jewish writer who draws repeatedly and emphatically from his Jewish heritage. For the most part, other writers have been subordinated to marginal status due either to their ethnicity or to the still burgeoning nature of Brazilian-Jewish prose. A notable example is Samuel Rawet (1929–1985), the proclaimed pioneer of Brazilian-Jewish writing, who encountered difficulties in terms of production and distribution, thereby drastically limiting the reception of his work. In other instances, language was the cause for literary segregation, evident in the use of Yiddish for theater, as by the very active Yiddish groups of São Paulo), and for fiction, as exemplified by the Brazilian-Yiddish writer Roza Palatnik. Whether in Yiddish or Portuguese, many texts with a focus on the immigrant experience impart a *Yiddishkeit* tradition that begs to be documented and interpreted. However, given the relatively recent development of modern Brazilian-Jewish expression, many writers are still unknown.

This current of Judaic fiction is notable for the uniqueness of Jewish voices speaking in the Portuguese language about the Brazilian experience. Brazilian literature of Jewish expression offers the contemporary reader an opportunity to appreciate the articulation of a Jewish identity within the Latin American context, particularly within the frame of Brazil's multicultural and multiracial society, where "to be or not to be" Jewish becomes not only a question of situational ethnicity but also a dilemma for Brazilian Jews facing an assimilationist national ideology and subtle expressions of prejudice that do not easily accommodate expressions of difference. Living in a predominantly Catholic nation of more than 150 million inhabitants, the upwardly mobile Brazilian-Jewish population, for the most part spread over three major Jewish communities in Rio de Janeiro, São Paulo, and Porto Alegre, represents a definite minority in the numerical as well as in the religious and cultural sense. Nonetheless, the Jewish presence in Brazil is culturally significant in its quiet contribution to the nation's socioeconomic and artistic spheres of influence. As a vibrant resource for understanding this phenomenon, Brazilian-Jewish writing attests to the dynamism of the Jewish gaze.

In terms of their insider/outsider stance, Brazilian-Jewish writers (predominantly Ashkenazim) may be considered negotiators or decentered dissenters in Brazil's national literature because they invariably approach their diasporist situation vis-à-vis the larger society from the perspective of the margin, thereby contrasting symbolically with what may be considered the center. On the other hand, their ethnic strategies (or situational ethnicity) often enable them to participate as part of the center or mainstream. Consequently, the Jewish gaze may project a myriad of meanings for such issues as immigration, racism, ethnicity, nationalism, memory, and identity as well as serve as a resource for debates on other stimulating topics such as cultural diversity, exile thinking, and postcolonialism. In other words, many of these writers comment on their own social history as a group as well as the sociopolitical forces directing the dominant or host society. As a result, their thematics invariably include thinking in relation to issues of displacement, alterity, belonging, difference, cross-culturalism, and anti-Semitism. In expressing these themes and questions, Brazilian-Jewish writers frequently focus upon the importance of language as a fount of endless interpretation, thus manifesting

an openness to indeterminacy and paradox along with an oxymoronic resistance to categorical closure so emblematic of Hebraic hermeneutics, that is, not autonomous but, rather, authentic to Jewish culture. The self-conscious, critical, and metacritical proclivities in their writings also point to their interest in grappling with provocative enigmas instead of facile solutions. As contemporary voices, these writers often challenge established nationalist norms and myths via unconventional and fantastic tropes. The scope of their writings reflects the testimonial, memorialist, and fantastic modes common to Latin American literature as well as the repercussions of living within a predominantly Catholic context. In addition, they are subject to the influences of European, African, indigenous, and a myriad of diverse immigrant cultures in Brazil, such as the Japanese. In much of this writing there emerges traditional narration as well as a new type of discourse that defies naturalist poetics, a common trait of many Brazilian canonical texts. Interestingly, Brazilian-Jewish writing frequently explores innovative forms and themes while acknowledging the time-honored heritage of Judaic culture with the fresh eyes and voices of the Latin American ethos.

The following list of authors, many considered to be lesser-known writers (except for the notable journalist and writer Alberto Dines), represents the rising literary population of Brazilian-Jewish expression. These authors grapple with such issues as assimilation and ethnic identity, memory and the Holocaust, immigration, dispersion, Yiddishkeit heritage, diasporic conditions, repression, Israeli-Brazilian relations, Jewish commerce, Jewish colonization, Jewish women, outsiders and insiders, social exclusion, and prejudice. This list represents a sample of contemporary writers: Bernardo Ajzenberg (b. 1959), Nelson Ascher (b. 1958), Roney Cytrynowicz (b. 1964), Zevi Ghivelder (b. 1934), Judith Grossman (b. 1931), Jacó Guinsburg (b. 1921), Jaime Lerner (b. 1959), Eliezer Levin (b. 1930), Elisa Lispector (1911–1989), Samuel Malamud (1908–2000), Jorge Henrique Mautner (b. 1941), Cíntia Moscovich (b. 1958), Roza Palatnik (1904–1979), Leonor Scliar-Cabral (b. 1929), Isaac Starosta (b. 1933), Paulo Wainberg (b. 1944), and Amália Zeitel (1933–1992).

The other notable writer of the last century, Samuel Rawet (1929–1985), became the actual precursor of modern Jewish writing in Brazil because he set the stage for a Brazilian-Jewish discourse in 1956 with his critically acclaimed collection of stories, *Contos do imigrante*. In several collections of short stories, essays, and novellas, Rawet's work continually focuses upon Jews and other marginalized voices in Brazil. Rawet's writing questions the attitude and treatment shown toward "ethnic others" who do not represent Brazil's Catholic culture and traditional customs. In short, Rawet's fiction calls attention to the difficulties of reconciling Jewish mores with Brazilian nationalist norms. His portrayal of Jewish and Yiddishkeit culture in Brazil, as well as the symbolic depiction of many immigrants and displaced individuals, reflects his being one of the first publicly acknowledged Brazilian-Jewish voices speaking in modern literature in the Portuguese language.

Born in Klimontow, a small Polish town and *shtetl* near Warsaw that was destroyed during World War II, Rawet emigrated to Brazil at the age of seven along with his family and settled in the northern lower-class suburbs of Rio de Janeiro. Frequently set in these disadvantaged suburbs of Rio de Janeiro, many of Rawet's stories depict Jewish protagonists struggling with their identity in the context of social alienation and prejudice. Dramatizing the bicultural conflicts that provoke social and psychological fragmentation, these stories question the absolutism of monocultural identity. Later, as an adult armed with an engineering degree, Rawet was to move to the new capital Brasília, where he worked alongside Oscar Niemeyer and his architectural associates in one of the most daring and pioneering ventures in world architecture. Issues of isolation, seclusion, and dislocation surface in many of his tales and reflect Rawet's own experience in the initial cultural desolation of life on the vast lonely plateau of Brasília. Travels to Europe and Israel inspired some of his other story collections, but for the most part, Rawet resided in Brasília, where he died in 1984. Recognized by Alberto Dines as the Brazilian inventor of the tales of Jewish exile, Rawet in his fiction manifests the difficulties and tribulations of displacement, cross-cultural conflict, and lives in dispersion. In their diverse singularities, his protagonists become the prototypical outsiders-within. In this sense, he developed the theme of Jewish immigration and cultural conflict into the broader and universal issue of strangeness and otherness experienced by all groups. His distinctive style, hermetic and dense, reflects the anguished intensity of troubled and misunderstood individuals. His innovative syntax and special use of time, space, and language for transmitting the feelings of dislocation, confusion, rage, and isolation point to the complex social web of being considered and treated as "other." While one may encounter touches of humor and social satire in some of his stories, the reader is confronted repeatedly with Rawet's ongoing philosophical pursuit of ontological questions.

Although Rawet's fame resides in his immigrant stories and their depiction of the struggles with the dominant culture, he also calls attention to intracultural conflict, thereby underscoring the potential dangers of rigid ethnocentrism. Moreover, with allusions to biblical stories such as the *akedah* of Abraham and Isaac, Rawet focuses upon the generation conflicts between fathers and sons as unending and irreconcilable. Inversion and irony also surface as modes for deconstructing the patriarchal and cultural myths that profess democratic harmony by attempting to cover up blatant prejudice, clandestine discrimination, and socially rooted authoritarianism. In short, these myths convey a false picture of the actual state of Brazilian race and ethnic relations. As overriding themes in all his prose, alienation, displacement, and marginalization become vehicles for challenging social stereotypes, absolutist thinking, society's rigid norms, and the status quo. Above all, Rawet's outstanding contribution to Brazilian literature is his heartfelt understanding and vivid evocation of the Brazilian-Jewish diaspora.

As the premier Brazilian woman writer of this century, Clarice Lispector (1925–1977) also deals with issues of dislocation by transposing her own sense of the uprootedness and unfixedness of life-in-dispersion in view of her own experience as an immigrant from what is now the Ukraine, as a resident of northeast Brazil and eventual migrant to Rio, and as one who spent many years living abroad as a diplomat's wife. Through her identity-quest narratives, she reclaims for herself and for her readers a form of expression representative of the ontological struggle she experienced in trying to understand the human condition, a compelling quest bordering on the metaphysical. In such works as *A Paixão segundo G. H.* [1964; The Passion According to G. H.], *Agua viva* [1973; The Stream of Life], and *A hora da estrela* [1977; The Hour of the Star], her narrators' monologues are frequently internal discourses on

or quests for the phenomenon of "being" and "being other" simultaneously. As a Jewish woman of spirit and an independent writer open to mystical reception, her narratives become spiritual quests that struggle with the mysteries of life. Transcending the concreteness of the written word, Clarice Lispector frequently evokes silence or what words are incapable of saying–the ineffable or the unsayable–a subject also linked to Judaic philosophy and religion. In this vein, the mystery of her writing reflects the hermeneutical idiom of the Old Testament in which the imperfections of language and meaning cause the relentless seeking of an answer, a hidden one that is unattainable for man because it rests with the divine.

Clarice Lispector's spiritual universe partially stems from a Jewish sensibility that relates metaphors and motifs frequently connected to the Judaic diaspora experience, from biblical times in the desert to the modern-day displacement of migration and immigration. Of course, while not exclusive to the Judaic experience, these motifs and images predominate among those Jewish writers who reflect on their ontological position of dislocation, where personal search and incessant questioning flourish. Two works that illustrate this Jewish cultural propensity are Lispector's *A paixão segundo G. H.* and *A hora da estrela*, narratives manifesting the passionate quest for identity as well as the sentiments resulting from psychological, social, and cultural exile.

By using the desert as a metaphor for illustrating the sense of displacement and possible redemption, Lispector's *A paixão* subtly develops the question of cultural, social, and ontological otherness and displacement. With images of the Wandering Jew and the ineffable, G. H.'s subjective and retrospective narrative alludes to the struggle in the desert and an individual's passionate search. In the novel, this quest is sparked by a minor domestic event, a Brazilian bourgeois's account of what happened when she entered the tiny quarters of her maid, who recently and unexpectedly left her employment. Ontologically invisible to G. H. prior to this experience, the maid and her room become a symbolic representation of otherness and the desert. Instead of finding a dirty mess as expected, G. H. is shaken to find the room as a clean quadrangle of white light, thereby upsetting her stereotypical view of what a mulatta maid's room should be. Furthermore, instead of encountering this space in its original unkempt state as a storeroom, G. H. sees how the maid transformed the tiny space into a "room of her own," subverting G. H.'s hierarchical notions of ownership. Ultimately, this experience forces G. H. to recognize her own blindness in seeing the maid merely as some dark, silent cultural other, at the expense of the latter's sense of self. In turn, G. H.'s "voyage within" dismantles her neatly constructed identity of immutable subjectivity and, especially, her well-ordered but false existential sense of self (her Sartrean *en-soi*, being in itself), which heretofore has never been challenged.

G. H.'s personalist narrative becomes a pathway toward depersonalization and deconstruction of the heroic, away from an obsessively subjective (narcissistic and selfish) ego, a behavior inimical to Jewish ethical behavior and its Golden Rule commandments. The age-old, exogenous social and cultural experience of the Jew as other is mirrored here in the discovery of the narrator's own alterity. With intertextual intimations of the Bible as well as Kafka and the subject of transformation/metamorphosis, Clarice Lispector's narrative is never too distant from the precepts of her ethnic and religious heritage. Furthermore, in terms of social and gender segregation, the protagonist G. H. has forsaken the identity of sameness that is so indicative of woman's traditional and insidious function in a society that relegates her solely to domestic roles. Here, G. H. is acknowledging her own alterity as a woman as well as the subalternity represented by the maid, which contributes to an enlightened sense of the human condition. And by extension, Clarice Lispector, the writer, drawing upon her own experience with gender, ethnicity, and displacement, dramatizes in this novel the condition of social exclusion and disregard or lack of recognition that plague lives that are segregated in insidious ways. In this vein, Paul Ricoeur's reading of identity is pertinent: He views identity as being only preoccupied with the self in opposition to "recognition," which integrates alterity, allowing for a dialectic of the self and the other, implying reciprocity. As G. H. becomes more socially conscious and engaged with the world beyond the selfish ego, she recognizes that a full life is one that involves living for others. While G. H.'s search is never-ending, its mini-revelations have guided her quest for enlightened narrative to the raw material of life and to an altered personal identity, one commensurate with perspectives found within, although in no way restricted to, Jewish culture. In this novel, Clarice Lispector brings her muted sense of social justice to the foreground in a spiritually evocative discourse that signals the need to acknowledge difference, or rather a sense of alterity, one frequently wanting in a society inured to the behavior of exclusion, often resulting from a dogged adherence to hierarchical structures and social taboos. Within this narrative, Clarice Lispector manifests revelations about race (the black other as subaltern), gender (female subjectivity), ethnicity (an implicit embedded Jewishness), and taboos (censured cultural behavior)–cultural signs that disclose aspects of the "performative" time of Brazil's everyday life.

In 1976, Clarice Lispector returned to her Northeastern roots in a short trip made one year prior to her death from cancer. She also made a metaphorical trip to this region through her unsophisticated, Northeastern, and seemingly anti-Maccabean heroine, Macabéa, of her last publication, the novella *A hora da estrela*. In revisiting her Northeastern roots by way of this ironic narrative with what I perceive to be subtle Judaic motifs, frequently challenged by the narrator, Clarice Lispector, it could be argued, was also returning more openly to her Jewish roots and to the various social classes she experienced in life. If we read this novel as a coming-to-terms with her Jewishness and with her strong sense of social justice, could we not recognize that her ethnic identity was expressed in a complex voice that transcended social realism and ethnic literature per se? As a writer interested in the metaphysics of the human condition, Clarice Lispector regarded ethnic literature as limiting and categorical. However, with this novella, critical commentaries began to emerge about her oblique use of Jewish myths and motifs. This new way of reading her fiction stemmed from this novella's symbolic use of the apocryphal Maccabean legend, personified in her eponymous protagonist Macabéa. Inspired by the biblical Maccabeans and martyrs who resisted Greek oppression in their refusal to disregard Jewish law, this novella was especially motivated by an image of a poor unknown girl who, by migration, "exiles" herself to Rio from the small and impoverished Northeastern state of Alagoas.

Here, Lispector dismantles the Jewish archetypes of the martyr and the oppressed by using the unheroic figure of Macabéa. Without diminishing the reader's sympathy for this socially and economically oppressed character, Lispector does diminish a facile picture of a protagonist's heroic idealization or glorification by depicting Macabéa's heroism as a form of dogged resistance: She simply endures and withstands. In readapting the Maccabean myth, Lispector points to the results of displacement and disregard (lack of recognition) in the context of the sociopolitical injustice and repression rampant among the millions of invisible others living in modern Brazil. The novella also allows the reader to perceive the human spirit in unexpected places and in nonheroic beings. In this vein, the novella also recalls Lispector's mystical, existential, and philosophical preoccupations because it deals with ontological, religious, and creative questions about the ethics of speaking for disadvantaged others; Jewish theodicy; Christian vows and promises; spiritism; artistic creation; women's roles; and social dislocation and deprivation. Moreover, by placing herself obliquely within the novella's multilayered narrative scheme of *récit* and *discours*, composed by her fictional upper middle-class male writer/narrator, Clarice evokes multiple readings by inciting empathy, recognition, and inclusion in light of the hardships and resistance of a displaced, deprived, and disregarded soul who is seriously disadvantaged by an unjust and inhuman social system. Given its enigmatic evocations for continual reinterpretation, the novella manifests midrashic tendencies that allude with great subtlety to Lispector's cultural debt to Jewish thinking. With its emphasis upon alterity, by prophesying the need to acknowledge difference in meaningful social ways, Clarice's quest for meaning, social justice, and interpretation becomes part of the signature of her cultural ideology and literary vision.

I have given this extended attention to Clarice Lispector, not because she is part of the excluded in Brazilian letters–for, as I have said earlier, she is the most important Brazilian woman writer of the twentieth century–but rather because her writing exemplifies the way in which Jewish writing has become part of the Brazilian mind and has contributed greatly to its complex development. No longer is the treatment of the immigrant experience or the typical Jewish themes of transplanted East Europeans of any significance. I would argue that Jewish writing has given Brazilian letters subtle introspective values about the exploration into identity, the need to leave the tight-knit community and consider humanity at large, and most of all, a deep probing into the meaning of social justice. It goes without saying that all of these concerns are shared by people of many languages and many cultures, but in Brazil, Jewish writers have been prominent in addressing these universal issues.

To conclude, Brazilian-Jewish writers address the cultural and social blind spots prevalent in their country. They underscore issues of displacement, exile, fragmentation, alienation, prejudice, alterity, and disregard as well as those of quest and change via innovative narratives that challenge unilaterally naturalist and mimetic dramatizations. Within their narrative quests, they claim a public space for the inclusion of difference by pointing to the gaps, fissures, and fractures related to cultural alterity. In this way, Brazilian-Jewish writing reflects the sociopolitical issues of equity and ethics.

Works Cited

Barreto, João Paulo. 2001. *Crônicas efêmeras: João do Rio na Revista da semana*, Ed. Niobe Abreu Peixoto, São Paulo: Oficina do Livro Rubens Borba de Moraes.

Barroso, Gustavo. 1937. *Judaismo, Maçonaria e Comunismo*. Rio de Janeiro: Civilização Brasileira.

Cascudo, Luis da Câmara. 1988. *Diccionário do folclore brasileño*. São Paulo: Editore da Universidade de São Paulo.

Cohen, Martin A., ed. 1971. *The Jewish Experience in Latin America*. Vol. 2. Waltham, MA: American Jewish Historical Society.

Dines, Alberto. 1992. *Vínculos do Fogo: Antônio José da Silva, o Judeu, e outras histórias da Inquisição em Portugal e no Brasil*. São Paulo: Companhia Das Letras.

Lesser, Jeff. 1995. *Welcoming the Undesirables: Brazil and the Jewish Question*. Berkeley: University of California Press.

Lispector, Clarice. 1964. *A Paixão segundo G. H*. Rio de Janeiro: Editôra do Autor.

———. 1973. *Agua viva*. Rio de Janeiro: Editora Artenova.

———. 1977. *A hora da estrela*. Rio de Janeiro: Livraria J. Olympio Editora.

Magalhães, Domingos José de. 1972 [1839]. *António José, o Poeta e a Inquisição*. Rio de Janeiro: Serviço Nacional de Teatro, Ministerio de Educação e Cultura.

Novinsky, Anita. 1972. *Cristãos Novos na Bahia*. São Paulo: Editôra Perspectiva.

Rawet, Samuel. 1956. *Contos do imigrante*. Rio de Janeiro: Livraria J. Olympio Editora.

Ricoeur, Paul. 1992 [1990]. *Onself as Another*. Trans. Kathleen Blamey. Chicago: University of Chicago Press.

Santareno, Bernardo. 1966. *O Judeu*. Lisbon: Edições Atika.

Teixeira, Bento. 1923. *Prospopea*. Preface by Afranio Peixoto. Rio de Janeiro: A. Pinto.

SECTION II
GENDER AND SEXUAL ORIENTATION IN THE HISTORICAL FORMATION OF THE CULTURAL IMAGINARY

CHAPTER 31

WOMEN WRITERS DURING THE VICEROYALTY

Josefina Muriel

What did female culture consist of in New Spain? It has been virtually excluded from literary histories on the subject: With the sole exception of Sor Juana Inés de la Cruz (1648–1695) (see **Figure 1**), there were three hundred years of silence on female culture between 1521 and 1821. Women who played an active role in the literary culture of the viceroyalty were assiduous transmitters of the cultural values that constituted their world, values that were so deeply rooted that they have survived to this day. Women who wrote during the viceroyalty belonged to a specific social group that included the middle class and the aristocracy, a group characterized by its economic status, cultural level, and social and geographical situations.

In terms of economic status, these women came from families that owned ranches or haciendas, were engaged in commerce, formed part of the viceregal bureaucracy, or held political positions such as governors, mayors, or aldermen. Some of them belonged to families that were supported by the fathers' professions as physicians, painters, printers, or musicians, for example. Rarely does one find nuns who came from the families of great businessmen, miners, or ennobled property owners. Women's economic status was invariably a determining factor in the acquisition of culture.

As a result of current knowledge on female education during the viceroyalty and the information yielded by the lives of the women writers studied, we have a general idea of the way women acquired culture. Three stages were involved, the first corresponding to what could be called basic education, which was what enabled women to share the essential values of Western-Catholic culture. This was based on the philosophical-theological explanation of human existence and its relationship to God. This meaning of life was taught to all women of any race and economic status through the catechism. These fundamental beliefs were lived in Christian families, whether those founded by young Indians educated by Gante, Zumárraga, Quiroga, Catalina de Bustamante and others who were dedicated to educating Indian youth during the sixteenth century, or those established by Spaniards, former conquistadors who had settled in the emerging cities, to which they brought their wives and children. These were all people whose Christian faith and customs were zealously protected by the Holy Office of the Inquisition.

Figure 1.

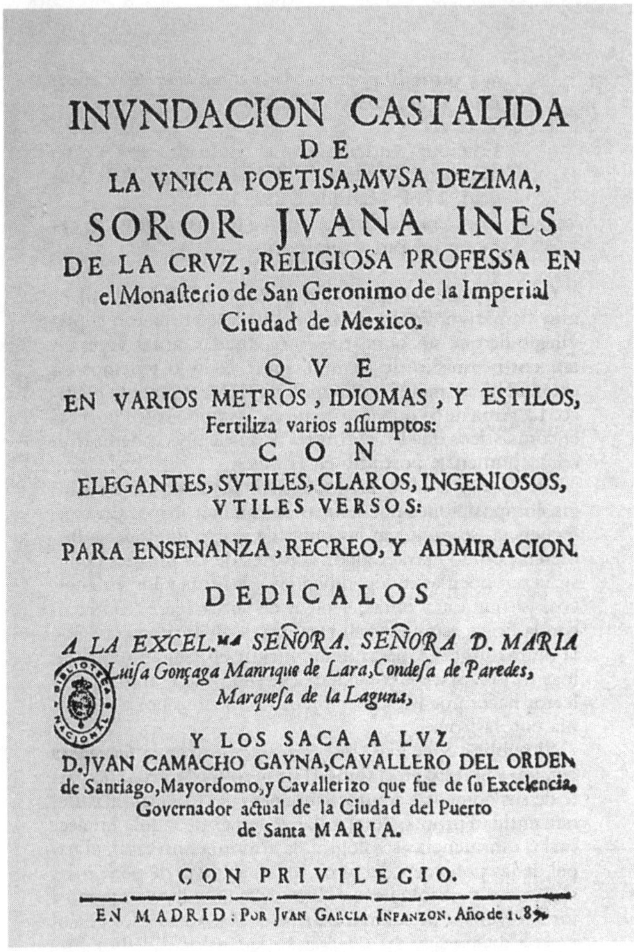

INVNDACION CASTALIDA
DE
LA VNICA POETISA, MVSA DEZIMA,
SOROR JVANA INES
DE LA CRVZ, RELIGIOSA PROFESSA EN
el Monasterio de San Geronimo de la Imperial
Ciudad de Mexico.
QVE
EN VARIOS METROS, IDIOMAS, Y ESTILOS,
Fertiliza varios assumptos:
CON
ELEGANTES, SVTILES, CLAROS, INGENIOSOS,
VTILES VERSOS:
PARA ENSENANZA, RECREO, Y ADMIRACION.
DEDICALOS
A LA EXCEL.MA SEÑORA. SEÑORA D. MARIA
Luisa Gonçaga Manrique de Lara, Condesa de Paredes,
Marquesa de la Laguna,
Y LOS SACA A LVZ
D. JVAN CAMACHO GAYNA, CAVALLERO DEL ORDEN
de Santiago, Mayordomo, y Cavallerizo que fue de su Excelencia.
Governador actual de la Ciudad del Puerto
de Santa MARIA.
CON PRIVILEGIO.
EN MADRID: POR JVAN GARCIA INFANZON. Año de 1.89.

(Courtesy of John P. Robarts Research Library, University of Toronto)

The second stage, which one could call basic culture, comprised the formative period of a girl's life, when she learned to read and write and learned the four rules of arithmetic and womanly skills. In addition to this cultivation of their intellect, women were taught the cultivation of the heart; in other words, she learned the practice of human virtues regarded as indispensable for living in the best way within a society that would place her under the tutelage of her father, husband, or brother, if she had one. This society would also give her the responsibility of bringing up her children and running the home, which included, particularly in rural areas, the moral responsibility of ensuring a decent life for the servants, slaves, and workers in her employ. Through this, women acquired a community responsibility, which, when properly discharged, raised them to the level of prototypes worthy of admiration. This second stage of a woman's education was provided in public schools; private schools, particularly those called *amigas* schools (boarding schools); convents; and community houses for lay sisters.

There was a third stage in a girl's education that was a preparation for a higher level of culture. These studies followed the personal interests of each student, and were virtually always directly paid for by the parents. Thus, students could choose to study what they liked, such as grammar, Latin, Greek, music, or painting. These classes were given by private tutors, who were usually graduates from the Real y Pontificia Universidad or teachers from university colleges, but they were always men. Their task was to open the doors to higher culture, to enable the students' personal interests to lead them into the world of humanities through reading. All these stages, however, reflected the deeply held view that the first, basic stage was all that a person really needed to be able to lead a decent life and achieve the spiritual end for which one had been created. During the first half of the sixteenth century, there were attempts to make the second stage of education available to all women. However, due to a series of problems whose analysis is beyond the scope of this study, this was eventually undertaken only in the capitals of the provinces and in towns with a certain degree of importance, and it was generally restricted to those of a fairly high economic status.

Public schools were free but scarce, meaning that parents had to send their daughters to private, fee-paying schools (*amigas*) or the colleges; community houses for lay sisters; or convents (all for boarders), in which, although tuition was free, there was a charge for the girls' board and lodging. There were obviously exceptions, since there were numerous scholarships as a result of charity work, but by no means were all women in New Spain able to reach this second stage of their education. Economic factors and the distance from rural centers made this unaffordable for the majority, and particularly for Indian girls. The third stage was attained only by a small group of women who had to have the approval of their fathers and a comfortable economic position as well as a personal interest (which itself was not that common because of a lack of incentives).

Although economic factors were extremely important, one should not overlook the geographical factors, which included the emergence of cities and the means of communication by which they were linked and their higher economic levels. Living in cities gave one the opportunity to go to school, to have private teachers, to purchase books, and to be in contact with cultural movements. Consequently, all women from rural areas were compelled to go to the cities to study; Sor Juana is a typical example, although there were many others.

In the cities, as in the capital of the viceroyalty, there were religious schools of higher education; these monasteries were places of higher learning, with well-stocked libraries where Augustinian, Dominican, and Franciscan friars, as well as members of other orders, wrote texts on history, philosophy, rhetoric, and medicine and where the young students were novices, brothers, relatives, or friends. All these cultural centers were linked to the larger society because their members were part of society and their works were produced for it. The books written there were read by the same people who flocked to the churches to listen to sermons of the preachers who were also university professors or teachers, for instance, at the Jesuit colleges in Mexico City, Puebla, Oaxaca, Valladolid de Michoacán, and Guadalajara or the schools of the Oratory of San Miguel el Grande.

Sitting under the dome of the cathedral of Mexico City, Puebla, or Antequera gave one the opportunity to listen to concerts by Zumaya, Franco, Jerusalem, or Vallados and to hear the melodious voices of the children of the *schola cantorum*. Living in a city meant being able to receive books that arrived from Spain and read the new authors published on the printing presses of New Spain (many of which were run by women). Living in the cities gave people the chance to find out about university life, to share publicly with the "Atenas Mexicana" the completion of a degree, and to take part in literary competitions. The cultural atmosphere of the cities was not only provided by the literary gatherings of the royal residences but also, and perhaps even more so, by those held in the houses of the middle class, to which the university graduates, lawyers, and doctors belonged. In the drawing rooms, in front of the ladies, the men commented on books that had arrived, discussed literary competitions, and spoke about the competition for university positions. These gatherings attracted scholars and artists alike, as well as members of the clergy. This is why, when we study the work of a particular woman writer, we find that she invariably developed as a writer in a city. To date, the largest number of early female writers have been found in Mexico City and Puebla, although they also existed in Oaxaca, Lagos, San Miguel el Grande, and possibly also in Guadalajara and Valladolid, although our knowledge of these places is insufficient to tell with any certainty.

Another extremely important factor in defining women writers as a specific group was social class. Although women with outstanding virtues, who are mentioned in chronicles or about whom biographies were written could be Spanish, *criolla*, *mestiza*, Indian, or even black (since virtue was admired in women, regardless of race), the same ecumenical openness was not extended to women writers. The ability to write required an education, which in turn implied belonging to the dominant group; consequently, women who were in a position to write were either Spaniards, *criollas*, or members of the Indian nobility.

Spanish women from the Peninsula were fairly scarce at this time. They were generally founders of institutions or women who, having taken up residence in the New World, established convents, about which they wrote chronicles or menologies. There were also a few female mystics (although we know nothing of their work), as well as a handful of musicians, *criolla* women constituted the main group. To understand who the *criollas* were, a few things must be clarified. Although a *criollo* is understood to be the child of a Spaniard born in America, this definition, which corresponds more to their legal status, is not really accurate in the context of the historical reality of New Spain: Many *mestizo* or mulatto children were in fact registered in the parishes as the descendants of Spaniards born several generations earlier, in order to free them from social restrictions. Thus, when a particular woman is said to be a *criolla*, this does not necessarily mean that she is the daughter only of Spaniards born here; she may have

Indian or *mestizo* forebears. Thus, the word *criollas,* in this essay, refers to women who were born in New Spain and formed part of its culture.

Their presence became evident during the second half of the sixteenth century, and throughout the period of the viceroyalty, they were the driving force behind culture (understood in the broadest sense). A world based on faith invariably produces saints, and the saints in New Spain were typically *criollas,* such as María de Jesús de Puebla (1579–1637); a religious society produces mystics and theologians, such as, in this case, the *criollas* María de San José (1656–1719) and María Anna Águeda de San Ignacio (1695–1756); a humanist culture necessarily produces poets, such as María de Estrada (b. 1620?) and Josefa Campos; a society that loves music, and that gave its women conservatories such as Las Rosas, produces musicians, such as the *criollas* Ana de Santa Catalina and Jerónima de la Trinidad (15th c.?–1616); and a humanistic-Christian culture, such as that which developed in New Spain, is capable of producing a literary genius who writes about the mysteries of the faith, in the midst of allusions to the Greek gods, and who is concerned about the scientific thought that was beginning to emerge. This genius, too, was a *criolla,* Juana Inés de la Cruz. The women who created Mexico's national cuisine were also *criollas.* As this implies, Indian women writers were a minority and were primarily biographers, writing within the convents created for the Indian nobility in the cities of Mexico, Morelia, and Oaxaca.

Consequently, we can say that the women who wrote during the viceroyalty constitute a social group defined by a series of factors that make them a cultural elite. However, they are not a uniform group. There are profound differences of personality among them, from which their themes, forms of expression, and literary interests are derived. An analysis of the themes of the works written by the women of New Spain also shows variations that reflect the changes in the viceroyalty's development. It is no coincidence that the first known work by a woman in New Spain was the chronicle of a convent, or that the first poem was the recollection of a mystic poet. All writing is the result of the cultural and social atmosphere of a given moment; no one can escape the historical context, a fact clearly reflected in women's writings.

The chronicles of the convents and girls' schools were always written by women, just as those of the friars' monasteries and schools were always written by men. However, there is a fundamental difference between the two. Whereas the friars always published their work, women only occasionally had their work published. As in the Middle Ages, the chronicles of the convents were handwritten and stored in convent archives and libraries. No one ever thought they would have other audiences. Some of these chronicles were published by men, such as those of the convents under the jurisdiction of a male religious order, such as the Franciscans or Dominicans. Fray Agustín de Vetancourt (1620–1700), in the third part of his *Teatro Mexicano* (1696), wrote a chronicle of all the convents that had depended or still depended on the Franciscan province of the Holy Gospel (such as those of La Concepción at the outset, and those of the Clarists later). Vetancourt fails to mention the fact that his chronicle was based on those written by the nuns of the respective convents to which he refers, merely citing the archive of the Convent of La Concepción, in order to lend greater value to his account of the founding of this first convent in America. In the Franciscan menology constituting Volume IV of the same work, Vetancourt mentions all the outstanding Clarists who lived in the convents in Mexico City, Pue-

bla, and Atlixco. Again, he fails to mention his sources, which were undoubtedly the writings of nuns at the very convents where the subjects of his biographies lived and worked.

Fray Alonso Franco, in the second and third part of the *Historia de la Provincia de Santiago de México de la orden de predicadores en la Nueva España* [1645; History of the Order of Preachers of the Province of Santiago in Mexico in New Spain], devotes several chapters to the convents and the lives of their outstanding residents. His text, too, is based on the chronicles written by the nuns and on the biographies that they themselves wrote. He does not admit this in so many words, but we can infer from certain references (such as those in which he says he no longer writes because the reports sent to him were lost) that he had access to the nuns' writings.

There are other chronicles devoted exclusively to convents that were later rewritten by men. These include *El trono mexicano* [1728; Mexican Throne] by Fray Ignacio de la Peña, a chronicle of the Capuchin monastery of St. Philip the Apostle, and the unpublished *Historia del convento de San José de Carmelitas* [History of the Carmelite Convent of Saint Joseph] by Fray Juan Bautista Méndez. The Franciscan Friar Antonio de la Rosa y Figueroa wrote the unpublished *Crónica sucinta del convento de Santa Clara de México* [Succinct Chronicle of the Convent of Saint Clare in Mexico], and Carlos de Sigüenza y Góngora (1645–1700) published the chronicle on the Conceptionist Convent of Jesús María, under the somewhat baroque title of *Parayso Occidental* [1684; Occidental Paradise].

All these chronicles were based on those that the nuns kept in handwritten form in their respective convents. Some male authors conceal the fact–Father Méndez barely confesses it in his unpublished chronicle–whereas others openly admit it, such as Carlos de Sigüenza y Góngora, when he notes in the prologue to his work:

Ocurrí al archivo del Real Convento, cuyos papeles se me entregaron y tambien varios cuadernos de autos y cédulas. Leí también las relaciones originales que de la fundación del Convento de San José de Carmelitas escribieron las V.V.M.M. Inés de la Cruz [1588–1663] y Mariana de la Encarnación [1571–1657] y la que de su vida dio aquélla al P. Gaspar de Figueroa, su confesor y con lo que de una y otra dejó dicho la M. Catalina de Cristo . . . Tuve también todo lo que de la V.M. Marina de la Cruz escribieron la V.M. Inés de la Cruz y los licenciados Francisco Loza y Pedro de la Mota y Escobar . . . varias noticias que de las V.V. Religiosas, de quienes se escribe, se me dieron por parte del Real Convento, en que trabajaron nimiamente la M.M María Antonia de Santo Domingo (que descansa en paz) y Petronila de San Joseph, actual abadesa del Real Convento. (Sigüenza y Góngora folio 2)

I consulted the archives of the Real Covento, whose members gave me their papers, as well as various notebooks of records and edicts. I also read the original reports on the foundation of the Convent of San José de Carmelitas by the Reverend Mothers Inés de la Cruz [1588–1663] and Mariana de la Encarnación [1571–1657], and the latter's account of her life, which she gave to Father Gaspar de Figueroa, her confessor, and Mother Catalina de Cristo's report on the lives of both these nuns . . . . I also had access to everything that Reverend Mother Inés de la Cruz and the lawyers Francisco Loza and Pedro de la Mota y Escobar wrote about Reverend Mother Marina de la Cruz . . . and various reports on the Venerable Nuns, given to me by the Real Convento, on which Reverend Mother María Antonia de Santo Domingo (may she rest in peace), and Petronila de San José, the present Abbess of the Real Convento worked meticulously.

Of all the chroniclers, Carlos de Sigüenza y Góngora is the one who writes the most respectfully and affectionately about the women's work. Unlike other men of his time, he admits that he was not unaware of the scorn of male wits toward women's writing. But this is a man who had the privilege of conversing through the bars of the convent parlor with the most erudite, virtuous, and scientific women of the time, such as Petronila de San José, with whom he coauthored *El Paraíso Occidental,* and the great Sor Juana Inés de la Cruz, with whom he discussed his concerns regarding the sciences, philosophy, and art. As a result of all this experience and his contact with other educated women, he acknowledged and respectfully gave credit to women's work, to the extent that at one point he stops writing, warning readers that he is handing over the completion of the text to the Conceptionist Inés de la Cruz (from the Convent of Jesus María and founder of the Order of Carmelites of Saint Joseph.)

Further bibliographical proof is available, but I think that these examples suffice to show that the chronicles of the convents published by men are always based on handwritten versions produced by the nuns. One should remember that, during the sixteenth century, the majority of works written by women were these chronicles of convents. This is understandable in view of the fact that this was the time of their foundation in the context of expansionist religious fervor. There was an intense awareness of the importance of establishing in the new lands these institutions, which were so highly appreciated in Europe. Let us recall, for example, the importance attained in both the Church and the Spanish state by the Monasterio de las Huelgas and its abbesses. There was a strong sense of the need to leave a record of who had established the convents and when, and their reasons for doing so. In other words, because these women possessed a historical sense, the chronicles recording this history were written. These chronicles were an important issue for the nuns, the schoolgirls, and the lay sisters who were the ones concerned with their writing. Thus, they copied them out time and time again, expanding and improving them, compiling previous writings, or sometimes asking male historians to write out in a coherent form what they had assembled or to express in a more elegant fashion what their predecessors had written simply and hastily.

At the same time as chronicles were being written, another genre–biography–developed. This was undoubtedly the most popular genre, one that managed to sustain the public's interest and was produced in the greatest numbers throughout the Colonial period. The reason for its popularity lay in the biographies themselves and in the reasons behind them, the need to show examples worthy of imitation and thereby to justify the existence of the institutions associated with them. This is why biographies only revealed the positive aspects of their subjects, in other words, what was worthy of imitation. It is not that the subjects were regarded as angels, since their struggle against passions, for instance, is mentioned, but rather that their vices are simply overlooked; one has the impression that the biographers merely presented an image of a spirit enveloped in a woman's skin (which is the only thing that proved her existence in this world). The biographers only mentioned their subjects' love of God and charity toward their fellow humans. Human love, even love of relatives, was absent as such.

Sex is depicted as a temptation, sometimes brutally and aggressively presented in demonic racialized images of blacks and mulattos, but always eventually subjugated by the triumphant virtue of chastity. Hatred, jealousy, envy, pride, anger, and gluttony, in short, all those age-old human sentiments, appear only in their opposite form, in other words, transformed into the virtues of love, humility, patience, and abstinence, in short, into the virtues of women who avoided human miseries in their everyday lives and went through life without being affected by them. To date, I have been unable to find a single biography written by a woman that focuses on the purely human values of her fellow humans, much less on any frivolous aspects of life. The only woman who dares to speak more frankly about the lives of the women of her time is Sor Juana, and even she uses the more impersonal form of the theater.

Such was the case from the sixteenth until the early nineteenth century. Changes began to emerge as this literary genre developed, however, such as the fact that the subjects of biographies were no longer only the descendants of noble families. This marked the beginning of a slight democratization: When the subjects actually did have noble forebears, the fact now had to be pointed out. Another significant modification in these narratives was the fact that the presence of the work of the devil was not as highly emphasized in the eighteenth-century biographies as it was in seventeenth-century ones (when male biographers attributed so much importance to the devil that this sometimes took up most of their work). The devil's existence was not denied later, but it was kept quite definitely in its place–in hell–and its presence failed to affect any visible daily activity. In this biographical genre, in which faith was the basis, there was never any critical spirit or doubt about facts that seem implausible to our current rational thinking. (These are facts that do not concern issues of dogma but actions in the real lives of the subjects of the biographies.) The colonial nuns, it should be noted, were not interested in writing the biographies of women who were not nuns, lay sisters, or schoolgirls. The biographies of lay women were the province of men alone.

The themes that appear in female poetry in New Spain are extremely varied, but their diversity clearly reveals the interests of women throughout the various centuries. Two *criollas,* Catalina de Eslava and María de Estrada Medinilla, give us a glimpse of female interests in New Spain: the first through a laudatory sonnet to a mystic poet (her uncle), whom she praised as much for his mysticism as for his poetry, and the second through her descriptive, secular poetry, in which she presents all the features of politico-juridical, religious, and cultural power in New Spain. This range, which began in the late sixteenth century and early seventeenth century, reveals the course that female poetry was to take during the following centuries. Thus, we find that the most widely developed poetry until the mid-eighteenth century was religious, even in literary competitions, since these were organized to celebrate canonizations, the arrival of relics, and the inauguration of convents. They were written by lay women and sisters alike. The writing of the Hieronymite nun, Sor Juana Inés de la Cruz, was so brilliant that it eclipsed the work of other women. The pleasure her poetry brought us has also made her into the alpha and omega of female culture.

Geniuses are unique and impossible to repeat; there is no point comparing them, and so this essay makes no attempt to do so. As a historian, however, I am interested in studying other women writers in order to investigate the cultural development of New Spain and to show how these women, secluded in their homes, convents, schools, or retreats, were an integral, active part of this *criollo* country whose culture was based on all the ideological principles imported through Spanish humanism. We do not know whether the first women who came to Mexico participated in the anonymous satirical poetry, consisting of couplets and popular ballads written against Cortés in the months following the conquest of Mexico City, but they may well have taken part because this genre of popular lyric did not require a high degree of culture, which these first European women certainly did not have, merely wit, which Spaniards have never lacked.

As for Sor Juana, her poetry was not restricted to religious or celebratory themes, although much of it was indeed religious and some was written to commemorate worldly festivities, such as the arrival of the viceroys (*Neptuno Alegórico*, 1689), or offer homages to the royal representatives and their wives, archbishops, university graduates, and cultured men of the time. However, she also dealt with subjects that were not explored in the female colonial poetry of the seventeenth century, philosophical-moral, historical, mythological, congratulatory, amatory, and burlesque themes. This clearly does not mean that others wrote only religious poetry; yet, since it elicited the greatest interest, it was the kind that was usually published. At a time when so much verse was produced, those who participated in literary contests undoubtedly wrote other poems; their creativeness is unlikely to have lasted merely for the duration of the competition, and their interests, since they were women of the world, could not have been purely mystical. Their festive, congratulatory, and amorous poetry must still be extant somewhere. Just as we have never seen the poem on bullfighting by María de Estrada Medinilla, I am sure there must have been countless poems on purely human themes that we have never seen because they were never published.

The last decades of the seventeenth century, when Charles III implemented the reforms of centralized authority, saw a change in the themes of female poetry that lasted until the end of the viceroyalty. Enlightened despotism led to a defense of the monarchy and the expulsion of the Jesuits, disturbing the previously unshakable Catholicism of the entire Spanish empire. In the king's presence, instead of arguing the rights and dignity of man, favors were requested–and granted–as a result of base praise. Once the monolithic bloc of common state-Church interests had been destroyed, the Inquisition focused more on political affairs than on Christian faith and customs. Irreligiousness was publicly expressed in the form of lampoons that satirized the Church, mocking dogmas, making fun of relaxed morals amongst the clergy. The king once ruled by the grace of God; given the absence of the latter, he now reigned as a result of the people's will. The theme of women's published poetry consequently shifted from God to the king and from the sacred to the political, which implied a reformulating of previously unshakable political ideas. There was a shift from respect and reverence for the viceroys–images of the king–to false, empty praise of the monarch and his representative. The competition in honor of Charles IV and the placing of his statue by the Viceroy Branciforte is a case in point.

Shortly afterward, the theme of America emerged, together with an awareness of Spanishness in the face of Napoleonic challenges. Another theme taken up by the women writers of New Spain was the rebellion against Calleja, the general, who could just as easily have been the viceroy. This new theme of "freedom and justice" would no longer emerge from the pens of educated ladies who had studied Latin, but instead from those who spoke Spanish badly and made spelling mistakes, that is, the ordinary women who fought for independence. With this theme the poetry of the viceroyalty came to a close; the verses on the triumph of the army of the Three Guarantees, penned by a Carmelite nun from Morelia, began the articulation of an independent Mexico.

Mysticism is a personal experience that occurs within a person, and therefore, when mystics record the results of their experience, they are providing a description of what they have achieved through this path of subjective knowledge. The mystic is moved by a desire to know God, a desire to achieve union with Him. This, in turn, entails the congruity of the human with the divine will. There can be no union with God if a discrepancy exists between God's will and that of humanity. For this reason, mystics strive, as far as their nature allows, to renounce everything that separates them from God, hence the sacrifices to master humanity's sinful tendencies and disorderly passions. This does not imply hatred of oneself, merely hatred of what differentiates and separates one from God. This total adaptation of humanity's will to that of God is what mystics seek in order to achieve the final beatific vision, which they begin to glimpse in their ecstasies and in their flights of spirit that translates into the love that captivates the senses, which the prophet Jeremiah called the seduction of Yahweh. This love bends human will, subjugating it until total surrender is achieved because the Lord is the most powerful Lover.

Spanish mysticism is undoubtedly one of the most important expressions of the Iberian renaissance. Through it one can see the constituent elements in their full scope. The religious, philosophical, humanistic, and popular interests of that ancestral Spanish culture are combined, reflecting a national interest in mystical expression. This is shown, as Aubrey F. G. Bell notes in his seminal *El renacimiento en España*, by the vast production of this type of work, which outstripped even the pastoral novel. Interest in mysticism was brought to New Spain by the early missionaries, bishops, and lay persons from Spain with their exuberant, colonizing, and evangelical Catholicism. The priest on that first Franciscan mission of 1524, Friar Martín de Valencia, was a mystic who retreated to the Caves of Sacromonte to be able to be alone with the Lord. The Augustinian friars, settlers who built towns and hospitals in the mornings and withdrew to the mountains to pray at night, were also mystics, as were those whom the Indians watched levitate in mystical rapture above the treetops. Gregorio López (1542–1596) was also a mystic who retreated to the caves of the Santa Fe Hospital in Tacubaya and subsequently in Oaxtepec, whence he fled from the visits of viceroys and archbishops. He was a mystic who studied the medicinal plants of the Indians at certain times and, at others, when he was inspired, commented on the Apocalypse.

Mystical literature was disseminated in order to foster a certain type of life. The first archbishop, Fray Juan de Zumárraga (1468–1548), was anxious that the Christian life advocated in New Spain should be more suited to simple people rather than scholars. To this end, Juan Estrada translated the *Ladder to Paradise* by the contemplative mystic St. John Climacus (died c. 649) into Spanish in Mexico, even before Fray Luis de León (1527–1591) did so in Spain. This is why it is by no means unusual that this was the first book printed in New Spain, nor that, despite the cost of printing and the scarcity of printing presses, the *Mística Teológica* by St. Bonaventure, which showed the true path to heaven, was printed three times during the sixteenth century (1546, 1549, and 1575). The works of Fr. Juan de los Angeles (1536–1609), Fr. Luis de León, Fr. Luis de Granada (1504–1588), the lay brother Juan de Ávila (1499–1569), San Juan de la Cruz (1542–1591), San Ignacio de Loyola (1491–1556) and others arrived continuously during the Colonial period, generally printed and bound, although occasionally in handwritten form.

Through their works, too, Spanish women writers inspired the production of a mystical literature in Spanish America. This type of literature appeared in Tunja, Colombia (with Mother Castillo), as well as among the nuns and lay sisters of Quito, Cuzco, Arequipa, Guamanga, Trujillo, Lima, and other places. The women of New Spain could not avoid this strong interest and, indeed, participated with an extraordinary enthusiasm that is reflected in the numerous biographies of nuns and lay women printed at that time and preserved in the other writings they left behind. Spanish, *criolla*, Indian, mulatto, and even black women formed part of this mystic movement, some merely experiencing it, others recording their mystical experiences on the order of their superiors.

The works of St. Teresa were avidly read, leading to the creation of convents that sought to imitate her life. The influence of this writer in New Spain also extended to male clergy and lay persons. Another writer of great importance was Mother María de la Antigua, through her work, *Desengaño a las religiosas y de las almas que tratan de virtud* [Disabuse of Religious Women and of Souls who Seek Virtue], widely disseminated in female institutions, colleges, and retreats. However, the person who wielded the greatest mystical influence, along with St. Teresa, was the venerable María de Jesús de Agreda (1602–1665). Her work, *La Mystica Ciudad de Dios* [The Mystical City of God], was reprinted seventy-two times in Europe and once in Mexico and twenty-seven times in a summarized form (see **Figures 2** and **3**). Seven editions of the latter were produced in New Spain. The work was so widely disseminated that there was not a single convent, college, community house for lay sisters, or retreat without several copies. Her influence on Spanish American women writers was decisive, even on its greatest figures, such as Sor Juana Inés de la Cruz in Mexico and Sor Francisca del Castillo in Colombia. Painters from the Colonial period have left fine portraits of María de Jesús de Agreda, whom they place next to the great visionaries and fathers of the Church. Thus, she often appears in the center with her mystical city, flanked by St. John with the Apocalypse on one side and St. Augustin with the City of God on the other.

Chroniclers refer to female mystical life as a fact from the third decade of the sixteenth century onwards, and explain it as one of the results of the first stage of evangelization. The fervor with which this was experienced was the Catholic response to the Reformation. The mystical writings with which we are familiar, however, emerged only at the end of the sixteenth century, reaching their peak in the seventeenth century and maintaining supremacy until the first half of the eighteenth century. By the second half of the eighteenth century, mystical writings had become rare, eventually disappearing during the last decades of the century. Apparently, by this time, women were more interested in action than contemplation. We should recall that it was at this time that religious orders emerged based on an active life, such as the Society of Mary, which founded the famous La Enseñanza school. A tendency toward secularization also began at this time with the creation of civil institutions, such as the Colegio de las Vizcaínas, which managed to escape archiepiscopal jurisdiction, and the shift into the civil sphere of marital problems and divorce suits, once the sole province of the Church.

One cannot categorically state, however, that the mystical life narrated by women writers had ceased to exist by the

Figure 2.

(Courtesy of John P. Robarts Research Library, University of Toronto)

eighteenth and nineteenth centuries; both the stories and their tellers existed in Mexico and throughout the Catholic world. However, this type of literature did become scarce, and tended to be stored away in monastic archives. It was no longer published because society showed little interest. This shift should be kept in mind when analyzing the change in mentality that took place between the sixteenth and nineteenth centuries in Mexico because one of the most accurate indicators of this is indeed mysticism, which reflects the most intimate expression of the spirit of the women who experienced it. With the exception of María Anna Águeda de San Ignacio, women mystics did not always seek to teach anyone. They did not necessarily wish their personal experiences to be directly transmitted to the public (in other words, to be printed), although they did want the spiritual directors, to whom they gave their works, to disseminate the forgiveness of God that they said they had experienced personally, thereby tacitly acknowledging that their personal experience was valid for others. Their wishes were fulfilled after their deaths, when their biographers included the texts of their writings in their biographies. The very fact that women dared to explore mystical-theological issues within the culture of New Spain proves that women were able to reach a high level of achievement if they so wished.

Figure 3.

(Courtesy of John P. Robarts Research Library, University of Toronto)

Theological issues as such demand an extremely high level of education and, at that time, required great personal bravery, given the zeal with which the Inquisition preserved its dogmatic purity. For this reason, only two women of proven intelligence dealt with the issues directly: Sor Juana Inés de la Cruz and María Anna Águeda de San Ignacio. The former did so in the seventeenth century, shielding herself artfully behind the freedom that poetry gave her writings (except the *Carta Athenagórica),* while at the same time freeing herself from the formalism, precision, and magisterial nature that theological responsibility might entail. However, the theological insights she offers in her poetry show us the profound, constant interest that theological issues held for her, issues that were always dealt with in keeping with the purest Catholic orthodoxy.

During the eighteenth century, María Anna Águeda de San Ignacio was also concerned with theological issues, which she regarded as the most important and the only ones worthy of interest. She wrote under the protection of the Bishop of Puebla, Domingo Pantaleón Álvarez de Abreu, with the aim of having her work published and used for teaching purposes. Thus, whereas Sor Juana confessed that she was not writing to

teach anyone anything, Sor María Anna wrote for precisely this reason. We know from various sources that other women ventured to write about these issues, yet their works are unknown because they were never published. The development of this theme required so much in terms of intellectual conditions, culture, and even lifestyle, as St. Thomas would say, that those who wrote on the subject were necessarily part of an extremely privileged elite.

Thus, if we were to devise a scale of the women writers of New Spain according to their cultural level, we would place those who wrote about cooking on the lowest and most popular level, chroniclers and biographers on the next step up, poets and mystics still further up, and theologians at the top. After the conquest and at the beginning of life in New Spain, the new settlers' families brought their own gastronomic interests in Spanish cooking with them, since by that time, the famous *Libro de los guisados y manjares* [Book of Stews and Special Foods] by the royal chef Ruperto de Nola had been published. In Mexico, they encountered Indian cookery, which had its own distinctive stamp, both in the ingredients used and in its broad range of flavors. The convergent (rather than parallel) development of these two cuisines during the viceroyalty proved to be yet another adventure in the process of discovering new things, which in this case involved gastronomy. Daring to eat unknown ingredients and trying the new flavors helped produce a new type of cuisine. Women from various social classes played an important role in the development of the gastronomy of New Spain: The women who had the dishes made and supervised their production were usually *criolla* or Spanish, while those who prepared them were usually Indian. Among their manuscripts, the *criollas* have left us the historical legacy of Mexican cooking, but it was the Indians who actually exercised a decisive influence over the creation of that cuisine. This combination of elements, using both native and imported ingredients to achieve new flavors, together with the attractive presentation of the final result, is an art linked to the spirit of the times, and, whether or not their creators were aware of it, one that lent to this culinary art a particular style. Thus, just as literary forms reflected the architectural lines of the Baroque, in Méndez Plancarte's happy turn of phrase, so culinary works, with their multifaceted flavors and rich presentation, constituted a baroque development that culminated in the masterpieces of Mexican cooking, such as chiles in walnut sauce or turkey in *mole.*

Few written testimonies remain of cooking in the family, the real crucible where the habits and flavors of two cultures were blended. Conversely, we do have more information about the cooking undertaken in female institutions. All nuns practiced the art of cooking to a greater or lesser extent, striving to create exquisite dishes to thank their benefactors, obtain favors, wine and dine bishops, and receive viceroys. When the convents' income dwindled as a result of poor administration or economic or political problems, the nuns survived on the sale of their most famous dishes. In Mexico City, the nuns of La Concepción baked mouth-watering pastries; those of San Bernardo produced all kinds of candies and preserves, in addition to confecting sponge fingers and fried and garnished tortillas for invalids. The nuns of La Encarnación were experts at making corn liquor and honey of roses. When the Convent of San Jerónimo, famous for its cuisine, founded the Convent of San Lorenzo, it took its culinary tradition with it, for it was famous for its almond-flavored sugar paste and caramels. The nuns at Santa Catalina made all kinds of sweets and pastries. Those at Santa Teresa (la Nueva) were famous for their rose-flavored pastries and *marquesotes,* or corn cakes, and the Capuchin sisters of Nuestra Señora de Guadalupe were renowned for confecting the most delicious chocolate in the city.

The nuns in Puebla were even more famous cooks, and their beautiful kitchens speak for themselves. At the Convento de Santa Rosa, while the theologian Sor María Anna Águeda was busy writing in her cell, other nuns in the kitchen concocted superb dishes, such as *mole poblano* (whose creation is traditionally attributed to Sor Andrea de la Asunción, a nun from the Dominican convent, although there is no documentary proof of this). This is also where the delicious chiles in walnut sauce, almond nougat, *leche de mamey,* and many other delicacies of Puebla's cooking were made. The sieved corn flour tamales from Santa Mónica were famous, as were the *yemas reales, alfajores* (a kind of pastry), the almond ring-shaped pastries, *polvorones* (sugar cookies), and *jamoncillos.* The mere mention of the Clarists' convent evokes memories of the Santa Clara *camotes,* subsequently naturalized by the city as *camotes de Puebla.* At the same time, their *tostaditas* and raisin puddings became famous. One can hardly forget the Carmelites in Puebla, with their fish in *adobo* (a sort of chili paste), Carmelite chicken, fish *a la teresiana,* pigeon and partridge stew, San Blas sauce, *alfajores de Luz,* and that mouth-watering dish, the nuns' delight, aptly called *Dulce del Cielo.*

Any history of Mexican cuisine should include the dishes created by these and many other nuns not mentioned here, such as those in Querétaro, the creators of the famous *puchas,* for dipping into chocolate, and those in Oaxaca, Chiapas, Michoacán, Nueva Galicia, and many other provinces, whose baroque creations made an important contribution to the art of dining in New Spain. Traditional dishes, those that emerged from these new combinations and exotic creations, were recorded in the recipe collections compiled by each nun for her personal use, as well as in the community cookbooks. The majority of these have, unfortunately, been lost. We know from the surviving cookery books, however, that women in the viceroyalty constantly jotted down their culinary discoveries. We are certain of the existence of a famous *Libro de Cocina del Convento de San Jerónimo* [Cookbook of the Convent of San Jerónimo's Kitchen], because it is mentioned by Sor Juana Inés de la Cruz in a dedicatory sonnet in the booklet she made for her sister, with a selection of its recipes.

The recipes that Sor Juana copied constitute the oldest manuscript of women's recipes that has ever been found. The poet's selection includes stews and sweets from the second half of the seventeenth century (Sor Juana Inés de la Cruz 1979). The value given to such works is shown by a beautiful, anonymous book written in Puebla in 1786, entitled *Arte de Cocina* [The Art of the Kitchen]. Its cover, a veritable calligraphic work of art in itself, is a pen drawing of a panoply of cooking utensils and ingredients common at the time. The drawing shows saucepans, casseroles, spoons, and ovens together with rabbit, turkey, partridge, fish, sausage, and so on. In short, there are such expressive decorative features that one can immediately guess at the appetizing content of the text. Who wrote this book? We do not know for sure, but since the nuns wrote on the order of their superiors and the title includes the phrase, "Written by order of my superior," one can assume that it was written by a nun from Puebla. The entire book is written in impeccable calligraphy imitating printed characters.

Other booklets and loose pages from convents, written in the eighteenth century and now found in private collections, have also been discussed. A complete recipe book from this century is held in the *Archivo General de la Nación* [General Archive of the Nation] and others undoubtedly exist–all anonymous. These recipe books also reflect the influence of the Enlightenment. Culinary knowledge was supposed to be an orderly compilation of gastronomic wisdom. This is what led an anonymous author to produce a *Diccionario de Cocina* [Kitchen Dictionary]. The work is handwritten and bound in the shape of an envelope, in brown leather, in the style of the time. Among the handwritten books produced by families, there is one entitled *Cuaderno de Guisados–Soy de María León de Gómez* [Cookbook–I belong to María León de Gómez]. It consists of five notebooks, each on different paper and in different handwriting. Some are from the eighteenth century and others from the early nineteenth century, showing how family culinary traditions were created through the writings of different generations.

During the nineteenth century, although they gradually began to emerge from anonymity, women continued to record recipes, even for cookbooks for domestic use, such as one by doña Clara Garnica, dated 1852 by the author; the *Libro de Cocina de la Señorita Guadalupe Ovando* [Miss Guadalupe Ovando's Cookbook], produced in 1857; or the *Recopilación de recetas y guisados* [Collection of Recipes and of Stews], compiled by Emilia Priani in 1864. The custom of sharing recipes with friends and relatives is reflected in another recipe book entitled "*Recetas de mi Lolita Chula*" [Recipes of my Dear Lolita], which begins with a delicate recipe for "Red snapper in pine nut sauce." What is interesting about these nineteenth century manuscripts is that they begin to show foreign influences, openly reflected in printed cookbooks.

Independence from Spain marked a significant change in Mexican gastronomy, as the country opened itself up to the world of international trade and thus cultural influences. At the same time as Mexico's unusual cooking began to be known abroad–as a result of the anonymous publication of a Mexican recipe book entitled *Arte nuevo de cocina y repostería* [New Art of Cooking and Baking]–recipe books with foreign recipes began to be produced in Mexico, such as an anonymous cookbook entitled *El cocinero mexicano–Colección de las mejores recetas para guisar al estilo americano y de las más selectas, según el método de las cocinas española, italiana, francesa e inglesa* [The Mexican Cook–Collection of the Best Recipes to Cook in the American Style and the Most Select Methods from the Spanish, Italian, French, and English Cuisines], published in 1831, and another anonymous cookbook entitled *La cocinera de todo del mundo* [Cooking from All the World], published in Puebla in 1843. People became aware that a change was taking place. Titles reflecting this began to appear, such as the anonymous *Nuevo y sencillo arte de cocina* [New and Easy Art of Cuisine], printed in 1836, and the *Novísimo arte de cocina* [The Newest Art of Cuisine], by Simón Blanquel, published in 1853.

Recipe books, which were not published at all during the viceroyalty (printed cookbooks were imported from Spain and only covered Spanish cooking), began to be widely published afterward. We know of seventeen editions of Mexican cookery books printed in Mexico in the nineteenth century, four of which were produced in Puebla, Morelia, and Guadalajara, and more undoubtedly exist. It was during this time that women began to sign their printed work. They began by calling their work *Cocina Mexicana*

[Mexican Cuisine] or "Written by a Mexican woman," thereby expressing their patriotism, so important at the time for the firm integration of the country in the face of foreign powers. Mexican women's patriotism was particularly acute in the provinces where the *Manual de Cocina Michoacana* [Manual of the Michoacan Cuisine], *La Cocina Poblana* [The Puebla Cuisine], and other works were published. The names of the authors, such as Vicenta Rubio and María Antonia Gutiérrez, subsequently appeared in the books published in the capital and the provinces. This century also saw the publication of numerous cookery books by men, all of which tended toward the gastronomic internationalization of Mexican cuisine. Cooks' dictionaries, the first of which was published by a woman in the eighteenth century, began to be produced by men in the nineteenth century, such as *El tesoro de la cocina* [Treasure of the Kitchen] and *Diccionario de las familias* [1866; Dictionary for Families; Anonymous]. However, these belong to a period of history that goes beyond the scope of this essay.

Knowledge of female culture in New Spain undoubtedly provides a broader, deeper, and more accurate view of Spanish-American history. Works written by women during the Colonial period provide valuable historical information. They give us more in-depth knowledge of family life in the various social classes and show how economic factors modify social and cultural status. These works depict the lifestyle of the middle class (*criollas*) in the countryside and the cities, describing the social function of blacks and mulattos, masters, servants, and slaves, as well as articulating women's dependence, which was stipulated by law and experienced in their relations with their authoritarian fathers and brothers and broken only through stubborn confrontations that led them to exercise their rights and choose the type of life they wished. The works describe the type of instruction given to women, from basic education to the high cultural levels available to the privileged classes. They mention the viceroys and the esteem in which they were held, the prestige of the high courts as administrators of justice, and the respect for culture symbolized by the university. They mention the wives of the viceroys, such as the one who promoted Sor Juana within Spanish literature, another who used her influence to obtain royal approval for the foundation of a monastery and who stitched the altar cloths of the future church in the palace, and a third who nursed a humble Carmelite and personally emptied the sick nun's chamber pots, without lessening her viceregal dignity. These women not only explain the importance of faith as a central feature in the constitution of New Spain but they also describe themselves as the transmitters of that faith, thus implying a way of life that embeds values in familial and institutional life (schools, convents, communities for lay sisters). They mention bishops, chaplains, missionaries, and confessors, and their relationship with them as directors of their spiritual lives, in this way revealing the profound influence of the Church on the social life of New Spain.

Yet these women writers have shown us all this without producing treatises on sociology, economics, or education, or analyzing political and religious situations. They did it by sharing their experiences with us, in other words, by telling us how they behaved in a given culture, civilization, and social environment at a particular time in history. In their accounts, material values (in other words, those which constitute civilization) emerge as the background to culture, although both are obviously linked in an inseparable bond, and spiritual values are so prominent that they become the very air that the societies to which they belong breathe. We sometimes find their language difficult to understand, so that even when they speak to us of freedom, justice, equality, truth, love, the meaning of life, and "the world" with all its material values (wealth and all the privilege linked to this), we are forced to analyze carefully the meaning of their words. In order to understand the specific meanings they have given these and other concepts, we have to go back to their times and view them within the context of Western Christian culture.

By way of example, when they talk of charity, they do not mean altruism but a rational act of solidarity. When they speak of freedom, they are not referring to political situations but to that which is inherent in the soul. We have to view them within this theological framework in order to realize that, when they speak of knowledge, understanding, counsel, scholarship, strength, piety, and fear of God, they are referring to the gifts of the Holy Spirit. When they write about virtues, they are not referring exclusively to human virtues, but rather to the supernatural gifts that are the fruit of these gifts, such as peace, patience, and charity. In short, we must realize that biographers, chroniclers, and mystics are engaged in a continuous relationship with what transcends this life. For this reason, the act of renouncing temporal matters has both meaning and value. Yet above all, one has to consider the place that each thing occupies within their lives, in other words, how they live and how they rate them themselves. Thus, through them we understand how these values constituted a way of life, that of New Spain.

There are, however, moments in their lives that focus so intensely on human values that they seem to transcend a specific time and place and acquire a universal validity, the same today as it was five hundred or two thousand years ago. Women's writing has shown what life guided by these values was capable of producing for New Spain. Thus, one can say that, according to the information yielded by the historical works of these women, much of the richness of architecture, painting, sculpture, and crafts, which today form part of the history of art, was due to women's intervention in various forms. Their accounts show the place women held in society as wives, mothers, heads of entailed estates, or title-holders as abbesses, founders, teachers, musicians, slaves, or servants, in other words, what society required from each of them according to their different functions. Women's literature in New Spain held the ideal woman to be one who was able to occupy the place that corresponded to her role with the greatest virtue (meaning Christian virtue). This position was never held by prostitutes or by the most attractive, beautiful, rich, or preeminent or by the finest poet or musician but by the woman with the greatest goodness. There was no point in being wise unless one was also good. This explains Sor Juana's wish to link knowledge and holiness as she wrote in her carols and Bishop Fernández de Santa Cruz's praising of her exemplary nun's life before he praises her intelligence and urges her to achieve greater perfection. It also explains the publication of the works of María Anna Águeda and the existence of a predominantly religious women's literature that reflected Spanish humanism and its renaissance.

Translation by Suzanne D. Stephens

Works Cited

Arte de Cocina. Escrito por Superior Mandato. 1786. Manuscript. Puebla: Virginia Armella de Aspe Collection.

Arte Nuevo de Cocina y Reposteria. Acomodado al uso mexicano. 1828. New York: En Casa de Lanza y Mendea and C. Impresores Libreros.

Bell, Aubrey F.G. 1944. *El renacimiento en España.* Trans. Eduardo Julia Martínez. Zaragoza: Editorial Ebro.

Blanquel, Simón. 1853. *Novísimo Arte de Cocina lo publica Simón Blanquel.* Mexico City: Imprenta de Tomás S. Guardia. Dolores Correa de García Granados Collection.

La cocinera de todo el mundo. 1843. Puebla: Imp. Juan Nepomuceno del Valle.

El cocinero mexicano. 1831–1834. 3 vols. Mexico City: Imprenta de Galván a cargo de Mariano Arévalo.

Diccionario de Cocina. N.d. Manuscript. Puebla: Virginia Armella de Aspe Collection.

Franco, Alonso, O.P. 1900. *Segunda parte de la historia de la provincia de Santiago de México. Orden de Predicadores en la Nueva España 1645.* Mexico City: Imprenta del Museo Nacional.

Garnica, Clara. 1852. *Libro de Cocina para el uso de la Señora Doña Clara Garnica.* N.p.: Carmen Pérez Salazar de Ovando Collection.

Juana Inés de la Cruz. 1979. *Libro de Cocina del Convento de San Jerónimo.* Selection and copy by Sor Juana Inés de la Cruz. Mexico City: Imprenta de la Enciclopedia Mexicana.

León de Gómez, Rosa María. N.d. *Cuadernos de Guisados.* Manuscript. N.p.: Virginia Armella de Aspe Collection.

María de Jesús de Agreda. 1709. *Mystica ciudad de Dios.* Antwerp: Henrico and Cornelio Verduggen.

Méndez, Juan Bautista. N.d. *Historia de la fundación del Convento de San José de Carmelitas.* Manuscript. N.p.: Archivo del Convento de San José, Private Collection.

Nuevo y sencillo arte de cocina. 1836. 2 vols. Mexico City: Imprenta de Santiago Pérez.

Nuevo y sencillo arte de cocina, repostería y refrescos dispuestos por una mexicana y experimentado por personas inteligentes antes de darse a la prensa. 1865. 3d ed. Mexico City: Imprenta de Luis Inclán.

Ovando, Guadalupe. 1857. *Libro de Cocina del uso de la Srita. Guadalupe Ovando.* N.p.: Carmen Pérez Salazar de Ovando Collection.

Peña, Ignacio de la, O.F.M. 1728. *El trono mexicano.* Madrid: Imprenta Francisco del Hierro.

Priani, Emilia. 1864. *Recopilación de recetas y guisados de Emilia Priani.* N.p.: Virginia Armella de Aspe Collection.

Recetas de mi Lolita Chula. N.d. N.p.: Carmen Pérez Salazar de Ovando Collection.

Rosa y Figueroa, Antonio de la. N.d. *Crónica sucinta del convento de Santa Clara de México.* Unedited manuscript which forms part of the Gómez de Orozco Collection. Mexico City: Biblioteca del Museo Nacional de Antropología de la Ciudad de México.

Sigüenza y Góngora, Carlos de. 1684. *Parayso occidental.* Mexico City: Imprenta Juan de Rivera.

El tesoro de la cocina. Diccionario de las familias. La cocina puesta al alcance de todas las inteligencias y fortunas. 1866. Mexico City: Imprenta Juan Nepomuceno del Valle.

Vetancourt, Agustín de, O.F.M. 1870. *Teatro mexicano.* Mexico City: Imprenta de Ignacio Escalante.

CHAPTER 32

SAINTS OR SINNERS?
LIFE WRITINGS AND COLONIAL
LATIN AMERICAN WOMEN

Kathleen Ann Myers

From its inception, the study of Colonial Latin American literature has been fraught with attempts to define and characterize the vast array of texts written during more than three hundred years of production. As a result of a boom in colonial studies that began around 1980, terms such as *colonial discourse* have frequently replaced *literature* in order to indicate the often nonliterary origins of the majority of texts we study: Historiographic, religious, and legal conventions–marked by ideologies and cultural contexts–informed textual production. As the idea of a purely literary canon has been revised, the field has changed dramatically. No longer limited primarily to the stories written by Spanish and *criollo* men, colonial discourse now includes many voices of women and nonwhite colonial subjects. Thanks in part to the new critical tools developed by feminist, subaltern, and cultural studies, we have begun to recognize the key role played by gender and caste in the establishment and evolution of Colonial Latin American society and culture.

In fact, a wealth of material by and about colonial women has been uncovered in the last two decades, drastically altering our view of Mexico's star poet Sor Juana Inés de la Cruz as writing alone in a wilderness of male clergy. With a few notable exceptions (such as Isabel de Guevara y Amarillis, as Josefina Muriel notes), women wrote primarily from the point of view of a religious woman. Exalted by society as *misioneras encerradas* ("cloistered missionaries"), these *beatas* ("devout women") and brides of Christ provided the viceregal capitals and urban areas, in particular, with a sense of identity within the universal Catholic Church. They were living examples of heroic virtue and helped to establish a Christian history on a continent where none had existed. In the process of founding convents and writing about their spiritual lives, women often dealt with some of the highest ranking men of church and state.

The seventeenth century was a particularly fertile time for the lives and stories of such memorable women as America's first saint, Rosa de Lima (1582–1617); America's most notorious transvestite, the "Lieutenant Nun" Catalina de Erauso (1582?–1650); Colonial Spanish America's most widely published poet, Sor Juana Inés de la Cruz (1648–1695); and one of New Spain's most popular *beatas,* the Asian Indian princess-slave Catarina de San Juan (1608?–1688). Diverse as their stories may be, however, each of these women, and others who will be discussed below, had to confront the basic Counter-Reformation life model for women: that of the virginal holy woman, the *perfecta religiosa.* All creatively engaged at some point with this script–though with vastly different outcomes– and all participated in the process of turning this lived experience into a textual life-writing tradition, the confessional, hagiographic life story. While some women wrote their own life stories or drew on the form to create a hybrid self-narrative, others were the subjects of formal biographical life stories written by male clergy. Thus we are dealing with a spiritual, didactic model of prescriptive behavior for women that had a dual textual result, the autobiography and biography life story. To understand this textual life model is to understand, perhaps, the richest, most prolific source, aside from legal records, for recovering the cultural constructs that informed women's self-conception and their key roles in helping to build Colonial society. To recognize the intricacies of this discourse–seeing it as a textual family, but not a monolithic discourse–we must factor in the role of chronology, geography, and relationships between men and women, between individuals and the institutions they represented.

Life Writings

Historians and literary scholars of the early modern period have frequently pointed to the emergence of a new phenomenon called, by some, an incipient autobiographical impulse and, by others, a new consciousness of a person's subjectivity (both in the sense of being an agent and as being an individual subjected to another's will or mandates). Its origins are traced to a spiritual model, dating as far back as Augustine's *Confessions* and the need to examine one's life and intentions before a God who judges them; to a feudal-based legal form (*relación*) that was available to anyone to justify his or her position and petition for justice; to a poetic sense of the self and subjective experience in the love poetry of Petrarch; and to a historiographical model derived from the clash between the personal experience of explorers during periods of European expansion and authoritative canonical texts about the world. Whether spiritual, bureaucratic, poetic, or historiographic in its origins, at the core of these life writings lies an increased sense of the value and authority of individual experience as it negotiated its own place within lived situations–such as confession, love, and conquest–that had been culturally codified.

This testimonial, experiential aspect of writing, in fact, characterizes the majority of colonial prose. On-site sixteenth-century historians of a New World posited their experience as authoritative in *relaciones* and histories, while indigenous Americans and *mestizos* responded to these foundational texts by creating an alternative viewpoint and discursive tradition. Seventeenth-century chroniclers reinterpreted the narratives of conquest to include an active role for themselves in colonizing America. Women joined the ranks to discuss their personal experiences as mystics and convent founders who worked hand-in-hand–though not always smoothly–with male confessors, chaplains, and bishops to found a New World paradise for Christianity.

The autobiographical, subjective impulse was given further impetus by developments within the embattled Catholic Church. It is well known that the Counter-Reformation established a series of religious and aesthetic guidelines that attempted to control anything that might further fracture Catholicism–in particular, any movement that might undermine the heavily

hierarchal Church and its central theological role as mediator between God and humankind. What may be less obvious, however, is that the Counter-Reformation's very
insistence on regulating individuals' lives and redefining
orthodoxy resulted in a proliferation of what we would call
today "life writings," a potpourri of short confessional *relaciones,* testimonial mystic accounts of prayer and ecstasy, and
the autobiographical and biographical life stories previously
mentioned.

These various subgenres were shaped by the formal, inves-
tigative processes initiated by the Church through the Holy
Office of the Inquisition and the Sacred Congregation of Holy
Rites, which conferred the status of official sanctity. Both
offices had been changed and formalized by a series of
reforms after the Council of Trent, and again under the
papacy of Urban VIII. And both offices—whether at the level
of the universal Catholic Church in Rome or at the local level
of Inquisitorial proceedings—sought through the direct testimony of hundreds of people to ferret out examples of the
New World's contribution to the Church (by heroic virtue) or
threats to it (by fakeries and heterodoxy). Much as the popular legal and quasi-legal form of the *relación* had given voice to
a wide range of lettered and relatively unlettered chroniclers
in the early years of the Conquest (for example, the writings
of Hernán Cortés and Bernal Díaz del Castillo), the ideology
and practices of canonization and inquisitorial proceedings
permeate period religious, spiritual discourse. Imitating sanctioned life and textual models became essential to one's spiritual practice and self-representation. And yet, as we will see,
the lines often blurred as models and antimodels swapped
places.

The role of official Church judges and mediators further
complicated a person's engagement with the Church's scripts
for good behavior. A defining element of early modern life
writings is the intrinsic petitions and apologies to superiors
they contain. An author wrote to justify the nature of his or
her individual experience to a privileged reader, who represented a political or religious institution that could judge the
writer according to ideal norms for his or her class, race, and
gender. The petition, therefore, nearly always had a concrete
demand (monetary reward, restoration of honor, or absolu-
tion of sins) as well as a more subtle plea—a sort of apology—in
which the individual asked to be taken back into the ideal community and seen as a model of heroic behavior, in spite of the
outward appearance of failings. Persuasion is the central rhetorical construct as the writer acknowledges the reader's power to
grant or deny the petition, or to condone or condemn the behavior. Although primarily a personal account, these documents
also had a potentially high public audience, if the addressee
decided to draw in other judges or to publish the account.
Spiritual accounts of personal experience further complicated
this dialogic, shifting engagement between subject-writer and
superior-reader by invoking God as the divine author and
ultimate judge.

One of the central changes initiated by the Council of
Trent was a renewed vigor in requiring frequent confession,
and its extension: written records of spiritual experience for
closer examination. The literary result of this encouragement
of self-examination and representation in the name of behavioral control depended in large measure on a person's class
and gender. Although there are several significant exceptions,
criollos dominated the religious-spiritual literary scene in
Spanish America, but peoples of other castes could provide

oral testimony in cases that examined possible sanctity or heresy. In general, women were officially restricted to writing
devotional texts—such as novenas and Stations of the Cross
that gave new living examples of already established practices—or confessional accounts, all based on their own experience of the spiritual path. Barred in theory from learned
theological discourse, women followed in the footsteps of the
Counter-Reformation saint par excellence, Teresa de Ávila
(1515–1582), with intertextual citings of previous religious
texts, introducing a discourse authorized by direct experience
of divine knowledge and will. Dialogical, heterogenous texts
emerged as women shuttled between imitations of authorized
Church texts and accounts of their own experience, between
the demands of the reader-confessor and their own consciences as they listened to God's voice within them.

Indeed, most of the accounts written by women were initiated by a cleric's request (nuns were considered *escritoras por
obediencia*—writers in obedience) and mediated after being
written, in order to be turned into official Church texts such
as hagiographic life stories and prayerbooks. The spiritual
pragmatics of this situation created a doubling of interlocutors, authors, and narrative ends. Although generally written
for confessional purposes—in order to find one's place before
God—the life story also invoked God as the ultimate addressee
and author. The act of reviewing and recording one's life
inspired the sinner to express not just remorse but the grati-
tude of one who could see God's merciful gifts manifested in
her life. As a result, God is directly or indirectly invoked as
the real Author of the life story as lived and recorded. Thus,
while initially confessional in purpose, the life story ultimately
could serve a didactic purpose: to persuade the reader(s) of
the ultimate goodness of the writer's life, shaped by the grace
of God. Both cleric and God are addressees, both nun and
God are authors, and the account itself served both confessional and didactic ends. The rhetorical matrix (structuring) of
the life story reflects these complex and at times competing
elements. The formal aspects of the life story as a genre
include (1) the rhetorical posture—which also reflected
Church precepts regarding religious women—of the *escritora
por obediencia,* and its accompanying rhetoric of silence,
humility, and holy ignorance; (2) the narrative structure of a
divine call to serve God (*vos me cogesteis*) and the purifying suffering (*imitatio Christi*) required to follow the path; and (3) the
characteristic shifts between confessing a life and defending it,
manipulating the narrative for persuasive and didactic ends.
All these elements are present—and stunningly effective—in
the foundational and most popular model for the feminine life
story, Teresa de Ávila's *Libro de la vida* (1588).

In chronological terms, we are dealing with the mid-Colonial
period, a period that reaches back to the late sixteenth-century building of the first convents, *beaterios,* and *recogimientos*
for women (see J. Muriel). This institutionalization of the
feminine religious colonization project flourished during the
seventeenth century but petered out by the mid-eighteenth
century as Bourbon reforms, the secularization of many
aspects of society, and, perhaps, the new trend toward professional writers emerged. In geographical terms, we are
dealing with a single empire and yet an enormous expanse
of territory that embraced often-distinct local customs and
historical circumstances. Although the authors of life writings (at least those that we have been able to recover to date)
are generally from urban centers and Spanish-based cultural
traditions (*criollo*), there are significant differences among

them, depending on the proximity to or distance from the metropolis and viceregal centers. In religious terms, it is important to note the often widely different ideological programs and concerns of orders and differences between cloistered nuns and lay *beatas*. The secular and regular clergy, for example, did not always see eye-to-eye, and the Jesuits were renowned for being demanding spiritual directors–promoting spiritual exercises that revolved around self-revelation. Here a woman's religious affiliation could strongly mark her self-representation and her biographer's representation of her.

Lay *Beatas*: Rules for Sanctity and Hagiography

Patron Saint of America, Rosa de Lima (1582–1617)

Interestingly, our first case frequently contradicts the very points the Counter-Reformation teachings most emphasized for the *perfecta religiosa*, and yet the lay holy woman, Rosa de Lima, is one of only two American women who reached the high altars of the Catholic Church during the Colonial period (see **Figure 1**). (The other was the seventeenth-century lay *beata* Mariana Jesús de Paredes.) Rosa was born Isabel Flores de Oliva to a *criollo* couple of modest means living in Lima only a few score years after its conquest by Pizarro. The story of America's first saint is one about the inconsistencies that prevailed throughout the Counter-Reformation period as Rome, Madrid, and colonial urban centers bickered about the role of popular piety and the new rules for sainthood, and the need to both create and control a fervent Catholicism in newly colonized lands. Rosa's life, as seen through canonization process documents (*procesos*) and hagiographic production, was one that both reinforced the codes for model religious behavior and opened a means for refashioning it in order to accommodate more individual life paths. It provides a backdrop against which to understand the varying interpretations, politics, and representations of holiness for Rosa's heirs.

According to hagiographic legend, Rosa's religious calling began at a young age and continued until her early death. As a five-year-old, the girl heard the life story of the popular medieval Italian mystic and third-order Dominican, Catherine of Siena (1347–1380), and soon began to imitate Catherine's Christocentric, ascetic, mystic life. Rosa built a hut in her backyard to lead a life as a semi-hermit and began practicing extreme self-mortification–something that would become one of the hallmarks of her sanctity. At age twelve, after a vision of Christ, Rosa gave herself in mystic marriage to him. Rosa associated first with the Franciscan order (circa 1603–1607) and then, more importantly, with the Dominican order (1607–1617), wearing its habit and following a typically Dominican schedule of prayer, readings, Mass, penances, and consultations with confessors. Besides modeling her life on that of Catherine of Siena, Rosa also was inspired by another hagiographical account, that of the recently beatified New Spanish lay hermit, Gregorio López (1542–1596). In addition, she studied doctrinal works by the Counter-Reformation author par excellence, Fray Luis de Granada (1504–1588), and consulted with Juan del Castillo, the first American author to publish commentaries on Teresa de Ávila's mystical texts. At one point in 1614, Rosa was examined informally by some clergy associated with the Inquisition, but all seemed to have concluded that Rosa was following an orthodox path.

Yet Rosa's life story flies in the face of the Counter-Reformation emphasis on strict obedience to Church superiors and on the enclosure in convents of religious women.

Figure 1.

(Courtesy of John P. Robarts Research Library, University of Toronto)

Rosa never entered the cloister–by some accounts repeatedly refusing to do so. She preferred her lay status, a status that allowed her relative freedom as she held religious gatherings in her home and had followers that she directed along the spiritual path. Rosa became a public figure, even in her semi-seclusion, as she was entrusted with interceding on behalf of the people of Lima as they fought off plague and infidels (such as the Dutch siege of the port in 1615). By Rosa's death at the age of thirty-one, she had become a key symbol for the city and for the Dominican order in particular. Throngs of people descended on the church that displayed her body, and officials immediately began collecting testimony for initiating canonization proceedings.

As scribes took down testimony from all sectors of society, especially by Dominicans, Rosa's group of male and female followers continued their spiritual work. Within several years, however, the steps toward canonization and the work of her followers were suspended as the Peruvian Inquisition examined Rosa's group for evidence of the heterodox practice of mysticism, or *alumbradismo* (a sect that claimed an individual could directly access the divine without the intercession of a priest). Inquisition authorities confiscated Rosa's writings and personal effects, including, by some accounts, a now-lost spiritual autobiography and poems. At the same time that this stumbling block was thrown in the road to Rosa's canonization at local levels, her case made the transatlantic crossing to the governing body for the Spanish colonies, the Council of the Indies in Seville. Now representatives of factions within the Dominican order, Lima clergy, the Spanish Crown, and the Vatican all vied to have their say. After several false starts and dramatic halts–the most significant being Rome's decision to initiate another round of testimony in the 1630s and the implementation and later waiving of Urban VIII's rule that a candidate for sainthood had to be dead for fifty years before he or she could be considered–Rosa's cause shot through the final hoops to sainthood. She was beatified in 1668, declared the Patron of America and the Philippines in 1670, and canonized in 1671.

Unlike Teresa de Ávila and other nuns we will study, Rosa left no autobiographical writings per se and very few works that are definitely from her hand. Recorded in the *procesos* and by early biographers, some religious poetry, songs, and prayers have been attributed to Rosa. The prayers revolve around the theme of God's magnificence and Rosa's love for God (for example, *Ejercicio Angélico* [Angelical Exercise]), and the songs involve word plays about her name; Rosa sang them as she spent hours playing the guitar in her room. Along with several formulaic letters, only two unusual collages, depicting the path to divine love, survive in her own hand. There are period references to a good deal more written material–notebooks that explain the collages, an autobiographical confessional account, and a collection of religious poetry–but none of this work seems to be extant. In fact, like many materials dealing with feminine religious experience, Rosa's emblematic collages were only rediscovered in the twentieth century, when the Dominican friar Luis Getino began looking through papers dealing with Rosa de Lima in the convent dedicated to her in Lima. Scholars speculate that other works may remain there, having perhaps been returned after either being confiscated by the Inquisition (1620s), sent to Rome for the canonization process (1630s), or hidden by the Dominicans themselves during a rift within the order (1620s).

While the prayers and songs attributed to Rosa in the *procesos* are often rather simple and echo period conventions, the collages testify to Rosa's creative imagining of the complex mystic process, later described in words by many other Spanish American nuns. *Las Mercedes* [The Mercies] or *Heridas del Alma* [Wounds of the Soul] consists of three hearts that are placed in a column to represent graphically the stages along the road to mystic union with God, and *La Escala Mística* is conceptualized as a fifteen-stage stairway of the mystic process. Both images are striking for their use of the Renaissance emblem tradition, primitive artistic quality, and intriguing use of iconography to describe the human experience of moving toward divine love. Moreover, they have been executed with originality and a good degree of understanding of mystic theology. Nonetheless, Rosa echoes the rhetoric of humility and ignorance, insisting that her mystic knowledge comes from direct experience of the divine, rather than book learning; she is quoted as stating: "confieso con toda verdad en presencia de Dios que todas las mercedes que he escrito así en los cuadernos como esculpindas y retratadas en estos dos papeles ni las he visto ni leído en libro alguno, solo í obradas en esta pecadora de la poderosa mano del Señor en cuyo libro leo que es Sabiduría Eterna" (Mujica Pinilla, 97) ("I confess in truth and in the presence of God that all that I have written in notebooks or on sculpted pieces and reported on in these papers is the work of this sinner and has not been copied from any book I read, guided as I was by the poweful hand of God in whose book I have read eternal wisdom").

The scarcity of writing by Rosa makes it impossible to know much about her own self-conception beyond this mystic love for God. Traditionally, hagiography has taken over the representation of Rosa and influenced how women would imitate her in future generations. The key biography to canonize Rosa in the sense of both a life and textual model was written as part of the canonization cause and was published in 1664 by one of the Dominican order's authors, Leonhard Hansen, *Vita mirabilis, mors pretiosa venerabilis Sororis Rosa de S. Maria limensis.* Soon translated into Spanish and found in nearly every Spanish American convent library in the seventeenth century, Hansen's *Life* of Rosa reconfigures first-hand canonization testimony (he himself never knew Rosa) according to the new demands for sanctity instituted in the first half of the century. He carefully notes his use of the new style, emphasizing historical method and avoiding the proclamation of miracles (this was now to be determined solely by Rome). Hansen's representation of Rosa, like that of Teresa de Ávila at the beginning of the century, significantly reconfigured Rosa's story and created an, at times, impossible model for women to follow. Her extreme mortification was exalted but officially discouraged. And even though Rosa was able to lead a life of heroic virtue in the world, lay status was officially frowned upon.

Rosa's extraordinary popularity throughout Spanish America reflects a double-focused movement: a certain competition with the Old World and a gelling of *criollo* identity from within, especially in the viceroyalties of Peru and New Spain (Mexico). She was not only the "fénix criolla" ("*criolla* phoenix") for Lima; Rosa was embraced by New Spaniards as well. The cult of the Virgin of Guadalupe was still in its infancy and Rosa was rapidly taken in as one of New Spain's own. When the New Spanish Dominican author, Sebastián de Santander y Torres, for example, gave the opening sermon for a new convent, he evoked Rosa as a model of both the heroism and dangers of a religious woman living outside the cloister, but he also pointed to her broader symbolic role as "nuestra criolla" ("our *criollo* woman"), triumphant against idolatrous practice. Another Dominican chronicler, Juan Meléndez, captures this common sentiment and representation of Rosa in his own hagiography of her, calling her the "redentor" ("redeemer") of the New World.

La China Poblana, Catarina de San Juan (1608?–1688)

Whereas Rosa de Lima inspired the largest number of works written about an individual living in America, another popular symbol of piety and local identity inspired the single most voluminous work to be published in Spanish America, in the heart of Puebla de los Angeles, the city that produced the largest number of hagiographic biographies (by this term we mean biographies of noncanonized people written in hagiographic style). Like Rosa de Lima, Catarina de San Juan was a lay *beata* who had been actively engaged with many of the highest ranking New Spanish church officials as well as having been a popular, if reclusive, figure among local citizens. In the year or so after her death, hundreds of people visited the chapel where the Asian-born holy woman had spent years of her life and lit candles to venerate her image. At the same time, an usually large number of New Spanish church officials were signing licenses to approve the first hagiographic biography of Catarina—eventually a triple-volume history written by the Jesuit Alonso Ramos, *Prodigios de la Omnipotencia y milagros de la Gracia en la vida de la venerable sierva de Dios Catharina de S. Joan* [1689, 1690, 1692; Marvels of the All Powerful and Miracles of the Divine Grace in the Life of the Venerable Servant of God, Catherine of St. John]. Among the clerics were Antonio Núñez de Miranda, who was the Inquisition's *calificador* (official) and the renowned Jesuit confessor of Sor Juana Inés de la Cruz, and Bishop Manuel Fernández de Santa Cruz, the famous addressee of Sor Juana's *Respuesta* [Answer].

In a turnaround from Rosa's time, the writing and publishing of a hagiographic life story had generally become the first step in launching a candidate into the rosters of official sainthood. Catarina de San Juan's cause, however, never made it beyond the life story to the stage of taking testimony. In fact, the biography apparently became the catalyst for debate about sanctity and blasphemy; the participants were local New Spanish inquisitors, Spanish inquisitors, Jesuits, and the devoted populace. Within three years of her death, the Inquisition of New Spain had prohibited the display of her portrait. By 1692, the Spanish Inquisition had banned the first volume of Ramos's work on the grounds that it was blasphemous; in a stunningly slow response, the Holy Office of New Spain followed suit four years later, demanding that all three volumes of Ramos's work be confiscated and ordering the altar dedicated to Catarina be boarded up. Yet, in these same years, the slim *Compendio de la vida y virtudes de la venerable Catarina de San Juan* 1692 [Compendium of the Life and Virtues of the Venerable Catherine of St. John] by the cleric José Castillo de Graxeda was allowed to circulate in New Spain. This transatlantic cross fire tells much about America's fight for officially sanctioned local religious figures and the difficulty of promoting local candidates.

By both biographers' accounts, Catarina de San Juan was just the sort of exotic figure to capture popular imagination in baroque Mexico. Born into a noble Asian family but kidnapped by Portuguese pirates at age ten, Catarina was sold in 1617 to a childless couple from Puebla who adopted her as a child-servant. Upon their deaths a decade later, she became a housekeeper for a priest, who married her to one of his Chinese slaves; she managed to preserve her virginity in spite of her husband's wishes. By the 1640s both husband and master had died, and Catarina was at last free to devote her life to Christ as a lay holy woman. She took no formal religious vows but lived a life of seclusion, prayer, and penance in a small room that a wealthy neighbor had given her across from her favorite church, run by the Jesuits. Taken under the wing of Jesuit confessors, Catarina lived the last four decades of her life following the contemplative life of a visionary, making prophecies about important political and ecclesiastic figures and occurrences in the Spanish empire. Upon her death in 1688, commoners and high-ranking officials alike declared that the octagenarian recluse had died in the odor of sanctity, a heavenly aroma bestowed upon God's chosen at their death.

Because of her illiteracy in Spanish, Catarina had never written about her spiritual experiences, but her Jesuit confessor Alonso Ramos recorded his vision of her life story, presented in an affective, florid style. The *Prodigios de la Omnipotencia y milagros de la Gracia en la vida de la venerable sierva de Dios Catharina de S. Joan* privileges Ramos's position as confessor and tells, as the title indicates, of abundant signs of divine favor. Although this relationship between spiritual daughter (subject) and confessor (author) was not unusual, Ramos carries it to an extreme, reconstructing Catarina's life story as an extravagant series of supernatural adventures filled with exotic, often erotic, elements.

Ultimately, Ramos's text appealed to the baroque literary taste for exotic manifestations of paradoxical phenomena–a slave of noble birth, a dark-skinned bride of Christ, a poor woman telling the king his future, and a virgin sleeping untouched by her lustful husband–but the author paid little heed to the Church's post-Tridentine conventions for hagiography. Besides tightening the definition of heresy, the Council of Trent had also stiffened the requirements for canonization following the rigors espoused by humanist historians, which, among other things, prescribed reliable witnesses and a stylistic decorum befitting historical truth. First, Ramos employs a dubious historical method, frequently ignoring Rome's rules about framing accounts with eyewitness testimony or corroboration. Second, Ramos's narrative of these visions allot extremely wide-ranging and prolific supernatural powers to a socially marginal woman.

The author of the second biography on Catarina de San Juan, Castillo de Graxeda, uses the same point of departure as Ramos: God authorizes his role as biographer via a vision that Catarina reported to Graxeda as her confessor. Although Castillo de Graxeda never reveals any knowledge of the 1692 Spanish edict that prohibited Ramos's first volume, the metadiscourse he employs about his narrative method points precisely to the problems Ramos's text encountered. From the outset Castillo de Graxeda signals that he takes very seriously his duty to keep to the verifiable facts, or the appearance of them. Rather than promoting the life story as *prodigioso* (marvelous) and full of miracles, as Ramos had, Castillo de Graxeda humbly calls his work a *compendio* (compendium). Castillo de Graxeda avoids describing revelations that might seem "indecent" or "dangerous," and he methodically demonstrates that he has not fallen prey to "vain credulousness"– all part of the Inquisition's charges against Ramos's book. Moreover, he creates a testimonial voice for Catarina by "transcribing" confessional conversations as he remembers them, and he even adds a verisimilar element by echoing her pidgin Spanish: "En verdad ángel mío, que vuesastedes dicen el verdad, y así echen ruego a Dios no me perda" ("In truth, angel of mine, you speak the truth, pray to God that I may be saved"). While both biographies draw on highly charged, exotic material to strike awe in readers and act as springboards for preaching, Castillo de Graxeda saved his text from the hands of the Inquisition, adhering closely to the new rules established for sainthood in the seventeenth century.

Yet Catarina de San Juan's life story was still a far cry from that of the typical Counter-Reformation saint. As Peter Burke notes, saints canonized between 1588 and 1767 generally were well-born offspring of white upper-class parents living in powerful countries (Italy and Spain dominate) and professed in important religious orders (primarily the Franciscans, Dominicans, and Jesuits). Most were founders of religious orders or missionaries, while a significant number of others were pastors or mystics, or were devoted to charitable works. The centralization and control of sanctity demanded that candidates conform to Rome's definition of holiness as judged by its examiners, which discouraged individualization and local cults. No doubt, the banning of her portrait, and, three years later, the closing of the popular oratory dedicated to her came from an attempt to discourage the popular cult that was forming around Catarina de San Juan.

Not a simple case of how one life or book was deemed heterodox, the story of the representation of Catarina de San Juan's life showcases the issues involved in studying colonial

Mexico, the Church, women, and religious discourse. Her case demonstrates how the lives of holy women helped define society of New Spain and therefore became targets of control by the Church hierarchy. The historical facts about and the writings by religious women themselves often faded away as official discourse took over to paint an ideal portrait, if hotly contested, one that might serve the ends of the institutional Church. Catarina, as a person, gets lost in the shuffle of Church politics and didactic ends. As was partially the case with Rosa de Lima, the true face and voice of an Asian woman who ended her final days surrounded by revering townspeople and clergy is impossible to recover; the facts are eclipsed first by a confessor's account that dramatized and eroticized Catarina's life story, and then by a second biographer who, by closely following the rules, turns her story into a generic paradigm of female sanctity. This almost legendary quality of Catarina's life was carried into nineteenth-century Puebla, when she became a symbol of local identity and renamed "La China Poblana" ("the Chinese woman living in Puebla").

The Enclosure of Religious Women and the Many Life Stories of Christ's Brides

As noted earlier, the perceived dangers of having mystic women and *beatas* "in the world," coupled with the fervent religious climate following in the wake of peninsular monastic reforms and the apogee of Spanish mysticism, led to a century or more in which large amounts of funds and public energy were devoted to founding convents. A byproduct was the flowering of convent writing in urban Spanish America (see Lavrin 1986, 1993 and Chapter 31 of this volume). Some were large, unreformed convents of relaxed or regular rule that housed hundreds of nuns, each typically having her own multi-room cell complete with a servant or slave. Others, adhering to Teresian Carmelite reforms, reinforced the vow of poverty by drastically reducing the number of nuns and servants living in a community and limiting living quarters to a small individual cell. In either type of convent, the rule required full-fledged nuns of the highest rank (black-veiled nuns, also known as nuns of *coro y canto* [choir and song]) to follow an often-strict schedule of daily prayer, labor, and spiritual examination. They spent hours in community prayer saying the Divine Office and could spend hours dedicated to their assigned *oficio* (duty) within the convent structure (for example, as novice director, nurse, accountant, wardrobe-keeper, or secretary) and to their individual spiritual growth. This last area, as can be imagined, provided the fertile terrain in which nuns might develop elaborate meditational and penitential practices, interior dialogues with supernatural beings, and self-revelatory points to be covered in mandatory weekly confession with their assigned male spiritual directors. It was during this spiritual process and contemplative time–and nearly always with a significant role played by the nun's spiritual director (to whom she had professed a vow of obedience)–that religious women wrote about their lives vis-à-vis their own understanding and interiorization of the model of the *perfecta religiosa*. The handful of women we examine subsequently are all nuns who held high administrative positions within this urban Spanish American convent system, spanning the viceroyalties of New Spain and Peru and the Reino de Nueva Granada.

Mystic Conqueror, Madre María de San José, Juana Palacios Berruecos (1656–1719)

The same New Spanish author who both exalted Rosa de Lima's heroic virtue and warned of the perils involved in imitating her wrote a hagiographic biography of the two-time convent founder and mystic writer, María de San José (see **Figure 2**). In his *Vida* (1723), Sebastián Santander y Torres creates a highly baroque verbal portrait of María as the symbolic equivalent of her great-grandfather, who had helped with the conquest of Mexico. Having taken the mandatory vow of perpetual enclosure, María became a spiritual conquistador who wrote and prayed from within convent walls. Although most of María's more than 2,000 pages of writing for her confessors were never published, they provided the raw material for Santander y Torres's biography. Only since the rediscovery of the autograph manuscript in 1984 have we had the luxury of being able to read María's own words and compare them with the official texts of her life. Whereas Rosa's case illuminates the close relationship between canonization processes and the genre of hagiography in the Counter-Reformation, María de San José's demonstrates the inextricable link between hagiography and the genre of spiritual autobiographical writings in the period. Inspired by saints' stories, María earnestly sought to imitate the extreme penances and lay mystic path of Rosa de Lima, on the one hand, and the ideal nun and author Teresa de Ávila, on the other. María wrote copiously about that experience under

Figure 2.

(Courtesy of John P. Robarts Research Library, University of Toronto)

obedience to clergy, who then rescripted her life story for others to live by. Her persistent imitation of the life prescribed for the *perfecta religiosa* serves as a touchstone for understanding the possibilities and limits of this model for *criolla* women.

As Rosa's canonization process was being renewed in Lima and Rome in the mid-seventeenth century, María was living on a rural hacienda on the outskirts of an Indian town in New Spain and was leading the life of a lay *beata*, having taken the third-order Franciscan habit. Born Juana Palacios Berruecos to cash-poor, landowning *criollos*, María, like Rosa, had been called to the religious life in a vision during childhood, had immediately begun an extreme ascetic practice, and eventually shed her given name upon devoting her life to Christ. But unlike Rosa, who by some reports had fought to stay out of the convent, María sought the safety of perpetual enclosure. In fact, she struggled for more than two decades to achieve her wish in the face of family conflict and financial straits—straits that would be aggravated by paying the hefty dowry required for entrance into most convents. Whereas Rosa had died at age thirty-one, María finally rejoiced at becoming "dead to the world" when she entered the reformed Augustinian Recollect Convent of Santa Mónica in Puebla, Mexico at the same age (1687). After professing final vows, María de San José could no longer leave the walls of the convent or see family and friends without a chaperon present and an iron grate between them. Her whole life was to be devoted to prayer without worldly concerns. After several years of initial conflict with other nuns and self-doubt over her vocation, María was promoted to convent founder and novice director for the new Convent of Nuestra Señora de la Soledad in Oaxaca (1697). There she lived the remaining two decades of her life and wrote copiously, in spite of having never received a formal education, not even in the rudimentary *amiga* system. The majority of her more than twelve volumes recording her spiritual experiences were composed in Oaxaca. Her writings comprise nearly all the religious prose genres officially available to nuns: a formal, confessional life story; informal diary-like *cuentas de conciencia* (often in lieu of confession or detailing a specific vision or prophecy); a chronicle of the founding of Nuestra Señora de la Soledad; devotional Stations of the Cross; and short biographical life stories of the virtues of confessors and novices.

As Maria began to set her life story to paper—first initiated by an order from the famous addressee of Sor Juana's *Respuesta*, Bishop Fernández de Santa Cruz—she was very aware of the long, complex Church process of spiritual discernment. Her style—earthy, often colloquial and, at times, clearly untrained (for example, she makes grammatical errors)—might easily be misunderstood by present day readers as a spontaneous, unlettered outpouring. Yet this lack of formal training disguises an encoding of nearly every aspect of her recorded experience. At the heart of Maria's journals, and especially of those reflecting more formal genres, such as the life story and *estaciones*, lies a carefully constructed narrative embedded with passages that echo the rules and guidelines for orthodoxy and holiness.

Volume I, Maria's most formal confessional life story, provides the key for understanding this process. She opens the volume with an authorizing history of the high-ranking churchmen of New Spain who had ordered, read, and officially registered her writings during more than a decade (circa 1691–1705). She also weaves in passages from Teresa de Ávila's own autobiographical life story, Hansen's *Life* of Rosa

de Lima, and other church texts, using their canonized voices to voice her own experience. Madre María recalls an ascetic practice closely related to the medieval models established by Catherine of Siena and imitated by Rosa. Although never mentioning either of their names in her extensive writing, Maria de San José follows Rosa's biography, almost verbatim at times, in describing the details of her fasting, retirement to a garden hut for prayer and mortification, secret help from Native Americans in her penitential practices, and mystic marriage to Christ. Moreover, whereas both Rosa and Maria had taken the third-order Franciscan habit for their first religious affiliation, María silences this fact in the first two versions of her account of her secular life. It is not until an account written several years before her death that she finally reveals in writing that from age fifteen to thirty-one she had been a Franciscan lay holy woman—a fact completely absent in her biographer's account. Perhaps more telling than the list of influences on her life as a *beata* are the mentions of models' once she had taken the veil: The two bodies of writing that figure most prominently are the life story and devotional writings of the founder of Maria de San José's order, Mariana de San José, and those of St. Teresa de Ávila. Running a distant third are Maria de la Antigua's *Estaciones*. Not surprisingly, the models in the convent were all Spanish nuns and writers who had come to represent Counter-Reformation teachings about the enclosure of religious women and the careful ecclesiastic monitoring of writing about the spiritual life.

In a much more potentially powerful—and, therefore, dangerous—move than imitating canonized models, Madre María turns to the convention of Divine Authorship. God Himself authorizes Maria's path, telling her: "Tu camino es mui parecido al de Santa Teresa" ("Your path is quite similar to that of Saint Teresa") and "No escribas ni una tilde más ni menos, que todo es de Mí" ("Do not write one comma more or less, for everything comes from Me"). This invocation and transcription of God's speech reveals a deeper encoding and textual process in Maria de San José's works: the mystic triad, the dynamic relationship between God as Author, nun as mystic scribe, and confessor as official Church intermediary. Writing becomes a balancing act: a confession and *apologia pro vita sua* before the eyes of God and His intercessor, a vehicle for revealing God's handiwork and goodness, and an outlet for the creative construction of the self that weaves together the personal and the ideal.

In this system, Maria is a writer only by obedience—to either God or confessor. Depending on her own narrative needs, however, Maria and her Sisters at times negotiated their positions as scribes by intertwining and playing off the confessor's and God's mandates. In a case in which María deviates from the narrative of her own life story to talk of a vision, she explains that while she was giving her confession, a sudden vision of Christ entered her thoughts. This dynamic interplay frames nearly every account in Maria's journals. Her text reveals how the genre of spiritual autobiography for Counter-Reformation visionary women is modeled on a literary-religious theory of *imitatio* and characterized by a dynamic overriding triad that plays off authority, obedience, and spiritual experience. The result is frequently a highly encoded autobiographical text, filled with conventional metaphors, turns of phrases, and themes, that nonetheless reflects the individual's negotiation of the various demands of a confessional account that depended on the language of devotional literature for its expression.

The success of the life story was often seen only later, if it was used for didactic ends, upon the nun's death. The Church would mine her manuscripts for quotes and prayers to be published within officially sanctioned forms–both to promote a model of holiness and to decrease the chances of a popular cult forming. These tactics often enjoyed considerable success. Santander y Torres's hagiographic biography of María, for example, went into two editions, and the rescripted version of María's *Estaciones*, which recounted her visionary experience of the Virgin Mary teaching her to pray the Stations of the Cross, went into four editions during the eighteenth century. In addition, the Bishop of Oaxaca, Angel de Maldonado, wrote a Latin tract officially proposing to Rome the initiation of a *proceso* for María's beatification. These texts painted Maria as a paragon of the virtues of obedience and simplicity of heart that could lead to intimate knowledge of God. Her life and texts, according to one Church canon, reflected María's role as an Erudite Chronicler for God. Despite this success at the local level in New Spain, to date no record of her cause has been found in Madrid or Rome. Sanctity was generally limited to a select few from the Old World as Europe tried to keep America under its thumb (see Rubial Garcia 1999).

The Mystic of Tunja, Madre Castillo, Francisca Concepción del Castillo (1671–1742)

Another sincere, devoted imitator of Rosa who became an abbess, mystic, and author lived in Tunja in the Reinado de Nueva Granada (present-day Colombia). In many ways, Madre Castillo's story parallels that of María de San José, both in her perseverance in attaining her spiritual goals and in the situation of her writing and strategies. Born into an influential family, Francisca Concepción del Castillo imitated Rosa de Lima as a girl and, by early puberty, she entered the Convento Real de Santa Clara. There Madre Castillo, as she came to be known, became a key figure in that convent's history as she rose to positions of power as a director of novices and, later, as abbess. During this time she wrote extensively, authoring her own compositions under obedience to her confessors and copying works from favorite authors (such as Sor Juana Inés de la Cruz and San Juan de la Cruz). Madre Castillo wrote essentially three distinct works that we know of: her formal *Vida* (1817), two miscellanies of spiritual accounts, *Afectos* (1843), and *Cuaderno de Enciso* [1844, Notebook for Spiritual Instruction]. Significantly, Madre Castillo's writings were not published until more than fifty years after her death, and she was not promoted by the Church in a biographical hagiography, which, as we have seen, would have been common for the women deemed most holy in the period. In fact, Madre Castillo's life and works are at the margins of the geographical centers and chronological period in which religious life stories flourished.

In many regards, Madre Castillo followed the, by now, time-worn rhetorical strategies of religious women who wrote about their life experiences, employing deftly interwoven passages from Church texts and a shifting center of authority through the theological and rhetorical construction of the mystic triad. But the Colombian nun had a much higher level of education than her Mexican counterpart, María de San José, and, as a new and important study of Castillo convincingly argues, the nun used short spiritual descriptions of her personal mystical experiences as a springboard for sermonic spiritual instruction, particularly in the little-studied *Cuaderno*

de Enciso (see McKnight). Madre Castillo's prose moves from recording autobiographical spiritual experiences to interpreting Sacred Scripture. She uses a mixture of narrative discourses from Carmelite contemplative mysticism, meditative practices of Saint Ignatius of Loyola, and sermons. As she does so, the pedagogical voice of a teacher emerges from the affective prose of the mystic, thus conflating a genre generally prohibited for women writers with one that was encouraged within limits.

Although Madre Castillo actively participated in convent founding in newer urban areas of Spanish rule and followed many period conventions for the *perfecta religiosa*, her life and works did not have the same impact on colonial society as those of her seventeenth-century and early eighteenth-century counterparts. Half a century after her death, however, Madre Castillo's texts seem to have served as a bridge into the nineteenth-century nation-building efforts, much as Catarina de San Juan's life had in Puebla; the Colombian nun's works were first published during this time. Where once nuns had served as proof positive of colonial Spanish America's parity with Europe, they were now being transformed into the voices that would announce and symbolize a new identity for independent Latin American countries. This is a factor that helps explain perhaps why Madre Castillo was one of the few nun-writers anthologized by twentieth-century literary critics such as Anderson-Imbert.

La Décima Musa, Sor Juana Inés de la Cruz, Juana Inés de Asbaje y Ramírez (1648–1695)

Within years of Madre Castillo's taking of the veil in Tunja, a storm was brewing over a nun's literary production in the cultural center of Spanish America, Mexico City: a storm that would culminate with an innovative use of the life story. The most famous nun of the Colonial period, Sor Juana Inés de la Cruz had written profane and sacred poetry, drama, and prose for decades at the behest of Church leaders and viceregal couples. Composing anything from sharply biting lines about men's contradictory demands of women to sublime devotional dramatic pieces, for years after her entrance into the cloister in 1669 Sor Juana seemed to have escaped the limits imposed on religious women. By 1690, she had acquired an extensive library and her fame had spread with the publication of her poetry (*Inundación Castálida*, Madrid 1689). Sor Juana's artistic and intellectual life also extended to frequent *tertulias* (literary gatherings) that she held in the convent *locutorio* (locutory), often attended by Mexico City's leading figures–among them a professor of mathematics and science, Carlos de Sigüenza y Góngora; two sets of viceregal couples; and the Puebla bishop Manuel Fernández de Santa Cruz, the same cleric who had initiated María de San José's writing career and had promoted Catarina de San Juan's biography. It was perhaps in one such forum for artistic and philosophical debate that Sor Juana first offered a logical critique of a theological point in a sermon by an influential Jesuit, António de Vieira (1608–1697). One of the interlocutors, by most accounts, Bishop Fernández de la Cruz, taken with the brilliance of the rebuttal, asked Sor Juana to record it for him on paper. Apparently without Sor Juana's consent, Bishop Fernández de Santa Cruz then published her thesis–originally titled *Crisis de un sermón* [Critique of a Sermon], but retitled by the bishop himself as the *Carta atenagórica* (Puebla 1690), a "Letter Worthy of Athena." In an outwardly contradictory move, Bishop Fernández de Santa

Cruz both promoted a nun's incursion into the forbidden terrain of theological debate and wrote a prologue in which he lightly admonishes Sor Juana for her literary pursuits and for not imitating the path of the *perfecta religiosa*.

Suggesting that Sor Juana follow the model of Teresa de Ávila and signing the prologue with the pseudonym *Sor Filotea* ("Sister Lover-of-God"), Bishop Fernández de Santa Cruz left his intentions enigmatic. What is clear, however, is that the publication unleashed a flurry of responses from both supporters and detractors as well as from Sor Juana herself, who would write several more letters to clarify her position. Sor Juana's response was to be the most famous Latin American woman's autobiography in the feminist debates of the twentieth century, *Respuesta a Sor Filotea de la Cruz* [1691; Response to Sor Filotea de la Cruz]. It is a stunning defense of her right as an individual, gifted by God, to follow intellectual and artistic pursuits, in spite of Church restrictions on women's learning. And in the *Respuesta*, she cunningly uses the central structuring and rhetorical devices of the life of the perfect religious woman to rescript a religious woman's portrait.

Born in 1648 in a small town a day's travel from Mexico City, Juana Inés de Asbaje y Ramírez, by her own account in the *Respuesta*, had a certain independence of spirit and precociousness; by age three, she tricked a teacher into letting her attend an *amiga* school with her sister, and she learned Latin in fewer than twenty lessons. When dreams of disguising herself as a man in order to attend the university in Mexico City and study science proved far-fetched, Juana set about studying the books in her grandfather's library—an inspiration that would later lead to her having one of the largest personal libraries in seventeenth-century New Spain. By about age ten, Juana left home to live with relatives in Mexico City and soon became a lady-in-waiting in the viceregal court. For nearly five years, she attended to the Vicereine and participated actively in ceremonial and social activities at court. Seen as something of a phenomenon by the court, Juana's exceptional gift for writing verse and accumulating knowledge became widely known and sought. By 1669, in order to avoid marriage and to have some daily time to read and write, she took the veil as a nun in the relaxed Heronymite Convent of Santa Paula in Mexico City. There she would serve in important positions teaching nuns and keeping the convent's financial records.

Moving between court and convent from within the cloister itself, through her writing Sor Juana participated in the thick of religious, civic, and cultural celebrations in Viceregal Mexico. Commissioned to write occasional verse for birthdays and funerals, popular musical verse (*villancicos*) for church feasts, courtly love poetry for literary contests (*certámenes*), one-act sacramental plays for Corpus Christi celebrations, prose descriptions of ceremonial arches to be erected for the entrance of a new viceroy, and theological rebuttals for a bishop, Sor Juana's corpus covers the gamut of popular and erudite, profane and sacred baroque literature. Beyond these official commissions, Sor Juana herself seemed to delight in writing about her quest for knowledge, *Primero Sueño* [First Dream], and about human relationships, devoting some of her most touching verse to her close friends.

In the very years that Sor Juana's literary works began to circulate widely in Spain and America, the exchange of letters that culminated in the *Respuesta* took place, provoking a controversy that spanned the Atlantic and ultimately led to Sor Juana's withdrawal from public life. With a somber backdrop

of floods, famine, and epidemics resulting in a public revolt against the viceroy, 1690 marked a shift in Sor Juana's luck with Church hierarchy. Sor Juana had already run head-on into conflict with her influential Jesuit confessor, Antonio Núñez de Miranda, the *calificador* who would approve the first biography of Catarina de San Juan. Their disagreement over Sor Juana's literary pursuits had resulted in the *Carta al Padre Núñez* [1682, Letter to Father Núñez] and the break in their relationship.

The *Carta al Padre Núñez* lays bare the internal structure and argument that Sor Juana later developed in the *Respuesta*. In unequivocal, unadorned language she pointed a finger at Núñez's misinterpretation of God's will and bids her confessor farewell in order to be able to continue on her path towards God:

> Dios que me crió y redimió, y que usa conmigo tantas misericordias, proveherá con remedio para mi alma, que esper[o] en su vondad no se perderá aunque le falte la dirección de V.R., que a el cielo hacen muchas llaves, y no se estrechó a un solo dictamen, sino que ay en él infinidad de manciones para diversos genios . . . . ¿Qué precisión ay en que esta salvación mía sea por medio de V.R.: ¿No podrá ser por otro? Restringióse y limitóse la misericordia de Dios a un hombre . . .? (*Carta al Padre Núñez*, 625–26)

> I pray that God who created and redeemed me and who has granted me so many favors will provide in his goodness for the salvation of my soul in spite of the fact that I will be deprived of your guidance, and that there be many keys to heaven, and that the way not be limited to one, but there be an infinite number for the diversity of peoples . . . what necessity is there that my salvation be by your guidance? Could there not be others? Can the mercy of God be restricted and limited to one man?

The authoritative role of the confessor is completely undermined as Sor Juana shows how he had blocked, rather than nurtured, God's presence in her life. Sor Juana continued to write with the protection of the viceregal court and even the encouragement of some members of the clergy.

A decade later the threats unleashed by the publication of the *Carta Atenagórica* (1690) moved Sor Juana to take a more public stand about the individual's right to develop God-given talents. She did not come to this point immediately, however. One month after Bishop Fernández de Santa Cruz's publication of the *Carta Atenagórica*, Sor Juana wrote him a letter, the recently rediscovered *Carta de Sor Serafina*. In a clever, if oblique, satirical wordplay, Sor Juana tells the bishop that he misinterpreted the target of her letter about the sermon. She was not critiquing its original author, she explains, so much as her own ex-confessor Núñez de Miranda.

Apparently the satirical *Carta de Sor Serafina* failed to quell the debate raised by the theological rebuttal—and may have only fanned the flames. Writing only a month later, Sor Juana's second letter to Bishop Fernández de Santa Cruz took a different tack. The *Respuesta* is a carefully crafted, highly rhetorical literary piece. Defying strict generic categorization, the letter is variously called a self-defense and autobiography. It has been most frequently studied for its clues to Sor Juana's psyche and poetic production, and, more recently, for its strategic dialogue with Church rules and history, dealing in particular with the themes of obedience and institutional hierarchy. Some critics have extended this idea of dialogue to the highly intertextual nature of the *Respuesta*, highlighting Sor Juana's careful rewriting of authors mentioned. Sor Juana also uses the ideological and rhetorical devices of her own previous letters and Fernández de Santa Cruz's prologue as intertexts that establish the foundation of her *Respuesta*. On one side is the central theology of free will, as expressed in the *Carta Atenagórica*, together with its application in personal terms within the spiritual director-daughter relationship, seen in the *Carta al Padre Núñez*. On the other side is Bishop Santa Cruz's invocation of Saints Paul and Teresa when discussing model behavior for women in the Church.

Taking full advantage of both the hybrid form of the letter and her own self-training in widely dispersed fields of knowledge, Sor Juana enters the ongoing secular debate of women's roles (*querelle des femmes*) and theological discussions about women in the church. Employing narrative structuring common to much discourse dealing with a person's defense (both the legal and religious form), Sor Juana rescripts the traditional outcome of the nun's life story. She builds her defense on the problematic situation of the woman writer who has taken a vow of obedience, depicting her own adherence to the virtues of the model nun. These include humility: "confieso desde luego mi ruindad y vileza" ("without hesitation I confess my baseness and infamy"); writing at the behest of others: "yo nunca he escrito cosa alguna por mi voluntad, sino por ruegos y preceptos ajenos" ("I have never written anything of my own free will but only in response to the pleas and requests of others"); ignorance: "los torpes borrones de mi ignorancia" ("the clumsy scribblings of my ignorance"); and suffering: "sufrir" ("to suffer"), "poca salud" ("poor health"), "repugnancia" ("repugnance"), and so forth. But the narrative core rests on the doctrinal teaching of the "estrechísima cuenta" ("narrowest of accountings") on Judgment Day that she, like all human beings, will have to make, an accounting of how she best employed her God-given talents. She argues that in following her "inclinación a las letras" ("inclination to letters") she has followed the prescribed path to salvation. Sor Juana begins her life story at essentially the same point as her Sisters—that of the Divine call (*vos me cogesteis*)—and follows much of the same process of following Christ's example (*imitatio Christi*), but she deliberately chooses a nonconventional way to justify her path, even shunning the culturally acceptable (though still dangerous) practice of following the mystic's path. Instead, Sor Juana underscores that a woman who has been bestowed with a good intellect should use it for the glory of God in perfecting herself and consequently be worthy of it, just as the woman who has been given visionary gifts should use them to know herself as God's servant. After all, she argues, all things issue from God. By employing the conventions of the life story for an alternative life story and apology for a perfect religious woman, Sor Juana deliberately both validates the use of the genre for religious women's self-representation and targets its narrow, often contradictory limits. Sor Juana uses the form of the life story not only as a mask to cover her assertive response to cultural expectations for women, but also to make clear through the use of the only culturally acceptable form of self-expression available to religious women the dilemma of the seventeenth-century woman writer. In a Baroque layering of forms and meaning, Sor Juana simultaneously employs the genre and rejects it as inadequate, displaying the faulty teachings about women that led to its conventions as she exposes the flaws of Church practices toward women. No longer simply the personal defense to a confessor found in her *Carta al Padre Núñez*, but by using the pedagogical and didactic possibilities of the life story, the *Respuesta* lays claim to a much broader agenda: the right to an education for all women who are so inclined.

The *Respuesta* became part of a much larger polemic that resulted in one of Sor Juana's defenders being summoned by the Inquisition; she herself was entered into a *proceso arzobispal secreto* ("archiepiscopal secret trial"), which led to the selling of her extensive library and the official renunciation of her literary career in 1693–1694. By 1695, Sor Juana was dead from an epidemic. Five years later, a Jesuit biographer, Diego Calleja, would publish a saintly version of Sor Juana's final years, depicting a prayerful, self-mortifying nun. It served also as a prologue to the posthumous publication of many of Sor Juana's most devotional works, *Fama y obras póstumas* [1700; Fame and Posthumous Works]. Recent archival finds, however, have shown that despite the Church's efforts to rescript Sor Juana's life into that of a model nun—in much the same way it had done with Rosa, Catarina de San Juan, and María de San José—Sor Juana continued her daring literary pursuits until her death. A newly rediscovered copy of an inventory taken upon her death reveals that Sor Juana did not fall silent during these final years; the inventory notes several notebooks of writings and numerous books in her library (see Trabulse 1997, 1999).

The numbers and ranks of players involved in Sor Juana's final years and the years immediately following her death bespeak the high stakes for controlling access to and interpretation of the Church's brides. The selective silencing of Sor Juana's life lasted until recently. Yet the very clarity and startling freshness of Sor Juana's own voice in her verse, drama, and letters ring out in her texts and have ensured that her voice has not been lost. Remarkably unmuddled and free of the ambiguity that often characterized nuns' writing as they walked the tenuous line between self, confessor, and God, Sor Juana's letters wittily exploited the full range of arguments, texts, and genres available to her.

In the same year that Sor Juana Inés died, New Spain's only published theological woman author was born, María Ana Aguilar Velarde, who became Sor María Anna Agueda de San Ignacio (1695–1756). Like many nuns, she had come from a *criollo* but somewhat impoverished background, had spent time as a lay holy woman living in the Beaterio de Santa Rosa in Puebla, and later had risen to become director of novices and prioress when the Beaterio was converted into a convent. Because her story and writings are treated in the other essay by Josefina Muriel in this volume (Chapter 31), they are mentioned here only to point to what appears to be a seeming mid-eighteenth century relaxation of Counter-Reformation guidelines regarding women's ability to be theological writers. Several of Sor María Anna's works were published during her own life time. Her two most noted works, *Devoción* [1791; Devotion] and *Mar de gracias* [1758; Sea of Graces], continue to employ the central stance of nuns' writings: the need to draw authority from direct spiritual experience rather than learned readings of texts (see Eich and Routt).

La Santa Comedianta, Ursula Suárez (1666–1749)

One of the most startling formal autobiographical life stories written by a nun during this later Colonial period was penned by a Clarist nun living in an urban area somewhat peripheral to the colonial centers of the empire, Santiago de Chile. Going beyond even Sor Juana's reformulation of the life story, Ursula Suárez's account turns the conventional model of holiness on its head by describing her propensity for laughing, tricking men, and engaging in provocative conversations with God. While writing for her confessor sometime around

1708 and using the dialogic structure of the mystic triad found in her Sisters' accounts, Ursula borrows heavily from picaresque narratives to rewrite the story of the *perfecta religiosa*. Born in 1666 to a fairly prominent family, Ursula lived with them for only twelve years before moving to the relaxed Clarist Convento de la Plaza, which at one point held around 500 women. Although we know little about Ursula's formal learning, she mentions teaching Latin to her Sisters, keeping financial records for the convent, and serving at one point as abbess (1721–1725). The sole text by Ursula that we have to date is her relatively recently published *Relación autobiográfica* [1984; Autobiographical Report]. Surely, however, letters from her years as abbess must remain on some archive shelves. Because we do not have the autograph manuscript of her life story, we must raise the perhaps unanswerable question that often accompanies the study of colonial texts: How faithful was the copyist to the original? The information about Ursula's life coincides exactly with secondary documents and the narrator demonstrates thorough knowledge of a nun's role, leading to the conclusion that her account is probably authentic.

Ursula's *Relación* is a baroque story of a sinner-saint who suggests that the life stories of nuns need not be so different from those of rogues. Using a lively, popular literary style that incorporates ballad and verse forms, folkloric elements, and extensive dialogue into her narrative, the Clarist nun recounts her life on the road to becoming God's first comedian saint. Never directly invoking the most legitimizing model for a writing nun, Teresa de Ávila, Ursula instead takes to new limits the saint's famous definition of prayer as talking directly with God, and she records numerous playful conversations between the divine master and his servant. This witty, dialogic exchange, in fact, is the most salient characteristic of the *Relación*. Without ever using the word *pícara* (trickster), but employing most of its possible synonyms (cheat, roamer, knave, prankster, etc.), Ursula depicts herself as a verbally playful, proud trickster for God.

In spite of the persistent thread of interior dialogue with God that Ursula records, her anecdotes are weighted toward the exterior happenings in her life. She shies away from Teresian descriptions of the spiritual path or a mystic discourse that attempts to describe deep, ineffable, spiritual transformations. Instead, Ursula's story depicts many vivid scenes of often conflictive encounters with people. The *Relación* diverges from confessional literature in its overlap with the picaresque narrative: scenes from daily life, the use of irony, the use of wit to trick others and challenge hierarchies, and a roguish central character.

Although Ursula had both a family of good social standing and, later, her own multi-room cell and material comforts in the convent, she ironically plays up the fact that, whether with family or her Sisters, she had to rely on her natural cleverness to help those around her obtain food, shelter, or clothing. She recalls how her mother used her as a go-between to obtain foodstuffs and cloth from Ursula's paternal grandmother. Even as a bride of Christ, Ursula used her feminine wiles on *devotos de monjas* (men who visited nuns and, in their devotion, donated money to the convent), as well as on an occasional bishop, to help maintain the convent. In a picaresque reworking of the hagiographic stories of saints who ignored threats from husbands or fathers in order to distribute food to the poor, Ursula secured food for her family and Sisters and tended to delight in the verbal games she had to play to accomplish her task.

Aware that she is working within the textual model for the *perfecta religiosa*, Ursula reworks mystical narrative strategies to achieve a multiple, often ironic, perspective on her life and text. In fact, Ursula argues that language is a woman's only weapon: "las mujeres sólo con palabras nos defendemos" (196) ("we women can only defend ourselves with words"). Before her spiritual conversion she had used verbal wit to better her family's and Sisters' economic circumstances; afterwards she also employed language to defend herself against Church hierarchies that imposed authority over her life and words. Language now becomes the tool for her *apologia pro vita sua*. The power of the word as wit is the basis for a *pícara*'s material gain and life story, and it is the site for a saint's mysticism, prophecy, and ecclesiastical authority. Ursula brings together these two seemingly irreconcilable traits because God had chosen her to be his "*comedianta*." When Ursula laments not being more like her Clarist models, the mystic nun and author Maria de la Antigua and Mariana de Escobar, God explains to Ursula the reason for this deviation: "Díjome mi Señor y Padre amantísimo: 'No he tenido una santa comedianta, y de todo hay en los palacios; tu has de ser la comedianta'" ("My beloved Lord and Father said to me: 'I do not have a holy playwright and there are multiple callings in the palace; you will be my playwright'"). Ursula portrays God as more human than is typical of convent writing, deviating from the conventional portrait of God in all His majesty granting a poor sinner mercy. Rather, God becomes the origin of her only sin–"engañar a los hombres" ("to deceive men"). He has allowed her to continue this "niñería" ("child's play") in making the convent rely on "devotos de monjas" ("devoted wealthy patrons" 178–79) for economic survival. After all, she argues like Sor Juana before her, all comes from God: "Señor, . . . me criastes . . . Todo es tuyo que yo nada tengo" ("Lord, you created me, all is yours, I do not have anything") (206).

By altering the exhortation to virtue and the idealized *perfecta religiosa* found in the life stories written by most nuns and by adding the scenes from daily life and the negative exemplarity found in the picaresque novel, Ursula challenges the male-female roles prescribed by society. The ideal female as silent, humble, obedient, and chaste portrayed in most life stories is reworked to include elements of the witty, sexually desirable *pícara* who champions her femininity and defends her right to talk. The typical nun writing confessional literature in this period would have justified her life as having been a good one, one that conformed to the Church's teachings and imitated the lives of the saints, thus providing a new exemplar. If there exists a subversive element in these life stories, as we saw earlier in the case of Madre María de San José, it usually derives from manipulations of the confessor's and nun's relationship and their respective relationships with God. With the exception of Sor Juana, the reframing of ecclesiastical hierarchy, however, rarely undermines the narrative impulse toward confession and exhortation to virtue. Clearly, such is not the case in Ursula's account. Just as Sor Juana drew on legal rhetoric and a multitude of intertexts to mount a defense that highlighted the shortcomings of the life and textual model of the *perfecta religiosa*, Ursula Suárez questions its precepts by pointing a finger at a patriarchal system that made women so dependent on men.

In the end, Ursula's own self-portrait presents an alternative to the saint or sinner models offered by the official Church for religious women. She is neither a holy mystic like

Sor María de la Antigua nor a heretic like the Peruvian Ángela Carranza (both cited by Ursula). The Clarist nun fashions her identity enough within limits to avoid being targeted by the Inquisition, but too far from them to avoid censure at one point in her life by the bishop (circa 1715), or, later, to be the focus of a hagiographic biography. Like Sor Juana, Ursula successfully deviated from strict interpretation of Church mandates for women because she was willing to risk censure in order to create an alternate path to the divine, and because, for years, she was well connected to influential clergy. The one case on record in which Ursula was punished coincided with the lack of support from a bishop. But unlike Sor Juana, Ursula lived for many more years and would later regain her power and become abbess of the convent when there was a change of bishops (1721).

La Monja Alférez [The Lieutenant Nun], Catalina de Erauso (1582?–1650)

As perhaps a coda to this account of the life stories written by and about religious women in Colonial Latin America, the *Vida i sucesos de la Monja Alférez* [*Lieutenant Nun*, 1996] points to two recurring themes: the way that these confessional life stories served as key textual defenses for women's lives, and the extent to which they could be turned into hybrid genres by being mixed with other autobiographical forms to create a new effect. As in the case of Ursula Suárez's account, we do not have the autograph manuscript for Catalina de Eruaso's story, so we cannot tell to what extent the manuscript may have been tweaked, but most critics agree that Catalina at least had a hand in this highly unusual autobiographical account. Probably drafted when Catalina was in Madrid and Seville requesting compensation for having served in the king's army and before she went on to Rome to seek approval for remaining dressed as a man, the account lies at the opposite end of the spectrum from Rosa de Lima's case, which was being examined by the Seville-based Council of the Indies in these same years (circa 1624).

Catalina de Erauso's *Vida i sucesos,* corroborated by several legal *relaciones,* recounts her tale of moving from life in a convent in Spain to that of a New World soldier and outlaw. Catalina had been born to a well-to-do family in the Basque country, entered her aunt's convent at the age of four, escaped before professing at age fifteen, donned male garb, and served as a page before embarking for America, where she worked at various occupations, including those of merchant and soldier. She also confessed to having maimed and killed many men. Finally caught and discovered to be a woman, Catalina confessed to the local bishop. He, in turn, demanded proof that she had never taken final and irrevocable vows as a nun, which required permanent enclosure. Thus, after years in battle against the fierce Araucano Indians, duels over gambling and ladies, and quick escapes, the lieutenant nun—as she came to be known—entered a Lima convent for several years while she awaited official confirmation from Spain that she had been a novice, but had escaped before being inducted into the ranks of Christ's brides. When the letter finally arrived, Catalina again rejected the nun's veil and put on trousers. But rather than take up her previous life on the frontier, she embarked for her homeland. There she spent the next six years initiating a series of petitions, and either dictating or writing her memoirs.

The admiration and astonishment expressed by the crowds that had gathered to witness Catalina's entrance into Lima and the ecclesiastical authorities who heard her confession were mere preludes to the sensation her story caused in Europe. Although both ecclesial and civil codes prohibited cross-dressing, the highest-ranking officials of Church and Empire granted Catalina's petition to remain dressed as a man. Her petition to the Crown, in fact, builds a case on a dual argument: the merits of her deeds as a soldier and the singularity of her position as a woman fighting in the army (see Vallbona 1992 and Merrim 1994). As recorded in Catalina's memoirs, the reactions of king and pope on hearing Catalina recount her story confirm that it was indeed the uniqueness of her position as a woman soldier–and, more importantly, an intact virgin–that brought her such success. Catalina de Erauso's life story reveals how religious, political, and literary codes shape the account of a woman who slipped through the cracks of society's confines for women and reemerged as a cultural phenomenon, due in large part to her successful negotiation of codes for femininity versus masculinity and the geography of the frontier.

Not surprisingly, as a soldier and an outlaw, the protagonist of the *Vida i sucesos* drew heavily on the popular narrative forms of the soldier's life with its record of services rendered and petition for reward, and the picaresque, with its focus on life at the margins of society. Like her soldier comrades, the one-time lieutenant opens her account with a simple statement of her parents' names and the year and place of her birth. Inscribing her account into an explicitly male genre that often imitated forensic (legal) factuality and brevity, as well as oral paradigms constructed for the first telling of the story to others, the life story provides a somewhat juridical listing of information about dates, names, titles, monetary sums, and distances traveled–the sort of information needed to make a case.

While maintaining the often lively, action orientation of the genre of the soldier's tale, Catalina undermines the exemplarity of the soldier's petitionary life story when she is not yet a quarter of the way into her story. Whereas many a *vida de soldado* (soldier's tale) recounts vicissitudes and failings, often criticizing certain aspects of society in the process, rarely is a soldier's tale so blatantly transgressive and parodic. Writing when the picaresque was already a well-established genre, Catalina's *Vida i sucesos* shares with it an emphasis on an unrepentant rogue. Although Catalina does not share the *pícaro*'s story of an illegitimate birth and truly living on the margins of society, she echoes the genre at a lexical level (chapter 12), at the level of emplotment (as she moves from master to master living by her wits), and at the ideological level (she mocks hard work in favor of "industria" ["cleverness"]. At one point, after escaping once again from the law, Catalina proclaims: "Que estos milagros suelen acontecer en estos conflictos i más en Yndias. Gracias a la vela industria" ("It just goes to show that persistence and hard work can perform miracles and it happens regularly–especially in the Indies") (chapter 10).

The narrator of the *Vida i sucesos* flaunts a different type of genre-gender blurring and rewriting in the final chapters, however. With the exception of a few short stints in jail, Catalina escapes serious consequences for her transgressive acts, but later–like all the women studied in this essay–at a certain crucial point in her life she comes face to face with a bishop. After killing the famous local figure known as "El Nuevo Cid" ("The New Cid") and hard pressed to escape, Catalina begins to confess. While still inscribed into picaresque literature with its examples of false confession, the narrative sequence blends with the spiritual or confessional autobiography, which is a genre that the picaresque parodies. Yet it is also a genre that empowers women to defend their life path. Catalina borrows elements from a nun's self-representation by capitalizing on its inherent struggle for control over the interpretation of the story told. This spiritual focus and the real mediation of a male Church superior set this genre apart from the picaresque and the soldier's tale. Catalina may have confessed to the bishop, but the literary representation of that process mixes the transformative power of confession with a highly condensed, parodic style that leaves the reader both laughing and perplexed at the meaning of this central scene:

Señor . . . la verdad es ésta: que soi muger; que nací en tal parte, hija de fulano i sutana; que me entraron de tal edad en tal Convento con fulana mi tía; que allí me crié; que tomé el hábito; que tuve noviciado; que estando para profesar, por tal ocasión me salí; que me fui a tal parte, me desnudé, me vestí, me corté el cabello; partí allí i acullá me embarqué, aporté, trahiné, maté, herí, malee, correteé, hasta venir a parar en lo presente i a los pies de Su Señoría Iustrísima.

(Chapter 20)

Señor . . . . the truth is this: that I am a woman, that I was born in such and such a place, the daughter of this man and this woman, that at a certain age I was placed in a certain convent with a certain aunt. . . . I left the convent for such and such a reason, went to such and such a place, undressed myself and dressed myself up again, cut my hair, traveled here and there, embarked, disembarked, hustled, killed, maimed, wreaked havoc, and roamed about until coming to a stop in this very instant, at the feet of Your Eminence.

No true spiritual transformation or conversion seems to have occurred; there is no account of repentance and the taking up of a new life.

In the next scene, Catalina draws on another theme of the nun's spiritual autobiography, which is the vow of chastity. Knowing proof of her virginity will be her trump card, Catalina invites the bishop to have matrons examine her. In the literary rendition of the scene, the narrator reports that Catalina is an "intact virgin" and implicitly mocks the insistence of both the Church and the genre that sexual purity begets and reflects spiritual wholeness and virtue. Here Catalina highlights her paradoxical situation as a sexually pure outlaw. The account meets the genre's requirement that transformation occur, but in the person of Catalina such a transformation is subverted both in purpose and outcome. No longer portraying a reconciliation between the individual and God, the narrative form becomes Catalina's safety net for her gender change. By echoing and yet radically altering the genre's central passage, which is the moment of conversion and confession before all, Catalina's spiritual transformation becomes her gender (re)transformation. Whereas the conventional nun's account bore witness to how a lowly woman's life overcame the limitations of her sex and revealed the shaping hand of the divine Author, the Monja Alférez's life altered that formula to bear witness to how a woman could undo "natural," God-given gender categories with approval by the pope himself.

In destabilizing the transcendent meaning of confessional literature, altering the male soldier's tale, and employing ruses common to both the *pícaro* and the *pícara*, Catalina goes beyond the simple blurring of literary and gender conventions to create a complex and ambiguous discursive matrix. Competing motives undermine traditional paradigms with

their narrow embodiment (both literally and figuratively) of self-representation and identity. Although all autobiographical writing of the period is a hybrid genre that moves between petition and authority, author and addressee, historical person and literary construct, the *Vida i sucesos* manipulates genres and their inherent gender-related rules to create a truly unique text, even to having a first-person narrator who fluctuates between using feminine and masculine adjectives to describe herself.

Remarkably, this tale became the fodder for some of the most dramatic male rescripting of a woman's life story. One Mexican broadside (1653) has Catalina falling desperately in love with another woman. In contrast, the Jesuit Diego de Rosales's *Historia general del Reino de Chile* [General History of the Kingdom of Chile, chapter 37], rewrites her life story as a nun who, because of her true religious vocation, ultimately returned to the cloister. Catalina, in fact, ended the final decades of her life in a very different manner from either fictional account. She took her payment from the king and her license to remain dressed as a man from the pope and returned to America. For the final twenty years of her life, she seems to have lived in relative obscurity, dressed as a man, calling herself Antonio de Erauso and dedicated to a life on the road as a muleteer who transported people and goods along the Royal Road from Veracruz to Mexico City.

Catalina's life showcases, in a perhaps surprising twist, the transatlantic, transgender political, religious, and cultural exchanges during the mid-colonial period. As rules and regulations were increasingly codified at institutional levels, individuals found ways to capitalize on gaps and inherent contradictions within codes in order to follow alternate life paths. Through the textual traditions that allowed–and even demanded that–these models and deviations from it be recorded, we glimpse a vibrant, spirited culture, one in which religion and society, men and women, colony and metropolis, were intimately engaged in a dynamic process. The narrative form for telling the story of the model *perfecta religiosa* was shaped according to a woman's own life, proximity to the centers of the viceroyalties, and chronological distance from the boom years of the genre. Whether we examine Rosa de Lima's defiance of Counter-Reformation dictates about the enclosure of women, Catarina de San Juan's spiritual power in spite of her caste, María de San José's insistence on her confessor's limited knowledge of divine will, Madre Castillo's incursion into the forbidden terrain of Scriptural interpretation, Sor Juana's construction of a woman's right to follow an intellectual path to God, Ursula Suárez's evocation of humorous portraits pleasing to God, or Catalina de Erauso's demonstration of a virgin woman's "masculine" valor on the frontier, we witness a variety of active, creative women who carved out roles for themselves within society. They wrote of their experiences and inspired male biographers to retell their stories.

The range of women studied helps us glimpse the commonalities and differences in these texts and points to the need to formulate a new critical model. As scholars have pointed out, many early modern Christian teachings and behavioral manuals had set the tone for viewing women as either saints or sinners who needed to be carefully controlled by male clergy. Women were either virginal, virtuous, obedient, and silent or they were the embodiment of demonic temptations of the flesh and spirit. Although a compelling paradigm, this dualistic model of the saint or sinner–until recently frequently repeated by twentieth-century historians and literary critics–fails to take into account the rich reality of women's lives beyond prescriptive norms. Too often we have configured women's self-representation as an either/or experience, as a highly conflicted self that moves only between the two extremes of self-abnegation and self-assertation. In other cases, we have gone further and suggested the notion of woman's unrepresentability, the idea that feminine autobiographical forms were mostly formal public contracts with no space for selfhood (see Smith). While these views have served us well for pointing to gender restrictions and difference, it is now crucial to move beyond these limits because they contain the variety of women's experiences and expression. Perhaps what we see emerging in place of these previous models are models of multiplicity, which at once honor the individual response to codified discourses for women and sets them into the broader context of colonial society.

Just as important as the need to formulate new critical frameworks for studying colonial women is the need to understand that the cultural significance of these *perfectas* and not-so-*perfectas religiosas* did not always die at the end of the colonial period. As suggested earlier, Madre Castillo's works were published for the first time in the nineteenth century, as evidence of an authentic Colombian voice, and Catarina de San Juan was renamed and regarbed to become the *China Poblana*, an icon for Puebla's new identity. Rosa de Lima also acquired several new iconographic depictions for both the independence movement and native Andean populations. Now, at the turn of the millennium, as Sor Juana has taken a firm hold again as a valued part of Mexican culture (her portrait is on one of the peso bills) and new voices are being heard, we are beginning to recognize these foundational narratives and sites for identity in Latin America–sites that even today hold significance as cultural and religious centers (Rosa de Lima's house, for example, is a sanctuary; María de San Jose's two convents are museums; and, fittingly, Sor Juana's cloister now houses a university). As this essay closes, we note only that this recuperation of texts and voices from the Colonial period and their reintegration into a complex historical-literary scene is still in its infancy. In the last two decades alone, important archival research has uncovered many of the manuscripts studied here. As these texts are reaching wider audiences both in the Spanish- and English-speaking worlds, no doubt the voices within them, if we but listen, will show us the way to continue to read and understand their riches.

Works Cited

Burke, Peter. 1984. "How to Be a Counter-Reformation Saint." *Religion and Society in Early Modern Europe 1500-1800*. Ed. Kaspar von Greyerz. London: George Allen and Unwin. 45–55.

Castillo Graxeda, José del. 1987 [1692]. *Compendio de la vida y virtudes de la venerable Catarina de San Juan*. Puebla: Bibliotheca Angelopolitana.

Eich, Jennifer Lee. 1992. "The Mystic Tradition and Mexico: Sor María Anna Agueda de San Ignacio." Dissertation. University of California, Los Angeles.

Erauso, Catalina de. 1992. *Vida i sucesos de la Monja Alférez: Autobiografía atribuida a Doña Catalina de Erauso*. Ed. Rima de Vallbona. Tempe: Center for Latin American Studies.

———. 1996. *Memoir of a Basque Transvestite in the New World. Catalina de Erauso*. Trans. Michele and Gabriel Stepto. Boston: Beacon Press.

Hansen, Fray Leonhardo. 1929. *Vida admirable de Sta. Rosa de Lima*. Lima: n.p.

Juana Inés de la Cruz, Sor. 1987 [1692]. "Carta de la Madre Juana Inés de la Cruz Escripta a el R.P.M. Antonio Núñez de la Compañía de Jesus." "La Carta de Sor Juana al Padre Núñez (1682)" Antonio Alatorre. *Nueva Revista Filología Hispánica* 335: 591–673.

———. 1994. *The Answer/La Respuesta*. Ed. and trans. Electa Arenal and Amanda Powell. New York: The Feminist Press.

———. 1996 [1691]. *Carta de Serafina de Cristo, 1691*. Ed. Elías Trabulse. Toluca: Instituto Mexiquense.

Lavrin, Asunción. 1986. "Female Religious." *Cities and Society in Colonial Latin America*. Ed. Louisa S. Hoberman and Susan M. Socolow. Albuquerque: University of New Mexico Press. 165–96.

María de la Antigua. 1699. *Estaciones de la passion del Señor que exercitava la V. M. Maria de la Antigua . . . y le mandó N. Señor las publicase para gloria Suya, memoria de Su SS. Passion y mayor aprovechamiento de las almas*. Mexico City: n.p.

Mariana de San Joseph. N.d. (In press). *Obras completas*. Ed. Teodoro Calvo de la Madrid. Madrid: Colección de Espirituales Españoles de la Fundación Española.

———. 1645. *Vida de la venerable M. Mariana de S. Joseph, fundadora de la recolección de monjas augustinas*. Ed. Luis Muñoz. Madrid: n.p.

———. 1723, 1773, 1782. *Estaciones que la Soberana Emperatriz de los Cielos Maria Santissima Nuestra Señora anduvo y eseñó a la Venerable Madre maria de San Joseph . . . sacadas de lo que escribe en su vida*. Puebla and Sevilla: n.p., 1723. Mexico City: n.p., 1773. Puebla: n.p., 1782.

McKnight, Kathryn Joy. 1997. *The Mystic of Tunja: The Writings of Madre Castillo, 1671-1742*. Amherst: University of Massachusetts Press.

Merrim, Stephanie. 1994. "Catalina de Erauso: From Anomaly to Icon." *Coded Encounters: Writing Gender and Ethnicity in Colonial Latin America*. Ed. Francisco Javier Cevallos-Candau et al. Amherst: University of Massachusetts Press. 177-205.

———. 1999. *Early Modern Women's Writing and Sor Juana Inés de la Cruz*. Nashville: Vanderbilt University Press.

Mujica Pinilla, Ramón. 1995. "El ancla de Rosa de Lima: mística y política en torno a la patrona de América." *Santa Rosa de Lima y su tiempo*. Ed. José Flores Araoz et al. Lima: Banco de Crédito del Perú. 53–211.

Muriel, Josefina. 1946. *Conventos de monjas en la Nueva España*. Mexico City: Editorial Santiago.

Myers, Kathleen A. 1993. *Word from New Spain: The Spiritual Autobiography of Madre María de San José (1656–1719)*. Liverpool: TRAC Liverpool up.

Ramos, Alonso. 1689–1692. *De los prodigios de la Omnipotencia y milagros de la Gracia en la vida de la venerable Sierva de Dios Catharina de S. Joan*. Vol. I, Puebla: n.p., 1689; Vol. II, Mexico City: n.p., 1690; Vol. III, Mexico City: n.p., 1692.

Rosales, Diego de. 1877-1878. *Historia general del reino de Chile*. Valparaiso: Mercurio.

Routt, Kristin Eva. 1998. "Authoring Orthodoxy: The Body and the Camino de perfección in Spanish-American Colonial Convent Writings." Dissertation. Indiana University.

Santander y Torres, Sebastián de. 1723. *Vida de la venerable madre Maria de S. Joseph, religiosa augustina recoleta, fundadora en los Conventos de Santa Monica de la Ciudad de Puebla, y despues en el de la Soledad de Oaxaca*. Mexico City: n.p.

Smith, Sidonie. 1987. *A Poetics of Women's Autobiography*. Bloomington: Indiana University Press.

Suárez, Ursula. 1984. *Relación Autobiográfica*. Ed. Mario Ferreccio Podestá. Santiago: Academia Chilena de Historia.

Teresa de Jesús, Santa. 1982. *Libro de la vida*. Ed. Dámaso Chicharro. Madrid: Cátedra.

Trabulse, Elías. 1997. "El silencio final de Sor Juana." *Universidad de México* 558: 11–19.

———. 1999. *De la muerte de Sor Juana*. Mexico City: CONDUMEX.

Vallbona, Rima de. 1992. "Introducción." *Vida i sucesos de la Monja Alférez: Autobiografía atribuida a Doña Catalina de Erauso*. Ed. Rima de Vallbona. Tempe: Center for Latin American Studies. 1–32.

CHAPTER 33

MYSTICS AND VISIONARIES
WOMEN'S WRITING IN EIGHTEENTH-CENTURY PORTUGUESE AMERICA

Leila Mezan Algranti

There is practically no record of private or domestic writing in Portuguese America. Whatever private diaries once existed have not survived, perhaps protected by modesty or by the shame of making public something that belonged to the private sphere and should therefore not be exposed to the gaze of the outside world. Nonetheless, some examples of domestic writing dating from the end of the colonial period do exist, the *Livros de Razão ou de Assentos* [Books of Reason or Good Judgment] among them; these were ledgerlike memoranda in which entries were made about certain family events, the daily purchase of products, or other sale transactions (Algranti 1997, 133). However, none of the few surviving domestic texts were written by women (Elias 249). For a long time it was believed that there was no surviving evidence of women's writing in pre-nineteenth-century Brazil. It is known, though, that, in a tradition dating back to medieval Europe, nuns and pious women habitually wrote to their confessors about mystical experiences, visions, and premonitions, generally at the confessors' request. Such writings were considered devotional Christian literature for the faithful, intended to develop feelings of devotion to God.

But although many records of lettered nuns who wrote about their own lives or the lives of their companions are readily available both in Portugal (Morujão 225) and in Spanish America (Franco), in Portuguese America this custom was practically unrecorded if it ever existed. Recently, however, some writings produced by nuns from Portuguese America have been located by Brazilian scholars in ecclesiastical and inquisitorial archives. They are letters to relatives and civil or religious authorities, *relatos de consciência* (accounts of conscience), written confessions of sorts directed to confessors and bishops. In his book, *Rosa Egipcíaca: uma Santa Africana no Brasil* [Rose of Egypt: An African Saint in Brazil], Luiz Mott mentions several of these letters as well as a five-hundred-page confession said to have been burned by her confessor, to whom Rosa had recounted her mystical experiences (Mott 1993, 491). Jacinta de São José, founder of the Carmelite order in Brazil, fared better with the letters of conscience she wrote to her spiritual advisers in Rio de Janeiro between 1747 and 1748. They have survived in the archives of the Lisbon Inquisition as partial documentation of a lengthy trial. Like Rosa, Jacinta was denounced to the Inquisition, and, in addition to her confessions, there are letters directed to the inquisitors as well as a full account of her life written for the Bishop of Rio de Janeiro, Dom Antônio do Desterro (Algranti 1998, 182). Written in the first person, these letters were strongly influenced by her reading of the lives of saints, a popular literary genre of the period.

Mother Jacinta de São José is therefore one of the few women of the Colonial period whose personal accounts of her own life have come down to us. This section proposes to outline her writings and consider a specific type of women's writing, one that most resembles the genres of autobiography and hagiography. In order to make known her project, she recorded "divine conversations" and "graces received" in writing to Rio de Janeiro's ecclesiastical authorities. Thus she was able to transmute intimate and private writing into something political and public. In a time when women were afforded precious few means of public expression, Jacinta's writings reveal important aspects of the female and religious culture of her day. Before we turn to the tenor of these writings, we should describe the trajectory of Jacinta's life and her "letters of conscience."

The Letters of Jacinta de São José

It was not unusual for women living in the cloisters to be enveloped by the mystical climate typical of the convents of the day, claiming to have visions of God and the devil (Schutte 11). Jacinta's visions, however, predate the beginning of her convent life, for according to her priest-biographers, the founder of the Brazilian Carmelite order was marked by the extraordinary from a tender age. Jacinta's life is narrated by her biographers in an edifying style; her qualities are clearly described with the intention of developing and increasing the reader's feelings of devotion to the saint, as is generally the case in hagiography (São José 112). Among the hagiographic elements that may be found in biographies of Jacinta as well as in her autobiographical writings are her early vocation, visions, ecstasies, physical suffering, and, especially, the work of foundation. The biographies are filled with descriptions of a saintly death and abound in confirmation of her exemplary life (São José 112). This is as it must be, for they aim to construct and preserve the memory of the founder of a religious order in Brazil. Let us explore this material to discover who Jacinta Rodrigues Aires was, however.

Jacinta was born in Rio de Janeiro in 1715 into a well-to-do family. According to her biographers, from an early age she manifested a desire to become a nun, a direction in which she was much encouraged by her father. After his death, however, her mother attempted to dissuade Jacinta from this purpose; she eventually left her mother's house, retiring to a small country house with her sister, Francisca, where they were soon joined by other young women to live on alms in the Carmelite tradition. Religious institutional life in Portuguese America of that time was made difficult by the Crown's settlement policy. Thus, Jacinta founded a lay institution, a house for recluses like others that existed in Southeastern Brazil, in hopes of someday receiving royal approval for its transformation into a convent (Algranti 1993, 72–81). Word of Jacinta's saintly reputation and the austerity of the life she led in the cloister of Santa Teresa spread throughout the city, moving the governor of Rio de Janeiro, Gomes Freire de Andrade, and eventually reaching the bishop, who joined him in supporting her project of a new convent within the city (Lisboa 401–403). By the time the monarch's authorization finally arrived in 1753, however, it established the foundation of a Franciscan convent, according to the wishes of the bishop, who

303

thought the Carmelite order too austere for the climate of Rio de Janeiro. Frustrated by this news and after further disagreement with her bishop, Jacinta fled to Lisbon in an attempt to obtain direct authorization for her Carmelite convent from the king.

Displeased by Jacinta's move, Dom Antônio do Desterro compiled a vast inventory of Jacinta's so-called visions (including letters she had written to her spiritual advisers and an account of her life he had in his possession), which he sent to the Inquisition, denouncing her as a false saint and an impostor (Inquisição de Lisboa 1753). He pronounced her lacking in humility for believing that her visions were of God when, possibly, they were of the devil. In Lisbon, Jacinta was merely interrogated by an experienced priest, to whom she never admitted having had visions even when questioned on the subject (Col), and, now armed with the authorization she had sought, she returned to her native city in 1756. The bishop, however, did not obey the royal command and indefinitely postponed the cloistered women's vows. Not until 1781, after the deaths of both Jacinta and Dom Antônio, did the Cloister of Santa Teresa in effect become the Convent of Santa Teresa (Algranti 1993, 21). Although she died without having fulfilled her dream of becoming a Carmelite nun, Jacinta has gone down in history as the order's Brazilian founder, her memory revered by Carmelite nuns for generations through biographies, foundation chronicles, and the letters of the founding mother. It is this group of letters, now preserved in the Lisbon Inquisition Archive, that we are interested in commenting upon briefly, for these "letters of conscience" and the *conta* (life story) that she wrote to the bishop about her life are documents that sustain the accusations made against her, several of her visions being recounted in them and written in her own hand (Inquisição de Lisboa 1753).

Whereas the trajectory of Jacinta's life is clearly intended by her biographers to edify, as is generally the case with hagiographies (Albert 10), Jacinta's autobiographical writings, on the other hand, are more baroque and less clear, suggesting that, although she was able to read, writing may not have come easily to her. This is perhaps due to the subject itself, but most probably proves she did not, indeed, ever fully master writing. At any rate, the surviving handwritten letters of conscience tell of several visions and conversations with God as well as of her divine mission to found a convent. In a letter dated 4 September 1749, she writes:

Quinta-feira, depois das seis horas, tive umas palavras substanciais, como impressas na alma, as quais me diziam que advertisse que estava com Ele e que com ele não temesse: que me vestisse da sua fortaleza que me dava. Depois tive uma visão, com certeza também que era de Deus; porém foi imaginosa . . . Nesta visão Deus assim lhe falou: Filha minha, . . . te chamei pelo caminho da minha cruz (. . .) quero que tomes a cruz por mim aos ombros: vê, quero que entres a acabar a minha obra, vê que te tenho dito que a quero a custa do teu trabalho . . . .

(Inquisição de Lisboa)

On Thursday, after six o' clock, I heard words of nourishment, they were imprinted upon my soul; which warned me that He was with me and that I should not fear him: that I should clothe myself in the fortitude he gave me. Later I had a vision which was also certainly of God . . . In this vision God said to me: My child . . . I have called you to my way of the cross . . . : put your shoulder to my cross; I want you to complete my task with your work . . . .

Within the context of her life, the work referred to in these visions is always the foundation of the convent. Jacinta clearly possessed no great literary gift–her writing was moved by a desire to communicate to her confessor (and, possibly, to a receptive audience) her subjective experience of love for God, as is typical of devotional literature. The experience of union with God is what the visionary yearns for from the beginning of her spiritual journey (Petroff 19) and is what she wishes to communicate to her readers and listeners. It is also a matter of revealing and declaring herself the equal of other visionary women and saints revealed by hagiography. Hence the resemblance of these writings to accounts of the lives of saints.

To consider Jacinta's writings as autobiography implies a discussion about the genre of biography and perhaps an amplification and modification of its definition. Petroff states that visionary writing presents an autobiographical impulse: that is, a desire to put into words the search for what might be designated as self and the discovery of this self in relation to God. But this self comes into existence through imaginary visions and dreams, as the texts reproduce a past experience that is renewed as description (Petroff 22). The issue becomes more complex when we observe that these writings are characterized by a double voice (one human, the other divine) and that, in recounting these dialogues, the visionary generally writes under the inspiration of the latter, but based on her own experiences and interpretations; that is, her work is an exercise of self-expression. Thus, autobiography seems to be the most adequate form by which to designate this type of writing, which thus takes on a public and markedly political character at a time when writing was predominantly a male prerogative and the education of women differed from that received by men.

Women's Writing and Political Choice

Women, who, like Jacinta, wrote devotional literature, especially in convents, were largely stimulated by mystical experience. In this sense it could be said that women's writing indicates representations and practices of the feminine, or of the female gender, in the specific field of the religiosity of that time; their devotions, visions, and their very act of writing were expressed differently from those of men. Visions were considered phenomena more frequently made manifest to women than to men (Petroff 2–20). But if Jacinta's writings failed to convince her inquisitors of any guilt, they disclose several characteristics of female devotional literature with which she may have been familiar. From the start, they illuminate the reasons that led women to write, the suffering caused by their visions, and even what and how they wrote. Another characteristic of this literature is the visionary's humility: Jacinta called herself a beast, an unworthy and incapable being. But, like other mystical women, she also spoke of the serenity of her union with God and the conflicts of her soul with the devil. While writing, Jacinta was perhaps unaware of her use of characteristic elements of visionary literature, though she fits perfectly what scholars have called the visionary archetype with its stages of visions. Nor, in sending letters to her spiritual adviser, was autobiography her stated intention, though she was indeed presenting an account of her life and what she believed to be a discovery about herself in relation to God.

What is striking about the writings of Jacinta and other mystics is the skill with which they were able to transform the apparent conformity and denial of the political induced by religious life into powerful weapons for carrying out their life projects, insofar as it was from their imaginary visions that mystics drew both their power and the arguments to fight for their objectives. They spoke with the authority of those who had seen to those who did not see; they challenged the limits imposed upon women of the day; they faced bishops and the hierarchy of the church but were apparently humble and submissive to divine will, to Church dogma, and to confessors. They frequently affirmed their rejection of fame and power, though, in fact, they did seek the protection and recognition of the community and of society in a politically planned and determined attitude. They wrote to their confessors or to civil authorities revealing intimate aspects of their lives (such as visions and premonitions) with the intent of giving visibility to their projects and obtaining the means to accomplish them.

Shrewdly, Jacinta did not reveal to her inquisitors the visions she had about the foundation, though she did expand upon them on several occasions–such as, for example, when she explains to her confessor that she had a revelation in which she saw Christ carrying the cross, "e tirando-a dos ombros, a largara sobre os dela, e dizendo-lhe: Filha, por mim carregarás e *te* será suave.Viu igualmente que ela com o Senhor estavam lançando o hábito a muitas donzelas.... junto delas uma grande multidão vestida do mesmo hábito, no meio das quais se achava uma matrona, venerada das outras" (São José 29) ("and taking it off his shoulders, lowered it onto hers, saying to her: 'Child, for me you shall carry this weight, and it will be light for you.' She also saw that with the Lord they were distributing habits to many maidens ... near them a large crowd, dressed in the same habit, in the midst of which was a matron, revered by the others"). It may be deduced that the matron was Saint Teresa de Ávila. Jacinta's difficulty in expressing in writing her imaginary intellectual visions is evident, for she asks permission from her spiritual guide to allow Padre Nunes (her confessor) to revise the account of her life that she was preparing for the bishop. It may be observed that there is, in this account, a selection of her visions, particularly those of the foundation, unlike those that occur in the account to Frei Manuel de Jesus (her confessor from 1744 to 1745) and served as a base for later biographies. In this account, Jacinta mentions other (childhood) visions and conversations with God and Saint Teresa. It would, therefore, seem that the account served a political purpose: namely to justify the vow she wished to profess and her mission as a Carmelite, at a time when her relationship with the ecclesiastical authorities of Rio de Janeiro was already most definitely compromised. This emphasis on her founding mission may also be seen in the letters she wrote between 1747 and 1748. A brief excerpt from the first letter to her spiritual adviser justifies this impression. In it Jacinta mentions an imaginary vision in which much blood flowed from a crucified figure who said that it had "que me vinha tirar do engano em que estava (de achar) que era tudo do demônio e mau espírito" ("come to dissuade me from my error [of thinking] that all was work of the devil and of evil spirits"), after which it vanished. Later, she heard voices threatening: "que já que não podia em nada me enganar (o demônio) e que tanto me fortalecia Deus, que ... se havia de meter no coração do *Senhor Bispo,*" (Inquisição de Lisboa 1753, Letter 1) ("God strengthened me that he [the devil] could not fool me in any way and I could enter the heart of the Lord Bishop"). One cannot fail to perceive the audacity of this vision, which clearly says that the devil stopped tormenting her personally because she was protected by God, but that he would torment

the Bishop in order to damage her. This was a way of saying that she no longer expected the bishop's collaboration in the founding of a Carmelite convent.

With regard to the vow to be professed in her convent, Jacinta tells the bishop in 1741 that she had "tendo eu já ordem de meu confessor para escrever tudo que tivesse por impulso, estando conversando com minha mãe ... tive uma coisa que se me começava a inflamar a alma, e logo tive umas palavras formais, com certeza que eram de Deus, que me diziam que escrevesse. Estava escrevendo sem saber o que, mas entendia o que escrevia, (era) o modo de vida que havíamos de ter" (Inquisição de Lisboa 1753, Letter 1) ("received orders from my confessor to write down everything on impulse, being engaged in conversation with my mother ... my soul became inflamed and I soon heard words and I was certain that they were from God; they told me to write. I knew not what I wrote but understood that this was the vow of the way of life we were to lead"). Thus Jacinta explained how, under divine inspiration, she composed the "Estatutos do Recolhimento de Santa Teresa" [Statutes for the Cloister of Saint Teresa], (Inquisição de Lisboa 1753). Although she thought they resembled the vows of Saint Francis, after reading them, her Franciscan confessor informed her that the vow she had written "era a mesma da Santa Madre" (Inquisição de Lisboa 1753, Letter 1) ("was the same as that of the Holy Mother [Saint Teresa]"). It may be inferred that, though this was not revealed until later, this vision preceded her dispute with the bishop. It seems obvious that both Jacinta's arguments and the image she held of herself–that of a woman honored by God whose mission it was to found the first Brazilian Carmelite convent–were skillful constructions. Her visions supplied the reasoning and the strength she needed to pursue her objectives and even to disobey her bishop. In her writing, Jacinta made use of devices that were characteristic of devotional literature, manipulating the known archetypes of female sainthood. She produced and reproduced the religious culture of her time and thereby imprinted political meaning on her writings while apparently seeking nothing beyond submission to divine intention. Jacinta's intimate writings reveal the image she constructed of herself as a founder, disseminated and nourished through centuries, which eventually prevailed over those who opposed her for, though she was once considered a saint by the people of Rio de Janeiro and by her biographers, her sainthood has not yet been confirmed by the Church.

Final Considerations

In the last decades, historians have sought to approach the so-called "excluded-of-history by exploring archives, rereading recognized and accepted historical sources, or finding new ones that allow us to hear new voices. Many recent studies reveal the wealth for sociocultural history of documents pertaining to judicial trials (Davis) and especially of inquisitorial trials (Ginzburg); these allow the recovery of lost worlds and heretofore forgotten historical agents. In this light, this study has sought to point out aspects of women's writing in the autobiographical writings of a Brazilian nun, which were preserved by the Inquisition of Lisbon. It is likely that other, similar investigations would allow us to hear the women of the colony even better. Ecclesiastical archives contain alternative sources of this type that might help in further uncovering the existence of women's writing during the Colonial period. The case of Mother Helena Maria (who also lived in the mid-eighteenth century), the founder of São Paulo's Convento da Luz, is another example which deserves to be remembered for, like Jacinta, she accomplished her foundational mission through written confessions to her spiritual guide and to the governor of São Paulo (Algranti 1993, 98–99). There is evidence that she also wrote an autobiography (Mott 2000, 12). It is now possible to hear the voices of the women of Portuguese America though, like whispers from a cloister, they have been muted and muffled by the rustle of nun's habits; these are the prisoners of memory and of the sentiments that led those women to the reclusive life.

Translation by Stephen A. Berg

Works Cited

Albert, Jean-Pierre. 1997. *Le sang et le ciel (Les saintes mystiques dans le monde chrétien)*. Paris: Aubier.

Algranti, Leila Mezan. 1993. *Honradas e Devotas: Mulheres da Colônia (Condição feminina nos conventos e recolhimentos do Sudeste do Brasil, 1750–1822)*. 2d. ed. Rio de Janeiro/Brasília, José Olympio/EDUNB, 1999.

———. 1997. "Famílias e Vida Doméstica." *Cotidiano e vida privada na América Portuguesa*. Ed. Laura de Mello e Souza. Coleção História da Vida Privada, dirigida por Fernando Novais. São Paulo: Companhia das Letras. 1: 83–154.

———. 1998. "Literatura religiosa e a biblioteca de uma mística Brasileira no século XVIII." *Revista Ciências Históricas* (Universidade Portucalense Infante D. Henrique) 12: 179–193.

Col, Padre. 1755. "Ofício do padre Col ao ministro do Ultramar sobre a inquirição de Jacinta de S.José." Arquivo do Convento de Santa Teresa no Rio de Janeiro, cópia de documento do Arquivo Ultamarino. 20-6-1755.

Davis, Natalie Zemon. 1983. *The Return of Martin Guerre*. Cambridge: Harvard University Press.

Elias, Maria José. 1966. "Transcrição do Caderno de Assentos do Coronel Costa Aguiar." Intr. and transcription of Maria José Elias. *Anais do Museu Paulista* 20: 179–348.

Franco, Jean. 1989. "Writers in Spite of Themselves: The Mystical Nuns of Seventeenth-Century Mexico." *Plotting Women: Gender and Representation in Mexico*. New York: Columbia University Press. 2–22.

Ginzburg, Carlo. 1987. *O queijo e os Vermes, o cotidiano e as idéias de um moleiro perseguido pela Inquisição*. Trans. Maria Betania Amoroso (text) and José Paulo Pes (poems). São Paulo: Companhia das Letras.

Inquisição de Lisboa. 1753. Processo 4423, Arquivos Nacionais da Torre do Tombo.

Lisboa, Balthazar da Silva. 1835. *Anais do Rio de Janeiro*. Vol. 7. Rio de Janeiro: Imprensa Estadual. 378–403.

Morujão, Isabel. 1995. "Contributo para uma bibliografia cronológica da literatura monástica feminina portuguesa dos séculos XVII e XVIII (Impressos)." *Lusitana Sacra. Revista do Centro de Estudos de História Religiosa* (Universidade Católica Portuguesa) 2nd series, 7: 253–338.

Mott, Luiz. 1993. *Rosa Egipcíaca: uma santa africana no Brasil*. Rio de Janeiro: Bertrand Brasil S. A.

———. 2000. "Martyrs, Confessor Saints and Blessed Women in Colonial Brazil." Conf. on Colonial Saints: Hagiography and the Cult of Saints in the Americas, 1500–1800. University of Toronto (May 12).

Petroff, Elizabeth Alvilda. 1986. *Medieval Women's Visionary Literature*. Oxford: Oxford University Press.

São José, Frei Nicolau. 1935. *Vida da serva de Deus Madre Jacinta de São José, carmelita descalça, fundadora do Convento de Santa Teresa no Rio de Janeiro*. Rio de Janeiro: Estudio de Artes Gráficas C. Mendes Junior.

Schutte, Ann Jacobson, ed. 1996. "Introduction." *Cecilia Ferrazi: Autobiography of an Aspiring Saint*. Trans. Ann J. Schutte. Chicago: Chicago University Press. 3–18.

CHAPTER 34

EXCLUSIONS IN LATIN AMERICAN LITERARY HISTORY

Debra A. Castillo

Juan Gelpí describes the concept of literary periods as an implicitly paternalistic model functioning as a mechanism of exclusion in which "generations revolve around a caudillo or boss, who becomes a kind of figurative father." Furthermore, Gelpí adds, "seldom have there been studies of the ideological implications" of this literary historical process (4). In reviewing traditional Latin American literary histories, both the workings of the process of exclusion and the mechanism's ideological subtexts are abruptly revealed when one contemplates the question of female writing culture. It would not be too much of an exaggeration to say that until the 1980s, nothing of the sort existed. Valdés and Valdés cite a figure of 93.7 percent of total pages dedicated to writing by men and 6.3 percent to women writers in Spanish literary histories through 1975 (72). Discussions of specific Latin American literatures support these statistics. Gelpí notes that, up until fifteen years ago, Julia de Burgos was the only woman discussed in Puerto Rican literary histories (3), and Cynthia Steele comments that "a patriarchal model, in fact, permeates much contemporary Mexican narrative, constituting a subtext that tends to be rendered invisible by virtue of its ubiquity" (26). Other such examples could be multiplied ad nauseum.

Before the "sudden explosion" of women writers on the Latin American literary scene during the decade of the 1980s, even the most assiduous historian of literature would be hard pressed to talk about a feminine literary culture beyond the three or four women—with the same names: Gabriela Mistral, Delmira Agustini, and Alfonsina Storni—grouped together in literary anthologies as a spurious community of the also-rans: *las poetisas.* This infinitesimal, marginalized category includes both the perversely lustful and the sweetly virginal, as well as that wonder of nature, Nobel-laureate Gabriela Mistral, who tends to be defined as both "virile" and "maternal" in the same breath. This essay, too, is complicit to some degree with such outdated structures to the degree that it operates under the false, but historically consistent, presumption of compulsory heterosexuality for all women writers, which has flattened out our understanding even of women like Gabriela Mistral, where revisionist feminist critics have quite correctly pointed out the role of the apparitional lesbian subtext in her work.

Thus, Sylvia Molloy quite rightly points to an originary instability in describing the woman writer, where the two words put in juxtaposition vibrate on the page as a scandalous oxymoron. Post-independence male writers allowed that scribbling ladies could legitimately produce affecting lyric poetry and could even contribute to schoolmarmish didactic texts. As Molloy reminds us, what they could not accept was the idea of a woman author—that is, a writer of intellectual power and cultural significance (108). What is curious and ideologically significant is that the existence of such women in pre-1980s literary history is both categorically denied and fiercely repressed, in such a manner that the inevitable return of the repressed figures the potency of the threat. If post-independence patriarchial culture posits that women cannot write

great literature (as in male-identified forms), it is also curious that such theoretically nonexistent forms must continually be decried and rejected.

To further complicate matters, while women have been traditionally prohibited from attempting male-identified cultural expressions, neither can they legitimately speak to the feminine experience; in Molloy's words "woman cannot write woman" in late nineteenth- early twentieth-century literature (109). Ironically the figure of "Woman" is the centerpiece of the *modernismo* aesthetic, so here too, the absence of women writers in a literary moment marked by "Woman" serves as a constant reminder of what must be ignored, erased, or remain ferociously repressed. Given such historical and ideological restrictions on masculinist understandings of female-authored texts, it is unsurprising that the few women who slip through this sanitary cordon are safely quarantined in their own little footnote or subject subheading, so that they avoid contaminating the main/male literary historical text.

The concern is a historical one, which Molloy anchors in the specific moment of literary *modernismo* in Latin America. However, the principle can be expanded—and in fact has been expanded in work by Magnarelli, Sommer, Masiello, and Franco, among others—to other periods and genres as well. In each case, these writers point to a certain dissonance in the canonical male literary text (for example: nineteenth-century national narratives in Sommer's case and Boom novels in Franco's) that operates as a surface feminization of the male text, while retaining a male-centered, even misogynistic aesthetic as a salient commonality in the deep structure of narrative. Here, too, as in the texts of *modernismo* that Molloy uses as her example, the apparent feminization of the male text serves the counter-function of limiting women writers even more forcefully to what Soledad Bianchi calls "the ghetto of sex" (26), writing "Woman" across the pages of traditional literary histories, while effectively de-authorizing women writers or limiting them to the canon's margins.

In the various proposals defining this project, Mario Valdés and the other members of his team point specifically to the challenges that feminism has posed to such traditional constructions of literary history. He and Linda Hutcheon write, for example, "What will inform all the discussions of these various historical problematics will be two important matters: an awareness of the once elided role of gender in each, and a reflexive self-questioning about the very terms and methods of analysis" (8). Hutcheon and Valdés quite rightly point to one of the most vexed questions involved in even the most self-questioning analysis, where the awareness of what has been "once elided" and needs to be recuperated inexorably requires us to reassert a rejected model, if only to say that it no longer applies. In Djelal Kadir's words, commenting on an earlier version of this chapter, "replication may well be an ineluctable quotient of any interrogation, revisioning, or rethinking.... Any reinvention of parameters is a revisitation." Of the many questions that need to be asked about such a self-reflexive interrogation, these are the questions that I want to pose and hold in abeyance in the background of the next few pages, giving the form of my inquiry its implicit (calculated) shape: If, as gender-conscious scholars posit, literary history is, by definition, a paternalistic form, then does "rethinking" the exclusion of women represent a return of the repressed (within the same structure) or a reinvention of parameters? How are the two alternatives propped upon each other as well as upon pre-existing and prejudicial constructions of the figure of women writers as figurative "Woman"?

Molloy, once again, offers a succinct point of departure for beginning an inquiry into these concerns: It may be argued that women, long represented by exaggerated images forged by male others, even as they question those images or as they construct defiant alternatives, fall inevitably into the trap of the very system of representation they shun. While this is partly (and inevitably) true, I would venture that what the woman writer takes from an androcentric system is not so much representation itself as certain representational strategies that she finds useful. This calculated reappropriation is not unrelated to the way a predominantly male literary establishment has viewed–and continues to view–women writers. One should keep in mind that in Latin America, critics have tended less to read the work of women authors than to dramatize the anomalies they attributed to them as persons (115).

Women authors, thus, frequently act in a conscious awareness of these exclusionary practices, and self-reflexively play upon them as drama, as mask, and as strategy. To cite a specific example, Rosario Castellanos's *Poesía no eres tú* [Poetry You Are Not] works within and against a (post) Romantic (Bécquer) literary tradition in which the female figures as poetic object but never a writing subject. There is, in this volume of poetry as a whole, a carefully calibrated, self-consciously calculated reappropriation and reinscription of these time-worn, identifiably masculinist, representational strategies. Reformulations of literary history–of the literary canon–need to take into consideration how, for writers like Castellanos, the supposition of exclusion has until very recently functioned in a paradoxical manner as a significantly productive point of departure for creative expression. One more catch-22: to rewrite literary history would be to write the power and poignancy out of many oppositional women's texts.

Let us remind ourselves of a very few basic structural constraints on women writers that have remained constant from post-independence times to the present: (1) Public literary culture, by definition, is male culture; thus, women's literary culture occurs most typically in specific, restricted spaces such as the women's periodical, the upper class women's literary salons or teas, or the contemporary workshops with an almost purely internal exchange of materials and little public resonance outside the group and its limited distribution network; (2) women readers are perceived by the literary establishment as slightly scandalous–frivolous or inadequate readers of mostly inferior texts written for them by other women; (3) oddly enough, however, women writers are harbingers of the potential dissolution of society, and prominent writers throughout the last 200 years have pontificated on the repercussions of taking women's texts too seriously–or, alternatively, not seriously enough. As the *Seminar* writers remind us, "the image of women as readers seems to pose little threat to this configuration: Reading counts as a form of consumption in bourgeois terms. The image of the women who writes, on the other hand, can be threatening." One index to the threat can be read in the precarious publication histories of women's fiction and female-run and woman-oriented presses, journals, and magazines such that "the short lives of most of the entries . . . attest to the hostile environment in which many of these publications were often carried out. The ephemeral character of many of the publications . . . should thus be read as a sign of struggle and scarcity" (Bergmann et al. 175, 178). What I will try to do in the following few pages is to look at the ways such intellectual and economic constraints have shaped some Latin American women's poetry and fiction.

Writing Culture

One important and inescapable condition of Latin American women's writing is that it has always been a largely elite enterprise. Most of the women who write do tend to belong to a single class: the bourgeoisie (as do most of the men, but that always seems more irrelevant somehow). Since the stereotypical "rich girl" is so easy to mock–much easier, in fact, than the stereotypical rich young man–her already-limited access to the literary forums is even more mediated by suspicion of her talents, her motives, and her character. When we look specifically at post-independence women's writing, it does not help, of course, that by and large the women writing socially committed work–the most visible contingent of "serious" writers–are intentionally and strategically duplicitous in their positioning with respect to the masculinist society around them. It is curious, however, that attacks on elite women's championing of social issues often take the form of critiques based on these women's presumed class affiliations and prejudices.

Beatriz Sarlo talks about the reformist thrust of much women's writing in post-independence Latin America, positing that "this trait may explain one of the strategies . . . that consists of the twofold movement of conquering spaces and reassuring men that their privileges and hegemony are not at stake in each movement" (232). Basically, then, the challenge for women is to decry gender inequalities while leaving male authority intact, to leave the private, domestic sphere without straying from their primary responsibilities to husband and children. These necessarily duplicitous gestures, while still part of some women's social and political repertoire to this day, are particularly evident in nineteenth- and early twentieth-century reformist literature, and no matter how many sops were thrown their way, the men were not fooled by them. In Masiello's words, "women were often perceived as straying from the family unit, . . . promoting activities that undermined larger state interests" (1990, 29). Some of the most interesting women writers of the early twentieth century respond to this accusation of straying from the national/family fold by choosing displacement. As Masiello notes, the novels by María Luisa Bombal (1910–1980; Chile), Norah Lange (1906-1973; Argentina), Teresa de la Parra (1889–1936; Venezuela) (see **Figure** 1), and others (we might add travel narratives such as Flora Tristán's (1803–1844) memoirs of her trip to her homeland of Peru as well) are deeply imbued with images of female homelessness: "They refused the unifying discourse that maintains the female body in place. . . . Female migration, travel, and orphanhood or abandonment thus provide the motivation for women's fiction of the 1920s" (Masiello 1990, 37).

What I would like to point out briefly with respect to these formulations, which seem to be absolutely correct and accurate, is the way in which the figure of the rebellious woman writer as well as the figure of the reformist fit within a particular

Figure 1.

Photograph of Teresa de la Parra (Ana Teresa Parra Sanojo, 1889-1936) c. 1924. (Courtesy of Beatriz González Stephan)

discursive field defined by spatial conceptions organized through a dominant, masculinist society. Thus, the reformist woman wants to "conquer" (male-associated activity) spaces formerly denied her, and proposes to do so through intact metaphors of placid domesticity which, whether assumed in good faith or as a duplicitous strategy, nevertheless force the structure of the text into the dominant culture's discursive space. The transgressive woman "strays" from this space (an ambivalent activity generally marked in dominant society by unacceptable sexual expression), and in so doing lays claim to the potentialities of travel: an activity strongly associated with educated white males. As James Clifford writes, tongue in cheek: "'Good travel' (heroic, educational, scientific, adventurous, ennobling) is something men (should) do. Women are impeded from serious travel. . . . 'Lady' travelers (bourgeois, white) are unusual, marked as special, . . . forced to conform, masquerade, or rebel discreetly within a set of normatively male definitions and practices" (105). In both cases, the woman writer's transgressive behavior falls within the boundaries of Latin American bourgeois culture.

Unsurprisingly, contemporary women writers have attempted to come to terms with this inherited impasse, struggling, as Molloy puts it, to cast literary, cultural, ethnic, and ideological groupings into the feminine mode (122). Rosario Castellanos (1925–1974), for one, implicitly recognizes and takes into account a tradition that marks women writers as bourgeois dilettantes and women readers as superficial and morally deficient. Her essay on María Luisa Bombal, openly marked as a celebration of the unexplored potentiality of the female reader and of the female novelist, proposes to exploit the familiar derogatory image, reversing the valoration so as to emphasize the slippery, unstable, performative qualities of Latin American feminine self-figuration:

> Cuando la mujer latinoamericana toma entre sus manos la literatura lo hace con el mismo gesto y con la misma intención con la que toma un espejo: para contemplar su imagen. Aparece primero el rostro . . . Luego el cuerpo . . . El cuerpo se viste de sedas y de terciopelos, que se adorna de metales y de piedras preciosas, que cambia sus apariencias como una víbora cambia su piel para expresar . . . ¿qué? Las novelistas latinoamericanas parecen haber descubierto mucho antes que Robbe-Grillet y los teóricos del *nouveau román* que el universo es superficie. Y si es superficie pulámosla para que no oponga ninguna aspereza al tacto, ningún sobresalto a la mirada. Para que brille, para que resplandezca, para que nos haga olvidar ese deseo, esa necesidad, esa manía de buscar lo que está más allá, del otro lado del velo, detrás del telón.
>
> Quedémonos, pues, con lo que se nos da: no el desarrollo de una estructura íntima, sino el desenvolvimiento de una sucesión de transformaciones. (Mujer 145)

When the Latin American woman takes a piece of literature between her hands she does it with the same gesture and the same intention with which she picks up a mirror: to contemplate her image. First the face appears. Then the body. . . . The body is dressed in silk and velvet, that is ornamented with precious metals and jewels, that changes her appearance as a snake changes its skin to express . . . what? Latin American women novelists seem to have discovered long before Robbe-Grillet and the theoreticians of the *nouveau roman* that the universe is surface. And if it is surface, let us polish it so that it does not present any roughnesses to the touch, no shock to the gaze. So that it shines, so that it sparkles, in order to make us forget that desire, that need, that mania, of looking for what is beyond, on the other side of the veil, behind the curtain.

Let us remain, therefore, with what has been given us: not the development of an intimate structure but the unenveloping of a series of transformations.

I am very taken by this image and wrote about it extensively in *Talking Back*, focusing on Castellanos's manipulation of a traditional metaphor of the bored, upper-class woman to intuit the startling possibilities of a feminine aesthetics as a radically different model for feminist politics. Castellanos's novel response to the figure of "Woman," then, is neither traditionally reformist nor traditionally rebellious; what she does with the abstraction is to adopt it, revalorize it, and read it against itself in a specular relationship that defines the woman author and her woman reader in the context of a field that includes, as it erases, the mediating presence of a masculinist tradition within which—and for which—it ostensibly and self-reflexively inscribes its primary image structure. Such diabolically complex tactics inform the apparently simple lyric forms of Castellanos' *Poesía no eres tú*, notably in much-cited poems such as her "Malinche." Sylvia Molloy has also intuited variations on an analogously defined performative practice in writers as diverse in national origin and genre as Elena Garro (1917–1998; Mexico; novel), Alfonsina Storni (1892–1938; Argentina; lyric poetry), and Rosario Ferré (b. 1938; Puerto Rico; short story), where she identifies a performative, against-the-grain reading of stereotypical female figures from classic mythology as the typical feature of a slippery, specular, feminist practice of reading and writing.

Molloy's analysis of Gabriela Mistral's (1889–1957) (see **Figure 2**) lamentably little-known poem "Electra in the Mist" offers a model of precise reading for the working of this trope (112–13); her findings could well be extended to some of the most exciting recent poetry dealing with reappropriations of the mythic poetic figure of Woman, such as work by poets as different as Myriam Moscona (b. 1955; Mexico; in her poetic reappropriation of biblical images like Eve and Lot's wife from a specifically Jewish tradition) and Nancy Morejón (b. 1944; Cuba; as in her use of Afro-Caribbean spirituality to rewrite the figure of the strong Afrocentric woman). In each case, we have works that are deliberately cast in the feminine and, with writers like Moscona and Morejón, who also attentive to the shaping experience of race and ethnicity, and whose works clearly reflect their necessary propping up and place within the dominant literary tradition, while at the same time they give that tradition an unusual twist. It is also worth note that, by the 1990s, such deliberately performative gestures that can trace their heritage back to the much-reviled poor little rich girl have opened out onto a scenario that includes complex and valid rethinkings of class and also of literary texts.

Numerous critics have commented on the role of women's writing in providing a space for marginalized peoples to enter into a national or international literary construction: Ur-texts in this regard include Clorinda Matto de Turner's (1852–1909) *Aves sin nido* [1889; *Torn from the Nest*, 1998], a denunciation of

Figure 2.

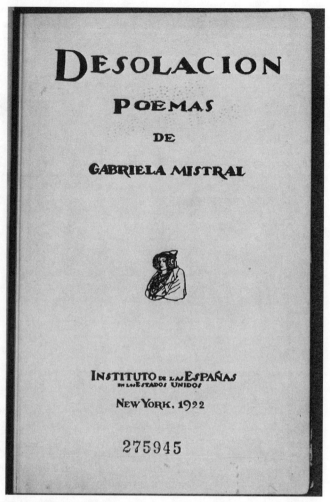

Photograph of cover of Desolacíon, 1922. *(Courtesy of John P. Robarts Research Library, University of Toronto)*

exploitative land tenure practices in Peru, which inaugurated the subgenre of the *indigenista* novel; and Cuban Gertrudis Gómez de Avellaneda's (1814–1873) *Sab* [1841], with its provocatively abolitionist sentiment and tale of miscegenated love. One alternative tracing of literary history would look more closely at these literary foremothers and trace their influence on contemporary literary practices, where an alliance, or at the very least a dialogue, between women of different races and classes frequently serves as the grounding trope of powerful contemporary narratives. Readily identifiable examples would include stories such as Rosario Ferré's (Puerto Rico) "Cuando las mujeres quieren a los hombres" ["When Women Love Men"]—which is really about women's relationships to each other across class and race boundaries—and Elena Garro's (1917–1998 Mexico) "La culpa es de los tlaxcaltecas" ["It's the Fault of the Tlaxcaltecas"]—in which a modern woman feels the weight of an indigenous past—or novels like Giaconda Belli's (b. 1948; Nicaragua) *Mujer habitada* [Inhabited Woman] and Laura Esquivel's (b. 1950; Mexico) megaphenomenon *Como agua para chocolate* [*Like Water for Chocolate*].

If we can say, however, relatively uncontroversially, that literature has class and race, we cannot make the same statement about gender, which remains as slippery as ever. Partly the problem is one of the relative isolation of women's literary production both in the diverse Latin American cultural contexts and in the various national and continental literary histories and anthologies. As long as the woman writer remains marginalized in/from the canon, it is impossible to talk about "women's" writing; all we can discuss are female conformists (defined in traditional texts as the typical woman writer, but always condescended to) and those reformers and rebels who exist as exceptions to a writing culture defined as male. Thus, for example, Soledad Bianchi suggests that in the 1980s "for the first time one can speak of women's writing, that way, in plural" (129), and Nelly Richard hints that only in the presence of such relative richness of field can we return to the question that has been exercising writers and critics for years: "Does writing have a sex?" Until achieving this critical mass, the question could not be submitted to a careful study, since it tended, says Richard, to be understood less as a theoretical concern than as the always already politically motivated construction of a thinker whose covert intention is to relegate women once again to a secondary and particularized position with respect to real literature, that is, writing by men. While the position is understandable in a literary historical context, Richard suggests that contemporary variations on the statement, "I'm not a woman writer; I'm a writer," are suspect on a number of grounds, including, most obviously, the political orientation of the author making the assertion (here the traditional close ties between pro-woman activism and feminist theorizing in Chile come very much to the fore). For herself, Richard proposes that feminist literary theory take into account and incorporate the dimension of "writing as textual productivity as well that of identity as a play of representations . . . in order to construct the 'feminine' as the signified and signifier of the text" (34).

A creative and rigorous grappling with these concerns would reshape our understanding of the field itself; in the extensions of her argument, Richard sees a necessary rethinking of all knowledge claims: not just literary but also scientific, not just academic but also social (21). Richard's politically-fraught understanding of the question "Does writing have a sex?" and her answer to that question in terms of the implications of assuming a distinct writing culture for women pose significant problems for further reflection, especially in the Chilean literary/political context that is the concrete referent for her meditations. Notably, she, too, subscribes to a theory relating women's textual production to a performative play of identity. In her work, however, the concept of performance has come a long, long way from the more naïve masquerades of the late nineteenth-century reformers who served as her foremothers; and yet, a more rigorous tracing of this literary history could well give us some clues as to the transnational and transhistorical construction of a women's writing culture outside the limited and limiting circles of salon, workshop, and proper feminine teas.

Easy Women/Tough Women

For the final section of this essay, I want to take another tack and look at another way of construing women's literary cultures. Traditional concepts of women's writing place authors in one of two typical spaces: (1) the subliterary and (2) the avant garde. Here too, we are dealing with conditions of struggle and scarcity, of the shaping effects of intellectual and economic constraints on women's poetry and fiction—but in a somewhat different forum. It is not altogether clear to me how women came to be associated both with the most facile and the most technically difficult literary forms, except as a reflection of reader prejudice and of dominant literary culture expectations playing themselves out across the body of women's writing. Thus, women's literary works tend to be assigned to one or the other of these discontinuous poles rather than to the rich spectrum associated with male writing. Thus too, we intuit the active forgetting and repression, the most blatant forms of exclusion, including outright misrepresentations of lines of influence leading back to women's writing.

A case in point is the relatively recent recovery of the potent impact of Elena Garro's work on Gabriel García Márquez and the "boom" in general, as well as upon the thought and poetry of Octavio Paz. Here is a woman whose work is gigantic in its own right, whose influence has shaped the two most recent literary Nobel Prize winners in Latin America, but who, until recently, has been written out of literary history or included only as a footnote. The subliterary forms (women's novels, lyric poetry) have been by one measure—sales—consistently and amazingly popular throughout the two centuries under analysis. This perennial "bestsellerdom" is so notorious that an argument could be made for the primacy of women's fiction as a national cultural form as against the less widely read products of the male imagination, which, one could argue, really circulate only among a narrow elite. Unfortunately, critics and literary historians have felt they can safely ignore such works, since they represent popular culture tastes rather than the more "refined" values of high art. Besides, as more than one feminist critic has noticed, regardless of subjective (or supposedly "objective") considerations of literary quality, when both the authors and the readers are female-identified, feminocentric projects get short shrift from the (male) critical establishment.

On the other hand, token women are consistently read into avant-garde movements, where their presence is fragmentary and marginalized. These writers tend to dissolve into the avant-garde as indistinguishable also-rans or, alternatively, as the bracketed exceptions to the rule. In neither case is the avant-garde woman writer read particularly well; whether absorbed or excluded, she is still an oddity, an exception. The contrast with the popular women writers is patent: low cultural capital versus high cultural capital; excellent local distribution versus a slight international distribution; high readership versus low readership. Only in one spot do these twain meet: In neither case is the woman writer given recognition or credit for innovative and influential theoretical or practical contributions to the larger (male) cultural construct. Yet, if arguably, the discussion in the previous section of this essay could be construed as defining a closed circuit of women's writing culture—a discussion between women, as it were—the same cannot be said with respect to popular culture and to the avant-garde, where a different model of circulation pervades the social scenario. Historical accuracy alone would seem to dictate a more equitable treatment in even the most traditional of literary studies.

In her tongue-in-cheek advice to Chilean women, *Diez cosas que una mujer en Chile no debe de hacer jamás* [Ten Things That a Woman in Chile Must Never Do], Elizabeth Subercaseaux (b. 1945) includes the following advice to the hopeful woman writer:

> Los hombres no la van a tomar en serio. . . . Si es escritora, los críticos se la van a tragar como una sandía, van a partir diciendo que su literatura es "inconsistente," "de gusto masivo," "facilona," sus personajes nunca tendrán "profundidad sicológica" y usted

siempre estará copiándole a alguien, que siempre será hombre, a Gabriel García Márquez, a Juan Rulfo, a Carlos Fuentes, a Julio Cortázar. Sus colegas escritores no van a leer sus libros. (69)

Men are not going to take you seriously. . . . If you are a writer, the critics will swallow you like a watermelon, they're going to start out saying your literature is "inconsistent," "for the masses," "easy," your characters will never have "psychological depth," and you will always be copying someone, who will always be a man: Gabriel García Márquez, Juan Rulfo, Carlos Fuentes, or Julio Cortázar. Your male counterparts will not read your books.

Of course, someone is reading these books that the male critical establishment has officially discarded as irrelevant or uninteresting, and so many someones have read books like those of Isabel Allende (b. 1942) and Laura Esquivel that the establishment has had to begin, at least, to rethink the role of the formerly ignored and much despised woman reader in shaping literary taste. These meditations have ranged from reassessing the history of what Fredric Jameson (referring to canonical male writers, of course) calls the "art romance" (113) to Octavio Paz's passionate and somewhat embattled "defensa de la literatura difícil" ("defense of difficult literature"), which includes furious denunciations of evil marketing ploys and unsophisticated reading strategies. As Sandro Cohen notes, "When *Like Water for Chocolate* sold over 10,000 copies, the writers of literary fiction got nervous; between 50,000 and 300,000 they began to fall back on disdain; with the 2,000,000 copies sold in the United States, they erased it from their map" (1996, 131). Male bestsellers have typically been received by the establishment as representing the best and finest Latin America has to offer; García Márquez (b. 1927) is the archetype of this phenomenon, and works like *El amor en los tiempos de cólera* [*Love in the Time of Cholera*] or *Del amor y otros demonios* [*Love and Other Demons*] are notable for their transparent attempt to appeal to the female reader, who is presumed to gobble up all books with "love" in the title. Female bestsellers, on the other hand, are constructed as a blot on the continental escutcheon and need to be ignored, explained away, or relegated to the dread class of "literatura lite" ("lite lit"). However, at some point it becomes overwhelmingly clear that traditionalist culture and literary critics are living in an embattled alternative reality. Jean Franco would add that Esquivel is now probably better known than García Márquez, making her the benchmark figure for Latin American fiction outside Latin America (1996, 226). If the implications of her statement are followed through to their radical conclusion, it would necessarily follow that the entire modern Latin American literary canon would undergo a complete dislocation, in which primacy would inescapably have to be given to women writers, with the male counterparts in a secondary, less vital, less path-breaking position.

Not all feminists, and certainly not all Latin American feminists, celebrate the seductions of the art romance. Tununa Mercado (b. 1939; Argentina), for example, criticizes the neoliberal market economy that propels many such works into "bestsellerdom"; Franco's excellent summary of her critique highlights Mercado's concern that "women's literature that relies on the seduction of traditional narrative despite its 'feminism' thus becomes a literature of accomodation with narrative seduction analogous to the seduction of the commodity" (1996, 228). For similar reasons, Chilean writer Diamela Eltit (b. 1949) critiques much of contemporary women's writing as counterproductive, as once more marginalizing women into

the ghetto space of romance even when the theme is ostensibly feminist (Franco 1996, 233–4).

Significantly, it is Diamela Eltit, whose work Nelly Richard calls "beyond a doubt the most explosive Latin American literature of these years" (42), who forcefully articulates the need to destabilize the edifice of literature, working from a hostility not only to art romance but to all traditional stories, and creating a new aesthetic rooted in the experience of marginalization and exclusion. Already in her early novels, as Kadir writes, Eltit "subjects the question of gender and gender constructs . . . into a rending critique that scorches historical commonplaces." This violence occurs both in reference to sociopolitical reality and at the level of syntax: "the Spanish language . . . is wrenched from its authoritative procedures, grammatical protocols, and rhetorical graces"(180). Her difficult and fragmentary texts tend to be associated with the avant-garde (however defined), but Eltit's choice of image and focus makes her work doubly difficult to read. In a roundtable on teaching, Mary Louise Pratt uses Eltit as an example of the problem of reading avant-garde texts in general: "As we were reading one of these writers, the Chilean Diamela Eltit, a batch of students refused to deal with the text. They had never encountered an avant-garde text: their backgrounds did not include Rimbaud, Pound, and so on, and they did not know how to read it" ("Teaching Literature" 105). Pratt points to an important concern in literary teaching and reminds us of the interdependence of pedagogical concerns with the literary canon; her students cannot read Eltit, she assumes, because they do not know their literary history. Interestingly enough, however, the line of descent Pratt so briefly outlines is a European male one marked by France (Rimbaud) and the United States (Pound).

Pratt reminds us of the internationalization of the avant-garde such that U.S. students, in order to read a contemporary Chilean woman, require a grammar and an aesthetics derived from European and U.S. men. In this respect, Pratt's comment reflects precisely the dilemma of those who attempt to rewrite literary history so as to depict more accurately the range of human expression by people from all parts of the sex-gender spectrum. At the same time, her brief comment opens onto a question involving how the avant-garde is constructed and understood. I would posit that even for the student familiar with Rimbaud and Pound, Eltit would cause a disquieting dislocation of expectations that could well relegate her once again to the realm of the almost-rans, the literary footnotes. For example, the central metaphor of *Vaca sagrada* [*Sacred Cow*] is menstruation, and no traditional literary historical understanding of avant-garde poetics either in the United States, Europe, or Latin America offers the reader any key to this particular symbolic cultural map. For this kind of international literary bloodline one would need to look to writers like Adrienne Rich (b. 1929) or Sandra Cisneros (b. 1954) rather than Ezra Pound (1885–1972); that is, the reader needs to have an understanding of what has been traditionally excluded from the avant-garde in order to reconstruct the tradition of an alternative avant-garde that problematizes the sacred cows of literature.

Similar arguments could be made with respect to many other writers loosely associated with the avant-garde. Thus, for example, as Elia Kantaris notes, the work of Uruguayan writer Armonía Somers (1914–1994) has consistently been met with bafflement and repulsion from the appearance of her first novel, *La mujer desnuda* [The Naked Woman] in 1950:

"From the very outset of her writing career, the pen name Armonía Somers became synonymous with scandal and moral outrage." Most famously, in canon-maker Ángel Rama's 1963 article where he describes Somers' work with adjectives like "uncanny," "disconcerting," "repulsive," "incredibly fascinating" (Kantaris 83–4). In Somers' works, too, like Eltit's, a woman's body serves as a focal point for symbolic mapping, and much of the fascination and disgust provoked in critics by the work has to do with the male-trained eye's response to all that bodily fluid. Likewise, Mexican poet Coral Bracho (b. 1951), whose connection to U.S.-based LANGUAGE poets has been much remarked, also specifically confronts the Mexican literary canon by exploding the conventions of erotic poetic imagery and combining in her poems lyric expression with explicit sexual language with scientific terms for a disconcerting and (for the traditionally trained reader) alienating effect. To construct an avant garde aesthetics that would permit a reading of such writers as these would be to recur to a literary canon giving pride of place to foremothers like Alfonsina Storni (1892–1938) whose poems, in Molloy's words, "use body fragments . . . for the purpose of self portraiture. These bare fragments are not synecdoches . . . . It is a way, finally, of wresting interpretive control from readers motivated by desire" (117). Similar comments could be made about many, many other writers associated with a feminocentric avant garde: Carmen Boullosa (b. 1954) in Mexico, for example, whose works have been met with excitement and puzzlement for the kinds of transvestite and transgendered positions of characters in novels such as her *Duerme* [Sleep], or Colombian Albalucía Ángel (b. 1939), whose technically difficult, highly political, and openly feminist novels have fallen into a critical near-vacuum.

Paradoxically, then, once again–as is the case with "lite lit"–the effort to exclude, or the effect of excluding, women writers once again propels them into the foreground as the most crucial (if underrecognized) constituent element of the form from which they are expelled. Avant-garde literature defines itself by its newness, its freshness; works like those of Eltit, Somers, Boullosa, or Ángel that do not yet have a pre-existing grammar are the sine qua non of the style. In terms of literary history, rectifying this patent omission or underrepresentation would require a rethinking of the entire project so as to take into account the way in which many of the most important innovative practices and theoretical advances have come from female authors' feminocentric texts.

Final Thoughts

This essay has concerned itself exclusively with women's writing culture in Latin America and the ways in which a Latin American(ist) feminist analysis helps to more accurately map the contours of a more complete literary history. A contributing factor to a more fruitful dialogue has been the literary feminists' growing awareness of the limited and shrinking market for literature, in Latin America as elsewhere, under pressure from television as the narrative genre of increasing preference, popular song as the preferred poetry, and *testimonios* as an ever-more heralded hybrid of oral and written cultures. U.S. Latin Americanist literary feminism is increasingly taking cognizance of popular culture forms and, as it moves closer to culture studies, there are opportunities for renewed connections with the strong tradition of well-developed, social science–based Latin American feminist theories. Curiously, the "lite lit"/avant-garde debate is reinscribed here once

again. Franco notes: "The class privilege of the intelligentsia has always posed a problem for Latin Americans, but in women's writing it becomes particularly acute since women writers are privileged and marginalized at one and the same time" (1992, 70). I would add to Franco's comment that privilege and marginalization act as floating signifiers that can be applied almost universally, with different valences, to widely different writers: Eltit is privileged (in the traditionally theoretical realms of the academy) and marginalized (in popular terms); Esquivel is also privileged (in popular culture, and in popular culture studies) and marginalized (in the academy), in precisely the opposite configuration. "Lite lit," thus, seems to offer a distinct advantage not only to the large number of female readers throughout the Spanish-speaking world, but also as the basis for social science–informed studies of popular culture. By implication then, the perceived hegemony of metropolitan thought will necessarily be broken up against more culturally sensitive local elaborations of theory. Latin American feminist sociology focusing on specific female cultures in specific regions–for instance, Norma Iglesias Prieto's (b. 1959) *La flor más bella de la maquiladora*, 1985 [*Beautiful Flowers of the Maquiladora*, 1997]–and the international literary market are slowly coming to accommodations, mutual recognitions, and fruitful collaborative efforts.

I agree with Nelly Richard that it is now impossible to talk about Latin America, even from within Latin America, without reference to metropolitan discourse: Her own metropolitan debt is very much apparent in her theoretically informed, rigorous analyses of feminist theory in the Chilean context. I am more optimistic than her, however, about the current situation, at least as it involves Latin American and Latin Americanist feminist culture workers. Thinkers throughout the Americas have become disillusioned with canonical theoretical models that were created out of and for other cultural conditions. Most importantly, the last few years have seen a widespread recognition of cultural basis and bias of a theoretical structure formerly imagined to be transparent and universal. While the power/knowledge relations remain severely unequal between theory talk and any kind of Latin American work, the most pertinent question for Latin Americanists seems to be how to rethink issues derived from Euro-American theoretical discourse so as to recontextualize them for a reality that we all know is vastly distinct from that of the Paris intellectual environment. This work is going forward in universities and research institutes throughout the Americas, and in many other sites and publications, where thinkers and theorists are finding a third way, neither rigidly local nor uncritically metropolitan, to speak and write literary history in the context of the active contributions of Latin American feminist thought.

Works Cited

Bergmann, Emilie et al. 1990. *Seminar on Feminism and Culture in Latin America. Women, Culture, and Politics in Latin America*. Berkeley: University of California Press.

Bianchi, Soledad. 1992. "Lectura de mujeres." In *Ver desde la mujer*. Ed. Olga Grau. Santiago, Chile: Cuarto Propio.

Castellanos, Rosario. 1984. *Mujer que sabe latín. . . .* Mexico City: Fondo de Cultura Económica.

———. 1988. *Poesía no eres tú*. Saint Paul, MN: Graywolf Press.

Castillo, Debra. 1992. *Talking Back: Toward a Latin American Feminist Literary Criticism*. Ithaca: Cornell University Press.

Clifford, James. 1992. "Traveling Cultures." *Cultural Studies*. Ed. Lawrence Grossberg, Cary Nelson, Paula Treichler. New York: Routledge. 96–112.

Cohen, Sandro. 1992. "Defensa de la literatura difícil." Special issue. *Vuelta*. 16.188.

———. 1996. "El escritor y los libros en tiempos de crisis: México, 1996." *Revista de literatura mexicana contemporánea* 1.2 :127–32.

Franco, Jean. 1992. "Going Public: Reinhabiting the Private." *On the Edge: The Crisis of Contemporary Latin Culture*. Ed. George Yudice, Jean Franco, and Juan Flores. Minneapolis: University of Minnesota Press. 65–83.

———. 1996. "Afterword: From Romance to Refractory Aesthetic." *Latin American Women's Writing: Feminist Readings in Theory and Crisis*. Ed. Anny Brooksbank Jones and Catherine Davies. Oxford: Oxford University Press. 226–37.

Gelpí, Juan G. 1993. *Literatura y paternalismo en Puerto Rico*. San Juan: Ed. de la Universidad de Puerto Rico.

Jameson, Fredric. 1981. *The Political Unconscious: Narrative as a Socially Symbolic Act*. Ithaca, NY: Cornell University Press.

Kadir, Djelal. 1993. *The Other Writing: Postcolonial Essays in Latin America's Writing Culture*. West Lafayette, IN.: Purdue University Press.

Kantaris, Elia Geoffrey. 1995. *The Subversive Psyche: Contemporary Women's Narrative from Argentina and Uruguay*. Oxford: Oxford University Press.

Magnarelli, Sharon. 1985. *The Lost Rib: Female Characters in the Spanish-American Novel*. Lewisburg, PA: Bucknell University Press.

Masiello, Francine. 1986. "Discurso de mujeres, lenguaje de poder: reflexiones sobre la crítica feminista a mediados de la decada del 80." *Hispámerica* 15.45: 53–60.

———. 1989. "Between Civilization and Barbarism: Women, Family and Literary Culture in Mid-Nineteenth Century Argentina." *Cultural and Historical Grounding for Hispanic and Luso-Brazilian Feminist Literary Criticism*. Ed. Hernán Vidal. Minneapolis: Institute for the Study of Ideologies and Literature. 517–66.

———. 1990. "Women, State, and Family in Latin American Literature of the 1920s." *Seminar on Feminism and Culture in Latin America. Women, Culture, and Politics in Latin America*. Ed. Emilie Bergmann et al. Berkeley: University of California Press. 27–47.

Molloy, Sylvia. 1991. "Introduction." *Women's Writing in Latin America*. Ed. Sara Castro Klarén, Sylvia Molloy, and Beatriz Sarlo. Boulder: Westview Press. 107–24.

Richard, Nelly. 1993. *Masculino/femenino: Prácticas de la diferencia y cultura democrática*. Santiago, Chile: Francisco Zegers.

Sarlo, Beatriz. 1991. "Introduction." *Women's Writing in Latin America*. Ed. Sara Castro Klarén, Sylvia Molloy, and Beatriz Sarlo. Boulder: Westview Press. 231–48.

Sommer, Doris. 1991. *Foundational Fictions: National Romances of Latin America*. Berkeley: University of California Press.

Steele, Cynthia. 1992. *Politics, Gender, and the Mexican Novel*, 1968–1988: *Beyond the Pyramid*. Austin: University of Texas Press.

Subercaseaux, Elizabeth. 1995. *Diez cosas que una mujer en Chile no debe de hacer jamás*. Santiago: Planeta.

"Teaching Literature in the Academy Today: A Roundtable." 1997. *PMLA* 112: 101–112.

Valdés, Mario J. and Linda Hutcheon. 1994. "Rethinking Literary History–Comparatively." *American Council of Learned Societies Occasional Paper*, No. 27. New York: ACLS. 1–13.

Valdés, María Elena de, and Mario Valdés. 1995. "Rethinking Latin American Literary History." *Latin America as Its Literature*. Ed. M.E. de Valdés, M.J. Valdés, and R.A. Young. New York: Council on National Literatures. 68–85.

CHAPTER 35

WOMEN WRITING IN
NONTRADITIONAL GENRES

María Elena de Valdés

Women writers in Latin America have traditionally been confined to a liminal space. As literate women they have been situated on the threshold of literary culture and, with a few brilliant exceptions, have looked in as readers, but have not entered as writers. This situation has changed radically in the last quarter of the twentieth century, but the liminality of their traditional place has remained both a historical heritage and a tensional force of empowerment, as explored in the preceding essays. The following historical examination of the alternative literature Latin American women have practiced throughout the long period of exclusion from literary culture assesses women's writing in the nineteenth and twentieth centuries in the so-called personal genres of writing: autobiography, memoirs, diary, and epistolaries. These genres have been practiced by men and women for centuries, but since women could pursue these modes of expression within the social restrictions on writing that governed most Latin American communities, they slowly became genres dominated by women.

A woman who wrote in her diary or wrote letters, the history of her family, or, indeed, her own life story, stayed within the social parameters of acceptable comportment. If Parisian middle-class society was shocked by the public display of independence by George Sand, it was only a surface expression of her deeper transgression of having entered into the literary domain of men. Latin American cultural centers were very remote from the Paris of George Sand, and in this world women cultivated the liminal space of the diary, letter, and life story and slowly built upon the powerful tension derived from liminality to bring forth creativity that finally burst forth in the work of writers like Victoria Ocampo, Rosario Castellanos, or Elena Poniatowska.

My examination of the liminal space of women writers will take up writers from Argentina, Cuba, and Mexico, and to a lesser degree writers from Bolivia, Chile, Colombia, Ecuador, Peru, Uruguay, Venezuela, and Central America. I will begin in the independence period and come up to our own time. In the last part I will also give a brief account of the role journalism has had in adding another threshold for women to cross. Just as the writing of canonical literature was a male domain, so was the newspaper. The fact that many Latin American women writers got their start in journalism is another indicator of how journalism continues to be a major force for change in Latin America.

As we have been seeing in the other essays in this section, the task of recognizing and describing the cultural imaginary of Latin American women is made extremely difficult because we have to begin with the deconstruction of the diverse currents of thought that have informed the literary and cultural histories of the past and have almost completely excluded–or at best marginalized–the writing of women, a practice that now stands out in vivid contrast to the literary histories of other cultures. There is no doubt that literary history has had a major role in the canon formation of the cultural imaginary of Latin America, but what concerns us here is how literary histories have affected participation. By excluding all but the most outstanding women writers such as Sor Juana Inés de la Cruz or Gabriela Mistral, these canon formations have contributed to the concept of separate feminine topics, style, and concerns that can be summed up as domestic issues, child rearing, and early education. Politics, economy, philosophy, history, and art were deemed to be either beyond the intellectual range of women or merely inappropriate because of social decorum. At the start of the twenty-first century it is clear that the decline in the influence of literary histories in the making of a national identity is due to many factors, but one of the most evident is the discrepancy between the cultural reality of Latin America and its historical representation.

It is commonplace to read in contemporary Latin American feminist criticism that women writers have been excluded or marginalized in literary history, and it is also generally agreed, as just noted, that literary history has played a major role in the canon formation of Latin American literature; therefore, we must conclude that the reality of Latin American literary cultures and its representations in the minds of its people stand far apart. But I would go further. The representation of a cultural imaginary that discounts one-half of the population as participants on the basis of gender must be challenged with the charge of misrepresentation. The data recently compiled on the literary histories of Latin America and the relative space allotted to women writers are revealing. The database concentrates only on histories purporting to cover all genres and all the Latin American countries of Spanish and Portuguese heritage. In the slightly more than 100 years of such literary histories (there were only national literary histories before 1893), the attention given to women has been scant, with only slight improvement in the last four decades. For example, Díez Echarri (1960) had 4,437 lines devoted to women writers; Iñigo Madrigal (1982) had 3,774 lines; Goic (1988), 4,328; but lamentably the trend toward inclusion did not continue. The 1996 history edited by González Echevarría and Pupo-Walker has only 2,474 lines on Latin American women writers spread over three large volumes. Although Marcelino Menéndez y Pelayo (1893) wrote about only twenty-one women in contrast to 858 men (i.e., 2 percent of the total number of writers), he wrote more than a passing remark when he did write about a woman. In total the Spanish scholar gave 1,086 lines to women writers. In that 1996 *Cambridge History* by González Echevarría and Pupo-Walker, in the volume covering the same period as Menéndez y Pelayo's work, forty-two women are mentioned in comparison to 1,062 men (4 percent). However, the total space allotted to these women writers was only 523 lines, less than half the space given in the 1893 history covering the same period.

There is considerable reduction of space allotted to women writers in the intervening years: Coester (1916), 331

315

lines; Barrera (1934), 40 lines; Torres Rioseco (1942), 407 lines; Leguizamón (1945), 1,216 lines; Bandeira (1949), 78 lines; Aubrun (1954), 82 lines; Anderson Imbert (1954), 1,428 lines; Bazin (1958), 122 lines; Díez Echarri (1960), 4,437 lines; Englekirk (1965), 269 lines; Lazo (1965), 52 lines; Henríquez Ureña (1966), 39 lines; Valbuena Briones (1967), 630 lines; Gómez Gil (1968), 693 lines; Henríquez Ureña (1969), 76 lines; Leal (1971), 206 lines; Schwartz (1971), 748 lines; Fernández Moreno (1972), 4 lines; Jean Franco (1973), 258 lines; Rodríguez Monegal (1977), 1,470 lines; Jozef (1982), 481 lines; Iñigo Madrigal (1982) 3,774 lines; Sánchez (1982), 210 lines; Bellini (1985), 1,200 lines; Peña Gutiérrez (1987), 300 lines; Goic (1988), 4,328 lines; Teodosio Fernández (1995), 333 lines; and, finally, González Echevarría and Pupo-Walker (1996), Volume 1: 523 lines, Volume 2: 1,243 lines, Volume 3: 708 lines, for a total of 2,474. The low point came in 1972 when the UNESCO history of Latin American literature (Fernández Moreno) reduced the space devoted to women writers to four lines, but we still have a long way to go to return to the coverage of Menéndez y Pelayo.

It is also instructive to examine the most extensive handbook of Latin American literature published to date in Spain, *Manual de la literatura hispanoamericana* (Pedraza Jiménez). The two volumes, covering the Colonial period to the end of the nineteenth century, give us the most accurate approximations of the state of the discipline today, some twenty-five years after the women's movement and in a time when women critics are more evident than ever. There are 3,390 creative writers and scholars cited in this publication; 180 of them are women. Obviously there is a mirage effect occurring today. When one reads the oft-quoted studies of so many women scholars and the revisionary studies of the past, one is tempted to think that radical change has come about; yet only 5.3 percent of this publication treats women, whether creative writers or scholars.

If we consider what Latin American literary history would be like if it included a higher percentage of women writers, we begin to realize that many, if not all, of the generalizations that emanate from a literary history would change and change radically; such questions as the representation of the quotidian or of women would clearly be open for reconsideration. But the larger question involves what is deemed to be historical material and what is not. Enrique Anderson Imbert stated in his *Historia de la literatura hispanoamericana* [1954; History of the Literature of Spanish America] that he was writing a history of the literary works themselves and would not be concerned with the culture that produced it. He certainly followed through on his stated intention. Today one would question whether such a history is a history at all. Does it not risk becoming an elaborate inventory of who did what and when? I contend that literary works must be contextualized in the literary culture that produced them, and none demands this more than the personal writing of autobiographies, memoirs, and diaries.

In assessing personal genres we must take some care to distinguish the public from the private spheres of textual intentionality. Both autobiography and memoir are written for the public sphere and, thus, the writer must perforce take a public stand on the issues, persons, and incidents she recounts. However, the diary and the epistolary form were for the most part not intended for public dissemination. These modes of writing are clearly in the private sphere,

whether the intended reader is oneself or the addressee of a letter. Therefore the publication of writing from the private sphere in a sense creates an unprotected text, which makes the writer extraordinarily vulnerable. An unknown body of material by Latin American women has remained in the private sphere for which it was written, but as these voices from the past begin to emerge in larger numbers, we will begin to redress part of the deficiencies of the construction of the cultural imaginary. The epistolary form is one of the richest unexplored areas of Latin American writing by women. The letter shares some of the intimacy of the diary, but it is arguably situated at the intersection of the private and the public, for it has been given up to its intended reader with an implicit trust that it will be respected as private communication, yet at the same time with the realization that there may well be additional readers, with or without the approval of the letter writer. We must nevertheless study those texts as being in the private sphere, for publication was not the purpose behind the writing. Some remarkable fictional hybrids published in recent years, however, indicate some of the possibilities that lie ahead. Elena Poniatowska's *Querido Diego, te abraza Quiela* [1978; *Dear Diego,* 1986] is an excellent example.

The inclusion of personal genres in literary history, especially those written by women, has great significance, not only as a way of establishing the presence of this mode of women's writing in the cultural discourse, but also as a formative part of the cultural imaginary.

There are not two distinct cultural discourses, one for men and another for women; such essentialism is naive and quite clearly ignores the texts themselves. Cultural discourse has multiple dimensions, and multiple forces are at work, but the almost complete rejection of a role for women in the making of a cultural imaginary is one of the most serious flaws in previous cultural histories. My approach to women's writing in the personal genres recognizes the particularities of each writer but also avoids the essentialist trap of purporting that women's writing is a closed code determined by sex. Without any pretension to being exhaustive, I do aim to observe the cultural diversities of Latin America.

The writer who narrates her life story in autobiography, recounts the specifics of persons and places in memoirs, or records her quotidian activity in a diary is not intent on the depiction of a historical situation; rather, she aims at describing her life experiences. In the case of the epistolary form, the writing is directly focussed on the addressee and the bonds the letter writer wants to establish or maintain with him or her. Performance art is the counterpart to such personal genres in theater. In this case the artist takes her body and her personal beliefs and fashions them into a theatrical presentation. Of course, each text and each performance in these personal genres represent singular, and thus very partial and limited, views of cultural reality; but it is equally evident that these personal viewpoints, when taken collectively, present extremely rich insights into women's participation in the making of the Latin American cultural imaginary (see Chapter 54, this volume).

It is necessary to take into account the double thrust of this essay: On the one hand, I want to examine the way these texts individually reflect the specific situation of women's lives, and, on the other, I want to study these texts collectively, as part of a cultural imaginary that heretofore has been constituted with huge exclusions. Therefore, this second direction involves not only the reconstruction of presence but also a rejection of historiographic absence.

For instance, the writer of a diary describes the situation in which she finds herself and, most importantly, what she has done—her actions—in response to the material and spiritual conditions in which she finds herself. The narrative is, in fact, organized as an explanation of what, how, and why the writer has done what she has. This description of action carries with it all the powers of observation, evaluation, and value judgment that constitute the observation and analysis of the flow of living. Nevertheless, these narrations, to a greater or lesser extent, often also convey certain intuitions that the writer herself does not understand. In some cases these enigmas are expressed in spiritual or religious terms or in metaphors, but in others simply as intimate thoughts.

The writer of an autobiography expands and augments this intertwining of the intimate and the observed that we find in the diary or in the life story. An autobiography has the added burden of making sense of a lifetime, of pointing out continuities, ruptures, and moments of crisis that have had long-lasting effects. In other words, the writer of an autobiography not only goes through the necessary process of selection, but she also has to account for the whole story; thus she must include elements of consistency building, primarily references back to points already made or forward to effects yet to be described.

Notwithstanding the structured nature of autobiography and the relatively basic and less formal structure of memoir and diary, in all three cases we must look at the works as texts and as witnessing a collective presence. A historical novel about a woman or a biography of a woman is different from an autobiography. Novel and biography are only distinguishable by the different truth claims the writer makes; the former can be an admixture of perceived facts and fictional reenactment, while the latter is restricted to what was said and what was done. However, in the case of autobiography both factual descriptions and imagining recollections are used because the truth claim is that the writer is writing about herself, as she has acted and as she thinks she has performed. The writer's text thus postulates that the telling of a life has a certain symbolic function with regard to living as a woman in the specific situations described. The autobiography therefore carries a symbolic weight beyond the limits of the individual.

Autobiography

The Latin American cultures that have the largest number of autobiographies by women are Argentina and Mexico, although the genre is present in all of Latin America. Of course, the circumstances of these women are quite varied, especially in earlier periods. Nevertheless, there are a few generalizations that can be made about women's autobiographies. They deal with the social and religious practices and duties that mark and situate the Latin American woman within a class structure of literate women. The credibility aimed at by the writer, and usually won, is the basis of the genre. Writers of the novel or the transcribed *testimonio* (e.g., Elena Poniatowska's *Hasta no verte, Jesús mío*) only permit a glimpse of intimacy, but the writer of the autobiography cannot hide behind narratological masks. Félix Martínez Bonati has described this partial revelation in the novel as a "qualitative process of world making that the reader accepts and shares." Or, as Doris Sommer writes in the case of Rigoberta Menchú's *testimonio,* "the persona of Rigoberta

cannot engage in intimacy because the *testimonio* is not about her but about her people." In the autobiography, by contrast, the writer must convince her readers that she has told them everything to the extent that she is able, or she will risk losing them.

In an autobiography the Latin American woman selects the quotidian that will be included in terms of the social class structures that govern her life. From this perspective, she both recalls events and incidents from her past and, at the same time, puts them in context for her reader. It is this general trait, above all others, that makes this genre so valuable for the reconstitution of the cultural imaginary that is representative of Latin America. One of the first autobiographies in Latin America is the work of the Cuban writer Gertrudis Gómez de Avellaneda (1814–1873). Her novels, plays, and poetry were published as soon as completed, with many reprintings and subsequent editions. Her autobiography was not published until 1907, thirty-four years after her death. It was published in Huelva, Spain, and later reprinted in Havana and Madrid in 1914. The autobiography of this writer went through several reprintings; the first extensive study was that of Carmen Bravo-Villasante in 1967. Her autobiography is notable, however, because it is written for a particular reader, Ignacio de Cepeda, "the love of her life." Although he married another woman, he kept Gómez de Avellaneda's autobiography and the letters she wrote him from 1839 to 1854 and instructed his wife to have them published after his death.

A large number of earlier autobiographies written by Latin American women are, at best, sources for the study of the way of life of the richest elite and are quite a vivid contrast to the far greater number of memoirs written by other women. For example, *Reminiscencias* is an autobiography of childhood and adolescence by the Argentinean Carlota Garrido de la Peña (1870–1912), written in 1888 and published in 1893; the narrative culminates in a description of courtship with the unique adventure of her young life, sharing a sugar pear with her fiancé. Another example of the elite's remembrances is Concepción Lombardo de Miramón (1835–1921), wife of Miguel de Miramón, Maximilian's strongest supporter among the military. Her autobiography describes life among the power elite during the short-lived French adventure in Mexico. Although the text covers the period from 1835 to 1917, it was not published until 1980. If we bear in mind that, in general, autobiography has been downplayed in Latin American literary histories, then we should not be surprised that women's autobiography rarely merits more than a passing remark. For example, the autobiography of José Vasconcelos has entered many of the more recent histories, as it should, but in contrast Victoria Ocampo's work only gets a few lines in González Echevarría and Pupo-Walker's 1996 history of Latin America. The resulting under-representation of women's autobiography puts the fairness and comprehensiveness of literary history into question.

The scholar who wishes to probe deeper into this little-studied genre must be prepared to go beyond the books actually entitled "autobiography." For example, the most important autobiography written by a woman in Latin American literature is the brilliant public defense *Respuesta/Answer* that Sor Juana Inés de la Cruz launched against the accusations of the Bishop of Puebla (see Chapters 31 and 32). The Uruguayan poet Juana de Ibarbourou's (1892–1979) autobiography is a one-hour lecture given in the Instituto de Altos Estudios in Montevideo in 1956, entitled "Autobiografía lírica." A similar case is the celebrated Puerto Rican writer Rosario Ferré's (b. 1938) autobiography, "La cocina de la escritura," [The Kitchen of Writing] which was published in *La sartén por el mango* [1984; The Frying Pan by Its Handle]. A more traditional form of publication, that is, as a book, usually only happens with a lifelong presence in the cultural life of a country, as was the case with the Argentinean Silvina Bullrich's (1915–1990) *Mis memorias* [1980; My Memoirs], recording fifty years of activism in women's rights.

The work of Victoria Ocampo (Argentina; 1890–1979) is an exemplary contribution to these personal genres written by Latin American women. In this case it is her autobiography and *Testimonios* that constitute the major work of this intellectual. The autobiography appeared posthumously in six volumes, and her *Testimonios* were published in ten volumes. The *Testimonios* should be considered the contextual complement to the autobiography. These sixteen volumes together constitute rich resource material for the historical study of the literary culture of Argentina and, indeed, of South America over more than half of the twentieth century. Victoria Ocampo had a leading role in the intellectual and artistic development of South America. She was at the center of cultural activity from the time she founded *Sur* in Buenos Aires (1931) to the time of her death at the age of eighty-nine in 1979. In the 1930s she saw *Sur* become the leading intellectual journal in Latin America. Her autobiography was printed by *Sur* in six volumes between 1979, the year of her death, and 1987. Her biographer, Doris Meyer, affirms that she often threatened to destroy the manuscript, and she relates that "Victoria Ocampo researched and described the intimate contradictions of her emotional and intellectual development as a young woman of the privileged class of Argentina. She concentrated her narrative on the years previous to the foundation of *Sur*. In these pages she wrote in order to recover the most critical experiences in her life as a woman, but her social education with all the constraints of discretion and reserve stood in the way of publication of these texts in her lifetime" (375). Ocampo gives a detailed account of the constant battle she had to wage as a woman in an intellectual world modeled by and for men only. A comparative reading of her autobiography and *La Respuesta a Sor Filotea de la Cruz* [*The Answer*] of Sor Juana Inés de la Cruz show how these are the foundational texts of women's autobiography in Latin America.

There was a sudden interest in autobiography in Argentina, in part perhaps prompted by the example of Victoria Ocampo's prolific outpouring of her life story as cultural witness. Such writers as Delfina Bunge de Gálvez, Argentina (1881–1952); Silvina Bullrich, Argentina (1915–1990); Norah Lange, Argentina (1906–1973); and María Rosa Oliver, Argentina (1898–1971) are examples. Lange, a contemporary of Ocampo, has also contributed to this genre with her autobiography, *Cuadernos de infancia* [1937; Notebooks of My Childhood], but it is not very revealing of its subject and primarily focuses on her family. Oliver's three volumes of autobiography, *Mundo, mi casa: Recuerdos de infancia* [1965; My World, My House: Remembrances of my Childhood], *La vida cotidiana* [1969; Quotidian Life], and *Mi fé es el hombre* [1981; I Believe in Man] offer us an interesting counterpoint to Ocampo's highly intellectualized life story.

Writing about Argentina in the 1930s, Oliver can say: "A medida que iba topando con sus problemas más mío sentía el país. Por pertenecer a él yo era en parte responsable de sus problemas" ("As I encountered Argentina's problems, my sense of belonging to it grew. As part of it, I was in part responsible for its problems") (364).

The Chilean Violeta Parra's (1917–1967) autobiography, *Décimas: Una autobiografía en versos* [Décimas: An Autobiography in Verse], is a text of some consequence. She was an extraordinary and gifted poet, artist, and ethnomusicologist. Her autobiography is written in verse and was published posthumously in 1970. Its discourse is as politically committed as she herself was during her life; her own life story is used to highlight her struggle against the widespread abuse of Latin American women. Parra writes about the world she knows and the place in it that women have been given. She condemns a society that honors women as wives and mothers and yet accepts rampant exploitation of women in the workplace, enforced pregnancy, abuse of young girls, and widespread dismissal of wife beating as mere domestic quarreling. She considers this abuse and violence the dark side of her cultural inheritance.

The list of autobiographies by women is much greater than generally assumed. The author of a 1991 study of autobiography in Latin America, Silvia Molloy, has only a rudimentary inventory; this is so, not because of any lack of scholarship, but because of the esoteric publishing practices of Latin America and the marginalized place in which all women's writing was situated until very recently. In addition to the new autobiographies published each year, there are also equal numbers of autobiographies from the past that have been recovered. Even if we leave out the autobiographical story (such as that of Mexican Guadalupe [Pita] Amor's (1920–2000) *Yo soy mi casa* [1957; I Am My House]) or the *testimonio* (which is of relatively recent development and is treated in full in Volume II of this history as a Latin American hybrid genre), we are still confronted with hundreds of writings by women in personal genres. Although there is sometimes a fine line between memoir and autobiography as written by women in Latin America, I think it is important to maintain the distinction that autobiography is the narrating subject's life story, whereas memoir is her description of times and places from her life. A few examples should suffice to indicate the range and diversity of women's autobiography in Latin America. *Benita* (1940) is the autobiography of Benita Galeana (1905–1995), a lifelong Mexican communist activist recounting the poverty into which she was born and the development of her political commitment. Celia Treviño Carranza (b. 1912), who published her *Mi atormentada vida* [1958; My Tormented Life], is from the opposite end of Mexico's social structure from Galeano; they are contemporaries and their autobiographies overlap; however, Galeano covers the period from 1910 to 1940 while Treviño Carranza recounts events in her life from 1912 to 1956. They are both women who broke out of social constraints, Benita as a political activist who does not achieve literacy until her mature years and Treviño, who was born into a distinguished family of musicians, becoming a noted violinist performing with the great symphony orchestras of the world. They share a sense of rebellion against the structures that would restrict them even though they live in two solitudes of Mexico's poor and affluent classes.

One of the most significant aspects of the cultural imaginary of any community, or conglomerate of communities like Latin America, is the sense of belonging. It is precisely because there are clear differences between the narrating subject's relation to his or her community that the exclusion of women's autobiography puts in question the multiple generalizations about national symbols and the sense of identity that have been proposed. One of the most extraordinary autobiographies written by a woman is Mexican Nellie Campobello's (1900–1986) *Las manos de mamá* [1937; *My Mother's Hands*, 1988]. It starts out as a biographical remembrance of her mother, but soon becomes the author's autobiography, especially focusing on her growth and development as an individual. She recreates the mother in order to be able to come to grips with her own identity as a woman independent of her mother, yet linked to her in a common sense of community. A recent development in this area is the series of short autobiographies by Mexican women writers published by UNAM and ECO. Such writers as Brianda Domecq (b. 1942), Esther Krause (b. 1954), Angelina Muñiz (b. 1936), Aline Petterson (b. 1938), María Luisa Puga (b. 1944) have appeared. Of course, these are commissioned autobiographies, written by professional women who have had success as writers.

In all the autobiographies examined here, the narrative is not conditioned by a specific objective, political or otherwise (with the possible exception of Violeta Parra's impassioned account of violence against women). These autobiographies constitute a contextualization of memory that aims, above all, to share the personal perspective with the writer's readers–other women–primarily other Latin American women. This mode of textual remembering has an almost unlimited range of expression. Women's autobiography tends to create a personal view of the material and social circumstances in which their life story has been played out. The emphasis is primarily on the integrity of the social group remembered, rather than on the unique point of view of the writer; for instance, Victoria Ocampo's entire first volume deals with her family's past four generations. Of course, a writer of autobiography has to situate himself or herself within the public social order and, therefore, draw upon a system of values and action that will permit the narration of the personal past. Women, just as much as men, write within an explicit or implicit sense of such social and ethical order, but in women's autobiography there is a tendency to concentrate on the quotidian. The primary goal shared by autobiographies written by women is to give a sense of aesthetic order to the material circumstances and the conditions of life. Latin America is a continent of the most varied political, social, and economic conditions; it is therefore difficult, if not impossible, to venture generalizations. Yet the particular aesthetic and ethical sense of order and the unswerving focus we have found in women's autobiography offer one such common ground. The underlying reason might be that there has been a common heritage of established roles for women in Latin America–whether in the home or in public life–simultaneous with the denial of a public voice. Although these conditions are not unique to Latin America and there are other cultures where more women wrote than in this one, there is a unique quality in these texts in their striving for the creation of a world that is like a private retreat. Without a doubt, the autobiographies examined offer a plethora of circumstances with concomitant information ranging from observation and appreciation to description, for example, of the botanical properties of plants.

Memoirs

The memoir is the oldest and most historically rich of the personal genres. It was well established in European letters before the conquest and soon became a New World mainstay, feeding the insatiable curiosity of European readers about the exotic Americas. It was therefore quite natural that lettered European women in the New World would contribute to this mode of writing. The demand for descriptions of the Americas in Europe far exceeded the supply, thus offering women an unprecedented opportunity to break through the barriers imposed on their writing. In dismissing this genre it is wise to distinguish the memoirs of European women and their encounter with America from the writing of memoirs by Latin American women who had been intellectually and spiritually formed in the Americas.

Every country in Latin America has produced memoirs written by women, and scores of them have been published since the eighteenth century. There are good reasons why this should be so: Since the memoir allows the writer to concentrate on her community rather than herself; it is usually intended for local readership, sometimes as limited as the family, and it does not demand great narrative skills. Therefore it would be fair to say its design and intentionality bespeak the writer's devotion to her community, and the genre often has no literary pretensions beyond vivid description. Nevertheless, I would like to claim a minor but significant role for these texts, for they contribute, as Debra Castillo has written, "to the still nascent emergence of women's voices into the public forum" (243). In addition to witnessing the collective writing presence of women, there are also particularly important memoirs by gifted writers. These remarkable texts are just as rare among men as among women; the difference is that a brilliant memoir by a man will get into literary history and one by a woman will not. A case in point is Margo Glantz (b. 1930) of Mexico and her uncommon *Las genealogías* [1981; *The Family Tree*, 1991], which turns family history into a memoir that speaks to the countless immigrants from Europe's tragic twentieth century. Yet, in the short article on life-writing in the 1996 *Cambridge History of Latin American Literature*, frivolous writing by the Guatemalan Enrique Gómez Carrillo or the "lighthearted chats" by the Argentinean Lucio V. Mansilla enter history, but Glantz does not even merit a passing mention. This history of Latin American literature still retains the heritage of exclusion: Volume II, "The Twentieth Century," has 586 pages of text of which only 22 pages treat women writers, and the index collapses the scant coverage even more. Silvina Ocampo is confused with her sister Victoria, thereby excluding another notable woman from this general guide. How important is one more text in a sea of hundreds of texts, for a literary history can never hope to be exhaustive? The importance in my mind is twofold: First and foremost, we must take into account the significance and achievement of a text within Latin America's literary culture; secondly, but also of importance, is the evidence of diversity as well as of the quotidian in the makeup of the literary culture. *Las genealogías* is a most valuable text on both scores. The immigration of Central European Jews to Latin America and the remarkable literary flowering of transplanted culture have long been excluded from literary history. Margo Glantz is important in her own right as a distinguished writer of fiction as well as scholarly works, and with this memoir she is part of the redressing of a double exclusion—of both women and immigrant populations.

Memoirs like the Mexican Nellie Campobello's (1900–1986) *Cartucho, relatos de la lucha en el norte de México* [1931; *Cartucho* 1988] recover specific memories regarding the Mexican revolution and all of the cruelty and violence of this period; the point of view is that of a young girl remembering. Of equal significance for Mexican historical background is Elena Garro's (1917–1998) *Memorias de España 1937* [1992; Memoirs of Spain 1937], in which she narrates the meeting of Latin American writers and intellectuals in solidarity with the Spanish republic at the "Second International Writers Congress for the Defense of Culture." The memoir is full of personal details about some of the most important writers of the Hispanic world. The sense of the times, the Spanish Civil War, the polarization of left and right in Europe, and the enthusiasm of youth are its highlights.

A number of memoirs consist of travel narrations, written with the supposition that the experiences of the places visited constitute the point of interest. Invariably, however, the strength of the memoir lies in the personality of the writer. Some of the Latin American women who have written travel memoirs are the Cuban María de las Mercedes Santa Cruz y Montalvo, Condesa de Merlin (1789–1852), *La Havane* [1844; Havana], the Colombian Soledad Acosta de Samper (1833–1913), "Recuerdos de Suiza" [Memoirs of Switzerland], the Peruvian Clorinda Matto de Turner (1852–1909), *Viaje de recreo: España, Francia, Inglaterra, Italia, Suiza, Alemania* [1909; Recreational Travel: Spain, France, England, Italy, Switzerland, Germany], the Cuban Dulce María Loynaz (1902–1997), *Un verano en Tenerife* [1958; A Summer in Tenerife], and more recently Silvina Bullrich (1915–1990), *El mundo que yo ví* [1969; The World That I Saw]. Other women writers of memoirs in the twentieth century whose work transcend the local are the Cuban Ofelia Rodríguez Acosta (1902–1975), *Europa era así* [1941; Europe Was Like This]; the Cuban Teté Casuso (b. 1912), *Panorama de México* [1938; Mexican Panorama] and *Recuerdos de un viaje a Europa* [1951; Memoirs of My Trip to Europe]; the Cuban Renée Méndez Capote (1901–1989), *Memorias de una cubanita que nació con el siglo* [1963; Memoirs of a Little Cuban Girl Born with the Century] and *Hace muchos años, una joven viajera* [1983; Many Years Ago, A Young Woman Traveler].

Among numerous memoirs in the nineteenth century, a hybrid of the memoir and the epistolary form was practiced with success by two Cuban writers at the end of the nineteenth century. Aurelia Castillo de González (1842–1920) and Catalina Rodríguez de Morales (1835–1894) write in letter format of their experiences traveling abroad. Rodríguez de Morales published her work in *El Album* from 1881 to 1882. Castillo de González published her texts in *El País* from 1889 to 1891 and then again in 1893; both collections were subsequently published as books. In 1997 the Cuban scholar Luisa Campuzano assembled and wrote an introduction to Castillo de González's *Cartas de México* [Letters from Mexico]. The Argentine Marta Lynch's (1925–1985) travel memoirs, *Apuntes para un libro de viajes* [1977; Notes for a Travel Book] represents the best of the memoir genre and was written for inclusion in general periodicals; the sketches are full of wit, keen observation of other ways, and a reflective look back on her own country.

An example of a European woman, a visitor to the Americas, who wrote memoirs about her American experiences, is Lina Beck Bernard (1824–1888), an Alsatian-Swiss who wrote in French about her role and observations regarding the foundation of Santa Fe in Argentina. She was a feminist who wrote for a European audience about her Argentinean experience, and did so largely through the perspective of the Swiss advocate of matriarchy, J. J. Bachofen. She published *Le Rio Parana: Cinq années de séjour dans la Confederée Argentine 1857–1862* [1864; Parana River: A Five Year Sojourn in the Argentinean Confederation 1857–1862]. Among the most significant memoirs of European women in Latin America is *Au Venezuela, 1876–1892. Souvenirs* [n.d.; In Venezuela. Memories] written by Yrcilia Leontine Perignon Roncajolo between 1879 and 1892 and published in Paris in 1895. Her commentary is unlike that of other European women traveling in the New World in that she passes over all aspects of culture and concentrates on detailed description of the physical geography of the Caribbean and Venezuela. She clearly writes to inform a specific readership in France. Another French woman who wrote a memoir about Venezuela was Jenny Tallenay (1860–1928), who published in Paris in 1884, but the younger Tallenay gives little more than naïve impressions in contrast to the methodical Perignon Roncajolo.

In contrast to the views expressed in other memoirs written by visitors to Latin America, which concentrate on the "exotic" dress, foods, and so on, Fanny Chambers Gooch Iglehart (1842–1913), who lived in Mexico from 1878 to 1885, wrote a memoir, *Face to Face with the Mexicans*, which is 584 pages long and has 200 sketches. She attempts to write a first-hand report on all aspects of life in Mexico. She never hides her vantage point as a North American woman who is part of the massive investment of U.S. capital during this period of the Díaz dictatorship. Her comments are a mixture of sentimental notions about the noble savage, sympathy for a friendly people, and deeply ingrained prejudices of moral and intellectual superiority. The memoir was published in 1887 and is dedicated to Porfirio Díaz. Other women's writings in America that should be noted include Mary Lester's memoir of her stay in Honduras, *A Lady's Ride Across Spanish*, published in her native London (1884); Cora Hayward Crawford from Denver, Colorado, also visits Mexico in 1886 and then publishes a memoir, *The Land of Moctezumas* (1890). This memoir stands in vivid contrast, for example, to Madame Calderón de la Barca's (1804–1882) description of Veracruz and Xalapa. Crawford is primarily overwhelmed by the color and richness of the flora. Of course, her observations are of the surface features of the tropical port of Veracruz because she could not speak Spanish. Finally, there was Ann Maudsley (1854–1939), a British woman who accompanied her archeologist husband to Guatemala and Honduras in a scientific expedition and wrote a detailed and careful memoir of the trip (1893–1894) that was published in London in 1894.

The second half of the twentieth century in Latin America has been beset by a new kind of warfare, one that no longer pits army against army or the national army against the insurrection, but rather one that throws the army up against the civil population in an effort to purge dissidence. The atrocities in Brazil in the 1960s, in Argentina, Chile, and Uruguay in the 1970s, and in El Salvador and Guatemala in the 1980s are a part of contemporary history. As is to be expected, personal genres reflect the political unrest of these nations, and women have not been silent. There are abundant noteworthy examples. One is the memoir (1990) written by Nidia Díaz (pseud., María Marta Valladares Mendoza, b. 1952) about her experiences of prison and torture in El Salvador; she was captured by United States assessors in April 1985 and was released 190 days later in exchange for the daughter of the Salvadorean strongman Napoleón Duarte. The entire memoir was tape recorded at one sitting and later transcribed. As in the case of the other memoirs, the text is not really about the subject. There is next to nothing about her personal life: The entire text is focused on the war, the fate of her fellow prisoners, the sadism of the army doctors and interrogator, and conditions in the cells where she was held.

Diaries

All personal genres have the common denominator of a shared personal experience, and, if the autobiography is the most reflexive with its evident retrospective of a life lived, and the memoir is the most clearly historical in its emphasis on narrating the quotidian of the community, the diary is the most immediate registration of experience. The diary's structure is that of the calendar, and entries are linked only by the presence of the writer. Because of the dominant focus on the here and now, the diary is perhaps the most subjective of personal genres. There is no attempt to sum up or achieve a sense of direction, since, for the most part, each entry is self-contained and is a direct response to immediate circumstances. Diary entries can range from the routine and commonplace to a lyrical emotional response. All in all, the diary offers both intimacy and the quotidian, and, in the hands of women who have had most forms of literary expression denied to them, it displays the occluded subjectivity of Latin American women. The traditional exclusion of women from literary history has not been redressed by the existence of hundreds of diaries written by women, because the diary by its very nature is a private form of writing and has not normally been published. The finding of these diaries, therefore, amounts to a discovery of literary gold in the archives. Arguably, statistical evidence of women's scant participation in Latin American letters exists and has been used to justify the exclusion of their writing from Latin American literary histories. But mounting evidence of heretofore unknown women's writing, especially in personal genres and, specifically, in diary form, challenges the still prevalent notion that Latin American women did not write. The texts I mention here are single links in the enormous chain that ties Latin American women of the past with the present. María Martínez de Nisser (1812–1872) took part in the civil wars of Nueva Granada (Colombia); in 1841 she kept a diary of her life as a front-line *guerrillera*. Born in Antioquía, first child of Spanish parents, she was given her early education by her father, a local school teacher. In 1825 she began to teach young women to read and write, and in 1831 she married Pedro Nisser, a Swede immigrant miner. In 1840 one of the bloodiest revolutions of the many Colombia has suffered was unleashed against the government of José Ignacio de Márquez. She began then to write *Diario de los sucesos de la revolución en la provincia de Antioquía* [Diary of the Events of the Revolution in the Province of Antioquía], which was published in 1843. The diary has 109 entries between 1

October 1840 and 22 May 1841. In it she deals with the details of the armed uprising and gradually shows her transformation from the role of observer to that of participant. Taking up the cause of defending the established government against the rebels in a world that rejected the opinion of a woman in the field of politics and war, she sought to capture the sense of the events as they happened. What began as a personal diary soon became a defense of her right to speak out on the issues that governed her life and those of all around her. The narrator weaves a text that is both private, in its references to her family and friends, and public, in her account of the hostilities and the final triumph of the government forces.

The publication of a diary is always a key factor in determining its perceived validity as witness to the events described. Diaries published by the writer constitute a conscious decision by the author to make a personal document public; this, however, is not the case with posthumous publications of diaries. We rarely are told whether the full text has been published. The remarkable fact that the diary written by Venezuelan Teresa de la Parra (1889–1936), *Diario de Bellevue-Fuenfría-Madrid* (1982), records only the most incidental aspects of her travels (1932–1936) and has nothing to say about her sentiments, opinions, ideas about her work, intimate reflections, and losing struggle with the disease that would kill her, can be explained by the fact that the diary was not published as it was written. For whatever reasons, it is the remains of a diary that we have been given in her published complete works.

Among the most interesting diaries in recent years is *Diario secreto* [1991; The Secret Diary] by Argentinean actor Norma Aleandro. This child's diary has fifty-three entries written in a precocious youth's language as she creates her intimate world which must be kept secret from the enemy, that is, the adults who want to control her. In the third entry, she writes: "He llegado hace doce años y sólo ahora estoy en condiciones de comenzar la lucha. Ya ha terminado mi crecimiento. Soy adulta hace dos días" ("I arrived twelve years ago and only now am I able to begin the struggle. I have finished growing up. Two days ago I became an adult") (17). Entry 29 reads: "No voy a ser sincera. No quiero decirles la verdad. Un día no tendrán poder sobre mi" ("I am not going to be sincere, I do not want to tell them the truth, one day they will not have power over me") (79). Or, witness the final entry: "Este diario va a terminar aquí por decisión unánime de Nosotros los Aliados y yo la Enviada" ("This diary is going to end here, by unanimous decision of We, the Allies, and I, the Sent One") (135). This kind of intimate diary has long been a kind of defense against the sense of inadequacy often felt in prepuberty and as the changes in the body begin to have their effect. In order to deny the need of the other, the young girl creates fictional others. The diary, therefore, serves not only as a personal defense against her own feelings of helplessness regarding her bodily changes but also works to offset the feelings of being dependent on parents and other adults. Her fantasy expresses the deeply rooted characteristics of self-sufficiency and independence in all of us, individually and collectively. Diaries written by women are now beginning to attain some readership because, as a body of texts, they present the full range of these private attempts at self preservation, which are, in most respects, as eloquent and moving as prose poems.

Among the numerous travel diaries written by European women in Latin America, a few stand out because the writers explore the cultural other with a directness uncommon in the usual light-hearted fare of wealthy travelers. Matilda Charlotte Fraser Houston (1815?–1892) was a British woman who visited Cuba and other Antilles in 1843 aboard a ship chartered in England. The ostensible reason for the trip was to take a retreat for reasons of ill health, but it soon becomes clear from her diary (published in 1844) that the Houstons were ardent abolitionists who wished to observe the practice of slavery first hand. The narration is personal and clearly intended for a British readership. She writes about the horror she experienced at witnessing the public flogging of a female slave and the repulsion she felt against all slaveholders. Another abolitionist, Rachel Wilson Moore, a Quaker from Pennsylvania, traveled through the Caribbean from December 1863 to May 1864, consistently speaking out against slavery but also advocating a nonviolent form of protest; *The Diary of Rachel Moore* was published in Philadelphia in 1867. On the other side of the slavery issue is the diary of Eliza McHatton-Ripley (1832–1912), a slave owner from Louisiana who was forced to flee when her lands were taken over by the Yankee army. She appears to have been the owner of a plantation in Arlington, and her husband was the administrator. In 1862 they crossed the border into Mexico, where they encountered "the civilizing influence of the French in Mexico." They proceeded to Cuba, and in 1865 they bought the sugar cane plantation "El desengaño" ["The Disillusionment"] and remained in Cuba for ten years. Her diary (published in New York in 1889, some fourteen years after it was written) records the struggle to make the plantation profitable.

The controversy surrounding María de las Mercedes Santa Cruz y Montalvo, better known as Condesa de Merlin (1789–1852), is over whether she is Cuban or French (she wrote in French) and whether she had any valid first-hand knowledge of Cuba, since she departed when she was twelve and returned only for a few months in 1840, thirty-eight years later; all this is beside the point. The singular fact is that this cultivated, French-educated woman chose to write about Cuba: first her memoirs of childhood, *Mes douze premières années* [1831; My First Twelve Years], immediately translated into Spanish and published in Philadelphia and later incorporated as the first part of *Souvenirs et mémoires de Madame la Comtesse Merlin: souvenirs d'une Créole* [Memoirs of Madame the Countess of Merlin: Memoirs of a Criolla]; then her major work, *La Havane* [1844; Havana] in three volumes (a reduced, censored Spanish version, *Viaje a la Habana* [A Trip to Havana], was published with a prologue by Gómez de Avellaneda). It is anachronistic to expect her to see Cuba in any way other than as a woman of her social class, education and, of course, such long residence in Paris. Her interest in Cuba and her observations on the state of the colony are deeply penetrating and focused on the status of *criolla* women. She tends to idealize *criolla* women, in contrast to the European women who suffer the sad consequences of marriage. This is without a doubt the view of an outsider who had a lifelong fascination with the place of her birth.

There are, of course, as many reasons for writing a diary as there are diaries. Some diaries are intimate records of lives lived. Others recall an important period in the writer's life. One such collection of diaries are those written by Ecuadoran Manuela Sáenz (1793–1859) about her life with Simón Bolívar. The diaries cover significant periods in their life together. Manuela Sáenz met Simón Bolívar when he entered Quito in triumph in 1822, became his lover and companion until 1830, the year of Bolívar's death. She outlived him by twenty-six years, leaving two diaries, "Diario de Quito" ["The Quito Diary"], written during May and June 1822 and "Diario de Paita" ["Paita Diary"], which dates from July 1840 to the end of May 1846. The diaries, together with her letters to Bolívar, present a vivid picture of this strong-willed, daring woman. (Elena Poniatowska has written a singular appreciation of these documents.)

Epistolary Genres

Collections of letters have been compiled for many reasons and under the most diverse of circumstances. However, what they all share is the creation of the letter writer's persona, which is quite different from the textual self of autobiography or the more random identity based on events of the diary writer. In this case the writing is directed to a specific reader whose relationship to the letter writer is always in the background. Latin American women have been prolific letter writers throughout history. The scarcity of the surviving collections of correspondence is due to the fact that only in very special circumstances have these letters been preserved, whatever their intrinsic value. The main categories of letters cannot be merely designated by the subject matter—such as letters of travelers from Europe, women of the aristocracy describing the New World, love letters of important people, and, more recently, letters by famous women. A far more fruitful approach is to distinguish those collections of letters that are complete exchanges (i.e., to and from the letter writer and the addressee), from collections wherein only the letters of the correspondent are contained. A second consideration of some importance is distinguishing between compilations made by the writer herself and collections compiled by others. The former is informed by a structural element of autobiography, the latter of biography.

I have already mentioned María de las Mercedes Santa Cruz y Montalvo, Condesa de Merlin, daughter of a Spanish aristocratic family, who left Cuba (where she was born in 1789) in 1801 not to return until 1840, and then visit for only two months. She wrote thirty-six letters in French in 1844, which were published almost immediately in the volumes of *La Havane* in Paris and Brussels; in these she reflects on her social status as well as her political attachment to the Spanish monarchy. But the epistolary genre has had an impact on Latin American literature in other ways: not only in the epistolary novel, such as Mexican Elena Poniatowska's (b. 1933) *Dear Diego*, or letters that are included in novels, as in Mexican Sara Sefchovich's (b. 1938) *Demasiado amor* [Too Much Love], but also by the publication of private correspondence, which has been quite accurately seen as a way of rescuing the voice of significant women who participated fully in the literary culture of their day, but whose written work has been marginalized.

María Antonieta Rivas Mercado (1900–1931) of Mexico wrote one of the most passionate sets of letters in Latin American literature to the painter Manuel Rodríguez Lozano. She was, until her suicide in 1931, at the center of Mexican artistic activity, whether in Mexico City, New York, or Paris. Her fortune was spent in sponsoring journals, theater groups, and painters. From September 1929 to her death in 1931 she became a fervent supporter of José Vasconcelos in his campaign for the presidency of Mexico. She wrote Rodríguez Lozano eighty-seven letters in three years, making quite explicit her love for him, her desire to be his lover, and, finally, her reluctant acceptance of a platonic relationship. She not only admired him, but she became so infatuated that she was on the verge of complete self-denial.

One of the most striking recent epistolary publications is that of Rosario Castellanos (1925–1974) of Mexico to her husband, Ricardo Guerra, and her son Gabriel Guerra Castellanos Cartas a Ricardo [1994; Letters to Ricardo]. The letters were preserved by the addressees and were returned to the author, who entrusted them to her close friend, Raúl Ortiz y Ortiz. The compilation and transcription was done by Juan Antonio Ascencio. Elena Poniatowska wrote the prologue for the publication twenty years after the death of Rosario Castellanos. The preface Rosario Castellanos herself wrote for the Mexican publication of Pierre Choderlos de Laclos's epistolary novel, Les liaisons dangereuses, can serve well as a summation for this personal collection: The expression of human sentiments transcends the specific in the quest for human fulfillment in the struggle against prejudice and against social institutions that tend to diminish such feelings, to subordinate them to vested interests, to make them lose their authenticity. Through this epistolary form appears a literary portrayal of the complex woman Rosario Castellanos was.

Another example of the contemporary resurgence of this genre is the publication of Cartas que no se extraviaron [1997; Letters that Did Not Go Astray] by the Cuban poet Dulce María Loynaz (1902–1997). As in the case of Castellanos, Loynaz herself is responsible for the collection of the letters. In this case it is unfortunate that the entire correspondence was not preserved, since it was the writer herself who recovered the letters she had written. The first part covers correspondence from 1932 to 1942, ranging from letters to close friends to letters to Juan Ramón Jiménez in 1936 and Gabriela Mistral in 1938. The second part of the collection covers the twenty years (1971–1991) of correspondence with her biographer Aldo Martínez Malo, in which she responds to his multiple queries about her life and work.

Juana Borrero (1877–1896), a brilliant Cuban modernist poet who only lived nineteen years, wrote one of the longest and most ardent set of letters in the history of Latin American literature, published posthumously in two large volumes, 100 years after her death. The major part consists of 230 love letters the Cuban poet wrote to her fiancé, Carlos Pio Uhrbach, sometimes hours after having last seen him, during the last months of her life, from Key West, Florida, where she died after a short illness. The letters are full of passion, desire, and expressions of love. The letters grow in intensity after 18 January 1896, when the Borrero family leave for Key West, where Juana will die on March 20. The language is lyrical, full of modernista tropes], but nevertheless reveals the extreme sense of longing for the beloved, characteristic of romantic poetry. In contrast to Juana's passionate prose, the addressee's responses, although full of devotion and pledges of love, are perfunctory. One of the most intense letters is entirely written in her own blood. Another poet, the Uruguayan

Delmira Agustini (1886–1914) also wrote letters, published as Correspondencia íntima [1969; Intimate Correspondence], that come close to Borrero's passion but with the difference that Agustini's is a sexual love that devours her.

Among the important correspondence involving visitors to Latin America are the fifty-four letters written from Mexico by Fanny Erskine Inglis, better known as the Marquesa Calderón de la Barca (1804–1882), to her family in Scotland from 1839 to 1842. At the insistence of her friend William Prescott, her letters were published in London and Boston in 1843 to resounding success. She was a well-read, educated woman with a keen intelligence, a good observer with a heightened sense of irony and not a little Eurocentric arrogance.

The Chilean Gabriela Mistral (1889–1957) wrote letters all of her adult life; she wrote to the great figures of the time, to friends, acquaintances, and family. Some of this vast repertoire has been collected: her letters to Lydia Cabrera, her long correspondence with Alfonso Reyes, forty letters to Eduardo Barrios from 1915 to 1922, and forty-five letters to her friend Joaquín García Monge from 1921 to 1934. A closer look at the Mistral-Reyes correspondence will give a good sense of Mistral, the letter writer. It begins at Mistral's initiative with a routine matter of requesting his permission for the use of some of his writings in the textbook she had prepared, Lecturas para mujeres [1923; Readings for Women]. The correspondence is renewed in 1926 with a request for his help in a lecture tour she plans in the United States. By 1929 she is involved in the politics of educational reform in Mexico under Vasconcelos as Minister of Education. Once again Mistral asks for Alfonso Reyes's advice. By 1930 there is a mutual trust and friendship between the two writers. They now address each other by first name, but they still maintain the formal pronoun usted. They exchange news, notices of their work, and poetry; they are both deeply involved in the cultural defense of Latin America. Mistral tells Reyes that he must take over the intellectual leadership of Latin American culture. After Gabriela Mistral is awarded the Nobel Prize, she begins a campaign to nominate Alfonso Reyes that ends in 1949, when she is told that the award will henceforth be reserved for creative writers. The letters after 1949 on her part are more and more personal letters of affection and news of her struggle with blindness caused by diabetes. She wrote her last letter to Reyes in December 1955 shortly before her death; Reyes answered on the last day of December 1955. All in all, the correspondence is filled with the cultural politics of Latin America over the two most important decades of resurgence, the explosive 1930s and the 1940s.

Journalism

The most consistent publishing of women's periodicals in Latin America has been in the three larger countries, Argentina, Brazil, and Mexico, where there has been some form of women's publication since the end of the colonial period in the nineteenth century. In the rest of Latin America women's periodicals have existed since the beginning of the twentieth century with another upsurge in the 1930s. Since the rebirth of women's movements in the 1980s, there has been some form of women's press in every country in Latin America.

The prevailing idea in most literary historical commentaries of the nineteenth century is that women's publications were a kind of pink ghetto limited to the trivialities of domestic concerns. That this should be so is hardly surprising because literacy for women was thought appropriate for the bourgeoisie, but writing and the empowerment it implies could be seen as threatening. The idea of a woman writing about politics, the economy, or conditions in the workplace was considered an aberration; yet, there is mounting evidence that contests the long-standing image that women's concerns were limited to the domestic.

As women's networks of print culture developed, the types of publication fell into two categories. On the one hand, there were women's periodicals that were edited by men and concentrated on fashion, cosmetics, and serialized novels; occasionally women writers were included, but male writers also used women's names. In the other major category were periodicals devoted to women's rights and the demand for a public voice on the political issues of the day; these were constantly under attack by their male opponents, who compared women editors to loose women or unrestrained spinster gossips. In Argentina, Manuel Irigoyen went so far as to start up a magazine purportedly written by women, but with the sole purpose of destroying *La Aljaba* (Buenos Aires, 1830–1831), a journal, published by Petrona Rosende de Sierra (1787–1845) devoted to the struggle for the recognition of women's rights in the civil code. Published in Buenos Aires, Irigoyen's pseudo-women's magazine, *La Argentina* (1830–1831) apparently won the battle as the true voice of Argentinean women and forced *La Aljaba* to close down after eighteen issues. In Mérida, Mexico, Rita Cetina Gutiérrez started *La siempreviva* (1870-80), a newspaper focused on the defense of women in the public sphere, offering information on hygiene and health, and educating women on proper nutrition and child care. In Brazil Senhorina da Motta Diniz published *O sexo Femenino* (1873–74; 1875–76; 1889–96). The battle cry was that Latin America would show the world the way toward better education for women. As female readership increased in Brazil, so too did the presses that served women. Virgilina de Souza Selles published and edited *Revista Feminina* in São Paulo from 1914 to 1927, with a run in the range of 20,000 to 25,000 copies. In terms of the literary culture of Latin America the influence of Victoria Ocampo's *Sur* is unparalleled. From 1931 until her death in 1979, she published and directed this journal, which became one of the most important publications in the Hispanic world.

One of the principal founders of a women's network of communication (and advocacy) was Juana Manuela Gorriti (1816–1892). She was exiled from her native Argentina in 1840 and went to Lima, where she helped promote women's journalism and founded the newspaper *La alborada de Lima*. In 1850 she returned to Argentina and started the literary journal *La alborada del Plata*; it carried a section devoted to women's issues from around the world and provided the model that many women's magazines would follow.

One of the most remarkable women of the nineteenth century in Latin America was the Colombian Soledad Acosta de Samper (1833–1913), one of the first in South America to advocate higher education for women and, in general, women's right to be heard on all issues. She published thirty-seven novels, forty-nine short stories in newspapers and journals of the day, and fifty-nine articles, mostly on women's rights. This prolific writer also published

four plays and twelve travel memoirs; in her lifetime she founded and directed five newspapers. She also translated ten studies and novels from English, French, and German. Her travel memoirs, like her other writing, are concerned with the status of women everywhere, but especially in Latin America. Her greatest impact on Latin American culture was perhaps her editorial contribution to an alternative journalism. At a time when women who dared publish in their own name were scorned and considered not fit for proper social circles, Soledad Acosta de Samper founded a women's journal: *La mujer* which was published twice a month from September 1878 to May 1881 and was run entirely as a women's cooperative. This journal still stands as one of the most innovative and politically aggressive in promoting women's rights.

The Peruvian, Clorinda Matto de Turner (1852–1909), was another nineteenth-century leader in women's rights. Although she is best known for her novel *Aves sin nido* [1889; *Torn from the Nest*, 1998], she also organized and participated in a literary salon from 1877 to at least 1887, and all her life wrote for newspapers. In 1889 she was the chief editor and director of *El Peru ilustrado*, and in 1892 she founded a feminist press and the newspaper *Los Andes*. Another Peruvian, Carolina Freyre de Jaimes (1827–1881) founded the newspaper *El Album*, which ran from 1860 to 1874 in Lima and La Paz. Claudia Lars, an El Salvadoran whose pseudonym was Carmen Brannon (1899–1974) directed a publishing house and the magazine *Cultura* in El Salvador. Janet Greenberg has assembled a listing of 373 women's periodicals in Latin America.

In order to summarize two centuries of woman's advocacy journalism, we should examine writings in certain periods: first, the situation before 1800; second, the years of the wars of independence and the aftermath, 1840–1860; and every twenty years since then to the present. These postindependence groupings are merely divisions of convenience and do not indicate anything more than that, but they will allow us to get an idea of the scope and numbers involved throughout Latin America.

In the period before 1800, Bernarda Calderón published irregular broadsheets in Mexico City between 1641 and 1684. During the chaotic period of the wars of independence, nine new women's periodicals appeared: three in Argentina, one in Brazil, one in Cuba, and four in Mexico. A network was beginning to take shape. After the independence turmoil, the next twenty years, 1840 to 1860, saw a proliferation of publications by women: six journals were published in Argentina, five in Brazil, a new journal in Colombia, one in Cuba, nine in Mexico, two in Peru, and one in Puerto Rico. This was the period of bold and innovative pioneers like Juana Manuela Gorriti (Argentina and Peru), Juana Manso (Argentina and Brazil), Gertrudis Gómez de Avellaneda (Cuba), and Clorinda Matto de Turner (Peru). The time of national foundation, 1860 to 1880, saw a setback in most Latin American countries in terms of women's publishing. Only Brazilian publishing grew; there were ten women's periodicals during this period. During these years publishing in Argentina and Mexico declined, but new journals started up in Colombia and Chile. The end of the century, 1880 to 1900, was a time of renewal in every country. Unprecedented growth in population took place in Argentina, as European immigrants poured in; by the turn of the century there were twelve women's periodicals in the country. By contrast, Mexico had only two; the Porfirio Díaz dictatorship was not a good time for feminist writing.

From the beginning of the twentieth century to 1920 was also a period of slow growth. New women's periodicals that had started in Montevideo before the turn of the century continued, and by 1920 there were three still being published; seven continued in Argentina; Mexico had two, and Brazil was down to only one. The two decades from 1920 to 1940 marked the turning point in women's periodicals in Latin America: forty-five were published during this period. Argentina was again in the lead with sixteen; a noteworthy addition was *La vanguardia femenina* (1946), published by Alicia Moreau de Justo in Buenos Aires. Mexico was second with nine. In Cuba in 1930 Rosa María Trejo was editor of the *Boletín de la Alianza Nacional Femenina*; in 1938 Silvia Planas was director of *Letras,* which had a large number of women on the staff. Surprisingly, Brazil maintained only one, and there were no periodicals in Bolivia, Chile, the Dominican Republic, Guatemala, Honduras, or Venezuela. The period of the Second World War and the economic prosperity that benefited much of Latin America did not translate into a gain in women's publications. Bolivia was the only country showing growth in this area. The others merely held on.

From 1960 on, the development of the women's network has been continuous. In 1980 there were forty-five women's publications, no longer concentrated in one or two countries but spread over seventeen countries in Latin America.. The explosion in this area came as the women's movement began to make inroads in Latin America. By 1990 there were 145 women's periodicals published in Latin America, and they were in every country except Guatemala and Honduras, which were caught up in bloody civil wars. But even war-torn El Salvador managed to published two journals that year.

In terms of readership, organizational network, and distribution, the journals from Argentina, Brazil, Chile, Mexico and Peru led the way. Mexico had fourteen, including Mexico City's highly successful *fem.* (1976) and the intellectual *debate feminista* (1990), also published in Mexico City; Argentina had seventeen journals, Brazil, eighteen, Chile, fifteen, Peru, eighteen, and Colombia shot up to eleven from only one a decade before. But the comeback award goes to Cuba, which had not had a woman's journal since 1940, and by 1990 had eight, showing how writers like Nancy Morejón were clearly in touch with the rest of Latin America. Representative of a resurgent militancy among women journalists in the 1970s was the series of interviews conducted in 1976 and 1977 by Esther Andradi and Ana María Portugal of Peru and eventually published as a collection with the title *Ser mujer en el Perú* [1978; To Be a Woman in Peru].

Women journalists have concerned themselves with art and literature but also with politics, social issues of the day, crime, education, and the economic situation. They have crusaded for women's right to vote and to have access to education, but also, with equal or ever greater commitment, they have been in the forefront of the demand that human rights violations be ended. Individual Latin American journalists of distinction are numerous. I have only mentioned some of those who have founded and contributed to an alternative press when the existing mainline papers and journals excluded or marginalized their opinion because of gender barriers. These are the women who made sure these barriers were cracked, split, and, finally, breached.

Works Cited

Acosta de Samper, Soledad. 1879-1880. "Recuerdos de Suiza." *La Mujer* 3: 109-283.

Agustini, Delmira. 1969. *Correspondencia íntima.* Estudio, ordenación y prólogo Arturo Sergio Bisca. Montevideo: Biblioteca Nacional.

Aleandro, Norma. 1991. *Diario secreto.* Buenos Aires: Emecé Editores.

Amor, Guadalupe. 1957. *Yo soy mi casa.* Mexico City: Fondo de Cultura Económica.

Anderson Imbert, Enrique. 1954. *Historia de la literatura hispanoamericana.* 2 vols. Mexico City: Fondo de Cultura Económica.

Andradi, Esther and Ana María Portugal, comp. 1978. *Ser mujer en el Perú.* Lima: Ediciones Mujer y Autonomía.

Aubrun, Charles Vincent. 1954. *Histoire des lettres Hispano-Américaines.* Paris: Armand Colin.

Bandeira, Manuel. 1949. *Literatura Hispano-Americana.* Rio de Janeiro: Irmaos Pongetti.

Barrera, Isaac J. 1934. *Literatura Hispanoamericana.* Quito: Imprenta de la Universidad Central.

Bazin, Robert. 1958. *Historia de la literatura americana en lengua española.* Buenos Aires: Editorial Nova.

Beck Bernard, Lina. 1864. *Le Rio Parana: Cinq années de séjour dans la Confédérée Argentine, 1857–1862.* Paris: De Grassart. Trans. José Luis Busaniche, *Cinco años en la Confederación Argentina, 1857–1862.* Buenos Aires: El Ateneo, 1935.

Bellini, Giuseppe. 1985. *Historia de la literatura hispanoamericana.* Madrid: Castalia.

Borrero, Juana. 1967. *Epistolario.* 2 vols. Havana: Academia de Ciencias de Cuba. Instituto de Literatura y Lingüística.

Bullrich, Silvina. 1969. *El mundo que yo vi.* Buenos Aires: Editorial Merlin.

——. 1980. *Mis memorias.* Buenos Aires: Emecé.

Bunge de Gálvez, Delfina. 1938. *Viaje alrededor de mi infancia.* Buenos Aires: Imprenta López.

Calderón de la Barca, Madame. See Inglis, Frances Erskine.

Campobello, Nellie. 1931. *Cartucho, relatos de la lucha en el norte de México.* Xalapa, Mexico: Eds. Integrales.

——. 1937. *Las manos de mamá.* Mexico City: Ed. Juventudes de Izquierda.

——. 1988. *Cartucho; and My Mother's Hands.* Trans. Doris Meyer and Irene Matthews. Intr. Elena Poniatowska. Austin: University of Texas Press.

Castellanos, Rosario. 1984. "Las amistades peligrosas." *Juicios Sumarios.* Vol. II. *Ensayos sobre literatura.* Mexico City: Fondo de cultura económica. 9–18.

——. 1994. *Cartas a Ricardo.* Prologue by Elena Poniatowska. Mexico City: Consejo Nacional para la Cultura y las Artes.

Castillo, Debra. 1992. *Talking Back: Toward a Latin American Feminist Literary Criticism.* Ithaca, New York: Cornell University Press.

Castillo de González, Aurelia. 1891. *Un paseo por Europa. Cartas de Francia (Exposición de 1889). De Italia y de Suiza. Pompeya (Poemita).* Havana: La propaganda literaria.

——. 1895. *Un paseo por América. Cartas de México y de Chicago.* Havana: Imprenta La Constancia.

——. 1997. *Cartas de México.* Ed. Luisa Campuzano. Mexico City: Redacta.

Casuso, Teresa (Teté). 1938. *Panorama de México.* Mexico City: n.p.

——. 1951. *Recuerdos de un viaje a Europa.* Havana: La Verónica.

Coester, Alfred Lester. 1916. *The Literary History of Spanish America.* New York: Macmillan.

Crawford, Cora Hayward. 1890. *The Land of Moctezumas.* Troy, N.Y.: Neins and Knight.

Díaz, Nidia. 1990. *Nunca estuve sola*. Buenos Aires: Ediciones Dialéctica.

Díez Echarri, Emiliano and José María Roca Franquesa. 1960. *Historia de la literatura española e hispanoamericana*. Madrid: Aguilar.

Englekirk, John et al. 1965. *An Outline History of Spanish American Literature*. 3d ed. New York: Appleton Century Crofts.

Fernández, Teodosio. 1995. *Historia de la literatura hispanoamericana*. Madrid: Editorial Universitas.

Fernández Moreno, César. 1972. *América Latina en su literatura*. Paris: UNESCO.

Ferré, Rosario. 1984. "La cocina de la escritura." *La sartén por el mango*. Ed. Patricia Elena González and Eliana Ortega. Puerto Rico: Huracán. 137–54.

Franco, Jean. 1973. *A Literary History of Spain: Spanish American Literature Since Independence*. New York: Barnes & Noble.

Galeano, Benita. *Benita*. 1940. Mexico City: Editorial Extemporáneos. Engl. trans. Amy Diane Prince. 1994. Pittsburgh: Latin American Literary Review Press.

Garrido de la Peña, Carlota. 1893. *Reminiscencias*. Santa Fé: Nueva Epoca.

Garro, Elena. 1992. *Memorias de España 1937*. Mexico City: Singlo Veintiuno Editores.

Glantz, Margo. 1981. *Las genealogías*. Mexico City: Martín Casillas. Engl. trans. Susan Bassnett. *The Family Tree*. London: Serpent's Tail, 1991.

Goic, Cedomil. 1988. *Historia y crítica de la literatura hispanoamericana*. Barcelona: Editorial Crítica.

Gómez de Avellaneda, Gertrudis. 1969. *Diario de amor: autobiografía, cartas a Ignacio de Cepeda*. Havana: Instituto del Libro.

Gómez Gil, Orlando. 1968. *Historia crítica de la literatura hispanoamericana, desde los orígenes hasta el momento actual*. New York: Holt, Rinehart and Winston.

González Echevarría, Roberto, and Enrique Pupo Walker, eds. 1996. *The Cambridge History of Latin American Literature*. 3 vols. New York: Cambridge University Press.

Greenberg, Janet. 1990. "Toward a History of Women's Periodicals in Latin America: A Working Bibliography." *Women, Culture, and Politics in Latin America*. By Emilie Bergmann et al. Berkeley: University of California Press. 182–231.

Henríquez Ureña, Pedro. 1966. *A Concise History of Latin American Culture*. Trans. and with a supplementary chapter by Gilbert Chase. New York: Frederick A. Praeger.

———. 1969. *Las corrientes literarias en la América hispánica*. Mexico City: Fondo de Cultura Económica.

Houston, Matilda Charlotte Fraser. 1844. *Texas and the Gulf of Mexico; or, Yachting the New World*. London: John Murray.

Ibarbourou, Juana de. 1968. "Autobiografía lírica." *Obras completas*. 3d ed. Madrid: Aguilar. 1364–1368.

Iglehart, Fanny Chambers Gooch. 1887. *Face to Face with the Mexicans*. New York: Fords, Howard & Hulbert.

Inglis, Frances Erskine (Marquesa Calderón de la Barca). 1843. *Life in Mexico: During a Residence of Two Years in That Country*. London: Chapman.

Iñigo Madrigal, Luis, ed. 1982. *Historia de la literatura hispanoamericana*. Madrid: Cátedra.

Jozef, Bella. 1982. *História da Literatura Hispano-Americana*. Rio de Janeiro: Francisco Alves.

Juana Inés de la Cruz. 1994. *The Answer/La respuesta*. Ed. and trans. Electa Arenal and Amanda Powell. New York: The Feminist Press.

Lange, Norah. 1940. *Cuadernos de infancia*. Buenos Aires: Editorial sudamericana.

Lazo, Raimundo. 1965–1967. *Historia de la literatura hispanoamericana*. 2 vols. Mexico City: Editorial Porrúa.

Leal, Luis. 1971. *Breve historia de la literatura hispanoamericana*. New York: Alfred A. Knopf.

Leguizamón, Julio A. 1945. *Historia de la literatura hispanoamericana*. 2 vols. Buenos Aires: Editorial Reunidas.

Lester, Mary (pseud. Maria Soltera). 1884. *A Lady's Ride Across Spanish Honduras*. London: William Blackwood. Trans. Anita Herzfeld. *Un viaje por Honduras*. 2d ed. San José: Editorial Universitaria Centroamericana, 1982.

Lombardo de Miramón, Concepción. 1980. *Memorias de Concepción Lombardo de Miramón*. Mexico City: Editorial Porrua.

Loynaz, Dulce María. 1958. *Un verano en Tenerife*. Madrid: Aguilar.

———. 1997. *Cartas que no se extraviaron*. Pinar del Río, Cuba: Fundación Jorge Guillén.

Lynch, Marta. 1977. *Apuntes para un libro de viajes*. Buenos Aires: Castor y Pollux.

Martínez Bonati, Félix. 1992. *"Don Quixote" and the Poetics of the Novel*. Trans. Dian Fox. Ithaca, N.Y.: Cornell University Press.

Martínez de Nisser, María. 1843. *Diario de los sucesos de la revolución en la provincia de Antioquía*. Bogota: Imp. de Benito Gaitan.

Matto de Turner, Clorinda. 1909. *Viaje de recreo: España, Francia, Inglaterra, Italia, Suiza, Alemania*. Valencia: F. Sempere y compañía.

Maudsley, Anne Cary Morris, and Alfred Percival Maudsley. 1894. *A Glimpse at Guatemala and Some Notes of Ancient Monuments of Central America*. London: John Murray.

McHatton-Ripley, Eliza. 1889. *From Flag to Flag: A Woman's Adventures and Experiences in the South During the War, in Mexico, and in Cuba*. New York: D. Appleton and Company.

Méndez Capote, Renée. 1976. *Memorias de una cubanita que nació con el siglo*. Havana: Bolsilibros Unión.

———. 1983. *Hace muchos años, una joven viajera*. Havana: Editorial Letras Cubanas.

Menéndez y Pelayo, Marcelino. 1893. *Antología de poetas hispano-americanos*. Madrid: Real Academia Española.

Merlin, María de las Mercedes Santa Cruz y Montalvo, condesa de. 1831. *Mes douze premières années*. Paris: Gautier-Laguionie.

———. *La Havane*. 1844. 3 vols. Paris: Librairie d'Amyot; Bruxelles: Société Belge de Librairie haumen et cie.

———. 1844. *Viaje a la Habana*. Prologue by Gertrudis Gómez de Avellaneda. Madrid: Imprenta de la Sociedad Literaria y Tipográfica.

Meyer, Doris. 1990. *Against the Wind and the Tide*. Austin: University of Texas Press.

Mistral, Gabriela. 1991. *Tan de usted: epistolario de Gabriela Mistral con Alfonso Reyes*. Ed. Luis Vargas Saavedra. Santiago de Chile: Hachette, Ediciones Universidad Católica de Chile.

Molloy, Sylvia. 1991. *At Face Value: Autobiographical Writing in Spanish America*. Cambridge: Cambridge University Press.

Moore, Rachel Wilson. 1867. *The Diary of Rachel Moore*. Philadelphia: Edward Zell.

Núñez Cabeza de Vaca, Alvar. 1932. *Naufragios y comentarios*. Madrid: Espasa-Calpe.

Ocampo, Victoria. 1941–77. *Testimonios*. Vol. 1. Madrid: Revista de Occidente, 1935; Vols. 2–10, Buenos Aires: Sur.

———. 1979–1987. *Autobiografía*. 6 vols. Buenos Aires: Ediciones Revista Sur.

Oliver, María Rosa. 1965. *Mundo, mi casa: Recuerdos de infancia*. Buenos Aires: Falbo Librero Editor.

———. 1969. *La vida cotidiana*. Buenos Aires: Editorial Sudamericana.

———. 1981. *Mi fé es el hombre*. Buenos Aires, Ediciones Carlos Lohlé.

Parra, Teresa de la. 1982. "Diario de Bellevue-Fuenfría-Madrid (1931–1936)." *Obra (Narrativa-Ensayos-Cartas)*. Ed. Velia Bosch. Caracas: Biblioteca Ayacucho. 447-70.

Parra, Violeta. 1970. *Décimas: autobiografía en versos chilenos*. Santiago de Chile: Nueva Universidad/Pomaire.

Pedraza Jiménez, Felipe B., ed. 1991. *Manual de la literatura hispanoamericana*. 2 vols. Berriozar, Spain: Cénlit Ediciones.

Peña Gutiérrez, Isaías. 1987. *Manual de la literatura latinoamericana*. Bogota: Educar Editores.

Poniatowska, Elena. 1969. *Hasta no verte, Jesús mío*. Mexico City: Ediciones Era.

———. 1986. *Dear Diego*. Trans. Katherine Silver. New York: Pantheon Books.

———. 1993. "Manuela Sáenz." *Patriota y amante de usted. Manuela Sáenz y el Libertador.* Ed. Carlos Alvarez Saá. Mexico City: Editorial Diana. 245–54.

Rivas Mercado, María Antonieta. 1975. *87 cartas de amor y otros papeles.* Xalapa, Mexico: Universidad Veracruzana.

Rodríguez Acosta, Ofelia. 1941. *Europa era así.* Mexico City: Editorial Botas.

Rodríguez de Morales, Catalina. 1881–1882. "Impresiones de viaje. Páginas Intimas." *El Album* (Matanzas, Cuba) 15 July–30 August.

Rodríguez Monegal, Emir and Thomas Colchie. 1977. *The Borzoi Anthology of Latin American Literature.* 2 vols. New York–Knopf.

Roncajolo, Yrcilia Leontine Perignon. 1895. *Au Venezuela, Souvenirs 1876–1892.* Paris: Paul Dupont. Trans. *Recuerdos.* Maracaibo: Universidad del Zulia, 1968.

Saénz, Manuela. 1993. "Diario de Quito." "Diario de Paita." *Patriota y amante de usted. Manuela Sáenz y el Libertador.* Ed. Carlos Alvarez Saá. Mexico City: Editorial Diana. 21–53, 57–91.

Sánchez, Luis Alberto. 1982. *Nueva historia de la literatura americana.* 6th ed. Valparaíso, Chile: Ediciones Universitarias de Valparaíso, Universidad Católica de Valparaíso.

Santa Cruz y Montalvo, María de las Mercedes. See Condesa de Merlin.

Schwartz, Kessel. 1971. *A New History of Spanish American Fiction.* 2 vols. Coral Gables, Fla.: University of Miami Press.

Sefchovich, Sara. 1990. *Demasiado amor.* Mexico City: Editorial Planeta.

Sommer, Doris. 1988. "'Not Just a Personal Story': Women's *Testimonio* and the Plural Self." *Life/Lines: Theorizing Women's Autobiography.* Ed. Bella Brodzki and Celeste Schenck. Ithaca, N.Y.: Cornell University Press, 107–30.

Tallenay, Jenny. 1884. *Souvenirs de Venezuela: notes de voyage.* Paris: E. Plon, Nourrit. Trans. René L. F. Durand. *Recuerdos de Venezuela.* Caracas: Ediciones del Ministerio de Educación, 1954.

Torres Rioseco, Arturo. 1942. *The Epic of Latin American Literature.* New York: Oxford University Press.

Treviño Carranza, Celia. 1958. *Mi atormentada vida.* Mexico City: Editorial Jus.

Valbuena Briones, Angel. 1967. *Literatura hispanoamericana.* 3d ed. Barcelona: G. Gilli.

CHAPTER 36

BRAZILIAN WOMEN
LITERATURE FROM THE NINETEENTH TO THE TWENTIETH CENTURIES

Lucia Helena, Sylvia Oroz, and Sylvia Paixão

At the dawn of the nineteenth century, literature, art, and society are closely articulated, and literary production is interwoven with the social, political, and economic construction of the nation-state. Benedict Anderson's considerations of this specific aspect in *Imagined Communities* (1983) are of importance. When the nation-states were formed, the bourgeois imaginary implanted not only its disciplines (historiography, among them) and institutions (of which the most directly related to the condition of women would be the bourgeois nuclear family), but also a metaphorical network of images that led to the exclusion of women from public life and their restriction to the private domain.

Manifestly, one of the leading metaphors of this exclusion relates woman to the earth-mother, a tutelary image which appears quite powerfully among us in José de Alencar's (1829–1877) (see **Figure 1**) *Iracema* (1865), that emblematic novel of nationhood. In poetry, this image is also the integrating force of the work of Narcisa Amália (1852–1924), whose themes create further images of the country's construction, in addition to an animizing of nature, often associated with the female body and the representation of woman. It is not easy, in these representations, to perceive any strong connection of women to the public space; in Narcisa Amália's poetry, women are always related to the private, to inwardness, and to intimacy. When she turns outward, the movement coincides with "natural" relations, that is, it is engulfed by nature, which is truly capable of representing the external.

In the twentieth century this same movement occurs also in the poetry of Gilka Machado (1893–1980), above all in *Sublimação* 1938 [Sublimation], as well as in Luciano Salce's 1954 film version of Dinah Silveira de Queiroz's (1910–1978) 1946 novel *Floradas na Serra* [Mountain Blossoms], in which illness, as part of the external world, dominates the female subject, leading to her death by the forces of nature. Nonetheless, when the same illness befalls the male subject, the protagonist's partner, he succeeds in escaping with his life. In Salce's film, we see the illness/body relationship in the form of an asymmetrical punishment involving the man and the woman, as she is more severely punished (with death) than he. This movie melodrama deals with the spectator's feelings about reality; that is, it deals with sentiments but not with meanings, as may be observed in the following dialogue between the actors Jardel Filho and Cacilda Becker:

J. F. - Você estava partindo.
C.B. - E você estava chegando.
J. F. - Pobre, doente, cheio de ressentimento.
C.B. - E agora?
J. F. - Agora, você está aqui mas eu prefiro ficar sozinho.
C.B. - Por quê?
J. F. - Porque não posso apaixonar-me. O amor é uma fraqueza e eu já tenho duas: a doença e a pobreza.

JF: You were going.
CB: And you were arriving.
JF: Poor, sick, and resentful.
CB: And now?
JF: Now you're here but I'd just as soon be alone.
CB: Why?
JF: Because I can't be in love. Love is a weakness and I already have two of those: illness and poverty.

(Oroz 1992, 169)

Even if the phenomenon of exclusion as linked to the marking of gender should be seen in its historicity, its reach extends beyond the bourgeois panorama, as described in Teresa de Lauretis's critical study of cultural gender specification (3–31) which is based on Yuri Lotman's study of mythical narrative typologies. The hero, founder of culture and institutions, and active subject is always male, while modalities of passivity and of obstacles in the form of dangerous savage forces are the feminine domain. But there is an aspect of cultural gender specification not discussed by either de Lauretis or Lotman: that of woman's transformation into a form of sensuality invented by and for man, for example. The theme of woman as an object of male desire, especially in cinema, reaches its zenith in the 1940s. Women are represented as divas, goddesses, and stars. In narratives that allude to the mythical, as in those studied by Lotman, those forces of the feminine are not transformed into obstacles, but neither do they constitute active principles related to cultural institutions, propaganda, and circulation of power. In star-system cinema, women appear in an ethereal mist, so that the same passivity observed by Lotman and, *a posteriori*, by de Lauretis reappears in new conjunctions. Despite the emphasis on the undeniable contributions (albeit sometimes silent and very often silenced) of women in historical construction, the passive images persist.

This passivity related to sensuality is the result not only of the cinematic elaboration of the twentieth century or even the literary fashion of the middle of the nineteenth century, the so-called naturalist period of Brazilian literature, which spans at least two decades (the 1880s and 1890s), but also possesses interesting characteristics that point, however, to complications in woman's relationship with passivity and her exclusion from being a driving force, a protagonist of the historical process. Passivity, for example, plays no part in the world of Leoni, the lesbian prostitute of Aluízio Azevedo's (1857–1913) *O Cortiço* [1890; *A Brazilian Tenement*, 1926]. The portrayal of the transgressive female prostitute, whom romanticism redeemed through love in José de Alencar's *Lucíola* (1862), receives another jolt from naturalism. The introduction of the character of the female prostitute, a lesbian transgressor whose acts are both reprehensible and forbidden, erases the Manichean relationship established between the hero and society: When the transgressor enters the scene, the itineraries of both hero and heroism are dramatically altered.

In film and in melodrama specifically, the transgressive female was a modernizing element. She produced a new model

Figure 1.

of opposition to the self-sacrificing, faithful Penelopes of the arts of waiting and passivity. This transgressor represented the sick side of society, that is to say, disorder installed as a "deviation" in the positivist order of emblematic modernity, as represented by the cinema between 1930 and 1950 (Oroz 1994, 107–24). The transgressive woman is not necessarily a prostitute, in the sense of obtaining a profit through sale of her body: She makes money that is not used for domestic needs and does not represent virtue, altruism, renunciation, self-sacrifice, or generosity. These models (the prostitute, the woman who deals with nondomestic money, and the woman who rejects those virtues foreseen and accepted by the social mores) make up the three prototypes of female transgressors. They function in opposition to the bourgeois family model and, within the dramatic structure itself, as obstacles that generate action. Rather than construct a new gender identity, the transgressor in a sense incorporates the patriarchal model. In Mexican cinema, the adaptation of Rómulo Gallegos's *Doña Bárbara* is a good example of this; in Brazilian cinema, the example is Humberto Mauro's *Argila* [Clay].

Excluded as much by historiography as by the symbolic structure that presides over the social imaginary, the representation of women in this culture has repeatedly been relegated to what is private or to what is incapable of producing knowledge or even unable to relate to the world of rationality and

objectivity. Women are seen as incapable of generating institutions, even though they may serve these as a uterus for the deposit of the virile seeds which will come to implant them.

In discussing the concepts of historiography, the canon, literature, and literary genres outside their articulation with gender specificity, it is clear that exclusion is also present. In Brazil, it appears to be circumscribed differently than elsewhere with the marking of gender, the male bourgeois construction of institutions and political power. In Brazil, the emergence of feminine artistic production has been present since the end of the nineteenth century through art exhibitions, teaching, journalism, literature, and the arts in general. Brazil establishes its imaginary versions of nationality based on such novels as José de Alencar's *Iracema* (1865) and *O Guarani* [1857; The Guarani], in which there are visible barriers of cultural gender specification (see **Figure 2**). Thus, it is not surprising that the phenomenon of the historical exclusion of women appears in imitation of Europe before the nineteenth century. The late twentieth century brings with it the emergence of cultural studies both inside and outside Brazil, along with the spread of feminism, women's studies, and investigations into literature and sexuality. In Brazil work on these interests did not really get under way until the 1970s.

The invisible violence of exclusion is manifest in the canon constructed by literary historiography. The selection established is only apparently natural; its normally hidden criteria represent the values of institutions that both formed and were

Figure 2.

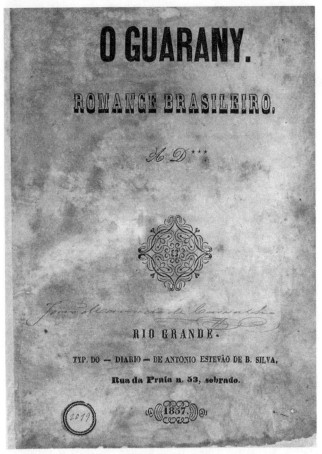

formed by the nation-states and were also formed *by* them, in a complex process of multiple reversibility. In the light of this canon, the privileged female characters are represented in relation to the forces of nature, and not to those who preside over institutions. In José de Alencar's emblematic novel, until the native Indian Iracema meets Martim, the white warrior, she remains the untouched virgin of Tupã, a priestess who therefore holds power within the tribe's religious structure. On the other hand, the very same Iracema, after meeting the one who is to become her lover, becomes pregnant and dies alone in childbirth. In the heart of the jungle, she waits for the return of the white warrior who has gone to war, and when he returns, she perishes like the flower when its bulb is removed. She returns, therefore, to a state of nature from which she had never, in truth, departed. Her encounter with Martim and her amorous surrender to him newly marked the loss of her priestly power.

When considered today, a certain ambivalence characterizes female figures like Iracema, who are both powerful and dominated at the same time. This is an ambivalence that they have always possessed but that canonical criticism reduced and transformed into the stock character of the submissive passive woman. In this sense, the canon and its exemplary readings reify the multidirectional social forces of the nineteenth century. If in the twentieth century the challenge to exclusion remained stifled by the power of the canon and its apparently unchallenged establishment (readily meeting the demands of both the expectations of the elites who erected it and the hegemonic profile desired by the nation-state), the late twentieth century did not lack for frequently subterranean expressions of the conflict between the culture of the excluded—women, blacks, natives, homosexuals, the poor, and whoever else need be named in composing an image of the periphery of power—and the official discourse that represents them. The first opening up of channels of expression for the excluded was a phenomenon of the 1960s.

Brazilian literature and film represent opposite trajectories that variously express a conflict between the literary text, and the sacralization process that dominates it, and its filmic adaptation. This conflict can be found in filmic adaptations ranging from the character of *Iracema* (1865) to Clarice Lispector's (1925–1977) (see **Figure 3**) Macabéa of *A Hora da Estrela* [1977; *The Hour of the Star*, 1986]; from the romantic conceit of "dying for love" (*Iracema*) through to the Parnassian "To *hear* stars, you say?" (*A Hora da Estrela*) all the way to Ana Cristina César's (1952–1983) *A teus pés* [At Your Feet]. The trajectories range from *Lábios Sem Beijos* [1929; Lips without Kisses] to *O Ébrio* [1946; The Drunkard] and to the *chanchada* genre. (The *chanchada* is a uniquely Brazilian film genre whose heyday extends from the late 1930s to the very early 1960s. It is a mixture of slapstick and farce, heavily laced with musical numbers.) An examination of this trajectory reveals, for instance, a tradition of praising women's world as a private space in which sentimental love and sadomasochism coexist. Dedication and infinite suffering are demanded by and of women as melodramatic manifestations of the ideas either that only through love can anything be constructed or that love equals pain. The historical trajectory of this notion can be demonstrated through the expression of the dominant themes, principally, the paradigms of the silent suffering woman, the inspiring muse, and the controlling medusa. Female characters under male tutelage become a construct within the cultural imaginary, from whence come both literary

and cinematic manifestations. Thus, the home, the street, the body, the marriage vow, and the sadomasochistic relationships of femininity's internal melodrama are not only themes but also the very configuration of a cultural imaginary, one in which the social and individual presence of women is linked, with astonishing frequency, to melodramatic and sadomasochistic content. These configurations are related to the idea that, in both bourgeois and popular culture, melodrama is a popularized form of tragedy (Hauser 254) that structures the affective ties of the urban culture of modernity in Latin America. But this melodramatic tension also structured the nineteenth century imaginary in the guise of serials (*feuilletons*). In this sense, melodrama becomes a form of double exclusion *par excellence*. It both expresses a sensibility dear to the excluded and is itself an excluded manifestation.

An Iracema motif is subterraneously inscribed in the Brazilian cultural imaginary, taken up by popular culture in different modalities; if examined carefully, it offers us an interesting profile of the literary representation of women's exclusion. The native is taken from her "home" and passes from Tupã (as we have seen, she was the virgin who guarded the secret of Jurema and who officiated religious ceremonies) into the arms of Martim, the virile white warrior. This passage from priestess in her own domain to warrior's beloved involves a progressive loss of identity moving toward being engulfed by the nature she represents. When, at the novel's end, her death is described with the phrase "all things pass on earth," the new religious paradigm of Christianity, the Catholic Mass, the new state, and the new civilization are all founded upon the melodrama experienced by a character who has lost herself in love and who dies as a consequence. Excluded, Iracema returns to the womb of an "eternal feminine," which remains as a generative, atemporal, ahistorical humus.

Iracema is part of a historical process. Three twentieth-century writers (Clarice Lispector, Márcia Denser (b. 1949), and Sônia Coutinho (b. 1939) explore this Alencarian matrix and vigorously subvert the canonical construct of that powerful network of persuasive metaphors of gender that merge, on the one hand, nature, woman, and emotions and, on the other, science, man, and rationality. Within the complex network of this dichotomous representation of women and men, representations of women are restricted to the emotional realm of a lesser, quotidian life, while representations of men are linked to the construction of institutions, laws, rules, and the behavioral profiles of rights and duties.

An example of the corrosion of this dichotomous discourse, however, may be seen in *Laços de Família* [1960; translated into English by Giovanni Pontiero as *Family Ties*, 1990], one of Clarice Lispector's earliest short story collections. These stories may be read as "versions of a single developmental tale that provides patterns of female possibilities, vulnerabilities and power in Lispector's world" (Peixoto 296). Ten of the book's thirteen stories examine problems faced by women, whether as adolescents confronting the fantasy or reality of sex (as in "Preciousness"), or as mature women who relate precariously to the family and to themselves (in "Love"), or even as venerable old women observing the failure of family ties (in "Happy Birthday"). The remaining stories focus on similar problems but have male characters as protagonists ("The Dinner," "The Beginnings of a Fortune") and, in one of them, an animal is allegorized ("The Buffalo"). This set of stories engenders a sort of evolving narrative that appears to articulate the development of people from

Figure 3.

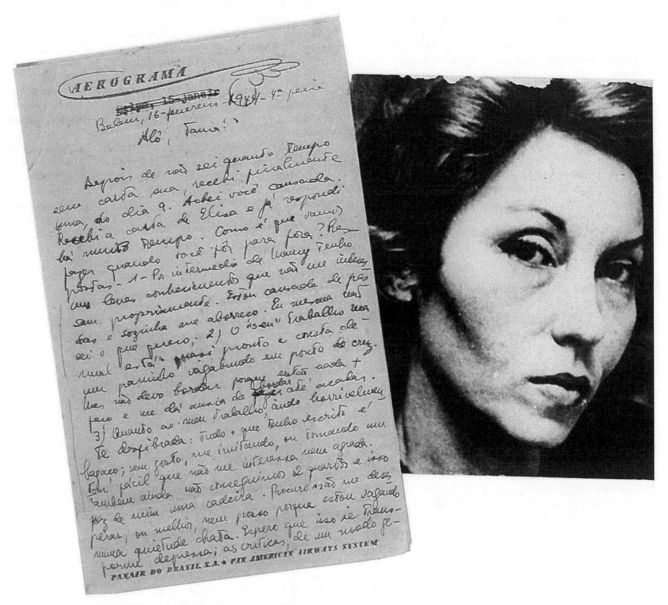

(Courtesy of the John P. Robarts Research Library, University of Toronto)

adolescence to old age. And, with the exception of the story about the smallest woman in the world, they insist on themes of the lack of fulfillment and the impotence of persons incapable of generating their own autonomy, caught in intricate technologies of gender in which the silent but powerfully corrosive violence of the familial context is always emphasized. In one story after another, narratives strategically "repeat" images of men and women projected by the patriarchal model, which ideologically provides the stories' gender patterns. This technique forces the reader to take a stand about what "common sense" dictates to be appropriate roles for husbands and wives, men and women, parents and children. As if obsessively and innocently stockpiling images, Lispector's texts dismantle the supposed innocence and truth of these projected images and deconstruct beliefs in the pre-existing essences of religious faith, subjectivity, and truth. It is as if her characters, starting out from the patriarchal universe where these essences are conceived as *a priori* and natural, had been

dragged the length of their textual journey to the progressive destabilizing of their apparent internal and familial peace.

Compared to the author's later texts, this collection concentrates more on the examination of a specific social stratum (the middle-class bourgeois nuclear family) with its fears, myths, and impossibilities. Adopting an apparently realist discourse, Lispector's narrator proceeds with caution. She does this by structurally duplicating, through what first appears to be a realist narrative, the way of being of these average families in an apparently representational text that simultaneously causes this mimetic model to be subverted by free indirect discourse and by subtle techniques of interior monologue that deconstruct the model. Lispector also makes use of patriarchal patterns in the images she elects to destabilize: These are the very patriarchal premises that entrap her characters.

In most of the stories, an opposition is established between external and internal space. Doubled in significance, these spaces simultaneously also represent extra-literary reality (as signs of a concrete physical world) and the unconscious, a force without boundaries (as signs of the character's delirium and secret longings). In "Love," "The Imitation of the Rose" and "The Mystery in São Cristovão," nature appears as a metaphor for the unconscious and powerful secret forces with which the protagonists maintain a timorous contact. In "The Imitation of the Rose," Laura sees in flowers, and in what they represent (the potent ardor of great beauty and perfection), the forces that set loose her delirium outside the four walls within which she is enclosed–according to unwritten, albeit extremely powerful laws of the gender divisions of both the society and the nuclear family to which she belongs. In "Love," Ana sees, in the blind man and in the nonurban landscape of the Botanical Garden, the force of incandescence that replaces, albeit temporarily, the internal dimensions of her world made up of kitchen, home, husband, and children. In "Mystery in São Cristovão," the hyacinths in the garden and the three masked men are the magical elements leading to the white hairs that appear on the adolescent's head after what is implied to have been a night of sexual initiation. Opposing such binary paradigms, in which social and domestic prescriptions imprison the character whose unconscious world requires liberation, Clarice Lispector's narrator depicts characters whose patterns of imprisonment are stratified so as to reveal themselves as extremely powerful barriers, impossible to overcome, except in a few moments of epiphany (as in "Love"), or in madness, another form of imprisonment (as in "The Imitation of the Rose").

The richness of Lispector's text lies precisely in the absence of the promise of salvation or happy endings, which give the expected simulacrum of freedom or ingenuously promise women redemption in spite of family entrapment. Rather, the narrative presents power relations and the construction of gender as constructing a complex network of incessantly crisscrossing discourses whose destabilized patterns nevertheless point to continuous mobility that purported a totality of reality. Beyond the existentialist epistemology that was being discussed during the 1950s and 1960s, Clarice Lispector offers in her works, at the end of the century, a contemporary reflection on gender that has become central in the academic world and in larger intellectual circles.

In *O último verão de Copacabana* [1986; The Last Summer in Copacabana], Sônia Coutinho deals in another manner and from another perspective with these same subjects. In the fourteen stories that make up the collection, she examines the melodramatic universe of the representation of the feminine in which women are customarily confined. The characters are propelled by a pathetic, tragic sense of existence which becomes melodramatic through the idealization of Copacabana, the mythical city of glamour, and the quest for a happy ending, yearned for by these women. Their tragedy comes from the impossibility of realizing their desires, as Coutinho's stories undermine these artificial ideals. In this way, these women's lives are engaged as an erotic experience, a "forma de conhecimento: destilação, gota a gota, de um cotidiano ao mesmo tempo inviável e o único possível, feito de solidão, incomunicabilidade, devastação interior, obsessões" ("form of knowledge: the drop by drop distillation of a daily life at once inviolable and yet the only one possible, made of loneliness, lack of communication, internal devastation, obsessions") (Coutinho 1986, dust jacket).

The story "Every Lana Turner has her Johnny Stompanato" is an admirable narrative synthesis of Coutinho's

work. It is built around an initial reference to Lana Turner, the actress-and-myth, but takes the reader through a successive unfolding of this image into multiple others of deglamorized women. It speaks to us of an other, from the absence of self that is the other. This is an empty space without name or biography. Among the main characters, the mythical Lana Turner multiplies indefinitely into various women's names, creating a game in which (as Madame Bovary was to Flaubert) this Lana Turner becomes "myself" to the second woman, to the other, to the mirror: "Folheava uma revista, na varandinha de seu apartamento, quando se deparou, num repentino susto de reconhecimento, com o retrato não muito antigo de Lana, numa reportagem nostálgica sobre grandes estrelas do passado" ("On the small veranda of her apartment, she leafed through a magazine. In a sudden start of recognition she found herself face to face with a fairly recent picture of Lana in a nostalgic article about the great stars of the past") (Coutinho 1986, 4–5).

Far removed from the housewife or the nuclear family that prevails in Lispector's book, the women in Coutinho's gallery function independently outside the home, and are capable of throwing themselves into disturbing professional and sexual experiences. The narrative seeks to investigate a secret reality of hidden meaning, permanently subject to transformations. In making use of the figure of Lana Turner, the narrative gathers two characteristic views of Coutinho's women: In the first, harsh reality is in the conflict with dream; the second is the mythologizing of consumer society. Thus, the book simultaneously deconstructs two images of women: the romantic figure of a woman in a provincial setting, and the glamorous image of a woman in a large metropolis who is lost in the brightness of neon lights and her own incomplete identity. In the short story in question, this opposition is clarified in the image of the "little veranda," which signals the intimacy and shelter of the home, in opposition to Copacabana, the omnivorous big city neighborhood setting, which becomes an allegorized character in the search for glamour.

The result of this procedure is that the reader is led to perceive a kind of ludic behavior typical of contemporary society, where television sells images that people embody without knowing why they do so, compelled by forces at once internal and external, both tempting and frightening. In the case of Coutinho's work, however, these images are sold to educated, well-informed, avowedly single women–frequently actresses and journalists–with a clearly outlined professional profile. In addition, the game these women play is a sort of ventriloquism wherein the search for identity is an erasure. There are no essences, only mythologies. (There is an intertextual link worth noting to Manuel Puig's characters, primarily based on movie melodrama.)

For these women, the exercise of living is realized in speaking or just in going from day to day–as if they were another. This is living like a ventriloquist's dummy as the ventriloquist skillfully speaks without moving his lips, persuading the listener that it is the dummy that speaks. This empty lifestyle is not just individual but collective: This social ventriloquism characterizes a world that continuously externalizes images of simulacrum, with its indefinite duplicating reflection and incessant slippage of signification. In this world, the identity obsessively sought by the characters is barred. Coutinho's technique and her theme both speak precisely of this emptiness. The very structure of her narrative seeks to imitate the social structure represented by the characters. The landscape of which this world speaks is paradigmatic; most of the time, a glamorous city–Copacabana, Hollywood, New York–attracts the character and sets off a compensatory fantasy, which sets up a contrast to another, utterly dull city, that represents the figuration of the anonymous everyday life from whence the characters come.

Steering clear of pretentiousness, Coutinho adopts a subtle and bitter irony as the sharp tool with which she dissects, in sometimes tiny slices, the heavy burden of myth that envelops the imaginary of her characters. This bitterness usually befalls the character whenever she appears about to be caught in the web of romantic idealizations about women. And, undoing the possible happy endings of modern woman's encounter with her own self or the discovery of an alleged identity obliterated by social *a prioris*, Coutinho's characters struggle with the conscious desolation of their solitude and the price customarily paid for trying to avoid it. A woman feeling her loneliness on a Saturday afternoon is depicted as menaced by a vicious bite.

Insisting, like Coutinho, on the depiction of modern woman who only laterally inhabits the space of the bourgeois nuclear family, Márcia Denser creates Diana Marini, a composite female character in whom a contradictory and divided being is represented, one who questions cultural heritage, subjectivity, and the new places occupied by women in contemporary society. "Tigresa" ["Tigress"] is the eighth story in the 1986 collection titled *Diana Caçadora* [Diana the Huntress]. Marini is the protagonist of three other stories in this book, and the protagonists of the remaining stories (identified by a simple "I") are variant versions of her: an economically independent but emotionally immature (and sometimes unstable) upper middle-class woman from the Southeast of Brazil.

Diana Marini is a woman of many faces. A successful journalist, she works for an advertising agency and is also a writer. In "Tigresa," she is getting ready to leave her office when she receives a telephone call from a fan:

–Li teu conto na revista. Achei você sensacional. Você deve ser uma mulher incrível. Preciso te conhecer.
–Claro, respondi, irrefletidamente impostando o tom condescendente de ídolo para o fã. Meu ego estremecera até as raízes.
(Denser 1986, 121–2)

"I read your short story in the magazine. I thought you were sensational. You must be an incredible woman. I must meet you." "Sure," I replied, unthinkingly adopting the condescending tone of idol to fan. My ego was shaken to its roots.

From the very first lines, the reader is aware of Diana's duplicity: a hunter, strong and independent, yet capable of being prey to another hunter, in this case a fan. A sexual and professional go-getter, Diana represents a complex and paradoxical version of male-female relations: On the one hand, she competes with men in her workplace and is their equal outside the limits of the four walls of her home; on the other hand, even though she is over thirty, she lives with her parents. Unlike Clarice Lispector's Lauras, Anas, and Macabéas, or the multinamed, melancholy characters of Sônia Coutinho, there is something grotesque about the hedonistic and independent yet fragile, solitary, and immature Diana Marini. The narrative tends to underline her quasi-neonaturalistic sexuality, as if to indicate that, within a repressive society, her search for liberation implies dramatizing and fulfilling sexuality at the limits of the grotesque. According to this very mark,

in "Welcome to Diana" (the title is in English even in the Brazilian original), another story from the same collection, the character is treated like a prostitute by Fernando, who gives her seven hundred dollars after they have had sex in a São Paulo motel.

Alcoholism, sexual brutality, and both hetero- and homosexual experiences are among Diana Marini's regular practices. In "Ladies First" (another title in English), the homosexual allusion strategically accentuates, through the character's search for identity, the deconstructive nature of Márcia Denser's perspective. The narrator describes the "Ladies Drinks Bar" as a very dark place, but after half an hour, when Diana's pupils have grown used to it and she has actually begun to make out her surroundings. It is still a good while before she manages to realize that the slim youth seated at the next table is a woman, and that the chubby guy in the checkered suit, two tables away, is another woman. The narrator stresses Diana's growing confusion about who really is a woman; she tells herself that "Eu, por exemplo, era uma mulher, não restava a menor dúvida. Ou restava?" (Denser 1986, 90–91) ("There could not be the slightest doubt that I, for example, am a woman. Or could there?").

This fragment by Denser both emphasizes and erases the usual fixed binary opposition of the gender system, since the slim youth is a woman and the chubby guy in the checkered suit is another woman. The expected binary opposition is dislocated and readers' expectations are thus redirected, leaving them face to face with much more complex human classifications, intensified by the lingering question: "There could be no doubt that I, for example, am a woman. Or could there?" The naturalist manner of the description of the "Ladies Drinks Bar" underlines the questioning of Diana Marini's subjectivity as much as it condenses her awareness of the complexity of gender relations. In this sense, Denser's characteristically postmodern use of the grotesque is a means of promoting the erosion of traditional values in a self-destructive and highly consumerist urban society whose simulacrum is life in the metropolis of São Paulo. Beyond being a meditation on subjectivity and a close look at men's and women's places in society, what Denser's narrative debates is the very category of representation and, consequently, of her depiction of the concept of gender. Denser questions the gender system's repressive ideology and rejects the male patriarchal desire to pin woman down to a stable and stabilizing identity. She succeeds in unmasking the gender patterns of a certain social stratum. By pointing out the accumulated repressive binary oppositions in Diana Marini's everyday world (the hunter/the hunted, active/passive, hetero/homo, masculinity/femininity, etc.), Denser's fiction indicates that the security of social prescription and for female characters' subjectivity is weakened. Furthermore, these women move within a network of relationships that cause the subject to lose her mythical image as depicted in the masculine paradigm (i.e., Alencar's fiction), but instead finds herself to be fragmented as well as imprisoned by patriarchal chains. Her fiction depicts the decentering of this subject and dismantles the ideology of gender that allowed the stable, binary allocation of masculine and feminine.

This aspect of Denser's writing questions a series of interconnected concepts usually associated with liberal humanism: certainty, transcendence, unity, truth, fulfillment, and so on. Denser once again takes up these concepts in order to question them–not merely to deny them, but to strip representation from them through human experience as filtered by literature. Paradoxically, her texts both reinstate and discard these ideas by destabilizing them. This occurs also when Denser resorts to metafiction, wherein the critical meaning lies beyond mere self-referentiality. In "Relatório Final" ["Final Report"], for instance, Denser gives us an example of a productive union between metalanguage and a critique of the gender system. In the following fragment, the narrative correlates literary flux to the metaphor of bleeding, articulating the body of literature with the gender-specific body, proposing them both anew as asymmetrical fluxes, able to provide the grounds of a new debate on traditional gender relations:

> E tudo isso quer dizer literatura: a requintada crueldade de poder observar as próprias vísceras expostas refletidas no espelho e imaginando não ser as nossas, como se este refletisse a humanidade toda agora [. . .] como o olho cego da câmara fotográfica, as lâminas frias da cortina que fecha e abre a objetiva, o vidro da lente, inopinadamente a sangrar, a sangrar, amigos, a sangrar, o fluxo maldito chamado literatura, a sangrar. . .
> (Denser 1986, 140)

> And all of this means literature: the refined cruelty of being able to observe one's own entrails reflected in the mirror and imagine that they do not belong to us, as if the mirror now reflected all humanity [. . .] like the blind eye of a camera, the cold blades of the curtain that opens and shuts the lens, the crystal of the lens, unexpectedly bleeding, bleeding, my friends, bleeding, the accursed, bleeding flux called literature. . .

Through self-referential writing, Denser seeks not only to proclaim a text's autonomy, self-sufficiency, or transcendence, but also to narrate contingency itself. In Denser's fiction, there is a banishment of the absolute, of transcendental values, of the mythological universality of gender marking and its validity as truth. In the above-quoted fragment, the "accursed, bleeding flux called literature" may be equated to another flux opened up by the textual mesh. If, in Brazilian literature (e.g. Alencar's *Iracema*), the Brazilian soil has become the representation of the nontransforming principle of a culture constructed in the masculine, in "Diana the Huntress" it is caught in a perspective that alerts us to the ideological nature of these representations that reify into an exercise of power through the mechanisms of cultural gender specification.

Like the women she depicts, the themes of Denser's fiction are paradoxical. On one hand, the elements of imprisonment (the idealizations, the compensatory fantasies, and the prescriptions of the gender system) develop dialectically within their opposites (the character's awareness of her loneliness and internal division, like a price to be paid for freedom and independence). On the other hand, the movement directed to the search for identity and liberation always turns against itself, indicating that freedom and identity are not social products but processes, a continual movement that counterpoints restrictive forces, whether social or individual.

Through their critical engagement, these three writers show themselves to be ill at ease in the patriarchal tradition with which they are engaged in dialogue. They are writing within a state of renewed perspectives and making important contributions to critiques of patriarchy and of the mythologies of bourgeois humanism. Their texts question and criticize the technology of gender, which created the images of earth mother and of women confined within the boundaries of home and family—now obsessively problematizing

this subject (Lispector), now erasing it and relating it to new compensatory myths of postmodern society, which will also be corroded (Coutinho and Denser). Lispector's narratives (as well as those of the other two) promote the deconstruction of two fundamental notions. In the first place, by dealing with the subjects of identity and subjectivity outside the confines of an exclusive binarism, they destabilize certain gender stereotypes. Secondly, their works contain a dialogue with those nineteenth-century protagonists, the heirs of Iracema, secluded in the world of the ruling lords and in the myth of a biologically determined opposition between the sexes. In Lispector's work, this takes place through a demonstration of the ambiguity of family ties as ties both of affection and of powerful neurosis, ties that may unite and yet be capable of imprisoning (while the narrative works to help undermine the reader's passive acceptance of belief in the immutable values of family "peace"). Sônia Coutinho does not deal explicitly with woman's search for freedom from her confining ties to the nuclear family (since her characters, free women, nostalgically navigate the frontier between past and present), but she nonetheless examines, with great subtlety, the weight of guilt and anxiety that those characters must bear as they try to make their painful break.

We would do well to remember that an exemplary number of films made by women in Brazil and in Latin America insist on this very subject; witness the films of Ana Carolina (Brazil), Maria Luísa Bemberg (Argentina), and Sara Gómez (Cuba), among others. Coutinho undermines, through sharp, ironic narratives, the myths that nourish her characters. Yet they are deeply divided women: extremely free, yet idealizing not only the glamour of Copacabana but also that of the romantic fulfillment they never attain. Thus, she creates characters who are internally torn by feelings of loneliness and harsh melancholy, caught in an anxiety generated by the break they cannot manage to achieve. The value of Coutinho's contribution lies precisely in the subtle delicacy with which she faces the following dilemma: Identity and freedom do not occur in the form of a totality without gaps; nor do they lead to beatific fulfillment. Her gallery of female characters know this. Márcia Denser's narrative does not naively pretend to liberate women, but she does suggest that the workings of gender cannot just be redeemed or ignored. Her fictions present gender relations as a complex network of structures that point to the "labirinto especular no qual continuo vagando, os pés feridos nos meus próprios cacos, armadilhas obstinadas a me reter, infinitamente, destruir-me, reconstruir-me, incessantemente" (Denser 1986, 29) ("specular labyrinth in which I continue to drift, my feet wounded on the shards of myself, obstinate traps that detain me, infinitely, destroy me, reconstruct me, incessantly").

The writing of Clarice Lispector, Sônia Coutinho, and Márcia Denser is part of a new system of cultural signification. Their fiction exposes the multiple burdens of woman's exclusion, as much in the public space as in the self-awareness of the construction of woman's own destiny. They articulate new possibilities for working the powerful discursive machine that dynamizes and constructs the cultural imaginary and engenders a new positioning from which to discuss the multiple subjectivity of a subject organized according to the feminine, separate from the idea of *woman* as an essence inherent to all women. In this sense, to reinforce the notion of woman as other is still insufficient, as observed by Heloísa Buarque de Holanda in her introduction to *Tendências e impasses* [Trends and impasses] (13). Progressively, twentieth-century Brazilian writers are engaged with this matter. Since 1930, the narratives of Raquel de Queiroz (1910–2003), for instance, have included the precise marks of the process of women's emancipation. The same might be said of her contemporary Patrícia Galvão, the famous Pagu (1910–1962), author of the proletarian novel *Parque industrial* [1931?; Industrial Park], and co-editor, with Oswald de Andrade (1890–1954), of the Communist newspaper *O homem do povo* [The Man of the People], in which, through the humor of her comic strips, an ardent communist militancy is displayed. As for the women characters created by Raquel de Queiroz, not only in *O Quinze* (1930), but also in *João Miguel* (1932), *Caminho das Pedras* [1937; Stone Road], *As Três Marias,* [1939; *The Three Marias,* 1963] and, most recently, in *Memorial de Maria Moura* [1992; Memorial of Maria Moura], her texts present "a double anti-repressive discourse, for both class and oppressed gender speak in them. In the roster of peasant or lumpen proletariat dramas we see a parade of the afflicted, of widows and of women whose children have died or been killed. And we see also the trajectory of the inmates or militants who pay their dues in a social prison" (Duarte 82). Despite the fact that gender issues are not her most frequent themes, Lygia Fagundes Telles (b. 1923) is another important figure in the narrative presentation of women's profiles in literature.

Starting in the second half of the twentieth century, and especially during the years following the 1960s and 1970s, political stands proliferated, pointing not only to the presence in Latin America of the main feminist lines of dissent—Anglo-American and French—but also to the attempt to consider the subject in political terms both from a social angle and through the textual politics of Latin America. These women, through their construction of feminine subjectivity in literature, are political voices in Latin America. This politicizing impulse is responsible for the inclusion in the writings of contemporary women of themes such as racism, antisemitism, imperialism, colonialism, and the emphasis on class differences, both within specifically feminist debates and in recent literary production (Buarque de Holanda 16).

Brazilian feminist writing has covered a good deal of ground since the image of the "caged bird" present in the narratives of Sônia Coutinho or the one suggested by the oppressive atmosphere of Lya Luft's (b. 1938) *As parceiras* [1980; The Partners], and *O quarto fechado* [1984; *The Island of the Dead,* 1986]. These are narratives which started off as protests against the social imprisonment of women and later evolved in the direction of an open eroticism and lesbianism, as is also the case in the collections edited by Márcia Denser (1982 and 1985), in which we may call particular attention to the texts of Cecília Prada, Edla Van Steen (b. 1936), Judith Grossman (b. 1931), Julieta de Godoy Ladeira (b. 1935), Lya Luft, Myriam Campello, Olga Savary (b. 1933), Rachel Jardim (b. 1928), Renata Pallotini (b. 1921), Sônia Nolasco Ferreira, and Tânia Faillace (b. 1939). Eroticism in Brazilian women's writing has been an expression of women's repossession of their sexuality. The female body is portrayed as a textual space of women's sexual pleasure, not limited or constrained by the male construction of gender within a patriarchal framework. In this line of writing, we might single out Luíza Lobo's (b. 1948) *Sexameron* (1997).

From the literature of the 1960s to that of the present, the recovery of identity has been a constant theme in women's writing. The female subject looks in the mirror and the entire semantic charge of what she sees comes to the fore in what are often obsessive expressions of a search for identity: Witness Helena Parente Cunha's (b. 1929) novel *A mulher no espelho* [1983; *Woman between Mirrors,* 1989], and also the character Lory in Clarice Lispector's *Uma aprendizagem ou O livro dos prazeres* [1969; *The Apprenticeship, or The Book of Delights,* 1986], as well as Lya Luft's *As parceiras* [The Partners].

Clarice Lispector, Lya Luft, Sônia Coutinho, Zulmira Tavares Rodrigues, and, more recently, Marilene Felinto (b. 1957) have all responded to the problems of identity within a discourse in which the female subject's gaze dramatizes the oscillation of woman from the condition of subject to that of object, "constructing a new way of relating to men, themselves balanced today upon a tightrope of uncertainties, as undecipherable and enigmatic as she herself. In the novels *Atire em Sofia* [1989; Shoot Sofia], and *O caso Alice* [1991; The Alice Case], Sônia Coutinho underscores characteristics already observable in her short stories and privileges a destructive feminine circulating within a deterritorialized space, covering countless literary references" (Viana 173). The subjects of identity, of duplicity, of oscillating profiles and minds are also of interest to Nélida Piñon (b. 1937), another important Brazilian writer. In the story "I Love My Husband," published in the collection *No calor das coisas* [1980; In the Heat of Things], Piñon exposes the enfolding, destructive reality of love ritualized by everyday life and the cliché of bourgeois marriage. According to Rita Terezinha Schmidt, "[the] protagonist, who is also the narrator, establishes from the outset a double perspective: at times, representing herself as the object of class and gender socialization, she reproduces patriarchal ideology; and at other times she subverts the ideological code by subtly setting herself outside its reach. Since the borderlines between representation and transgression are not always too clear, ambiguity and irony emerge as the distinctive characteristic of a double character and, inevitably, of this duplicity's very discourse" (213).

Another noteworthy narrative trend, as we have seen in other chapters of this volume, is that of the memoir, as in, for instance, Ana Maria Machado's (b. 1942) text, *Tropical sol da liberdade* [1988; Tropical Sun of Freedom]. Within the developmental line of memory associated with facts and social history, these memoirs are narratives of witness (testimony), more striking in Latin America's Spanish-speaking countries than in Brazil, where they are best represented by Carolina Maria de Jesus's (1914–1977) text, *Quarto de despejo* (1960) and Maura Lopes Cançado's (b. 1930) *Diário do hospício* [1979; Madhouse Diary]. In the same memorialist vein, yet more closely articulated with the political issues of the 1970s, Eliane Maciel's *Com licença, eu vou à luta* [1983; Excuse Me, I'm Off to Work] comes readily to mind.

Among the writers of short stories, novelists, and poets who emerged in the years from the 1960s to the present day, there is one other noteworthy trend: Many of them have turned to writing books for children and for the youth market. This was the case not only with Clarice Lispector, but also with Ana Maria Machado, Marina Colasanti (b. 1937), Ruth Rocha (b. 1931), and Roseana Murray (b. 1950), among others.

In concluding, it is worth noting that in writing by Brazilian women it is not only in the prose works that the image of the bird in search of freedom persists. The poetry of Gilka Machado (1893-1980), for instance, had already engaged in a dialogue with this figural tradition: "Wings, I wish I had wings to fly." If, over the last twenty years, however, eroticism as an expression of that freedom has been a trademark of women's writing in Brazil, it is important to inquire whether this trend has continued in the new generation of women writers at the end of the twentieth century, especially in the light of women's recent and multiple victories in the social, political, and artistic fields. The metaphor of the "caged bird," yearning for empyrean flight, common in women's poetry since Gilka Machado, is enfeebled in the image of the everyday life of the housewife, as she moves through kitchen, living room, and back yard. The grotesque is often part of the world of women's poetry, and the domestic space is portrayed critically, albeit without rancor: "a vida é o varal/de onde tombam os sonhos" (Murray; "life is the clothesline from which dreams fall"); "Estendo toda a manhã/meu varal de estrelas e/saio" (Silva; "Every morning I put up my clothesline of stars/and go out") "Verdadeiramente teatral/com quarenta lençóis/Secando em meu varal" (Guimarães; "Truly theatrical/with forty sheets/drying on my clothesline").

In 1985, Yêda Schmaltz (b. 1941) published *Baco e Anas Brasileiras* [Brazilian Bacchus and Annas]. Her poetry navigates a familiar domestic world in search of the forbidden and the sinful, generating "edible" poems which speak of onions, trifles, savories, and pastries: "Sou mais/as doces peras/mudas/dos meus seios" ("Rather I am/the sweet, mute pears/of my breasts"). In "Monguba Flower," eroticism overflows in running fruit juices, revealing the poetry and thematizing the obscene and forbidden side of the woman's world, abandoning traditional poetic themes using transgressive language which, while breaking limits, penetrates to the intimacy of women directly and without guilt. With Suzana Vargas (b. 1955), the domestic world is reconstructed in language that criticizes with irony and humor the private world traditionally attributed to women: "Meu país é uma/casa onde o/dono/verifica constantemente/nas tampinhas de refrigerantes/a chegada dos prêmios/(patins? Vitrolas?)/E a mulher/Come doces de/abóbora/formato coração/Comprados/Furtivamente/À revelia da engorda" (*Sem recreio*; "My country is a/house where the/owner/constantly checks/soda pop bottle caps/for the arrival of prizes/(skates? Record players?)/And the woman/eats heart-shaped/pumpkin sweets/furtively/purchased/ignoring the fattening"). Women's everyday life seen as an admixture with the sacred–which does not occur in the poetry of the 1990s–is a recent trend, but one already foreshadowed by Adélia Prado (b. 1932), whose poetry of everyday life presents the sacred and the profane as dual ways of experiencing poetry and other things in a life devoid of glamour. The intensity of this work derives from an unexpected yet magnificent surrender to the dull side of domesticity.

To conclude this essay, we would like to review briefly, recent women's poetry in Brazil; first by mentioning those poets whose work has been internationally recognized. we can single out outstanding poets such as Ana Cristina César (1952–1983), Adélia Prado, Astrid Cabral (b. 1936), Hilda Hilst (b. 1930), Leila Miccolis (b. 1947), Lélia Coelho Frota (b. 1937), Myriam Fraga (b. 1937), Neide Archanjo (b. 1940), Olga Savary (b. 1933), and Orides Fontella (b. 1940). Secondly, we also want to acknowledge a number of other poets whose work has not yet been fully recognized but in qualitative terms

have made a significant contribution; these include Cláudia Roquette-Pinto, Marisa Bueloni, Elizabeth Veiga, Lu Menezes, Clara Goés (b. 1956), Rita Moutinho (b. 1951), Roseana Murray (b. 1950)and Suzana Vargas (b. 1955).

Translation by Stephen Berg

Works Cited

Alencar, José de. 1886. *The Honey Lips: A Legend of Brazil.* Trans. Isabel Burton. London: Bickers.

—. 1943 [1857]. *O guaraní.* Rio de Janeiro: H. Antunes.

—. 1979 [1865]. *Iracema.* São Paulo: EDUSP.

Anderson, Benedict. 1983. *Imagined Communities: Reflections on the Origin and Spread of Nationalism.* London: Verso.

Azevedo, Aluízio. 1968 [1890]. *O cortiço.* São Paulo: Livraria Martins.

Buarque de Holanda, Heloisa, ed. 1994. *Tendências e impasses; o feminismo como crítica da cultura.* Rio de Janeiro: Rocco.

Cançado, Maura Lopes. 1979. *Diario de Hospicio.* Rio de Janeiro: Record.

César, Ana Cristina. 1982. *A teus pés.* São Paulo: Brasiliense.

Coutinho, Sônia. 1986. *O último verão de Copacabana.* Rio de Janeiro: José Olympio.

—. 1989. *Atire em Sofia.* Rio de Janeiro: Rocco.

—. 1991. *O caso Alice.* Rio de Janeiro: Rocco.

Cunha, Helena Parente. 1985. *A mulher no espelho.* 2nd ed. São Paulo: Arte Editora.

Denser, Márcia. 1986. *Diana Caçadora.* São Paulo: Global.

— ed. 1982. *Muito prazer: Contos eróticos femininos.* 3rd ed. Rio de Janeiro: Record.

— ed. 1985. *O prazer é todo meu. Contos eróticos femininos.* 2nd ed. Rio de Janeiro: Record.

Duarte, Eduardo de Assis. 1995. "Raquel de Queiroz–Literatura, Política no Feminino." *Mulher e Literatura: Anais do V Seminário Nacional.* Org. Constância L. Duarte. Natal: UFRN. 81–85.

Guimarães, Thaís. 1986. *Jogo de cintura.* 2nd ed. Belo Horizonte: Roma, Dubloso.

Hauser, Arnold. 1964. *Historia social de la literatura y el arte.* Trans. A. Tovar and Varas-Reyes. 2 vols. Madrid: Guadarrama.

Jesus, Carolina Maria de. 1960. *Quarto de despejo.* São Paulo: Livraria Francisco Alves.

Lauretis, Teresa de. 1987. *Technologies of Gender: Essay on Theory, Film, and Fiction.* Bloomington: Indiana University Press.

Lispector, Clarice. 1960. *Laços de família.* Rio de Janeiro: Editora do Autor.

Lobo, Luíza. 1997. *Sexameron.* Rio de Janeiro: Relume-Dumará.

Lotman, Yuri. 1977. *The Structure of the Artistic Text.* Trans. Gail Lenhoff and Ronald Vroon. Ann Arbor: Department of Slavic Languages and Literatures.

Luft, Lya. 1980. *As parceiras.* Rio de Janeiro: Nova Fronteira.

—. 1984. *O quarto fechado.* Rio de Janeiro: Guanabara.

Machado, Ana Maria. 1988. *Tropical sol da liberdade.* Rio de Janeiro: Nova Fronteira.

Maciel, Eliane. 1983. *Com liçenca, eu vou à luta: (é ilegal ser menor?).* Rio de Janeiro: Codecri.

Murray, Roseana. 1988. *Paredes vazadas.* Rio de Janeiro: Memórias Futuras.

Oroz, Sylvia. 1992. *Melodrama: O cinema de lágrimas da América Latina.* Rio de Janeiro: Rio Fundo.

—. 1994. "O discurso da transgressão feminina no cinema: o melodrama latino-americano dos anos 30 e 40." *Letterature d'America.* Rivista Trimestrale. 14 (Roma, "La Sapienza"), 57–8:107–124.

Peixoto, Marta. 1983. "Family Ties: Female Development in Clarice Lispector." *The Voyage In: Fictions of the Female Development*. Ed. Elizabeth Abel, Marianne Hirsh and Elizabeth Langland. Hanover, New Hampshire: University Press of New England. 287–303.

Piñón, Nélida. 1980. "I Love My Husband." *O calor das coisas: contos*. Rio de Janeiro: Editora Nova Fronteira. 57–68.

Queiroz, Dinah Silveira de. c1969. *Floradas na serra 1939–1969*. Rio de Janeiro: J. Olympio.

Schmaltz, Yêda. 1985. *Baco e Ana brasileiras*. Rio de Janeiro: Achiamé.

Schmidt, Rita Terezinha. 1995. "Os Estudos Sobre Mulher e Literatura no Brasil: Percursos e Percalços." *Mulher e Literatura: Anais do V Seminário Nacional*. Ed. Constância L. Duarte Natal: UFRN.175–87.

Silva, Maria Abadia. 1987. *Cabeça cauda*. Rio de Janeiro: n.p.

Vargas, Suzana. 1983. *Sem recreio*. Rio de Janeiro: Achiamé.

Vianna, Lucia Helena. 1995. "Por uma Tradição do Feminino na Literatura Brasileira." *Mulher e Literatura: Anais do V Seminário Nacional*. Ed. Constância L. Duarte. Natal: UFRN. 168–74.

CHAPTER 37

CONSTRUCTING THE PLACE OF WOMEN IN BRAZIL'S NORTHEASTERN REGION

Luzilá Gonçalves Ferreira

Closely interwoven with the history of Brazil's nation building, the history of the Northeastern region is clearly defined by the persistent and effective participation of women. More than in any other region of the country, women in the Northeast have a defining omnipresence both in the private space of home–as organizers of the family circle, which was central for creating and sustaining a country undergoing a process of formation–and in the public space of political performance. The presence of women runs through centuries of Brazilian history and extends over the physical space of a landscape that was witness to the birth of a nation, from the years of discovery to the colonial period and the rise of the independence movement. Furthermore, the participation of women in the public space of the community took place both in the coastal regions of the country and in the remote inland settlements, which only belatedly became generative cultural centers.

Dominique Wolton has suggested three possible subdivisions of the place where individuals may perform and act at the heart of the *polis*: a common space related to circulation and expression, a public space where discussion can take place, and a political space where decisions may be taken. According to these subdivisions, we could say that by exploding the private space of the home, Northeastern women were able to act effectively inside the space of circulation and expression, the space for discussion, and even inside the more political space of decision taking.

Indeed, during the first century after colonization, a woman controlled the destiny of the city of Pernambuco–"captain" Dona Brites de Albuquerque. This woman, referred to as "illustrious" by the poet Bento Teixeira in his poem "Prosopopéia," was the wife of Duarte Coelho and governed the captaincy of Pernambuco for nearly thirteen years whenever her husband was away: from 1540 to 1541, from 1553 to 1560, from 1572 to 1573, and finally during 1579 and 1582. During the period of Dutch domination, there were several women remarkable for their resistance to the invaders, either fighting shoulder to shoulder with the men, like Dona Clara Camarão, or defending their village when men were away, like the heroic women of Tejucupapo. However, there were also those who, following the example of Anna Paes D'Altro, believed that Brazilians would be better off under a Dutch government and fought for their presence in Brazil. Anna Paes, close friend of Count Maurício de Nassau, had married two Batavian officers in succession and christened her children as Protestants; she rejected the Luso Brazilians and collaborated with the Dutch army. The final battle took place on her sugar plantation, called Casa Forte, on August 17, 1645.

The presence of women was equally significant during the emergence of settlements both in the coastal regions and inland, for it was women who often donated the plot where the chapel or church would be built and around which would develop the village or future city. This is the case, for instance,

with the city of Garanhuns, founded by Dona Simoa Gomes. In the more developed urban centers, like Recife, women often donated the physical space and the means for building hospitals, convents, and schools. Such was the case in 1684, when Dona Inês Barreto de Albuquerque, together with her husband Dom João de Sousa, "noble cavalier of His Majesty's house," pledged herself to build on her land a hospital "for the welfare of the poor and forsaken, in their sickness," as well as other buildings, offices, churches, and houses. The village of Poço da Panela, close to Recife, grew around the chapel built in October 1770 by a widow, Ana Maria Clara, in return for the restoration of her health.

Throughout the years of colonization, along the coastal area called *Zona da Mata* (Bushland), many sugar plantations–which constituted the main source of wealth in the region–were managed by women. They organized the economic and social life of the communities alongside their husbands or even on their own when a husband died or was too weak. For instance, at the death of her husband (and, again, between 1563 and 1567), Branca Dias, a New Christian persecuted by the Inquisition, devoted herself to cultivating her sugar plantation in Camaragibe, not far from Recife, on a land grant from the King of Portugal as a *sesmaria* (a piece of uncultivated land granted in order to be cultivated). Another example is that of Dona Francisca da Rocha Wanderley, who had a strong grip on her plantation in Sirinhahém and who, legend has it, used to free the prisoners who entered her lands if they shouted "Valei-me dona Francisca" ("Come to my aid, Dona Francisca!").

Inland, in the arid regions of the *agreste* and the *sertão*, women were active participants in the life of the community and produced material and symbolic goods. When they were not managing the plantations and estates, they took part in the life of the family, deciding marriages, christenings, choosing the name and even the surname of sons, daughters, and grandchildren–family surnames in which the name of the husband was often lost. Sons and husbands were often named in relation to the women themselves, like Severino, Dona Flor's husband, who is called Severino de Flor, and her own children. Many family names in the region were created this way. These women also organized the main family celebrations, such as weddings, in which close and distant relatives were reunited. They were also the axis around which moved the slaves who received orders, or the girls of the family who were learning how to sew, embroider, or cook (whenever servants were difficult to find). At night, it was not unusual to gather the whole family and household together in order either to pray at the family's shrine or to read serialized stories, popular romances, or novels by fashionable authors. When they knew how to read, women were the ones to instruct children. They were also in charge of the events and ceremonies related to birth and death. It was their duty to care for women in labor, newborn children, and sick and dying people, as well as to organize the burial wake, and to attend to the corpses when either the priest or the man of the house was not present. Regarding domestic economy, women were active participants in the accumulation of the family's wealth. Sheep and goats were under their supervision, as was the management of the production of milk, the making and selling of cheese, and the production of meat for internal and external consumption. In the fields, women worked alongside men in agriculture, weeding, tilling the soil, and planting. These activities—which make real matriarchs of these women—were carried out throughout the centuries and continue to exist up to now in the more distant and isolated villages of the region.

Therefore, it is not surprising that women also took part in spiritual and intellectual activities. For instance, Rita Joana de Souza, the first Brazilian woman poet, was born in 1696, in the city of Olinda, Pernambuco and died at twenty-two years of age. She is known to have written a number of poems and a "Tratado de Filosofia Natural e Memórias Históricas" [Treatise of Natural Philosophy and Historical Memoirs], both of which have been lost. One of her contemporaries also lived in Olinda: Lourença Tavares de Hollanda, a "matron with a big name and huge talent," according to historian Fernandes Gama. Her dates of birth and death are not known, and nothing remains of her poems; we have only four letters written to Portuguese authorities interceding for her brothers, who had been taken prisoners in the Mascates War. (Mascate was a derogatory name given to the Portuguese inhabitants of Recife by Brazilians living in Olinda. It gives the name to the Mascates War, which started in 1710 in Pernambuco.)

Maria Firmina dos Reis (1825–1917), who can be considered as the first Brazilian woman novelist, was also born in this region, in the state of Maranhão. Teacher, journalist and poet, she left, among other works, an abolitionist novel that radically differs from other contemporary books in its treatment of slavery and black people. Indeed, Úrsula, published in 1859, is certainly the only abolitionist novel in which the good slave is not the one who has a "white soul," who adopts the religion of his masters, or who somehow adapts to the new land. He is rather a man who remains faithful to his origins, and who considers Africa his real homeland. Túlio, the slave who helps the protagonist, is as brave and generous as his white master and is fully aware of his spiritual freedom for, as the author states, nobody can enslave the human mind. Maria Firmina is equally careful in creating the figure of the woman slave. She eludes the stereotype common to most novels written by men: her female slave is not the sensual and licentious mulatto woman, such as Rita Bahiana, portrayed by the naturalist Aluízio de Azevedo (1857–1913), but an individual committed to her own origins and fighting to build her own identity.

Throughout the nineteenth century, Northeastern women struggled hard in order to be heard and to gain a place in the literary world. Hundreds of women writers published their poems in journals and magazines; even if the aesthetic value of the works is sometimes doubtful, they remain as witnesses to a lively imaginary world. However, it is mainly in journalism that women managed to enter the public space of exchange and discussion. The first newspaper for women was born in this region, O Espelho das Brazileiras [The Brazilian Woman's Mirror] and was published in Olinda in 1832, probably by Nísia Floresta, who would later translate the work of Mary Wollstonecraft and become the friend of Auguste Comte. The publishing house had a dynamic role to play in the vindication of the rights of women to be instructed, to speak freely, and to participate in the struggle for the abolition of slavery and for the establishment of the Republic. The names of three women stand out: Pórcia Constança de Mello (1824–1894), Maria Amélia de Queiroz (1860?–1923) and Maria Augusta Meira de Vasconcelos (1872–193?). Pórcia was the owner of a printing press that supported the Republic and editor of a newspaper, A Rosa [The Rose], which in 1890 asked the other (male) "robust newspapers" for permission to contribute, with a woman's voice, to the "great work of civilization." The title of the newspaper is misleading, because the rose has thorns, and it was precisely in the section called "Thorns" that the criticism of patriarchal society became mordant. There were attacks, for instance, on the lecturers of Recife's Faculty of Law, who, having granted the degree of Bachelor to a woman, did not allow her to practice a profession that, they claimed, was not appropriate to feminine modesty. Maria Amélia de Queiroz was the most important abolitionist and republican orator. A woman with a vast humanist culture, she struggled to end the monarchy and to introduce democracy that, for her, was the system which granted men dignity because it gave them the right of education. The law student with the bachelor's degree defended by Pórcia was Maria Augusta Meira de Vasconcelos, poet and chronicle writer who fought, through the newspapers, a long and difficult battle with her former teachers for her right to practice the profession she had chosen. She lost the struggle.

Maria Augusta Meira de Vasconcelos and Maria Fragoso (1866–1947) were the first women to obtain a law degree in Brazil and, a few years later, another woman once again fractured a male tradition: In 1922, the poet Martha de Hollanda (1903–1950) fought to gain an electoral card, a battle that would turn out to be quite useless: Women were given the right to vote only ten years later. There were other pioneering women as well. The Academy of Letters of Pernambuco was the first in Brazil to accept a woman as a full member: the poet, lecturer and feminist Edwiges de Sá Pereira (1885–1954). In a sense, she was preceded by the poets Joanna Tiburtina de Silva Lins (1840–1905) and Francisca Izidora (1855–1918), who had been acting as "correspondent associates" of the same Academy at the turn of the century. The pioneering work of these women culminated with the writing of the novelist Rachel de Queiroz (1910–2003), who, in 1930, published a book that marked the start of the Brazilian regional novel, entitled O Quinze. Born in Ceará and working as a journalist from the age of sixteen on, she pictures the harshness of the lives of the inhabitants of the Northeastern region suffering from draught, in a forceful, simple, and direct narrative. Throughout the years, this author has never betrayed her vocation as a chronicler of Brazilian life—paying heed to the weaknesses and small successes of people—just as she has never betrayed her vocation as regional novelist. Her last published work, O Memorial de Maria Moura [1992, Memoirs of Maria Moura], tells the story of a nineteenth-century Brazilian woman who, living in a hostile, patriarchal society, decides to control her own fate: She becomes the leader of a gang by overpowering its male members, in order to build her own world by conquering lands and people.

There is still much to say about the participation of women in this region of Brazil, about the ways in which they broke through the boundaries of the private space that was their fate, and about how they managed to penetrate the public space of action and speech. In the meantime, it is enough to remember the path they traveled and how, even if they acted on the margins of history, this path allowed them to open the channels of expression and action for today's Brazilian women.

Translation by Nair Ma. Anaya Ferreira

Works Cited

Gama, Fernandes. 1977. *Memórias Históricas da Provincia de Pernambuco.* 2nd ed. Vol. II. Recife: Public State Archives.

Queiroz, Rachel de. 1992. *O Memorial de Maria Moura.* São Paulo: Editora Siciliano.

Reis, Maria Firmina dos. 1977. (1859). *Úrsula.* Reedition Resgate Collection. Rio de Janeiro: Presença Prómemória. INL.

Wolton, Dominique. 1996. "Espace public: un concept à retravailler." *Études.* Paris. February. 187–98.

CHAPTER 38

WRITING AGAINST THE GRAIN
AN OVERVIEW OF TWENTIETH-CENTURY LESBIAN LITERATURE IN LATIN AMERICA

Elena M. Martinez

Lesbian Latin American writing designates a body of texts that articulate implicitly or explicitly lesbian themes and perspectives. This definition highlights content over the sexual orientation of the writer. In this essay, *lesbian* refers to women who experience erotic as well as emotional connections with other women.

Homophobia has used many strategies for dismissing lesbian experiences. Critics and readers have minimized and undermined lesbian views through the assumption that lesbian discourse is personal and belongs to a private space. Works presenting lesbian motifs and issues are, however, political and public in that they challenge societal power structures and criticize existing (heterosexual) institutions. Moreover, this type of literature is political because it denotes not only a sexual orientation but also a network of complex cultural and social relations. By refusing to submit to the sexual and gender dispositions that characterize heterosexual cultural norms, lesbian works suggest rebellion and become a threat to male authority and dependency at the same time that they encourage transformations in culture and society. In the essay "Lesbianism: An Act of Resistance," Cheryl Clarke stresses the political value of lesbianism. She argues that, no matter how lesbians live their lesbianism, they rebel against submission to men and proclaim their autonomy (128).

Over the past two decades there has been an increased interest in lesbian literature in North American universities. In Latin America, however, where a body of lesbian literature indeed exists and continues to grow, silence is still the norm. Responding to social restrictions and impositions, lesbian writers have used euphemisms to disguise their meanings or to communicate them in a secretive manner. Through the use of codes and a language of reticence, these writers have articulated lesbian meanings, as Bonnie Zimmerman and Lillian Faderman have already noted with regard to U.S. lesbian authors. As Faderman states, writers purposely encode lesbian subject matter so it needs to be deciphered by the reader who has knowledge of the writer's homosexuality (1994, 445). Because of the way these lesbian meanings have been hidden and transformed into socially acceptable forms in the texts, they have been easily overlooked.

The purpose of this essay is to offer an overview of twentieth-century lesbian Latin American literature. Because of the silence that has prevailed and continues to prevail regarding non-normative sexuality in Latin America, one writes against the grain in describing a tradition of lesbian literature in a society in which the history of lesbianism has yet to be rescued from denial and silence. The first part of this essay deals with what Faderman terms "the literature of the closet," that is, literature written during the first part of the twentieth century that implicitly, either through textual strategies or through its thematic concerns aided by a biographical reading, articulates lesbian themes or sensibilities. Part two of this essay addresses the more explicit treatment of lesbian themes and motifs in texts from the 1970s to the present. As we shall

see, this more explicit literature presents four major thematic concerns: the erotic, the autobiographical, the self-reflexive, and the sociopolitical. Because these themes are intertwined in many of the texts (poetic as well as narrative), their classification within these four categories resists easy identification.

Writers of the first part of the twentieth century thematized lesbianism through the employment of specific strategies. Among the most prominent are: a speaker who places herself as an outsider, as either a psychological or social exile; the thematization of the mirror and the double; a particular employment of female/male pronouns or, on the contrary, the omission of pronouns that mark gender; the sexual ambiguity of speakers or characters. Literature of the second part of the twentieth century becomes more open in its presentation of lesbianism. Some of the salient features of this literature are: the treatment of lesbian love intertwined with a formal self-reflexivity; lesbian love and sociopolitical issues; the revision of classical western myths to challenge heterosexual interpretations; an openly erotic discourse that portrays the union of a female "I" with the "you" or the "I" and the "she"; themes of sisterhood and female bonding; the employment of a celebratory tone to speak about love or the presentation of the painful experience of unrequited love.

The poetry of Sor Juana Inés de la Cruz (1648–1695) inaugurated a Latin American tradition of encoding a lesbian sensibility. Sor Juana Inés de la Cruz—the religious name of the Mexican Juana de Asbaje—is well known for her lyrical and philosophical poetry, essays, and drama. Her love poems (dedicated to such women as the Countess of Paredes), as well as her antagonism toward men, have provided a basis for lesbian readings of her works and life. Poems such as "En que describe racionalmente los efectos irracionales del amor" [In which she describes rationally the irrational effects of love], "Filis," "Divina Lysi mía" [My Divine Lysi], "Detente, sombra, de mi bien esquivo" [Stop, Shadow of My Disdainful Beloved], and "Envía las Pascuas de Resurrección" [Easter Greetings, My Lady] may be read as the encoding of a lesbian love discourse because they indeed represent women's poetry dedicated to and inspired by women.

In recent years a key literary figure from the first decades of the twentieth century, Gabriela Mistral (Chile, 1889–1957; pseud. of Lucila Godoy), has begun to be rescued for a lesbian tradition by textual readings and biographical interpretations. The work of Mistral is a good example of the "literature of the closet." On the one hand, it reflects her identification at different levels with other women. However, critics have ignored the female friendships in Mistral's life, stressing instead the desolation caused by the death of a male lover. Her poetry has only recently been the subject of lesbian literary approaches. (For contributions to the study of Mistral's poetry as part of a lesbian tradition, see Lanzarotti, Horan, and Fiol-Matta).

Lesbianism is encoded in Mistral's poetry through the treatment of certain themes, as well as the avoidance of pronouns

341

that mark gender. Frustration, prohibition, absence, and exile all thematize the marginal position of lesbians in society. In poems such as "País de la ausencia" [Land of Absence], "Dios lo quiere" [It Is God's Will], and "Todas íbamos a ser reinas" [We Were All Going to Be Queens], the poetic voice is characterized by a tragic view of love that seems to refer to non-normative forms of sexuality. In "País de la ausencia" the speaker speaks from a position of marginalization and exile. These themes of exile and absence have been used in lesbian literature to symbolize psychological conditions rather than merely geographical ones. Exile can be read as a metaphor for the disenfranchisement of lesbians in a society that is hostile to unconventional forms of love and desire.

Whereas the texts of Sor Juana Inés and Mistral belong to the "literature of the closet," the works of Alejandra Pizarnik (Argentina, 1936–1972) and Cristina Peri Rossi (Uruguay, b. 1941) are more explicit in their articulation of lesbian discourses. Pizarnik's works, characterized by a concern with the process of writing poetry, mix an erotic discourse with self-reflexivity. La condesa sangrienta [The Bloody Countess], a volume of eleven prose vignettes based on Valentine Penrose's Erzébet Bathóry: La Comtesse Sanglante (1963), recounts the torture and murder of young women by Countess Bathóry. Here torture, death, power, and lesbian eroticism are intertwined. In the section "El espejo de la melancolía" [The Mirror of Melancholy], the homosexual tendencies of the countess are referred to: "Speaking of mirrors, no one was ever able to confirm the truth of the rumors about the countess's homosexuality. We will never know whether she ignored the tendency or, on the contrary, admitted it as a right she accorded herself along with all the other rights. Essentially, she lived submerged in an exclusively feminine universe" (Graziano 100). In some poems, Pizarnik has encoded lesbian meanings through the use of female and masculine pronouns. Poems such as "Cenizas" [Ashes], from Las aventuras perdidas [The Lost Adventures], employ the masculine pronoun. In other poems, the repeated themes of displacement and exile, as well as a tragic view of love, may be read (as in the case of Mistral) as an encoding of lesbian themes and a marginalized sensibility.

The writings of Pizarnik's Uruguayan contemporary, Cristina Peri Rossi, are characterized by her critical view of institutions, her use of irony, the speakers' or characters' sexual ambiguity, and an insistence on transgressive acts. Her poetry collection Evohé (1976), a source of controversy when published, is an example of the strategy of using male/female pronouns to encode lesbian desire. Here, a male speaker expresses desire for the female body. Moreover, one of the epigraphs of the collection, a poem by Sappho, is an obvious reference to lesbianism ("Once again: Eros, sweet and bitter, invincible monster, tortures me"). Through its use of male and female pronouns, Evohé masks lesbian eroticism. In some instances this encoding leads to an abundance of clichés and stereotypical relationships between the male and the female. Thus the strategy's purpose is twofold: It allows Peri Rossi to articulate her feelings for a woman, and it also inscribes a critique of male/female coupling. In fact, the adoption of a male voice by Peri Rossi in Evohé is an attempt to erase the gender categories so deeply inscribed in literature. This gesture of articulating lesbian eroticism through the use of male and female pronouns allows the speaker to discuss lesbian eroticism using the forms of heterosexual longing, thus encoding the poet's desire for another woman. The strategy of transforming and hiding meanings and themes to avoid political censorship has been a common strategy used by marginalized writers everywhere, but as Peri Rossi acknowledged in an interview with John Deredita, her recourse to this strategy has been particularly pronounced (Deredita 134).

In Evohé, Peri Rossi's speaker establishes connections between the female body and language and poetry, words and women, and the poet and the lover. This collection presents the male speaker's desire to find refuge in words after disappointments with women. The speaker, who is not willing to be seduced by the charm of words, connects women's seductive charms with the power of language. Throughout the collection, the words "woman" and "language" are interchangeable. Typographical innovations allow for linguistic openness as a metaphor for diversity in sexual pairings. At times, Peri Rossi suggests the interchangeability of the erotic and the poetic by inverting the words in a phrase. This strategy breaks with the reader's expectations: "The woman pronounced and the word possessed" (Evohé 37). On other occasions, the speaker establishes a dialogue between consecutive poems: "Women come from afar/to console male poets/for words' deception," and in the next poem: "Words come from afar/to console us/for women's deception" (Evohé 19). Even though the text compares words with women, the category of gender is being linked with the origins of poetic discourse. Women's eroticism overpowers language and poetry. In poems like "Silencio" [Silence], the poet goes beyond the dichotomy "nature/civilization" and subordinates literature to the female lover.

In 1979's Lingüística general [General Linguistics], Peri Rossi again investigates the relationship with regard to meaning, grammar, and gender categories. Whereas in Evohé Peri Rossi uses a system of encoding homoeroticism and love, in Lingüística general the theme of lesbianism is overtly addressed as the poet moves from secret encoded meanings to an openly lesbian sexual discourse. In several of the poems in this book ("Haendeliana," "Dolce Stil Nuovo," "Dolce Stil Nuovo II," "3ra. Estación: Campo de San Barnaba," and "4ta. Estación: Ca Foscari") the poet explores lesbian love. In "3ra. Estación: Campo de San Barnaba" the speaker is characterized by her conscious transgressions. The desire to transgress a law has political value; here, a lesbian subjectivity is clearly expressed, as the female speaker proclaims her love for another woman:

Esta noche, entre todos los normales,
te invito a cruzar el puente.
Nos mirarán con curiosidad
—estas dos muchachas—
y quizás, si somos lo suficientemente sabias,
discretas y sutiles
perdonen nuestra subversión
sin necesidad de llamar al médico
al comisario político o al cura.

Tonight, along with all the normal people,
I invite you to cross the bridge.
They'll stare at us
—these two girls—
and perhaps, if we are wise,
secretive, and subtle enough
they will forgive our subversion
without calling in the doctor,
the commissar, or the priest.

Here the expressions "among the normal people" and "to cross the bridge" clearly refer to a sexuality that has traditionally been seen as subversive.

In "4ta. Estación: Ca Foscari" the poet continues her exploration of love between women. The speaker emphasizes the sameness of female bodies and the interchange of the women's clothes, bodies, and identities. Love is presented through this exchange of identities and the reciprocity of their feelings:

Te amo como mi semejante
mi igual mi parecida
de esclava a esclava
parejas en subversión
al orden domesticado
Te amo esta y otras noches
con la señas de identidad cambiadas
como alegremente cambiamos nuestras ropas
y tu vestido es el mío
y mis sandalias son las tuyas
Como mi seno
es tu seno.

I love you as my sister
my equal, my double
slave to slave
partners in revolt
against domestic order
I love you tonight and other nights
trading birth marks
the way we joyfully exchange our clothes
and your dress is mine
my sandals yours
my breast
your breast.

In "A los poetas . . . " ["To the Poets"], one of the poems of Peri Rossi's *Diáspora* (1976), the speaker confronts a male-oriented tradition that has objectified women. This poem presents a woman who makes public her lesbian identity. Here the woman-object assumes the role of subject and makes a political statement. The public announcement of the speaker's lesbianism—in English and in French (an indirect allusion to English and French feminisms)—is a reaffirmation of her sexual orientation and of her identity.

The 1980s witnessed the emergence of other lesbian poetic voices in Latin America. Joining the voices of Pizarnik and Peri Rossi were those of the Argentineans Diana Bellessi (b. 1944) and Mercedes Roffé (b. 1954), the Puerto Rican Nemir Matos (b. 1949), and the Mexican Sabina Berman (b. 1953). Some of the poetry by Bellessi, Roffé, and Berman presents the theme of lesbian identity through a self-reflexive discourse; other poems are characterized by the sheer enjoyment of lesbian sensuality. Bellessi's poetry collection *Eroica* (1988) presents a strong lesbian erotic discourse, a celebration of sexual and emotional relationships among women. It is a work of passion and desire for the female body. Throughout the book's eight sections, the speaker unites eroticism with the pleasure of the word. The poems praise different parts of the female anatomy, emphasize the senses, and link body and text. In "El texto" ["The Text"], "El Magnificat," and "Intempesta Nocte" ["Stormy Night"], the speaker describes lesbian sexual encounters up to the moment of orgasm. In one of the most accomplished sections of the book, "Dual," the poetic voice recalls, as in Peri Rossi's "4ta. Estación: Ca Foscari," the reciprocity of desire of the two women lovers, a theme that is articulated through the unification and the interchangeable positions of the "you" and the "I."

As in "Dual" and "4ta. Estación Ca Foscari," the reciprocity of the lovers' desire is also a thematic feature of the poetry of Nemir Matos, who Carlos Rodríguez Matos has asserted was the first Puerto Rican poet to textualize lesbianism openly (216). Her poetry, like some of Peri Rossi's works and Bellessi's *Eroica,* privileges eroticism. In it, the speaker dwells on her lover's body and desires, as well as on her own. Powerful erotic images compare the female body to elements of nature. In her poem "Oleajes" [Ocean Swells], from *Las mujeres no hablan así* [Women Do Not Speak Like That], the speaker describes a sexual encounter between two women. A feature of this lesbian discourse is the use of a colloquial language to speak about sex in a way that challenges poetic tradition as well as social convention—a point alluded to in the collection's title. *Lunas* [Moons], a 1988 poetry collection by the Mexican poet, playwright, novelist, and actress Sabina Berman, offers an erotic writing of the lesbian body. In this collection, as in *Evohé* and *Eroica,* eroticism and poetic discourse are closely linked. Like Matos, Berman defies traditional language forms in order to inscribe the oppression of women. She plays with the Spanish-language conventions of grammatical gender and explores the linguistic possibilities of including feminine forms of speaking about women's physical and emotional experiences.

A tone of celebration of the female body and of lesbian encounters prevails in the poetry of Peri Rossi, Bellessi, Matos, and Berman. But the lesbian love poetry of Mercedes Roffé distances itself from the celebration of the sensual, erotic aspect of lesbian relationships to articulate the painful experience of the absence of the lover. In Roffé's *Cámara baja* [The Lower Chamber], the lesbian theme is encoded in the articulation of a tension between the spheres of the female and the male and is elaborated through a series of oppositions: mother/father; aunt/uncle; female lover/male lover; a Jewish girl/boy. In two of the poems of this collection, "Entierra, entierra" [Bury It, Bury It] and "Almita mía" [My Beloved], the tension between female and male becomes associated with the speaker's quest for the definition of her sexual orientation. In the closing poem of the book, the speaker expresses her rebellion against women's oppression. Roffé's collection of poetry entitled *La noche y las palabras* [Words and Night] presents the theme of the absence of love and its relationship to the process of writing. This collection, like Sylvia Molloy's celebrated novel *En breve cárcel* [*Certificate of Absence,* 1989] and Nancy Cárdenas's *Cuaderno de amor y desamor* [Book of Love and Absence of Love], emerges as a cathartic exercise for the loss of the lover. The tone of intimacy used by Roffé's speaker expresses, in a self-contained manner, her desolation over the loss of her lover.

Several of the collections by Cuban poet Magaly Alabau (b. 1945) present a vein of lesbian eroticism linking women's identity, psychology, and the body. For instance, in her *Electra/Clitemnestra*, a highly charged poetry collection, the female body is portrayed as the paramount object of desire. In her second book, *Hermana* [Sister], the representation of lesbian eroticism is transformed into an emotional bonding as well as a physical connection. However, the erotic discourses in these two collections are distinct, as they correspond to different definitions of eroticism. Nevertheless, they are both expressions of a lesbian sensibility. *Electra/Clitemnestra* and *Hermana* are lesbian texts in the sense that they highlight intense sexual and emotional relationships between women. Whereas in *Electra/Clitemnestra* Alabau explores aspects of rivalry and competition within the context of a mother-daughter relationship marked by erotic tension and desire, in *Hermana* the poet explores the relationship of twin sisters, one who left the country and lives in exile and the other who stayed behind and lives in a mental institution, another form of exile. The idea of "twin sisters" recalls one of the expressions used to designate "romantic friendships" among women in the nineteenth century: "kindred spirits" (as Faderman has noted in the context of nineteenth-century North American writers). Following Faderman's hypothesis, the title *Hermana* works as a metaphor for a lesbian lover.

Lesbian eroticism in *Electra/Clitemnestra* supposes a re-reading of classical Greek myths. Readers witness a development in the relationships among the mythical female protagonists from *Electra/Clitemnestra* to *Hemos llegado a Ilión* [1992; Ilium]. The former collection, as its title indicates, explores the relationship between Electra and her mother, Clytemnestra. *Hermana* alludes to the myth of Orpheus, the return to a past to rescue the speaker's muse (a sister or a lesbian lover). *Hemos llegado a Ilión* evokes the myth of Demeter and Persephone. In Alabau's poetry, the female heroines, who in the classical stories act for the sake of the patriarchal family, are instead carrying out a personal quest for power or the satisfaction of their sexual desire. In *Electra/Clitemnestra*, Alabau explores Electra's feelings of anger and jealousy; she has killed her mother, not to reestablish the order of the patriarchal home, but rather to take revenge against the woman who failed to reciprocate her feelings. Electra acts out of jealousy, since Clytemnestra has a male lover. In her re-reading of the myth, Alabau rejects avenging the father's death as a significant motif in the story.

The erotic discourse in *Electra/Clitemnestra* articulates diverse views on eroticism and is characterized by two themes: the centrality of violence and the superiority of female sexuality. The lovemaking of Clytemnestra and Medusa, as presented in poem VII, is characterized by violence. All images in this poem denote great passion mixed with rage, jealousy, and fury:

> Medusa la restriega y la desnuda,
> la latiga, la sacude y la alza.
> Se le monta en el cuello,
> le embarra la cara.
> Lengua con lengua,
> espuma roja, espesa.
>
> (20)
>
> Medusa scrubs her and strips her,
> lashes her, shakes her, and holds her up.
> She mounts on her neck,
> muddies her face.
> Tongue against tongue
> thick red foam.

Through the use of powerful, vivid language, Alabau imbues Medusa with an erotic lesbian strength. In this poem, Medusa is the one who seeks out Clytemnestra and finds her sitting in her room. Clytemnestra's house is transformed into the site of lesbian sexual encounters, as Medusa approaches Clytemnestra and they make love:

> Se tiran en una cama larga
> Medusa monta un caballo largo
> el techo las aplasta
> y se unen
> y se unen

> y se aman
> y se cortan de dientes
> Medusa le entra por la boca,
> por la espalda, y grita.
>
> (20)
>
> [they] fling themselves down on a long bed
> Medusa mounts a long horse
> the roof crushes them
> and they unite
> and they unite
> and they love one another
> and they bite each other
> Medusa enters her mouth,
> from behind, and cries out.

The reciprocity of the lesbian lovers' actions is indicated by the parallelism of the words "y se unen" [and they unite] and "se aman" [and they love]. Here, the speaker focuses on the power of the sexual encounter. In other poems, traditional phallic symbols such as serpents, trunks, and horns are included in the context of a lesbian relationship. Sex between the female protagonists is viewed first as a struggle and then as a moment of perfection. It is linked to a new beginning or the rebirth of Mycenae: "Dos mujeres vibran, se amoldan/ mueren abrazadas/y ya no hay heridas ni cráteres./Micenas renace" [Two women vibrate, mold to each other/die in an embrace/and there are no more wounds, no craters/Mycenae is reborn] (20).

In Alabau's book *Hemos llegado a Ilión*, the mother-daughter relationship is evoked through the re-elaboration of the myth of Demeter and Persephone. This myth is at the center of the work of Jungian feminist writers who value the archetype of the Great Goddess and the role of the mother (Purkiss 451). It is a story of separation and love that reinforces the idea of female connection. Demeter searches for her daughter and effects her return through her own divine power. In *Hemos llegado a Ilión*, the speaker travels back to her native land to see her mother. The journey back to the speaker's country is a journey to Averno, associated with the underworld and with Persephone. *Electra/Clitemnestra*, *Hermana*, and *Hemos llegado a Ilión* all reclaim relationships among women: mothers, daughters, sisters, and friends. In Alabau's poetry, however, the mother-daughter and sister-sister relationships are metaphors for female erotic pairings.

In *Cuaderno de amor y desamor* by the Mexican poet and playwright Nancy Cárdenas (1934–1994), the poetic voice clearly states the affective-erotic specificity of its discourse, a lesbian one in which the female speaker is invoking a woman lover. There are poems—or several moments of the long poem, since the entire book can be considered one poem— that come together in a rich synthesis through the use of the words "amor/ desamor" (love and absence of love) taken from the title of the book. The poems of the first part, in the tradition of Monique Wittig's *The Lesbian Body,* are dedicated to the joy of erotic and affective relationships between women. They are a celebration of the lesbian body, praising the physical, as well as the intellectual and emotional, characteristics of the female lover. Cárdenas's text presents a clear relationship between lesbian eroticism and poetic discourse. The need to write emerges from encounters with the speaker's lover: "your visits are good for me/they leave me filled with poems" (47). Cárdenas is aware that the expression of lesbian love is a political act, and throughout the book we find the desire to claim a lesbian poetic space from which the lesbian subject may articulate her experiences. The cyclical structure of *Cuaderno de amor y desamor,* as well as the articulation in one long poem of various repeated motifs, allows for an aggressive continuum–"todo fluye: nunca nos hemos separado" (43) [everything flows:/we have never been separated]– and it also lends fluidity to the reading. Moreover, it textualizes the nonauthoritarian character of this lesbian discourse and the recurrent theme of love in Cárdenas's poetry from 1984 until her death in 1994.

The works of the Puerto Rican poet Luz María Umpierre (b. 1945) are part of the literary production of Latinas in the United States. In addition to the treatment of racial and ethnic issues, during the 1980s Latina lesbian writers introduced themes of the marginality imposed on them because of their sexual orientation. Chicana and Puerto Rican women stand out among the Latina writers who produced this type of literature. While lesbian motifs begin to appear in her early poetry collections–*Una puertorriqueña en Penna* [1979; A Puerto Rican in Penna], *En el país de las maravillas* [1982; In Wonderland], and . . . *Y otras desgracias. And Other Misfortunes* . . . (1985)–it is in *The Margarita Poems* (1987) that Umpierre clearly articulates both a lesbian erotic discourse and the political consciousness of her situation as a Puerto Rican in the United States. Echoing the Chicana writer Cherríe Moraga's (b. 1952) title *Loving in the War Years: lo que nunca pasó por sus labios* (1983), Umpierre asserts the need to break the silence and to speak openly about her sexual orientation: "First of all, I needed to say, to speak, 'lo que nunca pasó por mis labios,' that which I had not uttered, and which was being used as a tool in my oppression by others, murmured behind closed doors, brought up as an issue to deny me my rights by those enemies who read my poetry too well. What I needed to verbalize is the fact that I am, among many other things, a Lesbian. Second, I wanted to communicate in some viable form with some One who came to represent all women to me" (1). *The Margarita Poems,* like the works of other Latinas, is characterized by bilingualism and biculturalism. The collection includes nine poems, five of which are in English: "Immanence," "No Hatchet Job," "The Statue," "Only the Hand that Stirs Knows What's in the Pot," and "Título: En que trata de lo que es y no hay mah ná." Three poems are in Spanish: "Madre," "Ceremonia Secreta," and "Transcendence." The last poem, "The Mar/Garita Poem," is in both English and Spanish.

In "Madre," Umpierre, like Alabau in *Electra/Clitemnestra,* explores the conflictive dimension of biological and sexual bonding among women. The speaker's maternal search is both literal and metaphorical: She looks for both her mother and a literary role model. Here, the traditional maternal body is transformed and eroticized as the speaker finds her absent mother in the bodies of a plurality of female lovers. The lesbian relationship is presented through the use of a female "I" and a female "you" as Umpierre had already elaborated in such previous poems as "Transference" and "Clímax," from her collection . . . *Y otras desgracias. And Other Misfortunes* . . . (1985).

Lesbian prose writers in Latin America have been less prolific than their poetic counterparts. Prominent novels presenting lesbian characters or perspectives or allowing for a lesbian interpretation include: Reina Roffé's *Monte de Venus* (1976), Sylvia Molloy's *En breve cárcel* [1981; translated by Daniel Balderston as *Certificate of Absence,* 1989], Albalucía Angel's *Las andariegas* [1984; The Wandering Women], Rosamaría

Roffiel's *Amora* (1989), and Sara Levi Calderón's *Dos mujeres* [1990; *The Two Mujeres,* 1991]. Very different from one another, these novels either present lesbian motifs encoded in the theme of solidarity among women, as can be seen in Angel's *Las andariegas,* or are openly lesbian, like the groundbreaking *Certificate of Absence.* Despite differences in the presentation of lesbian themes and in the use of literary techniques, these works share some features: concern for the autobiographical, the search for a common past, female bonding, and the need to forge a lesbian space.

One novel written in the biographical mode is *Monte de Venus* [1976; Mount of Venus] by Reina Roffé (Argentina, b. 1951). A novel censored by the Argentinean government due to its portrayal of political problems and lesbianism, *Monte de Venus* has two main plot lines. One, narrated in the third person, relates experiences in a school for adults. It explores the relationships and amorous intrigues among the students and the repressive atmosphere of the school, a mirror image of the political situation in Argentina during the 1970s. The second plot revolves around Julia Grande, whose life experiences articulate the lesbian's marginality in a homophobic society. Despite the stereotyping and the tragic view of lesbianism presented in *Monte de Venus,* its open portrayal of sexual and erotic encounters between women, as well as its articulation of the lack of understanding and tolerance toward different expressions of sexuality, make a political statement that calls for society's acceptance of lesbianism.

Certificate of Absence, by the literary critic Sylvia Molloy (Argentina, b. 1938), has a double plot: It articulates the story of a lesbian love affair, as well as the process of writing about it. The novel's erotic discourse, like that of Alabau's *Electra/Clitemnestra,* follows French notions of eroticism, especially those proposed by Georges Bataille and Monique Wittig. Bataille and Wittig's notions of eroticism differ, of course; the former proposes a view that is male-centered and heterosexist, while the latter presents a lesbian perspective. However, Bataille and Wittig do agree on two issues: first, that violence is an essential element of the erotic experience and, second, that it is textualized through the fragmentation of the body. For both Bataille and Wittig, partners in the sexual act become unified; the "I" and the "you" are interchangeable as a result of communication; there is the dissolution of the "I," and the discontinuance of space and time during the erotic experience. In *Certificate,* Molloy underscores the notion of female bonding through the identification of the "I" and the "she." Furthermore, by relating the "I" and the "she" through violence and dissolution, Molloy keeps the discourse of love open, thus preventing the novel from falling victim to melodramatic views on love and female bonding. In the end, the conjunction of a passionate lesbian erotic text and a discourse on female-centeredness defines the novel and lends it its singularity.

The relevance of passion is stressed by the bookcover of the Spanish version, which features a reproduction of Michelangelo's "Woman Kneeling Down with the Instruments of Passion." The various definitions of "passion" highlight the elements of violence and intensity present in the novel. Passion is defined as an intense and overpowering emotion; an eager outreaching of mind toward some special object or an ardent affection for someone; a fit of intense and furious anger, rage; any transport of excited feeling and violent agitation. The female protagonist's need to write about her love life emerges from the absence of love and the pain caused by her lover's abandonment. Writing is, for the woman, an exercise with a dual purpose: It helps the protagonist recover her lost lover, and it allows her to purge herself of the feelings she has for her earlier lover. The woman attempts to recall the feelings of the affair and at the same time to liberate herself from them.

Certificate not only exists as a result of the rupture of a lesbian love relationship, but it also presupposes a separation from a heterosexual literary tradition. Thus, the novel is based on the tension between several oppositional forces. The specific tension that characterizes the writing and the eroticism in the text is synthesized through the mythological figure of Diana the huntress. In *Certificate,* as in *Électra/Clitemnestra* and *The Margarita Poems,* female mythological figures are re-read as symbols of lesbian culture. In one of the most singular dreams in the novel, the protagonist's father asks her to go to Ephesus to see Artemis, the goddess of fertility. However, the father's message, which is ambiguous, confuses the protagonist: She is unsure whether she is being asked to worship or to destroy Artemis. Instead of going to see the goddess of fertility, the protagonist realizes she prefers to see Diana. This act of paternal disobedience is necessary for the lesbian writer who blazes her own trail, rather than following an established path.

It is not accidental that the first part of *Certificate* ends with the dream of Artemis and the motif of fertility. The mythological figure of the huntress remains at the center of the novel (as the search for other women and the discourse of desire and violence have been at the core of the narration). The dream connects the literary and the lesbian erotic discourses by reaffirming the lesbian meanings of the text and destroying heterosexual alternatives. Thus, the first part of the novel symbolizes a female journey in search of the significance of fecundity. Procreativity is linked, in the case of the lesbian writer, not to her body and the institution of motherhood, but rather to literary practice inspired by lesbian desire and love. The ungovernable huntress contrasts with the fixed, imposing image of fertility represented by Artemis:

> She prefers another Artemis, another Diana–the free huntress, not weighed down by a breastplate of fertility–though no fixed sanctuary seems to have been built to her. Indeed, she delights in the small, firm breasts of that other Diana, barely visible beneath the tunic her sixteenth-century celebrants give her in their paintings and statues. Poised for action, armed with bow and arrow and attended by hounds, she is on the move: not burdened by the clustering stone breasts of her mothering counterfigure, the huge image at Ephesus, symbol of fertility. No, this other Diana, the one she prefers, the free Diana–is not fertile. Ungovernable, she tantalizes with her always desirable, always unreachable body: if there is something fertile about her it is the challenge itself, which nourishes her. (57)

Through the protagonist's preference for the violent and erotically charged goddess, Molloy privileges lesbian existence and identifies violence with writing. Therefore, her passion for writing and the primacy of lesbian eroticism and meanings are brought forth through the novel's motif of Diana the huntress. Wittig and Sande Zeig have pointed out the mythological figure's relevance for lesbian culture. In *Lesbian Peoples: Material for a Dictionary,* they assert: "[Diana the huntress:] Most recent name of Artemis, the only known Amazon goddess to whom all the lesbian peoples remained attached after the time of the amazons, writing poems and celebrations in her name. Diana was represented as a goddess of the horned moon, hunting with bow and arrows. She was celebrated in Etruria during the beginning of the Iron Age as the

one who calls to arms once again the amazons who, in that obscure time, had already begun to scatter. Each of those eager to rejoin the dispersed amazons consecrated her daughter to Diana" (Wittig and Zeig 43). In Molloy's novel the protagonist's interest in Diana is based on her defiant character and multiplicity: "She would like to see herself in harmony, in a happy conjunction, with Diana, toward Diana, through *multiplicity and contradiction*" (118; emphasis added). Through the writer's identification with Diana, she breaks with impositions and expectations of gender roles, since males have traditionally been associated with the ability to hunt and kill while females have been identified with the capacity to reproduce and nurture. Her identification with the huntress underlines the woman's preference for mobility, change, action, and aggression instead of the passive role that has been assigned to her. The mythological figure of Diana the huntress represents not only action and aggression, but also sensuality. Lesbians' lives presuppose a detachment from heterosexual norms of love, desire, and the institutions of marriage and motherhood. Identified with what Diana represents, *Certificate*'s love discourse is characterized by violence, ambiguity, and elusiveness.

In *Las andariegas* (1984), the Colombian writer Albalucía Angel (b. 1939) re-reads the myths of the Amazons while establishing a dialogue with Wittig's *Les Guérillères. Las andariegas* is a text that breaks with literary conventions by including elements of essay and poetry within the novelistic form, as well as breaking with the role that women have traditionally played by centering on the Amazon women. The novel stresses the need for women to bond with other women in order to claim a space and a tradition that have been denied to them as well as to reframe women's experiences in a different cultural context.

Unlike *Certificate of Absence,* Rosamaría Roffiel's (b. 1945) novel *Amora* (1989) presents a unifying view of lesbian love and eroticism. The novel's dedication–"to all women who dare to love women"–states its lesbian as well as its autobiographical nature. The main plot is concerned with lesbian love: Indeed, the novel's title attempts a new definition of love as it is synthesized in the word "amora." In addition to telling a love story from a lesbian point of view, the novel intertwines a reflection upon women's position of inequality in Mexican society. The feminist discourse, elaborated through a chorus of female voices, touches upon such issues as the lack of recognition of women, the prohibition of sexual pleasure, and the limitations imposed upon women's sexual behavior and sexual orientation. Love in the "feminine mode" stresses emotional intimacy and solidarity among women. The emphasis on emotions and the significance of building a lesbian community are essential aspects of *Amora.* Solidarity among women, along with a sense of a lesbian collectivity that provides the women with a sense of identity, is central to this work. The lesbian characters, Mariana, Citlali, and Lupe, live together as a family. Their relationship is based on equality, which contrasts with the inequality that prevails in the male/female relationships in the novel. These women represent a group committed to working together against sexist forms of socialization.

In *Amora,* there are two chapters that are essential to the discourse of love and sensuality: "Somos mujeres, y nos gusta serlo" [We Are Women and We Love Being Women] and "El amor es una cosa esplendorosa" [Love Is a Splendored Thing]. In these two chapters, the dialogues between Lupe and Claudia allow for a discussion of the need to redefine love and sexuality from a lesbian perspective. This redefinition would separate itself from the stereotypical constructions that have identified lesbian love as unfulfilling and tragic, as well as from a conception of love and sexuality that excludes emotional attachment:

> [A]memos diferente, sin cortarnos las venas, sin amenazar con tirarnos desde un puente en el periférico, terminar vomitando en Garibaldi o bajándole la novia a la amiga nada más para que vean qué chingona vengo este año, es decir, no amemos así como dicen que amamos las lesbianas, como si fuéramos la versión femenina del Charro Negro. (*Amora* 33–34)

> [L]et's love differently, without slashing our veins, without threatening to jump off an overpass, or end up vomiting in Garibaldi Square or laying a friend's lover just to prove how tough we are; that is, let's not love following a lesbian stereotype like a female version of the Mexican charro.

Roffiel's novel makes a claim for a lesbian form of sexuality, integrating sexual pleasure with emotions, spirituality, and other aspects of life. The importance of feelings in *Amora* is manifested in the abundance of romantic scenes in which the lovers share confessions, listen to music, have long conversations, and enjoy the atmosphere of romance and intimacy. Lovemaking takes place in an idealized space in which a celebration of the bodies and the senses prevails. Intimate moments are romantically described: "Moon water, cool, tipped with silver. Embroidered sheets. Shroud of light. Mother of pearl bed. Two women. Two. Facing each other in this unique game that is love" (71–72).

In 1990 the Mexican sociologist Sara Levi Calderón (b. 1942) published *Dos Mujeres,* an autobiographical novel that stirred controversy because of its portrayal of lesbian encounters. It is the portrait of Valeria, a thirty-nine-year-old Mexican "petit bourgeois" of Jewish heritage and a divorced mother who, discovering her sexual orientation, narrates a lesbian love affair. The novel has a testimonial value as a coming-out experience in contemporary Mexico. Moreover, *Dos mujeres* relates the oppression suffered by lesbians and society's strategies to silence and marginalize non-normative forms of sexuality. Indeed, despite the work of the women's movement, lesbianism and lesbian literature are still unspeakable in Latin America.

Works Cited

Alabau, Magaly. 1986. *Electra/Clitemnestra*. Concepción, Chile: Libros del Maitén.

——. 1986. *La extremaunción diaria*. Barcelona: Ediciones Rondas.

——. 1989. *Hermana*. Madrid: Editorial Betania.

——. 1991. *Hemos llegado a Ilión*. Madrid: Editorial Betania.

——. 1992. *Hermana/Sister*. Bilingual edition. Trans. Anne Twitty. Madrid: Editorial Betania.

——. 1993. *Liebe*. Bilingual edition. Trans. Anne Twitty. Miami: La Torre de Papel.

Angel, Albalucia. 1984. *Las andariegas*. Barcelona: Argos Vergara.

Bataille, Georges. 1986. *Eroticism: Death and Sensuality*. Trans. Mary Dalwood. San Francisco: City Lights Books.

Bellessi, Diana. 1988. *Eroica*. Buenos Aires: Ediciones Ultimo Reino/Libros de Tierra Firme.

——. 1992. *El jardín*. Buenos Aires: Bajo la Luna Nueva.

Berman, Sabina. 1988. *Lunas*. Mexico City: Editorial Katún.

Cárdenas, Nancy. 1994. *Cuaderno de amor y desamor*. Mexico City: Colección Sentido Contrario, Hoja Casa editorial.

Clarke, Cheryl. 1981. "Lesbianism: An Act of Resistance." *This Bridge Called My Back. Writings by Radical Women of Color.* Ed. Cherríe Moraga and Gloria Anzaldúa. New York: Kitchen Table: Women of Color Press. 128–38.

Deredita, John F. 1978. "Desde la diáspora: entrevista con Cristina Peri-Rossi." *Texto Crítico* 9: 131–42.

Faderman, Lillian. 1981. *Surpassing the Love of Men: Romantic Friendship and Love Between Women from the Renaissance to the Present*. New York: William Morrow.

——. 1994. "In the Closet: The Literature of Lesbian Encoding." *Chloe Plus Olivia: An Anthology of Lesbian Literature from the Seventeenth Century to the Present*. Ed. Lillian Faderman. New York: Viking Penguin. 441–46.

Fiol-Matta, Licia. 1995. "The School Teacher of America: Gender, Sexuality, and Nation in Gabriela Mistral." *¿Entiendes? Queer Readings, Hispanic Writings*. Ed. Emilie Bergmann and Paul Julian Smith. Durham, N.C.: Duke University Press. 201–29.

Graziano, Frank, ed. 1987. *Alejandra Pizarnik: A Profile*. Trans. María Rosa Fort, Frank Graziano and Suzanne Jill Levine. Durango, Colo.: Longbridge-Rhodes.

Horan, Elizabeth Rosa. 1994. "Gabriela Mistral." *Latin American Writers on Gay and Lesbian Themes. A Bio-Critical Sourcebook*. Ed. David William Foster. Westport, Conn.: Greenwood Publishers. 221–35.

Juana Inés de la Cruz, Sor. 1956. *Obras completas. Lírica personal*. Ed. Alfonso Méndez Plancarte. Vol 1. Mexico City: Fondo de cultura económica.

Lanzarotti, Claudia. 1992. "Sospechosa para todos." *APSI* (Santiago de Chile) 418: 30–33.

Levi Calderón, Sara. 1990. *Dos mujeres*. Mexico City: Editorial Diana.

——. 1991. *The Two Mujeres*. Trans. Gina Kaufer. San Francisco: Aunt Lute Books.

Matos, Nemir. 1981. *Las mujeres no hablan así*. Rio Piedras, Puerto Rico: Editorial Atabex.

Mistral, Gabriela. 1983. *Poesías de Gabriela Mistral*. Mexico City: Editores Mexicanos Unidos.

Molloy, Sylvia. 1981. *En breve cárcel*. Barcelona: Editorial Seix Barral.

——. 1989. *Certificate of Absence*. Trans. Daniel Balderston with the author. Austin: University of Texas Press.

Moraga, Cherríe. 1983. *Loving in the War Years: Lo que nunca pasó por sus labios*. Boston: South End Press.

Peri Rossi, Cristina. 1971. *Evohé. Poemas Eróticos*. Montevideo: Girón editorial.

——. 1978. *Diáspora*. Barcelona: Lumen.

——. 1979. *Lingüística general. Poemas*. [Valencia]: Editorial Prometeo.

Piznarik, Alejandra. 1971. *La condesa sangrienta*. Buenos Aires: Aquaris.

——. 1986. "The Bloody Countess." *Other Fires: Short Fiction by Latin American Women*. Trans. and ed. Alberto Manguel. New York: Clarkson N. Potter. 70–87.

Purkiss, Diane. 1992. "Women's Rewriting of Myths." *The Feminist Companion to Mythology*. Ed. Carolyne Larrington. New York: Harper and Collins. 441–57.

Rodríguez Matos, Carlos. 1994. "Luz María Umpierre." *Latin American Women Writers on Gay and Lesbian Themes. A Bio Critical Sourcebook*. Ed. David William Foster. Westport, Conn.: Greenwood Press. 434–36.

Roffé, Mercedes. 1987. *Cámara baja*. Buenos Aires: Ediciones Ultimo Reino.

——. 1996. *La noche y las palabras*. Buenos Aires: Bajo la Luna Nueva.

Roffé, Reina. 1987. *Monte de Venus*. Buenos Aires: Ediciones Corregidor.

Roffiel, Rosamaría. 1989. *Amora*. Mexico City: Editorial Planeta Mexicana.

———. 1986 [1994]. *Corramos libres ahora*. Mexico City: Femsol.

Umpierre, Luz María. 1979. *Una puertorriqueña en penna*. [San Juan: Masters].

———. 1985. . . . *Y otras desgracias. And Other Misfortunes* . . . Bloomington, Ind.: Third Woman Press.

———. 1987. *The Margarita Poems*. Bloomington, Ind.: Third Woman Press.

———. 1990. *En el país de las maravillas (In Wonderland)*. 2d ed. Berkeley: New Earth Publications.

Wittig, Monique. 1971. *Les Guérillères*. New York: Viking Press.

———. 1975. *The Lesbian Body*. Trans. David Le Vay. Boston: Beacon Press.

Wittig, Monique, and Sande Zeig. 1979. *Lesbian Peoples: Material for a Dictionary*. New York: Avon Press.

Zimmerman, Bonnie. 1981. "What Has Never Been: An Overview of Lesbian Feminist Criticism." *Feminist Studies* 7.3: 451–75.

CHAPTER 39

SECRETS AND TRUTHS

Daniel Balderston

Xavier Villaurrutia (1903–1950) writes in the first stanza of his "Nocturno de los ángeles" (Nocturne of the Angels/L.A. Nocturne, 1936; all translations mine):

Se diría que las calles fluyen dulcemente en la noche.
Las luces no son tan vivas que logren desvelar el secreto,
el secreto que los hombres que van y vienen conocen,
porque todos están en el secreto
y nada se ganaría con partirlo en mil pedazos
si, por el contrario, es tan dulce guardarlo
y compartirlo sólo con la persona elegida.

One could say that the streets flow sweetly in the night.
The lights are not so bright as to reveal the secret,
secret known to the men who come and go,
they are all in the secret
no one would gain anything from having it shatter
when it is doubly sweet to keep it
and share it only with the chosen one.

Here we might recall Eve Kosofsky Sedgwick's reflection on "open secrets" in the first chapter of *Epistemology of the Closet*: "In the modern cultures of the West, same-sex desire is still structured by its distinctive public/private status, at once marginal and central, as *the* open secret" (22), and that hiding it is "a performance initiated as such by the speech act of a silence" (3). Similarly, in *The Novel and the Police*, D. A. Miller asserts: "I can't quite tell my secret, because then it would be known that there was nothing really special to hide, and no one really special to hide it. But I can't quite keep it either, because then it would not be believed that there was something to hide and someone to hide it" (194). Miller later quotes a character from Oscar Wilde: "[secrecy] is the one thing that can make modern life mysterious and marvelous. The commonest thing is delightful if one only hides it" (195).

There are many Latin American texts that could say with Villaurrutia that everyone is in on the secret (and has a stake in keeping it that way). Even one of the founding texts of Latin American gay literature, the novel *La pasión y muerte del cura Deusto* [1924; Passion and Death of the Priest Deusto] by the Chilean writer who called himself Augusto D'Halmar (1880–1950), tends to take refuge in assertions of this kind: "lo nuestro no tiene solución en esta tierra" (259) ("our love has no solution in this world,". The exceptions to this rule, Adolfo Caminha's (1867–1897) *Bom Crioulo* [1895; Good Creole] and the play *Los invertidos* [1914; The Inverts] by José González Castillo (1885–1937) do call "inversion" and "pederasty" by their names, but they do so–and we should recall that these are texts written under the tutelage of the naturalism of Emile Zola, with its discourse of the medicalization of sexuality–from the outside, from the vantage point of scientific truth. The nascent literature of homosexuality, from D'Halmar to the Mexican group Contemporáneos, instead chooses to evade these pseudoscientific categories, preferring to speak from silence.

There is surely no better example of this structure of the "open secret" than the famous short story "El hombre que parecía un caballo" [1914; "The Man Who Looked Like a Horse"] by the Guatemalan writer Rafael Arévalo Martínez (1884–1975), inspired in the ambiguous relationship he had

with the Colombian poet who would later call himself Porfirio Barba Jacob (but who in this period used the pseudonym Ricardo Arenales, much closer to the name of the character in the story, the "señor de Aretal"). What is of interest in this story is not so much the fact that it alludes to homoerotic desire, but the identification, on the part of both Arévalo Martínez and Barba Jacob, with the characters in the story, and the manner in which this identification insinuated itself into literary gossip (and literary history, as we shall see later on) but also into the two writers' "self-fashioning," to use Stephen Greenblatt's term. What is never made explicit in the story becomes so in the public threats that Barba Jacob makes after the story's publication, although nothing was to come of those threats, no doubt because Barba Jacob enjoyed the notoriety pressed upon him by his sometime friend. This is, then, an "outing" story, with the curious effect that the intended victim was to forge a new identity around the caricature of himself in the text (see Balderston 1997).

José Lezama Lima (1910–1976) writes of this in *Paradiso* (1966), in the famous dialogue in Chapter 9 in which Fronesis, Foción, and Cemí debate the nature of homosexuality and the contributions of homosexuals to history and culture:

Recuerde usted aquel poeta Barba Jacob, que estuvo en La Habana hace pocos meses, deber haber tomado su nombre de aquel heresiarca demoníaco del XVI, pues no sólo tenía semejanza en el patronómico sino que era un homosexual propagandista de su odio a la mujer. Tiene un soneto, que es su ars poética, en el que termina consignando su ideal de vida artística, "pulir mi obra y cultivar mis vicios." Su demonismo siempre me ha parecido anacrónico, creía en el vicio y en las obras pulidas, dos tonterías que sólo existen para los posesos frígidos. (252)

You remember that poet Barba Jacob, who was in Havana a few months ago: he must have taken his name from that notorious sixteenth-century heretic, since he resembled his precursor not only in name but also in that both were homosexual propagandists for the hatred of women. He wrote a sonnet, his *ars poética*, in which he defines his literary ideal as "polishing my work and cultivating my vices." His demonism always seemed anachronistic to me: He believed in vice and in polished works, two idiocies that exist only for frigid maniacs.

The portrayal of Porfirio Barba Jacob (1883–1942) as a "propagandist" for homosexuality owes a great deal to the caricature of him that appeared a half-century earlier in Arévalo Martínez's story. It is interesting that, in Lezama's Catholic, neo-baroque take on these questions, "propaganda" (a word whose origin, as is well known, has to do with the Roman Catholic Church) is taken as wholly negative. There are gay characters in *Paradiso*–Foción is the most important–who fall in love only then to suffer in silence. "Open secrets" are preferred to publicity (here called "propaganda").

And yet, this tendency is not the only one that existed in Latin America in the years prior to the 1960s and 1970s (decades that marked important changes in this discourse, as we shall see). In the most important text of a different kind, the essay "Ballagas en persona" [1955; "Ballagas in Person"], by another great Cuban writer of those years, Virgilio Piñera

(1912–1979), the following is stated: "Si los franceses escriben sobre Gide tomando como punto de partida el homosexualismo de este escritor; si los ingleses hacen lo mismo con Wilde, yo no veo por qué los cubanos no podemos hablar de Ballagas en tanto que homosexual. ¿Es que los franceses y los ingleses tienen la exclusiva de tal tema?" (194). ["If the French write about Gide taking his homosexuality as a point of departure, if the English do the same with Wilde, I cannot see why we Cubans cannot speak of Ballagas as a homosexual. Or do the French and English have exclusive rights to this topic?"].

It is interesting to note that the poems by Ballagas that Piñera cites most frequently as products of the conflicted sexuality of the Cuban poet, "Elegía sin nombre" and "Nocturno y elegías," adhere closely to the rhetoric of "open secrets" that we saw in the poem by Villaurrutia.

"Elegía sin nombre" opens with epigraphs from Whitman and Cernuda, a signal to the gay reader to keep an eye out for the expression of homosexual feelings, but the dominant note in the poem is that of the rhetoric of silence:

¡Ya es mucho parecerme a mis palidas manos
y a mi frente clavada por un amor inmenso,
frutecido de nombres, sin identificarse
con la luz que recortan las cosas agriamente!
¡Ya es mucho unir los labios para que no se escape
y huya y se desvanezca
mi secreto de carne, mi secreto de lágrimas,
mi beso entrecortado!

(142)

It is already so much to resemble my pale hands
and my forehead pierced by a great love,
fruiting with names, not spoken
with the light that cuts bitterly through things!
It is already so much to join lips so that
my secret of flesh, my secret of tears,
my interrupted kiss,
not come out, flee, are swept away!

In these verses, we note the repetition of the word "secret," the absence of grammatical signs indicative of the gender of the "immense love"–an ambiguity that is maintained nearly throughout the poem–and the fact that the loved one remains "unidentified." The most open verses in the poem are these:

Así anduvimos luego uno al lado del otro,
y pude descubrir que era tu cuerpo alegre
una cosa que crece como una llamarada
que desafía al viento,
mastil, columna, torre,
en ritmo de estatua
y era la primavera inquieta de tu sangre
una músima presa en tus quemadas carnes.

(143)

Thus we walked one next to the other,
and I could see that your happy body
was a thing that grew like a flame
defying the wind,
mast, column, tower,
with the rhythm of a statue,
and that the restless springtime of your life
was a captive music in your burning flesh.

Here the synecdoche obviously links the "happy [or gay?] body" of the beloved with his erect phallus ("mastil, columna,

torre" 'mast, column, tower'), while the masculine pronouns ("uno al lado del otro" 'one next to the other') suggests that the beloved is male.

"Nocturno y elegía" ("Nocturne and Elegy"), the next poem in *Júbilo y fuga* (Jubilation and flight), opens with the following lines:

Si pregunta por mí, traza en el suelo
una cruz de silencio y de ceniza
sobre el impuro nombre que padezco.

(145)

If he asks for me, trace on the ground
a cross of silence and ashes
over the impure name that I bear.

And the following stanza begins:

No le digas que lloro todavía
acariciando el hueco de su ausencia
donde su ciega estatua queda impresa
siempre al acecho de que el cuerpo vuelva.

(145)

Don't tell him that I still weep
hugging the emptiness of his absence
where his blind statue imprinted itself
always waiting for the body to return.

Like the references to silences and secrets, this allusion to the statue–what the body of the beloved leaves in memory, a memory as much physical as mental–forms part of a code that is repeated in various gay poets of Ballagas's generation. It is present, for instance, in Villaurrutia's "Nocturno de la estatua" (Nocturne of the statue) and in various of his other poems, as well as in the fourth poem of Salvador Novo's *Nuevo amor* (New love), which reads:

Junto a tu cuerpo totalmente entregado al mío
junto a tus hombros tersos de que nacen las rutas
de tu abrazo,
de que nacen tu voz y tus miradas,
claras y remotas,
sentí de pronto el infinito vacío de tu ausencia.
Si todos estos años que me falta
como una planta trepadora que se coge del viento
he sentido que llega o que regresa de cada contacto
y ávidamente rasgo todos los días un mensaje que nada
contiene sino una fecha
y su nombre se agranda y vibra cada vez
más profundamente
porque su voz no era más que para mi oído,
porque ciega mis ojos cuando aparta los suyos
y mi alma es como un gran templo deshabitado.
Pero este cuerpo tuyo es un dios extraño
forjado en mis recuerdos, reflejo de mí mismo,
suave de mi tersura, grande por mis deseos,
máscara
estatua que he erigido a su memoria.

(86)

Beside your body offered completely to mine
beside your taut shoulders where the routes
of your embrace are born,
where your voice and your clear,
remote glances are born,
I suddenly felt the infinite emptiness of your absence.
If all the years that remain to me

like a climbing plant that grasps onto the wind
I have felt arriving or returning at every touch
and I avidly scratch each day for a message that
contains nothing but a date
and his name gets larger and vibrates ever
more deeply
because his voice speaks to no ear but my own,
because he blinded my eyes when he turned his aside
and my soul is like a great empty temple.
But this body of yours is a strange god
forged of my memories, a reflection of myself,
soft in my tautness, large to my desire,
mask
statue that I have erected to his memory.

It is striking that the same vocabulary—absence, body, statue, memory, blindness—is at the heart of the Ballagas poems and of those of the Contemporáneos. If Neil Bartlett, in his remarkable book *Who Was That Man? A Present for Mr. Oscar Wilde* (39–59), has been able to reconstruct the "language of flowers" that the contemporaries of Wilde—and Proust—used as coded speech, so we can suspect that in the 1930s and 1940s something similar happened with the language of statues, at least in the Spanish-speaking world, and that the legacy of this tradition would be the famous concept of *imago* in Lezama.

It is pathetic and yet amusing that this language of concealment, or interrupted discourse among the chosen few, should come to be the prevailing note of the final paragraphs of the preface that Osvaldo Navarro wrote for the edition of Ballagas's poems that was published by Editorial Letras Cubanas in 1984, which is full of such silliness as:

Por eso, en alguna reunión de amigos inteligentes y sensibles, en la unión de alguna pareja que disfruta esa magnífica y unánime soledad que se produce entre un hombre y una mujer enamorados, alguien, algún amigo, o uno de los dos en la pareja, recordará de pronto un verso de Ballagas, y todos, y ellos dos, tendrán de pronto la noción precisa de que en el hombre hay algo de inmortal y eterno, algo bello y real que vive con nosotros y que el poeta nos lo advierte, porque el poeta es el único humano que muere antes de morir y uno de los pocos que nos ayuda a vivir mas allá de la muerte. (40)

That is why, in a gathering of sensitive, intelligent friends, during the union of a couple that enjoys that magnificent and harmonious solitude that happens when a man and a woman are in love, someone, some friend, or one of the members of the couple will suddenly remember a verse by Ballagas, and the two of them will suddenly have the precise notion of what in man is immortal and eternal, something beautiful and real that lives in us and that the poet informs us about, because the poet is the only human being who dies before dying and one of the few who helps us live after death.

The paragraph before this depends completely on the rhetoric of secrets—messages whispered through half-open doors, bouquets of flowers offered—while the second clarifies, rather clumsily, that "the union of a couple" is properly defined as (and limited to) the union of "a man and a woman in love," so that the reader will not suffer any unwelcome surprise, not be led on by any degree of ambiguity. But as Piñera clarifies, even this sort of heterosexual union was a motive of anguish for Ballagas, who "llega a la mujer y al hijo muy diferentemente de lo que lo haría el hombre heterosexual" (198) ("approaches his wife and son in ways very different from how a heterosexual man would do"). Piñera notes that in the period in which the poet wrote the two elegies mentioned,

1937–38, "Ballagas acaba de salir, como quien dice, de un amor fracasado con una persona de su mismo sexo (prefiero expresarme así y no con el método elusivo de Vitier–'los amantes sin saberlo, son empujados por el destino hacia el fatal encuentro'–que provocará burlonas sonrisas en los amigos y enemigos del poeta)" ("Ballagas had just come out, so to speak, of a failed affair with a person of his same sex [I prefer to express myself that way and not in Vitier's elusive fashion– 'the lovers, without knowing it, are impelled by fate toward their fatal meeting'–that surely provokes joking smiles among the friends and enemies of the poet]." Piñera comments that when "Elegía" appeared "ciertos homosexuales de capilla" ("some militant homosexuals") thought "¡Por fin alguien nos representa!" ("Finally someone represents us!") and "ciertos intelectuales de capilla" ("certain militant intellectuals") in their turn thought: "Es poesía 'engagé', ya el uranismo cubano tiene su profeta" (198) ("This is engaged poetry; finally Cuban perversion has found its prophet,". And he clarifies that when Ballagas marries and has a son ten years later, "esas 'reinas' y esos 'plumíferos', incapaces de medir la larga agonía que es una década de escrúpulos de conciencia, convierten el 'crédito' concedido al poeta en 'descrédito', el activo en pasivo" (199) ("those queens and those scribblers, incapable of sensing the long anguish that is a whole decade of scruples of conscience, convert the 'credit' granted the poet into 'debit,' the active into passive"). Given the sense that these final adjectives have in the world of male homosexuality, this phrase breaks definitively with the rhetoric of silence, secrets, flowers, and statues.

So it is not unreasonable to say that the fundamental break in the treatment of the topic of homosexuality in Latin America takes place—rather secretly, since the article did not circulate all that widely—in this 1955 article by Piñera. In outing Ballagas (posthumously), in saying in "Ballagas en persona" that it is important to speak of his tortured homosexuality and the false heterosexuality he used to conceal it, Piñera—against the Origenistas, and especially against Lezama and Cintio Vitier (b. 1921)—made it possible for other writers fifteen years later (in Cuba, Antón Arrufat [b. 1935] and Reinaldo Arenas [1943–1990], and elsewhere in the continent, Luis Zapata [b. 1951], Manuel Ramos Otero [1948–1990], Néstor Perlongher [1949–1992], Darcy Penteado [1926–1990], João Silverio Trevisan [b. 1944]) to live their homosexuality more openly and to deal with the theme outside the tortuous labyrinths of previous generations. Though little known outside of Cuba in the 1950s, and though not collected into a book until Arrufat and Carlos Bonfil gathered Piñera's poetry and criticism into a volume published in Mexico City in 1994, Piñera's 1955 article did not actually produce this change of tone and approach, but it is evident that by insisting on speaking openly of Ballagas's homosexuality, Piñera (like Genet and Isherwood in the same period) anticipated in an isolated sense the striking change that was to occur in a more general way some fifteen or twenty years later. But the act of naming the other, of saying "I cannot see why we Cubans cannot speak of Ballagas' homosexuality," is not yet a public declaration of the writer's own homosexuality, and does not yet configure a public, collective identity from which one can speak.

In this regard one certainly thinks of Manuel Puig, who names homosexuality in *El beso de la mujer araña* [*Kiss of the Spider Woman*]–in the footnotes–and who forces the reader to associate the analytical discourse of the notes with the dialogue on top of the page between Molina and Arregui. At the same time he makes fun of the rhetoric of open secrets in the final footnote, in which the author disguises himself as a woman, speaking through the invented Danish doctor, Anneli Taube, author of a book on sexuality and revolution. Puig and his novel–and the success that the characters have had in their successive incarnations in fiction, theater, cinema, and musical comedy–have no doubt done more than any other Latin American author and text to spark interesting and subtle discussions of the topic of homosexuality. If we were to repeat the experiment that Neil Bartlett proposes in his book on Wilde (26) of conducting a survey asking a Latin American sample to name one famous homosexual in the continent, much more than the name of Arenas or Sarduy or Perlongher or Ramos Otero, no doubt Puig's name would come up, even though he himself denied the existence of homosexual and heterosexual identities.

If a moment ago I mentioned a series of writers for whom it has proved easy or natural to define themselves as homosexual or incorporate a gay thematics openly in their work, then I think one figure who is of particular interest is the Venezuelan poet Armando Rojas Guardia (b. 1949). Since the publication of his book-length essay *El dios de la intemperie* [1985; The God of Inclemency], through *El calidoscopio de Hermes* [1989; The Kaleidoscope of Hermes], as well as in his poetry, Rojas Guardia has done as much as anyone to foster an intelligent and interesting discussion of the relations between homosexuality and other spheres of life, and of the ways in which an open gay sexuality can become part of a complex worldview. And he has done it in a relatively unusual sphere, certainly unusual in Latin America: in the religious sphere, and specifically within the Roman Catholic tradition, inscribing his reflections in the rich Catholic tradition of confessional literature.

In *El dios de la intemperie*, the homosexual topic emerges, in a rather heterodox way, from a discussion of spiritual experience. Rojas Guardia asserts that from such experience, especially mystic experience, "brota, en cierta forma, una estética" ("in a sense, an esthetic springs forth," (39). He mentions Pasolini's film "Teorema," in which "el misterioso huésped . . . trastorna . . . la vida de todos . . ., convoca a éstos al desierto, al lugar de la más absoluta desnudez, un lugar simbólico en mitad del cual el hombre encuentra el contacto con una epifanía llameante, con el grito de la última desgarradura" (46) ("the mysterious guest turns everyone else's life inside out, bringing them together in the desert, in the place of utter nakedness, a symbolic place in the midst of which man encounters a burning epiphany, with a rending cry"). He then refers openly to "mi específico carácter homosexual" (84) ("my specific homosexual nature), and comments:

La vida espiritual del homosexual se enfrenta, en el marco de la sociedad regida por la Norma heterosexual y patriarcal, a específicos peligros. Como no existen paradigmas positivos para el eros homoerótico, la existencia homosexual se gesta en la entraña de una trampa mortal: la tácita vinculación que va estableciéndose en el inconsciente entre cuerpo, goce, vida de los sentidos, erotismo, por un lado, y, por otro, satanismo, imagen bufonesca de la atracción hacia personas del mismo sexo, criminalidad latente, malignidad radical. (84–85)

The spiritual life of the homosexual is confronted, within the framework of a society ruled by a heterosexual and patriarchal norm, with specific dangers. Just as positive paradigms do not exist to talk about homoerotic love, so homosexual existence comes to be within the confines of a lethal trap: the tacit links in

the unconscious between the body, pleasure, the life of the senses, the erotic, on the one hand, and satanism, a clownish image of same-sex attraction, latent criminality, radical evil, on the other.

Since a large part of this book tells of the author's experience in mental hospitals, the importance of the link between homosexuality and madness is perhaps emphasized more than the wished-for positive images. He later summarizes: "Mi homoerotismo me ha conducido a la heterotopía" ("My homoerotic feelings have led me to a heterotopia"), a term he defines, after de Certeau, as "el lugar otro, fuera-de-la-ley" ("the other place, outside the law") (106). And he therefore defines desire as "no . . . simplemente una epifanía de la afirmación de sí" (127) ("not simply an epiphany in the affirmation of the self) but as "la búsqueda del Otro, del Otro como tal Otro, como absolutamente Otro" ("the search for the Other, for the Other as Other, as absolutely Other").

Four years later, in "Pequeña serenata amorosa" ["Little Amorous Serenade"] in *El calidoscopio de Hermes* (1989), he deepens his discussion of this topic, but now with regard to a less metaphysical Other: "Junto a él percibo con exactitud por qué soy homosexual. El presencializa ante mí, y mas aún, dentro de mí, un acorde de la ternura. Pero este acorde es esencialmente viril: sólo un hombre puede manifestarlo" (143–44) ("When I am with him I know precisely why I am homosexual. He makes present for me, or better still, inside of me, a note of tenderness. But this note is essentially male: only a man can make it manifest"). And he later comments: "Para el homosexual, constituye empresa titánica construir la espiritualidad de una pareja. Y ello porque pertenecemos a una especie amorosa para la que no existe, diseñado, un orden cultural" (152) ("For the homosexual, it is a titanic enterprise to construct a spiritual dimension to a relationship. And that is because we belong to a loving species for which a defined cultural order does not exist"). It seems to me that the almost unique contribution of Rojas Guardia to Latin American discussions of the topic of homosexuality is his insistence on the changes–the wrenching changes, as witnessed by his experience of mental illness, but also changes that fascinate due to his insistence on a spiritual dimension to homoerotic desire–necessary to produce a future world in which homosexual love might be accepted in society and might discover positive features currently obscured by fear and rejection. He is a Utopian thinker, something rarely seen in the continent and in his milieu.

The passages from speaking of a secret in which all are invested to naming homosexuality, and from there to naming oneself as homosexual, are long, slow processes, though they do crystallize around a few moments, as we have seen. And it is interesting that they should have happened in Latin America at roughly the same time as elsewhere: Piñera's essay is from 1955, and *Paradiso* and *El lugar sin límites* [Place Without Limits] are from the late 1960s, a little before Stonewall and the gay liberation movements. The liberation movements are explicitly named in the footnotes to *El beso de la mujer araña*, and the works of Luis Zapata and Néstor Perlongher are unimaginable without them. And I believe that the possibility of writers naming themselves as gay has depended on the existence of the international movements (and of the national ones, however small), that even the Catholic and spiritual homosexuality of Armando Rojas Guardia, for example–his reflection on the gay couple in "Pequeña serenata amorosa," in which he yearns for social rituals that would foster the spiritual dimension in homosexual relationships–could not be expressed if it were not for the prior move from the individual to the collective, and from the linking of the personal and the political.

Literary histories of Latin America have rarely dealt with issues of sexuality, much less homosexuality, either with regard to literary works or to their authors. In what remains here I would like to look at a few examples of how literary historians have gone to considerable lengths to avoid saying anything about these issues, and of how revealing their statements—and their silences—have been in defining the prejudices that are at work in the construction of literary canons. "Discrimination" is a double-edged word, connoting both the faculty of good taste and the marginalization of everything that the arbiter of taste would prefer not to deal with, and not to have others see, hear mentioned, or read. Unfortunately, standards of what is fit to be read and commented upon have been profoundly conservative in Latin American literary studies, perhaps even more than in the literature itself.

It is revealing to see what literary historians have had to say about Augusto D'Halmar, in particular on his novel *La pasión y muerte del cura Deusto* (1924), the tragic story of the love between a Basque priest and a gypsy altar boy in Seville. In the several dozen literary histories I examined, the words "homosexual" or "homoerotic" are rarely used to describe the love, and some of the descriptions of the contents of the novel are hopelessly off the mark. The following, by the Peruvian critic Augusto Tamayo Vargas (from his *Literatura en Hispano América*, 1973; Literature in Hispanic America) is better than most, but he refers to the wrong (?!) title by D'Halmar:

En *Juana Lucero* [sic], D'Halmar dota su prosa de una imaginación brillante, de un refinamiento sensual y busca el exótico ambiente de una Sevilla mórbida y pagana para amores homosexuales, dentro de un colorismo que venía del decadentismo modernista y avanzaba hacia el imaginismo de vanguardia. Oscar Wilde y D'Annunzio se veían tras sus narraciones poéticas. (306)

In *Juana Lucero* [sic], D'Halmar endowed his prose with brilliant imagination, with sensual refinement, and sought out the exotic space of a delicate, pagan Seville as the backdrop for homosexual love, within a coloration that derives from modernista decadence and that points forward to the imagism of the avant garde. Oscar Wilde and D'Annunzio can be glimpsed in his poetic narration.

Fernando Alegría, in his *Historia de la novela hispanoamericana* [3rd ed., 1968; History of the Hispanic American Novel], says that D'Halmar and another Chilean writer, Edgardo Garrido Merino, "analizaron aspectos recónditos del alma española sin batir tantas castañuelas" (127) ("analyzed hidden aspects of the Spanish soul without clicking on so many castanets")—though Sylvia Molloy has noted, in a brilliant paper on D'Halmar, that it is precisely the febrile rhythm of castanets that accompanies the love story in the novel. Alegría devotes considerable space to D'Halmar in his history, but when he gets to the text that interests us he writes simply that this is "su mejor novela: *Pasión y muerte del cura Deusto* (1935); en ella combina estilo y perspicacia psicológica para analizar el desarrollo de una extraña pasión que une a un cura y a un niño" ("his best novel, *Pasión y muerte del cura Deusto* (1935), in which style and psychological perspicacity combine to analyze the growth of the strange passion that link a priest and a boy") (127). Orlando Gómez Gil, in his *Historia crítica de la literatura hispanoamericana* [1968; Critical History of Hispanic American Literature], summarizes the plot of the novel, which he calls "la extraña pasión de un jovencito de pueblo y un cura" ("the strange passion of a country youth and a priest") (472), notes the influence of Wilde, Flaubert,

Maupassant, Daudet, and D'Annunzio, and concludes: "La obra vale, tanto por el lenguaje muy estilizado como por el análisis sicológico de los personajes de este drama de pasiones extrañas y morbosas" (472) ("The work matters, as much for its stylized language as for the psychological analysis of characters in a drama of strange and morbid passions"). Maximino Fernández Fraile, in his *Historia de la literatura chilena* [1994; History of Chilean Literature], is quite vague in his reference to "la relación ambigua y fuerte entre un joven y un adulto" (2: 356) ("the ambiguous and strong relationship between a youth and an adult"), while the "camino de la evasión" (2: 356) ("path of evasion") he mentions is as applicable to his own text (published, to be sure, by the Salesian Order) as it is to D'Halmar. But the prize for the silliest discussion of the novel is easily won by Enrique Anderson Imbert, in his *Historia de la literatura hispanoamericana* 2nd revised ed., [1970; History of Hispanic American Literature]:

Transcurre en Sevilla, en 1913. Una Sevilla de turista. Una Sevilla pagana aun en sus fiestas religiosas. Y nos cuenta tres años de amistad equívoca, escabrosa, entre un cura y un vasco adolescente. El análisis psicológico es menos fino que la pintura de una atmósfera mórbida, "decadente", tal como gustaba a los modernistas. La vida eclesiástica no es austera: rodean al cura toreros, trapecistas de circo, pintores, tonadilleras, poetas. El mismo Deusto es músico; su amado Pedro Miguel, cantor y bailarín. Más esteticismo que psicologismo, más oscarwildismo que proustianismo en la descripción de ese amor que, "llegado al límite" no puede prolongarse. (460)

It is set in Seville in 1913. A tourist Seville. A Seville still pagan in its religious holidays. And it tells us of a questionable, risqué, three-year friendship between a Basque priest and an adolescent. The psychological analysis is not as fine as the delination of a morbid, "decadent," atmosphere of the type that pleased the modernists. The ecclesiastical life is not austere: The priest is surrounded by bullfighters, trapeze artists, painters, songsters, poets. Deusto himself is a musician; his beloved Pedro Miguel, a singer and dancer. There is more aestheticism than "psychology," more Oscar Wildeism than Proustianism in the description of a love that, "having reached its extreme," can no longer be prolonged.

Anderson Imbert never explains why he considers the matter of the novel "scabrous" and "morbid;" he seems to be fighting straw men in his discussion of the priest's lack of austerity, and his plot summary gives little inkling of Deusto's melodramatic suicide beneath the train that is carrying Pedro Miguel off to Madrid. Indeed, one has to wait until 1997 for a direct reference to both the theme of the novel and to the author's sexuality. In Verity Smith's *Encyclopedia of Latin American Literature*, Darrell B. Lockhart notes:

Recently . . . there has been a renewal of interest in his writing because of the open treatment of homoerotic themes found throughout the majority of his texts. In the past this topic, as well as the author's own sexuality, conveniently had been glossed over, mentioned in highly euphemistic terms, or neatly explained away by most critics, in spite of an often overt textual presence . . . . The work that most openly addresses this issue, *La pasión y muerte del cura Deusto*, contains all the characteristics of a tragic love story. The novel was written during the author's residence in Spain, and it takes place in Seville. The basic plot revolves around the personal conflict between religiosity and homosexual desire as experienced by a Basque priest who finds himself overwhelming[ly] attracted to an Andalusian boy. His desire eventually leads him to commit suicide rather than succumb to his physical yearnings and a love that must not be. (259)

It is sad to think that D'Halmar's novel had to wait more than seventy years to be described frankly in these terms, and interesting to reflect on the fact that literature has been more unfettered than literary criticism in Latin America. When discussing "El hombre que parecía un caballo," several of the literary histories note the relation of the story to gossip and intrigue, and many comment on Arévalo's "zoomorph" fiction, but almost none are clear about the homoerotic content of the text. Orlando Gómez Gil writes that Arévalo "presenta una caricatura del gran poeta colombiano Miguel Angel Osorio, más conocido por Porfirio Barba Jacob" (495) ("presents a caricature of the great Colombian poet Miguel Angel Osorio, better known as Porfirio Barba Jacob").

With regard to the Contemporáneos group in Mexico, no literary history I examined (except for specialized ones like David William Foster's reference works on gay and lesbian writing in Latin America, and the Gay Sunshine Press anthologies of Latin American writing) mentions the sexuality of most of the members of the group, the importance of homoerotic themes in their writing, or the ferocious polemics against them by the *estridentistas*, Diego Rivera, Manuel Maples Arce, Arqueles Vela, and others, which included a public campaign against the presence of "individuos de moralidad dudosa" ("individuals of uncertain morality"), "afeminados" ("effeminate men"), and "hermafroditas" ("hermaphrodites") in the postrevolutionary civil service. The closest reference to the issue is José Juan Arrom's brief mention, in his survey of the work of the group, of the representation of "un caso de manía obsesionante causada por fuerzas sexuales reprimidas" ("a case of obsessional mania caused by repressed sexual forces" (15) in a novel by Agustín Lazo, a member of the group who was much better known as an artist.

The only canonical work discussed in numerous literary histories in a way that makes the mention of homosexuality impossible to avoid is José Lezama Lima's *Paradiso* (1966). Because several central chapters of the novel are focused on "deviant" sexuality of several varieties, especially the famous Chapter 9 (the dialogue among Foción, Fronesis, and Cemí on homosexuality), the issue was difficult to avoid. Emir Rodríguez Monegal is celebratory in his "Tradition and Renewal" in César Fernández Moreno's *Latin America in its Literature* (1980) of the "creation of a summa" in the novel which is at once "a story of costumbrista appearance [and] a treatise about the heaven of childhood and the hell of sexual perversions" (107). Ramón Xirau, in "Crisis of Realism" in the same volume, says that Lezama's novel "narrates innocence and violence, ingenuousness and sexual deviations, delves deeply into evil, depravation and horror, mocks history and substitutes myth in its place" (149), though Fernando Alegría (in "Antiliterature," again in the same volume), attacks the novel as shapeless and chaotic, ruled by a "sexual time and a belly which thinks" (185). Haroldo de Campos, in the entry on "Beyond Exclusive Languages," celebrates *Paradiso* (1966) and Guimarães Rosa's (b. 1908–1967) *Grande Sertão: Veredas* (1956) as both baroque books, and mentions the sexual ambiguity in the latter work, but does not mention the presence of these issues in *Paradiso*. Kessel Schwartz, in *A New History of Spanish American Literature* (1971), is rather more explicit when he says that this novel "combines the real and the absurd in a new way, mixing magic and madness, hallucinations and visions, history and poetry, reality and dreams, memories of memories, erotic encounters, multiple fornications, phallic rituals, adultery, and debates on homosexuality, on which the novelist probably has more to say than any other Spanish American writer" (205), though rather peculiarly he summarizes: "To an average reader the novel may seem like a decided defense of homosexuality" (206), which begs the question of who this "average reader" might be. Randolph Pope, in his chapter of the *Cambridge History of Latin American Literature*, writes that "Long philosophical discussions on homosexuality bog down a few later chapters" (2: 275), a statement that suggests a critical distaste with homosexuality, or philosophy, or both.

Piñera's essay on Ballagas seems to be as unknown to literary historians as Piñera's work was to them, with the exception of historians of the theater, who could not but mention his pioneering role in the Cuban theater and in bringing to Latin America some aspects of the "theater of the absurd." I have seen no reference to homosexuality in discussions of Piñera or of Ballagas in the literary histories I have examined. What could certainly be claimed as the first frank discussion of homosexuality in Latin American literary criticism is mysteriously absent from accounts of Latin American literary history, even when both the author of the essay and its subject are writers whose works are dealt with in the histories.

The centrality of homosexuality and homophobia to the works of José Donoso (1925–1996), especially *El lugar sin límites* (1967), is also conspicuously absent from the references to Donoso in the histories, except for Randolph Pope's reference to the transvestite character (Manuela) and "a truck-driver who is a violent repressed homosexual" (Pancho) in his essay on the Boom novel in the *Cambridge History of Latin American Literature* (2: 271–72). Most of these focus on *El obsceno pájaro de la noche* [1970; *The Obscene Bird of Night*, 1973], but not on the range of sexual expression in that novel, while references to *El lugar* tend to be in passing. Kessel Schwartz again is fairly forthright in his descriptions (but somewhat obtuse in his language) when he calls the Japonesita (little Japanese girl) "the daughter of a 'fairy'" and asserts that the novel "reaffirms the ambivalence of hetero- and homosexual relationships and the sexual and physical violence each human being nurtures within his soul" (159).

As for the newer, and much more explicit, gay literature of Latin America, much of it is too recent to be discussed much in the literary histories examined. Few historians have dealt forthrightly with the presence of gay themes in very transgressive ways, but those few are worth mentioning. David William Foster's *Handbook of Latin American Literature* (1987) refers (rather oddly, to my taste) to "the new gay and proletarian subgenres" (400). The *Historia de la literatura hispanoamericana* [1985; History of Hispanic American Literature] by Teodosio Fernández, Selene Millares, and Eduardo Becerra refers frankly to the presence of homosexual themes in the works of Puig, Zapata, Perlongher, Moro, and others. The *Cambridge History of Latin American Literature*, edited by Roberto González Echevarría and Enrique Pupo-Walker, is curious in that occasional reference is made to these authors, particularly in Gustavo Pellán's essay on recent developments in the novel, but only as part of a discussion of "novels that break with Spanish American literary and historical stereotypes by giving voice to the experience of women, homosexuals, and Jews" (2: 283), or later, "In two decades since 1970 the greater prominence of women novelists . . . of Jewish/Spanish American writers . . . and of a whole generation of university-educated novelists with lower-middle-class or proletarian background . . . and of homosexual writers such as

Reinaldo Arenas ... Manuel Puig, and Severo Sarduy ... who defy Spanish American machismo by writing openly about homosexuality in their novels, has resulted in a far less homogenous outlook than ever before" (2: 298–99). There is a further brief discussion of Arenas by William Luis (2: 539). Verity Smith's *Encyclopedia of Latin American Literature* (1997) is exemplary in this respect, however.

To conclude, then, although Latin American writers first begin to write of gay love more than a hundred years ago, and although there are a series of important (and canonical) works from 1914 to the late 1960s that hinge on what Borges once termed, in a very different context, "la inminencia de una revelación, que no se produce" ("the imminence of a revelation that does not take place"), and there are important works from the 1970s to the present that are explicit in addressing these issues (sometimes in very transgressive ways, as in the works of Perlongher and Lamborghini), nevertheless literary historians have been much more cautious about naming names, about frankly describing the contents of texts, and about analyzing the construction of homosexual–and heterosexual (and other)–desire in Latin American writing. If there has been a flirting with open secrets in the last century of literary works from the region, in literary criticism, and even more strikingly in literary history, there has been a conspiracy of silence. If it were not for the important work in the last few years of such critics as Oscar Montero, José Quiroga, David William Foster, Jorge Salessi, and–most valiantly, and most importantly–Sylvia Molloy, the silence of the previous generations of scholars would still smother us. It is important to speak out, and to speak frankly, and to teach this material, to make, in Paulo Freire's famous phrase, a "pedagogy of the oppressed."

Works Cited

Alegría, Fernando. 1966. *Historia de la novela hispanoamericana.* 3rd ed. Mexico City: Ediciones de Andrea.

Anderson Imbert, Enrique. 1970. *Historia de la literatura hispanoamericana.* 2nd rev. ed. 2 vols. Mexico City: Fondo de Cultura Económica.

Arévalo Martínez, Rafael. 1997. *El hombre que parecía un caballo y otros cuentos.* Ed. Dante Liano. Paris: Colección Archivos.

Arrom, José Juan. 1977. *Esquema generacional de las letras hispanoamericanas: Ensayo de un método.* Bogotá: Instituto Caro y Cuervo.

Balderston, Daniel. 1997. "Amistad masculina y homofobia en 'El hombre que parecía un caballo". *El hombre que parecía un caballo y otros cuentos de Rafael Arévalo Martínez.* Ed. Dante Liano. Paris: Colección Archivos. 331–37.

Ballagas, Emilio. 1984. *Obra poética.* Selección y prólogo Osvaldo Navarro. Havana: Editorial Letras Cubanas.

Bartlett, Neil. 1988. *Who Was That Man? A Present for Mr. Oscar Wilde.* London: Serpent's Tail.

D'Halmar, Augusto. 1924. *La pasión y muerte del cura Deusto.* Berlin, Madrid, and Buenos Aires: Editorial Internacional.

Fernández, Teodosio, Selena Millares, and Eduardo Becerra. 1995. *Historia de la literatura hispanoamericana.* Madrid: Editorial Universitas.

Fernández Fraile, Maximino. 1994. *Historia de la literatura chilena.* 2 vols. Santiago: Editorial Salesiana.

Fernández Moreno, César, Julio Ortega, and Iván A. Schulman, eds. 1980. *Latin America in its Literature.* Trans. Mary G. Berg. New York: Holmes & Meier.

Foster, David William. 1987. *Handbook of Latin American Literature.* New York: Garland.

Gómez Gil, Orlando. 1968. *Historia crítica de la literatura hispanoamericana: Desde los orígenes hasta el momento actual.* New York: Holt, Rinehart and Winston.

González Echevarría, Roberto and Enrique Pupo-Walker. 1996. *Cambridge History of Latin American Literature.* 3 vols. Cambridge: Cambridge University Press.

Lezama Lima, José. 1988. *Paradiso.* Recop. Cintio Vitier. París: Colección Archivos.

Miller, D. A. 1988. *The Novel and the Police.* Berkeley: University of California Press.

Novo, Salvador. 1961. *Poemas.* Mexico City: Fondo de Cultura Económica.

Piñera, Virgilio. 1994. *Poesía y crítica.* México City: Consejo Nacional para la Cultura y las Artes.

Puig, Manuel. 1976. *El beso de la mujer araña.* Barcelona: Seix Barral.

Rojas Guardia, Armando. 1985. *El dios en la intemperie.* Caracas: Editorial Mandorla.

——. 1989. *El calidoscopio de Hermes.* Caracas: Alfadil Ediciones.

——. 1993. *Antología poética.* Caracas: Monte Avila.

Schwartz, Kessel. 1973. *A New History of Spanish American Fiction.* 2 vols. Coral Gables: University of Miami Press.

Sedgwick, Eve Kosofsky. 1990. *Epistemology of the Closet.* Berkeley: University of California Press.

Smith, Verity, ed. 1997. *Encyclopedia of Latin American Literature.* London: Fitzroy Dearborn.

Tamayo Vargas, Augusto. 1973. *Literatura en Hispano América.* 2 vols. Lima: Ediciones Peisa.

Villaurrutia, Xavier. 1974. *Obras.* Ed. Miguel Capistrán, Alí Chumacero, and Luis Mario Schneider. Mexico City: Fondo de Cultura Económica.

NOTES TOWARD A HISTORY OF HOMOTEXTUALITY IN BRAZILIAN LITERATURE

Denilson Lopes

The history of what we could call "homotextuality" in Brazilian literature is still to be written, despite the many articles and theses that have begun to discuss the subject. Even a fundamental work on Brazilian homosexuality like *Devassos no Paraíso* [Perverts in Paradise] by João Silvério Trevisan (b. 1944), in which an outline of this form of cultural production is included, does not go much beyond an introductory gathering of facts. The initial and therefore leading question for this work goes back to the classic but inevitable ones: In what way does a homoerotic critical perspective add to our understanding of Brazilian culture, and how has the representation of homosexuality affected (or not) the basic structure of Brazilian literature?

I begin from the assumption that sexuality is part of a text's definition and not only with respect to ideology or biography or even through the determination of erotic topoi (see Stockinger 136). Frequently and justly the claim is made that the history of oppressed groups rescues a memory that is fundamental to our understanding of the price that has been paid for writing mainstream history. Moving beyond resentment or the mythifying of a history of resistance, the construction of alternative memories constitutes a central political reference point for the development of any multicultural society. In this sense, the normalization of heterosexuality in Brazil, disguised as apparent sexual flexibility (whether on the part of the elites or the popular classes) takes on a new significance. A way is now open to understand the relations among social and political power, sexuality, and the various social processes of exclusion, at the level of both individual and national identities. If the split between homosexuality and heterosexuality has been central to the Western modernizing process since the nineteenth century, as has been argued, what then are the specific outlines of a Brazilian gay problematic?

For this purpose, this study—which does not intend to be exhaustive, yet seeks to be as complete as possible—is an investigation of how the issue of homoerotic relations emerges through literary characters, behaviors, and themes. Even if homosexuality is not a determining factor in the plots of the works studied or its representation only repeats the stereotypes of official ideologies, it is important, at least in the beginning, not to disregard these literary moments, for they are traces (or ruins) of a repressed, residual history. Clearly, this preliminary investigation is not sufficient. It is needed, though, to try to lay out the groundwork that has made possible the decisive emergence in contemporary literature of a significant homotextuality, that is, homotextuality beyond that portrayed in isolated works. For this reason, I will entertain certain possibilities for literary criticism within the framework of a homoerotic historiography. These will attempt to deconstruct the homosexuality/heterosexuality dualism, in full awareness of the difficulties in the face of the lack of a specific theoretical bibliography on the topic that might help overcome the various problems involved in writing such a history or even in conducting case studies, in the anthropological or sociological mode, that might contribute to it. For example, any division according to literary genres seems artificial in that the discourses on homosexuality move among various genres, although certain representations are more visible in one genre than in another (like the imaginary pedophile in the lyric or the sex change theme in comedy). It is also important not to fall into microanalytic summaries or facile biographisms. Without simply repeating contextualist views or reflection theories, it is imperative to define a historical perspective that is constructed by identifying groups of works and articulating axes, and not simply using thematic categories that are so vague that they are lost in the mists of ahistoricity. Therefore, it is necessary here to develop networks of affinity without violating the specificity of separate texts. This task of delineating genealogies should furnish new elements for the analysis of particular works that would otherwise remain not very visible or even invisible.

This mapping of homotextuality in Brazilian literature will proceed through the identification of aesthetic categories (camp), genres (letters, diaries), spaces (the closed institution, in Erving Goffman's sense of the term, like the boarding school and the armed forces; proscribed places, like boarding houses or nightclubs; more private places, like the bedroom; those resulting from the conquest of open-air space—the streets of the city), and figures (the ambiguity of the timid adolescent, the transvestite, the masculine woman, the bachelor/spinster, the bisexual). These latter are associated with the constructing power of the gaze and of desire when confronted with those less institutionalized and more marginalized practices (within the ideology of reproduction) such as masturbation, voyeurism, pornography, and promiscuity, among others. The purpose here, then, is to outline a history of discontinuities and dispersions, of the simultaneity of distinct homotexts, without a strong commitment to chronology or to the reified unity of the work or of the canon.

The exclusion of homotextual issues from Brazilian criticism and literary history must be examined in a nuanced way in order to understand the tentative emergence of both a critical perspective and a different literary production in the present, in addition to understanding the reasons for the silences of the past (such as the fear of stigmatization and exclusion from the establishment). To avoid imposing simplifying anachronisms on the past, it is fundamentally important to establish a two-way movement between past and present, which may bring works from the past up to date and make those of the present seem less isolated. It is also crucial not to impose on Brazilian literature the standards of identity politics that may already be old-fashioned in the North American context. The challenge is to consider the complexities and the hybridisms, both in politics and in the political vision of works of art, especially at a time when one seeks change in the general public sphere and not just to ensure specific rights that are not certain or assured in a minority situation. Two other points should be made before beginning. In the new context of gay and lesbian studies, one must also acknowledge the particularity of lesbian exclusion, which is even greater than that of gay men, both in literary and critical production, without, however, creating for lesbians an isolated ghetto. In addition, the homoerotic identity must be studied in all its fragility and performativity, instead of as any essential nature.

One can speak of the emergence of a homotextual prose in Brazil with the rise of literary naturalism, a fact that has implications for the representation of the homosexual up to the present time. In the novel *O Bom Crioulo* 1895 [The Good Black], by Adolfo Caminha (1867–1897), today praised in Brazil and abroad as a pioneering work, the representation of homosexuality is not only a circumstantial fact or something produced through stereotypes (as we shall see is the case in so many other works of Brazilian literature in the twentieth century), but it becomes a central element in the narrative. The novel presents the ship as a central space; as "homoidentities" (all of them marked by ambiguity), it offers the gay macho, the adolescent, and the masculine woman. The association of maritime life with homosexuality already has a significant place in the international gay imaginary, from the writings of Jean Genet and Kenneth Anger to the drawings of Tom of Finland. But in *O Bom Crioulo* this association is not at all linked to voyeurism or the cult of the body. On the contrary, this is the story of a quest for freedom. The protagonist, the black Amaro, at first finds in the navy liberation from his condition as a slave on the plantations. Even the rigid discipline of the navy, whose violence is already made clear to us in the first chapter where the lash is used as punishment, does not stifle his search for identity as both a man and a *free* man. Amaro, the "Good Black," becomes strong in body and character and is respected by all. But after ten years of hard work he discovers that his routine labor has turned into a new prison. It is at this moment that the encounter between Amaro and the cabin boy Aleixo takes place.

Pedagogical and protective instincts prompt Amaro to become a mentor to the young Aleixo, introducing him to the life of a sailor. At the same time his growing desire for the boy opens up a new horizon for the lonely sailor, who is still a virgin at the age of thirty (79). The most free expression of this desire occurs in the attic of a boarding house in Rio de Janeiro, in an ordinary room turned into a "museu de cousas raras" (106) ("museum of rare things"), filled with objects and furniture in the Rococo style (93)–suggesting a taste for artifice that will crystallize later in "camp." However, this is also a space of freedom even if private, a pause in life spent on the sea, where this "amizade inexplicável" (67) ("inexplicable friendship") can be shown as existing without bounds. The landlady's intrusion as Aleixo's lover causes this "pequena família" ("small family's") paradise of an orderly and calm life (94) to fall apart. Before this, Amaro and Aleixo walk "braço a braço" ("arm in arm") on the street (84), and the landlady Carolina accepts Amaro, without any problem, as not being an "homem para mulheres" ("man for women") (91–2). Although the novel appeared at a time when the diffusion of pretentiously pseudoscientific legal and medical discourses identified homosexuality as a mental disease and a crime, there is little sign of this discourse in the novel itself. The narrator does take on the task of simultaneously explaining and censoring the characters, however, identifying the relation between Amaro and Aleixo as a "delito contra natureza" (74) ("crime against nature"), "gozo pederasta" ("pederastic pleasure"), or "semelhante anomalia" (78) ("deviation"), but still allowing the story to be told. Curiously for a novel marked by naturalism, the amorous discourse ranges from erotic fury, seen in the animal metaphors affirming the split between masculine and feminine, to a more romantic representation of the adoration and devotion that Amaro vows to Aleixo, which culminate in a tragic finale like that of many great love stories.

It is this tragic love that the novel portrays, a love stronger than desire and even life itself. This love story is the great victory of the novel, a victory that overcomes the prejudices of a rigidly hierarchical society by means of the noblest amorous discourse, presented as emerging from a character who is black, poor, and homosexual. For his part, Aleixo is in the end emancipated from his role as object of desire, as voiceless fetish, as "carnalidade grega" (73) ("Greek carnality"). He leaves behind the timidity of the androgynous adolescent–he is discussed in such terms as "faltavam-lhe os seios para que ... fosse uma mulher" (98) ("he lacked the breasts ... to be a woman") and is seen as "uma rapariga que se vai fazendo mulher" (99) ("a girl who is turning into a woman,")–for the shamelessness or pragmatism of the adult who would not hesitate to exchange Amaro for another who could offer him more (110). For Aleixo, Amaro is an "uma boa criatura" (111) ("good person"), but one for whom the esteem he feels is not "uma sangria desatada que não acabasse nunca" (109) ("a continuous bleeding that never ends"). Amaro becomes for Aleixo "o que um animal de estima é para seu dono–leal, sincero, dedicado té o sacrificio" (151) ("what a pet is for its owner–loyal, sincere, dedicated to sacrifice"), and, finally, a burden (153–54). The complexity and ambivalence of desire are also expressed in Amaro, in his desire to "encontrar rapariga de sua cor" (129–30) ("find a girl of his own color") and in the melancholy realization that "neste mundo a gente vive enganada. . . . Quanto mais se estima uma pessoa, mais essa pessoa trata com desprezo" (125) ("in this world we live deceived. . . . The more you like someone, the more that person treats you with scorn"). In Amaro, however, passion only ceases with death, passing through the degradation of drink, humiliation, and the violence of being beaten up in public and hospitalized. He moves further and further from the "liberdade absoluta de proceder, conforme o seu temperamento, amor físico por uma criatura do mesmo sexo que o seu, extraordinariamente querida como Aleixo" (153–54) ("absolute freedom of conduct, according to his disposition, physical love for a person of his same sex, extraordinarily dear as Aleixo"): Aleixo had initiated Amaro into love and made him "sofrer as amarguras de uma vida de condenado" (158) ("suffer the bitterness of the life of a condemned man"). The hospital, clearly far from being a place of rest, becomes more like a prison for Amaro, even a true hell in which the inner emptiness is not attenuated even with the healing of the body. Amaro's end is thus marked by a resignification of space: the city becomes a labyrinth and the room, which had been an "espaço de felicidade" ("space of happiness"), ends up being "o túmulo de suas ilusões" ("the tomb of his illusions"). The ending avoids close-ups and details: We see only Aleixo's dead body, but not the fight that caused it, while Amaro is imprisoned definitively by the sounds and power of the city.

This image of the sailor in his exclusively masculine environment–with its "corpos indistintos no convés" (72) ("indistinguishable bodies on the deck")–has had some influence on Brazilian literature, as in the phantom apparition of Gasparino Damata in the novella, "O Marinheiro" ("The Sailor") by Caio Fernando Abreu (1948–1996), in *Triângulo das Águas* [1983; Triangle of Waters], or in the mixture of violence and masculine bonding in "A Hora do Aço" ["The Hour of Steel"] by the same author, in *Ovelhas Negras* [1993; Black Sheep]. We might also identify a later development of this sailor fetish in the fascination for strong lower-class men. This theme suggests less a (transvestite) attraction to an excess of masculinity than a representation of the ambiguity of relations between men, relations that range from a nonproblematic bisexuality, like that of the German in *Lábios que Beijei* [1992; Lips I Have Kissed] by Aguinaldo Silva (b. 1944), to a depiction that barely masks a hidden or repressed homosexual identity, as in "Revelação" ["Revelation"] by Harry Laus (b. 1922). It is important to remember that the association of violence with sexual relations between men is an especially important one, notably in representations of homosexuality among the popular classes and particularly among marginal groups, as can be seen in Jorge Amado's (1912–2001) *Capitães de Areia,* [1937; Sand Captains] and Plínio Marcos's (b. 1935) "Barrela" ["Deceit"]. A version of this sailor image also appears in the figure of the outsider or foreigner in contemporary fiction, portrayed as a drifter in the work of João Gilberto Noll (b. 1946) and Bernardo Carvalho (b. 1960) or as lonely and alone in the stories of Silviano Santiago (b. 1936) and Caio Fernando Abreu.

In the "mulher-homem" ("man-woman") (118) figure of Carolina, who sees in Aleixo "algo feminino" ("something feminine") (153–4), can be seen a protoimage of the lesbian as a strong, active woman, defined either by her sexual behavior (as with the prostitute who seduces Pombinha in Aluísio Azevedo's [1857–1913] *O Cortiço* [1890; The Slum]) or by being associated with the traditionally masculine world of work and power–as in the tradition of warrior-maids, from Domingos Olímpio's (1850–1906) *Luzia-Homem* [1903; Lucy the Man] to Diadorim in *Grande Sertão: Veredas* [1967, *The Devil to Pay in the Backlands,* 1963] by Guimarães Rosa (1908–1967).

As opposed to the frank explicitness of the relations between Aleixo and Amaro and their direct language, Raul Pompéia's (1863–1895) *O Ateneu* [1888; The Academy], published only eight years before *O Bom Crioulo,* offers an exemplary literary representation of the sexuality of the ruling classes, for this fell victim to an even greater critical silence than the aforementioned homotextual works. With this novel another frankly masculine, closed space is established: the boarding school, where an existential apprenticeship of the protagonist takes place that is fundamental to the development of his emotional and sexual identity. O *Ateneu* is much more virulent than *O Bom Crioulo* in its criticism of social control and punishment. From the beginning, the question of sexuality is developed in relation to that of power in such a way that the division between male and female students is also a division between the misogynist and the homophobic, between the strong and the weak. This sexualized power makes every relationship one of dependency and, indeed, a form of violence in which "os rapazes tímidos, ingênuos, sem sangue" ("the timid, naïve, bloodless boys") are called "as meninas" ("the girls"), the "sexo da fraqueza" ("weak sex") (28), as the intellectual student Rebelo announces to the protagonist at the beginning. With the imposition of this duality, the sensitive protagonist Sérgio will oscillate between one and

the other extreme, from being protected by the oldest student Sanches to being the solitary, independent outsider. He shows a tendency toward the masculine pole at the end, after the breakup of his unique friendship with Egberto (the only relationship among equals presented in the text). It is as if sexual ambiguity were something to be tolerated only in adolescence: "certa efeminação pode existir como um período de constituição moral" (72) ("a certain effeminacy can exist as a period of moral constitution"). Even then, it is tolerated only with difficulty, as a test in the formation of the character of a young man inserted into a society rigidly divided (and ranked) between masculine and feminine; consequently, sexual ambiguity dare not be spoken of, and those who defy this rule are violently silenced, as seen in the public trial of Cândido. For the good of the reigning concept of morality, private friendships that cross the line of sexuality do so at the risk of their breaking up, as happens with Sérgio and Egberto.

The same can be said of other stories in Gasparino Damata's (b. 1918) collection, *Histórias de Amor Maldito* (1967): Mário de Andrade's (1893–1945) story "Frederico Paciência" (1947), for example, and in a subtler and more delicate form, Harry Laus's (b. 1922) "Prelúdio" [1989; "Prelude"]. In an equally subtle but more ironic form, the theme appears in "Pílades e Orestes" by Machado de Assis (1839–1908) and in *O Encontro Marcado* (1956; The Date], by Fernando Sabino (b. 1923). In the stories of Renard Perez (b. 1928), with their tone of ambiguous homosociality or latent homosexuality, at times there is some suspicion or mystery associated with masculine meetings, such as the "secret pulsation" (90) in "A visita" [1979; "The Visit"], while in "Sábado" [1979; "Saturday"] a stranger in the night turns out to be the protagonist's friend. In "A Bebedeira" [1976; "The Bender"], as well as in "Briga de Bar" [1979; "Bar Brawl"], the bar is seen as a traditional space of masculine affirmation. There are also moments of masculine bonding in "Banca do Jornal" [1979; "Newsstand"] and "A Farra com Benedito" [1973; "The Spree with Benedict"]. Making explicit what was not said by Renard Perez in "Irmãos da noite" ["Night Brothers"], Caio Fernando Abreu's "Madrugada" ["Early Morning Hours"], published in *Inventário do Ir-remediável* [1970; Inventory of the Ir-redeemable], appears as a text that shows homophobia to be a basic part of these masculinized spaces. The establishment of a game of seduction and fascination between a heterosexual and a homosexual man is also an interesting departure from the world of homophobia as depicted in "Futebol Americano" ["American Football"], in *Banquete* [Banquet], by Silviano Santiago.

Pompéia's (1863–1895) criticism of boarding schools points to what he presents as a hypocritically concealed "uma egeminação mórbida" ("morbid effeminacy"), a "letargia moral" ("moral lethargy,") (35). If the relationship of submission that Sanches expects of Sérgio is frankly condemned, the half-platonic, half-fraternal relations that are established between Bento and the protagonist are presented with greater tolerance. As an adult, Sérgio (the narrator of the novel) frankly says of Bento: "Estimei-o femininamente, porque era grande, forte, bravo; porque me podia valer; porque me respeitava, quase tímido, como se não tivesse ânimo de ser amigo" (72) ("I thought of him in a feminine way, because he was big, strong, brave; because he could appreciate me; because he respected me, almost shyly, as if he didn't have the energy to be a friend"). Sérgio is a "dama romanceira" ("romance lady") and Bento a "gentil cavalheiro" ("gentle knight") (84) in a relationship that ends up in an "briga ines-perada" (106) ("unexpected fight"), an explosion of unnamed desire, after which Bento leaves the school. The novel attacks, therefore, the weak virility of this space, its permissiveness masked as false morality that values mostly appearances and the power of money.

Yet something is represented here beyond the "comédia colegial dos sexos" (105) ("school comedy of the sexes"), the form in which the seduction games of adolescents are critically portrayed. Through the relationship between Sérgio and Egberto, an idealized view of friendship is restored–"tudo que nos pertencia era comum" (111) ("we shared everything")–in which the relationship comes to seem like a romantic idyll in a world of violence, an idyll again that ends under the shadow of the manifestation of desire. Egberto is involved in the scandalous expulsion of Cândido, who had relations with Emílio, another boarding school student. In the embarrassed silence between Egberto and Sérgio after the scandal, Sérgio feels attracted to the director's wife. Egberto becomes "uma recordação" (117) ("a memory"), and friendship a "coisa insu-ficiente" ("insufficient thing"), as if he needed something more, which only a woman could give him–a "selvageria amordaçada de afetos" (121) ("muzzled savagery of affec-tions"). The passage concludes with the exclusion of any ambiguous desire. The physical destruction of the Academy at the end is the destruction of a space in which homosexuality, despite unfavorable circumstances, could be experienced, even in a homophobic environment. In this sense, if the school is both a microcosm and the result of the society of which it is a part, as the teacher Cláudio argues (128), the place of homosexuality is only in the silenced margins. Whenever it expresses itself openly, it can only be excluded.

The boarding school as both a space of exclusion and, at the same time, a space of possibility for homosexuality reappears in the stories "Inventário do Primeiro Dia" ["Inventory of the First Day"] and "A Última Vez" ["The Last Time"] by Autran Dourado (b. 1926); in the mini-novel with short chapters entitled *Internato* [1951; Boarding-School] by Paulo Hecker Filho (b. 1926); and with an exacerbated sexuality, overloaded with Baroque tones, in *Em Nome do Desejo* [1985; In the Name of Desire] by João Silvério Trevisan (b. 1944). The relationship between teacher and student is also portrayed in a beautiful story by Autran Dourado, "História Natural" [1954; Natural History], which goes beyond an apology for the amoral aestheticism à la Wilde offered in *O Ateneu* (82) and *O Renascer do Jacinto* [Jacinto's Rebirth] by Francisco Igreja (b. 1949).

The androgynous adolescent, who oscillates between angel and pervert, has many incarnations. I have already spoken of Aleixo of *O Bom Crioulo*; in addition to him and to Marcelo of "História Natural," there are many characters notable for the fascination their young bodies arouse. These range from the allegorical perspective of "O Iniciado do Vento" [1954; The Initiate of the Wind] by Aníbal Machado (1894–1964), in which desire is translated through the association of the fascination for the boy with that for the wind, to the more naturalistic narrative of initiation of the adolescent to sexual life through a relationship with an older man, as in "Aprendizado" ["Apprenticeship"] and "O Anjo da Avenida Atlântica" ["The Angel of Atlantic Avenue"] by Luiz Canabrava (b. 1926), or in "Juca" by Amador Ribeiro Neto, with its more direct sensual appeal, of ancient origin, going back to the Greek pedophilic imaginary.

This, in particular, is part of a less strong, yet more and more visible, trend in Brazilian lyric poetry, from the tender "Sonnet" of Mário de Andrade to the poems of Valdo Mota (b. 1959), less appreciated for their homoerotic reading of the Bible and the mystical tradition than for their unpretentious colloquialisms. We should not forget to mention Roberto Piva's (b. 1937) delirious, disordered search for "imensa e delicada adolescência" ("huge and delicate adolescence") (1981, XVII) in the wild, modern city (as captured in Pasolini's films) where "os garotos de subúrbio são anjos" ("the boys from the outskirts are angels"). See, too, the works of Antônio Cícero (b. 1945), Roberto Corrêa dos Santos (b. 1949), and Pedro Paulo Sena Madureira (b. 1947) on this theme. As Mario de Andrade writes in his "Sonnet,"

Tudo o que há de milhor e de mais raro
Vive em teu corpo nu de adolescente,
A perna assim jogada e o braço, o claro
Olhar preso no meu, perdidamente.

All that is finer and rarer
Lives in your naked adolescent body,
The leg sprawled like that and the arm, the clear
Look fixed on mine, desperately.

Roberto Piva (b. 1937) writes:

vou moer teu cérebro. Vou retalhar tuas
coxas imberbes & brancas
vou dilapidar a riqueza de tua
adolescência. vou queimar teus
olhos com ferro em brasa.
vou incinerar teu coração de carne &
de tuas cinzas vou fabricar a
substância enlouquecida das
cartas de amor.
[Music of Bach in the background.]

(XIV, 1981)

I will gnaw your brain, I will shred your
young white thighs.
I will squander the wealth of your
adolescence. I will burn your
eyes with a red-hot iron.
I will incinerate your heart of flesh &
from your ashes I will manufacture
the crazed substance of
love letters.

And, in the words of Valdo Mota (b. 1959), in "Waw" (1996):

Tem que ver o papo
de que sou o pai
que você não teve.
Faça-me de pai,
de mãe e de quantos
irmãos necessite
o seu desamparo

There is something to the talk
about my being the father
that you never had.
Make me a father,
a mother and as many
brothers and sisters
as your defenselessness requires.

In "Pier Paolo," Italo Moriconi (b. 1953) adds:

Ah, carne, curva de um músculo,
Talhar o *ragazzo* transcendental
Em cada face imperfeita.

Ah, flesh, curve of a muscle,
Carve the transcendental *ragazzo*
On every imperfect face.

After the great novels of the end of the nineteenth century, and with the advance of modernity, homotextuality presents itself in a less obvious form; it is present in stories and poems, but it does not constitute a homoerotic aesthetic, a gay art. Yet, before entering decisively into a discussion of the modernist period, I must bring up one name that deserves to be remembered as offering a different alternative to those mentioned here: João do Rio (1881–1921). In at least two of his stories, "Histórias de Gente Alegre" ["Stories of Merry People"] and "O Bebê de Tarlatana Rosa" ["The Pink Tarlatana Baby"], public space is the setting, and in particular the worldly space of high society. Here, the representation of homosexuality takes on a decidedly decadent, turn-of-the-century tone; associated with perversion; homosexuality is distanced from the standards of bourgeois morality and thus attractive. (See "Cidade do Vício e da Graça" ["City of Vice and Grace"] by Ribeiro Couto [1898–1963] and the carnival setting of "Terça-Feira Gorda" ["Mardi Gras"] by Caio Fernando Abreu in *Morangos Mofados* [1982; Moldy Strawberries], in which the apparently permissive environment of carnival explodes into homophobic violence.) Whether with the caustic irony of João do Rio, who perhaps finds only a lesser follower in Darcy Penteado (1926–1990) in *A Meta* [1976; The Aim], or with the humor that situations of sexual confusion evoke in the plays of Henrique Coelho Neto (1864–1934) (e.g. "Mistérios do Sexo" ["Mysteries of Sex"]) and later, in a more sophisticated form, in "Qorpo Santo" ["Holy Body"], homosexuality almost had its fashionable moment in the *belle époque*. We should also recall that the figure of the affected queer–as something between laughable and pathetic–recurred often, from the work of Nelson Rodrigues (1912–1980) to plays and television soap operas.

It is no overstatement to say that, in the literature of high modernity at the end of the nineteenth century and the beginning of the twentieth, possibilities that existed for the construction of a homoerotic art were not developed further. "Homotexts" here predominantly take the form of short stories rather than novels; they also tend to appear as isolated phenomena in the works of certain writers. Silence predominates and, when visible, homosexuality is represented in ridiculed stereotypes or in images of homoerotic desire as something impossible, fated to fail. Perhaps, in terms of all these works taken as a whole, one can even speak of the decisive emergence of only one new figure of homoerotic identity: the guilty man, marked by a strong religious or existential anguish. It is in this line of development that we can situate some of the works of Otavio de Faria (1908–1980), with his characters tortured by sin, and, in a minor way, those of Walmir Ayala (b. 1933), with his humiliated defeatism. The same is true of Lúcio Cardoso's (1913–1968) masterpiece *Crônica de uma Casa Assassinada* [1959; Chronicle of a Murdered House], where the apparent solidity of a patriarchal family is corroded by a family line attracted to alternative sexualities, which includes a female ancestor who dressed like a man (the horsewoman Maria Sinhá), a foreign woman with a strong personality (Nina), and the last of the

heirs (the androgynous adolescent André). This line climaxes in Timóteo, the transvestite isolated in his room, wearing his mother's clothes, while his body swells into shapelessness, destroyed by the search for truth and beauty. A character masterfully interpreted by Carlos Krober in *Timóteo,* the film adaptation made by Paulo César Saraceni in 1971; he incarnates the centrality of artifice in the constitution of a homoerotic identity and aesthetic.

The work of Samuel Rawet (1929–1985) is situated beyond the Catholic sphere, but still within the framework of a deep existential anguish marked by guilt, as in his story "O seu minuto de glória" [1967; "Your Minute of Glory"]. Rawet is of the opinion that to speculate on anguish is worse than anguish itself. This same position also incorporates another important figure in the literary representation of homosexuality: the bachelor, who, in the well-known work of Gasparino Damata, *Os Solteirões* [The Bachelors], is presented in a more colloquial way, but who in Rawet's work, incarnates the burden of uncommon solitude in the midst of a world of vain expectations. The protagonist bitterly comes to the conclusion that the man for whom he has been waiting all his life has already come and gone, without his knowing how to recognize him and perhaps having inadvertently humiliated him.

Passing to the 1960s, it seems that "foi então que aquela coisa que ele mal ousava chamar amor, transformou-se em amor" (Ayala 265) ("it was then that that thing he hardly dared call love was transformed into love"). Finally, the city streets become a space of visibility for gay characters, whether presented in libertarian, "pamphletarian," or neonaturalist manners (mixing the question of sexuality with the social, economic, and political wounds of a country that has increasingly developed a modernizing project of exclusion, in the shadow of an authoritarian regime): For the marginalized individual the displacement is to have, simultaneously, freedom from condemnation and an impetus to individual, idiosyncratic growth (Stockinger 139–44). It is at this moment that the first collections that privilege the gay question in Brazilian literature appear, even though they are not exclusively homotextual: *Histórias do Amor Maldito* [1967; Stories of Cursed Love], edited by Gasparino Damata, and *Erotismo no Conto Brasileiro* [Eroticism in the Brazilian Short Story], edited by Edilberto Coutinho. As the author of the preface of *Histórias,* Octávio de Freitas Jr., reminds us (in a tone attuned to the 1960s), what is important about the book is that it "exposes human dramas that articulate the problem of existential legitimacy *vis-à-vis* conventional structures," asking whether in the future "there will still be accursed loves" (13). Other collections followed: one edited in English by Winston Leyland, focusing on gay Latin American literature (1979, 1989), as well as a more recent one featuring contemporary Brazilian short-story writers, *O Amor com Olhos de Adeus* [1995; Love with the Eyes of Goodbye], edited by José Carlos Honório, all a sign of interest in Brazil and abroad in this subject–from the 1960s to the present.

Authors such as Luiz Canabrava (*O Sexo Portátil* [1968; The Portable Sex]), Darcy Penteado (*Crescilda e os Espartanos* [1977; Crescilda and the Spartans]), and Aguinaldo Silva have offered direct neonaturalist narratives, without the intervention of pseudoscientific gay discourses, that represent the search for an image beyond self-negation: "Estou farto de ser um espelho. Sim, espelho, porque quando nos olhavam, no fundo da minhas órbitas nada mais viam senão sua própia imagem" (Silva, *Primeira carta* [First Letter] 78) ("I'm fed up with being a mirror. Yes, mirror, because when they looked at us, deep in my eyes they saw nothing else but their own image"). To say out loud what one is, in a libertarian way, seems to mark the end of the era of silence. "Agora sou realmente um só, o mais forte, aquele que pode dizer sem medo e responder quando perguntado" (Silva 106) ("Now I am really only one, the strongest, he who can say without fear and answer when asked–I")–even if daily life is much harder, especially for those who are thrown into a world apart, a "desordenado império" (107) ("disordered empire"). These authors move between a literature too confined in its intention to document the reality of the *bas-fonds* and an intellectual fascination with possible allegorical readings. Other works investigate the association between political repression and sexual repression, as it is manifest both on the part of conservatives and at the core of the leftist movement. Political activity takes place in frankly masculine worlds, as in the novel *Nivaldo e Jerônimo* (1981) by Darcy Penteado. But there are also narratives of the poignant liberation of the senses, such as *Meu Corpo Daria um Romance* [1984; My Body Would Make a Novel] by Herbert Daniel (1946–1992), or less conventional works like João Silvério Trevisan's *Testamento de Davi Deixado a Jonathan* [1976; David's Will Left to Jonathan] and Silviano Santiago's *Stella Manhattan* (1985), which escape the prevalent neonaturalistic and allegorical styles.

The work of Glauco Mattoso (b. 1951) brings together themes of abject marginalization and parody, giving new force to his frankly obscene poetry with its homoerotic traces. In Brazil this more peripheral kind of poetry begins with the works of Gregório de Matos (1633?–1696), and includes the poems of Laurindo Rabelo (1826–1864) and the recently rediscovered work of Paulo Velloso (1909–1977), as well as that of Jaime (b. 1908) and Guilherme Santos Neves (b. 1906), in *Cantáridas e outros Poemas Fesceninos* [Spanish Flies and Other Obscene Poems]. In *Memórias de um Puteiro* [1982; Memoirs of a Brothel] by Glauco Mattoso, as in *Jornal Dobrábil* [Folding Newspaper], there is a strong fascination with the scatological. The centrality of the organic and corporeal persists, with a focus on feces and genitals, the penis and anus: "A merda é mais universal que o Esperanto. As bocas têm muitas línguas; o cu apenas uma" (24) ("Shit is more universal than Esperanto. Mouths have many tongues; the asshole has only one"). The very acts of writing and thinking are associated with bowel movements (25, 42, 49). Excrement is presented not only as remains, residuum, but, in an inversion, as centrally important and thus associated with minorities, whose struggle is considered "greater" (40). This text appropriates the leftist jargon of the 1970s, putting in García Lorca's mouth the following provocation: "Tres cosas solas en el mundo, que el heterosexual no comprenderá nunca: libertad, igualdad y fraternidad" (48) ("there are only three things in the world which the heterosexual will never understand: liberty, equality, fraternity"). It is in the spiritualization of excrement that the very secret of art lies (29), he argues. In the "Coprophagic Manifesto" he writes:

Ó merda com teu mar de urina
com teu céu de fedentina
tu és meu continente terra fecunda onde germina
minha independência minha indisciplina.

(43)

O shit with your sea of urine
With your sky of stench
you are my continent fertile earth where
my independence my indiscipline germinates.

A parallel "impurity" from the textual point of view is encountered in the systematic cultivation of plagiarism, quotation, and explicit self-quotations–the gestures of an anarchic *bricoleur*, denier of the values of originality and novelty that guide avant-garde discourse. His ferocious humor deconstructs elevated or grandiloquent diction: "Dorme com menininhos e amanhecerás borrado. Dorme com meninões e amanhecerás porrado" (23) ("Sleep with little boys and tomorrow thou shalt wake up beshitted. Sleep with big boys and tomorrow thou shalt wake up beaten up").

Against this background we can situate the passage of a marginal homotextuality more and more toward the center of contemporary Brazilian literature, especially in the presentation of affective alternative networks both to "reprosexuality [which] involves more than reproducing, more even than compulsory heterosexuality; it involves a relation to self that finds its proper temporality and fulfilment in generational transmission" (Warner 9) and to "repro-narrativity," the "notion that our lives have in some way more meaning because they are inserted in a narrative of generational succession" (7). The latter has been used historically to affirm the succession of brilliant heterosexual writers (whose brilliance may have nothing to do with questions of sexuality).

It was the need to come to terms with generations, with childhood and adolescence (in the context of the family and morality) in intimate narratives, which made the timid adolescent another important figure: Witness *Limite Branco* [1971; White Limit] by Caio Fernando Abreu, *Aquele Rapaz* (1990) by Jean-Claude Bernardet (b. 1936), and the novellas published by Silviano Santiago (especially "Father and Son") in *Duas Faces* [Two Faces]. Adolescence is referred to both generically and explicitly in the story "Sobreviventes" ["Survivors"], as "a dor coletiva dos que perderam a voz" (38) ("the collective pain of those who have lost their voice") (in *Troços e Destroços* by João Silvério Trevisan). These are texts, in general, that are part of their authors' early development–sometimes clumsy, sometimes foolish, sometimes beautiful, but always necessary not only for the achievement of their more mature works, but for the imploding of the spaces of exclusion and the dominant stereotypes. "Sargento Garcia" ["Sergeant Garcia"] by Caio Fernando Abreu (in *Morangos Mofados*, 1982) takes up once again the figure of the adolescent, but this is one who is already engaged in life. Apprehension does not prevent sexual initiation from occurring; sex is neither glamorized nor traumatizing. Similarly, in "Pequeno Monstro" ["Small Monster"], from the collection *Os Dragões não conhecem o Paraíso* [Dragons Do Not Know Paradise], the sensation of the adolescent protagonist that he is different is undone when he meets an older cousin, with whom he has his first sexual experience, a fleeting encounter that liberates him from an internal prison; memory remains encrusted on his body as sperm is on his hands: "Sozinho na sala, em silêncio, eu não era mais monstro. Fiquei olhando minha mão magra morena, quase sem pêlos. Eu sabia que o primo Alex tinha ficado para sempre conmigo. Guardado bem aqui, na palma da minha mão" (146) ("Alone in the room, in silence, I was no longer a monster. I stared at my thin, brown, almost hairless hand. I knew that cousin Alex had been with me forever. Kept right here, in the palm of my hand").

When the utopian and rebel energies that agitated the 1960s and part of the 1970s began to lose force, a postmodern scene, constituted and interpreted by homoerotic desires and energies, emerged: spaces between possible melancholy and joy, sexual uncertainty and the fear of AIDS, loneliness and tenderness, deterritorialization and the search for new types of relations. It is in this context that one can place the work of Caio Fernando Abreu, Silviano Santiago's book, *Keith Jarrett in the Blue Note* (1996), as well as works by José Carlos Honório (b. 1946), João Gilberto Noll, and Bernardo Carvalho, the lyrics of Cazuza and Renato Russo, the poems of Ana Cristina César (1952–1983), and some of the stories of Edilberto Coutinho (b. 1938).

The tone of this work ranges from a certain subtlety and lightness to the dry but elevated style of José Carlos Honório's work, with its atmosphere of doubt and dissent:

o momento
para dizer
coisas banais
não é este

   (Atravessar [Crossing] 96)

the moment
to say
vulgar things
is not this one

Céu Nu e a Biruta [1990; Naked Sky and the Nutty Woman] by the same author, at its best, attains a threshold of poetic prose in which ambiguity is achieved by concision; at its worst, it borders on self-reflexive verbosity. Its grandiloquent phrases and explanatory discourses suspend the narrative flow. This is done deliberately to mark introspection and mild epiphanies, in which the body is rarefied and made insubstantial, as in "Lim," "Quando se parte: Até" ["When One Leaves: Till"], "A Possibilidade" ["The Possibility"], or even more expressively, in the poetic encounter between the protagonist and a boy in "Armando": "Ele bonito e em estado de achar bonito. Tudo é diferente então: tudo passa a ser mágico. Não tocável" (13) ("He's good-looking and in a state of mind to think so. Everything is different then: everything becomes magical. Untouchable"). This story returns to the homoerotic environment of a ship, but here the look replaces the touch: "Na cozinha Mando era olhado por um menino que só gostou de olhá-lo" (13) ("In the kitchen, Mando was gazed at by a boy who only liked to look at him"). The whole effort of understanding the desire of the other, of a communication beyond desire itself, is concentrated in the gaze. The gaze can even substitute for the written or spoken word, but its evanescence persists. Not only do the two protagonists have the same name–Armando, split into Ar and Mando–but beyond any play of doubles or Platonic fusion of lovers, everything seems to be deindividualized: These are figures without names or faces. Even touch, when it occurs, sacrifices the body to the generic image: "Mando levou poucos instantes para abraçar com as duas mãos a se confundirem, Ar. As costas e o beijo. A boca" (22) ("Mando took a few moments to embrace Ar with both hands to the point of becoming enmeshed. Their backs and the kiss. The mouth").

But the corporeal body is not always ignored. AIDS as a theme in the homotextual context appears rarely, but it is powerful when it does–in works by the militant Herbert Daniel (1946–1992), especially his "Annotations on the Margin of Living with AIDS," or in the direct, pressing *A Doença–Uma Experiência* (1996) of Jean-Claude Bernardet (b. 1936) with its imaginary dialogue between the narrator in the present, victim of an unnamed disease (like AIDS, in the beginning), and a mad

uncle already dead (thereby establishing an association between the marginal figures of the insane and gay). In the work of Abreu, the metamorphosing presence of AIDS (in "Anotações sobre um Amor Urbano" ["Notes on an Urban Love"] in *Ovelhas Negras*, [1995; Black Sheep]) does not have the function of masking the disease, as Susan Sontag might argue in her *AIDS and its Metaphors*, but of pointing to an emotional lack. The desire to maintain human contact persists, nonetheless. It is opposed both to the "eu aceito, eu me contento com pouco" ("I accept, I am contented with little") and to the "eu quero muito, eu quero mais, eu quero tudo" (205) ("I want a lot, I want more, I want everything,"); it is not afraid to say "gosto muito de você gosto muito de você gosto muito de você" (207) ("I like you very much I like you very much I like you very much"). There is a constant search for that "que não está completo sem o outro" (204) ("which is not complete without the other"): "amanhã não desisto: te procuro em outro corpo, juro que um dia eu encontro. Não temos culpa, tentei. Tentamos" (208) ("tomorrow I don't give up: I look for you in another body, I swear that one day I'll find you. We are not guilty, I tried. We tried"). This is a strategy of survival that, one might say, is an ethical one: "Tantas mortes, não existem mais dedos nas mãos e nos pés para contar os que se foram. Viver agora, tarefa dura. De cada dia arrancar das coisas, com as unhas, uma modesta alegria; em cada noite descobrir um motivo razoável para acordar amanhã" (207) ("So many deaths, there are no more fingers or toes to count those who have gone. To live now is a difficult job. Day after day to wrest a modest joy from things; every night to discover a sensible reason to wake up tomorrow"). The series of chronicles published in *Pequenas Epifanias* (1996), especially "Última Carta para além dos Muros" ["Last Letter Beyond the Walls"], offers a public announcement of being HIV-positive in a direct, emotional tone: "Aceito todo dia. Conto para você porquê não sei ser senão pessoal, impudico, e sendo assim preciso te dizer: mudei, embora, continue o mesmo. Sei que você compreende" (103) ("I accept every day. I tell you because I only know how to be personal, immodest, and so I need to say: I have changed, but I remain the same. I know you understand"). Good-byes are said, people go on living, torn between the love of life and the melancholy of time that passes.

In our contemporary time of sexual and emotional uncertainty, AIDS is not only an affirmation of the outsider status of the homosexual but the redefinition of his affectivity. The streets, acting now as more than a space for furtive encounters, translate the uncertainty and instability of desire: "I picked this boy from the hollowness of the night/between a corner and old anguish" ("Noturno" ["Nocturne"] in *Quase Sertão* [Almost Backlands], by Ítalo Moriconi [b. 1953]). Or, even more simply put, "preciso da rua/e de seus vértices que não se deixam agarrar" ("I need the street/and its vertices which do not let them be clasped"; "O Belo não é senão a Promessa da Felicidade" ["The Beautiful Is Nothing If Not a Promise of Happiness"], in *Quase Sertão*). The city is no longer just the scene of desire; desire itself cannot be separated from it. Beyond these spaces, in the portrayal of the tension that exists in the uncertainty that makes for possible encounters and lack of encounters between nonidentities, in the confusion between journeys and the desire for home and stability, perhaps the most typical representations are those of João Gilberto Noll. In the 1980s, this writer offered the most successful Brazilian version of the "road movie" aesthetic, with its emotions conveyed in dry images and terse vocabulary. In the general picture of pansexuality, the question remains whether homosexuality really is implied in the encounters he describes between men and boys in "Alguma Coisa Urgentemente" ["Something Urgently"] (in *O Cego e a Dançarina* [1980; The Blind Man and the Dancer]) or in *Rastros de Verão* [1986; Remains of Summer], in the exacerbated desire of *A Fúria do Corpo* [1981; Fury of the Body], or even in the play of masculine doubles in *Bandoleiros* [1985; Bandoleers]. But certainly his latest novel, *A Céu Aberto* [1996; Under the Open Sky], constructs a dreamlike, elliptical, and decidedly homoerotic universe of a dislocated war in which spatial uncertainty is related to the uncertainty of desire.

Somewhere between an epistolary novel and a television soap opera, as the jacket of the book itself points out, *Os Histéricos*, by Jean-Claude Bernardet and Teixeira Coelho (b. 1944), looks to a horizon of fragile identities, incorporating questions of homoeroticism in the redefinition of more complex affectivities. The game of letters, of encounters and lack of encounters, turns the characters into mutant beings, depending on who is speaking and who is looking for meaning and communication. The form of the letter is anachronistic in the world of the telephone and the computer, at the same time as it plays with the idea of sincerity and intimacy, as Ana Cristina César also shows in *A Teus Pés* [1982; At Your Feet]. The "hysteria" of the title of Bernardet and Coelho's work comes from the exacerbation of the affections ("por que recusar o melodrama, se é a única constante que resta de tudo que fazemos?" [172] ["why reject melodrama, if it is the only constant that is left in everything we do?"]), of theatricality ("Nunca quis ser ator, embora eu seja um grande ator" [175] ["I never wanted to be an actor, although I am a great actor"]), which leads to weariness ("Cansei, só isso. Não exatamente de você: devo ter me cansado de mim através de você" [175] ["I am tired, that's all. Not exactly of you: I must have got tired of myself through you"]), and of a lack of control that is also an opening up of possibilities ("Um choro por tudo e por nada, um choro por uma imensa felicidade, uma devastadora e minúscula tristeza" [185] ["A cry for everything and for nothing, a cry for a vast happiness, a devastating and minute sadness"]). It is the related tension between artifice and excess that sets the tone in "A Valorização" ["The Valuing"], by Bernardo Carvalho, in *Aberração* [1993; Aberration], through the absolute artificiality of the character called ae (15–16) and his last wish to spend all his money on releasing hot air balloons in the middle of the Amazon forest, with only the narrator as witness (14, 26). This excessive, useless gesture is recounted by the narrator, who is somehow both accomplice and heir, but it is also a gesture of memory and a coming to terms with the past. We know from the beginning that "esta é uma história de bicha velha. Sempre fui um velho homossexual, desde garoto, e sei muito bem todo o ridículo que isso acarreta. ae sempre foi um mau-caráter, desde garoto, desde quando o conheci" (12) ("This is a story of an old faggot. I was always an old homosexual, from boyhood, and I know very well the ridicule that this causes. ae was always a bad man, from boyhood, from when I met him").

This question of memory is also central to Bernardo Carvalho's latest book *Os Bêbados e Sonâmbulos* [The Drunks and the Sleepwalkers], in which the protagonist has a disease that makes him forgetful. At the same time, however, a desperate search for an evanescent past and present, for a fragile identity, is taking place. That fragility is carried through to the narrator (appearing as a character in the second part), who is adrift between desires and deaths: "Cada morte me despertava uma nostalgia de vida alheia. Eu não ter sido aquela pessoa" (122) ("Every death awakens in me a nostalgia for others' lives, for not having been that person"). This is a narrator-writer who is ultimately lost in passion, lost in another, who always throws himself into the world without reflection, merely moving between spaces and lovers: "Ao conhecê-lo, anulei-me por completo, perdi os meus valores em nome dos dele, sexo e dinheiro, as únicas coisas que existem no mundo, era verdade. Todos os sentidos que até então tinham sustentado a minha vida desapareceram. De mim não sobrou nada. Só ele" (123) ("When I met him, I completely annihilated myself, I lost my values in the name of his, sex and money, the only things that exist in the world, it was true. All the good sense that until then had sustained my life disappeared. Nothing remained of me. Only him"). This is a world of seeking and waiting, which only ends with death.

Holding on to humanity amidst open and ever present violence is a related theme captured by Ayala: "Adotei a delicadeza como última arma num mundo de ameaça e agressão permanentes" (*Poemas do amor maldito* [Poems of Condemned Love] 8) ("I used gentleness as the last weapon in a world of permanent threat and aggression"). The first collection of stories of Caio Fernando Abreu, *Inventário do Ir-remediável*, written in 1969 and revised for publication again in 1995, is worth noting on this count; the stories are written in a style somewhere between Clarice Lispector's intimate manner and a more allegorical mode. The sincerity and emotionality, which would be strong traits in his future writing, already appear here, even if under the aegis of fear, in a world where "ver é permitido mas sentir já é perigoso" (15) ("seeing is permitted but feeling is already dangerous"): "existir me dói feito bofetada" (117) ("to exist hurts me like a blow"). This is once again an adolescent world, inhabited by loneliness and pain, as in "Domingo" ["Sunday"] or "Meio Silêncio" ["Half-Silence"]: "É tudo tão bonito que me dói e me pesa" (96) ("It is all so lovely that it hurts and weighs on me"). But already the encounter with others begins to overcome loneliness, even in mumbled words and timid gestures: "Ergue o braço lentamente, afunda as mãos nos cabelos do outro. E de súbito um vento mais frio os faz encolherem-se juntos, unidos no mesmo abraço, na mesma espera desfeira, no mesmo medo. Na mesma margem" (98) ("Raise your arm slowly, dig your hands into the hair of the other. And suddenly a colder wind makes them contract together, united in the same embrace, unmade in the same waiting, in the same fear. In the same margin"). The refusal of life's loneliness and the desire to escape to somewhere a long way from home also appear as themes in *Limite Branco* [White Limit], the author's first novel (1971). Here fragments of memories mixed with diary entries come together in a melancholic account of a sensitive adolescent: "Hoje não me sinto menos só, apenas meio triste" (82) ("Today I do not feel less alone, only a bit sad"). *O Ovo Apunhalado* [1975; The Stabbed Egg], offers allegorical fantasies, like those of the solitary protagonist of "Réquiem por um Fugitivo" ["Requiem for a Fugitive"], waiting for an angel. Both an oppressive environment and a countercultural climate pervade these stories of solitude and fantasy, almost to the brink of making homosexual difference heroic, as in the allegorical "Eles" ["They"]. In "Retratos" ["Portraits"], the encounter of an old civil servant and a hippie boy echoes the story of Thomas Mann's Tadzio and Aschenbach in *Death in*

Venice in which the youth shows the older man that his life is a kind of death. Here it occurs through successive portraits that the youth makes of the older civil servant; at each meeting, he draws him away from his daily life, from the limitations of a bureaucratic existence and a false morality imposed by neighbors. The countercultural context achieves a more poetic register in "Uma História de Borboletas" ["A Butterfly Story"] (in *Pedras de Calcutá* [Stones of Calcutta]), where an asylum is the space in which two friends, incapable of living in the ordinary world, end up: "Mas eu sabia que eles não admitiriam: quem havia visto o que eu vira não merecia perdão. Além disso, eu tinha desaprendido completamente a sua linguagem, a linguagem que também tive antes, e, embora, com algum esforço conseguisse talvez recuperá-la, não valia a pena, era tão mentirosa, tão cheia de equívocos" (106) ("But I knew they wouldn't allow it: Whoever had seen what I had seen didn't deserve forgiveness. Besides, I had completely unlearned their language, the language I had before, and although with some effort I could have perhaps recovered it, it wasn't worth it, it was so deceitful, so full of errors"). The difficulty in communicating, this time because of paranoia, also appears as a theme in "Diálogo" ["Dialogue"], the opening story of *Morangos Mofados*.

The maturity of Abreu's work is most evident in the creation of affirmative characters ready for life; he moves beyond the excessive intellectual references of his work in the 1960s and 1970s, as can be seen in the shamelessly emotional, almost fairy-tale "Aqueles Dois" ["Those Two"] (in *Morangos Mofados*), in which a different love emerges little by little from ordinary everyday life as an unexpected occurrence. There is here no exaggeration; everything seems to contribute to moving the characters into their ambiguous situation, somewhere between friendship and love. On a related theme, "Pela Noite" ["At Night"], a novella published in *Triângulo das Águas* [1984; Triangle of the Waters] about the encounter of two men on a Saturday night, presents a quest for love in full awareness that time is passing. "Peças de museus, nossas emoções. Todas as emoções" (188) ("Museum pieces, our emotions. All emotions"), Santiago says: "Medo de ficar só, medo de não encontrar, medo de AIDS. Medo de que tudo esteja no fim, de que não exista mais tempo para nada" ("Fear of being alone, fear of not finding, fear of AIDS. Fear that everything is at an end, that there is no more time for anything"). Pérsio adds: "E da grande peste. Mas hoje não, *agora* não. Agora só tenho vontade de galinhar um poco" (189) ("And of the great plague. But not today, not *now.* Now I feel like putting out a little"). Between Santiago's melancholy and Pérsio's merriness, a whole panoply of emotional possibilities opens up.

Perhaps the story that best makes the transition to a realm beyond these works filled with allegories, nameless characters, and a withdrawal into introspection is "Os Dragões não Conhecem o Paraíso" ["The Dragons Do Not Know Paradise"] (in the book of the same title). There, a permanent play of ambiguities exists between the existence and nonexistence of dragons and around the question of whether the narrator has or does not have a dragon. This ambiguity is used not to conceal the character's life, but to take it to the limits of what is reality and what is imagination. The dragon, as a negative version of the angel found in some contemporary narratives, appears here as an image of lightness and the sublime, but also, in a different form, as an image of artifice. But far from coming from a harmonious paradise, the dragon is a being

from a world of conflict, seeming to carry in himself the very need to be abandoned, as pure chimera, so that reality may take over. The narrator notes: "Desde que o mandei embora, para que eu pudesse enfim aprender a grande desilusão do paraíso, é assim que sinto: quase sem sentir. . . . Agora apenas deslizo, sem excessivas aflições de ser feliz" (156) ("Ever since I sent him away, so that I could at last learn of the great disillusion of paradise, this is how I feel: almost without feeling. . . . Now I merely glide along, with no excessive worries about being happy"). But the affirmation of life is made in the act of writing stories that are "totalmente verdadeira, mesmo sendo totalmente mentira" (157) ("totally true, even being a total lie"). These are stories of love and friendship that together create joy in the midst of contemporary uncertainty: "Cansado do amor que sinto, e num enorme esforço que aos poucos se transforma numa espécie de modesta alegria" (157) ("Tired of the love I feel, and in an enormous effort that gradually turns into a kind of modest joy").

The important phenomenon of camp must also be addressed in this context. It can be identified in the spectacularization of the everyday, as in *Stella Manhattan*, by Silviano Santiago, or "Fotografias" ["Photographs"], in *Morangos Mofados*, and "Os Sapatinhos Vermelhos" ["The Red Shoes"] in *Os Dragões não Conhecem o Paraíso*. The possibility of a camp homoerotic aesthetics—that is, moving beyond any biographical facts about the author or the presence of gay characters in the work—is evident in "Mel e Girassóis" ["Honey and Sunflowers"] (in *Os Dragões*), in which a shameless sentimentalism echoes the fascination melodrama holds not only for a female public but also for gays. Caio's early texts are similarly campy: the frank melodrama of "A Maldição dos Saint-Marie" ["The Curse of the Saint-Maries"] or the anti-fairy tale "O Príncipe Sapo" ["The Frog Prince"], published in the collection *Ovelhas Negras*, 1995. Here, in the paradisiacal space of a beach vacation, emotions are not corroded by irony but smoothed over through artifice with a scene from a Hollywood movie, filled with sentimental music and lively dialogue: "Virou de costa, debruçou'se na janela, feito filme: Doris Day, casta porém ousada. Então ele veio por trás: Cary Grant, grandalhão porém mansinho" (113) ("He turned his back, leaned on the windowsill, like a Doris Day film: chaste but not so bold. So he came up from behind: Cary Grant-like, big but tame"). In "Onírico" ["Dreamlike"] (in *Ovelhas Negras*), a modern fairy tale turns into a camp performance of Bovaryism, a tendency that is often present in women's representation but finds far less resonance in gay imaginary constructions. The same is true of its masculine counterpart, the mixture of reality and fantasy known as "Quixoticism" (see the return to Don Quixote in "O Homem e a Mancha" ["The Man from La Mancha"], published in *Teatro Completo* [1997; Complete Dramatic Works]). In an insensitive world, the expression of love, even in this kind of camp fantasy, represents "certa espécie de vitória. Mas tão dúbia que parece também uma completa derrota" (239) ("a certain kind of victory. But so dubious that it also looks like a total defeat"). It is in *Onde Andará Dulce Veiga?* [1990; Where Is Dulce Veiga?], subtitled "a B novel," that the camp sensibility takes on more unpredictable dimensions. Here we find more than the melancholic climate of so many films of the 1980s, from neo-road to neo-noir movies, or constant references to films and their stars; from the look of the reporter-detective, saturated with images and information, to the construction of the diva who disappears, we plunge into a world of images as an act of learning. The search for the singer undertaken by the aging protagonist is touching and grandiloquent even in its gentleness; it is a search for identity amid virus and violence. In "Caçada" ["Hunt"] (in *Pedras de Calcutá*), we enter the space of discos, clubs, and bars that we saw earlier, but now presented differently. The dizziness and the fragmentation created by the way the actual words follow one another echo the swiftness of the characters' (mis)encounters and the intersecting of speeches and noises. In "O Rapaz mais Triste do Mundo" ["The Saddest Boy in the World"] (in *Os Dragões*), the bar is a space where a fleeting encounter between two solitary men takes place before an almost voyeuristic narrator. Strangers to themselves, they are strangers in the world they inhabit: "Alto da noite, certa loucura, algum álcool e muita solidão" (67) ("Late at night, a certain madness, a little alcohol, and a lot of loneliness").

As this suggests, the resignification of home and family in some contemporary North American gay fiction–as spaces no longer of oppression but of emotional connection–seems *not* to be very visible in Brazilian literature. An interesting exception to this would be *Meu Corpos Daria um Romance* [My Body Would Make a Novel], by Herbert Daniel, where there is a movement from the dissatisfaction of sex in public ("Tudo bem, você goza garoto. Mas e o amor? L'amour, morou?" [162] ["Very well, you come, my boy. But love? L'amour, get it?"]), even if liberating ("Quando comecei a freqüentar os lugares de pegação, abusei de trepar anonimamente, perdendo minha noção de individualidade egoísta para ser estritamente corpo genitalizado, sedutor e seduzido, em fodas gostosíssimas e nada além do que o gosto inominado da foda" [327] ["When I began to go to the pick-up spots, I did too much anonymous balling, losing my notion of selfish individualism to become strictly a genitalized body, seducer and seduced, in great fucks and nothing beyond the unnamed taste of the fuck"]), to the constitution of more stable relationships ("Procuramos–e não é fácil–formar um par, sem estabelecer um compartimento que nos isole, mas compartilhar a vida. Vivemos juntos e namoramos outros" [228] ["We try–and it's not easy–to be a couple, without establishing a division that isolates us, but to share life. We live together and make love to others"]). In the story by Caio Fernando Abreu, "Triângulo em Cravo e Flauta Doce" ["Triangle in Harpsichord and Flute"] (written in 1971 and published in *Ovelhas Negras*), what predominate are solitude and furtive encounters. In *Keith Jarrett in the Blue Note*, by Silviano Santiago, the fragile ego of the aging narrator-protagonist is represented in the use of the second-person pronoun to explore subjectivity without fear of being exposed. Such formal sophistication is not used to conceal emotion, but instead to emphasize daily solitude in the uncertainty of memories, phone calls, places, and people. Encounters and dis-encounters are (re)lived as possibilities: "Se você nunca soube quando tudo começou, como vai poder adivinhar como tudo vai terminar? é o que você se pregunta" (147) ("If you never knew when it all began, how could you guess how it will all end? That is what you ask yourself"). What does not seem to change, though, is the sense of solitude in the absence of the beloved. As he writes in *Cheiro Forte* [Strong Smell]:

As sombras indistintas
que carrego comigo
(olho para a pilha delas, milhares)
Os ombros não suportam mais.

(19)

The indistinct shadows
that I carry with me
(I look at the pile of them, thousands)
The shoulders bear no more.

Solitude is seen as the penultimate space before death. The everyday consolidates as a daily struggle. "At that time, my only daily occupation was to try not to die" (*Ovelhas Negras* 243):

Boca faminta
de si mesma.
Para o beijo? não,
para a morte
de todos os segundos.

(Cheiro Forte 9)

Mouth hungry
for itself.
For the kiss? No,
for the death
of every second.

This is not the survival of past ideals, but survival in relation to those who died before us, survival in relation to those parts of us that have also gone. There remains "alguma coisa amarga, alguma coisa assim: *no se puede vivir sin amor*" ("something bitter, something like this: you cannot live without love," "Sobre o Vulcão" ["Over the Volcano"], *Ovelhas Negras* 243). There is simply the search for the other, in the passing of time and places, in uncertainty: "Aos caminhos, eu entrego o nosso encontro" ("To the paths, I hand over our encounter," "Bem Longe de Marienbad" ["Very Far from Marienbad"], *Ovelhas Negras* 41). It is as if death were the last possibility of dialogue, exchange, or conversation:

A morte nunca é agora;
é sempre:
    não nasce,
    não morre:
dádiva de um corpo
    para outro corpo

(Cheiro Forte 10)

Death is never now;
it is always:
    it isn't born,
    it doesn't die:
gift of one body
    to another body

But the dialogue *does* continue. Gay literature continues to be written in Brazil, expressing all these diverse themes in all these diverse styles: "gift of one body/to another body."

**Translation by Glaucia Renate Gonçalves
and Tom Burns**

Works Cited

Abreu, Caio Fernando. 1982. *Morangos Mofados*. São Paulo: Brasiliense.

——. 1984. *Triângulo das Águas*. Rio de Janeiro: Nova Fronteira.

——. 1988. *Os Dragões não Conhecem o Paraíso*. São Paulo: Companhia de Letras.

——. 1995 [1968]. *Inventário do ir-remediável*. 2nd ed. Porto Alegre: Sulina.

——. 1995. *Ovelhas Negras*. 2nd ed. Porto Alegre: Sulina.

——. 1996 [1977]. *Pedras de Calcutá*. 2nd ed. São Paulo: Companhia das Letras.

———. 1997. *Pequenas Epifanias*. Porto Alegre: Sulina.

Amado, Jorge. 1989. *Capitães de Areia*. 69th ed. Rio de Janeiro: Record.

Andrade, Mário de. n.d. "Soneto". *De Paulicéia Desvairda a Café (Poesias Completas)*. São Paulo: Círculo do Livro. 263.

———. 1967. "Frederico Paciência." *Histórias do Amor Maldito*. Org. Gasparino Damata. Rio de Janeiro: Gráfica Récord Editora. 81–100.

Assis, Joaquim Maria Machado de. 1968. [1958]. "Pílades e Orestes." *Histórias do Amor Maldito*. Org. Gasparino Damata. Rio de Janeiro: Gráfica Récord Editora. 151–60.

Ayala, Walmir. 1967. "Taís." *Histórias do Amor Maldito*. Org. Gasparino Damata. Rio de Janeiro: Gráfica Récord Editora. 253–67.

———. 1969. "Depoimento de um antologiado a guisa de prefácio" *Poemas do Amor Maldito*. Org. Gasparino Damata and Walmir Ayala. Brasilia: Coordenada Editora de Brasilia. 7–10.

Azevedo, Aluísio. 1968. *O Cortiço*. São Paulo: Livraria Martins Editora.

Bernardet, Jean-Claude. 1990. *Aquele Rapaz*. São Paulo: Brasiliense.

———. 1996. *A Doença. Uma Experiência*. São Paulo: Companhia de Letras.

——— and Teixeira Coelho. 1993. *Os Histéricos*. São Paulo: Companhia de Letras.

Caminha, Adolfo. n.d. [1896]. *O Bom Crioulo*. Rio de Janeiro: Ed. De Ouro.

Canabrava, Luiz. 1967. "Aprendizado." *Histórias do Amor Maldito*. Org. Gasparino Damata. Rio de Janeiro: Gráfica Récord Editora. 109–19.

———. 1968. *O Sexo Portátil*. Rio de Janeiro: Gráfica Récord Editora.

Cardoso, Lúcio. 1979. *Crônica de uma Casa Assassinada*. Rio de Janeiro: Nova Fronteira.

Carvalho, Bernardo. 1993. "Atores." *Aberração*. São Paulo: Companhia de Letras. 117–31.

———. 1993. "A valorização." *Aberração*. São Paulo: Companhia de Letras. 11–26.

———. 1996. *Os bêbados e os sonâmbulos*. São Paulo: Companhia de Letras.

César, Ana Cristina. 1982. *A Teus Pés*. São Paulo: Brasiliense.

Cícero, Antônio. 1996. *Guardar*. Rio de Janeiro: Gráfica Récord Editora.

Coutinho, Edilberto, ed. 1980. *Erotismo no Conto Brasileiro*. Rio de Janeiro: Civilização Brasileira.

Damata, Gasparino, org. 1968 [1967]. *Historias de Amor Maldito*. 2d ed. With preface by Octávio de Freitas Jr. Rio de Janeiro: Gráfica Récord Editora.

——— and Walmir Ayala, org. 1969. *Poemas do Amor Maldito*. Brasília: Coordenada.

Daniel, Herbert. 1984. *Meu Corpo Daria um romance. Narrativa Desarmada*. Rio de Janeiro: Rocco.

———. 1992. "Anotações à margem do Viver com AIDS." *SaúdeLoucura*. 3–20.

Dourado, Autran. 1957. "Três Histórias do Internato ('Inventario do 1º Dia', 'A Última Vez' e 'A História Natural'")." *Nove Histórias em Grupo de Três*. Rio de Janeiro: José Olympio. 175–248.

Hecker Filho, Paulo. 1951. *No Internato*. Porto Alegre: Fronteira/RGS.

Honório, José Carlos. 1992. *Atravessar teu Corpo*. São Paulo: Ars Poética.

———, org. 1995. *O Amor com os Olhos de Adeus. Antologia do Conto Gay Brasileiro*. São Paulo: Transviatta.

Igreja, Francisco. 1986. *O Renascer do Jacinto*. Rio de Janeiro: Romance.

Luft, Lya. 1988. *Exílio*. Rio de Janeiro: Rocco.

Mattoso, Glauco.1982. *Memórias de um Pueteiro: as Melhores Gozações*. 2d ed. Rio de Janeiro: Trote.

Moriconi, Ítalo. 1996. *Quase Sertão*. Rio de Janeiro: Diadorim.

Mota, Valdo. 1996. *Bundo e outros poemas*. Campinas: Editora da Unicamp.

Perez, Renard. 1979. *Irmãos da Noite*. Rio de Janeiro: Civilização Brasileira.

Piva, Roberto. 1981. *20 Poemas com Brócolis*. São Paulo: Massao Ohno/Roswith Kempf.

Pompéia, Raul. 1988 [1888]. *O Ateneu*. 7th ed. São Paulo: Ática.

Rawet, Samuel. 1967. "O Seu Minuto de Glória." *Histórias do Amor Maldito*. Org. Gasparino Damata. Rio de Janeiro: Gráfica Récord Editora. 215–17.

Rio, João do [João Paulo Barreto]. 1910. "O Bebê de Tarlatana Rosa." *Dentro da Noite*. Rio de Janeiro: H. Garnier. Estadual do Livro. 153–64.

———. 1910. "Histórias de Gente Alegre." *Dentro da Noite*. Rio de Janeiro: H. Garnier. 25–39.

Rosa, João Guimarães. 1967. *Grande Sertão: Veredas*. Rio de Janeiro: José Olympio.

Sabino, Fernando. 1977. *O Encontro Marcado*. Rio de Janeiro: Record.

Santiago, Silviano. 1985. *Stella Manhattan*. Rio de Janeiro: Nova Fronteira.

———. 1995. *Cheiro Forte*. Rio de Janeiro: Rocco.

———. 1996. *Keith Jarrett no Blue Note*. Rio de Janeiro: Rocco.

Silva, Aguinaldo. 1975. *Primeira Carta aos Andróginos*. Rio de Janeiro: Pallas.

———. 1993. *Lábios que Beijei*. São Paulo: Siciliano.

Stockinger, Jacob. 1978. "Homotextuality: A Proposal." *The Gay Academic*. Org. Louie Crew. California: ETC. 135–51.

Trevisan, João Silvério. 1986. *Devassos no Paraíso*. São Paulo: Max Limonad.

———. 1976. *O Testamento do Jônatas deixado a David*. São Paulo: Brasiliense.

———. 1985. *Em Nome do Desejo*. São Paulo: Max Limonad.

———. 1997. *Troços e Destroços*. Rio de Janeiro: Record.

Warner, Michael. 1991. "Fear of a Queer Planet." *Social Text* 29.9:3–17.

PART THREE

PLURALITY OF DISCOURSE IN LATIN AMERICAN CULTURE

SECTION I
INTRODUCTION: POLITICAL, SCIENTIFIC, AND RELIGIOUS DISCOURSES

Eneida Maria de Souza and Raúl Antelo

We begin with the presupposition that thinking about literature beyond its traditional limits means giving it a new threshold, conceiving of it by starting with and then moving away from its conventional, unconditional, and intransitive character. Yet, because literature is at the same time a mode of subjective experience, to rethink its history is to rethink the modes of discernment of certain theological-social fables that permeate its process. If, for example, we take up the adventure of modernity, we necessarily perceive the paradoxical quality of this as an identity fable, for the writing is contested, repeatedly, by the materiality of the reality: Latin American literature has been timidly whispering for the better part of five centuries. Out of this paradox arise two consequences. The first is that Latin American literature until well into the twentieth century has been a nonparticipant on the world stage because it has dealt with manifestations that say absolutely nothing about the reality of life in the Latin American continent. The second is that Latin American literature lost its speech at birth because, in the understanding of the dominant, national-liberal ideology (always so impregnated with categories such as universal values–i.e., Western European values–or genius and the singularity of expression), the literature of the Latin American lettered elite was a pale imitation of metropolitan models, and given the crushing weight of imitating the great world prose of Europe, it was with very few exceptions sterile, apathetic, empty, and largely ignorant of its own culture, peoples, and lands. The excitement in Latin American literature has been the story of the manipulation of its meager effort; it has been the point of contact between the theological-philosophical constraints of the colonized and the political-cultural dream of liberation within the boundaries of the postcolonial state.

It is also worth considering that the very emergence of Latin America on the international scene corresponds to the development of modernity as a social drama. Western civilization–this fiction represented by ourselves, we who exist as self-inventions of the human being insofar as we project the intolerability of the immediate Dionysian passion onto the tolerable and the mediated–is what invents Latin America today as a constructed space, starting from the dialectic of the tolerable and the intolerable, in other words, as a space of the unlimited semiosis of the modern. This civilization arises less as the harmonious continuation of European ideals than as the shrinking of that logic of rational control that is exasperated every time the Western Enlightenment process collapses.

In the final analysis, Latin American culture never ceases to reopen the question of the validity of the truth-claim and of the possibilities of a free examination of opinions. We all remember the elliptical Kantian condemnation of religious practices, notably of the bloody, inquisitorial *autos-da-fé*, in his discourse on the Enlightenment. It is not difficult to prove that, two centuries later, against the logic of moral reason in the search for truth, evil born out of ignorance casts a new light by which we can understand the self-poeticizing of collective life. Therefore, not only does the present political and social situation of Latin America reveal the crude and the abject, but the reality of Latin American culture is also seen in its inexhaustible heterogeneity.

If we accept these presuppositions, an analysis of these different discourses (philosophical, political, religious) indicates a dialogue between peripheral and metropolitan modernities, largely because of the degree of receptivity to imported theories on the American continent. The continuous exchange of transcultural formations offers one of the most important means for creating a scenario of shared experiences as social, economic, and cultural changes highly influence the interpretation given to foreign borrowings and their application in each region of Latin America. With the current advance of cultural studies, it is clear that theoretical perspectives, interpretive pluralism, and the relativization of hegemonic power have increased, which is demonstrated by the diversity and the quality of discursive interventions on the world scene. The five chapters in this section attest to that fact.

Alongside these discursive transformations, other theoretical frames have been invoked by these essays, notably the growing weakening of the influence of scientific reasoning over the last two decades of the twentieth century, keeping epistemology in check as the universal basis of knowledge and causing the emergence of particularized rationalities and specific theoretical approaches. Throughout the last century, the discourse of positivist science, with its deliberate intention of reconstructing totalities, has shown itself to be inappropriate, a fact that demanded a gradual change in paradigms and analytical frameworks. The preeminent place given to modern science, together with the imposition of systems control in the everyday life of ordinary people as well as the financial-industrial drive for globalization, have been challenged by a radical questioning of all received knowledge, thus valuing incompleteness and openness as constructive principles.

367

Yet, in order to analyze the intervention of political, scientific, and religious discourses in Latin America, it is appropriate to discriminate among and describe the truth claims in the various types of discourses involved. Already at the beginning, that is, from the seventeenth- and eighteenth-century colonial period to the nineteenth-century liberal order, it is possible to note the elaboration of a rhetoric of citizenship at four points: the didactic imperative colonial discourse; the self-conscious linking of emancipatory discourses in journalism and state institutions at the beginning of the nineteenth century; the utilization of the utopian imagination and the pedagogical-disciplinary role of intellectuals throughout the Independence period, and, last, the postulating of the nation as involving an association of secularism, scientism, and institutional modernization.

Starting from this premise, Adriana Rodriguez Pérsico, for example, has concentrated on the similarities and divergences of elements of this rhetoric, as seen through specific fictional regimes: the discourse of science, in its biological and psychiatric variants (the latter necessarily associated with the discourse of positivism); the sociological discourse, centered either on the social body or on the movement of the masses; the discourse of occultism—an antipositivist imaginary, but at the same time an indication of cultural hybridizations that have persisted since the colonizing process began (as Silvia Delfino demonstrates in her analysis of the use and value of mimesis and translation in the formation of a Latin American cultural subject); the discourse of the nation (regional and continental, obsessed with homogenization and voluntarism); the aestheticizing discourse (the life of the artist in opposition to instrumental utilitarianism; its anti-bourgeois result); and, finally, the discourse of desire, understood as transgression or trespassing of bodily discipline.

How has the state reacted to the rhetoric of the citizen? Aparecida Paiva's essay on Catholic discourse in Brazil illuminates this debate. This discourse held a veto on literary creation; any literary text that was judged to obstruct the formation of sound minds, as guided by "conscience," was banned. This feature was transposed to a veto and was imposed by the positivist pseudoscientific discourse on Brazilian society. The close connection between modernization and nationalism in Brazil at the beginning of the twentieth century also counted on the cooperation of the State and the Church for the consolidation of educational and moralistic programs and in the creation of strong institutions bent on the practice of such principles. The State's large-scale importation of European clerics coincided with the need to expand religious ideology in colonized countries, mainly through the dissemination provided by the press and the written word.

It is impossible to approach these issues without paying attention to the powerful effort toward cultural homogenization undertaken by the State and its institutions. The work of Rachel Esteves Lima notes the place of the essay in the development of post-World War II cultural thought; once scientism and the control of the rationalist order lost their dominance, this genre returned to the scene but under a different guise, although it retained some features of its former style (such as the experimental character of the presentation of theories), but the locus of enunciation of the subject within discourse reversed the positivist spirit of treatises and disciplinary models that ruled over the search for truth in the modern process of knowledge construction. The most recent breakup of disciplinary boundaries in the late twentieth century has contributed decisively to re-establishing an interdisciplinary approach within the humanities. Although there is always the risk of falling into a globalized lack of differentiation, such a critical position, nevertheless, reintegrates knowledge into a horizon of expectations that relativizes the hierarchical verticality of disciplines.

In all these cases we have witnessed a series of attempts to associate knowledge and power in making the public space autonomous, but at the same time, and imposing equally unceasing pressure, Latin American literary culture has engaged in developing an alternative biopolitics. As has been observed, the miscellaneous discourse of the chronicle subverts the apparent transparency of the rhetoric of citizenship as the beginning of Independence, producing a series of discourses that have shaped Latin American cultural heterogeneity in the transition to modernity. The contribution of Claudia Gilman shows that this miscellaneous system of rhetoric provides us, however, with a point of departure for understanding the present-day breaking away from modernity. More than the complexity of modernity, one notes the perplexity of the accelerating pace of change in contemporary life. A positivist identity fiction in the first half of the century affirmed the subject, but we now have cynical arguments that question its existence. New post-identity crises are thus grasped at the moment of the subject's inflection, which ultimately gives way to negation. Once more, the concept of translation helps us to outline the continuity with the retrospective reconstruction proposed here, and figures like those of the centaur (the strongman) or the cannibal (the nationalist), used as operative concepts, lose the bizarre quality they might have had in the miscellaneous systems of high modernity to affirm a double value: the exhaustion of evaluation, and the decline in validity of the universals that orchestrated the construction of national citizenship in Latin America.

In their double value, fictional representations in Latin America not only allow but begin to demand an allegorical reading for their occult or neglected representations. In other words, they claim the content of truth of narrative knowledge through insistence on the local character of discourses and on the mode of bringing this knowledge up to date by means of testimonial accounts and no longer by conceptual descriptions. The narrative construction of political knowledge is conspicuous from the point of view of the literary text and its interpretation. The task of re-establishing a new order for rationality employs above all narrativity, considered as one of the possible places for truths to emerge. Meaning, traditionally understood as the product of a conceptual network, is now purged of certainties and shares the creative force and instability of metaphorical articulations.

At what point does this type of heterogeneous religious hyperceremonial of the present Latin American culture touch on the politics of truth inherited both from the Iberian colonial tradition and Church domination during the period of state formation? To answer the question, we could argue with Lacan that, while no religion is true, Christianity is the one that comes closest to the truth insofar as it does not imply contemplation or immovable knowledge, but rather a dramatic intervention of the crucified Christ and the discovery that there are two: God and Man. What is important in this case is to understand the consequences of this ambiguity: It reinforces, on the one hand, the process of rupture of representations, and it helps us, on the other hand, to understand that truth circulates without being represented or without exhausting its semiotic potential. What the excessive religious hyperceremonial enacts today is a hypothesis of true capability, that is, of a truth claim that is not factual or empirical but virtual (not taken place), poetic (metaphorical), and infinite (political rhetoric).

These hypotheses–which we reencounter in the unifying sermons of Padre Vieira, in the populist sovereignty of Tomas Antônio Gonzaga and Juan Bautista Alberdi, in the political fiction of Sarmiento or Euclides da Cunha, and even in the allegories of the avant-garde–are all established retrospectively in place of any attempt to know the original thought. In this intersection of past and present, we have, in the last analysis, the interpretive elements of Latin American modernity. More than that, we have also the three elements of what we might call the Latin American political fiction–bringing together history, art, and religion. There are at least three components to this fiction. First, there is an analysis of the modern world in terms of material resources with the assertion of infinite abundance of natural resources. Second, there is a standard exegesis of

historical events that entails the religious doctrine of double meaning: redemption through Christ and the irruptive notion of miracles. Third, within the formal dogma of divine intervention, an unmistakable interpretive axiology takes control.

It is only by returning to a basic historical logic that we can rethink the history of Latin America's literary culture and develop a postevent historical concept of experience on which to confer meaning and thus avoid the category errors of the past, which have either mistaken the formal-empirical description of the event for the truth of the lived experience or constructed a self-serving fiction and claimed it as historical truth. Latin American intellectual discourse at the start of the twenty-first century oscillates constantly between a utopian vision that has appropriated the Other and a postutopian vision associated with the voiding of the validity of all discourse depicting human experience.

**Translation by Glaucia Gonçalves
and Thomas LaBorie Burns**

CHAPTER 41

THE RHETORIC OF LATIN AMERICAN NATIONALISM FROM THE COLONIAL PERIOD TO INDEPENDENCE

Silvia Delfino

It is common knowledge that Latin American literary cultures are grounded in the interaction among philosophical, literary, and cultural modalities from Europe and the United States of America. This interaction has been one of translation and appropriation that transformed European concepts and ideas in the local literary cultures of Latin America.

This trans-Atlantic appropriation formed part of the institutional cultural configuration of Latin American countries and slowly developed into a national discourse, or a citizens' religion, as the Argentine Esteban Echeverría (1805–1851) liked to call it. This transformative appropriation of European (especially French, English, and Spanish) cultural modalities is often disparaged by current commentators who appear not to recognize that this process served to produce Latin America's cultural uniqueness. On the one hand the resulting hybrid Latin American culture made the symbolic excess of the Baroque intelligible in universal terms, and on the other it made the national cultural differences from Mexico to Argentina compatible because of their common foundational base. Latin American heterogeneity therefore does not refer to interchangeable differences but rather to the specific cultural reformulation brought about by the pressure of the suppressed native American elements that became the primary transformative agents.

Once these tensions have been recognized, one may begin to address the different regional problems, starting with the conflict between cultural institutions, the diverse and often incompatible articulations of discourses and practices, including the formation of esthetic precepts and the numerous controversies concerning the constitution of social and political life, in order to ask how one cultural order was legitimated and served as a map of possible meanings for shared social experiences. In this respect, Latin American criticism has reexamined the configuration of cultural canons, in which the ambivalence between the modern and the traditional, the new and the obsolete, the secular and the religious, narrates a historical continuity that organizes the disparate times and shiftings of borders. Raúl Antelo has studied this difficult transmutation of the "confusion of races and tongues" that has been, ever since the seventeenth century, one of the most productive metaphors in Latin American culture, standing at once for the normative view and for decentered and deviant displacement (see Antelo 1994). The change in the social significance of these conflicts can be traced back to the distinct status religion, science, and politics held when one took persuasion and consensus-making into account. These differences have left their mark on many areas of discourse that contest the relationship of subject to community—and it is these that may be regarded as revealing the rhetoric of citizenship in Latin American culture. It follows that this rhetorical practice creates space for reflecting upon the limits of languages, discursive practices, and knowledge, which determine the forms of order, authority, and power, as well as the rules governing the production and reception of cultural genres through a hierarchy of sensitivities, pleasures, and virtues.

The aim of this section is to historicize the constitution of cultural canons on our continent by comparing two rhetorical devices, ridicule and praise, which contest the relationships among discourse, ethics, and politics. Whereas praise is predictably expressed in genres of abstract or general utterance (the ode, the hymn, demonstrative essays of philosophical or scientific import) at the top of the normative stratum, ridicule undermines this status hierarchy by displacing censorship, decorum, and the approved uses of laughter and ridicule in insult, imprecation, and invective. These forms forge models of reciprocity between sectors and forms of communal identity by foregrounding cultural and political differences. This creates problems that involve, on the one hand, devising a concept of culture perceived as part of a common history and, on the other, specifying the variable status of the discourses of knowledge, ethics, politics, and religion that are constructed once the core conflictive situation has been taken into account. We shall attempt to redefine the specific link between culture and politics by examining a series of verbal acts and figurations that run through the relationships among practices, knowledges, and meanings. Linda Hutcheon points out that the complex functions of irony–like ridicule and sarcasm–move from the "minimal affective charge" of mere trivializing to the "maximum affective charge" of powerful collaboration between inclusionary and exclusionary views (Hutcheon 37–56). In this resides irony's critical edge, which affects as much the ironist as the audiences through the burst of energy that redefines rhetoric as the specific connection between language, knowledge, and action.

In this way, the diverse maps marking the boundaries of the authority of religious, scientific, and political discourse in cultural and educational institutions can be reconstructed by undertaking a comparative study of both the history of esthetic ideas and institutional controversies. These render visible both the persistence of and the variations in the procedures of appropriation and displacement, which are based on the tension between formal equality before the law and the inequality and discrimination concerning the distribution of rights, the eligibility to participate and to enjoy social opportunities. Fundamentally, this history can be interpreted on the basis of the translation and subsequent appropriation of concepts from the scientific, political, and religious discourse of Europe and the United States. The concepts appropriated from high European culture (the universal notions of liberty, equality, and fraternity of the Age of Enlightenment) were enunciated and generalized as a national culture when translated by symbolic practices or literary genres that not only set them in a new and different context but also established specific relationships among the cultural levels involved. A comparative approach reveals several possible patterns for the constitution of cultural canons on this continent between the Colonial period and emancipation. This would permit us to historicize the following four things.

1. The ways in which the acts of appropriating and translating genres and cultural practices affect the production of a conflictive concept of the singularity of Latin American culture, in which praise and ridicule were interfused at the time of colonization. The aporia thus constituted oscillated between an exaltation of the grandeur of the American continent and its innocence, nobility, and exoticism on the one hand, and contempt for and condemnation of its cultural and institutional emptiness on the other, given that these very features demonstrated its barbarity, primitivism, and vacuity. Antonio Cándido argues that the national cultural canons laboriously postulated in Latin America during the nineteenth century exalted a naturally hypostatized distinction, thereby constructing what he calls a "compensatory particularity" in light of the discouraging paradox of immense natural riches and dearth of secular institutions (Candido 1976).

2. The way in which this state of affairs is positioned through translation and cultural criticism passes through the intersection of opposites, at times complementary to each other. That juncture is expressed through terms such as *backwardness, savagery,* and *barbarity.* This contradictory notion has been generally attributed to uncontrollable excess; it also produces a picturesque singularity once the principles of secularization, rationality, and social differentiation have been channeled through the ambivalent processes of economic and political modernization.

3. The way in which the specific material conditions can be interpreted in the different configurations of this aporia, as they displace and define the status of the discourses of knowledge, religion, and politics, proves determinative.

4. The extent to which the struggle to delimit the status of these discourses appears to plot a map of dominant meanings.

In this sense, if our critical approach focuses on specificity, we can study the different components of this aporia, in which the opposites of ridicule and praise are interfused. Our purpose is to discover not what they represent or reveal of the makeup of an objective and natural social order, but how they formulate the specific material configurations in the relations between culture and historical conditions. This may result in a rereading of the periodization that displaces the four philosophic/institutional nuclei that are considered the great moments of transformation in the history of Latin American culture, that is, (1) the relations among religion, philosophy, and political administration under the colonial model from the sixteenth to the eighteenth century; (2) the change in these relations among journalism, literary, legal, and scientific institutions as seen in emancipatory discourses during the first half of the nineteenth century; (3) the recording and exalting of ethnic and geographic peculiarities in order to propose a natural uniqueness that articulated a civilizing esthetic difference (the wisdom of the imagination), the intellectuals' representation of their experiences of this singularity (and their pedagogical and political role); and (4) the attempt to construct a national cultural canon postulated as an objective order–by joining together laicism, positivism, and the institutional modernization of the liberal and conservative states at the end of the nineteenth century.

Historical studies and literary criticism have studied these as moments of rupture and transition. I would argue that they are worth reexamining in order to study the representations of primitivism, barbarity, picturesqueness, and civilization, and the possible rearticulations of struggle in the figures of *mestizaje,* acculturation, indigenousness, hybridity, and transculturation, as well as the unstable configuration of the link between inequality and difference during moments of social crisis. However, my express interest lies not in the social significance of such configurations but in the cultural operations implied in their production as the provisional resolutions for conflicts involving pacts, institutions, and roles. In these disputes, the difference in scope and effectiveness of edicts and orders, legal constitutions, hymns and praise songs, diatribe, insult, and ridicule cannot be determined by one poetic theory alone. When it comes to constituting cultural canons, Latin America cannot be thought of as a homogeneous entity; similarly, the differences among its material and historical features cannot be conceptualized as autonomous and restrictive in ethnic and regional terms. In fact, their institutionalization, which entails reaching some form of resolution, indicates both the designation and the crisis that is its very condition of being. Thus, these configurations do not reveal Latin American cultural specificity so much as the effect produced by the historical conceptualization of these crises as instances of the relations among theory, criticism, and their own historical circumstances.

Translation, Censorship, and Grievance

In *Imperial Eyes* Mary Louise Pratt argues that the conquest of South America, Mexico, Central America, and the Caribbean (not only by Portugal and Spain, but also by Great Britain, France, and Holland) led to the reinvention of Europe through narratives of self-assertion. The physical and ethnic diversity of the New World was dressed up in exotic apparel and conceived as a source of incommensurable riches and as a heroic challenge to the religious faith, the knowledge, and the administrative abilities of this civilization. In this sense, the narratives written by the explorers, priests, and regents worked on two levels: To the European patrons they offered an efficacious yardstick for calculating, estimating, and registering expectations, and to the conquered peoples they moved instruments of exegesis, conversion, and domination. The indigenous translators, guides, and intermediaries were represented as educable children. Rhetoric thus functioned as an economy of naming, with the Baroque style providing the ceremonial complexities to the relations among religion, philosophy, and political administration during the sixteenth and seventeenth centuries. During the eighteenth century, however, the so-called Euroamericans attempted to recontextualize the relationship between alterity and representation by means of both consensus-making and institutions that mediated the liberalization imposed by the Spanish and Portuguese economies and the need to maintain their privileged status above the mulattos, *mestizos,* black people (free and slaves), indigenous peoples, and *zambos* or sambos. During the European crisis of 1809, which led to the downfall of the Spanish viceroyalties, the transfer of the Portuguese court to Brazil, and the commercial crisis and espionage in Cuba, religion, nationalism, and modernization continued to be, according to Jean Franco, the most extensive "narrative systems" (Franco 1989). These produced both integration and stratification in terms of gender, ethnicity, and, to a certain extent, religion and culture that could be seen in journalism, in literary and scientific organs, and even in the legal constitutions' emancipatory discourses, which became the site for distribution of shared authority. The possible alliance between apostolic authority and rational persuasion highlights three points: first, the rewriting of notions of the common good as dogma; second, the impact on the division of literary genres (such as the romance of chivalry, the picaresque novel, the philosophical sermon, and the *costumbrista* play); and, finally, the ways in which these displacements collaborated to legitimize patriotic societies, clubs, literary circles, and political groupings.

The cultural history of Latin America demonstrates that the many periodicals, which had a broad circulation, were one of the means of exploiting tensions between European dominance and the attempts at self-government in colonial cities. As one might expect, these scientific, philosophical, and literary periodicals published odes and songs of praise to Latin-American nature, translations of European philosophy and, revealing an anxious desire for reciprocity, accounts of the European and North American scientists' and explorers' adventures on the continent. These travel narratives were circulated as forms of self representation, particularly through the images rendered by Alexander von Humboldt and Aimé Bonpland, together with economic reports and philosophical debates, in the colonial social gatherings known as *tertulias*. At the same time, the growing group of *criollo* intellectuals, dependent on the arrival of new books from across the sea and on their own ability to translate and publish, fought against censorship, which proved to be rather ineffective toward the end of colonial rule (even if newspapers did have to show their Imprimatur license on the front page until the nineteenth century). For this reason, the efforts by the colonial powers to control these publications exposed the contradictions between a need for publicity and a desire to regulate the powers' own excess of exploitation through religious censorship. One can observe this tension in the rhetorical practices in political declarations in the periodicals; the contradictions, however, also produced and sustained the possibility of opening a space for the debate about the ethical authority of the Independence movements.

These publications (some official and bureaucratic, others clandestine and censored, because of their pamphleteering, subversive content) serve as the basis for a possible mapping of the intersections, alliances, and hostilities between European-ness (in this case, Spain and Portugal) and American-ness, as well as among the different languages (French, Dutch, English, Guaraní, Quechua, Mayan, Nahuatl, and Zapotec). The interrelation of science and a discourse of emancipation is to be found in such works as *El amigo del país* [Friend of the Nation], *El patriota* [The Patriot], *El telégrafo mercantil rural político económico e historiográfico* [The Mercantile, Rural, Political, Economic, and Historiographic Telegraph] which combine references to Voltaire, Locke, or Newton with the fables and burlesque satires of the colonial Baroque. The odes and songs in praise of Latin-American nature (*Oda al Paraná* in the River Plate or *Vila rica* in Bahia) can be compared with the nativistic descriptions that the Jesuits had bequeathed to America upon their expulsion in 1767. For instance, Fray Rafael Landívar's (1731–1793) bucolic description in Latin (1782; *Rusticatio mexicana*) transfers not only the mysticism of nature but also the hybridity of language by grafting indigenous designations onto the Latin and by using American Spanish terms that contrast sharply with Castilian usage. Other examples of this kind of nativistic transformation are

the Venezuelan Andrés Bello's (1781–1865) "Canción a la agricultura en las zonas tórridas" [1826–27; "Ode to Agriculture in the Torrid Zones"] and Sarmiento, Bello, and Bolívar's polemics on grammar and vocabulary. The celebration of American nature—its plains, saltpeter deposits, jungles, and mountains—as being more than human in scale, on the one hand, reproduced the animistic vision that the priests of the former Jesuit American domain had developed in a kind of lived syncretism as one of the conditions for possible emancipation. On the other hand, as mimetic translation, this celebration contrasted with the colonials' urbanization and mercantilism, which championed the founding of scientific academies, universities, and *Sociedades de Beneficiencia* or Benevolent Societies.

The balance and redistribution of the controlling roles of religion and science in the relations among the Church, the metropolitan administration, and the local élite are exemplified by the expulsion of the Jesuits in 1767. This move resolved the Spaniards' problems of centralizing the Church and of forming an alliance with the *criollos*, who regarded the white viceregal authority as the suppressor of the uprisings of the mulattos, *mestizos*, blacks, indigenous peoples, and sambos. It is hardly surprising that the exiled Jesuits often pronounced libertarian diatribes against the pedagogical crusade undertaken by the Benedictine and Franciscan scribes, who translated Descartes and Rousseau, purging them of their heretical metaphysical propositions. Such is the case of Fr. Benito Jerónimo Feijoo (1676–1764). He succeeded in reconciling religious belief and scientific knowledge in his *Teatro crítico universal o Discursos varios en todo género de materias para desengaño de errores comunes* [1726; Universal Critical Theater or Varied Discourses in Every Kind of Matters for Disproving Common Errors], in which he proposed that a moderate rationalism be added to the espousal of both the experimental method and theological doctrine. This gesture inspired Mariano Moreno (1778–1811) of the Río de la Plata region to translate Rousseau's *The Social Contract* for elementary schools, after eliminating the heresies the philosopher was purported to be guilty of. Under this moderate version of Enlightenment, doctrine, sovereignty, and collusion were invoked to reconcile the interests of physiocracy, free trade, and mercantilism with reason and empirical observation, while never acting contrary to the religious or administrative authority of the viceroyalty.

In this respect, historiography indicates that the Age of Enlightenment did not begin in Latin America at the time of the insurrections of the nineteenth century but at the time of the Bourbon Reform of the Viceroyalty of New Granada, New Spain, Peru, and Río de la Plata and the Pombaline Reform of 1759 in Brazil, both of which gave a certain impetus to modernization. For this reason, Caracas, Buenos Aires, Santa Fé de Bogotá, Havana, Bahia, Rio de Janeiro, São Paulo, and Minas Gerais were perceived as secularized cities. This cosmopolitanism gave South American travelers the opportunity to return the Europeans' exploratory gesture by producing their own publications in Europe—and not just for diplomatic reasons. Such was the case of Hipólito José da Costa Pereira Furtado de Mendoça (1774–1823), who published the *Correio Brasiliense* in London from 1808 to 1822, and of Domingos José Gonçalves de Magalhaes (1811–1882), who published *Niterói, Revista Brasiliense* in Paris in 1836. The best representative of this elusiveness is the Venezuelan Francisco de Miranda (1750–1816). During his travels through Africa and the Caribbean, especially Jamaica, and his many visits to Great Britain, he assumed the Jekyll-and-Hyde role of statesman and conspirator, disclosing plots and schemes of revolt against the Spaniards at the Foreign Office in London and in lodges and secret societies (which would then circulate his publications in Latin American cities from Mexico to Buenos Aires and Montevideo). As a result, the legislative power over press censorship and the banning of books was at once enforced and undermined by such publishing practices as authorial anonymity, pseudonymity, falsification, and ghost editors. This made possible the production of underground translations; in 1794, Antonio Nariño (1760–1823), a civil servant in New Granada, privately published the Spanish translation of the French revolutionary text *Declaración de los derechos del hombre y del ciudadano* [Declaration of the Rights of Man and of the Citizen], which was read throughout the viceroyalty. A group of nativist poets from the Brazilian state of Minas Gerais, however, suffered a different fate when in 1789 they joined an insurrection under the banner of *Inconfidencia.* One of them, Tomás Antônio Gonzaga (1744–1807?), a Portuguese civil servant who was appointed judge of Vila Rica, wrote a series of burlesque satires against the idleness and corruption of the colonial administration, which led to his imprisonment and subsequent exile to Angola, where he died. Thus, civil servants, diplomats, and censors played their parts in this drama of colonization, which, after 1808, had no authority to answer to, whether it be the Spanish Crown or the Pombaline empire. Christopher Columbus, Hernán Cortés, Humboldt, and Bonpland versus Francisco de Miranda, Andrés Bello (1781–1865), Tomás de Gonzaga, Domingo F. Sarmiento (1811–1888): a play, indeed, of distorting mirrors insofar as these ideological conflicts signal as much the dramatization of national sovereignty as the manipulation of political principles. If Latin America was a jungle of signs, falsification and duplicity were strategies for making other voices heard and for making ethical discretion a complement of secrecy. The judge listened and spoke as a foreigner but was not perceived as such. The key to the secret lay in an extreme awareness of class difference, which defined the issues at stake: new subjectivities and practices that had as their aim the public administration of honor. Hence, the play of ethnic, religious, and gender differences became a means of domination.

The relation of censorship and disclosure to audience permits us to interpret the historical traces of ridicule and irony in an episode often quoted by critics because translation is presented in it as a contextualized experience. I am referring to the publication of *El lazarillo de ciegos caminantes* [1776; El Lazarillo: A Guide for Inexperienced Travelers between Buenos Aires and Lima] in Peru, a picaresque tale written in the form of a journal or guidebook for travelers, which was apparently signed by an indigenous writer, although it was actually written by Alonso Carrió de la Vandera (b. ca. 1706), a Spaniard who traveled through the Americas from Mexico to Peru, Buenos Aires, and Montevideo. He was the administrator in charge of sending the Jesuits to Spain after their expulsion; as a reward, he was appointed Inspector of the staging posts on the postal route between Lima and Buenos Aires. Emilio Carilla describes how Carrió de la Vandera, disillusioned by intrigue and the tense political situation, decided to publish his story, granting authorship to a real indigenous person, Don Calixto Bustamente Carlos Inca, who used the pseudonym of Concolorcorvo and assumed the role of his "companion and clerk" (Carilla in Carrió de la Vandera iii). He also falsified the date and place of publication: It appeared in Lima

between 1775 and 1776, but Carrió claimed it was published in Gijón in Spain in 1773. Even if it is not a picaresque novel *per se,* his "clerk" ironically discusses some of the classical conditions of the picaro's code of honor during the Spanish Golden Age or *Siglo de Oro* by contrasting the racially pure Indian with the Spaniards, blacks, and *mestizos* who had interbred with the indigenous peoples. This interbreeding reduces, as he says, "the number of pure Indians." And he adds:

> Yo soy indio neto, salvo las trampas de mi madre, de que no salgo por fiador. Dos primas mías coyas conservan la virginidad, a su pesar, en un convento del Cuzco en donde las mantiene el rey nuestro señor. Yo me hallo en ánimo de pretender la plaza de perrero de la catedral de Cuzco, para gozar inmunidad eclesiástica y para lo que me servirá de mucho mérito el haber escrito este itinerario, que, aunque en Dios y en conciencia lo formé con ayuda de vecinos, que a ratos ociosos me soplaban a la oreja, y cierto fraile de San Juan de Dios, que me encajó la introducción y los latines, tengo a lo menos mucha parte en haber perifraseado lo que indica el visitador en pocas palabras. Imitando el estilo de éste, mezclé algunas jocosidades para entretenimiento de los caminantes para quienes particularmente escribí.
> (Carrió de la Vandera 115–16)

> I am a pure Indian, save my mother's escapades, for which I cannot stand surety. Two noble cousins of mine kept their virginity, to their misfortune, in a convent in Cuzco where the good Lord looks after them. I am the dog warden of Cuzco cathedral so that I may enjoy ecclesiastical immunity and earn the credit due to me for having written this itinerary, in which, although by God and my conscience I gave it shape with the help of neighbors, who in idle moments whispered in my ear, and a certain friar of *San Juan de Dios* who lumbered me with an introduction and the Latinisms, I played a great part by paraphrasing in a few words what the visitor indicated. Imitating his style, I added a jocular touch for the entertainment of the travelers for whom I was particularly writing.

This jocular touch refers to the text's verbal misprisions and the way in which the different groups of Indians, *mestizos, criollos, gauderios,* and *gachupines* (Spaniards who had settled in the colonies) questioned these misprisions and responded to them. For this reason, the narrator, from the ethnically pure stance he has appropriated, can ridicule the history of displacement: Insults to nationality, race, and gender form a list of linguistic spells and superstitions, which he uses to justify his authority to express contempt in a literary mode. Nevertheless, this list also gives a profile of the reader he is apparently addressing:

> Así como los escritores graves, por ejemplo, el Plomo, y aún los más leves, v.g. el Corcho, dirigen sus dilatados prólogos a los hombres sabios, prudentes y piadosos, acaso por liberarse de sus críticas, yo dirijo el mío, porque soy peje entre dos aguas, esto es, ni tan pesado como los unos, ni tan liviano como los otros, a la gente que por vulgaridad llaman de la hampa o cáscara oscura, ya sean de espada, carabina y pistola, ya de bolas, guampar y lazo.
> (Carrió de la Vandera 116)

> Thus, just as such serious writers as the *Plomo* [Lead], or even the more light-hearted, such as the *Corcho* [Cork], address their expansive prologues to wise, prudent and pious men, perhaps to free themselves from the burden of their criticism, so I address my own, because I am an angler fish steering a middle course, that is, not so dense as some or so light-hearted as others, to people who are commonly known as criminals or blackguards, whether with a sword, carbine, or pistol or with bolas, horn, or lasso.

In her analysis of this text, Karen Stolley compares two episodes in which the relation between language and situation is not only humorous but also reveals the Indian's linguistic gift as he speaks Spanish and carefully weighs his astuteness in this Colonial confusion of tongues. In the *Informe oficial de viaje de Inspector de Postas* [Official Account of the Travels of the Inspector of Staging Posts], the Inca Concolorcorvo, who is probably a *mestizo* and is made a *lazarillo* or guide for parodic purposes, passes on tricks to the traveler in order to warn him about the wily ways of such manipulators as the corrupt priests, who, in the case of the Jesuits, praise the Indians for virtues they have never had in order to construct an empire of their own in the Americas. Immoderation and excess are associated with the wastefulness of the *gauderios* as opposed to the prodigality and innocence of the Spaniards, who, acting in good faith, are deceived. The invocation of moral principle is used to make his case against the Jesuits while disproving his connivance with his alleged community of readers when he gives advice on how to dominate the Indians and servants when on one's travels:

> El que quisiere caminar más haga lo que cierto pasajero ejecutó con un indio guía. En la primera cruz que encontró hizo su adoración y echó su traguito y dio otro al indio que iba arreándole una carguita, y le hizo doblar el paso. Llegó a otra cruz, que regularmente están éstas en los trivios o altos de las cuestas. Luego que divisó la segunda cruz y se acercó a ella, dijo al español: caimi, cruz, y detuvo un rato la mula de carga hasta que el español bebió y le dio el segundo trago; llegó, finalmente, a una pampa dilatada de casi cuatro leguas, y viéndose algo fatigado a la mitad de ella, dijo el indio: español, caimi cruz. Se quitó el sombrero para adorarla y dar un besito al porito, pero no vio semejante cruz, por lo que se vio precisado a preguntar al indio dónde estaba la cruz, que no la divisaba. El indio se limpió el sudor del rostro con su mano derecha, y con toda celeridad levantó los brazos en alto y dijo: caimi, señor. El español que era un buen hombre, celebró tanto las astucias del indio que le dobló la ración, y el indio quedó tan agradecido que luego que llegó al tambo, refirió a los otros mitayos la bondad del español, y al día siguiente disputaron todos sobre quién le había de acompañar. (Carrió de la Vandera 108–109)

He who would journey on should do what one traveler did with his Indian guide. Upon first seeing a cross, he blessed himself, had a drink, gave one to the Indian who was goading his mule, and then made him go twice as fast. He reached another cross; they are usually on the slopes or hilltops. When he had sighted this second cross and drawn near to it, he said to the Spaniard, *caimi*, cross, and hung around with his pack mule until the Spaniard took a draft and gave him one; finally, halfway across a long pampa of almost four leagues, the Indian, finding he was rather weary, said: Spaniard, *caimi*, cross. He took his hat off to bless himself and kiss the stake, but since there was no sign of a cross, he felt he had to ask the Indian where the cross was, that he could not see it. The Indian wiped the sweat off his face with his right hand and swiftly raised his arms and said: *caimi, señor.* The Spaniard, who was a good man, was so charmed by the Indian's astuteness that he doubled his rations, and the Indian was so grateful that when he arrived at the inn, he told the other Indian slaves of the Spaniard's kindness, and the following day there was a general dispute as to who should be his companion.

In this case, translation, as a carefully calculated physical act, dismantles, on the one hand, the false exchange of tongues for retribution and obedience. On the other, it shows the slipperiness of an ironic procedure: The cross episode camouflages the object and allows anything similar to suffice as resemblance (the arms raised in the form of a cross). However, the ironic distance created by translation changes color in the second episode examined by Stolley, which runs as follows:

> . . . pidiendo unos soldados de Cortés forraje para sus caballos, y viendo los indios que aquellos prodigiosos animales apetecían la yerba verde, recogieron la punta de algunas plantas que hoy llamamos maíz, . . . y al tiempo de entregar los hacecillos, dixeron: Mahi, señor, que significa "Toma, señor", de que infirieron los españoles que nombraban aquella planta y a su fruto maíz, y mientras no se hizo la cosecha, pedían siempre los soldados maíz para sus caballos, porque lo comían con gusto, . . . y en lo sucesivo continuaron los mismos indios llamando maíz al fruto, . . . por lo que les pareció que aquél era su verdadero nombre en castellano. (Carrió de la Vandera 327)

. . . when some of Cortés's soldiers asked for feed for their horses, the Indians, noting that those prodigious animals hungered for grass, picked the spikes off some of the plants we now call maize, . . . and as they gave them the bundles, they said: "*Mahi,* señor," which means "take, señor," from which the Spaniards inferred that they called that plant and its grain "maize." The soldiers always asked for "maize" for their horses, because the animals ate it with such gusto . . . and the Indians themselves began calling the grain "maize," . . . because they thought that that was its real name in Castilian.

The mistake in this translation exchange is not produced by reversibility but by the dominance of one language over another. The Quechua word not only names an object that does not exist in Spanish but is then also displaced by an accidentally invented Castilian name and is even adopted by the Indians themselves–a symbolic enactment of extermination and conversion in an exchange of unequals. Jean Franco has detected this articulation of figures of dominance in the controversial role played by La Malinche, Cortés's indigenous companion and translator, during the conquest of the Aztec Empire. Concolorcorvo, in his Inca guise, proposes the possibility of almost total assimilation, so long as his astute ridicule of translation practice ensures his survival.

The plural histories of these verbal acts of translation do not indicate mere proliferation or symbolic excess, however. At the heart lies the conflict of translation as a displacement of the distribution of names and places recorded in the debates about the granting of citizenship by means of patrial lineage (that is, defining the difference between homeland and nation). José Luis and Luis Alberto Romero have compiled, in *El pensamiento político de emancipación* [1977; Political Thinking of Independence], a corpus of texts dealing with this issue. In 1792, the Jesuit Juan Pablo Viscardo (1748–1798), a Peruvian by birth, wrote, while living in London under the protection of the British government, a *Carta a los Españoles Americanos* [Letter to American Spaniards] three hundred years after the discovery of America. One could argue that this letter took the opposite route from that of the Lazarillo's travel journal. It was first translated into French, and then the English version was published in Philadelphia in *The Edinburgh Gazette.* Only after the author's death was it sent to the Venezuelan Francisco de Miranda, who published it and circulated it throughout Latin America:

> El sacrificio hecho a la España de nuestros más preciosos intereses, ha sido mérito con que todos ellos pretenden honrarse para excusar las injusticias con que nos acaban. Pero la miseria en que la España misma ha caído, prueba que aquellos hombres no han conocido jamás los verdaderos intereses de la nación y que han procurado solamente cubrir con este pretexto sus procedimientos vergonzosos; y el suceso ha demostrado que nunca la injusticia produce frutos sólidos. A fin de que nada faltase a nuestra ruina y a nuestra ignominiosa servidumbre, la indigencia, la avaricia y la ambición han suministrado siempre a la España un enjambre de

aventureros, que pasan a la América resueltos a desquitarse allí con nuestra sustancia de lo que han pagado para obtener sus empleos. (Viscardo 53)

The religious sacrifice made to Spain of our most treasured traditions has been the claim all have made in order to excuse the injustice of our destruction. But the poverty with which Spain is afflicted proves that those men never reached an understanding of the real interests of the nation and merely used this pretext to hide their shameful procedures; and the outcome has demonstrated that injustice never yields a good harvest. To ensure that nothing be spared to impose our downfall and our ignominious servitude, destitution, avarice, and ambition have always supplied Spain with a swarm of adventurers who come to America determined to enrich themselves and take compensation for whatever they have paid to obtain their posts.

This letter not only forms part of a predictable series of claims on the part of the banished Jesuits but also highlights the possible insult of being dis(-)placed from the center of nomination. For this reason, the following reference to the connection between nation, nature, and conversion denounces the conquest as a deceptive operation that condemns the Spanish nation:

Renovando todos los días aquellas escenas de horrores que hicieron desaparecer pueblos enteros, cuyo único delito fue su flaqueza, convierten el resplandor de la más grande conquista en una mancha ignominiosa para el nombre español. Así es que, después de satisfacer el robo, paliado con el nombre de comercio, a las exacciones del gobierno en pago de sus insignes beneficios y a los ricos salarios de la multitud innumerable de extranjeros que, bajo diferente denominación en España y América se hartan fastuosamente de nuestros bienes, lo que nos queda es el objeto continuo de las asechanzas de tantos orgullosos tiranos, cuya rapacidad no conoce otro término que el que quieren imponerle su insolvencia y la certidumbre de la impunidad. Mientras que en la corte, en los ejércitos, en los tribunales de la monarquía se derraman las riquezas y los honores a extranjeros de todas las naciones, nosotros sólo somos declarados indignos de ellos e incapaces de ocupar aun en nuestra propia patria unos empleos que en rigor nos pertenecen exclusivamente. La gloria que costó tantas penas a nuestros padres, es para nosotros una herencia de ignominia y con nuestros tesoros inmensos no hemos comprado sino miseria y esclavitud. (Viscardo 54)

Reliving every day those scenes of horror when entire communities disappeared, whose only crime was their frailty, converted the splendor of the greatest conquest into an ignominious blemish on the Spanish nation. That is, after the satisfaction of theft, concealed under the name of trade, the demands of the government in payment for their illustrious benefits and the wealth of the highly paid stream of foreigners, who, under a different category in Spain and America, gorge themselves extravagantly on our riches, what remains is the continual object of the traps set by so many arrogant tyrants whose greed knows no other end than that which their insolvency and certainty of impunity impose on them. Whereas wealth and honors are lavished upon foreigners from all nations in the court, the army, and crown counsel, we are simply declared unworthy of such distinction and incapable of holding, even in our own homeland, certain posts that strictly speaking belong exclusively to us. From the glory for which our fathers paid such a price we have inherited dishonor, and all we have bought with our immense treasures is poverty and slavery.

Playing honor off against infamy, the Jesuit priest, a "pure Peruvian," challenges not only the power to humanize the indigenous peoples and convert them to Christianity, but also the authority to administer the riches of the continent, which he claims for Spanish America. The different language of the legal counsel, of planners and strategists, displaces religious discourse as a form of knowledge, and he is empowered by this displacement to make a subversive declaration to the authorities that banished him. This rhetoric constructs ethical disapproval, which, grounded on complaints and recriminations, articulates a social duty as a way to advocate sedition.

This is the rhetoric of numerous petitions and representations made to the European and colonial authorities. In these reports, the *criollos* not only claim posts as parliamentary deputies but also contest the status of local people in the governing bodies. These are the issues addressed by Camilo Torres (1766–1816), who wrote a *Representación a la Suprema Junta Central de España* [Report to the Supreme Central Council of Spain] in 1809 at the request of the Santa Fe de Bogotá Council. Even though the city council eventually decided not to submit this work but to file it away, the text, known and renamed as the *Memorial de Agravios* ("Petition of Grievance"), was widely circulated. This petition fuses memory and language for the purpose of condemning the distribution of power granted to *criollos* and Spaniards, and establishes a principle that recontextualizes the opposition between excess and lack, placing the affluence of the continent on the side of mercantile interests and its diversity on the side of proportional representation, in order to demonstrate the need for a change in the posts granted:

Las Américas, Señor, no están compuestas de extranjeros a la nación española. Somos hijos, somos descendientes de los que han derramado su sangre por adquirir estos nuevos dominios a la corona de España; de los que han extendido sus límites y le han dado en la balanza política de la Europa una representación que por sí sola no podía tener. Los naturales conquistados y sujetos hoy al dominio español son muy pocos o son nada en comparación de los hijos de europeos que hoy pueblan estas ricas posesiones. (Torres 29)

The Americas, my Lord, is not a continent of foreigners to the Spanish nation. We are the children, the descendants of those who shed their blood to acquire these new dominions for the Spanish Crown; of those who expanded their frontiers and gave Spain a representation in the political balance of Europe that she would not have obtained otherwise. The conquered indigenous peoples subjected today to Spanish rule are few in number or a mere nothing in comparison with the children of Europeans who now inhabit these rich possessions.

The petition denounces exploitation and domination by bureaucrats and speculators:

Es preciso tener presente que cada Virreinato de América se compone de muchas provincias que algunas de ellas valen más por sí solas que los reinos de España. En cuanto a la ilustración, la América no tiene la vanidad de creerse superior ni aun igual a las provincias de España. Gracias a un gobierno despótico, enemigo de las luces, ella no podía esperar hacer rápidos progresos en los conocimientos humanos. . . . La imprenta, el vehículo de las luces y el conductor más seguro que las puede difundir, ha estado más severamente prohibido en América. . . . En vano se diría que las noticias adquiridas por el gobierno podrían suplir este defecto: ellas serán siempre vagas e inexactas, cuando no sean inciertas y falsas. . . . Los gobernantes de América, principalmente los que ocupan sus altos puestos han venido todos, o los más, de la metrópolis: pero con ideas de volverse a ella a establecer su fortuna . . . El no sufre las trabas del comercio que le imposibiliten hacer su fortuna. El no ve criar a sus hijos sin educación y sin letras. Su mesa se cubre con los manjares que brinda el suelo pero no sabe de las extorsiones que sufre el indio condenado a una eterna esclavitud y a un ignominioso tributo que le impuso la injusticia y la sinrazón. El, en fin ignora los bienes y los males del pueblo que rige en donde sólo se apresura a atesorar riquezas para trasplantarlas al suelo que le vio nacer. Doce millones de hombres con distintas necesidades en distintas circunstancias, en tan distintos climas y con diversos intereses necesitan de distintas leyes. Vosotros no las podéis hacer, nosotros nos las tenemos que dar. (Torres 38)

It is worth bearing in mind that each American Viceroyalty is made up of many provinces and that some of them are worth more in their own right than the Spanish domains. In relation to the Enlightenment, the Americas would never be so vain as to believe themselves superior or even equal to the Spanish provinces. Thanks to a despotic government, an enemy of enlightenment, she cannot hope to make rapid progress in human knowledge. . . . The press, the transmitter of enlightenment and the surest means by which it may be circulated, has been severely censored in America. . . . In vain they say that the news the government offers can make up for this shortcoming: it is always vague and inexact, if not dubious and incorrect. . . . The American governors, principally those who have held the highest posts, all, or nearly all, come from the metropolis and entertain the idea of returning to settle down with their fortune. . . . He [a governor] is not afflicted by the misfortunes of commerce which would deny him the possibility of making his fortune. He does not have to see his children brought up without education and letters. His table is spread with the delicacies of our land but he has no knowledge of the extortions which are the affliction of the Indians condemned to eternal slavery and to the ignominious tribute that imposed unwarranted injustice upon them. In the end, he ignores the wrongs and the rights of the country he governs, in which he merely hastens to amass riches so that he can take them back to the land of his birth. Twelve million men who have different needs and a diversity of interests in different circumstances and such different climates obviously need different laws. You cannot make these, we have to provide them.

The salient characteristics of this public writing aroused individual passions about collective interests and established a moral and esthetic hierarchy in an attempt to redress humiliation. In 1811, Camilo Henríquez (1769–1825), a Chilean friar renowned for his sermons, wrote a Proclamation (under the anagrammatic pseudonym of Quirino Lemachez) about the inevitability of emancipation, foregrounding philosophical knowledge rather than the covetousness and foolishness of the viceregal bureaucrats:

A la participación de esta suerte os llama ¡Oh, Pueblo de Chile! el inevitable curso de los sucesos. El antiguo régimen se precipitó en la nada de que había salido por los crímenes y los infortunios. Una superioridad de las armas del dañar y los atentados impusieron el yugo a estas provincias; y una superioridad de fuerzas y luces las ha librado de la opresión. . . . Las reliquias miserables de un pueblo vasallo y esclavo como nosotros quienes o su situación local o política del vencedor no ha envuelto todavía en el trastorno universal; este resto débil situado a más de tres mil leguas de nuestro suelo ha mostrado el audaz e importante deseo de ser nuestro monarca. . . . Entonces las provincias chilenas, animadas del vigor y magnanimidad que inspira la libertad y la sabiduría de las leyes, gozando ya de una gran población de hombres robustos, opusiera de un modo terrible el número y aliento de sus naturales, de sus caballos y el cobre de sus minas. . . . A la ilustración del entendimiento deben unirse las virtudes patrióticas, adorno magnífico del corazón humano: el deseo acreditado de la libertad, la disposición generosa de sacrificar su interés personal al interés universal del pueblo; en el momento en que se constituye un hombre legislador por el voto y la confianza de sus conciudadanos, deja de existir para sí mismo y no tiene más familia que la gran asociación del estado. (Henríquez 220)

Oh, Chile! I summon you to take part in this destiny, this inevitable course of events. The old regime plummeted to nothingness from which it had risen through crime and misfortune. Superior weapons to wound and attack these provinces imposed the yoke upon them; and superior strength and learning has liberated them from oppression. . . . The miserable remains of a country of enslaved vassals like ourselves which, whether because of the local conditions or the victor's political circumstance, have not yet become embroiled in universal upheaval; this enfeebled remnant situated more than three thousand leagues from our land has demonstrated a brazen and importunate desire to be our monarch. . . . But the Chilean provinces offered mighty opposition, roused by the fervor and magnanimity which liberty and knowledge of law inspire, its great number of robust men, the sheer strength and spirit of its people, horses, and the copper of its mines. Enlightenment and understanding should become one with patriotic virtues, with that magnificent accessory of the human heart: the justified desire for liberty, the generous disposition to sacrifice one's personal interests for the universal interests of the country; when a person becomes a statesman because he has the vote of confidence of his fellow countrymen, he will cease to exist as an individual and will have no other family than the great alliance of the state.

The use of imprecation as a verbal act gives us the chance to analyze episodes that politically sanction different acts of verbal violence. *Libertad o Muerte* [Liberty or Death] in what Jean Jacques Dessalines had written as a heading in the *Proclama de Haití* [Proclamation of Haiti] of 1804 that was subsequently incorporated into the flag of the new nation. This proclamation began with the summons:

Ejército Indígena: Ciudadanos indígenas, hombres, mujeres, niños, pasead la mirada sobre todas las partes de esta isla; buscad en ella vosotras a vuestros maridos, vosotras a vuestros hermanos, vosotros a vuestras hermanas. . . . Marchemos sobre otras huellas; imitemos a los pueblos que llevando su celo hasta el porvenir y temiendo dejar a la posteridad un ejemplo de bajeza, han preferido ser exterminados antes que borrados del concierto de las naciones libres. Combatid hasta el último suspiro por la independencia de nuestro país. (Dessalines 85)

Indigenous army, indigenous citizens, men, women, children, cast your eye over every part of this island; seek in it yourselves and your spouses, yourselves and your brothers, yourselves and your sisters. Let us advance along others' tracks; let us follow those peoples who, bearing their zeal to the future and fearing leaving to posterity a lesson of vileness, would rather be exterminated than be eliminated from the community of free nations. Fight to the death for the independence of our country.

The call for independence turned sedition into a pact for patriotic commitment and appealed to indigenousness as an essential natural trait of the nation. In 1808, Fray Melchor de Talamates (1765–1808) published (under a pseudonym) his *Representación Nacional de las Colonias* [National Representation of the Colonies], dedicated to the Mexican *ayuntamiento* [city council]. Under the subtitle of *Discurso filosófico* [Philosophical Discourse], this representation produced the double move from insult to summons and, again, to imprecation:

Si por razones de una fina y consumada prudencia no tomásemos la resolución de declararnos independientes, debemos al menos manejarnos desde ahora de manera que la Europa toda tema nuestra resolución. Tiemble ese continente, abrigo de los errores, perfidias y calamidades de esos monstruos sanguinarios, devastadores del género humano, al saber que se le va a obstruir el canal por donde se le comunican abundantemente nuestra riqueza. Sepa también el pérfido y vil usurpador, que ha querido subyugar a la noble y generosa España, que las Américas, felices por sí mismas, con sus inagotables riquezas de todo género y teniendo por muros las aguas inmensas del océano, no podrán ser sorprendidas de sus falsos halagos, mentirosas promesas y ofertas impotentes, no serán intimidades de su feroz arrogancia, ni darán jamás el imprudente paso de quedar expuestas, por reconocer precipitadamente otra autoridad al ignominioso abatimiento de postrarse a sus despreciables plantas. (Talamates 99)

If for reasons of acute and consummate prudence we resolve not to declare our independence, we should at least handle ourselves in such a way from now on that the whole of Europe will fear our resolve. That continent, that haven of the mistakes, treachery, and calamities caused by those bloodthirsty monsters, destroyers of the human race, trembles in the knowledge that the channel through which our riches are so copiously conveyed to it is going to be blocked. The treacherous and vile usurper [Napoleon], who has wanted to subjugate noble and generous Spain, well knows that the Americas, happily self-reliant with inexhaustible riches of every kind and bulwarked by immense oceanic waters, cannot be surprised by false flattery, dishonest promises and ineffective offers, will not be intimidated by ferocious arrogance, will never take the imprudent step of remaining exposed, by rushing headlong into recognizing another authority to the ignominious abasement of bowing before any despicable design.

These texts show that the Napoleonic invasion of Spain in 1808 engendered a conflict not only of power, but, above all, of sovereignty; religious discourse was put in the position of promoting a move toward the new doctrine of the sovereign country. Thus, when insult is a sign of connivance, it can be used to explore the different aspects of the interrelations between personal experience and society, as well as the principles that produce the symbolic modes of delimitation and interpellation.

This is the case of José Joaquín Fernández de Lizardi (1776–1827) who, precariously balancing exposition and secrecy, published *El Pensador Mexicano* [The Mexican Thinker] between 1813 and 1816, taking the name from a Spanish newspaper (*El Pensador Madrilense*) of the end of the eighteenth century that had translated part of the French Encyclopedia. In order to evade the control of the Imprimatur, he wrote the *costumbrista* story of a young follower of his master under the title of *El periquillo sarnieto* (1815) or *The Itching Parrot*, which is generally considered the first Latin American novel. Lizardi used the occasion of the Viceroy's birthday to ask for the repeal of the edict that permitted military commanders to interfere in the trial of the revolutionary clergy. As a result, freedom of the press was suspended and Lizardi was imprisoned on 7 December 1813. From then on he wrote under the pseudonym of the *pensador mexicano* and branched out to contribute to another periodical, *Alacena de Frioleras*, in which he sustained his tone of ridicule and continued to exchange insults with other writers, but abstained from challenging religion by focusing instead on a criticism of manners in articles on behavior in *tertulias* and theaters, on the cleanliness of streets and the changes in fashions imported from overseas. In issues 13 and 14 of *El Pensador Mexicano* of 1814, he attempted to gain a pardon by grounding an argument on the premise that there was a difference between patriotic priests and traitors. He tried to convince the ecclesiastical tribunal that the true heretics were "under disguise" within the Church. Instead of turning away from religion, they aspired to reform it, which revealed their "sacrilegious, impious, and openly heretical tone." On the contrary, the errors of the poor, the Mexican thinker argued, cannot be considered heresy, but blind faith and humble piety:

¿Dejará esta misma iglesia de incomodarse con la multitud de espantos, revelaciones y milagros que se esparcen en el pueblo cada día por la ignorancia de algunos fieles sencillos? ¿Ignorará esta sapientísima Asamblea presidida siempre por el espíritu de la verdad infalible, los requisitos necesarios que debe tener todo suceso para clasificarse de milagroso? . . . De que el pueblo vulgar amontone prodigios y milagros apócrifos creyendo que son verdaderos, no se sigue otra cosa que un exceso de piedad y devoción o, cuando más, unas mentiras oficiosas que no pueden pasar de unos pecados veniales indeliberados; pero si se le prohíbe poner sus figuritas de plata y cera en los nichos de los santos, . . . este mismo vulgo declinará al otro extremo, esto es, en exceso de impiedad; y persuadido de que todo milagro es falso o imposible, se negará a la creencia de los más autorizados, entrando en este número los que hizo el mismo Jesucristo. (Fernández de Lizardi 239)

Would this same Church stop feeling uneasy about the many rumors of fears, revelations, and miracles spread day by day throughout the country by the ignorance of simple believers? Would this verily wise Assembly presided over by the spirit of infallible truth cast to one side the essential ingredients that each event classified as a miracle ought to have? . . . That the common people amass what they believe are true apocryphal prodigies and miracles can only be a sign of extreme piety and devotion, or, at least, officious lies that cannot be other than unintentional venial sins; but if they are forbidden to put their silver and wax figures in the saints' niches, . . . they will tend to the other extreme, that is, to irreverent impiety; and persuaded that no miracle can be true or possible, they will refuse to believe in those that are sanctioned, including among these those of Jesus Christ.

Cabildos, Tertulias, and Periodicals

The periodical at this time strove to differentiate truth from deceit and burlesque imitation from ennobling mimesis. *Conversaciones entre un Payo y un Sacristán* [Conversations between a Peasant and a Sacristan], published by Lizardi from 1824 to 1825, analyzes the relation between language and rhetoric concerning the political ethics of the distribution of social roles. In this final act of reconciliation between the peasant and the religious man (both probably alter egos of Lizardi himself), the conversation proposes a project for the Constitution. The peasant says to the sacristan: "no somos literatos, que usted no pasa de un sacristán ni yo de un ranchero" (300) ("we are not learned men, you are no more than a sacristan and I a farmer"). And the sacristan replies: "eso no me espanta: rancheros he visto yo que parecen literatos y literatos que parecen rancheros; con que zas, manos a la obra y vamos a organizar la república a nuestro modo. Usted se llama cámara de senadores y yo cámara de diputados: entre los dos discutimos nuestras proposiciones y luego que estemos acordes fijamos los artículos respectivos" (300) ("That does not scare me: I have seen farmers who are like learned men and learned men who are like farmers; with that spirit, hands on the job, we are going to organize the republic in our way. You are the Senate and I am the Chamber of Representatives: between these two we can discuss our proposals and once we have agreed we can set down the respective articles"). Later, when they attempt to identify the various figures who would sustain the constitution, the sacristan settles the argument by outlining the most united community possible: "Por qué no han de ser ciudadanos todos los extranjeros? Son ciudadanos todos los hombres que sean útiles de cualquier modo a la república sean de la nación que fuesen" (Fernández de Lizardi 300) ("Why should the foreigners not be citizens? All men who serve the republic in any way are citizens, wherever they come from").

This conversation highlights a common critical assumption that in the emancipatory projects, roles in the public sphere were viewed according to two conflicting models: whereas the conservative *criollos* attributed the welfare of the nation to Church, land, and tradition, the so-called liberals regarded modernity as the true writer of interests. Both views were legitimized by the Wars of Independence as means of achieving a higher state of civilization. The early patterns of this historical process indicated, nevertheless, that in Latin America the equating of cultural canons with nation was complicated by the intrinsic relation between conquest and an imposed tongue. The colonists were more interested in centralizing political power than in defining national boundaries. In turn, the emancipatory movements revealed different experiences of what was intended to be organized dispersion, and which gave rise to other methods of defining social integration. Once again, a new displacement occurs: on the one hand, certain aspects of the discourse constructed an audience or general public of new citizens and, on the other, a debate invoking both ridicule and praise provided a space for discussing the sectorial interests that specified the requirements for order and general welfare.

Josefina Ludmer has argued that a particular treatment of universal concepts of community is a salient characteristic of the gaucho literature of the Río de la Plata region and especially of the way in which literature and the state are interrelated. A gaucho's rendering of such universals as fatherland, liberty, and equality presupposes that (1) the subject is both singer and patriot and (2) his voice and register appear in the text and comply with a series of metrical and rhythmical conventions. This implies that translation is a history not merely of the traits of popular culture but of the institutional exploitation of the gaucho's voice in cultivated verse. It is further assumed that (3) this passage through the conventions of written poetry is analogous to the gaucho's rites of passage through the army, concerning, first, his voice and, second, the legality of Wars of Independence and the gaucho's integration into the civilizing process of the liberal state.

Both official and partisan journalism offered a privileged space for foregrounding these debates. Here are visible the traces of the configurations of public opinion that made it possible for the liberals and the conservatives to legitimize constitutional projects, alliances between provinces, federal agreements, and so forth. The discussions on authority focused on the modes of integration and necessitated a concept of the nation that was closely related to the models of federalism or confederation. The satiric nature of the partisan press gave rise to new semantic fields that produced signs both of recognition and of the construction of identities that we might provisionally call "local" in that they referred to provinces, towns, and cities. The lyrics, ballads, and satiric *décimas* can be read as serving the function of giving prominence to the pacts that pronounced that all the land belonged to all the people, which the constituent assemblies and congresses had debated on Independence. In these periodicals ridicule generally created a tension (whether in their regular pages or in their highbrow supplement) between didactic and humorous essays, which highlighted the artifice of the notion of the political adversary, if not of the periodicals themselves. The voices of the patriot and the people were seen as a sign of resistance on the part of a certain group that defined itself as representing the public good. As one periodical of a literary society, translating Benjamin Constant, stated: "Entre nosotros se ha celebrado un tratado entre la autoridad y la razón... en el cual los hombres ilustrados dicen a los depositarios del poder legítimo... vosotros nos sostendréis con toda la protección de la ley y nosotros circundaremos vuestras instituciones con la fuerza de la opinión" (Constant qtd. in *La abeja argentina* 33) ("We have celebrated an agreement of authority and reason... in which enlightened men say to those in legitimate power: ... you will defend us under the protection of the law and we shall uphold your institutions with the force of public opinion"). The problem grew more serious, however, in those genres in which the balance between need for evidence and requirement of decorum was achieved only at a certain cost. Whereas hymns and praise songs held the highest place in the hierarchy, fables and illustrated satires were more threatening because they ridiculed private traits in order to exalt the general law. In this sense, the censorship hearings revealed that ridicule acted as a sign of the dynamism of public opinion. For this reason, titles such as *El Patriota* [The Patriot], *El Amigo del país* [The Friend of the Nation], *El Correo mercantil, económico y político* [The Mercantile, Economic, and Political Mail], and *La Gaceta* [The Gazette] point to a struggle against the authority of the proclamations, edicts, religion, and censorship. The function of a form of translation as simultaneous displacement can be observed, as we have seen, in the writers' use of strategies such as pseudonymity and anonymity to combat censorship.

Within this struggle between different discursive practices, the re-vision of these strategies and of the ways in which they function in specific contexts also presupposes the reconstruction of the disputes about the configuration of a shared language that would define the degree of ridicule. Whenever a particular version of the common good is offered, laughter acts as a mechanism for rationalizing it, while also indicating the limits of possible dissent. One needs to create the appropriate atmosphere and language so that concepts can be transformed into a pact of coexistence. In this respect, the interrelation of ridicule and praise helps one to examine how humor regulates and re-accommodates probability and contingency in the act of deciding among the multiple versions of the common good. Once one has recognized the many different conceptions of the common good, one can argue that laughter demonstrates the supremacy of an order that includes the rest, giving to each a certain position–the participants who discern the ridicule are empowered. This test becomes a criterion that legitimates and confirms the existing norms of the community, while attempting to extend it on the basis of the friendly agreement implied by shared laughter.

In 1822, a story published anonymously in the periodical *El Centinela* of the Río de la Plata region represented an unusual dialogue between a lawyer and an Augustinian priest on the subject of specters and phantoms. The skeptical lawyer would like the priest to recognize the impossibility of the existence of what cannot be appreciated by the senses. Enthusiastically, the priest insists: "¿Cómo no he de creer? ¡La otra noche yo mismo he visto un espectro! ¡Tan claro como os veo a vos mismo!" ("Why shouldn't I believe it? I saw a ghost the other evening. As clearly as I see you!"). When asked what the ghost looked like, the priest replies: "¿Qué se yo? Parecía medio cerdo... medio zorra..." ("How would I know? It looked a bit like a pig... a bit like a fox...."). The mention of this similarity ends the discussion when the lawyer replies triumphantly: "¡Quite usted padre; se habrá asustado usted de su propia sombra!" ("Stop it, father. It is your own shadow that is frightening you!" (qtd. in *El Centinela* 1822b, 33).

It is precisely this kind of mockery used for the purposes of reasserting a necessary agreement that lies behind the defense of Juan Cruz Varela (1794–1839), an official journalist of the liberal government of Rivadavia in the Río de la Plata region and a ghost writer for newspapers closed for their satirical excesses. A dispute about the permissible degree of ridicule in the national language dominated the struggle between different literary practices. The fear of the masses produced a shift by means of which offensive behavior and language were transformed into civilizing traits and, thus, esthetic objects.

It thus appears that ridicule acts as a means of regulating and re-accommodating inequalities in the institutionalization of discourse. It is a question of redefining obedience as a reciprocal pact of understanding. Humor as a characteristic of a particular sensibility points to a change of position in language. Laughter is used in this move to collectivity as both an esthetic convention and a strategy of political prudence. If this act of consensus making is to have the necessary effect, however, it has to be continually updated. Those who feel that they have to participate in the cross fire of insult and diatribe should not only demonstrate the unrecognized virtues of their discredited arguments but also their ability to handle language. Perhaps the strength of diatribe lies precisely in this play of precariousness and shrewdness and in the futility of it all. One can detect this characteristic in the tone of those periodicals, which, obsessed by politics, opened spaces for debate around the censorship hearings.

The history of journalism in Latin America records an episode indicative of this trend. It tells of the banning of *Antón Peluca, Padre de la Señora doña María Retazos, ausente en Santa Fe* [Antón Peluca, Father of Doña María Retazos, Absent in Santa Fe], written by Juan Cruz Varela, which appeared as a single issue on 27 January 1824 and was seized because of the seriousness of the offenses. Instead of appearing in court himself, Varela sent in his place a very well-dressed person who proceeded to make the public laugh. The alleged writer confirmed his authorship. When the panel of judges contested his statement, because it was well-known that he was illiterate, he replied that he could not deny this, and for this reason he had not written the periodical but dictated it. After the laughter from the public gallery had subsided, the strawman was sentenced to spend a period of two months twenty leagues from the city, while the Varela brothers continued to divide their time between writing official journalism in *La Gaceta de Buenos Aires* and composing highly imaginative satires. This is one example of the way in which the censors' hearings revealed the notion of ridicule as a sign of the dynamism of public opinion. The same can be seen in *El Granizo*, the burlesque supplement of *El Porteño*, a critical newspaper in which articles written by the delegates of the Constituent Assembly of 1826 were published:

En materia de desprecio, como en materia de infamia, no hay más tribunal que la Opinión. . . . La picota es en Inglaterra una pena infamante y, sin embargo, todos saben que el autor de un libelo condenado a ella, hace pocos años, pasó la hora de su condena recibiendo parabienes de todo el pueblo de Londres. . . . Los que cuenten con la opinión, no teman al ridículo.
(qtd. in *El Centinela* 1822a, 116)

On the subject of derision, as on the subject of infamy, there is no other tribunal than Opinion. . . . In England the pillory is an infamous penalty, but everyone knows that a lampoonist condemned to it, only a few years ago, spent the hour of his punishment being congratulated by all and sundry in London . . . . Those who have opinion on their side do not fear ridicule.

Nationalism as a World Participation

Sometimes an emblem is used to articulate the meaning of political differences. Consensus and harmony may attempt in this way to make sense of the void created by insult. The Argentine Juan Bautista Alberdi (1810–1884) wrote in the periodical *La Moda*: "cuando una idea política adopta un color por emblema y esta idea se levante sobre todas, el color que la simboliza en manos del espíritu público no tarda en volverse moda" (Alberdi 154) ("when a political idea adopts a color as its emblem and this idea is elevated above all others, the color symbolizing it will soon become fashionable among the public-spirited"). By appealing to both the private and the public sphere, the accessory trait unites them, thereby becoming itself part of a code for interpreting meaning; that is, the emblem is legitimized by a new subjectivity, the masses that so concerned Juan Cruz Varela: "Tal es entre nosotros el color punzó, emblema de la idea federativa, es a la vez un color político y un color a la moda; lo lleva el pueblo en sus vestidos, los lleva el poder en sus banderas, contando así con una doble autoridad de la que sería ridículo pretender sustraerse" (Alberdi 154) ("Bright red is such an important color for us; it is an emblem of the federation, a political color and a fashionable color; people use it in their dress, power uses it on its flags, thus revealing the dual authority it would be ridiculous to negate").

In a similar way, translation operates as a symbolic act of displacement and as a cultural object. In 1839, Mariquita Sanchez de Mendeville refused to let Juan Manuel de Rosas's secret police raid her home, stating that her husband was a French diplomat *and* that she "was the most patriotic of us all, that she had helped build the country and its liberty," according to the soldier's story. Rosas made his apologies for this frustrated attack, but not before sardonically complaining that it would have helped if the lady in question had decided upon her nationality. She was *criolla* by birth, English by her first marriage, and, finally, French, as she had claimed: "Conocí antes una María Sanchez buena y virtuosa federal. La desconozco ahora en el billete con tu firma que he recibido de una francesita parlanchina y coqueta" (qtd. in Zavalía Lagos 168) ("María Sanchez, as I knew her, was a good and virtuous federalist. I can no longer recognize her in this description that I have received from this indiscreet and flirtatious little French woman"). José Mármol (1817–1871) used a similar tact in his *Semblanza de Manuela Rosas* [1851; Semblance of Manuela Rosas], when he cautioned his readers that this was his "Primer ensayo sobre esta vida, tan famosa sin desearlo tan singular sin merecerlo" (Mármol 8) ("first essay on Manuela Rosas, so unwittingly famous, and so undeservedly unique"). In his character sketch, Mármol endeavored to separate the person from the public image and infamous name. Adriana Rodríguez Pérsico (1992) argues that Sarmiento too grounds the relationship between fiction and politics in his work on the construction of what she calls "biographies of barbarity" in order to describe the connections between institutions, subjects, and social control.

In constructing the uniqueness of Latin American culture, artists record and celebrate its ethnic and geographic peculiarities in order to propose its so-called natural uniqueness. This aesthetic perception of emptiness and excess articulates distinguishing features which are at once abstract and atemporal, and thus universally significant. The Romantic critical tendency to abstract the general from the particular is yet another means of marrying the personal or private sphere to public interests. One offspring of this union is precisely the social category of the masses. As an excess beyond the control of the ethics of the Independence movements, this links ideals with individual passions through the archetypal figure of "the people." Because liberty is the political principle ruling customs and social conventions, it becomes the ideal of democracy in that the fatherland, together with the people, is the highest form of belief, establishing, as noted at the beginning, a "citizen's religion."

Laymen and the Clergy: A Conflict of Shared Authority

At the time of modernization during the upheaval at the end of the nineteenth century, the impulse to secularization was the dominant state model promoted in the press, on the rostrum, and in clubs; this involved liberalism, conservatism, and the relations between the two in a project that required free will and authority. Instead of reproducing the fin-de-siècle dispute between believers and atheists, between *modernistas* and positivists, it would be more interesting to see this as a change in the rhetorical emphasis on persuasion and consensus making. The discourses of the period were not concerned with antithesis and contradiction so much as with the variable and dynamic figure of a correlation between equality and shared sovereignty. During the period of emigration, whether from Europe to the Americas or within the continent, new challenges to and tensions in the relative status of religion, knowledge, and administration appeared. As I have suggested, the rhetoric of citizenship had articulated and, to a certain degree, absorbed different struggles against different authorities. The dispute between laicism and the Church predictably focused on two main issues: state control of worship as a private observance, and the authorities' exploitation of religion in their attempt to centralize, through immigration laws, the newcomers' means of participation. Anticlerical discourse demonstrated this tension: the figure of the priest as an intruder, conspirator, or renegade gave rise to this variety of terms of condemnation, which served as signs of sedition. However, secularization tended to limit this violence to a conflict of means of persuasion. For this reason, seeming insult may blind us to the elusive practices of the redistribution of authority. The violence of ridicule among equals here displaced the conflict of linguistic and racial diversity by establishing both a hierarchical order for the different genres in culture and an intelligibility that depended on the actors and the stage. A dual idea of morality emerged: on the one hand, citizenship as a civil status, which should be regulated and administered by the state, and, on the other, religious worship as private ethics.

The model of centralizing and controlling public life implied a definition not only of the subject but also of his or her rights to intervene in political matters. Restrictions on ecclesiastical power did not, under this model, so much circumscribe its control as create a new configuration of private life. We are well aware that the state seized control of the public life of citizens by means of those instruments that weighed and calculated social changes: the Church lost control of such matters as statistics, fiscal processes, judicial procedures, education, calendars, births, marriages, and deaths. To it was left the control of spiritual life. One consequence was a change in the spaces available for the discussion of issues, which became at once more open to the world and more private; another concerned the constitution of a domain of public life that separated itself from the state in order to guarantee the basic principles of liberalism: freedom of thought and of association in commerce, and the right to private property. In the public sphere, the political press became a private, and even family, business. Ridicule was transformed into a ritual, a form of discussion among like-minded persons.

From the second half of the nineteenth century, the effect of this shift in the national language caused public debate in *tertulias* or social gatherings, cultural circles, and periodicals, that national language was seen as the place where meanings derived from collective experiences crystallized. Consensual pressures demanded not only a realignment of genres and cultural practices, but also their conversion. The aim was to formulate a rhetoric that would articulate both expectation and disillusionment. At the turn of the century, this rhetoric was clearly represented in the cultural canons forming the cornerstone of national tradition. In 1882 the Andean surveyor Joaquín Víctor González (1863–1923), who was a specialist in border litigation, wrote *La Tradición Nacional* [The National Tradition], arguing that under its civilizing impetus, culture could sustain and consolidate religions, popular beliefs, forms of organization, and government. The author proposed displacing the status of religious discourse in relation to that of knowledge and of politics, which was constructed on the basis not of an antinomy but of a union of belief and action in light of the national state of affairs. Instead of linking culture with modernity, *La Tradición Nacional* aimed to recuperate the essential national traits in language, history, and art that incite the spirit. The consolidation of nationality could, moreover, be analyzed according to the structuring principles of this evolving national spirit. Tradition thus recuperated feelings and even superstitions, which it elevated to a category of exemplary testimony. The national writing spirit reached from the pre-Hispanic peoples to the theater of future redemption, thereby differentiating but also linking one culture that emerged from brute nature's, pure beauty, and another lyrical culture that represented civilized nature.

Fabricio Forastelli has studied this same conflict in the historical construction of the nation in the correspondence of the historian Vicente Fidel López (1815–1903) (*La Gran Semana de Mayo* [The Great Week of May]):

Publicamos con este título un legajo viejo de cartas que encontramos en el baúl de la parda Marcelina Horma. Las cartas no son evidentemente originales, sino copias de una misma letra, firmadas con simples iniciales, que llevan las fechas del 20 al 31 de mayo de 1810. Carecen, por consiguiente de autenticidad, pero presentan un grande interés no sólo porque se puede conjeturar por sus iniciales, que están escritas o atribuidas a personas muy conocidas en aquel tiempo (Fidel López 15)

We publish under this title an old legacy of letters that we found in the trunk of the half-breed Marcelina Horma. Clearly, the letters are not original, but are copies, all in the same hand, merely signed with initials, and bear the dates of 20 May to 31 May 1810. Consequently, they lack authenticity but are most interesting because one can speculate about the initials, which were attributed to very well-known people of the time.

Rather than arguing legitimacy setting up an antagonism between autochthonous Americans and *criollos*, the historian focuses on the issues of unreliable authorship and lack of authenticity. In Forastelli's opinion, this offers the possibility that, on the one hand, the elderly woman in whose trunk the letters were found might be elevated to the status of a founder of the fatherland (like Mariquita Sánchez, who does indeed embody the patrician lady). On the other hand, these issues shed light on the anxiety caused when historians attempt to reconstruct documents from the past. Sylvia Molloy and Francine Masiello have studied this link between autobiography and figurations of authority from the perspective of gender difference as part of the discourses of hygiene, police identification, and criminology. Skits, serials, and *costumbrista* stories also highlighted the triviality of politics in light of the conflict between nationality and money, but did succeed in creating a rhetoric that outlined a path to national recovery, which controlled thwarted expectations and any recourse to authoritarianism. Problems of race, gender, religion, and nationality in sentimental novels, skits, and serials were weighed against the path to perfection usually demanding the death of any tainted object. Carlos Monsiváis has argued the relationship between comic farce and nationalism is not one of disenchantment but rather the rearticulation of discontent through ridicule and humor.

As stated earlier, a type of burlesque reflection on the endeavors to concentrate the economy, order, and stability led to a decentering in which diversity would challenge the prescriptiveness of mainstream writing with a new strangeness of language and image. In 1881, the Cuban poet José Martí (1853–1895) wrote in *La Revista Ilustrada,* published in New York:

> El aldeano engreído cree que el mundo entero consiste en su aldea. Siempre que él pueda ser alcalde, humillar el rival que le roba la novia o agregar ahorros en su caja fuerte, considera que el orden universal es correcto, inconsciente de los gigantes de botas de siete leguas que pueden aplastarlo.... Este hombre presuntuoso siente que la tierra fue hecha para servirle de pedestal ... y acusa a su tierra nativa si sus junglas vírgenes no ofrecen constantes medios para viajar alrededor del mundo. (Martí 55)

> The arrogant villager believes that the entire world consists of his village. So long as he can be chairman of the parish council, humiliate his rival who stole his girlfriend, and put savings in his strongbox, he considers universal order quite correct, unaware as he is of the giants wearing seven-league boots who can crush him.... This pretentious man feels that the earth was made to serve him as a pedestal ... and he condemns his homeland if its virgin jungles do not constantly provide him with the means for traveling around the world.

The impassioned and ironic articles that Martí published in newspapers in Venezuela, Cuba, Argentina, and New York conversed with such vanguard literary movements as modernism, creationism, and ultraism. They proposed a common "continental citizenship" and articulated a critical distance between tradition and the avant-garde. The fin-de-siècle decadentism of ultraism and *modernismo* displaced the religious vision in the sublimated conflict of aesthetics. One only has to recall the famous "Palabras preliminares" [Preliminary Words] that the Nicaraguan writer Rubén Darío (1867–1916) wrote as a dedication in his *Prosas profanas* [*Lay Hymns*] of 1896:

> ¿Hay en mi sangre alguna gota de sangre de Africa, o de indio chorotega o nagrandano? Pudiera ser a despecho de mis manos de marqués, más he aquí que veréis en mis versos princesas,

reyes, cosas imperiales, visiones de países lejanos e imposibles; ¿qué queréis? Yo detesto la vida y el tiempo en que me tocó nacer.... Si hay poesía en nuestra América, ella está en las cosas viejas: en Palenke y Utlatán, en el indio legendario y en el inca sensual y fino, y en el Gran Moctezuma de la silla de oro. Lo demás es tuyo, demócrata Walt Whitman. Buenos Aires, Cosmópolis. (Darío 8)

> Is there in my veins a drop of African blood, or of Chorotega or Nagrandano blood? It might be that, in spite of my fine aristocratic hands, there is more in my poems than meets the eye, princesses, kings, imperial things, visions of far-off and unattainable lands. What would you like? I hate the life and times I was born to.... If there is poetry in our America, it is in the old things: in Palenke and Utlatán, in the legendary Indian and the fine and sensual Inca, and in the Great Motecuhzoma of the golden chair. The rest is yours, Walt Whitman, the democrat. Buenos Aires, Cosmopolis.

Cosmopolitanism and nationhood, revolution and the quest for recognition constituted, as Beatriz Sarlo suggests, a program for cultural transformation. In 1924, the Peruvian Carlos Mariátegui (1894–1930) repositioned the relation between the avant-garde and nationalism in his article *Lo nacional y lo exótico* [The National and the Exotic]:

> La suposición de que nuestra juventud está seducida por miradas extranjeras o teorías exóticas surge de la interpretación superficial de la relación entre nacionalismo y socialismo.... En Perú, aquellos que representan e interpretan la "peruanidad" son los poetas vanguardistas.... Los poetas argentinos son un interesante ejemplo: todos ellos se han nutrido de la estética europea. Todos, o casi todos, han viajado en alguno de los vagones del Expreso Grand Europe que para Blaise Cendrars, Valery Larbaud y Paul Morand es, indudablemente, el vehículo de la unidad europea tanto como uno de los elementos indispensables de la nueva sensibilidad literaria. Sin embargo, a pesar de esta infusión de cosmopolitismo, esa ecuménica concepción del arte, los mejores de estos artistas vanguardistas son, aún, los poetas más argentinos. La argentinidad de Girondo, Güiraldes, Borges, etc., no es menos evidente que su cosmopolitismo.... Observamos el mismo fenómeno en la literatura peruana.... Vallejo es tan indígena como peruano, es una prueba más que, en esos viajes cosmopolitas y ecuménicos por los que somos tan reprochados, estamos, de manera creciente, descubriéndonos a nosotros mismos. (Mariátegui 135)

> The supposition that our youth is seduced by a foreign gaze or exotic theories arises from a superficial interpretation of the relation between nationalism and socialism.... In Peru, those who represent and interpret "Peruvianness" are the avant-garde poets.... The Argentine poets are an interesting example: They have all been nourished by European aesthetics. All, or nearly all, have traveled in one of the cars of the *Grand Express Européen,* which for Blaise Cendrars, Valéry Larbaud, and Paul Morand is undoubtedly the vehicle for European unity as well as one of the indispensable elements of a new literary sensibility. Nevertheless, despite this infusion of cosmopolitanism, this ecumenical conception of art, the best of these avant-garde artists are still the most Argentine poets. The Argentineness of Girondo, Guiraldes, Borges, and so forth is no less evident than their cosmopolitanism.... We observe the same phenomenon in Peruvian literature.... Vallejo is as indigenous as he is Peruvian, one more sign that, on these cosmopolitan and ecumenical journeys for which we have been so reproached, we are forever discovering ourselves.

The repertoire of a national tradition, which is a self-reliant and totalizing system, permits us, on the one hand, to interpret the cultural canon as a quest for the picturesque which neutralizes differences. On the other, the conventions of this cultural canon reveal the point at which they themselves are no longer viable; for this reason, a culture always fails in its attempt to constitute itself as an objective order. In turn, the cultural critic, as the Latin American avant-garde suggests, works with a form of cultural translation as an intersection of elements. In this sense, mestizaje, acculturation, and hybridity are not peculiar to Latin American culture but are generalized conceptual and historical configurations that enable us to formulate the connection between cultural criticism and cultural viability. A twofold reading of the material relationship between language and actions is thus possible: heterogeneity versus stratified participation. Heterogeneity represents the differences in economic orders, legal organizations, and symbolic systems of the relation between Europe and America; stratified participation represents the local kinds of inequality that regulate differences. We can thus imagine the challenge for cultural criticism in a Latin American context at the present time: Instead of positing itself as a disclosing force, it should propose a reflection on the place itself as a rewriting of the interconnections between knowledge, beliefs, and the elaboration of an approach to the subject that demonstrates its competence to act upon and intervene in culture.

Translation by Charlotte Broad

Works Cited

Alberdi, Juan Bautista. 1977. *Escritos satíricos y de crítica literaria.* Buenos Aires: Academia Argentina de Letras.

Alonso, Carlos J. 1990. *The Spanish American Regional Novel. Modernity and Autochthony.* Cambridge: Cambridge University Press.

Antelo, Raúl. 1993. "Cartografías." *Revista de Lengua y Literatura. Universidad Nacional del Comahue* 13/14 (Noviembre): 79–86.

———. 1994. "Biografía de la infamia y la imaginación." *La imaginación histórica en el siglo XIX.* Ed. Lelia Area y Mabel Moraña. Rosario: UNR Editora. 193–201.

Altamirano, Carlos, and Beatriz Sarlo. 1997. *Ensayos Argentinos. De Sarmiento a la vanguardia.* Buenos Aires: Centro Editor de América Latina.

Brunner, José Joaquín. 1988. "América Latina. Cultura y Modernidad." *Un espejo trizado. Ensayos sobre cultura y políticas culturales.* Santiago de Chile: FLACSO.

Candido, Antonio. 1976. *Literatura e Sociedade.* São Paulo: Editora Nacional.

Carrió de la Vandera, Alonso ("Concolorcorvo"). 1973. *El Lazarillo de Ciegos Caminante.* Ed. Emilio Carilla. Barcelona: Editorial Labor.

Chiaramonte, Jose Carlos. 1971. *Nacionalismo y liberalismo económicos.* Buenos Aires: Solar Hachette.

———. 1991. "El mito de los orígenes en la historiografía Latinoamericana." *Cuadernos del Instituto Ravignani.* Instituto de Historia Argentina y Americana Dr. Emilio Ravignani, Facultad de Filosofía y Letras, Universidad de Buenos Aires. 1–90.

Constant, Benjamin. 1960. *La abeja argentina* 9, 1:33. Buenos Aires: Senado de la Nación, Biblioteca de Mayo.

Cueto, Marcos. 1989. *Excelencias científicas en la periferia.* Lima: Grade Concitec.

Darío, Rubén. 1963.. "Palabras Preliminares." *Prosas Profanas.* Buenos Aires: Huemul. 8.

Dessalines, Jean Jacques. 1977. "Acta de Independencia de Haití y Proclama (1804)." *Pensamiento político de la emancipación.* Ed. José Luis Romero and Luis Alberto Romero. Caracas: Biblioteca Ayacucho. 84–7.

El Centinela. 1822a. Num. 9 (22 September). Buenos Aires: Senado de la Nación, Biblioteca de Mayo. 116.

———. 1822b. Num. 16 (14 October). Buenos Aires: Senado de la Nación, Biblioteca de Mayo. 33.

Fernández de Lizardi, José Joaquín. 1968. *Obras. III Periódicos.* Ed. María Rosa Palazón and Jacobo Chencinsky. Mexico City: Univerisidad Nacional Autónoma de México.

Fidel López, Vicente. 1960. *La Gran Semana de Mayo.* Buenos Aires: EUDEBA.

Franco, Jean. 1989. *Plotting Women: Gender and Representation in Mexico.* New York: Columbia University Press.

González, Aníbal. 1993. *Journalism and the Development of Spanish American Narrative.* New York: Cambridge University Press.

Henríquez, Camilo. 1977. "Proclama (1811)." *Pensamiento político de la emancipación.* Ed. José Luis Romero and Luis Alberto Romero. Caracas: Biblioteca Ayacucho. 220–24.

Hutcheon, Linda. 1994. *Irony's Edge: The Theory and Politics of Irony.* London: Routledge.

Laclau, Ernesto. 1986. *Política e ideología en la teoría marxista.* Mexico City: Siglo XXI.

Lechner, Norbert, ed. 1987. *Cultura política y democratización.* Santiago de Chile: CLACSO, FLACSO, ICI.

Ludmer, Josefina. 1988. *El género gauchesco: un tratado sobre la patria.* Buenos Aires: Sudamericana.

Mariátegui, José Carlos. 1970. *Peruanicemos al Perú.* Lima: Empresa Editora Amauta.

Mármol, José. 1972. *Asesinato del Sr. Dr. D. Florencio Varela.* Buenos Aires: Manuela Rosas, Casa Pardo.

Martí, José. 1960. "Nuestra América." *Ensayos.* Buenos Aires: Austral Espasa Calpe. 55–8.

Masiello, Francine. 1992. *Between Civilization and Barbarism. Women, Nation, and Literary Culture in Modern Argentina.* Lincoln: University of Nebraska Press.

Molloy, Sylvia. 1990. *At Face Value: Autobiographical Writing in Spanish America.* Cambridge: Cambridge University Press.

Monsiváis, Carlos. 1988. *Escenas de pudor y liviandad.* Mexico City: Grijalbo.

Moreno, Mariano. 1943. *Escritos.* Vol. 2. Buenos Aires: Estrada.

Panesi, Jorge. 1995. "Cambaceres, un narrador chismoso." *Revista Interamericana de Bibliografía: El reverso de la tradición: transformaciones culturales en la literatura argentina del siglo XIX.* 45. 3:339–46.

Pratt, Mary L. 1992. *Imperial Eyes: Travel Writing and Transculturation.* London: Routledge.

Prieto, Adolfo. 1988. *El discurso criollista en la formación de la Argentina moderna.* Buenos Aires: Sudamericana.

Rama, Angel. 1984. *La ciudad letrada.* Montevideo: Fundación Internacional Angel Rama.

———. 1985. *La crítica de la cultura: América Latina.* Ed. Saul Sosnowski and Tomás Eloy Martínez. Caracas: Biblioteca Ayacucho.

Rodríguez Pérsico, Adriana. 1992. *Un huracán llamado progreso. Utopía y autobiografía en Sarmiento y Alberdi.* Washington: OEA INTERAMER.

Romero, José Luis 1976. *Latinoamérica: las ciudades y las ideas.* Buenos Aires. Siglo XXI.

——— and Luis Alberto Romero. 1977. *Pensamiento político de la emancipación.* Vol. 1. Caracas: Biblioteca Ayacucho. 2 vols.

Sarlo, Beatriz. 1988. *Una modernidad periférica: Buenos Aires. 1920 y 1930.* Buenos Aires: Nueva Visión.

Schwarz, Roberto. 1992. *Misplaced Ideas: Essays on Brazilian Culture.* London: Verso.

Sommer, Doris. 1991. *Foundational Fictions: The National Romances of Latin America.* Berkeley: University of California Press.

Stolley, Karen. 1992. *El Lazarillo de Ciegos Caminantes: un itinerario crítico.* Hanover: Ediciones del Norte.

Talamates, Melchor de. 1977. "Representación Nacional de las Colonias. Discurso filosófico. Conclusión. (1808)." *Pensamiento político de la emancipación*. Ed. José Luis Romero and Luis Alberto Romero. Caracas: Biblioteca Ayacucho. 98–9.

Torres, Camilo. 1977. "Memorial de Agravios (1809)." *Pensamiento político de la emancipación*. Ed. José Luis Romero and Luis Alberto Romero. Caracas: Biblioteca Ayacucho. 25–42.

Valdés, Mario J. 1992. "Why Comparative Literary History?" *Comparative Literary History as Discourse*. Ed. M. J. Valdés. Bern: Peter Lang. 3–22.

Valdés, Mario J., and Linda Hutcheon. *Rethinking Literary History Comparatively*. ACLS Occasional Paper 27. New York: American Council of Learned Societies, 1994.

Viñas, David. 1974. *Literatura argentina y realidad política*. Buenos Aires: Ediciones Siglo XX.

Viscardo, Juan Pablo. 1977. "Carta a los españoles americanos (1792) (Selección)." *Pensamiento político de la emancipación*. Ed. José Luis Romero and Luis Alberto Romero. Caracas: Biblioteca Ayacucho. 51–8.

Zavala, Iris M. 1989. "Representing the Colonial Subject" *1492–1992: Re/Discovering Colonial Writing*. Ed. René Jara and Nicholas Spadaccini. Minneapolis and Oxford: University of Minnesota Press. 323–48.

Zavalía Lagos, Jorge A. 1986. *Mariquita Sánchez y su tiempo*. Buenos Aires: Plus Ultra.

CHAPTER 42

THE RHETORIC OF CITIZENSHIP IN MODERNITY

Adriana Rodríguez Pérsico

Dilemmas of Modernity

If one had to compile a dictionary of modernity, the following entries might serve to create a list of basic indicators: transformation, crisis, speed, novelty, fragmentation, science and progress, utopias, technologies, mass media, urbanization, multitudes, democratization, anarchy, rationalization, subjectivization, and decadence. For the purposes of this study, we shall focus on only one aspect: the changes and transformations that occurred in the late nineteenth and early twentieth century that, in social practice, translated into a web of disorienting sentiments marked by a generalized sensation that combined euphoria and malaise. In a world that was becoming globalized, this feature pointed to a common heritage, at least in western Europe and the Americas. We need only examine the connections drawn by Marshall Berman in *All That Is Solid Melts into Air* (1982). Describing the second phase of modernity–the first lasted from the beginning of the eighteenth century until the French Revolution–Berman implies that the late-nineteenth-century public still recalled what spiritual life was like in a world that was not yet modern. Ideas of modernization and modernity emerged and developed on the basis of this internal dichotomy: the modern and the premodern, this sensation of being out of balance derived from living in two worlds at the same time.

For Berman, the intellectual relationship between Nietzsche and Marx is linked to the idea that every element is impregnated by its opposite. One might, therefore, think that the end of the century invested the written word with the function of inventing hierarchies in a reality that was perceived as chaotic. This feeling of crisis, of experiencing one order that was dying and another that was beginning to emerge, produced the desire for classification in discourse. Paul Bourget may have summarized another important part of modern thought in his theory of decadence, a term he uses to characterize contemporary society in *Essais de la psychologie contemporaine* [Essays on Contemporary Psychology]. He argues that, as in a living organism, the predominance of the individual over the collective led to anarchy. Bourget thus equates nature with society and language: "A decadent style is one in which the book's unity breaks down as a result of the sentence's independence and the sentence's making way for the non-related word" (19–20). This concept originally gained currency through Nietzsche's interpretation of Wagner and especially through Baudelaire–whom the German philosopher regarded as the master of decadence and whose work he discovered in Nice in 1883.

Modernity, Modernism, and Modernization in Latin America

Once the formation of the political and legal structures of Latin American states had been completed, the main challenge was to incorporate these incipient markets into the world economy. The period from 1870 to 1920 was therefore one of drastic political, social, economic, and cultural transformations. Among these *fin-de-siècle* changes, the rapid growth of urban centers was perhaps the most spectacular. José Luis Romero notes: "The world market's preference for countries that produced raw materials and that were consumers of manufactured products was undoubtedly what led to the rapid growth of a varied population in a number of Latin American cities, which in turn created sources of employment in the latter and created a hitherto unknown level of activity, which hastened the trends that would attempt to eliminate the colonial past to make way for modern lifestyles" (248). The Argentinian historian has linked European and North American imperialist policies to a specific type of economic model: the rapid development of major economic centers that would control the various sectors of the periphery, with the consent of the local leading classes. Between approximately 1850 and 1900, Latin America's population doubled from thirty million inhabitants to just over sixty million (see Sánchez Albornoz in Chapter 7, this volume). The waves of immigration, most evident in Argentina, Brazil, and Uruguay, increased exponentially from 1880 to the end of the century. The year, 1880, therefore, can serve as a tentative and obviously arbitrary date for the beginning of the peak of the modernizing project in Latin America.

To a certain extent, the democratization of everyday life reflected the vibrant spirit of the times. Changes followed one after another with breathtaking speed: new macro-economic models, the demographic explosion, great social mobility, the configuration of hitherto unknown social strata such as the industrial proletariat, the development of the middle classes, the growth of cities (to the detriment of the countryside), the expansion of the press, the spread of education, and the coexistence of various distinct European, Asian, and American cultures together with the shift from a culture of the elite to a culture of the masses. Paradoxically, in Latin America, modernization involved both an opening and a closing, and thus a somewhat ambivalent intellectual attitude, since, on the one hand, the period was extolled as a symbolic time of progress, on the other, there was a sense of loss and of the threatening aspects of this same modernity. Economic modernization does not necessarily coincide with aesthetic modernism, and indeed, in Latin America, they developed at very different rates. In *Las máscaras democráticas del modernismo* [1985; The Democratic Masks of "Modernismo"], the Uruguayan critic Angel Rama (1926–1983) explores the formation of Latin American cultures in the superposition and coexistence of different forms of aesthetics. In this part of the world, the accumulative nature, which, in Rama's view, configures the peculiarity of Latin American cultural processes, can be detected in the proliferation of a specific *fin-de-siècle* discourse. This aesthetic heterogeneity can be interpreted as the driving force behind the need to posit models of intelligibility to counter a fragmented reality. During the extended period of modernization (1880–1920), Rama detects an initial moment, which he calls enlightened culture, from the middle of the

384

1870s onwards. Here, the role of the intellectuals (who still belonged to the elite) proved crucial and, rather like the traditional men of letters who had figured in Latin American life from Colonial times, these intellectuals performed a variety of functions, serving as journalists, educators, politicians, and occasionally military men. Born ideologues and circumstantial artists, they were admirers of positivism and realism.

The 1880s marked a second period of democratized culture, when young people joined the daring modernizing project. Although still aware of the fact that they were an elite, the majority were literate, self-taught, and mistrustful of any kind of institutional instruction. They preferred the thought-provoking, literary atmosphere of cafés to the scientific aspect of university classrooms, and the busy streets to the cloistered atmosphere of academies and athenaeums. The new generation filled the ranks of the rapidly expanding press, writing chronicles or producing impressionistic criticism. In a happy turn of phrase, Olavo Bilac (1865–1918) captured the subtleties of the genre: "Os cronistas são como os bufarinheiros, que levam dentro das suas caixas rosários e alfinetes, fazendas e botões, sabonetes e sapatos, louças e agulhas, imagens de santos e baralhos de cartas, remédios para a alma e remédios para os calos, breves e pomadas, elixires e dedais" ("The chroniclers are like the peddlers who carry in their cases rosaries and pins, cloth and buttons, bars of soap and shoes, dishes and needles, images of saints and decks of cards, medicines for the soul and medicines for calluses, papal sermons and creams, elixirs and thimbles") (19). Somewhat skeptical and adventurous, they read about contemporary issues, yet had a marked preference for lyric poetry or short stories. They willingly accepted the French legacy of Parnassianism and Symbolism, particularly from 1890 onwards, while regarding themselves as the heirs of the Romantics.

In Spanish America, *modernismo* occupied a dominant position. Some literary historians believe it began in 1888 with the Chilean publication of Nicaraguan Rubén Darío's (1867–1916) *Azul* [1888, Blue], a groundbreaking work which included Parisian-style short stories in addition to poetry with a strong Parnassian tendency. Others set its origin as far back as 1882, the year when Cuba's José Martí (1853–1895) published *Ismaelillo*. In *Azul*, Darío used the term *modernity* in a broad, ambiguous sense to describe the Mexican, Ricardo Contreras. In 1890, when he described a meeting with Ricardo Palma, he used the concept as a sign of belonging to the *modernistas,* and thus thereafter denoted the style of a group of writers. At this stage, the work of these modern writers linked imagination, beauty, freedom, and political risk-taking: All traits derived from a search for their main value, novelty, and regeneration. Many among Darío's group had indeed made a profession of their modernist faith. It was a reaction to a culture that, in their view, had already become passé; this profession of faith was an expression of a *fin-de-siècle* anarchic idealism, a search for individual accents, and a means of counteracting the materialism of the times. The aim was to find a contemporary voice–often achieved by appealing to a remote, legendary past, now made originary in the context of the 1890s; the aim was to elevate the sign of what was unique and impossible to repeat and set it against the debasement of the mass-produced culture of the world market.

Traditionalist detractors of these writers gave the adjectives *modern* and *modernista* a negative connotation. They equated *modernista* texts with a decadentism that resulted in a disturbing combination of characteristics: lapses into affectation, a pronounced rejoicing in the exotic, the cultivation of artificiality, a frivolous weakness for French literature, and a love of the Bohemian life–drowning in alcohol or bloated with drugs. The critique was so strong that, in 1894, Darío distanced himself from the excesses of *modernismo* in his article "Pro domo mea," published by *La Nación*. In the foreword to *Prosas profanas* [1896 and 1901; Profane Prose], he subsequently launched another attack, emphasizing his distance from these frivolous imitators.

But without a doubt, Darío's aestheticism also presupposed a vehement rejection of the culture of the market. Julio Ramos attributes this gesture to the discovery of a new function for literature. When literature loses its political function as national foundation and the once homogenous republic of letters shatters into a thousand parts, literature consequently modifies its place of enunciation within society. While they wrote for major newspapers (Martí and Darío, for example, were correspondents for *La Nación*, while Machado de Assis [1839–1908] and Olavo Bilac wrote for the *Gazeta de Noticias),* these artists questioned the professionalization of writers and scorned established canonical literature, although they accepted the fact that it was this new market that had created a space permitting a type of enunciation that was totally alien to the positivist spirit of the beginning of the twentieth century. In a *crónica de saudades* [chronicle of longing]–symptomatically, the same genre as Raúl Pompeia's (1863–1895) *O Ateneu* [1888; The Athenaeum]–Olavo Bilac recalls the moment when he broke with Machado de Assis: "Tudo para mim era o ponto de partida de um sonho" ("For me, everything is a point of departure for a dream") (54). Writing for a newspaper meant more than simply earning money; it implied achieving literary consecration. Midway between the festive register and touches of nostalgia (and using as a symbol of his devotion to the press an amorous relationship with a young woman), the chronicler describes the position of writers in the cultural field and explains the pioneering task of the professionalized writer: "A minha geração, se não teve outro mérito, teve este, que não foi pequeno: desbravou o caminho, fez da imprensa literária uma profissão remunerada, impôs o trabalho" (56) ("If my generation had no other merit, it had this one, which was not small: It pioneered the way to make the publishing of literature a paid profession; the work itself demanded it").

Yet it is reductive to describe the end of the nineteenth century only within the narrow constraints of aestheticism or to restrict it to artistic superficiality. This was also a time marked by an international political viewpoint for Latin America, a change accentuated in response to the 1898 war between the United States and Spain. The *novecentistas* (as the writers of the early 1900s were later known) extolled national or supranational identities as a response to the war as well as to various independence commemorations. The ebbing of Spanish influence was offset by a cultural and historiographic outpouring that increased between 1880 and 1882; the publication of Menéndez Pelayo's (1856–1912) *Historia de los heterodoxos españoles* [History of Spanish Heterodoxy] was recognized as symbolic of a metaphysically eternal Spain. In Latin America, the spiritualist movement of Arielism reached its peak with the publication of José Enrique Rodó's (1871–1917) *Ariel* (1900), an essay based on a classical culture that deliberately erases the indigenous features of Latin America and imagines a Eurocentric, white America. But there was also a powerful response from José Martí, who revalued the *mestizo* condition of the continent in his "Nuestra América." Darío also demonstrated his political Latin Americanism on numerous occasions. In 1887, his *Canto a las glorias de Chile* [Song in Praise of the Glory of Chile] reflected the grandiloquence of patriotic poetry. Subsequently, in the foreword to *Prosas profanas,* he set Latin American identity in a golden past that shines in the Mayan ruins and in the tragic history of the last Aztec emperor, Moctezuma, while he carved out his own aesthetic-political position in an erotic metaphor that alludes to his native wife and his French lover. Latin American sentiments are also evident in the poems of *Cantos de vida y esperanza* [1905; Songs of Life and Hope].

Whether *mestizo* or classical, Indian or white, for the *modernistas,* Latin America is undoubtedly the counterpart to the United States, as symbolized in the dichotomy that sets Ariel against Calibán, or genius and beauty against the inhumanity of materialism. The exaltation of what was national presaged the climate of the Independence Centenaries. In 1910, Darío joined the festivities for the century of emancipation with a lengthy poem entitled "Canto a la Argentina" [1914; Song in Praise of Argentina], in which Latin Americanist motifs resound. The challenge of constructing an identity of one's own continued with the local responses to the avant-gardes of 1920; thus, the question of identity adopted the form of a tension between nationalism and cosmopolitanism.

Conflictive Subjectivities and "Knowable Communities"

If subjectivity and historicity are two concepts that partly define modernity in Latin America, then the end of the nineteenth century witnessed the gestation of an enunciative subject who renounced the historical, and what Eurocentric aesthetics promoted as universal, ideals of beauty. The artists, although all in very different ways, accepted the challenge of being created as subjects-in-discontinuity, looking to the historicity of art rather than its ideologies, and forging a literature for the future, which was also the Latin American society of the future. The period of modernization saw an intensification of juxtaposed contrasts in everyday experiences. In the cultural field, this process manifested itself as a sort of discursive vertigo. This literature, both narrative and lyric poetry, was steeped in a conflict between fragmentation and the nostalgia of unity. Many different ways of signifying heterogeneity have come to represent this chaotic period. In the space opened by the literature of the end of the nineteenth century and the beginning of the twentieth century, types of identities corresponding to different historical conjunctures were no sooner articulated when they were confronted; identities that maintained close links with the land and tradition coexisted with others that were closer to the new industrialized age. Different textualities establish identities– whether collective, generic, personal, or cultural–around certain fictitious identities: the artist, the prophet, the madman, the delinquent, the *femme fatale,* the mass, the people.

A brief glance at this heterogeneity reveals the presence of a discourse of science, with its two variants (medical discourse and psychiatric discourse, which overlap with juridical-legal discourse); sociological discourse (which focuses particularly on the study of multitudes and the relations between man and the environment); a fantastic and esoteric discourse (or a discourse of the sciences of the occult); a discourse of the nation or the continent (with its search for cultural, national, or supranational identity); an aesthetic discourse (which focuses on the artist's imagination); a religious discourse (which was heavily influenced by prophetic language); a discourse of desire (which created *fin-de-siècle* erotica); and a discourse of novelties or current events (which revealed an interest in everyday life in the cities through newspaper articles). Let us focus, for the moment, on two of these types of textualities: on the one hand, the desire to exalt an irreplaceable subjectivity– the artist; on the other hand, and serving as a counterweight to this individualism, a Latin American or nationalistic discourse that brings back the idea of collectivity. The common denominator of both types was the presence of heroes, who would be desperate artists, political leaders, or prophetic writers.

The end of the century witnessed what we could call a veritable passion for the witnessing gaze. The hegemony of the gaze marked the wish to take in everything. A whole range of genres was created to express this: travel writing, detective novels, newspaper articles, and treatises on criminology, physiology, and psychiatry. The glance that the writer-artist, physician, psychiatrist, or prophet cast at an object pointed to the invention of "knowable communities," the description of a "society selected by a selected point of view" (Williams 246). The fact that these types of discourse reduced and restricted these knowable communities, established their geographical and symbolic limits, prescribed their spaces, and gave them their characters, enabled what was strange to become familiar or, at least, describable and thus suitable for narration. In *The Country and the City,* Raymond Williams holds that myth and revolution are two ideas typical of the city. Through them, one could interpret much of *fin-de-siècle* Latin American literature. Myth is not opposed to history, but complements it, because it entails a distancing from an excess of historical awareness in order to approach aesthetic experience. Myth is the space where the individual rediscovers the community through recounting a collective history assumed by a hero whose existence displays a positive or negative value that has to do with group life. Nietzsche, in his essays on Wagner, notices that myths contain a political element. In this respect, myth functions as a nucleus of cohesion; in aesthetic terms, a renewed mythology acts as a magnet for social integration. And when Baudelaire writes about Wagner, he notes that myth has a narrative effectiveness that history lacks. If myth is the opposite of reason, as yet unlicensed reason will lodge in the positivist discourse expressed in case histories. In this respect, end-of-the-nineteenth-century myths could be said to include the prophet (the writer's double), the decadent artist, the *femme fatale* (the prostitute, Salomé), the angel woman, the multitudes, the people as a national subject and as a collective (Latin American identity). The other privileged gaze was that of the physician-psychiatrist and the jurist, who minutely analyzed cases and specified in detail the favorite object of *fin-de-siècle* science: the abnormal, including madmen, homosexuals, and delinquents. Etymology tells us that the word "case" means event or happening; in other words, a particular matter or an unusual history can be made exemplary. Retelling cases implies a sort of representative iteration and condensation. In this respect, the scientific discourse that examined cases carried out a diagnosis and proposed means of social defense. The political implications can be seen in the frequent confusion between invalids, anarchists, and immigrants. Aesthetic forms of discourse were sometimes set against scientific discourse, highlighting the division between the spheres; at other times, they came together in the space of the so-called sciences of the occult, a veritable passion of the era and the other side of positivism.

The Myth of Modernity

When Baudelaire urged artists to submerge themselves in the unknown to find what was new, he was articulating an activity that was inherent to the modern subject. In his analysis of modernity, several topics delineate decisive aspects in his thinking about *fin-de-siècle* culture: the admiration of barbarity; the praise of artifice and make-up; work with tradition and history; the protest against imitating, copying, and realism; the particularity of beauty; and the undeniable presence of the subject in the production of a play. In order to describe the importance of art, Baudelaire portrayed the writer as the painter of modern life. Life and historicity were the raw materials. In referring to the double aspect of custom—the artistic and the historical—he found an opportunity "to establish an historical and national theory of beauty" (685). In this, he was following the already-famous concept of the beautiful as a compound of one eternal invariable element and another relative, circumstantial element. At another time, modernity would share these attributes, a time that articulated its own beauty in the description of urban life.

Baudelaire's (male-oriented) version of the artist's subjectivity linked men of the world, men of the multitudes, and children: in other words, the cosmopolitan man, the dandy, the son of transition, and a traveler through different geographies and cultures; the curious, impertinent creature who took the pulse of the feverish era and extracted from it its energies; the child who contemplated the most insignificant things with recently acquired powers of observation. Yet astonishment does not prevent contradictions. Baudelaire toyed with the idea of epochal barbarity, which he regarded as a kind of gaze designed to take in the whole, a gaze that scorned the small detail and any objectivity. Far from legitimizing modernity in making a break with and forgetting the past, the artist believed he was the heir to the grand tradition re-examined from the present perspective of his passionate modernization the mark of the *subject-of*, the sense of breadth and nobility introduced into the chain of history. Continuing these reflections, one could say that the modern artist was inexorably a barbarian, and that therein lay the effectiveness of his practice: a historical being who learned a method and a logic from his forebears and expressed those feelings and teachings in a summation in which intimacy was coupled with childish excitement. With these concepts, one can trace the outlines of a sensibility marked by the negation of conventions, the rejection of what has already been established, the search for beauty, the vertigo and the futility of modern experience, and, sometimes, a sense of the division between the hopes of future utopias and the skeptical melancholy over what has been lost. Literature assumes responsibility for the tensions that arise between a subjectivity marked by dispersion and elitism and the emergence of a political order in the process of democratization, upset by the presence of a thitherto unknown social agent, the masses. In his preface to *Cantos de vida y esperanza* [1905; Songs of Life and Hope], Rubén Darío confesses, somewhat plaintively, "Yo no soy un poeta para las muchedumbres pero sé que indefectiblemente tengo que ir a ellas" (1977, 243) ("I am not a poet for the masses, but I know that I must unfailingly go to them").

In the prologue to the poem "Al Niágara" [1882; To Niagara] by the Venezuelan Juan Antonio Pérez Bonalde (1846–1892), Martí explores similar contemporary ambiguities: "Y hay ahora como un desmembramiento de la mente humana.

Otros fueron los tiempos de las vallas alzadas; éste es el tiempo de las vallas rotas. Ahora los hombres empiezan a andar sin tropiezos por toda la tierra; antes apenas echaban a andar, daban en muro de solar de señor o en bastión de convento" (Martí 1989, 208) ("And now, it is as though there is a dismembering of the human mind. The time of raised barricades is long past; this is the time of smashed barricades. Now men begin to walk freely over the earth; before, no sooner had they begun to walk than they bumped into the wall of a mansion or the bastion of a convent"). He also highlights the consequences of the democratization of life, a sort of decentralization of intelligence, which passed over individual genius in favor of collective mediocrity. Martí traces the confrontation between the times and aesthetics, placing an art created by giants next to one produced by dwarfs. The feeling of being in between a moment already past and another moment that has not yet happened points to the brevity and the vertigo of modernity in art. Martí rejects both ornamental lyricism and the dramatic epic and turns to the land of his native Cuba (but, in general, of the tropics), with the force of passion found only in the greatest of Romantics. Through metaphorical shifts between society and nature, Martí shakes up the old order. The modern conditions of life are amassed by the poet in a masterful summary: There is an economic order, but also a religious and aesthetic order that have to be replaced. This time, he praises modernity: "La batalla está en los talleres; la gloria, en la paz; el templo, en toda la tierra; el poema, en la naturaleza" (Martí 1989, 210) ("The battle is to be found in workshops; there is glory in peace; temples are the entire earth, and poetry is in nature itself"). Martí expressed his (lay) position against falsity and masks, and for a heroism of modern life, an order that, although it failed to dispel hierarchies, postulated a combination of high and low, old and new, large and small. Although there were forms and times that were worn out, there was also a future whose protagonist was a new social subject: the masses—always regarded somewhat ambiguously.

With his customary succinctness, Darío also captured the conflicts of modernity in many of his stories. Irony and mockery, the hallmarks of Darío's prose, shine through "El velo de la reina Mab" [Queen Mab's Veil] or "El rey burgués" [The Bourgeois King]. Trivialized by abridged school versions, "El velo de la reina Mab" in its full force illustrates a crossroads of art. Its protagonists are four poor artists who, despite having received precious gifts, fail to realize their ideal. Individual anguish is made to represent the problems of contemporary art and artists: In the case of the *sculptor*, it involves the burden of choosing a model—Fidias—who belongs to the culture of an earlier era. The *painter*, who complains of the laws of the market and seeks the false success of the salons, suffers from eclecticism. (As Baudelaire would say, an eclectic is a man without passion.) The distance between art and life is reflected in the crowd's lack of understanding of the *musician's* idiom. Finally, the dangers of anachronism are encoded in the *poet's* choice of archaic forms such as the epic, lyric songs, or eclogues. Without pathos, the text works the image of the starving artists, eliciting an understanding smile in the ending, where the recourse to a deus ex machina—the intervention of the fairy—turns unhappiness into illusion.

On the basis of the oxymoron in its title, "El rey burgués" reviews the conditions of art in an upside-down world: The institution of patronage, the separation between true and circumstantial art, the idolization of money, and the prostitution of artists. The bourgeois king silences the impassioned discourse of the poet, who prophesies revolutions and envisages an austere form of art that will prefer content to form and act in accordance with the violent times that are approaching. The king condemns him to the greatest humiliation possible–not to exchange words for meals, but food for remaining silent. In "Historia de mis libros" [1916; "Story of My Books"], Darío interprets the story symbolically, as the protest of the artist-dreamer against insensitive, uncultured wealth. Angel Rama (1926–1983), however, offers a less linear interpretation because the king, despite his ignorance, lives in the midst of the most sublime refinement. Conversely, the poet, who depicts himself as a Whitmanian prophet, has no readers: "La mordacidad sobre el lujo refinado del rey burgués no es mucho mayor que la aplicada al poeta harapiento porvenirista" (Darío 1977, xxii–xxiv) ("The biting criticism of the refined luxury of the bourgeois king is hardly more severe than that directed at the ragged poet, with his hopes vested in the future").

The Artist's Imagination

The *fin-de-siècle* egos of some (increasingly irrelevant) poets slid down the slippery paths of exoticism. They adored esoteric words; they aspired to fantastic and cabalistic spiritual secrets; they wandered though urban landscapes, observing the multitudes; they amused themselves with the recovery of recondite words, only to fall suddenly back into the language of the commonplace; they ridiculed academic art and mocked the public's feelings. Elaborate artificial constructs and iconoclasm were their favorite games, superficiality and brilliant conceits their style. These poets lacked a social function and failed to reconcile the disparities of their own lives, which seemed as artificial and divided as the objects that peopled their symbolic universes.

Gómez Carrillo (1873–1927) filled his life and his texts with these characteristics of the turn of the century. In his book of memoirs, *En plena bohemia* [In the Midst of Bohemian Life], which includes "Treinta años de mi vida" ["Thirty Years of My Life"], he saunters ironically through the commonplaces of Parisian bohemia. Free of any hint of tragedy, he plucks his famous characters out of the sanctuaries of poetry, placing them in everyday settings such as the café or dinner with friends. In his work, the characters are at odds with each other since their only common bonds are negative ones. The object of his writing is not aesthetic production, but rather a portrayal of poets from a perspective that aims at demystification, yet wherein praise is not absent. Gómez Carrillo chooses his eccentrics carefully, and establishes some distance from Ruben Darío's *Los Raros* through his ironic tone. His depiction of Verlaine, "the king of the Bohemians," borders on parody but, at the same time, is inclined to be compassionate. Verlaine had been promoted as mythological character of immortal stature. This is why Gómez Carrillo's chronicler rejects the heroic, mythic portrait in favor of the image of a mischievous, amusing, almost-childlike man. When Verlaine asks one of his neighbors for his "little red ribbon"–the badge of the *Légion d'Honneur*–the gesture involves neither solemnity nor rancor, but merely expresses a sort of childish delight with the object, beyond its value or symbolic meaning.

In contrast to Gómez Carrillo, Darío regards his *aristoi* with admiration, seriousness, and compassion. In Verlaine, he traces the outlines of a wounded subjectivity that medical discourse is unable to describe. In the work, "Paul Verlaine," positivist rationality emerges in all its destructive, hyberbolic

simplification (Darío 1952, 46–51). When Darío transcribes a fragment of Max Nordau's *Degeneración* [Degeneration] that presents "a most abominable portrait" of the French poet, the descriptive exaggeration makes a caricature of the man, yet leaves Verlaine's work intact. In order to portray Verlaine's abnormality, wherein the supreme greatness of his poetry must stand alongside the most horrific misery of his life, Darío chooses the hagiographic genre. Verlaine's miserable life fits into the genre of the lives of saints who attained God in spite of a life in which they were goaded by the devil and tempted by the pleasures of the flesh and of the world. According to this genre, the greatest sinner can be the chosen one. Opposites such as saint and sinner are eliminated the moment extremes meet in his work: Verlaine, the "eternal prisoner of desire," is also the "hermit of the Lord" in his poetry. The existential space of illness is also that in which genius develops, and the space of crowds in the city is also the space of introspection in this image of the artist. This tragic figure of the past gives voice to others from the most varied social circumstances: the vulgar public, the rich bourgeois, the geniuses, the morally damned, the aristocrats, the paupers, saints, madmen, heroes, and devils–all come together in the poet's vision.

We know that literary criticism can make any figurative element into a political symbol. This is certainly true of Sylvia Molloy's interpretation (1992), in which she links desire to ideology in the chronicles that Darío and Martí wrote about Oscar Wilde or when she stresses the political power of the affectation of *fin-de-siècle* artists. In introducing Wilde, Gómez Carrillo blends together grotesqueness and futility, sexuality and arrogance. Nevertheless, his depiction of Wilde grows in stature when he describes Wilde's obsession with the figure of Salomé. The English writer juxtaposes foolishness and geniality: "And they certainly mocked. They made fun of the others and themselves gently, subtly, and even childishly" (192). Gómez Carrillo reveals what Martí, in his chronicle on Wilde, conceals: that undefined sexuality that, in the pages of *En plena bohemia*, operates as a sine qua non for writing. Wilde's art is contained in the oxymoron of inspired foolishness. After hearing the story of Salomé from Rémy de Gourmont, the writer gives artistic creation preference over historical fact. The privileged status given to fiction reveals a rejection of objectivism and his defense of subjectivity that permeates every aspect of life. Latin American *modernismo* produced a system of representation that despised mimicry and amalgamated fetish, masks, makeup, and the colorfulness that ends in parody; *modernismo*'s poetic space is saturated with cultural references to the unusual and the dissonant. Its aesthetics can be summarized in Darío's advice: Create artificial roses that smell of spring.

Benjamín interprets the bourgeoisie's desire to accumulate objects as a means of offsetting the diminishment of private life in large cities (61–62). These collected objects, with their sentimental value, hoard the impressions of their owners. In the same way, *modernista* writers could be said to reflect this bourgeois attitude to objects. *Modernista* poets make a desperate attempt to collect words and to take possession of them in order to protect them from profane eyes and ears. Language becomes a fetish. From this perspective, Gwen Kirkpatrick regards *modernista* language as a "fetishistic insistence on the bodily form" (8). The capacity for suggestion of fetishistic power lies in its appeal to what is manufactured and artificial: Objects are emptied of their physical density and are presented as object-signs (8). Artists often assume this role in the texts; their actions construct the new sensibility, cutting it out of a world of carefully chosen objects overloaded with the meanings that the subject gives them. Linked to experience, these objects contain the marks of the ephemeral time of the event through which they are defined as objects in an intimate, sacred ritual. This practice gives esoteric meanings to the objects which, having been depleted of their lexical significance, acquire the outlines of the fantasies of their new owners.

Rubén Darío reflects this attitude in his portrait of Eduardo Dubus. Darío concentrates on key points of an aesthetic that separates art from politics. This position, which affirms the irreconcilability of the two spheres, implies the negation of the market, contempt for the public, and the idea of a book as a beautiful, useless jewel, in which only the initiate can recognize themselves and from which the ignorant are excluded. Thus, Dubus' *Quand les violons sont partis* [When the Violins Have Gone] is declared to be the opposite of real book publication. Darío writes: "Cuando la publicación de su libro-bijou (. . .)–libro especial defendido de los hipopótamos callejeros porque era de subscripción y no se vendía en las librerías–los pocos, los que le comprendieron, le saludaron como a uno de los más ricos y brillantes poetas de la nueva generación" (1952, 144) ("This jewel-book was a special book protected from the hippopotamuses of the street because it was only available by subscription and was not sold in bookstores; a very few, those who understood it, greeted him as one of the most brilliant and talented poets of the new generation"). Distinguishing a real jewel from worthless trinkets requires an expert. The violin chords, which are unheard by the rest, are reserved for those who perceive the differences.

The New Prophets

"Depending on whether one is for or against, one moves away from the center to find the x," says Nietzsche, referring to the situation of the *fin-de-siècle* subject. While Baudelaire inspired *modernistas* with a passion for the most radical experiences, Nietzsche, through Zarathustra, paved the way for the advent of superman. What was Zarathustra laughing about? That laugh, expressing neither pain nor joy, causes astonishment in the reader, a mixture of thunderstruck interrogation, overflowing vitality, and contained skepticism. Contemplating the present world, Zarathustra laughs at the sublime and the weak, recoiling from the spirit of heaviness. He therefore recommends abandoning the sublime and heroic. Only then can one take the path toward beauty suggested by the coming of superman. Zarathustra, so focused on the future, is an exile from every country. In the dwelling of thought–that place in the wilds that encourages reflection–the pilgrim sings a song against the limits imposed on man by the moral values of good and evil. Only those who, of their own volition, walk the path that has yet to be outlined are freed from the spirit of heaviness, an obvious criticism of conformity and self-satisfaction. Zarathustra invites others to engage in a practice that involves "concentrating and uniting everything which, in man, is nothing more than fragment and enigma and terrifying chance" (139). He goes on to define himself: "As a poet, as a redeemer of chance, I have taught them to be the creators of the future and, by creating, to save all that once existed" (139). The artist is therefore depicted as an interpreter of signs, an artifice of future language and a creator of history. The prophet preaches in solitude, and is only heard by a few; his audience is not the multitude.

Several compositions by Rodó, José Asunción Silva (1865–1896), Darío, Martí, Leopoldo Lugones (1874–1938) and Graça Aranha (1868–1931)–in many respects, the predecessor of Brazilian modernism–provide the conditions for enunciating the prophecy of the year 1900. We should add that the Messianic gesture and the spiritualistic tone lasted in Brazilian culture until well into the 1920s. The Symbolist legacy is evident in Río de Janeiro with Tasso da Silveira (1895–1968), whose ideas contrasted sharply with both the *Revista de Antropofagia* [The Review of Antropophagy] and the *Escola da Anta* [School of Anta] of Plínio Salgado (1895–1975) and Menotti del Picchia (1892–1988). The latter writers, in part inspired by the Mexican José Vasconcelos' (1881–1959) idea of a cosmic race, promulgated a Brazilian national identity based on miscegenation. The discourse of the 1920s, in sharp contrast to the turn of the century, is highly political; it depicts the present as an improvement over the past and predicts a better future. Writers comment on the processes of modernization and the place of progress, reason, faith in the role of literature, and the social function of the writer (in that order). With the exception of a few nihilists like Silva, they develop a concept of history as a record of an inexorable move toward a better world. They bet on a prophetic word that is seen as successful in Darío and Martí, is declared a failure in Silva, is said to be the beginning of a new social order in Rodó and Graça Aranha, but is inverted in Lugones. In the cultural imaginary, the prophet represents the writer's alter ego, a rebel who discerns the exact state of things. He is brought close to prophetic knowledge by the revelation of secrets and the clarification of moments of servitude, as well as through his social function of guiding the multitudes from his central position of mediation between an inarticulate people and their history. The artist, thus, is the interpreter of cultural and political reality.

Rubén Darío's poem "El porvenir" (1885, "The Future") contains certain recurrent elements taken from the Apocalypse: the Last Judgment, the call of the archangel, and humanity appearing before a severe God who stands in judgment. Darío also borrows from apocalyptic literature a way of approaching the incessant terror of crisis and moving toward the notion of living in an era of transition with the hope of renewal (see Kermode). Following the oldest literary conventions, "El porvenir" begins with a prayer to the deity for inspiration. Instead of the gods of Olympus, the modern poet appeals to the human capacity to think, which anxiously seeks appropriate expression. The poet, representing the act of writing, provides an anthropomorphized version of history; the poet becomes history. Past, present, and future are personified as archetypes, and they file past the divine judge. An old man, a worker, and an angel exemplify the three phases of humanity on the road to perfection. This allegorical interpretation of history focuses on an imagination that condemns the wars of the past, gives new value to the present time of work and revolution, and predicts a fulfilling future within the harmony of art. The characters from other times, members of "the race of Cain," are audacious warriors, bloody conquerors, and, also, all of the defeated. Much like the science fiction about a postnuclear world, this apocalyptic landscape consists of cities in ruins in the desolate panorama of a descent into primitive survival as the legacy of the death of the gods.

In Darío, the present is marked by struggles that will drastically change the course of history. All changes bear the seal of modernity: Schools replace temples, the law takes the place of the arbitrary rule of kings, reason tames nature, and the power of intelligence opens up unsuspected paths for thought. "'El porvenir' refiere contiendas libertarias que hacen coincidir el trabajo con el intelecto: golpea el yunque la falange obrera y escribe la falange pensadora" (Darío 1977, 51) ("'The Future' refers to struggles for freedom, which make work coincide with the intellect: the workers' phalanx strikes the anvil/and the thinking phalanx writes"). The heroes of the period are the anonymous and collective-of-the-people. Or they have proper names: Simon Bolívar, Víctor Hugo. This is where the geography of America begins to be outlined; a fertile nature replaces the area of ancient cities crushed beneath the clash of arms. The history being made in the present is that of the liberation from the tyranny of the idols and the installation of the empire of truth; royal prerogatives and superstitions give way to the force of reason and the building of the future. There are, however, always doubts, which are a threatening presence. "El porvenir" ends with an accumulation of stereotypes that praise the universal peace that will soon be achieved when ethnic groups and cultures manage to draw together within a utopian America based on the ideals of heroism, love, and art. Around the idea of modernity and on the basis of common battles fought, the prophets will re-establish a framework of social justice for all. Darío contrasts myth and history: Myth breaks up the past and the present, while history traces a line of continuity between the past and the future.

Lugones, however, sees only indifferent masses and the death of Darío's myth of the modern positive spirit. *Las montañas del oro* [1897; The Gold Mountains] includes verses that refer to the disappearance of God, a fact that, in the view of the people, implies freedom. The lyric voice argues against this popular equation of a godless universe with one free of all constraints. Using a form of pedagogy suitable for children, he sees the death of God as the death of transcendence. The lyric voice makes proposals, dispensing advice and giving warnings, which the crowd, as yet immature, scorns. The poet-prophet of *Las montañas del oro* predicts the destiny of the writer; given the blindness of the masses, he will move away from the people to place himself "on the side of the stars" as an intermediary between God and the people, sometimes becoming God himself–a God who thinks–and therefore suspending the fulfillment of his mission. The opposite of the warlike Whitman, who understands the voice of the people, Lugones, the poet, turns a deaf ear to the word that affirms the triumph of science and industry, the forgetting of religion, the path of progress and education, and the advent of a new age of reason and freedom:

> He aquí el nuevo dogma!
> Dios, lacerante yugo,
> Es el primer tirano i el primer verdugo.
> La libertad le niega, la ciencia le suprime:
> La libertad que alumbra, la ciencia que redime.
> A destronarle, picas!
> Guerra a Dios! Muerte al mito!
>
> *(Lugones 1947, 15)*

> Here's the new dogma!
> God, the lacerating yoke,
> Is the first tyrant and the first executioner,
> He forbids freedom and suppresses science:
> Freedom that enlightens, science that redeems,
> Dethrone him, pikemen!
> Make war with God! Death to the myth!

The poet lectures the militants of "modern worship," giving faith back its redemptive dimension:

> Pueblo, sé poderoso, sé grande, sé fecundo;
> Abrete nuevos cauces en este Nuevo Mundo;
> . . .
> Borra de tus encías la hiel de todo insulto;
> I haz que las hostias sean, en tu moderno culto,
> No de carne sangrienta sino de dulce trigo. (16)

> People, be powerful, be great, be fertile;
> Open up new channels in this New World;
> . . .
> Erase from your gums the gall of all insults;
> And ensure that the hosts, in your modern worship,
> Are not made of bloody flesh but of sweet wheat.

The flattery of inflated verses that purport to dissuade rebellion and quell disobedience is even more surprising when one recalls that, the same year, Lugones, together with Ingenieros, founded the socialist newspaper *La Montaña,* in whose pages we find: "Y bien: es por esto que va a haber Revolución. Nosotros que sufrimos del dolor de la servidumbre, hemos proclamado la Libertad. Queremos derribar nuestra cárcel, toda! Queremos que desaparezca el orden social que es nuestra cárcel. Y nuestra aspiración va desde el granero a la academia" ("There is going to be a Revolution. We, who suffer the pain of servitude, have proclaimed Freedom. We want to tear down our prison. We want to eliminate the social order that is our prison. And our aspirations range from the granary to the academy") (Ingenieros and Lugones 61).

In the attempt to create a totality, this literary mission driven by prophetic passion appealed, at times, to Nietzschean Caesarism, adding fragments of the emerging nationalistic ideology. Political utopia and idealized love appear in *De sobremesa* [1895; After Dinner Conversation] by the Columbian José Asunción Silva (1865–1896); these two means of salvation are both eventually aborted in his brand of nihilism. The protagonist–a blend of decadent aesthete, successful entrepreneur, and enlightened despot–dreams of a dictatorial fantasy, a state project that dissolves social institutions through violence. In the beginning, there was culture: In the midst of a sublime landscape, his senses heightened by a fast of several days, Fernández dreams up his project in the form of blood-curdling pictures which stir up ghosts of the past and "recuerdos de lecturas remotas" ("memories of distant readings"). The program is made up of an accumulation of modernizing postulates: industrialization, immigration, highways, factories, railways, bridges, and education, culminating in the splendid words, "Luz! Más luz!" ("Light! More light!") (Silva 121). During the bloody journey, national cultural identity is outlined through a hodgepodge mix that includes the traditions of indigenous legends, the epic song of the Wars of Independence, the praise of a fertile nature, and the desires for the future fatherland. The tireless experimenter proffers a form of subjectivity that hovers between genius, crime, and madness and is consolidated only in heterogeneity. The crux is to destroy all existing social standards until even sexual certainties vacillate. At the same time, Fernández reaffirms the Latin American cultural legacy, the eternal struggle between civilization and barbarity. This dichotomy explodes into a multiplicity which, even at the risk of destroying its own identity, paradoxically facilitates access to a singularity that erases both sexual limits and the borders between nature and culture.

Social prophecy, so markedly unsuccessful in Silva, triumphs in Martí. In *El Poeta Walt Whitman* [The Poet Walt Whitman], published in 1887 in *El Partido Liberal* in Mexico and in *La Nación* in Argentina, Martí links art and society by declaring that literature describes collective history more fully than does historical discourse because writing a history of literature involves exploring community life. Martí focuses on the great social achievements of human effort in North America. The chronicle sketches the image of Whitman as a prophet in harmony with nature, even in its most uncontrollable aspects: an artist and an art dedicated to life. Insofar as this poet hero, in his isolation, questions cultural institutions that minimize human creativity, his voice sounds a discordant note in the university cloisters. Openly challenging academic dodges and shortsightedness, the text sets in motion a conception of a true, totalizing art that emerges from the profound harmony between man and nature. The hymn sung by the prophet emphasizes the themes of work and health, which contrast with the Latin American cultural features so deeply affected by weakness and futile academicism. The spokesman for a young, different culture, a veritable Titan of modernity, Whitman offers humanity a new faith. On the basis of this affinity, he is portrayed as being exceptionally powerful: "cuando se le compara a esos poetas y filósofos canijos, filósofos de un detalle o un solo aspecto; poetas de aguamiel, de patrón, de libro; figurines filosóficos y literarios" (1989, 268) ("when he is compared with feeble poets and philosophers, philosophers of a detail or a single aspect; poets of sugared water, formula poets, bookish poets; mere philosophical and literary figures"). In vigorous prose that alternates between opposition and exhortation, Martí moves from art to religion, giving them a similar status. He adds juridical and even philosophical aims to the transcendental dimension in his rapprochement between reason and faith. He finally offers a defense of poetry as a fundamental human need and, establishing a hierarchy, he puts poets at the head of society. Under the poets, he places the masses, who, without spiritual leaders, lose their bearings. The alliance between the artist and the people culminates in an attitude of openness that manages to reconcile diverse elements: "El es de todas las castas, credos y religiones, y en todas encuentra justicia y poesía" (271) ("The poet belongs to all casts, creeds, and religions, and in all of them, he finds justice and poetry"). In 1887, in Martí's view, the prophetic word had already been spoken.

Ten years later, Rodó thought that this word had yet to be uttered. *El que vendrá* [1897; The One Who Is to Come] took stock of the literary state of the century; to his review of the past, he added an interpretation of the future and a verdict on the present. Inasmuch as experience is synonymous with art, the prophet who will redeem life is the artist of the new word. The current period, adrift in solipsism and indifference, is viewed as an interregnum of uncertainties. Nevertheless, from the lowest point, the hope of the messianic word arises: "tiene por cáliz el alma de todos los tiempos en que recrudecen el dolor y la duda" (Rodó *El que vendrá* 13) ("its chalice is the soul of all the times in which pain and doubt are exacerbated"). Rodó coincides with other *Modernistas* in depicting the century as a series of battles of ideas and excited masses. Between the century's dawn and dusk, literary movements file by that are, for the essayist, really philosophical systems that attempted to answer vital questions. Rodó initially relegated prestigious aesthetic concepts to the background–the inflexibility of Parnassians, Symbolists, and decadents alike. Diagnosis

subsequently gives way to interpretation, however, as Rodó questions the prophet, the "*sublime vengador*" (sublime avenger) or "*apóstol dulce*" (sweet apostle) of the future: "De qué nos hablarás, revelador, para que nosotros encontremos en tu palabra la vibración que enciende la fe, y la virtud que triunfa de la indiferencia, y el calor que funde el hastío?" (14) ("What will you speak to us about, revealer, that will enable us to find in your words the spark that ignites faith, the virtue that triumphs over indifference, and the heat that dissolves boredom?"). In the last paragraphs, in his visionary gesture, Rodó follows the path of the mystics. On sensing the divine presence, the spirit still challenging doubt, pursues it. However, the pilgrimage does not end with finding it. In 1897, humanity was still a "caravan of decadence," an image already used by Lamartine and Gautier, and, also, by Darío in "La página blanca."

Somewhat different is the mood in *Chanaan* (1902) by Graça Aranha, an uneven novel in which, through the dialogue of its characters–two immigrant friends, Lentz and Milkau–the thesis of the survival of the fittest (using violent means) contrasts with that of victory through the integration of peoples. While Lentz discusses Nietschean and Darwinist arguments, Milkau posits an evolutionary humanitarianism that predicts the discovery of a promised land. When, on rescuing the innocent María and helping her to escape from prison, Milkau decides to act out of love and disinterest; he embarks on a journey of no return that forces him to wander in search of an ideal society from Bavaria to Brazil, from Brazil to an egalitarian Utopia that keeps receding before him like the horizon:

> Não te cances em vão. . . . Não corras. . . . E inutil. . . . A terra da Promissão, que eu te ia mostrar e que tambem anceoso buscava, não a vejo mais . . . Ainda não despontou à Vida. Paremos aqui e esperemos que ella venha vindo no sangue das gerações redimidas. Não desesperes. Sejamos fieis à doce illusão da Miragem. Aquelle que vive o Ideal contrae um emprestimo com a Eternidade . . . Cada um de nós, a somma de todos nós, exprime a força creadora da utopia (. . .). (359)

> Do not tire yourself in vain. . . . Do not run. . . . It is useless . . . . The promised land, which I was going to show you and that I anxiously searched for, I can no longer see . . . Let us stop here and let us wait for life to come in the blood of the redeemed generations. Do not despair. Let us be loyal to the sweet illusion of the mirage. The person who lives the ideal enters into a contract with eternity. Each of us, all of us express the creative forces of utopia
> (. . .).

Prophecy thus links up with the desire to forge a Latin American cultural and political identity. Writers fulfill the prophecies and embody the figure of the prophet who speaks a common language, telling stories of identity. Martí was to do this in "Nuestra América," Rodó in *Ariel*, Darío in certain texts in *El canto errante* [1907; The Song of the Wanderer] and *Canto a la Argentina*, Lugones in *La guerra gaucha* [The Gaucho War] and *El payador* [1916; The Ballad Singer], while in 1930 Plínio Salgado (1895-1975) would do the same in his novel *O Esperado* [The One Awaited]. Prophetic discourse prepared the way for discourses of Latin America (or "Nuestra América" 'Our America'), and in some cases, for the nation; the prophet anticipated the Americanist or nationalistic writer.

Stories of Collective Identity

A People for a Nation

Latin Americanist and subsequently nationalistic discourses were regarded as the translators of the intimate connection that existed between the different planes of community life. The enunciatory subject revealed its history by recovering specific values from the past that were then projected towards the future. These discourses strung together disperse elements; they re-established the unity of time and space, fitting a collective subject (guided by soldiers, scientists, politicians, and scholars) into their movable borders. If fetishism involves private history, with individual means transferred to certain objects of desire, public community discourse differs because it deals with conflicts distributed throughout a society. It seeks to trace the outlines of a future history on the basis of reflections on decadence, using, virtually without exception, the remains of other cultures and other histories. Although many such discourses appeal to archaic features, they also bear the sign of modernity when they voice threats that are only implied in other countries. From a mass of these texts, we can cull a few problems that configure the political matrix of the literature: how to classify or integrate new cultures, which strategies to employ in the modernizing process, what cultural policies to adopt toward forms of imperialism, what values should be preserved and recovered from traditional culture, the place of art and the artist in the new order ruled by exchange values, and how to describe relations in mass societies. These types of community discourse and their utopian variants serve to offset modernity, by aiming at the totality that the latter rejects.

Revolutionary, anarchist, socialist, and rebel: This is how Rubén Darío greeted the young poet Leopoldo Lugones, who arrived in Buenos Aires in 1896, and whose only letters of presentation were his strange verses and emphatic prose. Although the epithets did not suffice to permit his inclusion in *Los raros* (Darío chose the Cuban Martí to represent Latin America), Lugones undoubtedly adopted a messianic pose with great success. In his work, the development of a nationalistic and epic discourse parallels that of a fantastic discourse that incorporates both positivist explanations and the heterodoxies of occultism. Sometimes, Lugones the *modernista* presages the theorists of nationality: *La guerra gaucha* (1905) is a text that juxtaposes *modernista* discourse and the ideology of a patriotic *criollo* nationalism. The most startling characteristic of this work was the lies with which Lugones retells the wars of liberation. The lament for the lost unity of Spanish America prompts him to an impossible return to the classic epic—knowing that its replacement would be a short story. The literary problem that had to be solved was how to produce an epic in the twentieth century that would transmit the didactic fervor of the genre. Lugones responded with his own formula, by taking *modernista* resources to an extreme, and writing in a way that Jorge Luis Borges (1899–1986) disliked–in other words, by using all the words in the dictionary and inventing new ones for good measure.

On the basis of the analysis of Lugones's organicist metaphors, María Teresa Gramuglio interprets the figure of Güemes in *La guerra gaucha* as the supreme leader capable of organizing the war and thinking about politics at the same time; the *caudillo* was the symbolic head while the *gauchos* were reduced to a mute body, producing an organic whole. Yet, although the voice of the gaucho had been virtually elided and the narrator possessed the only authoritative voice (portraying himself as the creator of national memory), there are other heroes and heroines. And herein lies an important twist. Examples include the patriotic Indians—one of the few positive representations of them in Argentine literature—and the patriotic

witch, placed in the foreground in the story entitled "Castigo." There is also the patriotic idiot in "Vado," and the Indian sacristan in "Dianas." Read in sequence, the stories imply that war was a collective, supportive undertaking. This absence of the gaucho's own voice may be linked to the idea of the collective nature of a national struggle, but there is also an undeniable aim of homogenizing the distinct and plural into one national voice. The voice of the nation thus moves effortlessly between populism and authoritarianism.

Immanuel Wallerstein holds that the concept of "the people" holds the key to the past. The first two decades of the twentieth century are a favorite period for a nationalistic discourse of restoration of past glory or the redemption of thwarted greatness. Both terms–restoration and redemption–are stock terms in nationalistic rhetoric and are used extensively in *La Guerra Gaucha* by the lettered narrator. Although the text eliminates the voice of the gaucho, the text does highlight the vast number of skills he possesses: singing, animal tracking, popular medicine, animal training, tiger hunting, fighting, the manufacture of weapons, and silverwork. The so-called *montoneros* were defined particularly by remaining silent and resisting all adversity. This collective subject is individualized in the last story in the figure of Güemes, the leader who links all subjectivities into one image that fused the hero with the fatherland. In a number of texts, Lugones condenses national identity into a handful of values: civilization, patriotism, freedom, and justice. Transformed into epithets, these operate like a matrix of gaucho identity as outlined in *El payador* (1916). The essay traces the making of Argentine identity through the figure of the gaucho, who was, by then, eliminated except in fiction. The Argentine character is said to be the result of the embodiment of these universals in a representative body like the *montoneros* and the particular gaucho expression based on a constructed collective geography and history.

Constructed on the basis of analogies and genealogies, from the outset, *El payador* reveals its intention to articulate an Argentine identity as as well as its constituent elements:

> Producir un poema épico, es, para todo el pueblo, certificado eminente de aptitud vital; porque dicha creación expresa la vida heroica de su raza. Esta vida comporta de suyo la suprema excelencia humana, y con ello, el éxito superior que la raza puede alcanzar: la afirmación de su entidad como tal, entre los mejores de la tierra. Ello nada tiene que ver con la magnitud del suelo perteneciente, ni con la cantidad de población, porque se trata de un estado espiritual al cual llamamos el alma de la raza. (18)

> The creation of an epic poem is for an entire people; it is an eminent certificate of vital aptitude, because this creation expresses the heroic life of its race. This life entails supreme human excellence and through it, the greatest success that the race can achieve: the affirmation of its identity as such, to be among the finest on earth. This has nothing to do with the extent of the land it possesses, or with the size of its population; it has everything to do with a spiritual state, which we call the soul of the race.

The name of the author is erased to emphasize the collective nature of the work; the subject is the people to whom this description corresponds. Nationality transcends the body, yet its immateriality is visible in a particular soil and in an individual character.

While Domingo Faustino Sarmiento (1811–1888) equated gauchos with barbarity, Lugones regarded them as the "héroe(s) y civilizador(es) de la pampa" (36) ("heroes and civilizers of the pampa"). And although both agreed on the radical difference between gauchos and Indians, their works point to several other enemies of the people. While Sarmiento is entirely Eurocentric ethnically and culturally, Lugones' prose points to at least two enemies: the Indian, who is stigmatized as having subhuman features; and the immigrant, who appears briefly in his prose, already depicted as a bird of prey in the 1880s. Nationalistic discourse sketched exemplary types which, in the case of *El payador,* are summarized in the phrase: "modelo de vida integral" ("his life was the model of a full life"), "Ha muerto era un hombre" ("He lived. He died. He was a man,") (62)–so goes the epitaph the essayist proposes for the hero's tomb. In addition to his private qualities, the gaucho, as the personification of male heroics, also has distinctive social attributes: serenity, courage, and vigor, which blend with frankness, loyalty, and generosity. His identity is a combination of the variety of roles he has taken on–gaucho-soldier, gaucho-poet, gaucho-civilizer, and gaucho-worker, together with a handful of chivalrous attitudes bequeathed to future generations. The writer manages to insert himself into the group by undertaking the task of interpreting the legacy of the gaucho. First, Lugones nationalizes the gaucho poet, investing him with the function of the making of a national literature; then he inserts him into a universal system of values in order to construct the cultural identity of Argentina by linking José Hernández's (1834–1886) *Martín Fierro* (1872) to an ancient heritage of courage, freedom, and poetry. Lugones devotes several paragraphs to the national character of the language of the poem, another topic dear to Latin American nationalism at this time. Through its etymological explorations, the text concludes that the language of the poem, and consequently of the gaucho, is derived from Latin; its predecessors are identified as Spanish popular literature, collections of ballads, and the picaresque novel–mainly because of the close links all of these genres maintained with the people. The other feature to note, besides linguistic archaism, is virility: The national language is said to be an original, primitive, masculine language.

Ricardo Rojas's (1882–1957) nationalism is distinguished from that of Lugones by its pursuit of more democratic ideals, which translate into strategies that encourage combination rather than separation, integration rather than exclusion. He is, however, careful to establish limits to the Argentine capacity to absorb differences, since, "Todo ha de ser argentino sobre la tierra argentina!" (148) ("Everything on Argentine soil must be Argentine!"). In *Blasón de plata* [1912; Silver Blazon], whose intertexts are the early colonial chronicles–El Inca Garcilaso's (1540–1616) *Comentarios reales* (1609 and 1616) and legends of the oral tradition–regional identity that dates back to a foundational Guaraní myth telling of the birth of the community. To prevent war, the two heirs, Tupí and Guaraní, divided the territory, one taking the north, the other the south. In this text, Rojas reinterprets this first of the many dismemberments that would take place. In the long history of the region, seen through the topos of envy and fratricide from the story of Cain and Abel, discord appears to be the recurring fate of its people. (This is also what we read in Mario de Andrade's (1893–1945) *Macunaíma* (1928): the duel between "o herói sem nenhum caráter" ["the hero without any character"] and his brother Jiguê).

In addition to *Blasón de plata*, Rojas wrote other nationalistic essays of note: *La restauración nacionalista* [1909; Nationalist Restoration], *La argentinidad* [1922; Being Argentine] and *Eurindia* (1924). In each of these, he describes three traditions:

the Indian, the Spanish, and the Argentine revolutionary traditions, which at the same time serve him to divide the history of Argentine literature into distinct periods. He begins with the Colonial period; follows it with the Gaucho, the exiled, and then a new period, the "Modern," which is the period of the convergence between the one before and cosmopolitan individualism. This last option determines his linguistic policy, which is, above all, one of an integration of all forms of discourse. But his vision of integration was also territorial: The map it outlined went far beyond existing borders, restoring the boundaries of Argentina to those of the ancient Inca civilization, the original space that is also the foundational place of a culture and certain appropriate political forms. In Rojas, nationality is a sort of variation on the expanded American spirit. *Blasón de plata* questions the "territorial conscience of the people." Regardless of the differences, the land is the center of belonging, investing people with its energy, overwhelming them and, like a mother, giving birth to them; it is the origin from which all the signs of culture are traced: "Cualquiera sea el idioma de nuestro patronímico o la genealogía de nuestros padres, un parentesco espiritual nos asemeja, por el solo hecho de nuestro gentilicio y de nuestra cuna, a todas las generaciones que antes de nosotros hayan respirado en la tierra argentina" (98) ("Regardless of the language of our surname or the genealogy of our parents, a spiritual kinship brings us together, because of the mere fact of our shared heritage and our common origin, that ties us to all the generations before us who have ever lived on Argentine soil").

The writer takes possession of the voice of memory: "La tierra que habla por la voz de sus poetas, ha evitado que se realizara también el círculo del humo del olvido" (72) ("The land, which speaks through the voice of its poets, has also prevented the formation of the cloud of smoke of oblivion"). Rojas retells the myth in which Viracocha orders the Inca to unify the peoples under a single government, religion, and language; he sees his role as writer determined by this injunction, and his essays can be read as his form of fulfillment of this ancient command. If the nation is the result of successive strata of communities, national history is a continuum that is enriched by numerous legacies. This is how both the collective identity of the people and the personal identity of the writer come together. When Rojas says that Tupac Amaru's "lengua cortada por los extranjeros predica todavía la restauración" (89) ("tongue, cut out by foreigners, still preaches the restoration of the Inca throne"), his position is successor to Tupac Amaru. He, as writer, must speak on behalf of the fallen Indian leader who is unable to do so and so he calls upon him to bolster his spirit against threats from the outside world. In order to create a national identity for the future, Rojas must eliminate Sarmiento's dichotomy of civilization and barbarity. He proposes a complementary relationship between "exoticism" and "Indianism"; the name of the new fatherland, "Eurindia," contains the best features of both legacies. In this respect, this essay challenges the stereotype of the brutalized Indian established by earlier writing. Rojas believed that, although colonial discourse homogenized the enormous heterogeneity of the peoples when it attempted to construct a national genealogy, it did assert certain peculiarities that made distinctions in what had been presented as the same. Thus Rojas asserted that the Inca civilization had a great culture and a warrior's courage for confronting foreigners; above all, they possessed a feeling of belonging and a sense of the fatherland.

Another line of argument about nationality arises from the struggles for independence based on the universal principles of the Rights of Man promulgated by the French Revolution. This argument would therefore seem to imply that "*criollo*," "Patriot," and "American" are synonyms. However, at the end of the essay, Rojas's discourse turns into a harangue. He now addresses an audience of immigrants, anarchists, and communists, creating a warning in a threatening tone through the use of the imperative and the insistence of anaphora:

> Renuncien, pues, los extranjeros de la inmigración a torcer esa ley de la vida en el planeta, fundamento de razas y de patrias. Renuncien igualmente a ello los anunciadores de una fraternidad materialista, que no sería sino la convivencia de hombres heterogéneos en una sorda hostilidad babélica. Póngase unos y otros del lado de esta fórmula nueva y racional, revelada por la historia; fórmula que es indianismo cuando mira a la tierra y a la raza, y que es nacionalismo cuando mira al Estado y a la civilización. (150)

> Foreign immigrants, you must relinquish your attempts to distort the law of life on earth, the basis of all races and fatherlands everywhere; renounce all your proclamations of a materialistic brotherhood, since such a situation would be nothing more than the coexistence of heterogeneous men in a deaf, Babelian state of mutual hostility. All of you must support the new rational formula revealed to us by history, a formula that is Indianism, which, when it looks at the earth and the human race, creates nationalism and, when it considers the State, produces civilization.

To move to another example of nationalistic discourse, Antonio Candido considers the lengthy, polemical work of Sílvio Romero (1851–1914) as turbulent agitation and an unstable image of the nation. In Romero's view, those who criticize his work should interpret culture and produce evaluative judgments with the aim of changing the status quo:

> A nós que temos vivido de contrafações indigestas, a nós que não temos vida própria, que somos um dos povos mais deteriorados do globo; que, espécie de contrabandistas do pensamento, não temos a força das grandes conquistas e das grandes verdades da ciência, só a crítica, a tão desdenhada crítica, nos pode preparar um futuro melhor. (3)

> Those of us who have lived in indigenist imitation, those of us without our own life, we are one of the most deteriorated people of the globe; as a kind of a smuggler of thought, we do not have the strength of the great conquests, nor of the truths of science—just criticism, the disdained criticism, that can prepare us for a better future.

The conflict of ideas in Romero leads to vacillating attitudes, ranging from the exaltation of patriotism to a radical pessimism when the subject is Brazil. He alternates racist positions with sympathy for cultural and ethnic miscegenation; he ventures to adopt democratic positions without relinquishing a certain distrust of the people. He praises German nationalism to offset the predominant influence of France, while still remaining faithful to certain Gallic cultural ideas of individual freedom. He expresses socialist ideals, while declaring the impossibility of their implementation in Brazil; he proposes the need for scientific objectivity in cultural criticism, while suggesting evaluative tasks for this in the future (Ventura 75).

Romero was a staunch defender of national causes. He attacked the false picturesqueness of romantic Indianism and proposes *mestizaje* as the only future of Brazilian culture. The unifying function of miscegenation and the adaptation of *mestizos* to an environment that is uniquely their own serve as the scaffolding for the creation of Brazilian nationality. As a supporter of diversity, he accepts the importance of the environment and the acceptance of diverse ethnic groups; yet, in order to dilute excessive group determinism, he calls for a privileged place to be given to the individual: "que em cada homem é uma resultante obscura de toda a evolução cósmica e humana, a resultante de um passado indeterminado pela complexidade inexplicável de sua indefinita duração" (40) ("that each person is the obscure result of the entire cosmic and human evolution, the result of an indeterminate past of unexplainable complexity and uncertain endurance"). In political commentary that resembles the statements of Borges in the 1920s, this Brazilian writer bases nationality on subjective, intimate aspects: "um caráter nacional não se procura, não se inventa, não se escolhe; nasce espontaneamente, bebe-se com o leite da vida, respira-se no ar da pátria" (29) ("one does not look for national character, it is not invented, it is not chosen; it is born spontaneously, it is to be drunk with the milk of life, it is breathed in the air of our country"). And although he is far removed from Borges' sense of precision on the matter (that is, nationality as an exploration of a characteristic tone of voice, a particular use of language), Romero shares Borges' similar views on nationalism's fatal condition, a fatality that is cultural in Borges but racial in Romero: "Tal diversidade manifesta-se também nas literaturas e, por isso, a determinação do caráter nacional nas letras não é um capricho; senão a comprovação de um fato" (30) ("Such diversity is also manifested in literature, and, for that reason, the determination of the national character in literature is not a whim, but the confirmation of a fact"). For Romero, the key lies in the perspective taken in writing about or interpreting cultural models. Above all, in establishing the foundation of a Brazilian transformation in which Portuguese, black, and Indian elements combine, Romero defends a Brazilian identity that is not the sum of these three elements but something different, something unique: a new race, not African, European, or Indian, but only Brazilian. Romero considers American cultures as hybrid creations of heterogeneous elements living together. Far from being limited to genes, race is a slippery notion that involves various historical and cultural processes. But spheres overlap to such an extent that features are exchanged from one race to another and "inferior forms" are eventually eliminated by a gradual whitening: "Those qualities of ethnic character are the foundation and strength of our literary nationalism" (31).

In 1910, Manuel Gálvez (1882–1962) paid homage to the Centenary of the May Revolution against Spain in the *Diario de Gabriel Quiroga* [The Diary of Gabriel Quiroga], a veritable catalog of nationalistic rhetoric. Nearly incomprehensible pages trace a sort of ethnography that posits a return to tradition. The fictitious author—an iconoclastic mix of skeptical bohemian, Nietzschean apprentice, and folkloric archaeologist—turns into an obstinate patriot after a trip to Europe. But the grotesque seriousness of Gálvez's incongruous amalgamation of notions of nation becomes pathetic irony in Lima Barreto's (1881–1922) *Triste fim de Policarpo Quaresma* [1911; *The Patriot*, 1978], whose main character is also engaged in the ignoble profession of being a patriot. This text is the opposite of a nationalistic discourse; the novel's action follows a path that goes from initial idealism to profound disillusionment. Quaresma is a passionate reader, a modern reincarnation of Don Quixote, who discovers the history of Brazil through books, not through experience, forgetting the lesson that Cervantes (1547–1616) gave the world: Don Quixote's idealism, born out of reading, was considered madness by all, including his narrator. In his journey to discover his roots, Quaresma exhausts the local libraries, which do give him the essence of nationalism; he moves on to the study of the Tupí language and Indian customs, investigates the popular music of the *modinhas*, devotes himself to farming, but finally comes up against the disaster of war, which thrusts him violently into a crude reality. The narration underlines the loneliness of the eccentric whose inability to adapt to the times and the environment invariably leads to the asylum or death. When a guitarist suggests to him finding relief in dreams, Quaresma replies: "Consola, talvez; mas faz-nos também diferentes dos outros, cava abismos entre os homens" (61) ("Dreams console, perhaps, but they also makes us different from others, they create abysses between men").

In a distorted world, only children can undertake heroic actions. Using doubled structures, but escaping the grip of stereotypes, Lima Barreto takes society's pulse and finds that salvation is in the hands of the common people. He takes refuge in an affective alliance of common people and rejects the verbal promises of the saviors of the fatherland, and the proximity of resurrection (the name Quaresma, meaning Lent, indicates this potential anticipation). This is an affective rather than a political alliance among those who are ordinary people: the immigrant Coleoni, the popular artist with the obvious name (Ricardo Coracão dos Outros), the average, idealistic man (whose disappearance reveals the necessary aim of a tradition that rejects change), and the woman who flouts convention–these form a collective that does not take refuge in rhetorical hyperbole. In the dénouement, the vague hope is transferred from Quaresma to the young Olga: "Tinha havido grandes e inúmeras modificações. Que fora aquele parque? Talvez um charco. Tinha havido grandes modificações nos aspectos, na fisionomia da terra, talvez no clima . . . Esperemos mais, pensou ela; e seguiu serenamente ao encontro de Ricardo Coração dos Outros" (182) ("There had been large and countless modifications in the appearance, in the land's physiognomy, maybe even in the weather. We expect more, she thought; and she continued serenely to her meeting with Ricardo Coração dos Outros"). This irritating silence may have been responsible for the silence that surrounded the novel when it began to be published as a serial in the *Jornal do Comércio*.

A People for a Continent

In Rubén Darío's *El canto errante* (1907), the poet is a demiurge with different Latin American accents. As lyric voice, he links the past and the future of this part of the world by choosing two means of retelling history–from the perspective of a future paradise and old Indian legends. There is also a special place for salutations to Utopia and prayers to heroes. If Latin American writing brings together heterogeneous material, it is because the mission of the wandering poet-minstrel is to traverse the diversity of geographies and engage the multiplicity of events. The poet adapts to times and cultures by turning into a time traveler who crosses through modernity or returns to previous eras by covered wagon, car, gondola, horse, canoe, or train. These changes are aesthetic and political and entail retelling the past using traditional literary forms but from a modern ideological perspective. In *Tutecotzimi*, the ideas of social revolution and justice are transported to an Indian past modeled on a concept of wisdom in which the people, as the true sovereign, punish the tyrant and anoint a common man as king, who then sings a Mexican song about

peace and work. Darío sketches the roles that exist in society for the poet and the people at the end of the century: the poet is the prophetic voice, but he must reach the people and make an alliance with them. The people as sovereign can thus achieve justice. Darío interprets the recent history of Latin America through the multiple conflicts between tyranny and law, and he outlines an ideal geography that satisfies both the material and physical needs of the people, thus redrawing the political map of Latin America.

Darío was annoyed by nihilism, but even more by the pompous pretentiousness of the patriotic spirit, even though he himself had indulged in such writing at one time. When he became melancholic, he produced his manacled poetry; when he had to forge an identity for himself, he preferred sarcasm and duplicity: "Abuelo, preciso es decíroslo: mi esposa es de mi tierra; mi querida de Paris" ("Old man, I must tell you, my wife is a fellow countrywoman; my mistress is from Paris") (1977, 180). Beauty does not shout, it prefers halftones; identity is not recited, it is sought in the monuments of ancient or modern culture, in Palenque, Utatlán, or Buenos Aires. A multiple sense of belonging often emerges in his work, crystallizing in *Canto a la Argentina*. In it, Argentina is his adopted country, and he traces the outlines of a Utopia which includes the extremes: modernity and tradition, rural life and the city, the immigrant urban masses and the rural population, popular legends and lettered poetry, the Wars of Independence with their anonymous heroes and soldiers, all framed by the national anthem. The image of the promised land links the past to the future in a continuum of time in which both local and foreign traditions join the present of machines and industrialization to participate in the construction of a single national history placed under the aegis of universal rights of man. The Americanist discourse is twofold: It reaffirms traditions, while embracing modernity.

The struggle between the spiritual side of life and materialistic concerns was reworked in a *fin-de-siècle*, anti-imperialist literary code, and had its greatest expression in Rodó's *Ariel* (1900). The Shakespearean opposition of Prospero and Caliban, so often employed by European thinkers, became, in Latin American hands, the framework for an evolutionary history of ideas and cultures in conflict. The savage with an imposed language and culture eventually rebels against his master; but in Rodo's hands, Prospero is still the guardian of truth and Caliban is still learning. Rodó had no doubts: America must be Latin and, to avoid any errors, he clarified what this meant: It involved the overlapping of the legacies of Greco-Latin culture–order, hierarchy, and respect for creative genius–with the egalitarian spirit of Christianity. *Ariel* is a program for vital regeneration that links culture and society and in which aesthetics functions as the means of achieving moral ends. The old master hands over his legacy to youth in order to fulfill his mission of articulating the liberating premises of culture for the people. The master solves the current enigmas for his disciples by taking a leap forward, which is, in fact, a leap backward, since he finds the ideal in the restoration of the Greco-Roman heritage of the Latin world.

The wise Prospero speaks in the future tense, so much so that he ends each of his themes with a moral of hope. When he judges the century, literature–with its abundance of European references and shortage of American names–provides him with essential clues, as he outlines in detail the processes that have led to "disminución de *juventud interior y de energía*" (Rodó 1919, 32) ("a reduction of inner youth and energy"). The word implied but not said is obviously *degeneration*, here replaced by *reduction*. But this denunciation, which has been avoided at the cultural level, emerges when the essay changes tack and confronts the political system. Democracy–"the ignoble predominance of numbers"–is therefore judged severely. Through a series of strategies that use (in a gesture reminiscent of Sarmiento) everything that will further the current arrangement–from the liberal politics advocating popular education to the argumentative legitimization of Darwinian science–Rodó expresses a conditional acceptance of democracy by incorporating the struggle for the ideal of spiritual values within a hierarchical structure. At the end, the closing scene justifies the dignity of the guide to the future: "Mientras la muchedumbre pasa, yo observo que, aunque ella no mira al cielo, el cielo la mira. Sobre su masa indiferente y oscura, como tierra del surco, algo desciende de lo alto. La vibración de las estrellas se parece al movimiento de unas manos de sembrador" (Rodó 1919, 144) ("As the crowd passes by, I can see that, although the crowd is not looking at the sky, the sky is looking at it. Over its dark, indifferent mass, like furrowed land, something descends from on high. The vibration of the stars resembles the movement of the sower's hands"). The social values are forthcoming from above.

Contrary to *Ariel*, the anti-imperialist discourse of Martí's "Nuestra América" solves the enigma of Latin American identity. In answer to the question, "Who are we?", Martí responds vehemently; by attacking the very concept of race: "No hay odio de razas, porque no hay razas" (17) ("There is no hatred between races because there are no races"). He thus incorporates ethnic struggles into the fight for freedom. Martí has no doubts: America is *mestizo*, not European, or African, or Indian. For this reason, his Latin American history is a history of the combatants of the Wars of Independence. The "soul of the earth" or the "continental soul" moves away from all ideological essentialism, focusing instead on the feasibility of armed or intellectual liberation. The position of the speaker is quite clear: "Con los oprimidos había que hacer causa común, para afianzar el sistema opuesto a los intereses y hábitos de mando de los opresores" (14) ("With the oppressed, one had to fight for a common cause, find a way to strengthen a system that was opposed to the interests and ruling customs of the oppressors"). Using harsh terms and turbulent prose, the Cuban appeals to the political class to correct past historical distortions. He warns of the historical errors to which decontextualized ideas lead and calls for the establishment of a national political leadership. The reinterpretation of Sarmiento's dichotomy of civilization versus barbarism transfers what is foreign and what is Cuban into political and cultural dichotomies. Martí draws interpretative clues from the lives of the oppressed, continuing the story in "Madre América": "¿Y como no recordar, para gloria de los que han sabido vencer a pesar de ellos, los orígenes confusos y manchados de sangre de nuestra América? (. . .) Del arado nació la América del Norte, y la española, del perro de presa" (22–23) ("Our America: And how could one not fail to recall those who have been able to overcome the legacy of the confused, bloodstained origins of our America? North America was born from the plow and Spanish America from the hunting dog"). In this approach to history, which sometimes slips into antimodern posturing, there is also a place devoted to modernization: Latin America is also a place of books, newspapers, railways, and cities.

Heroes and Martyrs of Science

The pseudoscientific search for the distinguishing ethnic and racial features that would establish national identity returns to haunt society as racism. A strong taste for the esoteric runs opposite to the scientific spirit of the period. Faced with a decadent world, *fin-de-siècle* people found a suitable antidote in mysticism. The appetite for mystery is general; it appears in the heart of the fiction of everyday events, and in the return of fairy stories–by Gutiérrez Nájera (1859–1895) or Darío himself–or in the popular legends of spirits and ghosts. At other times, it involves stories where a diffuse animism anthropomorphizes nature. Some texts display theosophic principles, spiritualist beliefs, and Pythagorean mysteries, interwoven with anarchist or Masonic beliefs. In spite of differences in detail, a certain common thread holds together this eclecticism: the belief that invisible, cosmic forces dominate life. Both matter and spirit are seen as manifestations of a single animistic force; the cosmos is constantly changing, but the expert who manipulates these forces is identified as the artist who penetrates the world of the occult (Fraser 125). Occultism has a long history in Europe. Of course, in Latin America, one of its most widely publicized aspects was spiritualism; this expansion was largely due to the work of Allan Kardec and the foundation of the American Society of Theosophy by Mme. Blavatsky. In the nineteenth century, Victor Hugo was a spiritualist, while William James, Théophile Gautier, and Stéphane Mallarmé were also interested in these doctrines. Poe regarded himself as a medium, and Yeats believed in the spiritual world. In Latin America, occult doctrines and ideas impassioned intellectuals and public figures such as Martí, Darío, Amado Nervo, Francisco Madero, and João do Río, to name but a few.

In Rio de Janeiro, the interest of the Baudelairean-Symbolist poets focused on Kardecism and the Rosicrucian movement, but it was in Buenos Aires that Latin American occultism reached its peak. Its popularity at the end of the century is borne out by numerous articles and testimonies published in the popular magazine *Caras y Caretas*. Alfredo Palacios (1878–1965), Leopoldo Lugones (1874–1938), José Ingenieros (1877–1925), and Emilio Becher (1882–1921) all were avid followers of Theosophy. In 1897, *La Syringa*, named by Rubén Darío, was published by a sort of literary coterie that attracted young Bohemians, many with Masonic affiliation. Darío himself, Florencio Sánchez (1875–1910), Leopoldo Lugones, José Ingenieros, and Enrique García Velloso (1880–1938) were part of this secret society. In a series of thoughtful reflections on these issues, Jorge Salessi has chosen the work and life of Ingenieros to illustrate some of the strategies used for inclusion in and exclusion from the group. In referring to the activities of this society, Salessi reports the testimony by Héctor Agosti: "La Syringa sometía a sus miembros a numerosas pruebas de iniciación que eran motivo de tremendas bromas a costa de algunos aspirantes a genio, que se suponían ungidos con las dotes de los 'syringos'" (*La Syringa* subjected its members to several tests of initiation, which led to tremendous practical jokes at the expense of certain aspirants who believed they were blessed with the gifts of the *Syringos*") (144). Occultism was organized around the axis of religion and science, either to create a sort of tension between the two or to propose a type of knowledge that confronted hegemonic positivism. The conflict between science and faith is the matrix of *La Extraña Muerte de Fray Pedro* [The Strange Death of Fray Pedro], published by Darío in Paris in 1913. The story tells of the alienation of a friar caused by his attempts to prove the existence of God by using X-rays. Science is the modern devil in the guise of a priest who places the fatal instrument in Fray Pedro's hands. The story has the transparency of an apodictical truth and an exemplary ending in which triumph and death converge. The experiment is tautological and re-establishes the truth of religion by using scientific methods to verify what the doctrine teaches: the sacred Host is the body of Christ.

Far removed from Darío's levity, Lugones takes up the idea of the imminent destruction of those who exceed the limits of the knowable world, or of those who, lacking sufficient knowledge, tempt cosmic forces. Lugones' *Las fuerzas extrañas* [1906; The Strange Forces] is a book that lends itself equally to a political and an esoteric interpretation. If in *La guerra gaucha* there is the need for a leader to direct social forces (and the figure of the military commander fills this gap), in *Las fuerzas extrañas* Lugones' prose links the fantastic and the esoteric to an extreme nationalistic discourse, which clearly anticipates his eventual shift toward Fascism in the 1930s. The idea of a great spiritual force structures these stories. More than just stories involving supernatural phenomena or ancient surroundings, of speakers coming from ancient times, or containing biblical references, the central idea here is that of the release or containment of the force and the dreadful consequences that will befall humanity by the destruction of cosmic unity. In "Un fenómeno inexplicable" [An Unexplainable Phenomenon], a passion for science links the narrator and an Englishman who challenges the relationship of physical causality in order to support the hypothesis that even a minimal amount of physical displacement may cause disaster.

"Yzur," perhaps his best story, brings together various strands of his nationalistic discourse, combining it with Darwinian evolutionary ideas. A monkey is the "pedagogical subject" par excellence–malleable material–which is obliged to learn, through extreme coercion, the language of its owner. The point where the animal achieves its greatest humanization–namely, in the acquisition of language–causes its death; but before it breathes its last breath, it utters the terrible words that reflect the success of its owner: *"Amo, agua. amo, mi amo . . ."* (1993, 166) ("Master, water. master, my master . . ."). The text depicts a history of submission through violence, the victory of the strong over the weak, as well as the act of supreme resistance by the dominated creature: the monkey remains silent until the end of his life. When he dies, he expresses his own fleeting triumph over his master. In *"Los caballos de Abdera,"* the fundamental harmony between mankind and nature is disturbed by social ills such as the gradual gain in bourgeois values, esoteric refinements and empty banalities, and moral perversions of all kinds, which have an alienating effect on the natural world. An indifferent society has disturbed the natural order, causing an attack on society by the displaced hordes. The final battle is between the enraged hordes and Hercules, a combination of mythological hero and Nietzschean superman. In an unexpected inversion, it is an unconquered nature that rescues decadent society from the chaos it has brought on itself. The narrative provides a detailed account of the latent dangers of the animal-like masses when they seek to free themselves from their natural place through wanton destruction.

Rebellion and the tyranny of science are the main themes of the novel *O alienista* [The Alienist], which Machado de Assis includes in *Papeis Avulsos* [1882; Doubtful Papers]. With skepticism and caustic humor, the narrator brings together two types of revolutions–the scientific and the social–or, rather, he mocks both of them by creating absurd situations: the scientific deliriums of an emerging discipline of psychiatry and the manipulation and control of the masses by unscrupulous individuals. Legitimized by the prestige conferred on him by having studied in Europe, Dr. Simão Bacamarte inaugurates the Casa Verde, a lunatic asylum. Obsessed with establishing the exact boundaries between reason and dementia, the psychiatrist tests typologies into which virtually all types of behaviors fit. Yet by expanding the concept of madness to any modification in behavior, the physician transforms the asylum into a prison in which the majority of citizens are confined. When terror takes hold of the city, its inhabitants plan the first rebellion, led by the barber, hungry for public authority. The narrator notes sardonically, "A ação podia ser restrita,–visto que muita gente, ou por medo, ou por hábitos de educação, não descia à rua; mas o sentimento era unânime, e os trezentos que caminhavam para a Casa Verde,–dada a diferença de Paris a Itaguaí,–podiam ser comparados aos que tomaram a Bastilha" (35) ("Action could be restricted, since many people, out of fear or out of manners, would not step down into the street; but the sentiment was unanimous, and the three hundred people who walked to Casa Verde,–given the difference between Paris and Itaguaí–could be compared to the ones who overtook the Bastille") . In this short fable on power that anticipates, albeit in a derisive manner, the technologies of control and discipline theorized by Foucault; a few deft strokes suffice to lay bare the authoritarian, oppressive features of modern science, while exposing the niggardly interests of the ruling classes, their longing for power, their shady business dealings, their cowardliness, their manipulation of the masses, their facile deception through pseudodemocratic discourse, and the general lack of awareness of basic information. Science and the enacted laws to control behavior contradict common sense to such an extent that the counselor who suggests that the psychiatrist is the true lunatic ends up in the mental hospital himself. The story ends with the voluntary acceptance of an upside-down world, since the asylum is not demolished–nor is Simão Bacamarte punished. The incongruities of scientific thought–the limits of reason–are revealed the moment the physician reverses his hypotheses in such a way that normal people appear to be insane. When traditional social virtues such as modesty, tolerance, loyalty, and generosity become madness, the world is upside down. Finally, a victim of his own theory, the psychiatrist decides on his own confinement, believing absolutely in the correlation between perfection and madness; since he has attained perfection, he must be mad. Subtleties like this abound in Machado's work. *O alienista* is a summary of his main novels: *Memórias Póstumas de Brás Cubas* [The Posthumous Memoirs of Brás Cubas], *Quincas Borba*, *Dom Casmurro*, and *Esaú e Jacó*, among others. The significance of these texts in Brazilian letters cannot be overestimated, for Machado de Assis reveals not only the irrationality of a supposedly rational discourse, but the opacity and confusion of social and institutional relations in the modern world.

Suspicious Multitudes

The *fin-de-siècle* Latin American writer had an aversion to mediocrity, but an even greater aversion to mass culture. Multiple perspectives, including literary, political, sociological, biological, and psychological, deal with the masses and seek to elucidate the blind power of an always devastating, faceless social force personified by the wild mob. Gustave Le Bon establishes the stereotype of the masses in his "Psychologie des foules" [Psychology of the Masses], an essential reference during the early decades of the twentieth century. The comparison between the members of the masses and the cells of a living organism becomes a commonplace, together with other features such as the obliteration of the sense of individual responsibility; the supremacy of unpredictable sentimentality over rational personal interest; behavior as a result of contagion and high suggestibility; the dangerous and barbarous nature of the abandonment of the individual subject to the will of the mob; the elimination of intellectual debate in favor of emotionalism, a mental state deemed homologous with the life of primitives and children; and the desire to be dominated by a master leader, a desire that prefers illusion to truth. The impact of this theory was so great that, as late as 1921, Freud used Le Bon's ideas as the basis for his essay "The Psychology of the Masses." However, although Freud followed Le Bon, he also established a new view with his concept of libido in his analysis of group psychology. The collective psyche has such powerful affective links that panic is only produced when these links begin to crack. Freud saw the birth and development of the gregarious instinct in the need for justice; this implies that we deny ourselves certain things, such as taking another person's possessions, so that the rest of the group will also have to renounce them as well in the interest of harmonious coexistence.

This theme takes on discriminatory inflections in discourses that touch on madness, politics, and crime. The essays of the Argentine positivists are, in this respect, paradigmatic. At the start of the organization of the workers' movement, in which the anarchists played a decisive role, the social hygienists envisaged crime as a disease affecting the whole social body. In Argentina, discriminatory policies culminated in the Law of Residence, which authorized the expulsion of any foreigner accused of threatening the established order. In 1905, Moyano Gacitúa's *Delincuencia argentina* [1905; Argentine Delinquency] certified that the social imaginary of the immigrant, criminal, or agitator took shelter in urban anonymity in order to achieve perverse ends: "Immigrants do not disperse in the country; an excessive number of them crowd into the capitals, applying for nonexistent jobs; they flood the streets, struggling desperately to survive, living outside of wedlock and in promiscuity with their fellow country-folk, fostering strikes and disorder, and both acting as agitators at the same time being easily agitated" (Salessi 116).

José María Ramos Mejía (1849–1914) contrasted the physical and moral health and well-being of the multitudes of the revolution and independence era with the degradation of the subsequent immigrant masses. We should, however, keep in mind that this racist psychopathology does not begin with Ramos Mejía, but goes back to Sarmiento and his depiction of the racial struggle between Indians and Spaniards as a war between barbarism and civilization. Darwinism was now incorporated into a myth of origin that took on the form of a racial struggle, along the same lines developed earlier by Sarmiento. From *Facundo* to *Las multitudes argentinas* [1898; The Argentine Multitudes], an early historically derived view of nationality declined into a version that would stress only "the biological and psychopathological component, supported by the theory of degeneration" (Vezzetti 94). In *Las multitudes argentinas*, Ramos Mejía offers two analytical views:

that of the politician and that of the psychiatrist. Both undertake a social diagnosis on the basis of an examination of past history. This social diagnosis involves a sort of biological positivism that draws ideas from the natural sciences into the social and political fields in order to explain the phenomenon of the masses. He begins with a description of the transformations and functions of the masses in Viceregal times and during the Wars of Independence, shows how they were used by Rosas to sustain tyranny, and finally arrives at a description of the modern multitudes. The book, "a transformist fable" in the words of Vezzetti, portrays an Argentine history with a biological positivist bias in describing the changing roles of this collective subject, at once feared and desired; this is an attempt to capture the protean identity of the Argentine masses. The barely concealed aim is to devise principles of understanding on which to base strategies of governability.

According to the ideas then in vogue, the multitude reacts with emotive and instinctive behavior. Within it, the (male) subject buries his individuality in order to reduce himself to the anonymity of the "carbon-man," a simple chemical element capable of combining with others. This is the same author who feminizes the masses, describing them as little more than impulse and disorganization: "Por eso éstas son impresionables y veleidosas como las mujeres apasionadas, puro *inconsciente*, (. . .) porque la multitud es sensual, arrebatada y llena de lujuria para el placer de los sentidos. No raciocina, siente" (33) ("That is why they are impressionable and fickle, like passionate women, pure *unconsciousness*, (. . .) because the multitude is sensual, impetuous and full of lust for the pleasure of the senses. It does not reason, it feels"). Yet the multitude is also the *pharmakon*, the remedy and the poison. This ambivalent condition comes from the occasions on which it has fallen to the masses to act: Historical circumstances and political options determined and oriented both continuities and breaks. Heroic or vile, Ramos Mejía's view is twofold. On the one hand, he moves away from a linear historical conception; on the other, there is an evolutionary sense to his social metamorphoses: Just as the arrogant bird emerged from the reptile, so the emancipatory masses emerged from the colonial multitude.

Although the youthful masses grew up and achieved their maturity in the struggles for freedom, they also effected a brutal separation from the immigrants, the absolute other: "crepuscular," "larval," "el pesado palurdo que no siente como nosotros" (206) ("crepuscular, larval, the tiresome yokels who do not feel the way we do"). After the period of large scale immigration in the late nineteenth century, the masses became deformed. The foreigner was turned into the dwarf who moved around in a territory that did not belong to him: "Le veis cruzar la calle cuajada de gente bien dispuesto al *titeo* y a los manotones, asentando con aplomo terrible su pata alpatargada de paquidermo" (209) ("You see him cross a street full of similar people, eager to engage in primitive expressions of recognition, as he drags his heavy, sandaled pachyderm's foot along"). This grotesque xenophobia—which added the figure of the deformed dwarf of stunted development to the figures of the criminal and the madman—was somewhat diluted through the proposal that education could be a solution in the long run. Although the first generation may have been irredeemable, Ramos Mejía anticipated the nationalization of the coming generations through the schools and the inculcation of love for national symbols. Education was to offset inheritance, to such an extent that the essay was able to predict their human future with professorial seriousness: "Hay que observar a los niños de los últimos grados, para ver cómo de generación en generación se va modificando el tipo del inmigrante *hecho gente*" (213) ("One should observe the children in the higher grades to see how the physiognomy of immigrants, now fully humanized, is modified from generation to generation"). Although the inauspicious presence of the immigrant may be neutralized by these means, a shadow lies in wait at the end and imposes itself with the eloquence of hyperbole. The threat is called politicization; its protagonists are the socialist masses.

As if to offset this collection of social stereotypes, there are some well-written pages dedicated to minor participants in history: stories of women's lives, muleteers, farm workers, friars, and victims of the Inquisition. Summarizing the protohistory of emancipation, these types contain *in nuce* the future cultural identity of Argentina whose mainstay is the resistance to established power. Rummaging through documents and old histories, the essayist concludes:

> De repente ese *espíritu de rebelión* se amortigua o se interrumpe, y como uno de esos hilos de agua cristalina que discurren por la pendiente y que luego de ocultarse penetrando en el corazón de la montaña, surgen de nuevo inesperados pero más anchos y voluminosos, así parece que en el curso de los siglos entra aquél en la tierra patria a recibir sus fluidos jugosos y brotar a la superficie para no perderse jamás. (43)
>
> This *spirit of rebellion* is deadened or interrupted, but like one of those streams of crystalline water that slide down the slope and, after disappearing into the mountain, suddenly re-emerge, but much larger and more voluminous; so it seems that during the course of the centuries, a man returns to his fatherland to receive his essential fluids and re-emerge on the surface never to be lost again.

A key work of the period was *Os Sertões* [1902; *Rebellion in the Backlands*, 1944] by the Brazilian Euclides da Cunha (1866–1909), a tragic and dialectic vision of the Canudos rebellion in which two types of society, coastal and inland, and two periods, republican modernity and millenarian anachronism, are contrasted. The Republican positivism of Euclides, acquired at military school, gives *Os Sertões* a discourse alternating between sociological analysis and denunciation. Progressive convictions about the end of retrograde social elements give way to harsh criticism of the government for the massacre of the *jagunços*. Nevertheless, despite its evident sympathy for the conquered, the work is riddled with contradictions. Euclides attributes rebellion to racial factors rather than political conjunctures since, from his point of view, the identity of the *mestizo* is established in the struggle between races, one superior and the other inferior, which predominates. In a discourse tinged with racial and psychological determinism, which often echoes Sarmiento's *Facundo*, the influence of the environment on man, the similarity between the *jagunços* and the Bedouins, themes of madness, fanaticism, and the belief in a mysterious world as a popular platform for the caudillo, and the use of legends and popular stories—all establish a biography of conversion that turns out to be an aleph of society. The generic hybridity of *Os Sertões* posits the thesis that the community and the leader complement each other. The multitude creates the leader in its own image, by investing him with its own characteristics. A projected image and human oxymoron, Antonio Maciel is a bedeviled saint.

Oscar Terán regards positivism as a cultural movement for the construction of the nation. Since establishing links between the economy and politics requires cooperation and consensus, the dominant Argentinian sectors ponder how best to incorporate the immigrant masses into the regime of the working class and what means can be used to nationalize them. The disciplining of the immigrant, it is argued, can best be attained both by enacting mandatory public education and through specific cultural policies that would be informed by the new sciences, psychiatry and criminology, and would restrict the forces of madness, crime, and violence. Thus positivism medicalized law and, at the same time, regarded any social element that did not adapt to these national policies as pathological (Terán 22–23). In the midst of urban chaos, criminologists promoted a suspicion of the immigrant in order to distinguish appearance from the truth, for it was evident to them that criminal behavior could be concealed under the guise of madness in order to deceive the law. One should recall Ramos Mejía's *Los simuladores del talento* [1904; Simulators of Talent] or *La simulación de la locura* [1900; The Simulation of Madness] as well as *La simulación en la lucha por la vida* [1904; The Simulation in the Struggle for Life] by José Ingenieros, an essay whose ideology owes much to Molière's *Le malade imaginaire*. During the first decade of the twentieth century, Ingenieros' interests focused on criminology and psychiatry, an area in which he held public posts. The pathological structure of the multitude is linked to social Darwinism in *La simulación en la lucha por la vida*. His medical-legal eye glimpses the symptoms of simulators and draws up a scale ranging from the use of simulation as a strategy for coping with the environment of the criminal alibi. An apodictical Ingenieros notes: "Todos los hombres son simuladores, en mayor o menor grado, siendo ello indispensable para la adaptación de la conducta a las condiciones del medio. Pero la simulación es la nota dominante en el 'simulador característico', en quien la simulación es el medio preferido en la lucha por la vida" (169) ("All men are simulators, to a greater or lesser extent, since this is essential for adapting behavior to one's surrounding conditions. Yet simulation is the key note in the 'characteristic simulator' in whom simulation is the preferred means in the struggle for life"). Nevertheless, with persistent optimism, Ingenieros predicts a reduction of fraud as a result of the advance in culture that would cause a reduction in the need for the existential struggle by fostering solidarity. His prose describes the spaces of simulation and the types of simulations, incorporating anti-Semitic prejudice into the struggle between races, the repressive state in the class struggle, female pretense in the struggle between the sexes, the deception of political leaders and other groups, and colorful professions that include lawyers, jewelers, carpenters, and priests. At the end of the book, the arguments begin to ease, since the wisdom of the specialist who has penetrated these secrets brings camouflaged realities up to the surface.

Another Purpose?

The real world has become a fable, opines Friedrich Wilhelm Nietzsche in *The Twilight of the Idols* (1889). If absolute truth is replaced by particular truths, if science is unable to provide all the answers to human questions, and if history no longer follows the perfect path to progress, then all that remains is art. If we accept, with Baudelaire, that art makes a translation to life, the possible forms of organizing and lending meaning to cultural phenomena are rhetoric, fables, or legends. At the end of the nineteenth century, these fables are retold by combining the idealistic and the skeptical, the immoral and the moral, and are recounted in redemptive or discriminatory accents in discourses where the defense of modernity is punctuated by a criticism of the era impregnated either with nostalgic memories of a golden past or with palpitating utopic futurism.

Swans are said to be most beautiful at the point of death. In a series of "heterodox digressions," as Carlos Reyles (1868–1938) calls his essay "La muerte del cisne" [1910; "The Death of the Swan"], the Uruguayan writer identifies the causes of his social malaise: the nihilistic doctrine of the triumph of force, the praise of gold, and the decadence of the Latin culture. In tones ranging from anger to nostalgia, passing through cynicism, Reyles portrays a somber future:

> Entre mil tabulaciones, el curioso se pregunta, si está a punto de convertirse en realidad palpitante la transmutación de valores anunciada por el terrible profesor de Basilea, y si la Fuerza, como principio de la moral y medida de todas las cosas, no amenaza de muerte, a pesar de la Conferencia de la Haya y del humanitarismo, las entidades de las filosofías espirituales: Justicia, Derecho, Bien, Mal. (7–8)

> In the midst of a thousand tribulations, the curious wonder whether the transmutation of values announced by the terrible professor from Basel [Nietzsche] is about to come true, and whether Force, as a principle of morality and a measure of all things, is not, despite the Hague Conference and the Conference on Humanitarianism, issuing a death threat to the entities of spiritual philosophy: Justice, Law, Good, Evil.

Although historians despise repetition and vicious circles, the contradictions of the end of the nineteenth century guide the present ones: The crisis of representation, the refusal to think on the basis of totalizing models, the loss of the notion of a complete subject and Utopian dreams—all speak of a past that could hardly be more contemporary.

Translation by Suzanne D. Stephens

Works Cited

Andrade, Mario de. 1988. *Macunaíma o héroi sem nenhum carácter*. Ed. Telê Porto Ancona Lopez. Florianópolis: Colecção Arquivos.

Barreto, Lima [Afonso Henrique]. 1994. *Triste fim de Policarpo Quaresma*. São Paulo: Atica.

Baudelaire, Charles. 1976. "Le peintre de la vie moderne." *Oeuvres Complètes*. Paris: Gallimard, Bibliothèque de la Pléiade.

Benjamín, Walter. 1980. *Poesía y capitalismo. Iluminaciones 2*. 2d ed. Trans. and prologue by Jesús Aguirre. Madrid: Taurus.

Berman, Marshall. 1988. *All That Is Solid Melts into Air: The Experience of Modernity*. New York: Penguin Books.

Bilac, Olavo. 1996. *Vossa Insolência. Crônicas*. Ed. Antonio Dimas. São Paulo: Companhia das Letras.

Bourget, Paul. 1937. *Essais de Psychologie Contemporaine*. Paris: Librairie Plon.

Candido, Antonio. 1978. "Introducção." *Teoria, crítica e histórica literária*. By Sílvio Romero. Ed. Antonio Candido. São Paulo: EDUSP. i–xxx.

Cunha, Euclides da. 1995. *Os Sertões. Campanha de Canudos*. Rio de Janeiro: Francisco Alves.

Darío, Rubén. 1952. *Los raros*. Buenos Aires: Espasa-Calpe.

——. 1976. "Historia de mis libros." *Autobiografías*. Prologue by Enrique Anderson Imbert. Buenos Aires: Marymar. 155–78.

——. 1977. *Poesía*. Prologue by Angel Rama. Caracas: Biblioteca Ayacucho.

——. 1988. *Cuentos Completos*. 2d ed. Mexico City: Fondo de Cultura Económica.

Fraser, Howard. 1992. *In the Presence of Mystery: Modernist Fiction and the Occult*. Chapel Hill: University of North Carolina Press.

Freud, Sigmund. 1922. *Group Psychology and the Analysis of the Ego*. Trans. James Strachey. London: International Psycho-Analytical Press.

Gálvez, Manuel. 1932. *El general Quiroga*. Buenos Aires: La facultad, J. Roldaín y cía.

Gómez Carrillo, Enrique. N.d. *Treinta años de mi vida. Libro 2. En plena bohemia*. Madrid: Editorial "Mundo Latino."

Graça Aranha, José Pereira da. 1902. *Chanaan*. Rio de Janeiro: H. Garnier.

Gramuglio, María Teresa. 1997. "La primera épica de Lugones." *Prismas. Revista de historia intelectual* (Universidad Nacional de Quilmes) 1:157–63.

Ingenieros, José. 1990. *La simulación en la lucha por la vida*. Buenos Aires: Losada.

——. and Leopoldo Lugones. 1996. *La Montaña. Periódico socialista revolucionario–1897*. Buenos Aires: Universidad Nacional de Quilmes.

Kermode, Frank. 1967. *The Sense of an Ending: Studies in the Theory of Fiction*. London: Oxford UP.

Kirkpatrick, Gwen. 1989. *The Dissonant Legacy of Modernismo*. Berkeley: University of California Press.

Le Bon, Gustave. 1921. *Psychologie des foules*. Paris: Felix Alcan.

Lugones, Leopoldo. 1947. *Las montañas de oro*. Buenos Aires: Ediciones Centurión.

——. 1979. *El payador*. Caracas: Biblioteca Ayacucho.

——. 1992. *La guerra gaucha*. Buenos Aires: Losada.

——. 1993. *Las fuerzas extrañas. Cuentos fatales*. Intro. Noé Jitrik. Buenos Aires: Espasa-Calpe, Austral.

Machado de Assis, Joaquim Maria. 1993. *O alienista*. São Paulo: Principio.

Martí, José. 1980. *Nuestra América*. Intro. Pedro Henriquez Ureña. Buenos Aires: Losada.

——. 1989. *Obra literaria*. 2d ed. Caracas: Biblioteca Ayacucho.

Molloy, Sylvia. 1992. "Too Wilde for Comfort: Desire and Ideology in Fin-de-Siècle Spanish America." *Social Text* 31/32. 10: 187–201.

——. 1994. "La política de la pose." *Las culturas de fin de siglo en América Latina*. Ed. Josefina Ludmer. Rosario: Beatriz Viterbo. 128–37.

Nietzsche, Friedrich. 1985. *Así hablaba Zaratustra*. Trans. Juan Fernández. Buenos Aires: Siglo Veinte.

Rama, Angel. 1985. *Las máscaras democráticas del modernismo*. Montevideo: Fundación Angel Rama.

Ramos, Julio. 1989. *Desencuentros de la modernidad en América Latina: Literatura y política en el siglo XX*. Mexico City: Fondo de Cultura Económica, Tierra Firme.

Ramos Mejía, José M. 1977. *Las multitudes argentinas*. Buenos Aires: Editorial de Belgrano.

Reyles, Carlos. N.d. *El canto del cisne*. Paris: Librería Paul Ollendorff.

Rodó, José Enrique. N.d. *El que vendrá*. Montevideo: Claudio García & Cía.

——. 1919. *Ariel*. Ed. Leopoldo Alas (Clarín). Madrid: n.p.

Rojas, Ricardo. 1954. *Blasón de plata*. Buenos Aires: Losada.

Romero, José Luis. 1986. *Latinoamérica: las ciudades y las ideas*. 3d ed. Buenos Aires: Siglo Veintiuno.

Romero, Sílvio. 1978. *Teoria, crítica e histórica literária*. Ed. Antonio Candido. São Paulo: EDUSP.

Salessi, Jorge. 1995. *Médicos maleantes maricas*. Rosario: Beatriz Viterbo.

Silva, José Asunción. 1992. *De sobremesa*. Buenos Aires: Losada.

Terán, Oscar. 1986. *En busca de la ideología argentina*. Buenos Aires: Catálogos.

Ventura, Roberto. 1991. *Estilo Tropical: História cultural e polêmicas literárias no Brasil*. São Paulo: Companhia das Letras.

Vezzetti, Hugo. 1983. *La locura en la Argentina*. Buenos Aires: Folios.

Wallerstein, Immanuel. 1988. "La construction des peuples: racisme, nationalisme, ethnicité." *Race, Nation, Classe. Les identités ambigües*. Ed. Immanuel Wallerstein and Etienne Balibar. Paris: Edit. La Découverte. 95–116.

Williams, Raymond. 1973. *The Country and the City*. London: Chatto and Windus.

CHAPTER 43

THE STRUGGLE OVER THE PRINTED WORD
THE CATHOLIC CHURCH IN BRAZIL AND SOCIAL DISCOURSE

Aparecida Paiva

The Press in Brazil and Church-State Relations

Although it is not possible to lay out all major elements of the Catholic Church's discourse on the control over reading matter, we can at least review some of them here in context. Central to this endeavor will be Father Pedro Sinzig (1875–1952), a German Franciscan friar, naturalized Brazilian, director of the publishers Editora Vozes of Petrópolis for twelve years, and author of sixty-five books, including biographies, novels, and musical and didactic works. It is through his writings that we can reconstitute part of the discourse of, specifically, the Catholic censorship of reading in Brazil at the beginning of the twentieth century. There is no doubt that the Catholic Church learned, in the last decades of the *belle époque*, to recognize the significance and power of the printed word. At the same time, it realized that the question of appropriate reading material was at the center of the issue and that the Church needed to address it. The concern with reading, which increased at the end of the nineteenth century, was linked to a number of historical factors. The development of the press, along with a literature of republican or socialist ideology, made intellectuals at different levels of power impatient. This was a time when secular certainties were wavering and the traditional social models were no longer guarantees of order. The contradictions and conflicts that arose from the clash between the Church and modernity were expressed in the discourse on the control of reading matter. The political debate that violently shook the emerging Republic found in print–whether book or newspaper–the vehicle for its independent expression.

This discourse of the Catholic ban on certain publications has to be considered in light of the times and the threat some writing represented to the established authority of the Church. The first move to control reading material was overt censorship, imposed through the publication of the *Index Librorum Prohibitorum,* a list of prohibited books which was first published in 1559 by the Sacred Congregation of the Roman Inquisition with all the self-assurance of those who claim to have the truth. (The last revision was in 1946 and the last reprinting was in 1966; it has not been reissued.) The second move, specific to Brazil and in which Sinzig takes part, corresponds to the initiative of some of his representatives who took upon themselves the job of being the Brazilian censors; they published guides and commentaries to detail and make specific the prohibition. Let us consider now the discourse of this group of priests who spared no effort in the task of prescribing reading norms for Brazilian Catholics. What is fundamental to the present analysis is that Sinzig's work reveals the political issues of Brazil's international relations through the specific problem of the institutional reorganization of the Church in Brazil. The singularity of this

discourse–the elements of the Brazilian context and the ways in which they are represented, taken together–offers a number of possible directions to take in any analysis of Church authority. Here the analysis will not be limited to the simple recognition of social forms, economic structures, and political organizations in which Sinzig's and, in a certain way, the Church's efforts, took place; nor will it seek to interpret Catholic policy in terms of its religious significance. Rather it tries to understand the specific character of religious censorship within Brazilian social and cultural formations. Without disregarding either political-economic factors or strictly religious concerns, the aim of this analysis is to understand the workings of the sociocultural system of representations used by Sinzig to confront these realities and the language he used symbolically to transform reality.

Historical Background

The "religious question," as the 1874 conflict between the Church hierarchy and the monarchy in Brazil became known, was the result of a particular set of factors: The development of Ultramontanism in the Vatican, its impact on certain members of the Church hierarchy in Brazil, and the reactions of the imperial government, which, at the beginning of the First Republic, culminated in the official separation of Church and State. This was an attempt to abandon colonial Catholicism and adopt a more European policy. The disputes between Ultramontanists and Liberals had ended up undermining the power of the Church by 1870. In response to this debate and similar ones which raged in Europe, the First Vatican Council (1879) established the dogma of papal infallibility. The Papacy sought, thus, to affirm itself as a spiritual power, and since then, the central directive offices of the Church in Rome have not spared any efforts in promoting the mystical cult of the figure of the Pope and his spiritual prestige. In his important 1988 study, *A elite eclesiástica brasileira* [The Brazilian Ecclesiastical Elite], Sérgio Micelli pertinently analyzes this tumultuous period of transition. According to him, compromises were being made on all levels. The Brazilian authorities sought to attend to the most relevant demands of the Church: First, the Church sought to strengthen itself as a legal entity on such matters as the regulation of property ownership and control over the educational system and other strategic areas such as publishing. Thus it hoped to be able to guarantee its continuing dominance. It is important to emphasize that the ecclesiastical elite sought political alliances with dominant groups and parties who were willing to defend its prerogatives in the parliament. The ecclesiastical organization, therefore, found the means to recover a large part of the political and institutional ground that had been lost with the separation of Church and State and, in this way, got around the measures imposed by the provisional government, which had hoped to contain the Church's political influence. Education had been secularized, religion had been eliminated from the curriculum, and the federal and state governments were forbidden to underwrite religious schools. None of this, however, prevented the Church from rendering educational services and from constituting the principal source of new schools under the expansionist policy of the new government. Secondary schools became the most dynamic and profitable lever of ecclesiastical power. The founding of secondary schools for boys and girls became one of the concerns of the government and the oligarchic leaders, even in the most backward states, but governments could not bear the financial and institutional burden imposed by employing a large number of new teaching and administrative staff. The absence of appropriate public policies in the educational area made state governments vulnerable and gave the upper hand to some important local groups who were favorably disposed to the Church.

Also, according to Micelli, the accelerated expansion of these opportunities for investment in the secondary school market (and the resulting importation of European clergy) was possible only because of the severe restrictions imposed on religious orders in their countries of origin: "não fora a penosa conjuntura de perseguições religiosas de que estavam sendo vítimas algumas das mais importantes ordens religiosas da Europa, o desenvolvimento organizacional da Igreja brasileira ficaria consideravelmente comprometido" (Micelli 72) ("if it had not been because of the grievous context of religious persecutions of which some of the most important religious orders in Europe were the victims, the organizational development of the Brazilian Church would have been set back considerably"). The Brazilian Church, therefore, after the official separation from the State, was torn between two social forces whose demands sometimes proved to be contradictory: On one side, the Vatican, imposing a radical model of centralization; on the other, the well-off benefactors, the State governments and leaders, wanting to contain Church influence on temporal matters but, at the same time, giving the Church almost a free hand in the educational system. The strength of the Vatican directives on the training of the clergy was undeniable, but so were the connections of the ecclesiastical elite with the holders of local and State power. At the height of the institutional restrengthening of the Church, its connections with the Vatican were tightened even more through a process known as "Romanization." This notion reaffirmed that one of the alternatives (if the Church were to survive as a dominant force) was to take very strong positions in the face of a troubled world, with the dangers that beset it everywhere at the end of the nineteenth century and, most evidently, after the First World War. The secular hegemony of the Church was threatened with the growing secularization of large sectors of national life.

After the establishment of the Republican regime, the State took a position of official indifference and neutrality on religious questions. The separation of Church and State thus forced the Church to find another channel through which it could exercise power and influence the country. This separation, however, was only relative. The fact was that the Church and the State had similar goals, although for very different reasons: The State found it expedient to allow the Church to dominate education, and the Church saw this as an opportunity to regain influence. The supranational institutional power of the church was one of the important elements behind its influence. Church leaders made certain that this development had not appeared to take place in the Colonial period out of the total dependence of the Church on the structures of the State, and the State, for its part, did not wish to use its limited resources to promote the development and expansion of a religious institution. After the coming of the Republic, the fundamental objective for the Church was to strengthen its place as a national institution. Consequently there was a marked increase in the number of dioceses and a new distribution of the territorial divisions of parishes, all accompanied by the increase and improvement of pastoral authority—all part of the Church's plan of action in Brazil. The founding of new diocesan seminaries, the reopening of monasteries, and the recruiting of European monks, nuns, and priests to occupy vacant posts and strengthen the ranks of the secular clergy reveal the efforts of Brazilian bishops, with the encouragement of the Holy See, to move toward independence from State authority. With this, the so-called process of "re-Europeanization," begun at the end of the Colonial era, was greatly intensified in the early years of the Republic. The improvement in the quality of education and the training of the national clergy in the seminaries that already existed or would be built were the main concerns of the Catholic hierarchy.

If the Church aimed at developing institutionally as a means of exercising its influence, the fact remained that it was a "denationalized" institution. If, on the one hand, the Brazilian Church had closer relations with Rome in this period, maintaining intense direct contact with it and following its directives more closely than ever, on the other, this connection in itself had its dangers, since the guidance of the Holy See did not often conform to Brazilian reality. Withdrawn from that reality on account of its being "Romanized," the Church was also increasingly excluded from the public domain. An indisputable figure in reorganizing the Brazilian Catholic church was Dom Leme, who, on becoming Assistant Archbishop and Apostolic Administrator of Rio de Janeiro in 1921, immediately began to set in motion a new organizational movement of the Catholic laity. His intense efforts to increase the influence of the Church lasted the entire twenty years he held this position. His main objective was to assemble groups of isolated and dispersed laymen and to transform them into a laity of the elite: An efficient, disciplined organization for collaboration with the Church hierarchy in the formation of a new Brazil. The results of these efforts did not take long to become manifest. The creation of the Catholic Confederation of Rio de Janeiro, founded at the end of 1922, had about 420 associations affiliated with it by 1924, all of which took on the implementation and coordination of the multiple initiatives of the lay apostolate. The creation of the magazine *A Ordem* [The Order] in 1921, and of the Centro Dom Vital [Don Vital Center] in Rio de Janeiro in 1922, besides being notable examples of the beginnings of the Catholic lay movement, are fundamental for understanding the project of Dom Leme. Assisted by Jackson de Figueredo (1891–1928), he set out to attract the intellectual elites of Rio de Janeiro to the movement. Jônatas Serrano (1885–1944), Heraclito Sobral Pinto (1893–1991), Hamilton Nogueira (1897–1981), Father Arlindo Vieira (1897–1967), Alceu Amoroso Lima (1893–1983), and Father Leonel Franca (1893–1948) are among those who joined the project and became members of the Center, which, by this time, was already expanding to other state capitals. Therefore, the Centro Dom Vital and its vehicle, *A Ordem*, are the two exemplary enterprises in which at least two objectives were pursued: To join together the Catholic laity and to enlarge the prestige and influence of the Church within the ranks of Brazilian intellectuals.

A Ordem, in the very choice of its name (which was not by chance), reveals the tendencies of the moral and political project of the group that brought it into being. It symbolizes the intention of the Catholic elite, led by Jackson de Figueiredo, at once to promote and maintain the national order with the aid of religion and also to identify itself with the "cada vez mais altissonantes do governo brasileiro em favor da ordem" (Azzi 6) ("ever louder appeals for order made by the Brazilian government"). This revealed the common interests of the two institutions: According to the view of both the political and religious authorities, new forces existed which were turning into political movements that were meant "a desagregar a unidade política e religiosa de nação" (Azzi 10) ("to disintegrate the political and religious unity of the nation"). From its creation in 1922, the Centro Dom Vital, along with Cardinal Dom Leme himself, was responsible for several other lay movements: Ação Universitária Católica (Catholic University Action), Confederação Nacional dos Trabalhadores Católicos (National Confederation of Catholic Workers), Confederação da Imprensa Católica (Confederation of the Catholic Press), Juventude Universitária Católica (Catholic University Youth), Juventude Feminina Católica (Catholic Feminine Youth), Juventude Operária Católica (Catholic Workers Youth), etc. All these movements prepared the coming of the Ação Católica Brasileira (Brazilian Catholic Action), made official in 1923 and directly encouraged by Pope Pius XI, representing an important instrument for mobilizing the laity in support of the Church throughout the nation. This movement was embraced by seventy bishops throughout the country and, by about 1937, became the coordinating agency of all the other lay movements.

In September 1938, the Ação Católica Brasileira began the monthly publication of a newsletter entitled *Ação Católica* [Catholic Action], which became its official organ under the direction of Alceu Amoroso Lima, with the job of censor falling to Father Leonel Franca, who also contributed articles. In the opening contribution to the publication, Alceu Amoroso Lima announced to Catholics that the country "que ingressa numa fase das mais críticas de sua existência" ("was in one of the most critical phases of its existence"), and that they should therefore unite their efforts to promote the true religion and not lose their determination or stand by in the face of the "dificuldades de vida e perplexidades políticas dos dias que vivemos" (in Franca 6) ("difficulties of life and political perplexities of the present times"). The command to Catholics was to act. These "perplexities," which had been pointed out and discussed by Catholic thinkers for some time, were now more pressing, in part owing to the shock waves caused by a general world crisis. The policies of Ação Católica for Catholic action are present in all the main publications of the group but would become the object of greatest (or at least, most emphatic) reflection in the writings and lectures of Father Leonel Franca. The unconditional and militant actions of this priest were immediately followed by the rest of the group. In the understanding of this Catholic thinker, the problems of the economic, political, social, and moral order could be reduced to problems of human nature and, therefore, would require "Soluções humanas inspiradas num conceito da natureza e dos sentidos do homem" ("human solutions inspired by the concept of the nature and feelings of man") (Franca 630). Based on this idea, Father Leonel Franca's concern was to establish that the great crisis of modern society was a crisis of the moral and

spiritual values experienced by man. An organic view of society and of man is evident everywhere in his writing. In his diagnosis of modern society, there were no discussions of collective experience; his traditional single vision of the world always prevails. He left no room for a transition from the present to a better stage. He rejected the possibility of any adaptation of the old agencies to the new demands of contemporary life. He was not an optimist with regard to the future. In his view the pressing challenge consisted of valuing moral experience, repudiating the decadent formulas of a corrupted civilization, creating a group around Catholic ideals, strengthening spiritual values, and thereby avoiding disorder in all social institutions, especially the Catholic family: "No plano das instituições sociais a 'familia', envenenada pelo individualismo, atraiçoa a sua missão e nos lares sem berço deixa extinguir-se a chama da vida" (78) ("the family, poisoned by individualism, betrays its mission and in homes with no cradle lets the flame of life be extinguished").

The confirmation of this ideology would come with the encyclical *Quadragesimo Anno* of Pope Pius XI, who put the Vatican seal of approval on this project, maintaining the defense of the family to be strictly tied to the right of self-sufficiency and continuation, which must be assured and guaranteed by the State. The ideals of Leonel Franca and of the Pope were distinct, but acted as corollaries to each other, both on the model of the Holy Family. The nonintervention of the state in the basic social groups–family, school, business, unions–left all open to the Church's influence and power. The encyclical proposes that the state should fulfill its function as coordinating agent of the various groups and social classes with a view to their common good. This notion is defended by Alceu Amoroso Lima, who conceived of a corporate state based on Catholic principles. This aspect of Catholic interpretation can be associated with other questions about the family that were seen in social and political dimensions as the importance of the new Church-State relation. In the perspective of the Catholic movement, if the economic order alters positions of people owing to its own dynamic, the state should abstain from interfering in the domestic functions of the family, just as the social order (the family), organized on the basis of privilege and position acquired and confirmed by tradition, cannot try to take over political functions. Thus, the appropriation of family life by the state is constantly challenged; it is already inscribed deeply in Catholic thought. The integration of the family into the political structure does not necessarily imply the right of the state to deal with the family in an arbitrary way. Moreover, the family is integrated into the state, not to serve it but to have the state serve the family. This is the sense of Alceu Amoroso Lima's reflections, aware, as he was, of the reality of modern times, which, in his opinion, brought in their expansion "o veneno do individualismo, levando à desagregação familiar" (43) ("the poison of individualism, leading to family disintegration"). In Brazil, one of the consequences of this conception was an endless, ever renewed discussion among Catholics that this "onda de individualismo" ("wave of individualism") would always put at risk "os quadros tradicionais da família cristã" ("the traditional role of the Christian family,"). The introduction of divorce and birth control were immediately denounced as two elements of domestic disintegration "em especial a alta burguesia" ("especially affecting the upper bourgeoisie") (Lima 132).

The choice of this specific debate by Catholics was not arbitrary; certainly journalists of the period discussed it frequently. Starting from the presupposition that the wealthier social classes would best be able to maintain the stability of the home and raise large families "para maior glória de Deus" ("for the greater glory of God"), journalists denounced them as precisely the ones who were responsible for the decrease in births. For Alceu Amoroso Lima, the bourgeoisie in general was the class that most "traiu as leis naturais da vida" ("betrayed the natural laws of life") (42) . From a Catholic perspective, following the Christian model of society, divorce and birth control were immoral policies. Thus, militant Catholics were not able to assimilate the countless changes occurring in various sectors of society. Modern society, it was claimed, was lost, immersed in a serious crisis of moral order because it had lost its Christian values; the bourgeoisie had forgotten the essential truth that the sole purpose of man was the salvation of his soul. The question of the salvation of the soul–the great moral question that was put to Catholics–stimulated both long discussions and the Church's successive prohibitions of a number of social policies.

Petrus Sinzig: The Apostle of Good Press

It is in the wake of these events that Editora Vozes of Petrópolis is to be placed, including its newspapers and magazines, as well as the censorship project that Pedro Sinzig would develop. Whether dealing with directors, editors, writers, or reporters, the question for him was, above all else, the problem of the "crisis of conscience" brought on by the purported wave of materialism that destroyed spiritual values and invaded every level of social life. His dominant ideal was "tentar vencer o puro materialismo e naturalismo de nossa época. Pois nós já perdemos hoje em dia o centro, o equilíbrio, a justa medida" (14) ("to try to defeat the materialism and naturalism of this period. For today we have already lost the center, the balance, the right measure"). No civilization can achieve continuity and durability if it does not have a very clear concept of humanity and of life or a true, integral humanism. What did Sinzig do to make this Christian humanism happen in his time? How did he exercise his apostolate and spread his message? Sinzig employed all the modern means, putting them all to work toward these goals: He brought together the press, cinema, and political advocacy and implemented his message by means of a nearly epic struggle in the attempt to form consciences through the written word and visual imagery. What is interesting in Sinzig's work is that it was based both on the lay movement and the organizational structure of the Brazilian ecclesiastical hierarchy. From the early (1916) text *Reminiscências de um Frade* [Memoirs of a Friar] to the many works that followed, tracing Sinzig's intellectual development is indispensable for anyone who wishes to investigate his work as censor. He designed his project demanding the fulfillment of Christian precepts under the moral authority granted by the church. His dream of "moralizing" Brazilian society involved an attempt to make Catholic morality the cornerstone of the Christian's relation to written, especially literary, production. Within the organizational machinery of the Church, Sinzig wrote as its legitimate "organic" intellectual. He belonged to the most influential sector of the Church and did the systematic intellectual work of recording, transcribing, and publishing documents, articles, newspapers, and magazines. He worked to synthesize collective memory in a considerable effort to eliminate any "tendentious" printed material, to rebut anticlerical arguments, and resist the proselytism of the competing Freemasons, Protestants, and spiritualists; in short, he condemned everything that, in his opinion, was contrary to Catholic doctrine.

In this way Sinzig put together his *Através dos romances: guia para as consciências* [Review of Novels: A Guide for Consciences], published for the first time in 1915, a guide that was composed of critiques of a great number of fictional works with the aim of recommending them (or not) to readers, according to their adherence to the precepts of the Catholic Church. For this purpose, Sinzig divided them into three distinct categories: (1) good books, recommended for healthy reading, which perfectly obeyed these precepts; (2) books recommended with restrictions, those "que não prejudicam o leitor adulto sensato que o lesse por algum justo motivo" (2) ("that do not harm the sensible adult reader who reads them for a valid reason"), although they could be dangerous if read indiscriminately; (3) dangerous books, whose reading was a poison to the souls of their readers and that definitely contaminated the cultured or uncultured spirit, and were to be rigorously labeled "literary garbage." The prohibition guide was, therefore, transformed into the ideal project, the sign of Catholic censorship reaching the readers, giving them "infallible" guidance. For the restless censor, the guide also suggested the possibility of spreading healthy reading, giving him the illusion of the Church's control: Spreading its moral values to be shared by all according to Catholic precepts, but prepared to deal with the challenges imposed by the proliferation of publications. From this perspective, the censor compiled 21,553 entries on novels, putting them in alphabetical order, with only 381 referring to Brazilian novels, written by 148 writers (out of the 6,657 commented on). Of these Brazilian novels, 328 were written by 127 men and 53 by women. The most well-known male writers who were proscribed were Aluísio de Azevedo (1857–1913), José de Alencar (1829–1877), Joachim Maria Machado de Assis (1839–1908), and, among the foreigners, Gustave Flaubert and Emile Zola. (These authors will be commented on in more detail later on.) The censorship proposed by Sinzig was distinct from others of its type: It was a "modern" guide, well put together, capable of "Neutralizar de algum modo os grandes males que podem produzir as más leituras dos maus livros e principalmente dos maus romances" (*A Resposta* 52) ("neutralizing in some way the great evils that the reading of bad books and mainly of bad novels can produce").

Sinzig assembled this condensed guide, convinced of the importance of the novel as either a good or bad influence on readers. He made this work a weapon of his apostolate. His main goal ("guiding consciences") was literally and morally to guide Christians by not allowing Catholic homes to be invaded by the corrupting poison of "literary garbage." The great themes that he would condemn were in keeping with the concerns of the Catholic movement of this time: "naturalismo na literatura, crimes, suicídios, amor livre, adultério" (Sinzig 8) ("naturalism, crimes, suicide, free love, adultery"). This mission was a response to his perceived imperative of protecting the people from a literary sewer. Courage and action were needed, and he would guide the consciences of Christians bewildered by the outpouring of novels at the turn of the century. He would distinguish between good and bad books for the common readers, the innocent spectators who allowed themselves to be affected by their imagination, giving way to emotions and feelings that could be so ruinous to their Catholic faith. He would control this dangerous literary production–the immoral novel–which, to attract even more readers, was ready to transgress all moral values. He would maintain vigilance over the reading of fiction, a growing danger from the second half of the nineteenth century on, since it had attained a privileged role during leisure hours (which, in former times, were dedicated to pious reading); it filled heads with dreams instead of religious meditation. He would recover the only legitimate use for reading: Moral elucidation, which would also propagate the authorized word of the Church. He would create a means of control over the book efficient enough to allow Catholic readers to confront the challenge of modern times, so that they could read for their moral fulfillment and live according to the teachings of the Church.

As a great number of studies have shown throughout history, the Catholic Church has always considered reading a dangerous practice, and one of the results of this presupposition has been its constant warning to Catholics of the high risk to the salvation of their souls if they were not aware of the traps set by the written text. And, as guardian of the dogma of faith, the Church delegated the task of evaluating good and bad reading to its representatives. This strict control of the printed word was considered not only a right but a duty of the Church. The act of choosing reading matter according to Catholic precepts was the responsibility of the Catholic scholar who is as close as possible to dogma but is also accustomed to methods of rhetorical persuasion, and who also has institutional knowledge; who thus, in a selective way, could promote publication and transmission of morally uplifting works. The written word could be an illusion, but a much more dangerous illusion when it contributed to the suppression of moral conviction, or when it deceived through artifice. The question of the printed word and its uses is at the center of the cultural and religious changes the Western world has undergone since the Council of Trent (1545). And, although the teachings of the Church on what literature is and what it should be have remained much the same since the fifteenth century (always emphasizing the didactic character of good literature as character formation), to allow literature to be a living continuation of the Christian tradition, at the end of the nineteenth century, the Church was forced to change its approach by confronting the proliferation of texts (books, newspapers, pamphlets, etc.), the rapid growth of educational facilities, and the swift increase in literacy. The reaction of the hierarchy of the Church was to attempt to control reading on a more popular level than had heretofore been necessary (see Chartier and Herbrard). The social divisions between lettered and unlettered, between readers and nonreaders, continued, but the press had acquired social status and a presence in the political and cultural arena. The Catholic authorities who examined reading matter in the last decades of the nineteenth century could not escape the impact of the crisis caused by the Church's loss of power. This crisis was also tied to the secularization of schools and the break with traditional structures of everyday life. Nevertheless, the Church still made an all-out effort to resist the divisive forms of modernity, but it gradually discovered that its failure to control life was the result of its loss of authority.

It is in this effort at resistance that the Church invested its front-line fighters who propagated the discourse of censorship, of banning bad books, of prescribing good books and, in most cases, of condemning much more than promoting. By endorsing a conception of reading matter that confuses literature and apologetics, the Church reaffirmed that the task of transmission of the word of God involved a solemn obligation to protect the faithful. As an institution the Church tried to maintain the status quo but, because of this institutionalized conservatism, the church established a negative relationship with cultural production as a whole. In this sense, Sinzig's discourse is not the Church's only discourse, but it is an expression of one of its dominant currents. His guide to banning, therefore, echoes condemnations dating from the medieval church. It is a guide for those who claim the right to determine the reading of other people, according to Christian morality. Our particular interest in this form of control here is that one can see in it, not only the effects of a moralistic and intransigent censorship, but also the claim that Brazil's reading public was, according to Sinzig, more fragile than others and for this very reason had to be protected so as to preserve innocence and faith.

This guide for controlling reading matter, produced by the Brazilian Catholic Church, avoided direct confrontation with European publishers, because it was intended for the domestic hunting down of bad books. The prohibition would be made in the public arena so as to prevent the poison from entering the home. This public struggle made explicit that there was no longer any way of sustaining the ideal that the only necessary readings for a Christian were the Gospels and the lives of the saints. The novel, for its part, occupied a major place in the list of dangerous books at the turn of the last century. It was the novel that had to be torn from the hands of women. In this reading practice, recreation, entertainment, and the fantasy it makes possible had taken the place of immediate moral enlightenment. For Sinzig, it would be better to accept the book, to reflect on its use, to learn to evaluate it and, thus, to distinguish among the countless books available in the market those that contribute to a sound mind and a Christian heart and conscience. Or, at the very least, one could learn to accept the harmless ones. Sinzig was clearly concerned with the diffusion of the book and with mass media communications, and he particularly wanted the church to gain "control" of this process, or at least participate in it. The Brazilian guide for readers is closely modeled on *Romans à lire et romans à proscrire* [Novels to Read and Novels to Proscribe] by the French priest Father Louis Bethléem (1869–1940). With respect to this work, Jean Hebrard has commented: "It will surpass 120,000 copies, which is an apparently unique bibliographic event of its kind and has become a sort of reference guide used beyond Catholic circles" (in Chartier and Hebrard 420). Bethléem was basically concerned with two points: To guide the mass of the faithful confused by the overabundance of printed material and, on the other hand, to establish the Catholic Church's authority as a force strong enough that its influence could carry weight effectively in the public sphere, both in the political arena and in the publishing market. Both Bethléem and Sinzig counted on a great many collaborators: Laymen participated actively in the project (literary critics, journalists, writers), sometimes using pseudonyms. This was a group of Catholics whose target was not the vices usually opposed by the leagues of virtue (prostitution, alcoholism, etc.) but the immorality of the printed word, which seduced hearts and intoxicated minds. There is no doubt that this movement proved the extraordinary power that the censors attributed to the printed word.

It mattered little, therefore, whether "Catholic criticism" obeyed aesthetic and literary standards or not. These guides were compiled in republics (France and Brazil) motivated by the will to instruct, in a social space dedicated to the multiple forms of print and in which the Church found itself on the verge of losing its authority if it could not take a leading role and exert influence on print culture. It was a question of out-doing the adversary, turning its own weapons against it. The clergy, which was lettered by its training, had to take up and maintain the Catholic press as a work of faith, working to connect the development of a reading public to the Church's sphere of influence, facing the cultural and political problems of "democracy"–or risk becoming irrelevant. This meant an important change in the functions of priests: After having been preachers, then schoolmasters, they now had to become journalists. That was what happened to Sinzig and to Beth-léem. (In November 1911, Bethléem was designated by his bishop to dedicate himself full-time to this "hygienic" press, guided by morality and religion.)

The assumption defended by Sinzig and inspired by Beth-léem was that books were dangerous; but the more serious presupposition was that Catholic readers were weak willed and often naïve. The book and the press then became doubly dangerous because they could now reach a majority of the population, thereby producing a crisis of values. The insulated Catholic family was now vulnerable to seduction by a world whose culture was definitely no longer organized around religious faith and Catholic moral order. Therefore, it was necessary to select books that could work for the propagation of the Christian faith and its values, ensuring the continued role of parental guide for the Church and, at the same time, doing everything possible to remove dangerous reading from the Catholic home.

The Rules of Censorship

The practice of censorship that was to be performed by Sinzig during this period can be grasped through the structure of his guide. Paratextual resources made up the first part of the book: This was a kind of collection of opinions, suggestions, and statements that have pointed out not only his opinion regarding the guide, but also indirectly indicated the way he would like it to be read. Sinzig intended to insert the Catholic reader, his privileged addressee, into his idea of moral order; it was his aim that the reader would gain a Christian viewpoint on the world at large and its press. He gave attention to the technical, visual, and physical aspects of books standardized, in a way, into a set of rules that were intended to mould the reader's "conscience" through the constant reminder of the guide's relation to the sacred teachings of the Church. Once his authority had been established, he set up the rules by which the readers would regard the entries. Thus legitimized by "divine" power, with the support of "earthly" power, Sinzig had a great moral role to play, at least according to his own point of view: To restore the dignity of the literary tradition against the "mad" undertakings of the book merchants; to safeguard the decency of the Brazilian Catholic vis-à-vis the danger of the licentious novel and the "rage to read" that characterized the new century; to help those who tried to reconcile Catholic morality with their desire to read. He was convinced that, in the question of reading, religious indifference was the true threat. To read is always to be indoctrinated, and the work of protecting readers was a task of patient education in building up their reserves of moral judgment. With this in mind, Sinzig wrote his ten small chapters, oriented by a pedagogical strategy to situate readers in the work of reading as a jury passing judgment on the novels they had not read (as well as those they had read that had put them in danger). His purpose was to develop an attitude towards reading in readers and insisted that all the faithful were to use his guide in all of their encounters with the printed word.

That evil has many sources seems to be the thread that links the ten chapters. Evil intent can be in the author, the publisher, or the bookseller. It is up to readers, with the aid of the *Guide for Consciences*, to defend themselves and to prevent evil from propagating, thereby preserving the basic Christian values proposed by the censor: Innocence and faith. Besides the emphasis on the evil consequences of the morally bad book, Sinzig was also particularly concerned with "popular" crime fiction, which, in his view, was even more dangerous because of its greater readership. This concern also set up a tension in the ten chapters between the fallibility of other views and the infallibility of his own regarding the sensuous and moral appeal of books. Sinzig was conscious of literature's incredible range of freedom because of its limitless deployment of the imagination. He inquires: "Também os livros, geralmente, se apresetam apetitosos. Cuasam às vezes verdadeira fome e avidez de leitura. Será tão mau isto?" (10) ("Books are also generally appetizing. They sometimes cause a true hunger and greed for reading. Can this be so bad?"). We know his response: Give the people nourishment, not poison.

Throughout the guide there is a recurrent use of the organic metaphor of the tree of life and of the "natural" growth of sin that will eventually kill the tree. His ideological discourse, with its positivist vision, is illustrative of a mix in Brazilian national culture of that period. The attempt to control literary production, and reading, points in the direction of the militant action of the Catholic organizations in Brazilian society. The *Guide to Consciences*, above all, aimed to defend social Christian morality and to strengthen it through an integrated consideration of politics and culture, religion and literature. Undoubtedly, Sinzig tried to lead a national project on reading and morality, promulgating healthy growth as obedience to Catholic precepts, and finally trying to influence social reorganization along Catholic principles. The books displayed in the windows of large bookstores were seen as objects of explicit seduction, attracting innocent souls and corrupting them. It may be said that Sinzig's text contained within it a contradiction, for at the same time that he condemns literary seduction, he creates his own seduction through a language full of the diverse discourses that reverberate in the collective cultural imaginary: Parables, popular as well as learned dialogues, popular histories as well as the official history of the Church, cinema (especially those films he considered uplifting), and journalism. This seduction also had a peculiar feature that was the direct relation of the book to the body: Sinzig's text explores aroma, color, touch, and the visual. Effectively, the sensory appeal competes with the moral appeal so that, together in dialectic expression, they reach the objective aimed at by censorship: To convince the reader of the importance of following the teachings of the Church.

Of course, all of Sinzig's writing constitutes highly prejudiced opinion offered under the illusion of infallibility. Regarding morality, on what basis can he make his numerous value judgments? And when Catholic dogma is not in question, what certainty can he have that his opinion is that of the Church? Did the Church have to make a statement on everything printed? For Sinzig, however, there was no doubt: In times of disorder and confusion, the responsible clergy must speak loudly and clearly. It is only within his ideal concept of Christian reading that one can understand his enterprise and the excesses to which he was driven. He asked: Why do we read? For amusement, instruction, education. How should we read? Slowly, seriously. What should we read? Books that observe aesthetic qualities but fundamentally express a Christian moral point of view. Amusement is tolerated; instruction requires teachers; education is the only true end. The aesthetic point of view becomes "useless," in Sinzig's opinion, if the "decisive" moral point of view is not observed. From these rules, some Christian principles of reading that he defended so vigorously can be deduced. First was renunciation, understood as a strict observance of all Christian duties with regard to the sins of the flesh: Catholics cannot succumb to the fear of not appearing up to date or the fear of ridicule; they must resist without concern the snobbery of amoral sophisticated readings, the trap of ephemeral successes, the seduction of the appearance of books, and the repeated insistence of advertising. Second, they must accept the precepts of Church authorities. There should be no reading of books from the *Index Librorum Prohibitorum* or those condemned in his guide, no reading of books that do not have any value. Third, there was to be only one morality, not two—one for the "simple people" and another for "adults." "Educated" people could not consider themselves exempt from observing the church's bans. Even if the degree of danger in reading was relative, for each of these groups, it was necessary to restate that all had the duty to obey. It was the unassailable and universal truth contained in the Church's teachings that authorized Sinzig's book to risk "with no fear" entering the terrain of literature, specifically fictional narrative.

He maintained that one needed to read to strengthen one's inner life and advance toward one's salvation: The meditation on holy books was, however, the "only true" act of reading, an act that prolongs the act of prayer. This linkage of reading and prayer had been a part of monastic life at least since Saint Benedict. A patient, assiduous reading, carried out with concentration and with many rereadings, was precisely what occurred in the reading of the catechism. It was, therefore, the catechism to which one must return, and this was recommended especially for girls, who would one day be mothers. With time, however, the irresistible rise of the novel diminished the virulence of his dismissal of the trivial and sensuous. Yet, Sinzig was convinced that offense was the best defense; the resolute offensive had always been the secret of victory, he felt. Sinzig concentrated on two strategies. First, he aimed to defend his critical conception against those who accused him of "strict moralism." He argued: "este livro dirige-se não tanto oas letrados, e sim às consciências" (19) ("this book is directed not so much to the lettered as to Christian consciences"). The second aim was even simpler: It was always necessary to show everywhere that it was only the *moral* criterion he applied, since his criticism found its meaning and its basis only in the Catholic religion.

But how could someone who had always preached renunciation regarding fictional narrative, believing in the virtues of prohibition as he professed to do, have thrown himself into a bibliographical adventure which led him to read so much without worrying about his own morality? Of what special immunity did he feel he possessed in order to go, without sin or dishonor, through the maze of writings that he forbade others to read? What fascination, what passion of the collector could sustain this frantic work of endless reading and cataloguing? His cataloguing according to the criterion of religious morality was a vain effort: Because it was a cataloguing enterprise (and not because it was moralizing), it was an enterprise of nonreading. This process, in effect, forced one to separate each work from the contexts of its reception, ignoring that the value of the text cannot be known

except through the experience of the reader. And the predictable effect of this effort of objectification was that the cataloguing often revealed the cultural prejudices, the tastes, and the methods of the one who assembled the files. Apparently, the success of Father Bethléem—and, in a certain way, of Sinzig—proved that his thinking was shared by many people. This singular enterprise of the early twentieth century is an extraordinary documentary source of the attempt to influence and control the cultural imaginary in Brazil. Many other priests, some contemporary with these censors and others not, chose to write, to establish newspapers, or to write an alternative Christian literature—that is to promote writing, not ban it. This relation to writing thus reveals important fissures in the inner Catholic world. The work done by Sinzig and his collaborators (literary critics such as Perillo Gomes and even writers recognized as important novelists who are studied even today, such as Amélia Rodrigues [1861–1926] and Hilda Leite Guimarães [1860–1916], besides countless teachers in religious schools who aided in propagating the guide for banning) gives us concrete evidence about the distance in both laity and clergy between an attempt to control the cultural imaginary and the dominant modes of publication during the rest of the century.

When Banning Produces Temptation

What if we accept Sinzig's invitation and go beyond his commentary? If one were indeed to go through the 21,553 entries and manage to review each of his judgments, it would be a greater folly than that of the one who compiled them and put them in alphabetical order. Surely, there is no way to escape the trap. The vast labyrinth of the guide is interminable because of the sheer volume of entries; it is impossible to evaluate it in any meaningful way. The seduction is already at work; going through the pages of his guide, it is as if we were hurled back to a monastery of the Middle Ages with its enclosed space, breathing the air of fear, as we encounter the countless books Sinzig has decided to prohibit. One can imagine Sinzig as a reader of so many sinful books that they insinuate themselves into the mind of this reader-censor through their passionate display of sensuality, licentiousness, and false gods. The poison ends up being transformed into an antidote. Yes, the book is poison and antidote; it is attractive and perverse.

For people who were educated in religious schools and were trained to follow the text step by step with the commentaries of their teachers, the most disturbing aspect of the guide was not the existence of disreputable or impious books, but the way in which Sinzig commented on the condemned books. The entries show an almost constant repetition of the binary opposition of good–bad, condemned–approved, dangerous–inoffensive book. A predominantly negative terminology is established. What attracts attention most, however, is the economy of words, when dealing with books that are approved, and the extraordinary refinement of details when dealing with the condemned books. There can be no doubt that the approved books are merely tolerated and that the condemned books have been read carefully. For the approved books, the terms used are: Inoffensive, decent, profitable, useful, moral, genuinely Catholic, approved by the ecclesiastical authorities, interesting, healthy, very delicate, worthy of praise, instructive, recommendable, and worthy of a place of honor in all libraries. For the condemned books, the terms are: Passionate, amoral, bold, abject, antihygienic, anticlerical, banal, bizarre, low, concupiscent, cynical, vulgar, shameless, dishonest, deplorable, scandalous, eccentric, extravagant, erotic, exciting, enervating, harsh, frivolous, fatalistic, inappropriate, immoral, unable to be narrated, untruthful, unworthy, wicked, filthy, impure, indecent, impious, and on and on.

Sinzig is especially concerned with what he considered to be the most fragile and innocent reading public–women. Ironically, they may have been tempted to read these books because of this very stream of verbal improprieties. He claims that women "[se] apaixonam loucamente pelas más leituras como pela morfina e pelo baile" (8) ("fall madly in love with bad reading as they do with morphine and dancing"). How could one not fall prey to this seduction if the commentaries on the good books are sparse and the only concern is emphasizing their moral value, and those on the condemned books offer such highly inviting summaries. An avid bookseller could not have promoted "forbidden fruit" more effectively. Is it a case of self-flagellation on the part of the censor or is he himself seduced? Here is an example:

> ALBERTINA BERTA. A leitura do romance *Exaltação* é extremamente perigosa. É a história de um desordenado espírito concuspicente, obsedado pelo erotismo insaciável de quem não quer perder tempo em divagações que não concorram para satisfação carnal de sua luxúria. . . . Em tudo a escritora descobre a ânsia muito animal da fusão dos sexos. . . . É um labirinto, uma reunião complexa de cenas sem lógica, sem seriação e sucessão, onde as figuras andam às tontas num jogo de cabra-cega e as cenas se baralham até uma confusão inominável. . . . O ambiente social onde se movem essas figuras corre parelha com a psicologia dessas personagens. É todo vicioso e mau.

> *(Sinzig 30)*

> ALBERTINA BERTA. The reading of the novel *Exaltação* [Exaltation] is extremely dangerous. It is the story of a disordered concuspicent spirit, obsessed with the insatiable eroticism of one who wastes no time in anything that does not contribute to the carnal satisfaction of her lust. . . . The writer discovers in everything the animal anxiety of the fusion of the sexes. . . . It is a labyrinth, a complex network of scenes with no logic, order or succession, where the characters stagger about in a game of blind man's bluff and the scenes are shuffled into an indescribable confusion. . . . The social environment in which these characters move is like their psychology. It is all corrupt and evil.

At the end of the nineteenth century, Brazilian women were for the first time going beyond the private sphere of the home and were engaged in activities that were not formerly condoned: They were now students, teachers, clerical workers; their lives were now greatly diversified. In the entries that comment on novels written by women, Sinzig offers some clues to the educational processes and the socialization experienced by women at the end of the nineteenth century. From the reading of these entries, one can discern the transgressions that these women writers committed in their writing regarding Catholic morality; the fact that these books were published with women readers as the intended audience was, of course, cause for alarm.

Sinzig, therefore, was right to be extremely concerned. For the universal Catholic Church, worldly women posed a major threat to the stability of the modern family. This social change in the status of women triggered countless manifestations in defense of the stable and cohesive Christian family. The concept of the Christian family was taken as the "mother-cell" of society, the base of the social edifice, and so the destabilization of the family institution would have dire consequences for all of society, especially putting at risk the very continuity of the exercise of power and influence that the Church had

enjoyed for centuries. To defend and preserve the stability of the family against every kind of disintegration would therefore guarantee peace and harmony in society (as a complex of families) and, in the last instance, the survival of the Church itself as an institution. It was natural, given this desire for absolute control over the lives of women, that the readings they had access to and were produced by them be rigorously censored. The mimetic novel, according to Sinzig, had the power to alter people's behavior and was dangerous especially when depicting women, who were, in his view, more susceptible to such influences. Another entry reads today like the blurb the publisher would print on the back cover of a sensational paperback edition:

> *A carne* de Júlio Ribeiro. É um dos romances mais obscenos que mancham a literatura brasileira. Um rapaz que se hospeda em casa de uma família, no interior, que é provocado insistentemente por uma rapariga sem educação, e a seduz. Este romance é de um realismo brutal, pornográfico, pintando quadros infames, da mais desbravada imoralidade.

> *(621)*

> *A carne* [Flesh], by Júlio Ribeiro, is one the most obscene novels ever to stain Brazilian literature. A boy boards with a family in a small town and is insistently provoked by a girl with no education until she seduces him. This novel contains brutal, pornographic realism, painting lewd pictures of the most untamed immorality.

Sinzig did not condemn all fictional narrative, but he did fight relentlessly against naturalism, a literary movement that was dominant in Brazil, as in the rest of Latin America, at the time when he first published his guide. It is for this reason that the two foreign authors he most condemns are Zola and Flaubert:

> Zola é o representante mais forte do naturalismo no romance, que não recua de descrever o que há de mais baixo e animal no homem, pelo que é muito prejudicial. Suas obras são tão ignóbeis que até seus amigos acabaram por ter náuseas delas. Assim diz o Pe. Betheléem. Tos os seus livros estão no Índex.

> *(631)*

> Zola is the strongest representative of naturalism in the novel, a man who does not shrink from describing whatever is lowest and most animalistic in man, and for this reason he is very destructive. His works are so ignoble that even his friends eventually were sickened by them. So says Father Bethléem. All his books are on the *Index*.

> Flaubert. Discípulo de Balzac. Foi tão realista na descrição de cenas ambíguas e imorais que ser romance *Mme Bovary* foi impugnado diante do tribunal. Seus livros não podem ser lidos por quem preza a moral cristã.

> *(Sinzig 41)*

> Flaubert, a disciple of Balzac, was so realistic in the description of ambiguous and immoral scenes that his novel *Madame Bovary* was attacked in a court of law. His books cannot be read by anyone who values Christian morality.

Sinzig traces the heirs of this literary movement in Brazil, exhaustively citing the most celebrated: "Aluísio de Azevedo, da Academia Brasileira. Foi o iniciador, no Brasil, do naturalismo. A maior parte dos livros deste escritor procura assunto na prostituição, no crime e no escândalo" (79) ("Aluísio de Azevedo, of the Brazilian Academy, was the initiator of naturalism in Brazil. Most of the books of this writer find their subjects in prostitution, crime, and scandal"). These commentaries are of a moral character, and are always aggressive and virulent in tone.

The condemnation is swift and absolute, especially when the writers are antipapal, combat religion, or offer calumnies against the monastic orders. Only books that come from the Catholic ranks are approved.

There was strong political sense in Sinzig's censorship. If literary tradition (and even the intellectual tradition in a broad sense) needed, from his point of view, to come under Catholic control, politics could not escape judgment; perhaps politics should be censored too, for Brazilian politics were so ridden with the vices of immorality, utilitarian interests, and petty politicking that only the Church could reform it. But it was the Catholic censorship of novels that was characterized by an attempt to forge an absolute link between Catholic moral values and everyday life; this was literature as social moralization. It is this trait that makes this prohibition guide a major document for the history of reading in Brazil.

**Translation by Glaucia Gonçalves
and Thomas Burns**

Works Cited

Azzi, Riolando, ed. 1983. *Vida religiosa no Brasil* . São Paulo: Paulinas.

Chartier, Anne Marie and Jean Hebrard. 1991. *Discours sur la lecture (1880–1980)*. Paris: Centre Georges Pompidou.

Franca, Leonel. 1951. *A crise do mundo moderno*. Rio de Janeiro: Agir.

Lima, Alceu Amoroso. 1940. *A família e a questão social*. São Paulo: Ação Social.

Micelli, Sérgio. 1988. *A elite eclesiástica brasileira*. Rio de Janeiro: Bertrand do Brasil.

Paiva, Aparecida. 1997. *A voz do veto: a censura católica à leitura de romances*. Belo Horizonte: Autêntica.

Sinzig, Pedro. 1923. *Através dos romances: notas sobre 21.553 livros e 6.657 autores; guia para as consciências*. Petrópolis:Vozes.

CHAPTER 44

SCIENTIFIC DISCOURSE IN BRAZIL AND INTELLECTUAL EXCHANGE

Rachel Esteves Lima

Exhibiting the fine irony that distinguished him in Brazilian national literature, Joaquim Maria Machado de Assis (1839–1908), in his story *Teoria do medalhão* [Theory of the Medallion], expresses (as few can) some ideas that would recur in the Brazilian intellectual sphere, not only in the nineteenth century but also (and especially) throughout the twentieth: The absence of original thinking, the lack of commitment to scientific inquiry or the search for knowledge, the indifference to effective change in society, and the presence of merely decorative cultural manifestations, which were nothing but strategies for social climbing. Here, the advice offered by the father to his son entering adulthood is the means by which the author criticizes a sociocultural system that is only apparently modern. This is a society characterized by talk and the abuse of rhetorical artifices that characterize public eulogy and the personal dimension of social relations as well as the indiscriminate use of foreign expressions and scientific and philosophical terminology. What is missing is any real force capable of transforming social structures. The highly praised progress of the country represented, in Machado's thinking, only a façade in which the ornamental nature and the anti-reflective spirit of letters in Brazil, besides creating a social condition wherein acquiring prestige was the only goal of the individual, also diverted attention from the precariousness of the economic, social, political, and cultural development of the country. Brazil showed a superficial, "imported progress, superimposed upon an agricultural country" (Faoro 172). It was all cosmetic effect and not real social process.

The picture painted by Machado de Assis has been the object of analysis by a great number of scholars of Brazilian culture, and one can say that today a consensus still persists that the intellectual culture of Brazil is characterized by a hypertrophy of rhetoric and a noncritical acceptance of foreign ideas. In the nineteenth century, this critique can be traced to the books of Manoel Bonfim (1868–1932); in the first half of the twentieth century, to the works of Sérgio Buarque de Holanda (1902–1982), João Cruz Costa (1904–1978), and Fernando Azevedo (1894–1974); until the 1950s and currently, to the work of Antonio Candido (b. 1918), Roberto Schwarz (b. 1938), and Luiz Costa Lima (b. 1937).

The choice of the above authors does not merely correspond to chronological order but also to the debate with the rather questionable division that some historians of ideas have explicitly or implicitly established that marks an intellectual rupture passing from an *ideological* model of Brazilian problems to a *scientific* model. Such a distinction presupposes a break from or an assimilation of imported theories in the analysis of Brazilian problems. This development, it is proposed, has led Brazilian intellectuals to the racist ideas that were in vogue at the end of the nineteenth century, and replacing them, from the middle of the twentieth century onwards with contributions from modern sociology, especially those of Marxist tendencies. This

position is not actually justified, because current critics constantly resort to the ideas of those who preceded them, and also because it implies an unconditional embracing of the notion of scientific objectivity, which presents the contemporary theoretical model to the interpreter as being the *truth*–although it is, in fact, the substitution of one ideology for another (Ventura 60).

The development of historical and sociological studies in Brazil has, in fact, ended up by questioning the historian's premise that a servile imitation of European ideas has predominated in the Brazilian intellectual life of the nineteenth century. Even the mixture of historicism and social psychology that marks the work of Sérgio Buarque de Holanda, Fernando Azevedo, and João Cruz Costa as part of the so-called "Analysis of National Formation" movement does not prevent them from understanding that the process of cultural transplantation does not take place in a passive way, without any selectivity or adjustments. This realization is at the basis of Buarque de Holanda's conviction that we live an experience without a simile and of Cruz Costa's theory which argues that imitation is a "natural and universal social phenomenon," that "does not occur without deformation, which in itself constitutes originality" (Costa 5–6). The questioning of the notion that there was a literal appropriation of racist ideas in the evolutionist approach at the end of the nineteenth century in Brazil has been pursued vigorously by Antonio Candido in his analysis of evolutionism in the work of Silvio Romero (1851–1914). According to Candido, Romero managed to escape the fatalism decreed by biological and social determinism, which presupposed an irreversible backwardness of colonized countries in relation to European civilization, by mitigating this determinism with Comte's positivist idea that transformations in society are a matter of development of ideas and institutions: "Silvio never again lost the positivist concept that ideas are what determine social evolution, and by one of those combinations, strange at first sight, but fertile in the philosophical naturalism of the nineteenth century, he connected it to the strict physical-biological determinism of a Taine or a Buckle. Physical-biological selection is slow and, although it determines the state of ideas, the latter, in their turn, go from effects to causes and ultimately determine the ideological situation of the moment" (Candido 1988, 51).

There is in Silvio Romero's thought a theoretical adjustment, in an effort to synthesize divergent positions, that finally determines the role reserved to the intellectual in Brazilian society. The educated class did not simply try to produce a copy of the European models, which would only reflect on the inappropriateness of European discourse and the lack of fit with the social structure it should reflect, as Roberto Schwarz's theory of "misplaced ideas" suggests (1981, 13–28). In the construction of Schwarz's ideological models, there was no room for mere imitation: "The European systems of thought were integrated in a critical and selective way, according to the political and cultural interests of the educated classes, concerned with adjusting foreign ideas to local reality. Scientific racism took on an *internal* function, not coinciding with imperialist interests, and was transformed into a conservative and authoritarian instrument for defining the social identity of the master class and ruling groups before a population considered ethnically and culturally inferior" (in Ventura 60).

At the end of the nineteenth century, the optimistic vision of a "lost paradise" that had permeated reflections on the New World had already exhausted its power in the Western imaginary; in its stead the evolutionist theories that universalized the notion of progress and constituted a project of a general science of order, as Michel Foucault has called it, ended up by generating an atomosphere of pessimism on the American continent. This, in the end, turned out to be quite useful for the educated class. It is in this period, for example, that the Brazilian museums were at their zenith, presenting themselves not only as a locus for exhibiting the commemorative markers of national memory, but also (and mainly) as a space for establishing physical anthropology, based on natural history. Following the model of European institutions, the National Museum in Rio de Janeiro, the Goeldi Museum in Pará, and the Paulista Museum based their research on an encyclopedic and taxonomic vision which fulfilled a specific function in the Brazilian environment. "Beginning with the flora and fauna to arrive at man, by collecting, analyzing, classifying, ranking, and exhibiting, the museums seemed to offer a little 'science in order,' in a society lacking classifications" (Schwartz 1981, 60).

The racial issue takes on an important role in the Brazilian science produced at the end of the nineteenth century and the beginning of the twentieth, guiding the research that established a homology between biological and cultural development. Thus, the consciousness of backwardness would have as a result the legitimation of intellectuals as an elite holders of knowledge, while at the same time it would distance them from the working classes. This response to "backwardness" represented for the country as a whole the only alternative in the creation of a modern Brazil. Today we recognize the importance of scientific positivism in the thought of the Brazilian educated class, recovering its contribution to the development of a national project "based on the competence, real or presumed, of technicians" (Carvalho 35).

The naturalist and positivist doctrines, therefore, informed the "civilizing" process of Brazilian intellectuals and scientists and directed them in the construction of a modern nation. If, in literature, naturalism fulfilled its role of describing the origin and the essence of Brazilianness, philosophical positivism, in its turn, provided the technicians and scientists with what they felt were objective instruments with which to exercise a disciplinary control over society:

In other words, positivism offered them a "method," made of these scientists "missionaries of progress," "priests of learning," transformed science into the only path to attain the full health of the "social body," "civilization." It was necessary, however, according to these intellectuals, to "intervene," "organize," "make healthy," "prevent" in order to avoid the "dangers," "excesses," "faults," and "deviations" that threatened the environment, culture, and the individual, that is, the realization of the main goal: "the full making of the nation." This doctrine, therefore, took on for this new generation of thinkers, scientists–writers–intellectuals, a fundamental meaning.

It was developed in the ideological matrix, at the point of departure for those who had been committed to the "march toward progress." It contributed to the ascension of these individuals to the condition of intellectuals vis-à-vis the state and legitimized their interventions (Herschmann 56–57).

The regulation of public and private life, as implemented from the end of the nineteenth century up to the end of the Second World War, is often illustrated by metaphors that refer to the purification of the organic body: "Thought of as a living organism, according to this imaginary construction the social body should be protected, cared for, and cleansed through countless methods and even surgical intervention to extirpate its sick parts, its chancres and tumors" (Rago 167). Three figures stand out in this process: The engineer, the public health physician, and the educator. In this period of the beginnings of economic development (which, in fact, began the process of industrial modernization of the country), the nation needed the work of these professionals, who were responsible for containing and organizing the daily practices of the emergent proletarian classes.

A central role in the beginning of the construction of modern Brazil was played by a series of institutions: The Escola Politécnica do Rio de Janeiro (Polytechnic School of Rio de Janeiro), which originated in the Academia Real Militar (Royal Military Academy), founded by Dom João VI in 1810; the Schools of Medicine of Bahia and Rio de Janeiro; and the Instituto de Manguinhos (Manguinhos Institute of Experimental Pathology). These institutions, founded at the turn of the nineteenth century, created the image of the scientist as hero: A man trained to plan, organize, and control, through scientific methods, both public and private spaces. The engineers had the task of repairing the city streets, of building factories, workers' houses, and villages, and of instituting rational techniques in the workplace. The doctors had the task of making the spaces of human agglomeration sanitary–the streets, plazas, factories, and homes–by diffusing habits of hygiene and public health, of regenerating and moralizing customs through a scientific discourse that, in the case of Legal Medicine, was often based on current racist eugenic concepts. Thus, the disciplining of society was achieved by establishing moral values, which would ensure the continuity of the capitalist process, in part by restricting the freedom of organization of individuals and their intimate relationships. The repression of popular demonstrations, prostitution, homosexuality, and free sexual relations had as its counterpart the organization of the nuclear family, the regulation of marriages, the distancing of woman from the work force, the building up of the myth of motherly love, and the sanctity of childhood (Herschmann and Pereira; Rago).

From the 1920s on, there is a split between the figures of the *bacharel* (scholar, lawyer) and the *doutor* (doctor, technician), two roles that, until that time, had worked together rather harmoniously, since a cultural market structured around a consistent division of intellectual labor was not yet in effect. These two figures embody and synthesize the contradictory roles played by the two elements responsible for establishing the European cultural tradition in Brazil, according to Cruz Costa: Respectively, the Jesuit and the intellectual adventurer. He works from the typological approach of a Weberian base as established in *Raízes do Brasil* [Roots of Brazil], a work published in 1936 by Sérgio Buarque de Holanda. He presupposes the existence within collective life of two systems of opposed values (although not irreconcilable in practice) represented by the ethics of the worker and of the intellectual. In Cruz Costa's analysis, as well as in that of Azevedo and Buarque de Holanda, the ethics of work is not emphasized, since it was a question of rethinking (from a modern perspective interested in understanding what distinguished Brazil from economically developed countries) the particularities of the Brazilian sociocultural formation as it developed from a colonial-slaveholding basis. These thinkers combined a historical approach with a literary knowledge and an anthropological theory, and this is reflected in the essay as the form of choice for the exposition of their ideas: "It is the historical essayism of ethnic causes, of geographical parallel causes and psychological subcauses" (Bosi ii). The work of these authors thus remains indebted to the juxtaposition of science and art characteristic of the essay, a medium that illustrated the rejection of subjectivity in order to attain a disciplined objectivity of historical discourse.

Thus the analyses of Buarque de Holanda, Azevedo, and Cruz Costa corroborate the picture sketched by Machado de Assis in the story to which I alluded at the beginning of this text. Until the beginning of the nineteenth century, "literary inflation" (Candido 1980, 132) contaminated every aspect of social life and vulgarized belles-lettres; the results of this could be observed on a general level in the appropriation of rhetorical resources by politicians, jurists, and doctors. These historians cite four factors as being at the origin of this discursive tendency, which prevented the development of the reflective and speculative capability of Brazilian thought:

1. Education based on scholastic humanism with literary features, introduced initially by Jesuit teaching and later carried on by the law schools

2. The pragmatic spirit, a legacy of the Portuguese, which was manifest in immediatism, in improvisation, and in empiricism;

3. The slaveholding basis of the economy, which contributed to the horror of manual labor and elevated oratorical talent as a mark of social distinction

4. The patrimonialist economic formation, based on the lack of distinction between the public and the private, which resulted in an excessive attachment to individualism

Antonio Candido also recognizes the significance of literature in Brazilian social life, but does not think that the cultivation of literary discourse would have, in itself, prevented the development of the technoscientific spirit, as the thinkers mentioned above believed. According to him, literature served, until recently, as a palliative measure in a country devoid of institutions of sociocultural research, taking over the task of revealing Brazilian reality and, at the same time, shaping the national consciousness.

These ideas have been reworked more recently by Luiz Costa Lima, for whom the lack of autonomy of the Brazilian intellectual system results precisely from the commitment of the thinkers and intellectuals to the mission of documenting and constituting the nation. The confusion between literature and pedagogy and the absence of theoretical reflection in Brazil are the target issues in the work of this critic, who in "Da existência precária: O sistema intelectual brasileiro" ["On Precarious Existence: The Brazilian Intellectual System"], an article published in 1978, supports Buarque de Holanda's position by suggesting the existence of a correlation between the development of an engaged political culture, disseminated through platform speeches, and the authoritarian, patrimonial profile of Brazilian colonialism. The culture developed here

would be perceived as a strategy for projecting the identity both of the nation and of the intellectual, now elevated from the status of an uprooted European to that of doutor (doctor) (3–29). In Sociedade e discurso ficcional [1986; Society and Fictional Discourse], Costa Lima, now pondering the reasons that led to the formation of the documentary canon in the literature not only of Brazil but of the entire Latin American continent, would take up again the work of Sérgio Buarque de Holanda, associating it with studies by Habermas and Koselleck. Based on his reading of these authors, Costa Lima argues that the emergence of public opinion, indispensable to the rise of an autonomous intellectual system in countries where the bourgeois revolution has been completed, is at the same time the result of the dissociation of the public and private spheres (Habermas) and of a process of internalization of the law (Koselleck), through which ethics and a rational morality are assimilated.

As Sérgio Buarque de Holanda had already suggested, in Brazil the process of the socialization of individuals was not a consequence of the bourgeois public sphere but of the family clans, who had maintained the patriarchal relations proper to the oligarchic system that prevailed in the country at least until the 1930s. In this regime, individuals remained prisoners of private interests, not internalizing a morality capable of transforming them into citizens of a nation; they revealed no capability of establishing a distinction between an impersonal, polished language appropriate to the public space and a personalized, cordial language that ought to be restricted to private relations. Instead of defining the essence of the Brazilian citizen, cordiality would therefore refer to a "socio-psychological formation inadequate to the age of the bourgeoisie" (Lima 124). Nondocumentary or self-reflexive literature and original critical thinking could arise only with the emergence of the bourgeoisie and the creation of cultural institutions that opposed the state, pressuring it to take class interests into consideration. Thus, the conservative face of Brazilian modernity is betrayed, according to Costa Lima's analysis, not only by the participation of the modernist intellectuals in cultural projects created under authoritarian states but also by the very form they produced: A literature of foundation. The literature "of purification" (Candido 1980, 133) became feasible only when it could already count on a cultural market structured and compartmentalized in disciplinary terms, and it was in this direction that Brazilian intellectuals went when they committed themselves to a project for cultural development in which education played a fundamental role: "For the intelligentsia, structuring cultural space meant the possibility of creating modern institutions, open to the spirit of renewal and research, and, at another level, institutions capable as well of removing it from isolation, of spreading its message and of creating a 'market,' not necessarily or exclusively in the economic sense of the term, but also in the sense of a place where ideas are exchanged: In short, the loci for the foundation, the recognition, and the expansion of its social identity and even of its 'mission' in society" (Martins 80).

It is not our intent to deliver sterile value judgments that define which is the richest, more sophisticated, or more critical type of literature—a discussion that almost always tends to become an apology for the self-reflexive art of the European avant-garde. This apology, besides reifying the benefits originating in the progress of developed countries, seems to lament (more in aesthetic than in properly social and economic terms) the noncompletion of the bourgeois revolution on the Latin American continent. This position also does not consider the fact that modernism generated countermodern narratives as well, which questioned bourgeois rationality both in Europe and in the tropics. In addition, in that space, intellectual status is defined by the possibility of social intervention and of believing nowadays in the universal values created by the autonomy of one field in relation to others. As the sociologist Pierre Bourdieu says, it seems a regression to the modern paradigms that presuppose the specialization of knowledge. What does interest me is how to understand the ambiguity of the role of Brazilian intellectuals vis-à-vis modernity, which–in different ways, evidently–conferred identity on them, both in the center and at the periphery of capitalism.

The process of creating cultural institutions that would lead to the "autonomy" of the intellectual field in Brazil also illustrates this ambiguity. The Brazilian university, created late (not until 1934), would follow the idealist model of the modern German university, which presupposed the metaphysical unity of knowledge and learning in a disinterested perspective; but, having been founded either by the state or by elite segments of the liberal bourgeoisie who were ambitious to achieve power, it had as its primordial aim the formation of an elite capable of taking charge of the country's future. In this way it broke with the two characteristics of higher education at that time: Literary and rhetorical discourse, embodied in the *bacharel*, and the spirit of assiduity, which predominated in the professional schools that formed the *doutor*. The Faculties of Philosophy, Science, and Letters, planned to be the model for the institutions created after 1934, can be characterized as bringing together teaching and research activities and by an encyclopedic vision that would allow them to, in theory, engage every branch of human knowledge.

The positivist belief in the power of ideas continued to dominate the goals of the emerging Brazilian bourgeoisie. One may conclude from the prophetic words of Júlio Mesquita Filho (1892–1969), one of the founders of the University of São Paulo, that his concern for the state's loss of public power with the Revolution of 1930 and the São Paulo Uprising of 1932 was well placed. He reasoned: "Conquered by arms, we knew too well that only through science and perseverance of effort would we regain the hegemony we enjoyed for long decades in the Federation" (qtd. in Fávero 60). Political motivations were certainly at the heart of the desire to establish a model that would grant a central place to the human sciences–which had already revealed their entrenched anachronistic character and their ineffectiveness in the very context in which they had originated (the elite lettered bourgeoisie) when confronted with the developmentalism of capitalist forces. The proliferation of disciplines would, both in the European continent and, since the 1960s, in Brazil, lead to the creation of autonomous institutes, interested in research in pure science, and a growing process of specialization, which would make the acquisition of a humanistic culture of a universal character more and more difficult to achieve or even plan.

The containment of the literary caprices of Brazilian students and the development of a reflective, critical spirit were to be tasks for the European professors hired by the Rio and São Paulo universities to found a scientific tradition in the country. In the human sciences, this role would predominantly fall to the French, who would have to tame the empty erudition, the superficial encyclopedism, and the facile brilliance of their students' expositions. Professors like Claude Lévi-Strauss, Roger Bastide, Pierre Deffontaines, Pierre Monbeig,

Fernand Braudel, Jean Maugüé, among others, hired since 1934 by the Universidade de São Paulo (USP), were responsible for introducing a new intellectual attitude that professed the use of scientific research techniques, the valuing of personal reflection, the definition of clear methodological criteria, and an investment in the research of Brazilian reality. As Paulo Arantes reminds us in his memoir-chronicle:

> . . . à sombra da modesta revolução cultural que vinha se desenrolando em São Paulo a partir dos anos 30, assistíamos a uma curiosa *Aufklärung* temporã, na qual a autonomia encarnada pela *Selbstdenken* (a máxima que mandava pensar por si mesmo) era aos poucos conquistada com os "ingredientes tomados avidamente aos estrangeiros." Seguramente o lado menos conservador de nossa modernização retardatária. (79)

> . . . in the shadow of the modest cultural revolution that had been unfolding in São Paulo from the 1930s on, we witnessed a curious premature *Aufklärung*, in which the autonomy embodied in the *Selbstdenken* (a maxim that demanded one to think for oneself) was little by little gained with the "ingredients avidly taken from foreigners." It was surely the least conservative side of our retarded modernization.

Some of these professors would later become famous in their specialties on the international scene. But it was Jean Maugüé–who fled the rigidity of specialization and who retired in France simply as a *lycée* professor–who formed the most important generation of students at USP. He led the development of a social model for the criticism of Brazilian culture. Maugüé's connection with this tradition is emphasized in practically all the texts of the *Clima* group. (*Clima* was the title of a publication at the beginning of the 1940s of a group of young people that included, among others, Antonio Candido, Ruy Coelho (1920–1990), Paulo Emílio Sales Gomes (1916–1977), Décio de Almeida Prado (1917–2000), Lourival Gomes Machado (1917–1967), and Gilda de Mello e Souza (b. 1919). With Maugüé, these students refined the essayist diction that characterizes their works and that conveys a style of thinking that proceeds by allusions and attempts, through reminiscences and the reading of the *fait divers*, to establish an ordering of cultural facts.

The essay, a hybrid genre characterized by Adorno as an effective means for the interpretation of individual experience, but which the *Clima* group elaborated as an expression of collective experience as well, goes back to the art of rhetoric, here understood as an artifice that facilitates communication. Thus, the essay demands not only vast erudition, but also an ability to establish transversal connections among several fields of knowledge and to make possible the subjective expression of cultural experience. Belonging to a segment of the *petit-bourgeoisie* that had already accumulated a reasonable symbolic capital, the young people of *Clima*, with degrees in philosophy and the social sciences, could put into practice an interdisciplinary approach, proposing a bridge between research activity and art criticism, and, in a certain way, resisting the growing process of specialization in São Paulo's university environment.

The ambiguous character of the essay has been the object of reflection of some work that has recently been dedicated to coming to terms with the Brazilian historiographical tradition from the 1930s onward. On analyzing the work of Gilberto Freyre (1900–1987), Ricardo Benzaquém de Araújo finds that the preference for this genre has attenuated the conflicts in the social order that the author of *Casa grande & senzala* [1933; *The Masters and the Slaves*, 1946] sought to depict. Freyre's

414 RACHEL ESTEVES LIMA

work offered an excessive approximation to the object of study, the sensation of authenticity furnished by the assembling of documentary sources and personal reminiscences, and the search for orality that would allow the intellectual to synthesize through writing the "diglossia" (a term used by Ángel Rama [1926–1983] to refer to the coexistence, in Latin American societies, of a cultivated language intended for writing and a private language for popular and informal daily use) would have contributed to create the "climate of ethical ambiguity" (Araújo 185–208). The ambivalence of the essay form is also the focus of Célia Pedrosa in her 1994 analysis of Antonio Candido's work. Considering it a "dangerously ambiguous instrument, both revealing and mystifying," the author points out the genre's commitment, in its Brazilian version, to defining the national identity. According to her, the essay was: "the first form of Brazilian intellectual production explicitly to take on the *hybrid* character of its language, in the same way that it is the first to point out hybridism as a fundamental component of our nationality. And this theme points both to the dissipation of and the confrontation with our contradictions, the mixture of affect and rationality, imagination and observation, expressiveness and referentiality, and is also seen to have a double effect" (167).

For the *Clima* group, the essay fulfilled the function of maintaining the "harmonious sharing and exchange of ideas between literature and social studies" (Candido 1980, 134), which would be responsible for the formation of a Brazilian documentary canon in the period prior to the specialization of knowledge. In its institutional reformulation, the essay could not, however, maintain the same level of influence that had characterized the genre's original form as the prose of ideas; there was now a certain commitment to method as well as ideas. Studying the role played by the members of the periodical in the São Paulo and Brazilian cultural environment, Heloisa Pontes states that they "turned criticism into a link between the Brazilian intellectual tradition, strongly impregnated with essayism, and the academic style ingrained in the university" (284). What was not appropriated became an obstacle to be overcome by both disciplines, in a struggle for autonomy. The same conflict experienced in other cultures between the culture of reason and the culture of feelings was also reproduced in Brazil. According to Wolf Lepenies, "this conflict characterized the European social sciences as a 'third culture,' which oscillated between 'scientificism,' eager to imitate the natural sciences, and a hermeneutic position closer to the discipline of literature" (11).

In the field of sociology, the protagonist's role in this struggle would fall to Florestan Fernandes, responsible for the formation of the second generation of social scientists who would initially achieve the hegemony for that discipline in USP's School of Philosophy and would attain, with the ascension of Fernando Henrique Cardoso to the nation's presidency in 1994, the highest aim envisioned by the São Paulo university. Working beside Antonio Candido, during the period when the latter worked in the Department of Social Sciences of USP, Fernandes participated in academia through his search for conceptual precision and methodological rigor and his refusal to compromise with the essay genre. A disciple of Roger Bastide and Emílio Willems, Fernandes incorporated both the French anthropological perspective and especially the structural-functionalist paradigm of English anthropology, especially in the works he wrote when he moved to Sociology after Roger Bastide's departure.

Distancing himself from the works initially begun under Bastide's supervision, which did not make any sharp distinction between ethnology and sociology, from the 1950s onward, Florestan Fernandes began to work toward a growing specialization of the social sciences. Around him, a group of researchers gathered to give an eminently scientific cast to the investigations made in the sociological and political spheres, investing in the structural analysis of Brazilian society and abandoning the French orientation, which still offered space for the analysis of symbolic productions. The use of North American scientific paradigms was responsible for a "polarization established by sociologists, in the course of the 1950s, between activities considered scientific and those classified as cultural" (Pontes 315). The abandonment of ethnological studies was perhaps based on the same motives that had led Florestan Fernandes to avoid essayism, a genre that was more appropriate to the expression of cultural facts. Besides having a modest social background and thus being deprived of the financial and symbolic capital that gave one the erudition necessary to succeed in the analysis of the symbolic field, Fernandes felt, moreover, that in Brazil "essayism and the literary style of writing are committed to the state's vision of culture" (in Arruda 133). Thus: "contrary to his department colleagues–Lourival Gomes Machado, Ruy Coelho, Antonio Candido, and even Aziz Simão, who, although closer to the profile of the sociologist, were also dedicated to literary criticism–Florestan set himself to really transform sociology into a science, sacrificing fluency and didacticism in favor of an intellectual standard in which the strictness of terminology, a listing of bibliographical sources, and empirical and theoretically based analysis ruled. In the words of Antonio Candido, 'he revolutionized the situation. After him, amateurism, the more-or-less, and in writing, essayism were no longer possible'" (Esteves Lima 119).

From then on, research themes returned to the structural factors of Brazilian underdevelopment, substituting a predominantly Weberian and Marxist basis for the ethnoanthropological perspective of sociology in the analysis of the peculiarities of the social and economic formation of the country. From this point on, racial studies would be part of the study of social classes. This research, which at the end of the 1960s would yield the formulation of the theory of dependency, instituted the standard of academic rigor and scientific neutrality that had been aimed at and was differentiated from the research done by the intellectuals at the Instituto Superior de Estudos Brasileiros (Higher Institute of Brazilian Studies–ISEB) in Rio de Janeiro. Created by the federal government to foster the analysis of the obstacles that prevented national development and to develop alternatives to help overcome such obstacles, the ISEB claimed industrialization as the fundamental strategy to bridge the gap between modern and archaic Brazil. In addition, the ISEB related economic development to the development of a national consciousness, which would lead its intellectuals to take up an engaged position, which was understandable since they were so close to power.

At USP, on the other hand, the liberal legacy of its illustrious founders and the demand for scientific objectivity contributed to the intellectuals' retreating before any type of commitment of a national or popular kind. Commenting on the approval by these professors on a primarily educational development, Alfredo Bosi ironically says:

Science, obtained with so much labor, in the end duplicated with the sign of its authority the common sense of the oppressed man who sees the sad but fatal price of civilization in the maladies of the present, which in this case is mistaken for the subproduct of capitalist development. The moral attitude that then informed university studies would like for this price not to be so high, but it could not go beyond a pious vow. *Vae Victis!* In other words: The most coherent culture was doing reconnaissance work on empirical reality, which was presented as a series of "facts" or of "traits" peculiar to a moment of acceleration of the capitalist system within and outside of Brazil. Occupied with the objective picture of the "transition of the traditional to the modern," it could not have seen that "pure" science went together with the course of domination, whence its air of a precocious necrology of the object studied. (vii)

With no place in the social sciences, a large part of the *Clima* group found shelter in the *Letras* (language and literature) courses, where, besides Antonio Candido, Paulo Emílio Salles Gomes and Décio de Almeida Prado, they also encountered an institutionalized space to give continuity to their work of cultural criticism in the areas of literature, cinema, and theater. But in the field of literary studies, the process of autonomization had also already begun, a fact reflected even in the obligatory status of the newly created discipline "Literary Theory" in the *Letras* courses, to which Antonio Candido transferred his allegiance at the beginning of the 1960s. Organizing the Department of Literary Theory and Comparative Literature of the University of São Paulo, the author of the *Formação da Literatura Brasileira* [Formation of Brazilian Literature] paradoxically revealed his opposition to the process of specialization, implemented in the other *Letras* courses precisely through the discipline that he would introduce into the university. The approach he used, that one should teach by closely following the text without too much theorizing, shows well the amount of resistance to theoretical activity that was more explicitly observed in other courses of *Letras* in the country. At the same time, this proposal also presupposed an emphasis on critical activity by conditioning the study of literature to textual reading, which would form the value judgments of the analyst in a "scientific" way, legitimating his or her power in the intellectual system.

Besides showing a greater desire for communication in his teaching, the choice of the essay genre by Antonio Candido is also indicative of this resistance to exposing the theoretical basis of his interpretation:

> In what refers to the didactic concern, it can be said that the essayism of Antonio Candido takes on the form of a dialogue with the average reader to be instructed by the author-professor, attempting to honor a commitment to clarity and accessibility of language and the subject about which he writes. Perhaps from this concern of his, a certain purposeful carelessness arises in the exposition of the theoretical principles of his analyses, which, in the last instance, is also, according to Adorno, characteristic of the essay. But such a practice can result in a naturalization of the ideas transmitted by the essay, which seem not to depend on any theoretical-methodological viewpoint, presenting themselves as unquestionable "truths" and therefore as ideology.
> (Esteves Lima 118)

The resistance to theory in the 1970s gave rise to the debate about structuralism, which once again brought to the surface the problem of cultural dependence. The controversy began with an article by Roberto Schwarz, sociologist and disciple of Candido in the *Letras* course at USP, in which he ironically criticizes the importation of immanentist theories

that predominated in the courses in Rio de Janeiro. In presenting his "Nineteen Principles for Literary Criticism," Schwarz draws a caricature of a critic who, differing from the approach at USP, anchored his analyses in the most recent theories in vogue on the international scene. Symptomatically, the reiteration of one of his principles points to the core issue of the discussion: "Do not forget: Marxism is a reductionism and is surpassed by structuralism, phenomenology, stylistics, the American New Criticism, Russian formalism, aesthetic criticism, linguistics, and the philosophy of symbolic forms" (Schwarz 1978, 93–94).

The first response to this provocation, which is now commonplace in Brazil, was published in 1975, in the article "*Quem tem medo de teoria*" [Who's Afraid of Theory], by Luiz Costa Lima (1981, 193–98), the greatest spokesman for anthropological structuralism in Brazil. But as in almost all of his work, this critic has sought to reveal the authoritarian trait of a literary system committed to the pedagogical mission, where the intellectual makes a pact with the ideology of national identity, which leads him to fear that "theoretical inquiry is nothing more than a kind of escapism" (Lima 1981, 14). This fight over intellectual space omits the fact that in the decade of the 1970s, even at USP, the belief in a "scientific" perspective of literary analysis predominated, always mediated by imported theories, with the specificity, in the case of Candido and Schwarz, of the coexistence of an inherent theorizing of literature and a sociological tradition, at that moment committed to a Marxist approach, which presupposed as much as structuralism the objectivity and the consequent suppression of subjectivity.

In 1957, João Cruz Costa inquired about the meaning taken on by positivism in the spiritual and political history of the country, considering it as an ideology that still plays a role in Brazilian life. If its theoretical principles fell into disuse, the same cannot be said of the myth that was formed, thanks to it, around the power of ideas. According to the author, positivism would be, perhaps, a "symbol of the deep contradictions that are part of the national destiny" (275). To corroborate this position, this essay is trying to emphasize that these contradictions are manifested precisely in the incorporation of scientific discourse by intellectuals as a strategy to confer identity simultaneously on themselves and on the nation. As an imported ideology, like all others, positivism was selected (and not merely copied) as the doctrine that would be the basis of the modern project of the educated class of the country at the end of the nineteenth century and would justify even today the power it wields in conducting the destiny of the country. In this sense, far from being a symptom of the mental laziness of Brazilian thinkers, positivism was an instrument used for the creation of a social imaginary that considers technoscientific knowledge an indispensable condition for generating progress and the future elimination of social inequalities.

The breaking of this pact implies, therefore, the questioning of the notion of progress, justified by modern Western reason, which, in a dependent society, has made difficult the establishment of the distinction between pure and applied science, even before the birth of *big science* (Schwartzman 1979, 20). The prevailing nationalist character in the projects of institutionalization and the disciplinary compartmentalization of knowledge has legitimated the predominantly organic profile of the Brazilian intellectual class, often leading it to collaborate with authoritarian governments (see Fernandes). Taking on the ambiguous role of the intellectual seems to be the only alternative to a critique of its practice, thus initiating reflection that is not sub-ordinate to the interests of the ruling classes. This thought is only made possible, however, from an interdisciplinary perspective, which is a product, in the final instance, of the "internal erosion of the principle of the legitimacy of knowledge" (Lyotard 82).

Beginning with this paradigm, Silviano Santiago, in the article, "A pesar de dependente, universal" [Universality in Spite of Dependency], suggests that imitation of the continent cannot be transcended only through historical discourse, which, after all, would illustrate Western rationality, but from the joining of history with anthropology. For if history leads us to think, as Roberto Schwarz reminds us (1987), that the mimicking of European discourse by the intellectual is associated with a privileged situation, from which minorities are excluded, anthropology, for its part, denounces the fact that the incorporation of these minorities into the process of Western development is made at the cost of its destruction:

> In the ambivalent situation of its cultural being lies the ethical drama of the Brazilian intellectual in relation to the minorities of Latin America. Its comprehension of these minorities by historical materialism has to pass through their total and definitive integration into the process of the Westernization of the world; their comprehension by anthropological thought has to question this historical integration, so that they do not continue to live a "fiction" imposed as determinant of their past and their future disappearance. The pact between the Latin American man and Western history is a difficult one, unless one resorts to certain determinations of a developmentalist type, where the ideological praxis of progress is taken as capital. (Santiago 1982, 18)

On stating that the greatest contribution offered by Latin America to Western culture is the systematic destruction of the concepts of unity and purity (1982, 18), Santiago theorizes and effects a flight from identity discourses, breaking simultaneously with the disciplinary rigor and with false polarizations of the self and the other, which have made up the discourse of the intellectual in the tropics.

The return of essayism in contemporary times, as a substitution for the treatises and monographs that prevailed in the academic environment to the beginning of the 1980s, illustrates exactly the overthrow of the positivist spirit and the disciplinary schemes that ruled the search for autonomy in the modern process of knowledge construction. A risky, hybrid genre, having already deviated in the Brazilian experience (as was seen in the modern chronicle of origins and identity), the essay, by contrast, questions the principles of objectivity and scientific neutrality, refusing, through the exposition of subjective experiences, a rigid distinction between the public and private spheres by which Western reason was structured. The essay is thus revealed as index of the incomplete bourgeois revolution or of Brazilian postmodernity *avant la lettre*. Rehabilitated by the history of thought, the essay mixes genres by shuffling literature, documentation, and the accounts of daily life, just as it does with various types of knowledge. It refuses any totalizing synthesis, and is characterized by interdisciplinarity, discontinuity, and transitoriness; and always seeks a new reordering of the cultural facts. Thus, it refuses the pretension of being characterized as truth and displays the nature of the construction of all discourse.

With the discrediting of the hermeneutic analysis of the literary work, the critical text no longer claims to be objective proof and admits its partiality and incompleteness. The recognition of the ephemeral character of all knowledge leads critics

to concern themselves less with *what* to say and more with *how* to say it. Located between theory and art, the essay shapes a space in which subjects can enact their knowledge as a spectacle, using for this purpose various fictional strategies, which give a narrative quality to critical discourse. It is necessary, however, to take care that the use of the genre does not mean only a relapse into the exposition of mere points of view, which would represent a return to a critical impressionism that did nothing more than construct and make famous the figure of the creative genius. This image can also be revealed in textual criticism, at least when it clings to the superficiality of commentary and the aesthetic experimentation of language. The essay, in these circumstances, would stop denouncing, in Adorno's words, "the illusion that thought can escape that which is *thesei*, culture, and be that which is *physei*, natural" (175).

In affirming the primacy of the text in the act of interpretation, proposing a criticism that is situated on the inside, manifested by the anxiety of using language, and justified only by the pleasure of the text; some works at present go in the opposite direction of the essay as defined by Adorno: They end by invoking a reification of the concept of literature and establishing merely an "instrumentalist" relation with language. In this case, the projection of subjectivity takes on a nostalgic connotation, and the mimicking of literary procedures succeeds only in displaying the narcissism of a writer who cannot discern the difference between the self and the image reflected by the text.

It is certain that themes privileged in the contemporary world favor the representation of the "ego-history" or the "biotext" in textual criticism. The discourses of minorities and especially the discourse of personal memory often present a potential for treating the body openly–a topic that was censored for so long–which is an extremely positive point of the postmodern position. What is questioned is the ontologization of these discourses by an interpretive activity that is based only on the erotic experimentation of language, leaving aside the contextualization that could lead to a result capable of calling into question the forces that perpetrated this censorship. Only by refusing to convey any projection of identity can the essay achieve this goal, thereby constituting an effective means for the criticism of ideology.

Translation by Glaucia Gonçalves
and Thomas LaBorie Burns

Works Cited

Adorno, Theodor W. 1986. "O Ensaio como Forma." *Theodor W. Adorno*. Ed. Gabriel Cohn. Trans. Flávio R. Kothe, Aldo Onesti, Amélia Cohn. São Paulo: Ática. 167–87.

Arantes, Paulo Eduardo. 1994. *Um Departamento Francês de Ultramar: Estudos sobre a Formação da Cultura Filosófica Uspiana (Uma Experiência nos Anos 60)*. São Paulo: Paz e Terra.

Araujo, Ricardo Benzaquen de. 1994. *Casa-Grande & Senzala e a Obra de Gilberto Freyre nos Anos 30*. Rio de Janeiro: Guerra e paz: Editora 34.

Arruda, Maria Arminda do Nascimento. 1995. "A Sociologia no Brasil: Florestan Fernandes e a 'Escola Paulista'." *História das Ciências Sociais no Brasil*. Vol. 2. Ed. Sergio Miceli. São Paulo: Sumaré/FAPESP. 107–231.

Azevedo, Fernando de, ed. 1994. *As Ciências no Brasil*. Rio de Janeiro: Ed. Universidade Federal do Rio de Janeiro.

——. 1996. *A Cultura Brasileira*. Rio de Janeiro: Ed. Universidade Federal do Rio de Janeiro; Brasília: Universidade de Brasília.

Bosi, Alfredo. 1985. "Um Testemunho do Presente." *Ideologia da Cultura Brasileira (1933– 1974)*. Ed. Carlos Guilherme Mota. São Paulo: Ática. i–xvii.

Bourdieu, Pierre. 1996. *As Regras da Arte; Gênese e Estrutura do Campo Literário*. Trans. Maria Lucia Machado. São Paulo: Companhia de Letras.

Candido, Antonio. 1980. "Literatura e Cultura de 1900–1945." *Literatura e Sociedade*. São Paulo: Companhia Editora Nacional. 109–138.

——. 1988. *O Método Crítico de Silvio Romero*. São Paulo: Edusp.

Carvalho, José Murilo de. 1987. *Os Bestializados; O Rio de Janeiro e a República que Não Foi*. São Paulo: Companhia de Letras.

Costa, João Cruz. 1967. *Contribuição à História das Idéias no Brasil*. Rio de Janeiro: Civilização Brasileira.

Faoro, Raymundo. 1976. *Machado de Assis: A Pirâmide e o Trapézio*. São Paulo: Companhia Editora Nacional.

Fávero, Maria de Lourdes. 1980. *Universidade & Poder; Análise Crítica, Fundamentos Históricos* (1930–1945). Rio de Janeiro: Achiamé.

Fernandes, Ana Maria. 1990. *A Construção da Ciência no Brasil e a SBPC*. Brasília: Ed. UnB/ANPOCS/CNPq.

Freyre, Gilberto. 1956. *The Masters and the Slaves*. Trans. Samuel Putnam. New York: Knopf.

Herschmann, Micael M. 1994. "A Arte do Operatório: Medicina, Naturalismo e Positivismo 1900–37." *A Invenção do Brasil Moderno; Medicina, Educação e Engenharia nos Anos 20–30*. Ed. Micael Herschmann and Carlos Alberto Messeder Pereira. Rio de Janeiro: Rocco. 43–65.

Holanda, Sergio Buarque de. 1977. *Raízes do Brasil*. Rio de Janeiro: José Olympio.

Lepenies, Wolf. 1996. *As Três Culturas*. Trans. Clara Cescato. São Paulo: Edusp.

Lima, Luiz Costa. 1981. *Dispersa Demanda*. Rio de Janeiro: Francisco Alves.

——. 1986. *Sociedade e Discurso Ficcional*. Rio de Janeiro: Guanabara.

Lima, Rachel Esteves. 1997. "A crítica Literária na Universidade Brasileira." Diss. Belo Horizonte: Universidade Federal de Minas Gerais.

Lyotard, Jean-François. 1989. *A Condição Pós-Moderna*. Trans. José Bragança de Miranda. Lisboa: Gradiva.

Machado de Assis. 1979. "Teoria do Medalhão." *Obra Completa*. Vol. 2. Ed. Afrânio Coutinho. Rio de Janeiro: Nova Aguilar. 288–95.

Martins, Luciano. 1987. "A Gênese de uma *Intelligentsia*: Os Intelectuais e a Política no Brasil (1920–1940)." *Revista Brasileira de Ciências Sociais* 2.4:65–87.

Pedrosa, Célia. 1994. *Antonio Candido: A Palavra Empenhada*. São Paulo: Edusp; Niterói: Eduff.

Pontes, Heloísa. 1996. "Destinos Mistos: O Grupo Clima no Sistema Cultural Paulista (1940– 1968)." Diss. São Paulo: Universidade de São Paulo.

Rago, Margareth. 1985. *Do Cabaré ao Lar; A Utopia da Cidade Disciplinar: Brasil 1890–1930*. Rio de Janeiro: Paz e Terra.

Rama, Angel. 1985. *A Cidade das Letras*. Trans. Emir Sader. São Paulo: Brasiliense.

Santiago, Silviano. 1978. "O Entrelugar do Discurso Latino-Americano." *Uma Literatura nos Trópicos; Ensaios sobre Dependência Cultural*. São Paulo: Perspectiva. 11–28.

——. 1982. "Apesar de Dependente, Universal." *Vale quanto Pesa*. Rio de Janeiro: Paz e Terra. 13–24.

Schwartzman, Simon. 1979. *Formação da Comunidade Científica no Brasil*. São Paulo: Companhia Editora Nacional; Rio de Janeiro: Finep.

——. 1981. *Ciência, Universidade e Ideologia; A Política do Conhecimento*. Rio de Janeiro: Zahar.

Schwarz, Roberto. 1978. *O Pai de Família e Outros Estudos*. Rio de Janeiro: Paz e Terra.

——. 1981. *Ao Vencedor as Batatas*. São Paulo: Duas Cidades.

——. 1987. "Nacional por Subtração." *Que horas são?* São Paulo: Companhia das Letras.129–55.

Ventura, Roberto. 1991. *Estilo Tropical: História Cultural e Polêmicas Literárias no Brasil*. São Paulo: Companhia das Letras.

CHAPTER 45

BIO-POLICIES UNDERGOING TRANSFORMATION
BODIES AND IDEAS OF AMERICAN IDENTITY

Claudia Gilman

What is the scheme of philosophical, political, and religious discourses produced by Latin America after the vertigo of modernization? This issue is primarily framed as an inquiry into the limits of present-day discursive reality. Where does Latin America's present actually begin? One should note that "America" in fact means–the western hemisphere at various stages of its history (yet not at all of these stages, since this is not merely a cartographic issue but one that involves grasping a conceptual entity), which means that proposing an interpretative threshold also involves proposing some type of continuity as regards tradition. In other words, our attitude towards the Latin American present is fundamentally one of an unyielding distance or difference as regards the supposedly transtemporal essence of what is Latin American.

The idea of "American" is, as we know, a constellation that first emerged during the colonies' struggles for emancipation through specific enunciation strategies. It was taken up again, for the second time, and within the cultural sphere, by the *fin-de-siècle modernista* movement in literature, spread throughout the continent by the itinerant Darío. It was subsequently reflexively explored on the basis of the obsessive establishment of the topic of identity, and finally taken up, with the destruction of national borders, on the basis of the wave of revolutions that began in 1959 with the triumphal entry into Havana of the guerrilla commanders of the Sierra Maestra.

Through its dissemination, the density of the Latin American reality merely proves the constant, unoriginal presence of an ontological differentiation. What is unusual about this peculiar construction of identity, therefore, only acquires its paradoxical singularity in politics, knowledge, and beliefs, inasmuch as they cease being unusual and interrelated, in various ways, with the categories of time, tradition, and return. Each of these openings of borders (colonial subjugation, the republican order, cosmopolitan modernization, the civic revolution, and the purely political affirmation of a Great Fatherland) constitutes a veritable break or fold in the main space of the continent which left its traces on the development of Latin Americanist political discourse.

The slowness with which Latin Americans regarded themselves as part of the Americas even after 1810 was much in evidence; it was never the allegory of a "Sleeping Beauty." The idea of Latin America did indeed change, expand, and shrink its field of reference, defining itself in terms of a derivative, proliferating heterogeneity. One of its clearest components is that it is relational and thus is linked to the derivative, imitative, dependent, and peripheral nature (to establish a chronological and conceptually overdetermined list) of its relationships, first with Europe and subsequently with the United States and with the rest of the nations that, throughout the world, emerged as a result of struggles against colonialist

metropolises. The relational aspect of its composition also involves the inversion and multiple phrasing of such newer terms as authenticity, originality, independence, centrality, and historical prominence, as well as the elaboration of more complex configurations for the symbolic negotiation of the opposition to the derivative, imitative, dependent, and peripheral. They are undoubtedly ironic (in other words, modern) elaborations, inasmuch as apparently opposing terms are subjected to the historically dynamic and are forged together in dialectic relationships.

The cultivators of linear history have arguably failed in their interpretative discourses because they did not wish to see the superposition of times, cultures, and strata that actually characterize Latin America and so suggested the need to elaborate other instruments for organizing a homogenous critical discourse. In taking up these well-known ideas of Angel Rama, I do not urge the cancellation of the categories and concepts devised to provide an account of Latin American history, but rather emphasize the danger of categorical fossilization, which prescribes similarities and differences established by the same concepts and categories that have served to explain them. It is a question, then, of either going beyond them or opting for silence: Following routes that are not always new (but rather only suggested, left in historical latency) or else noticing that there is nothing left to be said. The prison-house of language is the greatest obstacle to these reinterpretations, and it is hardly surprising, then, that international artists sensitive to this problem, such as Antonin Artaud, Georges Bataille, or Sergei Eisenstein–all bewitched by Latin American reality–can serve as emblems for expressing not only the gap between language and thought but also the continuous need to find bridges to span them, however precarious these bridges may prove.

Ezequiel Martínez Estrada (1895–1964), the Argentine "radiographer" of the Pampas, or Octavio Paz (1914–1998), tracing the minute labyrinths of solitude or the nameless narrator in *Los pasos perdidos* [1953; *The Lost Steps,* 1956], Alejo Carpentier's (1904–1980) novel, agree when they perceive the Latin American world (and perhaps the world itself) as mindless agglutination and historical stratification, with no center, with simultaneous temporalities, about to emerge in any crack in time or space. Paz's Mexican descriptions can therefore be allegorically extended to the rest of the continent, a land where not only different races and languages but also various historical levels coexist. It is also a place where various eras confront, ignore, or devour each other in the same space or are separated by a few kilometers. If the continent is therefore the site of derivative spatial-temporal heterogeneity (in other words, a place where nothing coincides with itself), not only does it therefore favor repetition, but the responses themselves tend to be recurrent. However, within the same resources, the course or route of a definition of what is "Latin American" is outlined. This is a non-nostalgic concept of the tradition itself in which the establishment of its existence is constantly hurled into the vacuum of the future–which provides the necessary energies for its very construction. As a pluralistic conglomerate of unrelated events, Latin America defies narrative description in its specific historical unspeakableness. To offer an analogy: We know that the Hubble telescope reveals current images of now-extinct objects. One might justifiably ask, are they really extinct? We see their symptoms with our own eyes: Yesterday they were merely stars; today they are light. The long, interminable dialogue or murmur of culture shows that absolutely nothing has just died or been born. No novelty is absolutely novel. There is no death that cannot survive in phantasmagoria.

The militant Latin Americanist groups of the 1920s that emerged as a result of the university reform movement were exact contemporaries of the continental artistic vanguards. The two also coincided on their nationalistic concerns and many of their accounts of identity. Their artistic discourses of regionalism and avant-gardism, in principle, make them opposite to each other. In his detailed anthology of Latin American vanguards, Jorge Schwartz explains why he excludes the regionalist manifesto of Gilberto Freyre (1900–1987), which, for many years, was regarded as a representative product of the 1920s–that is, until Freyre himself admitted having written it in 1952. Yet Jorge Luis Borges (1899–1986) had already alerted us to the epistemological value of falsifications: Should we refuse, in the name of a confession that pays tribute to "historical truth," to question the conditions that make the links between a document and an era real? Freyre's manifesto *seemed* to form part of a constellation of the 1920s; the empirical fact that delayed it for three decades ought not to erase the traces of its credible belonging to a climate of ideas.

We know that Latin American literary vanguards comprise a multiplicity of paradoxes, paradoxes that are undoubtedly included within the framework of the insistent reflection on Latin American identity that is broader and more extended in time. We know that the literary form of the essay played a leading role in this process, as borne out by such works as *Radiografía de la pampa* [1933; *X-Ray of the Pampa,* 1971] by Ezequiel Martínez Estrada, *Historia de una pasión argentina* [1937; *History of an Argentine Passion,* 1983], by Eduardo Mallea (1903–1982), *Retrato do Brasil* [1928; Portrait of Brazil] by Paulo Prado (1869–1943), *Raízes do Brasil* [1936; Roots of Brazil] by Sergio Buarque de Holanda (1902–1982), *Interpretação do Brasil* [1947; *Brazil: An Interpretation,* 1945] by Gilberto Freyre, *Guatemala, las líneas de su mano* [1955; Guatemala, The Lines of Its Hand] by Luis Cardoza y Aragón (1904–1992) or *Laberinto de la Soledad* [1950; *Labyrinth of Solitude,* 1961] by Octavio Paz. In order to explain the power exerted by the essay from the definition of this Latin American identity (situated moreover, within the general framework of *modernismo*), Richard Morse, for example, is obliged to frame the successive as simultaneous, positing the existence of a landscape that, towards the end of the 1920s, would lead modernism to orient itself initially from an aesthetic to an ideological point of view.

Within this interpretation, for example, Mario de Andrade (1893–1945), the author of *Macunaima* (1928), would navigate the transition between both aesthetic and ideological moments and would also explain the social orientation of the Northeastern modernism of Gilberto Freyre and Graciliano Ramos (1892–1953). The theme of identity, amply developed through the essay form, would, thus, be explained not only by the diagnostic possibilities of the genre but also by the fact that its authors tended to be more critical of the *status quo* and more respectful of the aspirations of the dispossessed. Jorge Schwartz also postulates this shift from the aesthetic to the social, exemplifying it in the trajectories of Pablo Neruda (1904–1973) and César Vallejo (1892–1938); this itinerary leads from the avant-garde to socialism and includes the abandonment of experimentalism and submersion in social action by Oswald de Andrade (1890–1954) and the reformulation of the aesthetic-ideological project of Martínez Estrada. Critics would appear to have detected something like the structure of the double helix in the modernist DNA in the fact that this movement constitutes *both* an aesthetic and an ideological project (either simultaneously or in successive chronological stages). It is true that modernism certainly constitutes a complex and contradictory phenomenon, implying both a criticism and a celebration of modernity itself. But the greater degree of attention given to the avant-garde aesthetics of modernism may have been a result of the brilliance of modernism itself as well as of an affinity with scholarly sensibilities. Here, perhaps, are the remains of a will to tradition that seeks to continue the task of modernization that literally exploded in the 1960s in literature, in the streets, in the mountains, and in the jungle. Since then, in the eyes of Latin American criticism, modernism has constituted a central aesthetic category that sometimes overshadows other expressions of experiences, political fables, quests, and explorations that, while not always prized, were also important at the time.

It is useful to note, however, that the heightened ideological tension of the late 1920s and early 1930s was not unique to Latin America. This period can be regarded as the era of the international ideological civil war, when the fate of the world seemed to depend on Spain, the symbol of this global struggle. Undoubtedly, the period between the Week of Modern Art in São Paulo in 1922 and the Red Communist Rebellion led by Luis-Carlos Prestes (1890–1990) in November 1935 saw a number of significant historical events that modified the shape of the world, such as the Wall Street crash on 29 October 1929 and the subsequent collapse of the world capitalist economy, at least for a time. The fall in prices wrecked the economies of Argentina, Bolivia, Brazil, Chile, Colombia, Cuba, Mexico, Paraguay, Peru, Uruguay, and Venezuela–in other words, all the countries whose foreign trade was based on certain raw materials. Halperín Donghi noted that, although the crisis created a brusque anticlimax following half a century of economic expansion, it is also necessary to consider the particularity of local cycles, which, on more than one occasion, had already been completed before the end of the stage that would come to a close in the 1930s. (The historian's observation was intended to warn of the complexity and particularity of periodization.) One of the results of the Great Depression was that it banished economic liberalism for half a century and thus modified state models. During 1930 and 1931, twelve Latin American countries underwent a change of government or regime, ten of which occurred as a result of military coups. The collapse of world economies was followed by a period of war, heralded by Lugones in Lima in 1924, on the occasion of the centenary of the battle of Ayacucho.

The First World War put an end to the illusion of the inevitable rise of modernity at the very center of the model; this failure was borne out by the panorama of unfulfilled promise of the elites who controlled the Latin American economy and political development. On the one hand, as we know, historians have set the decline of the positivist paradigm between 1910 and 1920 (Leopoldo Zea). The incisiveness of the diagnosis of Western decadence offered by Spengler is borne out by the readiness of Latin America to agree with his conclusions. Be that as it may, it is not unlikely that the disintegration of the center opened up the possibility of postulating new centers or simply eliminating the center as the basis of the existence of differences. If Latin American identity is made up of a plurality of unrelated events, if its essential heterogeneity is to be found in its origins, if there is no longer a modernization program, and civic representation collapses; then the problem will lie in the adherence to a national tradition and the role of personal loyalties and relationships played out on a national scale. In other words, the redefinition of tradition opens up the very possibility of a breakdown in meaningful interpersonal relationships in quotidian reality. This factual or empirical nonrelationship can be seen as a resistance to change and the denial of the irreversibility of historical time.

It is in this respect, and only this, that Latin America was able to travel in a new and opposite direction, as the Peruvian physiologist Carlos Monge Medrano (1884–1970) wrote to his son, comparing his trip to Europe as a student to his journeys abroad from 1929 onwards, as a way to explain the results of his discovery. The *journey in the opposite direction* meant that, henceforth, it was he, the American, who would be listened to rather than listen. Likewise, this new journey was linked, in various accounts, to a review of the theories of the inferiority of the native population of Latin America and the persistent reflection on the specific identity of the Latin American social body. This journey in a new direction assumes the introduction of various new modes of order. In the intellectual sphere, it involved the abolition of the scientific view of the inferiority of the native. By way of illustration of this view, one should recall that in 1921, an expedition of U.S. and British scientists led by the physiologist Joseph Barcroft carried out observations on the effects of altitude on the human body, using the expedition members, none of whom was accustomed to the altitude, as reference. Their conclusion stated that human acclimatization to altitude was virtually impossible and that the Indians' physical and mental capacities were therefore reduced by anoxia. Dennis Jourdanet, a French physiologist, had conducted studies of this nature in Mexico during the second half of the nineteenth century and had reached similar conclusions: Mexicans were an anemic race due to the lack of oxygen in the blood experienced by the inhabitants of the plain when they were in high places, which kept them in a permanent state of weakness.

It was precisely to refute this thesis that, in 1927, Monge Medrano organized an expedition to the Andes in order to prove that the concept of normality might have other meanings; he thereby revealed the existence of physical and physiological mechanisms that Andean men had developed over the centuries in order to acclimatize to the low oxygen pressure at high altitudes. The description of the loss of acclimatization to altitude was internationally recognized as an autonomous clinical entity and since 1928 has been known as Monge's Disease, in honor of his scientific-cultural crusade to vindicate Andean men.

It is clear that both Barcroft and Monge held certain beliefs before they undertook their work. Traveling in the opposite direction required not only knowledge but an idea of one's destiny. Each state of society is capable of conducting a certain type of science: Since the ancient religion of Babylon demanded the exact prediction of celestial events, it is hardly surprising that Babylonian science should have encouraged the study of astronomy. Likewise, in order to break with the scientific view of the scientific inferiority of the Indian, which they did not believe, a group of Peruvian scientists responded with the discovery of the hematological mechanisms that functioned at high altitudes. Needless to say, this discovery coincided with the moment when the question of the native in Latin America was being reconsidered; it also established the basis for turning Peru into an immense, first-rate laboratory where human physiology at high altitudes would be studied. Thus, European and North American aviators would want to discover the secrets of the highland Indians for their work in the dangerous skies of the Second World War. Something powerful was being produced in America, or so they suspected in Europe, when, after the Nobel Prize for medicine and physiology awarded to Bernardo Houssat in 1947 for his discovery of the complex interlocking of hormonal effects, many believed that the strength of the German pilots was due to the Argentine exportation of suprarenal glands to the Axis countries. This widespread pseudoscientific fable appeared to be based in part on European notions of what was Latin American. The belief that the Germans' superpowers were due to the effects of a sort of druidic potion originating in a place that combined the unknown, exoticism, and distance reflects a European, central perspective (Bataille, Caillois, Artaud) on the regenerative powers of the primitive.

At the same time, from an aesthetic point of view, there was a parallel and similar attempt to repeat and recover essential cultural elements through the reappraisal of black and indigenous art in Latin America. This was expressed by David Alfaro Siqueiros (1896–1974) in his *Manifesto de Barcelona* [Barcelona Manifesto] in 1921; in the inclusion of pre-Columbian art in the constructivist universalism of Joaquín Torres García (1874–1949); in the Afro-Americanism of Candido Portinari (1903–1962) and Wilfredo Lam (1902–1982); in the Latin Americanist *negrismo* of Nicolás Guillén (1902–1989) and his *mestizo* poetry; in the Brazilian manifestos, including both *Antropofagia* [Anthropophagy] and *Pau Brasil* [Brazil Wood] as well as *Verde Amarelo* [Green Yellow]; in the Argentine *criollo* avant-garde; and last, but not least, in the poetry of César Vallejo (1892–1938).

There was also a manifesto of a new political order in the student rebellion movement. In 1917, there was a general strike of junior and senior high school students that extended throughout Uruguay, transferring its epicenter (in 1918) to the Argentinean province of Córdoba. This movement spread in expanding waves throughout the continent, creating a new Latin American generation, which, according to José Carlos Mariátegui (1894–1930), was the result of the proletarianization of the middle class. The social and economic conditions of the future educated classes of the continent had therefore been radically transformed. In 1924, the Uruguayan Carlos Quijano (1900–1984), one of the major promoters of Latin Americanist thought and ideologies, founded in Paris a general association of Latin American students, together with José Ingenieros (1877–1925) and Victor Raúl Haya de la Torre (1895–1979).

Yet there was also an affirmation of miscegenation as the demographic evidence of a new social order, visible, for example, in José Vasconcelos (1881–1959), whose journey through the continent in 1922, as the leader of the revolutionary Mexican delegation, enabled him to create bonds of sympathy and establish the bases of his theory of ethnic unification on which he would expand in *La raza cósmica* [1925; *The Cosmic Race,* 1979] and *Indología: una interpretación de la cultura iberoamericana* [1926; Indology: An Interpretation of Contemporary Iberoamerican Culture]. According to his theories, the Amerindians had belonged to the Atlantean race of red men, which prospered and then irreversibly declined after fulfilling their particular mission. For Vasconcelos, the Inca and Aztec empires, far from being the high expression of that culture, were merely its decaying remains. In keeping with José Enrique Rodó (1871–1917) or Eduardo Paulo da Silva Prado (1860–1901), Mexicans saw the antagonism between Latin Americans and Anglo–Saxons as the true historical conflict. History's secret plan indicated that the red Atlanteans, from whom the Indians descended, would never reawaken and that the days of the pure whites, the conquerors of today, were also numbered. A new period was approaching, that of the fusion and blending of peoples. America, the oldest and newest continent in the world, was destined to be the cradle of the fifth race, the highest of all lineages, which would reveal the fundamental feature of a Spanish-American idiosyncratic identity. Unlike its predecessors, this race would not have a precarious historical mission but would become a definitive race, an integral race, the synthesis of all peoples. There would be no need to elaborate a political program along racial lines, since peoples of different races would develop their own natural policies, governed by enlightened passion: Marriage, as a result of pleasure and attraction, would be a work of art, capable of eliminating the ugliness of the earth. Vasconcelos's aesthetic-amorous evolutionism reinterpreted the disturbing present in terms of a Utopian future that would heal all wounds. He thereby affirmed that miscegenation would not be denied as the regenerative destiny of the Americas.

We can, therefore, see that this derivative heterogeneity of what was "Latin American" has historically exerted two types of pressure. The force exerted by tradition takes its direction from a relationship with the given and the inherited. Conversely, the power of centrifugal forces is derived from a ceaseless attempt to reinterpret these traditions. In culture, in society, in the regions, and on the map, the existence of a serious conflict of racial and political order begins to emerge, one that translates, in the first place, into bodies, as nontransferable results of policies and history. From this came a need to determine who the parents were—if one wished, as indeed was the case, to acknowledge one's brothers. This search required the discontinuous verticality of alliances in order to understand the continuous horizontality of the present, the mere result of a historical process. In his letter from Jamaica, Simón Bolívar (1783–1830) took it upon himself to record the time that had elapsed, in terms of human mutation, between the arrival of the European (and the conquest) and the emancipation of Latin America, stating that they had barely preserved vestiges of what they were in earlier times, that they were neither Indians nor Europeans, but rather an intermediate species between the legitimate owners of the country and the Spanish usurpers.

According to Octavio Paz, at the center of Mexican history lies orphanhood; hence the obstinate, interminable search for origin and filiation. The fact that orphanhood is not solely a Mexican notion is borne out by the Argentine rancher, patron, and writer Ricardo Güiraldes (1886–1927), who wrote *Don Segundo Sombra* (1926), a *criollo* modernista novel, the subject and

enigma of which is the *gaucho,* or homeless person (in popular language, a person who does not know his parents, or who has not been recognized by them). The development of the novel is driven by the dilemma of affiliation, which, despite being formally resolved in the end (the homeless gaucho turns out to be the illegitimate son of the owner of the ranch), fails to resolve the real problem of paternity, whose economic, ethical, cultural, and physical functions multiply without complementing each other. The dilemma also affects the author himself, Güiraldes, which is why he dedicated the novel to the gaucho–"to the gaucho in me." The aesthetic depiction of rural life does not detract from the dilemma of orphanhood through which the text raises the question of paternity. It is no coincidence that, shortly before being deported to the gas chamber, a war orphan, Benjamín Fondane (1898–1944), sought the origin of his tragedy in a film version of this very text, to which, working with Victoria Ocampo, he tried to give a Russian flavor by exploring the issue of emptiness and existential crisis.

Naturally, by tracing one's lineage, with all its political, cultural, economic, social, ethnological, and historical nuances, Fondane reveals the selective nature of what is understood as representative and typical of a people. What differs from one group to another is undoubtedly the genealogy. Whether or not one agrees, the denotative tension of the Other as barbarous shows what a shifting concept foreignness is. So much so, in fact, that one can draw an arc between what is foreign and what is native. The density of what is otherness lies precisely in the fact that, from the point of view of power, one never knows the Other or exactly what the Other wants. However, one is always suspicious of his actions and fears the consequences, revealing a specific fantasy that attributes an all-embracing power to the desires of the Other seen as a homogeneous threat. By attributing a will, a direction, and a common objective to the Other, the discriminating fantasy enables the threatened to escape from an unbearable situation. This unbearable situation is one in which the Other never ceases to make demands on "us" (the dominant, entitled elite), one in which "we" are unable to translate the desires of the Other into an unequivocal language and a specific demand; this is the allegory of the insatiable blackmailer who will exploit his victim endlessly.

The crisis of identity is, therefore, transformed into the Other's endless demands and, finally, into the emergence of what is sinister. From the Hispanicism of José Vasconcelos and Pedro Henríquez Ureña (1884–1946) (correlative to Freyre's views on the Portuguese colonizer), spanning the indigenism of Mariátegui, the vindication of the Haitian Creole in Jean Price-Mars (1876–1969), the double forswearing of Martínez-Estrada's predecessors and Paulo Prado's scorn for the policies of the Brazilian colonizer, a wide arc of dissent cuts through this idea of a focus on the origins of national identity, the family, and the state. To understand Latin America implies an intense review of the demographic order that nuances any appraisal and perception of the human and physical component of social matters; the gamble on the future, implicit in Juan Bautista Alberdi's (1810–1884) motto of "to govern is to populate" and explicitly taken up by Mariátegui, thus becomes an acceptance of the hybrid. The ideology that promoted mass immigration from Southern Europe to South America had two faces: The desire for a new white hybrid and the operation that implied annihilating the indigenous and now surplus population in the pursuit of modernizing projects.

It is, therefore, clear how Latin American politics are linked to the logic of breeding; this, however, does not belie the Platonic theory of politics. *Nomos* (the law) and *nomeus* (the shepherd) show the genealogy of a pastoral power wielded over a flock with a salvational intention and a categorical imperative. While the pastor divides and classifies, in other words, selects, the law attributes, gives lessons, and interprets bodies and spaces. The virtually infinite Latin American territorial expanse, during the lengthy period when land was the principal source of wealth, created a relationship with cruelty and with blood that undoubtedly went beyond the moment of positivism. Conversely, in lands where there were barely any industries, the new masses of immigrants would be directed by a populist leader, the true pastor of consciences. It is impossible to attribute these ideological developments to traditional thinkers alone. One should recall, by way of an example, that while condemning demographic statements which expressed the expectation that an Indian emancipation would result from an active cross between the aboriginal race with white immigrants (a form of sociological naïveté), Mariátegui shows how this naïveté was the order of the day in expectations surrounding the new future of Latin America. The majority view stated that the future of Latin America depended on the fate of miscegenation. The racism of sociologists regarding the *mestizo* (as established by Le Bon) was followed by a Messianic optimism that invested this same *mestizo*, the Other, with the hope of liberating the continent.

A Marxist such as Mariátegui rejects the promise, the prophecy, and the future predicted for a people left to their fate and removed from the truly political will to action. Modernity, in his view, is hegemony, and, in the final analysis, sovereignty. Yet this does not cause Mariátegui to diminish the importance of bodies and their hybridity. His emphasis on the economic decisions concerning the Peruvian situation and the means of resolving the latter is based, perhaps involuntarily, on the unpolluted permanence of Indian populations. If the Indian, as an organic member of society and culture, can find the key to modern civilization on his own, his capacity for political, social, and economic struggle is also due to his survival: According to Mariátegui, the biological material of the Tahuantinsuyo has remained unchanged after four centuries.

One could say that, in every case, following the era of the modernizing social laboratory, there is a need to observe results and evaluate gains and losses. The most obvious result of the latter is the existence of visible remains, like the corporeal human mass that emerges from the demographic policies of the learned elites. The most obvious proof of the failure of these policies created by the Liberal imagination is provided by Carlos Bunge (1875–1918) when, in *Nuestra América* [Our America], he is compelled to condone the effects of elements as disparate and difficult to manipulate as smallpox, alcoholism, and tuberculosis because of their ability to decimate the Indian and African populations.

A population of mixed race, urban poor, and immigrants came together in the cities and formed extended systems of mediation and negotiation between the main demographic entities of Indians, blacks, Spaniards, and some of the most recent European arrivals. These ubiquitous presences forced the reflection, affirmation, or rejection of the impact of history on bodies. Yet those who do so have looked at themselves in the mirror; their own bodies have also been closely observed. Leopoldo Lugones (1874–1938) had successfully exalted the

gaucho as an emblem of nationality in a social world comprising new *othernesses* (in *El payador* [1916; The Ballad Singer]) and even managed to ignore Bolívar's declaration "we are neither Indian nor European" in order to postulate that the *mestizos* were the Others. The visibility of his hybrid nature escaped him: Lugones sought to control the uncontrollable by defining a stable and therefore abstract *mestizo*. He was constantly troubled by his negation of himself as a *mestizo*; for a time, the *mestizo* served as the basis of class distinction for the patrician learned and urban elites. The same thoughts are expressed by Alfonso Reyes (1889–1959) in the first issue of *Sur* in his self-portrait: His physical features are those of an Indian, but, he states, his mind is European. This, then, was what constituted being a living contradiction in terms, the amphibian of miscegenation, neither fish nor reptile.

Human existence, it was stated over and over again, depended on codes of behavior, rules of control in civilized society, but where there had been order, there was now an uncontrolled mindless palpitation, the pulse of which continued in a social body that was brain-dead. Even the traditional life and death split was no more. The split was now between normal life and a horrendous inert life, a kind of living death, a machine-like nonlife that controlled the state apparatus as a mob. In his own way, and before Freud, Martínez Estrada accurately pointed out the distance between idea and matter, the hiatus between past and present, when he wrote, in his poem *Argentina* (1927), that the meek, foundational efforts of the fathers of the nation was an idea and not of flesh and blood. The lack of representation of death in the unconscious became a postulation of the phantasmagoric nature of history in psychologists' discourse on the national character.

Failing to take these paradoxes into account, the thought about the past, present, or future identity of Latin America made abundant use of a rhetoric of biology, thus making a lexical link with the positivism against which it railed. As in Vasconcelos's prophecy, in many cases, it metaphorically implied the creation of cell tissue that would be the new biological man. The writers who offered their prophecies or criticisms spoke at length of the attention to bodies and miscegenation as one of the most important features of the present. Like the Cuban Virgilio Piñera (1912–1979) in *La carne de René* [1952; The Flesh of René], the Ecuadorian Jorge Icaza (1906–1978) in *Huasipungo* (1934) subsequently framed his denunciation in the rhetoric of nausea: Not merely flesh, but rotten, diseased, stinking flesh. His list of what was foul was almost limitless.

Endless variations on this theme emerged, arising from the examination of the hybrid social body, Gilberto Freyre (1900–1987), in his preface to *Casa grande & senzala* [1933; The Masters and the Slaves, 1946], held that everything seemed to depend on him and his generation, and that, of all the problems, none concerned him as deeply as miscegenation. Perhaps Gilberto Freyre, even more than Fernando Ortiz (1881–1969), best evaluated the mixture of bodies of heterogeneous origin in the American continent: He regarded the difference between race and culture as fundamental. This crucial differentiation had already been expressed in *Raza y Cultura* [Race and Culture], a speech delivered by Pedro Henríquez Ureña on Columbus Day in 1934 that, as the Dominican pointed out, could well have been called the day of Hispanic culture. In Freyre's terms, this operation involved discriminating between the effects of purely genetic relationships and those involving social influences. This radical expansion and displacement of genetic and social causes is far from evident. In order to acquire scientific status, as Freyre proposes, it is impossible to break completely with the models and blood laws imposed by racist versions of positivism. Freyre himself used the regulating framework of Wissler's theories of bio-chemical content, the economic determinations of Marxism, the psycho-physiological studies by Walter Cannon and Arthur Keith, and even agreed with Francisco José de Oliveira Viana (1883–1951) who, in *Evolução do Povo Brasileiro* [Evolution of the Brazilian People], had written an apology for the white groups in his country based on the hypothesis that the tropical climate per se was capable of making northern Europeans degenerate.

Gilberto Freyre's attempts at synthesis and erudition can be seen from the heterogeneity of his acknowledgments: Hacienda owners, former slaves, colleagues, libraries, archives, museums, sugar mill owners, his own relatives, and the relatives of barons and viscounts—a world shot through by antagonisms whose harmonious coexistence was possible only in books. One could say that, in order to avoid succumbing to the alienation of the subject, paying attention to bodies required close observation of the (Freudian) primary scene in Latin America. In a famous and fairly recent song, Silvio Rodríguez, the singer-songwriter of the group Nueva Trova Cubana, dreamt about serpents. Paulo Prado, Octavio Paz, Martínez Estrada, Gilberto Freyre, Carlos Mariátegui, and Price-Mars dreamt of wolves, as in the famous dream of the "Wolf Man" analyzed by Freud, in which several of these animals, high up in the branches of a walnut tree and absolutely immobile, stare fixedly, terrorizing the dreaming four-year-old. Freud interprets this image as the child's view of the sexuality of his parents. This disturbing fixed gaze can be made doubly perturbing in Spanish and Portuguese, since these languages can supplement the visual aspects of the dream, representing, as in a concrete poem, the eyes in the vowels that spell out the word: l-O-b-O.

This is why it is not only a question of knowing who our parents are but of seeing what they have done with their sexuality: As Octavio Paz said, the question of origin was the secret center of anxiety and anguish. Paulo Prado entitles the first chapter of *Retrato do Brasil* [Portrait of Brazil] "Luxúria" ["Lust"]. This Edenic paradise was the Brazilian territory where the Portuguese colonizers, as violent adventurers, arrived to unleash the exuberance of youth, exercise their desires, and satisfy their sexual appetite. Fired up by the nudity of the Indian women, they multiplied their purely animal unions; their immorality seemed literally terrifying and absolutely limitless.

The essays of Gilberto Freyre (from a less traumatic although no less explicit perspective), Martínez Estrada, Mariátegui, and Octavio Paz focus on the Conquest, describing as rape the first physical contact, provoked by the shortage of white women, between the conquistadors and the Indian women. Thus, the population of the Americas is the direct result of violence: *Mestizos* were engendered in infamy, while the imputation of this carries repugnance of one who satisfies his fleshy appetites, as Martínez Estrada dramatically suggests. The population bears the stigma of these irregular unions, which, over time, would turn the past into a time of accumulated shame. The time that has elapsed since this era of shame is described best through the genre of the essay, undertaken as an essential task for understanding the present. The shame of the past assumes the form of trauma. The unusual persistence of Cortés and La Malinche in the Mexican imagination and sensibility, as Paz suggests, shows that they are more than

historical figures; they are the symbols of a secret, unresolved conflict, the meeting with *Reality*. In this respect, it would even be worth drawing up a provisional typology. Mariátegui and Martínez Estrada are situated at opposite ends of the political spectrum when dealing with the role of human will. Whereas the former deploys all the forces of rationality to explain the Peruvian situation, the latter places the degradation of history (or its irremediable impossibility) within the natural and cosmic order. Indeed, both regard the conquistador as an anachronism in Latin America by defining him as a medieval man. Yet, although one sets the conquered land in a more ancient prehistory rather than in the context of the cosmos, the other regrets the eradication of a social plenum (Incaic communism) by invaders from an even more archaic society.

The Hybrids of Civilization and Barbarity, Nature and Culture

The cultural discourse on the difference and conjunction between natural procreation and systematic control over human production in the name of anthropological selection techniques reflects an ideological victory for ideologues of planned population control. There are some who believe that Nietzsche exaggerated when he promulgated the idea of the breeding of man (*Verhaustierung*) on the basis of state control. However, there is no doubt that a project such as this constitutes a peculiar example of hybridism, firstly because it proposes, in the short term, the elimination of all distinguishing signs of difference, and secondly, because (unlike an earlier mindless exercise of the religious salvational, imperial power, in which pastoral power was exercised by bio-cultural instincts with no empirical goal) toward the end of the nineteenth and throughout the twentieth century, the idea of human procreation without a program of breeding is replaced by the state agency that plans the hybrids. In Latin America, Domingo Faustino Sarmiento (1811–1888) brutally inscribed the awareness of two irreconcilable modes of order in the divided Latin American body within the continent's cultural and political memory. The opposition between civilization and barbarity, which has proved particularly mobile and rich in its various connotations, continues to exert an extraordinary fascination in the political, scientific, and demographic elaboration of the continent. In practical terms, the Comtean watchwords of order and progress describe the building of bridges capable of ensuring the human and cultural flow between a civilized Europe and a Latin America that was barbarous yet wished to stop being so.

By inventing a ghostly godfather, Ricardo Güiraldes domesticates the terrible shadow of Facundo, whom Sarmiento exorcises at the beginning of his famous text. He takes him to his home, uses him *pro domo sua*, introducing him into his own inner gaucho self, the gaucho within him. The negotiation between the two radically different orders of civilization and barbarity, culture and nature, spirituality and materiality, humanity and animality is achieved here by reducing the different profiles of each of the terms. The result is not strictly a synthesis, since a complete suture could not exist between these poles that history has forced to move in both directions at once, which are thus quite barbarous and quite civilized at the same time. It is hardly surprising that this revision should coincide with the much-quoted revelation of Walter Benjamin—avid reader, like Martínez Estrada, of the writings of George Simmel (the source, in fact, of the idea that there are no documents of culture that are not also documents of barbarity).

Paradoxically, positivism, which emphasized social determinism and the natural laws of evolution, also carried the illusion of the conquest as dominating nature through technological and scientific progress in America, the same way that positivists had sought to control demography in Latin America. The antipositivist reaction would emphasize the illusory nature of this conquest, which, even today, is far from complete. In Peru, the only thing that is well defined is nature, notes Mariátegui bluntly. Not that far removed from the convictions of Euclides da Cunha (1866–1909) or Martínez Estrada, he suggests that land is the definitive truth, the first and the last. If supremacy over nature is synonymous with modernizing rationality, the revenge of the forces that resist all domination must be expressed, or rather, is what must be expressed. The survival strategy of a Hansel and Gretel spoiled by Liberalism assumes, beyond the evident evil of the world, a stable, terrestrial area in which stones, roads, and maps indicate visible paths. Yet Latin America seems to emerge as an unstable living space in which all traces of planned urbanization are erased not only by the overwhelming, uncontrolled power of nature but also by the Latin American man, who turns the confrontation into a personal wager, which he will lose. Hence the convergence of nature as a force that swallows up man's meager efforts, or conversely, Brazilian anthropophagy and the explicit return to nature, and all the forms of the natural environment that overwhelms man from earthquakes to the tropical rainforest and the hurricanes of the Caribbean. These novels, *La Vorágine* [1924; *The Vortex*, 1945] by José Eustasio Rivera (1888–1928), *Los pasos perdidos* [1953; *The Lost Steps*, 1956] by Alejo Carpentier (1904–1980), and *La casa verde* [1967; *The Green House*, 1968] by Mario Vargos Llosa (b. 1936), nearly always feature a place where tracks are erased and roads can be walked along only once.

Nature constantly reveals its double valency: Its possibilities of destruction and creation, its untamed power and its beneficent sustenance of life. Like the jungle in *La Vorágine*, it is the source of rubber that will establish the country's wealth, and of swallowing up the protagonist together with his wife and son, but not his story, recovered thanks to Clemente Silva. It may involve extremes, as shown by the voyage through time embarked on by the narrator of Carpentier's *Los pasos perdidos* as he goes deeper into the Venezuelan jungle. When he tries to retrace his steps, he fails, for the route back cannot be traversed. This double valency is both symbolic and economic: Barbarous nature is the main provider of the resources that incorporated Latin America into international trade. However, this poorly managed natural wealth could be exhausted in the expansive cycle of the economy, often destroying the fertility of the land, as in the case of the coffee and sugar plantations, and forcing the Latin American economy to be dependent on international prices for its export products. This primary order or disorder, in many cases unforeseen (such as the wealth of guano in Peru, excremental richness par excellence), reveals the living nature of merchandise and the identity derived from it. This, in turn, has led to an entire system based on materiality and on the primary nature of subsistence: Eating and excreting, performing all one's bodily functions without shame, and even transgressing the taboos that established civilization, as in the Anthropophagous Movement.

Just as anoxia produced by altitude develops compensatory mechanisms in the blood, culture develops similar mechanisms for defining, creating, and inventing a figure to describe the hybrid. Beyond the projects of social transformation suggested by the Liberal program, this bet on barbarity, skillfully expressed by Alfonso Reyes' redundancy (the amphibian of miscegenation) also appears in the wager on the regenerating power of nature expressed by Oswald de Andrade and Martínez Estrada, for whom barbarity and civilization are two centripetal and centrifugal forces of a system in equilibrium. On the basis of these contradictory data, of affirmation and resistance, remains of transplanted colonial illusions of empire or authenticity, reconciled if not domesticated by modernization, one of the hybrids of mythological imagination that have most forcefully intervened in the history of the continent begins to emerge on the contemporary scene. Encyclopedias, dictionaries, and compilations of beliefs bear out the view expressed by Jorge Luis Borges in *Libro de los seres imaginarios* [1967; Book of the Imaginary Beings]: That the terrible image of the centaur lies at the origin of the American conquest, based on the belief that, for the Indians, who were unfamiliar with horses, Pizarro's or Hernán Cortés's soldiers were physically joined to their steeds. The Latin American centaur, on which the imaginative vision of the hybrid would be based, was the centaur at the agonizing moment of taming, at the painful and still unstable moment of metamorphosis. Colt and rider resembled a wounded centaur, as Martínez Estrada tells us in his poem on horse training, in the brutal melee of the rodeo where steer, horse, and man are indistinguishable.

Unlike what we find in Greek and Hellenistic iconography, the Latin American hybrid does not ride Apollo's horses or tolerate a third person on his mount. He finds identity in the very process of his always unstable alloy, threatened by a horse's plunge or his lack of experience. His concern is for what creates a hybrid being, rather than hybridization itself. It is Santos Luzardo, the civilizer and barbarian in *Doña Bárbara* (1929) by Rómulo Gallegos (1884–1969), and it is also Doña Bárbara and the raped mother described by Octavio Paz. The conclusion is similar to the experience of Macunaíma in the city: The final thought that men were machines and machines, men. We are thereby distancing ourselves from humanism. Human selection obviously creates unease, yet it is no less true that abandoning this possibility, as in the times of the original impotency when this power was delegated to God or others, far from resolving the issue, prevents the understanding that man is not necessarily man's friend. On the contrary, recent cultural history shows that, for his fellow men, man represents the highest power, which produces not only purely modernist malaise in culture, but a postmodernist abandonment of the notion of humanism.

In Latin American cultural history, the images of the cannibal and the centaur indicate the process of the combination of bodies. Both figures emerge as a process, never as a product. (Hence the obsession with the horse-training scene, correlative to the obsession with the primary scene.) The Latin American barbarian, who is, at the same time, a remnant of a lost civilization, is perceived in nature and also in the masses, in other words, as what can be trained and harnessed, the thing whose voice can be transformed into the howl of a bleeding animal, as in Jorge Icaza's *Huasipungo*. The "animalization" and "naturalization" of man and his body no longer fulfills even the basic conditions of reproduction of the social order. The Indian masses produce and die; they build a highway over the marsh, which has been drained at a massive cost to human life. The type of naturalism represented by *Huasipungo* is worth reviewing, particularly the consideration of the reproductive or mimetic nature of the Indian language. This is presented as an absolutely zero degree of language, in other words, a purely affective language: The only language that can be transformed into the howl of a bleeding animal. This line of development includes the animal transformation of the narrator in Clarice Lispector's work (1925–1977): She takes animal transformation beyond modernism. Lispector's narrative is devoid of all mimetic experience—in the quasi-cockroach, G. H, and Macabea, the quasi-rat. She pushes the human body beyond all mimetic registers and into a primeval sense of life. In this hybrid of the masses and nature, one can also see the type figures of political domination. In many Latin American countries, the space devoted to the rider, in the fable of the horse-trainer, will be simultaneously or successively occupied by popular leaders and armies, men on horseback and their battles. The instability of power in this constant struggle for dominance leads to the creation of the *cacique* type, in which one strongman is indistinguishable from another.

The 1960s and 1970s: The Period of Revolution

For heuristic purposes of analysis, one can establish an outline of the periods of the construction of Latin American identity. If the mode of order of modernity declared that the future was now, and its successors were concerned only with changing the present and abolishing the centrality of political power in an emancipatory social revolution modeled on the Cuban revolution as in the version of Ernesto (Che) Guevara (1928–1967): The present is the struggle, and the future will be ours. *El socialismo y el hombre nuevo en Cuba* [Socialism and the New Man in Cuba], Guevara's famous text, written during his trip to Africa, is in fact a letter sent to Carlos Quijano for publication in the Uruguayan weekly *Marcha* (directed by Quijano from 1939). It is not a historical curiosity but rather an important indicator of how this Latin Americanism served as mediation between José Ingenieros's (1877–1925) progressive ideas of the late nineteenth century and Che Guevara's vision of the twenty-first century, heralded by the creation of a publishing house of that name Siglo Veintiuno Editores during the 1960s.

From the 1960s onwards, Latin America formed new political blocs with other regions, citing a new diagnosis and focusing on new relationships: The illness/identity to be resolved was called "dependency," and the program to cure this was a new means of insertion in the world, one that took on itself the task of "liberation"; the result of this worldwide involvement reaching from Africa and the Middle East to America would be a future identity, this time a full one. By going in an already-defined direction, Latin America would no longer be a "way of living" but would have a "position" in the world, and would claim its long-demanded rights. The response to the challenge of this new, inevitable, and imminent liberation was the figure of the new Latin American man. Its definitive version, in both theory and practice, was conceived by Ernesto Guevara, one of the most enduring symbols of Latin America's new moment ushered in by the Cuban revolution. In it, the idea of *hybris* underlying the Nietzschean *Übermensch* re-emerges.

Man would be the *locus* of this renovating metamorphosis; he would no longer be defined by his physical features but by his relationships. This is the oppressed man described by Paulo Freire (1921–1997), exploited and dominated, one of the "outcasts of the world" to whom he devotes his *Pedagogía del oprimido* [1970, *Pedagogy of the Oppressed*, 1970]. Or this is the

bandit proclaimed by his compatriot, Hélio Oiticica, through the motto "seja bandido, seja herói" ["be he bandit, be he hero"]. Unlike Vasconcelos's new man, founded in the expectation of the biological force of miscegenation, the current image shifts to the new and, as yet, undetermined man: The human being who will arise in the future, based on the struggle of liberation and sacrifice. This future man who responds to the Latin American hour of revolution implies a new type of family line. His code is not genetic or even eugenic, but purely ideological. This new family of man possesses the strength of will and does not develop in segments. Its prefigurement is to be seen in warriors, individual men who have produced a mutation in themselves: A physical mutation for resisting inclemency and obstacles, a spiritual mutation that leads to the giving of the self to the cause of the liberation of human forces capable of fully developing in a radically transformed society.

Latin American political thought comes back to reality in the force and persuasiveness of liberation theology, which also arose during this period. Camilo Torres (1929–1966), priest and guerrilla leader assassinated in 1966, caused a major shift in thinking when he said that whoever was not a revolutionary was guilty of mortal sin. The hopes of transcendence were secularized in the new man: The violence of the Christian apocalypses shifted to an understanding—until then hypocritically concealed behind the rhetoric of submission that the church had promulgated—of violence as a constituent feature of politics, all politics.

The period of the 1960s and 1970s constitutes an era with its own historical density and fairly precise limits, separating it from the constellations immediately before and after it, surrounded, in turn, by thresholds that enable it to be identified as a temporal and conceptual entity in its own right. The Cuban revolution, the decolonization of Africa, the Vietnam war, the civil rights movement in the United States, and the various outbreaks of youth rebellion allow one to postulate a set of institutional, political, and socioeconomic relationships without which it is extremely difficult to imagine how the perception could have arisen that the world was about to change and that intellectuals would have a role in this transformation, either as its spokesmen or as an inseparable part of its own revolutionary energy. During the 1960s and 1970s, according to the manifestos and declarations that proliferated at the time, the logical unfolding of the dialectic materialist view of history appeared to be inevitable, and it was expressed in the emergence of an accelerated sense of time, whose best metaphor is that of the furious chariot of history that trampled the hesitant underfoot. This was a moment when politics gave meaning to various practices and structured a generalized perception of the inevitable and longed-for transformation of the world of institutions, subjectivity, art, and culture. This is the perception within which truly groundbreaking events, such as the Cuban Revolution, were interpreted.

The belief in the inevitability of socialism went hand-in-hand with the idea that it (rather than capitalism) embodied the historical rationality of modernity: The domination of the majority by the minority was, for many intellectuals, a reality that was not only ethically unacceptable but an affront to intelligence. The world in general and Latin America in particular seemed convinced of the imminence of a radical change in the world and in man. Even in the United States, on 12 May 1966, Senator Robert Kennedy gave a televised speech in which he publicly acknowledged what seemed to be obvious to the left: A revolution was imminent in Latin America. Even the Church, affected by the climate of the times, transformed its pastoral discourse. New laws, new pastors. New *nomoi,* new *nomia.* Indeed, from the papacy of John XXIII onwards, when the encyclicals *Mater et magistra* (15 May 1961) and *Pacem in terris* (11 April 1963) were proclaimed, the Church introduced what was known as *aggiornamento* ("bringing up to date"). As a result, official ecclesiastic discourse was permeated by reinterpretations of the mandate of charity. As part of this modernization by the Vatican Council, Paul VI defined the moment as a *new era* in history, one characterized by the gradual worldwide spread of profound changes. The Church, thereby, increased its contacts with the African and Latin American continents. The climax of this strategy was the General Latin American Episcopal Conference in Medellín (1968), where the Pope was received with a speech confirming that an abnormal situation existed in Latin America, where the dignity of human beings was ignored and where vast masses were still awaiting the sign of their redemption. Those calm promises of peaceful coexistence, endorsed by the meeting at Camp David between Kennedy and Khrushchev, failed to consider the geographical breadth of the world map: Africa, Latin America, and Asia were the scene of a revolutionary wave that swept much of the world. The decolonization of Africa, the Cuban revolution, and Vietnamese resistance undoubtedly served as a radical denial of the predictions of those who, shortly beforehand, had predicted the end of revolutionary ideologies.

Yet the new political and intellectual agenda proposed the rejection of all colonial powers, postulating an anti-imperialism that, without rejecting the idea of national sovereignty and liberation, coexisted with the expectation that the world revolution had already begun. The conviction that the scenario of history was changing and that it would thereafter unfold in the Third World also gained currency. These expectations concerning peripheral revolutionary possibilities were periodically renewed in discourses that were virtually harangues. There was a shift from a Eurocentric, Western, or North Atlantic perspective to one of polycentricism. Third-World leaders were constructing a new revolutionary theory for new actors with new battles to fight. Although the perception of new antagonisms failed to eliminate the class struggle, it underlined other elements in conflict. Terms such as oppressive and oppressed nations, developing or developed nations involved new perspectives on domination and exploitation, suggesting that the rebellion of the proscribed and outsiders, the exploited and the persecuted of other races and colors, the unemployed and the unemployable was revolutionary, even if their consciences were not. Che Guevara expressed a similar idea: The military avant-garde could trigger the conditions for a revolution even though subjective conditions were not ripe.

The explanatory category of imperialism was invoked with renewed force to explain why the revolution had not begun in the societies of advanced capitalism as Marx had predicted. According to this explanation, the lack of proletarian revolutions in developed countries was due to the material well-being enjoyed by even the least privileged classes as a result of the exploitation of colonies, new and old. Intellectuals, too, stated that capitalist countries had weakened the revolution and the social conflict at the heart of societies, because they had improved the living standards of their proletariat through the exploitation of the impoverished masses of Africa, Asia, and Latin America. It was also believed, however, that this

situation was drawing to a close. The dependent countries had also acquired an awareness of the struggle that they would have to wage to liberate themselves and, consequently, to create the conditions that would make a proletarian revolution inevitable in the central (industrialized) countries.

At the conceptual level, the theory developed by Latin American sociologists and economists, and subsequently known as the dependency theory, proved crucial. These analyses emerged as a result of a double matrix: They were rooted in the interpretation of the Economic Commission for Latin America (ECLA)–inspired by Raúl Prebisch–of the growing deterioration of the terms of exchange between underdeveloped countries, which produced raw materials of "low aggregate value," and industrialized countries. In this respect, the creators of the dependency theory believed that a fundamental starting point would be to refute the hypothesis that development in peripheral countries would necessarily involve repeating the evolutionary stages of the economies of the central countries. To this end, they sought to elaborate an integrated development model in which development and underdevelopment were viewed as two, mutually necessary sides of the same coin, rather than as successive stages in a universal development model. Dependency theory was also based on a Marxist matrix, a reinterpretation of Lenin and his concept of imperialism.

The crisis in political thinking also affected trust in the revolutionary role of the Soviet Union, the residual leader of the socialist camp, which, at that time, was vying for leadership with an emerging China. In fact, the anti-Communists, who believed that the decline of the Cold War would put an end to the lengthy fight for hegemony between the two major world powers (since it had come to be known as "peaceful coexistence"), had failed to perceive that there were new revolutionary energies that were not derived from the old Communist parties. Indeed, none of the existing Communist parties or states seemed to be the ideal place for promoting a Third World revolution. Despite the fact that over half the world had been won over by socialism, the party of professional revolutionaries created by Lenin was dedicated to the defense of the thesis of socialism in a single country.

The nationalistic component of the new Latin American left, together with the characteristics of Communist parties on the continent, which always toed the Soviet Union Communist Party line, showed the need for a new road to progress. If the militants themselves started from the basis that it was essential to fight against party dogma, those who had never followed party guidelines would find this theoretical struggle even less traumatic. The condemnation of the new left by Communist party leaders was emphatically rejected by critical intellectuals who no longer accepted the criteria of undisputed authority, or felt that their social importance had declined. For militants of the new Latin American revolutionary causes and also for their intellectual fellow travelers, the widespread discredit of both the democratic-bourgeois political systems and the traditional Communist parties led to the conviction that only a violent revolution could produce genuine socialism. Violence thus acquired its central status in the political life of leftist militants and intellectuals. The perception that the social order itself was based on violence enabled revolutionary counterviolence to be set against the violence of the oppressors. Moreover, even the central conflict of modernization–the tension between universe and region–was legitimized by this code. The unjust violence of the colonial order was followed, in a story such as *A hora e a vez de Augusto Matraga* [1946; The Hour and Time of Augusto Matraga] by João Guimarães Rosa (1908–1967), in which the protagonist goes through a religious conversion and commits himself to holy violence.

Establishing the start of the 1960s and 1970s period is far simpler than determining when it ended. In 1997, in a review of his own political life and its trajectory, Régis Debray dubbed the leftist militancy a "spectral community," meaning that it had evolved around a completely mistaken ideological or blind view of the world. For this Frenchman, the 1960s and 1970s constituted the last transformation of Marxism, which, whether reformulated or orthodox, had served as the main theoretical signpost for the era. This era constituted the great frustration of expectation, the swan song of educated culture in Latin America and the world. We know for a fact that the world revolution failed to take place. Were this leftist community, so powerful in its production of discourse and so convincing regarding the changes it heralded, and this period, when the masses mobilized to a thitherto unprecedented degree, the result of baseless illusion? If, in Débray's view, the left was mistaken, might not the succession of military coups and brutal waves of repression have been a response based on the very conviction that the revolution was imminent (and therefore had to be combated)? Were the forecasts mistaken, or was the use of force modified to suppress existing revolutionary impulses?

These questions cannot be answered, yet must be raised. Many protagonists and witnesses of this period are currently reviewing the beliefs and convictions they held then. This is borne out by the growing mass of books and research on the period that reveal a considerable degree of sympathy for the revolution that never materialized and show that the interpretation of this period has not yet been concluded. Yet, although a period can be defined by a conceptual framework that can be expressed at a given moment, the end of a period is linked to a powerful redistribution of discourses and a transformation of the paradigm itself that can or cannot be discussed. In 1971, in Bolivia, General Hugo Banzer overthrew his colleague Torres, whose populist national government was supported by much of the left. Between 1971 and 1974, Banzer consolidated a repressive regime that was strikingly similar to those of other Latin American dictators. In 1973, the overthrow of Salvador Allende's socialist government in Chile marked the end of one of the experiences that had fed the expectations of regional transformation. At the same time, in Uruguay, the president-elect Bordaberry, who had come to power in 1971, defeating the leftist Frente Amplio in the elections, curtailed civil rights in a process that was further expanded when Aparicio Méndez was deposed as a de facto president in 1976. In August 1975, the Peruvian general Morales Bermúdez defeated another general, Velasco Alvarado, who had been supported by important leftist intellectuals and even militant former guerrillas and whose government had undertaken an agrarian reform to the detriment of large landowners. In March 1976, another military regime took over in Argentina, beginning a wave of repression that reached hitherto unknown levels in that country. The military dictators' brutal coercion imposed the nature and limits of discourse by force, taking repression of all dissent to extremes and silencing them by censorship or murder (see **Figure 1**).

Figure 1.

Photograph of one of the 'Mothers of the Plaza de Mayo' Buenos Aires. (Courtesy Juan Villegas)

To return to the Church, it is useful to note that the Church also yielded to the imposed silence of the period. Many of the terms that had held a particularly important significance were re-interpreted. The encyclical *Evangelii nuntiandi*, promulgated by Paul VI, the Medellín pope, redefined in far less political terms the awkward connotations of the word "liberation" that had been emblematic of that Colombian conference. In many respects, this period can be regarded as a crisis of hegemony in the Gramscian sense; in other words, as a crisis in the habitual nature of the pact between the dominators and the dominated, producing a tie between antagonistic forces. An emblematic metaphor, *the old dies without allowing the new to be born*, sums this up. It involves a crisis of trust that affects all parties, includes all organs of public opinion—particularly the press—and is disseminated throughout civil society. It implies, in the last analysis, that the ruling class no longer performs its economic, political, and cultural function of propelling society as a whole forward. As a result, the ideological structure that lends the ruling class cohesion and hegemony tends to collapse. One should recall that the construction of hegemony is a necessary condition for a dominant class to become a ruling class, which in turn tends to undermine the very ideology that lent it cohesion and hegemony. Indeed, Gramsci had already pointed out that the collective awareness of the subaltern classes should not necessarily become a revolutionary awareness and warned that the politicization of the subaltern classes had less likelihood of success, given that these classes did not have the same ability to reorient and reorganize themselves as quickly as the ruling classes. In the modern world, the most frequent examples of crisis resolution of this nature are usually regressive; in other words, they end with the recomposition of the previous political structure. In a situation of this nature, the dominant sectors always have more alternatives; the recomposition of civil society; the use of political society through the use of the state apparatus in order to quash the reaction of the subaltern classes or to separate them from their intellectuals by force, political attraction, or Caesar-like solutions in which providential or charismatic men emerge. At times like these, both camps are equally strong, yet neither has an absolute possibility of winning.

Beyond knowing whether a crisis of hegemony effectively took place, there is no doubt that, one way or another, the international left interpreted the general process of politicization, together with other signs, as though it was actually facing a crisis of this nature, particularly in Latin America. Indeed, through their media channels, critical intellectuals and militants announced the imminent end of capitalism, whose agony could be read in the events of Vietnam and the replacement of the dollar standard in Europe, the rejection of U.S. politics by significant groups of liberal intellectuals in the United States; and the emergence of black power and other movements was regarded as proof, in the words of the much-quoted Martí, of the poverty that corrupts from the very entrails of the monster. For leftist militants and intellectuals, it was significant that the American army, with all its paraphernalia and professional training, should have lost a war in which all its prestige as a superpower was at stake against a poorly armed group of amateur combatants.

For this reason, if the era can be regarded in Gramscian terms as a crisis of hegemony, its closing coincided with the recomposition of the old method of hegemonic domination, which foundered together with the revolutionary expectations that had characterized its beginning. This hypothesis allows one to posit a second point when the crisis ended: The process of the death of the old without the birth of the new implies the end of a future that could have been possible, a future that had been meticulously outlined by successive generations of society. In this respect, the era came to an end when this future was called a Utopia when, in the words of Dante, the doors of the future were closed.

Translation by Suzanne D. Stephens

Works Cited

Andrade, Mario de. 1988. *Macunaíma. O herói sem nenhum caráter.* Edição crítica Telê Porto Ancona Lopez. Florianópolis: Coleção Arquivos.

Bolívar, Simón. 1984. "Carta de Jamaica." *Contestación a la Carta de Jamaica.* Ed. Simón Becerra Rondón. Caracas: Comité Ejecutivo del Bicentenario de Simón Bolívar. 85–120.

Borges, Jorge Luis with Margarita Guerrero. 1967. *El libro de los seres imaginarios.* Buenos Aires: Editorial Kier.

Buarque de Holanda, Sérgio. 1936. *Raízes do Brasil.* Rio de Janeiro: Olympio.

Bunge, Carlos Octavio. 1905. *Nuestra América. (Ensayo de psicología social).* Buenos Aires: Valerio Abeledo.

Cardozo y Aragón, Luis. 1955. *Guatemala, las líneas de su mano.* Mexico City: Fondo de Cultura Económica.

Carpentier, Alejo. 1953. *Los pasos perdidos.* Mexico City: Ed. y Distribución Iberoamericana de Publicaciones.

Debray, Régis. 1996. *Loués soient nos seigneurs: Une education politique.* París: Gallimard.

Freire, Paulo. 1970. *Pedagogía del oprimido.* Montevideo: Tierra nueva.

Freud, Sigmund. 1948. "Historia de una neurosis infantil." *Obras Completas.* Volumen II. Madrid: Biblioteca Nueva.

Freyre, Gilberto. 1937. *Nordeste.* Rio de Janeiro: Olympio.

———. 1947. *Interpretação do Brasil: Aspectos da Formação Social Brasileira como Processo de Amalgamento de Raças e Culturas.* Rio de Janeiro: Olympio.

———. 1992. *Casa-Grande & Senzala.* Rio de Janeiro: Editora Record.

Gallegos, Rómulo. 1986. *Doña Bárbara.* Ed. Luis Harss and Alberto Blasi. Buenos Aires: Biblioteca Ayacucho, Hyspamérica.

Gramsci, Antonio. 1984. *Notas sobre Maquiavelo, sobre la política y sobre el estado moderno.* Trans. José Aricó. Buenos Aires: Nueva Visión.

Guevara, Ernesto. 1987. "El socialismo y el hombre nuevo en Cuba." *El socialismo y el hombre nuevo.* Ed. José Aricó. 7th ed. Mexico City: Siglo XXI. 3–18.

Guimarães Rosa, João. 1946. "A hora e vez de Augusto Matraga." *Ficção completa.* Rio de Janeiro: Editora Nova Aguilar. 429–462.

Güiraldes, Ricardo. 1926. *Don Segundo Sombra.* Buenos Aires: Proa.

Halperín Donghi, Tulio. 1997. *Historia contemporánea de América Latina.* Quinta reimpresión. Mexico City: Alianza.

Henríquez Ureña, Pedro. 1978. *La utopía de América.* Caracas: Biblioteca Ayacucho.

———. 1998. "Raza y cultura hispánica." *Ensayos.* Ed. José Luis Abellán and Ana María Barrenechea. Mexico City: Fondo de Cultura Económica. 319–25.

Icaza, Jorge. *Huasipungo.* 1930. Buenos Aires: Las grandes obras, Espasa Calpe.

Lispector, Clarice. 1964. *A Paixão Segundo G.H.* Rio de Janeiro: Editôra do Autor.

———. 1977. *A Hora da Estrela.* Rio de Janeiro: Livraria J. Olympio Editora.

Lugones, Leopoldo. 1916. *El payador.* Buenos Aires: Otero.

Mallea, Eduardo. 1939. *Historia de una pasión argentina.* Buenos Aires: Espasa–Calpe.

Mariátegui, José Carlos. 1928. *Siete ensayos de interpretación de la realidad peruana.* Lima: Amauta.

Martínez Estrada, Ezequiel. 1947. "Argentina." "La doma." *Poesía.* Buenos Aires: Argos. 143–59, 165–66.

———. 1991. *Radiografía de la Pampa.* Ed. Leo Pollman. Madrid: Archivos CSIC.

Ortiz, Fernando. 1978. *Contrapunteo cubano del tabaco y el azúcar.* Caracas: Biblioteca Ayacucho.

Paz, Octavio. 1959. *El laberinto de la soledad.* Mexico City: Fondo de Cultura Económica.

Piñera, Virgilio. 1995. *La carne de René.* Havana: Ediciones Unión.

Prado, Eduardo Paulo da Silva. 1997. *Retrato do Brasil.* Ed. Carlos Augusto Calil. São Paulo: Companhia das Letras.

Ramos, Graciliano. 1938. *Vidas secas.* Rio de Janeiro: José Olympio.

Reyes, Alfonso. 1931. "Compás poético." *Sur* 1: 64–73

Rivera, José Eustasio. 1976. *La vorágine.* Caracas: Biblioteca Ayacucho.

Sarmiento, Domingo Faustino. 1921. *Facundo (Civilización y barbarie).* Buenos Aires: Librería "La Facultad."

Torres García, Joaquín. 1984. *Universalismo constructivo.* Madrid: Alianza.

Vasconcelos, José. 192? *La raza cósmica. Misión de la raza iberoamericana. Notas de viajes de la América del Sur.* París, Madrid, Lisboa: Agencia Mundial de Librería.

———. 1958. *Indología: una interpretación de la cultura iberoamericana contempóranea.*

Obras completas. Mexico City: Libreros mexicanos unidos. 2: 1069–303.

Viana, Francisco José de Oliveira. 1956. *Evolução do povo brasileiro.* Rio de Janeiro: Livraria José Olympio Editora.

Zea, Leopoldo, ed. 1993. *América Latina en sus ideas.* Mexico City: Siglo XXI.

SECTION II
ORALITY AND LITERATURE
Introduction
Eugenia Meyer

Everything in Latin America involves language: power and freedom, domination and hope. Yet although the language of barbarity wishes to subject us to the linear determinism of time, the language of imagination seeks to destroy that fatality by freeing the simultaneous spaces of what is real.

(Carlos Fuentes 58)

In the past, orality was regarded as primitive, as folklore, or as the merely popular, in contrast to written texts, whereas today historians and social scientists are aware of the need to recover the richness of oral traditions as a part of history. It is difficult to ignore the paradox that historiography (in other words, historical writing) is a combination of two antonymous terms: that is, knowing and writing (Certeau 58). Because the potential intelligibility of the past undoubtedly lies in the space between doing and saying, the permanent link between social action and historical speech therefore determines the various kinds of new directions in the humanities and social sciences. Saying displays the variations of sensations, experiences, and even fiction that stand behind the written narrative with its great historical significance. Consequently, the relationship between the word and the world concerns not only linguistics or poetics but a wide range of social disciplines, including history, which attempt to explore the relationships between discourse as action and the "universe of discourse" (Jakobson 349)–in other words, the problem of the relationship between words and the world.

When social scientists study language in an interdisciplinary fashion, they find over and over again that language and culture are inextricably linked and that language, whether oral or written, can be conceived only as a social product. In this respect, popular culture is primarily expressed in oral language, which, from the moment it is written down, transcends symbolic representation and becomes a document, an instrument in creating history. It is a commonplace to observe that writing precedes history and orality comes before writing, but what is often overlooked is that, at the end of the twentieth century, the majority of the world's languages exist only in the spoken form (Kress 65). Carlos Fuentes has pointed out that "adopting a radical position towards their own past, Latin American writers undertake a review on the basis of evidence: the lack of a language. The old obligation to make denunciations becomes a far more complex task: the critical elaboration of everything that is not said in our history of lies, silence, rhetoric, and academic complicity. Inventing a language involves saying everything that history has kept secret. A continent of sacred texts, Latin America feels an urgent need for a profanation that will express four centuries of a sequestered, marginalized, and unknown language. This resurrection of a lost language requires a diversity of verbal explorations, which is one of the signs of the health of today's Latin American novel" (58).

The case of Latin America is undoubtedly significant, both because of the richness of its pre-Columbian cultures and because of the dogged attitude of its peoples in redefining and reinforcing the value of their orality. It would be difficult to explain contemporary Latin American literature without the ingredient of these multiple forms of orality, which become constant witnesses and, indeed, protagonists. Many American peoples have managed to preserve and defend their worldviews, so different and remote from those imposed by homogenizing European and Eurocentric political rule, precisely on the basis of both particular forms of orality and their own languages. Indeed, the survival of multiple cultures is based on their distinct ways of life, their understanding of nature, and the transmission of their values and beliefs through their original literatures, handed down orally from generation to generation.

Over a decade ago, Paul Verdevoye pointed out the obvious: a close relationship that exists in Latin America between literature and the realities of the environment (45–46). In this respect, the influence of orality on literary culture has been considerable, as the recovery of testimonies has had an impact on the written literature of these countries. Folklore, history, and geography are crucial elements for the understanding of orality. In the sphere of Latin American literature, both fiction and the re-creation of everyday reality abound in local phraseology, old wives' tales, vendors' cries, proverbs, popular tales, and various forms of narrativity that reflect the creative individuality and pluralism of the multiple and varied forms of Latin American literature. One outstanding feature is the richness and diversity of its myths, which teach us a great deal about the societies from which they originate, help to reveal the ways communities function, and provide the raison d'être for their beliefs, customs, and institutions. In short, myths serve to define a certain modus operandi of the human spirit, "so constant over the centuries and so widespread that they can be regarded as fundamental, meaning that one can search for them in other societies" (Lévi–Strauss 577).

This is how the inventiveness and thought of the producers of various literary genres, whether essays, novels, short stories, or poetry, are formed. All of them contain an underlying partial and perhaps unconscious discourse, reflecting the ideology of the author and the author's community and providing a glimpse of the common discursive universe with which he or she identifies, through an elementary sense of belonging. The individual or collective imagination investigates and probes into an unusual common cultural heritage; at the same time, it reinstates the natural ambiguity of language. A propos of this exploitation of natural polysemy, one has to distinguish the role of literature as a historical source (White 1992). Since we know that all texts have a certain degree of subjectivity, we should accept the fact that literary works can also serve as a form of representation in which one can observe spaces, times, personages, and persons involved in purportedly human action that could have been, although it may never have been.

The combined forces of history, anthropology, and ethnology are means through which one can recover orality (understood as a substantial element in the construction of historical memory) and therefore accept the intimate relationship between oral narration and what Unamuno called *intra-historia*, the history of everyday matters, the day-to-day struggle, the unimportant facts, on the basis of which various individual or collective-social paths are taken. This aim goes hand in hand with the need to emphasize the *long duration* (to borrow a term from Braudel) of this type of history compared with the history punctuated by events as the sole referents of historical narrative. By observing and analyzing the ways of thinking and behaving inscribed in language use and ignoring the rhetoric imposed on them, the interpretation of the various modes of discourse, whether oral or written, acquires more clarity.

It would seem then that silence can become direct expression, that those with no written history did indeed conquer their own spaces, and that a new kind of history is possible, one that gets rid of monumental deeds, depersonalized events, the great actions of heroes, and, consequently, also the great failures. The aim is not to avoid the narrative of events, but to recover everything that contributes to solid reflections on the exploratory, analytical, and expressive functions of historical constants. The Annales school in Paris has contributed major studies in this line, and in these volumes we aim to do the same for the literary cultures of Latin America.

One of the distinctive features of contemporary history is that it is based on the existence and experience of witnesses of the events studied, thereby forcing the historian to be vigilant and alert, waiting to see what will happen when historical events are contextualized. Indeed, not only is every written text, every essay, every publication subjected to the criticism and judgment of the scientific community to which it belongs, but the protagonists of the historical events being recorded can discuss the emerging historical record, having the advantage of their presence at the time of the occurrence of the events, and can contribute to the debate on what really happened. There is therefore a double requirement for the historian, because representing historical events effectively means proposing "a past whose material and mental reality cannot be fully reconstructed, and recognizing the historian's individual intelligibility which arranges a set of events so as to give them meaning. But it also means having to tell the *truth*, in the awareness that it is only possible to approach

truthfulness (*one* form of truth), which is above all, but not only, the discursive and rational part of the past" (Voldman 80).

The verbal source of the accounts of ordinary life compels historians to acknowledge that there are other perspectives and responsibilities than those that prevailed in the written accounts of the past. The importance of all this lies in being able to choose the participatory level at which one wishes to remain and in knowing the reasons and limitations, the nature and consequences of one's choices. The need then arises to intercede on behalf of *that other history,* which, in the case of Latin American countries, is based on instruments that are better suited to their local idiosyncrasy and thus adapted to national specificities and tasks rather than to any universal precepts. To some extent, these instruments have begun to gather up the loose threads of the dense fabric created by the Amerindian informants who shared their knowledge with the evangelizers and conquerors, thereby vindicating the oral tradition of their peoples by transcribing the original history of Mesoamerica. These instruments were used to gather information from peasants and workers, ordinary men and women; they attempt to restore numerous connections between the economic structures and ideological and legal-political infrastructures from which different interpretations can be made of the historical process of this century.

Jan Vansina emphasizes the coherence of the oral tradition among the peoples of Africa; the history of Latin America also draws on its oral cultural heritage, handed down from generation to generation. We should also stress the conscious efforts by Latin American peoples continuously to revalue and enrich their oral history; these efforts protect and defend the oral tradition behind written history—always tinged by the partiality and subjectivity of the clergy, who have insisted on preserving it without having been totally faithful to the original version. Narrating events is an inherent part of human nature. We narrate, communicate, preserve, invent, diversify, modify, and enrich knowledge; we unburden ourselves; and from these multiple sources history is constructed by the historian. Oral literature can be conceived as a collective creation in the sense that, regardless of its authorship, spoken discourse is appropriated by its receivers, who decode the message the moment it is received, in accordance with their personal and subjective way of understanding what has been narrated, so that they in turn become the senders of a new discourse, and so on.

Walter J. Ong, commenting on Homeric Greek culture, observes: "In an oral culture knowledge once acquired had to be constantly repeated or it would be lost: fixed formulaic thought patterns were essential for wisdom and effective administration" (24). Anyone familiar with the Mesoamerican oral tradition and its transcriptions into writing during the early Colonial period will recognize the full applicability of these comments to New Spain. It is ironic indeed that humanist Spain, which so idealized ancient Greece, would be the instrument of intolerance toward and destruction of much of the Amerindian oral tradition. When discourse is printed, and therefore fixed, a specific phenomenon takes place; by effectively eliminating the physical presence and the act of appropriation that the receiver performs in oral transmission, printing also cancels out the possibilities of remaking the past by turning the receiver into a sender of knowledge.

There are other basic characteristics of the oral tradition that are lost or radically changed in a written culture. The oral text displays a structure of addition of data, unlike written structures with their predilection for principal and subordinate information. The oral text tends to be aggregative and redundant, more concerned with conserving than with innovating; knowledge is considered precious. An oral tradition will thus place high value on the skill of old men and women who specialize in conserving the past and in telling the stories that are foundational to the community. The written text can and often does completely transcend the time and place of composition and is therefore incomplete in a way that an oral text within its community can never be. Thus, in its written form, literary creation becomes a highly individual, personal process both for writer and reader, and through it, originality becomes much more important than in an oral tradition. Conversely, in a written culture such as ours, anonymous, collective creation that is transmitted orally becomes devalued and marginalized. Thus, original, oral, formulaic production, which once maintained a permanent link between producer and receiver, is pushed into the background, regarded as belonging to the anonymous masses, and condemned to disappear as ephemeral. Current scholarship contradicts this opinion, for oral literature is today regarded as an ongoing cultural phenomenon, representative of Latin American national majorities, a fact that has prevented it from being considered subliterary. We should, however, realize that the very nature of oral literature hinders its study; as a result, very few compilations of oral texts have been published that take their peculiar features into account and treat them as literary creations. It is therefore essential not only to study oral literature closely but to reconsider its place within Latin American cultures (Mariscal 343–54).

Oral literature reflects an inheritance that is constantly renewed in transmission and grows, enriched by the community's historical knowledge—interpreting, judging, analyzing, and thereby incorporating current events. Its most recurrent themes include stories with a mythical element that explain a people's origins or sanction the behavior of community members. Some contain tales of the adventures of people who are clearly identified with the community itself, as preserved through testimonial stories that refer to everyday practices and activities, everyday history as expressed in poems, songs, and *corridos*. Raphael Samuel used to say that the aim of popular history was "to bring the limits of history closer to people's lives" (15). The historian's attention generally used to focus on structures and technology, favoring political events and ignoring reflections about the general population, unless assumed by an epic national tradition. Indeed, from the 1920s, attempts have been made to broaden the basis of history, increase the scope of its study, use new materials, and offer new maps of knowledge. This broader conception associated with Bloch, Braudel, and the Annalists constitutes an alternative to traditional political history, which was consistently transmitted through structured discourse, with the inevitable ideological bias that reflected the interests of the particular group in power.

This is the background to the recovery of the oral tradition—life stories, testimonies, and multiple forms of orality, understood as a means of giving coherence to the spontaneous tales of protagonists as everyday individuals with commonly felt desires. What is valued in the oral tradition is the depiction of the times in the life of each individual and the significance of these times in collective history. The triad of orality, oral tradition, and life stories spans the entire range of cultural expression, for every society is determined by its collective experiences. Thus these refer to communal life, education, art, communication, everyday matters, attitudes and, more recently, in keeping with modernity, ideologies and gender issues. They therefore emphasize the cyclical nature of social life, its general features, and its close relationship to the repetition of these acts in a social system. What is surprising is the frequency with which they occur, regardless of the accuracy with which they are observed or described (Barth 1969). In this respect, the question of hierarchy and equality, similarity and differences, becomes particularly important. Recovering, safeguarding, and preserving direct and personal testimony, on the basis of life stories, heuristically recovering the inherited baggage of the oral tradition, of the so-called *peoples without history,* and incorporating them into the narrated histories of ordinary men and women and anonymous protagonists—such is the function of orality in Latin America. Attempting, in short, on the basis of words and silences, emotions and tears, to catch a glimpse, perhaps as intruders, of our own otherness. Thus it is that we perceive the interaction between the voice of the oral narrator and the listener.

Our work in this history of literary culture starts with the deconstruction of memory, whether individual or collective, in order to reconstruct history in a scholarly adventure in which geography, linguistics, sociology, and anthropology join forces to compile an integral history in which time and space are regarded as fundamental elements. I am referring here to the proposal articulated by the General Editors, Valdés and Hutcheon, understood as a means of raising the multiple fabrications of the past to a conscious critical level that will permit what we could call the verbalization of writing, thereby evoking a means of philosophizing, a style of political thought, and a form of criticism and analysis, or to borrow Derrida's idea that truth is, in the last analysis, a changing, unclaimed exchange of messages, with no origin or addressee (Derrida 1980). By unleashing this memory and discovering reminiscences, one advances along three essential paths: the path of identification with collective and individual symbols; the path of the specification of the dynamics, causes, ruptures, and manipulations and of the reconfirmation of memories in a narrative that assumes its complicity with what is believed or imagined, what is recreated or told; and, finally, the path that attempts to narrate what is to be preserved.

There are certainly differences between the happening of an event and the memory of it; but how can one describe an event without involving individual and collective recollections? How can one stop time and depict an event as complete? Indeed, unleashing memory and bringing it to the surface become in themselves the initial actions of constructing history.

Recovering oral sources for literature sometimes assumes a subordinate, auxiliary function to documentary evidence; but, like the latter, oral testimony should meet the criteria of reliability, representation, and documentation. At the start of the twenty-first century, we recognize that "Historians work over significations—discourse—already achieved, already ideologized, their collective acts determined by the maintenance of the historian's privilege: that the form of story is compatible with every mode of intellection, yet transcendent to critical thought" (Cohen 326).

The historical past of a literature as recorded in national literary histories is often full of a false loftiness that can be demythologized only through an exhaustive analysis of ideological and social processes. In contrast to a version of the past determined by "the interests of power, and therefore mutilated, censored, deformed, the masses provide a more solid image, an image befitting their aspirations and one which reflects the real richness of their past" (Chesneaux 40). Our collective aim in these volumes is therefore to approach literary culture as broadly as possible. Indeed, the aim in the first half of the twentieth century was to create a critical front to oppose positivist historicism and to seek a genuinely effective relationship with other social disciplines in order to reinforce a comparative approach. One should also note, albeit in passing, the experience of the historian who, when faced with living sources, feels compelled to take unexpected positions and even recognize passions, and ultimately to *question* history. It is therefore a question of experience and one that is profoundly human. Literary history must also make room for documents from experience, in addition to historical analysis.

There is no such thing as an innocent historian or an unbiased history, just as there are no innocent readers; we are never removed from the reality that surrounds us. In short, distrust of theoretical proposals, like that of a comparative literary history, immediately comes up against a critical and personal position that challenges theory and experience. Hence the development of a freer form of history, whose interpretive function must be permanently subjected to experimentation and rational scrutiny. The danger of the researcher's naïveté or passionate romantic defense of causes continues to persist, as does the certainty that objectivity cannot be achieved and that partiality is permanent. If this were not the case, then history would be meaningless, and literary history would be a mere catalogue of names and works.

Every day, we experience having to cope with all kinds of sources. Some we locate, others we discover, and others we have often been forced to create. We should not forget that all these sources have an underlying ideological bias and a political aim, and it is precisely here that one should embark on the unavoidable task of deconstructing individual and collective memory in order to construct the history of literary culture. The uses and abuses of memory, the historical formulations after the fashion of ideologies and false consciences, cannot be avoided. However, if the historian's aim is not to serve as a channel for predetermined political interests but rather to rescue various voices and expressions from oblivion, then we shall be able to recognize the multiple crossroads and options offered by this deconstruction of memory. We should no doubt rethink the idea that "history is for analyzing the present better, so that we can design a better future" (Fontana 143), because the old formulae in which we had deposited our hopes have been disproved. The long path taken during the second half of the twentieth century, following the influence of new forms of history (or rather new forms of conceiving history) and new specializations (economic, political and social history, not to mention macro- and micro-histories, as well as the -isms of historicism, scientism, positivism, Marxism, structuralism, feminism, and even postmodern revisionism) has proved the need to return to the old task of proposing a history free of dogmatism, one that will abandon ties with any type of catechism, in short, as Mercedes Vilanova has said, "a history without adjectives" (95).

The use of testimonies as a representation of memory, the confrontation between stories and personal and collective memories (understood either as a natural elaboration or as a political construction, at set times or under set circumstances) reveals a series of conditions, options, and intentions, as well as needs, that have been arranged and constructed on the basis of specific interests. The aim, then, is to discover the origin and guiding thread of these representations in order to understand or discover the self-serving apologies of authority hidden in these processes.

Here we should also meditate on the artificial nature of recreating the versions we recover from the past, and the loss of the original aim of the person who first transmitted them. Who wishes to tell us something, and how far is he prepared to reveal himself? What do we hear and what do we want to hear? How do we feel gratified by these stories that comprise the historical story of a community's identity?

The intimate relationship between memory, time, and history finds its greatest expression in stories that, whether oral or written, become literary expression. To a certain extent, lived reality becomes the essence of narrative discourse, whether mythical, historical, or fictional (see White). If memory fades and time inexorably places a particular slant on events, the need to recover this permanent inheritance of the word and communication in its most pristine form suggests orality's multiple relations. In the simplest gestures–the sound of a drum, wind instruments that exhale expression and sentiment, rudimentary poems, litanies, couplets, *corridos*–or even in certain refined poetic forms, we find the basis of that orality that allows us to travel back and forth through time for the sake of a common history. This underscores the permanent link between history and literature as a constant theme of historical work, in order to establish an overall theory that will incorporate language through narrative discourse and temporality (Ricoeur 1995). It is Paul Ricoeur who underlines the importance of the framework, understood as a sequence of scattered events that configure symbolic representation, through the language of the experience of time.

In its earliest version, namely orality, narrative allows historians, who rarely come face to face with their object of analysis, to reconstruct an event or a series of situations and grants them the unusual privilege of interrogating the document, making it speak, and perhaps meeting it, in order to throw a "working hypothesis at it" (Ricoeur 1990, 25). Thus historians first attempt to understand what has happened, in order to satisfy themselves and then be able to explain it to others. The point is that all this is achieved within the sphere of verbal expression, through words. Orality therefore acquires another dimension, consolidating its permanent and indissoluble link with history. It would not be feasible to return to the idea of a narrative history of literary culture, presented as a neutral form of explanation, devoid of any ideological bias. The alternative aim that governs the present work is to recover various forms of discourse, expressed as perspectives of individual memory, such as the identification and changing dimensionality of historical subjects, in order to enable the deconstruction of collective memory to recover the inherent plurality and heterogeneity of history. Nor can we assume that the historian's task is reduced to offering a linear, orderly explanation. The historian should instead seek the hybridity provided by a coherent summary of politics, society, and literary culture, acknowledging that the protagonists are flesh-and-blood creations. This is where the pluralistic richness of orality comes into its own. In this respect, as one can see, we have come a long way from the original age of innocence to the current state of historical research.

The point, then, is to avoid futile attempts at finding arguments to defend the recovery of testimonies, and to stop hiding behind our uncompromising support of the recovery of orality as the ultimate goal of our commitment as historians. We should not allow the trees to obscure the forest of possibilities and intentions in the alterable and renewable course of history. Ambition should not trick us into thinking that we can achieve total, absolute knowledge. For, as Ricoeur wrote, indeed, the point is to listen to alternative forms of subjectivity, reappraising conditions, events, and circumstances in order to process individual and collective memories and their political uses and embark on the task of creating a history of literary culture in movement, inasmuch as it is and continues to be a humanistic discipline. The aim, in short, is to attempt to create another type of history, one that is multiple, diverse, polyphonic, and complex, and which strives to recover the richness of orality. Such, then, is the underlying aim of the work of those who took part in the adventure of recovering or deconstructing this part of literature, which includes some of its prehistory and some of its destiny, namely orality. Indeed, as Roland Barthes notes, there is no place "without language, one cannot contrast language, whether verbal or merely verbose, with a pure, appropriate space that would be the sphere of what is real and truth, a space outside language. Everything is language, or rather, language is everywhere. It runs through reality; there is no reality without language" (Barthes 168).

And if language is reality, recovering this sense of the real obliges historians and critics alike to search its origins. To do this, we suggest a type of geography that befits our aims: in other words, an undoubtedly subjective but transparent and rational formal order that would enable us to regard orality on the basis of its roots. Thus, our focus spans five major areas: Mesoamerica, the Caribbean, the Andean high plateau, the far south of the continent, and Brazil. Through it, we have attempted to trace the development that spread from Mexico to the Central American countries, while observing the experience of blacks and their influence on both the Caribbean mainland and its islands; we have explored the high plateau, where we sought to recover the Andean experience, before returning to the path that enabled us to reflect on orality in the far south of the continent, in Chile, Uruguay, Argentina; our journey ends in the rich and varied experience of Brazil. Our overall goal was obviously to present an overview of the origin, the reason behind, and the meaning of our natural orality, its performance, permanence, and survival, as well as its profound, indissoluble links as a source of inspiration, as a protagonist of contemporary Latin American literature, in order to create and tell a new and different history.

> Whether said or written, words advance, and are written one after another in their own space: a sheet of paper, a wall of air. They wander hither and thither, following a path: they slip by, like time. . . . There is no beginning, nor end, everything is the center. There is no before or after, no forward or backward, no outside or inside: everything lies within everything else. (Paz 133)

Translation by Suzanne D. Stephens

Works Cited

Barth, Fredrik. 1969. *Ethnic Group and Boundaries: The Social Organization of Cultural Difference.* Boston: Little, Brown.

Barthes, Roland. 1985. *El grano de la voz. Entrevistas 1962–1980.* Trans. Nora Pasternac. Mexico City: Siglo XXI Editores.

Braudel, Fernand. 1953. *El mediterráneo y el mundo mediterráneo en la época de Felipe II.* Trans. Mario Monteforte Toledo, Wenceslao Roces, and Vicente Simón. Mexico City: Fondo de Cultura Económica.

Certeau, Michel de. 1985. *La escritura de la historia.* Trans. Jorge López Moctezuma. Mexico City: Universidad Iberoamericana.

Chesneux, Jean. 1993. *¿Hacemos tabla rasa del pasado? A próposito de la historia y de los historiadores.* Trans. Aurelio Garzón del Camino. Mexico City: Siglo XXI Editores.

Cohen, Sande. 1988. *Historical Culture: On the Recording of an Academic Discipline.* Berkeley: University of California Press.

Derrida, Jacques. 1980. *La carte postale de Socrate à Freud et au-delà.* Paris: Aubier-Flammarion.

Fontana, Josep. 1992. *La historia después del fin de la historia. Reflexiones después del fin de la historia.* Barcelona: Crítica (Serie General no. 225).

Fuentes, Carlos. 1980. *La nueva novela hispanoamericana.* Mexico City: Cuadernos de Joaquín Mortiz.

Jakobson, Roman. 1981. *Ensayos de lingüística general.* Trans. Josep M. Pujol and Jem Cabanes. Barcelona: Seix Barral.

Kress, Gunther. 1983. "Los valores sociales del habla y la escritura." *Lenguaje y control.* Ed. Roger Fowler, Bog Hodge, Gunther Kress, and Tony Trew. Trans. Valente Reyes. Mexico City: Fondo de Cultura Económica. 65–88.

Lévi-Strauss, Claude. 1981. *Mitologías IV: El hombre desnudo.* Trans. Juan Almela. Mexico City: Siglo XXI Editores.

Mariscal Hay, Beatriz. 1992. "Creación y tradición en la literatura oral de México." *Reflexiones lingüísticas y literarias.* Vol. 2: *Literatura.* Ed. Rafael Olea Franco and James Valender. Mexico City: El Colegio de México. 343–54.

Ong, Walter J. 1982. *Orality and Literacy: The Technologizing of the Word.* London: Methuen.

Paz, Octavio. 1974. *El mono gramático.* Barcelona: Seix Barral.

Ricoeur, Paul. 1990. *Historia y verdad.* Trans. A. Ortiz García. Madrid: Encuentro.

———. 1995. *Tiempo y narración.* Trans. Agustín Neira. Mexico City: Siglo XXI Editores.

Samuel, Raphael. 1984. *Historia popular y teoría socialista.* Trans. Jordi Beltrán. Barcelona: Grupo Editorial Grijalbo (Crítica #134).

Valdés, Mario J., and Linda Hutcheon. 1994. *Rethinking Literary History—Comparatively.* ACLS Occasional Paper no. 27. New York: ACLS.

Vansina, Jan. 1965. *Oral Tradition: A Study in Historical Methodology.* Chicago: Aldine.

Verdevoye, Paul. 1984. "Literatura e identidad en América." *México en el Arte.* Ed. Federico Alvarez. Trans. Cintia Russo. Mexico City: Instituto Nacional de Bellas Artes, Cultura, SEP. 45–47.

Vilanova, Mercedes. 1995. "Historia sin adjetivos." *Historia y fuente oral. Por una historia sin adjetivos.* Ed. Mercedes Vilanova. Barcelona: Universitat de Barcelona. 95–116.

Voldman, Danièle. 1992. "La importancia del verbo. Homenaje a François Bèdarida, 14 de mayo de 1992." *Historia y fuente oral. Andalucía. Invención y realidad.* Ed. Mercedes Vilanova. Barcelona: Universitat de Barcelona. 171–76.

White, Hayden. 1992. *El contenido de la forma. Narrativa, discurso y representación histórica.* Trans. Jorge Vigil Rubio. Buenos Aires: Paidos.

CHAPTER 46

THE HISTORY OF ORAL LITERATURE IN MEXICO

Leonardo Manrique Castañeda

It might seem futile, not to say pretentious, in a work on literature–in this case, the comparative history of Latin American literary cultures–to offer a few comments on what should be understood by oral literature. Some clarification is required, however, because scholars sometimes overlook the distinction made by various peoples and cultures between what qualifies as literature and what does not, regardless of what they call it. Choosing not to see a difference between literary oral production and everyday, utilitarian verbalization is probably the result of a desire to eliminate the old, pernicious habit of regarding as literature only the written production of authors considered to be classical. In Mexico, for example, texts in various Amerindian languages have recently been edited as oral literature, including texts derived from virtually any type of field recordings–conversations, descriptions, certain short stories, narrations of the authors' lives, or anecdotes–which are evidently useful to the study of language but, in my view, only occasionally merit being called literature.

In a commendable attempt, in *Comparative History of Latin American Literary Cultures,* to situate literatures in their broadest historical and cultural contexts (thereby managing to avoid, as has usually been the case, focusing merely on their best-known writers–which has excluded Amerindian languages or what was written by immigrants, women, or others who were not acknowledged as cultural participants), the editors of this work have taken literature to mean any verbal discourse, together with its most obvious connotations of verbal works in many different languages (Valdés and Hutcheon 1994; Hutcheon et al. 1996).

Because for native Spanish speakers the word *literature* is obviously linked to that for *letters,* although one may not know exactly how (the same is true of the equivalents in Portuguese and French for speakers of those languages), it has been generally assumed that if a language has no letters, it cannot have a literature. In present-day Mexico, even among Spanish-language teachers, there is a widespread belief that the Amerindian languages spoken in the country are "dialects"–a term that has the connotation of being an incomplete and therefore inferior language–based on the arguments that these languages are not written, have no literature, are spoken by very few people, are not the main language of any country, and so forth. It should be pointed out that this derogatory concept of dialect was formed in the nineteenth century. Works written during the three centuries of the Colonial period referred to the various native forms of speaking as languages, as shown by the titles I have selected (with one title from each century): *Arte para aprender la lengua mexicana* [Skills to Learn the Mexican Language], written in 1547 by Fr. Andrés de Olmos (ca. 1491–1571?), although not published until 1875; *Doctrina y enseñança en la lengua maçahua* [1637; Doctrine and Teaching of the Maçahua Language] by Diego de Nájera Yanguas (1580–1635); and *Noticia de la lengua huasteca, que en beneficio de sus nacionales . . . da Carlos de Tapia Zenteno . . .* [1767; Report on the Huasteca Language, Which, in Support of Its Speakers, . . . is Offered by Carlos de Tapia Zenteno . . .].

Regardless of the origins of this contempt for the country's Amerindian languages, an issue that warrants further exploration, the fact is that today there is a general tendency to recognize the value of minority or subordinate languages and cultures (whether ethnic groups, migrants, the proletarian classes, or women), together with the right of these groups to express their culture, language, and habits and to defend them from others or change them in accordance with their own interests. The struggle for these rights and for a positive appraisal of the work of these groups has not been easy or brief. For some decades now, anthropologists and linguists have fought on behalf of minorities–which is not to say that certain individuals from these groups had not fought just as much and even earlier, but simply that the very fact that they belonged to these groups, which were unappreciated, meant that their highly justified, well-argued protests went unheard, and were regarded as nonsense or as making unreasonable claims, characteristic of ignorant, uneducated people. External support proved extremely useful, not to say essential, at the start of this struggle. The difficulties encountered in achieving a positive appraisal of the forms of expression through which minorities are identified and reaffirmed have sometimes led to an equally extreme, opposing position. All that is required is for a linguistic form or habit to have been recorded in a minority group (or by a person from one of these groups) for it to be automatically regarded as an expression of one of the values of this minority. This position overestimates these expressions as much as the opposite position underestimates them. These minority groups obviously value some things and not others, both in their verbal production and in their material objectives. That is why it is an exaggeration to regard all verbal discourse as literature.

Most verbal discourse consists of the everyday, practical, and utilitarian use of language. Business transactions, the distribution of the tasks involved in a particular job, the exchange of news, the teaching and discipline of children, instructions on various procedures, mundane conversations, or simply gossip are all forms of verbal discourse that can hardly be considered literature, either by those who produce them or those who receive them, because they usually lack the aesthetic components–often not expressly formulated–necessary to make them literature. Literary verbal production–whether oral or written–is that which speakers of a particular language regard as beautiful, elegant, well expressed, forceful, or emotional. In the majority of cases, they find it impossible to define and simply feel that certain verbal constructions are better than what most people utter every day. Similarly, they are aware that although someone may occasionally produce literature (regardless of the meaning that what we have defined as literature here has in each language), there are certain persons in their community who produce literary discourse more frequently than others.

According to the cultural patterns of each people, there are certain forms of discourse which one would expect to be literary works, although their quality varies in every case and, in the view of those present, they may not always attain the expected level. One example would be the speeches given by the priest or the godfather on the occasion of a girl's fifteenth birthday, among the popular classes in Mexico, or imposed upon newlyweds at their wedding ceremony. Another might be the language used during a Tzotzil trial (a language from the Mayan family, from the Yaxché group, spoken in Los Altos de Chiapas, in Mexico), in which both defendants and accusers must use certain forms of expression regarded as expressions of eloquence appropriate to the circumstances (see Nash 1968). There are also other oral texts, however, that come closer to a people's identity, such as the recited language used by a Lacandon when telling of the origin of the world, which has characteristic forms that are very different from the colloquial speech used in everyday conversations (Bruce 1976–77, 391). Gossen (270) says that the Chamulas use the phrase "ancient words" to describe the narrations that deal with the first three successive creations (a feature common to the Mesoamerican system of beliefs) and that are easily distinguished from the new words that correspond to recent events, gossip, verbal duels, and other genres that do not invoke or specifically mention supernatural beings. The list of possible examples is endless; suffice it to say that they are fragments of language produced in special ritual or quasi-ritual circumstances, or concerned with sacred matters.

Although most oral expression utilizes the resources of the everyday language, there is nearly always a certain usage that preserves the ancient forms of a language, is not fully understood by much of the society in which it is produced, and is sometimes even completely unintelligible, or merely formulaic. (Apparently, grammatical studies of Sanskrit and Greek began as attempts to explain these already antiquated forms.) Conversely, literary language is subtly different from that which is spoken every day. Precisely because they involve different formal arrangements of the same verbal material and follow the same grammatical rules, these distinctions cannot easily be described by the speakers of this language or by scholars of oral literary phenomena (such as linguists or men of letters). Certain features, however, are commonly found in oral literatures throughout the world. These include repetition, usually in pairs; obviously everyday verbal exchange contains repetition (to clarify misunderstandings, reinforce an order, etc.), but this is occasional, whereas oral literature resorts frequently and universally to dual structures—which are not always exactly the same—as a means of expression, which may originally have been a mnemonic device. Also frequent are rhythmic forms, which, according to both ancient and recent information, were accompanied by musical instruments and sometimes by dance. If both of these were used to reinforce people's memories, then another aspect of this rhythmic characteristic would seem to have been its use in linking human beings to supernatural beings (such as gods or spirits). It goes without saying that meter in its multiple variants and the reiteration of sounds (rhyme and alliteration) characterize the creation not only of poetry but also, to a certain extent, the prose of many, if not all, oral literatures.

These formal features, which are open to analysis (though that is no easy task, as we have already seen) can be described as external features, because it is not necessary to be a speaker of a particular language to be able to perceive them in a particular literary piece in that language. Other elements that lend oral literature its "literary" nature are the internal features felt by those who speak the language, but which are more difficult for observers who do not speak the language to understand, particularly if they are traditional forms. These internal features are common in literature and include classical tropes such as metaphor, metonymy, and synecdoche. Other internal features include the subject or theme of a piece, as well as the genre under which it is classified; it is because every culture has its own catalogue of genres and classification of themes (a description of the genres in Nahuatl oral literature will be provided later) that these tend to be internal.

External or internal criteria serve to determine the fact that certain verbal fragments are literary whereas others are definitely not literary (merely everyday speech or just words), and these constitute the opposite ends of a continuum. Societies usually use other expressions that are somewhere between these two extremes, and usually closer to one end or the other. This intermediate area includes riddles, proverbs, fairy stories (or similar tales of fantasy), anecdotes (whether edifying or not), jokes, and other types of text that most people know and whose verbal formulae they can repeat (including many sayings and riddles) or retell—with certain fixed forms—as well as those that do not have a rigid structure. In any case, although genres with a fixed structure may be modified each time they are repeated, they are re-created every time they are uttered, and linguistic communities are aware that while certain individuals are skillful re-creators of oral literature, others are capable of destroying the most sublime myth, the most fascinating story, the most amusing anecdote. The gifted men and women of letters might be known by other names locally, such as storytellers, narrators, and so on.

Oral Literature and Oralized Literature

If we agree that there is an oral literature, which can be recognized by formal (external) and internal features, then the literature of peoples who never had a writing system as such was necessarily oral. A true writing system is one that graphically encodes oral language in a univocal fashion and that, when read, reconverts what is written into oral language, always in the same form. Despite what many people believe, it does not matter whether the features of writing (graphemes) are abstract or pictorial figures; both are found in writing systems and in nonwritten recording systems (see Manrique 1989, 1996a, 1996c). At a later stage we shall have the opportunity to examine whether written Amerindian literatures existed.

Literatures that have never been written down are necessarily oral literatures, as many literatures were before they had the benefit of a writing system—whether created by the people themselves or received from elsewhere and adapted with varying degrees of success. At the same time, among the literatures that do justice to the etymology of the word (in that they were written), there is a type that I would like to call *oralized*, because it initially existed in a written form, through which it reached a particular society, but it has been transmitted orally for many years now—adopting along the way all the forms favored by orality, such as constant variation, the inclusion of motifs or episodes from other pieces, and the creation of verbal ornaments. This would appear to be the case with certain stories narrated in autochthonous languages that are very close to certain traditional European stories (and even include certain cultural elements characteristic of Europe and unrelated to the Indian way of life). This implies that they were imported, probably in written form, and then translated and perpetuated in an oral form. An incontrovertible example is the French fairy story "La belle et la bête" ["Beauty and the Beast"] (*Cihuanton huan yólcatl* in Nahuatl), which Fernando Horcasitas (1978) found among the 105 oral narrations in Nahuatl compiled or recorded during the twentieth century. Forty-two percent of these are basically Indian, although they incorporate non-Indian elements, while a larger proportion (44 percent) are primarily European narrations; the remaining 14 percent were not classified. The literatures of societies with a writing system known only to a very small group and unknown to the vast majority are also often oralized. In these cases, literature has a dual identity: It is written for a few and oral for the rest, and this sometimes gives rise to two parallel literatures in a single language community (as was apparently the case of the pre-Hispanic Amerindian literatures of Mesoamerica).

The characteristics of oral literature that fundamentally distinguish it from written literature are its evanescence and its constant mutation. A piece of oral literature exists only during the time it is being emitted; it has the transitoriness of natural language. A common saying in Mexico refers to this characteristic–"words are carried away by the wind"–a feature that, according to Hockett (1960), is one of the thirteen features of natural human languages. Some of these features are shared by the communication systems of other animal species, while other features of natural language are absent from other communication systems (whether used by humans or by other living beings). Thus, the only way of finding out about an example of oral literature is to be present when it is produced (although this makes it almost impossible to study). Even though societies possess the means of perpetuating oral literature among their members, researchers do not; particularly if the sample they wish to analyze is not part of their own native language, they are able to commit only a few features of the object of their interest to memory. Although these fragments may be written down, this transcription is no easy task. The researcher may ask the narrator (reciter, singer) to repeat what he or she is interested in more slowly, in order to record it at the much slower tempo of writing as opposed to that of spoken language. Not infrequently–I myself have experienced this–the informant then produces an abridged version, omits pieces that he or she thinks are repetitive, and finds it difficult to remember the entire text when not performing it at the usual rhythm. Asking informants to write down a particular literary piece–either because they are already able to write or because they have learned to do so especially for the occasion–does not completely eliminate problems of transcription by the researcher and increases the number of spelling mistakes. In short, the greatest problem in writing down what was originally oral literature lies in enclosing it "in the well-lit prison of the alphabet" (Garibay 1953, 1:15) by fixing it and stripping it of its supra-linguistic features.

There is, therefore, a paradox in the study of oral literature, an entity that is fluid, constantly innovative, and living. It cannot be studied in the way it is usually produced, meaning that it has to be recorded; but making the recording shackles the oral literature and makes it lose its vitality. It becomes set, without its essential nature: Orality. Sound recording (now magnetophonic, previously accomplished on disks) has the advantage over writing of being able to record nuances that are lost by the latter, which is why it should be recommended, without forgetting that oral literature recorded in this way will inevitably remain fixed, invariable, and mummified and that, for the purposes of its study and especially its dissemination, it nearly always ends up as a purely alphabetical transcription.

The Pre-Hispanic Literatures of Mesoamerica

Why focus on the pre-Hispanic literatures of Mesoamerica rather than Mexico? Because Mexico, the country now known by that name, has existed as such (with more or less the same area and culture) only since the middle of the last century. One of the chief merits of this comparative history of Latin American literary cultures is probably its attempt to focus precisely on this type of problem by writing an open history, through various approaches, that examines literary institutions and culture in light of the conditions in which they took place. In the early sixteenth century, nearly two-thirds of what is now the northern part of Mexico was inhabited by nomadic tribes, and only the southern third saw the splendor of high culture; the latter obviously did not stop at today's borders but extended throughout several of the countries in what is now Central America. Anthropologists and historians have called these high cultures and the geographical area they occupied Mesoamerica. Approximately three-quarters of Mesoamerica lay in what is now Mexico, which alone is sufficient reason for our concern with Mesoamerican Amerindian literatures, the indigenous forerunners of literary history in Mexico and the neighboring Central American countries.

Mesoamerica possesses a long history: Archaeological evidence has been found of man's presence in Mexican territory 22,000 years ago and of the processes that made these gatherers and large game hunters adopt farming and village life, which, in about 2,000 BCE, formed the basis of the development of the Mesoamerican cultural system. It would be impossible to summarize here the complex development of Mesoamerica, from its origins to its state at the time of the arrival of the European conquerors. (In other publications [e.g. Manrique 1990, 1998], I demonstrate the parallels between linguistic and archaeological history.) A shared material history (the establishment of agriculture as the basis of sustenance, the emergence of capital cities with village constellations, the existence of warring states, etc.) also led to a shared ideological history. Belief systems (concerning the structure of the world, gods, and other supernatural beings), political systems, and systems of social organization are very similar throughout Mesoamerica. In some cases, it is possible to say how a particular feature emerged and how it spread to other peoples, although one generally sees only a parallel history.

Despite this homogeneity, there was great regional diversity. Although there was always a god of rain, the style of his representations varies, and whenever we have access to writings about his powers, these details also vary. The belief in various successive creations is pan-Mesoamerican, although in some cases there were said to have been four and in others five. The supreme lords (who were also high priests and semidivine governors) are typical of Mesoamerica, but the title they were given in each language implied a different concept. In Nahuatl they were known as *huey tlahtoani* ("great one who talks"), in Yucatec Mayan as *halach uínic* ("true man"), and so on. Part of the regional diversity within Mesoamerican unity lay in the multiplicity of languages spoken. There were no fewer than eighty, which can be grouped into fourteen families. (The actual list of the names of these languages totals more than a hundred, although a careful analysis shows when a single language was given several names–as if, for example, we were to use the terms Argentinean, Bolivian, and Mexican to denote the various types of Spanish, with their obvious dialectal variations, spoken in their respective countries or even within the same country as this dialectical map of Mexico demonstrates [see **Map 1**].) Languages within the same family have a number of broad similarities, due partly to the preservation of features from the parent language from which the new languages were born, and partly to shared innovations. (Huichol and Nahuatl resemble each other in the same way as Spanish and French do, while Cora and Huichol are more similar, like Spanish and Portuguese. In any case, they are classified as languages if they are not mutually intelligible.) However, languages from two different families are completely distinct. When there is a remote linguistic relationship between families, they are known as phyla. Languages in the Oaxacan family (Mixtec, Zapotec, Popoloca, etc.) have a slight similarity to those of the Otopame family (Otomí, Matlatzinca, Pame, etc.), comparable to that which exists between Spanish and Russian, members of two families within the Indo-European phylum. In other cases, there is no discernible relationship: Nahuatl, Yucatec Mayan, and Otomí, for example, are as different as Spanish, Finnish, and Chinese. Despite this degree of linguistic variety, native Mesomerican literatures have certain similarities. Some of these would appear to be universal features of oral literatures; others are probably due to the fact that they were produced in worlds that were socially and ideologically similar, while still others may be the reflection of a more or less shared literary history.

Any brief characterization of Mesoamerican society and culture will necessarily be insufficient, but it is worth attempting to provide an overview of the circumstances in which pre-Hispanic literature was created. Mesoamerican peoples based their subsistence on agriculture, often with the help of complex irrigation systems, which, nonetheless, depended on the abundance of rain. Many of the gods (of rain, rivers, fire, and plants) were linked to cultivation, the farming cycle, and nature: The gods of heavenly bodies (the Sun, the Moon, Venus, the other planets, and the constellations), the calendar, the "owners" of animal species, the hills, and so on. The population lived in hierarchical settlements: State capitals, cities dependent on those capitals, subordinate villages, and small hamlets. Those who lived in smaller units, such as towns and city districts, were related by marriage and, in addition to farming, often produced a particular form of handicraft from their village, such as pottery, stonework, sculpture, gold and silver work, or fine feather work.

Society was divided into two strata: The ordinary people (farm laborers and craftsmen) and those whom the conquerors called nobles and lords, whose particular configuration in each state was sometimes markedly different. In greatly simplified terms, the nobles were the dominant stratum, which provided each nation with its rulers, priests, judges, and military leaders and exacted tribute from the common people in kind or in the form of labor. Just as there were two

Map 1.

(Courtesy Beatriz Garza Cuarón)

social strata, there were several conceptual dualities that opposed and complemented each other in the universe, such as heavenly versus netherworlds or north versus south (west and east were also opposed, as were up and down), and day and night. There were double (male and female, or light and dark) or quadruple gods (two times two, etc.). All these gods were propitiated and nourished by the people, led by the lords, who made greater personal sacrifices. It was the lords who knew about the gods, the stars, time, and the fate of individuals, peoples, and kingdoms through a complicated calendar that combined solar and Venusian cycles, a vigesimal numbering system, and the number 13, recorded in special books which only they could read.

The centuries from approximately CE 1100 to 1500 saw an increase in wars, which led to conquests, alliances, new sources of tribute, and what have been called empires. At the time of the Spaniards' arrival, the Mexicas (more generally known as Aztecs) in the dual city of Tenochtitlan-Tlatelolco, allies of the lords of Tetzcoco and Tlacopan, had built a vast empire with control over nearly half of Mesoamerica. The ancient cities of Tenochtitlan and Tlatelolco occupy a mere two thousandths of the total area (in the center) of today's enormous Mexico City. Tlacopan, now known as Tacuba, just over 6 kilometers to the west, was absorbed many years ago by the megalopolis, which now extends as far as Tetzcoco, some thirty kilometers to the east. The great pyramid of Tenochtitlan had two temples on its summit, one dedicated to the sun god of war, Huitzilopochtli, the other to Tlaloc, the god of rain. The principal market was in Tlatelolco, where "every day, there are over sixty thousand souls to be found buying and selling; where there are all kinds of merchandise found in all the lands (brought by the Tlatelolcan traders)" (Cortés 63.) It was not unusual, therefore, that Nahuatl, the language of the Mexicas, spoken in many regions even before the time of their empire, should have become the lingua franca throughout virtually all of Mesoamerica. The important role of the Aztecs and their language meant that this was the first tongue to be studied by the Franciscan missionaries. The role played in Cortés's conquest by the interpreters Jerónimo de Aguilar and Doña Marina is well-known. The former, who was shipwrecked, reached the coast of Yucatan and, by the time Cortés rescued him, could already speak Maya, the lingua franca of the entire region, which he could translate into Spanish and vice versa. The latter (also called La Malinche) was handed over to Cortés together with other women in Tabasco, where Mayan and Nahuatl were spoken. Marina was fluent in both, meaning that she could translate from Nahuatl into the Mayan spoken by Aguilar and from the latter into Spanish. The popular image of La Malinche is that of a traitor to her people: Current Mexican Spanish has a term, *malinchista,* to describe a person who prefers foreign over Mexican things.

At the same time, the oldest *Arte* (i.e., grammar) of an American language was being created. Fr. Andrés de Olmos, who reached Mexico in 1528, was given the task of writing about its antiquity and compiling the *Arte de la lengua mexicana,* which he completed on 1 January 1547. He also compiled a number of *huehuetlatolli,* examples of eloquent discourse. Other friars also recognized the value of this literature, much of which they transcribed, thereby enabling us to examine it more closely. Let us begin with a look at some of its principal formal features. Nahuatl literature, like other oral literatures from Native America as well as other parts of the world, abounds in various forms of repetition, a useful means of remembering texts. Generally speaking, a phrase is repeated only once, producing parallel phrases. (Given the impossibility of showing all the types of parallelism recognized by scholars, I have included a number of examples at the end of this paragraph, numbered consecutively, for easy reference.) A sentence can be repeated, changing one or more words (in other words, the syntactic framework is preserved, with a few lexical changes); in semantic parallelism, the same idea is expressed in different words, using another syntactic construction (as far as the grammar of the language permits, obviously). In order to appreciate these formal details, it is essential to give examples in the native languages (translations of Nahuatl to Spanish are by Leonardo Manrique, by Garibay [1953–54], León Portilla [1996b], García Quintana [1974], which were the sources for the English translation given here):

1. *Auh niman anyazque in ompatlapco*
Auh niman anyazque in amilpampa
Y luego irás hacia el lejano oriente
Y luego irás hacia las parcelas de riego [el sur]
And then you will go to the far east
And then you will go to the irrigation plots [the south]

2. Ica nichoca
nicnotlamatía
por eso lloro
por eso causo compasión
That is why I weep
That is why I inspire compassion

3. Xochiquétzal in quéchol, mahuilía
mahuili onxochitla icpacan, ohuaya
ohuaya
Zan coyachichinaya nepápan xochitlin
mahuilía mahuili onxochitla icpacan,
ohuaya ohuaya
El quéchol [cierta ave roja] de Xochiquetzal
se deleita, se deleita sobre flores,
sólo chupa en muchas flores,
se deleita, se deleita sobre flores,
The roseate spoonbill from Xochiquetzal
takes pleasure, takes pleasure in
ohuaya flowers,
it only sucks many flowers,
it takes pleasure, it takes pleasure
in ohuaya flowers

(Cantares Mexicanos leaf 61)

4. Amoxtlincueponi ye no hueh, huiya
huiya huiya
cuícatl notlátol, aya, xóchitl ninotlayócol
Libro que florece es mi tambor,
mi canto es mi palabra, *aya,* es flor mi pensamiento
A book that flowers is my drum,
my word is song, *aya,* my thought is a flower

(Cantares mexicanos leaf 24)

Example 5 shows the great richness obtained through the reiterated use of paired sentences in a continuous text, by resorting to synonyms, syntactical variations, contrasts, and reinforcements:

5. *Ihuan ma ticmocuitlahui ma ítech timoma*
   in tianquiztli ihuan in apan;
   in opan ma timoquetza, ma timotlali
   in oncan ca, oncan nemi,
   ihuey iteiya, ihuey itecuaya,
   in tlacatecólotl
   yéhuatl in tecíhuauh, yéhuatl in tetlácauh,
   in teaxca, in tetlatqui

   Y guárdate de permanecer
   en el mercado ni en el río
   en el camino no te detengas, no te sientes
   [porque] ahí está, ahí vive, [ahí tiene]
   sus grandes lugares para beber y comer gente,
   el hombre-búho
   Esto es la mujer ajena, el esposo ajeno,
   las cosas de otra gente, los bienes de otros

   And avoid remaining
   in the market or the river;
   do not stop on the way, do not sit down
   [because] he's there, he lives there, [that's where he has]
   his great places to drink and eat people,
   the owl-man
   that is the woman of another, the spouse of another,
   the things of other people, the goods of others

Also highly characteristic of Nahuatl literature are what have been called *difrasismos,* or metaphors consisting of two elements. Metaphors, a common device of ordinary language frequently used in literature (whether oral or written), often contain expressions that are difficult to understand. For example, in *Beowulf* [see Edmonson 1978], an expression like "the master of what glitters in the fishes' path" is equivalent to "king," yet this is not a complex metaphor, but rather a chain of simple metaphors: Kings own gold, gold is "what glitters" and is thought to abound on the seabed, while "the fishes' path" is a metaphor for "sea." Conversely, the two elements of a *difrasismo*–not just one of them–constitute the Nahuatl metaphor; some are transparent, and one scarcely needs knowledge about the aboriginal culture to understand them, as shown in examples 6–10:

6. *in tlilli, in tlapalli*
   la tinta negra, la tinta roja: escritura, y de ahí sabiduría
   black ink, red ink: writing, hence knowledge

7. *in tetl, in cuáhuitl*
   la piedra, el palo: el castigo
   stone and stick: punishment

8. *Ca nauh, ca notlácual*
   Es mi bebida, es mi comida: de esto vivo
   It is my drink, it is my food: That is what I live on

9. *mixtitlan, ayauhtitlan*
   de entre las nubes, de entre la niebla: no se sabe de dónde
   from amid the clouds, from amid the mist: from who-knows-where

(This *difrasismo* was followed by *oquizaco,* "it has come," which is very similar to the expression "caído del cielo" [literally, fallen from heaven, meaning a "godsend"], commonly used and understood in present-day Mexico.)

10. *in macehuallu, in ilhuilli*
    el que merece, el que vive al día: gente común
    he who is deserving, he who lives from hand to mouth: common people

The meaning of some *difrasismos* requires knowledge of certain aspects of pre-Hispanic Mesoamerican culture, although they are generally fairly easy to understand. Witness:

11. *in nontlan, in itzcatlan*
    lugar de mudez, lugar de frío: el mundo de los muertos
    place of muteness, cold place: the world of the dead

12. *cuitlapilli, atlapilli*
    cola y alas de ave: gente común
    the bird's tail and the bird's wings: ordinary people

13. *in chalchíhuitl*
    la piedra preciosa: persona noble, preciada
    precious stone: noble, esteemed person

14. *in atl, in tépetl*
    el agua, el cerro: pueblo o ciudad
    the water and the hill: town or city

15. *yollotli, eztli*
    corazón, sangre: cacao
    the heart and the blood: cacao

(Sahagún, [6, ch. 43, 454–66] explains that this metaphor refers to the fact that if an ordinary person drank it he would die, because chocolate, due to its high price and scarcity, was reserved for nobles. Bernardino de Sahagún [1500?–1590] may have suggested this explanation of something about which he was unable to obtain specific information.)

Difrasismos were not absolutely invariable formulae but were often subjected to grammatical inflection or else abbreviated; example 14 above, for instance, is used more commonly in narrative as *altépetl,* rather than the *in atl, in tépetl* form, although *atloyan tépetl* is also found in a description of Tenochtitlan, to emphasize the fact that the city was surrounded by water.

Alliteration is another literary device overlooked by previous studies, yet clearly evident in examples 16 and 17 (in the former, boldface and underscoring are used to mark the groups with alliteration: hual. . . . hual. . . . hue. . . . huan. . . . hua. . . . hue; tococ. . . . coco. . . . lotoc. . . . yotoc; **tzi**. . . . **tzi**. . . . **tza**. . . . tzi):

16. *Hualiatotoc hualcocoliloya*
    in atl in tépetl Huexo**tzi**nco
    tzihuantlan **tza**cualotoc
    in tlacochahuayotoc
    in Huexotzinco ya ohuaya Huexotzinco,
    People watch with envy, people watch with anger
    the city of Huexotzinco
    is surrounded by clubs of thistle
    and besieged by darts
    oh *ohuaya,* Huexotzinco

    (Cantares mexicanos leaf 12 r.)

17. *Nican mitohua motenehua ynquenin oacico, ocallaquico inhuehuetque*
    inmitohua motenehua Teochichimeca Aztlan tlacamexitin
    Chicomoztoca yntlaltemoco, yntlamaçehuaco. . .
    Here they say, here they tell how they arrived, how the ancients, as they are called, arrived, they are called Teochichimecs, people of Aztlan, Chicomoztoc Mexicans, when they came in search of land, when they came to deserve lands.

In example 17, a fragment of the first part of the *Crónica Mexicáyotl* [Alvarado Tezozómoc], alliteration is partly produced by the use of parallel forms with the same syntactic structure, as can be vaguely seen in its translation.

All these formal characteristics are found in two main genres, which the Nahuas called *cuícatl* and *tlahtolli,* each with its own distinctive features. The former, translated as song, is approximately equivalent to what the Western world knows as poetry, while *tlahtolli*, meaning word or discourse, resembles what we call prose. *Cuícatl* were almost always accompanied by musical instruments, foremost among which was the *teponaztli* (a wooden double-reed wind instrument) which, when properly played, produced four tones. This is what the four syllables *to, co, ti,* and *qui,* appearing in different combinations at the beginning of the poems in the *Cantares Mexicanos* would seem to refer to, such as the one entitled "This is where the kettledrum poems begin": "*Tico, tico, toto, toco, auh icontlatiuh cuícatl tiquiti, titito, titi.*" ("*Tico, tico, toto, toco,* and the poem is accompanied by *tiquiti, titito, titi.*"). The verses often end with meaningless syllables that must have been used to provide rhythm and assonance. (In order to distinguish the lexical elements [words] from these syllables–nonlexical codas [Kartunnen and Lockhart 1980]–the Nahuatl words in the examples are written in italics and the codas in roman letters, while in the translations, roman letters are used for the English and italics for the codas such as *ohuiya* [in examples 3 and 16], *ohuiya, huiya, aya, iya, ya,* etc.) These elements also, though less frequently, appear in the middle (18) or at the start of a verse (20), while one or two syllables occasionally appear in the middle of a word (19).

18. Cannelpa tonyazque yn aic timiquizque
    huiya *ma ççan ni chalchíhuitl* . . .
    ¿A dónde pues iremos, que nunca moriremos?
    huiya Aunque fuera yo de jade . . .
    Where shall we go then, never to die?
    (*huiya*) Even if I were made of jade . . .

19. *toconya*chihua (instead of *toconchihua*), *tonaya*tlatoa
    (instead of *tontlatoa*).

There is a marked tendency for the verses to appear in pairs, which often form groups of four pairs (eight verses) or multiples of eight. Despite the efforts of various researchers (such as Garibay 1953–1954; Kartunnen and Lockhart 1980; and León Portilla 1983), the issue of poems with a different number of verses has yet to be fully resolved, while several aspects concerning the rules of metrics and musical accompaniment are still pending future research. The songs and dances, which sometimes accompanied these songs, were taught at three types of temple schools built by the Aztecs. The children of the common people (*macehualtin*) learned at the *telpochcalli*, at which they boarded "for their teaching and education"; the sons of the nobles and lords (*pipiltin, tlatohque*) studied at the *calmécac*. Both classes, together with women, attended the "House of Songs," *Cuicacalli*, because singing and music played a key role at the religious ceremonies held every twenty years, and in some of them, a special role was assigned to the boys from the *telpochcalli* or *calmécac*. (Unfortunately, there is no room here to provide details of the copious information compiled by Sahagún [1988] and presented by López Austin [1994].) The *macehualtin* were presumably just as capable as their lords of composing songs, but all the *cuícatl* that have survived are exclusively the work of the dominant group, of whom we know the names of several of their *cuicapicque* or "makers of songs." The most famous of these was Nezahualcóyotl, and there was also a princess among them (see León-Portilla 1966). Apparently, there was a stock of verses that the poets used in various songs or in variations of the same song, so that one of the principal features of the great poets was that they actually created new expressions.

It is difficult to know how many types of *cuícatl* the pre-Hispanic Nahuas recognized. On the basis of the designations given to many of the songs, there might have been twenty; but if they are classified by theme (as in Garibay 1953–54 and León Portilla 1983), they total fewer than ten. One of the classifications they themselves did recognize was the divine songs. According to Sahagún (qtd. in López 1994, 46), "[In the *calmécac*,] they were taught all the verses of the songs to be sung, which were known as divine songs." Two examples are given below of fragments of *teocuícatl*, hymns dedicated to the gods (the spelling has been modernized in each case) as a sample of the literary form of these songs. (Unfortunately, there is no room to illustrate the other types of songs in the same way.)

20. *Teteu innan icuic*
    Ahuia *cozáhuic xochitla oyacueponca*
    yehua tonana teumechaue
    moquizican Tamohuancha
    huayia, ahuayia, yiao, yia, yieo
    aye, aye, ayia, ayiaa
    Ahuia *iztac xochitla oyacueponca*
    yehua tonana teumechaue
    moquizican Tamohuanchan
    uayia, ahuayia, yiao, yia, yieo
    aye, aye, ayia, ayiaa
    Song to Teteoinnan
    Ahuia, yellow flowers opened.
    She is our mother, the masked one;
    you are a native of Tamoanchan.
    huayia, ahuayia, yiao, yia, yieo
    aye, aye, ayia, ayiaa
    Ahuia, white flowers opened.
    She is our mother, the masked one;
    you are a native of Tamoanchan.
    huayia, ahuayia, yiao, yia, yieo
    aye, aye, ayia, ayiaa

Note the meaningless words at the beginning and end of each verse.

It is obviously "extremely difficult, not to say impossible, to understand a particular literature without knowing about the ideas and institutions of the people from which it originates" (Garibay 1992, 207), although, at the same time, literature sheds light on the institutions and ideas of a particular people. As regards *Song to Teteoinnan*, one should recall that its name means Mother of the Gods; the colors of the flowers may refer to those that were associated with the points of the compass; Tamoanchan was a semi-legendary, paradisiacal region.

21. *Chicomecóatl icuic*
    Chicomolótzcin, xayamehua,
    ximizotía, acatonan
    titechicnocahuazqui
    tiahiuya
    mochan tlallocan nohuiya
    Song to Chicomecóatl
    Venerable Seven Ears of Corn, arise.
    Wake up! Ah, 'tis our mother,
    we will be left as orphans.
    You are going now
    to your home, to Tlalócan.

There are also many songs extolling wars and the conquests of the lords. Some of these are unequivocally known as "songs of war" (*yaocuícatl*, from *yáotl* meaning war), while others are songs of eagles or tigers, *cuauhcuícatl* and *ocelocuícatl*, undoubtedly a reference to the military orders or ranks of tigers and eagles. There are, however, no differences as regards formal features or content that clearly distinguish these from the former. It is worth noting that the relatively high frequency of all these types accurately reflects the militaristic nature of the empire created by the Mexica *tlatoani* (lords), in whose palace there were musicians waiting to perform in front of them or accompany them in their songs and dances or to compose new songs in their honor or for their pleasure. These would have included songs referring to flowers, friendship, and other pleasures of life called *xochicuícatl*, "songs of flowers," which would appear to be the same as the songs of spring or *xopancuícatl*.

Written in a contrasting tone to the above were the *icnocuícatl*, songs of abandonment, which lament the helplessness and loneliness of the poet; but since this abandonment is regarded as common to all mankind, the songs often question the role of humanity in this world and our relationship to the gods. Several song names refer to a more physical and carnal form of pleasure, such as *cuecuechcuícatl*, songs of mischief, *ahuilcuícatl*, songs of pleasure, and *cococuícatl*, songs of turtledoves, the latter being decidedly erotic. Certain other names would appear to be titles of actual compositions, rather than indicators of genre. For example, the poem *Chalcaciuhuacuícatl*, "Song of the Women of Chalco," which draws a parallel between amorous approaches and battle maneuvers, would be a *cococuícatl*. Others are called *cuextecáyotl, huexotzincayot....* (in the style of the *cuexteca, huexotzinca....*) which imitate a foreign style. (Literary historians are familiar with similar cases, such as the dissemination of the sonnet.) Models of these Nahua songs "in the style of" have not survived; nor have I been able to discern a characteristic, particular form of each of them. These may, however, have been recognized genres. For example, we can assume that the *Cuextecáyotl cuícatl* was a song of happiness, because the Mexicas used to say that the *cuexteca* were particularly lecherous. The "Song in the Style of Huexotzinco" for example, may have been a war poem, and so on. Finally, names such as *otoncuícatl* (songs of Otomís), *tochcuícatl* (song of rabbits) and other similar names would appear to be very specific designations.

Formally speaking, *tlahtolli* are all the words or speeches that do not have to be adjusted to rhythms or meters (which entails, as we have seen, inserting syllables or words as fillers or providing musical accompaniment) characteristic of the songs, although a certain accentual rhythm can sometimes be detected. This absence of meter gave the artist the freedom to pursue other forms. Most *tlahtolli* possess a narrative structure or logical development that the *cuícatl* lack. The breadth of meaning of the Nahuatl word *tlahtolli* makes it difficult to tell which genres were recognized in pre-Hispanic times, but it is worth making the effort. The name *teotlahtolli*, divine words (which is how Sahagún had translated it, strictly meaning "words [referring to the] gods"), was given to the narrations concerning the origins and events of the gods and demigods, which implies the beginnings of the worlds (remember that several suns came into being one after another), and those about matters concerning nature or human beings. By way of example, a typical fragment taken from Sahagún (vol. 1, book 3, ch.1) is given below.

22.   *Uncan mitoa in quenin otzintique inteteuh*
  Inquenin tzintique inteteuh incan
  patzinque, amo uel macho, ca
  ieiehoatl inpanica in oncan
  Teutihuacan, quitoa incanin yniquin
  inco iouaian oncan mocentlalique,
  in ixquichtin teteu, yoan mononotzque,
  inaquin tlatlquiz, inaquin tlamamaz,
  Inaquin tonatiuhiez.

Del principio que tuvieron los dioses
Del principio de los dioses, no hay clara ni verdadera
  relación, ni aun se sabe nada,
mas lo que se dice es que hay un lugar que se
  dice Teotihuacan, y ahí de tiempo
todos los dioses se juntaron
y hablaron diciendo
¿Quién ha de gobernar y regir al mundo?
¿Quién ha de ser sol?

Of the origin of the gods,
Of the origin of the gods, there is no clear
  or true report; nor is anything known,
but what people say is that there is a place
  called Teotihuacan, and there,
from time immemorial,
all the gods gathered,
and spoke saying,
"Who will govern and rule the world?"
"Who will be the sun?"

Another genre was that of the *huehuetlatolli*, meaning ancient words, recorded by the author of the first known grammar of the Nahuatl language. The term consists of the root *huehue*, meaning old or ancient, and *tlatolli*, meaning "word, discourse, what is spoken" (from the root *tla' tol*, generally written by omitting the glottal occlusive consonant between the *a* and the *t*, although nowadays, it is represented in this position by an *h*, meaning that *tlatol-, tlahtol-* and *tlàtol* are all graphic variations of the same root). Therefore this word could equally correctly be translated as "ancient words," "words of the elders," or "ancient histories." Note that the first two imply the same thing in Nahuatl thought, because ancient words (or words of the ancients) are preserved by society's elders. The former figure frequently in Book 6, on Moral Philosophy, of Sahagún's work, where Sahagún did not call them *huehuetlatolli*, but rather *tenontzaliz tlatolli*, "words of advice." Fr. Juan Bautista (1555–ca. 1613), who studied them in depth, published them as *Huehuetlatolli. Pláticas morales de los indios para doctrina de sus hijos, en mexicano* [Huehuetlatolli: Moral Advice of the Indians in Order to Teach Their Children, in the Mexican Language] in 1600. These "words of the ancients" were used to exhort, advise, encourage, and support ordinary people at critical moments (such as birth, marriage, childbirth, illness, admission to temple schools). They were also used for congratulating or consoling the lords at key points in their lives (on their ascension to the throne, on the death of a relative, or at the start of a campaign) and for consoling the people in the event of natural disasters, famine, or epidemics. The *huehuetlatolli* showed the Nahuas' appreciation of skillful verbal expression. Indeed, the lord or the governor was the *tlatoani*, "he who spoke [par excellence]." Example 5 shows the first words of "A father's exhortation to his son" recorded by Olmos; fragment 23, from the first *huehuetlatolli* by Fr. Juan Bautista, begins with metaphors, *difrasismos*, and other elegant forms common in Nahuatl oral literature:

23.   *Nopiltze, nocozque, noquetzale*
  otiyol, otitlácat, otimitlalticpacquixtico....
  Auh mixco, mocpac, otitlachixque
  in timonanhuan, in timottahuan;
  ihuan immahuihuan, immotlahuan,
  immohuayolque omixco
  mocpac tlachixque,
  ochocaque, otlaocoxque,
  mopantzinco in ic otiyol
  inic otitlacat in tlaticpac

My son, my necklace, my precious, feather,
you were conceived, you were born, you appeared on
   earth. . . .
We have taken care of you,
your mother, your father,
and your aunts and uncles,
your relatives,
have taken care of you;
they all cried
and were moved
when you were born, when you appeared on this earth. . . .

(After the second line, Fr. Juan Bautista adds *in tlalticpac in totecuyo omitzyocox, omitzpic, omitztlacatili in ipalnemohuani in Dios* ["It was Our Lord, God, our creator, who formed and created you and made you be born"], thereby lending a clearly Christian meaning to what was a discourse belonging to another universe of beliefs. Yet even here, he is able to employ terms that were already used in pre-Hispanic times, such as *totecuyo* "our lord," *ipanemohuani* "the omnipresent one" (literally, "lord of near and far").

A third genre would be the *tlatlatlauhtiliz tlatolli*, "words of entreaty" aimed at the gods, which were not that different in form from the *huehuetlatolli*. We cannot be certain that the advice to a lord, who was, after all, a god, was any different from what we hear in the prayers for the Mexicas. It seems likely that, by the time of the Mexicas, a genre had been consolidated which narrated the events of the lords and events in antiquity. We know that there are examples classified as *yehuecauh tlatolli* (translated as "history of ancient things," or literally, "words about the past"); many historical reports written during the Colonial period may have emerged from the fusion of this tradition with that of European-style history. There are other expressions incorporating the term *tlatolli* that do not appear to designate literary genres but seem instead to be descriptions of various uses of words: *in tonalli itlatlatollo* "words [that predict] destiny" are the forecasts made according to a person's day of birth; the wizards or sorcerers naturally uttered for their spells *nahuallatolli* "words of witchcraft" that may have corresponded to the *teyollo cualiz tlatolli*, which Molina's dictionary renders as "sorcerers' words for killing" (literally, "words to eat up a person's heart"). In contrast, *tlaquetzalli, zazanilli,* and perhaps *machiotlatolli* do seem to designate recognized forms.

According to Molina, *tlaquetzalli* means "legend, fable"–in other words, popular stories and narrations. Sahagún offers "a few *zazaniles*. . . . which are like riddles in our language" (1988, Vol. 1, Book 6, chapter 42):

24. *Çaçantleino:*
    texcatzintli
    acxoyacaletica.
    Ixtelolo

    ¿Qué cosa y cosa:
    un espejo
    que está en una casa de ramas de pino?
    El ojo.

    What [thing] is
    a mirror
    in a house with pine branches?
    The eye.

As one can see from this, Nahua uses the *zazantleino* form (just as Sahagún uses "Riddle"), whereas present-day Mexican Spanish uses "Qué casa y cosa" "What [thing] is . . . and . . . ," among other formulas. (I have separated Sahagún's continuous text to make it easier to compare it with the translation.)

25. *Çaçantleino:*
    xoxouhqui xicalzintli
    momochitl ontemi
    Ilhuícatl

    ¿Qué cosa y cosa:
    una jícara azul sembrada
    de maíces tostados que se llaman momochitl?
    El cielo.

    What [thing] is
    a blue gourd covered
    in toasted maize kernels called *momochitl?*
    The sky.

Because this riddle includes things characteristic of the aboriginal culture that are unfamiliar to Europeans, it should be pointed out that *momochitl*, "toasted maize kernels," are what English speakers know as popcorn. In order to understand other riddles, it is necessary to have more information on the native way of life. For example, some riddles are impossible to understand unless one knows what loincloths looked like and how they were worn.

Because Sahagún uses the Spanish word *adagio* (adage) within one Nahuatl text, the Mexicas presumably did not have a word for the equivalent form. The Spanish-Nahuatl section of Molina's vocabulary does not contain *adagio* or its equivalents, "saying," "aphorism," or "proverb," which undoubtedly existed. It is interesting that Sahagún gives the Nahuatl and, instead of translating it, provides a similar Spanish saying, together with a complementary explanation where necessary (26, 27):

26. *Tlatolli itlácual*
    Salta como granizo de albarda/Es nolimetángere
    Las palabras son su alimento
        que salta apenas se le dice una palabra áspera
    It jumps like hot bacon/It's a touch-me-not.
    Words are his sustenance.
    He winces when anyone addresses him harshly.

27. *Campa xonpati*
    Fui por lana y vine trasquilado
    ¿Dónde irás a convalecer?
    I went to get wool, but instead got fleeced.
    Where will you go to convalesce?

There are various references to certain plays by the pre-Hispanic Mexicas. In some of the monthly celebrations (the 365-day calendar had eighteen twenty-day months and five days of reflection, the *nemontemi*), certain episodes of the gods' lives were dramatized; in other cases, the actors, disguised as animals, represented legendary events, while in others, they performed "farces" in which they imitated members of other ethnic groups or certain occupations (see Horcasitas 1974). However, there does not seem to have been a distinct theatrical literary genre; instead, these performances were understood as sets of dramatized *cuícatl* (with their dances and music) and *tlahtolli*.

As a result of the copious documentation available, we have been able to explore in depth the environment in which Nahuatl oral literature emerged in the years prior to the Conquest. We know less about the other pre-Hispanic autochthonous literatures, although enough to understand that Mesoamerican societies and their literatures shared certain general patterns. Nahuatl is one of the languages comprising the Uto-Aztecan language family, whose members extended from the area occupied by particular languages toward the north, along the Western Sierra Madre and its environs well into what is now the United States. Nahuatl was the only member of this language family in Mesoamerica; and in spite of certain dialectal variations, all the speakers of this language could understand each other. (Cora and Huichol may have occupied a marginalized Mesoamerican region, but Cahita, Tepehuán, and other languages were almost certainly outside Mesoamerica by this time.)

All the languages–over twenty–in the Mayan family (also known as Maya-Quiché) were spoken in Mesoamerican territory. (Manrique [1998] presents the classifications of the languages of Mesoamerica and northern Mexico, as well as distribution maps of the language families.) We have no information on the pre-Hispanic literatures of most of these, although they were presumably similar to the Mayan Yucatec (from the Yucatan peninsula) and Quiché (spoken in the highlands of Guatemala) literatures, given the similarities between these and Nahua literature, despite linguistic differences. This phenomenon occurs in language contact areas, in view of the fact that the extremely prolonged contact between languages from different families means that they influence each other– just as their speakers influence each other culturally, politically, and ideologically–so that they eventually resemble each other. (Other language contact areas outside Mesoamerica include the Balkans, several regions in India, and northern Scandinavia.)

Part of the Mayan language family developed a proper writing system–in other words, a means of graphically codifying oral language, so that on being decodified (read) it would always, invariably, produce the same utterance in oral language (see Manrique 1989)–but this was only used in the lowlands, not in the highlands. (This is probably because there were more structural similarities between the languages that adopted it than between the latter and the languages of the highlands [see Bricker 1986]). Epigraphic writing (on stelae, lintels, and staircases) was used to record precise dates. (There is no room here to explain the complexities of the Mayan calendar; suffice it to say that they recorded the days that had elapsed since a hypothetical moment–a date in 3013 BCE–by recording, for greater accuracy, the precise days of the lunar phases, synodic periods of Venus, and other specific events made possible by their extensive knowledge of astronomy; this method determined the length of the solar years more accurately than our current calendar does.) They also recorded the lives and feats of the *halach uinic,* the lords of the city-states (constantly at war), some of whom, during the course of history, extended their hegemony over groups of minor domains, only to be subjugated by others at a later date. (See the dynasties of the various Mayan cities, such as Copán, Tikal, Palenque, Calakmul, and Naranjo, and the heroic battle feats of their respective lord-gods studied by Schele and Freidel [1992].)

Books (known as codices) were also written, of which three, the Dresden, Madrid, and Paris codices, are legible. The Grolier codex (whose antiquity is doubted by some researchers) contains only calendrical records, meaning that it cannot actually be read as a book. Other codices, found during archaeologists' explorations (for example, in Altun Ha, Belize) cannot be opened to be read. There are also samples of inscriptions on jade or shell jewels, or painted on pottery vessels, giving the name of the person who commissioned the work, the scribe, or the person who received it as a gift. The writing on these pieces presumably may sometimes have been literary, although it has yet to be fully deciphered. All the sections of the codices contained "glyphic sentences" consisting of a certain number of hieroglyphs that are repeated and a (nearly always) smaller number of hieroglyphs that vary from sentence to sentence and that immediately recall those repetitions we have seen in oral literature. (It is perhaps unfortunate that similar patterns can be found in forecasts that depend on dates and even in mathematical formulas, the least literary form of writing, which constitute the main content of the codices, since these can hardly qualify as literary expressions. Inscriptions on jewels and vessels are more likely to be literary.)

Unlike Nahua literature, which was compiled by European missionaries, Mayan literature was recorded in the Roman alphabet by the Mayan Indians themselves. The oldest manuscript extant (dating from the first half of the sixteenth century) is probably that of the *Cantares de Dzibalché* [Poems of Dzibalché] (see Barrera Vázquez 1965). Other examples of recorded Mayan Quiché and Mayan Yucatec literature date from the seventeenth and eighteenth centuries. These may also have been written in the early Colonial period and subsequently copied, after the originals had deteriorated. We know from literature written in the Roman alphabet since the sixteenth century that the formal resources of Mayan literatures overlapped considerably with those used in Nahuatl oral literature, such as the repetition of sentences in a different way, but based on the same idea (28) or the use of complementary sentences (29).

28. *Are, u xe'oher tzih*
    Uaral k' iche, u bi.
    Uaral x-chi qa tz' iobah ui
    X-chi qa tikiba ui' oher tzih . . . .
    Esta es la raíz de la palabra antigua,
    aquí está lo quiché nombrado.
    Aquí, pues, escribiremos,
    iniciaremos las palabras antiguas. . . .

(Popol vuh 3)

This is the root of the ancient word,
this is how it is said in Quiché.
Here then, we shall write,
we shall begin the ancient words . . . .

29. *U caah h-tippil zazilil*
    kin tut haal caan
    T-cu bin u bin bey nohol bey t-xaman,
    bey t-lakin, bey xan t-chikin.
    Tuma tal u zazil yokol cabilil eh hook chen.
    X-kuuluuch yeet maaz
    yeet chiic h-k . . . x-dzunun
    cu yaalcab t-cuchil
    Va a surgir la luz del sol en el
    horizonte.
    Va y va, así por el sur como por el norte,
    así por el oriente como por el poniente
    Viene su luz sobre la tierra obscura.
    Las cucarachas y los grillos
    y las pulgas . . . y las mariposas nocturnas
    corren a sus madrigueras.

(H-kay baldzam "Song of the Minstrel", Barrera Vázquez, Cantares de Dzibalché 66)

The light will emerge on the
horizon.
It goes and goes south and north,
east and west
Its light shines on the dark earth.
The cockroaches and crickets
and the fleas and the moths
run to their dens.

Difrasismos abound, though some use referents different from the Nahua one to give the same idea. In the *Popol vuh*, "born and engendered" means "noble," "orphan" means an ordinary person (whereas the Mexicas used "precious stone, quetzal feather" and "he who is deserving, he who lives from hand to mouth"), and "older and younger brothers" means "everyone" (both nobles and the common people). The content of these *difrasismos* would seem to reflect the preponderance of kinship relationships in Mayan societies. Others are closer to those of the Mexicas, such as "hill and valley" for "native village" and certain authors (e.g., Edmonson 1978) believe them to be of Mexica origin, although they may be common to all Mesoamerica.

The Mayan peoples undoubtedly had several literary genres, but it is not easy to know which ones they acknowledged and which characteristics they gave each one. All the languages mention "songs." (It was possible here to give the terms in the native language when only one language, Nahuatl, was involved, but it would be pointless and cumbersome to provide them in several Mayan languages. To give a brief example, "song" is *kay* in Yucatec Maya and *bix* in Cakchiquel, while "dance" is rendered as *okot* and *xaho*, respectively.) However, there is no word for "poems." For this reason Colonial commentators assumed that poetry was unknown to the Mayan people, in spite of ample evidence to the contrary in the inventive dialogues and reciting couplets during dances. This type of composition was generally intoned, presumably with musical accompaniments. In Yucatec Mayan, songs generally rhymed in groups of three verses, and one of the rhymes was often assonant; alliteration was also used:

30. *Kin kuilancail*
     t-cah nahlil
     U caah h-tippil
     zazilil kin
     tut haal caan.

We are not certain about the metrics used, but they apparently preferred verses of four syllables (or double this, i.e., eight) with certain rules for counting those with three or five as four (although they did not use words or empty syllables as fillers). It is even more difficult to work out the metrics of the songs (assuming that they are in fact songs) written on the vessels. (It is worth consulting the work of the Russian scholars Knórozov and Yershova, although some experts believe that the sound value attributed to the glyphs is not always accurate and disagree with their interpretations [Knorozov and Yershova 1992a, b; Yershova 1992a].)

The "epic poems," of which only a dozen exist–very few in comparison with those that have survived in Nahuatl–have names that suggest a theme (perhaps a subgenre) similar to those of the Mexica. There are prayers (example 31, a minute fragment, like the rest; the gods were not the same as those of the Mexicas, although not completely different), warriors' songs (example 32), another one "about flowers" (example 33), in addition to those on love, along with the gloomiest

laments. Despite this variety, they were all intended to be used in the *colomché,* a complex theatrical dance.

31. I yumileex, cin
     taa cheen chin
     chin u taanil
     inuich dzooc
     in uileech ta cuch
     temen titech
     cin kubic tu tuliz
     inuolal . . . .

     (Barrera Vázquez, Cantares de Dzitbalché 46)

     Padres míos: yo
     vengo completamente
     inclinada la frente
     de mi rostro . . . .
     a verte en tu lugar
     porque a ti
     entrego por entero
     mi voluntad . . . .

     My parents: I
     come to you
     with my forehead
     completely lowered . . . .
     to see you in your place
     because to you
     I fully submit
     my will . . . .

32. *ci zuuzma y yee ahuul*
     aci xaabcheil t-ma u zumil
     a puuma dzamaa maalob
     yiitz x-catzim tuut kuuk
     mel u yiit uchilbil a huul

     (Barrera Vázquez, Cantares de Dzitbalché 77)

     Bien es afilado la punta de la flecha
     bien has puesto en el palo la cuerda
      de tu arco; puesta tienes buena
     resina de *catzim* en las plumas
     del extremo del asta de tu flecha.

     You have sharpened your arrow-head,
     You have strung your bow well,
     You have put good
     Acacia gum on the feathers
     On the end of your arrow.

33. Calicil h-zaay
     c-yalcu . . . ben
     lail kaxil chiich
     cu hoopz cu kay
     tumen heeb
     ziamcen utzilil.

     (Barrera Vázquez, Cantares de Dzitbalché 66)

     Mientras las hormigas rojas
     se apresuran,
     estos pájaros silvestres
     comienzan su canto
     porque el rocío
     [les] da felicidad
     While the red ants
     hurry,
     These wild birds
     begin their song,
     because the dew
     makes [them] happy.

The term which in several Mayan languages refers to the rough equivalent of what we call prose is *dzib,* in other words, writing. (There is a term for word or language–*t'an* in Yucatec Mayan, *tzih* in Cakchiquel, etc.–which can form compounds, such as good [and bad] words; they mean to speak or to prattle, but never discourse or text.) These include narrations on the origins of the universe or the deeds of the gods (example 34, in the *Popol vuh)* as well as stories of the past (the life and deeds of the lords, incidents in the lives of peoples), with information on the exact dates involved. Indeed, the versions that exist in the Roman alphabet always immediately recall the reading of glyphic writings (example 35).

34. *Ta x-pe q' ut u tzih uaral*
    X-ul k-uq ri Tepeu Q' uq' Kumatz
    uaral chi q' equmal, chi' aqabal
    X-ch' au r-uq ri Tepeu, Q' uq Kumatz
    x-e ch' a q' ut
    Ta x-e naohinik ta x-e bizonik,
    Ta x-e riqo k-ib:
    x-ki kuch ki tzih, ki naoh
    Ta x-k-alah, ta x-ki k' uxilah k-ib
    x-e uinaqi tah
    ta x-k-alah puch uinaq.
    Ta x-ki naohih u tzuqik,
    u uinaqirik chee, q' aam,
    u tzukuxik puch k' azilem,
    uinaquirem . . . .

    (Popul vuh 10–11)

    This is how the word came,
    It came to Tepeu and Gucumatz,
    there in the darkness, in the night.
    He spoke to Tepeu and Gucumatz,
    and they spoke to each other.
    And thought and consulted each other;
    they reached an agreement:
    they joined their words and thoughts.
    Then they decided, agreed
    that there should be a population,
    that man should appear.
    Then they agreed on the surgimento, emergence,
    and creation of trees and bushes
    and the birth of life
    and humanity . . . .

This fragment (example 35) from the *Historia de los Xiu* (cf. *Crónica de Oxkutzcab)* omits the version in the native language for reasons of space. The numbers of the katuns (periods of twenty years) follow each other in descending order, with all the odd numbers–the highest being 13–followed by the even numbers, due to the complex way they are designated.

35. Este dicho katún
    dejaron su tierra y su casa: Nonoualcan.
    Ahí estaban los Tutul Xiu
    al oriente de Zuiná.
    La tierra de donde vinieron:
    Tulapa Chichunauhtlan.
    Fueron cuatro los katunes que caminaron,
    hasta que llegaron aquí
    Holonchantepeu y sus vasallos.
    Así aparecieron en esta tierra.
    Fue el ocho ahau,
    sucedió el seis ahau,
    el cuatro ahau,
    el dos ahau
    Un año menos que cien años
    estuvieron ahí, en Chacnouitán.

    Ochenta y un años,
    porque el primer año
    del trece ahau
    sucedió que llegaron aquí,
    a la tierra.
    Ochenta y un años
    en total caminaron.
    Salieron de su tierra
    y llegaron aquí,
    a la tierra de Chacnouitán.
    Ocho ahau,
    seis ahau,
    dos ahau.
    Llegó a Chacnouitán Ah Mekat Tutul Xiu

    (Sodi 29–30)

    On this katun,
    they left their land and their house: Nonoualcan.
    There were the Tutul Xiu
    to the east of Zuina.
    The land whence they came:
    Tulapa Chichunauhtlan.
    Holonchantepeu and his vassals
    walked for four katuns
    until they arrived here.
    Thus they appeared on this earth.
    It was 8 Ahau,
    it happened on 6 Ahau,
    on 4 Ahau,
    on 2 Ahau.
    They were there in Chacnouitán
    for a year less than a hundred years.
    Eighty-one years,
    because the first year
    of 13 Ahau
    it so happened that they reached this point,
    the land.
    They walked a total of
    eighty-one years.
    They left their land
    and arrived here,
    in the land of Chacnouitán.
    Eight Ahau,
    Six Ahau,
    Two Ahau.
    Ah Mekat Tutul Xiu reached Chacnouitán.

Precise information exists on theatrical representations among the Maya. Fr. Diego de Landa (1524–1579) notes that in Chichén Itzá (already in ruins when he saw it), there were two platforms for these ritual dramatizations opposite the pyramid of Kukulcán. The pieces he mentions have not survived; they were of a humorous or mocking nature, "He who carries the hill," "The white-mouthed macaw" (a metaphor for falsity), and "The white-headed boy." Others combined dance with the acting out of occupations such as: "Painted with indigo," referring to the fishermen, "Dance of the Physicians," and "Dance of the Warrior." There was one work in Quiché, *Rabinal Achí,* "The Lord of Rabinal." (It is impossible to include a significant extract from *Rabinal Achí* here, but it is extremely well known; see Acuña 1975, 1978.) Obviously, most of these performances involved the dramatization of sacred events (such as, for example, the successive creations, the journey of the divine twins to the underworld, fights between groups of gods or the victories of the divine lords of this world), with dances and comic performances being inserted into this type of episode. Nowadays, on the occasion of the patron saint's day, Amerindian peoples celebrate with dances and certain performances, although these are usually the dramatization of mystery plays of European origin, and the dances–a form of prayer–are removed from the context they had in pre-Hispanic times. This ancient theater probably finds a better parallel in the performances of the *Ramayana* and other sagas in the Hindu religion. Entertainment was not the sole purpose of theater, but the people, who often participated in the dramatizations, found moments of recreation within these religious celebrations.

One can only regret the lack of materials in other Mesoamerican languages comparable even to those available in Mayan Yucatec and Mayan Quiché languages, not to mention those in Nahuatl. A few examples do exist in certain languages, but they are so small that they are difficult to analyze. General descriptions are available, however, of dances in certain villages or participation in performances. From these external data and the little that can be examined in the language itself, one can infer that literary genres and expressive resources were common throughout Mesoamerica, although the speakers of languages with very different structures obviously adapted features taken from other literatures to their own language, which in turn influenced their own creations (remember that in Nahuatl poetry, "In the style of. . . . " refers to a particular nation). This lengthy shared history is what lent unity–if not absolute uniformity–to the culture and literatures of the area.

During the first half of the sixteenth century, the Amerindian peoples were forcibly subdued by the Europeans. The Spanish and Portuguese Conquests were particularly important in the history of Latin American literatures, although the French also played a significant role. Conversely, the colonizing actions of both England and Holland can virtually be ignored. A well-known, anonymous *icnocuícatl* (36) expressed (here in Spanish translation) the grief and pain felt at the destruction of the ancient world:

36. Con esta lamentosa y triste suerte
      nos vimos angustiados.
      En los caminos yacen dardos rotos,
      Los cabellos están esparcidos.
      Destechadas están las casas,
      enrojecidos tienen sus muros.
      Golpeábamos, en tanto, los muros de adobe
      y era nuestra herencia una red de agujeros.
      Con los escudos se protegían, pero,
      los escudos no pueden resquardarlos de la soledad

      (León Portilla 2002, 160–161)

      We were distressed
      by this lamentable, sad fate.
      The paths were strewn with broken darts,
      and scattered hair.
      The houses had lost their roofs
      and the walls were red . . . .
      Meanwhile, we beat the adobe walls,
      and our legacy was a network of holes.
      They protected themselves with shields,
      but the shields could not protect them from loneliness.

The greatest catastrophe ever experienced by this continent was the drastic change from pre-Hispanic to European ways of life. The old universe was replaced by a new universe; all civilized order was disturbed, including religion, political organization, and social systems; the prevailing worldview

was destroyed and replaced by another. Never again, not during the Wars of Independence or the revolutions, would there be such a profound transformation. The changes were not instantaneous, however, and certain features of the ancient tradition survived within the new scheme, partly as a result of the resistance put up by the natives–now reduced to the status of subjects–and partly because their institutions were adapted by the conquistadors to meet the new circumstances. During the Colonial period, the Spanish literary tradition was superimposed over native literatures. Both cultural forms contained oral expressions to which we do not have access, precisely because of their transitory nature (one of their distinctive features). To have some idea of these, one is obliged to resort to indirect references and comparing what is known about previous literatures and current oral literary expressions, as well as consulting the occasional written record, but this obviously deprives us of what was undoubtedly much more prevalent in a living yet transient oral form.

It is commonly held that during Spanish rule, the Indian ruling classes (of whom songwriters were members) disappeared–hence the belief that during the Colonial period, literary production became the province of the lower classes (*macehualtin, uinicoob,* etc.). However, as we have seen earlier, if all the pre-Hispanic poems that have survived are the work of the nobility, then one can assume that ordinary people also composed their own works and continued to do so during the Colonial period. Moreover, the Indian nobility did not disappear, although it lost part of its status and was subjected to Spanish rule. It is true that the survival of the Indian nobility was not without its problems, as shown by the abundant evidence submitted by the Indians in order to be recognized as nobles and enjoy the privileges (different taxes, being entitled to carry a sword, etc.) granted by the Spanish Crown. There are also documents in which the common people denounced impostors who, posing as nobles, exploited them. These would-be nobles were sometimes denied their rights or reduced to the rank of plebeians. The Colegio de Santa Cruz de Tlatelolco (founded in 1536) did educate the sons of the nobility in the Spanish style, and we know that certain students wrote songs for the new religion.

Below are two songs of abandonment written in Colonial times, one in Yucatec Mayan (example 37), the other in Nahuatl (example 38), lamenting the loss of their forebears' traditions. Although the names of the authors are not known, they could just as easily have been nobles as plebeians.

37. *Okolbil kay* (extract)
      . . . . ua hayppel haab ua katun kin maan
      le u kinil uay te cahobaaleil
      h-nucuuch chaac uinicoob
      latioob liiz u paakleil
      u uchben cahob helah c-ilic . . . .
      . . . .*uay helah taan c-iliic ttuch*
      men ttuch yokol canal uitzoob
      u thanil baalbaal lail c-iliic hela . . . bax
      alan ton tum men h-uuchben uinicob
      uay, t-cahale uay, t-lume ti c-dziic

      (Barrera Vázquez, Cantares de Dzitbalché 42)

      Canto de lamento
      . . . . cuántos años o katunes han pasado
      desde cuando vivieron aquí en estos pueblos
      los grandes y poderosos hombres,
      aquellos que erigieron los muros

de los antiguos poblados que ahora miramos,
[cuyas ruinas] ahora vemos elevarse
aquí y allá, sobre altas pirámides.
Su significado vemos hoy. . . lo que
nos fue dicho por los antiguos,
hombres de aquí, de nuestros
pueblos, de nuestra tierra. . . .

Song of Lament
. . . . how many years or katuns have elapsed
since great powerful men
lived here in these towns,
those who erected the walls
of the ancient cities we now see,
[whose ruins] we now see rise
here and there above the high pyramids.
We see their meaning today.
What the ancients told us, men
from here, from our
villages, from our land. . . .

As this poem forms part of the *Cantares de Dzibalché,* written by Indians in the mid-sixteenth century to record the speeches in the play *Kolomché,* the "lament" may already have existed during the pre-Hispanic era, although its theme and tone were undoubtedly perfectly suited to the lament genre because of the subjugation caused by the Conquest.

38. *Ca iuh otechilhuitiaque in*
    huehuetque,
    totahuan, tocolhuan
    ¿Auh, quen? ¿Cuix ilcahuiz,
    cuix polihuiz
    in otechmachtitiaque huehuetque?

    (Serna I, 62)

    Porque así nos dejaron dicho los
    ancianos,
    nuestros padres, nuestros abuelos
    ¿Pero, cómo? ¿Acaso tendrá que olvidarse,
    tal vez deberá perderse y acabarse
    lo que enseñado nos dejaron
    los ancianos?

    Because this is what the
    ancients said,
    our parents, our grandparents.
    But surely not? Are they things
    that our forebears handed down
    to us to be forgotten, perhaps lost
    and destroyed?

These words were recorded by Jacinto de la Serna (d. 1691?), who, in the seventeenth century, gathered materials for a series on what he regarded as surviving superstitions that were contrary to the Catholic faith. They are part of an Indian's oral response, which has been preserved by chance. Poems written to praise and celebrate the new (only) God, Christmas, and the Virgin Mary have also been preserved, and the identity and place of origin of the authors are sometimes known. We shall not concern ourselves with them here, because they are not oral poems; one can, however, reasonably assume that similar compositions existed but were never written down.

The chronicles, petitions, evidence, and legal and economic documents written in native languages, often accompanied by parallel registers recorded in picto-glyphic characters, may fit in another part of this study, but they cannot strictly be considered literary creations (and besides, the very fact of being written places them outside the scope of oral literature). These documents include the *Crónica Mexicayotl,* a history which begins in a style that seems to reflect the oral repetition of the ancient *yehuecauh tlatolli,* which would perhaps justify their inclusion as an example of oral literature. Later on, their author Fernando Alvarado Tezozómoc (1530?–1600?) presents lengthy genealogies that may correspond as much to a Mesoamerican tradition (many codices deal with this issue) as to a European one.

Throughout the Colonial period, there were two opposing views of the languages that should be used in evangelization. The Crown favored the use of Spanish, whereas the missionary friars preferred the native languages of their parishioners. The Crown attempted to implement Antonio de Nebrija's (1444?–1522) theory that, throughout history, every empire has always been linked to one particular language. There was also a more practical reason: Colonial administration was easier in a single language, which is why the use of Nahuatl as a lingua franca was extended beyond its original limits. Despite repeatedly ordering the use of Spanish, however, the Spanish monarchs never really opposed the missionaries' wishes. For their part, the missionaries were inspired by St. Paul's strategy of attracting neophytes in their native languages. Because they are nonliterary written works, we will not concern ourselves here with the widespread publication of grammars and bilingual dictionaries, brief examples of which are available in Manrique (1990, 1996b). At the time, grammars were called *Arts,* while dictionaries were known as *vocabularies.* Their obvious didactic purpose was to prepare the missionaries for oral preaching. It is unlikely, although not impossible, that these tomes would have had a literary form, and attempts may indeed have been made to achieve this.

However, parallel to these works of linguistic research, there were also pseudo-oral literary creations. I have called these works pseudo-oral because they were intended to be delivered from the pulpit as speeches, which is why they were carefully written, imitating the native oral literature. Proof that the friars were fully aware of the literary value of the "epic poems," the "words of the ancients," and other forms of discourse lies in the compilations they produced (which we have used in our discussion of pre-Hispanic literatures) in which there is no shortage of notes on the elegance, elevation, or beauty of what they record. The friars also noticed the Indians' appreciation of these forms of expression, which is why they used them as paradigms for what they themselves produced. By way of an example, I include here an extract from a Christmas sermon (example 39) written by Sahagún (qtd. in Baudot 71):

39. *Ynin teotlahtolli notlaço*
    pilhuane axcan omihto
    yquac intimochintin yxtlapach
    otiuetzque
    otiuetzque, cenca uey cenca
    mauiztic tlahtollo,
    yn Jesus Cristo Dios ypiltzin tlacati
    ompa in Bethleem Juda ytechpohui. . . .
    Yn axcan nopiltzine açotiquitoa,
    ynin cayehuecauh omochiuh,
    cuixnotopanpa ynaxcan tinemi.
    Tlaxiccaqui nopiltze, maciui yeuecauh
    Omochiuh. . . ¿intemaquixtiliztli cuixpoliuh
    auh in temaquixtiani cuixotech

motlalcauili?
Ca niman amo, caynyehuatzin
temaquixtiani totlan moyetztica
ynican tlalticpac. . . .
Auh yn axcan intiteta
yntitenan. . . . ticnonotzaz yn mopiltzin. . . .
tiquilhuiz . . . Yn tonatiuh, ayctimoteotiz,
ca çatlanextli amo yolli, amo tlacaqui,
amo tlachia, amo tlequimati . . . .

Esta palabra divina se dirige
ahora a mis hijos
queridos, a vosotros que vagáis
cabizbajos,
esta palabra es harto sabia y harto
nueva
Jesus Cristo hijo de Dios nació
allá en Bethleem que es tierra de Judea. . . .
Ahora, hijo mío, quizá digas que
 esto ocurrió hace mucho tiempo,
que vivimos ahora por casualidad.
Escucha, hijo mío, hace tiempo ocurrió
. . . ¿La redención desapareció
acaso, así el redentor acaso se fue
lejos?
Aún no es tiempo,
el redentor él mismo está aquí cerca
de nosotros, en la tierra. . . .
Así pues ahora, tú que eres padre,
tú que eres madre. . . . llamarás a tu hijo
le dirás . . . [Al] sol nunca lo divinizarás,
ya que la luz no vive, no entiende,
no ve, no sabe. . . .

This divine word is now intended
for my beloved sons,
to you, who look crestfallen,
this word is wise and new.
Jesus Christ, the son of God,
was born there in Bethlehem, in the land of Judea. . . .
Now, my son, you may say that
this happened many years ago,
that now by chance we are living.
Listen, my son, it happened a while ago. . . .
Did redemption disappear?
Did the redeemer by chance go
far way?
It is not yet time,
the redeemer himself is here,
near us, on earth. . . .
So now, you who are a father,
you who are a mother. . . . will call your son
and tell him you will never extol the sun
for the light no longer lives, it does not understand,
it cannot see, it does not know. . . .

This brief extract may be too short to show fully the links with ancient literature, but one should note the adoption of Nahuatl terms even for Christian concepts, as well as the usual devices–parallelisms, repetitions, and so forth. (The case of the *huehuetlatolli* published by Fr. Juan Bautista (1555–ca. 1613) is slightly different; see example 29).

Another instrument of evangelization favored by the friars–no doubt because of the popularity of these performances among the Indians–was the scenic dance, theatrical play, or farce. Although the performances themselves were obviously oral, the speeches in the mystery plays were written down so that they could be carefully memorized; whereas for certain farces, all one had to do was to give the actors a rough guide as to what they were to say, and they would improvise. Alternatively, the Indians were allowed to perform one of their traditional heathen plays, provided all signs of worship of the ancient gods had been previously expurgated. The plays with the greatest doctrinal implications had to be written in a language that was entirely free of any suspicion of heresy. There were plays on the Old Testament (as a prefiguration of the New Testament) such as *La caída de nuestros primeros padres* [The Fall of Our First Parents], on the life of Christ, including, among many others, *La anunciación* [The Annunciation] by Fr. Juan Bautista, who published the *huehuetlatolli*, and *La Comedia de los Reyes* [The Play of the Magi]. Other plays were more symbolic in tone, such as *La ruina de Jerusalén* [The Destruction of Jerusalem] or *La conquista de Rodas* [The Conquest of Rhodes]. Farce was the name given to theater meant only for entertainment, often tinged with mockery. There are also records of a play involving a mock hunt, in a landscape with an artificial forest and boulders.

Not far removed from this theater were what the conquistadors called popular and ritual dances, which were not purely choreographical arrangements but instead formed part of dramatized performances during pre-Colonial times and were therefore accompanied by dialogues and speeches. The missionaries occasionally attempted to banish these plays, aware that (particularly when they were performed at night) they were the last remaining traces of a religion they were trying to eradicate. On other occasions, however, they adapted them to the new Christian pantheon, and even introduced the *Danza de los moros y cristianos* [Dance of the Moors and Christians], and an adapted version of the latter, *Danza de la conquista* [Dance of the Conquest], both symbolizing Spanish supremacy.

At this point, it is worth recalling the Spanish oral literature of the sixteenth and seventeenth centuries and noting that, like many other institutions, it too accompanied the conquistadors and settlers. However, the matter requires some clarification, because these forms have been deeply rooted in popular customs ever since that time. Profane oral literature primarily included ballads, songs, stories, fables, and exemplary tales. The ballad tradition is ancient, yet it has always had the same function: To narrate notable deeds or the exploits of popular heroes. It began in approximately the thirteenth century with the *chansons de geste*, such as *Cantar del mío Cid* [c. 1207; *The Poem of Mio Cid*], and developed in Spain with ballads on the wars between the Christians and Moslems. It then, incorporated in the sixteenth-century amatory and pastoral themes, particularly in the work of renowned authors who imitated the popular genre. Ballads were written in praise of Hernán Cortés, and there were undoubtedly far more on other heroes and subjects, the words of which have now literally gone with the wind, because they were oral productions.

There is little direct evidence of specific stories or fables, yet the presence of examples of an unquestionably European tradition in current oral literature is sufficient proof that they were imported, although whether during the Colonial period or at a later date is not clear. There is, however, one notable exception. Eight other pieces were bound together with the manuscript of the *Cantares mexicanos*. The heading of one of them reads *Nican ompehua yçaçanillatolli yn qui tlali ce tlamatini ytoca Esopo. . . .* ("This is the beginning of the fables [literally, "little stories for entertainment"] that a wise man named Aesop gave as an example. . . . "). In the Nahua translation, the animals in the fables were adapted to Mexican fauna. For example, the word *acuetzpali* (alligator) was used instead of crocodile, *cóyotl* (coyote) replaced wolf, while *tecuanimiztli* (puma) was used instead of lion. These manuscripts were the painstaking work of an erudite friar from the beginning of the Colonial period, and they do not appear to have achieved wide currency.

Popular ritual-religious literature undoubtedly produced a vast amount of ten-line stanzas, eulogies, traditional Spanish Christmas carols (*villancicos*), and so on. It is impossible to tell whether some of the compositions that appear in works written in Spanish during the Colonial period were the original creation of the authors to whom they were attributed or whether they were compiled by the latter from anonymous popular compositions. To cite just one example: Sor Juana Inés de la Cruz (1648–1695) wrote several carols in Spanish and, according to Horcasitas (1980), "her eighth carol, *Ensaladilla*. . . . [Small Salad] consists of a felicitous combination of four voices which take turns speaking in Spanish, Nahuatl, Latin, and a sort of gibberish spoken by a Black." Scholars assume that Sor Juana Inés composed the parts in the first three languages—there is no doubt that she was perfectly capable of doing so, as she was fluent in them—yet it does not seem to have occurred to anyone that she might have incorporated a popular composition into her own work, which was often done and indeed continues to be done, as it is regarded as legitimate.

The nineteenth century saw the independence of Latin American countries and the development of their respective national identities. There were of course antecedents to this, by which I mean the Indian rebellions, particularly during the eighteenth century, which proclaimed the expulsion of the Europeans and often the establishment of an Indian kingdom. (There is no point going into detail here about the independence of the United States, the French Revolution, and the Napoleonic invasion of Spain.) These were also exceptions, but one is justified in saying that, during the first quarter of that century, countries freed themselves of their European metropolises, while the following three quarters of a century saw lengthy struggles between *caudillos* who defined the features of each country, even as they fought for power. In Mexico, the struggle for independence began in 1810 and ended eleven years later, although it tended in the end to reinforce the privileges of the powerful classes. Peasants, miners, certain craftsmen, those who operated the wool mills (primitive textile factories where petty criminals and recently-subjected Indian rebels alike carried out their sentences) and the *pelados* (the dispossessed urban population; the term is used today to mean "a person of the lowest class, with no education, who uses obscene language") who had formed the insurgent armies as a means of achieving social and economic benefits rather than political independence, were still prepared to follow the *caudillo* who offered them what they wanted. They therefore supported Agustin de Iturbide's (1783–1824) bid to have himself crowned emperor, but subsequently joined the forces that overthrew him, and fought for thirty years in favor of either the Federalist Liberals or the centralist Conservatives. It was not that they lacked political ideals, but rather that their struggle was more of a social nature.

The country experienced a similar degree of instability during the two foreign invasions: That of the United States (1846–1848), which stripped Mexico of half its territory, and the French invasion (1861–1867), which defended the emperor of Austrian origin, Maximilian (1832–1867), with unrest continuing even after the republic had been restored. In an overview of oral literature, political events, presented extremely schematically here, are less important than social events, which are obviously linked to the former to a certain extent. Armed struggles obviously did more for the adoption of Spanish by the Indians than all the viceregal government's previous, and admittedly not very energetic, efforts. The short-term contact between speakers of different languages who joined a particular group of fighters forced them to use Spanish as a *lingua franca,* as a result of which it became the language of the country. However, Nahuatl continued to be the Indian language with the largest number of speakers, and to a certain extent, symbolized all that was Indian—which was why Maximilian made an effort to learn it. In the meantime, political transformations stripped the Indian communities of their communal lands, which swelled the large estates of the powerful landowners. As members of the rural proletariat, the Indians were despised, as were their languages.

These political changes apparently marked the end of oral literary creation in indigenous languages. This end was only apparent, however, because some of the literary forms we know of from the pre-Hispanic era and the Colonial period in Indian languages have continued to this day, and this would not have been possible if they had disappeared during the nineteenth century, although they were certainly ignored until the end of the century. Examples of oral literature in Spanish, often of a political nature, are also scarce (yet, see example 40).

40. Canto de Chinaca
 Yo soy libre como el viento,
 pero tengo dignidad
 adoro la libertad
 con todo mi corazón.
 Y de orgullo el alma llena,
 declaro de buena gana
 que soy pura mexicana,
 nada tengo de español

 The *Chinaca's* Song
 I am as free as the wind,
 but I have dignity;
 I adore freedom,
 with all my heart.
 And with my heart full of pride,
 I willingly declare
 That I'm fully Mexican,
 Without a drop of Spanish blood.

A *chinaco,* by the way, was a member of one of the irregular forces that fought for Benito Juárez (1806–1872) and the Liberals (against the French at one time); a *chinaca* is the name of his woman companion. These two strophes were sung by guerrillas during the Reform War; anti-French verses were added subsequently.

These oral forms sometimes provided news of fighting and obviously extolled the insurgent *caudillos* (example 41). Many must have been lost, although strangely enough, example 41 survived as evidence against a man accused of being an insurgent and is now held at the Archivo General de la Nación (*Infidencias* section, vol. 52, 20–22).

41. Cantares dedicados al cura Morelos
Que Calleja para Cuautla
con su ejército marchando
a las orillas llegó
pero a las trincheras ¿cuándo?

¡Viva Morelos,
viva su nombre
al mundo asombre su gran valor!

Divina Guadalupana:
con esos preciosos dedos
¡échale tu bendición
al señor cura Morelos!

¿Dónde están, tropas del rey,
vuestro denuedo y valor,
si los han de hacer correr
los que gritan: carbón sior?

Epic Poems Dedicated to the Priest Morelos
Calleja set off for Cuautla,
marching with his army,
and reached the shores,
but what about the trenches?

Long live Morelos!
Long live his name!
Let his bravery astonish the world!

Divine Lady of Guadalupe:
with your lovely fingers
cast your blessing
on Father Morelos!

So much for the king's troops,
with their daring and bravery,
if they are routed by those
who shout, "Charcoal, sir?"

This refers to the resistance of José María Morelos's (1765–1815) troops, besieged in Cuautla by the viceregal army in 1812. Obviously, a full understanding of the pieces that narrate real events, whether historical or anecdotal, requires a transcription of the complete work, which reasons of space prevent here, as well as additional information, in many cases.

Written in the opposite spirit to these is a broadsheet (example 42) narrating an event. This may already have been anonymous by that time. It offers an example of the damage caused by disobeying the authorities, a sin committed by the insurgents, and was published by the Imperial Press in 1822. It contains a long prologue whose central idea is that if a man is unable to control himself (by obeying the authorities and respecting the project for a moderate monarchy) then he would be a victim of a disastrous chain of events that would drag him violently to the edge of the precipice:

42. Suceso acaecido en el pueblo
de Tlalmanalco en 1815
Los hijos inobedientes
oigan, aunque no les cuadre,
lo que sucedió a un mancebo
que no obedecía a su padre.

En fin, se llegó a enmendar,
dando admiración y espanto
¡oh incomprensibles arcanos
de un Dios justo, de un Dios santo!

Era este joven bizarro
de los patriotas de Chalco
y estaba de guarnición
con otros en Tlalmanalco.

Volvieron los emboscados
donde esta, muy feroces,
y le apagaron la sed
a puñaladas atroces.

Aquí aparece, señores,
se cumplió la maldición
que este mozo se había echado
como dije otra ocasión.

Y para que Dios os libre
de estas malas ocasiones,
obedezcan a sus padres
y no se echen maldiciones.

(Colin 8–15)
Event that took place in the
town of Tlalmanalco in 1815.
Disobedient sons, although
this may not apply to you,
listen to the tale of a lad
who disobeyed his father.

He finally mended his ways,
causing surprise and dismay,
oh incomprehensible mysteries,
of a just and holy God!

This gallant young man
was one of the Chalco patriots
stationed at a garrison
with others in Tlalmanalco.

The men lying in ambush
came back, very fierce,
and they quenched his thirst
by stabbing him viciously.

This it seems, gentlemen,
was the fulfillment of the curse
that this young man had brought upon himself,
as I said on another occasion.

And so that God will spare you
these unfortunate moments
obey your parents
and don' t bring a curse upon yourselves.

It is fascinating to see the reflection of popular compositions–example 43 appears to have been genuinely composed by the people–in written literature: Several nineteenth-century politicians were poets and writers who composed ballads (44) and songs (45) imitating these, although these were adopted by anonymous singers, which explains the variations produced by their oral transmission.

43. Corrido de Nicolás Romero (c. 1865)
Viene Nicolás Romero,
como valiente y osado,
con Aureliano Rivera
que al *mocho* ya ha derrotado.

Es impetuoso y ardiente
y combate con valor
al francés y al mexicano
que se ha unido al traidor.

en cien acciones de guerra
como valiente ha lucido,
Michoacán ya fue testigo
de sus hechos singulares.

"Ahora sobre ellos, muchachos!"
grita Nicolás Romero,
"Vamos a derrotarlos
cual manada de borregos!"

(Mendoza 1954, 9)

The Ballad of Nicolás Romero
Here comes Nicolás Romero,
so brave and daring,
with Aureliano Rivera
who has already defeated the *mocho*'s troops.

He is impetuous and passionate
and fights bravely
against the French and Mexican
who has joined the traitor.

In a hundred minor battles
he has fought bravely,
Michoacán has already witnessed
his unusual feats.

"Go get 'em boys!"
shouts Nicolás Romero,
"We' re going to destroy them
like a herd of sheep!"
. . .

44. Los cangrejos
Cangrejos, al combate,
cangrejos, a compás,
un paso pa' delante,
doscientos para atrás.

Casacas y sotanas
dominan dondequiera,
los sabios de montera
felices nos harán.

. . .

En ocio el artesano
se oculta por la leva;
ya ni al mercado lleva
el indio su huacal.

(Kuri-Aldana and Mendoza, 84–85)

The Crabs
Crabs, into the fight,
crabs, keep in step,
one step forward,
two hundred back.

Riding coats and cassocks
govern everywhere,
the wise men in cloth caps
will make us happy.

Forced to be idle, the craftsman
hides to avoid the draft;
now not even the Indian
Takes his wooden crate to market.

This is a fragment of the most popular song of the time, which is why it had many variations. The words were written by Guillermo Prieto (1818–1897), a journalist (pen-name Fidel), Minister of Finance under Juárez, whom he accompanied on his tour of the republic, a politician and prolific writer.

45. Adiós a mamá Carlota,
La nave va en los mares,
botando cual pelota:
Adiós, mamá Carlota,
adiós, mi tierno amor.

. . .

Acábanse en Palacio
tertulias, juegos, bailes;
agítanse los frailes
en fuerza del dolor.

. . .

Y en tanto los chinacos
que ya cantan victoria,
guardando tu memoria
sin miedo ni rencor.

(Mendoza 1939, 623)

Farewell, to mother Carlota,
The boat sets out to sea,
bobbing up and down like a ball.
Farewell, mother Carlota,
good-bye my sweet love.

The Palace has seen the end
of gatherings, games and dances;
the friars tremble,
wracked with grief.

And meanwhile the *chinacos*
are already shouting victory,
preserving your memory
with no fear or malice.

The words are by Vicente Riva Palacio (1832–1896), military man, historian, and liberal politician. Carlota was the empress, a Belgian princess married to Maximilian. This literature written by educated persons was sometimes set to popular tunes, so that they would be easily adopted by the people, the majority of whom were uneducated or even illiterate. The authors of these verses, published in the newspapers of the time, indicated whether they should be sung to the music of *La paloma* [The Dove] or *Los enanos* [The Dwarfs], or even *Xochipitzáhuac,* the traditional wedding music of certain Nahua villages. Thus, certain lettered creations became oral literature.

The first decade of the twentieth century in Mexico saw the culmination of the historical processes of the previous century. Porfirio Díaz managed to stabilize the country, at a cost of thirty years of dictatorial exercise of power (1876–1911, minus the four years of Manuel González's presidency). He enjoyed the support of the army, the Church, and above all the landowners (who were now also the new industrialists), as well as foreign investors. The Reform Laws included the disentailment of religious communities' property. These aimed to make the large estates accumulated by religious orders more productive, but they were also applied to the communal lands of the Indians, depriving them of their peasant way of life. During the *Porfiriato,* the companies responsible for marking out the boundaries of Mexican land greatly increased this plundering. Admittedly, a railroad network was built, agriculture was diversified, silver production increased, and oil production and industrialization began, but this mainly benefited those who were already powerful landowners, or foreign capital. The peasants became laborers, exploited even further by the *tiendas de raya* (exchange shops), as they received their salaries in vouchers that could only be exchanged for goods available at the hacienda's own shop. Industrial workers suffered the same exploitation as workers in the rest of the world at that time: Disproportionately long shifts, low wages, denial of the right to strike, child and female labor, and so forth. This background description helps to explain why the political revolution begun in 1910 by Francisco I. Madero (elected president in 1911, deposed and assassinated in 1913) soon turned into a social movement. Madero's failure to meet popular demands fanned social unrest. The triumph of the revolution led by Carranza led to the constituent congress of Querétaro (1917) but did not put an end to the armed movements, which continued until after 1920.

Oral literature began to be compiled in the late nineteenth century, particularly by foreign scholars interested in researching the Indians and their languages; there are also testimonies of oral literature in Spanish, although more as a spontaneous product than as an object of scholarly study. Although clear records are not always available of the preservation of literary forms in native languages during the nineteenth century, the fact that they are still alive today is proof of their survival. Genres that had existed since pre-Hispanic times have survived, in addition to some from European and African traditions. Since there is some doubt as to which of these were ancient genres, it would be just as naive to attempt to prove that they all have current expressions; instead, let us examine some examples of the most characteristic genres.

Nowadays, it is still possible to hear various "Words [about] the gods." One may think that the Lacandon example 46 (Bruce 1974) continues to remain so close to its pre-Hispanic roots because it is used by people who, in many ways, have maintained an ancient lifestyle. However, almost identical examples are found among the Tzotziles (example 47) who, moreover, classify them as ancient words, in contrast to the new words, which do not mention or invoke supernatural beings–reminiscent of the distinction made by the Mesoamericans between "divine words" and others (see Nash 1968; Bruce 1976–77). However, it is not always easy to make this distinction, as certain themes or issues (for example, etiological matters, or those that attempt to provide moral teaching) may be deeply rooted in the most highly venerated words about the gods–such as the rabbit imprinted on the Moon–or in amusing or droll stories, particularly because they have been blended with oral literature that originated outside Native America.

46. Päy tan Kacoch. . . .
    Lati' , Kacoch u ku. . . .
    Mäna' an kax,
    mäna' an che,
    mäna' an tunich
    Chen lu' um yetel ha'. . . .
    `Pachil Äkyantho',
    Hacbäykyum tooppih. . . .
    Yan u tzicbal yetel catulo'

    (Bruce 1974, 17–18, 19)

    En el principio existió Kacoch. . . .
    Kacoch es su dios de ellos. . . .
    No había bosque,
    no había árboles,
    no había piedras,
    sólo tierra y agua. . . .
    Después Äkyantho
    y Hachäkyum nacieron. . . .
    y acordaron entre ellos.

    In the beginning was Kacoch. . . .
    Kacoch is their god. . . .
    There was no forest,
    there were no trees,
    there were no stones,
    only earth and water. . . .
    Afterwards Äkyantho
    and Hachäkyum were born. . . .
    and they agreed among themselves.

47. *Lik la sbek' batel ti nab,*
    k' alal la ti sbek' batel ti nab,
    ta huhot xokon banamil.
    puru *xa la banamil kom ta* ora
    pero puru *la stanleh.*

    (Bruce 1974, 20)

    Comenzó a barrer el mar,
    cuando hubo barrido al mar,
    la tierra estaba vacía en todas direcciones.
    Ahora sólo quedó la tierra, nada más
    sólo los llanos, nada más.

    He began to sweep the sea,
    when he had swept the sea,
    the earth was empty in all directions.
    Now only the earth was left, nothing else
    only the plains, nothing else.

Moral tales, as Fr. Juan Bautista called them, have also survived. These are recited at key points to people undergoing rites of passage: Birth, first communion, marriage, the assumption of civil or religious posts, etc. (example 48).

48. Juan, *iidzy ti iidzi n mih ha' a yiyny,*
    ká n nehwi' iyyitzi minaa n o' ogibitzy.
    Ë paady kyixpi nima' a' awa' any
    neh waad m tzina' ayy m huugy' aty
    É neh waad m utzy ahkxy m gwén' aty

    Juan, ya estoy viejo,
    no sé cuando me muero.

    Y así quiero decirte
    cómo debes vivir la vida
    y cómo cuidar a tus hermanos menores.

    I am old, now, Juan,
    I don' t know when I'll die.

    So I want to tell you
    how you must live your life
    and take care of your younger brothers and sisters.

Van Haitsma and Van Haitsma (1976) (qtd. Bricker and Edmonson [1996]), slightly modified this extract. Mije is virtually unintelligible for those accustomed to Spanish and English spelling, but it seemed appropriate here not to restrict the examples to Nahuatl or Mayan languages.

Prayers or words of supplication are also transmitted orally, whether uttered in the temple or in other sacred places, such as caves, peaks, cliffs, or springs, either alone or as part of complex ceremonies, such as dances. These are directed to God and the angels and saints of the Catholic Church and often incorporate words in Spanish (and sometimes even Latin words or those of Hebrew origin–*amén*) into the sentences. Stories, fables, or narrations for entertainment continue to be part of oral literature, handed down from generation to generation. The themes, characters, and development of some of them are totally or partially found in the pre-Hispanic literature compiled at the beginning of the Colonial period, thereby indicating their Indo-American origin. Nowadays, however, certain typically European fairy stories are told in Indian languages (although, according to certain scholars, some of the former are originally Asian), together with animal fables (whether indigenous, European, or African) and stories about witches. As one would expect, there is no shortage of merging and influencing. Several contain a moral or exemplary teaching. It is sometimes difficult to determine the time and way in which those of external origin became part of the repertory of Indian languages. For example, the French fairy story "La belle et la bête" ["Beauty and the Beast"] compiled in Tepoztlan in 1920 (known as *Cihuanton huan yolcatl* in Nahuatl [Horcasitas 1978, 188]), cannot date from before the nineteenth century, but how did it get to Tepoztlan? We also know of riddles, sayings and proverbs, and other forms of word play, such as what are known as *albures* or puns in Mexico: Words with a double meaning, one of which nearly always has a sexual connotation, often used in verbal duels. Bricker and Edmonson (232) record an Otomí pun. In pre-Hispanic times these may have been thought of as a single genre (*zazanilli* would be the general term for this in Nahuatl).

While it is not easy to distinguish the genres of oral prose, it is even more difficult to classify the genres of poetry. Firstly, in the majority of Indian languages, poetry continues to be called chant or song as it was in pre-Hispanic times (and according to Weitlaner and Soustelle 1935, among the Otomí, poetry is nearly always set to music, although it is occasionally recited). Secondly, the detailed classification of genres that existed in Nahuatl (which may, moreover, have been different in other languages) seems to have been lost, although we know less of these songs. Those that have survived as distinct genres include the songs to the gods, which are today translations of sacred Christian songs; love songs, which are more or less equivalent to the old songs of flowers or spring; and the songs of abandonment (example 49).

49. Bimá mândé bizogaua,
    hyegidama, gahôna man' á.
    hyegiadû bigota rajú.
    Bimá mândé, bizogathó.
    Maxidadû gamá mangú,
    gahômba rajú.

    (Soustelle 245)

    Yesterday she went away and left me here;
    it doesn't matter that she's gone, I'll find another.
    Let her die for all I care, her sister is still here.
    She went away yesterday, she just left me.
    Even if she dies, I'm going home,
    I'll look for her sister.

Throughout the Otomí region, there are songs beginning with the words *bimná mândé* ("she went away yesterday") followed by a form of the verb "to leave." The theme of abandonment (reminiscent of the *icnocuícatl* of the ancient Mexicas) is recurrent, despite the fact that the singer goes on to say that he does not care very much and that he intends to console himself with the sister of the woman who left him. Finally, one should also remember that some Indian communities value the quality of the discursive forms used in certain formal situations, such as trials or debates to nominate authorities. Since they are not regarded as everyday speech and their quality (or lack of it) is used to determine the decision eventually made, they should probably be regarded as literature (see, for example, Nash 1968).

Obviously, all forms of oral literature in Indian languages that are still current were just as popular (if not more so) at the beginning of the twentieth century and during the 1910 Revolution. During the early years of the revolutionary regimes, their value was recognized and they were used, in Spanish versions, to lend force to Mexican nationalism. Indian features permeated the plastic arts (mural paintings, engravings by the *Taller de la Gráfica Popular* [Workshop of Popular Graphics], etc.), music (although the *Sinfonía India* by Chávez and the work of other composers have no words, songs in native languages were taught at primary schools), and even literature, as shown by the fact that Amerindian stories were given the same importance as other literatures in *Lecturas clásicas para niños* [Classical Readings for Children], published by the Ministry of Public Education between 1924 and 1925. This pronounced nationalism was subsequently eschewed, because it was thought that Indian languages and cultures hindered the country's progress. Efforts were therefore made to integrate them into a poorly defined national culture; only a few scholars, and obviously the Indians themselves, continued to appreciate these oral literatures. Since the mid-nineteenth century, speaking an Indo-American language has carried a stigma that has marked its speakers, who have been exploited and discriminated against as a result. It is hardly surprising, therefore, that many Indians should have attempted to hide their knowledge of these languages or that they should have prevented their children from learning their mother tongue.

In recent years, the world has acknowledged the right of Indian minorities to preserve and cultivate their customs and languages. The Mexican experience has contributed to this recognition: As a result of the efforts of linguists, anthropologists, and Indian social activists, primary education for Indian children has been bilingual and bicultural since 1960. The concept has gradually been refined, and teaching materials improved. Nowadays, some writers compose literary works in their native languages (in prose and poetry, example 50), which sometimes follow the oral models and may eventually become a source of new oral expressions. However, the spread of literacy has meant that the little that was transmitted orally until recently is not now recorded in written form, causing it to lose its fundamental features.

50. *Xmoquixtli' un mitl* (extract)
    Zan xquita' tonahli'
    uan xquita' cuacalaqui'
    uan cuaquiza'.
    aman in motonal
    uan xcauili' mitl
    maya' ipan tonahli'.

    (Ramírez Celestino 210)

    Sólo ve al sol
    y ve cuando se oculta
    y cuando aparece,
    ahora éste es tu día
    y deja a la flecha
    que se vaya hacia el sol.

    He only sees the sun
    and sees when it hides
    and when it appears
    Now it is your day
    and let the arrow
    fly toward the sun.

During the nineteenth century, ballads became *corridos*, compositions that narrate events the singer thinks are worth telling (examples 51 and 52), praise the deeds of popular heroes such as bandits (example 53) or military ringleaders (example 54), or describe examples of altruism, love (often thwarted), unusual crimes, and such in verses that are nearly always octosyllabic, with varying rhyme schemes arranged in four-line verses. This means of spreading news among mainly illiterate people obviously flourished during the turbulent periods of *caudillismo*, particularly during the Mexican Revolution.

51. *Corrido de la explosión de Tultenango*
El veinticinco de marzo,
del treinta y seis presente,
un carro con dinamita
ha matado a mucha gente.

Los edificios volaron,
todititos por doquiera,
piernas, brazos y cabezas
se volaron muy afuera.

El veinticinco de marzo,
ni me quisiera acordar
que en la estación Tultenango
tal desgracia fue a pasar.

Un carro con dinamita
que estaba en esa estación,
fue causa de la desgracia
y hoy lo siente la nación.

(Colin 105–6)

"Ballad of the Explosion in Tultenango"
On March the twenty-fifth,
in nineteen thirty-six,
a train car carrying dynamite
killed a lot of people.

The buildings blew up,
bits flew everywhere,
legs, arms, and heads,
were scattered far and wide.

On March the twenty-fifth,
I wish I could forget,
in Tultenango station,
this tragedy occurred.

A train car carrying dynamite
that was in the station
was the cause of the tragedy
that's now felt by the nation.

52. *Detalles del* TERRIBLE TERREMOTO *que hizo cimbrar a toda la República.*
Año de mil novecientos
cincuenta y siete al contar,
hay lágrimas en mis ojos,
no me quisiera acordar;
sufrió México un temblor
que hoy es luto nacional.

Domingo veintiocho de julio,
a las tres de la mañana,
occurrió el terremoto
que en ruinas nos dejaría,
pues su fuerza arrolladora
todito lo destruía. . . .

(public domain)

"Details of the DREADFUL QUAKE That Shook the Entire Country"
In the year nineteen
fifty-seven, by the calendar
there are tears in my eyes,
I wish I could forget;
Mexico had a quake
and the nation's now in mourning.

On Sunday, July twenty-eighth,
at three o' clock in the morning,
the earthquake struck
that would leave us in ruins,
since its overwhelming force
destroyed everything in its path. . . .

This fragment of the *corrido* was printed on an anonymous broadsheet. The title or heading, in capital letters, shows the general nature of the *corridos* and the exaggeration to which several resorted: The earthquake was felt in Mexico City and the neighboring states, particularly towards the Pacific Ocean, but certainly not "throughout the entire country." This *corrido* is a relatively late one, but others have been written far more recently. The genre, although less popular than before, still exists.

53. *Corrido de Jesús Cadenas*
Voy a cantar un corrido,
prestadme vuestra atención,
que mataron a Cadenas
sin tenerle compasión.

En el estado de Coahuila
había un hombre muy valiente
que robaba donde quiera
y no le temía a la muerte.

Era don Jesús Cadenas
el que los tenía azorados,
Porque era astuto ladrón
y jefe de los malcriados.

Cinco años fue militar
del gobierno federal,
cuando dejó la carrera
no halló mejor que robar.

Un último golpe dio,
en Hidalgo del Parral,
se robó quince mil pesos
y un buen caballo alazán.
. . .
El jefe de armas le dijo,
"Caíste en mi tribunal,
de quince muertes que debes
con una vas a pagar."
. . .
Le siguieron persiguiendo,
hasta que al fin lo agarraron,
lo llevaron a Saltillo
en donde lo ejecutaron.

Ya con esta me despido
blancas flores de azucena,
ya les canté a mis amigos
el fin de Jesús Cadenas.

(Stanford 50)

"Ballad of Jesús Cadenas"
I'm going to sing a ballad,
so pay attention, please,
they up and killed Cadenas
and showed no mercy there.

In the state of Coahuila
there lived a boastful man
who robbed high and low
and had no fear of death.

It was Jesús Cadenas
who had them all confused,
for he was a clever thief
and leader of ruffians.

Five years he served the army
of the federal government,
but when he left the army,
he turned his hand to theft.

He pulled off his last heist
in Hidalgo del Parral,
he stole fifteen thousand pesos
and a fine sorrel horse.

The Head of the Army said,
"You've landed in my court,
the fifteen deaths you caused
you'll pay for with just one."

They followed him all over,
until they tracked him down,
they took him to Saltillo,
and there they cut him down.

With that I take my leave
with white Madonna lilies,
now I've told my friends
the end of Jesús Cadenas.

Here is one of the many *corridos* (rather than variations of a single *corrido,* which also exist) referring to the same person. Given the impossibility of including complete poems, below is a transcription of approximately a quarter of the poem to provide a better idea of the structure of this type of *corrido.*

54. *De la toma de Zacatecas*
Voy a cantar estos versos,
de tinta tiene sus letras,
voy a cantarles a ustedes
la toma de Zacatecas.

Mil novecientos catorce,
mes de junio veintitrés,
fue tomado Zacatecas
entre las cinco y las seis.

Gritaba Francisco Villa
en la estación de Calera:
"Vamos a darle la mano
a don Pánfilo Natera."

"On the Capture of Zacatecas"
I'm going to sing these verses,
their words are written in ink,
I'm going to sing you a song
on the fall of Zacatecas.

In nineteen fourteen,
on June the twenty-third,
Zacatecas was seized
between five and six p.m.

Francisco Villa cried out
in the station at Calera:
"We're going to give a hand
to Don Pánfilo Natera."

(Mendoza 1954, 50–52)

This is one of the many *corridos* that extolled Francisco Villa (1878–1923) by focusing on his battle exploits.

Although illiteracy was fairly common, it was gradually reduced as a result of schooling. This in turn led to the widespread publication and circulation of broadsheets: Single sheets of paper, preferably in loud colors, containing the words of a *corrido,* together with a striking woodcut, which were sold for very little. Thus, the *corridos* were recorded in writing, without losing any of their popularity. This form of dissemination was not new. The most highly venerated religious images were printed, often together with a rondel or a prayer, while etchings of national heroes or notable villains were also circulated. It is interesting to speculate on how the anonymous literary creations that were originally passed on by word of mouth were compiled and printed on broadsheets, while the texts of the latter, which sometimes had been composed by writers of deserved fame, were then circulated orally by the people, who in turn subjected them to numerous variations.

Even at the end of the last decade of the twentieth century, oral transmission of the various popular literary expressions had not been lost. Prayers, religious songs, fairy stories, legends, puns, jokes, poems, and songs are still being learned by hearing and then repeating them with the help of people's memories. However, dissemination is usually achieved through the written or printed word or even through means that our grandparents never dreamt of, such as phonograph records or compact discs, or magnetic tapes and digital recordings.

Translation by Suzanne D. Stephens

Works Cited

Acuña, René. 1975. *Introducción al estudio del Rabinal Achí.* Mexico City: Universidad Nacional Autónoma de México, Centro de Estudios Mayas (Cuadernos 12).

——. 1978. *Farsas y representaciones escénicas de los mayas antiguos.* Mexico City: Universidad Nacional Autónoma de México, Centro de Estudios Mayas (Cuadernos 18).

Alvarado Tezozómoc, Fernando. 1975 [c. 1609]. *Crónica Mexicáyotl.* Mexico City: Universidad Nacional Autónoma de México, Instituto de Investigaciones Históricas (Primera serie prehispánica 3).

Archivo General de la Nación [de México]. Ramo *Infidencias.* Vol. 25, folios 20-22.

Barrera Vázquez, Alfredo, ed. and trans. 1965. *El libro de los Cantares de Dzibalché.* Mexico City: Instituto Nacional de Antropología e Historia (Colección científica 9).

Baudot, Georges. 1978. "Un huehuctlatolli desconocido en la Biblioteca Nacional de México." *Estudios de cultura náhuatl* 13: 69–87.

Bautista, Fray Juan. c. 1600. *Huehuetlatolli. Pláticas morales de los indios para doctrina de sus hijos, en mexicano.* N.p.: n.p.

Bricker, Victoria Reifler. 1986. *A Grammar of Mayan Hieroglyphs.* New Orleans: Tulane University, Middle American Research Institute (Publication 56).

—— and Munro S. Edmonson. 1996. "Las coplas indígenas de México." *Historia de la literatura mexicana, desde sus orígenes hasta nuestros días.* Vol. 1: *Las literaturas amerindias de México y la literatura en español del siglo XVI.* Ed. Beatriz Garza Cuarón and Georges Baudot. Mexico City: Siglo XXI, Universidad Nacional Autónoma de México. 207–40.

Bruce, Robert D., ed. and trans. 1974. *El libro de Chan K'in.* Mexico City: Instituto Nacional de Antropología e Historia (Colección Científica 12).

——. 1976-1977. "The Popul Vuh and the Book of Chan K'in." *Estudios de la cultura maya* 10: 173-208.

Cantares mexicanos. 1994. Ed. Miguel León Portilla. Facsimile edition of the anonymous 16th century ms. In the National Library of Mexico. Mexico City: Universidad Nacional Autónoma de México.

Colin, Mario. 1972. *El corrido popular en el Estado de México.* Mexico City: Biblioteca Enciclopédica del Estado de México, 25.

Cortés, Hernán. 1961. *Cartas de relación de la conquista de México.* Mexico City: Espasa-Calpe Mexicana.

Coto, Thomás de. 1983. *Thesaurus verborum. Vocabulario de la lengua cakchiquel, u [el] guatemalteca, nuevamente hecho y recopilado con summo estudio, travajo y erudición.* Ed. René Acuña. Mexico City: Universidad Nacional Autónoma de México, Instituto de Investigaciones Filológicas.

Crónica de Oxkutzcab. N.d. Original ms. Peabody Museum. Reproduced by William Gates and C. P. Bowditch [also called *Crónica Xiu*].

Edmonson, Munro S. 1978. "Los Popul Vuh." *Estudios de cultura maya* 11: 249–66.

García Quintana, Josefina. 1974. "Exhortación de un padre a su hijo. Texto recogido por Andrés de Olmos." *Estudios de cultura náhuatl* 11:137–82.

Garibay Kintana, Ángel Maria. 1953-1954. *Historia de la literatura náhuatl.* 2 vols. Mexico City: Porrúa.

——. 1992. *Historia de la literatura náhuatl.* Mexico City: Porrúa.

Gossen, Gary H. 1978. "The Popul Vuh Revisited: A Comparison with Modern Chamula Narrative Tradition." *Estudios de cultura maya* 11:267–83.

Hockett, Charles F. 1960. "The Origin of Speech." *The Origin of Man.* Special volume of *Scientific American* 203.3: 89-96.

Horcasitas, Fernando. 1974. *El teatro náhuatl. Épocas novohispana y moderna.* Mexico City: Universidad Nacional Autónoma de México, Instituto de Investigaciones Históricas.

——. 1978. "La narrativa oral náhuatl." *Estudios de cultural náhuatl* 13:177–209.

——. 1980. "La danza de los tecuanes." *Estudios de cultura náhuatl* 14:239–86.

Hutcheon, Linda, Djelal Kadir, and Mario J. Valdés. 1996. "Collaborative Historiography: A Comparative Literary History of Latin America." American Council of Learned Societies Occasional Paper No. 35. New York: ACLS.

Juana Inés de la Cruz. 1975. *Obras completas.* Mexico City: Porrúa.

Karttunen, Frances, and James Lockhart. 1980. "La estructura de la poesía náhuatl vista por sus variantes." *Estudios de cultura náhuatl* 14: 15–64.

Knórozov, Yuri, and Galina Yershova. 1992a. "Profecia del sacerdote." *Arqueología (Revista de la Coordinación Nacional de Arqueología del Instituto Nacional de Antropología e Historia)* 8: 45–54.

——. 1992b. "Sacerdotes astrónomos mayas." *Arqueología (Revista de la Coordinación Nacional de Arqueología del Instituto Nacional de Antropología e Historia)* 8: 55–61.

Kuri-Aldana, Mario, and Vicente Mendoza Martínez, ed. 1990. *Cancionero popular mexicano.* 2 vols. Mexico City: Dirección General de Publicaciones/Dirección General de Culturas Populares del Consejo Nacional para la Cultura y las Artes.

Landa, Diego de. 1966. *Relación de las cosas de Yucatán.* Intro. Angel María Garibay K. Mexico City: Porrúa.

Lecturas clásicas para niños. 1984 [1924–1925]. 2d ed. [facsimile]. 2 vols. Mexico City: Comisión Nacional de los Libros de Textos Gratuitos.

León-Portilla, Miguel. 1966. *Trece poetas del mundo azteca.* Mexico City: Universidad Nacional Autónoma de México, Instituto de Investigaciones Históricas (Serie de cultura náhuatl, monografías 11).

——. 1983. "*Cuícatl y tlahtolli.* Las formas de expresión en náhuatl." *Estudios de cultura náhuatl* 16: 13–108.

——. 1996. "Literatura en náhuatl clásico y en las variantes de dicha lengua hasta el presente." *Historia de la literatura mexicana, desde sus orígenes hasta nuestros días.* Vol. 1: *Las literaturas amerindias de México y la literatura en español del siglo XVI.* Ed. Beatriz Garza Cuarón and Georges Baudot. Mexico City: Siglo XXI, Universidad Nacional Autónoma de México. 131–83.

——, ed. 2002. *Visión de los vencidos. Relaciones indígenas de la conquista.* Mexico City: Universidad Nacional Autónoma de México.

López Austin, Alfredo, ed. 1994. *Educación Mexica. Antología de documentos sahaguntinos.* Mexico City: Universidad Nacional Autónoma de México, Instituto de Investigaciones Antropológicas (Serie antropológica 68).

Manrique Castañeda, Leonardo. 1989. "Ubicación de los documentos pictográficos de tradición náhuatl en una tipología de sistemas de registro y escritura." *Memoria del Primer Coloquio de Documentos Pictográficos de Tradición Náhuatl.* Mexico City: Universidad Nacional Autónoma de México, Instituto de Investigaciones Históricas (Serie de cultura náhuatl, Monografías 3). 159–70.

——. 1990. "Pasado y presente de las lenguas indígenas de México." *Estudios de lingüística de España y México.* Ed. Violeta Demonte and Beatriz Garza Cuarón. Mexico City: Universidad Nacional Autónoma de México/ El Colegio de México.

——. 1996a. "Hay que andarse por los cerros. (Comentarios en torno al grafema N15)." *Segundo y tercer coloquios de Documentos Pictográficos de Tradición Náhuatl.* Mexico City: Instituto Nacional de Antropología e História (Colección Científica 249). 99–112.

——. 1996b. "Historia de las lenguas indígenas de México." *Historia de la literatura mexicana, desde sus orígenes hasta nuestros días.* Vol. 1: *Las literaturas amerindias de México y la literatura en español del siglo XVI.* Ed. Beatriz Garza Cuarón and Georges Baudot. Mexico City: Siglo XXI, Universidad Nacional Autónoma de México. 51–83.

——. 1996c. "Métodos de recopilación y análisis de textos pictográficos." *Memorias. Jornadas Filológicas 1995.* Mexico City: Universidad Nacional Autónoma de México, Instituto de Investigaciones Filológicas (Ediciones especiales 7). 241–48.

——. 1998. "Historia de las lenguas y arqueología." *Historia Antigua de México.* 2nd ed. Ed. Linda Manzanilla and Leonardo López Luján. Mexico City: Universidad Nacional Autónoma de México/Instituto Nacional de Antropología e Historia/Miguel Ángel Porrúa.

Mendoza, Vicente T. 1939. *El romance español y el corrido mexicano: estudio comparativo.* Mexico City: Ediciones de la Universidad Nacional Autónoma.

——. 1954. *El corrido mexicano.* Mexico City: Fondo de Cultura Económica.

Molina, Alonso de. 1944 [1571]. *Vocabulario en lengua castellana y mexicana.* Madrid: Ediciones Cultura Hispánica.

Nágera Yanguas, Diego de. 1637. *Doctrina y enseñanza en la lengua maçagua.* Mexico City: Juan Ruyz.

Nash, June. 1968. "Rhetoric of a Maya Indian Court." *Estudios de cultura maya* 8: 239–96.

Olmos, Andrés de. 1993 [1547]. *Arte y lenguas mexicana.* Facsimile ed. Ed. Ascención and Miguel León Portilla. Madrid: Ediciones de Cultura Hispánica.

Popul Vuh. The Book of Counsel: The Popol Vuh of the Quiche Maya of Guatemala. 1971. Ed. Munro S. Edmonson. New Orleans, LA.: Middle American Research Institute, Tulane University.

Ramírez Celestino, Alfredo. 1983. "Cuatro poemas en náhuatl de Xalitia. (Con presentación de Leonardo Manrique Castañeda)." *Estudios de cultura náhuatl* 16: 207–17.

Sahagún, Bernardino de. 1956. *Historia general de las cosas de Nueva España: Primera versión íntegra del texto castellano del manuscrito conocido como Códice Florentino.* Vols. 1–2. Ed. Angel María Garibay Kintana. Mexico City: Porrúa.

——. 1988. *Historia general de las cosas de Nueva España: Primera versión íntegra del texto castellano del manuscrito conocido como Códice Florentino.* Vols. 1–2. Ed. Alfredo López Austin and Josefina García Quintana. Madrid: Alianza Editorial.

Schele, Linda, and David Freidel. 1990. *A Forest of Kings: The Untold Story of the Ancient Maya.* New York: Quill/William Morrow.

Serna, Jacinto de la. 1953. *Tratado de las idolatrías, supersticiones, dioses, ritos, hechicerías y otras costumbres gentílicas de las razas aborígenes de México.* 2d ed. Ed. Francisco del Paso y Troncoso. 2 vols. Mexico City: Ediciones Fuente Cultural.

Sodi, Demetrio. 1982. *Textos mayas. Una antología general.* Mexico City: Secretaria de Educación Pública/Universidad Autónoma de México.

Soustelle, Jaques. 1996. "Literatura otomí." *Historia de la literatura mexicana, desde sus orígenes hasta nuestros días.* Vol. 1: *Las literaturas amerindias de México y la literatura en español del siglo XVI.* Ed. Beatriz Garza Cuarón and Georges Baudot. Mexico City: Siglo XXI, Universidad Nacional Autónoma de México. 241–52.

Stanford, E. Thomas. 1974. *El villancico y el corrido mexicano.* Mexico City: Instituto Nacional de Antropología e Historia.

Tapia Zenteno, Carlos de. 1767. *Noticia de la lengua huasteca, que en beneficio de sus nacionales de orden del Ilmo. Sr. Arzopispo [sic] de esta santa iglesia metropolitana, y a sus expensas, da Carlos de Tapia Zenteno.* Mexico City: Imprenta de la Bibliotheca Mexicana.

Valdés, Mario J. 1997. Letter to the collaborators of the *Comparative History of Latin American Cultures* (October 28).

—— and Linda Hutcheon. 1994. *Rethinking Literary History–Comparatively.* American Council of Learned Societies Occasional Paper No. 27. New York: ACLS.

Van Haitsma, Julia Dieterman, and Willard Van Haitsma. 1976. *A Hierarchical Sketch of Mixe as Spoken in San José el Paraíso.* Norman: Summer Institute of Linguistics.

Weitlaner, Roberto, and Jacques Soustelle. 1935. "Canciones otomíes." *Journal de la Société des Américanistes* 27: 304–24.

Yershova, Galina. 1992. "Lírica maya en la antigüedad." *Arqueología (Revista de la Coordinación Nacional de Arqueología del Instituto Nacional de Antropología e Historia)* 8: 27–44.

CHAPTER 47

AFRICAN ORALITY IN THE LITERARY CULTURE OF THE CARIBBEAN

Luz María Martínez Montiel

Delimitation of the Cultural Area of the Caribbean

For the purposes of this essay, the Caribbean includes not only the set of islands in the sea of the same name but also the mainland territories of Guyana, Surinam, French Guiana, Colombia, and the Atlantic coast of Venezuela. Described as the most colonized region in America, it has been dominated by Europe, and so it has Spanish, English, French, Dutch, and Portuguese influences. This explains the cultural diversity that includes several common economic and historic elements within one sea. The most important of these elements were the first encounters among blacks, whites, and Indians; the area subsequently has been called the America of plantations or Afro-America. As such, it includes the northeast coast of Brazil, the southern United States (Florida and Louisiana), and the coasts of the Gulf of Mexico: Veracruz, Tabasco, Campeche, and Yucatán. However, in this essay we refer mainly to the Antillean archipelago.

As an area with shared economic and cultural features, the Caribbean was created following the European colonization, which caused the total or partial extinction of an aboriginal population, created economic systems to establish a plantation economy, and, given the demand for cheap labor, introduced the importation of African slaves to be sold in the American colonies. The slave trade transported twenty million human beings from all regions of Africa to the New World. After the Colonial period, the region increased its population with immigrants mainly from India and China. As a result, the Caribbean has come to be regarded as a synthesis of humanity. It is essential to realize, however, that the Spanish colonies in the Caribbean, as well as the English and Portuguese colonies, bore similarities to the mainland colonies established by European powers throughout the continent. Nowadays, certain countries in the Antilles, such as Cuba, the Dominican Republic, and Puerto Rico, for example, are fully identified with what is known as Latin America, although this does not prevent the Caribbean from being regarded as an area with common cultural features due to its African roots. In the islands off the African coast, the Portuguese had already established sugar plantations; in the Antilles, the Spaniards cultivated the same crop, taking advantage of the similar environmental conditions, soil, rainfall, forestry resources, and suitable temperatures. The plantation system was adopted by the English and the French, who achieved enormous yields in their colonies. According to the figures available for the late eighteenth century (1790), the Antilles produced enough for the world's entire sugar consumption. This high yield was primarily due to the system of slavery to which the Africans were subjected.

The demographic factor explains the economic and cultural evolution in the area. Other crops besides sugar called for slave labor, such as tobacco and indigo, which also required the contribution of white settlers' labor, particularly during the early stages of colonization. What is of interest here is the ethnic proportion of the Caribbean populations. In 1640, for example, there were 52,000 whites in Barbados and 6,000 slaves, while in Martinique and Guadeloupe, there were 15,000 whites. As sugar production increased, so did the slave population; in 1680, there were 40,000 slaves in Barbados, production had risen to 8,000 tons annually, and the white population had fallen to 2,000, including planters and land and slave owners. By the mid-seventeenth century, Barbados was the most prosperous and highly populated colony in America, and by the end of the century, it was the most highly populated in the entire continent, importing 1,400 slaves annually. During this period, the English colonies in the United States had only 30,000 slaves, whereas Brazil had a total of 600,000. There were a total of 450,000 slaves in the French and British Caribbean together as opposed to 400,000 in the Spanish American Caribbean. The growth of the plantations paralleled the population increase; both increases were determined by the importance of sugar production rather than through conflicts between European powers. This demand for sugar production determined the number of slaves imported; the seventeenth and eighteenth centuries proved crucial to Caribbean demography and the American colonies in general.

African Presence, Orality, and Transculturation

The African slaves imported during four centuries of Atlantic slave-trading came from the villages of western Sudan, equatorial Africa, and the Angolan region; their ethnic origins have been reconstructed through research conducted over the past five decades. It should be said, however, that despite the fact that these cultures have been a factor in defining the identity of much of America, the studies undertaken to date on African ethnic groups, although numerous, are still insufficient. Systematic research on Afro-Caribbean cultures has not been undertaken in several Latin American countries. Africanness in America is generally approached through demographic studies based exclusively on the sometimes unreliable figures of slave demography for historical reconstruction. The study of orality in sub-Saharan or black Africa, as the area of black peoples was called, has been approached from various angles depending on the experts in different disciplines who have taken an interest in the issue. Specialists in folklore consider these forms of cultural expression the remnants of traditional forms that have now disappeared; ethnologists view them as a reflection of contemporary society and a means of teaching or transmitting group values, and Freudian psychiatrists regard them as the expression of psychological problems. African oral literature is all this at the same time, yet one should not forget that myths, stories, proverbs, and even riddles are above all a collective creation and should be considered as such. Understanding African oral literature requires analyzing its form and content using a multidimensional approach. This source of culture should be studied according to the lines that define it rather than those used in literary criticism in general.

Each text offers scholars numerous possibilities of analysis that link the works of oral literature to other aspects of the same culture. The language, lexicon, and syntax are factors that, because of their dimension in traditional orality, make the latter a richer form of expression than everyday spoken language. Oral language contains opening and closing formulas, particular modalities, onomatopoeia, diminutives, and augmentatives, among other devices. A distinction is made between fixed and free genres. In the fixed genres, the text, by definition, remains unchanged (as in proverbs, enigmas, and spells), and the language is therefore archaic. In free genres, however, the formulation may change (as in short stories or tales). These narrative systems also contain variables that depend on the narrator and his or her audience. Some stories are mimed and constitute pretheater. No narrator transmits a text received through the oral tradition word for word; the richness and diversity of spoken literature lies in this very freedom. Certain societies have a tradition of intervening, as a group, during the re-creation of a story or a narration (for example, during the narration of stories by two or more people, animation, choruses, sung tales, or sung histories).

The grammar of a story implies a narrative structure, such as the sequence in which it should be repeated. The language of stories offers an infinite variety of vocabulary, depending on the oral tradition of the society that has produced the work. It is said that there is no society in the world that does not have a stock of this type of creation transmitted through the cultural tradition. In some societies more than others, these forms are preserved and stem from the need to keep alive certain elements of culture that would not be preserved in any other way. This is true of the stories and genealogical reconstructions preserved in Africa for centuries and associated with the important (and in some cases mythical) actions of the cultural heroes of each ethnic group. This is the heritage entrusted to the *Griots*, the prodigious oral *Peul* historians of the Mande peoples in West Africa. In the vocabulary of narration, the actors—men, animals, plants, genies, and so on—have a particular place and symbolic value in each society. These elements can be used to create a repertory of metaphors and metonymies. Actions and gestures can be either universally understood or specific to a particular society. The narrator's accessories (jewels, clothes, disguise, etc.) also have a symbolic value. All myths (and many stories are remnants of myths) must be deciphered because they contain implicit messages. Stories, as the reduction of a cosmogony that sometimes contains an omission (collective in the case of a myth, individual in that of a story), are deciphered during the course of their repetition. Next to the implicit messages lie the explicit messages, which do not have the same importance because they do not modify the internal structure of the text; the function of the explicit motifs is to indicate the end of the story, the account, or a genealogical reconstruction. Symbolism is multifarious in stories; stories transmit the messages in an indirect fashion using a coded language, symbolism, which can reduce or intensify the internal conflicts of a society.

This essay is not the place to discuss matters concerning written African literature; suffice it to say that modern genres are undoubtedly based on traditional ones, although the point is that modern genres project the black African world beyond its limits, thereby incorporating it into the concert of nations. Thus, since the middle of the century, the broad dissemination of African thought has been accomplished through the theater, where epic or political themes have been explored. Traditional representations (music and dance), which have been widely disseminated from the outset, have exercised an influence over scenic art throughout the world. In addition to those already mentioned, the genres of poetry (both combative and militant), realist novels, metaphysical and allegorical novels, and others where the African personality achieves international levels are flourishing. It goes without saying that the earliest recognition of African oral literature dates to the beginning of European occupation of the black continent. Missionaries and explorers referred to the literature of the "blacks" when they finally understood the fables, historical legends, stories, and, in general, everything that surrounded the orality of the African peoples. Orality, though, was a weapon used to combat the devastating effects of colonialism. The Africans employed it as a living means of preserving their traditional cultures; in time, the newly independent countries, shaking off the dead weight of Europe, were able to reconstruct their ancestry and projects for a national culture. The "books" of age-old African experiences were preserved in the memory of the elders. It is often said that when an old man dies, a library is lost.

Research on orality obviously has to resort to linguistics and must be based on a thorough knowledge of the society concerned and its value systems and categories of space (in which the borders of the supernatural are located) and time (a historical deed rapidly becomes legendary).

The unwritten history of the African peoples can be found in the unconscious forms of social life, in other words, through the analysis of cultural facts and the genres of oral literature. Orality is what enables a profound study of social structure by restoring historicity to a society without writing. We should, however, admit that history and historical awareness do not always coincide, which is part of the problem with the relationship between history and anthropology. Nonetheless, once one realizes that every society has a culture and a history, an historical awareness begins to emerge. This awareness emerges from the overcoming of ethnic divisions in a country, giving rise to the patient reconstruction of time sequences with the help of all the auxiliary sciences such as archaeology, ethnobotany, glottochronology, and ethnology.

Orality is not merely a reflection of the society from which it emanates; it can also reveal the internal, social, and psychological contradictions that become perceptible through words. Distinguishing the major themes of the oral literature of a nation with its variants permits a comparison with the texts of European, African, American, and Asian folklore and reveals, through exploring its classical mythologies, the profile of the particular "humanism" of a people and its degree of participation in what we could call universal "humanism." Having reached this point, it is worth identifying—as a means of bringing discussions of orality in Afro-America up to date—the two factors on which orality in the Caribbean is based: The first is the replacement of African elements by others derived from colonial domination, and the other is the retention and persistence of the features of origin. Regarding the former, colonized peoples use the colonial language to express their desires; here, a feature of the imposed culture can also be liberating. Likewise, the construction of creole languages on the basis of an African model functions as an archive in which the essential contents of an African imaginary, idealized in people's memories, are preserved. The second factor–persistence–is substantial and indispensable, so essential that the depths of the African soul can be plumbed only by studying it in detail; its major form is the drum. Only rarely, and not until recently, have Western historians and ethnologists approached–and not always reliably–the study of percussive rhythm as a substitute for writing in Africa.

Drums constitute a link with the past; as a means of communication, dance accompaniment, and transmitting sacred or profane messages, the drum was the guardian of the "memory-recollection," the name given to Africans' ability to maintain the values of their tradition and the keys to their identity by handing them down from generation to generation, thereby unifying collective emotions. Dance cannot take place without drums; the latter provides the sound writing that the dancer must follow when he or she aurally reads what it dictates. "Drum writing," adds Jahn, "can spread news more quickly than graphic writing" (262). In order to understand the semantic value of the drum, one has to refer to the African languages, which are phonic systems with layers of sound that give words a different meaning according to the pitch of the vowels. Without special modifications, most writing systems are not very suitable for writing grave, acute, or intermediate tonalities, particularly the latter, since no discrete writing system contains signs to represent a continuum of pitch. But drums faithfully reproduce the necessary tonal character of African languages. As Jahn explains: "The language of the drum is the immediate, natural reproduction of language; it is an intelligible form of 'writing' for anyone with sufficient practice, except that instead of being designed to be seen, it is intended to be heard. Just as young Europeans at school learn to link optical signs using their sight, so young Africans used to have to learn the art of capturing the acoustic signs of the drum" (262).

There are many sizes and shapes of drums, depending on the purpose for which they are intended in the many different societies in which they are used. Thus, there are Yoruba drums in Cuba and Brazil, and in Guyana, Surinam, and French Guiana there are as many varieties of drums as there are groups that still use them, originating from the Congo, Benin, Ghana, Angola, Sierra Leone, Guinea, and Gambia. Throughout the world, making a drum requires a ritual that consecrates it as an instrument for calling up the spirits, invoking the gods, summoning the community, and even marking the rhythm to be followed by the dancers and the steps they must perform. Thus, choreographies should be understood as another code written in body language, but absolutely nothing can take place without orality, whether spoken or sung.

In traditional cultures–regarded as such even after the impact of colonialism–European researchers, specifically the French, have classified black African oral literature starting from the evidence of the vitality of cultural creations that provide a glimpse of a new form of humanism. Thus, archetypes are established using African categories, eliminating conflict by making an interpretation from within the oral traditions. Paradigms are also established; the paradigm of oral literature that exalts mythical Africa and corresponds to the traditional world also includes stories and chronicles regarded as historical. A psychological interpretation shows how the mythical contents of stories and legends are based on social reality.

This genre contains a transposition in which animals are given human behavior and nature is granted the gift of the word. The most realistic narration is not strictly based on reality, and the most fantastic story has a minimum of reality. These creations obviously reflect the social fabric within which they are produced; the variations of a story are explained by sociological and psychological changes. In other words, myths are lived–they are simply experiences that become set narrations. In this oral genre, it is possible to find signs of social changes because changes are much more easily incorporated into stories than into myths, which are generally retold more or less word for word. There are no myths without ritual and no rituals without myth; in other words, a myth is a form of oral ritual, hence its inalterability.

Orality in Cultural Spaces of African Latin Americans

As shown by the figures on slave trade, the African factor was and is demographically dominant among the Caribbean populations. The cultures that developed there, as a result of the encounter between Europeans and Africans once the native population had been exterminated, have therefore been under the determinant sign of Africanness. This predominance, however, should not lead us to ignore the aspects of European transculturation that contributed to the process of cultural formation as a whole. Although we should not be surprised to find traces of African civilizations in America, we must not attempt to preserve them to such an extent in our analyses that they become isolated from the global context in which they are immersed; the collective imagination of the early slave generations contained the bases that enabled it to survive despite the deculturizing action of slavery. At the beginning of their lives in strange lands, the Bozales, first-generation Africans, suffered the dispersion of their families, which destroyed the kinship systems and the unity of their lineage; subsequent sexual unions inevitably meant a mixing with other men and women alien to their culture, and so part of their heritage was diluted in their offspring. Their lifestyle disappeared, and parts of their language and customs were replaced by those of their masters. Yet at the same time that slaves were forced to assimilate the culture of their masters, they were segregated and prevented from integrating with them. In order to be able to survive in this social abyss, blacks resorted to the legacy of their ancestors. They managed to create a slave culture with what they had retained of Africa together with what they managed to assimilate from the dominant culture, from the universe that received them. This cultural *mestizaje* that took place throughout America was predominantly African in certain regions, whereas in others the Indian matrix prevailed. In all of them, however, European culture held sway, supported by a system of forced acculturation. In no case was there an absence of an original culture; nor did it totally disintegrate. By black cultures, we mean those in which African features survived and that, when integrated into the system, animated the lives of the people in their communities throughout the hemisphere. In all Afro-American expressions of culture, original African elements make their way into those of Indian or European origin, although the same can be said of Indian-*mestizo* or Euro-American culture. The same culture is involved, but in some cases African aspects prevail and in others, Indian or European. Yet there is one undeniable fact: Afro-America was the crucible in which the three roots of the continent were fused in a variety of ways. The originality of Afro-America lies in the fact that it is a transit culture; it still contains the roots that gave birth to it.

Transculturation is a process by which new forms of knowing and feeling (collective representations) in a system that is also new (taking culture as a whole, including economics, society, and knowledge) give rise to a new civilization.

The African men and women captured by the slave traders were transported by ships to be sold as mere merchandise. Despite their being members of advanced societies and developed civilizations, they possessed less military power than the Europeans. They brought with them their gods, their beliefs, and the knowledge acquired in their societies of origin. From the start of their lives as slaves, they strongly opposed not only the regime of forced labor but the system of values and beliefs imposed on them by colonialism. In using their creative force to save their heritage, they managed to reconstruct part of their folklore, their customs, and their culture. This vitality revealed the power of orality in African traditions, since the way this magnificent, intangible heritage has been transmitted for five centuries was through the word. The transculturation of African languages adapted to European ones produced creole languages, in which poetry and narrative abound, in addition to myths and legends, fables, and other popular genres.

Particularly worth noting is the francophone area of the Caribbean, whose cornerstone is Haiti, the site of a great slave revolution, the first in the American continent. The remaining French possessions, including Guadeloupe and Martinique, remained until recently under a colonial system that gave them a special status: French Caribbean poetry and literature amply transcended their limits by becoming a literature of cultural revindication, the first of its kind in the colonized world. This produced an awareness of peoples stigmatized by the color of their skin; subsequently the Negritude movement demanded recognition of the values of the black world and its contributions to universal culture. This ideology, which originated in the Antilles but spread from the French capital, urged all the blacks in the world to recover their dignity and ancestral values. In France, during the period from 1930 to 1950, intellectuals, including Sartre, joined Césaire and Senghor, the Negritude poets, thereby converting this movement into a veritable wave of *mise en valeur* of everything that was black. Meanwhile, Picasso and other painters proclaimed the renovation of art through the formal values of African sculptures. Since 1906, so-called Primitive Art took the lines and outlines of African art that expressed a relationship between the balanced masses and the richness of volume in masks and sculptures. Both movements emerged from the popular sphere to achieve the level of fine arts (Martínez Montiel 6).

There was yet another forerunner to Negritude. A century after the Haitian revolution, in the midst of the U.S. occupation of Haiti between 1915 and 1934, Jean Price Mars (1876–1969) produced *Ainsi parla l'oncle* [1928; So Spoke the Uncle], an extraordinary compilation of oral traditions that configured the reinterpretation of the universe and the emergence of blacks in the world of slavery. The Martinican Aimé Césaire (b. 1913), together with the Senegalese Léopold Sédar Senghor (1906–2001), actually rediscovered Negritude after the term appeared in 1939 in Césaire's *Cahier d'un retour au pays natal* [Return to My Native Land]. Since then, a theory has been created around Negritude, conceived as ideological liberation (understood as any action of rebellion or struggle against all forms of oppression and imposition). This position enabled men of African ancestry not to reinterpret the West

through a black mentality, as Herskovits believed, but to adapt to the conditions of struggle in America by transforming Western cultural schemes to meet their profoundly emotional links to Africa.

This is borne out by the existence of creole and Voodoo, conceived as the original forms of rebellion expressed in both language and religion as well as in folklore and art. Despite the fact that colonization introduced European technology, which submerged the material expressions of African culture, the latter reemerged in wooden sculptures, paintings, and textiles. In the syncretic process, African religious values and those of the West have acquired new dimensions and performed different functions from those they had in their respective original cultures. (Militant Negritude is also close to a syncretic religious practice.) Being an intellectuals' movement, Negritude, together with its doctrine, spread to Africa via Europe (mainly France). There are thus various forms of Negritude from the Antilles and Africa, with various trends and currents. As a diversified movement, it can appear in progressive forms or in the shape of dangerous dogmas that threaten to become new forms of alienation. According to Depestre:

> There is an irrational, reactionary, mystical Negritude that propels its projects into the sphere of ideological impostors and serves as the cultural basis for the neo-colonialist penetration of our countries. It involves a new myth that deliberately tries to conceal the socioeconomic factors that have conditioned the situation of alienation and oppression of blacks in our societies. This Negritude fails to take into account the radical disorder of social relationships in the African, Asian, Antillean, and Latin American Third World in general. This Negritude has stopped being a legitimate form of rebellion opposed to the contemptible manifestations of racist dogma and now poses as a mystical operation that tends to dissimulate the presence in the historical scenario, in Africa and the Antilles, of black members of the bourgeoisie, who, in Haiti, for example, became the dominant class long ago. (1978, 16)

The passionate search for black identity as a factor of recognition in the Afro-American world is active in literature, painting, music, and all forms of popular culture and formal academic culture; these works and authors constitute the enormous cultural stock of the Caribbean. There would be no point in making lists of these authors and their works, some notable and famous, others anonymous and popular; what remains true is that, whether inside or outside Negritude as a movement, Caribbean culture, both before and after its intellectualization, is a reality that is constantly fed by the everyday lives of its peoples.

Orality in the Sacred Sphere

Of all collective manifestations, the clearest example of the strength and preservation of traditions is religiosity. It not only reflects the African legacy but also is a code of rules and precepts applied for social control. Within this scheme, Afro-Caribbean religions have preserved three existing planes within their conception of the universe: First, the supreme being; second, living creatures (nature and men); and third, the intermediate plane or sphere of spirits, genies, and deities, who act in man's everyday life as messengers between men and the supreme being. The oral systems used to invoke the divinities (saints, *orishas*, or spirits) are mainly constructed using creole languages. Each deity has its form of worship, its offerings or sacrifices, and its dances and drumbeats, but the main discourse (in spells) exists orally. During the ceremonies, the initiates go into a trance in which they serve as a receptacle for the divinities, who use their voices to express themselves to humans. Religious rituals are far different from what ignorance and prejudice have claimed.

In practice, Afro-Caribbean cults should be interpreted as a means of re-emigration; through the trance, blacks return to their African homeland. They enter their native land–speaking the language of their ancestors–invoke their gods, and are possessed by them. At the climax of the ceremonies, when everything ceases to exist in order to give way to the voice of the *orishas*, the sacred space is recovered and the person returns, in a state of altered consciousness, as a result of what is said, sung, and danced. Without the proper oral formula, the possessed man will be lost and fail to arrive–and yet be unable to return either. On the subject of orality in the *fon* language, Janheinz Jahn notes:

> Voodoo! Word of obscure vowels, and muffled, resounding consonants. Voodoo! Mysterious and nocturnal sound of drums in the lands of Haiti, a sound that terrifies tourists, reminding them of a series of horrors read somewhere: voodoo, idolatry, witchcraft, infernal visions, black mass with cannibalistic sacrifices, Voodoo, the quintessence of depravation, of all the vices and horrors, the witches' Sabbath of the nether powers and ineradicable heresy. How much truth is there in all this? (349)

To this Alfred Métraux replies:

> This legend is far older. It dates to the Colonial period in which it was the result of fear and loathing; one cannot be cruel and unjust with impunity. The anxiety that develops in those who abuse force often takes the form of imaginary terrors and demented obsessions. The master despised his slave, yet feared his hatred. He treated him like an animal yet distrusted the occult powers attributed to him. (11)

By transforming Voodoo into magic, the cult's priests in the Mississippi Delta have become mere quacks, with a fair share of charlatans who entertain New Orleans tourists by selling them all kinds of amulets and "magic" objects. This spurious Voodoo, adulterated by its distance from its sources, was taken to the northern United States as part of the cultural baggage of the black emigrants, during the mobilization from south to north, both between and after the two World Wars. This explains why it is found in New York, Philadelphia, and Pittsburgh, where it coexists with jazz and blues, which also emigrated from the south.

Orality in the Social Sphere

The religious brotherhoods paved the way for syncretism; once the *orishas* had been put on the same level as the Catholic saints, the Afro-Brazilian and Afro-Cuban cultures stopped being purely African and developed new forms, equally close to both Catholicism and the African world. In this religious duality, what was African was often associated with evil and sin. Despite this, Africans adopted Catholicism, while whites infiltrated the cults of "blacks." The numerous *terreiros* and *reglas de ocha* diversified throughout the country, their names varying from one region to the next; thus, independently, with no precise links between each other, the *candomble* developed in Bahía, the *xangós* in Recife, the *macumbas* in Río de Janeiro, the *vodus* in Maranhao, and the *batuques* in Porto Alegre. *Santería* took hold throughout Cuba, whence it spread to the United States and, since the mid-twentieth century, to Spain and to Costa Rica, Santo Domingo, and other Latin American countries.

Once Brazil was declared a republic, the repression of cults intensified, particularly in the capital, Río de Janeiro, where *macumba* was forced into hiding, far more so than in the past. This led to a simplification of the ritual, and foreign elements found their way into the heart of the doctrine. The suppression of certain original elements, however, paradoxically implied the proliferation of divinities whose origin was no longer African or even Roman Catholic. The cults were enriched by the spirits of the *caboclos*, a practice of Amerindian origin, and varied practices of witchcraft, often with European origin (see Pereira de Queiroz). As part of this incorporation of new elements, the cults began to attract followers from all racial and social sectors; whites frantically embraced what they had once scorned, drawn by the need to solve the problems of poverty, unemployment, or family conflicts. In other words, cults began to function as a form of collective consultation of the forces of the next life, where orality was seen as the sole means of communication with the deities.

The second half of this century saw the emergence of a new form of Afro-Brazilian cult: *umbanda*, which took elements of Catholic origin with an African base, with additions from Alan Kardek's spiritualism and certain elements regarded as being of Indian origin. *Umbanda* spread from the cities of Río de Janeiro and São Paulo to the rest of the country, gaining adepts at all social levels of the urban population; in the late 1970s, the number of *umbandistas* was estimated at twenty million throughout Brazil. Unlike previous cults, which were transmitted through the oral tradition, *umbanda* had a series of doctrinal texts that became the book of this religion. It is useful to point out here that the emergence of *umbanda* coincided with the rise of *mestizos* and blacks who encouraged this cult once they had reached the middle and upper middle classes; in *umbanda*, the social rules that separated the different ethnic groups were broken. There seem to have been more women than men, but an equal proportion of Jews, Arabs, whites, and blacks. During the ceremonies, drums (*atabaques)* were beaten, but without any particular rhythm or in the style of either *candomble* or *macumba*. Since *umbanda* has a written doctrine, intellectuals and "sages" arose who were entrusted with the responsibility of determining the dogmas and liturgy. This cult therefore has an organization, is widely publicized, and exercises a great influence over the Brazilian masses. It continues to be the bastion of Africanness and a means of resisting the homogenizing assimilation in which the original values of the population of African ancestry are at stake.

Orality in Resistance, Rebellion, and Liberation

The blacks' struggle has been intense since the liberation movements, and through their political participation in the various fronts, they have attempted to improve their living conditions. They subsequently have become active agents of change in the struggle for civil rights and in the unending commitment to the fight against racism–progressing or being forced to retreat, according to external or internal factors that either helped or hindered their aspirations. Creole folklore, as Bastide calls it, originated in America as a result of the social relations between slaves and their masters–the product of the feelings of one group toward the other and the coercive means whites used to acculturate blacks. The forms of this folklore maintained their Africanness, yet their contents included the slaves' new reality: Plantations, forced submission, pain, and rebellion, which transformed the oral tradition from accounts of daily life, stories, or myths into a folklore of fugitive rebels. Since it was spontaneous, rather than inherited from African folklore, it was disseminated by means of orality in every country whose population had African roots. One example, as we have seen, was the Negritude movement; another was *myalism* and the Rastafarian movement. However, the influence of Marcus Garvey's (1887–1940) doctrine on the messianic movements of popular expression during this century was significant. Garvey was a militant nationalist born in Jamaica who combined the principles of Pan-Africanism with Negritude–both the result of the intellectual activity of black Americans–which, as mentioned earlier, began in the early twentieth century and culminated in the 1930s, giving rise to new trends such as Rastafarianism.

As a result of Garvey and other Antillean and American intellectuals such as W. E. B. Du Bois (1868–1963) and Aimé Césaire (b. 1913), the new black struggle began with the following weapons: The revindication of the values of African culture, the dignity of blacks as the heirs to their culture, and racial pride. The blacks were no longer working in the *palenques* and through organized rebellion, since they were legally free, but in the cultural sphere, where they were still denied entry and discriminated against. In the relationship between fugitives and orality, it is useful to recall that in Africa, any human activity and any movement of nature lies in the word, which is a creative force like water and fire, as well as a life force, as found in a seed. As has often been said, the word links the living with the dead and the deities; it is the engine that initiates and continues the movement of all things. According to Jahn, Amma is the great procreator who engendered the world through the semen of the word. It is a well-known fact that in Africa, no poison or protection is effective without the word. Spells, creation, and magic formulas liberate supernatural forces and place them at the service of men.

In addition to resistance to forced labor, the runaway slave movement was a form of cultural resistance whose organization was based on ethnic identity but admitted indigenous factors with which it coexisted. This did not imply the total assimilation of one group by another but instead the natural emergence of norms and patterns as a form of synthesis. One could call this "runaway slave culture" a model of the fusion of cultural elements and lifestyles resulting from the semi-isolated, syncretic process. The latter element should be stressed, since no runaway community was absolutely incommunicado; we know that many of them maintained trading links and contacts with the rest of the colonial population from which certain influences resulted. This explains why the runaway slave movement preserved both ancient African cultural features and those derived from the slave regime of the Colonial period. Both have now disappeared, yet they are still present in the oral tradition as legends.

Criollo languages developed in the Caribbean as a basic part of runaway slave culture. Escaped slaves coming together to form small communities had a need to create a common language that would overcome cultural diversity, resist isolation, and thus enhance their survival. *Criollo* was a synthesis of West African language fused together with French and with loan words from English and Spanish. The tonality, however, was African. It is ironic that this creation of former slaves came to be the domestic language of the white population. The traditional genres of oral cultures flourished in creole: stories of heroes, fables, proverbs, and songs. This literature came to be a detailed record of the historical process of these former slaves and their communities, a collective memory handed down from parents to children (see Arnold, Vol. 1). Edith Efron adds:

> It is an independent, well integrated language, full of color and flavor which prefers poetic images to abstractions, rich in proverbs and maxims, with a singing, musical expression. Its vocabulary is French, and composed of words that were poured into the slave's language by the first buccaneers, planters and French colonists who brought their French dialects from Normandy, Picardy, Brittany and Anjou to Hispaniola. Indian words also enriched the language, often to describe local fruits, flowers and animals. A large number of African words concerning customs and religious beliefs, meals, foods and household objects, have remained in the creole language. Many characteristic Africanisms are prominent in creole, notably the repetition of words to indicate emphasis. (in Franco 244)

In order not to neglect other Caribbean cultures, one should also mention the oral tradition in the Dutch Caribbean, which, in addition to traditional genres, has preserved the *Cumfa*, which contains the invocation of the gods in religious cults. The African origin of many of these oral texts that interpret the universe and are handed down from generation to generation is the Ivory Coast and other regions along the west coast of Africa. Few dances and songs have retained such a high degree of Africanness as those of Guyana, particularly those of the so-called jungle communities protected from foreign influences. The bush blacks, famous for their purely African culture, are the descendants of runaway slaves who hid in the forest amid rivers and waterfalls, where they developed an economy of self-sufficiency, organizing themselves on the basis of traditions preserved since the time of slavery.

Among these oral texts created in slavery and exile, the word, as in Africa, is extraordinarily powerful. Through the word, ordinary events acquire a degree of sacredness. This is manifested in key formulas (which confirms the fact that even though Africans did not bring any form of writing to the New World, it was not because they lacked one, since several writing systems were invented by the peoples of the southern Sahara) used in limited areas at first and then widely disseminated. It is thought that, due to the lack of materials that could be preserved for a long time, such as papyrus, blacks maintained a system of oral transmission that was more durable than any written material and was therefore adopted as a means of communication. They developed an original language that achieved extraordinary levels of complexity in Africa, a language that was far more effective than and superior to writing as a means of communication. Jahn explains:

> If we extend the concept of writing to a little beyond what is included in the word derived from "write" and adopt the European custom of understanding the concept on the basis of its aim rather than the means involved, and define writing as the "signs produced which man uses to communicate," we find that the language of the drums is also writing. Seen from this point of view, African culture is therefore not a pre-literate culture. Both Western and African cultures had writing systems; the former, alphabetic writing, the latter, drum writing. (260–61)

The majority of Afro-American cultures preserved the use of drums in both religious cults and profane celebrations. It was only in the British colonies of North America that blacks were deprived of them; Protestant slave owners, with a great deal of intuition, prohibited drum beats, presuming that without them the African gods would not rush to assist their children. Meanwhile, evangelized blacks replaced these instruments by following the beat with their hands and feet during religious services. Subsequently, musical creativity would bring back the drums by recreating the various popular genres of musical bands, particularly in the south, where the popular blues and jazz genres would later emerge as an expression from New Orleans in which creole—the same as that spoken in Haiti—was used.

The complex relationship between drums and words is sometimes produced as a dialogue and sometimes as a parallel discourse, but the crux of this relationship is that the oral text serves as an echo of the source of sound. Indeed, the characteristic feature of the drum lies in its percussion techniques, meaning that a narration may be organized by percussion and repercussion. A Bantu lullaby provides an example of this:

1. Kuku!
2. Kugu kuku!
3. Nyo mee
4. Ma soo mabolwe!
5. Andogsul
6. Gwet gwa temb ki!

This piece, consisting of six phrases, the first two of which reproduce the song of a bird in the forest, is a well-known song among all the inhabitants of the jungle in Cameroon. The scheme is as follows: 1-2 slowly twice, 1-2-3-4 quickly four times. Even beforehand, at the melodic and rhythmic level, we notice that the second phrase is a double echo of the first, since the first phrase in two time corresponds to the second in four time; its reproduction may be accompanied by a rhythmic and melodic expansion. Likewise, the rhythm of the first phrase corresponds to the acceleration of the quick beat that echoes the phrases alternately. Within this relationship, the rhythm corresponds to the oral text, since the latter is constructed on the basis of the basic percussive rhythm, repeated from the beginning to the end of the text. Other kinds of rhythmic instruments include maracas, clavés, achereke, and so on. Known throughout the Spanish Caribbean, they have even been incorporated into symphony orchestras.

On the Caribbean mainland, black Brazilian festivities, sociologically regarded as contributing to community integration and black self-affirmation, were held for four days, during which samba schools played the chief role in inverting values: Blacks were transformed from a subjected to a ruling people. By institutionalizing the blacks' popular culture and making it official, white society regarded it as a complement of its own, stripping itself of its leading role:

> At the same time that this phenomenon took place, at other levels, various other specific groups were formed, as a result of other contradictions, and the cycle began again. A form of contradictory, dialectic independence/intermittence takes place among these groups, while competitive society seeks to marginalize them socially, by disorganizing or whitening these groups, destroying their role as a form of resistance and transforming them into appendices of the dominant classes. (Moura 189)

As Moura points out, however, black arts and popular culture stand out within this interethnic competition. They are present in painting, music, dance, literature, theater, and the cinema. As hundreds of artists and the new politico-cultural movements have shown, blacks have overcome inequality and have coped with changes, supported by their tradition and the vitality of their creative spirit. Again and again, since Colonial times, their African heritage has been renovated, invented, re-created, and relocated. All of this constitutes their heritage, which has been handed down from generation to generation.

The Spanish Caribbean

As in the United States, the influence of Protestantism produced a syncretism in the religious songs of black English-speaking Antilleans: Their rhythm was impregnated with the ancestral African heritage. It accompanied blacks in their everyday lives and in religious songs. Blacks of Antillean origin from Limón, Costa Rica, were predominantly influenced by Anglican, Baptist, and Methodist Protestant churches, to which parareligious sects, such as lodges, *pocomía*, and obeah, were added. In lodges, brotherhood and philosophical speculation were compulsory practices, with members primarily seeking the prestige and company of their coreligionists. *Pocomía* was a minority cult of self-styled witch doctors who defended themselves from their enemies. Obeah consisted of a series of practices administered by people with supposedly supernatural powers, which they used to defend or to attack. All this reveals the inclination of blacks to ritualize and sanctify certain moments in the life cycle. Since they are extremely religious by tradition, sensitive to any religion and respectful of any belief, they preserve their African heritage in plural forms. Today in Costa Rica, interethnic relationships are asymmetrical: At school, work, and in public life, there is prejudice against blacks, regardless of whether or not they have attained higher levels of instruction or technical or scientific training. Blacks even despise their own cultural heritage, as a result of social pressure or ignorance. This is exacerbated by the disintegration of families, as a result of poverty and emigration due to economic reasons.

The world of sugar plantations, alluded to in the fine arts in the Spanish Caribbean, is as inseparable from blacks as banana growing is from Central America. Sugarcane growing has been preserved to this day, and any reference to it is not merely a reference to the past, since culture and single-crop farming are still the pillars of life in Cuba. Within this context, remnants of African customs have been preserved to a remarkable degree; particularly important to note here is the role of black assemblies during the Colonial period. Groups of slaves from the same place of origin offered mutual assistance and fraternal help to each other. These social spheres were maintained through orality, rites, dances, and other traditions. At one point, the gods from one nation even coexisted with those of another. Within this ethnic diversity of Bantu and Sudanese groups, the dominant culture was the Yoruba culture of the Dahomean and Nigerian regions; many from here were sent to the Spanish and Brazilian Caribbean during the final stage of slave trading in the nineteenth century. Since the basic characteristics of each group were preserved, it was apparently possible to distinguish between the contributions of the Yoruba, the Congo, the Arara, and the Carabalis in Cuba.

In the eighteenth century, a modified form of black ritual music found its way into dance halls, and the art of proverbs, sayings, and ballads, in various hybrid forms resulting from miscegenation, was practiced at every level of society. The cotillion appeared in 1794, followed immediately by the *habanera*, genres already cultivated by the humble popular black musicians, who introduced African rhythm into white dances. It has been said that words and drums are two constants in Caribbean Africanness, which makes it essential to stress the core of these two elements: Rhythm. As a result of the internal dynamism that shapes it, rhythm is the architecture of being, as Senghor calls it, a vital force like blood, a vibration which moves people at the most intimate level. It is the language or mode of discourse of a collectivity, even when it permits individual creativity. By enlightening the spirit, rhythm is materialized through sounds and words. It is expressed through colored lines, sculpture, painting, or architecture, with an emphasis on poetry, drum beats, dance movements, and also all the concrete expressions of African spirituality. Sentiment and rhythm are inseparably intertwined, as a result of which it is said that Africa has provided more emotional than rational cultures and that the spiritual reserves of mankind lie in this continent. As an essential element, rhythm gives words life and makes them effective; it is their procreator. The rhythmic word of God, according to Senghor, created the world. Because of their rhythm, drumbeats are more than just sounds; they are essentially language. They can be the voice of one's ancestors; their magical words can be used to construct the image of a *loa*, induce a trance, or structure a poem cadenced by accents.

In Cuba, the stock of the African language in the eighteenth century, particularly the Yoruba language, was jealously guarded in the notebooks owned by the officiants of the various cults. It has been proved that many of these notebooks were the old account books of the sugar refinery offices. What is not clear, although one could hazard a guess, is how these account books came to be owned by blacks. By this time, mulattos and blacks had attained a certain degree of social mobility and occupied positions of responsibility in the sugar mills, sometimes even becoming foremen and overseers. It would not have been unusual, given the opportunity, for them to have learned to write, either to fulfill the supervision tasks assigned to them or to leave for future generations a written account of traditional tasks, ancient history, myths, and fables, in short, all the historical heritage of their experience, which, preserved in these notebooks, can be consulted to this day. Studies of these notebooks have confirmed the phonetic alterations of the Spanish spoken in Cuba, as well as the introduction of words and concepts into nouns, adjectives, verbs, and place names of African origin. At the same time, it is assumed that the Spanish of the colonists was already a language with elements of Afro-Arab origin, introduced during the many centuries of North African presence in the peninsula.

The interethnic relations that took place in the various regions of the New World among the descendants of the three basic nuclei had various moral, religious, and legal frameworks that governed the lives of the three peoples. The image of the slave or blacks varied considerably according to the era and the specific circumstances of each colony. This contributed to their unequal integration in colonial societies once they had obtained their freedom, since their immediate future also depended on their integration. The former slaves were integrated into the community, where they could exploit their creativity and talent, and this necessarily required new forms of acculturation. (This process has been marked by the vitality and permanence of African systems in resisting the continuous pressure of depersonalization by those to whom they were subjected.)

Following the elimination of racial divisions, mulattos–the offspring of white and black parents–became part of *mestizo* societies, yet an unrepentant form of racism continued to classify blacks into an absurd range of tones from "extremely black" to "blue-black," "ashen black," "faded black," "purple," and "red." Deive notes:

> The terms *prieto* and *moreno* date to colonial Mexico. They are less pejorative and socially more acceptable than the word *negro*. The second term is used as a euphemism in *Lazarillo de Tormes* and other classic Spanish works, and continues to be used as such in Santo Domingo today, despite the fact that in the past it was used to refer to free blacks as opposed to slaves, referred to exclusively as *negros*. (157)

As in virtually all the American colonies, in the Spanish-speaking regions throughout the Colonial period, royal officers purchased blacks in shipments to undertake major public works. In addition to the construction and repair of fortifications and roads, blacks were employed in the dockyards and for the transport of heavy loads. On the few occasions when Indians came to own blacks, the latter were employed in building bridges, roads, and churches. As colonial institutions, hospitals and town councils were also slave owners; there, blacks were assigned the hardest physical tasks, only rarely being trained as town criers, messengers, or porters. Domestic slavery in haciendas was undoubtedly the form of captivity in which blacks were treated the most humanely. As household members, they obviously received kinder and more benign treatment and may even have been moderately content. This form of slavery is similar to that of blacks in Europe prior to the Colonial period. In America, ownership of domestic slaves afforded Europeans prestige and comfort. As members of the master's household, thanks to acculturation and education, slaves were able to incorporate some of their original features, making their integration less violent. Within their sphere, domestic slaves ensured the survival of their beliefs, despite the fact that slaves from the same ethnic group or who were related were usually separated as soon as they embarked or were sold individually for fear of rebellions. Nevertheless, in black assemblies, brotherhoods, and haciendas, the authorities supported the trend to group together blacks from the same nation so that, having identified each other, they would undertake tasks requiring a collective effort more effectively. One can logically assume, however, that in the shelter of their homes (rather than in brotherhoods and councils), slaves did become attached to the families that fed, clothed, and educated them.

Urban domestic blacks undoubtedly assimilated the culture of their masters readily, and transmitted it to their peers; think of the wet nurses and ladies' maids who in turn influenced whites through their words and beliefs. At this point, it is worth recalling the circumstances that enabled African women to prolong their maternity through their masters' children. José Luciano Franco refers to them in these terms: "In her later years, the black woman became the ayah and amah, the ruler of the family and the children's governess. The mistress entrusted her with the running of the house, the disciplining of the servants and the religious education of the latter and her children; in short, she became a 'matron,' respected and obeyed by all." (14). Given that domestic slavery also fostered the influence of slaves over their masters, black nannies were a constant theme in *costumbrista* literature and poetry, characterized by the idyllic accounts of whites raised by their ayahs, who in turn introjected their beliefs into the dominant society, sharing the protection of their ancestral gods with their wards. Urban slaves were found in the majority of Latin American cities, particularly during the last two centuries of the Colonial period. They were also concentrated in nearby rural areas with access to major communication routes. Since they were sometimes prohibited from living in towns, groups of blacks with no fixed employment plundered Indian communities. This form of existence has been called "vagrancy," since those involved had no clearly defined status; the classless also lacked any clear social position. This experience was very different from that of the individual or collective runaway slaves, which has already been described in detail.

Other forms of stratification among slaves were defined, within the *esclavonías* or complements of slaves, by their level of autonomy and knowledge. The first stratum was measured by the degree of trust the master deposited in a particular slave by granting him or her positions of privilege and power over other slaves; the knowledge that some individuals possessed of African culture and language placed them in a superior position among those of their community. Knowing how to read and write the European language and understanding the world and reality of the masters also gave them more autonomy and status. Wizards and witch doctors also enjoyed great prestige among the slaves, which, although not acknowledged by the master, gave them power over him. Their control of the supernatural meant that they were both feared and solicited by the master himself. This biculturalism was a factor that enabled slaves to achieve positions of command when they acted as cultural mediators, particularly in domestic service in which there were Indians as well as blacks. By speaking the European language, they created an interethnic link among Indians, whites, and blacks; bilingualism gave them immense prestige with individuals of the same condition as themselves. Many blacks in domestic service learned and eventually mastered the cultured forms of European poetry (such as quatrains and décimas), which were subsequently incorporated into popular language; *decimistas* or improvisers, as they were known in the Spanish Caribbean, used rhyming oral texts to sing while they danced, giving them rhythmical variations with which the local traditions of the various communities in this area have been created.

Caribbean Afro-Hispanic Literature Vis-à-Vis Orality

The vast panorama of literary production in the Caribbean offers numerous works in various European languages in addition to those produced in creole languages. Apropos of this, it is worth noting the approach that certain scholars have taken to folk literature or oral literature. The term "literary folklore" generally includes all artistic expressions, in either prose or verse, with stable structures that are preserved in different versions and transmitted in a predominantly oral and anonymous form, according to the traditional norms of each folk group. Within literary folklore, a distinction is commonly made (based on formal characteristics) between the allegorical of narrative in prose and other forms, such as poetry, proverbs, riddles, and so on. Prose narrative includes the forms and genres regarded as major, such as myths, legends, and stories, and minor, such as jokes and anecdotes, family sagas, memoirs, personal work experiences, and so on (see Moedano Navarro). In the African scheme, the traditional genres of orality correspond to what are regarded as major genres in literary folklore. What has been described in this essay as creole folklore also belongs to it; in other words, the creations of Afro-American peoples have been reinterpreted to incorporate their creator's Africanness and have thereby kept folklore in force until the present.

We should now, therefore, refer to the Afro-Caribbean production that specialists have called black or *negrista* literature,

in keeping with the theory of Negritude. The Spanish- and Portuguese-speaking Caribbean is characterized by the vital attitude blacks have toward life, art, and literary creation, as is well known and evident in the poetry of Cuba's Nicolás Guillén (1902–1989):

Tu vientre sabe más que tu cabeza
y tanto como tus muslos.
Ésa
es la fuerte gracia negra
de tu cuerpo desnudo

("Madrigal")

Your belly knows more than your head
and as much as your thighs.
That
is the powerful black grace
of your nude body

Due to the miscegenation between blacks and Europeans, since Indians were merely part of the past of collective memory, there is an overflowing of sensuality in music and dance, which has extended to the literary production of other poets who, regardless of the color of their skin, acknowledge the power of Negritude:

¡Ahí vienen los tambores!
Ten cuidado, hombre blanco, que a ti llegan
para clavarte su aguijón de música
Tápate las orejas,
cierra toda abertura de tu alma
y el instinto dispón a la defensa;
que en la torva noche de Nigricia
te picara un tambor de danza o guerra
su terrible ponzoña
correrá para siempre por tus venas.

(Luis Palés Matos, "Tambores")

The drums are coming!
Watch out, white man, because they're coming
to pierce you with their music.
Put your hands over your ears,
close every opening in your soul
and put your instinct on the defensive;
because if, in the fierce night of Blackness,
a dance or war drums bite you,
its terrible poison
would course through your veins forever.

According to Miguel Barnet (b. 1940), Christopher Columbus was prophetic when he said that Cuba was an island of very sweet air and words, for he seemed to prophesy what would be the essence of Cuba's economy and life. Barnet continues:

Because weren't the most valuable aspect of our music and our dances, the *maní, yuca, garabato, macuta,* the Ocha dances, the *caringa* and the *zapateo,* danced in the grounds of the sugar mills? And didn't the best of our rumba, *columbia* and *yambú,* arise in the main sugar-producing area in the wide Colón plain? Don't our fables, with their intrinsic anthropomorphous sense attributed to Cuban fauna, our Yoruba mythology, the only mythological body we really possess, the most highly prized oral literature of the sugarcane peasants, constantly refer to the world of the sugar mills and their habitat? Don't the *danzón* and the *son* come from areas that are rich in sugar, where the plantation system was the mainstay of the economy? Don't the most famous *huarachas* in our comic theater refer at some point to life in the sugar mills, the master, the overseer, the foreman and the slave? Didn't the first

Cuban press develop as a result of commercial dealings involving sugar? Our fiction, our light genres, our poetry; as Cintio Vitier said in his poem, "La Zafra," the aroma of the sugarcane harvest-time epitomized the tragedy of the Cuban people. And didn't Nicolás Guillén, in "Elegía a Jesús Méndez," express all the drama of our pseudo-republic? (14)

Blacks first appeared in Cuban literature in 1608, the date of the first document in which they were the protagonists, "Espejo de paciencia" [Mirror of Patience]. In *costumbrista* literature, blacks formed the accompanying chorus that faithfully reflected their condition. By the nineteenth century, certain philanthropists had begun to write against slavery and the maltreatment of blacks; men of letters produced sentimental pieces about the "resignation" of blacks (disproved by the numerous rebellions and uprisings), which were re-created in dramas, novels, or burlesque poems in which blacks were buffoons with African accents who made audiences laugh in comic sketches. The nineteenth century saw the emergence of social criticism, most acutely expressed in comedies and *guarachas*, within the framework of the frequent slave uprisings leading up to the major rebellion in 1868. A compilation of *guarachas* published in 1963, taken from a 1882 edition, shows the diversity of ethnic groups on the island; the protagonists, far from being fictional, were real people.

The Mexican Caribbean, which since the beginning of the Colonial period has undergone numerous influences from the Spanish Antilles, displays a cultural diversity in which loans from Cuba and Puerto Rico are highly evident in oral literature. Whereas this influence is only barely noticeable in the popular genres of the states with mestizo and Indian majorities (Tabasco, Campeche, Yucatán), in Veracruz there are noticeable traces of Afro-Cuban culture. This is due firstly to the presence of African slaves, who arrived from the sixteenth century onward in areas where there was no Indian population, and secondly to the migrations of Cubans (the majority of whom were blacks), who reached the Port of Veracruz in the seventeenth through nineteenth centuries, bringing their popular traditions with them. These then became established all along the Sotavento coast. The *Chuchumbé* was a Cuban dance that crossed the sea and, from the seventeenth century onwards, was established in this port city. It was accompanied by "obscene" verses, and its choreography included "lascivious" movements that scandalized the Church authorities, who forbade it. Rhymed genres became an essential ingredient of the *fandango,* whose verses were composed as a form of chronicle, criticism, and irony, characteristic of local culture.

The recently coined term Afro-Caribbean immediately suggests a geographical and social context, an unmistakable ethnicity, which gives it a mark of Africanness; an undeniable diversity, but also a common essence, is contained in this compound word (see **Figure 1**). The Caribbean is rhythm, tropical beauty, and creativity, and its people use their ingenuity in their demands for independence and in their fight for freedom from the greed that oppresses them. There are *ñañigos* (the members of secret societies) with their drums, the spells of the *congos,* the religious invocations, and all the oral genres that fill the chapters of literature. In this expression of Afro-Caribbean creativity, the life of its protagonists reflects the passions, suffering, and enjoyment of the black peoples. Poetry, like narrative, reflects the search for identity, the national motifs, and the need to recognize oneself in Spanish America or Latin America; Alberto Insúa's (1883–1963) *El negro que tenía el alma blanca* [1922;

Figure 1.

Photograph of Cuban street singer in 'Bodeguita de medio'. (Archive of the author)

The Black Man Who Had a White Soul] marked the beginning of the fictionalized pages of social ethnology.

This work was followed by others of similar quality, invariably tracing the blacks' progress: *El reino de este mundo* [1949; The Kingdom of this World] by Alejo Carpentier (1904–1980); *Pobre negro* [1937; Poor Black Man] by Rómulo Gallegos (1884–1969); *Manuel Piar: El caudillo de dos colores* [1987; Manuel Piar: The Strongman of Two Colors] by Francisco Herrera Luque (1927–1991); *Pedro Claver, el santo de los esclavos* [1950; Saint Peter Claver, the Slaves' Saint] by Mariano Picón Salas (1901–1965); and Lino Novás Calvo's (1905–1983) *El negrero: vida novelada de Pedro Blanco Fernández de Trava* [1933; The Slave Trader: The Novelized Life of Pedro Blanco Fernández de Trava]. At the same time that this writing stimulated the study of black society, it also emphasized the other coexisting world and thus racial inequality. The exaltation of African roots and the struggle of the slaves' descendants were also explored by poets, such as the Dominican Manuel del Cabral (1907–1999), the Cuban Nicolás Guillén, and the Puerto Rican Luis Palés Matos (1898–1959), who was mentioned earlier. In terms of intellectual production, this poetic-narrative trend sought to create ethnic-national pride based on the values of Africanness. Spain recognized that this literature, produced by the sons of Africa, was a new art form that eschewed fantasy in favor of revealing the Afro-American soul, while clamoring for its recognition. This avant-garde movement produced major writers who created a profound literature containing the beginnings of a dialogue between older traditions and the newer voices of Latin American narrative. The many works of the past two centuries depict not only blacks but also Indians and *mestizos* resulting from the process of miscegenation. One writer who stands out because of his vast knowledge of Antillean culture is Alejo Carpentier. His work includes music, oral traditions, rituals, and everything that belonged to the world of European surrealism, which was represented by André Bréton, Pablo Picasso, Tristán Tzara, and Jorge de Chirico, the principal theoretical exponents of this cultural movement.

In Afro-Hispanic oral literature, colonial society is denounced by its blacks and mulattos–its offspring of blacks and Indians or Spanish. From rebellion emerged the history of their tragedy in slavery, their ancestral uprootedness, with the burden of suffering, degradation, and denial of their identity. In their own words, these defenseless heroes sought to obtain their freedom, protected only by gods who, like them, lived in exile. Latin American blacks have managed to endure the harsh existence of slavery and forced acculturation, leaving the chronicle of their experience in the oral tradition recorded in social narrative and ethno-poetry.

Translation by Suzanne D. Stephens

Works Cited

Arnold, A. James, ed. 1994. *A History of Literature in the Caribbean.* Vol. 1. *Hispanic and Francophone Regions.* Amsterdam: J. Benjamins.

Barnet, Miguel. 1979. *La cultura que generó el mundo del azúcar.* Havana: Revolución y Cultura.

Bastide, Roger. 1967. *Las Américas negras: Las civilizaciones africanas en el Nuevo Mundo.* Trans. Patricio Azcárate. Mexico City: Alianza Editorial.

Carpentier, Alejo. 1967. *El reino de este mundo.* Barcelona: Editorial Seix Barral.

Césaire, Aimé. 1960. *Cahier d'un retour au pays natal.* Preface by Petar Guberina. Paris: Présence africaine.

Deive, Carlos Esteban. 1978. *El indio, el negro, y la vida tradicional dominicana.* Santo Domingo: Museo del Hombre Dominicano.

Depestre, René. 1978. *Problemas de la identidad del hombre negro en las literaturas antillanas.* Mexico City: Cuadernos de Cultura Latinoamericana, Universidad Nacional Autónoma de México.

Franco, José Luciano. 1968. *La presencia negra en el Nuevo Mundo.* Havana: Cuadernos Casa de las Américas.

Gallegos, Rómulo. 1970 . *Pobre negro.* Buenos Aires: Espasa-Calpe Argentina.

Guillén, Nicolás. 1972. "Madrigal." *Obra poética 1920–1958.* Havana: Instituto Cubano del Libro. 39–40.

Herrera Luque, Francisco J. 1987. *Manuel Piar: Caudillo de dos colores.* Caracas: Pomaire.

Herskovits, Melville Jean. 1938. *Acculturation: The Study of Culture Contact.* New York: J. J. Augustin.

Jahn, Janheinz. 1963. *Las culturas neoafricanas.* Mexico City: Fondo de Cultura Económica.

Martínez Montiel, Luz María. 1997. *La plástica africana.* Mexico City: Afroamérica México A.C.

Moedano Navarro, Gabriel. 1975. "Los estudios literarios de folklore literario en Prosa." *Boletín 2 del Departamento de Investigación de las Tradiciones Populares.* Mexico City: S.E.P., Dirección General de Arte Popular. 5–33.

Moura, Clóvis. 1977. *O Negro de bom escravo a mau cidadão.* Rio de Janeiro: Conquista.

Novás Calvo, Lino. 1944. *El negrero: Vida novelada de Pedro Blanco Fernández de Trava.* Buenos Aires: Espasa-Calpe Argentina.

Palés Matos, Luis. 1968. "Tambores." *Poesía 1915–1956.* Intr. Federico de Onís. San Juan, PR: Universidad de Puerto Rico. 244–45.

Pereira de Queiroz, Maria Isaura. 1981. "Religious Evolution and Creation: The Afro-Brazilean Cults." Trans. Jeanne Ferguson. *Diógenes* 115 (Fall): 1–21.

Picón Salas, Mariano. 1950. *Pedro Claver, el santo de los esclavos.* Mexico City: Fondo de Cultura Económica.

Price-Mars, Jean. 1973. *Ainsi parle l'oncle.* Ottawa: Lemeac.

CHAPTER 48

ORALITY AND LITERATURE IN THE PERUVIAN ANDEAN ZONE

José Antonio Giménez Micó

It is paradoxical that any findings, recordings, or studies of oral expression must be registered in one way or another–in writing, or by some other means of fixing orality (whether audio or audiovisual). Consequently, the preservation of orality contrasts with at least one of its main features, its spontaneity–in other words, the fact that it can only be undertaken in the present, together with the fact that it is continuously updated and transformed in each new performance, thanks to the enriching and undoubtedly complex tension between memorization and improvisation (Calvet 43 ff.). Although folklorists, ethnologists, and anthropologists are aware of this paradox today, this does not mean that they have found a solution to the problem. At the same time, ethno-historians who choose to concern themselves with this issue must deal with a complementary problem: Orality does not necessarily follow a linear conception of temporality. This problem is concretely expressed, for example, in the difficulty of dating so-called oral texts, whose "origin and chronology can only be determined on the basis of the date of compilation when they were recorded in writing" (Alcina Franch 25).

In attempting, if not to solve these problems, then at least to reformulate them according to the parameters of a hermeneutic literary history, we will have to begin by establishing a distinction between the two types of reception of oral expression, which we shall call direct and deferred or indirect. Direct reception is that which the public undertakes at the time of the performance and is characterized by being ephemeral, unique, and impossible to repeat. Deferred reception is that to which access may be obtained at a later date, thanks to the recording (whether written, audio, or audiovisual) of these direct receptions. Historians of oral literature can obviously concern themselves only with the second type of reception, because, although they may have caused or contributed to direct reception, their first action will have been to record the latter and work on it a posteriori on the basis of this result. Deferred reception implies, in effect, resorting to the material supports through which specific, unique forms of oral expression have been successfully or poorly recorded. The point is to make people aware that these supports are not oral texts as such, even though we call them this for reasons of practicality, but rather mediators or written residues, as Beyersdorff calls them (213–14), or even *simulacra* in the sense this term is used by Marc Angenot: As "a second object presenting a gradual difference with a class of primary objects which keeps certain components (which enhance identification) without presenting all the axiomatic features which practice confers on them" (73). They are simulacra, in this case, of oral phenomena that took place at another time, in another context, and for another purpose. At the same time, though, they are phenomena that continue to take place, not only in remote places, but just around the corner in any Latin American city.

Simulacra, as understood here, are permanent objects that replace the fleeting phenomena of direct reception in an obviously imperfect fashion, yet have the enormous advantage (characteristic of literalness) of being able to be gathered, preserved, reproduced, catalogued, analyzed, and reinterpreted. Their usefulness therefore lies in their ability to be recontextualized (to be transmitted and reproduced), which performances lack. Simulacra are obviously the instruments used by our lettered culture to appropriate oral culture in general, particularly that of popular and indigenous cultures. From a hermeneutic point of view of knowledge through interpretation, which implies the ethical position of attempting to open oneself up to otherness, recognition of this appropriation proves to be not only legitimate but also fertile and, in any case, essential.

The written simulacra of oral phenomena or oral simulacra attest to the enormous distance that separates us from the oral expressions they represent, and, precisely because of this, they become (from our hermeneutic perspective) the bridges through which historian-interpreters can explore the past or the other presents, on the basis of their own present and the discursive position they occupy in their cultural environment. Rather than attempting to reconstruct these othernesses, investigators will formulate predictive hypotheses about the moment or the time of its first performance, provided this proves useful to its study (for a description of the concept of predictive hypothesis, see Schoenfel and Traub 281). At other times, what may be of interest is not so much the unrecoverable origin of the production of oral expressions but, rather, certain moments of their reproduction, in which they have been refunctionalized. In any case, regardless of the point of view adopted, the hermeneutical historian must assume that "no one is situated outside history and no one can assume that he is free of his own experience. Texts from the past, or those from a specific tradition, are never understood in the past; they are understood in the present, in the light of the reader's experience" (Valdés 28).

Pre-Hispanic Period

We have already referred to the dubious possibility of dating oral expressions; as José Alcina Franch stated a few years ago: "Some of the works to which we shall be referring could be classified as Colonial, others as being from the National period, and others as being from our time. However, this is not that significant since the most important fact is that, despite the undoubtedly valuable contributions from Spain, the Quechua cultural tradition continues to exist among the people" (25). If we add the facts that "we have virtually no knowledge of the history of popular and indigenous literatures" (Cornejo Polar 20), and "we lack the archives to document the evolution of Andean literary discourse during the past four centuries" (Lienhard, 1992, 40), then referring to the history of pre-Hispanic Andean oral literature, in other words, the history of the deferred reception of the latter, becomes even more problematic, since the only access we have to it are colonial sources, which, despite referring to the "antiquities of this kingdom," may say more about the Colonial period than the earlier one. As Kenneth Mills points out:

In the Andes, because historians for the most part lack sources equivalent to the splendid historical and geographical information contained within the few Mesoamerican codices that date from just before and after the arrival of the Europeans in the Mexica realm, it is necessary to employ the "regressive method" so well known to historians of European popular culture, among other fields. One must learn what one can of earlier, pre-Hispanic histories by cautiously reading backward from later, colonial sources. (47–48)

Some chroniclers, such as Fernando Montesinos or Diego de Castro Titu Cussi Yupanqui, state that Andean archives and libraries once existed, but there are certainly no traces of pre-Hispanic phonetic representation in the Andes. The Andean societies did have material supports for the representation of ideas, the so-called ideographic quipus (in addition to the numerical quipus, which were used for various calculations and administrative purposes). Quipus were made out of a series of colored strings and knots, the arrangement of which constituted a sophisticated semiotic system that has so far proved indecipherable (see **Figure 1**).

El Inca Garcilaso de la Vega (1539–1616) and Joan de Santa Cruz de Pachakuti Yamqui Salcamaygua (end fifteenth century), together with presumably all or most informants, were the "descendants of the Cuzcan aristocracy. These included the *Inkaruna,* who served as priests in the court (*Willaq uma*), the keepers and interpreters of records (*Khipukamayuq*), and the reciters and versifiers of lyrical genres (*Harawiikuq*)" (Beyersdorff 218). The Khipukamayuq was the only person able to interpret the signs that the Harawiikuq represented, in the double sense of the term interpretation: Understanding and application or bringing up to date. In this respect, the Inca archives and libraries can be said to have existed, and even to have lived and died, in the literal sense of the word; they were composed of the people who assumed these undoubtedly prestigious functions. The fact that these quipus were ideographic rather than phonetic certainly invalidates previously accepted ideas, according to which the oral tradition, based exclusively on memory, was restricted to word-by-word transmission over generations of a single, invariable text, recorded in the memories of the members of the collectivity. In fact, "there are a few cases where–it seems–this is indeed done (though more likely over the years than over generations), but by and large, the most striking characteristic of oral as opposed to written literature is precisely its variability. . . . By its very nature, oral literature is changeable; it cannot be checked by reference back to a written standard" (Finnegan 69). One could call this erroneous conception of orality the "Fahrenheit 451 syndrome" in the sense that it assumes that peoples with traditions other than the written tradition have a lack of the latter and are, therefore, in a situation of intrinsic inferiority determined by their lower degree of evolution, rather than by circumstantial relations of domination.

Through the works of the first two lexicographers of Quechua, the *Lexicon o vocabulario de la lengua general del Perú* (1560) by Fr. Domingo de Santo Tomás (1499–1570) and the *Arte y diccionario quechua-español* (1608) by Fr. Diego González Holguín (b. 1552), it is possible to draw up a brief catalogue of various types of Quechua dances and songs from the Colonial era that, although probably already adapted to the new reality implied by the disintegration of Tawantinsuyu, undoubtedly continued the Inca tradition in some way or another. The *Lexicon* "contained only the terms required by the catechization of the time and therefore includes only terms that refer to the

Figure 1.

Andean quipu. (Courtesy of Denise Y. Arnold and Juan de Dios Yapita)

musical and choreographic aspects of the *Qhaswa* (dancing in chorus), *Waynu* (dancing by couples), and *Taki* (the singing of repetitive phrases or music and dance)" (Beyersdorff 215). At the same time, *Arte y diccionario,* in addition to a fair number of entries related to different forms of expressing oneself orally and whose very existence gives an idea of the importance of art in oral communication in pre-Hispanic Andean society, also contains references to twelve forms of verses and various subgenres of the latter (for a non-exhaustive list of this poetics, see Harrison 78–79).

At the same time, several colonial missionaries and chroniclers referred to myths, legends, historical events, or festivities during which dances, songs, and recitals of all kinds of poems and plays were performed. In her "incomplete report of the chroniclers who, in some way or another bequeathed their pre-Hispanic Peruvian literature to us," María Zulema Zevallos mentions eleven:

Juan de Betanzos . . . recounts many war or religious rituals. . . . Martín de Morúa tells us the beautiful legend of the Idyll of the beautiful and discreet Chuquillanot, the daughter of the Sun and the shepherd Acohrapha. . . . Cristóbal de Molina transcribes sacred *jaillis,* such as the "First Prayer to the Maker" and

"Rogation to Wiracocha for the good of the Inca." Blas Valera [through the intermediary of El Inca Garcilaso, who copied] his precious manuscript "Sumaj Ñusta," dictated to him from a quipu by a *quipucamayo* and the "Prayer to the Sun by all the Incas . . ." We are indebted to Anello Oliva for the post-diluvian myth of the Chinchaysuyo and the legend of Chunta Huacho. . . . Cieza de León speaks to us of the Spanish Conquest and of the existence of the Oracle of Camay in Chincha. . . . Sarmiento de Gamboa tells us the fable of the Origin of the Inca of Cuzco. . . . Through his chronicles, Father Arriaga narrates the myth of creation in Huacho and Végueta. . . . Marcos de Niza describes the Flood of Chinchaysuyo . . . [,] while Father Las Casas and the chronicler Santillán were primarily concerned with describing the Coricancho and its wealth. (Zevallos 108–10)

On the basis of this material, several researchers have established an extremely fragmentary poetics of pre-Hispanic literary production.

We have already referred to the "songs," which would form part of a narrative-poetic art. As far as dramatic art is concerned, the person who has studied this in the greatest depth is the Bolivian Jesús Lara, who refers to two perfectly differentiated genres: The *wanka*, intended to recall the deeds of the Inca and other illustrious personalities, and the *aránway*, which describe episodes of everyday life:

The lack of exact equivalents in Spanish enabled Garcilaso and other authors to refer to the *wanka* and the *aránway* as though they were fully synonymous with European tragedy and comedy. Yet the only similarity between the *wanka* and tragedy is that both involve illustrious personalities. The *Wanka* lacks the tragic mood and unfortunate ending essential to tragedy. The *wanka* is a page from history rather than a description of great misfortune. The *aránway* was closer to comedy, differing only from the latter in its admission of music and song. Music and song, elements that were alien to comedy, enjoyed enormous prestige in not only the *aránway* but also the *wanka*. (Lara 1989, 16)

(We should point out that Spanish sixteenth- and seventeenth-century comedy did include music and song, contrary to what Lara believed [see, for example, Aubrun 19 ff.]. However, this in no way invalidates the pertinent observation of the erudite Bolivian.)

It should also be borne in mind, despite the relatively numerous references to pre-Hispanic oral literature, that only five chroniclers provide transcriptions of specific oral productions, totaling a mere forty-five. Available documentation on pre-Hispanic literature is limited, not only because of its meagerness but also, perhaps, because of its predominantly aristocratic nature, since "the chroniclers . . . did not concern themselves with the songs of the common people" (Beyersdorff 219); the only exception may be Felipe Guamán Poma de Ayala (1524?–1613). One should add that, unlike the Spanish empire, the Inca empire never sought to homogenize the great cultural diversity of its territory, comprising numerous macro-ethnic groups with their own habits, customs, and languages (see Rostworowski 17 ff.). The furthest they ever went was to impose Quechua as the lingua franca, or rather to acknowledge the fact that it served this purpose, since the language had been used for centuries in the trade relations between the various communities (see Torero 145–50).

The Colonial Period, 1530–1650

In 1550, a royal decree stipulated that, since "even in the most perfect language of the Indians, they are unable to explain the mysteries of our Holy Catholic Faith properly . . . , it would be advisable to introduce the Spanish language." As a result

of this "the Indians were to be given teachers, to teach those who wished to learn it of their own accord, in the way that was least unpleasant and costly to them" (Torero 195). Yet reality, both stubborn and complex, would take it upon itself to thwart the imperial plans of Charles I. Quechua not only did not become less important during the sixteenth and seventeenth centuries; it extended to areas that it had thitherto never penetrated (Potosí, Quito, Santiago del Estero, and part of the Amazon), to the point where the priests called it "Indian Latin." The Spaniards, extremely few in comparison with the Indians, soon discovered the impossibility of imposing Spanish, as well as the virtues of the "general language," which enabled them, more than with any other language, to extend their colonial rule, from the purely military point of view as well as the commercial and, obviously, the religious (see Glave 455): "It was only from this utilitarian perspective that they [the Spanish] showed interest in learning it, turning it into a refined instrument of domination, particularly as regards the ideological imposition of the new ruling class" (Cerrón Palomino 42). One should recall that, at the time of the Conquest, the Indians comprised an extremely complex social network in which, for example, most non-Cuzcans regarded Cuzcans as their oppressors.

The expansion of Quechua, with the subsequent (extremely relative) dissolution of the various local identities into one Indian voice (which, as a result of colonization, would also include that of the popular sectors of Hispanic and African origin), far from preventing, actually facilitated the establishment of a diglossia between Spanish and autochthonous languages, which, in general terms, reflected the division between writing and orality:

In the Indian and marginalized subsocieties, the oral system continued to dominate, as a "low variant" of the "disglossic" system. There was no fusion between the two, nor could there have been; it is impossible to blend the pen or the typewriter with the human voice.

Each one of these systems represents the pure state, a collective "cultural style": that of orality being collective, that of writing individual. Although the two cultures were partly modified as a result of a long, unequal dialogue, something also changed in the social function of communication systems. As a result of its marginalization, the oral system lost the state validity it had acquired during the pre-Hispanic period. As a system of local communication, however, it did not experience any profound transformation. (Lienhard 1992, 112–13)

The progression of the principal languages of the dominated peoples, precisely when the latter had reached the lowest point of submission, together with the relative autonomy of these cultural practices, in which orality continued to play a key role, can be fully understood only if one takes into account the complexity of the relations established in any colonial situation. The dichotomy between oppressors and oppressed certainly existed and obviously had devastating effects, but one should resist the temptation to reduce this to a simple deterministic dichotomy that clumsily traces the dialectic of master and slave, according to which the oppressor imposes his language, culture, religion, and worldview by force on a population that can only yield or openly rebel. We know it was not that simple. The diversity and specificity of each of the former colonies prove that the thin, homogenizing layer of colonial society poorly concealed its ambiguities, subtle resistance, apparent subjugation, syncretism, and various hybridities (invariably imperfect assimilations), interpretative conflicts, mutual misunderstandings, mutual contaminations, appropriations of the opposite discourse, and unconscious transformation of their own discourse; in short, an always problematic zone of contact (in the sense of Pratt 1992), in which the identities of the colonized and those of the colonizers were forged, were modified, and became more complex. All this was due to the bicultural or multicultural dialogue, always asymmetrical and often dysphoric, which the different groups were obliged to maintain with each other, whether they liked it or not.

The broad discursive field linked to religions (rather than just one religion) undoubtedly constituted the best sphere for appreciating the constant negotiation between the various identities that took place during the vice-royalty, since it was in the religious sphere that assimilation was most aggressive and most subtle. It was precisely the priests who were the most enthusiastic about learning native languages, to the point where, "since the Council of Lima in 1584, the learning and use of Quechua were inevitable requirements of the administrative apparatus" (Baquerizo 61). This Third Council produced the first printed book in the entire Peruvian Vice-royalty: *Doctrina Christiana* or *Catecismo para instrucción de los Indios y las demás personas, que han de ser enseñadas en nuestra santa Fe* [1584, Christian Doctrine or Catechism for the Instruction of the Indians and Other Persons Who Are to Be Instructed in Our Holy Faith], published in Spanish, Quechua, and Aymara. A third of the document, subsequently published as *Tercer Catecismo y Exposición de la Doctrina Cristiana por Sermones* [Third Catechism and Exposition of Christian Doctrine for Sermons] was tantamount to an admission, on the part of the Church, of the futility of the tactic, thitherto employed, of regarding the Indians as sheets of blank paper on which they could simply write the Spanish language and Catholic faith. The *Tercer Catecismo* was primarily intended for

> "los curas y doctrineros de indios," los cuales como lo había demostrado repetidas veces la experiencia, no siempre se encontraban preparados para ejercer con eficacia el difícil ministerio de la predicación entre los indígenas. El desconocimiento de las lenguas indias, junto a la negligencia de algunos en el cumplimiento de este oficio y la falta de adaptación a las características psicológicas de la nueva feligresía, obstaculizaban continuamente la marcha de la evangelización. (Durán 344)

> priests and catechists among the Indians, who, as experience had proved on countless occasions, were not always prepared to exercise effectively the difficult ministry of preaching among the Indians. Ignorance of the Indian languages, together with the negligence on the part of some as regards the fulfillment of their duties and the lack of adaptation to the psychological characteristics of the parishioners, continuously hindered the progress of evangelization.

Little did it matter that the *Tercer Catecismo* blamed the "limited intelligence of the Indians" for preventing priests from preaching to them about "exquisite things, or in a lofty style, as though one were preaching in a court or a university" (Durán 345). What is interesting to note is that, despite all its prejudices, the Church was forced to admit that, in order to establish the necessary contact, it would have to adapt to what Durán called the psychological features of its involuntary parishioners. Thus, in addition to advocating the use of the native language, it was recommended that parish priests inform themselves of the idolatrous beliefs of the Indians, in order to be able to use "certain similes of the things they used" (Durán 345). As a result of this, an impressive quantity

of information on autochthonous rituals has been preserved (see Mills, Vol. 3, Ch. 11). Even more significantly for our purposes, the collection of sermons recommends that the missionaries adapt their oratory art to criteria that they believed–rightly or wrongly–would be able to seduce their audience, since they would be instantly recognized:

> Importa en los sermones usar de cosas que provoquen y despierten el afecto, como apóstrofes, exclamaciones y otras figuras que enseña el arte oratoria. . . . Y aunque esto es general a todos, muy especialmente se experimenta que los indios, como gente de suyo blanda, en sintiendo en el que les habla algún género de afecto, oyen y gustan y se mueven extrañamente. Porque ellos entre sí mismos en su lenguaje tienen tanto afecto en el decir, que parece a quien no les conoce pura afectación y melindre. (qtd in Durán 346)

> It is important in the sermons to use things that provoke and inspire affection, such as apostrophes, exclamations, and other figures taught by oratory art. . . . And although this is true for everyone, it is particularly true of the Indians, who, being a naturally sensitive people, if they feel that someone is talking to them about affection, they pay attention and experience pleasure and move strangely. Because, among themselves, in their language, they use words that are so full of affection that a person who is unaccustomed to them thinks that they are nothing more that affectation and affectedness.

In addition to their sermons, the priests utilized another powerful form of propaganda machinery, which also sought to appropriate orality in the way it was used by the Indians: Catechistic theater, which, for the same reasons of adaptation, "in some cases . . . not only made use of the language but also of certain ritual forms of the Indians" (Lienhard 1992, 53). According to the hypothesis of Teodoro L. Meneses, who, like Jesús Lara, based his view on the references by the chroniclers to the existence of a pre-Colonial theater, in order to undertake the elaboration of this "ethno-fiction" or "fabrication of a fictitious, clearly instrumental Indian discourse" (Lienhard 1992, 55), the priests would have proceeded to re-elaborate certain Inca *wankas*:

> Official Inca theater was utilized by the catechists, who simply changed the themes. Vernacular motifs were replaced by religious-Christian cultural concerns of the Evangelizers. Short allegorical plays on pious biblical themes were performed in the churches during the religious festivities like popular theater. Thus, the theater of evangelization was encouraged during the first stage of the Colonial period, where, in some cases, the themes of ancient Inca *wankas* were occasionally used in *autos sacramentales* (religious plays). (Meneses 7–8)

Most Colonial Quechua literature–in other words, written and erudite literature–consisted mainly of allegorical *autos sacramentales* and other kinds of plays. These texts were often composed by priests, missionaries, and catechists (cf. Baquerizo 62 ff.). *El rapto de Proserpina y Sueño de Endimión* [The Abduction of Proserpina and the Dream of Endymion], *El Hijo Pródigo* [The Prodigal Son], *Usca Páucar,* and *El pobre más Rico* [The Richest Poor Man] are some of the best-known works of this literature. Quechua and even the Indian oral tradition were undoubtedly utilized by the priests in charge of Indian parishes in their "policy of subjugation and exploitation" (Baquerizo 61), rather than "out of the desire to preserve native values" (62). However, it had an unintentional side effect, so to speak: The willy-nilly contribution to the preservation-transformation (albeit under conditions of absolute debasement) of at least some of these values was the only way of establishing the necessary dialogue that would enable the men of the cloth to attempt to incorporate the Indians into the Christian value system. The "blank paper" proved to be a palimpsest.

It is difficult to gauge the exact scope of these practices. What we can say is that they made an enormous contribution to Andean syncretism, understood not merely as a problem-free "fusion" but rather as a subtle mechanism, whether conscious or otherwise, of resistance, enabling the Indians to preserve an identity that was constantly being transformed, through the interpretation of thitherto unknown signs through the grid of their own cultural imagination. In this respect, Martin Lienhard refers to the semantic re-orientations that both missionaries and Indians had to apply to these alien cultural features (1992, 108–10). Flores Galindo, who, in order to explain this phenomenon, borrowed the term *disjunction* from iconographic theory, provides numerous examples of this "encounter between the features of pre-Hispanic divinities and the representations of Christianity":

> The figure of the crucified Christ, for example, sometimes acquired the dark features of an underground divinity such as Pachacamac, who had the power to make the earth shake: the Christ of Miracles in Lima, the Christ of Luren in Ica, and the Lord of the Earthquakes in Cuzco. This path led to the images of Christ-the-pauper and Christ-the-Indian, such as those which can still be seen to this day on the walls of the Church of St. Christopher of Rapaz, probably painted by a mestizo between 1722 and 1761: Christ is shown being whipped and tortured by Indians dressed as Spaniards. (43–44)

That syncretism—which is a constant process, rather than a result—should constitute a "source of profound conceptual ambiguities which may eventually be maintained more or less consciously as a mechanism of resistance in front of the oppressor" (Ansion 50) and should not lead one to the false conclusion that what is established between colonizers and the colonized is a dialogue of the deaf in which neither subject is affected. There is obviously some truth in this, but it is more useful to regard syncretism (and, in general, any phenomenon linked to the "contact zone") as an ambiguous area in which the various social actors contradict each other, appropriate the material and symbolic tools of the others, misinterpret their semic components by applying their own discursive models to them and, precisely because they fail to understand the signs and symbols of the adversary, contribute to their modification. This constant process of widespread mutual misunderstanding (to use Maingueneau's concept) gradually transforms the perception that each side has of the other and, inevitably, of itself. One of the many examples of this is the widely documented belief of Catholic priests in something that was completely alien to their dogma, such as the *Huacas*:

> The Huacas, a synonym of what was sacred in the Andes, were converted into devils by the extirpators' imagination. . . . The Spaniards also believed that the idols talked. They accepted this version. Yet, in those cases, they regarded them as incarnations of the devil, the evil spirit dominating the souls of the Indians. In this veritable crusade to extirpate idolatry, Catholic priests were overwhelmed by an imagination peopled with devils and the desire to exorcise. (Flores Galindo 104, 98–99)

This is mentioned as a means of countering the widespread tendency to regard acculturation in a single direction, as though the American Western culture had been a mere transplant, implant, or appendix of European culture that would have remained intact for centuries. What actually happens when one society imposes its political, military, economic,

and therefore cultural domination on another is that "in this meeting the victor himself is transformed because in order to impose his will he must take into account the society he has in front of him and adapt to it" (Ansion 48). This is precisely why Mary Louise Pratt defines *transculturation*–once this notion, like dialogue, has been stripped of any idealization–as a characteristic phenomenon of contact zones (6–7).

This perspective provides a better understanding of the disagreements among the various historians and social researchers who have studied the colonial period. According to some, this was a period of "rapid acculturation, easy collaborationism between Spanish and Indian attitudes which tended to dissolve autochthonous political and social systems" (Burga 1990, 585). Others believe that, "[i]n the long term, Indian resistance and adaptation strategies within Colonial society have enabled units of local organization and Indian culture to survive, despite their enormous internal transformations, throughout these centuries of European domination" (Larson 189). On the basis of the perspective adopted here, these positions appear to be complementary rather than diametrically opposed. The point is that the Indians or *mestizos* in contact with the Spanish emissaries and subsequently with the Europeanized *criollos* or *mestizos* found that collaboration was the most effective form of resistance; this is what Franklin Pease has accurately termed "consensual or consenting resistance" (105 ff.). Given the need to participate in the new society, the various colonized subjects, particularly the *caciques* or village headmen, who were the most exposed to contact, developed not one but a series of specific strategies to enable them to "enter and leave modernity," to use García Canclini's apt phrase, strategies that inevitably seem ambiguous when viewed from an overall perspective.

Understandably enough, then, most *caciques* were forced to perform two functions: Collaboration (which legitimized them in the eyes of the new authorities) and resistance (which performed the same function in the eyes of their own group). The counterpart of this ambiguous form of survival is provided by the ambivalence of the priests (and authorities in general) toward the various Indian cultural expressions, particularly during the first two centuries of the Colonial period. This ambiguity ranges from ineffective total repression (the extirpation of idolatries) to the more subtle, although not necessarily more effective tolerance (since imposition might backfire) with respect to differences, which was particularly evident in the authorization and even promotion of various popular festivities:

> The formula discovered by the colonial regime was based less on a single message (other than to eliminate and marginalize the expressions regarded as diabolical in religious terms) than on the possibility of what one might call the "range of voices" characteristic of baroque esthetics. Colonial life, until the early decades of the Bourbon dynasty, was ruled by the acceptance and maintenance of cultural differences, which had been previously adapted to colonial circumstances, as a means of exercising power through a pact. (Estenssoro 182–83)

Thus, at the same time as, yet very far from, the erudite literature written in Quechua mentioned earlier, there was a continuation of the "artistic forms, such as the theater or folkloric choreographic representations, and the transmission of a Quechua tradition" (Glave 476). And, in addition to the continuation of their own traditions, they re-elaborated foreign elements according to their own cultural patterns. This was true, for example, of the *autos sacramentales* that literally flooded the Andean streets and plazas during the festivities of Corpus Christi and that, over time, "were assimilated by the Qosqoruna folklore [and that of other zones], creating a Spanish-Quechua hybrid of this form of theater. To this day, the feast of Corpus Christi is performed with *chinkachikuy, pantanakuy, santusuway*, puppet shows, dances and *autos sacramentales*" (Avendaño1 145).

Popular festivities witnessed the re-emergence of the phenomenon of disjunction or semantic re-orientation so that–for example–what the authorities thought was a pious fiesta in praise of the Virgin of the Assumption became the "diabolic" adoration of Pariacaca and Champiñamoco. With memories of *Taki Ongoy* probably still fresh, it is hardly surprising that a festival of this sort, held in 1608 in the village of San Damián (Huarochirí) should have triggered a campaign for the extirpation of idolatries, which would last until 1670 and, at far more irregular intervals, until the eighteenth century (Mills 52–53). As mentioned earlier, the campaigns aimed at eradicating the Indian religions paradoxically ensured, however problematic the sources may be, the conservation of valuable ethnographic information about this culture that was intended to be eliminated. Researchers have also discovered what Martin Lienhard has called the "verbal recording of contemporary reality by interposed compilers" who appear, for example, in "the Quechua manuscript traditionally attributed to Francisco de Ávila (ca. 1573–1647) or in various anti-idolatrous reports, written mainly during the second half of the seventeenth century" (1992, 73). This Quechua manuscript, which incidentally contains a "collection of mythology very different from Inca mythology, since it belonged to the Chinchaysuyo who were always extremely disinclined to total imperial subjugation" (Zevallos 94), is the most elaborate simulacrum preserved from this period:

> The untitled Quechua manuscript, beginning with the words: *Runa yndio niscap Machoncuna naripa/pacha quill casta yachan mancarca chayca* . . . was discovered in the late sixteenth century in the province of Huarochirí, belonging to the archdiocese of Lima, Perú, by the Cuzcan priest Francisco de Ávila, and preserved among his papers in vol. no. 3169 of the Biblioteca Nacional de Madrid, together with two additional or supplementary texts on the same issues and an incomplete, free translation by Francisco de Ávila of the first six chapters of the manuscript. (Rama 5)

José María Arguedas (1911–1969), who translated the complete manuscript into Spanish in 1966, notes that "the narrative may have been dictated by more than one informant, according to which village is being described, or was written by someone with firsthand knowledge, not as observer but as a participant of the matter being recorded" (*Prologue* 1975, 10); subsequently, an excellent English translation was published by Salomón and Urioste). This text is a bi-cultural product typical of the colonial period whose hybridity is expressed, at the content level, by an explanation of the Andean worldview, which had already incorporated various Christian elements; and, at the formal level, in the blend of marks of oral and written registers, largely attributable to the interaction between an Indian informant of popular extraction and a cultured mediator. The following quotation, taken from Arguedas's prologue to his Spanish translation, is of particular interest because it reflects the survival of an Andean orality that lettered culture–including, one has to admit, the present contribution to a history of oral literature–barely glimpses, although it obviously can and must be considered:

> En algunos pasajes se nota que el lenguaje es escrito, como en el caso del Prefacio y la mayor parte de los nombres de los capítulos, pero el torrente del lenguaje del manuscrito es oral. Este torrente cautiva. . . . La materia de la lengua oral transmite un mundo de hombres, dioses, animales, abismos, caminos y acontecimientos como únicamente lo sentimos en los cuentos quechuas oídos en nuestra infancia a los famosos narradores indígenas. (1975, 10–11)

In some passages, it is obvious that the language is a written language, as in the case of the Preface and most of the names of the chapters, but the flow of the language in the manuscript itself is oral. This flow captivates. . . . The subject matter of oral language transmits a world of men, gods, animals, abysses, paths, and events in a way that is only felt in the Quechua stories heard in our childhood from famous Indian narrators.

The Colonial Period from 1650 to the Republican Period

Popular festivities offer a privileged position from which it is possible to observe the problematic dialogue (or pact, to use Estenssoro' s term), or consensual resistance (Pease) between colonizers and colonized. These celebrations were officially Catholic and "aesthetically regarded as identical to the Spanish ones" (Estenssoro 182); they were allowed outwardly to express the Andean cultural heritage, particularly the iconic and the musical, in which orality obviously played an important role. As noted earlier, they were permitted, provided the authorities were unable to prove that they had deviated from the function of merely representing the cultural diversity assigned to them. The problem was that "the fiesta itself became a space that had been won and conquered by Indians, and in the cities by blacks too, who were able to impose their culture merely by being listened to" (Estenssoro 183). Listened to: Therein lies the starting point of an oral literature that, having lost the legitimizing function of the system of power that it had enjoyed during the pre-Colonial period, now became necessarily rebellious, if not actually clandestine, on the basis of the principle that "if the dominant class monopolized the techniques of writing, everything that concerns orality turns into an object of repression, and oral poets, wrongly or not, become the spokesmen of the oppressed" (Zumthor 218). It is hardly surprising, then, that Manuel Burga should have attributed the origin of what he and Alberto Flores Galindo call the "Andean Utopia" to this festive atmosphere:

> During the second half of the seventeenth century, the Indian elites performed the roles of Inca and Rumiñahui, and the acculturated Indians or freed slaves dressed up as Spaniards. This performance gradually became a ritual mechanism that praised what was Inca and mocked what was Spanish. . . . This is how this ritual became the vehicle that would lead to the birth of the Andean utopia through the memorization of what was Inca, its subsequent idealization, and the attempt to construct a unified Indian identity. (Burga 52–53)

The Andean utopia, articulated first in the mid-seventeenth century, "responds to the need to reinforce symbolic forms of legitimization in order to offset the wearing out of the socioeconomic function" (Saignes 646). It does not, therefore, constitute an attempt to preserve the order that existed prior to the arrival of the Spaniards, but instead represents a typically Colonial invention within this tradition:

> In the Andes, the paradigm and the alternative to colonial order were identified with the land of the Inca: the empire was recreated in the popular imagination. A relatively short period of Andean history, during which state coercion had been imposed

on the peoples and regions, was converted into a long period during which there was no hunger, wealth was fairly distributed, and there were no continuous waves of epidemics–the opposite to the image of the colonial world. These conceptions did not arise automatically as a reflex response to the Conquest. They were the result of a process in which elements of Andean and Western thought sometimes converged and at other times clashed: myth and history, writing and oral traditions, priests and peasants, intellectuals and popular classes. (Flores Galindo 87)

The Andean utopia is obviously a key motif in the Andean cultural imagination and therefore in the pre-figurative dimension of its oral literature, as borne out by the abundance of popular dramas that updated the death of the Inca Atahuallpa (cf. Lienhard 1988, 46; 1992, 75, and Lara 1989, 15), performed in the plazas of various villages during the patron saint's day festivities (and which continue to be performed, as will be seen below). The drama *Ollantay,* whose first known written version dates from the second half of the eighteenth century, is the only simulacrum from this oral literature that has been preserved from this period.

The vitality of these expressions of popular literature, together with the cohesion they contributed to the formation of a common Andean identity, could not have been more obvious from the mid-eighteenth century onwards, when the enlightened Colonial authorities, for the benefit of the *criollo* elites, attempted to put a stop to any externalization of popular culture. This coincided with the outbreak of various Indian rebellions led by *caciques* who had experienced a considerable reduction of their share of power in recent years. The rebellion led by Túpac Amaru II was the last straw for colonial power:

> The Túpac Amaru rebellion marked a break in the authorities' tolerance of Indian cultural manifestations. The sentence passed by the [Inspector General] Areche banned two important aspects: theatrical representations of the Inca theme (including music and melancholy song) and the use of traditional instruments such as the *pututus.* However, the most tangible result of the defeat of the Túpac Amaru movement lay in the public image of the Indian elite as a group, and in the lack of external attributes that defined and identified them as such. (Estenssoro 188)

The independence movement, led by the *criollos* a few years later, was based on these Andean movements, as well as those of *mestizos* and blacks. The struggle for emancipation produced two poets, both of whom died in combat, whose cultured poetry was inspired by Andean oral literature: The Quechua Juan Wallparrimachi Mayta (1793–1814), who wrote *Karuncharay* (c. 1810) in his native language, "a notoriously colonial and written poem" (yet whose "versification . . . was less contaminated by the Spanish tradition" [Lienhard 1992, 163], meaning that it can be regarded, like the *Ollantay,* as a written re-elaboration of oral Quechua songs of the nobility), and Mariano Melgar (1790–1815), who produced a Spanish version of the oral poetry of the time, the *yaraví,* which in turn was a *mestizo* Arequipu re-elaboration of the pre-Colonial *Harawi:*

> It was Mariano Melgar who recovered a pre-Hispanic form of oral communication, turning it into his intimate songs known as *yaravíes.* By recovering a form of expression of Indian origin and popular impact and form, Melgar became a forerunner, fortunately recorded by literary criticism, of the local and popular voices that kept an alternative culture alive in the Republic. (Glave 474)

Although the popular sectors of the new nations continued to update and re-elaborate oral literature in the form of songs, legendary-mythical stories, and dramatic and choreographic representations, this failed to elicit any interest on the part of the *criollos.* At the same time, Quechua began to lose ground progressively, since the "ruling classes in Peru no longer needed the Quechua language for their social relations with the Andean people, as the Spanish colonialists had done" (Baquerizo 61). It is true that on 10 January 1825 Simón Bolívar declared to the Peruvian Congress that the Liberation Army had given back to the sons of Manco Capac the freedom of which Pizarro had deprived them (see Chang-Rodríguez 369.) By resorting to the glorious pre-Colombian past (while conveniently ignoring the current situation of Indians, blacks, and *mestizos*), the *criollos* legitimized their own emerging discourse, through which they could construct national identities anchored in a foundational time and space that would enable them to destroy their links with the former metropolis. The *criollos* restricted themselves to occupying the space left vacant by the Spaniards, without managing to modify the latter's archaic social system, which explains why "the rebellion of the Indians," which "lasted throughout the colonial period . . . was not quelled by the establishment of the Republic" (Arguedas 1989 *Canto,* 1). The new situation of internal colonialism established with the creation of the new Spanish-American states enabled the new elites to draw up modern national projects, based on those of France and England or the recently formed United States, in which any element regarded as non-European was immediately marginalized.

The Twentieth Century

By the end of the nineteenth century, certain *criollo* voices, particularly the newly emerging *mestizo* class, had begun to be interested in the Indian problem, although from a position in which the same civilization/barbarity binary used by the most conservative *criollo* elites–blind to any forms of popular cultural expression, particularly Indian–continued to exist. Thus, for example, "in his speech commemorating national day (1888), don Manuel [González Prada] declared that Peru was mainly populated by semi-civilized Indians who, if taught how to read and write, would very soon recover their human dignity" (Chang-Rodríguez 370). A similar thing happened with Clorinda Matto de Turner (1852–1909), especially as regards her *Indianista* novel *Aves sin nido* [1889; *Torn from the Nest,* 1998], whose aim, she declares in the preface, was to remember "that in the country there were brothers who suffered, exploited in the dark night of ignorance and martyred in the darkness that cried out for light" (10). The fact that this brave denunciation of the Indians' situation–which nevertheless continued to assume their barbarity–led to her excommunication and exile, is indicative of the darkness in which the ruling classes lived as regards alternative popular culture.

The twentieth century saw a progressive reappraisal of the Indian and the *mestizo,* culminating in the *indigenismo* of the 1920s and 1930s (see Zapata 152–62). Thus, in 1938, the Universidad Nacional Mayor de San Marcos re-established the chair of Quechua and began to publish colonial plays. In 1905, the intellectual, philologist, folklorist and journalist Adolfo Vienrich published *Azucenas quechuas* [1905; Quechuan Lilies] in Tarma, his adopted city, followed, a year later, by *Apólogos quechuas* [1906; Quechuan Eulogies], works that recorded in writing the living oral literature of the central zone (Jaujam Concepción, Huancayo, and Puno) in their original version, together with a Spanish translation. In the preface to *Azucenas,* Vienrich establishes an important connection between precolonial literature and contemporary popular oral literature:

> The ignorance in which we live regarding Inca literature is profoundly disconcerting, since the few works and fragments that have been preserved do not suffice to recapture the glorious past of this noble Quechua race . . . Although several deny the existence of these expressions . . . , this literature exists, as borne out by the declarations of primitive historians that comedies and tragedies were performed; and even today, in the Indians' gatherings and fiestas, one hears their songs, their dialogues, their stories, their fables and their religious traditions. (Vienrich 14)

Other researchers—foremost among whom were José María Arguedas (1938, 1949, 1965, 1969), José María Arguedas and Francisco Izquierdo Ríos (1947), Jesús Lara (1947), José María Benigno Farfán (1952), Sergio Quijada Jara (1957), Gabriel y Gloria Escobar (1981), and Jesús Armando Cavero Carrasco (1985)—continued the line begun by Vienrich in subsequent decades. Through them, one is able to glimpse the fundamental role played by oral literature in the continuous revitalization of the collective Andean memory. Thus, for example, in his numerous articles on popular songs, the novelist and anthropologist José María Arguedas insists that these are not "archaic songs, handed down from generation to generation; virtually all of them are the creations of the Indian and *mestizo* people of today, composed in their current language, Quechua, and with many Spanish words . . . ; they are, therefore, the expression of the lives of contemporary Indian and *mestizo* peoples" (Arguedas 1989a, 22). These songs always exist in a creative tension between the preservation of repressed or marginalized cultural expressions and their updating through the appropriation of hitherto alien elements:

> Los españoles trajeron al mundo indio la bandurria y la guitarra. El indio dominó rápidamente la bandurria; y en su afán de adaptar este instrumento y la guitarra a la interpretación de la música propia–wayno, k'aswa, araskaska, jarawi . . . –creó el charango y el kirkincho, a imagen y semejanza de la bandurria y de la guitarra. El arpa y el violín fueron conquistados por el indio tal como lo recibieron de los invasores. Ahora el arpa, el violín, la bandurria, el kirkincho y el charango, son, como la quena, el pinkullo, la antara y la tinya, instrumentos indios. Alma y alegría de las fiestas. O cuando entra la pena a las casas y a los pueblos, el charango y el kirkincho lloran por el indio, con tanta fuerza y con la misma desesperación que la quena y el pinkullo.
> (Arguedas 1989 *Indios*, 41)

> The Spaniards introduced the bandore and the guitar into the Indian world. The Indians soon mastered the bandore, and in their desire to adapt this instrument and the guitar to the interpretation of their own music–*wayno, k'aswa, araskaska, jarawi* . . .– they created the *charango* and the *kirkincho,* in the image and likeness of the bandore and the guitar. The harp and the violin were mastered by the Indians just as they received them from the invaders. Now the harp, the violin, the bandore, and the *charango* are Indian instruments, like the *quena,* the *pinkullo,* the *antara,* and the *tinya.* They are the soul of *fiestas.* Or when sorrow strikes families and villages, the *charango* and the *kirchinko* weep for the Indian, with the same force and despair as the *quena* and the *pinkullo.*

Arguedas has also mentioned an oral theater performance, which he was fortunate enough to attend, in the 1930s. This reference is doubly interesting in that it links popular twentieth century literature to the *aránway* (a pre-Incan popular form of theater described by Jesús Lara on the basis of references drawn from the chronicles). The author and director of the company that performs it is a highlander "of pure Spanish

stock," effectively debunking the ethnic determinism that provided the basis for the theory of dualism dominant in the Peruvian discursive universe for so many years:

> Gabriel Aragón . . . belongs to the Aragones of San Pablo de Cacha, an ancient family, of pure Spanish stock, the only family with the right to represent the White King at the Twelfth Night celebration held in San Pablo on January 6th.
> . . . Gabriel Aragón is blind and cannot write *waynos,* far less his plays. And this is why he travels from village to village with a group named after him, consisting entirely of Indians. Every musician in the group is also an actor. Yet since there is no script or anything written, Aragón has explained the plot and the motif of the plays to the Indians in his group and he too is an actor.
>
> All of Aragón's works are in Quechua and describe the lives of the Indian people. That is why the Indians in his group have no need of scripts; on stage, they portray their own lives in the world, creating and improving on the work each time they perform it. I have seen these plays by Gabriel Aragón. In the district of Combapata, with a thousand inhabitants, in a large hall with no furniture, where all the spectators had to stand. Nearly all those who filled the hall were Indians, and followed the development of the play with an interest and an anxiety I had never seen. The lives of the Indian people were being depicted there, in that rustic scenery, just as they were, without the least distortion, or any exaggeration or artifice, and portrayed by illiterate Indian actors who neither spoke Spanish nor understood it properly and who, through the fact of having to play their own lives, simply experienced it, what they were and why they suffered and enjoyed themselves wherever they were. (Arguedas 1989a, 53–54)

However, what undoubtedly stands out in all the fieldwork undertaken by anthropologists and other social researchers is their constant recourse to this Andean utopia, which, according to the widespread view of the specialist, has constituted a fundamental motif in the Andean imaginary since the eighteenth if not the mid-seventeenth century. The Andean utopia is expressed in a trend that involved performances (whether dramatic, musical, or choreographic) representing the death of Atahuallpa as well as in a narrative trend, the so-called "Inkarrí cycle."

In 1952, Jesús Lara came across a pamphlet announcing the performance of a play called *Relato del Inca* [Story of the Inca]. This modest pamphlet immediately aroused his curiosity, since all the data seemed to indicate its similarity to a recited piece performed annually in the village of Toco (Cochabamba) on the occasion of their patron saint's day festivities. Lara knew the *Danza de Toco* thanks to the novel *Valle* (1943) by Mario Unzueta, which includes a detailed description of the fiesta and even incorporates a Spanish translation of the libretto of the *Danza.*

Lara, assuming "that the work would at least contain the same themes as those discovered by Unzueta" (1989, 18), immediately went to see a performance of the *Relato del Inca.* Once the performance was over, he asked the cast of players for a copy of the text. The latter not only agreed but, to Lara's astonishment, encouraged him "to introduce any corrections or additions he saw fit into the text. At the same time, we kept telling them that documents of this sort deserved every respect and should not be touched in the least" (1989, 19). And it is that the performers of oral literature have always known that the greatest faithfulness to orality lies precisely in the adaptation of any of its elements (whether specifically oral, thematic, proxemic, or choreographic) to the ever-changing circumstances of each new enunciation. The actors told him that, like the *Danza*, this work had been performed since time immemorial in a village, San Pedro de Buena Vista (Charcas de Potosí) in this case, to celebrate the New Year.

This type of play was first performed at the beginning of the Colonial period, and was always linked to the catechizing work of the Church:

Parades and plays on Incan themes invariably accompanied the Potosí festivities [in] celebrations such as the rebuilding of the Church of the Society of Jesus in 1590, the 1608 Corpus financed by the "Criollos of Potosí," the novena period of the Immaculate Conception in 1622, the Canonization of St. Ignatius of Loyola in 1624, or a private wedding in 1642.

. . . The "dances of the Conquest" enabled the Indians to rationalize their defeat (one should recall the premonitory dreams of the Inca), while confirming their condition as "conquered peoples." Moreover, the role of the religious orders, particularly that of the Jesuits, is a vital element in understanding this "theater of evangelization." (Saignes 639–41)

This was undoubtedly the function that the civil and religious authorities wished the celebrations to have. Whether the rest of the population actually viewed them in this way is another matter. It is reasonable to assume that many spectators applied this principle to the disjunction or semantic reorientation that we referred to earlier, to the point that they actually re-functionalized these festivities, turning them into the nucleus of a broad, Andean utopia.

From the mid-eighteenth century onwards, the contempt of the enlightened Spanish and *criollo* elites towards everything that came from the "common people" meant that, in the urban environment, this type of representation, like so many other festive popular expressions, was either prohibited or grossly instrumentalized for the greater glory of the Metropolis. This happened, for example, during the fiesta held in honor of Charles IV in Lima in 1789, where, "instead of the dances and representations of the Inca dynasty . . . a mask with the figure of twelve Indians eliminated any possible symbolic ambiguities about the Indian presence. In it, there was a young man who was left in charge of the twelve Indians as lackeys . . . , a symbol of the Spanish monarchy" (Estenssoro 189). But it is obvious that the Incas' plays, particularly those concerning the execution of Atahuallpa, continued in various Andean villages, as their performance to this day attests.

Jesús Lara and Mario Unzueta opened up research into the numerous contemporary folkloric expressions that dramatize the death of the Inca in various ways. Thus, for example, Mily Ahón Olguín de Iriarte and Francisco E. Iriarte Brener undertook an exhaustive formal study on "The Drama of Atahualpa in the Province of Cajatambo" in which they compiled various versions of this popular celebration in thirteen localities in this area (75). At the same time, Rogger Ravines refers to *Los Ingas, drama en verso* performed in the district of Chilia in the province of Pataz, in the district of La Libertad, during the feast of Our Lady of the Rosary (40); and *Los Incaicos* from the same department, "a dramatic poem [which] is a substantially altered, modified and adapted version of another which we do not know" (57); and the Quechua-Spanish drama, *Prendimiento y degollación del Inca,* performed in Llamellín, the capital of the province of Antonio Raimondi, the district of Ancash, during the feast of the Immaculate Conception, the patron saint of the village, on December 8th each year" (18). In the next passage, Ravines refers to the popular extraction of the actors, as well as the handing down of the notebooks:

The leading actors, generally peasants or *mestizos* from the popular classes, rehearse their roles for several months, under the supervision of the steward of the fiesta and the "rehearser.". . . The version that has been transcribed has been taken from one of the notebooks of don Lucio Tarazona, "a well-known rehearser" from Llamellín, dated 1895, which, at the same time, is a copy of another 1860 "notebook." Don Lucio Tarazona, a native of Huari, was born in 1900. A pyrotechnist and a blacksmith by trade, he sometimes worked as a manual laborer. He has devoted his life to rehearsing drama, since he himself "was an actor during his youth." His notebook was given to another rehearser in 1933. (18)

Certain researchers decided not to work from the notebooks (which, provided extremely fragmentary information on the "text" itself and very little or none on the rest of the semiotic systems accompanying the linguistic system, if, indeed, they even existed) but instead, from their own interpretations as direct receptors of the performance. This was the case of Henrique Urbano, who described and commented on the *Inca wit'uy* or the death of the Inca, which he probably saw in the late 1970s or early 1980s (he fails to specify which) "in a small village near Yuca, a few kilometers outside the city of Cusco, during the annual feast of the patron saint in October (1981, 97). In the mid-1980s, two Peruvian researchers, Manuel Burga and Alberto Flores Galindo also decided to undertake ethnohistorical field work on these expressions of popular oral literature in central Peru, as part of their joint project *La utopía andina* [The Andean utopia] financed by UNESCO. According to these analysts, in the central region of Perú, "we have never encountered this popular drama as a theatrical or even virtually theatrical performance, but primarily as dances performed by members of the chorus who, with the intervention of the entire village, perform the tragedy of Atahuallpa as part of the patron saint's day festivities" (Burga 1988, 27). In August 1984, they attended one of these fiestas, the fiesta of Chiquián, the capital of the province of Bolognesei, in the district of Ancash, which lasted a whole week. Their acute observations need no commentary:

The expenses of the organizers of the festivities totaled millions. The principal families feel proud and enthusiastically welcome visitors. According to their version, the fiesta is extremely democratic; no-one is excluded and everyone can dance and eat as they would at home. The message apparently transmitted by the festivities is one of a *mestizo* country, in which their opposing traditions have been reconciled and the Western and Andean aspects of the country have blended. Conflict is excluded; it simply does not exist. At the end, the Inca and the Captain (the name given to Pizarro) embrace and dance in the latter's house. The next day, they watch a bullfight together, in the Spanish style, in other words, in a square, with a bullfighter brought in from Lima and volunteers from the public. (Flores Galindo 69–71)

In these fiestas, the most important roles or positions are those of the Inca and the Captain. This must have been the original hierarchy, although today the positions have been reversed:

the most important and costly role is that of the Captain. He is the favorite of the *mishtis* in the central sierra. The post of Inca requires fewer expenses and is generally performed by poor peasants or simply the least powerful members of each rural locality. This current ritual contrasts with the complex ritual that accompanies the Inca: a striking, sumptuous costume, with the accompaniment of the *pallas* and a string ensemble playing apparently very Indian music. (Burga 1988, 29)

The day of the capture, a ritual fight is held between the attendants of the Inca and the Captain: Some on foot and others on horseback. They start at the outskirts of the village, march through the main street to the center and thence to the plaza, where a bullfight is held the next day. Throughout the route (approximately fifteen blocks long), the rival groups throw sweets at each other. The sweets are in fact sugar-coated pebbles which can hurt the opponents. Up to this point, the representation has tried to respect the chroniclers' version of the capture of Atahuallpa; the night before, the Captain and his attendants, like Pizarro and his troops, do not sleep. They ride in and begin their final pursuit of the Inca in the afternoon at about 4 P.M., eventually capturing him in a plaza surrounded by rockets, which explode, at the same time as clarinets and trumpets are heard, in the midst of a smell of gunpowder, smoke, and general confusion. However, the fight is an occasion for tensions to be relieved and for faithfulness to history to be ignored. The Captain's fight against the Inca turns into a fight with everyone apparently against everyone else; in fact, however, it is a fight between some the residents of Lima with whom the people identify most closely, rich against poor, with the *mestizos* and whites on one side and Indians on the other. Sugar-coated pebbles are soon abandoned in favor of direct blows. National integration is not well served when one of the Captain's attendants, who presides over the court carrying the Peruvian flag, uses it as a lance to attack those who are trying to unhorse him and hit him. Tempers flare. A horse attacks the crown. Whips crack. They eventually reach the Plaza which they are supposed to circle twice, although newcomers to Lima who are unfamiliar with the ritual push the Captain so that he takes hold of the Inca and captures him, giving him a thorough beating in the process. By the end of the day, the Inca is extremely annoyed, meaning that he will not attend the general festivities. However, the next day, he forgets his animosity and attends the bullfight:

> Ending up with the bullfight–where the next Captain will be designated–is a way of affirming that Peruvian culture is predominantly Spanish. Miscegenation does not mean balance but the imposition of some over others. The discourse on the past serves to confirm the predominance of Chiquián over the neighboring villages, although this precarious situation can be deduced from a representation in which everyday events prevail over historical fidelity. The biography of the Andean utopia is not divorced from the class struggle. (Flores Galindo 69–75)

This last phrase, "the biography of the Andean utopia is not divorced from the class struggle," is echoed in Burga's remark that "ritual ... not only transmits a memory, a worldview and an identity; it also reproduces the social order and legitimizes hierarchies" (1988, 24). Oral literature (like written, in fact), rather than presenting an idealization or a single static or dualistic vision of society, presents one that is so close to the constant re-ordering of it and "is restricted" to reproducing the conflicts of the representations and interpretations of society, that it allows "everyday events to prevail over historical fidelity" (75). Therein lies its strength and its weakness.

Closely linked to the various collective representations of the death of Atahuallpa, the Inkarrí (both myth of creation and Messianic utopia) has been widely documented in field work, particularly since 1955, when the ethnological expedition led by Oscar Nuñez del Prado discovered this figure in the hacienda community at Q'ero. The "Inca King" (a hybrid divinity with features drawn from both Jesus Christ and the Inca Atahuallpa and Tupac Amaru) was quartered by "Españarri," "Pizarro," "the Spanish Inca," or "the president," according to the known versions, and different parts of his body were buried in various places; his head is growing, and when the parts of his body are put back together again, it will produce the new *Pachacutiy*, the reversal of the world will take place and the Inca order will rule again. (For an overview of the various studies on the Inkarrí, see Urbano 1986, 4.)

As in all deferred reception, particularly when (as in the case of the Inkarrí) direct reception does not take place in its natural context but at the behest of the researcher, one might well ask how much of the proposed meaning is in fact that of the interpreting informer or of the lettered mediators themselves. Scholars have tried to give the "myth of Inkarrí" revolutionary connotations, particularly in the nationalistic context of the Left during the 1970s, when most studies on the Inkarrí were produced (see Flores Galindo 23). And they certainly exist, at least in some of its expressions. Yet it is much more than that, as shown by the sometimes contradictory versions recorded, depending on the region or social condition of the Indians and *mestizos* interviewed, in other words, depending on the particular context of the informant. A few years ago, Henrique Urbano said, particularly as regards the myth of Inkarrí, that "the majority of the studies published to date on the ancient myth fail to suggest any thesis that might guide us in the search for a global scheme of interpretation" (1986, 9). The point is that the Andean cultural imaginary is dynamic and contradictory, exactly like that of any other collectivity. This means that it would be fruitless to attempt to reduce it to a logical scheme of representation. Some people think that the Inkarrí constitutes irrefutable proof of the "persistence of completely original cultural molds based on the traditional system of collective values and representations" and, consequently, that "waiting for a future in which the Quechuas will experience a new period of florescence and, once free, will live in abundance, has remained unaltered over time" (Curatola 72). Restricting a people to its original unalterable molds, however worthy the jailer's intentions, hardly constitutes a favor. However, the extreme diversity of the material compiled on the Inkarrí and, according to some observers, "the scant enthusiasm for the possible emergence of the Inca" expressed by "the Andeans, in their discourse and their acts" (Ortiz Rescaniere 213–14) prevents one from reaching the same conclusions as Curatola.

The Inkarrí, or rather the multiple changing Inkarrí circulating in the Andean discursive universe through the most varied cultural formations and practices, composes a key figure in the Andean oral literary pre-figuration and, as such, contribute to the constant construction of the identity of this collectivity. In a recent study documenting the path from "the Utopian Inca to that of contemporary popular tradition," Alejandro Ortiz Rescaniere (208-19) mentions three very different examples of the use of this figure: That of the Inkarrí Quechua competing with the Aymara Collarí to establish cultural or even regional differences between the two groups; the traditional version of the Inkarrí vs. Españarrí recorded in Quechua from a *mestiza* lady in Ayacucho (here Collarí is depicted as the wife of Inkarrí); and the third, which a charlatan (of which there are so many in the Plaza San Martín de Lima) once recounted in Spanish, over a period of months, to the delight of passers-by.

Much could be said of a discourse that blends elements from so many and such different spheres of the popular imaginary. Let us simply point out, like Ortiz Rescaniere, that the playful parodying of key elements of Andean history and mythology serves as a "criticism of the situation of the

Andean migrants" (218) who compose the majority of the audience. And, incidentally, it is symptomatic of the "advance of Andean culture" from "the shanty towns, a veritable cultural melting pot," to "the central areas of the city of Lima, forcing the bourgeoisie to relocate both spatially and socially," which, however, did not enable them to "completely resist the massive influence of Indian culture" (Zapata 181–83), a culture that gradually infiltrated a city that, until a few years ago, was so proud of its *criollo* features. As noted by Ortiz Rescaniere, who attended several comic performances and noticed the transformations introduced on each occasion, the discourse reflects "living feelings, common to Ecuadorians, Bolivians, and Peruvians, and not only those who inhabit the marginalized districts of their cities." To this end, a repertoire of themes is used that, like the feelings they evoke, "are complex and reversible, according to the contexts, and re-edit or echo other discourses and feelings from the past" (217). It would be difficult to find a more apt description of oral literature.

Translation by Suzanne D. Stephens

Works Cited

Ahón Olguín de Iriarte, Mily and Francisco E. Iriarte Brenner. 1985. "El drama de Atahualpa en la provincia de Cajatambo." *VI Congreso Peruano del Hombre y la Cultura Andina*. Ed. Francisco E. Iriarte Brenner et al. Lima: Universidad Inca Garcilaso de la Vega. 73-134.

Alcina Franch, José. 1989. *Mitos y literatura quechua*. Madrid: Alianza.

Angenot, Marc. 1985. *Critique de la raison sémiotique: fragment avec pin up*. Montreal: Université de Montréal Press.

Ansion, Jean-Marie. 1984. *Démons des Andes: la pensée mythique dans une région des Andes péruviennes (Ayacucho)*. Louvain-la-Neuve: Université Catholique de Louvain.

Arguedas, José María. 1949. *Canciones y cuentos del pueblo quechua*. Lima: Huascarán.

——. 1965. *Poesía quechua*. Buenos Aires: Ed. Universidad de Buenos Aires.

——. 1969. *Cantos quechuas*. Santiago: Ed. Universitaria.

——. 1975. "Prólogo." *Dioses y hombres de Huarochirí*. Comp. by Francisco de Avila. Trans. José María Arguedas. Mexico City: Siglo XXI. 9–18.

——. 1989a. [1938]. *Canto kechwa con un ensayo sobre la capacidad de creación artística del pueblo indio y mestizo*. Lima: Horizonte.

——. 1989b. *Indios, mestizos y señores*. Lima: Horizonte.

——. and Francisco Izquierdo Ríos. 1947. *Mitos, leyendas y cuentos peruanos*. Lima: Ministerio de Educación Pública.

Aubrun, Charles V. 1968. *La comedia española (1600–1680)*. Madrid: Taurus.

Avendaño, Ángel. 1993. *Historia de la literatura del Qosqo: del tiempo mítico al siglo XX*. 3 vols. Qosqo: Municipalidad del Qosqo.

Avila, Francisco de, comp. 1975. *Dioses y hombres de Huarochirí*. Trans. José María Arguedas. Mexico City: Siglo XXI.

Baquerizo, Manuel J. 1981. "El quechua en el mundo andino de hoy." *Allpanchis*. 17-18: 61–76.

Beyersdorff, Margot. 1986. "La tradición oral quechua vista desde la perspectiva de la literatura." *Revista Andina*. 1: 213–36.

Burga, Manuel. 1988. *Nacimiento de una utopía: muerte y resurrección de los incas*. Lima: Instituto de Apoyo Agrario.

——. 1990. "La emergencia de lo andino como utopía (siglo XVII)." *Allpanchis*. 35–36: 579–98.

Calvet, Louis-Jean. 1984. *La tradition orale*. Paris: Presses Universitaires de France.

Cavero Carrasco, Jesús Armando. 1985. "El Qarawi y su función social." *Allpanchis*. 25: 233–70.

Cerrón Palomino, Rodolfo. 1980. *El quechua: una mirada de conjunto*. Lima: Centro de Investigación de Lingüística Aplicada.

Chang-Rodríguez, Eugenio. 1984. "El indigenismo peruano y Mariátegui." *Revista Iberoamericana*. 127: 367–93.

Cornejo Polar, Antonio. 1989. "Los sistemas literarios como categorías históricas: elementos para una discusión latinoamericana." *Revista de crítica literaria latinoamericana*. 29: 39–58.

Curatola, Marco. 1986. "Mito y milenarismo en los Andes: del *Taki Ongoy* a *Inkarrí*" *Allpanchis*. 10: 65–92.

Durán, Juan Guillermo. 1982. *El catecismo del III Concilio Provincial de Lima y sus complementos pastorales (1584-1585)*. Buenos Aires: El Derecho.

Escobar, Gabriel and Gloria Escobar. 1981. *Huaynos del Cusco*. Cusco: Garcilaso.

Estenssoro, Juan Carlos. 1992. "Modernismo, estética, música y fiesta: élites y cambio de actitud frente a la cultura popular. Perú 1750-1850." *Tradición y modernidad en los Andes*. Ed. H. Urbano. Cusco: Centro de Estudios Regionales Andinos Bartolomé de las Casas. 181–95.

Farfán, José María Benigno. 1952. *Colección de textos quechuas del Perú: sobretiro de la Revista del Museo Nacional*. Vol. 16–20. Lima: Instituto de Estudios Etnológicos.

Finnegan, Ruth. 1988. *Literacy and Orality: Studies in the Technology of Communication*. Oxford: Basil Blackwell.

Flores Galindo, Alberto. 1987. *Buscando un Inca: identidad y utopía en los Andes*. Lima: Instituto de Apoyo Agrario.

García Canclini, Néstor. 1990. *Culturas híbridas: estrategias para entrar y salir de la modernidad*. Mexico City: Grijalbo.

Glave, Luis Miguel. 1990. "Grito de pueblos silenciados. Intermediarios lingüísticos y culturales entre dos mundos: historia y mentalidades." *Allpanchis*. 35–36: 435–513.

Harrison, Regina. 1982. "Modes of Discourse: The *Relación de antigüedades deste reyno del Pirú* by Joan de Santacruz Pachacuti Yamqui Salcamaygua." *From Oral to Written Expression: Native Andean Chronicles of the Early Colonial Period*. Ed. R. Adorno. New York: Syracuse University Press. 65–99.

Lara, Jesús. 1947. *La poesía quechua*. Mexico City: Fondo de Cultura Económica.

——. 1989. *Estudio preliminar: tragedia del fin de Atawallpa. Atau Wallpaj p'uchukakuyninpa wankan*. Cochabamba: Ediciones del Sol.

Larson, Brooke. 1990. "Casta y clase: la formación de un campesinado mestizo y mercantil en la región de Cochabamba." *Allpanchis*. 35–36: 187–222.

Lienhard, Martin. 1988. "Pachacutiy Taki." *Literaturas más allá de la marginalidad*. Eds. Th. Bremer and J. Peñate Rivero. Giessen: AELSAL. 38–52.

——. 1992. *La voz y su huella: escritura y conflicto étnico-cultural en América Latina 1492–1988*. Lima: Horizonte.

Maingueneau, Dominique. 1984. *Genèses du discours*. Brussels: Pierre Mardaga.

Matto de Turner, Clorinda. 1889. *Aves sin nido*. Buenos Aires: Felix Lajouane.

Melgar, Mariano. 1971. *Poesías completas*. Lima: Academia de la Lengua.

Meneses, Teodoro L. 1983. *Teatro quechua colonial: antología*. Lima: Edubanco.

Mills, Kenneth. 1997. *Idolatry and Its Enemies: Colonial Andean Religion and Extirpation 1640-1750*. Princeton, N.J.: Princeton University Press.

Ortiz Recaniere, Alejandro. 1992. *El quechua y el aymara*. Madrid: Mapfre.

Pease, Franklin. 1981. "Continuidad y resistencia de lo andino." *Allpanchis*. 17–18: 105–18.

Pratt, Mary Louise. 1992. *Imperial Eyes: Travel Writing and Transculturation.* London: Routledge.

Quijada Jara, Sergio. 1957. *Canciones del ganado y pastores.* n.p.: Huancayo.

Rama, Ángel. 1975. "Introducción." *Dioses y hombres de Huarochirí.* Comp. by Francisco de Avila. Trans. José María Arguedas. Mexico City: Siglo XXI. 7–8.

Ravines, Rogger. 1985. "Dramas coloniales en el Perú actual." *VI Congreso Peruano del Hombre y la Cultura Andina.* Org. Francisco. E. Iriarte Brenner et al. Lima: Universidad Inca Garcilaso de la Vega. 13–71.

Ricoeur, Paul. 1991. "Appropriation." *A Ricoeur Reader: Reflection and Imagination.* Ed. Mario J. Valdés. London: Harvester Wheatsheaf. 86–98.

Rostworowski, María. 1990. "Las macroetnias en el ámbito andino." *Allpanchis.* 35–36: 3–28.

Saignes, Thierry. 1990. "Es posible una historia 'chola' del Perú?: acerca de *Nacimiento de una utopía* de Manuel Burga." *Allpanchis.* 35–36: 635–57.

Salomón, Frank and George L. Urioste. 1991. *The Huarochirí Manuscript: A Testament of Ancient and Colonial Andean Religion.* Austin: University of Texas Press.

Schoenfeld, Mark and Valerie Traub. 1996. "Forum." *PMLA.* 111: 280–82.

Torero, Alfredo. 1980. *El quechua y la historia social andina.* Havana: Editorial de Ciencias Sociales.

Unzueta, Mario. 1943. *Valle.* Cochabamba: La época.

Urbano, Henrique. 1981. "Del sexo, incesto y los ancestros de Inkarrí: mito, utopía e historia en las sociedades andinas." *Allpanchis.* 17–18: 77–103.

———. 1986. "Presentación: discurso mítico y discurso utópico en los Andes." *Allpanchis.* 10: 3–14.

Valdés, Mario J. 1995. *La interpretación abierta: introducción a la hermenéutica literaria contemporánea.* Amsterdam: Rodopi.

Vienrich, Adolfo. 1961. *Apólogos quechuas por unos parias.* Lima: Lux.

———. 1970. *Azucenas quechuas.* Huancayo: Casa de la Cultura de Junín.

Wallparrimachi, Mayta Juan. 1947. "Cuatro poemas de Walparrimachi." In *La poesía quechua.* Ed. Jesús Lara. Mexico City: Fondo de Cultura Económica. 182–86.

Zapata, Roger. 1989. *Guamán Poma, indigenismo y estética de la dependencia en la cultura peruana.* Minneapolis: Institute for the Study of Ideologies and Literature.

Zevallos, María Zulema. 1990. *Sondeando en la literatura autóctona peruana.* Lima: Minerva.

Zumthor, Paul. 1983. *Introduction à la poésie orale.* Paris: Seuil.

CHAPTER 49

ARGENTINA, CHILE, AND URUGUAY
A HISTORY OF LITERARY ORALITY

Eva Grosser Lerner and Eduardo Lucio Molina y Vedia

Oral literature in what is now Argentina, Chile, and Uruguay dates back to before the Spanish Conquest of America. By oral literature we mean ritual pieces, legends, or invocations that are not written down but spoken and often sung, as well as lyrics, poems, and stories; these are "texts" that are sometimes only oral and at other times, though originally part of the oral tradition, were eventually printed. These texts represent linguistic universes full of human emotions, descriptions of landscapes and customs, and narrations of experiences or adventures–all displaying an aesthetic sense of the quality and importance of performance. The oldest material we have on record was produced, or at least compiled, in its entirety after the arrival of the Spanish. In some cases, we have only fragments, testimonies given by aboriginals and recorded by members of colonizing expeditions or by their descendants, the *criollos* during the first stages of the Colonial period. In other cases, the texts are modern compilations of traditional oral texts by speakers of native languages, including some that are becoming extinct. Through these, we get glimpses of a pre-Hispanic past. Important testimonies in indigenous languages that are available today are the result of the recent recovery or compilation of texts that trace verifiable links and interactions between orality and written literature. Beyond these modern texts, the corpus of oral literature begins with the narrations of participants in the campaigns of Conquest and continues with the recovery of Indian oral traditions by lettered members of the colonizing groups, usually clerics and subsequently by the contrapuntal singers of the rural ballad, which then developed into the oral or, subsequently, printed literature of the *payadores* and the gaucho. This reconstructed orality is prolonged as a national idiom in response to the great European migrations of the nineteenth century and becomes a basis for the contemporary language of theater, cinema, and popular songs, from the folkloric to the most up-to-date.

Original Historical and Sociocultural Features

A common characteristic of the area usually known as the Southern Cone was the scant population at the time of the arrival of the conquistadors; even the Mapuches in Chile, who had assimilated agriculture and cattle raising as a result of their contact by groups from the Incan empire, had sparse settlements. The ethnic groups that inhabited this vast area of what today is South America were not only illiterate but were also nomads, hunters, gatherers, and subsistence farmers. In some cases (such as the Charrúas and Guaraníes, who occupied what is now Northern Uruguay, Paraguay, the present Rio Grande do Sul state in Brazil, and the northeast Chaco of Argentina) they were cannibalistic; in other words, they were far removed from the high Incan, Mayan, or Toltec cultures. The vicissitudes of the Conquest turned the European settlers themselves into cannibals. Fr. Luis de Miranda, who in 1536 experienced the misery and horror of the first founding

of Buenos Aires, when starving in a besieged country house that the Indians set partially aflame with their burning arrowheads, left these lines on the cannibalism that took place among the conquistadors (which has been confirmed by other testimonies):

> La carne de hombre también la comieron;
> Las cosas que allí se vieron no se han visto en escritura.

> *(quoted in Horacio Salas 13)*

> They also ate the flesh of men;
> The things seen there have not been seen in literature.

Totemism and Magic

Aníbal Barrios Pintos, in *Los aborígenes del Uruguay* [1958; The Aboriginals of Uruguay], quotes the testimony of the Portuguese navigator Pedro López Souza, who, in 1531, described the Charrúas of what is now Uruguay:

> [. . .] salieron de tierra hacia mi, cuatro almadias (balsas) . . . Se reunieron pronto conmigo; traían arcos, flechas y azagayas (lanzas pequeñas) de palo . . . venían con muchos penachos y pintadoss de mil colores . . . sin mostrar miedo y con mucho placer nos abrazaban a todos . . . hablaban guturalmente . . . sus almadías tenían 10 a 20 brazas de largo y media braza de ancho [una braza = 1,67 metros], hechas de madera de cedro muy bien trabajadas: remaban con unas palas muy largas que en su extremo tenían penachos y borlas de plumas . . . remaban cuarenta hombres de pie . . . mandaron una almadía con pescado; yo les mandé cascabeles, cristales . . . quedaron tan contentos y mostraban tanto placer que parecían locos . . . venían detrás de nosotros que íbamos con viento muy fresco a popa. Estos hombres son tan grandes y robustos y parece que tienen mucha fuerza. Las mujeres son todas muy bien parecidas. (quoted in Antón 14–15)

> . . . four boats sailed toward me. . . . [T]hey quickly came up alongside me; they were carrying bows and arrows and small lances made from sticks. . . . [T]hey came wearing many plumes and painted in a thousand colors . . . ; showing no fear and great pleasure, they embraced us all. . . . [T]hey spoke gutturally. . . . [T]heir boats were 10 to 20 *brazas* long and half a *braza* wide [one *braza* = 1.67 m], made from finely carved cedar; they rowed with very long oars with plumes and feather tassels at the ends . . . forty men, standing up, rowed. . . . [T]hey sent a boat with fish; I sent them jingle bells and glass, and they were so happy that they seemed demented. . . . [T]hey rowed hard behind us even though we had a stiff breeze astern. These men are so tall and robust and seem to be very strong. The women are all handsome.

According to the geologist, geographer, and anthropologist Danilo Antón (1996), "los pueblos pampas vivían en clanes de unos 50 a 100 integrantes, tenían un jefe elegido y formaban confederaciones con otros clanes para defenderse o atacar a otros grupos" (15) ("the pampas peoples lived in clans of fifty to a hundred members; they had an elected chieftain and formed confederations with other clans to defend themselves or attack other groups")–which would have been exactly the case in the expulsion of the first settlers of Buenos Aires. Antón goes on to say, "[. . .] cada grupo de la pampa tenía su propio tótem; hay referencias, por ejemplo, de que los bohanes tenían como tótem el venado, y es probable que cada uno de los otros grupos estuviera unificado (entre otras cosas) por un tótem común. Hay además referencias a tótems clánicos (de cada toldería) y tótems individuales" (16) (". . . each pampas group had its own totem; there are references, for example, to the fact that the *bohanes* had a deer as their totem, and it is likely that each of the other groups was united, among other things, by a common totem. There were also references to clan totems of each Indian camp and individual totems"). In describing the totemic and magical stage in the development of human societies, John D. Bernal emphasizes the importance of obtaining the required daily food supply, which was dependant on the animals and plants around them, which were of course subject to the sometimes extreme variations in climate; this highly vulnerable way of life could only be overcome by the invention of agriculture. He then goes on to explain:

> Nevertheless he thought he could persuade and fool Nature to help him by methods which worked with his fellow tribesmen and with the animals he hunted. *Magic* was evolved to fill in the gaps left by the limitations of technique. By making each useful animal or plant the *totem* of a particular tribe or section of a tribe, by the use of images, symbols, and imitative dances, the primitive tribesmen believed that the animal or plant could be encouraged to flourish and multiply. (76)

In terms of historical evolution, it is estimated that a period of three to four millennia separated the stages of development of the Indians of the extreme American south from those of the principal pre-Columbian civilizations (which flourished in what are now Mexico, Central America, and Peru). This general lack of sedentary development facilitated the capture of these sparsely populated southern territories; it was relatively easy to mount effective campaigns to dominate, assimilate, and destroy the natives. Beyond our knowledge of the employment of native peoples (together with the African slaves) in South America's southern regions as exploited labor, scant evidence of these peoples survived, and the legacy of Indian cultures was reduced to minimal expression, in sharp contrast with the Andean region and Mexico.

The main features of literature—its suggestive, expressive power, its conceptual dimension, and its beauty and sensitivity, in short, its "poetic function" in the words of Roman Jakobson— have, from the outset, been inseparable from the powers of language itself. Although there most certainly must have been some prayers, fables, songs, or oral accounts among the Indian peoples of the southern area considered here (all of whom had no writing), no verbal testimony of their pre-Hispanic past has been left, no evidence that would reveal the extent of their literary culture. Stories or poems compiled after the European conquest and disseminated much later (some only recently—particularly in Mapuche, Guaraní, Aymara, and Quechua) in some cases take us back to that South American past, partially reviving their mythologies, or rather what is left of them in the memory of the current descendants of these ethnic groups, virtually all of whom have been acculturated or are becoming monolingual speakers of Spanish and Portuguese. We can reasonably assume that some of these oral texts—as has happened throughout history with all nomadic peoples, hunters, gatherers, and fishermen—can be linked to rites of passage, prayers, or religious songs intended to give meaning to life, relieve suffering, help people cope with the crisis of the inscrutability of destiny, or banish evil (see Clifford Geertz)—as well as to obtain food, whether through magical invocations or through descriptions of hunting experiences or techniques.

The Italian researcher Carlo Ginzburg notes that what characterizes venatic knowledge is the ability to work back from apparently insignificant empirical data, such as faint tracks, to a complex reality that cannot be experienced directly; these data are arranged by the observer in such a way that they can give rise to a narrative sequence whose simplest formulation would be: Someone went by there. And he adds:

> . . . perhaps the very idea of narration, as opposed to enchantment, spells and invocations, originally emerged in a society of hunters, from the experience of deciphering animal tracks. The hunter had been the first to "tell stories" because he was the only one able to read a coherent series of events in the mute (although not imperceptible) tracks left by the prey. This indicative or prophetic paradigm reveals the oldest gesture in the intellectual history of mankind: that of the hunter squatting down in the mud examining the tracks of his prey. (120)

Thus, early man emerges as not only a hunter of prey but also a hunter of symbols because behind the track, the indication, lies the sign. Ginzburg convinces us that the metaphor of *reading* animal tracks is perhaps the verbal condensation of a historical process that led, over an extremely long time span, to the invention of writing. According to Bernal, there was a use of sounds that predated language; the sounds were used by birds and other animals to produce actions or indicate an emotional mood or the willingness to undertake certain acts. At the same time, gestures from the totemic system of beliefs operated in dances, speech, and literature, which eventually spawned references to the "magic of words." There would also have been a true criterion of human language, in which a descriptive element was superimposed over the so-called magical element for action, two modes that blended extremely slowly (Bernal 76).

Ginzburg's and Bernal's reflections would seem to confirm a tale told by the Indian narrator Luis Cuaterno and translated freely from Mapuche or Araucanian a few years ago by the linguist Ana Fernández Garay (1994). The original dialectal variant of the Mapuche of these short stories was already becoming extinct at the time and probably no longer exists in the community of Anecón Grande, part of the Argentinian Patagonian province of Río Negro. A few examples follow:

> Dicen que el tigre pasó por ahí. Tenía cuatro cachorros. Mientras él se paseaba, un viejo lo estaba observando. El viejo le dijo al tigre: "Sígueme". Entonces tomó un palo y lo plantó en el suelo. Después, se sacó la ropa y con ella vistió al palo. El tigre se acercó creyendo que era el viejo y éste aprovecho para apuñalarlo por atrás. Finalmente, le sacó el cuero. (Fernández Garay 287)

> They say that the tiger passed by there. It had four cubs. An old man watched it as it walked by. The old man said to the tiger, "Follow me." Then he took a stick and stuck it in the ground. Then he took off his clothes and draped them over the stick. The tiger approached the stick, thinking it was the old man, who took advantage of the situation and stabbed the tiger in the rear, and then skinned it.

This theme is repeated in another story in which a test of hunting skills must be passed to obtain the Daughter of the Sun and the Moon:

Acá nació Elal. Su abuela lo crió. Se hizo hombre y dominó todas las cosas. Partió en busca de la Hija del Sol y de la Luna. Ya no va a volver a soplar el mar. La abuela le adviente del peligro. "Te puede agarrar a vos y a tu caballo." Pero Elal estaba con los ojos abiertos.

Al llegar al toldo de Sol y de Luna, una muchacha lo hace entrar al lugar donde se hallaba la única hija de ambos. El Sol y la Luna le exigen una serie de pruebas. Una de ellas es traerles un guanaco macho para hacer una bolsa con el cuero del cogote. Supera todas las exigencias y los padres de la joven reconocen sus poderes. Finalmente abandona a la joven en el mar luego de sacarle su collar. (Fernández Garay 322)

Elal was born here. His grandmother raised him. He became a man and ruled over all things. He set off in search of the Daughter of the Sun and the Moon. The sea-wind will no longer blow. His grandmother warned him of the danger. "It can seize you and your horse." But Elal's eyes were wide open.

When he reached the canopy of the Sun and Moon, a girl led him into the place where their only daughter sat. The Sun and the Moon subjected him to a series of tests. One of them was to bring them a male *guanaco* to make a purse out of the skin of its nape. Elal passed all the tests, and the young girl's parents acknowledged his powers. In the end, he left the young girl in the sea after removing her necklace.

Before the Conquest: Without Testimonies

According to Albert Rex González and José A. Pérez (1976), the most accurate datings show that man's arrival in America dates back over 30,000 years, but the oldest remains in the south of the continent are no more than 11,000 years old. Antón agrees with the first date yet surmises that the oldest remains might be between 12,500 and 15,000 years old. In what was formerly the southern region of the Viceroyalty of Peru and, from 1776 onward, of the New Viceroyalty of the River Plate, there were no Indian cities; nor were any traces of graphic representation of language found. The closest equivalents to the high civilizations of the Andes and Mesoamerica are traces of a primitive, rough industry in the fertile valleys of the northeast of Argentina and the north of Chile, which were at that time peripheral provinces dependent on the Incan empire. There was also a greater demographic density in these southern dependencies. The inhabitants engaged in a horticultural economy with irrigation, which suggests a relatively higher cultural level than their neighbors in the Chaco region.

According to ethno-historical references, the total Indian population in the mid-sixteenth century was approximately 350,000 in what is now Argentina and Uruguay—a similar figure to the current Indian population, according to official censuses. Conversely, the Araucanians or Mapuches in what is now Chile were estimated at one million, and this size proved to be a decisive factor in their partial shift to the Argentinian pampas, the conquest of other Indian groups, and the stiff resistance they put up to the Spanish invaders and subsequently to the republican armies on either side of the Andes. The resistance of the Mapuches was such that they continued fighting until the end of the nineteenth century, when they were eventually pacified on one side of the Andes by the Chilean army and on the other by the so-called "Desert Campaign" led by General Julio Argentino Roca. *Una excursión a los indios ranqueles* [1870; *An Expedition to the Ranquel Indians*, 1997] by General Lucio Victorio Mansilla (1831–1913) provides a detailed account of part of this story, in which descriptions of bloody massacres were interspersed with tales of Machiavellian negotiations, in what was a tracing of the ethnohistory of one of the conquered peoples. It shows how the effective incorporation of the vast Patagonian region known as The West began barely a century ago. Another revealing theme in the common past of the Southern Cone prior to the Conquest is demography. In what are now Argentina and Uruguay, stable populations of over 2,000 existed only in the northeast, while the rest of Patagonia was inhabited by a number of groups not larger than fifty to a hundred individuals, living in Indian camps, such as the remaining nomadic Charrúa and Guaraní populations that moved around territories in the northeast and south of Brazil. The Indians of the Pampas—the vast, fertile plains covering Uruguay and part of the horizontal central strip of Argentinian territory—gathered together only to launch their fearsome raids, with hundreds and sometimes thousands of warriors, as widely described in the literature and oral testimonies of the nineteenth century.

Successful Recoveries: The Yasi-Yatere, A Guaraní Legend

Despite the lack of direct sources, stories recorded by researchers at various times in history have enabled us to reconstruct certain expressions of literary orality, whose origins, however, cannot be accurately dated; nor is it possible to place them either before or after the Conquest or to determine the extent of ancient or modern features. One of these stories evokes the bewitching seductiveness of the mermaid, that fabulous sea nymph, half woman, half fish, whose song misdirects sailors, according to a European tradition already present in Homer's *Odyssey*. It also recalls the *ciguanaba*, an equally fantastic creature in the stories and popular legends of Central America, a representation of a ghost in the image of an extraordinarily beautiful woman who appears to peasants in the woods. The ethnographer Juan Bautista Ambrosetti (1865–1917) in *Supersticiones y leyendas* [1947; Superstitions and Legends] recalls that, while staying in a maté dealer's hut near the Tacurú-Pucú stream, in the Argentine province of Misiones, he discovered, on waking, that the women there had been unable to sleep because they had heard the whistle of the Yasi-Yateré. He goes on to say that some people believed that a bird uttered the terrifying whistle, while others said that it was

Un enano rubio, bonito, que anda por el mundo cubierto con un sombreo de paja, y llevando un bastón de oro en la mano. Y agrega: "Su oficio es el de robar niños de pecho, que lleva al monte, los lame, juega con ellos y luego los abandona allí, envueltos en isipós (enredaderas). Las madres, desesperadas al notar su falta y guiadas por sus gritos, generalmente los encuentran en el suelo; pero desde ese día, todos los años, en el aniversario del rapto del Yasi-Yateré, las criaturas sufren ataques epilépticos. Según otros roba a los niños no para lamerlos sino para enseñarles su oficio de raptor, y no falta también quien asegura que no sólo roba a las criaturas sino también a las muchachas bonitas, las que son a su vez abandonadas, y el hijo que nace de esa unión, con el tiempo, será Yasi-Yateré.

(Ambrosetti 50–1)

A handsome, blond dwarf who went through the world wearing a straw hat and carrying a gold walking stick in one hand. And he adds, "His job was to steal infants, to take them into the hills, lick them, play with them, and then leave them there, wrapped in vines. The anguished mothers, realizing they had been taken away and guided by their cries, usually found them on the ground; but from that day on, every year, on the anniversary of the kidnapping by Yasi-Yateré, the children suffered epileptic attacks. According to others, the dwarf did not steal the children to lick them but to teach them the kidnapper's trade, while others said that he not only stole babies but also pretty girls, whom he also abandoned, and that the child who was born of this union would eventually become Yasi-Yateré.

Ambrosetti also describes superstitions from the Misiones region concerning funerary practices, sexual love, animals, rural chores, games, plants, and therapeutic beliefs, as well as folk tales from the Calchaqui valleys in the northeast of Argentina about coca, the *Pacha Mama*, vicuña hunting, and the carnival. "Men and women," he says of the Calchaqui carnival, "sing in unison and entertain themselves for hours, repeating the same music, while cups of liquor are passed from hand to hand. They previously soaked themselves with buckets of water or disfigured their faces and clothes with handfuls of starch, flour, and colored paint, and set off rockets, with which they engage in a carnival celebration" (Ambrosetti 75). In his description of Pampas folklore, Ambrosetti mentions popular superstitions about rain, therapeutic cures, rural veterinary cures, and signs of misfortune. He places particular emphasis on the role of the toad, in various forms, in curing headaches or toothaches or as an antidote for snakebites. He also underlines the prophetic nature of the song of the partridges, reflected in several versified proverbs.

In 1965 the researcher León Cadogan recovered an important Guaraní oral poem. The Mexican cultural historian Alfredo López Austin glossed it as follows:

El Creador, utilizando su vara-insignia, de la que hizo brotar llamas y tenue neblina, creó el lenguaje. Este lenguaje, futura esencia del alma enviada a los hombres, participa de su divinidad. Crea después el amor al prójimo y los himnos sagrados. Para formar un ser en el cual depositar el lenguaje, la divinidad, el amor y los cantos sagrados, crea a los cuatro dioses que tienen ombligo y a sus respectivas consortes, que enviarán a la tierra el alma de los hombres. (Cadogan and Austin 53)

The Creator, using his staff of office, from which he brought forth flames and a soft mist, created language. This language, the future essence of the soul, was sent to men by the Creator, and they shared in his divinity. He then created love of one's fellow men, and sacred hymns. In order to form a being in which to deposit language, divinity, love, and the sacred hymns, he created four gods with navels and their respective consorts, who will send a soul to men on Earth.

Here are some fragments of Cadogan's free translation:

El verdadero padre ñamandu, el Primero,
de una pequeña porción de su propia divinidad,
de la sabiduría contenida en su propia divinidad,
hizo que se engendrasen llamas y tenue neblina.
Habiéndose erguido concibió el origen
del lenguage humano
e hizo que formara parte de su propia divinidad.
Antes de existir la tierra,
en medio de las tinieblas primigenias,
antes de tenerse conocimiento de las cosas,
creó aquello que sería el fundamento
del lenguage humano
y concibió el origen del amor al prójimo
y un solo himno sagrado.
Reflexionó profundamente sobre a quién hacer partícipe
de las series de palabras que componían
el himno sagrado

y creó a quienes serían compañeros
de su divinidad,
creó los ñamandu de corazón valeroso,
al verdadero Padre ñamandu,
a la futura verdadera Madre de los ñamandu,
con el reflejo de su sabiduría, el Sol,
y les impartió conciencia de la divinidad.
Por haber asimilado la sabiduría divina
de su propio Primer Padre,
después de haber asimilado el lenguaje humano,
de haberse inspirado en el amor al prójimo,
de haber asimilado las series de palabras
del himno sagrado,
después de haberse inspirado en los fundamentos
de la sabiduría creadora, a ellos también llamamos
excelsos verdaderos padres de las palabras-almas,
excelsas verdaderas madres de las palabras-almas.

(Cadogan and Austin 54–7)

The true Ñamando father, the First,
out of a small portion of his divinity,
out of the knowledge contained in his own divinity,
created flames and a soft mist.
Having stood up, he conceived the origin
of human language
and made it part of his own divinity.
Before the earth existed,
in the midst of the original darkness,
before there was knowledge,
he created what would be the basis
of human language
and conceived the origin of the love of one's neighbor
and a single sacred hymn.
He thought deeply about whom he should choose
to share the series of words that made up
the sacred hymn
and created those who would be the companions
of his divinity,
he created the Ñamandu with the brave hearts,
the true Ñamandu father,
and the future true mother of the Ñamandu,
with the reflection of his knowledge, the Sun,
and gave them an awareness of divinity.
Through assimilating the divine wisdom
of his own First Father,
and after having assimilated human language,
and been inspired by the love of one's neighbor,
after having assimilated the series of words
from the sacred hymn,
after having being inspired by the basis
of the knowledge of creation, we also called them
the sublime fathers of word-souls,
and the sublime mothers of word-souls.

Other texts from Guaraní literature recorded by Cadogan include the *Primitivas costumbres del colibrí* [The Ancient Customs of the Hummingbird], *La primera tierra* [The First Earth], *Las llamas y la neblina del poder creador* [The Flames and the Mist of the Power of Creation], *El diluvio* [The Flood], *La nueva tierra* [The New Earth], and *Las aventuras de un Dios* [The Adventures of a God], among other matters. A special chapter is dedicated to *Cuentos, leyendas y cantos infantiles* [Short Stories, Legends, and Children's Stories].

In Anecón Grande, the Argentinian linguists Ana Fernández Garay and Lucía Golluscio recorded a series of rogations and sacred Mapuche songs for linguistic analysis (1978). These were oral pieces delivered at various points in the *camaruco,* an annual religious ceremony lasting three or four days in which the Mapuches of Argentina and Chile gather together, among other things, to ask for good weather (rain) and good health. (Anecón Grande is a village set on the slopes of the Andes, over three thousand feet above sea level, in an arid, isolated zone.) One of the rogations treats the god like a friend with whom one can share maté: "Dame bienestar, tomemos mate juntos. Oh, Viejo Creador de gente; oh, Viejo Creador. Tú posees la vida, oh, Viejo Creador Fecundo, Viejo Creador Fecundo. Tú posees la vida, oh, Viejo Creador Fecundo, Viejo Creador Fecundo. Tomemos mate juntos, dijo. Dame comida." ("Give me well-being, let us drink maté together. Oh, old creator of people; oh, Old Creator. You possess life, oh, old fertile Creator, Old Fertile Creator. You possess life, oh, Old Fertile Creator, Old Fertile Creator. Let us drink maté together, he said. Give me food," Fernández Garay and Golluscio 109).

In *Textos orales en mapuche del centro-sur de Chile* [1984; Oral Texts in Mapuche from South-Central Chile], the linguist Adalberto Salas reproduces the following story from traditional literature, recorded by Manuel P. Loncomil Coñuenao:

Había una vez un hombre. Este hombre enviudó. Quería mucho a su mujer. Quedó muy triste y sufriendo mucho. Le hizo el funeral a su mujer y la sepultó en el cementerio. Pero se dijo a sí mismo: "¿Cómo podría ver de nuevo a mi mujer?" dijo. Entonces: "Voy a ir al cementerio y estaré allí observándola, ya que se dice que los difuntos salen para ir a otro sitio. Si eso fuere cierto, volveré a verla, aunque no más sea un ratito", dijo el hombre. Entonces, fue al cementerio a quedarse allá. Se quedó tendido junto al sepulcro donde estaba su mujer. Así pasó una noche. Cuando ya estaba por amanecer regresó a su casa y a la noche siguiente volvió a ir; ahí alojó, y luego, casi al amanecer, regresó a su casa. A la noche siguiente volvió a ir. Entonces, cuando ya estaba a punto de ser medianoche, el ataúd produjo un ruido. Inmediatamente el hombre despertó y miró hacia donde estaba sepultada su mujer y la vio venir hacia él. Corrió a abrazarla. "¡Qué bueno que has resucitado! Volvamos a la casa", le dijo a su mujer. Pero ella le dijo: "No regresaremos a la casa. Yo he muerto; salí del sepulcro, pero nunca jamás he de volver a la casa. Sufro mucho de verte en esto. Vuelve tú solo porque yo ya me voy a otra parte, a una tierra muy lejana, y para llegar allá más rápido debo irme volando", dijo la mujer. Pero el hombre le respondió: "Yo iré contigo", le dijo. "¿Pero cómo vas a poder ir si yo voy volando?", dijo la mujer. "De todos modos iré", dijo el hombre. La mujer le contestó: "Bueno, iremos los dos. Caminando iremos los dos por un sendero angosto", se le dijo al hombre. "Pero no te cansarás", se lo dijo. "No me cansaré", dijo él. Empezaron a caminar los dos siguiendo un sendero angosto. Casi al amanecer entraron en un gran bosque. En medio del bosque había un pequeño claro. La mujer le dijo al hombre: "Aquí comeremos algo; tú te quedarás durmiendo todo el día. A mi no me verás más porque yo me transformaré en carbón. No te vayas a ninguna parte; quédate esperándome, porque cuando vuelva a anochecer me pondré en pie nuevamente y me transformaré en gente", le dijo ella. El hombre creyó e hizo lo que había dicho su mujer. Estuvo durmiendo todo el día, y cuando oscureció, a la llegada de la noche, se sentó la mujer y volvió a ser ella misma. Nuevamente el hombre se alegró mucho al volver a ver a su mujer. Entonces comieron algo y "Vamos" se dijeron. Caminaron siguiendo nuevamente el mismo sendero angosto. Este relato mítico concluye cuando tras un mes o dos arriban a una gran isla donde habitan los muertos, que se convierten en carbón, y ella se despide de él: "Regresa. Anda allá a ver a tu gente, pero no te quedarás allá por mucho tiempo. Pronto volverás acá. Es casi como si ya estuvieras viniéndote." (42–59)

There was once a man who was widowed. He had loved his wife deeply, and when she died he became very sad and suffered a great deal. He organized a funeral for his wife and buried her in the cemetery. But he said to himself, "How could I see my wife again?" Then he said, "I shall go to the cemetery and watch her there, since they say that the dead leave to go somewhere else. If that is true, then I shall see her again, even if only for a little while," said the man. So he went to the cemetery. He lay down next to the grave where his wife lay. . . . Then, just before midnight, the coffin made a noise. The man woke up, and looked towards the place where his wife was buried and saw her coming towards him. He ran to embrace her. "I'm so glad you have come back to life. Let's go home," he said to his wife. But she replied, "We can't go home. I have died. I came out of the grave but I shall never go home. . . . But the man replied, "I shall go with you," he said. But how are you going to be able to come if I'm going to fly?" asked the woman. "I'll go anyway," said the man. The woman replied, "Well, let the two of us go then. The two of us will walk along a narrow path," she said to the man. . . . So they ate something and then said, "Let's go." They took the same narrow path again. This mythical tale ends when, after a month or two, they reach a large island inhabited by the dead, who turn into charcoal, and the wife bids farewell to her husband saying, "Go back. There you will see your family, but you won't be there for long. You'll be back here soon. It's almost as though you were already on your way here."

Salas explains that the most striking traditional Mapuche literary expressions are in narrative genres, such as the *epeo,* or fictional tales (either mythical or about animals) and the *nutram,* or stories about an event described as it actually happened. He suggests that the level of "formalization of narrative works is low, in the sense that there would seem to be no fixed text for each composition. Indeed, the structure of the text depends more on idiosyncratic factors (whether the narrator is good or bad) and occasional factors (such as different versions by the same narrator)" (18). The mythical *epeo* have a somber tone; their universe is that of sorcerers, devilish creatures, and the dead. The animal *epeo* are much lighter in tone and more like fables; the fauna of the Mapuche habitat interact in an anthropomorphized form with allegorical behavioral stereotypes (cunning, physical strength, ingenuity, etc.).

During the three centuries between the Conquest and Independence, given the late introduction of the printing press and widespread illiteracy, orality was the dominant means of development for the European languages as well. In the American encounter with various Indian languages, Spanish and Portuguese popular narratives were diversified by incorporating and creating words, prosodic features, syntactic inflections, and semantic fields that enriched the originals and introduced various new cultural identities. These processes began to be incorporated in the early stories of the Conquest, through which the new American realities were conveyed to Europe. Missionaries' grammars not only were translated into the Indian languages but also worked to propagate Christian doctrine; there were soon catechisms, confessionals, religious canticles, talks, and sermons in the Indian languages. But there were also other texts that shed light on the lives and customs of the native peoples, especially the narratives of Quechua, Aymará, Guaraní, and Mapuche cultures. Pre-Columbian legends and myths, together with Indian formulas and ritual songs, only survived the reduction of the very languages and ethnic groups that had produced them in fragmented form. In some cases the languages disappeared entirely, as in the case of the Kunza or Atacameño, spoken in areas that are now part of Argentina and Chile, and the Tehuelches or Patagonians. Later, at the end of the Colonial period, as we shall see shortly, the *payador* emerged as the primary storyteller, particularly during the first century of republican history, though losing ground by the first quarter of the twentieth century and only managing to survive in the present day. In the nineteenth century, however, the *payador* was the main figure in literary orality in the southern extreme of the American continent. Accompanied by a guitar and performing in front of a popular audience, he competed with others for honor in the art of improvised versification.

The author of the first regional literary testimony, fundamentally oral in nature despite being printed in book form, was, strangely enough, a Bavarian. The seafaring adventurer Ulrich Schmidel (1510–1579?), who traveled throughout the area for nearly two decades (between the ages of twenty-four and forty-four), was the son of a noble family in Bavaria. He enrolled as a foot soldier in the fleet of the Spanish governor Pedro de Mendoza en route to the Río de la Plata estuary. He was not a chronicler proper but a mercenary who wrote down his memoirs. *Wahrhafftige Historien einer wunderbaren Schiffart* [True Stories of a Marvelous Sea Voyage] was first published in German in 1567 and translated into Spanish several times, most recently by Klaus Wagner (1986) under the title of *Relatos de la Conquista del Río de la Plata y Paraguay (1534–1554)* [Tales of the Conquest of the River Plate and Paraguay (1534–1554)]. In the preface, Wagner states that "reading the stories, one has the feeling that Schmidel did not actually write them down; or at least, it is not a reflective text. It is as though he were telling the story to an audience gathered around him" (Schmidel 14). Written in a conversational style, the text does not skimp on the details of the horrendous massacres or the enslavement of the conquered peoples, as well as the numerous adventures that marked the exploration and conquest from the Argentine pampas and the Gran Chaco to the borders of Peru; it mentions, in fact, the author's presence at the founding of Buenos Aires and Asunción. It also tells of the bloody wars against the Charrúa chieftain Tabaré, taken up three centuries later (in the form of an Indian legend) in a romantic, epic poem written by Uruguayan Juan Zorrilla de San Martín (1855–1931).

Schmidel's account reveals a wry sense of humor and irony, qualities that doubtless proved invaluable during his two decades of American adventures. For instance, he recalls that the Carios took up their bows and arrows and gave a traditional welcome; in another example, the Indians attacked fifty Spaniards while they were eating, and blessed their food in such a way that none was spared. Irony is also evident in his description of the episode involving young maidens and Domingo Martínez de Irala (1486–1557), a Spanish conquistador who was the Governor of River Plate. It so happened that the Maipais Indians, in order to ingratiate themselves with the invaders, offered Irala three young women, who, however, wasted no time in escaping from the governor. Schmidel notes with guileless malice: "Shortly after midnight, our captain general had lost his three damsels, perhaps because he was unable to satisfy all three" (46). Schmidel is not an historian or a chronicler, much less an analyst of the events that took place in River Plate at the beginning of the Conquest. He is simply a man who had extraordinary adventures for someone of his time and origins, who had the good fortune to survive and who, at the end of his life, felt the need to convey them to his fellow countrymen, who may well have asked him

to do so. His story is strongly autobiographical in nature and is the first and only narrative by an eyewitness of the events referred to.

It is an actual, direct account, despite the clumsiness of expression, and thus contrasts with the official accounts of the majority of Spanish chroniclers, with the notable exception of Bernal Díaz del Castillo (1492–1584), who, like Schmidel, was a mere soldier who happened to participate in unprecedented events. In this strange, fantastic threatening world, where the Indians sometimes, he humbly admits, shared their meager portions of fish and meat, he focused on the food: Thistles, hearts of palm, yam, cassava, groundnuts, and many other roots and fruits from which the natives made their wine. He also described the fauna: Boars, swine, viscachas, elk, chickens, and geese. He was especially interested in the women, "the Jarayes, beautiful and very loving, affectionate and passionate. They walk around naked and are beautiful. And they may even sin in the dark" (55). He also tells of the siege and burning of the Buenos Aires settlement at the end of June 1536, almost five months after its foundation in February of the same year. (The city was re-established in 1580 by Juan de Garay, who died at the hands of the natives, just like the discoverer of the Río de la Plata, Juan Díaz de Solís, half a century earlier.) Schmidel too describes the attack of the first Buenos Aires: "The Indians attacked us with great force, with nearly twenty-three thousand men from four different nations: Querendies, Bartenies, Charrúas, and Timbúes. Their aim (and intention) was to kill us all but, praise be to Almighty God who wished to save the majority of our men, out of all the captains, subalterns, and other soldiers, only thirty were killed. When they besieged Buenos Aires, some attacked it, while others shot blazing arrows onto the houses, which, since they had straw roofs, immediately went up in flames, with the exception of the Captain General's house, which was the only one covered in tiles" (86–87). Five hundred and sixty men remained of the 2,500 with whom Mendoza had set out from Spain; the rest died, mainly of starvation.

A significant testimony, although it seems exaggerated and fantastic, was *Argentina*, a long narrative subtitled *Historia del descubrimiento, Conquista y población del Río de la Plata* [History of the Discovery, Conquest, and Settlement of the River Plate], a handwritten copy of which was produced in 1612 by Ruy Díaz de Guzmán (1558?–1629), who was said to have been a direct descendant of a conquistador and himself a self-styled conquistador. The text erroneously records the date of the arrival to the Río de la Plata by Juan Díaz de Solís (which was in 1516, rather than 1512). Solís gave the name Mar Dulce [Sweet Water Sea] to this 36,000 square kilometer estuary formed by the mouths of the great Paraná and Uruguay rivers. That same year, while attempting to disembark in the Río de la Plata island of Martín García, the discoverer died at the hands of the Charrúa Indians, who are reputed (according to William Robertson in 1840) to have fed on his body and those of the group accompanying him; after this the rest of the expedition fled in its two caravels. The episode is alluded to by Jorge Luis Borges (1899–1986) in his poem *Fundación mítica de Buenos Aires* [1929; Mythic Foundation of Buenos Aires]. Robertson, following the Spanish historian Antonio de Herrera y Tordesillas (1559–1625), comments: "The Spaniards had intended to make a landing but Solís and many from his crew were killed by the natives who, in full view of the ships, cut up the bodies of the Spaniards and ate them up after having roasted them" (quoted in Guzmán 218).

This tradition of written texts reflects an underlying orality because their authors were not writers but soldiers who related their adventures in the New World, including adventures and sayings of everyday life. In contrast, writing is a style replete with metaphors and rhetorical figures, we find one of the most outstanding figures who stood out as both a poet and a soldier, a native of Madrid, Alonso de Ercilla y Zúñiga (1533–1594). His great epic poem *La Araucana,* composed in royal octaves and published in three parts in 1569, 1578, and 1589, praises the heroic deeds of the Spanish Conquest of Chile, led by the Captain General Pedro de Valdivia, while extolling the bravery of the Mapuche Indians or Araucanians. This ethnic group, which occupied the central horizontal strip that crosses what is now Argentina and Chile–where, under the influence of the Incas, they had became sedentary and adopted agriculture (maize, potato) and cattle raising–proved to be exceptionally brave and constant in the war against the Spanish invaders. During the pre-Columbian era, the Mapuches (of whom approximately five hundred thousand descendants still survive, having more or less been assimilated into the national cultures of Argentina and Chile) traded with the Incan empire and, through it, with the Aztecs and the Maya via networks of main and alternative highways that criss-crossed the Latin American territory lengthwise along the coast of the Pacific Ocean. (Argentinean archaeologist Alberto Rex González is an authority on these networks, which included alternative networks for periods of intense rain and were equipped with their corresponding staging posts or hostels.)

One of the main characters in Ercilla y Zúñiga's poem is the conquistador Valdivia, who fought in Venezuela and subsequently in Peru under Pizarro and who went on to found Santiago de Chile in 1541 with 150 men. The other was the Araucanian leader Lautaro, whose forces captured and executed Valdivia in 1554, following a fierce battle at the Spanish fort of Tucapel, now the region of Arauco. The Mapuche chieftain, who, tradition has it, was born in 1535, was educated by the conquistadors to serve as an intermediary in the subjugation and enslavement of the natives. His rebellion (treason for the conquistadors, but a liberating awakening for the Araucanos) occupies a central position in the epic poem. *La Arcaucana* provides the following description of the Mapuche leader:

Fue Lautaro industrioso, sabio, presto,
de gran consejo, término y cordura,
manso de condición y hermoso gesto,
ni grande ni pequeño de estatura;
el ánimo en las cosas grandes puesto,
de fuerte trabazón y compostura;
duro los miembros, recios y nerviosos,
anchas espaldas, pechos espaciosos.
Por él las fiestas fueron alargadas,
ejercitando siempre nuevos juegos
de saltos, luchas, pruebas nunca usadas,
danzas de noche en torno de los fuegos:
había precios y joyas señaladas,
que nunca los troyanos ni los griegos,
cuando los juegos más continüaron,
tan ricas y estimadas las sacaron.

(58)

This Lautaro was industrious,
Wise and ready, shrewd and prudent,
Meek in manner, fair of gesture,

Neither stately nor enormous,
With a mind inured to greatness,
Fibrous and sedate in bearing,
Hard of limb, with sinews wiry,
Broad of shoulders, and full chested,
He prolonged the gay carousals
In ever new games of exulting,
Jumping, wrestling, tests amorphous,
Nightly dancing round the bonfires.
There shone glittering jewels and prizes,
Richer, of more precious value
Than were gained by Greeks or Trojans
In spectacular disportment.

(59)

Lautaro was defeated and killed in 1557 by the Spanish leader Francisco de Villagra, yet this figure lives on in the hearts and minds of those who fought for Independence, to such an extent that a secret lodge founded in Buenos Aires in 1812 by the generals José de San Martín, Bernardo O'Higgins, and Carlos de Alvear to prepare the continental fight against the Colonial forces was named after him. *La Araucana* is the first literary text from the south of the continent, yet it includes a series of stories and adventures that really happened, while incorporating an aesthetic and expressive dimension linked to popular language.

The Payador or "Contrapuntal Singer"

The *payador* was undoubtedly well known in the eighteenth century before the Independence revolutions and probably already existed in the seventeenth century. The classic version of this figure, however, was developed in the early nineteenth century; he was a contrapuntal singer who traveled through what is now Argentina, Chile, Paraguay, Uruguay, and the Brazilian state of Rio Grande do Sul and was the main propagator of the oral literature that predominated in the region until the beginning of the twentieth century and has survived, in residual form, to the present day. The themes covered by the *payadas* were increasingly (though not exclusively) linked to political and social events, inasmuch as the latter acquired historical relevance and public significance in everyday life. The word *palla* or *paya,* which in Chile meant the separation of a mineral extracted from a mine, gave rise to the term *payada,* an improvisation or lyrical composition in the form of a dialogue. Initially oral, although occasionally written down and printed, it was accompanied by a repetitive tune on the guitar, with the text serving as an exposition of the theme, or more commonly of a controversy, with alternating questions and answers. The *payador,* a figure who achieved the greatest popularity in the Río de la Plata areas, was originally a peasant who frequented country houses and popular meetings, improvising songs or *payas,* which he accompanied on his guitar, and becoming involved in bids with other *payadores* in verbal contests that sometimes ended in a change of status or even in bloody duels.

Gaucho authors wrote *payadas* to include in their works, even though this is a spontaneous and fundamentally improvised genre. Practice, however, meant that the *payador* sang prerehearsed and memorized lines with regular metrics and rhyme, which constituted a veritable self-made set of rules. The *payadores* themselves–who eventually became professional–wrote texts in which there was no opponent and that were more thought out and elaborate than those that the contingencies of a *payada* led them to perform. But perhaps the most genuine and celebrated expression of the genre was the *payada de contrapunto*–in other words, the versified confrontation of two bards. *El cantar del payador* [The Song of the Payador], compiled and prefaced by Beatriz Seibel (1988), contains the textual version of a meeting, held at the Teatro Florida de Pergamino, in the province of Buenos Aires in October 1894. The protagonists were Pablo J. Vázquez (1864–1897) and Gabino Ezeiza (1858–1916):

GE: Está fuerte y muy contento
     y de lejos se divisa
     que algo le falta al cimiento
     como a la torre de Pisa.

PV: Esto sólo es lo que usted arguye,
     es fácil de comprender
     de que ha llegado el momento
     y que me haga convencer.

GE: Que yo lo haga convencer,
     hay esta rara emergencia,
     si puede usted responder,
     pregúntele a la concurrencia.

PV: He llegado a una creencia
     y en su santuario llamé
     y allí he encontrado más fuerza
     para luchar con usted.

GE: Si es que ha encontrado más fuerza
     ya varia de opinión,
     fuerza puede hallarla ahora
     pero no tener razón.

PV: De que no tenga razón
     yo no le puedo objetar,
     pero no es usted, Gabino,
     quien me debe juzgar.

GE: Yo no lo puedo juzgar,
     pero no está calculando
     de que soy su adversario
     y que a mí me está peleando.

PV: Que yo lo estoy peleando
     pero con armas muy leales,
     usted debe demostrarme
     de que sí son desiguales.

GE: La desigualdad existe,
     bien se puede calcular,
     que yo improviso ligero
     y usted se pone a pensar.

PV: Es que me falta una cuerda
     y debo de estar atento,
     pues si una nota disuena
     se me trunca el pensamiento.

GE: Si es que le falta una cuerda
     entonces tiene razón,
     la cuerda del sentimiento
     que da tanta vibración.

PV: La cuerda del sentimiento
     no me falta según creo:
     al yo cantar con usted
     la he notado en su apogeo.

GE: La ha notado en su apogeo
     pero tan sólo voy,
     por más que tengo deseo,
     a no escucharla ahora hoy.

PV: Qué gran lástima mi amigo
     de que así desprecie el arte,
     porque así se constituye usted
     siendo juez y parte.

GE: Como juez ni parte soy
     bien se puede concebir,

que he venido aquí a luchar,
con nobleza a combatir.

PV: Si ha venido con nobleza
     si con nobleza ha venido,
     yo también en el mismo caso
     me encuentro muy decidido.
     Al interrumpir mi canto,
     voy a dejar la cuarteta,
     porque me dice el padrino:
     la sesión está completa.
     Y antes de que me repitan
     el sonar de la campana,
     voy a terminar, señores,
     diciendo yo hasta mañana.

GE: Con que será hasta mañana,
     justo es que razón no sobre,
     que puede darle las gracias
     a este auditorio tan noble.

(Seibel 45–47)

GE: He's strong and very happy
     but you can see from a mile away
     that he's missing a bit at the bottom
     like the leaning Tower of Pisa.

PV: That's your story,
     it's easy to understand
     that the time has come,
     to let you convince me.

GE: To let me convince you,
     there's an unusual emergency,
     if you can respond,
     ask those assembled here.

PV: I have acquired faith
     and I called upon its sanctuary
     and there I have found more strength
     to fight with you.

GE: If you have indeed found more force
     then you've changed your mind,
     You may find strength now
     yet not be right.

PV: I can't refute the fact
     that I may not be right,
     but you, Gabino,
     are not the one to judge.

GE: I cannot judge you,
     but what you have not realized
     is that I am your adversary
     and you're fighting against me.

PV: I am indeed fighting
     yet with very loyal weapons,
     and you must prove to me
     that they are unequal.

GE: Inequality does exist,
     as can indeed be proved,
     I improvise at speed
     but you start to philosophize.

PV: I'm missing a guitar string
     and I have to take great care,
     because if I play a wrong note
     I lose my train of thought.

GE: If you're missing a string
     then you're absolutely right,
     it must be the string of sentiment
     which gives so much vibration.

PV: I don't really think I'm missing
     the string of sentiment;
     because while singing with you,
     I've noticed it's in top form.

GE: You've noticed it's in top form
but I'll be on my way,
because what I really want,
is not to hear any more today.

PV: Well, it's a pity my friend
That you should scorn my art,
because that way you become
judge and jury all in one.

GE: Since I'm neither judge nor jury
you might well believe,
that I've come here to battle,
and to fight a noble fight.

PV: If you've come here with nobility,
with nobility you have come,
well, then in that case
I am absolutely determined.
By interrupting my song,
I shall leave the quatrain,
because my sponsor tells me:
the session is now complete.
And before they repeat
the sound of the bell,
I shall finish here, gentlemen,
saying, farewell until tomorrow.

GE: So until tomorrow 'twill be,
I won't disagree with that,
and instead would like to thank
this wonderful audience.

The most emblematic figure in the *payadas* and in oral culture generally was the River Plate gaucho, a social figure who emerged from the mix of European and Indian blood toward the end of the eighteenth century; he was a key figure in the Wars of Independence and early national organization, not only in the south of the continent but also in battlefields as far away as Bolivia, Peru, or Ecuador. Through the gaucho and his dramatic career–in which he gave everything without receiving or asking for anything–a new popular poetics emerged that incorporated voices and new turns of phrase drawn from everyday speech, which he in turn enriched with his own contributions. Here was a genre that eventually adopted classical literary forms and was published in book form without losing its original oral roots. Gaucho literature, like the Mexican *corrido*, is partly a tributary of the Spanish ballad, a poetic form that culminated in the fifteenth century and was originally the result of the fragmentation of medieval *chansons de geste* (and the division into two hemistichs of the sophisticated, sixteen-syllable verse). Its earliest origins can be traced to the rhapsodists of ancient Greece. The apogee in the River Plate pampas of this form of expression was initially represented by the anonymous *payador* and then by the urban poet: Exemplary exponents of this genre included Bartolomé Hidalgo (1788–1922) of Montevideo, Hilario Ascasubi (1807–1875) of Córdoba, Estanislao del Campo (1834–1880) of Buenos Aires, and José Hernández (1834–1886), also of Buenos Aires, whose *Martin Fierro* (1872, 1879) is regarded as the greatest representation of gaucho literature.

Typical gaucho themes included rebellion against injustice, praise of the vicissitudes of love, a deep sense of the vastness and beauty of natural landscapes, accounts of the fierce frontier wars against the Indians, patriotic rebellious passions about the internal struggles of the emerging republics, the magic of fantastic tales told around campfires, boasting of skill in horsemanship and roping, and predicting the weather by merely glancing at the sky; in short, these are poetic narratives of rough images in language that blends Spanish archaisms,

indigenous words, and neologisms. According to some critics, such as Rafael R. Rodríguez López, the proliferation of these themes "inspired a native form of mystical lyricism" (6). But without a doubt it was Rafael Obligado's (1851–1920) *Santos Vega*, based on the homonymous texts by Hilario Ascasubi and Bartolomé Mitre (1821–1906), that established the presence of the legendary personage based on a *payador* from Tuyú, in the province of Buenos Aires. Although his invincibility seemed diabolical, he was eventually defeated by an unknown young man, who was naturally the Devil himself or Modern Progress, according to an alternative interpretation that sees the poem as an allegory of the social conflict between the indigenous rural population in the open spaces of the Pampas and the large-scale European immigration. The immigrant farmer was a predictable victor at the end of the nineteenth and the beginning of the twentieth century; the introduction of the division of land into small plots; wire fencing, roads, electricity, and new work techniques within one generation made an anachronistic figure of the grave expert of the Pampas, the gaucho, once so indispensable. Yet as a myth, Santos Vega *el payador* is still alive and reappears periodically and mysteriously, instilling fear and respect in the peasants in the vast River Plate plains.

Mitre, the president of Argentina between 1862 and 1868, was an admirer of this mythic figure and wrote this poetic appraisal:

Santos Vega, tus cantares
no te han dado excelsa gloria
mas viven en la memoria
de la turba popular;
y sin tinta ni papel
que los salve del olvido,
de padre a hijo han venido
por la tradición oral.
Bardo inculto de la pampa,
como el pájaro canoro
tu canto rudo y sonoro
diste a la brisa fugaz
y tus versos se repiten
en el bosque y en el llano,
por el gaucho americano,
por el indio montaraz.
¿Qué te importa si en el mundo
tu fama no se pregona
con la rústica corona
del poeta popular?
Es más difícil que en bronce,
en el mármol o granito
haber tus obras escrito
en la memoria tenaz.

(quoted in Rodríguez López 109–116)

Santos Vega, your songs
have not given you great glory
yet they live in the memory
of the popular masses;
and with no ink or paper
to save them from oblivion,
they have been passed down from
father to son by the oral tradition.
Uncultured bard of the Pampas,
like the songbird,
your rough melodic song
you gave to the fleeting breeze
and your verses are repeated
in the forest and the plains,

by the American gaucho,
and the highland Indian.
What does it matter if in the
world, your fame is not proclaimed
with the rustic crown
of the popular poet?
Engraving your works in man's
stubborn memory took more than
it would have done to engrave
them in bronze, marble, or granite.

No works can be accurately ascribed to the mythical Santos Vega, he of great fame, who, according to legend, died of grief while singing of his love, like a bird in a tree, and strumming away furiously on his guitar. However, Mitre credited Obligado with the only verses attributed to the supposed *payador* of Tuyú, and these are reminiscent of a Spanish ballad.

In "La poesía gauchesca" [1932; Gaucho Poetry], Jorge Luis Borges held that the genre arose from nostalgic urban sentiment in Buenos Aires and Montevideo at the end of the nineteenth century, when the Wars of Independence (1810–1816), periods of internal anarchy (1829–1832 and 1835–1852), and finally the war against the Indians (1878–79) made the urban population identify with the idealized gauchos. Borges felt that the chance combination of these two vital cultures–the urban and the rural–and the astonishment that the one would produce epic heroics in the other, gave Argentina its first national expression: Gaucho literature. In 1969, Borges wrote in "Los gauchos" that:

> Hombres de la ciudad les fabricaron un dialecto y una poesía de metáforas rústicas. Pero también admitió, quizá contradictoriamente: [. . .] alguno, el escuchado, fue el payador. Cantaba sin premura, porque el alba tarda en clarear, y no alzaba la voz. Ciertamente no fueron aventureros, pero un arreo los llevaba muy lejos y más lejos las guerras. [. . .] No murieron por esa cosa abstracta, la patria, sino por un patrón casual, una ira o por la invitación de un peligro. Su ceniza está perdida en remotas regiones del continente, en repúblicas de cuya historia nada supieron, en campos de batalla, hoy famosos. (Borges 1974, 1001–2)

> Men of the city had invented a dialect for them, together with a form of poetry with rustic metaphors. Yet . . . the one who was listened to was the *payador*. He sang without haste, because it took a long time from dusk to dawn, and he did not raise his voice. They [the gauchos] were by no means adventurers, but rounding up cattle took them a long way from home and wars, even further. They did not die for an abstract cause, the fatherland, but rather because of a casual encounter, a fit of anger or a challenge to their honor. Their ashes are scattered in the remote regions of the continent, in republics of whose history they knew nothing and in battlefields that are now famous.

Martín Fierro by José Hernández (see **Figure 1**) is perhaps one of the few books in the history of Argentinean literature that was sold at the end of the last century in grocery stores together with sugar, maté, maize, and lentils. For decades, "I'll have a kilo of *maté* and a *Martín Fierro*," was the standard request of a massive clientele that showed little inclination for highbrow literature yet was immune to the barely disguised contempt behind the condescending praise that prestigious literary historians felt obliged to bestow on popular genres such as gaucho literature. Behind the poetic form with its rules of rhyme and metrics, *Martín Fierro* essentially constitutes a sort of sung narrative of an epic nature, although it differs from classic epics in that it is the story of a fugitive gaucho who lacks heroic stature and who is not favored by divine

Figure 1.

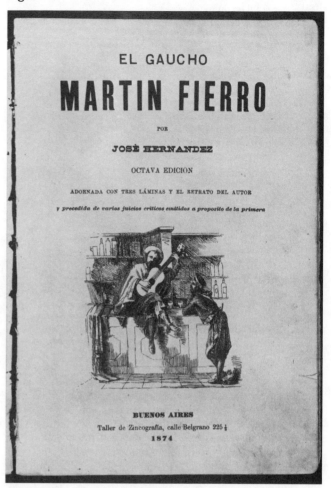

Photograph of cover 1874 8th edition of Martin Fierro (1872).
(Courtesy of John P. Robarts Research Library, University of Toronto)

intervention or a high political position. His simple descriptions of rural happiness–prior to the army levies to wage their campaigns to exterminate the Indians–are beautiful. The verse form most commonly used by Hernández is the sextet with octosyllabic lines and the following rhyme scheme: The first line is unrhymed; the second, third, and sixth lines rhyme; and the fourth and fifth lines have rhyming endings and sometimes rhyme within the verse.

The rapid urbanization of the Southern Cone, beginning with the development of Buenos Aires and Montevideo, radiating out from the River Plate areas and including Santiago on the other side of the Andes, coincided with the macroorganization of the modern state in Argentina, Chile, and Uruguay in the late nineteenth and early twentieth century. Against the background of an agricultural boom, together with the expansion of trade and industry, overwhelming demographic and technological changes accompanied enormous waves of immigrants, primarily from various European countries. This produced a mixture of races and cultures similar to that recorded in the United States as a result of the flow of immigrants that arrived in the port of New York during the same period. At the same time, the railroad had caused a veritable rural revolution, leading to an incipient managerial structure on the farms and a population shift from the countryside to the cities.

In the River Plate, one of the most striking results in the cultural sphere was the emergence of the tango–a sad thought that is danced, according to the poet and musician Enrique Santos Discépolo (1901–1951). In just over a century of existence, tango culture went through a number of stages. Initially it was purely instrumental music (the flute and the guitar), but subsequently it was sung. The history of the River Plate tango goes back to its Afro–Latin American roots, linking it to the *habanera,* the *milonga,* and the *candomble.* It was influenced by Andalusian dance music and the folk songs of the Pampas, as well as by the contributions of the immigrants, particularly Spanish and Italian, culminating in the inclusion of instruments such as the piano, the large accordion, and the violin. It subsequently developed into a concert genre with composers of the stature of Astor Piazzolla. And as far as the lyrics were concerned, forms and topics ranged from its initial playful picaresque structure to the high urban poetry of the 1930s, 1940s, and 1950s. Although the existence of tangos was recorded twelve years earlier, the oldest score to have been preserved is *El Talar,* by the Buenos Aires composer Prudencia Aragón, dated 1895. *La morocha,* with music by the Uruguayan Enrique Saborido and lyrics by the Argentine Angel Villoldo, was the first tango to have been sung, probably in about 1905. The tango was born in the brothels that existed to offset the lack of a female population; until approximately 1925, in other words during its first thirty or forty years of existence, the tango was a synonym of scandal, crime, and sin. It originally expanded on the outskirts of Buenos Aires and Montevideo, home to both lowlifes and the poorer of the city. It was nurtured in the suburbs, in tenement houses lit by kerosene lamps, in boardinghouse rooms, and in the humble dwellings where large families lived in cramped surroundings while the mothers cooked and the fathers had very little room to rest at the end of their working day. In the beginning, however, the tango's lyrics avoided the everyday life of the proletarian shantytowns, focusing instead on the experiences of marginality.

The brothel and lowlife origins of the tango did nothing to prevent its involvement, from the outset, with all the popular classes constituting the new River Plate population: Blacks who had survived Colonial slavery, the Wars of Independence, and internal wars that broke out during the nineteenth century; working-class men, who challenged each other in knife fights (whose movements prefigured dance); farm laborers driven from the countryside by modernization; and European immigrants, who, from the start, were imbued with a nostalgia for a vanished past. In time, the mythology of low-life marginalization lost ground within the sphere of tango poetry, while Lunfardo (River Plate slang) gained currency, as shown by the Buenos Aires poet Dante A. Linyera, whose real name was Francisco Bautista Rimoli (1902–1938).

The themes of the tango knew no limits, since they range from stories and portraits of important personages to urban and rural landscapes and reflections on the intimacy of feelings–in other words, a collage of local scenes, together with a profession of faith in what identity in a marginalized state should be. In 1923, Celedonio Flores (1896–1947) sang the praises of a new institution, the bachelor's flat, the refuge of lovers, friends, and tango-loving bohemians. There was also a rural version of tango lyrics that spoke of horses and the Pampas, as in *El cuarteador* by Enrique Cadícamo (b. 1906), who, after 1924, cultivated every possible version of the tango. Tango lyrics acquired an elevated status from the

1920s onward, when they began to incorporate a broad range of themes and stylistic motifs and resources that interacted with creative developments of music. Discépolo brought to tango a satirical, skeptical, straightforward, and even crude vision of his times that is sometimes strikingly contemporary, as in *Cambalache* (1935). Cátulo Gonzáles Castillo (1906–1975), wrote the heartrending lyrics of *La última curda,* in which drunkenness is a metaphor for despair and repeated failure in life. Another poet, Homero Manzi (1905–1951), painted an affectionate portrait of the Buenos Aires slums of the 1950s. With its enormous musical and literary richness, the tango transcends the framework of a popular genre. It is a means of coping with life, a view of the world that permeates everyday life and is omnipresent in the culture and poetry of the River Plate.

Other contemporary trends in the literary orality of the Southern Cone are drawn from folk production and the collection of urban songs of more recent origin. The Argentine Atahualpa Yupanqui (1908–1992), composer, guitarist, and singer, whose *Coplas del payador perseguido* [Couplets of the Pursued *Payador*] provide an up-to-date view of the genre, links his work to a message of social transformation. The tragic life of the Uruguayan Eduardo Mateo (1940–1990), entrapped by addictions and madness, produced two records regarded as classics, *Mateo sólo bien se lame* (1971) and *Mateo y Trasante* (1976). Another Uruguayan, Jaime Roos (b. 1953), composed *murga* (rhythmic carnival music) lyrics for voice, choir, and guitars accompanied by snare drums, bass drums, and cymbals. Called *Los olímpicos,* an ironic allusion to the Olympic football titles won by Uruguay in Colombes (Paris, 1924) and Amsterdam (1928), it speaks of the separations and perplexities of exile caused by the Southern Cone military dictatorships of the 1970s and 1980s. The late 1960s and early 1970s in Buenos Aires saw the emergence of a new popular urban genre that, for lack of a better term, was called progressive rock. Its lyrics reflected a new youth culture that unconsciously re-created its links with the past and the tradition of affirming an original identity. Although it was a local version of a world phenomenon, the existence of that oral historical background lent these productions a distinct musical and literary identity far removed from the imitations of successful groups that arose in other parts of the world.

Toward a New Orality

The last hundred years have seen an extraordinary worldwide increase in technologies, experiences, and instruments that, either directly or indirectly, have fostered dynamism and a dynamic role for orality in human communications and linked its characteristics, levels, and registers of language to those of the traditional literature of the academic world, libraries, bookshops, and groups of artists and intellectuals. Given the globalization of development in industrialized societies and large modern cities, this process is part of the emergence and increasing coverage of the new mass media and is related to the fact that the printed word is disseminated on a mass scale as a result of newspapers and the development of the publishing industry in general; furthermore, we have telephones, photography, record players, films (first silent, then talking), radios, tape recorders, television, satellites, and global information networking in real time through computers, to mention just some of the best-known factors cultures must deal with. If the visual, individual, silent reading of written texts has been a generalized habit for a mere two centuries (see Margit Frenk 1996), and if this relatively recent practice coexisted for centuries with reading aloud, singing, and recitation (before which reading was almost predominantly for oral performance), we should acknowledge and then analyze the fact that, at the beginning of this millennium under completely new circumstances we are not only experiencing the era of the image, as certain theoreticians such as Marshall McLuhan have pointed out, but also the re-emergence of a new form of orality.

It is a well-known fact that cultures with primary orality (in other words, those with no writing system) constituted the vast majority throughout history and that, in the remaining cultures, reading was virtually always the privilege of a fairly small group of elites, as continues to be the case throughout much of the world today. In ancient Greece and Rome, public and private places and buildings were devoted to reading aloud to "auditoriums" full of people. St. Augustin, a disciple of St. Ambrose, the bishop of Milan in 384, expressed concern in his *Confessions* at the unusual sight of the master in his cell, with a book, reading in silence, without articulating a single word. At the time, it was common to read aloud to grasp the meaning better, since there were no punctuation marks or even word divisions, and people also read aloud *together* to offset the problem of the scarcity of books. "The voice, with its material presence, lent meaning to a writing that, without it, was a dead letter," (4) says Frenk. And she adds that "the gestural and vocal expressiveness of the reader, reciter, or singer was equally important" (4). As late as the nineteenth century, the German poet Johann Wolfgang von Goethe used to say that "writing constitutes a poor use of language; reading to oneself in silence a poor substitute for spoken language" (qtd. in Frenk 3).

Yet, whereas in the past writing was the only way of preserving what speech and memory failed to capture (as in the Latin phrase *verba volant, scripta manent* [words fly, writing remains]), the situation today has changed radically. Given the new contemporary realities and technologies, one should seek to reassess the experience of orality–improvisation, the art of conversation, recitation, the sung word, reading aloud, and the general hearing of oral or written texts–considering all the varied and complex implications that phenomenon possesses. Readers of the past were, in fact, listeners, and those of today or of the near future often are or will be, perhaps increasingly so, listeners once again. This is shown, among other things, by the proliferation of literary circles, workshops, presentations, recitals, recordings, and literary radio and television spots that occupy an increasingly significant portion of the real consumption of texts by the mass public.

It is important to realize that texts meant for reading aloud, singing, or recitation are not written in the same way as those intended to be read in silence, with visual contact between a person and a text. It is one thing to write a text thinking of the sound of the words and making its structure and energy felt by an audience whose reception proceeds without interruption, with no possibility of returning to the previous paragraph, and quite another to work with the reliability, consistency, and ease of consultation of an object-book. Within this dichotomy, factors that come into play include the values of variety (in form and content), the linear and episodic structure of narrations where appropriate, the recourse to repetitions and redundancies to consolidate the text and make it accessible, and the search for a variety of effects in order to maintain the reader's or the audience's attention.

Frenk notes that at the physiological level no reading or writing is completely silent, and she quotes Alfonso Reyes (1889–1959) (*Tres puntos de exegética literaria* 1962): "*The ear, the larynx and the tongue . . .* internally perceive a phonetic repercussion, a movement and rhythm in verbal sequences" (3).

The oral is, whether or not we are aware of this, consubstantial with our experience as readers or writers because a text that is written or read (in one way or another) always includes a spoken or imagined sound. Specialists have measured the degree of tiredness of the vocal chords during these activities even when the voice is not used. A recent, positive result has been the revaluation of orality in the teaching of reading and writing. Orality and literature are as inseparable as speech and writing. To a certain extent, all literature is oral because it includes language read, whereas all orality contains, to a greater or lesser extent, literary elements by virtue of the poetic dimension inevitably involved in any linguistic act.

Translation by Suzanne D. Stephens

Works Cited

Ambrosetti, Juan Bautista. 1947. *Supersticiones y leyendas (Región misionera, valles calchaquíes, las pampas)*. Buenos Aires: Lautaro.

Antón, Danilo J. 1996. *Uruguaypirí*. Montevideo: Rosebud Ediciones.

Ascasubi, Hilario. 1955. *Santos Vega*. Buenos Aires: Editorial Jackson.

Barrios Pintos, Aníbal. 1958. *Los aborígenes del Uruguay*. Montevideo: Editorial Linardi y Risso.

Bernal, John Desmond. 1971. *Science in History*. Vol 1: The *Emergence of Science*. 4 Vols. Cambridge: MIT Press.

Borges, Jorge Luis. 1974. "Fundación mítica de Buenos Aires." *Jorge Luis Borges: Obras Completas*. Buenos Aires: Emecé Editores. 81.

———. 1974. "Los gauchos." *Jorge Luis Borges: Obras Completas*. Buenos Aires: Emecé Editores. 1001–2.

———. 1974. "La poesía gauchesca." *Jorge Luis Borges: Obras Completas*. Buenos Aires: Emecé Editores. 179–197.

Cadogan, León and Alfredo López Austin. 1978. *La literatura de los guaraníes*. 3d ed. Mexico City: Editorial Joaquín Mortiz, S.A.

Cancioneros. Letras de tango de José González Castillo, Cátulo Castillo, Celedonio Flores, Enrique Santos Discépolo, Homero Manzi y Enrique Cadícamo. 1977. Buenos Aires: Torres Agüero Editor.

Del Campo, Estanislao. 1942. *Fausto*. Buenos Aires: Editorial Guillermo Kraft.

Díaz de Guzmán, Ruy. 1882 [1612]. *Argentina, historia del descubrimiento, conquista y población del Río de la Plata*. Buenos Aires: C. Casavalle Editor.

Ercilla y Zúñiga, Alonso de. 1945. *Araucana: The Epic of Chile*. Trans. Walter Owen. Vol 2. Buenos Aires: Walter Owen.

Fernández Garay, Ana. 1994. *Testimonios de los últimos Tehuelches*. Buenos Aires: Instituto de Lingüística, Facultad de Filosofía y Letras, Universidad de Buenos Aires.

——— and Lucía Golluscio. 1978. "Rogativas araucanas." *VICUS Cuadernos, Lingüística II*. 103–32.

Frenk, Margit. 1996. "La lectura silenciosa y la lectura en voz alta." *Espacios* 2: 2–4.

Geertz, Clifford. 1981. *La interpretación de las culturas*. Madrid: Gedisa.

Ginzburg, Carlo. 1983. "Señales, raíces de un paradigma indiciario." *Crisis de la razón. Nuevos modelos en la relación entre saber y actividades humanas*. Ed. Aldo Gargani et al. Mexico City: Siglo XXI Editores. 55–99.

Hernández, José. 1978. *Martín Fierro*. Mexico City: Editores Mexicanos Unidos.

Jakobson, Roman. 1975. "Lingüística y poética." *Ensayo de lingüística general*. Trans. Josep Pujol and Jem Cabanes. Barcelona: Seix Baral. 347–95.

Mansilla, Lucio Victorio. 1955. *Una excursión a los indios ranqueles.* Buenos Aires: Editorial Jackson.

——. 1994. *Mis memorias y otros escritos.* Buenos Aires: Secretaria de Cultura de la Nación y Editorial Lugar.

Mateo, Eduardo. 1990. "Mateo sólo bien se lame." *Mateo clásico.* Vol. I, CD. Montevideo: Sondor.

——. 1990. "Mateo Trasante." *Mateo clásico.* Vol. I, CD. Montevideo: Sondor.

McLuhan, Marshall. 1962. *The Gutenberg Galaxy.* Toronto: University of Toronto Press.

Rex González, Alberto and José A. Pérez. 1976. *Argentina indígena en vísperas de la conquista.* Buenos Aires: Paidós.

Reyes, Alfonso. 1962. *La experiencia literaria: tres puntos de exegética literaria.* Vol. 14. *Obras completas.* 26 vols. Mexico City: Fondo de Cultura Económica.

Rimoli, Francisco Bautista [Dante A. Linyera]. 1980. *Autobiografía rasposa.* Buenos Aires: Torres Agüero Editor.

Robertson, William. 1840. *Historia de la América.* Barcelona: Edición Olivares.

Rodríguez López, Rafael R. 1943. Introduction and notes. *La poesía gauchesca en lengua culta.* Ed. Esteban Echeverría, Bartolomé Mitre, Juan María Gutiérrez and Rafael Obligado. Buenos Aires: Ciorda and Rodríguez Editores.

Roos, Jaime. 1992. *Selección 1.* CD. Montevideo: Mediocampo Producciones.

Salas, Adalberto. 1984. *Textos orales en mapuche o araucano del Centro–Sur de Chile.* Concepción: Editorial de la Universidad de Concepción.

Salas, Horacio. 1968. *La poesía de Buenos Aires: ensayo y antología.* Buenos Aires: Pleamar.

Schmidel, Ulrico. 1986. *Relatos de la conquista del Río de la Plata y Paraguay 1534–1554.* Trans. Klaus Wagner. Madrid: Alianza Editorial.

Seibel, Beatriz, ed. 1988. *El cantar del payador.* Buenos Aires: Ediciones del Sol.

CHAPTER 50

ORAL LITERATURE IN BRAZIL

Jerusa Pires Ferreira

It is urgent that the history of "oral literature" in Brazil be undertaken so that the richness and complexity of its oral genres, so lively and vigorous, can be understood. They constitute a living memory, as well as a continuous process of creation, re-creation, and adaptation by diverse cultural segments. Right from the start, there is a paradox: "literature" in this case means process, creation, and art, as well as a history of the printed word; "oral" refers to a condition, a poetics, a fate, a circuit, and a universe (including the oral/written aspects or a mixed orality), and to the vitality of a transmission of voice and gesture. We must therefore deal with both a history of dates and facts as well as a history of the paths of folk manifestations in Brazil at the turn of the last century. Yet, we are also confronted by a dynamic storehouse of memory that cannot be dated, a reserve whose origin is lost in the most remote of times. It has its own imaginary organization, with its own coherence, but often its principles of time-and-space construction seem chaotic by our standards of written texts.

In a country such as Brazil that came to literacy rather late and is still not completely literate, and given a colonial society with little printed material (the delays caused by social inequalities of various kinds), the role played by oral creation and transmission could only be strong; this is territory favorable to the development and continuity of the poetics of the voice. If we consider the vast distances and thus the regions that remained isolated, as well as the harsh conditions in which communities survived, and if we observe the cultural production of groups that are marginal to any kind of knowledge that requires reading and the other apparatuses of contemporary life, we find a Brazilian cultural imaginary that established itself and fully developed in oral culture. It joined together elements of many cultures–African, European, and Native American– and allowed, at its own pace, for the creation of a poetics to deal with this traditional legacy and the continuous creation and re-creation of "oral genres," which are transmitted by voice (or in some cases by writing that subsequently results in an oral presentation). In the oral tradition, the speaking human body is the *sine qua non*, as is the listening public that has knowledge of the repertory and the ways of performing it.

The Oral Genres

In order to situate the many possibilities that form an oral poetics, we can follow the complex plotting of the cultural imaginary as manifested through memory and performance. Throughout the years I have done research in this area, some points that have merited greater attention may serve as a kind of unifying magnet to avoid the dispersal, given such complexity: (1) the notion of matrix–which accounts for the several stages in the creation of the oral text, taking into account the processes and supports of orality and of printing; (2) the study of the construction of dialogues–in which speech acts are studied, whether in the oral to printed text or in the printed to oral one; and (3) the identification of several types of memory, the stability of certain forms, the intricate games of oral exchange, and most important, the process that determines what is selected or rejected, what is kept or discarded.

In accordance with the research of Paul Zumthor (1983, 1987), I began to observe the complexity of oral poetics, rejecting the notion of a simple formulaic embryo, of a single cell that repeats itself and thus accounts for an entire poetics. Inevitably I moved from studying the most prototypical and recurrent types of situations to observe how orality is re-created, conveyed, and made present, through gestures and the communicative energies of the body at a given social moment that involves actors and spectators with very distinct roles. If we refer to an archetypal construction that retains and transmits themes and prototypical, repetitive forms of expression, and if there are memories that crystallize certain genres of oral poetic expression (much more naturally formalized than the genres of written literature, because if they were not formalized, they would not have remained a part of memory), we must also pay attention to the dynamics, the mobility, and the nomadic nature of a kind of trans-memory. This is a creative circulation that makes each sequence, spoken aloud, go beyond the limits of genres and of definite forms and builds a link between lived time and that time that has shifted in memory. As we examine the continuity of oral forms, we must not ignore the relations between folk production and the groups that dominate the traditional cultures that are now undergoing rapid and profound changes.

We must acknowledge the miserable living conditions of people from the country migrating to the urban centers–isolated people in the big cities–where there is a loss of the sense of community and of a common culture. These cultural deprivations are what Lotman defines as non-culture (Lotman et al. 1975, 39–40). He refers to all that is not transformed into a patrimony of signs, a void that cannot be filled and that causes even the memory of genres to be lost, along with the expression of a poetic quality with which a culture is identified and that is its cohesive force. We can then recognize the significance of the memory of these genres and their transmission of a cumulative cultural legacy that provides a sense of community. Another important point is the relevance of an oral/written folk literature: The *cordel*, which is directly associated with its European origins and therefore functions at the same time as a universal and regional creation, an elaborate imaginary that cannot be traced beyond the last century and that constantly inserts the contemporary. We must also look at oral registers (e.g., song, ritual performance, local history, etc.), which, considering their place in historical time, will help us see these oral texts as important documents for the study of social life and the utopian or transforming projects revealed in folk creation and transmitted by oral literature.

Mythopoeics: Story and Chapbook; *Cordel* Literature

Here we will examine the mythic universe that flourishes in the narration of stories of wonder or enchantment, which contain an archeological repertory that refers back to the Indo-European narratives and have become today's oral folk stories–and, ultimately, the *folhetos* (chapbooks) that apprehend, adapt, and re-create these various themes. Yet, to study the oral folk story (so alive and active in Brazil) means to face many mysteries that go from the construction and continuation of complex cosmogonies to the performative act that is constituted by hearers and sharers of that art and, above all, the continuous insertion of common everyday practices that continue to be passed on in these treasures of human experience. In order to situate the folk story in the general territory of orality, we must note the perpetuation of situations associated with various rites and rhythms of social life, with nature, the agrarian world, and a whole new order that diminishes the gap between the individual and the collective, the social and the cosmic. This may seem like an abstraction, but little by little we can discern that in many parts of the world there are similar themes, topics, and processes, as if there were one great text hovering over it all, a sort of virtual narrative that, at a given moment, emerges and modernizes itself. This hypothetical great text, however, demands a living presence, a performance, and a heritage of the folk tale, brought to Brazil by the colonizers. This performance gives new meaning to what was given to the culture that re-creates it–offering contemporary challenges, complex mixtures of elements, choices of the storyteller, and solutions to local problems. What has been called an oral tale, a tale of enchantment, or magic and later a fairy tale–through various mediations–presents differences within its surprising unity, differences that subtly mark the individual, an inscribing of the historical into the mythical body, in the search for something fundamental to be transmitted. The tale in this world of orality bears the traces of many inscriptions, of successive stages of oral/written/printed transmission. The power of the storyteller must be emphasized here, the one whom traditional ethnology inadequately named the "informant," and before whom we are in awe, whether in the backlands of Brazil or in the cities. Intersemiosis, vocality, and the gestural are all combined to reach the senses of the hearers and participants through the transmission of stories that bring together children and adults and that allow the community to share a common tradition.

The art of storytelling is still very much alive in Brazil, as elsewhere. It is worth mentioning, however, that there is a remarkable exchange that takes place among oral texts. Some stories originate in ancient folk tales and often come together in the unexplained junction of many fragments of stories that somehow cling together. In this way, one story is transformed into another and so on, in succession, by parts of collective memory at play and by the demand for local compatibility (which makes one choice more viable than another). Here we are dealing with maintaining a repertory that, in a certain way, belongs to all and is a kind of meta-art: To tell a story is to make oneself heard and known, whereas hearing a story is to re-create what, more often than not, one has already heard and mastered. We cannot forget the work of compilation and writing on the part of the great collectors of the oral tale–Perrault, Anderson, Grimm, Afanassiev, Adolfo Coelho, Sílvio Romero, or Câmara Cascudo. Oral tales were passed on in the images and words of anthologies, in books transmitted to children, which in turn became printed matrices of oral storytelling (see Pires Ferreira 1995; 1997). They are, in turn, the point of departure for new oral creations. What seems important then is that these narrative arts fill great spaces in the imagination of the groups from which they originate, as well as in the modern imagination, preparing us for the challenges that await us. In them we find the power of the dialogue

between the universal and the regional in a creative, dramatic, and human process that explains, at this start of the new millennium, the continuing popularity of the storyteller.

There have been several attempts at classifying *cordel* chapbooks, notably the Casa de Rui Barbosa catalogue (1973). Those collections offer a poetics of the quotidian as transmitted by the chapbooks; this is a poetics of the most striking events (disasters, etc.) and as such can also be considered a kind of folk journalism. The situations that were considered more relevant in the life of a community are those that found their way into the chapbooks. As in the ancient literature of Europe, droughts, the visits of illustrious people, disasters, accidents, or any other unexpected event becomes part of tradition and is inherited and crystallized in repertories of immediate and striking events. It is impossible to underestimate the communicative function of such folk poetry since it processes the exceptionality and impact of news that capture hearers and generate new creations.

The Narrative Cycles

Cavalcanti Proença has claimed that medieval narrative cycles are still alive in Brazilian oral and folk poetry. The heroic deeds of Charlemagne and his peers are very popular and indeed omnipresent in the rural culture of Brazil. The printed text of the novella *A história do Imperador Carlos Magno* [The History of the Emperor Charlemagne] is a kind of countertext that determined the meaning of many oral texts, as I have tried to show in *Cavalaria em Cordel* [Chivalry in *Cordel*] (Pires Ferreira 1993). As for the popularity of the Arthurian cycle in the *cordel*, the notion of a courtly heroism is evident in tales of enchantment, mysterious combat, and the confronting of danger–all part of the Brazilian cultural imaginary (Pires Ferreira 1991, 53). In this scenario we also see enacted relations with the other world and the restoration of a threatened peace. Though these elements are part of the European courtly tradition, heroic deeds, mysteries, and evil confrontations constitute some of the most active aspects of this memory transmitted through writing/orality. So we have Lampião, Antônio Silvino, and Lucas da Feira (1807?–1849). In the same way, using narrative elements as similar in form as they are different in detail, we have the mythopoetic creation of the devout, of saints and holinesses, as in the well-known case of Padre Cícero and Padre Damião, whose lives have generated a number of oral texts. Political figures, such as Getúlio Vargas, Tancredo Neves (though to a lesser degree), or Juscelino Kubitschek, are portrayed in the manner of Lampião or Silvino, confronting the Last Judgment, which brings them to realms well beyond the rural world that hearken back to sects of medieval Christianity or ancient Gnosticism with São Pedro (Saint Peter) as the key figure.

The composition of narrative cycles that evoke the medieval world, knights in combat, and the courtly universe–all that is associated with glorious adventure–effectively dispels the frustration of the real. Another cycle one must not overlook is that of a *Teufel literatur*, an oral literature in which the devil represents a supernatural power that is everywhere. There is a cycle of deceived devil stories (Pires Ferreira 1996, 23), in which pacts, formulas for outwitting the devil, and certain tricks take us back to the picaresque and to trickster figures. When told aloud, these stories have a visual appeal, corroborated by countless pictures that contrast, for instance, the devil with saints, or that typify the apparition that has turned into an icon: The devil as a gentleman of means, a terrifying figure combining power and evil. Deeply rooted in fixed dialogue and in scenes that touch the religious world and at the same time are anchored in the picaresque, in deceit and malice, this figure is both an oral creation and an example of pure theatricality.

I have a sound recording of a blind woman who performed, to an extraordinary beat, Francisco de Sales Areda's (b. 1916) chapbook *O Ferreiro da Maldição* [n.d.; The Evil Blacksmith], a kind of Faust legend in which Promethean disobedience is incited. What comes to the rescue of the pact-maker is the eternal feminine, *A Compadecida* [The Compassionate], one of the most striking figures of the medieval tradition, who lives on in the backlands. The performance of a text-memoir such as this one emphasizes the ability of performing with a local accent that makes us realize the centuries of tradition and culture based on a kind of unity between the one who speaks and the one who receives the enunciation. In it we find together the oral folk tale and its re-creation in performance.

Naturally, when speaking of orality one must consider Mikhael Bakhtin's theory about the world of laughter. Parody, farce, buffoonery, and jokes all work to turn the real into the comic in a most lively poetic performance. This world reverses and subverts the heroic and the religious and, in my opinion, directly complements it. Although I acknowledge the importance of Bahktin's theory, I disagree with him when he claims that parody degrades the sublime (1974, 250). I prefer to remove the notion of degradation from the buffoon or from the excessive and obscene. Parody is often almost an aspect of the religious, in the same way that the sacred and the profane appear together in most rituals. Obscene pamphlets such as *História de João Demarcado* [The Story of João Demarcado], in which the hero fills the town with rivers of laughter, are indicators of very ancient rites. In others, one finds the comic, witty comments, or the occasional grotesque image. The origin of the Rabelaisian mode described by Bakhtin can be found in this folk universe and appears disguised in riddles and puns. Thus we have, for instance, an author that uses the signature H. Romeu and a title like *O Escravo que comeu sinhô* [The Slave Who Ate the Master] (Cuíca de Santo Amaro). One of the recurrent themes of this oral literature continues into the chapbook literature printed in São Paulo, for example, the texts of Boccaccio's *Decameron*, present in this tradition since Colonial times, as Câmara Cascudo demonstrates (1952, 189). What is interesting is how these circulate in the mobile oral genre clustered, condensed, or enlarged into one great text with various repertoires, like those of circus clowns. Some of them even become connected to adventures joining the comic to the sublime or evil. A whole universe, based in the *cordel*, oral folk tales, and the fragments of ritual languages, waits to be explored.

Romanceiro: The Narrative Song Collection

The romance has two contexts in this folk literature. The first is a broad one, related to the original meaning of the word (on which modern fiction is based), with elements like those of the great adventures of the courtly romances—in which case we speak of a romance chapbook, that is, one that tells a story in verse. A second designation is the traditional romance, a dramatized oral genre, spoken and sung, that experienced a unique development in the Iberian Peninsula, and in America achieved its full promise. This is deeply anchored in oral memory, in dramatic situations that contain fragments of tragedies or epic poems that were divided up and whose parts

gained their own autonomy, or even historical themes or parts of themes that continued their course, of transmission by word of mouth, in an incredible number of versions—as is the case of the romances *Juliana e D. Jorge* [Juliana and Don Jorge], *Conde Claros* [Count Claros], and *Donzela que vai à guerra* [The Maid Who Went to War], among many others. This material has been collected by folklorists and today is collected by researchers in cultural anthropology. In Brazil, the work of Bráulio do Nascimento is exemplary. However, there is still much to be collected.

Oral memory reconstructs, through tales and drama, old collections that would otherwise be lost. In memory and in song one finds human situations in which death, treachery, betrayal, and heroic deeds play a crucial role—a repertory of tragic situations, from martyrdom to incest or punishment to miracles, in these wonderful little dramatic pieces perpetuated in oral form. The *romanceiro* played an important role in the development of Brazilian literature for poets such as Cecília Meireles (1901–1965) or João Cabral de Melo Neto (1920–1999), who realized the power of this dramatic construction.

Prophecy

Prophecy is one of the most recurrent and popular types of oral poetry. In prophecy there is an exaggerated performance of the speech act, with a whimsical touch of divination. In prophecy, the future is predicted and the present is rendered as either apocalypse or a new beginning of another world to be restored, recomposed, or made just. Prophecy is one type of poetic creation of orality that takes over the popular realm and serves as the basis for its speeches and projects. It exists, therefore, in the dramatization of the voices—in recordings as well as in poetic texts, religious pamphlets, or narratives that echo the words of children still in their mothers' wombs or the voices of animals to warn us of a coming disaster. There is one prophecy put in the mouth of Antônio Conselheiro, leader of the Canudos Messianic movement, that is an intrinsic part of Brazilian culture. In it, nature is reversed: He says that the backlands will turn into sea, the sea into the backlands. Within this prophecy there is something that is inherent to the form: Utopian expectation, the desire for social justice.

The *cordel* chapbook, a printed genre of mixed orality written from a large repertory of oral matrices of the imaginary in which historical time is also inscribed, gathers together both the collective imagination and the personal construction of facts. In this case, we could say that, to a certain extent, it restores a kind of "vocigraphy," the echoes of voices associated with prophetic utterances: The recordings of people such as Antônio Conselheiro, for instance, whose voice was persuasive and somehow reached the soul without going through the mind. In fact, this is the field proper in which to explore the visionary quality of the voice in its restored dimension: From so many re-created and retold texts voices that were silenced are heard again, and energies are evoked that were once excited and then crushed. As we evoke them, we bring close to us the intensity of the conflicts in which they were involved. We cannot forget that voices, or group chants, are parts of sacrificial rites ranging from utopia to prophecy and are heirs to millenary imaginary constructions and convey a particular way of representing the world and therefore essentially inciting rebellion. Associated with this universe are the sacred practices, the prayers, and the chants, which, as they are performed, embody a religious belief and a celebration of life, an exorcism of death in the same way that, in rituals of death, the chants of the praise add to the celebration, carnivalize death, and confer on it the pursuit of the desired life, a continuous banquet, a utopic world of general well being, and life lived to the full as a response to death.

The World of Proverbs and the Worlds of Riddles

Both the proverb-world and that which, to a certain extent, is its opposite—the riddle-world—display a complementary relation of opposition that is indispensable to the universe of traditional orality and chapbooks. In one we find realization, in the other, doubt. In one there is a discovery, in the other, a search. The power of the well-established proverb is present in the poetics of the oral; in fact, the proverb has great poetic potential. The saying, the ready-made sentence, and the formulas of courtesy all carry a philosophical tone and often transmit the rhetorical legacy of the Baroque. This aphoristic proverbial matrix follows from several oral genres, at times balancing, delaying action, creating pauses, or even legitimating that which fabrication could not itself legitimate. In the Northeastern *cordel romance* (*romance* here meaning a story in verse, a collection of sententious sayings) is an inseparable component of the narrative. We recall, thanks to Auerbach's work (1950, 11) on Goethe and Schiller, that such sayings have an effect—related to performance and to the rendering and the fruition of the narrative—of delaying or of inserting a pause in the narrative action. They delay the action. In terms of the verse, they also have the function of marking rhythm and pauses. Greimas (1976, 208) made an observation that seems to me rather important when one thinks of how sayings and reflections are handled in the poetics of the oral: He noted that these expressions clearly distinguish themselves from the whole by means of a difference in performance. According to this view the speaker seems to abandon his or her own voice and borrows another, as if offering a citation. In the case of folk literature in verse, in *cordel* chapbooks the insertion of sayings and teachings confers mobility (contrary to what one might think) and helps avoid monotony. A recording of the reading of these poems by popular readers, and hearing them as they are repeated and read (that is, chanted) by the poets that composed them would be very enlightening.

When dealing with collective memory, we should mention the importance of what are called the "ABCs" as texts that link and condense information. Whether in the oral romance or in the printed pamphlet, the ABC represents a summary of repertories and documents that records details of social practices, contextualizes historical moments, and offers a prototype for recurrent facts or established practices. Ranging from epic to lyric themes (such as the ABCs of the Kiss or Love), these works narrate as well the successes or failures of economic trends—the ABC of Coffee. The writer Jorge Amado (1912–2001), in his popular novel *Tereza Batista* (1972), knows how to take advantage of the proverbial and allegorical tradition by creating his ABC of Bexiga, in which he tells the story of the plague in Buquim. The engravings of Calasans Neto correspond to the text that has been re-created from tradition in a quite correct way. On the other hand, there is the power of the games of deciphering, that is, the power of riddles, divinations, tongue twisters, puzzles, and children's games that we have also inherited. The world of gambling enters here with the numbers and their hidden meaning and the spatialization (geometry) of the body and gestures. As Julio Cortázar

(1914–1984) recalls in *Rayuela* [1963, *Hopscotch*], an entire exercise of memory is transformed into a wealth of language and a universe that unveils damnation (hell) or salvation (heaven). Charades, riddles, and divinations are practices that maintain themselves beyond the world of letters. In the texts of *Tutaméia* (1968), João Guimarães Rosa (1908–1967) was aware of this complexity. The *cordel* chapbooks gradually recover and assert the complexity of the games permeating the poetics of the oral, ranging from the world of incantations to the fascination with the unknown that was concealed and is through these texts transmitted or revealed. Another genre that also belongs to the religious world and more concretely to the history of sermons and examples are fables, edifying stories that appear in the pamphlets as *Trancosos;* (the name is an allusion to the Portuguese Gonçalo Fernandes Trancoso [1515–1596?] and his stories of instruction and example). Pamphlets of the mythical, which have a religious aim and present a moral, were called *Trancosos* by Luzeiro Publishers in São Paulo; among them, we find *O Ferreiro das Três Idades* [1980; The Blacksmith of the Three Ages], which tells of a pact made with the devil. To the general public, the term *trancoso* refers to this kind of collection of fables.

Singing

The song is one of the most recurrent genres in oral literature around the world, and it involves expertise and competence in the verbal simulation of combat, of men and voices engaged in verbal confrontation. Associated once with journeys in the backlands that included overnight stays in masters' houses, as Luis da Camara Cascudo (1898–1986) affirms (166) in his memorable *Vaqueiros e cantadores* [1984; Cowboys and Singers]. These songs that originated in rural Brazil have moved to cities and the realm of telecommunications and are now used for all kinds of purposes, such as political propaganda or commercials. All over Brazil, whether in the rustic backland or the gaucho world, the confrontation of voices and the challenge of wit take place and now are recorded and preserved through various means of diffusion. In São Paulo, where there are organized song duels, there is an association that schedules events. A few years ago in Paris, I met singers from Azerbaijan (the *aschiks*) involved in a kind of poetic contest that was very similar to the singing of the folk artists in Brazil. In this context "singer" is the name given to the contestants in the duels. Some poets, such as João Martins de Athayde (1877–1959), in order to distinguish the performer from the writer, use the term *poeta de bancada* (bench poet) to refer to those who write their pamphlets or even re-create their contests in writing (see Almeida 1979).

Indeed, this is a contest of mastery originating in medieval poetry. More related to the troubadour world than to contemporary art, the singing duel effects the consolidation and enrichment of voices in opposition, but the two voices become part of the same discourse and thus form a unit. Singing, which retains memory through exercise and skill, eliminates any notion of simplicity or artlessness in poetic form. Nothing is more elaborate than the transmission through performance of popular knowledge that is articulated in response to an adversary, whether as a means of displaying geographical knowledge by means of exercises that contain the names of rivers, countries, cities, and so on, or introducing literary tropes that challenge a whole body of mythological references.

Many years ago, when I came across the notorious *Peleja ou Discussão de João Athayde com Leandro Gomes* [1913; Duel or

Argument of João Athayde and Leandro Gomes], I knew that I had found a very special text in that it illustrated the obvious complexity of its genre and was performed by a composer–Athayde–who stands for the most important kind of Northeastern folk poetry (even if we could argue about the degree of creativity or invention of this artist or question his performance as a poet/editor). It is one of these invented songs, a piece written by a folk poet that simulates a dispute, a contest for mastery with someone who is his ideal rival. Some may refer to the author of such texts as an office or bench poet, trying to demonstrate that the improviser is one thing, the poet who writes down any so-called improvisation quite another. Although I believe these terms limit folk writing, I think they reveal the way in which this kind of literature is constructed. For instance, in "Marco Parahybano" [Marco from Parahyba], by José Adão (b. 1924), the poet makes himself very clear:

> Só sei cantar obra feita
> Por que não sou repentista
> Sou poeta pensador
> Que pouca fama conquista

> *(Adão Filho 42)*

> I only know how to sing a written piece
> Because I am no improviser
> I am a thinker poet
> Who wins no fame

In the case of Athayde's duel, one feels that he is quite aware both of the potential effects he can create in writing and also of the power of the oral contest for his audience. He constructs on the ground of intertextuality, taking explicit quotations from the most popular classics and well-known passages from other poets and, above all, from his purported rival. Various registers of culture are at play in this conscious game whose world of expression is shared by other folk poets as well as by his readers and hearers. "Marco," also composed by Athayde, is his oldest composition published as a chapbook. It tells the story of an odd contest, an imaginary duel in which the poet builds a fortress or castle, and it is up to his rival to take down piece by piece both the symbolic fortress and the argument he has developed. It is the imaginary duel taken to its highest level. "Marco," as a system of composition, is above all associated with the world of these duels, which illustrates both the game between writing and orality, improvisation, and minute elaboration and the sophistication of being able to write while incorporating oral nuances and of being able to create a writing that is addressed to the ears, a supposed speech to be read. From the point of view of communication, the impact of writing on a text that is both written and oral can be seen in several aspects of signification. There are many nuances in the exchange caused by the various types of alternating registers, as each purported singer tries to out-perform his rival. When writing a contest such as this, the poet offers, as a challenge to his imaginary rival, the richness of a virtual construct of order and thus generates, successively, new and suggestive intertextual allusions. In fact, each new text that is created produces a kind of echo effect, and there is always a response waiting to be made (Pires Ferreira 1991).

To return to our first example, the *Peleja*, the second part of the contest begins with the invitation to amuse or entertain or make merry. This invitation masks the beginning of the development of the opposite sequence, one in which mythological knowledge is conveyed. The line opens into a wealth of poetic questioning and the variations in representing everyday life through rhetorical procedures. It is up to the character Leandro to use the basic quatrain and to develop a semantic variation that is to be completed by Athayde:

> Uma nação reminada
> Uma morada distante
> Um porto na beira mar
> Um homem comerciante.

> *(Athayde 13–14)*

> A rebel nation
> A faraway dwelling
> A shoreline harbor
> A salesman.

The line that develops from this is intended, above all, to establish a correspondence of signification:

> A nação–dez fortalezas
> A homens–moradas
> A vapores–o porto.

> *(Athayde 14–15)*

> The nation–ten fortresses
> The men–dwellings
> The steamers–the harbor.

Here we have a constructive chiasmus–very common in this style–in which there is a descending sequence from the original quatrain and to which the ascending response is added. The inverted sequences oppose each other to create the progression and the meaning.

The Unmaking

The *décima corrida* (tenth race) or *desmancha* (unmaking) is a typical genre of Northeastern folk poetics, in which the first singer makes and the second one unmakes what the first has done, from back to front. These exercises prove the continuation of mastery and the preservation of the genre and make the notion of simplicity or spontaneity as the defining characteristic of folk literature seem ridiculous. What one really has is a form of traditional poetry, to a certain extent anachronistic and obviously naive at times by our standards, but one that has a high level of sophistication and structural complexity. To follow its development is constantly to need to consult the rules of rhetoric or the poetic arts. The fact that it involves making and unmaking, both in the last example and in "Marco," discredits the notion that pragmatism, usefulness, or some practical objective is the essence of folk art. The making-unmaking that João Cabral de Melo Neto would take as canonical in *Educação pela pedra* [1966; Education by Stone] exists in the dialogue-monologue forms of these folk poets, for whom poetry is the engine of the world, the exercise that makes the recovery of the ancestral possible, that is able to transmit beyond inspiration or poetic rage; it constitutes the rigorous knowledge of an office, the exact measure of the social meaning of the art.

For this reason, in the motto-gloss competition in which Athayde envisioned a contest with Leandro, as in so many other cases, the components of the constructed gradation are a carefully thought out ensemble, as an imagined picture:

> Dez fortalezas salvando
> Nove batalhões formados
> Oito generais armados
> Sete cornetas tocando

Seis pedras infernais queimando
Cinco tinas de gelada
Quatro casas de morada
Três comandantes de linha
Duas cidades vizinhas
Uma nação reminada

(Athayde 14)

Ten fortresses saving
Nine battalions aligned
Eight generals armed
Seven cornets sounding
Six infernal stones burning
Five tins of ice-cold drinks
Four houses for living
Three line commanders
Two neighboring towns
One rebel nation

The association of rebel with generals, battalions, cornets, and then hell and ice is politically significant. The poet, when building the epic gloss, tries to include signs from history–changing from guillotines, a probable legacy of the French Revolution, to Byzantine castles, suggesting more traditional stories:

Dez homens numa questão
Nove guilhotinas armadas
Oito oficinas fechadas
Sete minas de carvão
Seis crateras de vulcão
Cinco astros de levante
Quatro marés na varzante [*sic*]
Três estudantes ladinos
Dois castelos bizantinos
Uma morada distante.

(Athayde 14–15)

Ten men in a dispute
Nine armed guillotines
Eight workshops closed
Seven coal mines
Six volcano craters
Five men of insurrection
Four low tides
Three bright students
Two Byzantine castles
A distant dwelling.

These passages clearly permit different readings. On the one hand, there is the semantic universe of protest: Closed workshops, strikes, and punishment; on the other, there is the cosmic notion of promise. The juxtaposition has a great effect, which is related to the core concept of the motto: A rebel nation.

It is Leandro, as a character, who must compose as he plays for Athayde (who is usually pretentious because he is both creator and creature, but here is openly modest in relation to the man who is his model poet), whose words he must retain and repeat. The segments that we could call "gloss-chiasmus" correspond to each of the themes in a given motto, to each of the terms introduced at the beginning. As the composition becomes more and more complex, we note that the contest gradually diminishes and nearly disappears. The text becomes an arranged exercise, not a dialogue but a monologue in which a whole cultural repertoire is evoked and passed on with pleasure–a vision of a world, pictures from the memory of the poet, but most obviously an image of the creator himself involved in a complex task that

requires all conceivable creative processes, from the most simple to the most sophisticated:

Dez vapores da saída
Nove bandeiras içadas
Oito escotilhas fechadas
Sete trens fazem partida
Seis criaturas sem vida
Cinco paisanos a falar
Quatro botes a navegar
Três vagões cheios de gente
Duas colinas de frente
Um porto à beira Mar.

(Athayde 15)

Ten steamers departing
Nine flags hoisted
Eight hatchways closed
Seven trains leaving
Six lifeless creatures
Five civilians speaking
Four boats sailing
Three railway cars full of people
Two hills ahead
One shoreline harbor.

In this sequence a dynamic development involving the notion of transportation is represented by its means: Railway cars, trains, steamers, boats, and so on. The sequence also suggests revolution: War and its implications, soldiers and civilians, hoisted flags, and the sight of death. The original meaning of revolution–turning over–is implied here, again putting together the social and the cosmic levels in a progressive dynamic development–as if in a narrative countersong in which the life of the nation flows normally from the cosmic to the practical. Then, after the strike, peace is restored. In the calm after the storm, the social dimension prevails in the making of an inventory:

Oito poetas glosando
Sete patacas de pão
Seis metros de gorgurão
Cinco meninas galantes
Quatro sujeitos pedantes
Três despachantes ligeiros
Dois automóveis cargueiros
Um homem comerciante.

(Athayde 16)

Eight poets glossing
Seven pieces of bread
Six yards of fabric
Five graceful girls
Four arrogant men
Three swift clerks
Two freight trucks
One salesman.

Various elements here form part of one semantic group: The yards of fabric, the graceful, and the arrogant. And in all of this there is a perfect correspondence between complementary notions, illustrating the course of poetic organization in the handling of words:

tumulto–reminado
atuação–combate
paz–ordem

tumult–rebel
performance–combat
peace–order

A simplistic interpretation would present this duel as a poetic project that advocates accord or conformity. But one should remember that what might seem an accord could be the very terrain of a utopia that is never realized. This is really an example of how the poet's reflection on his time, his social space, and his proposal for social harmony develops. One clearly sees a game of contrasts with a concision and coherence that seem to point to a fundamental core in every contest. The domain of wordplay and verse is shown, for this is a composition intended for the ear, one that perpetuates itself because it is both collective and individual, and traditional and ever renewing, especially since it is based on poles of semantic difference that guarantee its preservation in memory.

Another interesting genre is the *mourão* (stanzas with dialogues of five, six, or seven verses) in which the poet, besides being a spokesman, is also an acrobat of rhyming and mnemonics. In São Paulo, there is also the powerful *cururu* (dance with a singing competition), and Amadeu Amaral (125) reminds us of the importance of ballads and song-rounds, which have an established status in the complex universe of folk music: The *moda de viola* (guitar song). The complexity of the oral tradition, considered in universal terms or from the perspective of a regional or national identity cannot be summarized as if it were a fixed repertory. In the case of Brazil, one needs to understand that this is an oral tradition of European origin, though permeated by elements of black and aboriginal cultures. In order to evaluate this flexible complex entity, one needs more than the instruments with which one approaches language. There are oral, visual, and gestural modes involved through which space and time are articulated. Time takes another course, organizing itself by multiple criteria that allow a range of possibilities, from the linear to the cyclical and to the visionary entropic. The sense of space is strongly connected to the notion of *territory* (Zumthor 1993, 81). In the case of folk poetry, whether it is oral or of a mixed oral/written/printed/made-oral form, a whole space of designation is constructed: That of seeing/hearing/pointing. Gesture is embedded in voice. Orality involves both vocality and sight. In dealing with oral poetry and its performance, the notion of performative sound systems cannot be ignored. Clapping, shouting, laughter, internally and externally created noises, and hesitations and silence that contextualize the emotional variations of those who recite and receive and the whole surrounding atmosphere of reception must be taken into consideration. This is what Deleuze (1969, 21–25) reminds us of when he comments on Freud's insistence on the acoustic origin of the superego.

In conclusion, it is clear that understanding the poetics of orality is important if we are to understand the achievements of collective memory, the body of a patrimony that contributes to literary culture. The legacy of orality in Brazil brings imaginary forces and unique variations of a culture into motion in the complex whole of a literary culture. This tradition is sharply undervalued if we take it as either picturesque or folkloric; and its study is also reduced if it is to be seen as the work of antiquarians, described by Alejo Carpentier (1979, 58) as pursuing the last signs of survival of practices that are no longer relevant. On the contrary, traditional orality is a great text with all the flexibility of continuous creative adaptation. Establishing a process of cultural translation, it recovers the popular in a form that has a greater affinity than do written texts with its expressive mode and therefore with the conception of a world of social interaction. Cascudo

(1984, 241) tells us that the *congos* (dramatic dances, according to Mário de Andrade [1893–1945]) at times include passages from operas and songs heard in the theater and later disseminated widely in these popular forms. The voices of the traditional high culture gradually move into the mass media, where they open the way to a lively and renovating reworking of the classical as popular.

We can then acknowledge the wholeness and coherence of this collective universe of signs and discover that we lose Brazil's cultural imaginary when we prefer to get only glimpses of the popular roots of this tradition. In the oral tradition, forms contain within themselves the memory of genres and of poetic configurations—past and present—that continuously cluster and reorganize themselves (Lotman 1990, 123). In its variety and fluidity, oral literature offers a scenario of social and cultural life as a flexible and moving whole. It is therefore difficult to study the chapbook apart from the songs and romances, for each one of them extends into the other. Research on oral literature puts in evidence details of the shared expertise and competence of an anonymous collectivity.

**Translation by Glaucia Gonçalves and
Thomas LaBorie Burns**

Works Cited

Adão Filho, José. 1921. *Marco parahybano.* Recife: Typ. Chaves.

Almeida, Atila Augusto F. de and José Alves Sobrinho. 1978. *Dicionário bio-bibliográfico de repentistas e poetas de bancada.* João Pessoa: Editora Universitária. 2 vols.

Amado, Jorge. 1972. *Tereza Batista: cansada de guerra.* São Paulo: Martins.

Amaral, Amadeu. 1976. *Tradições Populares.* 2d ed. São Paulo: Hucitec.

Andrade, Mario de. 1959. *Danças Dramáticas do Brasil.* São Paulo: Martins Fontes. 3 vols.

Athayde, João Martins de. 1985. *Peleja ou Discussão de João Athayde com Leandro Gomes.* São Paulo: Luzeiro.

Auerbach, Erich. 1950. *Mimesis: la representación de la realidad en la literatura occidental.* Trans. I. Villanueva and E. Imaz. Mexico City: Fondo de Cultura Económica.

Bahktin, Mikhail. 1974. *La cultura popular en la Edad Media y en el Renacimiento: El contexto de François Rabelais.* Trans. Julio Forcat and César Conroy. Barcelona: Barral.

Cabral de Melo Neto, João. 1997. *Educação pela pedra.* Rio de Janeiro: Editora Nova Fronteira.

Carpentier, Alejo. 1978. *Literatura e consciencia política na América Latina.* Trans. Manuel J. Palmeirim. São Paulo: Editora Global.

———. 1973. *Catalogue.* Rio de Janeiro: Casa de Rui Barbosa.

Cascudo, Luis Fernando da Câmara. 1952. *História da Literatura Brasileira: Literatura Oral.* Coleção Documentos Brasileiros. Vol. 6. Rio de Janeiro: José Olympio.

———. 1984. *Vaqueiros e cantadores.* São Paulo: EDUSP.

Cortázar, Julio. 1963. *Rayuela.* Buenos Aires: Sudamericana.

———. 1969. *Hopscotch.* Trans. Gregory Rabassa. New York: Pantheon Books.

Deleuze, Gilles. 1969. *La logique du sens.* Paris: Minuit.

Ferreira, Jerusa Pires. 1991. *Armadilhas da Memória. Conto e poesia popular.* Salvador: Fundação Casa de Jorge Amado.

———. 1993. *Cavalaria em Cordel. O passo das aguas mortas.* 2d ed. São Paulo: Hucitec.

———. 1995. "Matrices imprimées de l'oralité." *Frontières du Litteraire.* Ed. Zilah Bernd and Jacques Migozzi. Limoges: Pulim.

———. 1996. *Fausto no Horizonte.* São Paulo: Hucitec-EDUC.

———. 1997. "Matrices imprimeés de l'oral." *Le Roman populaire en question(s)*. Ed. Jacques Migozzi. Limoges: Pulim.

Greimas, Algirdas Julien. 1976. *Sémiotique et sciences sociales*. Paris: Seuil.

Guimarães Rosa, João. 1968. *Tutaméia*. 2d ed. Rio de Janeiro. Olympio.

Lotman, Yuri. 1975. *Analysis of the Poetic Text*. Ed. and trans. D. Barton Johnson. Ann Arbor, Mich.: Ardis.

———. 1990. *Universe of the Mind: A Semiotic Theory of Culture*. Trans. Ann Shukman. London: Taurus.

———. Boris A. Uspenskii and Remo Faccani, ed. 1975. *Tipologia della cultura*. Trans. Manila Barbato Faccani. Milano: Bompiani.

Nascimento, Bráulio and Cynéa Bouyer, ed. 1971. *Bibliografia do folclore brasileiro*. Rio de Janeiro Biblioteca Nacional, Divisão de Publicações e Divulgação.

Trancoso, Gonçalo Fernandes. 1974. *Contos e histórias de proveito & exemplo*. Ed. João Palma-Ferreira. Lisboa: Imprensa Nacional.

Zumthor, Paul. 1983. *Introduction à la poésie orale*. Paris: Seuil.

———. 1987. *La mesure du monde*. Paris: Seuil.

———. 1993. *A Letra e a voz*. Trans. Amálio Pinheiro and Jerusa Pires Ferreira. São Paulo: Companhia das Letras.

CHAPTER 51

TEXTUALITY AND TERRITORIALITY IN BRAZILIAN ORAL DISCOURSE

Ivete Lara Camargos Walty

In a world that bows to the power of the visual image and virtual reality, and in a society that still has large numbers of illiterate people–as well as whole groups with no writing at all–living alongside computers, it is important to examine the role of oral discourse and its relationships with other forms of discourse. Keeping in mind the aim of "rethinking Latin America's history of literary culture," it is important to ponder the place of oral literature: With regard to the other kinds of literature considered by us, because oral literature moves through diverse spaces, overcomes limits, and makes frontiers relative. The notion of transit is very important here because this essay starts from the premise that the narrative structures of discourse reflect a world picture. Consequently, the flexibility and interactivity of oral discourse reveal a moving, flowing world in permanent transformation, in spite of possible recurrences and constant repetitions. This is not in reference to the invariable narrative elements as suggested by Propp, but rather to the movement of what is being told and to the variations and modulations of discourse in its multiple enunciations. More than any other literary discourse, the narrative of Latin America or, at least, some of its best creations, becomes a place of interaction and exchange and has led to the production of theories such as Carpentier's "marvellous real," Lezama Lima's "gnostic space," Glissant's "poetics of relationship," Octavio Paz's "tradition of rupture" together with his notion of *otherness*, Silviano Santiago's "inter-place," and other theories that try to explain this open space of transit, interaction, and cultural exchange.

The purpose of this essay is to analyze the oral cultural productions–either audio-recorded or in written form–of certain Brazilian regions and to relate them to the productions that are recognized by the official canon, in order to observe their reverberations, their insertions, and their dissemination in other times and spaces. In this way, one can study the territoriality of oral Latin American discourse in its textual and social aspects, involving the establishment of the text–as an enunciative game–and its relationship with the institutions that determine it. To do this, we will examine the productions of the following Brazilian regions: Amazonia, represented here by a sample of some stories told by the Indian Pichuvy Cinta-Larga (d. 1988), as well as narratives gathered among the riverside population by a group of the University of Pará (Simões and Golder); narratives from the Jequitinhonha Valley and from the Minas Gerais region (Pereira); and narrations that circulate in the region of Outer Belo Horizonte (Laterza). In this way, these narrative flashes will metonymically outline certain strokes of Latin American cultural diversity in all its territorial mobility. More than privileging a structural or thematic analysis of the texts, the aim here is to study the relationship between textuality and territoriality, taking these two terms as interchangeable in so far as the text becomes territory and the territory becomes text. Thus, it is very important to use the relational concept of territorial categories, as Featherstone has suggested. A close reading of these stories–which constitute a significant sample of a wider corpus–reveals that they share certain elements that deserve to be considered. Among these are the tendency to make frontiers and dichotomies relative, and to start from the contradictions inherent in oral productions, whether recorded on tape, on video, or in books.

Word in Action

I will start with the *Histórias de maloca antigamente* [Stories of an Ancient Indian Village], told by Chief Pichuvy Cinta Larga, an Indian from Rondônia, northern Brazil, because these tales are the product of a society with no writing system and, thus, constitute what has been called primary orality in relation to civilized society. Indian narratives, especially those marked by a mythical time, reveal a constant interaction between cosmogony and eschatology, life and death, creation and destruction. Death is reversible because everything is in constant transformation and in permanent integration, as can be seen in the tale about some Indians killed by a panther who returned to life with the help of a deer. Each arrow–the metonymic image of the Indian and his cultural creation–is replaced by a bone, which is in turn transformed into an Indian: "Todo o tempo tinha arco com flechinha pra, quando osso virar índio, matar onça." ("All the time I have a bow with a little arrow ready; when the bone becomes an Indian, it kills the panther," 60). In the tale in which a woman gets inside an animal in order to escape from the owl (the lover who is chasing her), we have the human–animal integration in a literal and metaphorical way: "Mulher entrou dentro do pescoço do socó. (por isso socó tem pescoço grande, né?)" ("The woman entered inside the neck of the *socó*. [That is why the *socó* bird has a long neck, isn't it?], 65). Thus, there are no barriers between Indians and animals, between the forest and the hamlet, between high and low lands. The relationships among the Indians themselves and between the Indians, the animals, and the rest of the objects are determined by the transformation. All of them take part in this process and share its language: "Aí índio mandou logo o madrugada, né? Chamando ela. Cantava tudo de passarinho, né? Jacu, jacutinga, nambu . . . tudo ele cantava chamando madrugada. Aí madrugada chegou" (54) ("There the Indian summoned dawn, called the early sunrise. He sang like a little bird, didn't he? *Jacu, jacutinga, nambu* . . . all his being sang summoning dawn. Then dawn arrived.")

Such a symbolic transformation is the hallmark of a tribal community, characterized by the people's coming and going in their love affairs or in the sociopolitical relationships which are realized in the flexibility of the text. Indian territory is like its text: Mobile, with no fixed borders. It is a place where the path is made by treading on it–"Não tem isso dividir terra não.

Mesma terra, né? . . . Não é marcado terra nada. Tem nada! Só caminho–picada, né? Ninguém vai ir lá. Não tem caminho de lá longe não. Só caminho de maloca nossa . . ." (119) ("Here there isn't this thing of dividing the land, oh no. It's the same land, isn't it? . . . Land is not marked here. Land is not marked! There is only a path–opened by machete. Nobody's going there. There is no road from the outside, from beyond the land. Only the path of our *maloca*–of our Indian compound.")

Land reversibility corresponds to textual reversibility. A story ends and begins several times; the end is not conclusive: "Tem outra história de Pawo assim, sabe?" (43) (There is another Pawo story, you know?); "Então, história de Ngurá também. Outro Ngurá també́n que nome é Tiriri" (21) (And so, there is also another Ngurá story. Another Ngurá who is called Tirir). Everything is constantly emerging, starting again. Gerunds are the characterizing features of the texts: "Ele brilho brilhando todo pendurado de vagalume. Pequenininho . . . bem baixinho" (35) (It shines, shining, hanging with fireflies. Tiny . . . flying low); "Aí virou festa dançando dançando dançando, fazendo bebida de chicha" (74) (It turned into a party, dancing, dancing, dancing, preparing a *chicha* drink); "Coruja foi andando andando andando" (65) (Owl kept going, going, going). The notion of continuity, of movement–evident in the reiteration of the gerund form–is always present in the process of narrating the story, a process where past, present, and future interact. This transforms the very role of story-telling: "Eu tô vivo aqui, eu contar muito de história. Assim que eu faço pessoal meu (. . .). E muita vez que eu falava que índio tem lembrar como foi antigamente, como que velho contava pra nós, que velho conta muita história pra nós. Por isso eu conta muita história assim" (15) (I am alive here, I tell many tales. And so I create my own characters. . . . Many times I have said that Indians have to remember how life used to be in the past, how the old man used to tell us things, how the old man tells us stories. This is why I tell so many stories).

This enunciative interplay can also be appreciated in the drawings made by the Indians in order to illustrate their stories. These drawings show not only the overlapping of spaces, but also the physical linkage between man and animal in such a way that one becomes the extension of the other (see **Figure 1**).

The condition of gestation, of being pregnant, involving both humans and animals, gods and plants, symbolizes an integration of the universe. The body is the house in the world. Sexuality is the sign of life, of renewal. It is present in each segment of nature: "Primeiro ele transava o coco de castanha. Coco de castanha tem boca que cabia jibaca dele. Aí zup ficou lá dentro castanha. Gente nasceu dentro de castanha . . . ." (19) ("First he handled the *coco de castanha* (Brazil coconut). This coconut has such a mouth that a *jibaca* fits inside. There *zup* remained inside the nut. People were born inside the nut.") Apart from being reversible, the word-text is permeable. It does not go untouched because it embodies the trademark of the person who makes use of it. It is the inhabited word, the word which is impregnated and fecund. That is why it is ambivalent and ambiguous. This ambivalence becomes more evident when the original word comes together with the colonizer's word and speaks it. This is an adoption of both the colonizer's language and his technological means of communication, such as the printed book, which, instead of being intended for the other Indians, is made for literate non-Indians. Indians listen to these same stories but in a

different way, in other spaces, at specific times. Pichuvy Cinta Larga speaks about the customs of his culture that are established in the mixed language he uses to tell his stories, which circulate between spaces destined to oppose each other but which, in fact, unavoidably intersect. His personal language–a showcase of contradictions–incorporates the voices of his own people but, also, the words of the non-Indian.

Myth, the foundational narrative par excellence, embodies cosmogonic and eschatological signs and, when retold and literally relocated, incorporates another story or stories in an endless movement of the search for group identity, and thus shapes a nomad story. According to Featherstone, such a story would emphasize a relational understanding of the same places seen from a changing and multiple point of view. When a female Suruí Indian from Rondônia was asked to draw her house, she drew the same symbol used by the Indians of her tribe around their lips, the distinctive mark of their people. My house is me; my world is me. But also, I am my people. How would such a place be designed? Like the heart of the world? Or precisely the me but not me? Or me in space? It is important to examine some of the drawings created by the Yanomami Indians (see **Figure 2**): A pregnant woman, two pots, and the hamlet, all of them metonymies of the world, permeated by the energy of life. Is this the maximum possibility of interaction or centering? And where is the center? In the waves of vital energy of the Yanomami people, or in the web of their stories?

The photograph of a Yanomami room, or *shabono*, side by side with that of another room–requested by the Commission for the Creation of the Yanomami Park, a nongovernment organization, and designed by Leda Leonel, an architect from Minas Gerais (see **Figure 3**), shows the possible exchange in the middle of the Amazon forest between the vital force of the clay pots, the woman, and the hamlet and the cybernetic, technological world to which we belong. The aim of the project proposed by the architect is to integrate the Indian way of life and method of employing forest materials for construction with the technology of the so-called civilized world in order to build the Balawaú Health Post for Indians and non-Indians. All of this is part of a shared social action that characterizes the notion of orality as exchange, dialogue, and interplay and underlines the concept of a nation in process, determined by birth, as Hannah Arendt has said. Its creation embodies the idea of transformation, of change. Stories are told precisely because there is change. To walk and to talk are signs of orality in its moving and interacting process, as can be seen in Vargas Llosa's (b. 1936) book, *El hablador* [1987; *The Storyteller*, 1989], where Indian storytelling is presented: "Todos fueron antes algo distinto de lo que ahora son. A todos les sucedería algo que puede contarse" (1997, 189; ("Before, they were all something different from what they are now. Something happened to all of them that you could tell a story about," 196); "Aquí estamos. Yo en el medio, ustedes rodeándome. Yo hablando, ustedes escuchando. Vivimos, andamos. Eso es la felicidad, parece" (1997, 41; "Here we are. I in the middle, you all around me. I talking, you listening. We live, we walk. That is happiness, it seems," 40). To talk and to walk are also the ways of keeping the universe alive and of surviving physically and culturally.

The Procession or Giant Cobra

Those who have attended the procession of the Nazareth Candle in Belém do Pará, in Brazil's northern region, can testify to

Figure 1.

Pichuvy

(Archive of the author)

Figure 2.

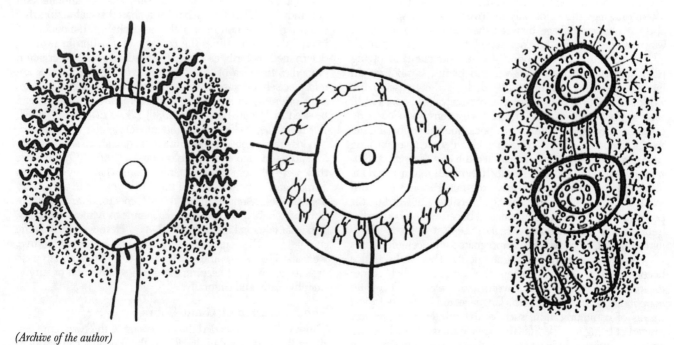

(Archive of the author)

Figure 3.

(Archive of the author)

the presence of the interactive movement we have been talking about, the expression of a cultural dialogue in the name of Christianity. People are joined together by a huge rope and crawl through the streets of the city paying tribute to the Virgin of Nazareth. In a show of faith, they carry miniatures of the goods acquired (or objects that represent the favors received) with the intervention of the Saint: Houses, ships, arms, legs . . . everything winds its way towards the city's basilica, like the giant cobra in the regional myth. The procession includes people from nearby towns and other Brazilian cities, and is seen by visitors from all over the country and indeed the world. The streets become the stage for a popular religiosity and bring together a variety of ethnic and social groups. The hands seizing the long rope, which form the huge cobra, engage in a silent embrace.

In giving expression to the large cobra, which inhabits both the rivers and the popular imaginary of the cities, the stories from the region converse with this particular religious celebration. This symbolic connection is also noted by other scholars, such as Paulo Nunes (b. 1944), a Pará poet, who writes about the diversity of cobra images in Belém, including those that appear in the stories told by his grandmother:

Belém, meus filhos, é cidade oca. Pode ver, não se pode fazer nela prédio muito grande. Sinão é capaz, diz-que, d'ela afundar. Me discurpem se conto isso, mas é verdade. E olhem só, esse tremor que teve aqui num dia desses, diz-que foi tremor de terra. Será? Acho que é coisa das rabudas, isso sim é que é. Tudo porque, vocês sabem, nas entranhas de Belém moram duas cobras. A Boiúna e a Cobra Norato. Uma mora nos porões da Sé, e outra nas funduras da Basílica. De quando em vez elas se mexem e provocam mor estrago. Qué vê só? Essa rachadura nas costas da Igreja de Nazaré, falam que é caminhão e ônibus passando . . . É nada! É mesmo a cobra que se arrepia e faz estremeção. Só peço em Deus quando as duas se verem cara a cara eu já tenha morrido. Nossa Senhora de Nazaré, cruz credo! Se a Boiúna da Sé e a Norato da Basílica se encontrá, axi porcaria, num quero nem tá viva prá contá os estragos! Chuu, já se foi Belém . . .
(Nunes, unpublished text)

Belém, my children, is an *oca* city. You can see, very tall buildings cannot be built here. Otherwise Belém might very well sink. I am sorry to be telling you this, but it is true. Listen, the tremor we felt some days ago, they say it was an earthquake. Can it be? I think it is a question of the long-tailed creatures, that's what it is. And the reason for this is, you know, that two cobras live in the depths of Belém–the *Boiúna* and the *Norato*. One lives in the basements of the Church of Nazareth, and the other in the foundations of the Basilica. From time to time they move and cause havoc. Do you want to see? That long crack on the side of the Church of Nazareth, they say it was caused by the buses and trucks that pass by. . . . Not at all! It is the cobra shivering and producing an earth tremor. I only wish to God that when the two cobras see each other in the face, I am already dead. Our Lady of Nazareth be blessed! If the Boiúna of the Church and the Norato of the Basilica come together, what the heck, I don't want to be alive to tell of the damages caused! Puf, Belém is gone . . . .

The discursive register that combines popular and colloquial speech moves between myth and technology, the sacred and the profane, and by using threatening interjections, expresses the fear characteristic of apocalyptic narratives. The presence of the cobras underneath the sacred territory of the churches is, thus, something exceptional to these people. Always present in the literature of the region, and already incorporated into canonized works, such as Raul Bopp's (1898–1984) *Cobra Norato* (1931), the cobras have become an element of cultural resistance, like the worms of Carpentier's (1904–1980) *Los pasos perdidos* [1953; *The Lost Steps*], which insist on existing amid technological progress and its detritus: Open sewers, downtrodden streets, seedy rooms, and insectlike people. Winding its way through a variety of spaces, oral narrative is what makes this process of engagement possible.

The tales compiled by the research group coordinated by professor Maria do Socorro Simões confirm this reading of the interplay of metamorphoses and of going beyond the borders. The *Cobra Norato* tale is characterized by ambiguity and by different levels of incantation. Norato "era, era, segundo a lenda, era um rapaz que também era encantado, numa cobra grande, e que, no Amazonas ele teve uma briga muito grande com outra cobra e, essa cobra furou o olho dele; ele era cego dum lado" ("was, according to legend, a lad transformed by magic into a huge cobra who had a big fight in the Amazon River with another cobra, which hurt him in one eye; he was half-blind," Simões and Golder 46). He has the characteristic features of mythical heroes, but his vision is different. Norato used to turn into a person and enjoyed dancing and reveling at night; people did not know who he was, and when they would look for him at a certain hour, he had vanished unnoticed, leaving no trace. The playful space that allows for the integration of animals and people reinforces the mystery involving the character in a way that is reminiscent of the stories of Eros and Psyche, Beauty and the Beast, or Cinderella. One story is interwoven with another in a playful interaction. The constant presence of water in all of these tales (here represented by a waterway) reinforces the uncertainty, the dislocation of space.

According to the narrator-witness, women can beget cobras and enchanted people, thus creating another type of ambiguity. A legendary figure can become the source of truth: "Seu Monteiro confirma a história da Cobra Norato: 'É uma história-verdade. Só isso'" (94) ("Mister Monteiro confirms the tale of the *Norato* Cobra: 'It is a truth-tale, only that.'"); "História-verdade que meu avô contava pra mim. É meu avô mesmo. Ele realmente conheceu ele, o Norato." (94) ("My grandfather used to tell me these truth-tales. And he really was my grandfather. He really knew Norato.") In so far as the narrator tries to make his word trustworthy by taking it back to the past or by projecting it into the future, the enunciative interplay dislocates speech. The tale "Vira, vira porco" ["Becoming a Pig"] tells about the transformation of a hunter into a pig as a punishment for his constant and indiscriminate hunting sprees: "Ele ia matando, esfolando lá no mato e deixando a carne estragar." (63) ("He went on killing and letting meat rot.") Turned into a pig, he lives among the pigs who protect the jungle. Human identity and superiority become relative in this transition between different species. The skin of the pig, placed on the body of the man, is a metonymy of the power of the jungle and of its resistance mechanisms. Several elements of the Pichuvy Cinta Larga tales are repeated here, such as the fact that Pawo, the protector of the jungle, turns Indians into pigs, a power which links the story to the Circe episode in Homer's *Odyssey*: "Agora teu pessoal vai virar porco lugar meu porco" (Cinta Larga 45)("Now your people will become pigs, they will be my pigs.")

Pawo controls his victim's word. When his victim wants to say something he says something else: "Quando meu primo tava láaaa longe . . . armou rede lá longe, aí Pawo vem deitar com ele. Aí ele quer falar: 'Pawo quer me matar'–assim ele quer–aí ele falou: 'trazer fogo pra mim!'–ele falou assim: 'traz fogo pra mim!'" (Cinta Larga 43) ("When my cousin was in a place, far, faaaar away . . . he opened a hammock, in a place far away. And there Pawo came to sleep with him. There, he wanted to say: 'Pawo wants to kill me'–that's what he wanted to say–but then he said: 'Bring me fire!'–that is how he spoke–'bring me fire!'") We have here an entity who travels between the hamlet and the jungle, the natural and the supernatural, the real and the imaginary, like the cobra, Norato. These tales play an important role in the organization of the text. They end and begin again, reinforcing the paratactic and reiterative structure: "Tem outra história de Pawo assim, sabe? Então é só isso, viu?" (Cinta Larga 43) ("There is another *Pawo* tale like this one, you know? It's not only this one, right?"); "Então, que ficou falada a história de Norato. Só isso" (Simões and Golder 98) ("And so, the tale of *Norato* has been told.") The play of metamorphoses itself goes through various transformations and thus both the mystery of the spells and the possibility of physical and cultural resistance are retained.

Clay Narrations

Several researchers have studied the tales of the Jequitinhonha valley, a mining region that has a wealth of cultural manifestations in spite of its poverty, which has led many of its inhabitants, especially men, to emigrate towards São Paulo and other southern areas in order to work in the sugarcane fields. Mainly told by elderly people, the stories narrated in the valley also have a dynamic and interactive nature. At a thematic level, we find multiple metamorphoses, as in the tales "O mestre do mio (milho)" ["The Corn Master"] or "Os treis cavalo incantado" ["The Three Enchanted Horses"]. In his struggle to survive, the hero has to undertake several tasks and, according to the tasks' degree of difficulty, he has to become a variety of animals. He takes from fish their flippers to swim in the river, from birds their wings to fly into the sky in order to escape from his pursuer, and so on. Borders clearly disappear. Thanks to secret knowledge or through the help of a magical amulet, he can overcome obstacles. Being at the margins of society, the protagonist faces these difficulties with cunning and skill, and defeats the giants who have power. As his reward he marries the daughter of a rich man, as in so many European and Middle Eastern fairy tales: "Aí o mestre virô um merguião e vup! Atrás do pexe. Pega aqui, pega ali. E o pexe veno que ele ia pegá, virô uma rola e vuô. O mestre virô um gavião e bateu atrás dessa rola. a rola viu que ele ia pegá, né?" (Pereira 107) ("There the master became a fish-eating duck and oops! He followed the fish. Followed it here, followed it there. And the fish, realizing that it was going to get caught, turned itself into a turtledove and flew away. The master became a hawk and pursued the dove. The dove saw that the hawk was going to get it, didn't it?")

The same kind of mobility of form can be seen in the ambiguous clay figures of the region. The women do not sign their works, but they are able to identify them because they do leave their marks on them. These figures combine the forms of people and animals, and most of them are female.

(see **Figure** 4). The anthropomorphic features introduce a dynamism to each clay figure; they represent movement through the waters of the sea or the heavens, and into the valleys or up the mountains; the figures are at once fantasy and reality. Thus they are both decorative and utilitarian in the information they contain. Women with huge bellies and tiny heads announce their social status and expose their greatness as the makers of life. (**Figure** 5). These clay narratives are also oral narrations in a sense: Fragile and yet sturdy, fixed but dynamic, they are interactive and regional, a means of cultural exchange. They represent that notion Mario de Andrade termed "sabença" (wisdom), a kind of learning clearly differentiated from the learning that has been institutionalized and accepted as cultured (as has been clearly demonstrated by Vera Felício Pereira when analyzing the region's tales).

Another recurring element in the oral tradition is the need to offer a testimony of the truthfulness of the tales: "Hoje ele mora lá, tá lá rico, o pai rico. Té pouco tempo que vi eles lá" (Pereira 107) ("Today he lives there, he is rich, and his father is rich. I saw them there a while ago.") The narrator invites reader-listeners to confirm his testimony, or else deliberately excludes them: "Nunca vi tanta coisa, num sabe? E foi aquela festona! Doce? Mas tinha otro pote de doce, fui, eu quiria trazê procês . . . E o que aconteceu cum esse doce?–A mesma coisa que acunteceu cum outro. Meus amigo, num vão cumê esse ingasga-gato nunca!" (Pereira 140) ("I've never seen so many things, you know? What a party it was! Dessert? They had another pot of pudding. . . . I even wanted to bring some to you . . . And what happened to that pot of pudding?–The same thing that happened to the others. My friends, you're never going to have this firewater, never.") The same tale becomes itself the shared pudding or the spirituous liquor which can be linked to a story which embodies another one, always beginning again, involving listeners to the point that the narrator modifies his own narration depending on the context of reception.

Tales or the Table?

Another distinctive mark of oral narration then, is the act of addressing the listener or reader, who is invited to take part, agree, reiterate, and become a witness. This is why research studies, such as that carried out by Moacyr Laterza Filho about the astonishing elements of the Minas Gerais narratives, establish the relationship of these oral narrations to convivial songs, both of which involve people assembled around abountiful table in a Minas town. When studying the spaces of the tales that deal with ghosts and apparitions, Moacyr Laterza states that the stories are like ghosts whose role is to scare the listeners, helping them thus to exorcize their own ghosts in the very moment of the telling of the stories. The enunciation is characterized by constant repetition and by the fact that there is an emphasis on the relativity of the location or the

Figure 4.

(Archive of the author)

Figure 5.

(Archive of the author)

possible origins of the tale. In its endless retelling, the story is constantly renewed–while being also permanent–putting into action its collective role. Laterza writes: "Thus, the sense of astonishment can be the listener's reaction to the telling of the tales. This brings into the foreground the role of the listener/reader as one of the narration's subjects. The tale itself constitutes the sense of astonishment, because it is precisely in the tales that supernatural entities come to life. It is through tales that the encounter between the souls of this world and the next occurs. The act of narration is what produces astonishment; by means of it, the suffering souls communicate with the living" (166).

This encounter between speakers and audience, between characters and listeners, takes place at different narrative levels and is in the relativized borders of the home–where ghosts appear–as well as outside it. It also takes place in the interplay between the natural and the supernatural, dream and reality, life and death, hero and antihero, the high and the low. Nothing is conclusive; everything is transformed overnight. The characters' movement is a metaphor of other kinds of movement and typifies the space of the threshold. This is why certain syntactic structures are clearly marked by the use of parataxis; repetitions are emphatic and ambiguities intensify the sense of mystery. All of the story happens in the context of an almost mythical atemporality realized in the ritual of

storytelling. Within the communicative process established in oral narrative, Laterza includes another interactive aspect–the movement between past and present, between tradition and the new elements brought about by new developments–and demonstrates that even if these tales travel around the world and are full of universalized stereotypes, they are still a feature of the identity of Minas Gerais. It seems that the temporal existence of ghosts diminishes as a consequence of the changes brought about by progress; it is as if ghosts stopped appearing because there is too much light around: "Existe! . . . Agora num . . . agora . . . eu num sei, porque o mundo evoluiu, que agora tudo tá diferente . . . esses trem tá" (Laterza 52) ("It exists! . . . Not now . . . now . . . I don't know, everything is different now because the world has changed . . . the machinery is there now.") The fact that this kind of narration persists demonstrates the prevalence of ghosts who converse with technological progress and insist on their continued presence in spite of the existence of mechanisms of exclusions. They are, thus, a form of resistance, even when they transmit certain elements that embody apparently procolonialist ideas.

In the tale of the fearless man, the image of a body formed by pieces falling from the roof of a haunted house can be interpreted as a metonymy of oral narrations in their own reiterative and fragmented circulation:

> Aí . . . apareceu uma voz. "Eu vô caí!" ele falô: "pode caí!" Caiu uma perna. Aí, "eu vô caí".ele falô: "pode caí." Caiu a otra perna. Aí foi: "eu vô caí." Ele: "pode caí. Pode caí o resto d'uma vez!" Aí caiu . . . o resto todo, sabe? . . . formô um homem, né?
> (Laterza 143) (story told by Antônio Camargos Neto, in the Esmeraldas region, 45 kilometers from Belo Horizonte).
>
> There . . . emerged a voice. "I'm falling down!" he said, "I can fall down!" A leg fell. "I'm falling down!" he said, "I can fall down!" The other leg fell. Then he said: "I'm falling down!" He said, "I can fall down! The rest will fall down!" And the rest fell down, you know? And it formed a man, you know?

The body cut in pieces has also been employed by Italo Calvino in his *Italian Fables* and by Pedro Nava (1903–1984), a Minas Gerais chronicler, in his book *Baú de ossos* [1972; Trunk of Bones]. It represents a fragmented memory of the disparable spaces of nomad history and constitutes a threat to the foundations of sedentary society, much in the same way that the cobras living underneath the churches of the city of Belém are a constant threat.

It does not matter that other countries also have oral narrations, nor that one country's tales are repeated in another country. What is important is that the idea of a fragmented body, for instance, does not have a fixed origin and that oral narrations are anonymous. Paradoxically, these stories constitute both a place of resistance and a space of intersection, like our hybrid and plural geographical spaces. In claiming a new marginal place of interrelationships, Latin America vindicates its oral cultures in the sense that it does not seek to be conclusive or unified, because it knows it is a simulacrum; it also knows it is fragmented. Both Latin American fiction and criticism can be read as an oral space, in this sense of being a space for exchange, interaction, and the encounter of dislocated and dislocating fragments. This is why Paul Zumthor states that the "predominance of oral communication is restricted to poor areas, to marginal regions which are linked today to popular culture" (30).

It is possible to ponder the significant–if not dominant–presence of an oral culture in so-called Latin America, either in

the form of primary orality or else as absorbed in written literature (or even in aware critical readings). Such reflection may
lead us to perceive this marginal space from a different point of
view, and to comprehend its position between resistance to colonization (in a broad sense) and acceptance of the rules of the
game. Once again, this sense of movement and interaction–
like that being developed in the area of Cultural Studies–offers
a new look at marginal regions, even if the perspective often
remains of a center that does not want to be one.

It so happens that academic writing merely repeats other
centralizing forces; it is only one critical tool among many
others. But since orality is always a de-centering process, it
can be seen to elude the recapitulating synthesis of academic
writing. This is why Pierre Lévy foretells the advent of
another kind of orality, created by the cybernetic hypertext,
offering a new collectivization of knowledge and new forms
in which to apprehend knowledge (3).

Latin America itself, in a sense, is an oral, written, and virtual text, like all the other regions of the earth. Latin America
is an oral text in the sense of its consciousness of movement,
transitivity, and its marginality, it is the collective product of
metaphors and cultural exchange. These are territories/texts
with mobile and interchanging frontiers that do not accept for
themselves the status of a fixed model but rather know they
are a construct in process, a discursive map of the rhizome of
its infinite conversational possibility. In this sense, it is important to remember the significant relationship, suggested by
Olga Valeska, between the Mexican tree-of-life clay sculptures (shown in **Figure 6**) and Latin American narrations, a
relationship that reveals the presence of a decidedly eccentric
order: Within the limits of their branches, life-outside-life is
established–a liminal space where censorship loses its power,
as does linear cause and effect reasoning. "And the forms of
all the bodies interweave in an embrace which is both erotic
and melancholic (con)fusing the borders of all polarities"
(Valeska 92). The tree of life, considered as an emblem of narrative, would also illustrate what I have here been calling
orality: The exchange between life and death, chaos and the
cosmos, the sacred and the profane, in the constant interplay
of transformations and metamorphoses that, even when being
crystallized in a written form, overcomes its borders, subverting order and invading other spaces. Words in action, a procession, a large cobra, a clay narration, mobile territories/
texts, in the voices of those who tell a tale and make a point.

Translation by Nair Anaya-Ferreira

Works Cited

Arendt, Hannah. 1994. *Sobre a violência*. Trans. André Duarte. Rio
de Janeiro: Relume-Dumará.

Bopp, Raul. 1975 [1931]. *Cobra Norato e outros poemas*. 10th ed. Rio
de Janeiro: Civilização Brasileira.

Calvino, Italo. 1997. *Fábulas italianas*. Trans. Nilson Moulin. São
Paulo: Companhia das Letras.

Carpentier, Alejo. 1987. *A literatura do maravilhoso*. Trans. Rubia P.
Goldoni and Sérgio Molina. São Paulo: Vértice.

——. 1994. *Los pasos perdidos*. Havana: Letras cubanas.

Cinta Larga, Pichuvy. 1988. *Histórias de maloca antigamente*. Ed. Ana
Leonel Queiroz, Ivete Walty and Leda Leonel. Belo Horizonte: SEGRAC.

Featherstone, Mike. 1997. *O desmanche da cultura. Globalização, pós-
modernismo e identidade*. Trans. Carlos Eugênio M. de Moura. São Paulo:
Studio Nobel.

Figure 6.

(Archive of the author)

Glissant, Édouard. 1981. *Poétique de la relation*. Paris: Gallimard.

——. 1994. "Le chaos-monde, l'oral et l'écrit." *Écrire la parole de nuit.
La nouvelle littérature antillaise*. Ed. Patrick Chamoiseau et al. Paris:
Gallimard. 111–29.

Laterza, Moacyr Filho. 1997. "Da plausibilidade dos fantasmas ou
Das histórias de assombração como fator de identidade cultural em
Minas Gerais." Diss. Belo Horizonte.

Lévy, Pierre. 1998. "A reencarnação do saber." *Folha de S. Paulo* 22. 2:3.

Lezama Lima, José. 1998. *A expressão americana*. Trans. Irlemar Chiampi.
São Paulo: Brasiliense.

Nava, Pedro. 1978 [1972]. *Baú de ossos*. 5th ed. Rio de Janeiro: José
Olympio.

Nunes, Paulo. 1997. *Belém e seus encantos de Cobra: leitura-audição de
meus afetos*. Belém.

Paz, Octavio. 1971. *Los signos en rotación y otros ensayos*. Madrid:
Alianza Editorial.

——. 1992 [1950]. *El laberinto de la soledad*. Mexico City: Fondo de
Cultura Económica.

Pereira, Vera Lúcia F. 1995. *O artesão da memória no Vale do Jequitinhonha*.
Belo Horizonte: Editora da UFMG/Editora PUC-MINAS.

Propp, Vladimir. 1983. *Morfologia do conto*. 2d ed. Trans. Jaime Ferreira
and Victor Oliveira. Lisboa: Veja.

Santiago, Silviano. 1978. *Uma literatura nos trópicos.* São Paulo: Perspectiva.

Simões, Maria do Socorro and Christhofe Golder, eds. 1995. *Belém conta.* Pará conta series. Belém: CEJUP/UFPa.

Valeska, Olga. 1998. "Miragem de olhares: a presença perturbadora do outro." Diss. Belo Horizonte.

Vargas Llosa, Mario. 1989. *The Storyteller.* Trans. Helen Lane. New York: Farrar, Straus, and Giroux.

——. 1997 [1987]. *El hablador.* Barcelona: Editorial Seix Barral S. A.

Zumthor, Paul. 1987. *La lettre et la voix. De la "littérature" médiévale.* Paris: Seuil.

SECTION III
THE MULTIPLICITY AND DIVERSITY OF DISCOURSES AND THEATRICALITIES: INTRODUCTION

Juan Villegas

Every literary history constitutes a process of inclusion and exclusion. Thus, the majority of the histories of Latin American theater have tended to focus on texts that were in some way representative of the most important Latin American problems, as defined by the social sector to which the historian belonged. In general terms, the texts selected have been those whose theatrical codes were identifiable with the aesthetic tendencies legitimized by that same social sector, and preferably established by the dominant trends in Europe. These perspectives have given rise to histories of Latin American theater predominantly based on works representative of the cultural preferences of the middle classes with European-minded aesthetic tastes. These histories tend to exclude works from the culturally nonhegemonic sectors of society or those that do not conform to a limited definition of theater. Only on rare occasions do they consider the various texts' theatrical qualities and historical contexts. Histories of Latin American theater, like those of Latin American cultures generally, have tended to be monocultural in outlook and principally based on written texts.

The culture of Latin America is constituted by a plurality of cultures whose legitimacy within the critical and historical discourses of hegemony—and, therefore, their inclusion or exclusion from official history—has varied according to political and economic transformations and to changes in the institutions with which the critical discourses, whether theoretical or practical, are linked.

The recent dilation of the concept of theater within the field of theory (Schechner 1985; De Marinis; Fischer-Lichte), has furnished instruments for the inclusion of theatrical forms from the marginal sectors of society into theatrical discourse. Today it is possible to understand "theater" as theatrical discourse, which is to say as a cultural product in which a transmitting group constructs a spectacle or performance with the aim of communicating with some audience. In the production of this performance, the transmitters employ the theatrical codes legitimized within their cultural system, adapting the codes to their intentions and the possibility of communicating the social imaginary and the appropriate message to the spectators. In ideal instances of the communicative process, the spectators possess the necessary competence to decipher the codes being employed and manipulated. For their part, the producers tend to employ those codes accessible to the spectators or the codes of the culture of the potential spectators. From this point of view, the communicative function of the performance, its addressees, and its context have varied in different cultures.

In the Latin American case, the ethnic determinant of cultural systems has played an important role in the configuration of the various theatrical traditions. While history has privileged the theatrical traditions rooted in the European cultures, these latter have coexisted with indigenous theatrical traditions—of an enormous variety—as well as with Afro-Latin American traditions. Indigenous theatrical traditions have generally been considered under the rubric of religious celebrations or native rituals. Much less attention has been paid to the theatrical traditions rooted in cultures of African origin or practiced by the descendants of the black slaves.

The history of Latin America is the product of a series of historical transformations in which the culturally productive sectors of society have been displaced. These historical transformations have justified the substitutions of the social groups for whom the cultural products were intended. In the case of theater, these displacements have given rise to significant transformations in the social imaginaries constructed and in aesthetic preferences. The displacements of the interests of the culturally productive sectors vis-à-vis the potential addressees, on the other hand, have given rise to differentiated discursive forms. Latin America has been and continues to be characterized by a vast conglomerate of cultures, a diversity that extends in many cases even to the linguistic differences between microcultures, as with the present-day indigenous languages, or between macrocultures, as is the case with the Spanish and Portuguese languages in Latin America and in Europe. Within this diversity the traditions of those social sectors wielding cultural hegemony have distinguished themselves as the determining cultures. This hegemony—rooted in political, economic, and military power—has, since 1492, by and large been linked to traditions of European origin. The alternative discourses, on the other hand, have been especially linked with the discourses produced by the cultural systems rooted in the diverse ethnicities that constitute the Latin American space or with those sectors in opposition to the political hegemonies.

To write a history of Latin American theater and theatrical traditions presupposes the description, in a series of synchronic sections, of the coexisting cultural discourses of the various culturally productive sectors, as well as that of their potential addressees. However, in this section we will employ multiple perspectives emphasizing the diachronic dimension. This choice is grounded in our assumption of the coexistence throughout the better part of Latin American history of three cultural macrosystems. Diachronically, the first perspective is constituted by the indigenous cultures, within which there has existed throughout history a plurality of microcultures. In this context we consider the work of Tamara Underiner on the recent animation of the Mayan theater in Guatemala and southern Mexico. The second point of reference is the macro-system of cultural hegemony, a system marked by an enor-mous diachronic variety and a plurality of forms and transformations. The third and last point of view is that of the Afro-Latin American cultures and their specific variations and distinct localizations. By virtue of its cultural and linguistic substrata, as well as for historical reasons, Brazil constitutes a macroculture of its own, which has undergone changes that, in a number of instances, are different from those experi-enced in the rest of Latin America. Thus, although we make

reference to the theatrical discourses of Brazil throughout our analysis, we have also included two essays specifically devoted to the theatrical manifestations of nineteenth- and twentieth-century Brazil.

Translation by Colman Hogan

Works Cited

DeMarinis, Marco. 1993. *The Semiotics of Performance.* Trans. Aine O'Healy. Bloomington: Indiana University Press.

Fischer-Lichte, Erika .1992. *The Semiotics of Theater.* Trans. Jeremy Gainer and Doris L. Jones. Bloomington: Indiana University Press.

Schechner, Richard. 1985. *Between Theater and Anthropology.* Philadel-phia: University of Pennsylvania Press.

CHAPTER 52

THE THEATER IN
PRE-HISPANIC AMERICA

Juan Villegas

The Macro-System of the Indigenous
Theatrical Traditions

The traditional European concept of theater has had negative consequences for the study of the cultural and theatrical discourses of Latin America. It has justified the exclusion of enormous sectors of theatrical production and has conditioned the study of some cultural productions under inadequate criteria. A surprising number of critics have denied the existence of theater in the pre-Hispanic period. Other critics, while expressing sympathy for the theatrical manifestations of that epoch, have implicitly assigned them a lesser status, since they do not correspond exactly to the criteria that are expected within a "real" theatrical tradition.

Luis Ordaz, in his *Aproximación a la trayectoria de la dramática argentina* (1992) [Approaches to the Evolution of Argentine Theatre], speaks of the antecedents of Latin American theater. He mentions the *Rabinal Achí* and *Fiesta del Sumamao* [Sumamao Festival] but later argues for their exclusion, noting "it can, nevertheless, be affirmed that theater as such disembarked in the territory of Argentina with the Spanish colonizers" (8). Moreover, by referring to structural elements, such histories make manifest the predominance of those concepts that stem from the dominant culture. There are critics, for example, who attempt to justify study of pre-Hispanic theater by arguing that a number of the elements emphasized by Aristotle as being essential to tragedy are present in these indigenous theatrical manifestations. Thus Carlos Espinoza Domínguez points out that "they avail themselves of what Aristotle defined as one of the most basic resources of the theater, imitation" (50).

From this perspective, there is in the dominant Western tradition a certain consensus surrounding the use of "theater" as a point of reference and the ensuing naming of other neighboring or related activities as modifications of the term. Thus, one frequently hears talk of pre-theatrical, para-theatrical, or post-theatrical forms. In other instances, the concepts of "ethnic" or "folkloric" theater are used. These adjectives exclude the theatrical forms in question from historical consideration or condition their examination from the point of view of the values of the aesthetic system pertaining to the hegemonic discourse. All these expressions seem to suggest that the activities being named have something in common with theater or the theatrical, while at the same time implying that there remains something that does not justify their qualification as such. In such cases, the concepts of "theater" and "theatrical" function as norms, determining how these activities will be defined or characterized. In this way, the characteristics assigned to the theater by the possessors of the discourse are established as the standard of achievement or value. The resulting ideological, historical, and political consequences can be of enormous significance. Awareness of the inadequacy of the term *theater* has given rise to the use of other expressions, such as "representations" or "ceremonial festivals." However, both of these alternatives are marked by limiting connotations. In anthropological studies of dances and rites, especially those carried out in the United States in recent years, the concept of *performance,* suggesting the act of staging a representation, has acquired a common currency.

The term *theatricality* allows us to liberate ourselves from the traditional connotations of theater, stimulates the understanding of culture as a process of the construction of images that shape and sustain the social imaginary, and furnishes us with instruments adequate to the comprehension of marginal cultures. "Theatricality" designates a system of communication in which the emphasis is placed on signs and visual representation. As with every communication system, theatricality serves a representative and a pragmatic function. The connotations of the signs emitted are determined by the cultural system in which they are lodged and, at the same time, conditioned by the aptitude of the potential addressees. Our supposition is that in each historical moment there coexist various theatricalities, some of which were legitimized and others delegitimized by the mechanisms of power. Understood in this sense, theatricality is not limited to what the Western tradition has called theater.

From this perspective, indigenous theatricalities constitute diverse systems of theatrical forms responding to the distinct cultures and historical and social conditions of indigenous peoples. The inclusion of these theatrical discourses in history involves understanding their functionality and meaning in accordance with the transformations in the power relations of the producers of these discourses. In the pre-Hispanic period the socially and culturally dominant class was the producer of these discourses, and their function was to stage and celebrate the reigning cosmological conceptions and to communicate a legitimized social imaginary to potential spectator-participants. Following the military, political, and cultural defeat of the indigenous societies, these discourses acquired new functions and new characteristics. Instead of challenging other cultures from a position of power, the predominant interrelation was oriented toward the European conquering culture and practiced from a position in the shadow of a destructive, assimilating, and imposing order. Under these new conditions, the indigenous cultural discourses became discourses of marginalization, constrained to employ the codes of the dominant culture in order to satisfy the exigencies of the powerful. Thus, the past appropriation by Spanish producers of theatrical discourses of elements from other cultures was now transformed into a syncratic means of absorption of these discourses by a subjected Indian population. Since the Spanish discursive producers belonged to the ruling sectors of a subjugated society and they directed their discourses at marginalized or defeated addressees, spectacles that were essentially the same as they had been in the past now acquired a different meaning: They constituted a validation of the past and functioned to maintain a cultural or cosmographic tradition. It is at this point that indigenous cultural discourses acquired an abiding hybrid character in which the indigenous residues or continuity traits varied according to the historical

515

contexts and the forms or presence of the dominant cultures. At the same time, cultural hybridity took different forms and was experienced to differing degrees in the distinct cultures of the indigenous sectors. While in some areas indigenous elements have almost disappeared, in others they have been conserved relatively intact. And in still other areas, indigenous practices have absorbed elements of other cultures, imparting to them an indigenous face or integrating them in such a way that they have become defining of what is the indigenous.

The pre-Hispanic cultural space was constituted by a plurality of cultures in which were mixed, as much synchronically as diachronically, dominant and marginal/dominated cultures, many of which were, at the time of the Spanish arrival, considered nonexistent or extinct. Each of these cultures possessed a plurality of theatricalities whose functions were distinct, one of which was religious. Theatricality comprehends a manipulation of space, personages, and their characterization as well as an orchestration of time, themes, tones, modes of performance, and other parameters. All this would be specific to the culture in question, its context, and the intentions of the producers. In Néstor García Canclini's analysis and description (1996), theatricalities must be understood as forms by which the ruling classes stage themselves. These theatricalities were manifest in a great diversity of cultural practices, from architecture to household utensils and tools, and from public spaces to mass spectacles. Such public spectacles filled a number of diverse functions, sometimes profane, sometimes religious or ritualistic. The majority of the histories of Latin American theater have emphasized the ritual-religious dimension, usually as a consequence of interpreting these cultures as primitive. The reality, however, was that in each of the different cultures theatrical discourses fulfilled a variety of functions, with codes and signs specific to the various distinct occasions.

Each of the theatricalities of the cultures that existed in what is now Latin America before the arrival of the Spanish had its own historicity and specific transformations. Each of the dominant indigenous cultures integrated, at various times, anterior or coexistent cultures, shaping the functional dimensions of the subdominant cultures to its own interests or social imaginaries. Knowledge of a number of these subdominant cultures either disappeared from the historical memory imposed by the dominant cultures or was transmitted to the first Spanish chroniclers or historians by representatives or informants, but always from the point of view of the reigning culture. Contemporary research has been uncovering information about the existence of a plurality of cultures and about their geographic extension, their economic bases, their social structures, social peculiarities, and cosmogonies. In the majority of cases, their histories have been partially retold on the basis of artifacts that have been either unearthed or otherwise conserved. These have constituted the raw materials for the reconstruction of their customs and cosmogonies. What has not been possible, however, is to reconstruct their theatricalities, their forms of presenting themselves in social spectacles, or the system of images constituting their social imaginary.

Although, as mentioned, some historians have denied the existence of the theater in pre-Hispanic cultures, few today question its diverse manifestations. As Eugenio Pereira Salas has declared, "in pre-Hispanic America, a specific concept of theater was cultivated, with designated sites, actors skilled in their craft, abundant resources, and a multiplicity of themes

and forms. The most notable examples were the Inca *taqui,* the Maya and Nahua *mitote,* and the *micehauliztli* of the Mexicas" (13). Referring to the *areitos* (songs of the pre-Hispanic cultures of the Caribbean and Central America), Rine Leal writes: "The *areitos* were, thus, a complex manifestation of aboriginal culture mixing song, dance, poetry, choreography, music, costumes, and pantomime orchestrated by the *tequina* or *coreuta . . .*" (9–10). For their part, María Bonilla and Stoyan Vladich emphasize the diversity of functions: "In addition, it appears that scenes of great humour were staged and that on these days the entire community participated in the event. The various themes ran the gamut from domestic subjects and agricultural problems to historical and mythological representations, and such spectacles thus constituted a kind of autochthonous cultural memory" (22). Descriptions of pre-Hispanic theatricalities–their collective modes of staging the social fabric of their culture and times–allow us to understand these societies, their structures and social relations, their social imaginaries, and their cosmogonies and how they were visualized.

The following sections will discuss representative aspects of the theatricalities and the theatrical discourses of the Aztec and Incan cultures. In the Aztec case, this principally concerns the ritual dimension of their theatricality; in the Incan case, it involves the employment of theatricalities and theatrical discourses as a means for the auto-legitimization of power.

Aztec Culture: Ritual as Theatrical Spectacle

In the land known today as Mexico there existed a wealth of theatrical activity, both ritual and profane. In his introduction to the *Rabinal Achí,* Francisco Monterde points to the existence of various zones of theatrical activity: "By the testimony of some of the Catholic priests, we know very well that in Mexico City and Cholula there were night-time theatrical representations, held in especially designated, elegantly decorated and ornamented open spaces. The performances were by preference comic, with spectacular costumes. Frequently masquerading as animals, the actors' characterizations (and speeches) amused the spectators to no end" (vii). María Sten has highlighted the importance of dance in these ceremonies: "Dances formed part of daily life and especially part of the ritual festivals" ("Ponte a bailar" ["Let's Dance"] 67). She has also noted that "both in space and time, in their movements as well as the colour of the costumes and the decorations, in the participation of the women together with or separate from the men, such ceremonies were marked by a hidden sense of being united with the cosmological principle. The dances had in addition another meaning of equal importance: The social and political" (67).

The majority of the theatrical and festive spectacles were tied to religious or ceremonial activities. Within this plurality, Martha Toriz has detailed the existence of certain ceremonies associated with the eighteen-month Aztec calendar, revealing their differences from and similarities with one another. Toriz's analysis centers on the theatricality of four festivals and has brought to light the specifically theatrical elements. She points out that to understand these spectacles it is necessary to have a grasp of pre-Hispanic Nahuatl religions since "indigenous religion is charged with a great number of symbolic elements with which we must familiarize ourselves" (15). These rites, she notes, made use of a multitude of theatrical elements, including scenography, dances, costuming, make-up, props, action, music, and song: "All the strata of Nahuatl society participated either as actors or spectators, and this fact has allowed us to understand how that society was structured and what functions were exercised within it" (15). Toriz concludes that these ritual festivals made use of an elaborate theatrical codification for the communication of their message. While some festivals involved the entire population, in others the warriors were the principal actors. Costumes varied considerably from one festival to another, as did the dances and the musical accompaniments. The system of codifications suggests that the festivals corresponding to specific months possessed their own distinct theatrical characteristics, subject to annual repetition.

Pedro Morales has also described the Aztec rituals from a perspective of theatricality and has highlighted a number of elements not mentioned by Toriz. He points out that the Huitzilopochtli festival, for example, "obeyed the conventional structuration of ritual, organized vis-à-vis determinate ends.... Thus ritual acts with spectacular characteristics served as an ideological instrument for the propagation of the religion professed by the dominant class" (44). Referring to the modes of characterization, he also points out that "among the Aztecs, the personification of the gods was buttressed to a considerable extent by what we today would call external characterization, which is to say, by recourse to objects adorning the human body that imparted to it a divine personality" (46). Morales notes the little-studied playful element: "The ludic factor was expressed in some Aztec rituals by means of games, races, chases, jocular confrontations and ritual thefts" (47). In sum, it must be stressed that these spectacles were massive, although the forms of participation varied widely.

The Legitimization of Power: Inca Theatricalities

The theatrical discourses and theatricalities of the Inca in Peru provide another perspective on the function of theatrical spectacles in pre-Hispanic Latin America. As was the case in Mesoamerica, there existed a great diversity of spectacles operating within the production of clearly established codes. A number of researchers in this area have revealed the existence of theatrical genres that they have attempted to identify with the genres of the Aristotelian tradition. These identifications are, however, erroneous, since the genres in question correspond to very different concept of the world. The *wancas,* for example, were predominantly historical spectacles, recounting the exploits of the Inca and the great figures of the empire. The *aranway,* on the other hand, represented episodes of daily life.

The descriptions left by the Spanish chroniclers suggest a markedly pragmatic dimension to Incan theater since they give evidence of how such performances were utilized by the system or social group in power to legitimize or construct a history that bestowed authority on their rule. A number of the spectacles, for example, concerned the origins of the Inca; others recounted the military victories of Huayna Capac; the coronation of Cusi Huascar, the twelfth Inca; and Atahualpa's insurrection and death: "All the spectacles belonged to this first group of massive, multi-day representations performed by the army en masse. They were distinguished by the exceptional splendour of the decorations and costumes, which served to underline the grandeur and the power of the empire. However, their plots were simple and the structures and roles were fixed by tradition" (Oleszkiewicz 19). Within the *aranway* tradition, themes were varied and various subgenres existed, among which the so-called *taquis* constituted one of the most important. It has been determined with

respect to the representational forms of the latter that the musical accompaniment was performed by women and the more theatrical part by men, and that they were elaborately decorated with floral arrangements and pluming.

Indigenous Theatrical Discourses during the Colonial Epoch

Although historians have noted the discontinuity of the indigenous theatrical practices during the Colonial epoch and the fact that there was a conscious effort on the part of the authorities to eliminate them, others have pointed out that indigenous theatrical practices nonetheless continued to exist. It is of course important to realize that the continuity of the representations took place within a different context, in terms of the conditions in which both the producers and the addressees of the discourses found themselves. During this epoch the producers no longer constituted a dominant power group, and thus even texts originally produced in the previous era had to have been viewed in a different light by the now vanquished social classes. In discussing indigenous participation in the theatrical spectacles of the Colonial era, we must consider both those spectacles produced independently by and for the natives—in continuity with the traditions described in the previous sections—as well as those orchestrated by the priests for indigenous audiences. This is to say that, within the new indigenous traditions, we must include the theatrical discourses favored by the Catholic priests inasmuch as these spectacles constituted a hybridization of a Christian message with elements and forms stemming from the Spanish medieval and the indigenous theatrical traditions.

Cultural Hybridization: The Church and the Theater of Evangelization

Many Colonial-era cultural and theatrical productions, with variants in the different countries, were linked to or produced by the ecclesiastical sectors and predominantly addressed to the indigenous population, who participated in great numbers. A plurality of forms arose conditioned by the producers—Church or state—and the ethnic and social diversity of the potential addressees. In this manner, the Jesuits, possessors of a clearly defined discourse, utilized theatrical procedures and images in accordance with the ethnic sectors to whom their discourse was directed: Guaraní, Aztec, Maya, Aymara, Quechua, and so on. In each instance, they tended to employ theatrical elements that were current within the theatrical competence of the practitioners and the theatricality of the addressees. Almost all the historians have stressed that Latin American theater arose from these practices. Walter Rela, for example, speaking of the origins of theater in Brazil, has connected it to the Jesuits' habit of employing theater as a means of instruction: "The [Society] of Jesus, from the moment of first contact, made use of theater as a way of seducing the natives into the mysteries of the Christian faith. Operating with a certain vision of the various regional differences in media, the Jesuits adapted native rituals, dances, and musical forms, and made use of the bounteous store of native myths, shaping those raw materials into simple dramatizations" (8). The position of Mario Cacciaglia is similar: "The originators of theatrical activity in Brazil were the Portuguese Jesuits of Coimbra who, fifty years after the discovery of Brazil, were sent as missionaries to the new land" (159).

Some historians have spoken of a theater of evangelization. According to Armando Partida, this was a type of theater produced by the priests, written in Nahuatl, and directed almost exclusively at the natives: "What is evident and of importance is that the union and interaction of the two cultures gave rise to an original form of religious theater which, formally speaking, is what we can consider the theater of the evangelization, the theater performed in Nahuatl: The first aesthetic fruit of the cultural interpenetration, independently considered from the religious and ideological content that both cultures brought to it" (26). Othon Arróniz, in contrast, includes within his comprehension of the theater of evangelization practically all the theater produced by the priests for indigenous audiences. Thus, Arróniz dedicates separate chapters to Franciscan, Dominican, and Jesuit theater. Arróniz also underlines the fact that the Spanish and Portuguese priests began their theatrical and catechizing labours as soon as they disembarked in America, pointing out that these efforts antedated the great development of Spanish theater many years later. He notes, for example, that the first mention of these theatrical labors comes in 1533, when "the history of the Golden Age theater had hardly commenced" (15).

These types of theatrical discourse shared a number of common characteristics across the various regions of Latin America and can be directly correlated with the zones in which a major indigenous population was resident or where religiously important spaces were located. They can also be correlated with the zones in which an indigenous theatrical tradition was able to supply artisans and actors for the staging of such discourses and in which familiarization with theatrical codes gave rise to a significant potential audience. On the other hand, such theatrical performances tended to be held during times that were, either for the population, the ethnic group, or the church, practically useful or functional. Thus, they were frequently celebrated during Catholic religious festivals or on the feast day of the patron saint of the city. At the same time, since the Church made use of the native religious spaces and festivals, many of the religious festivals coincided with indigenous celebrations.

These stagings often served to represent a part of the history of the indigenous populations or problems that they faced, and as such functioned as emblems of their history and, at the same time, were linked to pre-Hispanic theatrical forms. The performances were staged by indigenous actors and scenographers. History was adapted to suit the circumstances, and fiction was combined with reality. Specifically, the fiction of a previously fictionalized historical event–the Christian conquest of Jerusalem, for example–was identified with the Spanish Conquest (on the level of fiction) and concluded with the real (nonfictional) baptism of the natives. The representations relied on the cultural competency of the spectators–their knowledge, for example, of Cortés and Alvarado. Most of the productions were staged in the languages of the addressees. On some occasions they were bi- or trilingual, such as in the case cited by Bonilla and Vladich: "Rela mentions the representations staged by Padre Manuel de Nóbrega in Brazil: *Diálogos sobre a converzão dos gentíos* [Dialogues on the Conversion of the Gentiles] (1557–1558) and, between 1567 and 1570, Padre José de Anchieta's *La Pregação Universal* [The Universal Proclamation] in Piratininga and San Vicente, a piece staged in Spanish, Portuguese, and Tupi. . ." (26). The trilingual play, *Auto representando na festa de São Lourenço* [The Allegory of the Feast of St. Lawrence], "incorporated contradictions and conflicts pertaining to the historical moment of its staging. Thus, for example, among the principals of the

work are the devil Guaixará and Aimbiré, his servant, who continually attempt to deceive the people, events which are repeated in *Na festa do Natal* [The Feast of the Nativity]. It is significant that the names of the two devils are native, and even more so that they are the names of two great Tamollo chieftains, allied with the French, and sworn enemies of the Portuguese and their allies, the Tupi" (Rela 26).

As has often been noted, the natives supplied the manpower, and at times, between 1535 and 1575, in the Viceroyalty of New Spain there were special stages, open chapels decorated by indigenous artisans "consisting of a small central nave with ample lateral arcades spacious enough for a large audience" (Azor 21). The fact that the actors in these performances were native allows us to conjecture that a major part of the theatricality and body language was constituted on the base of indigenous theatrical codes, although the message of the texts was Christian. Thus, it is possible that in many cases each spectator deciphered the theatrical signs of the representation from the point of view of his or her respective ethnic social imaginary, an operation surely reinforced by other elements of the spectacle. According to Ileana Azor, "the natives brought to the productions, in addition, all the elements of scenography, costuming, and make-up. . . .There are descriptions by Spanish chroniclers marveling at the colour and diversity of indigenous decorations, and thus we must conclude that pre-Colombian culture had a significant presence in the colonial spectacles" (20).

The producers of these discourses belonged, of course, to the culture of the hegemonic discourses. One well known case was that of Juan de Espinosa Medrano, El Lunarejo [The Spotted-Face] (1620?–1688), a native born in a town near Cuzco who rose to high ecclesiastical office in the cathedral of that city. In his *El hijo pródigo* [The Prodigal Son], written in Quechua and performed before indigenous audiences in the Cuzco region, Espinosa Medrano rewrites biblical history with a native ambiance and characters: "In the work, the Young Son of a native family decides to traverse the world, seeking out new experiences. Against his father's wishes, he departs in the company of The Body, The Youth, and The Word of God, the latter constantly counseling him not to let himself be distracted by his other traveling companions" (Azor 38).

The Reutilization of Indigenous Traditions

The pre-Hispanic indigenous theatrical or spectacular tradition explains the rapid reutilization of the spectacles, which the priests produced in native versions. One example of this is the "Moors and Christians" mock-battle dances that can still be seen today, dances that the natives appropriated very early on. Studying this tradition in Guatemala, Matilde Montoya notes that examples and documents have been preserved showing that already by around 1630 to 1632 there were *moreros* and that "at that time they were charged with furnishing costumes for the indigenous dancers" (31). Montoya relates how, in the celebrations surrounding the opening and consecration of the Guatemala City Cathedral in 1680, "little boys and girls from the *highest aristocracy* of Guatemala learned dances and sported costumes representative of indigenous personages, evidence that there was fusion in the theatrical and dance performances of both cultures" (35).

Let us now turn to two examples that demonstrate the continuity of tradition, albeit a tradition whose variants were determined by the new historical conditions.

Ollantay, or the Reutilization of History

Although the text we have dates from 1853, and its problems are legion, *Ollantay* is an indigenous text, unquestionably addressed to natives since it was written in Quechua. As for the producers and the cultural and theatrical codes employed, these questions open up numerous problems. First published in 1853 (although there are references to a production of 1780), it has been translated into several languages. In addition, it has been "the cause of polemics between those who date it before the conquest and those who see in it elements of the Spanish Golden Age theatre" (Ripoll and Valdespino 421). In the Spanish version of the text, written in metrical verse, love and pride figure as motivations and there are associations with characters from the cloak-and-dagger play.

According to Ripoll and Valdespino, "it is the insurrectional spirit, the censure of tyranny and the defense of popular sovereignty, so incompatible with the absolutist Inca regime, which inclines us to think that it is not pre-Colombian" (421). However, this observation does not take account of the transformation of status from dominant culture to vanquished culture. What could be a legitimization of the powerful in the first case was, by implication, available for reuse by the vanquished in the second, a reutilization involving not only the transformation of the text but possibly an appropriation of codes and traits of the dominant culture as well. From the descriptions, it seems necessary to establish the relation between this text and the rebellion of Tupac Amaru, the Inca who in 1780 led an insurrection against the Spanish: "The play was staged with propagandistic aims in mind and, according to contemporary testimonies, done for the leader of the insurrection, with whom the protagonist of the drama shared a notable coincidence of convictions and attitudes. The protagonist's petition to Pachacútec for the hand of the princess can be read as symbolic of Túpac Amaru's petition at the high court [*Audiencia*] of Lima pressing his right to the throne of the empire, and even the settings–the youth of the rebel and that of the character–are grounded in a single geographic reality" (Ripoll and Valdespino 422). Read in this way, *Ollantay* is seen to reutilize the historical Quechua theater tradition in a new context, transforming it into an advocate of the rebellion and, especially, a vindicator of the new hero, Tupac Amaru (1738–1781).

The Rabinal Achí

The majority of critics and historians have considered the *Rabinal Achí* the sole remnant of the rich Mayan theater tradition. The text was called the *Rabinal Achí* by its discoverer, the French abbé Charles Etienne Brasseaur de Bourbourg, who published this version in 1862, although to the natives of Guatemala it is known as the *Xahoh Tun* or *Dance of Tun*. The composition of the work can be dated to the second half or even waning years of the fifteenth century, prior to the Conquest. It must be supposed that the nineteenth-century version has incorporated variants integrated over the course of the Colonial era.

A reading of the existing text can be carried out from one of two perspectives. In an archeological reading, attempting to reconstruct the original, the text can be considered part of a ritual ceremony whose origins are Mayan-Quiché and is thought, thus, to have functioned within the cosmological and cultural belief system of that culture. As Azor points out, "by virtue of its plot and structure, recounting the story of the sacrifice of an enemy prince, the *Rabinal Achí* is an exceptional example of the native tradition of religious representations"

(16). However, as with other texts of the past, the *Rabinal* is also open to a revisionist reading. This reading would focus on the text's semiotic potential in relation to those distinct historical moments that have changed the communicative situation, whether in terms of the social or cultural position of the producers and potential addressees or in terms of the transformations of the dominant cultures. From this point of view, it becomes clear that the staging of the work fulfilled one function when, during the period in which the Mayan-Quiché culture was the dominant culture, it was produced by the dominant class and quite another function when staged by and for natives in the period after the Conquest. In the latter case, performances of the text concern the staging by a marginalized group of a theatrical text belonging to that group. While in the first instance, representations of the *Rabinal* constituted an affirmation of a legitimized culture and ruling class, in the second instance they constituted affirmations of a dominated social group whose religion and system of values had been deprived of legitimacy by Colonial society. This reading can be seen, therefore, as constituting a potential process of social self-affirmation on the part of the marginalized, either by vindicating the buried or hidden tradition or by safeguarding the identity suppressed by the dominant power. In this latter instance, the text constitutes part of an alternative discourse to the theatrical discourse imposed by the culturally dominant one. In both cases, however, Mayan-Quiché codes of theatricality are employed and function within the transmission of the specific message of the two contexts, which differ radically.

The social imaginary conceived by the existing variant of the text is that of a fundamentally agricultural society with a stratified social structure, in which the military is subordinated to the civil authorities and the principal cause of warfare is the acquisition or defense of food supplies. The authorities and the army essentially function as defenders of the population's means of subsistence. Within this order, representatives of enemy societies are treated with great respect, being, in many aspects, very similar to the Mayan-Quiché: Society's heroes are warriors whose personal pride is founded on a code of service to the authorities, personal valor, prowess in combat, and recognition by others. Women have no stature in such a society, and compliance with social norms and codes is essential. The parameters of this social imaginary are manifest in the world constructed by the text as well as by its structures and the rhetorical effects it employs. The dramatic structure is one of a contest of wills between two protagonists. Stylistically, the text's discourses are reiterative, with characters repeating the discourses of other characters, and as such the protocolic or ritual nature of these discourses is emphasized. Other ritual characteristics include an emphasis on dialogue, as manifest in long speeches, and the use of dance. Emphasis is also placed on the enumerative quality or metonymy of the voice representing the character who is reproduced in the discourse. The characters' speeches are intercalated with dances incorporated into the action. The importance assigned to the voice reinforces the oral and public character of communication.

A number of the structural and theatrical codes of the *Rabinal* can be observed in other theatrical forms of a pre-Hispanic origin, both during the colonial epoch and even today. These can be taken as evidence that, despite the overwhelming presence of theatrical forms of European origin, indigenous theater traditions or those of a popular theater have continued, albeit hybridized with elements from theatrical discourses of Hispanic origin.

The Discourse of Social Resistance: El Güegüense

The process of reutilizing tradition can also be seen in the Maya text *El Güegüense*. Written in a mixture of the Nicaraguan Mangue dialect of Mayan and Spanish, the text was published for the first time in 1874 by C. H. Berendt. While the date of composition is unknown, historians have surmised it was sometime in the sixteenth to eighteenth centuries. "*El Güegüense* is, thus, one of the representative works of the Latin American and Caribbean theater. However, it is very much more than that. It is, in fact, nothing less than the first work, chronologically speaking, of that theater. On the one hand, its origins reach back to pre-Colombian theatrical traditions; on the other hand, the text has been rounded off with grafts from Hispanic theater, most likely in the first century of the colony, the sixteenth, or at some other time during the Colonial era. Born in the cradle of our miscegenation, it is, thus, a work of popular ingenuity; a work that, mestizo to the core, has maintained for centuries its relevance, conserved in memory and the oral tradition. . ." (Galich 11).

The text is marked by a number of satirical and parodic aspects: A popular (at times impudent) language, repetitions, and the recurrence of situations in variations. On the spectacular level, the most striking aspects of the play are its use of masks and dances: "Between the various speeches of *El Güegüense* the characters often break into dance. There are fourteen dances in all, each with their own style and melody, some of which are named: *Ronda* [Roundel], *Corrido* [Ballad], *San Martín*, *Son Antiguo* [Old Air], *Valona*, *Rujero*, and *Puerto Rico*" (Galich 14).

Indigenous Discourses in the Nineteenth Century

The political and economic transformations of the nineteenth century gave rise to changes in the conditions of the marginalized sectors in Latin America, as well as to changes in their modes of relation to the dominant sectors and in the cultural objects they produced in relation to their function within the various national projects. These projects, however, implied a notion of national unity that entailed an immersion in the hegemonic system, and thus the cultural isolation, exclusion, or submission of the nation's microcultures. While the cultural and theatrical productions of the indigenous sectors continued, directed either at the natives themselves or at the dominant sectors, so too did the marginality of the natives, both for ethnic and for economic reasons. Yet the nineteenth-century displacement of the producers of the theatrical discourses toward the agrarian oligarchy did not radically alter the indigenous theatrical discourses as they had been constituted during the Colonial era. In fact, it can be said that the appropriation of Spanish elements became an inherent element of the indigenous theatrical discourse. During the republican period, the indigenous sectors continued to mount theatrical productions in the form of religious festivals, modernizations of ancient dramas, or as representations of pre-Hispanic or Colonial era works. The manifestations in the various regions were diverse, as were their degrees of hybridization and the reutilization of Western cultural codes.

It can be stated that the indigenous traditions constituted the major root system of these manifestations and, since some

Figure 1.

'Dance of Moors and Christians', Basilica Virgen de Guadalupe, Mexico City. (Archive of the author)

of the productions were written in aboriginal languages, their principal addressees were the indigenous populations. In these spectacles, elements of the original verbal discourse were conserved, although altered or updated to the new conditions in which the producers of the discourses found themselves. In some instances during this period, however, the indigenous productions were versions of the dramas or spectacles that had originally been devised by the priests or had originated in the dominant discourses directed at the natives of the Colonial era. Thus, there would be texts in indigenous languages and texts in Spanish or Portuguese that reiterated representations, as mentioned above, such as the fall or conquest of Jerusalem, in the manner of the various versions of the "Moors and Christians" mock battles (see **Figure 1**). The major difference, however, appears to be that many of these dramas or spectacles, which in the Colonial period were directed or imposed by the ecclesiastical sectors, had by now become texts seen as representative of indigenous spectacular practices. Since these performances no longer fulfilled a function for those who exercised power, they now constituted instances of the appropriation of cultural objects.

In this light, Malgorzata Oleszkiewicz dedicated considerable labor to the analysis of a text that figures in the tradition of the death of Atahualpa. She points out that the different versions of the *Tragedia del fin de Atawallpa* [The Tragedy of Atahualpa's Death] "constitute a collective creation, works in progress that also depend on their interaction with the public and are subject to constant modifications" (57). Of all the various versions–this multiplicity being an index of the work's popularity–she notes that the Quechua variant recorded in

1871, known as the Chayanta version, manifests the "greatest purity of the Quechua language" and "has best retained the indigenous elements and perspective" (57).

Oleszkiewicz has enumerated several features of the work that correspond to an indigenous worldview: "the sacred and cosmic sense of nature" (59); the view that "each event in human life has its resonance in the world of nature, and that natural phenomena are tied to the relationships between human beings" (59); the belief that "in the Andean vision of the cosmos, nature is endowed with a sacredness" (59). She also points out a number of details that are revelatory of the indigenous perspective: "In his premonitory dreams, Atahualpa perceives the immanent danger symbolically, in terms of natural phenomena" (59); she adds to this list the manner in which the Spanish are described, "reflecting the natives' astonishment at the arrival of these odd beings" (61); the "incomprehension that reigned between the natives and the Spanish" (62); the "accentuation of the rapacity and duplicity of the conquistadors" (62); "[t]he contrast made between the covetousness and brutality of the Spaniards and the grandeur and generosity of the Inca" (63).

From a theatrical history perspective, it is important to point out that the tradition of Incan theater had not disappeared in nineteenth-century Peru. Nor had indigenous theater disappeared from the other Latin American countries with large indigenous populations, such as various parts of Mexico, Central America, Ecuador, Bolivia, Paraguay, and Brazil. The indigenous language was maintained in the staging of theatrical productions, and features that rendered such representations specifically indigenous were retained.

The Twentieth Century:
The Middle Classes in Power

The displacement of the sectors producing theatrical discourses toward the middle classes did not radically change indigenous theatricality or theatrical discourses, nor did it alter the marginal status of the natives in Latin America. In the first decades of the twentieth century, the marginal sectors that most interested the middle classes were the workers, although some attention was paid to the peasantry and the natives. In subsequent decades, when the dominant discourse began calling for social revolution, the indigenous sectors acquired a notable importance in some countries, and this gave rise to numerous programs of cultural practices aiming to validate the indigenous cultures. Within these projects, theatrical practices took on special signification in the process of recovering indigenous traditions. Finally, in recent years, political changes and the Catholic movements inspired by liberation theology, the Second Vatican Council, and the Puebla accords have led to an intensification of indigenous theatrical practices, thanks in part to the patronage of churches and governments.

The climate of protest and the postulates of social revolution gave rise in these years to the formation of theatrical groups, directed by representatives (in some cases called monitors) of political or religious institutions. The raison d'être of these groups was to communicate the institutions' message of social transformation or the supposed rescue of the popular traditions. There arose, thus, groups that were in effect adjuncts of the churches or unions, and whose fields of operation were the population at large, the slums, and the towns. While these groups tended to be under the direction of representatives of their patron organizations, the actors were by

and large natives. Although this arrangement seemingly allowed for the self-representation of the indigenous sectors, in general it tended to mediate that representation through the values of the union or church representative and his or her institution.

The Laboratorio de Teatro Campesino e Indígena de Tabasco [Tabasco Peasants' and Natives' Theater Laboratory] (founded in 1983) was an experiment rich in ideas. Under the inspiration of Julieta Campos, this project fostered the recuperation of the traditional arts. The Laboratory staged a spectacular version of García Lorca's (1898–1936) Bodas de Sangre [1933; Blood Wedding] in which an entire village was mobilized as the setting, villagers took on the roles of the drama, and the traditional music and choreography of the region were employed. The guiding idea behind this integration was to link the universal and the ethnically specific and thereby facilitate the diffusion and valorization of the local. The project was not limited to the production of the theatrical spectacle but included as well an array of pedagogic workshops covering a diversity of historical, cultural, and theatrical topics. Descriptions of the project seem to emphasize the insertion into the indigenous culture of elements of the dominant culture: "Theatrical training was based on the Stanislavsky system, adapted to indigenous characteristics. . . . Seventeen theoretical-practical workshops were held: Acting, voice, diction, memorization, textual analysis, genres, dramaturgy, dance, biomechanics, pantomime, make-up. . ." (Quemain 153).

During the late 1970s, large numbers began participating in this popular theater movement. On the level of theatrical discourses, one highly suggestive example is the establishment and longevity of the Teatro de la Fragua [The Forge Theater]. Founded by an ecclesiastic who is both a priest and the group's director, Teatro de la Fragua operates from a small village in Honduras, although its economic and political base is in the United States. In an interview included in a video distributed by the Jesuit Mission Bureau, the priest who directs the theater, Jack Warner, S.J., declares that he sees no contradiction in carrying out both secular and religious activities, since both contribute "toward the same thing, to make people realize themselves." In one of the theater group's reports, written by Billy Peña (1990), the group's objectives are explained. Father Warner arrived in Progreso, Honduras, in 1980 "and since then has dedicated all his efforts to directing the teatro, and to taking the teatro to the towns and villages. If the people don't go to the theater, the theater has to go to the people. . . ." After receiving training in "the dramatic arts at the Goodman Theater in Chicago," Warner, who was at that time greatly influenced by the Teatro Campesino [Peasant Theater], went to Honduras with the idea of starting a theater company. It seems that Warner's principal objective has been to develop the theater and to give the villagers the opportunity to express themselves: "The works that la fragua presents put the people in direct contact with their historical past as well as inspiring them to have faith in a better future" (tlf news/noticias tlf. Vol. XI, No. 3, September 1, 1990). From an ideological point of view, Teatro de la Fragua's notion of "self-realization" is a form of the self-affirmation advocated by the Catholic Church in present-day Latin America. While in such cases the indigenous theater is represented by indigenous actors for indigenous audiences, the principles and objectives of the new Catholic Church play a mediating role in the value systems, the social imaginary, and the theatricality given representation.

The Catholic Church is not the only player in this endeavor to transmit principles and values to the popular sector. Groups such as the *Elenco Teatro Libre del Paraguay* [Elenco Free Theater of Paraguay], for example, are also involved. This group is backed and partially financed by "a consortium of European churches." The group's publication, *Ñande Reko. Cuaderno de Literatura Popular* [Ñande Reko. Popular Literature Chronicle], describes itself as a "Publication of the Communitarian Cultural Action Program, Friendship Mission." It sees itself as part of a national program for the creation of a new Paraguay and emphasizes the marginal sectors, especially the peasantry and the natives, by celebrating the Guaraní language, myths, and rituals. During the Stroessner dictatorship, the objective of the group was to bring to fruition a program fusing democratization and evangelization. The group's texts seek to represent the history of Paraguay from pre-Hispanic times to the present; in them Guaraní characters speak Guaraní and the colonizers speak Spanish. While the pre-Hispanic space is represented as a paradisiacal one, in the contemporary period the descendants of the Guaraní are shunted into degraded marginalized spaces, have lost their culture, and only vaguely remember bits of their ancient myths. They are the victims of cultural and personal degradation as well as of the political and economic system. History, as it figures in the group's productions, is a process of progressive destruction of the Guaraní culture and continual spoliation of the culture and dignity of the first inhabitants of Paraguay. Within the potential plurality of forces capable of having contributed to this sad state of affairs, no mention is made of the Church, its proselytism, or religious impositions, and the vision propounded of Guaraní culture is one saturated with nostalgia and idealization. The Church does not figure in this representation as one of the forces that caused the destruction of the Guaraní culture. In actuality, therefore, such productions do not constitute self-representations of the indigenous sectors, but rather a representation of indigenous culture from the perspective of a Church that, for political and evangelical reasons, has erected a mythical construction of that culture (Villegas 1990).

The discourses of the socially and culturally marginal sectors manifested a variety of different forms of expression in this period. On the one hand, they continued the theatricalities of festivals and celebrations, traditions that to a greater or lesser extent were altered or transformed by the processes of transference or cultural reutilization of elements from the dominant cultures. On the other hand, there were new theatrical spectacles produced, in almost all cases sponsored or directed by representatives of the culturally hegemonic sectors. The indigenous sectors continued to produce the theatrical spectacles and celebrate the religious festivals in which the characteristic features of their theatricalities were manifest. In the contemporary period, the postmodern era, these discourses have maintained a complex interrelation with the dominant cultures, and their degree of cultural hybridization varies in accordance with their distance from the centers or their diffusion. One of the new developments of the period is the visibility that many of these festivals and theatricalities have received by means of national and international television. This phenomenon must be understood as an integration of the marginal ethnic sectors within the dominant cultures and the inclusion of the exotic and the visual within the postmodern, although these productions always preserve their dimension of being cultural products of the Other.

Television and video technology has made possible a double process, in which the colonization of ethnic cultures has been intensified and at the same time the visibility of indigenous theatricalities has increased. On the one hand, this visibility has contributed positively to political objectives. Unlike in the previous era, in which the middle classes appropriated indigenous culture as a model and symbol of political revolution, today the major emphasis is placed on the visuality of indigenous culture and, in some cases, on its picturesqueness. On the other hand, the current interest in ethnic rituals has been bolstered by interpretations of what is properly Latin American advanced by a number of philosophers and Christian thinkers who link the specificity of Latin America with religiosity (Larraín 169–83).

Continuity of Traditions

Numerous studies have been undertaken in the past few decades on the subject of popular cultures, many of which are linked with indigenous traditions. Speaking of the Colombian theater, Fernando González Cajiao has highlighted the "popular viewpoint," which he characterizes as "having developed outside of the official aesthetic channels and canons, either among indigenous groups who continue to be more or less autonomous, among blacks, or in mestizo communities where it is created spontaneously" (1986, 25). Such an orientation demonstrates that the theatrical traditions initiated in the pre-Hispanic and Colonial periods have continued into the present: "Indigenous and mestizo theater naturally integrates various genres: Theater, music, dance, performance. Neither solemnity nor histrionics are necessary: What is indispensable is the creativity capable of endowing characters with vitality. The tenor of these performances is not so much festive as celebratory. Their dramatic form is one in which the activity of the characters is recounted. In itself it is a syncretic representation that is renewed each year" (Escudero 22). And Teresa Gisbert, referring to Bolivia, points out that: "There exists in Bolivia a popular and indigenous form of theater–street spectacles taking place during the Carnivals of Oruro and the *Fiesta del Gran Poder* in La Paz–whose origins can be traced back to the sixteenth century. Nowadays, these works are composed of two parts: The drama representing the death of Atahualpa and the contest between the Archangel St. Michael and the demons" (212). Gisbert has also noted that one of the most frequently performed spectacles in the religious celebrations or festivities, the Devil's Promenade [*las Diabladas*], was "originally an *auto sacramental* allegory which, much like the mystery play, was represented in the streets accompanied by music and dance" (213). Today, she adds, they are rarely mounted, although their music and dances still exist, as well as the costumes, "which can be traced back to the uniform of the Roman legionnaire" (213).

Other researchers have detailed the existence of community dramas in which several of the motifs or circumstances of the old celebrations recur, albeit in a form hybridizing the Spanish and the indigenous, as was seen in previous centuries. Some maintain that certain indigenous theatrical traditions have been preserved in all their purity (see **Figure 2**). González Cajiao, for example, has spoken of unadulterated rustic theatrical representations. The various types he enumerates "are staged during a festival called the 'Dance of the *Cabrita*,' in honour of Mareiwa, the goddess of the rains. In addition to the music, dance, and song that accompany all the indigenous rituals, curiously, these representations are also accompanied by a narrator" (26).

In many cases the more common hybridized transformations are evident in the language, images, or visual representations. The greater part of these productions both conserve elements of indigenous theatricality and include aspects belonging to the dominant cultural traditions. There are materials susceptible to cultural appropriation as well as reutilization. In the "Moors and Christians" mock battles, for example, pre-Hispanic indigenous costumes have been replaced by elements that the popular imagination–derived from the Catholic tradition–has imposed. The figures with which the dancers' capes are decorated suggest a cultural insertion. In some cases, indigenous visual elements have been conserved, although their meaning no longer corresponds with the original meaning. Thus, in a spectacle produced by the *Teatro de la Comunidad Emiliano Zapata* [Emiliano Zapata Community Theater], witnessed in Cholula, Mexico, the cloaks of the Christian dancers sported Christian symbols–angels, virgins, crosses–while those of the Moors, in contrast, sported indigenous symbols such as the plumed serpent. In this same spectacle, other elements of modernization were present: Wireless microphones and loudspeakers allowed the words of the performers to be heard throughout the entire precinct. In addition, it could be seen that many dancers wore Nike running shoes under their traditional costumes, suggesting that comfort (the performances last several hours) was displacing tradition.

In recent years, the expansion of television and cinema has contributed to the integration of pre-Hispanic and modern visual cultures. Thanks to international television broadcasts, indigenous celebrations are more and more frequently employed as items of national and transnational consumption. Traditional religious celebrations have become the focus of attention of television broadcasters and educational channels, and it is now possible to watch these festivities without participating in them. In this way they are being transformed into spectacles of the hegemonic and popular sectors. The diffusion of cinema in the popular sectors since the 1930s and of television in recent decades has furnished new visual and choreographic materials, and that diffusion has had an impact on the visual construction or constitution of these ceremonies. Research on the dances of the *Fiesta de la Tirana* in Northern Chile, for example, has demonstrated how the festival has been permanently transformed and has revealed the role that other aspects of popular culture have played in the festival's aesthetic legitimization–aspects such as the utilization of 1940s cinema personalities in the creation of new dance groups dedicated to the Virgin or the transformation of the groups themselves. This kind of analysis has demonstrated the permeability of some of the popular festivals as well as the points of articulation between indigenous cultures and their hybridization with the dominant cultures (see Villegas-Silva).

The process of appropriation, however, has concerned not only the festivals and celebrations. It can also be seen in theatrical forms associated with the theater in the traditional sense of the word. The *Fragua Theater,* mentioned above, whose actors are of indigenous heritage and whose themes and motives are associated with the problems of the indigenous community or its traditions, has frequently made use of styles and gestural systems derived from the contemporary globalized world or contemporary visual arts. In one of their recent productions, *Un sueño nuevo* [A New Dream], raising the issue of what kind of future awaits the youth of the community, the troop's young actors employ gestures of happiness derived

Figure 2.

Dance of El Venado, Sinaloa, Mexico. (Archive of the author)

from youth culture or from U.S. sports culture picked up from televised U.S. basketball games.

Within the historical process of this schema of indigenous theatrical discourses and theatricalities, directed either at indigenous or nonindigenous communities, there is one constant: Elements of the theatricality or theatrical codes proper to the hegemonic cultures are subject to continuous utilization and reutilization in indigenous theatrical productions. This appropriation appears to be grounded in the aesthetic preferences of the indigenous sectors, since they select from the hegemonic and popular cultures those elements functional within their own representations or associated with their own culture, at times integrating them in such a manner that they appear to be essential to indigenous culture. One clear example of the system of refunctionalized appropriation can be seen in the use of the characters of the "Devil's Promenade" in many of the Andean spectacles. It has been documented that these devils originated in European medieval theatrical traditions.

In the pre-Hispanic period, Latin American indigenous theater and theatricalities carried out a plurality and diversity of functions within the hegemonic cultures, and the cultures that sustained them. This diversity is still present today, even though the Catholic Church, as a transnational and colonizing institution, has infused indigenous theatricalities with its own theatricality. In the contemporary epoch, while the forces of power on the national or transnational level are somewhat different–cinema and television above all–these forces have made available options that the cultural producers from the ethnic sectors have appropriated for the construction of their cultural and theatrical forms in response to given historical and social conditions.

Translation by Colman Hogan

Works Cited

Arróniz, Othon. 1979. *Teatro de evangelización de la Nueva España.* Mexico City: Universidad Nacional Autónoma de México.

Azor, Ileana. 1988. *Origen y presencia del teatro en nuestra América.* Havana: Letras Cubanas.

Bonilla, María, and Stoyan Vladich. 1988. *El teatro latinoamericano en busca de su identidad cultural.* San José, Costa Rica: Cultur Art.

Cacciaglia, Mario. 1986. *Pequena história do teatro no Brasil.* São Paulo: Editora da Universidade de São Paulo.

Escudero, María. 1988. "La Mama Negra del Ecuador." *Escenario de dos mundos. Inventario teatral de Iberoamérica.* Ed. Moisés Pérez Coterillo and Carlos Espinoza Domínguez. 4 vols. Madrid: Centro de Documentación Teatral. I: 18–22.

Espinoza Domínguez, Carlos. 1993. "Presencia náhuatl en el teatro mexicano en el siglo XIX." *Conjunto* (octubre): 49–54.

Galich, Manuel. 1993. "El primer personaje del teatro latinoamericano." *Conjunto* (octubre): 4–13.

García Canclini, Néstor. 1996. *Culturas híbridas.* Mexico City: Grijalbo.

Gisbert, Teresa. 1988. "Manifestaciones teatrales indígenas." *Escenario de dos mundos. Inventario teatral de Iberoamérica.* Ed. Moisés Pérez Coterillo and Carlos Espinoza Domínguez. 4 vols. Madrid: Centro de Documentación Teatral. I: 212–13.

González Cajiao, Fernando. 1986. *Historia del teatro en Colombia.* Bogotá: Instituto Colombiano de Cultura.

——. 1995. "El teatro callejero y la búsqueda del teatro popular." *Conjunto* 101: 24–32.

Larraín, Jorge. 1996. *Modernidad, razón e identidad en América Latina.* Santiago, Chile: Editorial Andrés Bello.

Leal, Rine. 1980. *Breve historia del teatro cubano.* Havana: Editorial Letras Cubanas.

Monterde, Francisco. 1995. "Prólogo." *Teatro Indígena Prehispánico.* Mexico City: Universidad Nacional Autónoma de México. v–xxiii.

Montoya, Matilde. 1970. *Estudio sobre el baile de la conquista.* Guatemala City: Editorial Universitaria.

Morales, Pedro. 1992. "Elementos preteatrales en los principales rituales aztecas." *Conjunto:* 42–59.

Oleszkiewicz, Malgorzata. 1995. *Teatro popular peruano: Del precolombino al siglo XX.* Warsaw: Ediciones CESLA.

Ordaz, Luis. 1992. *Aproximación a la trayectoría de la dramática argentina.* Ottawa: Girol Books.

Partida, Armando. 1992. *Teatro de evangelización en náhuatl.* Introductory study, selection and notes. Mexico City: Consejo Nacional para la Cultura y las Artes.

Peña, Billy. 1990. "Teatro La Fragua." *tlfnews/ noticias tlf* 11.3 (1 sept.). n.p.

Pereira Salas, Eugenio. 1974. *Historia del teatro en Chile.* Santiago: Ediciones de la Universidad de Chile.

Quemain, Miguel Angel. 1988. " El Laboratorio de Teatro Campesino e Indígena." *Escenarios de dos mundos. Inventario teatral de Iberoamérica.* Ed. Moisés Pérez Coterillo and Carlos Espinoza Domínguez. 4 vols. Madrid: Centro de Documentación Teatral. III:152–54.

Rela, Walter. 1980. *Teatro brasileño.* Montevideo: Instituto de Cultura Uruguayo.

Ripoll, Carlos, and Andrés Valdespino. 1973. *Teatro hispanoamericano. Antología crítica.* 2 vols. New York: Anaya Books.

Sten, María. 1992. "Ponte a bailar, tú que reinas." *El Público* 88 (enero–febrero): 65–69.

Toriz, Martha. 1993. *La fiesta prehispánica: Un espectáculo teatral.* Mexico City: CITRU.

Villegas, Juan.1990. "Cuarto Festival de Teatro Poblacional en Santiago." *Gestos* 9: 155–59.

Villegas-Silva, Claudia. 1995. *Apropiación de teatralidades en la Fiesta de la Tirana.* M.A. thesis. Tempe: Arizona State University.

CHAPTER 53

CONTEMPORARY MAYAN THEATER

Tamara Underiner

In the Mayan *Popol vuh,* one of the last acts the twin hero-gods perform, before earthly time begins, is an act of theatrical illusion. In a command performance staged for the lords of the underworld, the twin Xbalanque apparently beheads his brother, Hunahpu; cuts out his heart; and then brings him back to life. When the delighted lords demand that the trick be performed on them, the brothers oblige, but this time it is not an illusion. Thus the twins score a certain victory over the gods of death: They decreed that henceforth the lords of the underworld will "limit their attacks on future human beings to those who have weaknesses or guilt" (Tedlock 1985, 46).

Because the *Popol vuh* is, in large part, the story of how the creator gods and original humans worked to make the world safe for human habitation, we can see that in the worldview of the ancient Maya, the role of theater and illusion was no small one. Not only necessary for the well-being of humanity, it was, literally, a death-defying act. And although the theater in which Mayans have participated throughout their collective history has undergone a series of changes in aim, content, and structure, this aspect of it has remained: It has always carried a revolutionary potential in which the borders between representation and its material effects are crossed and recrossed.

For example, the only pre-Columbian drama still extant, the *Rabinal Achí* from what is now Guatemala, treats a conflict between two Mayan groups and implicitly makes a connection between cultural identity and the spirits of place (Monterde, Leinaweaver). In this dance drama, a warrior-prince from one town is captured in one of his many raids on another, in order to break the latter's monopoly on resources in the region. Because of his bravery, he is asked to join the ranks of his captor's warriors. His pride and sense of his own local identity prevent him from accepting the offer, choosing instead the fate of all such captives: Death by his captors. Most researchers have interpreted his end as a ritual sacrifice, arguing that it is both a representation and manifestation of the ritual aspect of pre-Hispanic performance. Dennis Tedlock, who witnessed a January 1998 performance in Rabinal, suggests an alternative theory, based on linguistic analysis and his readings of hieroglyphs representing similar events: That the death of the warrior is less a sacrifice, with its ritual–religious overtones, than a *political execution,* which in turn casts the play as an early example of sociopolitical theater–in this case, upholding the values of the Rabinal imperial imperative (Tedlock 1998).

Although the *Rabinal Achí* is the only extant example of a pre-Hispanic performance text, the evidence of monuments, codices, and letters sent home by the newly arrived military and missionary settlers in New Spain attests to the theatricality that attended all aspects of pre-Hispanic life. The letters described a variety of performance forms: Farces, comedies, jugglers, acrobats, magic shows, puppet shows, clowning, and elaborate spectacles in which wigged, masked, and costumed players enacted ritual stories. In Mexico, such activities were observed in the Aztec societies that dominated the north and

central regions, as well as in Mayan communities under their rule to the south and east. So talented were some of them at mimicry that they would be hired by Spanish officers to provide spoofs of the Spaniards for an evening's entertainments. Like Bali, pre-Hispanic Mexico could be described in Clifford Geertz's terms as a "theater state" (Durán, Frischmann 1991, Ravicz).

Spanish missionaries, too, were quick to capitalize on the performing talents of the natives, employing indigenous actors in vast spectacles of missionary theater that was aimed at converting the latter to Christianity and instructing them in its doctrines (Harris, Ravicz, Sten, Versenyi, Weiss). As an early example of intercultural performance, these spectacles generally followed the form of the Spanish mystery and morality plays, but they incorporated many elements of native theatricality. As María Sten suggests, "theatre was to the spiritual conquest of Mexico what the horses and gunpowder were to its military defeat" (14). At the same time (as was true also in the religious drama of contemporary Europe) creative actors and authors (many of them indigenous or *mestizo*) began to incorporate elements of farce and buffoonery into these performances, blending the lines between the sacred and the profane. In some plays, the friars' attempts to couch new ideas in familiar forms meant that they included (or allowed to be included) more pre-Hispanic practices than were comfortable to certain authorities. As a result, there are numerous records of attempts by both the Church and Crown in Spain to censor or even prohibit evangelical theater in New Spain (Ravicz, Weiss). However, awareness and enforcement of these censures was difficult and sporadic, and such drama flourished throughout the sixteenth century. So successful were the efforts at Catholicizing the natives that among Mayans today, all but a small group of a few hundred Lacandón Mayans living in the jungles of Chiapas are, at least nominally, Christian.

Ravicz, Bricker, Harris, and others report that "schismatic fragments" of these early plays still appear in the *fiesta* sketches, dances, and tableaus repeated yearly in indigenous communities throughout Mexico. Such performances manifest an ongoing negotiation between assimilation and resistance (Beezley et al.). On the one hand, they serve to reinforce indigenous Catholicism (although this is changing due to the effects of evangelical Protestantism and its converts in this century). That is because on the surface, they rehearse the same kinds of saint and Bible stories originally introduced by the Spanish in the sixteenth century, although within them there is wide room for burlesque and improvisation. On the other hand, as in all Carnival-like events, fiesta performances provide a site for the conventional forms of authority to be, at least temporarily, symbolically overturned. Thus, in many such sketches, the figure of the European is one of ridicule, excess, and lasciviousness–whether that figure is a *conquistador* or a Spanish bishop.

The power of these performances is not limited to the kind of "safety valve" function theorized most famously by Bakhtin. In some instances, as Victoria Bricker has illustrated in her studies of Mayan Carnaval celebrations in Chamula, Chiapas, they can also provide a site for an alternative historiography, as they tell a complex, cyclical history of the Mayans and their encounters with a series of "others." For Bricker, the fiesta is ultimately a restaging of historical ethnic conflict, hidden in the "thematic disjunction" between costume and role, between costume and action, and among elements of costuming. She finds no fewer than six historical events being dramatized at once in this superficially religious festival: (1) the Conquest; (2) the Cancuc revolt of 1712 (in which Tzeltal Mayans rebelled against the Church and state authorities for denying them cult worship of the Virgin); (3) the French intervention in Mexico's post-Independence struggles for self-governance (1864–1867); (4) the Chamulan uprising against *ladino*-dominated San Cristóbal de las Casas in 1867–70; (5) a boundary dispute with neighboring Guatemala; and (6) the Pineda revolt of 1920. These are all staged within the overarching structure of the Passion of Christ, which organizes the surface action and serves as the paradigm for all the other ethnic conflicts also represented. Thus, Carnaval is much more than a palimpsest of pre-Hispanic and evangelical theater. It is also a complex way of staging both history and the *notion* of history as being cyclical rather than linear, with events repeating themselves structurally if not literally. Such historiography is an important act of self-definition, since centuries of political marginalization and a related lack of educational access has meant that it is mostly those "others" who have written Mayan history "for" them. Finally, it's worth pointing out that since Bricker did her study in the 1970s, Carnaval has attracted increasing numbers of Mexican and international tourists, adding a new valence to this act of historical and cultural self-definition: If the audience is taken into consideration, the performance becomes intercultural as well as indigenous.

Most recently, multiple forms of contact between Mayans and non-Mayans, coupled with Mexico's more recent movements toward democracy and a global-facing, free-market economy, have raised urgent questions about the role of Mayans *as Mayans* in the country's future as well as its shared past, as the ongoing troubles in Chiapas illustrate (1994 and continuing). One less violent response to these questions has been the emergence of a new kind of text-based theater, self-identified as "Mayan" or as "indigenous" in Mayan-speaking areas of Mexico (Chiapas, Tabasco, and the Yucatán Peninsula). Heirs neither to an unbroken history of dramatic performance extending back to pre-Hispanic times (for that trajectory was redirected by Conquest) nor precisely to the unscripted *fiesta* performance tradition, these scripted dramas emerge from a richly ambivalent and peculiarly postmodern confluence of people, movements, texts, and technologies.

Accounts of this emerging theater, particularly that of Chiapas, have begun to appear in U.S. academic and critical anthologies (see Frischmann 1994b, 1995; Steele 1995; and Underiner), and several of the troupes have had the opportunity to tour their work internationally. But since much of this work originates in Mayan languages and are subsequently translated into Spanish, exposure is limited by theater scholarship's English-language bias in the United States, and by cultural elitism–tokenism in Spanish-speaking countries. Further,

no published version of these texts can ever capture their impact in performance, considering the history of essentializing representations of Mayan culture promulgated by the tourist trade and the mass media. This essay considers this new theatrical activity significant to an understanding not only of how theater is an agent of cultural self-definition and community-building among indigenous communities in Mayan Mexico, but also of how it negotiates complex relations among such communities, state governments, and non-Mayan researchers and artists.

One key problem for the study of such theater is a definition of the term "Mayan" itself. As anthropologist Quetzil Castañeda puts it, Mayan identity is one of those "fundamentally contested terms that have no essential entity outside of the complex histories of sociopolitical struggles" (13). As noted above, most of those complex histories have been written, managed and in key ways invented by those who had the power to do so, which most often have not included Mayans themselves. This is not to suggest, however, that "Mayan" identity has neither rhetorical meaning nor material reality for those so identified, even when they themselves choose other bases for self-identification, most often, but not always, by linguistic grouping (see King). Thus, in the past two decades, politically active indigenous individuals and groups, spurred by human rights movements worldwide and liberation theology closer to home, have begun strategically to deploy the term "Maya" as a call to collective agency in pursuit of full representation under Mexico's emergent democracy (Materne, Wearne).

Another problematic issue is that, to varying degrees, most Mayan theater troupes either work with non-Mayans or owe their start to such work in the past. Financially, many receive at least a nod of support from the Mexican government via its cultural bureaus, and some of them have received substantial sums from U.S. organizations like the Ford Foundation and Cultural Survival. Beyond the financial aspect, there has been quite a bit of cross-pollination of aesthetic material as well. Initially, some of the troupes came into being as a result of the efforts of the government-sponsored "Brigadas Teatrales" of the 1960s and 1970s, which (like the earlier cultural missionary work of the Cárdenas years) used theater as a means to bring rural communities into fuller participation in the Mexican national community by shaping plays about current sociopolitical concerns and training groups of local actors in the latest, university-inspired acting techniques. This kind of cross-pollination continues, as troupes receive creative direction and training by both non-Mayan Mexicans and U.S. theater artists–which helps, in turn, to improve their chances at international funding. As Kirsten Nigro suggests, the question of outsiders is both complicated and controversial: "For if nonindigenous people work with this theater, and if they attribute to it a sociopolitical rather than a ritualistic purpose, it is then questionable whether the result can be labeled 'indigenous.' For Estage Noël it cannot and should not be, whereas for others, the key is who performs rather than who promotes it . . . . Because of the presence of outsiders [in the Brigadas Teatrales] who were salaried by the government, it is not hard to see why there were and still are concerns here about cultural manipulation and hidden agendas and, if not that, at least about some well-intentioned but misguided notions concerning the kind of performance methods that are best suited to a rural, indigenous people . . ." (234–35)

It may seem, then, that many Mayans are caught, at least representationally, between a rock and a hard place. On the one hand, they are situated in a particular postmodern moment that questions the very possibility of coherent cultural identity, at a time in their own history of exclusion and marginalization in which they wish most to assert such an identity (Beverley). On the other, as the question of "outsiders" suggests, some have been criticized in their creative work for "not being Mayan enough." Mayan theater practitioners have developed a variety of responses to this dilemma, and their work registers its complexity, both onstage and off.

Take, for example, the work of "Lo'il Maxil" ("Monkey Business"), a troupe of Tzotzil- and Tzeltal-speaking Mayans working with Sna Jtz'Ibajom ("House of the Writer") in San Cristóbal de las Casas, Chiapas. Since 1989, their repertory has grown and changed, reflecting that tension between nostalgia for an imagined past and vision for an imaginable future that characterizes identity politics in the region. As described in more detail by Frischmann (1994b), the troupe began by dramatizing Mayan folktales in an effort both to encourage literacy in the mother tongues and to "take back" some of the stories collected and published in non-Mayan languages by visiting anthropologists. *El haragán y el zopilote* [1989; The Loafer and the Buzzard], and *A poco hay cimarrones?* [1990; Who Believes in Spooks?] are two moralistic tales that both entertain and teach lessons in proper gendered behavior. Soon the troupe began experimenting with retellings of local and national history. *Herencia fatal* [1991; Fatal Inheritance], based on a true story in a nearby Tzotzil village, deals with a land dispute that led to internecine murder. In the actual event, a pair of brothers who murdered a sister for her share of the family land escaped punishment; in the Lo'il Maxil version, justice prevails—significantly, without the need for intervention from authorities outside the village. Here, a clear message about indigenous autonomy and self-rule is reinforced.

Other plays are more overtly critical of non-Mayan participants in Mexico's shared history: *Vámonos al paraíso* [1993; Let's Go to Paradise], suggests that the abusive conditions on 1930s-era coffee plantations were returning in the 1990s, because earlier reforms were being erased in the face of bribery and deceit. Official history is critiqued in *Antorchas para amanecer* [1995; Torches for the Dawn], a play-within-a-play about the imposition of Spanish culture onto Mayan religious practices and an educational system that, in its attempts to bring all Mayans into a modern, Spanish-speaking Mexico has, in effect, further marginalized its non-Spanish speaking citizenry.

But the troupe's two most-requested plays, from their repertory of ten, best reflect the attempt to negotiate a place for the past in a difficult present. *Dinastía de jaguares* [1992; Dynasty of Jaguars], is an epic treatment of the fall of the classic Mayan civilization. Based on recent (and controversial) historical and anthropological theories about the possible causes for the intertribal warfare of that decline, the play "stresses unity and peaceful coexistence as the keys to strength and survival. The latter are closely linked to the perpetuation of key cultural elements: Customs, language, and rituals" (Frischmann, 1994b, 233–34), but the play's pre-Columbian setting allows it to operate at a distant—and therefore safe—distance: Removed from contemporary intercultural considerations. Far riskier is the 1994 *De todos para todos* [From All for All], which explores the

roots of an uprising very similar to the Zapatistas Rebellion of 1994. Developed within a month of the New Year's Day confrontation, it is concerned to reveal the injustice and inequity that fuel this ongoing conflict and to illustrate the danger to the whole of creation that such injustice can propagate. Its characters include a community of peasants displaced into the jungle by the greed and duplicity of *ladino* authorities; a chorus of jungle animals angered by their subsequent displacement by the peasants; an indigenous Earth Lord who is instrument of both revenge and reconciliation; a local shaman whose cures can only be temporary; and a character reminiscent of Subcomandante Marcos, who leads the peasants to take up arms. Their revolution is quickly aborted, however, by the intervention of the Earth Lord, whose impassioned plea for species-wide brotherhood nevertheless ends with a call that the "fight for indigenous peoples" continue. Thus the play walks a tenuous line between patriotism and revolution—staging the latter, even without endorsing it, is a risky move in post-1994 Mexico.

If on-stage Lo'il Maxil's work reflects a focus on Mayan culture and concerns, both historical and contemporary, offstage, the group is a more hybrid entity. It operates both multiculturally, since its members include representatives from Mayan communities that might otherwise consider themselves to be culturally distinct; and interculturally, through alliances with non-Mayan maskmakers, directors, puppeteers, and researchers. Thus Lo'il Maxil's work, celebrated everywhere as "Mayan theater," is, in fact, highly collaborative with artists and researchers trained in very different traditions. As a result, their emergent performance "tradition" reflects these diverse impulses and influences. Although the general action of the plays is generally developed collectively by the troupe, their non-Mayan resident playwright both shapes the plays and translates them into Spanish. In structure, they tend to follow the well-made play format (although they are typically more episodic than linear within it). The plays almost always feature masks and costume devices not traditional to the region; the U.S. director and maskmaker, Ralph Lee, who has directed every Lo'il Maxil production, frequently uses *commedia dell'arte*–style half-masks to mock non-Mayan villains in many plays. Now, some of the group members conduct mask-making workshops in indigenous communities. As a result, this theatrical convention (not indigenous to this part of Mexico, but mediated through Lee's own work in European and other indigenous traditions), is becoming a new signifier, in theater, of "Mayan" culture.

The plays are performed in Tzotzil or Tzeltal for local communities, in Spanish for audiences of tourists and international observers of the stalled peace talks, and for national and international theater festivals; they have also been published in a bilingual collection, *Renacimiento del teatro maya en Chiapas* (*Sna Jtz'ibajom*). Several of the plays have been professionally produced as videos, broadcast on state television, and made available to interested visitors and researchers. Thus, the audience for Lo'il Maxil's work has grown far beyond the original indigenous communities for whom it was targeted, to include non-Mayan Chiapans, international tourists and observers, and classrooms of students studying Mayan culture in the United States.

As the example of the dramatized folktales suggests, Lo'il Maxil's explorations of Mayan ethnic identity are rooted in traditional views of gender relations, and traditional gender dynamics tend to be reproduced in the group's day-to-day operations (Steele 1994). Although it is true that, traditionally, the kind of public profile attached to the acting profession goes decidedly against the grain of many Mayan communities' assessment of "proper" women's work, it is also true that more and more Mayan women are adopting active roles in the shaping of indigenous demands for peace and justice in Mexico's increasingly tense political and economic environment (Rojas). Thus, in 1993, two former Lo'il Maxil actresses, Petrona de la Cruz Cruz and Isabel Juárez Espinosa, formed an alternative troupe in order to address specifically the contemporary concerns of Mayan women in San Cristóbal and its surrounding communities. Called La Fomma, an acronym for "Empowerment of the Mayan Woman," this group, like Sna Jtz'ibajom, works collectively and is concerned to improve adult literacy in the region. A key difference is its focus, on-stage and off, on indigenous women's issues, work, and educational opportunities (Steele 1994).

In addition to providing free literacy and writing workshops, La Fomma solves the women's workload problem by also providing day care and after-school programs for their children and educational theater for both children and adults. Their plays treat themes specific to the realities these women face: Alcoholic and abusive spouses, poverty in the communities, sexual abuse of children, and the dilemmas faced by *campesinos* and *campesinas* who are forced to make their way in the cities—all from the perspective of their effects on the women and children. De la Cruz Cruz's plays, for example, are relentless in their portrayal of the limitations on women's choices in many communities. Her *Una mujer desesperada* [1991; A Desperate Woman], examines domestic violence as it relates to alcoholism and poverty in rural communities and the dependence of women upon men in a fundamentally patriarchal and authoritarian system. A more recent work, *Almas enjauladas* [1996; Caged Souls], is based on a true story of a nine-year-old girl whose impoverished and desperate parents sold her to a non-Mayan man to be his "wife" (de la Cruz Cruz often gathers her material by conducting ethnographic interviews with women in rural communities). Juárez Espinosa, whose writings have been collected in *Cuentos y teatro tzeltales* [Tzeltal Short Stories and Theater], is similarly relentless in her *Migración* [1993; Migration], a play showing how Mexico's ongoing economic crisis has forced many indigenous men to supplement subsistence farming with migrant work and unskilled labor in the cities, with particularly harsh trickle-down effects on women and children. Again, alcoholism, verbal abuse, masculine authoritarianism, and a lack of alternatives for the principal women are significant factors in the play's action.

Both tragedies explore and expose painful realities without offering much in the way of an escape route or call to positive action. But in the process of developing these works for the stage and in crafting the end-of-the-year sketches that La Fomma's participants perform for families and friends, La Fomma's significant contribution is in opening up a site for the articulation of these realities in a region where, for centuries, women have been accustomed to being neither seen nor heard. This is especially remarkable when one considers the centuries-old proscription on Mayan women performing at all, much less in men's roles, as the women of La Fomma do to meet their casting needs. Thus, both organizationally and representationally, the work of La Fomma has radical potential.

This potential has yet to be fully realized, although it has brought international attention (especially among feminists) to the group and its work. Like Lo'il Maxil, they have received funding from international sources, though to a lesser degree—both to bring theater artists to San Cristóbal for training, and to bring their work to audiences in the United States, Canada, Belgium, and Australia. But despite their international profile, the work of La Fomma remains underrecognized in Mexico, reflecting the double marginalization experienced by women in general and indigenous women in particular with regard to social power in Mexico (Steele "Indigenismo"). Finally, because their work troubles traditional definitions of Mayan culture, often targeting traditional patriarchal structures as a source of women's and children's misery, their message has yet to be fully embraced by many Mayans as well.

In one state to the east, Tabasco, another theater troupe has, for the past fifteen years, been gaining its own kind of notoriety. Called the Laboratorio de Teatro Campesino e Indígena, it was spearheaded by a non-Mayan director who had been engaged by the state government to develop a theatrical program similar to the Brigadas Teatrales among the Choles and Chontales of rural Tabasco. In its heyday, the LTCI developed a network of seven troupes throughout the state, and eventually expanded into other rural areas and some urban *barrios* as well. Now that the troupe is no longer supported by the Tabascan government, their operations have been scaled down considerably, but several of the network labs continue to make headlines.

The reason for the attention within Mexico, and in places as far away as Madrid and the Catskills, is the rather unique brand of theater that characterizes both the LTCI repertory and its working methods. Instead of following in the tradition of the Brigadas Teatrales by developing community theater based on sociopolitical issues, director María Alicia Martínez Medrano instituted a different kind of program. She invited whole communities to become involved in her theater as actors, directors, choreographers, dancers, composers, musicians, costume and set builders, and technicians. Those who accepted received a three-year training program that featured study in Mexican history, theater history, and training in an acting style that was a combination of Stanislavsky and Meyerhold, as mediated through the Japanese director Seki Sano (with whom Martínez Medrano trained). Then their skills would be utilized in spectacular productions based on plays from the Western tradition (*Romeo and Juliet, Bodas de sangre* [Blood Weddings]); those of Mexican playwrights (Garro's *La dama boba* [1963; The Foolish Lady]), Magaña's *Los argonautas* [1967; The Argonauts], Carballido's *La danza que sueña la tortuga* [The Dance the Turtle Dreams]); and works created for the labs by Martínez Medrano and—or alumni of the program (Martínez Medrano's *El Evangelio según San Mateo* [The Gospel According to Matthew] and Santos G. Pisté Canché's *La bruja y el pueblo* [The Witch and the Town] and *La tragedia del jaguar*, a collaboration between Martínez Medrano and LTCI participants Auldárico Hernández, Eutimio Hernández, and Martha Alicia Trejo (Madrid et al).

The repertory is notable not only for its variety (a combination of adapted classics, Mexican *indigenista* works, and locally developed tales), but also for its production style. The signature work in this style continues to be García Lorca's *Bodas de sangre*, which was developed in the remote community of

Oxolotán and subsequently staged in Mexico City, New York state, and Madrid. In it, Martínez Medrano and her cast of literally hundreds of Oxolotecans took Lorca's original tragic tale of passion and vengeance, and moved it from the Spanish countryside to the Tabasqueño cornfields. While remaining faithful to the original text, the LTCI version substituted machetes for the knives that play such a key part in the original. Also, they transformed the Lorcan moon into a more literal representation of Death who enters on horseback and is costumed in a manner reminiscent of Mexican Day of the Dead iconography; and they added other local touches that successfully evoke a rural Mexican community. Most important are the music and dances of a *campesino* wedding, and the festive dress appropriate for such an affair–practices that had been driven underground by the repressive policies of former Tabascan administrations, whose policies of enforced cultural assimilation had the effect of erasing these signs of "Indianness" throughout Tabasco (Bonfil Batalla). As a result, the Lorca text and the Oxolotecan *mise en scène* constitute a kind of hybrid performance that uses a Spanish text to recuperate a specifically local history. A similar process was at work in the LTCI version of *Romeo y Julieta*, transposed from Venice to the henequen plantations of the Yucatán peninsula and adapted to represent a historical conflict between two indigenous groups: The native Maya of Yucatán and the Mayo of northern Mexico, who had been forcibly removed by Porfirio Díaz to work on those plantations. In addition to localizing the scene and the action, the staging incorporated local music and dance to redefine the Bard's relevance for indigenous Mexican performers and audience members.

Within Mexico, LTCI's reception has been mixed. While from an aesthetic standpoint most critics applaud the results, this celebration is often accompanied by a troubling note of astonishment over the group's achievements *as* indigenous performers (Espinosa 1987, 1991, Vicente). From a sociopolitical standpoint, other critics are harsher. Some have criticized the rural programs for, as they put it, "taking the Indians out of their cornfields" and compelling whole communities to forget their *campesino* roots (Zúñiga). At its reactionary extreme, this criticism masks a racist desire to keep the indigenous in their socioeconomic and cultural place. In its more postcolonial manifestation, the concern is that Martínez Medrano's interest in staging what she refers to as "universal art" might really be masking a form of cultural imperialism, since it occurs in an environment overdetermined by asymmetrical relations of social and economic power. But even to answer the question of "whose interests are being served by this theater" is a complicated matter, and the voluntary participation of large numbers of indigenous performers remains undertheorized.

If the theatrical activity described so far is as intercultural as it is Mayan or indigenous, a final theatrical example suggests a different strategy of identity articulation, one that is far more resolutely local: The grassroots, community-based theater of the Yucatán Peninsula. For a variety of reasons–geographical location, political and economic history, climate, travel and tourism–the peoples of the Yucatan Peninsula have perhaps had more opportunity to interact with the rest of the world than have the other regions of Southern Mexico. Particularly since the early nineteenth century, the Peninsula has frequently been the first stop in Mexico for European business travelers–and theater companies–on their way to the capital (Muñoz). Despite official Yucatán's openness to international exchange, its Mayan populace has yet to enjoy full participation. Economic opportunities continue to be unevenly distributed according to ethnicity, and many Yucatec Mayans serve as the exploited underclass in an exploitative tourist industry. But in the villages off the tourist routes, community-based theater becomes an important site for cultural self-definition.

Although this theater is far less reliant on the contributions of non-community members, as a regional movement it, too, can trace its roots to state-sponsored theatrical programs in the 1960s and 1970s; many of its organizers were trained by professional theater artists from Mexico City and have gone on to provide their own forms of training within the community. Unlike that of the other troupes discussed here, however, this community-oriented theater operates as a free-time activity, rather than serving as a means of financial support for its participants. More importantly, according to Feliciano Sánchez Chan (a playwright, director, theater organizer, and compiler of a bilingual collection of Yucatecan plays developed over the past fifteen years), this theater is "done by groups who don't confine themselves to conventional spaces with lots of scenography, properties, lights and special costumes, and who don't necessarily express themselves through the works of great authors, but rather with texts created according to their own needs and starting with their own problems and reality–be these groups indigenous, campesino, popular, or community.... *Teatro comunitario* is an artistic–cultural activity that a given group of people develops, based on its own reality and creativity, utilizing elements from everyday life to express its own viewpoint on a given situation in its own communityand inviting everyone else in the community to reflect on those themes" (1992; my translation).

Such themes have included alcoholism, the emigration of youths to the cities, land scarcity and the resulting overwork of existing fields, inconsistent electrical service, games children play, the abuses of teachers who don't let their students speak Mayan in school, commercial concerns of farmers, communal land management, children and television, agricultural rites and traditional fiestas, the pueblo's oral storytelling traditions–in short, anything that comes to the attention of the troupe as worthy of dramatization. Most often, these works are developed in improvisation, performed in Yucatec Mayan, and written down only after the fact–if at all. The quotidian nature of these plays provides their audiences with a kind of representational three-dimensionality they very rarely see in the mainstream media and is in no way limited to idyllic caricatures of village life. Three recent plays, in particular, provide sustained analyses of the struggle to preserve local identity in an increasingly globalized environment.

Los aluxes is the collective creation of a community theater troupe in Oxkutzkab (a sizable community in the state of Yucatán) under the coordination and direction of Yucatec writer María Luisa Góngora Pacheco. In the exaggerated vocabulary of farce, it tells the story of a young man who has so far lost his connection to his village identity (largely through the influence of the media and his life in the city) that he arranges to sell its *aluxes* to a visiting *gringa*. (*Aluxes* are small creatures, somewhat like the fairyfolk of European lore, who benefit those who believe in them and torment those who don't.) In the play they serve as powerful symbols of local identity, disempowered when they are decontextualized as "dolls" by the tourist. Their absence wreaks havoc on the townspeople's health, and order is restored only when they demand that the young man return the money and retrieve the *aluxes*. Though the play is very funny, it still contains an important element of critical self-reflection, as the young man remains strangely unrepentant at the play's end. The community retrieves their *aluxes*, but they are also stuck with the young man—the play's stubborn symbol of mass-mediated, global culture. The play sounds a warning that, like this young man, the processes and problems of cultural change are not going to go away, and, more importantly, that they are the responsibility of the community itself to manage.

Community autonomy and accountability constitute a recurrent theme in the published work of Sánchez Chan. In *Las abejas*, the bees of the title become a powerful symbol in an epic play about conquest, greed, and community complacency—and complicity—with those who would impose their values from without. In the end, what is advocated is a blend of community autonomy and judicious cooperation with external agents, with an accent on the community's rigorous monitoring of the terms and limits of that cooperation.

Sánchez Chan's *Las langostas* [The Locusts] is another epic allegory advocating community autonomy in the face of encroaching global markets. Taking as its starting point a plague of locusts that devastated the Yucatán countryside in the 1940s, it suggests that contemporary over-reliance on junk food and Coca Cola—made irresistible through addiction to television, with its commercials—are the modern equivalent of such a plague, the cause of widespread malnutrition and illness in indigenous communities. This "modern locust" is literalized in a character whose costume is covered in snack wrappers and soda cans and who menaces the townfolk when they let their guard down. But rather than targeting Coke or *telenovelas* as the only culprits, the play is strong in its critique of local acquiescence in their consumptive power. Rallying together under the slogan "The pueblo that produces what it eats will never be manipulated," the community attempts to kill off the modern locust. But like *Los aluxes*, this play ends on an ambiguous note, as the locust comes back to life, hoots at the crowd, and runs off. The problem of global infiltration is not so easily managed, the play suggests, and ongoing vigilance on the part of the community will always be required.

As the examples of all these troupes suggest, the staging of Mayan cultural identities is a complex matter of local identification within an increasingly global and intercultural field of operations. If, in response to this complexity, their repertories reflect a kind of "strategic essentialism," to use Gayatri Spivak's term; it is also true that the results bear a different stamp from region to region and troupe to troupe. After a five-century hiatus, it is no longer accurate to say there is no such thing as Mayan theater. Rather, we might say that there is a proliferation of Mayan theatricality expressed in the most diverse forms.

Works Cited

Beezley, William H., Cheryl English Martin and William E. French, eds. 1994. *Rituals of Rule, Rituals of Resistance: Public Celebrations and Popular Culture in Mexico*. Wilmington, DE: SR Books.

Beverley, John et al., eds. 1994. *The Postmodernism Debate in Latin America*. Durham: Duke University Press.

Bonfil Batalla, Guillermo. 1996. *Mexico Profundo: Reclaiming a Civilization*. Trans. Philip A. Dennis. Austin: University of Texas Press.

Bricker, Victoria R. 1981. *Indian Christ, Indian King*. Austin: University of Texas Press.

Castañeda, Quetzil E. 1996. *In the Museum of Maya Culture: Touring Chichén Itzá*. Minneapolis: University of Minnesota Press.

Cruz Cruz, Petrona de la. *Una mujer desesperada*. MS in author's possession.

Durán, Diego. 1963. *Historia de las Indias de Nueva España e Islas de la Tierra Firme*. Mexico City: Editorial Porrua.

Espinosa, Tomás. 1987. "Imágenes del Laboratorio de Teatro Campesino e Indígena." *Expresión* 18 (mayo-junio): 6–9.

———. 1991. "Laboratorios de Teatro Campesino e Indígena de México: Tabasco, Yucatán y Sinaloa: el Renacimiento." *Conjunto* julio–sept.: 85–89.

Fomma, La. 1996. Author's interviews with founders and members, May–August, San Cristóbal de las Casas, Chiapas.

Frischmann, Donald H. 1991. "Active Ethnicity: Nativism, Otherness, and Indian Theatre in Mexico." *Gestos* 11 (abril): 113–126.

———. 1995. "Contemporary Mayan Theatre and Ethnic Conflict: The Recovery and (Re)Interpretation of History." *Imperialism and Theatre: Essays on World Theatre, Drama and Performance*. Ed. J. Ellen Gainor. London and New York: Routledge, 1995. 71–84.

———. 1994a. "*Misiones Culturales*, Teatro Conasupo, and Teatro Comunidad: The Evolution of Rural Theater." *Rituals of Rule, Rituals of Resistance: Public Celebrations and Popular Culture in Mexico*. Eds. Willian H. Beezley, Cheryl English Martin and William E. French. Wilmington, DE: SR Books. 285–306.

———. 1994b. "New Mayan Theatre in Chiapas: Anthropology, Literacy, and Social Drama." *Negotiating Performance: Gender, Sexuality, and Theatricality in Latin/o America*. Eds. Diane Taylor and Juan Villegas. Durham, N.C.: Duke University Press. 213–238.

———. 1990. *Nuevo Teatro Popular en México*. Mexico City: INBA.

García Lorca, Federico. *Bodas de sangre*. María Alicia Martínez Medrano, adaptor. Villahermosa: Edición especial imprimido por el Gobierno del Estado de Tabasco, 1986.

Geertz, James Clifford. 1988. *The Predicament of Culture: Twentieth Century Ethnography, Literature and Art*. Cambridge: Harvard University Press.

Harris, Max. 1993. *The Dialogical Theatre: Dramatizations of the Conquest of Mexico and the Question of the Other*. New York: St. Martin's Press.

Hernández Gerónimo, Auldárico, Eutimio Hernández Román, Martha Alicia Trejo Espinoza, and María Alicia Martínez Medrano. 1989. *La tragedia del jaguar*. Mexico City: Instituto de Cultura de Tabasco.

Juárez Espinosa, Isabel. 1994. *Migración. Cuentos y teatro tzeltales*. Mexico City: Editorial Diana, 1994.

King, Linda. 1994. *Roots of Identity: Language and Literacy in Mexico*. Stanford: Stanford UP.

"Laboratorio de Teatro Campesino e Indígena," internal document dated 1995, in LTCI archives, Mérida, Yucatán.

Lee, Ralph. Telephone interview, November 26, 1996.

Leinaweaver, Richard E. 1968. "Rabinal Achí." *Latin American Theatre Review* 1/2 (Spring): 3–53.

Lo'il Maxil, Sna Jtz'Ibajom. 1996. Author's interviews with members, May–August, San Cristóbal de Las Casas, Chiapas.

Madrid, María Elena, Sylvia Sambarino y Miguel Angel Piñeda, eds. 1987. *Laboratorio de Teatro Campesino e Indígena*. Villahermosa, Tabasco: DIF.

Martínez Medrano, María Alicia. 1996. Personal interviews, August 11, Tucta, Tabasco; Sept. 3–4, Mexico City; Sept. 7–8, Tlayacapán, Morelos.

Materne, Yves, ed. 1980. *The Indian Awakening in Latin America*. New York: Friendship Press.

Monterde, Francisco. 1955. *Teatro indígena prehispánico*. Mexico City: Universidad Nacional Autónoma de México.

Muñoz, Fernando. 1987. *El teatro regional de Yucatán.* Mérida: Grupo Editorial Gaceta.

Nigro, Kirsten F. 1994. "Twentieth Century Theater." *Mexican Literature: A History.* Ed. David William Foster. Austin: University of Texas Press. 213–42.

Ravicz, Marilyn Eckdahl. 1970. *Early Colonial Religious Drama in Mexico: From Tzompantli to Golgotha.* Washington, D.C.: Catholic University of America Press.

Rojas, Rosa. 1995. *Chiapas ¿y las mujeres qué?* Mexico City: Ediciones La Correa Feminista.

Sánchez Chan, Feliciano. 1992. *Manual de Teatro Comunitario.* Mexico City: Dirección General de Culturas Populares.

———. 1994. *Teatro Maya Contemporáneo I y II.* Mexico City: INI and SEDESOL.

———. 1996. Personal interviews, July–August

———. 1997. Personal interviews, December.

Sna Jtz'ibajom. 1996. *Renacimiento del teatro maya en Chiapas,* tomos I–III. Mexico City: Colección Letras Mayas Contemporáneas, Chiapas (INI).

Steele, Cynthia. 1993. "Indigenismo y posmodernidad: narrativa indigenista, testimonio, teatro campesino y video en el Chiapas finisecular." *Revista de Critica Literaria Latinoamericana* XIX, 38: 249–60.

———. 1994. "A Woman Fell into the River: Negotiating Female Subjects in Contemporary Mayan Theatre." *Negotiating Performance.* Eds. Diana Taylor and Juan Villegas. Durham, N.C.: Duke University Press. 239–56.

Sten, María. 1982. *Vida y muerte del teatro nahuatl.* Xalapa: Universidad Veracruzana.

Tedlock, Dennis. 1985. *Popul Vuh.* New York: Simon and Schuster.

———. 1988. "The *Rabinal Achí:* Continuity and Change in a Mayan Dance Drama." Presentation at University of Minnesota, Minneapolis, 8 Oct.

Underiner, Tamara. 1998. "Incidents of Theatre in Chiapas, Tabasco and Yucatán: Cultural Enactments in Mayan Mexico." *Theatre Journal* 50: 349–69.

Versenyi, Adam. 1993. *Theatre in Latin America: Religion, Politics, and Culture from Cortes to the 1980s.* Cambridge: Cambridge University Press.

Vicente Mosquete, José L. 1987. "Un Lorca indígena, ritual y campesino." Rev. of *Bodas de Sangre,* dir. María Alicia Martínez Medrano. LTCI. Chapultepec Park, Mexico City. El Público (Madrid) mayo: 57–63.

Wearne, Philip. 1996. *Return of the Indian: Conquest and Revival in the Americas.* London: Cassel.

Weiss, Judith A. 1993. *Latin American Popular Theatre: The First Five Centuries.* Albuquerque: University of New Mexico Press.

Zúñiga, Reynaldo. 1990. "'Teatro Campesino,' cortina de humo de corruptelas, malversación y degeneración." Photocopy of unidentified newspaper article, dated April 24, 1990, p. 48, in archives of Centro de Investigación Teatral Rodolfo Usigli, Instituto Nacional de Bellas Artes, Mexico City.

CHAPTER 54

PLURALITY AND DIVERSITY OF THEATER DISCOURSE

Juan Villegas

This essay presents a portrait of the theatrical discourses produced by the culturally hegemonic sectors in Latin America since the arrival of the Europeans. The emphasis here is placed on a description of the culturally productive sector or the cultural powers. From this perspective, three principal phases can be distinguished: The colonial period, in which the dominant sectors were constituted by the Spanish rulers, the Catholic Church, and the *criollos* (who, with time, would come to constitute the major cultural or administrative force); the independence era, which began with the nineteenth century and in which the *criollos*, predominantly representing the bourgeoisie of the Enlightenment, rose to power as a new upper class; and a third phase, commencing at the end of the nineteenth and the beginning of the twentieth centuries, in which the enlightened bourgeoisie was displaced by the new middle classes. During the twentieth century, it was the middle classes who produced the majority of the hegemonic cultural objects from a plurality and diversity of positions, manifest in the diverse political and cultural tendencies that characterize that group.

The Discourses of the Colonial Macro-System: The Legitimization of Power

The period traditionally named the colonial era dates from the arrival of the first conquistadors (around 1530) to approximately 1810, although in some countries this period extends to the end of the nineteenth century. It comprises, thus, almost 300 years and is a period in which the societies that would come to represent the diverse countries of Latin America underwent a number of transformations. These transformations occurred in economic conditions, the social constitution of the groups in power, cultural and religious influences, and the official politics of the various regions. At the same time, there were enormous differences among the regions, differences that were not constant throughout the period. For example, Mexico and Peru, since they were first established as viceroyalties, were characterized by a social sector dependent on the Crown and a cultural life much more closely linked to cultural activities in Spain. In some cases, the subjugation of the natives was achieved in the first decades; in others, war with the natives continued for many years. Whereas some indigenous groups maintained a strong economic and political power base (these sources of income giving them marked possibilities for cultural development), other groups inhabited impoverished regions and, thus, their cultural productions were marked by a much more pragmatic character.

José Juan Arrom has detailed a number of traits distinguishing the theater of the colonial era and its relation to Spanish influence. He notes that each colony had its own peculiarities: "The climate of the region, the lack or abundance of minerals, the density of the indigenous population, and even the greater or lesser degree of political stability, all

these were factors influencing the life of each colony and, thus, conditioning their theatrical activities" (25).

All Latin American cultural products of the colonial era must be seen as cultural objects of a colonized culture in which the politics of the center—whether it was Spain or Portugal—were determining (above all with respect to prohibitions) and explicit, as can be seen in the royal or ecclesiastical political and administrative policies. In principle, these were cultures governed from the mother country, and transformations effected in the political cultures of the periphery originated in changes first seen at the center. The greater part of the production of theatrical discourses during the colonial period thus lay in the hands of the ruling political or ecclesiastical classes, and the variations in these discourses were directly related to the interests of these two sectors. These groups produced theatrical discourses for the *criollo* sector as well as for certain sectors of the non-Hispanic cultures. In both cases, the intentionality of the theatrical productions, theatrical codes, and images varied considerably.

As seen in other sections, with the theatricalities of the colonizing power and the theatrical discourses directed at the members of that culture there coexisted a series of theatricalities and theatrical discourses produced by the indigenous sectors, the greater part of which reutilized pre-Hispanic traditions or fused them with the celebrations established by the religious and political powers. In addition, it was during this period that manifestations of the Afro-American culture began, above all in regions such as Cuba, Panama, and Brazil. Despite the regional differences and historical transformations, a number of common features can be enumerated. The discourse of the dominant sectors made use of both public theatricalities and theatrical discourses to communicate and impose their system of values. The Catholic Church constituted one of the ruling power's principal means of indoctrination and proselytization, and directed its energies at both the *criollo* and indigenous sectors. On the other hand, the economic power supporting and sustaining the spectacles was that of the political authorities (the viceroyalty, for example) and the town councils, as well as the Church. On many occasions guilds financed festivals that included theatrical spectacles. Finally, in all these countries, the Feast of Corpus Christi was the most important nucleus of theatrical productions; in a continuation of the European tradition, a great number of theatrical expressions or dramas were staged in the context of this Catholic festival. Within this multiplicity and diversity, and despite the transformations that had taken place over the centuries, the theatrical discourses of the hegemonic sectors have tended primarily to employ the theatrical codes of the legitimized culture. This is to say that, with regional variations, they utilize the codes of the Spanish theater—as adapted to the interests of the various centers and modified by the interests and specific intentions of the cultural producers in the distinct zones of the empire. Thus, it is possible to encounter Renaissance, Baroque, or Enlightenment elements, although naturally refunctionalized by their employment in the political culture of each space. All these codes clearly imply an audience competent in or familiar with the Spanish high culture of the epoch.

The Discourses of the Religious Powers: The Catholic Church

The first theater produced by the Spaniards in Latin America was that staged in the churches, a theater which was predominantly, although not exclusively, of a religious nature. The Catholic theatrical discourse constitutes one of the most important cultural discourses of the period, although, as the society of the conquest transformed into a civil society, a diminution was seen in its relevance, just as, in the same time period, a loss or diminution of the general importance of the Catholic Church was seen in the ruling sectors of Spanish society.

One of the discourses that was much practiced in the first years of the colony was that of divine pastoral literature, a transformation that had taken place in Spain at the end of the sixteenth and at the beginning of the seventeenth century. One example of this genre was Juan Pérez Ramírez' (b. 1544?) *Desposorio espiritual entre el pastor Pedro y la Iglesia Mexicana* [1574; Spiritual Betrothal between the Shepherd Peter and the Mexican Church], "written and staged to celebrate the consecration of Archbishop Moya de Contreras, the 8 December, 1574" (Ripoll and Valdespino 13). The influence of Juan del Encina (1468–1529?) on this work can be seen in its idealization of the shepherds, the bucolic ambiance, and the "music, dances, and popular allusions" with which it closes (13). The *Desposorio* belongs to the theatrical discourse of religious celebrations. The eulogy of the new Archbishop is rooted in the codes of pastoral literature, but a pastoral literature turned to the divine, incorporating elements belonging to the mystical tradition and saturated with biblical imagery, both from the Old and New Testaments. The Mexican church is described in pastoral terms ("*hermosísima pastora*" 'loveliest shepherd') and in the language of courtly poetry ("*mi señora*" 'my lady'), while the beneficiaries of the Archbishop's arrival are described in the literary vocabulary of shepherds (sheep, flocks, herds). The intertextual relation with courtly poetry is clear, as is the use of gemology as a source of comparison with the beautiful or the valuable. Other important stylistic elements pertaining to high literature include the use of the philosophic dialogue as a structuring device, citations in Latin, and phrases from psalms either sung by the shepherds or recited by some of the allegorical figures.

One of the other codes that recurs in the religious theatrical discourse of the period is that of biblical allegory. A fine example of this discourse is *Coloquio séptimo* [Seventh Colloquy] by Fernán González de Eslava (1534–1601), considered the most important dramatist of sixteenth-century Latin America. A Spaniard by birth, perhaps from Seville, González de Eslava was born in 1534, arriving in Mexico when he was in his twenties, where he was ordained to the priesthood; he died in 1601. In his drama, *De cuando Dios Nuestro Señor mandó al profeta Jonás que fuese a la ciudad de Nínive a predicar su destrucción* [How God, Our Lord, Sent the Prophet Jonah to Nineveh to Predict Its Destruction], he presented in a bold and picturesque form one of the principal characteristics of the theater of the epoch, anachronism. In the work, a number of contemporary figures take the stage as the traveling companions of the biblical Jonah: A Biscayan, a fool, and a Mexican married couple, she a "daughter of a conquistador."

Secular Discourses

One of the recurring dramatic forms in this early period is the *entremés*, or short farce interlude, employed as a parodic genre satirizing society. As it was employed in Latin America, this form demonstrates that its producers and receivers were familiar with the theatrical forms of the so-called minor genres of the Spanish theater and the possibility of taking pleasure in formal and stylistic details. The *entremés* contributed to the fashioning of a number of aspects of Latin American culture by facilitating the inclusion of popular figures and vocabularies as well as abundant references to history, geography, and the customs and manners of the period. Within the *entremés* tradition, one of the most notable authors was Cristóbal de Llerena (1545–1616), a Dominican priest. His text, known as the *Entremés*, was first performed by university students in the atrium of the Cathedral of Santo Domingo on the eighth day of Corpus Christi, 1588. It satirizes feminine frivolity, the shams of notaries, and the usury of merchants as well as criticizing the "venality and negligence of the colonial authorities" (Ripoll and Valdespino 33). The colloquial expressions it places in the mouths of the popular characters, such as the Fool or Clown, are specifically Latin American. The theatrical codes employed, however, are merely variations of Spanish theatrical forms.

The already mentioned Fernán González de Eslava is often cited in histories of Latin American theater for his skillful versification, the agility of his dialogue, and his Latin American references. These contextual allusions are noteworthy for the abundance of their types, customs, landscapes, and local figures; for their reference to the Viceroys, whom González de Eslava praised in his prologues or celebrated in a number of his colloquies; for the use of historical events as raw material for one or another of the themes of the plays; and, above all, for the large number of Mexicanisms in the language.

The epoch of the Colonial cultural system in Latin America is very long, and Colonial society underwent numerous significant changes during the period. Thus it is hardly surprising that, especially in the eighteenth century, other social sectors arose, producing cultural products, including literary and theatrical texts, whose social imaginary was different from the status quo and whose sustaining values envisaged other social systems. These cultural newcomers manifested a preference for French cultural codes; some have called this advent the beginnings of a *criollo* literature, others the opening of a new region of interests on the part of other social sectors. One of the most famous dramatists of the colonial era, and a practitioner of various theatrical forms, was *El Lunarejo* [The Spotted Face], by Pedro de Peralta Barnuevo (Peru, 1663–1743). The first use of French neo-Classical codes in Latin America can be traced to his works. An imitator of Corneille and Molière, *El Lunarejo* is "an example of how a single figure could be both a representative of the decadent baroque and a precursor of the neo-Classical current in Hispanic-American theatre" (Ripoll and Valdespino 385).

Sor Juana Inés de la Cruz and the Theater of the Colonial Discourse

Sor Juana Inés de la Cruz (1648–1695) is a fine example of the dominant tendencies of her times in her use of references to the discourse of hegemonic culture. In recent years, she has been the subject of intense interest on the part of Latin American feminist scholars. For many, her theatrical texts correspond both to the discourses of the Church and to those of entertainment proper to seventeenth-century Spain, albeit with moralizing overtones. Recent studies, however, have pointed out that the discourse of Sor Juana ultimately constitutes an alternative discourse. From this new perspective, what had appeared in her works to be an untransformed utilization of prior theatrical codes has become a utilization in which the function of those codes has been changed, thus endowing her works with a potentially subversive message. What is undeniable in her works is the dominant role that religious discourse plays; however, within that discourse it is possible to observe innovations that depart from the theatrical discourses of her epoch.

The Eulogy of the Eucharist in the Play El divino Narciso [The Divine Narcissus]

The motive for the eulogy in *El divino Narciso* (1692) is the meeting of Religion, Fervor (representatives of the Catholic religion), and the Spanish conquistador with Occident and America (representatives of indigenous culture), in which the former attempt to convert the latter to the Christian faith. One option is to convert them by force; the second is to convince them with words. The eulogy attempts to demonstrate that the second is the better course and that it had been used with great success throughout the history of the Church. According to Ileana Azor, "in addition to possessing a certain autonomy, thanks to the theme with which it treats, [the play] is especially significant given the serious and sincere intention of its author to dignify the 'idolatrous' cults of the Mexican natives" (31).

According to the edition of 1690, the text was not intended to be staged for native or *criollo* audiences in Latin America, but rather "to be performed at the Royal Court in Madrid. This explicit designation of potential addressees helps to explain a number of its features. What the text appears to want to demonstrate is the fallacy of conversion by force. Referring to the conversion of St. Paul, it emphasizes that similar means must be employed: Namely, to identify the traits or expectations the natives held with respect to their gods and to demonstrate that those characteristics can be found in the Christian God. This strategy involves giving a certain credence, whether real or apparent, to the natives, recognizing their beliefs, and promoting the Christian faith by substituting the Christian God and saints for the indigenous gods in the collective imaginary of the natives. From the point of view of the potential spectators, this identification-in-essence of the Catholic religion and native beliefs—even extending to the justification of human sacrifice, a practice that had permitted the Spanish to judge the natives as savages and that justified much of the Spanish violence against them—constituted a valiant stand with respect to the indigenous problem and the representation of natives within the hegemonic culture at a time when the persecution of heretics and religious heterodoxy was intensifying.

El divino Narciso forms part of an allegorical discourse in which the codes of a number of traditions come together: Greco-Latin, biblical, Renaissance, indigenous, and the rhetorical tradition of high Catholic theological culture. Although the dominant code of the text is the divine pastoral, potential spectators require, in addition, a familiarity with the tradition of patristic disputes. The strongest influence on Sor Juana's sacramental allegory is Calderón de la Barca (1600–1681), and the origins of *El divino Narciso* can be traced back to *Echo and Narcissus*. Other sources feeding into the text include the Greco-Latin tradition, the patristic tradition, the Song of Songs, the poetry of Garcilaso de la Vega (1503–1536) and San Juan de la Cruz (1542–1591), and especially the latter's "*Cántico espiritual*" [c. 1577; "Spiritual Canticle"].

The Cloak-and-Dagger Play

One of the most popular genres in the Latin American theater of this period was, as in Spain, the drama of intrigue or the cloak-and-dagger play. Once again the work of Sor Juana Inés de la Cruz is exemplary in this matter, notably her drama *Los empeños de una casa* [1692; *The House of Trials*, 1996]. During the colonial era, both in the colony and the mother country, the staging of dramas constituted an extensive spectacle that, in addition to providing entertainment, fulfilled a plurality of other social functions. Sor Juana's drama, for example, was, among other things, the occasion for a social homage. According to the Fontanara edition, "the drama was staged in 1683 during a celebration that Sor Juana organized for María Luisa Gonzaga, the wife of the Viceroy Tomás Antonio de la Cerda. The celebration was carried out with a great deal of pomp in the palace" (*Los empeños* 8). Schmidhuber has called the continuous staging of Sor Juana's spectacle—all its texts were written by Sor Juana—the *revelry* of *Los empeños*. The insertion or the analysis of the drama within the context of a larger spectacle, as opposed to a study of the text in isolation, has opened up new perspectives on Sor Juana's career as a woman of the theater. Most critics of the text have highlighted the existence of autobiographical passages, the meta-theatricality of the second one-act farce and the third act, the close relation of the play to the Golden Age drama of intrigue tradition, various elements of a potentially feminist politic, Sor Juana's fine use of language, the wealth of references to seventeenth-century high culture, the allusions to historical personages, and the drama's representation of Mexican culture, especially in the final *Soirée*.

Los empeños certainly belongs to the Spanish Golden Age tradition of the drama of intrigue and should especially be considered in the company of the works of Calderón de la Barca (1600–1681), although various historians have emphasized the influence of Lope de Vega (1562–1635). It employs many of the typical elements of the genre: Star-crossed lovers, reversals of fortune, hide-and-seek subplots, deceptions and complications, shadowy dealings, disguises, a command of theatrical space and a rapid dénouement. One traditional element, employed with an extraordinary mastery and frequency in the play, is the aside. Asides fulfill a number of functions, including foreshadowing, revealing the depth of the characters, and providing a window on the private thoughts, emotions, and reactions of the characters. More generally speaking, however, their function appears to be that of making the spectator or reader complicit, while furnishing him or her with information that in a certain sense explains the behavior or the speech of the other characters. The aside plays a key role in the dramatic development.

In addition to the fact that the work belongs to a theatrical genre legitimized within the Spanish-speaking cultured sectors, the circumstances of the performance and the implicit social imaginary of the work served to bolster the reigning power system. As in the classic theater, the social structure represented in *Los empeños* is that of the bourgeoisie, and the play makes recurrent use of certain motifs by which that class was represented in the theater: Preoccupations with honor and the marrying of daughters, sentiments of love, and the economic arrangements that justify behaviors–all representations that imparted certain values. In the shadow of the bourgeoisie there appears the strata of servants: Fulfilling subordinate functions and endowed with those preoccupations proper to the tradition, namely, economic self-interest and personal salvation. They are not interested in honor but rather in money and advantage. After the intrigues, harmony returns to the world, love triumphs, and honor is salvaged.

The Discourses Addressing European Audiences

An important part of the theatrical activity in Latin American countries during the colonial era was composed of productions imported from Europe, by and large from Spain and, in the case of Brazil, from Portugal. These visits by European theatrical groups contributed to the strong presence of European theatrical culture in Latin America. On the other hand, various playwrights received recognition and honors on the stages of the peninsula, although their works were little performed (or not at all) in Latin America. The majority of the histories of Latin American theater include discussions of Juan Ruiz de Alarcón (1581–1639) as a Mexican dramatist. At the same time, Spanish theater histories consider him to be one of the principal dramatists of the Spanish Golden Age. Born in Mexico around 1581, Alarcón studied both in Mexico and Spain. He took up residence in Spain around 1613 and there wrote almost all his works. Some modern critics have attempted to determine the "Mexican-ness" of his works. They have suggested a number of elements of his vocabulary and characterizations as fitting this bill. The truth is, however, that Ruiz de Alarcón wrote for the Spanish audiences of his time, in accordance with the theatrical codes of peninsular stagecraft and the preoccupations of the Spanish. His most renowned works are *Las paredes oyen* [1628; The Walls Have Ears] and *La verdad sospechosa* [1630; *The Truth Can't Be Trusted*, 1998]. It is usually pointed out that his principal themes are of a moral nature and that the most salient feature of his works is the psychological characterization of his characters.

The case of Antonio José Silva, or Judeu (1705–1739), is somewhat similar, as he is often mentioned as a distinguished Brazilian dramatist. Although born in Rio de Janeiro, his family moved to Lisbon when he was a child. In the judgment of Rela, however, "there is nothing in his plays linking them to the traits, expressions, norms, or themes then current in the Colony. . . . His comedies, maintaining the European characteristics of the epoch (wit, extravagant jokes, popular effects), are distinguished by their interesting worldly picturesqueness and by the irony of their language, a quality that made him famous in his time and is the source of his continuing interest today" (21). The majority of his plays were performed in Portugal, although in 1761 his *Anfitrião* [Amphitryon] was staged in Bahía.

The Nineteenth Century: Theatrical Discourses of the Enlightened Bourgeoisie

The cultural and theatrical macro-system that displaced the colonial order was a dynamic rather than a static system. Rooted in certain basic concepts of the Enlightenment, this new system, with specific variations in the various countries, prevailed until the first decades of the twentieth century. The independence process that took place during the years 1810–1820 in the majority of the Latin American nations constituted a major transformation in the cultural producers' value

systems, the function of those systems, and in aesthetic and cultural preferences. However, once again, we must point out the complexity of Latin American society: Although general historical tendencies are recognizable, the formation of such tendencies, as well as the historical, economic, social, and cultural conditions of the different emerging nations were really quite distinct.

The sector dominating cultural production in this period was the national bourgeoisie, a social class whose wealth stemmed from agricultural production and the development of industry and commerce, especially international commerce, frequently based on the export of primary or raw materials. This class linked its interests to those of the French, English, and U.S. bourgeoisies, establishing in this way their character as an exterior-oriented, socially hegemonic class whose value systems combined a sense of national identity and a sense of identity in cultural association with European cultures.

This period was marked by a new relation between the state and the production of culture in which cultural politics depended on the status of the reigning social sectors. During this time the Church lost its predominance in society, although in some regions it managed to maintain its political power through association with certain social groups. In some cases the separation of Church and state was only achieved at the end of the century. The cultural objects produced by the religious orders ceased to constitute a significant aspect of the legitimized culture in the majority of Latin American nations. In general terms we can describe this transition as the advent of a secular or, on occasion, antireligious culture. In the theatrical domain, the opening of the hegemonic discourses towards the exterior resulted in a utilization or reutilization of the theatrical codes legitimized in France and, to a lesser extent as the century progressed, in Spain: Romanticism, realism or the representation of social customs and manners. The dissatisfaction of some social sectors gave rise to a transformation in which literature became an institution questioning the social–and not the political– order, and assuming for itself a critical, satiric, or parodic position *vis-à-vis* the dominant values or social system. Only on rare occasions did this questioning of the system imply a desire for its destruction. On the other hand, economic arrangements and the general external orientation meant that some of the theatrical performances staged in Latin America were those of foreign companies on tour, although the frequency of such performances varied from region to region. Cuba, for example, received numerous Spanish touring companies, and the situation was somewhat similar in Argentina and Uruguay, countries that could be characterized as constituting a theatrical microculture.

Within the macrosystem two successive subsystems can be distinguished. The first arose in the early years of independence, when the dominant social sectors considered culture an instrument useful in the formation of republics. The neo-Classical, with inklings of Romanticism, was the aesthetic system of preference. The second subsystem was a characteristic of the established republics, dating from approximately the 1840s or 1850s to the end of the century, whose cultural preferences were Romanticism and the tradition of a drama of customs and manners. In each of these subsystems the hegemonic discourses coexisted with the marginal cultural systems that produced and utilized their own theatricalities and theatrical discourses, as we have seen.

The Subsystem of the New Theatrical Discourses of National Identity

The main groups producing theatrical discourses and determining the cultural production and the political cultures of Latin America in this period belonged to the political and economic sectors that had triumphed in the struggle for independence. Their initial impetus was to rupture with the cultural system dominating the final years of the colonial era. The majority of the theatrical practitioners actively participated in the social and political life of the times and, in general, integrated their theatrical activities into the process of historical transformation. This period was distinguished by its preference for neo-Classical aesthetic codes in accordance with the Enlightenment prescription that development and progress were to be founded upon education, defined as the cultivation of reason. Culture, in this schema, was viewed as an instrument fundamental to the formation of a new society, to the realization of its ideals and, consequently, to the constitution of national identity. From this perspective the theater would fulfill the important task of disseminating and validating the presuppositions of the new nations. This modernizing project was brought to fruition by means of the translation of European texts bearing on the issues of violence and oppression and by the creation of original works, although at times the story-lines were located in the historical past.

Camilo Henríquez (Chile, 1769–1825) wrote in exile two works that remained unstaged in his lifetime: *Camila o la patriota de Sudamérica* [1817; Camila, or The South American Patriot] and *La inocencia en el asilo de las virtudes* [1817?; Innocence in the Sanctuary of Virtues]. Henríquez, a priest who was very active in the Chilean independence movement and a member of the first provisional government, noted in a number of his writings the important function of theater in the education and consolidation of the new political system. *Camila* was written in 1817 in Buenos Aires, where Henríquez had taken refuge during the Spanish reconquest of Chile. An excellent interpretation of this text has been offered by María de la Luz Hurtado. The play, a love story, takes place in the native hamlet of Omaguas in the Ecuadorian jungle; its plot concerns the construction of a utopic world and seeks to diagnose the causes of society's ills. In the social imaginary underlying Henríquez's texts, the Spanish appear to represent the forces of evil and those educated in the Enlightenment tradition, the forces of good. According to Henríquez's vision, the Arcadia of the Latin American natives constitutes a utopic space. In *La inocencia en el asilo de las virtudes* Henríquez took the United States as a utopic model for the "scene of the action of a social drama in which the material and social advances of society are highlighted. Science and technology (steam engines, artificial street lights, factories) struck Henríquez as admirable means of creating a clean and ordered milieu and satisfying the necessities of life with a certain leisure and comfort" (Hurtado 47).

Another writer who participated intensely in the political life of the era was Juan Cruz Varela (Argentina, 1794–1839), who, among other things, was the Minister of Government and Foreign Affairs in the Bernardino Rivadavia administration. Cruz Varela's *Dido* (1832), dedicated to Rivadavia, was based on the classical story of the arrival of Aeneas in Carthage and the refuge offered him by Queen Dido, and it concerns the contest of passion, duty, and political destiny. Dido's tragic predicament is both that of the human condition—she is a woman overwhelmed by the passion and the rejection of her lover—and that of a political being, in that falling in love with a foreigner causes her to betray her royal office. In his selection of the episode, the tragic structure, the classical motives, the strophic form, and the images, Cruz Varela opted to employ the theatrical codes of neoclassicism, although he verges upon Romantic codes in the representation of inflamed passions, the use of dreams, and the description of a wild natural environment.

The Subsystem of the Republican Bourgeoisie

Histories of Latin American theater tend to point out that around 1840 the Romantic storm erupted. Once the Romantics were established, the culturally productive sectors as well as the potential theatrical addressees of the era began to utilize elements of the new theatrical tendency in a process of legitimizing their social, political, and cultural interests. Of the options available to Romanticism, the theater predominantly opted for a customs and manners aesthetic, ironically interrogating the values of the new society. The defining characteristic of this trend was a theatrical production whose cultural imaginary was rooted in a society sustained by money, principally coming from agricultural production, and whose principal point of representational reference was the family. These families were well-to-do, with servants and maids and lands or a spacious house in the town or the city. Often, the dramatic conflict centers around the marriage of a daughter—generally, the sole daughter. One recurring motif is that of the stranger or itinerant worker, who is usually painted in a negative light. The theatrical codes employed are those of the customs and manners plays, many of which were written in verse and whose endings were, in general, happy ones in which the true values of society triumph. Once the new national states were established, in the majority of the cases, the producers of the theatrical discourses of the hegemonic culture placed less emphasis on national values than on the customs and manners that the new society had established. The fundamental preoccupation was with the state of affairs among the well-off strata of the bourgeoisie, with little reference to other non-dominant sectors. While this tendency was colored by differentiating shades in each of the various countries, its fundamental features were common to them all.

In *Contigo pan y cebolla* [1833; Bread and Onions with You], Manuel Eduardo Gorostiza (Mexico, 1789–1851) leveled his irony at the French influence in Latin American culture, although his critique is neither bitter nor destructive. Despite his ironizing, however, Gorostiza's work ultimately redeems the society whose fundamental values remain unquestioned: Money, the happiness associated with economic well-being, the control of strong passions, and the ability of men to resolve the problems originating in their fantasies and exaggerated idealizations of women. Emphasis is placed on the ills of too much reading and the pernicious effects of new novels on young women. The image is one of a society founded upon money and lacking in any form of class conflict, and of a society in which, since the mother is absent, the father and the servants take over her various functions. The codes employed are those of the Spanish comedy of intrigue.

Preoccupations with the state or the national political project surface in historical dramas whose themes usually centered on the denunciation of tyranny or the abuse of political power. *El visitador de México* [1838; The Official Visitor to Mexico], by Ignacio Rodríguez Galván (1816–1842), is an excellent example of a theatrical discourse that questions political power from a point of view that will be taken up again and again in the history of Mexican theatrical discourses. This text opens a new and important dimension of the history of Latin American theater in that it seeks to represent the intellectual of the marginal sector and because its author belonged neither to the aristocracy nor to the powerful. Some critics have highlighted the fact that Rodríguez Galván was of indigenous origin; in addition, he was a bookseller by profession. The play was a smashing success when it premiered. Although Rodríguez Galván died very young, at the age of twenty-seven in Cuba, he received a great deal of recognition in his short lifetime and was awarded a diplomatic post.

The plot of this work centers on Alonzo Muñoz, a visiting representative of the King of Spain, and his attempts to seduce Celestina, happily married to Baltasar Sotelo. Despite all Muñoz's advances, however, Celestina resists. Although Rodríguez Galván considered his text to be an example of Romanticism and employed the majority of its codes, it is significant for his vision of a society in which the human being is capable of living in peace and realizing him- or herself within the ideal conditions of requited love. This ideal is destroyed by the intrusion of an outsider whose passion and intentions lead him to violence. The drama is marked by a complete separation between the *us* and the *other*, between the Mexican and the Spaniard, and emphasizes that the cause of misfortune is an envoy from the outside, not a member of the society. Throughout the play this antithesis is referred to and, in the third act especially, it is invested with major political significance when the behavior of the visitor, Muñoz, is identified with that of King Felipe. This contrast serves as a point of reference for the portrayal of a society obsessed with power, especially foreign power.

From Modernity to Postmodernity

Overview

The majority of the legitimized cultural production in Latin American countries in the twentieth century arose from the middle classes, despite the fact that, as a class, they acquired political power around the 1920s. This hegemony was maintained over the course of the entire century, and thus both education and culture bore the stamp of their interests and the transformations that these sectors underwent in each of the Latin American nations. By virtue of their status as politically ascendant at the beginning of the century, the middle classes became the spokespersons of the new systems of values and other new social and politically emergent groups. Over the course of the century their hegemony would be questioned by the emergence of other groups and by the identification of representatives of the middle classes with the anxieties or grievances of other sectors, especially the workers in the first decades of the century, peasants and other marginalized people in more recent decades. The greatest economic and cultural power in this period was the state, which established the norms of cultural operation. At the beginning of the century, and especially in the period following the encyclical *Rerum Novarum*, the Catholic Church contributed to raising the awareness of the middle classes about the material conditions of the workers and had an influence on the images shaping the social imaginary of the times. However, the Church was in no sense a determinant of the cultural objects consumed by the middle classes. In recent years the situation has changed radically, since the Church's new attitude toward the popular sectors–synthesized in Liberation Theology–has been manifest in the production of cultural objects from all sectors of society and in the validation of the cultures of the popular sectors.

The middle classes were neither politically or ideologically unified nor internally cohesive. Their representatives advocated a diverse array of platforms based on national or international projects in which the future of the various countries in question, the participation of the distinct social sectors, and the several political ideologies undergirding them often led to antithetical positions. The fervor of these ideological conflicts waxed and waned in accordance with national internal situations, the international context, and the position of transnational institutions (the Communist Party and the Church, for example). Over the course of the century, the mediating role that the transnational institutions played in the production of cultural objects intensified, especially in recent decades. These institutions have promoted cultural events or played an active role in their dissemination or legitimization.

With respect to theatrical discourses, the most salient changes have been the displacement of the interests of the producers' discourses and the incorporation of other social groups into both the production of the discourses and their intended audiences. This diversification has given rise to a plurality of theatrical discourses. In general terms, the theater continues to be seen as a vigorous mode of social communication, capable of raising awareness both in the minority as well as in the popular sectors. Although not mutually exclusive, four successive subsystems can be distinguished. Each of the four has entailed a displacement of the producing sectors' interests, a creation of distinct relations with their potential addressees, and the predominant use of specific theatrical codes. It goes without saying by now that each, in addition, is subject to national variations.

The system as a whole is characterized by an intensification of the use of technological procedures in theatrical production and, in some cases, the substitution of visual signs for verbal language, thus altering the production methods and the images of the dominant or marginal theatricalities. This tendency reached its apogee in the latest subsystem, a development that some theater historians and critics have considered as characterizing the postmodernity of Latin American theater. In each of the subsystems a greater acceptance and legitimization of the productions of the marginal sectors was witnessed, as well as an increase in the number of producers and intellectuals from the middle classes participating in the production of discourses produced by the marginalized. In this period, in addition to the natives and the Afro-Latin Americans, we also have to consider workers, urban dwellers, and women, since they have all begun, especially within the last subsystem, to produce theatrical discourses whose aims are markedly different from what has been previously seen. The traditionally marginalized ethnic sectors have not radically altered their positions, despite the fact that representatives of the groups in power have tended to pay more attention to them, either directly, through their own spokespersons, or through middle-class intellectuals advocating on their behalf. With respect to their theatrical discourses, these sectors have maintained their traditions of massive spectacles staged in the context of religious festivals or public rituals, even though there are clear differences between the indigenous sectors and the Afro-Latin American sectors. In the postmodern subsystem, an extraordinary dissemination and circulation of the spectacles produced by the marginal sectors has been effected by the new political interests of the majority, the Church's preoccupation with the marginalized, and the postmodern commodification of these spectacles as raw material for the mass communication media, above all national and international television.

The Subsystem of the Enlightened Bourgeoisie in Crisis

The majority of theater historians consider modern theater to have begun in the first years of the twentieth century, even though many of the elements of these theatrical discourses were in fact a final manifestation of the modernizing projects of the enlightened bourgeoisie. The representative texts of the period reveal a crisis of Enlightenment values and of the factors that had sustained the social order and economic system, and give evidence of the emergence of both new social sectors and dramatists conscious of the injustices of the existing system. The preferred cultural codes employed in this theater are Realism and Naturalism, especially as rooted in the tradition of Ibsen and Spanish Realism. One of the recurring themes in the plays of this period is the representation of a society in crisis over the inability of individuals or the social system to adjust to social and economic changes. In some cases, this crisis is represented as a conflict between the old landholders and the new generations and their new systems of production. This conflict affected both individuals and groups, although in both cases the protagonists are presented as the victims of the transformation. This motif is, of course, theatrically framed in accordance with the specific circumstances and ideological preferences of the producers.

Interpretations of the theatrical work of Florencio Sánchez (1875–1910) confirm his status as a representative of this subsystem, especially in his highlighting of the consciousness on the part of middle-class intellectuals of the misfortunes endured by other social sectors. As Castagnino points out, "in his shorter works Sánchez focused his theatrical spotlight directly on a deplorable social reality. The overcrowding of tenements, inhuman exploitation, the government's neglect of the urgent problems of immigration and immigrant housing are fixed features of his short dramas and farces" (147).

Sánchez's play *Barranca abajo* [Into the Abyss], first staged in 1905, has become one of the classic works of modern Latin American theater and is considered representative of the Realist-Naturalist current. The text pursues two themes: The transformation of the system of agricultural production and its effects on the individual who represents the system being superseded. The protagonist, Don Zoilo, an agrarian patriarch overwhelmed by debts, refuses to sell his lands and insists on working them in the same way he has always done. Backed by members of Don Zoilo's own family and forces representing the authorities, the prospective buyers push Don Zoilo over the edge, and at the end of the play he commits suicide. Only his consumptive daughter Robustiana, and Aniceto, who is in love with her, come to Don Zoilo's defense: "His personal plight can be seen as a symbol of a dispossessed class; however, at the same time the audience is shaken and disturbed by the tragedy of a man vanquished by destiny" (Arrieta, 4: 553–54).

Although the basic story situation is the same, *Pánuco 137* (1933) by Mauricio Magdaleno (Mexico, 1906–1986) suggests that this thematic motif can be reutilized and reshaped according to the historical conditions of each country. In this play, the plot centers on the conflict between the indigenous farmers, who prefer to continue cultivating their lands in the traditional way, and a U.S. company seeking to extract petroleum. This conflict serves to portray a Mexican society in which representatives of the institutions of power favor those economic transformations that are in accord with their own interests. Magdaleno, for his part, takes the side of the natives and denounces the reigning political system. The context of the motif's reutilization is thrown into relief when we recall that the text was written five years before the Lázaro Cárdenas administration nationalized the petroleum industry. It is in this light that Marcela del Río's comments are thought-provoking: "the potential addressees of the text were not the peasants, who Magdaleno knew to be marginalized and disqualified from gaining access to theatrical fora, but rather the ascendant petite-bourgeoisie public who had acquired the economic wherewithal to educate themselves and create for themselves a culture" (142). In addition, Del Río notes that Magdaleno's "text proposes an interpretation of the [Mexican] revolution that seeks to be the accepted interpretation in the official historical discourse" (142). Portraying the U.S. businessmen whose decisions are based on the firms' self-interest and the possibility of profit, Magdaleno refrains from condemning them. The real targets of his condemnation are the representatives of the Mexican power elite, since they are linked to criminal elements and since their primary motivation is not to serve their country but to line their own pockets.

A somewhat different case is that of *La viuda de Apablaza* [1928; Apablaza's Widow], by Germán Luco Cruchaga (Chile, 1894–1936). Critics (Rojo, Durán Cerda) have emphasized the play's relation to the Western tradition, its reutilization of the myth of Phaedra, and the incestuous character of the widow's passion for her stepson. María de la Luz Hurtado's analyses, on the other hand, has emphasized how the work casts light on the transformation of Chilean agricultural production. According to Luz Hurtado, in Cruchaga's representation of the transfer of the estate's management to the stepson and his subsequent death, we witness "the end of an epoch in the Chilean countryside and the advent of capitalist forms of production and labor relations. While these changes do not represent a more just or better way of life for the bulk of the Chilean peasantry, they do constitute a change in the forms of authority and in human relations, henceforth subordinated to the economic interests of the landowners" (91). Ñico, the protagonist, reorganizes the operation of the estate and its relations with the workers with a view to turning it into an economic enterprise, thus putting an end to the tradition of the master as the fountainhead of his workers' well-being or misfortune.

One important discourse of this subsystem, although there are significant national differences, has sought to portray the sectors marginalized in terms of economic well-being and to emphasize social conditions, the life of poverty and its effects, or the exclusion of some human beings from the benefits of modernization. Most of the discourses presenting or defending the problems of the proletariat were produced by intellectuals from the middle classes who shaped their texts to represent a proletarian point of view. This was done, in some cases, in conjunction with the political project of one or another of the international ideologies that, in this period, had begun to surface in Latin America or sometimes as part of a national project that implicated the emergent sectors in their realization.

La fragua [1912; The Forge], by Armando Discépolo (Argentina, 1887–1971), concerns a strike and its consequences and the various positions taken by the factory workers vis-à-vis the owners. The worker protagonist, Lorenzo, an Italian immigrant and idealist ready to sacrifice himself for the collective good, represents the anarchist ideas of social and human renovation. Previously persecuted and jailed, he returns to defend the workers' ideals and views the strike as a vehicle for obtaining the redress of their needs. In his interpretation of this play, Pellettieri states that "*La fragua* is the theatrical text where Discépolo most explicitly expounds his anarcho-socialist ideas by means of a humanitarian message based on an exaltation of the 'reasons of the heart'" (244).

Discépolo incorporated another sector of the proletariat in his drama *Mateo* (1923) [Matthew]. Like the enlightened bourgeoisie texts of the previous century, *Mateo* centers on the family; however, in this case it concerns the penniless family of an immigrant whose profession–he is a hackney coach driver–has been rendered obsolete. Certain aspects of the patriarch tradition are maintained, inasmuch as the father feels responsible for the well-being of the family and resorts to crime in order to sustain it. The dénouement, however, is optimistic: The sons (the new generation) begin to assume responsibility for the family, learning the new trades in demand in the new society, and one is left with a hopeful picture of the family's overcoming their impoverished condition. The sons have understood that certain professions are obsolete and that education is the only way to prepare for the contingencies of life in modern society.

The Subsystem of the Middle Classes in Power: New Modernization

The second subsystem commenced around the end of the First World War and stretched approximately into the 1950s. It was based on the affirmation of the ascendancy of the middle class to political power and brought with it proposals for new national projects envisaging the participation of workers as potential allies in that ascendancy or in its maintenance. Pedro Morandé has called this period one of "modernization": "During the 1920s and '30s there arose a generation of Latin American intellectuals who reflected on the challenges posed by the advent of mass society" (16–17). This general transformation was manifest in the domain of culture. In the case of theater, historians have noted that towards the third or fourth decade of the twentieth century, with some variation, significant changes in the texts and in the stagings of productions began to manifest themselves in various countries. Morandé notes, in addition, that a number of radical groups or movements arose, especially in Mexico, Argentina, Uruguay, and Chile. The most characteristic feature of these new groups (led by small cadres of intellectuals) was their call for replacing the old theatrical forms with new ones more in accord with new national projects. The new system of aesthetic preferences of theatrical discourses implied the ready acceptance of new aesthetic tendencies (Surrealism, Expressionism, and avant-garde ideas), or the validation of dramatists who appeared to be innovators (O'Neill, Pirandello). Art for art's sake theories and aesthetic ideas emphasizing the artistic object in place of its reflection or representation of reality became the vogue. These ideas implied a new conception of the human being and a different function for theater, especially with respect to elements of direction, acting, and staging. In the majority of cases in Latin America, however, the new tendencies did not annul the pragmatic character of the theatrical message with respect to the *hic et nunc* of the sociopolitical context in which the work was written or staged.

On the other hand, the new national projects entailed a rereading of history, thereby delegitimizing the past and justifying the new sectors in power. The quest to widen theatrical audiences to include other parts of the population necessitated the inclusion of discourses that made social conditions known and that then provoked a desire for change. These redemptive discourses promised the marginalized that they would receive the fruits of the social transformation that the new national projects sought to effect. These historical conditions gave rise to a plurality of discourses within the hegemonic sectors and altered the representational modes of the marginal sectors within these discourses.

Despite the enormous historical differences between countries, and despite their functioning within different contexts, creating significations specific to each of these different spaces, common theatrical codes were utilized within the hegemonic discourses. Critics have tended to speak of this historical moment and this group of theatrical producers as the "Generation of '27" or as the "Experimentalists." For his part, Grínor Rojo has characterized them as "the individuals who inaugurated this new sense of history. In their participatory universalism, in their certainty of being an active part of a general cultural crisis touching all the facets and geographic sectors of Western culture, I believe we can see the nucleus of their sensibilities. . . . It is the response of a new Hispano-American dramatic sensibility to a universal crisis of culture" (24–25). Frank Dauster, for his part, has characterized and historically located this moment as "the experimentalist one; it began towards the end of the 1920s, although in some countries there were prior manifestations" (1973, 25). He goes on to mention the most important groups: "Mexico, Teatro Ulises, 1928; Río de la Plata, Teatro del Pueblo, 1930; Cuba, the antecedents of the Cueva group, 1928. Even in Puerto Rico, where this movement took hold between 1938 and 1941, its roots can be traced back to the awakening of the conscience and the questioning of being a movement that in Puerto Rico has been baptized, in a highly significant manner, 'the Generation of 1930'" (1973, 25). In the case of Chile and Brazil, this theatrical renovation did not take hold until the 1940s.

One of the most frequently mentioned dramatists within this subsystem has been Xavier Villaurrutia (Mexico, 1903–1950). His new concept of human existence is evident in his *Parece mentira* [1933; You Don't Say]. This work incorporates a reflection on the truth of being and proposes multidimensionality and time-consciousness as the determinants of truth. The individual may embody various entities at the same time and may be seen from a multiplicity of perspectives, without abandoning his or her reality. In the play's dialogue, existentialist overtones can be heard, and shades of the Pirandello of *Six Characters in Search of an Author* can be glimpsed in the characters' on-stage process of becoming. Although the representational style appears realist, the dialogue and the characters intimate a subversion of realism in as much as they question their own validity and representations.

Another dimension of theatrical renovation was manifest in the so-called "Poetic Theater," a movement principally characterized by the avoidance of social issues, the construction of imaginary spaces unlinked to national historical circumstances (preferably medieval or exotic spaces), and an intensification of poetic language. A good example of this is

El pacto de Cristina [1945; Christine's Covenant] by Conrado Nalé-Roxlo (Argentina, 1898–1971). On the most traditional level, the play presents an antithesis between reality and illusion, distancing itself from immediate historical events. This perspective is reinforced by the play's medieval setting, its associations with the theater of García Lorca and Casona, its poetic language, its use of folkloric songs and lullabies, and its image of a conflict resolved. In the context of mid-1940s Argentina, however, the text's aesthetic plays a double role. On the one hand, it is artistically legitimized by appearing within a theatrical current that had acquired some prestige: It was during these years that Ortega y Gasset (1883–1955) visited Buenos Aires and that his reflections on the "dehumanization of art" had become fashionable. On the other hand, the text can be read as an allegory of good and evil in which the opposition reality-fantasy corresponds to a concrete social phenomenon: The fact that once human beings are prepared to risk their souls and reality for an illusion, that the very wager will unfailingly lead to the shattering of illusion. If we accept this hypothesis, *El pacto de Cristina* acquires an historical dimension: Both Peronism and Marxism could be seen as fantastic illusions that, ultimately, will destroy the creators and the disciples of those utopias. In this sense Nalé-Roxlo's texts must be viewed as dystopic.

Saverio el Cruel [1936; Saverio the Cruel], written by one of the founders of the Teatro del Pueblo, Roberto Arlt (Argentina, 1900–1942), represents another vein of the Latin American theatrical renovation in this era. Arlt incorporated into his works a number of renovative techniques: Metatheatricality, or theater-within-theater, a concept of both sane and insane character, and a theatrical space of the imagination. In *Saverio el Cruel* these techniques attend a questioning of the social and political regime of the moment, and imply a parody or satire of some of the contested values in the Argentina of the 1930s. Arlt interrogates the political power of the landholding class, mockingly ironizes the ascendant class of the industrial bourgeoisie, and questions in particular the idle younger generation, who enjoy the economic means and free time to isolate themselves from society in their games of leisure. This assertion is highly significant when we recall the numerous tracts and essays published in the epoch advancing the notion that education of the younger generation constituted the basis of new national projects (Rodó, Ingenieros, Ortega y Gasset). *Saverio el Cruel* also satirizes the merchant bourgeoisie and its potential transformation into an instrument of military power.

Another important dimension of cultural production at this time was the justification of national projects copiously documented in Latin American essays of the period. Nationalist discourses sought to give a sense and direction to history by interpreting the national projects. Two of Rodolfo Usigli's dramatic texts demonstrate a couple of the dimensions of questioning that interpretations of these projects were subject to. In *El Gesticulador* [1937; The Gesticulator], Usigli (Mexico, 1905–1979) challenged the accepted view of an episode of the Mexican revolution and put forth an interpretation of the truth of the official history. Usigli's *Corona de sombra* [written in 1943, premiered in 1947; Crown of Shadows] is an almost exemplary text, from the point of view of both its historical re-examination and its modernization of theatrical techniques. The story concerns the visit of the Historian to the elderly former Empress Carlota and reconstructs the period when Maximilian of Austria (1832–1867) was made Emperor of Mexico (1864–1867). The plot centers on the efforts of Carlota, Maximilian's wife, to secure European approval and support. The incident is related by means of intensely modern techniques (demonstrating Usigli's familiarity with theatrical tendencies in Europe), including a manipulation of times and the techniques with which they are linked, as well as the use of flashbacks, story-telling, and multiple narrators. In addition, Usigli employs a *mise-en-scène* in which multiple spaces coexist on a single stage, thus allowing, when accompanied by fadeouts, for displacements from one historical moment-space to another. The temporal perspective is that of the Historian's present. The dramatic structure of the play is based on this character's efforts to reconstruct the period and resolve the unanswered questions of the existing historical record. The analysis of the Historian, Erasmo Ramírez, and his function within the imaginary world of the text highlight a number of significant elements. According to him, the function of historical reconstruction is to fill in the cracks of history. Ramírez, whose physical resemblance to Benito Juárez (1806–1872) (President of Mexico, 1858–1872) is explicit, appears to represent the native dimension of the Mexican character. While the text, as a whole, declares its rejection of the Imperial imposition, in the end the Historian comes to understand and develops an understanding with Carlota. The text shows the two powerful foreigners coming to accept the values of the Mexican world, demonstrating their love of the country, and seeking to serve Mexico above all else. Despite having implemented a number of severe policies, these rulers ultimately feel a great affection for the Mexican people. We are shown how, within the context of a social class attempting to surrender Mexico to foreign interests, the emperor attempts to defend the nation's territorial integrity and to protect the people, despite the schemes of certain popular leaders. Viewing the United States as the enemy, the emperor and empress struggle to maintain the unity and indissolubility of Mexican space. The play's vision of the Church, as portrayed through various of its representatives, is negative, however.

This epoch witnessed a tendency that attained its most systematic realization in Mexico during the 1920s: State sponsorship of theatrical discourses was addressed to the popular or marginal sectors, seeking to educate those groups or to integrate them into the national projects. Under the auspices of the Secretary for Public Education's Cultural Missions project, this theatrical movement was carried out by a group of teachers who, integrating themselves into indigenous communities, sought to educate and inform the natives about the national projects. Within the context of the new socialist ideology, these pedagogical efforts sought to impart practical knowledge of history, first aid and medicine, agriculture and agronomy, among other things: "The theatre was one means of fostering in the peasantry a consciousness of the importance of their participation for the success of national development" (Chabaud 150). This movement thus gave rise to a great number of theatrical forms, running the gamut from the theater of political consciousness raising–the "*Teatro de Ahora*" ("Theater of Now"), for example–to a pedagogical theater offering instruction on the principles of health and hygiene.

The Discourses of the Alternative Sectors in the Macrosystem

The cultural practices of the hegemonic groups in the twentieth century manifest a greater and greater incorporation of and interrelation between cultural producers and marginalized cultures. The core interest in this period is in the proletarian sectors, now transformed into producers or privileged addressees of theatrical discourses. Within the discourses produced at the beginning of the century by the proletarian sectors, we should distinguish between the anarchist discourse, whose importance was greatest in the first decades, and the socialist discourse, which became more important from the 1920s and 1930s on, when, following the establishment of the Socialist and Communist Parties, anarcho-syndicalism began to lose its relevance among the workers.

Eva Golluscio de Montoya has analyzed the modes of production and signification of the anarchist theatrical discourses of this period, above all in the texts of Florencio Sánchez. In her numerous essays and her book, *Teatro y folletines libertarios rioplatenses (1895–1910)* [1996; Libertarian Theater and Serials in the Río de la Plata, 1895–1910], Golluscio de Montoya has demonstrated the intense theatrical activity of orchestral musicians and the anarchist-inspired workers' centers. Thanks to her research, we can speak of an anarchist discourse produced by the members but directed predominantly at the middle classes. In her opinion, the movement was "the privileged cultural activity of a core group of nonconformists. . . . It had an oral propagandistic quality and was the ideal vehicle for the diffusion of the Idea" (85). She goes on to add that "by far the largest number of the dramatic spectacles presented at the anarchist functions of the epoch made reference not only to the existence of texts (by national or foreign authors), but also to the lives of the audience, the actors and actresses who performed, the person in charge of staging the production (however modest it may have been), and the critics of the production, and also to the budgets for publicity, programs, and the hiring of materials necessary for the representation" (85–86). As Golluscio de Montoya notes, these spectacles were in fact highly complex undertakings: "The dramatic functions staged at the libertarian centers were only on rare occasions autonomous productions. They almost always integrated within one extended program hymns, conferences, union meetings, debates, theatrical plays, recitations, tombola, music–the theatrical representation constituted merely a link within a much more vast ensemble, that of militant activity" (86).

One of the great difficulties in the study of workers' theater is the retrieval of sources: It is not easy to find the texts of the works staged or even commentaries on them. Pedro Bravo-Elizondo has carried out excellent work in reconstructing the context and the circumstances of the socialist spectacles staged by workers in the north of Chile. His descriptions and numerous examples reinforce the picture detailed by Golluscio de Montoya in the sense that these types of productions constitute a central component of the cultural and political activities of socialist workers. Like their anarchist counterparts, these workers are organized in sociocultural centers and understand themselves to be integrated into a diversity of activities aiming at educating and raising the consciousness of workers as a whole under the slogan "*ayudar a transformar la actual sociedad*" ("to lend a hand and change society" Bravo-Elizondo 1986, 105). Within the context of national economic problems affecting the saltpeter workers at the end of the Second World War, the examples raised by Bravo-Elizondo suggest that the socialist workers' theater constituted an element of solidarity in difficult times. They also suggest that in general such theatrical activities are multi-faceted, involving entire families, and that they frequently occasion other social activities. In a number of the examples cited, the evening's performance ends with a "terrific social dance" (125).

From the Cold War to Postmodernity

From the end of the Second World War, the majority of the Latin American nations officially aligned themselves with the United States in the Cold War. Latin American leftist movements, in contrast, fell in with the eastern bloc and intensely promoted the mobilization of workers and peasants. This unstable sociopolitical situation led to a series of revolutionary *coups d'état*, either from the right or the left, in several Latin American countries, and to the growth and development of guerrilla movements and dictatorial governments. The most salient characteristic of this climate was a feeling of social anxiety on the part of some sectors and a corresponding feeling in other sectors that repression was necessary. In addition to the Cold War, other determinant historical events of the period were the Cuban Revolution and the series of military dictatorships in the region generally.

With respect to cultural production during this period, the middle classes tended to support those sectors that favored changes. It was also during this period that organized labor began to exercise its power on the various national stages and the marginal and popular sectors began to appear as participants or potential allies of the ruling classes. Parallel to these developments, Latin American cultural producers came under the strong influence of European cultural currents, giving rise to a theater of personal reflection and discontent with the human condition. This theatrical attitude made recourse to the styles and techniques of the existential theater or theater of the absurd as well as the theater of cruelty inspired by Artaud or, in its Latin American version, the theater of panic. The theatrical discourses of the middle classes tended either to be politically engaged or to show signs of a disillusionment with modernity, emphasizing either the absurd dimension of all human existence or the loneliness and abject condition of the individual in the new society. Characteristic features of this subsystem were its efforts to socialize theatrical production by means of what was called "collective creation," an emphasis and reflection on the process of the *mise-en-scène*, and the utilization of codes associated with Brecht's epic theater.

The dominant feature of the period was the utilization of the theater as a means of political struggle, which has been called the socialization of production, in which theatrical productions demonstrated a preference for the techniques stemming from Brechtian epic theater tradition. The current of political engagement gave rise to street theater groups predominantly addressing the popular or marginal sectors of society. At the same time, Latin American theater also witnessed an intensification of more general reflections on the human condition. This theatrical climate led to a number of declarations or manifestos on the function of theater in society, as well as its staging and direction. With respect to the latter, ideas based on the theories of Stanislavsky began to acquire a predominance. Although a number of theatrical theorists in Latin America reflected on the function of the theater, without a doubt the most influential and visible, both nationally and internationally, was Augusto Boal (1972, 74). One of the dramatists most representative of the revolutionary theater was Osvaldo Dragún (Argentina, 1929–1999). In a number of his texts, he made recourse to techniques that had been popularized by the Brechtian theater: The use of narrators, anti-dramatic structures, posters, placards, and song. One of the most revealing works in this current was Dragún's *Heroica de Buenos Aires* [Buenos Aires Heroics], awarded the Casa de las Americas Prize in 1966, based on Brecht's (1898–1956) *Mother Courage* (1941). In all of his work, a number of themes are highlighted. For example, Dragún's play *Y nos dijeron que éramos inmortales* [1962; And They Told Us We Were Immortal], on the bleak prospects confronting the younger generation in society, emphasizes the imperative of social transformation. Recounting the story of a conscript killed in a guerrilla attack, the play reconstructs his life and that of his friends, throwing into relief the conditions that led to his death and thereby portraying the senselessness of the life that bourgeois society promises the younger generation.

One of the most important dramatists of the period, associated not only with the collective theater movement, but with the new theater (Rizk) and the political theater as well, was Enrique Buenaventura (Colombia, b. 1925). Although it is a late text, Buenaventura's 1988 *Crónica* [Chronicle] is a fine example of the tendencies of social theater in this period. Based on an episode recounted by Bernal Díaz del Castillo (1492–1584) in the *Verdadera Historia de la conquista de Nueva España* [1632; *The Discovery and Conquest of Mexico*], and which Cortés mentions in one of his letters to the king, *Crónica* concerns the fate of two sailors, Gonzalo Guerrero and Jerónimo de Aguilar, who, fleeing the tyranny of Pedrerias Dávila, head for Jamaica and are shipwrecked on an island near Cozumel and made prisoners and slaves of the local Mayans. The play aims to recount the story of the conquest from an indigenous perspective–an extremely worthy aspiration at the time and even more valid in subsequent years in the context of the 500th anniversary of Columbus's voyage. Despite this intent, however, the play is marked by the fundamental fact that it seeks to speak in the name of the other, assuming and impersonating, making itself the spokesperson, of the voice of the vanquished. In this appropriation of voice, what is assigned to the defeated are the voice and ideas of the creators and producers. This message and intent must be seen within the ideological context of the times in which Buenaventura, an intellectual of the 1960s' and 1970s' Latin American left, associated with the Communist Party and the Marxist movement and, thus, strongly influenced by the contemporary European cultural trends, sought to disseminate a new truth.

Within these discourses we need to consider a current almost silenced at the time, but which would later acquire major importance: The current of disillusionment with socialist utopias. One exemplary text in this matter was *Rasga coração* [1974; Gash to the Heart], by Oduvaldo Viana Filho (1936–1974). According to Carmelina Guimaraes, "Vianninha envisioned his greatest work as a synthesis of an entire historical period, from 1930 to 1970, and as a retrospective of the most effervescent epoch in the entire history of republican Brazil. . . . The setting of *Gash to the Heart* recounts the perfecting of the authoritarian state–from the period of the New State (1937–1945) to the AI-5 law (December 1968)– and the ideological resistance to it" (25). Viana himself described the play, which he finished a couple of months before his death, as "the story of Manguarí Batalla, an anonymous freedom fighter who, after forty years of struggle for all that he deems new and revolutionary, is confronted by his son accusing him of being conservative, anachronistic, and out of touch. Interrogating these ideas, the play illuminates forty years of our political life" (33). This play was first staged with

great success by the founder of the Arena theater group, José Renato, in 1979, three years after Viana Filho's death.

Nationalist Preoccupations: The Case of Puerto Rico

The theatrical discourses of the Cold War period also reveal preoccupations with questions of nationalism, especially in those countries where conflicts over the definition of what is national remained in force. Such concerns were an issue for a number of Puerto Rican dramatists, René Marqués (1919–1979) in particular. The centrality of the theme of identity in Puerto Rican drama is an example of how specific historical circumstances have taken control of the general tendencies. The discourse of Marqués emphasizes a number of aspects bearing special significance for Puerto Rico: The influence of and dependence on the United States; the rustic and his immigration to the cities; Puerto Rican immigration to New York City; the shock of the meeting of two cultures. With respect to the theatrical codes employed by Marqués, some critics have pointed to his "naturalist techniques and nationalist thematics" in *La carreta* [1950; *The Wheelbarrow*, Dauster 102], while others have highlighted the great diversity of his other works in which he experimented with neo-naturalism, the absurd, expressionism, epic theater, poetic theater, and historical theater. The most openly political of his plays is *La muerte no entrará en palacio* [1956; Death Will Not Enter the Palace], which, critics have pointed out, bears a number of similarities with the life and times of the ex-Governor of the island, Luis Muñoz Marín. In *Un niño azul para esa sombra* [1960; A Blue Boy for That Shadow], Marqués threw the spotlight on the issue of culture shock; in this work the young protagonist, Michelín, finds himself caught between the cultural allegiances of his mother, oriented towards the United States, and those of his father, imprisoned for his political beliefs, which have their roots in the native culture and in aspirations for liberty. The protagonist is a "child prodigy and visionary, a 'blessed child' who understands the impossibility of his existence in a degraded and impoverished world. He represents the decay of the family–lovelessness, lack of communication–that leads to alienation. At the same time, however, the family situation is seen to be the product of social conditions in which the father, Michel, a 'visionary' of freedom and fighter for political liberty, is overwhelmed by the forces of oppression and finally destroyed by his inability to assimilate himself into the system of social degradation. By the play's end he too is a 'visionary,' but one whose visions have driven him mad and into the streets where he proclaims his truth to all New York" (Villegas 1989, 116).

The "European Schools"

During the reign of the postwar subsystem, the majority of the theatrical innovations seen in Latin America were linked to the dominant codes of the European hegemonic theater of the period, especially the theater of the absurd. This utilization of codes associated with the European "schools" did not, however, annul their social orientation in Latin America. Agustín Cuzzani (Argentina, 1924–1978) is considered by many a typical representative of the theater of the absurd. According to Suárez Radillo, "Cuzzani is, perhaps, of all the Argentine dramatists born in the heat of the independent theater movement, the dramatist most translated into other languages and whose plays have been staged in the greatest number of countries" (151). Two of Cuzzani's works have been the subject of extensive commentary: *El centroforward murió al amanecer* [1953; The Center-Forward Died at Dawn] and *Sempronio* (1958). According to Bravo-Elizondo, *El Centro-Forward* advances the proposition that "only liberty can justify the existence and happiness of the human being on this earth. The play's complex theme also addresses issues of the exploitation of the individual on the part of the institution, and the submission of the arts and sciences to personal rather than communitarian interests" (1975, 121). For its part, *Sempronio* takes up the question of atomic fallout but turns this issue toward a consideration of a potential transformation of Latin American society. The story concerns the absurd situation of Sempronio, a retiree whose hobby of stamp collecting inadvertently turns him into a radioactive source of energy after he is irradiated by the stamps in his collection from Hiroshima and Nagasaki. He becomes a kind of human battery powering all the electric radios and irons in the neighborhood. He feels that his life has been vindicated; we may say that his fate represents the triumph of the people. The absurdity of the situation is in the service of a social critique of the greed of big business and of the ambitions of the army, who, concerned only with their own interests, are oblivious of the state of things in the popular sectors of society. The text advances the notion that nuclear power is not in itself evil incarnate but rather something to be made use of. On the personal level, Sempronio is a kind of Everyman, since his electrical capacity functions only when he is happy and he is happy only when his existence has meaning, which is to say when he lives in collaboration with his neighbors.

Another distinguished work, winner of the Casa de las Americas theater prize in 1965 and considered by critics to be one of the most outstanding works of the theater of the absurd in Latin America, is *La noche de los asesinos* [1963; The Night of the Assassins] by José Triana (Cuba, b. 1931). Various interpretations of the play have been advanced, ranging from a denunciation of the (then) new Cuban regime to a representation of pre-Revolutionary Cuban society or the true conditions of the bourgeois family.

Anti-Dictatorial Discourses

The series of dictatorships that plagued Latin America in the Cold War period have been a point of reference for numerous narrative, lyric, essayistic, or theatrical texts. With respect to the theatrical discourses, many texts exist denouncing dictatorship, either in general terms or in specific instances. Roberto Athayde (Brazil, b. 1949) achieved tremendous international acclaim for his work *Apareceu a Margarida* [1973; Miss Margarita]. The play's protagonist, the teacher Margarita, makes use of the audience as if they were a group of students with whom she establishes a sadomasochistic relationship. The play is a fiery denunciation of political dictatorship, of the educational system, and of a society that sanctions the exercise of such forms of power. Although the list of Argentinean, Chilean, and Uruguayan plays on the subject of dictatorship is a long one, one of the classic texts of this subgenre is *El señor Galíndez* (1973) by Eduardo Pavlovsky (Argentina, b. 1933). The scene is set in a room that, however odd, is not very different from a room in any house or office building: "Furniture, a bed, various metal chairs, a table, a couple of cupboards, a mattress on the floor" (Dauster 1983, 157). The characters arrive and begin conversing in a very ordinary way about their privates lives and personal ambitions, which are not that different from anyone else's. As the action proceeds, however, the reader or the spectator begins to realize that this room is a torture chamber and that the characters are torturers by

profession. The order which they all serve is represented by the absent character of Señor Galíndez, who communicates with the characters on stage solely by telephone. According to Frank Dauster, the great international success of the play "was due to its exposition and denunciation of institutionalized torture in our world" (1983, 152).

One of the most obvious tendencies of the anti-dictatorial theater is its reutilization of classical texts, rereading or representing them as implicit denunciations of specific dictatorships. The dictatorships have tended not to subject classical texts to state censorship, out of a fear that such censorship could be interpreted internationally as an attack on culture. Thus, during various dictatorial regimes, works such as Lope de Vega's *Fuenteovejuna* and, especially, *Antigone*, either in translations from Sophocles or in contemporary adaptations, have frequently been performed on the Latin American stage. One of the most performed adaptations has been that of Griselda Gambaro (b. 1928), the Argentinean dramatist who has also written various other works denouncing dictatorial regimes, including *Los siameses* [1965; The Siamese], *El campo* [1967; The Camp], and *La malasangre* [1981; Bad Blood].

Street Theater

Although not exclusive to the post–World War II period, the use of street theater as a means of social communication witnessed an intensification in these years. The predominant addressees of this theater have been the popular sectors, whether urban dwellers or the rural peasantry. Street theater takes a number of forms and can be found in practically every region of Latin America. It has also exercised a profound influence on those theatrical forms produced by the marginalized. In general, it is a theatrical form seeking to effect social change and that, to varying degrees, aims at instructing or awakening the social conscience of its audiences. Groups practicing street theater are usually transitory ensembles, and they tend to make use of similar theatrical resources and employ similar forms of presentation, including a theatrical rhetoric somewhat akin to circus spectacles. Over time, many of the groups have become established and, in addition to their streetscape presence, they have become an obligatory feature at national and international theater festivals. Their objective is to attract and engage the masses in a kind of identification with their popular sector audiences. The majority of the members of these troupes have a solid professional training, are well aware of new theatrical movements and techniques, and are familiar with European theatrical trends. Often their models are North American or European troupes. The majority make use of materials similar to those used by The Bread and Puppet Theater; they have been influenced by the teachings of Grotowski and, in recent years, by Barba and his anthropological theater. In some cases, they have created actors' colonies of a sort, in which the members live a life entirely devoted to their physical, technical, and ideological training, a knowledge that the groups disseminate wherever they tour. Their galvanizing mission or function often leads these groups to project their own preoccupations onto their popular sector audiences. Their themes, whether anti-dictatorial, anti-oppression, pro-feminist, or even ecological, have varied according to the preoccupations of the various spaces from which they have arisen.

The System of Postmodernity: Dehistoricization and Demythification of Utopias

Although the tendencies of the previous years did not disappear, it is well known that in the 1980s the theatrical discourses of the hegemonic sectors experienced a number of significant changes. The historical, social, cultural and technological circumstances of Latin America capable of influencing the social imaginary of the producers of the hegemonic theatrical discourses also experienced significant changes. On the international level, the defining features of the Cold War era disappeared and the power of transnational corporations intensified. With respect to Latin American political life, a number of the dictatorial regimes ended, the planned or socialist economies tended to give way to market or free-market economies, and the economic presence of the giant international consortiums increased. In the domain of communications, the majority of the Latin American nations witnessed an intensification and diversification of the use of television as a means of communication, thus giving rise to determinant transformations in the dominant theatricalities and collective imaginaries. What was fashionable in the technological and international theatricalities also became increasingly influential in Latin America.

Postmodernity has become the dominant feature in the culture legitimized by the high cultural sector, and this has tended to transnationalize culture and to diminish or render obsolete the social or political function of cultural discourses. On the other hand, however, the democratization and expansion of the means of communication have opened the cultural playing field to numerous marginalized groups. The notion of women's liberation has intensified, not only in social life, but in political and other dominant discourses, resulting in the increased importance of women in the domains of work, politics, and cultural production. Latin American theater has felt the consequences of this globalization of culture and the increased influence of the transnationals: Its producers have intensified their use of technology as a theatrical medium, and certain of its local manifestations have acquired an international resonance through the participation of Latin American groups at international theater festivals. These transformations have especially resulted in an irruption of anti-historical or supposedly ahistorical discourses and an emphasis on innovation. The principal consequence of these has been a new formal experimentalism and a marked intensification of the integration of the visual arts and electronic and technological elements as important components of theatrical production. On the other hand, there has also been an expansion of the social sectors that produce theater, consume it, or have access to the hegemonic culture, especially through television. This has given rise to new patterns in the consumption or perception of the theatrical discourses.

Within the theatrical discourses dominant in the ruling sectors, the theater of historical events has experienced a tremendous revival, especially in the years leading up to and following the quincentenary of the "discovery of America," and this has been at the origin of a rereading and revision of the "discovery" and the Conquest. Although, for some critics and historians, postmodernity has been seen as an apolitical and less engaged discourse, the theatrical discourses considered postmodern in Latin America have tended to be engaged in a historical deconstruction of the official histories of most of the Latin American nations, questioning their heroes and, on many occasions, parodying the official reading of the past. At their core, the political function of these discourses has been that of undermining the foundations of the tradition that has sustained the ruling regimes. This iconoclasm has not been limited to the history of the Latin American nations; in some instances it has also included the deconstruction of the icons of the hegemonic culture of the West. In Mexico, for example, Vicente Leñero (b. 1933) has presented problematic representations of Morelos and Cortés. In the years prior to 1992, numerous works grotesquely magnified historical characters who had directly or indirectly participated in the "discovery" and the Conquest.

One of the most thought-provoking texts in this context has been *Acto cultural* [1977; Cultural Ceremony] by José Ignacio Cabrujas (Venezuela, 1937–1995). Critics have detailed the basic themes of Cabrujas's work: Mythic allusions and attempts to dismantle them, humor, caustic irony, and the fact that his entire *oeuvre* is an attempt to interpret his country. However, Cabrujas's theater is really much more a manifestation of a disenchantment with nationalist and utopian discourses. *Acto cultural* is dominated by attempts to destroy the myth of Venezuela the Great and to ridicule the values of national patriotism. The work subjects the intensified sentiment of nationality, based on an attachment to a given parcel of land, to interrogation, undermining the discourse of nationalism. It ridicules the culture that has arisen from this self-affirmation of collective self-esteem and this love of the local. All this is denounced as detritus of European culture and attacked for its verbal diarrhea, for its dissimulating or silencing of personal sentiment, for its repression of sensuality and sexuality, and for its emphasis on the theatrical and histrionic. *Acto cultural* ironizes the self-interpretation of the past, exemplified in the story of San Rafael de Ejido, and aggressively satirizes the neoclassical historical discourse on which the political discourse of the Latin American nationalities has been founded. In *El día que me quieras* [1979; Someday You'll Love Me], Cabrujas mocks and undermines the myth of a socialist utopia. Marco Antonio de la Parra (Chile, b. 1952) also satirizes utopian dreams, especially in his *La secreta obscenidad de cada día* [1984; The Secret Obscenity of Every Day]. The drama centers on two characters waiting on a bench opposite the entrance to a private high school for girls; their names identify them with two of the West's master narratives—Sigmund (Freud) and Karl (Marx). The two are characterized as sexual exhibitionists. At the end of the play it appears they are also terrorists who, machine guns primed, are waiting for someone to come out of a ceremony that has taken place in the college. Their dialogue both satirizes socialist utopias and mocks psychoanalysis.

Postmodern stagecraft entails an intensification of the use of contemporary technologies as an integral part of theatrical production. In many instances, the *mises-en-scène* are transformed into complex technological displays or into bold formal experiments. One of the most innovate directors in Mexico has been Luis de Tavira (b. 1948). Tavira has staged a number of the works of Vicente Leñero, some of whose texts are rooted in the potentiality of contemporary technology. One of Leñero's most thought-provoking texts, *Hernán Cortés*, is a sustained interrogation of history and historiography, addressing the issue of history as an ideological construction of the historian, the materials employed by historians, the selectivity and fragility of memory, and the means of writing. The work is technically demanding, requiring multiple stages, lighting and shadow effects, phantasmagoric visual constructions, displacements in time, as well as the coexistence of two historical moments separated by centuries in an atmosphere of formal or technological timelessness.

The New Feminist Theatrical Discourses

Although both the nineteenth and twentieth centuries were not without female dramatists, it has only been in recent years that there has arisen a critical preoccupation with establishing the criteria of the theatrical discourse of women. This period has witnessed the emergence of a group of dramatists and directors interested in producing theatrical discourses of difference. One of the emergent discourses in Latin America has been that established by women's theater groups and professionals, who, for the most part, are aware of the new feminist theories, who have put into practice an interrogation of patriarchal discourse in the theater, and who have proposed a theatricality specific to women's discourses. This questioning has been manifest not only in theoretical declarations but also in the formation of theater groups constituted exclusively or almost exclusively by women. Among the working principles of these groups are: A clear awareness of gender as a cultural construction, a consciousness that power is rooted in patriarchal discourse, and the championing of a subversive and vindicatory discourse in solidarity with other subversive and marginal discourses. These discourses seek to deconstruct the patriarchal one by throwing light on the fact that the dominant image of women in the theater is a product of the patriarchy and is reinforced by the recurrence of certain stereotypes emphasizing the sensuality, sexuality, or corporeality of women as victims. Proclaiming their liberation from existing theatrical practices and calling for the integration of various arts and disciplines, these groups have been able to construct irreverent theatrical spectacles and forge a multi-disciplinary theatrical practice.

These approaches are clear in a number of theatrical practices such as performance art and the frequent utilization of dance. Probably the most characteristic feature of this theater is the use of body language in place of speech. This feminist theatrical discourse is often associated with various features of postmodern theatricalities. Among their points of convergence are a utilization of popular cultural materials, the manipulation of stereotypes, the ironization or parody—with the intent to subvert—of images from the hegemonic culture, an emphasis on theatricality or meta-theatricality, a consciousness of the artistic object as a construction, a diminution of the importance of speech and an augmentation of the importance of images as means of communication, and the importance of silence. This proximity between postmodern techniques and procedures and those utilized by feminist theatrical discourses has conferred a cultural legitimacy on a discourse whose fundamental aspiration is to be subversive. Among the dramatic productions manifesting these characteristics, mention could be made of Jesusa Rodríguez and her group at *El habito* in Mexico City (see **Figure** 1), *La condesa sangrienta* [The Bloody Countess] by Grupo Rendijas from Mexico, *Barriendo sombras* [Sweeping Out the Shadows] by Grupo Ubu from Costa Rica, directed by María Bonilla, and the various productions mounted by Grupo KORE from Colombia.

One major difference between the women's theatrical discourses of this subsystem and the texts written by women in previous eras is the advent of a feminist consciousness. A number of dramatists have taken up feminist causes and produced texts that give clear evidence of a vindicatory or denunciatory stance. Among this group, we should note the recent work of Sabina Berman (Mexico, b. 1953) and, especially, the works of the Argentine dramatist Cristina Escoffet (b. 1945). Escoffet's productions are marked by a feminist infrastructure and have been highly praised for their themes, their use of language, irony, and parody, as well as for their innovative *mises-en-scène*. Her best known and most staged text, with productions in various countries, is *Concierto de señoritas* [1994; Young Ladies' Concert].

During this period critical discourse has also emphasized a feminist reading of the dramatists of the past, the most cited text in this context being *El eterno femenino* [1975; The Eternal Feminine] by Rosario Castellanos (Mexico, 1925–1974). While women have written plays and produced theater at other times, in the twentieth century the dramatists who have predominated have not expressed a feminist consciousness and have instead made use of the codes belonging to the dominant theatrical discourse of the era. Their texts, in general, have not been read from a feminist point of view. Such is the case with dramatists like Isidora Aguirre (Chile, b. 1919), Griselda Gambaro (Argentina, b. 1928), Luisa Josefina Hernández (Mexico, b. 1928), Elena Garro (Mexico, 1917–1998), Fanny Buitrago (Colombia, b. 1943), Gloria Parrado (Cuba, 1927–1987). These kinds of productions have been technically included in the postmodern current since they make use of numerous formal techniques and procedures that have been legitimated in postmodern theater.

International Theater Festivals or the Transnationalization of Cultures

García Canclini (1989) has very convincingly pointed out that the use of culture as an instrument of power cannot be limited to the State. The activity and visibility of Latin American theater has increased thanks to the profusion of festivals in the various Latin American countries and in Europe. Some historians like Marina Pianca have recounted this history in great detail. International theater festivals are not objective samples of the theatrical manifestations to be found in the countries represented. The assumption is that each festival performs a number of functions, both political and cultural. Among these functions are the self-legitimization of the organizing institutions and the cultural policies that sustain them, and the legitimization or de-legitimization of aesthetic and theatrical codes that correspond to these cultural policies. In addition, such festivals clearly also involve a legitimization of aesthetic forms.

The organization and sponsorship of a festival generally perform, implicitly or explicitly, a political function, by means of which the sponsoring country or organization hopes to justify or legitimate its own culture. This political function is manifest both in the selection of works or groups to be invited and in the image that the sponsoring body projects of itself. The selection process, thus, has more to do with the ideological interests of the organizers than with the represented theatricalities in themselves. The selection process naturally involves a system of aesthetic and ideological values bearing on the constitution of the power wielded by the organizing institution. One timely and representative example, the *Festival de Teatro de las Naciones* [Theater of the Nations Festival] held in Santiago, Chile, in April and May 1992, clearly demonstrated the cultural interrelation and political legitimization of a country on the international stage. This festival fulfilled an important political function for the country of

Figure 1.

Jesusa Rodríguez playing the devil in The Council of Love. *(Courtesy Jesusa Rodríguez)*

Chile, both nationally and internationally. From the national point of view, the emphasis was placed on the construction of an international image that would have an impact on the national sectors.

By placing Chilean democracy in an international spotlight, the festival sought to publicize the return of a free and unfettered cultural life to Chile. After twenty years of authoritarian rule, a period that the national and international oppositions had dubbed a "cultural blackout," the new government sponsored the *Festival Teatro de las Naciones* as a symbol of the Chilean cultural renaissance. After the dark years of military dictatorship, the light of democracy, and with it "the cultural eminence of the world," returned to Chilean society. The festival also constituted a demonstration that, after a period of cultural and international isolation, the country could return to the family of nations, proof not only that was it capable of organizing a congress and a festival but also that it could administer them like an enormous private enterprise, with an absolute efficiency and with a knowledge and expertise of all the systems that advances in communications and organization could provide. As such, the festival constituted an emblem of Chile's national entrepreneurial capabilities, although its symbolic import was directed less toward the interior and more toward the exterior. The Cádiz Festival represents another telling example of the political function of international festivals. Established in 1986 as part of the 1992 quincentenary celebrations, its objective was to highlight Spanish-Latin American relations and the

1992 festival as a "Meeting of Cultures" and to replace the connotations implicit in the notions of "discovery" and "conquest." When the 1992 festivities were over, however, Spain began to show more interest in joining the European Union and in forging links with the community of Mediterranean nations. The Cádiz Festival self-designated itself as the bridge between Latin America and Europe (see Pérez Coterillo et al.).

National and international festivals, especially those held in Europe, have constituted a nucleus of characteristically postmodern theatrical activities. For example, these festivals tend to erase national boundaries since the potential political content of a production or text in the context of its country of origin is diluted when performed in front of an international audience; the national character of spectacles becomes only a differentiating exoticism. From the point of view of the theatrical codes reigning in such festivals, it can be seen that they tend to promote contemporary theatrical trends and the search for theatrical codes that, paradoxically, aspire to blur the frontiers between national cultures or to reinforce the stereotypes of those cultures on a national level.

Translation by Colman Hogan

Works Cited

Arrieta, Rafael Alberto, ed. 1958–1960. *Historia de la literatura argentina.* 6 vols. Buenos Aires: Ediciones Peuser.

Arrom, José Juan. 1967. *Historia del teatro hispanoamericano (Epoca colonial).* Mexico City: Ediciones de Andrea.

Azor, Ileana. 1988. *Origen y presencia del teatro en nuestra América.* Havana: Letras Cubanas.

Boal, Augusto. 1972. *Categorias del teatro popular.* Buenos Aires: Ediciones Cepe.

———. 1974. *Teatro del oprimido y otras poéticas políticas.* Buenos Aires: Ediciones de la Flor.

Bravo-Elizondo, Pedro. 1975. *Teatro hispanoamericano de crítica social.* Madrid: Playor.

———. 1986. *Cultura y teatro obreros en Chile (1900–1930.)* Madrid: Meridión.

Castagnino, Raúl. 1963. *Sociología del teatro argentino.* Buenos Aires: Compendios Nova de Iniciación Cultural.

Chabaud, Jaime. 1988. "El teatro rural en México." *Escenario de dos mundos. Inventario teatral de Iberoamérica.* Ed. Moisés Pérez Coterillo and Carlos Espinoza Domínguez. 4 vols. Madrid: Centro de Documentación Teatral. III: 149–151.

Dauster, Frank. 1973. *Historia del teatro hispanoamericano. Siglos XIX y XX.* 2nd ed. Mexico City: Ediciones de Andrea.

———. 1975. "René Marqués y el tiempo culpable." *Ensayos sobre teatro hispanoamericano.* Mexico City: SepSetentas. 102–26.

———. Leon Lyday and George Woodyard, eds. 1983. *Tres dramaturgos rioplatenses: antología del teatro hispanoamericano del siglo XX.* Ottawa: Girol Books.

Dragún, Osvaldo. 1968. *Teatro.* Madrid: Taurus.

Durán Cerda, Julio. 1959. *Panorama del teatro chileno 1892–1959.* Santiago de Chile: Editorial del Pacífico.

Festival Iberoamericano de Teatro de Cádiz. 1995. Cádiz: Artes Gráficas Nueva.

García Canclini, Néstor. 1989. "La política cultural en países en vias de desarrollo." *Antropología y políticas culturales.* Ed. Rita Ceballos. Buenos Aires: República Argentina. 7–27.

———. 1996. *Culturas híbridas.* Mexico City: Grijalbo.

Golluscio de Montoya, Eva. 1987. "Elementos para una teoría libertaria." *Latin American Theater Review* 21: 85–94.

———. 1996. *Teatro y folletines libertarios rioplatenses (1895–1910) (Estudio y Antología).* Ottawa: Girol Books.

Guimarães, Carmelina. "Rasga corazón." *Conjunto* 76: 24–31.

Henríquez, Camilo. 1912. "La Camila o la Patriota de Sud-América." *Teatro dramático nacional.* Ed. Nicolás Peña. Biblioteca de Escritores de Chile. Santiago: Imprenta Barcelona. 1–39.

Hurtado, María de la Luz. 1997. *Teatro chileno y modernidad: Identidad y crisis social.* Irvine: Ediciones de *Gestos.*

Juana Inés de la Cruz. 1692. *El divino Narciso. Los empeños de una casa. Obras Completas.* Vol. 2. Seville: Tomás López de Haro.

Morandé, Pedro. 1987. *Cultura y modernización en América Latina: Ensayo sociológico acerca de la crisis del desarrollismo y de su superación.* Madrid: Encuentro Ediciones.

Pellettieri, Osvaldo. 1987. *La obra dramática de Armando Discépolo.* Buenos Aires: EUDEBA.

Pérez Coterillo, Moisés and Carlos Espinoza Domínguez, eds. 1988. *Escenarios de dos mundos. Inventario teatral de Iberoamérica.* Madrid: Centro de Documentación Teatral. 4 vols.

Pianca, Marina. 1990. *El teatro de nuestra América: Un proyecto continental: 1959–1989.* Minneapolis, MN: Institute for the Study of Ideologies and Literature.

Rela, Walter. 1980. *Teatro brasileño.* Montevideo: Instituto de Cultura Uruguayo.

Río, Marcela del. 1993. *Perfil del teatro de la revolución mexicana.* New York: Peter Lang.

Rizk, Beatriz J. 1991. *Buenaventura: La dramaturgia de la creación colectiva.* Mexico City: Escenología.

Rojo, Grínor. 1972. *Orígenes del teatro hispanoamericano contemporáneo.* Valparaíso: Ediciones Universitarias de Valparaíso.

Schmidhuber, Guillermo. 1996. *Sor Juana Dramaturga. Sus comedias de "falda y empeño."* Puebla: Benemérita Universidad Autónoma de Puebla.

Suárez Radillo, Carlos Miguel. 1975. *Temas y estilos en el teatro hispanoamericano contemporáneo: una experiencia radiofónica de difusión teatral.* Zaragoza: Editorial Litho Arte.

Villegas, Juan. 1989. *Nueva interpretación del texto dramático.* Ottawa: Girol Books.

CHAPTER 55

AFRO–LATIN AMERICAN THEATER

Juan Villegas

The introduction of slaves into Latin America dates from the earliest years of the colonies. Rolando Mellafe has pointed out that Hernán Cortés and Francisco Pizarro "received authorization to introduce considerable quantities of Negro slaves into their governments" (1964, 22). Despite this fact, José Juan Arrom, in his *Historia del teatro hispanoamericano (Epoca colonial)* [The History of Hispano-American Theater (The Colonial Epoch)], makes no reference whatsoever to the Afro-American sectors. The amplification of the concept of theater I have proposed in my introduction to this section obliges us to consider the theatricalities of these marginalized cultures within our history of Latin American theater.

Our hypothesis of the diversity of cultures coexisting in Latin America is confirmed when we take note of the existence of a series of theatrical discourses produced by the Afro-American ascendancy. The characteristic features of these discourses are the hybridization of the distinct African cultures from which the slaves came with the cultures of the geographic areas in which they were newly located and the cultures coexisting in these new spaces, and, to a greater or lesser degree, the integration of these hybridizations into the dominant cultures of these spaces. Within this cultural system a number of differentiated actualizations were seen, actualizations whose variety depended in part on the origins of the slaves brought into the zone in question as well as the differing degrees of the slaves' integration into or participation in the coexisting cultures of the majorities. Thus, it will be necessary for us to establish first an understanding of the African cultures that were the sustaining bases of the Afro–Latin American cultures.

Inés María Martiatu Terry has pointed out that, with respect to Cuba, there were at least four African cultures that were incorporated into Cuban culture at specific historical moments and under specific circumstances. Thus, the degree of purity or of hybridization varied:

> Following the almost total extinction of the indigenous population of the island, representatives of numerous African ethnic groups were brought to Cuba by the slave trade. However, from among these numerous groups, four in particular are well known to have contributed to the formation of the Cuban nation; it was their beliefs that gave rise to the creation of syncretic magico-religious systems of great cultural importance and whose force and validity have been preserved to this day. These four are: the Yoruba of Nigeria, the Calabar (also from southern Nigeria), the Bantu from the Congo-Zaire-Angola region, and the Fon, from Dahomey, first brought to Cuba by the slave trade and known as the Arará, and later arriving in an exodus from Haiti in 1791 as a result of the Haitian revolution, with a third wave arriving in the 1920s and 1930s as sugar cane laborers. (Martiatu Terry 97)

Patricia González, for her part, has detailed well the diversity and presence of their theatrical practices:

> In their assemblies the Afro-Cubans were able to preserve their gods or orishas, their language, their culture, and their religion. The Lucumí were no exception. In Yoruba culture the orishas

journeyed down different roads, which were really dramatic adventures and happenings, full of conflicts. The Yoruba pantheon revealed a series of unforgettable fables that reflected the social conditions of life and the community. Each orisha had his or her own characteristic gestures and movements, costumes, and makeup and comported him- or herself in a certain determinate way in the course of their dialoguing with the other orishas or the spectators. (29)

This diversity of origins and historical circumstances obliges us to retrace the original differences in order to better understand the specificities of the Afro–Latin American theatricalities, whether they be in Brazil, Cuba, Panama, or Venezuela. At the same time, however, the Afro–Latin Americans' modes of self-representation were conditioned by the modes of their representation in the dominant cultures. In the canonized arts and in the dominant sectors, peoples of African origin tended to be characterized pejoratively in a distorted, belittling, and mocking way, something that did not happen so consistently with the indigenous sectors. And in fact, as I have indicated elsewhere, certain indigenous groups were, at certain historic moments, even subject to idealizations. In contrast to the cultural discourses of the indigenous cultures of the Americas, the cultures of African origin in Latin America have been localized in certain zones. With respect to their theatricalities, cultures of African origin were most active in regions such as Cuba, Panama, and Brazil, although research into the latter two zones are very much less extensive because of a scarcity of written texts.

The Afro–Latin American cultural discourses, spectacles, and festivals constitute a cultural space that has been little investigated, often held in contempt, and constantly surveyed from the perspective of the cultures of European origin. The silence with which the dominant historical and critical discourses have treated the cultural discourses of the Afro–Latin American sectors appears to imply that either such sectors do not exist or that they have been reduced to a degree of primitiveness or naturalness that effectively annuls the complexity and variety of their practices. In some cases in the past, it is only by implication or allusion that we can even know of their existence. In the majority of cases, however, when the cultural productions of the hegemonic sectors do make reference to the Afro–Latin American sectors, mockery or satire predominate.

In the domain of theater, this subject can be viewed from two perspectives: From the point of view of the representations or spectacles produced by the practitioners of the cultures of African origin, or from the point of view of the modes of representation of these cultures and their practitioners transmitted through the hegemonic discourses. Historically speaking, studies of the representations of the former and the modes of representation of the latter have been connected to the political and economic interests of the dominant sectors or to the ideology of the producers of the historical or theatrical discourses at each given historical moment. In the majority of the dominant cultural productions, the marginalized Afro–Latin American was represented in a negative and stereotypical light that, in the nineteenth century, condensed into the image of the domesticated or depraved *negrito*.

Afro–Latin American theatrical productions and spectacles, however, involved a mode and function of representation that accorded with the conditions of these social sectors within the ensemble of society. Marginalization allowed them to conserve many of their original features or permitted those features to evolve within the new sociocultural context; at the same time, however, they also acquired new features as they integrated and hybridized with the dominant cultures.

One revealing case from this point of view is that of post-1959 Cuba, where, with the establishment of a relation between Cuban identity and Afro-Cuban-ness, the Afro-Cuban cultures have acquired an enormous importance. All too often, however, the critical perspective on this development has been an ethno-European one that represents the interests of the cultural powers that be. Rine Leal, for example, has noted that "Afro-Cuban ceremonies must be seen as *representations* of the struggles, aspirations, and the cultural syncretism of the black slaves who have been so unfairly treated," adding that they must be considered "practices going back to the origins of the theatre" (22). On the one hand, Leal does concede a singular importance to the *diablitos*, or demon dolls, represented in the Epiphany festivals: "On this day, centuries of Christian indoctrination fall away in the face of the energy and vitality of the various African groups that were enslaved and brought to the island. This festival is the exaltation of the Afro-Cuban religious values, their most fecund outward expression, their most spectacular liturgy" (22). However, on the other hand, Leal's limited concept of theater leads this critic to insist that "we stand more in front of a liturgy than a theatrical expression properly speaking. . . . However, it is possible to extract from the initiation ceremonies of the Yoruba or Lucumí the germ of a real theatrical expression that will be to Cuban theater what the Elysian mysteries are to European theater" (24).

Leal also details the theatricality of these representations by describing their dances, the use of choruses to comment on the action, their characteristic gestures and typical movements, their costumes and props, and the diversity of the representations rooted in various Afro-Cuban ethnic groups.

This Europeanizing perspective can also be seen in the numerous references made by Fernando Ortiz in his descriptions of aspects of the Afro-Cuban cultures. For example, when mentioning the religious practices of these groups, Ortiz assigns them degrees of development, implying a reading of the manifestations that is rooted in a Western religious concept. He often cites anthropological or ethnographic accounts in which black African cultures are inserted under the rubric of the primitive or uncivilized, such as his reference to John Lubbock, for example, "who has taught us how in the wild or uncivilized towns, and not only among the blacks, dance was a means of transcendence, serious and utilitarian, linked, like magical songs, to all the functions of tribal life" (202).

As a result of these tendencies, it is often necessary to read between the lines of historical descriptions in order to be able to characterize the Afro–Latin American theatricalities. One example of this is the narration of the festivities celebrating the coronation of Felipe V de Borbón, in 1701 in Venezuela, recounted in their totality by Azparren (1996,

111–15). Preoccupied with demonstrating the widespread acceptance of the new monarch, the informant describes in some detail the different social sectors participating in the celebrations. Toward the end of his account he observes: "Hasta los negros esclavos demostraron su alegría representando una comedia y jugando veinte toros a caballo, y en la tarde de este día también una cañas, cuya acción por ser de tan mísera y desdichada gente" ("Even the black slaves demonstrated their gaiety, performing a comedy and staging a game of twenty bulls on horses and, in the afternoon of the same day, a number of jousting tournaments. These were performed by such squalid and wretched figures," 1996, 114). The Afro-American theatricality described here does not correspond to a specific dramatic form of the ethnic group, but rather to a travesty or imitation of the Spanish theatricalities and festivities performed by the descendants of the Africans. However, they do serve as a clue to understanding the nature of participation in the festival whose ethnic division is clear. The narrator follows his description of "la hermandad de Nuestra Señora de Altagracia" ("the brotherhood of Our Lady of Supreme Grace") with the qualifying phrase, "que se compone de todos los pardos libres de esta ciudad" (113) ("which was composed of all the free mulattos of this city"). He notes their theatricality when he describes that they employed "un carro triunfal" ("a triumphal chariot"), "curiosamente compuesto" ("curiously put together"), "acompañado de todos ellos a caballo con hachas encendidas en las manos y adornados con lucidas galas" ("accompanied by men on horseback with burning axes in their hands and adorned in brilliant trappings"). This group arrived at the plaza accompanied by music and instruments as "enigmáticas figuras" ("enigmatic figures"), "que explicaban la majestuosa función a que se dedicaba" ("who explained the majestic function to which they were dedicated"). In such descriptions we are afforded a glimpse of a quite different theatricality.

Afro–Latin American Theatrical Forms and Spectacles

Afro–Latin American theatricality is manifest in a multiplicity of activities and, as we have seen was the case in Venezuela, in public ceremonies participation is signaled predominantly by dances and other ritual activities recognizable both by their gestures and by their decorations and masks. A number of forms have been specified as being most often associated or identified with the tradition of spectacles whose origins are African.

Dances and Dancing

One of the characteristic features of Afro–Latin American theatricality is the utilization of dance, although this characteristic is naturally not exclusive. Ortiz has described a variety of Afro-Cuban dances, certain of which are almost exclusively associated with the Afro-Cuban cultures: "In colonial Havana, the 'kill the snake' dance was especially popular among the blacks. . . . A procession of blacks leaping, dancing, and singing would wind its way through the streets of Havana carrying an enormous artificial snake, several meters in length, pausing in front of the largest houses to receive festive gifts" (284). Ortiz has also described other dances, including "Ogún Dances," "Inle Dances," "Babalú-Ayé Dances," and "Changó Dances," the latter reappearing in a number of contemporary performances. Changó is the god of virility, strength, and lightning, and his dances, marked by a great intensity of highly energetic movements, are either erotic or bellicose. According to Ortiz, Changó appears "dressed in red and white striped trousers and a short jacket, with a crown on his head which in Cuba today usually takes the castellated form of the heraldic crowns depicted on old murals, being influenced by the Catholic images of Saint Barbara with whom he is associated" (333).

Congo Rituals

Although Ortiz describes the theatricalities of African origin from the perspective of a Eurocentric anthropologist, his study is probably the most important to have been made on the subject and the most comprehensive. His Eurocentric perspective is observable in his assigning degrees of "advancement" to the religions he discusses. In the opinion of Ortiz, the congos in Cuba are ritual-magic forms, and he describes a number of their constituents (168–69). These rituals center on the sorcerer-priest, who carries out a series of invocations, each one of the various phrases of which plays a role in the drawing near of the divinity. Each phrase possesses its own accompanying gestures and movements. In some cases, the "rites are carried out collectively through participation of the initiates in the sect" (169). As to the drumming that accompanies the rites, "the rhythms are driving, and in order to emphasize them even more, various simple, fundamentally percussive instruments are employed, such as beating the ground with various magical, curved wooden sticks" (170).

Spirit Dolls (Mojigangas)

Although, according to the experts, this theatrical form arrived in the New World with the Spanish, it does constitute a spectacular form with black roots inasmuch as it originated long before the arrival of the Spaniards in America among the black slaves of the Seville region in Spain. According to González Cajiao, "the blacks of Andalucía would join the carnival processions sporting masks and carrying puppets and idols made of wood, messengers from the spirit world, which they called *mojigangas*" (28).

Masquerades

In general, these consist "in the physical incarnation of a spiritual entity (divinity or ancestor); in Africa masks are employed but, according to Gloria Triana, in the Americas these African masks (made from ivory, metal or wood) have entirely disappeared. These representations constitute an intercourse between humans and the divinities" (González Cajiao, 28).

Masked Dances

One of the masked dances discussed by Ortiz is known as the *kulona*. According to Ortiz's informant (one of the dancers), "the name *kulona* is perhaps only the Malinké or Mandingo adjective *kulona* or *lonna*, which in this case means 'wise' or 'well-educated' and is applied there to the priests or sorcerers. . . . He went around disguised in a primitive, vaguely symbolic, extravagant costume, and with a variety of decorations on his head, including feathers, horns, bonnets, crowns, or miters, brightly colored and decked with small bells, but his face was not hidden although daubed with stripes and rings under his eyes and other grotesqueries that distorted his features" (446).

Afro-American Theatricalities during the Colonial Epoch

Referring to the Colonial period, Azor has pointed out the necessity of taking "the first theatrical manifestations of the black culture [into account], however incomplete they may have been and however much they may have had the same religious and ceremonial objective that I have already mentioned, and that above all in those countries where the enslavement of blacks played an important role in economic life, namely, in Brazil and in Cuba" (23). Patricia González, for her part, is more forthright, affirming that "the black Cuban theater appeared on the island almost in parallel with the establishment of the importation of black slaves and integrated itself synthetically into the Catholic religious festivals, incorporating into it both rituals and dances from the Yoruba religion" (28).

For their part, Bonilla and Vladich place particular importance on the dance called *El juego de los congos* ("The Game of the Congos") or the *Baile del Terrible* ("Dance of the Dreadful"), information on which they have collected from the blacks of the Colón region in Panama. They declare that the dance had its origins in one of the several slave revolts that took place in what is today the Republic of Panama. Citing the work of Domingo Olmos, who has observed the dance's participants and their intentions, Bonilla and Vladich point out that evidence of the Christian teachings of the colonial political system can be observed in the dance. The congos have intentionally distorted, in a critical manner, those doctrines and political systems: "The motives and events can be seen in the drama or game . . . the mass flight of the slaves into the jungle, their arduous life there in the *fundación* or what they called the stockade, the brave struggle of the men against their pursuers and the adroit collaboration of the women, the behaviour of the slavers and the suffering of the slaves, the betrayal of some slaves, and the intervention of the spirits, whether good or evil" (31).

Noting that this dance appears in Cuban carnival celebrations, Mariartu Terry has pointed out that it originated in Epiphany festivities. She goes on to describe the importance of the African ethnic groups' participation in the celebrations: "On this day the military authorities in Havana permitted the slaves to parade organized in the various assemblies that represented the different *nations*. By means of dance, pantomime, music, and the public staging of mystery plays, these processions acquired a spectacular character. . . . The public who participated, the rich and the *Capitán General* himself, offered the blacks coins, known as *aguinaldos*. Even those blacks not part of the processions of the assemblies went out in the street masked, disguised as picturesque characters" (99). With respect to colonial Colombia, González Cajiao has recorded that Octavio Marulanda established the existence of spirit dolls (*mojigangas*) in the region of Cali, Valle del Cauca, although, referring to a 1717 event, the author surprisingly speaks of *indios*, or natives.

The Nineteenth and Twentieth Centuries

In the majority of the regions that were home to the descendants of the black slaves in the nineteenth century, Afro–Latin American theatricalities persevered, even in those instances where theater or performance was prohibited. In Cuba, for example, as Rine Leal notes, "the festivities of the free blacks or *horros* were strictly limited in 1792 and 1799, the slave law of 1842 prohibited musical and dance ceremonies in the slaves' dwelling quarters, while the 'colored persons' place' was systematically negated or relegated to the worst localities" (49–50).

Nor did the theatricalities of African origin disappear in the twentieth century. The presence of a number of their fundamental manifestations can be established. On the one hand, manifestations linked to the popular festivals that had arisen in previous centuries, or variants of them, continued. On the other hand, their inclusion within the dominant discourse constituted a process of validation or recognition of their significance within the cultures of Latin America or was used to valorize certain popular sectors. In the latter case, the producers were generally not Afro–Latin American, but rather researchers: Those who made use of anthropological research, or those who invited practitioners of the Afro–Latin American cultures to participate in some function or another. A third tendency was the formation of folkloric groups, frequently associated with researchers who sought to reconstruct or revitalize Afro–Latin American spectacular traditions. Within some hegemonic discourses, however, the grotesque, mocking, or satirical utilization of visual or anecdotal elements of the Afro–Latin American cultures continued unabated. (This latter tendency will not be considered in what follows.)

Festivities

A number of the features common to indigenous theatricalities can also be seen in Afro–Latin American theatricalities, including hybridization, their incorporation into religious festivals, and their becoming part of what are considered popular festivities. An example from Ecuador hints at a number of the processes involved in such cultural hybridization. In her research on the celebration known as "La Mama Negra" celebrated in the streets of Catacunga in the province of Cotopaxi, María Escudero has pointed out that at first glance this celebration seems to be a Holy Week procession. However, she observes that the celebration in homage to the Virgin of Mercy on September 24 "assembles . . . characters and symbols of diverse ethnic origin," and that the participants quickly "abandon the Catholic canticles, postures, attitudes, and corporative forms, transforming themselves into a popular festival" (18). Escudero's description and analysis point out the "clear evidence of the festival's Yoruba origins, the old myth of the African nations, resuscitated and annually proclaiming their validity in South America": "Yoruba I say, since the figure of the Black Mama is represented by a man, chosen for 'being one of the decent people,' which is to say, honest, healthy, generous, and–take note–a man seen as being in solidarity with his community. One of the figures of the Yoruba rite is bisexual and has twin sons. Her attire and the presence of the twins, as well as her ample breasts, make reference to customs situated outside the continent" (21–22). Escudero's description emphasizes the fact that this festival has produced a profound syncretism among the various ethnic groups of the region and is evidence of the presence of theatricalities of African origin in many of the regions' festivals and primarily Catholic religious celebrations.

The situation is very similar in some of the carnivals in those regions where black slaves were once an important part of the economy–Cuba, Brazil, Panama, and Peru. Rafael Brea has examined the African elements in the carnivals of Santiago de Cuba. He observes that these elements date from Colonial times, that they have been inserted into Catholic religious festivals (in this case that of Santiago), and that they have been syncretized with elements from other cultures: "they constitute at the same time the oldest African antecedent and the most defined of the celebrated Santiago

de Cuba *congas* and parades that Cubans have praised. Of course, the African presence is not limited to the masquerade groups, but includes much more extensive aspects related to the dances, the plastic arts, and, in a very special way, to the music" (23).

Afro–Latin American Cultures and Their Representatives in the Hegemonic Theatrical Discourse

Cultural Devalorization

The representation of Afro–Latin Americans in the dominant discourses has been quite different from that of the indigenous peoples. On the one hand, Afro–Latin Americans appear hardly at all in these discourses, and when they do, they are not characterized with the idealism that has tended to surround the representation of the natives. In some cases, such as in the "black-face," or *negritos,* theater in Cuba, they have been utilized as objects of ridicule or mockery. As Leal points out, "slavery, which runs through the backbone of our history, has negated the possibility of the black dramatic figure, relegating him to the role of the clown who of necessity shared the fate and misfortunes of the mulatto, the Chinese, the underclass, and the impoverished immigrants, by and large the Spanish *gallegos*" (49). Leal's description of the black-face theater is even more forceful: "If the Afro-Cuban theatrical expressions 'represented' the blacks as seen by black eyes, speaking and acting in their own idiom, presenting the theatrical image of their own culture and identity, the white authors will create its antipode in the figure of the *negrito,* which is to say, in the black character represented by white actors for a white audience, speaking in Spanish or in the broken Spanish of parody, and naturally demonstrating the point of view of the slave-owning culture" (30).

The Construction of Folklore

One aspect of the Afro-Cuban cultures that has been of interest to the hegemonic sectors, especially in the twentieth century, is the folkloric dimension, as a spectacle of the "other," with whom the Eurocentric spectator does not identify. Here the "other" loses his or her connotations of social critique or threat and is rendered an object contemplable from a distance. A part of this perspective includes religious festivals and festivities associated with what is considered to be specifically Afro-Latin American. Another part is represented by the formation of folkloric groups aiming to preserve or revitalize the traditions, creating in this way spectacles that are ultimately atemporal and ahistoric and which, in many cases, falsify the origins or the original meanings of the dances or spectacles. What ultimately is thought to be interesting about such constructions is the fact that they are visually pleasing and without social connotations. On the other hand, the culturally hegemonic sectors–especially in recent years–have begun to emphasize the representation of the various national cultures as hybrid cultures.

Legitimization of Afro-Latin American Culture and Rites

Although the representation of Afro-Latin Americans in Latin American theater and spectacles, as we have seen, has tended to be carried out from the perspective of the Eurocentric hegemonic discourses, in recent years a notable transformation has taken place. As in the case of the indigenous peoples, the dominant cultural discourse in Latin America has tended to embrace a deconstruction of the modes of representation of the marginalized and has attempted to construct other images of these same groups. Naturally, this transformation has been manifest in a diverse array of manners in the distinct microcultures, both on the social plane and in the domains of the plastic arts and theatrical representation. The Peruvian theater group *Raíces* (Roots), a troop employing street theater modalities, mounted several years ago a spectacle entitled *Los Fantasistas* (The Fantasists) parodying the characterizations made by the dominant ethnic groups in Peru. In its characterization of the "*morenos*" (dark ones), as Afro-Latin Americans are called in Peru, Peruvian society demonstrates its prejudices and stereotypes: The *morenos* are seen as a marginal group whose sole talent is for playing football.

An article in the *Los Angeles Times* (8 August 1988; A12–13) points out both the continuity of the cultures of African origin in Brazil and the wholly natural character of cultural hybridization. According to the author, "[t]he fusion of Catholic and Afro-Brazilian faith pervades this northeastern port city (of Belem) whose hundreds of baroque churches, legendary music and predominantly black population make it the nation's cultural soul" (12). The natural manner of this fusion has been called into question by a number of religious purists, since, according to the article, the practitioners cultivate African rites as part of the Catholic religious ceremonies without being aware of their relevance to one or the other of the two traditions. An especially suggestive case on the level of both society and theatrical representation is that of post-revolutionary Cuba, where the official political discourses have promoted a valorization of Afro-Cuban culture as an important constituent of what is Cuban or of what it means to be Cuban. The various modes of its presence include elements of magic, music, or dance affiliated with the Afro-Cuban culture. In the theatrical domain this tendency has been manifest in the inclusion of elements of Afro-Cuban figures or of elements of the Afro-Cuban culture or ethnicity as themes or important components of various theatrical works.

One of these modalities was employed in *Réquiem por Yarini* [1960; Requiem for Yarini] by Carlos Felipe (1911–1975), a play in which elements of Afro-Cuban rites were incorporated as integral to the dramatic development and in which ritual practices of the Changó cult were put on stage. According to Patricia Elena González: "*Réquiem por Yarini*, in addition to identifying the character Yarini with Changó, presents the world of the *santería* cult in all its vividness. The *santero* or priest of the play, Bebo la Reposa, casts shells in order to predict the fate of Yarini. In addition, the play presents Changó rituals, stages a ritual trance and a dialogue with the spirits and *orishas* or deities, perpetuating before the audience the world of the living and the dead in accordance with the Yoruba vision of the cosmos" (34). (See **Figure 1.**)

Folkloric Versions

In those countries where the presence of the Afro-Latin American ethnic sectors is strong, independent or government sponsored folkloric groups that seek to reconstruct or revitalize dances and musical forms have become institutionalized. One good example of this tendency is Cutumba, the Afro-Cuban Folkloric Ballet of Santiago de Cuba. Founded in 1961, Cutumba has taken advantage of the differences among the distinct regions of Cuba and the different traditions that have resulted from the different waves of immigration to the country at different moments of its history. Cutumba has, for example, recognized the importance of the Haitian immigrants to Cuban culture and, with them, the French influence in the greater process of Cuban hybridization. The characterization of Cutumba that appeared in the program of the *Festival Iberoamericano de Teatro de Cádiz* [Ibero-American Theater Festival of Cádiz] suggests a number of features applicable to other examples: "Recreating in its repertoire all these elements with a generosity and freshness characteristic of the tropics, Cutumba insinuates you into their festive vortex and at the same time claims an absolute respect for the folkloric bases of their works, handled with an artistic rigor and a clearly elaborated aesthetic that, in some instances, reaches remarkable theatrical heights" (144).

The process of "aesthetic elaboration" or "folklorization" implies splitting off or tearing away cultural practice from the present time and present historicosocial conditions. It implies carrying out transformations that are aesthetically justifiable—either from the perspective of the new producers, or as justified by virtue of their satisfying the ideological or aesthetic preferences of the potential audiences—but which do not necessarily correspond to the history or to the original spirit of the forms in question. A ritual dance extracted from the circumstances and conditions of its rite becomes merely a spectacle to be seen and enjoyed in accordance with the aesthetic conventions or expectations of satisfaction of the spectator. When this audience is an international one, the stylistic tendencies of modern dance frequently become a shaping factor of the folkloric work.

Figure 1.

Photograph of the representation of Changó during Carnaval, Santiago de Cuba.(Archive of the author)

Hybridism

A new perspective on Afro-Latin American cultures has been opened up by works that integrate myths of African origin with those from the dominant European cultures. This process was witnessed in *Las ruinas circulares* [The Circular Ruins], presented by the Teatro Buendía group from Cuba at the Ibero-American Theater Festival in Cádiz in 1995. This spectacle centered on a voyage in search of origins undertaken by the main characters, The Knight Errant and his Squire. Afro-Cuban elements were incorporated into the play via the bodies of the actors, all Afro-Cubans, who performed movements or ceremonies of a sacred character in the Yoruba cultures, reinforced by Yoruba songs, rites, and musical elements. The group's self-description in the Festival's program confirmed its self-awareness vis-à-vis the process: "To the rhythm of the Batá Drums, the legendary figures of the Knight Errant and his Squire, invoked by the black slave, are illuminated by a strange and hallucinatory light" (36).

Even more clear and complex was the hybridization manifest in Teatro Buendía's *Otra Tempestad* [*Another Storm*], which was premiered in Havana in 1997 and performed at the Ibero-American Theater Festival in Cádiz in 1998. On the foundation of Shakespeare's *The Tempest*, the director, Flora Lauten, constructed a complex story integrating characters from Shakespeare's theater—Macbeth, Shylock, Othello, Prospero, Caliban, and others—with figures from the African mythology of the Caribbean. In the opinion of the dramatist Raquel Carrió, "the fable concealed a play of theatricalities that called attention to a diverse series of referents. On the one hand, the texts of Shakespeare: The universe of the medieval and Renaissance chivalry *that was brought to the Americas*. On the other hand, the rites, the stories, the gestural and sonorous systems of the Yoruba and Arará cultures, cultures of African provenance transplanted into the Caribbean" (10). Various cultures of African origin have contributed to the shaping and structuring of the cultural plurality of Latin America. With respect to the theatrical and spectacular discourses, their gestural systems and theatricalities were subjected to distortion and parody by the hegemonic discourses of the past and by some social groups. This theatricality coexisted in the past, however, but in a position of marginalization *vis-à-vis* the dominant discourses and in a condition of hybridization *vis-à-vis* both the indigenous and the dominant cultures. In both cases it has been transformed and has reutilized the theatricalities of other cultures or has integrated itself into other cultures. In the present, in the process of the opening up of the culturally dominant sectors towards the marginalized sectors, these Afro-Latin American theatricalities are being utilized as means for the legitimization of the integration or potential integration into and the importance of the Afro-Latin American sectors in the history of Latin America.

In Summation

From pre-Hispanic times to postmodernity, the theater and the theatricalities of Latin America have constituted a key component of the coexistence, imbrication, and tensions and strains of the region's cultures. They also constitute in all probability one of the clearest evidences of the continual utilization, on the part of its cultural producers, of modes of self-representation and of the representation of the "other" on the stage of national and international collective life: The social sectors in power have constantly made continuous use of the theater to stage their rule and configure collective imaginaries. Theatricalities and theatrical discourses have constituted a key element of the coexistence of a plurality of cultures and social and ethnic sectors in Latin America, from the pre-Hispanic era to the present. The general tendency has been that the cultural practices of hegemonic groups produce a diversity of theatrical discourses in accordance with their potential addressees and the function that the producing sectors assign to these addressees within the various national projects. The culturally dominant groups utilize the theatrical codes of their own culture or reutilize the codes of the other cultures legitimized at the various distinct historical junctures. Generally, these legitimized cultures have been Spanish or European. In the colonial epoch, the dominant culture utilized or reutilized Spanish codes both to maintain the Spanish tradition and to legitimize their own culture within the colonies. At the same time the dominant culture made use of the theater and theatricalities in their efforts to impose their image of the world and their religion on the subjugated ethnic groups. For their part, while these latter preserved important elements of their own theatricalities, they also utilized—with varying degrees of hybridization—elements from the dominant culture. Already during the colonial epoch the indigenous sectors had appropriated important elements from the Spanish and Portuguese cultures, incorporating them into their own theatrical celebrations. These hybrid discourses and theatricalities ultimately constituted festivities and theatricalities that would come to be defining characteristics of the marginalized cultures in the nineteenth and twentieth centuries.

Translation by Colman Hogan

Works Cited

Arrom, José Juan. 1967. *Historia del teatro hispanoamericano (Epoca colonial)*. Mexico City: Ediciones de Andrea.

Azor, Ileana. 1988. *Origen y presencia del teatro en nuestra América*. Havana: Letras Cubanas.

Azparren, Leonardo. 1993. *Cabrujas en tres actos*. Caracas: Ediciones el Nuevo Grupo.

———. 1996. *Documentos para la historia del teatro en Venezuela. Siglos XVI, XVII Y XVIII*. Caracas: Monte Avila Editores Latinoamericana.

Bonilla, María, and Stoyan Vladich. 1988. *El teatro latinoamericano en busca de su identidad cultural*. San José, Costa Rica: Cultur Art.

Brea, Rafael. 1988. "Presencia africana en los carnavales de Santiago de Cuba." *Escenarios de dos mundos. Inventario teatral de Iberoamérica*. Ed. Moisés Pérez Coterillo and Carlos Espinoza Domínguez. 4 vols. Madrid: Centro de Documentación Teatral. I, 23–29.

Carrió, Raquel. 1998. "Ironías y paradojas del comediante. (Notas sobre el proceso de montaje de *Otra Tempestad*.)" *Conjunto* 109 (April–June): 10–16.

Escudero, María. 1988. "La Mama Negra del Ecuador." *Escenario de dos mundos. Inventario teatral de Iberoamérica*. Ed. Moisés Pérez Coterillo and Carlos Espinoza Domínguez. 4 vols. Madrid: Centro de Documentación Teatral. I: 18–22.

Festival Iberoamericano de Teatro de Cádiz. 1995. Cádiz: Artes Gráficas Nueva.

González, Patricia Elena. 1997. "Presencia de la cultura negra en el teatro cubano contemporáneo." *Tramoya* 53 (Oct.–Dec.): 28–38.

González Cajiao, Fernando. 1995. "El teatro callejero y la búsqueda del teatro popular." *Conjunto* 101: 24–32.

Leal, Rine. 1980. *Breve historia del teatro cubano*. Havana: Editorial Letras Cubanas.

Martiatu Terry, Inés María. 1992. "Teatro sagrado, teatro de dioses." *El Público* (Sept.–Oct.): 96–115.

Mellafe, Rolando. 1964. *La esclavitud en Hispanoamérica*. Buenos Aires: EUDEBA.

Olmos, Domingo. 1980. *La danza de los negros congos en la costa arriba de Colón*. Panamá: Universidad de Panamá.

Ortiz, Fernando. 1985. *Los bailes y el teatro de los negros en el folklore de Cuba*. Havana: Editorial Letras Cubanas.

CHAPTER 56

THEATRICAL FORMS AND THEIR SOCIAL DIMENSIONS IN NINETEENTH-CENTURY BRAZIL

João Roberto Faria

The chroniclers and travelers who wrote about Brazilian life during the colonial period at times refer to theatrical performances which they saw, generally on festive occasions, almost always recalling the poverty of the performance, the precariousness of the sets, and the amateurism of the actors. Strictly speaking, only after the arrival of Dom João VI and the Portuguese royal family in 1808 could theatrical art develop and improve in Brazil. In the first place, this is thanks to the incentive of D. João VI himself, who had a real theater built in Rio de Janeiro (before that, there were only modest so-called "opera houses"); he also brought theater companies with renowned actors from Portugal, such as Mariana Torres and Victor Porfírio de Borja. Second, the growth of cities, caused by the opening of the ports and the more frequent contact with European countries, created the material and intellectual conditions for the existence of this art form that demands a set of extraordinary factors: playwrights, plays, actors, and a public.

Naturally, during the early colonial period, Brazilian theater depended strongly on Portugal. It was from Lisbon that the repertory of original plays, or those translated from French, came to Brazil; the actors for the most part lived in Rio de Janeiro, and even a large part of the theater public was formed by the expatriates who had fled Napoleon's troops. In any case, the seeds of a Brazilian theater were planted. And if playwrights did not immediately emerge, at least the theater public in Rio de Janeiro grew larger, and the first actors born in Brazil began to take up their place on the stage. After these modest beginnings of theatrical activity, most notable for the performances of melodramas of a historical and political cast, a richer phase followed: In the 1830s, Brazil, having acquired its independence, began to respond to European Romantic ideas. Worthy of note, in this sense, is a long text published in the *Revista da Sociedade Filomática* [Review of the Philomatic Society] in 1833 entitled, "Ensaios sobre a tragédia" ["Essays on Tragedy"], in which three young intellectuals—Francisco Bernardino Ribeiro, Justiniano José da Rocha, and Antonio Augusto de Queiroga—identify tragedy as the genre that should be cultivated by Brazilian playwrights, instead of Romantic drama and melodrama. They, thus, reopened the debate that had shaken France in the 1820s and that culminated in the famous "Batalha do *Hernani*" ("Battle of the Hernani") with the victory of Romanticism. Brazilian academicians of the Law School of the Largo de São Francisco took up a position contrary to the European developments in the arts. But they were not alone; the first Romantics in Brazil never entirely broke with the neo-Classical education they had received.

João Caetano: Neo-Classical Tragedies, Dramas, and Melodramas

The most notable effect of the Portuguese presence on Brazilian stages was to arouse the theatrical vocation of João Caetano

(1808–1863), an actor who had his debut probably in 1827, as an amateur, and who, in 1833, was already at the head of his own theater company, working in Niterói and Rio de Janeiro. One may even say that the whole Romantic period of Brazilian theater turned around this imposing figure, who specialized in grandiose (and often merely grandiloquent) roles, especially those of the heroes of neo-Classical tragedies, melodramas, and Romantic dramas, which made up almost the whole of his repertory over more than thirty years of work. João Caetano was also an impresario, responsible for the choice of the plays put on by his theater company. This selection evidently, corresponded not only to personal preferences and artistic aspirations but also to the public taste, which to a great extent was molded by what was presented on stage.

A general review of João Caetano's repertory allows one to evaluate how decisive his contribution was for the development of Brazilian theater. It was Caetano who introduced Romanticism to Brazilian theater, with the staging, from 1836 on, of the French Romantics from Victor Hugo to Alexandre Dumas *père*. Going directly to France for his selection of the plays, he dispensed with the mediation of Portugal and put the Brazilian audience in direct contact with the most modern theatrical tendencies of the period. At the same time, however, the admiration that he had for the great French tragic actor, [Francois-Joseph] Talma (1763–1826), led him to stage some neo-Classical tragedies of the end of the eighteenth century: works by Antoine Vincent Arnaut, Vincenzo Monti, and Jean-François Ducis, among others. Ducis was also known for his adaptations of Shakespeare's plays to French neo-Classical precepts. João Caetano staged *Hamlet* and *Othello* in Brazil, obtaining one of his greatest successes with *Othello*.

From 1836 , for about ten years, Romantic drama and neo-Classical tragedy were offered alternately to the public of Rio de Janeiro. But this generic predominance was soon affected by another genre, one of a more popular appeal: melodrama. Though always important, it came to be Caetano's preferred form, either because it offered him roles that allowed for virtuoso performances or because it proved to be more profitable than the theatrical productions of the more established European repertoire. Authors like Victor Ducange, Anicet Bourgeois, Joseph Bouchardy, and Adolphe Dennery were continuously presented. The fact is that, by giving such importance to box-office appeal, the impresario buried his actor's dreams of artistic greatness; he had begun his career inspired by Talma and neo-Classical tragedy and ended it as a kind of Frédérick Lemaître of the tropics. (Lemaître was the greatest French actor of melodrama and was brilliant in countless Romantic dramas.)

The Rise of Dramatic Art

The French and Portuguese plays put on by João Caetano became the models for Brazilian playwrights. Curiously, it

555

was not Romantic drama that at first seduced writers and intellectuals. The play that inaugurates Brazilian playwriting is a tragedy by Gonçalves de Magalhães (1811–1882), *Antonio José, ou O poeta e a inquisição* [Antonio José, or The Poet and the Inquisition], staged by João Caetano in 1838 with great success. The author was already a well-known poet and had published a book of poems two years before. Gonçalves de Magalhães never completely freed himself from the Classical aesthetics that had formed him as a poet. The prologue he wrote for *Antonio José* is quite revealing of his aesthetic preferences, which tended toward the balance of the Classical form, always denying the so-called Romantic disharmonies. While claiming that he would like to conciliate the two dramatic systems, in the two tragedies he wrote the characteristics of neo-Classical tragedy are most evident and used to great effect at a time when this kind of theater was, in fact, dying. He used the French neo-Classical rules of the division into five acts; the unities of time, space, and action (followed rigorously); blank, decasyllabic verse, not alexandrines; and the unity of tone and a concern with the *bienséances*. It can be said that Gonçalves de Magalhães took from Romanticism only the idea of the creation of a national literature, to which he committed himself, as did the other writers of his generation.

The success of *Antonio José* (1838), which staged the death sentence of a Jewish comic playwright by the Inquisition, did not result in creating a Brazilian repertoire of tragedies. The genre was at a low ebb and was cultivated only sporadically by one writer or another, such as Joaquim Norberto de Souza e Silva (1820–1891) or Antonio Gonçalves Teixeira e Sousa (1812–1861). Melodrama had a greater appeal, and there were at least two important authors of this genre in this period: Luís Antônio Burgain (1812–1877) and Martins Pena (1815–1848). The former, French by birth but a long time resident of Brazil, wrote more than a dozen plays in Portuguese that were staged—at least two of them by João Caetano—and published. Martins Pena, although better known as a writer of comedies, did not have the same luck: He wrote five melodramas, which remained unpublished in his time, and only one of them was produced—without success.

The dramatic production of these two writers situates the reader in the dramatic universe that reigned on João Caetano's stage. The plays have entangled plots, full of surprises, extraordinary coincidences, a certain lack of verisimilitude, reversals of fortune, and extensive imaginative exaggeration. The formula, as always, came from France, where the genre had acquired its basic features, to a large extent already present in the works of Guilbert de Pixerécourt. The most important of these features is that the melodrama should always lead to just reward for virtue and punishment for crime. The heroes and heroines suffer the whole time in the hands of terrible and crafty villains, until a bombastic revelation or a surprising fact comes to change the course of events, guaranteeing the virtuous characters' happiness in the end. Manichean and moralistic, melodrama was a spectacle for the masses, and the people were enchanted by the vibrant dramatic action, strong emotions, sentimentalism, emphatic language, and eloquent gestures.

Brazilian theater of the early Romantic period offered another theatrical form that was also well-received by the public: the comedy of manners. In the same year of 1838, a few months after the production of *Antonio José*, João Caetano's theater company staged the first of a series of plays by

Martins Pena, *O juiz de paz da roça* (staged 1838) [The Rural Justice of the Peace]. With no dramatic pretensions, the author wanted merely to amuse the spectator with a simple plot. He wrote dozens of plays, all built around a young couple confronting numerous obstacles before attaining their final happy union. But, together with this plot, the play presented a description of the precarious workings of the justice system in the specific social context of Brazil. Despite the comic stylization and farcical resources, the realism of some scenes, of certain habits of the characters, and even of the clothes to be worn by characters (according to the stage directions), offered uncontestable proof of the author's skill at observation.

A fusion of the comedy of intrigue and the comedy of customs was the formula developed by Martins Pena, who was probably inspired by such great playwrights of comedy as Gil Vicente (1470–1536?), Molière (1622–1673), and Antônio José da Silva, "o Judeu" (1705–1739). Another factor to consider was that the one-act comic farce was characteristic of the Portuguese interlude, which was frequently staged by Portuguese theatrical companies that came to Brazil after the arrival of D. João VI. This was a short one-act play that completed the night's performance (whose main attraction was generally a neo-Classical tragedy, a drama, or a melodrama). Martins Pena found his voice in this minor comic genre. Skillful at creating complicated plots, situations, and characters, always with the aid of farcical resources—hiding-places, rows, disguises, misinterpretations, and so forth—he wrote more than two dozen highly amusing one-act comedies, bringing a good measure of "Brazilianness" to the stage in the process. Seen as a whole, the plays bring together the most varied themes and characters, forming such a wide and exact portrait of the customs of the country and the city of Rio de Janeiro that one of the main literary critics of the nineteenth century, Sílvio Romero, in a fit of enthusiasm, considered them authentic documents of the 1830s and 1840s.

Brazilian comedy was born, then, with Pena's comedies of manners. Though this form was not appreciated in the beginning, whether because the force of the prejudices of the Romantic writers and intellectuals of the period regarding low comedy or because of the secondary position it held at the time in Europe, the truth is that during the nineteenth century, the comedy of manners acquired enough prestige to draw a good number of playwrights to it, like Joaquim Manuel de Macedo (1820–1882), Joaquim José da França Júnior (1838–1890), and Artur Azevedo (1855–1908), among others. All these playwrights exploited the paths opened up by Martins Pena, introducing into longer plays his popular forms of comedy and at the same time continuing to bring some facets of Brazilian life to the stage.

The Theater of the Romantic Writers

It is curious to note that Brazilian theater, as a system composed of authors, works, actors, and public, was constituted during the Romantic period, but its first playwrights did not write Romantic dramas, as it would be logical to suppose at that historical moment of rupture with Classicism. The play that ought to have been the result of the fusion of tragedy and comedy, according to the formula prescribed by Victor Hugo in the "Preface" to *Cromwell* in 1827, only appeared in Brazilian dramatic literature in the middle of the 1840s, with the plays by Antônio Gonçalves Dias (1823–1864). Having lived in Europe, this playwright knew Shakespeare's works, the models of the Romantic dramatists, as well as German and French theater, like no other Brazilian writer of the time. The reading of his four dramas and of the "Prologue" he wrote for the finest of them, *Leonor de Mendonça* (1847), makes it clear that he had completely mastered the basic concepts of Romantic theater. Thus, he proceeded with total freedom in relation to the rules of Classicism, constructing a dramatic *oeuvre* in which several aspects of form and content specific to melodrama are present, such as the overwhelming force of passion. The dramatic material he used was based on the past—but on national histories rather than Greco-Roman antiquity. It must also be noted that he did not flinch from confrontation with controversial themes (such as incest), and attacked the social indifference to the moral or didactic purpose of art. He also cultivated the simultaneous presence of domestic scenes characteristic of comedy and violent scenes more common in tragedy, as well as the diffusion of dramatic action in time and space.

The differences between a drama like *Leonor de Mendonça* and the earlier Brazilian plays are striking. In the first place, prose advantageously replaces the blank verse that had been used by Gonçalves de Magalhães. The dialogues, free of pompous rhetoric, gained lyrical and emotional intensity. In *Antonio José*, one of the serious problems is that the love of the protagonist for Mariana is not sufficiently explicit and remains in the background. In contrast, in *Leonor de Mendonça*, as an authentic Romantic drama, love is the emotion that moves the characters and triggers the action. And when it is not love, it is hate—its next of kin. Unlike the melodramas of Burgain and Martins Pena with their wild plots and simplified characters, Gonçalves Dias's play offers surprising dramatic and literary quality. The manner in which the author introduces and develops the main conflict, around an adultery that does not take place, has unarguable sensitivity and beauty. The play also presents characters with psychological depth; the plot is built on impeccable logic; and, without question, it has both an elegant style and a balanced measure of emotion. *Leonor de Mendonça* is evident proof of the dramatic talent of Gonçalves Dias, but so are the other dramas he wrote: *Beatriz Cenci* (1844–1845), *Patkull* (1843), and *Boabdil* (1850). Despite the fact that these plays have minor flaws, his *oeuvre* stands out as the most representative of Romantic drama in Brazil. Unfortunately, though, the playwright's efforts were not appreciated in his time. His dramatic works never made it to the stage during the Romantic period and were never taken as a model for other playwrights. *Beatriz Cenci* was censored by the Dramatic Conservatory because it introduced the theme of incest, and *Leonor de Mendonça* was turned down by João Caetano.

Practically all the Brazilian Romantic writers, at some moment of their lives, dedicated themselves to the theater—some with greater diligence than others. After Gonçalves Dias, Joaquim Manuel de Macedo, is also worthy of mention, since he was already a novelist of some prestige when he wrote *O cego* [The Blind Man], a drama produced by João Caetano in 1849, and the comedy *O fantasma branco* [The White Ghost], staged in 1851. It was the beginning of a very diversified dramatic *oeuvre*, since the author tried several genres, always following the tendencies of the moment. In the case of *O cego*, the mixture of elements of neo-Classical tragedy and melodrama predominates in this hybrid play: Written in

verse, it is divided into five acts, reasonably faithful to the rule of the three unities, and with a plot constructed from worn-out dramatic situations. *O fantasma branco*, which the author called an "opera," is a farce with musical interludes in the action, very similar to the French *vaudeville*, which had already been staged in Rio de Janeiro. In this type of play with no intellectual pretensions, the burlesque, the jocular, situations bordering on the absurd, and the busy plots predominated, all with considerable music sung in arias, duets, trios, and in chorus. In this genre, Macedo also wrote *O primo de Califórnia* [1855; The California Cousin]—which is in fact an imitation of *L'oncle d'Amérique* [The American Uncle] of Augustin Scribe—and the highly amusing *A torre em concurso* [staged 1881; The Tower in the Contest].

About 1850, Manuel Antonio Álvares de Azevedo (1831–1852) became interested in the theater. But his only dramatic production was the play *Macário* (1850–1851) which escapes any classification. The poet himself took care to state in the preface that he did not know whether he had written a drama, a comedy, or a mere dialogue, considering it instead the result of a "confused inspiration," far from the ideal play he had in mind: something grand, which should bring together the ardent passions of Elizabethan theater, the imagination of the Spanish Golden Age theater, and the stark simplicity of Greek tragedy. Álvarez de Azevedo died very young and did not accomplish his writer's dreams. *Macário*, however, gives a good idea of what he could have done in the domain of dramatic art. A good first act develops around an encounter between a young Romantic poet and Satan, with intelligent and witty dialogues on life, death, love, women, illusions—all in the purest Romanticism of the Byronic manner. There is considerable theatricality in the first act, in which the action slides into the fantastic, but in the second act, unfortunately, this quality is lost. The good dialogues give over to long literary and philosophical discussions that would have been more appreciated in essay form.

Poets like Casimiro José Marques de Abreu (1839–1860), Luis José Junqueira Freire (1832–1855), and Fagundes Varela (1841–1875) also turned to the theater, without leaving any significant work. At different periods, at least three authors—Martins Pena, Macedo, and Bernardo Guimarães (1825–1884)—tried to create the Romantic drama of the Indian, but with no success. With the passing of time, theatrical Romanticism began to lose its appeal and, from 1855 on, was displaced by realism in Rio de Janeiro. Yet, Romantic drama, long after it had passed its day in France, still survived in Brazil. Important writers like José de Alencar (1829–1877) and Antonio de Castro Alves (1847–1871) showed they had learned well the lessons of Victor Hugo in their historical dramas such as *O jesuíta* [1861; The Jesuit] and *Gonzaga ou A revolução de Minas* [1867; Gonzaga, or The Revolution in Minas]. Before them, Agrário de Sousa Meneses (1834–1863) of Bahia and Paulo Eiró (1838–1871) of São Paulo had written, respectively, *Calabar*, in 1856, and *Sangue limpo* [Clean Blood], between 1859 and 1861. Rather belatedly in relation to the French models (Alexandre Dumas *père*'s *Henri III et sa cour* dates from 1829), historical drama arrived in Brazil, based on episodes of national history. Even though, in its formal aspects, this small late development is mixed with elements of neo-Classical tragedy and melodrama, the strict connection it has with the Romantic spirit cannot be denied. All the plays reveal the nationalist sentiment of their authors, who sought future greatness in the nation's history.

Realism

The transformations that Brazil underwent from 1850 on, a time during which the slave traffic stopped, are vast. Some cities benefited from the money that had previously been invested in the purchase of slaves, and they now began to grow, thanks to the multiplying of businesses, the expansion of trade that created jobs, the establishment of banks and small industries–thanks, in short, to all those activities that an emerging bourgeoisie was undertaking. The effect of this new public would soon reach the theater. In Rio de Janeiro, a certain dissatisfaction with João Caetano's repertory, considered anachronistic by young intellectuals who worked in the press, took concrete form in 1855, when the impresario Joaquim Heleodoro Gomes dos Santos created the Teatro Ginásio Dramático and began to put on a new type of play that had been having great success in France: the Realistic play of authors such as Alexandre Dumas *fils*, Émile Augier, Théodore Barrière, and Octave Feuillet. Once more, and it would not be the last time in the nineteenth century, the Brazilian audience enthusiastically applauded a French literary model.

Generally speaking, the Realistic play has none of the violent situations, sharp tensions, sentimentalism, and strong color of melodrama. Its universe is basically the life of the bourgeoisie, portrayed sympathetically by the authors, who try to create scenes and dialogues of the utmost naturalness. At the same time, the Realistic play has a moralizing trait. The prescription of ethical values, such as work, honesty, and marriage, is juxtaposed to the description of customs within a plot that contrasts the good and the bad in bourgeois society. "Realism" in this type of play is evidently relative, for the portrait of bourgeois society is always improved by the moralizing brushstrokes. The heroes, for example, are well-behaved fathers and mothers or young men and women who are emotionally well balanced. The love that is valued is no longer ardent passion but conjugal love, which must be calm and serene. The fact is that French playwrights, contrary to the idea of art for art's sake, made themselves into spokesmen of the bourgeoisie and wrote plays with the intent to defend their values and way of life. What contributed to this, besides the rather Manichean plot of good and evil, was the presence of the *raisonneur* character, an obligatory figure who comments on the dramatic action and conveys moral lessons to the other characters and to the audience. When French Realistic plays began to be produced in the Teatro Ginásio Dramático, various writers and intellectuals believed in the social power of this type of play and began to defend the idea that it was possible to create a national repertory with the same characteristics. The man leading the way was José de Alencar (1829–1877), who in 1857 wrote *O demônio familiar* [The Familiar Demon], *O crédito* [Trust], and *As asas de um anjo* [The Wings of an Angel], Realist plays that discussed on stage social problems such as domestic slavery, marriage for money, speculation, and prostitution. Taking Dumas *fils* as the model to be followed, the Brazilian writer reconciled naturalness and morality in his plays, putting the bourgeoisie on stage to defend its greatest institution: the family.

Alencar's example bore fruit. Between 1857 and 1865 a group of playwrights emerged, committed to making the theater an instrument of the regeneration and moral reform of society by means of the themes and forms of the Realist play. The Ginásio Dramático effectively produced most of these plays, driving forward in a decisive way the renewal of Brazilian playwriting–with the strong support of the public and press. Besides Alencar, the following authors and plays are important: Quintino de Sousa Bocaiúva (1836–1912), *Onfália* (1860) and *Os mineiros da desgraça* [1861; The Miners of Disgrace]; Joaquim Manuel de Macedo, *Luxo e vaidade* [staged 1860; Luxury and Vanity] and *Lusbela* (1862); Antonio Aquiles de Miranda Varejão (1834–1900), *A época* [1860; The Era], *A resignação* [1861; Resignation], and *O cativeiro moral* [1864; The Moral Jail]; Sizenando Barreto Nabuco de Araújo (1842–1892), *O Cínico* [1861; The Cynic] and *A túnica de Nessus* [1863; The Coat of Nessus]; Valentim José da Silveira Lopes (b. 1830), *Sete de setembro* [1861; September Seventh] and *Amor e dinheiro* [1862; Love and Money]; Francisco Pinheiro Guimarães (1832–1877), *História de uma moça rica* [staged 1861; Story of a Rich Girl]; Francisco Manuel Álvares de Araújo (1829–1879), *De ladrão a barão* [1862; From Thief to Baron]; Joaquim José da França Júnior (1838–1890), *Os tipos da atualidade* [1862; The Types of the Present]; Constantino do Amaral Tavares (1828–1890), *Um casamento da época* [1862; A Wedding of the Period].

This is not, of course, a high-level repertory in terms of quality. But some plays had an enormous critical and popular success, giving us a sense of the taste and tendencies of the period. In fact, the titles of the plays themselves indicate the subjects with which they deal. Some of them did not completely break away from Romanticism, since some aspects of Romantic theater remained, but became mixed with Realistic norms. Such hybrid theater is typical of a period of aesthetic renewal. Moreover, inspired by French Realistic theater, these works portray the customs of the Brazilian bourgeoisie and its liberal values. Contrary to what was seen in Romantic dramas and melodramas or in the comedies of Martins Pena, the main characters of Brazilian Realistic plays are lawyers, doctors, engineers, students, journalists, businessmen–that is, professionals and intellectuals who made up the emergent middle class in Rio de Janeiro. Thus, the audience could identify itself with the characters on the stage and applaud the efforts of the playwrights committed to displaying the most modern segment of Brazilian society.

Among the enthusiasts of these dramatic works, a very young critic at the beginning of a brilliant literary career stands out: Joaquim Maria Machado de Assis (1839–1908). The articles he published in the newspapers, *O Espelho* and *Diário do Rio de Janeiro,* show his commitment to Realistic theater and his belief in the theater as a civilizing art. Curiously, in his own dramatic works, he did not follow the model of a Dumas *fils* or an Augier. Perhaps he did not feel he was mature enough for the longer form of the Realistic play, which dealt seriously with the social questions of the time; he preferred at that time the brief form of the salon comedy, which he had certainly learned as a reader of Alfred de Musset and Octave Feuillet. In this genre, two basic characteristics predominate: vivacity of style and wit. It is therefore a short, elegant comedy that avoids any type of vulgarity or farce. In its original form it was almost a game, practiced in the French aristocratic salons at the end of the seventeenth century: The audience had to guess what the proverb concealed in the action was. Later, with Carmontelle in the eighteenth century and Musset in the nineteenth, the proverb appeared at the end of the play or even in its title. The dramatic works of Machado de Assis belong to this tradition. In *O caminho da porta* [1862; The Way to the Door], for example, the dramatic conflict is almost nonexistent, and the action turns around a widow who has several suitors and chooses none of them. The coded language, the witty dialogues, the irony, the jokes, and the characters representing the elite of Rio de Janeiro are the main features of this little play (produced in 1862) and of several others that followed it. It seems that Machado de Assis wished to carry on a close dialogue with the Realistic comedy then in vogue. In a lighter and more amusing way, using some resources of high comedy, he sought to show that there was, in Rio de Janeiro, a refined bourgeoisie with salons where intelligent prose and the taste for art were cultivated.

The Comic and Musical Theater

While the Realist play had its success in the Ginásio Dramático and seduced the main writers and intellectuals, another type of theatrical spectacle, based on joyfulness, light music, cunning, and the beauty of women, began to attract an audience less and less interested in so-called serious theater with its literary and edifying preoccupations. In the Alcazar Lyrique, created in 1859, the repertory, as well as the actors, came entirely from France and consisted of canzonets, comic scenes, comic duets, and, in general, small vaudeville skits. The theater as entertainment gradually undermined the work of the authors associated with the Ginásio, and many of them quit writing plays for the most varied reasons, including disappointment with the new directions that Brazilian theater had been taking. The last straw was the stupendous success of the operetta Orphée aux enfers, with music by Offenbach and a text by Hector Crémieux and Ludovic Halévy, which premiered at the Alcazar in February 1865 and ran for the entire year. The enthusiasm of the public signaled deep transformations in the theater in the years to come. During the ten or twelve years that followed, the main French operettas, from authors like Offenbach and Charles Lecocq, were produced and much applauded in Rio de Janeiro: The main effect of this was the emergence of a new comic genre, equally amusing, irreverent, and with a Brazilian touch: the operetta parody.

Orphée aux enfers opened in Paris in 1858. Arguably, it is a work in which the music is of more importance than the text. Of course, the burlesque parody of the myth of Orpheus is also quite funny. If in mythology we have the figure of a solitary, suffering poet and musician in love with his faithful wife Eurydice, in Crémieux and Halévy's text the parodic inversion makes Orpheus a bad fellow who hates his wife who, for her part, cheats on him with the shepherd Aristeu and other lovers. The plot, full of comic nonsense and malice, is, in fact, a pretext for the vibrant, joyful music that joins song and dance numbers (such as the famous can-can). The principle of the parodic operetta was delightfully appropriate for Brazilian authors. Offenbach's music was maintained, but the action was now set in Brazil. The one who first had the idea of creating a work of this kind was Francisco Correia Vasques (1839–1892), the most famous comic actor of the time. His Orfeu na roça [Orpheus in the Countryside], staged in 1868, shared the success of Orphé aux enfers. In the Brazilian parody, Orpheus is Zeferino Rabeca, the neighborhood barber, and Eurydice is Dona Brígida, a countrywoman who aspires to life at court. Other characters of the operetta, such as Cupid, Morpheus, and Hercules, take on hilarious names: Quinquim das Moças, Joaquim Preguiça, and Antonio Faquista. Total irreverence results from this plot, which sticks to the original text but is adapted to Brazilian customs and country types.

The fashion introduced by Vasques was much exploited. At a time when French operettas were staged in their original language, Brazilian versions actually multiplied. Offenbach's Barbe-Bleue [Bluebeard], for example, was transformed into Barba de milho [1869; Corn-Beard] in Augusto de Castro's (d. 1896) parody and into Joaquim Serra's (1838–1888) Traga-moças [1869; Fetch-Girls]. The most skillful Brazilian author of this type of play was Artur Azevedo, who nationalized the operetta after having great success with some parodies. The first was produced in 1876, A filha de Maria Angu [The Daughter of Maria Angu], a version of LeCocq's La fille de Mme. Angot. It was performed so often that, at one point, the author himself asked that its run be ended. Many other parodies followed, among which A casadinha de fresco [1876; The Newlywed Lady] and Abel, Helena (1877), adapted from LeCocq's La petite mariée and Offenbach's La belle Hélène. The experience acquired in these parodic works led Artur Azevedo to write original operettas. In Nova viagem à lua [New Voyage to the Moon] of 1877, he also took advantage of LeCocq's music but now included the Brazilian jongo, a dance and song of African origin. With Os noivos [1880; The Newlyweds] and A Princesa dos cajueiros [1880; The Princess of the Cashew-Trees], produced in 1880, the operetta became completely nationalized, since the music was written by Sá Noronha, a Portuguese composer who lived in Brazil.

In addition to operetta, another genre that enjoyed the public's favor was the fantastic play (in France, féerie). The plot is the mere pretext for action filled with tricks and surprises. It may be comic, allegorical, or have a moralistic basis, but there is no commitment to realism, with characters who are fairies, genies, devils, gnomes, and other supernatural beings. Generally speaking, the protagonist is blessed with a talisman with which he can overcome the obstacles put before him, so that his wishes are granted, whatever they may be. Thus, to give an example, in the féerie entitled As pílulas do diabo [1839; The Devil's Pills], by Ferdinand Lalou (d. 1850), and Auguste Anicet-Bourgeois (1806–1871), Laurent, the protagonist, in order to test the efficacy of his talisman—a pill that he swallows—points to a character and reveals his wish—that the other be transformed into a turkey: the stage directions call for this to occur on stage. The so-called changements à vue, which also transformed sets, were common in this genre. In A galinha dos ovos de ouro [1848; The Hen with the Golden Eggs], by Adolphe d'Ennery (1811–1899) and M. Clairville (1811–1879), which was performed in Rio de Janeiro, a room is transformed into a cave, a ballroom turns into a vast hell, old furniture becomes new and golden, a man turns into a rooster, and a series of extravagant wishes are granted.

As spectacle, the féerie appealed both to the eyes and ears of the audience. Besides the rich sets and costumes, the performances also included dance and musical numbers. But the ones who effectively brought to life the fantasy world of the féerie were the backdrop painters, the prop operators, the stage managers, the costume designers, and the scenographers. By means of extraordinary tricks, they were able to simulate on stage the eruption of volcanoes, a cyclone, hellfire, or a flood. In Brazil, apparently, theater professionals had no difficulties in putting on this type of play. Owing to the great popularity of these plays, not even a novel like O guarani [1857; The Guarani] escaped a magical adaptation, which was made in 1875 by José Alves Visconti de Coaraci (1837–1892) and Francisco Pereira da Silva. On stage, according to the newspaper advertisements, everything could be seen: a silver sea, an enchanted palace, a cliff with waterfall in the background, a moonlight effect, a ball, an explosion, a flood of the Paquequer River, and, finally, Peri and Ceci carried off by the current on the trunk of a palmtree.

Brazilian authors like Moreira Sampaio, Vincente Torres da Silva Reis (1870–1947), and Augusto de Castro wrote a few *féeries* that were produced at that time, but almost all of the repertory shown in Rio de Janeiro came from France and Portugal. While the audience amused itself and the impresarios made pots of money, the intellectuals lamented the turn Brazilian theater had taken, moving even further from literature and toward pure entertainment. Alencar, for example, strongly disliked the adaptation of *O guarani* and protested against the distortion of his work. Before him, on several occasions, Machado de Assis had already shown his displeasure with the situation. In the well-known article "Instinto de Nacionalidade" ["Instinct of Nationality"] of 1873, he used harsh terms to attack the dissipation of the Brazilian stage.

The comic and music theater, however, both continued their rise. In addition to the operettas and the *féeries*, a new genre was founded: the annual review. The first great success of this type of play took place in January 1884, with the production of *O mandarim* [The Mandarin], by Artur Azevedo (1855–1908). With the way now open–some prior attempts had not achieved good results–the authors of Brazilian reviews multiplied. Moreira Sampaio, Augusto de Castro, Antonio Valentin da Costa Magalhães (1859–1903), Vicente Reis, Oscar Francisco Leite, and Paranhos Pederneiras (1860–1890), among others shared the applause of the public with Artur Azevedo, the author of nineteen reviews. The annual review, as the name suggests, recapitulates the main events of the past year. Everything that was important or that had some impact–a political event, a crime, an invention, a new newspaper, the collapse of a bank, a literary work, a theatrical show, an epidemic–was staged in a comic treatment, sometimes with a critical or satirical bent. Like the operetta or the *féerie*, with which it is closely related (either because it requires eye-catching scenery, including the use of set changes, or because it has music and dance numbers), the annual review is also a light genre. Given its fragmented structure, one of its characters has the task of linking the separate parts that compose it: This is the *compère*, who comments on and explains the action to the audience. Another unifying means, besides the presence of the *compère*, is the use of a more sustained comic plot developed within the different parts and used to tie them together. Artur Azevedo, the most creative of the comic dramatists, favored this combination, as is seen, for example, in the review, *O tribofe* [1892; The Swindle]. Besides presenting what happened in 1891, commented on by the *compère*, the play achieves unity by the comic plot centered on the presence of a family from the countryside in Rio de Janeiro. In other words, at the same time that the spectator is amused at the adventures of the family, we see in retrospect the social, political, and cultural facts through the biting satire and caustic humor of Artur Azevedo, an attentive observer of Brazilian life at the end of the nineteenth century.

The theater that appealed to a mass public did not rely only on the operettas, the *féeries*, and the annual reviews.

Adaptations of successful serialized novels, as well as old and new melodramas, were regularly presented. Generally speaking, dramatic fashion set the tone, motivating the rise of the so-called *dramas de grande espectáculo* (spectacle-dramas) and mixed genres, such as the operetta-*féerie*, the fantastic drama, or the comic-fantastic review. Involved in this type of theater, Brazilian authors rarely wrote more serious plays or plays with real literary quality, and they were often no more than translators and adapters of foreign works. Artur Azevedo, once accused of having been the cause of the decadence of the Brazilian theater, defended himself by saying that when he arrived in Rio de Janeiro in 1873, the process was already underway, and the "serious" plays he wrote–like *A almanjarra* [1888; The Carriage], *A jóia* [1879; The Gem], *O badejo* [1898; The Fish], *O retrato a óleo* [staged 1902; Portrait in Oil]–never won over the public, which preferred his *bambochatas* (extravagances). Artur Azevedo in fact wrote some masterpieces of comic and musical theater, such as the burlesques *A capital federal* [staged 1897; The State Capital]–from the comic plot of *O tribofe*–and *O mambembe* [1904; The Amateur Actor]. Both plays, in a way, summarize what was going on in terms of theater at the time, since they brought together some characteristics of the comedy of manners, the operetta, and the *féerie*.

In addition to Artur Azevedo, the most outstanding writer in the comedy of manners was França Júnior. The legitimate successor of Martins Pena, skillful in managing low-comedy resources, he created very funny types and situations, often with a devastating critical impact. Among the two dozen comedies he wrote are *Como se fazia um deputado* [staged 1889; How a Government Representative Is Made] and *Caiu o ministério* [1882; The Ministry Has Fallen], delicious satires on Brazilian political practices; and *As doutoras* [1889; The Lady-Doctors], a comic but conservative observation on the first feminist manifestations in Brazil. Brazilian theater at the end of the nineteenth century also counted on the participation of Aluísio Azevedo (1857–1913), who wrote some plays by himself and co-authored several plays and annual reviews with his brother Artur, as well as others with Emílio Rouède (1848–1908). Although this part of the author's work is unknown today, it had some impact in the decade of the 1880s, especially because it was staged at a time when there was a great debate in intellectual circles over whether naturalism was possible in the theater. The productions in Portuguese of *Thérèse Raquin*, *L'Assommoir*, and *Nana* in 1880 to 1881 brought the world of Émile Zola to the Brazilian stage, but not the form of the naturalist drama. The adaptations of the novels did not manage to avoid the melodramatic excesses, as critics pointed out at the time. Even so, without a model, Aluísio Azevedo adapted *O mulato* [1881; The Mulatto] for the stage and wrote plays like *Um caso de adultério* [1890; A Case of Adultery], *O caboclo* [1886; The Countryman], and *Venenos que curam* [1885; Poisons that Cure]–the three co-authored with Emílio Rouède–introducing some features of the new literary movement in Brazilian theater. These attempts at serious drama, however, did not continue and did not bring about the formation of a dramatic repertory linked to naturalism. The hegemony of the comic and musical theater was complete in those times, to the joy of the public and the dejection of the intellectuals.

The Foreign Presence

Theatrical life in Brazil at the turn of the century was not only intense but extraordinarily rich and sophisticated, especially because of the presence of the great European celebrities on the stages of major cities such as Rio de Janeiro and São Paulo. In fact, from the arrival of D. João VI onward, Brazil began to receive foreign actors—mainly from Portugal, obviously, and later from Italy and France. But from the last decades of the nineteenth century and beyond, this intensified, turning out to be a profitable enterprise for the European dramatic companies, which were not intimidated either by the tiring Atlantic crossing or the risks of catching yellow fever. Only the prospect of large profits can explain, for example, the three voyages that Sarah Bernhardt, perhaps the greatest actress of her time, made to Brazil in 1886, 1893, and 1906. Acclaimed all over Europe, she surely did not need Brazilian applause for her glory. To understand better the arrival of the great foreign actors in Brazil, one needs to keep in mind that the theatrical season in the European capitals usually began at the end of September or the beginning of October and extended to the end of May or the middle of June. In the summer months, the bourgeoisie in Paris was almost entirely absent from the theater. With no work for three or four months, the actors of renown invited a few of their colleagues, formed a drama company, and came to America, giving performances in Rio de Janeiro, São Paulo, Porto Alegre, Buenos Aires, Montevideo, and occasionally other smaller cities.

A quick recording of the names that passed through in those times is surprising in both quantity and quality. From France, besides Sarah Bernhardt, came famous artists like Le Bargy, Coquelin Aîné, De Féraudy, Réjane, Suzanne Desprès, Jane Hading, and many others. From Italy, which had already sent Adelaide Ristori and the Shakespearean actors Tommaso Salvini and Ernesto Rossi, in 1869 and 1871 Brazil twice received Eleonora Duse, Sarah Bernhardt's great rival, and other excellent actors such as Adelaide Tessero, Clara Della Guardia, Giovanni Emmanuel, Ermete Novelli, and Ermete Zacconi. From Portugal came many dramatic companies from Lisbon and Porto and an even greater number of actors: Eduardo Brasão, Palmira Bastos, Adelina Abranches, Ângela Pinto, Chabi Pinheiro, and Cristiano de Sousa—not to mention the countless Portuguese impresarios and actors who lived in Brazil or who stayed there for long periods, dividing their professional life between the two countries. Finally, from Spain came the best companies doing zarzuelas, the theatrical genre closely related to operetta. Without a doubt, Brazilian audiences of the period had the privilege of seeing a great part of the best in European theater, both with respect to actors and dramatic literature. Authors acclaimed in Paris, like Victorien Sardou, Alexandre Dumas fils, Émile Augier,

Édouard Pailleron, Henry Meilhac, Ludovic Halévy, Alphonse Daudet, Émile Zola, Henri Becque, Edmond Rostand, Georges Feydeau, Eugène Brieux, Georges Ohnet; and many others (not necessarily French—like Ibsen, Sudermann, and D'Annunzio) had their works produced a great number of times, as well as the classic theater of Shakespeare, Racine, and Molière.

It is not easy to evaluate the consequences of such a significant foreign presence on the Brazilian stage. On the one hand, it is evident that theatrical life gained an extraordinary fascination, as if a piece of Europe moved to Brazil every year; on the other hand, it is hard to explain why this constant presence did not motivate the rise of richer and more up-to-date Brazilian drama than had existed in the earlier periods. Called on by the market to write plays for entertainment, Brazilian authors limited their aesthetic horizon and did not keep up with—even at times refused—the changes taking place in the European theater, which was undergoing a process of modernization.

**Translation by Glaucia Gonçalves
and Thomas LaBorie Burns**

Works Cited

Alencar, José de. 1960. *Obra completa.* 4 vols. Rio de Janeiro: Aguilar.

Alves, Castro. 1956. *Gonzaga ou A revolução de Minas.* Salvador: Progresso.

Assis, Machado de. 1982. *Teatro completo.* Rio de Janeiro: MEC/SNT.

Azevedo, Álvares de. 1982. *Macário.* Campinas: IEL/UNICAMP.

Azevedo, Artur. 1983–1995. *Teatro de Artur Azevedo.* 6 vols. Rio de Janeiro: MEC/INACEN.

Eiró, Paulo. 1949. *Sangue limpo.* São Paulo: Departamento de Cultura/Divisão do Arquivo Histórico.

Ennery, Adolphe d' and M. Clairville. 1861. *La poule aux oeufs d'or.* Paris: Beck.

França Júnior, J. J. de. 1980. *Teatro de França Júnior.* 2 vols. Rio de Janeiro: MEC/SNT.

Lalou, Ferdinand, and Augusto Anicet-Bourgeois. 1839. *Les pilules du diable.* Paris: Marchant.

Macedo, Joaquim Manuel de. 1979. *Teatro completo.* 3 vols. Rio de Janeiro: MEC/SNT.

Magalhães, Gonçalves de. 1865. *Tragédias.* Rio de Janeiro: Garnier.

Meneses, Agrário de Souza. 1955. "Calabar." *Dionysos* 6: 43–163.

Offenbach, Jacques. 1985. *La belle Hélène.* Choeurs et Orchestre du Capitole de Toulouse. Direction de Michel Plasson. Emi France: 2 cds.

———. 1987. *Orphée aux enfers.* Choeurs et Orchestre du Capitole de Toulouse. Direction de Michel Plasson. Emi France: 2 cds.

Pena, Martins. 1956. *Comédias.* Rio de Janeiro: MEC/INL.

———. 1956. *Dramas.* Rio de Janeiro: MEC/INL.

CHAPTER 57

DRAMATURGIES AND THEATRICALITIES

ASPECTS OF THE TWENTIETH-CENTURY BRAZILIAN LITERARY SCENE

Maria Helena Werneck and
Victor Hugo Adler Pereira

The roar of laughter that today overtakes the audience is a small reminder of the first successes of comedy writer Artur Azevedo (1855–1908); his vaudeville *O Mandarim* [The Mandarin] opened in 1883 and gave rise to "the laughter that shook Rio de Janeiro" (Magalhães Júnior 45). Authors tried their hand at a variety of dramatic genres, such as the revue, burlesque, or comedy of manners, in which they combined the presentation of everyday life and political events in Rio de Janeiro to great laughter and loud applause. This could be a brief description of the Brazilian theatrical scene throughout the first half of the twentieth century, a subject that until recently (Veneziano 84) was eclipsed by the notion that the first three decades of the twentieth century were just a waiting period for the great aesthetic revolution of 1943. In this way, historiography (Prado 1988, 14) has tended to assume the point of view of Alcântara Machado, writer, chronicler, and dramatic critic from 1923 to 1926, who could see only a "most unhappy Brazilian stage" (Machado 164). His sharp reviews took to task the genre of the comedy of manners, especially those plays that dealt with adultery plots in the style of "the little French comedies." He called for a renewed dramaturgy that could "testify to the change of habits and customs and could leave aside nineteenth-century Parisian characters, types, and plots that did not correspond to Brazilian reality" (Materno 46). Apart from considering the plays themselves, he seriously questioned both the quality of the repertoire and staging of foreign companies and those Brazilian actor-managers (such as Leopoldo Fróes, Procópio Ferreira, or Jaime Costa) who wanted to stage only those plays specially written for their own performing skills.

Following the reviews of the time, literary histories tend to emphasize the idea that, at the turn of the century, Brazilian theater seemed to await a modernizing renewal that did not take place until the 1940s, thanks to the participation of groups working with foreign directors and the success achieved by playwright Nelson Rodrigues (1912–1980) in *Vestido de Noiva* [1943; Wedding Dress]. Thus, Alcântara Machado's heated attack on the foreign domination of Brazilian dramaturgy fell on deaf ears, and a sense of Brazilianness is said to emerge in only popular genres, such as the revue, the burlesque, and the circus. This attitude was defiantly expressed in the following terms:

Que venham a farsa grosseira, a comédia de costumes, os galãs de pés do chão, as ingênuas do subúrbio, o folclore, o samba, o carnaval, a feitiçaria, o vernáculo estropiado, os dramas do sertão, flores de papel nos lustres, carapinhas, dentes de ouro, a fauna e o ambiente, graças e desgraças da descivilização brasileira. (Machado, quoted in Materno 47)

Let [the public] come—the rude farce, the comedy of manners, the uncouth beaux, the suburban ingenues, folklore, samba, carnival, witchcraft, the spoiled vernacular, rural dramas, paper flowers in the chandeliers, individuals with curly hair and golden teeth, the local animal life and environment, all the fortunes and misfortunes of Brazilian lack of civilization.

Yet, Álvaro Moreira (1888–1964)–a contemporary of Alcântara Machado (1875–1941)–was able to identify an original form of expression at the turn of the century, a kind of aesthetic renewal of Brazilian theater emerging out of comic genres. Moreira was in charge of the *Teatro de Brinquedo* [Toy Theater]. He proposed an original stage and dramaturgy that developed in the 1920s in a kind of dialogue with Oswald de Andrade's (1890–1954) anthropophagy theory. However, Moreira adapted Andrade's idea of Brazilian art consuming Brazilian reality by synthetizing the avant-garde experiences of international theater and choosing only the plays that could be made over by Brazilian dramaturgy through a form of internal cannibalism (Souza 116). In an interview given in 1929 for the *Revista de Antropofagia* [Anthropophagy Review] (see **Figure 1**), Moreira considered the musical farce *Forrobodó* [Dance of the Rabble] as the play that gave a new impetus to "our theater," a kind of "carnival follow-up in Rio de Janeiro" that was born in the Largo do Rocio, nowadays the Tiradentes Square: "A new theater was born out of the diverse races that have mingled into this race. A new theater that is original, direct, rude, natural, without manners, whimsical, producing laughter, half *capoeira*, half *fado*, extending language unwittingly, establishing types without realizing it" (Souza 116). Written by Luiz Peixoto (1889–1973) and Carlos Bittencourt (1890–1941), with music by Chiquinha Gonzaga, and staged by Pascoal Segreto's *Companhia de Revistas e Burletas do Teatro São José* [Company of Revues and Burlesques of the Theater of São José], the play was a success and made popular a variety of musical genres that had been eclipsed after the death of Artur Azevedo in 1908. Azevedo had been the great Brazilian revue writer of the nineteenth century; nevertheless, many of his plays had no more than flimsy plots with tongue-in-cheek humor aiming at belly laughs. In contrast, according to Álvaro Moreira, *Forrobodó* created new local lineage: "instant images of the city parade onto the stage, images of society, of the ways and customs of the common people of Rio de Janeiro and of the populace who live in the hills and districts where not even the Grand Dukes risk to travel" (quoted in Souza 124). The urban escapist utopia created at the end of the nineteenth century by Azevedo's revues (Süssekind 1986, 59) resulted from the particular atmosphere that prevailed in rather limited upper-class social and geographic environments. After several decades of these comedies, this utopia was either transferred to the small provincial towns or

Figure 1.

REEDIÇÃO DA REVISTA LITERÁRIA PUBLICADA EM SÃO PAULO - 1ª E 2ª "DENTIÇÕES" -1928-1929

(Courtesy John P. Robarts Research Library, University of Toronto)

else became a musical utopia in which various (idealized) segments of the population sang and danced. Between the 1940s and the 1950s it was a microscopic chronicle of urban daily life, where the utopia fell apart under the tyranny of a restricted sense of well being consisting of a provocative and only slightly disguised sensuality.

In these end-of-the-year revues, the sense of strangeness arising from rapid changes in urban life and historic changes became less threatening when the accelerated rhythm of a big city could be translated into a succession of pictures and short scenes in a staged display of the year's significant events; the squares, streets, and buildings, all well known by the audience, were reproduced on stage. Within a theater, this world did not frighten the viewer, who was protected by the "reassuring mirages of the capital" and marveled at the aesthetic effects of the *féerie* [fantastic effects] (Sussekind 1986, 75). What was staged was a sense of theatricality, which resulted from the combination of romantic fantasy with a naturalistic aesthetic of the visible, "thanks to the theatrical acceleration of history and of urban activity, the 'naturalism' of such scenes is covered by fanciful mutations, mythological sceneries, and various allegories" (Sussekind 1986, 75), as well as a number of musical pieces, both songs and dances. People who attended those musical farces or *burletas,* written by Luiz Peixoto and his contributors, were witnessing another kind of theatricality, one characterized by a multiplicity of intermingling characters (Silva 26) who gave a sense of variety to the stage. A carnival club situated in a small warehouse in the slums, a

horse circus, and a church atrium where St. John's Day is celebrated these are some of the places where people get together to have fun, prepare for a carnival parade, or commemorate a special date. But above all, they are gathering spaces. The stage presented a parade of changing revue tableaux; it did not show the movement of passers-by, in a smooth allegory of urban speed. On the contrary, it constantly turned one scene into another, even choreographing a fight (usually a *capoeira* or fight-dance). There was no proper sequence of episodes but rather a spinning-out of scenes structured only by singing and dancing. A *gafieira* (popular ballroom) seems to be the best metaphor for this dramatic genre—the place where the usual rules of conduct do not inhibit the liberty of dancing, which promotes a festive atmosphere, thus ending hostilities.

Luiz Peixoto's musical farce *Forrobodó* takes place in a *gafieira* of a Rio de Janeiro slum called Cidade Nova (formerly called Mangue). The plot deals with the prosaic subjects of chicken stealing and reveling at a *gafieira* called "Grêmio Recreativo Familiar Dançante Flor do Castigo do Corpo da Cidade Nova" [New City's Body-Punishment Flower Dancing and Recreative Family Guild]. The characters–a watchman, a rascal, a vain mulatto woman, a mulatto man turned poet, a Portuguese man, a journalist addressed as a man of significance, and another mulatto man who is a boastful *capoeira* fighter and his lover, the French Madame Petit-Pois–all enact a fast-moving plot where comic misunderstandings arise out of whims, jealousy, and frightening experiences. However, all these situations are usually saved by the joy of music and dance. Madame Petit-Pois summarizes best this ethos: "Après le Forrobodó. Maintenant je veux la dance. Viens comigue, maxixê" [After the Forrobodó, I want to go dancing. Come dance with me].

Throughout the 1920s and 1930s, the comedies of manners in Brazil had the purpose of nationalizing the French formula of the previous century. The stage setting was restricted to a dining room, a boarding house, or a private house; therefore, characters tended to group themselves around a family. Gastão Tojeiro (1880–1965), Oduvaldo Viana (1892–1972) and Armando Gonzaga (1889–1954) are the names of the playwrights who could exploit a single formula with a number of variations and were successful at it. In the play *Onde canta o sabiá* [1921; Where the Sabiá Bird Sings], both the routine and unexpected aspects of a suburban family's everyday life depend on the train's arrivals and departures as well as on an itinerant horse circus. Problems arise with the characters who have not been included in the family group: A jobless single man; an unemployed girl looking for a husband and being pursued by a passionate train station guard; a couple of married servants who comment upon the house's petty intrigues; and an unexpected guest–a Brazilian man very critical of the country's situation, who becomes a convinced nationalist thanks to the love of his woman, Nair. Far from the city–although influenced by it–the family defends itself against the antinationalist assault and the disruptions of love intrigues with the song of the sabiá bird, which becomes an allegory of Brazilianness and of domestic prosperity. The stage looks outward from the home to the outside world (the garden, the train station, the circus). It is constantly traversed by the in-and-out movements of the characters, thus offering a theatrical model of transition different from the common one of revues and musical farces (especially through the inclusion of songs in the comedy of manners). Because this play opened at the Trianon Theater, "it became known as the 'Trianon' genre" (Cafezeiro and Gadelha 347). It has several type-characters: The servants, the train guard who leaves his post in order to see his lover, the father who tries to get a civil service job for his nephew. The concentration of comic effects in one single character—what will distinguish the "actor dramaturgy"—had not yet developed (Magaldi *Panorama* 173).

This expression, *actor dramaturgy,* applies to those texts built around a single comic role that is larger than the rest. Invariably, the set does not go beyond representing a dining room, and the single important role is usually destined for a particular actor, the company owner. The organization of the text does not leave any doubt as to who is the star and, even more importantly, who is allowed to improvise. Literary historians condemned this dramatic format because, in their opinion, it delayed the appearance of the professional director on the Brazilian theatrical scene, a figure whose function was to guarantee a much more unified perspective to the performance. Thus it is that the comic protagonist (played by Leopoldo Fróes, Jaime Costa, and Procópio Ferreira) became the core of national theater (Prado 1988, 21). The prompter also became significant; new plays opened almost weekly, and therefore actors could neither rehearse nor learn their lines in a proficient way. Thus, the prompter became the lifeguard of the cast, and, facing the free disorder of improvisation, he constantly struggled to recover the text. The prompter's responsibility was, then, to ensure the smooth operation of the spectacle because he was also in charge of "organizing the lights and the curtains, as well as the sounds" (Brandão 1996, 12).

Besides the first central comic actors, there was also a mass of character actors who "tried to diversify their roles in their physical aspects by (inadequately) wearing wigs, which often ended up hanging from the side of the head; using false moustaches; and coarsely painting wrinkles on their faces. They made people laugh; the audience was won over by the unvarying regularity of their performances and by the ease with which they transformed their voices or their countenance" (Prado 1988, 21). These roles are part of a dramatic genre in which there were many characters involved in plots related to winning the favors of the powerful in order to obtain a job, an inheritance, or the love of a woman. Armando Gonzaga (*Ministro do Supremo* [1921; Minister of the Supreme Court]; *Cala a boca* [1925; Shut Your Mouth]) was an expert in this kind of plot, where one could find the most humble figures, such as servants, hired hands, and ingenues, both witty and meddlesome but with the best speeches and great opportunity to put into practice their comic repertoire of catch-phrases, gestures, and tics.

The comedy of manners dominated for three decades (1920s, 1930s, and 1940s), renewing itself thanks to the speed with which new productions were staged and the constant change of the teams of writers. Among them, Raimundo Magalhães Júnior (1907–1982) attained a great success by writing for Procópio Ferreira the play entitled *Essa mulher é minha* [1950; That Woman is Mine], an anachronistic survivor of the genre that managed to have over two hundred performances, was staged several times, and was transformed into a film. This was during a period in which the Companhia Vera Cruz had hopes of developing a modern cultural industry through certain playwrights who had become experts in writing for mass audiences. With only a few characters—a couple of devout spinsters, a brother with a double life, his lover, an employee who works in the family's butcher shop, and their

father, all immersed in the morality of a small town—the play succeeded thanks to the personality of Procópio Ferreira, who transformed an ugly and uncomely character into a romantic lover.

In the 1950s the comedy of manners seemed to lose ground against serious foreign drama and the modern dramaturgy of Nelson Rodrigues, Jorge Andrade (1922–1984), and the young playwrights of São Paulo's Teatro de Arena [Sand Theater]. In Rio de Janeiro, the movie theater area, called Cinelândia, and the theaters of Tiradentes Square were on the decline; thus, the genre had to reinvent itself in the southern districts of the city in very small theaters. So the comedy of manners persisted throughout the 1950s. Life in Rio was miniaturized, and humor penetrated the intimacy of the "small urban burgeois, of elegant habits" (Sampaio, qtd. in Dória 138). With his *Triologia do Herói Grotesco (A Inconveniência de ser Esposa; Da Necessidade de ser Polígamo; A Garçonière de meu Marido)* [Trilogy of the Grotesque Husband: The Inconvenience of Being a Wife; Of the Necessity of Being Polygamous; My Husband's Bachelor Flat], José da Silveira Sampaio's (1914–1964) dramaturgy offers simple roles and witty dialogue, always under his controlling presence on the stage in the roles of author, director, and actor. The trilogy was first presented in the Teatrinho Intimo do Leme [Leme's Intimate Little Theater] and then in the Teatro de Bolso [Pocket Theater], located in General Osório Square in the Ipanema area. One single intent unites the trilogy: "compõe-se o jogo da elegante permissividade dos enganados e enganadores" (Sampaio 5) [to offer a satire of those men and women who like to deceive others but hate being deceived]. In *A Inconveniência,* two friends find out that their respective wife and husband are having an affair. They decide to reverse the game, acting as if they had not been deceived but, quite the contrary, were the first ones to cheat on their respective spouses. The other plays turn the betrayal around until it becomes institutional. In *Da Necessidade,* a character named Petúnio creates, as an experiment, a polygamous group, whereas in *A Garçonière,* the husband gets confused when he realizes that his wife has become his lover, whom he meets every day in his bachelor's flat. In these simple but witty plots, Silveira Sampaio identifies the same kind of mixture to be found in "the nonsense of the Marx Brothers, French comedy, farce, and even the circus" (Doria 138). Caricature mingles with elements of psychological therapy, thus deforming characters and situations "occasionally streaked with expressionism" (Dória 138).

Contrary to the revues, which "overshadowed private elements in relation to the splendour of another character—public space" (Sussekind 1986, 39), Sampaio's pocket theater valued the internal spaces of the apartments located in Rio's southern area. Portraying few characters, four at most, his plays deal with the elegant permissiveness of deceivers and deceived, minimalizing the role of comedy to "apenas um roteiro para o espetáculo" (Sampaio 5) [merely an itinerary for the show]. Caricature here depends on plot and character, not on the classical comedy of manners. Working within such scanty dimensions, his resources consisted of occupying the stage for as little as possible and with only the absolutely necessary elements: "side panels were used for scenery in order to offer an idea of depth. All of this was well served by a careful use of lighting" (Dória 132). This minimalist harmony highlighted the presence of actor Silveira Sampaio, whose performances were marked by all kinds of exaggerated gestures using "the whole body of the performer, whose legs, arms, head, express themselves without restraint" (Dória 133) and making full use of the example of movie comedians such as Bob Hope and Jerry Lewis. Tall, thin, and with a small moustache, Sampaio filled the stage; there were other actors too, of course, elegantly and nostalgically dressed (Oliveira, quoted in *REDE* 34). Silveira Sampaio performed in order to conquer the audience, just as some authors wrote in the 1960s to conquer their readers: Think of Nelson Rodrigues in his journalistic short-story column, *A vida como ela é* [Life As It Is], and Stanislau Ponte Preta in his stories. For these three, the illusion of fidelity and the reality of unfaithful desire find their tragic and comic forms in the chronicles of everyday life in Rio de Janeiro.

Building a Modern Dramaturgy

From the Chanchada to the Brazilian Comedy Theater

The metamorphoses suffered by the comedy of manners went hand in hand with the transformations of Brazil's capital, Rio de Janeiro, as places of entertainment moved from the central area to the southern districts of the city. One of the consequences of this dislocation can be seen in the work of Silveira Sampaio, which focused on the destabilization of traditional married life and thereby addressed more general changes taking place in the patriarchal morality of Brazil; these social changes by and large corresponded to the concerns of a part of Rio's middle-class population for whom this process of change was most evident. Just as before, Brazilian comedy seemed to respond to both the introduction of new habits of everyday life and to the adaptation of the scenic arts to a new distribution of urban space. From this perspective, there was a sense of continuity in the transformation of certain comic genres and of the kind of theater concerned with the box office and the modernization of Rio de Janeiro. This process—already mentioned by Flora Sussekind in relation to the revues of Artur Azevedo (Sussekind 1977, 59)—also appears in the shows staged by the Jardel Jércolis company, called the Tro-ló-ló Company, as well as in the work of Walter Pinto (1913–1994) during the 1940s and 1950s; this was the modernizing period of Brazilian cultural life.

The success of these companies guaranteed the continuity of a theatrical tradition based on certain genres, such as the revue and the *chanchada* (a minor theatrical play whose aim is to produce laughter), or other less prestigious ones, such as the comedy of manners. Thus, Brazil saw the development of many new forms linked to these comic genres, whose protagonists were characterized by their virtuosity in improvisation, their skill in characterizing types, their contagious histrionic abilities, and their versatility in facial and bodily expression. Among the most brilliant actors with the longest careers are Dercy Gonçalves, Oscarito, and Grande Otelo; it is not a coincidence that the three shared an early formative training in the circus. The role of local mannerisms of speech was minimized in variety shows; instead, an outline of the scenes indicated the concern for articulating the text as spectacle (choreography of the dances, actor prompting, quick paced music, rapid-change scenography, and lighting—all fundamental aspects of Walter Pinto's company). The *chanchada* shows were based on parodying renowned plays. In spite of the possible clichés that could emerge from deconstructing the original texts, the symbolic significance of irreverently appropriating canonized works—which in themselves represented European cultural hegemony—contributed to the critical evaluation of the cultural canon in the 1960s. José Celso Martinez Correa was one of the spokesmen for this process of recovering the "cannibalistic"

nature of the *chanchada*, which was usually described as "rubbish." The pejorative term "chanchada" has its origins in the underworld slang of the River Plate region (31).

A successful play by Nelson Rodrigues, *Vestido de Noiva* [Wedding Dress], which opened in December 1943 and was recognized as a model of the innovative tendencies of Brazilian theater, actually became a matter of controversy among theater experts. On the one hand, some discussed the role to be played by the state in promoting theatrical activities: Many actor-managers considered that direct state intervention in financing the theater was detrimental, since it eliminated the box-office control exerted by the audience. On the other hand, some figures who were authoritative in forming public opinion condemned the technical backwardness of Brazilian theater reflected in the poor quality of stage productions and in the fact that, even in the 1940s, directors were not a common feature. Those who argued for the modernization of Brazilian theater considered that the absence of the director was a major issue because up to that point professional companies were dominated by the figure of the actor-manager, who promoted an attitude of self-promotion that badly affected the production of the play: The main actor tended to look for opportunities to upstage the cast and in general eliminate elements that could eclipse him. The gradual transformation of Brazilian drama in the search for an international standard was accompanied by an underlying concern for the purported nonexistence of an acceptable national theater.

This issue brought to the surface once again the question of the relationship between Brazilian dramaturgy and European culture. European directors exiled in Brazil during World War II gave Franco Zampari the opportunity to begin a process of theatrical modernization that, based on European cultural patterns, had two main venues: The Vera Cruz Movie Company and the Brazilian Comedy Theater. The incursion into the film business was a short one, but the stage company seriously influenced the patterns of artistic taste of audiences by training actors in the canonical traditions of European theater and by employing technical and mechanical devices in the sets that were unknown in the country up to that time. Among the foreign set designers who worked for the company were Aldo Calvo, Bassano Vaccarini, Túlio Costa, Gianni Ratto, and Mauro Francini. This foreign influence was later condemned in some artistic and cultural sectors as a diminishment of authentic Brazilian theater and as the cause of both its alienation from popular taste and the lack of communication with the kind of diversified audiences that had filled the variety shows—which, during the Vargas regime (1930–1945), included everyone from the President to the lower middle classes.

The Brazilian Comedy Theater, founded by business mogul Franco Zampari in 1948, was organized around a modernization proposal that imported European values. According to critic Sábato Magaldi: "The formula for having new patrons was simple: São Paulo's cosmopolitan outlook demanded the same kind of theatrical productions as those found in Paris, London, or New York" (Magaldi, *Panorama* 195). The consequences of this procedure were obvious: "Once foreign set designers, expressly hired abroad, took part in the setting, the idea was established of placing a stage experience intended for Paris before an avid São Paulo audience. . . . A play only needed to be successful in Paris or New York for it to be staged by the Brazilian Comedy Theater" (Magaldi, *Panorama* 195). Sometimes the cast did not even manage to read the original script (Magaldi, *Panorama* 177). Abílio Pereira de Almeida (1906–1977) was, in fact, the only playwright who definitely followed the lead of the audiences and the popular taste the audiences were looking after. The degree of influence exerted by the Brazilian Comedy Theater in forming professional actors and shaping the outlook of a bourgeois, middle-class audience–initially in São Paulo and later in Rio de Janeiro, the two cities that centralized the theatrical activities of the country in that period–can be measured by the success of renowned actors who performed in those two cities during the 1950s as well as by the prestige of certain theater companies that began there, such as the Nydia Lícia-Sérgio Cardoso Company, the Tônia-Celi-Autran Company, the Cacilda Becker Theater, and the Seven Theater–groups that established a refined professional practice by alternating the staging of clearly commercial plays with that of significant original works.

A Dramaturgy in Crisis

Nelson Rodrigues and Jorge Andrade are recognized by theater critics and historians as the great names in modern Brazilian drama. Another name that can be added to the list is that of Oswald de Andrade, who is responsible for one of the highlights of the 1960s with his 1967 staging of *O Rei da Vela* [The Candle King], directed by José Celso Martinez Correa, but who is considered by such a renowned critic as Sábato Magaldi (*Panorama* 190) as a kind of wasted dramatic talent. One of the little explored aspects of Oswald de Andrade's dramatic works, and one that helps to explain their permanence on the stage for decades, is the way in which his plays incorporated popular staging traditions into the representation of political and philosophical issues. This combination was not really acceptable within the narrow confines of Brazilian theater, which instead promoted guidelines on such issues as the rigid distinction between "serious theater" and "theater for a laugh" and the exclusion of grotesque elements and verbal or gestural violence from serious drama. This conservative feature paralleled the predominance of a patriarchal outlook in Brazilian society, which successfully protected itself from the threats posed by any kind of defiant attitude, above all coming from the world of show business; this was a society that could hardly stand the attacks against the family structure in the works of Oswald de Andrade. Even in the late 1960s, when there was a loosening of restrictions, the staging of one of his plays was viciously received, and some of the offended critics attributed the radical nature of the performance to the fact that the director José Celso Martinez Correa had distorted it (Pereira 177).

These three playwrights share the experience of having some of their plays banned and censored during the military regime because of their critical and defiant nature; but they also share a complex self-awareness of their own dramaturgy and of its possibilities in Brazil. These authors occupied a singular position among the intellectual elite of a country in which the theater was granted minimal conditions for survival, conditions that fluctuated between state censorship (and a consequent bargaining over resources) and the appeal of the market, which often led to immediate and unscrupulous profit-taking. Both the instability of the business and the episodic nature of its successes multiplied the difficulties in trying to maintain and develop Brazilian theater. The pressure to adapt plays to different kinds of audience was at times irresistible. This is perhaps the reason why these playwrights needed

to question the very nature and purpose of their theater, an attitude that modified the structure of their plays.

Jorge Andrade's metadramaturgy takes the form of an argumentation on the conditions needed to develop theatrical activities in the country. In the plays *Rasto atrás* [1965; Traces Left Behind] and *Sumidouro* [The Sewer]–written shortly after the 1964 military coup–this issue is related to a search for emotional integrity and financial resources, whereas in *As confrarias* [1968; The Guilds] the possibility of physical survival and of actually staging a play within the context of violent social repression is explored using the figure of an eighteenth-century actor. In this last play–which was the first included by Andrade in an anthology of his works, entitled *Marta, a árvore e o relógio* [1970; Martha, the Tree and the Watch]–the actor's social status seems to be symbolically determined by the decrepit and destitute condition of the social environment in which he appears. In this play actors are portrayed as mulattos, with no social standing, and placed in a liminal situation between blacks and whites, who were divided into powerful guilds. A sense of conflict is evident in the fact that José, the protagonist, does not see himself as someone of mixed race: "Meus olhos, meus cabelos, minhas feições diziam que eu era uma coisa; meu trabalho afirmava que era outra" (49) [My eyes, my hair, my features told me I was one thing; my job stated that I was something else]. This contradiction shows how difficult it was to determine both his social status as an actor and the roles that could be ascribed to it. This anomalous situation emerges recurrently in Andrade's works and has some autobiographical elements: He came from São Paulo's social aristocracy but was placed into a marginal position as an intellectual and a writer. At some points, the character's way of speaking offers a compensatory facet as a kind of romantic notion of the artist as an outcast. Aspects such as an awareness of a fragmented personality, a sense of uncertainty regarding social status, and an individual's realization that he or she can respond to the needs and yearnings of others around him or her are usually interlinked, as can be seen in the words of Marta, a spokeswoman in *As Confrarias*: "Quem consegue sentir os outros, se não os que vivem divididos em mil pedaços! Ele tinha muito de pardo. Daqueles que são estrangeiros em sua própia casa" (48) ("Who, if anyone, can sympathize with others better than those who are divided into thousands of fragments? He had many mulatto features. He was one of those persons who are foreigners in their own house").

Even in works that are not overtly autobiographical the issue of a loss of identity appears in several plots and in the way many protagonists are characterized. Some of Andrade's early plays, such as *O Telescópio* [1960; The Telescope] and *A Moratória* [1955; The Moratorium], focus on the decadence of the rural aristocracy of São Paulo during the coffee crisis. Andrade's solidarity with the representatives of the patriarchal order is a marked feature of his work, even when he introduces a character like the *bandeirante*–a person who went inland to search for mines or to enslave Indians. He compares Fernão Dias Pais's unrestrained search for emeralds with the existential struggle of an artist searching for his own identity in *Sumidouro*. The epic device of simultaneously superimposing characters from different periods serves as a form of continual commentary on the action. This temporal unfolding–which was identified ever since the success of *A Moratória* as a legacy of Nelson Rodrigues's innovations in Brazilian theater–offered Andrade the possibility both of exploring the nature of the hero and of passing a detached judgment upon all the characters, especially Fernão Dias. This character is an "alter ego" of the playwright but, unlike the latter, is aware neither of the historic process he is living in nor of the way it is going to end; his innocence is linked to an existential path whose meaning he cannot perceive. The playwright thus becomes an instance of truth for the historical character, who in turn becomes an existential allegory. The playwright's certainties turn him into a psychoanalyst of sorts, who interprets each episode of the saga, always stating that his authority emerges from a process of self-knowledge. This play is clearly related to Andrade's previous work *Rasto Atrás*, where the dramatist-character discovered the core of his identity both in the existential journey toward his past and in the process by which he came to terms with his father's image (Andrade 586).

In spite of the fact that Andrade introduces female characters of the lower classes into his last plays, *Confrarias* and *Sumidouro*, his symbolic commitment with the patriarchal order of society far exceeds such circumstantial details. Studies have pointed out that the concept of the subject that sustains and guarantees the predominance of that social order can be identified with the notion of an ego looking for its undivided essence. Jorge Andrade's dramaturgical project reveals a search for a purported source from which subjective conflicts emerge. Psychoanalysis has established the form of this classical lyricism of Chekhov (Szondi 20); so too is it useful in understanding the direction taken in the dramatic works of Jorge Andrade. The process of psychic unveiling results in the discovery of a nucleus related to an Oedipus-like set of problems. The dramatist-character acquires a wisdom based on overcoming the existential knot that constituted the struggle with the father figure and is thus allowed to lead the rest of the characters in their process of self-revelation. The narrator who offers this epic association operates much more like a psychoanalyst, a role that would be well known to the educated audiences to whom Andrade's plays were addressed, audiences who would also identify this kind of experience in films, books, or in their frequent visits to the increasing number of therapeutic couches of the 1950s. Borch-Jacobsen's (68) theoretical observation regarding the role of psychoanalysis in helping the ego to emerge strengthened is thus enacted in Andrade's plays, which answered the demands of an educated audience and brought Brazilian drama up to the international standards of psychological realism developed in the United States by Eugene O'Neill (1888–1953).

The link between Nelson Rodrigues's drama and psychoanalysis goes in a different direction; the same is true of his use of epic devices, more abundantly and variously employed than in Andrade's work. Even in his first play, *A Mulher Sem Pecado* [The Woman without Sin], which opened in 1942, the staging of attitudes related to jealousy has much to do with the psychological concerns that were in vogue among the intellectual circles of the period; however, the unusual ways of speaking of the characters and the daring construction of the plot dislocate the play from the axis of this kind of psychological realism. The psychological unfolding of Lídia, which emerges from the suggestions of Olegário, her jealous husband, constitutes a surprising discovery that offers a glimpse of Rodrigues's future work, characterized by the recurrent use of construction and deconstruction in games of conflicting subjectivities.

His second play, *Vestido de Noiva*, which made him famous, also had as point of departure a kind of psychological unfolding. Alaíde, the wife who follows the bourgeois conventions of the family, had been fascinated since childhood by Madame

Clessi, the prostitute. Alaíde's close encounter with death helps her to gain an understanding of her life. As in Andrade's work, the prostitute's presence acts as a dramatic device that assumes a psychoanalytic function by means of which episodes from the protagonist's life are presented and interpreted. Critical distance is also made possible by the temporal distance that exists between the two characters. In the same way that the ironic presentation of certain episodes in *A Mulher Sem Pecado* establishes a critical psychological dimension, so in *Vestido de Noiva* there is a deconstruction of such discourse by means of stage devices linked to psychoanalytical practices. For instance, the reliability of the character who is analyzing the lived images is questionable because it is presented like a carnivalized unfolding of the existential dissatisfaction. It could be argued that the same process takes place with Fernão Dias in *Sumidouro*, however, in Andrade's play the interpreter's discourse is granted a significant superiority and authority. In *Vestido de Noiva* there is a predominance of a polyphonic encounter between the perspectives derived from two symbolic spaces that are generally opposed in the existential experience of the middle classes: That of the family and that of prostitution. Even though the figure of the prostitute is presented as the desired inversion of the norms of domestic universe, it is also submitted to a corrosively ironic treatment. This is what happens in all the situations involving Madame Clessi's affair with a schoolboy, who ends up stabbing her to death because she refused to go to a picnic in Paquetá. The possibility of getting at the truth does not exist, a situation that becomes evident at the play's ending, a purely theatrical event that follows after the death of Alaíde. She hands the wedding bouquet to her sister Lúcia, and it is as if this act is symbolic both of triumph over the patriarchal order and of submission to it; this action announced not only the recognition of her banishment from the family but also the transmission to others of her sense of a story that is so characteristic of the feminine universe.

From a theater semiotics perspective, Fred Clark (21) has stated that "Nelson Rodrigues's plays distort old forms (such as naturalist drama or melodrama) by incorporating certain non-dramatic elements (films, fiction, journalism) in order to achieve innovative and provocative dramatic texts." Quoting Sábato Magaldi, Clark (101) also identifies the cinema as a clear source for the innovations introduced by Rodrigues. Magaldi's observations lead to a reflection upon the phenomena linked to gradual transformation of dramatic elements into epic ones, a transformation that Szondi (22) has defined as a recurrent element in modern theater. Nelson Rodrigues's appropriation of cinematographic techniques, as well as the fact that he had managed to make certain intellectual sectors of the audience sensitive to deeper psychological conflict, seem to imply that some radical transformations were taking place in theater culture, rather than showing any lack of knowledge of theatrical traditions on the part of the dramatist. Rodrigues looked for new expressive resources in order to overcome the difficulties of traditional drama in responding to new aesthetic issues, new forms of perception, and new subjectivities that emerged along with the development of the mass media at the end of the nineteenth century. How can it be forgotten that this process became more intense in Brazil precisely in the 1940s? (see Ortiz 1985.) The new modes of staging were developed not only because of new technical devices but also, and primarily, because they expressed a number of transformations in cinema, above all in what Gilles Deleuze (86) defined as visibilities, following Michel Foucault.

In any case, the presence and significance of epic devices in Nelson Rodrigues's dramaturgy seem to be much more related to a discussion on the limits of drama–which reflects a concern for the nature of language and its implications in human life–than to the search, as is the case with Andrade, for an autobiographical explanation or some kind of historic process that can be clearly defined. In the plays that followed *Vestido de Noiva*–which are considered by Sábato Magaldi as representative of "the search for the primitive unconscious, for archetypes, for ancestral myths, which had begun in *Álbum de Família* [1945; Family Album]– the appropriation of some elements characteristic of Greek tragedy works much more like a 'cliché-zation' of the genre" (1987, 15). Ângela Leite Lopes explains this process by stating that the dramatist captures the "tragic clichés in building his tragedies" (94). She asks: "Which are those clichés? The notions of fate, fatality, curse, vengeance; elements such as the chorus; a certain atmosphere. He will also revisit certain subjects such as incest or infanticide" (94). The increase in (and intensification of) these clichés is part of the driving force of this playwright's dramaturgy.

In *Álbum de Família*, the pathos created by certain elements–like the screams of a woman in childbirth which accompany the action, or the dialogue with its extreme aggression directed at hypersexuality–is only moderately toned down by the initial presentation of each of the scenes by means of a distancing device that urges the audience to consider a critical and ironic reading. Each scene is preceded by the display of an album's page, in which members of the family are described in an edifying speech by a "speaker," who points them out as examples of the respect shown to moral values. In the first stage directions, the playwright includes a "Nota Importante" ("Note of Interest") in which he explains: "O mencionado 'speaker,' além do mau gosto hediondo dos comentários, prima por oferecer informações erradas sobre a família" (521) ("Apart from the stinking bad taste of his comments, the abovementioned 'speaker' struggles hard to offer mistaken information about the family"). He adds: "O 'speaker' é uma espécie de 'opinião pública'" (521) ("The 'speaker' is a 'public opinion' of sorts"). In a sense, the use of these metadramatic devices in Rodrigues's theater anticipated the epic perspective that would be developed in the 1960s by Augusto Boal (b. 1931), leader of the Arena group, with the "Coringa System" (Prado 1987, 75).

Even in what is considered the first stage of Rodrigues's dramatic production, the notion of "public opinion" reveals itself as a major plot factor. In *Senhora dos Afogados* [1947; Lady of the Drowned] the action is counterpointed by a "chorus of neighbors," which makes observations and comments about the events but does not usually interact with the protagonists. After the success of *A Falecida* [1953; The Dead Woman]–a play in which he incorporates some characteristic features of Rio's life, something that he had been doing in his role as journalist/chronicler–two 1960 plays stand out by the way in which he explores the relationship between "public opinion" and the everyday life of the characters: *Bouca de Ouro* [Golden Mouth] and *Beijo no Asfalto* [Kiss on the Asphalt Road]. Both plays deal with situations in which the author can explore the formation of collective perceptions over the individual, as well as the role of the press in this process. In *Boca de Ouro*, which is closer to farce, the plot is quite schematic, built on the different versions given by D. Guigui, lover of a famous Madureira lottery seller, of the legends surrounding this

famous figure. In *Beijo no Asfalto*, the gratuitous act of a married man–who kisses a dying, recently run-over man on the mouth and is surprised by a corrupt reporter–becomes a nightmare that will completely ruin his life.

Perhaps one of the reasons why the plays of Nelson Rodrigues were so well received by audiences was his overall concern with concealing and revealing the secrets of human privacy, a subject that becomes an organizing element of his works and with which he responds to what Jean Baudrillard (28) identifies as the generalized "obscenity" of contemporary culture. Nelson Rodrigues seduced his audiences by ritualizing the unmasking of the most surprising aberrations within overtly conservative social environments (for instance, in rural areas in his first tragedies or Rio's suburbs in his later work). At the same time, his work explores the ways of perceiving and interpreting extreme situations, as well as questioning the discourses that characterize them. The play between "voyeurism" and the disappointment that follows, either when the truthfulness of the situation is questioned or else when the meaning of the episode is being discussed, is highlighted by certain dramatic devices, such as the intervention of an external point of view within the dramatic narrative, a device that–as Fred Clark (27) has pointed out–is quite significant in *A Falecida*. The internal observer's viewpoint is not absolute since it invites the audience to deconstruct the scene in order to recognize the devices with which it was built. The metadrama that takes place here is not an aestheticist project because, by seducing the audience to project itself into the action, the dramatist actually confronts it with the paradoxes inherent in the action staged and the ways of staging it.

The significance of Rodrigues's dramaturgy is not restricted to the fact that it contributed to the renewal of "serious drama" during the 1940s and 1950s. Rodrigues's success–not only in drama but also in the theatrical conceptualization revealed in his chronicles and his fiction as well–is reflected not only in his constant popularity among a wide audience but also in the fact that his work has not lost its force with time. The incorporation of certain technical devices and themes into Brazilian drama was certainly the result of a dialogue in which the author and the author's works could converse with the mass media. The complex and tight relationships between Rodrigues's work and the issue of obscenity, the critical incorporation of psychoanalysis, and the constant reprocessing of influential models and discourses all situate this author as a point of departure from which, even today, important controversies can take place, such as the crisis between the private and public spheres or the mechanisms of constructing subjectivity in Brazilian society.

Rebellion, Defiance, and Tyranny of the Self: Dramaturgies at the Turn of the 1970s

The transition between the 1960s and the 1970s was characterized by an increasingly strong censorship that had been imposed by the different states in a decentralized way since the 1964 military coup but in 1967 was concentrated in Brasília. In the new capital, censorship was tightened by means of the 1968 Fifth Institutional Act, which became the instrument to oversee cultural and artistic activities. According to one of the most important critics of the period, "censorship, either official censorship or self-censorship, became the protagonist of the national stage" (Michalski 33). Censorship was merciless toward the theater, cutting up whole parts of plays, banning complete works, and closing recently opened shows.

When the artist Maria Fernanda and the producer of Tennessee Williams's *A Streetcar Named Desire* received a thirty-day suspension and the play was banned, members of the other companies in Rio de Janeiro and São Paulo went on strike, and the most important figures of Brazilian theater held vigils on the front steps of the Municipal Theaters in both cities. As a result of the movement, the government was forced to offer a proposed law on censorship and to promise that it would stop interfering with the theater (Michalski 34). However, as Ian Michalski's chronicle reveals, the military president, General Costa e Silva, denied the very promises made by the government when he appeared on television in order to "indignantly comment on 'the immorality' of the play *Santidade* [Sanctity], written by José Vicente (b. 1945), and which has just been banned"; this opened the way to a wide slander campaign against the theater, a campaign which "insisted upon the 'immorality' of the shows and the number of four-letter words uttered on the stage" (Michalski 34).

Both José Vicente, the writer who provoked the General's anger, and Plínio Marcos (b. 1935), a polemical and successful novel playwright, went through the two decades writing plays that were the target of censorship because of their transgressive nature. Both, however, managed to maintain an independence from various larger aesthetic projects: The political theater of the group called Teatro de Arena de São Paulo, represented by Gianfrancesco Guarnieri (b. 1934) (*Eles não usam black-tie* [1958; They Do Not Wear Tuxedos]) and Augusto Boal (b. 1931) (*Revolução na América do Sul* [1960; Revolution in South America]), or the resistance theater represented by literary musicals (*Opinião* [1964; Opinion] and *Liberdade, Liberdade* [1965; Liberty, Liberty]) or historic musicals (*Arena conta Zumbi* [1965; Zumbi's Life According to Arena] and *Arena conta Tiradentes* [c1967; Tiradentes's Life According to Arena]) (Michalski 23). A third author, Oduvaldo Viana Filho (1936–1974), also called Vianinha, took part in the heroic struggle of the political drama of the Arena group but then went back to more traditional dramatic forms in the 1970s in order to explore the type of violence against personal and collective freedom during times of political and military repression and thus probe into the reality of social alienation. According to historian Décio de Almeida Prado, "with the almost simultaneous disappearance of the *Teatro de Arena* and the *Teatro Oficina*, which took place around 1972, a historical cycle came to an end" (Prado 1987, 119).

The plays of these three authors, José Vicente, Plínio Marcos, and Vaininha, differ from the mature works of Nelson Rodrigues in that they reinvented a genre that, from the turn of the century, focused on the "overcoming of the dialectic of interpersonal relations—continuously achieved and continuously destroyed by means of dialogue" (Szondi 22). Plínio Marcos's plays are notable for the hyperrealism of their dialogue, which turns into an aggressively corporeal form of contact between the characters. José Vicente explores the subjective depths of the characters' speech—which lead to religious confessions of evil. Vianinha goes back to a more rigorous form of drama by using self-reflective devices to bring out repressed violence. Even though they are quite different, the three authors all synthesize two theatrical tendencies from the 1960s that continued to the 1970s: The "aesthetics of the word" and the "theater of aggression" (Brandão 1983, 15).

In 1966, Plínio Marcos premiered *Dois Perdidos numa Noite Suja* [Two Lost in a Dirty Night], which was very successful in Rio over the next year. It tells about two characters who share poverty and solitude: They are unemployed and live on the sporadic money they receive as market porters. One of them migrated from the countryside and dreams of returning to a normal life and a steady job. The other is an outcast who has long been marginalized and has undergone a brutalizing experience of survival on the fringes of society. The cruelty society has shown toward them is replicated in their relationship, which is marked by hostile dialogue—"from slight jeers, passing through insults, derision, and scheming" (Prado 1988, 153). The aggressiveness of their speech—described by Ian Michalski as typical of "Brazilian popular slang, and showing a sense of authenticity that only Nelson Rodrigues had been able to articulate up to then" (32)—gradually turns into physical violence, and the play ends in theft and murder. Unlike the effect in naturalist drama, the dialogue here makes only indirect reference to a meager and harsh reality: The characters have no family, no social class or any kind of group that might give them traces of identity and offer some parameters of justice; this is the most basic struggle to retain some semblance of human existence. Facing each other, the two characters fight for the only available sign of dignity: A pair of decent shoes. Imprisoned by the dialogue's tension—and not by any pressure of social forces, such as a boss, company, or money—their rebellion is both diffuse and yet addressed to the other person. Thus, the power relations that prevail in society are either consolidated or inverted: The best is exploited by the worst; the strongest is exploited by the weakest (Prado 1988, 153). Their bodies are mouths that spit out slang and four-letter words; they also become the setting for the vilest human degradation.

The first play written by Plínio Marcos was compared by critics to Albee's *Zoo Story* and Beckett's *Waiting for Godot*, whereas the second, *Navalha na Carne* [1968; Razor Blade in the Flesh] was compared more to the Sartrean universe of *Huis-Clos*, a life absolutely deglamorized. Neusa Suely the whore, Wado the pimp, and Veludo the homosexual each creates his or her own hell. Aggression takes over the stage by means of the cruelty of words and physical force, thus giving shape to the only kind of communication available among the characters. Their portrayal as victims is derived from certain economic relationships epitomized in sexual activity. However, at the same time that they submit their bodies in exchange for survival, they do not withdraw from the little bit of pleasure they experience, and this is what in the end moves and humanizes them. Their identities lie precisely in this mixture of wretchedness and sexual redemption. Consequently, while operating within a direct mode of theatricality and a naturalistically threatening kind of realism, the dialogue leaves a margin for whatever can be found beyond this threatening plane. If there is obscenity expressed in "a drastic language" that "underlines and lays bare erotic relationships, and thus reduces them to the mere physical process" (Rosenfeld 146), then the dialogue, as a whole, points to a "dramatic transparency" that diverges from the audible and visible obscenity: "the ability to reveal the thought that cannot be uttered by speech" (Prado 1988, 218). Beyond the cruel and vengeful insults, one can sense the helplessness of aging, the lyricism of love, and an unrestricted sexual attraction born out of violence.

In *O Assalto* [1969; The Assault], the second play written by José Vicente, whose *Santidade* had been banned, the dialogue enacts with the same clash between characters but ends up being transformed into a pretext for lyrical expression; people are humanized by the desire for self-discovery and an intense communication with the audience. After work, a clerk and a floor cleaner face each other on the premises of a bank. On the surface, the plot deals simply with the issue of the oppression of the individual by the inhuman machinery of a capitalist company; however, according to Michalski, it goes further by mixing a variety of registers: "Starting from a simple naturalist staging of a bitter reality, José Vicente projects his play towards the grounds of existential relief and mystical exorcism" (quoted in Andrade 57). Even in his first play, *Santidade*, the issue of giving vent to feelings and the subject of mystical transcendence were already present. Labeled by the author himself as a "terrible" play, it deals with a former seminarist who discloses to his brother–himself about to take holy orders–the truth about his homosexuality and how he lives off a rich merchant. At the same time, this revelation acts as both an occasion for indignant derision against normal social rules and a vehicle to spread the belief that sex, practiced as prostitution, reveals the face of God.

In the case of *O Assalto*, the very title of the play becomes meaningful through the process in which Vitor, the clerk, tries to dominate Hugo, the sweeper. Provocative and seducing, Vitor induces the worker to rebel–which will result in a bank robbery, Hugo's sexual surrender, and his immolation. However, the act of assaulting the other involves transference of destructive anxieties: First from Vitor to Hugo and then from Vitor on himself. The process of psychic unfolding is presented as a necessary element of the theatrical dynamics through different forms of monologue. The process, then, is one of an "assault on the inner world," which was, in fact, the title of Sábato Magaldi's review of the play, which also considered another feature of the play: The strong autobiographical element, which at the time was reinforced by the existence of interviews with the playwright himself, introduced as a former bank clerk. Thus, personal experiences acquire an unexpected political nature insofar as the authenticity of both the text and the set–the room becomes a cold trunk (Braga 80) that echoes the confinement of the human form–influences the audience, which is in turn "assaulted" in a shared ritual of feelings and apprehensions resulting from the severity of the dictatorship and lost illusions about social change (Andrade 24). The tyranny of the self in José Vicente's works is thus mitigated through a dramaturgy that counts on communication with the audience and is based upon a form of increasing theatrical intensity so that the play shifts the inquiry toward the inner space of the spectators (Lima, 52). As a result of the impossibility of fighting against the repressive forces, art became generic "because dissatisfaction itself was generic, as if the oppressor lacked both name and history but were just an Oppressor" (Lima 52). Conflict and alienation are terms that disappear from the horizon of those (author, actors, spectators) who approach any artistic activity as a ceremony that permits a utopia, a free realm–"the inner realm of each human being where it is possible to act" (Lima 49).

At the same time that Plínio Marcos and José Vicente were concentrating on certain theatrical conventions–the former through the dissatisfaction aggressively materialized in the crudeness of the mise-en-scène; the latter projecting them upon the spectator through catharsis–Vianinha returned to professional drama "with the political purpose of questioning and enlarging those parameters, both in the sense of the perception of the audience and in the concrete sense of cultivating such an audience" (Damasceno 219), after having worked during the 1960s with the most important groups in Brazilian political theater (Arena, Opinião, CPC). His plays–*A longa noite de Cristal* [1969; Cristal's Long Night], *Corpo a Corpo* [1970; Hand-to-Hand], and *Alegro desbum* [1972; Happy-Go-Lucky]–close the theatrical circle of the two decades. The autobiographical *Rasga Coração* [1974; Tearing the Heart] rescues the power of a citizen's commitment against social injustice and that of the political activism of a militant within a political party. In the first three plays, Vianinha discusses the paths reserved for a left-wing militant intellectual committed to aesthetic projects linked to political utopias when the only alternative is to work for the communications industry. There is a simultaneous alienation from and fascination about the entertainment industry. He lives the contradiction between responsibility, artistic liberty, and marketing co-opting. It is a choice between indifference and annihilation. The three plays explore these three subjects, albeit using completely different dramatic forms. In *Rasga Coração*, the contradiction is enacted through the confrontation between two kinds of political engagement: Activism and protest of the countercultural kind. *A longa noite de Cristal* deals with the career of a television newscaster who becomes successful by unconditionally surrendering to the demands of the entertainment industry. In the end, he loses his friends and tries to commit suicide; he falls from the heights of success and ends up on a night radio program. In *Corpo a Corpo*, a monologue, the protagonist Viváqua experiences a night of rebellion and conflict generated by the possible resignation of a fellow publicist, his mentor and first protector. All through the night he reviews his own life and the way in which he has betrayed his family, his girlfriend, and his convictions; all of these issues come to the surface, destructively, as a result of a series of phone calls to settle accounts. At daybreak, the alert consciousness of the night is replaced by the illusion of being able to reconcile artistic freedom and unjustifiable acts of betrayal. *Alegro Desbum*, closer to farce and *boulevard* comedy, deals with the life of an advertising editor who plunges into the bohemian way of life and leaves behind his job and girlfriend to embrace the countercultural attitude of his times.

By turning to genres such as "existential urban drama" and comedy–the latter, a Brazilian genre with a long history of tradition and success–the playwright wants to create a "theater of connections, rigorous observation, precise images, complexity" (Viana, quoted in Damasceno 223). Vianinha reaffirms the position of a theater that had been obsessed with political reflection. Some unexpected changes in the initial mise-en-scène of *A longa noite de Cristal* resulted in its being interpreted as a moralistic play, one dealing with individual behavior. According to Leslie Damasceno, the characterization of the protagonist ended up turning him into a hero, in spite of the fact that the dialogue was carefully structured in order to generate a sense of both closeness and distance (which left open the possibility that actors could play more than one of the secondary roles) and that the stage offered a multiplicity of open spatial possibilities. Thus, instead of producing a critical challenge to the audience, there was a sense of identification (Damasceno 224). The experience of staging the *Cristal* script was fundamental for the production of *Corpo a Corpo,* which was "written as praxis to explain Vianinha's theoretical endorsement of the defiant dramatic conventions of the early 1970s" (Damasceno 231). The monologue brings to the surface a variety of registers, which include the aggressive speech of Plínio Marcos' characters and José Vicente's cathartic utterances. The single character, Viváqua, confronts disembodied voices in a flat where he makes and receives telephone calls all through one exhausting night. By means of this theatrical device, both the character's narcissistic isolation and the borders of a marginality that imposed the conflict are broken down; what is not broken down, however, is his inability to keep in touch with the people around him. The character's aggressiveness is symbolically divided into figures who act as counterpoints to him; however, he always turns against himself. In the play's preface, entitled "O meu corpo a corpo," Vianinha declares himself to be distant from the theater of aggression, even if he wants to find "the imperious necessity imposed by this theater" (Damasceno 232). Searching for a more emphatic and radical dramaturgy–one that absorbs by negatives–Vianinha began a period of premature maturity (he died in 1974) with the same drive as the other two playwrights, lacerating his own flesh in order to create works that are still capable of moving, thanks to his belief that on the stage the truth can neither be hidden nor silenced.

Against the silence of oblivion, *Rasga Coração* stages forty years of political life in Brazil–the 1935 communist insurrection, the regime of Getulio Vargas and his authoritarian New State, the democratic government, the period of a renewed faith in Brazil started by Juscelino Kubitschek, and the military dictatorship from 1964 to 1974, when the activities of the Brazilian Communist Party (to which the protagonist belongs) turn predominantly to trade union organization. This historical review is filtered by the remembrances of the character Manguari Pistolão, but this does not mean that the play's dramatic core is nostalgia. The historical references are presented in flashbacks that "produce a collage of historic moments which are in turn dramatized as they are lived and perceived by the characters" (Damasceno 254); following the pattern of psychological realism, these distancing flashbacks are generated by the unfolding of a conflict between the militant and his son. Past and present are intermingled in such a way that, starting from the everyday clash between generations, a gradual and painful process of self-criticism takes place inside the militant old man. At the same time, there is a serious reflection on the forms of revolution that take place everyday in social relations. Considered as "a popular anonymous hero" by the character Camargo Moço–one who "integrates the essential meaning of the action and interprets it for us, thus becoming a kind of dramatic link between the play and the audience" (Damasceno 258)–the protagonist embodies a double critical reconciliation with the political history of Brazil and with the role of theater, the place where "os homens se reúnem para contemplar a si mesmos" (Prologue to *Rasga Coração*) ("men come together in order to contemplate themselves").

The Death of the Theater

The gradual opening up that characterized the policies of the military regime in the late 1970s, with the subsequent relaxation and finally deactivation of the censorship mechanisms that prevailed during the dictatorship, gave rise to a certain perplexity. Issues related to the theater demanded new readings in the light of the terrible repression of cultural activities by the regime that came into power in 1964, a repression that reached its highest point in 1968 with the promulgation of the Fifth Institutional Act, the instrument by means of which terror was legalized: It banned any public manifestation that expressed a critical spirit or proposed to analyze the social and economic situation. After this, it was not possible to recover immediately–in the theater or in any other activity. The cultural production had been contaminated by the mechanisms provoked by the military regime–ranging from a simple dismantling of any critical sense to the creation of subterfuges for the transmission of information (as in the metaphors and euphemisms of popular music). There was also an increasing awareness of the fact that some problems faced in the fields of cultural production and diffusion reflected the cruel reality of Brazil's insertion in the modern world and revealed the historical consequences of the country's various historical stages and political models. Yet, the concern with censorship, both by direct police intervention and by more subtle methods, such as restricting production, brought the different sectors and individuals together; their differences became secondary to their common struggle against a powerful destructive enemy, thus reflecting a new attitude emerging toward the end of the dictatorship. In the meantime, it became possible to deal with topics that had been kept in the background, such as gender status and racial issues, which had reinforced and complemented the *economic* exclusionary mechanisms in Brazil (Santiago 11).

Until the late 1990s, the controversies within the theatrical and critical milieu continued to deal with the same issues that had been present since the 1940s: The means of state support, the level of production, and the audiences. Even today at the start of the twenty-first century, a director surrounded by a persistent aura of the avant-garde, such as Gerald Thomas, continues to define the features of his own theater and of his audience according to patterns that remind one of the arguments of that earlier period. Throughout the 1980s, a characterizing feature of Brazilian theater was the prestige achieved by some directors who staged quite personal experiences and were considered, in many of the public debates and assessments, to represent a tradition opposing the total commercialization of theater. Together with the dictatorship itself, television was seen as the main enemy of theatrical development because it promoted models of staging that differed from those of the theater and also because it was argued that television productions indirectly determined which actors got stage jobs, thus promoting both good and bad professional performers based on visibility rather than talent. Anatol Rosenfeld attributed Brazil's problems to the fact that concern for cinema and television came before the theater (Magaldi 1996, 10).

From the 1980s on, the kind of theater that was accepted by the channels of cultural legitimation in Brazil gave rise to two main issues: The nature of the projects proposed by directors that were considered as avant-garde and the substitution of theatrical technique for original dramaturgy. Regarding the first, it is evident that, among the main playwrights who emerged toward the end of the dictatorship, the prevailing focus was on theatrical language itself.

The significance for contemporary Brazilian theater of director Antunes Filho is intimately linked to the impact of his theatrical adaptations from other genres. Even in 1978, he considered that new adaptations were the only solution to the lack of new dramatic authors caused by the self-censorship imposed by the military regime (Novello 36). From 1980 onward, theatrical adaptations became one of the more characteristic forms of Brazilian theater. The starting point was the stage version, performed by the Pau-Brasil company and directed by Antunes Filho, of Mário de Andrade's (1893–1945) rhapsodic romance *Macunaíma* (1928). At that time, the director had heated arguments in a succession of newspaper interviews over the issue of faithfulness to the original work. In fact, he had created a method for studying and preparing the staging of the play, a method that included research of the sources used by Mário de Andrade in writing his own fiction (Novello 50). Antunes Filho's experience had a significant impact on theatrical circles, reinforcing an existing tendency and leading to the staging in Rio of more than 700 adaptations of literary works between 1978 and 1995. Some of the successful plays include Alfonso Henrique Lima Barreto's (1881–1922) *Triste fim de Policarpo Quaresma* [1911; *The Patriot* 1978], Clarice Lispector's (1925–1977) *Um sopro de vida* [1978; A Breath of Life], Manuel Puig's (1932–1990) *El beso de la mujer araña* [1976; *The Kiss of the Spider Woman* 1979], Rubem Fonseca's (b. 1925) *Lúcia MacCartney* (1969), João Guimarães Rosa's (1908–1967) *Corpo de baile* [1956; Chorus Line], and Virginia Woolf's (1882–1941) *Orlando* (1987).

Adapting literary works offered an important point of departure for the free creativity on the part of the directors. Sergio Sant'Anna's adaptation of Jules Verne's (1828–1905) novel, *Viagem ao Centro da Terra* [*Journey to the Center of the Earth*], was staged by Bia Lessa. In the printed program, a note explained that the director had not even read the novel on which the play was based, adding that "the text is significant, but only as one more element and on the same level as the set, the music, the actors; one more element in the theatrical process" (Novelo 182). The search for new means of theatrical expression was accompanied by Bia Lessa's endeavors to study quantum physics, working together with Antunes Filho, who introduced her to the theater. The dual investment was justified as a desire to inquire into new forms of rationality, and the theater was the instrument of that research. This eliminated any concern for, or commitment to, the social or political issues that had been the driving force of the preceding generations of Brazilian drama. Thus, there was, for instance, a tendency to choose internationally renowned foreign novelists as the point of departure of their research.

Several significant debates ensued over the perspective adopted in the process of adaptation regarding the impact on the Brazilian cultural milieu of the historical moment and of the variety of languages employed. To begin with, Antunes Filho's proposal to transform *Macunaíma* into a "universal" work that would transcend its immediate cultural references provoked a controversy, especially when it was compared with Joaquim Pedro de Andrade's film version, which was shown during the years of the military dictatorship and which, in its exploring of the popular traditions of the *chanchada*, was both very successful and itself the subject of heated debates. The same kind of "universalist" approach determined the 1981 show *Nelson Rodrigues, o Eterno Retorno* [Nelson Rodrigues, The Eternal Return]. Michalski considers that the staging of this play was influenced by German expressionist films and the experiences of Pina Bausch and concludes: "Therefore, there are no obvious symbolic images, nor any jargon typical of Rio. Antunes stated that he had created a Germanic show, and his definition is certainly relevant" (in Novello 98). Leaving aside the explanations of the director's concern for the universal and his use of archetypes (thanks to

his conversion to Oriental religiosity and then his subsequent attraction to Jung's theories), José Celso Martinez Correa argues for a link between Antunes' *Nelson Rodrigues, o Eterno Retorno* and his adherence to one of the main lines of Brazilian theater, represented by the Brazilian Comedy Theater (in Novello 97).

Antunes Filho's proposal to create a universal theater–a proposal full of contradictions–represents an attempt to overcome the tendency of Brazilian theater, starting from its first modernizing steps at the turn of the century, toward becoming the expression of a purely personal vision (Szondi 20). In the case of director Gabriel Villela, the search to go beyond the impasses of Brazilian theater can be seen in his endeavor to recuperate those authentic elements that still remain in popular cultural manifestations or that have not been polluted by the expansion of the cultural industry. In the meantime, the epic perspective of this director's work is characterized by a detachment from these manifestations caused by the loss of authenticity by urban audiences. In many of his creative stagings, the director appears as an object to be contemplated by the audience, in the compartment called "culture," in a museum-like way. Similarly, directors Moacyr Góes and Ulisses Cruz take into account an aesthetics of contemplation in which even the actor's performance is relegated to a secondary place in a very sophisticated set filled with mannequins. Director Gerald Thomas came to represent the new tendencies of Brazilian theater by staging extremely visual plays characterized by the daring mannequins and sets created by his wife Daniela Thomas. In 1968, the presentation of *Electra Concreta* [Concrete Electra] was controversial because of its innovative use of the set space and the mise-en-scène of tableaux representing Brazilian traditions. At the same time, he began to write fragmented spoken texts that would become one of the trademarks of his plays. Flora Sussekind (1996, 283) highlights the substitution of the primacy of the text as the center of dramatic creation for other aspects of theater, such as the actor's body, lighting, scenic objects, and sound. She establishes a parallel between the deconstruction of language in the plays of Gerald Thomas and those of Bia Lessa. This line of development is linked to the reconsideration of the role of the text in contemporary culture; this is a radical redimensioning, according to Fredric Jameson, of reality as texts (68).

The metatheatrality of Gerald Thomas and Bia Lessa–which deconstructs traditional representations of the subject– aims at establishing a barrier against the cultural industry, distancing itself from commercial theater and from the powerful television monopoly, and at making known different modes of representation. This task of symbolic "deinscription" has the perverse effect of condensing the interest of the plays in the figure of the director, who becomes a privileged character in the mass media vehicles destined for an audience that withholds the patterns of cultural legitimacy. The stage becomes a space of purely personal references, even when they claim to be international (a term that substitutes for the word "universal" in media obsessed with globalization). In this way, for instance, the deconstructing procedures of Gerald Thomas focus on many references to renowned works within restricted circles of Europe or the United States; that is, they focus on works relevant to a reduced segment of the symbolic goods market. Considering the extreme self-referentiality of this kind of theater, it is no coincidence that the publication of an academic anthology of the author's interviews is called *Um encenador de si mesmo: Gerald Thomas* [His Own Scenographer] (Fernandes 1996).

The deconstructing of the representations of subjectivity and of the conventional place of artistic work has an inverse effect in the context of the symbolic goods market, reproducing a process that is analogous to what Fredric Jameson (79) has seen in the work of some videomakers. The endeavor to flee the subjective nature of production or to escape from this flow of "ego-trip" in Brazilian drama—an attempt represented by the search for the universal in the archetype (Antunes Filho) or in popular traditions (Gabriel Villela)—points to an alternative space that is beyond theater as performance before an audience. One of the issues that, in our opinion, has not been discussed enough by the producers and apologists of the avant-garde experiences of this theater is the lack of desire and courage to abandon the sacred space of the stage (the continued use of the Italian-style stage) as well as conventional production patterns (such as the search for support from the government or from private companies, the latter linked to tax incentives). A symptomatic experience of the limits and difficulties of innovative initiatives in contemporary Brazilian theater was Gabriel Villela's 1996 mise-en-scène of *Morte e Vida Severina* [1956; A Severe Death and Life] written by João Cabral de Melo Neto (1920–1999). The plastic beauty of the show—creating a universe in which even the actors' bodies looked like popular crafts—the meticulous choreographic and vocal work, and the actors' interpretation put into question the relevance of the staging. The adaptation of Cabral's work echoed the mise-en-scène of Strindberg's *Sonhos* [Dreams], which was represented some months earlier by a group of actors from Bahia under Villela's direction. The parade of the world's sufferings—the subject of both plays—was choreographically explored in quite a creative way: In *Sonhos,* one of the impressive effects was created by a line of actors sitting in wheelchairs, acting as a counterpoint to the plot; whereas in *Morte e Vida Severina* considerable impact was produced through heaps of boxes framing the bodies, turning death into an everlasting presence that reflects João Cabral's other iconographic signs and his text. The presence of an epic structure, supported in both plays by the narrator commenting on and interpreting the dramatic action, symbolizes the search for the meaning of life—which is limited by the finding of answers leading only to a sense of resignation before human fate. The plays' sensory richness is touched by a certain melancholy that keeps inducing the audience to think about some of the impasses of the community in this historical stage as well as about the very meaning of the works. The plays evoke a magical world that feeds the senses of the spectators and gets them in touch with the sophistication of an extinguishing popular cultural source; however, in the end, the dramas offer only a personal lament for the conflict between the beauty of artistic creation and the horror of everyday life outside the stage. Quite often, the disquieting effect on audiences is that they are forced to conclude that the theater manages only to deplore shyly the degradation of this historic period, without actually being able to propose any daring vital alternatives.

Translation by Nair Maria Anaya Ferreira

Works Cited

Andrade, Ana Lúcia V. de. 1996. "A cena do eu: dramaturgia brasileira em 1969." Master's Diss. Rio de Janeiro: Post-Graduate in Theater: UNI-RIO.

Andrade, Jorge. 1986. *Marta, a árvore e o relógio.* Rio de Janeiro: Editora Perspectiva.

Baudrillard, Jean. 1977. *Oublier Foucault.* Paris: Editions Galilée.

Borch-Jacobsen, Mikkel. 1991. "The Freudian Subject from Politics to Ethics." *Who Comes After the Subject?* Ed. Eduardo Cadava. New York: Routledge. 61–78.

Braga, Reinaldo. 1995. "Cerejas, Assaltos, Assassinos, Selvagens, quatro espetáculos e dois cenógrafos no Teatro Ipanema." Master's Diss. Rio de Janeiro: Post-Graduate in Theater, UNI-RIO.

Brandão, Tânia. 1983. "A estática da palavra." *Ensaio/Teatro 5. Dramaturgia Brasileira Hoje.* 13–20.

———. 1996. "O antigo e o moderno no Teatro Brasileiro." *Teatro Brasileiro no século XX. Cadernos de Pesquisa em Teatro.* Ed. Tânia Brandão. Rio de Janeiro: UNI-RIO, Série Bibliografia. No.1 (July):11–18.

Cafezeiro, Edwaldo and Carmem Gadelha. 1996. *História do Teatro Brasileiro. De Anchieta a Nelson Rodrigues.* Rio de Janeiro: Editoras UFRJ; EDUERJ; FUNARTE.

Clark, Fred M. 1995. *Spectator, Character, Text: Semiotic Readings of Nelson Rodrigues' Theater.* Valencia: Albatros-Hispanófila ediciones.

Damasceno, Leslie H. 1994. *Espaço cultural e convenções teatrais na obra de Oduvaldo Vianna Filho.* Trans. Iná C. Costa. Campinas: Editora da UNICAMP.

Deleuze, Gilles. 1987. *Foucault.* Trans. José Carlos Rodrigues. Lisboa: Vega.

Dória, Gustavo A. 1975. *Moderno teatro brasileiro: crônica de suas raízes.* Rio de Janeiro: SNT/MEC.

Fernandes, Sílvia. 1996. *Memória e invenção: Gerald Thomas em cena.* São Paulo: Perspectiva/FAPESP.

Gonzaga, Armando. 1940. *Comédias.* Rio de Janeiro: Livraria Teixeira.

Jameson, Fredric. 1991. *Postmodernism, or, the Cultural Logic of Late Capitalism.* Durham: Duke UP.

Lima, Mariângela A. de 1979. "Quem faz o teatro." *Anos 70. Teatro.* Ed. Adauto Novaes. Rio de Janeiro: Europa. 42–73.

Lopes, Angela Leite. 1993. *Nelson Rodrigues: trágico, então moderno.* Rio de Janeiro: Editora UFRJ/Tempo Brasileiro.

Machado, Antônio de Alcântara. 1983. *Prosa preparatória & Cavaquinho e Saxofone.* Rio de Janeiro: Civilização Brasileira.

Magaldi, Sábato. N.d. *Panorama do Teatro Brasileiro.* Rio de Janeiro: MEC; DAC; FUNARTE; SNT.

———. 1987. *Nelson Rodrigues: dramaturgia e encenações.* São Paulo: Perspectiva.

———. 1996. "Tendências contemporâneas do teatro brasileiro." *Revista de teatro. SBAT - Sociedade Brasileira de Autores Teatrais.* 497/498: 4–12.

Magalhães Júnior, Raimundo. 1966. *Arthur Azevedo e sua época.* 3rd edition. Rio de Janeiro: Civilização Brasileira.

Martinez Correa, José Celso. 1979. "'A guinada de José Celso.' Entrevista a Tite de Lemos." *Arte em Revista.* São Paulo: Kairós Livraria e Editora. (May/August). 45–50.

Materno, Angela. 1994. "A crítica teatral de Alcântara Machado." *O Percevejo. Revista de Teatro, Crítica e Estética* 2, 2. Rio de Janeiro: Departamento de Teoria; Escola de Teatro; UNI-RIO. 44–47

Michalski, Ian. 1989. *O teatro sob pressão. Uma frente de resitência.* 2nd ed. Rio de Janeiro: Zahar.

Novello, Vera Angela. 1997. "Do herói sem caráter ao homem sem qualidades: estudos sobre a adaptação Literatura ao Teatro." Master's Diss. in Theater, University of Rio de Janeiro.

Oliveira, Roberta. 1997. "Gerald Thomas e seus 400 umbigos." *Jornal do Brasil.* March 21, 1997: B1.

Ortiz, Renato. 1988. *A moderna tradição brasileira.* São Paulo: Editora Brasiliense.

Peixoto, Luiz and Carlos Bittencourt. 1961. "Forrobodó." *Revista de Teatro* 73. Rio de Janeiro: SBAT. 322 (July–Aug.): 1–14.

Pereira, Victor Hugo Adler. 1995. "O Rei e as revoluções possíveis." *Oswald Plural*. Ed. Gilberto Mendonça Teles et al. Rio de Janeiro: Ed UERJ. 163–80.

Prado, Décio de Almeida. 1987. *Exercício Findo*. São Paulo: Perspectiva.

——. 1988. *O Teatro Brasileiro Moderno*. São Paulo: Perspectiva.

REDE. Revista da Rede Municipal de Teatros 1,1. Rio de Janeiro: Prefeitura da Cidade do Rio de Janeiro.

Rodrigues, Nelson. 1993. *Teatro completo*. Ed. and preface Sábato Magdali. Rio de Janeiro: Editora Nova Aguilar.

Rosenfeld, Anatol. 1993. *Prismas do Teatro*. São Paulo: Perspectiva.

Sampaio, Silveira. 1961. *Trilogia do Herói Grotesco*. Rio de Janeiro: Civilização Brasileira.

Santiago, Silviano. 1998. "Democratização no Brasil – 1979–1981 (Cultura versus Arte)." *Declínio da arte e ascensão da cultura*. Ed. Raúl Antelo et al. Florianópolis: Abralic/Letras Contemporâneas.11–25.

Silva, Daniel Marques da. 1998. "'Precisa arte e engenho até. . .' Um estudo sobre a composição de personagens tipos através das burletas de Luiz Peixoto." Master's diss. Rio de Janeiro: UNI-RIO.

Souza, Valder Gervásio Virgulino. 1992. "Álvaro Moreira e os Anos 20 no Rio de Janeiro." Master's diss. Rio de Janeiro UFRJ.

Sussekind, Flora. 1977. "Nelson Rodrigues e o fundo falso." *I Concurso Nacional de Monografias 1976*. Brasília: Ministério da Educação e Cultura. 7–42.

——. 1986. *As Revistas de Ano e a Invenção do Rio de Janeiro*. Rio de Janeiro: Nova Fronteira; Casa Rui Barbosa.

——. 1996. "A imaginação monológica." *Um encenador de si mesmo: Gerald Thomas*. Ed. Sílvia Fernandes and João Guinsburg. São Paulo: Perspectiva. 281–95.

Szondi, Peter. 1994. *Teoría del Drama Moderno (1880–1950); Tentativa sobre lo trágico*. Barcelona: Ediciones Destino.

Veneziano, Neyde. 1996. *Não adiante chorar. Teatro de Revista Brasileiro . . . Oba!* Campinas: Editora UNICAMP.

SECTION IV
TRANSFORMATIONS IN POPULAR CULTURE: INTRODUCTION

Mario J. Valdés

Time and Narrative (1983–1985) by Paul Ricoeur has produced one of the most important new approaches to cultural hermeneutics, a work that is destined to stand as foundational for this emerging discipline. In his reconsideration of Aristotle's mimesis, Ricoeur developed a tripartite concept of mimesis as figurative representation. This is a cycle of world-making in which we all participate. The action of representation is initiated with the encounter between the reader/listener and the text (i.e., configuration); this encounter bears fruit insofar as it develops the textuality of commentary and redescription by the reader/listener (i.e., refiguration). However, it should be clear that these manifestations of the cultural imaginary are possible only because of the pre-existing storehouse of cultural discourse that is common to both the producer and the receiver of the representation (i.e., prefiguration). The application of the concept of prefiguration will have far-reaching consequences in cultural hermeneutics, for the prefigurative constitutes nothing less than the cultural imaginary in which we live.

I quote some lines from volume I of Ricoeur's work: "Whatever the innovative force of poetic composition within the field of our temporal experience may be, the composition is grounded in a preunderstanding of the world of action, its meaningful structures, its symbolic resources, and its temporal character" (54). The richness in meaning of the prefigurative is the collective memory of the community. He adds: "To imitate or represent action is first to preunderstand what human acting is, in its semantics, its symbolic system, its temporality. Upon this preunderstanding, common to both poets and their readers, emplotment is constructed and, with it, textual and literary mimetics. It is true that within the domain of the literary work, this preunderstanding of the world withdraws to the rank of repertoire, to use the language of Wolfgang Iser in his *Act of Reading*: 'yet despite the break it initiates, *literature would be incomprehensible if it did not give a configuration to what was already a figure in human action*'" (64); (emphasis mine). What we now call popular culture is part of the prefigurative richness that is the mother-lode of Latin American literatures.

This section on the transformation of popular culture in Latin America has been organized in consultation with Carlos Monsiváis. Among the major areas of consideration we include public celebrations, especially religious festivals, and one of the Latin America's most important popular celebrations: Carnival. Another area we take up is that of the distinct but also related expressions of popular and mass culture. We also focus on the creation of Latin American hybrid genres such as the *cordel* from Brazil and the *corrido* from Mexico. We conclude with the most significant development in mass culture: the *telenovela* or soap opera.

The seven texts that make up this section are representative studies of the richness and diversity of Latin America's popular culture included here in order to build up the complex foundation of the cultural imaginary. Anticipating the query of whether or not such undoubtedly ordinary aspects of the cultural scene are relevant to the work of great writers like Sor Juana Inés de la Cruz, Domingo Sarmiento, Ruben Darío, or Carlos Fuentes, to name only some major figures, we must question the idea of the isolated genius with the hypothesis of the writer as a full participant in society.

The study of public celebration as a part of cultural history is a relatively new undertaking. Formerly research on religious festivals was almost entirely the domain of religious studies, and Carnival was primarily in the hands of anthropologists and folklorists. We have welcomed the work of older scholarship, but we have also sought to complement it with interdisciplinary approaches. This section highlights the significance of religious festivals in Brazilian society and interprets one of these popular festivals wherein the marginalized black population engulfs the mainstream, if only for a few days. In discussing popular culture and its roots in a people's traditions we run into the epistemological need to distinguish such manifestations of a community's culture from the popular mass-produced aspects of present-day urban culture such as comics, popular music, or pulp fiction.

European concepts of art coming into Latin America in the early twentieth century were not limited to generic development and formal innovation; they carried the much deeper message that value in art and literature was directly linked to progress or modernity, as it was called. In Latin America, paradoxically, this socially driven concept was linked to the Romantic idea of art as autonomous or pure. In 1924, Pedro Henríquez Ureña, one the finest cultural historians of the twentieth century in Latin America, wrote: "One should not think that what passes for culture today in this era of capital disguised as liberalism is anything more than the enclosed garden of exclusivist dilettantes given over to the cultivation of artificial flowers. . . high culture, anywhere but especially in Latin America, without popular culture would be false and ephemeral" (89).

Works Cited

Henríquez Ureña, Pedro. 1998. "La Universidad." *Ensayos.* Ed. José Luis Abellán and Ana María Barrenechea. Mexico City: Fondo de Cultura Económica, ALLCA XX. 87–108.

Iser, Wolfgang. 1978. *The Act of Reading.* Baltimore: Johns Hopkins University Press.

Ricoeur, Paul. 1984–1988. *Time and Narrative.* 3 vols. Trans. Kathleen Blamey and David Pellauer. Chicago: University of Chicago Press.

CHAPTER 58

LAUGHING THROUGH ONE'S TEARS
POPULAR CULTURE IN MEXICO

Carlos Monsiváis

The Origins: The Centuries of the Viceroyalty

During the three centuries of the viceroyalty, the basis of everyday life was formed by religion, by acquiring Spanish and the customs of Spain, and above all by obedience to the king of Spain and his representatives. Religion was the only (and omnipresent) explanation of reality: Thence we came, thither we were headed; there was faith and obedience, forgiveness and grace. The king was the intangible presence, the source of all gifts, whose remoteness increased the insignificance of his subjects and the relative greatness of his direct envoys. And the Church and the Spanish state manifested themselves through the great festivities that the masses then converted into part of their own world: The Birth of the Christ Child, the Crucifixion of the Beloved Son, the appearance of the Virgin of Guadalupe (from the end of the sixteenth century onward), the arrival of a new viceroy, the burning of heretics, the parading of images, and processions that honored the lengthy calendar of saints' days. In addition to these rites of initiation, there was the general pageantry that blinded the ragged masses and enforced the respect due to the majesties of this world and the next.

Saints and miracles, judges and *encomenderos* (landholders), conquest and catechization. For three hundred years, religion underpinned the understanding and government of the world. Vassalage was also an extension of belief: Those dominions that belonged to the Lord our God, and to Him alone, had been delegated by heaven to the Spanish Crown. This is why colonial life centered on the powers that formally represented divinity and the religious institutions that were an inseparable part of power. And the poles of personal and collective emotionality were subject to the whim of viceroys, *encomenderos,* and judges at one pole, and servitude to bishops and priests at the other. The feasts of the Church were proof of the insignificance of civil authority: There were celebrations for the enthronement of Corpus Christi, Holy Week, and the nativity of Christ for the benefit of contrite humble hearts, who thus were both programmed and engaged in genuine rejoicing.

He Made No Other Nation Like Mexico

Above all, the masses increasingly accepted Our Lady the Virgin of Guadalupe, the quintessence of realities and transfigurations, who, by virtue of the color of her skin and the depth of people's despair, was soon fully appropriated by the Indians and the groups that lived crowded together in the godforsaken areas of the Spanish and *criollo* city. God had not done the same for any other nation. A virgin became a racial mirror who showed the true miracle of the appearances at Tepeyac: By avoiding the Spaniards, La Guadalupana revealed herself to an Indian first. Guadalupe-Tonantzin: A form of syncretism that restored the dignity of dark skin was a strictly national phenomenon. Religiosity soon became the signal culture of a new Indian and *mestizo* people who retained and transformed their former gods, lavishly provided symbols, and laboriously constructed a worldview. Thereafter, devotion persisted amid political adjustments and social upheaval, ignoring liberal secularization and capitalistic modernization and linking religion to nationality–all in one fell swoop. You, the Virgin, exist thanks to us and we exist thanks to you. Praying to you means asking for favors from heaven and being aware that we are Mexican. Before the nation existed as such, it had already been heralded by the distinctive quality of its religious fervor.

In order to express itself in La Villa de Guadalupe, a relatively autonomous popular sentiment had recourse to mysticism and understanding of one's surroundings at any price. A unique culture emerged that would not tolerate any form of compromise; it took root in the exasperation of marginalized subsistence and made surrender to the sacred the principle of an identity. In the faith placed on the Virgin of Guadalupe there was something like the idea of a chosen people: "Hear us, little Mother: The unconditional love we profess to you is a prerequisite to becoming a nation." The plaintive cry goes like this, and we might well add: It is a nation that still does not know what it is, and a popular culture that will take centuries to call itself a nation, and a miserable existence wherein one's survival of human transgressions, abuse, and exploitation depends on one's links with the divine. On being forcibly converted, the Indians invented their own religion, from which they derived their sense of celebration and spectacle and the agglomeration-that-makes-it-all-worth-it. In monastery atria, in churches, and in the processions, they were taught both ethically and aesthetically, by contemplating the superb floats, dances, and inventions of Corpus Christi or Saint Hippolytus's day, and the solemn processions of the Viceroy, the High Court, the town councils, monastic orders, the clergy, the university faculty, the inquisitors, and the archbrotherhoods. The pageantry impressed the conquered and their children; the sumptuousness of the ornaments and images constituted a political program, while the procession itself was a form of mass media that broadcast images of total subjugation.

How else does one intimidate and persuade, if not through lavishness and profane organization? The show is virtually everything, and what it fails to cover is not recorded: The exhausting work, the lack of elementary rights, the way in which the pretense of enjoyment in freedom is forged from servitude. Profane festivities also contributed a sharp dose of theatricality. In *Torneos, mascaradas y fiestas reales en Nueva España* [Tournaments, Masquerades, and Royal Festivities of New Spain], Manuel Romero de Terreros (1880–1968) describes the famous fiesta of the mock war games played on horseback with sugar canes instead of lances; these exercises were copied from the old Moorish celebrations, which served as a pretext for gentlemen (riding with their stirrups short and their legs bent and luxuriously attired, carrying a lance in their right hand and a shield in their left) to be divided into squadrons of various liveries, called squads, each with its captain, in charge of four, six, eight, or more combatants. They rode into the square through various doors, to the sound of oboes, sackbuts, and other instruments, and in the most solemn games, each team was preceded by numerous pages leading mules that were carrying canes and were covered with brocatelle on one side. Once the teams had assembled in the center and handed their lances to their respective squires, they took up their canes and began the game, which consisted of various demonstrations of agility and skill in fighting with canes and defending themselves with their shields. There were numerous variations on this theme. The only constant was the variety of methods utilized by a Spanish minority to exorcise the tedium and boredom of the *criollos* and reaffirm the resignation of the Indian and mestizo majority, deprived of any initiative and confined to appropriating the amusements of the Spanish minority that they creatively copied and altered: Sports and popular spectacles of celebration, masquerades and bullfights, cockfighting, and to one side of all this, happiness, amidst such multitudes that rational people would flee. The majority stole the feast day celebrations from the Spanish and re-created something of the impulse of an exclusive society, converting virgins and saints into their basic interlocutors and amusing themselves with the memory of the Indian past and the elementary translation of what took place in the realm of the conquerors.

The Nineteenth Century

Family and Fantasy

From 1810 onward, the second decisive element (after religion) was the very notion of Independence. Being free men, escaping from serfdom, traveling at will throughout the country: These were novelties that were hard to internalize and that, again, were realized only by a minority who, in principle, constituted both the people and the nation. Yet before proceeding, we should ask ourselves whether popular culture or popular art was conceivable in nineteenth-century Mexico, in a country that was overwhelmingly rural and which, moreover, did not feel that *popular* was a suitable adjective for either culture or art? There were the handicrafts and tastes of the masses and entertainment for the rabble, and that was that. The "people," as far as one can gather from the testimony of narrators, chroniclers, and historians, were what would be called the middle class today. Among these sectors, whose lives and desire for revelry are described in some available accounts, the popular involved a sense of inferiority, fantasies of dissipation, and an imagination that was liberated and enslaved at the same time. During the nineteenth century, the popular was a social force that distrusted its own spontaneity, drew a modicum of security from the high numbers of its adherents, and accepted the fact that secularization did not affect its system of beliefs, even if it modified popular customs and diversified oral culture. As a form of popular expression, liberalism visibly bore fruit in songs and roundels, and subsequently in the growing discovery that religious matters were not to be found exclusively in churches. Astonishment gradually turned into a kind of grateful sorrow for the practice of politics in a lay religion.

The family was the basic nucleus of society, the nation, and popular culture. The family was an entity to which certainly not everyone had access (for the poorest and most marginalized in the nineteenth century, the family was a luxury or an aspiration), and love of God was strictly love of the family, the sphere which preserved and consolidated traditions and conservatively acclimatized any novelties. Christmas festivities and liturgy outside the churches took place in the open; there were communal celebrations in which children, who were ignored throughout the rest of the year, suddenly became visible; neighbors were incorporated into the family, as the latter was extended to include the neighborhood or the village. If the family was a protective organization in an inclement society, the relative humanization of collectivity was expressed through things that were both anecdotal and essential: The gaiety of the *posadas* (nine days of pre-Christmas celebrations), the diligent fulfillment of religious duties, and delight in sweets and games. The moments of collective splendor were both the reward for submission and the opportunity for community expression.

These conditions explain why the popular in the nineteenth century was the birthright of the middle classes, and they account for the difficulty of documenting the tastes and trends of the lower classes. What, for example, do we know of beggars, tramps, or the ragpickers of public refuse dumps? Julio Guerrero (1862–1937) describes them in *La genesis del crimen en México* [1906; The Genesis of Crime in Mexico]: They earned between twenty and forty centavos a day, were dirty and unshod; they aged extremely quickly and many had no idea of their paternity. As one moves up the social scale, however, there are similarly few opportunities for finding out about the points of view of soldiers or craftsmen. They barely had enough money to eat and dress; they amused themselves as best they could and as far as they were allowed; they were unrestrainedly promiscuous and lived a varied and not very orthodox form of religiosity, described in the verses in honor of a saint from Ixtacalco:

Glorioso San Miguelito.
Que es el santo más mejor.
Que muy poquito le falta
para ser madre de Dios.

(*Moisés González Navarro* 455)

Glorious St. Michael.
The best of all saints.
Who's only a hair's breadth away
from being the Mother of God.

Or witness the quatrain of a pastourelle recovered by Hugo Gutiérrez Vega (b. 1934):

Ya parió Maria
ya parió José,
parieron los pastores
y el Niño también.

Mary has given birth,
Joseph has given birth,
the shepherds have given birth
and so has the Christ child.

It fell to the big city to introduce elements of undisguised malice, and what was popular in the late nineteenth and early twentieth century was the result of an agreement between the reverent, lax multitudes and the established powers. Much of what was to become the urban temperament came, almost imperceptibly, from the masses expelled from civilized life as defined in the European manner: They covered themselves up with whatever they could find–rags; coarse cotton breeches and shirts; loosely fitting blouses, trousers, and broad hats; shawls and percale petticoats; and patent leather half-boots. Among these groups, women were not seen or allowed to speak; if they were fortunate, they would become wives. If not, they would become someone's common-law wife, in the shadow of dances and fits of drunkenness. Nevertheless, these marginalized groups derived pleasure from the city despite the odds. They experienced great food shortages, were illiterate, and alternated between drunkenness and disease. The only thing they produced were children; their entertainment depended on the generosity of their rulers, and so on, but–and Cantinflas was not the only proof of this–their struggles in the streets and alleys gave rise to popular culture.

The Transition: The Era of Porfirio Díaz

The aim was to unify Mexico and incorporate it into the concert of nations. Following the end of the extremely short period of the Restored Republic (1867–1876) and the consolidation of the lengthy dictatorship of Porfirio Díaz (1876–1910, except for a brief interval), the oligarchy needed the civilized trappings that would contrast, as far as possible, with the spectacle of the drunken, foul-smelling crowds, the landscapes of Indians' apathy, and the abysmal difference between themselves and Europe. Mexico, that highly disputed and visually hackneyed concept, must adopt *criollo* ways, cleansing itself of the noxious masses and the dead weight at the doors of progress. Porfirian culture rejected, ignored, and slandered the popular spirit, which it regarded as a mark of chaos or the influence of barbarity. Poets, historians, realist narrators, grammarians, and scientists reached an agreement: We shall not succumb to the double temptation of piety and nostalgia; we shall dispense with these voices and these lives, with their burden of poorly finished, insubstantial products, with no opportunity whatsoever of international recognition. In order for that "Mexico" to dazzle, we need an array of emotional and sentimental narcotics–positivism, oratory, Italian-style music, modernismo, medieval scholasticism, and Gallic culture–to keep the unbearable reality at bay. For the Mexicans of the time of Porfirio Díaz to shine, it was essential not to accept anything that was popular, or to accept it only if it was ennobled by the aura of foreigners' curiosity.

Even if the anonymous people of the end of one century and the beginning of the next had no money with which to bet or to pay for tickets, they were enthusiastic supporters of cockfighting and bullfights, and deeply resentful of the fact that gambling was prohibited in the Federal District. In their view, the most effective strategy was to turn everything into a great spectacle–everything from the arrival of an opera singer to don Joaquín de la Cantolla y Rico's acrobatics in a hot-air balloon. His every excursion was followed by delirious crowds who, on his descent, shouted "Long live Mr. de la Cantoya! Long live the Mexican eagle! Long live the autonomy of the fatherland! Long live the freedom of independent Anahuac!" For these workers and urban pariahs, what was popular consisted of the consumption of alcohol as a form of a license to speak; circuses with their range of wonders for children–clowns, the fly woman, the bearded lady (amusement and freak-shows); the increasingly lavish, touristlike commemorations of the dates of the consolidation of Independence and Reform–September 16, February 5, May 5, and April 2; the theater shows and performances in which the masses displayed their sense of humor and sexual desires. This hotchpotch of human flesh literally

lived in ghettoes, accepting that it was nonexistent in the nation, and emerging only under the protection of public license. If there was no carnival, then at least they turned what they could into a carnival. The cinema, primarily from the beginning of the twentieth century onward, although it initially met with resistance among those who regarded it as a diabolical invention, soon proved irresistibly attractive, and apparently reduced crime, the result of idleness; the gramophone players in the streets on Sundays entertained the peasants or Indians who had flocked to the capital to sell their wares. And, at another level, what was popular was religion.

The Other Version of the City

The nation became "decent" and submitted itself to the fabrication of a pompous legal mask. Trade increased and, in the cities already characterized by the buying and selling of food, large clothing stores with French names were set up, and by the 1880s, two hundred thousand people had made trade their main activity. The desire existed to create a Good Society and build a "decent city" within the city. This wish to ignore the popular for virtually the whole year demanded a critical review (never verbalized) of tradition, the continuous abasement of guilds, and a police force devoted to the elimination of visible poverty and to leaving the slums to their own devices–since there was nothing that could be regarded as culture there. Let the poor contemplate the poor and keep themselves entertained. In 1910, this was the most obvious inheritance of the majority of the inhabitants of the capital. This inheritance was divided into various main themes: Bullfighting, hot-air balloons, games of chance, cockfighting, *zarzuelas,* processions, parades, the worship of divas, and the adoration of poets. It was not necessary however, to have listened to a great opera singer or to know the work of a famous author. All that was required was the right spirit, the hijacking of prestige. Thus, what was popular was, nearly always, a re-creation of themes and behaviors imposed from abroad.

In the nineteenth century, what is known as "leisure" today–imagination, a sense of improvisation, voluntary or induced pleasures–depended, first, on religious and family training and, second, on ritual opportunities: Bullfighting, the ascent of hot-air balloons, *zarzuelas,* songs, local saints' feast days, and unusual spectacles–shootings and executions, processions, and parades. The liberal project of secularization was based on laws, elementary education . . . and the need for new "good" customs, that is, Eurocentric customs. Creators of popular art were not recorded; instead there were craftsmen, responsible workers who made no great distinction between nature and society, or between contingency and fatality. What culminated in the work of Vanegas Arroyo's Workshop and in the work of Manuel Manilla and José Guadalupe Posada was, in fact, an ancient tradition: A way to gladden people's hearts, to force them to become (productively) public, by heaping recognizable images on them–apparitions, crimes, national heroes, fantasies, *costumbrista* scenes, catastrophes, and fashionable events. What was popular was what caught people's attention: Entertaining, free shows that combined familiar landscapes, scenes of religious wonder, satires, oneiric explosions, and sexual insinuation. Craftsmen satisfied collective appetites and reserved the right to determine the shape their work took.

Posada: Repertoire of Emotions

José Guadalupe Posada was born in Aguascalientes in 1852 and died in Mexico City on 20 January 1913. His life included extreme poverty, a childhood that took place between the wars of intervention, the beginnings of an artistic life spent copying religious figures or the illustrations on playing cards, a stay at a drawing academy, and formative training in the workshop of the master craftsman Pedroza. His precocious technical expertise was soon in demand and El Jicote ("Periódico hablador pero no embustero, por un enjambre de avispas" ["A tattler but not deceitful newspaper, written by a swarm of bees"]) published remarkable lithographic cartoons by Posada aimed at a local tyrant. Censorship forced him first to León, Guanajuato, and subsequently to the capital. In 1889, at the age of thirty-seven, Posada set up a workshop there. He had already assimilated the early influences of both national and foreign Romantic illustrators, and demonstrated his skill in the use of black and white and a range of grays. He had also created numerous illustrations for *corridos,* indoor games, primers, songbooks, prayer sheets, and children's stories (see **Figure 1**, **Figure 2**, and **Figure 3**). He had produced religious and patriotic engravings; bullfight, theater, and circus posters; playing cards; book covers; and advertisements. Since the client is always right, he also produced advertisements for trains, yarn and textile factories, cigarettes, matches, and food products, all under adverse working conditions. In his indispensable sourcebook, *El folclore literario de México* (1929), Rubén M. Campos (1876–1930) describes the little workshop in which Posada received the most extraordinary job assignments. It was really a kind of closet in a passageway, more like a glass cage with broken glass and cardboard glued to the holes in the window panes. One visitor would request images for illustrating a prayer with indulgences; another would require illustrations of a lamb, chicken, or rabbit for a cookbook; still another would ask him to illustrate a dentist's handbill with a full set of teeth; and the list goes on and on: Hats for a local hat shop, cooking utensils, pharmacist's jars to illustrate remedies and patent medicine. Everything that was needed for a popular publicist was requested from Posada and to all he answered with the same smile of a simple man who happened to be a great artist of the people. Without hesitation Posada would set to work with his very basic tools, working without sketches–merely a glance to calculate the reduction or the amplification of the model. Antonio Vanegas Arroyo, his employer, tells of Posada's morning rounds: Every morning, before going to see Vanegas, Posada would visit other workshops, asking whether they needed any engravings. If the answer was yes, he extracted a chisel and the rest of his materials from the large pockets of his overcoat. There he would cut out the vignette or the portrait or whatever they needed. Having finished his work, he proceeded to the next printing press, where he would ask the same question (Toor, O'Higgins and Vanegas Arroyo, 14–16).

Vanegas Arroyo's workshop, with its doors hanging off their hinges, an old hand- or pedal-operated press, piles of cut paper, and walls covered in posters announcing cockfights, village bullfights, theater performances in huts or fleapits, and circuses in small squares, employed half a dozen tattered workers and two or three long-haired poets who wrote endless *corridos,* or serial novels. There, without expecting or demanding recognition, Posada worked in full view of the public, behind the shop window that faced the street. The young José Clemente Orozco (1883–1949) would stand there, entranced, for a few minutes, on the way to school, watching the engraver four times a day. This was the first spur to his

Figure 1.

Photograph of a José Guadalupe Posada woodcut of a popular song book. (Archive of the author)

imagination; it encouraged him to doodle his first cartoons on bits of paper, the first inkling of the existence of the art of painting. From then onward, he was one of the best clients of Antonio Vanegas Arroyo's printing shop. Vanegas Arroyo's operation was a veritable cross-section of the small printing trade at this time. The old house contained a varied and select supply of popular songs; collections of social greetings, jokes, magicians' tricks, riddles, and parlor games; cookbooks and books on confectionery and baking; collections of toasts for special occasions; poems for entertainers, patriotic speeches, puppet plays for children, fantastic legends, and romantic stories. Vanegas Arroyo was an extraordinary printer. He was familiar with, and promoted, variations in popular taste. He was aware of the pleasure derived from scandal and of the need for accessible reading matter, and for this reason, he indiscriminately published storybooks, recipe books, models for love letters, prophecies, patriotic stories, and "examples," or narrations with a moral epilogue designed to warn against the perils and pitfalls of passion, misery, and ignorance. Posada admirably captured the sense of Vanegas Arroyo's productions, discovering popular taste and expression in the most notable crimes and discerning modern-day fairy stories in celebrated bloody deeds: Not Sleeping Beauty in the forest

Figure 2.

Photograph of a Posada woodcut of a calavera "soldadera" on the cover of a song book. (Archive of the author)

Figure 3.

Photograph of the cover of a song book of popular songs, engraving by Posada. (Archive of the author)

or Puss in Boots, but "El horrorosísimo crimen del horrorosísimo hijo que mató a su horrorosísima madre" or "Una mujer que se divide en dos mitades, convirtiéndose en bola de fuego" ["The dreadful crime of the dreadful son who killed his dreadful mother," or "A woman who splits into two, turning into a ball of fire"].

What did the strictly popular engravers, such as Gabriel Vicente Gaona (Picheta) in Yucatán or Manilla and Posada in Mexico City, do? With talent, imagination, wit, and *costumbrista,* or patriotic loyalties, they drew attention to the visual achievements of those remote from academic art through their blend of recognized and recently invented procedures and their gaiety in depicting the real and the fantastic with the same zeal. It was a time of great experimentation. Without anyone's looking, without any demands for quality, a culture created a public, satisfying basic needs with great creativity. This was particularly true of the work of cartoonists, draftsmen, and engravers, the visual educators of a people who worked to replace the already endangered oral culture. Throughout the nineteenth century, in newspapers, journals, pamphlets, and broadsheets, a complex, nuanced art began to emerge. Broadsheets had a "ruin apariencia" ["appalling

appearance"] obtained from "imprentas de mala muerte, divulgadores cotidianos de corridos" ["dreadful printing presses, the everyday disseminators of *corridos*"] with images presenting executions by firing squad, burial processions, a skull and crossbones, a woman crying on a burial mound, a weeping willow in a cemetery, two old women insulting each other, two members of the rabble fighting with knives, the souls of purgatory in the midst of flames; there was always something funereal or scandalous or tragic, and so on and on it went. In this tradition, Posada, a tireless creator of forms, appropriated an imaginary space between reality and fantasy. His engravings (totaling approximately five to ten thousand) repeatedly stress the fact that what is social to the popular masses is what is natural to the community. The people are part of nature and form a collectivity that lacks the drive, malice, or sufficient information to be able to understand respectability and decorum and so finds the following entirely natural: Crime and the most tragic consequences of sin; desire without euphemism and vices without any sense of guilt; the limited forms of faith and customs on the edges of society; fear of death and love of morbid engravings; dictatorship and criticism of dictatorship; the confusion of history with stories of what has happened to well-known personalities; and the further confusion of historical events with miracles.

Everyday life was, therefore, an expanded form of nature. Posada, free from prejudice yet a victim of prejudice, paid the same attention to bizarre phenomena (a pig with a man's face, a fish's eyes, and a horn in the middle of his forehead, or a woman who gave birth to three children and four crocodiles), the appearance of the Virgin, or the "unforgettable shudders" provided by what was experienced on an everyday basis: Executions, daring deeds, bandits' exploits, kidnappings, assassinations, cataclysms, accidents, and successes in the bullring. The *Gaceta callejera* [Street Gazette] published *corridos* (ballads of local events) seven times a week, and when called in to illustrate one, Posada proved eclectic: He was both anticlerical and superstitious, a misogynist and a devotee of the Virgin, a supporter of the devil and respectful of the Church, an admirer of society's brigands and a frequenter of the Holy Lord of Chalma. And in these interminable dualities, he saw no contradiction because–in his own particular fashion–he regarded himself as a mediator, a bridge between the masses and reality, between information and deluded beliefs.

The *Gacetas callejeras* (the format proliferated) converted social upheaval into sensation; events were presented as so real that they seemed implausible, so near that–transfigured

by art or scandal–their remoteness was suddenly revealed: The bloody murder of María Antonieta Rodríguez, who killed her *compadre* (her child's godfather) by stabbing him ten times because he refused to succumb to her desires, or the crime of the Bejarno woman. The milieu surrounding Posada was, at that time, necessarily indifferent to artistic quality. It fed on passions that were shouted out at the top of one's lungs to establish one's existence, and gave vent to anger that chose the noisiest versions of justice and contradictory feelings. For this reason, somewhere along the way, criminal events stopped being collective scandals and became household legends. Once the victims had been forgotten and the initial shock had died away, all that remained was the story that was preserved by the engraver and retold in family conversations. Posada did not aim to become one of the people; nor was he completely unusual. Unlike Daumier or Goya, with whom he is frequently compared, he did not wish to be an artist, a title that would not have meant much to him. He regarded himself as a craftsman, or rather, he lived the life of the engravers of the time, who were recognized only through the demand for their work. An unmistakably popular genius, because of his capacity to transmit and materialize the new or buried greatness of the masses, Posada offered his clientele not the responsibility of artistic contemplation, but the happiness of the transfiguration of the real (see **Figure 4**).

Figure 4.

Photograph of Posada woodcut "Rebumbio de calaveras." Skeleton newsboys are selling traditional satiric poems, calaveras, on the Day of the Dead, November 2. (Archive of the author)

The Revolution and Its Scope

During the twentieth century, the determining cultural fact was the coexistence of the progress of the educated in society and the extent and depth of illiteracy. In 1910, a country with an illiterate majority recognized only sounds and images as being fully their own, and believed religiously in the written word (and–if pronounced majestically from a balcony–in the spoken word). As a result of oral culture, Patriotic History circulated (Independence was primarily the sum of the legends of Hidalgo, Morelos, and Allende), and in poetry, art *par excellence,* admiration was based on verbal musicality. The outbreak of the Mexican Revolution in 1910 radically changed both public and everyday private life, shifting large contingents from one side of the country to another, destroying certain types of inertia, and populating and depopulating Mexico City. After a decade of the appearance or reappearance of the populus in arms, the institutions that arose reflected on the city and culture-for-those-who-lack-it. There were high cultural events, available to a minority, but this was different from what took place on the streets, in festivities, in cinema halls, and in the theater. In vaudeville, with its comedians, singers, magicians, and tightrope walkers, the public accepted, with affection, that the image proffered there not only resembled real life but was the only conceivable one. Comic actors created stereotypes whose greatest merit was the active engagement of spectators; singers disseminated fashion, ensuring that their work had a national scope.

The revolution did not invent the country, yet its vigor lent the masses legendary characteristics for the first time. The revolutionary with the cartridge belt and thick voice, the murderous glare and criminal ignorance that barely hid his guileless soul, made his debut. Astonishment is a sign of discovery; in the middle of the forum, popular storytelling was in the forms of speech, the succession of stereotypes, and the imaginative faithfulness of the actor's wardrobe (for more on this, see Armando de María y Campos's intriguing *El teatro del género chico en la Revolución Mexicana* [1956; Vaudeville Theater in the Time of the Mexican Revolution]). The archetypes were already there, and nineteenth-century chroniclers merely offered verbal depictions of them. What was new was the shift from the *costumbrismo,* which apologized for existing, to the defiant pride of the new species. Spectators discovered and recognized themselves in their counterparts in the theater and applauded the novelty of their shift from landscape (at best) to characters–rather circumstantial perhaps, yet unmistakable. A qualitative shift took place: In the late nineteenth century, shows involved grotesque performances by seemingly primitive beings who tied themselves in knots and then unraveled themselves for the audience's pleasure. From 1911 onward, a people began to emerge amid the guffaws, accepting the humorous reduction of its existence. The repertoire now included gendarmes with drooping mustaches, saloon-bar drunks, scorned lovers, rustic cattle farmers (hyperprovincials), drunken Spaniards, poor wretches, young dandies, Indians from Xochimilco, and outsiders. From their balcony seats and boxes, the audience contemplated itself on stage for the first time and found solidarity in the recognition of these types. From the pit below, the plebeians had a wonderful time, because the merriment at the expense of one was the cause of enjoyment for all. As had happened during the viceroyalty, popular culture at this time also involved a concentration of multitudes. And vaudeville confirmed what the morals of the street had already shown: The gradual disappearance of a traditional vision, reflected in the great nineteenth-century novels, Luis G. Inclán's (1816–1875) *Astucia* [1865–1866; Guile] and *Los bandidos de Río Frío* [1889–1891; The Bandits of Río Frío] by Manuel Payno (1810–1894), which is the view summarized in the notion of the "Mestizo Mexico," of *criollo* reminiscences and regional combinations, of Guadalupanism and the orgiastic spirit. This vision disappeared and had to be mythically recomposed, since it depended primarily on outdated, dying forms. Although no one specifically pointed this out, the metamorphoses of authoritarianism, the true level of secularization, and the balance between repression and self-destruction were all expressed in popular taste. What from the outside appeared to be survival tactics for the masses from the inside comprised the founding requirements of a culture: Improvisation that imitated the customs and pastimes of the dominant class, undisguised sentimentalism, the confusion between *costumbrismo* and reality, and the interminable repetition of new discoveries.

Regional and local contributions were reduced by the growing influx of products from the capital, aided by technology from the 1920s onward. National society was composed of political institutions, certain traditions in crisis, some economic scaffolding, an interpretative monopoly on history (for which the State was responsible), and the certainty that, in a land of illiterates, what was popular was necessarily what was marked by distance from the centers of civilization. In response, the elite created a language to which it lent enormous prestige, for it expressed the spirit of saving a tradition (together with irritated depression at the emergence of the rabble). For those in power, the popular was not only nonexistent, but also degrading. Listen here, people, ignorance is the beginning and end of your social immobility. How could it possibly have been otherwise? Acknowledging that the masses had any merit at all would reduce the power of intimidation. Pathetic in their desire to be part of the metropolis, despotic in their response to the popular, the social elites shifted from scorn to indifference to distrust to aggression to apocalyptic suspicion to their current state of offended confusion and uneasiness.

An urban popular culture is a creation of the masses that have recently begun to savor their existence as a collectivity, and are anxious for visibility and desirous of increasing the distance from the tumultuous street scene. This cultural enterprise (in the anthropological sense of the word) lent the ill-fated flock (to paraphrase the poet Ramón López Velarde [1888–1921]) what their indifference to shootings and battles had given the peasant armies: Voice and shape. Temperament was recognized and adjusted to the scenarios, and the resulting sketches, by establishing attitudes through speech, legitimized them socially. If "society" was restricted to the comings and goings of an elite, these theater sketches expanded or, better still, postulated conditions for the expansion and conversion of this larger group into a national element. José Clemente Orozco (1883–1949), in his extraordinary *Autobiografía* [1945; Autobiography], attests to what he liked to call true proletarian art. It was in these popular theaters that the incredibly versatile Beristáin, Amparo Pérez, Rivas Cacho, and so many others served the popular masses with extraordinary originality and comic genius in such skits as "El pato cenizo" ["The Ashen Duck"], "El país de la metralla" ["The Country of the Machine Gun"], "Entre las ondas" ["In

Between the Waves"], "Los efectos de la onda" ["The Effects of the Waves"], and so many more. The script and even the music were secondary, since the art form was basically a comic improvisation of basic themes performed with a profound understanding of the public, thus giving the audience a few hours of respite from a hard life.

Prostitutes, laborers, government ministers, and the intelligentsia make up a gallery of types thrown into the staged frenzy of the skit, making their entry into the performance in keeping with the social trends of the day. The character of the *payo,* for example, an always dazzling figure, a bewildered peasant, as evident from his dress, for decades represented the scorn toward newcomers to the capital. Yet in real life, a marginalized person like this who felt he was being represented on the stage acquired an increased sense of his own value, because social invisibility has always been the first strategy of domination. Perhaps it is because of this that racism was accepted for so long by those it affected most. Indian peasants who laughed at the stereotypes of the poor little Indian, urban pariahs who were amused by comedians' mockery of them, and domestic servants who applauded the cruel parodies of themselves in the cinema all regarded marginalization as so invincible that it was enough that it even be taken into account at all. Orozco observes:

Uno de los lugares más concurridos durante el huertismo fue el Teatro María Guerrero, conocido también por María Tepache, en las calles de Peralvillo. Eran los mejores días de los actores Beristáin y Acevedo, que crearon ese género único. El público era de lo más híbrido, lo más soez del "peladaje" se mezclaba con intelectuales y artistas, con oficiales del ejército y de la burocracia, personajes políticos y hasta secretarios de Estado. La concurrencia se portaba peor que en los toros; tomaba parte en la representación y se ponía al tú por tú con los actores y actrices, insultándose mutuamente y alternando los diálogos en tal forma que no había dos representaciones iguales a fuerza de improvisaciones. Desde la galería caían sobre el público de la luneta toda clase de proyectiles, incluyendo escupitajos, pulque o líquidos peores y, a veces, los borrachos mismos iban a dar con sus huesos sobre los concurrentes de abajo. Puede fácilmente imaginarse qué clase de "obras" se representaban entre actores y público. Las leperadas estallaban en el ambiente denso y nauseabundo y las escenas eran frecuentemente de lo más alarmante. Sin embargo, había mucho ingenio y caracterizaciones estupendas de Beristáin y de Acevedo, quienes creaban tipos de mariguanos, de presidiarios o de gendarmes maravillosamente. Las "actrices" eran todas antiquísimas y deformes. (Orozco 1966, 37–38)

One of the most frequented spots in Huertista time [1912–1915] was the Theater María Guerrero, or as it was also called, María Tepache, in Peralvillo District. These were the best days of the actors Beristáin and Acevedo, who created a unique genre. The audience was utterly hybrid: The filthiest scum of the city mixed with intellectuals and artists, and with army officers, bureaucrats, politicians, and even secretaries of state. They conducted themselves worse than at bullfights; they pushed their way into the very performances, taking the most familiar tone with the actors and actresses, and insulting one another and making such changes in the dialogue that no two performances were alike. From the gallery above, all sorts of missiles fell onto the heads of those in the orchestra seats–spit, pulque, and even worse liquids; and sometimes the drunks themselves came tumbling down upon those below. It is easy to imagine the effects that actors and audience achieved between them. The fury of the rabble broke out in a dense and sickening atmosphere, and the spectacles were often of the most alarming sort. Yet, for all this, there was much wit and telling characterization. Beristáin and Acevedo were wonderfully good at taking off marijuana addicts, convicts, and policemen. The actresses were, all of them, terribly old and deformed.

The image that the people had of themselves (usually, as degrading, bothersome, and shy, as far as one can gather from available testimony), fueled a drive toward nationalism: This is what we are like and how we talk and act; our behavior is primarily derived from our nationality. The confusion between social and individual psychology is easily explainable; its main source was the presentation of popular types with whom people could identify and whom they could imitate both ironically and sincerely.

This is why the theater was so essential. It was a school of manners and expression for all social classes. In bourgeois theater, melodrama was the means for the discovery of scandalized sentiments at vaudeville theater performances; the masses enthused over shows that represented them to themselves. This is borne out by the chronicles: The most entertaining feature was the crowd itself, which, despite the burden of its limitations, amused itself. This–noticeable too among the bullfighting public–was evident in the smaller spaces of vaudeville. This popular theater had no pretensions to dramatic art or even passable musicality. The public was hungry for pornography and lewdness, which ranged from the cancan to the erotic sketch. Vaudeville as a refuge of coarse taste was also proof of vitality, as Luis G. Urbina (1868–1934) recognized. After the fall of Porfirio Díaz, theater slipped into history as an appendix to reactionary aggressiveness: Actors rebuked the democrat Francisco I. Madero and praised the dictator Victoriano Huerta. It did not matter: Right-wing slander was anecdotal in the public's search for freedom of expression, and what had been considered dispensable popular trash, namely the procession of lowlife types, released the pent-up energy previously seen only in popular celebrations.

La chingada (Explicit Language) as a Form of Liberation

Urban popular culture emerged from chaos. But what is chaos? Contradiction becomes counterpoint in Mexican popular culture. See, for example, the decoration of a pulqueria (bar serving a fermented drink made from the maguey plant) in one of Mexico City's most violent quarters, depicting an angel with a lyre standing over the maguey plant (see **Figure 5**). The alliance between the celebration of the grotesque, verbal ferocity, admiration of any form of virtuosity, theatricalization of city speech, and enthusiasm for the gifts of vulgarity. Swear words were the essential grammar of class, and the depiction of men on the dramatic stage was the result of an idiomatic impoverishment that was felt to be both an offensive and a defensive instrument. When censorship was eliminated for a few years, puns were enthusiastically deployed, while the use of obscenities allowed the public to express their sense of humor through sexual irony. The political message of the Revolution reignited an appetite for rebellion among the common people but in a much more intense fashion. This aggression ranged in expression from the burlesque of the rich to the open venting of sexual desire. Vaudeville and the circus offered a perennial carnival whose bases of enjoyment were sexuality and the mention of genitals (bellicose insinuation, sexual allusion, and vulgarity as the only available forms of expression). The popular classes used obscenity to counter the norms of the Porfirian era with its sense of prudery and sexual hypocrisy and thereby asserted their very existence.

From the viceroyalty to the era of Porfirio Díaz, the body was depicted only as sordid, something to be hidden, establishing thereby the tradition of concealment. During the

Figure 5.

Photograph of the decoration of a "pulqueria." Mexico City c. 1928.
(Archive of the author)

decade of the 1910s, during the brief suspension of traditional norms, the body became culturally visible with the rejection of the hypocritically worshipped Spirit, which had restricted all forms of corporeal authenticity to the carnal dissipation of the brothel. With the renewal of the Pantagruellian energies that Bakhtin found in the Middle Ages and the Renaissance, the lower half of the body re-emerged and became verbalized. It was soon subjugated once again, however, and relegated to the forbidden zones of language; but during the few years of its aggressive public presence, the body's nether region produced an avalanche of popular comedy, based on elementary factors (butt, testicles, vaginas, bellies, excrement, farts, etc.), as well as performances in which the female nude was offered as art in the service of onanism. In the theater, the glories of the nether regions that the gallery applauded were feted as a genuine epic of the popular.

At the same time, and with no contradictions (since every form of media expresses the historical and cultural times it is allowed to express by political and social censure), silent movies celebrated women's spirituality. Cinema marked the visual transformation of melodrama, whose public expanded and whose key characteristics were gradually modified. This was the kingdom of the prima donnas, of women whose beauty was proof of the effectiveness of technique and of the public's rapid adjustment to the morals of the patriarchy. In any case, what was striking in these silent movies was the minimal presence, outside of documentaries, of the Mexican Revolution as an aesthetic and thematic element. The decade of the 1920s attested to the efforts of the creators of the cultural

industry to make society decent, to provide it, through songs, movies, and plays, with a form of morals that was as ineffable as the songs of the Yucatan *trova* or the gestures of the divas. As the result of this vast ideological and commercial operation of isolation, the revolution was successfully prevented from being ideologically incorporated into the popular, except in the form of picturesque anecdotes or cinematographic mythologies.

Popular Music

The Spanish conquistadors felt they needed to eliminate Indian music and used Christianity to fight the use of ceremonial musical instruments. This implied the invariably partial banishment of *chirimias, teponaxtle,* and *huéhuetl* (flageolets, horizontal and vertical drums). Once sacred music predominated, the popular became an ecclesiastic by-product in the form of long, slow, sad hymns that were inevitably repetitive: "Mercy, my Lord, mercy and clemency, mercy and indulgence, mercy and pity." The late eighteenth century, however, saw the emergence of the *corrido,* a derivation of the ballad, which would become the rural genre *par excellence.* In the cities, the forerunner of what is now known as tropical music was persecuted because of its erotic content. The *chuchumbé* was prohibited from the pulpit for being scandalous obscene music, offensive to chaste ears; it was danced with a waggling of the behind, clasping, and embracing, and was sometimes danced belly to belly. In the mid-eighteenth century, pulque shops (dispensaries of a Mexican alcoholic drink derived from the agave plant) preceded saloon bars in the promotion of popular music. The clergy regarded them as the very image of hell, and in response, these demonic hovels permitted dancing to popular Cuban *sones,* a noise detested by the civil and church authorities, who favored the *jarabe tapatio* (Mexican hat dance), danced by modestly separated couples. The Wars of Independence restored forbidden rhythms; high society enjoyed the dances of Delicious Xenomania (mazurkas, polkas, and redowas); and Italian opera, the sediment of luxury and lyrical exaltation, was introduced. Sacred music was also affected by political fluctuations, while popular music was condemned by moralists as a vile, perishable genre, worthy of only the worst kind of people (Morales). For over a century, composers' struggles to nationalize European genres, particularly Italian ones, had repercussions on songs.

By 1840, a nationalistic trend had begun to emerge, reinforced by the wars of intervention (as seen in such liberal songs as "Los cangrejos" ["The Crabs"] and "Adiós Mamá Carlota" ["Goodbye Mama Carlota"]). Cultured musicians lavished praise on operas, romanzas, polkas, waltzes, marches, and songs; village string ensembles proliferated (including the Jalisco mariachi), while collections of songs and poems using novel methods were sold at fairs (having an assistant to attract attention, provide comments, and request financial contributions). Publishers disseminated *corridos* and popular songs with the help of organ-grinders, candy vendors, and small string ensembles. Female folk singers, the forerunners of *ranchera* singers, also began to emerge:

> Quieren morir tu ánima y tu estilo,
> cual muriéndose van las cantadoras
> que en las ferias, con el bravío pecho
> empitonando la camisa, han hecho
> la lujuria y el ritmo de las horas.

> (López Velarde, "Suave patria" 270)

Your spirit and style are dying out
like the vanishing goddess of song
in a country fair–indomitable bosom
challenging straining bodice–
who evoked lust along with life's rhythm.

For a song to gain popularity, it had to rely on the lay religion of the nineteenth century: Poetry, such as "Las golondrinas" ["The Swallows"] by Narciso Serradel or "Marchita el alma" ["Withered Soul"] by Antonio Zúñiga. If words and music were indistinguishable, as far as lyricism was concerned, the force of the song doubled. One particular rhythm, the waltz, promoted a type of sensitivity at whose center was a purity of spirit (the ecstasy of the listeners); "Dios nunca muere" ["God Never Dies"] by Macedonio Alcalá, "Sobre las olas" ["Over the Waves"] by Juventino Rosas, and "Vals poético" ["Poetic Waltz"] by Ricardo Castro articulated the harmony that confirmed social stability. The group consisting of Castro, Felipe Villanueva, and Gustavo Campa successfully opposed the prevailing Italianism; these musicians created the sordid but golden legend of Bohemia with its tragic lives of alcoholic frenzy (Juventino Rosas and Alcalá) and premature deaths (Villanueva, dead at 31). A growing public adored this music and, despite the exhortations of moralists, idolized the artists. Some of the compositions aimed at the elites were adapted to the needs of streets and *rancherías*. Marginalized life was celebrated in the songs of drunks, students, soldiers, marijuana smokers, braggarts, bandits, prisoners, beggars, cardsharps, cowboys, muleteers, sailors, tradesmen, and workers (see Mendoza): Quatrains referring to love affairs or political rebellion (usually with tragic endings) were committed to memory, and poetry within the whole range of oral culture was celebrated.

The nationalism unleashed by the Revolution found expression in songs that served as a bridge between romantic tradition and new experiences. In its renewed form, the *corrido* enjoyed years of success and fulfilled a specific plural role: Singing the heroic deeds of a people that recognized itself in violence, death deifying heroes and legends, sustaining the idea of history as a duel between political bosses, promoting an archetype of popular poetry, instilling pride in the revolutionary troops, narrating memorable battles, highlighting the figure of Pancho Villa, and serving as an abridged memory of the revolution. As Vicente T. Mendoza's compilations show, the *corrido* is a musical, political, and informative instrument, a system of connections in a country whose links have been severed. Fly, fly little dove, and tell the *corrido* that it simultaneously represents poetry, novels, history, military exploits, stories, and rumors. The soldiers' songs responded to this same tradition: *Cielito Lindo, La Cucaracha, La Adelita, La Valentina,* and *Joaquinita* shared in the joyful yet melancholy celebration, and recorded the emergence of women and their bravery in the history of Mexico. The *corrido* thus served a variety of purposes: It was popular poetry, composed with great lyrical skill; it provided a succession of metaphors that could be understood by all; it disseminated tragedies–this is what happened to the disobedient son, or to the rival brothers, or to Simón Blanco, or to that shameless hussy Rosita Alvírez, or to the brave Pancho Villa. In contrast to the anonymous breadth of *corridos,* romantic songs were didactic and offered warnings: This is how you should react if you are dying of love, say these phrases, or if you are abandoned (though the anecdote was omitted, the aim was to transmit a particular mood).

Mythicizing Memory

Political stability reinforced popular songs, which played an unforgettable supporting role in the new "national essence"–a requirement for the rediscovery of a country praised by intellectuals and politicians. From 1912 to 1913, the composer of cultured music Manuel M. Ponce (1882–1948) recovered and compiled the most interesting popular songs, gave concerts, and paved the way for what would become a cultural invention by the 1920s–the focusing on the evocation of the peasant world: "Adiós Mariquita linda" ["Goodbye Pretty Mariquita"] by Marcos Jiménez, "Canción Mixteca" ["Song of the Mixteca"] by José López Alvarez, and "La Casita" ["The Little House"] by Felipe Lleras presented a mythologizing of a changeless countryside that was disappearing thanks to forced migrations. Enthusiasm for "Mexican songs" (the genre that would become *ranchera* songs) was reignited; rural images were idealized and agrarian realities ignored. Ignacio Fernández Esperón and Tata Nacho composed "Adiós mi Chaparrita" ["Goodbye, My Little One"] and "La Borrachita" ["The Little Drunkard"]: "If he leaves the ranch, he'll soon be back." Nostalgia was the social link between what was lost and what was victoriously presented. There was a pressing need to recover what had been forgotten or destroyed by the city: The countryside, *criollo* customs, and collective and personal emotions. In the provinces, the popular was linked to the sensitivity of romantic poets (the sensitivity of the defeated class).

Old and New Nation, Old and New Customs

The three decades from the 1920s to the end of the 1940s saw significant change, as cultural nationalism used songs to provide stimuli for migrating groups. Without an up-to-date model, nostalgic songs were created. The aim was to establish an idyllic profile of a disappearing tradition and add it to the collective memory, thereby developing both a sensitivity and an industry. Some of the characteristic musical forms of this period were:

- The *danzón*, the quintessential sound of the brothels in the early twentieth century, became the forerunner of tropical music, which allowed the free contact of bodies; this was the dance form of popular fiestas.

- Rhythms from the United States (the swing, the boogie-woogie) instilled the idea of the contemporary and precipitated what had been unknown until then: acrobatic desire, the body as an allegory of speed.

- The *trova yucateca* pays homage to ecstasy provoked by the ideal of the purity of the soul. During the 1920s, the romantic verses that accompanied the melodies of Guty Cárdenas and Ricardo Palmerín, the work of highly skilled authors (Luis Rosado Vega, Antonio Méndez Bolio, Ricardo López Méndez), added poetry (the certifier of noble sentiments and exalted passions) to personal relations and also expressed the self-deceit and reticence felt toward urban frenzy: "I know I worship you in vain/and that my heart evokes you to no avail./Yet despite all this, I love you,/Despite all this, I adore you,/Although I may never be able to kiss you." The romanticism of traditional song offered the unreality without which everyday life lost its utopian possibilities.

Agustín Lara: The Empire of the Bolero

The son of a well-to-do family, a precocious artist whom a prostitute fatally infected with syphilis, Augustín Lara (1900–1970) was the author of dazzling lines and melodies disseminated in cabarets and homes alike. In 1926, his song "Impossible" (dedicated to a "woman of easy virtue") made him the leading exponent of a new sexualization. In vaudeville theaters and dance halls, in the eyes of a public that decided which songs would disappear and which would endure, Lara was the poet of the majority, a famous-man-living-a-marginalized-life who sang to prostitutes and surrendered fearlessly to sentimentalism. A national and nationalistic icon, a summarizer of trends, and a literary and melodic innovator (not necessarily in that order), Lara stopped the rise of the tango, increased the popularity of Mexican composers, idealized the (moderate) change of customs, and exalted a literary sensibility–a role which for many years had been played by contemporary poetry.

One hypothesis is that Agustín Lara was the product of the strictest Romanticism, and heir to Manuel Acuña. Despite his much-heralded contacts with *modernismo,* this constituted only a minute portion of his work. In Lara, what was even more important than the musicality of the lyrics of his songs was the combination of his figure and legend (uncontrolled popular culture) with what was overwhelmingly artistic. Art and life frequently overlapped in his work, and the Lara phenomenon forces us to confront the issue of kitsch. It is difficult to prove the irrelevance of any aesthetics of limits in societies where bad taste is the only form of taste supported. Is it true, as Adorno says, that composition listens for the listener? In cabarets and brothels, Lara's songs summarize the experience of the marginalized, serving as both an incentive and a confirmation. The commonplace is true; the technique of idolizing women is followed by an attempt to make the object of pleasure abstract, once it has been utilized, and the ritual includes avoiding any form of guilt. The deified prostitute protects what is familiar, exalts the patriarchy, and bespangles the prostitute herself with tears; thus the evocation of exploited lives is granted the warmth of the hearth.

The Pleiad of the Hearth

Agustín Lara consolidated his success during the 1930s. He was brilliant, excessive and metaphorical, unrepeatable and irreplaceable. Others appeared who lacked this extraordinary impact yet were nonetheless able to create a standardized taste. The following is a representative, although not exhaustive, list of their work: María Grever, "Júrame" ["Promise Me"]; Gabriel Ruiz "Usted" ["You"]; Consuelo Velázquez "Bésame mucho" ["Kiss Me More"], "Verdad amarga" ["Bitter Truth"]; Gonzalo Curiel "Vereda Tropical" ["Tropical Path"], "Incertidumbre" ["Uncertainty"]; Alberto Domínguez "Frenesí" ["Frenzy"], "Perfidia" ["Treachery"]; and for children, there was the work of Francisco Gabilondo Soler Cri-Cri, a melodist and story writer in the tradition of Iriarte, Samaniego, and Guillermo Prieto. The urban middle class gradually replaces the most traditional evocations of the beginning of the century. Movies, radio, and the record industry promoted an ideology, both essential and limiting, that instituted a minimal sense of the artistic: Easily memorized melodies, lyrics that never moved far away from Romanticism or *modernismo,* and a tendency to concentrate on amorous intensity. A related phenomenon was the ideological exploitation of music. Prime examples of cultural nationalism turned into melodrama were the *ranchera* songs, which denied the narrative and community spirit of the *corrido* and exalted the desperate monologue.

I Am an Elegant Charro, One of Those Esoteric Ones

In 1901, the pianist and composer Miguel Lerdo de Tejada founded the Orquesta Típica, dressing the musicians up as *charros,* and, in approximately 1928, the Mariachi Vargas left Tecalitlán, Jalisco, the natural seat of this group, and set off for Mexico City. The Mariachi's original instruments were two violins, a small guitar, a large guitar, harp, and drums. Both the ensemble and its attire gradually became more sophisticated: Drums were eliminated, as was the harp, and replaced by guitars, and, according to legend at the suggestion of Azcárraga himself, trumpets were added, an essential component for the expression of a lament that could be both displayed and enjoyed, and of the unequivocal transformation of a rural into an urban ensemble. The Mariachi–a sign of the folkloric idealization of the past–proved to be a sign of the commercialization of tradition: Nationality invaded aggressively and imposed itself on melodic quality and on the unintentionally humorous or inevitably poetic lyrics with their *costumbrista* descriptions. There was a shift away from the desolation of the country to commercial offerings that frequently became popular creations. (Nothing was dearer to listeners' hearts than the commercial songs of José Alfredo Jiménez.) Radio, television, and the (transnational) record industry modified the expressions of popular music, which had already been integrated into the national identity. Following the obvious crisis of agrarian reform and massive migrations to the cities, what was rustic was reinvented, and agricultural reality became a utopia that could be sung about and danced to, a version of the Rancho Grande that postponed the Last Judgment. No one cared about verisimilitude, and the countryside was only a diffuse hypothesis, commercialized in an equivalent process to the one that led from Jorge Negrete to Pedro Infante through Javier Solís, to Vicente Fernández and eventually to Juan Gabriel.

Ay, Jalisco, Don't Give In

The commercializing process underwent several stages:

1. The theatricalization of primitive sentiments, in which the performer was basically the message. The finest example of this was the great singer Lucha Reyes as "La Reina del Mariachi" ["The Queen of the Mariachi"]; the radio station XEW and RCA Victor promoted this exalted vision that endorsed localism, definitions of femininity ("like a good Mexican woman, I shall suffer pain in silence"), and in general the bravado that was part of the festive spirit. ("Borrachita de tequila, llevo siempre el alma mía"["My soul is always drunk on tequila"].) From her appearance and gravelly voice, from her use of Mariachi to represent a nation that witnessed tragedy, Reyes, the Daring Female, was the perfect creature of the new folklore. The combative spirit of the slums rose up in contrast to the sweetly "countrified" (Esparza Otero, Tata Nacho).

2. Prefabricated desolation. The lyrics of *ranchera* songs described a (shapeless) process and provided the lesson of a type of behavior. Subject–"Me cansé de rogarle" ["I got tired of begging her"]–was immediately followed by drama and the moral. The process: (1) story of abandonment: "Por tu amor que tanto quiero y tanto extraño" ["Because of your love that I want and miss so much"]; (2) existential collapse and desire for self-destruction: "Que me sirvan otra copa y muchas más" ["Give me another drink and a lot more besides"]; (3) illustration through an exemplifying instance: "Que me sirvan de una vez pa' todo el año" ["Give me another drink to last me for the rest of the year"]; (4) theological insistence: "Que me pienso seriamente emborrachar" ["I'm planning to get seriously drunk"]. Human relations are amalgams of destiny: the inherent evil of women meets the weakness of males.

3. A notorious fashion: "what was Mexican." The Latin-American success of *Allá en el Rancho Grande* [1936; *Back in the Rancho Grande*] revealed and expanded the market. If the *charro* was such a profitable symbol, it would be useful to provide him with challenging melodies and lyrics. A voice with operatic overtones, together with a tall rigid figure, were the ideal vehicles for the commercial exploitation of the gestures and morals of the hacienda during the era of Porfirio Díaz. Ernesto Cortázar (lyricist) and Manuel Esperón (composer) equipped Jorge Negrete with "¡Ay Jalisco, no te rajes!" "Cocula," and "Tequila con Limón" ["Ay, Jalisco, Don't Give In"; "Cocula"; "Tequila with Lemon"]. In songs and movies Negrete was a magnificent, albeit involuntarily parodic, portrait of the social beliefs of two decades, the male equivalent of Mae West in the United States. By emphasizing femaleness to the hilt, Mae West reduced it to the absurd. Negrete operated in a similar fashion as far as manhood, good looks, and boastful smiles were concerned. He seduced with his voice and disarming familiarity phrases: "¿Qué hay? ¿Se es o no se es?" ["What's up? Are you or aren't you?"]. However, Negrete benefited an industry in need of male archetypes.

Revenge on Request

Return trip: While one type of song, not necessarily old, represented tradition, because of its power to evoke and its proximity to the images of the *corrido,* another commercial trend, based on the experience of country-fair *lyriscista* and nineteenth-century Romantic poets, was responsible for an extraordinary period in *ranchera* songs. Foremost among these composers were Manuel Esperón, Chucho Monge, Tomás Méndez, and José Alfredo Jiménez. Outstanding singers included Pedro Infante, Lola Beltrán, Javier Solís, Lucha Villa, Vicente Fernández, Amalia Mendoza, and, in her own particular style, Chavela Vargas. A qualitative leap was made by the work of the composer and singer José Alfredo Jiménez (1926–1974), a superb lyricist, ahead of his time in popular poetry, a renovator of the stock of simple images that had become commonplace. As in the case of Agustín Lara, in José Alfredo's life, songs, autobiography, self-destruction, and confessions of defenseless marginality ("Yo sé bien que estoy afuera" ["I know very well that I am on the outside"]) blended with macho presumption ("Te solté la rienda" ["I loosened your reins"]). Like Lara, José Alfredo endured because of his great talent, helped somewhat for a time by his public behavior: Bohemia, dissipation, passion without hope. Through José Alfredo, an area of scenic nationalism began to emerge that included the patriotism of self-destruction and the delicacy of psychological shipwreck: "México, creo en tí, porque no creo en mí" ["Mexico, I believe in you because I don't believe in myself"]. And *ranchera* songs shifted from chauvinism ("Yo soy mexicano, mi tierra es bravía" ["I am Mexican, my country is fierce"]) to the distinctly individual:

Yo sé bien que estoy afuera,
pero el día que yo me muera,
sé que tendrás que llorar.
Dirás que no me quisiste,
Pero vas a estar muy triste,
y así te vas a quedar.

I know very well that I am on the outside,
but the day I die,
I know you'll have to cry
You'll say you didn't love me,
but you are going to be sad,
and so you will remain.

The *ranchera* song is the queen of posthumous victories.

Circle of Classes and Ages

The double edge of popular music includes one that has already been pointed out (learning sentimental language, the tradition of distress, multiclass links) and one that has prevailed since the 1960s: The passive, colonized adhesion to a form of consumption in which internationalizing taste fosters the illusion of an extremely modern life. Here is a brief list of some relevant phenomena of the period from 1960 to 1999:

- For "reasons of status," a significant portion of the middle classes hated the most representative genres (and corresponding social spheres) of traditional Mexico, restricting Romantic music to the life-forgiving region of memory. Whoever listened to it and was moved by it was exposed to an unforgivable anachronism. This lasted until approximately the beginning of the 1990s, when, protected by the nostalgia produced by the end of the millennium and the use of the *bolero* in movies such as Pedro Almodóvar's *La ley del deseo* [The Law of Desire] and Orlando Jiménez-Leal's *El super,* the bolero genre became a cultural passion. Records by outstanding performers (from Daniel Santos to Elvira Ríos, from Chelo Silva to Beny Moré, and María Luisa Landín to Olga Guillot) were re-edited; the "classics" were recorded in new versions (usually inferior in quality to the originals); and "old-fashioned" sensitivity was given a new lease on life. Any evaluation of a century of popular music in Spanish-speaking Latin America would place the bolero in a central position. Over a hundred years of a genre interested solely in love (the more futile, the more praiseworthy) produced a repertoire of highly talented lyricists who were masters of contemporary popular poetry, performers whose voices alone evoked entire life styles . . . and grateful generations who remembered them. The history of the *bolero* is precisely a survey of the happiness of families, couples, and solitary persons because, even though the lyrics concern the end of relationships and abandonment, the melodies praise the habit of happiness; together, they celebrate the personal and collective time in which loving suffering also gladdens. Millions of people will never be so forgetful that they will cease to be living anthologies of the *bolero*.

- Traditional methods of disseminating popular music disappeared. Vaudeville, once a great platform for launching songs, came to an end; street music was forbidden or disappeared; outstanding singers did emerge from television, but this medium failed to reflect the public's true opinion. However, there were some means of continuity: Compact discs have recovered the best of the past; street performers in subway cars choose the songs most closely linked to contemporary taste; theater and movie directors resort to *boleros* or *ranchero* songs to set the scene, since they already clearly function as a form of period decoration. This resistance is surprising, given the long period in which the survival of a repertoire was justified by arguing its need for those who could not afford to be modern.

Tropical Music: Drume negrita

The *danzón* was established in Mexico, via Veracruz, in the early twentieth century, and thereafter was essential to the erotic history of the people, to the anticipation, promise, or triumphal nonachievement of sexual intercourse. During the 1940s, a generation of Caribbean musicians, such as Mongo Santamaría, Cachao, Beny Moré, Rita Montaner, and Dámaso Pérez Prado, produced extraordinary pieces that were increasingly valued. In Mexico, from 1949 onward, Pérez Prado's mambos incorporated the intensity and permissiveness of the expanding city into music and dance. And the Sonora Matancera and its singers (Celia Cruz, Daniel Santos, Alberto Beltrán, Carlos Argentino, Celio González, and Bienvenido Granda) brought together magnificent and lusty voices with sensuality and choreographic energy. The mambo was followed by the cha-cha and years later by salsa, which incorporated jazz elements into rumba. Other rhythms prevailed among the popular classes in the *vallenato, cumbia, merengue,* and *guaracha.* The *cumbia* in particular attracted teenagers and youth in search of social pleasures, dancing skill, and proof of their physical stamina.

Thanks to music, an extremely broad sector of society revealed its aspirations, its frustrations, and its shrewdness in the face of oppression. *Cumbia* fans do not represent the degradation pointed out by the right, but merely the futility of pontificating about matters of musical taste in societies that, nonetheless, with hindsight, appear to have made extraordinarily accurate predictions. If they select national *cumbia* versions, in dreadful recordings or performed by extremely insignificant groups, it is not because they are unaware of the quality of Celia Cruz, Johnny Pacheco, Eddie Palmieri, Willy Colón, Oscar D'León, Rubén Blades, and musicians from the Fania recording company; it is because their choice of these groups corresponds to the peculiarity of tastes in urban atmospheres and in people's individual lives.

The Comic

And All Mexico Went "Gulp"

In the mid-1930s, the newspaper publisher José García Valseca decided to publish comics for the majority of the population who could not read. His project made sense: Absolute and functional illiteracy were so widespread that an industry could be created by taking them into account. The success of comic strips (first called *monitos* and then comics) for those who could not read, even if they knew the alphabet, was immediate. The cultural limitations of the public justified the elementary views and explanations and the augmenting of simple-mindedness and social, sexual, and racial prejudices. During the 1930s, the success of *Paquito,* the comic strip by García Valseca, confirmed the worth of his project. The comic strip presented a short story, an adventure, or a small melodrama taken from real life—all illustrated and with no more written text than the odd, very short dialogue. People who could barely spell and were not at all fond of reading would happily spend ten cents on *Paquito.* And people who could not read at all entertained themselves by following the visual story line of the illustrations, and would ask a relative or a friend to decipher the brief dialogues, although often within a few days, curiosity had already spurred them to learn enough of the alphabet to make them out themselves. *Paquito* was everywhere: In corner pulque bars, markets, neighborhoods, villages, and even farms. He soon acquired a little sister, Paquita, who was followed by the youngest child, Pepín. Demand was so great that corner shops and ice cream parlors bound collections of "Pepines," which they rented out for five cents to a varied population of children and adults who came in to read them or simply to look at the pictures. Thus, illiterates and quasi-illiterates had affordable publications and even an incentive—within range of their capacity—to learn to decipher the brief dialogues between the boy and the girl. Within a short time, *Paquito* achieved a circulation of an incredible 320,000 copies a day. Over ten thousand pesos' profit a day!

Comic strips initially had to be "comical" (i.e., humorous) and extremely nationalistic (e.g., the first acknowledged comic strip, *Don Lupito,* by Andrés Audiffred, published in the newspaper *Argos*). In 1921, *El Heraldo de Mexico* asked Salvador Pruneda to produce a series, *Don Catarino,* that blended the adventures of an extremely local Mexican *charro* with urban domestic situations. The *Don Catarino* formula solved the dilemma of Mexican originality; in order to differentiate themselves from foreign comics, the narrative formulas of comics in the United States were followed, but the local signs were intensified. If the speech was Mexican, or more typically still, from Mexico City, it did not matter that the creators of "cartoons" adopted the prevailing forms of the United States, and added extreme candor, fallible cleverness, and anecdotal awkwardness. Readers accepted these flaws with supportive smiles. The cartoonists did not feel they were artists, since no one regarded them as such. To become established, Mexican comics intensified certain expressions and customs, imitated vaudeville techniques, and emphasized highly Mexican situations, such as peasants' immigration to the capital and the rustic man's astonishment at city life. On their arrival in Mexico City, Mamerto and his wife embodied migratory fear. ("Hey, wifey, ain't this a pretty station?" Answer, "Oy think that 'ere in Mexico City, we're gonna get cross-eyed, Memerto.") And in order to make Mexican nationalism work, readers had to recognize themselves in the characters' expressions.

Comic strips and cartoons give literary chroniclers a new task of preserving and recognizing popular types or, in fact, stereotypes, to judge from their appearance. Through the "unimportant and the frivolous," virtual class miracles took place. In Acosta's *Chupamirto,* begun in 1932, a lumpen rogue, looking like a beaten man, with his trousers hanging down below his waist, his old undershirt, and shabby raincoat, was a centrally recognizable character in a way that was impossible in the literature of the time. (Shortly afterward, the movies presented Cantinflas as the pauper who makes us laugh.) The standard view was that poverty was a trap in which moral lessons lay in wait. Although this first generation of cartoonists did not distinguish itself with its social criticism, its *costumbrista* praise did lend marginalized characters and situations visibility, albeit precarious and involuntary; servants and bus drivers, flag sellers, balloon vendors, working-class courting couples, and the figure of Chupamirto would never have featured in the chronicles of the everyday life of the middle class.

Now That I Can Read, What Do I Read?

Making illiteracy the motivation does not translate automatically into childish comic strips. In those produced in the 1940s, for example, the language is varied and the plots can be extremely involved. This relative complexity was required to retain a reading public. Simplification was increasingly obvious in the drawings, as were the repetition of traditional morals and above all the attachment to the themes and obsessions of oral culture (or the cinema, the new version of oral culture). Comics easily became traditional reading matter for a mass audience, creating an industry that, in 1981, published nearly one hundred million comics, a record figure and one of the highest in the world (perhaps the highest in proportional terms). Functional illiteracy alone does not explain this growth. Comics undoubtedly served those who had nothing to read, but how did they persist in a universe governed by television and the shock of newer technology? Probably because of the need to read more than images and because of the summary of popular tastes that comics provide. In order to grow, a country needs to eliminate the dead weight of illiteracy, and the Mexican government has made an effort to do this. However, there still remains the literate population's need for knowledge. Learning how to read and write is the major means of social advancement, the key to providing us with an understanding of why we have lived in this way and why we deserve to live better. It hardly matters that there is no real love of reading, that there is no tradition of this, or any available incentives. What is basic here is the timid veneration of schools, and the acceptance of the myth of schooling that will make the poor rich.

Massive literacy campaigns were conducted in small towns, urban neighborhoods, suburbs, and working-class districts (the "slums" of the time), leaving behind a residue of frustration: Millions learned to read as best they could, and there they remained. These young people were only able to complete third, fourth, or sixth grade of elementary school, or fared poorly in middle school; life could not offer them any more, as they would say. However, through the comics life did grant them some skills, such as access to another universe, peopled with signs they happily deciphered, reminding them of a world of experience whose importance they accepted without admitting it. The cinema affected them differently; with comics, the social dream definitely took place through language.

The poor became literate, happily acquiring a new skill, albeit with difficulty; yet they did not know how to use their new gift. For example, millions of Indians, barely bilingual, were left adrift, not incorporated into a nation of *criollos* and *mestizos* as a result of their rejection by society on the one hand, and the desire to preserve their own lifestyle on the other. They had learned to read, yet they lacked books (with the exception of the Bible in certain cases), and the meagre provincial press offered them nothing. The alternative was comics: Relatively cheap, comics were easily understood and disseminated pleasant, amusing narrative schemes. This is usually where acculturation begins. For fifty years, comics in Mexico—an instrument of transition—were the main literary form available to millions of marginalized displaced people and émigrés. Armies of migrants left their towns and villages and settled in large Mexican cities and in the United States, and lived as best they could. Along the way, in bus stations, on trains, and in the squares as they waited for the "coyotes" (who ferried those without identification papers across the border), in the rest-periods during their ten-hour working days, and in the loneliness of fatigue, they devoured these poorly-made and badly printed booklets. And there they were confirmed in their prejudices, their fatal conclusions about reality. They could certainly read. But reading is an undertaking that requires time, support, and personal and public incentives; in this respect, the taste for reading is a privilege of class or vocation. For the poor and marginalized, books are an inhibiting force and bookshops sacred places. Yet, while reading a book may be slow, expensive, and difficult, consuming insignificant, swiftly read magazines is fast. Workers, the unemployed, housewives with no houses, children, and teenagers have used comics to eliminate their fear of books, have established their first, and nearly always last, relationship with literature, and have begun one of the intimate forms of learning about social life.

For All Generations

Nothing out of the ordinary: Comics demanded identification with plots, characters, and situations. Identification: The pauper recognizes himself in those who use similar words and live in familiar situations; the child mentally incorporates the deeds of his peers who grow up good-natured and noble in the midst of the ignominy of the slums; housewives are reflected in women who suffer, laugh out of impotence, and cry because they are unaware of any other way to express themselves. Identifying with the comic's offerings does not mean distancing oneself; it means reaffirming values, and mitigating the anguish of displacement and marginalization. For this reason, unlike U.S. comics, Mexican comics reject the idea of adjusting comics to the level of children. If adults read them, so will children. The formula "Suitable for children aged eight to eighty" is not out of the question. Age is unimportant to this industry.

Are there, nonetheless, aspects of comics that are specifically or primarily geared to children? During the early decades of the twentieth century, comic strips were included in newspapers to provide women, removed from politics, with the incentive to read something and be entertained. In the pursuit of success, newspaper editors required the imitation of U.S. models. The order was carried out, but almost immediately this adherence to U.S. formats was ignored, not so much in response to nationalist psychology, but as a means of gaining credibility. The popular classes had no use for intellectualized humor or national platitudes about future well-being, and less for sermonizing morality. Readers demanded all the vulgarity that censorship would allow, with a distinct preference for the picaresque and local characters and situations. Cartoons were not regarded as artistic or literary products, merely as scale models of melodrama or national humor. This process of adaptation led to the nationalization of an entertainment genre for children from the United States. Moreover, Mexico had no artists of the caliber of Alex Raymond (*Flash Gordon*), Burne Hogarth (*Tarzan*), or Hal Foster (*Prince Valiant*), none with the formal talent of Will Eisner (*The Spirit*); it had the equivalents, however, more with regard to inventiveness than to form, of the creators of *Li'l Abner*, *Pogo*, and *Peanuts*.

As a result of the reluctance to experiment and the hastiness with which the drawings were produced, there was a lack of fixed criteria. Notwithstanding its rivalry with U.S. comics, the industry did not court child readers and continued to produce comics for adults. (Only photonovels would modify this scheme, with their target audience of girls aged fourteen to nineteen and their wealth of programmed illustrations.) As proof of their loyalty to those over eighteen, Mexican comics continued to portray golden-hearted, unhappy prostitutes, gigolos who beat up and eliminated their victims, and settings of vice and redemption. And official censorship, which had been so strict for decades on such matters, was not concerned by the excesses of material "supposedly" for children. But censors were fully aware of what they were doing: The offensive comics would actually end up only in the hands of those adults who had already fallen. Children who were worth protecting would never read that sort of material, and, even if they did, they would read it differently. Similar tastes and opposing conclusions. Children would draw one lesson, while adults would draw another, completely different lesson from the same comic book, thereby proving that it was suitable for all generations. It helped the young to learn about collective dreams and moved adults to become resigned to their lot in life. The comics accepted this challenge because a public consisting entirely of children would not be sufficient; so they also aimed to fill in those areas of adult neglect, where those who read comics did not think that they were reading, but merely being entertained.

Between Ideology and a Joke

The comics industry followed the most absurd anti-Communist rallying cries, promoted and defended sexism, refused to engage in any form of experimentation, exploited fanaticism and superstitions, was terrified (since it was so unprofitable) of artistic drawing, and paid cartoonists and script writers miserable salaries; yet despite all this, during the period from 1930 to 1970, Mexican comics actively connected with their readers. Their covers–with tearful contrite faces, ignominious humor, magicians, and monsters apparently designed by an amnesiac ten-year-old–somehow connected, as far as possible during the permanent economic crisis, with collective experiences and beliefs. Not far removed from comics were the picture cards of saints and virgins that attested to a relationship with the sacred; the shameless excesses of melodrama were also not that far removed from reality. And the dynamics of comics and photonovels were not only or primarily understood from the perspective of ideology. More than a means of manipulation, this phenomenon can be seen as the result of the lack of alternatives. The abysmal quality of comics, photonovels, television, and populist cinema was accepted since there was nothing better available.

The most successful comics always included one or more of the following well-tested formulas:

- Melodramas of servants turned into bourgeois women (Cinderella), imbued with the fatalism of class; an impoverished situation redeemed by the generosity of the soul, while a wealthy milieu is imbued with familial hatred.

- Variations of the Ape Man with processions of monsters, multiform villains, snake pits, unexpected tigers, and helpful elephants–all distorted versions of Hollywood film plots.

- The simplistic treatment of childhood, which is either the psychological space of understanding of a society through suffering or the saddest banality.

- Variations on the superhero of U.S. comics with incredible mental powers, control of heavenly forces, mastery of oriental cultures, extrasensory perception, telekinesis, the capacity to get himself out of fixes, the gift of turning people into animals, and so on.

- Humorous series that exploit the popularity of comedians in vogue at the time, ranging from Cantinflas to the Chapulín Colorado. These regard vulgarity as the sole criterion for laughter but, at their best (Gaspar Bolaños' *Rolando el Rabioso* and above all, Gabriel Vargas' *La Familia Burrón*) renounce an impossible U.S. way-of-life in Mexico and attempt something freer: Comic delirium and a sense of unreality, caused by the narrowness of the medium, herald the replacement of traditional nationalism by humor derived from a pained, ironic affection toward a people and its customs.

- Witches' or ghosts' stories, inevitably linked to adultery and Satanism.

Given the small number of plots available, the vitality of these comics is astonishing. The basic narrative schemes had already existed since the 1930s, and new ones were extremely scarce, with the exception of the political work of Rius, whose extraordinary international success confirmed his didactic effectiveness and the persuasiveness of his humor. And readers from a rural background or living a marginalized urban existence regarded comics as a replacement for their oral tradition, guaranteed to satisfy their passion for the feats of heroes from an alternative calendar to that of saints, their need for coarse jokes, their fascination with never-ending stories (in the style of *A Thousand and One Nights*), their Manichean enjoyment of exemplary heroes and villains, and their taste for the reproduction in print of a type of speech that was somewhat similar to their own.

By the late 1980s, everything pointed to the extinction of Mexican comics: Children's annoyance at the abysmal quality of the products, their relatively high cost, the international transformation of the comic into an artistic genre, and the domination of television. Sales plummeted and all hope was abandoned. Then, unexpectedly, a subgenre took hold of the market, one that could be called "light porn" or "pornographic sketches," which did not dare to be fully pornographic for fear of censorship. Once again, comics recovered their massive readership through their new repertoire of physically exceptional beings, dialogues using lascivious slang, wonderful breasts and buttocks, bodily perfection, endless sex (without any depiction of the genitals), adultery that anticipated crimes, satanic possession, nymphomania and male sexopathy, rapes that were avenged by murder, schools dominated by orgies, and a cascade of acts of fellatio, cunnilingus, and the like. And the readership of these scandal sheets is, as in the past, a blend of children, teenagers, and adults. Only by reaching the limits of exploitative violence, this time sexual, did comics recover their massive readership.

Of Popular Culture and Mass Culture

Why do I call the products of an era of the cultural industry "urban popular culture"? Because in addition to the general commercialization and omnipresence of advertising, the masses have been intensely involved with films, comics, songs, radio programs, the circus, and vaudeville. The masses (still not called The People) have chosen their idols, their essential themes, their ultimate vocalists, the comedians from whom they have drawn a sense of humor and speech rhythms, the comic strips that have not allowed them to leave their childhood, and dance styles that have moved them to virtuosity. Pedro Infante became a myth, not because of the avalanche of advertising about him, but because of the friendliness and good looks with which millions identified, his tragicomic voice and authority, his endless romances, and his tragic end in a fatal crash flying his private plane. If María Félix was the sole symbol of female authority for so many years, it was not because of any decision on the part of the industry, but because of her blend of beauty and personality, her tumultuous life, and her exceptional appearance. By emphatically rejecting the virtuosity of tenors, Daniel Santos created the virtuosity of those who could only imitate Daniel Santos and, indeed, wanted to do so, as he revolutionized the songs of the slums. All of them, and many others (actors, actresses, singers, comedians, soccer players, boxers) constituted popular culture because they were both unique to it and could be expropriated by hundreds of thousands at the same time.

How did urban popular culture become a key tradition in the twentieth century? The answer should take the following psychological and cultural fact into account: In all societies, what is certain is what is known by everyone or virtually everyone. The admiration and habits of the multitudes constitute certainty in the midst of technological change, the disintegration of families, and the loss or modification of beliefs. Marginal cultural expression has an additional factor in its favor: The complicity of the mediator who disseminates it as a discovery that is then mass produced and finds a place "in people's hearts." There are two successive responses to mass culture and its spectacular programs, its singers on request, its forays into infantile humor, and its soap operas that keep entire nations in suspense. The first is unconditional surrender: Ecstasy prevails during the broadcasting of *El derecho de nacer* [The Right to Be Born] or *Simplemente María* [Simply Maria] or *Ave sin nido* [Bird without a Nest] or *Los ricos también lloran* [The Rich Also Cry]; young girls are reduced to tears by seeing a singer they have never heard; an entire society repeats comedians' phrases like a battle cry (Roberto Gómez Bolaños, el Chapulín Colorado, and El Chavo del Ocho are good examples of this). The second reaction is programmed amnesia. If the memory of generations of children is measured by television series ("When I was a child, I never missed . . ."), forgetfulness feeds on idols, comics, the plots and actors in soap operas. Television products are very famous because they will soon be forgotten. Only rarely does mass culture become real popular culture.

Just as mass culture only rarely becomes popular culture, television has never really replaced the cinema. During the 1930s and 1950s, moviegoers demanded of national cinema what U.S. movies failed to give it: Images of public virtues and private vices, and the reaffirmation of the very categories of vice and virtue. From the 1970s onward, audiences demanded from movies what was neither allowed by nor granted by television. If the country had apparently set its sights on modernity, in which the majority population was out of place, the films featured the mass audience's flaws: The men were womanizers, drunks, irresponsible, ignorant, and even despicable. They cursed, were dazzled by puns with sexual meanings, and made their sexual craving commonplace. Television, a middle-class show for all ages, is more distant, lacking coarsely realistic, violent sentiments. The cinema arouses viewers' feelings, particularly class pride or resentment. Millionaires in film are an unknown quantity, an arrogant and nearly always despicable abstraction, as opposed to the generosity of the poor who, since they have nothing to lose, are noble and authentic. Yet the sanctified spirit of the poor does not attract audiences, and, in order to succeed, the cinema has resorted to nude women, previously forbidden words, breaks with the social norms, leading permissiveness and heterodoxy. If television is based on a conceit of "family decency," cinema portrays what producers assume to be outbreaks of the collective unconscious. And thus the two media complement, rather than oppose, each other.

Somebody Stop That Landscape Wobbling (On Talking Pictures in Mexico)

In urban popular culture, cinema is a definitive influence, a university of beliefs and customs. Indeed, cinema offers the first overview of the country outside textbooks and the expansion of popular culture through technology. In the course of its three or four thousand films, the industry has offered (a rough guess) a handful of masterpieces, eighty to a hundred good films, hundreds of significant films saved by the cameramen, actors, settings, excellent technicians . . . and also a host of failures resulting from haste and awkwardness, pandering to machismo, intolerance, and racism. This type of cinema determines its public, the reverent or anxious masses who turn it into the main interpreter of the exaltations and fatalities of the race. And it maintains their liking for melodrama, both feeding and tempering their intolerance . . . and imperceptibly modifying them. And at the end of this process, an extremely significant part of Mexican cinema proves to be popular culture, because in a sense it has freed itself from its commercial aims and has revitalized its audience.

In fulfillment of its creative strategy and its system of expanding and retaining its public, Mexican cinema presents itself as a grand summary of the popular, its achievements, rituals, myths, prejudices, inclinations, attitudes to celebrations and mourning, and its search for "Mexicanness." The industry (producers, directors, screenwriters, actors, composers, and set designers) is primarily concerned with re-creating, reflecting, praising, or discreetly criticizing its public and its lifestyles, which the cinema enhances, modifies, and refines. Regardless of the definition of popular culture adopted (the institutionalized practices of communities, the catalogue of rituals and predilections, methods of resistance against established powers, the folkloric idealization of the realities of class, race and gender, or simply what is accepted by a large number of people), it is clear that the public is drastically transformed through its depiction in films and on radio and television. Until approximately 1960, Mexican popular culture was basically rural, with religious overtones, revealing a form of authoritarianism that had been profoundly interiorized. By 1999, it had become an urban culture, highly secularized as a result of technology and mass society, and with growing courage to criticize central authoritarianism. At the same time, a significant number of local religious and community forms continued to exist.

Mexican cinema exploited government indifference to public need, church censorship—which, *contrario sensu,* supported what it forbade—and the backwardness of the audience. Yet this does not fully explain its power of attraction, which has been in part complemented by the power of technology, the strength of oral culture, and real or functional illiteracy (which, for example, prevented people from following the Spanish subtitles quickly enough). The cinema, which was in no way regarded as an art, provided viewers with a fundamental incentive: The guarantee of an amusing or tearfully entertaining approach to the images of both the wider world and their particular locality.

The Golden Age of Mexican Cinema

In the twentieth century, popular culture in Mexico was transformed by what became known as the Golden Age of Mexican Cinema. To a very great extent, cinephiles (as all Mexicans are) drew their speech, their notion of appropriate behavior in family conflicts, their gestures, and their view of society and entertainment from the films of this period. It was, in fact the Golden Age of the public, rather than the cinema. On weekends, in the company of his or her family, each viewer knew exactly what to expect regarding group opinions and judgments, what produced mirth and what produced grief, what was beautiful and what was insignificant. As a result of the profound influence of the films of the Golden Age, the public once again became compulsively nationalized. What were some of the basic scenarios of the Golden Age that became the traditional places cherished by the public?

- The home (humble; otherwise it would inevitably become a bone of contention), presided over by the Virgin of Guadalupe, and by a poor, humble yet orderly sense of decoration.

- The cabaret, that moral hell and sensory heaven, where the prohibited was normalized and slightly unorthodox songs became hymns to dissipation, while tropical orchestras disseminated the libidinous sound that encouraged people to think about sex rather than the popular art of dance.

- The dance hall, the "Athenian agora of Tenochtitlan," where dance was the quintessential discourse of social relevance among those destined for anonymity.

- The saloon bar (preferably rural) as a peak experience, one of the three great sites of pain (the other two being shady churches and bedrooms in semidarkness), where the macho spirit was beaten into shape and the collapse of the soul was forged, fatal decisions were made, and the edicts of self-destruction (songs) were listened to.

- The historical scenes, fancy dress balls, and moving nationalist speeches and allegations of social justice recited without conviction.

- The countryside (the idyllic countryside, the campfire, the serenade), the great setting in which primitivism was indistinguishable from purity.

- The street where prostitutes lived (the red-light district), where the discovery of the opportunities of the city prevailed over desolation.

- The brothel, where noble souls wallowed in vice in order to be able to long for innocence.

- The neighborhood, as the society within reach of the poor, which required the following choral genres: melodrama, where the neighborhood meant fatality, and comedy, where the neighborhood was both beginning and end.

- Couples in bed: shameless confessions that appealed to the public's taste for voyeurism.

- Xochimilco: paradise lost; Jalisco: the paradise that defends its identity with manly bravado.

- The "Mexican gothic" hacienda: the secularization of the great beyond, expressed in the form of vampires, Aztec mummies, wolfmen, and priests who worshipped Huitzilopochtli.

- The boxing ring, as a metaphor for the struggle for life (or rather the opposite).

- The chapel, the parish, the confessional, a world understood through low voices, total prohibitions that grant one privilege; keeping one's gaze lowered.

This catalogue of themes, characters, and situations was circumscribed by a keen sense of certainty: The public was like that, not any other way. Come hither, mothers bathed in tears and self-pity, prostitutes who glimpse redemption through agony, priests who direct lives using simplistic techniques of good and bad, severe parents who are angry ambassadors of God at table, policemen who are as good as gold, gangsters who die by the sword because censorship demands their tragic deaths, families that disintegrate because no one warned them in time of the separation of souls and bodies, heroes and comic actors whose strength is derived, in the first analysis, from their similarity to the spectators, rumba dancers who make the cabaret tremble with their lascivious rhythms, disdainful *charros* from beaten-up saloon bars, revolutionaries who dig their own graves without checking on the size. Unintentionally satirical, intentionally humorous and sentimental, occasionally tragic, the repertoire of the formative decades of this cinema, from the 1930s to the 1950s, revealed the profound traits of the communities that supported it. According to these films, the popular culture of Mexico was generous, prejudiced, more emotional and less thinking, racist ("so they wouldn't get ideas above their station"), sanctimonious and yet scornful of sanctimoniousness, servile to the Master and the Barrister, as rebellious as it could be, fond of memorized jokes, and attentive to the subversive elements found in comedy.

The consolidation of the industry brought with it the need to imitate and assimilate that inexorable model, Hollywood. And the main attraction was the star system, which, more than any other element, transformed certain actors and actresses into authentic popular culture: The media and the public agreed to classify these exceptional beings as "myths":

Jorge Negrete, Dolores del Río, María Félix, Pedro Infante, Pedro Armendáriz, Mario Moreno Cantinflas, Joaquín Pardavé, Germán Valdés Tin Tan, Arturo de Córdova, Fernando Soler, Sara García, Ninón Sevilla. Their mythical status was derived less from their "inaccessibility" (conditions that only Dolores and María fulfilled) than from their archetypal roles and their transformation into collective symbols. Character actors were also essential. By dint of repetition, stereotypes became household figures, the irreplaceable neighbors or relatives of cinephiles. The consequences of this set of hallowed myths and stereotypes led Gilbert Seldes to remark: "We have noted that the immature and uncritical form the bulk of the movie audience; and it can therefore cause no surprise to find that most movies are made for them. For such audiences, simplicity is an essential and complex emotion that must not be aroused. Good and bad must be easily recognized and the audience must be able to answer for itself, without any hesitation, the question 'Whom are we rooting for?' . . . The true stereotype is internal as well as external" (22–23). The aesthetics of Mexican cinema were based on its resemblance to the ideal life of its audience, brought up on one idea: Custom is beauty's other name. Tradition marks the junction of the picturesque and the beautiful. Cinema helped society to rediscover its surroundings from a loving point of view.

A Commonplace: The Cinema as an Element of National Union

A lay state: A process of secularization that moved religious institutions (although not religious feelings) off center stage, a cinema that linked the profound convictions of the public to the imposition of modernity. The strong state was responsible for institutions, formal education, and the keys for interpreting politics, economics, and society. The only thing it left out was everyday life. The Church was responsible for hopes in the next world, while the cinema, radio, the record industry, comics, and then television were responsible for earthly illusions. The division of labor was as follows: The control of public life (work and politics) was the concern of the state; the ultimate meaning of life (what happened to people when they died) was the privilege of religion, whereas what people did in their free time was the responsibility of the cultural industry. Cinema proved decisive in national integration, as the mediator between the all-powerful state and the masses who are linked by sentimental nationalism, but who are a population without any sense of a democratic tradition. If a real political culture does not exist, then let laughter and tears flow. If high society excluded spectators, then let the cinema, radio, and comic strips create a society that would accept them. If there were no habit of reading, then let there be an abundance of visual alternatives. A public that did not travel and included a substantial number of illiterates and poor readers did not trust U.S. films to represent its experience. It chose its own cinema, knowing that it would provide it with irreplaceable features: The familiar turns of phrase, the scenes of poverty, faces-as-mirrors, the delights of melodrama, the poetic landscapes that they could afford to visit, and the music that accompanied them all day. The terra firma of Mexican cinema was both an implicit and an explicit idea: The nation was a prolongation of the family; the family was the truest representation of the nation. This nationalism and familial ideology were both real and slanderous, false and true. They expressed an autocratic state and were the result of political and social weakness in a majority that accepted everything that unified it.

The Mexican Revolution

A favorite perspective in the industry was that of the dramatic compassion of civilized man toward primitive man. The elite spectators, aware that they were far removed from primitivism, identified with the rejected past or viewed the revolutionary vulgarity with disdain. And they remembered the bellicose events between 1910 and 1917, the cavalry charges, the capture of cities, the fearlessness of the women soldiers, and the brazenness of the generals. The revolution was still profitable: What a feast for the eyes was that combination of dust and blood, shootings and forgiveness, Villa's trains and Porfirian farewells! Under the pretext of a homage to the Revolution, the industry celebrated machismo, made the past decent, and converted a social explosion into a landscape from a Western.

The main support for this sleight of hand was provided by Pancho Villa himself. He could not be made into a sacred figure; legend and truth were indistinguishable in his life; he did not found institutions like Carranza; he did not prove to be a stabilizing force, like Obregón and Calles; nor was he a pure martyr like Zapata. If that were not enough, he invaded Columbus, New Mexico, in the United States, wept at burials, had people shot first and asked questions later, inspired fanaticism among the troops, had a ringing name, was a social highwayman, and attracted the world's attention through his character and audacity. Thanks to Villa and *villismo*, the cinema used the Mexican Revolution without making the slightest commitment to it. And the public had an extraordinary symbol at its disposal.

Making Technique Sacred

The first clash was with the technical. To some extent, astonishment at the wonders of technology was the national definition of limitations. The shift from silent movies to talking pictures clarified this intuition: If we cannot generate our own technology, at least we can distinguish the most genuine form of reality, that of the screen. It does not reject us; it leads to instant identification; and it makes us share its idea of nation, family, and society. (Television inherited this lack of distinction between technological products and reality.) At this point, extraordinary changes took place in Mexico. A considerable amount of feudal residues disappeared; the right withdrew into its strongholds; *machismo* was nearly always an insulting term; and people did not go to the cinema for the reaffirmation of traditional certainties, but rather for the opposite: A glimpse of what was inevitably to come, lifestyles that frightened and then fascinated, and the transgressions that made this patriarchal, God-fearing country unrecognizable. If the cinema of the Golden Age created its public by giving everyday life a utopian aspect, the cinema of recent decades maintained the hopes of its audience by guaranteeing attention to its landscapes and situations (with distance and a certain amount of humor).

Myths: *Jorge Negrete, Pedro Armendáriz, Pedro Infante, Arturo de Córdova*

The industry made magnificent use of stereotypes: The Long-Suffering Woman, the Prostitute with the Heart of Gold, the Generous Macho, the Elderly Beau, the Comic (who entertains while he destroys), the Primitive Man (who aspires to justice), and the perfect representations of the Adam and Eve of the country paradise. Once embodied in actors, stereotypes became archetypes, an essential element for those at the opposite end of the spectrum from politics, history, and society. One of the most enduring and deep-rooted myths, or archetypes, is that of Pedro Infante, a figure who could not be exported, a man of the people who made his limitations his greatest virtue. If Infante represented losers as if being a loser were the most natural thing in the world, it was, among other things, because these audiences did not usually observe winners. Infante was the incarnation of the symbols and interlocutors of the people, originally a charming Macho who captivated and dazzled with his songs and charm. Today he is a sort of dynamic museum specimen of a vanishing Mexico, and he represents a country where people still had feelings with which their forebears could easily identify.

Jorge Negrete is a quintessential Macho, an operatic tenor who raised the level of *ranchera* songs, an arrogant version of the landowner who condescended to play humble characters, the emblem of a Spanish-speaking public that had discovered the advantages of combining good looks and machismo. In turn, Pedro Armendáriz represented the finest version of Mexicanness, with his lusty voice, his dominant presence, his gait of a general on his way to battle, and a face that could express anger as easily as adoration. And Arturo de Córdova, with the skills he had acquired during his time as a radio announcer, was the cultivated professional, the born seducer, the man tortured by his unconscious, the pre-Wildean cynic, the owner of a voice that was a declaration of cultural assets.

The Genre of Beginnings: Ranchera Comedies

The innovation that established Mexican cinema in popular culture was the *ranchera* comedy. In 1936 Fernando de Fuentes directed *Allá en el Rancho Grande* [Back on the Big Ranch], filmed by Gabriel Figueroa, with forgettable performances. This was a *ranchera* fantasy consisting of a romance in a "typical" hacienda of the 1920s and 1930s, three children who grew up together until class differences separated them, the theme of the nobility of the rural soul, the malevolent shadow of a go-between, a duel of songs, a challenge to personal and family honor, a horse race, and a happy ending. This elementary combination heralded the future of Mexican cinema, which did not lie in technical or artistic effect, but in the negotiated guilelessness of those who watched it (the basis of the Golden Age was the educational level with which producers credited their audience). *Allá en el Rancho Grande,* like the slew of imitations that followed, was based on the implicit hatred of Lázaro Cardenas's land reform, a utopian view of large landed estates, and praise of the submission of laborers and peasant women. But at the time of their release, spectators in Mexico and Latin America did not concentrate on the ideology but on perfect innocence. In 1936, despite the pressure of revolutionary nationalism, very few were affected by reactionary ideology. There was talk of class struggle and the proletarian masses filed by in the streets, but class and racial prejudices in the cinema failed to cause distress. What did *ranchera* comedies offer? Songs, archetypes, and stereotypes, an amusing idea of country life, a romantic plot, expressions that summarized their lifestyles, and more songs.

Atmospheres: Poverty

Mexican cinema made poverty its raison d'être, not for political, but for scenographic and budgetary reasons. Since it was useless to compete with Hollywood, to deal with the awkwardness of scripts and the lack of so-called stars, the flaws in the plots, the excess of improvisation, and the like did not matter. This misery produced an aesthetics that was passionately experienced by millions in Mexico and Latin America; given the poverty represented, there was no cultural or social intimidation. Lacking the money for super-productions, Mexican cinema sought to emphasize the lack of majestic scenery. Since they could not afford a Griffith or a Cecil B. DeMille, it was up to them to nationalize genres, formats, techniques for presenting the main figures, and unforgettable plots. Truth lay in repetition: By dint of seeing the same set and the same faces, viewers came to declare they were genuine; they had endured the procession of plots and situations and survived artistic disasters. After three or four basic plots had been repeated over and over, viewers were able to discover their identity by memorizing their own reactions: "I cry because I'm sentimental, I get indignant because I'm very manly, I laugh because I laughed at the same thing before." This strategy of circularity bred trust. What did not vary was worthy of credit and was called a family show; the phrase *family show* ended-up being a game of mirrors: Mexican families saw the reflection of their eternal unity in the cinema, while the industry took for granted the stability of the family, given its similarity to what took place on the screen. This illusion was not even shattered by the conviction that the cinema was the compulsory avant-garde of the period. Only the boom in independent television freed the cinema from its household concerns.

Myths: María Félix and Dolores del Río

Cruel beauty and untouchable beauty. The woman who demanded her place of honor (and dishonor) and the domination of men that extolled her person. The man-eater and the bird of paradise. Doña Bárbara and María Candelaria. If Dolores del Río had the fragility that turned beauty into invincible strength, María Félix was the female who turned into a male to survive and humiliate other women—those who were not beautiful, who lacked personality, or who were incapable of handling a whip. Both definitions of beautiful women concealed and deferred recognition of real women. What is attractive about both Dolores del Río and María Félix is the unrepeatable nature of their figures and their features and their star quality in an age when the cinema magnified and channeled the religious spirit. In an officially lay century, the cinema represented a mystical, or perhaps pagan, persistence of the adoration of virgins and goddesses, the transformation of heroes and heroines into cathedrals and statues, the canonization of the couple, the assumption and resurrection of the face, the beatific trembling in the presence of the evil and horror that, from the audience's seats, are revealed in characters such as Milagros Travestidos ("Milagros the transvestite") and in the appearances of our Bloodthirsty Lady. "We had faces then," is the proud declaration of the diva of silent movies, Norma Desmond (Gloria Swanson), in Billy Wilder's *Sunset Boulevard*, the film that marked Hollywood's transition from oneiric church to cultural passion. They certainly had faces then, bestowed by nature, re-created in the studios, and maintained through the sacrificial efforts of their owners . . . and a team of make-up artists, fashion designers, lighting directors, photographers, experts in the manipulation of light and shadow and in the technique that gave close-ups the gift of releasing and demanding our intimacy. Dolores and María are the most beautiful women of that century in Mexico, and *beauty* here is a term that blends manifest beauty and the art of appearance and willpower. No native has ever been as convincing (or unreal) as Dolores del Río in *Flor Silvestre*. No political boss has made his features as imperious as María

Félix did in *Doña Bárbara*. María and Dolores are brilliance transformed into ideas, and ideas that stay with us with overwhelming intensity.

Humor

In Mexican cinema, a comedian needs to do the following:

- Belong to the lower classes, beginning with his appearance, and to express this both verbally and socially. He must be likable but obedient, playful but strong-willed, roguish but honest. If, as a result of his theatrical training or temperament, the comic–as in the paradigmatic case of Joaquín Pardavé–plays parts of upper-middle- or middle-class characters, he must be evidently anachronistic. It was not until the 1960s, after the Golden Age, that a comic leading man, Mauricio Garcés, emerged ostensibly from the middle classes.

- Show not class conflict, but rather the limitations of the dispossessed: their shyness or false arrogance or mythomania. The point was to turn social resentment into obsequious folklore and to make humor a technique for stifling rebellious or turbulent impulses.

- Experience amorous conflicts in such a way as to make humor appear as an extension of feeling. Jokes are a parenthesis in emotion, while laughter hides tears (although not vice-versa).

- Maintain his principal attraction, in other words, his previous personality, which brought him to the cinema from the theater or the vaudeville or television (comics who began in the cinema are the exception). His original resources (expressions, voice, nickname, manners) are his ultimate resources in a medium that is reluctant to accept gags or visual jokes.

- Remain, whatever happens, in the same environment, going from slum to slum to slum (with a compulsorily short stay in the lap of luxury). And the majority, despite their proven talent, intervene as a counterpoint to the immaculate couple or the tragic couple. The great exceptions were Cantinflas and Tin Tan. During the 1930s, Cantinflas invented a form of speech–*ese decir que no se dice porque ya se dijo lo que nomás no y quién lo iba a decir* ("that speech which is not said because it has already been said what cannot be said and who would have said it")–that served as a radical identity for those who wished to feel different so that they could move up the social scale. The newspapers dubbed him "the immortal little bugger" and "the inspired mimic," and, in 1936 and 1938, Cantinflas showed the country the humor to be found in the verbal and gestural expressions of the poor. His first viewers admired him for his behavior, the way he related to others, and the way he trapped people, confusing them with his banter. Around him, another form of national unity operated, where the bourgeois, the middle class, and the working classes reveled in the novelty that was soon named after him: *cantinflismo*, or using a lot of words to say absolutely nothing. Cantinflas perfected the art of facial and verbal jerks (enigmatic mimicry): His eyebrows asked questions, his arms hung down dejectedly, and his body would gesticulate furiously confronted with the autonomous nature of verbs, nouns, and adjectives. During the years of his early triumph, this extravagant being who captured the astuteness and skill of the marginalized population in the capital was a revelation. In vaudeville and in light theater, everything about Cantinflas was dazzling: the humor, the mimicry, the charm, the irreverence of the "cheeky little bugger," the urban pariah (see **Figure 6**).

Sex and politics, spirituality and carnality, laughter and protests: Spectators happily lost themselves in the blend of the sensual, the comic, and the cheeky; the public, which, at the very mention of politics, returned to its original condition as the masses and elevated Cantinflas's sarcasm to the level of protests in the Plaza Mayor, rejoicing in the irreverence toward those at the top, those who were not mentioned by name but only by their function: "They can have their politicians and millionaires, but we'll hold our own when it comes to joking." Urban humor grew out of a blend of double meanings, wit, wordplay, and ambiguity. And while this sexualization of humor was watched carefully by the censors, Germán Valdés's Tin Tan was the exception that proved the rule. He ushered in a modern style that combined the Spanish spoken on the border (Spanglish), acting ability, humor drawn from upsetting solemnity, wearing a zoot suit or the youthful fashion of the day, the body language of a *fauno,* and a vocal style that exerted a powerful influence over his admirers. Tin Tan was a cultural forerunner of the "Chicanoization" of Mexico and a prologue to the popular culture of the twenty-first century.

Melodrama

The cinema provided the first inkling of globalization. However attractive Hollywood may have been, Latin-American audiences did not regard its products as the truth but rather as an intuition of a world, something that they wished would be true. Hollywood was an invitation to leave behind the feeling that the village, city, or country where one lived was a prison. During the Second World War, Mexico had the opportunity of competing in Latin America with a U.S. film industry that was otherwise absorbed by the war effort. It was an extraordinary

moment, and, in the public's eyes, Mexican films represented an extension of urban life never before seen, a blend of fantasy and voyeurism and a great learning experience. Thus, if anything, melodrama prepared one to live life to the full–in other words, melodramatically. Melodrama, definitely the central genre in Mexican cinema, initially used models from English and French theater, which it then poured into Hollywood molds. It soon tired of these thematic restrictions, opting instead for more sensational, tearful, exaggerated formulae that shed light on self-destructive behavior. Mexican melodrama scorned containment and was so excessive that it combined comedy, nightmare, *costumbrista* evocation, dreams, and puppet shows in one fell swoop. It enthusiastically depicted families as both heaven and hell at the same time, identifying passionate love with a wish to hurl oneself into the depths of Hades as can be revisited in *Maria candelaria* (see **Figure 7**). The crowning achievements of Mexican melodrama–*Nosotros los pobres* [1947; We the Poor] and *Ustedes los ricos* [1948; You the Rich], directed by Ismael Rodríguez with the quintessential proletarian couple, Pedro Infante and Blanca Estela Pavón–illustrate the industry's radical tenet: If the public does not suffer, it is disappointed and feels that it is watching a film, rather than what it should be watching, namely reality.

Figure 6.

Photograph of Mario Moreno (Cantinflas) with Joaquin Pardavé in Ahí está el detalle, *Azteca Films 1940. (Courtesy of Zuzana Pick)*

About Urban Popular Culture at the End of the Century

If it is true that today the energy expended by urban popular culture is intent on recovering achievements and trends of the past, then we have reason to hope. There has been a renewed burst of creativity in the exercise of ancient traditions; the frenzy of mass culture is being resisted and expressions of "high culture" are, recognizably, now popular culture. These include *El llano en llamas* [1954; *The Burning Plains*] and *Pedro Páramo* [1955] by Juan Rulfo (1918–1986), *El laberinto de la soledad* [1950; *The Labyrinth of Solitude*] by Octavio Paz (1914–1998), *Cien años de soledad* [1962; *One Hundred Years of Solitude*]

by Gabriel García Márquez (b. 1927), the work of Jaime Sabines (1926–1999), the architecture of Luis Barragán (1902–1988), the photography of Manuel Alvarez Bravo (1902–2002) and Nacho López (1923–1986), the work of Diego Rivera (1886–1957), Frida Kahlo (1907–1954), David Alfaro Siqueiros (1896–1974), José Clemente Orozco (1883–1949), and Rufino Tamayo (1899–1991), and most classical music, from Vivaldi and Bach to Mozart and Beethoven, to cite some irrefutable examples. Although mass culture reduces the vigor of popular culture, the addition of other hallowed expressions expands its sphere of action.

Translation by Suzanne D. Stephens

Figure 7.

Photograph of Pedro Armendariz and Dolores del Rio in Emilio Fernandez's Maria Candelaria, *Azteca Films 1943. (Courtesy of Zuzana Pick)*

Works Cited

Bakhtin, Mikhail. 1968. *Rabelais and His World.* Trans. Helen Islowksy. Cambridge: MIT Press.

Campos, Rubén M. 1929. *El folclore literario de México: Investigación acerca de la producción literaria popular (1525-1925).* Mexico City: Publicaciones de la Secretaria de Educación Pública.

García Márquez, Gabriel. 1967. *Cien años de soledad.* Buenos Aires: Sudamericana. 1970. *One Hundred Years of Solitude.* Trans. Gregory Rabassa. New York: Harper and Row.

González Navarro, Moisés. 1957. *El Porfiriato. La vida social.* Vol. 4 in *Historia moderna de Mexico,* 9 vols. Ed. Daniel Cosio Villegas. Mexico City: Editorial Hermes.

Guerrero, Julio. 1906. *La génesis del crimen en México: Estudio de psiquiatria social.* Paris: Vda. De C. Bouret.

Inclán, Luis Gonzaga. 1969. *Astucia: El jefe de los Hermanos de la hoja o los charros contrabandistas de la rama.* Mexico City: Porrúa.

López Velarde, Ramón. 1971. *Poesías completas.* Ed. Antonio Castro Leal. Mexico City: Porrúa. 1995. *Song of the Heart: Selected Poems by Ramón López Velarde.* Trans. Margaret Sayers Peden. Austin: University of Texas Press.

María y Campos, Armando. 1956. *Teatro del género chico en la Revolución Mexicana.* (Serie: Biblioteca del Instituto Nacional de Estudios Históricos de la Revolución 7) Mexico City: n.p.

Mendoza, Vicente T. 1982. *La canción mexicana: Ensayo de clasificación y antología.* Mexico City: Fondo de Cultura Económica.

Morales, Salvador. 1975. *Auge y ocaso de la música mexicana.* Mexico City: Editorial Contenido.

Orozco, José Clemente. 1962. *José Clemente Orozco: An Autobiography.* Trans. Robert. C. Stephenson and Introduction by John Palmer Leeper. Hartford: Connecticut Printers Inc.

——. [1945], 1966. *Apuntes autobiográficos.* Mexico City: Secretaría de Educación Pública, Subsecretaría de Asuntos Culturales.

Payno, Manuel. 1945. *Los bandidos del Río Frío.* Ed. Antonio Castro Leal. Mexico City: Porrúa.

Paz, Octavio. 1964. *El laberinto de la soledad.* Mexico City: Fondo de Cultura Económica.

Romero de Terreros, Manuel. 1918. *Torneos, mascaradas y fiestas reales en Nueva España.* (Serie: Cultura 7.4) Mexico City: n.p.

Rulfo, Juan. 1953. *El llano en llamas y otros cuentos.* Mexico City: Fondo de Cultura Económica.

——. 1955. *Pedro Páramo.* Mexico City: Fondo de Cultura Económica.

——. 1994. *Pedro Páramo.* Trans. Margaret Sayers Peden. London: Serpent's Tail.

Seldes, Gilbert. 1968. *The New Mass Media: Challenge to a Free Society.* Washington, D.C.: Public Affairs.

Toor, Frances, Paul O'Higgins and Blas Vanegas Arroyo. 1930. *Monografía: las Obras de José Guadalupe Posada, grabador mexicano.* Mexico City: Mexican Folkways.

CHAPTER 59

MASS CULTURE AND LITERATURE IN LATIN AMERICA

Ana María Amar Sánchez

The last half of the twentieth century was characterized by the appropriation of images and conventions associated with mass culture. Indeed, one might think of this period as the culmination of a process of expansion of popular narrative that began more than two centuries earlier. Currently, culture is not a totalitarian system that in some way organizes all production and reception but, in fact, a complex of discourses that are constructed in conflict, frequently in a contradictory manner, in a struggle to legitimize them as privileged forms of representation. Among these, mass culture has been one of the clearest factors contributing to the crisis and destabilization of the categories into which the arts had been customarily organized. Having revealed a multiplicity of aesthetic possibilities, mass culture has created fundamental changes in the idea of art itself. On the other hand, as avant-garde utopias collapsed, so did the polarity of consumerism and experimentation; in other words, the distinction between art and mass genres, the latter once considered agreeable and unproblematic, also collapsed. After the experimental text that produced the neo–avant-garde movements in the period designated as the end of modernity, one of the possible paths was to resume a tradition that battled within Latin American culture to win space and that has produced a continuous game of contact and distance with this avant-gardist trend, which it regards as its antithesis. In effect, the presence and development of popular forms have been constants in the literary history of Latin America, as is shown by the region's permanent link with nonliterary discourse, particularly popular genres that are almost always regarded as subliterary. These have influenced so-called "cultured" formats, producing modifications and changes in the canon. Therefore, much Latin American literature dramatizes a discursive fragmentation, an ambiguity and a relativism produced by this encounter between "highbrow" and "lowbrow" literature.

A popular genre *par excellence,* the serial story of the nineteenth century, is the point of departure for the majority of formats in contemporary consumer culture. The serial format (in installments) is repeated in the romantic novel, adventure stories, and detective fiction, among others genres, as well as being recognizable in the comic book and the soap opera. Even so, this by definition "lowbrow" format has been basic to the development of the Latin American novel of the twentieth century. It underpins the major part of the work of Roberto Arlt (1900–1942), Jorge Amado (1912–2001), and later, Manuel Puig (1932–1990), authors whose work can be considered as marking a breakthrough and revealing the influx of radical changes, therefore putting the system into crisis. The codes of popular and mass-produced storytelling mark the constitution of a narrative that would represent its opposite within the literary system: The struggle against convention, the opening up to new forms of expression, and the proposed aim of destroying any automatization of the reading experience.

In a similar manner, the influence of cinema is present in narrative technique, both in the montage approach to construction and in the use of its fictions, while the codes of radio, pop music, romance novels, social chronicles, and, particularly, advertising are also key elements. Novels organize themselves as spectacles, a characteristic of mass culture; in some cases language not only proposes "oral effects" but also explores all the elements present in the languages used in advertising and the media. In Luis Rafael Sánchez's (b. 1936) *La guaracha del Macho Camacho* [1976; *Macho Camacho's Beat* 1980], for example, redundancies, accumulations, and tautologies echo the rhythm and form of a "jingle" or information given over the radio.

To sum up, the seduction of the mass media and the sensory seduction (seen in phonetic games, obscene language, and rhythm) of certain popular forms are exaggerated. In texts of recent years, the experience of narrators and/or characters is permeated by the cultural codes of the mass media. But one also finds the most "highbrow" culture in this same network. A character in *La importancia de llamarse Daniel Santos* [1988; The Importance of Being Daniel Santos] by Luis Rafael Sánchez points out that "La modernidad se sitúa en las destrucciones que construyen, en la fragmentación como materia prima, en el vacío poblado de flechas direccionales" (78) ("Modernity is located in a kind of destruction that constructs, with fragmentation as the *materia prima,* in an emptiness guided by arrows"). These "arrows" connect one text with another, stretching toward other texts and permitting the continual construction of a map that goes nowhere.

This is the culmination of a long process already clearly established in the first novels of Roberto Arlt, particularly *El juguete rabioso* [1926; The Rabid Toy], one of the great achievements of the twentieth century in terms of productive contact between "highbrow" and "lowbrow" literary genres. This text extends the limits of Latin American narrative; it is part of a tradition of contact with popular genres and lays down the terms of the relationship that would be followed by other novels. One can see in the way Arlt works within these genres a coexistence of discourses that are employed at the same level, an appropriation of the formats at his disposal that work in synthesis as much with the canon of the moment as with what is antithetical to it, thanks to this inclusion of paraliterary genres. The canonical form is never repeated when these latter are included; rather, it deviates from both forms through inversion or the transformation of its functions or key elements. One could say that his work uses the structures of a number of genres to create a text that, in fact, breaks with them (and their ideological function); it exploits them, only to disarm them immediately. In this sense, it plays with the expectations of readers in terms of the known, seducing them and deceiving them at the same time. In an ambivalent movement, the text includes all these genres that both shape it and point out that it now is something else, a different discourse irreducible to all the other exploited forms.

In their canonical formats, popular and mass media genres are characterized by their rigorous fulfillment of the conventions of their formulas. Thus they give their public the sensation of familiarity, while simultaneously introducing minimal variations with which they maintain the reader's interest. All forms of popular culture work within the limits established between convention and novelty. Consequently, their texts cannot distance themselves too much from the formula, because then they run the risk that the reader will not recognize them. The aesthetics of modernity has been very severe on the products of mass culture on account of their serial and repetitive character. If good literature is defined, for many, by its capacity to break with the canon in which it takes a superior place, then popular genres do not appear to have any chance of entering into this domain. In contrast, post-modern aesthetics propose a new means of confronting the idea of repetition (Eco 1988, 138), incorporating a certain degree of transformative work with formulas and genres. This involves a usage that does not imply an intention to elevate the genre or a parody, but a pastiche in which these tensions and conflicts that always exist in the relationship between lesser and greater express themselves in a clear form. In each instance, the way in which these texts use the genres produces a distortion of the code used, a subversion of its elements, whether the system is narrative, discursive, or ideological. The "high art" text always has a double movement, ambiguous and contradictory: It integrates mass culture, but it cannot do anything but produce some kind of distancing from it. A continuous tension is produced, which is why the texts are read sometimes as parody and other times as lesser works within their author's oeuvre. In all cases, the narrative finds itself on the borderline (of genres and literature), exploring it in a situation of perpetual tension and questioning. There is also always a destabilizing use of mass culture, thanks to which the borders between those genres deemed lesser and greater, vulgar and avant-garde, lose their meaning. However, none of these can stop manifesting their difference, their belonging to another zone of culture. All reiterate the fatal gesture of any relationship with the lesser; integration exists to point out the difference between them and the irreducible distance that separates the two.

The Latin American Detective Novel at the End of the Century

The Latin American detective novel is perhaps one of the most interesting cases of this relationship. The genre, in its canonical form, establishes a strong seductive connection with the reader. A large part of this charm (and its addictive capacity) is generated through complicity and the pleasure of recognizing a shared code. Although each genre produces some kind of pleasure that is specific to it alone, the detective novel is defined and indeed particularly depends on this contact. Most critics agree on the fact that suspense is the form of pleasure that belongs to this genre (Palmer 1987; Porter). The need to unravel the enigma, discover who is the murderer and why and how he or she killed, seems to be the first element to capture the reader. It is certain that suspense is essential to pleasure, but such pleasure is not created only through the desire to know or the deductive capacity used to pit one's wits against the plot. Pleasure depends on the nexus established between the reader and the code as accomplices, the dialogue that supposes a wink of recognition in the face of each predictable element.

Even so, the history of the genre in Latin America is an example of its flexibility and the possibilities that lie beyond the formulaic. This is notable from the 1960s on through the influence of the "hard-boiled" North American detective novel. The Latin American versions of the genre contradict those detractors who accuse it of being a repetitive machine that both impoverishes and alienates. If the conventional detective story were programmed to repeat a norm, the best text would therefore be one that fulfills the rules of the canon most exactly. A whodunit would always be a particular creation with few variations, in fact, formulaic. This in turn is the indispensable requisite of a mass literature aimed at the escapism of an addicted reader who only desires to re-encounter the already known and once again feed his or her fantasies of a more interesting world. On the contrary, Latin American detective novels, in particular from Jorge Luis Borges (1899–1986) onward, have used the canonical forms, freely parodying them and integrating them with others. The history of the genre in Argentina is an example of this process. Borges parodies but also transforms the mystery story, using and questioning the elements that go into its construction. From these early years to the end of the century, the detective novel in Latin America has been defined by its ability to deform and exploit the variables implicit in the formulas. The history of the genre and its potential for transformation can be traced from Borges to Juan Sasturain (b. 1945) and Paco Ignacio Taibo II (b. 1949).

There is no doubt that one can encounter a transformative usage of some generic elements of the detective novel in other narrative forms. Part of the work of Friedrich Dürrenmatt the Swiss writer (1921–1990), notably *Justiz* [1985; *The Execution of Justice* 1989], *Der Auftrag* [1986; *The Assignment* 1988], and *Das Versprechen* [1958; *The Pledge* 1959], exemplify such appropriation. Even so, it is in Latin American literature that this process becomes systematic, where similar variations of the canon constantly repeat. José Pablo Feinmann has observed this tendency with reference to Argentinean literature: "What does it mean that we have written novels that are *more* or *less* than detective novels? It means that we have not *subjected* ourselves to the genre. The Argentine detective novel . . . has worked on the *borders* of the genre, not *inside* the genre" (1991, 164; author's italics). All works of detective fiction, whether of the mystery genre or *roman noir,* need a crime surrounded by mystery, inasmuch as suspense must sustain the investigation that the detective is undertaking. These canonical components admit modifications, and their variables define how the three conditions essential for the genre come together: Crime, truth, and justice. The whodunit tells the story of how, once the crime has been committed, the search for the truth develops and justice is restored. Each format, whether classic mystery or *roman noir,* resolves and defines the elements of the triangle in a different way. It is precisely these differences that define, from the classic to the "hard-boiled" narrative, a progressive politicization of the crime, different ways of representing it, diverse classes of crime, and different connections with the law. The genre articulates the relationships between these conditions; truth and justice will be possible only in relation to a certain degree of legality. Crime and the law make their play in complementary positions: The law decides whether there is a crime, whether there is truth, and whether justice will be done. The history of the genre has been one of sketching out the possibilities of these conditions from the epoch of the classic story with its domestic crimes, truths, punishments, and dependable laws to the present day (Chandler 221; Enzensberger 27).

Born in the nineteenth century, this genre was strongly linked to modernity and to positivist rationalism. Its faith in the system, in legal order, and in the triumph of reason and logic has gradually eroded during the twentieth century. The texts of the Argentine Rodolfo Walsh (1927–1977) mark the culmination of a process, initiated by Borges, of disintegration of certainties. In turn, the detective novel of the last decade of the twentieth century recuperates and emphasizes this tradition. These possibilities become the law of the genre in Latin American detective fiction. The texts represent the imaginary realm as well as resolve the conflicts and desires addressed by the genre by playing with the conditions of the system. Borges used and parodied the classic formula but also questioned the canon that is the secure resolution of the system: The discovery of the truth, the punishment of the guilty, and the carrying out of law and justice. With Walsh, this solid and tranquilizing reading definitively explodes; his testimonial narratives develop this tendency to the maximum. The close contact with journalism meant the culmination of this process of politicization of the crime and the transformation of relationships in the triad crime–truth–justice; in this way, the code and function of the genre were redefined. In the conclusion of his nonfiction story *Operación masacre* [1957; Operation Massacre], the narrator reveals himself as skeptical regarding justice and associates crime, the state, and impunity for the first time in Argentine detective literature: "el gobierno … aplicó retroactivamente … una ley marcial … y eso no es un fusilamiento. Es un asesinato" (Walsh 1972, 192–93) ("… the government … retroactively applied … a martial law … and this is not execution. It is assassination").

Despite the fact that this process is paradigmatic in Argentine literature, other Latin American whodunits from the end of the last century adopt the same play with the code. To read these stories is to see the genre in its transmutations and its connections with other discourses located within a very precise historical time. In the 1980s the detective novels by the Mexican writer Paco Ignacio Taibo II (b. 1949), the Brazilian Rubem Fonseca (b. 1925), and the Argentinean Juan Sasturain (b. 1945) create among them an exemplary pattern of the system in response to the possibility of constructing a Latin American version of the detective genre. The canonical texts are evident in their work as well as the "variations" that were created years before by Manuel Puig, Vicente Leñero (b. 1933), and Ricardo Piglia (b. 1941), among others. In the 1960s, when the stories of Raymond Chandler (1888–1959) and Dashiell Hammett (1894–1961) increased in impact, many asked about the possibilities of translation (in the double sense of the language and the genre having indubitable links with North American culture). Ricardo Piglia points out:

> Pensar la inserción de la literatura policial en la Argentina a partir de Walsh y de Goligorsky supone tener en cuenta los cruces entre traducir y escribir el género, entre adaptarlo y repetir sus fórmulas, … junto con la historia de ese traslado (con sus repeticiones, traiciones, parodias y plagios) era posible aventurar la hipótesis de otro uso, más secreto e indirecto de los temas y de los procedimientos … Esa es para mí la diferencia entre el uso de un género y su *remake*. (Piglia 1993, 8–9)

> To consider Walsh and Goligorsky's introduction of detective literature into Argentina supposedly takes into account the crossover between translating and writing the genre, between adapting it and repeating its formulas … together with the history of this transfer (with its repetitions, betrayals, parodies, and plagiarizing); it was thus possible to put forward the hypothesis of another, more secret and indirect usage of themes and procedures. … This is for me the difference between the use of a genre and its remake.

From then on, texts such as *Manual de perdedores* [1985; Losers' Handbook] by Sasturain, Fonseca's *Agosto* [1990; August] and "Romance negro" [1992; "Roman Noir"], or Taibo's *Sombra de la sombra* [1986; *The Shadow of the Shadow* 1991] have offered a response. The genre developed a creole version that permanently played (with intertextual allusion and humor) on the clichés of the code, while at the same time becoming politicized.

The detective novel at the end of the last century appears as a balance and settling of accounts with the genre. The texts are a reflection on the genre and its canonical rules, while simultaneously deforming them. Borges opened up the possibility of transforming the code in Latin America and gave an unthinkable twist to a genre that was both consoling and entertaining. His particular way of manipulating it produced a whole literary current that combined parody, transformation, and homage to past models; indeed his free and deviating use of formulas has threatened the very basis of the genre. The variations of the plot in his stories undermine the legality of convention and for this reason attract attention to it. The detective novel thus becomes a genre marked by a double complicity between writer and reader; there is the recognition of the code but also of the games with and divergences from it. Enjoyment is found in this simultaneous convergence between delight in the conventional and distance from it. From the 1960s onward, the allusion to the canonical and its deformation are both echoed in many stories. Texts such as Manuel Puig's *The Buenos Aires Affair* (1973) and *Los albañiles* [1964; The Bricklayers] by Vicente Leñero (b. 1933) use and displace elements such as the mystery, the investigation, or the crime. Puig's narrative is subtitled "detective novel," thereby preparing the reader for a code that will be systematically violated. All attempts to recognize the canonical are frustrated to the point where the crime turns out to be fiction or displaced. The novels of Leñero, not only *Los albañiles* but also *El garabato* [1967; The Scribble] and *Estudio Q* [1965; Studio Q], permeated as they are by the *nouveau roman*, distort the system, compromise the investigation, and question the possibility of discovering the truth. *Los albañiles,* presented as a complex of confessions to the detective by probable assassins, underlines the impossibility of achieving any kind of certainty and stresses the failure of the search in which detective and reader are equally matched. This last point is essential because the stories insist on their categorization as detective novels and capture the reader, while at the same time frustrating his or her sense of complicity. They insist on the code and focus attention on it, only to destroy it and debate its ideological basis.

From the 1980s on, this form of relationship with the detective novel became dominant. *La pesquisa* [1994; The Investigation] by Juan José Saer (b. 1937) is a clear homage to the genre. Saer himself writes, "volver a los orígenes del género podía ser una solución interesante no para parodiarlos, sino para tomarlos como punto de partida y avanzar a partir de ellos en mi propia dirección" (1997, 24) ("to return to the origins of the genre could be an interesting solution, not for purposes of parody but to take them as the point of departure and advance from there in my own direction"). Reflection and debate on the possible literary condition of the detective novel can be traced in texts such as Elvio E. Gandolfo's (b. 1947) "La reina de las nieves" [1982; "Queen of the Snows"], a tale that works freely with the elements of the genre and exemplifies the tension between usage and difference that characterizes these stories. The formula dissolves and becomes contaminated to constitute a new form that dilutes the canonic elements but does not stop returning and alluding to them. Numerous texts could be mentioned in this context: Osvaldo Soriano's (1943–1997) *Triste, solitario y final* [1973; Sad, Lonely, and Final] is an example of those texts that during this period initiated the link with the detective novel, and so is Mario Levrero's (b. 1940) serial story entitled *Nick Carter se divierte mientras el lector es asesinado y yo agonizo* [1975; Nick Carter Enjoys Himself While the Reader Is Assassinated and I Agonize]. This latter, beginning with the title, is the wildest and most extreme case of this play with the code.

Self-reflection and transformation is the basis for Taibo's *Sombra de la Sombra* and *La vida misma* [1987; Life Itself] and Sasturain's *Manual de perdedores,* and in Fonseca's texts it becomes a complex network. Narratives such as "Romance negro" (a true settling of accounts with the detective novel that exploits another possibility of failure to discover the truth from within the genre itself), *O caso Morel* [1973; The Morel Case], and *Vastas Emoções e Pensamientos Imperfeitos* [1989; Great Emotions and Imperfect Thoughts] work through all the alternatives of seduction and betrayal of the crime fiction formula. But they, in turn, link up with other codes and lead us to other networks of mass genres. *Vastas Emoções* in particular is a compendium of popular formulas: Detective fiction, adventure novel, love story, and mystery tale, all framed by the cinema, which seems to condense them all. In the same way, from its entrance into the marketplace as a newspaper serial, *Manual de perdedores* emphasizes its strong connection with the mass media (see **Figures** 1 and 2). Originally published in installments in the Buenos Aires newspaper *La voz* between January and May 1983, it was accompanied by Hernán Haedo's illustrations (which have remained in the book edition). These illustrations imitate the function performed in the serials of the nineteenth century (which also can be found in children's books), that is, enlivening the text by cutting the monotony of the written pages, helping the reader's imagination, and reinforcing generic stereotypes. But in *Manual* they also reveal their link with popular forms and their serial character.

Comic strips offer a story while possessing a more complex function than simple illustrations. They are not only a category of one of the most popular forms of mass culture. The comic strips used in this novel dialogue with the text and comment on it; they are clues and guides for the reader that point out the shared process that the story and the genre are following. In fact, a whole sequence of "Peanuts" runs through *Manual I* and acts as a self-referential system, discussing the construction of a novel, the clichés of detective stories, and the surprising changes in the code expected by the reader. In other words, as self-reflection through quotations from and unexpected twists of the genre, the comic reiterates the system of the story. In *Manual II,* the comic strips, with one exception by Hugo Pratt (1927–1995), are by the Argentinean scriptwriter Héctor Oesterheld (1919–1977), who disappeared in the last military dictatorship. The comic here becomes political: Nazi helmets and monsters appear; image and text accompany and underline the politicization of the story. In the last illustration, which opens the "Finale," the protagonist of a comic strip corresponding to Oesterheld's *Mort Cinder* (and drawings by A. Breccia) looks straight out at the reader and asks: "Is the past as dead as we believe?" This takes place in a game of multiple references between text, comic strip, and history.

Figure 1.

Etchenaik pensó que un detective era un hombre que camina por un pasillo hacia una puerta entreabierta con un revólver en la mano. Eso era él.

Photograph of woodcut from Juan Sasturain's Manual de perdedores. *(Archive of the author)*

Figure 2.

Un pasamontaña rojo que sólo dejaba libres unos ojos claros.

Photograph of woodcut from Manual de perdedores. *(Archive of the author)*

Manual is set up as a self-conscious text to an excessive degree, in a kind of fiesta of allusions for the reader familiar with the genre and happy in the role of accomplice. It opens with *film noir* and closes with the tango. All the action originates in and comes to a resolution through similarity to or difference from the codes. This play of allusions is repeated in the other stories and almost constitutes a narrative type in crime fiction at the end of the twentieth century. Thus the titles of the chapters hark back to novels, tangos, or cinema or simply indicate this complicity with the reader of detective novels (e.g. "Classic Chapter," "Obvious Cigarettes"). The titles of the famous stories that intertwine have the same function, for example, "Welcome Warrior of the Concrete Jungle" and "they wandered about there below like a deep sea filled with octopi or large fish"–clear allusions to W.R. Burnett's (1899–1982) *Asphalt Jungle* (1949) and to *Deep Water* (1966) by Patricia Highsmith (1921–1995), respectively. The story is presented openly as a copy of Don Quixote's quest, perhaps the Latin American version for the end of the twentieth century. While the imitation is clear in the antihero who follows the rules of the genre, the presence of the classic model is more complex and implies some differences. On the one hand, *Manual* quotes Cervantes's text, repeating the links between literature and life, the game of reality and fiction, and the failure inherent in the encounter between these two worlds. It follows his teachings by also returning to a popular genre at the height of its influence, with the difference being that, in this case, there is no attempt to destroy the popular form but rather a desire to include and revitalize it. The parodic alternative becomes more ambiguous and the difference the text proposes suggests a new reading of the classic: "Tendrían que leerlo de nuevo" (Sasturain I, 18) ("You must read it again").

The debate around the possibilities of a national version of the genre centers on issues of self-conscious reflection, the game of parody and its transformation in Latin America. Considering the genre and considering how to distance itself from its origins also form part of the same movement. The stories in *Seis problemas para don Isidro Parodi* [1942; Six Problems for Don Isidro Parodi 1981], by "Honorio Bustos Domecq"–Jorge Luis Borges and Adolfo Bioy-Casares (1914–1999)–constitute an exemplary paradigm. The imprisoned detective who drinks maté introduces irony into the classical formula while at the same time discussing its local possibilities. In this sense, from the 1950s on, Borges's position has been at the center of the debate: What identifies a nation has nothing to do with local color, he argued. From then on, those working in the genre have constantly worked to translate and convert Latin America into a backdrop for detective stories, but the focus is not on local color but on a notation that quotes and transforms a space, a culture, and a code. In this sense, *Manual* inspects the affiliation of the text carefully: "Más Hammett que Goodis, un poquito de Chase. ¿Usted leyó las cosas más recientes, Etchenique [...] Los argentinos: Tizziani, Sinay, Martini, Urbanyi, Feinmann, Soriano sobre todo... Algunos cuentos de Piglia también" (Sasturain I, 77) ("More Hammett than Goodis, a little Chase. Have you read the most recent things, Etchenique?... the Argentineans: Tizziani, Sinay, Martini, Urbanyi, Feinmann, Soriano above all.... Some stories by Piglia as well"). The movement toward including Argentinean authors, after mentioning the North American classics, implies the reclaiming of a legacy and includes the possibility of a Latin American detective story on a national level.

This Latin American version has generated debate on the possibilities of the genre itself within the region. For this reason, the texts become a play of allusions and differences with respect to the canon. All play with the reader's pleasure in and knowledge of the formula in order to disappoint subsequently with crimes for which the authorities are responsible, truths that are impossible to reveal, and punishments that will never be carried out. In each one, the distortion of the formula implies an ideological transformation of the premises that sustain the classic English story. This is what the detective of *Agosto* (who will be assassinated at the end of the story, the greatest betrayal of the norms) believes: "A lógica era, para ele, una aliada do policial ... havia uma lógica adequada à criminologia, que nada tenha a ver, porém, com premissas e deduções silogísticas à la Conan Doyle" (Fonseca 1990, 109) ("It was logical for him, an ally of the detective story... to have an adequate logic for criminology that has nothing to do with premises and syllogistic deductions in the style of Conan Doyle").

Likewise, in Taibo's *Sombra de la sombra*, the Chinese detective (in reality Mexican, even though he transforms the pronunciation of "r" into "l" in a comic echo of a long-standing tradition in North American detective fiction) states:

–... puedo sugeliles que lean a un esclitol inglés que se apellida Conan Doyle.
–¿Está traducido?
–No ... tiene un detective que siempre anda con un médico.
–Será que lo necesita. Como nosotros.
–No, lo siento, nada de ingleses todavía .... (Taibo 1986, 137)

"... I suggest that you all go and lead the books of an Englishman named Arthur Conan Doyle."
"Have they been translated?"
"No, ... He's got this detective that always goes around with a doctor."
"I suppose a detective needs a good doctor. We could use one, that's for sure."
"Sorry, friends, but I think that things are complicated enough with the Brits and the Frenchman we've already got to deal with." (Taibo 1991, 120)

Here, in condensed form, we find the problems of translation, quotation, and similarity and difference from the models, in other words, what constitutes a Latin American detective story. To quote, translate, and transform seem to define the work of these stories. One quotes, but it is necessary to make a "national translation" of the conventions. For this reason, to assimilate the need for the doctor in Conan Doyle and in this story does no more than accentuate the differences between the two. The function of a doctor for Holmes is very different from that for the four Mexican detectives, who are always in danger and on the point of being shot. The logical rigor is not the same either because coincidence and luck here replace rationality. Detectives who do not appear to be so, who do not see themselves in this role, and astonishing stories that require other methods to be resolved reveal a difference from convention established by the text in a very conscious way.

Possibly, "Romance negro" by Rubem Fonseca marks the culmination of this process of self-consciousness and self-reflection in regard to the detective novel. A tale whose theme is the genre itself and the possibilities that provide for the exploration of its limits, it explores and summarizes theoretical perspectives, polemics, and debates. In the framework of a "Festival de novela y film negros" ["Festival of the Novel and Film Noir"], an author of detective novels proposes a challenge: To discover the perfect crime, the one that he himself committed. Multiple secrets expose this as the extreme example of the genre. The author and protagonist is an impostor and the assassin of the true writer. The game of doubles and identities is also a variation on the Oedipal story—an element to be found in the origin of the genre. The constant presence of canonical topics does not help the reader arrive at any conclusion; on the contrary, the clues dissolve into ambiguity. The story undermines and destroys all the cores that sustain the classic certainties. Meanwhile the drama introduces suspicions about the existence of a crime that is improbable for the majority of people, while the narrator, the authority within the text, seems to accept the story of the presumed killer. The text has stretched the variables of the genre to their ultimate consequences, and the solution of the case becomes impossible. One cannot know the truth and solve crimes that perhaps have not been committed. This short story represents the high point of self-reflection on the conventions, and at the same time their maximum disintegration, inasmuch as the triad of crime, truth, and justice that sustains the genre loses all meaning. Fonseca here explores one of the alternatives of the extreme transformation of the canon. The other takes place in *Agosto*. Both explore the limits of a format. Set between self-consciousness and politicization, the detective novel with Fonseca offers new possibilities.

The play of quotations, the pleasure that goes with recognizing a cliché, and the enjoyment of the consumer of the genre, who simultaneously maintains a certain distance—all this conceals the fundamental distortion that these *fin de siècle* detective novels propose with respect to the canonical forms: The transformations, viewed as a literary game, give an unthinkable twist to a format that is traditionally consoling and entertaining and convert it into a political genre. In all cases, the genre transforms itself in its key elements: The detective, the investigations, the results, the fulfilling of justice, or the discovery of the truth. Even so the *crime* is the essential term that produces the political twist to the code. This is the constructive element of detective fiction; the crime idea is shared by all story types, for around it the variations of the canon organize and structure themselves. Palmer (1991) points out that crime in modern societies is always a challenge to the legitimacy of a social and moral order that is supposedly universal. Crime therefore represents the violation of a social limit. Its investigation is always with an intent to reinforce moral boundaries and punish whoever has transgressed the frontiers of the permitted. In this way, the genre in its canonic form not only allows a tranquilizing response, since order always triumphs, but also proposes a kind of limited, controllable, and explainable violence and criminality. The Latin American story shatters this pact, destroying the harmony among society-justice-law, in order to represent the crime as the product of political and social institutions. Not only does it destroy the order, but there is also no appeal to either legality or legitimacy. The relationships among crime, truth, and justice become thus more conflictive. From the era of the English detective story with its private murders and dependable deductions, crimes become increasingly politicized, with solutions that become more problematic. This relationship has become complicated because of the proliferation and the ambiguity of the offences: Private and public crimes become interwoven and confused. Private felonies are mixed with political misdemeanors, while the

criminals are supported by institutions that are themselves criminal. *Manual de perdedores, Agosto,* and *Sombra de la sombra* revise all the possibilities and place the action in very particular situations, such as the last Argentinean military dictatorship, the end of Getúlio Vargas' government in Brazil, and the Mexican Revolution, respectively.

This is one of the principal characteristics that differentiate these texts. The historical situations in which the stories of classical detective fiction take place hold little or no importance for the drama. The "hard-boiled" American story is linked to certain social conditions, but historical precision is not necessary. On the contrary, the texts mentioned above are intimately linked to very precise historical moments: Crimes, investigation, the possibility of access to the truth, or the meting out of justice are the result of certain political circumstances. Also, in this sense, they are heirs to Walsh's use of the genre in his nonfiction stories. The three novels offer a framework based somewhere between journalism and the detective novel, as established by Walsh in *Operación Masacre, Caso Satanovsky* [1973; The Satanovsky Case], and *¿Quién Mató a Rosendo?* [1969; Who Killed Rosendo?], and thereby establish one of the basic formats of the genre in the 1980s. They thus bring to a close the tradition of a whole century with a local response to the problems involved in the translation of the imported code: The Latin American version of the genre becomes political.

In this sense, *Manual de perdedores,* despite pointing out that "los años están entreverados a propósito" ("the years are jumbled together on purpose"), clearly locates the story and the position of the hero from the beginning: "una ráfaga que pasó por los diarios a mediados del setenta . . . después la oscuridad, el olvido junto a sátiros de poca monta o *las andanzas de los Falcon color mar turbio*" (Sasturain I, 12; author's italics) ("a wind that passed through the daily newspapers in the mid seventies . . . then obscurity, oblivion, together with insignificant little satires or *the adventures of the Falcon, the color of the foul sea*"). The development of the story at the time of the terrifying green Falcon of the military dictatorship set in "dirty war" establishes the situation, while simultaneously suggesting the possibility that the protagonist might be a *desaparecido* ("disappeared person"). While history interlaces with the plot like a nightmare in *Manual, Agosto* defines it in the same way with a quotation from Joyce in which history is "la pesadilla de la que estoy tratando de despertar" ("the nightmare from which I am trying to wake up"). And it is also, for one of the characters, the daughter of Getúlio Vargas, "uma estúpida sucessão de acontecimientos aleatórios, um enredo inepto e incompreensível de falsidades, inferências fictícias, ilusões, provoado de fantasmas" (Fonseca 1990, 304) ("a stupid succession of chance events, an inept and incomprehensible trap of lies, fictitious interferences, illusions, full of ghosts"). This description also fits the story; once again the detective novel convention is run through with historical events and the murders have confused motives, a mix of money, politics, and power. *Agosto* offers a framework of private and political crimes clearly taking place in the days prior to the suicide of Getúlio Vargas in August 1954. The novel has used history to create a fiction with a structure very close to the journalistic story. And, in this sense, it uses and reverses Walsh's legacy, since one is here dealing with a detective novel that uses history and journalism as a structural resource.

Taibo's *Sombra de la sombra* can be included in the same tradition, but it uses different strategies. Framed by two fragments, *Nota* [Note] and *Después de la novela* [After the Novel], the fiction is literally enclosed by journalism and history, in this case documentary information and an account of the revolutionary situation. In reality, there are two situations that intermesh here; the unfortunate present-day one originates in and is explained by the past recounted in the story. The text thus straddles two genres. The final observation, *Después de la novela*, which brings the dénouement to a close from another space that is now nonfictional, is signed and dated by the author, who in some way evaluates the events. The story takes place in April 1922, immediately after the Mexican Revolution, and narrates the historical moment when characters such as Artemio Cruz from Carlos Fuentes' (b. 1928) *La muerte de Artemio Cruz* [1962; *The Death of Artemio Cruz* 1964] come to the fore or educated men such as one of the main characters from Mariano Azuela's (1873–1952) *Los de abajo* [1915; *The Underdogs* 1963] begin to be successful. The text also proposes a retrospective review of the Revolution while including itself within this tradition. That past had given way to a present (1982–1985) in which "El hampa abandonó su marginalidad, coexistió con la ley, abandonó su exotismo y finalmente se institucionalizó como parte de la misma policía" (Taibo 1986, 248) ("The criminal underworld abandoned its marginality and exoticism, learned to coexist with the law, and finally became institutionalized as an integral part of the Mexican police force"; Taibo 1991, 227). In this sense, all these novels not only connect to very precise historical situations but also take up a position with regard to them.

Manual de perdedores, from its very title onward, marks an essential difference from the canon. "Habría que escribir un libro . . . de instrucciones para la derrota . . . . Porque hoy, a quién le vas a enseñar a ganar?" ("One should write a book . . . of instructions for defeat . . . . Because today, whom can you teach to win?"), comments the detective. The narrator clarifies by saying: "Y ya no hablaba de ajedrez . . . Hablaba de todo y algo más . . ." (Sasturain II, 151) ("And he was not discussing chess . . . He was discussing everything and something more"). This statement plays with the code of detective fiction involving the game of chess, a commonplace in the genre, in the context of the situation in which the story occurs (the last Argentinean military dictatorship). Not to be able to teach chess is not to master the rules of the game (and the genre) and to have to accept others in support of defeat. For this reason, the detectives of the three texts play other games that are not those of the convention. In *Sombra de la sombra* they do so literally, since they play dominoes, defined as "el gran deporte nacional" (Taibo 1986, 249) ("the great national pastime"; Taibo 1991, 228). Dominoes provide the framework for the story, which opens and closes with chapters entitled "Los personajes juegan dominó" ("In Which the Characters Play Dominoes"), elsewhere repeated as "Los personajes juegan dominó y se definen como mexicanos de tercera" ("In Which the Characters Play Dominoes and Accept Their Lot as Third-Class Citizens"); "Los personajes juegan dominó sobre un piano" ("In Which the Characters Play Dominoes on Top of a Piano"); and so on. The game and the action of the novel run parallel in an association that alludes to and differentiates itself at the same time from the conventions of detective fiction. Unlike chess, a purely rational game, the game here is influenced by politics: War, anarchy, and the narration all intermesh on the gaming

table. Playing, talking, keeping quiet, and joking have as much value for the game as for the plot of the detective story. Dominoes, a *national* game, has other rules that are scarcely logical and not very deductive, just as the detectives are far from the sure rational control of an Hercule Poirot.

The mathematical logic of chess, the exercise of the deductive capacity that it implies, has always been associated with detective fiction, particularly in the mystery story. The detective, like the chess player, dominates the game, knows how to move the pieces, and can predict the movements of the enemy and beat him. On the contrary, the detectives of these stories do not know how to deal with the new rules of the game. Their lack of knowledge and control over the situation means the disappearance of the main characteristic of the classic detective, who, in whichever variant of the formula, is the one who knows. As such, he holds the power as the figure representative of legal process. Even in the "hard-boiled" stories that feature loser characters such as Chandler's Marlowe, the detective continues to be a winner who arrives at the truth and achieves some kind of justice. In contrast, the heroes of these novels find themselves in an ambiguous situation as detectives. Like the protagonists of *Sombra*, they are not really detectives, or they are playing at being so. In that novel, four enthusiasts are trapped in a drama they do not understand because it is now not a question of professionals but a group of almost marginal survivors who confront the system into which the Revolution is becoming transformed.

In *Agosto* (1990), seemingly the closest to the canonical of these *romans noirs*, the detective/commissioner messes up the investigation, leaves the police force, and is murdered by the assassin for whom he has been searching from the beginning of the story. His death duplicates the suicide of Getúlio Vargas. Both deaths occur a few hours apart and both are prepared for from the beginning. They are connected, and in both cases the nexus between truth, justice, and crime will remain unresolved. The detective cannot solve anything; nor does he know, on dying, the identity of his killer and the cause of his death. Contrary to the classical detective fiction, the detective knows *less* than the readers and seems reduced to impotence. He is distant from both the web woven by the plot and the crimes committed. He does not *know*, nor is he *able to* exercise any power. In this mesh of stories that constitutes *Agosto*, the parallel destinies of Commissioner Mattos and Getúlio Vargas make both characters equal and incorporate them each as victim. Vargas commits suicide and Mattos is murdered, even though he is the only character given an ethical dimension in the story. For this reason, he is an isolated and defeated antihero in a political system that is in disintegration. His inadequacy and his break with the system (leaving the police force, he gives up his weapons and thus will have nothing with which to defend himself from his murderer) parallel the catastrophic development of the story. His death, an insignificant incident, is missed in the midst of the political chaos that follows Vargas's suicide. This change in the function and locus of the protagonist is essential. He has moved from the central space that he knows, where he has power and where the law acts in his favor. From their new marginal situation, these detectives no longer challenge the reader with their ingenuity; they do not play the game of intelligent deduction. The texts establish a new complicity with the readers—at least with some of them—and this is why they each become like a "manual of losers." (This title is appropriate for many stories, especially the three considered here.) They are books of instructions for defeat, as detective Etchenique proposes; he does not do anything more than follow the advice of one of the characters–a *desaparecido*–of *Respiración artificial* [1988; *Artificial Respiration* 1994]: "Hay que hacer la historia de las derrotas" (Piglia 1988, 18) ("One must write the history of defeats"). In this way a linkage and a common political function between these two texts is defined. As in *Respiración artificial*, the detective novels at the end of the twentieth century tell both other stories and an alternative history. They no longer provide a tranquilizing space for the reader; they sketch out other forms of consolation.

Every narration that deals with the law always presupposes in a certain way a form of legality according to which the characters act. The detective novel thematizes the connections between the plot and the law; each variation of this canonical combination implies a reflection on or an interpretation of the linkage between justice and legality. If, in the view of many critics, the detective novel is distinguished by narrating the process that goes from the crime to its punishment, the Latin American detective novel–by questioning this established process–destroys the rule of the genre and, at the same time, subverts any faith in the judicial system. The resolution of the crime through the triumph of the hero in the canonical detective novel reaffirms confidence in the law and represents the tranquilizing possibility of its reestablishment. For this reason, the systematic failure of the detectives in the contemporary Latin American detective novel introduces a disquieting insecurity that refers the reader back to the daily information in the newspaper. Perhaps for this reason the three writers maintain a strong connection with journalism, reinforcing, once again, their relationship with the police-witness texts of Rodolfo Walsh. In *Manual de Perdedores* the partial resolution of the case implies concealments and negotiations, dirty dealings in which the police are involved. In *Sombra de la sombra* the case is solved, but the truth never comes to light and the guilty party is not punished. *Agosto* exposes the greatest failure of the linking of crime–truth–justice. The text closes with an epilogue that wipes out every clue of the events: "A cidade teve um dia calmo. O movimiento do comércio foi considerado muito bom [. . .] Foi um dia ameno, de sol. A noite a temperatura caiu um pouco. [. . .] Vemos de sul a oeste, moderados" (Fonseca 1990, 349) ("The city has a calm day. Trading was considered to be very good . . . . It was a pleasant sunny day. The temperature fell a little during the night . . . . Moderate winds from South to West"). The journalistic informative style accompanies the review of the news of the day, the dissolving of political crimes, the hiding of the truth, and of course, the wiping out of all hope of justice.

The knowledge of what happened and who did it always ends up confused and partial. The truth in these tales is obtained in fragments. Obscure points are never clarified. The shattering of the classic certainties of the detective novel extends to the development of the story but also affects the possibilities for readers to solve the case; their bewilderment and insecurity now accompany those of the detective. It is a world in which there are no longer any precise boundaries between the good and the bad, and the latter occupy the legal position and power base of the former. The "truth" is the final product of a negotiation, what remains of a sum of losses and defeats. For this reason, the failure of the detective is crucial to this system. His character

is not only that of an antihero like that of the North American "hard-boiled" detective story (Marlowe, even though beaten up and skeptical, solves his cases) but also that of a failure who does not manage to put together fragments of information or to succeed in knowing all the truth. The impossibility of success in a world in which no level of power can be achieved emerges in the previously mentioned proposal of Etchenique in *Manual*: "Habría que escribir un libro útil, al alcance de todos, de instrucciones para la derrota" (Sasturain II, 151) ("One ought to write a useful book, accessible to all, of instructions for defeat"). With this loser concept, this impossibility of ever winning, the text takes on what is a characteristic of Latin American detective fiction at the end of the twentieth century. The majority of narratives from this period exemplify this failure, this loss of power suffered by the protagonist of crime fiction. Titles such as *Ni el tiro del final* [1981; Not Even the Last Shot] by José Pablo Feinmann (b. 1943), O. Soriano's *Triste, solitario, y final* (1973), and *No habrá final feliz* [1989; *No Happy Ending*] by Taibo are all indications of this form of the "losers' handbook." The novel that actually bears this name is the sum and synthesis of this: The detective has undergone a process of physical and psychic destruction; lame and one-eyed, "despistado, desconcertado y sorprendido . . . ya no juega a ganar, juega a sobrevivir y a seguir chingando" (Taibo 1989, 85) ("absent-minded, bewildered and surprised . . . he no longer plays to win, but to survive and carry on screwing up"). The character of the Mexican version of the failed detective is in many ways interchangeable with that of Etchenaik, and, like Mattos in *Agosto*, he too is murdered.

This failure of the detective parallels the lack of justice and the impossibility of knowing the truth when this involves political authority. In *Manual* this is clear in the solution of the cases that focus on the two women central to the narrative, La Loba and Cora, the vanished girl. Justice is done outside the law, in the case of the private crime, at the hands of La Loba. The woman who has hidden in the shadows throughout the plot and who appears only fleetingly in a few scenes is responsible for the conclusion and the fulfillment of justice beyond the law of men. Her body is present at the end and covers up an absence and another failure of justice: The disappearance of Cora's body and the impunity of those responsible. But the political crime, that of the military dictatorship, cannot be righted. La Loba appears at the end to repair the irremediable absence of Cora. She takes justice into her own hands because she is a mother and in some way takes vengeance not only for her son but also for the vanished Cora. From the beginning, La Loba is the figure of Justice. In this sense *Manual* is perhaps the most comforting text if one compares it with *Agosto*, whose conclusion leaves the reader with no way out. Thus it fulfills the traditional function of the genre but from another, very distinct perspective; it does not engender forgetfulness or an alienated consolation but rather redresses the horror of injustice on a symbolic level. In its turn, *Sombra de la sombra* suggests the hope of reparation through the text, since, as the journalist-detective Manterola points out, "quizá tenga alguna utilidad estar contando lo que pasa" (Taibo 1986, 113) ("maybe it's not such a bad thing to have somebody around to tell what happened"; Taibo, 1991, 99). Even so, we are reading the same story sixty years after the event, and this is proposed as the only compensation for injustice. The temporal distance that mediates between the present of the story and what is narrated dissolves all hope of reparation. Thus the usefulness of retelling the story is relativized.

The detective genre had and has the function of decentralizing high or serious literature. But this role implies not only the rescue of a popular form but also its distance from "good literature." More than any other literary form, crime fiction at the end of the twentieth century has taken on the responsibility of narrating history. Within its confines, a balance has been achieved in constructing the chronicle of the last thirty years of Latin American political life. A code, that is possibly one of the most formalized and fictional, represents specifically what is either not spoken about in other forms of discourse or not easy to discuss. Here at least, there is debate on the possibilities of justice and law in Latin American culture in this historical moment.

This is so much the case that, with multiple transformations, the majority of the narratives of these years, such as the work of authors as different as Ricardo Piglia, Roberto Drummond (1937–2002), or Ana Lydia Vega (b. 1946), are based on a crime story. At the end of the twentieth century, such fiction, complete with failed detectives who cannot solve anything, who are impotent when faced with the law, and who are lost in a tangled mess in which one can barely glimpse the truth, has abandoned the ingenuous confidence that surrounded the system and the law in the early days of the genre. Far from maintaining confidence in a tranquilizing and comfortable situation, they represent the story of a loss. The illusory confidence in institutions and systems, along with the possibility of a just order, has been eradicated. The tension that the texts under discussion maintain with the consoling populist formulas of the canonical detective story results in a variant of the genre that has changed the relationship with mass culture. Participating in it, enjoying it, this version of genre has also marked out a difference–in the political balance of an epoch and the representation of an impossible dream. In these interstices, narratives are constructed in which law and knowledge, as Foucault has already pointed out, go together and belong to others, to those who have the power to decide what is truth and what is justice.

Camp and Pop: The Establishing of a Canon

If one thinks of a Latin American literary canon established in the twentieth century with contributions by Roberto Arlt, Jorge Amado, Rodolfo Walsh, Manuel Puig, José Donoso (1925–1996), Gabriel García Márquez (b. 1927), and Luis Rafael Sánchez, among others, one can conclude that it was consolidated in recent years; indeed it has almost been "institutionalized." Already clearly prefigured by Puig, this new tradition broke through and became itself almost a canon with the work of Ana Lydia Vega, Roberto Drummond, and Luis Zapata (b. 1951). It is no coincidence that the latter recovered, exploited, and completed at the end of the century what Arlt began in 1926. Narratives such as Zapata's *En Jirones* [1985; In Tatters] and *El vampiro de la colonia Roma* [1979; *Adonis Garcia: A Picaresque Novel* 1981] and Vega's "Pasión de historia" [1987; "Passion of History"] are the apotheosis of popular seduction, and they are themselves seduced by *boleros*–media culture and popular commonplaces. But they also end up being the highest expression of the inevitable betrayal of and infidelity to popular culture, to the degree that Camp and Pop can be defined by the distance they generate from their contents, a distance that at the same time implies usage, inclusion, and integration, but above all difference. It is this difference, for example, that makes *El vampiro* a mix of autobiography, picaresque novel, serial story, romance, and something more–perhaps a literary novel–that simultaneously denies and affirms all these genres. Pop, Camp, and their aesthetic of bad taste allow the connection maintained by these texts with mass culture to be considered more clearly. In this sense, the last three authors mentioned above are exemplary: All have become canonical, and as such their texts exercise an authority that eliminates any notion of marginalization. Somehow these stories have triumphed in the struggle to create a new canon, and the periphery has become the center. From this very authority comes the complex problem of complicity posed by these texts. This is evident in the Camp material and in that delight in certain expressions of bad taste. (Such a phrase indicates the existence of a norm of good taste that has been displaced, but remains present.) The texts of Sánchez, Zapata, and Vega, like the films of Almodóvar, use the forms of mass culture: They know their seductive qualities and so place them at the center of their intertextual game. But complicity is established only with a reader capable of understanding the seductive aside, recognizing the rules of the game, and establishing an ironic distance (Eco 1984, 74). This connection between text and reader authorizes us to enjoy without guilt the bad taste, the *bolero* sentimentalism, and the romantic melodrama. We can allow ourselves to be seduced precisely because we know that our complicity with the text allows us to maintain the distance of difference. In other words, usage without the hierarchies of the highbrow and lowbrow art forms is a recognition of popular culture's seductiveness but with absolutely no innocence.

"I am strongly drawn to Camp, and almost as strongly offended by it. That is why I want to talk about it, and why I can." This quotation from Susan Sontag (276) has the virtue of condensing all the contradictions that cultured authors, critics, and readers experience with Camp, Kitsch, and Pop aesthetics. The relationships and the tensions between highbrow and lowbrow culture have always been complex, and their ambiguities become particularly evident when one is dealing with expressions of so-called bad taste. The tensions between seduction and rejection, and condemnation and pleasure, that are provoked by the lowbrow forms of expression, acquire notable relevance in the literature of the last thirty years, when contact with popular sources has become dominant. The texts of the Brazilian Roberto Drummond, the Mexican Luis Zapata, and the Puerto Rican Ana Lydia Vega condense a now long tradition, while at the same time sustaining it in their exploitation of mass culture and Camp and Pop aesthetics. Kitsch and Camp always have meant escapism, stereotypes, and bad taste. It is this latter feature that reminds us of an implicit norm of good taste. The theories around these expressions of lowbrow culture do not differ much from the most severe apocalyptic critiques of mass culture. Umberto Eco links the condemnation of Kitsch (and the eulogizing of art) to a necessity to extinguish the desire generated by this "shameful" expression. He defines it as a product that fabricates effects and wants to sell itself as artistic (1968, 83–140). From this perspective Kitsch comes to represent the worst of mass culture. An art of consumption, banal and vulgar, it never had aesthetic value. Camp then becomes an intellectual and snobbish aestheticization of Kitsch. Meanwhile, Pop is considered art composed from the materials (waste products) of mass culture (Ross 1989). Reflection on these three aesthetics is characterized by its slipperiness, its lack of rigorous criteria, and, in the majority of cases, by the restoration of oppositions such as highbrow/lowbrow and cultured/vulgar. Even in the cases in which works of Pop or Camp are recognized as more elaborate expressions that are in some way distanced from Kitsch, what is stressed is their frivolous and apolitical character. The ambiguity in defining boundaries between these two categories is confusing to those who confront all these forms with notions of art, originality, and beauty.

In critical essays on Camp and Kitsch the contradictions become acute when any kind of proximity to mass media is involved, and it seems that here the conflict of positions is more evident when a value judgment is called for. The diverse perspectives can be organized via a system of binary oppositions. Kitsch, in particular, presents itself as the negative pole of good taste, beauty, the canons of art, the avant-garde, the political, the moral, and the good. Some critics try to organize systems that in some way can determine what is or is not Kitsch or Camp. In the work of others, however, classifications oscillate, as the same qualities appear to define one or the other aesthetic. All agree that Kitsch and Camp are marked by stereotype, artifice, frivolity, and exaggeration. Most are also accustomed to relate it to a homosexual sensibility (Meyer). The debate on this last point repeatedly enters into the discussion and shows to what extent the variables used to define these aesthetics depend on subjective critical positions.

One interpretation, now classic, is that of Mihai Calinescu, who considers Kitsch a phenomenon of modernity and places it in opposition to the avant-garde. This results in a polarization in which the former is synonymous with vulgarity, repetition, and banality; in other words, it lacks the capacity to renew itself through experiment, as well as the commitment to change—both characteristics of avant-garde aesthetics. This opposition is common and repeats that of another classic, Clement Greenberg's *Avant-garde and Kitsch* (1939), which confronts the substitute commercial culture with genuine culture. Beyond the arguable subjectivism in the use of these descriptive adjectives, his perspective is notably different from that of Eco. It is possible to argue for a dialectic between avant-garde and Kitsch, given that the latter "se renueva y prospera aprovechando continuamente los descubrimientos de la vanguardia" (Eco 1968, 93) ("renews itself and prospers, continually taking advantage of avant-garde discoveries"). One could add that these texts also reveal an inverse dialectical relationship, for they use stereotypes and Kitsch clichés to construct an anticanonical narrative.

The critical positions on Kitsch and Camp aesthetics (and to a lesser extent those on Pop) form a mosaic of postures that could be grouped along two basic lines: Those concerned with aesthetic import (accusations of looking for effects, imitation, falsity) and those with ideological-political interests (manipulation of taste, consumerism, escapism). Both customarily come together in perspectives that verge on the ethically moralizing. In reality, not only do they install Kitsch as a phenomenon of modernity, but they are also readings conducted *from* the perspective of modernity. In recent years Postmodern perspectives have left to one side the aesthetic-ethical judgments in order to consider this as a cultural phenomenon that paradoxically is no longer the negative pole of genuine art. On the contrary, Frederic Jameson sees it as one of the expressions of the stylistic diversity and heterogeneity of the present day in which the oppositions that sustained judgments of bad or good taste have been eroded. From his perspective, Pop would be the art *par excellence* of our time, a form of expression in which the distinctions between experimental art and art for the masses loses all meaning (Jameson).

The texts of Vega, Drummond, and Zapata (like those of Sánchez, Puig, and many others) offer evidence of the seduction of popular forms. All explore and exploit the aesthetic of Camp and Pop cultures; they delight in bad taste and establish by it their complicity with the reader. All have created an aesthetic from fragmentation and *bricolage*, out of a play of quotations without hierarchy but also without innocence. These stories, more than those of any other genre, accentuate the paradox of the connection between highbrow and lowbrow. A perpetual balance exists between the difference from and the inclusion of that other culture. They establish a space that uses mass culture and deforms it at the same time. For this reason, they can combat accusations of apoliticalness, repetition, and vulgarity. This kind of narrative becomes political precisely in its use of depoliticized forms. Far from being in opposition to avant-garde movements, it has been in permanent connection to and exchange with them. Now, in fact, it occupies their place and their function. The capacity for experimentation, the gesture of transgression that always implied a political gesture, has taken up residence in these hybrid narratives. During the historical period of the avant-garde and the neo–avant-garde of the 1960s the texts of Arlt and Puig kept up a constant play of contact and difference, placing the literary system in crisis and producing changes in the canon. At the end of the twentieth century, the avant-garde utopias no longer seemed feasible, while other utopian expressions, specifically those of politicization and experimentation, did. These stories take responsibility for this function in a paradoxical fashion. They turn to bad taste, to Kitsch, to create a narrative that inverts the standard signs of frivolity or apoliticality. This gesture of simultaneous inclusion and difference implies a constant challenge to the canon at the same time as it launches a permanent struggle to occupy that space. Transgression and canonicity create a play of very conscious balances–and allusions–within these texts. The stories of Vega, Zapata, and Drummond are paradigms of this gesture, and above all, work out a tradition of the use of popular culture, recognizing its seductiveness and distancing themselves from it at the same time.

Camp or Kitsch strategies of displacement from the periphery to the center of the canon do not imply the elimination of the laws of good taste. Good and bad are present in these texts represented by encounter or fusion of two aesthetics. This involves a struggle to impose another canon, transgress the dominant one, or at least force the limits of what is accepted. Even so, a balancing game is perpetuated in which the ugly is recognized and separated from knowledge of the beautiful. It is therefore in these narratives that the strategies of seduction and the game of complicity with the receiver can be best observed. In contrast to the detective story, the seduction lies not only in the recognition of the formulas but also in the game of complicity with a reader who enjoys the cliché and bad taste and recognizes it as low. This is a game that oscillates between the seduction that the aesthetic provides and the recognition of a distance, a difference that the forms analyzed here concern themselves with establishing.

Ana Lydia Vega's story "Pasión de historia," (Passion for history) which opens the collection *Pasión de historia y otras historias de pasión*, belongs on the complex borderland that all contact with Kitsch or "bad taste" generates in art. It can be interpreted as a pivot or a point of intersection between the crime genre and texts connected with the aesthetic of Kitsch and Camp. This story fuses a multiplicity of popular forms of expression and does so ostentatiously. Vega is aware of the game, exposes it, and exploits the possibilities that it allows her. "Pasión de historia" could be considered as yet another variation on detective fiction at the end of the last century. Like Fonseca's "Romance negro," it can be read as an extreme case of the transformation and self-consciousness of the genre. In "Pasión," the crime novel undergoes a surprising turnaround with respect to its conventional form and crosses over into melodrama to create another way of reading history. The formula has also been transformed by another plot alternative: Women maintain their usual role (they end up murdered), but they are also the only ones who have the power of speech (between them, with the narrator as the center, they circulate letters, oral stories, novels, personal diaries, and newspapers). They alone hold the doubtful possibility of achieving the truth. This is essential to understanding how the story inverts another key point of the detective novel: The perspective from which readers implicate themselves in the plot. In this sense, this story has a very particular place in the detective novel at the end of the twentieth century; it brings together cases of women murdered for reasons of passion, and this is how it connects with the prime topics of melodrama and the gutter press as well as the detective novel: Crimes of passion, the vengeance of men who defend their honor, and stories whose truth depends on the testimony of women–and therefore seem hardly to be trusted.

The enigmas derived from these tales of passion (probable or real infidelities, vengeful, murderous husbands) are not solved but remain ambiguous. This ambiguity extends to the crime itself and so undoes the motive of the investigation and the search for the truth traditional in the detective genre. It thus leaves the melodrama apparently standing alone with the "history of passion" at the center. In the same way, the role of the detective that has been occupied by the narrator shifts. Even so, he is incapable of understanding the clues, including those that are linked to his own story; nor does he succeed in advancing the investigation. As in other police stories from this period, the character who takes on the search for the truth gets lost in the tangled web of the story. The reader's knowledge, in fact, exceeds his; he is not able to predict either danger or the plot's conclusion. None of the female characters has a clear perception of her situation, and each projects her life without taking into account the danger embodied in the masculine figures around her. The absence of the conventional return to order and justice leaves the women defenseless and introduces yet another variable in the structure of the detective conventions at the end of the twentieth century. Starting with the title (of the book and the individual story), it is clear that the contiguity and contact of diverse cultural levels ensure that highbrow and lowbrow come together to form a thread that runs through the story. As the narrator says, "para tejer el cuento" era necesario "un hilo que . . . pusiera a significar" (Vega 9) ("a thread that . . . could have significance is necessary to weave the story"). This particular thread unites two cultures and two different forms of knowledge, and the work of weaving is similar to the work that the reader must undertake, interweaving stories and tales of passion. History and the short story, the lie and melodrama–these make up these women's stories, throwing light on other ones and intermixing with multiple other genres such as the chronicle, journalism, and the detective novel.

The quotations and dedications that open "Pasión de la historia" maintain the same strategy, weaving a thread linking highbrow and lowbrow. Readers must be familiar with the subtle relationships among William Irish, Alfred Hitchcock, and Raymond Chandler beyond their shared writing in detective story and mystery genres. It is clear that the story relies on its readers' experience of film and literature. Both intermix to set up descriptions and to qualify and organize scenes, invoking diverse systems of cultural references, both highbrow and lowbrow: "the unexpected clash between the cultured and popular becomes one of its principal aesthetic strategies" (Barradas 554). The totality of the reading experience passes through this heterogeneous cultural sieve consisting of Daphne du Maurier, *Yocasta*, François Truffaut, Jean-Paul Sartre, and Simone de Beauvoir, *Nosferatu*, Brian de Palma, and Miss Marple. This encounter between diverse cultural levels involves a far more complex game than that of a simple pastiche of opposites. The ostensible use of Kitsch functions in the same way, for it is by definition part of an aesthetic generated from another, more ambivalent register. At first sight, Vega's stories seem a glorification of Kitsch, bad taste and lowbrow forms of expression, because of her vocabulary and her recourse to plots of the gutter press and melodrama. Her use of popular vernacular language and allusions to sexuality that border on the coarse does dominate the text; yet bad taste or Kitsch still functions as a space in which aesthetic and political issues are debated and confronted.

On the other hand, it must not be forgotten that this story was published in a collection of supposed "textimonies" by a women's publishing house called "*Seremos*" ("We Will Be"). The epilogue once again unites lowbrow genres with history and journalism at the same time as it makes the story we read synonymous with the novel that the narrator has been writing. Passion, history, journalism, and the detective genre are important to both. We, as the readers of the case of Malén, encounter a passionate melodrama but are also taken over by the sensationalism of the gutter press. Just as in the word-play of the title of the collection, the conclusion of the story links discourses of different value: Testimonials, journalism, crime fiction, and history all work with the notion of truth, even though their places in the "truth" hierarchy differs. Even so, for Ana Lydia Vega the equivalence between "pasión de historia" ("passion for history"? "passion for the truth of history"? or, taking the word in its etymological sense, "pain provoked by history"?) and "historias de pasión" ("stories of passion") is something more than a play on words. Whether invoking love, desire, or pain, the ambiguity of the title opens up a whole range of possibilities. The key that defines this "pasión de historia" (and allows for another reading) appears in the last story of the collection, *Sobre tumbas y héroes* (1961) [*On Heroes and Tombs* 1981]. This title echoes the highbrow literature of Ernesto Sábato (b. 1911), but the subtitle, "Folletín de caballería boricua" [Feuilleton of Boricua Chivalry], once again challenges the hierarchy and reintroduces the lowbrow. Here "pasión de historia" is at last defined. It is not "[. . .] la historia cipaya de los administradores coloniales, ni la de las mediocres maldades de metópolis madrastras . . . Sino la Intra-Historia, la canción de gesta de los supuestos derrotados"

(Vega 103) ("the history of colonial administrators in the pay of foreign powers, nor that of the mediocre evils of interfering metropolises . . ., but the intra-history, the *chanson de geste* of the apparently defeated"). The story relates the project of writing Puerto Rican history–telling the "other history"–and in its configuration mixing traditions and popular beliefs with the myths of mass culture. This is reflected in the room of the protagonist Don Virgilio, an unorthodox historian, where books, newspapers, papers, back numbers of *Volantín Nacional,* the Lares flag, and a poster of Libertad Lamarque in *Besos Brujos* [Bewitched Kisses] all come together. The concept of history has become complicated and the *passion off/for stories* ranges from those of melodrama to history; this text can only be read through our encounter with these various discourses. Thus, if it is still true that the victims are women, it should not be forgotten that they are also Puerto Ricans. "Pasión de historia" opens the way for this reading. To the extent that the narrator feels guilty "como acusada puertorra en corte federal gringa" (Vega 29) ("like a *puertorra* [slang for Puerto Rican woman] accused in a *gringo* Federal court"), something is added to her condition as a woman: Terms such as "island mammal," "Taíno princess," and "*puertorra*" underscore the Puerto Ricanness of the protagonists. The concept of nation is interwoven here with that of woman. If a woman's place is a space that needs to be won through constant struggle (the Woolfian "room of one's own" will cost the narrator dearly), the same is true of the Puerto Rican citizenship. When the time comes to seek asylum, she does not find a single room or space with in a national context: "pedir asilo en la embajada puertorriqueña (cuál?)" (Vega 30) ("ask for asylum in the Puerto Rican Embassy (which?)").

While the women are those with the threads of the story in their hands, their narrative capacity is exercised in stories that systematically have no conclusion or resolution. They cannot take them forward (just as the cases in the detective novels cannot be solved); they do not know enough. Their subjectivities are constructed from stereotypes; they reproduce them and repeat their clichés. Permeated by mass culture and fixed formulas, the characters resign themselves to contradiction in that ambiguous and elusive space that is also that of Kitsch. The stories of these women cannot be told: No one will be able to know the truth or know their identities; nor can the narrator explain, trapped in a world of formulas, aggressive stories, chronicles, soap operas, and melodramas. To her question, "¿Quién contaría a Malén, quién diría la verdad, si ella estaba muerta?" (Vega 21) ("Who would tell Malén, who would tell the truth, if she was dead?"), the story responds "Nadie" ("No one"). Another story has been constructed with the clichés of mass culture, a frustrated story, the story of the impossibility of narrating women's history. Whereas women have always been defined, reduced, and explained in romances and melodramas through stereotypes, here they remain as that otherness that escapes all comfortable resolution. The formulas of mass culture too seem to have failed.

But these women's stories also function as a mirror of history itself. The title of the book is a chiasmus that confronts, reflects, and balances history and melodrama. Popular forms create the space in which both feminine and national identity are debated. In this sense "tejer el cuento de Malén, la novela de Malén" ("to weave Malén's story, Malén's novel") is to try to write the Great Puerto Rican Novel, an attempt that remains interrupted because "cada día se iba enredando más la madeja de escenas sueltas, deshilachadas, donde siempre faltaba algo: la costura decisiva, el hilo que las pusiera a significar" (Vega 9) ("each day the skein of odd, frayed scenes are tangled, where there is always something missing: The decisive stitch, the thread that could give them meaning"). An unfinished national novel articulates identities that are still unsure (*shall we be* free women? *shall we be* an independent country?). History is sketched out through these narratives of passion, in other words, through mass culture. These lowbrow expressions are the threads that give the stories meaning. Their failure makes it impossible to end these stories and comfort oneself with them, but their seduction allows one to trace out *through them* that different space by means of which a political reading can be offered.

If all literature linked to mass cultural genres always establishes a seductive relationship with the reader, Pop explicitly sells seduction and sells it to a higher degree than other forms. Such are the first condition and the first advantage of the connection with the more immediate forms of expressions of mass culture. The attraction of their consumption derives from the recognition of their laws. As we have seen, in the contract established between reader and text, between pleasure and interest development depends on encountering the expected. Thus, in most popular genres the promise of seduction is rapidly diluted in the comforting fulfillment of this pact. The reader receives a fleeting pleasure, but the seduction is lost in satisfaction and confirmation of recognition. On the contrary, Pop narratives establish far more complex relationships of pleasure and seduction. The Pop aesthetic is composed of the most obvious mass expressions but establishes a tension whose greatest seduction lies in what is not resolved. It directly addresses the consumers of mass culture and assumes knowledge of media codes, especially visual ones. Pop artists seem euphorically to affirm the visual reality of mass culture and, in this sense, end up offering a radical critique of a highbrow aesthetic. But this does not mean an adhesion to or a total fusion with mass culture. The Brazilian novelist Roberto Drummond and the North American painter Roy Lichtenstein are paradigms of the Pop aesthetic, as well as being the most interesting examples of the use of similar strategies in two different artistic fields.

In his early work, Lichtenstein painted human figures as if reduced and constructed by a comic strip artist, invoking a known visual code that is enjoyed by many. Far removed from any kind of realism, his canvases represented what has already been represented, and such preexistent images were always products of mass culture. Lichtenstein's compositions, modeled upon previously drawn comic strips and saturated with strident colors, are integrated into the narrative system of separate scenes so typical of this art form. But they focus, as in a cinematographic close-up, onto faces and scenes that remain unresolved for the spectator. The dialogues are fragmented, decontextualized. The code has shattered at the exact point that sustains it; there no longer exists a narrative thread to guide us. Even so, the seduction of the images, these small fragments, is linked to and depends to a large extent on our experience as readers of comic strips. It plays with our desire to know and our knowledge of the code. The deception we feel establishes the difference between any comic and a Lichtenstein canvas. In fact, Lichtenstein quotes comics by including them in other contexts and thus establishes distance and another kind of seduction. In some cases, the dialogue in the balloons that accompany the image changes the sense completely. *The Engagement Ring,* for instance, leads spectators to a very different interpretation than the original scene from the comic "Winnie Winkle" suggested. Now there is no interest in following a plot; the image itself has exercised a new form of seduction. In fact the seductive capacity of the image is multiplied in that the figure, removed from its original context, opens up new alternatives to the imagination of spectators. The picture only harkens back to a code it shares with the reader, and its meaning is supported by this shared knowledge. The transcription of the familiar comic drawing, with its graphic technique made large, makes it strange without destroying its familiarity. This is one way to work with mass culture: The recognition and use of its seductive possibilities (possibilities the mass culture itself may not exploit, given that their seduction dilutes quickly into pleasure) and also alienation, the deception that generates another kind of connection that is undoubtedly more complex. Lichtenstein's images work with the stereotype of the comic strip and the banalized feelings of the characters (Waldman 113). They show and name very familiar details and objects that are social myths. The real object, mediated through myths and clichés, is diluted; it does not exist. We have only artifice, quotations, strategies.

The same strategic game is found in the narratives of Roberto Drummond. His work represents a specific project to construct a Pop literature, to make "uma literatura sem nenhum vínculo com a literatura tradicional"(1975, 3) ("a literature without any link to traditional literature"); in other words, to create texts that establish a new relationship with mass culture. The accumulation of elements of popular culture, such as advertising slogans, radio and television dialogues, and newspaper cuttings is condensed into a gesture that could be called nominative and thus very similar to the work performed by word and image in Lichtenstein's paintings. The name (of people, places, and brand names) not only functions as a cultural cliché that echoes a code and acts as a known reference for the reader but also becomes itself a component of the narrative. To narrate is to name and define through that name. Even so, paradoxically, the naming depersonalizes; nothing or no one has a secure identity in these stories. The proliferation and the shifting of names produce an effect of distancing. The sign is emptied of meaning. Naming functions in the same way as do Lichtenstein's enlarged figures and the phrases and names contained in the balloons of his paintings. Once again, the procedure that seems most clearly to indicate the sense of belonging to mass culture also provokes a differentiation.

In his "Coca-Cola cycle," which includes texts such as *A morte de D. J. em Paris* [1975; The Death of D. J. in Paris], *O dia em que Ernest Hemingway morreu crucificado* [1978; The Day That Ernest Hemingway Died Crucified], and *Sangue de Coca-Cola* [1981; Blood Made of Coca-Cola], Drummond offers a political reading of contemporary Brazil: "E eu provo um pouco do meu sangue: tem gosto de Coca-Cola ... o Brasil também tem sangue de Coca-Cola" (1981, 8) ("I taste a little of my blood; it tastes like Coca-Cola ... Brazil also has the blood of Coca-Cola"). This quotation opens the text and is printed onto an image of a Coca-Cola bottle turned upside down. The novel takes place on April 1, the date of the resignation of President Jânio Quadros and the victory of the military in 1964. The recording of this particular situation gives a political grounding to the text, where, at the same time, characters called Tyrone Power or Erika Sommer cross one another's paths. This nominative jungle does not assure us of

the familiar world in which names such as Coca-Cola, Hemingway, Kennedy, or Catherine Deneuve should suggest, because these individuals do not correspond to expected identities; they have shifted and lost their fixed media fascination. The short story, "Objectos pertencentes a Fernando B, misteriosamente desaparecido" ("Objects Belonging to Fernando B, Mysteriously Disappeared") from *A morte de D. J. em Paris*, is exemplary. We only know the vanished man through the inventory of his belongings. The emptiness of his identity is covered over by famous names and brands; the photo of "Catherine D." replaces that of the suspected murderers on a wanted poster. The sign (the photo) does not correspond to the object (the actress) and refers us to other identities, as unknown and unrecognizable as that of the protagonist. It is impossible to solve the probable crime, to discover its motive and perpetrator(s). The supposed transparent relation of objects to name falls apart, as does the genre of the detective story. Once again, as with Lichtenstein, identification is broken with a world that becomes increasingly confused and disquieting–the opposite of the security that consumer society promises.

"Dôia na janela" ["Dôia at the Window"], also from *A morte de D. J. em Paris,* can be read as a metaphor or synecdoche of the relationship established by Drummond's texts with mass culture: "Dôia gostava de olhar o anúncio luminoso da Coca-Cola e certas noites o único consolo de Dôia era aquela garrafa enchendo um copo de Coca-Cola" (1981; 21) ("Dôia liked to look at the lighted Coca-Cola sign, and on certain nights Dôia's only consolation was that bottle filling a glass of Coca-Cola"). But the protagonist is locked up in a psychiatric clinic and, from the window, her life, her experience and even her hallucinations are defined by advertisements and brand names. Her vision of the crucified Christ is of a man who looks like Robert Redford, wearing Lee jeans and Adidas shoes, and who is given a bottle of Coca-Cola on the cross. The world of the protagonist has been reduced to a window that opens onto a media world that is simultaneously seductive and deceptive. Similarly, in the title story, "A morte de D. J. em Paris" (1975), the protagonist creates her own Paris out of paper, posters, and photos in the basement of the house in which she lives. In other words, she has constructed an imaginary space, an illusion, where reality and illusion are confused. As in many expressions of mass culture, the individual lives in the illusion of possession and converts the artifice in which she or he is submerged into a spectacle. The episode thus functions as synecdoche of the way the story appropriates mass culture, for this is an appropriation that rapidly defamiliarizes and makes the daily signs of that culture become strange.

But Drummond's texts are especially associated with Lichtenstein's paintings because of their strong graphic presence. Their drawings, strongly influenced by the comic strip and by advertising design, integrate with the story; in fact they are stories in themselves. The poster designed by Elifias Andreato that accompanies *O dia em que Ernest Hemingway morreu crucificado* at the same time contains and subverts all the characteristic signs of this popular format. The faces of Kennedy and Marilyn Monroe are lost among others less familiar and among floating elements (mouths, shoes, animals) that are inexplicable outside the context of the novel. The first function of the poster as a form, that is, to offer a clear and recognizable message consumers can identify, dissolves. The cover of this same novel, designed by

E. Andreato, takes up and duplicates Drummond's aesthetic: An upside-down bottle of Coca-Cola acts as a cross on which Christ bleeds–in the same color as the spilt soft drink. The panel is shared with the celebrated image of Marilyn Monroe with her skirt blown up by uprushing air (from the film "The Seven Year Itch"). In its turn, this entire cover is based on Salvador Dali's "Corpus Hipercubicus." The image is thus composed of quotations and brings about the fusion of two cultures. It calls on the media format but dismantles its attraction, decontextualizing it and constructing a montage of figures in which their commercially seductive nature can no longer be recognized. In short, the images repeat the procedure followed by the texts: They create an initial impact and seduce by bringing in what is known and easily consumed by the reader, but they introduce some unsettling difference. In these hyperrealist formats, in the recognizable faces of actors or comic strip personalities and in the symbols of the media imaginary, there suddenly emerges some alien element that breaks up the identification and introduces difference. The deception experienced recalls that of viewing Lichtenstein's paintings, in which our hopes of following a story and knowing what has happened and to whom are frustrated. In these illustrations (which are pure code references), the Adidas shoes are torn, the brandname shirt has a bullet hole at breast level, the pretty girl with the touch of Greta Garbo has a set of false teeth in her hand, and a stream of liquid that seems to be blood pours from the Coca-Cola bottle. There is no comforting recognition or pure consumption. The text and the painting have trapped us; they have maintained a game of postponement and established a different space. It is in this both disappointing and, at the same time, pleasant space that these works are politicized.

A story such as Luis Zapata's *El vampiro de la colonia Roma*, when read after Puig's work, offers another interesting point of contact with mass media formats and is also an index of the space covered and the networks proposed by these texts. *El vampiro* establishes its affiliations clearly, exposing them and tracing a line of adhesions with which to define its identity: Interwoven with *boleros,* films, and clichés, the text immediately echoes the aesthetic of the stories of Manuel Puig and the films of Pedro Almodóvar. The Camp aesthetic, the codes derived from mass culture, Kitsch, and bad taste all mingle in this monologue/dialogue of the protagonist. Zapata's narrative is composed of this "formula" and incorporates "love stories" that are far removed from the romantic tradition; love, passion, romance, and lies seem to dominate his stories *(Ese amor que hasta ayer nos quemaba* [1989; That Love that Until Yesterday Burned Us], *En jirones* and *La más fuerte pasión* [1995; The Strongest Passion]). *El vampiro* also marks the crossing point and fusion of highbrow and lowbrow culture through its graphics and spatial organization. The intent to reproduce the phonetic reality of a story that is presented as a complex of tape recordings seems to point directly to these mass formats and their reproductive nature. A trick effect of "authentic" conversation (prior to all manipulation by the interviewer) is visually created by supposedly faithful graphic reproduction. Even so, these graphics that eliminate capital letters and the blank spaces that substitute for punctuation recall experimental texts with their constant self-reference to their condition as writing. Paradoxically, the same procedure, high and low, represents both, supporting the aim of maximum journalistic transparency and drawing attention to the material and spatial aspects of the text.

At the same time it is clear that the stories pick up on the picaresque tradition. On the one hand, this recall invokes a prestigious but also very popular Spanish tradition; on the other, it establishes its connection to one of the first milestones of Latin American literature in the twentieth century that made contact with the mass media, Roberto Arlt's *El juguete rabioso.* Zapata's novel traces a line that connects Arlt with Puig, Almodóvar, and a Camp aesthetic. The linking of a format that clearly owes much to Puig with a tradition rescued by Arlt suggests a sharing of the same contact with lowbrow forms and the recovery of marginal genres excluded from literature up to that point. But it also implies taking on, through Arlt, a genre that is not usually associated with the mass culture at the end of the twentieth century. The structure of *El juguete rabioso* intermixes a serial story, outlaw tales, and the picaresque. These expressions of popular culture constitute a story of initiation written at the zenith of the avant-garde period that opens up another path to understanding transgression and rupture. Arlt in the 1920s made the same move as Puig in the 1960s: He questioned the limits of the literary system and, through the insertion within it of lowbrow and derided formats, established a means of appropriating popular culture that would be a model for the rest of the century. Silvio Astier, the protagonist of *El juguete rabioso,* creates his identity from a stereotype, as would the characters of Manuel Puig later. From Oscar Masotta onward, the serial story, the picaresque, and the one-act farce would all organize their discourse around one essential point of reference: Betrayal. This could also be read as the text's "betrayal" of the popular genres, which it employs through distancing and creating thereby a new mode of connection with them. The quotations in *En jirones* offer a good example: A fragment of a song by Roberto Carlos, "Fiera herida" ("Wounded Animal"), brings both Kitsch and Camp aesthetics, with their delight in musical formats such as the *bolero,* into contact with a quotation from *El juguete rabioso.* This isolated citation "El recuerdo, semejante a un diente podrido, estaría en mí, y su hedor me enturbiaría todas las fragancias de la tierra" (Arlt 125) ("The memory, like a rotten tooth, would be in me, and its stink would foul all the perfumes of the earth") seems to allude to the love theme but in fact occurs at the moment when the protagonist prepares for his *betrayal* of a friend. Homage to a key text and author who deployed lowbrow formats, an allusion to the betrayal theme, and a reference to the most definitively picaresque novel, *El vampiro de la colonia Roma,* all come together in this quotation.

El vampiro can be read as a Postmodern version of the genre, however, because the formal similarities underline one supreme difference. The picaresque life of a servant with its changes of masters and employment has been displaced into the life of a homosexual who prostitutes himself. The chain of masters has been replaced by one of lovers and protectors. This difference establishes a clear distance from Spanish canonical texts while strengthening the link with Arlt's novel. In fact, it was in *El juguete rabioso* that a homosexual made his first appearance in a picaresque tale. While the quotation of Arlt opens *En jirones, El vampiro* also insists on this connection. The character who in *El juguete rabioso* only crosses the protagonist's path once is taken up and developed into the protagonist of the story.

This dialogue with tradition structures the text. Quotations from *Lazarillo de Tormes* and Fernández de Lizardi's (1776–1827) *El Periquillo Sarniento* [1816; *The Itching Parrot* 1942] open *Vampiro*. The double movement of inclusion and distancing is already set up in the opening of the tale in relation to the initiators of the genre in Spain and Latin America, but the divergence from the canon is signaled by the affiliation with Arlt, who was responsible for recuperating the form for literature in the twentieth century. *El Vampiro* seems to follow Francisco de Quevedo's (1580–1645) picaresque message in *El Buscón* [1604; *The Swindler* 1969] in proposing the impossibility of adjusting into another "world":

> el otro día leí en el periódico que una persona había entrado en contacto con seres extraterrestres y se había ido con ellos . . . me cae que yo sí me iba . . . y entonces sí 'adiós mundo cruel' como dice la canción . . . y pediría un deseo que no volviera nunca pero nunca por ningún motivo a este pinche mundo. (Zapata 1979, 222–23)

> the other day I read in the newspaper that a person had come into contact with extraterrestrials and had gone with them . . . I would like to have gone . . . and then yes "goodbye cruel world" as the song goes . . . and I would ask for a wish that I would never come back, never but never for any reason, to this blasted world.

This remark comes at the end of the novel, where no space seems to exist to satisfy the protagonist. Marginality and failure are resolved in an imaginary flight through the multiple clichés of mass culture. The flight to another world, literally in this case, drawing on the popular imaginary conception of extraterrestrials), corresponds to Buscón's desire to "journey to the Indies" and the ambiguous and highly controversial "And I left" that concludes *El Juguete*. In these stories, the journey, the way out, or the flight, even though destined to failure, is toward an imaginary destination that is more propitious, but in *El vampiro* there seems to be no place at all where the protagonist can improve his luck. This narrator/protagonist's identity and imaginary are formed in the point where the mass media and homosexual subjectivity cross. The two terms are confused in some scenes and together define the perspective of the character and the aesthetic of the story. On one hand, media culture explains and defines it. But above all, his sexuality is linked to the culture of the image; sex and cinema are linked with his own sexual initiation and in his definition as subject. Adonis García is the subject defined at the crossing point between homosexuality and the Camp aesthetic. This is also the place where the nonadjustment to life of the picaresque character takes a more political turn. The emptiness and lack are both voiced, "de repente me puse a pensar en mi vida y se me hizo . . . como que estaba formada por puros huecos no?" (Zapata 1979, 100) ("suddenly I thought about my life and it made me [feel] as if I was made out of just holes no?"), and duplicated by the blank spaces that replace the text's punctuation. This graphically and verbally expressed emptiness is also filled by Camp and Kitsch images: The hole, the fantasies, and dreams of castration and failure are rapidly covered over by media images.

The lack of conformity of the character with the world does not only refer to his sexual identity or his feelings of otherness and existential alienation. Adonis also faces the institutions that are most representative of the nation. In these, this difference condemns him to failure. Interwoven in accounts of his amorous adventures, the school, police, hospital, and prison are all rejecting political spaces whose power culminates in the final fragment, causing that search for the way out through the mass media imaginary. The fantasy departure allows him to separate himself from a world marked by the most representative symbols of the Mexican nation:

> llegaron los marcianos y me raptaron y nos fuimos bailando el cha cha cha . . . y adiós ángel de la independencia y adiós caballito y adiós monumento de la revolución . . . y después la república y el continente americano (Zapata 1979, 222–23)

> the martians arrived and abducted me and we went off dancing the cha cha cha . . . and good-bye angel of independence and goodbye little horse and good-bye monument of the revolution . . . and afterwards the republic and the american continent

The picaresque tradition is merged with the signs of a Camp aesthetic: *El Buscón* structures the unraveling of the history here, but Adonis imagines himself as a character by constructing himself a sign of the media and Kitsch culture. A culture that operates only on the periphery and a marginalized sexuality fuse for Adonis in a precise space and time (Mexico City in the mid-1970s). The novel articulates the nexus between homosexuality and politics: It makes sexual marginality political and does so by appropriating from the same culture that has constructed the identity of the protagonist. Consequently the use of the Camp and Kitsch aesthetic, dominant in the text, is by no means frivolous and apolitical. On the contrary, it is through them that homosexuality and politics come together. As in the other texts considered in this essay, political motives attributed to the media have been reversed, and mass culture ends up being the vehicle through which a possibility for the politicization of sexual marginality is proposed.

The imaginary that organizes this narrative is among those dominant in Latin American literature at the end of the twentieth century. The Kitsch reference and the invocation of the code of the consumer have become metaphors of an aesthetic that challenges marginalization. The new corpus is now extensive, with a large number of texts in which "passion, tears, and nostalgia" are "components of a subjectivity disqualified by the previous aesthetic and that emerges strongly in the contemporary novel" (Santos 46). For this reason, a story of the 1990s, such as *Parece que fue ayer* [1991; It Seems It Was Only Yesterday] by Denzil Romero (1938–1999) with its subtitle "crónica de un happening bolerístico" [Chronicle of a *Bolero* Happening], is an indication of how this tradition has consolidated and made itself each time more self-conscious and self-referential. The entire text ends up being a condensation of citations from popular culture. A manifesto on Camp, complete with questions by Carlos Monsiváis and definitions by Susan Sontag, that opens the novel constitutes a metanarrative whose object is to insist on a self-reflexive and metacritical dimension. Thus, at the close of the twentieth century, the gesture of adhesion to these forms of expression demonstrates the strength of a new canon. The literary system has included popular culture, and once again the struggle between highbrow and lowbrow begins, but now from *within* this consecrated space.

Translation by Jessica Johnson

Works Cited

Arlt, Roberto. 1980. *El juguete rabioso*. Buenos Aires: Losada, 1988.

Azuela, Mariano. 1960. *Los de abajo*. Mexico City: Fondo de Cultura Económica.

Barradas, Efraín. 1985. "La necesaria innovación de Ana Lydia Vega: preámbulo para lectores vírgenes." *Revista Iberoamericana* 51.132–133: 550–558.

Borges, Jorge Luis, and Bioy Casares (Honorio Bustos Domecq, pseud.). 1995. *Seis problemas para don Isidro Parodi*. Buenos Aires: EMECE.

Calinescu, Matei. 1987. *Five Faces of Modernity: Avant-Garde, Decadence, Kitsch, Postmodernism*. Durham, N.C.: Duke University Press.

Chandler, Raymond. 1980. "El simple arte de matar." *El simple arte de matar*. Spanish version by Jaume Prat, based on translation by Floreal Mazia. Barcelona: Bruguera. 196–216.

Drummond, Roberto. 1975. *A morte de D. J. em Paris*. São Paulo: Atica.

———. 1978. *O dia em que Ernest Hemingway morreu crucificado*. São Paulo: Atica.

———. 1981. *Sangue de Coca-Cola*. São Paulo: Atica.

Eco, Umberto. 1968. *Apocalípticos e integrados*. Trans. Andrés Boglar. Barcelona: Lumen.

———. 1984. "Lo posmoderno, la ironía y lo ameno." *Apostillas a El nombre de la rosa*. Trans. Ricardo Pochtar. Barcelona: Lumen. 71–82.

———. 1988. "La innovación en el serial." *De los espejos y otros ensayos*. Trans. Cárdenas Moyano. Barcelona: Lumen. 134–56.

Enzensberger, Hans Magnus. 1968. "Reflexiones ante una celda encristalada." *Política y delito*. Trans. Lucas Sala. Barcelona: Seix Barral. 7–34.

Feinmann, José Pablo. 1981. *Ni el tiro del final*. Buenos Aires: Pomaire.

———. 1991. "Estado policial y novela negra argentina." *Los héroes difíciles*. Ed. Jorge B. Rivera. Buenos Aires: Corregidor. 155–65.

Fonseca, Rubem. 1973. *O Caso Morel*. São Paulo: Artenova.

———. 1989. *Vastas Emoções e Pensamentos Imperfeitos*. São Paulo: Ed. Schwarcz.

———. 1990. *Agosto*. São Paulo: Ed. Schwarcz.

———. 1992. *Romance Negro e Outras Histórias*. São Paulo: Ed. Schwarcz.

Fuentes, Carlos. 1962. *La muerte de Artemio Cruz*. Mexico City: Fondo de Cultura Económica.

Gandolfo, Elvio E. 1982. *La reina de las nieves*. Buenos Aires: CEAL.

Greenberg, Clement. 1970. "The Vanguard and Kitsch." *Kitsch. An Anthology of Bad Taste*. Ed. Gillo Dorfles. London: Studio Vista. 116–26.

Jameson, Frederic. 1991. *Ensayos sobre el posmodernismo*. Trans. Esther Perez, Christian Ferrer, Sonia Mazzeo and Laura Klein. Buenos Aires: Imago Mundi.

Leñero, Vicente. 1964. *Los albañiles*. Barcelona: Seix Barral.

———. 1965. *Estudio Q*. Mexico City: Joaquín Mortiz.

———. 1967. *El garabato*. Mexico City: Joaquín Mortiz.

Levrero, Mario. 1992. *Nick Carter se divierte mientras el lector es asesinado y yo agonizo*. Montevideo: Arca.

Masotta, Oscar. 1965. *Sexo y traición en Roberto Arlt*. Buenos Aires: Jorge Alvarez.

Meyer, Moe. 1994. *The Politics and Poetics of Camp*. London and New York: Routledge.

Palmer, Jerry. 1987. "Thrillers." *Popular Fiction and Social Change*. Ed. Christopher Pawling. London: Macmillan. 76–98.

———. 1991. "Crime Fiction: The Genre Dimension." *Potboilers. Methods, Concepts and Case Studies in Popular Fiction*. London/New York: Routledge. 131–42.

Piglia, Ricardo. 1988. *Respiración artificial*. Buenos Aires: Sudamericana.

———. 1993. "Prólogo." *Las fieras*. Buenos Aires: Clarín/Aguilar. 7–11.

Porter, Dennis. 1983. "Backward Construction and the Art of Suspense." *The Poetics of Murder*. Ed. G. Most and W. Stowe. London and New York: Harcourt Brace Jovanovich. 327–40.

Puig, Manuel. 1973. *The Buenos Aires Affair*. Buenos Aires: Sudamericana.

Romero, Denzil. 1991. *Parece que fue ayer*. Caracas: Planeta Venezolana.

Ross, Andrew. 1989. *No Respect: Intellectuals and Popular Culture*. New York and London: Routledge.

Saer, Juan José. 1994. *La pesquisa*. Buenos Aires: Seix Barral.

———. 1997. "Un largo adiós al policial." *Clarín. Cultura y Nación*, October 27. 24.

Sánchez, Luis Rafael. 1976. *La guaracha del macho Camacho*. Buenos Aires: Ed. de la Flor.

———. 1988. *La importancia de llamarse Daniel Santos*. Hanover: Ed. del Norte.

Santos, Lidia. 1992–1993. "Des héros et des larmes. Le kitsch et la culture de masse dans les romans des caraïbes hispanophones et du Brésil." *Études Littéraires* 25.3: 39–48.

Sasturain, Juan. 1985/1987. *Manual de perdedores 1/2*. 2 Vols. Buenos Aires: Legasa.

Sontag, Susan. 1964. "Notes on 'Camp'." *Against Interpretation and Other Essays*. New York: Dell Publishing. 275–92.

Soriano, Osvaldo. 1986. *Triste, solitario y final*. Buenos Aires: Sudamericana.

Taibo II, Paco Ignacio. 1986. *Sombra de la sombra*. Mexico City: Planeta.

———. 1987. *La vida misma*. Mexico City: Planeta.

———. 1989. *No habrá final feliz*. Mexico City: Planeta.

———. 1991. *The Shadow of the Shadow*. Trans. William I. Neuman. New York: Viking Penguin.

Vega, Ana Lydia. 1987. *Pasión de historia y otras historias de pasión*. Buenos Aires: Ediciones de la Flor.

Waldman, Diane. 1993. *Roy Lichtenstein*. New York: Guggenheim Museum.

Walsh, Rodolfo. 1969. *¿Quién mató a Rosendo?* Buenos Aires: Tiempo Contemporáneo.

———. 1972. *Operación Masacre*. Buenos Aires: Ed. de la Flor.

———. 1973. *Caso Satanovsky*. Buenos Aires: Ed. de la Flor.

Zapata, Luis. 1979. *El vampiro de la colonia Roma*. Mexico City: Grijalbo.

———. 1985. *En jirones*. Mexico City: Posada.

———. 1989. *Ese amor que hasta ayer nos quemaba*. Mexico City: Posada.

———. 1995. *La más fuerte pasión*. Mexico City: Ed. Océano de México.

CHAPTER 60

LITERATURA DE CORDEL
LITERATURE FOR MARKET
AND VOICE

Idelette Muzart Fonseca dos Santos

During the early years of the twentieth century, the literature of chapbooks produced in Brazil became a complex literary system almost independent of the institutionalized literary system, with its own poets, publishing houses (which sometimes belonged to the poets themselves), circuits of distribution, and principally, its own public of readers, having little if any formal education, in rural areas and in the big cities. The 1865 chapbook discovered by Orígenes Lessa (1903–1986) confirms the existence of the publication of *folhetos de feira* (the traditional denomination of these chapbooks) in Recife in the state of Pernambuco. In the Iberian tradition of animal stories, however, some historical allusions bear witness to the fact that the works were either written or rewritten in Brazil. A few later references may be found to these chapbooks, which Sílvio Romero, always alert to oral and popular creation, disdainfully refers to as "worthless booklets."

Cordel literature was born at the end of the nineteenth century, more precisely after 1893, with Leandro Gomes de Barros's (1865–1918) publication of his poem, followed in the next decades by Francisco das Chagas Batista (1882–1930) and João Martins de Athayde (1880–1959) (Terra 1983, 17). It is worth noting that, with the exception of João Martins, these pioneers come from the same state (Paráiba) and even from the same microregion (Teixeira). The name of Silvino Pirauá de Lima (1848–1913) (frequently cited as one of the first authors of chapbooks) should be added to the list. Whereas Leandro and João Martins migrated to Vitória de Santo Antão and Recife, Francisco das Chagas Batista settled in his state's capital, where in 1913 he founded Popular Editora, to which Mário de Andrade (1893–1945) would pay vibrant homage in 1929 (quoted in Souza 1981, 28). Whether documenting the customs and myths of Brazilian rural life or recreating in writing an oral tradition inherited from Europe, the chapbook's multiple denominations betray its ambiguous identity.

The traditional term for this eight to forty-eight-page chapbook is *folheto de feira*. At the height of their popularity, some numbered sixty-four pages. The standard 11 cm × 16 cm format was imposed by the folds of the paper and the type of distribution. It is reminiscent of the single sheets of French *littérature de colportage* (Bollème 1971), the English chapbooks, and the Spanish *pliegos sueltos* share with these the same lightness and waywardness temporaly circumscribed by a place of meetings and interchange: The street, the market, the fair, the railway, or the bus station. In Brazil, the appearance of the term *literatura de cordel*, used to designate these leaflets, dates from 1879 and 1880. Sílvio Romero (1851–1914) was perhaps the first Brazilian to make use of the expression (Romero 257), inspired by the Portuguese example and the studies of Portuguese scholar Teófilo Braga (1843–1924). The term *cordel* had been in use in the region of Valencia since the thirteenth century to designate a string of (fine) twine. Its use extended throughout the Peninsula and, in the sixteenth century, there was frequent mention in Portugal of *teatro de cordel*. The term finally appears in Brazil at the end of the nineteenth century. Apart from its usage to designate the twine upon which the books were hung in markets and town squares, the word is part of a series of expressions referring to the specific product for sale: *cordel* farces or *cordel* theater, which refer exclusively to theatrical texts sold on the street—rare in Brazil, though quite commonplace in the Iberian peninsula—*cordel* bookstore, restricted to a commercial designation, and of course, *literatura de cordel* (*cordel* literature), a term that covers all literary works of popular and traditional origin exhibited for sale in a public place. Such generalization, however, comes relatively late (the *"cordel* farces" entry in *Caldas Aulete*, the first Portuguese dictionary, is dated 1881) and is scholarly in origin, both in Portugal and in Brazil. The *Great Portuguese and Brazilian Encyclopaedia* opts for a mixed solution: In addition to the term *literatura de cordel*, its entry for *folhetos de cordel* (*cordel* leaflets) briefly records description, authors, titles, and means of distribution before concluding with a reference to their near-extinction in Portugal. No mention is made of Brazilian chapbooks.

Despite protests from Brazilian scholars who rejected the use of an imported term imposed by a few lettered men upon a Brazilian popular reality (Horacio Almeida 6–7), the expression *literatura de cordel* gradually took on a level of generalization that made it official, leading the popular poets themselves to employ it. Prior to 1960, José Bernardo da Silva's publishing house in Juazeiro was called Literatura de Cordel; the poets of Bahia came together under the flag of the Brazilian Order of *Cordel* Poets. Poets and publishers alike appeared to want to adapt to the scholarly, lettered perspective of this marketplace literature, which continues to be purchased, read, and loved by the people. With its popularization, the scholarly denomination underwent changes. Articles and books now tend to erase the word *literature*. They speak simply of *cordel* to designate popular literature in verse, as well as the culture and worldview that allowed for the appearance and development of this unique literature for the unlettered, this writing that sings.

On the formal level, the chapbooks possess individual characteristics that distinguish them from the singing or oral improvisation known as *repente*. The simplification and homogenization of sung poetic modalities were consequences of this transition to writing. At the moment in the history of *cantoria* when the quatrain (almost exclusively the stanzaic form of past improvisations) gives place to the sextain, the *décima*, and other derivative forms, the chapbook establishes the sextain as the dominant stanzaic form. Writing therefore unifies the formal aspect, and creativity is thus reserved for the narration, or for the story told. Oral poetry, on the contrary, slowly relinquishes narrativity and chooses formal sophistication as a means of enhancing improvisation. Some of the older chapbooks were based on transcriptions of

614

traditional oral compositions from the Iberian or Brazilian *romanceiros*. This "writing of the voice" is not peculiar to Brazil: Since the sixteenth century, Spanish *literatura de cordel* had included various traditional stories whose publication in *pliegos sueltos* frequently included, for typographical reasons, lettered or popular songs as well as more "evolved" stories or modern stories (Garcia de Enterría 1973, 35). The transformation into writing of an orally created story was generally reserved for Brazilian stories. Whether *cantoria* or story, all things thus converge in the chapbook, a written poetic form that retains various oral features. But writing does not here represent the definitive fixing of oral tradition. The chapbook is part of this cultural dynamic and the circuit that replenishes and renews itself, from both the poetic and the narrative perspectives, through the oral tradition of *cantoria* and *contos* (stories).

Thus, storytellers from Paraíba organize their repertory into three categories: "Trancoso stories" (a term frequently used to designate stories from the oral tradition by referring to Portuguese author Gonçalo Fernandes Trancoso, 1515–1596?), chapbook stories, and short stories. If storytellers acknowledge having read many chapbooks, their free recreation of them make them traditional storytellers, unconcerned with preserving even the slightest feature of the original verses (Silveira 1998). The same creative freedom manifests itself in popular poets when they make use of various sources to enrich their narrative material. Thus Altino Alagoano (a pseudonym of Maria das Neves Batista Pimentel [1913–1995], one of the rare women authors of chapbooks) specialized in the *cordel* verse "translation" of novellas, novels, and serials such as Victor Hugo's (1802–1885) *Notre-Dame de Paris* (transformed into a leaflet under the title of *O corcunda de Notre-Dame* [The Hunchback of Notre Dame]) or *O violino do diabo* [The Devil's Violin], a verse re-creation of the homonymous prose novel by Enrique Pérez Escrich (1829–1897), a famous popular Spanish writer of the nineteenth century whose novels had impressive Brazilian editions (Mendonça 1993). In *cordel* literature, a single work of fiction may be the object of several adaptations or verse translations, as has been the case with Alexandre Dumas's (1802–1870) *Comte de Monte Cristo*, as freely adapted by João Martins de Athayde and later by José Costa Leite, in a less successful version (Santos 1997b). In this case, though, as in many others, film versions of the work in question and images from these films provide another source of inspiration for the new written narratives. During the 1940s and 1950s, motion pictures became an almost inexhaustible source of narratives and illustrations for book covers, which abound with photographs of Hollywood stars. Thus did Joan of Arc become a *cordel* heroine—by means of a cover photograph of Ingrid Bergman in the film of the same name.

Though intended to be read aloud, these texts continue to be perceived as oral texts. The spelling of a word may be transformed, and not always by ignorance, as the lettered reader might suppose, but more often to facilitate a rhyme or, more concretely, because of a typographical shortage. More important, modifications may lead to the elaboration of variants in a process identical to that of ordinarily transmitted oral literature. A fine example of this confusion between orality and *cordel* writing may be found in *O Soldado Jogador* [previous to 1918; The Gambling Soldier], written by Leandro Gomes de Barros and based on oral versions of an Iberian story. In creating the *cordel* book, the poet transformed the oral text. If the Iberian novel is still remembered, it is intermixed with variants of Leandro's text: The process of hybridity has been completed. The act of writing and the chapbooks themselves give rise in this way to the question of intellectual property. For the poets, one of the assertions of ownership occurs in the use of an acrostic in the poem's final stanza or the inclusion of the poet's name in the sixth line of the last sextain, as in the case of Bahian poet Rodolfo Coelho Cavalcante (1919–1986). The acrostic continues to be the most frequent "signature." Leandro Gomes de Barros used a seven-line stanza, corresponding to the seven letters of his name, even when the chapbook had been written in sextains. Poets generally compose one or more acrostics consisting of abbreviations of their names or combinations of initials from names and surnames (LEANDRO, JCLEITE, JBARROS, and so on). In fact, this graphic identification is a way to guarantee a book's material ownership. Similarly, around 1910, Leandro Gomes de Barros, whose stories were published by several publishing houses without license or royalty payments, published the following warning on the back covers of his chapbooks: "The author reserves rights of property" (*Literatura Popular em Verso Antologia 3* [Popular Literature in Verse Anthology 3] 281). Nonetheless, the notion of intellectual property remains confused, as evidenced by the following examples.

Who is the author of *Romance do Pavão Misterioso* [Tale of the Mysterious Peacock]? José Camelo de Melo Rezende (b. 1964) was a poet and *cantador* of the twenties from the state of Paraíba. Not being a good improvisationalist, he composed stories that he memorized and sang solo or with poet Romano Elias. Among these was the famous story of the mysterious peacock, a mechanical object built by an engineer at the request of a lovelorn youth. Half airplane, half helicopter, the object was kept in a small box that, when opened, took the form of a peacock. The youth later kidnaps his beloved against the will of her jealous father, who has kept her at home under lock and key. In 1927, José Camelo was forced to flee from Paráiba and, during his absence, the story was published in chapbook form, its authorship attributed to João Melchíades Ferreira. Years later, José Camelo wrote his own version in a chapbook published by Joaquim Batista da Sena with an accusatory introduction disclosing the tale's itinerary from voice to writing, an itinerary followed by many texts published prior to 1950:

> Quem quizer ficar ciente
> da história do Pavão
> leia agora este romance
> com calma e muita atenção,
> que verá que esta história
> é minha, e de outro não.
>
> Há muitos anos versei
> esta história e muitos dias
> fiz uso d'ela sozinho
> em diversas cantorias,
> depois dei a cópia dela
> ao cantor Romano Elias.
>
> O cantor Romano Elias,
> mostrou-a a um camarada
> –a João Melquiade Ferreira
> e este fez-me a cilada
> de publicá-la, porém,
> está toda adulterada.
>
> E como muitas pessoas
> enganadas têm comprado
> a diversos vendelhões

o romance plagiado
resolvi levá-lo ao prelo
para causar mais agrado.

Portanto, eu vou começar
a história verdadeira
na estrofe imediata,
e no fim ninguém não queira
dizer que ela é produção
de João Melquíades Ferreira:

—Na Turquia, há muitos anos
um viúvo capitalista
morreu deixando dois filhos:
Batista e Evangelista
mas todos dois eram João
sendo o mais velho o Batista.

Whoever wishes to know
the story of the Peacock
should read this story
calmly and carefully
and he will see that it
is mine, it belongs to me and to no other.

I set it to verse
many years ago
and made frequent use of it
in song contests,
after which I gave a copy of it
to singer Romano Elias.

Singer Romano Elias
showed it to a colleague
—to João Melquíades Ferreira
who tricked me
into publishing it, though,
it is much altered.

And since many folks
who were deceived bought
from peddlers
the plagiarized story
I have decided to bring it to press myself
and give them greater pleasure.

Therefore, I shall begin
the true story
in this very stanza,
and when it is over no one will want
to say it is the work
of João Melquíades Ferreira:

—Many years ago in Turkey
a capitalist widower
died and left two sons:
Batista and Evangelista,
though both were João,
and the eldest Batista.

(Almeida-Alves 1978, 235–36)

In fact, the José Camelo text presents precious few variations and, despite the episode's verification by several popular poets, a correction of the previously attributed authorship is only rarely made. *The Tale of the Mysterious Peacock* continues to be among the greatest of chapbooks, sold in marketplaces to this day, having inspired both a popular song and a television soap opera, though its true author remains unknown, forgotten, and even denied. Is this not the stuff of folklore?

After the death of Leandro Gomes de Barros, the publication of his chapbooks was kept up by his son-in-law Pedro Batista, brother of another famous poet, Francisco das Chagas Batista, who announced the sale of "*Folhetos de Leandro Gomes de Barros* at the Pedro Baptista Bookshop" in Guarabira, Paraíba. In August 1919 his publications already included an appeal to the police chiefs of the states of Pará and Ceará to denounce pirated editions of Leandro's books in those states, "sem a menor autorização da minha parte, proprietário legítimo de toda a obra literária deste poeta" (*Literatura Popular em Verso Antología 3* 132) [without the slightest authorization on my part as legitimate owner of all of this poet's literary work]. Faced with a legal and familial imbroglio, Leandro's widow sold the collection to another famous poet, João Martins de Athayde, who had settled in Recife in 1908 as proprietor of a printing press. He continued to publish Leandro's chapbooks along with his own, adding mention of "editor-proprietário: João Martins de Athayde" [publisher-owner: João Martins de Athayde] on the cover beneath the author's name. With each successive edition, as the cover stamp wore down, or was re-set to include a new illustration, both Leandro's name and the mention of "publisher-owner" disappeared. The new book was declared to be João Martins's. Marks of authorship were further erased with the frequent modification or suppression of the acrostic stanza (in many chapbooks, LEANDRO became SEANDRO). Scholars have considered João Martins's act to be theft and have attributed the near-totality of chapbooks signed João Martins to Leandro. If, on one hand, the former was also a great poet, with an *oeuvre* of his own, on the other hand, he published the work of other poets under his name by purchasing rights. Correct attribution of authorship, therefore, can only be made after a comparative analysis of different editions and the subsequent verification of textual transformations.

In fact, textual appropriation becomes so complete that the new owners somehow consider themselves coauthors. Partial rewritings thus occur, generally through the amplification (or expansion) of narrative sequences or the introduction of new episodes. *Proezas de João Grilo* may serve as an example. In it, Leandro Gomes de Barros created a picaresque character more complex and ambiguous than those in traditional stories, at once crafty and wise, adventurer and counselor to the king. At the hands of João Martins, the chapbook undergoes a textual growth that takes it from twenty-four to thirty-two pages. With the exception of a few metrical corrections, the new edition is characterized by the appearance of two new episodes: Verse rewritings of a known story in the case of the first and the narrative illustration of proverbs in the second. More complex still is the textual manipulation of *A Vida de Cancão de Fogo e o seu Testamento* [The Life of Cancão de Fogo and His Testament]. Leandro Gomes de Barros had written two separate stories with the same protagonist and published them as different chapbooks: The first, *A Vida de Cancão* [The Life of Cancão], came at the end of a chapbook titled *Apuros de um governo decahido* [previous to 1918; Predicaments of a Fallen Government]; the second was part of another chapbook called *Casamento a Prestação* [previous to 1918; Marriage on the Installment Plan] (*Literatura Popular em Verso Antologia 3* 135–52). In 1938 the two stories were collected in a single fifty-six-page volume and published by João Martins de Athayde (the chapbook now belongs to Fonds Raymond Cantel, Université de Poitiers). The considerable success of *Cancão de Fogo* led João Martins to commission the writing of additional episodes from his printer-proofreader Delarme Monteiro (Souza 1976, 13-14), for this would enable him to publish a two-volume edition (thirty-two pages each volume) of *Canção de Fogo*. Who is the author of the text we know today?

When an ailing João Martins retired after forty years of writing and publishing, the same phenomenon was repeated: The publishing house was purchased by José Bernardo da Silva, a poet and publisher from Juazeiro do Norte, in Ceará. For identical reasons, and with equal ease, José Bernardo became "publisher-owner," slowly undertaking the publication of work by João Martins under his own name. In the sixties, however, José Bernardo's daughters, heirs to both the printing press and the editorial catalogue, attempted to restore some of the books to their authors, once more differentiating between attributing individual cover credit to authors and publisher-owner. The reason for this restitution of authorship may have been the influence of modern editorial practices or perhaps a preoccupation with affirming the glory of Leandro Gomes de Barros, who had finally been recognized and proclaimed by academics as Brazil's greatest popular poet.

The *cordel* titles whose itineraries I have retraced here were distinguished by the quality of the three poets; yet throughout the twentieth century the publisher-owner's practice of purchasing rights and editions continued to be the general rule. Nowadays, works are officially registered by some poets, but such practice continues to be the exception among the poets and publishers of the Brazilian Northeast. In São Paulo, on the other hand, where Edições Luzeiro were founded (at one point they represented an important number of *cordel* publications), all publications are registered.

What remains of the popular concept of authorship as it existed in Leandro or João Martins? How to speak of appropriation or plagiarism in a universe that assigns a totally different meaning to these words? The originality of fiction does not constitute the fundamental characteristic of innovation and creation in oral accounts: It is diction that is dominant and that becomes the true cause of appropriation. The revival of a narrative scheme or the rewriting of a text known and appreciated by a community of reader-listeners allows the elaboration of a work no longer anonymous (as demanded by the designation "folklore") but "recognized" by all, even if the name on the book cover changes from one edition to the next. Through a gradual labor of collective appropriation, the work becomes a common part of a living cultural patrimony, no longer requiring an author.

Determining the role played by the chapbook in the life of the Northeastern reader, as well as its social dimensions, permits us to understand the perennial nature of this literature of the marketplace and its remarkable resistance to modern media. The chapbook is often compared to the *canards* and other nineteenth-century European *feuilles volantes*. It recounts social events (hunts, the-one-that-got-away fishing stories, floods, and natural disasters) or political ones (electoral victories or the life and death of important politicians). Nonetheless, the many magical/fantastic stories might also lead to a literature of pure fiction and escapism. These apparently contradictory perspectives converge as the chapbooks establish a passage between a harsh and often dramatic reality and an imaginary world that provides the key for an understanding of this reality. Such a passage serves as much to link the everyday world to dreams as it does to insert the magical/fantastic accounts into the ordinary world of everyday life.

The chapbooks thus constitute a new means of understanding reality: The comprehension of new social, political,

or technical problems is facilitated by poetic language and a familiar narrative structure, both of which have undergone a process of collective assimilation. In the language of the books, this "transformation" of the real, or of new types of fiction, may be perceived in accounts of current events as well as in the revival of traditional references for a new subject or for *cordel* adaptation of works belonging to the universe of lettered culture. If at times the *folheto de atualidade* [chapbook based on current events] may have made up for the absence of newspapers, throughout the twentieth century it played a different role. In comparison with newspapers or radio or (later on) with television, it presented events with a certain delay and situated them within a poetic framework, explaining or ridiculing them, but always helping readers to master the situation and thus free themselves from their fear of the unknown. This transformation of the dramatic event by the poet becomes particularly sensitive during important historical moments (such as world conflicts or the suicide of President Getúlio Vargas) or natural disasters. Thus, the great Recife flood of 1975 was the subject of several chapbooks that illustrated diverse ways of coming to grips with the reality (Santos 1979, 202–205). Some of these ways are:

- Divine punishment: The flood is added to Northeastern roster of hardships (hunger, disease, corruption, poverty) and appears as just punishment for the sins of man. Throughout the region's history, this traditional view of self-culpability may be found again and again, as in messianic movements, for example.

- Description and exhortation (call) to action: Rejecting a mystical dimension, this type of chapbook considers the event as natural disaster and its final civic admonition is directed to the rulers who neglected to take the needed measures to protect the population.

- Satire: A satirical dimension is always present and generally refers to events either subsequent or peripheral to the disaster, as in the case of the fear that gripped the population of Recife on the day after the Capibaribe's flood, when it was falsely rumored that a dam had broken. The flight of the terrified mob allowed the poet to depict a gallery of comic portraits of street types, in which he included himself and other poets and vendors and regulars of the São José Market. The chapbook suggests that readers should attempt to master this fear, the better to laugh at it and perhaps at their own discontent. It fully accomplishes the transfiguration of dramatic reality into a fiction that explains and justifies without seeking to erase harsh reality but instead includes it in another representation of the real: The poetic function *par excellence*. Traditional accounts, present in *literatura de cordel* under the guise of poetic rewritings, largely maintain their original narrative schemas. These are the so-called "books of the people" (*livros do povo*) cited by Sílvio Romero and examined by Luís da Câmara Cascudo in 1953. They are chapbooks found in the Bibliothèque Bleue de Troyes and in various other European chapbook literatures: The stories of Robert le Diable, Peter of Provence and the Beautiful Magalona, John of Calais, the Maiden Theodora, the Empress Porcina, and perhaps most importantly, the story of Charlemagne and the twelve peers of France.

These chapbooks continue to be successfully reprinted, despite the relative rarity of the characters of Peter of Provence and the Empress Porcina. However, beyond retelling history, these books provide models and literary types for all *literatura de cordel*. Thus, Robert le Diable, a symbol of courage in the service of evil, may be transformed, thanks to penitence and conversion, into a soldier of God; directly or indirectly, he inspires a series of chapbooks about demonic possession of both humans and animals. Similarly, Theodora represents a relatively rare model for the valorization of female intelligence, whereas praise of chastity and married bliss (Princess Magalona or the Empress Porcina) finds countless echoes in the vast catalogue of *literatura de cordel*'s love stories. The story of Charlemagne became the matrix for the adventure story (Ferreira 1979); in addition to heroic characters such as Roland, Olivier, and the other peers of France, it provided a view of social and interpersonal relationships assimilated to an ideal of loyalty, frankness, and purity. Books that tell the adventures of the *cangaceiros* (backwoodsmen) frequently make use of the sort of acid test provided by the evocation of Charlemagne or Roland:

> Eu choro a falta que faz-me
> todos os meus companheiros,
> qual Carlos Magno chorou
> por seus doze cavalheiros!
> Nada me faz distrair
> não deixarei de sentir
> a morte dos cangaceiros.
>
> I mourn the loss
> of all my companions,
> as Charlemagne mourned
> the loss of his twelve gentle men!
> Nothing can distract me from this,
> I cannot help but mourn
> the loss of my cangaceiros.
>
> *(Leandro Gomes de Barros,*
> *As Lágrimas de António Silvino*
> *por tempestade; quoted in*
> *Santos 1997a, 153–59)*

The traditional tale offers the poets a guaranteed epic, which allows them to elaborate their own stories of *cangaceiros*, cowpunchers, and other popular heroes, authenticated by references (implicit or otherwise) to its unanimously recognized model.

The appropriation of the traditional story undergoes acclimation and regionalization of its characters and action; thus, the king becomes a wealthy rancher and his daughter is called *princesa* (princess). The knight who attempts to win the hand of a princess becomes a brave and loyal gun-toting cowpuncher whose enemies, often the farmer-rancher's henchmen, oppose his idyll with the rancher's daughter. In the harsh reality of the backlands, the cowpuncher rarely marries the farmer's daughter, though he dreams of this always, and it is the dream that is taken up by the poet: From the perspective of chivalry, courage, and love triumphant, in his dreams the cowpuncher will triumph and wed the princess. Traditional stories are also at the root of picaresque characters, the rascals or *amarelos* (yellow ones, an allusion to both the sickly demeanor of the poor and an undefined miscegenation); Pedro Malasartes, João Grilo, Cancão de Fogo, and even Luis de Camões (1524?–1580) and Bocage, famous Portuguese poets, are "rediscovered" along with many others in the Brazilian domain (Santos 1993). According to Roberto da Matta (1979), they are metaphors for the Brazilian worker, who must learn versatility and adapatability in order to obtain employment or become a new avatar of a traditional type made famous by the Spanish *siglo de oro* [golden age]. The Northeastern picaresque is principally intended to make readers and listeners smile, as are the tall tales that oscillate between comedy and fantasy, such as João José da Silva's (1922–1997) *Vira-Mundo* series about terrifying and utterly implausible giants, with its stories of *Vira-Mundo, Chico Vira-*

Mundo, Gonçalinho Vira-Mundo, Bate Mundo, Lasca Mundo, Cava-Mundo, Fura-Mundo, the brave *Corta-Mundo,* and the great-granddaughter of *Vira-Mundo,* who, in turn, inspired Erotildes Miranda dos Santos's *Bravery of Chico Vira-Mundo* and Antônio Teodoro dos Santos's story of the *Brave Acaba-Mundo and the Black Serpent.* For genuine laughter and the satirizing of all and sundry (including themselves), the popular poets write wonderful tall tales of country bumpkins at odds with modern life in the big city, mother-in-law stories, or stories about cuckolded husbands, as well as an entire repertory of malicious anecdotes and downright dirty stories that completely dispense with any need for timid periphrasis (*histórias de safadeza e putaria*). However, they prudently avoid signing their real names to these and make use of pseudonyms such as H. Rei (read as *agarrei,* meaning "I grabbed her" in Portuguese—sexual intercourse is implied) or H. Romeu (read as *agarra o meu,* meaning "grab mine"–the penis is obviously implied here).

The third important aspect of the writing of the chapbooks can be seen in the existing relationship between the popular work and lettered culture. Some chapbooks are abridged, versified retellings of well-known works from both Brazilian and world literature. The previously mentioned *people's books* are popular rewritings of classical creations; however, these books were widely read in Brazil in adaptations that were already reductive simplifications of previous texts. On the other hand, given these narratives based on themes, motives, and narrative sequences of folk origin, it becomes extremely difficult to differentiate or distinguish clearly the rewriting of a given text in terms of the conscious (or unconscious) influence of other narratives of the same type. Poets may choose to versify, to translate into book(let) form, a chapbook known and recognized by the cultural elite but unknown by the popular public. Among other examples taken from Brazilian literature we may cite João Martins de Athayde's *Romance de Iracema, a Virgem dos lábios de mel* [1865; *Iracema: The Honey Lips, A Lengend of Brazil* 1886], based on the novel *Iracema; lenda do Ceará* [1865; *Iracema: The Honey Lips, a Legend of Brazil* 1886] by José de Alencar (1829–1877), or Francisco das Chagas Batista's *História da Escrava Isaura* [The Story of the Slave Isaura], from the book by Bernardo Guimarães (1825–1884). Among the rewritings of works from French literature presented in Brazil as newspaper serials we may cite *O Amor nunca morre* [Love Never Dies] by Maria das Neves Batista Pimentel (Altino Alagoano), a simplified rewriting of the Abbé Prévost's *Manon Lescaut,* and several chapbooks inspired by the work of Dumas, both father and son (*Le Comte de Monte-Cristo, Les Fréres corses,* and *La Dame aux Camélias*). These are usually love stories whose adaptations emphasize adventure and action. Their rewriting as chapbooks presents itself as a reduction of the original text, accomplished through the selection of representative excerpts or, less frequently, by a synopsis of the entire work. The transformation of language is even more radical and seeks to adapt both the level of the language and the vocabulary itself.

The tradition of the chapbook lives on as permanent entertainment, articulating oral poetry and offering improvisation and composition, writing and memory, and acting as a witness to popular literature's extraordinary capacity for adapting to permanently evolving conditions of production and dissemination. This literature had its golden age around 1880, just as Sílvio Romero was announcing its imminent demise. See, for example, the highly successful *Oscar and Amanda: Love and Virtue Trumphant,* 1913 (**Figure 1**). Since the 1970s, the appearance and considerable development of the mass media, Brazil's profound economic and social changes, and the impoverishment that resulted from a brutal urbanization have contributed to the disappearance of the traditional texts that still structured a large part of Brazilian popular literature in the previous generation. Thus, the sad predictions about the disappearance of *literatura de cordel* and, with it, the rural culture to which it belonged, seem about to come true. At the same time, scholars, anthropologists, linguists, sociologists, and historians are discovering and attempting to understand the extraordinary wealth of this literary universe (see Arantes 1982; Cantel 1993; Cavignac 1997; Curran 1973; Londres 1983; Peloso 1984; Slater 1984), which is still socially and culturally undervalued, remembering Michel de Certeau's statement that "the ethnographer or archaeologist appears at the moment when a culture is no longer able to defend itself" (62).

Translation by Stephen Berg

Figure 1.

Cover of Oscar and Amanda: Love and Virtue Triumphant *(1913). (Courtesy of Marlyse Meyer)*

Works Cited

Almeida, Áltila F. de, and José Alves Sobrinho. 1978. *Dicionário bio-bibliográfico de repentistas e poetas de bancada.* 2 vols. João Pessoa/Campina Grande: Editora Universitaria.

Almeida, Horácio. 1976. "Introdução à obra de Leandro Gomes de Barros." *Literatura Popular em Verso, Antologia II, Leandro Gomes de Barros 1.* Rio de Janeiro/Campina Grande: MEC, Casa de Rui Barbosa, Fundação Universidade Regional do Nordeste. 1–14.

Arantes, Antônio Augusto. 1982. *O trabalho e a fala (estudo antopológico sobre os folhetos de cordel).* São Paulo: Kairós/FUNCAMP.

Bollême, Geneviève. 1971. *La Bibliothèque Bleue, la littérature populaire en France du XVIe au XIXe siècle.* Paris: Julliard (Coll. Archives).

Cantel, Raymond. 1993. *La littérature populaire brésilienne.* Poitiers: Centre de Recherches Latino-Américaines.

Cascudo, Luís da Câmara. 1953. *Cinco Livros do Povo, Introdução ao estudo da novelística no Brasil.* Rio de Janeiro: José Olympio.

Cavignac, Julie. 1997. *La littérature de colportage au Nord-est du Brésil: de l'histoire écrite au récit oral.* Paris: Editions du CNRS.

Certeau, Michel de. 1974. *La culture au pluriel.* Paris: Union Générale d'Edition, 10/18.

Curran, Mark J. 1973. "A Sátira e a crítica social na literatura de cordel." *Literatura Popular em Verso, Estudos.* Vol. I. Rio de Janeiro: Casa de Rui Barbosa/MEC. 271–310.

Ferreira, Jerusa Pires. 1979. *Cavalaria em Cordel, o Passo das Águas Mortas.* São Paulo: Hucitec.

Garcia de Enterría, Maria Cruz. 1973. *Sociedad y poesia de cordel en el barroco.* Madrid: Taurus.

Literatura Popular em Verso, Antologia 3. Leandro Gomes de Barros, 2. 1977. Rio de Janeiro: MEC/Casa de Rui Barbosa; João Pessoa: Universidade Federal da Paraíba.

Londres, Maria José F. 1983. *Cordel: do encatamento às histórias de luta.* São Paulo: Duas Cidades.

Matta, Roberto da. 1979. *Carnavais, malandros e heróis: para uma sociologia do dilema brasileiro.* Rio de Janeiro: Zahar.

Mendonça, Maristela Barbosa de. 1993. *Uma voz feminina no mundo do folheto.* Brasília: Thesaurus.

Peloso, Silvano. 1984. *Medioevo nel sertão. Tradizione medievale europea e archetipi della letteratura popolare del Noedeste del Brasile.* Napoli: Liguori Editore.

Romero, Sílvio. 1977 [1888]. *Estudos sobre a Poesia popular no Brasil.* 2nd ed. Petrópolis: Vozes/Governo do Estado de Sergipe.

Santos, Idelette Muzart Fonseca dos. 1979. "La littérature populaire en vers du Nord-est brésilien." *Cause Commune 1979/1, Les Imaginaires II.* Paris: UGE-10/18.

———. 1993. "Pícaros e malandros no Cordel: uma galeria de tipos." *Revista Internacional de Língua Portuguesa* 9: 121–36.

———. 1997a. *La littérature de cordel au Brésil, mémoire des voix, grenier d'histoires.* Paris: L'Harmattan. [which includes a bilingual edition of 13 chapbooks].

———. 1997b. "Monte Cristo, du roman au livre de colportage: traduction poétique et populaire d'Alexandre Dumas au Brésil." *Le Roman Populaire en Question(s).* Ed. Jacques Migozzi. Limoges: PULIM. 499–520.

Silveira, Maria Claurênia Abreu de Andrade. 1998. *O carretel da memória, histórias fabulosas de um contador paraibano.* João Pessoa: Universidade Federal da Paraíba.

Slater, Candace. 1984. *A vida no barbate, a literatura de cordel no Brasil.* Rio de Janeiro: Civilização Brasileira.

Souza, Liêdo Maranhão de. 1976. *Classificação popular da literatura de cordel.* Petrópolis: Vozes.

———. 1981. *O Folheto popular, sua capa e seus ilustradores.* Recife: Massangana.

Terra, Ruth Brito Lemos. 1983. *Memória de Lutas: Literatura de Folhetos do Nordeste, 1893–1930.* São Paulo: Global Editora.

CHAPTER 61

RELIGIOUS CELEBRATIONS IN BRAZILIAN CULTURAL HISTORY

Marlyse Meyer

Excluded from the city, relegated to the periphery and subject to the absence of minimal urban comforts, excluded from education and school, and excluded from the ownership of land, the poor person, the one who does not succeed in being a Brazilian like me, is also excluded from the official history of Brazilian culture. And yet, like me, he or she is a product of history and occupies a precise place: The battered one of *History*. This is one who, like me, also produces culture, which is also Brazilian. One example, among so many, of this culture of the "other" is the series of religious festivals spread all over Brazil, which constitute, according to Duglas Teixeira Monteiro, the author of *Errantes do novo século* [Wanderers of the New Century], Brazilian culture itself but are, as such, ignored. They remain on the margins of the official history of national culture, but they are resilient, as though dug into the subsoil of Brazilian culture (see Meyer 1993). In effect, there is great wealth of cultural practices maintained and transmitted among these defeated people of history. These expressions are generally labeled under the category of folklore: Poems, songs, stories of events narrated in rudimentary verse and printed in chapbooks (called *cordel*), and those religious festivals described by scholars such as Luis da Câmara Cascudo, Edison Carneiro, Mário de Andrade, Theo Brandão, and many others. These cultural manifestations are a valuable source for Ariano Suassuna's work.

It can be said that these festive-religious practices, characteristic of "Baroque Catholicism" with elements of African and European paganism, were current practices throughout the entire Colonial period and continued through the nineteenth century, regardless of social circumstances. Historians such as Marta Abreu and others conclude that Brazilian Roman Catholic liturgy was notable for the spectacular external manifestations as displayed in the extravagant celebration of High Mass, in the grandiose funerals of clergy and Portuguese aristocracy, in the processions of patron saints, and in the religious festivals, such as Corpus Christi, where hundreds of people of the most varied social backgrounds enjoyed music, dance, masquerades, and fireworks. These festivals usually mixed sacred and profane practices, both in the outdoor celebrations and in those that took place inside the churches. In folk festivals today as well, there are numerous manifestations of the rich and singular inventiveness of the popular classes. The Baroque religious practices of the past are continued in the celebration of saints' days and their processions. They express the suffering and the transformations of collective memory that are the lot of the poor population in this society. These popular festivals–which have usually been excluded from a comprehensive view of Brazilian cultural history–are sometimes remembered in the official celebrations of Folklore Week. Their rhythms and melodies are rediscovered by contemporary musicians and dancers, studied by anthropologists, and thus return annually, in spite of the adverse conditions, with their own beauty and with a renewed charge of meaning. These manifestations have their own language; it is a language

expressed through melody, rhythm, and color. This is a language that acquires new meaning in its resistance to opposition; this meaning is not understood by all, in spite of the resplendent and simple beauty of the costumes and the liberating sounds of the rhythms and dances. I will return later to this gap in perception and response.

These festivals have their own calendar, distributed among three principal celebrations:

1. The Christmas cycle, from Christmas Eve to the Feast of the Magi (Epiphany), including the Circumcision of Christ, Good Jesus (January 1), and in some regions, stretching to January 20, the feast of Saint Sebastian

2. Festivals of the Divine Holy Spirit, which were, and continue to be in some locales, in September/October but today tend to be fixed on the official date of the Pentecost, that is, fifty days after Easter

3. June festivals, the celebrations of an ancient tradition, associated with the solstices, featuring bonfires and games

The feastdays of the patron saints may be added to the list, and those of the black saints: São Benedito (St. Benedict), often on May 13, and Nossa Senhora do Rosário (Our Lady of the Rosary), generally on its official date of October 7. But both kinds of festivals, like all the others, can be shifted both in time and in place, a characteristic of folkloric improvisation, as Roger Bastide reminds us in his fundamental work, *Sociology of Brazilian Folklore*. We should also include the great festival of São Jorge (St. George), which has surpassed its traditional position in the great procession of Corpus Christi on April 23 and is today associated with an Afro-Brazilian cult and, together with that of Iemanjá on December 31, is becoming a new popular Brazilian ritual. The celebration of Força de Santa Madre (Strength of the Holy Mother) is predominant in the black community but is inseparable from the popular Catholic calendar and devotions, which have the added invisible weight of the memory of Africa and the horror of the crossing of the ocean-tomb, as Leda Maria Martins points out.

There are carols and dances of the Magi during the Christmas season, followed by the Festivals of the Magi–all hybrid reincarnations of those traditional strolling groups and the European custom of soliciting alms. The Christian festivals, without a doubt, are the same as the festivals of the Divine Holy Spirit, cheered by cavalcades and a procession of giants and including feasting and eating sweets. There are also folk performances, such as c*ongos, ticumbis, cambindas, moçambiques, pontões, congadas, reinados,* and *catopés,* related to the black saints; *alardos* in the state of Espírito Santo celebrating São Sebastião (St. Sebastian); and *maracatús* in the state of Pernambuco. These lively manifestations of popular devotion make up the so-called profane part of the official religious festival, which takes place over a week–a *novena*–and closes with the solemn procession. They may or may not be incorporated into the solemn procession, depending on the good will of the priest or bishop (which might change from year to year). Popular dramas and dances, the ludic part of the religious celebration, constitute, in short, the carnivalization of the official festival. Devotion is not lacking, however, insofar as its participants are also the faithful, the devotees of the saint. Underlying the desire to celebrate is a worldview intrinsically linked to the mystery of longing for grace and the miracles requested through the intercession of the saints and guaranteed by the vow or promise, which literally obliges the festival to take place outdoors. The festival, dance, song, and beating of the drums are, in fact, the form through which devotion is materialized.

I want to focus primarily on the festival of Nossa Senhora do Rosário and São Benedito of Uberlândia, Minas Gerais, celebrated in 1987 (and examined in more detail in my article "In This Month of the Rosary: Questions of *Congos* and *Congadas*"). This was one year before the great official centenary celebration of the abolition of slavery in Brazil (1888). This will allow me to show that there is a gap in the perception and response of those who shared the same urban space in which the festival went on for several days. It is fitting to make a few observations on the *congada*, or *congos*, which are at the heart of the festivals, and to note the ambiguity of the very term *congada*. These are the great black festivals of Christian and civic practice. In some parts of Brazil, the feast of São Benedito is moved to coincide with May 13, the anniversary of the abolition of slavery. To heighten the sense of hybridity, Princess Isabel, who signed the emancipation law, is mistaken for St. Izabel, whose banner also appears at the festival. *Congos*, *congadas*, and *congados* are popular Brazilian performances of African themes but are inseparable from the adoration of a Catholic saint: Nossa Senhora do Rosário and São Benedito, in general; the Divine Holy Spirit, in some states. They are found all over Brazil, with variations in denominations, plots, and themes, which can be more or less reduced or modified with a greater or lesser number of components. The variations reflect the particularities of the group, the city, or the region where the festivals take place.

The ludic part of the Rosário and São Benedito festivities comprises, when complete–which happens less and less often–a *cortejo*, or procession, and an *embaixada*. In the procession, the different *ternos*, "bands" or groups–*moçambiques*, *marinheiros* [sailors], *catopés*, and *congos*, properly speaking– parade in ordered sequences, in their "uniforms" and with their respective choreographies and musical accompaniment. Sometimes only the "bands" of *congos* are left, a term that also designates the celebrants themselves and always includes the *conguinhos*, the children who learn by imitation the dances and the songs that they will retransmit some day. The *embaixada* consists of the dramatic part of the ceremony, which may intermingle with or depart from the procession in order to mime, sing, or dance a story whose plot and development are often indecipherable. The essential theme is the *embaixada* of the queen Ginga to a black potentate, sometimes Henrique, King Cariongo (never King of the Congo). There are variants in which the queen is not present but rather someone of greater power from the *embaixada*, who fights and defeats the local king. This *embaixada* can also, in some regions, follow the Carlos Magno [Charlemagne] and the twelve Peers of France model (also quite common in the rest of America and in the Caribbean), which is the battle between Christians and Moors. Sometimes there is a Carlos Magno Reis (*sic*) of the Congo. Whatever the theme–African or Carolingian–the *congada* reenacts the violence of wars manifested choreographically by the violent clashing of staffs and by

songs possessing a warrior spirit. However small the play, the battle structure is a constant. There is another form of *congado* without acted drama, whose procession is associated with the coronation of the King of the Congo, who is not the same as the one in the drama of the *embaixada* but a black man of a certain age, "of respectable manner and appearance," as the great folklorist Edison Carneiro says, a king who, on that day and for one year after, reigns with his queen as "of olden times under slavery, a temporary majesty."

The vanishing of memories, the presence of economic difficulties, migrations, and regional differences have clearly interfered in the, as it were, canonical ordering of the *congada*. What is important to point out (and this is true for all manifestations of the *congada*, even if it is reduced to a single band) is that, during the *novena*, without the formality of the parade, on the day of the saint the procession roams through the streets and is interrupted at certain moments by the master's whistle. The lines then confront one another and "do battle" with swords or staffs, while the *moçambiques* punctuate the action with bells tied to their ankles. The procession then continues to roam through all the streets in town. Historically, the *congos* had their moments of splendor. They were, for example, an integral part of the famous processions and retinues of the Triunfo Eucarístico in Ouro Preto in the middle of the eighteenth century, and they were a part of the festival of the marriage of royal princes in Bahia, according to a 1760 report by Francisco Calmon. The coronation of the King of the Congo, which also exists in Portugal (and coincides with the festival of the Santos Reyes of Cuba, described by Fernando Ortiz [335–36]), has taken place in Brazil since 1711.

The transformations of Brazilian society, the impoverishment of the mines, abolition, urbanization, the great modern agricultural system, industrialization, and so on led to the marginalization of the Brazilian black, as is well known. It is not difficult even today, traveling around the state of Minas Gerais, to identify the places where black people live: On the outskirts of town, however small it is, generally on a hill, around a modest church, such as São Benedito or Rosário, or around a more prominent church, in the case of Santa Ifigênia of Ouro Preto. One can observe the same thing in Goiás, in the Vale do Paraíba, and elsewhere. And it is there, in these out-of-the-way communities, that the memory and practice of the *congada* has remained, intermingling with the cultural manifestations of the poorest people–which explains why many white people who have become "black" by a shared poverty participate in it.

Yet, given the spatial realities of the *congada*, this isolation ends, or seems to end, at the time of the festival. The different bands literally take over the whole town during the *novena* preceding the great saint's day. The ritual of promises makes it obligatory to pay visits, carry the banner, and dance for all those who have fulfilled their promises. These visits are always rewarded with food and drink, not to speak of the community meals in houses spread all over the city (called *quartéis* [barracks] in Uberlândia), to which the bands make their way in the course of their march. Still to come at the end of the day, when they are dressed in their colorful uniforms, is the assembly in the plaza designated to them by tradition, in front of the church of Rosário or São Benedito, where, tireless for hours on end, they beat the drums, shake the bells, dance, jump acrobatically, and sing hymns in homage to the saint. The festival ends with a solemn procession, which also roams round the town and which closes the *novena*. And, contrary to what its folkloric dimension might make one believe–that they are theoretically fated to disappearance–these festivals exist in ever greater number, as the Federation of the Congos of Minas Gerais shows.

If not all these dances of Rosário and São Benedito offer the outside observer the same aesthetic pleasure as do those in Serro or Uberlândia, the discourse they all suggest cannot be ignored. It seems to me imperative, through all the variations from group to group or from year to year imposed by their daily problems, the interventions of power, and the fading of memory, to try and perceive, especially if there is no strong aesthetic emotion, what at first sounds like monotonous and unexpressive repetition; it is important not only to perceive in this monotony the repetitive fidelity to a tradition but also to hear a tenacious insistence on being and continuing to be: An affirmation of identity, as Carlos Rodrigues Brandão observed, in the case of the State of Goiás, in his *Peões, Pretos e Congos: Trabalho e Identidade Étnica em Goiás* [Peasants, Blacks, and Congos: Work and Ethnic Identity in Goiás]. One must know how to hear in order to hear what is spoken in this multiple, diffuse speech of the most diverse meanings, even when it is expressed in the old, traditional forms, or precisely thanks to this tradition, duly codified and recorded in the folklore manuals–so alike or so different, according to the situation of the group that dances, the place where they dance, and the changes in the group or outside it from year to year. Sometimes it is the only discourse or the only one known to speak of a situation of need or anger, whereas another kind of discourse is not used and perhaps never will be.

Yet, regarding the *congada*, which can be so visible in its evolution and so involving in the diversity of its rhythms, there is a deafness and blindness on the part of global society, even though sometimes this phenomenon may be mobilized in the ideology of national memory and cultural roots. This is what I have observed in the various festivals of São Benedito or Rosário since 1976, the period when I began to study this folk expression, and it was what I encountered again on the eve of the commemorative ceremonies of the Centenary of the Abolition, in October 1987, in Uberlândia at the festival in honor of Nossa Senhora do Rosário and São Benedito. It is exciting to see the festival spread out all over the city as its twelve "bands" or groups march, going and coming from the *quartéis*, paying their protocol visits, and assembling in the main plaza, happy and relaxed on the saint's day and dazzling on the following evening, with the decorating of the two poles set up on each side in front of the church in the very center of Uberlândia. The groups suddenly emerge from the sides and from behind, and are suddenly in front of us, sweeping us along if necessary, following the peaceful but imperious advance of the captain holding his command baton horizontally to make way. The bands follow one another alternately and together, dancing in place, waiting their turn, and passing again and again before the open doors of the little blue church. They sing and dance, like David before the arc, leaping acrobatically in a movement that seems to thrust forward the drums solidly tied to their waists, and they go on beating them while they perform their prodigious arabesques. They leap by themselves but also in groups of two or four in a mock-fight; they leap and raise drum to drum; bowed in a feline curve, the girls of the banner dance gracefully with joyous and fervent chants of Our African Lady. We feel vertigo from the sounds and rhythms that involve and fascinate us in their variety, engaging us in the frenzied beating of the huge drum marking time in an almost diabolical way,

the sonorous jumps of the *moçambiques*, and the booming of drums and tom-toms of the *catopé* while the rattle of the snare-drums of the *congos* resounds energetically and rhythmically. The body, overcome and shaken by the rhythm, surrounded by the other dancing bodies, is alive in all its senses. Then there is also the parade of embroidered hats, ribbons, mirrors, pieces of glass, helmets of kings, long skirts, and the braided and beribboned sticks, the aerial dance of the "sailors," all culminating in the raising and rhythmic crossing of the diversely adorned staffs of the *moçambiques*–and it is they who form the core–in the staffs' adornment and solemn, ceremonial bearing inside the church.

Before we can recover from the emotion, a new wave of bands arrives, which surrounds us in front, back, and sides, nearly running into each other, beating with increasing frenzy, in their eagerness to pass once more in front of the ever-open doors of the blue church and to jump and sing "Land of Angola" and recite the Rosary of Mary, saying "goodbye my lord/goodbye my lady/what a sad farewell/it is time to leave," as they go running through the streets, breaking up the group for the remainder of the year. One must here evoke the lines of the poet:

. . . loucura santa,
desabrochar do corpo em rosa súbita,
em penacho, batuque, diabo, mico,
. . .
a cambalhota em si, o riso puro,
o puro libertar-se da prisão
que cada um carrega em sua liberdade
vigiada, medida, escriturada.

. . . holy madness,
budding from the body a sudden rose,
a helmet-plume, a dance, a devil, a monkey,
. . .
the somersault in itself, the pure laugh,
the pure freeing oneself from the prison
that each one carries in his freedom
watched, measured, registered.

(Carlos Drummond de Andrade, "Ver e ouvir, sem brincar" [To See and Hear Without Taking Part] 157)

Paradoxically, all this beauty was as though invisible for the inhabitants of Uberlândia. In the plaza, there were practically no spectators. Professors and students from the local university, with one or two exceptions (one of them, enchanted by what he had seen, returned in 1988), were unaware of the city's customary festival, even though the Rosário Church is in the central part of town; this indifference, this absence of public participation, was surprising. The festival itself seemed more melancholic on this not-very-festive centenary anniversary of Abolition. When they were interviewed in 1987, professors, students (including the only two black women students in the course), and leaders and members of the *congado* bands, among whom were many young people, all were unanimous in recognizing the genuine efforts and interest of the dynamic Secretary of Culture and her staff. "She understands," said Ananias, leader of the company of the *moçambiques*. But, in general, the festival is ignored by the white segment of the population because, as one of the members of the *congo* said, "They pay us no attention because it's a black thing, a slave thing." Or as one of the black students said: "Since there was once a *quilombo* [slave-republic] here, they don't even want to hear about it."

Many young black people once held the same attitude, in the opinion of the captain of the *moçambique* band "Star of the East." And so it is a very positive and progressive turn to see the conscious and intense participation of young black people, many of them militant in the Movimento Negro Unificado [Unified Black Movement], the MNU, in this traditional celebration of Christian faith through African dance. As they say, it is a return to Brazilian and African origins, confirmation of an old identity that is now the affirmation of a new black consciousness. And it is also, as has already been noted, the only time of the year when they can occupy the city in which they are generally invisible. But whether it is seen as an expression of old things, an expression of tradition, and for that reason annually repeated on the appointed day, or as an affirmation of identity, which has therefore been rethought within modernity, the *congada* echoes in a void of reception, as if it had not occurred. It is not experienced by the dominant segment of society, which also cannot see the roaming of dozens of groups through the streets and its strong, progressive concentration in the plaza (the same sly, surreptitious form of urban movement by which the people arrived and occupied the plaza in the demonstration for the popular vote in Anhangabaú, in São Paulo). (See Marlyse Meyer and Maria Lúcia Montes, *Redescobrindo o Brasil: a festa na política* [Rediscovering Brazil: The Festival in Politics]). In fact, it is as if the *congada* celebrations of Nossa Senhora do Rosário and São Benedito were the festival-religious manifestations that confirm the exclusion of their black creators. One might object that this ignorance, this nonrecognition, has to do precisely with the traditional, old, and therefore out-of-date character of these cultural practices that are taken as folklore. One might protest, on the other hand, that the rejection of these celebrations does not take place because these are black celebrations since blacks are more and more recognized as participants in global society. This is especially so in the world of Afro-Brazilian religion, whether in its more popular form, *umbanda*, or in its more African form, *candomblé*. Nor is there any rejection of the known and appropriated black elements, which are today a part of Brazilian carnival.

The other symbol that I see in the language and presence of the *congos* in the city that is not perceived by the general population is the exclusion of the black from dominant society. I ask myself whether one of the reasons for this inability of the white person to see and hear this strong annual festive presence could be connected, in fact, to the rejection of the black occupation of the city: It is the nature of the *congo* to take over the whole city once a year. Is this strong physical presence of a majority normally excluded from social intercourse with others, one that is disseminated and invisible, some veiled threat of a formidable force from which the unconscious defends itself, leaving the rest of the population blind and deaf? And, in an extension of what happens with the *congada*, associated with the poor, excluded black Christian, made invisible so as not to bother good conscience and provoke fear, could not the same phenomenon of exclusion be seen in keeping the black out of the priesthood? This is an exclusion proven by facts and figures. There are few blacks in the Brazilian Catholic hierarchy. According to Dom José Maria, the "Pelé bishop" of Paraíba and one of the six black bishops in Brazil, if the proportion of this racial contingent were to correspond to that of the sixty million descendants of Africans in the country, among the 352 Catholic bishops in Brazil, at least 150 ought to be black. Among the 12,500 Brazilian priests, 200 descendants of Africans, at most, can be counted. In a 1988 interview, Dom José Maria stated that he had never suffered discrimination. "If I had been an ordinary black, perhaps I would have felt racism in the flesh," he said. "In Brazil, however, when a black man reaches a certain position, whether in soccer, in the economy, or in the church, he is seen as a white man." As this suggests, ten years ago incontestable changes occurred. Black people began to occupy new spaces, and not only in music. There are now black executives and other successful men and women, including among them those who present themselves as blacks, that is, those with full consciousness that prejudice is disallowed in Brazilian society. Ceabra, the "Collective of Afro-Brazilian Businessmen and Employers" in Brasília, and the beautiful and successful magazine *Raça Brasil* can be cited as examples of change. Cases in point are the election in 1996 of the first black mayor of São Paulo, the largest city in the country, and the election of the first black woman senator of the State of Rio de Janeiro, Benedita da Silva, later elected vice-governor of the same state in 1998.

According to the architect Dulce Maria Pereira, a militant in the black movement and president of the Fundação Palmares [Palmares Foundation], such changes, however, do not allow us to speak of a black middle class: "That is not true," she says; it would be so, if there were a complex of black families who moved upward socially. Instead, only some isolated groups have managed to rise. Brazilian society does not yet permit the great majority of the Brazilian population that is black to find a place for themselves. The very choice of Celso Pitta for the first black mayor of a city the size of São Paulo showed the ambiguity and complexity of the black/white relation in Brazilian society. His university degrees in economics, his use of technical language, his fine manners and British-cut clothes, and the soothing rationality of his voice reassured voters from the middle and upper income classes. They probably saw in Pitta that "white" man to whom Dom José Maria referred. But he is in fact black, and that guarantees for him the votes of the dispossessed classes as well–mostly brothers of color and also of black militants, in spite of obvious ideological divergences. The campaign attitude of the black/white Celso Pitta and his later government in relation to the black issue was one of ambiguous neutrality. This attitude had repercussions for all. Journalists, the media, and militants dealt only with the surface issue: The mayor is black, what do you know. And the main project of the campaign for the new administration was the continuity with, and not any change in relation to, the previous administration with its populist white mayor. In a strange gap of perception, it was (and is) not seen or said that, in this powerful city, the mayor, a successful economist, is black, but that black is also the color of poverty, the color of street boys, and the color of the primary suspects in a police roundup. And, outside the realm of humble service jobs, reinforcing invisibility, black is the color absent from the theater audiences, restaurant tables, and universities and intellectual colloquia.

But can we imagine the attitude of those privileged black executives and this first black mayor of the most progressive city in Brazil, who are the incarnation of modernity, rationality, and efficiency, to the exuberant and yet invisible festival of Nossa Senhora do Rosário in Uberlândia? Everything indicates that they would have shared that gap of perception with its white inhabitants. Could this blindness and deafness be attributed to a just rejection of the repetitive tradition in the name of modernizing efficacy? Or is it due to the refusal to hear the speech that is traditional but always changing, the speech of its ineluctable origins? It is the troublesome speech of exclusion that not even the festival conceals, perhaps out of sheer ignorance: The silence of official history prevents any moderately informed person from recognizing cultural manifestations relegated to the category of folklore and therefore mentioned only once a year. The answer is not simple, nor is the problem. But at the present time these examples of blindness and deafness are not hypothetical. The gap of perception cannot be explained by a rejection of so-called folkloric manifestations. We find the same blindness today, for example, regarding an event that is nationally celebrated and amply publicized in the media: The Good Friday celebrations. However, these same media ignore the fact that this celebration also takes place all over the country: In all the cult locations of *candomblé* and *umbanda* there is a "body-closing" ritual because "Jesus Christ died and the devil is loose" on Good Friday.

Another example of the conscious blindness and deafness of the media is related to a cultural practice of the young people from the poorer classes of Rio: Funk, a kind of "anthem of the poor youth of Rio." Their privileged space is organized around the funk dance with its promise of a reaction against the segregation of the city because, little by little, middle-class youth is sharing the same dances, music, and slang repertory. On the one hand, the articles in newspapers and specialized magazines, the statements of disk jockeys, and the research and conclusions of anthropologists all point to the value of funk music and dance because it strengthens the self-esteem of poor youth and promotes their greater social integration. On the other hand, the great opinion-making press gives the impression of funk music as socially intractable. Only the violence is perceived—as if the funk dance were not also a place of celebration, social mingling, exchange, and symbolic solidarity. Both the press and some sectors of the state apparatus favor an essentially punitive response to these cultural practices (see *Galeras Cariocas: Territórios de Conflitos e Encontros Culturais* [Rio Youth Groups: Territories of Cultural Conflicts and Encounters], edited by Hermano Vianna).

Yet, funk music has something to say to us who do not know how to listen. The architect and urbanist Manoel Ribeiro, knowledgeable about the funk movement and an activist for social integration in Rio de Janeiro, advocates that we listen to the songs in which the young people speak of racial segregation, bad living-conditions, crime, police violence, and the difficulty of earning money. He says that it is a culture that developed on the margins of public power, and many of these young people participate now in seminars on citizenship. The Festival of Nossa Senhora do Rosário of yesterday; funk and rap music of today; Good Friday celebrations; and religious, ludic, and festive manifestations, rhythms, dances, speech, gongs, and percussion—all cry out loud that the gap is the place of the black and of the poor in our society in the past and in the present (see **Figure 1**).

**Translation by Glaucia Renate Gonçalves and
Thomas La Bornie Burns**

Works Cited

Abreu, Marta. 1998. "Império do Divino: Festas Religiosas e Cultura Popular no Rio de Janeiro. 1830–1900." Diss. Campinas: UNICAMP.

Andrade, Carlos Drummond de. 1985. "Ver e ouvir, sem brincar." *Amar se aprende amando: Poesia de convívio e de humor*. Rio de Janeiro: Editora Record. 156–58.

Figure 1.

Children in the refugee camps of homeless peasants from the hacienda Cuiabá, Sergipe, Northeast Brazil, 1996. (Courtesy of Sebastião Salgado)

Bastide, Roger. 1959. *Sociologia do Folclore Brasileiro*. Trans. São Paulo: Anhambi.

Brandão, Carlos Rodrigues. 1977. *Peões, Pretos e Congos: Trabalho e Identidade Étnica em Goiás*. Brasília: Editora da Universidade de Brasília.

Calmon, Francisco. 1982. *Relação das faustíssimas festas* (1762). Rio de Janeiro: Funarte/INL.

Carneiro, Edison. 1982. *Folguedos tradicionais*. Rio de Janeiro: Funarte/INL.

Martins, Leda Maria. 1997. *Afrografias da mem ria: o reinado do Rosário em Jatobé*. São Paulo: Perspectiva.

Meyer, Marlyse. 1993. "Um Eterno Retorno: As Desbobertas do Brasil" and "Neste Mês do Rosário: Indagações sobre Congos e Congadas." *Caminhos do Imaginário no Brasil*. São Paulo: EDUSP. 161–69.

——, and Maria Lúcia Montes. 1985. *Redescobrindo o Brasil: A Festa na Política*. São Paulo: T. A. Queiroz.

Monteiro, Duglas Teixeira. 1974. *Errantes do Novo Século*. São Paulo: Duas Cidades.

Ortiz, Fernando. 1993. *Los bailes y el teatro de los negros en el folklore de Cuba*. Havana: Editorial letras cubanas.

Vianna, Hermano, org. 1997. *Galeras Cariocas: Territórios de Conflitos e Encontros Culturais*. Rio de Janeiro: Editora UFRJ.

CHAPTER 62

CARNIVAL

Félix Coluccio and Marta Isabel Coluccio

The name carnival has been the subject of much debate as to its origins. Joan Corominas gives the following etymology for Spanish *carnaval*: "*carnaval*, 1495, rare until the seventeenth century. Derived from the Italian *carnevale,* which was in turn derived from medieval Latin *carnelevare,* 1130, taken from *carnelevare* composed of *carne* [meat] and *levare* [to give up] in keeping with the beginning of the Catholic liturgy of the forty days of abstinence and mortification that mark the Lenten period leading up to Holy Week and Easter" (130).

In most Catholic countries today, carnival takes place during the three days preceding Ash Wednesday. There are no precise facts to record how the pagan festival of ancient Rome was transformed into the highly complex festival of carnival; it came to Latin America in the cultural baggage of the French, Spanish, and Portuguese colonizers. There are a number of studies, including J. G. Frazer's classic *The Golden Bough,* that delve into the pre-Christian origins of carnival:

> On the morrow, the twenty-fifth day of March, which was reckoned the vernal equinox, the divine resurrection was celebrated with a wild outburst of glee. At Rome, and probably elsewhere, the celebration took the form of a carnival. It was the Festival of Joy (Hilaria). A universal license prevailed. Every man might say and do what he pleased. People went about the streets in disguise. No dignity was too high or too sacred for the humblest citizens to assume with impunity. (407)

> The resemblance between the Saturnalia of ancient and the Carnival of modern Italy has often been remarked; but in the light of all the facts that have come before us, we may well ask whether the resemblance does not amount to identity. We have seen that in Italy, Spain and France, that is, in the countries where the influence of Rome has been deepest and most lasting, a conspicuous feature of the carnival is a burlesque figure personifying the festive season. (679)

Our interest in this essay, however, is to examine the general outline of the Latin American mutations and the symbolic power of carnival and the carnivalesque in the cultural imaginary.

Today, throughout Latin America, the carnival is superseded only by the Nativity of Christ in its importance. These two festivals are without doubt the most significant in the Latin American calendar; one is profoundly pagan and sensually oriented, and the other is spiritual, its enormous consequence derived from the celebration of Christ's nativity.

By the Middle Ages almost all Europe celebrated carnival. Masquerades and large numbers of vehicles decorated with flowers, pendants, and other adornments were common features, and the *carros navales* boasted splendid figureheads copied from real ships. The custom was introduced into the New World with the Conquest. Carnival soon began to acquire a distinct character in each country. Indeed, each region had, and continues to have, different ways of celebrating this festival in accordance with its particular geographical and ethnic features. In Argentina, enthusiasm for carnival has decreased considerably, but it is still observed in the center and northeast of the country. One rather original manner of celebrating the festival long ago in Buenos

Aires has been described by Alfred Ebelot. The landowners used to send six or seven proud *pingos* (fast horses) to Buenos Aires so as not to be without a mount during these three days, since some horses would die in the races. Extremely fast races were held all over the city, the competitors turning corners at top speed. Another form of entertainment consisted of hurling oneself at breakneck speed against a rider and crashing into his knees so as to force him off his mount. After these violent exercises, characteristic of a frontier culture that owed much to the tough way of life of the cattle rancher, an intermediary form of carnival took over in which water predominated over horsemanship and in which everyone frenziedly drenched his neighbor. This water game is prohibited today because of the abuses and incidents to which it gave rise. However, in the Federal Capital it is still permitted on the Avenida Costanera, but within certain hours and under discreet surveillance so as not to inhibit the original intention. Enthusiasm for the *corsos* (parades), which take place over five or more well-lit city blocks, has also declined. In some of the streets bread was baked in precariously set-up ovens and offered to the public who watched the show from the sidewalk. The custom continues to this day in Jujuy.

In Rioja and Catamarca, carnival is still known as *Chaya* and continues to be celebrated in the traditional way. *Vidalas* (plaintive folksongs), specific to carnival, are sung and spirits are cheered by foaming drinks of *aloja* (a variety of Argentinean beer) stored in vats. Also preparations are made with due anticipation to fill small paper bags with starch. These are opened during the fiestas and the contents smeared on the faces of young girls in particular, who, thus daubed, present a truly grotesque sight. An additional and obligatory detail is the bunches of basil used to decorate corsages and hats. The participants run through the streets singing *vidalas* they have composed during the weeks dedicated to harvesting carob beans. The celebrations conclude with battles of starch powder and popular dancing. In Santiago de Estero and, particularly, in the surrounding countryside, carnival achieves its most intense expression in the *trincheras,* a cleared space or pitch surrounded by tree trunks laid out horizontally and sustained by forked props at given intervals driven into the soil. The riders have to vault to enter the *trinchera,* skilled equestrians carrying their girlfriends behind them.

In some places in northeast Argentina, such as Recreo in Catamarca, the branding of sheep or goats takes place on Carnival Sunday. In contrast, this task is performed on the first day of carnival in villages on the Quebrada de Humahuaca, such as Maimará and Tilcara, prior to the *desentierro del carnaval.* This latter ritual involves the disinterment of the *diablo,* buried the previous year in a special place on the mountain. The next stage represents the devil's return to the world; in other words, it is the return to merrymaking. Thus they continue with relentless energy until the Sunday after Ash Wednesday, the day of the *entierro del carnaval,* which is performed to songs in the rhythm of "*carnavalito*" accompanied on *quenas* (reed flutes), *sícuris* (pipes), and drums. The *topamiento de las comadres* takes place over most of northeast Argentina, and its purpose is to celebrate *compadrazgo* or *comadrazgo*. The women make ready their best clothes and adornments, the *madrinas* making a particular effort. Meanwhile, the men attend to their horses and riding harness. The important ceremonial element is the *arco* (arch). These arches can be fixed or moveable and are made of branches, normally of willow, and planted either in the street or on a pathway. Two groups gather equidistant from the arch and, at a given moment, signaled by music, they slowly approach, marking time with a rhythmic step or just walking. The so-called *topamiento* takes place under the *arco* where the *compadres* and *comadres* of both groups embrace and gently "*topan*" (butt) each other's forehead. They then immediately exchange either real children or symbolic dough images of infants (*guaguas*). This dough, also used to make the crowns worn on the heads of the women, is wrapped in silk lace and white fabric to simulate diapers. From this moment they are "received" as *madrinas* or *padrinos*, one of the most sacred bonds that can link two families and that disappears only at death. Fireworks are set off, starch powder is thrown around, and sport is made with bunches of basil as a prelude to Carnival. It is worth mentioning that the arches are adorned with real flowers or paper ones and paper streamers or fruit, cheeses, pastry rings, and *guaguas*. The fiesta concludes with dances.

In other countries on the continent, carnival takes on an equally unique form. In Bolivia, for example, it achieves true splendor in Oruro. For ten or fifteen days prodigality abounds, evident in the music that is played tirelessly by multiple bands (and all at once, to general confusion), in the dances whose turns and jumps do not seem to tire the dancers, in the drinks that do not seem to quench a thirst that revives every instant, and in the quantity of sweets and dishes produced. The streets fill with crowds, while the music, initially heard clearly, degenerates into a general uproar. Embroidery and jewelry sparkle to the sound of jingle bells on the costumes and the jingling of spurs. Those on the balconies manifest their enthusiasm for the *diablos* whose bodies are covered by skintight clothing that elongates the torso and extremities; the dancer's costume displays complex designs embroidered in gold and silver with insets of sequins and colored glass. The artisans responsible for the masks and the embroidery of these costumes compete in both imagination and skill. A red handkerchief on the shoulders; strong, hard boots; spurs that drag on the ground; and a trident in one hand complete the outfit of each dancer. The wealthier put a greater value on costumes (that are expensive enough anyway) by hanging old silver coins on them. When the participants of the *diablada* arrive at a wide street they distribute themselves strategically and perform modern dances.

In Iquitos, Peru, after the days of madness, fiesta, and rejoicing, preparations are made to celebrate the end of carnival in a dignified manner. This particular ceremony is different from any other held on the continent. Various robust young men, some of whom have been making monotonous sounds on the fife, drums, or bass drum, are joined by others to make up a large carnival procession. Provided with machetes, all set out on Carnival Sunday or Monday for the jungle of Punchana, Nanay, Morona Cocha, or San Juan. There they select a tall, strong palm tree, which they fell rapidly. The fronds of this giant of the jungle are lopped, leaving only the crown like an elegant crest. The trunk is carried back to the village where they are all received by young and old, who noisily join them to create a strange parade. On arrival at the assigned spot they lay down the palm trunk and immediately set to digging a very deep hole. After the crown of the palm has been decorated with little mirrors, necklaces, small flags, handkerchiefs, small containers of hair gel, and other trinkets and baubles, the tree is set vertically into the earth, where it remains like some exotic migratory flag staff, the focus for the shouts, applause, and imprecations of the entire populace, who anxiously await the climax to this carnival. The *humisha* (the name for this palm tree, which will have the ephemeral glory of heralding the death of carnival) will remain thus decorated for a day. Shortly after midday on Tuesday, everyone returns to the scene to organize, quickly and skillfully, the *pandilla*. In two columns, men and women, arm in arm, jubilantly traverse all the streets of the town, attracting to their lively parade all those who make an appearance, even if it is only to take a look. The band enthusiastically surrounds the flag-bedecked *humisha*, dancing and panting with the effort and tipsy as a result of the liquor (*chicha*) with which they are kept well supplied so that the enthusiasm does not flag. One of the crowd approaches a girl passing in front at that moment and hands her a small axe, which she immediately gives to her companion, who rapidly delivers the first blow to the palm trunk. The axe passes from hand to hand, and the well-aimed blows fall until eventually the giant of the jungle begins to tremble, accompanied by the increasingly explosive enthusiasm of the members of the *pandilla* and those watching the spectacle. The last blow is reserved for the couple that has the obligation of preparing and presiding over next year's carnival. The trunk sways and falls noisily, and the dancers and the observers leap onto the fallen crown, trying to grab at something hanging there.

In Brazil, carnival has acquired such characteristics that one could say that it is now identified as the American carnival *per se*, particularly that of Rio de Janeiro. The Rio carnival is spoken about as if it were a dream that had become reality or has the potential to become real, an opportunity to experience confusion and loss of identity, as one is crushed amidst the noisy multitude of Plaza Once. There, for just a few days, the human race achieves a kind of equality, aware only of their physical condition; there, no one is more or less, and all have come together with the same purpose of satisfying appetites that are not precisely spiritual. And all this happens to the rhythm of the joyful and provocative sambas that hammer away hours and days without rest, as if an extraordinary apotheosis wished to confound both heaven and earth. In nineteenth-century Brazil, carnival celebrations were stratified along the lines of the Brazilian social structure. There were three carnivals in one: The *Grandes sociedades* were the domain of the upper class, the *Ranchos dos Reis* was for the middle class, and the *Blocos de Sujo* were for the lower class. The *Grandes sociedades* made their first appearance in 1855. The parade consisted of a masked marching group with numerous bands and, for the first time in carnival celebrations, a series of floats on which were satirical enactments of current events. The songs of the 1855 *Grandes sociedades* were also full of political satire. The middle-class *Ranchos* originated in Bahia and presented themes based on history and culture. The lower class *Blocos de Sujo* used whatever costumes they could improvise, but the ideas of upside-down, inside-out, good-bad, and death-life predominated.

There are a number of reasons why the carnival in Rio de Janeiro is unlike any other, but perhaps the most significant is that it has become an aspect of national identity, and the samba schools that perform every year have had official sponsorship since the 1930s. As in much popular culture, the samba in Brazil has been the subject of debate between those who want to innovate in order to appeal to the public taste and those who want to preserve the authentic. As early as the 1870s, there were complaints of a corrupt samba. The debate became heated when the *samba de morro* became the official samba and the samba schools became the center attraction of the Rio carnival. In 1933 the first subsidy was given to these samba schools by the mayor of Rio de Janeiro, and beginning in 1935, the parade of the samba schools was printed up in an official carnival program published by the mayor's office. In that year the newspaper *O Globo* sponsored the carnival parade and established the regulations for the participation of the samba schools, which included the "prohibition of all wind instruments and the requirement that each group have some women dressed as Bahianas" (Santos and Silva 63).

The Brazilian government was now firmly involved in the carnival in Rio de Janeiro, which was, of course, used for political ends. For example, under the nationalist government of Getúlio Vargas, the *Deixa Falas* samba school was asked to dramatize the "October Revolution" (the 1930 revolution that brought Vargas to power, not the Russian Revolution of 1917) in their entry in the carnival parade. In short, under the Vargas regime the carnival and the samba schools had been nationalized.

The politics of Brazil have changed many times in the last sixty years, but the dominance of the Rio carnival as a national symbol has grown in stature and acceptance. The *Mangueira* samba school, which to many Brazilians is the paragon of authenticity, recently gave resounding support to Bahia and Bahian musicians as the heart of samba and the carnival. In Rio's 1994 carnival the *Mangueira* presented a highly acclaimed homage to Gilberto Gil, Caetano Veloso, Gal Costa, and Maria Bethânia. In a recent book Hermano Vianna sums up the present situation:

> Although most Brazilians now prefer the music of Olodum (a contemporary cosmopolitan blend of rhythms sometimes identified with "Tropicalismo") to that of Rio's samba schools, the carnival of Rio de Janeiro remains the national festival par excellence. The elaborately staged parade in its Sambadrome is televised in full throughout Brazil, while the Bahian carnival appears only in quick news broadcasts of the crowded streets. This is not merely an imposition of the Rio-based *Globo* Television Network. For even without the broad popularity that it commanded in earlier decades the traditional samba of the Rio de Janeiro carnival continues to be an agent of national unification. Caetano Veloso himself said this in a recent interview:

> "Mangueira, and by extension, Rio de Janeiro, represent our national unity. Now that there's so much talk of separatism, it is good to strengthen Rio as a symbol of our nationality." (107)

Newton Freitas, author of some magnificent texts on Brazilian customs, has pointed out that someone said that, during the three days of Carnival, the Brazilians realize what they have dreamed about during the year. Perhaps. And as Brazilians dream more than anyone else of love, the Carnival is an expansion of their various ways of loving. Joyful and sad love, pathetic, ridiculous, tragic, and conventional love are all manifested here. Paradoxically, masks take advantage of distractions to permeate the streets with truth, streets that on normal days are permanently disguised. There is no work, and nothing is taken seriously; all that matters is singing and loving in excess.

Brazil is one of the richest countries in terms of Latin American popular culture, and Rio is the summation of this Brazil that spreads itself out to the four points of the compass. Rio unites and compresses populations that arrive from all parts of the country in search of something evanescent or remote that lives in the dreams of each Brazilian. And the years rework and rekindle these diverse elements that come together, revive, and perpetually flow back from the periphery to the center to make Rio the core of Brazil. It is therefore hardly strange that the Rio carnival is essentially a national fiesta that boosts the northern sense of humor, the southern suggestiveness, and the strength of the center. It includes the remotest parts of the extreme north and the extreme south, and ties them together firmly in a knot that is not undone until the days of madness have passed. Only then is there a recollection as to who is from the provinces and who is *carioca* (from Rio de Janeiro). While the show lasts, Brazil revolves around this axis, a mixture of *catereté*, samba, *catimbó, macumba,* and *batuqué*. In civic terms, the nation rests on Carnival Saturday and wakes up again on Ash Wednesday. At dawn the last straggler remembers that he has a family, a job, and a position in society. It is time to return from that tremendous flight from responsibility to the requirements of convention. This experience is also the source of social preconceptions: The rich returns to be rich and the poor to be even poorer. This clearly has its most wretched effect on days after carnival, when the poor man climbs up the hills with his broken tambourine, his shirt in tatters, wearing his black straw hat he had worn to play on the *batuques*. But he returns with an air of a duty performed. Let us make no mistake about it–the samba schools demand a great deal from the participants in the pageant. A young woman who danced in Rio de Janeiro's carnival reflected on the year-long preparations: "Samba is our family, our Sunday outing, our movies, our lover. It is all we really know of happiness" (Santos and Silva 35). The rich man, on the other hand, returns in a bitter spirit, nostalgic for a freedom that passed all too quickly. He seals himself up in his luxury apartment and begins to talk badly of carnival. As the saying goes, in his old age the devil becomes a hermit-saint.

In Panama, carnival festivities have substantially declined, as in most of Latin America outside Brazil. To a certain extent they have a great similarity with those held in the rest of the continent, in particular the dances celebrated under awnings, in beer gardens, on walks in the afternoons along the great Central Avenue, and, to finish, the parade of floats decorated with allegorical themes and the election of a carnival queen. No longer do the joyful rhythms fill the streets of the city; nor do the original disguises of past times that once gave a touch of color make an appearance. Panamanians recall with nostalgia their old-time carnivals that began on the Sunday with dances in Boyain and La Ciénaga, two neighborhoods in the capital, whose exuberance escalated to include all the corners of the city. Castillero points out that, from carnival Monday onwards, the city girls began to show off their *mudas* [clothes] of fine cambric and *coquito* embroidery and the many flowers that decorated their hair. They had the appearance of walking flowerpots that moved in the harmonious rhythm of the *dengues*. The climax of the festivities occurred on Tuesday. In the nineteenth century, at midnight the *tunas* (musical groups of instrumentalists and singers) made their appearance. As there was no electric light in the streets, each woman carried a handful of candles to light up the way and dripped wax on those who came near. At this stage the women were not taking care of the aesthetics of their costume; nor could the men keep their balance. And no one cared that the singers held a note too long and the musicians couldn't keep the rhythm— the louder the shouting, the happier the *tuna*. As it is customary to set off fireworks in the midst of the group, it was not surprising that some of the costumes also were singed, but no one complained, since an accident was part of the fiesta. The coming and going between the dance floors of the locality went on until dawn on Tuesday and sometimes lasted until the day was well advanced on Ash Wednesday. When the church bells rang for the Mass and the grave-faced priests, holding a plate of ashes in one hand, declaimed to those standing around, "*memento homo, qui pulvis eris*" [Remember, man, that thou art dust], more than one of the devout would rise with a black cross on the cheek instead of the forehead: Unable to hold his head upright, the result of exhaustion or the sugar cane spirits that were still churning in his stomach, he would not be able to maintain the required composure for the sacred and solemn act of the tremendous admonition.

In Cuba, carnival achieved its greatest expression in Santiago and Havana. Ortiz and Vasconcelos defended the celebration of carnival, especially in Havana, where as a spectacle it expressed an aesthetic blend of vividly colored outfits imitating fantastic or allegorical animals, emblematic floats, brilliant lanterns, music, and songs, all composed by anonymous and naturally inspired artists. When the Carnival group had resources, they built a float whose theme generally alluded to the name of the group: A sparrow hawk, a Turkish throne from Venice, or a *fiqui*. There were often a number of floats with very different themes, often patriotic. In the night parades, the floats were accompanied by lanterns that often provided exquisite lighting effects. These included colossal lamps with multiple arms pleasingly arranged and polychrome lanterns or images of palaces, ships, or monuments made of transparent material and brilliantly illuminated from within. The great portable lanterns were swung to the rhythm of the music and the singing of the crowds, creating an original and very lovely dance of light that in the tropical night constituted an exquisite spectacle of processional ritual that was both profoundly touching and truly unforgettable.

Of course. carnival is not a literary phenomenon, but it is deeply rooted in the artistic expression of Europe and subsequently in those areas of the Americas colonized by the Spanish, French, and Portuguese. Mikhail Bakhtin calls it syncretic pageantry. In Latin America it is the Brazilian carnival that has developed the richest symbolic language. Among the most basic of carnival symbols are the dualisms of high and low, birth and death, and blessing and curse, as seen in the uniting of opposites in the same figure—pregnant death, the front and back of the person reversed, fool as wise man, wise man as fool, or simply turning clothes inside out. The lavish costumes of the pageant have their own visual language of freedom from all of the quotidian restrictions. And then there is the music. It is a narcotic that brings about the single most important part of the carnival: This is a spectacle of participation, for everyone gets caught up into the festival. The extraordinary influence carnival has had on literature is not only descriptions of carnival but also the use of its symbolic language. The carnavalesque play of opposites is the most powerful undercurrent of Latin American literature, and it is

here that we find a clue as to the relation between public festival, especially carnival, and Latin America's literary cultures.

Among the numerous examples in twentieth-century literature, in Argentina the spirit of the carnival infuses Julio Cortázar's (1914–1984) *Rayuela* [1968, *Hopscotch*, 1991]. The Brazilian poet, Haroldo de Campos (1929–2003), recognizes that Cortázar created a novel inside out with the same exuberance that carnival has always shown in turning the world upside down. Campos's own poems are cited by Cuba's Severo Sarduy (1934–1993) as prime examples of carnival's mobility, a search for constant displacement, constant change, movement, and permutation of phonemes: "The Unsurpassable the laudable the notable the adorable/the grandiose the fabulous the phenomenal the colossal/the Unshitpastable the lowbabble the nauseable the malodorable/The ganglious the flatulous the fetoranimal the cutarsadical" (Sarduy 64). This delivers a clear, obvious, immediately discipherable, and effective message: The high and low of the human condition are completely and continuously reversible.

Although in Mexico, with the exception of port cities such as Mazatlán, Tampico, and Veracruz (see **Figure 1**), carnival has not been widely cultivated, there is a plethora of public celebrations in every region of the country, nominally in honor of the patron saint, that are the Mexican equivalent to carnival. The colonial governments of New Spain fostered these festivals as a form of control over the Amerindian population; however, what they never were able to fathom was that the *danzantes*, the musicians, and the masses of participants had turned them into rituals of resistance. This deeply ingrained aspect of popular culture has from time to time entered the literary work of Mexican poets and writers. Octavio Paz (1914–1998) was able to articulate these cultural forces in his *Laberinto de la soledad* [1950; *Labyrinth of Solitude*] and in his poetic constructs *Discos visuales* [1968; Visual Discs]. However, one of Mexico's most carnevalesque poets was José Juan Tablada (1871–1945) who turned Mexico's national icons upside down in his lines about the Eagle and the Armadillo:

El águila que lo perseguía
desde el azur adonde se cernía
Lo dio por muerto . . .
¡y a poco el armadillo al sol surgía
como un santo ermitaño del desierto!

Burló del águila la garra,
mas al fin convertido en guitarra
bajo la mano
llena de amor patrio
de la Tierra de Promisión
al pie del ídolo del atrio,
de un zapatista suriano,
¡El armadillo canta la canción!

(459)

From the blue, the avid
eagle took its prey for dead. . . .
later the Armadillo basked in the sun
like a hermit saint in the desert!

Having escaped the eagle's claws
the Armadillo wound up as a guitar
Beneath a hand of a Zapatista
from the south, full of patriotic love
of the Promised Land
in the idol's atrium
the Armadillo sings its song!

Figure 1.

Photograph of Carnival mask, Veracruz, Mexico. (Courtesy Mario J. Valdés)

Perhaps one of the most widely recognized aspects of carnival is its double-voicing, which augments and exaggerates the commonplace of expressing one's own views through another's words. Thus, when a woman appears in carnival with a costume of a very pregnant death-figure, there appear two contradictory symbolic languages that are linked together but are now expressed in the same figure. Carnival marks the reversal of up into down and down into up, but it also marks the expression of opposites. This is the spirit that dominates contemporary Latin American literature, as in the nonheroic hero of Gabriel García Márquez's (b. 1927) *Cien años de soledad* [1967; *One Hundred Years of Solitude*] or the originality of Jorge Luis Borge's (1899–1986) Pierre Menard's exact reproduction of Cervantes' prose. There is a plethora of theories that have been proposed to explain this phenomenon, but there is one basic fact that transcends all theories and that is that Latin America's literary culture is deeply rooted in its popular traditions and celebrations. In conclusion, we should note that festivals such as carnival are not spontaneous but rather traditional ways of responding to a harsh way of life. With the exception of Brazil, where carnival has become a national institution, in the rest of Latin America such festivities are not sanctioned, sponsored, or formally organized. Carnival everywhere allows for role reversals, and therein lies its appeal.

Translation by Jessica Johnson

Works Cited

Bakhtin, Mikhail. 1984. *Problems of Dostoevsky's Poetics*. Trans. Caryl Emerson. Minneapolis: University of Minnesota Press. 122–28.

Campos, Haroldo de. 1996. "Liminar: Para llegar a Julio Cortázar." *Rayuela* by Julio Cortázar Ed. Julio Ortega and Saúl Yurkievich. 2nd edition. Madrid: Colección Archivos. xv–xxii.

Castillero, Ernesto J. 1953. "Carnavales de antaño." *Antología ibérica y americana del folklore*. Ed. Félix Coluccio. Buenos Aires: Edit. Kraft. 233–36.

Corominas, Joan. 1961. *Breve diccionario etimológico de la lengua castellana*. Madrid: Gredos.

Cortázar, Julio. 1967. *Hopscotch*. Trans. Gregory Rabassa. London: Collins and Harvill.

——. 1991. *Rayuela*. Ed. Julio Ortega and Saúl Yurkiévich. Nanterre, France: ALLCA XXe.

Ebelot, Alfred. 1943. *La pampa*. Buenos Aires: Alfer y Vays.

Frazer, James George. 1951. *The Golden Bough. A Study in Magic and Religion*. Abridged edition. New York: Macmillan.

Freitas, Newton. 1943. *Maracatú–motivos típicos y carnavelescos*. Buenos Aires: Pigmalión.

García Márquez, Gabriel. 1967. *Cien años de soledad*. Buenos Aires: Sudamericana.

Ortiz, Fernando and Ramón Vasconcelos. 1940–46. "Las comparsas populares del carnaval habanero." *Estudios Afrocubanos*. Havana. 129–72.

Paz, Octavio. 1959. *Laberinto de la soledad*. 2nd edition. Mexico City: Fondo de Cultura Económica.

——. 1968. *Discos visuales*. Mexico City: Era.

Santos, Lígia and Marília Silva. 1980. *Partido da Portela*. Rio de Janeiro: Funarte.

Sarduy, Severo. 1986. "Towards Concreteness." *Latin American Literary Review. Special Issue on Brazilian Literature* 14 (Jan.-June): 61–69.

Tablada, José Juan. 1966. "El ídolo en el atrio," *Poesía en movimiento. Mexico 1915-1966*. Ed. Octavio Paz et al. Mexico City: Siglo XXI. 457–59.

Vianna, Hermano. 1999. *The Mystery of Samba: Popular Music and National Identity in Brazil*. Trans. John Charles Chasteen. Chapel Hill: University of North Carolina Press.

CHAPTER 63

POPULAR MEMORY AND THE COLLECTIVE IMAGINATION IN LATIN AMERICAN SOAP OPERAS

Jesús Martín-Barbero

Popular Genres and New Narratives Involving Identity

As part of his interest in modern popular genres, Gramsci proposed a new means of viewing popular, mass literature by suggesting that the analysis of serial novels "belonged more to the study of the history of culture than to that of literary history" (208). This marked the beginning of an approach to literature adopted by cultural studies in recent years, in other words, the analysis of the diversity of matrices and social conflicts linked by culture. By his statement, Gramsci meant particularly what he called national-popular literature, far closer to life and to nonerudite culture than to art inasmuch as it is less concerned with books than with oral narratives, which, like stories, sayings, fables, or proverbs, are intended, according to Benjamin (1973, 131–34) to be told rather than read. As far as literary criticism is concerned, popular mass stories are restricted to schematic forms, transparent conventions, and commercial standardization. Until recently, this approach involved an updated form of that old confusion between unlettered and uncultured, through which, from the eighteenth century onward, the enlightened elites affirmed the place of the people in politics while negating them in culture, turning the notion of lack of culture into the intrinsic feature that configured the identity of the popular sectors, an insult that covered their self-serving inability to accept the fact that there might be experiences and matrices of another culture in those sectors. In order to understand the cultural density of the conflictual relationship between television and popular culture a new type of criticism must be developed–capable of distinguishing among complex issues: The necessary denunciation of television's complicity with the manipulation of power and commercial interests; the strategic position occupied by television in the dynamics of the everyday culture of the majorities; the transformation of memories and sensibilities and the construction of the cultural imaginary within which people recognize themselves and through which they represent what they are entitled to expect and hope for. Whether we love it or loathe it, television today is both the most sophisticated device for shaping and co-opting popular tastes and one of the most important historical mediations that expresses the narrative, gestural, and scenographic matrices of the popular cultural world, understood not as the specific traditions of a people but rather as the hybridization of certain forms of enunciation, certain narrative skills, and certain dramatic and fictional genres of both Western cultures and the mestizo cultures of Latin American countries (Martín-Barbero 1983, 110–32).

At the same time, we must recognize the decisive presence of television in the popular collective imagination of Latin America, where what is involved is that strategic and most peculiar of all cultural battles fought in these countries, the battle of images. Studying the history of this battle in Mexico, Gruzinski wonders the following:

How can one understand the strategies of the dominators or the resistance tactics of the Indian peoples from the time of Cortés to the Zapatista guerrillas of the end of the twentieth century, from the runaway slave cultures of the Caribbean peoples to the baroque of the Carnival in Río without examining the history that takes us from the sixteenth century didactic Franciscan image of the City of God to the heroic mannerism of liberating imagery and the baroque didacticism of Mexican muralism to the electronic imagery of soap operas? How can one explore the fluctuations and changes in identities without delving into the hybridity of the collective imagination in which the conquered peoples gave shape to a visible form of their memories and reinvented their own history? The current recovery of the popular collective imagination through the television programming of Televisa (Latin America's largest network, based in Mexico City), which owes its success to a combination of archaism and modernity, can only be understood through the connections that link sensibilities to a social visual order in which traditions are altered but not abandoned, anticipating experiences in visual transformations which as yet have no discourse. This leads one to posit that "the current post-modern dis-order of the collective imagination–the deconstructions, simulacra, de-contextualizations, eclecticisms–refers to the baroque (or neo-baroque) device, whose links with religious images foreshadowed the electronic body linked to its technological prostheses: walkmans, videocassette recorders, computers." (204)

In the face of this historical battle between images, imagery, and the collective imagination, the Latin American intelligentsia has maintained its deep-seated distrust of images, which "the lettered city" (Rama), that is, the cultural establishment, has made every attempt to control by confining them to art or to the world of deceptive appearances and the remains of popular magic. Today, however, a new position is beginning to be adopted toward the visual image, based on the new cultural historiography, which, on the one hand, regards orality not only as a research instrument (for anthropology, for example) but also as a source of knowledge, and on the other, rediscovers the line of thought that includes Walter Benjamin's view (1983, 15–59) of the strategic nature of technologies, particularly those concerned with the production and reproduction of images, in the configuration of modern sensitivity and cities. This line of inquiry is connected to that of Heidegger on modernity by linking the question of technique to a world that is constituted by images, in other words, to modernity as the age of the images of the world. It extends as far as the innovative turn provided by Gianni Vattimo on the links between technology and society: "the direction in which technology moves is no longer a question of mastery of Nature by machines and instead it involves the development of information and communication about the world as an image" (94).

Acknowledging the dominance of the image and audiovisual experience in the current construction of stories concerned with identity is crucial to an understanding of the profound interpenetration–the complicity and complexity of relationships–that now occurs in Latin America between the orality that has survived as the primary cultural experience of the majority of Latin America's population and technological visuality, a form of secondary orality (Ong) that has been organized by the techno-perceptive grammars of radio, cinema, video, and television. However scandalous it may sound, it is an undeniable fact that the majority of the population in Latin America is becoming incorporated into and appropriating modernity without abandoning their oral culture, in other words, not by reading, but through the genres and narratives, languages and skills of the audiovisual industry and experience. Discussing the media in Latin America has therefore become an issue of anthropological inquiry. What is at stake here are the profound transformations in the everyday culture of the population's majority, particularly among some in the new generation who can read, yet whose reading is influenced by the plurality of texts and writings currently circulating. Consequently, the complicity between orality and visuality does not refer to the exoticness of a Third World illiteracy but rather to "the persistence of profound strata in the collective memory and mentality brought to the surface by brusque alterations in the traditional social fabric caused by the rapid pace of modernization" (Marramao 60).

It is therefore necessary to posit the conflict that, in my view, constitutes the essence of the most specific tensions between literature and television. Without disregarding the fact that these tensions are a peculiar expression of the continued strength of ideological inertias involving high and low culture when they are transferred to the field of power struggles fostered by academic spheres and labor markets, it is essential to provide at least a minimal historical perspective to shed light on the various levels of the conflict. Initial contact between television and literature in Latin America was inevitably hampered by a culturally subordinate conception of television: Faithfulness to the literary text took precedence over the peculiarities and possibilities of the language of television. Writers regarded television as a valuable means of expanding their production, its sole task being to disseminate their works, illustrating them with images subordinated to the narrative logic of writing and the written work. Writers' acceptance of television as a means of communication for their works was therefore initially marked by an attribution of precariousness to television language that turned it into a mere transcription. This implied, on the one hand, that television dramatizations were judged entirely by their faithfulness to the literary text, since audiovisual experimentation was regarded as a distorting element. On the other hand, the "nobler" the (origin of the) literary text, the higher the level television was thought to have achieved. Consequently, the value of what was shown was attributed to the literary worth of the text and ultimately to its author. As a result, the work of the mediator between novels and television, the adapter, now known as the scriptwriter, was totally ignored.

In the mid-1970s, the relationship between literature and television was upset by a double infidelity that led to the serialization stories introduced by some of the finest television scriptwriters who had already written scripts for radio serials. Adapting television scripts to the serial form of long-running U.S. productions, such as *Peyton Place* (known as *The Devil's Cauldron* in Spanish), enabled the visual grammar of the cinema to be used for television dramatization. The second infidelity occurred within television itself and involved the technologization/specialization of program direction, in other words, the construction of a specific language for television narration that permitted the aesthetic liberation required by television stories. This double betrayal of the model that subordinated the language of television to the literary text was what would permit the narrative innovations that, in the 1980s, would pave the way for modern Brazilian and Colombian soap operas particularly, both in the long format with daily episodes and in the series with weekly dramatizations. Yet the modernity of soap operas is due less to their content or expressive forms than to the professionalization of the scriptwriters' job, which is proof of their cultural recognition and consequently of the legitimization of their (albeit relative) aesthetic autonomy. The new relationship between television and literature, established by soap operas, was inserted into the new aesthetic experience of the urban masses: The hybridization of oral cultures with electronic visual forms subverting the hegemonic order of writing and authorship. Let us remember that the division into writing units (see Barthes) produced by serials in nineteenth-century Europe thwarted the recognition of serial writers as novelists because the idea of a "salaried writer" (see Escarpit 1974 and 1982) was inconceivable. This forced Balzac to conceal his authorship of the novels he wrote in installments in order to survive at certain moments during his life. At the end of the twentieth century, the institutional mediation of the market justifies the disregard for aesthetic transformations that television has introduced into the social system of writing: We are witnessing mestizo practices that mix/stain the "pure" inwardness of aesthetic experience with the outwardness of the demands fueled by the industrial and commercial conditions of production. Yet it is by assuming the dense blend of cultural forms with industrial formats, professional ideologies, and productive routines, creative twists with commercial stratagems, that the scriptwriter and director lend television-writing professional status and its own form of expressiveness.

Television and Culture: From Sensibilities to Discourse

Television, more than any other media, reflects the contradictions of Latin American modernity; at the same time as its basic model, that of enlightened modernity, is asserted, it is also seen to be heading for a crisis in the decentered modernity of television. Although the press may be a decisive forum of opinion for the leading economic sectors of society, it is still an economically and especially culturally inaccessible medium for the majority of the population in Latin American countries. Radio, connected to the cultural orality of these countries, played a decisive role in the mediation between the expressive-symbolic world of the countryside and the techno-instrumental rationality of the cities until the 1970s, but it has been displaced in this function by television. The modernity of television is somewhat contradictory in countries where the disproportion in the social space occupied by this media form–at least in terms of the importance acquired by what is shown on television–is, however, proportional to the lack of political forums for the expression and negotiation of social conflicts and the nonrepresentation of the majority population in the discourse of official culture, and moreover to the very real diversity and complexity of the lifestyles and feelings of the people. In other words, what matters amongst the general population is what has been shown on television, in spite of a lack of representation of the majority; but in countries with limited means of public debate, television has become the social arbitrator by default. This weakness of Latin American civil societies, the long political stalemates, and the profound cultural schizophrenia of the elites are what fuel the disproportionate capacity for representation that television has acquired. It has an ability to appeal that cannot be confused with audience ratings. It is not because the amount of time devoted to television is not significant but because the political or cultural importance of television cannot be measured in direct, immediate contact but only in terms of the social mediation achieved by its images. And this capacity for mediation is derived less from the technological development of this particular media form or the modernization of its formats than from what people expect and demand of it. This means that it is impossible to know what television does to people if we are unaware of the social and cultural demands that people make of television. These demands bring into play the continuous destruction and re-creation of collective identities and the ways in which they feed on and project themselves onto the representations of social life that television offers. Indeed, from Mexico to Brazil to Argentina, television attracts people more than any other medium, but the image of Latin American countries that appears on television is not only an image that has been deformed by the economic and political interests that support and shape this medium but also, paradoxically, the painfully everyday face of all kinds of violence, ranging from child abuse to the widespread presence of aggression and death on the streets.

At the same time, television has become a crucial aesthetic mediator in Latin America; despite the shortsightedness of business people and the prejudices of many of the creators themselves, it has attracted a great deal of national talent, ranging from theater and cinema directors and artists to groups working in popular culture and the new generations of video makers. In the gaps left by commercial television and given the possibilities opened up by cultural, regional, and local or community channels, television appears as a strategic space for the production and reproduction of the images that Latin American peoples form of themselves and through which they wish to be recognized by others. In Latin America, it is through television images that the representation of modernity becomes accessible to the majority on an everyday basis. These images intervene in the access to modern culture in the whole range of its lifestyles, languages, and rhythms; its precarious, flexible forms of identity; the discontinuities of its memory; and the slow erosion of cultural referents by globalization. It is these contradictory movements, then, that we need to explicate and understand.

The first of these contradictory movements concerns the role of the media, particularly television, in the Latin American formation of nationhood. Since Latin American states were turned into nations at the same time as they became modern countries, it is hardly surprising that one of the most contradictory aspects of their modernity lies in its projects concerning nationhood and in the disagreements surrounding what qualifies as national. During the 1920s, that which was considered national was a summary of cultural particularity and political generality that "transforms the multiplicity of desires of the various cultures into a single desire to participate in (or form part of) national sentiment" (Novaes, 10). During the 1940s and 1950s, nationalism was transmuted into forms of populism that extolled state intervention to the detriment of civil society; this intervention was justified as being a

modernizing force in both the ideology of the left and the policy of the right (see Garreton 1984). Conversely, since the 1980s, the affirmation of national modernity has been identified with the replacement of the state by the market as the agent responsible for creating hegemony, a move that profoundly reversed the original meaning of nationhood and led to a growing devaluation of what was national (see Schwarz).

What role have the mass media played in this process? Their position in the current wave of modernization is sharply different from what it was during the early phase of modernity, from the 1930s to the 1950s, characterized by the populist governments of Getulio Vargas (1883–1951, President 1930–1945) in Brazil, Lázaro Cárdenas (1895–1970, President 1934–1940) in Mexico, and Perón (1895–1974, President) (1946–1952) in Argentina. During that first stage of modernization, the media played a decisive role in the formation and dissemination of national identity and sentiment. The idea of modernity underpinning the project of constructing modern nations from the 1930s to the 1950s linked an economic project–the entry of national economies into an international market–to a politico-cultural one: Turning them into nations through the creation of a culture and a national identity. This project could only be achieved through communication between the urban masses and the state. The media, particularly radio, would become the spokesmen for the appeal from the state that converted the masses into the people and the people into a nation (Martín-Barbero 1987, 177–93). Radio in every country and the cinema in certain countries–Mexico, Brazil, and Argentina–introduced traditional rural cultures to the new, urban culture of mass society, incorporating elements of orality and expressivity from the former into the latter, thereby enabling them to make the shift from the expressive-symbolic matrix of the popular world to the informative-instrumental rationality on the basis of which modernity is organized (see Sunkel).

The process we are experiencing today is not only different but virtually the reverse: The mass media, co-opted and led by television, have become powerful agents of a culture-world that is being configured today, most explicitly in the perception of youth and in the emergence of cultures lacking any territorial memory, linked to the global expansion of the television, record, or video market. These cultures are linked to new sensibilities and identities, for instance, to shorter, more precarious time spans, endowed with a great plasticity in order to amalgamate ingredients from extremely varied cultural worlds that are permeated by discontinuities in which atavistic gestures, residues of modernism, and post-modern vacuums coexist. These new sensibilities are linked to the movements of technological globalization that are reducing the importance of the territorial and the traditional. Yet the devaluation of what was national is not only due to audiovisual cultures and the transformations that information technology has wrought on identities but also to the internal erosion produced by the liberation from the domination of local differences (Vattimo 79), particularly from regional and generational differences. Seen from a global perspective, what was national seemed provincial and loaded with paternalistic dead weight. Seen from the diversity of local cultures, what was national was identified with centralist homogenization and official stereotyping. What was national in the cultural sphere was overtaken in both directions. This does not mean, however, that it was no longer relevant in the cultural sense or that it was no longer the historical mediator of the people's long memories, which is precisely what makes communication between the generations possible.

retelling the plot. The periodicity of the episode and the structure of the series create a bridge between the time of the cycle–that of the story–and that of linear progress, in other words, that of the novel. The newspaper serial is a form of narration that, while retaining some of the characteristics of a short story, is about to become a novel.

The presence of the popular narrative matrix in newspaper serials is also linked to the above-mentioned "primitive" narration, which, according to Northrop Frye, operates from a vertical perspective, sharply dividing heroes from villains by abolishing ambiguity and forcing the reader to take sides. Yet these are heroes and villains whose separation symbolizes a "topography of experience" (Gubern 214) drawn from the contrast between two worlds: One that is outside the everyday experience of life, the world of happiness and light, security and peace, and one that is below it, the world of the devil and the dark, terror and the forces of evil. Ritualization is therefore not only linked to techniques but also to archetypes that, as Gubern notes, do not come from heaven, but from the sum of human experiences, from everyday pleasures and suffering. The persistence in soap operas of "primitive" narration attributes this story to a family of stories that is the opposite of "author's literature." From this perspective, it becomes clear that the narrative resources of the newspaper serial-melodrama are not only linked to industrial formats but to a different form of narrating. This does not imply ignoring the skill of cultural industries and the pressure of formats of ideologies but recognizing other ingredients that are symbolically effective. Although the inordinate number of entanglements and adventures is linked to the producers' interest in extending the story and obtaining the greatest profit from its success, it is also linked to readers' expectations and the narrative logic of "And then . . .," in other words, the priority of action over psychology. Likewise, the redundancy that aids the shift from one episode to another leads to the repetition and schematism underlying the processes of identification and recognition.

Newspaper serial melodramas reached Latin America by two means: Urban writing and oral stories. In 1870 in Argentina, Eduardo Gutiérrez (1851–1889) published the first great gaucho newspaper serial for the newspaper *La patria argentina*. Entitled *Juan Moreira*, it blended the rural with the urban: The characters and adventures drawn from the couplets of the *payadores* (gaucho storytellers), circulated in booklets and gazettes, came together with incidents taken from police files. This created a "dramatic border universe" (Rivera 1982, 9) that reflected the changes caused by early modernization in the late nineteenth century. Yet Latin American newspaper serials were also broadcast on the radio rather than published in the press. And their mediators would be the circus in Argentina and the collective reading at tobacco factories in Cuba. The "creole circus" (Seibel 1984), that special form of circus resulting from the combination of dance floor and scenery, acrobats and dramatic performances under the same big top, would be the sphere in which the gaucho mythology of newspaper serials would blend with the scenes of traveling comedians from which radio plays were derived. Radio soap operas in Argentina were known as *radiodrama* precisely because the actors who performed on radio came from the circus and traveled throughout the provinces performing radio plays so that people could *see* what they were hearing. In Cuba, from the late nineteenth century onward, cigar factory workshops were the scene of the reading aloud of history books and newspaper serial stories that would provide radio

soap operas with themes and forms. This practice, which originated in European monasteries and prisons, was introduced into the sheds of El Arsenal, whence it was transferred to the Azcárate and Partagás cigar factories. From 1936 onward, readers coexisted with the radio, in which Cuba was a pioneer, "until machines overcame the cigar factory reader-performers through the wireless, which broadcast reading on air" (F. Ortiz 126). This is how the radio soap opera (the *mother* of Latin American television soap operas) originated, incorporating popular listening into the creation of a sonorous expressiveness that would include the corporeal dimension of the art of narration, in other words, the exploration of the sensorial effects–tones and rhythms–of the story.

One aspect of radio soap operas that carried on into television soap operas was the predominance of retelling the story to someone else, with the redundancy this implied in establishing dramatic continuity from day to day. It also preserved the indefinite openness of the story, its openness as regards time–viewers know when it begins but not when it will end–and its sensitivity to outside events that occur during the course of the story. A dialogistic text or–according to a Brazilian version of the Bakhtinian proposal–a carnivalesque genre, the television soap opera is a story "in which the author, reader and characters constantly exchange positions" (DaMatta 96). This exchange confuses the story with real life, connecting viewers with the plot in such a way that they eventually end up nourishing it with their own lives, because what television soap operas discuss and what people say is not something that is said once and for all in the soap-opera text or revealed by answers to surveys. It is a message charged with silences, depicting the lives of people who are unable to express themselves–much less write. And there are other silences that observe and link the dialogue of the people with what happens on the screen. TV soap operas speak far less from their texts than from the inter-text created by their interpretations. Consequently, among the popular classes, people enjoy retelling soap operas far more than actually seeing them, because of the confusion between the plot and real life that is created in the retelling of the story. And within this confusion, which is perhaps what most scandalizes intellectuals, several types of logic are intertwined: The commercial logic of the productive system, that of standardization, but also of popular stories, ballads, and songs with choruses, in other words, "the serial nature of an aesthetics where recognition and repetition constitute a significant part of pleasure and where it is, therefore, a standard of value of symbolic assets" (Sarlo 155).

Finally, the cinema also inherited melodrama. In Hollywood, where the audiovisual grammar on which soap operas would be based was created, melodrama is a decisive genre. From Griffith to King Vidor, Elia Kazan, and Douglas Sirk, the cinema reinvented melodrama, reconverting it–as early nineteenth-century theatrical melodrama had–into a popular spectacle that mobilized the masses. "When spectators shouted Bravo or whistled, it was not to express their judgment of the quality of a performance, but rather to express their identification with the fate of the heroes they saw on screen. They appropriated–without passing judgment on them–the ups and downs of people endowed with a sort of reality that transcended the idea of representation" (García Riera 16). This is the same identification that underlies the passion aroused by television soap operas. If Latin American cinema is predominantly melodramatic, as borne out particularly by Mexican films, it is because cinematographic melodrama has intervened in the transition from the rural experience to popular urban culture. And it has achieved this by "connecting with the longing of the masses to be socially noticed" (Monsiváis 446). In the form of cinema, people were able to see themselves, beyond the films' reactionary content or schematic forms, because it was there that they found familiar faces, gestures, rhythms, forms of speech, colors, and landscape. A nationalistic, populist form of cinema par excellence, melodrama proved vital to the urban masses, who, through its images, were able to lessen the impact of cultural shock and, for the first time, were able to conceive of their country in their own image.

Television Narrative in an Era of Globalization

Until the mid-1970s, fiction programs on Latin American television channels were overwhelmingly dominated by series from the United States. This meant, on the one hand, that programs imported from the United States—mainly comedies and melodramatic or detective series—accounted for 40% of programming (see Varis). At the same time, these programs were shown at peak times, in the evenings during the week and all day long on weekends. In the late 1970s, the situation began to change: In the so-called lost decade of the 1980s—notorious for the social and political destabilization caused by the size of the external debt—the communications industry was the only one that really expanded. The number of television stations rose from 400 to 1,500; Brazil and Mexico acquired their own satellites; radio and television information companies created global networks via satellite; and even in the poorest countries in the region, cities were filled with satellite dishes, cable networks were set up, and regional television channels began to appear.

This was the point when national production began to expand and compete with series from the United States for prime time. Within an extremely short period of time, national soap operas in various countries—Mexico, Brazil, Venezuela, Colombia, Argentina, and Chile (and Brazilian, Mexican, or Venezuelan television soap operas in other countries)—completely replaced U.S. production (see Schneider-Madanes). From then until the beginning of the 1990s, soap operas became a strategic enclave of Latin American audiovisual production, both because of their importance in the television market and because of the role they would play in the cultural acknowledgment and recognition of these countries, at both the national and the international levels. Not only in Brazil, Mexico, and Venezuela (the main exporting countries) but also in Argentina, Colombia, Chile, and Peru, soap operas played a key role in national television production (see Portales 1987 and 1994), in other words, in the consolidation of the television industry, the modernization of its technical and financial processes and infrastructures, and in the specialization of its human resources: Script writers, directors, camera men, sound engineers, set designers, and editors (see R. Ortiz; González; Coccato). Soap opera production has also entailed a certain appropriation of the genre by each country, that is, its nationalization. Although the soap opera genre implies rigid stereotypes, dramatic plotting, and powerful constraints on its visual drama reinforced by the standardizing logic of the world television market, each country has made soap operas a specific junction between television and other cultural spheres such as literature, cinema, and theater. Most countries began by copying, in some cases actually importing, the scripts, as had happened years before with

radio soap operas, when, under the auspices of Colgate-Palmolive, scripts were imported from Cuba or Argentina. Dependence on the radio format and the concept of the image as a mere illustration of a spoken drama gradually disappeared as television became more professionalized and production teams gradually conquered the new environment by appropriating its new expressive possibilities. Thus soap operas became a conflictive yet fertile field for politico-cultural redefinitions: Whereas, in countries such as Brazil, first-rate theater actors, cinema directors, and prestigious leftist writers were incorporated into the production of soap operas, in other countries, television in general and soap operas in particular were rejected by artists and writers as a dangerous trap and the most degrading of professional spheres. Gradually, however, the crisis in the cinema and the fact that ideological extremism was surmounted led to the incorporation into television, particularly through soap operas, of many artists, writers, and actors, who contributed themes and styles that include key aspects of life and national cultures.

Thus, at the height of their creativity, Latin American soap operas testified to the internal dynamics of a pluralistic cultural identity. Variations in the genre were reflected in two highly differentiated narrative matrices and in multiple versions of both. One, on the basis of Cuban radio soap operas (see Bermúdez), a genre was created in which tragic destruction prevailed by incorporating only basic, elementary drives and feelings and excluding any ambiguity or historical complexity from the plot. Yet from 1968 onward, as a result of the Brazilian soap opera, *Beto Rockefeller,* a new matrix began to emerge that, without entirely destroying the melodramatic scheme, incorporated a degree of realism that permitted the telling of a quotidian narrative (Pignatari 61) and thus a link between the genre and the country. The first model constituted the secret of success of Mexican soap operas, such as *Los ricos también lloran* [The Rich Also Cry] or *Cuna de lobos* [Cradle of Wolves], and Venezuelan soap operas, such as *Topacio* or *Cristal.* Conversely, the Brazilian soap operas *La esclava Isaura* [The Slave Isaura] and *Roque Santeiro* and, to a lesser extent, the Colombian soap operas *Pero sigo siendo el rey* [But I Am Still the King] and *Caballo Viejo* [The Old Horse] owed their success to the second model. In Brazilian soap operas, the referential capacity of the various spaces and the moments of the country's history and its industrial transformation are depicted in images through a story that links the lengthy duration of the newspaper serial—the unfolding of the history of various generations—to the visual fragmentation of advertising discourse (see A. and M. Mattelart). In Colombian soap operas, realism is tinged with an irony that suggests the satirical-*costumbrista* tradition, which makes it possible to outmaneuver melodrama and rediscover the country in the sharp diversity of its regions—including the Andes, the Caribbean, and the plains—as not only a recognizable dimension of the nation's pluralism but also one that can be shared. It is precisely this narrative heterogeneity, which used to reveal the cultural diversity of Latin America, that globalization is reducing by attempting to achieve folkloric effects and empty stereotypes. And it was when soap operas mobilized and incorporated a larger number and a better quality of artists, writers, and critics, obtaining the largest audiences in the history of Latin American television, that their success became a springboard for their internationalization. Although this responded to a movement of activation and recognition of what was Latin American in the countries of the region, it also marked the beginning of a trend toward the standardization of formats that rapidly neutralized the signs of conflict between Latin American identity and heterogeneity.

The pioneer in this field was Brazil: TV-Globo internationalized soap operas by exporting their successes to Portugal from 1975 onward, and in the early 1980s they crossed geographical and political borders by introducing their soap operas into Spain, Denmark, England, and even Japan. In 1988, *La esclava Isaura* was rated the best television program in Poland over the previous ten years, while in the People's Republic of China, soap operas seduced a public of 450 million viewers. Meanwhile, Mexico's Televisa focused primarily on the Latin American sphere–and on the Hispanic sphere in the United States–and from the mid–1980s onward, it re-structured its international commercialization strategy by increasing its presence in Europe and Northern Africa through hugely successful series such as *Los ricos también lloran,* shown everywhere from Italy to Russia. Something similar has happened with the Venezuelan television productions, whose narrative simplicity and dramatic exaltation has recently found an enormous resonance and devoted audiences in the most varied and distant countries. In recent years, the opening of the world market to Latin American soap operas has also incorporated Colombian, Chilean, and Argentinian productions, revealing the degree of development achieved by national television companies. In the 1990s, however, the soap operas' modernity underwent drastic changes, abandoning creative experimentation and the re-creation of the collective imagination in favor of technological modernization, industrialization, and commercialization. Responding to the neoliberal openness, audience success transmuted the form to the international level but at the cost of an industrialization of melodrama, which led to the progressive erasure of the author's traces and the signs of identity that had been achieved. The new production conditions would totally eliminate the narrative craftsmanship that had made soap operas so responsive to the context of their production (for example, that the creativity of an actor and his empathy with viewers had sometimes obliged scriptwriters to transform the role and importance of a character by altering the original direction of the plot. Conversely, the "demands of casting, the links with an increasingly aggressive form of merchandising, the processes of advertising promotion, in other words, the feasibility of exporting and the emphasis on themes or approaches which, however narratively schematic and impoverished, would guarantee success" were reinforced (Rey 51).

Given these facts and the compulsive reducing of what can be valued to what succeeds in audience ratings alone that is becoming increasingly evident, perhaps now is the time to ask whether the globalization of markets signifies the dissolution of all real differences or reduction to recipes for an outdated form of folklore. Or is this same market–as shown by the international success of the Colombian soap opera *Café*–not in fact crying out for demanding processes of experimentation and innovation that would permit the insertion into the languages of a globalized sensitivity of a variety of narratives, gestures, and collective imaginaries in which the true richness of these peoples is expressed? Clues to the answer to this question, raised in Colombia, are found in the transfer of both the connection with the country and aesthetic experimentation from the narrative of daily soap operas to the narratives of weekly series. In the early 1990s television attracted several young cinema directors who introduced narrative and visual experimentation and portrayed

the social experience of Colombians at the end of this century on the small screen. On the one hand, dramatized reports on national life, light years away from the usual denunciatory pamphlets of the past, brought themes such as political corruption, the contradictions of guerrilla warfare, the cruelty of kidnapping, and the commercialization of the media. On the other hand, they depicted painful generation gaps, women's independence, and the new moral climate; they converted this demand for reality television into a new narrative proposal: Making television drama a forum for exploring the uncertainty of the contemporary soul, its frustrations, and its enlightenment, as if the response to globalization lay not only in the manifestation of differences but also in the exposure of the moral and political lies with which our societies protected themselves during the dark end of the twentieth century and in the revelation of the senselessness that threatens the entirety of our stories and cultures.

The Collective Imagination of Soap Operas and Memories of a Country

As García Márquez never tires of saying: "In the land of magic realism, reality exceeds fiction, eventually surpassing it to such an extent that, in such a country, novelists have no alternative but to change jobs" (20–23). In television, the opposite is true. Whereas news programs are filled with technological fantasy, thereby becoming "shows," it is in soap operas and plays that the country is accurately depicted. Whereas in news programs political or theatrical posturing is passed off as reality, or worse still, transmutes into hyperreality, the kind that eliminates the impoverished and dramatic reality we live in, soap operas and weekly drama actually portray the history (with a small h) of what happens, its mixtures of nightmares and miracles, the hybridization of its transformation and anachronisms, the orthodoxies of its modernization, and the deviations of its modernity.

The main encounter between soap operas and their countries of origin took place in the early 1980s, as part of the new method of producing soap operas (see Martín-Barbero 1992), whose starting point was a spoof of the genre started by *Pero sigo siendo el Rey*, a soap opera in which Colombians simultaneously made fun of the rules of the genre and the way they themselves were depicted in the sentimental caricature of *rancheras*. The ironic vein, which took up an old, satirical-*costumbrista* tradition of New Granadan origin, began to pierce the grandiloquence and rigidity of melodrama, freeing the plot from the weight of destiny and allowing the story to breathe–in other words, enabling the actions to have spatiotemporal density and the characters to be three-dimensional. From the coastal world of *Gallito Ramírez* to the urban subworld of Bogotá in *Las muertes ajenas* (The Death of Others), we are given access to the framework of humiliations and acts of revenge comprising the lives of those who struggle not only to survive but also to become someone. To this end, soap operas explore the opaque fabric in which social classes come into contact: The perversions of the rich that connect them to the lowest strata of society and the tactics employed by the poor to exploit the vices of the rich. By expanding the horizons of what was regarded as suitable material for soap operas, new professions, or rather new worlds, began to be included in the plots. Artists, boxers, and the dregs of society revealed new forms of social relationships, obscure relationships of solidarity and complicity and moral and cultural wedges that cracked open the false normality of society.

Open to the present and receptive to the movements of current social events, Colombian soap operas in the 1980s moved away from the great symbols of good and evil toward the ambiguities and routines of everyday life and the cultural expressivity of the regions comprising the country. Faced with the deceptive sociocultural map of the dichotomy between progress and backwardness, drawn by a form of modernization based on development, soap operas such as *San Tropel* or *El divino* (The Divine) showed us a map that expressed both the discontinuities and lack of coincidence *and* the proximity and exchange between modernity and tradition and between the urban and rural sectors of the country, with villages where social relations no longer have the simplicity–that is, the stability and transparency–of the rural and with city neighborhoods where people survive on the basis of solidarity and knowledge derived from the country. It is a map in which the vertical serfdoms of fiefs are blended with, rather than opposed to, the horizontalities produced by modern homogenization and the informalities of the city in which witchcraft coexists with biorhythms, and deeply rooted religious moralities exist alongside the scandalous expression of affection and sensuality. To the astonishment of many Colombians, a fabric of exchanges and ruptures was made visible for the first time, which, despite its schematism and ideological inertia, discussed the way in which certain forms of sociability survive or perish, the violence that is either suffered or resisted, the practical uses of religion, and the moral transactions without which it is impossible to survive in the city.

Enmeshed in this fabric, soap operas also revealed the other contradiction that both destroys and links our collective modernity: The lack of synchronization between national and regional affairs, the disintegrating centralization of a pluralistic country, and the regions' struggle to be recognized as constituent parts of the nation. From the Caribbean coast to the Valley of Cauca, including Antioquia and the banks of the Sinú, soap operas permitted an approach to regional aspects that, by overcoming caricature and resentment, depicted its inhabitants' diversity of styles as regards feeling, cooking, singing, and retelling their lives and stories. They portrayed cultures on the coast where magic was not something from another world but merely an aspect of this world, in which boxing can become a system of morals rather than a trade, and where the *vallenato* is still a ballad that turns everyday miraculous events into history. These soap operas also depicted cultures from the Valle del Cauca that portray the feelings and the erotic and aesthetic power of the people of the country. It becomes a country where power and conflicts are the result of women's (or homosexuals') knowledge that blends sexual attraction with the control of communication, whether gossip or the telephone exchange, where witchcraft outwits established religion, and a crude, elementary eroticism combines with a refined homosexuality to outwit machismo. Here female knowledge and power are in conflict not with modernity but with the incoherence of the economy and the ugly mess that men make of politics.

In a country such as Colombia that is both socially and culturally fragmented, the soap operas of the 1980s combined and blended what was rural with what was urban, the oldest region with the newest, together with the diverse regions within this country. And the soap operas' reconstruction of the national collective imaginary also included the encounter, or rather the intersection, between melodrama and fantasy and the lack of restraint of Macondo, which is what made *Caballo viejo.* The vastness of the Sinú

River, the voluminosity of Aunt Cena's body, the delirious hotchpotch of life personified by Reencarnación, and the multiplicity of knowledge and flavors combined by Epifanio split the seams of the melodramatic story, letting in the magic of the word and a secret blend of the local with the universal. In contrast to the purely functional or redundant use of the word in relation to the image in Mexican or Venezuelan soap operas, in *Caballo viejo,* words were thickened until they became a poetic image: Loaded with silence and expressed in monologues, the word enchants and connects popular sayings to metaphor in a reencounter between soap operas and the cultural orality of the country, and through it, with the writing that has by-passed grammar; it releases the secret magic, sensibilities and rhythms of the oral. The other broken seam that let in the experience of a man and a people, lost in a bend in the Sinú River, feels universal. It sets up a form of cultural osmosis that blends knowledge and tastes from east and west, philosophy and folk wisdom, and sayings from the countryside and Caribbean expressions. Outmaneuvering melodrama from the inside will create an openness to the wonders of Macondo within the realism of its unreality.

Translation by Suzanne Stephens

Works Cited

Abraham, Pierre, ed. 1974. *Le roman feuilleton. Europe: Revue littéraire mensuelle.* 542. Paris: Denoel.

Angenot, Marc. 1975. *Le roman populaire: recherche en paralittérature.* Montreal: Presses de l'Université du Quebec.

Barlozzetti, Guido, ed. 1986. *Il palinsesto: testo, aparati e géner della televisone.* Milano: Franco Agnelli.

Barthes, Roland. 1964. *Le degré zéro de l'écriture.* Paris: Gonthier.

Benjamin, Walter. 1973. "El narrador." Trans. Jesús Aguirre. *Revista de Occidente* 129:301–33.

Bermúdez, Manuel. 1979. "La radionovela: una semiosis entre el pecado y la redención." *Video-forum* (Caracas) 2:85–98.

Bourdieu, Pierre. 1990. *Sociologia y cultura.* Trans. Martha Pou. Mexico City: Grijalbo.

Brooks, Peter. 1974. "Une esthetique de l'étonement: le melodrame." *Poétique* 19:340–55.

Coccato, Mabek. 1985. "Apuntes para una historia de la telenovela venezolana." *Video-forum* (Caracas) 1–2:79–102; 99–118.

Costa, Pere-Oriol, José Manuel Perez Tornero, et al. 1996. *Tribus urbanas.* Barcelona: Paidos.

DaMatta, Roberto. 1985. *A casa e a rua. Espaço, cidadania mulher e morte no Brasil.* São Paulo: Brasiliense.

Dumur, Guy, ed. 1965. *Histoire des spectacles.* Paris: Gallimard.

Escarpit, Robert. 1974. *Hacia una sociologia del hecho literario.* Madrid: Cuadernos para el diálogo.

———. 1982. *Sociologia de la literatura.* Buenos Aires: Mirasol.

Ferreras, Juan Ignacio. 1972. *La novela por entregas.* Madrid: Taurus.

Frye, Northrup.1980. *La escritura profana.* Trans. Edison Simon. Caracas: Monte Avila.

García Marquez, Gabriel. 1996. "Gabo cambia de oficio." Entrevista de S. Cato, *Cambio16* (Bogota) 151: 20–23.

García Riera, Emilio. 1974. *El cine y su público.* Mexico City: Fondo de Cultura Económica.

Garreton, Manuel A. 1983. *La cuestión nacional.* Santiago: Ilet.

Goimard, Jacques.1974. "Quelques structures formelles du roman populaire." *Le roman feuilleton.* Ed. Pierre Abraham. Paris: Editions Denoel. 19–30.

———. 1980. "Le melodrame: le mot, la chose." *Cahiers de la cinematéque* (Perpignan) 28:12–27.

González, Jorge. 1990. *Las vetas del encanto-Por los veneros de la producción mexicana de telenovelas.* Mexico City: Universidad de Colima.

Gramsci, Antonio.1977. *Cultura y literatura.* Barcelona: Península.

Gruzinski, Serge. 1994. *La guerra de las imágenes. De Cristóbal Colón a Blade Runner (1492–2019).* Mexico City: Fondo de Cultura Económica.

Gubern, Román.1974. *Mensajes icónicos en la cultura de masas.* Barcelona: Lumen.

Heidegger, Martin. 1998. "Lenguaje de tradición y lenguaje técnico." Trans. D. Tatián. *Pensamientos sobre la técnica. Revista Artefactos* (Buenos Aires). 1:10–21.

Hoggart, Richard.1972. *The Uses of Literacy.* London: Penguin.

Maffesoli, Michel. 1990. *El tiempo de las tribus.* Barcelona: Icaria.

———. 1997. *Du nomadisme. Vagabondages iniciatiques.* Paris: Librairie Générale Française.

Martín-Barbero, Jesús. 1983. "Memoria narrativa e industria cultural." *Ensayos de teoría literaria* (Mexico). 10:59–74.

———. 1987 *De los medios a las mediaciones.* Barcelona: G. Gili.

———. 1992. *Televisión y melodrama.* Bogota: Tercer Mundo.

———. 1996. "De la ciudad mediada a la ciudad virtual." *TELOS* (Madrid) 44:52–64.

Marramao, Giacomo.1989. "Metapolítica: más allá de los esqemas binarios." Ed. X. Palacios and F. Jarauta. *Razón, ética y política.* Barcelona: Anthropos. 59–86.

Mattelart, Armand and Michèle Mattelart. 1987. *Le carnaval des images.* Paris: La Documentation Française.

Moles, Abraham A. 1978. *Sociodinámica de la cultura.* Buenos Aires: Paidós.

Monsiváis, Carlos. 1976. "Nota sobre la cultura mexicana en el siglo XX." *Historia General de México.* Ed. Bernardo García Martínez et al. Vol. 4. Mexico City: El Colegio de México. 303–457.

Novaes, Adauto. 1983. *O nacional e o popular na cultura brasileira.* São Paulo: Brasiliense.

Ong, Walter J. 1987. *Oralidad y escritura.* Trans. Angélica Scherp. Mexico City: Fondo de Cultura Ecónomica.

Ortiz, Fernando. 1973. *Contrapunteo cubano del tabaco y el azúcar.* Barcelona: Ariel.

Ortiz, Renato, et al. 1988. *Telenovela: história e produção.* São Paulo: Brasiliense.

Pignatari, Décio. 1984. *Signagem da televisão.* São Paulo: Brasiliense.

Portales Cifuentes, Diego. 1987. *La dificultad de innovar. Un estudio sobre las empresas de televisión en América Latina.* Santiago de Chile: Instituto Latinoamericano de Estudios Transnacionales.

———. 1994. *Utopias en el mercado. Teoría y práctica de una contribución democrática de la televisión.* Santiago de Chile: Ediciones del Ornitorrinco.

Rama, Angel. 1985. "La ciudad letrada." *Cultura urbana latinoamericana.* Ed. R. Morse and J. E. Hardoy. Buenos Aires: Clacso.

Reboul, Pierre. 1976. "Peuple Enfant, Peuple Roy, ou Nodier: melodrame e revolution." *Revue des Sciences Sociales* (Lille) 162: 46–59.

Rey, German. 1996. "Ese inmenso salón de espejos: telenovela, cultura y dinámicas sociales en Colombia." *DIA-LOGOS de la Comunicación* (Lima) 44: 21–6.

Rivera, Jorge B. 1980. *El folletín: la novela popular.* Buenos Aires: Centro Editor de América Latina.

Salcedo Silva, Hernando. 1981. *Crónicas del cine colombiano: 1897.* Bogotá: Valencia Editores.

Sánchez Biosca, Vicente. 1995. *La cultura de la fragmentación.* Valencia: Filmoteca.

Sarlo, Beatriz. 1987. "Lo popular como dimensión: tópica, retórica y problemática de la recepción." *Comunicación y culturas populares en Latinoamérica.* Mexico City: Federación Latinoamericana de Asociaciones de Facultades de Comunicación Social; Ediciones G. Gili. 152–61.

Schwarz, Roberto. 1983. "Nacional por sustracción." *Punto de vista* (Buenos Aires) 28: 15–23.

Schneier-Madanes, Graciela, ed. 1995. *L'Amérique Latine et ses télévisions. Du localau mondial.* Paris: Anthropos/Institut national de l'audiovisuel.

Seibel, Beatriz. 1984. *El teatro 'bárbaro' del interior.* Buenos Aires: De la Pluma.

Sunkel, Guillermo. 1985. *Razón y pasión en la prensa popular.* Santiago de Chile: Ilet.

Tortel, Jean, et al. 1970. *Entretiens sur la paralittérature.* Paris: Plon.

Varis, Tapio. 1973. *International Inventory of Television Programmmes: Structure and the Flow of the Programmes between Nations.* Tempere: University of Tempere.

Vattimo, Gianni. 1990. *La sociedad transparente.* Barcelona: Paidós.

Virilio, Paul.1989. *La máquina de visión.* Trans. Mariano A. Rato. Madrid: Cátedra.

———. 1995. *Vitesse de libération.* Paris: Galilée.

Zonabend, Françoise. 1980. *La memoire longue.* Paris: PUF.

CHAPTER 64

THE POPULAR IN THE CONFUSED REPUBLICS?

Carlos Monsiváis

The Wars of Independence led to the emergence (or promotion) of the new identities of countries that were now formally independent (in other words, what was specifically Peruvian, Bolivian, Argentinian, Paraguayan, Guatemalan or Mexican) and needed to be sustained with references and meanings. It fell to writers to supply them with symbols, legends, myths, historical realities, descriptions of customs–in short, the contents that ensure the ease of the civilizing aim. In the beginning, they realized they were mired in backwardness, for example, the inhumanity of *caudillos* (local strongmen) and the indifference of society. At the end of the nineteenth century, the poet Amado Nervo (1870–1919) held that, in Mexico, writers generally wrote for those who wrote. Men of letters had a select coterie who read them and whom they eventually made their sole public. The *gros public*, as the French called it, could neither afford nor understand their work, however simply it was written. What, then, could be more natural than for them to write for those who, even if they failed to pay for their work, did at least read it?

In defining the nature of those who do not read them, writers generally identify three basic nuclei: The majority of their peers (the elite, which, at that time, was not entirely illiterate), the people (who, in the nineteenth century, were virtually synonymous with the working classes, with a touch of the middle classes), and the lower classes, often regarded by the elite as the great obstacle to progress, whether Indians or urban poor. The people belonged to the nation, albeit distantly, whereas the lower classes did not. They lay outside society and comprised an anonymous group, overflowing with voices and picturesque, threatening faces that were therefore deeply allegorical. If Barbarity with a capital "B" was a rural matter (as Sarmiento rightly said) because of a close contact with the jungle and the plains that incorporated men into nature, then impiety unburdened itself onto those who, through their failure to belong to the respectable social categories, were only entitled, as shadows, to a *costumbrista* (local color) impression. Those who lacked any information, and therefore power, could only aspire to allegorical drawings, phrases as epitaphs, terrifying adjectives, and exorbitant or commiserative annotations.

It is not so much a question of authors as of literature. What prevented contempt for the unredeemed masses, driven by primary impulses and unaffected by change for a century and a half? The incessant turmoil, the *caudillos* who symbolized the possible government, the ephemeral or permanent tyrannies, the lack of publishers and bookshops, the exhausting subjugation to journalism, and everything that was identified with national backwardness or the limitations of peripheral countries, all exacerbated the hatred against this unprotected expression of barbarity, poverty. This is why those who have been trained in privileges abound in antipopular diatribes. They are aware of the situation: The limit of their pretensions is the lack of a public, and the marginalized position of their nations destroys their pretensions to universal fame. By

not being Europeans, writers have no internal market and can (if they wish) foresee the reactions of each of their readers in detail. Therefore, the common people are made the culprits. Francisco Bulnes (1847–1924), an intellectual at the court of the dictator Porfirio Díaz, detested the mob, not the common, street people but the proletarian, educated, cowardly, envious, dishonest, and dissolute mob; José Vasconcelos (1881–1959) declared that there is no meaner spectacle than that of a people inebriated with its own ineptitude, like a sick person declared past recovery who takes a fiendish delight in his wounds.

The finest nineteenth-century Mexican novel, *Los bandidos de Río Frío* [1889–1891; The Bandits of the Río Frío] by Manuel Payno (1810–1894), a brilliant survey of popular customs and language, is a mural project that includes, without too many distinctions, members of the middle class and flower sellers, police chiefs who lead the criminal classes and lawyers who are invariably crooked, heroes and murderers, and virgins and lascivious assassins. Yet no one entirely escapes the laws of the time, and Payno's realism derives from the fatalities of class and nation: There is no way out for those living in penury because their origin is their bad luck and poverty is a moral flaw, an ontological defect. And Payno realizes this: A novel is either popular or nothing, since the masses offer the only omnipresent human landscape. The idealization of misery (at once inescapable and redemptive) that would be proclaimed by literary and cinematographic melodrama was still a long way off, and no one imagined what experimental narrative would be like. Nineteenth-century novels were classist, existing as they did in a society of inescapable categories, where social mobility was the most unusual of all customs. Yet if there were no themes in this literature that were unrelated to the popular poverty, "people who were not decent" were only entitled to a (distant) symbolic location. What other representation was available to the marginalized, those who had been excluded from all forms of power, including the purchase of books?

Throughout the second half of the nineteenth century and the early part of the twentieth century, Latin America was forced to acknowledge that poverty constituted both social and sentimental injustice. The mere absence of goods did not in itself create paupers. For that, it was also essential to lead a servile existence. As metaphors for vice or resignation, backwardness or "misfortune from the cradle," paupers adorned novels of realism or naturalism like fallen angels; they lacked the aura of decency and were consumed by degradation or, more often, were born villainous and endorsed this stigma through being abandoned. According to the doxa realism, what was popular was synonymous with bad luck. According to naturalism, what was popular meant meanness, lack of control, unsavory odors, an immorality imposed by one's facial features and the color of one's skin, and a form of animalization created by the impulse to survive. In *Santa* (1903), the first bestseller in Mexico, Federico Gamboa (1864–1939) describes the common people, conveniently animalized, during the Independence Day celebrations:

Por dondequiera, vendimias, lumbraradas, chirriar de fritos, desmayado olor de frutas, ecos de canciones, fragmentos de discursos, arpegios de guitarra, lloro de criaturas, vagar de carcajadas, siniestro aleteo de juramentos y venablos; el hedor de la muchedumbre, más pronunciado; principio de riñas y final de conciliaciones; ni un solo hueco, una amenazante quietud; el rebaño humano apiñado, magullándose, pateando en un mismo sitio, ansioso de que llegue el instante en que vitorea su independencia. (92–93)

All around, as far as the eye could see, there were vendors' stalls, bonfires, the sizzling of food being fried, an intense smell of fruit, echoes of songs, fragments of speeches, arpeggios of the guitar, babies crying, laughter wafting through the air, a sinister flapping of curses and insults, the powerful stench of the crowd; the beginning of quarrels and the end of conciliation; not a single space, a menacing calm; the human herd crammed together, bruising itself, stamping the ground, anxious for the moment when they could cheer its independence.

Here we have a joyful reactionary, an intransigent enemy of the popular. Yet his extreme attitude represents that of an entire sector, albeit a less belligerent one. Gamboa describes scenes of poverty in the terrifying terms reserved for Gothic atmospheres in other literatures:

Para arribar a tan ruin anclaje, anduvo Santa la Ceca y la Meca, lo mediano y lo malo que las grandes ciudades encierran en su seno como cutáneo sarpullido que les produce un visible desasosiego y un continuo prurito, que únicamente la policía sabe rascar, y que contamina a los pobladores acomodados y los barrios de lujo. Es que se sienten con su lepra, les urge rascársela y aliviársela, y a la par despiértales pavor el que el azote, al removerlo, gane los miembros sanos y desacredite a la población entera. En efecto, si la comezón aprieta y la policía rasca, sale a la cara la lepra social, se ven en las calles adoquinadas, las de suntuosos edificios y de tiendas ricas, fisonomías carcelarias, flacuras famélicas, ademanes inciertos, miradas torvas y pies descalzos de los escapados de la *razzia*, que se escurren en silencio, a menudo trote, semejantes a los piojos que por acaso cruzan un vestido de precio de persona limpia. Caminan aislados, disueltas las familias y desolados los parentescos: aquí el padre, la madre, allí, el hijo por su cuenta, y nadie se detiene, saben dónde van, al otro arrabal, al otro extremo, a la soledad y a las tinieblas. (301–2)

In order to reach her humble destination, Santa chased hither and thither, walking through the mediocre, poor areas that great cities conceal in their midst like a skin disease that makes them visibly uneasy and gives them a permanent itch, that only the police can scratch and which contaminates well-to-do residents and fashionable districts. They feel they must scratch their rash to get rid of it, while, at the same time, they are terrified that by touching their rash, in their attempts to remove it, they will affect other healthy members and discredit the entire population. Indeed, if the rash becomes very severe and the police scratch it, then this social leprosy comes to the surface and paved streets, those with sumptuous buildings and elegant shops, are suddenly peopled with prisoners' faces, starving creatures, uncertain gestures, fierce grimaces and the bare feet of those who have escaped the police raids, who melt away in silence, often at a quick trot, rather like fleas that accidentally find themselves coming across a clean person with expensive clothes. They walk separately, since their families have broken up and all kinship links have been dissolved; the father walks in one direction, the mother in another, while the son goes off on his own. No one stops, since they know where they are going, to another slum, on the other side of the city, to loneliness and darkness.

Voracious Nature

Most readers of this narrative (regardless of class) equate the popular with the typical, and the close identification between the doubly anonymous masses and the popular is expressed through emphatic definitions (the finest example being the narrative of realism.) The pauper's heaven is an historical anecdote; sacrifice without any social reward is the commonplace of dissimulation, and while vulgar laughter is the language of incomprehension, ideals are the temples of resentment, and only the forced surrender to the times–the river that sweeps away everything in its path, the river of blood that redeems everything–justifies the poor in their anonymous martyrdom.

In the realist narrative of Peru, Colombia, Venezuela, Ecuador, and Mexico, those who tame nature pay for this deed by becoming part of cruel nature themselves. In Mariano Azuela's (1873-1952) *Los de abajo* [1915; *The Underdogs*, 1963], *Los caciques* [1917; *The Bosses*, 1972], *Las moscas* [1918; *The Flies*, 1972]; José Eustacio Rivera's (1888–1928) *La Vorágine* [1924; *The Vortex*, 1935]; Ciro Alegría's (1909–1967) *El mundo es ancho y ajeno* [1941; The World is Wide and Alien]; Rómulo Gallegos's (1884–1969) *Doña Bárbara* [1929], *Canaima* [1935], and *Cantaclaro* [1934]; Jorge Icaza's (1906–1978) *Huasipungo* [1934]; Rafael F. Muñoz's (1899–1972) *Vámonos con Pancho Villa* [1931; Let's Go with Pancho Villa] and *Se llevaron el cañón para Bachimba* [1941; They Took the Cannon to Bachimba]; Martín Luis Guzmán's (1887–1977) *La sombra del caudillo* [1929; The Shadow of the Strongman] and *El águila y la serpiente* [1928; The Eagle and the Serpent]; and in the series of short stories and novels that explore armed struggle, the devastation created by the large land owners and the intervention of North American and European companies, in dramas involving genocide and the conquest of the jungle and the mountains, a vision of the people begins to emerge. The people constitute an entity that was initially generous, but became perverted if it wished to intervene in reality. Deceived by the system, it disappeared without realizing its mistakes or successes or survived in bitterness and organically combined idealism and cruelty. In *Los de abajo*, an undoubted masterpiece, the narrative is complex and nuanced, exemplifying the ultimate reasons given by the peasants who go off to fight in the revolution because they have nothing to lose. Nevertheless, this description is contradicted by the author's reflections; in the words of his autobiographical character, the idealist Alberto Solís:

Hay que esperar un poco. A que no haya combatientes, a que no se oigan más disparos que los de las turbas entregadas a las delicias del saqueo; a que resplandezca diáfana, como una gota de agua, la psicología de nuestra raza, condensada en dos palabras: ¡robar, matar! . . . ¡Qué chasco, amigo mío, si los que venimos a ofrecer todo nuestro entusiasmo, resultásemos los obreros de un enorme pedestal donde pudieran levantarse cien o doscientos mil monstruos de la misma especie! . . . ¡Pueblo sin ideales, pueblo de tiranos! . . . ¡Lástima de sangre! (Azuela 1970, 72)

We must wait a while, until there are no men left to fight on either side, until no sound of shot rings through the air, save from the mob, as carrion-like it falls upon the booty; we must wait until the psychology of our race, condensed into two words, shines clear and luminous as a drop of water: *Robbery! Murder!* What a colossal failure we would make of it, friend, if we, who offer our enthusiasm and lives to crush a wretched tyrant, became the builders of a monstrous edifice holding one hundred or two hundred thousand monsters of the exactly the same sort. People without ideals! A people of tyrants! Vain bloodshed! (Azuela 1963, 81)

Realism as a Warning

During the first half of the twentieth century, novels abounded in characters that, according to the standards of civilized literature, lacked any significant psychology. How could they possibly have any if they had no refined customs or thought-provoking language, if, in short, they were poor? But these characters, who were only rarely fully individualized, were important inasmuch as they were victims who would subsequently become responsible for other people's suffering: Theirs are nomadic tragedies and ends without a conceivable beginning. With the emergence of novels, the majority of readers (including progressive ones) regarded these popular characters (with the easily frightened rhetoric of the time) as plenipotentiary envoys of the Thousand-headed Monsters, or else beings that were so simple-minded that they were not quite human. In this narrative practice, the popular meant that which could not avoid being what it was, the autonomy of fatalism, for this was characteristic of the multitudes without a conceivable future; it meant a certain cruelty, suicidal courage, sentimentalism, essential defenselessness, and candor that substituted for history and art among the poor. The ideological heritage (and the repertory of acclamation and curses) of the poor was nationalism, marking the most intimate contact between the popular and the nation. In these stories, the people represent the fury of the shifting sea, their only notable feature being their endless beginnings, their moving forward without ever arriving, and the fact that they advanced without the slightest change.

In the vertigo of destructive symbolism (*Canaima, Doña Bárbara, La Vorágine*), the condensation of what was outside one's own control, the intensity provided came at a high price, and the people existed only to be lifted up for a second by the forces that would inevitably crush them. "Jugué con mi corazón al azar y me lo ganó la Violencia" (5) [I had gambled away my heart and violence had won it (13)] Arturo Cova famously declared in Rivera's *La vorágine/The Vortex*. And popular characters gave in to violence without even having had the happiness of free will. Even if they had a heart to begin with, the determinism of poverty destroyed it.

From the beginning of the nineteenth century to the 1960s (and in some cases, up to the present), the second great approach to the popular took place in response to literary realism. In describing the circumstances of the common people, many of the finest Latin American writers reserved the right to use a classical language, since literary style meant spiritual distance. In order to contain the invasion of the masses, it was essential to erect the barricade of High Culture (which at that time was, roughly speaking, a ritual selection of the best of the canon of the West in French translation). A perfect example of this was the beautiful book of chronicles by Martín Luis Guzmán (1887–1977), *El águila y la serpiente* [The Eagle and the Serpent], in which the period of armed struggle in Mexico was re-created in a refined language, full of the bookish references, mythological allusions, and the verbal ennoblement of that Latin American nightmare: Neo-Classical rhetoric. Guzmán wrote about what he knew: revolutionary mobs destroying each other in a fit of drunkenness; Villa's lieutenant, Rodolfo Fierro, personally assassinating three hundred prisoners; and the honest revolutionary who challenged the barbarity of Villa's supporters facing the firing squad without spilling the ash from his cigar, while the National Palace served as the "virtual forum" of the revolutionaries for a few days. In the chapter entitled "A night in Culiacán," Guzmán describes the condition of the city in the days following the siege, with its abandoned houses, looted shops, desolation, and the inevitable "gloomy images": "Y una imagen se agita

entonces en la memoria, se apodera del espíritu y le comunica su estremecimiento: se ve a Eneas abrazando en vano la sombra de Anquises bañada de lágrimas que no mojan" (1941, 168–69) [And an image stirred in people's memories, taking hold of their spirit and transmitting its fear: Aeneas was seen, vainly embracing the shadow of Anchises, who was covered in tears that were dry to the touch].

Aeneas and Anchises appear in the Revolution, and the classical spirit redeems the theme of the populace. This salvation by the Greco-Latin past offered an idiomatic approach to tragedy from a "sculpted" language of the first order; the devastation barely concealed a doctrine that sought to become irrefutable: If allegories accurately captured the people, it was because the people were at best a mere allegory. What was popular was, above all, the area of archetypes and abstractions whose virtues were those of nobility in the depths of misfortune, and whose every character was always legion (all the poor were the same; every pauper was emblematic). The laborers who killed the boss to obtain reliable proof of their passage through life, the outcasts eager for a form of speech in which to hide from the impact of the city, the peasants, forgotten to such an extent that they had barely retained their own names, the prostitutes who gave up their hearts in return for syphilis, priests in remote villages whose only household furniture was their resentment against God, corrupt clerks, and so on every stereotype of realism testifies on behalf of the group known as the people. Not all this narrative descends to the level of clichés and the most vital aspects avoid being captured by mythology, but on the whole (as in many essays and articles published at this time) the people serve as a gallery of stereotypes.

The Concrete Jungle

"Earthy convictions" or narratives where nature is the protagonist, the active ferocity that opposes progress, are now complemented by urban stories and novels where the city is the "concrete jungle" that perpetuates nature's fury by other means. Characters are like "Dry leaves," or like "Fruit that has fallen from the tall, leafy tree of Life"; these marginalized characters delight in being frustrated in sordid landscapes, and they call their class origins a "condemnation" and convert their situation into a para-religious martyrdom. If they finally achieve happy endings, it is only against a backdrop of resignation. The determinism of poverty affects novels such as *Adán BuenosAyres* (1948) by Leopoldo Marechal (1900–1970) and *La región más transparente* [1958; *Where the Air Is Clear*, 1960] by Carlos Fuentes (b. 1928). No one disputes the fact that the popular realm is expressed, or rather, written and read, as consisting of "exchangeable beings" in scenarios where human will is unimportant. Other negative characteristics are added to this in novels and short stories, popular speech (required to do justice to the gestures and the changing meaning of key words) is perceived as vivacity without elaboration, a circular form of language that never distinguishes between premises and conclusions (called Cantinflismo). The customary opposition between the terms "culture" and "popular" is depicted as entirely natural. How can the cultural stamp of approval be given to those who are reluctant to elevate their spirit? This corresponds to the narrative battle in which some seek to keep the popular in its place (that is, in the corner with the other classist stereotypes), while others persist in re-creating (or reflecting, as it was called then) authentic forms of behavior. An immense faith is expressed in the intrinsic nobility of the people, a faith that can give rise to masterpieces and, inevitably, to a populist industry: If I capture the essence of the people (their typicality), I redeem them and ensure that my production is authentic. Liberals and conservatives, leftists and rightists all agree on one thing: The term "the people" refers to others, to what is alien and can only be dignified if it is in a landscape or exits in deference to tradition; it is degraded if it is merely a presence, combative if it is intimidated by circumstances, but usually docile.

Cinema and literature reached an agreement for a time. What was popular included types, situations, and unforgettable characters. The popular granted writers, regardless of whether they were aware of it or used it, the necessary data on the "National Being." In any case, what was popular was an entity that lacked any awareness of itself, or whose awareness had been usurped and ignored. By the 1950s, definitive works such as Juan Rulfo's (1918–1986) *El Llano en llamas* [1954; *The Burning Plain,* 1967] and *Pedro Páramo* (1955) shattered a cherished myth of the countryside as the last reserve of both cruelty and purity.

How Was Experience Perceived?

The modernization of Latin America, already irreversible since the 1940s, did not immediately modify the literary perception of what was popular. The age-old dogma that had condemned the poor (lack of wealth; original sin) was compounded by the condemnation of the ideologues that regarded mass man as the enemy, an abstraction that, in the last analysis, merely referred to ordinary men. Neither Gustave le Bon in *Psicología de la multitud* [1895; *The Crowd: A Study of the Popular Mind,* 1960] nor Ortega y Gasset in *La Rebelión de las masas* [1930; *The Revolt of the Masses,* 1932] offers a spokesman for capitalism, yet their preaching in favor of supreme individualism was opposed to any democratic faith. As late as the mid-twentieth century, the elites classified the majority of the inhabitants of Latin America as primitive and rejoiced in the theory of the ignorant, weak-willed people and the irredeemable mob. To support their thesis, they mentioned ephemeral tastes or the figures of popular consumption in films, comics, magazines, radio soap operas, and sports magazines. This degradation, that was joyfully assumed, reaffirmed the-sentence-on-the-wall: Poverty is a choice and whoever is born poor wants to continue to be poor, whether out of laziness, idleness, or the happiness granted by the simplicity of one's soul. (This is exacerbated in the case of Indians, the invisible people par excellence.) The emerging cultural industry attracted entrepreneurs anxious for new markets, literati in embryo or in decline, and intuitive young people in search of the mother lode of the future. In order to know what public they were targeting, they invented one and perfected the invention with news of their success. The psychology of the average spectator emerges on request, based on his or her prejudices and occasionally on his or her mythological judgment. And cinemagoers demanded to see themselves on screen, regardless of whether this had to be achieved through archetypes and stereotypes.

The City: The Punctuality of Backwardness

In cities, what constitutes social morals is increasingly individualistic faith or damaged memories, which is why urban conglomerations consist of limitations and unexpected scope, permissiveness, and prohibitions. And in defining the nature of cities, literature is as indispensable as is cinema.

The mythological influence of poems and novels is enduring, and if Joyce's Dublin, John Steinbeck's California, and William Faulkner's Yoknapatowpha County exist, Lima, Bogotá, Santiago, Buenos Aires, and Mexico City are also contemplated from the perspective of exclusively urban modernists and social realists. The first to define the city as a central character was the Argentinian Leopoldo Marechal. In *Adán BuenosAyres,* we are offered the definitive urban scenario:

> ¡Númenes de Villa Crespo, duros y alegres conciudadanos; viejas arpías gesticulantes, como gárgolas, porque sí o porque no; malévolos gruñidores de tangos o silbadores de rancheras; demonios infantiles, embanderados con los colores de River Plate o de Boca Juniors; carreros belicosos que se agitaban en lo alto de sus pescantes y se revolvían en sus cojinillos, para canturrear al norte, maldecir al sur, piropear al este y amenazar al oeste! ¡Y sobre todo vosotras, muchachas de mi barrio, dúo de tacones y risas, musas del arrabal con la tos o sin la tos de Carriego el poeta! (12–13)

> Inspiration of Villa Crespo, hard, merry fellow citizens; old shrews gesticulating like gargoyles, for one reason or the other; malevolent grumblers of tangos or whistlers of rancheras; childish devils, beflagged with the colors of River Plate or Boca Juniors; militant cart drivers who got worked up in their driver's seats and writhed in their saddle-bags, to hum to the north, curse the south, flatter the east and threaten the west! And above all, you girls in my neighborhood, those duos of high-heels and laughter, muses of the slums with or without the cough of Carriego the poet!

The slums, the neighborhood, the football fans, all were immensely popular. *Adán BuenosAyres* blended novelty (the city as the great revelation) with a language that was still linked to modernism and the epithets of republican oratory. And the great city (the triumph of the popular over the pretensions of the elite) was the totalizing character in Carlos Fuentes's *La región más transparente* [1958; *Where the Air Is Clear,* 1960], Fuentes incorporates a number of lessons, particularly those learned from John Dos Passos in *Manhattan Transfer* and the *USA* trilogy, where the central narration is nuanced by certain significant biographies, news reports, and the vision of the city as an immense mechanical desolation. Fuentes also uses pre-Hispanic and post-Cortesian symbols, has recourse to lyricism and abrupt generalizations ("En México no hay tragedia: todo se vuelve afrenta" [3] [In Mexico City, there is never tragedy, but only outrage]), and enumerates exhaustively and compulsively. Torrential cataloguing is his preferred method of representing Mexico City: "Su danza (nuestro baile) suspendida de un asta de plumas o de la defensa de un camión; muerto en la guerra florida, en la riña de cantina, a la hora de la verdad: la única hora puntual" (3) [your dance adangle from a feather plume and a bus fender. Dead in a flowering war, a bar scrap, at the hour of truth, the only timely hour]. The city here is not yet a synonym for urban destruction, the death of the environment, and overcrowding. Instead, it is an entity that heralds the customs that last one month, paving the way for weekly traditions. In a prophetic vein, Fuentes regards the city as a metaphorical whole:

> Ven, déjate caer conmigo en la cicatriz lunar de nuestra ciudad puñado de alcantarillas, ciudad cristal de vahos y escarcha mineral, ciudad presencia de todos nuestros olvidos, ciudad de acantilados carnívoros, ciudad dolor inmóvil, ciudad de la brevedad inmensa, ciudad del sol detenido, ciudad de calcinaciones largas, ciudad a fuego lento, ciudad con el agua al cuello, ciudad del letargo pícaro, ciudad de los nervios negros, ciudad de los tres ombligos. (1968, 10–11)

Fall with me on our moon-scar city, city scratched by sewers, crystal city of vapor and alkali forest, city witness to all we forget, city of carnivorous walls, city of motionless pain, city of immense brevities, city of fixed sun, ashing city of slow fire, city up to its neck in water, city of merry lethargy, city of twisted stinks, city rigid between air and worms, city ancient in light, old city cradled among birds of omen, city new upon sculptured dust, city in the true image of gigantic heaven. (1960, 4–5)

For Fuentes, *Where the Air Is Clear* is a novel with a Muralist perspective of painting the broad canvas and should therefore contain all the social classes and their urban redemption, cultured speech and slang, prostitutes and virgins, refined poets and movie producers, and debutantes and bus drivers. In this city on the verge of modern capitalism, or at least with some of the trappings of modern capitalism, somewhere between 1946 and 1952, everything is interlinked. Carnivals are a glimpse of masks that are more sincere than faces, and, without restraining their impulses, all social classes dance the conga in the early morning. Take, for example, the prostitute Gladys's visit to the city:

> Frente al Hotel del Prado, se topó con una comitiva de hombres altos y mujeres rubias, alhajadas, que fumaban con boquillas. Ni siquiera eran gringos, hablaban español . . . .
> –Rápido, Pichi, vamos a tomar taxi.
> –Voy, chéri. Déjame arreglarme el velo.
> –Nos vemos en casa de Bobó, Norma. No llegues tarde: para las orgías, puntualidad británica . . .
> –Y además, el canalla de Bobó cambia de la Viuda a Ron Negrita en cuanto se levantan los coros de las bacantes.
> –¡Chao, viejita!
> –Toot-toot.
> y parecían dioses que se levantaban como estatuas, aquí mismo, en la acera, sobre las orugas prietas de los demás, ¡qué de los demás!, sobre ella que estaba fundida, inconsciente, hermana de los vendedores de baratijas pochos, jafprais, berichip, de los de la lotería, de los voceadores, de los mendigos y los ruleteros, del arroyo de camisetas manchadas de aceite, rebozos, pantalones de pana, cacles rotos, que venía hollando la avenida. Pero en el siguiente puesto, entre uno de bolsas de cocodrilo y otro de cacahuate garapiñado, gastó dos pesos en una boquilla de aluminio. (1968, 16)

In front of the Hotel del Prado, she stumbled on a cluster of tall men and bejeweled blonde women who were smoking with [cigarette] holders. Even if they looked like gringos, they were speaking Spanish . . . .
"Hurry up, Pichi, we're taking a cab."
"Coming, *chéri.* Just let me fix my veil."
"We'll see you at Bobo's, Norma. Don't be late. For orgies, British punctuality."
"Aside from the fact that when the good-byes start, Bobo's fountains change from champagne to rum."
"*Ciao,* sweet."
"Toot-toot."
They looked like gods who had risen like statues, there on the sidewalk amid the wrinkles and troubles of lesser beings: And what beings! She herself, low as the lowest, sister to peddlers of cheap tourist junk, vendors of lottery tickets, newspaper boys, beggars and hacks, river of oil-stained undershirts, shawls, corduroy pants, broken sandals plodding the great street, wearing tracks in it. But at the second trinket stall, between one filled with fake alligator handbags and another where sugared peanuts were sold, she invested two pesos in an aluminum cigarette holder. (1960, 9)

Accumulation and torrents of data are shown in an economy of illusion and waste. What John Dos Passos does in *Manhattan Transfer* and Andrei Biely does in *Petersburg* is here magnificently applied to the Latin American macropolis. Chaos is a narrative magnet for those who regard the city as a living being. And the omnipresence of chaos is the preamble to the new fatalism; the obsessions that the city authorizes will never be spoiled. As Raymond Williams describes Wordsworth's insight into insecurity and profound subjectivity in *The Country and the City* (1973), it is when we most feel alienated in a world of strangers that we have the greatest need to take refuge in the images and signs around us in order to try to discover a sense of community. People have few of the usual means of appropriating keys to modern life: A personal relationship with technology, cinema, massification, music, and literature, the classical means. This is why, in Latin America, the most outstanding works are portraits of family and nation and also fulfill functions reserved for sociology, social psychology, and history.

As late as 1950, what was regarded as popular in Latin American literature was a matter of society register, rather than cultural. A writer as extraordinary as Roberto Arlt (1900–1942), with his *Los siete locos* [1929; The Seven Madmen] and *El juguete rabioso* [1926; The Rabid Toy], burst onto the scene with narratives that assumed the aesthetics that had previously been scorned. Within this universe of exclusions, one is struck by the contributions of Jorge Luis Borges (1899–1986), who blends the tango, the underworld, cabaret, and the inhabitants of the slums with mirrors, tigers, and eternities. For Borges, what was popular lay in the traditions of bravery, the virile excitability of the slums, and the myths of the individual as opposed to the mass man. And in addition to evoking the underworld, that literary and symbolic stock to which he selectively resorts, Borges preached the greatness of those cinema genres so despised at the time, such as Westerns and gangster movies, the epic source that continued (and preceded) Borgesian mythology.

Of all the forms of popular expression, Julio Cortázar (1914–1984) chose jazz, the music of rigorous improvisation, which incorporates high culture and returns it, in an enriched form, for daily enjoyment. From his homage to Louis Armstrong ("Louis, you great chronoscope"), Cortázar regarded jazz as the epitome of formal freedom, and in his masterpiece *El perseguidor* [1959; The Pursuer], Cortázar praises the "music of brothels and drugs." The self-destructive wandering of a character who might be Charlie Parker is partly metaphysical, and the comparison between squalid hotel rooms and low-down alleys with the improvisation in jazz is particularly caustic. In *Rayuela* [1963; *Hopscotch* 1966], a book that is both literary theory (a forum for the complicities of the reader) and an anti-dogmatic review of Western culture, jazz is responsible for a glimpse of the other side of the present: Armstrong is the best state of mind; Thelonius Monk, a condition of the spirit; and jazz is refinement, a civilized condition. It is interesting to compare *Rayuela* or *El perseguidor* with *On the Road* (1957) and *The Dharma Bums* (1958) by Jack Kerouac, the beatnik legend. For Cortázar, jazz was the most refined spiritual delight; for Kerouac, it was the rhythm of excess and the juggling of the senses. Both of them agree however in the high esteem in which they hold this music.

Regional Differences

Certain books and characters experienced the same fate as the poetry of *modernismo* in the late nineteenth and early twentieth centuries: Their success transcended the sphere of their specific readers. If in 1905 and 1915 even those who could not read recited Rubén Darío (1867–1916) and Manuel Gutiérrez Nájera (1859–1895), in 1985 and 1999, regardless of whether the poets and writers were aware of this, the masses were somewhat linked to artistic conceptions going from literature into cinema, from literature into television, and from literature into the record industry. The finest example of a writer who appropriates a piece of reality to make it his own is Gabriel García Márquez, (b. 1927). Ever since the publication of *Cien años de soledad* [1967; *One Hundred Years of Solitude*, 1970], hundreds of thousands of new readers have entered this novelist's world. Other writers have brought popular scenes into life through popular sounds, such as the Cuban sound of the characters of Cabrera Infante (b. 1929), the Puerto Rican sound of those in Luis Rafael Sánchez's (b. 1936) *La guaracha del Macho Camacho* [1976; *Macho Camacho's Beat* 1976] and *La importancia de llamarse Daniel Santos* [1988; The Importance of Being Daniel Santos], and the Mexican sound of the characters in Ricardo Garibay's (b. 1923) *Acapulco* (1979), *Las glorias del Gran Púas* [1978; The Glory of the Great Puas], Elena Poniatowska's (b. 1933) *Hasta no verte, Jesús Mío* [1969; *Here's to you, Jesusa!* 2001], *Fuerte es el silencio* [1980; Strong is Silence], and *Nada, nadie: Las voces del temblor* [1987; Nothing, Nobody: The Voices of the Mexico City Earthquake]; or José Agustín's (b. 1944) *De perfil* [1966; The Profile].

In 1967 Cabrera Infante published *Tres tristes tigres* [*Three Trapped Tigers* 1971] and reintroduced parody into the great literary genres in Spanish, not simply in the form of an amusing transposition of styles but parody in its finest sense of the essentialization of speech, thought, and literary tone. At its best, everything in *Three Trapped Tigers* is a parody: The forms of speech in Cuba, the satirical foray into nightlife, and Cuban literary styles. In depicting this labyrinth, simplified by the corruption and the police force of the dictatorship in Havana in the mid-1950s, Cabrera's baroque style attests to the impulse of a culture whose marginalization is destroyed by the demographic growth that brings indifference with it. In the sequence entitled "Ella cantaba boleros" [She Sang Boleros], Cabrera finds an emblem in Estrella, the obese tyrannical deity, both atrocious and magnificent at the same time, who transcends her immediate source of inspiration (Freddy, the Cuban chanteuse who died in exile, leaving just one memorable record) and includes all the women who filter emotions, legitimize wantonness, and lead to amorous ardor through the institutional means of records, juke boxes, radios, cabarets, parties, and memories, whether happy or painful. Estrella installs herself at the center of a universe of feverish lyrics and catchy tunes, verbal and melodic clichés where what is passionately experienced is balanced by the urgent need to see it memorably expressed:

Y sin música, quiero decir sin orquesta, sin acompañamiento comenzó a cantar una canción desconocida, nueva, que salía de su pecho, de sus dos enormes tetas, de su barriga de barril, de aquel cuerpo monstruoso, y apenas me dejó acordarme del cuento de la ballena que cantó en la ópera, porque ponía algo más que el falso, azucarado, sentimental, fingido sentimiento en la canción, nada de la bobería amelcochada, del sentimiento comercialmente fabricado del feeling, sino verdadero sentimiento y su voz salía suave, pastosa, líquida, con aceite ahora, una voz coloidal que fluía de todo su cuerpo como el plasma de su voz y de pronto me estremecí. Hacía tiempo que algo no me conmovía así y comencé a sonreírme en alta voz, porque acababa de reconocer la canción, a reírme, a soltar carcajadas porque era Noche de ronda y pensé, Agustín no has inventado nada, no has compuesto nada, esta mujer te está inventando tu canción ahora: ven mañana y recógela y cópiala y ponla a tu nombre de nuevo: Noche de ronda está naciendo esta noche. (1991, 67)

And without music, I mean, without orchestra, or accompaniment from radio record or tape, she started singing a new, unknown song, that welled up from her breast, from her two enormous udders, from her barrel of a belly, from that monstrous body of hers, and I hardly thought at all of the story of the whale that sang in the opera, because what she was putting into the song was something other than false, saccharine, sentimental or feigned emotion and there was nothing syrupy or corny, no fake *feeling* or commercial sentimentality about it, it was genuine soul and her voice welled up, sweet, mellow, liquid, with a touch of oil now, a colloidal voice that flowed the whole length of her body like the plasma of her voice and all at once I was overwhelmed by it. It was a long time since anything had so moved me and I began laughing at the top of my voice, because I had just recognized the song, laughing at myself, till my sides ached with the belly laughs because it was "Noche de Ronda" and I thought talking to Agustín Lara, Agustín, Agustín, you've never invented a thing, you've not ever invented a thing, you've never composed anything, for now this woman is inventing your song: when morning comes you can pick it up and copy it put your name and copyright on it again: "Noche de Ronda" is being born tonight. (1971, 62–63)

The popular was transformed and became known as the classical marginalized. If Cabrera Infante's starting point is cinematographic mythology, his readers have already been conditioned by the hegemony of television, its lack of hierarchies, its fragmentation of images, its sensuality by inference, its transfer of the meaning of reality to advertisements and its division of the world according to interest groups. As late as the 1960s, the authentically popular was a function of the rural expression. Subsequently, thanks to books such as *Three Trapped Tigers*, what was authentic could be found in the immoral realms of nightlife, in identification with cinematographic fantasy and collective dreams, and in the relation between urban life and cultural industry. The new literature, lacking any commitment to the criteria of conventional logic, revolved around national speech and archetypes or tastes that previously only warranted incidental attention. Influenced by Lewis Carroll and Vladimir Nabokov, Cabrera Infante concerned himself equally with the expression of feeling, the vitality of the Spanish–Cuban language, and the exploration of the picaresque. And the world he describes is eminently popular.

With judicious deliberation, the Argentinian Manuel Puig (1932–1990) uses Kitsch themes, scenes, vocabulary, and phrases in his early novels *La traición de Rita Hayworth* [1968; *Betrayed by Rita Hayworth*, 1971] and *Boquitas pintadas* [1969; *Heartbreak Tango*, 1973]. At that time, kitsch had neither the renown nor the false yet real prestige it enjoys today. In *Betrayed by Rita Hayworth*, Puig describes a massive phenomenon: The inauguration of modernity through the cinema that, between the 1930s and 1940s, erased the monotony of urban and rural lives. And the cinema, the core of life-that-is-worth-living, offered disconnected conversations, fragments of a verbal exercise that never ends, and situations of amorous defenselessness that are scenographies of poverty. With a hunter's stealth, Puig approaches the language of amorous simplicity and weakness, the malice and self-flagellation of popular intimacy, the set phrases that, once uttered, will become dramatic revelations, and the undoubtedly cheap sentimentalist talk that, by force of repetition, comes to mean something else. Above all, Puig approaches one of the achievements of oral culture, conversation, but transforms it into a strange epistolary, a flow of words that mark time in cities that are half-dead:

Y lo dibujé al que se casó con la tía de Alicita y me salió igual, que hice los dos ojos bien iguales grandes abiertos con pestañas y una nariz chica y la boca chica con los bigotes finitos y el pelo con el pico en la frente y sin raya como Robert Taylor, que el tío de Alicita si fuera artista haría que se casara con Luisa Rainer en El gran Ziegfeld en vez de que ella se muera, cuando está enferma y se está por morir y lo llama por teléfono al ex-esposo Ziegfeld no se ponga triste, y apenas es la mitad de la cinta pero ella no sale más porque se muere en seguida, y mucho mejor sería que en eso suena el timbre y Luisa Rainer va a abrir y es uno que se equivocó de puerta, que es el tío de Alicita, pero Luisa Rainer está tan cansada después de levantarse a hablar por teléfono que se desmaya ahí mismo en la puerta, y él entra y la levanta y llama en seguida al mandadero del hotel, porque están en un hotel de lujo, que es un chico sin padre, que el padrastro le pega. (1971b, 75)

I drew the guy who married Alicita's aunt and he came out exactly just like in real life. I made the two eyes the same, big and wide opened with eyelashes and a small nose and a small mouth with a thin mustache and his hair with the point in front and no part like Robert Taylor, and if Alicita's uncle were an actor, I'd have him marry Louise Rainer in *The Great Ziegfeld* instead of having her die, when she's sick and about to die and she makes a telephone call to her ex-husband Ziegfeld who left her for another woman and she tells him she's not sick any more so Ziegfeld won't get sad, and it's only the middle of the movie but you don't see her anymore because she dies right away, and it would be much better if at that moment the doorbell rings and Louise Rainer goes to open it and it's a guy who came to the wrong door and it's Alicita's uncle, but Louise Rainer is so tired after getting up to talk on the telephone that she faints right there at the door and he comes in and picks her up and calls the bellboy right away, because they're in a first-class hotel, he's a boy without a father and his stepfather hits him. (1971a, 58–59)

And so on, ad infinitum. Oh, Rita. Oh, Greta. Oh, Joan Crawford. Puig reiterates the scene that would become commonplace over the next few decades. Most of the time, we the viewers no longer come from the jungle or the savanna and are no longer defined by the shock of recognition of the concrete jungle; nor are we descended from traditions destroyed by capitalism. We come from dreadful, glorious films, from contrasting the darkness of our lives with the severe brilliance witnessed in those dark rooms and we make the world we inhabit a false mirror of these images; we want to expropriate idols and lessons from Hollywood, that happy native land of real, ideal solitary creatures. A moral can be drawn from the limbo inhabited by Puig's characters: In Salta or Boyacá, in Medellín or Santo Domingo, and in Irapuato or San Salvador, an initially technical detail (the disproportion of the close-up in exalting the female face) creates a different mentality. Greta Garbo, Ginger Rogers, Bette Davis, Katherine Hepburn, Barbara Stanwyck, Marlene Dietrich, and Dolores del Río offer privileged features, clothes, and ways of walking or smoking, converting singularity into a mass utopia; they are the onirical devastation that helps millions of people to move toward compulsory modernization. What was popular was what could be intentified with on screen.

In *Heartbreak Tango*, Puig strips away the false candor of pulp fiction, producing a ferocious parody of the language attributed to the people, while he examines feelings (now indistinguishable from sentimentalism) that provide the raw material of self-hypnosis and aspirations (Puig 1973). These are everyday acts and tragedies: Washing dishes, changing one's clothes, going out to buy bread, sitting down in front of the mirror, putting on lipstick and powdering one's nose, putting a hand under a girlfriend's blouse, waiting behind bars, and mistaking hunger for ambition:

Si supiera que la pobre Pelusa nunca comió milanesas y la noche que llovió tanto y no me podía volver a casa y la Felisa hizo milanesas, después cuando el señor me llevó en el coche después de cenar, me acosté con la Pelusa y le conté lo de las milanesas. La Pelusa me destapó la barriga y me pasó la mano fría por la barriga para ver si se tocaban las milanesas. (1971b, 28-9)

If you only knew that poor Fuzzy has never once had veal cutlets and the night it rained so hard I couldn't go home and Felisa made veal cutlets, and afterwards when Mister Berto took me home in the car after dinner, I went to bed with Fussy and told her about the cutlets. Fuzzy uncovered my tummy and ran her cold hand along my tummy to see if she could touch the cutlets. (1971a, 22)

Puig re-elaborates the traditional "Romantic" styles of Latin America (sighs, maneuvering between pillows, sexual harassment, and the arrival of Prince Charming, who is as decent and handsome as a movie star), using language that is neither above nor to one side of his characters, which neither deprives them of authority nor patronizes them. In *Heartbreak Tango*, Puig makes desolation a favorable atmosphere for tenderness. Here, the popular serves as an inexhaustible landscape for literary emotion.

The Sound of Experience

What does a society sound like? What noise does it make? Is it a dodecaphony, a waltz, acid rock, rap, or the rhythm of *son* and rumba dancers, sinuous, unending, and rattling? In *La guaracha del Macho Camacho* by Luis Rafael Sánchez, which, on one level, is the story of a hit song, literary reality does not follow a logical course; it is both simultaneous and contradictory, the meeting between a political discourse and a *guaracha* in the midst of demented traffic. To demonstrate this, Sánchez combines neoclassical rhetoric and *salsa*, a call to the distinguished patricians and terrific events. One of the verses in the song says, "La vida es una cosa fenomenal/tanto p'al de adelante/como p'al de atrás" [Life is a wonderful thing, both for the guy ahead and for the guy behind]. The complications of the plot, that enslaving *conga* that we in Mexico or San Juan, Puerto Rico, call Social Life, mean that everyday life is a bit too serious:

Cuestión de unos pagarés y el linolium y el jueguito de comedor que lo quiero de cromium: pincela lujos menores como una mesita velador cubierta con tapetito bordado, con repollito tejido. No es que vaya a pasarse la vida con El Viejo, El Viejo le produce náuseas. Pero El Viejo le remite el chequecito verde de las esperanzas. Seis meses: tanto tiempo sujetá no le piace. La ventaja de estar sujetá es la obligación de amanecer todos los días lo mismo: el lavao, el planchao, el cocinao. Por eso es que yo admiro a Iris Chacón: habla de la artista Iris Chacón y le da asma. Porque Iris Chacón no está sujeta más que al impulso bailotero de su cuerpo. Por la noche sueña que la artista Iris Chacón, envuelta en emanaciones guarachiles, viene a buscarla: quedito, callandito, secretera, la artista Iris Chacón le dice. Nunca sabe lo que la artista Iris Chacón quiere decirle porque despierta, ay deja eso, terminados los pagarés y si te vi ya no me acuerdo. Las cinco y: y qué más dá, los pies conjuntan una bullanga como si el eructo fuera la luz verde para el brinqueto, el eructo o la acojonante guaracha del Macho Camacho La vida es una cosa Fenomenal, guaracha que le prende el fogón a los que no están en nada. Los pechos golpean las costuras del brassier, ricamente nervudos aunque amasaditos en la base. Las caderas se dejan caer en remolinos y la cintura las recoge en remolinos. La cabeza dibuja uno, dos, tres círculos que se corresponden con los tres chorros de ventosidad regocijado que expelen las trompetas; una alegría ceremonial, culto oficiado en cada rincón del cuerpo, cuerpo elevado esta tarde a templo del sudor con nalgas briosas como ofrendas ovaladas y tembluzcas. (1982, 182–83)

A matter of a few IOUs and the linoleum and the little dining-room set I want in chrome: she sketches out minor luxuries like a night-table covered with an embroidered mat, with lace trim. It isn't as if she's going to spend her whole life with The Old Man. The Old Man makes her puke. But The Old Man sends her the little green check of hope. Six months: so much time being kept doesn't give her any *piacere*. The advantage of being kept is that the eats are kept. The disadvantage of being kept is the obligation of getting up every morning just the same: washing, ironing, cooking. That's why I admire Iris Chacón: she talks about Iris Chacón the performer and she gets an asthma attack. Because Iris Chacón isn't kept by anything except the danceable impulse of her body. At night, she dreams that Iris Chacón the performer, enwrapped in guarachile emanations, comes to get her: softlike, quietlike, secrety, Iris Chacón the performer tells her. She never finds out what Iris Chacón the performer wants to tell her because she wakes up, oh forget it, no more IOUs and if I saw you, I can't remember. Five o'clock and: so what difference does it make, her feet making a riot as if the belch were a green light of rollicking, the belch or Macho Camacho's bollocking *gauracha Life is a Phenomenal Thing*, a guaracha that lights the stoves of people who aren't anywhere. Her breasts surge against the seams of her bra, rich and sinewy although doughy at the base. Her hips fall into a grind and her waist picks up the grind. Her head outlines one, two, three circles that correspond to the three gusts of joyful windiness that the trumpets expel; a ceremonial joy, a rite officiated in every corner of her body, a body elevated this afternoon to a temple of sweat, with buttocks as ovalate and trembling offerings. (1980, 164–65)

Another Puerto Rican writer, Edgardo Rodríguez Juliá (b. 1946), has produced two excellent works, *El entierro de Cortijo* [1983; The Funeral of Cortijo] and *Una noche con Iris Chacón* [1984; A Night with Iris Chacon], in much the same vein.

At a given moment, when the forces of the left moved away, realist literature failed to convince its readers. How could one find "what was real" in sordidness, in people who wept every time they remembered they were poor, in agonies of misfortune at not having been born with a silver spoon in their mouths, in people frenetically railing against the trap from which they need to escape, this shanty town, these slums, this popular neighborhood? Who could possibly be interested in finding "what was real" in the hamlets submerged in mud, venereal disease, illiteracy, incestuous relationships, and the dramatic awareness of being? The popular required a different approach. The increase in educational level facilitated change and demanded a nonpatronizing approach towards the popular. It was not a question of approving or disapproving, but rather of understanding and describing without a paternalistic bias. In *Las glorias del Gran Púas*, Ricardo Garibay (b. 1923) chooses as protagonist for his story, a boxing idol and converts the boxer's everyday life into a battle, a struggle against windmills. Pursued by fame and hounded by the media, Rubén Olivares (El Púas) personifies the rites of passage from poverty to celebrity, at which point the author begins to play with the legend. El Púas is a living scandal and a means of retaliation for the millions of people who could never become living scandals, even if they wished to do so. If El Púas succeeded, then why subject oneself to any discipline, why not submerge oneself in pulque and marijuana, why not lead a life of dissipation before they box you in, and why not surround yourself with a court of drunkenness? Authorized by success, El Púas took only chaos (the incapacity to become civilized) seriously, fell in love with obscenity, the regenerative matrix, and converted his extreme experience as a macho, drunk, and drug addict into a perpetual flow of speech.

In *Hasta no verte, Jesús mío*, Elena Poniatowska treats speech both as source of biography and as worldview and so records the voice of a woman who lived through the Revolution, became progressively disenchanted, and eventually ended up in the same position she had been in at the beginning, with experience and resentment as her only possessions. What in Oscar Lewis's *The Children of Sánchez* (1961) tends to dissolve into the picturesqueness or fatalism of the culture of poverty, in Elena Poniatowska's reconstruction becomes suffering that is not confined to anecdotes. In her loneliness, Jesusa Palancares, a woman who has experienced the misery of generations, a revolutionary, servant, and worker, resorts to an aggressive language that is poetic in spite of itself in order to distance herself ironically from bitterness. Thus, she relates her progress through relentlessly tiring work, describing the fate of the poor with and without determinism, yet avoiding self-pity as far as possible:

Y desde entonces todos fueron fábricas y fábricas y talleres y changarros y piqueras y pulquerías y cantinas y salones de baile y más fábricas y talleres y lavaderos y señoras fregonas y tortillas duras y dale y dale con la bebedera del pulque, tequila y hojas en la madrugada para las crudas. Y amigas y amigos que no servían para nada, y perros que me dejaban sola por andar siguiendo a sus perras. Y hombres peores que perros del mal y policías ladrones y pelados abusivos. Y yo siempre sola, y el muchacho que recogí de chiquito y que se fue y me dejó más sola y me saludas a nunca vuelvas y no es por ai María voltéate y yo como lanzarina, encerrada en mi cazuela, y en la calle cada vez menos brava y menos peleonera porque me hice vieja y ya no se me calienta la sangre y se me acabaron las fuerzas y se me cayó el pelo y nomás me quedaron unas clavijas por dientes rascándome con mis uñas, pero ya ni uñas tengo de tantos uñeros que me salieron en la lavadera. Y aquí estoy ya nomás esperando a que den las cinco de la mañana porque ni siquiera duermo y nomás se me revela todo lo que pasé desde chiquilla, cuando anduve de guacha y sin guarache, haciéndole a la revolución como jugando a la gallina ciega, recibiendo puros trancazos, cada vez más desmadejada en esta chingadera de vida. (143)

And after that it was all factories and more factories and workshops and small shops and night-clubs and saloons, bars and dance halls and more factories and workshops and washing places and washer women and stale tortillas and endlessly drinking pulque and tequila and herb teas in the morning to get rid of your hangover. And friends who were good for nothing and dogs who would leave me to follow their bitches. And men who were worse than dogs and thieving policemen and abusive wretches. And I was always on my own, and the boy I took in as a baby went off, leaving me more lonely than ever, and it was good-bye, forever, and no, not there María, get lost, and there I was, as though I'd been evicted, shut up in my little room, and when I went out, I wasn't as tough or aggressive as before, because I got old, and I don't get so worked up about things anymore and I've used up all my strength, and my hair fell out and all I have left is a few pegs instead of teeth, and I have to scratch a living but I don't even have any nails left after all the ingrown nails I got from spending so much time washing clothes. So here I am, just waiting for it to be five in the morning, because I can't even sleep anymore, I just go over everything I've done ever since I was a young girl, when I worked as a look-out and went around without sandals, playing at the revolution without the faintest idea what I was doing and just getting hit and growing weaker and weaker in this god-awful life.

The Idols: "He's Just Like Me, Except that He Is So Good that He Doesn't Resemble Me at All"

Cinema idols, record and variety show idols–for a time, they were regarded as the representatives par excellence of the congenital ignorance and poor taste of the rabble. Taken as a whole, they offer a theory of popular culture, a series of ideal portraits of collectivities. Who today could replace Agustín Lara, Pedro Infante, José Alfredo Jiménez, and the Los Panchos trio in Mexico; Carlos Gardel in Argentina; Julio Jaramillo in Ecuador; Rafael Hernández, Pedro Flores, and Daniel Santos in Puerto Rico; or Celia Cruz and Beny Moré in the realm of tropical music? They have been and remain unique responses to the theme or problem of popular expressivity. The enduringness of these idols had made them such potent signs of Latin American identity that a growing literary trend has begun to exploit them, often venerating them in the process. José Alfredo's vision-of-the-conquered is recreated by the Colombian David Sánchez Juliao (b. 1945) in *Pero sigo siendo el rey* [1983; But I Am Still the King], whereas Celia Cruz is idolized by Umberto Valverde in *Celia Cruz, reina Rumba* [1981; Celia Cruz, Queen Rumba], and the Puerto Rican *bolero* composer is the core of Luis Rafael Sánchez's *La importancia de llamarse Daniel Santos*. In hundreds of stories, the main ingredient is pop culture itself, not the people or the industry that conditions them but the anomalous result of joining commercial ambition and artistic creation. The fervor for sentimental and sexual themes is reflected in sales figures (this is the enduring attraction of *cumbia, merengue, danzón, salsa, bolero, ranchera,* and *vallenato*), proving that, beyond the industry's promotional efforts, a social contract remains that grants one party (the Idol) the gift of providing lasting images and sounds for desires and obsessions, while the other party (the public/the people) is committed to reproducing and imaginatively adulterating the models available to it. Popular music, at its various levels, thus signifies the unfalsifiable authenticity of millions of people.

Among Autographs: The New Cultural Past

In the era of videocassettes, satellites, records, video music, walkmans, supershows, satellite dishes, virtual reality, cyberspace, Internet, and e-mail, technology provides a worldview that forces one to reconcile literary forms and popular taste. The glorification of popular forms is undoubtedly a fashion and, as such, will eventually be extinguished, thanks to opportunism, populist imitations, the reduction of *bolero* lyrics to philosophical aphorisms, prefabricated poetry, and stereotypical concepts of people. Or perhaps coarse sexual action or police realism will destroy it. But there is something that is nonetheless irreversible: Numerous classist prohibitions have disappeared and, as far as the enlightened sectors are concerned, there has been a considerable downscaling of the battle between high and popular culture as a result of the constant blending of the two ancestral adversaries. Nowadays, everything influences everything else, as Alfonso Reyes might have said if he had commented on realms so diverse as soap operas and unemployment and the *cumbias* dedicated to Macondo and the conversion of Picasso and Mozart into ultra-popular works and names.

The popular also primarily entails a generally self-assured approach to sexuality and the depiction of real human events that are often either denied or alluded to euphemistically. Suddenly, forbidden ideologies and behaviors and vocabulary once regarded as illicit begin to appear in literature. Popular new themes emerge: Clinging to the world through technology; the disappearance of the mysterious or sinful aura surrounding sexual matters; the standardized description of appetites and intercourse; government and police corruption as politics' homage to the cinema; mountains of condoms in rubbish dumps; and the existence of comics and CDs. The present and the past are perhaps both contained in the present. The past, read nowadays, reveals tensions, that is, different relationships from those traditionally assumed between reality and utopia and between literature and community life. And the present is also already contemplated in a nostalgic fashion; everything flashes by so quickly that it is impossible to capture emotions or hang on to a moment. New experiences give pleasure precisely because they are not novel. What is postmodern here is the evocation of the now-extinct worship of progress. One chooses an ideal world, the Chile, Costa Rica, or Peru that one would have liked to inhabit, and furnishes it with the relevant passions, dialogues, and reactions possible before the cultural industry produced its swiftly legitimized and authenticated results. In its own way, this is another form of magic realism, the return to the past as the marvelously real, as the time when what was popular actually existed. Nowadays, many Latin Americans increasingly feel that they are, after all, walking (or sedentary) museums of popular culture.

In an excellent essay, "Globalization and the Crisis in the Popular," Jean Franco analyzes the outlook for today: "The popular" was formerly an index of Latin American difference, a difference that was measured by *distance* from the metropolis by the class who were closest to the metropolis and that acted as the foundation for nationhood (the independent *gaucho*, the "authentic" rural population). But, equally, popular culture served as an index of "underdevelopment" (it was pre-Enlightenment, preliterate), of tradition as opposed to progress, backwardness as opposed to modernity, "malandragem" [trickery], "choteo" [mockery], and "relajo" [lack of discipline] as opposed to the work ethic (209). The popular is a sign of the time prior to globalization, when (although neoliberals may jeer) nations and national communities still existed. The popular is already an encounter between a happy past and memory. Now, suddenly, everything is a hybrid culture (to use Nestor García Canclini's expression) or an example of fusion (to use the term from the record industry) or syncretism (if one wishes to depict the Virgin of Guadalupe in a hologram). Modernity interprets tradition; the Third World is the postmodernists' hell, and neoliberals credit inequality, the most significant cultural aspect of Latin America, with the role of civilization (they're poor because that is their atavistic impulse). One is reminded of Juan Rulfo's remark: It is up to writers to contribute realism or unreality; what is really magical is the fact that readers actually exist.

Translation by Suzanne D. Stephens

Works Cited

Agustín, José. 1976. *De perfil.* Mexico City: J. Mortiz.

Alegría, Ciro. 1945. *El mundo es ancho y ajeno.* New York: F. S. Crofts & Co.

Arlt, Roberto. 1981. *El juguete rabioso.* Buenos Aires: Losada.

——. 1992. *Los siete locos.* Madrid: Cátedra.

Azuela, Mariano. 1931a. *Los caciques.* Mexico City: Ediciones "La Razón".

——. 1931b. *Las moscas.* Mexico City: Ediciones "La Razón".

——. 1963. *The Underdogs: A Novel of the Mexican Revolution.* Trans. E. Munguía, Jr. New York: Signet Classics.

———. 1970 [1915]. *Los de abajo: novela de la revolución mexicana*. Mexico City: Fondo de Cultura Económica.

———. 1972. *Two Novels of Mexico: The Flies. The Bosses*. Trans. Lesley Byrd Simpson. Berkeley: University of California Press.

Biely, Andrei. 1978. *Petersburg*. Trans. Robert A. Maguire and John E. Malmstad. Bloomington: Indiana University Press.

Borges, Jorge Luis. 1974. *Obras completas*. Buenos Aires: Emecé.

Bulnes, Francisco. 1960. *Toda la verdad acerca de la Revolución Mexicana. La responsabilidad criminal del presidente Wilson en el desastre mexicano*. Mexico City: Los Insurgentes.

Cabrera Infante, Guillermo. 1971. *Three Trapped Tigers*. Trans. Donald Gardner and Suzanne Jill Levine. New York: Marlowe & Co.

———. 1991 [1967]. *Tres tristes tigres*. Barcelona: Editorial Seix Barral.

Cortázar, Julio. 1967. *El perseguidor y otros cuentos*. Buenos Aires: Centro Editor de América Latina.

———. 1984. *Rayuela*. Madrid: Cátedra.

Dos Passos, John. 1925. *Manhattan Transfer*. New York: Harper.

———. 1937. *U.S.A.:1. The 42nd parallel; 2. Nineteen nineteen; 3. The Money*. New York: Modern Library.

Franco, Jean. 1999. "Globalization and the Crisis of the Popular." *Critical Passions: Selected Essays*. Ed. Mary. L. Pratt and Kathleen Newman. Durham, N.C.: Duke University Press. 208–220.

Fuentes, Carlos. 1960. *Where the Air Is Clear*. Trans. Sam Hileman. New York: Ivan Obolensky, Inc.

———. 1968 [1958] *La región más transparente*. Mexico City: Fondo de Cultura Económica.

Gallegos, Romulo. [1934]. *Cantaclaro*. Barcelona: Araluce.

———. 1942. *Doña Bárbara*. New York: Appleton-Century-Croft.

———. 1991. *Canaima*. Madrid: Ediciones de Cultura Hispánica.

Gamboa, Federico. 1927. *Santa*. Mexico City: Eusebio Gómez de la Puente.

García Canclini, Nestor. 1992. *Culturas híbridas: estrategias para entrar y salir de la modernidad*. Buenos Aires: Sudamericana.

García Márquez, Gabriel. 1970. *One Hundred Years of Solitude*. Trans. Gregory Rabassa. New York: Harper and Row.

Garibay, Ricardo. 1978. *Las glorias del Gran Púas*. Mexico City: Grijalbo.

———. 1979. *Acapulco*. Mexico City: Grijalbo.

Guzmán, Martín Luis. 1941. *El aguila y la serpiente*. Mexico City: Editorial Anahuac.

———. 1983. *La sombra del caudillo*. Mexico City: Editorial Porrúa.

Icaza, Jorge. 1937. *Huasipungo*. Quito: Editorial Atahualpa.

Kerouac, Jack. 1958. *On the Road*. New York: Viking.

———. 1986. *The Dharma Bums*. New York: Penguin.

Le Bon, Gustave. 1960. *The Crowd: A Study of the Popular Mind*. New York: Viking. [1928. *Psychologie des foules*. Paris: Felix Alcan.]

Lewis, Oscar. 1961. *The Children of Sánchez*. New York: Random House.

Marechal, Leopoldo. 1966. *Adán BuenosAyres*. Buenos Aires: Sudamericana.

Muñoz, Rafael F. 1935. *Vámonos con Pancho Villa*. Buenos Aires: Espasa-Calpe.

———. 1944. *Se llevaron el cañón para Bachimba*. Buenos Aires: Espasa-Calpe.

Nervo, Amado. 1951–52. *Obras completas*. Madrid: Aguilar.

Ortega y Gasset, José. 1930. *La Rebelión de las masas*. Madrid: Revista de Occidente.

Payno, Manuel. 1945. *Los bandidos del Río Frío*. Ed. Antonio Castro Leal. Mexico City: Editorial Porrúa.

Poniatowska, Elena. 1980. *Fuerte es el silencio*. Mexico City: Ediciones Era.

———. 1984. *Hasta no verte Jesús mío*. Mexico City: Ediciones Era.

———. 1988. *Nada, nadie: las voces del temblor*. Mexico City: Era.

Puig, Manuel. 1971a. *Betrayed by Rita Hayworth*. Trans. Suzanne Jill Levine. New York: E. P. Dutton & Co.

———. 1971b [1968]. *La traición de Rita Hayworth*. Barcelona: Seix Barral.

———. 1969. *Boquitas pintadas*. Buenos Aires: Sudamericana.

———. 1973. *Heartbreak Tango*. Trans. Suzanne Jill Levine. New York: Dutton.

Rivera, José Eustacio. 1935. *The Vortex*. Trans. Earle K. James. London: Putnam.

———. *La vorágine*. 1972 [1924]. Mexico City: Universidad Nacional Autónoma de México, Dirección General de Publicaciones.

Rodríguez Juliá, Edgardo. 1983. *El entierro de Cortijo (6 de octubre de 1982)*. Rio Piedras, P.R.: Ediciones Huracán.

———. 1986. *Una noche con Iris Chacón*. Río Piedras, P.R.: Editorial Antillana.

Rulfo, Juan. 1953. *El llano en llamas y otros cuentos*. Mexico City: Fondo de Cultura Económica.

———. 1994. *Pedro Páramo*. Trans. Margaret Sayers Peden. London: Serpent's Tail.

Sánchez, Luis Rafael. 1980. *Macho Camacho's Beat*. Trans. Gregory Rabassa. New York: Pantheon Books.

———. 1982 [1976]. *La guaracha del Macho Camacho*. Barcelona: Argos Vergara.

———. 1988. *La importancia de llamarse Daniel Santos*. Hanover, N.H.: Ediciones del Norte.

Sánchez Juliao, David. 1983. *Pero sigo siendo el rey (Sinfonía para lector y mariachi, opus l.)*. Bogotá: Plaza y Janés.

Sarmiento, Domingo Faustino. 1998. *Facundo or Civilization and Barbarism*. Trans. Mary Mann. New York: Penguin.

Valverde, Umberto. 1981. *Celia Cruz, reina rumba*. Bogota: La oveja negra.

Vasconcelos, José. 1958. *Obras completas*. Mexico City: Libreros Mexicanos Unidos.

Williams, Raymond. 1973. *The Country and the City*. London: Chatto and Windus.

SECTION V
CINEMA: CULTURAL DIALOGUES AND THE PROCESS OF MODERNITY

CHAPTER 65

CULTURAL DIALOGUES AND THE PROCESS OF MODERNITY

Julianne Burton-Carvajal and Zuzana M. Pick

A Thoroughly Modern Practice

Cinema, the hegemonic mode of cultural expression during the twentieth century in Latin America as elsewhere, is a multidimensional practice, absorbing and transforming the artistic and mass media modalities that preceded it, including literature and drama, music and dance, art and iconography, and photography and radio. How have particular forms, agendas, technologies, institutions, ideologies, policies, and practices–interacting at regional, national, continental, and international levels–contributed to the production, circulation, reception, impact, and understanding of the film medium in Latin America? How have these changed over time in relation to formal, artistic, technological, economic, social, political, and historical transformations?

As art form, mass-mediated entertainment, industrial practice, social engineering mechanism, ideological weapon, consolidator of citizenry and national identity, marketing machine, and component of an electronically ubiquitous *espacio audiovisual,* the film medium requires a multi-faceted approach if we are to understand its pivotal role as both expression and shaper of culture. Meeting the challenge to assess its impact likewise entails marshaling a range of comparative approaches. The method of analysis employed here explores several debates and antinomies that have been at the center of film-related debates–popular versus mass versus elite culture, forging the nation, industrial versus artisanal modes of production, regional cycles and metropolitan versus peripheral traditions, regionalism versus national consolidation, dependency versus transculturation, and commercial versus oppositional cinemas. It then considers various constructs employed to confer meaning and assign value to cinematic works and then finally, in the conclusion, looks beyond the modernity paradigm toward the film medium's evolving role in the third millennium.

Popular, Mass, or Elite Culture?

Within the panorama of Latin American cultural expression, film has been not simply a manifestation of mass or popular or high culture but, to varying degrees and at different times, all three of these. In its production and circulation, the cinema asserted itself as a preferred means of constructing and reinforcing social bonds among national, sub-national, and pan-national communities and of (re)defining the changing nature of those bonds. The medium was, in this sense, a great socializer–a laboratory and a catechism, in the apt and often-invoked characterizations of Mexican cultural critic Carlos Monsiváis, who was among the first to identify the medium's role as modernizer and nation-builder (1994, 7–10).

No national cinema tradition managed to sustain the chimeric goal of replicating Hollywood's studio-based, industrial model of film production (and neither, in the end, did Hollywood), but in the three countries that came closest to this persistent if impractical aspiration–Mexico, Brazil, and Argentina–cinema became the most important register of national/popular culture, in part through its ability to incorporate social types, costumes, customs, landscapes, and then later speech patterns and musical traditions, into composites that came to symbolize both the national and the popular. These composites–manipulated, often arbitrary, and even tendentious constructions–took on a life of their own in the sphere of reception. In Mexico during the 1930s, for instance, "the public plagarised the cinema as much as possible: Its way of speaking and gesturing, its humor, respect for institutions, and its typical perspectives on duties and pleasures . . ." (Monsiváis 1995, 117).

In the case of Mexican cinema, unrivaled dissemination throughout the Spanish-speaking world and Brazil helps explain why the very specific historical and cultural imaginary invoked was widely embraced throughout the Spanish-speaking world as an expression of a shared supranational imaginary. Whatever linguistic advantage that Mexican films held over films made in other languages among "the poorer sectors of large urban centers and in rural areas where illiteracy was the norm," it was the successful development and sustained reworking of autochthonous generic forms, such as the *comedia ranchera,* the revolutionary epic, and the urban melodrama, that won over audiences by merging the allure of the picturesque with the reassurance of the familiar (López 1994, 7).

After mid-century, television's successful conquest of the mass audience, combined with cinema's ever-escalating costs and declining returns, made film an increasingly elite form of expression. The occasional international commercial success of films from Mexico or Brazil, Argentina or Cuba, or Chile or Bolivia now occurs in a radically altered context, because these films now circulate as part of an international art cinema that "speaks with a different voice to a radically different audience" (López 1994, 12); they are relatively indifferent to national specificity and target privileged rather than popular audiences.

Forging the Nation

Introduced in most Latin American nations within a few years of its "invention" in 1895 as a form of mass entertainment, cinema soon established itself as one of the obligatory instances of both modernity and nationhood. From "technological wonder and curiosity," through "the desire for self-representation," to "the potential for profit," cinema's "ability to generate a classless 'mass' audience" was equated with an ability to generate "symbolically, the nation itself" (King et al. xix).

The earliest images filmed in Latin America by the Lumière operators, who were sent from Paris to criss-cross the nations and regions of the continent, served only to augment the heterogeneity of the parent company's programs. Before long, these very brief *vistas* or "views" were made almost exclusively by local operators, among them many European immigrants who would play a key role in documenting social and political events of national if not international significance. In Mexico, as the new medium entered its second decade, cinema "showed images of the Revolution that no literary equivalent could match" and "constituted a vernacular form for the representation of contemporary events" (Reyes 1995, 71). In Brazil, where the growth of exhibition coincided with the electrification of the country, newsreel and fictional films were aligned to images of progress registering not only changes in the urban landscapes but numerous local campaigns of social improvement (Galvão 1987, 53).

In no country has cinema been more central to the deliberate construction of a new, homogenizing national consciousness than in Mexico, a circumstance that is the product of multiple, overlapping determinants. Foremost among them is the coincidence in the 1930s of the ascendant phase of the newly sonorized film medium and the consolidation phase of the postrevolutionary regime. Yet film historian Aurelio de los Reyes argues that the nationalist impulse is inherent to the entire trajectory of Mexican filmmaking, in the uses to which the fledgling medium was put from the time of its introduction during the last decade of Porfirio Díaz's thirty-year regime as well as in his successors' eagerness, during the second and third decades of the twentieth century, to export on film "the richness and beauty, the civilized and useful aspects" of Mexican culture to a world already woefully misled by Hollywood's distorted representations of Mexicans (1983, 228).

A contrasting instance can be found in Brazil, where nationhood had been articulated until the 1930s through "the idea of a new nation with a great future" (Xavier 9). Particularly in its second and third decades, film production flourished in Brazil, but because it was inevitably tied to the economic and political realities of neocolonial dependency, cinema was subject to cyclical declines even in the pre–World War I period, when Hollywood-based distributors and exhibitors began to seize control of the national market, and more markedly in the wake of the introduction of sound in the 1930s. Incipient production from various regions of this vast country was chronically marginalized, creating a situation in which "American cinema so saturated the market and occupied so much space in the collective imagination . . . that it seemed to belong to us" (Salles Gomes 247). In the early 1950s, the collapse of the Vera Cruz film production company–the last major Latin

American initiative to implement an industrial production system–confirmed "the pervasive influence of underdevelopment" and brought about "alternative proposals [that] made underdevelopment the cornerstone of the very identity of Brazilian cinema" (Galvão 1995, 271).

Since World War II, in nearly every instance of sociopolitical transformation toward a more functionally inclusive conceptualization of the nation, cinema has been the instrument of choice in the (re)definition of the national project and the enlistment of previously excluded or underrepresented national constituencies. Among the historical turning points that emphasized the film medium were the following: The Castro regime in Cuba from 1959, peasant and student mobilizations in Brazil prior to the 1964 military coup, student and worker mobilizations in Mexico City that ended in the Plaza Tlatelolco massacre of 1968, the Popular Unity period under Salvador Allende's presidency in Chile (1970–73) and the decade preceding it, the Sandinista regime in Nicaragua (1979–1990), the Salvadorean civil war, postdictatorial processes of redemocratization in the Southern Cone nations during the 1980s, and Bolivia's ethno-democratic resurgence in the 1990s. Two of these historical conjunctures in particular, Cuban cinema of the 1960s and 1970s and Argentine cinema of the 1980s, offer exemplary instances of film as the means by which a revised national project can be both formulated and promulgated. The new social movements of the 1980s and 1990s–women's, indigenous, and environmental movements, for example–are also associated with this audiovisual imperative, though their medium of choice is increasingly video because of its lower costs and greater flexibility.

Industrial versus Artisanal Modes of Production

Latin American cinema practices have continuously oscillated between industrial aspirations and artisanal necessities. A significant number of recently rediscovered female film pioneers from the 1920s through the 1940s–for example, Brazil's Carmen Santos and Gilda de Abreu and Mexico's Mimi Derba, Adela Sequeyro, and Matilde Landeta–were involved in attempts to found production companies. Not surprisingly, their efforts turned out to be as ephemeral as those of their male counterparts; likewise, their mode of production was more artisanal than industrial in the end.

Even a country as tiny as Uruguay aspired to a national film industry as early as the late 1930s. Chile, having seen its high point of production with the fifteen features filmed in 1925, made a concerted attempt in the 1940s under the government agency Chile Films to produce for both domestic and export audiences, importing prominent talent from elsewhere in the hemisphere. Venezuela's Bolívar Films, founded in 1940 by Luis Guillermo Villegas Blanco, employed a similar transhemispheric strategy in the production of eight features between 1949 and the mid-1950s. In the 1960s, the appropriateness of the industrial model began to be questioned at the same time that critics started to emphasize the personalized signature of directorial expression (auteurism) over the characteristic studio stamp of formulaic genre pictures.

Mexico's major studios were founded over three decades, from Chapultepec (later Nacional Productora) in 1922 to Clasa in 1935, Azteca in 1937, Churubusco (co-funded by Hollywood's RKO Studios) in 1944, and San Angel Inn, precursor to the still-mighty televisual producer Televisa, in 1949. If the fifty features produced in 1938 suggested the imminent attainment of industrial stature for the Mexican effort, the drop to twenty-nine just two years later signaled the precariousness of an enterprise that would persistently cycle from boom to crisis. Successfully broadening its markets with assistance from the United States during World War II, Mexican studios increased production to between seventy and seventy-five films annually from 1943 to 1945, and to over 100 between 1949 and 1951. Yet the industry was riddled with problems and conflicts throughout even its most prolific decade, with assorted bankruptcies, mergers, and struggles between state and foreign interests continuing into the 1970s, when production entered into a prolonged decline. In the ensuing decade, major Mexican studios began to be broken up through sell-outs to foreign producers and reconversion to other uses. In the early 1990s, the government's renewed interest in promoting quality cinema as a prestige product was undermined by transformations in the distribution and exhibitions sectors brought about by the North American Free Trade Agreement, changes which prompted eventual passage of a new national film law at the end of the decade.

Neither Brazil nor Argentina, Mexico's only rivals in the hemisphere, saw sustained studio-based production on the Mexican scale, though at its short-lived highpoint in 1942, when fifty-six features were produced, Argentina employed 4,000 technicians in thirty studios. Production was curtailed the following year because the United States market, favoring allied Mexico and in retaliation for Argentina's official neutrality, refused to furnish raw film stock. Potential for postwar expansion was undermined by a series of military interventions, beginning with Juan Perón's in 1945 and continuing through the so-called *Proceso* (Process of National Reorganization) from 1976–1983. During these decades, filmmaking, along with other forms of cultural expression, was chronically curtailed by censorship, the only significant exceptions being brief effervescences in the early 1960s and again in the mid-1970s. Despite the notable resurgence of national film production with the return to democratic government and the abolition of censorship in 1983, the massive closing of theaters and decline in audiences has meant that even the most long-lived of the Argentine studios, Aries and Argentina Sono Film, have disappeared or been reconsecrated to the production of the more profitable *telenovelas* (televised soap operas).

In Brazil, Adhemar Gonzaga founded the Cinédia studios in 1930 in imitation of the Hollywood model. Rio de Janeiro's Atlantida studios saw their heyday in the 1940s and 1950s with the production of scores of carnival-linked *chanchadas*, an autochthonous parodic genre, usually musical, as adored by audiences as it was repudiated by critics. The last and most spectacular attempt at industrialization on the Hollywood model took place in Brazil in the late 1940s. His prestigious association with the French avant-garde and English documentary movements as well as Britain's respected Ealing Studios made Brazilian-born, European-educated Alberto Cavalcanti the top choice to take the helm of the state-of-the-art Vera Cruz film production company, an ambitious venture bankrolled by São Paulo's powerful Matarazzo investment group. The financial failure of this controversial initiative, which produced eighteen features between 1949 and 1954, generated much rancor and recrimination, particularly after the profits of its principle success on both the domestic and international markets, Lima Barreto's (1906–1982) *O cangaceiro* [1953; The Outlaw], went directly to the coffers of Columbia Pictures because Vera Cruz lacked its own distribution apparatus. According to the leading historian of São Paulo-based cinema, "Vera Cruz was historically the most complete realization Brazil has known of the film industry myth" (Galvão 1995, 271).

A set of industrial practices in even their more artisanal incarnations, the "moving pictures" soon increasingly required a powerful marketing engine. At the close of the twentieth century, the film medium, along with its once-rival television, was absorbed into an audiovisual space that integrates electronic and digital modes into an ever more omnipresent and omnivorous "visual culture."

Regional Cycles and Metropolitan versus Peripheral Traditions

Throughout continental Latin America, where people continue to self-identify primarily on the basis of their province or region, the existence of sporadic regional filmmaking traditions should not be overlooked. Sometimes these are associated with individuals: Humberto Mauro and the Cataguazes "cycle" in the Brazilian state of Minas Gerais during the 1920s and '30s, Manuel and Víctor Chambi's "Cuzco School" in Peru's ancient Inca capital in the 1950s, and Fernando Birri's Documentary School at Santa Fé in Argentina in the early 1960s. In other instances, a regional production center has focused the efforts of numerous individuals across one or more generations: Guadalajara, Mexico, in the late 1940s and again from the 1970s, thanks to the repertory efforts of independent screenwriter-director Jaime Humberto Hermosillo; Mérida as the foremost center of film school activity in Venezuela since the 1960s; Medellín and Cali as alternative centers for the production of commercial and oppositional cinema in Colombia; and the dozen regional film-producing centers in Brazil during the 1920s and again in the late 1940s, including Porto Alegre in the prosperous state of Rio Grande do Sul, a site that achieved renewed prominence since the 1980s through its Casa de Cinema and filmmakers of the caliber of Jorge Furtado *Ilha das Flores* [1989; *Isle of Flowers*].

Many film-producing nations in Latin America demonstrate both metropolitan and peripheral traditions in the evolution of commercial filmmaking activities (usually subordinated to the capital) as well as in the development of oppositional ones. Colombia provides a convenient example: The polemic between a Bogotá-based tradition associated with José María Arzuaga in the 1960s and the militant documentaries of Carlos and Julia Alvarez in the 1970s versus a Cali-based alternative associated with the playful irreverence and experimentation of Carlos Mayolo and Luis Ospina, dating from their memorable short *Agarrando pueblo* [1977; With the People].

A metropolitan-peripheral struggle in another register can be read in the reception trajectory of Venezuelan Margo Benacerraf's feature documentary *Araya* (1959), an intricately orchestrated chronicle of salt production on the remote peninsula of the same name. Because the postproduction and premier of this feature-length scripted documentary took place in France nearly two decades before its Venezuelan release, the generation of militant filmmakers and critics that coalesced in Caracas in the 1960s tended to regard *Araya* as an "exotic flower" that "made distant lands more distant," refusing to acknowledge the film's contribution to the evolution of a genuinely Venezuelan film-making tradition, even though the popular press consistently hailed it as a foundational film (Burton-Carvajal).

A comparable debate engaging colonizer-colonized dynamics arose in Brazil after the international success of *Orfeu negro* [1959; *Black Orpheus*] by Marcel Camus, a French film that introduced world audiences to Afro-Brazilian culture through the vehicle of Greek mythology. Based on a play first staged in 1956 by the Brazilian playwright, poet, singer, and diplomat Vinícius de Moraes, the film featured Brazilian music, including enduring songs by Antonio Carlos Jobim, actors from Abadias do Nascimento's Black Experimental Theater group, and professional samba performers. Still, its relationship to Brazilian culture continues to be a focus of debate four decades later. Robert Stam points out that *Black Orpheus* "deserves credit for transcending conventional Hollywood representations of Latin America" and for "emphasizing the blackness not only of Rio's carnival but also of Brazil, something that Brazilian films themselves had tended to shy away from" (175, 177).

As a new technology that wed entertainment with consumption, the cinema became the fullest expression of the attributes of modernity. On the horizon of technological innovations at the dawn of the twentieth century, film held by far the most promise because it combined ideas, techniques, and strategies of representation already manifest in other artistic, musical, and literary expressions. As Paulo Antonio Paranaguá pointed out, the early cinema in Latin America is closely linked to photography because photographers often became the artisan-pioneers of the new medium (69). Later, cinema converged with other fields of communication, sharing production and technical personnel, stars, and genres with the *teatro de variedades* in the 1920s, radio after the coming of sound, television in the contemporary period, and literary and para-literary genres and fashions throughout. Argentina offers a pertinent example of how film found a place within a remarkably fluid system of cultural production and circulation alongside magazines and serial novels. Beatriz Sarlo has observed that the growth of the Argentine industry in the 1930s depended as much on the popular appeal of the sentimental feuilleton and the tango as on the heterogeneity of audiences (171).

Dependency versus Transculturation

The film medium in Latin America has been central to the formulation of regional and pan-regional identities, to the redefinition of national and pan-national identity in times of crisis, and to the enlistment of generalized support for national (and pan-national) projects. As the key components of a mass visual culture, film and television structured the imaginary of modernizing developmentalism, socializing citizens of traditional societies by showing them how to act "modern" as they migrated to the swelling cities of the hemisphere. Three mass media in particular–radio, film, and television–were agents and promoters of technological innovation: By enticing consumers into consuming and performing what was expected of them, they helped unify patterns of consumption and behavior. Today, national projects, to the degree they persist at all, must compete with postnational and transnational paradigms to which the electronic media, supported by neoliberal economic policies and other globalizing forces, are currently (and very selectively) resocializing the citizenry.

As an imported technology, film inevitably invokes the dependency dynamics of center and periphery, colonizer and colonized. The concept of transculturation, first articulated in 1940 by the Cuban anthropologist and ethnographer Fernando Ortiz (usefully refurbished four decades later by the Uruguayan literary critic Angel Rama (1926–1983), and recirculated in the 1990s in connection with its republication in English with a new introduction by the Venezuelan

anthropologist Fernando Coronil) can be productively applied to the perennial debates about national/regional cultural autonomy with their concomitant denial, dismissal, or disparagement of foreign components. Applying to cinematic practices the notion of Latin American cultural production as always already transculturative offers a means of breaking out of dead-end dichotomies: National versus foreign, autonomous versus imposed, authentic versus inauthentic, or autochthonous versus hybrid. Film as expression, industry, and commodity exceeds borders. An understanding of cinematic practice as the transformed and transforming product of ongoing, selective, and self-renovating processes of transculturation also appropriately relativizes the perceived novelty of the globalization process, which, despite the current intensification of its pace and impact, is historically rooted in processes that predate the European conquest of the New World.

In most of Latin America, as previously stated, the first practitioners of the medium were not nationals but foreigners, Europeans whose temporary residency sometimes became permanent. These entrepreneurial artistic and technological pioneers tended to be members of the *criollo* elite whose undiluted European heritage conferred privileges reserved for the highest rungs of society in countries heavily stratified by race, caste, and class. Among the rare exceptions to this racial-ethnic hierarchy are Argentina's pioneering feature filmmaker José Agustín "El Negro" Ferreyra, a mulatto; Mexico's Golden Age director Emilio "El Indio" Fernández, who claimed to be descended from Indian stock; the indigenous Chambi brothers, who made ethnographic films in Peru during the 1950s; and the Mexican Matilde Landeta, the only woman in the forties and early fifties to have acquired status as a director, with such films as *Lola Casanova* (1948), *La negra Augustias* (1949) [*Black Augustus*], and *Trotacalles* (1951) [*Street Walkers*]. She was a proto-feminist in a male industry and society (see **Figure 1**).

The aspiration to an autonomous national filmmaking tradition is vexed not only by the founding presence of Europeans and, somewhat later, North Americans but also by the sustained nature of foreign contributions. Research into the originary moments of Colombian cinema, for example, emphasizes the continuity of Spanish influence: The first feature film *María* (1920) and the first talking feature *Flores del Valle* [1940; *Flowers of the Valley*] were both directed by the Spanish-born Máximo Calvo; the first film society was founded in Bogotá in 1949 by the Catalonian Luis Vicens; the country's first socially engaged film movement was initiated in the 1960s by another relocated Spaniard, José María Arzuaga; and the most prominent director of the present generation, Sergio Cabrera, is a first-generation Colombian of Spanish parentage (Castillo de Rodríguez 1995, 52–53). The historical and actual trans-nationality of countless producers, directors, and performers questions the viability of the category of the national "as the central axis of classical Latin American film histories and underscores the hybridity of all national cinemas" (López 78).

Transculturation as paradigm also accommodates several additional film-related phenomena characteristic of Latin America that cannot be made to fit comfortably into a dichotomized inside/outside perspective: Migrations of talent, international co-productions, exile and diasporic film production, and the rise of Latino cinemas in the United States. Examples of migrations of talent within Latin American cinemas are rife. Incipient film production in Brazil, Argentina, Mexico,

Figure 1.

Photograph of movie poster. (Archive of the authors)

Colombia, and elsewhere enlisted countless Europeans, primarily French, Italian, and Spanish. The first commercially successful Brazilian sound film, *Coisas Nossas* [1931; *Our Things*] was directed by, Wallace Downey from the United States, and the Vera Cruz experiment imported talent from across Europe and elsewhere. Mexican cinema assimilated technicians from the United States and Canada; performers from the Caribbean (Ninón Sevilla, María Antonieta Pons) and Argentina (Libertad Lamarque, Delia Garcés); and directors from Spain (Luis Buñuel, Luis Alcoriza), the Caribbean (Ramón Peón), South America (Tito Davison), the United States (Norman Foster), and even Eastern Europe (Arcady Boytler). The Argentine director Carlos Hugo Christensen directed influential features in both Venezuela and Chile before relocating permanently in Brazil, where he has sustained an unparalleled output that has, until very recently, received little critical attention because it falls across national and linguistic borders. Carmen Miranda and Dolores del Rio are the foremost examples of Latin American actresses successfully transplanted to Hollywood, where they were (re)cast, respectively, as ubiquitous pan-American and pan-ethnic signifiers.

Co-productions, often perceived as an instance of globalization, in fact have a venerable history, having been, for example, key to maintaining the international reach of Mexican cinema during its Golden Age in the 1940s and again fundamental to both the resurgence of Argentine cinema in the 1980s and the survival of Cuban filmmaking into the 1990s. Laura Podalsky has demonstrated how co-productions between Cuba and Mexico in the 1940s and 1950s "marked national differences rather than erasing them" by revealing "how nations define themselves against other nations" (65, 68). Countless new Latin American cinema projects depended on more or less formalized international co-production arrangements, from series sponsored by *Radio-Televisione Italiana* (RAI) in the 1970s and *Televisión Española* (TVE) in the 1980s. Before the collapse of the Soviet Union and related internal economic pressures curtailed the activities of Cuba's national film institute (the ICAIC), a significant percentage of new Latin American cinema output was the beneficiary of co-production support from Cuba, acknowledged or unacknowledged.

Latin American directors who have developed portions of their careers in involuntary exile include the Argentines Fernando Solanas, Octavio Getino, and Gerardo Vallejo, collaborators on *La hora de los hornos* [1968; *The Hour of the Furnaces*] and the related theorization of "third cinema"; Glauber Rocha, the brilliant and polemical exponent of Brazil's Cinema Nôvo; the Bolivian director Jorge Sanjinés, who filmed with indigenous populations in three other Andean countries before returning to his native Bolivia; and a significant proportion of Cuban filmmakers, including the brilliant Spanish-born cinematographer of the French New Wave, Néstor Almendros, who left Cuba in the early 1960s and Afro-Cuban director Sergio Giral, who departed in the early 1990s.

Chile offers the most notable example of a national cinema transcending its own borders and becoming diasporic in response to political events. The foundations of Chilean film culture prior to Salvador Allende's socialist coalition Popular Unity regime (1970–73) were disjunctive: An ill-fated attempt at government-sponsored commercial production (1938–49), followed by a dozen-year hiatus, and then a decade of escalating activity catalyzed by Dutch documentarist Joris Ivens's 1962 visit and truncated by the 1973 coup d'état. The massive exodus throughout that decade resulted in nearly 200 Chilean exile productions made in France, Italy, Spain, Holland, Belgium, Great Britain, Germany, Switzerland, the Soviet Union, Sweden, Finland, Romania, Canada, Cuba, Nicaragua, Mexico, Venezuela, Colombia, and the United States (See Valjalo et al.). Among the more prominent Chilean directors, Raúl Ruiz (see **Figure 2**) has earned himself a permanent niche in the French avant-garde scene based on his acclaimed films including *La colonia penal* (1971) [*The Penal Colony*]. Miguel Littín eventually returned to Chile a few years after his clandestine reentry to direct *Actas de Chile* [1986; *Documents from Chile*]; and Patricio Guzmán, who remains in Spain, revisited the traumatic events of the early 1970s a quarter-century later in *Chili la mémoire obstinée* [1997; *Chile, Obstinate Memory*], his poignant, multilayered excavation of fragments of the Popular Unity past in neoliberal Chile's present. If exile disperses, its reverse, *desexilio* or the painful process of return and reintegration, coalesces; both processes "expand conceptual and aesthetic boundaries" and "contribute to a decentering of views on identity, nationality and difference" (Pick 158).

A different kind of influx was experienced by Mexico in the 1930s, Cuba in the early 1960s, and Nicaragua in the early 1980s as newly inaugurated postrevolutionary regimes in each of these countries privileged film among their cultural priorities, recruiting international talent and accommodating

Figure 2.

Photograph from movie La colonia penal [The Penal Colony], *directed by Raul Ruiz, Chile, 1971. (Archive of the authors)*

offers of assistance and cooperation. The advent of sound sent scores of Mexican movie aspirants and technicians to Hollywood; inversely, it also incorporated scores of North Americans temporarily, and sometimes permanently, into the incipient Mexican industry. In the Cuban case, Italian neorealist screenwriter Cesare Zavattini, Dutch documentarist Joris Ivens, and French cinema verité director Chris Marker were among those whose visits to ICAIC left a decisive imprint.

Ancient territorial appropriations and ongoing population displacements have contributed to the emergence of independent Chicano and Latino cinemas. The former category has been decisively shaped by the small screen due to the preponderance within this tradition of made-for-television work largely financed through public funding agencies (see Noriega). Enduring Chicano features include Luis Valdez's *Zoot Suit* (1981), Robert Young's *The Ballad of Gregorio Cortés* (1982), Gregorio Nava's and Anna Thomas's *El norte* [1985; The North], comedian Richard Cheech Marín's *Born in East L.A.* (1987), as well as the postmodern "melo-docu-mystery" *The Devil Never Sleeps* (1995) by Mexican-born Lourdes Portillo. Arguably, the latter film is equally exemplary of the more diffuse category of Latino cinema, part of a compelling "subgenre" of diarylike meditations on location, identity, and origin that also includes Marilú Mallet's *Journal inachevé* [1982; *Unfinished Diary*] and Frances Negrón Muntaner's *Cruzando el charco* [1994; *Crossing the Puddle*].

Commercial versus Oppositional Cinemas

Reacting against formulaic studio production, a generation of viewers whose tastes were shaped by the film societies that proliferated in many Latin American cities after World War II (one chronology cites a dozen such organizations founded throughout Brazil between 1946 and 1951) attempted to carve out a space for personalized expression. These independent productions first registered as a phenomenon in Argentina with what has come to be called the Generation of the 1960s. Partly because few of these young turks succeeded in finding production support for subsequent features in a deteriorating political climate, this generation failed to coalesce into a movement, though its legacy endures in a handful of memorable features by directors such as Leonardo Favio and Chilean-born Lautaro Murúa.

Similar conditions existed in Brazil in the late 1950s and early 1960s, but there sporadic and geographically distant attempts to produce another kind of cinema did successfully coalesce into the paradigmatic new cinema movement, Cinema Nôvo, characterized by new modes and philosophies of production and a new aesthetics based on scarcity. Various models, selectively appropriated–Italian neorealism, the French New Wave, and assorted trends in Anglo-American documentary–were conjugated into a self-consciously contestatory national imaginary. Whether urban or rural, Brazilian society was most appropriately viewed from below. For the first time, the vaunted industrial model was abandoned by choice rather than by default.

The perhaps unjustly exaggerated failure of the Vera Cruz experiment, which carried a number of other production companies in its wake, triggered a concerted search for new models of production that resulted in the emergence of culturally significant independent cinema movements in Rio, São Paulo, Bahia, and Minas Gerais. The possibility of consolidating these centers into a nationwide movement was stimulated by film conferences that formulated and debated issues destined to remain dominant through successive decades, not just in Brazil but throughout Latin America, including the nature of the national audience, foreign domination of the domestic market, the nature and goals of popular cinema, and the role of the state in fostering national cinema. For the first time in Latin American film history, critical-theoretical reflection and the formulation of programmatic goals were linked to the examination of concrete conditions of production and reception.

Invoking the antithesis of the industrial model, Glauber Rocha turned a phrase attributed to Jean-Luc Godard into a Cinema Nôvo slogan: "with a camera in your hand and an idea in your head." Endorsing the prevalent trend to nationalization of the country's natural resources in echo of the nationalist-developmentalist rhetoric of the period, the brilliant young critic and cinephile from Bahia argued that "Brazilian art forms had to nationalize their modes of expression" (1963). Rocha's (1995) invocation of an "aesthetics of hunger" and of the violence that hunger engenders was translated into a stylistics and a thematics based on scarcity, as anticipated in documentaries such as Linduarte Noronha's *Aruanda* (1959) and quintessentially embodied in features such as Nelson Pereira dos Santos's *Vidas Secas* [1963; *Barren Lives*], a hauntingly timeless and austere saga of a migrant family in the drought-stricken Northeast.

The *politique des auteurs* invoked by a group of French critics about to take up directing found a fervent, politicized echo in Brazil. For Rocha and his contemporaries across the hemisphere, film was "not a tool but a metaphysics" (1963, 12), and their embracing of the medium was not a vocation but a quasireligious crusade aligned to protonationalist, anticolonialist, prorevolutionary goals. Though it inspired other oppositional film movements throughout Latin America, for all its creative energy, contentious cohesion, and international acclaim, Cinema Nôvo never succeeded in sustaining the popular response its advocates and practitioners sought because, as Randal Johnson has argued after sustained analysis, the transformations it cultivated remained incomplete and its relationship with the distribution-exhibition sector essentially adversarial.

Oppositional cinema in Latin America took as its point of departure not only the introduction of new content and the transformation of cinematic forms but also the transformation of the subjective and objective conditions of film production and consumption. Where dominant cinema prioritized exchange value (profit), oppositional filmmakers emphasized use value (social benefit). Where industrializing modes of production turned filmmakers into virtual piece-workers or managers, alternative approaches sought reintegrative, cooperative participation at all levels of the creative process. Where commercial practices required large amounts of capital and a complex, costly infrastructure (studio sets, professionally trained actors, polished screenplays, fixed shooting schedules, sophisticated equipment, and a specialized crew) oppositional filmmakers opted instead for simplification and spontaneity, using location shooting, nonprofessional actors, improvised scripts, and less technological mediation.

Where the structures and conventions of traditional filmmaking required passive, socially fragmented audiences, who did their viewing in the ritualized space of conventional movie theaters, oppositional filmmakers sought to transform diffusion and reception practices in order to encourage broader audience participation and response. Distribution strategies included bringing films to often remote target audiences through self-distribution, mobile cinema projects, or parallel circuits that utilized community rather than commercial spaces. Reception strategies included organized discussions and debates, the enlistment of indigenous narrators to reprise film content, and stylistic modifications in the films themselves in order to catalyze audience intervention. Political motivations coincided with a generalized moment of modernist self-consciousness among filmmakers worldwide. During the 1960s, for example, Cuba's national film institute (ICAIC) sought to cultivate demystificatory film literacy through its features, documentaries, newsreels, television shows, and public forums. Toward the end of that decade, Argentina provided the watershed example of the semiclandestine production and completely clandestine exhibition of the formally audacious epic documentary *La hora de los hornos* and the ambitious feature *Los traidores* [1973; *The Traitors*] by the rival Cine de la Base group.

Shaping Meaning: Genre

More a practical than a conceptual entity, genre is best understood as an institutionalized set of expectations based on economies of repetition and difference, a convenient if always provisional signpost for those who produce films and those who consume them. Comedy, epic, and melodrama are the three major (meta)generic categories of Latin American fictional filmmaking, with the disposition to melodrama powerful enough to subtend the other two. Particular subgenres, often hybridized, began to characterize the major national cinemas of Latin America with the coming of sound and the incorporation of regional musical traditions whose primary mass audience outlet prior to that time had been the still emergent medium of radio. These autochthonous subgenres include Argentine tango melodramas (which had their beginnings during the silent era when orchestras played behind the screen), Brazilian *chanchadas* with their carnival-inspired plots and celebratory sambas, Mexican *comedias rancheras* with their singing *charros* and mariachi bands, and Mexican cabaret melodramas with their imported Caribbean dance rhythms and signature boleros (love songs) by composer Agustín Lara. Epics inspired by history and folk heroes—Mexican revolutionaries, Brazilian bandits (*cangaceiros*), and Argentine gauchos—also configured characteristic subgenres, often indebted to the Hollywood western. Luis Buñuel's *Los olvidados* [1950; *The Young and the Damned*] is the most famous exponent of another characteristic subgenre, the street chronicle. Depicting the lives of indigent children, this subgenre has indirect antecedents in the early Venezuelan sound feature *Juan de la calle* [1941; *Homeless Juan*], among other examples. Scores of subsequent examples appeared throughout the century: Nelson Pereira dos Santos's neorealist-inspired *Rio, quarenta graus* [Brazil, 1955; *Rio, North Zone*], Leonardo Favio's autobiographical *Crónica de un niño solo* [Argentina, 1965; *Chronicle of a Solitary Child*], Lautaro Murúa's *La Raulito* (Argentina, 1975), Ciro Durán's *Gamín* (Colombia, 1978), Héctor Babenco's *Peixoto* (Brazil, 1980), Víctor Manuel Gaviria's *Rodrigo D* (Colombia, 1989), and José Joffily's *Quem matou Peixoto?* [Brazil, 1995; *Who Killed Peixoto?*].

Tending toward a verbal rather than the predominantly physical basis of early Hollywood slapstick, Latin American comedy, with deep roots in regional variety shows and popular theater genres, has traditionally served as a vehicle for celebrating local cum national idiosyncrasies, particularly through archetypal personae like those embodied, for example, by Mexico's Cantinflas (Mario Moreno) as the *pelado* (marginalized sub-proletarian) and Tin Tan (Germán Valdés) as the *pachuco* (urbanized northerner).

With the rise of alternative filmmaking practices centered around auteurism and more artisanal modes of production, genre pictures tended to be de-emphasized. While certain New Cinema producers reworked national generic traditions, many attempted to work "outside" genre by enlisting history as a "documentary" presence not only narratively but also stylistically. Most practitioners of New Latin American cinema believed history and melodrama to be at odds with one another and, throughout the 1960s and 1970s, shunned the latter in order to privilege the former, which they often called national reality and discerned in observable phenomena. The vehemence with which melodrama was rejected, glimpsed in Glauber Rocha's tendentious description of "old cinema's" characters as "pathological" in contrast to those of the "new cinema," which he described as "historical" (1963, 14), was given fullest rein in essays by Cubans Enrique Colina and Daniel Díaz Torres (1971 and 1978) and barely mitigated by Reynaldo González two decades later.

Elsewhere in Latin America during that interim, however, melodrama reasserted its deep-seated epistemological claims on the culture in new formats, not only in prime-time soap operas that claimed mammoth audiences across divisions of gender, age, and social class but also in feature films, many made or scripted by women directors. In María Luisa Bemberg's *Camila* (Argentina, 1984) and in Luis Puenzo's *La historia oficial* [1985; *The Official Story*] made the following year from Aída Bortnik's script, melodrama and history are no longer at odds. Instead, in the wake of a sustained and violent governmental assault on the rule of law and civil rights, melodrama was embraced in Argentina as an instrument of national catharsis. Political justice, rather than an abstract morality, became the secular substitute for the "absent sacred," which, in literary critic Peter Brook's theorization, is the generative impetus of melodrama. Similarly, Tizuka Yamasaki's *Patriamada* [1984; *Beloved Country*], a celebratory neofoundational feature made in Brazil during the analogous redemocratization process, recuperated melodrama in order to transcend and subjectivize documentary-based representations of the transition from military to civilian rule.

Documentary Realism, Illusionism, and History

Perhaps more than in other regions of the world, Latin America's deepest cinematic roots are documentary. The Argentine silent features *Nobleza gaucha* [1915; Gaucho Nobility, Eduardo Martínez de la Pera] and *El último malón* [1918; The Last Indian Raid, Alcides Reca] are emblematic. Using traveling shots from streetcars and trains, the former provided street-level views of the city and the countryside, whereas the latter combined fictional modes with on-site historical reconstruction and ethnographic documentary. The early Mexican serial feature *El automóvil gris* [Mexico, 1919; The Gray Automobile, Enrique Rosas] marks a moment of transition in which national (vernacular) rather than "universal" (Hollywood) narrative forms still hold sway. In his magisterial two-volume history of Mexican

silent cinema, Aurelio de los Reyes stresses the documentary orientation that characterized film's early decades in that country, postulating the still under-recognized uniqueness of a Mexican vernacular style that predated the increasing dominance of Griffith-inspired montage after 1916. Throughout the hemisphere, the very illusoriness of industrial aspirations often meant that even the most ambitious fictional efforts carried a documentary imprint, deliberately or not, because found locations had to be substituted for manufactured ones. With the notable exceptions of Mexico, when studio production was at its zenith, and the Perón era in Argentina, when filming in actual civic spaces was strictly prohibited, Latin American cinematography past and present often "carries a special feeling for real social space," an aesthetic register of economic exigencies (Chanan 116).

The emphasis on asserting the presence of history through the multiple modalities of documentary has been one of the many ways that realist discourses have dominated the Latin American feature film scene. Documentary realism, social realism, and critical realism are multiple ways of naming an insistence on reality as made up of external, observable phenomena. The diversification of the film-making ranks that began in the 1970s with the incorporation of female directorial talent on a significant scale (for the first time since the 1920s) and the widespread questioning of embattled political ideologies and agendas during the subsequent decade led to a heightened revaluation of subjectivity, fantasy, and emotivity, a shift that B. Ruby Rich has aptly identified as "from exteriority to interiority" (12).

Yet, on the other hand, ethnographic and sociological impulses remain strong, since the conceptualization of cinema as a catalyst for social change is closely associated with the medium's ability to register cultural differences. In all the countries where indigenous peoples and cultures survive in significant numbers, the history of the film medium is entwined with the representational histories of those indigenous populations. In areas such as the Caribbean, where the original populations were decimated, the ethnographic focus shifted to peasant cultures and other nonurban or subcultural social formations. Sociological and ethnographic impulses combined in the commitment to map the hidden, marginalized, forgotten sectors of the nation as part of the discovery and/or recovery of national identity, a kind of auto-ethnography in that it was undertaken within rather than across national borders and pretended to capture previously un(der)represented aspects of the national self.

By the 1970s filmmakers, such as the Brazilian Artur Omar, *Congo* (1977), and the Venezuelan Carlos Azpúrrua, *Listen, Caracas* (1978), had begun to call into question the directionality and authority of the ethnographic gaze. Since the 1980s, indigenous peoples have embraced video and cybermedia to author their own representations and to engage in dialogue with other indigenous peoples throughout the Americas and the world.

The commemoration in 1992 of 500 years of contact between Europe and the New World prompted renewed interest in the cosmovision of the continents' prior inhabitants, as explored for example in Nicolás Echeverría's *Cabeza de Vaca* (Mexico, 1989), Juan Mora Catlett's *Retorno a Aztlán* [Mexico, 1990; *Return to Aztlán*], and Luis Alberto Lamata's *Jericó* (Venezuela, 1991). Likewise in Brazil, filmmakers and video artists continue to expose and deconstruct official discourses that for over a century have idealized the Indian as emblem of national difference though long proscribing his/her presence on the screen, thereby contributing to a "multicultural project" that Robert Stam describes as "an attempt to restructure knowledge and cultural relations in function of an anti-racist perspective that assumes the radical equality of peoples, communities and cultures" (17).

A generalized suspicion of illusionism characterized the era of heroic militancy in Latin American cinema. Much of the stylistic innovation associated with the New Cinema period was a product of filmmakers' aggressive undermining of conventional dichotomies between documentary and fictional modes of representation, favoring the former in order to insert history all the more convincingly into the inescapably imaginary construct that is cinema. This is the case, for example, with three of the most celebrated Cuban films from ICAIC's most productive period. Tomás Gutiérrez Alea's *Memorias del subdesarrollo* [1968; *Memories of Underdevelopment*] is a fictional collage composed of fragments in every conceivable documentary register. Sara Gómez's *De cierta manera* [1974/79; *One Way or Another*], disrupts its cross-class, interracial love story with pseudosociological discourses and reconstructed biographies of social actors. Humberto Solás's *Lucía* (1969) puts the experience of women from three key periods at the center of the epic of Cuban history, using stylistic and subgeneric markers to "document" the dominant modes of perception characteristic of each era. Other examples (and modes) of writing history into fiction include Miguel Littín's *El Chacal de Nahueltoro* [Chile, 1969; *The Jackal of Nahueltoro*], a crime and punishment story that charges the national judicial system and the news media for the misdeeds of a social-discard-turned-serial-killer, the properly socialized civic subject, and finally the (at last comprehending) target of an executionary firing squad; Jorge Bodansky's *Iracema* (1974), a cinema verité-style allegorization of Amazonian development as prostitution; and Solveig Hoogesteijn's *Macu, la mujer del policía* [Venezuela, 1987; *Macu, the Policeman's Wife*], an intricately layered, on-site reenactment of an infamous Caracas murder case that tellingly turns the family romance inside out.

Deliberately counter- and anti-epic modes of (re)writing history are exemplified by the differently subjectivized approaches of Jorge Sanjinés in *El coraje del pueblo* [Bolivia, 1971; *The Courage of the People*] (see **Figure 3**), Leon Hirszman in his luminous adaptation of the literary classic *São Bernardo* (see **Figure 4**) (Brazil, 1972), Paul Leduc in *Frida: naturaleza viva* [Mexico, 1984; *Frida*], and María Luisa Bemberg in *Miss Mary* (Argentina, 1986) and *Yo, la peor de todas* [1990; *I, the Worst of All*]. Significantly, feminine experience lies at the narrative core of each of these films and seems inseparable from the innovative stylistic choices that contribute to their profound appeal. A gendered reckoning with history, and a reconceptualization of history as capable of reckoning with gender, reinvigorated cinematic expression in Latin America from the 1970s, not only in the films directed by the emerging cadre of female directors but also by their male counterparts mentioned above and others.

Carlos Sorín took a parodic approach to history as conventionally represented in the films of his own and the preceding generation; his *La película del rey* [Argentina, 1986; *The King's Movie*] simultaneously satirizes the historical epic, the national hero, the national revolutionary project, and the heroic model of independent filmmaking (though not without reinforcing conventional hierarchies of gender). In *Julio comienza en julio* [1978; *Julio Begins in July*] (see **Figure 5**), the only feature film released under Chile's seventeen-year dictatorship, director Silvio Caiozzi provides a deconstructive example, simultaneously enlisting and undermining realism

through a pervasive cognitive dissonance between the early twentieth-century mise-en-scène and sepia-toned photography on the one hand, and a hyper-modern shooting and editing style on the other.

The realm of psycho-subjectivity, only sporadically engaged in Latin American cinema, was memorably invoked in Sergio Toledo's *Vera* (Brazil, 1987) through televisual imagery of the exploding Challenger spaceship, cutaways to computer screens, and the vast warehouselike space in which the protagonist, who insists that she is a man in a woman's body, wanders among discarded objects at the end of the film. In *Sur* [1988; *South*] and *El viaje* [1993; *The Journey*], repatriated Argentine director Fernando Solanas reached beyond conventional cinematic realism to create poignant, sometimes humorous, metaphorical and poetic images (streets inundated with discarded paper, entire cities underwater) of stunning visual and emotional power. Similarly, recurrent visual hyperboles, such as an oversize neoclassical mansion, a pharaonic pyramid in the desert, and a flood of biblical proportions, ironize the realist register of *Jonas y la ballena rosada* [1995; *Jonas and the Pink Whale*], the brilliant directorial debut of Bolivan Juan Carlos Valdivia.

In the films *La reina de la noche* [1994; *Queen of the Night*], *La mujer del puerto* [1995; *Woman of the Port*], and *Profundo Carmesí* [1996; *Deep Crimson*], Mexican auteur Arturo Ripstein carries realism over the edge into gritty, sordid naturalism. Since *Frida: naturaleza viva*, Mexican director Paul Leduc has pursued nonlinear narration based on tableaux and musical forms in films such as *Barroco* (1989) and *Dollar Mambo* (1993) without recourse to spoken dialogue.

It should be stressed that New Cinema documentarists also questioned received wisdom regarding realist-based mechanisms of perception and cognition early and often, beginning perhaps with the parodic statistics of the opening voice-over of Fernando Birri's foundation social documentary, *Tire dié* [Argentina, 1958/1960; *Toss Me a Dime*], and the heavily decoupaged manipulations of music and image that became the early and influential signature of Cuban documentarist Santiago Alvarez. Other "beginnings" of documentary's epistemological self-doubt that remain less consecrated by history include Margot Benacerraf's *Reverón* (1956), a hallucinatory and elaborately choreographed approximation to the highly creative madness of a reclusive Venezuelan painter.

In *Hombres de Mal Tiempo* [Cuba, 1968; Men of Mal Tiempo], Argentine Alejandro Saderman used solarization, negative reversal, slow motion, and other experimental techniques to externalize subjective memory as evoked by five centagenarian veterans of Cuba's war for independence from Spain. Among numerous examples from Colombia's documentary tradition are the obsessively reiterative voiceover of Gabriela Samper's *Los santísimos hermanos* [1969; *The Most Holy Brotherhood*], the dreamlike first communion sequence in Marta Rodriguez and Jorge Silva's otherwise eminently social realist-style *Chircales* [1968/1970; *The Brickmakers*] (see **Figure 6**), and their haunting evocation of mythic peasant belief systems in *Nuestra voz de tierra, memoria y futuro* [1981; *Our Voice of Earth, Memory and Future*].

Numerous documentaries of the Chilean diaspora also use highly subjectivized modes. *Por debajo de la mesa* [Canada, 1983; *Under the Table*, Luis Osvaldo García and Tony Venturi], uses the visual metaphor of a hearing aid to evoke one illegal immigrant's sensation of nonpersonhood through assumed deafness. Valeria Sarmiento inserts cutaways to mariachi bands and Mexican movie idol balladeers in the film *Un hombre cuando es*

Figure 3.

Photograph from movie El coraje del pueblo [The Courage of the People], *directed by Jorge Sanjínes, Bolivia, 1971. (Archive of the authors)*

hombre [Germany/Costa Rica, 1983; *A Man When He's a Man*], an otherwise conventionally interview-centered survey of gender socialization and its consequences, in order to evoke the structures of sentiment that popular culture inculcates. Marilú Mallet's *Journal inachevé* [Canada, 1982; *Unfinished Diary*] transforms documentary into a diary form that bears/bares intimate testimony to the culturally dissonant interiority of exile.

Literary Influence

Like history, literature offers a rich substratum from which filmmakers can draw at will. One of the characteristics that differentiated the writers of Latin America's mid-twentieth century literary boom from preceding generations was their formative association with cinematic culture. Major figures such as Mexico's Carlos Fuentes (b. 1928), Juan Rulfo (1918–1986), and Luis Spota (1925–1985); Argentina's Manuel Puig (1932–1990), Julio Cortázar (1914–1984), and David Viñas (b. 1927); Brazil's Jorge Amado (1912–2001); Paraguay's Augusto Roa Bastos (b. 1917); Chile's José Donoso (1925–1996); Peru's Mario Vargas Llosa (b. 1936); and most famously, Colombia's Gabriel García Márquez (b. 1927) wrote for the screen and/or saw their works adapted to film. Leading twentieth-century writers who regularly practiced film criticism include Horacio Quiroga (1878–1937), Jorge Luis Borges (1899–1986), Alfonso Reyes (1889–1959), and Alejo Carpentier (1904–1980), all of whose efforts have been

recently anthologized and republished. In a rather whimsical affirmation of the persistent linkages between cinematic and literary expression, a specialist in the origins of Mexican film criticism compiled a charming volume of verse by famous and not so famous "poets who went to the movies" between 1915 and 1996 (Miguel).

Some of this mutual imbrication apparently dwells under the sign of paradox. Many of the great works of Latin American literature, most notoriously and deliberately García Márquez's *Cien Años de Soledad* [1967; *One Hundred Years of Solitude* 1972], continue to defy satisfactory embodiment in cinema. On the other hand, directors who produced monumental works from modest literary efforts include Luis Buñuel (*El* [He], based on the autobiographical "novel" by Mercedes Pinto) and Tomás Gutiérrez Alea (*Memories of Underdevelopment*, based on the semiautobiographical work by Edmundo Desnoes). Argentine director María Luisa Bemberg, who began her late-blooming career as a screenwriter and who engaged several leading authors as co-scriptwriters once she began directing, found the footing she needed to tackle the cinematic depiction of the life of Latin America's greatest intellectual, the Mexican nun Sor Juana Inés de la Cruz, in Octavio Paz's (1914–1998) brilliant biography cum cultural history cum literary reappraisal.

Other prominent directors who worked hand-in-hand with writers include Leopoldo Torre Nilsson, whose status as

Figure 4.

Photograph from movie São Bernardo, *directed by Leon Hirzman, Brazil, 1972. (Archive of the authors)*

Argentina's premier auteur is indebted to his sustained collaboration with his companion, the writer Beatriz Guido (1925–1988). Before establishing his ongoing partnership with screenwriter Paz Alicia Garcíadiego in 1985, Mexico's Arturo Ripstein collaborated on successive projects with an impressive array of writers including Gabriel García Márquez, José Emilio Pacheco (b. 1939), Manuel Puig, and Vicente Leñero (b. 1933). Matilde Landeta, the only woman director during the Golden Age of Mexican cinema, also grounded her film projects in works of literature, adapting two ethnographic novels by Francisco Rojas González (1904–1951) before collaborating with Luis Spota on her third feature.

Brazilian Cinema Nôvo, like its inspiration, Italian neorealism, defined itself in terms of national literary traditions, embracing in particular the unpretentious regionalism of Graciliano Ramos (1892–1953). A vogue for literary adaptations is sometimes associated with periods of repression, as in Argentina under General Juan Perón's regime (1945–1955) or Brazil under the long military dictatorship (1964–1984), when directors who did not choose to work elsewhere sought the cover and relative safety of literary prestige. In the latter case, when adapted to film, Mario de Andrade's (1893–1945) *Macunaíma*, the preeminent text from Brazil's 1920s Modernism movement inaugurated a second, Tropicalist phase of Cinema Nôvo characterized by allegorized excess and indirection, a codified response to the prevailing climate of repression (see Avellar).

Recent scholarship on the intricate interface between literary and cinematic expression includes Flora Süssekind's

Cinematografo de letras: Literatura, tecnica e modernização no Brasil [1987; *Cinematograph of Words: Literature, Technique and Modernization in Brazil*] and J. Patrick Duffey's *De la pantalla al texto: la influencia del cine en la narrativa mexicana del siglo veinte* [1996; *From Screen to Text: The Influence of Cinema on Mexican Narrative in the Twentieth Century*]. In their methodology and theoretical sophistication, both these works establish new standards for the perennial comparison of these intimately related modes of expression.

Canon Formation

Like the continent's literary production, Latin American cinema is subject to the construction and demolition of canons. As instruments of both national and transnational validation forged by various interdependent interventions (festival and televisual programming decisions, video and laserdisc producers, and the comments of reviewers in the popular press and of scholars in more ponderous publications such as this one), canons reflect and partake of historically and culturally specific pressures, agendas, and polemics. The impulse to canonize is always tendentious, inevitably revisionist.

In the frenzy to compile various lists of the "100 greatest films of the twentieth century" that accompanied the centenary of the film medium in 1995 and the advent of the third millennium, Latin American cinema was largely overlooked. One way to view the activity of socially concerned filmmakers and critics from the 1960s to the present might be the constitution of a counter-canon, the mapping of alternative itineraries of

Figure 5.

Photograph from movie Julio comienza en julio [July Begins in July] *directed by Silvio Caiozzi, Chile, 1978. (Archive of the authors)*

national and pan-national representation. The impulse to create such counter-canons is exemplified, for example, in the early 1960s by the retrospective embracing of "political" films such as Mario Soffici's *Prisioneros de la tierra* [Argentina, 1939; *Prisoners of the Soil*] or Argentina's New Wave director Leopoldo Torre Nilsson's *La casa del ángel* (1959) [*The Angel's House*], and *Fin de fiesta* (1960) [*The Party Is Over*] (see **Figure 7**), or in the 1990s by the recovery of "feminist" films such as Adela Sequeyro's *La mujer de nadie* [Mexico, 1937; *Nobody's Woman*].

Whether or not their products are recognized on international "best" lists, certain historical moments stand as watersheds of achievement for national and pan-national filmmaking in Latin America. The year 1943 in Mexico, for example, saw the release of the first two collaborations between Emilio Fernández and his unrivaled cinematographer Gabriel Figueroa (*María Candelaria* and *Flor silvestre* [Wild Flower], both starring a newly repatriated Dolores del Rio) as well as Fernando de Fuentes's *Doña Bárbara*, with the gorgeous María Félix in the role that fixed her forevermore as the ferocious, pan-Latin she-man, and Julio Bracho's influential cabaret melodrama *Distinto amanecer* [Different Dawn], starring the legendary Andrea Palma. Twenty years later, 1963 saw an equally compelling constellation emerge on the Brazilian film

scene, inaugurating Cinema Nôvo: Nelson Pereira dos Santos's *Vidas Secas*, Glauber Rocha's *Deus e o diabo na terra do sol* [*Black God, White Devil*], and Ruy Guerra's *Os fuzis* [*The Guns*].

The end of that decade saw the nearly simultaneous release of an inordinate number of landmark political films that challenged both their sociopolitical context and the film medium itself in radical ways, including *Yawar Mallku* [Bolivia, *Blood of the Condor*, Jorge Sanjinés], *Terra em transe* [*Land in Anguish*] and *Antonio das Mortes* [Brazil (see **Figure 8**), both by Glauber Rocha], *El Chacal de Nahueltoro* [Chile, *The Jackal of Nahueltoro*, Miguel Littín], *Memorias del subdesarrollo* [Cuba, *Memories of Underdevelopment*, Tomás Gutiérrez Alea], *Lucía* [Cuba, Humberto Solás], and *La hora de los hornos* [Argentina, *The Hour of the Furnaces*, Fernando Solanas and Octavio Getino].

The years 1984 to 1985 also produced a panoply of works that signaled new directions. A trio from Argentina included María Luisa Bemberg's antipatriarchal melodrama cum national allegory, *Camila*; Luis Puenzo's family melodrama cum national allegory, *La historia oficial*; and a meta-musical on the emotional dislocations of exile by Fernando Solanas, *Tangos: El exilio de Gardel* [Tangos: The Exile of Gardel]. Another trio from Brazil included Nelson Pereira dos Santos's *Memorias do carcere* [Prison Memoirs], Tizuka Yamasaki's *Patriamada*

Figure 6.

Photograph of the movie Chircales [Brickmakers] *directed by Jorge Silva and Martha Rodriguez, Colombia, 1967–1972. (Archive of the authors)*

[*Beloved Country*], and Eduardo Coutinho's *Cabra marcado pra morrer: Vinte anos depois* [*Man Marked to Die: Twenty Years Later*]. Three more films that also signaled new directions were Jorge Ali Triana's *Tiempo de morir* [Colombia, *Time to Die*], Paul Leduc's *Frida: naturaleza viva* (Mexico), and Fina Torres's *Oriana* (Venezuela).

Currently, critical scholarship seems committed to the revival of a neotraditional canon through a reconsideration of disparaged directors, disdained subgenres, and neglected stars. Commercial directors, such as the unclassifiable Carlos Hugo Christensen, whose career spanned four countries and two languages; the Argentine master of soft-core pornography, Armando Bo; and a number of less celebrated Mexican directors, have been the beneficiaries of renewed scholarly and (occasionally) popular interest. In 1990s Mexico, generalized nostalgia for the Golden Age of Mexican cinema, now half a century removed in time, has fueled the massive newsstand marketing of glossy, large-format memoir/biographies of movie idols such as María Félix, Jorge Negrete, Pedro Infante, Dolores del Rio, and Cantinflas.

Historiography

Historiographical debates and dilemmas have been central to the formation of the various discourses–political-ideological, critical, theoretical, and methodological–that circulate in and around Latin American cinematic traditions and practices. Most film histories bifurcate with the introduction of sound. As the film medium extends into its second century, the insufficiency of this two-part division becomes more patent.

The first century of Ibero-American film history can be divided into four general phases: The silent era, commercially focused cinemas of national consolidation, national/pan-national opposition movements, and the contemporary "postnational" moment, with its return to paradigms of quality and its embracing of hybridity. Like other historical subdivisions, these are heuristic conveniences and remain perpetually subject to modification, not to mention changing critical orthodoxy and other shifting fashions. Both commercial and oppositional film production escaped rigorous historical analysis from the 1960s into the 1980s because the anticommercial, anti-Hollywood ideology prevalent from the 1960s tended to dismiss the "old" Latin American cinema while presenting itself as the incarnation of history. It was only in the 1990s that international scholars began fully to engage all periods and genres.

Beyond Modernity

The recent focusing of international critical attention on questions of how cinema implicates and expresses the national has made it obvious that all cinemas, even that perennially dominant (and increasingly heuristic) construct known as Hollywood, are national cinemas; some have simply been more transparently–that is, hegemonically–national than others. In countries once referred to as dependent or peripheral, even in the most mighty among them, questions of cinema and nation(hood) are incomparably fraught because "a sense of national powerlessness generates a sisyphean struggle to conquer an elusive 'authenticity' [that must be] constructed anew with every generation" (Stam et al. 395). Haunted by specters of dependency and cultural colonialism, national cinemas throughout the postcolonial world have been habitually evaluated in terms of their service to national consolidation, or in terms of their furthering the cause of national development or liberation. Creative expression, both individual and generational, has been subordinated to the larger project of vindicating a national image. From the late 1960s through the 1980s in Latin America, a "continental project" unifying in its diversity and tied to the larger project of continental revolution was superimposed upon the conventional mandate to (re)assert the nation in cinematic terms.

Predictably, the notion that film culture has been (self-) mandated to (re)assert the nation has varied according to particular national, historical, and political conjunctures. The characteristically populist strain that flourished in Latin American nationalisms from the 1930s through the 1950s and occasionally beyond, a strain that reflected "the unfulfilled Latin American dream of a painless modernity" (Castañeda 43), conferred upon the artist-intellectual sector the role of representational agent of the national citizenry, mediator between the latter and the state as well as between the state and the extranational realm.

During this period, the Latin American nation was understood as composed of two incompatible populations: The *comprador* elites, a foreign-identified "anti-nation," and "the people," an amorphous category designated as the true

Figure 7.

Photograph from the movie Fin de fiesta [The Party Is Over] *directed by Leopoldo Torre Nilsson, Argentina, 1960.*
(Archive of the authors)

nation. The latter consisted of the excluded or marginalized masses, perceived as socially, economically, racially, ethnically, and often culturally other. Regarded as voiceless as well as socially invisible, "the people" were perceived to require the intervention of self-appointed mediators to give them voice and visibility. For three decades, this shared social imaginary was constitutive of the supraregional pan-nationalism that the New Latin American Cinema movement both catalyzed and reflected.

For roughly the same thirty-year period–from the takeover of Havana by the Fidelistas in 1959 to the electoral defeat of the Nicaraguan Sandinistas in 1990–the idea of armed revolution occupied center stage in the left's pageant of history, whereas the interpretive filter was provided by dependency theory. The revolution was to be anti-imperialist, anticapitalist, and hemispheric; hence it needed hemispherically viable forms of cultural expression. Film, foremost among these because its massive reception did not require the mediation of literacy, needed to be dissociated from its origins, both imperialist and capitalist, by an emphasis on anti-industrial, artisanal modes of production, on original and autochthonous (as opposed to derivative and dependent) models of expression, and on participatory activating modes of reception.

In addition to serving as inspiration for incipient oppositional film movements in other parts of Latin America, the Brazilian Cinema Novistas also provided a model for the struggle for state support, which, by the 1970s, would be seen as an essential precondition for the creation and survival of national cinemas. State intervention in the Brazilian film sphere dates from the first ineffectual protectionist measures (screen quotas in favor of national films) instituted under the populist regime of Getulio Vargas in the early 1930s. After the military coup of 1964, the state's role evolved from regulator of market forces to active producer-agent, providing low-interest loans and distribution advances.

In the planning stages since the mid-1950s, the National Film Institute was created in 1966 to promote distribution. In 1975, the two functions were merged under Embrafilme, which, over the following five years, partially financed a quarter of domestic production. In the mid-1980s the agency was restructured in order to mitigate the problematic overlap of cultural and commercial mandates. Then in 1990, along with a number of other state cultural agencies, Embrafilme was summarily abolished by incoming President Fernando Collor de Mello. An attitude of adversariness toward both producers and exhibitors implicit in Cinema Nôvo's auteur model is now recognized as a crucial factor in the "failure to develop a

Figure 8.

Photograph from the movie Antonio das mortes, *directed by Glauber Rocha, Brazil, 1969. (Archive of the authors)*

self-sustaining film industry with a strong financial basis in the support of the Brazilian public" (Johnson 115). In 1993, innovative audiovisual legislation designed to stimulate private sector funding through tax credits gave a huge boost to previously languishing Brazilian film production. After a brief flurry of new releases, including the international success of *Four Days in September* (1996) and *Central do Brasil* [1997; *Brazil Station*], an international liquidity crisis late in the decade applied the brakes.

Parallel trajectories of state intervention in and retreat from the film sector could be traced, not only in Argentina and Mexico, but also in Peru, Colombia, and Venezuela. From the 1970s, the escalating implementation of neoliberal economic doctrines and their socially regressive consequences have encouraged reprivatization, transnationalization, increased dependency, and diminished autonomy in the cultural sphere. Whatever the limitations of the various government film agencies, the vacuum created by their abolition has had disastrous consequences for the preservation and perpetuation of national cinemas across the hemisphere.

As film production and consumption have declined by as much as 90% in the principal film-producing countries (due to rising production costs, lack of infrastructural reinvestment, massive theater closings, and changing patterns of consumption), cultural access in the private domestic sphere (via television, cable, satellite, video distribution, etc.) has increased proportionately. Collective use of public space and basic forms of sociability and civility have declined as a result, while national identities are being reconfigured transnationally because–despite the expanding global reach of regional television monoliths such as Brazil's *TV Globo* and Mexico's *Televisa*–the forms of culture being consumed derive increasingly from a single extranational source, the United States. U.S. products dominate Latin American home video and cable markets, where space for national and hemispheric products shrinks to minuscule or nil. The North American Free Trade Agreement signals the further tipping of these perennially unbalanced scales: The 62% proportion of U.S. product on Mexican movie screens prior to NAFTA subsequently jumped to over 90%. The rapid expansion of cyberculture through Latin America, with its embedded dependence on knowledge of English, guarantees the reinforcement of U.S.-generated cultural expressions. Geo-economic realignments in the 1990s have transformed modes of cinematic consumption to a degree unimaginable only a decade before. Ever more costly to produce, films now have to recover investment in multiple media markets because the theatrical return is no longer sufficient; yet this goal grows more elusive in light of market saturation by U.S. products and limited access to costly new technologies.

The current trend to privatization and transnationalization of film, television, video, and other techno-cultures aggravates communicational dependency. The vacuum created by the dearth of national policies regarding cultural production and new technologies risks allowing the default privatization and mercantilization of everything from scientific research and artistic innovation to the symbolic construction of national history. This increasing de-territorialization of the audiovisual media is only minimally offset by re-territorialization: Regional radio and television stations, musical micromarkets, grassroots video movements, and specialized cable broadcasters, not to mention the quixotic efforts of two prominent national film archives at opposite ends of the southern hemisphere (Caracas and Montevideo) to operate commercial theaters dedicated exclusively to programming from Latin America.

In some nations of the hemisphere, the boundary between film and television production has been eminently permeable. Peruvian auteur Armando Robles Godoy abandoned feature filmmaking for television in the mid-1970s, whereas Venezuela's leading director, Román Chalbaud, has alternated successfully between film, television, and theater over his forty-year career. In Colombia, filmmakers such as Sergio Cabrera, Lisandro Duque, Carlos Mayolo, Jose Ali Triana, and Ciro Durán have worked prominently in television since the 1980s. In Mexico and Brazil, in contrast, the interface between television and film tends in the opposite direction as transnational giants like TV Globo and Televisa manufacture products designed to compete in the "prestige" cinema market, where film remains a perhaps increasingly vestigal index of national worth.

As sociologist of culture Néstor García Canclini has noted, the European Union's practice of consolidating film, television, and video under the unifying designation of "audiovisual space" correlates with both the increasing technological and aesthetic integration of the three media and with their practical integration in public habits of consumption (1997, 253). Distribution is now globally tied to television, video, and cable. In order to survive and prosper, filmmakers must cast their lot with their counterparts working in television, video, computer imaging, and other emerging technologies, guiding the evolution of state policy, largely still unformulated, in the realm of culture and communications.

The Argentine film law of 1994 stimulated film production financing through a tax on home videos and regulations that encourage co-production arrangements with television producers. Integration of these various media is configured in the change of nomenclature: From the Argentine National Film Institute (INC) to the National Institute for Film and Audiovisual Art (INCAA). In 1998, after months of debate, the Mexican senate approved new film legislation, shepherded through by well-known actress María Rojo, that guarantees theatrical releases to domestic productions within six months of their registration. In countries throughout Latin America, filmmakers have

united for decades to lobby for national film legislation, making them the only cultural sphere with a policy-formation precedent, a strategic advantage in the present rapidly changing cultural landscape.

What are the cultural implications of the hybridizations that transnationality and globalization will continue to produce? How will regional, national, and hemispheric identities reconstitute themselves in response to contemporary processes of transcultural hybridization? What will be the role of film and audiovisual culture in that process? Nestor García Canclini, the Argentine sociologist of culture long relocated to Mexico, sees multimedia and multicontextuality as two key notions for redefining the social role of film and other communications systems. The concept of identity that he proposes is "not only sociospatial but sociocommunicational" in its simultaneous articulation of local, national, and postnational referents. Constructs of identity, if they are to remain basic to cultural articulation, must evolve as part of an ongoing "coproduction" process (1997, 256–57).

At the dawn of the third millennium, even as the silver screen is everywhere upstaged by the computer screen, video and computers have become fundamental to the filmmaking process itself through on-line editing and the instant video replay that has replaced the overnight wait for the "rushes" to be processed in the lab. In Latin America, there is a marked overproduction of aspiring filmmakers. Where no film schools existed at mid-century, over thirty had come into existence by the 1980s. Established local image industries can only absorb a small fraction of these aspiring students. Yet, on the other hand, Latin America boasts some 300 million potential image consumers; the U.S. population adds an estimated 30 million "Latinos." The voracious expansion of televisual markets and broadcast slots serving this vast and varied population not only promises to keep the cinema of the past recirculating but also offers contemporary audiovisual producers a potential bilingual and bicultural audience that has barely begun to be tapped.

Works Cited

Avellar, João Carlos. 1994. *Brazilian Cinema and Literature*. São Paulo: Camara Brasileira do Libro.

Brooks, Peter. 1991. "The Melodramatic Imagination." *Imitations of Life: A Reader in Film and Television Melodrama*. Ed. Marcia Landy. Detroit, MI: Wayne State University Press. 50–67.

Burton-Carvajal, Julianne. 1999. "*Araya* Across Time and Space: Comparative Instances of Critical Reception and the Writing of National and International Film Histories." *Revisión del cine de los cincuenta. Revisioning Films from the Fifties*. Ed. Julianne Burton-Carvajal. Bilingual issue of *Nuevo Texto Crítico* 21–22: 206–34.

Castañeda, Jorge. 1993. *Utopia Unarmed: The Latin American Left after the Cold War*. New York: Knopf.

Castillo de Rodríguez, Irene. 1995. "Cien años de presencia de España en el cine colombiano." *España en Colombia: Revista de la Embajada de España* 3: 52–53.

Chanan, Michael. 1998. "Latin American Cinema in the 90s: Representational Space in Recent Latin American Cinema." *Visual Culture in Latin America*. Ed. John Mraz. Special issue of *Estudios Interdisciplinarios de América Latina y el Caribe* 9.1: 11–19.

Colina, Enrique and Daniel Díaz Torres. 1971. "Ideología del melodrama en el viejo cine latinoamericano." *Cine cubano* 73–74–75: 14–26.

———. 1978. "Ideology of Melodrama in the Old Latin American Cinema." *Latin American Film Makers and the Third Cinema*. Ed. Zuzana M. Pick. Ottawa: Carleton University Press. 46–70.

Duffey, J. Patrick. 1996. *De la pantalla al texto: la influencia del cine en la narrativa mexicana del siglo veinte.* Mexico City: UNAM.

Galvão, María Rita. 1987. "Le Muet." *Le cinéma brésilien.* Ed. Paulo-Antonio Paranagua. Paris: Centre Georges Pompidou. 51–65.

———. 1995. "Vera Cruz: A Brazilian Hollywood." *Brazilian Cinema.* Ed. Randal Johnson and Robert Stam. Expanded ed. New York: Columbia University Press. 270–80.

García Canclini, Néstor. 1997. "Will There Be Latin American Cinema in the Year 2000? Visual Culture in a Postnational Era." Trans. Adriana X. Tatum and Ann Marie Stock. *Framing Latin American Cinema: Contemporary Critical Directions.* Ed. Ann Marie Stock. Minneapolis: University of Minnesota Press. 246–58.

González, Reynaldo. 1990. "Lágrimas de celuloide." *Cine latinoamericano, años 30–40–50: Memoria del XI Festival del Nuevo Cine Latinoamericano.* Dir. Ivan Trujillo. Ed. Collection Irma Arcelina Espinosa García. Mexico City: Universidad Nacional Autónoma de México. 141–48.

Johnson, Randal. 1991. "The Rise and Fall of Brazilian Cinema: 1960–1990." Ed. Kathleen Newman. Special issue of *Iris* 13: 97–124.

King, John, Ana M. López, and Manuel Alvarado, ed. 1993. "General Introduction." *Mediating Two Worlds: Cinematic Encounters in the Americas.* London: British Film Institute. xvii–xxi.

López, Ana M. 1998. "Historia nacional, historia transnacional." *Horizontes del Segundo Siglo. Investigación y pedagogía del cine mexicano, latinoamericano y chicano.* Ed. Julianne Burton-Carvajal, Patricia Torres, and Angel Miguel. Mexico City: Imcine and Guadalajara: Universidad de Guadalajara. 75–81.

Miguel, Angel, ed. 1997. *Los poetas van al cine.* Mexico City: Juan Pablos Editor.

Monsiváis, Carlos. 1994. "Se sufre pero se aprende (El melodrama y las reglas de la falta de límites)." *El melodrama mexicano.* Guest ed. Gastón Lillo. Special supplement of *Archivos de la Filmoteca* 16: 6–19.

———. 1995. "Mythologies." *Mexican Cinema.* Ed. Paulo-Antonio Paranagua. Trans. Ana M. López. London: British Film Institute; Mexico City: Imcine. 117–27.

Noriega, Chon. 1998. "Un nuevo acercamiento histórico al cine chicano." *Horizontes del Segundo Siglo: Investigación y pedagogía del cine mexicano, latinoamericano y chicano.* Ed. Julianne Burton-Carvajal, Patricia Torres San Martín, and Angel Miguel. Mexico City: Imcine and Guadalajara: Universidad de Guadalajara. 82–93.

Ortiz, Fernando. 1995. *Cuban Counterpoint: Tobacco and Sugar.* Introd. (1947) Bronislaw Malinowski; new introd. Fernando Coronil. Trans. Harriet de Onís. Durham, N.C.: Duke University Press.

Paranaguá, Paulo Antonio. 1998. "Por una historia comparada del cine latinoamericano." *Horizontes del Segundo Siglo: Investigación y pedagogía del cine mexicano, latinoamericano y chicano.* Ed. Julianne Burton-Carvajal, Patricia Torres San Martín, and Angel Miguel. Mexico City: Imcine and Guadalajara: Universidad de Guadalajara. 67–74.

Pick, Zuzana. 1993. *The New Latin American Cinema: A Continental Project.* Austin: University of Texas Press.

Podalsky, Laura. 1994. "Negotiating Differences: National Cinemas and Co-productions in Prerevolutionary Cuba." *The Velvet Light Trap* 34 (fall): 59–70.

Reyes, Aurelio de los. 1983, 1993. *Cine y sociedad en México, 1896–1930.* Volume 1: *Vivir de sueños, 1896–1920.* Volume 2: *Bajo el cielo de México.* Mexico City: Universidad Nacional Autónoma de México.

———. 1995. "The Silent Cinema." *Mexican Cinema.* Ed. Paulo-Antonio Paranagua. Trans. Ana M. López. London: British Film Institute and Mexico: Imcine. 63–78.

Rich, B. Ruby. 1991. "An/Other View of the New Latin American Cinema." Ed. Kathleen Newman. Special issue of *Iris* 13: 5–28.

Rocha, Glauber. 1963. *Revisão crítica do cinema brasileiro.* Rio de Janeiro: Editora Civilização Brasileira. 1965. *Revisión crítica del cine brasileiro.* Prologue Angel Fernández-Santos. Havana: Ediciones ICAIC.

———. 1965. "Estética da fome." *Revista Civilização Brasileira* 3.

———. 1995. "An Esthetic of Hunger (New York, Milan, Rio de Janeiro, January 1965)." Trans. Randal Johnson and Burnes Hollyman. *New Latin American Cinema.* Volume I: *Theory, Practices, and Transcontinental Articulations.* Ed. Michael T. Martin. Detroit, Mich.: Wayne State University Press. 59–61.

Salles Gomes, Paulo Emílio. 1995. "Cinema: A Trajectory of Underdevelopment." *Brazilian Cinema.* Ed. Randal Johnson and Robert Stam. Expanded ed. New York: Columbia UP. 244–55.

Sarlo, Beatriz. 1993. "Modernity and Cultural Mixture: The Case of Buenos Aires." *Mediating Two Worlds: Cinematic Encounters in the Americas.* Ed. John King et al. London: British Film Institute. 164–74.

Solanas, Fernando and Octavio Getino. 1969. "Hacia un Tercer cine." *Tricontinental* 13. Havana: OSPAAL.

———. 1983. "For a Third Cinema." Trans. Julianne Burton and Michael Chanan. *Twenty-five Years of the New Latin American Cinema.* Ed. Michael Chanan. London: British Film Institute. 17–27.

Stam, Robert, João Luiz Viera, and Ismail Xavier. 1995. "The Shape of Brazilian Cinema in the Post-Modern Age." *Brazilian Cinema.* Ed. Randal Johnson and Robert Stam. New York: Columbia University Press. 387–472.

Stam, Robert. 1997. *Tropical Multiculturalism: A Comparative History of Race in Brazilian Cinema and Culture.* Durham, N.C.: Duke University Press.

Süssekind, Flora. 1987. *Cinematógrafo de letras: Literatura, técnica e modernização no Brazil.* São Paulo: Companhia das Letras.

Valjalo, David and Zuzana M. Pick, eds. 1984. *10 años de cine chileno, 1973–1983.* Special issue of *Literatura chilena* 8.1.

Xavier, Ismail. 1998. *Allegories of Underdevelopment: Aesthetics and Politics in Modern Brazilian Cinema.* Minneapolis: University of Minnesota Press.